Annotated Teacher's Edition

Fourth Course

HOLT Literature & Language Arts

Mastering the California Standards
Reading · Writing · Listening · Speaking

HOLT, RINEHART AND WINSTON
A Harcourt Education Company
Austin • Orlando • Chicago • New York • Toronto • London • San Diego

EDITORIAL
Project Directors: Kathleen Daniel, Mescal Evler
Project Editors: John Haffner Layden, Hester Weeden
Managing Editors: Marie Price, Mike Topp
Manager of Editorial Services: Abigail Winograd
Senior Product Manager: Don Wulbrecht
Executive Editor: Kristine E. Marshall
Senior Editor: Susan K. Lynch
Editorial Staff: Rob Giannetto, David Bradford, Terence Fitzgerald, Michael Fleming, Martin Fox, Mark Hughs, Michael B. Laus, Albert Rolls, Jennifer Schwan, Alan Shaw
Administrative Managing Editor: Michael Neibergall
Copyediting Supervisors: Mary Malone, Kathleen Scheiner
Copyeditors: Christine Altgelt, Cathy Baehler, Joel Bourgeois, Emily Force, Christine Han, Leora Harris, Julie A. Hill, Julia Thomas Hu, Jessica Keitlen, Jennifer Kirkland, Theresa Mysiewicz, Millicent Ondras, Dennis Scharnberg
Editorial Finance Managers: Lori De La Garza, Elizabeth LaManna
Editorial Support: Renée Benitez, Louise Fernandez, Danielle Greer, Bret Isaacs, Casey Kelley, Laurie Muir, Kristen Nastanski, Erik Netcher, Joie D. Pickett, Janet Riley, Margaret Sanchez, Thomas VerGow
Editorial Permissions: Carrie Jones, David Smith

ART, DESIGN, AND PRODUCTION
Director: Athena Blackorby
Senior Design Director: Betty Mintz
Design: Preface, Inc.
Composition and PrePress: Progressive Information Technologies, Inc.
Production Manager: Catherine Gessner
Production Coordinator: Richard Colicchio

COVER
Photo Credits: (Coin) The Art Archive/Jan Vinchon Numismatist Paris/Dagli Orti (A); (wreath) Araldo de Luca/CORBIS; (Palace of Fine Arts) Philip James Corwin/CORBIS.

Acknowledgments appear on page 1041, which is an extension of the copyright page.

Printed in the United States of America

ISBN 0-03-057372-6 3 4 5 048 05

Program Authors

Kylene Beers established the reading pedagogy for *Holt Literature and Language Arts.* A former middle-school teacher, Dr. Beers has turned her commitment to helping readers having difficulty into the major focus of her research, writing, speaking, and teaching. A Clinical Associate Professor at the University of Houston, Dr. Beers is also currently the editor of the National Council of Teachers of English journal *Voices from the Middle.* She is the author of *When Kids Can't Read: A Guidebook for Teachers Grades 6–12* and the co-editor of *Into Focus: Understanding and Creating Middle School Readers.* Dr. Beers is the 2001 recipient of the Richard Halle Award from the NCTE for outstanding contributions to middle-level literacy education. She has served on the review boards of the *English Journal* and *The Alan Review.* Dr. Beers currently serves on the board of directors of the International Reading Association's Special Interest Group on Adolescent Literature.

Lee Odell helped establish the pedagogical framework for writing, listening, and speaking for *Holt Literature and Language Arts.* Dr. Odell is Professor of Composition Theory and Research and, since 1996, Director of the Writing Program at Rensselaer Polytechnic Institute. He began his career teaching English in middle and high schools. More recently he has worked with teachers in grades K–12 to establish a program that involves students from all disciplines in writing across the curriculum and for communities outside their classrooms. Dr. Odell's most recent book (with Charles R. Cooper) is *Evaluating Writing: The Role of Teachers' Knowledge About Text, Learning, and Culture.* He is past chair of the Conference on College Composition and Communication and of NCTE's Assembly for Research. Dr. Odell is currently working on a college-level writing textbook.

Writers

Robert Anderson is a playwright, novelist, screenwriter, and teacher. His plays include *Tea and Sympathy; Silent Night, Lonely Night; You Know I Can't Hear You When the Water's Running;* and *I Never Sang for My Father.* His screenplays include *The Nun's Story* and *The Sand Pebbles.* Mr. Anderson has taught at the Writers' Workshop at the University of Iowa, the American Theater Wing Professional Training Program, and the Salzburg Seminar in American Studies. He is a past president of the Dramatists Guild of America, a past vice president of the Authors League of America, and a member of the Theater Hall of Fame.

John Malcolm Brinnin, author of six volumes of poetry that have received many prizes and awards, was a member of the American Academy and Institute of Arts and Letters. He was a critic of poetry, a biographer of poets, and for a number of years the director of New York's famous Poetry Center. His teaching career included terms at Vassar College, the University of Connecticut, and Boston University, where he succeeded Robert Lowell as Professor of Creative Writing and Contemporary Letters. Mr. Brinnin wrote *Dylan Thomas in America: An Intimate Journal* and *Sextet: T. S. Eliot & Truman Capote & Others.*

Flo Ota De Lange and **Sheri Henderson** Flo Ota De Lange is a former teacher with a thirty-year second career in psychotherapy, during which she studied learning processes in children and adults. Those careers led to her third career, as a writer.

Sheri Henderson brings to the program twenty years of experience as a California middle-school research practitioner and full-time reading and language arts teacher at La Paz International School in Saddleback Valley Unified School District. She regularly speaks at statewide and national conferences.

Since 1991, DeLangeHenderson LLC has published forty-three titles designed to integrate the teaching of literature with standards requirements and state and national tests.

Phyllis Goldenberg graduated from the University of Chicago and did graduate work in literature at Columbia University. She has over thirty years' experience as an educational writer and editor specializing in literature, grammar, and composition materials for secondary-school students. She is the author of a student guide to writing a research paper and the author and series editor of a grammar and composition program for middle- and high school students.

Madeline Travers Hovland, who taught language arts for several years, is a writer of educational materials. She studied English at Bates College and received a master's degree in education from Harvard University.

John Leggett is a novelist, biographer, and former teacher. He went to the Writers' Workshop at the University of Iowa in the spring of 1969. In 1970, he assumed temporary charge of the program, and for the next seventeen years he was its director. Mr. Leggett's novels include *Wilder Stone, The Gloucester Branch, Who Took the Gold Away?, Gulliver House,* and *Making Believe.* He is also the author of the highly acclaimed biography *Ross and Tom: Two American Tragedies* and of a biography of William Saroyan, *A Daring Young Man.* Mr. Leggett lives in Napa Valley, California.

Mara Rockliff is a writer and editor with a degree in American civilization from Brown University. She has written dramatizations of classic stories, collected in a book called *Stories for Performance.* She has also published feature stories in national newspapers and is currently writing a novel for young adults.

Diane Tasca, a graduate of Temple University, earned a doctorate in English from the University of Illinois. Over the past thirty years, Dr. Tasca has taught various college courses in composition, literature, and performance and has developed, written, and edited instructional materials for high school and college language arts textbooks. A member of the San Francisco Bay Area theater community, she has performed in numerous plays and assisted playwrights with the development of new dramatic works. She currently teaches drama at Foothill College in Los Altos Hills, California.

Senior Program Consultant

Carol Jago is the editor of CATE's quarterly journal, *California English.* She teaches English at Santa Monica High School, in Santa Monica, and directs the California Reading and Literature Project at UCLA. She writes a weekly education column for the *Los Angeles Times.* She is the author of several books, including three in a series on contemporary writers in the classroom: *Alice Walker in the Classroom; Nikki Giovanni in the Classroom;* and *Sandra Cisneros in the Classroom.* She is also the author of *With Rigor for All: Teaching the Classics to Contemporary Students; Beyond Standards: Excellence in the High School English Classroom;* and *Cohesive Writing: Why Concept Is Not Enough.*

ADVISORS

Cynthia A. Arceneaux
Administrative Coordinator
Office of Deputy Superintendent, Instructional Services
Los Angeles Unified School District
Los Angeles, California

Dr. Julie M.T. Chan
Director of Literacy Instruction
Newport-Mesa Unified School District
Costa Mesa, California

Al Desmarais
English Department Chair and Curriculum Specialist in Language Arts
El Toro High School
Saddleback Valley Unified School District
Lake Forest, California

José M. Ibarra-Tiznado
ELL Program Coordinator
Bassett Unified School District
La Puente, California

Dr. Ronald Klemp
Instructor
California State University, Northridge
Northridge, California

Fern M. Sheldon
K–12 Curriculum and Instruction Specialist
Rowland Unified School District
Rowland Heights, California

Jim Shields
Instructor
El Toro High School
Saddleback Valley Unified School District
Lake Forest, California

CRITICAL REVIEWERS

Oscar Browne
Lincoln High School
San Diego, California

Dara Mosher
Ramona High School
Riverside, California

Toni Lee Olson
Nogales High School
La Puente, California

Rod Warren
Martin Luther King High School
Riverside, California

FIELD-TEST PARTICIPANTS

Sandra J. Gilligan
Passaic High School
Passaic, New Jersey

Lee Lowery
Highlands High School
Fort Thomas, Kentucky

Pamela Rockich
Barberton High School
Barberton, Ohio

Ellen Schunks
North County High School
Bonne Terre, Missouri

Casey Williams
Highlands High School
Fort Thomas, Kentucky

Contents in Brief

Chapter 1

Mastering the California Standards

Mastering the California Standards

• Vocabulary Development • Informational Materials

Chapter 1 Plot and Setting

Synthesizing Sources

Chapter 2

Character

Using Primary and Secondary Sources

Chapter 2

Mastering the California Standards

Reteaching Lessons

Mastering the California Standards

• Vocabulary Development • Informational Materials

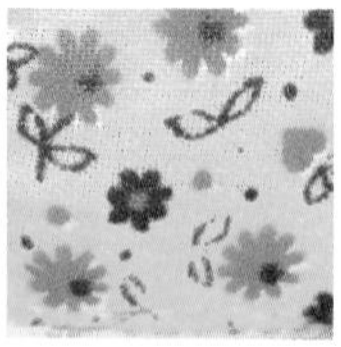

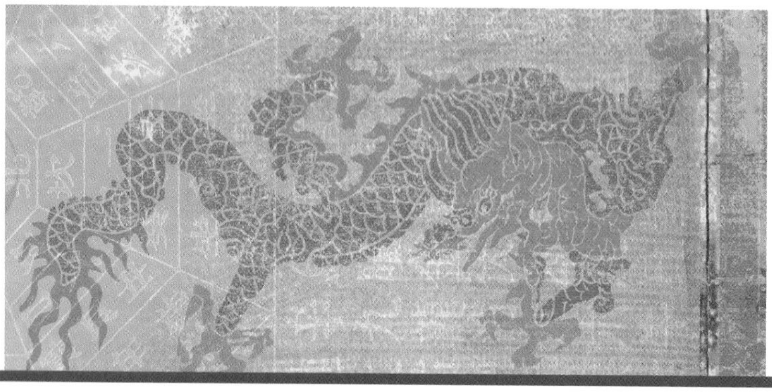

Chapter **3**

Narrator and Voice

Generating Research Questions

Chapter 3

Mastering the California Standards

Mastering the California Standards
• Vocabulary Development • Informational Materials

Chapter 4
Mastering the California Standards

Reteaching Lessons

Chapter 4

Comparing Themes
Evaluating Arguments: Pro and Con

Mastering the California Standards

• Vocabulary Development • Informational Materials

Mastering the Standards

CHAPTER REVIEW

Chapter 5 Irony and Ambiguity

Generating Research Questions and Evaluating Sources

Chapter 5

Mastering the California Standards

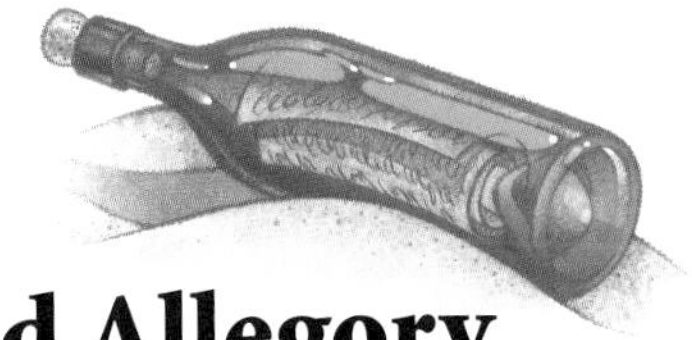

Chapter 6

Symbolism and Allegory

Synthesizing Sources

Chapter 6

Mastering the California Standards

Reteaching Lessons

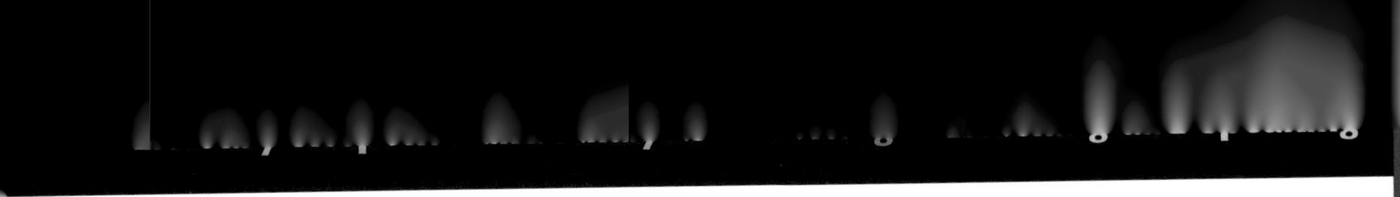

Chapter 7

Poetry

Chapter 7

Mastering the California Standards

Reteaching Lessons

Mastering the California Standards
• Vocabulary Development • Informational Materials

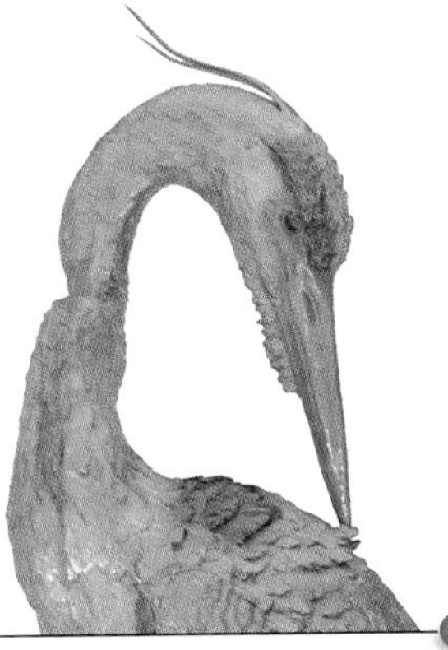

Chapter 8

LITERARY CRITICISM
Evaluating Style
Evaluating an Argument

Chapter 8
Mastering the California Standards

Reteaching Lessons

Chapter 9

LITERARY CRITICISM

Biographical and Historical Approach

Using Primary and Secondary Sources

Chapter 9

Mastering the California Standards

Reteaching Lessons

Mastering the California Standards

• Vocabulary Development • Informational Materials

Chapter 10 Drama

Evaluating an Argument

Chapter 10

Mastering the California Standards

Reteaching Lessons

Mastering the California Standards

• Vocabulary Development • Informational Materials

Mastering the Standards

CHAPTER REVIEW

Chapter 11

Consumer and Workplace Documents

Music on the E-frontier
by Flo Ota De Lange *and* Sheri Henderson

Resource Center

Chapter 11

Mastering the California Standards

Reteaching Lessons

Mastering the California Standards

• Vocabulary Development • Informational Materials

Skills, Workshops, and Features

Skills

Literary Response and Analysis Essays

Literary Skills

Mastering the California Standards

• Vocabulary Development • Informational Materials

Reading Skills for Literary Texts

Reading Matters

Reading Skills for Informational Texts

Vocabulary Skills

Workshops

Writing Workshops

Listening and Speaking Workshops

Features

A Closer Look

Grammar Link Mini-Lessons

Mastering the California Standards

• Vocabulary Development • Informational Materials

Standards Review and Test Practice

Test Smarts

Writer's Handbook

Selections by Genre

Fiction

Legend

Myth

Short Story

Drama

Comedy

Tragedy

Poetry

Bible

Nonfiction and Informational Materials

Autobiography

Biography

Diary

Encyclopedia Article

Essay

Eyewitness Account

Feature Article

Historical Article

Internet Article

Interview

Letter

Magazine Article

Mastering the California Standards

• Vocabulary Development • Informational Materials

Memoir

Newspaper Article

Op-Ed Article

Oral History

Play Review

Reflection

Speech

Textbook

Theory

Web Site

Consumer and Workplace Documents

STANDARDS CORRELATION BY CHAPTER

Note: For a chart that lists the text of all standards and also correlates the standards to the chapters, see pages 30–39.

CHAPTER	READING STANDARDS	WRITING STANDARDS	LISTENING AND SPEAKING STANDARDS
Chapter **1**	1.1, 1.2, 2.4, 3.6, Grade 8 Review 3.4	1.1, 1.2, 1.9, 2.1a–e	1.8, 1.9, 2.1a–d
Chapter **2**	2.5, 3.3, 3.4, Grade 8 Review 1.3	1.1, 1.9, 2.1a–e	
Chapter **3**	1.1, 1.2, 2.3, 3.9, Grade 8 Review 1.3, 3.4	1.3, 1.9, 2.3a–c, e, 2.4a–d	1.3, 1.6, 2.3a–g, 2.5a–d
Chapter **4**	1.1, 1.2, 2.8, 3.2, 3.5, Grade 8 Review 1.1, 1.3	1.2, 1.8, 1.9, 2.4a–d	1.1, 1.3, 1.5, 1.6, 2.5a–d
Chapter **5**	1.1, 1.3, 2.3, 3.8, Grade 8 Review 1.3, 2.7	1.1, 1.9	1.2
Chapter **6**	1.1, 2.4, 3.7, Grade 8 Review 1.3	1.1, 2.2a–d	1.4, 2.4a–d
Chapter **7**	1.1, 3.7, 3.9, 3.11, Grade 8 Review 1.1, 1.2, 3.1	1.1, 1.2, 1.9, 2.1c, e	1.7, 1.8, 1.9, 2.6a–c
Chapter **8**	1.1, 2.8, 3.11, Grade 8 Review 1.1, 1.3	1.2, 2.1a–e	
Chapter **9***	1.1, 1.2, 1.3, 2.5, 3.12, Grade 8 Review 1.2, 3.7	1.3, 1.4, 1.5, 1.6, 1.7, 2.3a–f	1.3, 1.7, 1.8, 1.9, 2.2a–f, 2.3a–c, f
Chapter **10**	1.1, 1.2, 2.8, 3.1, 3.10, Grade 8 Review 1.2, 1.3	1.1, 1.2, 1.4, 1.8, 1.9	1.1, 1.10, 1.11, 1.12, 1.13, 1.14
Chapter **11**	2.1, 2.2, 2.6, 2.7, Grade 8 Review 2.1	2.5a–d, 2.6a–d	
Writer's Handbook*		1.1, 1.3, 1.8, 1.9	

*Written and Oral English-Language Conventions:
Standard 1.5 is covered in Chapter 9.
Standard 1.3 is covered in the Writer's Handbook.

STANDARDS CORRELATION BY STANDARD

Standard Number	Text of Standard	Chapter(s)
DOMAIN	READING	
STRAND	WORD ANALYSIS, FLUENCY, AND SYSTEMATIC VOCABULARY DEVELOPMENT	
	Vocabulary and Concept Development	
1.1	Identify and use the literal and figurative meanings of words and understand word derivations.	Chapters 1, 3, 4, 5, 6, 7, 8, 9, 10
1.2	Distinguish between the denotative and connotative meanings of words and interpret the connotative power of words.	Chapters 1, 3, 4, 9, 10
1.3	Identify Greek, Roman, and Norse mythology and use the knowledge to understand the origin and meaning of new words (e.g., the word *narcissistic* drawn from the myth of Narcissus and Echo).	Chapters 5, 9
GRADE 8 REVIEW 1.1	Analyze idioms, analogies, metaphors, and similes to infer the literal and figurative meanings of phrases.	Chapters 4, 7, 8
GRADE 8 REVIEW 1.2	Understand the most important points in the history of the English language and use common word origins to determine the historical influences on English word meanings.	Chapters 7, 9, 10
GRADE 8 REVIEW 1.3	Use word meanings within the appropriate context and show ability to verify those meanings by definition, restatement, example, comparison, or contrast.	Chapters 2, 3, 4, 5, 6, 8, 10
STRAND	READING COMPREHENSION (FOCUS ON INFORMATIONAL MATERIALS)	
	Structural Features of Informational Materials	
2.1	Analyze the structure and format of functional workplace documents, including the graphics and headers, and explain how authors use the features to achieve their purposes.	Chapter 11
2.2	Prepare a bibliography of reference materials for a report using a variety of consumer, workplace, and public documents.	Chapter 11

Standard Number	Text of Standard	Chapter(s)
GRADE 8 REVIEW 2.1	Compare and contrast the features and elements of consumer materials to gain meaning from documents (e.g., warranties, contracts, product information, instruction manuals).	Chapter 11
	Comprehension and Analysis of Grade-Level-Appropriate Text	
2.3	Generate relevant questions about readings on issues that can be researched.	Chapters 3, 5
2.4	Synthesize the content from several sources or works by a single author dealing with a single issue; paraphrase the ideas and connect them to other sources and related topics to demonstrate comprehension.	Chapters 1, 6
2.5	Extend ideas presented in primary or secondary sources through original analysis, evaluation, and elaboration.	Chapters 2, 9
2.6	Demonstrate use of sophisticated learning tools by following technical directions (e.g., those found with graphic calculators and specialized software programs and in access guides to World Wide Web sites on the Internet).	Chapter 11
	Expository Critique	
2.7	Critique the logic of functional documents by examining the sequence of information and procedures in anticipation of possible reader misunderstandings.	Chapter 11
2.8	Evaluate the credibility of an author's argument or defense of a claim by critiquing the relationship between generalizations and evidence, the comprehensiveness of evidence, and the way in which the author's intent affects the structure and tone of the text (e.g., in professional journals, editorials, political speeches, primary source material).	Chapters 4, 8, 10
STRAND	**LITERARY RESPONSE AND ANALYSIS**	
	Structural Features of Literature	
3.1	Articulate the relationship between the expressed purposes and the characteristics of different forms of dramatic literature (e.g., comedy, tragedy, drama, dramatic monologue).	Chapter 10
3.2	Compare and contrast the presentation of a similar theme or topic across genres to explain how the selection of genre shapes the theme or topic.	Chapter 4

Mastering the California Standards

• Vocabulary Development • Informational Materials

Standard Number	Text of Standard	Chapter(s)
GRADE 8 REVIEW 3.1	Determine and articulate the relationship between the purposes and characteristics of different forms of poetry (e.g., ballad, lyric, couplet, epic, elegy, ode, sonnet).	Chapter 7
	Narrative Analysis of Grade-Level-Appropriate Text	
3.3	Analyze interactions between main and subordinate characters in a literary text (e.g., internal and external conflicts, motivations, relationships, influences) and explain the way those interactions affect the plot.	Chapter 2
3.4	Determine characters' traits by what the characters say about themselves in narration, dialogue, dramatic monologue, and soliloquy.	Chapter 2
3.5	Compare works that express a universal theme and provide evidence to support the ideas expressed in each work.	Chapter 4
3.6	Analyze and trace an author's development of time and sequence, including the use of complex literary devices (e.g., foreshadowing, flashbacks).	Chapter 1
3.7	Recognize and understand the significance of various literary devices, including figurative language, imagery, allegory, and symbolism, and explain their appeal.	Chapters 6, 7
3.8	Interpret and evaluate the impact of ambiguities, subtleties, contradictions, ironies, and incongruities in a text.	Chapter 5
3.9	Explain how voice, persona, and the choice of a narrator affect characterization and the tone, plot, and credibility of a text.	Chapters 3, 7
3.10	Identify and describe the function of dialogue, scene designs, soliloquies, asides, and character foils in dramatic literature.	Chapter 10
GRADE 8 REVIEW 3.4	Analyze the relevance of the setting (e.g., place, time, customs) to the mood, tone, and meaning of the text.	Chapters 1, 3
	Literary Criticism	
3.11	Evaluate the aesthetic qualities of style, including the impact of diction and figurative language on tone, mood, and theme, using the terminology of literary criticism. (Aesthetic approach)	Chapters 7, 8
3.12	Analyze the way in which a work of literature is related to the themes and issues of its historical period. (Historical approach)	Chapter 9
GRADE 8 REVIEW 3.7	Analyze a work of literature, showing how it reflects the heritage, traditions, attitudes, and beliefs of its author. (Biographical approach)	Chapter 9

Standard Number	Text of Standard	Chapter(s)
DOMAIN	**WRITING**	
STRAND	**WRITING STRATEGIES**	
	Organization and Focus	
1.1	Establish a controlling impression or coherent thesis that conveys a clear and distinctive perspective on the subject and maintain a consistent tone and focus throughout the piece of writing.	Chapters 1, 2, 5, 6, 7, 10, Writer's Handbook
1.2	Use precise language, action verbs, sensory details, appropriate modifiers, and the active rather than the passive voice.	Chapters 1, 4, 7, 8, 10
	Research and Technology	
1.3	Use clear research questions and suitable research methods (e.g., library, electronic media, personal interview) to elicit and present evidence from primary and secondary sources.	Chapters 3, 9, Writer's Handbook
1.4	Develop the main ideas within the body of the composition through supporting evidence (e.g., scenarios, commonly held beliefs, hypotheses, definitions).	Chapters 9, 10
1.5	Synthesize information from multiple sources and identify complexities and discrepancies in the information and the different perspectives found in each medium (e.g., almanacs, microfiche, news sources, in-depth field studies, speeches, journals, technical documents).	Chapter 9
1.6	Integrate quotations and citations into a written text while maintaining the flow of ideas.	Chapter 9
1.7	Use appropriate conventions for documentation in the text, notes, and bibliographies by adhering to those in style manuals (e.g., *Modern Language Association Handbook, The Chicago Manual of Style*).	Chapter 9
1.8	Design and publish documents by using advanced publishing software and graphic programs.	Chapters 4, 10, Writer's Handbook
	Evaluation and Revision	
1.9	Revise writing to improve the logic and coherence of the organization and controlling perspective, the precision of word choice, and the tone by taking into consideration the audience, purpose, and formality of the context.	Chapters 1, 2, 3, 4, 5, 7, 10, Writer's Handbook

Standard Number	Text of Standard	Chapter(s)
STRAND	WRITING APPLICATIONS (GENRES AND THEIR CHARACTERISTICS)	
2.1	Write biographical or autobiographical narratives or short stories:	Chapters 1, 2, 7, 8
a	Relate a sequence of events and communicate the significance of the events to the audience.	Chapters 1, 2, 8
b	Locate scenes and incidents in specific places.	Chapters 1, 2, 8
c	Describe with concrete sensory details the sights, sounds, and smells of a scene and the specific actions, movements, gestures, and feelings of the characters; use interior monologue to depict the characters' feelings.	Chapters 1, 2, 7, 8
d	Pace the presentation of actions to accommodate changes in time and mood.	Chapters 1, 2, 8
e	Make effective use of descriptions of appearance, images, shifting perspectives, and sensory details.	Chapters 1, 2, 7, 8
2.2	Write responses to literature:	Chapter 6
a	Demonstrate a comprehensive grasp of the significant ideas of literary works.	Chapter 6
b	Support important ideas and viewpoints through accurate and detailed references to the text or to other works.	Chapter 6
c	Demonstrate awareness of the author's use of stylistic devices and an appreciation of the effects created.	Chapter 6
d	Identify and assess the impact of perceived ambiguities, nuances, and complexities within the text.	Chapter 6
2.3	Write expository compositions, including analytical essays and research reports:	Chapters 3, 9
a	Marshal evidence in support of a thesis and related claims, including information on all relevant perspectives.	Chapters 3, 9
b	Convey information and ideas from primary and secondary sources accurately and coherently.	Chapters 3, 9
c	Make distinctions between the relative value and significance of specific data, facts, and ideas.	Chapters 3, 9

Standard Number	Text of Standard	Chapter(s)
d	Include visual aids by employing appropriate technology to organize and record information on charts, maps, and graphs.	Chapter 9
e	Anticipate and address readers' potential misunderstandings, biases, and expectations.	Chapters 3, 9
f	Use technical terms and notations accurately.	Chapter 9
2.4	Write persuasive compositions:	Chapters 3, 4
a	Structure ideas and arguments in a sustained and logical fashion.	Chapters 3, 4
b	Use specific rhetorical devices to support assertions (e.g., appeal to logic through reasoning; appeal to emotion or ethical belief; relate a personal anecdote, case study, or analogy).	Chapters 3, 4
c	Clarify and defend positions with precise and relevant evidence, including facts, expert opinions, quotations, and expressions of commonly accepted beliefs and logical reasoning.	Chapters 3, 4
d	Address readers' concerns, counterclaims, biases, and expectations.	Chapters 3, 4
2.5	Write business letters:	Chapter 11
a	Provide clear and purposeful information and address the intended audience appropriately.	Chapter 11
b	Use appropriate vocabulary, tone, and style to take into account the nature of the relationship with, and the knowledge and interests of, the recipients.	Chapter 11
c	Highlight central ideas or images.	Chapter 11
d	Follow a conventional style with page formats, fonts, and spacing that contribute to the documents' readability and impact.	Chapter 11
2.6	Write technical documents (e.g., a manual on rules of behavior for conflict resolution, procedures for conducting a meeting, minutes of a meeting):	Chapter 11
a	Report information and convey ideas logically and correctly.	Chapter 11
b	Offer detailed and accurate specifications.	Chapter 11
c	Include scenarios, definitions, and examples to aid comprehension (e.g., troubleshooting guide).	Chapter 11

Standard Number	Text of Standard	Chapter(s)
d	Anticipate readers' problems, mistakes, and misunderstandings.	Chapter 11
DOMAIN	WRITTEN AND ORAL ENGLISH-LANGUAGE CONVENTIONS	
STRAND	WRITTEN AND ORAL ENGLISH-LANGUAGE CONVENTIONS	
	Grammar and Mechanics of Writing	
1.3	Demonstrate an understanding of proper English usage and control of grammar, paragraph and sentence structure, diction, and syntax.	Writer's Handbook
	Manuscript Form	
1.5	Reflect appropriate manuscript requirements, including title page presentation, pagination, spacing and margins, and integration of source and support material (e.g., in-text citation, use of direct quotations, paraphrasing) with appropriate citations.	Chapter 9
DOMAIN	LISTENING AND SPEAKING	
STRAND	LISTENING AND SPEAKING STRATEGIES	
	Comprehension	
1.1	Formulate judgments about the ideas under discussion, and support those judgments with convincing evidence.	Chapters 4, 10
1.2	Compare and contrast the ways in which media genres (e.g., televised news, news magazines, documentaries, online information) cover the same event.	Chapter 5
	Organization and Delivery of Oral Communication	
1.3	Choose logical patterns of organization (e.g., chronological, topical, cause and effect) to inform and to persuade, by soliciting agreement or action, or to unite audiences behind a common belief or cause.	Chapters 3, 4, 9
1.4	Choose appropriate techniques for developing the introduction and conclusion (e.g., by using literary quotations, anecdotes, references to authoritative sources).	Chapter 6

Standard Number	Text of Standard	Chapter(s)
1.5	Recognize and use elements of classical speech forms (e.g., introduction, first and second transitions, body, conclusion) in formulating rational arguments and applying the art of persuasion and debate.	Chapter 4
1.6	Present and advance a clear thesis statement, and choose appropriate types of proof (e.g., statistics, testimony, specific instances) that meet standard tests for evidence, including credibility, validity, and relevance.	Chapters 3, 4
1.7	Use props, visual aids, graphs, and electronic media to enhance the appeal and accuracy of presentations.	Chapters 7, 9
1.8	Produce concise notes for extemporaneous delivery.	Chapters 1, 7, 9
1.9	Analyze the occasion and the interests of the audience and choose effective verbal and nonverbal techniques (e.g., voice, gestures, eye contact) for presentations.	Chapters 1, 7, 9
	Analysis and Evaluation of Oral and Media Communications	
1.10	Analyze historically significant speeches (e.g., Abraham Lincoln's "Gettysburg Address," Martin Luther King, Jr.'s "I Have a Dream") to find the rhetorical devices and features that make them memorable.	Chapter 10
1.11	Assess how language and delivery affect the mood and tone of the oral communication and make an impact on the audience.	Chapter 10
1.12	Evaluate the clarity, quality, effectiveness, and general coherence of a speaker's important points, arguments, evidence, organization of ideas, delivery, diction, and syntax.	Chapter 10
1.13	Analyze the types of arguments used by the speaker, including argument by causation, analogy, authority, emotion, and logic.	Chapter 10
1.14	Identify the aesthetic effects of a media presentation, and evaluate the techniques used to create them (e.g., compare Shakespeare's *Henry V* with Kenneth Branagh's 1990 film version).	Chapter 10

Standard Number	Text of Standard	Chapter(s)
STRAND	SPEAKING APPLICATIONS (GENRES AND THEIR CHARACTERISTICS)	
2.1	Deliver narrative presentations:	Chapter 1
a	Narrate a sequence of events and communicate their significance to the audience.	Chapter 1
b	Locate scenes and incidents in specific places.	Chapter 1
c	Describe with concrete sensory details the sights, sounds, and smells of a scene and the specific actions, movements, gestures, and feelings of characters.	Chapter 1
d	Pace the presentation of actions to accommodate time or mood changes.	Chapter 1
2.2	Deliver expository presentations:	Chapter 9
a	Marshal evidence in support of a thesis and related claims, including information on all relevant perspectives.	Chapter 9
b	Convey information and ideas from primary and secondary sources accurately and coherently.	Chapter 9
c	Make distinctions between the relative value and significance of specific data, facts, and ideas.	Chapter 9
d	Include visual aids by employing appropriate technology to organize and display information on charts, maps, and graphs.	Chapter 9
e	Anticipate and address the listener's potential misunderstandings, biases, and expectations.	Chapter 9
f	Use technical terms and notations accurately.	Chapter 9
2.3	Apply appropriate interviewing techniques:	Chapters 3, 9
a	Prepare and ask relevant questions.	Chapters 3, 9
b	Make notes of responses.	Chapters 3, 9
c	Use language that conveys maturity, sensitivity, and respect.	Chapters 3, 9
d	Respond correctly and effectively to questions.	Chapter 3
e	Demonstrate knowledge of the subject or organization.	Chapter 3
f	Compile and report responses.	Chapters 3, 9
g	Evaluate the effectiveness of the interview.	Chapter 3

Standard Number	Text of Standard	Chapter(s)
2.4	Deliver oral responses to literature:	Chapter 6
a	Advance a judgment demonstrating a comprehensive grasp of the significant ideas of works or passages (i.e., make and support warranted assertions about the text).	Chapter 6
b	Support important ideas and viewpoints through accurate and detailed references to the text or to other works.	Chapter 6
c	Demonstrate awareness of the author's use of stylistic devices and an appreciation of the effects created.	Chapter 6
d	Identify and assess the impact of perceived ambiguities, nuances, and complexities within the text.	Chapter 6
2.5	Deliver persuasive arguments (including evaluation and analysis of problems and solutions and causes and effects):	Chapters 3, 4
a	Structure ideas and arguments in a coherent, logical fashion.	Chapters 3, 4
b	Use rhetorical devices to support assertions (e.g., by appeal to logic through reasoning; by appeal to emotion or ethical belief; by use of personal anecdote, case study, or analogy).	Chapters 3, 4
c	Clarify and defend positions with precise and relevant evidence, including facts, expert opinions, quotations, expressions of commonly accepted beliefs, and logical reasoning.	Chapters 3, 4
d	Anticipate and address the listener's concerns and counterarguments.	Chapters 3, 4
2.6	Deliver descriptive presentations:	Chapter 7
a	Establish clearly the speaker's point of view on the subject of the presentation.	Chapter 7
b	Establish clearly the speaker's relationship with that subject (e.g., dispassionate observation, personal involvement).	Chapter 7
c	Use effective, factual descriptions of appearance, concrete images, shifting perspectives and vantage points, and sensory details.	Chapter 7

Your Road Map to Success: **Mastering the California Standards**

Students today enter their classrooms with a wide range of abilities and individual levels of preparation. Advanced students, English-language learners, students with learning disabilities, and students who have reading difficulties all converge in the language arts classroom with a need to build solid reading, writing, listening and speaking, and grammar skills. Teaching this broad scope of skills while addressing students' individual needs can be a challenge.

Designed for California Teachers and Students

The ***Holt Literature and Language Arts*** program has been designed specifically to help you address these critical skills and to guide your students toward mastery of the California English–Language Arts Content Standards. This carefully researched, comprehensive language arts program covers all the standards without losing sight of the central focus of the language arts classroom: to help all students become good readers and writers, appreciate literature, and embrace the power of the English language in all its forms.

Comprehensive and Coherent Structure

Holt Literature and Language Arts is based on current and confirmed research that suggests that curriculum, assessment, instruction, and organization should be aligned and integrated in any language arts program. This approach ensures that all students are given opportunities to achieve the essential knowledge and skills required by the standards and that students are introduced to these skills in a way that fosters confidence and promotes success.

Giving All Students Access to Language Skills

So that every student has a supportive environment in which to build language arts skills, the ***Holt Literature and Language Arts*** program provides alternative methods of planning, instruction, and assessment to help you differentiate instruction for your classroom's specific needs. Suggestions for modifying instruction to address the particular needs of advanced learners, special education students, English-language learners, or those who need more help building reading skills are included throughout the program.

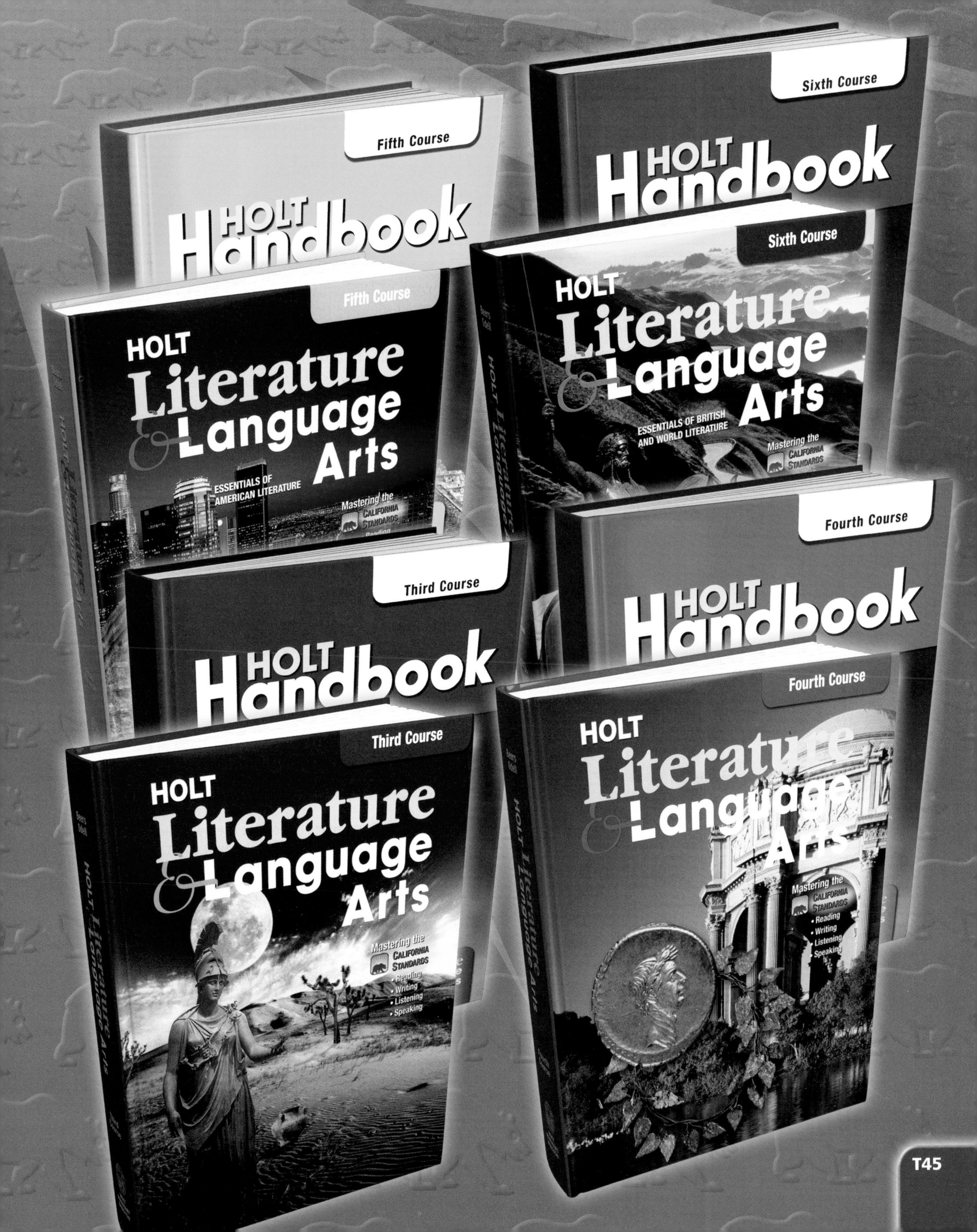
Fifth Course
HOLT Handbook
Sixth Course
HOLT Handbook
Fifth Course
HOLT Literature & Language Arts
ESSENTIALS OF AMERICAN LITERATURE
Mastering the CALIFORNIA STANDARDS
Sixth Course
HOLT Literature & Language Arts
ESSENTIALS OF BRITISH AND WORLD LITERATURE
Mastering the CALIFORNIA STANDARDS
Fourth Course
HOLT Handbook
Third Course
HOLT Handbook
Fourth Course
HOLT Literature & Language Arts
Mastering the CALIFORNIA STANDARDS
• Reading
• Writing
• Listening
• Speaking
Third Course
HOLT Literature & Language Arts
Mastering the CALIFORNIA STANDARDS
• Reading
• Writing
• Listening
• Speaking

MASTERING THE CALIFORNIA STANDARDS

Program Organization

Covering All the **Standards in the Language Arts**

The ***Holt Literature and Language Arts*** program is logically organized and systematically sequenced so that students build the skills and master the content required by the California standards. The ***Holt Literature and Language Arts*** *Student Edition* is the centerpiece for building the knowledge and skills required by the reading, writing, and listening and speaking standards. The ***Holt Handbook*** *Student Edition* is the primary tool for building the knowledge and skills required by the written and oral English-language conventions standards. Opportunities for practice and remediation and for reteaching, assessing, and connecting the standards are offered throughout the program.

Chapter 1

PLOT AND SETTING

GENERATING RESEARCH QUESTIONS

A story to me means a plot
where there is some surprise. . . .
Because this is how life is—
full of surprises.

—Isaac Bashevis Singer

Time Transfixed (1939) by René Magritte.
Oil on canvas (146.3 cm × 97.5 cm).
The Art Institute of Chicago.

Plot and Setting • Generating Research Questions 1

Mastering the California Standards in Reading, Writing, Listening, and Speaking

Contents in Brief

Contents A1

Mastering the California Standards
• Vocabulary Development • Informational Materials

Chapter 1 Plot and Setting
Generating Research Questions

A2 Contents

HOLT LITERATURE AND LANGUAGE ARTS

Mastering the California Standards in Reading

The chapters in ***Holt Literature and Language Arts*** are organized to cover the grade-level standards in vocabulary development, reading comprehension, literary response and analysis, writing, and listening and speaking. Each chapter includes a variety of informational materials related to the literary selections, multiple opportunities for students to master the standard, and a review section.

Two charts appear at the beginning of the ***Student Edition.*** The first chart, Standards Correlation by Chapter, lists every standard taught in the chapter. The second chart, Standards Correlation by Standard, shows where every standard is taught throughout the book. In addition, the text of the standards always appears on the page where it is taught so that students know which standard they are studying.

HOLT LITERATURE AND LANGUAGE ARTS

Mastering the California Standards in Writing, Listening, and Speaking

Each workshop offers a logical connection to either the literary or the informational selections studied and covers a different genre of writing. The workshops are directly correlated to standards instruction in writing strategies and writing applications. Each workshop includes direct instruction, sustained practice, and reinforcement of the standards. Assessment is aligned with the standards.

Writing Workshop

Writing an Autobiographical Narrative

Writing Assignment
Writing 2.1 Write an autobiographical narrative that reveals an experience's significance for you.

It is human nature to want to share what happe[n]
magazines and books—like this one—contain [...]
who want to share their meaningful life experien[c]
experience that is important to you with others b[y]
autobiographical narrative.

Prewriting

GO TO: go.hrw.com
KEYWORD: HLLA 9-1
FOR: Professional Model, Writer's Guides, and Reference Sources

Search Your Memory for Ex[...]

Magic Moments Your autobiographical n[...] on a specific, meaningful experience from your [...] some experiences that you might write about, j[...] visiting a specific place that was important to y[...] younger, thinking about the first time you did s[...] for example—or listing special occasions you re[...]

Choose an Experience

Do the Write Thing Ask yourself the foll[...] evaluate each experience that you thought of.

- Is this experience important to me? Why?
- What specific details can I give about this exp[...]
- Is the experience too private or embarrassing [...]

When you finish, look over what you wrote a[...] Choose the experience that brought out the mo[...] responses from you.

Writing 2.1 Write autobiographical narratives. **2.1b** Locate scenes and incidents in specific places. **2.1c** Describe with concrete sensory details the sights, sounds, and smells of a scene and the specific actions, movements, gestures, and feelings of the characters; use interior monologue. **2.1d** Pace the presentation of actions to accommodate changes in time and mood. **2.1e** Make effective use of descriptions of appearance, images, and sensory details.

Define Your Purpose and Au[...]

Your Side of the Story In an autobiogr[...] **purpose** is to relate the **sequence of events** that [...] experience and to express to your audience the [...] events. Your **audience** consists of the people yo[u] [...] autobiographical narrative. Ask yourself the qu[...] the next page to get a feel for your audience.

1. **Who is my intended audience?** Your audien[c]e [...] mates, teachers, friends, parents, or even tota[...]

66 Chapter 1 Plot and Setting • Generating Research Questions

2. **What will the audience need to know to understand the experience?** Plan to provide background information to help your readers understand your narrative, if necessary.

Gather Details

Let Your Memory Be Your Guide To search your memory for the details that will bring your narrative to life, answer the questions and use the tips in the chart below. List all of the vivid details you can recall about events, people, places, thoughts, and feelings. The second column contains details from one writer's answers to the questions.

Quick guide!

ADDING DETAILS

Questions/Tips	Examples
Events What sequence of events make up the experience? Were there important events that led up to or followed the experience? **TIP:** Match the **pace** of your narrative to the pace of the actual events—a quick pace for rapid events, a slow pace for more drawn-out events.	Sequence of events: walking in park, practicing building fires with Dad Later events: camp contest, camping in mountains
Places Where did the events happen? **TIP:** Use **concrete sensory details** to create effective images of the sights, sounds, and smells of the places you are describing.	city park on cool summer morning; wilderness; thickly leaved trees; pines and aspens; smell of trees
People Who was involved in the events? What did those people look like? What did they do and say? **TIP:** Use sensory details to describe **actions** and **gestures**. Use **dialogue,** actual words people say, to show each person's personality.	me—ages five, eleven, fourteen; Dad—young man dressed for work, wearing glasses; what Dad said as he taught me
Thoughts and Feelings What did I think and feel as the events unfolded? **TIP:** Use **interior monologue,** "thinking out loud," to share your thoughts with readers.	happiness during times with Dad; pleasure at collecting wood; luck for having such a dad; special bond

Organize Details

Ducks in a Row Now, take a look at the events that you listed. When you write your narrative, discuss the events in **chronological order,** or time order. Events that came before your experience will appear first in your narrative because they will help your audience

Writing Workshop: Writing an Autobiographical Narrative 67

HOLT HANDBOOK

The ***Holt Handbook Student Edition*** focuses on the written and oral English-language conventions required by the standards. The grammar, usage, and mechanics chapters are based on John Warriner's time-tested system for instruction: Teach students the rule, show examples of the rule in action, and provide immediate practice.

The ***Holt Handbook*** is divided into three main parts:

- **Part 1: Grammar, Usage, and Mechanics**
- **Part 2: Sentences**
- **Part 3: Resources**

CONTENTS IN BRIEF

Contents T3

MASTERING THE CALIFORNIA STANDARDS

Reading

Take a Road Trip to **Literary and Real-World Fluency**

Holt Literature and Language Arts prepares students to master the California reading standards by helping them build skills in reading comprehension, literary response and analysis, and vocabulary development. Each chapter offers culturally and historically significant literary works and a variety of high-interest informational pieces directly related to the literary selections—so that students understand how different structures are used to communicate meaning.

LITERARY RESPONSE AND ANALYSIS

Literary Response and Analysis

Illustrates one key literary standard that is developed in the chapter

Before You Read

Introduces standard instruction and reading skills students can apply to the upcoming selection

Directed-Reading Questions

Models the thinking and questioning strategies students need to build strong reading skills

Literary Response and Analysis

Guides comprehension of the selection and key literary standard with **Reading Check, Interpretation,** and **Evaluation** questions and a writing assignment. Links to **Writing Workshops** provide additional instruction for students

VOCABULARY DEVELOPMENT

Vocabulary Development

Focuses on the skills students need to build strong vocabularies with exposition and practice exercises

Test Practice

Tests mastery of multiple meanings, synonyms, or context clues using vocabulary learned from the chapter

READING COMPREHENSION INFORMATIONAL MATERIALS

Before You Read Informational Materials

Teaches essential skills students need to read, analyze, and evaluate informational texts

Consumer and Workplace Documents

Gives students practice with the kinds of reading they will need to navigate the real world

Read On

Helps students reach their goal of reading two million words annually with suggestions for independent reading of fiction and nonfiction

STANDARDS REVIEW

Provides standardized-test practice and a review of the chapter standards in reading, writing, listening and speaking, and vocabulary

Explore Multiple Avenues **to Reading Success**

U*niversal Access: Interactive Reading* offers alternative direct instruction in and practice of the grade-level standards taught in each chapter of ***Holt Literature and Language Arts.***

STUDENTS PRACTICE THE SKILLS OF GOOD READERS

Universal Access: Interactive Reading, a consumable worktext, offers students an interactive, hands-on approach to building reading, vocabulary, and literary-analysis skills.

SUPPORT THE STUDENT EDITION

Core Selections

from the *Student Edition* are reprinted interactively.

Students

- circle, underline, and respond in the margins
- focus on vocabulary, literary elements, and reading skills
- use graphic organizers to explore a selection

THE MOST DANGEROUS GAME

Richard Connell

PLOT

Underline the name of the island in line 4. What do you **predict** will happen in the story, based on this name?

Students might predict that Rainsford and Whitney will be shipwrecked on Ship-Trap Island.

"Off there to the right—somewhere—is a large island," said Whitney. "It's rather a mystery—"

"What island is it?" Rainsford asked.

"The old charts call it Ship-Trap Island," Whitney replied. "A suggestive name, isn't it? Sailors have a curious dread of the place. I don't know why. Some superstition—"

"Can't see it," remarked Rainsford, trying to peer through the dank tropical night that was palpable as it pressed its thick warm blackness in upon the yacht.

"You've good eyes," said Whitney, with a laugh, "and I've seen you pick off a moose moving in the brown fall bush at four hundred yards, but even you can't see four miles or so through a moonless Caribbean night."

6 Part 1 Chapter 1: Plot and Setting

BUILD INDEPENDENCE WITH ADDITIONAL READING

Literary selections not found in the ***Student Edition*** offer a literature-rich experience and extend students' practice.

Students

- acquire the habits of good readers
- practice reading and literary-analysis skills with new material
- gain additional practice with vocabulary development and standards

Standards Review

gives selection-specific review in standardized-test format.

Students

- review reading standards
- sharpen test-taking skills
- learn to analyze why answers are correct or incorrect

Crime on Mars

Arthur C. Clarke

WORD STUDY
Mars gets its name from the Roman god of war and destruction. Phobos (fō'bəs), the larger of Mars's two moons, gets its name from Greek mythology: Phobos is a son of Ares (Mars) and Aphrodite (Venus). *Phobos* is Greek for "fear."

SETTING
Setting is the time and place of a story. Underline the words in lines 5–6 that show *where* this part of the story takes place. *When* do you think this story takes place?
It takes place in the future.

WORD STUDY
Ocher (ō'kər) is a yellow or reddish-brown clay (line 9). Something that is ocher-tinted is dark yellow.

PLOT
Underline the clue in line 16 that suggests that the plot might be interrupted to flash back and tell what happened at an earlier time.

"We don't have much crime on Mars," said Detective-Inspector Rawlings, a little sadly. "In fact, that's the chief reason I'm going back to the Yard.[1] If I stayed here much longer, I'd get completely out of practice."

We were sitting in the main observation lounge of the Phobos Spaceport, looking out across the jagged sun-drenched crags of the tiny moon. The ferry rocket that had brought us up from Mars had left ten minutes ago and was now beginning the long fall back to the ocher-tinted globe hanging there against the stars. In half an hour we would be boarding the liner for Earth—a world on which most of the passengers had never set foot, but which they still called "home."

"At the same time," continued the Inspector, "now and then there's a case that makes life interesting. You're an art dealer, Mr. Maccar; I'm sure you heard about that spot of bother at Meridian City a couple of months ago."

"I don't think so," replied the plump, olive-skinned little man I'd taken for just another returning tourist. Presumably the Inspector had already checked through the passenger list; I wondered how much he knew about me, and tried to reassure myself that my conscience was—well, reasonably clear. After all, everybody took *something* out through Martian Customs—

"It's been rather well hushed up," said the Inspector, "but you can't keep these things quiet for long. Anyway, a jewel thief from Earth tried to steal Meridian Museum's greatest treasure—the Siren Goddess."

1. **the Yard:** popular term for "Scotland Yard," headquarters of the London Metropolitan Police.

40 Part 1 Chapter 1: Plot and Setting

OWN THE STORY

Crime on Mars

Time Line Time can be very confusing when you read a story within a story. Fill in the time line below, writing events from "Crime on Mars" in the order in which they happened.

Time	Event
Before the crime	An art collector hires Danny Weaver to steal Mars's greatest treasure—the Siren Goddess.
Friday afternoon	Danny checks into his hotel in Meridian West.
The next day	Danny checks out the museum.
That night	Danny hides in a gallery not open to the public.
After midnight	Danny works to remove the Siren Goddess and replace it with a replica.
Eight-thirty the next morning	The museum doors open, and the staff enters.

Standards Review

LITERATURE

Test Practice **The Most Dangerous Game**

Sharpen your test-taking skills. Complete the sample test item below. Then, check your answer, and read the explanation that appears in the right-hand column.

Sample Test Item	Explanation of the Correct Answer
Which of the following elements of **setting** does Rainsford *not* have to struggle against? A the ocean B quicksand C freezing cold D the jungle	The correct answer is *C*. Rainsford struggles against the ocean, encounters quicksand in the Death Swamp, and must fight through the jungle. There is no freezing cold; it is the tropics.

DIRECTIONS: Circle the letter of each correct response.

Reading Standard 3.4 (Grade 8 Review) Analyze the relevance of the setting (e.g., place, time, customs) to the mood, tone, and meaning of the text.

Reading Standard 3.6 Analyze and trace an author's development of time and sequence, including the use of complex literary devices (e.g., foreshadowing, flashbacks).

1. Which of the following passages from the story **foreshadows** danger?
   A "You've got good eyes," Whitney said.
   B "It will be light in Rio," promised Whitney.
   C "What island is it?" Rainsford asked.
   (D) "The old charts call it Ship-Trap Island," Whitney replied.
2. What is the **setting** for most of the action in this story?
   F A yacht
   G A castle
   (H) A jungle
   J The sea
3. Which of the following events happens first?
   A Rainsford kills Ivan.
   B Rainsford kills one of Zaroff's dogs.
   (C) Rainsford wounds Zaroff.
   D Rainsford dives into the sea.
4. Which of the following events happens last?
   (F) Rainsford and Zaroff fight in the bedroom.
   G Rainsford builds a Burmese tiger pit.
   H Rainsford builds a Malay man-catcher.
   J Rainsford falls overboard.

36 Part 1 Chapter 1: Plot and Setting

READ INFORMATIONAL AND REAL-WORLD TEXTS

Much of the reading students will do for life and for standardized tests will be nonfiction, informational pieces. Part 2 of ***Universal Access: Interactive Reading*** helps students develop the skills they need to read and analyze real-world texts such as magazine and newspaper articles, editorials, and essays. This section also offers vocabulary study and standardized-test practice.

TEACHING SUPPORT FOR TAILORING INSTRUCTION

Universal Access: Interactive Reading *Teacher's Edition* provides a variety of suggestions and plans to tailor instruction to your needs. This resource is divided into four sections:

- **Section 1: Guide to Teaching *Interactive Reading***
- **Section 2: Annotated Student Edition**
- **Section 3: Graphic Organizers**
- **Section 4: Transparencies for Modeling**

Discover Miles and Miles of **Program Reading Support**

Audio CD Library

Dramatic readings by professional actors bring to life nearly every reading selection in ***Holt Literature and Language Arts.***

Visual Connections Videocassette Program

Author biographies, interviews, historical summaries, and cross-curricular connections can motivate students and enrich and extend learning.

Audio CD Library: Summaries in Spanish

Recordings of summaries of virtually every selection in ***Holt Literature and Language Arts*** provide a valuable tool for English-language learners.

Audio CD Library: Selections in Spanish

Translations of key selections in ***Holt Literature and Language Arts*** assist students in reading and developing their own sense of a selection.

Vocabulary Development

- Exercises
- Worksheets
- Cumulative review

Progress Assessment: Reading, Vocabulary, and Literature

- Tests for each reading selection in the *Student Edition*
- Cumulative chapter tests

HRW LIBRARY

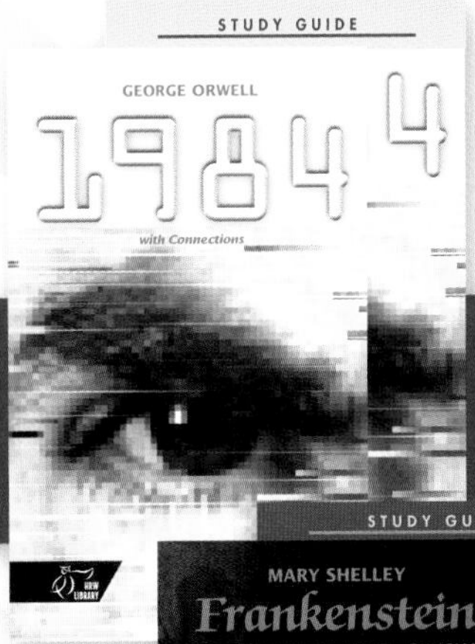

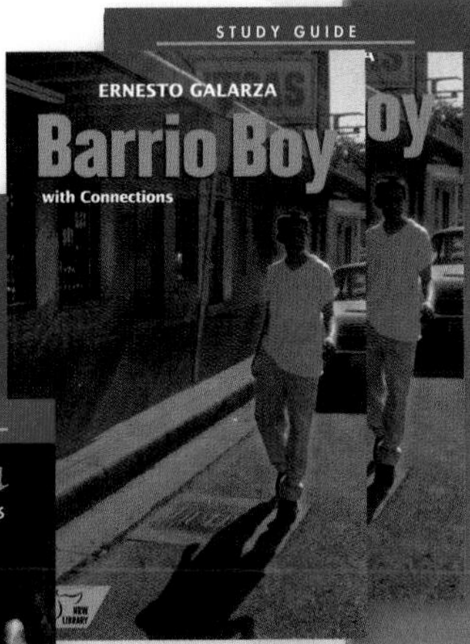

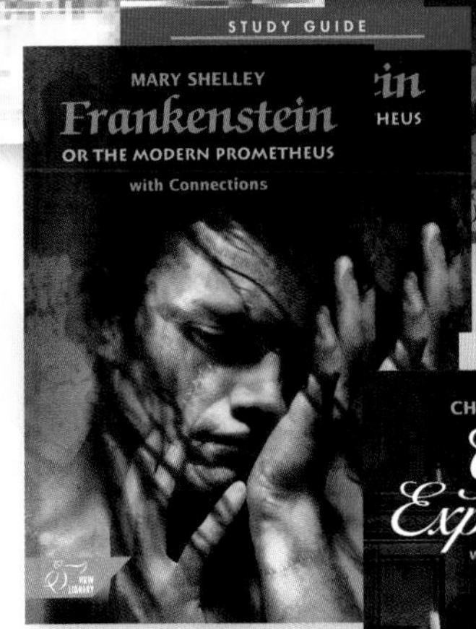

California HRW Library High School Titles

This extensive library program offers a comprehensive selection of the best literature for young adults, with readings drawn from a variety of cultures. Study guides help you motivate students and enhance their appreciation and understanding of classic and contemporary literature.

- A collection of titles ideal for helping students reach the annual two-million-word reading goal
- Connections that extend themes of core literature
- Connections drawn from essays, articles, interviews, and biographical sketches

Study Guides

This exceptional teacher resource provides the background, project suggestions, and vocabulary study that are so important to student involvement and understanding.

- Suggestions for differentiating instruction
- Reproducible masters for reading, vocabulary, and literary response

Give Students the "Write-of-Way" to **Standards Mastery**

Writing Workshops in each chapter of ***Holt Literature and Language Arts*** guide students through the writing process and help them master the California writing standards. Each workshop covers a different mode of writing, such as narration, persuasion, description, or exposition, and is a logical extension of the literary and informational materials covered in the chapter.

Prewriting

go.hrw.com

GO TO: go.hrw.com
KEYWORD: HLLA 9-1
FOR: Professional Model, Writer's Guides, and Reference Sources

Search Your Memory for Experiences

Magic Moments Your autobiographical narrative will be based on a specific, meaningful experience from your life. To come up with some experiences that you might write about, jog your memory by visiting a specific place that was important to you when you were younger, thinking about the first time you did something—rode a bike, for example—or listing special occasions you remember well.

Choose an Experience

Do the Write Thing Ask yourself the following questions to evaluate each experience that you thought of.

- Is this experience important to me? Why?
- What specific details can I give about this experience?

Prewriting

Step-by-step instruction helps students get started and think about the audience they want to reach. Additional guidance is available on the go.hrw.com Web site.

Quick guide

ADDING DETAILS

Questions/Tips	Examples
Events	
What sequence of events make up the experience? Were there important events that led up to or followed the experience? **TIP:** Match the **pace** of your narrative to the pace of the actual events—a quick pace for rapid events, a slow pace for more drawn-out events.	Sequence of events: walking in park, practicing building fires with Dad Later events: camp contest, camping in mountains
Places	
Where did the events happen? **TIP:** Use **concrete sensory details** to create effective images of the sights, sounds, and smells of the places you are describing.	city park on cool summer morning; wilderness; thickly leaved trees; pines and aspens; smell of trees
People	
Who was involved in the events? What did those people look like? What did they do and say? **TIP:** Use sensory details to describe **actions** and **gestures**. Use **dialogue**, actual words people say, to show each person's personality.	me—ages five, eleven, fourteen; Dad—young man dressed for work, wearing glasses; what Dad said as he taught me
Thoughts and Feelings	
What did I think and feel as the events unfolded? **TIP:** Use **interior monologue**, "thinking out loud," to share your thoughts with readers.	happiness during times with Dad; pleasure at collecting wood; luck for having such a dad; special bond

Quick Guide

Visually demonstrates to students what they need to do and provides examples they can emulate.

Writer's Framework

Shows students how to structure their papers

Writing

Writing an Autobiographical Narrative

A Writer's Framework

Introduction	Body	Conclusion
• Begin with an engaging opening. • Supply background information so readers understand the context of the narrative. • Hint at the significance of the experience.	• Discuss the sequence of events that make up your experience. • Discuss the important events that led up to or followed your experience. • Include plenty of details about people, places, and events.	• Look back at the experience from the present time. • Reflect on what you learned or how you changed as a result of this experience. • Reveal the significance of the experience.

A Writer's Model

A Campfire Girl

Do people make campfires anymore? I suppose they do, but building campfires is prohibited in many places now. Even if rangers do not ban campfires, environmentally aware people agree that no one should be allowed to pick the ground bare of wood and scar the land with fire rings. Still, I am a campfire girl at heart. Even though I dutifully use camp stoves in the mountains and in the campgrounds, I still love a small blaze to warm my hands, to dry soggy socks, and to stare into when the night sky, far from the glow of city lights, is deep black.

INTRODUCTION
Engaging opening
Background information
Hint at meaning

My love for campfires all started because of a leisurely stroll in a park in New York City. When I was a tidy little skirt-wearing five-year-old, my family lived in New York for a summer. My father and I would go out early, when it was still cool, to walk the dog. Dad would be dressed for work, his shoes treading the asphalt path as I happily did a quickstep along beside him.

BODY
First event of experience
People and place details
Feelings

One morning as my father threw sticks for the dog, I started picking up sticks of my own. Always ready to play and teach, my dad crouched down and said, "Here, let me show you the right way to build a campfire. Once you learn how, you can build a fire in the middle of a tornado." He took my sticks and helped me gather others, graduated in size from tiny twigs to hefty branches. Gently propping the twigs

Second event of experience
Dialogue
Specific action with sensory details

(continued)

Writer's Model

Demonstrates the workshop assignment with annotations to help students understand the structure and development of an essay

Universal Access: Writing, Listening, and Speaking

Designed to support instruction for students at various levels, this resource provides worksheets and transparencies to support instruction for each **Writing Workshop.** Transparencies include motivating visual **Writing Prompts.**

Grammar Link MINI-LESSON

Verb Tenses: What Time Is It?

The tense of a verb indicates the time of the action or the state of being expressed by the verb. Different tenses serve different purposes. "A Christmas Memory" is told in the present tense, although Capote uses the past and future tenses at times.

Tense	Example	Purpose
Present	"On the farther shore, Queenie shakes herself and trembles."	• expresses an action that is occurring now • shows a customary action • expresses a general truth
Past	"'I made you another kite.'"	• expresses an action that occurred in the past but is not occurring now
Future	"'Buddy, do you think Mrs. Roosevelt will serve our cake at dinner?'"	• expresses an action that will occur

PRACTICE

1. Choose two paragraphs without dialogue in the story. Rewrite them in the past tense. How does the change in tense change the feeling of the story? Why do you think Capote chose to write in the present tense?
2. Take a sample of your writing, and underline the verbs. Label each verb tense. Are your tenses consistent?

For more help, see Tense and Consistency of Tense in the *Holt Handbook,* pages 156–162.

Grammar Link

Shows students how to identify and correct common grammatical errors

Guidelines: Writing an Autobiographical Narrative

Evaluation Questions	Tips	Revision Techniques
1 Does the introduction include an engaging opening, background information, and a hint at the significance of the experience?	**Bracket** the engaging opening and background information. **Underline** the hint about the significance.	**Add** an engaging opening and background information. **Add** a sentence or two that suggests the significance of the event.
2 Does the narrative include details about events, people, and places?	**Circle** details. If you have fewer than three circles in each paragraph, revise.	**Add** details about events, people, and places to the paragraph. **Elaborate** on existing details with sensory language or dialogue.
3 Does the narrative include details about the narrator's thoughts and feelings?	**Highlight** sentences that contain the narrator's thoughts or feelings. If there isn't at least one such detail in the narrative, revise.	**Elaborate** on details by answering the questions, "What did I think?" or "How did I feel?" Consider using interior monologue.
4 Is the order of the events clear?	**Number** the events in chronological order.	**Rearrange** events in chronological order, if necessary, and **add** transitional words and phrases to show the order.
5 Does the conclusion discuss the significance of the experience?	**Underline** sentences in the conclusion that reveal the meaning of the experience.	**Add** sentences that indirectly or directly explain the importance of the experience.

Editor in Charge

Offers a three-step process with specific actions for students to take to locate and correct weaknesses in their papers

Style Guidelines

Evaluation Question	Tip	Revision Technique
Does the narrative include precise language?	Pick four sentences in each paragraph. In each, **circle** the nouns and adjectives. Are the nouns and adjectives vivid and precise?	**Replace** at least two imprecise nouns and adjectives per paragraph with more precise language. (Use a dictionary or thesaurus if necessary.)

Style Guidelines

Encourages students to revise their papers a second time for precise and effective language

MASTERING THE CALIFORNIA STANDARDS

Listening and Speaking

Widen the Road to **Excellent Oral Communication Skills**

Holt Literature and Language Arts prepares your students to master the California listening and speaking standards with workshops that guide students in delivering focused, coherent presentations and in evaluating a variety of oral and media communications. Each **Listening and Speaking Workshop** is tied to the **Writing Workshops** and thus focuses on a different kind of presentation, such as narration, exposition, persuasion, research, and response to literature.

Listening & Speaking Workshop

Participating in a Debate

Speaking Assignment
Listening and Speaking 1.5 With other students, stage a debate in which you present both sides of an issue.

"That's debatable" is an expression people often use to cast doubt on something that has just been said. If a statement is debatable, good arguments can be made both for and against it. While a persuasive essay or speech presents only one side of an issue, a **debate** involves two teams on opposite sides of an issue who publicly compete for the hearts and minds of an audience.

Prepare for a Debate

A Winning Proposition If you are asked to participate in a debate, you must first know what proposition you will be debating. A **proposition** focuses on one narrow, controversial issue. The proposition suggests a change in the **status quo**—the current state of things—and is worded as a **resolution.** An example of a proposition is "Resolved: That Chavez High School should build a parking lot west of the main soccer fields." Most often the person in charge of the debate assigns the proposition that the teams will debate.

Participants in a debate are usually also assigned a side of the proposition—pro (for) or con (against). If you are participating in a debate, your challenge is to present a good argument, based on solid reasoning, for your side of the issue—regardless of your personal feelings on the issue.

Who's Who? A traditional debate requires two teams of two people each, plus a chairperson in charge of running the debate.

Affirmative Team The **affirmative team** argues that the proposition should be accepted. Because the affirmative team argues for a change in the status quo, it has the **burden of proof**—an obligation to prove that change must be made.

Negative Team The **negative team** argues that the proposition should be rejected and that the status quo should remain unchanged.

Chairperson A **chairperson** rules over a debate, keeping the debate organized, courteous, and fair. A debater may appeal to the chairperson if he or she believes that the other team has broken any rules.

Research the Proposition To debate effectively, you must prepare by thoroughly researching the proposition. First, identify the differences between your position and the other team's position. These differences often revolve around the following questions.

- Is there a significant problem?
- What is causing the problem?

Listening and Speaking 1.5 Recognize and use elements of classical speech forms in formulating rational arguments and applying the art of debate. **2.5** Deliver persuasive arguments.

302 Chapter 4 Comparing Themes • Evaluating Arguments: Pro and Con

TESTS FOR EVIDENCE Quick guide

Evidence should have . . .	That means . . .
credibility	evidence should come from a source recognized as an authority on the subject. The source should be objective rather than biased toward one side of the issue.
validity	evidence should clearly support the position it is being used to support. Valid evidence should not be interpreted to support the opposite side of the issue.
relevance	evidence should have a close, logical relationship to the reason it supports. Relevant information is also recent enough to directly relate to the issue being addressed.

Quick Guide

Offers cogent tips, examples, and explanations to increase students' understanding and success

Present Your Ideas Your reasons and evidence will have the greatest impact if you are well prepared. As you speak, maintain eye contact with your audience and speak slowly, clearly, and loudly enough that everyone can understand you. Use your voice and facial expressions to emphasize important points.

Speaking in Turn A traditional debate follows this schedule. Each team member delivers one constructive and one rebuttal speech.

TRADITIONAL DEBATE SCHEDULE

First Part: Constructive Speeches		Second Part: Rebuttal Speeches
(10 minutes each)	Intermission	(5 minutes each)
1st Affirmative Team Speaker		1st Negative Team Speaker
1st Negative Team Speaker		1st Affirmative Team Speaker
2nd Affirmative Team Speaker		2nd Negative Team Speaker
2nd Negative Team Speaker		2nd Affirmative Team Speaker

Practice and Apply

Encourages students to follow easily understood steps to construct, deliver, and evaluate a presentation

And the Winner Is . . . Judges usually determine the winner of a debate. Occasionally, an audience may vote to determine the winning team. To make your own judgment about which team won a debate, answer the questions in the following chart. You can use the chart to evaluate both the affirmative and negative teams.

QUESTIONS FOR JUDGING A DEBATE

Content	Delivery
1. What arguments did the team provide to prove or disprove that a significant problem exists? Were these arguments effective? Explain why or why not.	1. How confident and well prepared were the speakers? How could they improve their delivery?
2. Did the team convince you that the proposition is or is not the best solution to solving the problem (if any exists)? Explain.	2. How well did each speaker maintain eye contact? How effective were the rate and volume at which each spoke?
3. What reasons and evidence did the team provide to support the case? How credible, valid, and relevant was the evidence?	3. Describe any incidents in which the speakers did not observe proper debate etiquette.
4. How did the team refute and rebut arguments made by the opposing team? Were the rebuttal speeches effective? Explain why or why not.	

PRACTICE & APPLY 5 Follow the steps in this workshop to plan, participate in, and judge a debate.

Listening and Speaking Workshop: Participating in a Debate 305

Writing, Listening and Speaking Videocassette Program

This package offers

- differentiated support and practice
- graphic organizers
- teaching transparencies
- videocassettes
- worksheets
- teaching notes

Holt Handbook: Your Road Map to Success in **Grammar, Usage, and Mechanics**

An integral part of the ***Holt Literature and Language Arts*** program, the ***Holt Handbook*** answers the call for students to master language skills at levels demanded by the twenty-first century. This invaluable handbook offers teachers and students a method for focusing on the written and oral English-language conventions required by the standards.

Give Your Students the Power of Language

Part 1: Grammar, Usage, and Mechanics helps students acquire the building blocks of language: words, phrases, clauses, and the knowledge of correct capitalization, punctuation, and spelling.

Part 2: Sentences is divided into three main areas of instruction: Writing Complete Sentences, Writing Effective Sentences, and Sentence Diagramming.

Part 3: Resources includes Manuscript Form, History of English, Test Smarts, and Grammar at a Glance.

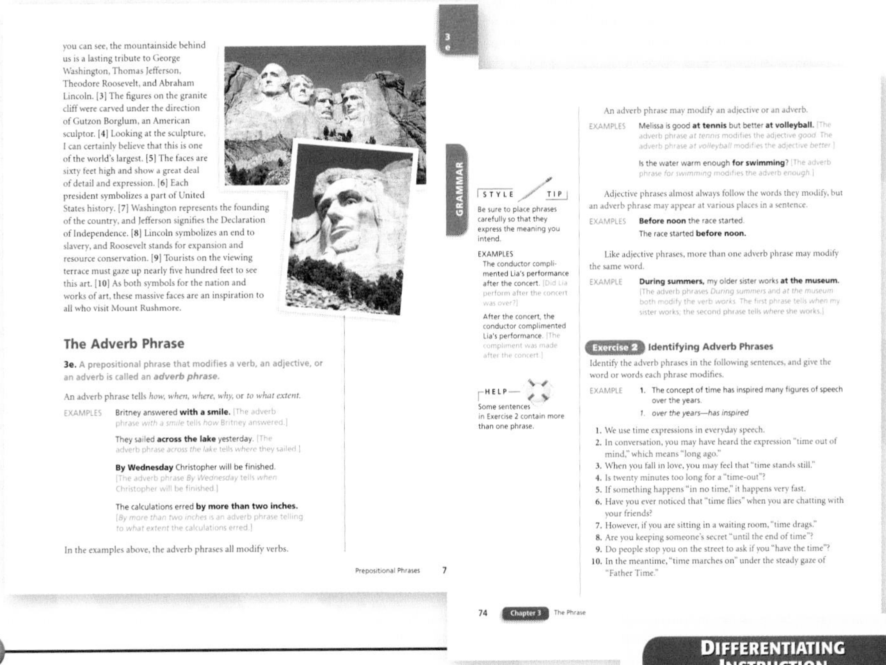
3
e

you can see, the mountainside behind us is a lasting tribute to George Washington, Thomas Jefferson, Theodore Roosevelt, and Abraham Lincoln. [3] The figures on the granite cliff were carved under the direction of Gutzon Borglum, an American sculptor. [4] Looking at the sculpture, I can certainly believe that this is one of the world's largest. [5] The faces are sixty feet high and show a great deal of detail and expression. [6] Each president symbolizes a part of United States history. [7] Washington represents the founding of the country, and Jefferson signifies the Declaration of Independence. [8] Lincoln symbolizes an end to slavery, and Roosevelt stands for expansion and resource conservation. [9] Tourists on the viewing terrace must gaze up nearly five hundred feet to see this art. [10] As both symbols for the nation and works of art, these massive faces are an inspiration to all who visit Mount Rushmore.

The Adverb Phrase

3e. A prepositional phrase that modifies a verb, an adjective, or an adverb is called an ***adverb phrase.***

An adverb phrase tells *how, when, where, why,* or *to what extent.*

EXAMPLES Britney answered **with a smile.** [The adverb phrase *with a smile* tells *how* Britney answered.]

They sailed **across the lake** yesterday. [The adverb phrase *across the lake* tells *where* they sailed.]

By Wednesday Christopher will be finished. [The adverb phrase *By Wednesday* tells *when* Christopher will be finished.]

The calculations erred **by more than two inches.** [*By more than two inches* is an adverb phrase telling *to what extent* the calculations erred.]

In the examples above, the adverb phrases all modify verbs.

Prepositional Phrases 7

GRAMMAR

STYLE TIP

Be sure to place phrases carefully so that they express the meaning you intend.

EXAMPLES

The conductor complimented Lia's performance after the concert. [Did Lia perform after the concert was over?]

After the concert, the conductor complimented Lia's performance. [The compliment was made after the concert.]

HELP

Some sentences in Exercise 2 contain more than one phrase.

An adverb phrase may modify an adjective or an adverb.

EXAMPLES Melissa is good **at tennis** but better **at volleyball.** [The adverb phrase *at tennis* modifies the adjective *good.* The adverb phrase *at volleyball* modifies the adjective *better.*]

Is the water warm enough **for swimming**? [The adverb phrase *for swimming* modifies the adverb *enough.*]

Adjective phrases almost always follow the words they modify, but an adverb phrase may appear at various places in a sentence.

EXAMPLES **Before noon** the race started.

The race started **before noon.**

Like adjective phrases, more than one adverb phrase may modify the same word.

EXAMPLE **During summers,** my older sister works **at the museum.** [The adverb phrases *During summers* and *at the museum* both modify the verb *works.* The first phrase tells *when* my sister works; the second phrase tells *where* she works.]

Exercise 2 **Identifying Adverb Phrases**

Identify the adverb phrases in the following sentences, and give the word or words each phrase modifies.

EXAMPLE 1. The concept of time has inspired many figures of speech over the years.

1. over the years—has inspired

1. We use time expressions in everyday speech.
2. In conversation, you may have heard the expression "time out of mind," which means "long ago."
3. When you fall in love, you may feel that "time stands still."
4. Is twenty minutes too long for a "time-out"?
5. If something happens "in no time," it happens very fast.
6. Have you ever noticed that "time flies" when you are chatting with your friends?
7. However, if you are sitting in a waiting room, "time drags."
8. Are you keeping someone's secret "until the end of time"?
9. Do people stop you on the street to ask if you "have the time"?
10. In the meantime, "time marches on" under the steady gaze of "Father Time."

74 Chapter 3 The Phrase

Warriner's Three-Step Approach to Learning Grammar

An English teacher for thirty years, John Warriner developed the original instructional approach used in the grammar, usage, and mechanics chapters. This logical approach is based on a three-step process:

- Teach students the rule.
- Show examples of the rule in action.
- Provide immediate practice and review to reinforce the skill.

Color-coding—rule in red, explanations in blue, and practice in black—makes instruction easy for students to follow.

Annotated Teacher's Edition: Suggestions That Keep All Students Involved

Suggestions for differentiating instruction are integrated into lessons to support all students.

Strategies are included to help students make connections between the sentence, grammar, usage, and mechanics skills you're teaching and the writing, science, and social studies skills they need to succeed in other classes.

DIFFERENTIATING INSTRUCTION

Special Education Students

Give students pictures of people running, playing, swimming, and so on. Have students working in pairs take turns asking one another to state what action is being performed and who is doing the action.

English-Language Learners

Japanese and Korean. In Japanese, the subject is always followed by the func
the
i (ee
gua
wor
be f
tion

CONTENT-AREA CONNECTIONS

Geography/Art

Planning a Cruise. Have students plan a cruise to a location they have studied. Suggest that students draw ornamental maps including geographic names that are correctly capitalized.

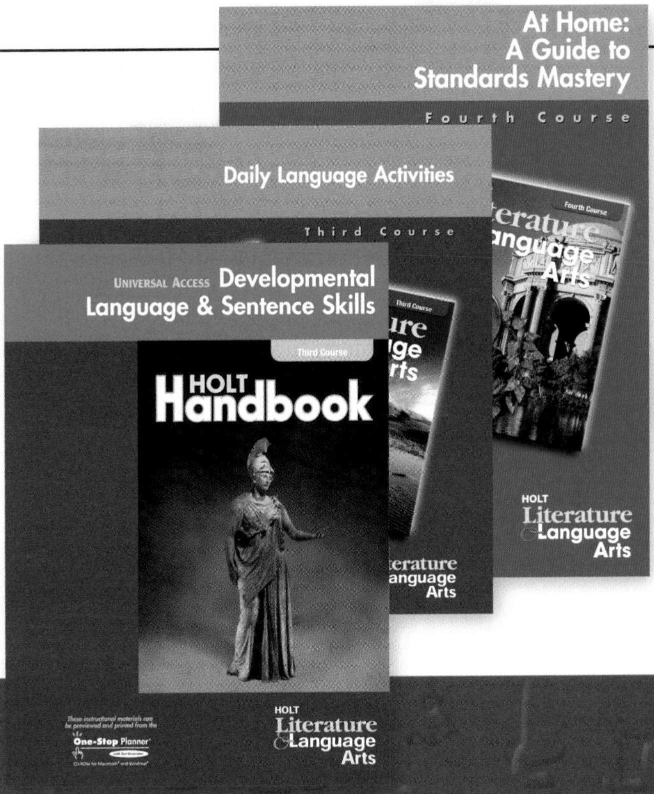

Additional Practice and Strategies to Help Students Succeed

Teaching resources for the program include

- *Universal Access: Developmental Language and Sentence Skills*
- *Language and Sentence Skills Practice*
- *Progress Assessment for the Holt Handbook*
- *Daily Language Activities*
- *Diagnostic and Summative Assessments: California Standards Mastery*
- *At Home: A Guide to Standards Mastery*

Technology resources for the program include

- *One-Stop Planner® CD-ROM with ExamView® Pro Test Generator*
- **go.hrw.com** Web site

Pave the Way Toward **Each Student's Success**

The ***Holt Literature and Language Arts*** program provides support to help you differentiate instruction for your classroom's specific needs so that every student has an equal opportunity to meet or exceed the California standards. This support is integrated throughout the program (in both the textbooks and the teaching resources), allowing you easy access to alternative methods of planning, instruction, and assessment.

DIAGNOSE AND ASSESS STUDENTS' NEEDS

Diagnostic and Summative Assessments

Determines students' levels of preparation and provides quarterly and summative assessment of standards mastery

Progress Assessment

Provides ongoing evaluations of students' skill development and understanding selection by selection

DIFFERENTIATING INSTRUCTION

REVIEW STANDARD

Special Education Students
Students may be overwhelmed if presented with the delivery techniques all at once. You may want instead to elicit from students the various techniques by playing for them a videotape of a speech and pausing the tape from time to time to ask students to comment on the speaker's delivery. Lead them to identify and discuss the techniques one by one as you write students' comments on the chalkboard. Ask students for their opinions on hether or not the techniques are fective. Then, have students work ith a helper to read the chart and etermine how the descriptions of e techniques match their own omments on the specific speech.

Annotated Teacher's Edition

Offers strategies and techniques to tailor instruction for advanced students, English-language learners, special education students, and learners having difficulty with content. Included are integrated assessments, guided practice, and links to alternative instruction.

DIFFERENTIATING INSTRUCTION

English-Language Learners
The punctuation of quotations differs greatly from country to country. Before students read **A Writer's Model,** you may want to review with them the standard American English conventions involving punctuating quotations. As students read the model they can identify the rules of punctuation the model's quotations follow.

OFFER SUPPORT FOR ALL STUDENTS

Universal Access: Interactive Reading

Offers students a consumable worktext to interact with reading selections.

- **Reading Strategy** helps students meet a California standard
- **Make the Connection** engages students and helps them interact with the text
- **Graphic Organizers** facilitate directed reading

Universal Access: Writing, Listening, and Speaking
Videocassettes and Worksheets

- Supports instruction and assignments in the *Student Edition*
- Includes worksheets, transparencies, and video segments for each **Writing Workshop** and each **Listening and Speaking Workshop**

Universal Access: Developmental Language and Sentence Skills
Support for the Holt Handbook

- Includes remedial worksheets for instruction, practice, and reinforcement of lessons in the ***Holt Handbook***
- Targets those students who have not yet mastered specific grammar, usage, and mechanics or sentence-skills concepts

Universal Access: Lesson Plans for Language Development

- Includes lesson plans with alternative teaching strategies
- Offers exercises for English-language learners and special education students

MASTERING THE CALIFORNIA STANDARDS

Assessment

Take the High Road to **Assessing Language Arts Proficiency**

Because assessment is so important in determining what to teach, how much your students are learning, and whether your students have achieved mastery, ***Holt Literature and Language Arts*** provides a complete standards-based assessment package that is fully integrated into the program. Carefully planned and sequenced assessment options throughout the *Student Edition, Annotated Teacher's Edition,* and assessment support materials provide the following:

- **Entry-level assessments**
- **Frequent ongoing assessments**
- **Summative assessments**

STANDARDS REVIEW

Literary Response and Analysis

Test Practice

Comparing a Theme Across Genres

DIRECTIONS: Read the following short story and poem. Then, read each multiple-choice question that follows, and write the letter of the best response.

What Happened During the Ice Storm

Jim Heynen

One winter there was a freezing rain. "How beautiful!" people said when things outside started to shine with ice. But the freezing rain kept coming. Tree branches glistened like glass. Then broke like glass. Ice thickened on the windows until everything outside blurred. Farmers moved their livestock into the barns, and most animals were safe. But not the pheasants. Their eyes froze shut.

Some farmers went ice-skating down the gravel roads with clubs to harvest pheasants that sat helplessly in the roadside ditches. The boys went out into the freezing rain to find pheasants too. They saw dark spots along a fence. Pheasants, all right. Five or six of them. The boys slid their feet along slowly, trying not to break the ice that covered the snow. They slid up close to the pheasants. The pheasants pulled their heads down between their wings. They couldn't tell how easy it was to see them huddled there.

The boys stood still in the icy rain. Their breath came out in slow puffs of steam. The pheasants' breath came out in quick little white puffs. Some of them lifted their heads and turned them from side to side, but they were blindfolded with ice and didn't flush. The boys had not brought clubs, or sacks, or anything but themselves. They stood over the pheasants, turning their own heads, looking at each other, each expecting the other to do something. To pounce on a pheasant, or to yell "Bang!"

Pages 306–309 cover **Reading Standard 3.2** Compare and contrast the presentation of a similar theme or topic across genres to explain how the selection of genre shapes the theme or topic.

306 Chapter 4 Comparing Themes • Evaluating Arguments: Pro and Con

ASSESSMENT LINKED TO INSTRUCTION

The *Student Edition* provides standards-review tests at the end of each chapter for ongoing assessment of reading, writing, and listening and speaking standards.

The *Annotated Teacher's Edition* helps teachers make informed instructional decisions and provides additional opportunities to monitor students' progress. Look for features labeled

- **Guided Practice**
- **Reading Mini-Lesson**
- **Preview Vocabulary**

GUIDED PRACTICE

Monitoring students' progress. To assess students' understanding of the story, ask them to create a two-column chart. Have them list the problems and difficulties Luis faces in the first column. Have students describe the way each problem is addressed or resolved in the second column.

ENTRY-LEVEL, ONGOING, AND SUMMATIVE ASSESSMENTS TO TEST FOR PROFICIENCY

Diagnostic and Summative Assessments: California Standards Mastery

- Includes entry-level tests (pretests of essential prior knowledge and skills)
- Includes tests (summative assessments required by California)
- Provides tools to monitor student progress through tracking student mastery and recording and analyzing scores

Progress Assessment: Reading, Vocabulary, and Literature

- Offers selection tests for reading comprehension, reading skills, literary elements, and vocabulary

Progress Assessment: Writing, Listening, and Speaking

- Includes assessment of writing, listening, and speaking standards in a variety of test formats, including standardized tests
- Provides scales and rubrics for each workshop assignment

Progress Assessment: Holt Handbook English-Language Conventions

- Contains chapter tests in standardized-test formats for the sentence and grammar, usage, and mechanics chapters in the ***Holt Handbook***

One-Stop Planner Test Generator

- Versatile and easy-to-use test generator provides easily edited, multiple versions of test items for each chapter in ***Holt Literature and Language Arts*** and the ***Holt Handbook***
- Provides a quick and useful way to find test items for each chapter in ***Holt Literature and Language Arts***
- Included as part of the ***One-Stop Planner CD-ROM*** program

One-Stop Planner®

with ExamView® PRO
Test Generator

Explore the World of **Technology and the Information Highway**

VISUAL AND VIDEO RESOURCES

Fine Art Transparencies

- Features stunning examples of classic and contemporary art to complement the selections in ***Holt Literature and Language Arts***
- Challenges students to analyze ideas and culture using transparencies of fine art
- Helps students explore literary characters and ideas through visual representations
- Encourages students to make cross-curricular connections

Daily Language Activities Transparencies

- Reinforces reading and writing skills covered in ***Holt Literature and Language Arts*** and grammar, usage, and mechanics skills covered in the ***Holt Handbook***

Writing, Listening and Speaking Videocassette Program

- Provides support and practice for the writing, listening, and speaking skills addressed in ***Holt Literature and Language Arts***
- Teaching Notes pages include suggestions for using Think Sheets, Independent Practice worksheets, Project-Planning Guides, transparencies, and video segments
- Includes a videocassette that provides models and practice for the Listening and Speaking assignments

Visual Connections Videocassette Program

- Enriches and extends course content with video segments for biographies, interviews, historical summaries, and cross-curricular connections
- Teacher's Manual includes background information, cross-curricular connections, additional video suggestions, bibliographies, and worksheets

CD-ROM RESOURCES

Audio CD Library

- Makes literature come alive with dramatic readings by professional actors. Includes nearly every reading selection in ***Holt Literature and Language Arts***

Audio CD Library: Summaries in Spanish

- Includes summaries of virtually every selection in ***Holt Literature and Language Arts*** to assist English-language learners in their language acquisition

Audio CD Library: Selections in Spanish

- Comprised of core selections, giving students an opportunity to listen to a selection in their home language before reading it in English

Audio CD Tutorial: Interactive Reading

- Gives students their own tutor as two voices guide them through ***Universal Access: Interactive Reading***

One-Stop Planner CD-ROM with ExamView Pro Test Generator

- Simplifies lesson planning and management
- Includes all the teaching resources for ***Holt Literature and Language Arts*** and the ***Holt Handbook***
- Includes printable program resources and an easy-to-use test generator
- Offers previews of all teaching resources, including assessments and worksheets linked to the *Student Edition*
- Launches directly to the **go.hrw.com** Web site

One-Stop Planner®
with ExamView® PRO
Test Generator

INTERNET RESOURCES

go.hrw.com

Internet references throughout the *Student Edition* direct students to a new Web site for California users of ***Holt Literature and Language Arts.*** This site provides standards-based activities and projects for each chapter and workshop and allows students to put their reading, writing, and listening and speaking skills into action.

When students see the **go.hrw.com** logo and a keyword in the textbook, they can go to the **go.hrw.com** site, enter the keyword, and connect instantly to activities and projects for the chapter or workshop they are studying. Additional references to the site appear in the *Annotated Teacher's Edition.*

MASTERING THE CALIFORNIA STANDARDS

Instructional Planning and Support

Your Road Map to Teaching **the Literature You Love and the Standards, Too**

Helping your students learn to appreciate and participate actively in building reading, writing, and grammar skills while guiding them to meet and exceed the California standards may seem like a Herculean task. That's why the ***Holt Literature and Language Arts*** program is so carefully sequenced and why the *Annotated Teacher's Edition* provides such easy-to-use planning resources. Now you can teach the literature you love and rely on resources built into ***Holt Literature and Language Arts*** to make planning for, integration of, and preparation for standards mastery an easy, integral part of your time in the classroom.

Instructional Sequencing That Helps You Cover It All

Holt Literature and Language Arts provides specific sequencing suggestions to ensure complete coverage of grade-level standards, prerequisite instruction, frequent and effective testing, and remediation and reteaching opportunities.

A variety of instructional options are carefully outlined in both the *Annotated Teacher's Edition* chapter interleaf pages and the resource ***On Course: Mapping Instruction.***

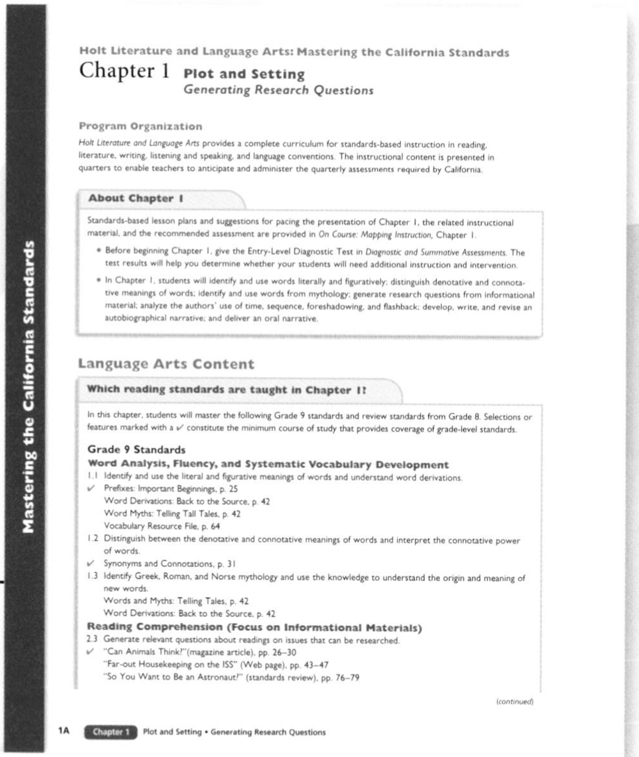

Mastering the California Standards

Holt Literature and Language Arts: Mastering the California Standards

Chapter 1 **Plot and Setting**
Generating Research Questions

Program Organization

Holt Literature and Language Arts provides a complete curriculum for standards-based instruction in reading, literature, writing, listening and speaking, and language conventions. The instructional content is presented in quarters to enable teachers to anticipate and administer the quarterly assessments required by California.

About Chapter 1

Standards-based lesson plans and suggestions for pacing the presentation of Chapter 1, the related instructional material, and the recommended assessment are provided in *On Course: Mapping Instruction*, Chapter 1.

- Before beginning Chapter 1, give the Entry-Level Diagnostic Test in *Diagnostic and Summative Assessments.* The test results will help you determine whether your students will need additional instruction and intervention.
- In Chapter 1, students will identify and use words literally and figuratively; distinguish denotative and connotative meanings of words; identify and use words from mythology; generate research questions from informational material; analyze the authors' use of time, sequence, foreshadowing, and flashback; develop, write, and revise an autobiographical narrative; and deliver an oral narrative.

Language Arts Content

Which reading standards are taught in Chapter 1?

In this chapter, students will master the following Grade 9 standards and review standards from Grade 8. Selections or features marked with a ✓ constitute the minimum course of study that provides coverage of grade-level standards.

Grade 9 Standards
Word Analysis, Fluency, and Systematic Vocabulary Development
1.1 Identify and use the literal and figurative meanings of words and understand word derivations.
✓ Prefixes: Important Beginnings, p. 25
Word Derivations: Back to the Source, p. 42
Word Myths: Telling Tall Tales, p. 42
Vocabulary Resource File, p. 64
1.2 Distinguish between the denotative and connotative meanings of words and interpret the connotative power of words.
✓ Synonyms and Connotations, p. 31
1.3 Identify Greek, Roman, and Norse mythology and use the knowledge to understand the origin and meaning of new words.
Words and Myths: Telling Tales, p. 42
Word Derivations: Back to the Source, p. 42
Reading Comprehension (Focus on Informational Materials)
2.3 Generate relevant questions about readings on issues that can be researched.
✓ "Can Animals Think?"(magazine article), pp. 26–30
"Far-out Housekeeping on the ISS" (Web page), pp. 43–47
"So You Want to Be an Astronaut?" (standards review), pp. 76–79

(continued)

1A Chapter 1 Plot and Setting • Generating Research Questions

CHAPTER 1 RESOURCES: READING

Planning
- *One-Stop Planner CD-ROM with Test Generator*
- *On Course: Mapping Instruction*
- *At Home: A Guide to Standards Mastery*
- *At Home: In Spanish*
- *Supporting Instruction in Spanish*

Reading
- *Interactive Reading*

Differentiating Instruction
- *Lesson Plans for Language Development*

Vocabulary
- *Vocabulary Development*
  - Cumulative Vocabulary Review, pp. 5–6

Grammar
- *Holt Handbook*
  - Tense and Consistency of Tense, pp. 156–162

Assessment
- *Progress Assessment of Reading*
  - Chapter Test

Planning Made Easy

Point-of-use references to chapter resources in the ***Holt Literature and Language Arts Annotated Teacher's Edition*** help you plan your lessons.

A Map to Chart Your Course

On-Course: Mapping Instruction: A Teacher's Guide for Planning charts the instructional path between ***Holt Literature and Language Arts*** and the ***Holt Handbook.***

- Includes planning charts that give overviews of the content covered for each quarter, chapter, and week
- Provides weekly lesson plans with annotated suggestions for the program features that address learners having difficulty, on-level learners, and advanced learners
- Offers a minimum course of study to ensure that standards are covered, because there is never enough time to do everything

One-Stop Planner®
with ExamView® PRO
Test Generator

Point and Click Your Way to Planning Lessons

The ***One-Stop Planner CD-ROM with ExamView Pro Test Generator*** is an all-in-one planning tool that includes all the teaching resources for ***Holt Literature and Language Arts*** and the ***Holt Handbook,*** as well as valuable planning and assessment tools.

Features of the ***One-Stop Planner*** include

- printable program resources
- easy-to-use test generator
- previews of all teaching resources, including assessments and worksheets linked to the *Student Edition*
- direct launch to the **go.hrw.com** Web site

Teaching resources are presented in point-and-click formats. To preview an assessment or to print out worksheets for your students, simply make your selection, and click your mouse.

The road to success lies ahead.

Holt Literature and Language Arts: Mastering the California Standards

Chapter 1 Plot and Setting
Synthesizing Sources

Program Organization

Holt Literature and Language Arts provides a complete curriculum for standards-based instruction in reading, literature, writing, listening and speaking, and language conventions. The instructional content is presented in quarters to enable teachers to anticipate and administer the quarterly assessments required by California.

About Chapter 1

Standards-based lesson plans and suggestions for pacing the presentation of Chapter 1, the related instructional material, and the recommended assessment are provided in *On Course: Mapping Instruction,* Chapter 1.

- Before beginning Chapter 1, give the Entry-Level Diagnostic Test in *Diagnostic and Summative Assessments.* The test results will help you determine whether your students will need additional instruction and intervention.
- In Chapter 1, students will identify and use words literally and figuratively; distinguish between denotative and connotative words; synthesize content from several sources; analyze and trace the development of time and sequence in a narrative; write an autobiographical narrative; and deliver an oral narrative.

Language Arts Content

Which reading standards are taught in Chapter 1?

In this chapter, students will master the following Grade 10 standards and review standards from Grade 8. Selections or features marked with a ✔ constitute the minimum course of study that provides coverage of grade-level standards.

Grade 10 Standards

Word Analysis, Fluency, and Systematic Vocabulary Development

1.1 Identify and use the literal and figurative meanings of words and understand word derivations.
✔ Word Analysis: Prefixes, p. 20
Analogies: Two Word Pairs with the Same Relationship, p. 29–30
Etymologies: Words Tell Their Stories, p. 42
Vocabulary Resource File, p. 54

1.2 Distinguish between the denotative and connotative meanings of words and interpret the connotative power of words.
The Power of Connotations, p. 54

Reading Comprehension (Focus on Informational Materials)

2.4 Synthesize the content from several sources or works by a single author dealing with a single issue; paraphrase the ideas and connect them to other sources and related topics to demonstrate comprehension.
✔ "Double Daddy" (newspaper article)
"Diary of a Mad Blender" (newspaper article)
✔ "The Child's View of Working Parents" (magazine article)
} pp. 21–29
"What Price Glory?" (standards review)
"Deprived of Parent Time?" (standards review)
} pp. 66–69

(continued)

(continued)

Literary Response and Analysis

3.6 Analyze and trace an author's development of time and sequence, including the use of complex literary devices.
"Plot: A Sequence of Events" (standards essay), pp. 2–3
✓ "Contents of the Dead Man's Pocket" (short story), pp. 4–19
"The Leap" (short story), pp. 31–41

Review Standard Grade 8

Reading 3.4 Analyze the relevance of the setting to the mood, tone, and meaning of the text.
"Setting: Putting Us There" (standards essay), pp. 44–45
"The Pedestrian" (short story), pp. 46–53

Which writing, and listening and speaking standards are taught in Chapter 1?

Writing Strategies

1.1 Establish a controlling impression or coherent thesis that conveys a clear and distinctive perspective on the subject and maintain a consistent tone and focus throughout the piece of writing.
Reflect on Your Experience, p. 58

1.2 Use precise language, action verbs, sensory details, appropriate modifiers, and the active rather than the passive voice.
Gather Details, pp. 56–57
Second Reading: Style, p. 62

1.9 Revise writing to improve the logic and coherence of the organization and controlling perspective, the precision of the word choice, and the tone by taking into consideration the audience, purpose, and formality of the context.
Evaluate and Revise Your Draft, pp. 61–62

Writing Applications

2.1 Write biographical or autobiographical narratives or short stories.

a. Relate a sequence of events and communicate the significance of the events to the audience.
Choose an Experience, p. 56

b. Locate scenes and incidents in specific places.
Gather Details, pp. 56–57

c. Describe with concrete sensory details the sights, sounds, and smells of a scene and the specific actions, movements, gestures, and feelings of the characters; use interior monologue to depict the characters' feelings.
Gather Details, pp. 56–57

d. Pace the presentation of actions to accommodate changes in time and mood.
TIP, p. 58
Organize Your Details, p. 58

e. Make effective use of descriptions of appearance, images, shifting perspectives, and sensory details.
Gather Details, pp. 56–57
Thoughts and Feelings, p. 57

Listening and Speaking Strategies

1.8 Produce concise notes for extemporaneous delivery.
Deliver Your Narrative, p. 65

1.9 Analyze the occasion and the interests of the audience and choose effective verbal and nonverbal techniques for presentations.
Deliver Your Narrative, p. 65

(continued)

(continued)

Speaking Applications

2.1 Deliver narrative presentations.

a. Narrate a sequence of events and communicate their significance to the audience.
Adapt Your Written Narrative, pp. 64–65

b. Locate scenes and incidents in specific places.
Adapt Your Written Narrative, pp. 64–65

c. Describe with concrete sensory details the sights, sounds, and smells of a scene and the specific actions, movements, gestures, and feelings of characters.
Adapt Your Written Narrative, pp. 64–65

d. Pace the presentation of actions to accommodate time or mood changes.
Deliver Your Narrative, p. 65

Review Standards Grade 8

Writing 2.1 Write biographies, autobiographies, short stories, or narratives.

a. Relate a clear, coherent incident, event, or situation by using well-chosen details.
Events, p. 57

Speaking 2.1 Deliver narrative presentations.

b. Reveal the significance of, and the subject's attitude about, the incident, event, or situation.
The Indispensable, p. 64

Instructional Planning and Support

Where do I find lesson plans, additional resources, and other teaching aids?

- This Annotated Teacher's Edition and *On Course: Mapping Instruction* provide direction in planning and implementing a complete California standards–based curriculum. These components also include instructions for diagnostic, progress, and summative testing; for presenting direct instruction of the standards; for differentiating instruction to provide universal access; and for locating and using the program's ancillaries.
- Lesson and workshop resources are referenced at the beginning of each selection or workshop, in the bottom margin of this teacher's edition.
- Reminders for using additional resources appear in this teacher's edition at point of use.
- The *One-Stop Planner* CD-ROM contains editable lesson plans and all print ancillaries, available in PDF format.

What if I don't have time to teach all of Chapter 1?

- Most standards can be taught with a minimum number of selections and features. In the chart on the preceding page, the core lessons you need in order to provide complete coverage of the chapter standards are identified with a ✓.
- *On Course: Mapping Instruction,* Chapter 1, lists lessons and activities that provide minimum standards coverage.

What provisions have been made for students who have additional class time scheduled in language arts?

- *Interactive Reading* provides for alternative direct instruction and practice of the grade-level standards taught in Chapter 1.
- *Universal Access: Writing, Listening, and Speaking,* Chapter 1, contains worksheets and transparencies that provide practice in and reteaching and reinforcement of the writing and listening and speaking standards in Chapter 1.
- *Universal Access: Lesson Plans for Language Development,* Chapter 1, provides alternative teaching strategies and additional worksheets designed specifically for English-language learners and special education students. Many of the suggestions and activities in this ancillary will also be helpful to students in the regular classroom who are having difficulty with particular skills.

Universal Access

How do I differentiate instruction to ensure that all my students master the standards?

Holt Literature and Language Arts provides comprehensive, differentiated instruction for all types of students.

- Most of the general instruction and teaching strategies in the Annotated Teacher's Edition are at grade level. These instructions will work well with the majority of your students.
- Point-of-use suggestions are provided for advanced learners, learners having difficulty, English-language learners, and special education students.
- *Interactive Reading* is designed to anticipate and remediate problems that students may experience in achieving mastery of the reading standards. See *Interactive Reading,* Teacher's Edition, Chapter 1, for information on using the reader to differentiate instruction.
- *Universal Access: Writing, Listening, and Speaking,* Chapter 1, contains worksheets and transparencies that provide practice in and reteaching and reinforcement of the writing and listening and speaking standards in Chapter 1.
- *Universal Access: Lesson Plans for Language Development,* Chapter 1 offers teaching strategies and additional worksheets designed specifically for English-language learners and special education students.

Assessment

How do I determine whether my students are making progress in mastering the standards?

Progress Assessment

- Use the Standards Reviews at the end of Chapter 1 for an informal assessment of the informational reading and writing standards.
- Use Chapter 1 tests from the *Progress Assessment* booklets to assess comprehension and progress on mastering the standards taught in this chapter.

Summative Assessment

The content of *Holt Literature and Language Arts* has been divided into quarters to allow you to administer the four summative tests required by California. Chapters 1–2 and related instructional material constitute the first quarter of instruction. At the end of Chapter 2, you may ask students to take the First-Quarter Test in *Diagnostic and Summative Assessments.*

Chapter 1

STANDARDS FOCUS

(For full text of standards taught in this chapter, see the Standards Correlation by Standard chart in the Student Edition.)

Grade-Level Standards

- Vocabulary Development 1.1, 1.2
- Reading Comprehension 2.4
- Literary Response and Analysis 3.6
- Writing Strategies 1.1, 1.2, 1.9
- Writing Applications 2.1a–e
- Listening and Speaking Strategies 1.8, 1.9
- Speaking Applications 2.1a–d

INTRODUCING THE CHAPTER

In this chapter, students will explore two building blocks of fiction—plot and setting. The stories demonstrate how writers present a sequence of events in order to create suspense and use techniques, such as flashbacks and foreshadowing, to shift a reader's attention to the past or future. The setting, too, can transport readers to the past or the future; or setting can establish an immediate, familiar present time and place. The stories also show how setting can create a mood.

Related articles about the hectic pace of contemporary life provide students with information and opinions to synthesize.

The chapter closes with an opportunity for students to write and present an autobiographical narrative.

CHAPTER 1 RESOURCES: READING

Planning
- *One-Stop Planner* CD-ROM with Test Generator
- *On Course: Mapping Instruction*
- *At Home: A Guide to Standards Mastery*
- *At Home: In Spanish*
- *Supporting Instruction in Spanish*

Media
- *Visual Connections*
  - Videocassette, Segment 1

Reading
- *Interactive Reading*

Differentiating Instruction
- *Lesson Plans for Language Development*

Chapter 1

PLOT AND SETTING

SYNTHESIZING SOURCES

If you're a writer, a real writer, you're a descendant of those medieval storytellers who used to go into the square of a town and spread a little mat on the ground and sit on it and beat a bowl and say, "If you give me a copper coin, I will tell you a golden tale."

—Robertson Davies

Men exist for the sake of one another. Teach them then or bear with them.—Marcus Antoninus, *Meditations* VIII:59 (1958) by Jacob Lawrence. Egg tempera on hardboard (20¾″ × 16¾″).

National Museum of American Art, Smithsonian Institution. Gift of the Container Corporation of America. Photo courtesy of Art Resource, New York. Artwork © Gwendolyn Knight Lawrence, courtesy of The Jacob and Gwendolyn Lawrence Foundation.

go.hrw.com

KEYWORD: HLLA 10-1

THE QUOTATION

Storytelling can be a form of teaching. Ask students if they can identify any stories that have taught them something important or memorable about their culture. How do these stories teach?

VIEWING THE ART

Jacob Lawrence (1917–2000), one of the most successful African American artists of our time, made art about the history and lives of American people. This painting is based on a quotation (used as the work's title) from Marcus Aurelius Antoninus, a Roman emperor and philosopher. As an experiment in advertising, the Container Corporation of America asked Lawrence and other prominent artists to produce paintings based on "the Great Ideas of Western Man." The series ran for nearly forty years and exposed people not only to ideas, but also to interesting art.

Resources Reminder

Assessment

- *Diagnostic and Summative Assessments*
  - Entry-Level Diagnostic Test

This assessment tests mastery of previous and grade-level standards.

Planning

- *At Home: A Guide to Standards Mastery*

Parent letters appear in this resource. Translations of these letters are found in *At Home: In Spanish.* Translations of selection summaries are found in *Supporting Instruction in Spanish.*

Reading

- *Interactive Reading*

The California framework requires students to read materials apart from in-class assignments. Additional readings are cited on the Read On page and on selected pages in the Student Edition.

Vocabulary

- *Vocabulary Development*
  - Cumulative Vocabulary Review, pp. 5–6

Grammar

- *Holt Handbook*
  - Case Forms of Personal Pronouns, pp. 145–154

Assessment

- *Progress Assessment of Reading*
  - Chapter Test
- *Diagnostic and Summative Assessments*
  - Entry-Level Diagnostic Test
- *One-Stop Planner* CD-ROM with Test Generator

Internet

- go.hrw.com (Keyword: HLLA 10-1)

STANDARDS FOCUS, pp. 2–3

(For the grade-level standard taught in this lesson, see Student Edition, p. 2.)

Prerequisite Standard

- Grade 7, Literary Response and Analysis 3.2 **Identify events that advance the plot and determine how each event explains past or present action(s) or foreshadows future action(s).**

Literary Focus: Plot

Choose a movie or a TV drama that your students have seen. Call on volunteers to identify the major events of the plot. Ask the following questions:

- Who is the main character?
- What is the basic situation?
- What complications or problems arise?
- What is the climax, or the most suspenseful moment?
- How is the problem resolved?

Point out to students that these events usually occur in sequence, or chronological order. Then, ask students, "Was the action interrupted at any point by a flashback to an earlier event?" and "Were there any clues that hinted at what would happen next?"

Literary Response and Analysis

Plot *by* John Leggett

A SEQUENCE OF EVENTS

Reading Standard 3.6 Analyze and trace an author's development of time and sequence, including the use of complex literary devices (e.g., foreshadowing, flashbacks).

How to Tell a Tale—In Sequence

This cartoon is funny—and it shows the nuts-and-bolts plot elements of any story. **Plot** is the sequence of related events that make a story hang together—it's what happens between "once upon a time" and "happily ever after." A plot will include characters who experience some problem or conflict (maybe facing a dragon), which is resolved in some way (maybe by a superhero). A complete story, of course, fills in the interesting details. It also takes place within a specific span of time.

The Building Blocks of Plot

1 A typical plot has four parts. The first part is the **basic situation** (sometimes called the **exposition**). The basic situation presents a main character who wants something very much and who encounters a conflict while trying to get it.

A young girl is cruelly treated by her jealous stepmother and stepsisters. She longs to go to the prince's ball, but all she has to wear is rags.

At this point the writer might develop the element of conflict further. Cinderella's stepmother might lock her in the cellar to keep her from going to the ball. That would be an **external conflict,** because it pits Cinderella against an *outside* force. If, however, Cinderella could go to the ball and hesitated out of shyness, she would experience an **internal conflict,** a struggle *inside* her own heart or mind.

2 In the next part of the plot, a series of **complications** arises, which causes new problems:

Cinderella's fairy godmother gets her an invitation to the ball, as well as a fashion makeover. There's a catch, however: If she isn't home by midnight, her gown will turn to rags and her coachmen into mice. At the ball the prince dances with Cinderella all night. At midnight she flees, losing her tiny glass slipper on the palace steps.

DIFFERENTIATING INSTRUCTION

Learners Having Difficulty

Plot. To help these students analyze plot, choose a volunteer to orally summarize the story line of a recent movie or a TV drama. Encourage students who are listening to stop the speaker each time they hear a description of the basic situation, an important event, the climax, or the resolution. Help students identify these plot elements by drawing a plot diagram on the chalkboard.

Activity. Have students copy the diagram and use it as a model to analyze the plot of another movie or TV show of their choice.

English-Language Learners

For more instruction on plot for English-language learners and special education students, see *Lesson Plans for Language Development,* pp. 3, 4.

3 The high point of the plot is the **climax,** the story's most exciting or suspenseful moment, when something happens that decides the outcome of the conflict. The climax of this tale takes place when the prince discovers that the glass slipper fits Cinderella's dainty foot.

4 The last part of the plot is the **resolution,** or **denouement** (dā′ no͞o·män′), when the problems are resolved and the story ends. In Cinderella's case she marries the prince in a fancy wedding, to which her wicked family is not invited. A more modern resolution to our story would suggest "they lived happily ever after, sort of" and would hint at what's behind the "sort of."

Timing Is Everything

The sequence of events described in Cinderella's tale is common to almost all stories. However, another important plot element remains to be considered: how the writer reveals the story's events within a span of time.

The usual way is to begin at the beginning and then tell about each event in the order in which it happens. This is called **chronological order.** However, writers also choose other techniques to manipulate time and control our feelings. To create **suspense,** for example, and to dramatize a moment of danger, they might slow time down—agonizingly. (You'll find this technique used in the following story, "Contents of the Dead Man's Pocket.")

Playing with Time

Writers also play with time by using **flashbacks,** in which the present action in a story is interrupted with a scene or scenes from the past. Flashbacks can reveal the past life of a character, explaining why someone is in a current situation. Some flashbacks cover a mere moment in time; others span many years. Sometimes writers also use **flash-forwards,** in which you visit a character's future.

With **foreshadowing**—another method for manipulating time—a writer plants clues that hint at something that will happen later in the plot. When you notice such a clue, you're drawn into the story: A clue that foreshadows danger, for example, will keep you on edge.

So whether writers have you looking back or thinking ahead, by playing with time, they hook you and draw you into their stories.

Practice

You can chart the **plot** of a story by using a diagram like the one below. Fill in a **plot diagram** for a fairy tale or a TV drama you know well. Television and movies make frequent use of **flashbacks** and **foreshadowing.** Insert those time tricks on your plot diagram as well.

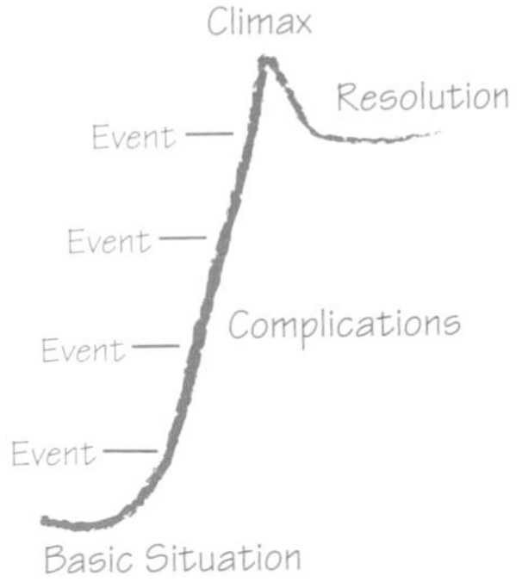

Practice

Possible responses for a plot diagram of "King Midas and the Golden Touch":

Basic Situation—King Midas is greedy for power and wealth. A god agrees to grant the king a wish. Midas asks for the power to turn anything he touches into gold.

Foreshadowing—The god warns Midas to be careful about what he wishes for because power can have unforeseen results. When Midas repeats his wish, the god grants it.

Event—Each living plant that the king touches in his garden turns to gold. Soon his garden is lifeless.

Event—Midas picks up a glass of wine to drink; the wine turns to gold.

Event—Midas picks up an apple to eat; it turns to gold.

Climax—Midas's beloved daughter rushes into the room and throws her arms around him. She is changed to gold.

Flashback—In grief, Midas goes into his garden and closes his eyes. He remembers a stroll that he and his daughter took in the garden. He remembers the pleasing scent of flowers. Then he opens his eyes, and everything around him is lifeless gold.

Resolution—Midas begs the god to take away his power; the god grants his new wish. Midas's daughter returns to life. Midas realizes that his real treasure is the love he shares with other living things.

Advanced Learners

Acceleration. This activity can help to move students toward the eleventh- and twelfth-grade Standard 3.5c, for which they evaluate historical influences that shape the plot of a work of fiction.

Activity. Have pairs of students choose a short story that is set during a particular time in history. After reading the story, have them research the historical period by using an encyclopedia. Next, ask students to re-read the story and identify any philosophical, political, religious, ethical, or social influences of the time period that relate to the story and its plot. Then, have each pair share their findings with the class, outlining the plot of their short story and explaining how the story reflects its historical period.

Apply

Encourage students to create their own "story template" cartoons, using four or five panels to sum up the parts of a plot. Students may want to choose a selection from this book or a story from their reading outside of the classroom. Have them label the panels that illustrate the four main parts of a plot—basic situation, complications, climax, and resolution.

STANDARDS FOCUS, pp. 4–20

(For grade-level standards taught in this lesson, see the citations on Student Edition pages.)

Prerequisite Standard

- Grade 7, Literary Response and Analysis 3.2 **Identify events that advance the plot and determine how each event explains past or present action(s) or foreshadows future action(s).**

Reading Skills

- Understand cause and effect.

Summary *at grade level*

Tom Benecke is conflicted by his career ambition and his desire to be with his wife. One night while his wife goes to the movies alone, he stays home to work in their eleventh-story apartment. As she leaves, a gust of wind blows a paper from his desk and through an open window. On the sheet are the irreplaceable results of two months' work. Seeing it drift onto a ledge, Tom decides to retrieve the paper. His perilous climb across the building's face is related step-by-step. As he grasps the paper, Tom sees the streetscape below and terror seizes him. The return trip is a fight against panic. Reaching the window, he inadvertently knocks it closed. He is unable to open it or maintain his perch indefinitely. His only hope is to smash the window with his fist, though this may topple him. Shouting his wife's name, he breaks the glass and climbs inside. He returns the sheet to the desk, laughing when it again blows out the window as he goes to find his wife.

Before You Read

Contents of the Dead Man's Pocket

Literary Focus

Time and Sequence: Ticktock . . .

Imagine a TV camera focused for eight hours on a sleeping teenager. TV producers have tried something like this, and the ratings for the experimental show were disappointing. The reason is simple: TV viewers, moviegoers, and story readers all want action. *Something* has to happen to the characters.

The series of related events that we all expect to find in a story is called the **plot.** Usually these events are told in **chronological order,** beginning with the first event and moving in sequence through a whole series of events until the story ends.

In "Contents of the Dead Man's Pocket," each event intensifies the reader's tension. To make the tension even stronger, the writer does something very interesting with time: He slows down the action so that you can almost feel the seconds ticking away. In fact, the time it takes to read the story probably matches the timing of the character's ordeal.

Reading Skills

Understanding Cause and Effect

A **cause** is the reason *why* something happens. An **effect** is the result of some event or action. Most causes and effects happen in chains, with cause leading to effect leading to another cause, and so on. As the plot of this suspenseful story unfolds, you'll be caught up in just such a chain of causes and effects. Indeed, many suspense-filled stories rely on edge-of-your-seat causes and effects that keep readers guessing.

Reading Standard 3.6 Analyze and trace an author's development of time and sequence.

Make the Connection

Quickwrite

Think of a time when you or someone you know felt almost paralyzed by fear. Where were you or the other person, and what happened? In your notebook, jot down some details about the tense situation.

Vocabulary Development

projection (prō·jek′shən) *n.:* something that juts out from a surface.

discarding (dis·kärd′iŋ) *v.* used as *adj.:* abandoning; getting rid of.

confirmation (kän′fər·mā′shən) *n.:* proof.

exhalation (eks′hə·lā′shən) *n.:* something breathed out; breath.

imperceptibly (im′pər·sep′tə·blē) *adv.:* in such a slight way as to be almost unnoticeable.

rebounded (ri·bound′id) *v.:* bounced back.

interminable (in·tur′mi·nə·bəl) *adj.:* endless.

irrelevantly (i·rel′ə·vənt·lē) *adv.:* in a way not relating to the point or situation.

incomprehensible (in·käm′prē·hen′sə·bəl) *adj.:* not understandable.

unimpeded (un′im·pēd′id) *adj.:* not blocked; unobstructed.

RESOURCES: READING

Planning

- *One-Stop Planner* CD-ROM with Test Generator
- *On Course: Mapping Instruction*

Media

- *Audio CD Library*
  - disc 1
- *Fine Art Transparencies*
  - Transparency 1

Reading

- *Interactive Reading*
  - Interactive version: "Contents of the Dead Man's Pocket"
- *Interactive Reading,* Teacher's Edition
  - Graphic Organizer: Story Map

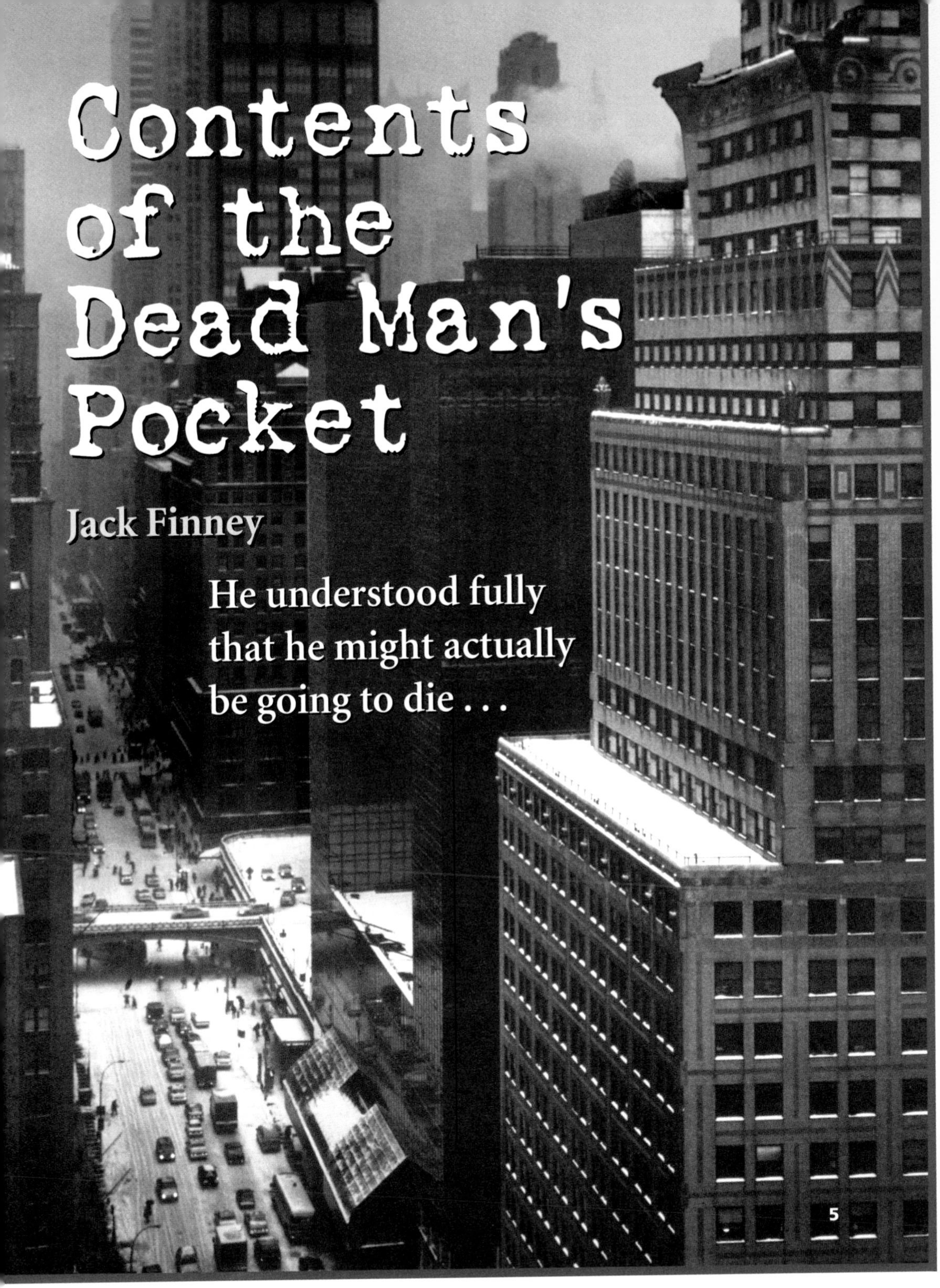

Contents of the Dead Man's Pocket

Jack Finney

He understood fully that he might actually be going to die . . .

PRETEACHING

Standards Starter

Motivate. Explain that the story's events occur over a period of minutes. Ask students to time how long it takes them to read the story. Challenge them to determine if reading the story takes more or less time than the story's events do.

Preview Vocabulary

For each of the underlined words below, have students choose the Vocabulary word on p. 4 that is closest in meaning.

1. The tent's overhang blocked a clear view of the stars. [projection, unimpeded]
2. The patient's respiration became gradually louder. [exhalation, imperceptibly]
3. Business recovered after the slump, but shedding excess inventory was costly. [rebounded, discarding]
4. The child's ceaseless babbling was charming but unintelligible. [interminable, incomprehensible]
5. The supporters extraneously claimed victory; only the ballots could offer evidence of who won. [irrelevantly, confirmation]

Assign the Reading

Most students will find the story compelling and the vocabulary and plot manageable. Less able readers may read in small groups. Since many of the sentences are long and complex, model for them the use of punctuation clues to enhance comprehension.

Differentiating Instruction

- *Lesson Plans for Language Development*
  - English-Language Learners, pp. 5–7, 26, 30
  - Special Education Students, pp. 8, 26, 30

Vocabulary

- *Vocabulary Development*
  - Vocabulary Worksheet, p. 1

Assessment

- *Progress Assessment of Reading*
  - Selection Test
- *One-Stop Planner* CD-ROM with Test Generator

DIRECT TEACHING

A Literary Focus
REVIEW STANDARD

Setting. What does Tom Benecke's use of a typewriter suggest about the time in which this story is set? [Possible response: The story is set at a time before home computers became popular.]

B Advanced Learners

Enrichment. After these students have read the story, ask them to identify clues that foreshadow later events. Students may note that the need to use force to open a window foreshadows a critical later event.

C Literary Focus
REVIEW STANDARD

Conflict. Remind students that conflict can take one of two forms—internal and external. What type of conflict is Tom facing? [He is experiencing an internal conflict. He is torn between going to the movies with his wife and working.]

D Vocabulary Development
GRADE-LEVEL STANDARD

Understanding word derivations. Point out that the prefix *un–*, meaning "not; opposite of," is derived from Old English. In this sentence, what is the meaning of the word *unannounced*? ["not disclosed; not made known"] What are some other words that use this prefix? [Possible responses: *unjust, unknown, unexpected.*]

At the little living-room desk Tom Benecke rolled two sheets of flimsy[1] and a heavier top sheet, carbon paper sandwiched between them, into his portable. *Interoffice Memo,* the top sheet was headed, and he typed tomorrow's date just below this; then he glanced at a creased yellow sheet, covered with his own handwriting, beside the typewriter. "Hot in here," he muttered to himself. Then, from the short hallway at his back, he heard the muffled clang of wire coat hangers in the bedroom closet, and at this reminder of what his wife was doing he thought: hot—guilty conscience.

He got up, shoving his hands into the back pockets of his gray wash slacks, stepped to the living-room window beside the desk and stood breathing on the glass, watching the expanding circlet of mist, staring down through the autumn night at Lexington Avenue,[2] eleven stories below. He was a tall, lean, dark-haired young man in a pullover sweater, who looked as though he had played not football, probably, but basketball in college. Now he placed the heels of his hands against the top edge of the lower window frame and shoved upward. But as usual the window didn't budge, and he had to lower his hands and then shoot them hard upward to jolt the window open a few inches. He dusted his hands, muttering.

But still he didn't begin his work. He crossed the room to the hallway entrance and, leaning against the doorjamb, hands shoved into his back pockets again, he called, "Clare?" When his wife answered, he said, "Sure you don't mind going alone?"

"No." Her voice was muffled, and he knew her head and shoulders were in the bedroom closet. Then the tap of her high heels sounded on the wood floor, and she appeared at the end of the little hallway, wearing a slip, both hands raised to one ear, clipping on an earring. She smiled at him—a slender, very pretty girl with light brown, almost blond, hair—her prettiness emphasized by the pleasant nature that showed in her face. "It's just that I hate you to miss this movie; you wanted to see it, too."

"Yeah, I know." He ran his fingers through his hair. "Got to get this done, though."

She nodded, accepting this. Then, glancing at the desk across the living room, she said, "You work too much, though, Tom—and too hard."

He smiled. "You won't mind, though, will you, when the money comes rolling in and I'm known as the Boy Wizard of Wholesale Groceries?"

"I guess not." She smiled and turned back toward the bedroom.

At his desk again, Tom lighted a cigarette; then a few moments later, as Clare appeared, dressed and ready to leave, he set it on the rim of the ashtray. "Just after seven," she said. "I can make the beginning of the first feature."

He walked to the front-door closet to help her on with her coat. He kissed her then and, for an instant, holding her close, smelling the perfume she had used, he was tempted to go with her; it was not actually true that he had to work tonight, though he very much wanted to. This was his own project, unannounced as yet in his office, and it could be postponed. But then they won't see it till Monday, he thought once again, and if I give it to the boss tomorrow he might read it over the weekend . . . "Have a good time," he said aloud. He gave his wife a little swat and opened the door for her, feeling the air from the building hallway, smelling faintly of floor wax, stream gently past his face.

He watched her walk down the hall, flicked a hand in response as she waved, and then he started to close the door, but it resisted for a

1. **flimsy** *n.:* thin paper used for typing carbon copies. Before computers and copying machines, copies of business communications were made with carbon paper.
2. **Lexington Avenue:** one of the main streets in New York City.

DIFFERENTIATING INSTRUCTION

Learners Having Difficulty

Invite learners having difficulty to read "Contents of the Dead Man's Pocket" in interactive format in *Interactive Reading* and to use the sidenotes as aids to understanding the selection. The interactive version provides additional instruction, practice, and assessment of the literature standard taught in the Student Edition. Monitor students' responses to the selection, and correct any misconceptions that arise.

Resources Reminder

Differentiating Instruction

- *Interactive Reading*
  - Interactive version: "Contents of the Dead Man's Pocket"

moment. As the door opening narrowed, the current of warm air from the hallway, channeled through this smaller opening now, suddenly rushed past him with accelerated force. Behind him he heard the slap of the window curtains against the wall and the sound of paper fluttering from his desk, and he had to push to close the door.

Turning, he saw a sheet of white paper drifting to the floor in a series of arcs, and another sheet, yellow, moving toward the window, caught in the dying current flowing through the narrow opening. As he watched, the paper struck the bottom edge of the window and hung there for an instant, plastered against the glass and wood. Then as the moving air stilled completely, the curtains swinging back from the wall to hang free again, he saw the yellow sheet drop to the window ledge and slide over out of sight. **E**

He ran across the room, grasped the bottom of the window and tugged, staring through the glass. He saw the yellow sheet, dimly now in the darkness outside, lying on the ornamental ledge a yard below the window. Even as he watched, it was moving, scraping slowly along the ledge, pushed by the breeze that pressed steadily against the building wall. He heaved on the window with all his strength, and it shot open with a bang, the window weight rattling in the casing. But the paper was past his reach and, leaning out into the night, he watched it scud[3] steadily along the ledge to the south, half plastered against the building wall. Above the muffled sound of the street traffic far below, he could hear the dry scrape of its movement, like a leaf on the pavement. **F**

The living room of the next apartment to the south projected a yard or more further out toward the street than this one; because of this the Beneckes paid seven and a half dollars less rent than their neighbors. And now the yellow sheet, sliding along the stone ledge, nearly invisible in the night, was stopped by the projecting blank wall of the next apartment. It lay motionless, then, in the corner formed by the two walls—a good five yards away, pressed firmly against the ornate corner ornament of the ledge by the breeze that moved past Tom Benecke's face. **G**

He knelt at the window and stared at the yellow paper for a full minute or more, waiting for it to move, to slide off the ledge and fall, hoping he could follow its course to the street, and then hurry down in the elevator and retrieve it. But it didn't move, and then he saw that the paper was caught firmly between a projection of the convoluted[4] corner ornament and the ledge. He thought about the poker from the fireplace, then the broom, then the mop—discarding each thought as it occurred to him. There was nothing in the apartment long enough to reach that paper.

It was hard for him to understand that he actually had to abandon it—it was ridiculous—and he began to curse. Of all the papers on his desk, why did it have to be this one in particular! On four long Saturday afternoons he had stood in supermarkets, counting the people who passed certain displays, and the results were scribbled on that yellow sheet. From stacks of trade publications, gone over page by page in snatched half hours at work and during evenings at home, he had copied facts, quotations, and figures onto that sheet. And he had carried it with him to the Public Library on Fifth Avenue, where he'd spent a dozen lunch hours and early evenings adding more. All were needed to support and lend authority to his idea for a new grocery-store display method; without them his **H**

3. **scud** *v.:* glide or move swiftly.

4. **convoluted** (kän′və·lo͞ot′id) *adj.:* intricate; coiled.

Vocabulary

projection (prō·jek′shən) *n.:* something that juts out from a surface.

discarding (dis·kärd′iŋ) *v.* used as *adj.:* abandoning; getting rid of.

DIRECT TEACHING

E Reading Skills

Understanding cause and effect. What caused the sheet of paper to fly out the window? [a gust of warm air from the hallway outside the apartment]

F Literary Focus GRADE-LEVEL STANDARD

Time and sequence. Why do you think the author provides such a detailed, step-by-step description of the paper's movement? [Possible responses: The yellow sheet is probably of great importance to Tom; this event will play a significant role in the plot.]

G Learners Having Difficulty

Using graphic aids. Most of the story's action takes place in the area described in these paragraphs. Encourage students to use the details provided here to make a sketch of the building's exterior. As they read further, students can refer to their drawings for help in visualizing story events. Suggest that they continue adding to their sketches as new details emerge.

H Reading Skills

Summarizing. Why is Tom upset about the loss of the paper? [The sheet contains the results of weeks of work on a personal project. He had hoped that this project would help him advance in the workplace.]

English-Language Learners

To help students visualize Tom's movement across the exterior of the apartment building, you may wish to use pictures to show the meaning of terms such as *mortar, casing, pane, sill, ornamental ledge, corner ornament, puttyless window edging, building face,* and *indented.*

Resources Reminder

For lessons designed for intermediate and advanced English-language learners, see *Lesson Plans for Language Development,* pp. 5–7, 26, 30.

Special Education Students

For lessons designed for special education students, see *Lesson Plans for Language Development,* pp. 8, 26, 30.

Advanced Learners

Enrichment. Finney's writing style may be characterized as having an almost cinematic, frame-by-frame quality.

Activity. Ask students to identify other fictional scenes that share this style. Have them bring in sample passages to read in a group setting and to analyze how the writers of these passages achieve this effect.

DIRECT TEACHING

A Literary Focus
REVIEW STANDARD

Conflict. What internal conflict is Tom experiencing here? [He is trying to rationalize the effect of the loss by convincing himself that the contents of the sheet weren't that important.]

B Literary Focus
REVIEW STANDARD

Suspense. Remind students that anxiety or uncertainty creates suspense. What questions have been posed in the reader's mind? [Possible responses: What consequences will the loss of the paper have? Will Tom try to retrieve the paper?]

C Reading Skills

Expressing an opinion. What does Tom's determination suggest about his willingness to take risks? [Answers will vary. Have students support their opinions.]

D Learners Having Difficulty

Finding details. Tom imagines that if the ledge were only a yard off the ground, the task of retrieving the paper would be easy. How high is the ledge? If you don't recall, look back at the beginning of the story to find out. [eleven stories]

E Literary Focus
GRADE-LEVEL STANDARD

Time and sequence. Ask students to describe the pace of this passage. How does it contribute to the feeling of suspense? [Tom's deliberate climb onto the ledge is related methodically, with each movement carefully described in sequence. This slow pace builds suspense because it emphasizes the caution with which Tom approaches his task, and this in turn emphasizes the dangerous consequences of a single misstep.]

idea was a mere opinion. And there they all lay, in his own improvised shorthand—countless hours of work—out there on the ledge.

For many seconds he believed he was going to abandon the yellow sheet, that there was nothing else to do. The work could be duplicated. But it would take two months, and the time to present this idea was *now,* for use in the spring displays. He struck his fist on the window ledge. Then he shrugged. Even though his plan was adopted, he told himself, it wouldn't bring him a raise in pay—not immediately, anyway, or as a direct result. It won't bring me a promotion either, he argued—not of itself. **B**

But just the same—and he couldn't escape the thought—this and other independent projects, some already done and others planned for the future, would gradually mark him out from the score of other young men in his company. They were the way to change from a name on the payroll to a name in the minds of the company officials. They were the beginning of the long, long climb to where he was determined to be—at the very top. And he knew he was going out there in the darkness, after the yellow sheet fifteen feet beyond his reach.

By a kind of instinct, he instantly began making his intention acceptable to himself by laughing at it. The mental picture of himself sidling along the ledge outside was absurd—it was actually comical—and he smiled. He imagined himself describing it; it would make a good story at the office and, it occurred to him, would add a special interest and importance to his memorandum, which would do it no harm at all.

To simply go out and get his paper was an easy task—he could be back here with it in less than two minutes—and he knew he wasn't deceiving himself. The ledge, he saw, measuring it with his eye, was about as wide as the length of his shoe, and perfectly flat. And every fifth row of brick in the face of the building, he remembered—leaning out, he verified this—was indented half an inch, enough for the tips of his fingers, enough to maintain balance easily. It occurred to him that if this ledge and wall were only a yard aboveground—as he knelt at the window staring out, this thought was the final confirmation of his intention—he could move along the ledge indefinitely.

On a sudden impulse, he got to his feet, walked to the front closet, and took out an old tweed jacket; it would be cold outside. He put it on and buttoned it as he crossed the room rapidly toward the open window. In the back of his mind he knew he'd better hurry and get this over with before he thought too much, and at the window he didn't allow himself to hesitate.

He swung a leg over the sill, then felt for and found the ledge a yard below the window with his foot. Gripping the bottom of the window frame very tightly and carefully, he slowly ducked his head under it, feeling on his face the sudden change from the warm air of the room to the chill outside. With infinite care he brought out his other leg, his mind concentrating on what he was doing. Then he slowly stood erect. Most of the putty, dried out and brittle, had dropped off the bottom edging of the window frame, he found, and the flat wooden edging provided a good gripping surface, a half inch or more deep, for the tips of his fingers.

Now, balanced easily and firmly, he stood on the ledge outside in the slight, chill breeze, eleven stories above the street, staring into his own lighted apartment, odd and different-seeming now.

First his right hand, then his left, he carefully shifted his fingertip grip from the puttyless window edging to an indented row of bricks directly to his right. It was hard to take the first shuffling

Vocabulary
confirmation (kän′fər·mā′shən) *n.:* proof.

sideways step then—to make himself move—and the fear stirred in his stomach, but he did it, again by not allowing himself time to think. And now—with his chest, stomach, and the left side of his face pressed against the rough cold brick—his lighted apartment was suddenly gone, and it was much darker out here than he had thought.

Without pause he continued—right foot, left foot, right foot, left—his shoe soles shuffling and scraping along the rough stone, never lifting from it, fingers sliding along the exposed edging of brick. He moved on the balls of his feet, heels lifted slightly; the ledge was not quite as wide as he'd expected. But leaning slightly inward toward the face of the building and pressed against it, he could feel his balance firm and secure, and moving along the ledge was quite as easy as he had thought it would be. He could hear the buttons of his jacket scraping steadily along the rough bricks and feel them catch momentarily, tugging a little, at each mortared crack. He simply did not permit himself to look down, though the compulsion[5] to do so never left him; nor did he allow himself actually to think. Mechanically—right foot, left foot, over and again—he shuffled along crabwise, watching the projecting wall ahead loom steadily closer. . . .

5. **compulsion** *n.:* driving force.

When he reached it, and at the corner—he'd decided how he was going to pick up the paper—he lifted his right foot and placed it carefully on the ledge that ran along the projecting wall at a right angle to the ledge on which his other foot rested. And now, facing the building, he stood in the corner formed by the two walls, one foot on the ledging of each, a hand on the shoulder-high indentation of each wall. His forehead was pressed directly into the corner against the cold bricks, and now he carefully lowered first one hand, then the other, perhaps a foot farther down, to the next indentation in the rows of bricks.

Very slowly, sliding his forehead down the trough of the brick corner and bending his knees, he lowered his body toward the paper lying between his outstretched feet. Again he lowered his fingerholds another foot and bent his knees still more, thigh muscles taut, his forehead sliding and bumping down the brick V. Half squatting now, he dropped his left hand to the next indentation and then slowly reached with his right hand toward the paper between his feet.

He couldn't quite touch it, and his knees now were pressed against the wall; he could bend them no farther. But by ducking his head another inch lower, the top of his head now pressed against the bricks, he lowered his right shoulder and his fingers had the paper by a corner, pulling it loose. At the same instant he saw, between his

DIRECT TEACHING

F Literary Focus REVIEW STANDARD

Setting. What might the apartment represent to Tom? What effect does its disappearance have on Tom? [Possible responses: The warm, well-lit apartment represents safety and security. The fact that it is now out of sight contributes to a rise in Tom's level of anxiety.]

G Literary Focus REVIEW STANDARD

Imagery. Ask students to identify sensory details that help the reader experience the scene being described. [Possible details: "shoe soles shuffling and scraping along the rough stone," "fingers sliding along the exposed edging," "buttons of his jacket scraping steadily along the rough bricks," "shuffled along crabwise."]

CONTENT-AREA CONNECTIONS

Social Science: Work and Family
Many people today feel the pressure of finding time for both their jobs and their families. While the number of hours worked has remained stable over the last fifty years, surveys show that people feel as if they are working longer. One reason may be the growing number of women in the workplace. With two parents working in more families, the total nonworking hours of many households have been reduced. Another cause is the blurring of the line between home and work. Home use of fax machines, computers, and the Internet make it harder to determine where work ends and home begins.

Small-group activity. Have students research and report on issues related to working hours, leisure time, telecommuting, and the intrusion of the workplace into the home.

DIRECT TEACHING

A Reading Skills

Understanding cause and effect. After purposely trying to avoid looking at the street below, Tom accidentally does so. What effect do you think this will have on him? [Possible responses: He may become frightened or suffer from vertigo; he may fall.]

B Literary Focus
GRADE-LEVEL STANDARD

Time and sequence. How much time has elapsed since Tom saw the paper fly out the window? [Responses will vary.]

C Literary Focus
GRADE-LEVEL STANDARD

Time and sequence. What happens to Tom in this "instant"? [For the first time he realizes just how far above the ground he really is and sees the precariousness of his position.]

D Reading Skills

Understanding cause and effect. What nearly causes Tom to fall? [Possible response: The realization that he is doubled over eleven stories above ground provokes an involuntary spasm of panic.]

E Literary Focus
GRADE-LEVEL STANDARD

Time and sequence. Ask students to comment on the relationship between the pace of the narrative and the level of suspense. What action is occurring at this moment? Is the suspense greater than it was before? [Possible responses: There is almost no physical action, yet the suspense has increased significantly. The reader is now uncertain whether any action by Tom, no matter how small, might lead to his death.]

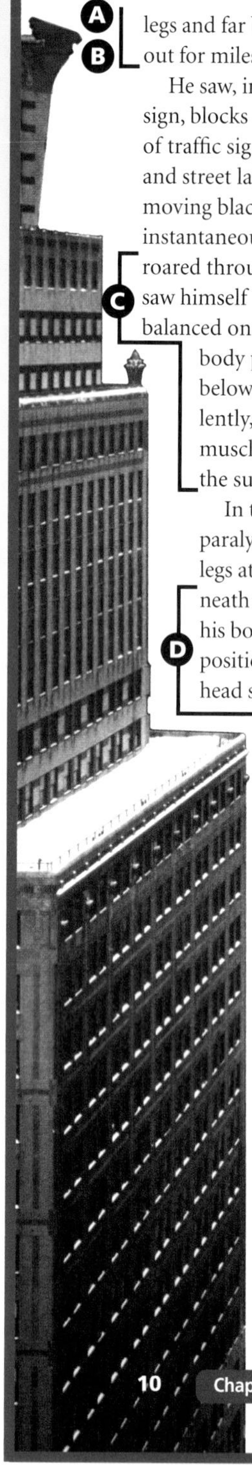

legs and far below, Lexington Avenue stretched out for miles ahead.

He saw, in that instant, the Loew's theater sign, blocks ahead past Fiftieth Street; the miles of traffic signals, all green now; the lights of cars and street lamps; countless neon signs; and the moving black dots of people. And a violent, instantaneous explosion of absolute terror roared through him. For a motionless instant he saw himself externally—bent practically double, balanced on this narrow ledge, nearly half his body projecting out above the street far below—and he began to tremble violently, panic flaring through his mind and muscles, and he felt the blood rush from the surface of his skin.

In the fractional moment before horror paralyzed him, as he stared between his legs at that terrible length of street far beneath him, a fragment of his mind raised his body in a spasmodic jerk to an upright position again, but so violently that his head scraped hard against the wall, bouncing off it, and his body swayed outward to the knife-edge of balance, and he very nearly plunged backward and fell. Then he was leaning far into the corner again, squeezing and pushing into it, not only his face but his chest and stomach, his back arching; and his fingertips clung with all the pressure of his pulling arms to the shoulder-high half-inch indentation in the bricks.

He was more than trembling now; his whole body was racked with a violent shuddering beyond control, his eyes squeezed so tightly shut it was painful, though he was past awareness of that. His teeth were exposed in a frozen grimace, the strength draining like water from his knees and calves. It was extremely likely, he knew, that he would faint, slump down along the wall, his face scraping, and then drop backward, a limp weight, out into nothing. And to save his life he concentrated on holding on to consciousness, drawing deliberate deep breaths of cold air into his lungs, fighting to keep his senses aware.

Then he knew that he would not faint, but he could not stop shaking nor open his eyes. He stood where he was, breathing deeply, trying to hold back the terror of the glimpse he had had of what lay below him; and he knew he had made a mistake in not making himself stare down at the street, getting used to it and accepting it, when he had first stepped out onto the ledge.

It was impossible to walk back. He simply could not do it. He couldn't bring himself to make the slightest movement. The strength was gone from his legs; his shivering hands—numb, cold, and desperately rigid—had lost all deftness;[6] his easy ability to move and balance was gone. Within a step or two, if he tried to move, he knew that he would stumble clumsily and fall.

Seconds passed, with the chill faint wind pressing the side of his face, and he could hear the toned-down volume of the street traffic far beneath him. Again and again it slowed and then stopped, almost to silence; then presently, even this high, he would hear the click of the traffic signals and the subdued roar of the cars starting up again. During a lull in the street sounds, he called out. Then he was shouting *"Help!"* so loudly it rasped his throat. But he felt the steady pressure of the wind, moving between his face and the blank wall, snatch up his cries as he uttered them, and he knew they must sound directionless and distant. And he remembered how habitually, here in New York, he himself heard and ignored shouts in the night. If anyone heard him, there was no sign of it, and presently

6. **deftness** *n.:* skillfulness; coordination.

DEVELOPING FLUENCY

Students need multiple exposures to unfamiliar words in order to make the process of reading them automatic.

Paired activity. Before students read the story, ask them to skim the text for unfamiliar words. Have them create personal glossaries by looking up and recording the definitions of the words. Then, have students share their glossaries with partners, making sure they both understand the meanings of all the words they have recorded. Students should write a sentence for each word that their partner recorded. Finally, before reading the story, they can exchange sentences and see if they still have difficulty with any of the words.

10 Chapter 1 Plot and Setting • Synthesizing Sources

Tom Benecke knew he had to try moving; there was nothing else he could do.

Eyes squeezed shut, he watched scenes in his mind like scraps of motion-picture film—he could not stop them. He saw himself stumbling suddenly sideways as he crept along the ledge and saw his upper body arc outward, arms flailing. He saw a dangling shoestring caught between the ledge and the sole of his other shoe, saw a foot start to move, to be stopped with a jerk, and felt his balance leaving him. He saw himself falling with a terrible speed as his body revolved in the air, knees clutched tight to his chest, eyes squeezed shut, moaning softly. **F**

Out of utter necessity, knowing that any of these thoughts might be reality in the very next seconds, he was slowly able to shut his mind against every thought but what he now began to do. With fear-soaked slowness, he slid his left foot an inch or two toward his own impossibly distant window. Then he slid the fingers of his shivering left hand a corresponding distance. For a moment he could not bring himself to lift his right foot from one ledge to the other; then he did it, and became aware of the harsh exhalation of air from his throat and realized that he was panting. As his right hand, then, began to slide along the brick edging, he was astonished to feel the yellow paper pressed to the bricks underneath his stiff fingers, and he uttered a terrible, abrupt bark that might have been a laugh or a moan. **G** He opened his mouth and took the paper in his teeth, pulling it out from under his fingers.

By a kind of trick—by concentrating his entire mind on first his left foot, then his left hand, then the other foot, then the other hand—he was able to move, almost imperceptibly, trembling steadily, very nearly without thought. **H** But he could feel the terrible strength of the pent-up horror on just the other side of the flimsy barrier he had erected in his mind; and he knew that if it broke through he would lose this thin artificial control of his body.

During one slow step he tried keeping his eyes closed; it made him feel safer, shutting him off a little from the fearful reality of where he was. Then a sudden rush of giddiness swept over him and he had to open his eyes wide, staring sideways at the cold rough brick and angled lines of mortar, his cheek tight against the building. He kept his eyes open then, knowing that if he once let them flick outward, to stare for an instant at the lighted windows across the street, he would be past help.

He didn't know how many dozens of tiny sidling steps he had taken, his chest, belly, and face pressed to the wall; but he knew the slender hold he was keeping on his mind and body was going to break. He had a sudden mental picture of his apartment on just the other side of this wall—warm, cheerful, incredibly spacious. And he saw himself striding through it, lying down on the floor on his back, arms spread wide, reveling[7] in its unbelievable security. The impossible remoteness of this utter safety, the contrast between it and where he now stood, was more than he could bear. And the barrier broke then, and the fear of the awful height he stood on coursed through his nerves and muscles. **I**

A fraction of his mind knew he was going to fall, and he began taking rapid blind steps with no feeling of what he was doing, sidling with a clumsy desperate swiftness, fingers scrabbling along the brick, almost hopelessly resigned to the sudden backward pull and swift motion outward and down. Then his moving left hand slid onto not brick but sheer emptiness, an impossible gap in the face of the wall, and he stumbled. **J**

7. **reveling** (rev′əl·iŋ) *v.* used as *adj.:* taking great pleasure or delight.

Vocabulary

exhalation (eks′hə·lā′shən) *n.:* something breathed out; breath.

imperceptibly (im′pər·sep′tə·blē) *adv.:* in such a slight way as to be almost unnoticeable.

DIRECT TEACHING

F Literary Focus
REVIEW STANDARD

Suspense. How does this passage build suspense? [Possible response: It helps the reader to visualize in minute detail the consequences of a misstep by Tom.]

G Reading Skills

Making inferences. Why is Tom astonished to feel the paper beneath his fingers? [Because of his panic, he had completely forgotten the reason why he had stepped out on the ledge in the first place.]

H Vocabulary Development
GRADE-LEVEL STANDARD

Understanding word derivations. Point out the word *concentrating.* Explain that the word is derived from the Latin prefix *con–,* which means "together," and the Latin root word *centrum,* meaning "center." Ask students how recognizing the word derivation might help them understand Tom's effort here. [Possible response: Tom is gathering all of his mental powers together into a common center; he is centering his mind.]

I Literary Focus
REVIEW STANDARD

Conflict. What is the only thing keeping Tom from reaching his apartment? [Himself; he should be able to reach the apartment easily if he can control his panic.]

J Reading Skills

Analyzing. What is happening to Tom? [He is panicking; he is losing his self-control.]

DIRECT TEACHING

A Learners Having Difficulty

Using graphic aids. To clarify students' understanding of the sequence of events in which Tom nearly falls, suggest that they make a storyboard, or a scene-by-scene representation of the principal events. Storyboards can cover the sequence of events that begins with the moment Tom stumbles, continuing through the events described on this page.

B Literary Focus GRADE-LEVEL STANDARD

Time and sequence. Why is it ironic that so little time has passed? [Possible response: To Tom, the minutes that have elapsed since he left the apartment must seem like an eternity.]

C Literary Focus REVIEW STANDARD

Suspense. Have students consider Tom's action in light of the story's title. How does it increase the reader's anxiety? [Possible response: Given the title "Contents of the Dead Man's Pocket," the action of putting the sheet inside his pocket forces readers to take seriously the possibility that Tom may wind up dead.]

D Reading Skills

Understanding cause and effect. Why is Tom stuck outside the window? What caused it to jam closed? [Tom's inability to control his fear caused the situation. He knocked the window shut during his panicked scramble to the sill.]

His right foot smashed into his left anklebone; he staggered sideways, began falling, and the claw of his hand cracked against glass and wood, slid down it, and his fingertips were pressed hard on the puttyless edging of his window. His right hand smacked gropingly beside it as he fell to his knees; and, under the full weight and direct downward pull of his sagging body, the open window dropped shudderingly in its frame till it closed and his wrists struck the sill and were jarred off.

For a single moment he knelt, knee bones against stone on the very edge of the ledge, body swaying and touching nowhere else, fighting for balance. Then he lost it, his shoulders plunging backward, and he flung his arms forward, his hands smashing against the window casing on either side; and—his body moving backward—his fingers clutched the narrow wood stripping of the upper pane.

A For an instant he hung suspended between balance and falling, his fingertips pressed onto the quarter-inch wood strips. Then, with utmost delicacy, with a focused concentration of all his senses, he increased even further the strain on his fingertips hooked to these slim edgings of wood. Elbows slowly bending, he began to draw the full weight of his upper body forward, knowing that the instant his fingers slipped off these quarter-inch strips he'd plunge backward and be falling. Elbows imperceptibly bending, body shaking with the strain, the sweat starting from his forehead in great sudden drops, he pulled, his entire being and thought concentrated in his fingertips. Then suddenly, the strain slackened and ended, his chest touching the windowsill, and he was kneeling on the ledge, his forehead pressed to the glass of the closed window.

Dropping his palms to the sill, he stared into his living room—at the red-brown davenport[8] across the room, and a magazine he had left there; at the pictures on the walls and the gray rug; the entrance to the hallway; and at his papers, typewriter, and desk, not two feet from his nose. A movement from his desk caught his eye and he saw that it was a thin curl of blue B smoke; his cigarette, the ash long, was still burning in the ashtray where he'd left it—this was past all belief—only a few minutes before.

His head moved, and in faint reflection from the glass before him he saw the yellow paper clenched in his front teeth. Lifting a hand from the sill he took it from his mouth; the moistened corner parted from the paper, and he spat it out.

C For a moment, in the light from the living room, he stared wonderingly at the yellow sheet in his hand and then crushed it into the side pocket of his jacket.

D He couldn't open the window. It had been pulled not completely closed, but its lower edge was below the level of the outside sill; there was no room to get his fingers underneath it. Between the upper sash and the lower was a gap not wide enough—reaching up, he tried—to get his fingers into; he couldn't push it open. The upper window panel, he knew from long experience, was impossible to move, frozen tight with dried paint.

Very carefully observing his balance, the fingertips of his left hand again hooked to the narrow stripping of the window casing, he drew back his right hand, palm facing the glass, and then struck the glass with the heel of his hand.

His arm rebounded from the pane, his body tottering, and he knew he didn't dare strike a harder blow.

But in the security and relief of his new position, he simply smiled; with only a sheet of glass between him and the room just before him, it was not possible that there wasn't a way past it. Eyes narrowing, he thought for a few moments about what to do. Then his eyes widened, for

8. **davenport** (dav′ən·pôrt′) *n.:* large sofa or couch.

Vocabulary
rebounded (ri·bound′id) *v.:* bounced back.

READING MINI-LESSON

Developing Word-Attack Skills
Use the selection word *trough* as the starting point for exploring the different sounds spelled with the letters *ough.* Call students' attention to the word, which appears on p. 9: "sliding his forehead down the *trough* of the brick corner." Point out that *trough* rhymes with the word *off.* The letters *ough* in *trough* stand for the sound /ôf/.

Activity. Have students identify the sound or sounds spelled by *ough* in the selection words that are listed below. Does *ough* stand for /ôf/ in any of these words? Are there any similarities between the sounds of *ough* in *trough* and in any of these words?

1. through [*ough* stands for /o͞o/]
2. though [*ough* stands for /ō/]

nothing occurred to him. But still he felt calm; the trembling, he realized, had stopped. At the back of his mind there still lay the thought that once he was again in his home, he could give release to his feelings. He actually *would* lie on the floor, rolling, clenching tufts of the rug in his hands. He would literally run across the room, free to move as he liked, jumping on the floor, testing and reveling in its absolute security, letting the relief flood through him, draining the fear from his mind and body. His yearning for this was astonishingly intense, and somehow he understood that he had better keep this feeling at bay.

He took a half dollar from his pocket and struck it against the pane, but without any hope that the glass would break and with very little disappointment when it did not. After a few moments of thought he drew his leg up onto the ledge and picked loose the knot of his shoelace. He slipped off the shoe and, holding it across the instep, drew back his arm as far as he dared and struck the leather heel against the glass. The pane rattled, but he knew he'd been a long way from breaking it. His foot was cold and he slipped the shoe back on. He shouted again, experimentally, and then once more, but there was no answer.

The realization suddenly struck him that he might have to wait here till Clare came home, and for a moment the thought was funny. He could see Clare opening the front door, withdrawing her key from the lock, closing the door behind her, and then glancing up to see him crouched on the other side of the window. He could see her rush across the room, face astounded and frightened, and hear himself shouting instructions: "Never mind how I got here! Just open the wind—" She couldn't open it, he remembered, she'd never been able to; she'd always had to call him. She'd have to get the building superintendent or a neighbor, and he pictured himself smiling and answering their questions as he climbed in. "I just wanted to get a breath of fresh air, so—"

He couldn't possibly wait here till Clare came home. It was the second feature she'd wanted to see, and she'd left in time to see the first. She'd be another three hours or— He glanced at his watch; Clare had been gone eight minutes. It wasn't possible, but only eight minutes ago he had kissed his wife goodbye. She wasn't even at the theater yet!

It would be four hours before she could possibly be home, and he tried to picture himself kneeling out here, fingertips hooked to these narrow strippings, while first one movie, preceded by a slow listing of credits, began, developed, reached its climax, and then finally ended. There'd be a newsreel next, maybe, and then an animated cartoon, and then interminable scenes from coming pictures. And then, once more, the beginning of a full-length picture—while all the time he hung out here in the night.

Vocabulary
interminable (in·tʉr′mi·nə·bəl) *adj.:* endless.

Direct Teaching

E English-Language Learners

Interpreting idioms. Tell students that the phrase *at bay* means "away" or "under control." Ask them to hypothesize about why Tom feels he must avoid feelings of yearning. [Possible response: Tom may feel that if he becomes distracted from finding a solution to his problem, he won't be able to successfully complete the task.]

F Literary Focus GRADE-LEVEL STANDARD

Time and sequence. How does the mention of what Clare is doing affect the reader's perception of time? [Possible response: The mention of Clare's mundane activity is jolting and in striking contrast to Tom's experience. While Tom's wife walks to the movies, he is risking his life and is experiencing disturbing emotions and thoughts. The contrast highlights the way that circumstances affect a person's perception of time and shows how dramatically life can change in an instant of time.]

3. thought [*ough* stands for /ô/]
4. rough [*ough* stands for /uf/]

Help students recognize that *trough* and *thought* both have the vowel sound /ô/ and that *trough* and *rough* both end with /f/. Invite students to brainstorm other words with the letters *ough* and to compare them with *trough, through, though, thought,* and *rough.*

Activity. Display these sentences. Have volunteers read each sentence aloud and suggest a word that rhymes with the underlined *ough* word. Students can consult a dictionary if necessary.

1. Snakes regularly slough off their skin. [Possible responses: rough, stuff.]
2. Stretch the pizza dough to fit the pan. [Possible responses: grow, thorough.]
3. The kitten clung to the bough of the tree. [Possible responses: brow, vow.]
4. Purple loosestrife grew in the slough. [Possible responses: due, few, view.]
5. The leader had to make a tough decision. [Possible responses: cuff, enough.]

Direct Teaching

Ⓐ Reading Skills

Making judgments. Have students evaluate Tom's assessment of his own predicament. Could a person withstand several hours outside the window without falling? [Most students will agree that no one could stay out on the ledge. Some students may say that with extreme effort, given the options, a person might stand a chance.]

Ⓐ He might possibly get to his feet, but he was afraid to try. Already his legs were cramped, his thigh muscles tired; his knees hurt, his feet felt numb, and his hands were stiff. He couldn't possibly stay out here for four hours or anywhere near it. Long before that his legs and arms would give out; he would be forced to try changing his position often—stiffly, clumsily, his coordination and strength gone—and he would fall. Quite realistically, he knew that he would fall; no one could stay out here on this ledge for four hours.

A dozen windows in the apartment building across the street were lighted. Looking over his shoulder, he could see the top of a man's head behind the newspaper he was reading; in another window he saw the blue-gray flicker of a television screen. No more than twenty-odd yards from his back were scores of people, and if just one of them would walk idly to his window and glance out. . . . For some moments he stared over his shoulder at the lighted rectangles, waiting. But no one appeared. The man reading his paper turned a page and then continued his reading. A figure passed another of the windows and was immediately gone.

In the inside pocket of his jacket he found a little sheaf of papers, and he pulled one out and looked at it in the light from the living room. It was an old letter, an advertisement of some sort; his name and address, in purple ink, were on a label pasted to the envelope. Gripping one end of the envelope in his teeth, he twisted it into a tight curl. From his shirt pocket he brought out a book of matches. He didn't dare let go the casing with both hands but, with the twist of paper in his teeth, he opened the matchbook with his free hand; then he bent one of the matches in two without tearing it from the folder, its red-tipped end now touching the striking surface. With his thumb, he rubbed the red tip across the striking area.

He did it again, then again, and still again, pressing harder each time, and the match suddenly flared, burning his thumb. But he kept it alight, cupping the matchbook in his hand and shielding it with his body. He held the flame to the paper in his mouth till it caught. Then he snuffed out the match flame with his thumb and forefinger, careless of the burn, and replaced the book in his pocket. Taking the paper twist in his hand, he held it flame down, watching the flame crawl up the paper, till it flared bright. Then he held it behind him over the street, moving it from side to side, watching it over his shoulder, the flame flickering and guttering in the wind.

There were three letters in his pocket and he lighted each of them, holding each till the flame touched his hand and then dropping it to the street below. At one point, watching over his shoulder while the last of the letters burned, he

14 Chapter 1 Plot and Setting • Synthesizing Sources

saw the man across the street put down his paper and stand—even seeming, to Tom, to glance toward his window. But when he moved, it was only to walk across the room and disappear from sight.

There were a dozen coins in Tom Benecke's pocket and he dropped them, three or four at a time. But if they struck anyone, or if anyone noticed their falling, no one connected them with their source, and no one glanced upward.

His arms had begun to tremble from the steady strain of clinging to this narrow perch, and he did not know what to do now and was terribly frightened. Clinging to the window stripping with one hand, he again searched his pockets. But now—he had left his wallet on his dresser when he'd changed clothes—there was nothing left but the yellow sheet. It occurred to him irrelevantly that his death on the sidewalk below would be an eternal mystery; the window closed—why, how, and from where could he have fallen? No one would be able to identify his body for a time, either—the thought was somehow unbearable and increased his fear. All they'd find in his pockets would be the yellow sheet. *Contents of the dead man's pockets,* he thought, *one sheet of paper bearing penciled notations—incomprehensible.* **B**

He understood fully that he might actually be going to die; his arms, maintaining his balance on the ledge, were trembling steadily now. And it occurred to him then with all the force of a revelation that, if he fell, all he was ever going to have out of life he would then, abruptly, have had. Nothing, then, could ever be changed; and nothing more—no least experience or pleasure—could ever be added to his life. **C** He wished, then, that he had not allowed his wife to go off by herself tonight—and on similar nights. He thought of all the evenings he had spent away from her, working; and he regretted them. He thought wonderingly of his fierce ambition and of the direction his life had taken; he thought of the hours he'd spent by himself, filling the yellow sheet that had brought him out here. *Contents of the dead man's pockets,* he thought with sudden fierce anger, *a wasted life.*

He was simply not going to cling here till he slipped and fell; he told himself that now. There was one last thing he could try; he had been aware of it for some moments, refusing to think about it, but now he faced it. Kneeling here on the ledge, the fingertips of one hand pressed to the narrow strip of wood, he could, he knew, draw his other hand back a yard perhaps, fist clenched tight, doing it very slowly till he sensed the outer limit of balance, then, as hard as he was able from the distance, he could drive his fist forward against the glass. **D** If it broke, his fist smashing through, he was safe; he might cut himself badly, and probably would, but with his arm inside the room, he would be secure. But if the glass did not break, the rebound, flinging his arm back, would topple him off the ledge. He was certain of that.

He tested his plan. The fingers of his left hand clawlike on the little stripping, he drew back his other fist until his body began teetering backward. But he had no leverage now—he could feel that there would be no force to his swing—and he moved his fist slowly forward till he rocked forward on his knees again and could sense that his swing would carry its greatest force. Glancing down, however, measuring the distance from his fist to the glass, he saw that it was less than two feet.

It occurred to him that he could raise his arm over his head, to bring it down against the glass. But, experimentally in slow motion, he knew it

Vocabulary

irrelevantly (i·rel′ə·vənt·lē) *adv.:* in a way not relating to the point or situation.

incomprehensible (in·käm′prē·hen′sə·bəl) *adj.:* not understandable.

DIRECT TEACHING

B Learners Having Difficulty

Questioning. Why wouldn't anyone else understand the contents of the yellow sheet? [It contains a jumbled assortment of scribbled notes, facts, figures, and quotations—all related to an independent project that Tom has yet to share with anyone.]

C Reading Skills

Understanding cause and effect. What effect does the realization that he might die have on Tom? [It provokes the revelation that he has wasted an irreplaceable portion of his life, sacrificing precious time with his wife for the sake of his ambition.]

D Literary Focus

GRADE-LEVEL STANDARD

Time and sequence. Have students note the manner in which the author reveals Tom's plan in order to maximize the suspense. First, he states Tom's intention to do something. Then he reveals that Tom has already had an idea, one that he didn't want to think about. Finally, the author slowly explains just what the idea is, detailing each step in the process that will be Tom's last chance to survive.

DIRECT TEACHING

A Literary Focus
REVIEW STANDARD

Imagery. What senses does the imagery in this paragraph appeal to? [*Imagery*—"drive a blow from the shoulder"; *Senses*—touch, sight. *Imagery*—"break through the heavy glass"; *Senses*—touch, sound. *Imagery*—"fingers of his other hand breaking loose"; *Senses*—touch, sight. *Imagery*—"nails scraping along the casing"; *Senses*—touch, sound.]

B Literary Focus
REVIEW STANDARD

Suspense. Have students discuss the ways in which the author prolongs and builds the suspense in the lead-up to this climactic moment. [Possible response: The reader is led through several false starts before the blow is actually delivered. First, Tom experiments with techniques. Next, he visualizes the punch and the terrifying consequences of failure. Then he readies himself once before halting. Finally, he draws back his arm two separate times before delivering the climactic blow.]

C Literary Focus
REVIEW STANDARD

Plot: Parallel episodes. What earlier episode do these events recall? How does this episode differ? [Possible response: This scene echoes the departure of Tom's wife, which sent the yellow sheet flying out the window the first time. This time, however, Tom is no longer worried about the sheet; he is joining his wife rather than working.]

D Literary Focus
REVIEW STANDARD

Conflict. How has Tom resolved his conflict? [Possible response: His indifference to the sheet—for which he risked his life—indicates that time with his wife will now take precedence over his career.]

would be an awkward blow without the force of a driving punch, and not nearly enough to break the glass.

A Facing the window, he had to drive a blow from the shoulder, he knew now, at a distance of less than two feet; and he did not know whether it would break through the heavy glass. It might; he could picture it happening, he could feel it in the nerves of his arm. And it might not; he could feel that too—feel his fist striking this glass and being instantaneously flung back by the unbreaking pane, feel the fingers of his other hand breaking loose, nails scraping along the casing as he fell.

He waited, arm drawn back, fist balled, but in no hurry to strike; this pause, he knew, might be an extension of his life. And to live even a few seconds longer, he felt, even out here on this ledge in the night, was infinitely better than to die a moment earlier than he had to. His arm grew tired, and he brought it down and rested it.

B Then he knew that it was time to make the attempt. He could not kneel here hesitating indefinitely till he lost all courage to act, waiting till he slipped off the ledge. Again he drew back his arm, knowing this time that he would not bring it down till he struck. His elbow protruding over Lexington Avenue far below, the fingers of his other hand pressed down bloodlessly tight against the narrow stripping, he waited, feeling the sick tenseness and terrible excitement building. It grew and swelled toward the moment of action, his nerves tautening. He thought of Clare—just a wordless, yearning thought—and then drew his arm back just a bit more, fist so tight his fingers pained him, and knowing he was going to do it. Then with full power, with every last scrap of strength he could bring to bear, he shot his arm forward toward the glass, and he said "Clare!"

He heard the sound, felt the blow, felt himself falling forward, and his hand closed on the living-room curtains, the shards and fragments of glass showering onto the floor. And then, kneeling there on the ledge, an arm thrust into the room up to the shoulder, he began picking away the protruding slivers and great wedges of glass from the window frame, tossing them in onto the rug. And, as he grasped the edges of the empty window frame and climbed into his home, he was grinning in triumph.

He did not lie down on the floor or run through the apartment, as he had promised himself; even in the first few moments it seemed to him natural and normal that he should be where he was. He simply turned to his desk, pulled the crumpled yellow sheet from his pocket, and laid it down where it had been, smoothing it out; then he absently laid a pencil across it to weight it down. He shook his head wonderingly, and turned to walk toward the closet.

C There he got out his topcoat and hat and, without waiting to put them on, opened the front door and stepped out, to go find his wife. He turned to pull the door closed and warm air from the hall rushed through the narrow opening again. As he saw the yellow paper, the pencil flying, scooped off the desk and, unimpeded by the glassless window, sail out into the night and out of his life, Tom Benecke burst into laughter and then closed the door behind him. ■ **D**

Vocabulary
unimpeded (un′im·pēd′id) *adj.:* not blocked; unobstructed.

FAMILY/COMMUNITY ACTIVITY

Ask students to share this story with their parents or other adult family members. After everyone has read the story, students may have family members discuss any difficulties they've had balancing workplace demands with the desire to spend more time at home. Have students ask the adults whether they have ever experienced moments of truth (perhaps less dramatic than that of Tom in the story), in which they realized that their families must take precedence over career ambitions. The adults might talk about how they have tried to rearrange their lives in order to maximize their time with loved ones. Ask volunteers to share with the class some of the responses they received. Remind students to get permission to share with the class their family members' responses.

Meet the Writer

Jack Finney

Space Aliens and Time Travel

Menacing alien plants hatch from pods, take human form, and gradually replace everyone—or almost everyone—in a small California town. Jack Finney (1911–1995) created this science fiction scenario in his second novel, *The Body Snatchers* (1955). The novel was turned into a horror-movie classic, *The Invasion of the Body Snatchers,* in 1956. For years, critics debated the secret meaning of the story—was it a protest against communism or a criticism of anti-Communist hysteria? Finney, a reclusive author who gave few interviews, had his own terse explanation: "I wrote the story purely as a good read."

Jack Finney, born Walter Braden Finney, was originally an advertising copywriter in New York City in the 1940s. Bored with his job, he began to write short stories in his spare time. When his stories began appearing regularly in popular magazines, such as *The Saturday Evening Post* and *Collier's*, Finney quit his advertising job to write full time. He published several collections of short stories and eight novels, five of which were made into movies.

Finney's second bestseller, *Time and Again* (1970), combines science fiction, mystery, and romance in a suspenseful time-travel adventure. In this tale a top-secret government project drafts Simon Morley, a young advertising illustrator in New York City, for an important mission that sends him back in time from 1970 to 1882. Finney's accurate, detailed picture of late-nineteenth-century Manhattan makes this novel a cult favorite, especially among those who love New York.

In commenting on the research needed to paint his meticulously realistic settings, Finney said,

> "I find a good thing to do is to get newspapers. . . . I look at anything that was going on. . . . I'm doing my best to give a feeling of what it was like. . . . That kind of stuff is fun, but that's also why it takes a long, long time."

For Independent Reading

You might want to read Finney's sequel to *Time and Again,* titled *From Time to Time* (1995). In the sequel, Morley is sent on another time-travel mission. This time he journeys back to 1912 to prevent the outbreak of World War I (in order to save the life of his young son) and to stop the sailing of the doomed R.M.S. *Titanic.*

GUIDED PRACTICE

Monitoring students' progress. To assess students' understanding of the selection, ask them to write a concise capsule review of the story, one that might appear in an in-brief section of a magazine or newspaper. Students should provide an overview of the plot, comment briefly on the writer's style, and express an overall opinion about the work.

Meet the Writer

Background. Much of the Milwaukee-born writer's work centered around the idea of time travel. Finney's 1986 collection *About Time* contains twelve short stories focused on this theme. Three decades earlier, the title tale of his collection *The Third Level* described a mysterious section of New York's Grand Central Terminal, where passengers could catch a train that ran back to the year 1894. The story displays Finney's vivid imagination, as well as his sense of humor.

Despite his fascination with time, Finney didn't expect his own writing to maintain its appeal for decades. He was both pleased and surprised by the enduring attraction of his works, such as *The Body Snatchers,* which was made into a movie three times. "You write a book, and you don't expect it to hang around," said Finney.

DIFFERENTIATING INSTRUCTION

Advanced Learners

Enrichment. Ask students to read several different short stories or novels by Finney and other writers that deal with the topic of time travel. Then, have them hold a panel discussion on the subject. Each student should give a brief presentation on the works that they have read. Preselect one student to serve in the role of a moderator. This student will direct the postpresentation discussion and use a prepared list of questions to initiate a comparison of the themes and ideas presented in the different works. Suggest that students enter *Jack Finney, Science Fantasy,* or *Science Fiction* as the keywords in an Internet search engine to find works on the subject of time travel.

Contents of the Dead Man's Pocket 17

Connection

Summary ⇔ *at grade level*

Kenneth Koch's poem echoes the dilemma faced by the protagonist of "Contents of the Dead Man's Pocket." In the poem the speaker claims that of three universal desires—love, a social life, and career success—there can only be time for two. He playfully spans the centuries to find support for his argument, questioning whether Michelangelo had time for a social life and noting that Homer lacked a girlfriend.

DIRECT TEACHING

A Reading Skills

Interpreting. According to the speaker, what do people want? [success and fulfillment in love, social life, and work] Does the speaker think it is possible to have all three of these things? [No, the speaker maintains that a person can only have two out of the three.]

B Learners Having Difficulty

Paraphrasing. Ask students to put this line into their own words. [Possible response: A day is too short.]

C Literary Focus REVIEW STANDARD

Allusion. Remind students that an allusion is a reference to something outside the text—often to a person, place, or event from history, religion, or mythology. What allusion does the speaker make to support the point that there isn't enough time for love, work, and friends? [The speaker alludes to masterpieces by Michelangelo, claiming that having created these works, the artist couldn't possibly have had time for a social life.]

CONNECTION / POEM

You want a social life, with friends

Kenneth Koch

(A) You want a social life, with friends,
A passionate love life and as well
To work hard every day. What's true
Is of these three you may have two
And two can pay you dividends
But never may have three.

There isn't enough time, my friends—
(B) Though dawn begins, yet midnight ends—
To find the time to have love, work, and friends.
(C) Michelangelo had feeling
For Vittoria and the Ceiling°
But did he go to parties at day's end?

Homer° nightly went to banquets
Wrote all day but had no lockets
Bright with pictures of his Girl.
I know one who loves and parties
And has done so since his thirties
But writes hardly anything at all.

11. Michelangelo . . . Ceiling: Michelangelo Buonarroti (1475–1564) was an Italian Renaissance painter, sculptor, and architect. He sculpted *La Vittoria* (or *Victory*) for the tomb of Pope Julius II and painted the famous ceiling of the Sistine Chapel at the Vatican in Rome.

13. Homer: ancient Greek epic poet (eighth or ninth century B.C.) credited with composing the *Iliad* and the *Odyssey*.

Connecting and Comparing Texts

Ask students to discuss whether or not Tom, the protagonist of "Contents of the Dead Man's Pocket," would agree with the sentiments expressed in "You want a social life, with friends." [Many students will say that after his near-death experience, Tom would certainly agree with the speaker of the poem. Some will note that Tom doesn't appear to have time for even two of the three realms of life discussed in the poem, since friends play no role in Finney's story.]

Literary Response and Analysis

Reading Check

1. **Summarize** the key events of the plot, being careful to identify **causes** and their **effects.** To indicate causes and effects, use words and phrases like *as a result, because of, then, thus, therefore.*

Interpretations

2. Like many stories, this one is built on choices made by the main character. What choice has Tom already made when the story opens? Why does he choose to risk his life to retrieve the paper?
3. Stories are also built on conflict. Does Tom experience **internal conflict, external conflict,** or both? Which is more compelling to you as a reader? Explain.
4. The story's events are told in **chronological order,** yet on page 13, Tom—and the reader also—is shocked to discover that only eight minutes have passed. How does Finney make time move slowly?
5. The two **settings**—ledge and apartment—are important in this story. How are they contrasted? How are you supposed to feel about each setting?
6. Name at least three ways in which Finney creates intense, hold-your-breath **suspense.** Consider the effects of the **setting** and the story's title. In your opinion, at what moment of the plot is the suspense greatest?
7. Based on Tom's actions at the very end of the story, what can you infer is the story's **theme** (its revelation about life)? How does the theme compare with that of Kenneth Koch's poem (see the ***Connection*** on page 18)?

Evaluation

8. Was the **resolution** of the story credible to you? Did you find Tom's actions believable?
9. What is your opinion of the premise of Koch's poem (See the ***Connection*** on page 18)? Can a person have all three—a social life with friends, a love life, and a successful career—or can you have only two? Be sure to give reasons for your opinion.

Writing

Just Add the Details

Look back at your Quickwrite notes, and replay the events in your mind's eye, as if you were watching yourself or the other person on a video. Take notes as you think about the sensory aspects of the scene—what could be seen, heard, touched, smelled. Then, write a **narrative** about the experience. Relate the events, and add enough sensory details to make readers feel they are there. You could draw out the suspense by imitating Finney: Describe each action and reaction of your character in exact detail, second by second.

Use "Writing an Autobiographical Narrative," pages 56–63, for help with this assignment.

Reading Standard 3.6 Analyze and trace an author's development of time and sequence.

Reading Check

1. Possible answer: Tom decides not to go out with his wife because he wants to work on a project. When she leaves, a gust of wind causes a paper to fly out his window onto a ledge. The paper is crucial to Tom's work; therefore, he climbs outside his eleventh-story apartment to retrieve it. A view of the street below causes him to panic. Then his fear-induced scramble back to his apartment causes him to jam the window shut. Tom risks falling by breaking the window and reenters the apartment. Since he now knows that his relationship is more important than work, he lets the paper blow away and leaves to find his wife.

INDEPENDENT PRACTICE

Literary Response and Analysis

Interpretations

2. Tom chooses to spend time on work rather than with his wife. Career ambition causes him to risk his life.
3. He experiences both. Internal conflicts include finding time for his wife and work and trying not to panic while out on the ledge. His attempt to break the window is an example of external conflict.
4. He describes in detail Tom's every thought, feeling, and action, slowing the pace of the narrative.
5. The warm, comfortable apartment is contrasted with the cold, dangerous ledge. The reader is expected to view the apartment as safe and hospitable, and the ledge as risky and foreboding.
6. Possible answer: The story's title raises the possibility of Tom's death. The setting, a narrow ledge eleven stories high, creates tremendous anxiety. Methodical pacing and vivid description of Tom's panic add to the suspense. Most suspenseful moments: when Tom loses control and scrambles along the ledge; when he poises himself to break the glass.
7. Possible answer: By nearly perishing, Tom realizes that his wife is more important to him than his job. The story's theme is "recognizing what matters most in life." Koch's poem advances a similar theme: Not everything one desires can be given equal attention, and one must therefore choose.

Evaluation

8. Many students will say that the resolution is credible. Some may find it odd that he so easily lets go of the paper for which he risked his life.
9. Some students will claim that a balance can be struck. Others will say that, inevitably, one or two of these must win out.

Vocabulary Development

Practice

1. Possible Answers
   - *projection.* *Etymology*—MFr < L *projectio.* *Prefix*—*pro–,* meaning "forward."
   - *discarding.* *Etymology*—OFr *descarter.* *Prefix*—*dis–,* meaning "to deprive of."
   - *confirmation.* *Etymology*—ME & OFr *confirmacion.* *Prefix*—*con–,* meaning "together."
   - *exhalation.* *Etymology*—L *exhalatio.* *Prefix*—*ex–,* meaning "out."
   - *imperceptibly.* *Etymology*—Fr < ML *imperceptibilis.* *Prefix*—*im–,* meaning "not."
   - *rebounded.* *Etymology*—ME *rebounden* < OFr *reboundir.* *Prefix*—*re–,* meaning "again."
   - *interminable.* *Etymology*—OFr < LL *interminabilus.* *Prefix*—*in–,* meaning "no."
   - *irrelevantly.* *Etymology*—ML < L *relevans.* *Prefix*—*ir–,* meaning "not."
   - *incomprehensible.* *Etymology*—< L *incomprehensibilis.* *Prefix*—*in–,* meaning "not."
   - *unimpeded.* *Etymology*—L *impedire,* "to entangle." *Prefix*—*un–,* meaning "not."
2. Responses will vary. Check that students' words contain each of the prefixes in the chart.
3. Possible answers: convert, invert, revert, subvert, extrovert, avert.

Resources Reminder

Vocabulary

- *Vocabulary Development*
  - Vocabulary Worksheet, p. 1
- *Lesson Plans for Language Development*
  - Vocabulary, pp. 26, 30

ASSESSING

Assessment

- *Progress Assessment of Reading*
  - Selection Test

Vocabulary Development

Word Analysis: Prefixes

Just by adding a few letters upfront, you can turn *appear* into *disappear, locate* into *relocate,* and *legible* into *illegible. Dis–, re–,* and *il–* are **prefixes,** word parts that attach to the front of a word or word root to change its meaning. The diagram on the lower right shows seven prefixes that attach to the root *–ject–* (from the Latin word *jacere,* "to throw") to create new English words. Learning the meanings of common prefixes can help you figure out the meanings of some unfamiliar words.

Spelling hint: When a prefix is added to a word, the spelling of the original word usually remains the same: *dis–* + *similar* = *dissimilar; extra–* + *ordinary* = *extraordinary.*

Word Bank

projection
discarding
confirmation
exhalation
imperceptibly
rebounded
interminable
irrelevantly
incomprehensib
unimpeded

Latin Prefix	Meaning	Example
com–, con–	together; with	conjunction
in–, il–, im–, ir–	no, not; in, into, on	inoperable
inter–	between, among; together	international
pre–	before	prefabricate
pro–	forward; defending	prolabor
re–	again	reexamine
sub–	under; below	subnormal
Greek Prefix	**Meaning**	**Example**
hyper–	above; more than normal	hyperactive
micro–	small	microorganism
mono–	one	monologue
ex–	away from; out	expand
Anglo-Saxon Prefix	**Meaning**	**Example**
a–	out; up	arise
with–	away; back; against	withstand
un–	not; opposite of	unable

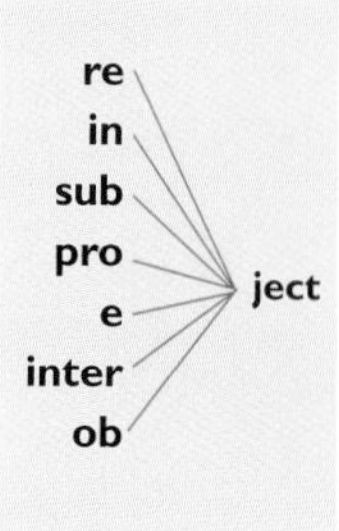

PRACTICE

1. Working with a partner, use a dictionary to find the **etymology**—word history—of the Word Bank words. Be sure to identify each prefix and its meaning. Remember that for some words that have prefixes, only the root word will be defined in the dictionary.
2. Work with a partner or team to think of as many other example words as you can for each of the prefixes in the chart.
3. Combine the root *–vert–* (from the Latin *vertere,* "to turn") with prefixes from the prefix chart to form new words.

Reading Standard 1.1 Understand word derivations.

RETEACHING

For another selection to teach Standard 3.6, see *Interactive Reading,* Chapter 1.

Before You Read INFORMATIONAL MATERIALS

Double Daddy ◆ Diary of a Mad Blender ◆ The Child's View of Working Parents

Synthesizing: Putting It All Together

When you are doing research or reading several articles on a topic, you want to **synthesize** the materials—that is, put it all together so that you can better understand the subject.

What's the best way to do that? Examine each source, and then compare the sources. Try following these steps:

- **Determine the message.** Look for each writer's **main ideas,** and take notes. For a difficult text or passage, try **paraphrasing,** or restating the sentences in your own words.
- **Look for supporting evidence.** As you read, be aware of how the writer supports each main idea. Does the writer offer facts, statistics, examples, anecdotes (brief stories about real people), or quotations?
- **Compare and contrast.** Note where each source agrees with or differs from the others on a topic or idea.
- **Make connections.** Relate each writer's message to other works you've read. Is the writer expressing the same ideas you found in other articles or books or even in a story or poem?
- **Put it all together.** When you have completed the above steps, you are ready to put everything together in a discussion about the topic. To practice **synthesizing,** you might write a research report, an editorial, a speech, or a letter. Be sure to acknowledge the source of the information or ideas that you cite.

Vocabulary Development

phenomenon (fə·näm′ə·nən) *n.:* observable event, fact, or circumstance.

chronic (krän′ik) *adj.:* constant; habitual.

trekked (trekt) *v.:* journeyed.

splicing (splīs′iŋ) *v.* used as *n.:* joining by inserting and binding together.

integrate (in′tə·grāt′) *v.:* combine; unify.

colleague (käl′ēg′) *n.:* fellow worker.

conviction (kən·vik′shən) *n.:* strong belief.

maximizes (mak′sə·mīz′iz) *v.:* increases as much as possible.

autonomy (ô·tän′ə·mē) *n.:* independence.

poignant (poin′yənt) *adj.:* emotionally moving; touching.

Connecting to the Literature

At the end of "Contents of the Dead Man's Pocket," Tom has decided to spend more time with his wife instead of overworking. In the articles that follow, different people comment on the difficulties of balancing time at work with time at home in today's busy world.

Reading Standard 2.4 Synthesize the content from several sources dealing with a single issue; paraphrase the ideas and connect them to other sources and related topics to demonstrate comprehension.

STANDARDS FOCUS, pp. 21–30

(For the grade-level standards taught in this lesson, see citations on Student Edition pages.)

Prerequisite Standard

- Grade 8, Reading Comprehension 2.6 **Use information from a variety of consumer, workplace, and public documents to explain a situation or decision and to solve a problem.**

Summary *at grade level*

Three short pieces focus on balancing work and home life. "Double Daddy" concerns stresses faced by working fathers. "Diary of a Mad Blender" is a humorous look at how one work-at-home mother tries to integrate work and family. "The Child's View of Working Parents" explores the issue from the children's perspective.

PRETEACHING

Selection Starter

Motivate. Have students vote on whether they agree with these statements. Tally the answers, and invite class discussion. Tell students that they will read about these issues.

1. If your boss expects you to work longer hours, you have to do it.
2. Fathers should put their jobs ahead of their families.
3. Fathers and mothers should share equally in childcare.
4. Both parents should have careers.

RESOURCES: READING

Planning

- *One-Stop Planner* CD-ROM with Test Generator
- *On Course: Mapping Instruction*

Media

- *Audio CD Library*
  - disc 2

Reading

- *Interactive Reading,* Teacher's Edition
  - Graphic Organizer: Synthesis Chart

Differentiating Instruction

- *Lesson Plans for Language Development*
  - English-Language Learners, pp. 9–11, 27, 31
  - Special Education Students, pp. 12, 27, 31

Vocabulary

- *Vocabulary Development*
  - Vocabulary Worksheet, p. 2

Assessment

- *Progress Assessment of Reading*
  - Selection Test
- *One-Stop Planner* CD-ROM with Test Generator

PRETEACHING

Preview Vocabulary

Have students answer the following questions to help them master the Vocabulary words on p. 21.

1. What phenomenon of family life today was seldom seen fifty years ago? [Mothers working.]
2. What should a sufferer of chronic lateness do? [Buy a watch.]
3. Where was the last place you trekked to? [Responses will vary.]
4. Why is splicing together enough time for career and family difficult? [Both are demanding.]
5. Provide an example of how to integrate entertainment and learning. [Read a book.]
6. Name a colleague of your teacher. [Other teachers.]
7. What conviction do you hold about how to succeed in life? [Education is the key.]
8. If a boy maximizes homework time, what happens to television viewing? [It reduces.]
9. Do most parents give their children enough autonomy? Explain. [Responses will vary.]
10. Identify a poignant movie scene. [Responses will vary.]

DIRECT TEACHING

A Reading Skills

Paraphrasing ideas. Have students paraphrase the message expressed in these paragraphs. [Possible response: Men as well as women now struggle to balance career and family.]

B Reading Informational Materials
GRADE-LEVEL STANDARD

Synthesizing content. Invite students to discuss what they have learned from other media and their own observations about how parents deal with child-care and workplace responsibilities.

NEWSPAPER ARTICLE

Double Daddy

from *The Denver Post*, September 5, 1999

Penny Parker

They struggle between the responsibilities of work and the needs of their families.

They have demanding jobs; they have children.

In some cases, they go to work before dawn, or take work home.

They race home to make it in time for their child's game, or play, or concert.

They worry that a business trip might take them away on their son's or daughter's birthday.

And surprise: They're men.

The Super Mom syndrome has jumped genders. Now it's working men who also want to be great fathers.

What has changed to make the working dad's life more stressful?

More is expected of fathers at home these days—and they expect more of themselves—but the demands of the workplace have, if anything, increased in recent years.

The phenomenon of "daddy stress"—as *Forbes* magazine dubbed it in a recent cover story—affects men from the executive office to the rank and file, and while a growing number of single dads may feel it most, married fathers are hardly immune.

"It's a familiar theme to women and not to men, and not to men's employers," said Linda Dunlap, chairwoman of the psychology department at Marist College in Poughkeepsie, N.Y., and an expert on families. "These men are saying, 'I'm working my tail off to get ahead, for the most part for my family, but I'm not spending time with my family. This doesn't make sense.' "

Ryan Streeter, a research fellow in the Welfare Policy Center at Hudson Institute in Indianapolis, calls the growing trend of men examining their roles as fathers "a national movement."

"There's been an increasing amount of literature, events, commercials, and public service announcements around the country in the last five years that have targeted the need for fathers to be engaged in their children's lives," Streeter said. "A group of largely men said it's time to take responsibility for their children not only economically, but emotionally and spiritually. There's a national consciousness around this matter."

The next step has to be a shift in the workplace mentality that says it's OK for a woman to take time off to stay home with a sick child or attend a child's football game, but it's not OK for a dad to do the same thing.

"It's popular to say there needs to be workplace flexibility for men," Streeter said, "but in general, corporations have the expectation for men to put business over family."

Brian Wills never set out to become a stay-at-home dad. It just worked out that way.

When he left his job in the marketing department of the *Denver Rocky Mountain News*

Vocabulary
phenomenon (fə·näm′ə·nən) *n.:* observable event, fact, or circumstance.

two and a half years ago, Wills says, he thought he'd pick up work as a freelance[1] copywriter for a while until a "regular job" came his way.

But because he was at home, Wills started "plugging into" more parts of his three children's lives. Now he's so engaged with their schedules and activities that he says he'd never go back to the corporate world.

On a typical recent day, Wills' focus was ferrets.[2]

His 11-year-old daughter Ashley wanted to take her ferrets to school for show and tell, and Wills' job was to ferry the ferrets back and forth.

A single dad who has remarried, Wills shares parental time and responsibilities with his ex-wife, who lives two miles away.

Three mornings a week, Wills and his oldest son, Eric, 15, work out at a health club together.

1. **freelance** *adj.:* not under contract for regular work but providing services independently.
2. **ferrets** *n.:* mammals about the size of a cat that are sometimes domesticated or used in hunting.

"That started to become a real important time of dialogue between us and has remained that," Wills said.

Once a week, Wills picks up Ashley at school and takes her out to lunch.

After school, Wills watches his sons, Eric and Ben, 12, practice in their rock band.

"They call me their band manager," Wills said, with more than a hint of pride.

Wills said he did time in the corporate rat race.

"In my 20s I really wanted to succeed in my job," he said. "I had a company car by the time I was 30. I was traveling a lot and never seeing my kids. Now it's become really precious for me in the sense that I know it's going to be somewhat short-lived."

Wills said he's gotten over his fear of being a freelancer, where he can't count on a regular income.

"I have a much greater fear about going into a stable income environment and losing time with my kids," he says. "That scares me way more." **C**

DIRECT TEACHING

C Reading Informational Materials
GRADE-LEVEL STANDARD

? Synthesizing content. In their attitudes toward work, how are Brian Wills and Tom Benecke (the protagonist of "Contents of the Dead Man's Pocket") similar? [Possible responses: Both were very ambitious in their careers, but both change their views. Both come to value the time spent with family more than career success.]

DIRECT TEACHING

A Reading Informational Materials
GRADE-LEVEL STANDARD

Synthesizing content. Have students compare and contrast the focus of this article with the focus of the previous article. [Possible response: Both articles focus on integrating work and personal life. Unlike "Double Daddy," this article does not appear to have a gender-specific focus. In addition, it deals with the role of technology in helping with work-home integration, an issue not treated in "Double Daddy."]

B Reading Skills

Classifying. What kind of details does the author use to illustrate the difficulties that she has while "integrating"? [She uses humorous personal anecdotes.]

NEWSPAPER ARTICLE

Diary of a Mad Blender

A Week of Managing Every Spare Minute

from *The Wall Street Journal,* March 22, 2000

Sue Shellenbarger

A It's one of the hottest work-life trends: integrating work and personal roles with the help of technology and flexible work setups.

I work from home, but there's certainly more I could do to integrate my work and my personal life. And as a chronic stretcher of deadlines whose home office looks like a landfill, I could use some help. So I trekked to a bookstore for an armload of time-management and life-balance books and tried some of their tips for a week. A few notes on the results follow.

Thursday. Heeding author Kathy Peel's advice to "never underestimate the potential of small snippets of time" (in *Be Your Best: The Family Manager's Guide to Personal Success*), I begin splicing work into unoccupied moments. I take my laptop to my son's dentist appointment and work in the waiting room. I edit a story on a treadmill at the gym, where I find it easy to slash the fat out of my copy.

Friday. To integrate some play with my work, I quit my office a couple of hours early, pack my cell phone and laptop, and drive my kids to a nearby ski area for a little night snowboarding. As I help my son with his bindings, a colleague calls on my cell phone to ask for sources for a story. Though I know the subject, I draw a blank. Somehow, the grandeur of my environment has idled the needed part of my brain.

After a stint on the slopes, I head to the lodge to work. My son bursts in. "Did you see me? I was bombing it!" he cries, thrilled by a rocket-fast run. Disappointed that I wasn't watching out the window, he leaves. At this moment, I realize, my presence is a pretense of little value to him. I'm actually consumed by work.

Monday. The experts suggest a laundry list of things to do while my computer is booting up. I love one bit of advice from *Family Education Today,* a newsletter: Write a postcard to a friend. But when I try taking a "minivacation," closing my eyes and breathing deep, I can't seem to relax.

B I try another tip: Meow loudly like a cat to firm your facial muscles. While I enjoy acting like an animal, our family Labrador, cat, and kitten gather in a puzzled circle around my chair. Then the kitten bites me in the ankle and runs away. I wonder what human co-workers would do.

Revved up to twitch speed, I pick up voice mail on my cell phone while driving my kids

Vocabulary

chronic (krän′ik) *adj.:* constant; habitual.

trekked (trekt) *v.:* journeyed.

splicing (splīs′iŋ) *v.* used as *n.:* joining by inserting and binding together.

integrate (in′tə·grāt′) *v.:* combine; unify.

colleague (käl′ēg′) *n.:* fellow worker.

DIFFERENTIATING INSTRUCTION

Learners Having Difficulty
You may wish to pair students as they read these three articles. Encourage them to take turns reading to each other. After students complete each article, have them work together to create an idea tree that identifies the main ideas (trunk) and supporting information (branches). To help the partners connect the articles to other sources, suggest that they discuss examples of people they know who illustrate the ideas.

Resources Reminder

Differentiating Instruction

- *Interactive Reading,* Teacher's Edition
  - Graphic Organizer: Synthesis Chart

English-Language Learners
Some students may have difficulty with the colloquialisms and work-related vocabulary in these articles. Ask them to use context to try to determine the meanings of terms, such as *flexible work setups, laundry list, slash the fat, X-Games of Extreme Integration,* and *give people an inch.* Ask volunteers to provide examples that help clarify these terms for other students.

home from school and listen to a time-management book on tape. Though I get it all done, my brain feels like Los Angeles after an earthquake.

Later, I discover that amid the self-imposed pressure, I forgot an editor's request that I review some copy that evening. I apologize, but the damage is done.

Tuesday. In *Take Back Your Time,* Jan Jasper advises getting little tasks done while watching television. I try opening mail and sorting work papers into stacks. I make a big dent in my office piles. But my daughter, who usually looks forward to watching TV with me, leaves the room.

Wednesday. By week's end, I am an also-ran in the X-Games of Extreme Integration. My experiment has indeed made me more efficient. My office is neater, and I'm embracing some of the integration tips permanently, such as writing some postcards during free moments and taking work with me to do while waiting in doctor's offices and other appointments.

But jugglers beware. It was far easier for me to splice more work into my week than to add time for rest and relationships. For me, at least, extreme integration is a rigged game—in favor of work.

And as I review my work, I agree, as James Gleick suggests in his 1999 book *Faster,* that the more I cram into my days, the stupider I get. My jampacked week has produced not one fresh idea or novel insight. Only after family needs force me to take a complete break does my mind kick back into a creative mode.

Maybe, as some management gurus suggest, my brain just needs a little cross-training. But in its current condition, it clearly needs a good long rest.

DIRECT TEACHING

C Reading Informational Materials
GRADE-LEVEL STANDARD

Synthesizing content. Ask students to paraphrase the author's conclusions about the value of the integration techniques she experiments with. [Possible response: Although they may help her work more efficiently, they do little to create more time for friends, family, or relaxation.] What advice do you think Brian Wills of "Double Daddy" would give her? [Possible response: Worry less about work, and spend more time with your children; this time of their lives is precious and will not come again.]

Resources Reminder
For lessons designed for intermediate and advanced English-language learners, see *Lesson Plans for Language Development,* pp. 9–11, 27, 31.

Special Education Students
For lessons designed for special education students, see *Lesson Plans for Language Development,* pp. 12, 27, 31.

Advanced Learners
Enrichment. Ask students to research how employers try to enhance their employees' abilities to balance work and home life by providing improved child-care, flextime, telecommuting, and personal leave programs.

Activity. Have students use the results of their research to write an essay that compares and contrasts the family friendliness of past and present workplace environments.

DIRECT TEACHING

A Reading Informational Materials
GRADE-LEVEL STANDARD
Synthesizing content. Remind students that a cliché is an overused expression that may contain a kernel of truth or describe something in an apt way. Ask if they agree that the description of working parents as jugglers is a cultural cliché, and have them support their opinions with examples. [Most students will agree, citing the portraits of parents trying to balance work and family in the previous two articles, as well as similar depictions of parents in popular culture. Students may note that the writer of "Diary of a Mad Blender" uses the expression.]

B Reading Informational Materials
GRADE-LEVEL STANDARD
? Synthesizing content. How will this examination of the subject differ from the previous two? [The previous two articles examined the issue from the perspective of the parents; this one will look at it from the perspective of the children.]

C Reading Informational Materials
GRADE-LEVEL STANDARD
? Synthesizing content. How do anecdotes from the two previous articles help support this conclusion? [In "Diary of a Mad Blender," the author reports on her son's and daughter's disappointment that though she is present she is not engaged in their activities. In "Double Daddy," Brian Wills tells of his becoming close to his children through involvement in their activities.]

MAGAZINE ARTICLE

The Child's View of Working Parents

from *Fortune,* November 8, 1999

Cora Daniels

A The image of working parents as jugglers long ago entered the gallery of cultural clichés. We know that balancing work and family life produces stress and guilt, not to mention the uncomfortable conviction that one day your child will cry to a therapist about how the baby sitter nursed her through the chickenpox. But what do children really feel about all this? That was the question that Ellen Galinsky, cofounder and president of the Families and Work Institute, set out to answer in her new book, *Ask the Children: What America's Children Really Think* **B** *About Working Parents.* Galinsky surveyed 1,023 children in the third through twelfth grades, as well as 605 employed parents. She had help designing the questions from her own daughter, Lara, who did one-on-one interviews with children of various backgrounds to find out what issues were important to them. Galinsky made some surprising discoveries. For one thing, children don't seem to mind that their parents work. But they do wish that when their parents were around, they were less tired and stressed. Galinsky found that the amount of time parents (both **C** mothers and fathers) spend with their children does matter, but so does the kind of time. Children who reported that their parents can focus on them when they're together were more likely to feel that their parents were good jugglers. And as Galinsky told *Fortune*'s Cora Daniels in a recent interview, when children have the chickenpox—or any illness—they really do want their parents around.

What did you find when you looked at spillover from family life to work life?

We asked parents, "How often have you been in a good mood at work because of your children?" Seventy-one percent said that they'd been in a good mood either often or very often at work because of their children. If you look at the people who say that they've been in a good mood at home because of their work, it's 37 percent. In fact, kids really energize us for work.

Do companies need to adopt new policies to help out?

People who work more tend to feel more stressed. But the real thing that's powerful is job pressure. You have deadlines that are difficult to meet; you have such a large amount of work, you can never get everything done. So the message to employers is to think about creating a work environment that maximizes people's productivity. We've tended to think of the main thing to do with children as helping to provide child care. That's important, but I think that for real return on investment, you need to think about creating an environment that helps people work in a more constructive way.

You also recommend that working parents be home when their child is sick.

Vocabulary

conviction (kən·vik′shən) *n.:* strong belief.

maximizes (mak′sə·mīz′iz) *v.:* increases as much as possible.

26 Chapter 1 Plot and Setting • Synthesizing Sources

In the early days when I was doing research on this subject, the conventional wisdom was that if you provide flexibility, employees will take a mile. We followed Johnson & Johnson through a process where it provided more flexibility, and it found that absenteeism went down. If you give people an inch, they give you an inch. If people have the flexibility to take care of family issues, they tend to be there for you when you need them as an employer. Give and take.

What can you tell about the next generation of workers?

A lot of business leaders I talk to think people aren't going to be willing to just get involved in the kind of frantic overwork that so many people do today. Children who have seen their parents struggle aren't going to be willing to do that. Not many people want to work harder than their parents. They might want to work as hard, but they don't want to work harder. People who are managing Generation X already feel there are some differences. Generation Xers want more autonomy; they're less willing to settle for less say in their jobs.

What is the bottom line of what kids are trying to tell us?

They're telling us that there is a problem, but it's not *that* we work, it's *how* we work. They worry about us. Two thirds of the kids worried about their parents at least some of the time, and mostly if we were tired and stressed. They often worried about our safety. Will we get to work safely? Will there be an accident? Will something go wrong? They are telling us to be there for them. And they're telling us—and I think this is perhaps one of the most poignant findings of the study—"If we act as if we don't want to talk, we may not know just how to tell you that we want to talk, but we really do. Don't set up the moment for the perfect quality time. Hang out with us, and then we'll warm up to it. And hang in there." **D**

Vocabulary

autonomy (ô·tän′ə·mē) *n.:* independence.

poignant (poin′yənt) *adj.:* emotionally moving; touching.

Direct Teaching

D Reading Skills

Summarizing. According to Galinsky, what do kids want from their working parents? [Possible response: Kids accept that their parents have to work. They don't need parents to try setting up artificial "quality time" situations; instead, kids want parents simply to be there for them in a natural way.]

Guided Practice

Monitoring students' progress. To assess students' understanding of the selections, have them answer the *5W-How?* questions for each of the selections.

Family/Community Activity

Have students work in small groups to design and conduct a survey on issues of integrating work and family life—similar to the one described in "The Child's View of Working Parents." Groups should choose particular kinds of respondents (for example, working parents, children, teachers with children) and then design a list of pertinent questions. Questions will depend upon the respondents chosen but might resemble the following items:

- What techniques help you maximize the quality time you have with your family?
- What workplace program or policy would most improve your ability to balance work and family needs?
- Do you think that your parents work too much?

Encourage students to display their results.

INDEPENDENT PRACTICE

Analyzing Informational Materials

Reading Check

1. "Double Daddy" deals with the difficulties working fathers face in balancing the demands of work and family.
2. The author provides a day-by-day account of her "mad" attempt to "blend" her work and family life.
3. Galinsky predicts that in the future, people will be less willing to be involved in frantic overwork.
4. Kids worry that their parents are often tired or stressed.

Test Practice

Answers and Model Rationales

1. **D** D is the best choice since "more than before" captures the article's focus on change. B is incorrect; the article states that "more is expected of fathers at home." C is not suggested in the article.
2. **F** Tom would agree since his experience taught him that time with his wife is more important than work. He did not acknowledge this before, so J is not correct. H is unlikely, given what he's been through.
3. **B** Galinsky includes statistics from interviews that she conducted with children and working parents. C is incorrect because she herself is the expert; she does not quote others. She does not provide anecdotes or examples from other countries, so students can eliminate A and D.
4. **G** While both articles discuss the stresses of parenting (F) and the goals of working parents (H), the important difference is the personal nature of the first article (G). The first article does not discuss other family members' points of view (J).

Analyzing Informational Materials

Reading Check

1. What conflict does "Double Daddy" deal with?
2. Explain the title "Diary of a Mad Blender."
3. In "The Child's View of Working Parents," what does Ellen Galinsky predict will be the next generation's attitude toward overwork?
4. According to Galinsky, why do kids worry about their working parents?

Test Practice

1. Which statement *best* summarizes the **main idea** of "Double Daddy"?
   - **A** Fathers need to work hard.
   - **B** Mothers don't need help.
   - **C** Kids should help parents more.
   - **D** Fathers are helping out more than before.
2. After experiencing the events of "Contents of the Dead Man's Pocket," what would Tom probably say about Linda Dunlap's quotation in "Double Daddy"?
   - **F** "I agree."
   - **G** "I disagree."
   - **H** "I have no opinion."
   - **J** "I always knew that."
3. What proof does Galinsky give to **support** her statements?
   - **A** Personal anecdotes
   - **B** Statistics from interviews
   - **C** Quotations from experts
   - **D** Examples from other countries
4. In what important way does "Diary of a Mad Blender" *differ* from "The Child's View of Working Parents"?
   - **F** It describes the stresses of parenting.
   - **G** It is based on the writer's own experiences.
   - **H** It supports the goals of working parents.
   - **J** It discusses other family members' points of view on working parents.
5. What is the **tone** of "Diary of a Mad Blender"? That is, what attitude does the writer take toward her subject?
   - **A** Sad
   - **B** Humorous
   - **C** Bitter
   - **D** Angry
6. Which phrase *best* describes the **topic** of all three articles?
   - **F** Daddy stress
   - **G** Mommy stress
   - **H** Flexible work setups
   - **J** Career-family conflict
7. The writers of all three articles imply that balancing work and family life is —
   - **A** unimportant
   - **B** impossible
   - **C** very easy
   - **D** not easy

Reading Standard 2.4 Synthesize the content from several sources dealing with a single issue; paraphrase the ideas and connect them to other sources and related topics to demonstrate comprehension.

5. **B** The writer's tone is clearly humorous.
6. **J** Although the first article concerns a father (F) and the second concerns a mother (G), these phrases do not capture the topic of all three articles. H also does not get attention in all three articles. Therefore, J is the best answer, since all of the articles concern career-family conflict.
7. **D** All three articles make strong arguments concerning the difficulties of managing work and family life. Not one of the articles states or implies that the task is unimportant (A), impossible (B), or easy (C).

8. Which of the following opinions is *not* expressed in any of the three articles?
   - **F** Life will soon be easier for working parents.
   - **G** Children are worried about their working parents.
   - **H** Corporations still expect men to put business before family.
   - **J** In the future, people will probably refuse to work as hard as their parents do now.

Application

Synthesize the three articles you have read by writing your own one-page article or editorial about the problems of balancing work and family life. Support your opinions or ideas by **paraphrasing** the articles, and make sure to acknowledge the source. Draw on other sources (such as Finney's story and Koch's poem) and on your own experiences. You might also want to interview your parents for their point of view and synthesize this information, including it in your article.

Vocabulary Development

Analogies: Two Word Pairs with the Same Relationship

In an **analogy** question, the words in one pair relate to each other in the same way as the words in a second pair. The words in the pairs may be synonyms (words with the same meaning) or antonyms (words with opposite meanings), or they may share some other relationship. Follow the steps below when you complete an analogy question:

DARK : LIGHT :: ________ : expensive

a. dear **b.** cheap **c.** costly **d.** bright

1. Identify the relationship between the words in the first pair. (In the example above, *dark* and *light* are opposites, or antonyms.)
2. Express the analogy in sentence or question form. ("*Dark* is the opposite of *light*, just as _______ is the opposite of *expensive*.")
3. From the choices available, choose the word that makes the second relationship the same as the first. (Look for a word that means the opposite of *expensive*. Choice b, *cheap*, is correct.)

(continued on next page)

Reading Standard 1.1 Identify and use the literal meanings of words.

8. **F** A quick scan of all the articles will reveal that only F was not expressed.

Test-Taking Tips

For more information on how to answer multiple-choice items, refer students to **Test Smarts.**

Double Daddy / Diary of a Mad Blender / The Child's View . . . 29

Vocabulary Development

Practice 1

2. chronic
3. conviction
4. autonomy
5. colleague
6. maximizes
7. trekked
8. poignant
9. splicing
10. phenomenon

Practice 2

1. part to its whole
2. thing to its category
3. thing to its characteristic
4. worker to his or her tool
5. thing to its characteristic
6. degree of intensity
7. thing to its category
8. degree of intensity

Resources Reminder

Vocabulary

- *Vocabulary Development*
  - Vocabulary Worksheet, p. 2
- *Lesson Plans for Language Development*
  - Vocabulary, pp. 27, 31

ASSESSING

Assessment

- *Progress Assessment of Reading*
  - Selection Test

RETEACHING

For another selection to teach Standard 2.4, see *Interactive Reading,* Part 2.

Analogies *(continued)*

The following chart shows some of the relationships you'll find in analogy test items and gives an example for each:

Type of Relationship	Example
Synonyms	QUICK : FAST :: loud : noisy
Antonyms	ENTER : DEPART :: build : destroy
Part of something to the whole	TOE : FOOT :: roof : house
Thing/object to a category it belongs to	ROBIN : BIRD :: maple : tree
Thing to the characteristic of the thing	BASEBALL : ROUND :: silk : smooth
Degree of intensity	GOOD : GREAT :: thin : emaciated
Worker to the tool the worker uses	PAINTER : BRUSH :: plumber : wrench

PRACTICE 1

Complete each analogy below with the word from the Word Bank that fits best. The first analogy has been done for you.

Word Bank
phenomenon
chronic
trekked
splicing
integrate
colleague
conviction
maximizes
autonomy
poignant

1. REWARD : PUNISH :: integrate : separate
2. STRONG : STURDY :: _____ : habitual
3. VIGOR : WEAKNESS :: _____ : disbelief
4. HOPE : DESPAIR :: _____ : slavery
5. FRIEND : PAL :: _____ : co-worker
6. SUPPORT : OPPOSE :: _____ : minimizes
7. CREEP : CRAWL :: _____ : journeyed
8. RARE : UNUSUAL :: _____ : touching
9. REPAIR : FIX :: _____ : joining
10. GHOST : INVISIBLE :: _____ : observable

PRACTICE 2

Using the chart above as a reference, identify the type of relationship in each of the following word pairs:

1. keyboard : laptop
2. Labrador : dog
3. children : young
4. writer : computer
5. earthquake : shaking
6. busy : frantic
7. ferret : mammal
8. fear : terror

30 Chapter 1 Plot and Setting • Synthesizing Sources

Before You Read

The Leap

Literary Focus

Flashback: Back to the Past

You're watching an exciting chase scene in a movie when suddenly the screen darkens and the main character becomes twenty years younger. What's happening? You're watching a **flashback,** a literary device that interrupts the present action in a story to show events that happened at an earlier time.

Flashbacks are effective for several reasons. They often add an emotional impact by showing the lasting effect of memory, and they can help you understand a character, especially a character's past. Flashbacks can also introduce an element of surprise or change the pace in a story.

In "The Leap" the narrator returns to the past more than once. As you read, be on the lookout for those time shifts.

Foreshadowing: Clues to the Future

Writers use another literary device, **foreshadowing,** to plant hints about events that will occur later in the plot. Look for words, images, or events in "The Leap" that seem to be clues to what lies ahead.

Reading Skills

Making Predictions

Part of the pleasure of reading a story is in **making predictions,** guessing what will happen to the characters as the plot moves ahead. You base your predictions on what you already know about the characters and their situation, along with what you know about how people behave in real life. Foreshadowing helps, too, if you're clever enough to recognize the writer's clues.

When you spot foreshadowing as you read "The Leap," use it to make a prediction about the characters and future events. The questions at the open-book signs ( ) should help you.

Make the Connection

Quickwrite

Has anyone ever acted courageously to help you? Maybe you yourself have acted bravely to help someone else. Why do you think people take risks to do what they think is the right thing? What is the reward? Jot down your thoughts on these complex questions about motivation and selfless behavior.

Vocabulary Development

encroaching (en·krōch′iŋ) *v.* used as *adj.:* advancing.

commemorates (kə·mem′ə·rāts′) *v.:* serves as a reminder of.

generate (jen′ər·āt′) *v.:* arise; come into being.

radiance (rā′dē·əns) *n.:* brightness; light.

extricating (eks′tri·kāt′iŋ) *v.* used as *n.:* releasing; disentangling.

illiterate (i·lit′ər·it) *adj.:* uneducated; unable to read or write.

constricting (kən·strikt′iŋ) *v.* used as *adj.:* limiting; confining.

tentative (ten′tə·tiv) *adj.:* timid; hesitant.

Reading Standard 3.6 Analyze and trace an author's development of time and sequence, including the use of complex literary devices (e.g., foreshadowing, flashbacks).

STANDARDS FOCUS, pp. 31–43

(For grade-level standards taught in this lesson, see the citations on Student Edition pages.)

Prerequisite Standard

- Grade 7, Literary Response and Analysis 3.2 **Identify events that advance the plot and determine how each event explains past or present action(s) or foreshadows future action(s).**

Reading Skills

- Make predictions.

Summary *above grade level*

In this story the narrator pays tribute to her elderly mother and finds strength to deal with her own challenges. The narrator's father has died, and she has returned to her childhood home to care for and read to her mother, Anna. The mother, now blind, once starred with her husband in a blindfold trapeze act. In flashbacks the narrator tells of her mother's three heroic "leaps"—her escape from death when lightning strikes the trapeze; her coping with the deaths of her first husband and her unborn child by learning to read and starting a new life; and her rescue of her young daughter (the narrator) from a burning house. The narrator reflects that directly or indirectly, each of these incidents gave her life, and takes heart from her mother's observation that falling gives a person time to think.

RESOURCES: READING

Planning

- *One-Stop Planner* CD-ROM with Test Generator
- *On Course: Mapping Instruction*

Media

- *Audio CD Library*
  - disc 2
- *Fine Art Transparencies*
  - Transparency 2

Reading

- *Interactive Reading,* Teacher's Edition
  - Graphic Organizer: Time Line

Differentiating Instruction

- *Lesson Plans for Language Development*
  - English-Language Learners, pp. 13–15, 28, 32
  - Special Education Students, pp. 16, 28, 32

Vocabulary

- *Vocabulary Development*
  - Vocabulary Worksheet, p. 3

Assessment

- *Progress Assessment of Reading*
  - Selection Test
- *One-Stop Planner* CD-ROM with Test Generator

PRETEACHING

Standards Starter

Build prerequisite skills. Ask students to suggest examples of flashbacks in movies. Discuss visual and auditory clues that a filmmaker may use to signal the beginning or end of a flashback (blurring of focus and changes in camera angle, lighting, music, or sets). Point out that in a similar way, authors use verbal clues to begin and end flashbacks in their writing. Examples include transitional words and phrases, shifts in verb tenses, sudden changes in imagery, and section breaks.

Preview Vocabulary

Use this exercise to help students master the Vocabulary words.

1. Why might illiterate people feel tentative about applying for a job? [Possible response: They might feel hesitant because they would be unable to read a job application.]
2. Identify the coin that commemorates Abraham Lincoln. [Students should identify a penny.]
3. Name several sources that generate heat and radiance. [Possible responses: sun, star, fire, lightbulb.]
4. If you were extricating a dog from a constricting situation, what might you be doing? [Possible response: disentangling its leash.]
5. How might townspeople respond to an encroaching flood? [Possible response: They might try to stop the advancing waters with sandbags.]

DIFFERENTIATING INSTRUCTION

Learners Having Difficulty

Modeling. To help students read "The Leap," model the reading skill of making predictions. Say, "Suppose you read that acrobats are performing in a circus tent when a lightning storm begins. You might predict that these performers are so daring that they will go on despite the danger." Encourage students, as they read, to ask themselves questions, such as "Which details hint at coming events?" and "What do I know about human nature that can help me guess what this character will do?"

Resources Reminder

Differentiating Instruction

- *Interactive Reading,* Teacher's Edition
  - Graphic Organizer: Time Line

English-Language Learners

These students may miss verbal clues that signal flashbacks. Suggest that they stay alert to shifts in verb tenses. Also, preteach specialized terms from the story. Using the illustrations, review the meanings of *trapeze, sequined costume, somersault, tent pole, guy wire, ringmaster, plumed helmets, midair, vaulted,* and *sawdust.*

My mother is the surviving half of a blindfold trapeze act, not a fact I think about much even now that she is sightless, the result of encroaching and stubborn cataracts.[1] She walks slowly through her house here in New Hampshire, lightly touching her way along walls and running her hands over knickknacks, books, the drift of a grown child's belongings and castoffs. She has never upset an object or as much as brushed a magazine onto the floor. She has never lost her balance or bumped into a closet door left carelessly open.

It has occurred to me that the catlike precision of her movements in old age might be the result of her early training, but she shows so little of the drama or flair one might expect from a performer that I tend to forget the Flying Avalons. She has kept no sequined costume, no photographs, no fliers or posters from that part of her youth. I would, in fact, tend to think that all memory of double somersaults and heartstopping catches had left her arms and legs were it not for the fact that sometimes, as I sit sewing in the room of the rebuilt house in which I slept as a child, I hear the crackle, catch a whiff of smoke from the stove downstairs, and suddenly the room goes dark, the stitches burn beneath my fingers, and I am sewing with a needle of hot silver, a thread of fire. **A**

MAKING PREDICTIONS

1. What clues in the last sentence hint at something to come? What might that event be?

I owe her my existence three times. The first was when she saved herself. In the town square a replica[2] tent pole, cracked and splintered, now stands cast in concrete. It commemorates the disaster that put our town smack on the front page of the Boston and New York tabloids.[3] It is from those old newspapers, now historical records, that I get my information. Not from my mother, Anna of the Flying Avalons, nor from any of her in-laws, nor certainly from the other half of her particular act, Harold Avalon, her first husband. In one news account it says, "The day was mildly overcast, but nothing in the air or temperature gave any hint of the sudden force with which the deadly gale would strike." **B** **C**

MAKING PREDICTIONS

2. The newspaper quotation creates suspense. What do you **predict** will happen? What effects might there be?

I have lived in the West, where you can see the weather coming for miles, and it is true that out here we are at something of a disadvantage. When extremes of temperature collide, a hot and cold front, winds generate instantaneously behind a hill and crash upon you without warning. That, I think, was the likely situation on that day in June. **D** People probably commented on the pleasant air, grateful that no hot sun beat upon the striped tent that stretched over the entire center green. They bought their tickets and surrendered them in anticipation. They sat. They ate caramelized popcorn and roasted peanuts. There was time, before the storm, for three acts. The White Arabians of Ali-Khazar rose on their hind legs and waltzed. The Mysterious Bernie folded himself into a painted cracker tin, and the Lady of the Mists made herself appear and disappear in surprising places. As the clouds gathered outside, unnoticed, the ringmaster cracked his whip, shouted his introduction, and pointed to the ceiling of the tent, where the Flying Avalons were perched.

1. **cataracts** (kat′ə·rakts′) *n.:* clouded areas on the lens of the eye that can cause partial or total blindness.
2. **replica** (rep′li·kə) *n.:* exact copy or reproduction.
3. **tabloids** (tab′lȯidz′) *n.:* newspapers that often feature sensational, exciting news stories.

Vocabulary

encroaching (en·krōch′iŋ) *v.* used as *adj.:* advancing.

commemorates (kə·mem′ə·rāts′) *v.:* serves as a reminder of.

generate (jen′ər·āt′) *v.:* arise; come into being.

DIRECT TEACHING

A Reading Skills

Making predictions. [Possible response to question 1: The clues "double somersaults and heart-stopping catches" hint at something exciting happening during a circus performance. "Crackle," "whiff of smoke," and "thread of fire" are clues that suggest a fire.]

B Literary Focus
GRADE-LEVEL STANDARD

Foreshadowing. In these lines, what hints does the narrator offer about events to come? [Possible responses: The hints "saved herself" and "disaster" suggest life-threatening events; the image of the splintered tent pole hints at a circus accident.]

C Reading Skills

Making predictions. [Possible responses to question 2: A dangerous storm will strike without warning during Anna's trapeze act. The effects may be that Anna's life will be in danger and that someone will be killed. The victim may be Harold Avalon, since he is her first husband.]

D Literary Focus
GRADE-LEVEL STANDARD

Flashback. Which sentence signals that the story is moving from the present to the past? ["That, I think, was the likely situation on that day in June."]

Resources Reminder

For lessons designed for intermediate and advanced English-language learners, see *Lesson Plans for Language Development,* pp. 13–15, 28, 32.

Special Education Students

For lessons designed for special education students, see *Lesson Plans for Language Development,* pp. 16, 28, 32.

Advanced Learners

Acceleration. Use the following activity to move students toward the eleventh- and twelfth-grade Standard 3.2, for which they analyze the way a selection's theme represents a view on life.

Activity. Have students meet in pairs to determine the story's theme. Suggest that in thinking about theme, they consider particularly the character of the mother, the daughter-mother relationship, and the meaning of the title. After students have chosen a theme, bring everyone back together to share their ideas and to discuss how the story's theme represents a view of life.

DIRECT TEACHING

A Literary Focus
GRADE-LEVEL STANDARD

Foreshadowing. At what coming tragedy does this quotation hint? [The phrase "lips destined 'never again to meet'" hints that Mr. Avalon will die.]

B Content-Area Connections
Science: Lightning

A lightning strike is a momentary but massive electrical current jumping between a negatively charged cloud and a positively charged object on the ground. Lightning may release up to twenty thousand amps of electrical power, with heat up to fifty thousand degrees Fahrenheit.

They loved to drop gracefully from nowhere, like two sparkling birds, and blow kisses as they threw off their plumed helmets and high-collared capes. They laughed and flirted openly as they beat their way up again on the trapeze bars. In the final vignette[4] of their act, they actually would kiss in midair, pausing, almost hovering as they swooped past one another. On the ground, between bows, Harry Avalon would skip quickly to the front rows and point out the smear of my mother's lipstick, just off the edge of his mouth. They made a romantic pair all right, especially in the blindfold sequence.

That afternoon, as the anticipation increased, as Mr. and Mrs. Avalon tied sparkling strips of cloth onto each other's face and as they puckered their lips in mock kisses—lips destined "never again to meet," as one long breathless article put it—the wind rose, miles off, wrapped itself into a cone, and howled. There came a rumble of electrical energy, drowned out by the sudden roll of drums. One detail not mentioned by the press, perhaps unknown—Anna was pregnant at the time, seven months and hardly showing, her stomach muscles were that strong. It seems incredible that she would work high above the ground when any fall could be so dangerous, but the explanation—I know from watching her go blind—is that my mother lives comfortably in extreme elements. She is one with the constant dark now, just as the air was her home, familiar to her, safe, before the storm that afternoon.

From opposite ends of the tent they waved, blind and smiling, to the crowd below. The ringmaster removed his hat and called for silence, so that the two above could concentrate. They rubbed their hands in chalky powder, then Harry launched himself and swung, once, twice, in huge calibrated[5] beats across space. He hung from his knees and on the third swing stretched wide his arms, held his hands out to receive his pregnant wife as she dove from her shining bar.

It was while the two were in midair, their hands about to meet, that lightning struck the main pole and sizzled down the guy wires, filling the air with a blue radiance that Harry Avalon must certainly have seen through the cloth of his blindfold as the tent buckled and the edifice[6] toppled him forward, the swing continuing and not returning in its sweep, and Harry going down, down into the crowd with his last thought, perhaps, just a prickle of surprise at his empty hands.

My mother once said that I'd be amazed at how many things a person can do within the act

4. **vignette** (vin·yet′) *n.:* short, memorable scene.

5. **calibrated** (kal′ə·brāt′id) *v.* used as *adj.:* measured.

6. **edifice** (ed′i·fis) *n.:* structure.

Vocabulary
radiance (rā′dē·əns) *n.:* brightness; light.

34 Chapter 1 Plot and Setting • Synthesizing Sources

of falling. Perhaps, at the time, she was teaching me to dive off a board at the town pool, for I associated the idea with midair somersaults. But I also think she meant that even in that awful doomed second one could think, for she certainly did. When her hands did not meet her husband's, my mother tore her blindfold away. As he swept past her on the wrong side, she could have grasped his ankle, the toe end of his tights, and gone down clutching him. Instead, she changed direction. Her body twisted toward a heavy wire and she managed to hang on to the braided metal, still hot from the lightning strike. Her palms were burned so terribly that once healed they bore no lines, only the blank scar tissue of a quieter future. She was lowered, gently, to the sawdust ring just underneath the dome of the canvas roof, which did not entirely settle but was held up on one end and jabbed through, torn, and still on fire in places from the giant spark, though rain and men's jackets soon put that out.

> **Even in that awful doomed second one could think.**

Three people died, but except for her hands my mother was not seriously harmed until an overeager rescuer broke her arm in extricating her and also, in the process, collapsed a portion of the tent bearing a huge buckle that knocked her unconscious. She was taken to the town hospital, and there she must have hemorrhaged,[7] for they kept her, confined to her bed, a month and a half before her baby was born without life.

Harry Avalon had wanted to be buried in the circus cemetery next to the original Avalon, his uncle, so she sent him back with his brothers. The child, however, is buried around the corner, beyond this house and just down the highway. Sometimes I used to walk there just to sit. She was a girl, but I rarely thought of her as a sister or even as a separate person really. I suppose you could call it the egocentrism[8] of a child, of all young children, but I considered her a less finished version of myself.

When the snow falls, throwing shadows among the stones, I can easily pick hers out from the road, for it is bigger than the others and in the shape of a lamb at rest, its legs curled beneath. The carved lamb looms larger as the years pass, though it is probably only my eyes, the vision shifting, as what is close to me blurs and distances sharpen. In odd moments, I think it is the edge drawing near, the edge of everything, the unseen horizon we do not really speak of in the eastern woods. And it also seems to me, although this is probably an idle fantasy, that the statue is growing more sharply etched, as if, instead of weathering itself into a porous mass, it is hardening on the hillside with each snowfall, perfecting itself.

MAKING INFERENCES

3. Notice what the narrator says about her sister and her sister's grave. How do you think the narrator feels about her sister?

It was during her confinement in the hospital that my mother met my father. He was called in to look at the set of her arm, which was complicated. He stayed, sitting at her bedside, for he was something of an armchair traveler and had spent his war quietly, at an air force training grounds, where he became a specialist in arms and legs broken during parachute training exercises. Anna Avalon had been to many of the places he longed to visit—Venice, Rome, Mexico, all through France and Spain. She had no family of

7. **hemorrhaged** (hem′ər·ijd′) *v.:* lost a great deal of blood.

8. **egocentrism** (ē′gō·sen′triz′əm) *n.:* self-centeredness.

Vocabulary

extricating (eks′tri·kāt′iŋ) *v.* used as *n.:* releasing; disentangling.

DIRECT TEACHING

C Literary Focus
REVIEW STANDARD

Characterization. What character traits do you see in Anna's behavior during the accident? [Possible response: She is quick thinking, resourceful, determined, and courageous.]

D Vocabulary Development
GRADE-LEVEL STANDARD

Understanding word derivations. The word *hemorrhaged* has the Greek root word *hem–* (*hemo–*), meaning "blood." What other medical terms do you know that have this root word? [Possible responses: hemoglobin, hemophilia, hemostat.]

E Learners Having Difficulty

Finding sequence of events. Students may need help following time shifts. The narrator interrupts the flashback to reflect on her changing attitude toward the stillborn baby. First, she recalls her childhood responses to visiting the baby's grave; next, she describes her responses as an adult.

F Reading Skills

Making inferences. [Possible response to question 3: Details such as "the carved lamb looms larger as the years pass" and "the statue is growing more sharply etched" suggest that her dead sister is becoming more prominent in the narrator's mind. Details such as "I think it is the edge drawing near . . . the unseen horizon" suggest that as the narrator grows older, she feels both closer to her sister and nearer to death.]

G Literary Focus
GRADE-LEVEL STANDARD

Flashback. What part of the mother's story will the narrator tell now? [Possible response: She will tell how her mother and father met, married, and began a family.]

CONTENT-AREA CONNECTIONS

History and Culture: The Circus

The kind of circus best known in Western culture was invented by Philip Astley (1742–1814) of England, who developed his talents as a horse trainer in the British army. In 1768, he was discharged from the army and began to make a living by performing tricks on horseback. He appeared in a circular arena called a *circus,* which allowed audiences to keep him in sight during the whole performance. For variety, he gradually added acrobats, tightrope walkers, jugglers, and clowns to his shows.

By 1800, circuses were opening throughout Europe. Catherine the Great invited one of them to set up a trick-riding school in St. Petersburg, and the circus tradition has flourished in Russia ever since. In 1793, a Scottish horseman named John Ricketts brought the first circus to the United States.

DIRECT TEACHING

A Advanced Learners

Acceleration. Have students analyze the metaphor the narrator uses to compare the trapeze act and the acts of reading and flying. [Readers, like trapeze artists, can "fly" beyond the limitations of a mundane, "earthbound" life.] Remind students that the story title is "The Leap," and ask them how the metaphor connects to the title and suggests a theme. [Possible response: The mother is not afraid to leap into the air or into the daunting task of learning to read as an adult. One theme may involve the courage or faith required to "fly."]

B Literary Focus
REVIEW STANDARD

Characterization. What does the narrator's return home to read to her mother suggest to you about the narrator's character traits? [Possible responses: The narrator is devoted to her mother; she is conscientious, kind, and loving; the narrator may be looking for encouragement to face her own "failed life."]

her own and was taken in by the Avalons, trained to perform from a very young age. They toured Europe before the war, then based themselves in New York. She was illiterate.

It was in the hospital that she finally learned to read and write, as a way of overcoming the boredom and depression of those weeks, and it was my father who insisted on teaching her. In return for stories of her adventures, he graded her first exercises. He bought her her first book, and over her bold letters, which the pale guides of the penmanship pads could not contain, they fell in love.

A I wonder if my father calculated the exchange he offered: one form of flight for another. For after that, and for as long as I can remember, my mother has never been without a book. Until now, that is, and it remains the greatest difficulty **B** of her blindness. Since my father's recent death, there is no one to read to her, which is why I returned, in fact, from my failed life where the land is flat. I came home to read to my mother, to read out loud, to read long into the dark if I must, to read all night.

Vocabulary

illiterate (i·lit′ər·it) *adj.:* uneducated; unable to read or write.

READING MINI-LESSON

Developing Word-Attack Skills

Remind students that in one-syllable words, a final e signals that the vowel sound is long. Illustrate this rule of pronunciation by using these selection words:

cape, gale, age	long *a*
times, miles, dive	long *i*
smoke, cone, rose	long *o*

Explain that this rule also applies to words with more than one syllable. Write the following words from the selection on the chalkboard. As you pronounce the words, point out that each word ends with e and has a long vowel sound in the last syllable.

trapeze	superannuate
concrete	creosote
concentrate	survive

Note that with multisyllable words, there are

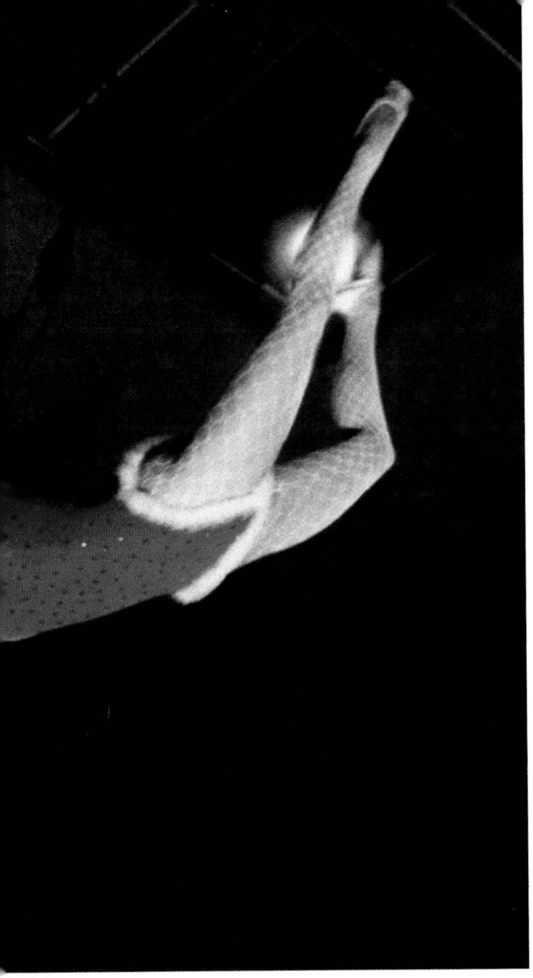

Once my father and mother married, they moved onto the old farm he had inherited but didn't care much for. Though he'd been thinking of moving to a larger city, he settled down and broadened his practice in this valley. It still seems odd to me, when they could have gone anywhere else, that they chose to stay in the town where the disaster had occurred, and which my father in the first place had found so <u>constricting</u>. It was my mother who insisted upon it, after her child did not survive. And then, too, she loved the sagging farmhouse with its scrap of what was left of a vast acreage of woods and hidden hayfields that stretched to the game park. **C**

I owe my existence, the second time then, to the two of them and the hospital that brought them together. That is the debt we take for granted since none of us asks for life. It is only once we have it that we hang on so dearly.

D I was seven the year the house caught fire, probably from standing ash. It can rekindle, and my father, forgetful around the house and perpetually[9] exhausted from night hours on call, often emptied what he thought were ashes from cold stoves into wooden or cardboard containers. The fire could have started from a flaming box, or perhaps a buildup of creosote[10] inside the chimney was the culprit. It started right around the stove, and the heart of the house was gutted. The baby sitter, fallen asleep in my father's den on the first floor, woke to find the stairway to my upstairs room cut off by flames. She used the phone, then ran outside to stand beneath my window.

When my parents arrived, the town volunteers had drawn water from the fire pond and were spraying the outside of the house, preparing to go inside after me, not knowing at the time that there was only one staircase and that it was lost. On the other side of the house, the superannuated[11] extension ladder broke in half. **E** Perhaps the clatter of it falling against the walls woke me, for I'd been asleep up to that point.

As soon as I awakened, in the small room that I now use for sewing, I smelled the smoke. I followed things by the letter then, was good at memorizing instructions, and so I did exactly what was taught in the second-grade home fire drill. I got up, I touched the back of my door before opening it. Finding it hot, I left it closed and stuffed my rolled-up rug beneath the crack. **F**

9. **perpetually** (pər·pech′o͞o·əl·ē) *adv.:* constantly.
10. **creosote** (krē′ə·sōt′) *n.:* oily deposit of tar, a byproduct of burning wood.
11. **superannuated** (so͞o′pər·an′yo͞o·āt′id) *adj.:* too old or worn-out to be of service.

Vocabulary
constricting (kən · strikt′iŋ) *v.* used as *adj.:* limiting; confining.

DIRECT TEACHING

C Reading Skills

Making inferences. Why do you suppose the mother insisted on staying in the town where the disaster occurred? [Possible responses: Her first child is buried there, and she wants to stay near the child's grave; she has already traveled extensively and has grown attached to her surroundings.]

D Literary Focus
GRADE-LEVEL STANDARD

Flashback. What shift in time begins with this paragraph? [The story jumps back to a third flashback in the more recent past, when the narrator was seven years old and the family house burned down.]

E Vocabulary Development
GRADE-LEVEL STANDARD

Understanding word derivations. The word *superannuated* comes from the Latin prefix *super–,* meaning "over; to an extreme degree," and the Latin root word *annus,* meaning "year." Something superannuated is worn out because it has existed for too many years; it is extremely old.

F English-Language Learners

Idioms. Point out to students the idiomatic phrase "followed things by the letter." Explain that the word *followed,* in this context, means "obeyed." To "follow by the letter" is to obey exactly, heeding each word or letter of instruction.

exceptions to the "final e equals long vowel" rule. Cite as examples *separate,* which has a long vowel sound in the final syllable when used as a verb but not as an adjective, and *magazine,* in which we hear a long e, not a long *i,* in the final syllable.

Activity. Write these pairs of words on the chalkboard. Have students read the pairs aloud and identify which word has a long vowel in the final syllable. Answers are underlined.

1. <u>confined</u> destined
2. edifice <u>suffice</u>
3. <u>calibrate</u> illiterate
4. tentative <u>survive</u>
5. opposite <u>exercise</u>
6. practice <u>entice</u>

DIRECT TEACHING

A Reading Skills

Making predictions. [Possible response to question 4: The mother will climb the tree and leap from it to the roof, then climb down into a window and rescue her daughter.]

B Literary Focus
GRADE-LEVEL STANDARD

Flashback. The sentence "I know that she's right" is a brief shift to the present. Where else in the story does the narrator mention the mother's comments about falling? [in the part about the trapeze accident] What is the effect of this flicker-in-time sequence? [Possible responses: It emphasizes that the house fire episode is a flashback; it tells what the episode means to the narrator.]

GUIDED PRACTICE

Monitoring students' progress. To assess students' comprehension of the story, have them compose a letter from the narrator to her mother. In the letter the narrator should tell her mother why she admires her, citing examples of the mother's past and present behavior.

I did not hide under my bed or crawl into my closet. I put on my flannel robe, and then I sat down to wait.

Outside, my mother stood below my dark window and saw clearly that there was no rescue. Flames had pierced one side wall, and the glare of the fire lighted the massive limbs and trunk of the vigorous old elm that had probably been planted the year the house was built, a hundred years ago at least. No leaf touched the wall, and just one thin branch scraped the roof. From below, it looked as though even a squirrel would have had trouble jumping from the tree onto the house, for **A** the breadth of that small branch was no bigger than my mother's wrist.

> **MAKING PREDICTIONS**
> 4. What do you **predict** the mother will do?

Standing there, beside Father, who was preparing to rush back around to the front of the house, my mother asked him to unzip her dress. When he wouldn't be bothered, she made him understand. He couldn't make his hands work, so she finally tore it off and stood there in her pearls and stockings. She directed one of the men to lean the broken half of the extension ladder up against the trunk of the tree. In surprise, he complied. She ascended. She vanished. Then she could be seen among the leafless branches of late November as she made her way up and, along her stomach, inched the length of a bough that curved above the branch that brushed the roof.

Once there, swaying, she stood and balanced. There were plenty of people in the crowd and many who still remember, or think they do, my mother's leap through the ice-dark air toward that thinnest extension, and how she broke the branch falling so that it cracked in her hands, cracked louder than the flames as she vaulted with it toward the edge of the roof, and how it hurtled down end over end without her, and their eyes went up, again, to see where she had flown.

I didn't see her leap through air, only heard the sudden thump and looked out my window. She was hanging by the backs of her heels from the new gutter we had put in that year, and she was smiling. I was not surprised to see her, she was so matter-of-fact. She tapped on the window. I remember how she did it, too. It was the friendliest tap, a bit tentative, as if she was afraid she had arrived too early at a friend's house. Then she gestured at the latch, and when I opened the window she told me to raise it wider and prop it up with the stick so it wouldn't crush her fingers. She swung down, caught the ledge, and crawled through the opening. Once she was in my room, I realized she had on only underclothing, a bra of the heavy stitched cotton women used to wear and step-in, lace-trimmed drawers. I remember feeling lightheaded, of course, terribly relieved, and then embarrassed for her to be seen by the crowd undressed.

I was still embarrassed as we flew out the window, toward earth, me in her lap, her toes pointed as we skimmed toward the painted target of the firefighter's net.

B I know that she's right. I knew it even then. As you fall, there is time to think. Curled as I was, against her stomach, I was not startled by the cries of the crowd or the looming faces. The wind roared and beat its hot breath at our back, and flames whistled. I slowly wondered what would happen if we missed the circle or bounced out of it. Then I wrapped my hands around my mother's hands. I felt the brush of her lips and heard the beat of her heart in my ears, loud as thunder, long as the roll of drums. ■

Vocabulary
tentative (ten′tə·tiv) *adj.:* timid; hesitant.

FAMILY/COMMUNITY ACTIVITY

You might invite a fire department representative to update the class about house and apartment fires, outlining the ways these fires start and spread and providing survival tips. Have students compare this information with the instructions that the narrator in "The Leap" followed as a child when she awoke to the smell of smoke. Encourage students to develop family fire evacuation plans if they have not already done so.

38 Chapter 1 Plot and Setting • Synthesizing Sources

Meet the Writer

Louise Erdrich

A Storytelling Tradition

When Louise Erdrich (1954–) was very young, her father paid her a nickel for every story she wrote, and her mother "published" the stories with construction-paper covers. "I had that kind of childhood where I didn't feel art was something strange," she recalls. "I felt that it was good for you to do it."

Erdrich, the oldest of seven children, grew up in a storytelling family in North Dakota. Both her German American father and her French Chippewa mother worked at an Indian boarding school. She described once in an interview how everyone in her family would tell stories.

"When I think what's a story, I can hear somebody in my family, my dad or my mom or my grandma, telling it. There's something particularly strong about a *told story.* You know your listener's right there, you've got to keep him hooked—or her. So you use all those little lures: 'And then . . . ,' 'So the next day. . . ,' etc. There are some very nuts-and-bolts things about storytelling. It also is something you can't really put your finger on. . . . The story starts to take over if it is good. . . . If it's good, you let the story tell itself. You don't control the story."

Erdrich, who started out as a poet, finished her first novel, *Love Medicine,* when she was twenty-eight. Although she had great difficulty finding a publisher for the book, it became a runaway bestseller and won the National Book Critics Circle Award in 1984. That story and many of her subsequent novels are set in the landscape of her childhood, in and around Turtle Mountain Reservation, North Dakota, where her grandfather was tribal chairman.

Although Erdrich continues to publish novels and short stories, she has branched out into nonfiction as well. In *The Blue Jay's Dance: A Birth Year* (1995), Erdrich writes about motherhood, marriage, family, writing, nature, and food during a year in which she awaits the birth of her daughter and then cares for her.

Meet the Writer

Background. To Louise Erdrich the titles of her stories and books are very important. She often thinks of a title first and then finds that it inspires ideas for characters and events. Erdrich says, "I think a title is like a magnet. It begins to draw these scraps of experience or conversation or memory to it. Eventually it collects a book." For her book about motherhood, she chose the title *The Blue Jay's Dance,* referring to a mother blue jay's way of protecting her young by dancing toward an attacker. Erdrich sees the blue jay's dance as a metaphor for "the sort of controlled recklessness that having children always is." Among her other titles are *The Beet Queen, Tracks,* and *The Bingo Palace.*

For Independent Reading

- Students intrigued by nonlinear storytelling may enjoy Sandra Benitez's *A Place Where the Sea Remembers,* an innovative novel of human resilience and courage in the face of misfortune.
- For students who like the parent-child relationship in "The Leap," recommend *One Writer's Beginnings,* Eudora Welty's delightful memoir of childhood and her strong, resourceful mother.
- Tales of brave, quick-thinking women abound in *Clever Gretchen and Other Forgotten Folktales,* retold by Alison Lurie.

DIFFERENTIATING INSTRUCTION

Advanced Learners

Enrichment. Tell students that many reviewers have praised Erdrich for her depiction of strong female characters; for her striking metaphors; and for her nonlinear storytelling, which creatively pushes the boundaries of chronological order.

Activity. Have students research reviews of Erdrich's fiction. Suggest that they use their library's online database of periodicals, entering *Louise Erdrich* as the keyword in their search. Direct them to find references to Erdrich's female characters, her use of metaphor, and her nonlinear storytelling and to apply these comments to "The Leap."

Connection

Summary at grade level

This article from Discovery.com tells of a 1944 fire that caused the worst circus tragedy in history. When the main tent of the Ringling Brothers Circus in Hartford, Connecticut, caught fire, it was packed with seven thousand spectators. Within six minutes the tent and everything inside was reduced to ash. Circus workers managed to rescue the animals but were unable to control the panicked crowds. Ironically, the U.S. Army had recently developed a chemical compound to fireproof tents but had refused the circus permission to use it. After the tragedy, the Army reversed its stance, and circus tents since then have been routinely fireproofed.

DIRECT TEACHING

A Learners Having Difficulty

Identifying cause and effect. Ask students to explain what safety measures the circus had in place to protect the animals. [Circus employees understood that the playing of "Stars and Stripes Forever" meant that a disaster had occurred and that it was their job to move the animals to safety.]

B Vocabulary Development

GRADE-LEVEL STANDARD

Understanding word derivations. Write the word *retardant* and its origin on the chalkboard—the Latin prefix *re–*, meaning "back"; the root word *tardare,* meaning "to delay"; and the suffix *–ant,* meaning "performing a specified action." Then, ask students to define the term *flame retardant* based on this word etymology. [Possible response: "holding back or delaying fire."]

CONNECTION / ARTICLE

The Day the Clowns Cried

R. J. Brown

The worst tragedy in the annals of circus history occurred during the afternoon show of the Ringling Brothers Circus on July 6, 1944, at Hartford, Connecticut. With nearly 7,000 people enjoying the performance, the big tent suddenly became engulfed in flames. As fire spread up the side walls and raced across the top of the tent, the bandmaster, Merle Evans, swung his band into the song "Stars and Stripes Forever"—the circus disaster tune. The sound of this tune moved all employees into high gear. The horses, elephants, the lions and tigers, were quickly led out of the tent out of danger. **A**

People stampeded toward the exit they had entered from. Unfortunately, this was the end on fire. Fire had not spread to the other end yet and employees tried directing them to that exit. In the panic, crowds still stampeded the end on fire. Three minutes later, the tent poles started collapsing and the roof—what was left—caved in. In six minutes total, almost all of the tent was burned completely and the entire area was nothing more than smoldering ashes. One hundred sixty-eight men, women, and children died as a result. Hundreds more were badly injured.

An important footnote to this fire story is the fact that the circus had tried unsuccessfully to obtain the necessary quantity of a new canvas flameproofing compound that was developed by the armed services. It was pointed out by the Army that no civilian concern was allowed the use of the compound. Soon after the fire, however, the Army approached Ringling's and granted them the necessary priority to obtain enough compound to fireproof their tents. From 1945 on, the circus tents were **B** treated with a flame-retardant compound.

—from *History Buff* on Discovery.com, October 31, 2000

Crowds flee the Ringling Brothers tent when it caught fire one summer day in 1944.

40 Chapter 1 Plot and Setting • Synthesizing Sources

Connecting and Comparing Texts

R. J. Brown's nonfiction article "The Day the Clowns Cried" tells of a real-life circus disaster reminiscent of the fictional lightning strike that changes Anna's life in Louise Erdrich's story "The Leap." Both Brown and Erdrich use vivid and poignant sensory images to draw readers into the action. Erdrich describes a trapeze artist who sees a blue glow of lightning through his blindfold and feels only empty air in his hands; Brown describes a bandmaster who directs musicians in "Stars and Stripes Forever" as circus workers lead their animals to safety, then try in vain to do the same for panicked spectators. Facts from the article might underscore Anna's heroism by emphasizing the fragility of the circus environment, the vulnerability of performers, and the need for quick, decisive action in this kind of emergency.

Literary Response and Analysis

Reading Check

1. Why has the narrator returned to her childhood home?
2. In a sentence or two, **summarize** the event that causes the end of the Flying Avalons' act.
3. How do the narrator's parents meet?
4. The narrator says she owes her mother her existence "three times." What are those three times?

Interpretations

5. Why is "The Leap" a good **title** for this story? Name all the leaps—both literal and figurative—that occur in the story.
6. Analyze the author's use of **flashbacks** by tracing the point where the story shifts from present to past and back again. Then, put the story's main events in **chronological order** on a time line. Begin with the day at the circus.
7. How are the different **flashback** episodes related to one another? What does the author's use of flashback add to the story that a strict chronological telling would not accomplish?
8. Find three examples of **foreshadowing** in the story. Did the clues help you make predictions about the story's outcome? Explain your answer.
9. What are the many ways in which the narrator's mother displays courage? What do her actions imply about her **character**?

Evaluation

10. Look back at your Quickwrite notes about people who behave courageously. Based on what you know about brave, selfless people, are the mother's actions **credible**? Explain your answer.
11. Compare the disaster in the story with the true-life disaster described in "The Day the Clowns Cried" (see the ***Connection*** on page 40). Do you think the real-life event would make a good topic for a story? Why?

Writing

Wild Woman?

Erdrich is known for her strong female characters. She has said of women,

> We are taught to present
> a demure face to the world,
> and yet there is a kind of
> wild energy behind it in
> many women that is
> transformational energy,
> and not only transforming to
> them but to other people.

Do you think the mother in "The Leap" fits the description above? Write a few paragraphs in which you support your **opinion.** Be sure to address each of the points in the statement: Does the mother seem outwardly demure and reserved? Does she have a hidden, wild energy? Is she able to transform, or change, herself and others? Include examples from the story to support your opinion.

Reading Standard 3.6 Analyze and trace an author's development of time and sequence, including the use of complex literary devices (e.g., foreshadowing, flashbacks).

INDEPENDENT PRACTICE

Literary Response and Analysis

Reading Check

1. She returns to care for and read to her blind mother.
2. Lightning strikes the circus tent pole during their act, and Harold falls to his death.
3. They meet when the father, a doctor, is asked to look at the mother's broken arm.
4. Mother survives accident; marries narrator's father; rescues narrator.

Interpretations

5. The story shows Anna's courage and skill. *Literal*—saves self; saves daughter. *Figurative*—goes on after loss of husband and baby; learns to read; remarries; copes with blindness and old age.
6. The story shifts to the past with "that day in June." *Brief shifts to present*—Narrator explains Anna's comfort "in extreme elements"; discusses Anna's views on falling; discusses sister's grave; tells of returning to read to Anna; reflects on debt to mother. *Chronological order*—lightning strikes tent; Harry dies; Anna survives; has stillborn baby; Anna meets second husband, learns to read, marries; narrator is born; Anna rescues narrator; narrator grows up, moves west; Anna loses sight; second husband dies; narrator returns.
7. The flashbacks describe the mother's acts of courage that made the narrator's life possible. The use of flashback conveys the impact of these events in the narrator's mind.
8. Possible answers: Images such as "needle of hot silver" and "thread of fire" foreshadow lightning and the burning house. The "deadly gale" and "lips destined 'never again to meet'" foreshadow Harold's death. The branch scraping the roof and a squirrel jumping foreshadow the mother's leap to save daughter.
9. She shows courage in surviving the circus accident, remarrying after losses, learning to read, rescuing her daughter, and coping with blindness and old age. Her actions show that she is loving, brave, and resourceful.

Evaluation

10. Possible answer: Like many people in an emergency, the mother acts bravely and selflessly.
11. Possible answers: Yes, if told from a survivor's point of view, the story would be suspenseful; no, because the disaster was so tragic.

Vocabulary Development

Practice

- *encroaching. Derivation*— < OFr *en–*, "into" + *croche*, "hook."
- *commemorates. Derivation*— < L *commemoratus* < *com–*, "together" + *memorare*, "bring to mind."
- *generate. Derivation*— < L *generatus*, "brought forth" < *genus*, "birth."
- *radiance. Derivation*— < L *radiatus* < *radius*, "ray."
- *extricating. Derivation*— < L *extricatus* < *ex–*, "out of" + *tricae*, "trifles or perplexities."
- *illiterate. Derivation*— < L *illitteratus* < *il–*, < *in–*, "not" + *litteratus*, "lettered."
- *constricting. Derivation*— < L *constrictus* < *com–*, "together" + *stringere*, "to pull tightly."
- *tentative. Derivation*— < L *tentativus* < *tentatus* < *tentare*, "to try."

Resources Reminder

Vocabulary

- *Vocabulary Development*
  - Vocabulary Worksheet, p. 3
- *Lesson Plans for Language Development*
  - Vocabulary, pp. 28, 32

Vocabulary Development

Etymologies: Words Tell Their Stories

Word Bank
encroaching
commemorates
generate
radiance
extricating
illiterate
constricting
tentative

An **etymology** (et′ə·mäl′ə·jē) traces a word's **derivation,** or origin. You can use a dictionary to find a derivation: It usually appears in brackets after the entry word's pronunciation and part-of-speech designation. The oldest form of the word will appear last. The dictionary should contain a section that explains the organization, abbreviations, and symbols used in its etymologies. Let's look at the beginning of a dictionary entry for the Word Bank word *commemorate.*

> **com·mem·o·rate** (kə·mem′ə·rāt′) ***vt.*** [< L *commemoratus*, pp. of *commemorare*, to call to mind < *com–*, intens. + *memorare*, to remind]

The entry tells us that *commemorate* derives from ("<") the Latin ("L") word *commemoratus,* which is a past participle ("pp.") of *commemorare,* Latin for "to call to mind." The entry further shows that *commemorare* is derived from *com–*, an intensive ("intens.")—a word that emphasizes a meaning—plus ("+") *memorare,* Latin for "to remind."

Some etymologies refer to a prefix and root word that combine to form the entry word, as in the entry below for the Word Bank word *illiterate:*

> **il·lit·er·ate** (i·lit′ər·it) ***adj.*** [L *illiteratus*, unlettered: see IN– & LITERATE]

The above entry tells us that the English word *illiterate* comes from the Latin ("L") word *illiteratus,* meaning "unlettered." The etymology also refers us to the prefix *in–* and the English word *literate.* When we look up *in–*, we find out that it is a prefix meaning "no, not, or without" and that it is spelled *il–* before the letter *l.*

A dictionary entry for *literate* reveals that the word derives from a Middle English word (*litterate*), which derives from a Latin word (*litteratus*), which derives from the Latin word for *letter:*

> [ME *litterate* < L *litteratus* < *littera,* LETTER]

Reading Standard 1.1 Understand word derivations.

PRACTICE

Use a dictionary to research the **derivation,** or origin, of the other Word Bank words. Write the oldest form of the word and the language from which it originally derived.

Grammar Link MINI-LESSON

Using Personal Pronouns—In the Right Places

The narrator of "The Leap" uses the first-person pronouns *I* and *me* to refer to herself. Using **personal pronouns** correctly in your writing can be tricky because there are two forms, or **cases,** and you need to choose the right form to fit each situation.

Nominative Case: I, you, he, she, it, we, they
Objective Case: me, you, him, her, it, us, them

Use a **nominative-case pronoun** if the pronoun functions as a subject or predicate nominative in a sentence.

He and I read "The Leap." [Pronouns are subjects: *He* and *I* carry out the action.]

The main characters are she and the mother. [Pronoun is a predicate nominative: *She* identifies the subject after a linking verb.]

Use an **objective-case pronoun** if the pronoun functions as a direct object, an indirect object, or the object of a preposition.

The firefighters saved the mother and her. [Pronoun is a direct object.]

The narrator tells us her mother's story. [Pronoun is an indirect object.]

The rescue seems unreal to him and me. [Pronouns are objects of preposition.]

PRACTICE

Edit and rewrite the following paragraph, correcting the personal pronouns. Hint: Not every pronoun needs to be corrected.

Julio told Carrie and I about a fabulous trapeze act he saw at the circus. Mara and him went to the circus last night and were astonished by what they saw. They described to the teacher and we the trapeze artists' daring tricks. Then him and Mara gave Carrie and I two discount tickets to the circus.

▶ **For more help, see Case Forms of Personal Pronouns in the *Holt Handbook,* pages 145–154.**

Grammar Link

Practice

(Corrected pronouns are in italics.) Julio told Carrie and *me* about a fabulous trapeze act he saw at the circus. Mara and *he* went to the circus last night and were astonished by what they saw. They described to the teacher and *us* the trapeze artists' daring tricks. Then *he* and Mara gave Carrie and *me* two discount tickets to the circus.

ASSESSING

Assessment

- *Progress Assessment of Reading*
  - Selection Test

RETEACHING

For another selection to teach Standard 3.6, see *Interactive Reading,* Chapter 1.

DIFFERENTIATING INSTRUCTION

Learners Having Difficulty

If you wish to give students additional practice with this skill, have them revise the following sentences so that all the pronouns are in the correct case. You may want to warn students that not every pronoun needs correction.

1. Her and her husband Harold are the Flying Avalons. [she]
2. Anna and him offered we in the audience a thrilling performance. [he, us]
3. When Anna and Harold flew through the air, everyone applauded she and him. [her]
4. "Me and my mother survived the leap from the burning house," the daughter explained. [I]
5. "To I and to others who saw her jump," said the daughter, "my mother is a hero." [me]

STANDARDS FOCUS, pp. 44–45

(For the review standard taught in this lesson, see Student Edition, p. 44.)

Prerequisite Standard

- Grade 6, Literary Response and Analysis 3.3 **Analyze the influence of setting on the problem and its resolution.**

Literary Focus: Setting

Ask students to describe the settings of some recent movies and television shows. Encourage them to mention works that are set in different times and places. Guide them to think about place, time, and social customs as elements of the setting. Discuss with them what feelings each setting is meant to evoke in viewers. Ask if each setting reveals anything about the characters.

Literary Response and Analysis

Setting *by* John Leggett

PUTTING US THERE

Where and When?

Is it possible for an interesting story to have no **setting** at all—that is, no indication of where or when the action takes place? Yes—if the characters and their situation are strong enough, they will hold our attention in empty space, just as a play presented on a bare stage can hold our interest.

In real life all events occur somewhere, so fiction specifies a setting most of the time. Think of how crucial setting would be in a story about a prisoner, in a story about castaways adrift on the Pacific, or in a story about a colony on Mars.

Setting puts us there—it gives us a feeling of being *in* the situation with the characters. Setting even includes people's customs—how they live, dress, eat, and behave.

Imagine a story that takes place in a town square in Honduras. The details of the setting should make us feel hot, sweaty, and thirsty. We should see the townspeople taking their afternoon siesta to escape the heat while the sun bakes the back of a little burro tethered beside the church. We should smell the *zozo,* the local delicacy of fish heads and banana skins, as it sizzles over charcoal.

Setting tells us not only *where* we are but also *when.* Setting can reveal a **time frame.** If the passing traffic is horse drawn, we can guess that we have gone back in time. An inch of new-fallen snow on a porch rail tells us it's winter. If the sun is just up over a pine ridge or if the *Ledger* is being tossed onto the front steps, it's early morning.

Grade 8 Review Reading Standard 3.4 Analyze the relevance of the setting (e.g., place, time, customs) to the mood, tone, and meaning of the text.

Details of setting give a story a kind of truth or believability. It is this realistic sense of place in fiction that gives us the joy of armchair travel—the chance to visit faraway places and times without ever leaving home.

Setting, Mood, and Tone

A more important function of setting, however, is to contribute to a story's emotional effect—its **mood,** or **atmosphere.** We all know that some settings can make us feel gloomy and others can make us feel cheerful. An autumnal setting can increase the sense of loss about a doomed love in a story. A spring setting can give a note of hope to a story of a girl's coming of age.

Details of setting can also help express **tone**—the writer's attitude toward a subject or character. Like a tone of voice, the writer's tone can be, for example, mocking or tender, joyful or nostalgic.

Here is a description of a rice paddy in Vietnam. How does it make you feel? How would you describe its **mood** and **tone**?

> His boots sank into the thick paddy water, and he smelled it all around him. He would tell his mother how it smelled: mud and algae and cattle manure and chlorophyll; decay, breeding mosquitoes and leeches as big as mice; the fecund warmth of the paddy waters rising up to his cut knee.
>
> —Tim O'Brien, from "Where Have You Gone, Charming Billy?" (page 621)

DIFFERENTIATING INSTRUCTION

Learners Having Difficulty

Setting. Show students a variety of photos that feature settings without people. Try to find photos of indoor and outdoor settings that reflect different moods. Discuss with students what mood they sense in each photo, what the details of the setting might reveal about people who inhabit that setting, and what potential conflicts might arise in each setting. Remind students that authors use words to create settings like the ones in the photos.

Advanced Learners

Acceleration. This activity can help move students toward the eleventh- and twelfth-grade Standard 3.3, for which they analyze the ways that tone, mood, and the "sound" of language achieve specific rhetorical or aesthetic purposes or both.

Elsewhere in the story this Vietnam jungle setting contrasts starkly with the young soldier's comforting memories of another setting, his home in Iowa. The mood and tone are different, and the emotional effect of that contrast is shattering.

He was pretending he was a boy again, camping with his father in the midnight summer along the Des Moines River. In the dark, with his eyes pinched shut, he pretended. He pretended that when he opened his eyes, his father would be there by the campfire and they would talk softly about whatever came to mind and then roll into their sleeping bags. . . .

Setting and Character

Setting also helps reveal **character.** We all affect our environment in one way or another, so a writer wishing to portray an untidy Alice will show us the mess in her bedroom: pajamas, hangers, and sneakers in a snarl on the floor of her closet; CDs and magazines strewn on the unmade bed. Even before we meet Alice, we know something about her.

Now consider Jim's room: a set of weights in one corner; a copy of the *Guinness Book of World Records* on the bedside table; school pennants, photographs of the basketball team, and a set of antlers on the wall; and a pair of boxing gloves hanging from a hook on the closet door. What do we know about Jim before he even steps into the story?

Setting and Conflict

Though in some stories, setting hardly matters, in others it provides the main **conflict** and can directly affect a story's meaning. In such a story, members of a polar expedition might fight the harshness of the arctic tundra and survive (or, alternatively, perish). In "Contents of the Dead Man's Pocket" (page 5), Tom's near-fatal struggle on the window ledge leads him to reevaluate the priorities in his life.

Practice

Work alone or with a partner to plan a story in which setting will play a major role. Use the chart shown here for your notes. It includes an example to help you.

Setting

Time: Late one winter night, early 1950s
Place: Run-down mansion in rural Scotland
Details of setting that affect mood or tone: Outside—dense fog; howling dog Inside—ticking clock; cold, damp rooms
Details of setting that reveal character: Bare rooms with few chairs; no rugs; dim light; hundreds of books in piles and bookcases
Details of setting that affect conflict and meaning: Isolated mansion; doors locked and barred

Practice

Possible chart:
Setting
Time—The present.
Place—A sandy beach at a seaside resort.
Details of setting that affect mood or tone—Sunny day, cool breeze, sparkling water, holiday crowds.
Details of setting that reveal character—Large, colorful beach umbrella shading a matching blanket; fashionable carryall with tubes of expensive sunscreen spilling out; floppy hat; beach robe; picnic basket; cooler.
Details of setting that affect conflict and meaning—Near blanket, beach volleyball court filled with boisterous players.

Apply

Encourage students to analyze the role of setting in a short story, which they have recently read, by making a chart like the one on this page.

Resources Reminder

Differentiating Instruction

- *Lesson Plans for Language Development*

For more instruction on setting for English-language learners and special education students, see *Lesson Plans for Language Development,* pp. 17, 18.

Activity. Encourage pairs of students to study the excerpt on p. 44 from "Where Have You Gone, Charming Billy?" Have them determine the paragraph's mood and tone and the author's purpose in writing it. Then, invite them to take turns reading the paragraph aloud, using tone of voice, emphasis, and cadence to express meaning. Finally, ask them to discuss how the paragraph's mood and tone and the "sound" of the language all work together to reflect the writer's purpose.

STANDARDS FOCUS, pp. 46–54

(For grade-level and review standards taught in this lesson, see the citations on Student Edition pages.)

Prerequisite Standard

- Grade 6, Literary Response and Analysis 3.3 **Analyze the influence of setting on the problem and its resolution.**

Reading Skills

- Determine the writer's purpose.

Summary *at grade level*

In this prophetic cautionary tale, Ray Bradbury creates a chilling portrayal of a society in which people are so isolated in their homes that a lone pedestrian is seen as a threat to the social order. The story's setting is an urban landscape in the year 2053. On a cold November night, Leonard Mead takes a walk alone through the city, as he has habitually done for ten years. He meets no one. Avoiding dog squads that harass walkers, he passes freeways that are totally deserted at night and tomblike homes where everyone watches TV. In this rigidly controlled city of three million people, there is one police car and no crime. When he is almost back home, Mead is stopped and interrogated by the robotic police car. Because he is exhibiting aberrant behavior as a pedestrian and because his profession—writing—isn't considered a real profession, he is driven away to the Psychiatric Center for Research on Regressive Tendencies.

Before You Read

The Pedestrian

Literary Focus

Setting and Mood

The **setting** of a story establishes the time and place of the action. Writers can also use setting to create a **mood,** or **atmosphere**—a subtle emotional overtone that can strongly affect our feelings. For example, settings can be used to suggest freedom, community, and peace. Settings can also be used to suggest control, isolation, and anxiety.

See what mood you sense in Bradbury's first paragraph. How does he use setting in the rest of the story to suggest his particular worldview?

Reading Skills

Does the Writer Have a Purpose?

Many fiction writers, poets, and dramatists have no **purpose** when they sit down to write other than to share a feeling or an experience, to re-create a world of their own making.

Ray Bradbury, however, is the kind of fiction writer who often writes for another purpose. Like many nonfiction writers, Bradbury tries to persuade us to accept his views on some issue.

To discover a writer's purpose, you must read closely. Take notes as you read. Look for **key passages** that directly express opinions. Watch for **loaded words.** Bradbury's comparison of the city to a graveyard in the second paragraph should immediately send you signals. In this story the **setting** relates closely to Bradbury's purpose and the story's meaning.

Grade 8 Review Reading Standard 3.4 Analyze the relevance of the setting (e.g., place, time, customs) to the mood and meaning of the text.

Make the Connection

Quickwrite

Bradbury's portrayal of a twenty-first-century world may raise as many questions as it provides answers.

What questions do you have now about what life will be like in 2053, when the story takes place? What predictions would you make? Write down your questions and ideas, and save your notes.

Background

In the early 1950s, Ray Bradbury was a young man living in southern California. He did not know how to drive, and he liked walking around his suburban neighborhood at night. Even back then such behavior was so rare that he was once stopped and questioned by the police. If an innocent walk was so suspicious in mid-twentieth-century America, Bradbury wondered how it might be viewed in the future. Then he wrote this story.

Vocabulary Development

manifest (man′ə·fest′) *v.:* appear; become evident. *Manifest* also means "show; reveal."

intermittent (in′tər·mit′'nt) *adj.:* appearing or occurring from time to time.

ebbing (eb′iŋ) *v.:* lessening or weakening. The ebb is the flow of water away from the land as the tide falls.

antiseptic (an′tə·sep′tik) *n.:* substance used to sterilize or to prevent infection.

regressive (ri·gres′iv) *adj.:* moving backward or returning to an earlier or less advanced condition.

46 Chapter 1 Plot and Setting • Synthesizing Sources

RESOURCES: READING

Planning

- *One-Stop Planner* CD-ROM with Test Generator
- *On Course: Mapping Instruction*

Media

- *Audio CD Library*
  - disc 2

Reading

- *Interactive Reading,* Teacher's Edition
  - Graphic Organizer: Setting Chart

Differentiating Instruction

- *Lesson Plans for Language Development*
  - English-Language Learners, pp. 19–21, 29, 33
  - Special Education Students, pp. 22, 29, 33

The Pedestrian

Ray Bradbury

A metallic voice called to him: "Stand still. Stay where you are!"

To enter out into that silence that was the city at eight o'clock of a misty evening in November, to put your feet upon that buckling concrete walk, to step over grassy seams and make your way, hands in pockets, through the silences, that was what Mr. Leonard Mead most dearly loved to do. He would stand upon the corner of an intersection and peer down long moonlit avenues of sidewalk in four directions, deciding which way to go, but it really made no difference; he was alone in this world of A.D. 2053, or as good as alone, and with a final decision made, a path selected, he would stride off, sending patterns of frosty air before him like the smoke of a cigar. **A**

Sometimes he would walk for hours and miles and return only at midnight to his house. And on his way he would see the cottages and homes with their dark windows, and it was not unequal to walking through a graveyard where only the faintest glimmers of firefly light appeared in flickers behind the windows. Sudden gray phantoms[1] seemed to manifest upon inner room walls where a curtain was still undrawn against the night, or there were whisperings and murmurs where a window in a tomblike building was still open.

1. **phantoms** (fan′temz) *n.:* ghosts; illusions.

Vocabulary

manifest (man′ə·fest′) *v.:* appear; become evident. *Manifest* also means "show; reveal."

Vocabulary

- *Vocabulary Development*
  - Vocabulary Worksheet, p. 4

Assessment

- *Progress Assessment of Reading*
  - Selection Test
- *One-Stop Planner* CD-ROM with Test Generator

PRETEACHING

Standards Starter

Motivate. Have students discuss movie scenes that have a mood, or atmosphere, of fear. Ask what details filmmakers use to create this mood. [Possible response: Filmmakers create an atmosphere of fear with details such as spooky music, darkness, shadows, a howling wind, and a creaky door.] Explain that such details establish a movie's setting—the time and place of the action—as well as the emotional tone. Point out that writers achieve similar effects with verbal description.

Preview Vocabulary

Have students read the definitions of the Vocabulary words on p. 46, and ask several volunteers to express each definition in their own words. Then, have students complete each of the following sentences with the correct Vocabulary word.

1. The beach seemed to widen as the tide was ______. [ebbing]
2. Through the fog, eerie shapes seemed to ______. [manifest]
3. The filmmakers created a wild, ______ scene of an earlier savage time. [regressive]
4. Alone on the dock, the fisherman grimaced as he splashed ______ on his wounded arm. [antiseptic]
5. ______ cries of gulls briefly broke the silence. [intermittent]

DIRECT TEACHING

A Literary Focus
REVIEW STANDARD

Setting and mood. Based on details in the opening paragraphs, how would you describe the setting? [The time is an evening in the future—November 2053. The place is a silent city.] How would you describe the mood? Which descriptive terms help to set the mood? [Possible response: The mood is ominous and dark. Descriptive terms include "graveyard," "gray phantoms," "whisperings and murmurs," and "tomblike."]

DIRECT TEACHING

VIEWING THE ART

Wayne Thiebaud (1920–) is a realist painter known for urban landscapes and paintings of ordinary objects. About his painting process, he says, "For me, realist painting is an alive confrontation. If you stare at an object, as you do when you paint, there is no point at which you can stop learning things about it."

Activity. Have students discuss the mood the painting creates for them. [Possible response: The mood is one of isolation. Students may note how the freeway cuts up the city.]

Freeway Interchange (1982) by Wayne Thiebaud. Oil on canvas.

DIFFERENTIATING INSTRUCTION

Learners Having Difficulty

Modeling. To help students read "The Pedestrian," model the reading skill of determining the writer's purpose. Say, "Suppose you read about houses described as 'tomb-like,' where people sit watching television 'like the dead.' These emotionally loaded words are tip-offs that the writer wants to persuade you not to live that way." As they read, encourage students to ask themselves, "What effect do these word choices have on me?"

Resource Reminder

Reading

- *Interactive Reading,* Teacher's Edition
  - Graphic Organizer: Setting Chart

English-Language Learners

Explain that Ray Bradbury wrote this story in the 1950s. At that time, Americans were just beginning to buy televisions and to move to newly built suburbs, where they were dependent on cars. Based on what he observed then, Bradbury wrote a story warning about life in the future.

48 Chapter 1 Plot and Setting • Synthesizing Sources

Mr. Leonard Mead would pause, cock his head, listen, look, and march on, his feet making no noise on the lumpy walk. For long ago he had wisely changed to sneakers when strolling at night, because the dogs in intermittent squads would parallel his journey with barkings if he wore hard heels, and lights might click on and faces appear and an entire street be startled by the passing of a lone figure, himself, in the early November evening.

On this particular evening he began his journey in a westerly direction, toward the hidden sea. There was a good crystal frost in the air; it cut the nose and made the lungs blaze like a Christmas tree inside; you could feel the cold light going on and off, all the branches filled with invisible snow. He listened to the faint push of his soft shoes through autumn leaves with satisfaction and whistled a cold, quiet whistle between his teeth, occasionally picking up a leaf as he passed, examining its skeletal pattern in the infrequent lamplights as he went on, smelling its rusty smell.

A "Hello, in there," he whispered to every house on every side as he moved. "What's up tonight on Channel 4, Channel 7, Channel 9? Where are the cowboys rushing, and do I see the United States Cavalry over the next hill to the rescue?"

The street was silent and long and empty, with only his shadow moving like the shadow of a hawk in midcountry. **B** If he closed his eyes and stood very still, frozen, he could imagine himself upon the center of a plain, a wintry, windless Arizona desert with no house in a thousand miles, and only dry riverbeds, the streets, for company.

"What is it now?" he asked the houses, noticing his wristwatch. "Eight-thirty p.m.? Time for a dozen assorted murders? A quiz? A revue? A comedian falling off the stage?"

Was that a murmur of laughter from within a moon-white house? He hesitated but went on when nothing more happened. He stumbled over a particularly uneven section of sidewalk. The cement was vanishing under flowers and grass. In ten years of walking by night or day, for thousands of miles, he had never met another person walking, not one in all that time.

He came to a cloverleaf intersection which stood silent where two main highways crossed the town. During the day it was a thunderous surge of cars, the gas stations open, a great insect rustling, and a ceaseless jockeying for position as the scarab beetles,[2] a faint incense[3] puttering from their exhausts, skimmed homeward to the far directions. But now these highways, too, were like streams in a dry season, all stone and bed and moon radiance.

He turned back on a side street, circling around toward his home. He was within a block of his destination when the lone car turned a corner quite suddenly and flashed a fierce white cone of light upon him. He stood entranced, not unlike a night moth, stunned by the illumination and then drawn toward it.

A metallic voice called to him:

"Stand still. Stay where you are! Don't move!"

He halted.

"Put up your hands!"

"But—" he said.

"Your hands up! Or we'll shoot!"

The police, of course, but what a rare, incredible thing; in a city of three million, there was only *one* police car left, wasn't that correct? Ever since a year ago, 2052, the election year, the force had been cut down from three cars to one. Crime was ebbing; there was no need now for

2. **scarab beetles:** stout-bodied, brilliantly colored beetles. Bradbury is using the term as a metaphor for automobiles.
3. **incense** (in′sens′) *n.:* here, smoke.

Vocabulary
intermittent (in′tər·mit′'nt) *adj.:* appearing or occurring from time to time.
ebbing (eb′iŋ) *v.:* lessening or weakening. The ebb is the flow of water away from the land as the tide falls.

DIRECT TEACHING

A Content-Area Connections
Culture: Television
Point out that in the 1950s, when this story was written, many popular television series were set in the Wild West, featuring cowboys or frontier conflicts.

B Vocabulary Development
GRADE-LEVEL STANDARD
Interpreting connotations. What do the words *wintry, windless, desert,* and *dry* suggest about Mead's impression of the urban landscape at night? [Possible response: These words suggest a lifeless, barren landscape.]

Resources Reminder
For lessons designed for intermediate and advanced English-language learners, see *Lesson Plans for Language Development*, pp. 19–21, 29, 33.

Special Education Students
For lessons designed for special education students, see *Lesson Plans for Language Development,* pp. 22, 29, 33.

Advanced Learners
Acceleration. Use this activity to move students toward the eleventh- and twelfth-grade Standard 3.3, for which they analyze how an author uses tone, mood, and style to achieve specific rhetorical purposes.

Activity. Have students discuss the story's themes of individuality versus conformity and alienation versus belonging. Ask students, "How does the author use descriptive details and dialogue to contrast Mead's individuality with others' conformity? How does the setting establish a mood of alienation? How does this mood relate to the theme and the writer's purpose?"

DIRECT TEACHING

A Reading Skills

Determining the writer's purpose. What is Bradbury's purpose for having the police say that writing is "no profession"? [Possible response: He is stressing that in this society, creativity is not valued.]

B Literary Focus
REVIEW STANDARD

Setting and mood. What words and phrases in this passage suggest a mood of death and despair? ["tomblike houses," "tombs, ill-lit," "people sat like the dead," "gray," and "never really touching them"]

VIEWING THE ART

James Doolin (1932–) creates a surreal feeling in his paintings by a process called staging. He finds that night landscapes are ideal vehicles for making staged spaces. In creating his paintings, he positions lights to suit a specific color and purpose—for example, playing "warm" places off "cool" places and "near" areas off "far" areas. The result is a theatricality that the artist finds very satisfying.

Activity. Compare this painting with *Freeway Interchange* on p. 48. [Possible response: One painting views highways from a distance; the other is a view from inside a vehicle.] Is there strange omission in Doolin's painting? [There is no driver.]

the police, save for this one lone car wandering and wandering the empty streets.

"Your name?" said the police car in a metallic whisper. He couldn't see the men in it for the bright light in his eyes.

"Leonard Mead," he said.

"Speak up!"

"Leonard Mead!"

"Business or profession?"

"I guess you'd call me a writer."

"No profession," said the police car, as if talking to itself. The light held him fixed, like a museum specimen, needle thrust through chest.

"You might say that," said Mr. Mead. He hadn't written in years. Magazines and books didn't sell anymore. Everything went on in the tomblike houses at night now, he thought, continuing his fancy. The tombs, ill-lit by television light, where the people sat like the dead, the gray or multicolored lights touching their faces, but never really touching them.

"No profession," said the phonograph voice, hissing. "What are you doing out?"

"Walking," said Leonard Mead.

"Walking!"

"Just walking," he said simply, but his face felt cold.

"Walking, just walking, walking?"

"Yes, sir."

"Walking where? For what?"

Highway Patrol (1986) by James Doolin. Oil on canvas.

Courtesy of Koplin Gallery, Los Angeles, CA.

READING MINI-LESSON

Developing Word-Attack Skills
Remind students that a final e in one-syllable words, like *cape,* and multisyllabic words, like *calibrate,* signals that the preceding vowel is long. In rare instances this is also true for a medial e. Point out that in *outrageous,* the medial e signals that the preceding *a* has a long sound and the g has the sound /j/.

Explain that in many words a medial e appears to be part of a vowel-consonant-e pattern, but in fact, the medial e is a syllable on its own. Show this using the selection word *avenue.* Point out that the word is not pronounced "āv′no͞o." It is pronounced "av′ə·no͞o." In *avenue,* the medial e is a syllable on its own with an unaccented vowel sound.

Point out that when a medial e precedes another vowel, as in *museum,* the e has the long sound /ē/.

Activity. Write the following words on the chalkboard. Ask students if the underlined e in each word signals that the preceding vowel is long, as in *outrageous*; is an unaccented syllable, as in *avenue*; or has a long e.

"Walking for air. Walking to *see*."

"Your address!"

"Eleven South Saint James Street."

"And there is air *in* your house, you have an air *conditioner*, Mr. Mead?"

"Yes."

"And you have a viewing screen in your house to see with?"

"No."

"No?" There was a crackling quiet that in itself was an accusation.

"Are you married, Mr. Mead?"

"No."

"Not married," said the police voice behind the fiery beam. The moon was high and clear among the stars and the houses were gray and silent.

"Wait a minute, I haven't done anything!"

"Nobody wanted me," said Leonard Mead with a smile.

"Don't speak unless you're spoken to!"

Leonard Mead waited in the cold night.

"Just *walking*, Mr. Mead?"

"Yes."

"But you haven't explained for what purpose."

"I explained: for air, and to see, and just to walk."

"Have you done this often?"

"Every night for years."

The police car sat in the center of the street with its radio throat faintly humming.

"Well, Mr. Mead," it said.

"Is that all?" he asked politely.

"Yes," said the voice. "Here." There was a sigh, a pop. The back door of the police car sprang wide. "Get in."

"Wait a minute, I haven't done anything!"

"Get in."

"I protest!"

"Mr. Mead."

He walked like a man suddenly drunk. As he passed the front window of the car, he looked in. As he had expected, there was no one in the front seat, no one in the car at all.

"Get in."

He put his hand to the door and peered into the back seat, which was a little cell, a little black jail with bars. It smelled of riveted[4] steel. It smelled of harsh antiseptic; it smelled too clean and hard and metallic. There was nothing soft there.

"Now, if you had a wife to give you an alibi," said the iron voice. "But—"

"Where are you taking me?"

The car hesitated, or rather gave a faint, whirring click, as if information, somewhere, was dropping card by punch-slotted card under electric eyes. "To the Psychiatric Center for Research on Regressive Tendencies."

He got in. The door shut with a soft thud. The police car rolled through the night avenues, flashing its dim lights ahead.

C They passed one house on one street a moment later, one house in an entire city of houses that were dark, but this one particular house had all of its electric lights brightly lit, every window a loud yellow illumination, square and warm in the cool darkness. **D**

"That's *my* house," said Leonard Mead.

No one answered him.

The car moved down the empty riverbed streets and off away, leaving the empty streets with the empty sidewalks and no sound and no motion all the rest of the chill November night. ■ **E**

4. **riveted** (riv′it·id) *v.* used as *adj.:* held together by rivets (metal bolts or pins).

Vocabulary

antiseptic (an′tə·sep′tik) *n.:* substance used to sterilize or prevent infection.

regressive (ri·gres′iv) *adj.:* moving backward or returning to an earlier or less advanced condition.

DIRECT TEACHING

C Learners Having Difficulty

Reading aloud. In this passage the speaker of the dialogue is not always identified. Have a pair of students read the dialogue aloud; if needed, help them identify who is speaking each line.

D Reading Skills

Determining the writer's purpose. What emotions do the words *brightly, illumination, square,* and *warm* suggest to you? [Possible response: They suggest warmth, hope, and solidity.] What might be the writer's purpose in describing Mead's house? [Possible responses: He describes it to reinforce the difference between Mead and the rest of society; he wants to emphasize that Mead is a light in the darkness; as Mead's lights shine into the darkness, the writer is suggesting the value of reaching out to others.]

E Advanced Learners

Acceleration. In this final paragraph, how does the writer use repetition both to create mood and to achieve his purpose? [Possible response: Repeating the words *empty* and *no* creates a mood of bleakness. The words also fulfill the writer's purpose of persuading readers that a society in which people isolate themselves is empty of meaning, value, and soul.]

sound, as in *museum*.

1. **skeletal** [unaccented syllable]
2. **permeable** [long e]
3. **molecule** [unaccented syllable]
4. **irreplaceable** [preceding long vowel]
5. **courageous** [preceding long vowel]
6. **linear** [long e]
7. **nucleus** [long e]
8. **monetary** [unaccented syllable]
9. **tenement** [unaccented syllable]
10. **petroleum** [long e]

GUIDED PRACTICE

Monitoring students' progress. Guide the class in answering these questions. Have students locate text details that support their responses.

True-False

1. Leonard Mead prefers television to walking. [F]
2. Homes in the city display bright lights at night. [F]
3. No one is in the patrol car. [T]
4. Mead stops and talks to people along his route. [F]
5. The desire to see the world and breathe fresh air is considered unnatural in the city. [T]

Meet the Writer

Background. Ray Bradbury says that he often begins his stories by thinking of the characters he wants to write about. "You can't have 'plot' and 'setting,' really, until you have a character who wants something with all his heart," he says. "The character, on his way to getting what he wants, be it love, survival, or destruction, will write your story for you."

For Independent Reading

- Students reading Bradbury novels might want to try writing their own science fiction stories. Recommend Bradbury's *Zen in the Art of Writing,* an exuberant guide to writing as an adventure. Bradbury leads writers to discover their own voices and to find unique ideas in their own minds.
- For a modern nonfiction account eerily reminiscent of Mead's experiences, suggest "Perfect Pitch" by David Remnick, first published in the February 12, 1996 *New Yorker.* This obituary of Russian poet Joseph Brodsky includes transcripts from his trial in the former Soviet Union for the "crime" of being a poet.

Meet the Writer

Ray Bradbury

The Man with the Child Inside

Ray Bradbury (1920–) calls himself "that special freak—the man with the child inside who remembers all." Bradbury was born in Waukegan, Illinois, and began writing when he was seven.

Bradbury sees himself as a magic realist (see page 586) and a disciple of Edgar Allan Poe (see page 428). He says that his lifelong hatred of thought control grows out of his sympathy for his ancestor Mary Bradbury, who was tried as a witch in seventeenth-century Salem, Massachusetts. Here is how his imagination grew:

"When I was three my mother snuck me in and out of movies two or three times a week. My first film was Lon Chaney in *The Hunchback of Notre Dame.* I suffered permanent curvature of the spine and of my imagination that day a long time ago in 1923. From that hour on, I knew a kindred and wonderfully grotesque compatriot of the dark when I saw one. . . .

I was in love, then, with monsters and skeletons and circuses and carnivals and dinosaurs and at last, the red planet, Mars.

From these primitive bricks I have built a life and a career. By my staying in love with all of these amazing things, all of the good things in my existence have come about.

In other words, I was *not* embarrassed at circuses. Some people are. Circuses are loud, vulgar, and smell in the sun. By the time many people are fourteen or fifteen, they have been divested of their loves, their ancient and intuitive tastes, one by one, until when they reach maturity there is no fun left, no zest, no gusto, no flavor. Others have criticized, and they have criticized themselves, into embarrassment. When the circus pulls in at five of a dark cold summer morn, and the calliope sounds, they do not rise and run, they turn in their sleep, and life passes by.

I did rise and run. . . ."

For Independent Reading

If you enjoyed "The Pedestrian," you might enjoy reading some of Bradbury's well-known novels. *The Martian Chronicles* describes the adventures of a colony of pioneers on Mars. *Dandelion Wine* paints a fantasy of a boy with special mental powers.

DIFFERENTIATING INSTRUCTION

Advanced Learners

Enrichment. Tell students that Ray Bradbury is a writer who has inspired passionate, lifelong fans. Many of them have formed online communities, where readers can share reviews, reflections, and ideas about their favorite Bradbury works.

Activity. Have students search the Internet for online fan clubs or message boards devoted to the works of Ray Bradbury. After they have independently read one of Bradbury's novels or short story collections, encourage them to submit their own online reviews or to initiate an online discussion about the work. Students may even want to set up their own Bradbury Web site or a message board linked to students in other high schools.

52 Chapter 1 Plot and Setting • Synthesizing Sources

Literary Response and Analysis

Reading Check

1. What ominous fact about this future society is **foreshadowed,** or hinted at, by the "buckling concrete walk" in the first paragraph? As the story develops, what else are you told about the **setting** of "The Pedestrian"?
2. Find the sentences and phrases that at first suggest that Leonard Mead is the only person living in this **setting** in A.D. 2053. Find the passage that reveals that there are other people living in this setting.
3. Explain Leonard Mead's "regressive tendencies."
4. Describe the police automaton's response when Mead says he is a writer.

Interpretations

5. Leonard Mead is the only human character in the story. Who—or what—appears to be in charge of this future world?
6. List several details that describe the houses Leonard passes and the evening streets. What **mood** do these details create?
7. What do you think Bradbury's **purpose** was in writing this story? How does the setting he chose help him achieve his purpose? Cite details from the story to support your answers.
8. Which of today's problems seem to have been eliminated from Leonard Mead's society? What does Leonard miss that we still enjoy today?
9. How is technology used to control Leonard's world? What point about technology and its power do you think Bradbury is making in this story? Find some key words, phrases, or events in the story to support your interpretation.

Evaluation

10. Do you think Bradbury is too pessimistic about technology? Support your opinion with details from the text and from the real world.

Writing

Picture the Setting

Use your imagination to help you describe the Psychiatric Center for Research on Regressive Tendencies that Leonard is sent to. Consider whether the researchers are human or robots, what they look like (including how they are dressed), and how the building is furnished. Be sure your **setting** creates a **mood** that fits with Bradbury's story.

Listening and Speaking

Debating the Future

Form a panel, and discuss what you think society will be like in 2053. Will technology isolate us from one another, as "The Pedestrian" suggests, or will technology be a force for good? Will individuals be more free or less free? Check your Quickwrite notes for other questions. Before you begin, assign a moderator, and establish rules for the panel. At the end of the discussion, audience members should prepare a **summary** of the panel's views and an **evaluation** of the participants' performances.

Grade 8 Review Reading Standard 3.4 Analyze the relevance of the setting (e.g., place, time, customs) to the mood and meaning of the text.

INDEPENDENT PRACTICE

Literary Response and Analysis

Reading Check

1. The sidewalk's disrepair shows that nobody uses it. The setting is a November night in 2053; roads are deserted; people numb themselves with TV; there is no crime; the city is patrolled by a single, robotic police cruiser.
2. Paragraph 1: ". . . he was alone in this world of A.D. 2053, or as good as alone." Paragraph 2: Phrases such as "walking through a graveyard" and "gray phantoms" suggest that Mead is the only one alive. Paragraph 3: We learn that he is not alone when faces appear at the windows.
3. Mead does things not done since technology changed society—he walks; he writes; he owns no television set.
4. It does not recognize his profession and calls him unemployed.

Interpretations

5. Machines.
6. Details include "gray phantoms," "tomblike," "silent and long and empty," "dry riverbed," "streams in a dry season," and "people sat like the dead." They create a mood of desolation and despair.
7. Possible answer: He is warning readers of addiction to technology, of abandoning individuality, and of alienation from the natural world. The deserted streets and dark houses of conformist TV watchers contrast with the lone individual who acts for himself. Details of setting that help Bradbury achieve his purpose include the deserted streets and the dehumanized police.
8. Crime and homelessness seem nonexistent. He misses contact with neighbors and freedom to walk about.
9. Possible answers: Automated police cars can stop and arrest people; television keeps people occupied at night. Bradbury's point may be that people must not let technology control them. Details that support this point of view include the "tomblike houses" where people "sat like the dead"; the automated police car with its back seat like "a little black jail."

Evaluation

10. Possible answers: He is too pessimistic because television and computers have made information easily accessible. He is not too pessimistic because people spend more time with television and computers than with each other.

Vocabulary Development

Practice 1

Possible Answers

- *Word*—manifest (verb). *Definition*—appear; reveal. *Sentences*—Only after his mother left did the baby's crying manifest a sorrow. New ideas began to manifest during our meeting.
- *Word*—intermittent (adjective). *Definition*—occurring from time to time. *Sentences*—While running, she experienced intermittent leg cramps. There were intermittent lightning flashes during the storm.
- *Word*—ebbing (verb). *Definition*—lessening or weakening. *Sentences*—The importance of mail is ebbing in today's digital world. My interest in the TV show was ebbing, so I turned it off.
- *Word*—regressive (adjective). *Definition*—returning to a less advanced condition. *Sentences*—For an adult, interest in cartoons may seem regressive. Some people show regressive behavior under stress.

Practice 2

Possible Answers

1. "Graveyard" in passage 1 and "gray phantoms" and "tomblike building" in passage 2 suggest death and isolation.
2. *Passage 1*—"And on his way he would see the cottages and homes with their dark windows, and it was not unequal to walking through *a peaceful, magical kingdom*." *Passage 2*—"Sudden *soft images* seemed to manifest upon inner room walls . . . or there were whisperings and murmurs where a window in a *serene structure* was still open."

Resources Reminder

Vocabulary

- *Vocabulary Development*
  - Vocabulary Worksheet, p. 4
  - Cumulative Vocabulary Review, pp. 5–6
- *Lesson Plans for Language Development*
  - Vocabulary, pp. 29, 33

Vocabulary Development

Vocabulary Resource File

PRACTICE 1

Begin a vocabulary resource file, starting with the words in the Word Bank. Put each word on an index card (or create a file on your computer). Use the example below as a model. Include a note to yourself to help you remember the word.

Word Bank
manifest
intermittent
ebbing
antiseptic
regressive

Word: antiseptic (noun)
Definition: substance used on the skin to prevent infection
Sentences: Before giving me the shot, the nurse swabbed my arm with an antiseptic.
After washing the cut, Dave applied iodine as an antiseptic.
Note: An antiseptic is used to kill bacteria on the outside of the body—on the skin. An antibiotic destroys bacteria inside the body.

The Power of Connotations

Certain words have emotional overtones, or **connotations,** that go beyond their literal meanings, or **denotations.** Consider the difference between the two words in the following pairs:

unusual/odd	young/immature	proud/smug
assertive/pushy	frugal/stingy	

In each pair the first word has more positive connotations than the second word. We might use the first word to describe ourselves but the second word to describe someone else. In fact, the British philosopher Bertrand Russell once gave a classic example of the different connotations of words: "I am firm. You are obstinate. He is a pig-headed fool."

Reading Standard 1.1 Identify and use the literal meanings of words.

Reading Standard 1.2 Distinguish between the denotative and connotative meanings of words and interpret the connotative power of words.

The following passages from "The Pedestrian" use words with strong **connotations:**

1. "And on his way he would see the cottages and homes with their dark windows, and it was not unequal to walking through a graveyard. . . ."
2. "Sudden gray phantoms seemed to manifest upon inner room walls . . . , or there were whisperings and murmurs where a window in a tomblike building was still open."

PRACTICE 2

1. Write down what you think is the strongest word or phrase in each of the numbered passages on the left. Then, describe briefly what the word or phrase suggests to you or how it makes you feel.
2. Rewrite each passage with words that have more positive connotations. The graveyard, for example, could become a sleepy village.

ASSESSING

Assessment

- *Progress Assessment of Reading*
  - Selection Test

RETEACHING

For another selection to teach Grade 8 Review Standard 3.4, see *Interactive Reading,* Chapter 1.

54 Chapter 1 Plot and Setting • Synthesizing Sources

Read On: FOR INDEPENDENT READING

FICTION

The Good Old Days

Jack Finney's flair for fast-paced time-travel stories with a comic edge is beautifully realized in his short story collection ***About Time.*** In these twelve tales you'll enter places where odd neighbors, magical coin collections, X-ray-vision eyeglasses, disappearing dogs, and candy bars made from unusual ingredients are your passports to the world of the past.

FICTION

Woman of Strength

Life in rural India is difficult for Rukmani and her family. Drought, disease, death, and desperate poverty threaten them at every turn. Yet Kamala Markandaya's ***Nectar in a Sieve*** is ultimately a story of hope—a beautiful tale of how a mother's strength, faith, and endurance manage to unite her loved ones in the worst of times.

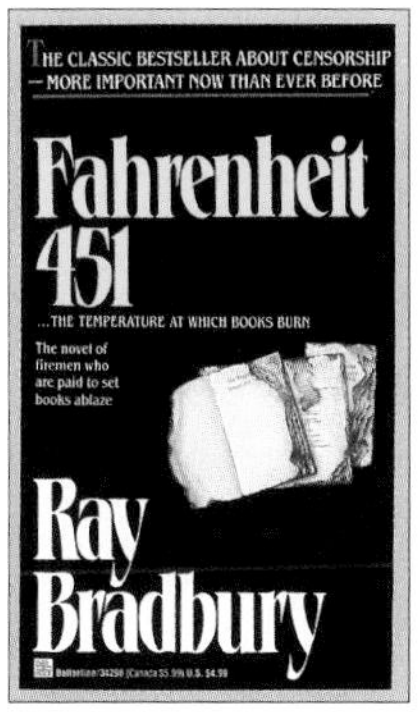

FICTION

Burning Books

A little knowledge is a dangerous thing in Ray Bradbury's futuristic world of ***Fahrenheit 451.*** People are forbidden to read, and any books that are found are immediately burned by "firemen." Then one day a fireman named Guy Montag begins to question the wisdom of what he's doing and soon discovers a secret and beautiful world he'd never dreamed of.

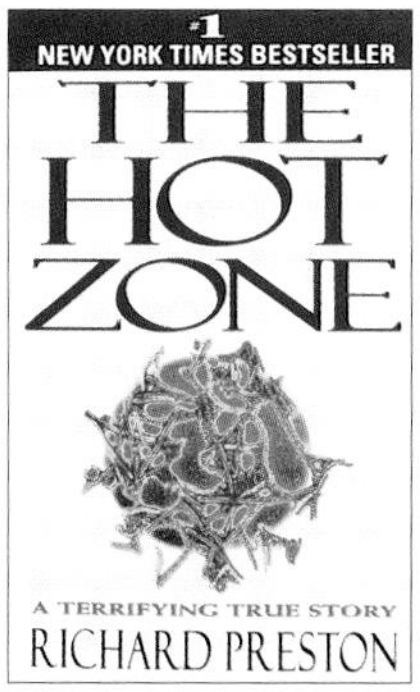

NONFICTION

A Very Close Call . . .

For a suspenseful and completely true story that even Stephen King found frightening, get ***The Hot Zone*** by Richard Preston. This nonfiction thriller focuses on a deadly virus that almost escaped from a research laboratory in Reston, Virginia. Find out how this tropical threat was brought under control—barely.

Read On

For Independent Reading

If students enjoyed the themes and topics explored in this chapter, you might recommend these titles for independent reading.

Assessment Options

The following projects can help you evaluate and assess your students' outside reading. Videotapes or audiotapes of completed projects may be included in student portfolios.

- **Book world.** Ask a student who has read *Fahrenheit 451* to chair a panel discussion about the value of reading and the importance of books. Invite students who have read *About Time, Nectar in a Sieve,* and *The Hot Zone* to join the panel. Have each student make a statement about why the book he or she read can make a difference to people in today's world. Invite them to discuss why a futuristic government might want to destroy books and how people's lives would be different if there were no books.
- **Make a map.** Suggest that students create a map that reflects the plot and setting of a book or story, devising descriptive symbols and labels to show where key plot events take place. Students can model their maps after various kinds of physical or special-purpose maps. For fictional locations, students can use imagination and details from the literature to create map elements.

Toward Reading Two Million Words Annually

Estimated Word Counts and Reading Levels of Read On Books:

Fiction			Nonfiction		
About Time	↔	72,800	*The Hot Zone*	↔	103,900
*Nectar in a Sieve**	↑	75,700			
*Fahrenheit 451**	↓	23,100			

***California Reading List Titles**

KEY: ↑ *above grade level* ↔ *at grade level* ↓ *below grade level*

PRETEACHING

Standards Starter

Motivate. To stimulate thought about personal reflection, explain that students have listened to or read stories about the experiences of others when the storytellers were young. Prompt students to identify someone who has shared personal experiences with them. Then, ask students to freewrite for ten minutes about that occasion. What did it teach them about the person? about themselves? about life?

Resources Reminder

To introduce the workshop, you may want to use the journal starters in *Writing, Listening, & Speaking* Teaching Notes.

DIRECT TEACHING

Consider Purpose and Audience

You may want to remind students that there is more than one form in which to present an autobiographical narrative. Some forms may be more appropriate depending on students' purpose and audience. For example, a journal entry might be an appropriate form to present a personal experience to a friend or family member. If the audience is a teacher, a formal essay is probably the most appropriate form for presenting information.

Writing an Autobiographical Narrative

Writing Assignment
Writing 2.1 Write a narrative about a significant autobiographical experience.

Somewhere, sometime, you've picked up a writer's account of a personal experience—something like, say, Sir Edmund Hillary's account of climbing Mt. Everest, your younger sister's account of the first day of first grade, or Sue Shellenbarger's account of her attempts to balance her personal and professional lives in "Diary of a Mad Blender"—and thought, "I've felt that way, too." People write **autobiographical narratives** to share their experiences and life lessons with others. What kind of experience do *you* have to share?

Prewriting

go.hrw.com

GO TO: go.hrw.com
KEYWORD: HLLA 10-1
FOR: Professional Model, Writer's Guides, and Reference Sources

Choose an Experience

Who Are You? To find an experience to use as the topic for an autobiographical narrative, begin by exploring the defining moments of your life—the experiences that have shaped who you are. Brainstorm a list of experiences you remember vividly. Then, jot down some notes about each one. Finally, look over your notes and choose the experience that stirs up the most vivid memories or feelings. Be sure to choose an experience you feel comfortable sharing with an audience.

Consider Purpose and Audience

Basic Considerations A basic principle of good writing requires you to keep two considerations—**purpose** and **audience**—in mind as you write, no matter what you're writing. Your purpose is to describe an experience that had a significant effect on your life. Provide your readers with the background information they will need to understand the significance of your experience fully. For example, introduce yourself as you were before the experience. Doing so will provide a hint about the effect the experience had on you.

Writing 1.0 Writing demonstrates students' awareness of audience and purpose. **2.1** Write autobiographical narratives. **2.1a** Relate a sequence of events and communicate the significance of the events to the audience.

Gather Details

Putting the Pieces Together The details of your experience are like the brightly colored pieces of a jigsaw puzzle. Put them together and they will create a vivid and coherent picture for your readers.

CHAPTER 1 RESOURCES: WRITING

Writing Workshop

Planning

- *On Course: Mapping Instruction*
- *One-Stop Planner* CD-ROM
- *Writing, Listening, & Speaking*, Teaching Notes, p. 1

Differentiating Instruction

- *Lesson Plans for Language Development*, pp. 23–24
- *Supporting Instruction in Spanish*

Practice

- *Writing, Listening, & Speaking*, Ch. 1

56 Chapter 1 Plot and Setting • Synthesizing Sources

Events First, brainstorm the **sequence of events** that is central to your narrative. Make sure that you **focus** the narrative by choosing only those events that are relevant to the experience. Then, list the events in a rough outline like the one below.

DO THIS

Events

1. I watched others practicing tae kwon do, the Korean martial art I had always wanted to learn, and imagined that I could do it, too.
2. I met an instructor who taught me techniques and encouraged me to practice hard.
3. I entered a competition.
4. My mom and dad saw me compete.

People and Places Close your eyes and walk yourself through the events you listed. Try to remember as specifically as possible the people and **specific places** involved in your experience. Jot down **factual details,** such as names, dates, and numbers; concrete **sensory details,** which have to do with the senses of touch, smell, hearing, sight, and taste; and the **specific appearances, gestures, actions,** and **dialogue** of the people involved, including yourself. Keep in mind that dialogue should be recorded as informally as it was spoken. For example, it can include slang and sentence fragments.

As you list details, jot down any **figurative language** (**similes, metaphors,** or **personification**) that will help you describe your experience more clearly and create more effective images. Also try to use precise **action verbs**—*paced* or *lurched* instead of *walked,* for example—to note events and actions. Take a look at part of the list that one student prepared about learning tae kwon do.

Reference Note

For more on **figurative language,** see pages 477–478.

Details about People and Places

Me—Shy, not very confident, age 13, physically scrawny and awkward

Gwen—College student, strong and swift, encouraging—"Hey, wallflower! Why don't you come help me practice some of my blocks?"

Thoughts and Feelings Your narrative should reveal what you thought and felt during your experience. In your rough outline, make some notes about your thoughts and feelings at each point. In your final draft, consider showing thoughts and feelings through **interior monologue,** or what you say to yourself in your head as the events of your narrative unfold. You may also want to **shift perspectives** by imagining the thoughts and feelings of other people in the narrative.

Writing 1.2 Use precise language, action verbs, and sensory details. **2.1b** Locate scenes and incidents in specific places. **2.1c** Describe with concrete sensory details the sights, sounds, and smells of a scene and the specific actions, movements, gestures, and feelings of the characters; use interior monologue to depict characters' feelings. **2.1e** Make effective use of descriptions of appearance, images, shifting perspectives, and sensory details.

DIRECT TEACHING

Integrating with Grammar, Usage, and Mechanics

As students begin their autobiographical narratives, they may have trouble with writing correct sentences. You may want to review the **Parts of Speech Overview** and **Parts of a Sentence** chapters in the *Holt Handbook.*

RETEACHING

GRADE-LEVEL STANDARD

People and Places

If students have difficulty incorporating factual details into their narratives, suggest that they draw maps of the settings of their autobiographical narratives. By visualizing and mentally walking through the rooms in the house, the areas of the yard, their neighborhood, or whatever the setting might be, students can generate more details for their essays. Students might note details directly on their maps or jot them down on a separate sheet of paper.

DIFFERENTIATING INSTRUCTION

Learners Having Difficulty

Students might benefit from telling their stories to one or more classmates who could write down the key details of the oral narratives. These details can then be given back to the speaker for use in his or her writing. Students can help the storyteller by asking questions that provide details for the writer to use. If possible, have each student serve as both a storyteller and a listener within a small group setting.

Reinforcement

- *Daily Language Activities*

Evaluation and Assessment

- *Test Generator* (*One-Stop Planner* CD-ROM)
- *Progress Assessment of Writing, Listening, & Speaking,* Ch. 1

Internet

- go.hrw.com (keyword: HLLA 10-1)
- Online assessments at go.hrw.com (keyword: HLLA)

CORRECTING MISCONCEPTIONS

Students using a flashback to organize the details of their narratives might incorrectly think that their introductions should contain their thoughts on the significance of their experiences. Caution them that even if they use the flashback technique, their remarks on the significance of the experience should be saved for the conclusion of the narrative.

Reflect on Your Experience

That Was Then, This Is Now An autobiographical narrative should convey the **significance,** or meaning, of the experience you describe. At the end, your readers should clearly understand the difference between who you were before the experience and who you became after it was over. To reflect on the meaning of your experience, think about what you were like before the experience, how you changed, and what you learned about yourself and about life in general.

DO THIS → Start reflecting on your experience by filling in a couple of simple sentences:

At first I ____________, *but afterward I* ____________.

I realized ______________.

The student writing about tae kwon do jotted the following sentences to express the meaning of her experience.

TIP Remember to signal the passage of time with **transitional expressions** such as *next, then, eventually, soon, the next day,* and so on.

> At first I was shy and lacked confidence, but afterward I was more self-assured. I realized that I had felt myself to be only a shadow of my older brother and sister, but now I had an accomplishment of my own to prove I was my own person.

Don't include these sentences in your narrative's introduction. Instead, use them to help you choose those details that contribute to a **controlling impression,** or central idea, about your experience. For example, the student writing about tae kwon do chose details to create the controlling impression that the sport gave her self-confidence and a sense of identity. Save any direct statement of the significance of your experience for the conclusion of your narrative—after your readers have had a chance to determine for themselves how the experience changed your life.

Organize Your Details

Following the Leader **Chronological order** is usually the easiest for readers to follow. However, a **flashback** is another effective way to organize a narrative: The narrative starts at the end and then "flashes back" to the earlier events that led up to that point.

Pace is also important to consider as you plan your essay. For example, quicken the pace of your narrative by using a series of short, to-the-point sentences to describe events that occurred rapidly. Slow your pace by using longer sentences to describe events that occurred slowly.

Writing 1.1 Establish a controlling impression and maintain a consistent focus throughout a piece of writing. **2.1d** Pace the presentation of actions to accommodate changes in time.

PRACTICE & APPLY 1 Choose a significant experience from your life as the subject of your autobiographical narrative. Then, plan the details of the narrative.

PRACTICE & APPLY 1

Guided and Independent Practice

Remind students that gathering details for their narratives may be an ongoing process. To relate an experience and its meaning effectively, students may need to add additional details as they work on their drafts.

To check that students have completed all the prewriting steps, have them organize their events, details, and controlling impressions in charts.

RESOURCES: WRITING

Practice & Apply 1

Guided Practice

- *Writing, Listening, & Speaking,* WS. p. 2

Reteaching and Modeling

- *Writing, Listening, & Speaking,* TP. 5
- *Writing, Listening, & Speaking,* WS. p. 3

Writing

Writing an Autobiographical Narrative

A Writer's Framework

Introduction	Body	Conclusion
• Start with an interesting opener. • Provide necessary background information. • Hint at the significance of the experience.	• Organize events so that they are easy to follow. • Include details about people, places, thoughts, and feelings. • Use figurative language and precise action verbs.	• Reflect on what the experience meant to you. • End with a direct statement of the significance of the experience.

A Writer's Model

Kicking Shyness

My whole way of looking at the world began to change around the time I turned thirteen. That May, my parents began taking the family to a local YMCA. At the time, although I didn't admit it to myself, I always seemed to live in the shadows of my older brother and sister. However, beginning with those hot summer days at the center, I started to lose track of what my brother and sister were doing—because for the first time in my life I was too busy doing my own thing.

INTRODUCTION
Interesting opener
Background information
Hint at significance

After about a month, I found a tae kwon do class at the YMCA and was mesmerized as I watched men and women, boys and girls practice moves and spar with each other. The room was filled with swishing, white uniforms and roaring *ki-hop* yells. I imagined I was one of these people, timing my strokes perfectly, blocking so gracefully, delivering the winning point at the last moment. In reality I spent weeks blending into the wall farthest from the class, shadowboxing at home behind locked doors, too afraid to join the others.

BODY
Event 1
Sensory details
Thoughts

Slow pace
Details about actions/Feelings

Then, after weeks of watching, one day it happened. The *sabom-nim* (instructor), a college student named Gwen who moved as if the law of gravity did not apply to her, called to me just as I was about to sneak out the door. "Hey, wallflower! Why don't you come help me practice some of my blocks?" she asked. I told her that I was not part of the class, but she insisted, saying, "I promise I'll only block your moves. No countermoves until you're ready—and I can teach you some other techniques, too."

Event 2
Details about appearance
Dialogue

(continued)

MODELING AND DEMONSTRATION

A Writer's Model

Since dialogue will add an important dimension to students' narratives, model correct punctuation of dialogue for them.

- Use quotation marks at the beginning and end of a direct quotation. ["I believe the test is on Friday."]
- Use a comma, a question mark, or an exclamation point to set off a quotation from the rest of the sentence. ["We are going to the movies on Saturday," said Dawn. "May I join you?" Holly asked.]
- Place question marks and exclamation points that belong to a quotation inside quotation marks. [My little sister shrieked, "This is absolutely the best gift!"]

Have student volunteers model correct punctuation by writing and correctly punctuating dialogue from their narratives on the chalkboard.

TECHNOLOGY TIP

Suggest that students use computer graphics software to create pictures or use word-processing software to create line drawings, such as maps or diagrams, to accompany their writing. Students may want to paste in clip art to add interest to their word-processor documents, or they may use a CD-ROM drive and software to download photographic images to include in their essays.

DIFFERENTIATING INSTRUCTION

English-Language Learners

Some students might settle for general verbs to describe actions, such as *looked* or *talked.* As a remedy, have students work with English-proficient partners, using a thesaurus to find synonyms, such as *contemplated, scrutinized, chatted,* or *jabbered.*

Resources Reminder

For more help with English-Language Learners, see *Lesson Plans for Language Development.*

DIFFERENTIATING INSTRUCTION

Advanced Learners

Acceleration. Use the following activity to move students toward Writing Standard 2.3a for grades 11–12. Allow students to explore the meaning of their experiences through acting or drawing. Students might visualize and quickly sketch how they felt and what they thought at the time of the experience. Then, they can sketch their current feelings and thoughts about it. If students wish to act out a scene, have them prepare dialogue and meet with partners. Students can take turns acting out each other's scenes. Have students refer to their sketches and scenes as they explain the meaning of the experience.

PRACTICE & APPLY 2

Guided and Independent Practice

To assess quickly that students' drafts follow the framework, ask students to use two different colored pens as they are drafting, one for writing and one to label the hinted significance in the introduction, the events in the body, the statement of significance in the conclusion, and one or two examples of transitional words, figurative language, and precise action verbs. Monitor progress by spot-checking as students draft.

(continued)

Figurative language
Rapid pace

If Gwen had not been so friendly, I might have tried to escape. Instead, I found myself on the mats, outfitted in all the cushioned protective gear. My knees were mashed potatoes. My heartbeat thundered in my head. My breath came in gasps. There was no escape. I tucked my head safely behind my pads. Now I was barely able to see. I moved haltingly forward, fearful and fascinated. After a few minutes, though, I started to relax and enjoy myself. "See?" Gwen said afterward. "Once you've loosened up, you're a natural." That was the right thing to say then, because I needed praise.

Event 3
Factual details

Figurative language
Dialogue

That night, I convinced my parents to let me enroll in the class. I memorized all the moves: *ahre maggi,* "down block"; *guligi cha-gi,* "hook kick"; *poom sogi,* "tiger stance"; and so on. Believe me, this "natural" never worked so hard in her life. There is no doubt about it—tae kwon do is a tough, aerobic workout. Sometimes my muscles felt like limp noodles by the end of the day. My friends thought I was crazy. "Here comes Jackie Chan," they would tease. Eventually, though, I was not just graceful but good enough to earn a yellow, then an orange, and later, a green belt.

Event 4
Factual details

Shifting perspective

Interior monologue

My mother still likes to tell the next part of this story. The following March, I had invited her, Dad, and my brother and sister to the center one Saturday for the spring tournaments—not telling them that I was competing. While they were looking for me on the bench, they were surprised to hear my name blared over a loudspeaker. Their shock was compounded when they finally noticed their younger daughter, poised confidently in the ring, waiting to spar in her first competition match. "I can't believe I'm here!" I remember thinking. I didn't win, but I did get my picture in the newspaper (a close-up of my determined face) and have the reward of my parents' amazed and proud faces.

CONCLUSION

Significance of experience

Looking back, I realize now that my parents did not need proof that I was worth something—*I* did. I needed an accomplishment all my own, and tae kwon do was it. I learned confidence and greater respect for myself, not from winning, but from trying. From then on, I felt like a real person, not just a shadow.

go.hrw.com

GO TO: go.hrw.com
KEYWORD: HLLA 10-1
FOR: Expanded Writer's Model and Student's Model

PRACTICE & APPLY 2 Use the framework on page 59 and the Writer's Model above to guide you as you write a first draft of your autobiographical narrative. Return to the Prewriting section to refresh your understanding of basic concepts.

RESOURCES: WRITING

Practice & Apply 2

Think Sheet

- *Writing, Listening, & Speaking,* WS. p. 4

Template

- *Writing, Listening, & Speaking,* WS. p. 5

Internet

- go.hrw.com (keyword: HLLA 10-1)

Revising

Evaluate and Revise Your Draft

Taking a Second Look Your task as a writer doesn't end once you've written your first draft. Now, with your readers in mind, evaluate and revise what you have written. Will they be able to follow the organization? Are your details vivid enough to set the scene? Reread your narrative at least twice—first to improve the organization and content of your draft and second to focus on style.

PEER REVIEW

Before you revise, ask a classmate to read your paper and suggest ways you might improve your content, organization, or style. You might ask, for example, if the meaning of your experience is clear.

First Reading: Content and Organization Use the following guidelines to evaluate and revise your autobiographical narrative. Because an autobiographical narrative is usually informal, check that you have consistently used first-person pronouns: *I, me, our,* and *we.* Also check on the **focus** of your narrative to make sure that each event you describe is relevant to the experience.

Guidelines: Writing an Autobiographical Narrative

Evaluation Questions	Tips	Revision Techniques
1 Does the introduction grab the reader's attention, provide background information, and hint at the meaning of the experience?	**Circle** the sentences in the introduction that capture the reader's attention. **Put parentheses around** background information. **Bracket** the hint at the meaning of the experience.	**Replace** the opening sentences with sentences that grab the reader's attention. **Add** background or a hint of the meaning of the experience.
2 Does the narrative include sensory and factual details that support the controlling impression?	**Underline** each sentence that begins a description of a separate event, person, or place. **Double underline** concrete details that support the controlling impression.	**Add** concrete sensory and factual details that support the controlling impression or **elaborate** on existing details.
3 Do the body paragraphs include descriptions of thoughts and feelings?	**Mark with a star** any sentences that describe thoughts and feelings.	**Add** or **elaborate** on details about thoughts and feelings.
4 Is the sequence of events in the narrative organized logically? Are all the events relevant to the experience?	**Number** the events in the narrative, looking for gaps or a confusing order. **Put an X** next to any irrelevant event.	**Reorder** the events in a way that will be clearer for the reader. **Cut** any events marked with an X.
5 Does the conclusion end with a statement of the significance of the experience?	**Highlight** any sentences that state why the experience was important to the writer.	**Add** sentences that clearly state the significance of the experience.

CRITICAL THINKING

Have students work with a partner to analyze and discuss the mood, or predominant feeling, expressed in each other's autobiographical narratives. Student may be able to suggest ways to improve each other's drafts so that readers may more easily re-create the mood expressed by the author in his or her reminiscence.

DIRECT TEACHING

Guidelines: Writing an Autobiographical Narrative

Advise students to use the **Guidelines** chart on this page as a think sheet by having them answer the questions in their notebooks. Explain that using think sheets to summarize their notes allows students to place their thoughts, observations, and questions on paper, which, in turn, helps improve the content and organization of their narratives.

REVIEW STANDARD

Elaboration

Remind students that when they elaborate, they need to add information, not just words. One way to do that in a personal reflection is to build on or flesh out existing details. Urge students to include fine detail in their writing by asking questions. How did the cat flex her paws? What did the clouds look like? Were the ants headed in random directions, or were they moving in a straight line? Fine detail in description makes writing vivid and memorable.

Writing Workshop: Writing an Autobiographical Narrative 61

Second Reading: Style A writer's style can be so dull that it lulls readers to sleep, or it can be so lively and engaging that readers regret coming to the end of the piece. During your second reading, focus on style—the way you express yourself. One common style problem in autobiographical narratives is **vague modifiers**—adjectives or adverbs that are ineffective because they don't create a precise mental image in readers' minds. For example, *firetruck red car* is more precise than merely *red car.*

editor in charge

Style Guidelines

Evaluation Question	Tip	Revision Technique
Are the modifiers specific enough to make the words they modify clearer or more vivid to readers?	**Put a jagged line** beneath each modifier and draw an arrow to the word it modifies.	**Replace** vague or ineffective modifiers with more specific or appropriate ones.

ANALYZING THE REVISION PROCESS

Study these revisions, and answer the questions that follow.

> The room was filled with swishing, white uniforms and ~~loud~~ roaring *ki-hop* yells. I imagined I was one of these people, timing my strokes perfectly, blocking so gracefully, delivering the winning point at the last moment. In reality I spent weeks blending into the wall farthest from the class, shadowboxing at home behind locked doors, too afraid to join the others.

replace

add

Responding to the Revision Process

1. Why does the writer replace *loud* in the first sentence?
2. What is the effect of the writer's addition to the last sentence?

Writing 1.2 Use appropriate modifiers. **1.9** Revise writing to improve the logic and coherence of the organization.

PRACTICE & APPLY 3 First, use the content and organization guidelines in this section to evaluate and revise those aspects of your narrative. Then, use the style guidelines to evaluate and revise the style of your narrative.

GUIDED PRACTICE

Responding to the Revision Process

Answers

1. The word "loud" is meaningless and unnecessary. The words "roaring *ki-hop* yells" are specific and effective.
2. The author's feelings are clearer.

PRACTICE & APPLY 3

Independent Practice

Have students form peer-review pairs to help revise each other's narratives. Students may answer the following questions as they read each other's narratives:

- Did the narrative keep my interest? Why or why not?
- What else would I like to know about the writer's experience?

Students should use the answers to these questions to guide their revisions.

62 Chapter 1 Plot and Setting • Synthesizing Sources

Publishing

Proofread and Publish Your Essay

A Smooth Finish Think about it: When you run across errors in spelling, punctuation, or grammar in something you're reading, you become distracted—you focus on the errors instead of what the essay or article means. To pave a clear path for your own readers, proofread your narrative carefully. It often helps to work with a partner.

It's a Small World, After All Writing an autobiographical narrative can give you insight into yourself you might never have achieved otherwise. Now, share that insight with others. Here are some ways to encourage others to read and respond to your narrative.

- Ask your teacher to arrange a "cultural exchange" of autobiographical narratives with a class in another part of the country or world. Look for the ways your experiences are similar—and different.
- Create a family memento by pasting or scanning old photos of your experience onto your narrative.
- Give or send a copy of your narrative to one of the people involved in the experience you narrated. Then, ask how he or she remembers the same experience.
- Turn your autobiographical narrative into a narrative poem told from the third-person point of view. Submit your poem to a literary magazine.

TIP A thorough proofreading will help you catch any problems in the **conventions** of standard American usage. Be especially sure to correct errors in **verb tense,** which often crop up when you are narrating a sequence of events. For more on **verb tense,** see page 188 in the *Holt Handbook*.

Reflect on Your Essay

Looking Back, Looking Forward Answering the following questions will help you think about what you have learned while writing your narrative and what you might do differently the next time you write one.

- Which prewriting step did you find most difficult? Do you think it will be easier for you the next time you write an autobiographical piece? Why or why not?
- While writing your narrative, what new insights did you have into the experience you chose as a topic?
- How was writing an autobiographical narrative different from the other kinds of writing you do in school? How was it similar?

PRACTICE & APPLY 4 Proofread your narrative for errors in the conventions of standard American grammar, usage, and mechanics before publishing it for an audience. Finally, answer the reflection questions above.

Resources Reminder

For help with writing assessment, see 6 Traits—Plus 1 in the "Scales and Sample Papers" section of *Progress Assessment of Writing, Listening, & Speaking.*

PRACTICE & APPLY 4

Guided and Independent Practice

As students read their peers' essays, ask them to check carefully for consistency in verb tense. To do this, students should read one paragraph at a time. In the margin they should note when the action takes place—past, present, or future. Then, they should use a highlighter to mark any verbs that are in the wrong tense. Spot-check to identify students who had difficulty with verb tense, and work with those students to make corrections.

RESOURCES: WRITING

Practice & Apply 3

Think Sheet

- *Writing, Listening, & Speaking,* WS. p. 7

Evaluation

- *Writing, Listening, & Speaking,* WS. p. 6

Practice & Apply 4

Assessment

- *Test Generator (One-Stop Planner* CD-ROM)
- *Progress Assessment of Writing, Listening, & Speaking,* pp. 3–5, 49–51

Internet

- Online assessments at go.hrw.com (keyword: HLLA)

PRETEACHING

Motivate. Ask students to think about the stories that are special to their families. Did their parents meet in a funny or ironic way? Did a member of the family have a particularly poignant "coming to America" story? Ask the students what value they place on these stories. Ask them how the stories that a family shares enhance the family's heritage. Tell them that they are going to deliver their narratives orally and that they should keep in mind that the narratives they share may one day be another of their families' valuable stories.

DIRECT TEACHING

GRADE-LEVEL STANDARD

The Big Picture

When students deliver their narratives after having shortened and simplified their sentences, they may have a tendency to rush their deliveries. Remind them of the importance of pace, and instruct them to vary their speaking rates to slow or accelerate the pace.

RETEACHING

REVIEW STANDARD

The Sands of Time

Reteach the concept of being concise by having students work backward from their written narratives to prepare concise notes for their oral presentations. First, have students highlight only the most significant events from their written narratives. Then, have them transfer these events to a simple sentence outline. Students can review their sentence outlines with peers to 1) make sure enough information remains so that the sequence of events can be followed and 2) make sure that the outlines are appropriately concise for use as base notes for an extemporaneous delivery.

Presenting a Narrative

Speaking Assignment
Listening and Speaking 2.1
Adapt your autobiographical narrative for an oral presentation to an audience.

A good storyteller is an artist who has a sense of pace, an eye for detail, and an ear for dialogue. It doesn't matter whether you are reading or hearing a story by such an artist. Your attention is riveted upon the story. There are differences between a written and an oral narrative, but they result from the difference between a reading and a listening audience. As you adapt your written autobiographical narrative for an oral presentation, keep your new audience in mind.

Adapt Your Written Narrative

The Big Picture Readers can always re-read a word, a passage, or an entire story until they understand it. Listeners can't. They must understand what a speaker says immediately. When you adapt your written narrative for an oral presentation, keep this simple fact in mind. Here are some things you can do throughout your adaptation to make it immediately understandable for your audience.

- **Simplify the vocabulary.** Substitute familiar words for words that might be unfamiliar to your audience.
- **Simplify sentence structure.** Find long, complex sentences in your written narrative and break them up into shorter sentences that get more directly to the point.
- **Use strict chronological order.** Readers can follow flashbacks and flash-forwards in a written narrative. Strict chronological order—a simple sequence of events—is easier for listeners to follow.

The Sands of Time If time limitations force you to adapt your written narrative by cutting it, be careful to retain the most important events. For example, if your written narrative includes transitional events—minor events that bridge the gaps between major events—keep the transitional events but cut the details used to describe them. If your written narrative includes an event that was part of the experience but had no role in making the experience significant, cut it.

The Indispensable Certain parts of your narrative are vital. Retain or strengthen the concrete sensory details that bring characters and action to life and that locate scenes and events in specific places, a strategy that allows your listener to visualize those characters, scenes, and events. Also retain the details necessary to create and maintain a controlling impression and those parts of your narrative that communicate the significance of your experience.

Listening and Speaking 2.1 Deliver narrative presentations: **2.1a** Narrate a sequence of events and communicate their significance to the audience. **2.1b** Locate scenes and incidents in specific places. **2.1c** Describe with concrete sensory details the sights, sounds, and smells of a scene and the specific actions, movements, gestures, and feelings of characters.

CHAPTER 1 RESOURCES: LISTENING & SPEAKING

Listening & Speaking Workshop

Planning

- *On Course: Mapping Instruction*
- *One-Stop Planner* CD-ROM
- *Writing, Listening, & Speaking*
  - Teaching Notes, p. 8
  - Project-Planning Guide, WS. p. 10

Think Sheet

- *Writing, Listening, & Speaking,* TP. 6

Differentiating Instruction

- *Lesson Plans for Language Development,* p. 25
- *Supporting Instruction in Spanish*

Hello and Goodbye Your oral presentation should be organized in the same introduction, body, and conclusion arrangement you used for your written narrative. The introduction and conclusion of an oral presentation are especially important.

- In the **introduction,** try to get the audience to identify with you—to think that they share common feelings and experiences with you. Make the introduction as intriguing and personal as possible.
- In the **conclusion,** try to make the significance of your subject clear and to make your listeners identify with your experience by thinking of similar significant experiences of their own.

Here are examples of techniques you can use to adapt the introduction and conclusion of your written narrative. If you use one of the techniques in the introduction, use another in the conclusion.

- Use an appropriate well-known quotation: "They say 'Every dog has its day.' I found out how true that is one Saturday three summers ago."
- Make an observation about life that hints at the importance of your experience: "I had always thought it was normal for the youngest child in a family to be completely without talent or skill."

Deliver Your Narrative

Prepare to Be Natural Once you've finished your adaptation, deliver it **extemporaneously** rather than from memory. Extemporaneous speakers rehearse their presentations thoroughly and refer briefly to a few written notes from time to time during their presentations.

To prepare to deliver your presentation extemporaneously, first write down the main events of your narrative and a few of the major details on note cards. If a particular piece of dialogue is important, write it down in its entirety. Then, arrange the note cards in the order in which you will use them.

Use All the Tools Speakers have verbal and nonverbal tools that a writer doesn't have. Speakers can use **gestures, facial expressions,** and **eye contact** to enhance their words. They can use their voices to **pace** the action in the narrative, slowing down or speeding up to mimic the action and accommodate changes in mood or time. They can use the **volume** of their voices to emphasize a point. A word or phrase said quietly can be as emphatic as a word or phrase said very loudly. Just be sure you always speak loudly enough to be heard.

PRACTICE & APPLY 5 Use the instructions in this section to adapt your written autobiographical narrative for an oral presentation. Rehearse your presentation until your delivery feels natural. Then, present your narrative to an audience.

Listening and Speaking 1.0 Students use gestures, tone, and vocabulary tailored to the audience and purpose. **1.8** Produce concise notes for extemporaneous delivery. **1.9** Choose effective verbal and nonverbal techniques (e.g., voice, gestures, eye contact) for presentations. **2.0** Students deliver polished extemporaneous presentations that combine the traditional rhetorical strategies of narration and description. **2.1d** Pace the presentation of actions to accommodate time or mood changes.

DIFFERENTIATING INSTRUCTION

Advanced Learners

Acceleration. Use the following activity to move students toward L&S Standard 1.4 for grades 11–12. To ensure that they are providing adequate detail for listeners to visualize specific places, scenes, and events, have students write two or three versions of each place description. They should use different types of sensory details and different figurative elements in each. Then, they should share the different versions with a peer and have the peer choose the one that most effectively re-creates the scene.

Learners Having Difficulty

To help students develop the introductions or conclusions of their presentations, instruct them to write one sentence that communicates the significance of the events in their narratives. Then, in groups of five, have students take turns sharing their sentences. After hearing a sentence, the group should search their memories for old sayings, famous quotes, or well-known resources that could serve as an introduction or conclusion.

PRACTICE & APPLY 5

Guided and Independent Practice

Allow students to choose partners who will help coach their deliveries. Partners should devise a simple set of signs to help the presenter. For example, pointing to the ear might mean "Speak up. I can't hear you." Placing a hand palm downward and pushing it toward the floor could mean "Slow down." Pointing to the eyes could indicate that the speaker needs to make eye contact with the audience. During the presentation, the speaker can look toward the partner for direction. Monitor students to make sure the signs they devise for each other are helpful and not elaborate to the point of distraction.

Evaluation and Assessment

- *Writing, Listening, & Speaking,* WS. p. 11
- *Progress Assessment of Writing, Listening, & Speaking,* p. 52
- *Diagnostic and Summative Assessments,* First-Quarter Test

Extension

- *Writing, Listening, & Speaking,* Videocassette Segment 1
- *Writing, Listening, & Speaking,* WS. p. 12

Internet

- go.hrw.com (keyword: HLLA)

Standards Review

Analyzing Informational Materials

STANDARDS FOCUS, pp. 66–69

(For the grade-level standard reviewed in this lesson, see Student Edition, p. 66.)

INTRODUCING THE STANDARDS REVIEW

Use this review to measure students' understanding of synthesizing information from different sources. If necessary, you can use the annotations to guide students in their reading before they answer the questions.

DIRECT TEACHING

A Analyzing Informational Materials
GRADE-LEVEL STANDARD

Paraphrasing ideas. What is this paragraph's main idea? [Possible response: It is difficult but important to balance the demands of work with the emotional fulfillment of home and family.]

STANDARDS REVIEW

Analyzing Informational Materials

Test Practice

Synthesizing Sources

DIRECTIONS: Read the following two articles. Then, read each multiple-choice question that follows, and write the letter of the best response.

Pages 66–69 cover **Reading Standard 2.4** Synthesize the content from several sources dealing with a single issue; paraphrase the ideas and connect them to other sources and related topics to demonstrate comprehension.

What Price Glory?

Len Lewis

Your flight is delayed for the third time this week, you have 22 e-mails and 10 voice messages since you checked one hour ago, and another late night will turn into another lost weekend of just trying to catch up—let alone getting ahead of the power curve.

If this seems like a familiar scenario,[1] it's one being played out every day in the industry by a cast of thousands. When playwright Arthur Miller created the character of Willy Loman,[2] the quintessential[3] road warrior, one character uttered the now famous line: "Attention must be paid." But attention to business and career at what price?

Clearly, success in an increasingly competitive and complex industry carries a stiff price. The question is, how much is too much?

Will the legacy of the late twentieth century be a generation of managers whose commitment and passion for career and company lead to emotional distress or boardroom burnout? When does an executive's total attention to business become his or her downfall? How many boards, committees, synergy or share groups can you sit on? And what is the point of diminishing returns when building a career makes you a better candidate for antidepressants, psychotherapy, and family counseling than a promotion?

A An overstatement? Perhaps! But the road to success for a new generation of managers is a bumpy one in terms of personal growth. Adding richness to daily life by striking a balance between home and office is the essence of a successful businessperson. Yet emotional connections to home and family and even oneself can be easily lost in a maze of meetings, workshops, committee work, or just the frustrating business of clearing the morning's e-mails.

1. **scenario** (sə • nerʹē • ō′) *n.:* outline of a play or movie or of any planned series of events.
2. **Willy Loman:** traveling salesman and the main character in Arthur Miller's 1949 play *Death of a Salesman.*
3. **quintessential** (kwin′te • sen′shəl) *adj.:* serving as a perfect example.

READING MINI-LESSON

Reviewing Word-Attack Skills

Activity. Display these sets of words. Have students identify the word that rhymes with the first word in each set.

1. trough	cough	tough	[cough]
2. bough	rough	brow	[brow]
3. through	clue	cloth	[clue]
4. though	grow	gruff	[grow]
5. dough	slow	brow	[slow]
6. enough	cough	rough	[rough]

Activity. Display these words. Have students identify the words in which the vowel in the underlined syllable is long.

1. heritage
2. imitate [long]
3. mitigate [long]
4. resonate [long]
5. instructive
6. herbicide [long]
7. instigate [long]
8. parade [long]
9. pantomime [long]
10. determine
11. intuitive
12. perspective
13. expedite [long]
14. generate [long]

Life outside the office is not a weakness. It's what makes people stronger. Taking the time to attend a school function or have dinner with a spouse or friend will not burst the new economic bubble. A child's hug after a bad day won't suffocate, but invigorate. And taking the time to decompress alone or with family—even if it means missing a conference or another meeting—won't derail years of hard work and dedication.

The solution to this dilemma won't be found in the hallowed halls of academia[4] or in the next workshop. It lies in a self-analysis of what we want to be. Maybe it is this self-analysis that has led so many food executives to walk away from 30-year careers into the arms of the new economy—for better or worse.

—from ***Progressive Grocer,*** **May 2000**

4. **academia** (ak'ə • dē'mē • ə) *n.:* academic world; colleges and universities.

Deprived of Parent Time?

Kim Campbell

Houses may be messier and parents may be sleepier, but that's a good sign for kids.

Across America, time spent in the company of children has become the holy grail[1] of working parents—and it appears to be well within their grasp. By curtailing everything from shut-eye to volunteer work to vacuuming, most moms and dads today are finding ways to put kids first, perhaps more consciously than in earlier eras.

"Anytime I'm not working, I'm with my kids," says Pamela Alexander, a manager at Ford Motor Company in Deerborn, Mich. To have more hours with their two girls, she and her husband hire out the housecleaning, and instead of giving time to charities, "I write big checks," she says.

With dual-income families now the norm, spending time with children requires more creativity than it did during the days of *Ozzie and Harriet.*[2] Solutions vary—from staggered job schedules, to one parent quitting work for a time, to dads picking up more of the child-rearing responsibility.

"We're in the midst of an evolution, not a revolution," says James Levine, director

1. **holy grail** (grāl): ultimate, hard-to-attain goal. According to medieval legend, the grail was a magical cup that Jesus drank from at the Last Supper.

2. ***Ozzie and Harriet:*** *The Adventures of Ozzie and Harriet* was a very popular TV show from the early 1950s to the mid-1960s.

DIRECT TEACHING

B Analyzing Informational Materials
GRADE-LEVEL STANDARD

Synthesizing content. Invite students to tell how they balance schoolwork with family life, volunteer or part-time work, and extracurricular activities.

C Analyzing Informational Materials
GRADE-LEVEL STANDARD

? Paraphrasing ideas. What is the author's solution to the problem? [Possible response: He recommends that individuals analyze what they really want in life. He believes that many will then cut back on work to make time for family, friends, and quiet time alone.]

Activity. Display these word pairs. Have students identify the word in which the underlined e is an unaccented syllable by itself.

1. comedy	comely	[comedy]
2. serenity	serenade	[serenade]
3. benefit	beneath	[benefit]
4. perennial	peregrine	[peregrine]
5. celebrate	celestial	[celebrate]
6. advantageous	adequate	[adequate]

Standards Review

DIRECT TEACHING

A Analyzing Informational Materials
GRADE-LEVEL STANDARD

Synthesizing content. How does this article's view of technology differ from the view "What Price Glory?" presents? ["What Price Glory?" discusses business technology, such as e-mail and voice mail, that creates additional responsibilities and deprives workers of family time. This article discusses kitchen technology, such as microwave ovens, that increases family time by simplifying household tasks.]

B Analyzing Informational Materials
GRADE-LEVEL STANDARD

Paraphrasing ideas. What ideas do the statistics in this paragraph support? [Possible responses: Today's working mothers spend about the same amount of time with their children as mothers did in the 1960s; today's fathers spend far more time with their children than fathers did in the 1960s.]

C Analyzing Informational Materials
GRADE-LEVEL STANDARD

Synthesizing content. How does this view of success compare with the view that "What Price Glory?" expresses? [Possible response: This view expresses what the author of "What Price Glory?" sees as ideal—"striking a balance between home and office is the essence of a successful businessperson." However, unlike Kim Campbell, Len Lewis does not see this happening today. He believes that overworked executives are finding too little time for family.]

of the Fatherhood Project at the Families and Work Institute in New York.

A Changes in technology and lifestyle patterns have certainly helped parents eke out more family time. Fast food and microwaves, for example, offer shortcuts for meal preparation. Children are also home less often than they used to be, being pulled out for activities like preschool, summer camp, and swimming lessons. Couples today also have fewer children than did their counterparts of recent decades, allowing for more parental "face time" per child.

B Thanks to such changes, mothers today spend about the same amount of time with their children as mothers did in the 1960s, according to new findings by Suzanne Bianchi, a sociologist at the University of Maryland in College Park. In 1998, women spent 5.8 waking hours with their children each day, versus 5.6 hours for mothers in 1965. Fathers did even better—increasing their time from 2.7 hours per day in 1965 to 4 hours in 1998.

Indeed, dads are the resource parents are drawing on most often to make up for the time women are spending at the office. Perhaps as a result, attitudes about men's role in the family are gradually changing.

C "When fathers define success today, it's no longer just in terms of being a breadwinner. It means being involved with the kids as well," says Dr. Levine, author of *Working Fathers.*

Many mothers say their husbands help with everything from folding laundry to picking up kids after school. Fathers' share of housework has increased in recent years, too, with men taking over some of the duties (although not half of them) from moms—both working and nonworking.

Luvie Myers, a stay-at-home mom in Winnetka, Illinois, says her husband can more easily leave work for a family event than a father could have in her parents' era. "Spending time with family is an excuse at work that people are willing to accept," she says.

—from *The Christian Science Monitor,* April 5, 2000

Using Academic Language

Review of Literary Terms
Reading Standard 3.6 and Grade 8 Review Reading Standard 3.4

Ask students to look back through the chapter to find the meanings of the terms listed at right. Then, have students show their grasp of these standards by citing passages from the chapter that illustrate the meanings of those terms.

Plot (pp. 2, 4); **Exposition** (p. 2); **External** and **Internal Conflict** (p. 2); **Complication** (p. 2); **Climax** (p. 3); **Resolution** (p. 3); **Chronological Order** (p. 3); **Flashback** (pp. 3, 31); **Foreshadowing** (pp. 3, 31); **Cause** (p. 4); **Effect** (p. 4); **Setting** (pp. 44, 46); **Time Frame** (p. 44); **Mood** (pp. 44, 46); **Tone** (p. 44).

1. The **main idea** of "What Price Glory?" is that busy executives —
   - **A** need more time to do their jobs well
   - **B** need to work more efficiently
   - **C** need to balance their home and office lives
   - **D** should change careers

2. In "What Price Glory?" the author's **attitude** toward the topic can *best* be described as —
   - **F** hesitant
   - **G** impassioned
   - **H** bitter
   - **J** indifferent

3. One of the **main ideas** of "Deprived of Parent Time?" is that fathers today —
   - **A** spend less time with their children than in the past
   - **B** spend more time with their children than in the past
   - **C** cannot juggle jobs and family life
   - **D** are conflicted over family roles

4. "Deprived of Parent Time?" includes all of the following types of **supporting evidence** *except* —
   - **F** quotations
   - **G** examples
   - **H** statistics
   - **J** opinion polls

5. Which article would you cite in a research report on boardroom burnout?
   - **A** "Deprived of Parent Time?"
   - **B** "What Price Glory?"
   - **C** Both articles
   - **D** Neither article

6. "What Price Glory?" *differs* from "Deprived of Parent Time?" because the former is based on —
   - **F** the author's opinion
   - **G** statistical research
   - **H** extensive interviews
   - **J** opinion polls

7. *Both* articles discuss the importance of —
   - **A** more efficient work schedules
   - **B** better child-care programs
   - **C** a shorter work week
   - **D** more quality time for families

8. Which of the following ideas is *not* discussed in *both* articles?
   - **F** Many working people are redefining the meaning of success.
   - **G** Spending time with children brings parents many rewards.
   - **H** Modern technology can help solve our time-crunch problems.
   - **J** Career success alone is not enough for a rich life.

Test-Taking Tips

Remind students to pay attention to italicized words in test questions. For example, the italicized word *except* in question 4 emphasizes that the correct answer choice will be something *not* found in the essay.

For more instruction on how to answer multiple-choice items, refer students to **Test Smarts.**

TestPractice

Answers and Model Rationales

1. **C** A is incorrect because the article suggests that busy executives already devote too much time to their jobs. B and D are discussed in the article but do not express the main idea.
2. **G** The author is clearly not being hesitant (F) or indifferent (J) to his topic, nor is he bitter (H).
3. **B** A goes against the data provided. C and D are incorrect because the article describes fathers who succeed at combining work and family life.
4. **J** The article cites no opinion polls.
5. **B** In "What Price Glory?" the term "boardroom burnout" is used. "Deprived of Parent Time?" does not cite negative effects of juggling home and office time.
6. **F** The author's opinions are expressed throughout "What Price Glory?"; it includes none of the other options.
7. **D** Neither article discusses A, B, or C. Both emphasize finding time for families.
8. **H** "Deprived of Parent Time?" cites time-saving technology, but "What Price Glory?" mentions technology that adds to work demands, reducing family time.

ASSESSING

Assessment

- *Progress Assessment of Reading*
  - Chapter Test

Review of Informational Terms
Reading Standard 2.4

Ask students to look back through the chapter to find the meanings of the terms listed below. Then, ask students to use those terms to explain how to synthesize content from several sources.
Synthesizing (p. 21); **Paraphrasing** (p. 21).

Test Practice

Vocabulary Development

Multiple-Meaning Words

Modeling. Model the answer to item 1. Say, "In the sentence from 'The Leap,' *object* is a noun meaning 'thing.' I can eliminate D, which uses *object* as a verb. In A, *object* is used as a grammatical term, and in B it means 'goal,' so I can eliminate A and B. Only in C does *object* mean 'thing.'"

Test Practice

Answers and Model Rationales

1. **C** See rationale above.
2. **G** In the sentence from "The Leap," *square* is a noun meaning "park or plaza." In F, *square* is an adjective; in H, it is a geometric term; in J, it is an arithmetic term.
3. **D** In the sentence from "The Leap," *form* is a noun meaning "kind." In A, *form* refers to a paper; in B, it is a verb meaning "mold"; in C, it refers to physical condition.
4. **J** The sentence from "The Leap" uses *practice* as a noun meaning "business." In F, *practice* means "habit." In G, it means "action done over and over to improve a skill." In H, *practice* is a verb.
5. **A** In the sentence from "The Leap," *heart* means "central part." In B it may mean "organ that pumps blood" or "source of emotions"; in C it refers to a playing card suit, and in D it refers to "basic quality."
6. **G** In the sentence from "The Leap," *roll* means "a loud reverberating sound." In F *roll* is a verb meaning "move back and forth." In H it means "move by turning." In J it means "piece of bread."
7. **D** In A, *act* means "a division in a play." In B, it means "behave." In C, it means "to serve as."

TEST PRACTICE

Vocabulary Development

Test Practice

Multiple-Meaning Words

DIRECTIONS: Choose the answer in which the underlined word is used in the same way as it is used in these sentences from "The Leap."

1. "She has never upset an object or as much as brushed a magazine onto the floor."
   - **A** In that sentence, *him* is the object of the preposition *to.*
   - **B** What is the object of this plan?
   - **C** That tiny carved statue is an object she treasures.
   - **D** Does anyone object to my suggestion?
2. "In the town square a replica tent pole, cracked and splintered, now stands cast in concrete."
   - **F** He ate three square meals a day.
   - **G** The park benches in the square are new.
   - **H** Rachel drew an uneven-looking square.
   - **J** The number four is the square of two.
3. "I wonder if my father calculated the exchange he offered: one form of flight for another."
   - **A** Please fill in this form, and sign it.
   - **B** In ceramics class we form clay into bowls.
   - **C** She was in great form for the race.
   - **D** Which is your favorite form of travel—cars, trains, or planes?
4. "Though he'd been thinking of moving to a larger city, he settled down and broadened his practice in this valley."
   - **F** It is her practice to walk every morning.
   - **G** Dara looks forward to band practice.
   - **H** Good musicians practice every day.
   - **J** His law practice covers two counties.
5. "It started right around the stove, and the heart of the house was gutted."
   - **A** The tallest buildings were in the heart of downtown.
   - **B** My heart skipped a beat.
   - **C** In this game a heart beats a diamond, spade, or club.
   - **D** At heart I think Len's very shy.
6. "There came a rumble of electrical energy, drowned out by the sudden roll of drums."
   - **F** The bad weather made the ship roll with the waves.
   - **G** She was frightened by the roll of thunder.
   - **H** He made sure to roll the dough on a flat, smooth surface.
   - **J** Sue ate a roll at breakfast.
7. "My mother once said that I'd be amazed at how many things a person can do within the act of falling."
   - **A** The play had only one act.
   - **B** Maria tried to act like an adult.
   - **C** He had to act as the committee chairman.
   - **D** Tony considered the gift an act of kindness.

Vocabulary Review

Use this activity to assess whether students have retained the chapter Vocabulary. Ask students to choose the word from the box that shares a root word with each word group listed.

imperceptibly	interminable	chronic
regressive	commemorates	

1. term, terminal, terminate, _____ [interminable]
2. memory, memorial, memorable, _____ [commemorates]
3. chronicle, chronological, chronometer, _____ [chronic]
4. digress, regress, regression, _____ [regressive]
5. perceive, perceptible, perceptive, _____ [imperceptibly]

Writing

Test Practice

DIRECTIONS: Read the following paragraph from a draft of a student's autobiographical narrative. Then, read the questions below it. Choose the best answer for each question.

(1) Even though I had a traumatic first experience, I still love riding horses. (2) I rode a trail horse named Potato who refused to follow the horse in front of him. (3) It was during a family vacation in Ruidoso, New Mexico, that I rode my first horse. (4) He kept stopping to eat the leaves and bushes on the side of the path through the forest, and we got separated from the group. (5) When I tried to go faster to catch up with everybody, Potato ran through some thick branches, and I was knocked off the saddle. (6) Luckily, I was more mad than hurt, so I grabbed the reins determinedly and got back on the horse. (7) By the end of the ride, Potato had begun to follow my directions, and I had learned how to control him.

1. Which of the following sentences could be added to the end of the paragraph to relate the significance of the experience?
   - **A** On the next family vacation, I was careful to pick a better horse.
   - **B** Riding horses is dangerous, and young children shouldn't participate.
   - **C** Learning to ride a horse wasn't easy, but it was worth it.
   - **D** Horses are the most obedient and trainable of animals.

2. Which sentences should be switched to better reflect chronological order?
   - **F** 1 and 7
   - **G** 2 and 3
   - **H** 4 and 5
   - **J** 6 and 7

3. To add sensory details, which sentence could the writer include?
   - **A** Being separated from the group on my first trail ride was scary.
   - **B** The forest was dense with fragrant evergreens that muffled the *clop clop* of the horses in front of me.
   - **C** Ruidoso is a small town nestled in the heart of New Mexico's southern Rocky Mountains.
   - **D** Potato was a stubborn seven-year-old quarter horse.

4. Which action verb would best replace the word *eat* in sentence 4?
   - **F** nibble
   - **G** drink
   - **H** consume
   - **J** smell

5. If you were presenting this passage as an oral narrative, how would your tone change over the course of the presentation?
   - **A** from embarrassment to sadness
   - **B** from happiness to disappointment
   - **C** from fear to relief
   - **D** from concern to triumph

RESOURCES: WRITING, LISTENING, & SPEAKING

Assessment

- *Test Generator (One-Stop Planner* CD-ROM)
- *Progress Assessment of Writing, Listening, & Speaking,* Ch. 1
- *Diagnostic and Summative Assessments,* First-Quarter Test

Internet

- Online assessments at go.hrw.com (keyword: HLLA)

Standards Review

Answers

1. C
2. G
3. B
4. F
5. D

APPLICATION

Storyboard

Homework

For homework, students can select a new event to share as a narrative. Then, have students create a storyboard (a series of sketches that depict important scenes that a filmmaker consults before filming) on a poster board or large sheet of butcher paper. The completed storyboard will resemble pages of a comic book, with dialogue and descriptions written below or beside each illustration. Students can display their storyboards in the classroom.

EXTENSION

Same Story, Free Verse

You may ask students to convert their autobiographical narratives into free-verse poems. Free-verse poems usually do not follow a regular pattern of rhythm or rhyme. The free-verse poem should focus on conveying the imagery and emotion of the event rather than the chronology of the event. Students should condense the event to its basic essentials and then use figurative elements to communicate it. Place words that need special emphasis at the beginning or the ends of lines.

Holt Literature and Language Arts: Mastering the California Standards

Chapter 2 Character
Using Primary and Secondary Sources

Program Organization

Holt Literature and Language Arts provides a complete curriculum for standards-based instruction in reading, literature, writing, listening and speaking, and language conventions. The instructional content is presented in quarters to enable teachers to anticipate and administer the quarterly assessments required by California.

About Chapter 2

Standards-based lesson plans and suggestions for pacing the presentation of Chapter 2, the related instructional material, and the recommended assessment are provided in *On Course: Mapping Instruction,* Chapter 2.

- In Chapter 2, students will extend ideas from primary or secondary sources through analysis, evaluation, and elaboration; analyze characters and methods of characterization; and write a biographical narrative.

Language Arts Content

Which reading standards are taught in Chapter 2?

In this chapter, students will master the following Grade 10 standards and review standards from Grade 8. Selections or features marked with a ✔ constitute the minimum course of study that provides coverage of grade-level standards.

Grade 10 Standards

Reading Comprehension (Focus on Informational Materials)

2.5 Extend ideas presented in primary or secondary sources through original analysis, evaluation, and elaboration.

✔ "Interview with Alice Walker" (interview)
"Interview with Nikki Giovanni" (interview)
"Thinkin' on Marryin'" (oral history)
"A Baby's Quilt to Sew Up the Generations" (newspaper article)
} pp. 88–95

Literary Response and Analysis

3.3 Analyze interactions between main and subordinate characters in a literary text, and explain the way those interactions affect the plot.

"Character Interactions: Relationships and Conflicts" (standards essay), pp. 96–97
✔ "Two Kinds" (short story), pp. 98–109
"By Any Other Name" (autobiography), pp. 112–119
"Powder" (standards review), pp. 130–133

3.4 Determine characters' traits by what the characters say about themselves in narration, dialogue, dramatic monologue, and soliloquy.

"Characters: The Actors in a Story" (standards essay), pp. 74–75
✔ "Everyday Use" (short story), pp. 76–86
"By Any Other Name" (autobiography), pp. 112–119
"Powder" (standards review), pp. 130–133

(continued)

(continued)

Review Standard Grade 8

Reading 1.3 Use word meanings within the appropriate context, and show ability to verify those meanings by definition, restatement, example, comparison, or contrast.

Clarifying Word Meanings: Look at the Context, p. 87

Clarifying Word Meanings: Comparison and Contrast, p. 110

Putting Words in Context: Cluster Diagrams, p. 120

Which writing standards are taught in Chapter 2?

Writing Strategies

1.1 Establish a controlling impression or coherent thesis that conveys a clear and distinctive perspective on the subject and maintain a consistent tone and focus throughout the piece of writing.
Create a Controlling Impression, p. 123

1.9 Revise writing to improve the logic and coherence of the organization and controlling perspective, the precision of the word choice, and the tone by taking into consideration the audience, purpose, and formality of the context.
Evaluate and Revise Your Narrative, pp. 127–128

Writing Applications

2.1 Write biographical or autobiographical narratives or short stories.

a. Relate a sequence of events and communicate the significance of the events to the audience.
Choose a Subject, pp. 122–123

b. Locate scenes and incidents in specific places.
Gather Details, pp. 123–124

c. Describe with concrete sensory details the sights, sounds, and smells of a scene and the specific actions, movements, gestures, and feelings of the characters; use interior monologue to depict the characters' feelings.
Gather Details, pp. 123–124

d. Pace the presentation of actions to accommodate changes in time and mood.
Plan Organization and Pacing, p. 124

e. Make effective use of descriptions of appearance, images, shifting perspectives, and sensory details.
Gather Details, pp. 123–124

Review Standard Grade 8

Writing 2.1 Write biographies, autobiographies, short stories, or narratives.

b. Reveal the significance of, or the writer's attitude about, the subject.
Create a Controlling Impression, p. 123

Instructional Planning and Support

Where do I find lesson plans, additional resources, and other teaching aids?

- This Annotated Teacher's Edition and *On Course: Mapping Instruction* provide direction in planning and implementing a complete California standards–based curriculum. These components also include instructions for diagnostic, progress, and summative testing; for presenting direct instruction of the standards; for differentiating instruction to provide universal access; and for locating and using the program's ancillaries.
- Lesson and workshop resources are referenced at the beginning of each selection or workshop, in the bottom margin of this teacher's edition.
- Reminders for using additional resources appear in this teacher's edition at point of use.
- The *One-Stop Planner* CD-ROM contains editable lesson plans and all print ancillaries, available in PDF format.

What if I don't have time to teach all of Chapter 2?

- Most standards can be taught with a minimum number of selections and features. In the chart on the preceding page, the core lessons you need in order to provide complete coverage of the chapter standards are identified with a ✔.
- *On Course: Mapping Instruction,* Chapter 2, lists lessons and activities that provide minimum standards coverage.

What provisions have been made for students who have additional class time scheduled in language arts?

- *Interactive Reading* provides for alternative direct instruction and practice of the grade-level standards taught in Chapter 2.
- *Universal Access: Writing, Listening, and Speaking,* Chapter 2, contains worksheets and transparencies that provide practice in and reteaching and reinforcement of the writing and listening and speaking standards in Chapter 2.
- *Universal Access: Lesson Plans for Language Development,* Chapter 2 provides alternative teaching strategies and additional worksheets designed specifically for English-language learners and special education students. Many of the suggestions and activities in this ancillary will also be helpful to students in the regular classroom who are having difficulty with particular skills.

Universal Access

How do I differentiate instruction to ensure that all my students master the standards?

Holt Literature and Language Arts provides comprehensive, differentiated instruction for all types of students.

- Most of the general instruction and teaching strategies in the Annotated Teacher's Edition are at grade level. These instructions will work well with the majority of your students.
- Point-of-use suggestions are provided for advanced learners, learners having difficulty, English-language learners, and special education students.
- *Interactive Reading* is designed to anticipate and remediate problems that students may experience in achieving mastery of the reading standards. See Interactive Reading, Teacher's Edition, Chapter 2, for information on using the reader to differentiate instruction.
- *Universal Access: Writing, Listening, and Speaking,* Chapter 2, contains worksheets and transparencies that provide practice in and reteaching and reinforcement of the writing and listening and speaking standards in Chapter 2.
- *Universal Access: Lesson Plans for Language Development,* Chapter 2 offers teaching strategies and additional worksheets designed specifically for English-language learners and special education students.

Assessment

How do I determine whether my students are making progress in mastering the standards?

Progress Assessment

- Use the Standards Reviews at the end of Chapter 2 for an informal assessment of the informational reading and writing standards.
- Use Chapter 2 tests from the *Progress Assessment* booklets to assess comprehension and progress on mastering the standards taught in this chapter.

Summative Assessment

The content of *Holt Literature and Language Arts* has been divided into quarters to allow you to administer the four summative tests required by California. Chapters 1–2 and related instructional material constitute the first quarter of instruction. At the end of Chapter 2, you may ask students to take the First-Quarter Test in *Diagnostic and Summative Assessments.*

Chapter 2

STANDARDS FOCUS

(For full text of standards taught in this chapter, see the Standards Correlation by Standard chart in the Student Edition.)

Grade-Level Standards

- Reading Comprehension 2.5
- Literary Response and Analysis 3.3, 3.4
- Writing Strategies 1.1, 1.9
- Writing Applications 2.1a–e

INTRODUCING THE CHAPTER

In this chapter's stories and poems, unforgettable characters spring to life and provide lasting insights on what it means to be human. In each selection, students will go inside the minds and hearts of the characters and recognize that they have feelings, motivations, disappointments, and dreams like those of real people. Two stories—"Everyday Use" and "Two Kinds"—explore conflicts between mothers and daughters. In "By Any Other Name," a young girl takes a stand when she is treated with disrespect in a clash between cultures. Poetry, an interview, and oral histories that are thematically linked to the fiction enable students to extend the connections between literature and life. The chapter closes with opportunities for students to write a biographical narrative.

CHAPTER 2 RESOURCES: READING

Planning

- *One-Stop Planner* CD-ROM with Test Generator
- *On Course: Mapping Instruction*
- *At Home: A Guide to Standards Mastery*
- *At Home: In Spanish*
- *Supporting Instruction in Spanish*

Reading

- *Interactive Reading*

Differentiating Instruction

- *Lesson Plans for Language Development*

Vocabulary

- *Vocabulary Development*
  - Cumulative Vocabulary Review, pp. 10–11

Chapter 2

CHARACTER

USING PRIMARY AND SECONDARY SOURCES

One cannot "make" characters. . . .
They are *found*.

—Elizabeth Bowen

Portrait of Dr. Gachet (1890) by Vincent van Gogh.
Oil on canvas (66 cm × 57 cm).

go.hrw.com
KEYWORD:
HLLA 10-2

Grammar

- *Holt Handbook*
  - Varieties of American English, pp. 518–519
  - Subordinate Clause Fragments, pp. 450–453
  - Clear Pronoun Reference, pp. 164–166

Assessment

- *Progress Assessment of Reading*
  - Chapter Test
- *One-Stop Planner* CD-ROM with Test Generator

Internet

- go.hrw.com (Keyword: HLLA 10-2)

THE QUOTATION

Remind students that characterization is one of the most difficult aspects of the writer's craft. Ask students what they think Bowen is referring to in the quotation. [Possible response: Bowen is suggesting that characters are not made by merely combining various human traits; they are discovered in the process of writing.]

VIEWING THE ART

Vincent van Gogh (1853–1890) transformed the world around him into paintings with an unprecedented brightness of color and rawness of painterly technique. This portrait is of Dr. Paul Gachet, a psychiatrist who took van Gogh into his house after the painter had suffered a nervous breakdown. The flower on the table is a foxglove, a plant that is used to make the drug digitalis. It may be a symbol of the doctor's profession.

Activity. Ask students to discuss who they think that the portrait tells us more about: van Gogh or Gachet? [Some students may think it tells more about van Gogh because of his stylistic transformations. Others may argue that the portrait primarily reflects Gachet's appearance and character.]

Resources Reminder

Planning

- *At Home: A Guide to Standards Mastery*

Parent letters appear in this resource. Translations of these letters are found in *At Home: In Spanish*. Translations of selection summaries appear in *Supporting Instruction in Spanish.*

Reading

- *Interactive Reading*

The California framework requires students to read materials apart from in-class assignments. Additional readings are cited on the Read On page and on selected pages in the Student Edition.

STANDARDS FOCUS, pp. 74–75

(For the grade-level standard taught in this lesson, see Student Edition, p. 74.)

Prerequisite Standard

- Grade 7, Literary Response and Analysis 3.3 **Analyze characterization as delineated through a character's thoughts, words, speech patterns, and actions; the narrator's description; and the thoughts, words, and actions of other characters.**

Literary Focus: Characters

Ask students to consider a well-known actor who plays a popular television character. Encourage students to list the ways that the actor changes in appearance, speech, and behavior to assume the role of the character. Point out that writers, like actors, often use characters' words and actions to reveal personality traits.

Literary Response and Analysis

Characters *by* John Leggett

THE ACTORS IN A STORY

What They Tell Us

Good fiction can tell us more about ourselves—about how human beings feel and behave in any imaginable situation—than just about any other form of art or science. Through fiction we can imagine how it feels to be a woman who has lived all her life on the prairie or glimpse how it feels to be a soldier lying wounded on a battlefield.

The revelations fiction offers lie largely in the element called **character**—that is, the story's actors. When the characters in a story behave in convincing ways, then we believe in them and maybe even love or hate them.

Creating Characters: How Do They Do It?

Writers reveal their characters' **traits,** or special qualities, either directly or indirectly. In **direct characterization** a writer simply tells us directly what the character is like.

Esmeralda was the most serious person in the school. She longed for fun but was afraid of disappointing her very serious aunt.

Reading Standard 3.4 Determine characters' traits by what the characters say about themselves in narration, dialogue, dramatic monologue, and soliloquy.

We would learn about Esmeralda in more subtle ways, however, if the writer were to use **indirect characterization.** With this technique a writer reveals characters' traits in the following five ways:

1 A character's **appearance** is a natural place for a writer to begin an indirect characterization.

Esmeralda, tall and thin, wore her mouse-brown hair pulled tightly back into a ponytail. She always dressed in a gray skirt and blouse and never wore jewelry.

This description says a lot about Esmeralda—we imagine a quiet, serious, perhaps shy person.

2 We can learn even more about Esmeralda when we hear her speak to other characters—through **dialogue.**

"Hey, Esmeralda, want to come with us to the movies tonight?" Ginger asked.

"Ooh, no," Esmeralda sighed. "My aunt would never allow it. She says I have to work on my research paper all weekend."

3 The writer can also take us into a character's mind to reveal his or her **private thoughts.** This is especially important when the **narrator** (the storytelling "I") is the main character. We eavesdrop on the narrator's thoughts—something we can never do in real life—and discover what that character wants or fears or worries about. If Esmeralda were the narrator, we might discover the following information:

"Why can't I be like other kids?" Esmeralda moped. She pressed her nose against the window. "I'd like to be out there with everybody else—laughing and skating and going to movies and just belonging."

4 In fiction as in real life, we learn a great deal about people by observing their **actions.**

DIFFERENTIATING INSTRUCTION

Learners Having Difficulty

Modeling. Model inferring Esmeralda's character traits from her words and thoughts by saying, "Esmeralda doesn't want to disobey her aunt, so I might infer that Esmeralda is obedient or dutiful. She also wishes she could have free time as other students have, so I might infer that she is fun loving or spirited."

Advanced Learners

Acceleration. Use this activity to move students toward the eleventh- and twelfth-grade Standard 3.5, for which they evaluate historical influences that shape characters in literature.

That afternoon, Leon ran to catch up to Esmeralda as she walked home. "Hey," he called excitedly and tapped her on the shoulder. She flinched—then looked away, blushing.

5 In one way or another most writers will reveal their characters through what they actually do and the **effects** those actions have on other characters.

Leon, puzzled, wondered why Esmeralda was so upset by his friendly gesture.

Dramatic Monologue and Soliloquy

Narrators who talk about themselves are found mostly in fiction, but they also appear in poetry and in plays. A form of poetry called **dramatic monologue** features a single character who addresses one or more silent listeners. From what this character says and the way it is said, we can infer his or her personality **traits.**

In plays we usually learn about character through dialogue and action. In a **soliloquy,** however, a character speaks his or her thoughts directly to the audience. Shakespeare's plays have many memorable soliloquies, such as Hamlet's famous "To Be or Not to Be" speech.

Flat, Round, and Stock Characters

Critics often use these terms to refer to fictional characters. A **flat character,** like a paper doll, is two-dimensional, with only one or two key personality traits: "Amy is extremely stubborn."

A **round character** has the three-dimensional qualities of real-life people, with many traits and complexities. In good fiction, writers include flat characters for a reason: Too many round characters would be distracting. Nonetheless, some flat characters are needed to get the story told.

Finally, a **stock character** is one who fits our preconceived notions about a "type" (for example, the mad scientist or the cruel-looking villain twirling his waxed moustache).

Stock characters are so familiar that as soon as we encounter any of their well-known traits, we can imagine the rest of their personalities. Of course, real people aren't like this—they are complex and unpredictable. What fascinates us in fiction are the characters who manage to confound our expectations yet still seem true to life.

Practice

Pick a character in a short story you have read. Review the story, and take notes in a chart like the one below. Identify two or three of the character's traits, and list the details in the story that illustrate those traits. Then, identify which literary device (such as narration, dialogue, or description) helped you identify each trait.

Character Traits	Supporting Details	Literary Device Used

Practice

Students' responses will vary.

For each trait that students list, they should include at least one corresponding detail from the story and at least one label (narration, description, dialogue) for the literary device that the detail exemplifies.

Possible responses for the character Mrs. Jones in "Thank You, M'am" by Langston Hughes:

- *Character Trait*—strength. *Supporting Details*—She's big and strong; she easily lifts, shakes, and drags the teenage boy. *Literary Device Used*—description of appearance; narration of actions.
- *Character Trait*—generosity. *Supporting Details*—She feeds the boy; she says she would have given him money if he'd asked. *Literary Device Used*—dialogue; narration of actions.
- *Character Trait*—trust. *Supporting Details*—She tells the boy about her life; she doesn't watch him every minute; he feels trusted. *Literary Device Used*—dialogue; narration of action and effects on other characters.

Apply

Homework

Have students scan literature they have read for examples of dialogues, dramatic monologues, or soliloquies that reveal character. Instruct each student to copy a brief example (or a portion of a longer example) and present it to the class. You may want to have students select and prepare their excerpts as homework.

Resources Reminder

Differentiating Instruction

- *Lesson Plans for Language Development*

For additional instruction on characters for English-language learners and special education students, see *Lesson Plans for Language Development,* pp. 35, 36.

Activity. Pair advanced learners, and have them list ten or twelve literary characters with whom they are familiar. Then, have the partners take turns role-playing and guessing the identity of the characters. The first student chooses a character from the list. Then, the student ad-libs a brief dramatic monologue in that person's voice, providing clues to the character's identity with personal and historical details. The second student guesses who the character is. Then the students reverse roles.

STANDARDS FOCUS, pp. 76–87

(For grade-level and review standards taught in this lesson, see citations on Student Edition pages.)

Prerequisite Standard

- Grade 7, Literary Response and Analysis 3.3 **Analyze characterization as delineated through a character's thoughts, words, speech patterns, and actions; the narrator's description; and the thoughts, words, and actions of other characters.**

Reading Skills

- Make inferences.

Summary *at grade level*

In this story, set in the 1960s, a mother tells about a visit from her daughter Dee, to the family's rural Southern home. Dee has adopted African dress and an African name, and she brings along a male partner who shares her Afrocentric ways. Narration and dialogue reveal character as tension builds among Mama, Dee, and the younger daughter Maggie, who is physically and emotionally scarred from a long-ago house fire. Dee disdains her family but wants their handmade household items, which she sees as valuable heirlooms. When Dee learns that the quilts she covets are promised to her sister, Dee becomes more determined to have them, arguing that Maggie would only "put them to everyday use." Maggie acquiesces, but Mama surprises even herself by defying Dee and presenting the quilts to Maggie.

Before You Read

Everyday Use

Literary Focus

Determining Characters' Traits: What They Say and Do

What would the world be like if we could read one another's minds? It can't happen in real life, but in fiction we step easily into characters' minds. When characters **narrate,** or tell their stories, we know their thoughts and feelings, and we get an idea of their **character traits**—their values, likes, dislikes, even their quirks.

We also learn about fictional characters by noticing what they say to other characters in the story's **dialogue.** In addition, as in real life, we notice what they do, the way they look, and what other people say about them.

You'll find these methods of character development in the next story. As you read, pay attention to what you learn about Mama and the other characters.

Reading Skills

Making Inferences About Characters

An **inference** is an intelligent guess based on evidence in the story and on what you already know. When making inferences about characters, you'll base many of your guesses on what they say and do. For example, here's what you can infer from just the first sentence of "Everyday Use": The narrator and someone named Maggie are expecting a female visitor. They've cleaned the yard especially for the visit, so it's obviously important to them. The phrase "made so clean and wavy" suggests that the narrator takes pride in a job well done. From just that one sentence you've made some inferences about character. Keep track of the other inferences you make as you read.

Pages 76 and 85 cover **Reading Standard 3.4** Determine characters' traits by what the characters say about themselves in narration, dialogue, and dramatic monologue.

Make the Connection

Quickwrite

"Everyday Use" takes place in the rural South during the 1960s, when values and ways of life were changing rapidly. The story concerns traditions and, in particular, some family heirlooms.

Many families have traditions or heirlooms that are handed down to the younger generation. Do you have any in your family? Jot down your feelings about maintaining family traditions.

Background

Quilting is an American folk art. In the South, quilts have a rich tradition influenced by African textile designs and historic American patterns. Quilts are often passed down in families for generations. Alice Walker, the author of "Everyday Use," is herself a longtime quilter.

Vocabulary Development

sidle (sīd′'l) *v.:* move sideways, especially in a shy or sneaky manner.

furtive (fur′tiv) *adj.:* acting as if trying not to be seen. *Furtive* also means "done secretly."

cowering (kou′ər·iŋ) *v.* used as *adj.:* drawing back or huddling in fear.

oppress (ə·pres′) *v.:* persecute; keep down by unjust use of power.

doctrines (däk′trinz) *n.:* principles; teachings; beliefs.

rifling (rī′fliŋ) *v.* used as *n.:* searching thoroughly or in a rough manner.

76 Chapter 2 Character • Using Primary and Secondary Sources

RESOURCES: READING

Planning

- *One-Stop Planner* CD-ROM with Test Generator
- *On Course: Mapping Instruction*

Media

- *Audio CD Library*
  - disc 3
- *Fine Art Transparencies*
  - Transparency 3

Reading

- *Interactive Reading*
  - Interactive version: "Everyday Use"
- *Interactive Reading,* Teacher's Edition
  - Graphic Organizer: Character Traits Chart

His Grandmother's Quilt (1988) by Phoebe Beasley. Collage.
Courtesy of the artist.

Everyday Use

For Your Grandmama

Alice Walker

I will wait for her in the yard that Maggie and I made so clean and wavy yesterday afternoon. A yard like this is more comfortable than most people know. It is not just a yard. It is like an extended living room. When the hard clay is swept clean as a floor and the fine sand around the edges lined with tiny, irregular grooves, anyone can come and sit and look up into the elm tree and wait for the breezes that never come inside the house.

Maggie will be nervous until after her sister goes: She will stand hopelessly in corners, homely and ashamed of the burn scars down her arms and legs, eyeing her sister with a mixture of envy and awe. She thinks her sister had held life always in the palm of one hand, that "no" is a word the world never learned to say to her.

PRETEACHING

Selection Starter

Motivate. Ask students how their families traditionally celebrate birthdays or special holidays. Invite students to identify any foods or objects that are important in these celebrations, such as a special menu, tablecloth, or decoration. Then, assign Make the Connection on p. 76.

Preview Vocabulary

Have students read aloud the Vocabulary Development words on p. 76. Then, have volunteers demonstrate the meanings of the words by doing the following exercises:

1. Role-play a cowering commoner who is trying to sidle up to a king.
2. Mime the actions of a furtive person rifling through your binder.
3. Explain briefly one of the political doctrines in the U.S. Constitution.
4. Dramatize a scene in which guards oppress a prisoner.

Assign the Reading

Homework

You may read the story as a class, up to the first break on p. 78. Ask students to list the character traits of Mama, Maggie, and Dee that are revealed up to this point. [Possible responses: *Mama*—large in size, tough. *Maggie*—homely, inadequate, insecure. *Dee*—successful, confident.] Students reading at or above grade level can read the rest of the story on their own and answer the Reading Check questions for homework. Monitor other students as they read in small groups.

Differentiating Instruction

- *Lesson Plans for Language Development*
  - English-Language Learners, pp. 37–39, 57, 61
  - Special Education Students, pp. 40, 57, 61

Vocabulary

- *Vocabulary Development*
  - Vocabulary Worksheet, p. 7

Assessment

- *Progress Assessment of Reading*
  - Selection Test
- *One-Stop Planner* CD-ROM with Test Generator

DIRECT TEACHING

A Reading Skills

Making inferences. From this dream, what can you infer about the relationship between the narrator and Dee? [Possible responses: The narrator wishes their relationship were warmer and more mutually gratifying; the narrator thinks that Dee would like her to be more sophisticated.]

B Literary Focus
GRADE-LEVEL STANDARD

Characters' traits. The narrator's activities are part of her rural way of life. What personality traits do you think her physical abilities reveal? [Possible responses: strength; endurance; down-to-earth practicality.]

C Literary Focus
GRADE-LEVEL STANDARD

Characters' traits. Mama's memories emphasize differences between Dee and Maggie and provide background for conflicts. What does Mama show about her closeness to her two daughters? [Possible responses: Mama feels closer to Maggie than to Dee. Maggie clings to Mama and needs her help, while Dee distances herself from Mama and their home and appears to stand in judgment of them.]

You've no doubt seen those TV shows where the child who has "made it" is confronted, as a surprise, by her own mother and father, tottering in weakly from backstage. (A pleasant surprise, of course: What would they do if parent and child came on the show only to curse out and insult each other?) On TV mother and child embrace and smile into each other's faces. Sometimes the mother and father weep; the child wraps them in her arms and leans across the table to tell how she would not have made it without their help. I have seen these programs.

Sometimes I dream a dream in which Dee and I are suddenly brought together on a TV program of this sort. Out of a dark and soft-seated limousine I am ushered into a bright room filled with many people. There I meet a smiling, gray, sporty man like Johnny Carson who shakes my hand and tells me what a fine girl I have. Then we are on the stage, and Dee is embracing me with tears in her eyes. She pins on my dress a large orchid, even though she had told me once that she thinks orchids are tacky flowers.

In real life I am a large, big-boned woman with rough, man-working hands. In the winter I wear flannel nightgowns to bed and overalls during the day. I can kill and clean a hog as mercilessly as a man. My fat keeps me hot in zero weather. I can work outside all day, breaking ice to get water for washing; I can eat pork liver cooked over the open fire minutes after it comes steaming from the hog. One winter I knocked a bull calf straight in the brain between the eyes with a sledgehammer and had the meat hung up to chill before nightfall. But of course all this does not show on television. I am the way my daughter would want me to be: a hundred pounds lighter, my skin like an uncooked barley pancake. My hair glistens in the hot bright lights. Johnny Carson has much to do to keep up with my quick and witty tongue.

But that is a mistake. I know even before I wake up. Who ever knew a Johnson with a quick tongue? Who can even imagine me looking a strange white man in the eye? It seems to me I have talked to them always with one foot raised in flight, with my head turned in whichever way is farthest from them. Dee, though. She would always look anyone in the eye. Hesitation was no part of her nature.

"How do I look, Mama?" Maggie says, showing just enough of her thin body enveloped in pink skirt and red blouse for me to know she's there, almost hidden by the door.

"Come out into the yard," I say.

Have you ever seen a lame animal, perhaps a dog run over by some careless person rich enough to own a car, sidle up to someone who is ignorant enough to be kind to him? That is the way my Maggie walks. She has been like this, chin on chest, eyes on ground, feet in shuffle, ever since the fire that burned the other house to the ground.

Dee is lighter than Maggie, with nicer hair and a fuller figure. She's a woman now, though sometimes I forget. How long ago was it that the other house burned? Ten, twelve years? Sometimes I can still hear the flames and feel Maggie's arms sticking to me, her hair smoking and her dress falling off her in little black papery flakes. Her eyes seemed stretched open, blazed open by the flames reflected in them. And Dee. I see her standing off under the sweet gum tree she used to dig gum out of, a look of concentration on her face as she watched the last dingy gray board of the house fall in toward the red-hot brick chimney. Why don't you do a dance around the ashes? I'd wanted to ask her. She had hated the house that much.

I used to think she hated Maggie, too. But that was before we raised the money, the church and me, to send her to Augusta[1] to school. She

1. **Augusta:** city in Georgia.

Vocabulary
sidle (sīd′'l) *v.:* move sideways, especially in a shy or sneaky manner.

DIFFERENTIATING INSTRUCTION

Learners Having Difficulty
Invite learners having difficulty to read "Everyday Use" in interactive format in *Interactive Reading* and to use the sidenotes as aids to understanding the selection. The interactive version provides additional instruction, practice, and assessment of the literature standard taught in the Student Edition. Monitor students' responses to the selection, and correct any misconceptions that arise.

Resources Reminder

Differentiating Instruction

- *Interactive Reading*
  - Interactive version: "Everyday Use"

English-Language Learners
To explain the term *everyday use,* you might contrast an ordinary chair used for practical purposes with an antique chair on display.

Resources Reminder

For lessons designed for intermediate and advanced English-language learners, see *Lesson Plans for Language Development,* pp. 37–39, 57, 61.

Special Education Students
For lessons designed for special education students, see *Lesson Plans for Language Development,* pp. 40, 57, 61.

used to read to us without pity, forcing words, lies, other folks' habits, whole lives upon us two, sitting trapped and ignorant underneath her voice. She washed us in a river of make-believe, burned us with a lot of knowledge we didn't necessarily need to know. Pressed us to her with the serious ways she read, to shove us away at just the moment, like dimwits, we seemed about to understand. **D**

Dee wanted nice things. A yellow organdy dress to wear to her graduation from high school; black pumps to match a green suit she'd made from an old suit somebody gave me. She was determined to stare down any disaster in her efforts. Her eyelids would not flicker for minutes at a time. Often I fought off the temptation to shake her. At sixteen she had a style of her own: and knew what style was. **E**

I never had an education myself. After second grade the school closed down. Don't ask me why: In 1927 colored asked fewer questions than they do now. Sometimes Maggie reads to me. She stumbles along good-naturedly but can't see well. She knows she is not bright. Like good looks and money, quickness passed her by. She will marry John Thomas (who has mossy teeth in an earnest face), and then I'll be free to sit here and I guess just sing church songs to myself. Although I never was a good singer. Never could carry a tune. I was always better at a man's job. I used to love to milk till I was hooked in the side in '49. Cows are soothing and slow and don't bother you, unless you try to milk them the wrong way. **F**

I have deliberately turned my back on the house. It is three rooms, just like the one that burned, except the roof is tin; they don't make shingle roofs anymore. There are no real windows, just some holes cut in the sides, like the portholes in a ship, but not round and not square, with rawhide holding the shutters up on the outside. This house is in a pasture, too, like the other one. No doubt when Dee sees it she will want to tear it down. She wrote me once **G** that no matter where we "choose" to live, she will manage to come see us. But she will never bring her friends. Maggie and I thought about this and Maggie asked me, "Mama, when did Dee ever *have* any friends?"

She had a few. Furtive boys in pink shirts hanging about on washday after school. Nervous girls who never laughed. Impressed with her, they worshiped the well-turned phrase, the cute shape, the scalding[2] humor that erupted like bubbles in lye. She read to them.

When she was courting Jimmy T, she didn't have much time to pay to us but turned all her faultfinding power on him. He *flew* to marry a cheap city girl from a family of ignorant, flashy people. She hardly had time to recompose herself.

When she comes, I will meet—but there they are!

Maggie attempts to make a dash for the house, in her shuffling way, but I stay her with my hand. "Come back here," I say. And she stops and tries to dig a well in the sand with her toe.

It is hard to see them clearly through the strong sun. But even the first glimpse of leg out of the car tells me it is Dee. Her feet were always neat looking, as if God himself shaped them with a certain style. From the other side of the car comes a short, stocky man. Hair is all over his head a foot long and hanging from his chin like a kinky mule tail. I hear Maggie suck in her breath. "Uhnnnh" is what it sounds like. Like when you see the wriggling end of a snake just in front of your foot on the road. "Uhnnnh."

Dee next. A dress down to the ground, in this hot weather. A dress so loud it hurts my eyes. **H** There are yellows and oranges enough to throw back the light of the sun. I feel my whole face warming from the heat waves it throws out.

2. **scalding** (skôld′iŋ) *v.* used as *adj.:* burning hot; here, biting or stinging.

Vocabulary
furtive (fʉr′tiv) *adj.:* acting as if trying not to be seen. *Furtive* also means "done secretly."

Direct Teaching

D Literary Focus
REVIEW STANDARD

Conflict. Why does Mama resent Dee's reading to her and Maggie? [Possible responses: She finds Dee overbearing; Dee makes Mama and Maggie feel "trapped and ignorant."]

E Reading Skills

Making inferences. What does Dee's desire for "nice things" and her confidence in overcoming disaster suggest about her? [Possible responses: Dee wants to rise above her poor rural upbringing; she is intelligent, determined, and already feeling entitled at a young age.]

F Literary Focus
GRADE-LEVEL STANDARD

Characters' traits. Details about a character's childhood add depth to characterization. What does Mama's narration tell you about her childhood? [Possible responses: She grew up in the 1920s and '30s; she has only a second-grade education; she was taught not to ask questions; she grew up doing farm labor and was good at it.]

G Advanced Learners

Acceleration. Why does the narrator emphasize the word *choose* in this context? [Possible responses: Mama is being ironic; she knows that she and Maggie have had no real choice about where they live.] How has the historical period influenced where the characters live? [Possible response: The racial segregation and discrimination of the times have severely limited Mama's and Maggie's choices.]

H English-Language Learners

Multiple meanings. Point out the word *loud,* and be sure students understand that here it means "offensively bright." Synonyms include *gaudy* and *garish.*

Advanced Learners

Acceleration. Use this activity to move students toward the eleventh- and twelfth-grade Standard 3.5, for which they evaluate historical influences that shape characters. Tell students that diction, or word choice, often reflects the times in which a character lives. For example, Dee says on p. 80, "I couldn't bear it any longer, being named after the people who oppress me." Her reference to oppression shows the influence of the 1960s civil rights movement on her character.

Activity. Have students identify diction that links the characters to their times.

DIRECT TEACHING

A Reading Skills

Making inferences. What can you infer about Maggie's feelings based on her actions when the man tries to hug her? [Possible responses: Her backing away suggests shyness; her "trembling" and "the perspiration falling off her chin" suggest fear and anxiety.]

B English-Language Learners

Building background knowledge. You might tell students that a Polaroid is a brand of instant-print camera that was fairly expensive in the 1960s.

C Literary Focus
GRADE-LEVEL STANDARD

Characters' traits. "Asalamalakim" is a greeting, not the man's name. Mama knows the difference but uses the term as his name in mild mockery of his appearance and mannerisms.

D Literary Focus
GRADE-LEVEL STANDARD

Characters' traits. All four characters in the story take part in this conversation. What do their words tell you about each of them? [Possible responses: Dee does not feel connected to her family's history and traditions in America; Mama is knowledgeable, insightful, and down-to-earth; Hakim is self-assured; Maggie is overwhelmed and inarticulate.]

E English-Language Learners

Building background knowledge. Explain that the Model A was one of the earliest American cars; few remained by the 1960s. Mama means that Hakim is looking at her as if she were quaint and out of date.

Earrings gold, too, and hanging down to her shoulders. Bracelets dangling and making noises when she moves her arm up to shake the folds of the dress out of her armpits. The dress is loose and flows, and as she walks closer, I like it. I hear Maggie go "Uhnnnh" again. It is her sister's hair. It stands straight up like the wool on a sheep. It is black as night and around the edges are two long pigtails that rope about like small lizards disappearing behind her ears.

"Wa-su-zo-Tean-o!" she says, coming on in that gliding way the dress makes her move. The short, stocky fellow with the hair to his navel is all grinning, and he follows up with "Asalamalakim,[3] my mother and sister!" He moves to hug Maggie but she falls back, right up against the back of my chair. I feel her trembling there, and when I look up I see the perspiration falling off her chin.

"Don't get up," says Dee. Since I am stout, it takes something of a push. You can see me trying to move a second or two before I make it. She turns, showing white heels through her sandals, and goes back to the car. Out she peeks next with a Polaroid. She stoops down quickly and lines up picture after picture of me sitting there in front of the house with Maggie cowering behind me. She never takes a shot without making sure the house is included. When a cow comes nibbling around in the edge of the yard, she snaps it and me and Maggie *and* the house. Then she puts the Polaroid in the back seat of the car and comes up and kisses me on the forehead.

Meanwhile, Asalamalakim is going through motions with Maggie's hand. Maggie's hand is as limp as a fish, and probably as cold, despite the sweat, and she keeps trying to pull it back. It looks like Asalamalakim wants to shake hands but wants to do it fancy. Or maybe he don't know how people shake hands. Anyhow, he soon gives up on Maggie.

"Well," I say. "Dee."

"No, Mama," she says. "Not 'Dee,' Wangero Leewanika Kemanjo!"

"What happened to 'Dee'?" I wanted to know.

"She's dead," Wangero said. "I couldn't bear it any longer, being named after the people who oppress me."

"You know as well as me you was named after your aunt Dicie," I said. Dicie is my sister. She named Dee. We called her "Big Dee" after Dee was born.

"But who was *she* named after?" asked Wangero.

"I guess after Grandma Dee," I said.

"And who was she named after?" asked Wangero.

"Her mother," I said, and saw Wangero was getting tired. "That's about as far back as I can trace it," I said. Though, in fact, I probably could have carried it back beyond the Civil War through the branches.

"Well," said Asalamalakim, "there you are."

"Uhnnnh," I heard Maggie say.

"There I was not," I said, "before 'Dicie' cropped up in our family, so why should I try to trace it that far back?"

He just stood there grinning, looking down on me like somebody inspecting a Model A car. Every once in a while he and Wangero sent eye signals over my head.

"How do you pronounce this name?" I asked.

"You don't have to call me by it if you don't want to," said Wangero.

"Why shouldn't I?" I asked. "If that's what you want us to call you, we'll call you."

"I know it might sound awkward at first," said Wangero.

"I'll get used to it," I said. "Ream it out again."

3. **Asalamalakim:** Asalaam aleikum (ä·sə·läm′ ä·lā′ko͞om′), greeting used by Muslims meaning "peace to you."

Vocabulary

cowering (kou′ər·iŋ) *v.* used as *adj.*: drawing back or huddling in fear.

oppress (ə·pres′) *v.*: persecute; keep down by unjust use of power.

CONTENT-AREA CONNECTIONS

History: Black Pride

Dee and Hakim reflect the values of the black power movement of the 1960s, which offered many African Americans a rediscovery of their African heritage through clothing styles, art, language, music, and religion. Previously some had valued lighter skin more than darker skin. This is shown in Mama's dream on p. 78 by her "skin like an uncooked barley pancake."

History: Civil War Service

Mama's mention of Great Grandpa Ezra's uniform on p. 82 reflects historical fact. More than 200,000 African Americans served in the military during the Civil War. Twenty-four were awarded the Medal of Honor.

Individual activity. Have students research African Americans who served in the Civil War.

Well, soon we got the name out of the way. Asalamalakim had a name twice as long and three times as hard. After I tripped over it two or three times, he told me to just call him Hakim-a-barber. I wanted to ask him was he a barber, but I didn't really think he was, so I didn't ask.

"You must belong to those beef-cattle peoples down the road," I said. They said "Asalamalakim" when they met you, too, but they didn't shake hands. Always too busy: feeding the cattle, fixing the fences, putting up salt-lick shelters, throwing down hay. When the white folks poisoned some of the herd, the men stayed up all night with rifles in their hands. I walked a mile and a half just to see the sight.

Hakim-a-barber said, "I accept some of their doctrines, but farming and raising cattle is not my style." (They didn't tell me, and I didn't ask, whether Wangero—Dee—had really gone and married him.)

We sat down to eat and right away he said he didn't eat collards, and pork was unclean. Wangero, though, went on through the chitlins and corn bread, the greens, and everything else. She talked a blue streak over the sweet potatoes. Everything delighted her. Even the fact that we still used the benches her daddy made for the table when we couldn't afford to buy chairs.

"Oh, Mama!" she cried. Then turned to Hakim-a-barber. "I never knew how lovely these benches are. You can feel the rump prints," she said, running her hands underneath her and along the bench. Then she gave a sigh, and her hand closed over Grandma Dee's butter dish. "That's it!" she said. "I knew there was something I wanted to ask you if I could have." She jumped up from the table and went over in the corner where the churn stood, the milk in it clabber[4] by now. She looked at the churn and looked at it. **F**

"This churn top is what I need," she said. "Didn't Uncle Buddy whittle it out of a tree you all used to have?"

"Yes," I said.

"Uh huh," she said happily. "And I want the dasher,[5] too."

"Uncle Buddy whittle that, too?" asked the barber.

Dee (Wangero) looked up at me.

"Aunt Dee's first husband whittled the dash," said Maggie so low you almost couldn't hear her. "His name was Henry, but they called him Stash."

"Maggie's brain is like an elephant's," Wangero said, laughing. "I can use the churn top as a centerpiece for the alcove table," she said, sliding a plate over the churn, "and I'll think of something artistic to do with the dasher." **G**

When she finished wrapping the dasher, the handle stuck out. I took it for a moment in my hands. You didn't even have to look close to see where hands pushing the dasher up and down to make butter had left a kind of sink in the wood. In fact, there were a lot of small sinks; you could see where thumbs and fingers had sunk into the wood. It was beautiful light-yellow wood, from a tree that grew in the yard where Big Dee and Stash had lived.

After dinner Dee (Wangero) went to the trunk at the foot of my bed and started rifling through it. Maggie hung back in the kitchen over the dishpan. Out came Wangero with two quilts. They had been pieced by Grandma Dee, and then Big Dee and me had hung them on the quilt frames on the front porch and quilted them. One was in the Lone Star pattern. The other was Walk Around the Mountain. In both of them were scraps of dresses Grandma Dee had worn fifty and more years ago. Bits and pieces of Grandpa Jarrell's paisley shirts. And

4. **clabber** (klab′ər) *n:* thickened or curdled sour milk.

5. **dasher** *n:* pole that stirs the milk in a churn.

Vocabulary

doctrines (däk′trinz) *n.:* principles, teachings; beliefs.

rifling (rī′fliŋ) *v.* used as *n.:* searching thoroughly or in a rough manner.

DIRECT TEACHING

F Learners Having Difficulty

Finding details. **Which detail tells you that Mama and Maggie are still using the churn to make butter?** [Possible response: The churn contains milk that has turned to clabber, which is a stage in the making of butter.]

G Reading Skills

Making inferences. **What do Mama's, Maggie's, and Dee's words suggest about the value of the churn to each of them?** [Possible responses: Maggie and Mama value it as a link to relatives they love; Mama also values its aesthetic beauty; Dee values it as an artifact to decorate her home.]

READING MINI-LESSON

Developing Word-Attack Skills

Explore the letter-sound correspondences in the selection word *limousine.* Point out that the last syllable of *limousine* has the *i*-consonant-e pattern, which usually means a long *i* sound, but the vowel sound here is an /ē/. Display the following examples of words in which the vowel sound in an *i*-consonant-e word is /ē/ instead of /ī/:

magazine elite figurine quarantine

Explain that these words all have French or Italian origins. Point out that *i* also stands for /ē/ when it comes before another vowel. Use the following words as examples:

euphoria experience
furious geranium

Activity. Display these sentences, and read them aloud. Have volunteers identify the word in which *i* before another vowel or the *i*-consonant-e spelling stands for /ē/. Answers are underlined.

1. They stared at the ancient machine.
2. It was a curious appliance.
3. It was scaly as a reptile and shiny as an automobile.
4. Our attraction to it was immediate.
5. There was nothing insidious about giving it a trial run.
6. But it hissed like a diabolical radio.

DIRECT TEACHING

A Literary Focus
REVIEW STANDARD

? Conflict. Why does Maggie slam the door when Dee asks for the quilts? [Possible responses: Maggie assumes that Dee will get her way, as she did with the churn; Maggie believes that Dee will simply take whatever she wants, and Mama will not stop her; Maggie is afraid to express her anger to Dee directly, so slamming a door from a distance is her way of showing it.]

B Literary Focus
GRADE-LEVEL STANDARD

? Characters' traits. Mama values the quilts, so why would she want them put to everyday use, which may damage them? [Possible responses: Mama is practical and may feel that if they're not used they're being wasted; she doesn't see the quilts as being precious artifacts the way that Dee does, and she knows that Maggie has the ability to make more.]

C Literary Focus
REVIEW STANDARD

? Conflict. How does Maggie handle the conflict with Dee over the quilts? [Maggie gives in without a struggle.] What does Maggie's approach to this conflict say about her? [Possible responses: Maggie feels inferior next to Dee so she doesn't try to compete with her. Her injuries have humbled her into holding a fatalistic view of life.]

D Reading Skills

? Making inferences. What effect do you think Mama wants her actions to have on Maggie? [Possible response: She wants Maggie to feel loved and entitled for a change and to know that she will not allow Dee to disparage them any further.]

---

one teeny faded blue piece, about the size of a penny matchbox, that was from Great Grandpa Ezra's uniform that he wore in the Civil War.

A "Mama," Wangero said sweet as a bird. "Can I have these old quilts?"

I heard something fall in the kitchen, and a minute later the kitchen door slammed.

"Why don't you take one or two of the others?" I asked. "These old things was just done by me and Big Dee from some tops your grandma pieced before she died."

"No," said Wangero. "I don't want those. They are stitched around the borders by machine."

"That'll make them last better," I said.

"That's not the point," said Wangero. "These are all pieces of dresses Grandma used to wear. She did all this stitching by hand. Imagine!" She held the quilts securely in her arms, stroking them.

"Some of the pieces, like those lavender ones, come from old clothes her mother handed down to her," I said, moving up to touch the quilts. Dee (Wangero) moved back just enough so that I couldn't reach the quilts. They already belonged to her.

"Imagine!" she breathed again, clutching them closely to her bosom.

"The truth is," I said, "I promised to give them quilts to Maggie, for when she marries John Thomas."

She gasped like a bee had stung her.

B "Maggie can't appreciate these quilts!" she said. "She'd probably be backward enough to put them to everyday use."

"I reckon she would," I said. "God knows I been saving 'em for long enough with nobody using 'em. I hope she will!" I didn't want to bring up how I had offered Dee (Wangero) a quilt when she went away to college. Then she had told me they were old-fashioned, out of style.

"But they're *priceless!*" she was saying now, furiously; for she has a temper. "Maggie would put them on the bed and in five years they'd be in rags. Less than that!"

"She can always make some more," I said. "Maggie knows how to quilt."

Dee (Wangero) looked at me with hatred. "You just will not understand. The point is *these* quilts, these quilts!"

"Well," I said, stumped. "What would *you* do with them?"

"Hang them," she said. As if that was the only thing you *could* do with quilts.

Maggie by now was standing in the door. I could almost hear the sound her feet made as they scraped over each other.

C "She can have them, Mama," she said, like somebody used to never winning anything or having anything reserved for her. "I can 'member Grandma Dee without the quilts."

I looked at her hard. She had filled her bottom lip with checkerberry snuff, and it gave her face a kind of dopey, hangdog look. It was Grandma Dee and Big Dee who taught her how to quilt herself. She stood there with her scarred hands hidden in the folds of her skirt. She looked at her sister with something like fear, but she wasn't mad at her. This was Maggie's portion. This was the way she knew God to work.

D When I looked at her like that, something hit me in the top of my head and ran down to the soles of my feet. Just like when I'm in church and the spirit of God touches me and I get happy and shout. I did something I never had done before: hugged Maggie to me, then dragged her on into the room, snatched the quilts out of Miss Wangero's hands, and dumped them into Maggie's lap. Maggie just sat there on my bed with her mouth open.

"Take one or two of the others," I said to Dee.

But she turned without a word and went out to Hakim-a-barber.

"You just don't understand," she said, as Maggie and I came out to the car.

"What don't I understand?" I wanted to know.

"Your heritage," she said. And then she turned

FAMILY/COMMUNITY ACTIVITY

Have students locate illustrations of quilts to display in the classroom. Then, invite someone skilled in quilting to visit the class to explain and demonstrate how quilts are made. Have the expert bring quilts to show, if possible. You might have your students welcome the guest by reading aloud the poem from "Hands: For Mother's Day" (p. 84) to him or her. Ask the expert to discuss the significance and history of quilt patterns, particularly those mentioned in "Everyday Use."

82 Chapter 2 Character • Using Primary and Secondary Sources

to Maggie, kissed her, and said, "You ought to try to make something of yourself, too, Maggie. It's really a new day for us. But from the way you and Mama still live, you'd never know it."

She put on some sunglasses that hid everything above the tip of her nose and her chin.

Maggie smiled, maybe at the sunglasses. But a real smile, not scared. After we watched the car dust settle, I asked Maggie to bring me a dip of snuff. And then the two of us sat there just enjoying, until it was time to go in the house and go to bed. ■

Meet the Writer

Alice Walker

Alice Walker and her daughter, Rebecca.

Writing All the While

Alice Walker (1944–), shown here with her daughter, Rebecca, was born in the small town of Eatonton, Georgia, the youngest of eight children. Her father was a sharecropper, and her mother worked as a maid. When she was eight years old, Walker was blinded in one eye by a shot from a BB gun. The resulting scar tissue made her painfully shy and self-conscious, and she spent her free time alone outdoors, reading and writing stories. With the aid of a scholarship for handicapped students, she attended Spelman College, a college for African American women in Atlanta. After two years, she transferred to Sarah Lawrence College in New York.

Women have always played an important role in Walker's life. She has said that she grew up believing there was absolutely nothing her mother couldn't do once she set her mind to it. So when the women's movement came along, she said that she was delighted because she felt it was trying to go where her mother was and where she had always assumed she would go.

Walker's third novel, *The Color Purple,* won the Pulitzer Prize for fiction in 1983 and was made into a popular movie. Walker has been a contributing editor of *Ms.* magazine and has been active in both the women's movement and the civil rights movement.

Walker has published short stories, poems, essays, and novels, so it comes as a surprise to learn that she never intended to be a writer.

"I just kind of found myself doing it. I remember wanting to be a scientist, wanting to be a pianist, wanting to be a painter. But all the while I was wanting to be these other things, I was writing. We were really poor, and writing was about the cheapest thing to do. You know, I feel amazed that I have been able to do exactly what I wanted to do."

For Independent Reading

In Search of Our Mothers' Gardens, a book of Walker's essays, has influenced many writers and many American women.

DIFFERENTIATING INSTRUCTION

Advanced Learners

Enrichment. Remind students that Walker's literary awards and honors include the 1983 Pulitzer Prize for fiction.

Activity. Suggest that students use a search engine to research Walker's Pulitzer Prize. Encourage them to find out what the 1983 awards committee said about Walker's prizewinning novel and to learn how Walker responded to receiving the prize. Have students report their findings to the class and share significant quotations.

GUIDED PRACTICE

Monitoring students' progress. Have students locate passages in the story that support their responses to these questions.

Short Answer

1. Where in Mama's dream does she meet Dee? [on a TV show]
2. How long did Mama attend school? [through second grade]
3. How does Maggie feel when Dee arrives? [nervous]
4. How will Dee use the churn top? [as a table centerpiece]
5. Who pieced the quilts that Dee wants? [Grandma Dee]

Meet the Writer

Background. Alice Walker lived in Mississippi and Georgia between 1965 and 1974, working for the civil rights movement and the Head Start program. Her daughter Rebecca, born in 1970, is also a writer. After living for a time in Brooklyn, New York, Walker moved to northern California.

For Independent Reading

Encourage students who read *In Search of Our Mothers' Gardens* to explore works by some of the African American writers Walker discusses in that volume, such as Zora Neale Hurston and Jean Toomer.

- For groundbreaking images of the lives of urban African Americans in mid–twentieth century, suggest *Selected Poems* by Gwendolyn Brooks.
- Fans of traditional American crafts will enjoy *The Foxfire Book,* edited by Eliot Wigginton, a 1960s collection of interviews with mountain craftspeople of rural Georgia.

Connection

Summary at grade level

This soliloquy, an excerpt from a prose poem, examines quilting as a metaphor for the experiences of many African American women. The speaker in the poem describes how "we" quilters take scraps discarded by "those with emotional options" and craft them into something "lovable" and "intrinsically worthwhile."

DIRECT TEACHING

A Reading Skills

Making inferences. From the words "dry, rough hands," what might you infer about the daily lives of the quilters in this poem? [Possible responses: They use their hands for physical work; they are not pampered.]

B Literary Focus
GRADE-LEVEL STANDARD

Characters' traits. In this soliloquy, the speaker in the poem says that quilters "survive on . . . the leftovers from a materially richer culture." What character traits of the quilters do the speaker's words emphasize? [Possible responses: resourcefulness; creativity; endurance.]

C Reading Skills

Making inferences. To whom do you think the "we" in the poem refers? Be ready to explain which parts of the poem support your inference. [Possible response: The phrases "Michelle-Angelo," "dry, rough hands," and "leftovers from a materially richer culture" support the inference that "we" refers to creative women living in poverty or oppression.]

CONNECTION / PROSE POEM

from Hands: For Mother's Day

Nikki Giovanni

Some people think a quilt is a blanket stretched across a Lincoln bed . . .[1] or from frames on a wall . . . a quaint museum piece to be purchased on Bloomingdale's[2] 30-day same-as-cash plan . . . Quilts are our mosaics . . . **A** **Michelle-Angelo's**[3] contribution to beauty . . . We weave a quilt with dry, rough hands . . . Quilts are the way our lives are lived . . . **B** **C** We survive on patches . . . scraps . . . the leftovers from a materially richer culture . . . the throwaways from those with emotional options . . . We do the far more difficult job of taking that which nobody wants and not only loving it . . . not only seeing its worth . . . but making it lovable . . . and intrinsically worthwhile . . .

1. **Lincoln bed:** probably a reference to a large, elaborately carved bed similar to one in the White House that is associated with President Abraham Lincoln (1809–1865).
2. **Bloomingdale's:** department-store chain.
3. **Michelle-Angelo:** tongue-in-cheek comparison to the famous Italian Renaissance artist Michelangelo Buonarroti (1475–1564).

Quilting Time (1986) by Romare Bearden.
Founders Society Purchase with funds from the Detroit Edison Company. © Romare Bearden Foundation/Licensed by VAGA, New York, NY.

Connecting and Comparing Texts

Like "Everyday Use," this excerpt presents images of strong, resilient women. The quilters in Giovanni's poem are not among "those with emotional options." Yet they take "that which nobody wants," find its potential, and transform it into quilts that are both useful and beautiful. Similarly, in "Everyday Use," Mama and Maggie have few options: They are bound by the limitations placed on them by racism and poverty. Yet they proudly defend their culture and their way of life in the face of one family member's shame. The ideas expressed in Giovanni's poem deepen the significance of the fact that Mama and Maggie are quilters, while Dee wants their quilts but wants to be free of the legacy that is truly attached to the quilts.

CONNECTION / Dramatic Monologue

Edgar Lee Masters's "Lucinda Matlock" is a famous ***dramatic monologue,*** *a type of poem in which a speaker (who is not the poet) addresses one or more silent listeners. Typically the speaker expresses deep thoughts or feelings. In this case the speaker is the spirit of Lucinda Matlock, who tells what she has learned about life's struggles during her many years as a wife and mother.*

© Hulton Archive.

Lucinda Matlock

Edgar Lee Masters

I went to the dances at Chandlerville,
And played snap-out° at Winchester.
One time we changed partners,
Driving home in the moonlight of middle June,
And then I found Davis.
We were married and lived together for seventy years,
Enjoying, working, raising the twelve children,
Eight of whom we lost
Ere I had reached the age of sixty.
I spun, I wove, I kept the house, I nursed the sick,
I made the garden, and for holiday
Rambled over the fields where sang the larks,
And by Spoon River gathering many a shell,
And many a flower and medicinal weed—
Shouting to the wooded hills, singing to the green valleys.
At ninety-six I had lived enough, that is all,
And passed to a sweet repose.
What is this I hear of sorrow and weariness,
Anger, discontent and drooping hopes?
Degenerate° sons and daughters,
Life is too strong for you—
It takes life to love Life.

---

2. **snap-out** *n.:* game in which a line of players holding hands makes sudden twists and turns, so that those players at the ends of the line are flung off.
20. **degenerate** (dē • jen′ər • it) *adj:* weak, in decline.

Connection

Summary at grade level

In this dramatic monologue, the character Lucinda Matlock looks back after death on her ninety-six years of life in the rural Midwest. Remembering play, love, work, and sorrow, she chastises younger generations for lacking the strength and wisdom to appreciate life.

DIRECT TEACHING

D Literary Focus
GRADE-LEVEL STANDARD

Characters' traits. What would you say are the speaker's character traits, based on her description of her activities? [Possible responses: liveliness; a nurturing nature; fidelity; strength; enjoyment of everyday life.]

E Learners Having Difficulty

Reading inverted sentences. What would be a more standard order for the words in this line? [Rambled over the fields where the larks sang]

F Reading Skills

Making inferences. Notice the words that Lucinda Matlock uses to describe dying. What do these words suggest about her attitude toward death? [Possible responses: She is matter-of-fact ("I had lived enough, that is all"); she accepts death peacefully, without fear or regret ("passed to a sweet repose").]

G Literary Focus
GRADE-LEVEL STANDARD

Characters' traits. What traits of the speaker are revealed in the last five lines of the poem? [Possible responses: strength, a critical or judgmental nature, insightfulness.]

The character of Lucinda Matlock in this poem is like the quilters characterized in "Hands: For Mother's Day" and like Mama in "Everyday Use." They are all strong women who have worked tirelessly, known only the simplest pleasures, endured pain and grief, and still found much to love in life. None of these women chooses to waste much time or energy on ". . . sorrow and weariness, / Anger, discontent, and drooping hopes." Hearing a younger generation complain, Lucinda Matlock rebukes the complainers as being "degenerate" and without resolve. She understands, as does Mama in "Everyday Use" and the quilters in "Hands: For Mother's Day," that to live fully, a person must deal with both the sorrow and the joy that life has to offer.

INDEPENDENT PRACTICE

Literary Response and Analysis

Reading Check

1. Dee is confident. She has lighter skin, nicer hair, and a fuller figure than Maggie. She is educated, wants nice things, and rejects her family heritage.
2. Maggie would use them as bedcovers; Dee would display them as works of art.
3. She was burned in a house fire.
4. She gives them to Maggie and offers Dee other quilts.
5. "'. . . backward enough to put them to everyday use'" (p. 82)

Interpretations

6. Possible answer: Mama shows she is tough, strong, and practical when she says "I can work outside all day . . ." She shows she appreciates her family heritage when she says, "Some of the pieces . . . her mother handed down to her."
7. Dee and Maggie have family heritage in common but differ in attitude toward it and themselves. Maggie is self-effacing and lives her heritage, saying "I can 'member Grandma Dee without the quilts." Dee is strong-willed and has an academic interest in her heritage. She wants to do "something artistic" with their things.
8. It means Dee has become successful. Signs of this include her sophistication and affluence.
9. *Agree*—Mama does not understand the value of the heirlooms. *Disagree*—Mama traces her family's history and treasures "everyday" objects.
10. Mama changes; she does "something [she] had never done before"; she stands up to Dee in favor of Maggie. Maggie changes; she feels deserving, and she smiles "a real smile, not scared" at Dee.

Literary Response and Analysis

Reading Check

1. According to Mama, how is Dee different from her and from Maggie?
2. What different uses would Maggie and Dee have for the quilts?
3. What terrible thing happened to Maggie when she was a child?
4. How does Mama choose to resolve the **conflict** over the quilts?
5. Find the passage in the text that explains the **title.**

Interpretations

6. Find passages in the story where Mama tells the reader about herself. Also, find passages of **dialogue** in which Mama reveals her character. On the basis of these passages, how would you describe Mama's **character traits**? Be sure to cite details in the story that support the traits you mention.
7. **Compare and contrast** Dee and Maggie. Find passages of **dialogue** about these characters, and make inferences about their **character traits.** What is the most significant thing they have in common? What's their most compelling difference?
8. Dee is referred to as the child who has "made it." What does that mean, and what signs tell you that she has made it?
9. Near the end of the story, Dee accuses Mama of not understanding their African American heritage. Do you agree or disagree with Dee? Why?
10. Has any character changed by the end of the story? Go back to the text, and find details to support your answer.

Reading Standard 3.4 Determine characters' traits by what the characters say about themselves in narration, dialogue, and dramatic monologue.

11. Do you think Dee would agree with the speaker in Nikki Giovanni's poem (see the ***Connection*** on page 84)? Why or why not?

Evaluation

12. Which character did you side with in the conflict over the quilts? Why?
13. This story occurs in a specific time, place, and culture. Could the conflict over traditions faced by this family be experienced by any family anywhere? What role do your heritage and family traditions play in your life today? (Look back at your Quickwrite notes.)

Writing

Two Strong Women

In a paragraph or two, **compare and contrast** Mama in this story with Lucinda Matlock in the **dramatic monologue** (see the ***Connection*** on page 85). Use a diagram like the one shown below to identify both characters' traits. Include what they say about themselves and what they say to others.

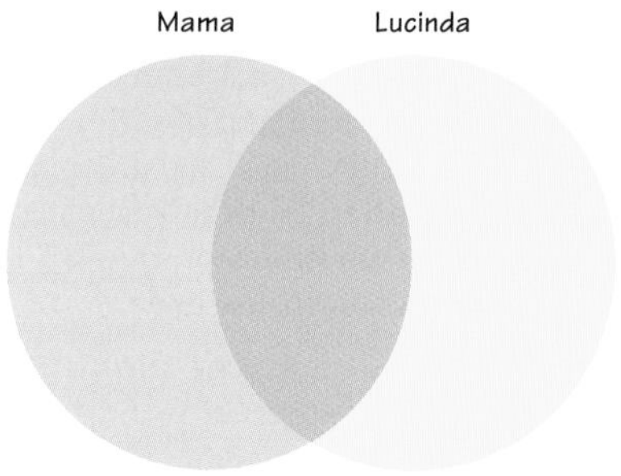

11. Yes; both see quilts as manifestations of the African American struggle. No; the speaker values the quilters, while Dee rejects them.

Evaluation

12. Possible answers: Maggie, because she was promised the quilts and loved their creator; Dee, because she sees their artistic value.
13. Some students may say that such conflicts are universal. Others may say that the events of the 1960s and the struggles of African Americans in the South make the Johnsons' conflict unique.

86 Chapter 2 Character • Using Primary and Secondary Sources

Vocabulary Development

Clarifying Word Meanings: Look at the Context

When you come across an unfamiliar word, don't focus on the word alone. Look at the big picture—the **context,** or the words and sentences surrounding the unfamiliar word. Writers often help you out by providing a built-in **definition,** a **restatement,** or an **example.**

DEFINITION Dee complains that Mama doesn't understand her heritage, **the traditions and culture of her ancestors.**

RESTATEMENT When Dee's old boyfriend Jimmy T marries another girl, Dee has to recompose herself, and it takes quite an effort before she can **get herself calmed down again.**

EXAMPLE Mama compares Maggie to a lame animal, **"perhaps a dog run over by some careless person,"** that sidles up to someone who is kind to it.

Word Bank
sidle
furtive
cowering
oppress
doctrines
rifling

The diagram below shows how one reader figured out the meaning of *sidle* by using various kinds of **context clues.**

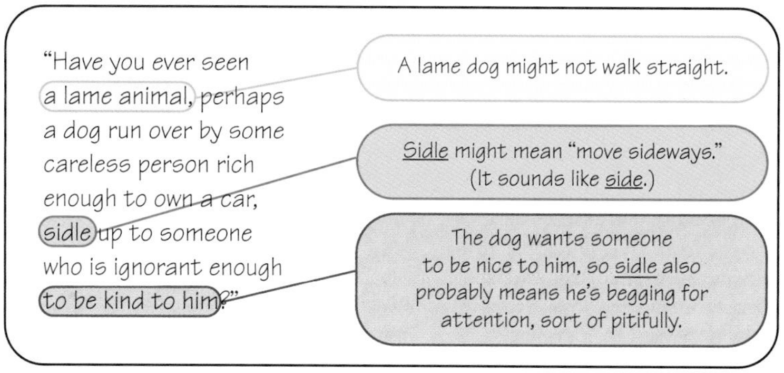

PRACTICE

1. Find the context for each of the other Word Bank words—the passage where each word appears in the story. Re-read the passage that the underlined word is in. Then, make a context diagram for each word.
2. For each of the words in the Word Bank, write one sentence with a definition, restatement, or example context clue that clarifies the word's meaning.

Grade 8 Review Reading Standard 1.3 Use word meanings within the appropriate context and show ability to verify those meanings by definition, restatement, or example.

Vocabulary Development

Practice

1. Possible Answers
- "Furtive boys . . . hanging about on washday" (p. 79). *Possible entries*—They hang about rather than visit. The laundry may conceal them. Maybe furtive means "stealthy."
- ". . . Maggie cowering behind me." (p. 80). *Possible entries*—Maggie is timid and tries to hide behind Mama. Cowering may mean crouching in fear.
- "I couldn't bear it any longer, being named after the people who oppress me" (p. 80). *Possible entries*— Slaves in the South were given English names by their owners. Dee (Wangero) resents this. To oppress people may be to deprive them of freedom.
- "'I accept some of their doctrines . . .'" (p. 81). *Possible entries*—He accepts the group's doctrines but not the actions. Doctrines may be beliefs.
- "Dee (Wangero) went to the trunk . . . and started rifling through it. . . ." (p. 81). *Possible entries*—She rifles through a trunk. She is searching for quilts. Rifling may be searching.

2. Possible Answers
- Lee tried to sidle past, hoping to slip by unnoticed.
- With a furtive, sneaky motion, the thief pocketed the watch.
- The victim was cowering like a frightened dog.
- The government began to oppress its citizens, restricting many of their rights and freedoms.
- Missionaries spread church doctrines—beliefs.
- Rifling through the closet, he looked for his jeans.

Resources Reminder

Vocabulary
- *Vocabulary Development*
  - Vocabulary Worksheet, p. 7
- *Lesson Plans for Language Development*
  - Vocabulary, pp. 57, 61

ASSESSING

Assessment
- *Progress Assessment of Reading*
  - Selection Test

RETEACHING

For a lesson reteaching Standard 3.4, see **Reteaching,** p. 939A.

Everyday Use 87

STANDARDS FOCUS, pp. 88–95

(For the grade-level standard taught in this lesson, see citations on Student Edition pages.)

Prerequisite Standard

- Grade 7, Reading Comprehension 2.6 **Assess the adequacy, accuracy, and appropriateness of the author's evidence to support claims and assertions, noting instances of bias and stereotyping.**

Reading Skills

- Use primary and secondary sources.

Summary *at grade level*

This selection includes examples of primary and secondary sources on American quilters and their work. In the primary sources (two interviews and one oral history), Alice Walker discusses her own quilting, Nikki Giovanni explores quilting as a metaphor, and another quilter relates how her quilting attracted her future husband. The secondary source, a newspaper article, reports on a modern extended family embracing the quilting tradition: A novice quilter gathers fabric pieces and family stories to welcome a first grandchild.

Before You Read INFORMATIONAL MATERIALS

Interview with Alice Walker ◆ Interview with Nikki Giovanni ◆ "Thinkin' on Marryin'" ◆ A Baby's Quilt to Sew Up the Generations

Primary and Secondary Sources

Primary Versus Secondary: What's the Difference?

The materials you find when researching historical information can generally be classified into two categories: primary sources and secondary sources.

- A **primary source** is original material, a firsthand account of information that has not been interpreted or edited by other writers. It may give us eyewitness testimony to an event or tell us the writer's own opinions and ideas on a subject. Oral histories, interviews, autobiographies, letters, speeches, editorials, eyewitness news reports, and literary works are examples of primary sources.
- A **secondary source,** on the other hand, is based on other sources. It contains information that is at least one step removed from an event and is usually retold, interpreted, or summarized by the writer. Secondary sources are often based on a variety of primary sources. Encyclopedia articles and most magazine articles are secondary sources; so are biographies, textbooks, reference books, and literary criticism. Most newspaper articles are secondary sources, unless they are firsthand accounts written at the time of an event, editorials, or opinion pieces.

Pages 88–93 cover **Reading Standard 2.5** Extend ideas presented in primary or secondary sources through original analysis, evaluation, and elaboration.

Using the Sources

The following steps can help you use the information in a primary or secondary source to learn about a topic:

- **Analyze.** Read the material carefully to figure out what's being said. Who is the speaker or writer, and who is the intended audience? What is the message, or **main idea**? What details support the main idea?
- **Evaluate.** How accurate or credible is the message? Do you agree with the writer's message? Look for clues that tell you if you are reading **opinions** or **facts.** Using a primary source, try to confirm the information in other primary sources or in secondary sources.
- **Elaborate.** When doing research, you'll want to elaborate on the information you find in your primary and secondary sources. When you **elaborate,** you add something, usually more details. You might offer your own ideas on the topic, or you might do further research. If you are using a secondary source, you can check to see whether it has a **bibliography** or a list of **works cited.** This will help you find out where to look for more information.

Connecting to the Literature

The central conflict in "Everyday Use" concerns some treasured family quilts. Quilting has long been an important folk art and cultural tradition in America. In the following primary and secondary sources you'll learn more about quilting. One source features Alice Walker, author of "Everyday Use," who is herself a quilter.

RESOURCES: READING

Planning

- *One-Stop Planner* CD-ROM with Test Generator
- *On Course: Mapping Instruction*

Media

- *Audio CD Library*
  - disc 3

Reading

- *Interactive Reading,* Teacher's Edition
  - Graphic Organizer: Analysis, Evaluation, and Elaboration Chart

Differentiating Instruction

- *Lesson Plans for Language Development*
  - English-Language Learners, pp. 41–43, 58, 62
  - Special Education Students, pp. 44, 58, 62

Assessment

- *Progress Assessment of Reading*
  - Selection Test
- *One-Stop Planner* CD-ROM with Test Generator

*Here are three **primary sources** and one **secondary source** on quilting. The first two selections are interviews, one with Alice Walker (the author of "Everyday Use") and one with Nikki Giovanni (the author of "Hands: For Mother's Day"). The next selection is an **oral history** of a quilter that was tape-recorded in the Southwest in 1975. She speaks a distinctive regional dialect that differs in many ways from standard English. The last selection, the secondary source, is a newspaper article about one family's modern version of the family-quilt tradition.*

INTERVIEW

PRIMARY SOURCE

Interview with Alice Walker

from *A Communion of the Spirits: African American Quilters, Preservers, and Their Stories*

Roland L. Freeman

Alice Walker at home with her quilts.

I asked Alice to talk first about the tradition of quilting in her family.
Well, my mother was a quilter, and I remember many, many afternoons of my mother and the neighborhood women sitting on the porch around the quilting frame, quilting and talking, you know; getting up to stir something on the stove and coming back and sitting down. **A**

The first quilt I worked on was the *In Love and Trouble* quilt. And I did that one when I was living in Mississippi. It was during a period when we were wearing African-inspired dresses. So all of the pieces are from dresses that I actually wore. **B** This yellow and black fabric I bought when I was in Uganda,[1] and I

1. **Uganda:** country in central Africa.

PRETEACHING

Selection Starter

Motivate. Tell students about a craft or skill that older relatives or friends taught you (for example, playing an instrument, repairing something, or cooking a certain food). Ask students to describe skills or crafts they have learned from older relatives or friends.

DIRECT TEACHING

A Reading Informational Materials

GRADE-LEVEL STANDARD

Using primary and secondary sources. How can you tell which words are the interviewer's questions and which are Alice Walker's responses? [The interviewer's questions are printed in boldface type.]

B Reading Informational Materials

GRADE-LEVEL STANDARD

Using primary and secondary sources. In this part of the interview, is Alice Walker providing facts or opinions? [facts] How might you verify them? [Possible response: Interview someone who knew her at the time.]

DIFFERENTIATING INSTRUCTION

Learners Having Difficulty
Be sure students understand that interviews and oral histories reproduce the speakers' exact words and speech patterns. Reassure students that in these three primary sources, the speakers' words are simple and conversational, though sentences may be long and rambling.

English-Language Learners
Point out that the word *quilt* can function both as a noun and as a verb (for example, a quilt and to quilt). The words *frame* and *stitch* from this selection also can function as both nouns and verbs. Ask students to list similar words.

Resources Reminder
For lessons designed for intermediate and advanced English-language learners, see *Lesson Plans for Language Development,* pp. 41–43, 58, 62.

Special Education Students
For lessons designed for special education students, see *Lesson Plans for Language Development,* pp. 44, 58, 62.

DIRECT TEACHING

A Reading Informational Materials
GRADE-LEVEL STANDARD

? Using primary and secondary sources. How would you state the main idea about quilting that Walker expresses in this paragraph? [Possible response: Quilting connects the quilter to family traditions and to herself.]

B Reading Informational Materials
GRADE-LEVEL STANDARD

Using primary and secondary sources. [Possible responses to question: Many students will agree that "making and creating" is empowering and rewarding. Those who disagree may say that making one's own things can be too time-consuming and labor-intensive.]

had a beautiful dress made of it that I wore and wore and wore and eventually I couldn't wear it anymore; partly I had worn it out and also I was pregnant, so it didn't fit, and I used that and I used the red and white and black, which was a long, floor-length dress that I had when I was pregnant with my daughter, Rebecca, who is now twenty-three. I took these things apart or I used scraps. I put them together in this quilt, because it just seemed perfect. Mississippi was full of political and social struggle, and regular quilts were all African American with emphasis on being here in the United States. But because of the African consciousness that was being raised[2] and the way that we were all wearing our hair in naturals[3] and wearing all of these African dresses, I felt the need to blend these two traditions. So it's a quilt of great memory and importance to me. I use it a lot and that's why it's so worn.

I asked her what happens when she sleeps under that quilt.
Oh . . . I am warm and I am secure and I am safe. I feel that I know how to create my own environment, and I know how to protect it. And I know how to choose it. I realize that my quilts are really simple, and yet, they give me so much pleasure, because even in their extreme simplicity they are just as useful as the most complex. And in their own way, they are beautiful because they do express what I was feeling and they clearly mark a particular time for me.

2. **the African . . . raised:** reference to the increased pride that many African Americans were taking in their African ethnic heritage in the early 1970s.
3. **naturals** *n.:* African American hairstyles that don't involve chemical straightening.

I asked her if she had made a quilt for her daughter.
No. I'm sure that she will make her own quilt. I'll be happy to leave her these if they are not worn out, which they will probably be, but I hope that she will make quilts for (A) her own grounding and her own connection to me and to her grandmother and to her great-grandmother. I've seen quilts that my grandmother made. They tended to be very serviceable, very heavy and really for warmth, and, well of course, beautiful. My daughter has a quilt that she travels with. It's just a beautiful simple quilt that she loves. I gave it to her because she just feels like you can't sleep under just any old thing. It's got to be something that is congenial[4] with your dreams—your dream sense, your dreamtime. I'm trying to think of where I got it. I think that I just bought it somewhere. I believe it is from Texas.

I asked Alice what she'd like to say to people in general about quilting.
That they should learn to do it. That they should think less about collecting quilts and give more thought to making them. Because, really, that is the power. It may do all kinds of good things, too, to collect what others have made, but I think it is essential that we know how to express, you know, our own sense of connection. And there is no better sense of understanding our own (B) creation than to create, and so we should do that.

EVALUATE
Do you agree with Walker's **opinion** that there is power in making and creating? Explain.

4. **congenial** *adj.:* agreeable; in accord.

DIFFERENTIATING INSTRUCTION

Advanced Learners
Acceleration. This activity can help to move students toward the eleventh- and twelfth-grade Standard 2.3, for which they verify and clarify facts presented in expository tests.
Activity. Suggest that students team up in threes or fours and consult a variety of documents to obtain information on quilting, in order to verify the facts in the selection. Have each group begin by listing facts about quilting that are presented in the selection. Then, have students research documents that can support and clarify these facts. Ask the teams to share their results with the class.

INTERVIEW

PRIMARY SOURCE

Interview with Nikki Giovanni

from *A Communion of the Spirits: African American Quilters, Preservers, and Their Stories*

Roland L. Freeman

I asked Nikki whether she had ever written about quilts.

I have used quilts as a metaphor. That's because I have a line in a poem called "Hands," which is a poem I wrote for Mother's Day. It says, "Quilts are the way our lives are lived. We survive on the scraps, the leftovers from a materially richer society." Quilts are such a—what's the word I'm looking for—banner to black women. Because what they ended up taking was that which nobody wanted, and making something totally beautiful out of it. Making something in fact quite valuable. At least to this day. But that's like the spirituals.° We took a bad situation and found a way to make a song. So it's a definite part of the heritage.

EVALUATE

Explain Giovanni's use of quilts as a metaphor. Do you think the metaphor is effective? Explain why or why not.

C

°**spirituals:** folk hymns created by African Americans in the South in the eighteenth and nineteenth centuries.

ORAL HISTORY

PRIMARY SOURCE

"Thinkin' on Marryin'"

from *The Quilters: Women and Domestic Art*

Patricia Cooper *and* Norma Bradley Allen

Back when I was a girl, quilts was something that a family had to have. It takes a whole lot of cover to keep warm in one of them old open houses on the plains.

When a girl was thinkin' on marryin', and we all done a lot of that, she had to start thinkin' on gettin' her quilts pieced. The way I done mine was real nice, I think. Papa had laid up a beautiful arbor[1] with the brush he had cleared from the land. It was set up a ways back of the house. Well, I jest went out under that arbor, set up my frame, and went to quiltin' outdoors. Now some thought that was real funny, but I sure thought it was nice.

D

Mama gave me one real beautiful quilt, a Lone Star[2] that she had done herself. I made

1. **arbor** *n.:* shady covering, usually made of plants.

2. **Lone Star:** traditional American quilt pattern, also known as the Star of Bethlehem. The pattern features an eight-pointed star made up of contrasting dark and light diamonds.

DIRECT TEACHING

C Reading Informational Materials

GRADE-LEVEL STANDARD

Using primary and secondary sources. Remind students that a metaphor is a comparison of two things that are not usually thought of as being related. [Possible response to question: Quilting, in which one transforms worn bits of cloth into warm and beautiful covers, is likened to black women's transforming the difficult circumstances of socioeconomic disadvantage into a strong and beautiful culture. Many students may feel that the metaphor is effective, citing Giovanni's statement that both feats involve "surviving on scraps." Other students may say that the metaphor is too complex or outdated.]

D Reading Informational Materials

GRADE-LEVEL STANDARD

? Using primary and secondary sources. Which details support the main idea that quilts were essential household items in this speaker's earlier years? [Possible responses: Houses on the plains, where she grew up, were "open," or drafty; it took a "lot of cover to keep warm"; young women planning to marry had to have several quilts for their new households.]

CONTENT-AREA CONNECTIONS

Art/Math: Quilt Designs

Many traditional quilt patterns have complex geometric designs and colorful names. Examples include Robbing Peter to Pay Paul, Flower Garden, Tumbling Blocks, Rebel Patch, and Double Ax. Some quilters use compasses and straightedges to make the pieces uniform and to ensure that pieces fit together properly.

Individual activity. Have interested students research and sketch quilt patterns. Encourage them to identify the geometric shapes they see in the patterns and to describe the arrangements of shapes that form the designs.

DIRECT TEACHING

Ⓐ Reading Informational Materials
GRADE-LEVEL STANDARD

Using primary and secondary sources. Which part of this sentence is fact and which is opinion? [*Fact*—"I married . . . when I was eighteen." *Opinion*—"the finest-looking young man for three counties around."] How might you evaluate the accuracy of the speaker's statement that she married at eighteen? [Check county records; interview her husband or others who knew her at the time.]

Ⓑ Reading Informational Materials
GRADE-LEVEL STANDARD

Using primary and secondary sources. [Possible responses to question: Young women could marry in their late teens; most dreamed of marriage; they could attend dances; they waited for men to initiate courtship; they worked regularly at handicrafts; they made household items to use when they married.]

Collection of Rowland and Eleanor Bingham Miller; photograph courtesy of Shelly Zegart.

Star of Bethlehem or *Lone Star* (1832) by Hannah Huxley. Cottons, pieced and appliquéd (112″ × 108″).

three by myself that I don't reckon were much to look at, but I was awful proud of them then. And that's what I set out with when I married my sweetheart. Now that's **Ⓐ** a story. You won't believe it to look at me now, but I married me the finest-looking young man for three counties around when I was eighteen. And I didn't meet him at no dance neither. I don't reckon I would have stood a chance there. These big size tens were never so graceful. They're just good strong platforms for standin' on.

Anyways, what I was doin' was settin' there under that quiltin' arbor one spring afternoon, April fourteenth, just quiltin' and dreamin' a dream on ever' stitch and just plannin' who might share 'em with me.

And this deep, fine voice says, "Pardon me, ma'am, but I've been seein' you out here ever' day for weeks and I jest got up my nerve to come over and speak to you and see what you were workin' on with such care."

Lordy, girl, I married him and, as I recall it now, that was the longest speech he ever said at one time to this day. **Ⓑ**

ANALYZE

What can you **infer** about women's lives in this speaker's community when she was young?

FAMILY/COMMUNITY ACTIVITY

Point out to students that quilting is one of many crafts and activities that were commonplace for earlier generations but are rarely practiced today. Ask students to interview people in the community who grew up in the 1930s or '40s. Their questions should focus on descriptions and uses of items once commonly found in the home but seldom seen today (for example, iceboxes, record players, or washboards) and on things once commonly made at home but usually bought ready-made today (for example, clothing such as socks and sweaters, toys such as kites and skateboards, or foods such as mayonnaise and ice cream). Ask students to present oral reports or create visual displays from their findings, with the permission of interviewees.

SECONDARY SOURCE

NEWSPAPER ARTICLE

A Baby's Quilt to Sew Up the Generations

from *The New York Times*, July 9, 2000

Felicia R. Lee

The stepgrandparents on the mother's side sent a photo of themselves in Pisa, Italy. Cousin Barbara sent a paraphrased quotation from *The Little Prince*[1] that said, "What is essential is invisible to the eye." From a maternal great-great-grandmother came a piece of her apron, on which was inscribed a cookie recipe.

Each contribution was attached to a fabric square and each is part of a quilt that Marilyn Webb, a writer who lives on the Upper West Side, is making for her first grandchild. The boy will be born to her daughter, Jennifer Kiefer, and her son-in-law, Jason Kiefer, in Manhattan Beach, California.

The people behind the 40 squares represent the modern version of an extended family tree that includes half siblings,[2] stepparents, and stepsiblings, as well as the usual branches. ●

● EVALUATE
Evaluate what the writer says about modern families. Do you agree or disagree?

D

The quilt, with a blue border of little dogs, is draped over a couch in Ms. Webb's dining room, an old-fashioned gift for a new kind of family. It is a family story literally stitched together at a time when so many families drift apart, connecting mostly by e-mail and telephone through marriages, remarriages, births, and deaths.

In January, Ms. Webb sent a letter to dozens of family members that read, in part: "Following a women's tradition that apparently dates back to the 1800s, if not way before, I'd like to make this new baby a welcome quilt in which he or she can be wrapped in the very fabric of our families' lives. A true family quilt and maybe a new family tradition."

C

In addition to a seven-inch square, the letter also asked family members to write a letter introducing themselves to the new child and telling him (they later found out it would be a boy) what was special about the fabric and design they were contributing.

And so the pieces of lives came by mail from all over the country. Scraps of tablecloths, shirts, baby blankets, bibs. Some of the pieces came from people connected to the baby by blood, some from people linked by marriage.

Ms. Webb used books to teach herself to make a quilt and turned her dining room into a sewing room.

She believes quilting is an idea for these times, as many people seek ways to have more family time and preserve family history.

"We lose track of where we came from. We lose track of the fabrics we wore, the cookie recipes, the fabric that covered the sofa in our parents' living room."

1. ***The Little Prince:*** classic children's book by Antoine de Saint-Exupéry (1900–1944).
2. **half siblings** *n.:* half sisters or half brothers.

DIRECT TEACHING

C Reading Informational Materials
GRADE-LEVEL STANDARD

? Using primary and secondary sources. What primary-source materials might the reporter have gathered for this article? [Possible responses: interviews with Mrs. Webb; observations of the quilt squares; studies of modern extended families.]

D Reading Informational Materials
GRADE-LEVEL STANDARD

Using primary and secondary sources. [Possible response to question: Many students will agree that families today connect primarily via telephone and e-mail. Some students will disagree that modern families "drift apart," citing their own tightly knit families or pointing out that telephone and e-mail help families to stay close despite physical distance.]

GUIDED PRACTICE

Monitoring students' progress. Have students brainstorm lists of possible primary and secondary sources for a report on a subject of interest to them, such as designing or making jewelry, ocean kayaking, or dancing professionally.

INDEPENDENT PRACTICE

Analyzing Informational Materials

Reading Check

1. *In Love and Trouble* was made from dresses she had worn that reflected her African heritage.
2. While she was quilting outdoors, he noticed her and came over to introduce himself.
3. She is making it to welcome her first grandchild, to preserve family history, and to start a new family tradition.

Test Practice

Answers and Model Rationales

1. **C** C is correct because it reflects Giovanni's overall concept. A and B are too general, and the idea in D is not expressed.
2. **H** Point out the word *all,* which shows that the best response is an idea found in each of the five sources. None refers to tediousness (F). Only the oral histories imply that quilting might be difficult (G). J is inaccurate; Giovanni makes it clear that quilting is low-cost.
3. **C** A, B, and D are all examples of primary sources.
4. **J** Students should recall that primary-source information can be confirmed by checking other sources.
5. **A** The oral history's conversational tone makes it most resemble an interview. A also happens to be the only primary source among the items listed. B, C, and D are all secondary sources.
6. **F** F is the best answer, as it is closely reflected in both the content and the title of the selection. G and H speak against quilting, which is clearly not the main idea of the piece. J is not mentioned in the selection.

Analyzing Informational Materials

Reading Check

1. What was the name of Alice Walker's first quilt, and what was it made from?
2. In "'Thinkin' on Marryin',' " how did the speaker meet the man she would later marry?
3. In "A Baby's Quilt to Sew Up the Generations," why is Marilyn Webb making her quilt?

Test Practice

1. Which statement best summarizes Nikki Giovanni's **main idea**?
   - **A** Quilts are beautiful.
   - **B** Quilts remind us of family and our heritage.
   - **C** African Americans created beauty with quilts and spirituals despite their bad circumstances.
   - **D** African Americans created quilts as a form of political and moral protest.

2. All of the quilters in these excerpts agree that quilting is —
   - **F** tedious
   - **G** difficult
   - **H** rewarding
   - **J** expensive

3. If you were writing a report on quilting and needed a **secondary source,** which would you choose?
   - **A** An autobiography of a quilter
   - **B** A collection of quilters' letters
   - **C** An encyclopedia article about quilting
   - **D** A speech about quilting

4. How can you **evaluate** whether the speaker in an oral history is telling the truth?
   - **F** By asking the interviewer
   - **G** By reading the text aloud
   - **H** By reading the text carefully
   - **J** By checking other sources

5. The **oral history** included here is most similar to which of the following kinds of sources?
   - **A** Interview
   - **B** Newspaper article
   - **C** Editorial
   - **D** Encyclopedia article

6. Which of the following *best* describes the **main idea** in "A Baby's Quilt to Sew Up the Generations"?
   - **F** A quilt can tie together an extended family living in many different places.
   - **G** Family quilts don't suit our modern styles.
   - **H** It's time to come up with new family traditions to replace older ones, like quilting.
   - **J** Many people own treasured family quilts.

Reading Standard 2.5 Extend ideas presented in primary or secondary sources through original analysis, evaluation, and elaboration.

7. In a secondary source such as a newspaper article, you can identify a speaker's exact words by observing the —
   A italic type
   B title and author of the source
   C paragraph breaks
   D quotation marks

8. If you were trying to find out what it might feel like to sew your own quilt, which kind of source would be *least* helpful?
   F An oral history
   G An interview
   H An encyclopedia article
   J A short story

Application

Plan a quilt that will show real-life events in your own life. Then, create some actual quilt squares (seven inches by seven inches) on white cotton fabric, on an old T-shirt, or even on a piece of paper. You can use permanent markers, fabric paint, or crayons to decorate your quilt squares. Your class can then assemble everyone's squares into a class quilt.

Grammar Link MINI-LESSON

Dialect: Nonstandard but Authentic

Language is a living thing—it changes over time and in different environments. The spoken form of a language can also differ in some cases from its standard written form.

The oral history "'Thinkin' on Marryin''" contains regional **dialect,** which is a way of speaking that is characteristic of a particular region or group of people. In this case the dialect can be heard in parts of the rural Southwest, where speakers typically don't pronounce the *g* in words ending in *–ing,* so that *morning* becomes *mornin'.* These speakers also use **colloquialisms,** or local expressions, like *reckon* (for *think*). **Nonstandard grammar** is also common, such as *they was* (instead of the standard *they were*).

In fiction a writer often includes regional dialect in dialogue to give a fuller, more precisely descriptive portrait of the characters or to give a more realistic sense of setting. In the oral history you have read here, the exact reproduction of the woman's speech patterns gives an authentic quality to the material.

PRACTICE 1

Look through the oral history, and find at least six examples of regional dialect. On a separate sheet of paper, write the standard-English equivalent next to each example. See the models below:

DIALECT	reckon
STANDARD ENGLISH	think
DIALECT	they was
STANDARD ENGLISH	they were

PRACTICE 2

Try this experiment: Take a paragraph from the oral history, and rewrite it in standard English, without the dialect. What is lost?

➤ **For more help, see Varieties of American English in the *Holt Handbook,* pages 518–519.**

7. D Students should recognize that quotation marks enclose speakers' exact words in newspaper articles.

8. H Point out the word *least* in the question. Students should realize that a factual source such as an encyclopedia does not include subjective impressions.

Test-Taking Tips

Tell students to check questions for key words, such as *not* and *all,* and to choose answers accordingly. For more information on how to answer multiple-choice items, refer students to **Test Smarts.**

Grammar Link

Practice 1

Possible Answers

1. *Dialect*—"She didn't never let nobody else touch her quilts." *Standard English*—She never let anyone else touch her quilts.
2. *Dialect*—"I can tell you how plain I recall the day." *Standard English*—I can tell you how plainly I recall the day.
3. *Dialect*—"Papa come in about that time." *Standard English*—Papa came in about that time.
4. *Dialect*—". . . one of them old open houses . . ." *Standard English*—one of those old open houses.
5. *Dialect*—". . . We all done a lot of that." *Standard English*—We all did a lot of that.
6. *Dialect*—"I was . . . settin' there under that quiltin' arbor." *Standard English*—I was sitting there under that quilting arbor.

Practice 2

Possible rewrite:

Anyway, I was sitting there under that quilting arbor one spring afternoon, April fourteenth, just quilting and dreaming a dream on every stitch and just planning who might share them with me.

[Students may say that the rewritten paragraph has lost some of its individuality, its regional identity, or its intimacy.]

ASSESSING

Assessment

- *Progress Assessment of Reading*
  - Selection Test

RETEACHING

For a lesson reteaching Standard 2.5, see **Reteaching,** p. 939A. For another selection to teach Standard 2.5, see *Interactive Reading,* Part 2.

STANDARDS FOCUS, pp. 96–97

(For the grade-level standard taught in this lesson, see Student Edition, p. 96.)

Prerequisite Standard

- Grade 8, Literary Response and Analysis 3.2 **Evaluate the structural elements of the plot (e.g., subplots, parallel episodes, climax), the plot's development, and the way in which conflicts are (or are not) addressed and resolved.**

Literary Focus: Character Interactions

Write the following questions on the chalkboard: "Why is she laughing at me?" "Why did he say that?" and "Why can't they just lighten up?" Remind students that we all spend a part of each day trying to figure out why people act the way they do, especially when the behavior isn't in keeping with what we know or expect. Invite students to imagine a loyal friend suddenly becoming harshly critical. Ask students what questions they might consider posing to try to understand the friend's behavior. [Possible responses: What else is going on in the friend's life? What feelings might be motivating the friend?] Point out that in a good story, the major characters are so believable that readers can ask—and answer—these same kinds of questions.

Literary Response and Analysis

Character Interactions *by* John Leggett

RELATIONSHIPS AND CONFLICTS

The Protagonist

A story that puts its emphasis on revealing character is likely to be a story of higher quality than a simple narrative with an action-packed plot. Of course, we all enjoy these plots: We are gripped by the adventures of the rancher who faces an army of flesh-eating ants, and we fear for the spy caught as a double agent. Yet the main concern of literature is more often the portrayal of character rather than action itself.

Most stories have a main character, called the **protagonist,** who is the focus of our attention. In a good story the protagonist is a realistic, complicated human being with just enough strengths, weaknesses, and contradictions to remind us of ourselves.

Conflict: It Drives the Plot

As a rule, a story's plot gets underway when the protagonist wants something and sets out to get it. The **antagonist** in a story is the character or force that blocks the protagonist from achieving his or her goal.

The **conflict** between the protagonist and the antagonist is what hooks our interest, creates suspense, and drives the plot of most stories. This struggle is an example of **external conflict,** since it involves a conflict between the protagonist and some outside force. This outside force might be another character or group, society as a whole, or even something in nature. In an **internal conflict** the protagonist wrestles with his or her own fear or worry or the need to make a decision.

Reading Standard 3.3 Analyze interactions between main and subordinate characters in a literary text (e.g., internal and external conflicts, motivations, relationships, influences) and explain the way those interactions affect the plot.

Protagonists and antagonists rarely inhabit a story alone. We also meet friends, neighbors, family members, even passing strangers. These **subordinate characters** may not seem as important as the protagonist, but they're in the story for a reason. The main character's relationship with a subordinate character helps to reveal the protagonist's character and may also help develop the story's conflict. (A young man refuses to fight with a bully despite his classmates' jeers. He is in conflict with the bully—his antagonist—as well as with his classmates—subordinate characters.)

Dynamic Characters and Static Characters

The protagonist of a story is almost always a **dynamic character**—someone who changes in an important way during the course of the story. By the end of the story, a dynamic character has gained a new understanding, made an important decision, or taken a crucial action. Dynamic characters are capable of growing, learning, and changing.

In contrast, subordinate characters are almost always **static characters,** exactly the same at the end of the story as they are at the beginning. Static characters do not necessarily represent failures of the writer's art. In good fiction static characters are supposed to be static. Too many characters undergoing important changes would be distracting, especially in a short story, where we want to focus on what is happening to the main character.

The change that a dynamic character

DIFFERENTIATING INSTRUCTION

Learners Having Difficulty

Character and conflict. Using the tale "The Boy Who Cried Wolf," guide students in identifying the protagonist [the shepherd boy], the antagonist [the wolf], the boy's motivations [he wants attention, and he must keep his sheep safe], and the conflict [the wolf attacks the flock, but the townspeople ignore the boy's cries]. Ask students whether the boy is a static or a dynamic character and how they know. [static, because it is not clear that he learns a lesson]

Advanced Learners

Acceleration. This activity can help to move students toward the eleventh- and twelfth-grade Standard 3.2, for which they analyze the way a theme represents a view on life and provide evidence to support the claim.

96 Chapter 2 Character • Using Primary and Secondary Sources

undergoes (he learns not to be so arrogant; she learns not to be so jealous of her younger sister) must be **believable.** It should not be some miraculous, magic-wand transformation that neatly wraps up the plot. When that change is believable, it provides the key to understanding the character and also the best clue to the story's **meaning.**

Motivation: What Makes Characters Tick

One of the ways writers make characters believable is by showing what **motivates** them to act as they do. Unless we understand *why* an otherwise dutiful daughter suddenly lashes out at her mother, her behavior will strike us as inconsistent and unbelievable. However, once we recognize the need the daughter is trying to satisfy (say, to punish someone—anyone she can get her hands on—for the way her boyfriend has been ignoring her), her behavior begins to make sense. She is no longer the two-dimensional "dutiful daughter" but seems more like a real person—someone who is usually kind but who is also capable of cruelty.

Writers seldom state a character's motives directly. (She screams at her mother because Bill, her boyfriend, has been flirting with Jana, her best friend.) Instead, writers imply what those motives are—maybe even scattering clues throughout the story—and trust their readers to make inferences about why their characters act the way they do.

Trying to understand the motivation of characters in literature can be as puzzling and as satisfying as trying to understand people's motives in real life. While we know that real people often surprise us with their behavior, we also know that there are probably reasons for what they do and say. In real life we may never find out what those reasons are. In fiction we do.

"O.K., so I dig a hole and put the bone in the hole. But what's my motivation for burying it?"

Practice

Work with a partner to analyze a short story you have read recently. Use this data bank:

Data Bank
Main character:
What main character wants (motivation):
Relationship with subordinate character(s):
Conflict:
Resolution:
How main character changes:

Practice

If students cannot think of a story to analyze, suggest that they use a well-known myth in which a character learns a lesson, such as "King Midas and the Golden Touch."

Possible diagram entries:

Main character—King Midas.

What main character wants (motivation)—gold.

Relationship with subordinate character(s)—He loves just one person in the whole world: his daughter.

Conflict—Acquires the golden touch but accidentally turns his daughter to lifeless gold.

Resolution—Gives up the golden touch; daughter returns to life.

How main character changes—Learns that some things (like love) are more important than riches.

Apply

Have students fill out a data bank diagram for a movie they all know. Then, in a class discussion, ask them to analyze the motivations of the protagonist and antagonist (Are they clear? Are they realistic?); to decide whether the protagonist is static or dynamic; and to evaluate whether the movie's conflict and resolution are believable.

Resources Reminder

Differentiating Instruction

- *Lesson Plans for Language Development*

For additional instruction on character interactions for English-language learners and special education students, see *Lesson Plans for Language Development,* pp. 45, 46.

Activity. Point out that readers can infer a story's theme by seeing how the main character changes. Have students add one more box labeled "Theme" to the data bank diagram they create for the Practice on p. 97. Ask each student to formulate a sentence for the Theme box, expressing a view or comment on life that is reflected in the conflict and the change of the main character. For example, if the main character first rejects but later accepts a new way of doing things, the theme statement might express the value of flexibility. Have students share and explain their statements of theme, presenting evidence to support their ideas.

STANDARDS FOCUS, pp. 98–111

(For grade-level and review standards taught in this lesson, see citations on Student Edition pages.)

Prerequisite Standard

- Grade 8, Literary Response and Analysis 3.2 **Evaluate the structural elements of the plot (e.g., subplots, parallel episodes, climax), the plot's development, and the way in which conflicts are (or are not) addressed and resolved.**

Reading Skills

- Make inferences.

Summary *at grade level*

In "Two Kinds" a conflict arises in a Chinese American family when a strong-willed mother bent on seeing her child succeed is confronted by an equally determined daughter, who simply wants to be herself. As her mother pushes her to be a prodigy, Jing-mei is motivated to please her but becomes demoralized and angry after several failures. When her mother signs her up for piano lessons, Jing-mei gives the appearance of going along with her mother's wishes; but privately she resists, and her performance at a local talent show is an embarrassing disaster. At the climax her mother demands that she practice more, and Jing-mei rebels, lashing out cruelly. Jing-mei clings to the right to fail and be unexceptional until, at age thirty, she gratefully accepts the family piano from her mother as a peace offering.

Before You Read

Two Kinds

Literary Focus

Conflict and Motivation: Blocked Desires

Conflict is struggle. In a story a conflict can be **internal**—inside a character's mind—or **external**—in the outside world. The deepest conflicts are both internal and external. You may, for example, have difficulty making an important decision yet argue with a parent who wants to make the decision for you.

Conflict and motivation are closely tied. When actors study their parts in a movie, they ask themselves and the director, "Why do I do this?" What they're asking about is **motivation,** or the reasons for a character's behavior. When a character is motivated to fulfill a certain desire and that desire is blocked in some way, a conflict occurs. Conflicts often arise in close relationships, where people are strongly motivated to influence each other—relationships like the one between the mother and daughter in this story.

Reading Skills

Making Inferences About Motivation

Reading Standard 3.3 Analyze interactions between main and subordinate characters in a literary text (e.g., internal and external conflicts, motivations, relationships, influences) and explain the way those interactions affect the plot.

Understanding motivation is important for anyone—actor or writer—who wants to create a convincing character, and it's important for readers too. To understand a character's motivation, you must make **inferences,** or intelligent guesses. You base your inferences on clues from the text. You think about the character's actions and words, and you observe how others react to the character. Using these clues—and your own life experiences with people—think about what motivates both Jing-mei and her mother in this story, which takes place in San Francisco's Chinatown in the 1960s.

Make the Connection

Quickwrite

Conflicts often arise between what we want to do and what others want for us. Has anyone ever expected you to do something you really didn't want to do? Write about your experience and how you felt before, during, and after it.

Vocabulary Development

prodigy (präd′ə·jē) *n.:* child of highly unusual talent or genius.

lamented (lə·ment′id) *v.:* said with regret or sorrow. *Lamented* also means "mourned for; regretted intensely."

listlessly (list′lis·lē) *adv.:* without energy or interest.

mesmerizing (mez′mər·īz′iŋ) *v.* used as *adj.:* spellbinding; fascinating.

discordant (dis·kôrd′′nt) *adj.:* clashing; not in harmony.

dawdled (dôd′′ld) *v.:* wasted time; lingered.

stricken (strik′ən) *adj.:* heartbroken; affected by or suffering from something painful or distressing.

fiasco (fē·as′kō) *n.:* total failure.

nonchalantly (nän′shə·länt′lē) *adv.:* without interest or concern; indifferently.

betrayal (bē·trā′əl) *n.:* failure to fulfill another's hopes. *Betrayal* also means "act of disloyalty; deception."

RESOURCES: READING

Planning

- *One-Stop Planner* CD-ROM with Test Generator
- *On Course: Mapping Instruction*

Media

- *Audio CD Library*
  - disc 4
- *Visual Connections*
  - Videocassette, Segment 2

Reading

- *Interactive Reading,* Teacher's Edition
  - Graphic Organizer: Motivation-Conflict Chart

Differentiating Instruction

- *Lesson Plans for Language Development*
  - English-Language Learners, pp. 47–49, 59, 63
  - Special Education Students, pp. 50, 59, 63

Two Kinds

Amy Tan

"I'll never be the kind of daughter you want me to be!"

My mother believed you could be anything you wanted to be in America. You could open a restaurant. You could work for the government and get good retirement. You could buy a house with almost no money down. You could become rich. You could become instantly famous.

"Of course you can be prodigy, too," my mother told me when I was nine. "You can be best anything. What does Auntie Lindo know? Her daughter, she is only best tricky." **A**

America was where all my mother's hopes lay. She had come here in 1949 after losing everything in China: her mother and father, her family home, her first husband, and two daughters, twin baby girls. But she never looked back with regret. There were so many ways for things to get better.

We didn't immediately pick the right kind of prodigy. At first my mother thought I could be a Chinese Shirley Temple.[1] We'd watch Shirley's old movies on TV as though they were training films. My mother would poke my arm and say, "*Ni kan*"—You watch. And I would see Shirley tapping her feet, or singing a sailor song, or pursing her lips into a very round O while saying, "Oh my goodness."

"*Ni kan*," said my mother as Shirley's eyes flooded with tears. "You already know how. Don't need talent for crying!"

1. **Shirley Temple** (1928–): child movie star who was popular during the 1930s. Mothers all across the United States tried to set their daughters' hair to look like Shirley Temple's sausage curls.

Vocabulary
prodigy (präd′ə·jē) *n.:* child of highly unusual talent or genius.

PRETEACHING

Selection Starter

Motivate. Chinese American culture plays a key role in the conflict and motivations of the characters in "Two Kinds." Before students read the selection, familiarize them with this context by showing them "Chinese Americans: Culture and Contributions," Videocassette, Segment 2.

Preview Vocabulary

To build students' familiarity with the Vocabulary words, give volunteers the following exercises:

1. Explain why a fiasco might occur if firefighters dawdled. [Possible response: If a fire crew wastes time, a fire can spread.]
2. Imitate a dog that lamented by making discordant sounds. [Students might howl.]
3. Demonstrate the difference between responding nonchalantly and responding listlessly. [Students should show a lack of interest, but in responding listlessly, they should also show a lack of energy.]
4. Name a media star who was stricken over a betrayal. [Students might name any recently jilted star.]
5. Why might an audience find it mesmerizing to see a prodigy perform? [Possible response: Usually it takes time to develop a skill, so it is fascinating to see someone very young who can already perform at a high level.]

DIRECT TEACHING

A Literary Focus
GRADE-LEVEL STANDARD

Conflict and motivation. What does this background suggest about the mother's reasons for urging her daughter to excel? [Possible responses: The mother wants her daughter to live the American dream; the mother wants to compensate for tragic losses she herself has suffered.]

Vocabulary
- *Vocabulary Development*
  - Vocabulary Worksheet, p. 8

Assessment
- *Progress Assessment of Reading*
  - Selection Test
- *One-Stop Planner* CD-ROM with Test Generator

DIRECT TEACHING

A Reading Skills

Making inferences about motivation. To model inferring the narrator's motivation, read aloud this passage describing Jing-mei's fantasies. Point out that a star ballerina gets special attention and that Cinderella starts out humble and ignored but ends up surprising everyone with her beauty. Then say, "From these clues and from my own experience, I can infer that the narrator would like to be the center of attention and surprise everyone with her hidden talents."

B Literary Focus
GRADE-LEVEL STANDARD

? Conflict and motivation. What motivates Jing-mei to try to become a prodigy as her mother wants? [Possible responses: she wants her parents' unconditional love and approval; she fears being reproached for being ordinary.]

C Literary Focus
GRADE-LEVEL STANDARD

? Conflict and motivation. How can you tell from this passage that the mother is determined? [She works hard, cleaning many houses each week; she has learned to read English; she reads many magazines, looking for a prodigy her daughter can outdo.] How does her determination affect the narrator? [It puts pressure on her.]

Soon after my mother got this idea about Shirley Temple, she took me to a beauty training school in the Mission district and put me in the hands of a student who could barely hold the scissors without shaking. Instead of getting big fat curls, I emerged with an uneven mass of crinkly black fuzz. My mother dragged me off to the bathroom and tried to wet down my hair.

"You look like Negro Chinese," she lamented, as if I had done this on purpose.

The instructor of the beauty training school had to lop off these soggy clumps to make my hair even again. "Peter Pan is very popular these days," the instructor assured my mother. I now had hair the length of a boy's, with straight-across bangs that hung at a slant two inches above my eyebrows. I liked the haircut and it made me actually look forward to my future fame.

In fact, in the beginning, I was just as excited as my mother, maybe even more so. I pictured this prodigy part of me as many different images, trying each one on for size. I was a dainty ballerina girl standing by the curtains, waiting to hear the right music that would send me floating on my tiptoes. I was like the Christ child lifted out of the straw manger, crying with holy indignity.[2] I was Cinderella stepping from her pumpkin carriage with sparkly cartoon music filling the air.

In all of my imaginings, I was filled with a sense that I would soon become *perfect.* My mother and father would adore me. I would be beyond reproach. I would never feel the need to sulk for anything.

But sometimes the prodigy in me became impatient. "If you don't hurry up and get me out of here, I'm disappearing for good," it warned. "And then you'll always be nothing."

Every night after dinner, my mother and I would sit at the Formica kitchen table. She would present new tests, taking her examples from stories of amazing children she had read in *Ripley's Believe It or Not,* or *Good Housekeeping, Reader's Digest,* and a dozen other magazines she kept in a pile in our bathroom. My mother got these magazines from people whose houses she cleaned. And since she cleaned many houses each week, we had a great assortment. She would look through them all, searching for stories about remarkable children.

The first night she brought out a story about a three-year-old boy who knew the capitals of all the states and even most of the European countries. A teacher was quoted as saying the little boy could also pronounce the names of the foreign cities correctly.

"What's the capital of Finland?" my mother asked me, looking at the magazine story.

All I knew was the capital of California, because Sacramento was the name of the street we lived on in Chinatown. "Nairobi!"[3] I guessed, saying the most foreign word I could think of. She checked to see if that was possibly one way to pronounce "Helsinki" before showing me the answer.

The tests got harder—multiplying numbers in my head, finding the queen of hearts in a deck of cards, trying to stand on my head without using my hands, predicting the daily temperatures in Los Angeles, New York, and London.

One night I had to look at a page from the Bible for three minutes and then report everything I could remember. "Now Jehoshaphat had riches and honor in abundance and . . . that's all I remember, Ma," I said.

And after seeing my mother's disappointed face once again, something inside of me began to die. I hated the tests, the raised hopes and failed expectations. Before going to bed that night, I

2. **indignity** (in·dig′nə·tē) *n.:* loss of dignity or honor.

3. **Nairobi** (nī·rō′bē): capital of Kenya, a nation in Africa.

Vocabulary

lamented (lə·ment′id) *v.:* said with regret or sorrow. *Lamented* also means "mourned or grieved for; regretted intensely."

DIFFERENTIATING INSTRUCTION

Learners Having Difficulty

Modeling. To help students read "Two Kinds," model the reading skill of making inferences about motivation. Say, "You learn that a woman has lost everything in a war. Knowing this and knowing human nature, you might infer that she is motivated to make up for what she lost." Have students consider this question as they read: What do this character's words and actions hint about the things she really wants?

English-Language Learners

Be sure students understand that the story is set in the 1960s in San Francisco and that the parents are Chinese immigrants. Explain that Amy Tan represents the mother's Chinese American dialect by omitting the articles *a, an,* and *the* from the mother's speech.

Resources Reminder

For lessons designed for English-language learners and special education students, see *Lesson Plans for Language Development,* pp. 47–50, 59, 63.

100 Chapter 2 Character • Using Primary and Secondary Sources

looked in the mirror above the bathroom sink and when I saw only my face staring back—and that it would always be this ordinary face—I began to cry. Such a sad, ugly girl! I made high-pitched noises like a crazed animal, trying to scratch out the face in the mirror.

And then I saw what seemed to be the prodigy side of me—because I had never seen that face before. I looked at my reflection, blinking so I could see more clearly. The girl staring back at me was angry, powerful. This girl and I were the same. I had new thoughts, willful thoughts, or rather thoughts filled with lots of won'ts. I won't let her change me, I promised myself. I won't be what I'm not.

Chinatown, San Francisco, at night.

So now, on nights when my mother presented her tests, I performed listlessly, my head propped on one arm. I pretended to be bored. And I was. I got so bored I started counting the bellows of the foghorns out on the bay while my mother drilled me in other areas. The sound was comforting and reminded me of the cow jumping over the moon. And the next day, I played a game with myself, seeing if my mother would give up on me before eight bellows. After a while I usually counted only one, maybe two bellows at most. At last she was beginning to give up hope.

Two or three months had gone by without any mention of my being a prodigy again. And then one day my mother was watching *The Ed Sullivan Show* on TV. The TV was old and the sound kept shorting out. Every time my mother got halfway up from the sofa to adjust the set, the sound would go back on and Ed would be talking. As soon as she sat down, Ed would go silent again. She got up, the TV broke into loud piano music. She sat down. Silence. Up and

Vocabulary
listlessly (list′lis · lē) *adv.:* without energy or interest.

DIRECT TEACHING

D Reading Skills

Making inferences about motivation. Why does the narrator become angry and determined to resist her mother's expectations? [Possible response: Her mother's disappointment makes the narrator miserable, then resentful. The narrator wants to find her own identity rather than keep trying unsuccessfully to fulfill her mother's ambitions for her.]

E Content-Area Connections

Culture: Popular Culture
Students may not know that *The Ed Sullivan Show* was one of the most popular variety shows of the 1950s and '60s. It introduced Americans to the Beatles and set a television ratings record with the appeareance of the rock-and-roll musician Elvis Presley.

Advanced Learners
Acceleration. Use the following activity to help move students toward the eleventh- and twelfth-grade Standard 3.2, which calls for them to analyze the way the theme of a selection represents a view or a comment on life.
Activity. Ask students to meet in small groups to discuss questions like these:

- What does the narrator want? How has she changed by the end of the story?
- How would you state the theme of the story?
- What is Amy Tan's opinion of the characters' behavior?
- What does this story reveal about the writer's attitude toward life and the world?

DIRECT TEACHING

A Reading Skills

Making inferences about motivation. Given what you know about the mother, what do you think she will be motivated to do after seeing this child perform on *The Ed Sullivan Show?* [Possible response: The mother will decide to have her daughter take piano lessons.]

B Reading Skills

Interpreting. How does the speaker know she has just said the wrong thing? [Possible responses: She knows how her mother feels and can predict her reactions; perhaps her mother's facial expression tells her.]

C Learners Having Difficulty

Finding details. Earlier the narrator said she "wasn't worried" about being forced to take piano lessons, because her family didn't own a piano and could not afford lessons. How does her mother overcome these obstacles? [She barters housecleaning services for weekly lessons and daily practice time with a retired piano teacher who lives in the building.]

D Literary Focus
GRADE-LEVEL STANDARD

Conflict and motivation. Why is the narrator so angry with her mother, even though her mother works so hard for her? [Possible responses: She feels that her mother's expectations are too high to meet; she wants to be accepted for who she is.]

E Literary Focus
GRADE-LEVEL STANDARD

Conflict and motivation. How does the mother explain her motivations? [She says she just wants to help the daughter fulfill her own potential.]

---

down, back and forth, quiet and loud. It was like a stiff embraceless dance between her and the TV set. Finally she stood by the set with her hand on the sound dial.

She seemed entranced by the music, a little frenzied piano piece with this mesmerizing quality, sort of quick passages and then teasing, lilting[4] ones before it returned to the quick, playful parts.

"*Ni kan,*" my mother said, calling me over with hurried hand gestures. "Look here."

I could see why my mother was fascinated by the music. It was being pounded out by a little Chinese girl, about nine years old, with a Peter Pan haircut. The girl had the sauciness[5] of a Shirley Temple. She was proudly modest like a proper Chinese child. And she also did this fancy sweep of a curtsy, so that the fluffy skirt of her white dress cascaded slowly to the floor like the petals of a large carnation.

> "I'm *not* a genius! I can't play the piano."

In spite of these warning signs, I wasn't worried. Our family had no piano and we couldn't afford to buy one, let alone reams[6] of sheet music and piano lessons. So I could be generous in my comments when my mother bad-mouthed the little girl on TV.

"Play note right, but doesn't sound good! No singing sound," complained my mother.

"What are you picking on her for?" I said carelessly. "She's pretty good. Maybe she's not the best, but she's trying hard." I knew almost immediately I would be sorry I said that.

"Just like you," she said. "Not the best. Because you not trying." She gave a little huff as she let go of the sound dial and sat down on the sofa.

The little Chinese girl sat down also to play an encore of "Anitra's Dance" by Grieg.[7] I remember the song, because later on I had to learn how to play it.

Three days after watching *The Ed Sullivan Show,* my mother told me what my schedule would be for piano lessons and piano practice. She had talked to Mr. Chong, who lived on the first floor of our apartment building. Mr. Chong was a retired piano teacher, and my mother had traded housecleaning services for weekly lessons and a piano for me to practice on every day, two hours a day, from four until six.

When my mother told me this, I felt as though I had been sent to hell. I whined and then kicked my foot a little when I couldn't stand it anymore.

"Why don't you like me the way I am? I'm *not* a genius! I can't play the piano. And even if I could, I wouldn't go on TV if you paid me a million dollars!" I cried.

My mother slapped me. "Who ask you be genius?" she shouted. "Only ask you be your best. For you sake. You think I want you be genius? Hnnh! What for! Who ask you!"

"So ungrateful," I heard her mutter in Chinese. "If she had as much talent as she has temper, she would be famous now."

Mr. Chong, whom I secretly nicknamed Old Chong, was very strange, always tapping his fingers to the silent music of an invisible orchestra. He looked ancient in my eyes. He had lost most of the hair on top of his head and he wore thick glasses and had eyes that always looked tired and sleepy. But he must have been younger than I

4. **lilting** *adj.:* with a light, graceful rhythm.
5. **sauciness** (sô′sē·nis) *n.:* liveliness.
6. **reams** *n.:* here, great amount. A ream of paper is about five hundred sheets.
7. **Grieg** (grĕg): Edvard Grieg (1843–1907), Norwegian composer. "Anitra's Dance" is from his *Peer Gynt Suite.*

Vocabulary
mesmerizing (mez′mər·īz′iŋ) *v.* used as *adj.:* spellbinding; fascinating.

READING MINI-LESSON

Developing Word-Attack Skills

Tell students that George Bernard Shaw once observed that there are so many different sound-letter correspondences in English that *fish* could just as well be spelled *ghoti—gh* for /f/, as in *cough; o* for /i/, as in *women;* and *ti* for /sh/, as in *action.* Point out that of the three letter-sound correspondences in *ghoti, ti* for /sh/ is the most common. It occurs in every word that ends with *–tion.* Ask students for examples of words that end with *–tion* (/shən/). Examples from "Two Kinds" include *expectations, mention, carnation,* and *motions.*

Point out that *ti* represents /sh/ in other contexts as well. Display the following words, and have students read them aloud:

patience partial sequential pretentious

102 Chapter 2 Character • Using Primary and Secondary Sources

thought, since he lived with his mother and was not yet married.

I met Old Lady Chong once and that was enough. She had this peculiar smell like a baby that had done something in its pants. And her fingers felt like a dead person's, like an old peach I once found in the back of the refrigerator; the skin just slid off the meat when I picked it up.

I soon found out why Old Chong had retired from teaching piano. He was deaf. "Like Beethoven!" he shouted to me. "We're both listening only in our head!" And he would start to conduct his frantic silent sonatas.[8]

Our lessons went like this. He would open the book and point to different things, explaining their purpose: "Key! Treble! Bass! No sharps or flats! So this is C major! Listen now and play after me!"

And then he would play the C scale a few times, a simple chord, and then, as if inspired by an old, unreachable itch, he gradually added more notes and running trills and a pounding bass until the music was really something quite grand.

I would play after him, the simple scale, the simple chord, and then I just played some nonsense that sounded like a cat running up and down on top of garbage cans. Old Chong smiled and applauded and then said, "Very good! But now you must learn to keep time!"

So that's how I discovered that Old Chong's eyes were too slow to keep up with the wrong notes I was playing. He went through the motions in half-time. To help me keep rhythm, he stood behind me, pushing down on my right shoulder for every beat. He balanced pennies on top of my wrists so I would keep them still as I slowly played scales and arpeggios.[9] He had me curve my hand around an apple and keep that shape when playing chords. He marched stiffly to show me how to make each finger dance up and down, staccato,[10] like an obedient little soldier. **F**

He taught me all these things, and that was how I also learned I could be lazy and get away with mistakes, lots of mistakes. If I hit the wrong notes because I hadn't practiced enough, I never corrected myself. I just kept playing in rhythm. And Old Chong kept conducting his own private reverie.[11]

So maybe I never really gave myself a fair chance. I did pick up the basics pretty quickly, and I might have become a good pianist at that young age. But I was so determined not to try, not to be anybody different, that I learned to play only the most earsplitting preludes, the most discordant hymns. **G**

Over the next year, I practiced like this, dutifully in my own way. And then one day I heard my mother and her friend Lindo Jong both talking in a loud bragging tone of voice so others could hear. It was after church, and I was leaning against the brick wall, wearing a dress with stiff white petticoats. Auntie Lindo's daughter, Waverly, who was about my age, was standing farther down the wall, about five feet away. We had grown up together and shared all the closeness of two sisters squabbling over crayons and dolls. In other words, for the most part, we hated each other. I thought she was snotty. Waverly Jong had gained a certain amount of fame as "Chinatown's Littlest Chinese Chess Champion."

"She bring home too many trophy," lamented Auntie Lindo that Sunday. "All day she play chess. All day I have no time do nothing but dust off her winnings." She threw a scolding look at Waverly, who pretended not to see her.

8. **sonatas** (sə·nät′əz) *n.:* musical compositions, usually for one or two instruments.
9. **arpeggios** (är·pej′ōz) *n.:* chords whose notes are played quickly one after another, rather than at the same time.
10. **staccato** (stə·kät′ō) *adv.:* with clear-cut breaks between notes.
11. **reverie** (rev′ə·rē) *n.:* daydream.

Vocabulary
discordant (dis·kôrd′'nt) *adj.:* clashing; not in harmony.

DIRECT TEACHING

F Vocabulary Development
REVIEW STANDARD

Context clues: Comparison and contrast. What comparisons in this passage can help you figure out the meaning of the word *staccato?* ["marched stiffly" and "like an obedient little soldier"]

G Literary Focus
GRADE-LEVEL STANDARD

Conflict and motivation. Looking back as an adult, the narrator thinks that she might have become a good pianist if she had tried. Why didn't she try? [She was determined not to excel because she felt that her mother was trying to change her; the narrator wanted to be accepted as the average person she thought she was.]

Help students make the generalization that *ti* represents /sh/ when *ti* precedes a vowel.
Activity. Write the following sets of words on the chalkboard. Have students read each set aloud and identify the word in which *ti* represents /sh/. Answers are underlined.

1. practical	<u>palatial</u>	particle
2. <u>potential</u>	tentative	identical
3. satisfy	<u>satiable</u>	satirical
4. pathetic	patina	<u>patient</u>
5. <u>auction</u>	authentic	autism
6. <u>initial</u>	intimate	institute
7. mantis	matinee	<u>martial</u>
8. contiguous	<u>contentious</u>	continual

DIRECT TEACHING

A Reading Skills

Making inferences about motivation. Why do the mothers complain about the "problems" they have with their daughters? [Possible response: It is their way of boasting indirectly.] What does this conversation tell you about one of the mother's motivations for pressuring Jing-mei to be a prodigy? [The mother is competing with her friend, whose daughter is a chess prodigy.]

B Literary Focus
GRADE-LEVEL STANDARD

Conflict and motivation. So far Jing-mei's mother has shown great determination to make her daughter a prodigy. Now we learn that Jing-mei may be just as determined to thwart her mother. How might their matching levels of determination heighten their conflict? [Possible response: If the mother keeps pushing Jing-mei to excel at piano, Jing-mei may rebel and refuse.]

C Advanced Learners

Acceleration. Tell students that a symbol stands for something beyond itself. "Pleading Child" is a real piece of music, but Tan also uses the title for symbolic value. How might the title "Pleading Child" symbolize Jing-mei's feelings? [Possible response: Jing-mei's resistance is a plea for the right to shape her own identity and for acceptance.]

D Reading Skills

Making inferences about motivation. As she is about to play, Jing-mei feels confident and excited, though earlier she acted as if she didn't care about performing. What do Jing-mei's thoughts suggest about her willingness to make her mother's dream come true? [Possible response: A part of Jing-mei still shares her mother's dream. Jing-mei is seduced by the fantasy of being loved and admired with no effort on her part.]

"You lucky you don't have this problem," said Auntie Lindo with a sigh to my mother.

A And my mother squared her shoulders and bragged: "Our problem worser than yours. If we ask Jing-mei wash dish, she hear nothing but music. It's like you can't stop this natural talent."

B And right then, I was determined to put a stop to her foolish pride.

A few weeks later, Old Chong and my mother conspired to have me play in a talent show which would be held in the church hall. By then, my parents had saved up enough to buy me a secondhand piano, a black Wurlitzer spinet with a scarred bench. It was the showpiece of our living room.

C For the talent show, I was to play a piece called "Pleading Child" from Schumann's[12] *Scenes from Childhood.* It was a simple, moody piece that sounded more difficult than it was. I was supposed to memorize the whole thing, playing the repeat parts twice to make the piece sound longer. But I dawdled over it, playing a few bars and then cheating, looking up to see what notes followed. I never really listened to what I was playing. I daydreamed about being somewhere else, about being someone else.

The part I liked to practice best was the fancy curtsy: right foot out, touch the rose on the carpet with a pointed foot, sweep to the side, left leg bends, look up and smile.

My parents invited all the couples from the Joy Luck Club[13] to witness my debut.[14] Auntie Lindo and Uncle Tin were there. Waverly and her two older brothers had also come. The first two rows were filled with children both younger and older than I was. The littlest ones got to go first. They recited simple nursery rhymes, squawked out tunes on miniature violins, twirled Hula-Hoops,[15] pranced in pink ballet tutus,[16] and when they bowed or curtsied, the audience would sigh in unison, "Awww," and then clap enthusiastically.

D When my turn came, I was very confident. I remember my childish excitement. It was as if I knew, without a doubt, that the prodigy side of me really did exist. I had no fear whatsoever, no nervousness. I remember thinking to myself, This is it! This is it! I looked out over the audience, at my mother's blank face, my father's yawn, Auntie Lindo's stiff-lipped smile, Waverly's sulky expression. I had on a white dress layered with sheets of lace, and a pink bow in my Peter Pan haircut. As I sat down I envisioned people jumping to their feet and Ed Sullivan rushing up to introduce me to everyone on TV.

And I started to play. It was so beautiful. I was so caught up in how lovely I looked that at first I didn't worry how I would sound. So it was a surprise to me when I hit the first wrong note and I realized something didn't sound quite right. And then I hit another, and another followed that. A chill started at the top of my head and began to trickle down. Yet I couldn't stop playing, as though my hands were bewitched. I kept thinking my fingers would adjust themselves back, like a train switching to the right track. I played this strange jumble through two repeats, the sour notes staying with me all the way to the end.

When I stood up, I discovered my legs were shaking. Maybe I had just been nervous and the audience, like Old Chong, had seen me go through the right motions and had not heard anything wrong at all. I swept my right foot out, went down on my knee, looked up and smiled.

12. **Schumann** (sho͞o′män): Robert Schumann (1810–1856), German composer.
13. **Joy Luck Club:** social club to which Jing-mei's mother and three other Chinese mothers belong.
14. **debut** (dā·byo͞o′) *n.:* first appearance in public of a performer.
15. **Hula-Hoops** (ho͞o′lə ho͞ops′): trademark for plastic hoops usually twirled around the hips.
16. **tutus** (to͞o′to͞oz′) *n.:* short skirts worn by ballerinas.

Vocabulary
dawdled (dôd′'ld) *v.:* wasted time; lingered.

CONTENT-AREA CONNECTIONS

History: From China to America

The character of Jing-mei's mother was formed in part by her experiences as a refugee during China's bloody civil war of 1946–1949, when Communists revolted against the Nationalist government. Chinese immigration to the United States had been limited by severe quotas. After China's fall to the Communists, however, more than 15,000 Chinese refugees were allowed to enter the United States in the 1950s and '60s.

Small-group activity. Have groups of students research China's civil war and the increase in Chinese immigration to the United States, especially to West Coast cities. Have groups prepare multimedia reports including photographs, maps, and graphs to show the effects of the war on China and the United States.

104 Chapter 2 Character • Using Primary and Secondary Sources

The room was quiet, except for Old Chong, who was beaming and shouting, "Bravo! Bravo! Well done!" But then I saw my mother's face, her stricken face. The audience clapped weakly, and as I walked back to my chair, with my whole face quivering as I tried not to cry, I heard a little boy whisper loudly to his mother, "That was awful," and the mother whispered back, "Well, she certainly tried."

And now I realized how many people were in the audience, the whole world it seemed. I was aware of eyes burning into my back. I felt the shame of my mother and father as they sat stiffly throughout the rest of the show.

We could have escaped during intermission. Pride and some strange sense of honor must have anchored my parents to their chairs. And so we watched it all: the eighteen-year-old boy with a fake mustache who did a magic show and juggled flaming hoops while riding a unicycle. The breasted girl with white makeup who sang from *Madama Butterfly*[17] and got honorable mention. And the eleven-year-old boy who won first prize playing a tricky violin song that sounded like a busy bee. **E**

After the show, the Hsus, the Jongs, and the St. Clairs from the Joy Luck Club came up to my mother and father.

"Lots of talented kids," Auntie Lindo said vaguely, smiling broadly.

"That was somethin' else," said my father, and I wondered if he was referring to me in a humorous way, or whether he even remembered what I had done.

Waverly looked at me and shrugged her shoulders. "You aren't a genius like me," she said matter-of-factly. And if I hadn't felt so bad, I would have pulled her braids and punched her stomach.

But my mother's expression was what devastated me: a quiet, blank look that said she had lost everything. I felt the same way, and it seemed as if everybody were now coming up, like gawkers at the scene of an accident, to see what parts were actually missing. **F** When we got on the bus to go home, my father was humming the busy-bee tune and my mother was silent. I kept thinking she wanted to wait until we got home before shouting at me. But when my father unlocked the door to our apartment, my mother walked in and then went to the back, into the bedroom. No accusations. No blame. And in a way, I felt disappointed. I had been waiting for her to start shouting, so I could shout back and cry and blame her for all my misery. **G**

17. *Madama Butterfly:* opera by the Italian composer Giacomo Puccini (1858–1924).

Vocabulary
stricken (strik′ən) *adj.:* heartbroken; affected by or suffering from something painful or distressing.

Direct Teaching

E Literary Focus
GRADE-LEVEL STANDARD

? Conflict and motivation. What do you think of the reasons the narrator gives to explain why her parents sat through the rest of the show? [Possible response: She is probably right, since they would not want to show everyone their embarrassment by getting up and leaving.]

F Reading Skills

? Making inferences about motivation. Why might the mother feel that "she had lost everything"? [Possible responses: Her hopes for and pride in her daughter have been destroyed; she has been embarrassed in front of friends she wanted to impress.] Why does Jing-mei feel that she too has lost everything? [Possible responses: She has lost the last vestige of the dream she and her mother shared; she has lost her mother's respect; she has hurt her mother; she has been humiliated.]

G Reading Skills

? Expressing an opinion. Who do you think is more to blame for Jing-mei's misery—her mother or she herself? Explain. [Possible responses: Her mother, because she pressured Jing-mei too much; Jing-mei, because she didn't really try to learn the piano.]

Music: European Composers
The nineteenth-century composers Edvard Grieg and Robert Schumann were important figures in the Romantic period of European music. The pieces mentioned in the story—"Anitra's Dance," from Grieg's *Peer Gynt Suite,* and "Pleading Child," from Schumann's *Scenes from Childhood,* are among the composers' better known works. Both are challenging for a first-year piano student.

Individual activity. Ask piano students to select pieces that are representative of these two composers. Then, have them make a short audiotape, play it for the class, and describe the challenges faced by a beginning pianist in learning such works.

I assumed my talent-show fiasco meant I never had to play the piano again. But two days later, after school, my mother came out of the kitchen and saw me watching TV.

"Four clock," she reminded me as if it were any other day. I was stunned, as though she were asking me to go through the talent-show torture again. I wedged myself more tightly in front of the TV.

"Turn off TV," she called from the kitchen five minutes later.

I didn't budge. And then I decided. I didn't have to do what my mother said anymore. I wasn't her slave. This wasn't China. I had listened to her before and look what happened. She was the stupid one.

She came out from the kitchen and stood in the arched entryway of the living room. "Four clock," she said once again, louder.

"You want me to be someone that I'm not!" I sobbed.

"I'm not going to play anymore," I said nonchalantly. "Why should I? I'm not a genius."

She walked over and stood in front of the TV. I saw her chest was heaving up and down in an angry way.

"No!" I said, and I now felt stronger, as if my true self had finally emerged. So this was what had been inside me all along.

"No! I won't!" I screamed.

She yanked me by the arm, pulled me off the floor, snapped off the TV. She was frighteningly strong, half pulling, half carrying me toward the piano as I kicked the throw rugs under my feet. She lifted me up and onto the hard bench. I was sobbing by now, looking at her bitterly. Her chest was heaving even more and her mouth was open, smiling crazily, as if she were pleased I was crying.

"You want me to be someone that I'm not!" I sobbed. "I'll never be the kind of daughter you want me to be!"

"Only two kinds of daughters," she shouted in Chinese. "Those who are obedient and those who follow their own mind! Only one kind of daughter can live in this house. Obedient daughter!"

"Then I wish I wasn't your daughter. I wish you weren't my mother," I shouted. As I said these things, I got scared. It felt like worms and toads and slimy things crawling out of my chest, but it also felt good, as if this awful side of me had surfaced, at last.

"Too late change this," said my mother shrilly.

And I could sense her anger rising to its breaking point. I wanted to see it spill over. And that's when I remembered the babies she had lost in China, the ones we never talked about. "Then I wish I'd never been born!" I shouted. "I wish I were dead! Like them."

It was as if I had said the magic words. Alakazam!—and her face went blank, her mouth closed, her arms went slack, and she backed out of the room, stunned, as if she were blowing away like a small brown leaf, thin, brittle, lifeless.

It was not the only disappointment my mother felt in me. In the years that followed, I failed her so many times, each time asserting my own will, my right to fall short of expectations. I didn't get straight A's. I didn't become class president. I didn't get into Stanford.[18] I dropped out of college.

For unlike my mother, I did not believe I could be anything I wanted to be. I could only be me.

18. **Stanford:** high-ranking university in Stanford, California.

Vocabulary

fiasco (fē·äs′kō) *n.:* total failure.

nonchalantly (nän′shə·länt′lē) *adv.:* without interest or concern; indifferently.

DIRECT TEACHING

A Literary Focus
GRADE-LEVEL STANDARD

Conflict and motivation. Remind students that both Jing-mei and her mother are very determined. Their conflict is now reaching its peak. Ask what students think will happen now if Jing-mei refuses to play the piano. [Possible response: She and her mother may have a big fight; neither one is likely to back down.]

B Literary Focus
GRADE-LEVEL STANDARD

Conflict and motivation. Ask students to paraphrase the opposing motives that mother and daughter express here. [Possible responses: Jing-mei wants her mother to accept her without imposing unrealistic expectations. The mother wants Jing-mei to be dutiful and obey unquestioningly.]

C Reading Skills

? Making inferences about motivation. What do you think motivates Jing-mei to refer so cruelly to the babies her mother lost? [Possible response: By saying the most hurtful thing she can think of, she pushes her mother to the breaking point, completely silencing her. She may feel that she has asserted her own identity by gaining much power over her mother.]

D English-Language Learners

Slang. Explain to English-language learners that *alakazam* is a nonsense word used by magicians to signal that something amazing is about to happen.

E Correcting Misconceptions

Flash-forward. Be sure all students recognize that the story now flashes forward to the future, when the narrator has grown up.

DEVELOPING FLUENCY

Mixed-ability group activity. The story's dramatic climax is perfect for reading aloud. Have students of mixed abilities meet in groups of three to read aloud the scene, with one student serving as narrator and each of the other students reading the dialogue of a character. Have the groups read the passage through two or three times, the first time for practice and the next time or two to develop fluency. Then, ask the students to discuss the motivations of the characters in the scene.

And for all those years, we never talked about the disaster at the recital or my terrible accusations afterward at the piano bench. All that remained unchecked, like a betrayal that was now unspeakable. So I never found a way to ask her why she had hoped for something so large that failure was inevitable.

And even worse, I never asked her what frightened me the most: Why had she given up hope?

For after our struggle at the piano, she never mentioned my playing again. The lessons stopped. The lid to the piano was closed, shutting out the dust, my misery, and her dreams.

So she surprised me. A few years ago, she offered to give me the piano, for my thirtieth birthday. I had not played in all those years. I saw the offer as a sign of forgiveness, a tremendous burden removed.

"Are you sure?" I asked shyly. "I mean, won't you and Dad miss it?"

"No, this your piano," she said firmly. "Always your piano. You only one can play."

"Well, I probably can't play anymore," I said. "It's been years."

"You pick up fast," said my mother, as if she knew this was certain. "You have natural talent. You could been genius if you want to."

"No, I couldn't."

"You just not trying," said my mother. And she was neither angry nor sad. She said it as if to announce a fact that could never be disproved. "Take it," she said.

But I didn't at first. It was enough that she had offered it to me. And after that, every time I saw it in my parents' living room, standing in front of the bay windows, it made me feel proud, as if it were a shiny trophy I had won back.

Last week I sent a tuner over to my parents' apartment and had the piano reconditioned, for purely sentimental reasons. My mother had died a few months before, and I had been getting things in order for my father, a little bit at a time. I put the jewelry in special silk pouches. The sweaters she had knitted in yellow, pink, bright orange—all the colors I hated—I put those in mothproof boxes. I found some old Chinese silk dresses, the kind with little slits up the sides. I rubbed the old silk against my skin, then wrapped them in tissue and decided to take them home with me.

After I had the piano tuned, I opened the lid and touched the keys. It sounded even richer than I remembered. Really, it was a very good piano. Inside the bench were the same exercise notes with handwritten scales, the same secondhand music books with their covers held together with yellow tape.

I opened up the Schumann book to the dark little piece I had played at the recital. It was on the left-hand side of the page, "Pleading Child." It looked more difficult than I remembered. I played a few bars, surprised at how easily the notes came back to me.

And for the first time, or so it seemed, I noticed the piece on the right-hand side. It was called "Perfectly Contented." I tried to play this one as well. It had a lighter melody but the same flowing rhythm and turned out to be quite easy. "Pleading Child" was shorter but slower; "Perfectly Contented" was longer but faster. And after I played them both a few times, I realized they were two halves of the same song. ■

Vocabulary
betrayal (bē·trā′əl) *n.:* failure to fulfill another's hopes. *Betrayal* also means "act of disloyalty; deception."

DIRECT TEACHING

F Reading Skills

Making inferences about motivation. Why do you think Jing-mei feels frightened? [Possible responses: She may feel guilty for hurting her mother; she may fear that she has lost her mother's love.]

G Literary Focus
REVIEW STANDARD

Resolution. How is the mother-daughter conflict resolved? [With the gift of the piano, mother and daughter accept each other's differences.] **Why does Jing-mei call the piano "a shiny trophy"?** [Possible response: She has won it on her own terms, without having to prove anything to her mother.]

H Advanced Learners

Acceleration. Have students consider what the narrator's final statement about "Pleading Child" and "Perfectly Contented" suggests about her understanding of herself. [Possible response: She has accepted her childish rebellion as well as her mature peace with her parents and recognizes that both are part of being human.]

GUIDED PRACTICE

Monitoring students' progress. Guide students in answering these questions. Have them cite passages that support their responses.

True-False

1. The mother devises tests to reveal her daughter's talents. [T]
2. Jing-mei dreams of being a concert pianist. [F]
3. Jing-mei's performance in the talent show is a huge success. [F]
4. Right after the show, the mother scolds Jing-mei. [F]
5. Jing-mei sells the family piano after her mother dies. [F]

FAMILY/COMMUNITY ACTIVITY

Assign students to interview adults in the community about the hopes and expectations that the adults' parents had for them. Suggest that they ask what the hopes and expectations were, how the interviewees felt about them at the time, and how they feel about them now. Have students (with interviewees' permission) take notes, write up their interviews, and share the results in class, comparing and contrasting the real-life stories with the conflicts in "Two Kinds."

Meet the Writer

Background. Commenting on her work as a writer, Tan notes, "You can come up with structures and ideas at first, but it's what you stumble across without self-consciousness that's new, exciting, and much more honest. These things are within you, in your life's experience and the way you perceive the world."

Tan's third novel, *The Hundred Secret Senses* (1995), reveals differences between American and Chinese ways of perceiving the world. On its publication, the interviewer Sarah Lyall noted that Tan "has an American practicality, but her life has been so marked by quirks of fate that she has gradually come to believe, as her Chinese mother does, that there are things in the world that can't be explained rationally." Thus, Tan has seen some of her dreams come true against all odds. On the negative side, she suffers from "mechanical difficulties": Like the character Kwan in *The Hundred Secret Senses,* Tan finds that in her presence, TV sets and television cameras inexplicably go haywire.

For Independent Reading

- To pique students' interest in *The Joy Luck Club,* mention that in other parts of the novel, Waverly Jong (a chess prodigy and subordinate character in "Two Kinds") is a feisty main character with surprising contradictions.
- For other stories that address identity and growing up, recommend *America Street: A Multicultural Anthology of Stories* (edited by Anne Mazer). This collection includes works by Toni Cade Bambara, Gish Jen, Francisco Jiménez, and Toshio Mori.

Meet the Writer

Amy Tan

Many Englishes

Amy Tan (1952–) says that she grew up with several Englishes. The Englishes were primarily American English and Chinese English. Tan was born in Oakland, California, two and a half years after her parents fled China's Communist revolution and settled in the United States. Although Tan's parents had wanted her to become a surgeon, with piano as a hobby, she got a master's degree in linguistics instead. Her first short story, written at a writers' workshop in 1985, was eventually published in *Seventeen.*

At the request of a literary agent, Tan next drafted a proposal for a novel based on the lives of four Chinese mothers and their American daughters. Then Tan left on a trip to China with her own mother, who had just recovered from a serious illness.

When she returned, Tan was amazed to find that her agent had obtained a sizable advance for a book she hadn't even written yet. She immediately devoted herself full time to writing *The Joy Luck Club*—a collection of related stories told from the points of view of four mothers and four daughters.

"When I wrote these stories, it was as much a discovery to me as to any reader reading them for the first time," Tan has said. "Things would surprise me. I would sit there laughing and I would say, 'Oh you're kidding!' It was like people telling me the stories, and I would write them down as fast as I could." Published in 1989 to rave reviews, *The Joy Luck Club* became an instant bestseller.

Afraid of failing after the huge success of *The Joy Luck Club,* Tan agonized over her second novel, *The Kitchen God's Wife* (1991). In writing that book, she says, she "had to fight for every single character, every image, every word." She needn't have worried. The novel, the story of a woman's harrowing life in pre-Communist China, was another blockbuster. Tan followed her first two successes with two more: *The Hundred Secret Senses* (1995) and *The Bonesetter's Daughter* (2001).

Here is what Tan says about being a writer who knows two cultures:

> "I am a writer. I am fascinated by language in daily life. I spend a great deal of my time thinking about the power of language—the way it can evoke an emotion, a visual image, a complex idea, or a simple truth. Language is the tool of my trade. And I use them all—all the Englishes I grew up with."

For Independent Reading

If you enjoyed "Two Kinds," you might want to read *The Joy Luck Club* (mentioned above), from which "Two Kinds" is taken.

DIFFERENTIATING INSTRUCTION

Advanced Learners

Enrichment. Amy Tan rejects efforts to pigeonhole her as an Asian American writer. She says, "I don't see myself, for example, writing about cultural dichotomies, but about human connections. All of us go through angst and identity crises. And even when you write in a specific context, you still tap into that subtext of emotions that we all feel about love and hope, and mothers and obligations and responsibilities."

Activity. Have students read two other stories from *The Joy Luck Club,* keeping in mind Tan's statements. Have them evaluate the stories, using Tan's own standards of what she hopes to accomplish.

108 Chapter 2 Character • Using Primary and Secondary Sources

Literary Response and Analysis

Reading Check

1. What does Jing-mei's mother want for her daughter?
2. How does Jing-mei feel about her mother's plans for her?
3. What happens when Jing-mei plays the piano in front of an audience?
4. What does Jing-mei say to hurt her mother in their last struggle over the piano lessons?

Interpretations

5. Identify the story's central **conflict,** and tell what causes it. What does the **main character** desire, and what blocks her from achieving it?
6. What **inferences** can you make about the mother's **motivation** for pushing Jing-mei to be a prodigy? Consider
   - the mother's life in China
   - her life in America
7. Why might Jing-mei's mother want her to keep playing the piano even after her disastrous performance? What kind of daughter does she really want Jing-mei to be?
8. How do you think other children might respond to the pressure to become a prodigy? What **inferences** can you make about Jing-mei's **character traits** from her response to her mother's pressure?
9. What do you think the **title** of the story means? How does Jing-mei's discovery concerning the two Schumann songs relate to the story's title?
10. Near the end of the story, Jing-mei says, "In the years that followed, I failed her so many times. . . ." What does she mean by that? Do you think author Amy Tan agrees with her? Why?

Evaluation

11. Do you think the demands and high expectations of others can make us want to fail (out of spite or hopelessness, perhaps), or do you think such expectations can motivate us to greater success? Explain your opinion, drawing examples from your own experiences and those of people you know. (Your Quickwrite notes may help you answer this question.)

Writing

Mother Versus Daughter

Do you think Jing-mei's mother is right to push Jing-mei so hard, or do you agree with Jing-mei that her mother's pride is foolish? Do you think that Jing-mei is cruel to her mother or that her mother is cruel to her? Write a paragraph or two analyzing the relationship between the mother and daughter. Support your statements with details from the story.

My Unforgettable Character

Amy Tan's story is interesting in part because it lets us meet some unusual characters. Write a **character sketch** of your own about a person you know—preferably someone you can observe. You might find a subject by thinking about the characters in "Two Kinds." Does anyone in the story remind you of someone in your own life? Use descriptive details to tell what your character looks like, how he or she acts, what characteristic things he or she says, what he or she likes to do. How do you know this person? Open your sketch with a sentence that hooks your readers' interest.

Use "Describing a Person," pages 540–547, for help with this assignment.

Reading Standard 3.3 Analyze interactions between main and subordinate characters in a literary text (e.g., internal and external conflicts, motivations, relationships, influences) and explain the way those interactions affect the plot.

INDEPENDENT PRACTICE

Literary Response and Analysis

Interpretations

5. Possible answer: Jing-mei wants her own identity and her parents' love. Conflict arises when her desires are blocked by her mother's expectations.
6. Possible answers: The mother is motivated by a need to overcome tragic losses; by pride; by love; by her belief in the American dream; and by competitiveness with Auntie Lindo.
7. Possible answers: She believes that Jing-mei has talent and just needs to try harder. She wants Jing-mei to be obedient and to achieve great success.
8. Possible answer: Some children respond well to pressure; others rebel. Jing-mei's rebellion shows independence, stubbornness and determination.
9. Possible answer: The title echoes the mother's statement that there are two kinds of daughters: dutiful and willful. The songs also relate to the title: Jing-mei is a pleading child who wants to be loved for herself; as an adult she is content to be herself and to stop fighting her mother's expectations.
10. Jing-mei means that she failed her mother because she didn't succeed where her mother expected. Some students will say that Tan agrees, because she makes it clear that Jing-mei hasn't lived up to her potential. Others will say that Tan disagrees, because she suggests that Jing-mei has succeeded by achieving peace within herself.

Evaluation

11. Students might note that high expectations must be realistic or failure is certain. Fulfilling high expectations requires support from others.

Reading Check

1. Jing-mei's mother wants her to be a prodigy.
2. At first Jing-mei is excited about the idea of being a prodigy, but her feelings change to discouragement and then to resentment.
3. Jing-mei plays one wrong note after another but cannot stop herself. The music sounds terrible.
4. Jing-mei says she wishes that she had never been born or that she were dead, like the two babies her mother lost in China.

Vocabulary Development

Practice

Possible Answers

- *prodigy. Synonym*—genius. *Antonym*—(none). *Sample sentence with context clues*—The math prodigy was hailed as a **genius.** [synonym]
- *lamented. Synonyms*—mourned, complained. *Antonyms*—rejoiced over, celebrated. *Sample sentence with context clues*—He lamented his bad attitude, **mourning** the chances he had lost. [synonym]
- *listlessly. Synonyms*—languidly, sluggishly. *Antonym*—energetically. *Sample sentence with context clues*—She approached the task listlessly but soon she began to apply herself more **energetically.** [antonym]
- *mesmerizing. Synonyms*—spellbinding, fascinating. *Antonyms*—dull, boring, uninspiring. *Sample sentence with context clues*—The first show was mesmerizing, but the next one was **dull.** [antonym]
- *discordant. Synonyms*—dissonant, unharmonious. *Antonyms*—harmonious, melodious. *Sample sentence with context clues*—Expecting to hear **melodious** music, the listeners were disturbed by the discordant sounds. [antonym]
- *dawdled. Synonyms*—dallied, idled, lazed. *Antonym*—hurried. *Sample sentence with context clues*—A few hikers dawdled on the trek, **idling** by a lake. [synonym]
- *stricken. Synonyms*—wounded, afflicted. *Antonyms*—unaffected. *Sample sentence with context clues*—Stricken by Jing-mei's cruel remarks, her mother had to **suffer** in silence. [synonym]
- *nonchalantly. Synonyms*—coolly, indifferently. *Antonyms*—passionately, ardently. *Sample sentence with context clues*—He spoke nonchalantly of his accomplishments, as if **indifferent** to his success. [synonym]

Vocabulary Development

Clarifying Word Meanings: Comparison and Contrast

Comparison means finding similarities and **contrast** means finding differences. How can you use these skills to help build your vocabulary?

Clues to a word's meaning can often be found in a sentence by identifying **synonyms** (words with *similar* meanings) or **antonyms** (words with *opposite* meanings). Look also for **signal words.** Words such as *similarly, like, as, also, too,* and *resembling* signal comparison. Words such as *although, but, yet, still, unlike, not, in contrast, instead,* and *however* signal contrast.

COMPARISON Jing-mei's mother had a stricken look, **like** a woman who was **heartbroken.**

CONTRAST Jing-mei's mother expected **loyalty** and **trustworthiness, not** betrayal, from her daughter.

Word Bank

- prodigy
- lamented
- listlessly
- mesmerizing
- discordant
- dawdled
- stricken
- fiasco
- nonchalantly
- betrayal

PRACTICE

Make a word map like the one below for each Word Bank word. First, list at least one synonym and, when possible, an antonym (many words do not have antonyms). Consult a dictionary and a thesaurus if necessary. Then, write a sentence clarifying each word's meaning. In your sentences, use synonyms or antonyms to compare and contrast the words' meanings.

fiasco

Synonyms: failure, disappointment

Antonyms: success, triumph

Sample sentence with context clues: Jing-mei's recital was a fiasco, unlike Waverly's chess match, which was a **triumph.** [antonym]

Grade 8 Review Reading Standard 1.3 Use word meanings within the appropriate context and show ability to verify those meanings by comparison or contrast.

- *betrayal. Synonyms*—treachery, disloyalty. *Antonyms*—loyalty, fidelity, allegiance. *Sample sentence with context clues*—Jing-mei's parents saw her failure as a betrayal, an act of **disloyalty** to them. [synonym]

Resources Reminder

Vocabulary

- *Vocabulary Development*
  - Vocabulary Worksheet, p. 8
- *Lesson Plans for Language Development*
  - Vocabulary, pp. 59, 63

Grammar Link MINI-LESSON

Main or Subordinate Clause: Can It Stand Alone?

A **clause** is a group of words that has a subject and a verb. A **main clause** (also called an **independent clause**) can stand alone as a sentence because it has a subject and a verb, *and* it expresses a complete thought.

MAIN CLAUSE — Jing-mei's mother argued with her daughter. [sentence]

A **subordinate clause,** on the other hand, has a subject and verb, but it does *not* express a complete thought, and so it cannot stand on its own as a sentence. A subordinate clause must be attached to a main clause to communicate a whole idea.

A subordinate clause that stands by itself is a sentence fragment. A **sentence fragment** does not express a complete thought.

SUBORDINATE CLAUSE — Because Jing-mei didn't want to be a prodigy. [sentence fragment]

Whenever you write, make sure that every subordinate clause is firmly attached to a main clause. The subordinate clause may come at the beginning of the sentence, at the end, or in the middle.

COMPLETE SENTENCE — Jing-mei's mother argued with her daughter because Jing-mei didn't want to be a prodigy.

PRACTICE

Edit and rewrite the following paragraph, correcting all errors in the use of subordinate clauses. (Make any capitalization and punctuation changes that are necessary as well.)

The plot of this story would not have been believable. If Old Chong, the piano teacher, weren't completely deaf. Anyone can hear the terribly wrong notes. Who listens to Jing-mei's playing. When she starts playing before a hearing audience. Jing-mei realizes for the first time what she has done. She feels terrible. Because she has humiliated herself and her parents.

➤ **For more help, see Subordinate Clause Fragments in the *Holt Handbook,* pages 450–453.**

Grammar Link

Practice

Possible Answer

The plot of this story would not have been believable if Old Chong, the piano teacher, weren't completely deaf. Anyone who listens to Jing-mei's playing can hear the terribly wrong notes. When she starts playing before a hearing audience, Jing-mei realizes for the first time what she has done. She feels terrible because she has humiliated herself and her parents.

ASSESSING

Assessment

- *Progress Assessment of Reading*
  - Selection Test

RETEACHING

For another selection to teach Standard 3.3, see *Interactive Reading,* Chapter 2.

DIFFERENTIATING INSTRUCTION

Learners Having Difficulty

Each of the following items contains a sentence and a fragment. Copy them on the chalkboard; then, have students combine the sentences and the fragment by making each fragment a subordinate clause.

1. Jing-mei's mother is sure. That Jing-mei can be a prodigy. [Jing-mei's mother is sure that Jing-mei can be a prodigy.]
2. When she fails her mother's tests. Jing-mei grows discouraged. [When she fails her mother's tests, Jing-mei grows discouraged.]
3. Jing-mei plays miserably at the talent show. Because she barely practiced. [Jing-mei plays miserably at the talent show because she barely practiced.]
4. Jing-mei avoids pursuing success. As she grows up. [As she grows up, Jing-mei avoids pursuing success.]
5. If you understand the end of the story. Explain it to me. [If you understand the end of the story, explain it to me.]

STANDARDS FOCUS, pp. 112–120

(For grade-level and review standards taught in this lesson, see citations on Student Edition pages.)

Prerequisite Standard

- Grade 7, Literary Response and Analysis 3.3 **Analyze characterization as delineated through a character's thoughts, words, speech patterns, and actions; the narrator's description; and the thoughts, words, and actions of other characters.**

Reading Skills

- Compare and contrast.

Summary *at grade level*

This autobiographical account, set in India, has two main characters: Santha, the protagonist, a bright but meek five-year-old, and her sister, Premila, an assertive and proud eight-year-old. When the girls are sent to the local British school, they get their first taste of British discrimination against Indians. The school's English headmistress immediately renames the girls Cynthia and Pamela. For the next week, Santha (Cynthia) is bemused by her split identity and by the school's alien customs and subtle racism. Soon a teacher makes an overtly racist comment, and Premila promptly collects Santha and marches home. The girls' mother agrees that they shouldn't go back. She hopes Santha didn't notice the racism. Santha did, but is able to distance herself, since it all involved that odd other girl—Cynthia.

Before You Read

By Any Other Name

Literary Focus

Character and Autobiography

You've seen how fiction writers use methods of **indirect characterization** to create characters that seem real. They *show* (rather than *tell*) what their characters look like and what they say, do, and think. So how does a nonfiction writer (in this case a writer of **autobiography**) reveal what her real-life characters are like? Notice how Santha Rama Rau brings her characters and their conflicts to life. Are her techniques the same as a fiction writer's, or are they different?

Reading Skills

Comparison and Contrast

When the sisters in this account enroll in a school run by teachers from England in their native India, they encounter cultural differences ranging from the different foods the students eat to more important conflicts of values and attitudes. As you read, **compare and contrast** these cultures and the different reactions of the sisters.

Reading Standard 3.3 Analyze interactions between main and subordinate characters in a literary text.

Reading Standard 3.4 Determine characters' traits by what the characters say about themselves in narration and dialogue.

Make the Connection

Quickwrite

How important is a person's name? How would you react if someone took your name away and then referred to you only by a number? Quickwrite your response in a few sentences.

Background

At the time of this account (around 1928), India was a colony of Great Britain, and educated Indians were expected to learn English in addition to their native languages. (Many languages are spoken in India.) The headmistress of Rama Rau's school is British, as are most of the students, children of British civil servants sent to India as colonial rulers.

The essay's title comes from William Shakespeare's play *Romeo and Juliet.* Juliet wishes that Romeo had a different surname because his family and hers are enemies. "What's in a name?" she asks. "That which we call a rose / By any other name would smell as sweet."

Vocabulary Development

precarious (pri·ker′ē·əs) *adj.:* in danger of falling down; unstable.

intimidated (in·tim′ə·dāt′id) *v.:* made afraid.

provincial (prə·vin′shəl) *adj.:* belonging to a province, especially a rural one; also, unsophisticated.

insular (in′sə·lər) *adj.:* isolated from one's surroundings; narrow-minded.

valid (val′id) *adj.:* meeting the requirements of established standards.

palpitating (pal′pə·tāt′iŋ) *v.* used as *adj.:* throbbing; quivering.

wizened (wiz′ənd) *adj.:* wrinkled and dried up.

sedately (si·dāt′lē) *adv.:* in a calm and dignified manner.

tepid (tep′id) *adj.:* neither hot nor cold; lukewarm.

peevishness (pē′vish·nis) *n.:* irritability.

RESOURCES: READING

Planning

- *One-Stop Planner* CD-ROM with Test Generator
- *On Course: Mapping Instruction*

Media

- *Audio CD Library*
  - disc 4

Reading

- *Interactive Reading,* Teacher's Edition
  - Graphic Organizer: Character Traits Chart

Differentiating Instruction

- *Lesson Plans for Language Development*
  - English-Language Learners, pp. 51–53, 60, 63
  - Special Education Students, pp. 54, 60, 63

"Suppose we give you pretty English names."

Santha Rama Rau (right), her older sister, Premila, and their dog in Simla, India, 1927.

By Any Other Name

Santha Rama Rau

113

PRETEACHING

Selection Starter

Build background. Tell students that in 1877, India was annexed to the British Empire under Queen Victoria. Indian independence movements quickly arose, but in the 1920s, when this account takes place, Britain still held firm control. India won its independence in 1947.

Preview Vocabulary

To familiarize students with the Vocabulary words listed on p. 112, have students work with partners on the following exercises.

1. Suppose you received a gift basket of wizened fruit. Use the word peevishness to describe your reaction. [Possible response: My dismay upon seeing the shriveled fruit changed to a feeling of peevishness at those who sent it.]
2. Describe a precarious situation that intimidated you. [Possible response: Before I made my first ascent, the idea of rock climbing frightened me.]
3. Explain the difference between a provincial attitude and an insular one. [A provincial attitude is generally unsophisticated, whereas an insular one is narrow-minded.]
4. Use the words sedately and tepid in a sentence about a character. [Possible response: Carrying a bucket of tepid water, the gardener walked sedately over to the drooping rosebush.]
5. Why might a palpitating heart provide a valid excuse for sitting out gym class? [Exercise may be unsafe if one's heart rate is too high.]

Vocabulary

- *Vocabulary Development*
  - Vocabulary Worksheet, p. 9

Assessment

- *Progress Assessment of Reading*
  - Selection Test
- *One-Stop Planner* CD-ROM with Test Generator

DIRECT TEACHING

A Literary Focus GRADE-LEVEL STANDARD

? Character and autobiography. What does the headmistress think of Indian culture and of her own English culture? [The headmistress is prejudiced. She looks down on Indian culture and believes her own culture is superior.] How does the author reveal what the headmistress is like? [Possible responses: She uses indirect characterization, letting readers "see" the headmistress's hypocritical smile and "hear" her condescending words.]

B Reading Skills

? Comparing and contrasting. What similarities and differences do you find in the mother's attitude toward the British and the headmistress's attitude toward Indians? [Both show racial bias. The mother expresses hers directly, the headmistress indirectly.]

C Learners Having Difficulty

Paraphrasing. Ask students to paraphrase this saying. [Possible response: Some people never change.]

At the Anglo-Indian[1] day school in Zorinabad to which my sister and I were sent when she was eight and I was five and a half, they changed our names. On the first day of school, a hot, windless morning of a north Indian September, we stood in the headmistress's study, and she said, "Now you're the *new* girls. (C) What are your names?"

(A) My sister answered for us. "I am Premila, and she"—nodding in my direction—"is Santha."

The headmistress had been in India, I suppose, fifteen years or so, but she still smiled her helpless inability to cope with Indian names. Her rimless half-glasses glittered, and the precarious bun on the top of her head trembled as she shook her head. "Oh, my dears, those are much too hard for me. Suppose we give you pretty English names. Wouldn't that be more jolly? Let's see, now—Pamela for you, I think." She shrugged in a baffled way at my sister. "That's as close as I can get. And for *you*," she said to me, "how about Cynthia? Isn't that nice?"

My sister was always less easily intimidated than I was, and while she kept a stubborn silence, I said "Thank you," in a very tiny voice.

We had been sent to that school because my father, among his responsibilities as an officer of the civil service, had a tour of duty to perform in the villages around that steamy little provincial town, where he had his headquarters at that time. He used to make his shorter inspection tours on horseback, and a week before, in the stale heat of a typically postmonsoon[2] day, we had waved goodbye to him and a little procession—an assistant, a secretary, two bearers, and the man to look after the bedding rolls and luggage. They rode away through our large garden, still bright green from the rains, and we turned back into the twilight of the house and the sound of fans whispering in every room.

Up to then, my mother had refused to send Premila to school in the British-run establishments of that time, because, she used to say, (B) "You can bury a dog's tail for seven years and it still comes out curly, and you can take a Britisher away from his home for a lifetime and he still remains insular." The examinations and degrees from entirely Indian schools were not, in those days, considered valid. In my case, the question had never come up and probably never would have come up if Mother's extraordinary good health had not broken down. For the first time in my life, she was not able to continue the lessons she had been giving us every morning. So our Hindi[3] books were put away, the stories of the Lord Krishna[4] as a little boy were left in midair, and we were sent to the Anglo-Indian school.

That first day at school is still, when I think of it, a remarkable one. At that age, if one's name is changed, one develops a curious form of dual personality. I remember having a certain detached and disbelieving concern in the actions of "Cynthia," but certainly no responsibility. Accordingly, I followed the thin, erect back of the headmistress down the veranda to my classroom, feeling, at most, a passing interest in what was going to happen to me in this strange, new atmosphere of School.

1. **Anglo-Indian:** English and Indian; also refers to the British colonists living in India.
2. **postmonsoon** *adj.:* after the monsoon, or seasonal heavy rains.
3. **Hindi:** official language of India.
4. **Lord Krishna:** in the Hindu religion, human form taken by the god Vishnu. Many Hindu stories recount episodes in the life of Krishna.

Vocabulary

precarious (pri·ker′ē·əs) *adj.:* in danger of falling down; unstable.

intimidated (in·tim′ə·dāt′id) *v.:* made afraid.

provincial (prə·vin′shəl) *adj.:* belonging to a province, especially a rural one; also, unsophisticated.

insular (in′sə·lər) *adj.:* isolated from one's surroundings; narrow-minded.

valid (val′id) *adj.:* meeting the requirements of established standards.

114 Chapter 2 Character • Using Primary and Secondary Sources

DIFFERENTIATING INSTRUCTION

Learners Having Difficulty

Modeling. Before students read "By Any Other Name," model how to examine differences between the two cultures, based on how the main characters behave. On the chalkboard, make a two-column chart with the headings "Indian Culture" and "British Culture." Then, read the first five paragraphs of the story aloud, and write the names Santha and Premila in the first column of the chart and Cynthia and Pamela in the second. As students continue reading the story in small groups, have them fill in the chart with examples of the girls' behavior that reflects the customs of each culture.

English-Language Learners

Tell students that during colonial rule, many British citizens lived for years in India but didn't adopt Indian customs.

Resources Reminder

For lessons designed for special education students and English-language learners, see *Lesson Plans for Language Development,* pp. 51–54, 60, 63.

The building was Indian in design, with wide verandas opening onto a central courtyard, but Indian verandas are usually whitewashed, with stone floors. These, in the tradition of British schools, were painted dark brown and had matting on the floors. It gave a feeling of extra intensity to the heat.

I suppose there were about a dozen Indian children in the school—which contained perhaps forty children in all—and four of them were in my class. They were all sitting at the back of the room, and I went to join them. I sat next to a small, solemn girl, who didn't smile at me. She had long, glossy black braids and wore a cotton dress, but she still kept on her Indian jewelry—a gold chain around her neck, thin gold bracelets, and tiny ruby studs in her ears. Like most Indian children, she had a rim of black kohl[5] around her eyes. The cotton dress should have looked strange, but all I could think of was that I should ask my mother if I couldn't wear a dress to school, too, instead of my Indian clothes. **D**

I can't remember too much about the proceedings in class that day, except for the beginning. The teacher pointed to me and asked me to stand up. "Now, dear, tell the class your name."

I said nothing.

"Come along," she said, frowning slightly. "What's your name, dear?"

"I don't know," I said, finally.

The English children in the front of the class—there were about eight or ten of them—giggled and twisted around in their chairs to look at me. I sat down quickly and opened my eyes very wide, hoping in that way to dry them off. The little girl with the braids put out her hand and very lightly touched my arm. She still didn't smile. **E**

Most of that morning I was rather bored. I looked briefly at the children's drawings pinned to the wall, and then concentrated on a lizard clinging to the ledge of the high, barred window behind the teacher's head. Occasionally it would shoot out its long yellow tongue for a fly, and then it would rest, with its eyes closed and its belly palpitating, as though it were swallowing several times quickly. The lessons were mostly concerned with reading and writing and simple numbers—things that my mother had already taught me—and I paid very little attention. The teacher wrote on the easel-blackboard words like "bat" and "cat," which seemed babyish to me; only "apple" was new and incomprehensible. **F**

When it was time for the lunch recess, I followed the girl with braids out onto the veranda. There the children from the other classes were assembled. I saw Premila at once and ran over to her, as she had charge of our lunchbox. The children were all opening packages and sitting down to eat sandwiches. Premila and I were the only ones who had Indian food—thin wheat chapatis,[6] some vegetable curry, and a bottle of buttermilk. Premila thrust half of it into my hand and whispered fiercely that I should go and sit with my class, because that was what the others seemed to be doing. **G**

The enormous black eyes of the little Indian girl from my class looked at my food longingly, so I offered her some. But she only shook her head and plowed her way solemnly through her sandwiches.

I was very sleepy after lunch, because at home we always took a siesta. It was usually a pleasant time of day, with the bedroom darkened against the harsh afternoon sun, the drifting off into sleep with the sound of Mother's voice reading a story in one's mind, and, finally, the shrill, fussy voice of the ayah[7] waking one for tea.

5. **kohl** (kōl) *n.:* dark powder used as eye makeup.

6. **chapatis** (chə·pät′ēz) *n.:* thin, flat bread.

7. **ayah** (ä′yə) *n.:* Indian for "nanny" or "maid."

Vocabulary

palpitating (pal′pə·tāt′iŋ) *v.* used as *adj.:* throbbing; quivering.

DIRECT TEACHING

D Reading Skills

Comparing and contrasting. Which details help you contrast the status of English children with that of Indian children at this school? [Indian children are in the minority, sit at the back of the room, and emulate the English children's way of dressing.]

E Literary Focus
GRADE-LEVEL STANDARD

Character and autobiography. How does the writer use indirect characterization to show the distress Santha feels when the English children laugh at her? [She describes Santha's actions—opening her eyes wide "to dry them off"—and shows how another Indian child responds to her, sympathetically touching her arm.]

F Literary Focus
GRADE-LEVEL STANDARD

Character and autobiography. At only five, Santha speaks, reads, and writes English, although it is not her first language. What character traits does this fact suggest? [Possible responses: intelligence, flexibility.] **Why might the word *apple* puzzle her?** [Apples may not be common in this tropical part of India.]

G Literary Focus
GRADE-LEVEL STANDARD

Character and autobiography. What has the author directly said and indirectly shown about Premila's character so far? [Possible responses: She is a responsible older sister; she is "less easily intimidated" than Santha; she is proud enough to resent having her name changed; she urges Santha to do what the others do, suggesting that Premila wants to be accepted by the other children.]

Advanced Learners

Acceleration. This activity can help to move students toward the eleventh- and twelfth-grade Standard 3.3, for which students analyze the use of irony.

Activity. Ask students to note examples of irony in characterization as they read "By Any Other Name." Have students share their notes in small groups, and encourage groups to discuss how the examples of irony affect their responses to the characters and the story. Have groups share their observations with the class.

DIRECT TEACHING

A Reading Skills

Comparing and contrasting. How would you contrast the attitude of Santha's family toward competitive games with that of the English children? [Possible response: The English children value competing hard and winning; Santha's family members value helping other players, including opponents.]

B Literary Focus GRADE-LEVEL STANDARD

Character and autobiography. How do Santha's and Premila's responses to their mother's question differ? [Santha has much less to say.] How does this contrast show the effect on Santha of having her name changed? [It shows that Santha feels as if the events happened to "Cynthia," not to her.]

C English-Language Learners

Puns. Explain that the expression *for donkey's years* involves a pun on *years* and *ears*. A donkey's ears are long, so *for donkey's years* means "for long years" or "for a long time."

D Advanced Learners

Acceleration. What irony do you find in Premila's character? [Most students will infer that Premila wants the sandwiches so that she and Santha will be eating the same kind of food as everyone else. She wants to fit in, yet she is also proud and independent.]

At school, we rested for a short time on low, folding cots on the veranda, and then we were expected to play games. During the hot part of the afternoon we played indoors, and after the shadows had begun to lengthen and the slight breeze of the evening had come up, we moved outside to the wide courtyard.

I had never really grasped the system of competitive games. At home, whenever we played tag or guessing games, I was always allowed to "win"—"because," Mother used to tell Premila, "she is the youngest, and we have to allow for that." I had often heard her say it, and it seemed quite reasonable to me, but the result was that I had no clear idea of what "winning" meant.

When we played twos-and-threes[8] that afternoon at school, in accordance with my training I let one of the small English boys catch me but was naturally rather puzzled when the other children did not return the courtesy. I ran about for what seemed like hours without ever catching anyone, until it was time for school to close. Much later I learned that my attitude was called "not being a good sport," and I stopped allowing myself to be caught, but it was not for years that I really learned the spirit of the thing.

When I saw our car come up to the school gate, I broke away from my classmates and rushed toward it yelling, "Ayah! Ayah!" It seemed like an eternity since I had seen her that morning—a wizened, affectionate figure in her white cotton sari,[9] giving me dozens of urgent and useless instructions on how to be a good girl at school. Premila followed more sedately, and she told me on the way home never to do that again in front of the other children.

When we got home, we went straight to Mother's high, white room to have tea with her, and I immediately climbed onto the bed and bounced gently up and down on the springs. Mother asked how we had liked our first day in school. I was so pleased to be home and to have left that peculiar Cynthia behind that I had nothing whatever to say about school, except to ask what "apple" meant. But Premila told Mother about the classes, and added that in her class they had weekly tests to see if they had learned their lessons well.

I asked, "What's a test?"

Premila said, "You're too small to have them. You won't have them in your class for donkey's years."[10] She had learned the expression that day and was using it for the first time. We all laughed enormously at her wit. She also told Mother, in an aside, that we should take sandwiches to school the next day. Not, she said, that *she* minded. But they would be simpler for me to handle.

That whole lovely evening I didn't think about school at all. I sprinted barefoot across the lawns with my favorite playmate, the cook's son, to the stream at the end of the garden. We quarreled in our usual way, waded in the tepid water under the lime trees, and waited for the night to bring out the smell of the jasmine.[11] I listened with fascination to his stories of ghosts and demons, until I was too frightened to cross the garden alone in the semidarkness. The ayah found me, shouted at the cook's son, scolded me, hurried me in to supper—it was an entirely usual, wonderful evening.

8. **twos-and-threes:** game similar to tag.
9. **sari** (sä′rē) *n.:* long piece of cloth wrapped around the body. One end forms a skirt; the other end goes across the chest and over one shoulder.
10. **donkey's years:** expression meaning "a very long time."
11. **jasmine** (jaz′min) *n.:* tropical plant with fragrant flowers.

Vocabulary

wizened (wiz′ənd) *adj.:* wrinkled and dried up.

sedately (si·dāt′lē) *adv.:* in a calm and dignified manner.

tepid (tep′id) *adj.:* neither hot nor cold; lukewarm.

READING MINI-LESSON

Developing Word-Attack Skills

Use the selection word *solemn* (p. 115) as a starting point for discussing silent letters. Write *solemn* on the chalkboard, and have students identify the letter in the word whose sound is not heard [*n*]. Have them name other words that end with the letters *mn*. [Possible responses: *autumn; hymn.*]

Remind students of other letter pairs in which one letter is silent: *gn*, as in *gnaw* and *sign*, and *mb*, as in *thumb* and *tomb*. Have students suggest additional examples for each silent letter pair. [Possible responses for *gn* are *gnome, gnu, gnarl, gnat, gnash, reign, align;* for *mb, bomb, crumb, dumb, jamb, lamb.*]

Explain that when a suffix is added to a word ending in a silent letter, that letter is often heard in the longer word. Illustrate this point with *solemn* and *solemnity.*

Activity. Display the following pairs of related words. Explain that the first word in each pair contains a silent letter, and ask students whether that letter is silent or is sounded out in the second word.

116 Chapter 2 Character • Using Primary and Secondary Sources

It was a week later, the day of Premila's first test, that our lives changed rather abruptly. I was sitting at the back of my class, in my usual inattentive way, only half listening to the teacher. I had started a rather guarded friendship with the girl with the braids, whose name turned out to be Nalini (Nancy in school). The three other Indian children were already fast friends. Even at that age, it was apparent to all of us that friendship with the English or Anglo-Indian children was out of the question. Occasionally, during the class, my new friend and I would draw pictures and show them to each other secretly.

The door opened sharply and Premila marched in. At first, the teacher smiled at her in a kindly and encouraging way and said, "Now, you're little Cynthia's sister?"

Premila didn't even look at her. She stood with her feet planted firmly apart and her shoulders rigid and addressed herself directly to me. "Get up," she said. "We're going home." **E**

I didn't know what had happened, but I was aware that it was a crisis of some sort. I rose obediently and started to walk toward my sister.

"Bring your pencils and your notebook," she said. **F**

I went back for them, and together we left the room. The teacher started to say something just as Premila closed the door, but we didn't wait to hear what it was.

In complete silence we left the school grounds and started to walk home. Then I asked Premila what the matter was. All she would say was, "We're going home for good."

It was a very tiring walk for a child of five and a half, and I dragged along behind Premila with my pencils growing sticky in my hand. I can still remember looking at the dusty hedges and the tangles of thorns in the ditches by the side of the road, smelling the faint fragrance from the eucalyptus trees, and wondering whether we would ever reach home. Occasionally a horse-drawn tonga[12] passed us, and the women, in their pink or green silks, stared at Premila and me trudging along on the side of the road. A few coolies[13] and a line of women carrying baskets of vegetables on their heads smiled at us. But it was nearing the hottest time of day, and the road was almost deserted. I walked more and more slowly, and shouted to Premila, from time to time, "Wait for me!" with increasing peevishness.

Interior of a historic mansion in Goa, India.

12. **tonga** *n.:* two-wheeled carriage.
13. **coolies** *n.:* unskilled laborers.

Vocabulary
peevishness (pē′vish·nis) *n.:* irritability.

Direct Teaching

E Reading Skills

Comparing and contrasting. Contrast the actions of Santha's teacher with those of Premila. Which details show that Premila wields authority well? [Possible response: Premila's posture and tone are more commanding than the teacher's; she ignores the teacher and gets away with it; Santha unquestioningly obeys Premila and disregards the teacher.]

F Advanced Learners

Acceleration. Irony occurs when events do not turn out the way you might reasonably expect. What irony do you find in the contrast between Premila's behavior and the teacher's? [Possible response: It's ironic that an eight-year-old marches into a classroom and takes control, leaving a teacher sputtering ineffectively.] **What effects do you think this irony creates in the story?** [Possible responses: emphasizes Premila's strong will; challenges the English sense of superiority; creates humor.]

1.	autumn	autumnal [sounded out]
2.	sign	signal [sounded out]
3.	climb	climber [silent]
4.	crumb	crumble [sounded out]
5.	bomb	bombard [sounded out]
6.	align	alignment [silent]
7.	limb	limber [sounded out]

Content-Area Connections

Culture: Indian Beliefs
Many belief systems and practices tolerantly coexist in India under the rubric of Hinduism. Both a culture and a religion, Hinduism incorporates all forms of beliefs without exclusion or exception. The importance of names among Hindus is demonstrated by a ceremony called Nāmakarana, which is held during the first month of a baby's life. Family members gather for this ritual to welcome the new baby. The mother places the infant in the father's lap, and the baby formally receives a name.

Direct Teaching

A Literary Focus
REVIEW STANDARD

Theme. Changing the Indian children's names is an attempt to change their culture as well—to Anglicize them. How effective is this attempt with Santha and Premila? [Possible response: It backfires. Premila, offended, becomes stubbornly resistant. Confused, Santha dismisses her "Cynthia" self as "peculiar" and feels "no responsibility" for her.]

B Literary Focus
GRADE-LEVEL STANDARD

Character and autobiography. What direct statements does Rama Rau make about herself here? [She says that she understood what had taken place at the school but "put . . . away" the whole experience because it happened to "Cynthia."]

Guided Practice

Monitoring students' progress. Offer students guidance in responding to the following comprehension questions.

True-False

1. Premila is intimidated by the British headmistress. [F]
2. The girls' parents are eager to send them to a British school. [F]
3. Santha pays little attention to the lesson because she has already learned most of the material. [T]
4. Premila is sent home because she cheats on a test. [F]
5. Santha regrets losing her new identity as "Cynthia" so soon. [F]

Meet the Writer

Background. Santha Rama Rau first came to the United States in 1941. A critic has praised Rama Rau's skill at "transcribing life to paper in terms of people, their talk, their manners and customs."

She spoke to me only once, and that was to tell me to carry my notebook on my head, because of the sun.

When we got to our house, the ayah was just taking a tray of lunch into Mother's room. She immediately started a long, worried questioning about what are you children doing back here at this hour of the day.

Mother looked very startled and very concerned and asked Premila what had happened.

Premila said, "We had our test today, and She made me and the other Indians sit at the back of the room, with a desk between each one."

Mother said, "Why was that, darling?"

"She said it was because Indians cheat," Premila added. "So I don't think we should go back to that school."

Mother looked very distant and was silent a long time. At last she said, "Of course not, darling." She sounded displeased.

We all shared the curry she was having for lunch, and afterward I was sent off to the beautifully familiar bedroom for my siesta. I could hear Mother and Premila talking through the open door.

Mother said, "Do you suppose she understood all that?"

Premila said, "I shouldn't think so. She's a baby."

Mother said, "Well, I hope it won't bother her."

A Of course, they were both wrong. I understood it perfectly, and I remember it all very clearly. But I put it happily away, because it had **B** all happened to a girl called Cynthia, and I never was really particularly interested in her. ■

Meet the Writer

Santha Rama Rau

A Stranger in Her Own Land

Santha Rama Rau (1923–) was born into one of India's most influential families but has spent most of her life in other lands. Her father was a knighted diplomat, her mother a social reformer. Santha Rama Rau made her first trip to England at the age of six and returned for a much longer stay when she was eleven. In 1939, as war was breaking out in Europe, Lady Rama Rau took her two daughters back to India for safety. Feeling somewhat like an outsider, she made a conscious effort to reorient herself to her homeland and her extended family, and she recorded her impressions in her first book, *Home to India* (1944). In 1947, she witnessed the turmoil of India's independence from Britain. Five years later she married an American and settled in New York City.

Rama Rau eventually published many insightful travel books, as well as two novels, *Remember the House* (1956) and *The Adventuress* (1970). She also adapted E. M. Forster's novel *A Passage to India* into a play. Her autobiography *Gifts of Passage,* from which this selection is excerpted, was published in 1961.

Content-Area Connections

History: Britain and India
The small rebellion described in "By Any Other Name" mirrors a greater rebellion occurring throughout India during the same period. Indians led by Mohandas Gandhi (1869–1948) were successfully undermining British colonial power by using nonviolent civil disobedience. (One facet of the rebellion was a refusal to attend British schools.) The nonviolent protest methods pioneered by Gandhi were later adopted by the U.S. civil rights movement of the 1950s and '60s.

Small-group activity. Have interested students form groups to do research on the lives and contributions of the leaders of Indian independence movements, such as Gandhi. Have the groups present their findings in oral reports with visuals.

118 Chapter 2 Character • Using Primary and Secondary Sources

Literary Response and Analysis

Reading Check

1. Why are Santha and Premila sent to the English school?
2. How does the headmistress react to their names? What does she do?
3. Name two ways in which the Indian girls who have been at the school awhile imitate the English girls.
4. Why does Premila take Santha out of school in the middle of the day?

Interpretations

5. What does the mother mean when she makes the remark on page 114 about burying a dog's tail? Do her daughters' experiences in school prove she is right or wrong? Explain.
6. **Compare and contrast** aspects of Indian life and values with the values promoted in the English school. What other examples of cultural differences do you find in this story?
7. The selection has two **main characters** (Santha and Premila) and two **subordinate characters** (the mother and the headmistress). How would you describe each character's traits? Find details of **characterization** to support your descriptions.
8. Based on the last paragraph, explain how Santha resolves her **conflict** with the headmistress.
9. How do you think Santha Rama Rau would answer Juliet's question "What's in a name?" How important do you think a person's name is to his or her sense of identity? (Look back at your Quickwrite notes from page 112—have your ideas changed? How?)
10. This story takes place more than seventy years ago and half a world away. Do you think events like these stemming from prejudice take place today in other settings? Explain. Then, express what you think is the story's **theme,** or insight about life.

Evaluation

11. Santha Rama Rau doesn't directly tell us her thoughts and feelings as she looks back on her experiences as a five-year-old. Do you think her story would have been more powerful, or less, if she'd stated her thoughts and feelings directly? Explain.

Writing

Between Two Worlds

Rama Rau had the experience of living in two cultures. Can you think of someone—a relative, friend, or neighbor—who has come to this country and has had to adapt to American ways? Write a short biographical narrative describing the person and some experiences he or she had. If you don't know anyone personally, research and write about an author such as Julia Alvarez or Judith Ortiz Cofer.

▶ **Use "Writing a Biographical Narrative," pages 122–129, for help with this assignment.**

Name Yourself

Think about a different name you'd choose for yourself. It might be a name you've sometimes wished you had; it might be a perfectly ordinary name that just happens to be different from yours. It might be a name you'd take if you lived in another culture. Visualize yourself as the bearer of that name. Then, write a brief **character sketch** of yourself with your new name.

Reading Standard 3.3 Analyze interactions between main and subordinate characters in a literary text and explain the way those interactions affect the plot.

Reading Standard 3.4 Determine characters' traits by what the characters say about themselves in narration and dialogue.

INDEPENDENT PRACTICE

Reading Check

1. Their mother can no longer teach them.
2. She claims that she is unable to pronounce their names. She gives them English names.
3. The Indian girls eat sandwiches and wear dresses.
4. Premila refuses to accept the discrimination against Indians.

Interpretations

5. Possible answer: She means that people's nature never changes. Her daughters confront prejudice, but their experiences do not prove her generalization.

Literary Response and Analysis

6. Indian customs and values include adapting to the heat, teaching by example, and showing consideration for others. The British, in contrast, maintain a cool-weather lifestyle, teach through drills and testing, and emphasize competition.
7. Possible answer: Santha is bright (perceives the racism at school) and meek (obeys Premila). Premila is "less easily intimidated," anxious to fit in (wants sandwiches), proud (rejects racism), and responsible (cares for Santha). Their mother is warm and direct (calls the British "insular"). The headmistress is prim and indirect (touts English names as "nice" and "jolly").
8. She rejects the identity that the racist headmistress has given her.
9. Rama Rau might say that a person's name is crucial to his or her self-image and identity. Some students will agree; others may maintain, with Juliet, that names are of secondary importance.
10. Prejudice is still evident around the world; ask students to cite examples from current events. Possible themes: Cultural diversity is valuable; maintaining one's sense of self can be an antidote to racism.

Evaluation

11. Possible answers: Some students will feel that Rama Rau heightens the impact of her story by leaving her reflections unstated. Others may wish that Rama Rau had stated her thoughts directly, so that readers would have a clearer sense of what she experienced.

Vocabulary Development

Practice

Possible Answer

intimidated. How would you feel if you were intimidated?—anxious; frightened. *What physical things can make you feel intimidated?*—tests. *What nonphysical things can make you feel intimidated?*—others' scorn; high standards. *What are some words that are opposite in meaning to intimidated?*—confident; unfazed.

Resources Reminder

Vocabulary

- *Vocabulary Development*
  - Vocabulary Worksheet, p. 9
  - Cumulative Vocabulary Review, pp. 10–11
- *Lesson Plans for Language Development*
  - Vocabulary, pp. 60, 63

Grammar Link

Practice

1. The British girls and the Indian girls eat sandwiches for lunch, but the Indian girls do not like the sandwiches.
2. Premila and Santha like the school at first, but soon Premila is angered by something that happens to her.
3. Premila and Santha enter the mother's room, and the mother talks to Premila about whether the incident had upset Santha.

ASSESSING

Assessment

- *Progress Assessment of Reading*
  - Selection Test

RETEACHING

For a lesson reteaching Standard 3.4, see **Reteaching,** p. 939A.

Vocabulary Development

Putting Words in Context: Cluster Diagrams

PRACTICE

Organize what you know about each word in the Word Bank (you can skip *precarious*) by making a cluster diagram like the one below. Work with a partner to brainstorm several questions that suggest **contexts** in which the word is used appropriately. Then, list words or phrases that answer your questions.

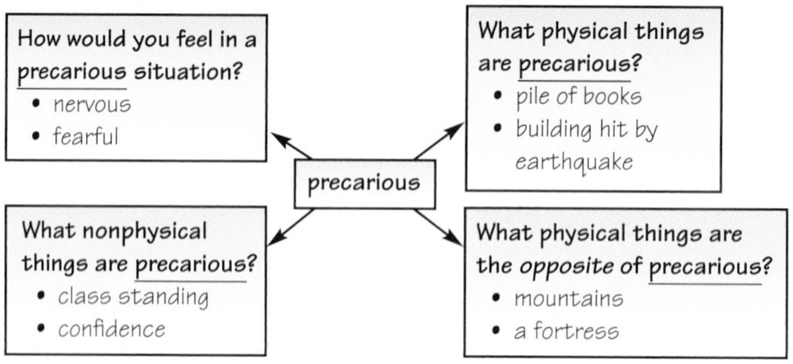

Word Bank

precarious
intimidated
provincial
insular
valid
palpitating
wizened
sedately
tepid
peevishness

Grammar Link MINI-LESSON

Grade 8 Review Reading Standard 1.3 Use word meanings within the appropriate context and show ability to verify those meanings by example, comparison, or contrast.

Who's Who? Making Pronouns Clear

Unclear pronoun reference, a common mistake, causes misunderstandings. A **pronoun** must clearly refer to its **antecedent,** the noun or pronoun that the pronoun replaces. Avoid unclear, or **ambiguous,** pronoun references, which occur when a pronoun can have more than one antecedent. One way to pin down your meaning is to replace the unclear pronoun with the noun to which it refers.

UNCLEAR Although Santha is five and her sister Premila is eight, she understands what happened. [Who understands—Santha or Premila?]

CLEAR Although Santha is five and her sister Premila is eight, Santha understands what happened.

PRACTICE

Reword the following sentences to correct any unclear pronoun references.

1. The British girls and the Indian girls eat sandwiches for lunch, but they do not like them.
2. Premila and Santha like the school at first, but soon she is angered by something that happens to her.
3. Premila and Santha enter the mother's room, and she talks to her about whether the incident had upset her.

For more help, see Clear Pronoun Reference in the *Holt Handbook,* pages 164–166.

120 Chapter 2 Character • Using Primary and Secondary Sources

Read On: FOR INDEPENDENT READING

FICTION

Money Isn't Everything

It's the mid–nineteenth century, and Catherine Sloper lives with her father in New York City's fashionable Washington Square. Catherine, a plain, awkward, and soft-spoken young woman, is generally thought to be "unmarriageable." When a poor but handsome suitor begins to court her, her father tries to end the relationship, believing that the young man has eyes only for the family fortune. Should Catherine listen to her father or to her heart? ***Washington Square,*** a novel by Henry James, reveals a woman's inner strength in a way that you might not expect.

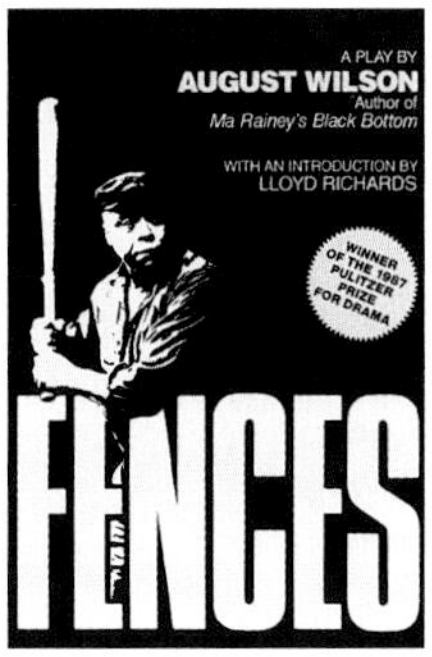

DRAMA

Father and Son

The father and son in August Wilson's 1987 Pulitzer Prize-winning play ***Fences*** have conflicting visions for the boy's future. Having once been excluded from baseball's major leagues because of his race, fifty-three-year-old Troy Maxson finds it difficult to encourage his son's ball-playing ambitions. Is he an overbearing dad, or is he just looking out for his son's best interests?

NONFICTION

Growing Up Despite It All

Gary Soto's ***A Summer Life*** reveals what it was like to grow up in a Mexican American family in California's San Joaquin Valley. In a series of funny and often touching essays, Soto focuses on topics like "The Shirt," "The Haircut," "The Drive-In Movies," "The Computer Date," and other vivid scenes and memories from a mischievous boy's life.

NONFICTION

The Smart One

Jade Snow Wong was one of many children in her parents' California home, but she was always regarded as the smart member of her family. She excelled in school and received tutoring from her father, learning the honorable, traditional ways of Chinese culture. However, Jade Snow's education afforded her the opportunity to have a life that the traditional Chinese girl didn't have. You can read about Jade Snow's struggle to unite her roots with her newfound American ways in her acclaimed autobiography, ***Fifth Chinese Daughter.***

Toward Reading Two Million Words Annually

Estimated Word Counts and Reading Levels of Read On Books:

Fiction			**Nonfiction**		
Washington Square	↑	23,100	*A Summer Life*	↓	41,100
Drama			*Fifth Chinese Daughter*	↔	99,100
*Fences**	↔	26,100			

*California Reading List Titles

KEY: ↑ *above grade level* ↔ *at grade level* ↓ *below grade level*

Read On

For Independent Reading

If students enjoyed the themes and topics explored in this chapter, you might recommend these titles for independent reading.

Assessment Options

The following projects can help you evaluate and assess your students' outside reading. Videotapes and audiotapes of completed projects may be included in students' portfolios.

- **Publish an online review.** Many online bookstores welcome reviews from readers. Instructions for submitting reviews are available at the Web sites. Invite students to review *Fences, A Summer Life,* or *Fifth Chinese Daughter* and to explain why they would or would not recommend the book for others their age.
- **Rate the movie.** Have students who read *Washington Square* view a video of the classic 1949 film *The Heiress,* based on the novel. Then, have students form pairs to stage a "television spot" in which they defend thumbs-up or thumbs-down ratings for the film's depiction of the motivations, conflicts, and relationships in the novel.
- **Role-play a support group for characters.** Encourage students who have read *Fences, Washington Square,* or *Fifth Chinese Daughter* to meet and role-play members of a support group for young people with difficulties. Have the students choose group members to play the main characters—Cory Maxson, Catherine Sloper, and Jade Snow Wong. Tell them that the "characters" should discuss problems they are having and the other group members should offer advice.

PRETEACHING

Standards Starter

Motivate. Ask students if they have ever seen a photograph of someone and thought, "This is a great picture. This captures [him or her] perfectly!" Ask some students to share examples of some favorite candid photos. What specific characteristics of the subject did the photograph capture? Tell students that they will be writing biographical narratives and that their goal will be to produce a piece of writing that effectively captures the essence of the person they write about, just as a quality photograph does.

Resources Reminder

To introduce the workshop, you may want to use the journal starters in *Writing, Listening, & Speaking* Teaching Notes.

CRITICAL THINKING

After students have listed a number of anecdotes for their narratives, suggest that they devise criteria for determining which anecdotes to use. Discuss as a class what makes one anecdote more successful than another, and help students turn this information into criteria. For example, students might note how anecdotes that make a clear point or that highlight a universal truth are most effective. Then, encourage students to use these criteria to evaluate which of their anecdotes would work best in their narratives.

Writing Workshop

Writing a Biographical Narrative

Writing Assignment
Writing 2.1 Write a biographical narrative about a person you know well, creating a controlling impression that communicates the significance of your subject.

Earlier in this chapter you read a fictional narrative—Alice Walker's short story "Everyday Use." In that story, the narrator sketches vivid portraits of her daughters by noting Maggie's thin, awkward arms and Dee's haughty walk. Now it's your turn to describe a person by writing a **biographical narrative,** a nonfiction account of someone who is important to you. In your narrative, you'll share anecdotes and concrete details that show how you feel about that person and your relationship.

Prewriting

GO TO: go.hrw.com
KEYWORD: HLLA 10-2
FOR: Professional Model, Writer's Guides, and Reference Sources

Choose a Subject

A Face in the Crowd To pick a subject for your biographical narrative, make a list of the most interesting people you know well. Picture the face of each person on the list and jot down what makes that person both interesting and **significant** to you. Then, list anecdotes—short, true stories—about each person on your list. Pick anecdotes that show why each person is meaningful to you. Look at how one writer took notes in a three-column chart.

Who	Significance	Anecdotes
Kelly	Her way of looking at life makes her interesting. She always helps me see a different side of things. We've been good friends since we both joined the Photography Club.	1. First notice of Kelly in middle school during a class discussion 2. My visit to Kelly's home 3. Kelly in the photography darkroom 4. Kelly's visit to my home
Aunt Thelma	Her wide-ranging knowledge makes her interesting. I've known her all my life.	1. Aunt Thelma teaching me to ride a bike 2. Aunt Thelma trying to teach me to sew 3. My trip to the museum with Aunt Thelma

Writing 2.1 Write biographical narratives.

CHAPTER 2 RESOURCES: WRITING

Writing Workshop

Planning

- *On Course: Mapping Instruction*
- *One-Stop Planner* CD-ROM
- *Writing, Listening, & Speaking,* Teaching Notes, p. 13

Differentiating Instruction

- *Lesson Plans for Language Development,* pp. 55–56
- *Supporting Instruction in Spanish*

Practice

- *Writing, Listening, & Speaking,* Ch. 2

122 Chapter 2 Character • Using Primary and Secondary Sources

Now, choose the subject from your list that prompts the strongest and most specific memories and feelings in you; when you write your biographical narrative, you'll need an abundance of details about your subject.

DO THIS

Create a Controlling Impression

Show, Don't Tell Because a biographical narrative is different from an essay, don't blurt out the importance of your subject in a traditional thesis statement. Instead, *hint* at your subject's significance in the beginning anecdote and let the rest of the anecdotes in your narrative—and the narrative as a whole—confirm the hint by creating a **controlling impression** of your subject, from which your readers can infer the subject's significance.

How do you create a controlling impression? The answer is in the **anecdotes** you narrate and the **details** you choose to include in each of them. For example, the student chose to write about her friend Kelly, whose significance is that she helps the writer see the world around her in different ways. The anecdotes and details in her narrative contribute convincingly to a single controlling impression of Kelly: She is generous in sharing her thoughtful and unique way of looking at the world around her.

Gather Details

Down to the Last Detail Create the controlling impression you desire by using **concrete sensory details**—details of sight, sound, smell, touch, and taste—to describe the actions, movements, and gestures of your subject. In addition, describe your thoughts and feelings about your subject and your relationship with that person. To share your thoughts and feelings, use **interior monologue**—the words you say to yourself in your head.

Also, use sensory details to describe the **specific places,** or **settings,** where each anecdote occurred. The sensory details you use will create **images** of place and time in your readers' minds and create a sense of the mood or atmosphere of the setting. For example, the writer of the sample narrative on page 125 included a description of birds in one setting—"their dark bodies distinctly silhouetted against the orange sun setting behind them"—to create an image that communicates an atmosphere of peacefulness and warmth.

Talk the Talk Using **dialogue** is another way to develop a controlling impression of your subject. Re-create your subject's own words and manner of speaking as exactly as you can. That means you can use slang and contractions. Using realistic dialogue in your paper will allow your readers to imagine a complete picture of your subject.

Writing 1.1 Establish a controlling impression that conveys a distinctive perspective on the subject. **2.1a** Relate a sequence of events and communicate the significance of those events. **2.1b** Locate scenes and incidents in specific places. **2.1c** Describe with concrete sensory details the sights, sounds, and smells of a scene and the specific actions, movements, gestures, and feelings of the characters; use interior monologue to depict the characters' feelings. **2.1e** Make effective use of sensory details.

DIRECT TEACHING

Integrating with Grammar, Usage, and Mechanics

As students start their biographical narratives, they may have trouble with phrases and clauses. You may want to review the corresponding chapters in the *Holt Handbook.*

DIFFERENTIATING INSTRUCTION

Learners Having Difficulty

Encourage students to bring to class photographs or other memorabilia relating to the subject of their biographical narrative to help them recall details about the person. Give students the option of including some of these items as part of their finished essays, if feasible.

Reinforcement

- *Daily Language Activities*

Evaluation and Assessment

- Test Generator (*One-Stop Planner* CD-ROM)
- *Progress Assessment of Writing, Listening, & Speaking,* Ch. 2
- *Diagnostic and Summative Assessments,* First-Quarter Test

Internet

- go.hrw.com (keyword: HLLA 10-2)
- Online assessments at go.hrw.com (keyword: HLLA)

RETEACHING

Pace Yourself

If students have difficulty with the concept of pacing and how it is influenced by sentence structure, read the introduction of two novels to the class. One novel should begin with lengthy, complex sentences and the other with short, fast-paced sentences. Ask students to identify the sentence structures and effects of each introduction.

PRACTICE & APPLY 1

Guided and Independent Practice

To guide students in organizing their impressions and feelings toward their subjects, encourage them to create graphic organizers such as word clusters or cause-and-effect diagrams. Word clusters can help students brainstorm descriptive details and label emotional responses they have when they think about their subjects. Cause-and-effect diagrams can help students see the results of the impact the subject has had on the student. Then, have them use this strategy as they complete **Practice and Apply 1** independently.

Look below at the notes the student took for the opening anecdote of her narrative. Notice how she divided her notes into categories.

> Anecdote 1
> - **Where and when:** three years ago in our overcrowded English classroom at Pinewood Middle School
> - **How Kelly looked:** dark red hair; wild curls escaping ponytail; infectious smile
> - **What happened:** Kelly explained to the class why a character everybody disliked was really a likable character.
> - **How Kelly acted:** Kelly spoke earnestly; she leaned forward and chopped the air with her hand for emphasis as she talked.
> - **What Kelly said:** "I *do* like him."
> - **What I thought:** I thought she looked friendly. Her explanation of the class's misunderstanding of the character gave me a glimpse into her unique way of seeing things.

Plan Organization and Pacing

Plot Your Course After collecting details, think of the most logical **organizational strategies** you can use to present those details. Most narratives are related in **chronological order,** beginning with the anecdote that occurred first and going on to the second, third, and so on. You will probably want to relate the **sequence of events** that make up an anecdote in chronological order, too. Within that framework, you may also want to organize some details **spatially,** or according to their location. For example, you might describe the setting of your aunt's wedding from left to right, top to bottom, or near to far. Alternatively, you could describe a friend's appearance from the top of her cinnamon-colored mop of a hairdo down to the tips of her aqua-blue painted toenails.

Pace Yourself Vary the **pace** of your narrative to show the passage of time or a change in the mood of your narrative. Pace can be conveyed by your choice of words and sentences. Short words and simple sentences are easier and quicker to read, so they speed up the events and make the mood seem hurried. Longer words and complex sentences tend to cause readers to slow down, drawing out the events and creating a serious mood.

Writing 2.1a Relate a sequence of events and communicate the significance of those events. **2.1d** Pace the presentation of actions to accommodate changes in time and mood.

PRACTICE & APPLY 1 Use the prewriting steps in this section to choose a subject and decide upon the controlling impression you want to create. Then, gather the details you will need and plan the organization and pace of your narrative.

RESOURCES: WRITING

Practice & Apply 1

Guided Practice

- *Writing, Listening, & Speaking,* WS. pp. 10, 11

Reteaching and Modeling

- *Writing, Listening, & Speaking,* TP. 6
- *Writing, Listening, & Speaking,* WS. p. 12

124 Chapter 2 Character • Using Primary and Secondary Sources

Writing

Writing a Biographical Narrative

A Writer's Framework

Beginning

- Open with an intriguing anecdote about your subject.
- Provide background information if necessary.
- Hint at the significance of your subject.

Middle

- Narrate anecdotes that contribute to a controlling impression of the subject.
- Include thoughts and feelings and concrete sensory details about people and places.
- Organize and pace your narrative logically.

End

- End with a memorable comment, image, or quotation that reinforces the controlling impression.
- Sum up the significance of your subject.

A Writer's Model

The View from a Different Angle

The first time I really noticed Kelly was during the first week of school at Pinewood Middle School three years ago. I spied her three rows over in English class and thought she looked friendly and confident. Her cinnamon-colored hair was pulled up in a haphazard ponytail from which a dozen mischievous curls had escaped. Her eyes crinkled merrily when she smiled.

BEGINNING
Background information
Details of appearance

Our class was discussing a character in the story we'd just read, someone who nearly everyone agreed was completely unlikable. Just then, Kelly raised her hand and said earnestly, "But I *do* like him." She leaned forward, emphatically chopping the air with her hands as she explained the ways she thought we had misunderstood the character. Slowly, our classmates began to nod in agreement. That was my first glimmer into Kelly's unique way of seeing things.

Opening anecdote
Details of speech, gestures
Hint at subject's significance

Later in the semester, we both joined the Photography Club and were matched as partners so we could share equipment. I hadn't realized that Kelly had a lot of her own photography equipment until she invited me over to try it out. When I arrived at her magnificent home—really a mansion—the first thing I noticed was a long hallway filled with pictures both old and new. I asked Kelly if the pictures in the hall had anything to do with why she wanted to be in the Photography Club. She looked puzzled for a minute, then smiled and

MIDDLE
Second anecdote
Details of setting and action

(continued)

DIRECT TEACHING

A Writer's Model

Point out the writer's use of vivid verbs, such as *spied, pulled,* and *crinkled.* Explain that vivid verbs turn "telling" statements into "showing" statements. Give students examples of overused verbs, and ask them to think of more specific, vivid synonyms, as in the following examples:

1. talked [rambled, mumbled, stuttered, chattered]
2. walked [strode, ambled, strutted]

DIFFERENTIATING INSTRUCTION

Advanced Learners

Acceleration. Use the following activity with students to move them toward Writing Standards 2.1c, e for grades 11–12. Suggest that students elaborate the details in their narratives by using metaphors, similes, and personification. For example, instead of simply writing "The weather was hot," students could elaborate with a simile ["The day was as hot as a frying pan"] or with personification ["The sun glared down on us"]. These forms of comparison will add a creative aspect to students' writing.

CORRECTING MISCONCEPTIONS

REVIEW STANDARD

Students may hesitate to include their own thoughts about the subjects of their biographical narratives. Stress to them that their thoughts are important and help individualize each essay—no one else sees the subject exactly as the author does or would write the same essay.

PRACTICE & APPLY 2

Guided and Independent Practice

Before students begin writing, point out to them that a narrative of this sort cannot be written according to a generic outline. Tell students that instead of confining certain elements to specific sections of the paper, they should sprinkle all of the following elements throughout their narratives:

- anecdotes
- details about subject's speech and gestures
- details of setting and action
- sensory details
- statements that contribute to controlling impression
- interior monologue

(continued)

Sensory details

Hint at controlling impression

Third anecdote

Sensory details

Writer's thoughts

Fourth anecdote

Details of setting

Writer's feeling

END

Interior monologue

Slow pace

Image

Summary of significance

said, "Not really, but what I *do* like about some of these pictures are the frames." I hadn't noticed them at all before, but it was true—some of the pictures had very intricate, hand-carved wooden frames around them. Kelly told me about the wood used in the frames, olive wood from hillside groves by the sea near her family's village in Italy. She described it so vividly that I could smell the salt in the air! As I came to know Kelly better, I realized that noticing the frame, as opposed to the picture, was just one way Kelly saw things differently.

In the same way, Kelly deliberated on the details of her work in the Photography Club. While I focused on the technical aspects of the camera, Kelly concentrated very intensely on the "art" of photography, especially in the darkroom. One time she spent hours bent over her work in the darkroom, developing a photograph of the moon rising at sunset. It came out beautifully, with both the moon and the sun appearing with almost exactly the same brightness against the sky. I knew I would never have her vision—or patience.

Although I didn't want to, I soon invited Kelly to my house. I was a little embarrassed because, well, my apartment seems sort of meager compared to a big house like Kelly's. I knew she had arrived when I heard her singing my name from my open bedroom window. When I looked down, she waved, and I ran down to let her in through the gate. When she came into my room, she made me flush with warmth as she praised the job I had done painting my room.

We sat on my bed, looking out my small, three-by-four window. "I wish we had a yard," I said as I looked down to the ground outside. "Like your family," I thought, more than a little jealous of Kelly's lush yard. Kelly replied by pointing out the sixth-story window to the expansive sky as a flock of Canada geese flew by. The birds moved in unison, their dark bodies distinctly silhouetted against the orange sun setting behind them. "You have the whole sky," she said. Kelly was always opening my eyes, teaching me to see the precious things I hadn't noticed and to understand the value of what I have instead of what I do not.

GO TO: go.hrw.com
KEYWORD: HLLA 10-2
FOR: Expanded Writer's Model and Student's Model

PRACTICE & APPLY 2 Using the framework on page 125 and the Writer's Model above, write the first draft of your biographical narrative. Return to the Prewriting section to freshen your understanding of basic concepts, as necessary.

RESOURCES: WRITING

Practice & Apply 2

Think Sheet

- *Writing, Listening, & Speaking,* WS. p. 13

Template

- *Writing, Listening, & Speaking,* WS. p. 14

Internet

- go.hrw.com (keyword: HLLA 10-2)

Revising

Evaluate and Revise Your Narrative

Methodical Mending Even the best editors can't revise a piece of writing after just one reading. To edit your draft thoroughly, read it at least twice. In the first reading, focus on content and organization. In the second reading, consider style.

First Reading: Content and Organization Using the questions in the following chart, carefully evaluate the content and organization of your narrative. As you work through the list, keep your **purpose** and intended **audience** in mind. Because the purpose of this biography is, in large part, to express your feelings and observations about your subject, your language may be **less formal** than in other papers you write in school. First-person pronouns and informal language, especially in dialogue, are acceptable here.

PEER REVIEW

Ask a classmate to read your narrative and suggest ways you might improve its content, organization, or style. For example, a classmate might suggest ways to better communicate the controlling impression of your narrative.

Guidelines: Writing a Biographical Narrative

Evaluation Questions	Tips	Revision Techniques
1 Does the narrative provide an interesting introduction to the subject and hint at the subject's significance to the writer?	**Underline** the vivid introduction of the subject. **Double underline** any hint of the subject's significance.	**Replace** the opening sentences with a striking or intriguing view of the subject. **Add** a hint about the subject's significance to you.
2 Do all anecdotes contribute to the controlling impression of the subject?	**Star** each sentence that begins a separate anecdote. In the margin **write a phrase** that tells the impression of the subject each anecdote gives.	**Cut** anecdotes that do not support the controlling impression. **Add** relevant anecdotes.
3 Are concrete sensory details used to describe all people and places? Are the writer's and others' thoughts and feelings described?	**Highlight** all concrete sensory details. **Check** the thoughts and feelings of the writer and others.	**Add** concrete sensory details or **elaborate** on existing details. **Add** thoughts and feelings of the writer and others.
4 Are anecdotes and descriptions organized logically?	**Number** the anecdotes narrated. **Bracket** each description of a person or setting.	**Reorder** incidents in chronological order or descriptions in spatial order.
5 Does the conclusion reinforce the controlling impression and sum up the subject's significance to the writer?	**Box** sentences enhancing the controlling impression. **Circle** sentences that sum up the subject's significance.	**Add** a final comment, quotation, or image to enhance the controlling impression. **Add** a clear statement of the subject's significance, if necessary.

DIFFERENTIATING INSTRUCTION

English-Language Learners

Since students' language may be less formal in an autobiographical narrative, they might benefit from a class exchange in which you provide relevant examples of colloquialisms and ask volunteers to give the standard English version of each expression. Then, have speakers of other languages offer examples of colloquialisms from their languages with translations so that students can see how informal phrases and word usage appear in other languages.

Resources Reminder

For more help with English-Language Learners, see *Lesson Plans for Language Development.*

DIRECT TEACHING

Guidelines: Writing a Biographical Narrative

Advise students to use the **Guidelines** chart on this page as a think sheet by having them answer the questions in their notebooks. Explain that using think sheets to summarize their notes allows students to place their thoughts, observations, and questions on paper, which in turn helps improve the content and organization of their narratives.

Elaboration

To help students elaborate on the details of their anecdotes, ask them to think of words or phrases that are characteristic of their subjects and to add these phrases to descriptions or include them in dialogue.

Writing Workshop: Writing a Biographical Narrative 127

MODELING AND DEMONSTRATION

GRADE-LEVEL STANDARDS

Second Reading: Style

One specific way for students to correct problems with overused adverbs is to eliminate adverbs from dialogue attributions. Model this strategy by writing this sentence on the chalkboard: "I missed the winning goal," he said disappointedly. Underline the word *disappointedly*, and point out its ineffectiveness; it tells rather than shows. Rewrite the sentence this way: "I missed the winning goal," he mumbled with shoulders stooped and eyes focused on the ground. Have students demonstrate understanding by revising these two sentences on their own paper. Allow volunteers to share their revisions with the class.

- "I have the winning ticket," she said excitedly.
- "We need to go that way," he said confidently.

GUIDED PRACTICE

Responding to the Revision Process

Answers

1. *Completely* is a more precise adverb than the overused adverb *very*. In the second sentence, *really* is deleted because it is an overused adverb, and it seems unnecessary as used here.
2. The addition helps create an image of Kelly in the reader's mind.

PRACTICE & APPLY 3

Independent Practice

Have students mark their revisions in colored pencil so you can quickly spot the changes and assess them. If students are using word-processing programs with a Revision feature, ask them to use it so that both the original text and the revision are visible.

Second Reading: Style During your second reading, focus your attention on the style of your narrative. Look carefully at the words you have chosen, particularly **adverbs,** words that modify verbs, adjectives, and other adverbs. Some adverbs are used so often that they have lost their punch. Use the following style guidelines to help you eliminate overused adverbs.

Style Guidelines

Evaluation Question	Tip	Revision Technique
Does the narrative contain worn-out adverbs?	**Highlight** worn-out adverbs, such as *very, really, awfully, rather, extremely,* and *somewhat.*	**Replace** the overused adverbs with more precise ones, or **delete** the adverbs.

ANALYZING THE REVISION PROCESS

Study these revisions, and answer the questions that follow.

Our class was discussing a character in the story we'd just read, someone who nearly everyone agreed was ~~very~~ *completely* unlikable. *(replace)* Just then, Kelly raised her hand and said ~~really~~ earnestly, "But I *(delete)* *do* like him." She *leaned forward, emphatically chopping the air with her hands as she* explained the ways she thought we had misunderstood the character. *(add)* Slowly, our classmates began to nod in agreement. That was my first glimmer into Kelly's unique way of seeing things.

Responding to the Revision Process

1. Why did the writer replace *very* with *completely* in the first sentence and delete *really* from the second sentence?
2. Why did the writer make the addition to the third sentence?

Writing 1.9 Revise writing to improve the precision of word choice by taking into consideration the audience, purpose, and formality of the context.

PRACTICE & APPLY 3 Using the guidelines in this section, evaluate and revise the content, organization, and style of your narrative. You may want to work with a classmate throughout the revision process.

RESOURCES: WRITING

Practice & Apply 3

Think Sheet

- *Writing, Listening, & Speaking,* WS. p. 16

Evaluation

- *Writing, Listening, & Speaking,* WS. p. 15

Practice & Apply 4

Assessment

- *Test Generator (One-Stop Planner CD-ROM)*
- *Progress Assessment of Writing, Listening, & Speaking,* pp. 6–10, 53–55

Internet

- Online assessments at go.hrw.com (keyword: HLLA)

Publishing

Proofread and Publish Your Narrative

Put Your Best Foot Forward You want your final draft to make a good impression, of course. To ensure that it does, carefully proofread it for errors in grammar, usage, and mechanics, and correct any mistakes you may find. When in doubt, consult a peer or your teacher.

May I Introduce You? You've worked exceptionally hard to capture the essence of your subject—what makes him or her a unique individual of great significance to you. Now, introduce your subject to the wider world with one of these suggestions.

- Give or send a copy of your narrative to your subject and ask for a response. In particular, you might ask if your portrait matches the way your subject sees himself or herself.
- Stage a group reading with other classmates. You might even hold your reading at a time when the people you have written about—or others who know them well—can attend.
- Submit your narrative to a student magazine. Many periodicals regularly publish biographical narratives. Ask your teacher or school librarian for the names of periodicals that publish biographical narratives.
- Exchange narratives with a peer from your English class. Then, discuss which literary characters have something in common with the subjects of your biographies. Be sure to offer specific evidence for your ideas.

TIP As you proofread, keep a sharp eye out for errors in the **conventions** of standard American English usage. In particular, watch for errors in punctuating dialogue, a common problem in biographical writing. For more on **using quotation marks,** see page 341 in the *Holt Handbook.*

Reflect on Your Narrative

A Backward Glance Before writing, you thought deeply about your subject and what makes him or her special to you. Now, reflect on the process of writing about that person. Use these questions to help you sort out your thoughts.

- What is your favorite line or passage in your narrative? Why?
- Did your view of your subject change as you worked on your narrative? Why do you think so?
- If someone wrote a biographical narrative about *you,* what controlling impression might it offer? Why do you think so?

PRACTICE & APPLY 4 If possible, collaborate with a classmate to proofread your narrative for errors in grammar, usage, and mechanics. Then, publish and reflect on your biographical narrative using the suggestions and questions above.

TECHNOLOGY TIP

Students may wish to preserve their biographical narratives in a multimedia format and include photographs and music.

Resources Reminder

For help with writing assessment, see 6 Traits—Plus 1 in the "Scales and Sample Papers" section of *Progress Assessment of Writing, Listening, & Speaking.*

PRACTICE & APPLY 4

Guided and Independent Practice

Monitor students' understanding by asking students to write a short list of grammar, usage, and mechanics errors they commonly find when proofreading their papers. Have them list strategies for correction. After briefly checking students' lists, take a quick poll to make sure each student has an idea for publishing his or her narrative. Then, have students complete **Practice and Apply 4** for independent practice.

Standards Review

Literary Response and Analysis

STANDARDS FOCUS, pp. 130–133

(For the grade-level standards reviewed in this lesson, see Student Edition, p. 130.)

INTRODUCING THE STANDARDS REVIEW

Use this review to assess students' grasp of the standards taught in this chapter. If necessary, you can use the annotations to guide students in their reading before they answer the questions.

DIRECT TEACHING

A Literary Focus
GRADE-LEVEL STANDARD

Conflict and motivation. What does the son want? [He wants to get to his mother's house for Christmas Eve dinner.] How is the father blocking the boy's wish? [He insists on staying for last-minute skiing in the fresh powder snow, instead of leaving on time.]

STANDARDS REVIEW

Literary Response and Analysis

Test Practice

Character

DIRECTIONS: Read the following short story. Then, read each multiple-choice question that follows, and write the letter of the best response.

Powder

Tobias Wolff

Just before Christmas my father took me skiing at Mount Baker. He'd had to fight for the privilege of my company, because my mother was still angry with him for sneaking me into a nightclub during our last visit, to see Thelonious Monk.[1]

A He wouldn't give up. He promised, hand on heart, to take good care of me and have me home for dinner on Christmas Eve, and she relented. But as we were checking out of the lodge that morning it began to snow, and in this snow he observed some quality that made it necessary for us to get in one last run. We got in several last runs. He was indifferent to my fretting.[2] Snow whirled around us in bitter, blinding squalls, hissing like sand, and still we skied. As the lift bore us to the peak yet again, my father looked at his watch and said, "Criminey. This'll have to be a fast one."

By now I couldn't see the trail. There was no point in trying. I stuck to him like white on rice and did what he did and somehow made it to the bottom without sailing off a cliff. We returned our skis and my father put chains on the Austin-Healy while I swayed from foot to foot, clapping my mittens and wishing I were home. I could see everything. The green tablecloth, the plates with the holly pattern, the red candles waiting to be lit.

We passed a diner on our way out. "You want some soup?" my father asked. I shook my head. "Buck up," he said. "I'll get you there. Right, doctor?"

I was supposed to say, "Right, doctor," but I didn't say anything.

A state trooper waved us down outside the resort. A pair of sawhorses were blocking the road. The trooper came up to our car and bent down to my father's window. His face was bleached by the cold. Snowflakes clung to his eyebrows and to the fur trim of his jacket and cap.

"Don't tell me," my father said.

The trooper told him. The road was closed. It might get cleared, it might not. Storm took everyone by surprise. So much, so fast. Hard to get people moving. Christmas Eve. What can you do?

My father said, "Look. We're talking about four, five inches. I've taken this car through worse than that."

The trooper straightened up, boots creaking. His face was out of sight but I could hear him. "The road is closed."

My father sat with both hands on the wheel, rubbing the wood with his thumbs. He looked at the barricade for a long time. He seemed to be trying to master the idea

1. **Thelonious Monk** (1917–1982): American jazz musician, famed as a pianist and composer; one of the creators of the bop style of jazz.
2. **fretting** *v.* used as *n.*: worrying.

Pages 130–133 cover **Reading Standard 3.3** Analyze interactions between main and subordinate characters in a literary text (e.g., internal and external conflicts, motivations, relationships, influences) and explain the way those interactions affect the plot.

Pages 130–133 cover **Reading Standard 3.4** Determine characters' traits by what the characters say about themselves in narration and dialogue.

READING MINI-LESSON

Reviewing Word-Attack Skills

Activity. Display the following words. Have students group them into three categories: those in which *i* represents /ē/; those in which *i* and the preceding consonant represent /sh/; and those in which *i* and the preceding letter represent /shē/.

precious [/sh/]	pretentious [/sh/]
previous [/ē/]	social [/sh/]
sociality [/shē/]	appreciate [/shē/]
grandiose [/ē/]	emaciated [/ē/]
credential [/sh/]	precarious [/ē/]
negotiate [/shē/]	satiate [/shē/]

Activity. Display these words. Have students identify the silent letter in each. Answers are underlined.

of it. Then he thanked the trooper, and with a weird, old-maidy show of caution turned the car around. "Your mother will never forgive me for this," he said.

"We should have left before," I said. "Doctor."

He didn't speak to me again until we were both in a booth at the diner, waiting for our burgers. "She won't forgive me," he said. "Do you understand? Never."

"I guess," I said, but no guesswork was required; she wouldn't forgive him.

"I can't let that happen." He bent toward me. "I'll tell you what I want. I want us to be together again. Is that what you want?"

I wasn't sure, but I said, "Yes, sir."

He bumped my chin with his knuckles. "That's all I needed to hear."

When we finished eating he went to the pay phone in the back of the diner, then joined me in the booth again. I figured he'd called my mother, but he didn't give a report. He sipped at his coffee and stared out the window at the empty road. "Come on!" When the trooper's car went past, lights flashing, he got up and dropped some money on the check. "Okay. *Vámonos.*"[3]

The wind had died. The snow was falling straight down, less of it now; lighter. We drove away from the resort, right up to the barricade. "Move it," my father told me. When I looked at him he said, "What are you waiting for?" I got out and dragged one of the sawhorses aside, then pushed it back after he drove through. When I got inside the car, he said, "Now you're an accomplice.[4] We go down together." He put the car in gear and looked at me. "Joke, doctor."

"Funny, doctor."

Down the first long stretch I watched the road behind us, to see if the trooper was on our tail. The barricade vanished. Then there was nothing but snow: snow on the road, snow kicking up from the chains, snow on the trees, snow in the sky; and our trail in the snow. I faced around and had a shock. The lie of the road behind us had been marked by our own tracks, but there were no tracks ahead of us. My father was breaking virgin snow between a line of tall trees. He was humming "Stars Fell on Alabama." I felt snow brush along the floorboards under my feet. To keep my hands from shaking I clamped them between my knees.

My father grunted in a thoughtful way and said, "Don't ever try this yourself."

"I won't."

"That's what you say now, but someday you'll get your license and then you'll think you can do anything. Only you won't be able to do this. You need, I don't know—a certain instinct."

"Maybe I have it."

"You don't. You have your strong points, but not . . . you know. I only mention it because I don't want you to get the idea this is something just anybody can do. I'm a great driver. That's not a virtue, okay? It's just a fact, and one you should be aware of. Of course you have to give the old heap some credit, too—there aren't many cars I'd try this with. Listen!"

I listened. I heard the slap of the chains, the stiff, jerky rasp of the wipers, the purr of the engine. It really did purr. The car was almost new. My father couldn't afford it, and

3. ***Vámonos*** (vä′mō • nōs): Spanish for "Let's go."
4. **accomplice** (ə • käm′plis) *n.:* partner in crime.

DIRECT TEACHING

B Literary Focus
GRADE-LEVEL STANDARD

Conflict and motivation. What is the father's motivation for disobeying the state trooper? [The father knows that if he doesn't return his son in time, the mother will be angry and will curtail his visitation privileges; the father wants to prevent that so that he can continue to see his son.]

C Literary Focus
GRADE-LEVEL STANDARD

Characters' traits. What character traits does the father demonstrate in this passage? [He shows that he is daring and has a sense of humor.]

1. arraignment
2. gnaw
3. jamb
4. pneumonia
5. deign
6. paradigm
7. solemn
8. feign
9. gnarled
10. mnemonic

Activity. Display these pairs. Ask students which word in each pair has a silent letter. Answers are underlined.

1. lumber — <u>plumber</u>
2. <u>phlegm</u> — phlegmatic
3. <u>hymn</u> — hymnal
4. limber — <u>climber</u>
5. <u>sign</u> — signature
6. <u>bomber</u> — bombard
7. <u>malign</u> — malignant
8. slumber — <u>dumber</u>

Standards Review

Direct Teaching

A Literary Focus
GRADE-LEVEL STANDARD

Characters' traits. **What character traits does the boy have that help him avoid conflicts?** [He always thinks ahead and makes plans; he's responsible.] **What character traits does the father have that help him overcome conflicts?** [He is charming and able to think quickly in difficult situations.]

B Literary Focus
GRADE-LEVEL STANDARD

Characters' interactions. **How does the boy's attitude toward his father change?** [The boy comes to appreciate his father's warmth, skill, and confidence and to trust him.] **How does this change in the boy's feelings help to resolve the story's conflict?** [The boy begins to share his father's zest for life; he stops worrying and starts enjoying the adventure in "fresh powder" as much as his father does.]

kept promising to sell it, but here it was.

I said, "Where do you think that policeman went to?"

"Are you warm enough?" He reached over and cranked up the blower. Then he turned off the wipers. We didn't need them. The clouds had brightened. A few sparse, feathery flakes drifted into our slipstream and were swept away. We left the trees and entered a broad field of snow that ran level for a while and then tilted sharply downward. Orange stakes had been planted at intervals in two parallel lines and my father ran a course between them, though they were far enough apart to leave considerable doubt in my mind as to where exactly the road lay. He was humming again, doing little scat riffs[5] around the melody.

"Okay then. What are my strong points?"

"Don't get me started," he said. "It'd take all day."

"Oh, right. Name one."

"Easy. You always think ahead."

True. I always thought ahead. I was a boy who kept his clothes on numbered hangers to ensure proper rotation. I bothered my teachers for homework assignments far ahead of their due dates so I could make up schedules. I thought ahead, and that was why I knew that there would be other troopers waiting for us at the end of our ride, if we got there. What I did not know was that my father would wheedle and plead his way past them—he didn't sing "O Tannenbaum"[6] but just about—and get me home for dinner, buying a little more time before my mother decided to make the split final. I knew we'd get caught; I was resigned to it. And maybe for this reason I stopped moping and began to enjoy myself.

Why not? This was one for the books. Like being in a speedboat, only better. You can't go downhill in a boat. And it was all ours. And it kept coming, the laden trees, the unbroken surface of snow, the sudden white vistas. Here and there I saw hints of the road, ditches, fences, stakes, but not so many that I could have found my way. But then I didn't have to. My father in his forty-eighth year, rumpled, kind, bankrupt of honor, flushed with certainty. He was a great driver. All persuasion, no coercion.[7] Such subtlety at the wheel, such tactful pedalwork. I actually trusted him. And the best was yet to come—switchbacks and hairpins impossible to describe. Except maybe to say this: If you haven't driven fresh powder,[8] you haven't driven.

5. **scat riffs:** short, improvised musical phrases in the style of scat, a kind of jazz singing.

6. **"O Tannenbaum":** title of a German Christmas carol, known in English as "O Christmas Tree."

7. **coercion** (kō · ʉr′shən) *n.:* use of force.

8. **powder** *n.:* light, dry snow, considered to be best for skiing.

Using Academic Language

Review of Literary Terms
Reading Standards 3.3 and 3.4

Ask students to look back through the chapter to find the meanings of the terms listed at right. Then, have students show their grasp of Standards 3.3 and 3.4 by citing passages from the chapter that illustrate the meanings of those terms.

Character (pp. 74, 96, 112); **Characterization** (pp. 74, 112); **Dialogue** (p. 74); **Dramatic Monologue** (p. 75); **Narration** (p. 76); **Protagonist** (p. 96); **Antagonist** (p. 96); **External and Internal Conflict** (pp. 96, 98); **Subordinate Characters** (p. 96); **Motivation** (p. 97).

Review of Informational Terms
Reading Standard 2.5

Ask students to look back through the chapter to find the meanings of the terms listed below. Then, ask students to use those terms to explain how to extend ideas presented in primary and secondary sources.

Primary Source (p. 88); **Secondary Source** (p. 88); **Analyze** (p. 88); **Evaluate** (p. 88); **Elaborate** (p. 88); **Bibliography** (p. 88); **Opinions** (p. 88); **Facts** (p. 88); **Main Idea** (p. 88).

1. Two adjectives that can be used to describe the father's **character traits** are —
   - **A** daring, humorous
   - **B** dull, hesitant
   - **C** mean, responsible
   - **D** fearful, serious

2. The father's drive down the mountain is **motivated** by his desire to —
   - **F** seek thrills no matter how great the danger
   - **G** prove his skill as a driver
   - **H** prove his concern for his son's safety
   - **J** keep his promise to his wife

3. The boy's mother, whom we never meet, influences the events of the **plot** since we infer that she might —
   - **A** punish the son for being late
   - **B** send out a search party
   - **C** celebrate Christmas without him
   - **D** prevent the father from seeing his son again

4. The relationship between which of the following characters in the story does *not* involve **conflict**?
   - **F** The father and the state trooper
   - **G** The father and the mother
   - **H** The son and his mother
   - **J** The father and his son

5. From what the **narrator** says about himself, which of the following statements can we infer?
   - **A** He misses his mother.
   - **B** He is very self-confident.
   - **C** He is a bully.
   - **D** He is a worrier.

6. From what the **narrator** says about his habits, we learn that he is —
   - **F** sloppy and reckless
   - **G** cautious and organized
   - **H** carefree and fun loving
   - **J** angry and depressed

7. When the son calls his father "rumpled, kind, bankrupt of honor, flushed with certainty," we can infer that the son —
   - **A** fears his father
   - **B** loves his father
   - **C** despises his father
   - **D** doesn't know his father well

8. The **dialogue** in the story between the father and son reveals the father's —
   - **F** love for his son
   - **G** need to be serious
   - **H** lack of self-confidence
   - **J** lack of humor

9. At the story's end the son feels —
   - **A** respect for his mother's judgment
   - **B** admiration for his father's skills
   - **C** an increase in self-confidence
   - **D** disappointment in his father

ASSESSING

Assessment

- *Progress Assessment of Reading*
  - Chapter Test

Test-Taking Tips

For more information on how to answer multiple-choice items, refer students to **Test Smarts.**

TestPractice

Answers and Model Rationales

1. **A** The father's actions show that he is daring, and his remarks show his humor.
2. **J** The father expresses his motive when he says, "She won't forgive me. . . . I can't let that happen."
3. **D** The father has already had to fight to see his son; the father states that he wants them to be together again.
4. **H** H is the only possible answer. Conflicts occur when the trooper stops the father (F); when the father battles the snow (G); and when father and son disagree about leaving on time (J).
5. **D** The narrator indicates that he is a worrier when he refers to "my fretting" and is anxious during the drive.
6. **G** The narrator reveals that he is so organized that he keeps clothes on numbered hangers and so cautious that he asks teachers for assignments far in advance.
7. **B** The boy's words suggest compassion and admiration. He is aware of his father's faults ("rumpled," "bankrupt of honor") but loves him anyway. D is wrong, since the boy's description of his father is accurate and perceptive. His words suggest neither fear (A) nor dislike (C).
8. **F** Students can eliminate G, H, and J because the father's dialogue sparkles with humor and self-confidence. He expresses love by saying that he wants to be with his son and by praising his son's virtues.
9. **B** At the end the boy calls his father "a great driver" and admires his skills.

Test Practice

Vocabulary Development

Context Clues

Modeling. Model the thought process of a good reader arriving at the answer to item 1 by saying, "I read that Maggie is shy and nervous. A—huddling in fear—is something a shy, nervous person might do. Also, the fact that Maggie is standing 'behind Mama's back' suggests that she is fearful. The other options don't fit."

Test Practice

Answers and Model Rationales

1. **A** See rationale above.
2. **G** Having a philosophy of life means living according to a set of principles.
3. **C** The context clue "desire to find" suggests a search. A, B, and D do not necessarily involve a search.
4. **G** The phrase "extraordinarily talented" is a clue that *prodigy* means "young genius."
5. **D** The context clue "tired and bored" points to a lack of energy.
6. **F** The context clue "painfully earsplitting" points to F, unharmonious. Melodious (G) and rhythmic (J) describe pleasing sounds. Popular music (H) covers many kinds of sounds.
7. **B** The clue "unlike the success" hints that *fiasco* is the opposite of success. The only option that is opposite to success is B, failure.
8. **F** Encountering "strange and unfriendly-looking" people might make someone feel afraid (F), not delighted (H). Being surprised (G) is not mentioned. Since there's no mention of conversation, being questioned (J) is incorrect as well.

TEST PRACTICE

Vocabulary Development

Test Practice

Context Clues

DIRECTIONS: Using context clues to help you, choose the answer that gives the best definition of the underlined word.

1. Always nervous and shy, Maggie was cowering behind Mama's back when Dee took their pictures. *Cowering* means —
   - **A** huddling in fear
   - **B** laughing with amusement
   - **C** making strange faces
   - **D** protesting loudly

2. Dee's boyfriend had built his philosophy of life on certain doctrines. *Doctrines* means —
   - **F** famous sayings
   - **G** principles
   - **H** relationships
   - **J** medical procedures

3. In her desire to find family heirlooms, Dee was caught rifling through Mama's belongings. *Rifling* means —
   - **A** slashing
   - **B** shooting
   - **C** searching roughly
   - **D** stealing

4. Jing-mei's mother wanted her to be a prodigy like Waverly Jong, who was an extraordinarily talented chess champion. *Prodigy* means —
   - **F** daughter
   - **G** young genius
   - **H** musician
   - **J** scholar

5. Jing-mei performed listlessly, her head resting on one arm. She seemed tired and bored. *Listlessly* means —
   - **A** without fear
   - **B** without embarrassment
   - **C** without talent
   - **D** without energy

6. Jing-mei played only discordant music, and Old Chong, her deaf teacher, had no idea how painfully earsplitting her playing sounded. *Discordant* means —
   - **F** unharmonious
   - **G** melodious
   - **H** popular
   - **J** rhythmic

7. Unlike the success Jing-mei had imagined, her performance was a fiasco that shamed her parents. *Fiasco* means —
   - **A** misunderstanding
   - **B** failure
   - **C** triumph
   - **D** surprise

8. Santha shyly entered the classroom of strange, unfriendly-looking students and was immediately intimidated by them. *Intimidated* means —
   - **F** made to feel afraid
   - **G** surprised
   - **H** delighted
   - **J** questioned

Vocabulary Review

Use this activity to assess whether students have retained the chapter Vocabulary. Ask students to complete each sentence with a word from the box.

provincial	furtive	lamented
intimidated	mesmerizing	

1. Santha, fascinated, found her playmate's long stories _____. [mesmerizing]
2. Confident and fearless, Jing-mei was not _____ by the audience. [intimidated]
3. Dee's lifestyle was urban and sophisticated; Mama's was rural and _____. [provincial]
4. Lucinda Matlock never complained or _____ her lot in life. [lamented]
5. Did anyone notice the _____ way the girls covertly eyed Premila's lunch? [furtive]

Writing

Test Practice

DIRECTIONS: Read the following paragraph from a draft of a student's biographical narrative. Then, answer the questions below it.

(1) Before my next-door neighbor became my friend, I saw her only once a day when she shuffled out of her house to get her mail. (2) Her appearance frightened me for a while. (3) One day I was locked out of my house after school and needed to borrow her telephone. (4) "She's going to slam this door right in my face," I thought as I knocked, but to my surprise she greeted me warmly and let me call my mom. (5) While I waited for my mother, my neighbor showed me her collection of glass animal figures and told me to keep the one I liked best. (6) I chose a tiny glass chameleon that changed colors as the light struck it from different angles—a reminder that appearances can be deceiving.

1. Which of the following techniques of narrative writing did the writer use in the first part of sentence 4?
- **A** imagery
- **B** sensory details
- **C** dialogue
- **D** interior monologue

2. To portray the setting of the passage better, the writer could
- **F** relate how scary it was to knock on the neighbor's door
- **G** describe the inside of her neighbor's home
- **H** tell what her neighbor was wearing
- **J** describe the writer's own room

3. Which additional character description would support the ideas in sentence 2?
- **A** My neighbor is retired and lives alone, but her son often visits.
- **B** She always holds a bright red leash with an excited white poodle bouncing at the end of it.
- **C** She talks to everyone and leaves little presents for the mail carrier.
- **D** Her wiry, wild, gray hair frames her dark eyes that dart suspiciously as she limps slowly to the mailbox.

4. Which clause could replace the last clause of sentence 6 and thus eliminate a cliché?
- **F** that beauty is in the eye of the beholder
- **G** that you shouldn't judge a book by its cover
- **H** that things appear very different from different perspectives
- **J** that the apple doesn't fall far from the tree

5. Which sentence could the writer add to summarize the significance of the subject?
- **A** I learned that my neighbor's appearance contrasts with her personality.
- **B** I learned that I live next door to a scary woman who is evil.
- **C** I learned that people's appearances sometimes reflect their natures.
- **D** I learned that my neighborhood is full of different and interesting people.

Standards Review

Answers

1. D
2. G
3. D
4. H
5. A

APPLICATION

When I Look at You, I See

Using the subjects from their biographical narratives, students should create attractive posters that convey the same type of information found in a biographical narrative. Each poster should contain images, phrases, colors, and textures that work together to present a controlling impression about the subject. Students may share their posters with the class and ask classmates to identify the controlling impression, based on words and images presented.

EXTENSION

A Personalized Greeting

For homework, have each student develop a free-verse poem that contains one or more of the anecdotes from his or her biographical narrative, along with an explanation of its significance to the writer. Students may or may not choose to share their poems with their subjects.

Homework

RESOURCES: WRITING

Assessment

- *Test Generator (One-Stop Planner* CD-ROM)
- *Progress Assessment of Writing, Listening, & Speaking,* Ch. 2
- *Diagnostic and Summative Assessments,* First-Quarter Test

Internet

- Online assessments at go.hrw.com (keyword: HLLA)

Holt Literature and Language Arts: Mastering the California Standards

Chapter 3 Narrator and Voice

Generating Research Questions

Program Organization

Holt Literature and Language Arts provides a complete curriculum for standards-based instruction in reading, literature, writing, listening and speaking, and language conventions. The instructional content is presented in quarters to enable teachers to anticipate and administer the quarterly assessments required by California.

About Chapter 3

Standards-based lesson plans and suggestions for pacing the presentation of Chapter 3, the related instructional material, and the recommended assessment are provided in *On Course: Mapping Instruction,* Chapter 3.

- In Chapter 3, students will identify and use words literally and figuratively; distinguish between denotative and connotative word meanings; generate relevant questions about readings; explain voice, persona, and choice of narrator and its affect on the text; write a problem and solution essay and deliver a persuasive speech.

Language Arts Content

Which reading standards are taught in Chapter 3?

In this chapter, students will master the following Grade 10 standards and review standards from Grade 8. Selections or features marked with a ✔ constitute the minimum course of study that provides coverage of grade-level standards.

Grade 10 Standards

Word Analysis, Fluency, and Systematic Vocabulary Development

1.1 Identify and use the literal and figurative meanings of words, and understand word derivations.
Suffixes: Meaningful Endings, p. 153
✔ Antonyms: Just the Opposite, p. 205

1.2 Distinguish between the denotative and connotative meanings of words.
Using a Thesaurus to Find Synonyms, p. 186

Reading Comprehension (Focus on Informational Materials)

2.3 Generate relevant questions about readings on issues that can be researched.
"Taste—The Final Frontier" (newspaper article), pp. 187–191
✔ "An Ancient Enemy Gets Tougher" (Internet article), pp. 206–210
"Local Hands on a New Space Project" (standards review), pp. 222–225

Literary Response and Analysis

3.9 Explain how voice, persona, and the choice of a narrator affect characterization and the tone, plot, and credibility of a text.
"Point of View: The Story's Voice" (standards essay), pp. 138–139
"By the Waters of Babylon" (short story), pp. 140–152
"The Storyteller" (short story), pp. 154–161
"The Cold Equations" (short story), pp. 163–185
✔ "Typhoid Fever" (autobiography), pp. 193–204

Review Standards Grade 8

Reading 1.3 Use word meanings within the appropriate context, and show ability to verify those meanings by definition, restatement, example, comparison, or contrast.
Using Context Clues, p. 162; Word Mapping: How to Own a New Word, p. 192

Reading 3.4 Analyze the relevance of the setting to the mood, tone, and meaning of the text.
"By the Waters of Babylon" (short story), pp. 140–152

Which writing, and listening and speaking standards are taught in Chapter 3?

Writing Strategies

1.3 Use clear research questions and suitable research methods to elicit and present evidence from primary and secondary sources.
Investigate the Problem and Solutions, p. 213

1.9 Revise writing to improve the logic and coherence of the organization and controlling perspective, the precision of the word choice, and the tone by taking into consideration the audience, purpose, and formality of the context.
Evaluate and Revise Your Draft, pp. 217–218

Writing Applications

2.3 Write expository compositions, including analytical essays and research reports.
- a. Marshal evidence in support of a thesis and related claims, including information on all relevant perspectives.
Build an Argument, p. 214
- b. Convey information and ideas from primary and secondary sources accurately and coherently.
Investigate the Problem and Solutions, p. 213
- c. Make distinctions between the relative value and significance of specific data, facts, and ideas.
Build an Argument, p. 214
- e. Anticipate and address readers' potential misunderstandings, biases, and expectations.
Consider Purpose and Audience, p. 212
- f. Use technical terms and notations accurately.
Build an Argument, p. 214

2.4 Write persuasive compositions.
- a. Structure ideas and arguments in a sustained and logical fashion.
Organize Your Analysis, p. 214
- b. Use specific rhetorical devices to support assertions.
Build an Argument, p. 214
- c. Clarify and defend positions with precise and relevant evidence, including facts, expert opinions, quotations, and expressions of commonly accepted beliefs and logical reasoning.
Build an Argument, p. 214
- d. Address readers' concerns, counterclaims, biases, and expectations.
Consider Purpose and Audience, p. 212

Listening and Speaking Strategies

1.3 Choose logical patterns of organization to inform and to persuade, by soliciting agreement or action, or to unite audiences behind a common belief or cause.
Adapt Your Written Analysis, pp. 220–221

1.6 Present and advance a clear thesis statement and choose appropriate types of proof that meet standard tests for evidence, including credibility, validity, and relevance.
Adapt Your Written Analysis, pp. 220–221

Speaking Applications

2.3 Apply appropriate interviewing techniques.
- a. Prepare and ask relevant questions.
Adapt Your Written Analysis, pp. 220–221
- b. Make notes of responses.
Adapt Your Written Analysis, pp. 220–221
- c. Use language that conveys maturity, sensitivity, and respect.
Adapt Your Written Analysis, pp. 220–221

(continued)

(continued)

d. Respond correctly and effectively to questions.
Adapt Your Written Analysis, pp. 220–221

e. Demonstrate knowledge of the subject or organization.
Adapt Your Written Analysis, pp. 220–221

f. Compile and report responses.
Adapt Your Written Analysis, pp. 220–221

g. Evaluate the effectiveness of the interview.
Adapt Your Written Analysis, pp. 220–221

2.5 Deliver persuasive arguments.

a. Structure ideas and arguments in a coherent, logical fashion.
Adapt Your Written Analysis, pp. 220–221

b. Use rhetorical devices to support assertions.
Adapt Your Written Analysis, pp. 220–221

c. Clarify and defend positions with precise and relevant evidence, including facts, expert opinions, quotations, and expressions of commonly accepted beliefs and logical reasoning.
Adapt Your Written Analysis, pp. 220–221

d. Anticipate and address the listener's concerns and counterarguments.
Adapt Your Written Analysis, pp. 220–221

Review Standards Grade 8

Writing 2.4 Write persuasive compositions.

b. Present detailed evidence, examples, and reasoning to support arguments, differentiating between facts and opinion.
Legs to Stand On, p. 214

Speaking 2.4 Deliver persuasive presentations.

c. Anticipate and answer listener concerns and counterarguments effectively through the inclusion and arrangement of details, reasons, examples, and other elements.
Make a Statement, p. 214

Instructional Planning and Support

Where do I find lesson plans, additional resources, and other teaching aids?

- This Annotated Teacher's Edition and *On Course: Mapping Instruction* provide direction in planning and implementing a complete California standards–based curriculum. These components also include instructions for diagnostic, progress, and summative testing; for presenting direct instruction of the standards; for differentiating instruction to provide universal access; and for locating and using the program's ancillaries.
- Lesson and workshop resources are referenced at the beginning of each selection or workshop, in the bottom margin of this teacher's edition.
- Reminders for using additional resources appear in this teacher's edition at point of use.
- The *One-Stop Planner* CD-ROM contains editable lesson plans and all print ancillaries, available in PDF format.

What if I don't have time to teach all of Chapter 3?

- Most standards can be taught with a minimum number of selections and features. In the chart on the preceding page, the core lessons you need in order to provide complete coverage of the chapter standards are identified with a ✔.
- *On Course: Mapping Instruction,* Chapter 3, lists lessons and activities that provide minimum standards coverage.

What provisions have been made for students who have additional class time scheduled in language arts?

- *Interactive Reading* provides for alternative direct instruction and practice of the grade-level standards taught in Chapter 3.
- *Universal Access: Writing, Listening, and Speaking,* Chapter 3, contains worksheets and transparencies that provide practice in and reteaching and reinforcement of the writing and listening and speaking standards in Chapter 3.
- *Universal Access: Lesson Plans for Language Development,* Chapter 3 provides alternative teaching strategies and additional worksheets designed specifically for English-language learners and special education students. Many of the suggestions and activities in this ancillary will also be helpful to students in the regular classroom who are having difficulty with particular skills.

Universal Access

How do I differentiate instruction to ensure that all my students master the standards?

Holt Literature and Language Arts provides comprehensive, differentiated instruction for all types of students.

- Most of the general instruction and teaching strategies in the Annotated Teacher's Edition are at grade level. These instructions will work well with the majority of your students.
- Point-of-use suggestions are provided for advanced learners, learners having difficulty, English-language learners, and special education students.
- *Interactive Reading* is designed to anticipate and remediate problems that students may experience in achieving mastery of the reading standards. See *Interactive Reading,* Teacher's Edition, Chapter 3, for information on using the reader to differentiate instruction.

- *Universal Access: Writing, Listening, and Speaking,* Chapter 3, contains worksheets and transparencies that provide practice in and reteaching and reinforcement of the writing and listening and speaking standards lessons in Chapter 3.
- *Universal Access: Lesson Plans for Language Development,* Chapter 3 offers teaching strategies and additional worksheets designed specifically for English-language learners and special education students.

Assessment

How do I determine whether my students are making progress in mastering the standards?

Progress Assessment

- Use the Standards Reviews at the end of Chapter 3 for an informal assessment of the informational reading and writing standards.
- Use Chapter 3 tests from the *Progress Assessment* booklets to assess comprehension and progress on mastering the standards taught in this chapter.

Summative Assessment

The content of *Holt Literature and Language Arts* has been divided into quarters to allow you to administer the four summative tests required by California. Chapters 3–5 and related instructional material constitute the second quarter of instruction. At the end of Chapter 5, you may ask students to take the Midyear Test in *Diagnostic and Summative Assessments.*

Chapter 3

STANDARDS FOCUS

(For full text of standards taught in this chapter, see the Standards Correlation by Standard chart in the Student Edition.)

Grade-Level Standards

- Vocabulary Development 1.1, 1.2
- Reading Comprehension 2.3
- Literary Response and Analysis 3.9
- Writing Strategies 1.3, 1.9
- Writing Applications 2.3a–c, e; 2.4a–d
- Listening and Speaking Strategies 1.3, 1.6
- Speaking Applications 2.3a–g, 2.5a–d

INTRODUCING THE CHAPTER

The stories in this collection, all eye-openers, expand the vistas of both mind and heart. "By the Waters of Babylon" and "The Storyteller" tantalize readers with surprising plot twists. "The Cold Equations" and "Typhoid Fever" follow young people through harrowing situations and will leave readers profoundly moved. Each story is told from a different point of view, and the text builds students' awareness of the effects of variations in narration and voice by exploring these differences. Nonfiction essays that follow "The Cold Equations" and "Typhoid Fever" pick up intriguing topics from the stories. These essays are used to teach students how to generate workable research questions. At the end of the chapter, students will have the opportunity to write an essay that analyzes problems and solutions, and to give a persuasive speech.

CHAPTER 3 RESOURCES: READING

Planning

- *One-Stop Planner* CD-ROM with Test Generator
- *On Course: Mapping Instruction*
- *At Home: A Guide to Standards Mastery*
- *At Home: In Spanish*
- *Supporting Instruction in Spanish*

Reading

- *Interactive Reading*

Differentiating Instruction

- *Lesson Plans for Language Development*

Vocabulary

- *Vocabulary Development*
  - Cumulative Vocabulary Review, pp. 17–18

Chapter 3

Narrator and Voice

GENERATING RESEARCH QUESTIONS

What I am trying to achieve is a voice sitting by a fireplace telling you a story on a winter's evening.

—Truman Capote

Let Me Help (1953) by Anna Mary Robertson ("Grandma") Moses.
Oil on panel (18″ × 22″).

go.hrw.com
KEYWORD: HLLA 10-3

137

THE QUOTATION

What does the quotation suggest about Capote's goal as a writer? [Possible response: He tries to create a narrative voice that is intimate and warm—something his readers can cozy up to.]

VIEWING THE ART

Anna Mary Robertson Moses (1860–1961), better known as Grandma Moses, was an untrained artist who began painting seriously in her seventies. Her scenes of an idealized, rural past captured the attention of mid-twentieth-century Americans who yearned for simpler times. During the forties and fifties, Grandma Moses became a media celebrity and held a lucrative contract to turn her paintings into fabric designs and greeting cards.

Activity. Ask students to explain the title of this painting, *Let Me Help.* [The painting's foreground shows a community of people who may be helping one another during the winter.]

Resources Reminder

Planning

- *At Home: A Guide to Standards Mastery*

Parent letters appear in this resource. Translations of these letters are found in *At Home: In Spanish.* Translations of selection summaries appear in *Supporting Instruction in Spanish.*

Reading

- *Interactive Reading*

The California framework requires students to read materials apart from in-class assignments. Additional readings are cited on the Read On page and on selected pages in the Student Edition.

Grammar

- *Holt Handbook*
  - Sentences Beginning with *There* or *Here,* p. 44
  - Sentences Asking Questions, p. 44
  - Agreement of Subject and Verb, pp. 108–113
  - Run-on Sentences, pp. 454–457
  - Quotation Marks, pp. 341–346

Assessment

- *Progress Assessment of Reading*
  - Chapter Test
- *Diagnostic and Summative Assessments*
  - First-Quarter Test
- *One-Stop Planner* CD-ROM with Test Generator

Internet

- go.hrw.com (Keyword: HLLA 10-3)

STANDARDS FOCUS, pp. 138–139

(For the grade-level standard taught in this lesson, see Student Edition, p. 138.)

Prerequisite Standard

- Grade 7, Literary Response and Analysis 3.5 **Contrast points of view (e.g., first and third person, limited and omniscient, subjective and objective) in narrative text and explain how they affect the overall theme of the work.**

Literary Focus: Point of View

Read aloud an account of a high-profile sporting event from the sports section of your local newspaper. Then, ask students how the account would be different if it had been written by one of the players. Write students' responses on the chalkboard. [Possible responses: The player would use the pronoun *I* and might tell what he or she experienced during the game; the account would be more subjective than objective.] Explain that a story told by a participant in the action has a first-person point of view; a story told by someone outside the action has a third-person point of view.

Literary Response and Analysis

Point of View *by* John Leggett

THE STORY'S VOICE

Omniscient Point of View: Know It All

Point of view—the vantage point from which a writer tells a story—has a powerful effect. The traditional vantage point is the **omniscient** (äm·nish′ənt) **point of view.** The **omniscient** ("all-knowing") **narrator,** a godlike observer who knows everything that is going on in the story, can see into every character's heart and mind—and tell us what each character is thinking. This storyteller is altogether outside the story's action.

> A newly married pair had boarded this coach at San Antonio. The man's face was reddened from many days in the wind and sun. . . . From time to time he looked down respectfully at his attire. He sat with a hand on each knee, like a man waiting in a barber's shop. The glances he devoted to other passengers were furtive and shy.
>
> The bride was not pretty, nor was she very young. She wore a dress of blue cashmere with small reservations of velvet here and there, and with steel buttons abounding. She continually twisted her head to regard her puff sleeves, very stiff, straight, and high. They embarrassed her.
>
> —Stephen Crane, from "The Bride Comes to Yellow Sky"

Reading Standard 3.9 Explain how voice, persona, and the choice of a narrator affect characterization and the tone, plot, and credibility of a text.

First-Person Point of View: "I" Speaks

At the opposite extreme from the omniscient point of view is the **first-person point of view.** In stories told in the **first person,** an "I" tells the story. This "I" also participates in the action, usually as the main character. (Literary critics often use the term **persona** to refer to this fictional first-person narrator.) The first-person point of view presents only what the "I" character sees, hears, knows, thinks, and feels. Suppose, for instance, Stephen Crane had the bride telling her own story.

> We boarded the Pullman car at San Antonio and sat stiffly in the plush seat. I was so nervous, and I noticed that my new husband seemed ill at ease. Did he regret our marriage already? I felt myself falling in love with his shyness.

A first-person narrator may or may not be **credible** or **reliable**—that is, he or she may not be objective, honest, or even perceptive about what's happening. In fact, the whole point of a story told from the first-person point of view may lie in the contrast between what the narrator tells us and what the writer allows us to understand in spite of the narrator.

Third-Person-Limited Point of View: Zooming In

Between the two extremes of the omniscient and first-person points of view lies the **third-person-limited point of view.** Here the story is told by an outside observer, who frequently refers to characters with third-person pronouns *(he, she, they).* Unlike the omniscient narrator this narrator views the action from the vantage point of one character, and plot events are limited to what this character experiences or observes. Suppose Crane used a third-person-limited narrator

DIFFERENTIATING INSTRUCTION

Learners Having Difficulty

Point of view. Help students understand how the choice of a first-person narrator affects what a reader learns, as well as the tone and voice of a story. From your own point of view, narrate events that occurred during a recent class period. Then, ask two volunteers to tell, from their points of view, what happened during the same class period. Finally, have students list differences in the three narratives, focusing on information, tone, and voice.

Advanced Learners

Acceleration. In order to move students toward the eleventh- and twelfth-grade Standard 3.3, for which students analyze the ways that tone and mood achieve specific aes-

138 Chapter 3 Narrator and Voice • Generating Research Questions

to tell his story and zoomed in on the husband:

He was a working man—a sheriff—and dressed in a new suit for the first time in his life. His face was like a map, full of lines from exposure to the sun. He was terrified of what he'd done—married a woman he hardly knew—but pleased with himself and his quiet bride.

Determining a Story's Point of View

When you read fiction, ask the following five questions about point of view:

1. Who is telling the story?
2. How much does this narrator know and understand?
3. How much does this narrator want me to know?
4. Can I trust this narrator?
5. In what ways would the story be different if someone else were telling it?

Voice: Hearing the Writer

Voice refers to the writer's distinctive use of language in a story, the choice of words (**diction**), and the attitude expressed (see **tone,** below). In fact, all the stylistic decisions a writer makes in a story contribute to the writer's voice. Although a writer's voice may evolve or vary, it tends to be consistent and recognizable from work to work.

In fiction a narrator can also be said to have a voice, as expressed by his or her way of speaking, use of language, and tone. The voice the author gives a narrator can strongly influence the story's tone and believability and even its plot. Imagine, for example, if "Everyday Use" were narrated by a meek, listless character with no gift for observation, description, or speech.

Tone: It's an Attitude

Tone is the attitude a speaker or writer takes toward a subject, a character, or the reader. Like the tone of a spoken voice, the tone of a story may be sympathetic, critical, ironic, humorous, tragic, hopeful, bitter, and so on.

Point of view has a tremendous effect on a story's tone. A story told from the perspective of a madman who hates everyone but his saintly mother will be different in tone from the same story told by the saintly mother herself. It will be still more different from the story told by an outside narrator who can penetrate the mysteries of both mother and son.

Practice

Take a story you've read recently, and do the following exercises:

- Imagine the story as told from a different point of view, and write the opening paragraphs.
- Explain how changing the point of view affects the story.

Practice

- *Possible rewrite of the third paragraph of "Everyday Use" in third-person-limited point of view*—Sometimes Mama dreams a dream in which she and Dee are suddenly brought together on a TV program of this sort. Out of a dark and soft-seated limousine, Mama is ushered into a bright room filled with many people. There she meets a smiling, gray, sporty man like Johnny Carson who shakes her hand and tells her what a fine girl she has. Then they are on the stage, and Dee is embracing Mama with tears in her eyes. Dee pins on Mama's dress a large orchid, even though she had told Mama once that she thinks orchids are tacky flowers.
- *How the change in point of view affects the story*—Even though the third-person narrator tells the story from Mama's viewpoint, the tone feels less intimate because the story is being told by an outsider instead of by Mama.

Apply

To emphasize the importance of point of view, have students rewrite a fairy tale from a different point of view, such as "Goldilocks and the Three Bears" from the bears' point of view or "Cinderella" from a stepsister's point of view.

Resources Reminder

Differentiating Instruction

- *Lesson Plans for Language Development*

For more instruction on point of view for English-language learners and special education students, see *Lesson Plans for Language Development,* pp. 65, 66.

thetic purposes, discuss the relationship between tone (the narrator's attitude) and mood (the emotional atmosphere in a story). Point out, for example, that a series of events narrated in an admiring tone may set a mood that is very different from one set by the same series of events narrated in a sarcastic tone.

Activity. Have students present a brief narrative twice, such as how they got to school this morning. They should use two different points of view and two different tones. Encourage students to change their diction, pitch, and intonations to suit the attitudes they want to express. Then, have them describe the mood established in each version.

STANDARDS FOCUS, pp. 140–153

(For grade-level and review standards taught in this lesson, see citations on Student Edition pages.)

Prerequisite Standard

- Grade 7, Literary Response and Analysis 3.5 **Contrast points of view (e.g., first and third person, limited and omniscient, subjective and objective) in narrative text and explain how they affect the overall theme of the work.**

Reading Skills

- Draw conclusions.

Summary *at grade level*

This classic vision of a post-apocalyptic world creates suspense by using a naive first-person narrator to describe a ruined civilization that the narrator does not understand, but that the reader gradually realizes is the city of New York after the Great Burning. The narrator—John, a young priest—lives in a primitive tribal world. He decides to journey to the Place of the Gods, a great city in ruins. Chased by wild dogs, he escapes into one of many tall buildings and stays the night there. During the night, he sees a stunning vision of the city alive and at its height, then witnesses its destruction. In the morning he finds the body of a "god" who once lived there, and he realizes that the gods were actually human beings. When John returns home, his father says that the truth about the place must be revealed gradually. John agrees, musing, "Perhaps, in the old days, they ate knowledge too fast."

Before You Read

By the Waters of Babylon

Literary Focus

First-Person Point of View: "I" Tells the Story

When a story is told from the **first-person point of view,** two important things happen. First, we share immediately in the narrator's experience and feelings. Second, we know *only* what the narrator knows. All that we learn about the story's events and the other characters comes from the narrator's observations.

Writers often choose the first-person point of view to create a sense of intimacy, as if the narrator were a friend talking directly to us. In other words, writers create a **persona,** which is a "mask" or voice for their fictional narrator. (The term *persona* comes from the Latin word for *mask.*)

Sometimes a writer will purposely use an unreliable narrator, one that the reader suspects can't be trusted, to report events. In this story, Benét uses the point of view to limit our knowledge—we know only what the narrator tells us as he makes his journey to the Place of the Gods.

Grade 8 Review Reading Standard 3.4 Analyze the relevance of the setting to the mood and meaning of the text.

Reading Standard 3.9 Explain how voice, persona, and the choice of a narrator affect characterization and the plot and credibility of a text.

Setting: Where and When

The **setting** of a story is the time and place in which the action occurs. Writers use setting in various ways: to create a **mood,** or atmosphere (such as gloomy, peaceful, or ominous); to help reveal character; and sometimes to provide the story's main conflict. In "The Cold Equations" (page 164), for example, the characters are in conflict with their setting—the cold, harsh, and dangerous frontier of space. As you read, think about the role the setting plays in this story.

Reading Skills

Drawing Conclusions: Detective Work

When you read mystery stories and other stories that present a puzzle, as "By the Waters of Babylon" does, you must act like a detective. You must look for clues and draw **conclusions** about what certain details in the story mean. As you read this story, be especially alert to clues to the **setting.** Read carefully the descriptions of objects and places. Think about what the narrator and the writer may *not* be telling you. Then, throw your own experience and knowledge into the mix as you try to solve the story's puzzles. Remember: Like a detective, you'll have to keep monitoring and revising your conclusions as new clues surface.

Make the Connection

Quickwrite

In Benét's fantasy you'll accompany John, the narrator, as he catches glimpses of a past civilization. Using what you know of world history, jot down some of the reasons why civilizations might disappear. What role do people play in their destruction?

Background

The title of this story is an **allusion,** or reference, to Psalm 137 in the Bible. The psalm tells of the Israelites' sorrow over the destruction of their Temple in Zion (a reference to Jerusalem) and their enslavement in Babylon. The psalm begins,

> By the waters of Babylon, there
> we sat down and wept, when we
> remembered Zion.

RESOURCES: READING

Planning

- *One-Stop Planner* CD-ROM with Test Generator
- *On Course: Mapping Instruction*

Media

- *Audio CD Library*
  - disc 5

Reading

- *Interactive Reading*
  - Interactive version: "By the Waters of Babylon"
- *Interactive Reading,* Teacher's Edition
  - Graphic Organizer: Narrator Chart

By the Waters of Babylon

Stephen Vincent Benét

At night, I would lie awake and listen to the wind—it seemed to me that it was the voice of the gods.

The north and the west and the south are good hunting ground, but it is forbidden to go east. It is forbidden to go to any of the Dead Places except to search for metal, and then he who touches the metal must be a priest or the son of a priest. Afterward, both the man and the metal must be purified. These are the rules and the laws; they are well made. It is forbidden to cross the great river and look upon the place that was the Place of the Gods—this is most strictly forbidden. We do not even say its name though we know its name. It is there that spirits live, and demons—it is there that there are the ashes of the Great Burning. These things are forbidden—they have been forbidden since the beginning of time.

My father is a priest; I am the son of a priest. I have been in the Dead Places near us, with my father—at first, I was afraid. When my father went into the house to search for the metal, I stood by the door and my heart felt small and weak. It was a dead man's house, a spirit house. It did not have the smell of man, though there were old bones in a corner. But it is not fitting that a priest's son should show fear. I looked at the bones in the shadow and kept my voice still. **A**

Then my father came out with the metal—a good, strong piece. He looked at me with both eyes but I had not run away. He gave me the metal to hold—I took it and did not die. So he knew that

141

PRETEACHING

Standards Starter

Build prerequisite skills. To review point of view, ask a volunteer what he or she did last weekend. Write the sentences on the chalkboard, using the pronoun *I*. Then, ask another student to summarize what the first volunteer did. Write the sentences on the chalkboard, using the pronouns *he* or *she*. Label the first group of sentences "First Person," and underline the *I* in each sentence. Explain that when a person tells his or her own story, the story is told from the first-person point of view. Label the other group of sentences "Third Person," and underline the *he* or *she* in each sentence. Explain that when someone tells another person's story, the story is told from the third-person point of view. Then, have students read and discuss the Literary Focus.

Assign the Reading

Homework

You might ask volunteers to read the first two pages of the story aloud and make sure students understand who is telling the story [the son of a priest], what kind of society the narrator lives in [a primitive one with few resources], where the narrator is going [to the Place of the Gods, the ruins left after the Great Burning], and why [to learn more about the Dead Places and what they mean]. Students reading at or above grade level can then continue independently, answering the questions on p. 152 for homework, while readers having difficulty can work in small groups with you.

DIRECT TEACHING

A Literary Focus
GRADE-LEVEL STANDARD

? First-person point of view. How do you know that this narrative is being told from the first-person point of view? [Possible responses: The narrator uses the pronoun *I*, and we see all the events through his eyes; we know only what the narrator knows.]

Differentiating Instruction

- *Lesson Plans for Language Development*
  - English-Language Learners, pp. 67–69, 92, 98
  - Special Education Students, pp. 70, 92, 98

Assessment

- *Progress Assessment of Reading*
  - Selection Test
- *One-Stop Planner* CD-ROM with Test Generator

DIRECT TEACHING

A Reading Skills

Drawing conclusions. The author does not reveal where the story is set, but you can learn about the setting from clues he provides. What conclusions can you draw so far about the setting? [Possible responses: It may be another planet or an imaginary place; it may be earth in the future, after some calamity has destroyed civilization.] What clues lead you to your conclusion? [The narrator and his people are primitive and superstitious; they collect metal from an advanced civilization's ruins, where they also find books that they struggle to understand.]

B English-Language Learners

Building background knowledge. You might introduce the noun *ritual,* saying it means "a set of ceremonial activities." Explain that this story includes references to religious rituals that are fictional but based on traditions common to many cultures.

I was truly his son and would be a priest in my time. That was when I was very young—nevertheless, my brothers would not have done it, though they are good hunters. After that, they gave me the good piece of meat and the warm corner by the fire. My father watched over me—he was glad that I should be a priest. But when I boasted or wept without a reason, he punished me more strictly than my brothers. That was right.

A After a time, I myself was allowed to go into the dead houses and search for metal. So I learned the ways of those houses—and if I saw bones, I was no longer afraid. The bones are light and old—sometimes they will fall into dust if you touch them. But that is a great sin.

I was taught the chants and the spells—I was taught how to stop blood from a wound and many secrets. A priest must know many secrets—that was what my father said. If the hunters think we do all things by chants and spells, they may believe so—it does not hurt them. I was taught how to read in the old books and how to make the old writings—that was hard and took a long time. My knowledge made me happy—it was like a fire in my heart. Most of all, I liked to hear of the Old Days and the stories of the gods. I asked myself many questions that I could not answer, but it was good to ask them. At night, I would lie awake and listen to the wind—it seemed to me that it was the voice of the gods as they flew through the air.

We are not ignorant like the Forest People—our women spin wool on the wheel, our priests wear a white robe. We do not eat grubs from the tree, we have not forgotten the old writings, although they are hard to understand. Nevertheless, my knowledge and my lack of knowledge burned in me—I wished to know more. When I was a man at last, I came to my father and said, "It is time for me to go on my journey. Give me your leave."

He looked at me for a long time, stroking his beard, then he said at last, "Yes. It is time." That night, in the house of the priesthood, I asked for and received purification. My body hurt but my spirit was a cool stone. It was my father himself who questioned me about my dreams.

He bade me look into the smoke of the fire and see—I saw and told what I saw. It was what I have always seen—a river, and, beyond it, a great Dead Place and in it the gods walking. I have always thought about that. His eyes were stern when I told him—he was no longer my father but a priest. He said, "This is a strong dream."

B "It is mine," I said, while the smoke waved and my head felt light. They were singing the Star song in the outer chamber and it was like the buzzing of bees in my head.

He asked me how the gods were dressed and I told him how they were dressed. We know how they were dressed from the book, but I saw them as if they were before me. When I had finished, he threw the sticks three times and studied them as they fell.

"This is a very strong dream," he said. "It may eat you up."

"I am not afraid," I said and looked at him with both eyes. My voice sounded thin in my ears but that was because of the smoke.

He touched me on the breast and the forehead. He gave me the bow and the three arrows.

"Take them," he said. "It is forbidden to travel east. It is forbidden to cross the river. It is forbidden to go to the Place of the Gods. All these things are forbidden."

"All these things are forbidden," I said, but it was my voice that spoke and not my spirit. He looked at me again.

"My son," he said. "Once I had young dreams. If your dreams do not eat you up, you may be a great priest. If they eat you, you are still my son. Now go on your journey."

I went fasting, as is the law. My body hurt but not my heart. When the dawn came, I was out of sight of the village. I prayed and purified myself, waiting for a sign. The sign was an eagle. It flew east.

DIFFERENTIATING INSTRUCTION

Learners Having Difficulty

Invite learners having difficulty to read "By the Waters of Babylon" in interactive format in *Interactive Reading* and to use the sidenotes as aids to understanding the selection. The interactive version provides additional instruction, practice, and assessment of the literature standard taught in the Student Edition. Monitor students' responses to the selection, and correct any misconceptions that arise.

Resources Reminder

Differentiating Instruction

- *Interactive Reading*
  - Interactive version: "By the Waters of Babylon"

English-Language Learners

Make sure students understand that the setting is meant to be a mystery. To figure out what the Place of the Gods is and why it is in ruins, readers must gather clues and draw conclusions from them. To get students started, hint that the Place of the Gods is an actual place in the United States.

Lake George with Crows (1921) by Georgia O'Keeffe. Oil on canvas (28″ × 25″).

National Gallery of Canada, Ottawa. Gift of the Georgia O'Keeffe Foundation, Abiquiu, New Mexico, 1995.

DIRECT TEACHING

VIEWING THE ART

Georgia O'Keeffe (1887–1986) was one of America's most innovative modernist artists. She is best known for works that abstracted the natural world, with distinct lines; vivid patterns; and clear, light hues. In this painting broad areas of color convey the expansiveness and the vibrant landscape of Lake George, New York, with suggestions of water, sky, hills, crows, and vegetation.

Resources Reminder

For lessons designed for intermediate and advanced English-language learners, see *Lesson Plans for Language Development,* pp. 67–69, 92, 98.

Special Education Students

For lessons designed for special education students, see *Lesson Plans for Language Development,* pp. 70, 92, 98.

Advanced Learners

Enrichment. Tell students that the narrator of a story becomes the voice that we hear telling the story. When authors choose a first-person narrator, they must make the voice, or speaking style, of the narrator suit his or her character. If the words and ideas don't fit the narrator's personality or background, the story loses credibility.

Activity. As students read the story, encourage them to record the words and images that best fit the narrator's character.

DIRECT TEACHING

A Advanced Learners

Enrichment. The narrator's voice, or style, is marked by the use of simple sentences with brief clauses and short words. How does this voice suit his character? [Possible response: He is innocent, unsophisticated, and only slightly educated—the voice echoes the way such a person might speak and think.]

B English-Language Learners

Elliptical constructions. Point out the elliptical construction "my journey clean." The verb *was* is missing; the reader must fill in this word to make sense of the sentence.

C Reading Skills

Drawing conclusions. What clues about the Place of the Gods does this passage give you? [Possible responses: Huge, ruined roads lead to it; its ruined buildings are "too big to be houses"; it lies on the other side of a great river called the Ou-dis-sun.] What conclusions can you draw so far about the Place of the Gods? [Possible responses: It was a metropolis surrounded by highways and bordered by a major river; the buildings are probably skyscrapers. Some students may already suspect that the Ou-dis-sun is the Hudson River.]

D Literary Focus
GRADE-LEVEL STANDARD

First-person point of view. What internal conflict is revealed by the narrator's thoughts before he enters the city? [Possible responses: He is torn between going forward and going back; he fears death if he enters the city, but his spirit will never be at peace until he explores the Place of the Gods.]

Sometimes signs are sent by bad spirits. I waited again on the flat rock, fasting, taking no food. I was very still—I could feel the sky above me and the earth beneath. I waited till the sun was beginning to sink. Then three deer passed in the valley, going east—they did not wind[1] me or see me. There was a white fawn with them—a very great sign.

I followed them, at a distance, waiting for what would happen. My heart was troubled about going east, yet I knew that I must go. My head hummed with my fasting—I did not even see the panther spring upon the white fawn. But, before I knew it, the bow was in my hand. I shouted and the panther lifted his head from the fawn. It is not easy to kill a panther with one arrow but the arrow went through his eye and into his brain. He died as he tried to spring—he rolled over, tearing at the ground. Then I knew I was meant to go east—I knew that was my journey. When the night came, I made my fire and roasted meat.

It is eight suns' journey to the east and a man passes by many Dead Places. The Forest People are afraid of them but I am not. Once I made my fire on the edge of a Dead Place at night and, next morning, in the dead house, I found a good knife, little rusted. That was small to what came afterward but it made my heart feel big. Always when I looked for game, it was in front of my arrow, and twice I passed hunting parties of the Forest People without their knowing. So I knew my magic was strong and my journey clean, in spite of the law.

Toward the setting of the eighth sun, I came to the banks of the great river. It was half a day's journey after I had left the god-road—we do not use the god-roads now, for they are falling apart into great blocks of stone, and the forest is safer going. A long way off, I had seen the water through trees but the trees were thick. At last, I came out upon an open place at the top of a cliff. There was the great river below, like a giant in the sun. It is very long, very wide. It could eat all the streams we know and still be thirsty. Its name is Ou-dis-sun, the Sacred, the Long. No man of my tribe had seen it, not even my father, the priest. It was magic and I prayed.

Then I raised my eyes and looked south. It was there, the Place of the Gods.

How can I tell what it was like—you do not know. It was there, in the red light, and they were too big to be houses. It was there with the red light upon it, mighty and ruined. I knew that in another moment the gods would see me. I covered my eyes with my hands and crept back into the forest.

> Everywhere there are the ruins of the high towers of the gods.

Surely, that was enough to do, and live. Surely it was enough to spend the night upon the cliff. The Forest People themselves do not come near. Yet, all through the night, I knew that I should have to cross the river and walk in the places of the gods, although the gods ate me up. My magic did not help me at all and yet there was a fire in my bowels, a fire in my mind. When the sun rose, I thought, "My journey has been clean. Now I will go home from my journey." But, even as I thought so, I knew I could not. If I went to the Place of the Gods, I would surely die, but, if I did not go, I could never be at peace with my spirit again. It is better to lose one's life than one's spirit, if one is a priest and the son of a priest.

Nevertheless, as I made the raft, the tears ran out of my eyes. The Forest People could have killed me without fight, if they had come upon me then, but they did not come. When the raft was made, I said the sayings for the dead and painted myself for death. My heart was cold as a frog and my knees like water, but the burning in my mind would not let me have peace. As I pushed the raft from the shore, I began my death song—I had the right. It was a fine song.

---

1. **wind** (wind) *v.:* detect the scent of.

144 Chapter 3 Narrator and Voice • Generating Research Questions

"I am John, son of John," I sang. *"My people are the Hill People. They are the men.*
I go into the Dead Places but I am not slain.
I take the metal from the Dead Places but I am not blasted.
I travel upon the god-roads and am not afraid. E-yah! I have killed the panther, I have killed the fawn!
E-yah! I have come to the great river. No man has come there before.
It is forbidden to go east, but I have gone, forbidden to go on the great river, but I am there.
Open your hearts, you spirits, and hear my song. Now I go to the Place of the Gods, I shall not return.
My body is painted for death and my limbs weak, but my heart is big as I go to the Place of the Gods!"

E

All the same, when I came to the Place of the Gods, I was afraid, afraid. The current of the great river is very strong—it gripped my raft with its hands. That was magic, for the river itself is wide and calm. I could feel evil spirits about me, in the bright morning; I could feel their breath on my neck as I was swept down the stream. Never have I been so much alone—I tried to think of my knowledge, but it was a squirrel's heap of winter nuts. There was no strength in my knowledge anymore and I felt small and naked as a new-hatched bird—alone upon the great river, the servant of the gods.

F

Yet, after a while, my eyes were opened and I saw. I saw both banks of the river—I saw that once there had been god-roads across it, though now they were broken and fallen like broken vines. Very great they were, and wonderful and broken—broken in the time of the Great Burning when the fire fell out of the sky. And always the current took me nearer to the Place of the Gods, and the huge ruins rose before my eyes.

I do not know the customs of rivers—we are the People of the Hills. I tried to guide my raft with the pole but it spun around. I thought the river meant to take me past the Place of the Gods and out into the Bitter Water of the legends. I grew angry then—my heart felt strong. I said aloud, "I am a priest and the son of a priest!" The gods heard me—they showed me how to paddle with the pole on one side of the raft. The current changed itself—I drew near to the Place of the Gods.

When I was very near, my raft struck and turned over. I can swim in our lakes—I swam to the shore. There was a great spike of rusted metal sticking out into the river—I hauled myself up upon it and sat there, panting. I had saved my bow and two arrows and the knife I found in the Dead Place but that was all. My raft went whirling downstream toward the Bitter Water. I looked after it, and thought if it had trod me under, at least I would be safely dead. Nevertheless, when I had dried my bowstring and restrung it, I walked forward to the Place of the Gods.

G

It felt like ground underfoot; it did not burn me. It is not true what some of the tales say, that the ground there burns forever, for I have been there. Here and there were the marks and stains of the Great Burning, on the ruins, that is true. But they were old marks and old stains. It is not true either, what some of our priests say, that it is an island covered with fogs and enchantments. It is not. It is a great Dead Place—greater than any Dead Place we know. Everywhere in it there are god-roads, though most are cracked and broken. Everywhere there are the ruins of the high towers of the gods.

H

How shall I tell what I saw? I went carefully, my strung bow in my hand, my skin ready for danger. There should have been the wailings of spirits and the shrieks of demons, but there were not. It was very silent and sunny where I had landed—the wind and the rain and the birds that drop seeds had done their work—the grass

DIRECT TEACHING

E Learners Having Difficulty

Reading aloud. The narrator interrupts the story to give the exact words of his song. Have a volunteer read it aloud. **What do readers learn about the narrator from having the exact words of the song, as opposed to a summary?** [Possible responses: his name; an inside view of his religion; the extent of his fear, faith, and courage.]

F Advanced Learners

Enrichment. **What metaphor and simile does the narrator use here?** [*Metaphor*—His knowledge is "a squirrel's heap of winter nuts." *Simile*—He feels as "small and naked as a new-hatched bird."] **How do these figures of speech fit his character?** [They show his closeness to nature and the intensity of his feelings.]

G Reading Skills

Drawing conclusions. **By this point, the writer has given several clues about the setting. What might the Bitter Water, the river, and the Place of the Gods be?** [Accept reasonable guesses without revealing the answers—the Atlantic Ocean, the Hudson River, and New York City.] **Look for more clues as you read, and revise your conclusions when you find new evidence.**

H Learners Having Difficulty

Questioning. **What does the narrator mean by "my skin ready for danger"?** [Possible response: His skin prickles with fear.]

DEVELOPING FLUENCY

Small-group activity. The scene in which John crosses the river (p. 145) is a good choice for a choral reading. Divide students into small groups, and assign paragraphs to individual readers. Suggest that after each individual reading, the group read part of John's song (p. 145) together. For example, they could use the following lines as a refrain:

"E-yah! I have killed the panther, I have killed the fawn! / E-yah! I have come to the great river. No man has come there before."

Direct Teaching

A Reading Skills

Drawing conclusions. Who does the statue represent? [George Washington] **What clues lead to your conclusion?** [Possible responses: Washington wore his hair long and "tied back like a woman's." The inscription "ASHING" is what might be left of the name Washington on the cracked half of the stone.]

B Reading Skills

Making inferences. Why does eating from the "enchanted boxes and jars" often cause death? [Possible response: The food has been contaminated by whatever destroyed the city.]

grew in the cracks of the broken stone. It is a fair island—no wonder the gods built there. If I had come there, a god, I also would have built.

How shall I tell what I saw? The towers are not all broken—here and there one still stands, like a great tree in a forest, and the birds nest high. But the towers themselves look blind, for the gods are gone. I saw a fish-hawk, catching fish in the river. I saw a little dance of white butterflies over a great heap of broken stones and columns. I went there and looked about me—there was a carved stone with cut-letters, broken in half. I can read letters but I could not understand these. They said UBTREAS. There was also the shattered image of a man or a god. **A** It had been made of white stone and he wore his hair tied back like a woman's. His name was ASHING, as I read on the cracked half of a stone. I thought it wise to pray to ASHING, though I do not know that god.

How shall I tell what I saw? There was no smell of man left, on stone or metal. Nor were there many trees in that wilderness of stone. There are many pigeons, nesting and dropping in the towers—the gods must have loved them, or, perhaps, they used them for sacrifices. There are wild cats that roam the god-roads, green-eyed, unafraid of man. At night they wail like demons but they are not demons. The wild dogs are more dangerous, for they hunt in a pack, but them I did not meet till later. Everywhere there are the carved stones, carved with magical numbers or words.

I went north—I did not try to hide myself. When a god or a demon saw me, then I would die, but meanwhile I was no longer afraid. My hunger for knowledge burned in me—there was **B** so much that I could not understand. After a while, I knew that my belly was hungry. I could have hunted for my meat, but I did not hunt. It is known that the gods did not hunt as we do—they got their food from enchanted boxes and jars. Sometimes these are still found in the Dead Places—once, when I was a child and foolish, I opened such a jar and tasted it and found the food sweet. But my father found out and punished me for it strictly, for, often, that food is death. Now, though, I had long gone past what was forbidden, and I entered the likeliest towers, looking for the food of the gods.

I found it at last in the ruins of a great temple in the midcity. A mighty temple it must have been, for the roof was painted like the sky at night with its stars—that much I could see, though the colors were faint and dim. It went down into great caves and tunnels—perhaps they kept their slaves there. But when I started to climb down, I heard the squeaking of rats, so I did not go—rats are unclean, and there must have been many tribes of them, from the squeaking. But near there, I found food, in the heart of a ruin, behind a door that still opened. I ate only the fruits from the jars—they had a very sweet taste. There was drink, too, in bottles of glass—the drink of the gods was strong and made my head swim. After I had eaten and drunk, I slept on the top of a stone, my bow at my side.

When I woke, the sun was low. Looking down from where I lay, I saw a dog sitting on his haunches. His tongue was hanging out of his mouth; he looked as if he were laughing. He was a big dog, with a gray-brown coat, as big as a wolf. I sprang up and shouted at him but he did not move—he just sat there as if he were laughing. I did not like that. When I reached for a stone to throw, he moved swiftly out of the way of the stone. He was not afraid of me; he looked at me as if I were meat. No doubt I could have killed him with an arrow, but I did not know if there were others. Moreover, night was falling.

I looked about me—not far away there was a great, broken god-road, leading north. The towers were high enough, but not so high, and while many of the dead houses were wrecked, there were some that stood. I went toward this god-road, keeping to the heights of the ruins, while the dog followed. When I had reached the

CONTENT-AREA CONNECTIONS

Social Studies: New York City Landmarks

The "great temple" where John finds food is Grand Central Terminal, a huge railroad terminal in Midtown Manhattan. Completed in 1913, the terminal is known for its main concourse, a masterpiece of Beaux-Arts design, which features arched windows, marble staircases, chandeliers of gold, and a ceiling painted blue-green, with constellations in gold leaf and 2,500 flickering lights to represent the stars. The station also houses shops and restaurants. Beneath the ground floor are other levels, more shops, and tunnels for arriving and departing trains. Threatened with partial demolition in the 1960s, Grand Central Terminal was preserved and recently underwent a major restoration.

Small-group activity. Invite small groups of students to become archaeologists of the future and explore the site of a landmark in your area. Have students describe the mysterious site and their feelings as they explore it. They might challenge classmates to guess the place.

god-road, I saw that there were others behind him. If I had slept later, they would have come upon me asleep and torn out my throat. As it was, they were sure enough of me; they did not hurry. When I went into the dead house, they kept watch at the entrance—doubtless they thought they would have a fine hunt. But a dog cannot open a door and I knew, from the books, that the gods did not like to live on the ground but on high.

I had just found a door I could open when the dogs decided to rush. Ha! They were surprised when I shut the door in their faces—it was a good door, of strong metal. I could hear their foolish baying beyond it but I did not stop to answer them. I was in darkness—I found stairs and climbed. There were many stairs, turning around till my head was dizzy. At the top was another door—I found the knob and opened it. I was in a long small chamber—on one side of it was a bronze door that could not be opened, for it had no handle. **C** Perhaps there was a magic word to open it but I did not have the word. I turned to the door in the opposite side of the wall. The lock of it was broken and I opened it and went in.

Within, there was a place of great riches.

Within, there was a place of great riches. The god who lived there must have been a powerful god. The first room was a small anteroom—I waited there for some time, telling the spirits of the place that I came in peace and not as a robber. When it seemed to me that they had had time to hear me, I went on. Ah, what riches! Few, even, of the windows had been broken—it was all as it had been. The great windows that looked over the city had not been broken at all though they were dusty and streaked with many years. There were coverings on the floors, the colors not greatly faded, and the chairs were soft and deep. There were pictures upon the walls, very strange, very wonderful—I remember one of a bunch of flowers in a jar—if you came close to it, you could see nothing but bits of color, but if you stood away from it, the flowers might have been picked yesterday. It made my heart feel strange to look at this picture—and to look at the figure of a bird, in some hard clay, on a table and see it so like our birds. Everywhere there were books and writings, many in tongues that I could not read. The god who lived there must have been a wise god and full of knowledge. I felt I had right there, as I sought knowledge also.

Nevertheless, it was strange. There was a washing-place but no water—perhaps the gods washed in air. There was a cooking-place but no wood, and though there was a machine to cook food, there was no place to put fire in it. Nor were there candles or lamps—there were things that looked like lamps but they had neither oil nor wick. All these things were magic, but I touched them and lived—the magic had gone out of them. **D** Let me tell you one thing to show. In the washing-place, a thing said "Hot" but it was not hot to the touch—another thing said "Cold" but it was not cold. This must have been a strong magic but the magic was gone. I do not understand—they had ways—I wish that I knew.

It was close and dry and dusty in their house of the gods. I have said the magic was gone but that is not true—it had gone from the magic things but it had not gone from the place. I felt the spirits about me, weighing upon me. Nor had I ever slept in a Dead Place before—and yet, tonight, I must sleep there. When I thought of it, my tongue felt dry in my throat, in spite of my wish for knowledge. Almost I would have gone down again and faced the dogs, but I did not.

I had not gone through all the rooms when the darkness fell. **E** When it fell, I went back to the big room looking over the city and made fire. There was a place to make fire and a box with wood in it, though I do not think they cooked there. I wrapped myself in a floor-covering and slept in front of the fire—I was very tired.

DIRECT TEACHING

C Reading Skills

Drawing conclusions. What might the "long small chamber" and the "bronze door that could not be opened" be? [an apartment hallway and an elevator door] **What clues lead you to your conclusion?** [Possible responses: Elevator doors are made of metal, and they have no handles; apartment hallways are long and narrow.]

D Literary Focus
GRADE-LEVEL STANDARD

First-person point of view. Dramatic irony occurs when readers know something that the character does not. How does the use of a first-person point of view create dramatic irony here? [The narrator is mystified by the things in the apartment, but readers recognize them as common furnishings and appliances.]

E English-Language Learners

Interpreting idioms. Be sure students understand that the idiomatic expression *darkness fell* means "night came."

DIRECT TEACHING

A Advanced Learners

Acceleration. **What simile does the narrator repeat here to describe his experience?** [He feels drawn out of his body "as a fish is drawn on a line."] **How well does this figure of speech fit his character?** [Possible response: It fits well, because it is another nature image and because it emphasizes the mystical power of the spirits in which he believes.]

B Learners Having Difficulty

Summarizing. **Have students pause in their reading and paraphrase what is happening in this episode.** [Possible response: The narrator may have fallen asleep. He dreams—or has a vision—of the city as it was before it was destroyed.]

C Reading Skills

Drawing conclusions. **What has happened to the city?** [It was hit by weapons of mass destruction, perhaps nuclear bombs.] **What clues help you draw your conclusion?** [Possible responses: The narrator sees a vision of war unlike any known in his primitive culture. Fiery weapons come from the sky, as if by plane or missile, with a poisonous mist (perhaps fallout or toxic gas) that contaminates the site for years.]

Now I tell what is very strong magic. I woke in the midst of the night. When I woke, the fire had gone out and I was cold. It seemed to me that all around me there were whisperings and voices. I closed my eyes to shut them out. Some will say that I slept again, but I do not think that I slept. I could feel the spirits drawing my spirit out of my body as a fish is drawn on a line.

Why should I lie about it? I am a priest and the son of a priest. If there are spirits, as they say, in the small Dead Places near us, what spirits must there not be in that great Place of the Gods? And would not they wish to speak? After such long years? I know that I felt myself drawn as a fish is drawn on a line. I had stepped out of my body—I could see my body asleep in front of the cold fire, but it was not I. I was drawn to look out upon the city of the gods.

It should have been dark, for it was night, but it was not dark. Everywhere there were lights—lines of light—circles and blurs of light—ten thousand torches would not have been the same. The sky itself was alight—you could barely see the stars for the glow in the sky. I thought to myself, "This is strong magic," and trembled. There was a roaring in my ears like the rushing of rivers. Then my eyes grew used to the light and my ears to the sound. I knew that I was seeing the city as it had been when the gods were alive.

That was a sight indeed—yes, that was a sight: I could not have seen it in the body—my body would have died. Everywhere went the gods, on foot and in chariots—there were gods beyond number and counting and their chariots blocked the streets. They had turned night to day for their pleasure—they did not sleep with the sun. The noise of their coming and going was the noise of many waters. It was magic what they could do—it was magic what they did.

I looked out of another window—the great vines of their bridges were mended and the god-roads went east and west. Restless, restless were the gods, and always in motion! They burrowed tunnels under rivers—they flew in the air. With unbelievable tools they did giant works—no part of the earth was safe from them, for, if they wished for a thing, they summoned it from the other side of the world. And always, as they labored and rested, as they feasted and made love, there was a drum in their ears—the pulse of the giant city, beating and beating like a man's heart.

Were they happy? What is happiness to the gods? They were great, they were mighty, they were wonderful and terrible. As I looked upon them and their magic, I felt like a child—but a little more, it seemed to me, and they would pull down the moon from the sky. I saw them with wisdom beyond wisdom and knowledge beyond knowledge. And yet not all they did was well done—even I could see that—and yet their wisdom could not but grow until all was peace.

> Now I tell what is very strong magic.

Then I saw their fate come upon them and that was terrible past speech. It came upon them as they walked the streets of their city. I have been in the fights with the Forest People—I have seen men die. But this was not like that. When gods war with gods, they use weapons we do not know. It was fire falling out of the sky and a mist that poisoned. It was the time of the Great Burning and the Destruction. They ran about like ants in the streets of their city—poor gods, poor gods! Then the towers began to fall. A few escaped—yes, a few. The legends tell it. But, even after the city had become a Dead Place, for many years the poison was still in the ground. I saw it happen, I saw the last of them die. It was darkness over the broken city and I wept.

All this, I saw. I saw it as I have told it, though not in the body. When I woke in the morning, I was hungry, but I did not think first of my hunger, for my heart was perplexed and

CONTENT-AREA CONNECTIONS

Science/History: The Atomic Age

Surprisingly this story seems to describe the aftermath of a nuclear war, although Benét wrote it before nuclear weapons were created. "By the Waters of Babylon" was first published in 1937. At that time, atomic theory was still young, and the idea of an atomic bomb had occurred to only a few physicists. It was not until 1939 that Albert Einstein brought the possibility to the attention of President Franklin D. Roosevelt, and the information remained top-secret. America's Manhattan Project to develop the first atomic bomb began in 1942. The public knew nothing of atomic weapons until the bombing of Hiroshima in 1945; awareness of the effects of fallout came only afterward.

Small-group activity. Have interested students research the 1945 controversy among Manhattan Project leaders over whether—and how—to use the atomic bomb. Then, invite students to take the roles of key figures (such as Gen. Leslie Groves, J. Robert Oppenheimer, Albert Einstein, and Niels Bohr) and stage a panel discussion. Have them quote lines from Benét's prophetic story in their discussion.

148 Chapter 3 Narrator and Voice • Generating Research Questions

Radiator Building—Night, New York (1927) by Georgia O'Keeffe. Oil on canvas (48″ × 30″).

Alfred Stieglitz Collection, Carl van Vechten Gallery of Fine Arts, Fisk University, Nashville.

DIRECT TEACHING

VIEWING THE ART

Georgia O'Keeffe (1887–1986) lived in New York in the 1920s and married Alfred Stieglitz, a photographer and a promoter of modern art. Intrigued by the city around her, she painted the skyscrapers being constructed during the building boom of the 1920s. The twenty-two-story American Radiator Building, designed by architect Raymond Hood in 1924, features a Gothic style and is covered in stark black granite. O'Keeffe wrote, "One can't paint New York as it is, but rather as it is felt." Her painting emphasizes the lights and shadows of the building's dramatic silhouette, while the steam on the painting's right side suggests the organic, abstract shapes of her paintings derived from nature. With an ironic touch, O'Keeffe substituted her husband's name for a neon advertisement's words.

Activity. Like O'Keeffe, the narrator of "By the Waters of Babylon" juxtaposes images of the city with images derived from nature. For example, bridges are "great vines." Ask students for more examples of this imagery. [Possible responses: The sound of the living city and its people are "the rushing of rivers" and "the noise of many waters"; "the pulse of the . . . city" beats "like a man's heart"; people "ran about like ants."]

READING MINI-LESSON

Developing Word-Attack Skills

Remind students of this mnemonic: "When two vowels go a-walking, the first one does the talking." Point out that although this applies to the vowel digraphs *ai, ea,* and *oa,* the opposite is often true with *ei* and *ie*, for example, *field* and *feisty.* In *field, i* comes first, but the sound is a long e. In *feisty,* e comes first, but the sound is a long *i.*

Next, compare the words *believe* and *receive.* Both words have the sound of a long e, but it is spelled with *ie* in *believe* and *ei* in *receive.* The mnemonic "*I* before e except after *c*" describes this phenomenon.

Then, compare the words *purified* and *studied.* Both have *ie,* but the letters stand for a long *i* in *purified* and a long e in *studied.* In both words, *ie* is the result of adding *–ed* to a base word that ends with *y.* The sound of *ie* is the same as the sound of *y* in the base word.

Activity. Have students read each word and indicate if the letters *ei* or *ie* stand for a long e or a long *i* sound.

1. shriek [ē] **3.** brief [ē] **5.** seismic [ī]
2. heist [ī] **4.** priest [ē] **6.** grief [ē]

DIRECT TEACHING

(A) Reading Skills

Drawing conclusions. Invite students to share their conclusions about the setting of the story and their evidence. See how many identified the city as New York.

GUIDED PRACTICE

Monitoring students' progress. Guide the class in answering these questions. Have students find text passages to support their responses.

True-False

1. The narrator's father is a priest, and he enters the Dead Places to find metal. [T]
2. The narrator is guided to the Place of the Gods by the Forest People. [F]
3. The narrator crosses the river on a raft. [T]
4. A man living in the Place of the Gods tells the narrator about the Great Burning. [F]
5. The narrator decides to return one day with his people to the Place of the Gods. [T]

confused. I knew the reason for the Dead Places but I did not see why it had happened. It seemed to me it should not have happened, with all the magic they had. I went through the house looking for an answer. There was so much in the house I could not understand—and yet I am a priest and the son of a priest. It was like being on one side of the great river, at night, with no light to show the way.

Then I saw the dead god. He was sitting in his chair, by the window, in a room I had not entered before and, for the first moment, I thought that he was alive. Then I saw the skin on the back of his hand—it was like dry leather. The room was shut, hot and dry—no doubt that had kept him as he was. At first I was afraid to approach him—then the fear left me. He was sitting looking out over the city—he was dressed in the clothes of the gods. His age was neither young nor old—I could not tell his age. But there was wisdom in his face and great sadness. You could see that he would have not run away. He had sat at his window, watching his city die—then he himself had died. But it is better to lose one's life than one's spirit—and you could see from the face that his spirit had not been lost. I knew that, if I touched him, he would fall into dust—and yet, there was something unconquered in the face.

That is all of my story, for then I knew he was a man—I knew then that they had been men, neither gods nor demons. It is a great knowledge, hard to tell and believe. They were men—they went a dark road, but they were men. I had no fear after that—I had no fear going home, though twice I fought off the dogs and I was hunted for two days by the Forest People. When I saw my father again, I prayed and was purified. He touched my lips and my breast, he said, "You went away a boy. You come back a man and a priest." I said, "Father, they were men! I have been in the Place of the Gods and seen it! Now slay me, if it is the law—but still I know they were men."

He looked at me out of both eyes. He said, "The law is not always the same shape—you have done what you have done. I could not have done it my time, but you come after me. Tell!"

I told and he listened. After that, I wished to tell all the people but he showed me otherwise. He said, "Truth is a hard deer to hunt. If you eat too much truth at once, you may die of the truth. It was not idly that our fathers forbade the Dead Places." He was right—it is better the truth should come little by little. I have learned that, being a priest. Perhaps, in the old days, they ate knowledge too fast.

Perhaps, in the old days, they ate knowledge too fast.

(A) Nevertheless, we make a beginning. It is not for the metal alone we go to the Dead Places now—there are the books and the writings. They are hard to learn. And the magic tools are broken—but we can look at them and wonder. At least, we make a beginning. And, when I am chief priest we shall go beyond the great river. We shall go to the Place of the Gods—the place newyork—not one man but a company. We shall look for the images of the gods and find the god ASHING and the others—the gods Lincoln and Biltmore[2] and Moses.[3] But they were men who built the city, not gods or demons. They were men. I remember the dead man's face. They were men who were here before us. We must build again. ■

2. **Biltmore:** New York City hotel.
3. **Moses:** Robert Moses (1888–1981): New York City public official who oversaw many large construction projects, such as bridges and public buildings.

FAMILY/COMMUNITY ACTIVITY

Most states and many local communities have agencies responsible for responding to natural and technological disasters. These agencies' activities are coordinated by the Federal Emergency Management Agency (FEMA). Have students research emergency response plans for your community. If possible, invite community leaders to come in and address the class on how to prepare for and respond to natural and technological disasters.

Meet the Writer

Stephen Vincent Benét

Mr. American History

According to one biographer, Stephen Vincent Benét (1898–1943) "wrote short stories for money and poetry for love." Yet despite his preference for poetry, some of Benét's stories have remained his best-known works. The story you have just read, "By the Waters of Babylon," first appeared as "The Place of the Gods" in *The Saturday Evening Post* magazine in July 1937. Benét later changed its title.

Benét was the grandson of an important general and the son of a well-known colonel who instilled a love of literature and American history in his children. (Benét's brother and sister also became writers.) With this background it's not surprising that Benét turned to American history, folklore, and legend as topics for his stories and poems. *John Brown's Body* (1928), a book-length narrative poem about the fiery abolitionist who led an attack on Harper's Ferry in 1859 and was hanged for treason, won Benét the Pulitzer Prize for poetry.

Benét always emphasized the importance of clear style. He advised one young writer,

"Don't use four adjectives when one will do. Don't use five long words to say, 'We were happy.' 'It rained.' 'It was dark.' Write of the simple things simply."

For Independent Reading

"The Devil and Daniel Webster," probably Benét's most widely anthologized story, pits the real-life American statesman and orator Daniel Webster against the devil in a fierce struggle to save the soul of a New Hampshire farmer. The story won the O. Henry Award in 1937 and was made into an opera, a play, and a movie.

Meet the Writer

Background. Born in Bethlehem, Pennsylvania, Stephen Vincent Benét attended a military academy from the age of ten and read widely in military history. At the time of his death, he was writing an epic poem about the American West. He finished the first volume, *Western Star,* for which he was posthumously awarded his second Pulitzer Prize in 1944.

In his long poem *Litany for Dictatorships,* published the year before "By the Waters of Babylon," Benét wrote a line that could be the theme of this story: "We thought, because we had power, we had wisdom."

For Independent Reading

- If students choose to read "The Devil and Daniel Webster," encourage them to compare the ideas that Daniel Webster expresses about civilization with the ideas conveyed in "By the Waters of Babylon."
- For another view of an apocalyptic future, suggest Jack London's classic story "The Scarlet Plague."
- Students who enjoy the voice of a naive first-person narrator will appreciate *To Kill a Mockingbird* by Harper Lee.
- For advanced learners, you might suggest Barbara Kingsolver's *The Bean Trees,* which switches between chapters written in the first and third person.

DIFFERENTIATING INSTRUCTION

Advanced Learners

Enrichment. Tell students that writings about cataclysmic events that end civilization are sometimes called apocalyptic literature. (Apocalypse is another name for the biblical book of Revelation, in which John the Evangelist describes a vision of the end of the world.) Other authors of apocalyptic stories include Edgar Allan Poe, H. P. Lovecraft, Ray Bradbury, and Nathaniel Hawthorne.

Activity. Ask students to meet as a group and brainstorm a list of stories they have read or films they have seen that deal with this topic. Ask them to discuss characteristics that the stories or films share.

INDEPENDENT PRACTICE

Literary Response and Analysis

Reading Check

1. Main events include purification ritual and dream; sightings of eagle and deer; killing panther; finding knife; crossing river; seeing statue of ASHING; exploring temple; being chased by dogs; exploring apartment; experiencing visions of the city; finding the "dead god" and realizing that he was a man.

Interpretations

2. Possible answers: god-roads are highways; high towers are skyscrapers; ASHING is a statue of George Washington; Great Burning is a war; caves and tunnels are subways.
3. Benét reveals details only gradually and indirectly. The setting also reveals John's courage and intellectual curiosity.
4. The use of first-person point of view lets readers identify with the thoughts and feelings of a young hero braving the unknown. The point of view sets a tone of wonder at what humans can achieve and of sorrow at their failings.
5. Possible answer: John sees that the man in the apartment is not a god. The first-person point of view lets readers share his response to the discovery.
6. The narrator's persona is innocent and curious. This helps the reader see civilization in a different light.
7. Answers will vary. Accept any reasonable response.
8. Possible answer: They didn't learn to use their knowledge wisely. Opinions will vary.
9. John, like the psalm's writer, sits near a river and mourns the loss of a great city.

Evaluation

10. Possible answers: Yes, because there is still no end to the threat of nuclear war; no, because we have defenses to prevent the complete destruction of civilization.
11. Many students will have guessed the setting and found the clues easy or just difficult enough. Students lacking knowledge of New York may consider the clues insufficient.

Literary Response and Analysis

Reading Check

1. Imagine that you are John, the narrator, telling the Hill People about your journey. Briefly **summarize** the **main events** of your journey, either orally or in writing.

Interpretations

2. To understand what is really happening in this story, you have to **draw conclusions** based on the writer's clues and your own experience and knowledge. What do you think John is really seeing (and how are you able to tell) when he describes these elements of the story's **setting**?
   - the god-roads
   - the high towers of the gods
   - the statue of ASHING
   - the Great Burning
   - the caves and tunnels
3. How does Benét use **setting** to create a **mood** of suspense and hold our interest? What does this particular setting (the time, place, and culture) reveal about John's character?
4. How does Benét's use of the **first-person point of view** affect what the reader knows about John and about what happens in the story? How does it affect the **tone** of the story?
5. Find a place in the story where John achieves a breakthrough, and explain what he discovers. How does the **first-person point of view** help you appreciate his breakthrough?
6. How would you describe the **persona** Benét has created for the narrator, John? Why is it important that someone like John tell this story?
7. At what point in the story did you first begin to guess what the Place of the Gods was?
8. Near the end of the story, John says, "Perhaps, in the old days, they ate knowledge too fast." What do you think he means? Are we "eating knowledge" too fast today? Explain.
9. The background on page 140 explains the biblical **allusion,** or reference, in the story's **title.** Now that you have read the story, explain how the words of the psalm connect to it.

Grade 8 Review Reading Standard 3.4 Analyze the relevance of the setting to the mood and meaning of the text.

Reading Standard 3.9 Explain how voice, persona, and the choice of a narrator affect characterization and the tone, plot, and credibility of a text.

Evaluation

10. Benét wrote this story in 1937, before the first atom bomb was built. World War II and the cold war are over now. Do Benét's warnings about the complete destruction of a civilization still have relevance? Why? (Your Quickwrite notes may help you answer.)
11. Do you think Benét made the secret of the Place of the Gods too easy to guess or too hard, or were the clues just difficult enough? Explain.

Writing

Babylon II?

What happened to the city that John calls the Place of the Gods? Write a **prequel,** a story of the events that led up to "By the Waters of Babylon." You might write your story from the **first-person point of view** of the man John finds "sitting looking out over the city," or you might write the story in the form of the man's last journal entries.

▶ **Use "Writing a Short Story," pages 602–609, for help with this assignment.**

152 Chapter 3 Narrator and Voice • Generating Research Questions

Vocabulary Development

Suffixes: Meaningful Endings

It's suffixes that change *say* into *sayings* and *true* into *truly.* A **suffix** is a word part (a group of letters) that is added to a word or word root to change the word's meaning and, often, its part of speech. Suffixes are tacked on to the end of a word. The most common suffixes are those that we use to create noun plurals and verb forms (*–es, –s, –ed, –ing, –en*) as well as adjectives and adverbs (*–er, –est, –ly*).

When you find an unfamiliar word, look for suffixes that provide clues to how the **root** (the base element of the word) changes. The chart below gives meanings and examples for some common suffixes and combining forms (a combining form is a kind of suffix). Remember that some suffixes have more than one meaning.

Latin Suffixes	Meaning	Example
–fy (forming *v.*)	to make; to become	liquefy
–ious (forming *adj.*)	characterized by	rebellious
–ity (forming *n.*)	state or condition of being	prosperity
–ous (forming *adj.*)	characterized by	dangerous
Greek Suffixes / Combining Forms	**Meaning**	**Example**
–cracy (forming *n.*)	form of government; rule by	democracy
–gram (forming *n.*)	something written or recorded	telegram
–logy (forming *n.*)	science or study of	zoology
–phobia (forming *n.*)	fear of	claustrophobia
Anglo-Saxon Suffixes	**Meaning**	**Example**
–wise (forming *adv.*)	in a direction or manner	clockwise
–dom (forming *n.*)	domain or dominion fact or state of being	kingdom wisdom
–hood (forming *n.*)	state or condition the whole group of	childhood priesthood
–some (forming *adj.*)	like; tending to be	lonesome

PRACTICE 1

Choose five suffixes from the chart. Then, work with a partner to list all the additional examples you can think of that use each suffix. Exchange your completed lists with those of another team.

PRACTICE 2

The words below are from the story. Each contains a suffix that is not on the chart above. Make a similar chart for these words. If you need help determining the meaning of a suffix, check a dictionary.

enchantments   wilderness   doubtless   wonderful

Reading Standard 1.1
Understand word derivations.

Vocabulary Development

Practice 1

Possible Answers

- *–ity. Examples*—necessity, originality, popularity, individuality, ability, possibility.
- *–ous. Examples*—glamorous, spacious, hilarious, ridiculous, ingenious.
- *–logy. Examples*—biology, anthropology, etymology, psychology, radiology.
- *–hood. Examples*—neighborhood, brotherhood, sisterhood, motherhood, statehood.

Practice 2

Possible Answers

- *–ment. Meaning*—act, process, or fact of being. *Example*—excitement.
- *–ness. Meaning*—quality or condition of being. *Example*—nervousness.
- *–less. Meaning*—without. *Example*—careless.
- *–ful. Meaning*—full of. *Example*—beautiful.

Resources Reminder

Vocabulary

- *Lesson Plans for Language Development*
  - Vocabulary, pp. 92, 98

ASSESSING

Assessment

- *Progress Assessment of Reading*
  - Selection Test

RETEACHING

For a lesson reteaching Standard 3.9, see **Reteaching,** p. 939A. For another selection to teach Standard 3.9, see *Interactive Reading,* Chapter 3.

STANDARDS FOCUS, pp. 154–162

(For grade-level and review standards taught in this lesson, see citations on Student Edition pages.)

Prerequisite Standard

- Grade 7, Literary Response and Analysis 3.5 **Contrast points of view (e.g., first and third person, limited and omniscient, subjective and objective) in narrative text and explain how they affect the overall theme of the work.**

Reading Skills

- Determine author's purpose.

Summary *at grade level*

In this satirical tale the omniscient narrator has two characters tell stories within a larger frame story. The frame story involves three children, their aunt, and a bachelor, who are all sharing a compartment on a train. It is a hot day, the next stop is an hour away, and the children are fidgety. The bachelor becomes annoyed at them, and the aunt begins to tell a story to quiet the children. The children listen to the story and then declare that the aunt's moral tale—about a very good girl who is rescued because of her goodness—is "stupid." The bachelor concurs, so the aunt challenges him to tell a story. He begins what seems to be a similar story, about a "horribly good" girl who always wears her medals for obedience, punctuality, and good behavior. The clanking of these medals ultimately leads to her being devoured by a wolf. The children pronounce that this story is "beautiful." The aunt scolds the bachelor, telling him that he has "undermined . . . years of careful teaching."

Before You Read

The Storyteller

Literary Focus

Omniscient Point of View: Knowing It All

An **omniscient** ("all-knowing") narrator plays no part in the action of a story. Instead, the narrator is an all-knowing observer who has the power to reveal the thoughts, feelings, and motives of every character and sometimes comments directly on the characters. Unlike stories written from the first-person point of view, stories with an omniscient point of view generally give us a more reliable perspective. We are in the hands of an all-knowing narrator, whom we are usually inclined to trust.

Satire: Isn't It Ridiculous?

Satire is any writing that ridicules the shortcomings of people or institutions in an attempt to bring about a change. Greed, injustice, cruelty, stupidity, and deceit are all targets of the satirist. Satire often uses both exaggeration and humor to invite laughter at someone's expense. As you read this story, try to figure out whom or what Saki is ridiculing.

Reading Skills

Does the Writer Have a Purpose?

Saki and other writers of humorous stories seem to create works that are pure entertainments. However, many of these writers, including Saki, often have a more serious purpose than simply to entertain their readers. To discover the purpose in a tale like "The Storyteller," you have to read closely. Look for key passages or loaded words that reveal the author's attitude toward the characters. Notice which characters Saki seems to poke fun at and which ones he seems sympathetic toward.

Reading Standard 3.9 Explain how the choice of a narrator affects characterization and the plot, and credibility of a text.

Make the Connection

Quickwrite

What do you expect from a children's story—a happy ending, a strong moral, surprising reversals? Think back to your favorite stories and books from when you were very young, and try to figure out why they captured your interest. Jot down your ideas.

Vocabulary Development

sultry (sul'trē) *adj.:* hot and humid; sweltering.

persistent (pər·sist'ənt) *adj.:* continuing.

diversion (də·vʉr'zhən) *n.:* something that distracts the attention.

resolute (rez'ə·lo͞ot') *adj.:* determined.

petulant (pech'ə·lənt) *adj.:* impatient; irritable; peevish.

deplorably (dē·plôr'ə·blē) *adv.:* very badly.

conviction (kən·vik'shən) *n.:* strong belief; certainty.

retort (ri·tôrt') *n.:* sharp reply.

assail (ə·sāl') *v.:* attack.

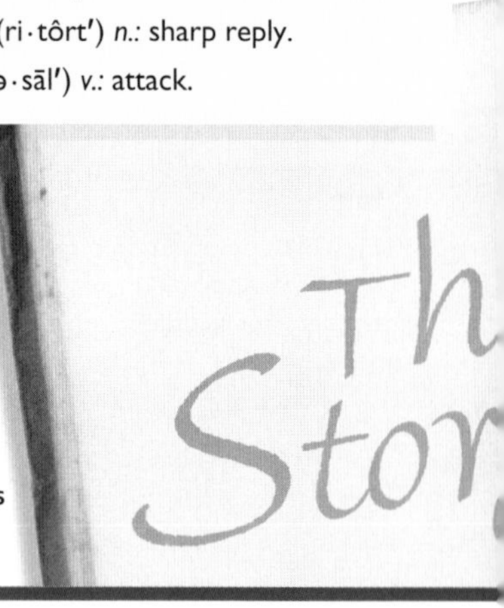

RESOURCES: READING

Planning

- *One-Stop Planner* CD-ROM with Test Generator
- *On Course: Mapping Instruction*

Media

- *Audio CD Library*
  - disc 5
- *Fine Art Transparencies*
  - Transparency 4

Reading

- *Interactive Reading,* Teacher's Edition
  - Graphic Organizer: Narrator Chart

The Storyteller

Saki

It was a hot afternoon, and the railway carriage was correspondingly sultry, and the next stop was at Templecombe, nearly an hour ahead. The occupants of the carriage were a small girl, and a smaller girl, and a small boy. An aunt belonging to the children occupied one corner seat, and the further corner seat on the opposite side was occupied by a bachelor who was a stranger to their party, but the small girls and the small boy emphatically occupied the compartment. Both the aunt and the children were conversational in a limited, persistent way, reminding one of the attentions of a housefly that refused to be discouraged. Most of the aunt's remarks seemed to begin with "Don't," and nearly all the children's remarks began with "Why?" The bachelor said nothing out loud. **A**

"Don't, Cyril, don't," exclaimed the aunt, as the small boy began smacking the cushions of the seat, producing a cloud of dust at each blow.

"Come and look out of the window," she added.

The child moved reluctantly to the window. "Why are those sheep being driven out of that field?" he asked.

"I expect they are being driven to another field where there is more grass," said the aunt weakly.

"But there is lots of grass in that field," protested the boy; "there's nothing else but grass there. Aunt, there's lots of grass in that field."

"Perhaps the grass in the other field is better," suggested the aunt fatuously.[1]

"Why is it better?" came the swift, inevitable question.

1. **fatuously** (fach′o͞o·əs·lē) *adv.:* foolishly.

Vocabulary

sultry (sul′trē) *adj.:* hot and humid; sweltering.

persistent (pər·sist′ənt) *adj.:* continuing.

Differentiating Instruction

- *Lesson Plans for Language Development*
  - English-Language Learners, pp. 71–73, 93, 99
  - Special Education Students, pp. 74, 93, 99

Vocabulary

- *Vocabulary Development*
  - Vocabulary Worksheet, p. 12

Assessment

- *Progress Assessment of Reading*
  - Selection Test
- *One-Stop Planner* CD-ROM with Test Generator

PRETEACHING

Selection Starter

Motivate. Have students name some of their favorite books or movies and explain why they like them. Then, have students brainstorm a list of characteristics of a good story. When students finish, ask them to complete the Quickwrite activity.

Preview Vocabulary

Have students work in pairs to complete the following exercise involving the Vocabulary words on p. 154.

1. Explain what you would do to make yourself comfortable during a sultry day.
2. Describe a situation in which you were persistent and eventually achieved your goal.
3. What would be a good diversion for a young child?
4. How would you know if someone was truly resolute?
5. In what situations might you find petulant children?
6. Tell about a time when you saw someone behaving deplorably.
7. Express your strongest conviction.
8. If someone said your haircut looked bad, what would be your retort?
9. How would you assail a castle?

DIRECT TEACHING

A Reading Skills

Determining author's purpose. Remind students that the way characters are introduced can provide clues as to the author's purpose. Why do you suppose Saki describes the aunt as "belonging" to the children? [Possible response: to emphasize the children's importance in the story; to suggest that they are in control.]

DIRECT TEACHING

A Literary Focus
GRADE-LEVEL STANDARD

Point of view. Remind students that point of view is the vantage point from which the writer tells a story. Is Saki's narrator a first-person, third-person-limited, or omniscient narrator? [omniscient] What detail reveals the narrator's omniscience? [Possible response: The narrator says what is in the aunt's mind—the bachelor is a hard, unsympathetic man.]

B Vocabulary Development
REVIEW STANDARD

Context clues. Ask students to describe the situation leading up to this reference to a "communication cord" and then explain what they think it might be. [The bachelor is irritated and looks at the cord. A communication cord is linked to a bell or buzzer that summons the train's conductor.]

C Literary Focus
GRADE-LEVEL STANDARD

Narrator's effect on characterization. Readers are inclined to trust an omniscient narrator. However, such narrators also have biases, which are often revealed in the specific words they use. Who is this narrator biased against? Find at least three words or phrases that support your answer. [Possible response: The narrator is biased against the aunt; words or phrases might include *unenterprising, deplorably uninteresting, lamely.*]

"Oh, look at those cows!" exclaimed the aunt. Nearly every field along the line had contained cows or bullocks, but she spoke as though she were drawing attention to a rarity.

"Why is the grass in the other field better?" persisted Cyril.

The frown on the bachelor's face was deepening to a scowl. He was a hard, unsympathetic man, the aunt decided in her mind. She was utterly unable to come to any satisfactory decision about the grass in the other field.

The smaller girl created a diversion by beginning to recite "On the Road to Mandalay."[2] She only knew the first line, but she put her limited knowledge to the fullest possible use. She repeated the line over and over again in a dreamy but resolute and very audible voice; it seemed to the bachelor as though some one had had a bet with her that she could not repeat the line aloud two thousand times without stopping. Whoever it was who had made the wager was likely to lose his bet.

"Come over here and listen to a story," said the aunt, when the bachelor had looked twice at her and once at the communication cord.[3]

The children moved listlessly toward the aunt's end of the carriage. Evidently her reputation as a storyteller did not rank high in their estimation.

In a low, confidential voice, interrupted at frequent intervals by loud, petulant questions from her listeners, she began an unenterprising and deplorably uninteresting story about a little girl who was good, and made friends with every one on account of her goodness, and was finally saved from a mad bull by a number of rescuers who admired her moral character.

"Wouldn't they have saved her if she hadn't been good?" demanded the bigger of the small girls. It was exactly the question that the bachelor had wanted to ask.

"Well, yes," admitted the aunt lamely, "but I don't think they would have run quite so fast to her help if they had not liked her so much."

"It's the stupidest story I've ever heard," said the bigger of the small girls, with immense conviction.

"I didn't listen after the first bit, it was so stupid," said Cyril.

The smaller girl made no actual comment on the story, but she had long ago recommenced a murmured repetition of her favorite line.

"You don't seem to be a success as a storyteller," said the bachelor suddenly from his corner.

The aunt bristled in instant defense at this unexpected attack.

"It's a very difficult thing to tell stories that children can both understand and appreciate," she said stiffly.

"I don't agree with you," said the bachelor.

Vocabulary

diversion (də·vʉr′zhən) *n.:* something that distracts the attention.

resolute (rez′ə·lo͞ot′) *adj.:* determined.

petulant (pech′ə·lənt) *adj.:* impatient; irritable; peevish.

deplorably (dē·plôr′ə·blē) *adv.:* very badly.

conviction (kən·vik′shən) *n.:* strong belief; certainty.

2. **"On the Road to Mandalay":** long poem in dialect by the English writer Rudyard Kipling (1865–1936). The first line is "By the old Moulmein Pagoda, lookin' eastward to the sea."
3. **communication cord:** on a train, signal used in emergencies to call the conductor.

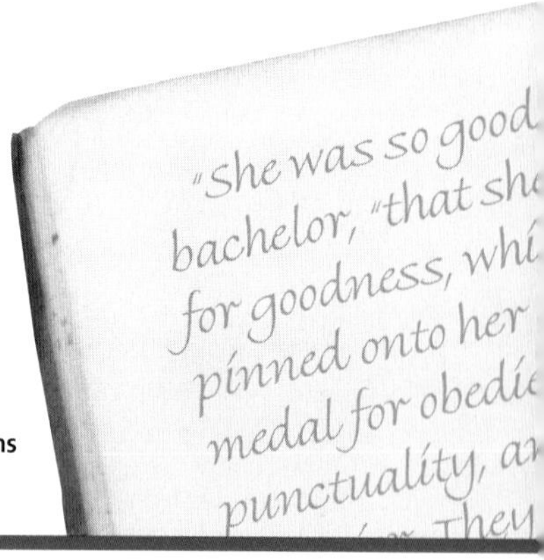

DIFFERENTIATING INSTRUCTION

Learners Having Difficulty

Modeling. To help students read "The Storyteller," model the reading skill of determining author's purpose. You might say, "This story is entertaining to read, but that is not the only reason Saki wrote it. He is also making serious comments about people like the aunt and the stories they tell children. What point do you think Saki is making by comparing the conversation of the aunt and the children to a 'persistent housefly' in the opening paragraphs?" [He is suggesting that their conversation is annoying.] As they read, encourage students to note key passages or loaded words that may reveal Saki's more serious purpose.

English-Language Learners

Students may need help with some of the British terms in this story. Have students give contemporary American English equivalents to British terms such as "railway carriage" [train car], "bullocks" [male cattle], "in instant defense" [defensively], and "tales of infant life" [children's stories]. Encourage students to check the footnotes for help with

"Perhaps *you* would like to tell them a story," was the aunt's retort.

"Tell us a story," demanded the bigger of the small girls.

"Once upon a time," began the bachelor, "there was a little girl called Bertha, who was extraordinarily good."

The children's momentarily aroused interest began at once to flicker; all stories seemed dreadfully alike, no matter who told them.

"She did all that she was told, she was always truthful, she kept her clothes clean, ate milk puddings as if they were jam tarts, learned her lessons perfectly, and was polite in her manners."

"Was she pretty?" asked the bigger of the small girls.

"Not as pretty as any of you," said the bachelor, "but she was horribly good."

There was a wave of reaction in favor of the story; the word horrible in connection with goodness was a novelty that commended itself. It seemed to introduce a ring of truth that was absent from the aunt's tales of infant life.

"She was so good," continued the bachelor, "that she won several medals for goodness, which she always wore, pinned onto her dress. There was a medal for obedience, another medal for punctuality, and a third for good behavior. They were large metal medals and they clicked against one another as she walked. No other child in the town where she lived had as many as three medals, so everybody knew that she must be an extra good child."

"Horribly good," quoted Cyril.

"Everybody talked about her goodness, and the Prince of the country got to hear about it, and he said that as she was so very good she might be allowed once a week to walk in his park, which was just outside the town. It was a beautiful park, and no children were ever allowed in it, so it was a great honor for Bertha to be allowed to go there."

"Were there any sheep in the park?" demanded Cyril.

"No," said the bachelor, "there were no sheep."

"Why weren't there any sheep?" came the inevitable question arising out of that answer.

The aunt permitted herself a smile, which might almost have been described as a grin.

"There were no sheep in the park," said the bachelor, "because the Prince's mother had once had a dream that her son would either be killed by a sheep or else by a clock falling on him. For that reason the Prince never kept a sheep in his park or a clock in his palace."

Vocabulary
retort (ri·tôrt′) *n.:* sharp reply.

Direct Teaching

D Literary Focus
REVIEW STANDARD

Characterization. At first, the girl in the aunt's story and the girl in the bachelor's story seem to be similar. How is Bertha similar to the girl in the aunt's story? [Possible response: She is very good—always truthful, obedient, clean, and polite.] What is the first clue that Bertha and the story about her will be different? [Bertha is "horribly good."]

E Advanced Learners

Acceleration. What does the phrase "horribly good" suggest to you? [Possible response: A person who is smug, a perfectionist, or too willing to ingratiate oneself.] You may wish to explain that "horribly good" is an oxymoron, or a combination of two contradictory words. Ask students for other examples of oxymorons, such as deafening silence, cheerful pessimist, wise fool.

F Literary Focus
GRADE-LEVEL STANDARD

Narrator's effect on credibility. Point out that the bachelor becomes an omniscient narrator for his story about Bertha. How do the children respond to the omniscient narrator and his explanation of why there are no sheep in the park? [Possible response: They trust the narrator; they embrace his explanation because it's fun and unexpected.]

---

other idioms and to consult a dictionary of idioms if they can't figure out unfamiliar words and phrases from the context.

Resources Reminder

For lessons designed for intermediate and advanced English-language learners, see *Lesson Plans for Language Development,* pp. 71–73, 93, 99

Special Education Students

For lessons designed for special education students, see *Lesson Plans for Language Development,* pp. 74, 93, 99.

Advanced Learners

Acceleration. Use this activity to move advanced learners toward the eleventh- and twelfth-grade Standard 3.1, for which they analyze characteristics of subgenres.

Activity. Have small groups of students discuss what Saki is criticizing, how he uses humor to do it, and what aspect of humanity he hopes to improve. After the discussion, students may write a brief analysis of Saki's use of the satire subgenre.

DIRECT TEACHING

A Reading Skills

Hypothesizing. Why do you think the bachelor has the Prince decide to have pigs instead of flowers in his park? [Possible response: He knows the children will like the unconventional idea of a park full of pigs.]

B Literary Focus
GRADE-LEVEL STANDARD

Satire. Remind students that satire is a kind of writing that ridicules human weakness or folly. Common targets of satire are greed, injustice, or cruelty. To help students identify Saki's unusual target of satire, ask them how Bertha feels about her goodness as she enters the park. [very proud] How does she feel about her goodness at the end of the passage? [She regrets being so good.] What is Saki satirizing? [Possible response: Morality that is based on convenience is satirized.]

The aunt suppressed a gasp of admiration.

"Was the Prince killed by a sheep or by a clock?" asked Cyril.

"He is still alive, so we can't tell whether the dream will come true," said the bachelor unconcernedly; "anyway, there were no sheep in the park, but there were lots of little pigs running all over the place."

"What color were they?"

"Black with white faces, white with black spots, black all over, gray with white patches, and some were white all over."

The storyteller paused to let a full idea of the park's treasures sink into the children's imaginations; then he resumed:

"Bertha was rather sorry to find that there were no flowers in the park. She had promised her aunts, with tears in her eyes, that she would not pick any of the kind Prince's flowers, and she had meant to keep her promise, so of course it made her feel silly to find that there were no flowers to pick."

"Why weren't there any flowers?"

"Because the pigs had eaten them all," said the bachelor promptly. "The gardeners had told the Prince that you couldn't have pigs and flowers, so he decided to have pigs and no flowers."

A There was a murmur of approval at the excellence of the Prince's decision; so many people would have decided the other way.

"There were lots of other delightful things in the park. There were ponds with gold and blue and green fish in them, and trees with beautiful parrots that said clever things at a moment's notice, and hummingbirds that hummed all the popular tunes of the day. Bertha walked up and down and enjoyed herself immensely, and thought to herself: 'If I were not so extraordinarily good I should not have been allowed to come into this beautiful park and enjoy all that there is to be seen in it,' and her three medals **B** clinked against one another as she walked and helped to remind her how very good she really was. Just then an enormous wolf came prowling into the park to see if it could catch a fat little pig for its supper."

"What color was it?" asked the children, amid an immediate quickening of interest.

"Mud-color all over, with a black tongue and pale gray eyes that gleamed with unspeakable

READING MINI-LESSON

Developing Word-Attack Skills

Write the selection word *petulant* in syllables on the chalkboard: pet-u-lant. Ask students to read each syllable in isolation. [/pet/, /yo͞o/, /lant/] Then, write *petulant* as a whole word. Read the word aloud (pech′ə•lənt), and have students note what happens to the sound of the letter *t*. Help students recognize that the *t* in *petulant* has the sound /ch/, which is usually spelled with the digraph *ch*.

Write the following word pairs with similar spellings on the chalkboard, and have students compare the sound of *t* in each pair.

fort, fortune	text, texture
act, actual	fat, fatuous

Encourage students to make a generalization about the effect of the letter *u* on the letter *t*.

Activity. Point out that when *t* is followed by *u*, it does not always have the sound /ch/. In each set below, have students identify the word in which *t* stands for /ch/.

1. petulant	petunia	[petulant]
2. costume	posture	[posture]
3. congratulate	gratitude	[congratulate]
4. opportunity	aperture	[aperture]
5. perpetual	perpetuity	[perpetual]

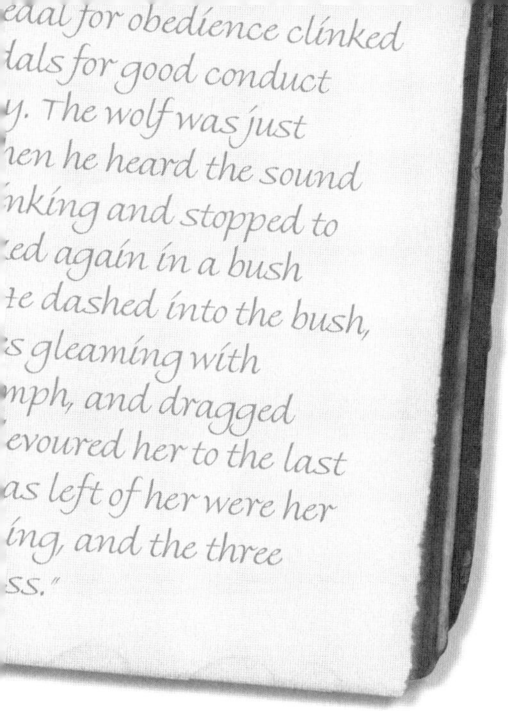

ferocity. The first thing that it saw in the park was Bertha; her pinafore[4] was so spotlessly white and clean that it could be seen from a great distance. Bertha saw the wolf and saw that it was stealing toward her, and she began to wish that she had never been allowed to come into the park. She ran as hard as she could, and the wolf came after her with huge leaps and bounds. She managed to reach a shrubbery of myrtle bushes and she hid herself in one of the thickest of the bushes. The wolf came sniffing among the branches, its black tongue lolling out of its mouth and its pale gray eyes glaring with rage. Bertha was terribly frightened and thought to herself: 'If I had not been so extraordinarily good I should have been safe in the town at this moment.' However, the scent of the myrtle was so strong that the wolf could not sniff out where Bertha was hiding, and the bushes were so thick that he might have hunted about in them for a long time without catching sight of her, so he thought he might as well go off and catch a little pig instead. Bertha was trembling very much at having the wolf prowling and sniffing so near her, and as she trembled the medal for obedience clinked against the medals for good conduct and punctuality. The wolf was just moving away when he heard the sound of the medals clinking and stopped to listen; they clinked again in a bush quite near him. He dashed into the bush, his pale gray eyes gleaming with ferocity and triumph, and dragged Bertha out and devoured her to the last morsel. All that was left of her were her shoes, bits of clothing, and the three medals for goodness."

"Were any of the little pigs killed?"

"No, they all escaped."

"The story began badly," said the smaller of the small girls, "but it had a beautiful ending."

"It is the most beautiful story that I ever heard," said the bigger of the small girls, with immense decision.

"It is the *only* beautiful story I have ever heard," said Cyril.

A dissentient[5] opinion came from the aunt.

"A most improper story to tell young children! You have undermined the effect of years of careful teaching."

"At any rate," said the bachelor, collecting his belongings preparatory to leaving the carriage, "I kept them quiet for ten minutes, which was more than you were able to do."

"Unhappy woman!" he observed to himself as he walked down the platform of Templecombe station; "for the next six months or so those children will assail her in public with demands for an improper story!" ■

4. **pinafore** (pin′ə·fôr′) *n.:* apronlike garment that little girls used to wear over their dresses.

5. **dissentient** (di·sen′shənt) *adj.:* dissenting; disagreeing.

Vocabulary
assail (ə·sāl′) *v.:* attack.

Direct Teaching

C Literary Focus
GRADE-LEVEL STANDARD

Narrator's effect on plot. What do you think will happen to Bertha? Support your answer with details from the story and with what you know about the narrator. [Possible responses: Bertha might escape because the wolf can't see or smell her in the myrtle. Bertha will not escape because the narrator knows the children will enjoy having a good girl meet an untimely end.]

D Literary Focus
GRADE-LEVEL STANDARD

Satire. Saki uses irony for the purpose of satire. What is comically ironic about Bertha's fate? [Her medals for goodness lead to her demise.] What is Saki satirizing in "The Storyteller"? [Possible responses: self-righteousness; stories with a moral; sheltering children from the truth.]

E Literary Focus
GRADE-LEVEL STANDARD

Theme. What theme, or perception about human nature, do you think Saki wants to share with readers? [Possible responses: The morality of convenience is not a truly respectable morality; stories with unrealistic morals and happy endings are not useful for teaching young people how to behave.]

Developing Fluency

Mixed-ability group activity. This story is perfect for a mixed-ability group to read aloud. Have more fluent students take the parts of the bachelor and the narrator, while less fluent students take the parts of the children. Have groups read the story aloud from the point where the bachelor begins his tale (p. 157). Some groups may choose to perform their readings for a younger class.

Family/Community Activity

The aunt and the bachelor have different opinions about how to rear children. The aunt tells a story that conveys a view of children as she feels they should be, while the bachelor tells a story that imparts a truth—that even good children may meet a ruinous end. You may want to ask students to survey family or community members to find out who agrees more with the aunt and who agrees more with the bachelor. Invite students who want to report their findings to the class to do so. Make certain those students who present to the class have gotten permission to share their findings.

GUIDED PRACTICE

Monitoring students' progress. Guide the class in answering these true-false questions. Direct students to locate passages in the text that support their answers.

True-False

1. Two girls, a boy, and their aunt and uncle share a train compartment. [F]
2. Neither the children nor the bachelor like the aunt's story. [T]
3. Bertha gets to go to the park because she is so good. [T]
4. Bertha's medals for goodness cause her to be eaten by the wolf. [T]
5. The children think the bachelor's story is mean. [F]

Meet the Writer

Background. Saki's childhood years had a great influence on his stories. The strict aunts who raised him served as models for some of his characters. His aunt Augusta, for example, inspired a character in "Sredni Vashtar," in which an overbearing aunt comes to a gruesome end. Two mischievous young men, Reginald and Clovis, are the heroes of a series of short stories, in which they take revenge on the adult world. These men are also thought to be drawn from aspects of Saki's childhood.

As an adult, Saki worked as a foreign correspondent for London's *Morning Post.* He traveled throughout southern central Europe and Russia, reporting such acts of violence and revolution as the 1903 assassination of the king and queen of Serbia. He was nearly shot in St. Petersburg in January 1905, on a day when the Russian army opened fire on a crowd of demonstrators. Critics have speculated that this early exposure to violence contributed to the edge of cruelty and brutality that lies under the genteel and humorous surface of Saki's stories.

Meet the Writer

Saki (Hector Hugh Munro)

An Unusual Sense of Humor

Saki is the pen name of Hector Hugh Munro (1870–1916), who was born in Burma, the son of a British military officer. His mother died before he was two, and he and his older brother and sister were raised in Devonshire, England, by their grandmother and two strict aunts. (We find bad-tempered aunts in several Saki stories, including "The Storyteller.")

From an early age, Munro displayed an unusual temperament and sense of humor. In her biography of Munro, his sister Ethel recalls their childhood and describes Munro's mischievous delight in getting a well-behaved playmate in trouble:

> "He saw to it that Claud did all the things we must never do, the easier to accomplish since his mother would be indoors tongue-wagging with Granny and the aunts. Poor Claud really was a good child, with no inclination to be anything else, but under Hector's ruthless tuition . . . he put in a breathless day of bad deeds.
>
> And when Aunt Tom (Charlotte she was never called), after the visitor's departure, remarked, 'Claud is not the good child I imagined him to be,' Hector felt it was the end of a perfect day."

Munro was a sickly child and had little formal schooling until he was sent to a boarding school at fourteen. "You can't expect a boy to be vicious till he's been to a good school," Munro wrote somewhat acidly in one of his stories.

At twenty-three, Munro returned to Burma to join his father and older brother. He took a police job arranged by his father but fell ill at once and returned to England a little more than a year later.

Early in his writing career he worked as a political satirist and a foreign correspondent for various newspapers. Eventually he found a wide audience for his humorous, satiric, and often cynical short stories.

Munro took his pen name from the Persian poem the *Rubáiyát of Omar Khayyám,* which was popular in England at the time. Saki is the name of the cupbearer, the servant who fills the wine cups.

Though Munro was forty-three when World War I began, he enlisted in the British army, eager for "the excitement of real warfare." He was killed on the front lines in France by a German sniper.

For Independent Reading

You can enjoy more of Saki's delicious twists in these short stories: "The Open Window" (about a girl whose story terrifies a visitor), "The Schartz-Metterklume Method" (in which a mischievous aristocrat plays a devious trick on an unsuspecting family), and "Sredni Vashtar" (about a boy's revenge on his overbearing guardian).

DIFFERENTIATING INSTRUCTION

Advanced Learners

Enrichment. Tell students that Saki lived during the Victorian era. He satirizes the puritan attitudes of the time, but not all Victorian tales were excessively moralizing.

Activity. Have students find out more about Victorian children's stories. Suggest that they enter *Victorian children's literature, Aunt Judy's Magazine, Alice's Adventures in Wonderland, At The Back of the North Wind,* or *The Secret Garden* as keywords in an Internet search engine. After students complete preliminary research, have them choose one piece of Victorian children's literature to read and summarize for the class. Students may wish to conclude by saying whether this is the sort of literature Saki is satirizing in "The Storyteller."

160 Chapter 3 Narrator and Voice • Generating Research Questions

Literary Response and Analysis

Reading Check

1. This is a **frame story,** in which one or more stories are told within another. Describe the **basic situation** that provides the frame for both the aunt's and the bachelor's stories.
2. In the aunt's story, why is the little girl saved? How do the children respond to the aunt's story?
3. What is the first "ring of truth" that the children notice in the bachelor's story?
4. In the bachelor's story, why does Bertha come to an unhappy end?

Interpretations

5. How would the story be different if either the aunt or the bachelor, rather than the **omniscient narrator,** were telling it from the **first-person point of view?** What would be lost?
6. What a vastly superior storyteller the bachelor is! He supplies both logic and information as he builds his extraordinary setting for Bertha's downfall. What surprises does he fill the park with? Why do you think he is able to make these surprises seem believable to the children?
7. When the bachelor calls Bertha "horribly good," the children are shocked and delighted. Find other **key passages** and **loaded words** that reveal the writer's **tone,** or attitude, toward the aunt, the bachelor, and their stories. What do you think Saki's **purpose** was in writing this story?
8. What would you say is the **theme,** or message, of the bachelor's story? How about the aunt's? Consult your Quickwrite notes to see how each story measures up to your own ideas of what's important in children's literature.
9. In what ways can "The Storyteller" be considered a **satire**? What is Saki ridiculing? How does he use humor and exaggeration to make his point? Support your answers with examples from the story.

Literary Criticism

10. Respond to the following comment by Saki's biographer, A. J. Langguth. Cite examples from the story to support your opinion.

> By now Hector was carving his stories with a keen blade, suffering no extraneous word or commonplace phrase. He had reached that degree of proficiency where the humor came less from his jokes than from the precision of each sentence.

Writing

Imagine a Park

Suppose you were telling a story about someone who could equip a park with unusual or unexpected attractions. Write a paragraph **describing** an imaginary park setting—one that is very different from the parks that we are used to.

Reading Standard 3.9
Explain how the choice of a narrator affects characterization and the tone, plot, and credibility of a text.

INDEPENDENT PRACTICE

Literary Response and Analysis

Reading Check

1. Five people are in the same train car on a sultry afternoon. The adults tell stories to distract the children.
2. The girl is saved because she is good. The children question the moral of the story and conclude that the story is stupid.
3. Bertha is "horribly good."
4. Bertha's medals clang and attract the wolf's attention.

Interpretations

5. Possible answer: If the aunt or bachelor were to tell the story from the first-person point of view, it would reflect their biases. With any first-person narrator, the reader would not know what the other characters are thinking.
6. Possible answer: Surprises include the choice of pigs over flowers, colorful fish, parrots that say clever things, and hummingbirds that hum popular tunes. The surprises are believable because the bachelor knows what appeals to children, and he speaks with confidence.
7. Possible answer: The writer's tone is revealed when the aunt answers "weakly" and "fatuously" and her story is called "unenterprising and deplorably uninteresting." On the other hand, there is a "wave of reaction in favor" and "a murmur of approval" for the bachelor's story. Saki's purpose is to poke fun at the excessive moralizing that is evident in children's stories at the time.
8. Possible answer: The theme of the bachelor's story is that goodness is not always rewarded. The theme of the aunt's story is that goodness *is* rewarded.
9. Possible answer: The story is considered a satire because it ridicules simplistic moral tales. Saki uses humorous details in the bachelor's story, such as a park that has pigs but no flowers, and he uses irony in the final scene when the clanging of Bertha's medals lead to her death.

Literary Criticism

10. Possible answer: Saki's humor comes from his precise words and sentences. For example, when Saki writes, "The bachelor said nothing out loud" on p. 155, the reader imagines what he must be saying to himself.

Vocabulary Development

Practice

Possible Answers

1. *sultry. Meaning*—hot and humid. *Sentence clue*—"bright August afternoon." *Story clue*—"hot."
2. *persistent. Meaning*—lingering. *Sentence clue*—"would never go away." *Story clue*—"refused to be discouraged."
3. *diversion. Meaning*—entertainment. *Sentence clue*—"welcome." *Story clue*—"recite 'On the Road to Mandalay.'"
4. *resolute. Meaning*—stubborn; decisive. *Sentence clue*—"never leaving." *Story clue*—"repeated."
5. *petulant. Meaning*—irritable. *Sentence clue*—"sharp, nagging questions." *Story clue*—"loud."
6. *deplorably. Meaning*—appallingly. *Sentence clue*—"everyone was angry." *Story clues*—"unenterprising," "uninteresting."
7. *conviction. Meaning*—strong belief. *Sentence clue*—"great willpower." *Story clue*—"immense."
8. *retort. Meaning*—sharp reply. *Sentence clue*—"bad-tempered clerk." *Story clue*—aunt's dialogue.
9. *assail. Meaning*—overwhelm. *Sentence clue*—situation of reporters gathered. *Story clues*—"'Unhappy woman!'" "demands."

Resources Reminder

Vocabulary

- *Vocabulary Development*
  - Vocabulary Worksheet, p. 12
- *Lesson Plans for Language Development*
  - Vocabulary, pp. 93, 99

Grammar Link

Practice

1. *Subject*—sheep. *Verb*—Were.
2. *Subject*—flowers. *Verb*—weren't.
3. *Subject*—they. *Verb*—were.
4. *Subject*—ponds. *Verb*—were.

Vocabulary Development

Using Context Clues

PRACTICE

Explain the meaning of each underlined word, and point out the **context clues** in the sentence that helped you guess the meaning. Then, go back to Saki's story, and see if you can find context clues for the same underlined words. Write down any clues that you find.

Word Bank
sultry
persistent
diversion
resolute
petulant
deplorably
conviction
retort
assail

Grade 8 Review Reading Standard 1.3 Use word meanings within the appropriate context and show ability to verify those meanings.

1. The bright August afternoon was typically sultry.
2. It was a persistent problem, one that would never go away.
3. The whole event became a welcome diversion for the bored onlookers.
4. He was resolute about never leaving his beloved boyhood home.
5. The girl's sharp, nagging questions were both petulant and rude.
6. Everyone was angry that she behaved deplorably.
7. She was a woman of great willpower and conviction.
8. The bad-tempered clerk gave the customer a quick retort.
9. The lawyer feared reporters would assail her as she left the courtroom.

Grammar Link MINI-LESSON

Inverted Order: Verbs Before Subjects

English sentences have a usual order: subjects first, then verbs. Some sentences, though, use **inverted order**—that is, the subject follows the verb. Inverted order is often used in questions and in sentences or clauses that begin with the word *here* or *there*. (Sometimes a sentence in inverted order will begin with a phrase or an adjective or adverb.) In these examples from "The Storyteller," the subject is underlined, and the verb is in boldface type:

"**Was** she pretty?"

"There **were** lots of other delightful things in the park."

PRACTICE

For each sentence, first find the subject. Then, choose the verb that agrees with the subject.

1. "(Were/was) there any sheep in the park?"
2. "Why (wasn't/weren't) there any flowers?"
3. "What color (was/were) they?"
4. "There (were/was) ponds with gold and blue and green fish in them. . . ."

▶ **For more help, see Sentences Beginning with *There* or *Here* and Sentences Asking Questions in the *Holt Handbook*, page 44.**

ASSESSING

Assessment

- *Progress Assessment of Reading*
  - Selection Test

RETEACHING

For a lesson reteaching Standard 3.9, see **Reteaching**, p. 939A. For another selection to teach Standard 3.9, see *Interactive Reading*, Chapter 3.

Before You Read

The Cold Equations

Literary Focus

Third-Person-Limited Point of View

Like the omniscient narrator, the narrator of a story written from the **third-person-limited point of view** stands outside the action and refers to all the characters by name or as *he* or *she.* Unlike the omniscient narrator, however, this narrator zooms in on the thoughts, actions, and feelings of only *one* character. We almost never know what the others are thinking.

This point of view is popular with modern writers because it combines the possibilities of the omniscient point of view with the intense, personal focus of first-person narration. In "The Cold Equations" the third-person-limited narrator provides a calm voice in an increasingly tense, emotional situation.

Reading Skills

Monitoring Your Reading: Questioning

Good readers ask questions as they read—whether they're reading a detective story or a serious novel. As you read "The Cold Equations," answer the questions at the open-book signs. They will serve as a guide for you to ask additional questions of your own as you read. You may keep wondering what is going to happen next in this suspenseful tale. You may have questions about the characters and the unusual setting and circumstances or about the choice of narrator. You may even have questions about Godwin's use of science.

Make the Connection

Quickwrite

Nobody gets through life without having to make hard decisions. What kinds of choices might have difficult consequences no matter what we decide to do? Freewrite about such a choice. How would you make a decision when faced with such a hard choice?

Vocabulary Development

inured (in·yo͞ord′) *v.* used as *adj.:* accustomed to something difficult or painful.

increments (in′krə·mənts) *n.:* small increases.

recoiled (ri·koild′) *v.:* drew back in fear, surprise, or disgust.

paramount (par′ə·mount′) *adj.:* supreme; dominant.

annihilate (ə·nī′ə·lāt′) *v.:* destroy; demolish.

irrevocable (i·rev′ə·kə·bəl) *adj.:* irreversible; incapable of being canceled or undone.

immutable (i·myo͞ot′ə·bəl) *adj.:* unchangeable; never changing or varying.

ponderous (pän′dər·əs) *adj.:* heavy and slow moving.

apprehension (ap′rē·hen′shən) *n.:* dread; fear of a future event.

ineffably (in·ef′ə·blē) *adv.:* indescribably; inexpressibly.

Reading Standard 3.9
Explain how the choice of a narrator affects characterization and the tone, plot, and credibility of a text.

STANDARDS FOCUS, pp. 163–186

(For the grade-level standards taught in this lesson, see citations on Student Edition pages.)

Prerequisite Standard

- Grade 7, Literary Response and Analysis 3.5 **Contrast points of view (e.g., first and third person, limited and omniscient, subjective and objective) in narrative text and explain how they affect the overall theme of the work.**

Reading Skills

- Monitor your reading.

Summary *above grade level*

In the year 2178, Barton pilots a one-person spacecraft toward the planet Woden, carrying serum that is the only hope for six fever-stricken explorers from Earth. A third-person-limited narrator reveals Barton's thoughts and feelings as he finds evidence of a stowaway and realizes he must jettison the person, since any extra weight will deplete fuel and cause the craft to crash. The stowaway is eighteen-year-old Marilyn Cross, who longs to see her brother Gerry on Woden. Torn by her innocence and racing against time, Barton slows fuel use and contacts his commander. Yet he cannot overcome the cold equation: Either she alone dies, or eight people will die. Marilyn writes letters to her family, briefly speaks with Gerry, then enters the air-lock and is blown into space.

RESOURCES: READING

Media

- *Audio CD Library*
  - disc 6
- *Fine Art Transparencies*
  - Transparency 5

Reading

- *Interactive Reading,* Teacher's Edition
  - Graphic Organizer: Narrator Chart

Differentiating Instruction

- *Lesson Plans for Language Development*
  - English-Language Learners, pp. 75–77, 94, 100
  - Special Education Students, pp. 78, 94, 100

Vocabulary

- Vocabulary Development
  - Vocabulary Worksheet, pp. 13–14

Assessment

- *Progress Assessment of Reading*
  - Selection Test
- *One-Stop Planner* CD-ROM with Test Generator

PRETEACHING

Selection Starter

Motivate. To demonstrate how the narrator can affect the tone of a text, have students write a paragraph describing a life-saving rescue in outer space. First, have students write from the third-person-limited point of view of the rescue team's captain. Then, have students rewrite the paragraph, describing the same events from the first-person point of view. Ask volunteers to read their paragraphs aloud. Discuss with the class how the change of point of view affects the tone.

Preview Vocabulary

Discuss the Vocabulary words and their meanings from p. 163. Then, use these exercises to familiarize students with the words.

1. Stage a scene in which characters have recoiled at the thought that something might annihilate them.
2. Give an example of an immutable circumstance that might cause apprehension.
3. Describe a change that seems to proceed in ineffably small increments.
4. Which irrevocable constitutional right is of paramount importance to you?
5. Describe a ponderous animal becoming inured to the hardships of a long journey.

Assign the Reading

Homework

Read the first few pages of the story aloud as a class, up to ". . . must be punished" on p. 167. Students reading at or above grade level can then finish the story independently and answer the Reading Check questions as homework, while you work with students having difficulty.

THE COLD EQUATIONS

Tom Godwin

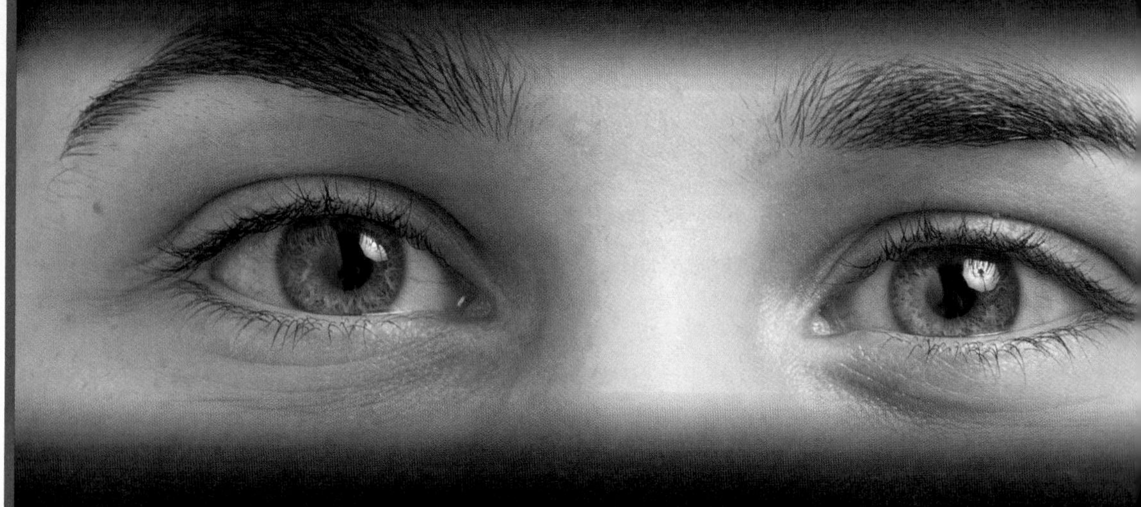

It was the law, and there could be no appeal.

He was not alone.

There was nothing to indicate the fact but the white hand of the tiny gauge on the board before him. The control room was empty but for himself; there was no sound other than the murmur of the drives—but the white hand had moved. It had been on zero when the little ship was launched from the *Stardust;* now, an hour later, it had crept up. There was something in the supply closet across the room, it was saying, some kind of a body that radiated heat.

164

DIFFERENTIATING INSTRUCTION

Learners Having Difficulty

Modeling. To help students read this story, model the reading strategy of questioning. Say, "Suppose I read a story in which the main character is referred to as 'he' and is not given a name. I might ask myself, 'Why doesn't the author reveal this character's name?' Asking questions like this alerts me to story details and to the author's purpose." Encourage students to note questions that occur to them as they read the story.

English-Language Learners

Let students know that this story features some made-up terms, including *Woden* and *Mimir* (imaginary planets), *kala* (an imaginary insect), and *Gelanese* (an imaginary language).

It could be but one kind of a body—a living, human body.

He leaned back in the pilot's chair and drew a deep, slow breath, considering what he would have to do. He was an EDS pilot, inured to the sight of death, long since accustomed to it and to viewing the dying of another man with an objective lack of emotion, and he had no choice in what he must do. There could be no alternative—but it required a few moments of conditioning for even an EDS pilot to prepare himself to walk across the room and coldly, deliberately, take the life of a man he had yet to meet.

He would, of course, do it. It was the law, stated very bluntly and definitely in grim Paragraph L, Section 8, of Interstellar Regulations: *"Any stowaway discovered in an EDS shall be jettisoned immediately following discovery."*

It was the law, and there could be no appeal.

QUESTIONING
1. The story opens with suspense and conflict. What do you **predict** will happen next?

It was a law not of men's choosing but made imperative by the circumstances of the space frontier. Galactic expansion had followed the development of the hyperspace drive, and as men scattered wide across the frontier, there had come the problem of contact with the isolated first colonies and exploration parties. The huge hyperspace cruisers were the product of the combined genius and effort of Earth and were long and expensive in the building. They were not available in such numbers that small colonies could possess them. The cruisers carried the colonists to their new worlds and made periodic visits, running on tight schedules, but they could not stop and turn aside to visit colonies scheduled to be visited at another time; such a delay would destroy their schedule and produce a confusion and uncertainty that would wreck the complex interdependence between old Earth and the new worlds of the frontier.

Some method of delivering supplies or assistance when an emergency occurred on a world not scheduled for a visit had been needed, and the Emergency Dispatch Ships had been the answer. Small and collapsible, they occupied little room in the hold of the cruiser; made of light metal and plastics, they were driven by a small rocket drive that consumed relatively little fuel. Each cruiser carried four EDSs, and when a call for aid was received, the nearest cruiser would drop into normal space long enough to launch an EDS with the needed supplies or personnel, then vanish again as it continued on its course.

The cruisers, powered by nuclear converters, did not use the liquid rocket fuel, but nuclear converters were far too large and complex to permit their installation in the EDSs. The cruisers were forced by necessity to carry a limited amount of bulky rocket fuel, and the fuel was rationed[1] with care, the cruiser's computers determining the exact amount of fuel each EDS would require for its mission. The computers considered the course coordinates, the mass of the EDS, the mass of pilot and cargo; they were very precise and accurate and omitted nothing from their calculations. They could not, however, foresee and allow for the added mass of a stowaway.

QUESTIONING
2. What questions do you have about the story's **basic situation** and the details of its **setting**?

The *Stardust* had received the request from one of the exploration parties stationed on Woden, the six men of the party already being stricken with the fever carried by the green kala midges and their own supply of serum destroyed by the tornado that had torn through their camp.

1. **rationed** (rash′ənd) *n.:* distributed.

Vocabulary
inured (in·yo͞ord′) *v.* used as *adj.:* accustomed to something difficult or painful.

DIRECT TEACHING

A Literary Focus
GRADE-LEVEL STANDARD
Third-person-limited point of view. What makes it clear to you that this story has a third-person narrator? [The narrator stays outside the action of the story and calls the main character "he."]

B English-Language Learners
Jargon. Point out the terms *interstellar* (among the stars), *jettisoned* (ejected from a ship), *galactic* (of a galaxy, especially the Milky Way), and *hyperspace* (space beyond three dimensions). Explain that these terms are part of the jargon of science fiction, astronomy, and space travel.

C Reading Skills
Questioning. [Possible responses to question 1: There will be a fight; the person in the closet will sabotage the ship; the pilot will be ejected; an alien life-form will emerge from the closet.]

D Literary Focus
REVIEW STANDARD
Setting. When and where is this story set? [The story is set in the future, somewhere in space, aboard a small spacecraft.]

E Reading Skills
Questioning. [Possible responses to question 2: How far in the future is this supposed to be? Where in the universe are they? How could a collapsible ship made of light metal and plastic withstand space travel? Why didn't the heat sensor show the stowaway's presence before the EDS took off?]

Special Education Students
For lessons designed for English-language learners and special education students, see *Lesson Plans for Language Development,* pp. 75–77, 78, 94, 100.

Advanced Learners
Acceleration. Use this activity to move students toward the eleventh- and twelfth-grade Standard 3.1, in which they analyze characteristics of subgenres.

Activity. Tell students that science fiction is a subgenre of fantasy, which often involves speculation about the future. In "The Cold Equations" (published in 1954), Godwin speculated about the future of space travel. Have students jot notes on the role that his speculations play in the story. For example, how might the plot be affected if Godwin had known of a compact fuel source for the EDS?

DIRECT TEACHING

A Learners Having Difficulty

Breaking down difficult text. Help students break down this complex key passage. First, define *mass* as "quantity of matter," *infinitesimal* as "too small to be measured," and *deceleration* as "slowing." Explain that the paragraph is describing the effects of a fuel shortage on the EDS. Ask students what the effects would be. [The ship wouldn't be able to slow down and would slam into the planet in a gory crash.]

B Reading Skills

Making inferences. Who are the seven others who would be killed if the stowaway stayed onboard? [The pilot and the six explorers, who need the serum to live, all will die if the ship crashes.]

C Advanced Learners

Acceleration. How do the author's speculations about the future of space travel help to create the story's conflict? [Possible response: The limited fuel capacity Godwin imagines for the EDS gives rise to the law about stowaways that underlies the story's conflict.]

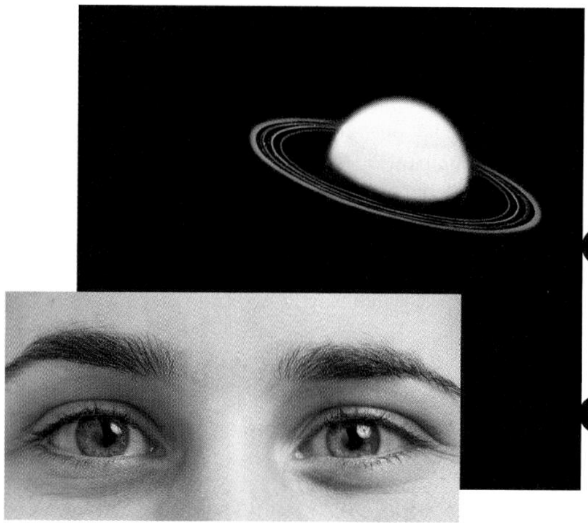

The *Stardust* had gone through the usual procedure, dropping into normal space to launch the EDS with the fever serum, then vanishing again in hyperspace. Now, an hour later, the gauge was saying there was something more than the small carton of serum in the supply closet.

He let his eyes rest on the narrow white door of the closet. There, just inside, another man lived and breathed and was beginning to feel assured that discovery of his presence would now be too late for the pilot to alter the situation. It *was* too late; for the man behind the door it was far later than he thought and in a way he would find it terrible to believe.

A There could be no alternative. Additional fuel would be used during the hours of deceleration[2] to compensate for the added mass of the stowaway, infinitesimal increments of fuel that would not be missed until the ship had almost reached its destination. Then, at some distance above the ground that might be as near as a thousand feet or as far as tens of thousands of feet, depending upon the mass of ship and cargo and the preceding period of deceleration, the unmissed increments of fuel would make their absence known; the EDS would expend its last drops of fuel with a sputter and go into whistling free fall. Ship and pilot and stowaway would merge together upon impact as a wreckage of metal and plastic, flesh and blood, driven deep into the soil. **B** The stowaway had signed his own death warrant[3] when he concealed himself on the ship; he could not be permitted to take seven others with him.

He looked again at the telltale[4] white hand, **C** then rose to his feet. What he must do would be unpleasant for both of them; the sooner it was over, the better. He stepped across the control room to stand by the white door.

"Come out!" His command was harsh and abrupt above the murmur of the drive.

It seemed he could hear the whisper of a furtive movement inside the closet, then nothing. He visualized the stowaway cowering closer into one corner, suddenly worried by the possible consequences of his act, his self-assurance evaporating.

"I said *out*!"

He heard the stowaway move to obey, and he waited with his eyes alert on the door and his hand near the blaster at his side.

The door opened and the stowaway stepped through it, smiling. "All right—I give up. Now what?"

It was a girl.

He stared without speaking, his hand dropping away from the blaster, and acceptance of what he saw coming like a heavy and unexpected physical blow. The stowaway was not a man—she was a girl in her teens, standing before him in little white gypsy sandals, with the top of her brown, curly head hardly higher than his shoulder, with a faint, sweet scent of perfume coming from her, and her smiling face tilted up so her

2. **deceleration** (dē·sel′ər·ā′shən) *n.:* act of slowing down.

3. **death warrant:** anything that makes someone's death inevitable.

4. **telltale** *adj.:* revealing what is meant to be hidden.

Vocabulary
increments (in′krə·mənts) *n.:* small increases.

CONTENT-AREA CONNECTIONS

Culture: Gender Roles
The young woman character in "The Cold Equations" is portrayed as not belonging on the harsh space frontier. In actuality, women have played key roles in international space programs from the outset. The first woman in space was the Soviet cosmonaut Valentina Tereshkova (1937–), who spent nearly three days orbiting the Earth in 1963 aboard the *Vostok 6*. In 1983, Sally Ride (1951–) became the first American female astronaut to travel in space. Her mission on the space shuttle *Challenger* involved pharmaceutical research and launching communications satellites. She also helped to test the shuttle's remote manipulator arm.

Small-group activity. Ask students to work in groups of three to research the role of women in space exploration. Encourage groups to consider not only astronauts but also scientists who have contributed to the program.

eyes could look unknowing and unafraid into his as she waited for his answer.

QUESTIONING
3. What questions would you ask the stowaway?

Now what? Had it been asked in the deep, defiant voice of a man, he would have answered it with action, quick and efficient. He would have taken the stowaway's identification disk and ordered him into the air lock. Had the stowaway refused to obey, he would have used the blaster. It would not have taken long; within a minute the body would have been ejected into space—had the stowaway been a man.

He returned to the pilot's chair and motioned her to seat herself on the boxlike bulk of the drive-control units that were set against the wall beside him. She obeyed, his silence making the smile fade into the meek and guilty expression of a pup that has been caught in mischief and knows it must be punished.

"You still haven't told me," she said. "I'm guilty, so what happens to me now? Do I pay a fine, or what?"

"What are you doing here?" he asked. "Why did you stow away on this EDS?"

"I wanted to see my brother. He's with the government survey crew on Woden and I haven't seen him for ten years, not since he left Earth to go into government survey work."

"What was your destination on the *Stardust*?"

"Mimir. I have a position waiting for me there. My brother has been sending money home all the time to us—my father and mother and me—and he paid for a special course in linguistics I was taking. I graduated sooner than expected and I was offered this job in Mimir. I knew it would be almost a year before Gerry's job was done on Woden so he could come on to Mimir, and that's why I hid in the closet there. There was plenty of room for me and I was willing to pay the fine. There were only the two of us kids—Gerry and I—and I haven't seen him for so long, and I didn't want to wait another year when I could see him now, even though I knew I would be breaking some kind of a regulation when I did it."

I knew I would be breaking some kind of a regulation. In a way, she could not be blamed for her ignorance of the law; she was of Earth and had not realized that the laws of the space frontier must, of necessity, be as hard and relentless as the environment that gave them birth. Yet, to protect such as her from the results of their own ignorance of the frontier, there had been a sign over the door that led to the section of the *Stardust* that housed the EDSs, a sign that was plain for all to see and heed: UNAUTHORIZED PERSONNEL KEEP OUT!

"Does your brother know that you took passage on the *Stardust* for Mimir?"

"Oh, yes. I sent him a spacegram telling him about my graduation and about going to Mimir on the *Stardust* a month before I left Earth. I already knew Mimir was where he would be stationed in a little over a year. He gets a promotion then, and he'll be based on Mimir and not have to stay out a year at a time on field trips, like he does now."

There were two different survey groups on Woden, and he asked, "What is his name?"

"Cross—Gerry Cross. He's in Group Two—that was the way his address read. Do you know him?"

Group One had requested the serum: Group Two was eight thousand miles away, across the Western Sea.

"No, I've never met him," he said, then turned to the control board and cut the deceleration to a fraction of a gravity, knowing as he did so that it could not avert the ultimate end, yet doing the only thing he could do to prolong that ultimate end. The sensation was like that of the ship suddenly dropping, and the girl's involuntary movement of surprise half lifted her from her seat.

"We're going faster now, aren't we?" she asked. "Why are we doing that?"

DIRECT TEACHING

D Reading Skills

Questioning. [Possible responses to question 3: Who are you? How did you get in? Why are you here? Don't you know the law?]

E Literary Focus
GRADE-LEVEL STANDARD

Third-person-limited point of view. The author has the girl speak for herself here; the third-person-limited narrator can't know these things about her. What is the effect of "hearing" the girl's words, as opposed to having a narrator report these facts about her? [Possible responses: Her words humanize her and reveal her personality; they allow readers to identify with her more easily, since she doesn't mean anyone any harm.]

F Reading Skills

Questioning. What questions occur to you at this point? [Possible responses: Why wasn't there a stronger warning? Why wasn't the area gated off and locked? Is there any way to save her? How will she react when she learns what the penalty is?]

G Literary Focus
GRADE-LEVEL STANDARD

Third-person-limited point of view. What do the pilot's thoughts—knowing that he can't prevent what must happen but trying to delay the inevitable—reveal about his feelings toward the girl? [Possible responses: He doesn't want to eject her; he pities her; he wants to protect her.]

DIRECT TEACHING

A English-Language Learners

Multiple meanings. These students may not be familiar with the meanings of the words *model* (exemplary) and *keep* (food and lodging fees) as used in this passage. You might define the words as they are used here, then have students list other meanings that they know for *model* and *keep.*

B Content-Area Connections

Literature: Classical Allusions
In Greek mythology, the golden fleece is wool of pure gold that was taken from a magical winged ram. The search for the golden fleece was the quest of Jason and the Argonauts, who faced many adventures and tests before (with the help of Jason's future wife, Medea) finally seizing the fleece from the oak tree where it had been nailed.

He told her the truth. "To save fuel for a little while."

"You mean we don't have very much?"

He delayed the answer he must give her so soon to ask, "How did you manage to stow away?"

"I just sort of walked in when no one was looking my way," she said. "I was practicing my Gelanese on the native girl who does the cleaning in the Ship's Supply office when someone came in with an order for supplies for the survey crew on Woden. I slipped into the closet there after the ship was ready to go just before you came in. It was an impulse of the moment to stow away, so I could get to see Gerry—and from the way you keep looking at me so grim, I'm not sure it was a very wise impulse. But I'll be a model criminal—or do I mean prisoner?" She smiled at him again. "I intended to pay for my keep on top of paying the fine. I can cook and I can patch clothes for everyone and I know how to do all kinds of useful things, even a little bit about nursing."

There was one more question to ask:

"Did you know what the supplies were that the survey crew ordered?"

"Why, no. Equipment they needed in their work, I supposed."

Why couldn't she have been a man with some ulterior motive? A fugitive from justice hoping to lose himself on a raw new world; an opportunist seeking transportation to the new colonies where he might find golden fleece[5] for the taking; a crackpot with a mission. Perhaps once in his lifetime an EDS pilot would find such a stowaway on his ship—warped men, mean and selfish men, brutal and dangerous men—but never before a smiling, blue-eyed girl who was willing to pay her fine and work for her keep that she might see her brother.

5. **golden fleece:** The reference is to the Greek myth of Jason and the Argonauts, who sailed to a faraway land to capture a golden sheepskin.

DEVELOPING FLUENCY

Individual activity. After students have read "The Cold Equations," tell them to scan the story for sentences and phrases that strike them as being memorable and that can be combined to form poems. Direct students to list their findings and to review them to see what themes are suggested. [Possible themes include students' views on technology, hopes for the future of humanity, and speculations about what space exploration might teach.] Tell students to choose appropriate phrases and sentences from their lists and to compose their poems. (In students' poems, these sentences and phrases need not appear in the same order as they did in the story.) You might ask students to read their finished poems aloud to the class, or you might post the poems on a classroom bulletin board.

He turned to the board and turned the switch that would signal the *Stardust*. The call would be futile, but he could not, until he had exhausted that one vain hope, seize her and thrust her into the air lock as he would an animal—or a man. The delay, in the meantime, would not be dangerous with the EDS decelerating at fractional gravity.

QUESTIONING
4. The **third-person-limited point of view** lets us witness the pilot's inner conflict. What do you learn about him in these last two paragraphs?

A voice spoke from the communicator. "*Stardust*. Identify yourself and proceed."

"Barton, EDS 34GII. Emergency. Give me Commander Delhart."

There was a faint confusion of noises as the request went through the proper channels. The girl was watching him, no longer smiling.

"Are you going to order them to come back after me?" she asked.

The communicator clicked and there was the sound of a distant voice saying, "Commander, the EDS requests . . ."

"Are they coming back after me?" she asked again. "Won't I get to see my brother after all?"

"Barton?" The blunt, gruff voice of Commander Delhart came from the communicator. "What's this about an emergency?"

"A stowaway," he answered.

"A stowaway?" There was a slight surprise to the question. "That's rather unusual—but why the 'emergency' call? You discovered him in time, so there should be no appreciable danger, and I presume you've informed Ship's Records so his nearest relatives can be notified."

"That's why I had to call you, first. The stowaway is still aboard and the circumstances are so different—"

"Different?" the commander interrupted, impatience in his voice. "How can they be different? You know you have a limited supply of fuel; you also know the law as well as I do: 'Any stowaway discovered in an EDS shall be jettisoned immediately following discovery.'"

There was the sound of a sharply indrawn breath from the girl. "*What does he mean?*"

"The stowaway is a girl."

"*What?*"

"She wanted to see her brother. She's only a kid and she didn't know what she was really doing."

"I see." All the curtness was gone from the commander's voice. "So you called me in the hope I could do something?" Without waiting for an answer he went on, "I'm sorry—I can do nothing. This cruiser must maintain its schedule; the life of not one person but the lives of many depend on it. I know how you feel but I'm powerless to help you. You'll have to go through with it. I'll have you connected with Ship's Records."

The communicator faded to a faint rustle of sound, and he turned back to the girl. She was leaning forward on the bench, almost rigid, her eyes fixed wide and frightened.

"What did he mean, to go through with it? To jettison[6] me . . . to go through with it—what did he mean? Not the way it sounded . . . he couldn't have. What did he mean—what did he really mean?"

Her time was too short for the comfort of a lie to be more than a cruelly fleeting delusion.

"He meant it the way it sounded."

"*No!*" She recoiled from him as though he had struck her, one hand half raised as though to fend him off and stark unwillingness to believe in her eyes.

"It will have to be."

"No! You're joking—you're insane! You can't mean it!"

6. **jettison** (jet′ə·sən) *v.:* throw overboard, usually used in reference to goods.

Vocabulary
recoiled (ri·koild′) *v.:* drew back in fear, surprise, or disgust.

DIRECT TEACHING

C Reading Skills
Questioning. [Possible responses to question 4: He has a kind heart; he is touched by the girl's naiveté, friendliness, and good intentions; he doesn't want to kill her.]

D Literary Focus
REVIEW STANDARD
Suspense. The author creates suspense in this passage by describing Barton's actions and the communicator's sounds, without explaining Barton's thoughts. What added effect do the girl's unanswered questions have? [Possible response: They heighten the suspense.]

E Literary Focus
GRADE-LEVEL STANDARD
Third-person-limited point of view. Unlike an omniscient narrator, the third-person-limited narrator can't report the thoughts or feelings of anyone but Barton. The narrator can report the girl's actions, but only as Barton perceives them. Judging from the girl's actions, what do you think she has just realized? [She has just realized that the commander is saying Barton must eject her from the ship.] What feelings do her actions suggest? [fear, horror, disbelief]

DIRECT TEACHING

A Reading Skills

Questioning. [Possible responses to question 5: Barton will defy the commander and find a way to save the girl; she will fight; she will try to take over the ship, and everyone will die; her brother will devise a way to rescue her.]

B Literary Focus
GRADE-LEVEL STANDARD

Third-person-limited point of view. Barton sees the girl as "small and limp like a little rag doll" and observes that "all the protesting and disbelief" seem to have left her. What do his perceptions suggest that the girl is feeling now? [Possible responses: resignation, hopelessness.]

C Learners Having Difficulty

Clarifying. To help students follow this dialogue, be sure they understand that Records is the job title of the clerk in the Ship's Records department. Ask students, "Who is saying, 'Here's your data . . .'?" [Barton]

D Literary Focus
GRADE-LEVEL STANDARD

Third-person-limited point of view. The narrator reports that Barton struggles to keep "the thickness out of his voice." What does this inside information tell you about Barton's feelings? [Possible response: He is so upset by the situation that his voice is affected.]

E Literary Focus
GRADE-LEVEL STANDARD

Third-person-limited point of view. What do the italics indicate here? [They indicate Barton's thoughts, not his words.]

"I'm sorry." He spoke slowly to her, gently. "I should have told you before—I should have, but I had to do what I could first; I had to call the *Stardust*. You heard what the commander said."

"But you can't—if you make me leave the ship, I'll *die*."

QUESTIONING
A 5. How do you **predict** the story will end? What do you think will happen to the stowaway?

"I know."

She searched his face, and the unwillingness to believe left her eyes, giving way slowly to a look of dazed horror.

"You know?" She spoke the words far apart, numbly and wonderingly.

"I know. It has to be like that."

B "You mean it—you really mean it." She sagged back against the wall, small and limp like a little rag doll, and all the protesting and disbelief gone. "You're going to do it—you're going to make me die?"

"I'm sorry," he said again. "You'll never know how sorry I am. It has to be that way and no human in the universe can change it."

"You're going to make me die and I didn't do anything to die for—I didn't *do* anything—"

He sighed, deep and weary. "I know you didn't, child. I know you didn't."

"EDS." The communicator rapped brisk and metallic. "This is Ship's Records. Give us all information on subject's identification disk."

He got out of his chair to stand over her. She clutched the edge of the seat, her upturned face white under the brown hair and the lipstick standing out like a blood-red cupid's bow.

"*Now?*"

"I want your identification disk," he said.

She released the edge of the seat and fumbled at the chain that suspended the plastic disk from her neck with fingers that were trembling and awkward. He reached down and unfastened the clasp for her, then returned with the disk to his chair.

C "Here's your data, Records: Identification Number T837—"

"One moment," Records interrupted. "This is to be filed on the gray card, of course?"

"Yes."

"And the time of execution?"

"I'll tell you later."

"Later? This is highly irregular; the time of the subject's death is required before—"

D He kept the thickness out of his voice with an effort. "Then we'll do it in a highly irregular manner—you'll hear the disk read first. The subject is a girl and she's listening to everything that's said. Are you capable of understanding that?"

There was a brief, almost shocked silence; then Records said meekly, "Sorry. Go ahead."

He began to read the disk, reading it slowly to delay the inevitable for as long as possible, trying to help her by giving her what little time he could to recover from her first horror and let it resolve into the calm of acceptance and resignation.

E "Number T8374 dash Y54. Name, Marilyn Lee Cross. Sex, female. Born July 7, 2160." *She was only eighteen.* "Height, five-three. Weight, a hundred and ten." *Such a slight weight, yet enough to add fatally to the mass of the shell-thin bubble that was an EDS.* "Hair, brown. Eyes, blue. Complexion, light. Blood type O." *Irrelevant data.* "Destination, Port City, Mimir." *Invalid data.*

He finished and said, "I'll call you later," then turned once again to the girl. She was huddled back against the wall, watching him with a look of numb and wondering fascination.

"They're waiting for you to kill me, aren't they? They want me dead, don't they? You and everybody on the cruiser want me dead, don't you?" Then the numbness broke and her voice was that of a frightened and bewildered child. "Everybody wants me dead and I didn't *do* anything. I didn't hurt anyone—I only wanted to see my brother."

READING MINI-LESSON

Developing Word-Attack Skills

Use the selection word *annihilate* to introduce the silent *h*. Write the word in syllables on the chalkboard: *an-ni-hi-late.* Beneath each syllable, write its pronunciation: /ə/, /nī/, /ə/, /lāt/. Have students identify the letter that is silent.

Point out that the letter *h* is often silent at the beginning of a word or syllable. Ask students to give examples of words in which the initial *h* is silent. Possibilities include *hour, heir, honor,* and *honest.*

Write these words on the chalkboard. Read each word aloud, and ask students to tell if the sound of *h* is heard in the word.

exhaust [no] exhale [yes] vehement [no]
nihilism [no] coherent [yes] graham [no]

Activity. Write the following sentences on the chalkboard. Have students identify all the

words with a silent *h*. Answers are underlined.

1. His friend exhorted him to act hurry.
2. He was exhilarated by the hilarity of the situation.
3. The heir would inherit a ninety-year-old touring car.
4. The ancient vehicle had a mahogany dashboard.
5. The owner was too inhibited to exhibit his emotions.

DIRECT TEACHING

A Learners Having Difficulty

Re-reading. Some students may remain puzzled about why the ship does not carry enough extra fuel for this emergency. Encourage them to re-read the fourth and fifth paragraphs on p. 165 to understand this key part of the story's conflict.

B Literary Focus REVIEW STANDARD

Suspense. Marilyn's desperate questions heighten the suspense at this point; the reader, too, is "leaning forward a little" to learn the answer.

C Reading Skills

Questioning. Do you agree with the idea conveyed in this sentence? [Possible responses: Yes, because certainty about one's fate can help bring acceptance and peace; no, because when there is no hope, one's fear and dread can only increase.]

D Literary Focus REVIEW STANDARD

Suspense. The author builds suspense by making Barton uncertain of how long Marilyn has to live. When a character who has to make a hard decision is uncertain, the reader is even more uncertain.

"It's not the way you think—it isn't that way at all," he said. "Nobody wants it this way; nobody would ever let it be this way if it was humanly possible to change it."

"Then why is it? I don't understand. Why is it?"

"This ship is carrying kala fever serum to Group One on Woden. Their own supply was destroyed by a tornado. Group Two—the crew your brother is in—is eight thousand miles away across the Western Sea, and their helicopters can't cross it to help Group One. The fever is invariably fatal unless the serum can be had in time, and the six men in Group One will die unless this ship reaches them on schedule. These little ships are always given barely enough fuel to reach their destination, and if you stay aboard, your added weight will cause it to use up all its fuel before it reaches the ground. It will crash then, and you and I will die and so will the six men waiting for the fever serum."

It was a full minute before she spoke, and as she considered his words, the expression of numbness left her eyes.

"Is that it?" she asked at last. "Just that the ship doesn't have enough fuel?"

"Yes."

"I can go alone or I can take seven others with me—is that the way it is?"

"That's the way it is."

"And nobody wants me to have to die?"

"Nobody."

"Then maybe— Are you sure nothing can be done about it? Wouldn't people help me if they could?"

"Everyone would like to help you, but there is nothing anyone can do. I did the only thing I could do when I called the *Stardust*."

"And it won't come back—but there might be other cruisers, mightn't there? Isn't there any hope at all that there might be someone, somewhere, who could do something to help me?"

She was leaning forward a little in her eagerness as she waited for his answer.

"No."

The word was like the drop of a cold stone and she again leaned back against the wall, the hope and eagerness leaving her face. "You're sure—you *know* you're sure?"

"I'm sure. There are no other cruisers within forty light-years; there is nothing and no one to change things."

She dropped her gaze to her lap and began twisting a pleat of her skirt between her fingers, saying no more as her mind began to adapt itself to the grim knowledge.

It was better so; with the going of all hope would go the fear; with the going of all hope would come resignation. She needed time and she could have so little of it. How much?

The EDSs were not equipped with hull-cooling units; their speed had to be reduced to a moderate level before they entered the atmosphere. They were decelerating at .10 gravity, approaching their destination at a far higher speed than the computers had calculated on. The *Stardust* had been quite near Woden when she launched the EDS; their present velocity was putting them nearer by the second. There would be a critical point, soon to be reached, when he would have to resume deceleration. When he did so, the girl's weight would be multiplied by the gravities of deceleration, would become, suddenly, a factor of paramount importance, the factor the computers had been ignorant of when they determined the amount of fuel the EDS should have. She would have to go when deceleration began; it could be no other way. When would that be—how long could he let her stay?

"How long can I stay?"

He winced involuntarily from the words that were so like an echo of his own thoughts. How long? He didn't know; he would have to ask the

Vocabulary
paramount (par′ə·mount′) *adj.:* supreme; dominant.

172 Chapter 3 Narrator and Voice • Generating Research Questions

ship's computers. Each EDS was given a meager surplus of fuel to compensate for unfavorable conditions within the atmosphere, and relatively little fuel was being consumed for the time being. The memory banks of the computers would still contain all data pertaining to the course set for the EDS; such data would not be erased until the EDS reached its destination. He had only to give the computers the new data—the girl's weight and the exact time at which he had reduced the deceleration to .10.

"Barton." Commander Delhart's voice came abruptly from the communicator as he opened his mouth to call the *Stardust*. "A check with Records shows me you haven't completed your report. Did you reduce the deceleration?"

So the commander knew what he was trying to do.

"I'm decelerating at point ten," he answered. "I cut the deceleration at seventeen fifty and the weight is a hundred and ten. I would like to stay at point ten as long as the computers say I can. Will you give them the question?"

It was contrary to regulations for an EDS pilot to make any changes in the course or degree of deceleration the computers had set for him, but the commander made no mention of the violation. Neither did he ask the reason for it. It was not necessary for him to ask; he had not become commander of an interstellar cruiser without both intelligence and an understanding of human nature. He said only, "I'll have that given to the computers."

The communicator fell silent and he and the girl waited, neither of them speaking. They would not have to wait long; the computers would give the answer within moments of the asking. The new factors would be fed into the steel maw[7] of the first bank, and the electrical impulses would go through the complex circuits. Here and there a relay might click, a tiny cog turn over, but it would be essentially the electrical impulses that found the answer; formless, mindless, invisible, determining with utter precision how long the pale girl beside him might live. Then five little segments of metal in the second bank would trip in rapid succession against an inked ribbon and a second steel maw would spit out the slip of paper that bore the answer.

QUESTIONING
6. Do the technological and scientific details seem believable to you? What questions would you ask the author?

The chronometer[8] on the instrument board read 18:10 when the commander spoke again.

"You will resume deceleration at nineteen ten."

She looked toward the chronometer, then quickly away from it. "Is that when . . . when I go?" she asked. He nodded and she dropped her eyes to her lap again.

"I'll have the course correction given to you," the commander said. "Ordinarily I would never permit anything like this, but I understand your position. There is nothing I can do, other than what I've just done, and you will not deviate[9] from these new instructions. You will complete your report at nineteen ten. Now—here are the course corrections."

The voice of some unknown technician read them to him, and he wrote them down on the pad clipped to the edge of the control board. There would, he saw, be periods of deceleration when he neared the atmosphere when the deceleration would be five gravities—and at five gravities, one hundred ten pounds would become five hundred fifty pounds.

The technician finished and he terminated the contact with a brief acknowledgment. Then, hesitating a moment, he reached out and shut off the communicator. It was 18:13 and he would have

7. **maw** *n.:* huge, all-consuming mouth.

8. **chronometer** (krə·näm′ət·ər) *n.:* instrument for measuring time scientifically.

9. **deviate** (dē′vē·āt′) *v.:* turn aside or away from a given course of action or practice.

DIRECT TEACHING

E Literary Focus
GRADE-LEVEL STANDARD
Third-person-limited point of view. The limited narrator can't know the commander's feelings, but Barton notices that the commander doesn't mention the violation of the rules. What does the commander's actions reveal about his feelings? [Possible response: The commander wants to buy time for Marilyn as much as Barton does.]

F Literary Focus
GRADE-LEVEL STANDARD
Theme. What view on technology does this passage convey? [Possible responses: Technology is cold and heartless; the more dependent we become on technology, the less room there is for human emotions.]

G Reading Skills
Questioning. [Possible response to question 6: No, the details do not seem credible because they do not reflect current computer technology; the computers are too bulky, lack monitors, and print answers on slips of paper. Possible questions: If the EDS has only enough fuel to land, how will it leave again? Did computers or spacecraft exist when you wrote this story? How did you get your ideas?]

H Learners Having Difficulty
Summarizing. What time is 19:10 on the twelve-hour clock? [7:10 P.M.] Summarize what will happen at 19:10. [Barton must begin decelerating to land. This will increase the effect of Marilyn's weight, so that in order to have enough fuel, he must eject her then.]

DIRECT TEACHING

A Literary Focus
GRADE-LEVEL STANDARD

? Third-person-limited point of view. What is the significance of Barton's going over these facts in algebraic terms, using *h, m,* and *x*? [Possible response: These terms recall the "cold equations" of the story's title. Barton is torn by the conflict between the equations of the laws of physics and the human struggle for survival.]

B Reading Skills

Questioning. [Possible response to question 7: We learn about Marilyn through Barton's perceptions of her and through what she says. We learn that she is afraid and that she wants to live. Marilyn feels that no one is assisting her and that the people involved are not concerned with her well-being.]

nothing to report until 19:10. In the meantime, it somehow seemed indecent to permit others to hear what she might say in her last hour.

He began to check the instrument readings, going over them with unnecessary slowness. She would have to accept the circumstances, and there was nothing he could do to help her into acceptance; words of sympathy would only delay it.

It was 18:20 when she stirred from her motionlessness and spoke.

"So that's the way it has to be with me?"

He swung around to face her. "You understand now, don't you? No one would ever let it be like this if it could be changed."

"I understand," she said. Some of the color had returned to her face and the lipstick no longer stood out so vividly red. "There isn't enough fuel for me to stay. When I hid on this ship, I got into something I didn't know anything about and now I have to pay for it."

She had violated a man-made law that said KEEP OUT, but the penalty was not for men's making or desire and it was a penalty men could not revoke. A physical law had decreed: *h amount of fuel will power an EDS with a mass of m safely to its destination;* and a second physical law had decreed: *h amount of fuel will not power an EDS with a mass of m plus x safely to its destination.* **A**

EDSs obeyed only physical laws, and no amount of human sympathy for her could alter the second law.

"But I'm afraid. I don't want to die—not now. I want to live, and nobody is doing anything to help me; everybody is letting me go ahead and acting just like nothing was going to happen to me. I'm going to die and nobody *cares.*" **B**

> **QUESTIONING**
> 7. Since this story is told from Barton's **point of view,** how do we learn about Marilyn? What do we learn about her in this paragraph?

"We all do," he said. "I do and the commander does and the clerk in Ship's Records; we all care and each of us did what little he could to help you. It wasn't enough—it was almost nothing—but it was all we could do."

"Not enough fuel—I can understand that," she said, as though she had not heard his own words. "But to have to die for it. *Me* alone . . ."

How hard it must be for her to accept the fact. She had never known danger of death, had never known the environments where the lives of men could be as fragile and fleeting as sea foam tossed against a rocky shore. She belonged on gentle Earth, in that secure and peaceful society where she could be young and gay and laughing with the others of her kind, where life was precious and well guarded and there was always the assurance that tomorrow would come. She belonged in that world of soft winds and a warm sun, music and moonlight and gracious manners, and not on the hard, bleak frontier.

"How did it happen to me so terribly quickly? An hour ago I was on the *Stardust*, going to Mimir. Now the *Stardust* is going on without me and I'm going to die and I'll never see Gerry and Mama and Daddy again—I'll never see anything again."

He hesitated, wondering how he could explain it to her so she would really understand and not feel she had somehow been the victim of a reasonlessly cruel injustice. She did not know what the frontier was like; she thought in terms of safe, secure Earth. Pretty girls were not jettisoned on Earth; there was a law against it. On Earth her plight would have filled the newscasts and a fast black patrol ship would have been racing to her rescue. Everyone, everywhere, would have known of Marilyn Lee Cross, and no effort would have been spared to save her life. But this was not Earth and there were no patrol ships; only the *Stardust*, leaving them behind at many times the speed of light. There was no one to help her; there would be no Marilyn Lee Cross smiling from the newscasts tomorrow.

DIFFERENTIATING INSTRUCTION

Advanced Learners

Enrichment. When Tom Godwin's story "The Cold Equations" was published in 1954, computers took up whole rooms and space travel was still a dream. Given the scientific and technological information available at the time, Godwin's prescience was remarkable.

Activity. Divide students into small groups, and suggest that they use available technology—such as CD-ROMs, videos, DVDs, and the Internet—to learn specifics about the development of technology and space exploration since the early 1950s. Groups might focus on topics such as the evolution of computers, early satellites, space probes to other planets, the Hubble telescope, the space shuttle, space stations, and manned landings. Direct each group to present its findings in a letter to Godwin, sharing information he would have been interested in or commenting on the accuracies and inaccuracies of his vision in "The Cold Equations."

Marilyn Lee Cross would be but a poignant memory for an EDS pilot and a name on a gray card in Ship's Records.

"It's different here; it's not like back on Earth," he said. "It isn't that no one cares; it's that no one can do anything to help. The frontier is big, and here along its rim the colonies and exploration parties are scattered so thin and far between. On Woden, for example, there are only sixteen men—sixteen men on an entire world. The exploration parties, the survey crews, the little first colonies—they're all fighting alien environments, trying to make a way for those who will follow after. The environments fight back, and those who go first usually make mistakes only once. There is no margin of safety along the rim of the frontier; there can't be until the way is made for the others who will come later, until the new worlds are tamed and settled. Until then men will have to pay the penalty for making mistakes, with no one to help them, because there is no one *to* help them."

"I was going to Mimir," she said. "I didn't know about the frontier; I was only going to Mimir and *it's* safe."

"Mimir is safe, but you left the cruiser that was taking you there."

She was silent for a little while. "It was all so wonderful at first; there was plenty of room for me on this ship and I would be seeing Gerry so soon. I didn't know about the fuel, didn't know what would happen to me. . . ."

Her words trailed away, and he turned his attention to the viewscreen, not wanting to stare at her as she fought her way through the black horror of fear toward the calm gray of acceptance.

Woden was a ball, enshrouded in the blue haze of its atmosphere, swimming in space against the background of star-sprinkled dead blackness. The great mass of Manning's Continent sprawled like a gigantic hourglass in the Eastern Sea, with the western half of the Eastern Continent still visible. There was a thin line of shadow along the right-hand edge of the globe, and the Eastern Continent was disappearing into it as the planet turned on its axis. An hour before, the entire continent had been in view; now a thousand miles of it had gone into the thin edge of shadow and around to the night that lay on the other side of the world. The dark blue spot that was Lotus Lake was approaching the shadow. It was somewhere near the southern edge of the lake that Group Two had their camp. It would be night there soon, and quick behind the coming of night the rotation of Woden on its axis would put Group Two beyond the reach of the ship's radio.

He would have to tell her before it was too late for her to talk to her brother. In a way, it would be better for both of them should they not do so, but it was not for him to decide. To each of them the last words would be something to hold and cherish, something that would cut like the blade of a knife yet would be infinitely precious to remember, she for her own brief moments to live and he for the rest of his life.

He held down the button that would flash the grid lines on the viewscreen and used the known diameter of the planet to estimate the distance the southern tip of Lotus Lake had yet to go until it passed beyond radio range. It was approximately five hundred miles. Five hundred miles; thirty minutes—and the chronometer read 18:30. Allowing for error in estimating, it would not be later than 19:05 that the turning of Woden would cut off her brother's voice.

The first border of the Western continent was already in sight along the left side of the world. Four thousand miles across it lay the shore of the Western Sea and the camp of Group One. It had been in the Western Sea that the tornado had originated, to strike with such fury at the camp and destroy half their prefabricated buildings, including the one that housed the medical supplies. Two days before, the tornado had not existed; it had been no more than great gentle masses of air over the calm Western Sea. Group One had gone about their routine survey work,

Direct Teaching

C Vocabulary Development
GRADE-LEVEL STANDARD

Literal meanings of words. The word *poignant* comes from the Latin verb *pungere,* which means "to prick or pierce." In English, *poignant* can mean "physically painful," "upsetting," or "touching." Which meaning of *poignant* does this passage express? [Possible response: upsetting.] What word could be a synonym for *poignant* in this context? [Possible response: distressing.]

D English-Language Learners

Building background knowledge. Be sure students know that the letter *h* in the word *hourglass* is silent. You might sketch an hourglass on the chalkboard and ask students why an hourglass is an appropriate image for the story. [An hourglass is appropriate because time is important to the story's outcome.]

E Reading Skills

Questioning. What new questions arise at this point in the story? [Possible responses: Will Marilyn have time to talk to her brother before she dies? Will she decide not to talk with him even if there is time? Will he fight to save her life? How will Barton respond to a tearful goodbye between Marilyn and her brother?]

unaware of the meeting of air masses out at sea, unaware of the force the union was spawning. It had struck their camp without warning—a thundering, roaring destruction that sought to annihilate all that lay before it. It had passed on, leaving the wreckage in its wake. It had destroyed the labor of months and had doomed six men to die and then, as though its task was accomplished, it once more began to resolve into gentle masses of air. But, for all its deadliness, it had destroyed with neither malice nor intent. It had been a blind and mindless force, obeying the laws of nature, and it would have followed the same course with the same fury had men never existed. **A**

Existence required order, and there was order; the laws of nature, irrevocable and immutable. Men could learn to use them, but men could not change them. The circumference of a circle was always pi times the diameter, and no science of man would ever make it otherwise. The combination of chemical A with chemical B under condition C invariably produced reaction D. The law of gravitation was a rigid equation, and it made no distinction between the fall of a leaf and the ponderous circling of a binary star system. The nuclear conversion process powered the cruisers that carried men to the stars; the same process in the form of a nova would destroy a world with equal efficiency. The laws *were,* and the universe moved in obedience to them. Along the frontier were arrayed all the forces of nature, and sometimes they destroyed those who were fighting their way outward from Earth. The men of the frontier had long ago learned the bitter futility of cursing the forces that would destroy them, for the forces were blind and deaf; the futility of looking to the heavens for mercy, for the stars of the galaxy swung in their long, long sweep of two hundred million years, as inexorably[10] controlled as they by the laws that knew neither hatred nor compassion. The men of the frontier knew—but how was a girl from Earth to fully understand? *h amount of fuel will not power an EDS with a mass of m plus x safely to its destination.* To him and her brother and parents she was a sweet-faced girl in her teens; to the laws of nature she was *x*, the unwanted factor in a cold equation. **B** **C**

QUESTIONING

8. What do you think of this view of humans and the "laws of nature"?

She stirred again on the seat. "Could I write a letter? I want to write to Mama and Daddy. And I'd like to talk to Gerry. Could you let me talk to him over your radio there?"

"I'll try to get him," he said.

He switched on the normal-space transmitter and pressed the signal button. Someone answered the buzzer almost immediately.

"Hello. How's it going with you fellows now—is the EDS on its way?"

"This isn't Group One; this is the EDS," he said. "Is Gerry Cross there?"

"Gerry? He and two others went out in the helicopter this morning and aren't back yet. It's almost sundown, though, and he ought to be back right away—in less than an hour at the most." **D**

"Can you connect me through to the radio in his copter?"

"Huh-uh. It's been out of commission for two months—some printed circuits went haywire[11] and we can't get any more until the next cruiser **E**

10. **inexorably** (in·eks′ə·rə·blē) *adv.:* in an unchanged manner.

11. **haywire** *adj.:* out of order.

Vocabulary

annihilate (ə·nī′ə·lāt′) *v.:* destroy; demolish.

irrevocable (i·rev′ə·kə·bəl) *adj.:* irreversible; incapable of being canceled or undone.

immutable (i·myo͞ot′ə·bəl) *adj.:* unchangeable; never changing or varying.

ponderous (pän′dər·əs) *adj.:* heavy and slow moving.

DIRECT TEACHING

A Literary Focus
GRADE-LEVEL STANDARD

Third-person-limited point of view. Why do you think Barton's mind now dwells on the tornado and its origins? [Possible response: The tornado destroyed Group One's medical supplies, making his trip necessary. If not for the tornado, he would not be facing this terrible decision.]

B Literary Focus
GRADE-LEVEL STANDARD

Theme. This long paragraph conveys the story's theme. How would you state the paragraph's main idea? [Possible responses: The laws of nature are unbendable and do not play favorites; humans are powerless against nature's laws.]

C Reading Skills

Questioning. [Possible responses to question 8: It is accurate, since natural disasters result from impersonal forces that we can do little about; it's chilling; it suggests a challenge of harnessing nature's forces to protect humanity.]

D Literary Focus
REVIEW STANDARD

Suspense. How does the author draw out the suspense at this point? [Possible response: Gerry is unreachable for about an hour, and Marilyn has only an hour left to live. The reader wonders whether Gerry will return in time to talk to his sister one last time.]

E Reading Skills

Questioning. Do you find it believable that Gerry's radio is broken now, when his sister desperately needs to talk to him? [Possible responses: Yes, the author made it clear that colonies seldom receive supplies, so things that break stay broken; no, it seems contrived to heighten suspense.]

DIFFERENTIATING INSTRUCTION

Learners Having Difficulty
Students struggling with the relatively complex content and wording of "The Cold Equations" may benefit from an opportunity to restate the story's main events in a different context.
Activity. Place students in groups of three to five, and direct each group to create an article for Marilyn's hometown newspaper about what has happened to her. They should include at least one photo, map, or sketch to accompany the article. Some group members might take care of the writing; others might handle art and layout.

stops by. Is it something important—bad news for him, or something?"

"Yes—it's very important. When he comes in, get him to the transmitter as soon as you possibly can."

"I'll do that; I'll have one of the boys waiting at the field with a truck. Is there anything else I can do?"

"No, I guess that's all. Get him there as soon as you can and signal me."

He turned the volume to an inaudible minimum, an act that would not affect the functioning of the signal buzzer, and unclipped the pad of paper from the control board. He tore off the sheet containing his flight instructions and handed the pad to her, together with pencil.

"I'd better write to Gerry too," she said as she took them. "He might not get back to camp in time."

She began to write, her fingers still clumsy and uncertain in the way they handled the pencil, and the top of it trembling a little as she poised it between words. He turned back to the viewscreen, to stare at it without seeing it.

She was a lonely little child trying to say her last goodbye, and she would lay out her heart to them. She would tell them how much she loved them and she would tell them to not feel bad about it, that it was only something that must happen eventually to everyone and she was not afraid. The last would be a lie and it would be there to read between the sprawling, uneven lines: a valiant little lie that would make the hurt all the greater for them.

Her brother was of the frontier and he would understand. He would not hate the EDS pilot for doing nothing to prevent her going; he would know there had been nothing the pilot could do. He would understand, though the understanding would not soften the shock and pain when he learned his sister was gone. But the others, her father and mother—they would not understand. They were of Earth and they would think in the manner of those who had never lived

CONTENT-AREA CONNECTIONS

Mathematics: Mathematical Formulas
In "The Cold Equations," Barton uses mathematical formulas to compute his spacecraft's fuel consumption. Laws of physics and chemical reactions can often be represented in mathematical terms.

Individual and whole-class activity. Invite interested students to extend their reading by researching some of the mathematical equations used to compute the effects of gravity. If possible, ask a student who is proficient in math to teach a lesson on how to apply these formulas.

DIRECT TEACHING

A Reading Skills

Questioning. How would you answer this question? [Possible responses: They might be enraged; they might not blame him when they learn of the circumstances.]

B Literary Focus GRADE-LEVEL STANDARD

Third-person-limited point of view. From this glimpse into Barton's thoughts, would you characterize him as logical or illogical, or would you choose a different adjective? [Possible responses: He is trying to be logical, but failing; he is emotional.]

C Advanced Learners

Enrichment. The pencil is described as "whispering." Why is this personification fitting? [Possible response: It shows the quiet of the ship and the intimacy of Marilyn's writing.]

D Literary Focus GRADE-LEVEL STANDARD

Third-person-limited point of view. The narrator can't report what Marilyn feels. What do her words to Barton reveal about her feelings for her family? [Possible responses: She feels concern; she wants them to know that she thought of them during her last hour.]

E Reading Skills

Questioning. Do you agree with Barton's statement? Why or why not? [Possible response: No, because cowardice usually implies a lack of moral strength or an inability to face one's fears. Marilyn is afraid of death but does not let her fear overwhelm her; she faces death with courage and dignity.]

where the safety margin of life was a thin, thin line—and sometimes nothing at all. What would they think of the faceless, unknown pilot who had sent her to her death?

They would hate him with cold and terrible intensity, but it really didn't matter. He would never see them, never know them. He would have only the memories to remind him; only the nights of fear, when a blue-eyed girl in gypsy sandals would come in his dreams to die again. . . .

He scowled at the viewscreen and tried to force his thoughts into less emotional channels. There was nothing he could do to help her. She had unknowingly subjected herself to the penalty of a law that recognized neither innocence nor youth nor beauty, that was incapable of sympathy or leniency. Regret was illogical—and yet, could knowing it to be illogical ever keep it away?

She stopped occasionally, as though trying to find the right words to tell them what she wanted them to know; then the pencil would resume its whispering to the paper. It was 18:37 when she folded the letter in a square and wrote a name on it. She began writing another, twice looking up at the chronometer, as though she feared the black hand might reach its rendezvous[12] before she had finished. It was 18:45 when she folded it as she had done the first letter and wrote a name and address on it.

She held the letters out to him. "Will you take care of these and see that they're enveloped and mailed?"

"Of course." He took them from her hand and placed them in a pocket of his gray uniform shirt.

"These can't be sent off until the next cruiser stops by, and the *Stardust* will have long since told them about me, won't it?" she asked. He nodded and she went on: "That makes the letters not important in one way, but in another way they're very important—to me, and to them."

"I know. I understand, and I'll take care of them."

She glanced at the chronometer, then back to him. "It seems to move faster all the time, doesn't it?"

He said nothing, unable to think of anything to say, and she asked, "Do you think Gerry will come back to camp in time?"

"I think so. They said he should be in right away."

She began to roll the pencil back and forth between her palms. "I hope he does. I feel sick and scared and I want to hear his voice again and maybe I won't feel so alone. I'm a coward and I can't help it."

"No," he said, "you're not a coward. You're afraid, but you're not a coward."

"Is there a difference?"

He nodded. "A lot of difference."

"I feel so alone. I never did feel like this before; like I was all by myself and there was nobody to care what happened to me. Always, before, there were Mama and Daddy there and my friends around me. I had lots of friends, and they had a going-away party for me the night before I left."

Friends and music and laughter for her to remember—and on the viewscreen Lotus Lake was going into the shadow.

"Is it the same with Gerry?" she asked. "I mean, if he should make a mistake, would he have to die for it, all alone and with no one to help him?"

"It's the same with all, along the frontier; it will always be like that so long as there is a frontier."

"Gerry didn't tell us. He said the pay was good, and he sent money home all the time because Daddy's little shop just brought in a bare living, but he didn't tell us it was like this."

"He didn't tell you his work was dangerous?"

"Well—yes. He mentioned that, but we didn't understand. I always thought danger along the

12. **rendezvous** (rän′dā·vo͞o′) *n.:* appointed meeting; here, the movement of a clock's hand to the next digit.

178 Chapter 3 Narrator and Voice • Generating Research Questions

frontier was something that was a lot of fun; an exciting adventure, like in the three-D shows." A wan smile touched her face for a moment. "Only it's not, is it? It's not the same at all, because when it's real you can't go home after the show is over."

"No," he said. "No, you can't."

Her glance flicked from the chronometer to the door of the air lock, then down to the pad and pencil she still held. She shifted her position slightly to lay them on the bench beside her, moving one foot out a little. For the first time he saw that she was not wearing Vegan gypsy sandals, but only cheap imitations; the expensive Vegan leather was some kind of grained plastic, the silver buckle was gilded iron, the jewels were colored glass. *Daddy's little shop just brought in a bare living. . . .* She must have left college in her second year, to take the course in linguistics that would enable her to make her own way and help her brother provide for her parents, earning what she could by part-time work after classes were over. Her personal possessions on the *Stardust* would be taken back to her parents—they would neither be of much value nor occupy much storage space on the return voyage. **F**

"Isn't it—" She stopped, and he looked at her questioningly. "Isn't it cold in here?" she asked, almost apologetically. "Doesn't it seem cold to you?"

"Why, yes," he said. He saw by the main temperature gauge that the room was at precisely normal temperature. "Yes, it's colder than it should be." **G**

"I wish Gerry would get back before it's too late. Do you really think he will, and you didn't just say so to make me feel better?"

"I think he will—they said he would be in pretty soon." On the viewscreen Lotus Lake had gone into the shadow but for the thin blue line of its western edge, and it was apparent he had overestimated the time she would have in which to talk to her brother. Reluctantly, he said to her, "His camp will be out of radio range in a few minutes; he's on that part of Woden that's in the shadow"—he indicated the viewscreen—"and the turning of Woden will put him beyond contact. There may not be much time left when he comes in—not much time to talk to him before he fades out. I wish I could do something about it—I would call him right now if I could."

"Not even as much time as I will have to stay?"

"I'm afraid not."

"Then—" She straightened and looked toward the air lock with pale resolution. "Then I'll go when Gerry passes beyond range. I won't wait any longer after that—I won't have anything to wait for."

Again there was nothing he could say.

"Maybe I shouldn't wait at all. Maybe I'm selfish—maybe it would be better for Gerry if you just told him about it afterward."

There was an unconscious pleading for denial in the way she spoke and he said, "He wouldn't want you to do that, to not wait for him." **H**

"It's already coming dark where he is, isn't it? There will be all the long night before him, and Mama and Daddy don't know yet that I won't ever be coming back like I promised them I would. I've caused everyone I love to be hurt, haven't I? I didn't want to—I didn't intend to."

"It wasn't your fault," he said. "It wasn't your fault at all. They'll know that. They'll understand."

"At first I was so afraid to die that I was a coward and thought only of myself. Now I see how selfish I was. The terrible thing about dying like this is not that I'll be gone but that I'll never see them again; never be able to tell them that I didn't take them for granted; never be able to tell them I knew of the sacrifices they made to make my life happier, that I knew all the things they did for me and that I loved them so much more than I ever told them. I've never told them any of those things. You don't tell them such things when you're young and your life is all before you—you're so afraid of sounding sentimental and silly. But it's so different when you have to die—you wish you had told them while you

DIRECT TEACHING

F Literary Focus
GRADE-LEVEL STANDARD

Third-person-limited point of view. How does Barton's observation of these details add to our understanding of Marilyn? [Possible responses: We learn more about her background and values; her family is of modest means, close, hardworking, and admirable; she is responsible and determined.]

G Literary Focus
GRADE-LEVEL STANDARD

Third-person-limited point of view. If Barton knows that the cabin temperature is normal, why does he agree with Marilyn? [Possible responses: He does not want to upset her further by disagreeing; he understands why she feels cold; he is acknowledging the "coldness" of their situation.]

H Literary Focus
GRADE-LEVEL STANDARD

Third-person-limited point of view. Barton notices "an unconscious pleading for denial" in the way Marilyn speaks. What does his observation reveal about Marilyn—and about himself? [Possible response: It shows that Marilyn needs reassurance, and it shows that Barton has grown very sensitive to her feelings.]

Direct Teaching

A Reading Skills
Questioning. [Possible responses to question 9: Marilyn is no longer lighthearted; she has lost her naiveté, but she has found the courage to face death. Barton is less detached and stiff than he originally seemed; he has found a way to bend the rules; he comforts Marilyn, and he talks with her about emotional issues such as life, death, and love.]

B English-Language Learners
Verb usage. Tell students that when a form of the verb *to keep* is used before an *–ing* word, it indicates continuous or repeated action—for example, "Lee *kept tripping* over the dog" and "If the dog *keeps lying* there, Lee *will keep tripping* over it."

C Literary Focus
GRADE-LEVEL STANDARD
Third-person-limited point of view. The narrator can't report directly how Gerry feels about Marilyn. What does this anecdote reveal about Gerry's feelings for his sister? [Possible responses: It shows that he feels protective of her; that he cares deeply about her; that he will fight anyone who stands in the way of her happiness.]

D Reading Skills
Questioning. Encourage students to share any questions that arise in their minds as they read this graphic passage. [Possible responses: Are these details accurate? Why does the author include these images? Why is Marilyn aware of such details?]

could, and you wish you could tell them you're sorry for all the little mean things you ever did or said to them. You wish you could tell them that you didn't really mean to ever hurt their feelings and for them to only remember that you always loved them far more than you ever let them know."

"You don't have to tell them that," he said. "They will know—they've always known it."

"Are you sure?" she asked. "How can you be sure? My people are strangers to you."

"Wherever you go, human nature and human hearts are the same."

"And they will know what I want them to know—that I love them?"

"They've always known it, in a way far better than you could ever put in words for them."

> **QUESTIONING**
> 9. How have the main **characters** changed since we first met them?

"I keep remembering the things they did for me, and it's the little things they did that seem to be the most important to me, now. Like Gerry—he sent me a bracelet of fire rubies on my sixteenth birthday. It was beautiful—it must have cost him a month's pay. Yet I remember him more for what he did the night my kitten got run over in the street. I was only six years old and he held me in his arms and wiped away my tears and told me not to cry, that Flossy was gone for just a little while, for just long enough to get herself a new fur coat, and she would be on the foot of my bed the very next morning. I believed him and quit crying and went to sleep dreaming about my kitten coming back. When I woke up the next morning, there was Flossy on the foot of my bed in a brand-new white fur coat, just like he had said she would be. It wasn't until a long time later that Mama told me Gerry had got the pet-shop owner out of bed at four in the morning and, when the man got mad about it, Gerry told him he was either going to go down and sell him the white kitten right then or he'd break his neck."

"It's always the little things you remember people by, all the little things they did because they wanted to do them for you. You've done the same for Gerry and your father and mother; all kinds of things that you've forgotten about, but that they will never forget."

"I hope I have. I would like for them to remember me like that."

"They will."

"I wish—" She swallowed. "The way I'll die—I wish they wouldn't ever think of that. I've read how people look who die in space—their insides all ruptured and exploded and their lungs out between their teeth and then, a few seconds later,

180 Chapter 3 Narrator and Voice • Generating Research Questions

they're all dry and shapeless and horribly ugly. I don't want them to ever think of me as something dead and horrible like that."

"You're their own, their child and their sister. They could never think of you other than the way you would want them to, the way you looked the last time they saw you."

"I'm still afraid," she said. "I can't help it, but I don't want Gerry to know it. If he gets back in time, I'm going to act like I'm not afraid at all and—"

The signal buzzer interrupted her, quick and imperative.

"I wanted to see you," she said again. "I wanted to see you, so I hid on this ship—"

"You *hid* on it?"

"I'm a stowaway. . . . I didn't know what it would mean—"

"*Marilyn!*" It was the cry of a man who calls, hopeless and desperate, to someone already and forever gone from him. "What have you done?"

"I . . . it's not—" Then her own composure broke and the cold little hand gripped his shoulder convulsively. "Don't, Gerry—I only wanted to see you; I didn't intend to hurt you. Please, Gerry, don't feel like that—"

"Gerry!" She came to her feet. "It's Gerry now!"

He spun the volume control knob and asked, "Gerry Cross?"

"Yes," her brother answered, an undertone of tenseness to his reply. "The bad news—what is it?"

She answered for him, standing close behind him and leaning down a little toward the communicator, her hand resting small and cold on his shoulder.

"Hello, Gerry." There was only a faint quaver to betray the careful casualness of her voice. "I wanted to see you—"

"Marilyn!" There was sudden and terrible apprehension in the way he spoke her name. "What are you doing on that EDS?"

Something warm and wet splashed on his wrist, and he slid out of the chair to help her into it and swing the microphone down to her level.

"Don't feel like that. Don't let me go knowing you feel like that—"

The sob she had tried to hold back choked in her throat, and her brother spoke to her. "Don't cry, Marilyn." His voice was suddenly deep and infinitely gentle, with all the pain held out of it. "Don't cry, Sis—you mustn't do that. It's all right, honey—everything is all right."

Vocabulary

apprehension (ap′rē·hen′shən) *n.:* dread; fear of a future event.

Direct Teaching

E Literary Focus
REVIEW STANDARD

Suspense. What remains uncertain in the story, now that it is clear that Marilyn will get to speak to Gerry? [Possible responses: how much time they will have to talk; whether Gerry will try to save her life; what Barton and Marilyn will do once the conversation is over.]

F Literary Focus
GRADE-LEVEL STANDARD

Third-person-limited point of view. The third-person-limited narrator can't report what Gerry is thinking or feeling. Why do you think Gerry says that everything is all right? [Possible responses: He is trying to comfort Marilyn; he is over his initial reaction to the news; he wants Marilyn to know he isn't going to be angry or critical.]

CONTENT-AREA CONNECTIONS

History: Space Pioneers

As Tom Godwin foresaw, pushing back the frontiers of outer space is an exacting enterprise that leaves little margin for error. The U.S. space program has had its share of heroes and tragedies.

Small-group activity. Group together students who are interested in space exploration so that they can conduct research about the history of the U.S. rocketry and space programs, perhaps beginning with Wernher von Braun and continuing up to the present. Have students create posters highlighting the contributions of heroic scientists and astronauts.

DIRECT TEACHING

A Reading Skills

Questioning. **Why does Marilyn defend Barton, the man who is about to kill her? Do you find her attitude surprising? Why or why not?** [Possible responses: It is surprising and makes her seem almost too good; it is not surprising because they have grown close through their ordeal and because we know Marilyn is tenderhearted.]

B Reading Skills

Questioning. **What questions occur to you as Marilyn turns toward the air lock?** [Possible responses: How can she do it? What will she think in there? Will Barton have a change of heart? Will he switch places with her? Will some outside event, such as an asteroid hitting the EDS, change everything?]

C Literary Focus
GRADE-LEVEL STANDARD

Third-person-limited point of view. **Which detail shows Barton—and readers—that Marilyn is frightened?** [A pulse in her throat shows that her heart is pounding.] **How would the effect change if Barton were the first-person narrator and reported, "I saw that the poor girl was terrified, and it broke my heart"?** [Possible responses: It would be clearer; it would seem melodramatic; it would save readers the work (or deprive them of the pleasure) of inferring how Barton feels.]

"I—" Her lower lip quivered and she bit into it. "I didn't want you to feel that way—I just wanted us to say goodbye, because I have to go in a minute."

"Sure—sure. That's the way it'll be, Sis. I didn't mean to sound the way I did." Then his voice changed to a tone of quick and urgent demand. "EDS—have you called the *Stardust*? Did you check with the computers?"

"I called the *Stardust* almost an hour ago. It can't turn back; there are no other cruisers within forty light-years, and there isn't enough fuel."

"Are you sure that the computers had the correct data—sure of everything?"

"Yes—do you think I could ever let it happen if I wasn't sure? I did everything I could do. If there was anything at all I could do now, I would do it."

A "He tried to help me, Gerry." Her lower lip was no longer trembling and the short sleeves of her blouse were wet where she had dried her tears. "No one can help me and I'm not going to cry anymore and everything will be all right with you and Daddy and Mama, won't it?"

"Sure—sure it will. We'll make out fine."

Her brother's words were beginning to come in more faintly, and he turned the volume control to maximum. "He's going out of range," he said to her. "He'll be gone within another minute."

"You're fading out, Gerry," she said. "You're going out of range. I wanted to tell you—but I can't now. We must say goodbye so soon—but maybe I'll see you again. Maybe I'll come to you in your dreams with my hair in braids and crying because the kitten in my arms is dead; maybe I'll be the touch of a breeze that whispers to you as it goes by; maybe I'll be one of those gold-winged larks you told me about, singing my silly head off to you; maybe, at times, I'll be nothing you can see, but you will know I'm there beside you. Think of me like that, Gerry; always like that and not—the other way."

Dimmed to a whisper by the turning of Woden, the answer came back:

"Always like that, Marilyn—always like that and never any other way."

"Our time is up, Gerry—I have to go now. Good—" Her voice broke in midword and her mouth tried to twist into crying. She pressed her hand hard against it and when she spoke again the words came clear and true:

"Goodbye, Gerry."

Faint and ineffably poignant and tender, the last words came from the cold metal of the communicator:

"Goodbye, little sister . . ."

She sat motionless in the hush that followed, as though listening to the shadow-echoes of the **B** words as they died away; then she turned away from the communicator, toward the air lock, and he pulled down the black lever beside him. The inner door of the air lock slid swiftly open to reveal the bare little cell that was waiting for her, and she walked to it.

C She walked with her head up and the brown curls brushing her shoulders, with the white sandals stepping as sure and steady as the fractional gravity would permit and the gilded buckles twinkling with little lights of blue and red and crystal. He let her walk alone and made no move to help her, knowing she would not want it that way. She stepped into the air lock and turned to face him, only the pulse in her throat to betray the wild beating of her heart.

"I'm ready," she said.

He pushed the lever up and the door slid its quick barrier between them, enclosing her in black and utter darkness for her last moments of life. It clicked as it locked in place and he jerked down the red lever. There was a slight waver of the ship as the air gushed from the

Vocabulary
ineffably (in·ef′ə·blē) *adv.:* indescribably; inexpressibly.

182 Chapter 3 Narrator and Voice • Generating Research Questions

lock, a vibration to the wall as though something had bumped the outer door in passing; then there was nothing and the ship was dropping true and steady again. He shoved the red lever back to close the door on the empty air lock and turned away, to walk to the pilot's chair with the slow steps of a man old and weary.

Back in the pilot's chair he pressed the signal button of the normal-space transmitter. There was no response; he had expected none. Her brother would have to wait through the night until the turning of Woden permitted contact through Group One.

It was not yet time to resume deceleration, and he waited while the ship dropped endlessly downward with him and the drives purred softly. He saw that the white hand of the supply-closet temperature gauge was on zero. A cold equation had been balanced and he was alone on the ship. Something shapeless and ugly was hurrying ahead of him, going to Woden, where her brother was waiting through the night, but the empty ship still lived for a little while with the presence of the girl who had not known about the forces that killed with neither hatred nor malice. It seemed, almost, that she still sat, small and bewildered and frightened, on the metal box beside him, her words echoing hauntingly clear in the void she had left behind her:

I didn't do anything to die for. . . . I didn't do anything. . . . ■

QUESTIONING D
10. What is your response to the story's ending?

Meet the Writer

Tom Godwin

A Sci-fi Pioneer

Tom Godwin (1915–1980) had a difficult start in life. He had to leave school after third grade because of family problems, and he suffered from a curvature of the spine. He later tried to earn a living in two very different fields—as a prospector and as a writer of science fiction.

Godwin lived for many years in various small towns in the Mojave Desert in southeastern California—a harsh environment that many people might consider as alien as outer space. Perhaps his surroundings influenced his first sci-fi stories, which appeared in 1953 in a pioneering sci-fi magazine called *Astounding Science Fiction.*

When "The Cold Equations," his most popular and controversial short story, appeared in the August 1954 issue of *Astounding,* many readers were shocked and angry. They wanted Godwin's "problem story" to have a happy ending, a last-minute way of saving the young stowaway.

Godwin published more than a dozen short stories and several novels, including *The Survivors* (1958) and *The Space Barbarians* (1964), but none of his works caused the stir of "The Cold Equations." His later writing continued to explore similar themes about the harsh indifference of nature to human survival.

DIRECT TEACHING

D Reading Skills
Questioning. [Possible responses to question 10: It's powerful because it's haunting and realistic; it's depressing—a rescue would have been more uplifting.]

GUIDED PRACTICE

Monitoring students' progress. Guide students in responding to these comprehension questions.

Short Answer

1. How does Barton discover the presence of the stowaway? [A heat sensor reveals it.]
2. How much control does Barton have over the course of his spacecraft? [Very little; it's preset by computer, and he is not authorized to make changes.]
3. Why does Marilyn steal onboard? [She follows a sudden impulse to see her brother on Woden.]
4. What consequences does Marilyn expect? [to be fined, to be taken back to the *Stardust,* or to be reprimanded]
5. What is Barton able to do for Marilyn? [He buys her an hour by slowing the ship, and he connects her with her brother by radio.]

DIFFERENTIATING INSTRUCTION

Advanced Learners

Enrichment. Tell students that *Also sprach Zarathustra* (*Thus Spoke Zarathustra*), a tone poem by the German composer Richard Strauss (1864–1949), was made popular by the 1968 film *2001: A Space Odyssey.* This music has since become clichéd for its overuse in films about space exploration, though Strauss was not thinking of space travel when he composed it. Instead, he was intrigued by the philosopher Friedrich Nietzsche's idea of the *Übermensch,* a creative superperson. In *Also sprach Zarathustra,* Strauss tries to capture Nietzsche's ideas musically. (Zarathustra is another name for Zoroaster, founder of a pre-Islamic Persian religion.)

Activity. Play for students the famous opening segment of *Also sprach Zarathustra* by Richard Strauss. Ask students why this music might or might not be effective for a film version of "The Cold Equations."

Connection

Summary ⟺ *at grade level*

The first-person speaker in this poem envisions a future in which technology has become one with nature. The speaker imagines that humans will be able to return to a natural paradise and live in harmony with animals, "all watched over by machines of loving grace."

DIRECT TEACHING

A Reading Skills

Questioning. What questions occur to you when you read the phrase "mutually programming harmony"? [Possible responses: What does that mean? How could animals program computers? Is the speaker serious or facetious?]

B Literary Focus
GRADE-LEVEL STANDARD

First-person point of view. What makes it clear that this poem is written from the first-person point of view? [Possible response: The speaker refers to himself or herself as "I."]

C Literary Focus
GRADE-LEVEL STANDARD

Theme. Do you think the speaker in the poem would describe the computers in "The Cold Equations" as "machines of loving grace"? Why or why not? [Possible responses: No, because they have no compassion and can't save Marilyn's life; yes, because the speaker seems to have a positive view of computers.]

CONNECTION / POEM

All Watched Over by Machines of Loving Grace

Richard Brautigan

I like to think (and
the sooner the better!)
of a cybernetic° meadow
where mammals and computers
A live together in mutually
programming harmony
like pure water
touching clear sky.

B I like to think
(right now, please!)
of a cybernetic forest
filled with pines and electronics
where deer stroll peacefully
past computers
as if they were flowers
with spinning blossoms.

I like to think
(it has to be!)
of a cybernetic ecology
where we are free of our labors
and joined back to nature,
returned to our mammal
brothers and sisters,
C and all watched over
by machines of loving grace.

3. **cybernetic** (sī′bər·net′ik) *adj.:* having to do with computers.

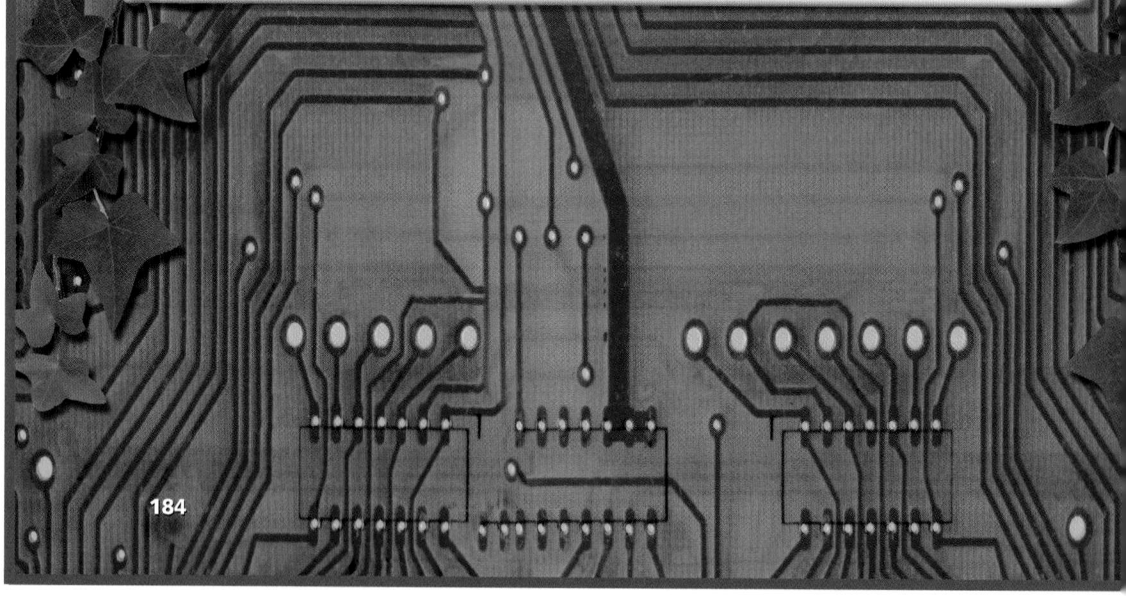

184

Connecting and Comparing Texts

Tom Godwin's short story "The Cold Equations" and Richard Brautigan's poem "All Watched Over by Machines of Loving Grace" provide two views on the future of technology. "The Cold Equations" paints a scientifically credible future in which the demands of space exploration result in a proliferation of technology that crowds out human values, leaving no margin for human error or compassion. "All Watched Over by Machines of Loving Grace" suggests the opposite; it paints a future in which technology has merged with nature, and computers whir "as if they were flowers" in peaceful forests and meadows, somehow keeping all living things in harmony. In the poem's wistful (or tongue-in-cheek) future, computers free humans from labor to rejoin "our mammal brothers and sisters," and computers themselves become compassionate, tending the world with "loving grace."

Literary Response and Analysis

Reading Check

1. **Summarize** the main events of this story in a paragraph. Open with a note describing the **setting,** and then tell who the **characters** are and what their **problem** is. Be sure to explain how the problem is resolved.

Interpretations

2. What is the source of the story's **suspense**—that is, what questions kept you turning the pages? Did you have questions that the story didn't answer? Explain.
3. This story contrasts life on earth with life on the space frontier. In what important ways are those **settings** different? Do you find Godwin's space frontier believable? Why or why not?
4. Find the passage toward the middle of the story that explains its **title.** What are the "cold equations"? What other **images** of coldness can you find in the story?
5. Why do you suppose Godwin chose the **third-person-limited point of view** instead of making Barton the **first-person narrator**? How does the third-person-limited point of view affect the story's **tone, plot,** and **believability**? For help answering, try rewriting a brief passage in Barton's first-person voice.
6. How believable are Marilyn's choice to stow away and her later responses to her fate? If you were in her situation, how do you think you would react? Be sure to check your Quickwrite notes.
7. Do you think that Godwin and Brautigan (see the ***Connection*** on page 184) have similar or different attitudes toward technology? Explain your answer.

Evaluation

8. On page 167, we learn that Barton would have immediately carried out the regulation to eject the stowaway if it had been a man. What do you think of this attitude?
9. "The Cold Equations" was published in 1954, at a time when technology was far less advanced than it is now. Today we are living in what, to Godwin, was the future (though not as far in the future as the story is set). Do you think the technological "future" is turning out to be as cold and harsh as Godwin predicted? Explain your answer with specific examples from your own experience.

What Godwin Predicted	Today's Reality

Writing

The Best Solution?

Do you agree that Barton has no choice but to let Marilyn die? Consider the problem presented in the story, and write a **problem-solution essay** in which you develop and support your ideas about what could have been done differently in "The Cold Equations."

▶ Use "Analyzing Problems and Solutions," pages 212–219, for help with this assignment.

Reading Standard 3.9
Explain how the choice of a narrator affects characterization and the tone, plot, and credibility of a text.

INDEPENDENT PRACTICE

Literary Response and Analysis

Reading Check

1. Possible answer: The setting is a space shuttle in the future. Barton, the pilot, is on a mission to a space colony. Marilyn, a stowaway, wants to see her brother in the colony. The ship doesn't have enough fuel for the added weight. Either Marilyn must be ejected or the ship will crash. Barton tries to save her but must jettison her from the ship.

Interpretations

2. The main question is "Will Marilyn survive?" An unanswered question might be "How will Barton get off Woden?"
3. The frontier lacks the resources that support compassion on Earth. Possible answer: Godwin's use of data and scientific principles makes the setting credible.
4. The main passage is the second paragraph, p. 176. "Cold equations" are scientific formulas that cannot be changed. Other images of coldness include the cold hatred Barton imagines from Marilyn's parents; Marilyn's feeling cold; her cold hand; and the cold metal of the communicator.
5. The third-person-limited narrator is a cool, impersonal voice, setting an authoritative, credible tone.
6. Possible answers: Marilyn seems unrealistically naive; her quick acceptance of her impending death is not credible; her impulsive decision to stow away is true to life because many young people are impulsive.
7. Some students may say the authors' attitudes are opposite: Godwin sees technology as heartless, while Brautigan envisions machines with compassion. Others may feel that Brautigan's tone is facetious and the authors' attitudes are similar.

Evaluation

8. Possible answers: Barton's attitude is biased; his attitude is reasonable because the context suggests that by the word *man* he means a threatening adult.
9. Possible answer: In contrast to Godwin's predictions, much of today's technology is quite "friendly." Examples might include hand-held computers, ATMs, and computerized devices to aid those with disabilities.

Vocabulary Development

Practice

Possible Answers

- *increments. Sentence*—"Additional fuel would be used . . . increments of fuel. . . ." *Synonym*—amounts.
- *recoiled. Sentence*—"She recoiled . . . as though he had struck her. . . ." *Synonyms*—flinched, shrank.
- *paramount. Sentence*—". . . the girl's weight would . . . become, suddenly, a factor of paramount importance. . . ." *Synonyms*—dominant, supreme, primary, highest.
- *annihilate. Sentence*—". . . a . . . destruction that sought to annihilate all that lay before it." *Synonyms*—destroy, eradicate.
- *irrevocable. Sentence*—"Existence required . . . laws . . . irrevocable and immutable." *Synonyms*—irreversible, fixed, set, permanent.
- *immutable. Sentence*—(See above.) *Synonyms*—changeless, unvarying.
- *ponderous. Sentence*—"It made no distinction between the fall of a leaf and the ponderous circling of a binary star system." *Synonyms*—heavy, cumbersome.
- *apprehension. Sentence*—"There was sudden and terrible apprehension. . . . " *Synonyms*—fear, dread, anxiety, foreboding.
- *ineffably. Sentence*—"ineffably poignant and tender . . ." *Synonym*—inexpressibly.

Resources Reminder

Vocabulary

- *Vocabulary Development*
  - Vocabulary Worksheet, pp. 13–14
- *Lesson Plans for Language Development*
  - Vocabulary, pp. 94, 100

Grammar Link

Practice

1. *Subjects*—Marilyn, her brother. *Verb*—is.
2. *Subjects*—Barton, his supervisors. *Verb*—were.
3. *Subject*—men. *Verb*—are.

Vocabulary Development

Using a Thesaurus to Find Synonyms

A **synonym** is a word that has the same or nearly the same meaning as another word. To find synonyms, writers use a **thesaurus** (a dictionary of synonyms). Most thesauri list synonyms based on a word's different shades of meaning, or **connotations.** You might want to look at all the synonyms and follow the cross-references given until you find the exact meaning you want to convey. See the example.

Word Bank

inured
increments
recoiled
paramount
annihilate
irrevocable
immutable
ponderous
apprehension
ineffably

inured → **Sentence in story:** He was . . . inured to the sight of death.

inured → **Synonyms:** callous, insensitive, hardened, hard-hearted

Reading Standard 1.2 Distinguish between the denotative and connotative meanings of words.

PRACTICE

Using a thesaurus, make **synonym charts** like the one above for the other Word Bank words. Before you list a synonym, check to be sure that it fits the meaning of the Word Bank word as it is used in the story.

Grammar Link MINI-LESSON

They Always Agree—Subject and Verb

One of the most common errors that people make in their writing and speaking has to do with subject-verb agreement. The rule is simple: **Singular subjects take singular verbs; plural subjects take plural verbs.** The trick is to find the subject and determine its **number.**

1. The number of the subject is not changed by a phrase following the subject.

   The dials in the EDS control room were flashing.

2. Singular subjects joined by *or* or *nor* take a singular verb.

   Neither Barton nor his supervisor wants to carry out the rules.

3. When a singular subject and a plural subject are joined by *or* or *nor,* the verb agrees with the subject nearer the verb.

   Neither Barton nor his supervisors want to eject the girl.

PRACTICE

Identify each subject below, and determine its number. Then, choose the correct verb.

1. Marilyn or her brother (is/are) going to die.
2. Neither Barton nor his supervisors (was/were) willing to make an exception to the rule.
3. The men on the EDS team (is/are) obliged to eject Marilyn.

Tip: When you proofread your writing, always check the subject o each sentence, and be sure the verb agrees with it in number.

For more help, see Agreement of Subject and Verb in the *Holt Handbook,* pages 110–113.

186 Chapter 3 Narrator and Voice • Generating Research Questions

ASSESSING

Assessment

- *Progress Assessment of Reading*
  - Selection Test

RETEACHING

For a lesson reteaching Standard 3.9, see **Reteaching,** p. 939A. For another selection to teach Standard 3.9, see *Interactive Reading,* Chapter 3.

Before You Read INFORMATIONAL MATERIALS

Taste—The Final Frontier

Generating Research Questions

When you set out to do a research project, your first, crucial step is to generate good research questions that will yield specific, relevant information. To help jump-start your questions, you may want to read a general encyclopedia article about your subject.

Helpful Hints

Here are some guidelines for generating productive research questions from materials you read:

- **Stay focused.** Don't write a long list of questions that cover everything you could possibly ask about a broad, general subject. Instead, zoom in on one aspect of your subject, and stick to questions about your narrowed topic. Try to identify the **main idea** of your topic to focus your questions better.
- **Check the subheads.** In an informational article, subheads indicate smaller divisions of the article's subject. They may give you ideas for a limited topic to research.
- **Do what reporters do.** Research questions that can be answered with yes or no will get you nowhere. When reporters investigate a story, their questions begin with *who, what, where, when, why,* and *how?* (For example, Who are the people involved? What happened?) Asking these ***5W-How? questions*** will lead you to specific information.
- **Be realistic.** Ask questions that you think you can find answers to with the resources available to you.

To sum up: Your first research task is to generate productive questions. Keep your questions on target (focused on your limited topic), and make them specific.

Vocabulary Development

breached (brēcht) *v.:* broken through.

palatable (pal′it·ə·bəl) *adj.:* tasty; fit to be eaten or drunk.

rancid (ran′sid) *adj.:* stale or spoiled.

mutiny (myo͞ot′′n·ē) *n.:* rebellion or revolt against authority.

impoverished (im·päv′ər·isht) *v.* used as *adj.:* poor; without funds.

habitat (hab′i·tat′) *n.:* person's environment or living space.

judicious (jo͞o·dish′əs) *adj.:* wise and careful.

metabolism (mə·tab′ə·liz′əm) *n.:* process by which living organisms turn food into energy and living tissue.

arresting (ə·rest′iŋ) *adj.:* interesting; striking.

Connecting to the Literature

Someday the space travel and colonization of other planets that is described in "The Cold Equations" may become a reality. Will space travelers be able to eat tasty and fresh foods, which until now have been missing from space missions? The following article discusses the plans and recipes that scientists are currently cooking up.

Reading Standard 2.3 Generate relevant questions about readings on issues that can be researched.

STANDARDS FOCUS, pp. 187–192

(For grade-level and review standards taught in this lesson, see citations on Student Edition pages.)

PRETEACHING

Preview Vocabulary

Use this exercise to build students' familiarity with the Vocabulary words on p. 187.

1. Why would eliminating all traffic lights not be a judicious decision? [Possible response: Cars would crash into one another.]
2. Name two foods you do not consider palatable. [Possible response: figs and tripe.]
3. Name one U.S. president who had an impoverished childhood. [Possible response: Lincoln.]
4. How would the crew of a ship stage a mutiny? [Possible response: by ousting the captain and taking command of the ship.]
5. When does butter get rancid? [Possible response: when it spoils.]
6. Name an astronauts' habitat. [a spaceship]
7. If a fortress has been breached, what has happened to it? [Possible response: It has been broken into.]
8. What sounds might a cat consider arresting? [Possible response: mouse squeaks.]
9. How does lack of exercise affect your metabolism? [It slows it down.]

RESOURCES: READING

Media
- *Audio CD Library*
  - disc 7
- *Fine Art Transparencies*
  - Transparency 6

Reading
- *Interactive Reading,* Teacher's Edition
  - Graphic Organizer: 5 W's and H Chart

Differentiating Instruction
- *Lesson Plans for Language Development*
  - English-Language Learners, pp. 79–81, 95, 101
  - Special Education Students, pp. 82, 95, 101

Vocabulary
- *Vocabulary Development*
  - Vocabulary Worksheet, p. 15

Assessment
- *Progress Assessment of Reading*
  - Selection Test
- *One-Stop Planner* CD-ROM with Test Generator

PRETEACHING

Summary ⇔ *at grade level*

In this newspaper article, Esther Addley describes the appalling food that is standard fare for space travelers. She surveys the history of space cuisine ("mush in a tube"), examines current challenges of feeding astronauts, and speculates about possibilities for improvements (hydroponic farms on the moon or Mars).

Selection Starter

Motivate. Ask students what they would like to eat during a voyage in space. Would they choose comfort foods? gourmet fare? ethnic treats? Elicit a number of responses. Then, ask students to read Connecting to the Literature on p. 187 and to list questions that arise as they read the article.

DIRECT TEACHING

A Reading Informational Materials
GRADE-LEVEL STANDARD

? Generating research questions. What are two *5W-How?* research questions suggested by the second paragraph? [Possible responses: What are American astronauts' favorite and least favorite space foods? How has the presentation of space foods improved since the 1960s?]

B Reading Informational Materials
GRADE-LEVEL STANDARD

? Generating research questions. How might you revise the question "Did Filippi manage to improve the food on Mir?" to make it more useful for research? [Possible response: Reword it as a *5W-How?* question, such as "What foods did Filippi prepare for the astronauts on Mir?" or "How did the astronauts respond to Filippi's menu items?"]

NEWSPAPER ARTICLE

Taste—The Final Frontier

from *The Guardian*, April 21, 2000

Esther Addley

Yuri Gagarin's first trip into space on April 12, 1961, was a brief one, which is perhaps just as well. If he'd stayed up any longer than his brief 108-minute orbit, he might have started getting peckish.[1] And since no one had any idea whether humans could swallow in zero gravity, he hadn't been allowed to take any food. The Soviets were ignoring the recommendations of the British interplanetary society in 1939, which advised that astronauts should be fattened up in advance, then given a daily pound of butter while on board to fulfill their calorific needs.

A Space nutrition has completed several missions of its own in the four decades since the final frontier was breached, and the popular image of high-protein slop that tastes like liquidized cardboard is now largely outdated. But while the presentation may have improved, astronauts broadly agree that food in space has remained pretty awful since John Glenn returned from his mission in 1962 demanding a real sandwich instead of mush in a tube.

The way we feed ourselves in space has actually changed very little. Foods are freeze-dried and vacuum-packed to weigh next to nothing; when you feel like lunch you select a sachet,[2] add water, stir, and suck it out of the carton. Delicious.

The main challenge in cooking for long-haul astronauts, as anyone who has taken a transatlantic flight will know, is making the food palatable. NASA is careful to supply every vitamin, mineral, and calorie an astronaut requires, calculated to the minutest scale. But that doesn't mean it tastes nice. French astronaut Jean-Loup Chrétien described the Russian prepacked pot noodles on Mir as tasting like "rancid almonds"; his **B** countryman Richard Filippi was so appalled at the menus that he devised a culinary art he called "gastronautics" to cater to the space station's final missions. "It was clearly unacceptable that a Frenchman should eat poorly in space," said Filippi. "Something had to be done." Astronauts, he figured, are like armies; they march—or spacewalk—on their stomachs.

Rehydratable food.

It's not just that astronauts are fussy eaters. Russian cosmonauts were rumoured at one point to be close to mutiny, so bad

1. **peckish** *adj.:* chiefly British for "slightly hungry."
2. **sachet** (sa·shā′) *n.:* small bag.

Vocabulary

breached (brēcht) *v.:* broken through.

palatable (pal′it·ə·bəl) *adj.:* tasty; fit to be eaten or drunk.

rancid (ran′sid) *adj.:* stale or spoiled.

mutiny (myo͞ot′'n·ē) *n.:* rebellion or revolt against authority.

DIFFERENTIATING INSTRUCTION

Learners Having Difficulty

Point out Addley's use of dry humor, as in her deadpan reference to the bizarre recommendations of the British interplanetary society (p. 188, first paragraph), her ironic comment "Delicious" (p. 188, third paragraph), and her image of astronauts "training tomatoes up their mass spectrometers" (p. 190, fourth paragraph).

English-Language Learners

Tell students that Yuri Gagarin (1934–1968) and John Glenn (1921–) were two of the first people to orbit the earth. You might also introduce the words *slop* (tasteless, watery food), *mush* (thick, soft matter), and *fussy* (hard to please).

was the food provided by their impoverished space agency. "It is extremely important that you have a varied diet in space," says Jean Hunter, associate professor of agricultural and biological engineering at Cornell University. "Food assumes an especially large role in psychological support of the crew. The astronauts are living in a habitat that doesn't change from day to day, so the most reliable source of variety in those conditions comes from the food."

The main gripe, unsurprisingly, is that nothing is fresh. Despite the introduction of refrigeration facilities, a locker of fresh apples and oranges will last only 48 hours. Then it's back to cartons, cans, and hot water, at least until a considerate shuttle drops by.

The solution? Grow the crops yourself. As well as providing variety, space crops would allow a future colony to be more self-sufficient. And it's not such a distant prospect. NASA has been investigating for some years the possibility of growing crops in space—artificially lit, watered, and temperature-controlled, of course. The atmosphere of Mars, 95% carbon dioxide, could be relatively easily managed for grain or vegetable production, the byproduct oxygen being used to produce water combined with imported hydrogen. And if the claims of ice having been discovered on the moon prove true, agriculture galactic[3]-style could really be in business.

C

Enter Hunter and her colleagues at Cornell. Raw grain or potato, after all, is unlikely to prove any more popular than in freeze-dried form. What astronauts will need is recipes, culinary tips, a cookbook. And this month 16 volunteers completed the first extended trial of moon food, for 30 days eating nothing but food that could, in theory, be grown and harvested on the moon or Mars.

D

"We developed more than 200 recipes using plants that could be grown in a lunar colony, in hydroponic cultures (that is, using nutrient-enriched fluid instead of soil) with artificial lighting, and looked at the ways they would have to be processed to turn them into food that people would want to eat," says Hunter.

Considering the restrictions on which plants can be cultivated—they need to be short, high yielding, and require little maintenance—the potential variety of diet is impressive. Rice, wheat, potato, sweet potato, tomato, and other vegetables are all seen as prime candidates. Soy

(From left to right) Mission Specialist Robert A. R. Parker, Payload Specialist Ronald A. Parise, and Commander Vance D. Brand enjoy a meal aboard the space shuttle *Columbia*.

3. **galactic** *adj.:* having to do with the Milky Way or another galaxy.

Vocabulary

impoverished (im·päv′ər·isht) *v.* used as *adj.:* poor; without funds.

habitat (hab′i·tat′) *n.:* person's environment or living space.

Direct Teaching

C Reading Informational Materials
GRADE-LEVEL STANDARD

Generating research questions. Revise the question "How does diet affect astronauts?" to make it more focused. [Possible responses: What psychological symptoms do astronauts show when their diet is not varied enough? What changes in diet bring about an improvement in astronauts' psychological well-being?]

D Reading Informational Materials
REVIEW STANDARD

Identifying the main idea. What are Jean Hunter and her colleagues working on? [Possible response: They are creating and testing recipes using plants that could be grown on the moon.]

Resources Reminder
For lessons designed for intermediate and advanced English-language learners, see *Lesson Plans for Language Development,* pp. 79–81, 95, 101.

Special Education Students
For lessons designed for special education students, see *Lesson Plans for Language Development,* pp. 82, 95, 101.

Advanced Learners
Enrichment. Encourage students to describe Esther Addley's writing style. You might challenge students to compare her style with the speaking style of Jean Hunter, whom Addley quotes. [Addley's style is imaginative and ironic; Hunter's is straightforward and intellectual.] Invite students to discuss how Addley's style affects their responses to the article. Does her style capture their interest, confuse them, make facts more memorable or less memorable, or have some other effect?

DIRECT TEACHING

A Reading Informational Materials
GRADE-LEVEL STANDARD

? Generating research questions. How might you use information from these paragraphs to narrow the focus of the question "What will space food be like in the future?" [Replace vague phrases such as "space food" and "be like" with more specific words. Possible responses: What factors limit the variety of plants that could be grown in space? What are some of the dietary restrictions and requirements of space travelers?]

GUIDED PRACTICE

Monitoring students' progress. Sketch a three-stage rocket on the chalkboard, drawing each stage as a box big enough to write in. Label the bottom box "Space Foods: The Past," the middle box "Space Foods: The Present," and the top box "Space Foods: The Future." Help students come up with major points from the article to list in each box.

beans would give oil and milk; meat substitute could be made from wheat. With judicious use of flavoring, believe the researchers, the food produced could be extremely tasty. Sweet potato pancakes, lentil loaf sandwiches, or chocolate soy candy, anyone?

Rupert Spies, senior lecturer at the university's school of hotel administration and developer of most of the recipes, admits to being frustrated that all Mars menus must be low in salt, but says he got round it by adding A "a lot of herbs." "The lack of salt is very important because it affects the metabolism in space. Salt and bone loss is a very specific issue if you are in microgravity."

Captain Loren J. Shriver, mission commander, pursues several floating chocolate candies on the flight deck of the space shuttle *Atlantis*.

At this stage, of course, all the recipes are necessarily vegan[4]—tethering a cow to a star-spangled banner on the surface of the moon is not yet a viable option. But not all animal protein will eventually need to be imported. "It is a very, very long way off until we will be farming animals in space," says Hunter. "But it does seem likely that the first meat animals will probably be fish, such as carp, because they can be grown in a closed system with very low water use."

The prospect of allotments[5] or fish farms dotted across the surface of Mars is an arresting one. But it is unlikely that astronauts will be training tomatoes up their mass spectrometers[6] for a while yet. And it will take considerably longer before they can cut ties with mother earth altogether.

"It's not worth attempting to be fully self-sufficient as a colony," says Hunter. "There are so many other things you'd have to bring from earth, you might as well bring some food as well." Exhausted astronauts might well agree. The average man requires 2.5 pounds of food a day. Tell an astronaut that he has to head off to the inflatable pod, harvest some grain, shell, grind, and cook it, and he might settle for powdered steak sandwich after all.

4. **vegan** (vē'gən) *n.* used as *adj.:* strictly vegetarian; not containing any animal products.

5. **allotments** *n.:* in Britain, small plots or parcels of public land set aside for growing vegetables or flowers.
6. **mass spectrometers** (spek·träm'ət·ərz): instruments used by scientists to identify chemical substances.

Vocabulary
judicious (jo͞o·dish'əs) *adj.:* wise and careful.
metabolism (mə·tab'ə·liz'əm) *n.:* process by which living organisms turn food into energy and living tissue.
arresting (ə·rest'iŋ) *adj.:* interesting; striking.

Analyzing Informational Materials

Reading Check

1. What is the astronauts' main complaint about food in space?
2. Why do astronauts use freeze-dried food instead of fresh vegetables and fruits?
3. How might colonists on Mars grow fresh vegetables and raise carp?

Test Practice

1. Which sentence states this article's **main idea**?
   - **A** Astronauts' meals are freeze dried and vacuum packed.
   - **B** Fresh vegetables may someday be grown aboard spaceships.
   - **C** Space nutritionists are trying to solve the problem of unappetizing food in space.
   - **D** A new recipe book has been compiled for astronauts who are vegetarians.

2. If you were researching the latest developments in food for U.S. astronauts, which question would provide the *most* relevant information?
   - **F** How is food freeze-dried?
   - **G** What is the history of hydroponic agriculture?
   - **H** Do U.S. astronauts still complain about food on extended space missions?
   - **J** What foods did U.S. astronauts eat during the last three space missions?

3. "What input have astronauts had in the most recent experiments on space food?" is a more useful research question than "Has space food changed since the 1960s?" because —
   - **A** it is a broad, general question about growing food on Mars
   - **B** it will yield specific information
   - **C** it can be answered *yes* or *no*
   - **D** it is about future events

4. Which of the following research questions is *not* related to the issues in this article?
   - **F** How might grains and vegetables be grown on Mars?
   - **G** What would be needed for astronauts to grow fresh vegetables aboard a space flight?
   - **H** Who would pay for constructing lunar colonies?
   - **J** In a Martian or lunar colony, how might residents get food?

Reading Standard 2.3 Generate relevant questions about readings on issues that can be researched.

Application

Write five **research questions** about humans in space. Your questions may further explore space nutrition or a related topic that this article has made you curious about. Then, get together with three or four classmates to evaluate one another's questions. Decide which questions seem likeliest to yield good research results.

INDEPENDENT PRACTICE

Analyzing Informational Materials

Reading Check

1. Their main complaint is that nothing is fresh.
2. Fresh vegetables and fruits keep for only two days in space.
3. Plants might be grown with artificial light, in nutrient-enriched fluid instead of soil. Carp might be raised in a closed system with little water use.

Test Practice

Answers and Model Rationales

1. **C** A and B are supporting details, not the main idea. D, another detail, does not appear in the article. Thus, C is correct.
2. **J** Students should immediately eliminate H, a yes-or-no question. F and G are far too general. J is focused on the topic.
3. **B** The first proposed research question is not general (A), is not a yes-or-no question (C), and is not about the future (D).
4. **H** Students should recall that issues mentioned in the article include growing food in space (G) and on the moon and Mars (F and J) but *not* funding (H).

Test-Taking Tips

For more information on how to answer multiple-choice items, refer students to **Test Smarts.**

Application

Make sure students' questions are focused, specific, and researchable. You may want to create a checklist, based on the Helpful Hints on p. 187, for students to use when evaluating research questions.

Vocabulary Development

Practice

Students' semantic maps will vary, but they should include questions that can be answered with definitions, examples, synonyms, antonyms, applications, and possible sentences.

Possible semantic map:
breached. Definition—broken through. *What are three things that might be* breached?—a dam or a wall; a social barrier; a border. *What is the opposite of* breached?—left intact; preserved; maintained. *What are some synonyms for* breached?—penetrated; violated. *When could a wall be described as* breached?—when someone climbs through a gap in it; when a drill goes through it; after it's hit by a wrecking ball. *What are some example sentences?*—When water breached the dam, the valley was flooded; Jackie Robinson breached the color barrier in major-league baseball; Enemy troops breached the border.

Resources Reminder

Vocabulary

- *Vocabulary Development*
  - Vocabulary Worksheet, p. 15
- *Lesson Plans for Language Development*
  - Vocabulary, pp. 95, 101

ASSESSING

Assessment

- *Progress Assessment of Reading*
  - Selection Test

RETEACHING

For another selection to teach Standard 2.3, see *Interactive Reading,* Part 2.

Vocabulary Development

Word Mapping: How to Own a New Word

Word Bank
breached
palatable
rancid
mutiny
impoverished
habitat
judicious
metabolism
arresting

Sometimes you can figure out a word from its context, but sometimes you can't. On page 188, the writer gives **context clues**—spread over three sentences—to help you understand what the word *palatable* means:

> "The main challenge in cooking for long-haul astronauts, as anyone who has taken a transatlantic flight will know, is making the food palatable. NASA is careful to supply every vitamin, mineral, and calorie an astronaut requires, calculated to the minutest scale. But that doesn't mean it tastes nice."

Making a **semantic map,** or **meaning map,** can help you pin down the meaning of a new word. Here is a sample map for the word *palatable.* Note how the questions, answers, and examples show the word in action and help to clarify its meaning.

palatable

What are three foods I find especially palatable?
- baked ziti
- chicken fajitas
- fresh fruit salad

What makes foods palatable?
- good taste
- seasoning
- texture
- good cooking

What's the opposite of palatable?
- inedible
- disgusting
- bad-tasting

What are some synonyms for palatable?
- tasty
- appetizing
- good-tasting

Definition: pleasant or acceptable to the taste; fit to be eaten or drunk

What are some example sentences?
- Nothing can make burned toast palatable.
- Homemade chicken soup is a palatable way to treat a cold.
- Carla finds every kind of pasta palatable.

Grade 8 Review Reading Standard 1.3 Use word meanings within the appropriate context and show ability to verify those meanings by definition, restatement, example, comparison, or contrast.

PRACTICE

With a partner, divide the remaining Word Bank words so that you each have four. Then, make a **semantic map** for each of your words. You may need to create some of your own questions and answers. When you finish, share your maps with those of your partner.

192 Chapter 3 Narrator and Voice • Generating Research Questions

Before You Read

Typhoid Fever

Literary Focus

Voice: The Sound of the Author

In literature the term **voice** refers to our sense of the writer who has created the work. (In fiction it can also refer to our sense of the narrator.) Writers express their voices by their distinctive use of language, including their **diction** (the kinds of words they choose), the complexity or simplicity of their sentence structure, and the **tone,** or attitude, that they take toward their subject and characters. In his memoirs, Frank McCourt uses a unique voice to tell his tragic story of growing up poor in Ireland. Read a passage aloud, and you'll hear McCourt's strong, true voice spring to life.

Reading Skills

Evaluating Credibility: Testing/Trusting Memory

"People are always asking, how does he remember so much," McCourt told an interviewer, "and how much is an Irish storyteller's embroidery?"

Credibility means "believability." How can you judge the credibility of an autobiography? Can adults remember exact conversations, events, and thoughts that took place when they were ten years old? Is factual accuracy important, or is it the significance of an event that's of greater interest? Keep all these questions in mind as you read "Typhoid Fever." Does it ring true to you? Could any of the story's facts be checked?

Make the Connection

Quickwrite

What do you remember from your childhood that is important, unusual, or funny? Make some notes about an early memory; think as a child. Ideas might come to you if you begin like this, in the present tense and the first person: "I am seven years old . . ." or "I'm in a playground . . ."

Background

Angela's Ashes is Frank McCourt's gritty, moving memoir of growing up in Limerick, Ireland, in the 1930s and 1940s. McCourt's family lived in a filthy, overcrowded slum, and bacterial diseases such as typhoid fever and diphtheria were common.

Typhoid fever, caused by contaminated food or water, wastes the whole body. Diphtheria, spread by contact with an infected person, starts with a sore throat and can end in suffocation. Because both infections spread easily, people with these illnesses are quarantined. In Ireland they were isolated in "fever hospitals." Most of these hospitals were run by the Catholic Church and staffed by nuns. McCourt caught typhoid fever at age ten and was sent to a fever hospital.

Vocabulary Development

induced (in·do͞ost′) *v.* used as *adj.:* persuaded; led on.

potent (pot′′nt) *adj.:* powerful; convincing.

torrent (tôr′ənt) *n.:* violent, forceful rush.

clamoring (klam′ər·iŋ) *v.* used as *adj.:* crying out; asking.

Reading Standard 3.9 Explain how voice and the choice of a narrator affect characterization and the tone, plot, and credibility of a text.

STANDARDS FOCUS, pp. 193–205

(For the grade-level standards taught in this lesson, see citations on Student Edition pages.)

Prerequisite Standard

- Grade 8, Literary Response and Analysis 3.6 **Identify significant literary devices (e.g., metaphor, symbolism, dialect, irony) that define a writer's style and use those elements to interpret the work.**

Reading Skills

- Evaluate credibility.

Summary *at grade level*

Speaking in the voice of himself as a ten-year-old, Frank McCourt recalls recovering from typhoid in a Limerick hospital. Allusions to Ireland's struggle against British oppression and to the McCourts' poverty contribute to the grimness of the setting: a hospital where laughing and singing are prohibited and conversation among patients is discouraged. Against the bleakness, young Frank savors the delights of language: Patricia, the dying girl in the next room, whispers comic impressions of nuns and nurses and recites from the ballad "The Highwayman"; the illiterate orderly Seamus sings pub songs on the sly and "carries poems in his head"; and, a line from Shakespeare in a smuggled book feels to the boy "like having jewels in my mouth."

RESOURCES: READING

Media

- *Audio CD Library*
  - disc 7

Reading

- *Interactive Reading,* Teacher's Edition
  - Graphic Organizer: Narrator Chart

Differentiating Instruction

- *Lesson Plans for Language Development*
  - English-Language Learners, pp. 83–85, 96, 102
  - Special Education Students, pp. 86, 96, 102

Vocabulary

- *Vocabulary Development*
  - Vocabulary Worksheet, p. 16

Assessment

- *Progress Assessment of Reading*
  - Selection Test
- *One-Stop Planner* CD-ROM with Test Generator

Preteaching

Standards Starter

Build prerequisite skills. Remind students that the term *diction* refers to an author's choice of words. Demonstrate the difference diction makes by asking students to compare these two sentences: *That guy is stupid. That gentleman's intellectual faculties are weak.*

Preview Vocabulary

Have students read the Vocabulary words and definitions on p. 193. Then, ask the following questions:

1. How might a child be induced to pick up her toys? [Possible response: Promise her a story.]
2. If kittens are clamoring for attention, what are they doing? [Possible response: meowing.]
3. How might somone feel after hearing a torrent of abuse? [Possible response: resentful, hurt.]
4. What might make a batch of hot sauce more potent? [Possible response: chili peppers.]

Direct Teaching

A Literary Focus GRADE-LEVEL STANDARD

Voice. What impression of the narrator is created in the first few paragraphs? How does McCourt create that impression? [Possible response: Frank is polite and quiet; he sometimes gets confused and doesn't understand what is happening. McCourt uses simple language appropriate to a ten-year-old.]

TYPHOID FEVER

from Angela's Ashes

Frank McCourt

Yoo hoo, are you there, typhoid boy?

The room next to me is empty till one morning a girl's voice says, Yoo hoo, who's there?

I'm not sure if she's talking to me or someone in the room beyond.

Yoo hoo, boy with the typhoid, are you awake?

I am.

Are you better?

I am.

Well, why are you here?

I don't know. I'm still in the bed. They stick needles in me and give me medicine.

What do you look like?

I wonder, What kind of a question is that? I don't know what to tell her.

Yoo hoo, are you there, typhoid boy?

I am.

What's your name?

Frank.

That's a good name. My name is Patricia Madigan. How old are you?

Ten.

Oh. She sounds disappointed.

But I'll be eleven in August, next month.

Well, that's better than ten. I'll be fourteen in September. Do you want to know why I'm in the Fever Hospital?

I do.

I have diphtheria and something else.

What's something else?

They don't know. They think I have a disease from foreign parts because my father used to be in Africa. I nearly died. Are you going to tell me what you look like?

I have black hair.

You and millions.

I have brown eyes with bits of green that's called hazel.

You and thousands.

I have stitches on the back of my right hand and my two feet where they put in the soldier's blood.

DIFFERENTIATING INSTRUCTION

Learners Having Difficulty

Modeling. To help students read "Typhoid Fever," model the reading skill of evaluating credibility. Say, "Suppose you read that the main character of 'Typhoid Fever' was allowed only one visitor a week in the hospital. You might say to yourself, 'That seems unlikely, but whether or not it is literally true, the author's remembering it this way shows how alone he felt.'" Encourage students to ask themselves as they read, "What sense of the author's experience does this detail create?"

English-Language Learners

Tell students that in this selection, Frank McCourt records dialogue without using quotation marks. He also re-creates the effect of spoken language by running many thoughts together in a single long sentence and by spelling some words as they would be pronounced in Irish dialect. Read aloud for students Seamus's first monologue on p. 195, which begins, "He says, I'm not supposed to be bringing anything." Help students break this long sentence into parts.

194 Chapter 3 Narrator and Voice • Generating Research Questions

Oh, did they?

They did.

You won't be able to stop marching and saluting.

There's a swish of habit and click of beads and then Sister Rita's voice. Now, now, what's this? There's to be no talking between two rooms especially when it's a boy and a girl. Do you hear me, Patricia?

I do, Sister.

Do you hear me, Francis?

I do, Sister.

You could be giving thanks for your two remarkable recoveries. You could be saying the rosary.[1] You could be reading *The Little Messenger of the Sacred Heart*[2] that's beside your beds. Don't let me come back and find you talking.

She comes into my room and wags her finger at me. Especially you, Francis, after thousands of boys prayed for you at the Confraternity.[3] Give thanks, Francis, give thanks.

She leaves and there's silence for awhile. Then Patricia whispers, Give thanks, Francis, give thanks, and say your rosary, Francis, and I laugh so hard a nurse runs in to see if I'm all right. She's a very stern nurse from the County Kerry and she frightens me. What's this, Francis? Laughing? What is there to laugh about? Are you and that Madigan girl talking? I'll report you to Sister Rita. There's to be no laughing for you could be doing serious damage to your internal apparatus.

She plods out and Patricia whispers again in a heavy Kerry accent, No laughing, Francis, you could be doin' serious damage to your internal apparatus. Say your rosary, Francis, and pray for your internal apparatus.

Mam visits me on Thursdays. I'd like to see my father, too, but I'm out of danger, crisis time is over, and I'm allowed only one visitor. Besides, she says, he's back at work at Rank's Flour Mills and please God this job will last a while with the war on and the English desperate for flour. She brings me a chocolate bar and that proves Dad is working. She could never afford it on the dole.[4] He sends me notes. He tells me my brothers are all praying for me, that I should be a good boy, obey the doctors, the nuns, the nurses, and don't forget to say my prayers. He's sure St. Jude pulled me through the crisis because he's the patron saint of desperate cases and I was indeed a desperate case.

Patricia says she has two books by her bed. One is a poetry book and that's the one she loves. The other is a short history of England and do I want it? She gives it to Seamus, the man who mops the floors every day, and he brings it to me. He says, I'm not supposed to be bringing anything from a diptheria room to a typhoid room with all the germs flying around and hiding between the pages and if you ever catch dipteria on top of the typhoid they'll know and I'll lose my good job and be out on the street singing patriotic songs with a tin cup in my hand, which I could easily do because there isn't a song ever written about Ireland's sufferings I don't know and a few songs about the joy of whiskey too.

1. **rosary** *n.:* group of prayers that Roman Catholics recite while holding a string of beads.
2. ***The Little Messenger of the Sacred Heart:*** religious publication for children.
3. **Confraternity:** here, a religious organization made up of nonclergy, or laypersons.
4. **dole** *n.:* government payment to the unemployed; also, money or food given to those in need.

DIRECT TEACHING

B Literary Focus
REVIEW STANDARD

Characterization. The narrator tells Patricia that he was given a transfusion of blood donated by soldiers. What does Patricia's response reveal about her? [She has a quick wit.]

C Content-Area Connections
History: World War II

In Europe, World War II lasted from 1939 to 1945. Ireland did not enter the war. England, heavily bombed and forced to divert almost all of its resources to the war effort, suffered severe food shortages.

D Literary Focus
GRADE-LEVEL STANDARD

Tone. The janitor Seamus (shā′mus) is a colorful character. What tone does his first speech establish? [a humorous tone]

Resources Reminder
For lessons designed for intermediate and advanced English-language learners, see *Lesson Plans for Language Development,* pp. 83–85, 96, 102.

Special Education Students

For lessons designed for special education students, see *Lesson Plans for Language Development,* pp. 86, 96, 102.

Advanced Learners

Enrichment. After students read the selection, have them re-read the quotation by Shakespeare and the paragraph following it (p. 196), in which Frank compares reciting the lines to "having jewels in my mouth." Ask students to think of lines from literature that give them the same feeling. Encourage them to check lines of which they are unsure, and suggest that they include favorite lines from McCourt's memoir. Then, guide them in analyzing the elements that make the lines appealing: sound effects, imagery, diction, balance, and so on.

DIRECT TEACHING

A Content-Area Connections

History: Irish Rebellion
The lyrics of "Roddy McCorley" pay tribute to an Irish hero of the Wolfe Tone Rebellion of 1798, one of many unsuccessful Irish rebellions against British rule.

B Reading Skills

Evaluating credibility. In evaluating the credibility of an autobiography, it is important to take the setting into consideration. How credible is McCourt's recollection of the hospital rules about laughing and singing? [Possible response: He was very young at the time and may not recall the rules exactly after so many years. Still, given what we know about the strictness of Irish Catholic nuns in the 1940s, the recollection is credible.]

C Literary Focus
GRADE-LEVEL STANDARD

Voice. How does McCourt re-create the voice—the speaking style and viewpoint—of a ten-year-old boy? [He uses rambling sentences strung together with *and*; he has the narrator call Seamus "an old man of forty."]

D Reading Skills

Drawing conclusions. What do the narrator's thoughts reveal about him? [Possible responses: He recognizes the quality of Shakespeare's work, even though he is only ten years old; he loves words and language; he likes to read; his thoughts seem to point to his future career as a teacher and writer.]

E Content-Area Connections

Literature: Nonsense Poem
"The Owl and the Pussycat" is a famous nonsense poem by the English humorist and illustrator Edward Lear (1812–1888).

Oh, yes, he knows Roddy McCorley. He'll sing it for me right enough but he's barely into the first verse when the Kerry nurse rushes in. What's this, Seamus? Singing? Of all the people in this hospital you should know the rules against singing. I have a good mind to report you to Sister Rita.

Ah, don't do that, nurse.

Very well, Seamus. I'll let it go this one time. You know the singing could lead to a relapse in these patients.

When she leaves he whispers he'll teach me a few songs because singing is good for passing the time when you're by yourself in a typhoid room. He says Patricia is a lovely girl the way she often gives him sweets from the parcel her mother sends every fortnight.[5] He stops mopping the floor and calls to Patricia in the next room, I was telling Frankie you're a lovely girl, Patricia, and she says, You're a lovely man, Seamus. He smiles because he's an old man of forty and he never had children but the ones he can talk to here in the Fever Hospital. He says, Here's the book, Frankie. Isn't it a great pity you have to be reading all about England after all they did to us, that there isn't a history of Ireland to be had in this hospital.

The book tells me all about King Alfred and William the Conqueror and all the kings and queens down to Edward, who had to wait forever for his mother, Victoria, to die before he could be king. The book has the first bit of Shakespeare I ever read.

I do believe, induced by potent
circumstances,
That thou art mine enemy.

The history writer says this is what Catherine, who is a wife of Henry the Eighth, says to Cardinal Wolsey, who is trying to have her head cut off. I don't know what it means and I don't care because it's Shakespeare and it's like having jewels in my mouth when I say the words. If I had a whole book of Shakespeare they could keep me in the hospital for a year.

Patricia says she doesn't know what induced means or potent circumstances and she doesn't care about Shakespeare, she has her poetry book and she reads to me from beyond the wall a poem about an owl and a pussycat that went to sea in a green boat with honey and money and it makes no sense and when I say that Patricia gets huffy and says that's the last poem she'll ever read to me. She says I'm always reciting the lines from Shakespeare and they make no sense either. Seamus stops mopping again and tells us we shouldn't be fighting over poetry because we'll have enough to fight about when we grow up and get married. Patricia says she's sorry and I'm sorry too so she reads me part of another poem[6] which I have to remember so I can say it back to her early in the morning or late at night when there are no nuns or nurses about,

5. **fortnight** *n.:* chiefly British for "two weeks."

6. **part . . . poem:** The reference is to "The Highwayman" by the British poet Alfred Noyes (1880–1958). The poem is based on a true story about a highwayman who fell in love with an innkeeper's daughter in eighteenth-century England. Highwaymen, who robbed wealthy stagecoach passengers, were at that time popular romantic figures.

Vocabulary

induced (in·do͞ost′) *v.* used as *adj.:* persuaded; led on.

potent (pōt′'nt) *adj.:* powerful; convincing.

196 Chapter 3 Narrator and Voice • Generating Research Questions

CONTENT-AREA CONNECTIONS

History: Ireland and England
The long history of conflict between Ireland and England began in 1171, when King Henry II of England forced the lords of Ireland to accept him as their king. However, over the next few hundred years, English influence in Ireland declined. In 1541, Henry VIII had the Irish Parliament declare him king of Ireland and tried unsuccessfully to establish Protestantism in Ireland. Later English monarchs maintained his policy by seizing Irish land and giving it to English and Scottish settlers, creating the Protestant majority that exists to this day in Northern Ireland. By 1704, Irish Catholics held only about one seventh of the land in all of Ireland. They could not purchase or inherit land. They could not be members of the Irish Parliament or army. Even their right

The wind was a torrent *of darkness among the*
gusty trees,
The moon was a ghostly galleon tossed upon
cloudy seas,
The road was a ribbon of moonlight over the
purple moor,
And the highwayman came riding—
Riding—riding—
The highwayman came riding, up to the old inn
door.

He'd a French cocked-hat on his forehead, a
bunch of lace at his chin,
A coat of the claret velvet, and breeches of
brown doeskin,
They fitted with never a wrinkle. His boots were
up to the thigh.
And he rode with a jeweled twinkle,
His pistol butts a-twinkle,
His rapier hilt a-twinkle, under the jeweled sky.

Every day I can't wait for the doctors and nurses to leave me alone so I can learn a new verse from Patricia and find out what's happening to the highwayman and the landlord's red-lipped daughter. I love the poem because it's exciting and almost as good as my two lines of Shakespeare. The redcoats are after the highwayman because they know he told her, I'll come to thee by moonlight, though hell should bar the way.

I'd love to do that myself, come by moonlight for Patricia in the next room not giving a hoot though hell should bar the way. She's ready to read the last few verses when in comes the nurse from Kerry shouting at her, shouting at me, I told ye there was to be no talking between rooms. Dipththeria is never allowed to talk to typhoid and visa versa. I warned ye. And she calls out, Seamus, take this one. Take the by. Sister Rita said one more word out of him and upstairs with him. We gave ye a warning to stop the blathering but ye wouldn't. Take the by, Seamus, take him.

Ah, now, nurse, sure isn't he harmless. 'Tis only a bit o' poetry.

Take that by, Seamus, take him at once.

He bends over me and whispers, Ah, I'm sorry, Frankie. Here's your English history book. He slips the book under my shirt and lifts me from the bed. He whispers that I'm a feather. I try to see Patricia when we pass through her room but all I can make out is a blur of dark head on a pillow.

Sister Rita stops us in the hall to tell me I'm a great disappointment to her, that she expected me to be a good boy after what God had done for me, after all the prayers said by hundreds of boys at the Confraternity, after all the care from the nuns and nurses of the Fever Hospital, after the way they let my mother and father in to see me, a thing rarely allowed, and this is how I repaid them lying in the bed reciting silly poetry back and forth with Patricia Madigan knowing very well there was a ban on all talk between typhoid and diphtheria. She says I'll have plenty of time to reflect on my sins in the big ward upstairs and I should beg God's forgiveness for my disobedience reciting a pagan[7] English poem about a thief on a horse and a maiden with red lips who commits a terrible sin when I could have been praying or reading the life of a saint. She made it her business to read that poem so she did and I'd be well advised to tell the priest in confession.

The Kerry nurse follows us upstairs gasping and holding on to the banister. She tells me I better not get the notion she'll be running up to this part of the world every time I have a little pain or a twinge.

There are twenty beds in the ward, all white, all empty. The nurse tells Seamus put me at the far end of the ward against the wall to make sure I don't talk to anyone who might be passing the door, which is very unlikely since there isn't

7. **pagan** (pā′gən) *adj.:* here, non-Christian.

Vocabulary
torrent (tôr′ənt) *n.:* violent, forceful rush.

DIRECT TEACHING

F Learners Having Difficulty

Reading aloud and summarizing. To help students understand why Frank would be enthralled with the poem, read these two stanzas aloud, and then ask students to summarize the content.

G Reading Skills

? Evaluating credibility. Tell students that one way to evaluate credibility is to look for consistency. A text in which a subject is handled consistently is likely to be more credible than one containing inconsistencies. Does the description of the nurse's reaction seem credible? Why or why not? [Possible responses: Yes, since it has already been shown that talking between rooms is forbidden and that the nurse is a stickler for rules; no, Frank's fear of the nurse may have distorted his perceptions.]

H English-Language Learners

Dialect. Point out that in the nurse's dialect, *ye* means "you" and *by* is "boy."

to practice Catholicism was restricted. During the 1700s, some rights were restored to Catholics, but Britain retained tight control over the country. In 1801, Ireland was officially incorporated into the United Kingdom. The Irish did not win independence from Great Britain until 1937 when they adopted a new constitution that declared Ireland to be "a soverign, independent, democratic state." The remaining ties to the British Commonwealth were cut by the Republic of Ireland Act of 1948. Northern Ireland is still under British control.

Mixed-ability group activity. Assign students of differing abilities to small groups to research some of the many Irish rebellions against British rule (such as the Easter Rebellion of 1916), and other events on Ireland's long road to independence (including the decisions that led to the separation of Northern Ireland from Ireland).

DIRECT TEACHING

A Content-Area Connections

History: The Potato Famine Blight, a plant disease, caused the failure of Ireland's potato crop, which led to the great famine. One million people died, and nearly two million emigrated as a result of the famine.

B Literary Focus
GRADE-LEVEL STANDARD

Voice. Up to this point the narrator has seemed naive, confused at times, and intimidated by some of the adults around him. What dimension does this passage add to his voice? [Possible response: He is perceptive, aware of the nurse's cruelty, and compassionate toward Patricia.]

C Literary Focus
GRADE-LEVEL STANDARD

Diction. In this passage, the author has chosen words that reflect Seamus's class and education level. Which words and phrases give the reader a sense of who Seamus is? [Possible responses: "right oul' witch"; "not bloody likely"; "when you're what? ten going on eleven?"; "never heard the likes of it."]

D Literary Focus
GRADE-LEVEL STANDARD

Voice. The somewhat bitter and mocking tone of this sentence contrasts sharply with the innocent, childlike voice that predominates in the selection. What is its effect on the reader? [Possible response: It conveys a sense of the author's sorrow at the tragic events of the past.]

E Vocabulary Development
REVIEW STANDARD

Antonyms. Tell students that one way to reinforce their knowledge of a word's meaning is to think of an antonym for it. What is an antonym for *perfidy*? [Possible responses: faithfulness, loyalty.]

another soul on this whole floor. She tells Seamus this was the fever ward during the Great Famine[8] long ago and only God knows how many died here brought in too late for anything but a wash before they were buried and there are stories of cries and moans in the far reaches of the night. She says 'twould break your heart to think of what the English did to us, that if they didn't put the blight[9] on the potato they didn't do much to take it off. No pity. No feeling at all for the people that died in this very ward, children suffering and dying here while the English feasted on roast beef and guzzled the best of wine in their big houses, little children with their mouths all green from trying to eat the grass in the fields beyond, God bless us and save us and guard us from future famines.

Seamus says 'twas a terrible thing indeed and he wouldn't want to be walking these halls in the dark with all the little green mouths gaping at him. The nurse takes my temperature, 'Tis up a bit, have a good sleep for yourself now that you're away from the chatter with Patricia Madigan below who will never know a gray hair.

She shakes her head at Seamus and he gives her a sad shake back.

Nurses and nuns never think you know what they're talking about. If you're ten going on eleven you're supposed to be simple like my uncle Pat Sheehan who was dropped on his head. You can't ask questions. You can't show you understand what the nurse said about Patricia Madigan, that she's going to die, and you can't show you want to cry over this girl who taught you a lovely poem which the nun says is bad.

The nurse tells Seamus she has to go and he's to sweep the lint from under my bed and mop up a bit around the ward. Seamus tells me she's a right oul' witch for running to Sister Rita and complaining about the poem going between the two rooms, that you can't catch a disease from a poem unless it's love ha ha and that's not bloody likely when you're what? ten going on eleven? He never heard the likes of it, a little fella shifted upstairs for saying a poem and he has a good mind to go to the *Limerick Leader* and tell them print the whole thing except he has this job and he'd lose it if ever Sister Rita found out. Anyway, Frankie, you'll be outa here one of these fine days and you can read all the poetry you want though I don't know about Patricia below, I don't know about Patricia, God help us.

He knows about Patricia in two days because she got out of the bed to go to the lavatory when she was supposed to use a bedpan and collapsed and died in the lavatory. Seamus is mopping the floor and there are tears on his cheeks and he's saying, 'Tis a dirty rotten thing to die in a lavatory when you're lovely in yourself. She told me she was sorry she had you reciting that poem and getting you shifted from the room, Frankie. She said 'twas all her fault.

It wasn't, Seamus.

I know and didn't I tell her that.

Patricia is gone and I'll never know what happened to the highwayman and Bess, the landlord's daughter. I ask Seamus but he doesn't know any poetry at all especially English poetry. He knew an Irish poem once but it was about fairies and had no sign of a highwayman in it. Still he'll ask the men in his local pub where there's always someone reciting something and he'll bring it back to me. Won't I be busy meanwhile reading my short history of England and finding out all about their perfidy.[10] That's what Seamus says, perfidy, and I don't know what it means and he doesn't know what it means but if it's something the English do it must be terrible.

8. **Great Famine:** refers to the great famine in Ireland from 1845 to 1849, when failed potato crops resulted in the starvation and death of about one million people.

9. **blight** (blīt) *n.:* kind of plant disease.

10. **perfidy** (pur′fə·dē) *n.:* treachery; betrayal.

198 Chapter 3 Narrator and Voice • Generating Research Questions

He comes three times a week to mop the floor and the nurse is there every morning to take my temperature and pulse. The doctor listens to my chest with the thing hanging from his neck. They all say, And how's our little soldier today? A girl with a blue dress brings meals three times a day and never talks to me. Seamus says she's not right in the head so don't say a word to her.

The July days are long and I fear the dark. There are only two ceiling lights in the ward and they're switched off when the tea tray is taken away and the nurse gives me pills. The nurse tells me go to sleep but I can't because I see people in the nineteen beds in the ward all dying and green around their mouths where they tried to eat grass and moaning for soup Protestant soup any soup and I cover my face with the pillow hoping they won't come and stand around the bed clawing at me and howling for bits of the chocolate bar my mother brought last week. **F**

No, she didn't bring it. She had to send it in because I can't have any more visitors. Sister Rita tells me a visit to the Fever Hospital is a privilege and after my bad behavior with Patricia Madigan and that poem I can't have the privilege anymore. She says I'll be going home in a few weeks and my job is to concentrate on getting better and learn to walk again after being in bed for six weeks and I can get out of bed tomorrow after breakfast. I don't know why she says I have to learn how to walk when I've been walking since I was a baby but when the nurse stands me by the side of the bed I fall to the floor and the nurse laughs, See, you're a baby again.

I practice walking from bed to bed back and forth back and forth. I don't want to be a baby. I don't want to be in this empty ward with no Patricia and no highwayman and no red-lipped landlord's daughter. I don't want the ghosts of children with green mouths pointing bony fingers at me and clamoring for bits of my chocolate bar. **G**

Seamus says a man in his pub knew all the verses of the highwayman poem and it has a very sad end. Would I like him to say it because he never learned how to read and he had to carry the poem in his head? He stands in the middle of the ward leaning on his mop and recites,

Tlot-tlot, *in the frosty silence!* Tlot-tlot, *in the echoing night!*
Nearer he came and nearer! Her face was like a light!
Her eyes grew wide for a moment; she drew one last deep breath,
Then her fingers moved in the moonlight,
Her musket shattered the moonlight,
Shattered her breast in the moonlight and warned him—with her death.

He hears the shot and escapes but when he learns at dawn how Bess died he goes into a rage and returns for revenge only to be shot down by the redcoats.

Blood-red were his spurs in the golden noon; wine-red was his velvet coat,
When they shot him down on the highway,
Down like a dog on the highway,
And he lay in his blood on the highway, with a bunch of lace at his throat.

Seamus wipes his sleeve across his face and sniffles. He says, There was no call at all to shift you up here away from Patricia when you didn't even know what happened to the highwayman and Bess. 'Tis a very sad story and when I said it to my wife she wouldn't stop crying the whole night till we went to bed. She said there was no call for them redcoats to shoot that highwayman, they are responsible for half the troubles of the world and they never had any pity on the Irish, either. Now if you want to know any more poems, Frankie, tell me and I'll get them from the pub and bring 'em back in my head. ■

Vocabulary
clamoring (klam′ər·iŋ) *v.* used as *adj.:* crying out; asking.

DIRECT TEACHING

F Reading Skills

Evaluating credibility. Does young Frank really see "people in the nineteen beds"? [Possible response: He imagines them so vividly that it's as if he sees them.] **What is the truth behind his imaginings?** [Possible response: He is terrified of his new surroundings.]

G Reading Skills

Interpreting. Children respond in various ways to adversity. They may become resentful, mistrustful, withdrawn, or fearful; they may display compassion, courage, or resilience. Which, if any, of these words would you use to describe young Frank's behavior, and why? [Possible responses: compassion (for Patricia); courage (in his determination to walk); resilience (in his memorizing literature as a source of comfort); fearful (of the visions he sees of the victims of the famine).]

GUIDED PRACTICE

Monitoring students' progress. Guide the class in answering these true-false questions. Ask students to find passages in the text that support their responses.

True-False

1. Frank catches typhoid fever from Patricia. [F]
2. Seamus smuggles a book to Frank. [T]
3. In the Fever Hospital no laughing or singing is allowed. [T]
4. Frank's family visits every day. [F]
5. Frank never finds out what happens to the highwayman in the poem. [F]

DEVELOPING FLUENCY

Peer-tutoring activity. Pair each struggling reader in the class with a more advanced reader for echo reading. Tell each pair to pick a passage of dialogue from the story. Ask the more advanced reader to read the passage first; then, have the struggling reader read it again.

FAMILY/COMMUNITY ACTIVITY

Suggest that students and their family members discuss experiences they've had in hospitals, either as patients or as visitors. Students might read the selection aloud to family members and then write a description of changes in hospital care since the time in which the story is set.

Meet the Writer

Background. *Angela's Ashes* may be the most famous memoir of the McCourt family of Limerick, but it isn't the only one. Long before Frank McCourt wrote his book, he and his younger brother Malachy, who also emigrated from Ireland to the United States, used to reminisce about their childhood days in Ireland. Around 1980, they were inspired to take their stories to the stage. In a small theater in New York City, they began presenting their stories in an improvisational performance. They called the show *A Couple of Blaguards.* ("Blaguards" is the Irish pronunciation of *black-guards,* meaning "scoundrels.") Their mother, Angela McCourt, saw the performance before she died in 1981. According to Malachy, she stood up halfway through the show and said, "It didn't happen that way! It's all a pack of lies!" At first the brothers performed without a script. Later both Frank and Malachy wrote memoirs based on the material. The two-man show has now been scripted and is performed by professional actors.

For Independent Reading

Suggest to students planning to read *Angela's Ashes* that they think about why the author chose that title. You might also recommend *Reading in the Dark,* by Seamus Deane, a fictional account of an Irish Catholic boyhood in postwar Northern Ireland.

Meet the Writer

Frank McCourt

"We Were Street Kids"

Frank McCourt (1930–   ), who regards himself as more a New Yorker than an Irishman, was born in Brooklyn, New York, the first child of Irish immigrants. When Frank was four, the McCourts made a bad decision—to move back to Ireland, where they lived in worse conditions than those they had fled in Brooklyn. Eventually Frank's father abandoned his wife, Angela, and their three surviving children.

Frank McCourt returned to New York City at age nineteen. Nine years later he began teaching writing to high school students. Encouraged by his students to write about his own experiences (see the ***Connection*** on page 201), he finally published his first book, *Angela's Ashes,* when he was sixty-six. The book dominated best-seller lists, won the 1997 Pulitzer Prize and the 1996 National Book Critics Circle Award for autobiography, and was made into a movie.

A sequel to his first novel, titled *'Tis* (1999), recounts McCourt's life as a young man in New York City, where he held a variety of jobs, from housekeeping at a hotel to acting to unloading meat trucks.

When he was asked how he found such humor in his poverty-stricken childhood, McCourt replied:

> "When you have nothing—no TV, no radio, no music—you have only the language. So you use it. We were street kids—we saw the absurdity and laughed at it. And we were fools; we were always dreaming. Bacon and eggs—we dreamed of that."

For Independent Reading

Don't miss the rest of *Angela's Ashes,* McCourt's moving, searing memoir of his growing-up years, or its sequel, *'Tis.*

DIFFERENTIATING INSTRUCTION

Advanced Learners

Enrichment. Though Frank McCourt considers himself more a New Yorker than an Irishman, his formative years were spent in Ireland during the 1930s and 1940s.

Activity. Have students find out more about the political, social, and literary scene in Ireland during McCourt's youth. Suggest that they enter *Irish literature* and *Frank McCourt* as keywords in an Internet search engine.

The Education of Frank McCourt

Barbara Sande Dimmitt

"Yo, Teach!" a voice boomed. Frank McCourt scanned the adolescents in his classroom. It was the fall of 1970 and his first week of teaching at Seward Park High School, which sat in the midst of dilapidated tenement buildings on Manhattan's Lower East Side. McCourt located the speaker and nodded. "You talk funny," the student said. "Where ya from?"

"Ireland," McCourt replied. With more than ten years of teaching experience under his belt, this kind of interrogation no longer surprised him. But one question in particular still made him squirm: "Where'd you go to high school?" someone else asked.

If I tell them the truth, they'll feel superior to me, McCourt thought. *They'll throw it in my face.* Most of all, he feared an accusation he'd heard before—from himself: *You come from nothing, so you are nothing.*

But McCourt's heart whispered another possibility: maybe these kids are yearning for a way of figuring out this new teacher. *Am I willing to risk being humiliated in the classroom to find out?* **A**

"Come on, tell us! Where'd you go to high school?"

"I never did," McCourt replied.

"Did you get thrown out?"

I was right, the teacher thought. *They're curious.* McCourt explained he'd left school after the eighth grade to take a job.

"How'd you get to be a teacher, then?" they asked.

"When I came to America," he began, "I dreamed bigger dreams. I loved reading and writing, and teaching was the most exalted profession I could imagine. I was unloading sides of beef down on the docks when I decided enough was enough. By then I'd done a lot of reading on my own, so I persuaded New York University to enroll me."

McCourt wasn't surprised that this story fascinated his students. Theirs wasn't the kind of poverty McCourt had known; they had electricity and food. But he recognized the telltale signs of need in some of his students' threadbare clothes, and sensed the bitter shame and hopelessness he knew all too well. If recounting his own experiences would jolt these kids out of their defeatism so he could teach them something, that's what he would do.

A born storyteller, McCourt drew from a repertoire of accounts about his youth. His students would listen, spellbound by the gritty details, drawn by something more powerful than curiosity. He'd look from face to face, recognizing a bit of himself in each sober gaze.

Connection

Summary at grade level

This biographical article links McCourt's years as a high school English teacher to the writing of his first book, when he was in his sixties. McCourt encouraged his students to "find your own voice and dance your own dance." Before he could take his own advice, however, he had to battle insecurities created by a childhood of poverty and abandonment. His students guided him with their questions and inspired him with the courage and candor of their writing.

DIRECT TEACHING

A Reading Skills

Evaluating credibility. Dimmitt describes McCourt's thoughts. Where might she have found this information? How could you check its accuracy? [Possible responses: She might have found her information by interviewing McCourt, by reading letters he wrote, or by talking with friends in whom he had confided. The information could be checked by asking McCourt or by finding the same information in writings by McCourt.]

Connecting and Comparing Texts

Whereas "Typhoid Fever" offers a glimpse of McCourt's childhood, "The Education of Frank McCourt" provides a look at the adult he became. Dimmitt's essay reveals the strengths McCourt developed, as well as the scars left by his childhood ordeals. McCourt became a creative and compassionate teacher whose sense of humor never left him. He was able to learn from his students as well as to teach them, so that ultimately he could develop the talent underlying the love of language he discovered as a ten-year-old in Limerick's Fever Hospital. In the process of becoming oneself, this essay suggests, does not end when one reaches eighteen or twenty-one, or even fifty or sixty; rather, it is a lifelong process.

Direct Teaching

A Reading Skills

? Expressing an opinion. What do you think of McCourt's teaching methods? [Possible responses: He seems to respect his students' struggles; he tries to reach them at their own level and encourage them to go further; he is too easy on them; he doesn't realize how hard it is to move from speaking to writing.]

B Literary Focus
GRADE-LEVEL STANDARD

? Voice. This article clearly conveys the voice of its subject, Frank McCourt. What sense of the writer, Barbara Sande Dimmitt, do you get? [Possible response: She is a matter-of-fact reporter of information who is sympathetic to McCourt's struggles and admires his achievements.]

Since humor had been the McCourts' weapon against life's miseries in Limerick, he used it to describe those days. "Dinner usually was bread and tea," he told the students. "Mam used to say, 'We've got our balanced diet: a solid and a liquid. What more could we want?'"

The students roared with laughter. . . .

A One day McCourt lugged a tape recorder to class. "We're going to work on writing. Each of you will tell a story into this," he announced. McCourt then transcribed the stories. One boy described the time he was climbing down a fire escape past an open window when an awful smell hit him. "There was a body in the bed," McCourt typed. "The corpse was all juicy and swollen."

McCourt handed back the essay the next day. "See? You're a writer!"

"I was just talking," the boy protested. "I didn't write this."

"Yes, you did. These words came out of your head. They helped me understand something that was important to you. That's what writing's about. Now, learn to do it on paper." The boy's shoulders squared with pride.

The incident reminded McCourt of something that had happened at college. A creative-writing professor had asked him to describe an object from his childhood. McCourt chose the decrepit bed he and his brothers had shared. He wrote of their being scratched by the stiff stuffing protruding from the mattress and of ending up jumbled together in the sagging center with fleas leaping all over their bodies. The professor gave McCourt an A, and asked him to read the essay to the class.

B "No!" McCourt said, recoiling at the thought. But for the first time, he began to see his sordid childhood, with all the miseries, betrayals, and longings that tormented him still, as a worthy topic. *Maybe that's what I was born to put on the page,* he thought.

While teaching, McCourt wrote occasional articles for newspapers and magazines. But his major effort, a memoir of 150 pages that he churned out in 1966, remained unfinished. Now he leafed through his students' transcribed essays. They lacked polish, but somehow they worked in a way his writing didn't. *I'm trying to teach these kids to write,* he thought, *yet I haven't found the secret myself.*

The bell rang in the faculty lounge at Stuyvesant High School in Manhattan. When McCourt began teaching at the prestigious public high school in 1972, he joked that he'd finally made it to paradise. . . .

The bits and pieces that bubbled into his consciousness enlivened the stories he told in class. "Everyone has a story to tell," he said. "Write about what you know with conviction, from the heart. Dig deep," he urged. "Find your own voice and dance your own dance!"

On Fridays the students read their compositions aloud. To draw them out, McCourt would read excerpts from his duffel bag full of notebooks. "You had

202 Chapter 3 Narrator and Voice • Generating Research Questions

such an interesting childhood, Mr. McCourt," they said. "Why don't you write a book?" They threw his own words back at him: "It sounds like there's more to that story; dig deeper. . . ."

McCourt was past fifty and painfully aware of the passage of time. But despite his growing frustration at his unfinished book, he never tired of his students' work.

Over the years some talented writers passed through McCourt's popular classes. Laurie Gwen Shapiro, whose first novel will be published in the spring, was one of them. He decided she was coasting along on her technical skills. "You're capable of much more," McCourt told her. "Try writing something that's meaningful to you for a change."

Near the end of the semester, McCourt laid an essay—graded 100—on Laurie's desk. "If Laurie is willing to read her essay," he announced to the class, "I think we'll all benefit."

Laurie began to read a portrait of love clouded by anger and shame. She told of her father, partially paralyzed, and of resenting his inability to play with her or help her ride a bicycle. The paper shook in her trembling hands, and McCourt understood all too well what it cost her to continue. She also admitted she was embarrassed by her father's limp. The words, McCourt knew, were torn straight from her soul.

When Laurie finished, with tears streaming down her face, the students broke into applause. McCourt looked around the room, his own vision blurred.

These young people have been giving you lessons in courage, he thought. *When will you dare as mightily as they?*

It was October 1994. Frank McCourt, now retired, sat down and read his book's new opening, which he had written a few days before and still found satisfying. But many blank pages lay before him. *What if I never get it right?* he wondered grimly.

He stared at the logs glowing in the fireplace and could almost hear students' voices from years past, some angry, some defeated, others confused and seeking guidance. "It's no good, Mr. McCourt. I don't have what it takes."

Then Frank McCourt, author, heard the steadying tones of Frank McCourt, teacher: *Of course you do. Dig deeper. Find your own voice and dance your own dance.*

He scribbled a few lines. "I'm in a playground on Classon Avenue in Brooklyn with my brother Malachy. He's two, I'm three. We're on the seesaw." In the innocent voice of an unprotected child who could neither comprehend nor control the world around him, Frank McCourt told his tale of poverty and abandonment.

—from *Reader's Digest,* November 1997

DIRECT TEACHING

C Content-Area Connections

Literature: A McCourt Student Laurie Gwen Shapiro's novel *The Unexpected Salami* was published in 1998. Frank McCourt might have been pleased to see one critic's comment that Shapiro's prose "marches along smartly to its own arrhythmic, offbeat beat."

D Reading Skills

? Comparing and contrasting. How would you compare the adult Frank McCourt with the young Frank of "Typhoid Fever"? [Possible responses: Both seem fearful yet determined; both love language; the adult McCourt seems more interested in helping others; the adult McCourt seems more concerned about protecting his privacy, though he finally did write his book.]

INDEPENDENT PRACTICE

Literary Response and Analysis

Reading Check

1. He has typhoid fever; she has diphtheria and "something else."
2. He is moved to another floor as punishment for talking to Patricia.
3. Frankie recovers and gets ready to go home.
4. Patricia dies.
5. Seamus finds someone at the pub to recite the poem, and he memorizes the last two verses and recites them for Frankie.

Interpretations

6. The highwayman's dress indicates a fashion and flair that contrasts sharply with Frankie's world. The poem inspires the children's fantasies.
7. He learns that he can endure much; that literature can be a source of strength; that he loves Shakespeare; that his sense of humor is a boon.
8. McCourt's voice is that of a naive child. He describes events from a child's point of view and presents the narrative in a stream-of-consciousness style with dialect.
9. The tone is matter-of-fact with touches of humor. This tone helps create the voice of an innocent, naive child struggling with difficult circumstances.
10. Patricia's mimicking the nurse; the character of Seamus; Frank's "review" of "The Owl and the Pussycat"; the nurse's urging Frank to "have a good sleep for yourself"; Seamus's wife's comments about "The Highwayman." Possible answers: The blend of comedy and pathos is true to life; the comedy makes these painful events more bearable for readers and perhaps for the writer.
11. Answers will vary; students should support their answers with examples from the selections.

Evaluation

12. Possible answers: The story is not credible, because the nurse and the nun are one-dimensional and their actions seem implausibly cruel, bordering on abuse. Also, it's unlikely that the writer would remember so much dialogue after so many years. The selection is a credible description of a young boy's inner reality. The behavior of the nurse and the nun is credible because children, especially poor children, were treated more cruelly then.

Literary Response and Analysis

Reading Check

1. Why are Frankie and Patricia in the hospital?
2. Why is Frankie moved to another floor?
3. What happens to Frankie in the end?
4. What happens to Patricia?
5. How does Frankie learn the remaining verses of "The Highwayman"?

Interpretations

6. How do the lines from "The Highwayman" contrast with the stark reality of the fever hospital? Why do you think the poem appeals to the two children?
7. What do you think Frankie discovers about himself in the hospital? Be sure to consider the role that language—and, especially, poetry—plays in this story.
8. Frank McCourt repeatedly told his students, "Find your own voice" (see the ***Connection*** on page 201). When McCourt found his voice, his memoirs took off. How would you describe that **voice**? How does he create it?
9. What adjectives would you use to describe the **tone** of this memoir? How does tone help create McCourt's **voice**?
10. The Kerry nurse asks sharply, "What is there to laugh about?" Find two examples of **comic relief** in McCourt's memoir. How do you feel about the use of comedy in such a sad story?
11. Explain why you would—or would not—want Frank McCourt as a writing teacher. Base your answer on what you learn about him in "Typhoid Fever" and in the ***Connection*** on page 201.

Reading Standard 3.9
Explain how voice and the choice of a narrator affect characterization and the tone, plot, and credibility of a text.

Evaluation

12. How credible do you think "Typhoid Fever" is, and how much of it seems like "embroidery"? Support your opinion with examples from the text.

Writing

Putting Us There

Frank McCourt puts us right inside a young boy's head, right in his Fever Hospital bed, right in the midst of a pack of colorful characters. Review the notes you made for the Quickwrite about a childhood memory. In a short **autobiographical incident,** make that memory come alive by answering these questions:

- Who was there?
- What did people say?
- How did you feel?
- Did anything comical happen?

Help the reader enter your scene.

Use "Writing an Autobiographical Narrative," pages 56–63, for help with this assignment.

Listening and Speaking

Live from Limerick!

"Typhoid Fever" is full of interesting characters, each with a unique way of speaking: Frankie, Patricia, Sister Rita, the Kerry nurse, Seamus, even Seamus's wife. It also contains singing and poetry recitations. With a group, plan, practice, and present to the class an **oral reading** of part of "Typhoid Fever." Try to include some of the parts that include lines from "The Highwayman."

204 Chapter 3 Narrator and Voice • Generating Research Questions

Vocabulary Development

Antonyms: Just the Opposite

PRACTICE

An **antonym** is a word that has the opposite or nearly opposite meaning of another word. Choose the best antonym for each word in capital letters. This exercise format will give you practice for taking standardized tests. Remember: You're looking for the best antonym—*not* **synonym** (word with the same meaning).

Word Bank
induced
potent
torrent
clamoring

1. INDUCED
a. persuaded
b. attempted
c. increased
d. discouraged

2. POTENT
a. impossible
b. weak
c. strong
d. safe

3. TORRENT
a. trickle
b. flood
c. law
d. tornado

4. CLAMORING
a. creating
b. whispering
c. opening
d. studying

Reading Standard 1.1 Identify and use the literal meanings of words.

Grammar Link MINI-LESSON

Usage and Style: Creating Voice

To help create the distinctive **voice** of his memoir, McCourt decided not to use standard punctuation and quotation marks. He wanted us to sense that we are overhearing someone's thoughts. He also wanted to represent realistic **dialect,** the characteristic way people talk in different regions. To appreciate the effect, read these passages aloud.

1. "Patricia says she doesn't know what induced means or potent circumstances and she doesn't care about Shakespeare, she has her poetry book and she reads to me from beyond the wall a poem about an owl and a pussycat that went to sea in a green boat with honey and money and it makes no sense and when I say that Patricia gets huffy and says that's the last poem she'll ever read to me."
2. "We gave ye a warning to stop the blathering but ye wouldn't. Take the by, Seamus, take him.
   Ah, now, nurse, sure isn't he harmless. 'Tis only a bit o' poetry."

PRACTICE

Suppose you are a very diligent editor in the publishing house that has accepted McCourt's manuscript. Your job is to "clean up" his writing, to make it conform to accepted usage. Correct the passages on the left. Correct spelling, and punctuate sentences for clarity. Compare your edited manuscripts in class. What has happened to McCourt's voice?

For more help, see Run-on Sentences, pages 454–456, and Quotation Marks, 341–345, in the *Holt Handbook.*

Vocabulary Development

Practice

1. d
2. b
3. a
4. b

Resources Reminder

Vocabulary

- *Vocabulary Development*
  - Vocabulary Worksheet, p. 16
  - Cumulative Vocabulary Review, pp. 17–18
- *Lesson Plans for Language Development*
  - Vocabulary, pp. 96, 102

Grammar Link

Practice

Possible Answers

1. Patricia says she doesn't know what induced means, or potent circumstances, and she doesn't care about Shakespeare. She has her poetry book. From beyond the wall she reads to me a poem about an owl and a pussycat that went to sea in a green boat with honey and money. It makes no sense. When I say that, Patricia gets huffy and says, "That's the last poem I'll ever read to you."
2. "We gave you a warning to stop the talk, but you wouldn't. Take the boy, Seamus. Take him."
   "Ah, now, Nurse, surely he is harmless. It is only a bit of poetry." The "cleaned-up" passages no longer convey McCourt's voice.

ASSESSING

Assessment

- *Progress Assessment of Reading*
  - Selection Test

RETEACHING

For a lesson reteaching Standard 3.9, see **Reteaching,** p. 939A. For another selection to teach Standard 3.9, see *Interactive Reading,* Chapter 3.

STANDARDS FOCUS, pp. 206–210

(For the grade-level standard taught in this lesson, see citations on Student Edition pages.)

Summary *at grade level*

This Discovery Web page explores the history of tuberculosis and describes the workings of the bacterium that causes the disease. Evidence of the disease has been found in stone age skeletons; the current death rate from the disease is put at two to three million people per year. The writer describes the effect of the TB bacterium on the body; she explains how the disease spreads and why it has proved difficult to eradicate. Internal, external, and multimedia links offer additional information.

PRETEACHING

Selection Starter

Build background. Ask students whether they recall having a tuberculosis test during a routine physical exam. Tell them that doctors screen for this disease because it produces few symptoms until later stages. Although it is less prevalent in the United States now than it was in the early years of the twentieth century, when patients were sent to special hospitals for long stays, the disease still kills two to three million people worldwide every year.

Before You Read INFORMATIONAL MATERIALS

An Ancient Enemy Gets Tougher

Researching Information

Once you have thought of several good research questions, it's time to search for answers. Consult as many reliable sources as you can in a library and on the Internet.

In a Library

Here are some useful library resources:

- **Reference materials** include encyclopedias, atlases, almanacs, and biographical sources, such as
  Encyclopaedia Britannica
  The Times Atlas of the World
  The World Almanac and Book of Facts
  Contemporary Authors
- **Other nonfiction books,** such as biographies, autobiographies, and works by experts on history and science, may be found in a library catalog.
- Use the subject index in the *Readers' Guide to Periodical Literature*—a print index—or an online index to find **periodicals,** such as newspaper and magazine articles.
- **Computer databases** may provide access to sources you can't reach on a home computer.

The Internet

Here are some Internet research tips:

- **Use Web sites.** You can go directly to a Web site if you know its URL (uniform resource locator), or address.
- **Use search engines.** If you don't know the address of the Web site you want, use one or more search engines. Enter a **search term,** and the engine will respond with sites having that term. If you get too many or unrelated results, use a more limited search term.
- **Evaluate sources.** Are you reading someone's opinion on a bulletin board, a home page by a high school student, or data from a government agency's site? Learn to evaluate each Web source. Is its creator reliable, expert, and objective? Is the site updated frequently?

Reading Standard 2.3 Generate relevant questions about readings on issues that can be researched.

Using a Web Site

Here are some common Web-site features:

- The **table of contents,** usually located near the top or at the side of a page, lists the site's other pages.
- Highlighted or underlined **links** connect you to other sources of information on your topic. Click on **internal links** to reach other pages in the same Web site. Click on **external links** to go to different Web sites.
- **Multimedia and interactive features** link you to sound and video components and allow you to interact with other users of the Web site.

Connecting to the Literature

In "Typhoid Fever" the narrator recounts his ordeal with typhoid fever. This Web page discusses another terrible disease that has long been a part of human history. It begins with a reference to the biblical tale of David and Goliath. David was a small shepherd boy who defeated the giant Goliath.

RESOURCES: READING

Planning
- *One-Stop Planner* CD-ROM with Test Generator
- *On Course: Mapping Instruction*

Media
- *Audio CD Library*
  - disc 7

Reading
- *Interactive Reading,* Teacher's Edition
  - Graphic Organizer: 5 W's and H Chart

Differentiating Instruction
- *Lesson Plans for Language Development*
  - English-Language Learners, pp. 87, 97, 102
  - Special Education Students, pp. 88, 97, 102

Back Forward Stop Reload Search

Location: http://www.discovery.com/exp/epidemic/tb/tb.html

An Expedition with the American Museum of Natural History

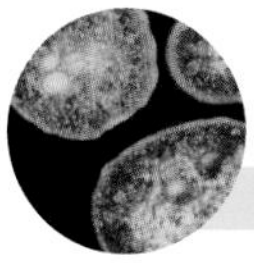

Title of Web page

EPIDEMIC! ON THE TRAIL OF KILLER DISEASES

TB THE DISEASE THAT WON'T GO AWAY

The struggle between critters that cause disease and humans is a long one, and it's unlikely to end any time soon.

An Ancient Enemy Gets Tougher

Karen Watson

Title and author of article

It's easy to think of David and Goliath when faced with the size of the creature that kills more people through disease than any other in the world. It's so small that it's invisible to the eye. Even viewed under a souped-up microscope it doesn't look like much—a tiny, capsule-like thing that could be a sprinkle on a frosted cake.

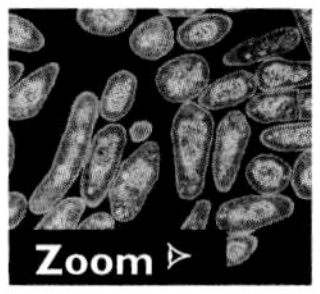

A

Yet the microorganism that causes tuberculosis has felled millions through a terrible wasting of the body—it takes just one bacterium to start what ultimately could become a fatal infection. For thousands of years, this invisible David has been knocking down human Goliaths in shocking numbers.

Stone Age skeletons unearthed in Britain and Germany show tell-tale TB damage. Egyptian tomb portraits include images of hunchbacks curled by spinal TB. Scribes from ancient Hindu, Babylonian, Assyrian, Chinese, Greek, and Roman cultures all describe the signs and symptoms of what in more modern times came to be called "consumption."

lick on **multi-nedia** **nk** for udio or sual fea-ures.

Follow TB's trail through time.

B RealVideo 28.8 (RealPlayer required) | RealVideo 56.6 | Quicktime

In 1908, when the American Museum of Natural History in New York opened its international exhibition on TB, people stood in lines that wrapped around the block to find out more about the disease that devastated families. Nearly 100 years later, as the museum launches a major new exhibition, "Epidemic! The World of Infectious Disease," TB remains a killer. These days, 2 to 3 million people a year die from tuberculosis worldwide, according to the World Health Organization. Someone somewhere is infected every second.

nternal **nks** (in ed) in he text ake you o related ages on he Web ite.

Is the little guy that packs a TB wallop out to get us? Do any of the microscopic critters that cause infectious diseases—the oddball zoo of viruses, bacteria, and protozoa—really want to see us dead?

The **Table of Contents** identifies other diseases covered on this Web site.

- TB
- Flu
- Polio
- Dengue
- Hanta

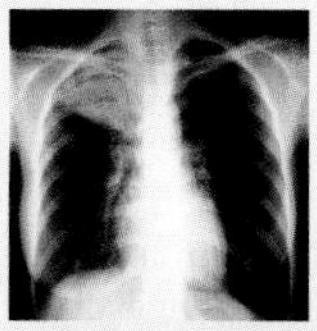

Fight the Invaders

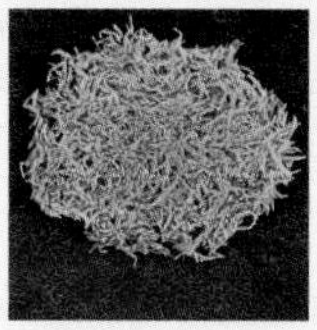

Hidden Enemies

Ask the Experts

Name That Creature

Go Inside a Virus

Tales of a Survivor

Views from Space

Disease Alert!

C

Click on one of these **internal links** on the side to go to a related page on this Web site.

DIRECT TEACHING

A Reading Informational Materials
REVIEW STANDARD

Researching information. If you click on the Zoom label, you will see an enlargement of the photograph and a caption explaining the picture. How would you return to this page? [You can return to this page by clicking on the Back button.]

B Reading Informational Materials
REVIEW STANDARD

Researching information. RealPlayer is software that allows you to access audio and video files. If you click here, your computer will download the software and play the audio or video file.

C Reading Informational Materials
GRADE-LEVEL STANDARD

Generating questions. Clicking on the phrase "Ask the experts" in either one of these places will take you to a page where you can submit your own question to an expert. Although this feature was available only for a limited period after the page was created, later visitors to the site could read the experts' answers to questions that had been submitted. What question would you submit? [Possible response: What are the symptoms of TB?]

Assessment

- *Progress Assessment of Reading*
  - Selection Test
- *One-Stop Planner* CD-ROM with Test Generator

DIRECT TEACHING

A Reading Informational Materials
REVIEW STANDARD

Researching information. When you use a Web site for research, keep a record of the URL, which allows you to return to the site without using a search engine.

Back Forward Stop Reload Search

Location: http://www.discovery.com/exp/epidemic/tb/tb.html **A**

No, say scientists. These inhabitants of a vast microworld are just out to make a living. It just so happens that the living is on us.

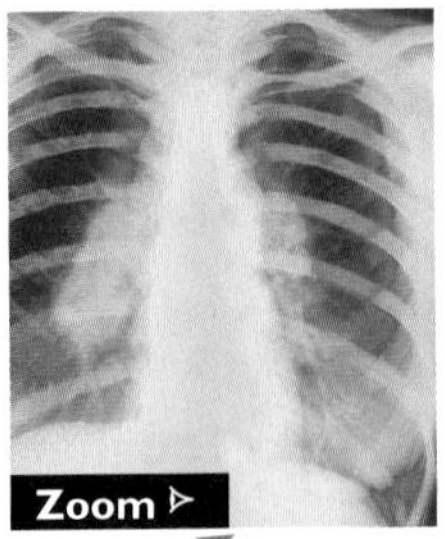

Take the TB "bug." It likes us for some reason, along with a startling collection of other animals. Lions, tigers, sheep, cows, guinea pigs, dogs, and cats are a few. Name it, and it likely gets the disease. Why? For some reason, the TB bacterium actually prefers life inside one of the body's defenders. It makes a living from an immune system cell that normally munches up such invaders.

Click on **zoom** for enlargement of photo and more information.

Ask the experts **about TB and our struggles with it.**

Breathe in an airborne TB bacterium and it typically lands in the lungs. There, immune system cells quickly surround it and wall it off, forming a firm white ball the size of a pinhead. Inside this ball, the bug persists, perhaps for years. Exactly what happens there remains unclear, and most people with the TB bug inside them never experience the disease or become infectious themselves. Their body successfully keeps the invader in check.

But if there's a glitch in the body's defense system, and it doesn't work quite right, these once tiny balls can grow, some to the size of a baseball, as the bacteria inside them reproduce. These balls can erupt, spreading bacteria to other parts of the body through the blood. More balls, or "tubercles," grow, eventually clogging up the way the body does its daily business.

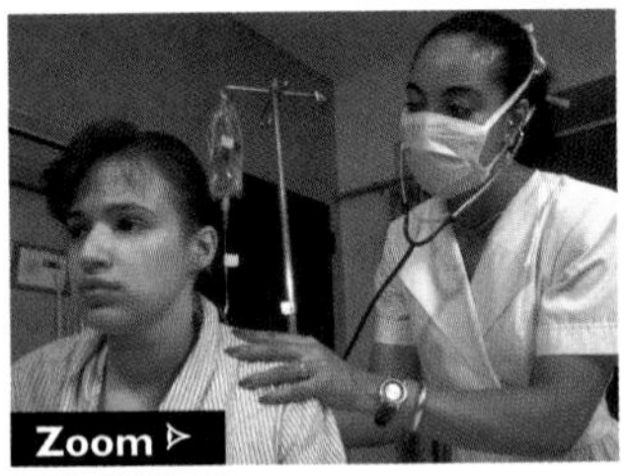

Every time someone sick with TB sneezes or coughs or exhales, they help the bacterium out. "Spreading is survival for the bug," says Dr. Ann Ginsberg, a TB scientist with the National Institute of Allergy and Infectious Diseases.

Hear about how tough **TB is to tackle.**

(RealPlayer required)

So why haven't we figured out a way to knock TB off the planet? The bug that scientists now call *Mycobacterium tuberculosis,* which long ago made a successful jump from living in dirt to living off animals, has turned out to be quite a survivor.

It hides well in humans—nearly 2 billion people are thought to carry the bacterium these days, though they show no signs. When symptoms do pop

DIFFERENTIATING INSTRUCTION

Learners Having Difficulty
If students are confused or distracted by the number of elements on the page, suggest that they skim through the left column and its visuals first and then examine the other elements on the page.

Advanced Learners
Enrichment. Remind students that consulting several sources will help them achieve the best research results.
Activity. Have students find several other print and electronic sources of information about tuberculosis and evaluate the reliability of each source.

208 Chapter 3 Narrator and Voice • Generating Research Questions

Back Forward Stop Reload Search

Location: http://www.discovery.com/exp/epidemic/tb/tb.html

up, they are easily confused with those of other illnesses. The bug lives off lots of other animals besides humans, and it has so far proved to be a tricky adversary when it comes to the creation of an effective vaccine, says Dr. Rick O'Brien, chief of research and development of TB elimination at the Centers for Disease Control and Prevention.

In cities worldwide, though mostly in Africa and East Asia where the disease is most prevalent, TB now has a new ally of sorts in the virus that causes AIDS. It weakens the immune system, giving TB a kick-start.

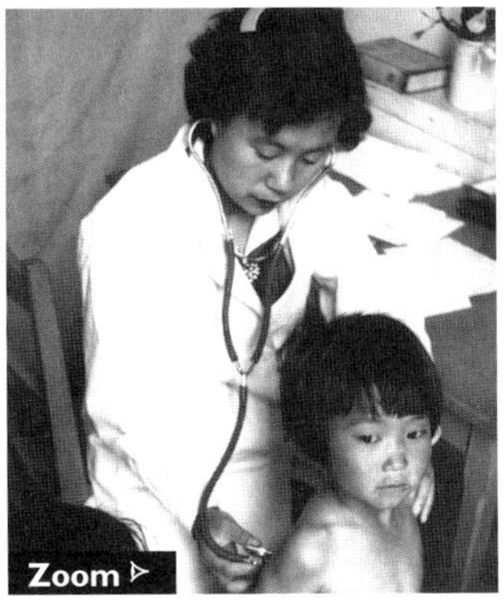

This has doctors and researchers worried, since it creates a double disease-whammy in places where people were just getting a handle on TB. Moreover, those who have the disease must take a special combination of antibiotics for at least six months. If they don't complete their treatment, they risk nurturing new strains of drug-resistant TB.

The deceptively tiny David carries a big bag of survival tricks.

Got a question about TB? Ask the experts.

Find out what happens when a microbe invades your body: Fight the Invaders.

Turn to Disease Alert! for the latest on outbreaks.

EPIDEMIC!

TB Flu Polio Dengue Hanta At the Museum
Disease Alert Tune In

EXPEDITIONS

http://www.discovery.com/exp/epidemic/tb/tb.html **B**

For more about TB:

Centers for Disease Control and Prevention

World Health Organization

National Tuberculosis Center, NJ

National Tuberculosis Center, NY

National Tuberculosis Center, CA

National Institute of Allergy and Infectious Diseases

Click on these **external links** to leave the Web site and go to other Web sites with related information. Phrases such as "For more about . . ." or "Other Sources" often identify these links.

DIRECT TEACHING

B Reading Informational Materials
REVIEW STANDARD

Researching information. This information enables readers to determine how recent the information is and to evaluate the credibility of the source. What indications are there that the source is reliable? [Possible responses: Discovery Communications Inc. is an established business of many years. Content provided by such reputable institutions as the American Museum of Natural History and the Pan American Health Organization should be reliable.]

GUIDED PRACTICE

Monitoring students' progress. Suggest that students make cluster diagrams recording facts about tuberculosis that they learned from this Web site. Then, have them list the main categories they used in their cluster diagrams. [Possible responses: History of TB, TB Today, How Humans Get TB, Why TB Is Hard to Combat.]

INDEPENDENT PRACTICE

Analyzing Informational Materials

Reading Check

1. Stone age skeletons; Egyptian tomb portraits; and ancient texts.
2. Two to three million people die of TB annually. Nearly two billion people may carry the bacterium.
3. When the bacteria lands in the lungs, immune cells wall it off, forming a tiny ball. If the body's defense system doesn't work properly, the balls can spread the bacteria.

Test Practice

Answers and Model Rationales

1. **D** TB is deadly only if the immune system malfunctions.
2. **G** G is the most specific. F, H, and J are too broad.
3. **B** B is the only choice that includes the word *ask*.
4. **G** G is correct because the online library would be up-to-date and very reliable.
5. **A** A health organization would have the most statistics.
6. **J** J is the only answer that specifically refers to a virus.

Application

Students' questions should be specific. Students' should rate scientific, academic, and government sources as the most reliable.

Test-Taking Tips

For more information on how to answer multiple-choice questions, refer students to **Test Smarts.**

Analyzing Informational Materials

Reading Check

1. What evidence do scientists have that tuberculosis is an ancient disease?
2. How widespread is tuberculosis today?
3. What happens when a tuberculosis bacterium enters a human body?

Test Practice

1. If you want to research why TB is still deadly, which of the following questions would be *most* relevant?
   - A What have stone age skeletons revealed about TB?
   - B How many species of animals can contract TB?
   - C Why is TB currently most common in Africa and East Asia?
   - D How does the human immune system function?
2. If you are using a **search engine** to learn about treating TB in domestic cats, which **search term** would probably yield the *best* results?
   - F Tuberculosis
   - G Tuberculosis in cats
   - H Pet care
   - J Preventing tuberculosis
3. Which **link** would you use to ask questions about TB?
   - A Disease Alert!
   - B Ask the Experts
   - C Fight the Invaders
   - D Hidden Enemies
4. Which source would provide the *most* reliable information about the latest methods of treating TB?
   - F An interview with an emergency-room doctor
   - G The online National Library of Medicine of the U.S. National Institutes of Health
   - H A research paper by a high school senior
   - J An article on tuberculosis in an encyclopedia for young readers
5. Which source would have the *most* recent statistics on TB worldwide?
   - A The statistics department of the World Health Organization
   - B A women's health magazine
   - C A book on TB written in 1998
   - D An encyclopedia article on TB
6. To find out about viruses, which **link** would be *most* helpful?
   - F Tales of a Survivor
   - G Views from Space
   - H National Tuberculosis Center, CA
   - J Go Inside a Virus

Reading Standard 2.3 Generate relevant questions about readings on issues that can be researched.

Application

Imagine that you are writing an article on TB or another disease. Write **questions** that focus on one aspect of your topic, and look for answers on the Internet or in a library. Keep a list of the sources you explore, and rate their usefulness.

ASSESSING

Assessment

- *Progress Assessment of Reading*
  - Selection Test

RETEACHING

For another selection to teach Standard 2.3, see *Interactive Reading,* Part 2.

210 Chapter 3 Narrator and Voice • Generating Research Questions

Read On: FOR INDEPENDENT READING

FICTION

Stories with a Twist

Surprise endings and outrageous characters abound in the stories of Saki (H. H. Munro). Two of Saki's best-known protagonists, Reginald and Clovis, are rebellious youths who make fun of polite society with mischievous thoughts and deeds. Their bird's-eye view of everything from far-away lands to their neighbors' parlors can be glimpsed in the stories in ***The Complete Saki.***

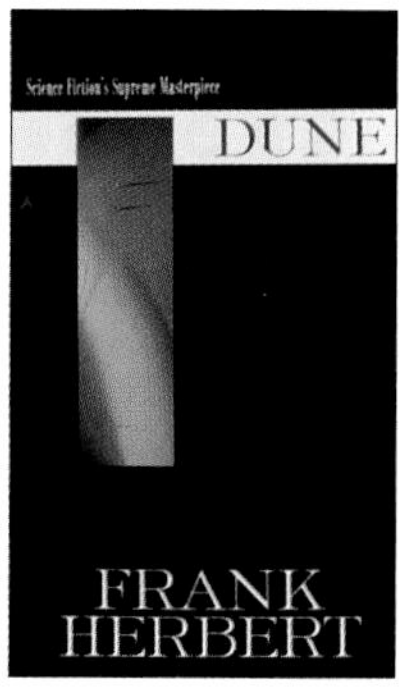

FICTION

Sand, Sand, Everywhere

Frank Herbert's classic science fiction novel ***Dune*** takes place on the strange desert planet Arrakis. There, under the shifting sands, live enormous worms that produce a precious life-sustaining spice valued throughout the universe. The young hero, Paul Atreides, must defend his noble family in a struggle to the death with rivals over control of the spice.

NONFICTION

A Special Friendship

"We understand each other. I let him go wherever he wishes and always he takes me where it is I wish to go." Such is the narrator's description of his faithful donkey, who brings a kind of enchantment to his small Spanish village. Juan Ramón Jiménez, winner of the 1956 Nobel Prize in literature, creates a tribute to friendship and the imagination through the deceptively simple autobiographical prose poems in ***Platero and I.***

NONFICTION

Countdown to Terror

Hiroshima, by the Pulitzer Prize–winner John Hersey, gives us a moment-to-moment look at what happened on August 6, 1945, the day the United States dropped the first atomic bomb on Hiroshima, Japan. In 1946, Hersey visited Hiroshima and interviewed survivors. The product of that visit is this detailed, compelling narrative that takes us into the minds of six people who relied on wits and luck to survive that terrible day.

Toward Reading Two Million Words Annually

Estimated Word Counts and Reading Levels of Read On Books:

Fiction			Nonfiction		
The Complete Saki	at grade level	364,800	*Platero and I**	at grade level	8,000
*Dune**	below grade level	222,600	*Hiroshima**	above grade level	29,700

*California Reading List Titles

KEY: *above grade level* *at grade level* *below grade level*

Read On

For Independent Reading

If students enjoyed the themes and topics explored in this chapter, you might recommend these titles for independent reading.

Assessment Options

The following projects can help you evaluate and assess your students' outside reading. Videotapes or audiotapes of completed projects may be included in students' portfolios.

- **Deliver a comic monologue.** Have students write and present a monologue incorporating the funniest comments made by one of the recurring characters, Clovis or Reginald, in *The Complete Saki.* Encourage students to adopt the character's gestures, tone, and mannerisms.
- **Build a 3-D map.** Suggest that students create a 3-D map of the planet Arrakis, the setting of *Dune,* depicting physical features of the landscape and sites of key events.
- **Create a poster.** Have students design a poster entitled "A Year in Andalusia," based on imagery from *Platero and I.* Encourage students to note details that convey the mood of Platero's village at different times of year. Have them choose the four most evocative images for the poster.
- **Review a review.** Have students find reviews of *Hiroshima.* On its publication in 1946, just a year after the bombing, the book created a sensation. A number of reviews appeared when Hersey died (1993) and on the fiftieth anniversary of the book's publication (1996). Have students evaluate one review and support their opinions with details from *Hiroshima.*

Analyzing Problems and Solutions

Writing Assignment
Writing 2.4 Write an essay in which you analyze a problem and try to persuade your readers to accept the solution you think is best.

Have you ever tried to convince someone that you have a good solution to a common problem? Perhaps you didn't face the kind of dilemma that the pilot does in Tom Godwin's "The Cold Equations." However, like the pilot, you may have found that arguing convincingly first means analyzing the problem before you can explain it to others. To **analyze** a problem, break it into its parts in order to understand it better. Then, present what you believe to be the best solution and try to persuade others to accept your solution.

Prewriting

GO TO: go.hrw.com
KEYWORD: HLLA 10-3
FOR: Professional Model, Writer's Guides, and Reference Sources

Find a Problem to Analyze

Problems, Problems, Problems Solving problems is not an activity reserved for geometry or physics classes. To choose an interesting problem—one that matters both to you and to your readers—read a weekly newsmagazine or watch the national and local news on TV. Browse the Web for information about government and community groups devoted to solving problems, or check the editorials in your local newspaper. Then, make a list of possible topics. Keep in mind that your topic should be one for which you could write a 1,500-word essay.

Consider Purpose and Audience

Best of All Your **purpose** for writing is **expository**—that is, to analyze the problem and the possible solutions. You also want to **persuade** your **audience,** or readers, that the solution you think is best is the one they should adopt. Before you begin your analysis, however, ask yourself, "What does the audience already know about the problem?" and "What **expectations** might my audience have about possible ways to solve this problem?"

Thinking beforehand about how much your audience knows or how your audience might solve the problem may help you sort through the possible solutions. Also, brainstorm any possible objections—or **counterclaims**—that your audience might raise to the solutions you consider. Addressing any **concerns** your audience may have—any **biases** and **misunderstandings**—will later help you convince your audience that your proposed solution is best.

Writing 1.0 The writing demonstrates students' awareness of the audience and purpose. **2.0** Students combine the rhetorical strategies of exposition and persuasion to produce texts of at least 1,500 words each. **2.3** Write expository compositions, including analytical essays. **2.3e** Anticipate and address readers' potential misunderstandings, biases, and expectations. **2.4** Write persuasive compositions. **2.4d** Address readers' concerns, counterclaims, biases, and expectations.

PRETEACHING

Standards Starter

Motivate. Arrange students into three groups and present each group with one of the following hypothetical problems.

- There are traffic jams every afternoon at a traffic light near your school.
- Your dog keeps discovering new ways to escape from the backyard.
- Between your part-time job and extracurricular activities, you have less and less time for homework.

Have group members discuss probable causes of the problem they are assigned and develop three possible solutions. Then, have group spokespeople present their problems and solutions to the class for discussion. Point out to students that analyzing problems and finding solutions is something everyone does in his or her day-to-day life, often without even realizing it.

Resources Reminder

To introduce the workshop, you may want to use the journal starters in *Writing, Listening, & Speaking* Teaching Notes.

DIRECT TEACHING

Consider Purpose and Audience

Remind students that there is more than one form in which to present a problem analysis. Some forms may be more appropriate depending on students' purpose and audience. For example, a brief letter or e-mail to the editor of a newspaper or magazine might be an appropriate form to present a problem and solution to the periodical's readership. If the audience is a teacher, a formal persuasive problem-solution analysis with more than just adequate support is probably the most appropriate form.

CHAPTER 3 RESOURCES: WRITING

Planning

- *On Course: Mapping Instruction*
- *One-Stop Planner* CD-ROM
- *At Home: A Guide to Standards Mastery,* p. 15
- *At Home: In Spanish*
- *Writing, Listening, & Speaking,* Teaching Notes, p. 21

Differentiating Instruction

- *Lesson Plans for Language Development,* pp. 89–90
- *Supporting Instruction in Spanish*

Practice

- *Writing, Listening, & Speaking,* Ch. 3

212 Chapter 3 Narrator and Voice • Generating Research Questions

Investigate the Problem and Solutions

First Things First Before you can persuade others that one solution is the best, you first need to explain the problem. One of the best ways to explain a problem is to provide answers to the *5W-How?* questions as one student did in the following chart.

DO THIS

Problem: Teenagers' poor driving practices	
Who is affected by the problem?	Parents, teenagers, police, insurance companies, doctors, and the general public are affected.
What has already been done about the problem?	Lawmakers may license teenagers in stages, only after a training period of several weeks.
Why is the problem occurring?	Teenagers lack driving experience and are faced with many new distractions on the road.
When did this problem become evident?	The problem has probably been around as long as teenagers have been driving.
Where is this a problem?	It's a national—maybe even worldwide—problem.
How does this problem affect me and my audience?	Bad driving puts everyone at risk.

To find answers to the *5W-How?* questions, do research in the library or on the Internet, or interview someone who is knowledgeable about the problem. If the problem is local, observe it directly. Remember to take careful notes from your sources so that you can convey the information and ideas accurately and coherently.

What Works While you are researching the problem, you should be researching solutions as well. Ask yourself, "What solutions have been suggested or attempted? What were the outcomes of the solutions?" The information you gather through your research should help you decide which solution you think may be the best for the problem.

What Works for You After you've analyzed the problem and gathered information about the possible solutions, look back over your notes. Do you agree with any of the proposed solutions, or do you have another solution to offer for the problem? Look at the following proposed solutions to the problem of teenagers' poor driving records and one student's own solution.

Solution 1: Institute a graduated licensing program. (Disagree)
Solution 2: Raise driving age to eighteen. (Disagree)
My solution: Develop high school driving safety clubs.

TIP As you do research to answer the *5W-How?* questions, record facts and quotations that you can use as **evidence** in your analysis of the problem. Be sure to record the page numbers and source title of direct quotations.

Writing 1.3 Use clear research questions and suitable research methods to elicit and present evidence from primary and secondary sources. **2.3b** Convey information and ideas from primary and secondary sources accurately and coherently.

MODELING AND DEMONSTRATION

Investigate the Problem and Solutions

Lead students through the process of completing a chart on a sample problem such as people who cause accidents because they are talking on cell phones while driving. Many of the answers to the *5W-How?* questions will parallel those in the chart given for "Teenagers' poor driving practices." After you have used students' suggestions to model the chart on the chalkboard, ask for volunteers to demonstrate their own answers to the chart questions for the problems they are considering as topics.

DIRECT TEACHING

First Things First

If students do research on the World Wide Web, you should keep in mind that Internet resources are sometimes public forums, and their content can be unpredictable.

GRADE-LEVEL STANDARD

Investigate the Problem and Solutions

Before students contact potential interview subjects, share the following interview strategies. Students should:

- remember that in an interview they will play two roles, one as listener and one as speaker
- respect the interview subject's opinions
- ask follow-up questions if they do not understand an answer
- monitor the subject's nonverbal communications (posture, facial expressions, and gestures)
- evaluate what the interview subject says

For further interview guidelines, direct students to the chart on pp. 220–221.

Reinforcement

- *Daily Language Activities*

Evaluation and Assessment

- *Test Generator (One-Stop Planner* CD-ROM)
- *Progress Assessment of Writing, Listening, & Speaking,* Ch. 3

Internet

- go.hrw.com (keyword: HLLA 10-3)
- Online assessments at go.hrw.com (keyword: HLLA)

Writing Workshop: Analyzing Problems and Solutions 213

CORRECTING MISCONCEPTIONS

When students write in a formal tone, they may be tempted to write words they do not understand, arranged with a convoluted, overwrought syntax. Tell students that they should use their own words as they write and that the tone of their writing should be formal enough to be taken seriously but not so much that their writing is stuffy, confusing, or dry. It may help students to write with a specific audience member in mind, such as the school principal, a TV anchorperson, or a government representative.

CRITICAL THINKING

REVIEW STANDARD

Students may come into contact with many first-person accounts in their research, ranging from tabloid articles to Web sites. Caution students that they must evaluate which sources are valid. Have students form small groups to create guidelines for "expert testimony" and the reliability of sources. *What makes a source reliable? What makes a source unreliable?* When the groups have finished their lists, have them choose spokespeople to share their guidelines with the class.

PRACTICE & APPLY 1

Guided and Independent Practice

Monitor students' understanding by having each complete an informal outline you may quickly check. Students should write their thesis statements at the top of a blank page, underlining the problem and circling the solution. A numbered list of their supporting points should follow. Then, have students complete **Practice and Apply 1** for independent practice.

Reference Note

For more on **rhetorical devices,** see page 295.

Build an Argument

Supporting Devices Give strong **reasons** to support your choice of solutions. Your reasons may include **rhetorical devices**—logical, emotional, and ethical appeals. **Logical appeals** provide solid reasoning. **Emotional appeals** use language to inspire strong feelings. **Ethical appeals** address the readers' sense of right and wrong and establish the credibility of the writer.

TIP Use evidence to build a persuasive case with **logical reasoning.**

Legs to Stand On To back up your reasons and convince readers to accept your solution, use your collected **evidence** or gather additional evidence. Provide information that is precise and relevant to the point you are making. Here are different kinds of evidence you can use.

Quick guide!

KINDS OF EVIDENCE

Facts are pieces of information that can be proven correct by testing or by consulting reliable sources. **Statistics** are facts expressed with numerical information.

Examples are specific instances of an idea or situation.

Expert opinions are statements by people who are considered experts in their fields. The opinion may include quotations or paraphrases of their ideas.

Anecdotes are brief personal stories that illustrate a point.

Commonly accepted beliefs are those beliefs shared by the writer and audience.

Case studies are examples from scientific studies.

Analogies are comparisons showing the similarities between two unrelated ideas or facts.

Write Your Thesis Statement

Make a Statement Generate a **thesis statement** that makes readers aware of the problem you are discussing and the solution you think is best. For example, one student's thesis statement was "Teens can take action to correct their poor driving practices by forming driving safety clubs."

Writing 2.3a Marshal evidence in support of a thesis and related claims. **2.3c** Make distinctions between the relative value and significance of specific data, facts, and ideas. **2.4a** Structure ideas and arguments in a sustained and logical fashion. **2.4b** Use specific rhetorical devices to support assertions. **2.4c** Clarify and defend positions with precise and relevant evidence, including facts, expert opinions, quotations, and expressions of commonly accepted beliefs and logical reasoning.

Organize Your Analysis

Put Things in Order To present your analysis of the problem and the solution you recommend in a logical progression, use **chronological order:** Tell how the problem has developed over time, what solutions have been proposed, and what the best solution is for the future. Use **order of importance** if you want your most important idea to fall at the end.

PRACTICE & APPLY 1 Follow the instructions on the previous pages to analyze a problem, decide on the solution you think is best, and support your ideas with evidence.

RESOURCES: WRITING

Practice & Apply 1

Guided Practice

- *Writing, Listening, & Speaking,* WS. pp. 22, 23

Reteaching and Modeling

- *Writing, Listening, & Speaking,* TP. 8
- Writing, Listening, & Speaking, WS. p. 24

214 Chapter 3 Narrator and Voice • Generating Research Questions

Writing

Analyzing Problems and Solutions

A Writer's Framework

Introduction

- Catch your audience's attention with an interesting anecdote or example.
- Provide background information if necessary.
- Include a thesis statement that identifies the problem and mentions the solution you think is best.

Body

- Analyze the problem.
- Explain the proposed solutions and present the solution you think is best.
- Use reasons, evidence, and rhetorical devices to support your analysis.
- Address readers' counterclaims.

Conclusion

- Remind readers why your solution is best.
- Issue a call to action for readers to participate in your solution to the problem.
- Restate your thesis in a new and different way.

A Writer's Model

Licensed AND Safe!

Teenagers, has something like this happened to you? You are driving through the neighborhood in your car, talking to your friends and changing the radio station. As you round a corner, a car that you didn't see crashes into you with a terrifying *crunch!* Everyone is okay, but the car is a wreck. While this unfortunate scenario is all too common for teenage drivers, it is a problem that can be solved. Teens can take action to correct their poor driving practices by forming driving safety clubs that increase teens' awareness of driving safety.

INTRODUCTION — Attention-grabbing anecdote; Thesis statement

The problem of poor driving practices is not a new one for teens, nor is it limited to one area of the country. Although national studies show that teenage males may be more prone to accidents involving speed, a large percentage of fatal accidents for teen passengers occur with both male and female teenage drivers. Such a problem puts everyone at risk, affecting parents, teenagers, police, insurance companies, and the general public.

BODY — Analysis of problem; Evidence: Fact

Why is this problem occurring? Of all the factors contributing to teens' poor safety record, a lack of driving experience is probably the leading cause of accidents involving teenagers. Frank Rodriguez, driving instructor for All Right Driving School, says, "A newly licensed driver needs about six more months of regular, non-stress

Further analysis; Evidence: Expert opinion

(continued)

DIFFERENTIATING INSTRUCTION

Advanced Learners

Enrichment. Have students reread the opening paragraph of **A Writer's Model,** noting the way the author changes direction at the end of the first paragraph by moving the reader from complacency to the realization that a problem exists. Remind students that this is an effective way to stimulate an audience and move them to consider possible solutions.

RETEACHING

GRADE-LEVEL STANDARD

A Writer's Model

If students struggle with readability, lead a class discussion on how they can use certain devices to make their essays more readable. Students may notice that the thesis statement of **A Writer's Model** is given in a separate paragraph and not at the end of the first paragraph, as is customary. Furthermore, the reasons supporting the writer's best solution are given together in one paragraph, instead of separately. Point out to students that just as important as an essay's reasoning is its *readability*—the writer's clear subordination of less important points under more important ones, and his or her skillful transitions between ideas. Use **A Writer's Model** to show the ways in which the writer of the model uses different methods such as rhetorical questions and transitional words to guide the reader through the argument.

TECHNOLOGY TIP

Students may notice in **A Writer's Model** the use of italics (line four) and capital letters (title). Point out that students using a word-processing program to prepare their essays can use similar devices to direct their readers' attention. Caution students, however, to use such strategies sparingly in order to avoid wearing out their effect—in **A Writer's Model,** there are only two such examples in the entire essay.

PRACTICE & APPLY 2

Guided and Independent Practice

Monitor students' progress by asking the following questions as they organize their essays.

1. How do you plan to order the main point and the key points within it?
2. Why does that order seem most effective?

Considering such questions will ensure not only that students have experimented with the organization of their essays but also that they have evaluated the different versions effectively.

Then, assign **Practice and Apply 2** for independent practice.

(continued)

Evidence: Statistics	driving to develop confidence and skills." Once licensed, however, teens are often too unfamiliar with the roads and too distracted by conversation, food, music, and cell phones to drive safely. Studies show that half of all teenage drivers have an accident within a year of getting a license, and more than six thousand teenagers die in auto accidents every year.
Solutions already proposed Counterclaims addressed	The solutions offered for this problem vary widely. Many lawmakers are pushing for a graduated licensing program to grant driving privileges over several months. Other lawmakers simply want to raise the driving age to eighteen, an age at which they believe teenagers will be more responsible. However, these solutions don't satisfy the multitude of mature, safe teenage drivers who desire freedom and depend on their cars for transportation to work or school. For those teens, raising the driving age or complicating the licensing requirements is more of a punishment than a solution to a problem.
Best solution Reason, with logical appeal Evidence: Anecdote Reason, with ethical appeal Evidence: Example	Teens can best address the problem of their poor driving practices by forming safe-driving clubs. Such clubs would increase teen drivers' awareness of safe driving practices. When I joined the Safe Driving for Teens Club, I helped print and distribute local street maps and brochures with tips for good driving habits. My club also developed an informative Web page with statistics about teenage driving, suggestions for parental supervision of teen driving, and advice for teens about driving in hazardous conditions. Our Web page received two community-service awards. Establishing safe-driving clubs for teens is also the right thing to do. Clubs like Safe Driving for Teens encourage teens to be safe drivers. More clubs like these should be started in school districts around the nation.
CONCLUSION Importance Emotional appeal Call to action Restatement of thesis	The problem of poor teenage driving practices is a serious one, but it can be reckoned with by the student community. If you don't want to see yourself or a friend hurt in an accident or wait until you're eighteen to drive, join an organization dedicated to increasing and improving teen responsibility on the road. By coming together to share and spread information on responsible driving, we can all work to make our communities safer places to live and drive.

GO TO: go.hrw.com
KEYWORD: HLLA 10-3
FOR: Expanded Writer's Model and Student's Model

PRACTICE & APPLY 2 Use the framework on page 215 and the Writer's Model above as guides to write a first draft of your problem-solution analysis. Remember to investigate your problem and the possible solutions before you build an argument and support it with reasons and evidence.

RESOURCES: WRITING

Practice & Apply 2

Think Sheet

- *Writing, Listening, & Speaking,* WS. p. 25

Template

- *Writing, Listening, & Speaking,* WS. p. 26

Internet

- go.hrw.com (keyword: HLLA 10-3)

216 Chapter 3 Narrator and Voice • Generating Research Questions

Revising

Evaluate and Revise Your Draft

Take a Second Look How do good writers produce such polished work? They revise their drafts—often more than once—to make the final product the best it can be. Use the following guidelines to evaluate and revise the content and organization of your problem-solution analysis. Use the guidelines on page 218 to improve the style of your analysis.

PEER REVIEW

Before you revise, ask a peer to read your paper and to evaluate your use of precise and relevant evidence.

First Reading: Content and Organization Use the chart below to evaluate the content and organization of your analysis. As you answer the evaluation questions, put yourself in your audience's place. Make sure that you have adequately explained the problem and given a sensible solution.

Guidelines: Analyzing Problems and Solutions

Evaluation Questions	Tips	Revision Techniques
1 Does the introduction grab the reader's attention?	**Circle** any attention-grabbing sentence or sentences.	**Add** an attention-grabbing opener—such as an anecdote or example.
2 Does the thesis statement identify the problem and suggest the solution you think best?	**Underline** the thesis statement. **Double underline** the solution you suggest as the best one.	**Reword** your thesis statement to present the problem clearly and to suggest the solution you think best.
3 Does the essay provide a clear and complete analysis of the problem?	**Highlight** the sentences that show the analysis of the problem.	**Elaborate** upon the problem with a complete analysis. **Add** details to make the problem clear.
4 Does the essay address any counterclaims that readers may have?	**Bracket** the sentence that addresses a counterclaim that readers may have.	**Add** a sentence or sentences to address readers' counterclaims.
5 Does the essay present the best solution and provide reasons and evidence to support it?	**Put a star** beside the best solution. **Draw arrow brackets** around the reasons and supporting evidence.	**Add** reasons to support the best solution. **Elaborate** with facts or statistics, an expert opinion, or example.
6 Does the conclusion restate the thesis of the essay? Does it contain a call to action?	**Label in the margin** the sentence that restates the thesis of the essay. **Put a check** beside the call to action.	**Reword** a concluding sentence to restate the thesis. **Add** a call to action.

DIFFERENTIATING INSTRUCTION

English-Language Learners

Students may benefit from working with partners or in small groups when answering the revision questions. You can also discuss the guidelines during individual conferences. Clarify any points that students do not understand, explain what they need to revise, and brainstorm possible revisions with them.

Resources Reminder

For more help with English-Language Learners, see *Lesson Plans for Language Development.*

DIRECT TEACHING

GRADE-LEVEL STANDARD

Elaboration

Point out to students that perhaps their strongest support should address their readers' counterclaims. They may be able to evaluate their success in this area themselves, but peer review is a particularly good time for them to make sure they have responded to their readers' expectations. As students locate additional reasons and evidence to support their proposed solutions, encourage them to use the keyword function on computerized searches, whether in an online library catalog, an online reference source, or a Web site. *You need to be aware that Internet resources are sometimes public forums, and their content may be unpredictable.*

Writing Workshop: Analyzing Problems and Solutions 217

Second Reading: Style When you are sure that you have presented a clear, thorough analysis of the problem and solutions, read your analysis again to concentrate on its style. Your analysis should excite readers and prepare them for action. Nothing will make readers tune out faster than **clichés**—tired, overused expressions, such as "the real thing" or "make a difference." Use the following guidelines to eliminate clichés from your essay.

Style Guidelines

Evaluation Question	Tip	Revision Technique
Does the essay include clichés?	**Draw a wavy line** under any phrases that sound familiar. Revise any underlined phrases.	**Replace** clichés with straightforward or original language.

ANALYZING THE REVISION PROCESS

Study these revisions, and answer the questions that follow.

replace — Teens can ~~take matters into their own hands~~ *best address the problem of their poor driving practices* by forming safe-

add — driving clubs. Such clubs would increase teen drivers' awareness *of safe driving practices.*

elaborate — *When* I joined the Safe Driving for Teens Club, *I helped print and distribute local street maps and brochures with tips for good driving habits.*

Responding to the Revision Process

1. How did replacing the cliché improve the first sentence?
2. Why do you think the writer added information after the second sentence?
3. How did the additions to the last sentence strengthen the evidence the writer used?

Writing 1.9 Revise writing to improve the logic and coherence of the organization and controlling perspective and the precision of word choice by taking into consideration the audience, purpose, and formality of the context.

PRACTICE & APPLY 3 Use the guidelines in this section to revise the content, organization, and style of your analysis of a problem and its solution. Make sure that you have included reasons, evidence, and rhetorical devices. Remember also to read through your paper and eliminate any clichés you may find.

GUIDED PRACTICE

Responding to the Revision Process

Answers

1. Replacing the cliché makes the sentence more specific and informative.
2. The addition helps describe the proposed solution.
3. The elaboration gives an example of a solution.

PRACTICE & APPLY 3

Independent Practice

Before students revise, ask them to

- describe in their journals the revisions they need to make;
- examine the peer-review comments and determine whether the intended audience is clear. If not, students should revise their essays to address the audience more accurately.

Then, assign **Practice and Apply 3** for independent practice.

218 Chapter 3 Narrator and Voice • Generating Research Questions

Publishing

Proofread and Publish Your Analysis

A Real Fixer-Upper If you want to be taken seriously, your analysis must be as error-free as possible. Set your analysis aside for a day or two so that you can look at it again with fresh eyes. Then, proofread it thoroughly and eliminate mistakes in grammar, usage, and mechanics.

Put the Gears in Motion Your analysis cannot help solve the problem unless you share it with others. Try one or more of the following ideas to find an audience for your analysis.

- Create a "problem bank." Gather copies of your class's problem-solution analyses, put them into a binder, and ask your school librarian to place the binder in the library for use as a problem bank. Other students at your school who are interested in problem solving and analyzing problems can use the problem bank as a resource.
- Schedule a debate. If your school has a debate team, share your essay with the debate coach, and ask him or her to consider using your problem as the topic for a schoolwide debate. This may help generate solutions that you may not have considered.
- Form a task force if your problem is school related. Does your problem directly affect students at your school? Is it something the students may be able to solve? If so, submit your analysis of a problem to your school newspaper and, with the school administration's permission, invite students, teachers, and parents to form a task force to put the solution you analyze into action.

TIP As you read your analysis, make sure that your sentences follow the **conventions** of American English. For example, avoid sentence fragments—groups of words that are not sentences. Take note of each sentence, and ask yourself, "Does the sentence have a subject? Does it have a verb? Does it express a complete thought?" For more information on **sentence fragments,** see page 446 in the *Holt Handbook*.

Reflect on Your Analysis

Look Back After you have completed your analysis, take a moment to answer the following questions and find out what you have learned from this writing experience.

- What new ideas or information did you discover about the problem you researched?
- What kind of evidence did you find most helpful in writing your problem-solution essay? Explain your response.

PRACTICE & APPLY 4 Use the instruction on this page to proofread your analysis, share it with a wider audience, and reflect on what you have learned. Keep track of any responses you get from your audience about your essay.

Resources Reminder

For help with writing assessment, see 6 Traits—Plus 1 in the "Scales and Sample Papers" section of *Progress Assessment of Writing, Listening, & Speaking.*

PRACTICE & APPLY 4

Guided and Independent Practice

To help students understand how to use the reflective questions as a self-check, model on the chalkboard possible answers to the **Look Back** questions. Then, ask students to submit their reflections with the final copies of their essays.

RESOURCES: WRITING

Practice & Apply 3

Think Sheet

- *Writing, Listening, & Speaking,* WS. p. 28

Evaluation

- *Writing, Listening, & Speaking,* WS. p. 27

Practice & Apply 4

Assessment

- *Test Generator* (*One-Stop Planner* CD-ROM)
- *Progress Assessment of Writing, Listening, & Speaking,* pp. 9–11, 56–58

Internet

- Online assessments at go.hrw.com (keyword: HLLA)

PRETEACHING

Motivate. Ask students if they know someone who is a good persuasive speaker—either a friend or family member or a politician or public figure who speaks very convincingly. Ask volunteers to share with the class their examples of convincing speakers and to identify the qualities these people have in common. You might suggest to students that while some qualities may be outwardly apparent, such as the speaker's confidence, the preparation and hard work that have led to that confidence may not be obvious but are nevertheless important.

DIFFERENTIATING INSTRUCTION

Learners Having Difficulty

Provide students with the following tips to help them make their persuasive speeches interesting and successful.

- **Be enthusiastic.** If you show interest, your audience most likely will, too.
- **Know your speech well.** Plan where to add emphasis or to refer to a visual.
- **Speak from notes,** not from memory or from a script.
- **Maintain eye contact** to keep your listeners involved.
- **Speak with feeling,** and vary your rate of speaking, volume, and pitch.

Allow students time to practice using the tips in small groups.

TECHNOLOGY TIP

If the equipment is available, have students compose their speeches on computers and make visuals they can either print as overhead transparencies or display on a projected computer screen. The visuals will help students create more professional presentations.

Giving a Persuasive Speech

Speaking Assignment

Listening and Speaking 2.5 Adapt a written analysis into a formal persuasive speech that addresses a problem and presents a solution.

Do you remember the last public speech you heard? Chances are it was a persuasive speech that presented the speaker's solution to a common problem. Public officials—from city mayors right up to the President—and professionals in business usually take great care in crafting speeches that will convince their audiences to agree on an action or unite behind a common belief or cause. You can convince an audience, too, by adapting the problem-solution analysis you have just completed into a persuasive speech.

Adapt Your Written Analysis

Make a Statement Your **purpose** in giving a persuasive speech is to point out a particular problem and to convince an **audience** that you have the best solution for it. To help you begin adapting your problem-solution analysis, follow these suggestions.

- Rewrite your thesis, if necessary, to make clear for your listeners your opinion about the problem and the solution you propose as the best. (The thesis of a persuasive speech is an **assertion**—a statement that identifies the issue and expresses your opinion about it.)
- Read your analysis aloud and time yourself. Add or subtract information to clarify your assertion and to remain within the time limit. Simplify the explanations of the problem and solutions, if necessary.
- If you find that you need more information, gather more details through research or interviews. By interviewing others, you may gain additional **reasons** and **evidence** to support your proposed solutions, or you may learn of other **concerns** and **counterarguments** your listeners will have. The following chart provides guidelines for conducting interviews.

TIP Reasons may include rhetorical devices—logical, ethical, or emotional appeals. For more on **evidence** and **rhetorical devices,** see pages 214 and 295.

Listening and Speaking 1.6 Present and advance a clear thesis statement and choose appropriate types of proof. **2.3** Apply appropriate interviewing techniques. **2.5** Deliver persuasive arguments. **2.5b** Use rhetorical devices to support assertions. **2.5c** Clarify and defend positions with precise and relevant evidence. **2.5d** Anticipate and address the listener's concerns and counterarguments.

Quick guide

GUIDELINES FOR CONDUCTING INTERVIEWS

Before the interview

- Select a reliable source for your interview and set up a time that is convenient for the other person to meet you.
- Make a list of questions to ask. Make sure the questions are arranged in a logical order and require more than yes or no answers.

(continued)

CHAPTER 3 RESOURCES: LISTENING & SPEAKING

Planning
- *On Course: Mapping Instruction*
- *One-Stop Planner* CD-ROM
- *Writing, Listening, & Speaking*
  - —Teaching Notes, p. 29
  - —Project-Planning Guide, WS. p. 31

Think Sheet
- *Writing, Listening, & Speaking,* WS. p. 32

Differentiating Instruction
- *Lesson Plans for Language Development,* p. 91
- *Supporting Instruction in Spanish*

220 Chapter 3 Narrator and Voice • Generating Research Questions

(continued)

During the interview

- Arrive on time. Ask the other person's permission to use a tape recorder or a video recorder. Also, be ready to take handwritten notes of responses.
- Listen carefully. Be respectful and sensitive if you ask follow-up questions. Respond politely and effectively if the interviewee asks you a question to show that you have knowledge of the subject.

After the interview

- Review your notes and write a summary of the material you have gathered.
- Send a note expressing your appreciation for the interview.
- Evaluate the effectiveness of your interview: What would you change?

Save the Best for Last As in your written analysis, the order of your speech should be coherent and logical. Begin with your thesis statement so that your audience is aware of your opinion. Then, provide background information and present the best solution with the reasons and evidence that show why this solution is the best. Arrange the reasons in **order of importance,** presenting the strongest reason last. End your speech with a call to action.

Rehearse and Deliver Your Speech

Speak Up, Speak Out For a formal presentation, memorize and then deliver your speech. Use only brief notes to help you. To help you gain confidence and to learn effective delivery techniques, rehearse your speech in front of a mirror or a few friends to help you maintain eye contact as you speak. Practice speaking loudly, slowly, and expressively enough to make your arguments clear even to listeners at the back of the room. Use standard American English for your formal presentation.

Ask for a Response After you deliver your speech, ask for feedback on your content and delivery techniques. Have your classmates answer questions such as, "What concerns or counter-arguments did you have that the speaker did not address?" or "What was especially effective in the speaker's delivery and why?" Evaluate the responses to your questions so that you can make adjustments the next time you deliver a speech.

PRACTICE & APPLY 5 Plan and practice giving a formal persuasive speech by adapting your problem-solution analysis. Deliver the speech in front of an audience and ask for feedback to help your future presentations.

Listening and Speaking 1.3 Choose logical patterns of organization to persuade, by soliciting agreement or action, or to unite audiences behind a common belief or cause. **2.0** Students deliver polished formal presentations that combine the traditional rhetorical strategies of exposition and persuasion. **2.3a** Prepare and ask relevant questions. **2.3b** Make notes of responses. **2.3c** Use language that conveys maturity, sensitivity, and respect. **2.3d** Respond correctly and effectively to questions. **2.3e** Demonstrate knowledge of the subject or organization. **2.3f** Compile and report responses. **2.3g** Evaluate the effectiveness of the interview. **2.5a** Structure ideas and arguments in a coherent, logical fashion.

Evaluation and Assessment

- *Writing, Listening, & Speaking,* WS. p. 33
- *Progress Assessment of Writing, Listening, & Speaking,* p. 59
- *Diagnostic and Summative Assessments,* First-Quarter Test

Extension

- *Writing, Listening, & Speaking,* Videocassette Segment 2
- *Writing, Listening, & Speaking,* WS. p. 34

Internet

- go.hrw.com (keyword: HLLA)

DIRECT TEACHING

GRADE-LEVEL STANDARD

Save the Best for Last

Provide students with the following outline for organizing their problem-solution speeches.

Analyzing Problems and Solutions
I. Introduction: State the thesis.
II. Body A. Present evidence of the problem. B. Present the solution. C. Present counterarguments.
III. Conclusion: Give a call to action.

RETEACHING

If students have trouble gaining confidence about speaking in front of an audience, you may want to ask students to express their fears about public speaking and then brainstorm with students ways in which they can react to such problems. Sharing their fears can help students be more comfortable speaking in public, and discussing the strategies in advance can also give them some peace of mind.

PRACTICE & APPLY 5

Guided and Independent Practice

Monitor students' understanding by reviewing with them the guidelines in the chart on this page. Have students discuss the elements of each in detail, and make sure every student takes part in the discussion. Then, assign **Practice and Apply 5** for independent practice.

Standards Review

Analyzing Informational Materials

STANDARDS FOCUS, pp. 222–225

(For the grade-level standard reviewed in this lesson, see Student Edition, p. 222.)

INTRODUCING THE STANDARDS REVIEW

Use this review to assess students' ability to generate research questions that are relevant to their reading.

DIRECT TEACHING

A Analyzing Informational Materials
GRADE-LEVEL STANDARD

? Generating relevant research questions. What questions could you ask to learn more about the space station? [Possible responses: Which sixteen nations helped to build it? How was it built? Who paid for it? What are the advantages of conducting experiments in space?]

Analyzing Informational Materials

Test Practice

Generating Research Questions

DIRECTIONS: Read the following article. Then, read each multiple-choice question that follows, and write the letter of the best response.

Local Hands on a New Space Project

Seema Mehta

Crystal capsules prepared by UC Irvine[1] scientist Alexander McPherson and schoolchildren across the United States are scheduled to be launched into space this morning on the shuttle *Atlantis,* destined for the International Space Station, a gigantic laboratory taking shape about 200 miles above earth. **A**

The station is a 16-nation effort led by the U.S. that should be completed in 2005. The finished lab, which will house scientists, should be as big as a football field and would weigh 1 million pounds on the ground.

Students helping with experiments for the International Space Station prepared solutions to grow crystals like the ones pictured here.

The growing of protein crystals is the first experiment aboard the massive lab. Protein crystals, used for new HIV inhibitors, cancer drugs, nonpolluting laundry detergent, and more, grow better in the low-gravity environment of space.

Pages 222–225 cover **Reading Standard 2.3** Generate relevant questions about readings on issues that can be researched.

1. **UC Irvine:** University of California campus at Irvine.

READING MINI-LESSON

Reviewing Word-Attack Skills

Activity. Display the following words. Have students group them into two categories: words with a long e sound and words with a long *i* sound. Ask students to underline the letters that represent the long vowel sound in each word.

retrieve [e] seize [e] siege [e]
diesel [e] belie [i] belief [e]
feisty [i] fiend [e] poltergeist [i]
fief [e] grievance [e] leisure [e]

Activity. Display these words. Have students underline the letter or letters that represent the *ch* sound in each word. Answers are underlined.

1. architecture
2. cultural
3. maturation
4. unfortunate

High school students working with solutions at NASA's Marshall Space Flight Center in Huntsville, Alabama. Their samples will be carried by the space shuttle *Atlantis* for experiments on the International Space Station.

About 150 of the 500 crystal samples being sent up were made by students in California, Alabama, Florida, and Tennessee. A total of 87 California students and teachers participated, most in Los Angeles and Orange counties.

"Our intention is not just to use the space station as a lab, but as a scientific classroom for the United States," McPherson said.

McPherson said student participation is a key element, because today's students are tomorrow's scientists. He traces his own interest in science to his youth.

5. lecture
6. intellectual
7. situation
8. perpetuate
9. recapitulate
10. picturesque
11. caricature
12. instinctual

Activity. Display these word pairs. Have students identify the word with a silent *h* in each pair. Answers are underlined.

1.	exhort	cohort
2.	prohibit	exhibit
3.	exhilarate	hilarity
4.	inherit	heir
5.	disheveled	dishonored
6.	hickory	vehicle
7.	vehement	hemoglobin
8.	exhaust	exhale

Standards Review

DIRECT TEACHING

A Analyzing Informational Materials
GRADE-LEVEL STANDARD

Generating relevant research questions. What ideas for a limited research topic do this subhead and the following two paragraphs suggest? [Possible responses: What statistics exist to prove that students aren't going into math and science? How has the ISS project affected participating students' attitudes toward science?]

B Analyzing Informational Materials
GRADE-LEVEL STANDARD

Generating relevant research questions. What questions can you think of about possible applications of NASA's protein crystal projects? [Possible responses: How are protein crystals used to study genetic defects? What information from the crystals can be used in making medicines, insecticides, herbicides, and detergents?]

C Analyzing Informational Materials
GRADE-LEVEL STANDARD

Generating relevant research questions. If you could e-mail Alexander McPherson, what questions would you ask him about his work? [Sample responses: How did you get involved with the space station and with planning for students' participation in space experiments? How can my school get involved?]

Test-Taking Tips

For instruction on answering multiple-choice items, refer students to **Test Smarts.**

A Mission to Excite Kids About Science

A "Since I grew up in Orlando, I saw all the early missions. I've been following the space program since Alan Shepard went up in the early 1960s," he said.

But today, "the students are simply not going into science and mathematics—they think it's too hard or intimidating or not interesting," he said. "We're trying to turn that around. Science is the most interesting thing in the world."

Researchers and the students, working under McPherson's direction, sealed chemicals into small tubes that were then frozen to minus 320 degrees Fahrenheit. Scientists placed the samples into thermoslike containers that are kept cool with liquid nitrogen. Once in orbit, the nitrogen naturally boils off, thawing the samples and allowing the protein crystals to begin growing, according to the National Aeronautics and Space Administration.

The crystals will remain in orbit until October, when they will be retrieved by another manned space shuttle.

Once the crystals are brought back to earth, scientists will use X-rays to deduce the detailed atomic structure of the molecules.

B Such studies have significant implications for humans because information gathered from the crystals can ultimately be used for manufacturing pharmaceuticals[2] and to learn more about human ailments such as genetic defects.[3]

C "Those protein molecules are extremely important because they are the major biochemical element of all living tissue," said McPherson, who has been involved with NASA protein crystal projects since 1984. He received the agency's Exceptional Scientific Achievement Medal in 1999. "We can use our knowledge of those to design new drugs."

The information also has applications in the manufacturing of insecticides,[4] herbicides,[5] and industrial products, such as laundry detergents that use enzymes.[6]

—from the *Los Angeles Times,* September 8, 2000

2. **pharmaceuticals** (fär′mə•so͞ot′i•kəls) *n.:* medicines.
3. **genetic defects:** disorders carried in the body's genes that can be passed from parent to child.
4. **insecticides** (in•sek′tə•sīdz′) *n.:* substances used to kill insects.
5. **herbicides** (hur′bə•sīdz′) *n.:* substances used to destroy plants, especially weeds.
6. **enzymes** (en′zīmz′) *n.:* here, synthetic proteins used to create kinds of chemical reactions.

Using Academic Language

Review of Literary Terms
Reading Standard 3.9

Ask students to look back through the chapter to find the meanings of the terms listed at right. Then, have students show their grasp of Standard 3.9 by citing passages from the chapter that illustrate the meanings of those terms.

Point of View (p. 138); **Omniscient Narrator** (pp. 138, 154); **First-Person Point of View** (pp. 138, 140); **Third-Person-Limited Point of View** (pp. 138, 163); **Credibility** (pp. 138, 193); **Voice** (pp. 139, 193); **Tone** (p. 139).

1. Which research question is *most* relevant to the information in the article?
   - **A** What have scientists deduced about the atomic structure of the molecules of a protein crystal?
   - **B** What techniques do master teachers use to make science and math more appealing to high school students?
   - **C** What is the history of the U.S. space program?
   - **D** Who is Alan Shepard?

2. Which research question would probably yield the *most* relevant information about future experiments planned for the ISS?
   - **F** What is the likelihood of future experimentation in space?
   - **G** How profitable is experimentation on the ISS?
   - **H** What do scientists hope to learn from space experiments?
   - **J** What are the research plans for the ISS for the next two years?

3. Which of the following research questions about protein crystals is the *most* narrow and focused?
   - **A** Why are protein crystals important?
   - **B** What are the results of some recent experiments in space?
   - **C** How will the information gained from protein-crystal research be used practically?
   - **D** What are the different types of crystals, and how does each grow?

4. If you were using a search engine on the Internet to try to find out more about the research experiment described in this article, which search term would probably be *most* helpful?
   - **F** UC Irvine
   - **G** Space science
   - **H** International Space Station
   - **J** Exceptional Scientific Achievement Medal

5. To find out the design of the ISS (what it looks like), which resource would be the *most* helpful?
   - **A** A recent magazine article about experiments aboard the ISS
   - **B** The ISS NASA-sponsored Web site
   - **C** An encyclopedia article about Alexander McPherson
   - **D** A book about the history of the U.S. space program published in 1997

6. For conducting further Internet research on the ISS, which kind of Web site would probably provide the *most* reliable source of information?
   - **F** A government-agency site on the U.S. space program
   - **G** A former astronaut's personal Web site
   - **H** The Web site of a graduate student in molecular science, the subject of which is growing crystals in space
   - **J** A popular author's Web site, the subject of which is space exploration and experiments in space

TestPractice

Answers and Model Rationales

1. **B** The article's title and subhead show that it focuses on student participation in the crystal project and on stimulating students' interest in science; B is most relevant to this focus.
2. **J** F and H are too general; they do not refer to the ISS. G refers to the ISS, but focuses on profits rather than research plans. Only J focuses on plans for experiments on the ISS.
3. **C** A, B, and D are all broad. B does not mention protein crystals and is weakened by the vague phrase "some recent." D mentions crystals but not specifically protein crystals. A mentions protein crystals but is still less focused than C, which zeroes in on an aspect of protein crystal research relevant to the article.
4. **J** Search engines work best with fairly narrow terms. *Space science* (G) is far too broad, as are *UC Irvine* (F) and *International Space Station* (H). *Exceptional Scientific Achievement Medal* (J) is the narrowest and would most quickly lead to further information under the keyword *Alexander McPherson.*
5. **B** A focuses on ISS experiments, not on the design of the ISS. C focuses on a person, not on the ISS. D is not recent enough to include information about the ISS. Therefore, B is correct.
6. **F** Of the four choices, only F is likely to have information about ISS that is up-to-date, authoritative, and unbiased and therefore reliable.

Review of Informational Terms
Reading Standard 2.3

Ask students to look back through the chapter to find the meanings of the terms listed below. Then, ask students to use those terms to explain how to identify research resources. **Reference Materials** (p. 206); **Periodicals** (p. 206); **Computer Databases** (p. 206); **Search Engine** (p. 206); **Links** (p. 206).

ASSESSING

Assessment

- *Progress Assessment of Reading*
  - Chapter Test
- *Diagnostic and Summative Assessments*
  - First-Quarter Test

Test Practice

Vocabulary Development

Synonyms

Modeling. Model the thought process of a good reader arriving at the answer to 1. Tell students, "*Conviction* means 'strong belief.' Even though *annoyance, skill,* and *disapproval* make sense in the sentence, they don't mean 'strong belief,' so B, C, and D are incorrect. Since *certainty* can mean 'strong belief,' A is correct."

Test Practice

Answers and Model Rationales

1. **A** See rationale above.
2. **G** *Petulant* means "rude" or "quarrelsome." Only G is close in meaning to these words.
3. **D** *Resolute* means "having a fixed purpose," which is consistent only with *determined* (D).
4. **J** *Paramount* means "above all others." F, *little,* is nearly the opposite in meaning. G and H are not close in meaning to *paramount.* Only *supreme* (J) is close in meaning.
5. **C** *Irrevocable* means "impossible to change." A and B are unrelated. D is an antonym. Only C, *irreversible,* is close in meaning.
6. **G** *Annihilate* means "reduce to nothing," which is close in meaning to G, *destroy.*
7. **A** *Immutable* means "incapable of changing." Only *unchanging* (A) is close in meaning.
8. **G** *Induced* means "led by persuasion or influence," so G is correct.
9. **A** Though some find Shakespeare's poetry *difficult* (C), *pleasing* (D), or *harsh* (B), these words do not have the same meaning as *potent,* "having force or influence."

TEST PRACTICE

Vocabulary Development

Test Practice

Synonyms

DIRECTIONS: Choose the best synonym for the underlined word in each sentence.

1. In "The Storyteller" the little girl criticizes the aunt's story with great <u>conviction</u>.
   - A certainty
   - B annoyance
   - C disapproval
   - D skill

2. The children's questions are loud and <u>petulant</u>.
   - F intelligent
   - G ill-tempered
   - H repetitive
   - J comical

3. The smaller girl keeps repeating the line of poetry over and over in a stubborn and <u>resolute</u> way.
   - A creative
   - B dreamy
   - C ridiculous
   - D determined

4. In "The Cold Equations" the stowaway's weight is of <u>paramount</u> importance.
   - F little
   - G relative
   - H usual
   - J supreme

5. The laws of nature are <u>irrevocable</u>.
   - A complicated
   - B universal
   - C irreversible
   - D changeable

6. A tornado threatened to <u>annihilate</u> the Group One camp on Woden.
   - F strike
   - G destroy
   - H close
   - J rearrange

7. An example of an <u>immutable</u> natural law is the force of gravity, which pulls toward the earth's center.
   - A unchanging
   - B powerful
   - C unfamiliar
   - D unproven

8. The first lines from Shakespeare that young Frank reads are, "I do believe, <u>induced</u> by potent circumstances, / That thou art mine enemy."
   - F overcome
   - G persuaded
   - H defeated
   - J upset

9. Frankie finds Shakespeare's poetry very <u>potent</u>.
   - A powerful
   - B harsh
   - C difficult
   - D pleasing

226 Chapter 3 Narrator and Voice • Generating Research Questions

Vocabulary Review

Use this activity to determine whether students have retained the chapter Vocabulary. Ask students to complete each of the analogies below with a Vocabulary word from the box.

mutiny	deplorably	impoverished
torrent	ponderous	

1. poor : ______ :: busy : industrious [impoverished]
2. gale : breeze :: ______ : trickle [torrent]
3. ______ : admirably :: slowly : quickly [deplorably]
4. bright : radiant :: weighty : ______ [ponderous]
5. renegades : ______ :: musicians : concert [mutiny]

Writing

Test Practice

DIRECTIONS: Read the following paragraph from a draft of a student's problem-solution analysis. Then, read the questions below it. Choose the best answer to each question.

(1) Asthma is a chronic lung disease that causes episodes of coughing, wheezing, and shortness of breath. (2) It can be triggered by allergens such as pollen and mold, and for that reason many doctors have recommended staying inside to prevent lung irritation. (3) By performing specific exercises to strengthen your lungs, you can manage asthma attacks and be able to live a more active life as well. (4) Asthma can be a pain in the neck, but it doesn't have to control your life.

1. To support the ideas in sentence 3, the writer could
   - **A** provide an expert opinion on why air-cleaning devices are important
   - **B** describe the other environmental factors that lead to asthma attacks
   - **C** relate in detail the precise breathing activity that should be performed
   - **D** include facts that prove the effectiveness of breathing exercises

2. Which sentence, if added, would express an emotional appeal that would support the thesis?
   - **F** Don't let asthma attack your social life—exercise and fight back!
   - **G** Some of the U.S. athletes in the 1996 Olympics may have had asthma.
   - **H** Stay inside to avoid the perilous allergens that assault your lungs.
   - **J** Because of sports-induced asthma, I can't play basketball anymore.

3. To address a reader's concern that exercising with asthma could be dangerous, the writer could
   - **A** provide an expert opinion stating that exercising with asthma is helpful
   - **B** tell readers to do more research on the topic
   - **C** tell readers that they shouldn't be concerned if they don't have asthma
   - **D** provide a list of professional athletes from all sports

4. Which of the sentences below would best replace sentence 4 in order to eliminate the use of clichés?
   - **F** Asthma can be a serious disease, but not as bad as other diseases.
   - **G** Asthma can be a serious disease, but it doesn't have to conquer you.
   - **H** Asthma can be a serious disease, and there's nothing you can do about it.
   - **J** Asthma can be a serious disease, but exercising can put you on cloud nine.

5. What might the student do to adapt the analysis into a persuasive speech?
   - **A** cut the introduction to save time
   - **B** read directly from note cards
   - **C** provide additional information that relates to the audience
   - **D** make arguments more complex so as to impress the audience

Standards Review

Answers

1. **D**
2. **F**
3. **A**
4. **G**
5. **C**

APPLICATION

Letter to the Editor

Have students work at home to adapt their analyses into a letter to the editor of a local or school newspaper. (They can also use the skills they have honed in this workshop to write a letter on a new topic.) Point out to students that their letters will necessarily be shorter than their essays and thus should include only their strongest reasons and appeals. Students can look on the editorial pages of the newspapers for examples their letters should follow.

Homework

EXTENSION

Analyze a Literary Character's Problems

For homework, ask students to analyze the problems of a favorite literary character. Have students make a chart in which they describe the character's basic situation, the conflict, any complications, the climax, and the resolution. Then, have volunteers present their findings to the class in a brief oral presentation.

Homework

RESOURCES: WRITING, LISTENING, & SPEAKING

Assessment

- *Test Generator (One-Stop Planner* CD-ROM)
- *Progress Assessment of Writing, Listening, & Speaking,* Ch. 3
- *Diagnostic and Summative Assessments,* First-Quarter Test

Internet

- Online assessments at go.hrw.com (keyword: HLLA)

Chapter 4 Comparing Themes
Evaluating Arguments: Pro and Con

Program Organization

Holt Literature and Language Arts provides a complete curriculum for standards-based instruction in reading, literature, writing, listening and speaking, and language conventions. The instructional content is presented in quarters to enable teachers to anticipate and administer the quarterly assessments required by California.

About Chapter 4

Standards-based lesson plans and suggestions for pacing the presentation of Chapter 4, the related instructional material, and the recommended assessment are provided in *On Course: Mapping Instruction,* Chapter 4.

- In Chapter 4, students will identify and use words literally and figuratively; distinguish between denotative and connotative words; evaluate the credibility of a claim; compare and contrast themes across genres and works that express a universal theme; design and publish documents; write a persuasive essay and debate an issue.

Language Arts Content

Which reading standards are taught in Chapter 4?

In this chapter, students will master the following Grade 10 standards and review standards from Grade 8. Selections or features marked with a ✔ constitute the minimum course of study that provides coverage of grade-level standards.

Grade 10 Standards

Word Analysis, Fluency, and Systematic Vocabulary Development

1.1 Identify and use the literal and figurative meanings of words, and understand word derivations.
Word Meanings—Yes or No?, Figurative Language—Don't Take It Literally, p. 242
Synonyms and Antonyms, p. 253
Mapping a Word's Origin, Word Roots, p. 271
Use a Word, and "Own" It, p. 292

1.2 Distinguish between the denotative and connotative meanings of words, and interpret the connotative power of words.
✔ In Other Words: Synonyms and Connotations, p. 282

Reading Comprehension (Focus on Informational Materials)

2.8 Evaluate the credibility of an author's argument or defense of a claim by critiquing the relationship between generalizations and evidence, the comprehensiveness of evidence, and the way in which the author's intent affects the structure and tone of the text.
✔ "If Decency Doesn't, Law Should Make Us Samaritans" (op-ed article)
"Good Samaritans U.S.A. Are Afraid to Act" (op-ed article) } pp. 284–291

Literary Response and Analysis

3.2 Compare and contrast the presentation of a similar theme or topic across genres to explain how the selection of genre shapes the theme or topic.
"Theme: What Does It Mean?" (standards essay), pp. 230–231
Comparing Universal Themes, pp. 232–254
Comparing a Theme Across Genres, pp. 255–283
✔ "And of Clay Are We Created" (short story), pp. 256–270
✔ "The Man in the Water" (essay), pp. 272–281
"What Happened During the Ice Storm", "Gracious Goodness" (standards review), pp. 306–309

(continued)

(continued)

3.5 Compare works that express a universal theme, and provide evidence to support the ideas expressed in each work.
"Theme: What Does It Mean?"(standards essay), pp. 230–231
Comparing Universal Themes, pp. 232–254
"Catch the Moon" (short story), pp. 233–241
"The Bass, the River, and Sheila Mant" (short story), pp. 243–252

Review Standards Grade 8

Reading 1.1 Analyze idioms, analogies, metaphors, and similes to infer the literal and figurative meanings of phrases.
Figurative Language—Don't Take It Literally, p. 242

Reading 1.3 Use word meanings within the appropriate context, and show ability to verify those meanings by definition, restatement, example, comparison, or contrast.
Jargon: Legalese—Words That Lawyers Use, p. 292

Which writing, and listening and speaking standards are taught in Chapter 4?

Writing Strategies

1.2 Use precise language, action verbs, sensory details, appropriate modifiers, and the active rather than the passive voice.
Second Reading: Style, p. 300

1.8 Design and publish documents by using advanced publishing software and graphic programs.
Proofread and Publish Your Essay, p. 301

1.9 Revise writing to improve the logic and coherence of the organization and controlling perspective, the precision of the word choice, and the tone by taking into consideration the audience, purpose, and formality of the context.
First Reading: Content and Organization, p. 299

Writing Applications

2.4 Write persuasive compositions.

a. Structure ideas and arguments in a sustained and logical fashion.
Organize Your Essay, p. 296

b. Use specific rhetorical devices to support assertions.
Voice of Reason, p. 295

c. Clarify and defend positions with precise and relevant evidence, including facts, expert opinions, quotations, and expressions of commonly accepted beliefs and logical reasoning.
Types of Evidence, p. 295

d. Address readers' concerns, counterclaims, biases, and expectations.
Support Your Opinion, p. 295

Listening and Speaking Strategies

1.1 Formulate judgments about the ideas under discussion and support those judgments with convincing evidence.
Tests for Evidence, p. 303

1.3 Choose logical patterns of organization to inform and to persuade, by soliciting agreement or action, or to unite audiences behind a common belief or cause.
Organize Your Debate Information, p. 304

1.5 Recognize and use elements of classical speech forms in formulating rational arguments and applying the art of persuasion and debate.
Research the Proposition, pp. 302–303

1.6 Present and advance a clear thesis statement and choose appropriate types of proof that meet standard tests for evidence, including credibility, validity, and relevance.
Prepare for a Debate, p. 302–303

(continued)

(continued)

Speaking Applications

2.5 Deliver persuasive arguments.

a. Structure ideas and arguments in a coherent, logical fashion.
Conduct the Debate, pp. 304–305

b. Use rhetorical devices to support assertions.
Prepare for a Debate, pp. 302–303

c. Clarify and defend positions with precise and relevant evidence, including facts, expert opinions, quotations, and expressions of commonly accepted beliefs and logical reasoning.
Prepare for a Debate, pp. 302–303

d. Anticipate and address the listener's concerns and counterarguments.
Conduct the Debate, pp. 304–305

Review Standards Grade 8

Writing 2.4 Write persuasive compositions.

c. Provide details, reasons, and examples, arranging them effectively by anticipating and answering reader concerns and counterarguments.
Consider Your Purpose and Audience, pp. 294–295

Speaking 2.4 Deliver persuasive presentations.

c. Anticipate and answer listener concerns and counterarguments effectively through the inclusion and arrangement of details, reasons, examples, and other elements.
Organize Your Debate Information, p. 304

Instructional Planning and Support

Where do I find lesson plans, additional resources, and other teaching aids?

- This Annotated Teacher's Edition and *On Course: Mapping Instruction* provide direction in planning and implementing a complete California standards–based curriculum. These components also include instructions for diagnostic, progress, and summative testing; for presenting direct instruction of the standards; for differentiating instruction to provide universal access; and for locating and using the program's ancillaries.
- Lesson and workshop resources are referenced at the beginning of each selection or workshop, in the bottom margin of this teacher's edition.
- Reminders for using additional resources appear in this teacher's edition at point of use.
- The *One-Stop Planner* CD-ROM contains editable lesson plans and all print ancillaries, available in PDF format.

What if I don't have time to teach all of Chapter 4?

- Most standards can be taught with a minimum number of selections and features. In the chart on the preceding page, the core lessons you need in order to provide complete coverage of the chapter standards are identified with a ✔.
- *On Course: Mapping Instruction,* Chapter 4, lists lessons and activities that provide minimum standards coverage.

What provisions have been made for students who have additional class time scheduled in language arts?

- *Interactive Reading* provides for alternative direct instruction and practice of the grade-level standards taught in Chapter 4.
- *Universal Access: Writing, Listening, and Speaking,* Chapter 4, contains worksheets and transparencies that provide practice in and reteaching and reinforcement of the writing and listening and speaking standards in Chapter 4.
- *Universal Access: Lesson Plans for Language Development,* Chapter 4, provides alternative teaching strategies and additional worksheets designed specifically for English-language learners and special education students. Many of the suggestions and activities in this ancillary will also be helpful to students in the regular classroom who are having difficulty with particular skills.

Universal Access

How do I differentiate instruction to ensure that all my students master the standards?

Holt Literature and Language Arts provides comprehensive, differentiated instruction for all types of students.

- Most of the general instruction and teaching strategies in the Annotated Teacher's Edition are at grade level. These instructions will work well with the majority of your students.
- Point-of-use suggestions are provided for advanced learners, learners having difficulty, English-language learners, and special education students.
- *Interactive Reading* is designed to anticipate and remediate problems that students may experience in achieving mastery of the reading standards. See *Interactive Reading,* Teacher's Edition, Chapter 4, for information on using the reader to differentiate instruction.
- *Universal Access: Writing, Listening, and Speaking,* Chapter 4, contains worksheets and transparencies that provide practice in and reteaching and reinforcement of the writing and listening and speaking standards in Chapter 4.
- *Universal Access: Lesson Plans for Language Development,* Chapter 4, offers teaching strategies and additional worksheets designed specifically for English-language learners and special education students.

Assessment

How do I determine whether my students are making progress in mastering the standards?

Progress Assessment

- Use the Standards Review at the end of Chapter 4 for an informal assessment of the informational reading and writing standards.
- Use Chapter 4 tests from the *Progress Assessment* booklets to assess comprehension and progress on mastering the standards taught in this chapter.

Summative Assessment

The content of *Holt Literature and Language Arts* has been divided into quarters to allow you to administer the four summative tests required by California. Chapters 3–5 and related instructional material constitute the second quarter of instruction. At the end of Chapter 5, you may ask students to take the Midyear Test in *Diagnostic and Summative Assessments.*

Chapter 4

STANDARDS FOCUS

(For full text of standards taught in this chapter, see the Standards Correlation by Standard chart in the Student Edition.)

Grade-Level Standards

- Vocabulary Development 1.1, 1.2
- Reading Comprehension 2.8
- Literary Response and Analysis 3.2, 3.5
- Writing Strategies 1.2, 1.8, 1.9
- Writing Applications 2.4a–d
- Listening and Speaking Strategies 1.1, 1.3, 1.5, 1.6
- Speaking Applications 2.5a–d

INTRODUCING THE CHAPTER

In this chapter the selections are grouped by theme, giving students an opportunity to compare different treatments of similar ideas. The first two stories develop the universal theme of adolescent love but arrive at very different conclusions. Then, students read a powerful short story and an essay that explore why some people put the lives of others above their own in moments of great danger and crisis. Next, students critique and evaluate arguments of two op-ed pieces that deal with the theme of good Samaritans. Finally, students will have a chance to express their own ideas by writing persuasive essays and by participating in debates.

CHAPTER 4 RESOURCES: READING

Planning

- *One-Stop Planner* CD-ROM with Test Generator
- *On Course: Mapping Instruction*
- *At Home: A Guide to Standards Mastery*
- *At Home: In Spanish*
- *Supporting Instruction in Spanish*

Reading

- *Interactive Reading*

Differentiating Instruction

- *Lesson Plans for Language Development*

Vocabulary

- *Vocabulary Development*
  - Cumulative Vocabulary Review, pp. 24–25

Chapter 4

Comparing Themes

EVALUATING ARGUMENTS: PRO AND CON

There are only two or three human stories, and they go on repeating themselves as fiercely as if they had never happened before.

—Willa Cather

The Couple at the Eiffel Tower by Marc Chagall (1887–1985). Oil on canvas.
Giraudon/Art Resource, New York.

KEYWORD: HLLA 10-4

229

THE QUOTATION

Tell students that when Willa Cather refers to "stories," she probably means universal themes that recur as part of the human condition. Ask why these stories might seem like they repeat themselves "fiercely as if they had never happened before." [Possible response: Every time an individual experiences a challenge, that person feels as if it is happening for the first time.]

VIEWING THE ART

The lyrical paintings of **Marc Chagall** (1887–1985) combine the innovations of modern art with his whimsical sensibility and his interest in folk art. Born in Vitbrsk, Belarussia, Chagall moved to France in 1910, where he spent most of his life. This fanciful painting emphasizes Chagall's playful approach to life in Paris. Note how he positioned small houses nestled into the levels of the tower and placed trees growing out the painting's sides.

Activity. Chagall's choices of color are idiosyncratic. What mood do they create? [The mood might be described as playful or romantic.]

Resources Reminder

Planning

- *At Home: A Guide to Standards Mastery*

Parent letters appear in this resource. Translations of these letters are found in *At Home: In Spanish*. Translations of selection summaries appear in *Supporting Instruction in Spanish*.

Reading

- *Interactive Reading*

The California framework requires students to read materials apart from in-class assignments. Additional readings are cited on the Read On page and on selected pages in the Student Edition.

Grammar

- *Holt Handbook*
  - Run-on Sentences, pp. 454–456
  - Verbals and Verbal Phrases, pp. 70–80
  - Uses of Subordinate Clauses, pp. 93–101

Assessment

- *Progress Assessment of Reading*
  - Chapter Test
- *One-Stop Planner* CD-ROM with Test Generator

Internet

- go.hrw.com (Keyword: HLLA 10-4)

STANDARDS FOCUS, pp. 230–231

(For grade-level standards taught in this lesson, see Student Edition, p. 230.)

Prerequisite Standard

- Grade 8, Literary Response and Analysis 3.5 **Identify and analyze recurring themes (e.g., good versus evil) across traditional and contemporary works.**

Literary Focus: Theme

Choose a popular movie or an episode from a TV drama that most students have recently seen. Work with the class to develop a statement of its theme, or what the story reveals about life. Ask students, "What is the main conflict of the story?" "How is it resolved?" "Does the main character grow or change in any way?" "What does he or she learn about human nature and life?" and "Does the title of the work offer any hints about the theme?" Call on volunteers to suggest a theme for the work. If they express different plausible ideas, point out that a work can have more than one theme.

Literary Response and Analysis

Theme *by* John Leggett

WHAT DOES IT MEAN?

Pages 230–254 cover **Reading Standard 3.2** Compare and contrast the presentation of a similar theme or topic across genres to explain how the selection of genre shapes the theme or topic.

Pages 230–231 and 254–283 cover **Reading Standard 3.5** Compare works that express a universal theme and provide evidence to support the ideas expressed in each work.

An Insight About Life

I once read a student's story that was full of action—two mountain climbers were about to plunge down a ravine, a skier was schussing into peril, and a killer was waiting in the valley below. Despite all this action and intrigue, however, the story was uninteresting because the action didn't seem to have any meaning.

A story's characters and events take on significance only when we recognize what they mean to us. In other words, all the elements of a good story must add up to a **theme**—an idea or insight about life and human nature that gives the story meaning. Themes are important to all forms of literature, and similar themes can often be found in different **genres**—in stories, novels, plays, poems, even in nonfiction.

What Do We Mean by Theme?

The theme of a work of literature is really its root. Theme is unseen and usually unstated, yet it is vital. It gives meaning to the characters and events, and at the same time it reveals the writer's personal attitude toward the world, toward how people should behave and how they actually do behave.

Theme is neither a summary of the plot (what happens) nor the work's subject (which might be boxing or prospecting for gold). Rather, theme is what the writer *means* by everything he or she has set down. A theme may give us insight into some aspect of life that we have never really thought about before, or it may make us understand something we always knew but never realized we knew.

Another student's story I once read was a good story, about a girl who finds her car broken into and her stereo stolen. The girl is crazy with rage, and all she can think to do is to call up an ex-boyfriend because she believes he'll know what to do. He does. He calms her, gets the car fixed, and talks her out of her anger.

As I read the story, I realized that the girl is still in love with her ex-boyfriend, though he is no longer in love with her, and the story is really about *that* misfortune. In the end the girl accepts both facts. I realized, with all the force of sudden revelation, that the heroine has been undergoing a major growing-up experience: She has learned to accept loss.

Now *that's* a theme. Telling that by means of a story is much more memorable and emotionally compelling than simply stating the story's theme: "One of the lessons that everyone must learn in growing up is how to deal with loss."

Discovering a Theme

It's often difficult for a reader to state the theme of a literary work. (Remember that the writer has had to write the whole work to get that theme across to us.) Yet the attempt to put a theme into words can often help us understand the work more fully. Here are some guidelines for discovering and stating a theme:

1 One of the best ways to discover the theme of a literary work is to

DIFFERENTIATING INSTRUCTION

Learners Having Difficulty

Modeling. Unlike setting and character, which usually have some explicit explanation in the text, theme can be subtle and may become a frustrating puzzle to many readers. Model how to discover theme by discussing a familiar fairy tale, such as "Cinderella." Point out that the main character is a generous, loving person and that the main conflict is between her and her stepmother, who is cruel, spiteful, and jealous. Cinderella's personality does not change, but her circumstances do. Explain that the conflict is resolved when the lowly Cinderella becomes the belle of the ball and a royal princess. Students should realize that the story's theme, or central idea about human nature, deals with goodness being rewarded and evil being punished. Then, ask students to form small groups and make a general statement of the theme. You may also have them work on discovering the theme of other tales, such as "John Henry" or "Beauty and the Beast."

Advanced Learners

Acceleration. Use the following activity with advanced students to move them ask how the protagonist *changes* during the course of the story. Often what this character learns about life is the truth the writer wants to reveal to the reader.

2 Because conflict is so central to most literature, a good clue to theme is how the conflict is resolved.

3 Another way to discover the theme is to think about the title of a work, which often—but not always—has a special significance and hints at the theme.

4 We must use at least one complete sentence to state a theme. In other words, a theme must be a statement about the subject of the work rather than a phrase such as "the rewards of old age." (Sometimes you can reword this kind of phrase to form a sentence: "Old age can be a time of great satisfaction.")

5 Remember that a theme is not the same as a moral, which is a rule of conduct. In getting at theme, we should ask ourselves, "What does this work reveal?" rather than "What does this work teach?" Thus, it is a mistake to reduce a theme (at least a serious writer's theme) to a familiar saying or cliché, such as "Crime doesn't pay." A theme is usually a much more complex and original revelation about life.

6 A theme must be expressed as a **generalization** about life or human nature; it should not refer to specific characters or events in the work. Themes are often **universal**—that is, they apply to people everywhere—because people all over the world have common desires, needs, and experiences. We all know about love and loss, dreams and dashed hopes.

7 There is no single correct way to state the theme of a literary work. If there are thirty-five students in your English class, for instance, there will probably be thirty-five distinct ways of putting a story's central insight into words. Your classmates may also have several different ideas about what the story's major theme is. In fact, if a story or work of literature is rich and complex, it may have more than one theme.

Practice

Choose a story you have recently read that meant something to you. Using a chart like the one below, go step by step to discover, and then state, the story's theme. Compare your statement of the theme with the statements of classmates who have chosen the same story.

Steps to a Theme
How the main character changes:
How the conflict is resolved:
What the title suggests:
What, in general, the story reveals about life or people:
The story's theme:

toward the eleventh- and twelfth-grade Standard 3.2, for which they use textual evidence to analyze how a theme presents a comment on life.

Activity. Challenge students to create statements of theme for one or more works that the class has already read. Ask students to share their theme statements and to defend their interpretations by citing details from the texts. Allow students time to review the works for supporting passages. Encourage students to rework their statements of theme based on their reexaminations of the stories.

Practice

Students' responses will vary. Sample chart responses based on Ray Bradbury's short story "The Pedestrian":

How the main character changes—During the course of the story, Mr. Mead learns that his eccentric view of technology is not socially acceptable and that he will be punished for having an imagination, for not accepting technology as others have, and for taking walks at night.

How the conflict is resolved—Because of his thinking and behavior, Mr. Mead is confined to a psychiatric center.

What the title suggests—There is only one pedestrian in the story's setting. This makes the sole pedestrian unusual or aberrant.

What, in general, the story reveals about life or people—When people grow dependent on technology, they may sacrifice their individuality or imagination.

The story's theme—Technology can be beneficial, but if it gets out of control, it can restrict both imagination and individual freedom.

Apply

Homework

To illustrate that a story's theme can be expressed in a number of ways (or that a story can have more than one theme), you may want to give advanced students the following homework assignment. Have each student fill in a "Steps to a Theme" chart for "Catch the Moon," this chapter's first selection. As a group, students can then compile their individual entries and list them on a group "Steps to a Theme" chart to be displayed in the classroom.

Resources Reminder

Differentiating Instruction

- *Lesson Plans for Language Development*

For more instruction on theme for English-language learners and special education students, see *Lesson Plans for Language Development,* pp. 103, 104.

STANDARDS FOCUS, pp. 232–254

(For the grade-level standard taught in this Comparing Universal Themes lesson, see citations on Student Edition pages.)

Prerequisite Standard

- Grade 8, Literary Response and Analysis 3.3 **Compare and contrast motivations and reactions of literary characters from different historical eras confronting similar situations or conflicts.**

Comparing Universal Themes

Overview

This feature introduces an opportunity for students to read two short stories on a timeless subject—falling in love. In these stories, students will meet characters who share some of their problems and concerns. Although the subjects are similar, these short stories contain different characters, settings, conflicts, resolutions, and themes.

The first story, "Catch the Moon" by Judith Ortiz Cofer, involves a boy dealing with anger about his mother's death and conflicts with his father. It is the boy's love for a girl that helps him heal.

The second story, "The Bass, the River, and Sheila Mant," involves a boy who can impress a girl only if he gives up something important to him. His choice leads him to an important realization.

After students have read these short stories, they will be asked to write a comparison-contrast essay (p. 254). Before students begin reading, encourage them to copy the chart on this page and fill it in with details as they read. Explain that they will need to refer to their chart later, when they write an essay that compares and contrasts these fictional works.

Literary Response and Analysis

Comparing Universal Themes

"Catch the Moon" . . . . *by* Judith Ortiz Cofer . . . short story . . . page 234
"The Bass, the River, and Sheila Mant" . . . *by* W. D. Wetherell . . . . . short story . . . page 244

A Universe of People and Themes

People all over the world and throughout time have shared common emotions, concerns, and experiences—it's what makes us human. We all want to be loved; we have hopes and dreams; we cope with loss, death, and disappointment. Our universal concerns are reflected in literature as **universal themes.** These broad themes come up again and again in literature, yet each writer gives a personal insight, or "twist," to these themes.

Love—You Can't Live with It, and You Can't Live Without It

Love is such a universal experience that sayings about it pepper our everyday conversation. Writers have explored the theme of love for thousands of years. The next two stories are about falling in love. You'll need to read on to find out how each story treats that universal experience.

Although we talk of love as a universal theme, remember that the theme of a work of literature is never expressed with a single word but rather in a complete sentence that makes a statement about life. For example, the theme of a story would never be stated simply as "love." Instead, the statement of the theme would express a view of love, such as "Love, despite its joys, also brings sorrow."

Pages 232–254 cover **Reading Standard 3.5** Compare works that express a universal theme and provide evidence to support the ideas expressed in each work.

Reading Skills

Comparing and Contrasting Themes

For help comparing the themes in these two stories, review the guidelines for discovering and stating theme on pages 230–231. After you have read and discussed each story, fill in comments about the story's plot, characters, and theme in a chart like the one below. Then, turn to page 254.

	"Catch the Moon"	"The Bass, The River, and Sheila Mant"
Main character		
Changes main character undergoes		
Conflict between characters		
How conflict is resolved		
How character's change relates to theme		
How conflict relates to theme		
Statement of theme		

DIFFERENTIATING INSTRUCTION

Learners Having Difficulty

Suggest that students use this chart as a worksheet. Students can keep track of character, conflict, changes, and theme by filling in the columns while they read. Point out that students can change or update their responses when they encounter new details in the text. Have students review their charts after finishing both stories.

Before You Read

Catch the Moon

Literary Focus

Theme and Character

A story's **theme** is the message it communicates about life or people. When you're trying to determine the theme, keep your eyes on the **main character.** How the main character changes and what he or she learns are important clues to the theme. The change in the main character may be an outside change that everyone can see or an inner change—perhaps a sudden realization—that only the main character and the reader can recognize.

Reading Skills

Making a Generalization

When you state the **theme** of a story or another work of literature, you state it as a **generalization**—a broad statement that takes into account all the details in the text, not just one. Generalizations help people make sense of the world. Just think how complicated life would be if we couldn't make generalizations about natural laws (wet climates produce lush foliage) or about people (everyone wants to be loved). As you read this story, think about what generalizations the characters and events suggest to you.

Make the Connection

Quickwrite

Does falling in love change a person? What might motivate someone in love to behave as he or she would never have behaved before? Quickwrite about your ideas. You might think about your own experiences and observations as well as about love stories you have read or seen in the movies.

Vocabulary Development

harassing (har′əs·iŋ) *v.* used as *n.:* bothering; troubling.

dismantled (dis·mant′'ld) *v.:* took apart.

vintage (vin′tij) *adj.:* dating from a time long past.

ebony (eb′ə·nē) *adj.:* dark or black.

sarcastic (sär·kas′tik) *adj.:* mocking; taunting; in a manner that makes fun of something or someone.

relics (rel′iks) *n.:* objects or things from the past that may have special meanings or associations, sometimes religious ones.

Pages 232–254 cover **Reading Standard 3.5** Compare works that express a universal theme and provide evidence to support the ideas expressed in each work.

STANDARDS FOCUS, pp. 233–242

(For grade-level and review standards taught in this lesson, see citations on Student Edition pages.)

Prerequisite Standard

- Grade 8, Literary Response and Analysis 3.5 **Identify and analyze recurring themes (e.g., good versus evil) across traditional and contemporary works.**

Reading Skills

- Make a generalization.

Preview Vocabulary

Use these questions to build understanding of the Vocabulary words on p. 233.

1. What might you say to someone who is harassing you? [Possible response: "Please leave me alone."]
2. Where are old cars dismantled? [Possible response: a junkyard.]
3. Where could you buy vintage furniture? [Possible response: in an antique store.]
4. If the sky is ebony in color, what time of day is it? [Possible response: nighttime.]
5. Why might someone make a sarcastic remark? [Possible response: to be insulting or funny.]
6. In what line of work do people search for relics? [Possible response: archaeology.]

RESOURCES: READING

Media

- *Audio CD Library*
  - disc 8

Reading

- *Interactive Reading*
  - Interactive version: "Catch the Moon"
- *Interactive Reading,* Teacher's Edition
  - Graphic Organizer: Theme Map

Differentiating Instruction

- *Lesson Plans for Language Development*
  - English-Language Learners, pp. 105–107, 128, 133
  - Special Education Students, pp. 108, 128, 133

Vocabulary

- *Vocabulary Development*
  - Vocabulary Worksheet, p. 19

Assessment

- *Progress Assessment of Reading*
  - Selection Test
- *One-Stop Planner* CD-ROM with Test Generator

PRETEACHING

Selection Starter

Motivate. Discuss the phrase *moment of understanding* with students. Ask volunteers to relate experiences that made them see something or someone in a different way. Have students look for moments in the story that cause Luis to see things differently.

Summary ⇩ *below grade level*

The story's main character is Luis Cintrón, a troubled teenager being raised by his widowed father. He has just spent six months in detention for breaking and entering. One afternoon, Luis is stunned by the arrival of a beautiful girl named Naomi. She is looking for a vintage hubcap. Her parents own a local funeral home, the place where the funeral service for Luis's mother took place. That night, Luis borrows his father's car and drives to the funeral home. He remembers his mother and breaks down in tears. Seeing his outburst, Naomi shows Luis a sketch that she has drawn of him. Luis returns to the junkyard. After a long search, he finds the hubcap that Naomi wants and hangs it by her window. It's the first positive thing he's done in a long time.

DIRECT TEACHING

A Literary Focus GRADE-LEVEL STANDARD

Theme and character. How does Luis feel about his stay in juvenile hall? What do his reactions say about him? [Possible response: He seems to think the punishment was undeserved. Excuses such as "he didn't even take anything" and "he did it on a dare" indicate that Luis doesn't take responsibility for his actions.]

CATCH THE MOON

Judith Ortiz Cofer

Luis watched the most beautiful girl he had ever seen.

Luis Cintrón sits on top of a six-foot pile of hubcaps and watches his father walk away into the steel jungle of his car junkyard. Released into his old man's custody[1] after six months in juvenile hall—for breaking and entering—and **A** he didn't even take anything. He did it on a dare. But the old lady with the million cats was a light sleeper, and good with her aluminum cane. He has a scar on his head to prove it.

Now Luis is wondering whether he should have stayed in and done his full time. Jorge Cintrón of Jorge Cintrón & Son, Auto Parts and Salvage, has decided that Luis should wash and polish every hubcap in the yard. The hill he is sitting on is only the latest couple of hundred wheel covers that have come in. Luis grunts and stands up on top of his silver mountain. He yells at no one, "Someday, son, all this will be yours," and sweeps his arms like the Pope blessing a crowd over the piles of car sandwiches and mounds of metal parts that cover this acre of land outside the city. He is the "Son" of Jorge Cintrón & Son, and so far his father has had more than one reason to wish it was plain Jorge Cintrón on the sign.

1. **custody** *n.:* term describing the legal responsibility of one person for another.

DIFFERENTIATING INSTRUCTION

Learners Having Difficulty

Invite students having difficulty to read "Catch the Moon" in interactive format in *Interactive Reading* and to use the sidenotes as aids for understanding the selection. The interactive version provides additional instruction, practice, and assessment of the literature standard taught in the Student Edition. Monitor students' responses to the selection, and correct any misconceptions that arise.

Resources Reminder

Differentiating Instruction

- *Interactive Reading*
  - Interactive version: "Catch the Moon"

English-Language Learners

Provide a description of the function of an auto salvage yard, the setting for much of the story's action. Explain that cars that have been "totaled," or damaged so severely that they

234 Chapter 4 Comparing Themes • Evaluating Arguments: Pro and Con

Luis has been getting in trouble since he started high school two years ago, mainly because of the "social group" he organized—a bunch of guys who were into harassing the local authorities. Their thing was taking something to the limit on a dare or, better still, doing something dangerous, like breaking into a house, not to steal, just to prove that they could do it. That was Luis's specialty, coming up with very complicated plans, like military strategies, and assigning the "jobs" to guys who wanted to join the Tiburones.

Tiburón means "shark," and Luis had gotten the name from watching an old movie about a Puerto Rican gang called the Sharks with his father. Luis thought it was one of the dumbest films he had ever seen. Everybody sang their lines, and the guys all pointed their toes and leapt in the air when they were supposed to be slaughtering each other. But he liked their name, the Sharks, so he made it Spanish and had it air-painted on his black T-shirt with a killer shark under it, jaws opened wide and dripping with blood. It didn't take long for other guys in the barrio[2] to ask about it.

Man, had they had a good time. The girls were interested too. Luis outsmarted everybody by calling his organization a social club and registering it at Central High. That meant they were legal, even let out of last-period class on Fridays for their "club" meetings. It was just this year, after a couple of botched jobs, that the teachers had started getting suspicious. The first one to go wrong was when he sent Kenny Matoa to *borrow* some "souvenirs" out of Anita Robles's locker. He got caught. It seems that Matoa had been reading Anita's diary and didn't hear her coming down the hall. Anita was supposed to be in the gym at that time but had copped out with the usual female excuse of cramps. You could hear her screams all the way to Market Street.

2. **barrio** (bär′ē • ō) *n.:* in the United States, a Spanish-speaking neighborhood.

She told the principal all she knew about the Tiburones, and Luis had to talk fast to convince old Mr. Williams that the club did put on cultural activities such as the Save the Animals talent show. What Mr. Williams didn't know was that the animal that was being "saved" with the ticket sales was Luis's pet boa, which needed quite a few live mice to stay healthy and happy. They kept E. S. (which stood for "Endangered Species") in Luis's room, but she belonged to the club and it was the members' responsibility to raise the money to feed their mascot.[3] So last year they had sponsored their first annual Save the Animals talent show, and it had been a great success. The Tiburones had come dressed as Latino Elvises and did a grand finale to "All Shook Up" that made the audience go wild. Mr. Williams had smiled while Luis talked, maybe remembering how the math teacher, Mrs. Laguna, had dragged him out in the aisle to rock-and-roll with her. Luis had gotten out of that one, but barely.

His father was a problem too. He objected to the T-shirt logo, calling it disgusting and vulgar. Mr. Cintrón prided himself on his own neat, elegant style of dressing after work, and on his manners and large vocabulary, which he picked up by taking correspondence courses[4] in just about everything. Luis thought it was just his way of staying busy since Luis's mother had died, almost three years ago, of cancer. He had never gotten over it.

All this was going through Luis's head as he slid down the hill of hubcaps. The tub full of soapy water, the can of polish, and the bag of rags had been neatly placed in front of a makeshift table made from two car seats and

3. **mascot** *n.:* person, animal, or thing kept by a group or team as its symbol or for good luck.

4. **correspondence courses** *n.:* courses of study conducted through the mail.

Vocabulary

harassing (har′əs·iŋ) *v.* used as *n:* bothering; troubling.

Direct Teaching

B Literary Focus
GRADE-LEVEL STANDARD

Theme and character. What does Luis's involvement in the gang say about his character? Does it show that he has negative traits, positive traits, or a complex mix of both? [Possible response: Although they get him into trouble, Luis's gang activities demonstrate his virtues as well as his faults. Clearly, he has a quick mind and leadership ability, traits that would serve him well if positively applied.]

C Reading Skills

Making a generalization. First, Luis outsmarts everybody by registering his gang as a social club. Later, he has to "talk fast" to stay out of trouble. What generalization could you make about Luis's actions? [Possible responses: Luis is trying to prove that he can outwit the adult establishment at school. Luis is rebelling against adult authority.]

D Literary Focus
GRADE-LEVEL STANDARD

Theme and character. What do you learn about Luis from this passage? [Possible response: Luis is dealing with a variety of serious issues. He has lost his mother and is having difficulty in his relationship with his father.]

cannot be repaired, are taken to salvage yards to be dismantled. Usable parts from the cars are sorted for sale, and the remainder becomes scrap metal. People with old or antique cars often go to salvage yards to obtain hard-to-find parts.

Special Education Students

For lessons designed for special education students and English-language learners, see *Lesson Plans for Language Development,* pp. 105–108, 128, 133.

Advanced Learners

Acceleration. This activity can help to move advanced learners toward the eleventh- and twelfth-grade Standard 3.2, for which they support their analysis of the way a story's theme represents a view of or comment on life.

Activity. Point out that "Catch the Moon" introduces timeless themes that relate to love, loss, and generational conflicts. Have students review the story and write a statement of its theme, noting supporting details from the text. Then, have students defend their choice of theme by citing evidence from the story in a small-group discussion.

Direct Teaching

A Vocabulary Development
GRADE-LEVEL STANDARD

? Figurative language. What kind of figure of speech is the phrase "like a smooth wood carving," and how do you know? [It is a simile, because it contains the word *like*. Similes use words such as *like* and *as* to compare unlike things.] How does the simile help you visualize the girl? [Possible response: Comparing her to a wood carving helps readers picture her smooth brown skin, her elegant shape, and her poise.]

B Learners Having Difficulty

? Monitoring students' progress. Be sure students recognize Luis's attitude toward the work he must perform for his father. Why does Luis toss the wrench? [Possible responses: He tosses the wrench to demonstrate his annoyance at having to follow his father's orders or to attract attention to his rebellious quality.]

a piece of plywood. Luis heard a car drive up and someone honk their horn. His father emerged from inside a new red Mustang that had been totaled. He usually dismantled every small feature by hand before sending the vehicle into the *cementerio,*[5] as he called the lot. Luis watched as the most beautiful girl he had ever seen climbed out of a vintage white Volkswagen Bug. She stood in the sunlight in her white sundress waiting for **A** his father, while Luis stared. She was like a smooth wood carving. Her skin was mahogany, almost black, and her arms and legs were long and thin, but curved in places so that she did not look bony and hard—more like a ballerina. And her ebony hair was braided close to her head. Luis let his breath out, feeling a little dizzy. He had forgotten to breathe. Both the girl and his father heard him. Mr. Cintrón waved him over.

"Luis, the señorita here has lost a wheel cover. Her car is twenty-five years old, so it will not be an easy match. Come look on this side."

B Luis tossed a wrench he'd been holding into a toolbox like he was annoyed, just to make a point about slave labor. Then he followed his father, who knelt on the gravel and began to point out every detail of the hubcap. Luis was hardly listening. He watched the girl take a piece of paper from her handbag.

"Señor Cintrón, I have drawn the hubcap for you, since I will have to leave soon. My home address and telephone number are here, and also my parents' office number." She handed the paper to Mr. Cintrón, who nodded.

"Sí, señorita, very good. This will help my son look for it. Perhaps there is one in that stack there." He pointed to the pile of caps that Luis was supposed to wash and polish. "Yes, I'm almost certain that there is a match there. Of course, I do not know if it's near the top or the bottom. You will give us a few days, yes?"

Luis just stared at his father like he was crazy. But he didn't say anything because the girl was smiling at him with a funny expression on her face. Maybe she thought he had X-ray eyes like Superman, or maybe she was mocking him.

"Please call me Naomi, Señor Cintrón. You know my mother. She is the director of the funeral home. . . ." Mr. Cintrón seemed surprised at first; he prided himself on having a great memory. Then his friendly expression changed to one of sadness as he recalled the day of his wife's burial. Naomi did not finish her sentence. She reached over and placed her hand on Mr. Cintrón's arm for a moment. Then she said "Adiós" softly, and got in her shiny white car. She waved to them as she left, and her gold bracelets flashing in the sun nearly blinded Luis.

Mr. Cintrón shook his head. "How about that," he said as if to himself. "They are the Dominican owners of Ramirez Funeral Home." And, with a sigh, "She seems like such a nice young woman. Reminds me of your mother when she was her age."

5. **cementerio** (se·men·te′rē·ō) *n.:* Spanish for "cemetery."

Vocabulary
dismantled (dis·mant′'ld) *v.:* took apart.
vintage (vin′tij) *adj.:* dating from a time long past.
ebony (eb′ə·nē) *adj.:* dark or black.

236 Chapter 4 Comparing Themes • Evaluating Arguments: Pro and Con

Hearing the funeral parlor's name, Luis remembered too. The day his mother died, he had been in her room at the hospital while his father had gone for coffee. The alarm had gone off on her monitor and nurses had come running in, pushing him outside. After that, all he recalled was the anger that had made him punch a hole in his bedroom wall. And afterward he had refused to talk to anyone at the funeral. Strange, he did see a black girl there who didn't try like the others to talk to him, but actually ignored him as she escorted family members to the viewing room and brought flowers in. Could it be that the skinny girl in a frilly white dress had been Naomi? She didn't act like she had recognized him today, though. Or maybe she thought that he was a jerk.

Luis grabbed the drawing from his father. The old man looked like he wanted to walk down memory lane. But Luis was in no mood to listen to the old stories about his falling in love on a tropical island. The world they'd lived in before he was born wasn't his world. No beaches and palm trees here. Only junk as far as he could see. He climbed back up his hill and studied Naomi's sketch. It had obviously been done very carefully. It was signed "Naomi Ramirez" in the lower right-hand corner. He memorized the telephone number.

Luis washed hubcaps all day until his hands were red and raw, but he did not come across the small silver bowl that would fit the VW. After work he took a few practice Frisbee shots across the yard before showing his father what he had accomplished: rows and rows of shiny rings drying in the sun. His father nodded and showed him the bump on his temple where one of Luis's flying saucers had gotten him. "Practice makes perfect, you know. Next time you'll probably decapitate[6] me." Luis heard him struggle with the word *decapitate*, which Mr. Cintrón pronounced in syllables. Showing off his big vocabulary again, Luis thought. He looked closely at the bump, though. He felt bad about it.

"They look good, hijo,[7]" Mr. Cintrón made a sweeping gesture with his arms over the yard. "You know, all this will have to be classified. My dream is to have all the parts divided by year, make of car, and condition. Maybe now that you are here to help me, this will happen."

"Pop . . ." Luis put his hand on his father's shoulder. They were the same height and build, about five foot six and muscular. "The judge said six months of free labor for you, not life, okay?" Mr. Cintrón nodded, looking distracted. It was then that Luis suddenly noticed how gray his hair had turned—it used to be shiny black like his own—and that there were deep lines in his face. His father had turned into an old man and he hadn't even noticed.

"Son, you must follow the judge's instructions. Like she said, next time you get in trouble, she's going to treat you like an adult, and I think you know what that means. Hard time, no breaks."

"Yeah, yeah. That's what I'm doing, right? Working my hands to the bone instead of enjoying my summer. But listen, she didn't put me under house arrest, right? I'm going out tonight."

"Home by ten. She did say something about a curfew, Luis." Mr. Cintrón had stopped smiling and was looking upset. It had always been hard for them to talk more than a minute or two before his father got offended at something Luis said, or at his sarcastic tone. He was always doing something wrong.

Luis threw the rag down on the table and went to sit in his father's ancient Buick, which was in mint condition. They drove home in silence.

After sitting down at the kitchen table with his father to eat a pizza they had picked up on

6. **decapitate** (dē·kap′ə·tāt′) *v.:* cut off the head of.

7. **hijo** (ē′hō) *n.:* Spanish for "son."

Vocabulary
sarcastic (sär·kas′tik) *adj.:* mocking; taunting; in a manner that makes fun of something or someone.

Direct Teaching

C Literary Focus
GRADE-LEVEL STANDARD

Theme and character. Have Luis's emotions changed in the three years since his mother's death? [Judging from the trouble Luis gets into, the thoughts he expresses, and his relationship with his father, it seems that he is still angry.]

D Learners Having Difficulty

Monitoring students' progress. Remind students that the changes a main character undergoes are often clues to a story's theme. Ask students to summarize what they have learned about Luis's character up to this point in the story. [He is a rebellious teenager who was jailed for breaking and entering. He resents having to work in his father's junkyard and is angry that his mother died. He is suddenly interested in Naomi.] Suggest that students pay close attention to any changes that occur in Luis as a result of his encounter with Naomi.

E Literary Focus
GRADE-LEVEL STANDARD

Theme and character. What is notable about Luis's feeling? [This is the first time Luis has shown remorse for something he has done; he feels some sympathy for his father.]

F Reading Skills

Making a generalization. What generalization can you make about Luis's attitude toward his father before this realization? [Luis resented his father and paid little attention to the changes his father was undergoing.]

DIRECT TEACHING

A Reading Skills

Making a generalization. Consider this interaction as well as the details of earlier interactions with his father. What generalization can you make about how Luis communicates with his father? [Possible response: Luis is not very communicative with his father. Perhaps he truly doesn't know where he wants to go, but in general, he tells his father as little as possible.]

B Advanced Learners

Enrichment. Ask students to consider what this simile comparing Luis's father to King Midas, a figure from Greek mythology, suggests about Luis's father. [Possible responses: Just as Midas turned common objects into gold, Luis's father has turned his wife's everyday items into museum pieces. Luis's father is coping with loss by memorializing his wife through the things she used and touched, rather than by taking more life-affirming action.]

the way home, Luis asked to borrow the car. He didn't get an answer then, just a look that meant "Don't bother me right now."

Before bringing up the subject again, Luis put some ice cubes in a Baggie and handed it to Mr. Cintrón, who had made the little bump on his head worse by rubbing it. It had GUILTY written on it, Luis thought.

"Gracias, hijo." His father placed the bag on the bump and made a face as the ice touched his skin.

They ate in silence for a few minutes more; then Luis decided to ask about the car again.

"I really need some fresh air, Pop. Can I borrow the car for a couple of hours?"

"You don't get enough fresh air at the yard? We're lucky that we don't have to sit in a smelly old factory all day. You know that?"

"Yeah, Pop. We're real lucky." Luis always felt irritated that his father was so grateful to own a junkyard, but he held his anger back and just waited to see if he'd get the keys without having to get in an argument.

A "Where are you going?"

"For a ride. Not going anywhere. Just out for a while. Is that okay?"

His father didn't answer, just handed him a set of keys, as shiny as the day they were manufactured. His father polished everything that could be polished: doorknobs, coins, keys, spoons, knives, and forks, like he was King Midas counting his silver and gold. Luis thought his father must be really lonely to polish utensils only he used anymore. They had been picked **B** out by his wife, though, so they were like <u>relics</u>. Nothing she had ever owned could be thrown away. Only now the dishes, forks, and spoons were not used to eat the yellow rice and red beans, the fried chicken, or the mouth-watering sweet plantains that his mother had cooked for them. They were just kept in the cabinets that his father had turned into a museum for her. Mr. Cintrón could cook as well as his wife, but he didn't have the heart to do it anymore. Luis thought that maybe if they ate together once in a while things might get better between them, but he always had something to do around dinnertime and ended up at a hamburger joint. Tonight was the first time in months they had sat down at the table together.

> It had GUILTY written on it.

Luis took the keys. "Thanks," he said, walking out to take his shower. His father kept looking at him with those sad, patient eyes. "Okay. I'll be back by ten, and keep the ice on that egg," Luis said without looking back.

He had just meant to ride around his old barrio, see if any of the Tiburones were hanging out at El Building, where most of them lived. It wasn't far from the single-family home his father had bought when the business starting paying off: a house that his mother lived in for three months before she took up residence at St. Joseph's Hospital. She never came home again. These days Luis wished he still lived in that tiny apartment where there was always something to do, somebody to talk to.

Instead Luis found himself parked in front of the last place his mother had gone to: Ramirez Funeral Home. In the front yard was a huge oak tree that Luis remembered having climbed during the funeral to get away from people. The tree looked different now, not like a skeleton, as it had then, but green with leaves. The branches reached to the second floor of the house, where the family lived.

For a while Luis sat in the car allowing the memories to flood back into his brain. He

Vocabulary
relics (rel′iks) *n.:* objects or things from the past that may have special meanings or associations, sometimes religious ones.

READING MINI-LESSON

Developing Word-Attack Skills

Write the word *tome* on the chalkboard. Explain that *tome* is a synonym for *book* and is often used to identify a large scholarly book. Have students read the word aloud. Tell students that the final e in *tome* indicates that the *o* is long.

Next, write the word *epitome* on the chalkboard. Note that although the last three letters in the word are the same as in *tome,* they are pronounced differently. Ask a volunteer to read *epitome* aloud: /ē•pit′ə•mē′/. Explain that in *epitome,* the final e does not signal a long *o*. Instead, it is part of the final syllable and has its own sound: /ē/.

Point out that several words used in English have a final pronounced e. In words with Greek or Latin origins, like *epitome,* this final e has a long e sound. In words with French origins, like *cafe,* the e has a long *a* sound, which may be indicated by an accent.

Activity. Write the following list of words on the chalkboard. Ask volunteers to read the words aloud and state whether the final e is pronounced as a long e or a long *a*. Have them consult a dictionary if necessary.

238 Chapter 4 Comparing Themes • Evaluating Arguments: Pro and Con

remembered his mother before the illness changed her. She had not been beautiful, as his father told everyone; she had been a sweet lady, not pretty but not ugly. To him, she had been the person who always told him that she was proud of him and loved him. She did that every night when she came to his bedroom door to say goodnight. As a joke he would sometimes ask her, "Proud of what? I haven't done anything." And she'd always say, "I'm just proud that you are my son." She wasn't perfect or anything. She had bad days when nothing he did could make her smile, especially after she got sick. But he never heard her say anything negative about anyone. She always blamed *el destino,* fate, for what went wrong. He missed her. He missed her so much. Suddenly a flood of tears that had been building up for almost three years started pouring from his eyes. Luis sat in his father's car, with his head on the steering wheel, and cried, "Mami, I miss you."

When he finally looked up, he saw that he was being watched. Sitting at a large window with a pad and a pencil on her lap was Naomi. At first Luis felt angry and embarrassed, but she wasn't laughing at him. Then she told him with her dark eyes that it was okay to come closer. He walked to the window, and she held up the sketch pad on which she had drawn him, not crying like a baby, but sitting on top of a mountain of silver disks, holding one up over his head. He had to smile.

The plate-glass window was locked. It had a security bolt on it. An alarm system, he figured, so nobody would steal the princess. He asked her if he could come in. It was soundproof too. He mouthed the words slowly for her to read his lips. She wrote on the pad, "I can't let you in. My mother is not home tonight." So they looked at each other and talked through the window for a little while. Then Luis got an idea. He signed to her that he'd be back, and drove to the junkyard.

Luis climbed up on his mountain of hubcaps. For hours he sorted the wheel covers by make, size, and condition, stopping only to call his father and tell him where he was and what he was doing. The old man did not ask him for explanations, and Luis was grateful for that. By lamppost light, Luis worked and worked, beginning to understand a little why his father kept busy all the time. Doing something that had a beginning, a middle, and an end did something to your head. It was like the satisfaction Luis got out of planning "adventures" for his Tiburones, but there was another element involved here that had nothing to do with showing off for others. This was a treasure hunt. And he knew what he was looking for.

Finally, when it seemed that it was a hopeless search, when it was almost midnight and Luis's hands were cut and bruised from his work, he found it. It was the perfect match for Naomi's drawing, the moon-shaped wheel cover for her car, Cinderella's shoe. Luis jumped off the small mound of disks left under him and shouted, "Yes!" He looked around and saw neat stacks of hubcaps that he would wash the next day. He would build a display wall for his father. People would be able to come into the yard and point to whatever they wanted.

Luis washed the VW hubcap and polished it until he could see himself in it. He used it as a mirror as he washed his face and combed his hair. Then he drove to the Ramirez Funeral Home. It was almost pitch-black, since it was a moonless night. As quietly as possible, Luis put some gravel in his pocket and climbed the oak tree to

DIRECT TEACHING

C Reading Skills

Comparing and contrasting. Compare this description of the mother's attitude toward Luis with the one he attributes to his father. [Possible response: Luis's mother provided unconditional support. In contrast, Luis's father is frequently offended and thinks that Luis is "always doing something wrong."]

D Literary Focus GRADE-LEVEL STANDARD

Theme and character. What is important about this moment? [It is the first time Luis has allowed himself to express grief over his mother's death.]

E Literary Focus GRADE-LEVEL STANDARD

Theme and character. Why are Luis's actions surprising? [Luis is willingly sorting auto parts, something he previously resented doing.]

F Learners Having Difficulty

Questioning. What is Luis trying to find? [the wheel cover that Naomi wants]

1. catastrophe	[long e]	**6.** syncope	[long e]
2. pâté	[long *a*]	**7.** facsimile	[long e]
3. finale	[long e]	**8.** hyperbole	[long e]
4. protégé	[long *a*]	**9.** cliché	[long *a*]
5. calliope	[long e]	**10.** aborigine	[long e]

FAMILY/COMMUNITY ACTIVITY

Encourage students to find out more about ways in which people come to terms with the death of a close friend or a family member. Invite students to talk to family members about their experiences with handling loss. You might also invite a counselor or staff member from a local hospice or a survivors' organization to speak with your class.

DIRECT TEACHING

A Literary Focus
GRADE-LEVEL STANDARD

Theme and character. What do Luis's actions say about the way he has changed? [Before, Luis was too angry to do anything positive. Now he has overcome his anger. He wants to help others, particularly the girl he loves.]

GUIDED PRACTICE

Monitoring students' progress. To assess students' understanding of the story, ask them to create a two-column chart. Have them list the problems and difficulties Luis faces in the first column. Have students describe the way each problem is addressed or resolved in the second column.

Meet the Writer

Background. Judith Ortiz Cofer refuses to be constrained by limits of geography, culture, or genre. Having lived in disparate locations from Puerto Rico and New Jersey to Georgia, she often writes about the difficulties of bridging American and Puerto Rican cultures. Cofer describes herself as "Latina wherever I am"; she notes that she sometimes feels pressure to write in Spanish but chooses to write in English, "the language of the country my parents brought me to."

For Independent Reading

- If students choose to read *An Island Like You: Stories of the Barrio,* have them note particularly the main characters and themes of the stories. What similarities, if any, do the characters in Cofer's tales share? What common themes are presented in the stories?
- For other stories about characters who bridge two cultures, you might recommend *The Circuit: Stories from the Life of a Migrant Child* by Francisco Jiménez.

the second floor. He knew he was in front of Naomi's window—he could see her shadow through the curtains. She was at a table, apparently writing or drawing, maybe waiting for him. Luis hung the silver disk carefully on a branch near the window, then threw the gravel at the glass. Naomi ran to the window and drew the curtains aside while Luis held on to the thick branch and waited to give her the first good thing he had given anyone in a long time. ■

Meet the Writer

Judith Ortiz Cofer

Bridging Cultures

Judith Ortiz Cofer (1952–) has always traveled between two cultures. She was born in Puerto Rico and began her visits to the United States mainland when she was four. Whenever her father, a career navy man, was overseas, his family would return to Puerto Rico. Then, when he sailed back to the States, his family would rejoin him in Paterson, New Jersey.

Cofer grew up listening to her grandmother's fascinating *cuentos* (Spanish for "stories") and soon knew that she wanted to write.

"When I was growing up, I absorbed literature, both the spoken *cuentos* and books, as a creature who breathed ink. Each writer provided poems, novels, taught me that language could be tamed. I realized that I could make it perform. I had to believe the work was important to my being: to use my art as a bridge between my cultures. Unlike my parents, I was not always straddling. I began crossing the bridge, traveling back and forth without fear and confusion."

Cofer writes from 5:00 to 7:00 A.M. before her day begins as wife, mother, and professor of English and creative writing at the University of Georgia in Athens. First known as a poet, she has said, "I'm still hoping to write that one poem that will outlast me." Among her works are a novel, *The Line of the Sun* (1989); a book of personal essays, *Silent Dancing* (1990); and two collections of prose and poetry, *The Latin Deli* (1993) and *The Year of Our Revolution* (1998).

For Independent Reading

If you enjoyed this story, try reading Cofer's *An Island Like You: Stories of the Barrio* (1995). The anthology includes "Catch the Moon" and other stories about the experiences of Puerto Rican teenagers growing up in the United States today.

DIFFERENTIATING INSTRUCTION

Advanced Learners

Enrichment. Tell students that Judith Ortiz Cofer has spoken and written extensively on the pleasures and difficulties of her dual heritage and the experience of reconciling two different cultures.

Activity. Encourage students to find out more about Cofer and her views on trying to bridge cultures through writing. To find articles, interviews, and essays by or about the writer, suggest that students enter the keywords *Judith Ortiz Cofer* and *Puerto Rico* into an Internet search engine.

Literary Response and Analysis

Reading Check

1. Why is Luis working for his father?
2. Who are the Tiburones, and what does their name mean?
3. What "treasure hunt" does Luis go on late one night?
4. Find the passage that explains the story's title.

Interpretations

5. Describe Luis's attitude at the beginning of the story toward his job in his father's junkyard. How has his attitude changed by the end of the story? Why?
6. What role does Naomi play in the story? What **character traits,** aside from her beauty, make her attractive to Luis?
7. Even though she has been dead for almost three years, the mother plays an important role in this story. How does she continue to influence Luis and his father? Why do you think Luis is able to cry "a flood of tears" when he does?
8. How does Luis's relationship with his father change in the story? Do you think it will continue to change? Support your answers with evidence from the story.
9. In light of the changes Luis undergoes and the reasons for those changes, what would you say is the story's **theme,** or broad **generalization** about life? Remember to state the theme as a complete sentence.

Evaluation

10. How believable is the change that Luis undergoes? Look back at your Quickwrite notes to see whether his behavior fits your ideas about the things people do for love.

Literary Criticism

11. In an essay about cultural awareness titled "I Am Latina Wherever I Am," Judith Ortiz Cofer says:

> I believe my role as an artist is to build bridges. To unite us with the world and fellow beings.

Do you think "Catch the Moon" accomplishes Cofer's goal of building bridges between cultures? Does the story express **universal** concerns and **themes**? Explain your answers.

Writing

Memory and Imagination

Cofer gives us her writing formula:

> I follow cuentos, memories, characters that take me back to moments of being in my life. I recreate the scenes of my youth and transform them with my imagination.

Test Cofer's technique. Reach into your memories, and pull out one actual scene—a real event and a character or two—and don't forget to add your imagination. Make up details, vary what really happened, and write a short piece of what Cofer calls "creative nonfiction," a hybrid of reality and imagination.

Pages 232–254 cover **Reading Standard 3.5** Compare works that express a universal theme and provide evidence to support the ideas expressed in each work.

INDEPENDENT PRACTICE

Literary Response and Analysis

Interpretations

5. At first, Luis resents having to work in the junkyard and ridicules his father's business. Luis's search for the hubcap changes his feelings. He comes to understand his father's satisfaction.
6. Naomi's appearance leads Luis to the funeral home, where he confronts his emotions over his mother's death. It also triggers his search for the hubcap. Luis is attracted to Naomi because of her poise and compassion.
7. Possible answer: The absence of his mother is one of Luis's difficulties, particularly in his relationship with his father. Luis cries because of the strong emotions stirred by his memory of his mother.
8. Luis's attitude changes from one of resentment to one of appreciation. Luis's intention to build a display wall for his father's business suggests that Luis's relationship with his father will improve.
9. Possible themes: Love can help people overcome their problems. People must confront the pain of loss.

Evaluation

10. Possible answer: The changes in Luis are plausible. Once he acknowledges the pain associated with his mother's death, he is able to manage his anger and to love again.

Literary Criticism

11. Possible answer: Yes, Cofer accomplishes her goal. While focusing on the experiences of a Puerto Rican teenager, Cofer demonstrates the universal nature of concerns such as love, family, and loss.

Reading Check

1. Luis works for his father because it is one of the conditions for his early release from juvenile hall.
2. The Tiburones are members of Luis's gang. *Tiburones* is the Spanish word for "sharks."
3. Luis searches through a mountain of hubcaps for the vintage wheel cover that Naomi wants.
4. The fourth paragraph on p. 239 explains the title. The wheel cover that Luis finds for Naomi is "moon-shaped."

Vocabulary Development

Practice 1

1. No; a kind person would not bother or upset a child.
2. No; when a clock is in pieces, it no longer functions.
3. Yes; a very old dress could be described that way.
4. No; ebony-colored hair would be very dark.
5. Yes; sarcasm is often bitter or insulting.
6. Yes; many museums contain artifacts from the past.

Practice 2

Possible Answers

1. *Expressions*—simile, metaphor. *Sentence*—He made a sweeping gesture over the piles of junked cars and mounds of metal parts.
2. *Expression*—idiom. *Sentence*—I am working extremely hard.
3. *Expression*—metaphor. *Sentence*—Keep the ice on that swelling.

Resources Reminder

Vocabulary

- *Vocabulary Development*
  - Vocabulary Worksheet, p. 19
- *Lesson Plans for Language Development*
  - Vocabulary, pp. 128, 133

ASSESSING

Assessment

- *Progress Assessment of Reading*
  - Selection Test

RETEACHING

For a lesson reteaching Standard 3.5, see **Reteaching,** p. 939A. For another selection to teach Standard 3.5, see *Interactive Reading,* Chapter 4.

Vocabulary Development

Word Meanings—Yes or No?

PRACTICE 1

Be sure to justify your yes-or-no answers to these questions.

1. Would you expect a kind person to be harassing a child?
2. If you dismantled a clock, would it still tell time?
3. Could a dress be described as vintage?
4. Would a blonde's hair be described as ebony?
5. Would a sarcastic person hurt people's feelings?
6. Could you find relics in a museum?

Word Bank
harassing
dismantled
vintage
ebony
sarcastic
relics

Figurative Language—Don't Take It Literally

Figurative language is language that is not meant to be taken literally. Here are three common types of figurative language:

- An **idiom** is an expression that is peculiar to a language and cannot be understood from the literal definitions of its words.
  "The old man looked like he wanted to walk down memory lane." [When you take a walk down memory lane, you're not literally walking anywhere—you're just recalling fond memories.]
- A **simile** uses the word *like, as, than,* or *resembles* to compare two unlike things.
  "The tree looked different now, not like a skeleton, as it had then, but green with leaves." [How can a tree look like a skeleton? When it is down to its "bare bones"—its trunk and branches.]
- A **metaphor** compares two unlike things by saying that something is something else. It also omits the word *like, as, than,* or *resembles.*
  "Luis Cintrón sits on top of a six-foot pile of hubcaps and watches his father walk away into the steel jungle of his car junkyard." [The jumbled auto parts are compared to a densely overgrown jungle.]

Grade 8 Review Reading Standard 1.1 Analyze idioms, analogies, metaphors, and similies to infer the literal and figurative meanings of phrases.

Reading Standard 1.1 Identify and use the literal and figurative meanings of words.

PRACTICE 2

Tell whether each underlined expression is an **idiom,** a **simile,** or a **metaphor.** Then, write a sentence that expresses the same idea in literal, not figurative, language. Which sentence do you prefer? Why?

1. "He yells at no one, 'Someday, son, all this will be yours,' and sweeps his arms like the Pope blessing a crowd over the piles of car sandwiches and mounds of metal parts. . . ."
2. "'That's what I'm doing, right? Working my hands to the bone.' . . ."
3. "'I'll be back by ten, and keep the ice on that egg.' . . ."

242 Chapter 4 Comparing Themes • Evaluating Arguments: Pro and Con

Before You Read

The Bass, the River, and Sheila Mant

Literary Focus

Theme and Conflict: Struggle Toward Meaning

Often the **theme** of a story—its message about life—is directly tied to the main character's **conflict,** or struggle, and to how that conflict is resolved. Remember that a conflict may be **external** (a show-down with another character or a struggle with nature) or **internal** (a struggle between competing desires or between two aspects of a character's personality). Internal conflicts force us to choose, and that choice can be agonizing.

In this story the main character is caught up in both external and internal conflicts. Watch to see how he deals with them and what the story's ending suggests about its theme.

Reading Skills

Making Inferences About Character Motivation

Why do characters act the way they do? In order for a story to be convincing, we need to be able to infer the characters' **motivations**—the causes of their behavior. Literary characters, like real-life people, are motivated by their wants and needs. As you read this story, see if you can infer the narrator's motivations for the choices he makes. Do his motivations seem believable?

Make the Connection

Quickwrite

Think back to some time when you had to give up one thing for something else. Write down what happened. Looking back, do you feel that you made the right choice? Do you have any regrets? Explain.

Vocabulary Development

denizens (den′ə·zenz) *n.:* inhabitants or occupants.

pensive (pen′siv) *adj.:* dreamily thoughtful.

dubious (do͞o′bē·əs) *adj.:* doubtful; not sure.

antipathy (an·tip′ə·thē) *n.:* feeling of hatred; powerful and deep dislike.

filial (fil′ē·əl) *adj.:* pertaining to or due from a son or a daughter.

surreptitiously (sur′əp·tish′əs·lē) *adv.:* stealthily; sneakily.

conspicuous (kən·spik′yo͞o·əs) *adj.:* obvious or easy to see.

concussion (kən·kush′ən) *n.:* powerful shock or impact.

luminous (lo͞o′mə·nəs) *adj.:* glowing; giving off light.

quizzical (kwiz′i·kəl) *adj.:* puzzled; questioning.

Pages 232–254 cover **Reading Standard 3.5** Compare works that express a universal theme and provide evidence to support the ideas expressed in each work.

STANDARDS FOCUS, pp. 243–253

(For the grade-level standards taught in this lesson, see citations on Student Edition pages.)

Prerequisite Standard

- Grade 8, Literary Response and Analysis 3.5 **Identify and analyze recurring themes (e.g., good versus evil) across traditional and contemporary works.**

Reading Skills

- Make inferences about character motivation.

Summary *at grade level*

The story's narrator recalls a summer on a New England river when he obsessively fished and admired the older girl next door, Sheila. One day he asks Sheila to a dance and picks her up in his canoe. When the boy moves to conceal his fishing rod, a huge bass strikes. As Sheila talks, the narrator faces external conflict (keeping the bass on the line a secret), as well as the internal conflict of deciding whether he wants Sheila or the bass more. These conflicts are clues to the story's theme, which deals with the necessity of making choices. The narrator chooses romance, secretly cutting the fishing line at the story's climax. However, Sheila leaves the dance with a college boy. The older, reflective narrator calls his choice a mistake that he has never repeated.

RESOURCES: READING

Planning

- *One-Stop Planner* CD-ROM with Test Generator
- *On Course: Mapping Instruction*

Media

- *Audio CD Library*
  - disc 8
- *Fine Art Transparencies*
  - Transparency 7

Reading

- *Interactive Reading,* Teacher's Edition
  - Graphic Organizer: Theme Map

Differentiating Instruction

- *Lesson Plans for Language Development*
  - English-Language Learners, pp. 109–111, 129, 134
  - Special Education Students, pp. 112, 129, 134

Vocabulary

- *Vocabulary Development*
  - Vocabulary Worksheet, p. 20

Assessment

- *Progress Assessment of Reading*
  - Selection Test
- *One-Stop Planner* CD-ROM with Test Generator

Selection Starter

Motivate. Ask students if they have ever had to make a choice in a win-win situation, in which both options were equally appealing. Have a volunteer describe such a situation and tell why having two appealing options can make it especially hard to choose. Then, have students complete the Quickwrite activity.

Preview Vocabulary

Have students complete each of the following sentences with the correct Vocabulary word from p. 243.

1. In the days leading up to the debate, ______ between the two rivals increased. [antipathy]
2. Thinking about her future on graduation day, my sister remained in a ______ mood. [pensive]
3. Since James nearly failed math, I am ______ about him pursuing a career in science. [dubious]
4. The hurricane destroyed the flimsy houses, leaving their ______ homeless. [denizens]
5. We easily found Jeremy in the crowd because his purple hat made him ______. [conspicuous]
6. I hoped no one would notice when I ______ reached for a third helping. [surreptitiously]
7. Forget about ______ loyalty, Dad. I'm not sharing my dessert! [filial]
8. The ______ shattered windows blocks away. [concussion]
9. The teacher gave me a ______ look when I asked to teach the class. [quizzical]
10. Her face was ______ with pride when she received the award. [luminous]

Assign the Reading

Homework

You may wish to review the selection Vocabulary words in class; then, assign the story to be read independently as homework.

The Bass, the River, and Sheila Mant

W. D. Wetherell

I never made the same mistake again.

244

DIFFERENTIATING INSTRUCTION

Learners Having Difficulty

Modeling. To help students read "The Bass, the River, and Sheila Mant," model the reading skill of making inferences about a character's motivation. Tell students to suppose they read that a character denies or lies about something important to him or her. Based on what they know about human behavior, students might infer that the character is trying to please or impress someone else. Encourage students to draw on their own experiences as they read, asking themselves questions such as "Why is the character acting this way?"

English-Language Learners

Students may not know the specialized terms related to swimming, fishing, and boating. You might preview the footnoted boating terms, as well as such swimming terms as *laps, flutter kick, crawl,* and *tuck and a half,* and

There was a summer in my life when the only creature that seemed lovelier to me than a largemouth bass was Sheila Mant. I was fourteen. The Mants had rented the cottage next to ours on the river; with their parties, their frantic games of softball, their constant comings and goings, they appeared to me denizens of a brilliant existence. "Too noisy by half," my mother quickly decided, but I would have given anything to be invited to one of their parties, and when my parents went to bed I would sneak through the woods to their hedge and stare enchanted at the candlelit swirl of white dresses and bright, paisley skirts.

Sheila was the middle daughter—at seventeen, all but out of reach. She would spend her days sunbathing on a float my Uncle Sierbert had moored in their cove, and before July was over I had learned all her moods. If she lay flat on the diving board with her hand trailing idly in the water, she was pensive, not to be disturbed. On her side, her head propped up by her arm, she was observant, considering those around her with a look that seemed queenly and severe. Sitting up, arms tucked around her long, suntanned legs, she was approachable, but barely, and it was only in those glorious moments when she stretched herself prior to entering the water that her various suitors found the courage to come near.

These were many. The Dartmouth heavyweight crew would scull[1] by her house on their way upriver, and I think all eight of them must have been in love with her at various times during the summer; the coxswain[2] would curse them through his megaphone, but without effect—there was always a pause in their pace when they passed Sheila's float. I suppose to these jaded twenty-year-olds she seemed the incarnation of innocence and youth, while to me she appeared unutterably suave, the epitome[3] of sophistication. I was on the swim team at school, and to win her attention would do endless laps between my house and the Vermont shore, hoping she would notice the beauty of my flutter kick, the power of my crawl. Finishing, I would boost myself up onto our dock and glance casually over toward her, but she was never watching, and the miraculous day she was, I immediately climbed the diving board and did my best tuck and a half for her and continued diving until she had left and the sun went down and my longing was like a madness and I couldn't stop.

It was late August by the time I got up the nerve to ask her out. The tortured will-I's, won't-I's, the agonized indecision over what to say, the false starts toward her house and embarrassed retreats—the details of these have been seared from my memory, and the only part I remember clearly is emerging from the woods toward dusk

1. **scull** (skul) *v.:* row, as a rowboat.
2. **coxswain** (käk′sən) *n.:* person steering a racing shell and calling out the rhythm of the strokes for the crew.
3. **epitome** (ē·pit′ə·mē′) *n.:* embodiment; one that is representative of a type or class.

Vocabulary
denizens (den′ə·zənz) *n.:* inhabitants or occupants.
pensive (pen′siv) *adj.:* dreamily thoughtful.

DIRECT TEACHING

A Reading Skills

Making inferences about character motivation. Based on this first sentence, what inferences can you make about the narrator's major interests at this time in his life? [Possible response: He loves fishing; he likes a girl named Sheila Mant.]

B English-Language Learners

Understanding idioms. Students may need help with the idiomatic expressions *all but* and *out of reach.* Tell them that *all but* means "nearly" or "just about." Explain that the literal meaning of *out of reach* is "beyond how far a person can reach" but that the phrase has the figurative meaning of "unobtainable." Taken together, the two idioms indicate that the seventeen-year-old girl is beyond what a fourteen-year-old boy might reasonably hope for in a girlfriend.

C Literary Focus
GRADE-LEVEL STANDARD

Theme and conflict. What internal conflict obsesses the narrator all summer long? [He wants to ask Sheila on a date but fears rejection.]

such fishing terms as *rod, reel, plug, casts, lure, let out line,* and *flared gills.* You might also provide photos of anglers and their gear to help students visualize the action.

Resources Reminder

For lessons designed for intermediate and advanced English-language learners, see *Lesson Plans for Language Development,* pp. 109–111, 129, 134.

Special Education Students

For lessons designed for special education students, see *Lesson Plans for Language Development,* pp. 112, 129, 134.

Advanced Learners

Acceleration. Use the following activity with advanced learners to move them toward the eleventh- and twelfth-grade Standard 3.2, for which they use textual evidence to analyze how a theme represents a comment on life.

Activity. After students read the story, ask them to share their interpretations of the theme in small groups. Have them identify details that support their interpretations.

DIRECT TEACHING

A Reading Skills

Making inferences about character motivation. Why doesn't the narrator just say "mounted my reel on my spinning rod"? Why do you think he also names the manufacturer of each item? [Possible response: Often when someone unnecessarily provides a brand name, it indicates that the item in question is of high quality. The narrator is probably quite proud of his equipment; it means a lot to him.]

B Learners Having Difficulty

Questioning. Why does the narrator lower his fishing gear into the water as he paddles to the Mants' dock? [He does it automatically, because he's used to fishing whenever he's in the canoe.] Suggest that students pay attention to the effects of this action as they continue to read the story.

while they were playing softball on their lawn, as bashful and frightened as a unicorn.

Sheila was stationed halfway between first and second, well outside the infield. She didn't seem surprised to see me—as a matter of fact, she didn't seem to see me at all.

"If you're playing second base, you should move closer," I said.

She turned—I took the full brunt of her long red hair and well-spaced freckles.

"I'm playing outfield," she said, "I don't like the responsibility of having a base."

"Yeah, I can understand that," I said, though I couldn't. "There's a band in Dixford tomorrow night at nine. Want to go?"

One of her brothers sent the ball sailing over the left-fielder's head; she stood and watched it disappear toward the river.

"You have a car?" she said, without looking up.

I played my master stroke. "We'll go by canoe."

I spent all of the following day polishing it. I turned it upside down on our lawn and rubbed every inch with Brillo, hosing off the dirt, wiping it with chamois[4] until it gleamed as bright as aluminum ever gleamed. About five, I slid it into the water, arranging cushions near the bow so Sheila could lean on them if she was in one of her pensive moods, propping up my father's transistor radio by the middle thwart[5] so we could have music when we came back. **A** Automatically, without thinking about it, I mounted my Mitchell reel on my Pfleuger spinning rod and stuck it in the stern.

I say automatically, because I never went anywhere that summer without a fishing rod. When I wasn't swimming laps to impress Sheila, I was back in our driveway practicing casts, and when I wasn't practicing casts, I was tying the line to Tosca, our springer spaniel, to test the reel's drag, and when I wasn't doing any of those things, I was fishing the river for bass.

Too nervous to sit at home, I got in the canoe early and started paddling in a huge circle that would get me to Sheila's dock around eight. **B** As automatically as I brought along my rod, I tied on a big Rapala plug, let it down into the water, let out some line, and immediately forgot all about it.

It was already dark by the time I glided up to the Mants' dock. Even by day the river was quiet, most of the summer people preferring Sunapee or one of the other nearby lakes, and at night it was a solitude difficult to believe, a corridor of hidden life that ran between banks like a tunnel. Even the stars were part of it. They weren't as sharp anywhere else; they seemed to have chosen the river as a guide on their slow wheel toward morning, and in the course of the summer's fishing, I had learned all their names.

I was there ten minutes before Sheila appeared. I heard the slam of their screen door first, then saw her in the spotlight as she came slowly down the path. As beautiful as she was on the float, she

4. **chamois** (sham′ē) *n.:* soft leather used for polishing.
5. **middle thwart:** brace across the middle of a canoe.

246 Chapter 4 Comparing Themes • Evaluating Arguments: Pro and Con

was even lovelier now—her white dress went perfectly with her hair, and complimented her figure even more than her swimsuit.

It was her face that bothered me. It had on its delightful fullness a very dubious expression.

"Look," she said. "I can get Dad's car."

"It's faster this way," I lied. "Parking's tense up there. Hey, it's safe. I won't tip it or anything."

She let herself down reluctantly into the bow. I was glad she wasn't facing me. When her eyes were on me, I felt like diving in the river again from agony and joy.

I pried the canoe away from the dock and started paddling upstream. There was an extra paddle in the bow, but Sheila made no move to pick it up. She took her shoes off and dangled her feet over the side.

Ten minutes went by.

"What kind of band?" she said.

"It's sort of like folk music. You'll like it."

"Eric Caswell's going to be there. He strokes number four."[6]

"No kidding?" I said. I had no idea whom she meant.

"What's that sound?" she said, pointing toward shore.

"Bass. That splashing sound?"

"Over there."

"Yeah, bass. They come into the shallows at night to chase frogs and moths and things. Big largemouths. *Micropterus salmoides*,"[7] I added, showing off.

"I think fishing's dumb," she said, making a face. "I mean, it's boring and all. Definitely dumb."

Now I have spent a great deal of time in the years since wondering why Sheila Mant should come down so hard on fishing. Was her father a fisherman? Her antipathy toward fishing nothing more than normal filial rebellion? Had she tried it once? A messy encounter with worms? It doesn't matter. What does is that at that fragile moment in time I would have given anything not to appear dumb in Sheila's severe and unforgiving eyes.

She hadn't seen my equipment yet. What I *should* have done, of course, was push the canoe in closer to shore and carefully slide the rod into some branches where I could pick it up again in the morning. Failing that, I could have surreptitiously dumped the whole outfit overboard, written off the forty or so dollars as love's tribute. What I actually *did* do was gently lean forward, and slowly, ever so slowly, push the rod back through my legs toward the stern where it would be less conspicuous.

It must have been just exactly what the bass was waiting for. Fish will trail a lure sometimes, trying to make up their mind whether or not to attack, and the slight pause in the plug's speed caused by my adjustment was tantalizing enough to overcome the bass's inhibitions. My rod, safely out of sight at last, bent double. The line, tightly coiled, peeled off the spool with the shrill, tearing zip of a high-speed drill.

Four things occurred to me at once. One, that it was a bass. Two, that it was a big bass. Three, that it was the biggest bass I had ever hooked. Four, that Sheila Mant must not know.

"What was that?" she said, turning half around.

"Uh, what was what?"

6. **strokes number four:** rows in the fourth position on a sculling crew.
7. ***Micropterus salmoides:*** scientific name for a large-mouth bass.

Vocabulary

dubious (do͞o′bē·əs) *adj.:* doubtful; not sure.

antipathy (an·tip′ə·thē) *n.:* feeling of hatred; powerful and deep dislike.

filial (fil′ē·əl) *adj.:* pertaining to or due from a son or a daughter.

surreptitiously (sʉr′əp·tish′əs·lē) *adv.:* stealthily; sneakily.

conspicuous (kən·spik′yo͞o·əs) *adj.:* obvious or easy to see.

DIRECT TEACHING

C Literary Focus
GRADE-LEVEL STANDARD

Theme and conflict. Point out that the narrator has gotten his wish and Sheila is accompanying him to the dance. What new problem does the narrator face? [Possible response: Sheila seems quite unimpressed by his canoe. His date isn't getting off to a good start.]

D Reading Skills

Making inferences about character motivation. Note that *strokes number four* is a sculling term. Who might Eric Caswell be? [He might be one of the Dartmouth crew team members who scull by Sheila's house.] Why might Sheila mention him? [Possible response: She might want the narrator to know that she is more interested in Eric than in the narrator.]

E Literary Focus
REVIEW STANDARD

Characterization. What do Sheila's comments about fishing show about her character? [Possible responses: She is not afraid to express strong negative feelings; she is self-absorbed and insensitive; she has not noticed the narrator's fishing rod and does not understand that his knowledgeable statements about bass suggest that he probably fishes.]

F Literary Focus
GRADE-LEVEL STANDARD

Theme and conflict. What internal conflict does the narrator now face? [He is torn by two desires—catching the biggest bass he has ever hooked and keeping Sheila from knowing that he fishes.]

DIRECT TEACHING

A Advanced Learners

Acceleration. Ask students what the details in this passage indicate about the narrator. [Possible response: When he tells Sheila that she hears a bat, he is lying about something important to him; by denying his "every instinct," he is behaving unnaturally.] **From the narrator's behavior, what generalization about life could you make?** [Possible response: When people try to please someone else, they might end up denying their own sense of self.]

B Literary Focus
REVIEW STANDARD

Characterization. What do Sheila's thoughts about choosing a college reveal about her personality? [Possible responses: She is rather shallow; she seems more concerned about parties and skiing than about academics.]

C Literary Focus
GRADE-LEVEL STANDARD

Theme and conflict. What physical struggle does the narrator face? [He has hooked a large bass that is strong enough to pull the canoe backward. It takes all the narrator's strength to keep the fish on the line and the canoe in the middle of the river, away from rocks and weeds.]

"That buzzing noise."

"Bats."

She shuddered, quickly drew her feet back into the canoe. Every instinct I had told me to pick up the rod and strike back at the bass, but there was no need to—it was already solidly hooked. Downstream, an awesome distance downstream, it jumped clear of the water, landing with a concussion heavy enough to ripple the entire river. For a moment, I thought it was gone, but then the rod was bending again, the tip dancing into the water. Slowly, not making any motion that might alert Sheila, I reached down to tighten the drag.

While all this was going on, Sheila had begun talking, and it was a few minutes before I was able to catch up with her train of thought.

"I went to a party there. These fraternity men. Katherine says I could get in there if I wanted. I'm thinking more of UVM or Bennington.[8] Somewhere I can ski."

The bass was slanting toward the rocks on the New Hampshire side by the ruins of Donaldson's boathouse. It had to be an old bass—a young one probably wouldn't have known the rocks were there. I brought the canoe back into the middle of the river, hoping to head it off.

"That's neat," I mumbled. "Skiing. Yeah, I can see that."

"Eric said I have the figure to model, but I thought I should get an education first. I mean, it might be a while before I get started and all. I was thinking of getting my hair styled, more swept back? I mean, Ann-Margret?[9] Like hers, only shorter."

She hesitated. "Are we going backward?"

We were. I had managed to keep the bass in the middle of the river away from the rocks, but it had plenty of room there, and for the first time a chance to exert its full strength. I quickly computed the weight necessary to draw a fully loaded canoe backward—the thought of it made me feel faint.

"It's just the current," I said hoarsely. "No sweat or anything."

I dug in deeper with my paddle. Reassured, Sheila began talking about something else, but all my attention was taken up now with the fish. I could feel its desperation as the water grew shallower. I could sense the extra strain on the line, the frantic way it cut back and forth in the water. I could visualize what it looked like—the gape of its mouth, the flared gills and thick, vertical tail. The bass couldn't have encountered many forces in its long life that it wasn't capable of handling, and the unrelenting tug at its mouth must have been a source of great puzzlement and mounting panic.

Me, I had problems of my own. To get to Dixford, I had to paddle up a sluggish stream that came into the river beneath a covered bridge. There was a shallow sandbar at the mouth of this stream—weeds on one side, rocks on the other. Without doubt, this is where I would lose the fish.

"I have to be careful with my complexion. I tan, but in segments. I can't figure out if it's even worth it. I wouldn't even do it probably. I saw Jackie Kennedy[10] in Boston, and she wasn't tan at all."

Taking a deep breath, I paddled as hard as I could for the middle, deepest part of the bar. I could have threaded the eye of a needle with the canoe, but the pull on the stern threw me off, and I overcompensated—the canoe veered

8. **UVM or Bennington:** University of Vermont or Bennington College, Bennington, Vermont.

9. **Ann-Margret** (1941–): movie star who was very popular at the time of this story.

10. **Jackie Kennedy** (1929–1994): First Lady during the administration of President John F. Kennedy; greatly admired by the public for her dignity and sense of style.

Vocabulary
concussion (kən·kush′ən) *n.:* powerful shock or impact.

READING MINI-LESSON

Developing Word-Attack Skills

Remind students to think of the following when they are trying to pronounce an unfamiliar word:

- what sounds the letters represent
- how the word breaks into syllables
- which syllable to stress most

Write the Vocabulary word *surreptitiously* on the chalkboard, and demonstrate how to break the word into syllables, reminding students that every syllable has one vowel sound: sur-rep-ti-tious-ly.

Remind students that when the letters *ti* precede another vowel, they usually stand for the sound /sh/. Have students read the separate syllables in *isolation.* Then, have them put the syllables together to pronounce the whole word and decide which syllable is said with the greatest stress.

Activity. Have students write these words in syllables and underline the syllable that is said with the greatest stress. Encourage students to consult a dictionary as needed.

1. incommunicative [in com <u>mu</u> ni ca tive]
2. imperturbable [im per <u>turb</u> a ble]
3. repugnant [re <u>pug</u> nant]
4. defenestration [de fen es <u>tra</u> tion]
5. perpendicular [per pen <u>dic</u> u lar]

left and scraped bottom. I pushed the paddle down and shoved. A moment of hesitation . . . a moment more. . . . The canoe shot clear into the deeper water of the stream. I immediately looked down at the rod. It was bent in the same tight arc—miraculously, the bass was still on.

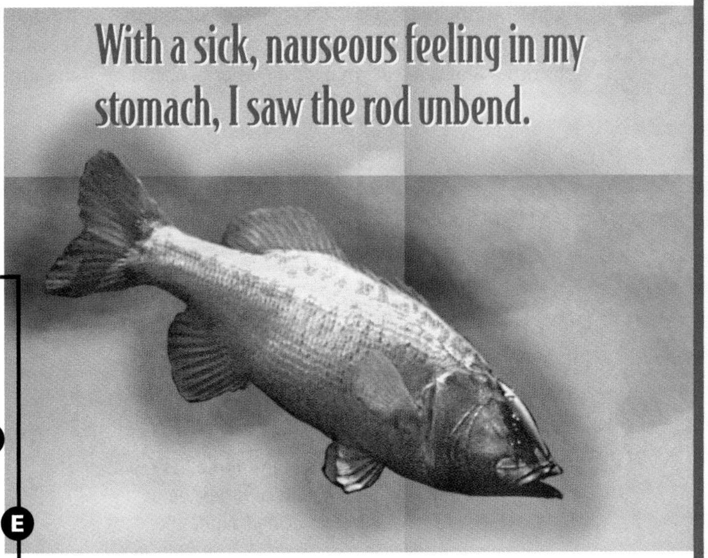

The moon was out now. It was low and full enough that its beam shone directly on Sheila there ahead of me in the canoe, washing her in a creamy, luminous glow. I could see the lithe,[11] easy shape of **D** her figure. I could see the way her hair curled down off her shoulders, the proud, alert tilt of her head, and all these things were as **E** a tug on my heart. Not just Sheila, but the aura she carried about her of parties and casual touchings and grace. Behind me, I could feel the strain of the bass, steadier now, growing weaker, and this was another tug on my heart, not just the bass but the beat of the river and the slant of the stars and the smell of the night, until finally it seemed I would be torn apart between longings, split in half. Twenty yards ahead of us was the road, and once I pulled the canoe up on shore, the bass would be gone, irretrievably gone. If instead I stood up, grabbed the rod, and started pumping, I would have it—as tired as the bass was, there was no chance it could get away. I reached down for the rod, hesitated, looked up to where Sheila was stretching herself lazily toward the sky, her small breasts rising beneath the soft fabric of her dress, and the tug was too much for me, and quicker than it takes to write down, I pulled a penknife from my pocket and cut the line in half.

With a sick, nauseous feeling in my stomach, I saw the rod unbend. **F**

11. **lithe** (līth) *adj.:* flexible; limber.

"My legs are sore," Sheila whined. "Are we there yet?"

Through a superhuman effort of self-control, I was able to beach the canoe and help Sheila off. The rest of the night is much foggier. We walked to the fair—there was the smell of popcorn, the sound of guitars. I may have danced once or twice with her, but all I really remember is her coming over to me once the music was done to explain that she would be going home in Eric Caswell's Corvette.

"Okay," I mumbled.

For the first time that night she looked at me, really looked at me.

"You're a funny kid, you know that?"

Funny. Different. Dreamy. Odd. How many times was I to hear that in the years to come, all spoken with the same quizzical, half-accusatory tone Sheila used then. Poor Sheila! Before the month was over, the spell she cast over me was

Vocabulary
luminous (lo͞o′mə·nəs) *adj.:* glowing; giving off light.
quizzical (kwiz′i·kəl) *adj.:* puzzled; questioning.

DIRECT TEACHING

D Literary Focus
REVIEW STANDARD

Imagery. Why do you think the writer includes these details about Sheila's appearance? [Possible response: The details indicate that the narrator's attention is veering away from the bass and back to Sheila. The narrator's internal conflict is intensifying.]

E Literary Focus
GRADE-LEVEL STANDARD

Theme and conflict. What two tugs or "longings" make the narrator feel "split in half"? [The narrator's longing for Sheila and his longing to catch the bass make him feel "split in half."] **According to the narrator, what more general aspects of life do Sheila and the bass represent?** [Sheila represents a sophisticated social world the narrator wants to share; the bass represents his longing to be close to nature.]

F Literary Focus
GRADE-LEVEL STANDARD

Theme and conflict. How does this image of the unbending rod resolve the story's conflict? [Possible response: Since the fish is now gone, the narrator can turn his attention to Sheila. However, he immediately recognizes by his "sick, nauseous feeling" that he has made the wrong decision.]

6. apprehensive [ap pre hen sive]
7. acculturation [ac cul tur a tion]
8. circumference [cir cum fer ence]
9. hallucinatory [hal lu cin a to ry]
10. corpuscle [cor pus cle]

FAMILY/COMMUNITY ACTIVITY

Ask students to share this story with their families. Students can discuss with parents and older family members the topic of making important decisions.

Encourage students to ask questions, such as the following: "What was one of the toughest choices you ever had to make?"; "Looking back, do you feel that you made the right decision?"; and "What did you learn about yourself during the decision-making process?"

DIRECT TEACHING

A Literary Focus
GRADE-LEVEL STANDARD
Comparing universal themes. The story provides an important insight: Even when people make the wrong choice, they have the opportunity to learn from their mistakes and make better choices in the future. Urge students to consider this idea with respect to some of the choices Luis makes in "Catch the Moon" (p. 234).

GUIDED PRACTICE

Monitoring students' progress. Guide the class in answering these questions. Direct students to locate passages in the text that support their responses.

Short Answer

1. What is the story's setting? [summer, on a river in New England]
2. What are the narrator's two passions? [fishing and Sheila Mant]
3. Who else notices Sheila Mant? [the Dartmouth rowing crew, specifically Eric Caswell]
4. Where does the narrator ask Sheila to go with him? [to a dance]
5. At the end of the story, what does Sheila call the narrator? ["a funny kid"]

Meet the Writer

Background. Wetherell has been praised for revealing his characters' inner lives. For *The New York Times,* critic Michiko Kakutani wrote, "He shows us how their secret hopes and fears collide with external events, how conflicting emotions can cut off all possibilities of spiritual fulfillment."

gone, but the memory of that lost bass haunted me all summer and haunts me still. There would be other Sheila Mants in my life, other fish, and though I came close once or twice, it was these secret, hidden tuggings in the night that claimed **A** me, and I never made the same mistake again. ■

Meet the Writer

W. D. Wetherell

An Eye for Detail

W. D. Wetherell (1948–) lives in New Hampshire. He was born in Mineola, New York, and earned a bachelor's degree at Hofstra University, on Long Island. Like many writers he has worked at various jobs—he has been a magazine editor, a movie extra, a teacher, a journalist, and a tour guide. Wetherell's works have won numerous awards, including the O. Henry Award, the Drue Heinz Literature Prize, and a fellowship in fiction from the National Endowment for the Arts. "The Bass, the River, and Sheila Mant" won the 1983 PEN Syndicated Fiction Prize. Having read this story, you won't be surprised to learn that Wetherell has also written essays about nature and fishing.

In one essay he relates a "fish story" with an ending quite different from the one you just read. In the Pacific Northwest his wife asked him to take a photograph of her and the fish she had caught.

"And I did, and as I focused the lens, the fog lifted, and behind her I saw the snowbanks and glacier and cliffs that framed the pond, revealing themselves only now when the moment was perfect. I held the camera steady until the beauty of the water and the woman and the trout came together, then—the moment captured—I crossed over the logs and took my wife by the hand."

250 Chapter 4 Comparing Themes • Evaluating Arguments: Pro and Con

It's Raining in Love

Richard Brautigan

I don't know what it is,
but I distrust myself
when I start to like a girl
a lot.

It makes me nervous.
I don't say the right things
or perhaps I start
to examine,
evaluate,
compute
what I am saying.

If I say, "Do you think it's going to rain?"
and she says, "I don't know,"
I start thinking: Does she really like me?

In other words
I get a little creepy.

A friend of mine once said,
"It's twenty times better to be friends
with someone
than it is to be in love with them."

I think he's right and besides,
it's raining somewhere, programming flowers
and keeping snails happy.
That's all taken care of.

BUT
if a girl likes me a lot
and starts getting real nervous
and suddenly begins asking me funny questions
and looks sad if I give the wrong answers
and she says things like,
"Do you think it's going to rain?"
and I say, "It beats me,"
and she says, "Oh,"
and looks a little sad
at the clear blue California sky,
I think: Thank God, it's you, baby, this time
instead of me.

The Heart in Bliss (1992) by Jim Dine. Oil, enamel, pencil, and wood fragment on canvas ($82\frac{1}{2}'' \times 86\frac{7}{8}''$).

Connection

Summary at grade level

For the speaker in Richard Brautigan's poem, falling in love can often mean temporarily losing one's sense of self-confidence. When concerned with impressing a girl whom he likes, the speaker becomes nervous about everything he says and does.

DIRECT TEACHING

VIEWING THE ART

Jim Dine (1935–) is an American artist known for his painted explorations of ordinary objects and icons including tools, bathrobes, and hearts.

Activity. Ask students to discuss the meaning of the painting's title. [Students may indicate that the painting captures the complexity of human emotions such as bliss.]

B Reading Skills

Comparing and contrasting. Have students note how the speaker's remark that he becomes "creepy" echoes the words of the narrator of "The Bass, the River, and Sheila Mant," who says that in similar situations he gets called "funny," "different," and "odd." Why might this happen to them? [Possible response: In situations where they are trying to impress someone, both the speaker and the narrator behave unusually because they are filled with insecurity, causing them to act and speak in ways that are not true to themselves.]

C Reading Skills

Analyzing details. Why does the poet mention "the clear blue California sky"? [Possible response: The clear sky indicates that rain is not a strong possibility. It is likely that the girl is nervous and searching for things to talk about.]

Connecting and Comparing Texts

Encourage students to compare the feelings expressed by the speaker of the poem with those experienced by the narrator of "The Bass, the River, and Sheila Mant." How does this poem reflect some of the central issues confronted by the narrator of that story? [The poem echoes the story's focus on what happens to a person's self-confidence when he is trying to win the object of his infatuation.] Ask students to also explain how the two works differ. [Possible responses: Unlike the narrator of "The Bass, the River, and Sheila Mant," the speaker of the poem also tells of a moment when the tables are turned and the speaker is the one who makes someone else nervous.]

INDEPENDENT PRACTICE

Literary Response and Analysis

Reading Check

1. The narrator tries to summon up the courage to ask Sheila Mant to go on a date with him.
2. He knows the bass is very large from the way his rod bends when the fish is hooked.
3. The narrator doesn't tell Sheila because she has just said that she thinks fishing is dumb.
4. Sheila essentially ignores the narrator, leaving him for an older boy.

Interpretations

5. The title contains the elements of his internal conflict (choosing between the bass and Sheila Mant) and his external conflicts (with the bass and the river).
6. The climax occurs at the moment when the narrator decides to cut the line and let the fish get away.
7. The narrator is motivated by two desires: to catch the biggest bass he has ever hooked and to impress the object of his affection, Sheila Mant. Some students may say his choice of the girl over the fish is believable because he has been obsessed with her for most of the summer; others may say that his love of fishing makes his choice unlikely.
8. Possible answer: The "secret, hidden tuggings in the night" refer to the pull of the bass on the line and his attempt to hide it from Sheila. The narrator means that he has never again made the mistake of not being true to himself in order to please others.
9. Possible themes: We learn from our mistakes; we must be true to who we are. The narrator's final statements support these responses.

Literary Response and Analysis

Reading Check

1. At the beginning of the story, what does the narrator try to find the courage to do?
2. How does the narrator know the bass on his line is very large?
3. Why doesn't the narrator tell Sheila that he has caught the bass?
4. How does Sheila behave toward the narrator when they get to the dance?

Interpretations

5. How does the story's **title** suggest the narrator's **external** and **internal conflicts**?
6. What is the story's **climax**—the moment of greatest excitement, when the conflict is resolved?
7. What two conflicting desires, or **motivations,** does the narrator have? Is his choice between them believable? Explain your answers.
8. What do you think the "secret, hidden tuggings in the night" are that the narrator mentions in the last sentence? What mistake has he never repeated?
9. Express the story's **theme** in one or more sentences. Remember that the theme makes a general statement about life and people. Find evidence in the story to support the theme.

Pages 232–254 cover **Reading Standard 3.5** Compare works that express a universal theme and provide evidence to support the ideas expressed in each work.

Evaluation

10. Does the narrator's experience remind you of any personal experience with making a difficult choice? Looking back, are you now happy with your choice? Explain. (Be sure to check your Quickwrite notes.)
11. Some readers object to the **characterization** of Sheila Mant as a beautiful airhead, a stereotype. How would you respond to this criticism?
12. Would you recommend this story to other students? Rate the story on a scale from zero (worst) to ten (best). Give at least three reasons for your rating. Consider the plot, the characters, and the theme.

Writing

Poem Versus Story—Alike and Yet . . .

Although "It's Raining in Love" (see the ***Connection*** on page 251) is a poem and "The Bass, the River, and Sheila Mant" is a story, the two works are similar in many ways. Write a paragraph or two in which you **compare** the conflicts of the narrators and the way the conflicts relate to the themes of the two works. In what ways are the themes similar? In what ways are they different?

Comparing Themes
For a writing assignment comparing the themes in "Catch the Moon" and "The Bass, the River, and Sheila Mant," see page 254.

Evaluation

10. Some students may say that they, like the narrator, learned from a mistake. Others may say that they were happy with their decisions.
11. Possible answers: The character does have stereotypical qualities, but some people are in fact that shallow; the narrator may portray Sheila negatively in order to save face over his inability to win her; the characterization adds humor to the story.
12. Some students will rate the story highly, noting its plausible plot, its appealing main character, and its realistic account of a teenager's struggle with hard choices. Others will be less impressed, citing the flat portrayal of Sheila, an inability to relate to the narrator's passion for fishing, and the need for the narrator to state the theme at the end.

Vocabulary Development

Synonyms and Antonyms

PRACTICE

Synonyms are words with similar meanings. **Antonyms** are words with opposite meanings: *warm/cool, happy/sad.* Make a synonym or antonym map for each Word Bank word. *Filial* has been done for you. Not all words have antonyms, so make antonym maps for these words: *dubious, antipathy, surreptitiously, conspicuous,* and *luminous.* For the rest of the words, make synonym maps.

filial → Synonym: daughterly

filial: A good parent has earned filial respect.

Synonym: daughterly: She showed her father a daughterly devotion.

Word Bank
- denizens
- pensive
- dubious
- antipathy
- filial
- surreptitiously
- conspicuous
- concussion
- luminous
- quizzical

Reading Standard 1.1 Identify and use the literal meanings of words.

Grammar Link MINI-LESSON

Stop That Run-on Sentence

A **run-on sentence** is made up of two or more sentences that are separated by a comma or are not set off with any punctuation. Here are three strategies for correcting run-ons:

1. Separate the run-on into two sentences.
   RUN-ON The narrator cuts the bass loose, he regrets it later.
   CORRECT The narrator cuts the bass loose. He regrets it later.
2. Change the run-on sentence to a compound sentence by using either a comma and a coordinating conjunction (such as *and, but, or,* or *so*) or a semicolon.
   CORRECT The narrator cuts the bass loose, but he regrets it later.
   CORRECT The narrator cuts the bass loose; he regrets it later.
3. Turn one sentence into a subordinate clause.
   CORRECT Although the narrator cuts the bass loose, he regrets it later.

PRACTICE

Act as an editor, and rewrite the following paragraph. Use all three strategies for correcting run-on sentences.

Sheila wanted to drive to the dance the narrator said they'd go in his canoe she didn't seem very happy about it, on the way to the dance all she did was talk about herself. They got to the dance, the narrator cut the bass loose, he didn't see Sheila much that night he didn't take her home probably that was their last date.

For more help, see Run-on Sentences in the *Holt Handbook,* pages 454–456.

Vocabulary Development

Practice

Possible Answers

- *denizens. Synonym*—residents. *Sentence*—The residents of the cabins are friends.
- *pensive. Synonym*—reflective. *Sentence*—The reflective boy thought about his mistakes.
- *concussion. Synonym*—jolt. *Sentence*—The jolt from the blow knocked him down.
- *quizzical. Synonym*—curious. *Sentence*—Sheila gave the odd painting a curious look.
- *dubious. Antonym*—certain. *Sentence*—I am certain that I exist.
- *antipathy. Antonym*—love. *Sentence*—I share the narrator's love for fishing.
- *surreptitiously. Antonym*—openly. *Sentence*—The boy openly watched the rehearsal.
- *conspicuous. Antonym*—unobtrusive. *Sentence*—The unobtrusive boy disturbed no one.
- *luminous. Antonym*—dull. *Sentence*—The silver tray was dull until he polished it.

Resources Reminder

Vocabulary

- *Vocabulary Development*
  - Vocabulary Worksheet, p. 20
- *Lesson Plans for Language Development*
  - Vocabulary, pp. 129, 134

Grammar Link

Practice

Possible Answer

Sheila wanted to drive to the dance. When the narrator said they'd go in his canoe, she didn't seem very happy about it. On the way to the dance, all she did was talk about herself. Just before they got to the dance, the narrator cut the bass loose. He didn't see Sheila much that night, and he didn't take her home. That was probably their last date.

ASSESSING

Assessment

- *Progress Assessment of Reading*
  - Selection Test

RETEACHING

For a lesson reteaching Standard 3.5, see **Reteaching,** p. 939A. For another selection to teach Standard 3.5, see *Interactive Reading,* Chapter 4.

The Bass, the River, and Sheila Mant 253

Writing a Comparison-Contrast Essay

Writing Tips

Explain to students that comparing and contrasting are two skills that we use on an everyday basis. Point out that whenever we discuss with a friend the strengths and weaknesses (or similarities and differences) of two sports teams, movies, or CDs, we are engaging in comparison-and-contrast analysis.

Emphasize that effective comparisons are strengthened by elaboration, or the use of specific details. For example, it is easy to say "Movie A is a much better movie than movie B," but there's no evidence to back up the statement. The argument is made stronger by citing specific scenes, aspects of the plot, bits of dialogue, or acting performances.

After reviewing the lesson with students, point out that the elements in the chart are just a sample. Students may choose to use these elements or different ones in their own essays. If they choose to use different elements, their essays should still use block organization and address the themes of both stories.

Writing a Comparison-Contrast Essay

Comparing Universal Themes

Now that you have read "Catch the Moon" and "The Bass, the River, and Sheila Mant," you can compare the themes of the two stories in a comparison-contrast essay. When you write a **comparison-contrast essay,** you use the skills of **comparing** (finding similarities) and **contrasting** (finding differences).

Gather Your Information, and Organize It

Go back to your chart on page 232, in which you compared different elements of the two stories. It should give you plenty of information to use in writing your essay.

There are two main methods for organizing a comparison-contrast essay. One is the **block method,** which you will practice in this exercise. The other is the **point-by-point method,** which you will practice on page 283.

The Block Method

With this organization you discuss each of the *stories,* one at a time. First you write about the elements of one story. Then you discuss the same elements in the same order for the second story. The chart on the right gives an example of how to organize your comparison-contrast essay using the block method.

Pages 254–283 cover **Reading Standard 3.5** Compare works that express a universal theme, and provide evidence to support the ideas expressed in each work.

Use Three Basic Parts

Like most essays, comparison-contrast essays have three parts:

1. The **introduction,** usually a single paragraph, provides the title, author, and necessary background. It also includes your **thesis statement,** in which you explain briefly how the themes are alike or different.
2. The **body** of your essay is the part where you explain the information you've gathered in your chart. Make sure you discuss at least two different elements for each story. You might want to devote a separate paragraph to each story.
3. In the **conclusion,** sum up your major points, and add a new thought or a personal response.

Elaborate: Get Down to Specifics

You should elaborate on every general statement you make, using details, examples, and quotations from the stories.

For more help writing comparison-contrast essays, see pages 382–389.

Block Method	
Story 1: "Catch the Moon"	
Element 1:	Main character
Element 2:	Main conflict and resolution
Element 3:	How character changes
Element 4:	Theme
Story 2: "The Bass, the River, and Sheila Mant"	
Element 1:	Main character
Element 2:	Main conflict and resolution
Element 3:	How character changes
Element 4:	Theme

DIFFERENTIATING INSTRUCTION

Learners Having Difficulty

To help students better understand block organization in a comparison-contrast essay, you may wish to provide them with photocopies of a model essay. Use two different colored highlighters to demonstrate how the author organizes the essay. Use one color to highlight text that refers to the first object of comparison and the other color to highlight text that refers to the second. Explain that the thesis statement and the conclusion refer to both works and are not highlighted. As students review the essay, have them note how the author addresses the same elements for each work in the same order.

You might also suggest that students use the highlighting method as a way of editing rough drafts of their own essays. By highlighting text that refers to "Catch the Moon" and text that refers to "The Bass, the River, and Sheila Mant" in different colors, students can check if they have used the block method correctly. They can also quickly see whether they have given equal attention to both stories.

Literary Response and Analysis

Comparing a Theme Across Genres

How Does Genre Affect Theme?

You'd probably agree that reading a short story about heroism affects you differently from reading a newspaper article or a poem about it. Why? For help understanding how genre shapes your reactions, consider the following:

- **How does the choice of genre relate to the author's purpose for writing?** For example, nonfiction authors usually want to examine an issue or make a point. Fiction authors want to share their particular insights into life. Poets often want to convey a theme in an intensified way.
- **What is the theme, or main idea, and is it stated or implied?** Generally in nonfiction the author states a main idea rather directly. In a story or poem, however, the author usually implies the theme, which can often make it more difficult for the reader to figure out.
- **How does the author use the characteristics of the genre to support the theme, or main idea?** For example, nonfiction authors usually supply facts and examples as support. Fiction authors use characters, conflict, point of view, and other literary elements to develop their themes. Poets often rely on imagery, figurative language, and mood.

Exploring a Theme

The short story and the essay you are about to read treat a similar theme and topic. Each centers on a person who heroically and unselfishly goes out of his way to help others. These selections are from different genres, and you'll be examining how the choice of genre shapes the theme and topic.

Reading Skills

Comparing and Contrasting a Theme Across Genres

For help comparing the themes in these two works, review the essay on theme on pages 230–231. After you have read and discussed each selection, fill in comments in a chart like the one below. Then, turn to page 283.

	"And of Clay Are We Created"	"The Man in the Water"
Genre		
Author's purpose		
How genre relates to purpose		
Theme or main idea (stated or implied)		
How elements of genre support theme or main idea		

Pages 255–283 cover **Reading Standard 3.2** Compare and contrast the presentation of a similar theme or topic across genres to explain how the selection of genre shapes the theme or topic.

STANDARDS FOCUS, pp. 255–283

(For the grade-level standard taught in this Comparing a Theme Across Genres lesson, see citations on Student Edition pages.)

Prerequisite Standard

- Grade 8, Literary Response and Analysis 3.3 **Compare and contrast motivations and reactions of literary characters from different historical eras confronting similar situations or conflicts.**

Comparing a Theme Across Genres

Overview

In this feature, students will be asked to compare a theme across genres by reading a work of fiction and a work of nonfiction that center around the notion of heroism. This introduction will help them to understand the ways in which genre and theme influence each other.

The first of the paired selections is a short story by Isabel Allende. Although the story is based on a factual event, Allende fictionalizes it and uses the techniques of fiction writing, such as setting, character, and plot, to share her insights and to make a point.

The second major selection is Roger Rosenblatt's essay, "The Man in the Water." Again, the subject is an act of heroism, but this time the subject is treated by an essayist who uses the techniques of nonfiction writing to share his ideas and to make his point.

After reading the selections, students are guided in writing a comparison-contrast essay, in which they determine similarities and differences between the work of fiction and the work of nonfiction.

STANDARDS FOCUS, pp. 256–271

(For the grade-level standards taught in this lesson, see citations on Student Edition pages.)

Prerequisite Standard

- Grade 8, Literary Response and Analysis 3.5 **Identify and analyze recurring themes (e.g., good versus evil) across traditional and contemporary works.**

Reading Skills

- Determine an author's purpose.

Summary *above grade level*

In 1985, a volcanic eruption and ensuing mudslides killed more than twenty thousand people in Colombia. Allende uses these facts as a framework for a work of fiction about a thirteen-year-old girl, named Azucena, who struggles to survive. Trapped in the mud that has killed her family, Azucena becomes the symbol of the tragedy to the world while television reporter Rolf Carlé struggles to free her. Rolf's girlfriend, who watches him and Azucena on televised news reports, narrates the story. Over several days, Rolf attempts to rescue Azucena with ropes, poles, and repeated calls for assistance, but her body is firmly held by the debris and the dead below. During the long, cold nights, he reassures the girl that she will be rescued while horrors from his own childhood unexpectedly confront him. He recalls a wartime concentration camp and being brutally beaten by his father. After his rescue attempts fail, Rolf accepts that Azucena will die and stays with her until she sinks beneath the mud, but he is badly scarred by the event. The narrator realizes that the experience has changed him in some fundamental way and that she must wait for his emotional wounds to heal before he can truly come back.

Before You Read

And of Clay Are We Created

Literary Focus

Fact Versus Fiction

You are about to read two versions of the same event in different **genres** (a short story and a newspaper article). Allende's story, a work of **fiction,** sounds so convincingly real that you might think it a **nonfiction** report of what actually happened. As you read the two accounts, think about how they differ and how they are alike.

Theme and Purpose

Fiction writers with an important message to convey have powerful tools at their disposal—especially **theme.** Determining the theme of a work of literature often gives us a good idea of the author's purpose for writing—and vice versa. Theme and purpose often go hand in hand.

Reading Skills

Determining an Author's Purpose

The three most common broad purposes of writing are **to inform** (for example, in a newspaper article), **to persuade** (in a persuasive essay), and **to entertain** (in a short story). Often, though, fiction writers want to do more than entertain us. Allende took a real event and fictionalized it. What was her purpose? To figure it out, ask yourself why this subject was important to her and what she wants us to think about it. The questions at the open-book signs will help you.

Pages 255–283 cover **Reading Standard 3.2** Compare and contrast the presentation of a similar theme or topic across genres to explain how the selection of genre shapes the theme or topic.

Make the Connection

Quickwrite

Do you agree or disagree with the following statements? Explain why, and give an example. Save your notes.

- People are helpless when a natural disaster hits.
- Most people would risk their lives to try to save a stranger.

Background

On November 13, 1985, the long-dormant Nevado del Ruiz volcano erupted in Colombia, South America. Molten rock and hot gases melted the volcano's thick ice cap and sent deadly mudslides down its slopes. More than 23,000 people died in the disaster—most of them in a village called Armero (är·me′rō).

Vocabulary Development

subterranean (sub′tə·rā′nē·ən) *adj.:* underground.

magnitude (mag′nə·to͞od′) *n.:* greatness or size.

presentiments (prē·zent′ə·mənts) *n.:* forebodings; feelings that something bad is about to happen.

tenacity (tə·nas′ə·tē) *n.:* stubborn persistence and determination.

equanimity (ek′wə·nim′ə·tē) *n.:* calmness; composure.

fortitude (fôrt′ə·to͞od′) *n.:* firm courage; strength to endure pain or danger.

ingenuity (in′jə·no͞o′ə·tē) *n.:* cleverness; originality; skill.

resignation (rez′ig·nā′shən) *n.:* passive acceptance; submission.

pandemonium (pan′də·mō′nē·əm) *n.:* wildly noisy, chaotic scene.

commiserate (kə·miz′ər·āt′) *v.:* show or express sympathy.

RESOURCES: READING

Planning

- *One-Stop Planner* CD-ROM with Test Generator
- *On Course: Mapping Instruction*

Media

- *Audio CD Library*
  - disc 9
- *Visual Connections*
  - Videocassette, Segment 3

Reading

- *Interactive Reading,* Teacher's Edition
  - Graphic Organizer: Theme and Genre Chart

Differentiating Instruction

- *Lesson Plans for Language Development*
  - English-Language Learners, pp. 113–115, 130, 135

PRETEACHING

Selection Starter

Motivate. Ask students to name a recent natural disaster that has been in the news. Have students volunteer everything they know about it, including what individuals and organizations did to help and the number of people who were affected. After the discussion, ask students to complete the Quickwrite activity.

Preview Vocabulary

To reinforce students' understanding of the Vocabulary words, have them match subjects with words. Ask students to choose the Vocabulary word that would be most likely to be used in referring to each subject below. Then, call on volunteers to use the subject and word in a sentence.

1. a fortuneteller [presentiments]
2. a leader calming an unruly crowd [equanimity]
3. a student abjectly accepting a failing grade [resignation]
4. size of an earthquake on the Richter scale [magnitude]
5. an inventor [ingenuity]
6. a search-and-rescue dog following a scent [tenacity]
7. New York City's Times Square on New Year's Eve [pandemonium]
8. a memorial service [commiserate]
9. a subway system [subterranean]
10. a firefighter [fortitude]

Assign the Reading

Homework

To introduce the story to the class, have one student read aloud the quotation by Allende on p. 257 and another student read the first paragraph of the story. Allow learners who are having difficulty to read the story in pairs while others read independently. You might assign the Connection feature on pp. 267–269 as homework.

- Special Education Students, pp. 116, 130, 135

Vocabulary

- *Vocabulary Development*
  - Vocabulary Worksheet, p. 21

Assessment

- *Progress Assessment of Reading*
  - Selection Test
- *One-Stop Planner* CD-ROM with Test Generator

DIRECT TEACHING

A Literary Focus
GRADE-LEVEL STANDARD

Fact versus fiction. This is the first paragraph of a short story. How is the language different from what you would expect to find in a factual article? [Possible response: The language is more poetic and emotional. Imagery such as "the weeping of orphans and wails of the injured" and "the unbearable image of the head budding like a black squash" are subjective impressions that would not appear in a factual piece.]

B Reading Skills

Determining an author's purpose. Remind students that clues to an author's purpose are often found in the details. Call students' attention to Allende's choice of words, such as *telluric vomit, viscous soup,* and *desert of mire,* that force the reader to focus on the repellent aspects of the eruption's aftermath.

[Possible response to question 1: The author's purpose is to inform the reader about the enormity of the disaster and to persuade the reader of its horror.]

C Literary Focus
REVIEW STANDARD

Point of view. From what point of view is this story being told? [the first-person point of view] What is the narrator's relationship to Rolf? [She is his girlfriend or wife.] You may wish to tell students that the narrator, unnamed here, is Eva Luna and that this story is the last one in Allende's collection *The Stories of Eva Luna.*

They discovered the girl's head protruding from the mudpit, eyes wide open, calling soundlessly. She had a First Communion name, Azucena.[1] Lily. In that vast cemetery where the odor of death was already attracting vultures from far away, and where the weeping of orphans and wails of the injured filled the air, the little girl obstinately clinging to life became the symbol of the tragedy. The television cameras transmitted so often the unbearable image of the head budding like a black squash from the clay that there was no one who did not recognize her and know her name. And every time we saw her on the screen, right behind her was Rolf Carlé,[2] who had gone there on assignment, never suspecting that he would find a fragment of his past, lost thirty years before.

First a subterranean sob rocked the cotton fields, curling them like waves of foam. Geologists had set up their seismographs[3] weeks before and knew that the mountain had awakened again. For some time they had predicted that the heat of the eruption could detach the eternal ice from the slopes of the volcano, but no one heeded their warnings; they sounded like the tales of frightened old women. The towns in the valley went about their daily life, deaf to the moaning of the earth, until that fateful Wednesday night in November when a prolonged roar announced the end of the world, and walls of snow broke loose, rolling in an avalanche of clay, stones, and water that descended on the villages and buried them beneath unfathomable meters of telluric[4] vomit. As soon as the survivors emerged from the paralysis of that first awful terror, they could see that houses, plazas, churches, white cotton plantations, dark coffee forests, cattle pastures—all had disappeared. Much later, after soldiers and volunteers had arrived to rescue the living and try to assess the magnitude of the cataclysm,[5] it was calculated that beneath the mud lay more than twenty thousand human beings and an indefinite number of animals putrefying in a viscous soup.[6] Forests and rivers had also been swept away, and there was nothing to be seen but an immense desert of mire.[7]

AUTHOR'S PURPOSE
1. What is the **author's purpose** in this paragraph?

When the station called before dawn, Rolf Carlé and I were together. I crawled out of bed, dazed with sleep, and went to prepare coffee while he hurriedly dressed. He stuffed his gear in the green canvas backpack he always carried, and we said goodbye, as we had so many times before. I had no presentiments. I sat in the kitchen, sipping my coffee and planning the long hours without him, sure that he would be back the next day.

He was one of the first to reach the scene, because while other reporters were fighting their way to the edges of that morass[8] in jeeps, bicycles, or on foot, each getting there however he could, Rolf Carlé had the advantage of the television helicopter, which flew him over the avalanche. We watched on our screens the footage captured by his assistant's camera, in which he was up to his knees in muck, a microphone in his hand, in the midst of a

1. **Azucena** (ä·sōō·sā′nä): Spanish for "lily."
2. **Rolf Carlé** (rôlf kär·lā′).
3. **seismographs** (sīz′mə·grafs′) *n.:* instruments that measure and record earthquakes and other tremors.
4. **telluric** (te·loor′ik) *adj.:* of or from the earth.
5. **cataclysm** (kat′ə·kliz′əm) *n.:* disaster; great upheaval causing sudden, violent changes.
6. **putrefying in a viscous soup:** rotting in a thick mixture.
7. **mire** *n.:* deep mud.
8. **morass** (mə·ras′) *n.:* bog or swamp.

Vocabulary

subterranean (sub′tə·rā′nē·ən) *adj.:* underground.

magnitude (mag′nə·tōōd′) *n.:* greatness or size.

presentiments (prē·zent′ə·mənts) *n.:* forebodings; feelings that something bad is about to happen.

DIFFERENTIATING INSTRUCTION

Learners Having Difficulty

Modeling. To help students read "And of Clay Are We Created," model the reading skill of determining an author's purpose. Read the first two sentences of the story aloud. Then, say to students, "Allende fictionalized the real girl, Omaira Sanchez, into the character named Azucena. Her purpose may have been to create a heart-rending contrast between the flower that grows in the mud (azucena, or lily) and the terrible fate of a girl (Azucena) buried to her neck in mud." Have students write a response to the following question: "What do you suppose is the value of fictionalizing aspects of the event?"

English-Language Learners

Clarify that this story is based on a real event. Have students access the Internet and other news archives for reports on the catastrophic eruption of Mount Ruiz on November 13, 1985. Students may read newspaper and magazine reports in both English and their native language for factual content. Then, they might discuss elements

The Nevado del Ruiz volcano after eruption, Colombia (1985).

Photograph by J. Marso.

bedlam[9] of lost children, wounded survivors, corpses, and devastation. The story came to us in his calm voice. For years he had been a familiar figure in newscasts, reporting live at the scene of battles and catastrophes with awesome tenacity. Nothing could stop him, and I was always amazed at his equanimity in the face of danger and suffering; it seemed as if nothing could shake his fortitude or deter his curiosity. Fear seemed never to touch him, although he had confessed to me that he was not a courageous man, far from it. I believe that the lens of the camera had a strange effect on him; it was as if it transported him to a different time from which he could watch events without actually participating in them. When I knew him better, I came to realize that this fictive distance seemed to protect him from his own emotions.

Rolf Carlé was in on the story of Azucena from the beginning. He filmed the volunteers who discovered her, and the first persons who tried to reach her; his camera zoomed in on the girl, her dark face, her large desolate eyes, the plastered-down tangle of her hair. The mud was like quicksand around her, and anyone attempting to reach her was in danger of sinking. They threw a rope to her that she made no effort to grasp until they shouted to her to catch it; then she pulled a hand from the mire and tried to

9. **bedlam** (bed′ləm) *n.:* place or situation filled with noise and confusion (from the name of an old insane asylum in London).

Vocabulary

tenacity (tə·nas′ə·tē) *n.:* stubborn persistence and determination.

equanimity (ek′wə·nim′ə·tē) *n.:* calmness; composure.

fortitude (fôrt′ə·to͞od′) *n.:* firm courage; strength to endure pain or danger.

DIRECT TEACHING

D Vocabulary Development
GRADE-LEVEL STANDARD

Root words. Call students' attention to the word *corpses,* and ask for its meaning. ["dead bodies"] Have students look up *corpse* in a dictionary to determine its root word. [L *corpus,* meaning "body"] Ask students to suggest related words. [Possible responses: *corporation,* "a group of people acting as one body"; *corps,* "a body of persons associated with one another"; *corpulent,* "a large or stout body."]

E Reading Skills

Making inferences. How does Rolf Carlé's profession affect the way he handles his emotional life? [Possible responses: Rolf's profession, especially his camera, helps him keep his feelings at a distance; by observing rather than participating, he protects himself from strong feelings and creates a barrier between himself and other people.]

F Reading Skills

Expressing an opinion. Why do reporters risk their lives to cover battles and other disasters? Does this characterization of Rolf Carlé help to explain their motives? Why or why not? [Possible responses: Yes; like Rolf, journalists may feel that they are not personally involved or threatened but simply doing their work. No; journalists are thrill seekers who want to be in the thick of the action so they can experience and feel more than their share of what life has to offer.]

of the coverage that may have inspired Allende to write this story.

Resources Reminder

For lessons designed for intermediate and advanced English-language learners, see *Lesson Plans for Language Development,* pp. 113–115, 130, 135.

Special Education Students

For lessons designed for special education students, see *Lesson Plans for Language Development,* pp. 116, 130, 135.

Advanced Learners

Acceleration. This activity can help to move students toward the eleventh- and twelfth-grade Standard 3.2, for which they analyze the ways that a story's theme can represent a view of life.

Activity. As they read, have students take notes about the story's themes. After reading the story, have students review their notes, choose the main theme, and look back through the story for passages that support that theme.

Direct Teaching

A Literary Focus
GRADE-LEVEL STANDARD

Fact versus fiction. How does this detail about the other members of Azucena's family affect the mood of the story? [This grotesque detail makes her plight all the more horrible and increases the mood of fear and dread.] Have students make a note of this passage and compare it to similar details in the newspaper report about the tragedy on pp. 267–269.

B Reading Skills

Identifying the narrator. [Possible response to question 2: Rolf Carlé's girlfriend is narrating the story. She is able to witness the action because she watches the televised newscasts, as well as reports by other journalists.]

C Literary Focus
GRADE-LEVEL STANDARD

Theme and purpose. Remind students that conflict is an important element of fiction and that the outcome of a conflict often gives clues about the theme of a story. What is the major conflict in the story at this point? [It is an external conflict—the struggle against time to free Azucena from the mud.] How might different resolutions of this conflict change the theme? [Possible responses: If Rolf frees Azucena, the theme might be an uplifting idea about heroic altruism; if time runs out and Azucena dies despite Rolf's efforts, the theme might concern the futility of human struggle against nature.]

move, but immediately sank a little deeper. Rolf threw down his knapsack and the rest of his equipment and waded into the quagmire, commenting for his assistant's microphone that it was cold and that one could begin to smell the stench of corpses.

"What's your name?" he asked the girl, and she told him her flower name. "Don't move, Azucena," Rolf Carlé directed, and kept talking to her, without a thought for what he was saying, just to distract her, while slowly he worked his way forward in mud up to his waist. The air around him seemed as murky as the mud.

It was impossible to reach her from the approach he was attempting, so he retreated and circled around where there seemed to be firmer footing. When finally he was close enough, he took the rope and tied it beneath her arms, so they could pull her out. He smiled at her with that smile that crinkles his eyes and makes him look like a little boy; he told her that everything was fine, that he was here with her now, that soon they would have her out. He signaled the others to pull, but as soon as the cord tensed, the girl screamed. They tried again, and her shoulders and arms appeared, but they could move her no farther; she was trapped. Someone suggested that her legs might be caught in the collapsed walls of her house, but she said it was not just rubble, that she was also held by the bodies of her brothers and sisters clinging to her legs. **A**

"Don't worry, we'll get you out of here," Rolf promised. Despite the quality of the transmission, I could hear his voice break, and I loved him more than ever. Azucena looked at him, but said nothing.

> **NARRATOR**
> **B** 2. Who is telling this story? What device enables the **narrator** to witness the action at Armero?

During those first hours Rolf Carlé exhausted all the resources of his ingenuity to rescue her. He struggled with poles and ropes, but every tug was an intolerable torture for the imprisoned girl. It occurred to him to use one of the poles as a lever but got no result and had to abandon the idea. He talked a couple of soldiers into working with him for a while, but they had to leave because so many other victims were calling for help. The girl could not move, she barely could breathe, but she did not seem desperate, as if an ancestral resignation allowed her to accept her fate. The reporter, on the other hand, was determined to snatch her from death. Someone brought him a tire, which he placed beneath her arms like a life buoy, and then laid a plank near the hole to hold his weight and allow him to stay closer to her. As it was impossible to remove the rubble blindly, he tried once or twice to dive toward her feet, but emerged frustrated, covered with mud, and spitting gravel. He concluded that he would have to have a pump to drain the water, and radioed a request for one, but received in return a message that there was no available transport and it could not be sent until the next morning. **C**

"We can't wait that long!" Rolf Carlé shouted, but in the pandemonium no one stopped to commiserate. Many more hours would go by before he accepted that time had stagnated and reality had been irreparably distorted.

A military doctor came to examine the girl, and observed that her heart was functioning well and that if she did not get too cold she could survive the night.

"Hang on, Azucena, we'll have the pump tomorrow," Rolf Carlé tried to console her.

Vocabulary

ingenuity (in′jə·no͞o′ə·tē) *n.:* cleverness; originality; skill.

resignation (rez′ig·nā′shən) *n.:* passive acceptance; submission.

pandemonium (pan′də·mō′nē·əm) *n.:* wildly noisy, chaotic scene.

commiserate (kə·miz′ər·āt′) *v.:* show or express sympathy.

Content-Area Connections

Science: Volcanoes

Mount Ruiz is located in the Cordillera Central, the highest Andean range in Colombia, containing peaks more than seventeen thousand feet tall. In the 1985 eruption that this story is based on, the snow and ice that covered the volcano melted and mixed with great mudflows that cascaded down the slopes, burying the town of Armero. According to accounts, the first mudflows were icy cold; subsequent mudflows were fiery hot.

Small-group activity. Have a small group of students research some aspects of volcanoes raised by this story. Topics may include how volcanic eruptions can be predicted, how volcanoes are formed, classification of volcanic activity, and information about Nevado del Ruiz. Have students share their research by collaborating on a magazine article or staging a televised report.

260 Chapter 4 Comparing Themes • Evaluating Arguments: Pro and Con

"Don't leave me alone," she begged.

"No, of course I won't leave you."

Someone brought him coffee, and he helped the girl drink it, sip by sip. The warm liquid revived her and she began telling him about her small life, about her family and her school, about how things were in that little bit of world before the volcano had erupted. She was thirteen, and she had never been outside her village. Rolf Carlé, buoyed by a premature optimism, **D** was convinced that everything would end well: the pump would arrive, they would drain the water, move the rubble, and Azucena would be transported by helicopter to a hospital where she would recover rapidly and where he could visit her and bring her gifts. He thought, She's already too old for dolls, and I don't know what would please her; maybe a dress. I don't know much about women, he concluded, amused, reflecting that although he had known many women in his lifetime, none had taught him these details. **E** To pass the hours he began to tell Azucena about his travels and adventures as a newshound, and when he exhausted his memory, he called upon imagination, inventing things he thought might entertain her. From time to time she dozed, but he kept talking in the darkness, to assure her that he was still there and to overcome the menace of uncertainty.

That was a long night.

> "Don't leave me alone," she begged.

Many miles away, I watched Rolf Carlé and the girl on a television screen. I could not bear the wait at home, so I went to National Television, where I often spent entire nights with Rolf editing programs. There, I was near his world, and I could at least get a feeling of what he lived through during those three decisive days. I called all the important people in the city, senators, commanders of the armed forces, the North American ambassador, and the president of National Petroleum, begging them for a pump to remove the silt, but obtained only vague promises. I began to ask for urgent help on radio and television, to see if there wasn't *someone* who could help us. Between calls I would run to the newsroom to monitor the satellite transmissions that periodically brought new details of the catastrophe. While reporters selected scenes with most impact for the news report, I searched for footage that featured Azucena's mudpit. The screen reduced the disaster to a single plane and accentuated the tremendous distance that separated me from Rolf Carlé; nonetheless, I was there with him. The child's every suffering hurt me as it did him; I felt his frustration, his impotence. Faced with the impossibility of communicating with him, the fantastic idea came to me that if I tried, I could reach him by force of mind and in that way give him encouragement. I concentrated until I was dizzy—a frenzied and futile activity. **F** At times I would be overcome with compassion and burst out crying; at other times, I was so drained I felt as if I were staring through a telescope at the light of a star dead for a million years.

I watched that hell on the first morning broadcast, cadavers of people and animals awash in the current of new rivers formed overnight from the melted snow. Above the mud rose the tops of trees and the bell towers of a church where several people had taken refuge and were patiently awaiting rescue teams. Hundreds of soldiers and volunteers from the Civil Defense were clawing through rubble searching for survivors, while long rows of

DIRECT TEACHING

D Vocabulary Development
GRADE-LEVEL STANDARD

Root words. Point out the phrase "buoyed by a premature optimism." Ask students for a paraphrase, such as "hoping too soon for a favorable outcome." Then, have a student look up the word *optimism* in a dictionary and write its root word and meaning on the chalkboard. [L *optimus,* meaning "best"]

E Advanced Learners

Acceleration. Elicit from students the multiple layers of storytelling that are occurring at this point. [Rolf's stories to Azucena; the narrator's story about Rolf and Azucena; Allende's story about all of the above] What theme does the prevalence of storytelling suggest to you? Cite evidence to support your idea. [Possible theme: People use storytelling as a way to sustain themselves and to make sense of tragic events. The theme is supported by the following evidence: Rolf believes that his stories will help reassure Azucena; Rolf is also trying to reassure himself; Allende may have written this story to give meaning to the tragedy.]

F Literary Focus
GRADE-LEVEL STANDARD

Theme and purpose. What is being compared in this simile? [The narrator compares her feelings of frustration and separation to the sensation of looking through a telescope and seeing light from a long-dead distant star.] What does the comparison suggest? [Possible response: The simile ominously suggests that there is little anyone can do and that Azucena may not survive.]

DEVELOPING FLUENCY

Mixed-ability group activity. Direct students' attention to the second paragraph of the story, which describes the disaster. First, have them read the passage silently as you read it aloud. Then, place students in groups, seated in circles if possible. Have students go around the circle, each carefully reading one sentence of the paragraph. Remind them to pause at commas and semicolons, as well as at end punctuation. Encourage students to make the paragraph flow as smoothly as possible. Assist students with the pronunciation of difficult words when necessary.

DIRECT TEACHING

A Reading Skills

Determining an author's purpose. [Possible response to question 3: The author wants readers to feel the horror of the tragedy and the helplessness of those who watch and want to help but can't because of logistic or bureaucratic setbacks.]

B Literary Focus
GRADE-LEVEL STANDARD

Theme and purpose. How does the journalists' equipment contrast ironically with the availability of other supplies in the disaster area? [Possible response: The journalists have every gadget, but essential medicine and pumps to drain the water are not available.] What developing theme does this support? [Possible response: The theme that life is often unfair and that people's priorities are sometimes misguided.]

C Content-Area Connections

Literature: *The Thousand and One Nights*

This allusion is to the Arabian collection *The Thousand and One Nights.* According to legend, a sultan had vowed revenge on all women because his first wife betrayed him. Each night he took a new wife, and the next morning had her killed. One wife, Scheherazade, tells him fantastic tales that she promises to finish the following night, thereby ensuring that she will live another day. She so entertains him that he revokes his decree.

---

ragged specters[10] awaited their turn for a cup of hot broth. Radio networks announced that their phones were jammed with calls from families offering shelter to orphaned children. Drinking water was in scarce supply, along with gasoline and food. Doctors, resigned to amputating arms and legs without anesthesia, pled that at least they be sent serum and painkillers and antibiotics; most of the roads, however, were impassable, and worse were the bureaucratic obstacles that stood in the way. To top it all, the clay contaminated by decomposing bodies threatened the living with an outbreak of epidemics. **A**

AUTHOR'S PURPOSE

3. What do you think the author wants us to feel about the tragedy at Armero?

Azucena was shivering inside the tire that held her above the surface. Immobility and tension had greatly weakened her, but she was conscious and could still be heard when a microphone was held out to her. Her tone was humble, as if apologizing for all the fuss. Rolf Carlé had a growth of beard, and dark circles beneath his eyes; he looked near exhaustion. Even from that enormous distance I could sense the quality of his weariness, so different from the fatigue of other adventures. He had completely forgotten the camera; he could not look at the girl through a lens any longer. The pictures we were receiving were not his assistant's but those of other reporters who had appropriated Azucena, bestowing on her the pathetic responsibility of embodying the horror of what had happened in that place. With the first light Rolf tried again to dislodge the obstacles that held the girl in her tomb, but he had only his hands to work with; he did not dare use a tool for fear of injuring her. He fed Azucena a cup of the cornmeal mush and bananas the Army was distributing, but she immediately vomited it up. A doctor stated that she had a fever, but added that there was little he could do: antibiotics were being reserved for cases of gangrene.[11] A priest also passed by and blessed her, hanging a medal of the Virgin around her neck. By evening a gentle, persistent drizzle began to fall.

"The sky is weeping," Azucena murmured, and she, too, began to cry.

"Don't be afraid," Rolf begged. "You have to keep your strength up and be calm. Everything will be fine. I'm with you, and I'll get you out somehow." **B**

Reporters returned to photograph Azucena and ask her the same questions, which she no longer tried to answer. In the meanwhile, more television and movie teams arrived with spools of cable, tapes, film, videos, precision lenses, recorders, sound consoles, lights, reflecting screens, auxiliary motors, cartons of supplies, electricians, sound technicians, and cameramen: Azucena's face was beamed to millions of screens around the world. And all the while Rolf Carlé kept pleading for a pump. The improved technical facilities bore results, and National Television began receiving sharper pictures and clearer sound; the distance seemed suddenly compressed, and I had the horrible sensation that Azucena and Rolf were by my side, separated from me by impenetrable glass. I was able to follow events hour by hour; I knew everything my love did to wrest the girl from her prison and help her endure her suffering; I overheard fragments of what they said to one another and could guess the rest; I was present when she taught Rolf to pray, and when he distracted her with the stories I had told him in a thousand and one nights beneath the white mosquito netting of our bed. **C**

When darkness came on the second day, Rolf tried to sing Azucena to sleep with old Austrian

10. **specters** *n.:* ghostlike figures.

11. **gangrene** (gaŋ′grēn′) *n.:* death or decay of flesh, usually caused by disease.

READING MINI-LESSON

Developing Word-Attack Skills

Activity. Write the selection word *soldiers* on the chalkboard, and ask students to read it aloud. Point out that the word *soldiers* almost qualifies as a sight word because of the unique spelling for the sound /j/: *di.*

Review with students the following conventional spellings for the sound /j/:

- *g* as in *gentle* and *gist*
- *ge* as in *page* and *courageous*
- *dge* as in *edge* and *ridge*

Ask students to offer additional examples of words with each of these /j/ sound spellings. Then, write these words on the chalkboard. Have volunteers read the words aloud and identify the letters that stand for the sound /j/. Answers are underlined.

imagination	adjective	gymnasium
regional	strategic	tragedy
allegiance	surgeon	gorgeous

Activity. Display these pairs of words. Have students read each pair, identify the word with the sound /j/, and tell the letters that stand for the sound. Answers are underlined.

1.	stranger	anger
2.	emigrant	emergent
3.	conjugate	congregate
4.	soldier	moldier
5.	contagious	contiguous

folk songs he had learned from his mother, but she was far beyond sleep. They spent most of the night talking, each in a stupor of exhaustion and hunger, and shaking with cold. That night, imperceptibly, the unyielding floodgates that had contained Rolf Carlé's past for so many years began to open, and the torrent of all that had lain hidden in the deepest and most secret layers of memory poured out, leveling before it the obstacles that had blocked his consciousness for so long. He could not tell it all to Azucena; she perhaps did not know there was a world beyond the sea or time previous to her own; she was not capable of imagining Europe in the years of the war. So he could not tell her of defeat, nor of the afternoon the Russians had led them to the concentration camp to bury prisoners dead from starvation. Why should he describe to her how the naked bodies piled like a mountain of firewood resembled fragile china? How could he tell this dying child about ovens and gallows? Nor did he mention the night that he had seen his mother naked, shod in stiletto-heeled red boots, sobbing with humiliation. There was much he did not tell, but in those hours he relived for the first time all the things his mind had tried to erase. Azucena had surrendered her fear to him and so, without wishing it, had obliged Rolf to confront his own. There, beside that hellhole of mud, it was impossible for Rolf to flee from himself any longer, and the visceral[12] terror he had lived as a boy suddenly invaded him. He reverted to the years when he was the age of Azucena, and younger, and, like her, found himself trapped in a pit without escape, buried in life, his head barely above ground; he saw before his eyes the boots and legs of his father, who had removed his belt and was whipping it in the air with the never-forgotten hiss of a viper coiled to strike. Sorrow flooded through him, intact and precise, as if it had lain always in his mind, waiting. He was once again in the armoire[13] where his father locked him to punish him for imagined misbehavior, there where for eternal hours he had crouched with his eyes closed, not to see the darkness, with his hands over his ears, to shut out the beating of his heart, trembling, huddled like a cornered animal. Wandering in the mist of his memories he found his sister Katharina, a sweet, retarded child who spent her life hiding, with the hope that her father would forget the disgrace of her having been born. With Katharina, Rolf crawled beneath the dining room table, and with her hid there under the long white tablecloth, two children forever embraced, alert to footsteps and voices. Katharina's scent melded with his own sweat, with aromas of cooking, garlic, soup, freshly baked bread, and the unexpected odor of putrescent[14] clay. His sister's hand in his, her frightened breathing, her silk hair against his cheek, the candid gaze of her eyes. Katharina . . . Katharina materialized before him, floating on the air like a flag, clothed in the white tablecloth, now a winding sheet, and at last he could weep for her death and for the guilt of having abandoned her. He understood then that all his exploits as a reporter, the feats that had won him such recognition and fame, were merely an attempt to keep his most ancient fears at bay, a stratagem[15] for taking

"I'm with you, and I'll get you out somehow."

12. **visceral** (vis′ər·əl) *adj.:* intuitive or emotional rather than intellectual.

13. **armoire** (är·mwär′) *n.:* large cupboard for holding clothes.

14. **putrescent** (pyo͞o·tres′ənt) *adj.:* rotting.

15. **stratagem** (strat′ə·jəm) *n.:* plan or scheme for achieving some goal.

Direct Teaching

D Content-Area Connections

History: The Holocaust
This passage is an allusion to the Holocaust. During World War II, approximately six million Jews were executed by the Nazis. The majority of the Jews were murdered in gas chambers. Rolf Carlé's buried memories of these events, which occurred during his childhood in Europe, come flooding back.

E Literary Focus GRADE-LEVEL STANDARD

Theme and purpose. Allende uses the tools of fiction, including characterization and flashback, to develop theme. Ask students to consider how Rolf's relationship with Katharina has influenced his current involvement with Azucena. How might the parallels between Katharina and Azucena hint at a theme of the story? [Possible response: Both girls are victims of circumstances beyond their and Rolf's control, though he tries to do what he can for them. This possibly points to a theme about the often unalterably tragic nature of life.]

Content-Area Connections

Culture: Allusion
After students have read the story, encourage them to look up passages from the Bible that mention clay (Isaiah 45:9, Romans 9:21, and Daniel 2:31–46). Have them also research world religions and myths for references to humans being created from earth (or clay or dust) and being returned to earth.

Individual activity. Ask students to explain what their research suggests about the meaning of the story's title and what it implies about the story's overall theme. You may wish to have students present their findings to the class by preparing and giving an oral report or by writing and reading a short essay.

DIRECT TEACHING

A Literary Focus
GRADE-LEVEL STANDARD

Theme and purpose. What does Rolf Carlé's "moment of truth" suggest about another possible theme of the story? [Possible response: No matter how hard people try to suppress their most painful feelings, they will always surface in moments of truth.]

B Reading Skills

Understanding characterization. [Possible response to question 4: The details of Rolf Carlé's childhood are important because they reveal what he's been repressing all these years and because they provide a connection between Azucena and him, between her present tragedy and his tragic past.]

C Reading Skills
GRADE-LEVEL STANDARD

Determining an author's purpose. What is ironic about the visit of the President of the Republic? [He pretends to be concerned but does nothing to help; in reality, he offers only platitudes, clichés, and threats. He seems unmoved by Azucena's plight, even though she is right in front of him.] What is the author's purpose in including this scene? [Possible responses: To inform and persuade readers of the callousness of some public officials; to demonstrate that Rolf Carlé is so fraught with desperation and frustration that he will dare to interrupt his nation's highest official to plead for a relatively simple, though critical, tool to rescue Azucena.]

refuge behind a lens to test whether reality was more tolerable from that perspective. He took excessive risks as an exercise of courage, training by day to conquer the monsters that tormented him by night. But he had come face to face with the moment of truth; he could not continue to escape his past. **A** He *was* Azucena; he was buried in the clayey mud; his terror was not the distant emotion of an almost forgotten childhood, it was a claw sunk in his throat. In the flush of his tears he saw his mother, dressed in black and clutching her imitation-crocodile pocketbook to her bosom, just as he had last seen her on the dock when she had come to put him on the boat to South America. She had not come to dry his tears, but to tell him to pick up a shovel: the war was over and now they must bury the dead.

B CHARACTERIZATION
4. Why are these details about Rolf's childhood important?

"Don't cry. I don't hurt anymore. I'm fine," Azucena said when dawn came.

"I'm not crying for you," Rolf Carlé smiled. "I'm crying for myself. I hurt all over."

C The third day in the valley of the cataclysm began with a pale light filtering through storm clouds. The President of the Republic visited the area in his tailored safari jacket to confirm that this was the worst catastrophe of the century; the country was in mourning; sister nations had offered aid; he had ordered a state of siege; the Armed Forces would be merciless, anyone caught stealing or committing other offenses would be shot on sight. He added that it was impossible to remove all the corpses or count the thousands who had disappeared; the entire valley would be declared holy ground, and bishops would come to celebrate a solemn mass for the souls of the victims. He went to the Army field tents to offer relief in the form of vague promises to crowds of the rescued, then to the improvised hospital to offer a word of encouragement to doctors and nurses worn down from so many hours of tribulations.[16] Then he asked to be taken to see Azucena, the little girl the whole world had seen. He waved to her with a limp statesman's hand, and microphones recorded his emotional voice and paternal[17] tone as he told her that her courage had served as an example to the nation. Rolf Carlé interrupted to ask for a pump, and the President assured him that he personally would attend to the matter.

I caught a glimpse of Rolf for a few seconds kneeling beside the mudpit. On the evening news broadcast, he was still in the same position; and I, glued to the screen like a fortuneteller to her crystal ball, could tell that something fundamental had changed in him. I knew somehow that during the night his defenses had crumbled and he had given in to grief; finally he was vulnerable. The girl had touched a part of him that he himself had no access to, a part he had never shared with me. Rolf had wanted to console her, but it was Azucena who had given him consolation.

I recognized the precise moment at which Rolf gave up the fight and surrendered to the torture of watching the girl die. I was with them, three days and two nights, spying on them from the other side of life. I was there when she told

16. **tribulations** (trib′yə·lā′shəns) *n.:* miseries or sufferings.
17. **paternal** *adj.:* fatherly.

FAMILY/COMMUNITY ACTIVITY

The image that prompted Allende to write this story (that of Omaira Sanchez stuck in the mud) was broadcast and printed everywhere for about a week in November 1985. Have students ask older family or community members if they recall the image. Students should ask these people if they remember the place of the disaster, its cause, and what happened to the girl. Have students report their findings to the class.

264 Chapter 4 Comparing Themes • Evaluating Arguments: Pro and Con

him that in all her thirteen years no boy had ever loved her and that it was a pity to leave this world without knowing love. Rolf assured her that he loved her more than he could ever love anyone, more than he loved his mother, more than his sister, more than all the women who had slept in his arms, more than he loved me, his life companion, who would have given anything to be trapped in that well in her place, who would have exchanged her life for Azucena's, and I watched as he leaned down to kiss her poor forehead, consumed by a sweet, sad emotion he could not name. I felt how in that instant both were saved from despair, how they were freed from the clay, how they rose above the vultures and helicopters, how together they flew above the vast swamp of corruption and laments. How, finally, they were able to accept death. Rolf Carlé prayed in silence that she would die quickly, because such pain cannot be borne. **D**

By then I had obtained a pump and was in touch with a general who had agreed to ship it the next morning on a military cargo plane. But on the night of that third day, beneath the unblinking focus of quartz lamps and the lens of a hundred cameras, Azucena gave up, her eyes locked with those of the friend who had sustained her to the end. Rolf Carlé removed the life buoy, closed her eyelids, held her to his chest for a few moments, and then let her go. She sank slowly, a flower in the mud. **E**

> **AUTHOR'S PURPOSE AND THEME**
> 5. What does the tragic ending suggest about the **author's purpose** and the story's **theme**?

You are back with me, but you are not the same man. I often accompany you to the station and we watch the videos of Azucena again; you study them intently, looking for something you could have done to save her, something you did not think of in time. Or maybe you study them to see yourself as if in a mirror, naked. Your cameras lie forgotten in a closet; you do not write or sing; you sit long hours before the window, staring at the mountains. Beside you, I wait for you to complete the voyage into yourself, for the old wounds to heal. I know that when you return from your nightmares, we shall again walk hand in hand, as before. ■

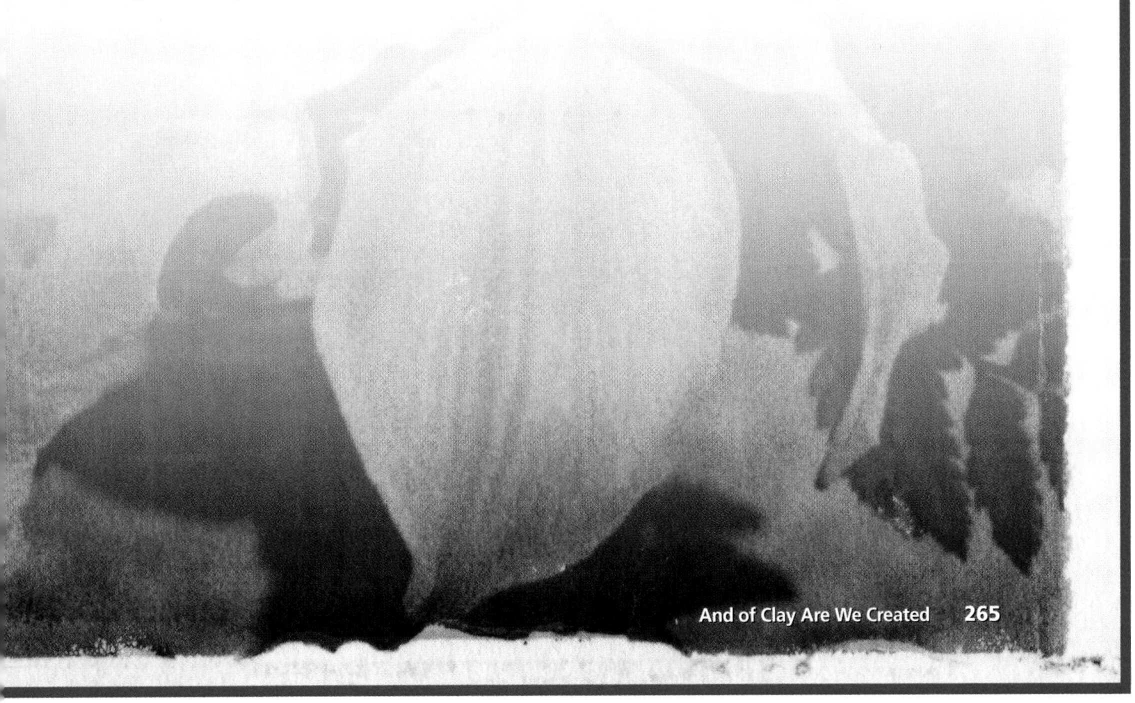

DIRECT TEACHING

D Literary Focus
GRADE-LEVEL STANDARD

Paradox. A paradox is a seeming contradiction that reveals a truth. What is paradoxical about the narrator's conclusion in this paragraph? [The paradox, or apparent contradiction, lies in the fact that the acceptance of death frees both Azucena and Rolf from despair.]

E Reading Skills
Determining author's purpose and theme. [Possible response to question 5: The tragic ending suggests that the author's purpose is to persuade us that humans are not all-powerful in the face of a cataclysmic event. It suggests that the story's theme is that people often fall short, despite their best efforts, and that even would-be heroes, such as Rolf Carlé, are reminded of their limitations.]

GUIDED PRACTICE

Monitoring students' progress. Guide the class in answering these comprehension questions. Direct students to locate passages in the text that support their responses.

Short Answer

1. How many lives were lost in the eruption? [more than twenty thousand]
2. What does Rolf Carlé need in order to free Azucena? [a pump]
3. Who is Katharina? [Rolf's sister]
4. What does the President of the Republic tell Azucena? [that her courage is an example to the nation]
5. After three days and two nights, for what does Rolf pray? [that Azucena will die quickly]

Meet the Writer

Background. When Allende was still a journalist in Chile earning some acclaim for her columns, she was invited to lunch by the poet Pablo Neruda. He told her, "You are a horrible journalist. But—you are a wonderful storyteller! You have the imagination of a great writer." In spite of this early encouragement, it was not until Allende was nearly forty years old that she began to fully explore her gifts as a writer of fiction. Allende found it difficult to find a publisher for her first novel, *The House of the Spirits.* But the novel was finally accepted by a publisher in Spain and appeared in 1982, ultimately becoming a bestseller all over the world. One of Allende's more recent works, *Paula,* is a memoir written in honor of her terminally ill daughter.

On her Web site, Allende explores the paradoxes of writing fiction. She writes, "The first lie of fiction is that the author gives some order to the chaos of life: chronological order, or whatever order the author chooses. As a writer, you select some part of a whole; you decide that *those* things are important and the rest is not. And you will write about those things from your perspective. Life is not that way. Everything happens simultaneously, in a chaotic way, and you don't make choices. You are not the boss; *life* is the boss. So when you accept as a writer that fiction is lying, then you become free; you can do anything."

Meet the Writer

Isabel Allende

"I Am a Story Hunter"

Isabel Allende (ēs'ä·bel ä·yen'de) (1942–) describes herself as a "good listener and a story hunter" who reads newspapers to search for story ideas. Allende vividly recalls the Armero disaster:

> "Thousands perished, but the world remembers the catastrophe specifically because of Omaira Sanchez, a thirteen-year-old girl who was trapped in the mud from the slide. . . . Her eyes staring from the television screen have haunted me ever since. I still have her photograph on my desk; again and again I studied it, trying to comprehend the meaning of her martyrdom."

Three years after Armero, Allende wrote the story you have just read. Thoughts of Omaira would still not leave her, though, and four years later, as her own daughter lay dying, Allende says she "finally could decipher the message in those intense black eyes: patience, courage, resignation, dignity in the face of death."

Allende was born in Lima, Peru, where her father served as a diplomat for the Chilean government. When her parents divorced, three-year-old Isabel returned with her mother to her grandparents' home in Santiago. She eventually became a journalist, conducting TV interviews, writing for a feminist magazine, and making documentary films.

Her uncle, Salvador Allende, president of Chile, was killed during a military takeover of the government in 1973. Isabel and her husband and children soon fled to Caracas, Venezuela. For the thirteen years they lived there in exile, Allende wrote columns for a Venezuelan newspaper. In 1987, she moved to the United States, where she taught literature at several colleges. She now lives in California.

In 1981, Allende began writing a long goodbye letter to her ailing grandfather, who was nearly one hundred years old and preparing to die. That letter grew into her first novel, *The House of the Spirits* (1982), which became an international bestseller. Her next three novels established her reputation as a major writer: *Of Love and Shadows* (1984), *Eva Luna* (1988), and *The Stories of Eva Luna* (1990), from which "And of Clay Are We Created" is taken.

DIFFERENTIATING INSTRUCTION

Advanced Learners

Enrichment. Allende has said that she belongs to the first generation of Latin American writers who grew up reading other Latin American writers. She says her most important literary influences were "the great writers of the Latin American boom of literature."

Activity. Have students find out more about the "Latin American boom." Suggest that they enter *Latin American literature* or *Latin American writers* as keywords in a search engine and then list ten prominent Latin American authors. Students may wish to choose one author to research in detail and present a biographical sketch to the class.

CONNECTION / NEWSPAPER ARTICLE

This newspaper article is an account of the real event in Armero, Colombia, that inspired Allende's story. Her character Azucena is based on Omaira Sanchez.

Ill-Equipped Rescuers Dig Out Volcano Victims; Aid Slow to Reach Colombian Town

Bradley Graham

Frank Fournier/Contact Press Images.

Thirteen-year-old Omaira Sanchez was trapped in a mudflow from the Nevado del Ruiz eruption. Rescue workers could not manage to release her from the hardening mud and debris, and she died within forty-eight hours.

ARMERO, Colombia, Nov. 15, 1985—From beneath the rubble of what was Armero, now a mass of broken concrete slabs and twisted corrugated metal, of scattered belongings and crushed bodies buried under brown watery slush, came the cries today of survivors alive two days after a volcanic eruption caused a flood of mud that swallowed this town.

But few were here to save them.

A Officials in Bogota, who had declared a national emergency after the eruption Wednesday of Nevado del Ruiz volcano, reported that aid had begun to arrive from the United States, Europe, and international agencies. But only a tiny amount of material and a small number of volunteers have arrived so far to this main scene of disaster.

Relief workers, laboring in hot, humid

Connection

Summary at grade level

In this *Washington Post* newspaper article, the reporter relates what he hears and sees in Armero, Colombia, two days after the eruption of Mount Ruiz. Much of the article gives details of the desperate situation in and around the stricken village. The article also relates the stories of two survivors—a farmer who is finally pulled from under his collapsed house and a young girl who is buried up to her neck in mud. It was this girl, Omaira Sanchez, who inspired Allende to write the story that students have just read.

DIRECT TEACHING

A Literary Focus
GRADE-LEVEL STANDARD

Fact versus fiction. Both the newspaper article and the short story describe the setting in the first few paragraphs. How does genre influence the description in the news article? [Possible response: The description of setting is factual, clear, rich in detail and even in tone, telling exactly what the reporter saw and heard.] How is this description similar to and different from that in "And of Clay Are We Created"? [Possible response: Allende's description is also rich in detail, but the words she uses are more emotional.] Which description do you find more effective? Explain. [Students' answers will vary.]

Direct Teaching

A Reading Skills

Comparing and contrasting. What details in this paragraph are similar to the details Allende uses in her story? [Possible responses: An official declares Armero "holy ground"; few people and little equipment are available to help survivors.]

B Literary Focus
GRADE-LEVEL STANDARD

Theme and purpose. This paragraph introduces two examples of the lengthy, arduous process of rescuing victims. How are the two victims different? How are their situations similar? [Gomez is a 34-year-old man; Sanchez is a 13-year-old girl. He is imprisoned by boards, while she is stuck in mud and concrete.] Why do you think Allende chose the girl rather than the man as the victim in her story? [Possible responses: The girl's situation is more dramatic; a reader will have more sympathy for a young girl; Gomez survives, while Sanchez dies tragically.]

weather amid the rising stench of spoiled food and decomposing bodies, said there was a desperate shortage of supplies and personnel. As they worked, more tremors and rumbles were felt from the volcano.

Government and relief officials estimated that as many as 20,000 people may have died in the disaster, and thousands more have been injured. But those on the scene stressed that a complete casualty count would not be possible for a long time.

Walter Cotte of the Red Cross said many of the dead were buried in mass graves without being photographed or fingerprinted. One relief official said it would probably be necessary to declare Armero "holy ground," leaving many of the dead buried where they died. Hastily constructed tent hospitals were set up in the nearby towns of Mariquita, Lerida, and Guayabal, civil defense officials said, but there were few helicopters to carry the victims there, and no roads were passable in the narrow Andean valleys near Armero. "We don't have the help we need," said Raul Alferez, who is in charge of the Red Cross medical unit here. "We need people, we need equipment, but we have next to nothing."

The magnitude of what has to be done is overwhelming. What was once a picturesque country city of 25,000 people is now a mangled mass of junk and corpses.

In the low hills above the city, several hundred people have camped in makeshift huts with tin roofs. They are the lucky ones, those who managed somehow to escape the waves of hot mud and debris[1] that swept through Armero.

But they were not being evacuated. Relief officials said priority for seats in the nine or ten helicopters ferrying people to and from the disaster site was given to the injured.

On the northwest side of Armero, several bulldozers were pushing back the mud, trying to open a road into the town. But it could be days before emergency land vehicles can reach here.

The Red Cross has set up a tent and evacuation area in a clearing several hundred yards from where the mud stopped. Only five medics and fifteen volunteers made up the Red Cross team today, according to Alferez. Also helping in the rescue effort here were about ten blue-suited Air Force members and about the same number of orange-suited Civil Defense workers. Yesterday, emergency teams pulled survivors off the roofs and trees where they had climbed to escape the avalanche. Today, the rescuers searched for those buried alive in the mud.

Alferez estimated that 1,000 people could be trapped alive in the city's ruins. An Argentine medic participating in the relief effort, 23-year-old Alejandro Jimenez, guessed that there could be 2,000.

As of early this afternoon, Alferez, who was not keeping exact records, said about 65 injured survivors had been found and flown out today.

But there is no organization, no plan, to search for the living. It is a hit-or-miss operation. Survivors have been located most often when their screams or cries were heard by passersby.

Once survivors are found, the process of freeing them is a lengthy, arduous effort.

One team of workers spent much of this morning trying to pry a 34-year-old man from his collapsed house while, a few yards away, another team chest-deep in water sought desperately to lift to safety a 13-year-old girl whose feet were pinned by fallen concrete.

1. **debris** (də·brē′) *n.:* rubble; broken glass, stone, and other materials resulting from destruction.

Connecting and Comparing Texts

Allende says that she often uses news reports as inspiration for her stories. Have students make a list of all the details from this newspaper article that appear in some way in "And of Clay Are We Created." Then, have students focus on one or two details that Allende changed. Have them analyze why Allende changed the details and how the changes served her purpose for writing the short story. Students may write a short essay focusing on Allende's purpose in writing this story, using the changes she made to details as illustrations of her purpose.

268 Chapter 4 Comparing Themes • Evaluating Arguments: Pro and Con

The man, Efrain Gomez Primo, a peanut farmer and candy vendor, was stuck under his collapsed house. He talked about his ordeal as rescue workers hacked away with machetes[2] at the boards that imprisoned him.

He said the walls of his house fell in Wednesday night as he was trying to flee the raging current. After the volcanic storm had subsided, he said, he started screaming for help. His brother found him at 6:30 yesterday morning and told him not to worry, that the Red Cross, Civil Defense, and Army were on their way. The brother never returned.

A Civil Defense worker who arrived soon afterward lacked the necessary tools and left. It was not until late this morning that a rescue squad arrived.

By then, a middle-aged woman, who had been caught in the wreckage with him and was in great pain through last night, had died. Her corpse lay facing up on a sheet of tin.

"I'm half dead," he said, as the effort to free him began. No one had given him anything to eat or drink for more than 36 hours. Gasping for air, he exclaimed, "I can barely breathe."

When he was finally pried loose and carried to the evacuation zone, medics had no splint for Gomez's broken right leg. They tied a strip of cardboard around it.

Just a few yards from Gomez was the girl, Omaira Sanchez. She had been found just after dawn yesterday by an Air Force officer working in the rescue campaign. The first problem was how to pry loose the stiff arms of the girl's dead aunt, who had grasped the child the night of the tragedy. **C**

Sanchez said the waters of the ravaging Lagunilla River had prevented her aunt from opening the door of their house. All during that stormy night, before she died, the aunt kept apologizing for not having managed to rush the family to freedom, the niece recalled.

The girl's eyes were bright red and swollen. When rescue workers called for an anesthetic,[3] there was none.

She asked for cookies, but there were none of those either. Somehow the girl managed to stay calm and lucid,[4] closing her eyes in pain at times, breaking into tears at other moments.

She would wrap her hands around the neck of a rescue worker standing in the water in front of her and try, with all her might, to tear herself free of whatever was keeping her feet pinned down. But she could not budge.

Workers dug around her, lifting out huge blocks of broken concrete. Rescuers feared that rising water would drown the girl if they couldn't get her out soon. Her head was just above the water line.

Watching the desperate attempts to save the girl, Alferez, the Red Cross chief, shook his head in despair.

"This makes one feel useless," he said. "What can we do?" **D**

—from *The Washington Post,* November 16, 1985

2. **machetes** (mə·shet′ēz) *n.:* large blades used to cut underbrush and crops like sugar cane.

3. **anesthetic** (an′es·thet′ik) *n.:* drug used to eliminate pain.

4. **lucid** (lo͞o′sid) *adj.:* clearheaded.

DIRECT TEACHING

C Literary Focus
GRADE-LEVEL STANDARD

Fact versus fiction. This newspaper article and the short story both include the detail of dead relatives holding the girl down in the mud. What is different about the news account and Allende's account of this detail? [Allende says it was the girl's brothers and sisters who were gripping her legs; the news report states that her aunt's arms were around her.] What was the reporter's purpose in recording this detail? [to inform] What was Allende's purpose in changing it? [Possible responses: to provide a poignant, dramatic story; to persuade the reader of the horror of the situation.] Explain which account you find more compelling and why. [Students' responses will vary.]

D Reading Skills

Finding the main idea. Like fiction writers, news reporters also make decisions about which details to include in their articles to better convey their main idea. Why do you think the reporter chose to end the article with this quotation? [Possible responses: It may have reflected a general attitude of people at the scene; it may have reflected the reporter's attitude.] How does the quotation contribute to the main idea of the report? [Possible response: The quotation emphasizes the main idea of the helplessness that people often feel in the face of overwhelming tragedy.]

INDEPENDENT PRACTICE

Literary Response and Analysis

Reading Check

1. After a volcanic eruption, rivers of mud bury a town.
2. She is trapped in mud.
3. He tries to pull her free; he struggles with poles and ropes; he puts a tire beneath her arms; he tries to remove rubble; he tries to get a pump.
4. She calls officials and asks for help on radio and television.
5. She dies.

Interpretations

6. Azucena is a victim; Rolf is her would-be rescuer. She gives him her fears, and he gives her encouragement.
7. Allende wanted to explore the disaster with more depth and emotion than would be possible in a nonfiction account. Her purpose is to inform the reader about the horror and to persuade us that sometimes the best efforts fail.
8. Like clay, human beings come from and return to the earth; there is utility, beauty, and fragility both in objects made of clay and in human life.
9. The world is full of horrors, but we still find ways to care for one another and value life while facing devastating losses.
10. *Story. Purpose*—to inform, entertain, persuade. *Point of view*—first person. *Tone*—emotional, personal. *Descriptive details*—many. *Figurative language*—often used, sometimes overblown. *Theme*—Although the world is full of horror, we must still care for each other.
    Article. Purpose—to inform. *Point of view*—third person. *Tone*—matter-of-fact. *Descriptive details*—fewer. *Figurative language*—not used. *Main idea*—The enormity of the disaster at Armero made rescue efforts hopeless.

Evaluation

11. Most people would try to help, but many might become less involved.
12. Yes; the image of Azucena in this terrible situation and Rolf's efforts to save her make the story very dramatic and moving. No; the language is overly emotional, and dragging in Rolf's memories of the past seems unnecessary to the outcome.

Literary Response and Analysis

Reading Check

1. Describe the event that occurs before the story begins.
2. Describe Azucena's situation when the story opens.
3. Summarize Rolf Carlé's efforts to save Azucena.
4. How does the narrator try to help Azucena?
5. At the end of the story, what happens to Azucena?

Interpretations

6. What is the relationship between Rolf and Azucena? What do they give to each other?
7. Why do you think Allende chose to write a story about the events described in the newspaper article, rather than a nonfiction account? What do you think her **purpose** is in this story?
8. What do you think the **title** of the story means?
9. Consider Rolf's efforts to help Azucena and what happens to Rolf and Azucena at the end. Then, in a sentence or two, express what you think is the story's **theme,** its insight or message about life.
10. **Compare and contrast** Allende's story with the newspaper account of the same events (see the ***Connection*** on page 267). Think about how the choice of **genre** affects how the story is told. Consider especially these elements:
    - writer's purpose
    - point of view
    - tone
    - descriptive details
    - figurative language
    - theme or main idea

    Which account do you find more moving? Which do you find more informative? Explain why.

Pages 255–283 cover **Reading Standard 3.2** Compare and contrast the presentation of a similar theme or topic across genres to explain how the selection of genre shapes the theme or topic.

Evaluation

11. Look back at your Quickwrite notes. Do you think most people would behave as Rolf Carlé does? Explain why or why not.
12. Allende has written:

> Writing a short story is like shooting an arrow; it requires the instinct, practice, and precision of a good archer . . . and good luck—to hit the bull's eye.

In your opinion, has she hit the bull's-eye with this story? Support your evaluation by referring to details in the story.

Writing

Tell It Again

Retell the events of the Armero disaster in still **another genre.** You might write a poem or song, an interview with a survivor, or journal entries that Rolf Carlé might have written after the disaster.

You Are a Story Hunter

Take a newspaper article from today's paper, and use it as the basis for a **short story.** Elaborate on the facts in the article with believable characters, dialogue, sensory details, and figurative language. Feel free to change or add characters and plot events. Before you start writing, decide on your purpose, and choose the point of view that you think will be most useful for that purpose.

Vocabulary Development

Mapping a Word's Origin

Every word has a history, which you can discover by checking its **etymology,** or **origin,** in a dictionary. (Since etymologies trace a word's history backward in time, the oldest form of the word is normally listed last.) Here is a word map for *subterranean:*

subterranean

Word origin: Latin *terra,* meaning "earth"

Related words:
terrain
terrace
terrarium

Meaning of word: underground

Sample sentences:
- A seismograph measures subterranean tremors.
- Animals that live in subterranean caves are often blind.

Word Bank
subterranean
magnitude
presentiments
tenacity
equanimity
fortitude
ingenuity
resignation
pandemonium
commiserate

PRACTICE 1

For each word in the Word Bank, work with a partner to make a word map like the one for *subterranean.* (Hint: For some words the dictionary may send you to another word to find the origin.)

Word Roots

When you trace word origins, you find that many words come from common roots. A **root** is the part of a word that carries its core meaning. The chart below lists some common Greek and Latin roots.

Greek Roots	Meaning	Example
–log–	study or science of	anthropology
–poly–	many; much	polygon
–therm–	heat	thermometer
Latin Roots	**Meaning**	**Example**
–cred–	belief; trust	credibility
–fid–	belief; faith	confidential
–luc–, –lum–	light	lucid, luminous
–vid–, –vis–	see; seeing	video, revise

PRACTICE 2

List as many example words as you can for each Greek or Latin root in the chart. Get together in a small group to compare lists.

Reading Standard 1.1
Understand word derivations.

ASSESSING

Assessment
- *Progress Assessment of Reading*
  - Selection Test

RETEACHING

For a lesson reteaching Standard 3.2, see *Interactive Reading,* Chapter 4.

Vocabulary Development

Practice 1

Possible Answers

- *magnitude. Origin*—L *magnus,* "great." *Related words*—magnify, magnate. *Meaning*—size.
- *presentiments. Origin*—L *prae–,* "before," plus *sentire,* "to feel." *Related words*—sentient, prescient. *Meaning*—feelings that something will happen.
- *tenacity. Origin*—L *tenere,* "to hold." *Related words*—tenable, tenant. *Meaning*—stubborn determination.
- *equanimity. Origin*—L *aequus,* "even," plus *animus,* "mind." *Related words*—animate, equality. *Meaning*—composure.
- *fortitude. Origin*—L *fortis,* "strong." *Related words*—fort, fortify. *Meaning*—strength to endure.
- *ingenuity. Origin*—L *ingenuus,* "freeborn." *Related words*—ingénue, disingenuous. *Meaning*—cleverness, originality, skill.
- *resignation. Origin*—L *resignare,* "to unseal or cancel." *Related words*—resign, sign. *Meaning*—passive or unresisting acceptance.
- *pandemonium. Origin*—Gr *pan,* "all," plus *daimon,* "spirit." *Related words*—demon, pandemic. *Meaning*—wild uproar.
- *commiserate. Origin*—L *com–,* "with," plus *miserari,* "to pity." *Related words*—misery, compare. *Meaning*—sympathize.

Practice 2

Possible answers: *log*ic; *poly*syllable; *therm*al; in*cred*ible; *fi*delity; *lum*inary; *vis*ta

Resources Reminder

Vocabulary
- *Vocabulary Development*
  - Vocabulary Worksheet, p. 21
- *Lesson Plans for Language Development*
  - Vocabulary, pp. 130, 135

And of Clay Are We Created 271

STANDARDS FOCUS, pp. 272–282

(For the grade-level standards taught in this lesson, see citations on Student Edition pages.)

Prerequisite Standard

- Grade 8, Literary Response and Analysis 3.5 **Identify and analyze recurring themes (e.g., good versus evil) across traditional and contemporary works.**

Reading Skills

- Summarize the main idea.

Summary *at grade level*

In this personal essay, journalist Roger Rosenblatt reflects on the heroic actions of a few people after a plane hit a bridge and crashed into the icy waters of the Potomac River in the winter of 1982. Rosenblatt calls the disaster "two forms of nature in collision: the elements and human character." He examines the heroism of two helicopter rescuers who risked their lives to lower a lifeline to the five survivors in the water and of a bystander who jumped in to drag another survivor to shore. His essay, however, focuses on the selfless actions of one of the crash victims, the anonymous "man in the water," who saved the lives of others by passing the lifeline to them, one by one. He then slipped into the water and drowned. In the actions of this anonymous "man in the water," Rosenblatt sees the best of Everyman, the triumph of humanity and altruism over the impersonal and indifferent forces of nature.

Before You Read

The Man in the Water

Literary Focus

Essays: Thinking on Paper

The subject matter of today's **personal** (or **informal**) **essays** is as wide as human experience—from the mysteries of the cosmos to the clothes dryer's habit of eating socks. The tone can range from serious and thoughtful, as in the essay you're about to read, to comic, as in essays by James Thurber, Dave Barry, and Erma Bombeck.

Essays are thought journeys. Essay writers take a subject—any subject—and examine it from different perspectives, like looking at an object through a telescope, then a microscope, and then a kaleidoscope. Essayists, writing about their own thoughts and feelings, touch us because they are writing about us all.

The Main Idea

When Roger Rosenblatt sat down to write about the man in the water, he probably had his **main idea** in mind—the insight or message he wished to communicate about the tragedy. He was not writing a news article in which he'd have to report the facts of the event. Instead, he wanted to talk about something important that he saw in the incident. He had an idea to share.

Pages 255–283 cover **Reading Standard 3.2** Compare and contrast the presentation of a similar theme or topic across genres to explain how the selection of genre shapes the theme or topic.

Reading Skills

Summarizing the Main Idea

When you **summarize** an essay, you state its most important idea in your own words. You should also cite some of the essay's key **supporting details.** To find the **main idea** of Rosenblatt's—or any—essay, look for key statements that express the writer's opinion.

Make the Connection

Quickwrite

In your notebook, define *hero* and *heroism* in a sentence or two. Then, list some people, past or present, famous or ordinary, whom you regard as heroes. Briefly tell why you think each person is a hero. Save your notes.

Background

The disaster described in this essay occurred on Wednesday, January 13, 1982, in the late afternoon. Washington, D.C., was blanketed in wet snow flurries when Air Florida Flight 90 took off from Washington (now Ronald Reagan) National Airport. Just after takeoff the plane hit the Fourteenth Street Bridge during rush hour, crushed five cars and tipped over a truck, and then crashed into the Potomac River. Seventy-eight people died, including four motorists. Of the seventy-nine people aboard the plane, only five survived—four passengers and one flight attendant. The probable cause of the accident was ice on the plane's wings.

Vocabulary Development

flailing (flāl′iŋ) *v.* used as *adj.:* waving wildly.

extravagant (ek·strav′ə·gənt) *adj.:* excessive; showy.

abiding (ə·bīd′iŋ) *adj.:* continuing; lasting.

pitted (pit′id) *v.:* placed in competition.

implacable (im·plak′ə·bəl) *adj.:* relentless; not affected by attempts at change.

272 Chapter 4 Comparing Themes • Evaluating Arguments: Pro and Con

RESOURCES: READING

Planning

- *One-Stop Planner* CD-ROM with Test Generator
- *On Course: Mapping Instruction*

Media

- *Audio CD Library*
  - disc 9
- *Fine Art Transparencies*
  - Transparency 8

Reading

- *Interactive Reading,* Teacher's Edition
  - Graphic Organizer: Theme and Genre Chart

Differentiating Instruction

- *Lesson Plans for Language Development*
  - English-Language Learners, pp. 117–119, 131, 136

Like every other person on that flight, he was desperate to live.

The MAN in the WATER

Roger Rosenblatt

- Special Education Students, pp. 120, 131, 136

Vocabulary

- *Vocabulary Development*
  - Vocabulary Worksheet, p. 22

Assessment

- *Progress Assessment of Reading*
  - Selection Test
- *One-Stop Planner* CD-ROM with Test Generator

PRETEACHING

Selection Starter

Motivate. Call students' attention to a recent news story about a disaster, such as an earthquake or a tornado. Have students discuss whether they would risk their lives to help strangers in the event of a similar disaster. After the discussion, have students complete the Quickwrite activity.

Preview Vocabulary

Have students read aloud the definitions of the Vocabulary words on p. 272. Then, ask them to choose the Vocabulary word that best fits in each of the following sentences:

1. Their battle to survive the storm shattered people's ______ trust in nature. [abiding]
2. The boats, ______ about in the rough waters, had to be tied tightly to the pier to protect them from severe damage. [flailing]
3. The breakwater could no longer withstand the ______ force of the battering waves. [implacable]
4. The rescuers ______ themselves against the floodwaters. [pitted]
5. After the storm, people were stunned by the sun's ______ display of warmth and beauty. [extravagant]

Assign the Reading

Homework

To introduce students to the voice of the essayist and his frequent use of complex sentences, you may wish to read the first paragraph aloud. Then, invite learners who are having difficulty to read the essay in small groups. As you monitor their work, have other students in the class read the essay independently and note statements that seem to be key in identifying the main idea. For homework, assign the Connection pieces, pp. 278–280, to all students.

DIRECT TEACHING

A Literary Focus
GRADE-LEVEL STANDARD

Personal essay. Remind students that a personal essay is just that—personal. This means there is a person behind it and that the essay reflects that particular person's thoughts, feelings, attitudes, and opinions. What event is Rosenblatt concerned about in this essay? [a plane crash] What are his thoughts and feelings about the event so far? [The crash was terrible but not unusual or unique.]

B Vocabulary Development
GRADE-LEVEL STANDARD

Synonyms and connotations. Point out the word *collision*. How are the connotations of this word different from those of its synonym *conflict*? [Possible responses: *Collision*, implying direct contact, is more concrete and violent than *conflict*. *Collision* also brings to mind the airplane's crash.]

C Literary Focus
GRADE-LEVEL STANDARD

Comparing a theme across genres. Remind students to note the similarities and differences between this essay and Allende's short story as they read. Ask them to consider how the elements of genre are related to each writer's purpose.

As disasters go, this one was terrible but not unique, certainly not among the worst on the roster of U.S. air crashes. There was the unusual element of the bridge, of course, and the fact that the plane clipped it at a moment of high traffic, one routine thus intersecting[1] another and disrupting both. Then, too, there was the location of the event. Washington, the city of form and regulations, turned chaotic, deregulated,[2] by a blast of real winter and a single slap of metal on metal. The jets from Washington National Airport that normally swoop around the presidential monuments like famished gulls were, for the moment, emblemized[3] by the one that fell; so there was that detail. And there was the aesthetic clash[4] as well—blue-and-green Air Florida, the name a flying garden, sunk down among gray chunks in a black river. All that was worth noticing, to be sure. Still, there was nothing very special in any of it, except death, which, while always special, does not necessarily bring millions to tears or to attention. Why, then, the shock here?

Perhaps because the nation saw in this disaster something more than a mechanical failure. Perhaps because people saw in it no failure at all, but rather something successful about their makeup. Here, after all, were two forms of nature in collision: the elements and human character. Last Wednesday, the elements, indifferent as ever, brought down Flight 90. And on that same afternoon, human nature—groping and flailing in mysteries of its own—rose to the occasion.

Of the four acknowledged heroes of the event, three are able to account for their behavior. Donald Usher and Eugene Windsor, a park-police helicopter team, risked their lives every time they dipped the skids[5] into the water to pick up survivors. On television, side by side in bright blue jumpsuits, they described their courage as all in the line of duty. Lenny Skutnik, a 28-year-old employee of the Congressional Budget Office, said: "It's something I never thought I would do"—referring to his jumping into the water to drag an injured woman to shore. Skutnik added that

1. **intersecting** *v.* used as *adj.:* cutting across.
2. **deregulated** *v.* used as *adj.:* removed from government control; here, an ironic reference to the disorder caused by a winter storm.
3. **emblemized** (em′blə·mīzd′) *v.:* represented; symbolized.
4. **aesthetic** (es·thet′ik) **clash:** unpleasant visual contrast.
5. **skids** *n.:* long, narrow pieces used in place of wheels for aircraft landing gear.

Vocabulary
flailing (flāl′iŋ) *v.* used as *adj.:* waving wildly.

DIFFERENTIATING INSTRUCTION

Learners Having Difficulty

Modeling. To help students read "The Man in the Water," model the reading skill of summarizing the main idea. Read the second paragraph aloud and then close the book. Say, "From what I've read so far, I think Rosenblatt's main idea is that there are two forms of nature—the natural world and human nature—and that in times of disaster, human nature can rise to the natural world's challenge." Encourage students as they read to jot down notes about Rosenblatt's main idea and to periodically summarize what they think Rosenblatt most wants to convey about this tragedy.

English-Language Learners

Rosenblatt calls the heroic passenger "the man in the water," "our man," and "man in nature," transforming the individual into an archetype. Be sure students understand that the word *man* can also mean "humankind." You might ask them to explain how this usage could cause confusion and to suggest alternatives that would clarify the meaning.

Resources Reminder

For lessons designed for intermediate and

"somebody had to go in the water," delivering every hero's line that is no less admirable for its repetitions. In fact, nobody had to go into the water. That somebody actually did so is part of the reason this particular tragedy sticks in the mind.

But the person most responsible for the emotional impact of the disaster is the one known at first simply as "the man in the water." (Balding, probably in his 50s, an extravagant moustache.) He was seen clinging with five other survivors to the tail section of the airplane. This man was described by Usher and Windsor as appearing alert and in control. Every time they lowered a lifeline and flotation ring to him, he passed it on to another of the passengers. "In a mass casualty, you'll find people like him," said Windsor. "But I've never seen one with that commitment." When the helicopter came back for him, the man had gone under. His selflessness was one reason the story held national attention; his anonymity[6] another. The fact that he went unidentified invested him with a universal character. For a while he was Everyman, and thus proof (as if one needed it) that no man is ordinary. **D**

6. **anonymity** (an′ə·nim′ə·tē) *n.:* unknown identity.

Vocabulary
extravagant (ek·strav′ə·gənt) *adj.:* excessive; showy.

A Closer Look

Black Box: Air Florida Flight 90

The following conversation took place just before the crash of Air Florida Flight 90. It was recorded on the plane's black box, later retrieved from the wreckage.

Copilot. It's been a while since we've been de-iced.
Pilot. Think I'll go home and . . .
Copilot. Boy . . . this is a losing battle here on trying to de-ice those things . . . a false sense of security, that's all that does.
Pilot. That, ah, satisfies the Feds. Right there is where the icing truck, they oughta have two . . .
Copilot. Yeah, and you taxi through kinda like a carwash or something.
Pilot. Hit that thing with about eight billion gallons of glycol . . .
Copilot. Slushy runway. Do you want me to do anything special for this or just go for it?
Pilot. Unless you got anything special you'd like to do.
Copilot. . . . just take off the nose wheel early like a soft-field takeoff . . . I'll pull it [the throttle] back to about one point five . . . supposed to be about one six depending on how scared we are . . . *(laughter)*

[*The plane is cleared for takeoff at 3:59 P.M., 45 minutes after its last de-icing.*]

Copilot. God, look at that thing.
Copilot. That doesn't seem right, does it?
Copilot. Ah, that's not right.
Pilot. Yes, it is, there's eighty.
Copilot. Naw, I don't think that's right.
Copilot. Ah, maybe it is.
Pilot. Hundred and twenty.
Copilot. I don't know. . . .
Pilot. Come on, forward. . . .
Pilot. Just barely climb.
Speaker Undetermined. Stalling, we're [falling].
Copilot. Larry, we're going down, Larry.
Pilot. I know it.

[*Sound of impact*]

DIRECT TEACHING

D Content-Area Connections

Literature: Everyman
Everyman was originally an allegorical character in *The Summoning of Everyman,* an English morality play of the 1400s. Today Everyman refers to any ordinary person who symbolizes the whole human race.

A Closer Look

Point out that the black box transcript has no main idea. Ask students why this is so. [Possible responses: It is raw data; it has not been composed by an author.] Remind students that data has no inherent main idea until an author shapes it. An author could use the transcript, the statistics, or both to express many ideas about the crash. Ask students what main ideas they might choose from the data to organize into a poem. [Possible responses: Loss of life is tragic; nature is harsh; disaster can strike suddenly.]

advanced English-language learners, see *Lesson Plans for Language Development,* pp. 117–119, 131, 136.

Special Education Students
For lessons designed for special education students, see *Lesson Plans for Language Development,* pp. 120, 131, 136.

Advanced Learners
Acceleration. Use the following activity to move students toward the eleventh- and twelfth-grade Standard 3.2, which requires that they use textual evidence to support a claim.
Activity. Have students create a chart with the head "Nature Versus Humanity." Under the head, have them cite the pages and lines of the essay that support its main idea.

DIRECT TEACHING

A Literary Focus
GRADE-LEVEL STANDARD

Personal essay. In what way does the essayist express his own insights in these paragraphs? [The essayist puts readers inside the mind of the man in the water during his last moments of life.] How effective is this method? [Possible responses: It enables readers to experience the man's thoughts and feelings and to recognize that he was much like themselves. It enables Rosenblatt to reveal his insight—that the man's sacrifice was deliberate; this, in turn, makes the man's actions more real and poignant.]

B Reading Skills

Summarizing the main idea. Here, Rosenblatt summarizes the main idea that the man's actions suggest to him. Why, in Rosenblatt's view, were people so riveted by the disaster? [Possible responses: because the man's actions affirm something wonderful in human nature; because people need to see the good in humanity as much as the crash survivors needed a lifeline.]

A Still, he could never have imagined such a capacity in himself. Only minutes before his character was tested, he was sitting in the ordinary plane among the ordinary passengers, dutifully listening to the stewardess telling him to fasten his seat belt and saying something about the "No Smoking" sign. So our man relaxed with the others, some of whom would owe their lives to him. Perhaps he started to read, or to doze, or to regret some harsh remark made in the office that morning. Then suddenly he knew that the trip would not be ordinary. Like every other person on that flight, he was desperate to live, which makes his final act so stunning.

For at some moment in the water he must have realized that he would not live if he continued to hand over the rope and ring to others. He *had* to know it, no matter how gradual the effect of the cold. In his judgment he had no choice. When the helicopter took off with what was to be the last survivor, he watched everything in the world move away from him, and he deliberately let it happen.

Yet there was something else about our man that kept our thoughts on him, and which keeps our thoughts on him still. He was *there,* in the essential, classic circumstance. Man in nature. The man in the water. For its part, nature cared nothing about the five passengers. Our man, on the other hand, cared totally. So the timeless battle commenced in the Potomac. For as long as that man could last, they went at each other, nature and man; the one making no distinctions of good and evil, acting on no principles, offering no lifelines; the other acting wholly on distinctions, principles, and, one supposes, on faith.

B Since it was he who lost the fight, we ought to come again to the conclusion that people are powerless in the world. In reality, we believe the reverse, and it takes the act of the man in the water to remind us of our true feelings in this matter. It is not to say that everyone would have acted as he did, or as Usher, Windsor, and Skutnik. Yet whatever moved these men to challenge death on behalf of their fellows is not peculiar to them. Everyone feels the possibility in himself. That is the abiding wonder of the story. That is why we would not let go of it. If the man in the water gave a lifeline to the people gasping for survival, he was likewise giving a lifeline to those who observed him.

The odd thing is that we do not even really believe that the man in the water lost his fight. "Everything in Nature contains all the powers of

Vocabulary
abiding (ə·bīd′iŋ) *adj.:* continuing; lasting.

CONTENT-AREA CONNECTIONS

Literature: The Hero
In classical literature of all cultures, the hero is an individual who is faced with a challenge that often results in a struggle between good and evil.

Whole-class activity. The man in the water altruistically gives his life for others. In a discussion, challenge students to determine differences between heroic altruism and unhealthy self-sacrifice. Then, have students brainstorm one list of literary characters that show heroic altruism and another list of characters who show unhealthy self-sacrifice. Ask students to discuss how the man in the water is similar and different from these characters. Explore disagreements and overlaps.

Nature," said Emerson. Exactly. So the man in the water had his own natural powers. He could not make ice storms, or freeze the water until it froze the blood. But he could hand life over to a stranger, and that is a power of nature too. The man in the water pitted himself against an implacable, impersonal enemy; he fought it with charity; and he held it to a standoff. He was the best we can do. ■

C **Vocabulary**

pitted (pit′id) *v.:* placed in competition.

implacable (im·plak′ə·bəl) *adj.:* relentless; not affected by attempts at change.

Meet the Writer

Roger Rosenblatt

Searching for the Good and the Mysterious

Roger Rosenblatt (1940–) says that an expression of mystery characterizes his best essays and stories.

"Often I will wait to write till the last possible minute before deadline, hoping not to solve a particular mystery, but to feel it more deeply. 'The Man in the Water' . . . was written in forty-five minutes, but I brooded about it for many days. . . .

Three full days that air crash led the evening news. I came to believe that the man in the water was the reason, yet no one had said so because he had done something people could not understand.

In too many ways the piece shows that it was written in forty-five minutes, but it resonated with readers at the time because it dwelt on the mystery of an act that people did not understand, or want to understand. Certain stories people do not want to understand. The mystery makes them feel closer to one another than would any solution."

Rosenblatt has had a career's worth of practice as a columnist and editorial writer for publications including *The New Republic, The Washington Post,* and *Time.* He appears regularly on PBS's *The NewsHour with Jim Lehrer* as a commentator on current issues.

Rosenblatt, who has a doctorate degree in English and American literature from Harvard University, began his career teaching literature and writing at Harvard before turning to journalism. In 1996, he returned to teaching as professor of English at Southampton College on Long Island.

He has written and coauthored more than a dozen books, among them *Children of War* (1983), *Witness: The World Since Hiroshima* (1985), *The Man in the Water: Essays and Stories* (1994), and *Rules for Aging* (2000). Many of Rosenblatt's books and essays show his search for the redeeming aspects of human existence and its mysteries.

DIRECT TEACHING

C Literary Focus
GRADE-LEVEL STANDARD

Comparing a theme across genres. Ask students to think about how they might summarize the contrast between Rosenblatt's main idea and Allende's theme. [Possible response: Rosenblatt believes that human beings are not powerless against nature, while Allende shows that many are often terribly powerless.]

GUIDED PRACTICE

Monitoring students' progress. Guide the class in answering these comprehension questions. Direct students to locate passages in the text that support their responses.

Short Answer

1. What heroic thing did the man in the water do? [He saved strangers' lives at the expense of his own.]
2. Which two qualities of the man made him fascinating in Rosenblatt's opinion? [selflessness and anonymity]
3. What two forces are contrasted in the essay? [humanity and nature]
4. What is the victory of the man in the water? [His selflessness and concern for others is a victory over the indifference of nature.]

Meet the Writer

Background. Rosenblatt has written that Americans' sense of irony is vanishing. "Everyone is taken at his or her word. Not that people have to mean what they say; they merely have to sound that way. . . . Why does the disappearance of irony matter? Because when people lose their sense of irony, they forfeit their ability to be teased out of adamancy; thus they also lose the chance to change their minds."

FAMILY/COMMUNITY ACTIVITY

Roger Rosenblatt appears occasionally on *The NewsHour with Jim Lehrer,* a public television evening newscast. Ask a member of the school or community who regularly watches the program to videotape a segment or segments on which Rosenblatt appears. Play the video for the class. Then, invite students to compare and contrast their responses to Rosenblatt's oral and written essays. What similarities do they notice between the way he writes and the way he speaks? How do the televised images that he has chosen to accompany his oral essay add to or subtract from students' interest in his words? Encourage students to express their opinions of Rosenblatt's reflections.

Connection

Summary at grade level

A traveler is attacked by thieves who rob him and leave him half dead. Soon a priest and then a Levite see the victim but pass along without helping. Finally, a Samaritan passes by. He gives the injured man first aid and takes him to an inn. The next day, the Samaritan leaves the innkeeper with some money and tells him to care for the man. The parable ends by asking who of the three men was the true neighbor.

DIRECT TEACHING

A English-Language Learners

Archaic diction and word order. Explain that although words and word patterns have changed since the King James Bible was published in 1611, readers should be able to use context clues to figure out the meanings.

B Content-Area Connections

History and Culture: The Samaritan

Today the phrase *good Samaritan* has become a general term used to describe a person who helps another unselfishly. The meaning of the words would have been quite different for Jesus' Judean audience. Although Judea and Samaria were near each other, people from these areas disliked each other. The Judeans would have expected the priest (a powerful upper-class Judean) or the Levite (an associate of priests) to help a wounded man. When Jesus says that the person who helped the man was not a Judean, but a despised Samaritan, his audience would have been shocked and angry. Only a few would have gone home to reconsider their prejudices.

CONNECTION / BIBLE PARABLE

*A **parable** is a brief story that teaches a lesson about life. In this well-known parable from the Bible, the lesson is about helping others.*

The Parable of the Good Samaritan

The Good Samaritan (1890) by Vincent van Gogh, after Delacroix. Oil on canvas.

Rijksmuseum Kröller-Müller, Otterlo, the Netherlands.

A A certain man went down from Jerusalem to Jericho and fell among thieves, which stripped him of his raiment[1] and wounded him and departed, leaving him half dead.

And by chance there came down a certain priest that way, and when he saw him, he passed by on the other side.

And likewise a Levite,[2] when he was at the place, came and looked on him and passed by on the other side.

B But a certain Samaritan,[3] as he journeyed, came where he was, and when he saw him, he had compassion[4] on him and went to him and bound up his wounds, pouring in oil and wine, and set him on his own beast and brought him to an inn and took care of him.

And on the morrow when he departed, he took out two pence and gave them to the host and said unto him, "Take care of him, and whatsoever thou spendest more, when I come again, I will repay thee."

Which now of these three, thinkest thou, was neighbor unto him that fell among the thieves?

—Luke 10:30–36, from the King James Bible

1. **raiment** (rā′mənt) *n.:* archaic word for "clothing."
2. **Levite** (lē′vīt′): member of the ancient Israelite tribe of Levi.
3. **Samaritan** (sə•mer′ə•tən): person from Samaria, a region neighboring ancient Israel.
4. **compassion** *n.:* pity for the sufferings of others.

Connecting and Comparing Texts

Point out to students that they have just read texts from three different genres (short story, essay, and parable) and that each text features a good Samaritan. Have students work in small groups to consider the actions of the Samaritan in each selection. Ask them to decide which selection had the greatest impact on them and why.

Activity. Have students write a short essay explaining how the Samaritan figures in Rosenblatt's essay and Allende's story are similar to or different from the Samaritan in the parable. Does it matter that the Samaritan saved a life and went on to live, while the man in the water saved lives but died, and Rolf did not save a life at all?

A State Championship Versus Runner's Conscience

John Christian Hoyle

A light drizzle and fog fill the vast margin between gray clouds and muddy ground. The temperature is 42 degrees. The weather envelops and entices me and my six cross-country teammates as we exit the school van.

Our previous performance under similar atmospheric conditions was impressive. It got us here—the final meet of the season, the high school state championship. Physically and mentally, we are overprepared. We're cocky.

Jogging toward the starting line, I feel the eyes of our competition burn into my back. I reciprocate[1] glares while laughing at a joke a teammate shares. I savor knowing that these 180-odd runners know we are the team to beat. I feel powerful. **C**

As we stretch ligaments, I catch a glimpse of our coach smiling—a configuration his mouth and cheeks are not used to. He knows

1. **reciprocate** (ri·sip′rə·kāt′) *v.:* return; exchange.

Connection

Summary *at grade level*

In this personal essay, the writer recalls an incident that occurred when he ran for his high school's cross-country team. After a winning season, his team goes to the state championship. Before the race, the coach tells the team that they have a good chance of winning and that they should not let anyone down. The writer begins the race strongly, and as he runs along a remote portion of the course, he sees an injured runner. He glances at his watch as he runs by, noting that he is making good time, but suddenly he stops in his tracks, torn between helping the hurt runner and winning the race for his team. Then the two runners' eyes meet, and the writer realizes that he has no choice but to stop and help. Many runners pass by. Finally, a man comes to help the injured boy, and the author finishes the race. His coach and teammates are waiting for him at the finish line, wondering what has happened. His coach belittles him for stopping to help. The writer concludes that he did the right thing by following his conscience.

DIRECT TEACHING

C Reading Skills

Making predictions. Will the author's team win the race? Use details from this passage to support your answer. [Possible responses: Yes, because they are "the team to beat." No, because they are "overprepared" and "cocky."]

DIRECT TEACHING

A Literary Focus
REVIEW STANDARD

Conflict. Ask students to name the type of conflict that the author is experiencing and to describe it. [The writer is experiencing internal conflict; he is debating with himself on whether to stop and help the hurt runner.] At what point is the conflict resolved, and what is the resolution? [When the runners' eyes meet, the author knows that he will stop to help and will consequently lose the race.]

B Vocabulary Development
GRADE-LEVEL STANDARD

Synonyms and connotations. Point out the author's use of the word *fellow* to describe the injured runner. How might the connotation have changed if the author had used the word *person* instead? [Possible response: The word *fellow* seems personal and friendly, while *person* comes across as cool and distant.]

C Reading Skills

Summarizing the main idea. Ask students to state in their own words what they consider to be the main idea of this essay. [Possible responses: You should help others, even if friends and authority figures disagree; you have to follow your conscience and do what you think is right.]

the probability of our placing first is better than excellent.

"This is the best opportunity your school has ever had to win a state title," he says in a gruff voice. "Don't let the school down. Don't let me down. Don't let your teammates down. And most importantly, don't let yourselves down."

Coach is still speaking. But I've stopped listening. I dream of the big, shiny trophy.

We take our places: The gun fires. As I accelerate, I inhale deep breaths. Most of the racers are behind me. I'm hitting my stride. A strong finish is mine.

Rounding a corner of a remote leg of the winding course, my eyes zero in on a runner in red shorts. He's sitting down, crying in pain, clutching his foot. I sidestep him and glance at my watch. I'm making good time. I take comfort in knowing there's one fewer runner ahead of me.

A But suddenly I freeze. Cold. I'm breathing heavily. My mind tells my legs to keep moving. But I don't. I swivel around, spotting the downed runner. He's now lying on his back—in the mud. I'm about 20 feet from him. I think for a moment. Do I help? Will someone else in the pack stop to help? Can I come back or send someone when I cross the finish line? I'm losing precious minutes. The agony on his face disturbs me. He's in trouble. Our eyes connect, and at this moment the race has ended for me. Arguments against helping become moot.[2] I can think of nothing other than helping this fellow. **B**

I help him to his feet. We look for someone else to help, but no one does. About 25 runners have whizzed by. Finally, two or three minutes later, a man comes to take over for me.

"Finish the race," he encourages. "Finish the race!" I do. When I cross the finish line, my coach and teammates are waiting to find out what happened.

"Where were you?" Coach asks in a tone that would have dwarfed Lombardi.[3]

I explain.

"You what?" he says, tossing his arms in the air in disbelief. "You stopped to help someone."

"Yes," I mumble sheepishly. "It seemed right. I'm sorry."

He laughs at me. His face is fiery red. The six-hour ride back takes days in my mind. It's lonely and silent. Drum beats from headphones are the only sounds that break the stale air.

My team placed fourth. Almost three weeks will go by until Coach speaks to me. Sports make my world revolve. It seems everyone thinks I failed, that I should have breezed by the guy.

C I think about it a lot, even now, several years later. Did I do the right thing? Was it worth it?

Yes, because when his eyes connected with mine, my conscience demanded that I stop and help. Though I had to think about it for a moment, I couldn't keep running. I would have felt awful if I had—and that would have smoldered in my mind a lot longer than the disapproval of Coach and my team. Basking in personal glory on the altar of ego, I figure, is never worth it.

—from *The Christian Science Monitor*, February 5, 1999

2. **moot** *adj.:* no longer worthy of consideration; pointless.

3. **Lombardi:** Vince Lombardi coached the Green Bay Packers football team from 1959 to 1967 and led them to five championships.

280 Chapter 4 Comparing Themes • Evaluating Arguments: Pro and Con

Connecting and Comparing Texts

Ask students to compare the themes or main ideas of "And of Clay Are We Created," "The Man in the Water," "The Good Samaritan," and this essay. How are the main ideas the same and different? [Possible responses: The main idea or theme of all the selections is that it is good to help others. "The Man in the Water" has another overarching main idea of man versus nature.] Ask students what Hoyle's purpose may have been in writing this piece. [Possible response: The essay relates the author's good deed while warning against "basking in personal glory on the altar of ego."]

Activity. Ask students to write a short essay analyzing Hoyle's possible motivations in writing this essay. Have them address the question of whether a first-person tale about an altruistic action is more or less powerful than a third-person telling of such a tale.

Literary Response and Analysis

Reading Check

1. Briefly describe the disaster.
2. According to Rosenblatt, the disaster was a clash between "the elements, indifferent as ever," and what else?
3. Besides the man in the water, who are the three other heroes, and what does each one do?
4. Describe what the man in the water looks like and what he does. What ultimately happens to him?

Interpretations

5. According to Rosenblatt, the man in the water symbolizes the **conflict** between human beings and nature. How does Rosenblatt characterize nature? How does nature differ from the man in the water?
6. Rosenblatt says that the man in the water is proof that "no man is ordinary." What do you think he means by this?
7. **Summarize** Rosenblatt's most important points, and state his **main idea**. Which passages support this idea most effectively?
8. Briefly state what you think is the **theme** of Rosenblatt's essay. In this case, is the theme the same as the main idea? Explain why or why not.
9. How is John Hoyle, the author of "A State Championship Versus Runner's Conscience" (see the ***Connection*** on page 279), like the Samaritan in the Bible parable (see the ***Connection*** on page 278)? How are they both like the heroes in Rosenblatt's essay? Are all these people good Samaritans? Explain your responses.

Evaluation

10. How would you react in a situation in which you might save a stranger's life but would risk losing your own? Talk about your responses to what the four heroes in Rosenblatt's essay did.
11. The final two paragraphs of the essay make specific points about human nature. Explain in your own words what Rosenblatt is saying, and then give your opinion of his ideas.

Writing

Right or Wrong?

Think about the writer of "A State Championship Versus Runner's Conscience" (see the ***Connection*** on page 279). Did he do the right thing? Write a **persuasive essay** in which you argue either that he should have helped the other runner *or* that he should have been more loyal to himself, his team, and his school. Be sure to include a thesis statement and supporting details.

Use "Writing a Persuasive Essay," pages 294–301, for help with this assignment.

My Hero

Create a brief **biographical sketch** of one of the heroes you listed in your Quickwrite notes. Show your hero in his or her surroundings, and tell a little about the person's life and why he or she is a hero to you.

Comparing Themes

For a writing assignment comparing the themes in "And of Clay Are We Created" and "The Man in the Water," see page 283.

Pages 255–283 cover **Reading Standard 3.2** Compare and contrast the presentation of a similar theme or topic across genres to explain how the selection of genre shapes the theme or topic.

INDEPENDENT PRACTICE

Literary Response and Analysis

Interpretations

5. Possible answer: Nature is indifferent, while the man in the water is caring and principled.
6. Possible answer: The man in the water becomes extraordinary through his selfless actions. Like him, everyone has the potential to act in an extraordinary way.
7. *Summary*—By sacrificing his life to save strangers, the man in the water shows human potential. Everyone has a capacity for caring that defies the indifference of nature. *Main idea*—Altruism is a powerful part of human nature. *Support*—Paragraphs 2, 7, 8, and 9.
8. Possible answer: Altruism is a powerful part of human nature. The main idea and theme are the same because Rosenblatt uses the story to illustrate the larger theme of altruism.
9. Possible answer: They both give help to a person in need. They are also like the heroes in Rosenblatt's essay who selflessly help others. All are good Samaritans to differing degrees. The man in the water may be considered the greatest Samaritan because he sacrifices the most.

Evaluation

10. Some students might say they would risk their lives, as Usher, Windsor, and Skutnik did, but would not deliberately give their lives for a stranger, as the man in the water did.
11. Possible answer: Rosenblatt is saying that the man in the water doesn't really lose the fight with nature, because it's also natural for humans to care for others. Most students will agree that Rosenblatt's ideas are uplifting.

Reading Check

1. An airplane taking off in cold, snowy weather hit a bridge and crashed into the Potomac River, killing all but five passengers.
2. human nature
3. Donald Usher and Eugene Windsor use a helicopter to lift survivors out of the water. Lenny Skutnik jumps into the water and drags a woman to shore.
4. He is balding, in his fifties, and has a large mustache. He passes the lifeline on to other passengers rather than using it himself. He drowns before he can be rescued.

Vocabulary Development

Practice

Possible Answers

1. *Flailing* indicates struggle, while *waving* can sound casual.
2. *Extravagant* indicates style, while *large* simply refers to size.
3. Unlike *lingering, abiding* adds a positive connotation of enduring.
4. *Pitted* suggests deep resolve; *set* is a more neutral term.
5. Unlike *firm, implacable* suggests that any pleas for compassion would be useless.

Resources Reminder

Vocabulary

- *Vocabulary Development*
  - Vocabulary Worksheet, p. 22
- *Lesson Plans for Language Development*
  - Vocabulary, pp. 131, 136

Grammar Link

Practice 1

Possible Answer

The description of the man in the water (p. 275) might be inflated as shown: With hair that was becoming more than a bit sparse; middle-aged, between the ages of forty-nine and sixty-five; with a fairly unusual-looking moustache.

Practice 2

You may wish to review students' rewritten prose.

ASSESSING

Assessment

- *Progress Assessment of Reading*
  - Selection Test

RETEACHING

For another selection to teach Standard 3.2, see *Interactive Reading,* Chapter 4.

Vocabulary Development

In Other Words: Synonyms and Connotations

PRACTICE

Reading Standard 1.2 Distinguish between the denotative and connotative meanings of words and interpret the connotative power of words.

Word Bank
flailing
extravagant
abiding
pitted
implacable

From a number of **synonyms,** Rosenblatt chose the words that had the **connotations**—the emotional overtones—he wanted. Answer the questions below about his word choices.

1. Rosenblatt says that in the aftermath of the crash, human nature found itself "groping and flailing in mysteries of its own." Why wouldn't *waving* have the same effect as *flailing?*
2. The author mentions the man's "extravagant moustache." Why is *extravagant* a more effective word to use than *large?*
3. What does *abiding* add to the author's conclusion about the "wonder of the story" that *lingering* wouldn't convey?
4. The man in the water "pitted" himself against nature. Why wouldn't substituting *set* for *pitted* work as well?
5. Why would the author call nature *implacable* rather than *firm?*

Grammar Link MINI-LESSON

Say It Straight: Eliminating Wordiness

Knowing when and how to use clauses and phrases is important because they can add information and variety to your sentences. Don't overdo them, though, and create a wordy disaster. Compare these two sentences, for example:

1. Every time, hoping to rescue him, they lowered a lifeline and flotation ring and hoped that he would allow himself to be rescued out of the water; but he conveyed the rescue device to yet another one of the passengers who had been in the plane with him, waiting in the water to be rescued after the crash.
2. ROSENBLATT
   "Every time they lowered a lifeline and flotation ring to him, he passed it on to another of the passengers."

Rosenblatt's sentence is not only much better than the first sentence; it was also harder to write. That's because it's easier to be wordy than concise. In your writing, don't add too many phrases and clauses to a sentence.

For more help, see Verbals and Verbal Phrases, pages 70–81, and Uses of Subordinate Clauses, pages 93–101, in the *Holt Handbook.*

PRACTICE 1

Pick another short passage from "The Man in the Water," and inflate it as in the first example. (By rewriting good, spare prose, you'll appreciate what makes it good.) Then, ask a partner to streamline the passage. Compare the shortened version with Rosenblatt's. Did your partner come close to finding the original amid the wordiness?

PRACTICE 2

Take a piece of prose you're working on or a piece from your writer's portfolio. See whether you can improve it by doing some pruning.

282 Chapter 4 Comparing Themes • Evaluating Arguments: Pro and Con

Writing a Comparison–Contrast Essay

Comparing a Theme Across Genres

Now that you have read Allende's story and Rosenblatt's essay, you can compare their themes in a comparison-contrast essay. When you write a **comparison-contrast essay,** you use the skills of **comparing** (finding similarities) and **contrasting** (finding differences).

Gather Your Information, and Organize It

For help writing your essay, go back to the chart you completed on page 255.

There are two main methods for organizing a comparison-contrast essay. The one you will practice here is the **point-by-point method.** (The **block method** was covered on page 254.)

The Point-by-Point Method

With this organization you discuss the *elements,* one at a time. You might discuss the author's purpose in work 1 and then the author's purpose in work 2, and so on for other elements. The chart on the right shows an example.

Use Three Basic Parts, and Elaborate

As with most essays, use three basic parts:

- **introduction**—includes background and **thesis statement**
- **body**—includes a separate paragraph for each element
- **conclusion**—sums up and adds a personal comment

Be sure to **elaborate** on every general statement you make; use details, examples, and quotations from the selections.

Revise Your Essay

Revise your paper after peer evaluation or self-evaluation. Ask yourself:

- Does the thesis statement clearly state the main point of the essay?
- Does the essay elaborate on the elements of both selections?
- Does the essay follow point-by-point organization? Is each point about an element in work 1 followed by a point about that element in work 2?
- Is the conclusion clear and effective?

▶ **For more help writing a comparison-contrast essay, see pages 382–389.**

Point-by-Point Method
Element 1: How Genre Relates to Author's Purpose
Work 1: "And of Clay Are We Created" Work 2: "The Man in the Water"
Element 2: Theme/Main Idea and Whether Stated or Implied
Work 1: "And of Clay Are We Created" Work 2: "The Man in the Water"
Element 3: Genre Elements That Support Theme/Main Idea
Work 1: "And of Clay Are We Created" Work 2: "The Man in the Water"

Pages 255–283 cover **Reading Standard 3.2** Compare and contrast the presentation of a similar theme or topic across genres to explain how the selection of genre shapes the theme or topic.

Writing a Comparison-Contrast Essay

Writing Tips

You may wish to share with students this tip from professional writers: If you don't understand your subject well, you won't be able to write about it well. Suggest that before students begin writing their comparison-contrast essays, they make themselves thoroughly familiar with the two selections. Encourage students to re-read the story and essay. As they do, they may fill in or add to their chart from p. 255. Explain that the details on this chart can serve as a convenient outline for their essays. They should refer to it as they write each new paragraph.

DIFFERENTIATING INSTRUCTION

Learners Having Difficulty

To give students practice at eliminating wordiness (p. 282), ask them to prune these inflated sentences based on Rosenblatt's prose. Have them compare their versions.

If you rate this disaster with others, this one was truly terrible, but it was not the only disaster of its kind, and it was not even the very worst of all the many airplane crashes that have taken place in the United States.

Review key literary terms, such as *genre, subject* (or *topic*), *theme, main idea,* and *author's purpose,* to help students compare the two selections (p. 283).

Advanced Learners

Point out that elements of fiction may creep into essays and memoirs, while works of fiction might incorporate real people, places, and events.

STANDARDS FOCUS, pp. 284–292

(For grade-level and review standards taught in this lesson, see citations on Student Edition pages.)

Prerequisite Standard

- Grade 8, Reading Comprehension 2.7 **Evaluate the unity, coherence, logic, internal consistency, and structural patterns of text.**

Summary *at grade level*

In these two essays the authors address the issue of whether the United States should enact "Good Samaritan" laws that would legally obligate people to help others in emergency situations.

Writers Allred and Bloom cite the alleged behavior of the paparazzi who did not come to Princess Diana's aid after her car accident as an example of behavior that is illegal under French law. In the United States, on the other hand, there is no law that requires passersby to assist a victim. However, there are laws that allow people who act as good Samaritans to be sued. Although the authors devote most of their essay to arguing for legislation, they end by appealing to our "moral responsibility" to aid others.

In the second essay, Sjoerdsma argues that Americans should *not* be obligated by law to help others. She points out that our law is based on English common law, which emphasizes individualism and does not require one person to aid another in an emergency, unless a special relationship exists between the two, such as parent-child or doctor-patient. She believes that we cannot legislate morality. Her arguments, supported by logical appeals, include a call to protect good Samaritans who act without the force of law compelling them to do so.

Before You Read INFORMATIONAL MATERIALS

If Decency Doesn't, Law Should Make Us Samaritans • Good Samaritans U.S.A. Are Afraid to Act

Evaluating Arguments: Pro and Con

Are You Convinced?

It's hard to get through a day without someone trying to persuade you, usually through an **argument,** a series of statements designed to convince you of something. For starters, consider politicians' speeches and all the editorials in newspapers. Often you are faced with opposing arguments (pro and con) on an issue, as in the two opinion essays you are about to read. How can you evaluate all these arguments? Whose position is believable and backed up by evidence, and whose isn't?

The following questions and the chart on the next page will help you evaluate the **credibility,** or believability, of an author's argument.

Pages 284–289 cover **Reading Standard 2.8** Evaluate the credibility of an author's argument or defense of a claim by critiquing the relationship between generalizations and evidence, the comprehensiveness of evidence, and the way in which the author's intent affects the structure and tone of the text.

1. **What's the claim or opinion?** If you're reading a persuasive piece, first read through it to get the big picture—the whole idea of what the writer is saying. Then, determine the author's **claim,** which is also called an **opinion.** This opinion is often stated in the form of a **generalization** (a broad statement that covers many situations). For example, this is a generalization that states an opinion: "Every eligible citizen should be required to vote."
2. **What's the support?** Here are some common ways in which authors support their views:

   Logical appeals. Logical appeals include convincing reasons and evidence.

   Reasons are statements that explain *why* the author holds an opinion. (For example, this statement includes a reason for the author's opinion: "Citizens should be required to vote because only then will elected officials represent all the people.")

   Evidence is the specific information that is used to back up a reason. Remember that evidence must be **relevant** to the reason—that is, it must be directly and logically related to it. Remember, too, that every generalization, in order to be believable, should be backed up by evidence.

   The types of evidence most frequently used include

   - facts
   - statistics (number facts)
   - examples
   - quotations or opinions by experts

   Emotional appeals. Arguments can also be supported by emotional appeals. These appeals stir feelings such as happiness or anger in readers. Authors often use emotional appeals because they know that our emotions may override our reason. You should be wary of a writer who mainly uses emotional appeals in an argument. Emotional appeals are usually accomplished through

   - loaded words (words with strong emotional connotations, or associations)
   - anecdotes (brief stories or personal accounts of an event or happening)

RESOURCES: READING

Planning

- *One-Stop Planner* CD-ROM with Test Generator
- *On Course: Mapping Instruction*

Media

- *Audio CD Library*
  - disc 9

Reading

- *Interactive Reading,* Teacher's Edition
  - Graphic Organizer: Argument-Evaluation Chart

Differentiating Instruction

- *Lesson Plans for Language Development*
  - English-Language Learners, pp. 121–123, 132, 137
  - Special Education Students, pp. 124, 132, 137

284 Chapter 4 Comparing Themes • Evaluating Arguments: Pro and Con

Evaluating an Author's Argument

Claim or Opinion	
Logical Appeals	
Reason 1	
Evidence	
Reason 2	
Evidence	
Emotional Appeals	
Loaded words, etc.	

3. **Is the evidence comprehensive?** Evidence can make or break an argument, so an author must provide sufficient evidence to back up generalizations and to make an argument convincing. Ask yourself whether the author has done his or her job. If the argument is filled with emotional appeals but no relevant evidence is presented, you need to ask yourself why. Could it be there is no real evidence to support the author's claim?
4. **What's the author's intent?** Consider the author's intent. Does he or she hold a biased or prejudiced interest in the topic and have an ax to grind, or is the author trying to present a reasoned, objective-sounding argument? Note how the author's intent affects the **tone.** For example, an angry or insulting tone should send up red flags, telling the reader that the author's argument is based more on opinion or strong feeling than on evidence.

➤ **For more about persuasive writing, see "Writing a Persuasive Essay," pages 294–301, at the end of this chapter.**

Vocabulary Development

allegations (al′ə·gā′shənz) *n.:* in law, assertions, or positive statements, made without proof.

depraved (dē·prāvd′) *adj.:* immoral.

liability (lī′ə·bil′ə·tē) *n.:* legal obligation or responsibility to make good a damage or loss.

rationalizations (rash′ən·ə·lə·zā′shənz) *n.:* seemingly reasonable excuses or explanations for one's behavior—but not the real reasons.

solidarity (säl′ə·dar′ə·tē) *n.:* complete unity in a group or organization.

callous (kal′əs) *adj.:* unfeeling.

feigning (fān′iŋ) *v.:* pretending.

immunity (i·myo͞on′ə·tē) *n.:* freedom from a legal obligation.

construed (kən·stro͞od′) *v.:* interpreted.

indemnifies (in·dem′ni·fīz′) *v.:* in a legal sense, protects.

Connecting to the Literature

Rolf Carlé in "And of Clay Are We Created" and the selfless hero in "The Man in the Water" are examples of people helping others in situations of extreme danger. The following two articles discuss whether such help should be required by law.

Vocabulary

- *Vocabulary Development*
  - Vocabulary Worksheet, p. 23

Assessment

- *Progress Assessment of Reading*
  - Selection Test
- *One-Stop Planner* CD-ROM with Test Generator

PRETEACHING

Selection Starter

Motivate. Have students imagine that they came upon an injured person in a parking lot. What would they do? Go over and help? Ignore the person? Call 911? Have students discuss the pros and cons of each option.

Preview Vocabulary

To reinforce students' understanding of the Vocabulary words, have them write their responses to the following questions. (Possible responses are given.)

1. What might happen to a person who was found to be feigning solidarity with her employer while passing trade secrets to a rival firm? [She might be fired.]
2. Give an example of an action that is callous and depraved. [treating a dog cruelly because it barks too much]
3. What rationalizations might a teenager use to counter her mother's allegations that she spends too much money on music? [She might say that she is studying music so that she can play her guitar better; she might say that she is working to improve her knowledge of the history of jazz.]
4. A driver has automobile liability insurance. Would that give him immunity from prosecution if he recklessly caused an accident? Explain. [Automobile liability insurance might pay for the damage he caused but would not protect him from prosecution.]
5. A man has sued a bleach-manufacturing company for damage to his laundry. As the judge construed the law, the warning label on the bottle of bleach indemnifies the manufacturer against frivolous lawsuits. Did the judge favor the man or the manufacturer? Explain. [The judge interpreted the law to mean that the manufacturer could not be sued in a case like this.]

If Decency Doesn't . . . / Good Samaritans U.S.A. . . . 285

DIRECT TEACHING

A Reading Informational Materials
GRADE-LEVEL STANDARD

Evaluating evidence. According to the essay, France has a "Good Samaritan" law; however, this did not cause the paparazzi to help the injured Princess Diana. Do you think this anecdote is an effective beginning for an essay in favor of "Good Samaritan" laws? Explain your answer. [Possible responses: Yes, because if the paparazzi are prosecuted, this may serve as an example to others. No, because in spite of the law, people did not help Diana and the others who were injured.]

B Reading Informational Materials
GRADE-LEVEL STANDARD

Evaluating emotional appeals. [Possible response to question 1: Loaded words include *bleeding, injured, and dying; shocked the world and offended our deepest sense of decency; depraved image of people trying to make a buck off the dying;* and *grievous injury or death.*]

OP-ED ARTICLE

If Decency Doesn't, Law Should Make Us Samaritans

from the *Houston Chronicle*, September 18, 1997

Gloria Allred *and* **Lisa Bloom**

Witnesses' allegations that paparazzi[1] stood by and snapped photos while Princess Diana[2] and her companions were bleeding, injured, and dying, rather than aiding the accident victims, have shocked the world and offended our deepest sense of decency.

A If the photographers did so, they may be charged with violating France's "Good Samaritan"[3] law requiring people to assist others in distress. Yet in the United States there is no civil or criminal law[4] requiring a bystander to come to the aid of another. If the accident had occurred in the United States, the paparazzi could not have been charged with violating any law as a result of photographing rather than assisting. If any good is to come of the Princess Diana tragedy and the depraved image of people trying to make a buck off of the dying, it should be a call to change U.S. law to require each of us to render at least minimal assistance, where possible, to those at risk of suffering grievous injury or death. B 1

1 EMOTIONAL APPEALS
What **loaded words** can you find in the first two paragraphs?

For example, it is not too much to ask that we call the police or an ambulance when we come upon a major car accident with severely injured people. In that situation a few minutes' delay can be the difference between life and death.

The American "no duty to come to the aid of another" rule has been criticized by legal scholars, yet the issue has generally been ignored by the public. It should insult our values to think that a healthy adult could come upon a baby drowning face down in an inch of water and walk right by when a mere nudge would save the baby's life. Law students are taught that if someone is choking on a chicken bone in a restaurant, not only are other patrons not required to give the Heimlich maneuver,[5] call an ambulance, or

1. **paparazzi** (pä′pä·rät′tsē) *n.:* photographers (especially intrusive photographers who take candid pictures of celebrities).
2. **Princess Diana:** Diana, Princess of Wales (1961–1997), who was killed in a highly publicized car crash in Paris on August 31, 1997. Photographers were later criticized for taking photos of the accident without trying to help the victims.
3. **Good Samaritan:** someone who unselfishly helps others in need. The term comes from a Bible parable (see page 278).
4. **civil or criminal law:** Civil law is the body of law relating to individuals' private rights; criminal law deals with crimes and their punishments.
5. **Heimlich maneuver:** emergency technique used to remove something blocking a person's windpipe by delivering a sudden, sharp, upward blow to the abdomen below the ribs.

Vocabulary
allegations (al′ə·gā′shənz) *n.:* in law, assertions, or positive statements, made without proof.
depraved (dē·prāvd′) *adj.:* immoral.

DIFFERENTIATING INSTRUCTION

Learners Having Difficulty
Modeling. To help students evaluate the credibility of an argument, write a statement on the chalkboard about which students may have strong feelings—for example, "It should be mandatory for everyone to learn a foreign language." Then, invite students to come up with several logical appeals and several emotional appeals, along with evidence, to support the argument. Write these on the chalkboard, and invite students to debate the merits of each piece of evidence. Then, ask students to decide whether they agree or disagree with the statement on the chalkboard, using their evaluation of the credibility of the evidence.

Resources Reminder
Reading
- *Interactive Reading,* Teacher's Edition
  - Graphic Organizer: Argument-Evaluation Chart

English-Language Learners
Because of the many legal terms used, reading these essays may be particularly challeng-

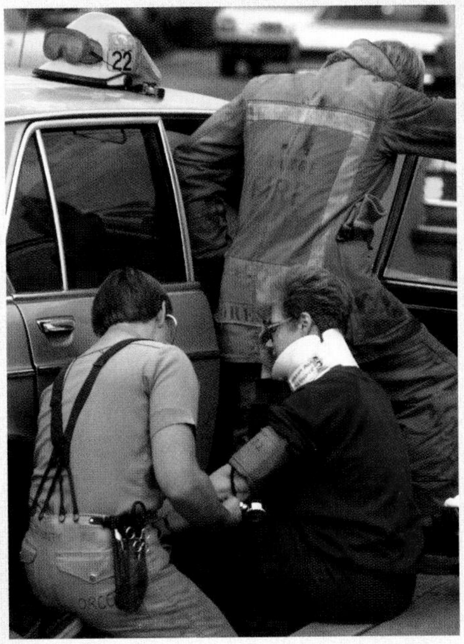

A paramedic assists an accident victim at the scene of a car crash.

do CPR,[6] but in fact the other patrons could, without violating any law, even dance around the gasping victim, singing, "Chicken bone! Chicken bone! Choking on a chicken bone!" ❷

> **C** **❷ EVALUATING TONE**
> What **tone** does this paragraph have? What phrases and sentences create the tone?

Under American law, liability generally exists for action, not inaction. We are each responsible for the harm we cause to others due to the lack of reasonable care. If my careless actions, however innocent, injure you, you have the right to sue me for your damages. Yet even if I maliciously, hatefully, and with evil intent stand by and watch you die without giving simple assistance, there is no legal remedy. This is indecent and should be changed. It is time to join with countries like France and insist that there be legal consequences for turning one's back on someone in desperate need. ❸

> **❸ EVALUATING EVIDENCE** **D**
> What is the author's main **generalization** in this paragraph? What **evidence** supports it?

Why do so many people ignore the needs of accident and crime victims? Rationalizations range from fear that getting involved will be unduly time consuming or cause personal injury to the Good Samaritan to doubts as to what to do in a crisis. While the untrained should not attempt medical assistance, it takes so little time and effort to phone paramedics.[7]

The real reason people don't reach out is because they feel disconnected from strangers in need. Yet the child at risk, the injured motorist, the choking restaurant patron could be any one of us or our loved ones. If each of us recognized a moral responsibility to come to the aid of others, we would all gain the benefits of a stronger and safer community. ❹

> **❹ EVALUATING EVIDENCE** **E**
> What **types of evidence** have the authors used to support their argument in this article? Cite examples of each type.

6. **CPR:** short for "cardiopulmonary resuscitation," an emergency first-aid technique using cardiac massage and mouth-to-mouth breathing to keep someone alive.

7. **paramedics** (par′ə•med′iks) *n.:* people who are trained to provide emergency medical services.

Vocabulary

liability (lī′ə · bil′ə · tē) *n.:* legal obligation or responsibility to make good a damage or loss.

rationalizations (rash′ən · ə · lə · zā′shənz) *n.:* seemingly reasonable excuses or explanations for one's behavior—but not the real reasons.

ing for students who are learning English. You may wish to pair these students with advanced readers. Have the partners read the essays together, pausing after each sentence to discuss and paraphrase its meaning and to demonstrate the meaning of terms such as *Heimlich maneuver.*

Resources Reminder

For lessons designed for intermediate and advanced English-language learners, see *Lesson Plans for Language Development,* pp. 121–123, 132, 137.

Special Education Students

For lessons designed for special education students, see *Lesson Plans for Language Development,* pp. 124, 132, 137.

DIRECT TEACHING

C Reading Informational Materials
GRADE-LEVEL STANDARD

Evaluating evidence. Remind students that *tone* is conveyed through a writer's choice of words and examples. [Possible response to question 2: The tone is fervent and emotional. Evidence may include "baby drowning face down" and "dance around the gasping victim, singing, 'Chicken bone.'"]

D Reading Informational Materials
GRADE-LEVEL STANDARD

Evaluating evidence. [Possible response to question 3: The authors' main generalization is that there should be legal consequences for not helping someone in need. The evidence that supports their argument is that those who do help others can be sued if they unintentionally cause harm while those who stand by and do nothing to help are not liable.]

E Reading Informational Materials
GRADE-LEVEL STANDARD

Evaluating evidence. [Possible response to question 4: The authors use many emotional appeals in the first, second, and third paragraphs, including phrases with loaded words such as *trying to make a buck off the dying,* and a hypothetical scenario in the fourth paragraph in which someone walks past a baby who is drowning in an inch of water. They also use logical appeals, such as facts (liability exists for action, not inaction) and examples (the person who acts may be sued, whereas the person who does nothing and allows a person to die may not be sued).]

DIRECT TEACHING

A Reading Informational Materials
GRADE-LEVEL STANDARD
Paraphrasing generalizations. [Possible response to question 1: U.S. law favors the individual, whereas European law favors society.]

B Vocabulary Development
GRADE-LEVEL STANDARD
? Legalese. Can you figure out the meaning of the word *mandating*? How? [Possible response: The word *mandating* means "requiring" or "ordering." The fact that this passage is discussing legal obligations helps to suggest the meaning of *mandating*, as does the word *imposing*, which means "establishing something or forcing something upon another."]

C Reading Informational Materials
GRADE-LEVEL STANDARD
Evaluating evidence. [Possible response to question 2: Today good Samaritans in the United States risk not only being ambushed and injured but also being sued by the person they tried to help.]

D English-Language Learners
Slang. The sentence that begins, "All states have 'Good-Sam' statutes, but 'they're all over the place,'" may confuse some students. Point out that Good-Sam is an abbreviation for "good Samaritan." Then, explain that "all over the place" means that they are all very different from one another.

OP-ED ARTICLE

Good Samaritans U.S.A. Are Afraid to Act

from *The Virginian-Pilot,* September 15, 1997

Ann Sjoerdsma

On the streets of Paris and other European cities, as we've learned since Princess Diana's fatal crash on August 31, passersby—even pursuing paparazzi—are required by law to assist victims of accidents. To be "Good Samaritans."

On the streets of most-towns, U.S.A., passersby who happen upon an accident—even physicians—can look the other way, ignore the victims. We have no legal obligation to assist.

A Thanks to our English common-law origins,[1] Americans have a legal system strong on individualism, whereas Europeans, whose "civil law" is Roman, prize social solidarity. ❶

> **❶ PARAPHRASING GENERALIZATIONS** In your own words, explain the **generalization** the author makes here.

B Increasingly, however, in reaction to cases of callous indifference, states such as Minnesota and Wisconsin are mandating citizen help in emergencies. They are imposing on us a duty to assist, provided we don't put ourselves at risk.

As much as I'd like to encourage compassion and community, I think it's too late to legislate such morality. It's too late because it's too dangerous. This isn't France.

The Good Samaritan of Biblical parable didn't have to fear that the man he found beaten and robbed in the road was feigning injury and might ambush him. He also didn't have to worry about being sued. Today's Good Samaritan U.S.A. does.

C Instead of compelling reluctant or even incompetent people to intervene, we should concentrate on protecting Good Samaritans who act now, without force of law. ❷

> **❷ EVALUATING EVIDENCE** What two **reasons** has the writer previously given to support the opinion in this paragraph?

D All states have "Good-Sam" statutes, but "they're all over the place," says Ken King of the Dallas-based American College of Emergency Physicians.

In general, if a Good Samaritan does what a "reasonable person"—in France, he's called a *bon père de famille*[2]—would do under the circumstances, he won't be held liable in negligence[3] for any harm he may cause the accident victim.

But he still might get sued.

Let me back up a bit. . . .

At common law there was no duty to

1. **English common-law origins:** reference to the English system of laws based on custom, usage, and legal decisions that forms the basis of the American legal system.

2. **bon père de famille** (bôn per də fä·mē'y'): French expression for "good family man."
3. **liable in negligence:** legally responsible to pay for loss or damage caused by *not* doing something.

Vocabulary

solidarity (säl'ə · dar'ə · tē) *n.:* complete unity in a group or organization.

callous (kal'əs) *adj.:* unfeeling.

feigning (fān'iŋ) *v.:* pretending.

288 Chapter 4 Comparing Themes • Evaluating Arguments: Pro and Con

render aid to a person in an emergency. A man could sit on a dock, smoke a cigar, and watch a person drown without risking any civil or criminal liability.

But there were exceptions.

A key one was a "special relationship" between the victim and the would-be rescuer. Certain people have a duty of care toward others because of their relationship, usually one of dependency: the physician toward his patient, the shopkeeper toward his customer, the employer-employee, parent-child.

If that man on the dock were a lifeguard, he'd have to dive in. Duty would call.

But suppose the man on the dock—or a passerby on the road—attempts to rescue the victim, does a poor job of it, and actually worsens the situation? Can he just quit? Others may have held up their rescues in reliance on his efforts.

No, a non-duty can become an affirmative duty after a person chooses to intervene. At common law, interfering had its price. Which is why we have "Good Samaritan" statutes[4] —to make it clear that good-faith efforts voluntarily undertaken by would-be rescuers, especially physicians, who lobbied for these laws, are protected and encouraged.

California passed the first Good Samaritan law in 1959.

Ironically, however, these statutes, which typically do not grant absolute immunity, have confused the issue. Why? Because they have to be construed, and when lawyers are around, interpretations of seemingly clear terms multiply.

North California law shields from civil liability "any person who renders first aid or emergency assistance" at a motor-vehicle accident unless the person's actions amount to "wanton[5] conduct or intentional wrongdoing."

Though it may seem unlikely that Good Samaritans would act wantonly, the term is subject to a lawyer's spin. And what exactly are the limits of "first aid" and "emergency assistance"?

Virginia, which has exemplary[6] Good-Sam laws covering a variety of personnel and crises, indemnifies "any person who, in good faith, renders emergency care or assistance, without compensation"[7] to injured people at an accident, fire, or other "life-threatening emergency."

Does this law safeguard doctors?

Though physicians without "a duty to treat" (based on an existing doctor-patient relationship) rarely get sued for their emergency treatment, lawyers can be creative about arguing that such a duty has arisen.

I wish we could do as the French do. But our nation is much too litigious[8] and dangerous. The "duty to assist" criminal laws that Minnesota and Wisconsin have enacted are largely symbolic, and likely to be selectively enforced.

For Americans, moral conscience, not legal duty, remains the best guide to emergency aid. But if ever there were an argument for a cellular phone, the plight of the Good Samaritan is it. ❸

❸ EVALUATING EVIDENCE
Cite **evidence** the writer has given in her article to support the **generalizations** made in these last two paragraphs. **E**

4. **statutes** (stach′o͞ots) *n.:* laws.
5. **wanton** (wänt′'n) *adj.:* deliberately harmful; immoral.

6. **exemplary** (eg · zem′plə · rē) *adj.:* serving as a good example; worth imitating.
7. **compensation** *n.:* payment.
8. **litigious** (li · tij′əs) *adj.:* quick to sue.

Vocabulary

immunity (i · myo͞on′ə · tē) *n.:* freedom from a legal obligation.

construed (kən · stro͞od′) *v.:* interpreted.

indemnifies (in · dem′ni · fīz′) *v.:* in a legal sense, protects.

DIRECT TEACHING

E Reading Informational Materials
GRADE-LEVEL STANDARD

Evaluating evidence. [Possible responses to question 3: One generalization is that the United States is too litigious and dangerous to have laws requiring people to assist others. Evidence to support this generalization includes these facts: A person might feign injury in order to ambush the helper; the helper might be sued; people even sue doctors who give them emergency treatment. A second generalization is that conscience, not law, is the best guide to aiding those in need of emergency help. Evidence for this generalization is that the law did not work to help Princess Diana in France.]

GUIDED PRACTICE

Monitoring students' progress. Have students draw a circle in the center of each of two blank pieces of paper. In one circle, have students write, in their own words, the main argument of the first essay, and in the other circle, the main argument of the second essay. Then, have students draw four lines radiating from each circle. On each line they should write one piece of evidence that the author(s) used to support the main argument.

FAMILY/COMMUNITY ACTIVITY

Ask students to list the Vocabulary Development words and other legal terms in the essays, such as *violating the law, intent, civil and criminal law, mandating, legislate morality, liable in negligence, statutes, lobbying for laws, civil liability, 'wanton conduct or intentional wrongdoing,'* and *litigious.* Tell students to make sure they understand the meaning of each term or phrase. Then, suggest that students invite their family members to join them in watching a television program concerning criminals and the law. Ask students to listen during the program for the words on their lists and to discuss with their families the meanings of these terms. Later, in class, students may compile a glossary of legal terms as a help in understanding written documents and televised dramas on the subject of law and order.

INDEPENDENT PRACTICE

Analyzing Informational Materials

Reading Check

1. Both opinion pieces were written in response to the death of Princess Diana.
2. Citizens are required to assist others who are in distress.
3. Under common law, people are not legally obliged to assist a stranger in an emergency.
4. Wisconsin, Minnesota, California, North Carolina, and Virginia

Test Practice

Answers and Model Rationales

1. **C** Students should easily eliminate B because the authors do not address riskiness. A and D are incorrect because the authors are making the opposite point.
2. **G** The description of a baby's drowning is clearly an appeal intended to stir feelings of outrage. Since the event is hypothetical, it is not fact or a quotation, so H and J can be eliminated. Since the event is unlikely, F is also incorrect.
3. **C** Some of the words in the other choices, such as *evil, indecent,* and *depraved,* are emotionally loaded and have negative connotations.
4. **J** Students can eliminate F and G because they are supporting evidence, not the main idea. H is incorrect because the author states that people should make their own decisions about helping others.

Analyzing Informational Materials

Reading Check

1. What event prompted the writing of both opinion pieces?
2. Explain France's good-Samaritan law.
3. Under common law, what is a person's duty when it comes to helping a stranger in an emergency?
4. Which states are mentioned in the articles as having good-Samaritan laws, or statutes?

Test Practice

1. Which statement best expresses the writers' main **claim** in the first selection ("If Decency Doesn't, Law Should Make Us Samaritans")?
   - **A** People should be liable only for damage they do through their actions.
   - **B** Helping others is very risky.
   - **C** There should be a good-Samaritan law requiring everyone to help others.
   - **D** In a free society no one should be required by law to help people in need.
2. In the first selection the baby drowning in an inch of water is an example of—
   - **F** a logical appeal
   - **G** an emotional appeal
   - **H** a fact
   - **J** a quotation
3. Which of the following quotations from the first selection does *not* contain **loaded words**?
   - **A** "maliciously, hatefully, and with evil intent"
   - **B** "This is indecent. . . ."
   - **C** "no duty to come to the aid of another"
   - **D** "the depraved image of people"
4. In the second selection ("Good Samaritans U.S.A. Are Afraid to Act"), what is the author's main **claim**?
   - **F** Americans don't need laws to behave morally.
   - **G** Trained paramedics, not bystanders, should help accident victims.
   - **H** Everyone has an absolute duty to help others in distress.
   - **J** Americans don't help strangers because they fear being hurt or sued.

Reading Standard 2.8 Evaluate the credibility of an author's argument or defense of a claim by critiquing the relationship between generalizations and evidence, the comprehensiveness of evidence, and the way in which the author's intent affects the structure and tone of the text.

290 Chapter 4 Comparing Themes • Evaluating Arguments: Pro and Con

5. In the second selection the author expresses disappointment because the state laws that have been passed protecting good Samaritans—
   - **A** are not consistent for every state
   - **B** are unnecessary
   - **C** have not been passed in enough states to evaluate their effectiveness
   - **D** confuse the issue because they are subject to varying legal interpretations

6. In the second selection the references to North Carolina and Virginia good-Samaritan laws are examples of—
   - **F** facts
   - **G** loaded words
   - **H** anecdotes
   - **J** statistics

7. To support her **argument,** the author of the second selection relies most heavily on—
   - **A** quotations from experts
   - **B** emotional appeals
   - **C** examples and facts
   - **D** statistics

8. Both articles seem to blame the difficulties in helping accident victims in the United States on the—
   - **F** U.S. legal system
   - **G** lack of adequate paramedic services
   - **H** decline of values and religion in the United States
   - **J** high number of car accidents on U.S. highways

Application

In a short essay, evaluate the **credibility** of the **arguments** in the two opinion pieces you have just read. First, summarize the writers' main **claim** in each piece. Then, evaluate the **evidence** and other support the writers used in their arguments. Finally, tell which article you found more convincing, and explain why.

5. D The author does not make the points cited in B and C. Though she does make the point in A, it is not what disappoints her.

6. F In these references the author quotes the states' laws, so they are examples of facts. The references do not include loaded words or statistics, so students can eliminate G and J. H is incorrect because no stories are told about the laws.

7. C D is incorrect because the author cites no statistics. While she does use some quotations and emotional appeals (A and B), she relies most heavily on examples and facts.

8. F While the lack of paramedic services and the decline of values (G and H) are touched upon, they are not blamed for the difficulties. The large number of accidents (J) is not mentioned at all.

Test-Taking Tips

For more information on how to answer multiple-choice items, refer students to **Test Smarts.**

If Decency Doesn't . . . / Good Samaritans U.S.A. . . . 291

Vocabulary Development

Practice 1

1. liability
2. indemnifies
3. allegations
4. immunity

Practice 2

Possible Answers

1. The depraved man enjoyed his victims' suffering.
2. I'm not using my problems as rationalizations for my irresponsible behavior.
3. In a show of solidarity, the whole class voted alike.
4. You hurt my feelings with your callous statement about my cat's weight problem.
5. While daydreaming about her future, Doris feigned interest in her teacher's lecture.
6. My words about landfills were wrongly construed to mean that I do not support recycling.

Resources Reminder

Vocabulary

- *Vocabulary Development*
  - Vocabulary Worksheet, p. 23
  - Cumulative Vocabulary Review, pp. 24–25
- *Lesson Plans for Language Development*
  - Vocabulary, pp. 132, 137

ASSESSING

Assessment

- *Progress Assessment of Reading*
  - Selection Test

RETEACHING

For a lesson reteaching Standard 2.8, see **Reteaching,** p. 939A. For another selection to teach Standard 2.8, see *Interactive Reading,* Part 2.

Vocabulary Development

Jargon: Legalese—Words That Lawyers Use

If someone trips over your outstretched foot, falls, and breaks a leg, are you *liable*—or are you *indemnified?* If that person sues you, are you the *plaintiff* or the *defendant?* Law—like every profession, hobby, and sport—has its own **jargon,** or specialized vocabulary. You already know a lot of legalese (the jargon that lawyers use) from watching TV shows and movies about crime, detectives, and courtroom trials.

Word Bank

allegations
depraved
liability
rationalizations
solidarity
callous
feigning
immunity
construed
indemnifies

PRACTICE 1

Choose between these Word Bank words to fill in the blanks below: *allegations, liability, immunity, indemnifies.* Use **context clues** to figure out which word goes where.

1. The judge charged the defendant with ____________ for the damages.
2. Are you sure this insurance policy __________ the homeowner against losses caused by flooding?
3. She offered no documents or other proof to support her __________ of wrongdoing at her place of employment.
4. The defendant asked for ____________ in exchange for testifying against members of his gang.

Use a Word, and "Own" It

PRACTICE 2

Grade 8 Review Reading Standard 1.3 Use word meanings within the appropriate context and show ability to verify those meanings.

Reading Standard 1.1 Identify and use the literal meanings of words.

When you can use a word correctly, you should feel that you "own" it. Follow the instructions below for each item, writing at least one sentence that uses the underlined word.

1. Use the word *depraved* in a sentence from a movie review of a violent horror film.
2. Use the word *rationalizations* in a note to your teacher explaining why your research paper is a week late.
3. Write a sentence from a TV newscast reporting a landslide election victory in your community; use the word *solidarity.*
4. In a letter to a friend, use the word *callous* in a sentence explaining why your feelings are hurt.
5. Describe a person who is feigning interest in a boring speech.
6. Write a sentence a politician might use who felt her remarks had been misinterpreted; use *construed.*

292 Chapter 4 Comparing Themes • Evaluating Arguments: Pro and Con

Read On: FOR INDEPENDENT READING

FICTION

"It Is a Far, Far Better Thing . . ."

Sydney Carton is a lazy ne'er-do-well who is disappointed by the course his life has taken. Charles Darnay is a French nobleman whose good deeds can't save him from a certain death. These two men's lives are at the heart of Charles Dickens's ***A Tale of Two Cities***—a novel about the passion, power, and discord of the French Revolution and an unlikely hero who sacrifices everything for a friend.

This title is available in the HRW Library.

FICTION

Forbidden Love

When Shinji first glimpsed Hatsue resting on the sand at twilight, he thought she was the most beautiful girl he had ever seen. What begins as an awkward friendship soon blossoms into a relationship of great tenderness and trust. Soon the young couple's families are doing everything to tear them apart—and Shinji must prove his worth at great risk to himself. Set in a small Japanese fishing village, Yukio Mishima's ***The Sound of Waves*** is one of the great love stories of the twentieth century.

FICTION

A Navajo Romance

Oliver La Farge's ***Laughing Boy*** takes us back to the American Southwest in 1915. Laughing Boy is an idealistic young man who follows the traditional ways of his Navajo culture. The woman he loves, Slim Girl, has been stripped of her heritage and forced to attend white-run schools. These two young people enter into a marriage marked by miscommunication and strife. Will their love be enough to hold them together, or will a fateful turn of events be their undoing?

NONFICTION

Stormy Weather

What began as a routine swordfishing expedition became a nightmare for six young fishermen from Gloucester, Massachusetts. A freakish combination of three weather systems resulted in ***The Perfect Storm***—a monstrous tempest with one-hundred-foot waves that overpowered the *Andrea Gail*'s crew on one fateful night in October. This riveting true story by Sebastian Junger boasts many heroes: the fishermen, the search-and-rescue crews, and the courageous families of the men who vanished at sea.

Read On

For Independent Reading

If students enjoyed the themes and topics explored in this chapter, you might recommend these titles for independent reading.

Assessment Options

The following projects can help you evaluate and assess your students' outside reading. Videotapes or audiotapes of completed projects may be included in students' portfolios.

- **Make a mobile.** Invite students to gather or make objects significant to the theme of a novel or nonfiction work. Direct them to assemble these objects into a mobile and to write an explanation of how each object relates to the theme. Have them present their work to the class.
- **Write song lyrics.** Have students compose songs exploring their reflections on the theme of a novel or nonfiction work. They may set their songs to existing melodies or to their own melodies. Have students perform their songs or play audiotapes of them for the class.
- **Create a correspondence.** Tell students to imagine that they are corresponding with a character in a novel. Have them write a series of letters to and from the character. Each letter should include comments and questions about and insights into the novel's characters, events, and theme.

Toward Reading Two Million Words Annually

Estimated Word Counts and Reading Levels of Read On Books:

Fiction			Nonfiction		
*A Tale of Two Cities**	↔	119,000	*The Perfect Storm**	↔	83,500
The Sound of Waves	↓	56,400			
Laughing Boy	↑	79,600			

***California Reading List Titles**

KEY: ↑ *above grade level* ↔ *at grade level* ↓ *below grade level*

PRETEACHING

Standards Starter

Motivate. Ask students to think of the one rule that is observed at their home or school that they would most like to change. List several of their responses on the chalkboard. Have volunteers suggest the methods they would use for changing the rule. Afterwards, discuss persuasive essays as a means for trying to bring about change. Ask students under what circumstances persuasive essays would be effective. [Students might say *to critique or encourage an action by the school board or to convince parents to allow more freedom in a special circumstance.*]

Resources Reminder

To introduce the workshop, you may want to use the journal starters in *Writing, Listening, & Speaking* Teaching Notes.

DIRECT TEACHING

Integrating with Grammar, Usage, and Mechanics

As students start their persuasive essays, they may have trouble using pronouns and verbs correctly. You may want to review these chapters in the *Holt Handbook.*

GRADE-LEVEL STANDARD

Consider Your Purpose and Audience

You may want to remind students that there is more than one persuasive method. Some methods may be more appropriate depending on students' purpose and audience. For example, a letter might be an appropriate method for presenting information to a school administrator, but if the audience is a teacher, an essay is probably a more logical method.

Writing a Persuasive Essay

Writing Assignment
Writing 2.4 Write a persuasive essay on an issue about which you have a strong opinion.

In Roger Rosenblatt's essay "The Man in the Water," you read about several heroes who made a difference for crash victims in the frozen waters of the Potomac River. Have you ever wanted to make a difference? Perhaps you want to change laws governing an endangered species' habitat or motivate people to do volunteer work in your community. Writing a persuasive essay on an issue is one way to turn your ideas into a reality and to make a difference in others' lives.

Prewriting

go.hrw.com

GO TO: go.hrw.com
KEYWORD: HLLA 10-4
FOR: Professional Model, Writer's Guides, and Reference Sources

Choose an Issue

Powerful Beliefs By definition, an **issue** is something about which people have opposing opinions. As you choose an issue to write about, keep in mind that you will probably not convince anyone to agree with you if you do not feel strongly about the issue you choose. To find an issue that matters to you, watch television news shows for current issues, or brainstorm with classmates about issues that affect your school or community.

State Your Position

No Fence-Sitting Allowed You've chosen an issue. Now make your position, or opinion, on the issue absolutely clear by writing a focused **opinion statement** that names the issue and states your position on it. The following notes show the opinion statement one student wrote.

[position] [issue]
State government should not create a law to limit the noise levels coming from car stereos.

Writing 1.0 Students write coherent and focused essays that convey a well-defined perspective and tightly reasoned argument. The writing demonstrates students' awareness of the audience and purpose. **2.4** Write persuasive compositions.

Consider Your Purpose and Audience

Rabble-Rousing Once you've written an opinion statement, your **purpose** for writing should be clear—to convince others to share your opinion or to take the action you recommend. Next, consider who your **audience** will be. Obviously, you don't need to worry about people who agree with you. Instead, you need to concern yourself with those who either disagree with you or have no opinion at all. Consider this audience by answering the questions on the next page.

CHAPTER 4 RESOURCES: WRITING

Writing Workshop

Planning

- *On Course: Mapping Instruction*
- *One-Stop Planner* CD-ROM
- *At Home: A Guide to Standards Mastery,* p. 17
- *At Home: In Spanish*
- *Writing, Listening, & Speaking,* Teaching Notes, p. 35

Differentiating Instruction

- *Lesson Plans for Language Development,* pp. 125–126
- *Supporting Instruction in Spanish*

Practice

- *Writing, Listening, & Speaking,* Ch. 4

- **What are my audience's concerns?** Think about **biases,** or prejudices, your audience might have. Be prepared to address any objections, or **counterarguments,** readers may propose.
- **What are my audience's expectations?** Your audience will expect a tightly reasoned **argument** that includes solid reasons supported by evidence. Read on to learn how to meet this expectation.

TIP Readers' counter-arguments can also be called **counterclaims.**

Support Your Opinion

Voice of Reason Strong **reasons** are the foundation of a persuasive argument. The reasons you give to back up your opinion statement will communicate your perspective on the issue and show why you think your opinion is correct. Your reasons should include the **rhetorical devices** of logical appeals, emotional appeals, and ethical appeals.

- **Logical appeals** speak to your readers' minds. They rely on your audience's ability to be reasonable and to use their common sense.
- **Emotional appeals** speak to readers' emotions, such as sympathy, fear, and hope.
- **Ethical appeals** appeal to your readers' ethics, or moral values. They rely upon commonly accepted beliefs or values. For example, honesty and fairness are values that most people accept as worthwhile. A writer uses an ethical appeal to establish that he or she is **credible,** or trustworthy.

TIP Your teacher may want you to include more logical appeals than emotional or ethical appeals in your essay.

Trust the Evidence It's not enough to state your opinion and tell why people should agree with you. You also need to provide **evidence** that supports your reasons. You can gather evidence through research or by interviewing local experts on your topic. The chart below shows the kinds of evidence you can look for while researching.

TYPES OF EVIDENCE *Quick guide!*

Facts	information that can be proven true. Some facts are in the form of **statistics,** or numerical information.
Examples	specific instances of an idea or situation
Expert opinions	statements (either **quotations** or **paraphrases**) by people who are considered experts on the issue
Analogies	comparisons that show the similarities between two otherwise unrelated facts or ideas
Case studies	examples from scientific studies
Anecdotes	brief, personal stories that illustrate a point

Writing 2.4b Use specific rhetorical devices to support assertions. **2.4c** Clarify and defend positions with precise and relevant evidence. **2.4d** Address readers' concerns, counterclaims, biases, and expectations.

DIFFERENTIATING INSTRUCTION

REVIEW STANDARD

Learners Having Difficulty

To help students better understand the concept of logical appeals, guide them through the process of developing a logical appeal. Have students come up with opinion statements they feel strongly about, and write a few examples on the chalkboard. Then, ask each student to pick one opinion statement and think of a reason and evidence to support it. [A sample opinion statement: Taxes should be raised on sales of cigarettes. Reason: Smoking is bad for your health. Evidence: Smoking causes cancer and lung disease (fact).]

CORRECTING MISCONCEPTIONS

Students may mistakenly believe that any sort of emotional appeal makes a persuasive essay more effective. Point out to students that appeals with too much emotion can weaken the effectiveness of their essays (for example, "Only an ignorant person would believe . . ." or "If you care about anyone besides yourself, you will . . ."). You may want to have student pairs check the effectiveness of each other's emotional appeals.

MODELING AND DEMONSTRATION

Types of Evidence

To model the strategies in the chart, choose a position on an issue and write examples of each strategy on the chalkboard. Then, have a student volunteer demonstrate the same strategies by using his or her own persuasive essay topic.

Reinforcement

- *Daily Language Activities*

Evaluation and Assessment

- *Test Generator (One-Stop Planner* CD-ROM)
- *Progress Assessment of Writing, Listening, & Speaking,* Ch. 4
- *Diagnostic and Summative Assessments,* Midyear Test

Internet

- go.hrw.com (keyword: HLLA 10-4)
- Online assessments at go.hrw.com (keyword: HLLA)

DIRECT TEACHING

Evidence

To help students create a chart to give support to their opinion statements, have them use a visual organizer such as the following one.

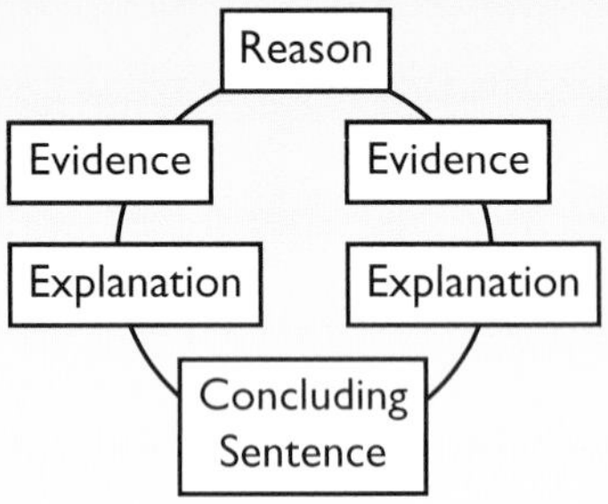

RETEACHING

The Importance of Order

If students have trouble organizing their essay, you might try the following activity. Find two or three simple persuasive paragraphs from the editorial page of a newspaper. For each paragraph, list the sentences out of correct order on the chalkboard. Have students reassemble each paragraph in order of importance.

PRACTICE & APPLY 1

Guided and Independent Practice

Have students write down three issues and opinion statements, and then have them choose the one with the strongest support. Monitor student progress by spot-checking with individuals to be sure that they

1. have selected an appropriate issue
2. are clear about which side to represent
3. feel strongly enough about the issue to write an effective essay

Then, have students complete **Practice and Apply 1** for independent practice.

Make sure that all of your evidence has the three *R*'s. It should be

Relevant—tied closely to your issue

Reliable—from trustworthy sources

Representative—not all from one or two sources

In the chart below, a student lists several reasons—containing logical, emotional, and ethical appeals—to explain why a law should not be passed to limit the noise levels of car stereos. She also gives at least two pieces of evidence for each of her reasons.

Opinion: The state government should not create a law to limit the noise levels coming from car stereos.

Reasons	Evidence
There are laws about disturbing the peace that cover this situation. (contains logical appeal)	**Fact:** Noise pollution laws exist. **Expert opinion:** Sheriff Tharpe says that he just enforces existing laws.
A law like this will add to the burden of overworked police. (contains emotional appeal)	**Fact:** information from newspaper article about police-staffing shortages **Anecdote:** John's father, Deputy Marquez, working double shifts **Expert opinion:** Deputy Marquez: officers spend too much time enforcing misdemeanor laws.
Singling out noise from car stereos is a form of discrimination. (contains ethical appeal)	**Fact:** Other public noises are loud but do not have laws against them. **Examples:** the noise at football games and other places

DO THIS

Create a chart like the one above in which you list the reasons and evidence that you will give to support your opinion statement.

Organize Your Essay

The Importance of Order The way you organize your essay is important to its effectiveness. Most writers of persuasive essays arrange their reasons in **order of importance.** Some writers feel that it is important to grab the audience's attention immediately by beginning with the strongest reason. Others feel that it is more effective to put the strongest reason last to leave the audience with a powerful last impression. Decide which order you prefer, and number the reasons in your support chart in the order in which you want to present them.

Writing 2.4a Structure ideas and arguments in a sustained and logical fashion.

PRACTICE & APPLY 1 Follow the instructions in this section to choose an issue, write an opinion statement, gather support, and organize your ideas.

RESOURCES: WRITING

Practice & Apply 1

Guided Practice

- *Writing, Listening, & Speaking,* WS. p. 36

Reteaching and Modeling

- *Writing, Listening, & Speaking,* TP. 9
- *Writing, Listening, & Speaking,* WS. p. 37

296 Chapter 4 Comparing Themes • Evaluating Arguments: Pro and Con

Writing

Writing a Persuasive Essay

A Writer's Framework

Introduction	Body	Conclusion
• Grab your readers' attention by asking a question, relating an anecdote, or presenting a startling statistic. • Give background information so readers understand the issue. • Give an opinion statement that clearly states your position on the issue.	• Give at least three reasons that support your opinion statement. • Make sure your reasons reflect logical, emotional, and ethical appeals. • Organize the reasons in an effective way to reach your audience. • Provide at least two pieces of evidence for each reason.	• Restate, but do not repeat, your opinion. • Summarize the reasons for your opinion if you like. • Include a call to action that tells readers what they can do to help change a situation.

A Writer's Model

Music to Whose Ears?

Warm spring weather had finally arrived. I got in the passenger seat of my brother's car. He got in the driver's seat. We rolled down the windows, and he popped a CD in the stereo, turned up the volume, and headed out for the lake. This is a recipe for a great feeling and harmless fun, right? Some state senators do not think so. They have proposed a law that bans car speakers above a certain size and sets legal volume levels. This law is misguided and unfair. State government should not create a law to limit the noise levels coming from car stereos.

INTRODUCTION Attention-grabbing opener

Background information

Opinion statement

Some people may think that a law should be passed because they believe loud car stereos are a public nuisance—or even dangerous. However, existing state laws already cover the problem of loud noises. According to Richard Tharpe, Hamilton County sheriff, "Right now we can arrest people for disturbing the peace, and state law even sets noise pollution levels. So a new law just doesn't seem necessary." In addition, if a stereo causes a traffic accident—which Tharpe notes is uncommon and hard to prove—the driver can be charged. However, in the past five years, only one such accident has been reported. To institute the proposed law, then, is simply unnecessary.

BODY/Addresses counterargument

First reason: Logical appeal

Expert opinion

Fact and statistic

(continued)

DIRECT TEACHING

Conclusion

Stress that students should not include any new information in their conclusions. Although a *P.S.*-type of addition might be acceptable in a friendly letter, it is not acceptable in an essay that the writer has had time to revise. Adding new information will only make the writer appear disorganized.

A Writer's Model

Point out the writer's use of the word *However* to begin the second sentence of the second paragraph. This follows the mention of a counterargument, and it directs the reader back to the writer's position on the issue.

(continued)

Second reason: Emotional appeal Fact Anecdote Expert opinion	Another reason the legislature should vote down this proposal is that it will add to the burden of already overworked police. A number of towns and cities in the state have admitted to staffing shortages. In fact, Deputy Dennis Marquez, the father of a close friend, has had to work double shifts the last six months in order to ensure that all patrols are covered. According to Deputy Marquez, this shortage results from officers spending too much of their time enforcing misdemeanor laws similar to the proposed ban on loud car stereos. Just because serious crime is no longer on the rise, the police should not have to add another misdemeanor to their workload. Do they really have time to point decibel monitors at passing cars?
Third reason: Ethical appeal Fact and examples	The most compelling reason to put a halt to this proposal is that setting legal limits on the volume of car stereos is a form of discrimination. After all, many other public noises are just as loud. Parades and rallies often use high-volume sound trucks. Radio stations broadcast live from stores and parking lots. Loudspeakers, bands, and cheering crowds at football games can be heard for blocks. For example, the cheering during last week's victorious game against the Tigers could be heard as far away as 135th Street. Also, what about the noise from tools? I have been awakened from a peaceful sleep on many Saturday mornings by neighbors' lawnmowers, yet I see no proposals for laws to regulate noise made under these circumstances. Why should car stereos be singled out?
CONCLUSION Restatement of opinion Summary of reasons Call to action	We all want our streets to be calm and safe, but the senators' approach is misguided. An existing law already addresses the problem, and creating a new one would cause more work for police officers. In addition, the new law would not take into account other noises. A law restricting the volume of car stereos is unnecessary and unfair, and each of us should write or call our legislators to say so.

PRACTICE & APPLY 2

Guided and Independent Practice

Call individual students to confer about their essays. Check to see that each student has an introduction with a clear opinion statement, a body with three reasons supporting the opinion, and a conclusion that restates the opinion.

Have students complete **Practice and Apply 2** independently.

go.hrw.com

GO TO: go.hrw.com
KEYWORD: HLLA 10-4
FOR: Expanded Writer's Model and Student's Model

PRACTICE & APPLY 2 Now it's your turn to draft a persuasive essay. As you write, clearly state your opinion and use the strongest reasons and evidence to provide support. Make sure you organize the support in a way that will persuade your readers. Refer to the framework on page 297 and the Writer's Model above as guides.

RESOURCES: WRITING

Practice & Apply 2

Think Sheet

- *Writing, Listening, & Speaking,* WS. p. 38

Template

- *Writing, Listening, & Speaking,* WS. p. 39

Internet

- go.hrw.com (keyword: HLLA 10-4)

298 Chapter 4 Comparing Themes • Evaluating Arguments: Pro and Con

Revising

Evaluate and Revise Your Paper

The Once-over, Twice Revising is possibly the most important part of the writing process. Read your paper at least twice. In the first reading, focus on the content and organization, using the guidelines below. In the second reading, focus on your essay's style, using the guidelines on page 300.

PEER REVIEW
Exchange your essay with a classmate. He or she may be able to spot reasons that need more evidence to support them.

First Reading: Content and Organization Use the chart below as a **think sheet.** The questions, tips, and revision techniques can help you look for ways to improve the content and organization of your persuasive essay. As you revise, consider your audience, purpose, and tone. Make changes that will appeal to your audience, match your purpose, and enhance a formal tone.

Guidelines: Writing a Persuasive Essay

Evaluation Questions	Tips	Revision Techniques
1 Does the introduction grab the reader's attention and give background information on the issue? Does it present a clear opinion statement?	**Put a check mark** by sentences that get the reader interested. **Put a star** by sentences that give background information on the issue. **Underline** the opinion statement.	**Add** an interesting statement and background information. **Add** an opinion statement that clearly states your position on the issue.
2 Does the essay include at least three reasons? Do the reasons contain logical, emotional, or ethical appeals?	**Highlight** each reason. **Draw a box** around the part that indicates a logical, emotional, or ethical appeal.	**Add** reasons that appeal to readers' logic, emotions, or ethics.
3 Is each reason supported by at least two pieces of relevant evidence?	**Circle** each piece of evidence (facts, examples, and so on). **Draw an arrow** from each item to the reason it supports.	**Add** evidence to support your reasons. **Rearrange** evidence so it is in the paragraph with the reason it supports.
4 Are the reasons organized effectively?	**Number** reasons in the order of their importance. If the order seems illogical or ineffective, revise.	**Rearrange** the reasons by putting the most important reason first or last.
5 Does the conclusion restate the opinion on the issue? Does it include a call to action?	**Underline** the sentence that restates the writer's opinion. **Put a check mark** next to sentences that make a call to action.	**Add** a restatement of your opinion on the issue. **Add** a call to action.

DIRECT TEACHING

Elaboration

Encourage students to elaborate their essays by adding description. For instance, if students are arguing in favor of a change in the way something is done, they could describe the situation before and after the change and use sensory words and details to appeal to the reader's senses.

Writing Workshop: Writing a Persuasive Essay 299

GUIDED PRACTICE

Responding to the Revision Process

Answers

1. The added sentence provides transition between a counterargument and the writer's argument.
2. The writer changed the last sentence from passive to active voice.

PRACTICE & APPLY 3

Independent Practice

You may want to have students revise their essays in the following way.

1. Form circles of four students each.
2. Pass papers to the person on the left.
3. Read the paper for content, marking comments at the beginning of the paper.
4. Pass papers to the left again and read for organization, marking comments at the end of the paper.
5. Pass papers once more and read for style, marking comments in the side margin.

Confer privately with those students who need significant revisions while others complete **Practice and Apply 3** for independent practice.

Second Reading: Style To be persuasive, you must present your ideas forcefully. To maintain a powerful tone, avoid using too many passive sentences, in which the subject does not perform the action in the sentence. Instead, use the **active voice** to spur readers to action. The guidelines below can help you turn passive sentences into active ones.

editor in charge

Style Guidelines

Evaluation Question	Tip	Revision Technique
Does the essay include active-voice sentences?	**Put a minus sign** above each subject that does not perform the action in its sentence.	**Rewrite** sentences so that the subject of the sentence performs the action of the verb.

ANALYZING THE REVISION PROCESS

Study these revisions, and answer the questions that follow.

> Some people may think that a law should be passed because they believe loud car stereos are a public nuisance—or even dangerous. *However, existing state laws already cover the problem of loud noises.* According to Richard Tharpe, Hamilton County sheriff, "Right now we can arrest people for disturbing the peace, and state law even sets noise pollution levels. So a new law just doesn't seem necessary." In addition, if *a stereo causes* ~~an accident is caused by a stereo~~ *a traffic accident*—which Tharpe notes is uncommon and hard to prove—the driver can be charged.

add

rewrite

Responding to the Revision Process

1. Why did the writer add the sentence before the quotation?
2. Why did the writer revise the last sentence?

Writing 1.2 Use the active rather than the passive voice. **1.9** Revise writing to improve the tone by taking into consideration the audience, purpose, and formality of the context.

PRACTICE & APPLY 3 Use the guidelines on these pages to evaluate and revise the content, organization, and style of your essay. If a peer reviewed your essay, consider his or her comments, too.

300 Chapter 4 Comparing Themes • Evaluating Arguments: Pro and Con

Publishing

Proofread and Publish Your Essay

One More Time Don't ruin the impact of your well-crafted words by letting little mistakes show up in your final draft. Review your paper to make sure it is free of mistakes in grammar, spelling, and punctuation. If you find it hard to inspect your own paper for these mistakes, trade papers with a partner and examine each other's work closely.

A Wider Audience You cannot persuade anyone if you are the only one who reads your essay. Take the next step in making your opinion heard by publishing your essay. Here are some ideas to help you gain a wider reading audience for your persuasive essay.

- Submit your paper to the opinion page of your school or local newspaper.
- Submit your essay to a local Internet bulletin board where public exchanges are welcome.
- Turn your persuasive essay into a pamphlet that contains photos or graphics by using publishing software or graphic programs. With your teacher's permission, distribute pamphlets to your classmates.
- With a partner who opposes your position, debate the issue you chose for your essay. For more on **participating in a debate,** see page 302.

Reflect on Your Essay

Take a Deep Breath Now that the hard work is over, think about your essay and the process you used to create it. Answering the following questions can help you think about the process of writing a persuasive essay and identify ways you and others use persuasion outside this class.

- Which of the reasons in your paper do you think is the weakest or least convincing? How could you revise the reason or the evidence that supports it to make it more convincing?
- How did you go about finding reasons to support your opinion or evidence to support your reasons? For what other types of writing might you use the same process for gathering support?
- How do you see logical, emotional, and ethical appeals used in other areas of life such as at home, on television, and in politics?

PRACTICE & APPLY 4 First, proofread your essay. Then, choose one of the options above to publish your essay for an audience. Finally, answer the reflection questions.

TIP Check that you have used English-language **conventions** properly. For example, if you include a quotation from an expert as a piece of evidence, don't forget to use quotation marks properly. For more on **quotation marks,** see page 341 in the *Holt Handbook.*

COMPUTER TIP

For more on **incorporating graphics,** see *Designing Your Writing* in the *Writer's Handbook.*

Writing 1.8 Design and publish documents by using advanced publishing software and graphic programs.

DIRECT TEACHING

A Wider Audience

If students publish their essays on the World Wide Web, *you need to be aware that Internet resources are sometimes public forums, and their content can be unpredictable.*

Resources Reminder

For help with writing assessment, see 6 Traits—Plus 1 in the "Scales and Sample Papers" section of *Progress Assessment of Writing, Listening, and Speaking.*

PRACTICE & APPLY 4

Guided and Independent Practice

After students proofread their essays, monitor them as they reflect on their essays. You might consider the following suggestions.

1. Ask students to think of two people or groups to whom they would like to present their essay.
2. Have students write down a plan for presenting their essay to both audiences. The plan should include the format for presenting the essay: Will it be written, as in a letter or article, or will it be presented orally, as in a speech or announcement?
3. Encourage students to share their essays and then informally report the results to the class.

RESOURCES: WRITING

Practice & Apply 3

Think Sheet

- *Writing, Listening, & Speaking,* WS. p. 41

Evaluation

- *Writing, Listening, & Speaking,* WS. p. 40

Practice & Apply 4

Assessment

- *Test Generator* (*One-Stop Planner* CD-ROM)
- *Progress Assessment of Writing, Listening, & Speaking,* pp. 12–14, 60–62

Internet

- Online assessments at go.hrw.com (keyword: HLLA)

Writing Workshop: Writing a Persuasive Essay 301

PRETEACHING

Motivate. Ask students to think of a time when they have been involved in an argument to defend a position or to argue against another position. Point out that a debate is a controlled, or formal, argument. Tell them that they will learn procedures and rules for debating, some of which they can use to keep discussions from becoming unfair.

DIRECT TEACHING

GRADE-LEVEL STANDARD

A Winning Proposition

You might wish to write some of these sample propositions on the chalkboard.

Resolved, That the United States should adopt a national day-care program.

Resolved, That athletes should not be required to practice or play in an outdoor area when the temperature is above 90 degrees.

Resolved, That public safety is more important than personal freedom.

Participating in a Debate

Speaking Assignment

Listening and Speaking 1.5 With other students, stage a debate in which you present both sides of an issue.

"That's debatable" is an expression people often use to cast doubt on something that has just been said. If a statement is debatable, good arguments can be made both for and against it. While a persuasive essay or speech presents only one side of an issue, a **debate** involves two teams on opposite sides of an issue who publicly compete for the hearts and minds of an audience.

Prepare for a Debate

A Winning Proposition If you are asked to participate in a debate, you must first know what proposition you will be debating. A **proposition** focuses on one narrow, controversial issue. The proposition suggests a change in the **status quo**—the current state of things—and is worded as a **resolution.** An example of a proposition is "Resolved: That Chavez High School should build a parking lot west of the main soccer fields." Most often the person in charge of the debate assigns the proposition that the teams will debate.

Participants in a debate are usually also assigned a side of the proposition—pro (for) or con (against). If you are participating in a debate, your challenge is to present a good argument, based on solid reasoning, for your side of the issue—regardless of your personal feelings on the issue.

Who's Who? A traditional debate requires two teams of two people each, plus a chairperson in charge of running the debate.

Affirmative Team The **affirmative team** argues that the proposition should be accepted. Because the affirmative team argues for a change in the status quo, it has the **burden of proof**—an obligation to prove that change must be made.

Negative Team The **negative team** argues that the proposition should be rejected and that the status quo should remain unchanged.

Chairperson A **chairperson** rules over a debate, keeping the debate organized, courteous, and fair. A debater may appeal to the chairperson if he or she believes that the other team has broken any rules.

Research the Proposition To debate effectively, you must prepare by thoroughly researching the proposition. First, identify the differences between your position and the other team's position. These differences often revolve around the following questions.

- Is there a significant problem?
- What is causing the problem?

Listening and Speaking 1.5 Recognize and use elements of classical speech forms in formulating rational arguments and applying the art of debate. **2.5** Deliver persuasive arguments.

CHAPTER 4 RESOURCES: LISTENING & SPEAKING

Listening & Speaking Workshop

Planning

- *On Course: Mapping Instruction*
- *One-Stop Planner* CD-ROM
- *Writing, Listening, & Speaking*
  - — Teaching Notes, p. 42
  - — Project-Planning Guide, WS. p. 45

Differentiating Instruction

- *Lesson Plans for Language Development,* p. 127
- *Supporting Instruction in Spanish*

Evaluation and Assessment

- *Writing, Listening, & Speaking,* WS. p. 46
- *Progress Assessment of Writing, Listening, & Speaking,* pp. 63–64

302 Chapter 4 Comparing Themes • Evaluating Arguments: Pro and Con

- Would this proposition solve the problem?
- What would the proposition cost (in time, money, or other resources)?

Next, develop specific **reasons,** which may include rhetorical devices, that will show people why they should support your side of the proposition. In turn, you must also find **proof**—evidence to support each reason. Three types of evidence commonly used in debates are defined below.

Facts and Statistics **Facts** are statements that can be proven true. **Statistics** are information based on numbers. For example, the following statistic might support an argument proposing a new school parking lot: "Our parking lot has 150 spaces, yet 297 teachers, staff, and students drive to school."

Specific Instances **Specific instances** are examples that illustrate a point, such as, "Parents who come to school during school hours have said that they had to park their cars blocks away on residential streets."

Testimony **Testimony** includes comments or opinions from people who have studied or experienced the problem. Here is an example of supporting testimony: "According to Principal Cho, 'School parking is a serious problem. Students with after-school jobs need to drive rather than take the bus. We don't have enough space for all of them.'"

Be sure that all evidence—facts, statistics, specific instances, and testimony—that supports your reasons meets the tests in the chart below.

TIP Additional types of evidence you can use are case studies, anecdotes, and analogies. For more on **types of evidence,** see page 295.

TESTS FOR EVIDENCE (Quick guide)

Evidence should have . . .	That means . . .
credibility	evidence should come from a source recognized as an authority on the subject. The source should be objective rather than biased toward one side of the issue.
validity	evidence should clearly support the position it is being used to support. Valid evidence should not be interpreted to support the opposite side of the issue.
relevance	evidence should have a close, logical relationship to the reason it supports. Relevant information is also recent enough to directly relate to the issue being addressed.

Listening and Speaking 1.1 Formulate judgments about the ideas under discussion and support those judgments with convincing evidence. **1.6** Choose appropriate types of proof that meet standard tests for evidence. **2.5b** Use rhetorical devices to support assertions. **2.5c** Clarify and defend positions with precise and relevant evidence.

CRITICAL THINKING

REVIEW STANDARD

Students must present facts and statistics in a valid context, but remind them that they do not have to remain defenseless in the face of a damaging statistic. For example, a statistic might reveal that 10 percent of students at Lincoln High School failed a class in the first semester, but only 4 percent failed the previous year. That information is damaging for a team documenting the school's improvement. Inform students that such a team should look for additional statistics to lessen the effect of the damaging one. For example, what if, during the same period, dropout rates decreased by 10 percent? The higher failure rate might have been a byproduct of more students staying in school, even when they were having difficulties.

- *Diagnostic and Summative Assessments,* Midyear Test

Extension

- *Writing, Listening, & Speaking,* Videocassette Segment 3
- *Writing, Listening, & Speaking,* WS. p. 47

Internet

- go.hrw.com (keyword: HLLA)

RETEACHING

Organize Your Debate Information

If students have difficulty identifying and organizing their debate information, find portions of newspaper articles that each present two sides of an issue. Allow students to work in groups of three or four on one article. Students should identify the proposition, list the reasons for and against, and make note of the evidence used by both sides. Ask the groups to read their articles to the other groups and to share their findings. Then, provide time for the class to discuss whether each group was accurate and thorough in its examination.

DIFFERENTIATING INSTRUCTION

Special Education Students

Some students may have difficulty presenting their speeches before an audience. You may want to suggest one of the following.

1. Offer students the alternative of working with a helper to record their speeches on videotape or audiotape. They can then play the tapes later for the class to evaluate.
2. Students could practice their speeches with a helper before giving them to the class.

Resources Reminder

For more help with Special Education Students, see *Lesson Plans for Language Development.*

Organize Your Debate Information

To Each Its Own Organize the reasons and evidence you find into three categories.

- **Constructive arguments**—support for your side
- **Refutations**—attacks on the other side's position
- **Rebuttals**—material that answers challenges to your position

Constructive Speeches A traditional debate is divided into two parts: **constructive speeches** and **rebuttal speeches** (which include both rebuttals and refutations).

First, teams make **constructive speeches,** which build their arguments for or against the proposition.

- If you are presenting a constructive speech for the **affirmative** (pro) side of an issue, you should provide two to four reasons for your position, each reason backed with strong evidence.
- To present a constructive speech for the **negative** (con) side of an issue, plan to defend the status quo. In other words, your speech should make clear either that no problem exists or that any existing problem can be corrected through existing solutions. Again, you will use reasons and evidence to build your position.

TIP Because time for rebuttal speeches is short, focus only on the most important points the opposing team made, not on everything they said.

Rebuttal Speeches After the constructive speeches, both teams make **rebuttal speeches.** In spite of their name, rebuttal speeches should include both rebuttals and refutations. In a **rebuttal** you rebuild your own arguments that the other team has damaged, while in a **refutation** you attempt to disprove your opponents' constructive arguments. Effective refutations focus on these elements:

- **Quantity**—Does the other team provide enough evidence?
- **Quality**—Is the other team's evidence credible, valid, and relevant?
- **Reasoning**—Has the other team drawn logical conclusions based on the evidence?

Making an effective rebuttal speech depends on your ability to listen to the opposing team's arguments and respond with convincing arguments and evidence of your own.

Listening and Speaking 1.0 Students formulate adroit judgments about oral communication. **1.3** Choose logical patterns of organization to persuade. **2.5a** Structure ideas and arguments in a coherent, logical fashion. **2.5d** Anticipate and address the listener's concerns and counterarguments.

Conduct the Debate

Present Yourself As a debater, you must follow proper **debate etiquette.** No matter what your opponent may say, you should remain respectful and courteous, avoiding sarcasm and personal attacks. Be polite. It is traditional to refer to other debate participants with terms such as "the first affirmative speaker" or "my worthy opponent."

304 Chapter 4 Comparing Themes • Evaluating Arguments: Pro and Con

Present Your Ideas Your reasons and evidence will have the greatest impact if you are well prepared. As you speak, maintain eye contact with your audience and speak slowly, clearly, and loudly enough that everyone can understand you. Use your voice and facial expressions to emphasize important points.

Speaking in Turn A traditional debate follows this schedule. Each team member delivers one constructive and one rebuttal speech.

TRADITIONAL DEBATE SCHEDULE

First Part: Constructive Speeches		Second Part: Rebuttal Speeches
(10 minutes each)	Intermission	(5 minutes each)
1st Affirmative Team Speaker		1st Negative Team Speaker
1st Negative Team Speaker		1st Affirmative Team Speaker
2nd Affirmative Team Speaker		2nd Negative Team Speaker
2nd Negative Team Speaker		2nd Affirmative Team Speaker

And the Winner Is . . . Judges usually determine the winner of a debate. Occasionally, an audience may vote to determine the winning team. To make your own judgment about which team won a debate, answer the questions in the following chart. You can use the chart to evaluate both the affirmative and negative teams.

QUESTIONS FOR JUDGING A DEBATE

Content	Delivery
1. What arguments did the team provide to prove or disprove that a significant problem exists? Were these arguments effective? Explain why or why not.	**1.** How confident and well prepared were the speakers? How could they improve their delivery?
2. Did the team convince you that the proposition is or is not the best solution to solving the problem (if any exists)? Explain.	**2.** How well did each speaker maintain eye contact? How effective were the rate and volume at which each spoke?
3. What reasons and evidence did the team provide to support the case? How credible, valid, and relevant was the evidence?	**3.** Describe any incidents in which the speakers did not observe proper debate etiquette.
4. How did the team refute and rebut arguments made by the opposing team? Were the rebuttal speeches effective? Explain why or why not.	

PRACTICE & APPLY 5 Follow the steps in this workshop to plan, participate in, and judge a debate.

DIFFERENTIATING INSTRUCTION

GRADE-LEVEL STANDARD

Advanced Learners

Enrichment. Teams can also compete using the Lincoln-Douglas debate format.

Affirmative	6-minute constructive speech
Negative	3-minute questioning of the Affirmative
Negative	7-minute constructive speech and refutation
Affirmative	3-minute questioning of the Negative
Affirmative	4-minute rebuttal speech
Negative	6-minute rebuttal speech and summary
Affirmative	3-minute rebuttal speech and summary

The Lincoln-Douglas format is named in honor of Abraham Lincoln and Stephen A. Douglas, who in 1858 participated in a series of debates while running for the U.S. Senate in Illinois. The format pits one affirmative speaker against one negative speaker.

PRACTICE & APPLY 5

Guided and Independent Practice

Monitor students as they plan the debate. You might use these steps.

1. Have class brainstorm resolutions.
2. Assign six students to debate each resolution.
3. Have groups randomly assign two team members to argue the affirmative position, two team members to argue the negative position, and an alternate for each side who participates fully in preparing for the debate.
4. Allow preparation time.
5. Stage the debate. Alternates can serve on a panel of judges.

Listening and Speaking Workshop: Participating in a Debate 305

Standards Review

Literary Response and Analysis

STANDARDS FOCUS, pp. 306–309

(For the grade-level standard reviewed in this lesson, see Student Edition, p. 306.)

INTRODUCING THE STANDARDS REVIEW

Use this review to assess students' grasp of the effects of genre in shaping theme. If necessary, you can use the annotations to guide students in their reading before they answer the questions.

DIRECT TEACHING

A Literary Focus
GRADE-LEVEL STANDARD

? Setting and conflict. How does the story's setting create conflict? [Possible response: The rural ice storm makes the pheasants helpless, permitting farmers to "harvest" them and inspiring the local boys to do the same.]

B Reading Skills

? Making predictions. What do you think will happen to the pheasants? Why do you think so? [Possible responses: The boys will harm the pheasants, since children often mimic adults; the boys will save the pheasants, since children often have more sympathy for animals than adults have.]

C Literary Focus
GRADE-LEVEL STANDARD

? Point of view. From what point of view is the story told? How can you tell? [The point of view is third person omniscient. The narrator uses third-person pronouns for all the characters and reveals what all of them are thinking.]

STANDARDS REVIEW

Literary Response and Analysis

Test Practice

Comparing a Theme Across Genres

DIRECTIONS: Read the following short story and poem. Then, read each multiple-choice question that follows, and write the letter of the best response.

What Happened During the Ice Storm

Jim Heynen

Pages 306–309 cover **Reading Standard 3.2** Compare and contrast the presentation of a similar theme or topic across genres to explain how the selection of genre shapes the theme or topic.

One winter there was a freezing rain. "How beautiful!" people said when things outside started to shine with ice. But the freezing rain kept coming. Tree branches glistened like glass. Then broke like glass. Ice thickened on the windows until everything outside blurred. Farmers **A** moved their livestock into the barns, and most animals were safe. But not the pheasants. Their eyes froze shut.

Some farmers went ice-skating down the gravel roads with clubs to harvest pheasants that sat helplessly in the roadside ditches. The boys went out into the freezing rain to find pheasants too. They saw dark spots along a fence. Pheasants, all right. Five or six of them. The boys slid their feet along slowly, trying not to break the ice that covered the snow. They slid up close to the pheasants. The pheasants pulled their heads down between their wings. They couldn't tell how easy it was to see them huddled there.

The boys stood still in the icy rain. Their breath came out in slow puffs of steam. The pheasants' breath came out in quick little white puffs. **B** Some of them lifted their heads and turned them from side to side, but they were blindfolded with ice and didn't flush. The boys had not brought **C** clubs, or sacks, or anything but themselves. They stood over the pheasants, turning their own heads, looking at each other, each expecting the other to do something. To pounce on a pheasant, or to yell "Bang!"

READING MINI-LESSON

Reviewing Word-Attack Skills

Activity. Display the following sets of words. Have students identify the word in each group in which the final e is not silent. (Correct answers are checked.) Tell students to consult a dictionary if necessary.

1.	epitome ✓	aerodrome	metronome
2.	envelope	antelope	calliope ✓
3.	safe	cafe ✓	chafe
4.	engine	aborigine✓	tangerine
5.	simile ✓	missile	domicile
6.	archetype	apocalypse	apostrophe ✓
7.	finite	finale ✓	famine
8.	sabotage	portage	protégé ✓
9.	tamale ✓	morale	molecule
10.	antidote	cyclone	hyperbole ✓

Things around them were shining and dripping with icy rain. The barbed-wire fence. The fence posts. The broken stems of grass. Even the grass seeds. The grass seeds looked like little yolks inside gelatin whites. And the pheasants looked like unborn birds glazed in egg white. Ice was hardening on the boys' caps and coats. Soon they would be covered with ice too.

Then one of the boys said, "Shh." He was taking off his coat, the thin layer of ice splintering in flakes as he pulled his arms from the sleeves. But the inside of the coat was dry and warm. He covered two of the crouching pheasants with his coat, rounding the back of it over them like a shell. The other boys did the same. They covered all the helpless pheasants. The small gray hens and the larger brown cocks. Now the boys felt the rain soaking through their shirts and freezing. They ran across the slippery fields, unsure of their footing, the ice clinging to their skin as they made their way toward the blurry lights of the house. **D** **E**

DIRECT TEACHING

D Literary Focus
GRADE-LEVEL STANDARD

Plot. Was the conflict resolved in the way you expected? [Students' responses will depend on their earlier predictions. Many will be surprised that the boys decide to protect the pheasants rather than kill them.]

E Literary Focus
GRADE-LEVEL STANDARD

Theme. What lesson do you think the boys learn from their experience? [Possible response: It can be rewarding to sacrifice one's own comfort to help a vulnerable creature in danger.]

Activity. Display the following words. Have students divide each word into syllables (indicated here by slashes). Have students use a dictionary to check their work.

1. ter/ri/to/ri/al
2. in/sus/cep/ti/ble
3. com/mon/al/i/ty
4. man/u/mis/sion
5. re/ar/range/ment
6. re/as/sim/i/late
7. re/ap/pear/ance
8. de/com/pres/sion
9. mor/ti/fi/ca/tion
10. in/con/sis/tent

Activity. Display the following pairs of words. Have students identify the word in each pair that has the sound /j/. (Answers are checked.)

1. guardian gerund ✓
2. pagan pageant ✓
3. lung lunge ✓
4. contagious ✓ contiguous
5. stinger stingy ✓

Standards Review

Direct Teaching

A Literary Focus
GRADE-LEVEL STANDARD

Comparing settings. How do the setting of this poem and the setting of "What Happened During the Ice Storm" compare? [Possible response: Both works are set outdoors, in nature. The story is set in a rural area during a winter storm; the poem is set at a beach in good weather.]

B Literary Focus
GRADE-LEVEL STANDARD

Point of view. From what point of view does the speaker narrate the events of the poem? How can you tell. [The point of view is first person. The speaker uses the first-person pronouns *we* and *my*.]

C Literary Focus
GRADE-LEVEL STANDARD

Plot. The speaker tells a story in a few short lines. What are the main events of the story? [Possible response: Two people at the beach see an injured seabird fall. They remove a barbed hook from its cheek and wing, and the bird flies safely away.]

D Literary Focus
GRADE-LEVEL STANDARD

Comparing themes. What lesson does the speaker learn from the encounter with the royal tern? [Possible response: Helping a wild creature in danger can be deeply satisfying.] How does this theme compare with the theme of "What Happened During the Ice Storm"? [Possible response: Both involve the emotional rewards of helping animals in danger.]

Reteaching

For another selection to teach Standard 3.2, see *Interactive Reading*, Chapter 4.

Gracious Goodness

Marge Piercy

On the beach where we had been idly
telling the shell coins
cat's paw, crossbarred Venus, china cockle,
we both saw at once
the sea bird fall to the sand
and flap grotesquely.
He had taken a great barbed hook
out through the cheek and fixed
in the big wing.
He was pinned to himself to die,
a royal tern with a black crest blown back
as if he flew in his own private wind.
He felt good in my hands, not fragile
but muscular and glossy and strong,
the beak that could have split my hand
opening only to cry
as we yanked on the barbs.
We borrowed a clippers, cut and drew
out the hook.
Then the royal tern took off, wavering,
lurched twice,
then acrobat returned to his element,
dipped,
zoomed, and sailed out to dive for a fish.
Virtue: what a sunrise in the belly.
Why is there nothing
I have ever done with anybody
that seems to me so obviously right?

Using Academic Language

Review of Literary Terms
Reading Standards 3.2 and 3.5

Ask students to look back through the chapter to find the meanings of the terms listed at right. Then, have students show their grasp of Standards 3.2 and 3.5 by citing passages from the chapter that illustrate the meanings of those terms.

Theme (pp. 230, 233); **Genres** (p. 230); **Universal Themes** (pp. 231, 232); **Comparing** (pp. 254, 283); **Contrasting** (pp. 254, 283).

Review of Informational Terms
Reading Standard 2.8

Ask students to look back through the chapter to find the meanings of the terms listed

1. In "What Happened During the Ice Storm," which element is important in establishing the **theme**?
   A Setting
   B Dialogue
   C Point of view
   D Tone

2. Which of the following influences provides the main source of **conflict** in the short story?
   F The boys' sympathy for the birds
   G The farmers' actions
   H The pretty landscape
   J The boys' fear of the birds

3. In "Gracious Goodness" the **narrator** seems to experience —
   A conflict
   B boredom
   C satisfaction
   D regret

4. One way the story *differs* from the poem is in the story's —
   F unexpected ending
   G humorous tone
   H first-person narration
   J outdoor setting

5. Which word *best* describes the **tone** of the poem?
   A angry
   B ironic
   C sad
   D reflective

6. Which statement *best* describes the common **theme** of both selections?
   F Helping others can be a rewarding experience.
   G Nature is both inspiring and terrifying.
   H No matter what we do, death comes to all living things.
   J Life is full of unexpected turns.

7. Despite their different **genres,** these two selections share a basically similar —
   A setting and plot
   B plot and cast of characters
   C point of view and theme
   D theme and subject matter

8. How does the **genre** of each selection affect the way the **theme** is developed?
   F Since the poem is shorter, its theme is not as rich.
   G Since the poem is shorter, it expresses its theme and subject matter more compactly.
   H The story can reveal characters' thoughts, but the poem cannot.
   J Since the poem has no plot, its theme must be inferred from imagery.

below. Then, ask students to use those terms to explain how to evaluate the credibility of an author's argument. **Argument** (p. 284); **Credibility** (p. 284); **Generalization** (p. 284); **Logical Appeals** (p. 284); **Reasons** (p. 284); **Evidence** (p. 284); **Emotional Appeals** (p. 284); **Author's Intent** (p. 285).

Test-Taking Tips

Point out that some questions ask students to compare elements common to two selections. Students should consider how each answer choice applies to both works; the correct choice will fit both. For more instruction on answering multiple-choice questions, refer students to **Test Smarts.**

TestPractice

Answers and Model Rationales

1. **A** Students can eliminate B, since there is no dialogue, and C, since the theme could as easily be established by a first-person narrator. The story's matter-of-fact tone (D) belies the theme's emotional content. The setting forces the boys to the decision that establishes the theme.
2. **F** The farmers' actions (G) set an example for the boys. The landscape (H) does not affect the boys, and they show no fear of the birds (J). Sympathy (F) is the main source of the boys' conflict.
3. **C** Lines 24–26 may imply some regret (D), but the speaker's main feeling is satisfaction (C). The speaker is not bored (B) or conflicted (A) by the bird's plight.
4. **F** The story does not have a humorous tone (G) or a first-person narrator (H), and both works have an outdoor setting (J). The story has a surprise ending; the poem does not.
5. **D** The speaker's attitude is straightforward, the opposite of ironic (B). It is not overridingly angry (A) or sad (C). The speaker is reflective about this and other experiences (D).
6. **F** Only F states a lesson learned by characters in both works. J is suggested by the story but not the poem. Neither G nor H is suggested by the works.
7. **D** The two works' plots are somewhat similar, but their settings (A), characters (B), and points of view (C) differ. Both works focus on animals in trouble and convey the theme that helping animals is emotionally rewarding.
8. **G** Students can eliminate H because the speaker in the poem reveals her thoughts, F because the poem's imagery makes its theme rich, and J because the poem has a simple plot and a stated theme.

Test Practice

Vocabulary Development

Multiple-Meaning Words

Modeling. Model the answer to 1 by saying, "In the sentence, as in A, *current* means 'flow of liquid.' In B, it means 'flow of electricity'; in C, 'contemporary'; and in D, 'course.'

Test Practice

Answers and Model Rationales

1. **A** See rationale above.
2. **J** In the sentence, *break* means "change" (J), not "pause" (F), "fracture" (G), or "chance" (H).
3. **B** In the sentence, *plane* means "two-dimensional surface" (B), not "airplane" (A), or "level" (C). Nor is it a tool (D).
4. **J** In the sentence, *bear* means "tolerate" (J), not "steer" (F), "keep" (G), or "show" (H).
5. **B** In the sentence, *figure* means "person" (B), not "body" (A), "number" (C), or "value" (D).
6. **J** In the sentence, *tone* means "spirit" (J), not "mode" (F), "shade" (G), or "condition" (H).
7. **C** In the sentence, *exercise* refers to strengthening an intangible attribute (C), not physical activity (A and D), or the practice of an academic skill (B).

ASSESSING

Assessment

- *Progress Assessment of Reading*
  - Chapter Test

TEST PRACTICE

Vocabulary Development

Test Practice

Multiple-Meaning Words

DIRECTIONS: Choose the answer in which the underlined word is used in the same way as it is used in each numbered sentence from "And of Clay Are We Created."

1. "I watched that hell on the first morning broadcast, cadavers of people and animals awash in the current of new rivers formed overnight from the melted snow."
   - A They paddled against a swift current.
   - B Turn off the electric current before you install the new light switch.
   - C She is critical of current government policies.
   - D What was the general current of the discussion?

2. "Despite the quality of the transmission, I could hear his voice break, and I loved him more than ever."
   - F He took a break from studying.
   - G A break in a pipe caused the leak.
   - H "Give me a break," she told the wildly barking dog.
   - J There was a sudden break in the singer's high note.

3. "The screen reduced the disaster to a single plane and accentuated the tremendous distance that separated me from Rolf Carlé; nonetheless, I was there with him."
   - A We heard a plane circling overhead.
   - B A picture painted on a flat plane can nevertheless look three-dimensional.
   - C Her comments brought the discussion to a higher plane.
   - D Use a plane to smooth rough boards.

4. "I could not bear the wait at home, so I went to National Television, where I often spent entire nights with Rolf editing programs."
   - F Remember to bear to the right.
   - G He tried to bear in mind the cost.
   - H The project will soon bear results.
   - J She could bear the pain with dignity.

5. "For years he had been a familiar figure in newscasts, reporting live at the scene of battles and catastrophes with awesome tenacity."
   - A Models must have a slender figure.
   - B She was a famous figure in history.
   - C The skater completed a figure eight.
   - D The figure for the sale was very high.

6. "Her tone was humble, as if apologizing for all the fuss."
   - F He set a moral tone for the others.
   - G The painting had a rich tone of red.
   - H Exercise can improve muscle tone.
   - J He always has a friendly tone.

7. "He took excessive risks as an exercise of courage, training by day to conquer the monsters that tormented him by night."
   - A Rowing is a form of exercise.
   - B That grammar exercise is too easy.
   - C Losing an election is an exercise in humility.
   - D Lorna is practicing a finger exercise on the piano.

Vocabulary Review

Activity. Have students select the correct Vocabulary word to complete each sentence.

denizens	flailing	feigning
dismantled	tenacity	

1. The ______ of the lake included bass, catfish, and turtles. [denizens]
2. With great ______, we spent the summer trying to catch bass. [tenacity]
3. The canoeist's wildly ______ paddle churned the water. [flailing]
4. We quickly ______ our fishing equipment and stored it in the car. [dismantled]
5. ______ a broken wing, the bird lured the fox away from her nest. [Feigning]

Writing

DIRECTIONS: Read the following paragraph from a draft of a student's persuasive essay. Then, read the questions below it. Choose the best answer to each question.

(1) Every day, children are bombarded with violent behavior on TV, and parents need to take action to protect their children. (2) With each passing year, the amount of violence on TV increases dramatically. (3) Watching too much TV has negative effects on children's health. (4) However, parental monitoring of TV programs is not enough. (5) Not only should parents remove televisions from the reach of vulnerable children, but they should also explain to those children that they are only allowed to watch TV with an adult.

1. Which sentence could be added to the paragraph as evidence to support the claim that there is too much violence on TV?

- **A** A recent study shows that 85 percent of cable TV contains violence.
- **B** Most of the violent programming comes on late at night.
- **C** Think about the violence in the television shows you watch.
- **D** Many parents do not watch television with their children.

2. How might the writer address the bias of some readers who think parental monitoring is a reasonable solution?

- **F** by telling them that their opinion will be discussed in detail at a later time
- **G** by ignoring their opinion
- **H** by providing evidence—only 38 percent of parents monitor their children
- **J** by restating his position

3. If the writer wanted to add an emotional appeal, which sentence would be most appropriate?

- **A** Children should read books.
- **B** Many TV shows contain violence.
- **C** Removing televisions from the reach of children is very important.
- **D** Children often mimic what they see on TV—with harmful results.

4. Which of the following sentences should be deleted to improve the organization of the evidence?

- **F** 1
- **G** 2
- **H** 3
- **J** 5

5. If you were listening to the paragraph in a debate, which of the following would best state the speaker's position?

- **A** The amount of violence on TV rises each year.
- **B** Violent episodes are shown on many channels.
- **C** Parents should not allow children to watch TV unsupervised.
- **D** Children should not watch prime-time shows.

Standards Review

Answers

1. A
2. H
3. D
4. H
5. C

APPLICATION

Conduct an Interview

For homework, have interested students contact the office of a local political leader and set up an interview with his or her speechwriter. Students could ask the speechwriter about his or her writing strategies and present their findings in the form of an oral presentation.

EXTENSION

Perform a Recitation

Point out to students that most speeches have an element of persuasion in them. Have interested students memorize a powerful persuasive speech (they might find one in a book of speeches in the library), paying attention to its logical and emotional appeals. Once they have committed the speech to memory, have them perform a recitation for the class. Then, have the class recall appeals from the speech that seem particularly effective.

RESOURCES: WRITING, LISTENING, & SPEAKING

Assessment

- *Test Generator* (*One-Stop Planner* CD-ROM)
- *Progress Assessment of Writing, Listening, & Speaking*, Ch. 4
- *Diagnostic and Summative Assessments*, Midyear Test

Internet

- Online assessments at go.hrw.com (keyword: HLLA)

Holt Literature and Language Arts: Mastering the California Standards

Chapter 5 Irony and Ambiguity

Generating Research Questions and Evaluating Sources

Program Organization

Holt Literature and Language Arts provides a complete curriculum for standards-based instruction in reading, literature, writing, listening and speaking, and language conventions. The instructional content is presented in quarters to enable teachers to anticipate and administer the quarterly assessments required by California.

About Chapter 5

Standards-based lesson plans and suggestions for pacing the presentation of Chapter 5, the related instructional material, and the recommended assessment are provided in *On Course: Mapping Instruction,* Chapter 5.

- In Chapter 5, students will identify and use words literally and figuratively; identify and use words from mythology; generate relevant questions; interpret and evaluate the impact of ambiguities, subtleties, contradictions, ironies, and incongruities; and maintain a consistent tone and organization throughout a piece of writing.

Language Arts Content

Which reading standards are taught in Chapter 5?

In this chapter, students will master the following Grade 10 standards and review standards from Grade 8. Selections or features marked with a ✔ constitute the minimum course of study that provides coverage of grade-level standards.

Grade 10 Standards

Word Analysis, Fluency, and Systematic Vocabulary Development

1.1 Identify and use the literal and figurative meanings of words, and understand word derivations.
✔ Analogies: Parallel Word Pairs, p. 365
✔ Word Clues: Greek and Latin Roots and Relations, p. 373
Word Roots and Their Families, p. 380

1.3 Identify Greek, Roman, and Norse mythology, and use the knowledge to understand the origin and meaning of new words.
Words from Mythology: So That's Where That Word Comes From, p. 348

Reading Comprehension (Focus on Informational Materials)

2.3 Generate relevant questions about readings on issues that can be researched.
✔ "Explorers Say There's Still Lots to Look For" (newspaper article), pp. 366–372
"The Last Frontier" (standards review), pp. 390–393

Literary Response and Analysis

3.8 Interpret and evaluate the impact of ambiguities, subtleties, contradictions, ironies, and incongruities in a text.
"Irony and Ambiguity: Surprises and Uncertainties" (standards essay), pp. 314–315
"Lamb to the Slaughter" (short story), pp. 316–326
"R.M.S. Titanic" (historical article), pp. 328–347
✔ from "Into Thin Air" (magazine article), pp. 349–364
"Notes from a Bottle" (short story), pp. 374–379

(continued)

Review Standards Grade 8

Reading 1.3 Use word meanings within the appropriate context, and show ability to verify those meanings by definition, restatement, example, comparison, or contrast.

Using Context Clues, p. 327

Word Maps: Showing Words in Action, p. 348

Technical Vocabulary—Widgets, Whatsits, Thingamajigs, p. 365

Words in Context: Clues All Around, p. 373

Reading 2.7 Evaluate the unity, coherence, logic, internal consistency, and structural patterns of text.

"R.M.S. Titanic" (historical article), pp. 328–347

Which writing, and listening and speaking standards are taught in Chapter 5?

Writing Strategies

1.1 Establish a controlling impression or coherent thesis that conveys a clear and distinctive perspective on the subject, and maintain a consistent tone and focus throughout the piece of writing.

Organize Your Essay, p. 384

1.9 Revise writing to improve the logic and coherence of the organization and controlling perspective, the precision of the word choice, and the tone by taking into consideration the audience, purpose, and formality of the context.

Evaluate and Revise Your Draft, pp. 387–388

Listening and Speaking Strategies

1.2 Compare and contrast the ways in which media genres cover the same event.

Choose a News Event, pp. 382–383

Review Standard Grade 8

Writing 1.0 Students write clear, coherent, and focused essays. The writing exhibits students' awareness of audience and purpose. Essays contain formal introductions, supporting evidence, and conclusions. Students progress through the stages of the writing process as needed.

Comparing Media Genres, p. 382–389

Instructional Planning and Support

Where do I find lesson plans, additional resources, and other teaching aids?

- This Annotated Teacher's Edition and *On Course: Mapping Instruction* provide direction in planning and implementing a complete California standards–based curriculum. These components also include instructions for diagnostic, progress, and summative testing; for presenting direct instruction of the standards; for differentiating instruction to provide universal access; and for locating and using the program's ancillaries.
- Lesson and workshop resources are referenced at the beginning of each selection or workshop, in the bottom margin of this teacher's edition.
- Reminders for using additional resources appear in this teacher's edition at point of use.
- The *One-Stop Planner* CD-ROM contains editable lesson plans and all print ancillaries, available in PDF format.

What if I don't have time to teach all of Chapter 5?

- Most standards can be taught with a minimum number of selections and features. In the chart on the preceding page, the core lessons you need in order to provide complete coverage of the chapter standards are identified with a ✔.
- *On Course: Mapping Instruction,* Chapter 5, lists lessons and activities that provide minimum standards coverage.

What provisions have been made for students who have additional class time scheduled in language arts?

- *Interactive Reading* provides for alternative direct instruction and practice of the grade-level standards taught in Chapter 5.
- *Universal Access: Writing, Listening, and Speaking,* Chapter 5, contains worksheets and transparencies that provide practice in and reteaching and reinforcement of the writing and listening and speaking standards in Chapter 5.
- *Universal Access: Lesson Plans for Language Development,* Chapter 5 provides alternative teaching strategies and additional worksheets designed specifically for English-language learners and special education students. Many of the suggestions and activities in this ancillary will also be helpful to students in the regular classroom who are having difficulty with particular skills.

Universal Access

How do I differentiate instruction to ensure that all my students master the standards?

Holt Literature and Language Arts provides comprehensive, differentiated instruction for all types of students.

- Most of the general instruction and teaching strategies in the Annotated Teacher's Edition are at grade level. These instructions will work well with the majority of your students.
- Point-of-use suggestions are provided for advanced learners, learners having difficulty, English-language learners, and special education students.
- *Interactive Reading* is designed to anticipate and remediate problems that students may experience in achieving mastery of the reading standards. See *Interactive Reading,* Teacher's Edition, Chapter 5, for information on using the reader to differentiate instruction.
- *Universal Access: Writing, Listening, and Speaking,* Chapter 5, contains worksheets and transparencies that provide practice in and reteaching and reinforcement of the writing and listening, and speaking standards in Chapter 5.
- *Universal Access: Lesson Plans for Language Development,* Chapter 5 offers teaching strategies and additional worksheets designed specifically for English-language learners and special education students.

Assessment

How do I determine whether my students are making progress in mastering the standards?

Progress Assessment

- Use the Standards Reviews at the end of Chapter 5 for an informal assessment of the informational reading and writing standards.
- Use Chapter 5 tests from the *Progress Assessment* booklets to assess comprehension and progress on mastering the standards taught in this chapter.

Summative Assessment

The content of *Holt Literature and Language Arts* has been divided into quarters to allow you to administer the four summative tests required by California. Chapters 3–5 and related instructional material constitute the second quarter of instruction. At the end of Chapter 5, you may ask students to take the Midyear Test in *Diagnostic and Summative Assessments.*

Chapter 5

STANDARDS FOCUS

(For full text of standards taught in this chapter, see the Standards Correlation by Standard chart in the Student Edition.)

Grade-Level Standards

- Vocabulary Development 1.1, 1.3
- Reading Comprehension 2.3
- Literary Response and Analysis 3.8
- Writing Strategies 1.1, 1.9
- Listening and Speaking Strategies 1.2

INTRODUCING THE CHAPTER

In this chapter, students will encounter irony and ambiguity. In factual narratives, they will follow the ironic twists and turns that led to the sinking of the *Titanic* and to the climbing of Mount Everest. In a suspenseful tale by Roald Dahl, students will meet a character who shows surprising strength. As students read the ambiguous "Notes from a Bottle," they will have to make inferences about what happens in the story.

Students will also have the opportunity to expand their understanding of the world of information by generating research questions and evaluating sources. The chapter culminates with an opportunity for students to compare media genres by writing an essay comparing coverage of a single news event by two different news media.

CHAPTER 5 RESOURCES: READING

Planning

- *One-Stop Planner* CD-ROM with Test Generator
- *On Course: Mapping Instruction*
- *At Home: A Guide to Standards Mastery*
- *At Home: In Spanish*
- *Supporting Instruction in Spanish*

Reading

- *Interactive Reading*

Differentiating Instruction

- *Lesson Plans for Language Development*

Vocabulary

- *Vocabulary Development*
  - Cumulative Vocabulary Review, pp. 31–32

Chapter 5

Irony and Ambiguity

GENERATING RESEARCH QUESTIONS AND EVALUATING SOURCES

irony is bitter truth
wrapped up in a little joke

—H. D.

The Human Condition (1934) by René Magritte. Oil on canvas.
Peter Willi/SuperStock.

go.hrw.com
KEYWORD: HLLA 10-5

313

THE QUOTATION

Explain to students that irony is a contrast between the way things seem and the way they really are. Say, "Suppose a teacher announces a surprise quiz on a day you haven't studied, and you groan, 'Oh, great!' Your exclamation is an example of irony. You really mean that the situation is just the opposite of 'great.'"

Point out to students that someone who says "Oh, great!" but means the opposite is making "a little joke" about "bitter truth." Tell students that they will encounter irony in several of the selections in this chapter.

VIEWING THE ART

René Magritte (1898–1967) was a surrealist artist. Employing a style of deadpan realism, his paintings explored ideas about the world and the way it is represented. *The Human Condition* is ironic because it depicts a painting of the landscape outside that physically blocks the view of the actual landscape.

Activity. Ask students what makes the viewer assume that the scene behind the painting is the same as what is depicted on the canvas. [We assume this because objects seem to continue on and off the canvas.]

Resources Reminder

Planning

- *At Home: A Guide to Standards Mastery*

Parent letters appear in this resource. Translations of these letters are found in *At Home: In Spanish.* Translations of selection summaries are found in *Supporting Instruction in Spanish.*

Reading

- *Interactive Reading*

The California framework requires students to read materials apart from in-class assignments. Additional readings are cited on the Read On page and on selected pages in the Student Edition.

Grammar

- *Holt Handbook*
  - Active Voice and Passive Voice, pp. 199–203
  - Comparison of Modifiers, pp. 218–223

Assessment

- *Progress Assessment of Reading*
  - Chapter Test
- *Diagnostic and Summative Assessments*
  - Midyear Test
- *One-Stop Planner* CD-ROM with Test Generator

Internet

- go.hrw.com
(Keyword: HLLA 10-5)

STANDARDS FOCUS, pp. 314–315

(For the grade-level standard taught in this lesson, see Student Edition, p. 314.)

Prerequisite Standard

- Grade 8, Literary Response and Analysis 3.6 **Identify significant literary devices (e.g., metaphor, symbolism, dialect, irony) that define a writer's style and use those elements to interpret the work.**

Literary Focus: Irony and Ambiguity

Show students a variety of comical and political cartoons. Discuss the elements that make each cartoon funny or thought provoking. Help students to understand that a surprising and unexpected comment or action often provides the basis for humor in cartoons. Stress that the meanings of political cartoons are often ambiguous, causing the reader to thoughtfully interpret the information before arriving at the cartoonist's point.

Literary Response and Analysis

Irony and Ambiguity *by* John Leggett

SURPRISES AND UNCERTAINTIES

Good stories entertain us and offer some insight into human experience, those joys and sorrows that are common to us all. For the magic of storytelling to work, the story must first persuade us that it is lifelike, which often means full of surprises and uncertainties. After all, we know that our own expectations are rarely fulfilled as we imagined they would be and that the future remains unknown. In fiction the representation of such surprises and uncertainties is often achieved through the use of **irony** and **ambiguity.**

Verbal Irony: Meaning Something Else

There are three kinds of irony, each of which involves some kind of contrast between expectation and reality. **Verbal irony**—the simplest kind—is being used when someone *says* one thing but *means* the opposite. The man who remarks "You sure can pick 'em" to his friend whose team finished last or the woman who says "Fine day for a picnic" in the middle of a torrential rainfall is using verbal irony. When we recognize verbal irony, we often laugh in appreciation.

Situational Irony: Reversing Expectations

Situational irony is much more important to the storyteller than other kinds of irony. It describes an occurrence that is not just surprising; it is the *opposite* of what we expected. In an ironic situation what actually happens is so contrary to our expectations that it seems to mock human intentions and the confidence with which we plan our futures. The ironic possibility that some haughty rich man will come begging from us tomorrow or that a woman who is dreading tonight's party will meet her future husband there keeps life interesting.

Situational irony cuts deeply into our feelings. When irony is put to work in fiction, it is often what touches us most. Irony can move us toward tears or laughter because we sense we are close to the truth of life.

Dramatic Irony: Withholding Knowledge

Dramatic irony is the kind of irony that occurs when *we* know what is in store for a character but the character does not know. This is called dramatic irony because it's so often used in plays and films. In an action movie, for example, we know (but the hero doesn't know) that one of the cables of the elevator she's about to enter has been cut.

Dramatic irony is used in novels and short stories too. What about Little Red Riding Hood knocking innocently on Grandma's front door? We know about the wolf under Grandma's bedclothes, wearing her bonnet, but Little Red is unaware of the toothy surprise that awaits her.

Dramatic irony adds to our enjoyment of a story because it mimics life, which is forever pulling surprises on us. Irony of all kinds is somehow enormously satisfying,

Reading Standard 3.8 Interpret and evaluate the impact of ambiguities and ironies in a text.

DIFFERENTIATING INSTRUCTION

Learners Having Difficulty

Have students work in small groups to discuss stories that they have read. Have them identify at least two stories in which the outcome was different from what the reader was led to expect. Ask students to explain these ironic outcomes to the class.

English-Language Learners

For more instruction on irony and ambiguity for English-language learners and special education students, see *Lesson Plans for Language Development,* pp. 139, 140.

Advanced Learners

Acceleration. The following activity can help to move students toward the eleventh-perhaps because we know instinctively that our carefully laid plans, ambitions, and strivings often come to little, whereas good luck (or bad) often finds unlikely targets.

Ambiguity: Multiple Meanings

While irony presents an outcome that is the opposite of what we expect, **ambiguity** offers us a choice of more than one meaning or interpretation. Ambiguity keeps us guessing, wondering, and reflecting. In an ambiguous story the choices are up in the air, but they are also ours for the taking. Think of the bright young singer who, after a terrible struggle, conquers the entertainment world and wins admiration and fame. By the end of the story, she is surrounded by fair-weather friends who insist she leave her past behind, including a boyfriend deeply troubled by her success. The confused hero then goes away alone on a long trip—and we are left to puzzle over her future. The point of ambiguity is to make us figure out our own interpretation of a story, our own reactions, based on the clues we uncover.

Ambiguity is not only rooted in a particular event or an ending, though. An ambiguous **theme** or **mood** can filter its way through an entire story. Is the tale of a nineteenth-century boy who becomes gravely ill from working in the coal mines—yet somehow retains his cheerful outlook—a moral lesson in keeping a positive attitude through hardship? Is it a comment on the society whose labor practices made him ill in the first place? Is the mood upbeat, tragic, or both? The opinions may vary from reader to reader as each finds a different answer within the delicate workings of the story.

Ambiguous stories generally linger in our minds the longest, because ambiguity challenges our imaginations. It gets us thinking and feeling, and it encourages us to talk about our reactions—to share our thoughts and ideas with others. What better purpose can a story have than that?

Practice

Imagine that you have been asked to contribute to a book that examines the many sides of irony, titled *The Irony of It All!* Review the discussion of irony in this essay, and use the chart below for a guide. Then, for each of the three types of **irony**—**verbal, situational,** and **dramatic**—come up with an example. Describe each example in a brief paragraph that you will contribute to the book. Be imaginative, but make sure your ironies ring true to life.

Verbal irony	Say one thing but mean the opposite	Example:
Situational irony	What happens is the opposite of what is expected	Example:
Dramatic irony	We know something a character does not know	Example:

and twelfth-grade Standard 3.3, for which they analyze ways in which irony achieves specific rhetorical or aesthetic purposes or both.

Activity. Remind students that satire is a type of writing that ridicules human weakness, vice, or folly in order to bring about social reform. Then, ask students to consider the relationship between irony and satire. Suggest that they identify examples of satirical stories, movies, and television shows and explain the role of irony in creating satire in each.

Practice

Students' responses will vary.

Verbal irony—A dancer is nervously making her entrance onto the stage when she trips and falls. Her partner helps her to her feet and whispers, "That was a really graceful move!" This is an example of verbal irony because both dancers know that a fall is the opposite of a graceful dance movement.

Situational irony—Many people are familiar with the poem "Casey at the Bat." In this poem the reader shares the crowd's excitement as a close baseball game draws to an end. It appears that mighty Casey will not get a chance to bat, but he finally approaches the plate, at which point "from that gladdened multitude went up a joyous yell." The reader is led to believe, along with the fans, that Casey will get a hit and win the game for his team. At the end of the poem, however, the reader learns that the "mighty Casey has struck out." This is an example of situational irony; the outcome of the game is the opposite of what the reader has been led to expect.

Dramatic irony—O'Henry's short story "The Gift of the Magi" is a classic example of dramatic irony. In this story, a young couple gets by with very little money. As Christmas approaches, each worries about not being able to afford a gift for the other. The young woman decides to sell her long, beautiful hair to buy a fob chain for her husband's treasured pocket watch. The young man sells his watch to buy an elegant set of tortoiseshell combs for his wife's beautiful hair. The reader, unlike the characters, is aware that the young man and young woman are each selling the very thing that the other hopes to enhance with her or his gift.

STANDARDS FOCUS, pp. 316–327

(For grade-level and review standards taught in this lesson, see citations on Student Edition pages.)

Prerequisite Standard

- Grade 8, Literary Response and Analysis 3.6 **Identify significant literary devices (e.g., metaphor, symbolism, dialect, irony) that define a writer's style and use those elements to interpret the work.**

Reading Skills

- Make predictions.

Summary *at grade level*

This darkly humorous story is a modern, yet classic tale of irony and suspense. Mary Maloney eagerly awaits her husband Patrick's arrival home from work. When he finally arrives, it is obvious that something is wrong. He tells his wife that he is leaving her, presumably for another woman. Shocked beyond reply, Mary begins cooking dinner. She grabs a large leg of lamb from the freezer. Suddenly she feels a desire to lash out. She walks up behind her husband and hits him on the head with the frozen meat, killing him. Then she shoves the leg of lamb into a hot oven. To establish an alibi, she goes out to the market and calmly asks the shopkeeper for potatoes and peas for her husband's dinner. When she returns home, she calls the police, pretending to have just discovered her husband's body. Hours later, as the police search for the murder weapon, Mary begs them all to eat the leg of lamb she has cooked so that it won't go to waste. The story ends with a final ironic twist as the police officers consume the leg of lamb, all the while discussing the mysterious disappearance of the murder weapon.

Before You Read

Lamb to the Slaughter

Literary Focus

Two Kinds of Irony

The story you are about to read starts out with a pleasant domestic scene that suddenly turns sinister. It's not scary the way a horror film is, but there are plenty of strange twists and surprises.

As you read the story, see if you can find both situational irony and dramatic irony. **Situational irony** occurs when something that happens is the opposite of what we would normally expect to happen or would find appropriate. In **dramatic irony** the reader knows something important that some or all of the characters do not know.

Reading Skills

Making Predictions

When you read a story or a novel, your brain automatically darts ahead, wondering, "What's next? Then what happens? And then what? How will it end?" Part of the fun of reading comes from your providing answers—guesses—to these "what's next" questions. You **make predictions** based on what you know about the story's characters and events and what you know about real-life people.

Stories with **ironic** twists, turns, and surprises are deliciously satisfying for making predictions. As you read this story, jot down your predictions—whenever you think you know what's coming next.

Reading Standard 3.8 Interpret and evaluate the impact of ironies in a text.

Make the Connection

Quickwrite

Have you ever heard someone described as going "like a lamb to the slaughter"? The saying comes from the Bible, which describes many instances of lambs used as sacrifices. Dahl chose that biblical **allusion,** or reference, as the **title** of his story. Knowing that, what do you think this story might be about? Jot down your ideas.

Vocabulary Development

anxiety (aŋ·zī′ə·tē) *n.:* state of being worried or uneasy.

placid (plas′id) *adj.:* calm; tranquil.

luxuriate (lug·zhoor′ē·āt′) *v.* (used with *in*): take great pleasure.

administered (ad·min′is·tərd) *v.* used as *adj.:* given; applied.

premises (prem′is·iz) *n.:* house or building and its surrounding property.

consoling (kən·sōl′iŋ) *v.* used as *adj.:* comforting.

hospitality (häs′pi·tal′ə·tē) *n.:* friendly, caring treatment of guests.

316 Chapter 5 Irony and Ambiguity • Generating Research Questions and Evaluating Sources

RESOURCES: READING

Planning

- *One-Stop Planner* CD-ROM with Test Generator
- *On Course: Mapping Instruction*

Media

- *Audio CD Library*
  - disc 10

- *Fine Art Transparencies*
  - Transparency 9

Reading

- *Interactive Reading*
  - Interactive version: "Lamb to the Slaughter"
- *Interactive Reading,* Teacher's Edition
  - Graphic Organizer: Irony Chart

Lamb to the Slaughter

Roald Dahl

"It's the old story. Get the weapon, and you've got the man."

The room was warm and clean, the curtains drawn, the two table lamps alight—hers and the one by the empty chair opposite. On the sideboard behind her, two tall glasses, soda water, whisky. Fresh ice cubes in the Thermos bucket.

Mary Maloney was waiting for her husband to come home from work.

Now and again she would glance up at the clock, but without anxiety, merely to please herself with the thought that each minute gone by made it nearer the time when he could come. There was a slow smiling air about her, and about everything she did. The drop of the head as she bent over her sewing was curiously tranquil. Her skin—for this was her sixth month with child—had acquired a wonderful translucent[1] quality, the mouth was soft, and the eyes, with their new placid look, seemed larger, darker than before.

1. **translucent** (trans·lo͞o′sənt) *adj.:* glowing; clear.

Vocabulary
anxiety (aŋ·zī′ə·tē) *n.:* state of being worried or uneasy.
placid (plas′id) *adj.:* calm; tranquil.

Differentiating Instruction

- *Lesson Plans for Language Development*
  - English-Language Learners, pp. 141–143, 163, 168
  - Special Education Students, pp. 144, 163, 168

Vocabulary

- *Vocabulary Development*
  - Vocabulary Worksheet, p. 26

Assessment

- *Progress Assessment of Reading*
  - Selection Test
- *One-Stop Planner* CD-ROM with Test Generator

PRETEACHING

Standards Starter

Motivate. To introduce dramatic irony, ask students if they have ever felt like calling out a warning to a character in a movie, such as "Don't open that door!" or "Run! They're right behind you!"

Ask volunteers to describe movie scenes that evoke such a response because viewers know more than the character does. Explain that this technique is called dramatic irony. Discuss the use of this technique to build suspense. Students should realize that dramatic irony keeps viewers on the edge of their seats, wondering whether characters will figure out the truth in time to affect the outcome of the plot.

Preview Vocabulary

Have pairs of students take turns reading aloud the definitions of the Vocabulary words listed on p. 316. To reinforce their understanding of the words, have the pairs work together on the following exercises:

1. Use your facial expressions and body language to show signs of anxiety. Then, show the expression of a placid person.
2. Draw a picture of vacation surroundings in which you might luxuriate.
3. Tell how a nurse may have administered a flu vaccination.
4. What consoling words might you offer to a friend who has just lost a competition?
5. Explain how you would extend hospitality to a houseguest.
6. Draw a map of your school's premises.

Assign the Reading

Homework

This story's vocabulary and sentence structure will pose little difficulty for most students, so you may wish to assign the story to them as homework. Learners who are having difficulty might read the story as partners with a peer tutor.

DIRECT TEACHING

A Learners Having Difficulty

Monitoring students' progress. How does Mary feel about her husband? [She loves him very much.]

B Reading Skills

Making predictions. How can you tell that something is disturbing Patrick? [He gulps down his drink in one swallow. He issues terse commands and one-word replies to his wife. His wife finds this behavior unusual.] What do you think will happen next? [Possible responses: Mary will try to find out what is bothering Patrick. Patrick will deliver some bad news.]

C Literary Focus
GRADE-LEVEL STANDARD

Interactions between characters. What can you tell about Mary's relationship with her husband from this dialogue? [Mary is very dutiful and solicitous of her husband's needs. She is very eager to please him. She seems afraid to challenge his behavior or to ask him what is wrong.]

When the clock said ten minutes to five, she began to listen, and a few moments later, punctually as always, she heard the tires on the gravel outside, and the car door slamming, the footsteps passing the window, the key turning in the lock. She laid aside her sewing, stood up, and went forward to kiss him as he came in.

"Hullo, darling," she said.

"Hullo," he answered.

She took his coat and hung it in the closet. Then she walked over and made the drinks, a strongish one for him, a weak one for herself; and soon she was back again in her chair with the sewing, and he in the other, opposite, holding the tall glass with both his hands, rocking it so the ice cubes tinkled against the side.

A For her, this was always a blissful time of day. She knew he didn't want to speak much until the first drink was finished, and she, on her side, was content to sit quietly, enjoying his company after the long hours alone in the house. She loved to luxuriate in the presence of this man, and to feel—almost as a sunbather feels the sun—that warm male glow that came out of him to her when they were alone together. She loved him for the way he sat loosely in a chair, for the way he came in a door, or moved slowly across the room with long strides. She loved the intent, far look in his eyes when they rested on her, the funny shape of the mouth, and especially the way he remained silent about his tiredness, sitting still with himself until the whisky had taken some of it away.

"Tired, darling?"

B "Yes," he said. "I'm tired." And as he spoke, he did an unusual thing. He lifted his glass and drained it in one swallow although there was still half of it, at least half of it left. She wasn't really watching him, but she knew what he had done because she heard the ice cubes falling back against the bottom of the empty glass when he lowered his arm. He paused a moment, leaning forward in the chair, then he got up and went slowly over to fetch himself another.

"I'll get it!" she cried, jumping up.

"Sit down," he said.

When he came back, she noticed that the new drink was dark amber with the quantity of whisky in it.

"Darling, shall I get your slippers?"

"No."

She watched him as he began to sip the dark yellow drink, and she could see little oily swirls in the liquid because it was so strong.

C "I think it's a shame," she said, "that when a policeman gets to be as senior as you, they keep him walking about on his feet all day long."

He didn't answer, so she bent her head again and went on with her sewing; but each time he lifted the drink to his lips, she heard the ice cubes clinking against the side of the glass.

"Darling," she said. "Would you like me to get you some cheese? I haven't made any supper because it's Thursday."

"No," he said.

"If you're too tired to eat out," she went on, "it's still not too late. There's plenty of meat and stuff in the freezer, and you can have it right here and not even move out of the chair."

Her eyes waited on him for an answer, a smile, a little nod, but he made no sign.

"Anyway," she went on, "I'll get you some cheese and crackers first."

"I don't want it," he said.

She moved uneasily in her chair, the large eyes still watching his face. "But you *must* have supper. I can easily do it here. I'd like to do it. We can have lamb chops. Or pork. Anything you want. Everything's in the freezer."

"Forget it," he said.

"But, darling, you *must* eat! I'll fix it anyway, and then you can have it or not, as you like."

She stood up and placed her sewing on the table by the lamp.

Vocabulary
luxuriate (lug·zhoor′ē·āt′) *v.* (used with *in*): take great pleasure.

DIFFERENTIATING INSTRUCTION

Learners Having Difficulty
Invite learners having difficulty to read "Lamb to the Slaughter" in interactive format in *Interactive Reading* and to use the sidenotes as aids to understanding the selection. The interactive version provides additional instruction, practice, and assessment of the literature standard taught in the Student Edition. Monitor students' responses to the selection, and correct any misconceptions that arise.

Resources Reminder

Differentiating Instruction

- *Interactive Reading*
  - Interactive version: "Lamb to the Slaughter"

English-Language Learners
To help these students read the story with greater ease, you may wish to review some of the crime-related terminology that they will encounter. These words include *detective, sergeant, police station, policemen, precinct, police photographer, penalty, murderer, fingerprints, corpse, weapon,* and *heavy blunt instrument.*

"Sit down," he said. "Just for a minute, sit down."

It wasn't till then that she began to get frightened.

"Go on," he said. "Sit down."

She lowered herself back slowly into the chair, watching him all the time with those large, bewildered eyes. He had finished the second drink and was staring down into the glass, frowning.

"Listen," he said. "I've got something to tell you."

"What is it, darling? What's the matter?"

He had now become absolutely motionless, and he kept his head down so that the light from the lamp beside him fell across the upper part of his face, leaving the chin and mouth in shadow. She noticed there was a little muscle moving near the corner of his left eye.

"This is going to be a bit of a shock to you, I'm afraid," he said. "But I've thought about it a good deal and I've decided the only thing to do is tell you right away. I hope you won't blame me too much."

And he told her. It didn't take long, four or five minutes at most, and she sat very still through it all, watching him with a kind of dazed horror as he went further and further away from her with each word.

"So there it is," he added. "And I know it's kind of a bad time to be telling you, but there simply wasn't any other way. Of course I'll give you money and see you're looked after. But there needn't really be any fuss. I hope not anyway. It wouldn't be very good for my job."

Her first instinct was not to believe any of it, to reject it all. It occurred to her that perhaps he hadn't even spoken, that she herself had imagined the whole thing. Maybe, if she went about her business and acted as though she hadn't been listening, then later, when she sort of woke up again, she might find none of it had ever happened.

"I'll get the supper," she managed to whisper, and this time he didn't stop her.

When she walked across the room she couldn't feel her feet touching the floor. She couldn't feel anything at all—except a slight nausea and a desire to vomit. Everything was automatic now—down the steps to the cellar, the light switch, the deep freeze, the hand inside the cabinet taking hold of the first object it met. She lifted it out, and looked at it. It was wrapped in paper, so she took off the paper and looked at it again.

A leg of lamb.

All right then, they would have lamb for supper. She carried it upstairs, holding the thin bone-end of it with both her hands, and as she went through the living room, she saw him standing over by the window with his back to her, and she stopped.

"For God's sake," he said, hearing her, but not turning round.

"This is going to be a bit of a shock to you, I'm afraid," he said.

DIRECT TEACHING

D Reading Skills

Making predictions. Why is Mary suddenly frightened? [Her husband is behaving oddly and seems about to reveal something important.] What do you think is about to happen? [Possible response: Patrick is about to tell Mary some bad news.]

E Learners Having Difficulty

Finding details. How can you tell that Patrick is feeling nervous and perhaps ashamed? [He keeps his head down and doesn't look at Mary. There is a muscle twitching by his eye.]

F Reading Skills

Making inferences. What seems to be Patrick's biggest concern as he delivers this news? [He is most concerned about himself, especially his job. He doesn't want Mary to challenge his decision or to make any trouble. He doesn't seem concerned about Mary at all.]

G Vocabulary Development
REVIEW STANDARD

Context clues. Based on the context of the sentence, what do you think the word *nausea* means? [being sick to one's stomach]

H Reading Skills

Making predictions. What do you think Mary is going to do next? [Students may correctly predict that Mary will strike her husband with the leg of lamb.]

Resources Reminder

For lessons designed for intermediate and advanced English-language learners, see *Lesson Plans for Language Development,* pp. 141–143, 163, 168.

Special Education Students
For lessons designed for special education students, see *Lesson Plans for Language Development,* pp. 144, 163, 168.

Advanced Learners
Acceleration. Use this activity to move advanced learners toward the eleventh- and twelfth-grade Standard 3.3, for which they analyze the ways in which irony achieves specific rhetorical purposes.

Activity. Have students review the last two pages of the story, in which the author sets the scene for the dramatic irony of the ending. Then, have them discuss what effect the author intends these scenes to have on the reader. Is his purpose to shock, outrage, or amuse? Have students point out specific details that support their views.

DIRECT TEACHING

A Literary Focus
GRADE-LEVEL STANDARD

? Situational irony. Why is Mary's violent action so unexpected? [She has always loved her husband deeply; up until now she has seemed gentle, solicitous, and submissive toward her husband.]

B Learners Having Difficulty

? Monitoring students' progress. What is Mary planning to do next? [She is planning to go to the market, pretending to prepare dinner for her husband, in order to establish an alibi for the time of the murder.] **What is her motivation for this plan?** [She is worried about what will happen to her unborn baby if she is convicted of the murder.]

C Literary Focus
GRADE-LEVEL STANDARD

? Interactions between characters. Why is Mary talking so much and giving the grocer so much information? [Possible responses: She wants to appear natural and relaxed, as if nothing is wrong. She wants the grocer to be able to back up the lies she plans to tell the police.]

"Don't make supper for me. I'm going out."

At that point, Mary Maloney simply walked up behind him and without any pause she swung the big frozen leg of lamb high in the air and brought it down as hard as she could on the back of his head.

She might just as well have hit him with a steel club.

She stepped back a pace, waiting, and the funny thing was that he remained standing there for at least four or five seconds, gently swaying. Then he crashed to the carpet.

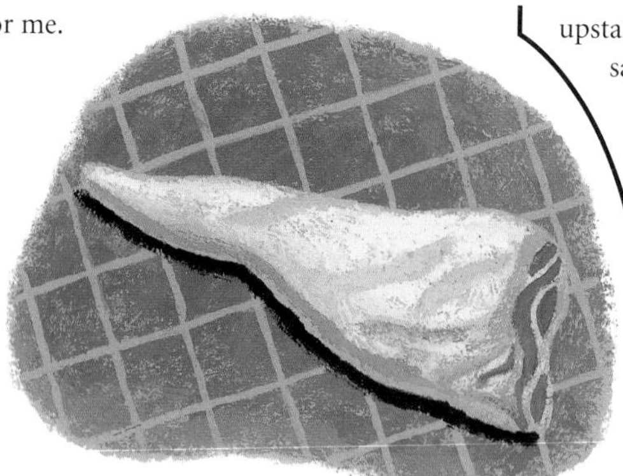

"I got a nice leg of lamb, from the freezer."

A The violence of the crash, the noise, the small table overturning, helped bring her out of the shock. She came out slowly, feeling cold and surprised, and she stood for a while blinking at the body, still holding the ridiculous piece of meat tight with both hands.

All right, she told herself. So I've killed him.

B It was extraordinary, now, how clear her mind became all of a sudden. She began thinking very fast. As the wife of a detective, she knew quite well what the penalty would be. That was fine. It made no difference to her. In fact, it would be a relief. On the other hand, what about the child? What were the laws about murderers with unborn children? Did they kill them both—mother and child? Or did they wait until the tenth month? What did they do?

Mary Maloney didn't know. And she certainly wasn't prepared to take the chance.

She carried the meat into the kitchen, placed it in a pan, turned the oven on high, and shoved it inside. Then she washed her hands and ran upstairs to the bedroom. She sat down before the mirror, tidied her face, touched up her lips and face. She tried a smile. It came out rather peculiar. She tried again.

"Hullo Sam," she said brightly, aloud.

The voice sounded peculiar too.

"I want some potatoes please, Sam. Yes, and I think a can of peas."

That was better. Both the smile and the voice were coming out better now. She rehearsed it several times more. Then she ran downstairs, took her coat, went out the back door, down the garden, into the street.

It wasn't six o'clock yet and the lights were still on in the grocery shop.

"Hullo Sam," she said brightly, smiling at the man behind the counter.

"Why, good evening, Mrs. Maloney. How're *you*?"

"I want some potatoes please, Sam. Yes, and I think a can of peas."

The man turned and reached up behind him on the shelf for the peas.

C "Patrick's decided he's tired and doesn't want to eat out tonight," she told him. "We usually go out Thursdays, you know, and now he's caught me without any vegetables in the house."

"Then how about meat, Mrs. Maloney?"

"No, I've got meat, thanks. I got a nice leg of lamb, from the freezer."

"Oh."

"I don't much like cooking it frozen, Sam, but I'm taking a chance on it this time. You think it'll be all right?"

CONTENT-AREA CONNECTIONS

Science: Forensics

Tell students that the use of science to solve crimes is called forensics. At the time this story was written, forensic scientists were limited to techniques such as autopsies and fingerprinting. Today, DNA testing has become an important way of identifying criminals.

Small-group activity. Have small groups of students research the history and techniques of fingerprinting and DNA testing as these processes are used in criminal investigations. Suggest that they explore what the detectives could have learned from the murder weapon in the story, both at the time the story is set and today. Invite students to present their findings to the class in an oral report.

"Personally," the grocer said, "I don't believe it makes any difference. You want these Idaho potatoes?"

"Oh yes, that'll be fine. Two of those."

"Anything else?" The grocer cocked his head on one side, looking at her pleasantly. "How about afterwards? What you going to give him for afterwards?"

D "Well—what would you suggest, Sam?"

The man glanced around his shop. "How about a nice big slice of cheesecake? I know he likes that."

"Perfect," she said. "He loves it."

And when it was all wrapped and she had paid, she put on her brightest smile and said, "Thank you, Sam. Good night."

"Good night, Mrs. Maloney. And thank *you*."

And now, she told herself as she hurried back, all she was doing now, she was returning home to her husband and he was waiting for his supper; and she must cook it good, and make it as tasty as possible because the poor man was tired; and if, when she entered the house, she happened to find anything unusual, or tragic, or terrible, then naturally it would be a shock and she'd become frantic with grief and horror. Mind you, she wasn't *expecting* to find anything. She was just going home with the vegetables. Mrs. Patrick Maloney going home with the vegetables on Thursday evening to cook supper for her husband. E

That's the way, she told herself. Do everything right and natural. Keep things absolutely natural and there'll be no need for any acting at all.

Therefore, when she entered the kitchen by the back door, she was humming a little tune to herself and smiling.

"Patrick!" she called. "How are you, darling?"

She put the parcel down on the table and went through into the living room; and when she saw him lying there on the floor with his legs doubled up and one arm twisted back underneath his body, it really was rather a shock. All the old love and longing for him welled up inside her, and she ran over to him, knelt down beside him, and began to cry her heart out. It was easy. No acting was necessary. F

A few minutes later she got up and went to the phone. She knew the number of the police station, and when the man at the other end answered, she cried to him, "Quick! Come quick! Patrick's dead!"

"Who's speaking?"

"Mrs. Maloney. Mrs. Patrick Maloney."

"You mean Patrick Maloney's dead?"

"I think so," she sobbed. "He's lying on the floor and I think he's dead."

"Be right over," the man said.

The car came very quickly, and when she opened the front door, two policemen walked in. She knew them both—she knew nearly all the men at that precinct—and she fell right into Jack Noonan's arms, weeping hysterically. He put her gently into a chair, then went over to join the other one, who was called O'Malley, kneeling by the body. G

"Is he dead?" she cried.

"I'm afraid he is. What happened?"

Briefly, she told her story about going out to the grocer and coming back to find him on the

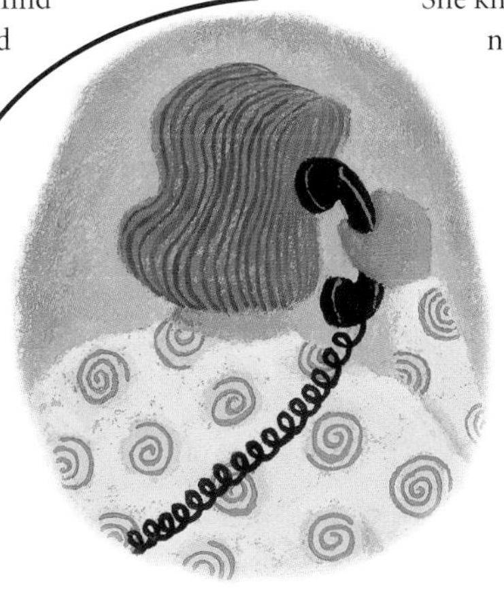

"Quick! Come quick! Patrick's dead!"

DIRECT TEACHING

D Literary Focus
GRADE-LEVEL STANDARD

Dramatic irony. What makes this scene an example of dramatic irony? [The reader knows that Patrick is dead, but the grocer does not. He is recommending a dessert for a dead man.]

E Advanced Learners

Enrichment. Mary Maloney has just murdered her husband and is now carrying out a clever plan to escape punishment, yet most readers find her a sympathetic character. How does the author create sympathy for Mary? [Possible responses: In the beginning the author establishes that Mary is a sweet, loving wife who does everything she can to please her husband, yet Patrick cruelly betrays her and seems to have no concern for her feelings. After the murder, Mary is motivated primarily by concern for her unborn child. Even then, she doesn't seem to be filled with hatred or anger toward her husband. The way Mary talks to herself to keep her spirits up is appealing.]

F Reading Skills

Evaluating. Do you find Mary's behavior in this scene believable? Why or why not? [Possible responses: Yes, because she really did love her husband before she found out about his betrayal and his plans to leave her. No, someone who has just been treated as cruelly as Mary would not feel love and sorrow for the person she killed.]

G Vocabulary Development
REVIEW STANDARD

Context clues. Based on the context of this sentence, what do you think the word *hysterically* means? [uncontrollably; wildly]

Social Sciences: The Justice System
Encourage students to imagine that Mary Maloney later feels guilty and confesses her crime. Ask them to speculate on how her case might be handled in court.
Small-group activity. First, divide the class into small groups to research the roles played by defense attorneys, prosecutors, judges, juries, police officers, and expert witnesses in criminal trials. Then, have students role-play the trial of Mary Maloney, concluding with a verdict from the jury and sentencing by the judge.

DIRECT TEACHING

A Literary Focus
GRADE-LEVEL STANDARD

Dramatic irony. Why is this passage an example of dramatic irony? [The reader knows that Mary has just told the police where the murder weapon is, but the police don't realize this.]

B Literary Focus
REVIEW STANDARD

Point of view. From what point of view is the story told? [It is told in third-person-limited point of view. The reader knows Mary's thoughts but not those of the police.] How does this point of view create suspense? [Like Mary, the reader must infer what the police are thinking from what Mary sees them do and from what she overhears them say.]

C Literary Focus
GRADE-LEVEL STANDARD

Interactions between characters. Do the police seem to suspect that Mary might be the murderer? How can you tell? [No, they are treating her kindly, as a grieving widow. Once they verify her alibi with the grocer, they believe her story that she was out shopping when the murder occurred.]

D Literary Focus
GRADE-LEVEL STANDARD

Interactions between characters. What other reason might Mary have for wanting to stay in the room? [She wants to be able to observe the police while they search for the murder weapon. She wants to overhear their conversation about who may have committed the murder.]

E English-Language Learners

Briticisms. Make sure students understand that in British English a *spanner* refers to a wrench and a *torch* refers to a flashlight.

floor. While she was talking, crying and talking, Noonan discovered a small patch of congealed[2] blood on the dead man's head. He showed it to O'Malley who got up at once and hurried to the phone.

Soon, other men began to come into the house. First a doctor, then two detectives, one of whom she knew by name. Later, a police photographer arrived and took pictures, and a man who knew about fingerprints. There was a great deal of whispering and muttering beside the corpse, and the detectives kept asking her a lot of questions. But they always treated her kindly. She told her story again, this time right from the beginning, when Patrick had come in, and she was sewing, and he was tired, so tired he hadn't **A** wanted to go out for supper. She told how she'd put the meat in the oven—"it's there now, cooking"—and how she'd slipped out to the grocer for vegetables, and come back to find him lying on the floor.

"Which grocer?" one of the detectives asked.

B She told him, and he turned and whispered something to the other detective who immediately went outside into the street.

In fifteen minutes he was back with a page of notes, and there was more whispering, and through her sobbing she heard a few of the whispered phrases—". . . acted quite normal . . . very cheerful . . . wanted to give him a good supper . . . peas . . . cheesecake . . . impossible that she . . ."

C After a while, the photographer and the doctor departed and two other men came in and took the corpse away on a stretcher. Then the fingerprint man went away. The two detectives remained, and so did the two policemen. They were exceptionally nice to her, and Jack Noonan asked if she wouldn't rather go somewhere else, to her sister's house perhaps, or to his own wife who would take care of her and put her up for the night.

No, she said. She didn't feel she could move even a yard at the moment. Would they mind awfully if she stayed just where she was until she felt better? She didn't feel too good at the moment, she really didn't.

Then hadn't she better lie down on the bed? Jack Noonan asked.

D No, she said. She'd like to stay right where she was, in this chair. A little later perhaps, when she felt better, she would move.

So they left her there while they went about their business, searching the house. Occasionally one of the detectives asked her another question. Sometimes Jack Noonan spoke to her gently as he passed by. Her husband, he told her, had been killed by a blow on the back of the head administered with a heavy blunt instrument, almost certainly a large piece of metal. They were looking for the weapon. The murderer may have taken it with him, but on the other hand he may've thrown it away or hidden it somewhere on the premises.

"It's the old story," he said. "Get the weapon, and you've got the man."

Later, one of the detectives came up and sat beside her. Did she know, he asked, of anything in the house that could've been used as the weapon? Would she mind having a look around **E** to see if anything was missing—a very big spanner,[3] for example, or a heavy metal vase.

They didn't have any heavy metal vases, she said.

"Or a big spanner?"

She didn't think they had a big spanner. But there might be some things like that in the garage.

2. **congealed** (kən·jēld′) *v.* used as *adj.*: thickened; made solid.

3. **spanner** *n.*: British English for "wrench."

Vocabulary

administered (ad·min′is·tərd) *v.* used as *adj.*: given; applied.

premises (prem′is·iz) *n.*: house or building and its surrounding property.

DEVELOPING FLUENCY

Mixed-ability group activity. Pair an advanced learner with either a learner having difficulty or an English-language learner. Have the two students take turns reading the story aloud together. Encourage them to stop after each page to discuss any predictions they made or any unexpected twists they encounter in the plot.

READING MINI-LESSON

Developing Word-Attack Skills

Write the selection word *extraordinary* on the chalkboard. Point out that *extraordinary* is made up of two smaller words: *extra* and *ordinary*. Remind students that when the two words are combined, their pronunciation changes: *extra* (eks′trə) and *ordinary* (ôrd′'n·er′ē) become *extraordinary* (ek·strôrd′'n·er′ē). Stress and sound changes

They were looking for the weapon.

The search went on. She knew that there were other policemen in the garden all around the house. She could hear their footsteps on the gravel outside, and sometimes she saw the flash of a torch through a chink in the curtains. It began to get late, nearly nine she noticed by the clock on the mantel. The four men searching the rooms seemed to be growing weary, a trifle exasperated.

"Jack," she said, the next time Sergeant Noonan went by. "Would you mind giving me a drink?"

"Sure I'll give you a drink. You mean this whisky?"

"Yes, please. But just a small one. It might make me feel better."

He handed her the glass.

"Why don't you have one yourself," she said. "You must be awfully tired. Please do. You've been very good to me."

"Well," he answered. "It's not strictly allowed, but I might take just a drop to keep me going."

One by one the others came in and were persuaded to take a little nip of whisky. They stood around rather awkwardly with the drinks in their hands, uncomfortable in her presence, trying to say consoling things to her. Sergeant Noonan wandered into the kitchen, came out quickly and said, "Look, Mrs. Maloney. You know that oven of yours is still on, and the meat still inside."

"Oh *dear* me!" she cried. "So it is!"

"I better turn it off for you, hadn't I?"

"Will you do that, Jack. Thank you so much."

When the sergeant returned the second time, she looked at him with her large, dark, tearful eyes. "Jack Noonan," she said.

"Yes?"

"Would you do me a small favor—you and these others?" **F**

"We can try, Mrs. Maloney."

Vocabulary
consoling (kən·sōl′iŋ) *v.* used as *adj.:* comforting.

DIRECT TEACHING

F English-Language Learners

Idioms. Make sure students understand that the idiomatic phrase *do me a small favor* means "perform a small act of kindness for me."

occur when *extra* and *ordinary* are combined.

Explain that pronunciation also changes when a suffix is added to a word. Demonstrate this by writing the words *peculiar* and *peculiarity* on the chalkboard and reading them aloud. Help students recognize that the syllable *cul* gets the greatest stress in *peculiar* (pi•kyo͞ol′yər), while in *peculiarity* the syllable *ar* is said with the greatest stress: (pi•kyo͞o′lē•er′ə•tē)

In a similar way, compare the pronunciations of *luxury* (luk′shə•rē) and *luxuriate* (lug•zhoor′ē•āt).

Activity. Write these pairs of words on the chalkboard. Have volunteers read the words aloud and circle the syllable said with the greatest stress. Answers are underlined.

1. ridicule — ridiculous
2. punctual — punctuality
3. strategy — strategic
4. habit — habitual
5. ethnic — ethnicity
6. tragedy — tragedian

Direct Teaching

Ⓐ Literary Focus
GRADE-LEVEL STANDARD

Dramatic irony. In what sense will the police be doing Mary a favor by eating up the leg of lamb? [They will be disposing of the murder weapon, the only clue indicating that Mary committed the murder.] Why do the police agree to this request? [They are hungry, and they believe that they are merely providing some comfort to a grieving widow by accepting her hospitality.]

Guided Practice

Monitoring students' progress. Guide the class in answering these comprehension questions. Direct students to locate passages in the text that support their responses.

Short Answer

1. How and why does Mary murder her husband? [She hits him on the back of the head with a frozen leg of lamb because he has just told her he is leaving her.]
2. What does Mary tell the grocer after the murder? [She tells him she is cooking dinner for her husband and that she needs some vegetables to go with the leg of lamb she is cooking.]
3. Why do the police spend several hours at the Maloney house after the murder? [They are searching for the murder weapon.]
4. What "small favor" does Mary ask the police to do for her? [She asks them to eat up the leg of lamb that she has been cooking for dinner.]

"She *wants* us to finish it. She said so. Be doing her a favor."

"Well," she said. "Here you all are, and good friends of dear Patrick's too, and helping to catch the man who killed him. You must be terrible hungry by now because it's long past your supper time, and I know Patrick would never forgive me, God bless his soul, if I allowed you to remain in his house without offering you decent hospitality. Why don't you eat up that lamb that's in the oven? It'll be cooked just right by now."

"Wouldn't dream of it," Sergeant Noonan said.

"Please," she begged. "Please eat it. Personally I couldn't touch a thing, certainly not what's been in the house when he was here. But it's all right for you. It'd be a favor to me if you'd eat it up. Then you can go on with your work again afterwards."

Ⓐ There was a good deal of hesitating among the four policemen, but they were clearly hungry, and in the end they were persuaded to go into the kitchen and help themselves. The woman stayed where she was, listening to them through the open door, and she could hear them speaking among themselves, their voices thick and sloppy because their mouths were full of meat.

"Have some more, Charlie?"

"No. Better not finish it."

"She *wants* us to finish it. She said so. Be doing her a favor."

"Okay then. Give me some more."

"That's the hell of a big club the guy must've used to hit poor Patrick," one of them was saying. "The doc says his skull was smashed all to pieces just like from a sledgehammer."

"That's why it ought to be easy to find."

"Exactly what I say."

"Whoever done it, they're not going to be carrying a thing like that around with them longer than they need."

One of them belched.

"Personally, I think it's right here on the premises."

"Probably right under our very noses. What you think, Jack?"

And in the other room, Mary Maloney began to giggle. ■

Vocabulary
hospitality (häs′pi·tal′ə·tē) *n.:* friendly, caring treatment of guests.

Family/Community Activity

Invite a police officer to talk to the class about the investigation of crime scenes, the collection of evidence, and the arrest and charging of suspected criminals. You might ask your guest to read "Lamb to the Slaughter" before addressing the class and then to comment on the conduct of the police in the story.

324 Chapter 5 Irony and Ambiguity • Generating Research Questions and Evaluating Sources

Meet the Writer

Roald Dahl

Master of the Delightfully Sinister

When Roald (ro͞o′äl) Dahl (1916–1990) was fifteen, a teacher in a British boarding school wrote on his report card: "A persistent muddler. Vocabulary negligible, sentences malconstructed. He reminds me of a camel." So much for accurately assessing Dahl's talents, for he became one of Britain's most popular writers of children's fiction and adult short stories, famous for his delightfully sinister fantasies.

The son of Norwegian parents, Roald Dahl was born in the south of Wales. Though his father died when Dahl was four, the family remained in England so the children could go to English schools, which his father had thought the best in the world. Dahl hated the boarding schools, which he began attending when he was nine. He recalled "just rules, rules and still more rules that had to be obeyed."

In 1934, when he graduated from prep school, Dahl turned down his mother's offer to send him to college. Instead, he took a job with an oil company and was sent to Tanzania, in East Africa. When World War II broke out, Dahl joined the British Royal Air Force in Nairobi as a fighter pilot, and he was badly injured when his plane crash-landed in the Libyan desert. In 1942, he was assigned as assistant air attaché to the British embassy in Washington, D.C. There he began writing, at first about his wartime experiences. "As I went on," he later said in an interview, "the stories become less and less realistic and more fantastic."

Dahl became especially interested in children's stories. In his first effort, *The Gremlins* (1943), he claimed to have coined the word for the imaginary gnomes that sabotage fighter planes and bombers, causing them to crash. Dahl's most successful children's books, inspired by the long bedtime stories he used to tell his five children, are *James and the Giant Peach* (1961) and *Charlie and the Chocolate Factory* (1964).

Dahl crafted his tales carefully, often spending six months on a single story. He once wrote this comment about being a writer:

"A person is a fool to become a writer. His only compensation is absolute freedom. He has no master except his own soul, and that, I am sure, is why he does it."

For Independent Reading

Want to learn more about the early life of the author? In *Boy: Tales of Childhood* (1984), Dahl relates his memorable boyhood experiences.

Meet the Writer

Background. Roald Dahl once observed that his daily work ritual consisted of writing for several hours in a small shed in his yard. He described sitting in an old armchair with a sleeping bag pulled up to his waist and his feet resting on a battered old suitcase. Beside him he always kept a jar full of six pencils, a thermos of coffee, and an electric pencil sharpener. Dahl claimed that his inspiration for "Lamb to the Slaughter" came to him at a dinner party at which he and writer Ian Fleming joked about the toughness of the lamb they were served.

For Independent Reading

In *Boy: Tales of Childhood,* Roald Dahl offers glimpses of early experiences that played a part in shaping some of his fiction. For example, he tells of holding a temporary position as a chocolate tester in a famous candy factory.

Students who enjoyed the irony and suspense of "Lamb to the Slaughter" may also enjoy the following short story collections:

- *The Lottery and Other Stories* by Shirley Jackson. Jackson's ironic, often darkly humorous tales of suspense have a sensibility similar to that found in Dahl's best work.
- *The Twilight Zone: Complete Stories* by Rod Serling. Serling, master of the ironic twist, adapted nineteen of his favorite dramas from his classic TV series for this collection.

DIFFERENTIATING INSTRUCTION

Advanced Learners

Enrichment. Tell students that Roald Dahl was one of those rare writers who was equally successful writing for both children and adults.

Activity. Have students research reviews of Dahl's fiction for children and for adults. Have them compare and contrast the strengths and weaknesses that reviewers have identified in his writing for each audience. Suggest that students enter *Roald Dahl* and *reviews* as keywords in an Internet search engine.

INDEPENDENT PRACTICE

Literary Response and Analysis

Reading Check

1. She deeply loves him.
2. Her husband says he is leaving her.
3. She wants to establish an alibi.
4. They think an intruder murdered him while Mary was at the store.

Interpretations

5. Possible answer: He is leaving Mary for another woman.
6. Possible answers: *Irony*—Meek, loving Mary murders her husband. *Clue*—She holds the leg of lamb like a club. *Irony*—Mary coolly goes to the grocer's to create an alibi. *Clues*—She was a detective's wife and wants to save her unborn child.
7. The police eating the leg of lamb provides dramatic irony because readers know the police are unwittingly destroying evidence of Mary's crime. Students may say that this is more powerful because readers realize that the seemingly innocent wife will get away with her crime.
8. Dramatic irony—readers know that Mary is really asking the police to unwittingly destroy the murder weapon, while the police think they are helping her.
9. Students may have predicted the murder and the weapon when Mary held the leg of lamb like a club and stopped upon seeing her husband's back. They may have predicted how Mary would dispose of the weapon when she asked for a "small favor."
10. "Lamb to the slaughter" usually refers to the sacrifice of an innocent, but here it suggests both the murder weapon and the irony of Mary, the innocent lamb, killing her husband.

Evaluation

11. Possible answer: No, the story is a fable of the innocent and meek overcoming the guilty and powerful. Mary's revenge and cleverness at concealing it do not fit her character. The police are gullible to fall for her tricks.

Literary Criticism

12. Possible answer: Dahl wants us to see Mary as an innocent victim of her husband's cruel betrayal and to feel that Patrick deserved his punishment, just as Mary deserved to triumph over him. Dahl lets us know Mary's feelings.

Literary Response and Analysis

Reading Check

1. At the beginning of the story, what do we learn about Mary's feelings for her husband, Patrick?
2. What happens to upset Mary?
3. Why does Mary go out to the grocer's?
4. What do the police think happened to Patrick?

Interpretations

5. Dahl does not tell us the exact details of what Patrick tells Mary. What can we **infer** that Patrick tells her?
6. Cite two examples of **situational irony** in the story. What clues, or **foreshadowing,** if any, does Dahl give to prepare us for the unexpected?
7. How does Dahl also make use of **dramatic irony**? Which did you find more powerful—the dramatic irony or the situational irony? Explain why.
8. Find the passage in which Mary asks the police officers to do her a "small favor" and eat the lamb. What kind of **irony** is at work here?
9. Look back at the notes you made as you read the story to see when, if at all, you **predicted** the following developments:
   - that Mary would murder her husband
   - what Mary would use for a weapon
   - how Mary would dispose of the weapon
10. Now that you have read the story, what do you think the **title** means? Is it appropriate? Is it **ironic**? Check your Quickwrite notes, and then explain your answers.

Reading Standard 3.8 Interpret and evaluate the impact of ambiguities and ironies in a text.

Evaluation

11. Do you think Dahl intends his characters and plot to be **credible**? Explain your answer.

Literary Criticism

12. Children, Dahl said,

> invariably pick out the most gruesome events as the favorite parts of [my] books. . . . They don't relate it to life. They enjoy the fantasy. And my nastiness is never gratuitous. It's retribution. Beastly people must be punished.

In your opinion, what does Dahl want us to think about Mary and the murder of her husband? How does he manage to make us react as we do?

Writing

Analyzing Character

What do you make of Mary's giggling at the end of the story? This ending is somewhat **ambiguous** and hard to interpret. On the one hand, you might think it shows a newly revealed, more sinister side to her nature. On the other hand, you might think it merely reflects her need for a small release from the great stress and strain of her recent experience. Perhaps you have yet another interpretation. Write a brief **character analysis** of Mary as she is depicted throughout the story. Be sure to explain what you think Mary's giggling at the end reveals about her.

326 Chapter 5 Irony and Ambiguity • Generating Research Questions and Evaluating Sources

Vocabulary Development

Using Context Clues

PRACTICE 1

Fill in the blanks below by using the **context clues** in each sentence and then choosing the Word Bank word that best fits each context.

Later in life, Roald Dahl complained that life at school was hardly calm and _______. Instead of discovering a pleasant atmosphere of _______, he lived in constant _______ over all the rules that had to be followed. He especially disliked the awful punishments that were ________ if any rules were broken. He couldn't even ______ in a chat in the dormitory—it was forbidden. When asked by his mother if he wanted to continue his education at university, he revealed his wish to leave the school's ________ and get a job far away—in China or Africa. He found his dream of future travel ______ during that difficult time.

Word Bank
- anxiety
- placid
- luxuriate
- administered
- premises
- consoling
- hospitality

PRACTICE 2

Now, identify the context clues in each sentence that helped you guess the correct missing word.

Grammar Link MINI-LESSON

Active or Passive Voice

Verbs that express action can be used in either the **active voice** or the **passive voice.**

ACTIVE Mary cooked the leg of lamb.
[The action is done *by* the subject, *Mary.*]

PASSIVE The leg of lamb was cooked.
[The action is done *to* the subject, *the leg of lamb.* The doer of the action is not even mentioned.]

For most kinds of writing, you are better off using the active voice, which is stronger and more direct. Use the passive voice only when you don't know the performer of the action or when you wish to conceal or give less emphasis to the performer.

PASSIVE According to the detective, Mr. Maloney was hit in the back of the head with a heavy object.
[The detective does not know who hit Mr. Maloney.]

PRACTICE

Rewrite the following paragraph so that all the verbs are in the active voice. (You may have to add new subjects for some sentences.)

Mary Maloney was told some shocking news by her husband. He was then killed by Mary with a frozen leg of lamb. The house was thoroughly searched, but nothing suspicious was found. Mary and the grocer were carefully questioned by detectives. The dreadful leg of lamb was cooked, and the murder weapon was eaten by the hungry detectives. The identity of the murderer was not guessed by the police. In fact, Mary was never suspected as the murderer.

► **For more help, see Active Voice and Passive Voice in the *Holt Handbook,* pages 199–203.**

Grade 8 Review Reading Standard 1.3 Use word meanings within the appropriate context and show ability to verify those meanings.

Vocabulary Development

Practice 1

placid, hospitality, anxiety, administered, luxuriate, premises, consoling

Practice 2

Possible Answers

- "a pleasant atmosphere" for *placid* and *hospitality*
- "Instead of discovering a pleasant atmosphere" and "all the rules that had to be followed" for *anxiety*
- "awful punishments were" for *administered*
- The words "couldn't even" and "forbidden" are clues for *luxuriate,* since readers know that Dahl would have enjoyed a chat.
- "his wish to leave the school's" for *premises*
- "his dream" and "difficult time" for *consoling*

Resources Reminder

Vocabulary

- *Vocabulary Development*
  - Vocabulary Worksheet, p. 26
- *Lesson Plans for Language Development*
  - Vocabulary, pp. 163, 168

ASSESSING

Assessment

- *Progress Assessment of Reading*
  - Selection Test

RETEACHING

For another selection to teach Standard 3.8, see *Interactive Reading,* Chapter 5.

Grammar Link

Practice

Possible Answer

Mary Maloney's husband told her some shocking news. Mary then killed him with a frozen leg of lamb. Police detectives thoroughly searched the house, but they found nothing suspicious. Detectives carefully questioned Mary and the grocer. Mary cooked the dreadful leg of lamb, and the hungry detectives ate the murder weapon. The police did not guess the identity of the murderer. In fact, they never suspected Mary as the murderer.

STANDARDS FOCUS, pp. 328–348

(For grade-level and review standards taught in this lesson, see citations on Student Edition pages.)

Prerequisite Standard

- Grade 8, Literary Response and Analysis 3.6 **Identify significant literary devices (e.g., metaphor, symbolism, dialect, irony) that define a writer's style and use those elements to interpret the works.**

Reading Skills

- Understand text structures.

Summary *at grade level*

In this thoroughly researched article, written for *Harper's Magazine* in 1934 (twenty-two years after the *Titanic* sank), Hanson W. Baldwin combines an objective exposition of the facts with skillful narrative techniques, including subjective language. This combination of storytelling and reporting highlights the dramatic and situational ironies of the great ship's untimely demise. The story begins as the *Titanic* sets sail for New York from Southampton, England, on Wednesday, April 10, 1912. On Sunday, the *Titanic* receives warnings of ice ahead, but they are ignored. Baldwin breaks off in midsentence to start his second section, which deals with the ship's collision and the terrible hours between impact and sinking. The third section relates the immediate aftermath of the sinking, including the eventual rescue of people in lifeboats. The fourth section tells how the world learned of the disaster, first through garbled wireless messages from the rescue ships and then from eyewitnesses after the 711 survivors arrived in New York. Baldwin's final section deals with official investigations into causes of the catastrophe.

Before You Read

R.M.S. Titanic

Literary Focus

Irony: It's Unexpected

The following account of the *Titanic*'s maiden voyage illustrates both **situational irony** (which occurs when what happens is the opposite of what we expect to happen or should happen) and **dramatic irony** (which occurs in literature when the reader knows something important that the characters do not know).

The passengers on the *Titanic,* including the great ship's builders and its financial backers, believed that they were on an unsinkable vessel. Their confidence, or arrogance, is one of the great ironies of twentieth-century history. Even the naming of the ship is ironic. The Titans were ancient Greek gods possessing enormous size and incredible strength. For eons they reigned supreme in the universe, according to Greek mythology. Perhaps those who named the ship had forgotten that even the Titans did not rule forever.

Grade 8 Review Reading Standard 2.7 Evaluate the structural patterns of text.

Reading Standard 3.8 Interpret and evaluate the impact of ironies in a text.

Objective and Subjective Writing

This account of the sinking of the *Titanic* may remind you of other disaster stories. When reporting on a catastrophe, different writers may begin with the same facts yet present the event in vastly differing ways.

In **objective writing** only the **facts** are included; the writer's views aren't revealed. Those facts, however, can be presented in an engaging and compelling manner. In **subjective writing** the writer adds his or her **opinions,** judgments, or feelings. As you read, determine Baldwin's approach. What stance does he strike immediately in his first paragraph?

Reading Skills

Understanding Text Structures

The sinking of the *Titanic* involved a complex series of actions occurring within a few hours. In writing his account of the disaster, Baldwin uses the **headings** I–V as **text structures** to organize and divide that complicated rush of events. Each numbered part covers a different stage in the tragedy. Another chronological text structure is the notation of time—as the minutes tick by in Part II. These reminders build suspense and help you keep stark track of the unfolding disaster.

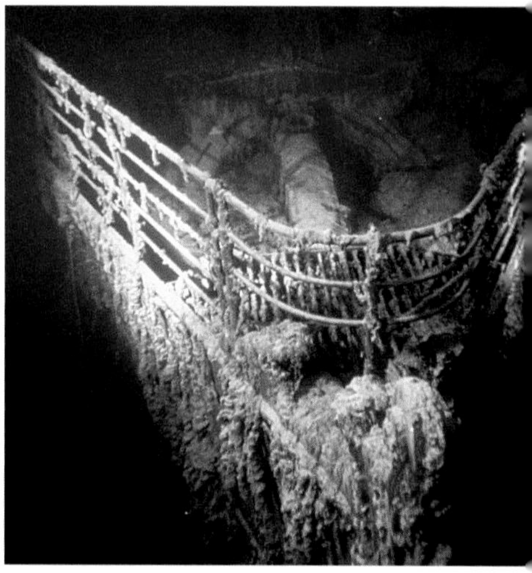

The *Titanic,* underwater 375 miles southeast of Newfoundland, in the summer of 1991.

RESOURCES: READING

Planning

- *One-Stop Planner* CD-ROM with Test Generator
- *On Course: Mapping Instruction*

Media

- *Audio CD Library*
  - disc 10
- *Visual Connections*
  - Videocassette, Segment 4

Reading

- *Interactive Reading,* Teacher's Edition
  - Graphic Organizer: Irony Chart

Differentiating Instruction

- *Lesson Plans for Language Development*
  - English-Language Learners, pp. 145–147, 164, 169

The *Titanic's* captain, E. J. Smith.

Make the Connection

Quickwrite

Choose any kind of disaster—a sinking ship, an earthquake, a raging tornado, a flood, an avalanche. Put yourself there. Write briefly about how you think you'd feel and what you'd do. Save your notes.

Background

The following article on the *Titanic* disaster was written by Hanson Baldwin in 1934. Baldwin's account was based on exhaustive factual research at the time, including a review of ship logs and other records as well as numerous interviews.

Since the publication of this landmark article, public fascination with the *Titanic* disaster has continued to grow, and more information has been revealed. For example, a pioneering underwater exploration of the wreck in 1986 was unable to find a three-hundred-foot gash in the ship, which Baldwin described. Instead, divers in a mini-submarine saw buckled seams and separated plates in the ship's hull, which are probably what caused the ship to flood and sink.

Vocabulary Development

superlative (sə·pʉr′lə·tiv) *adj.:* supreme; better than all others.

ascertain (as′ər·tān′) *v.:* find out with certainty; determine.

corroborated (kə·räb′ə·rāt′id) *v.:* supported; upheld the truth of.

quelled (kweld) *v.:* quieted; subdued.

poised (poizd) *v.* used as *adj.:* balanced; in position.

perfunctory (pər·fuŋk′tə·rē) *adj.:* not exerting much effort; unconcerned.

garbled (gär′bəld) *v.* used as *adj.:* confused; mixed up.

recriminations (ri·krim′ə·nā′shənz) *n.:* accusations against an accuser; countercharges.

pertinent (pʉrt′'n·ənt) *adj.:* having some connection with the subject.

vainly (vān′lē) *adv.:* without success; fruitlessly.

PRETEACHING

Standards Starter

Build background. To review the two types of irony found in this article, you may wish to ask students what they know about the *Titanic,* eliciting the fact that it sank on its first voyage. Explain that this knowledge is the basis of all dramatic ironies found in the article, since dramatic irony occurs when the reader knows something that the people involved do not. Then, review the definition of the term *situational irony:* a situation in which what actually happens is the opposite of what would be expected to happen.

Preview Vocabulary

Have students work in pairs to read the definitions of the Vocabulary words. Then, have volunteers write the following words in columns on the chalkboard. Ask students to match each word in the left column to its synonym in the right column.

1. superlative [c]	**a.** situated
2. ascertain [d]	**b.** subdued
3. corroborated [e]	**c.** unequaled
4. quelled [b]	**d.** determine
5. poised [a]	**e.** supported
6. perfunctory [f]	**f.** apathetic
7. garbled [g]	**g.** muddled
8. recriminations [j]	**h.** relevant
9. pertinent [h]	**i.** hopelessly
10. vainly [i]	**j.** blame

- Special Education Students, pp. 148, 164, 169

Vocabulary

- *Vocabulary Development*
  - Vocabulary Worksheet, p. 27

Assessment

- *Progress Assessment of Reading*
  - Selection Test
- *One-Stop Planner* CD-ROM with Test Generator

PRETEACHING

Assign the Reading

Homework

After students have read the Before You Read pages, suggest that they flip through the article and identify its main text structures. [Roman numeral headings, spacing between paragraphs, and references to times and dates] You might then assign those reading at and above grade level to read the article independently, perhaps beginning it in class and then continuing it as homework. Learners having difficulty might work in small groups to read and discuss one section of the article at a time.

To help prepare students for what they will read, point out that the events of the article occurred in 1912. At that time the radio and telegraph were the most advanced means of communication available to ships at sea, and the only way to get from Europe to America was by ship.

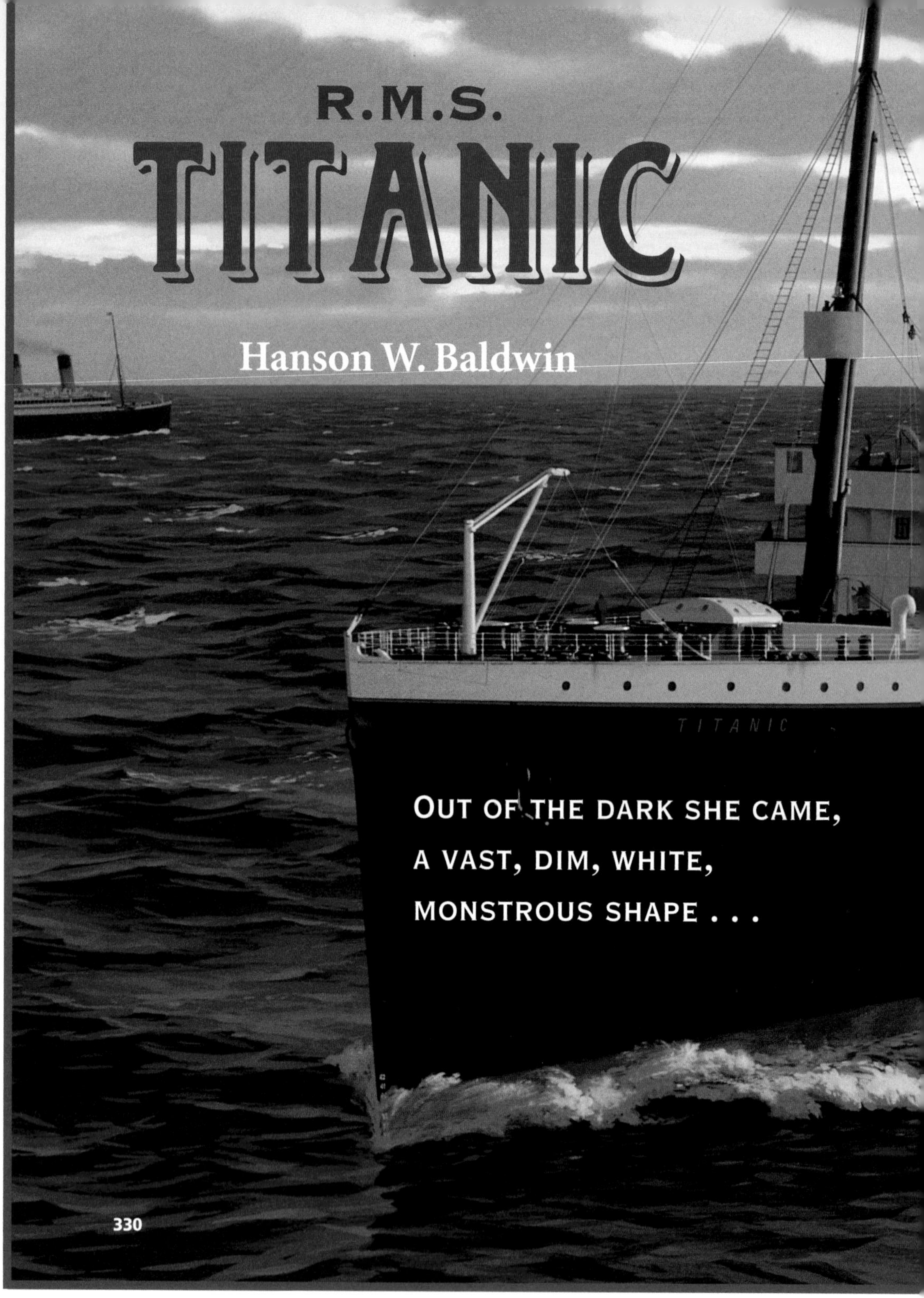

R.M.S. TITANIC

Hanson W. Baldwin

OUT OF THE DARK SHE CAME, A VAST, DIM, WHITE, MONSTROUS SHAPE . . .

330

DIFFERENTIATING INSTRUCTION

Learners Having Difficulty

Modeling. To help students read "R.M.S. Titanic," model the reading skill of using text structures. Say, "In this account the author uses certain text structures to organize information. First, he divides the article into five main sections that are identified with Roman numerals. Then to show a change in the action, he puts extra space between some paragraphs. Finally, he uses references to dates and time to help readers follow events." Point out examples of these structures, and encourage students as they read to use them to keep track of events.

English-Language Learners

In order for students to fully understand this story, they must be able to use context clues to guess the meanings of many unfamiliar words and phrases—some ship jargon, some archaisms. Before students begin reading, you may wish to sketch a ship on the chalkboard and label its parts: the bow, stern, hull, keel, deck, portholes, crow's-nest, funnels, and hold. Also, label the fore, aft, port, and starboard. Have students apply the terms to the illustration on pp. 330–331.

I

The White Star liner *Titanic,* largest ship the world had ever known, sailed from Southampton on her maiden voyage to New York on April 10, 1912. The paint on her strakes[1] was fair and bright; she was fresh from Harland and Wolff's Belfast yards, strong in the strength of her forty-six thousand tons of steel, bent, hammered, shaped, and riveted through the three years of her slow birth. **A** **B**

1. **strakes** *n.:* single lines of metal plating extending the whole length of a ship.

Direct Teaching

A Reading Skills

Understanding text structures. What text structure does Baldwin use to begin his article? [the Roman numeral heading I] **Based on these first two sentences, what do you predict this first section will be about?** [Possible responses: It may be about the first part of the *Titanic*'s first voyage. It may introduce the ship's design, crew, and passengers.]

B Literary Focus
GRADE-LEVEL STANDARD

Dramatic irony. In light of what students know about the fate of the *Titanic,* how does this description create dramatic irony? [Possible responses: Words such as *fair, bright, fresh,* and *strong* belie the disaster to come; readers know that the *Titanic* will turn out not to be so strong; its birth may have been slow, but readers know that the ship's death will be fast.]

Resources Reminder

For lessons designed for intermediate and advanced English-language learners, see *Lesson Plans for Language Development,* pp. 145–147, 164, 169.

Special Education Students

For lessons designed for special education students, see *Lesson Plans for Language Development,* pp. 148, 164, 169.

Advanced Learners

Acceleration. Use this activity to move advanced learners toward the eleventh- and twelfth-grade Standard 3.3, for which they analyze the use of irony to achieve specific rhetorical or aesthetic purposes or both.

Activity. After students have read the article, have them review it for instances of irony. Then, ask them to consider the following questions:

- How does the use of irony serve the author's purposes?
- What impact does irony have on the mood of a scene or on the reader's emotions?
- What impact does the use of irony have on the theme of the work?

You may wish to have students discuss these questions in small groups.

DIRECT TEACHING

A Vocabulary Development
GRADE-LEVEL STANDARD

Word origins: Greek mythology. Call on a volunteer to explain that the sister ships were both named for Greek gods. [*Titanic* is derived from the Titans, giant gods who once ruled the earth. *Olympic* comes from the Olympian gods, who lived on Mount Olympus and who overthrew the Titans.]

B Literary Focus
GRADE-LEVEL STANDARD

Dramatic irony. What irony do you see in this description? [Possible responses: The ship in fact turned out to be the least safe; it was more a deathtrap than a lifeboat.]

C Literary Focus
GRADE-LEVEL STANDARD

Dramatic irony. How does mentioning the "men, women, and children" aboard the ship create dramatic irony? [The reader knows the terrible fate awaiting so many of these men, women, and children, although they themselves do not.]

D Literary Focus
GRADE-LEVEL STANDARD

Dramatic irony. What is ironic about the immigrants being on their way to "the land of promise"? [Possible response: Readers know that their hopes of a better life will not be realized, as very few passengers in steerage will survive the disaster.]

E Reading Skills

Understanding text structures. How do the extra spaces between paragraphs (in two places on this page) help readers keep track of events? [Possible response: The first space indicates a change in location: The *Titanic* has left the dock and passed through the English Channel. The second indicates a gap in time: The narrative has jumped from Thursday night to Sunday morning.]

There was little fuss and fanfare at her sailing; her sister ship, the *Olympic*—slightly smaller than the *Titanic*—had been in service for some months and to her had gone the thunder of the cheers.

But the *Titanic* needed no whistling steamers or shouting crowds to call attention to her superlative qualities. Her bulk dwarfed the ships near her as longshoremen singled up her mooring lines and cast off the turns of heavy rope from the dock bollards.[2] She was not only the largest ship afloat, but was believed to be the safest. Carlisle, her builder, had given her double bottoms and had divided her hull into sixteen watertight compartments, which made her, men thought, unsinkable. She had been built to be and had been described as a gigantic lifeboat. Her designers' dreams of a triple-screw[3] giant, a luxurious, floating hotel, which could speed to New York at twenty-three knots, had been carefully translated from blueprints and mold loft lines at the Belfast yards into a living reality.

The *Titanic*'s sailing from Southampton, though quiet, was not wholly uneventful. As the liner moved slowly toward the end of her dock that April day, the surge of her passing sucked away from the quay[4] the steamer *New York,* moored just to seaward of the *Titanic*'s berth. There were sharp cracks as the manila mooring lines of the *New York* parted under the strain. The frayed ropes writhed and whistled through the air and snapped down among the waving crowd on the pier; the *New York* swung toward the *Titanic*'s bow, was checked and dragged back to the dock barely in time to avert a collision. Seamen muttered, thought it an ominous start.

Past Spithead and the Isle of Wight the *Titanic* steamed. She called at Cherbourg at dusk and then laid her course for Queenstown. At 1:30 P.M. on Thursday, April 11, she stood out of Queenstown harbor, screaming gulls soaring in her wake, with 2,201 persons—men, women, and children—aboard.

Occupying the Empire bedrooms and Georgian suites of the first-class accommodations were many well-known men and women—Colonel John Jacob Astor and his young bride; Major Archibald Butt, military aide to President Taft, and his friend Frank D. Millet, the painter; John B. Thayer, vice president of the Pennsylvania Railroad, and Charles M. Hays, president of the Grand Trunk Railway of Canada; W. T. Stead, the English journalist; Jacques Futrelle, French novelist; H. B. Harris, theatrical manager, and Mrs. Harris; Mr. and Mrs. Isidor Straus; and J. Bruce Ismay, chairman and managing director of the White Star Line.

Down in the plain wooden cabins of the steerage class were 706 immigrants to the land of promise, and trimly stowed in the great holds was a cargo valued at $420,000: oak beams, sponges, wine, calabashes,[5] and an odd miscellany of the common and the rare.

The *Titanic* took her departure on Fastnet Light[6] and, heading into the night, laid her course for New York. She was due at quarantine[7] the following Wednesday morning.

Sunday dawned fair and clear. The *Titanic* steamed smoothly toward the west, faint

2. **bollards** (bäl′ərdz) *n.:* strong posts on a pier or wharf for holding a ship's mooring ropes.
3. **triple-screw:** three-propellered.
4. **quay** (kē) *n.:* dock.
5. **calabashes** (kal′ə·bash′əz) *n.:* large smoking pipes made from the necks of gourds.
6. **Fastnet Light:** lighthouse at the southwestern tip of Ireland. After the Fastnet Light there is only open sea until the coast of North America.
7. **quarantine** (kwôr′ən·tēn) *n.:* place where a ship is held in port after arrival to determine whether its passengers and cargo are free of communicable diseases. *Quarantine* can also be used for the length of time a ship is held.

Vocabulary
superlative (sə·pʉr′lə·tiv) *adj.:* supreme; better than all others.

332 Chapter 5 Irony and Ambiguity • Generating Research Questions and Evaluating Sources

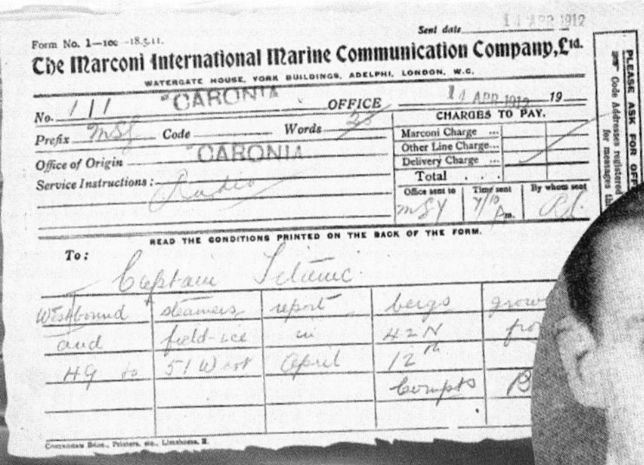
Form No. 1—100 —18.5.11.

Sent date 14 APR 1912

The Marconi International Marine Communication Company, Ltd.

WATERGATE HOUSE, YORK BUILDINGS, ADELPHI, LONDON, W.C.

No. 111 "CARONIA" OFFICE 14 APR 1912 19

Prefix MSG Code Words 23

Office of Origin "CARONIA"

Service Instructions: Radio

CHARGES TO PAY.

Marconi Charge

Other Line Charge

Delivery Charge

Total

Office sent to MGY | Time sent 7/10 pm | By whom sent

READ THE CONDITIONS PRINTED ON THE BACK OF THE FORM.

PLEASE ASK FOR OFFICIAL ... Code Addresses registered for messages ...

To: Captain Titanic

Westbound	steamers	report	bergs	grow[lers]
and	field-ice	in	42 N	fro[m]
49 to	51 West	April	12th	
			Compts	B[arr]

Message from the *Caronia*, warning of icebergs and tracts of floating ice.

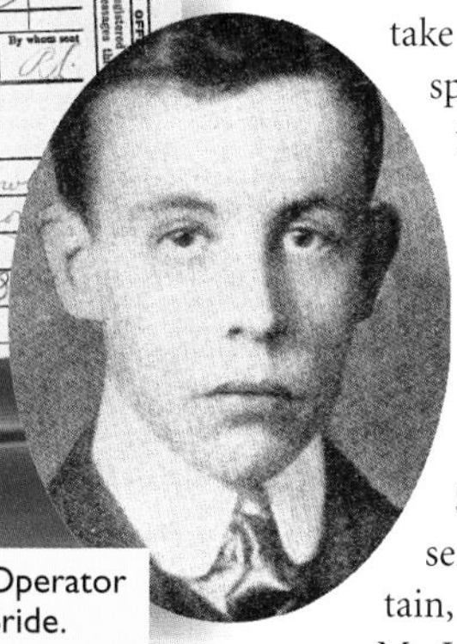

Second Operator Harold Bride.

streamers of brownish smoke trailing from her funnels. The purser held services in the saloon in the morning; on the steerage deck aft[8] the immigrants were playing games and a Scotsman was puffing "The Campbells Are Coming" on his bagpipes in the midst of the uproar.

At 9:00 A.M. a message from the steamer *Caronia* sputtered into the wireless shack:

> Captain, *Titanic*—Westbound steamers report bergs growlers and field ice 42 degrees N. from 49 degrees to 51 degrees W. 12th April.
> Compliments—Barr.

It was cold in the afternoon; the sun was brilliant, but the *Titanic,* her screws turning over at seventy-five revolutions per minute, was approaching the Banks.[9]

In the Marconi cabin[10] Second Operator Harold Bride, earphones clamped on his head, was figuring accounts; he did not stop to answer when he heard *MWL,* Continental Morse for the nearby Leyland liner, *Californian,* calling the *Titanic.* The *Californian* had some message about three icebergs; he didn't bother then to take it down. About 1:42 P.M. the rasping spark of those days spoke again across the water. It was the *Baltic,* calling the *Titanic,* warning her of ice on the steamer track. Bride took the message down and sent it up to the bridge.[11] The officer-of-the-deck glanced at it; sent it to the bearded master of the *Titanic,* Captain E. C. Smith,[12] a veteran of the White Star service. It was lunchtime then; the captain, walking along the promenade deck, saw Mr. Ismay, stopped, and handed him the message without comment. Ismay read it, stuffed it in his pocket, told two ladies about the icebergs, and resumed his walk. Later, about 7:15 P.M., the captain requested the return of the message in order to post it in the chart room for the information of officers.

Dinner that night in the Jacobean dining room was gay. It was bitter on deck, but the night was calm and fine; the sky was moonless but studded with stars twinkling coldly in the clear air.

After dinner some of the second-class passengers gathered in the saloon, where the Reverend Mr. Carter conducted a "hymn singsong." It was almost ten o'clock and the stewards were waiting with biscuits and coffee as the group sang:

> O, hear us when we cry to Thee
> For those in peril on the sea.

On the bridge Second Officer Lightoller—short, stocky, efficient—was relieved at ten o'clock by First Officer Murdoch. Lightoller had talked with other officers about the proximity of ice; at least five wireless ice warnings had

8. **aft** *adv.:* in the rear of a ship.
9. **Banks:** Grand Banks, shallow waters near the southeast coast of Newfoundland.
10. **Marconi cabin:** room where messages were received and sent by radio.
11. **bridge** *n.:* raised structure on a ship. The ship is controlled from the bridge.
12. Smith's initials were actually E. J., not E. C.

DIRECT TEACHING

F Learners Having Difficulty

Finding details. In which direction is the *Titanic* traveling? [west] What are westbound ships ahead of the *Titanic* seeing? [ice of various sorts] What action does the *Titanic's* crew take when they receive notice of the ice from other ships? [none] Why do you think none of these messages are heeded? [Possible responses: The captain and crew are complacent because the ship is considered "unsinkable." Some members of the crew are preoccupied.]

G Reading Skills

Paraphrasing. Baldwin uses the archaic phrase "rasping spark" to refer to wireless transmissions. Paraphrase this sentence in contemporary language. [Possible response: About 1:42 P.M., a radio message came through.]

H Literary Focus GRADE-LEVEL STANDARD

Dramatic irony. How does the group's choice of song create dramatic irony? [The group members do not suspect what the reader knows: Soon these people will be "in peril on the sea."]

I Literary Focus GRADE-LEVEL STANDARD

Situational irony. What might one reasonably expect the captain and officers to do in response to the repeated warnings about ice ahead? [Possible responses: alter course; reduce speed.] How is their actual response an example of situational irony? [Possible response: They do the opposite of what one might expect, holding the course at full speed.]

DIRECT TEACHING

A Reading Skills

Using text structures. Why do you think that Baldwin breaks off in midsentence and creates a major break at this point? [Possible responses: To build tension and suspense; to signal that this is where the waiting stops and the disaster begins; to emphasize the importance of the first sighting of the iceberg.]

B Literary Focus
GRADE-LEVEL STANDARD

Objective and subjective writing. This section opens with eerie sensory images: a sudden, looming, deadly shape and the chilling clang of alarm bells. What are the objective facts of the paragraph? [Fleet saw the iceberg and struck three bells. Then he called the bridge.] What words are emotionally charged? ["vast," "monstrous," "deadly," "ghastly thing," "frantically"] What does the subjective writing achieve? [Possible responses: It engages readers emotionally. It helps readers visualize the iceberg's impact on Fleet, the lookout.]

C English-Language Learners

Idioms. Point out that the main meaning of the phrase *dead ahead* is "straight ahead." Explain that in this context, the phrase has another, literal meaning that allows the phrase to foreshadow the death that will ensue after the ship hits the iceberg.

reached the ship; lookouts had been cautioned to be alert; captains and officers expected to reach the field at any time after 9:30 P.M. At twenty-two knots, its speed unslackened, the *Titanic* plowed on through the night.

Lightoller left the darkened bridge to his relief and turned in. Captain Smith went to his cabin. The steerage was long since quiet; in the first and second cabins lights were going out; voices were growing still; people were asleep. Murdoch paced back and forth on the bridge, peering out over the dark water, glancing now and then at the compass in front of Quartermaster Hichens at the wheel.

In the crow's-nest, lookout Frederick Fleet and his partner, Leigh, gazed down at the water, still and unruffled in the dim, starlit darkness. Behind and below them the ship, a white shadow with here and there a last winking light; ahead of them a dark and silent and cold ocean.

There was a sudden clang. "Dong-dong. Dong-dong. Dong-dong. Dong!" The metal clapper of the great ship's bell struck out 11:30. Mindful of the warnings, Fleet strained his eyes, searching the darkness for the dreaded ice. But there were only the stars and the sea.

In the wireless room, where Phillips, first operator, had relieved Bride, the buzz of the *Californian*'s set again crackled into the earphones:

Californian: "Say, old man, we are stuck here, surrounded by ice."

Titanic: "Shut up, shut up; keep out. I am talking to Cape Race; you are jamming my signals."

Then, a few minutes later—about 11:40 . . .

II

Out of the dark she came, a vast, dim, white, monstrous shape, directly in the *Titanic*'s path. For a moment Fleet doubted his eyes. But she was a deadly reality, this ghastly *thing*. Frantically, Fleet struck three bells—*something dead ahead.* He snatched the telephone and called the bridge:

"Iceberg! Right ahead!"

The first officer heard but did not stop to acknowledge the message.

"Hard-a-starboard!"

Hichens strained at the wheel; the bow swung slowly to port. The monster was almost upon them now.

Murdoch leaped to the engine-room telegraph. Bells clanged. Far below in the engine room those bells struck the first warning. Danger! The

Lookout Frederick Fleet.

First Operator Jack Phillips.

CONTENT-AREA CONNECTIONS

Geography: Mapping the Route
Show students a large wall map or globe to familiarize them with the general path of the *Titanic* and other transatlantic ships.
Paired activity. Have students use a map to trace the course of the *Titanic* from Southampton, England, to Cherbourg, France, to Queenstown (County Cork, Ireland) and across the north Atlantic toward the Grand Banks. Tell them to find 41°46' N, 50°14' W, the coordinates where the ship sank. Then, have them use the map's scale to calculate how far the ship had come and how far it still had to go before reaching New York.

History: Music of the Times
Popular music of this time period included ragtime, a lively type of music characterized by a strong syncopation in the melody.
Whole-class activity. You may wish to play recordings of Scott Joplin's works and other ragtime selections. ("Alexander's Ragtime Band" is one of the pieces that *Titanic* survivors recalled hearing.) Also, play recordings of the hymns mentioned in Baldwin's article: "Nearer My God to Thee,"

334 Chapter 5 Irony and Ambiguity • Generating Research Questions and Evaluating Sources

indicators on the dial faces swung round to "Stop!" Then "Full speed astern!" Frantically the engineers turned great valve wheels; answered the bridge bells . . .

There was a slight shock, a brief scraping, a small list to port. Shell ice—slabs and chunks of it—fell on the foredeck. Slowly the *Titanic* stopped.

Captain Smith hurried out of his cabin.

"What has the ship struck?"

Murdoch answered, "An iceberg, sir. I hard-a-starboarded and reversed the engines, and I was going to hard-a-port around it, but she was too close. I could not do any more. I have closed the watertight doors."

Fourth Officer Boxhall, other officers, the carpenter, came to the bridge. The captain sent Boxhall and the carpenter below to ascertain the damage.

A few lights switched on in the first and second cabins; sleepy passengers peered through porthole glass; some casually asked the stewards:

"Why have we stopped?"

"I don't know, sir, but I don't suppose it is anything much."

In the smoking room a quorum[13] of gamblers and their prey were still sitting round a poker table; the usual crowd of kibitzers[14] looked on. They had felt the slight jar of the collision and had seen an eighty-foot ice mountain glide by the smoking-room windows, but the night was calm and clear, the *Titanic* was "unsinkable"; they hadn't bothered to go on deck.

But far below, in the warren of passages on the starboard side forward, in the forward holds and boiler rooms, men could see that the *Titanic*'s hurt was mortal. In No. 6 boiler room, where the red glow from the furnaces lighted up the naked, sweaty chests of coal-blackened firemen, water was pouring through a great gash about two feet above the floor plates. This was no slow leak; the ship was open to the sea; in ten minutes there were eight feet of water in No. 6. Long before then the stokers had raked the flaming fires out of the furnaces and had scrambled through the watertight doors in No. 5 or had climbed up the long steel ladders to safety. When Boxhall looked at the mailroom in No. 3 hold, twenty-four feet above the keel, the mailbags were already floating about in the slushing water. In No. 5 boiler room a stream of water spurted into an empty bunker. All six compartments forward of No. 4 were open to the sea; in ten seconds the iceberg's jagged claw had ripped a three-hundred-foot slash in the bottom of the great *Titanic*.[15]

Reports came to the bridge; Ismay in dressing gown ran out on deck in the cold, still, starlit night, climbed up the bridge ladder.

"What has happened?"

Captain Smith: "We have struck ice."

"Do you think she is seriously damaged?"

Captain Smith: "I'm afraid she is."

Ismay went below and passed Chief Engineer William Bell, fresh from an inspection of the damaged compartments. Bell corroborated

13. **quorum** (kwôr′əm) *n.:* number of people required for a particular activity—in this case, for a game.
14. **kibitzers** (kib′it·sərz) *n.:* talkative onlookers who often give unwanted advice.

15. An underwater expedition to the *Titanic* wreck in 1986 led by the explorer Dr. Robert Ballard revealed loosened or buckled seams in the ship's hull but no three-hundred-foot gash. Ballard concluded that the collision of the ship with the iceberg caused the buckling of the seams and a separation of the hull's plates, which in turn allowed water to enter the ship and sink it. This theory explains why survivors said they barely felt the fatal collision when it occurred.

Vocabulary

ascertain (as′ər·tān′) *v.:* find out with certainty; determine.

corroborated (kə·räb′ə·rāt′id) *v.:* supported; upheld the truth of.

DIRECT TEACHING

D Literary Focus
GRADE-LEVEL STANDARD

Situational irony. This is the collision that sinks the *Titanic*. What irony do you find in the description? [Possible responses: One would expect the collision to be a great, shattering event. Instead, the words *slight, brief,* and *small* make it seem like a little scrape.]

E Reading Skills

Understanding text structures. Why is this brief passage set off? [to call attention to the moment that seals the ship's doom]

F Reading Skills

Analyzing. How do crew members and passengers respond to the collision? [calmly; complacently] What role do you think complacency has played so far in the disaster? [Possible responses: If the captain, officers, and radio operators hadn't been so complacent about iceberg warnings, the collision might not have happened; complacency led to carelessness, which caused the collision.]

G Literary Focus
GRADE-LEVEL STANDARD

Objective and subjective writing. With matter-of-fact exposition, Baldwin takes us step by step along the starboard side, describing the damage. With what subjective narrative technique does he end the paragraph? [He uses figurative language; he creates an implied metaphor comparing the iceberg to a monster whose "jagged claw" has slashed the ship.]

"Autumn," and "Eternal Father." Encourage students to analyze the mood created by each musical selection.

Science: The Radiotelegraph
Italian engineer Guglielmo Marconi (1874–1937) invented the radiotelegraph, or wireless telegraphy, in 1895; he won the 1909 Nobel Prize in physics for his work. The technology was still in its infancy in 1912, when the *Titanic* sank. Baldwin uses the now archaic phrases "Marconi cabin" and "Marconi men" to describe the radio room and the radio operators.

Small-group activity. Have small groups of students each choose a different form of wireless communication to research—from the radiotelegraph to present-day wireless devices. Have them report their findings to the class.

DIRECT TEACHING

A Literary Focus
GRADE-LEVEL STANDARD

Symbolism. As references to the blue spark of the radio call recur, the spark comes to symbolize something larger. Ask students to suggest what it may symbolize. [Possible responses: hope for rescue; life itself.] Suggest that students stay alert for references to the spark and notice how they relate to the probability of rescue and the hope for survival.

B Reading Skills

Speculating. Lifeboat drills were standard procedure; why do you suppose none were held on the *Titanic*? [Possible responses: No one thought they were needed since the ship was supposed to be unsinkable; maybe they had been postponed amid the fanfare of the first voyage.]

C Reading Skills

Understanding text structures. Call students' attention to the time notations that now open many paragraphs. How do these notations clarify the narrative for the reader? [Possible responses: They show the order of events; they show how quickly or slowly things happen.] Also call students' attention to the fact that Baldwin shifts from past to present tense, heightening the feeling of immediacy.

D Literary Focus
GRADE-LEVEL STANDARD

Situational irony. How is this event an example of situational irony? [Possible responses: One would expect the radio operator to stay on duty all night; one would expect the *Californian,* the nearest ship, to be of most help.]

the captain's statement; hurried back down the glistening steel ladders to his duty. Man after man followed him—Thomas Andrews, one of the ship's designers, Archie Frost, the builder's chief engineer, and his twenty assistants—men who had no posts of duty in the engine room but whose traditions called them there.

On deck, in corridor and stateroom, life flowed again. Men, women, and children awoke and questioned; orders were given to uncover the lifeboats; water rose into the firemen's quarters; half-dressed stokers streamed up on deck. But the passengers—most of them—did not know that the *Titanic* was sinking. The shock of the collision had been so slight that some were not awakened by it; the *Titanic* was so huge that she must be unsinkable; the night was too calm, too beautiful, to think of death at sea.

Captain Smith half ran to the door of the radio shack. Bride, partly dressed, eyes dulled with sleep, was standing behind Phillips, waiting.

"Send the call for assistance."

The blue spark danced: "CQD—CQD—CQD—CQ—"[16]

Miles away Marconi men heard. Cape Race heard it, and the steamships *La Provence* and *Mt. Temple.*

The sea was surging into the *Titanic*'s hold. At 12:20 the water burst into the seamen's quarters through a collapsed fore-and-aft wooden bulkhead. Pumps strained in the engine rooms—men and machinery making a futile fight against the sea. Steadily the water rose.

The boats were swung out—slowly, for the deckhands were late in reaching their stations; there had been no boat drill, and many of the crew did not know to what boats they were assigned. Orders were shouted; the safety valves had lifted, and steam was blowing off in a great rushing roar. In the chart house Fourth Officer Boxhall bent above a chart, working rapidly with pencil and dividers.

12:25 A.M. Boxhall's position is sent out to a fleet of vessels: "Come at once; we have struck a berg."

To the Cunarder *Carpathia* (Arthur Henry Rostron, Master, New York to Liverpool, fifty-eight miles away): "It's a CQD, old man. Position 41–46N.; 50–14 W."

The blue spark dancing: "Sinking; cannot hear for noise of steam."

12:30 A.M. The word is passed: "Women and children in the boats." Stewards finish waking their passengers below; life preservers are tied on; some men smile at the precaution. "The *Titanic* is unsinkable." The *Mt. Temple* starts for the *Titanic;* the *Carpathia,* with a double watch in her stokeholds, radios, "Coming hard." The CQD changes the course of many ships—but not of one; the operator of the *Californian,* nearby, has just put down his earphones and turned in.

The CQD flashes over land and sea from Cape Race to New York; newspaper city rooms leap to life and presses whir.

On the *Titanic,* water creeps over the bulkhead between Nos. 5 and 6 firerooms. She is going down by the head; the engineers—fighting a losing battle—are forced back foot by foot by the rising water. Down the promenade deck, Happy Jock Hume, the bandsman, runs with his instrument.

12:45 A.M. Murdoch, in charge on the starboard side, eyes tragic, but calm and cool, orders boat No. 7 lowered. The women hang back; they want no boat ride on an ice-strewn sea; the *Titanic* is unsinkable. The men encourage them, explain that this is just a precautionary measure: "We'll see you again at breakfast." There is little confusion; passengers stream slowly to the boat deck. In the steerage the immigrants chatter excitedly.

A sudden sharp hiss—a streaked flare against the night; Boxhall sends a rocket toward the sky. It explodes, and a parachute of white stars lights

16. **CQD:** call by radio operators, inviting others to communicate with them.

336 Chapter 5 Irony and Ambiguity • Generating Research Questions and Evaluating Sources

Molly Brown (nicknamed "unsinkable" by the Associated Press) helped row a lifeboat and nurse survivors.

Colonel John Jacob Astor, wealthy hotel owner, went down with the *Titanic*.

up the icy sea. "God! Rockets!" The band plays ragtime.

No. 8 is lowered, and No. 5. Ismay, still in dressing gown, calls for women and children, handles lines, stumbles in the way of an officer, is told to "get the hell out of here." Third Officer Pitman takes charge of No. 5; as he swings into the boat, Murdoch grasps his hand. "Goodbye and good luck, old man."

No. 6 goes over the side. There are only twenty-eight people in a lifeboat with a capacity of sixty-five.

A light stabs from the bridge; Boxhall is calling in Morse flashes, again and again, to a strange ship stopped in the ice jam five to ten miles away. Another rocket drops its shower of sparks above the ice-strewn sea and the dying ship.

1:00 A.M. Slowly the water creeps higher; the fore ports of the *Titanic* are dipping into the sea. Rope squeaks through blocks; lifeboats drop jerkily seaward. Through the shouting on the decks comes the sound of the band playing ragtime.

The "Millionaires' Special" leaves the ship—boat No. 1, with a capacity of forty people, carries only Sir Cosmo and Lady Duff Gordon and ten others. Aft, the frightened immigrants mill and jostle and rush for a boat. An officer's fist flies out; three shots are fired in the air, and the panic is quelled. . . . Four Chinese sneak unseen into a boat and hide in the bottom.

1:20 A.M. Water is coming into No. 4 boiler room. Stokers slice and shovel as water laps about their ankles—steam for the dynamos, steam for the dancing spark! As the water rises, great ash hoes rake the flaming coals from the furnaces. Safety valves pop; the stokers retreat aft, and the watertight doors clang shut behind them.

The rockets fling their splendor toward the stars. The boats are more heavily loaded now, for the passengers know the *Titanic* is sinking. Women cling and sob. The great screws aft are rising clear of the sea. Half-filled boats are ordered to come alongside the cargo ports and take on more passengers, but the ports are never opened—and the boats are never filled. Others pull for the steamer's light miles away but never reach it; the lights disappear; the unknown ship steams off.

The water rises and the band plays ragtime.

1:30 A.M. Lightoller is getting the port boats off; Murdoch, the starboard. As one boat is lowered into the sea, a boat officer fires his gun along

Vocabulary
quelled (kweld) *v.:* quieted; subdued.

DIRECT TEACHING

E Literary Focus GRADE-LEVEL STANDARD

Dramatic irony. What ironic details do you find in these paragraphs? [Possible responses: The women who want to avoid a "boat ride on an ice-strewn sea" don't know that drowning in an ice-strewn sea is the alternative; the breakfast that the men mention is far from the reality of what will come; the band plays breezy ragtime as if at a party, not a tragic disaster.]

F Reading Skills

Drawing conclusions. What would happen to the ship's radiotelegraph if the steam boilers stopped functioning? [Possible response: Apparently the radio runs on electricity from steam-driven dynamos; if the boilers stopped producing steam, the radio wouldn't work and the calls for help couldn't be sent.]

STANDARD REVIEW

Denotations and connotations. Remind students that when skilled writers of narrative choose a word, they consider its connotations—the emotions and associations that the word suggests. The connotations help to make character descriptions and action sequences compelling.

Activity. Ask students to take turns reading aloud narrative paragraphs on p. 337, from the "1:30 A.M." paragraph through the "2:00 A.M." paragraph on p. 339. As each paragraph is read, have listeners jot down the words whose emotional impact seems strongest. After the reading, have students share the words they have listed, discussing their connotations and their effects on the narrative.

DIRECT TEACHING

VIEWING THE ART

Point out that the illustration is photo-realistic, yet it also conveys the horror and tragedy of the *Titanic*'s sinking.

Activity. Discuss with students the artist's use of the following elements to convey emotion:

- Composition: The sinking ship takes up the majority of the illustration and even obscures much of the sky.
- Color: Somber shades suggest fear and sorrow. Small brighter areas on the ship and in the foreground highlight vulnerable-looking human forms in danger.
- Line: Angled lines of the ship and its rigging stand out grotesquely against the horizontal lines of the calm sea and the expanse of the placid sky, emphasizing the surreal quality of the disaster.

338 Chapter 5 Irony and Ambiguity • Generating Research Questions and Evaluating Sources

DEVELOPING FLUENCY

Mixed-ability group activity. The sections of the story that include dialogue are excellent portions for students to read aloud. Divide students into three or four groups, and have each group choose a passage of the story that includes dialogue. Have students take parts, including the role of narrator. Then, ask them to practice reading through the passage a number of times, experimenting with different volumes and tones of voice. Have the groups perform their excerpts for the class.

the ship's side to stop a rush from the lower decks. A woman tries to take her Great Dane into a boat with her; she is refused and steps out of the boat to die with her dog. Millet's "little smile which played on his lips all through the voyage" plays no more; his lips are grim, but he waves goodbye and brings wraps for the women.

Benjamin Guggenheim, in evening clothes, smiles and says, "We've dressed up in our best and are prepared to go down like gentlemen."

1:40 A.M. Boat 14 is clear, and then 13, 16, 15, and C. The lights still shine, but the *Baltic* hears the blue spark say, "Engine room getting flooded."

The *Olympia* signals, "Am lighting up all possible boilers as fast as can."

Major Butt helps women into the last boats and waves goodbye to them. Mrs. Straus puts her foot on the gunwale of a lifeboat; then she draws back and goes to her husband: "We have been together many years; where you go, I will go." Colonel John Jacob Astor puts his young wife in a lifeboat, steps back, taps cigarette on fingernail: "Goodbye, dearie; I'll join you later." **A**

1:45 A.M. The foredeck is under water; the fo'c'sle[17] head almost awash; the great stern is lifted high toward the bright stars; and still the band plays. Mr. and Mrs. Harris approach a lifeboat arm in arm.

Officer: "Ladies first, please."

Harris bows, smiles, steps back: "Of course, certainly; ladies first."

Boxhall fires the last rocket, then leaves in charge of boat No. 2.

2:00 A.M. She is dying now; her bow goes deeper, her stern higher. **B** But there must be steam. Below in the stokeholds the sweaty firemen keep steam up for the flaring lights and the dancing spark. The glowing coals slide and tumble over the slanted grate bars; the sea pounds behind that yielding bulkhead. But the spark dances on.

The *Asian* hears Phillips try the new signal—SOS.

Boat No. 4 has left now; boat D leaves ten minutes later. Jacques Futrelle clasps his wife: "For God's sake, go! It's your last chance; go!" Madame Futrelle is half forced into the boat. It clears the side.

---

17. **fo'c'sle** (fōk′səl) *n.:* forecastle, front upper deck of a ship.

DIRECT TEACHING

A Advanced Learners

Acceleration. Ask students to consider the implications of irony on the theme or main idea of the article. Explain that irony is important because it often adds a deeper level of meaning—it makes the reader pause and think about the nature of life and the turns that may be in store for us. Ask students what point about human nature Baldwin might be making here. [Possible response: Tragic situations can reveal people's true character. In the face of disaster, they can become courageous and altruistic, as Mrs. Straus and Colonel Astor demonstrate, or they can become brutal and devoid of compassion, as shown by the use of force to prevent steerage passengers from reaching the lifeboats.]

B Literary Focus

GRADE-LEVEL STANDARD

Objective and subjective writing. Have students identify the subjective and objective parts of this sentence. [*Subjective*—"She is dying." *Objective*—"her bow goes deeper, her stern higher."] Ask students to rewrite the first part of the sentence using objective language. [Possible response: The ship is sinking.]

STANDARD REVIEW

Analyzing cause and effect. Remind students that many events have multiple causes, which create multiple effects. In a complex event, such as the *Titanic* disaster, an incident can set off a cause-and-effect chain. A cause leads to an effect, which in turn becomes the cause of a new effect. For example, the gash in the hull causes water to pour in; the water floods boiler rooms and causes the ship's steam system to malfunction; the malfunctioning system causes a deafening roar of escaping steam, which obscures the crew's orders.

Activity. Have students re-read pp. 331–334 and list two long-term causes and two immediate causes of the collision.

Activity. Have students re-read Parts II and III and trace a cause-and-effect chain set in motion by any one incident.

Direct Teaching

A Reading Skills

Analyzing. Why do you suppose Baldwin abandons formal English here and uses the slang term "brains him"? [Possible responses: It shows that people are operating on instinct at this point; it's jarring, like the jarring actions that Baldwin describes.]

B Reading Skills

Interpreting. In the face of disaster, some people are carrying on with their activities: Gentlemen are exercising in the gym; mail clerks are trying to save the mail; band members are playing. How would you interpret the motives of the people who are behaving this way? [Possible responses: Some people may still expect to be rescued, while others may have given up hope of rescue. Some may be denying the reality of the situation, and some may be trying to distract themselves. The band members may be playing to help give other people spiritual comfort.]

C Reading Skills

Comparing and contrasting. Ask students to discuss why this man's retort is so different from the "women and children first" attitude that people maintained earlier. [Possible response: People are more desperate now that they know the ship will sink and death in the icy water is imminent.]

D Reading Skills

Understanding text structures. How long has it been since the *Titanic* hit the iceberg? Scan the time notations on pp. 334–341 to find out. [A little more than two and a half hours have elapsed.]

There are about 660 people in the boats and 1,500 still on the sinking *Titanic.*

On top of the officers' quarters, men work frantically to get the two collapsibles stowed there over the side. Water is over the forward part of A deck now; it surges up the companionways toward the boat deck. In the radio shack, Bride has slipped a coat and life jacket about Phillips as the first operator sits hunched over his key, sending—still sending—"41–46 N.; 50–14 W. CQD—CQD—SOS—SOS—"

The captain's tired white face appears at the radio-room door. "Men, you have done your full duty. You can do no more. Now, it's every man for himself." The captain disappears—back to his sinking bridge, where Painter, his personal steward, stands quietly waiting for orders. The spark dances on. Bride turns his back and goes into the inner cabin. As he does so, a stoker, grimed with coal, mad with fear, steals into the shack and reaches for the life jacket on Phillips's back. Bride wheels about and brains him with a wrench.

2:10 A.M. Below decks the steam is still holding, though the pressure is falling—rapidly. In the gymnasium on the boat deck, the athletic instructor watches quietly as two gentlemen ride the bicycles and another swings casually at the punching bag. Mail clerks stagger up the boat-deck stairways, dragging soaked mail sacks. The spark still dances. The band still plays—but not ragtime:

> Nearer my God to Thee.
> Nearer to Thee . . .

A few men take up the refrain; others kneel on the slanting decks to pray. Many run and scramble aft, where hundreds are clinging above the silent screws on the great uptilted stern. The spark still dances and the lights still flare; the engineers are on the job. The hymn comes to its close. Bandmaster Hartley, Yorkshireman violinist, taps his bow against a bulkhead, calls for "Autumn" as the water curls about his feet, and the eight musicians brace themselves against the ship's slant. People are leaping from the decks into the nearby water—the icy water. A woman cries, "Oh, save me, save me!" A man answers, "Good lady, save yourself. Only God can save you now." The band plays "Autumn":

> God of Mercy and Compassion!
> Look with pity on my pain . . .

The water creeps over the bridge where the *Titanic*'s master stands; heavily he steps out to meet it.

2:17 A.M. "CQ—" The *Virginian* hears a ragged, blurred CQ, then an abrupt stop. The blue spark dances no more. The lights flicker out; the engineers have lost their battle.

2:18 A.M. Men run about blackened decks; leap into the night; are swept into the sea by the curling wave that licks up the *Titanic*'s length. Lightoller does not leave the ship; the ship leaves him; there are hundreds like him, but only a few who live to tell of it. The funnels still swim above the water, but the ship is climbing to the perpendicular; the bridge is under and most of the foremast; the great stern rises like a squat leviathan.[18] Men swim away from the sinking ship; others drop from the stern.

The band plays in the darkness, the water lapping upward:

> Hold me up in mighty waters,
> Keep my eyes on things above,
> Righteousness, divine atonement,
> Peace and everlas . . .

The forward funnel snaps and crashes into the sea; its steel tons hammer out of existence swimmers struggling in the freezing water. Streams of sparks, of smoke and steam, burst from the after funnels. The ship upends to 50—to 60 degrees.

18. **leviathan** (lə·vī′ə·thən) *n.:* biblical sea monster, perhaps a whale.

Content-Area Connections

Science: Hypothermia

As students begin Part III, explain that the water temperature at the site of the sinking of the *Titanic* was about thirty degrees Fahrenheit, a temperature at which the human body quickly ceases to function.

Whole-class activity. Use ice cubes and salt to reduce a container of water to a temperature of thirty degrees Fahrenheit. Then, allow volunteers to place their hands briefly in the container and to describe the initial shock of the water and the sensation of growing numbness. Some students may wish to follow up on this experience by researching the physiological damage caused by hypothermia.

340 Chapter 5 Irony and Ambiguity • Generating Research Questions and Evaluating Sources

Down in the black abyss of the stokeholds, of the engine rooms, where the dynamos have whirred at long last to a stop, the stokers and the engineers are reeling against the hot metal, the rising water clutching at their knees. The boilers, the engine cylinders, rip from their bed plates; crash through bulkheads; rumble—steel against steel.

The *Titanic* stands on end, poised briefly for the plunge. Slowly she slides to her grave—slowly at first, and then more quickly—quickly—quickly.

2:20 A.M. The greatest ship in the world has sunk. From the calm, dark waters, where the floating lifeboats move, there goes up, in the white wake of her passing, "one long continuous moan."

III

The boats that the *Titanic* had launched pulled safely away from the slight suction of the sinking ship, pulled away from the screams that came from the lips of the freezing men and women in the water. The boats were poorly manned and badly equipped, and they had been unevenly loaded. Some carried so few seamen that women bent to the oars. Mrs. Astor tugged at an oar handle; the Countess of Rothes took a tiller. Shivering stokers in sweaty, coal-blackened singlets and light trousers steered in some boats; stewards in white coats rowed in others. Ismay was in the last boat that left the ship from the starboard side; with Mr. Carter of Philadelphia and two seamen he tugged at the oars. In one of the lifeboats an Italian with a broken wrist—disguised in a woman's shawl and hat—huddled on the floorboards, ashamed now that fear had left him. In another rode the only baggage saved from the *Titanic*—the carryall of Samuel L. Goldenberg, one of the rescued passengers.

There were only a few boats that were heavily loaded; most of those that were half empty made but perfunctory efforts to pick up the moaning swimmers, their officers and crew fearing they would endanger the living if they pulled back into the midst of the dying. Some boats beat off the freezing victims; fear-crazed men and women struck with oars at the heads of swimmers. One woman drove her fist into the face of a half-dead man as he tried feebly to climb over the gunwale. Two other women helped him in and staunched the flow of blood from the ring cuts on his face.

One of the collapsible boats, which had floated off the top of the officers' quarters when the *Titanic* sank, was an icy haven for thirty or forty men. The boat had capsized as the ship sank; men swam to it, clung to it, climbed upon its slippery bottom, stood knee-deep in water in the freezing air. Chunks of ice swirled about their legs; their soaked clothing clutched their bodies in icy folds. Colonel Archibald Gracie was cast up there, Gracie who had leaped from the stern as the *Titanic* sank; young Thayer who had seen his father die; Lightoller who had twice been sucked down with the ship and twice blown to the surface by a belch of air; Bride, the second operator, and Phillips, the first. There were many stokers, half naked; it was a shivering company. They stood there in the icy sea, under the far stars, and sang and prayed—the Lord's Prayer. After a while a lifeboat came and picked them off, but Phillips was dead then or died soon afterward in the boat.

Only a few of the boats had lights; only one—No. 2—had a light that was of any use to the *Carpathia,* twisting through the ice field to the rescue. Other ships were "coming hard" too; one, the *Californian,* was still dead to opportunity.

Vocabulary

poised (pɔizd) *v.* used as *adj.:* balanced; in position.

perfunctory (pər·fuŋk′tə·rē) *adj.:* not exerting much effort; unconcerned.

DIRECT TEACHING

E Reading Skills

Understanding text structures. Why do you suppose Baldwin chooses this point to end his second major section and begin his third? [Possible response: Tension and horror peaked with the sinking; now Baldwin shifts his focus to the aftermath of the disaster.]

F Correcting Misconceptions

Writers usually are encouraged to be consistent in their use of verb tenses, but Baldwin bends the rules to great effect. He switches to the present tense as he chronicles the *Titanic*'s end; doing so increases the urgency of those final two hours. Now, as the account's falling action begins, he returns to the less-urgent past tense.

G Literary Focus
GRADE-LEVEL STANDARD

Subjective and objective writing. Which parts of this paragraph seem objective (fact based) and which seem subjective (emotion based)? [Possible responses: Facts about people's actions and about how full the boats were are objective; emotion-laden modifiers, such as "perfunctory," "moaning," "fear-crazed," "half-dead," and "feebly," give the paragraph a subjective cast.]

Science: Icebergs

The article may spark students' interest in learning more about icebergs.

Small-group activity. Invite students to prepare and present oral reports about icebergs. Among the questions they might consider in relation to "R.M.S. Titanic" are the following items:

- How do icebergs form?
- How far south might the *Titanic* have had to sail to avoid icebergs in mid-April?
- How can an iceberg rip through tons of steel?
- How do ships deal with the threat of icebergs today?

DIRECT TEACHING

A Literary Focus
GRADE-LEVEL STANDARD

Symbolism. The image of the dancing blue spark recurs here, although the *Titanic* has gone down. Do you think the spark still suggests hope? [Possible responses: No, because the *Titanic* has sunk; yes, because other ships are still trying to come to the rescue.]

B Learners Having Difficulty

Monitoring students' progress. Make sure students understand that the "moaning cries" were from the people in the water who had hoped for rescue. The fact that their cries have died means that they too have died. The only survivors are those lucky enough to have gotten into a lifeboat.

C Reading Skills

Understanding text structures. Part III deals with the rescue of the survivors. What does it appear that Part IV will deal with? [Possible response: It will deal with what happens to the survivors and how the world learns of the disaster.]

D Reading Skills

Understanding text structures. What does this paragraph indicate that the fifth and final section of Baldwin's article will cover? [It will cover investigations into the disaster and deciding who was to blame.]

A The blue sparks still danced, but not the *Titanic*'s. *La Provence* to *Celtic:* "Nobody has heard the *Titanic* for about two hours."

It was 2:40 when the *Carpathia* first sighted the green light from No. 2 boat; it was 4:10 when she picked up the first boat and learned that the **B** *Titanic* had foundered.[19] The last of the moaning cries had just died away then.

Captain Rostron took the survivors aboard, boatload by boatload. He was ready for them, but only a small minority of them required much medical attention. Bride's feet were twisted and frozen; others were suffering from exposure; one died, and seven were dead when taken from the boats, and were buried at sea.

It was then that the fleet of racing ships learned they were too late; the *Parisian* heard the weak signals of *MPA,* the *Carpathia,* report the death of the *Titanic.* It was then—or soon afterward, when her radio operator put on his earphones—that the *Californian,* the ship that had been within sight as the *Titanic* was sinking, first learned of the disaster.

And it was then, in all its white-green majesty, that the *Titanic*'s survivors saw the iceberg, tinted with the sunrise, floating idly, pack ice jammed about its base, other bergs heaving slowly nearby on the blue breast of the sea.

IV

C But it was not until later that the world knew, for wireless then was not what wireless is today, and garbled messages had nourished a hope that all of the *Titanic*'s company were safe. Not until Monday evening, when P.A.S. Franklin, vice president of the International Mercantile Marine Company, received relayed messages in New York that left little hope, did the full extent of the disaster begin to be known. Partial and garbled lists of the survivors; rumors of heroism and cowardice; stories spun out of newspaper imagination, based on a few bare facts and many false reports, misled the world, terrified and frightened it. It was not until Thursday night, when the *Carpathia* steamed into the North River, that the full truth was pieced together.

Flashlights flared on the black river when the *Carpathia* stood up to her dock. Tugs nosed about her, shunted her toward Pier 54. Thirty thousand people jammed the streets; ambulances and stretchers stood on the pier; coroners and physicians waited.

In midstream the Cunarder dropped over the *Titanic*'s lifeboats; then she headed toward the dock. Beneath the customs letters on the pier stood relatives of the 711 survivors, relatives of the missing—hoping against hope. The *Carpathia* cast her lines ashore; stevedores[20] looped them over bollards. The dense throngs stood quiet as the first survivor stepped down the gangway. The woman half staggered—led by customs guards—beneath her letter. A "low wailing" moan came from the crowd; fell, grew in volume, and dropped again.

Thus ended the maiden voyage of the *Titanic.* The lifeboats brought to New York by the *Carpathia,* a few deck chairs and gratings awash in the ice field off the Grand Bank eight hundred miles from shore, were all that was left of the world's greatest ship.

V

D The aftermath of weeping and regret, of recriminations and investigations, dragged

19. **foundered** *v.:* filled with water, so that it sank; generally, collapsed; failed.

20. **stevedores** (stē′və·dôrz′) *n.:* persons who load and unload ships.

Vocabulary

garbled (gär′bəld) *v.* used as *adj.:* confused; mixed up.

recriminations (ri·krim′ə·nā′shənz) *n.:* accusations against an accuser; countercharges.

342 Chapter 5 Irony and Ambiguity • Generating Research Questions and Evaluating Sources

on for weeks. Charges and countercharges were hurled about; the White Star Line was bitterly criticized; Ismay was denounced on the floor of the Senate as a coward but was defended by those who had been with him on the sinking *Titanic* and by the Board of Trade investigation in England.

It was not until weeks later, when the hastily convened Senate investigation in the United States and the Board of Trade report in England had been completed, that the whole story was told. The Senate investigating committee, under the chairmanship of Senator Smith, who was attacked in both the American and the British press as a "backwoods politician," brought out numerous pertinent facts, though its proceedings verged at times on the farcical.[21] Senator Smith was ridiculed for his lack of knowledge of the sea when he asked witnesses, "Of what is an iceberg composed?" and "Did any of the passengers take refuge in the watertight compartments?" The senator seemed particularly interested in the marital status of Fleet, the lookout, who was saved. Fleet, puzzled, growled aside, "Wot questions they're arskin' me!" **E**

The report of Lord Mersey, wreck commissioner in the British Board of Trade's investigation, was tersely damning.

F The *Titanic* had carried boats enough for 1,178 persons, only one third of her capacity. Her sixteen boats and four collapsibles had saved but 711 persons; 400 people had needlessly lost their lives. The boats had been but partly loaded; officers in charge of launching them had been afraid the falls[22] would break or the boats buckle under their rated loads; boat crews had been slow in reaching their stations; launching arrangements were confused because no boat drill had been held; passengers were loaded into the boats haphazardly because no boat assignments had been made.

G But that was not all. Lord Mersey found that sufficient warnings of ice on the steamer track had reached the *Titanic,* that her speed of twenty-two knots was "excessive under the circumstances," that "in view of the high speed at which the vessel was running it is not considered that the lookout was sufficient," and that her master made "a very grievous mistake"—but should not be blamed for negligence. Captain Rostron of the *Carpathia* was highly praised. **H** "He did the very best that could be done." The *Californian* was damned. The testimony of her master, officers, and crew showed that she was not, at the most, more than nineteen miles away from the sinking *Titanic* and probably no more than five to ten miles distant. She had seen the *Titanic*'s lights; she had seen the rockets; she had not received the CQD calls because her radio operator was asleep. She had attempted to get in communication with the ship she had sighted by flashing a light, but vainly.

"The night was clear," reported Lord Mersey, "and the sea was smooth. When she first saw the rockets, the *Californian* could have pushed through the ice to the open water without any serious risk and so have come to the assistance of the *Titanic.* Had she done so she might have saved many if not all of the lives that were lost.

"She made no attempt." ■

21. **farcical** (fär′si·kəl) *adj.:* absurd; ridiculous; like a farce (an exaggerated comedy).
22. **falls** *n.:* chains used for hoisting.

Vocabulary

pertinent (purt′'n·ənt) *adj.:* having some connection with the subject.

vainly (vān′lē) *adv.:* without success; fruitlessly.

DIRECT TEACHING

E English-Language Learners

Dialect. Students may be puzzled by the dialogue of Fleet, the lookout. Explain that he is British and that these words are an attempt to reproduce the sound of his cockney accent. Ask students to try to figure out what his words would be in standard English. ["What questions they're asking me!"]

F Literary Focus
GRADE-LEVEL STANDARD

Objective and subjective writing. Ask students to determine whether this paragraph includes only factual information or reveals the writer's opinions and feelings. [The paragraph is factual and objective.] Then, have students comment on why Baldwin may have chosen to provide this information objectively. [Possible responses: The factual evidence is damning enough without the author's needing to inject his personal opinions. Giving readers the facts and letting them draw their own conclusions makes the evidence more stark and powerful.]

G Literary Focus
GRADE-LEVEL STANDARD

? Objective and subjective writing. In what way is this paragraph objective? subjective? [Possible responses: It's objective in its statistics and its detailed list of causes; it's subjective in that the cumulative effect of the list creates a feeling of horror at the needless loss of life.]

H Reading Skills

? Expressing an opinion.

Do you consider Lord Mersey's condemnation of the *Californian* objective or subjective? [Possible responses: Objective, because Mersey cites facts; subjective, because the facts are mixed with speculation.]

FAMILY/COMMUNITY ACTIVITY

This account of the sinking of the *Titanic* will remind different people of different disasters they have experienced directly or indirectly. Encourage students to seek out and interview members of their family or community about the disaster story that is clearest in their memory. Invite students to tell the class about one of their interviewees' memories of a disaster and how it affected him or her. Remind students to get permission from interviewees before relating their stories.

GUIDED PRACTICE

Monitoring students' progress. Guide the class in answering these comprehension questions. Direct students to locate passages in the text that support their responses.

Short Answer

1. Why was the *Titanic* considered unsinkable? [It had a double bottom and sixteen watertight compartments.]
2. Did the appearance of ice surprise the *Titanic*'s captain and crew? [No; several nearby ships had radioed warnings of ice.]
3. Why was it especially unfortunate that the *Californian* did not respond to the *Titanic*'s distress calls? [The *Californian* was the ship nearest to the *Titanic*.]
4. After the collision, why were some passengers unaware that the ship was sinking? [Possible responses: They were asleep, and the shock of the collision was so slight that they were not awakened; the sinking was gradual.]
5. List two criticisms of the *Titanic* in the investigators' report. [Possible responses: excessive speed in dangerous waters; too few lookouts; too few lifeboats; no lifeboat drills; haphazard loading and manning of lifeboats.]

Meet the Writer

Background. In a letter to Baldwin, Karl Baarslag, a radio operator and fellow student of the *Titanic*, wrote: "Evans [of the *Californian*], in my opinion is the world's most unfortunate radio operator in that he might have saved 2,200 lives had he stayed up fifteen minutes longer. . . . [He] had been up and continuously on duty from 7 A.M. until 11:20 P.M., long past the usual time for him to go off watch. His ship was stopped by ice for the night; the crew, except for a few on watch, were turned in, and there was no reason for him to continue on any longer. Even a $20 a month radioman is entitled to some sleep."

Meet the Writer

Hanson W. Baldwin

Journalist and Seaman

Hanson W. Baldwin (1903–1991) was one of America's great journalists. He graduated with an ensign's commission from the U.S. Naval Academy at Annapolis. After only three years of service aboard battleships, Baldwin resigned from the Navy and launched a career as a military correspondent and editor. His longest hitch was with *The New York Times.*

During World War II Baldwin covered battles in North Africa and the D-day invasion of Normandy. His series of articles on the war in the South Pacific won him a Pulitzer Prize in 1943. After the war, he reported on the second atomic bomb test at Bikini Island, on guided-missile and rocket-firing installations, and on the organization of U.S. military forces in the nuclear age.

Relatively early in his writing career (1934), Baldwin wrote an article for *Harper's Magazine* about the sinking of the *Titanic,* which had occurred twenty-two years earlier. His research was thorough: He pieced together information from ship logs, from interviews with survivors, and from written reports detailing the ship's design and launching. The subject of the *Titanic* was by no means new for Baldwin's readers. The sinking of the "unsinkable" ship had been fictionalized, sensationalized, and sentimentalized many times before 1934. Nevertheless, Baldwin's article became a textbook example of excellent reporting. His fast-paced account, with its mixture of factual details and irony, makes the disaster and all the human foibles associated with it seem tragically real again.

DIFFERENTIATING INSTRUCTION

Advanced Learners

Enrichment. In 1912, when the *Titanic* sank, William Howard Taft was president; ragtime was a hot craze in music; the radio (called "the wireless") and telegraph were high tech; steam still powered most engines; and ships were the only means of travel between Europe and America. This was all recent history when Baldwin wrote his article, yet all had changed by the time he died in 1991.

Activity. Have students research on the Internet one aspect of life and how it changed during Baldwin's lifetime. Suggest that they enter *telegraph, steam engine,* or *ragtime* as keywords in a search engine. After researching the topic, students may then report to the class.

The lifeboats of the "unsinkable" Titanic *carried fewer than one third of the approximately 2,200 people aboard. A U.S. Senate investigating committee in 1912 found that a total of 1,517 lives were lost—a high proportion of them poor passengers who were far below deck, in steerage. Here are two eyewitness accounts of survivors:*

J. Bruce Ismay, director of the White Star Line.

A Fireman's Story

Harry Senior

Mrs. J. Bruce Ismay.

I was in my bunk when I felt a bump. One man said, "Hello. She has been struck." I went on deck and saw a great pile of ice on the well deck before the forecastle, but we all thought the ship would last some time, and we went back to our bunks. Then one of the firemen came running down and yelled, "All muster for the lifeboats." I ran on deck, and the captain said, "All firemen keep down on the well deck. If a man comes up, I'll shoot him."

Then I saw the first lifeboat lowered. Thirteen people were on board, eleven men and two women. Three were millionaires, and one was Ismay [J. Bruce Ismay, managing director of the White Star Line; a survivor].

Then I ran up onto the hurricane deck and helped to throw one of the collapsible boats onto the lower deck. I saw an Italian woman holding two babies. I took one of them and made the woman jump overboard with the baby, while I did the same with the other. When I came to the surface, the baby in my arms was dead. I saw the woman strike out in good style, but a boiler burst on the *Titanic* and started a big wave. When the woman saw that wave, she gave up. Then, as the child was dead, I let it sink too.

I swam around for about half an hour, and was swimming on my back when the *Titanic* went down. I tried to get aboard a boat, but some chap hit me over the head with an oar. There were too many in her. I got around to the other side of the boat and climbed in.

"The *Titanic* orphans"—Edmond (age two) and Michel (age three) Navratil.

Connection

Summary at grade level

This feature provides two eyewitness accounts of the sinking of the *Titanic*—the first by a fireman who jumped into the water and narrowly survived and the second by a woman in a lifeboat who saw the *Titanic* sink.

DIRECT TEACHING

A Learners Having Difficulty

Using context clues. From clues in this paragraph and from your reading of "R.M.S. Titanic," what do you think *fireman* means in this context? [Possible responses: someone who works with the ship's engines or furnaces; someone who stokes the engine.]

B Literary Focus
GRADE-LEVEL STANDARD

Objective and subjective writing. How would you evaluate the first paragraph of this eyewitness account? Is it objective or subjective? [The description is clear, detailed, and even in tone, telling exactly what Senior saw and heard. It is objective.]

C Reading Skills

Comparing and contrasting. Do you notice any details that conflict with Baldwin's report? [Possible response: Baldwin states that there were only twelve people in the first lifeboat and that Ismay left the *Titanic* later in another lifeboat.] **Whose account are you inclined to believe?** [Possible responses: Senior's, because he was there and saw it; Baldwin's, because he probably has more than one source to back up his statements.]

R.M.S. Titanic 345

DIRECT TEACHING

A Reading Skills

Understanding text structures. To Mrs. Bishop, it seemed that she watched from a distance for "a couple of hours" before the *Titanic* sank. According to Baldwin, how much time actually went by between the launching of the first lifeboat and the sinking of the *Titanic*? Scan the time notations in Part II to find out. [about an hour and a half]

B Reading Skills

Drawing conclusions. From what you know about Mrs. Bishop and where she was as the ship sank, what can you conclude about her socioeconomic class? [Possible response: She was probably of the upper classes because she was in one of the first lifeboats and could report the ship sinking from a mile away. Also, her characterization of the "great black mass of people in the steerage" echoes the cliché of "the great unwashed masses" and suggests that Mrs. Bishop considers steerage passengers beneath her.]

C Reading Skills

Comparing and contrasting. What details in Mrs. Bishop's account are similar to details Baldwin used in his article? [Possible responses: the gradual slanting down of the bow; the eventual acceleration of the tilt; the rush of the passengers to the stern; the almost perpendicular position of the ship before it sank] How does information at the beginning of the second to last paragraph differ from information provided by Baldwin on p. 340? [Possible responses: Baldwin says that the *Titanic*'s light went out several minutes before it sank; Mrs. Bishop says, "The lights continued to burn till it sank."]

From a Lifeboat

Mrs. D. H. Bishop

Ruth Becker and her brother Richard survived in separate lifeboats.

We did not begin to understand the situation till we were perhaps a mile or more away from the *Titanic.* Then we could see the rows of lights along the decks begin to slant gradually upward from the bow. Very slowly, the lines of light began to point downward at a greater and greater angle. The sinking was so slow that you could not perceive the lights of the deck changing their position. The slant seemed to be greater about every quarter of an hour. That was the only difference.

In a couple of hours, though, she began to go down more rapidly. Then the fearful sight began. The people in the ship were just beginning to realize how great their danger was. When the forward part of the ship dropped suddenly at a faster rate, so that the upward slope became marked, there was a sudden rush of passengers on all the decks toward the stern. It was like a wave. We could see the great black mass of people in the steerage sweeping to the rear part of the boat and breaking through into the upper decks. At the distance of about a mile, we could distinguish everything through the night, which was perfectly clear. We could make out the increasing excitement on board the boat as the people, rushing to and fro, caused the deck lights to disappear and reappear as they passed in front of them.

Marion Wright from Somerset, England, married her fiancé when she arrived in New York City.

This panic went on, it seemed, for an hour. Then suddenly the ship seemed to shoot up out of the water and stand there perpendicularly. It seemed to us that it stood upright in the water for four full minutes.

Then it began to slide gently downward. Its speed increased as it went down headfirst, so that the stern shot down with a rush.

The lights continued to burn till it sank. We could see the people packed densely in the stern till it was gone. . . .

As the ship sank, we could hear the screaming a mile away. Gradually it became fainter and fainter and died away. Some of the lifeboats that had room for more might have gone to their rescue, but it would have meant that those who were in the water would have swarmed aboard and sunk them.

Connecting and Comparing Texts

To help students compare these eyewitness accounts to the article by Hanson W. Baldwin, have them consider the following points:

- The eyewitness accounts capture the subjective experience of "being there" in the most literal sense, from the point of view of one survivor. How does this differ from Baldwin's account? [His account tells the entire story.]
- Baldwin crafts his article carefully, with attention to literary elements, such as irony; the eyewitness accounts are less artful.

Why might these accounts be called amateur snapshots? [They focus on a narrow experience. They are up-close pictures of the event, clear and rich in detail.]

Literary Response and Analysis

Reading Check

1. According to the Baldwin article, what caused the *Titanic* to sink?
2. Why didn't the closest ship rush to the rescue?
3. Why weren't the lifeboats full?
4. Cite two heroic acts and two cowardly acts that took place aboard the *Titanic.*

Interpretations

5. Baldwin uses numbered **headings** as **text structures** to organize his article. Briefly summarize what is covered in each numbered part. Why are these divisions logical?
6. Find as many examples as you can of **irony**—both **situational** and **dramatic**—in this story of the *Titanic.* Which instance of irony do you think is the most incredible?
7. Baldwin combines a **chronological** account (a **narrative,** or story) with **factual** information (**exposition**). What do you think is his **purpose** in combining these two types of writing?
8. What techniques does Baldwin use to create drama and **suspense** in this story, whose outcome we already know? Notice, for example, the switch to present-tense verbs in Part II. What other devices help make the article as compelling as a fast-paced adventure novel?
9. Baldwin returns many times to the music played by the ship's band. What **moods** are suggested by the music? What other examples of **repetition** can you find?
10. What truths about human nature can you **infer** from this story and from the survivors' accounts (see the ***Connection*** on page 345)?

Evaluation

11. After reading about the events on board the *Titanic,* as well as the ***Connection*** on page 345, how do you think (or hope) you would have acted if you'd been a passenger? a crew member? Look back at your Quickwrite to see whether you've changed your mind about how you'd behave in a catastrophe.
12. Baldwin spent hundreds of hours reading reports, ships' records, eyewitness accounts, and court proceedings. How **objective** or **subjective** do you think Baldwin's report is? Explain your evaluation.

Writing

Summary of a Disaster

Write a one-page **summary** of "R.M.S. Titanic," including the most significant facts and Baldwin's most important conclusions. Before you begin writing, **outline** the article, showing what Baldwin covers in each of the five numbered sections. Include with your summary a graphic organizer in the form of a **time line** to show the major events in the disaster.

Titanic Update

We now know that Baldwin's article contains errors (such as Captain Smith's initials and the description of a three-hundred-foot gash that later exploration has not been able to find). Using the Internet and recent books and articles on the subject, determine what other information has been revealed about the *Titanic* since the Baldwin article was written. Record your findings in a **brief report**.

Grade 8 Review Reading Standard 2.7 Evaluate the structural patterns of text.

Reading Standard 3.8 Interpret and evaluate the impact of ironies in a text.

INDEPENDENT PRACTICE

Literary Response and Analysis

Interpretations

5. Possible answers: *Part I*—events leading to collision. *Part II*—collision and sinking. *Part III*—aftermath and rescue. *Part IV*—world learns of the disaster and survivors arrive in New York. *Part V*—investigations. The divisions follow chronological order and break down a complex event.
6. Possible answers: the ignored iceberg warnings; the *Californian* told to "shut up" when it warned of ice; the *Californian*'s operator removing his earphones only minutes before the *Titanic* radioed for help; the lifeboats being launched half empty.
7. Possible answer: to engage the reader by telling a story while presenting factual information.
8. Possible answers: using transcripts of radio messages; minute-by-minute narrative of events; foreshadowing the ice; instances of dramatic irony.
9. The ragtime suggests levity; the hymns suggest somberness. Another example of repetition: the blue spark suggests hope.
10. Possible answers: tendency toward complacency that can prove disastrous; people have a capacity for cowardice and heroism.

Evaluation

11. Possible answers: fearfully, levelheadedly, confusedly, heroically.
12. Possible answers: objective, in that the article is full of facts; subjective, in that Baldwin engages the reader's feelings and reveals some of his own.

Reading Check

1. An iceberg gashed its hull.
2. Its radio operator had gone to bed just before the *Titanic* began calling for help.
3. Passengers were at first unwilling to get in the lifeboats; officers feared that full boats would break the ropes that lowered them into the water; loading was confused.
4. Possible answers: *Heroic*—stokers and engineers continued to work; Mrs. Straus turned back to be with her husband; women rescued a swimmer. *Cowardly*—a stoker tried to steal Phillips's life jacket; some people in lifeboats beat away drowning swimmers.

Vocabulary Development

Here are possible word-map answers for some Word Bank words.

Practice 1

- *ascertain. Meaning*—find out with certainty; determine. *How would you ascertain something?*—by looking for answers; by running tests. *What kinds of things might you ascertain?*—why a car won't start; why someone is ill. *Original Sentence*—You don't need a mechanic to ascertain that the car is out of gas.
- *quelled. Meaning*—quieted; subdued. *How might you quell someone's anxiety?*—by talking calmly and reassuringly. *What kinds of things might be quelled?*—a baby's crying; a person's anxiety. *Original Sentence*—I quelled her anxiety about the test by reassuring her that it would be easy.
- *poised. Meaning*—balanced; in position. *How might you feel when you are poised?*—alert, ready. *When might an athlete be poised?*—at the start of a race; when about to shoot a basketball. *Original Sentence*—Poised at the starting line, the runners waited for the starting gun to fire.

Practice 2

1. *panic. Modern meaning*—sudden, overwhelming fear or terror.
2. *echo. Modern meaning*—the repetition of a sound caused by reflected sound waves.
3. *narcissism. Modern meaning*—love of self; egocentrism.
4. *tantalize. Modern meaning*—to tease by keeping out of reach something desirable.

Resources Reminder

Vocabulary

- *Vocabulary Development*
  - Vocabulary Worksheet, p. 27
- *Lesson Plans for Language Development*
  - Vocabulary, pp. 164, 169

Vocabulary Development

Word Maps: Showing Words in Action

PRACTICE 1

You can pin down a new word's meaning by asking—and answering—questions about it. Work alone or with a partner to make a **word map** like the one below for *superlative* for the other words in the Word Bank. The questions you ask will vary.

Word Bank
superlative
ascertain
corroborated
quelled
poised
perfunctory
garbled
recriminations
pertinent
vainly

superlative

What kinds of things might you call superlative?
- delicious dinner
- great movie
- actor's performance

Meaning
- supreme
- better than all others

How would you feel if someone called your work superlative?
- complimented
- flattered
- happy

Original Sentences
- Jeff did a superlative job of painting the kitchen.
- The conductor complimented Sheila for her superlative trumpet solo.

Words from Mythology: So That's Where That Word Comes From

Grade 8 Review Reading Standard 1.3 Use word meanings within the appropriate context and show ability to verify those meanings.

Reading Standard 1.3 Identify Greek mythology and use the knowledge to understand the origin and meaning of new words.

Many words in English derive from the myths of ancient Greece. For example, ***Titanic,*** as you read earlier, comes from the Greek myth of the Titans. ***Ocean*** is another word that comes from the myth of the Titans. Ocean, or Oceanus, was lord of the great river (also called Ocean) that was believed to circle the earth.

PRACTICE 2

Match the words below to the numbered items that follow. Then, use a dictionary to define the modern meaning of the words. (For more about words from mythology, see pages 672 and 684–685.)

echo	panic
narcissism	tantalize

1. Pan, the Greek god of shepherds, was depicted as half-man and half-goat. His great shout struck fear in humans.
2. Echo was a nymph, a kind of goddess. She angered the goddess Hera, who took away her power to speak, except to repeat what others said. Echo was in love with a youth who rejected her, and she pined away for him until all that was left was her voice.
3. Narcissus, a beautiful youth loved by all the nymphs who saw him, rejected them, and they prayed for revenge. In answer to their prayers, the goddess Nemesis made him fall in love with his own reflection.
4. Tantalus, a king who stole the food of the gods, was punished with eternal hunger and thirst while food and drink were kept just out of his reach.

ASSESSING

Assessment

- *Progress Assessment of Reading*
  - Selection Test

RETEACHING

For another selection to teach Standard 3.8, see *Interactive Reading,* Chapter 5.

Before You Read

from Into Thin Air

Literary Focus

Ironies and Contradictions That Spell Real-Life Disaster

In this true story of climbers struggling on Mount Everest, Murphy's law seems to have taken hold: "If there's a possibility that something can go wrong, it will." As you read, look for examples of **situational irony**—when the opposite of what's expected or appropriate occurs.

Look also for the real-life **contradictions** and **incongruities** that lead to disaster—instances in which people don't do what they say they will do or when things don't come together as they should. For example, expedition leader Rob Hall contradicts his own rule of an absolute cutoff time for reaching the summit. These and other fateful twists combine to spell tragedy for the climbers.

Reading Skills

Understanding Cause and Effect

A **cause** is the reason why something happens; an **effect** is the result of some event. A single effect may have several causes, and a single cause may lead to many effects.

Everything that happens in this tragic story is connected by a complex pattern of causes and effects, many of which are filled with **irony.** As you read, look for the causes that led to the disasters on Mount Everest. Look for the effects of certain decisions made by the climbers. The questions at the open-book signs will help you.

Make the Connection

Quickwrite

Can you imagine yourself standing on the 29,035-foot top of the world? The cold has numbed your body, the altitude has dulled your brain, and you are exhausted beyond belief. Now you have to get down—the most dangerous part of the climb.

Jon Krakauer, the author of this magazine article, lived through that experience. Why do you think some people, like Krakauer, are so drawn to climbing mountains? Would you like to do it? Briefly jot down why you would or wouldn't.

Vocabulary Development

deteriorate (dē·tir′ē·ə·rāt′) *v.:* worsen.

innocuous (i·näk′yo͞o·əs) *adj.:* harmless.

notorious (nō·tôr′ē·əs) *adj.:* famous, usually in an unfavorable sense.

benign (bi·nīn′) *adj.:* here, favorable or harmless.

apex (ā′peks′) *n.:* highest point; top.

crucial (kro͞o′shəl) *adj.:* extremely important; decisive.

speculate (spek′yə·lāt′) *v.:* think; guess.

traverse (trə·vurs′) *v.:* cross.

jeopardize (jep′ər·dīz′) *v.:* endanger.

tenuous (ten′yo͞o·əs) *adj.:* weak; slight.

(continued)

Reading Standard 3.8 Interpret and evaluate the impact of contradictions, ironies, and incongruities in a text.

STANDARDS FOCUS, pp. 349–365

(For grade-level and review standards taught in this lesson, see citations on Student Edition pages.)

Prerequisite Standard

- Grade 8, Reading Comprehension 3.6 **Identify significant literary devices (e.g., metaphor, symbolism, dialect, irony) that define a writer's style and use those elements to interpret the work.**

Reading Skills

- Understand cause and effect.

Summary *at grade level*

Krakauer's report covers seventy-two hours in May 1996, when he was part of one of several commercial Mount Everest expeditions that culminated in the mountain's worst tragedy to date. As his account opens, he stands at the summit. Ironically, Krakauer is too ill and spent to savor the experience—he stays only a few minutes. Dropping into an unexpected blizzard and depleted of his oxygen supply, he struggles to reach the safety of Base Camp; others, including several of his hiking mates, wait too long to descend—and die. Krakauer reveals the many incongruities of the ill-fated expeditions and provides important details about what went wrong and why. He implicitly points out the contradictions of the burgeoning "ready-made adventure" industry that played a part in the disaster.

RESOURCES: READING

Planning
- *One-Stop Planner* CD-ROM with Test Generator
- *On Course: Mapping Instruction*

Media
- *Audio CD Library*
  - disc 11

Reading
- *Interactive Reading,* Teacher's Edition
  - Graphic Organizer: Situational Irony Chart

Differentiating Instruction
- *Lesson Plans for Language Development*
  - English-Language Learners, pp. 149–151, 165, 170
  - Special Education Students, pp. 152, 165, 170

Vocabulary
- *Vocabulary Development*
  - Vocabulary Worksheet, p. 28

Assessment
- *Progress Assessment of Reading*
  - Selection Test
- *One-Stop Planner* CD-ROM with Test Generator

PRETEACHING

Selection Starter

Build background. Students may enjoy Krakauer's account more if you provide them with additional information about the mountain's initial "conquerors." In 1953, Sir Edmund Hillary and Tenzing Norgay were part of a British team led by Lord John Hunt. Before Hillary and Norgay reached the summit, Hunt and two other team members had climbed to within four hundred feet of it and then descended, leaving a cache of supplies that would later sustain Hillary and Norgay. After the successful climb, Hunt told a reporter that one cannot speak of "conquering" a mountain. "The relationship between a man and what he does on a mountain is one of humility," explained Hunt. ". . . [T]o feel that you've conquered them is a presumption."

Preview Vocabulary

Have students read the definitions of the Vocabulary words on p. 349. Ask several volunteers to use each word in a sentence. Then, have students use the words to solve the following acrostic. The hidden words name two small items that play big roles in life-and-death struggles in the selection.

1. _ _ n _ _ _
2. _ _ u _ _ _ _
3. _ _ t _ _ _ _ _ _ t _
4. _ _ _ _ _ r _ _
5. _ _ _ u _ _ _

[Answers 1–5: benign, crucial, deteriorate, traverse, tenuous; hidden word: glove]

6. _ o _ _ _ _ _ _ s
7. i _ _ _ _ _ _ _ _
8. _ _ _ c _ _ _ _ _
9. _ _ o _ _ _ d _ _ _
10. _ _ e _

[Answers 6–10: notorious, innocuous, speculate, jeopardize, apex; hidden words: ice ax]

Background

Hot Story, Cold Mountain

The man who said he wanted to climb Mount Everest "because it's there," George Leigh Mallory, disappeared in a mist near the summit in 1924. The first recorded conquest of the 29,035-foot peak was achieved by Edmund Hillary of New Zealand and Tenzing Norgay of Nepal in 1953. Since then more than 1,300 climbers have reached the summit, but about 170 have lost their lives to the mountain.

The journalist who wrote this magazine article barely escaped with his life. In 1996, *Outside* magazine financed Jon Krakauer's climb, which he undertook as a client of a commercial expedition. The day he reached the summit of Everest, eight other climbers (including Krakauer's tour leader) died on the mountain. (This is the riskiest form of **participatory journalism,** in which a reporter takes part in the events he or she is reporting.)

Since the May 1996 tragedy, more and more people have caught Everest fever, some paying as much as seventy thousand dollars for a guided climb. Although many of these climbers are experts, some are inexperienced—a problem that creates grave dangers.

Making a Climb

Everest expeditions ascend the mountain in stages. From Base Camp, at 17,600 feet, they make short trips up and down to acclimatize, or get used to higher elevations. This process may last several weeks before the final climb to the top, which is also done in stages. Krakauer's group made camp at 19,500 feet, 21,300 feet, 24,000 feet, and 26,000 feet. The area above 25,000 feet is known as the Death Zone. Here the air is so poor in oxygen that it's almost impossible for climbers to make rational decisions.

Some of the Climbers Involved in the Tragedy

New Zealand–Based Team	American-Based Team	IMAX Film Crew
① Rob Hall, *leader; head guide*	Scott Fischer, *leader; head guide*	David Breashears, *leader; film director*
② Mike Groom, *guide*	Anatoli Boukreev, *guide*	Ed Viesturs, *climber; film talent*
③ Andy "Harold" Harris, *guide*	**Taiwan Team**	
④ Doug Hansen, *client*	"Makalu" Gau Ming-Ho, *leader*	
⑤ Jon Krakauer, *client; journalist*		
⑥ Yasuko Namba, *client*		
⑦ Beck Weathers, *client*		
Lhakpa Chhiri Sherpa, *climbing Sherpa*		

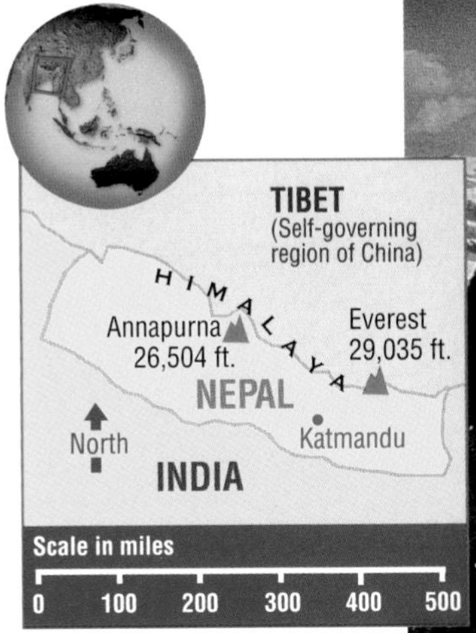

Members of Jon Krakauer's expedition team, led by Rob Hall. The numbers identify the team members named in the list of expedition members on page 350.

Homework

Assign the Reading

You may wish to assign sections of the long narrative account as independent reading for students at most ability levels. Before assigning the reading to English-language learners and learners having difficulty, you may wish to preview the selection in class, familiarizing students with the history and geography of the Mount Everest expeditions and discussing selection Vocabulary.

Ask students to study the picture on p. 352, read the caption, and think about the title of the article. Invite them to make predictions about what the article will deal with. [Possible responses: climbers who try to reach the top of Mount Everest and die in the attempt; the business of making money to guide the climbers; the high cost, both financial and physical, of making the climb and surviving.]

DIRECT TEACHING

A Learners Having Difficulty

Using graphic aids. To help students follow the selection, have students work in pairs to list the people labeled in the photograph. Explain that these people play significant roles in the selection. Tell students to stay alert for references to each person as they read and to add brief notes to their lists, tracking each person's experiences. Also, encourage students to refer back to the map in order to follow the progress of the climbers.

As an alternative, you might have students photocopy the photodiagram and the list of climbers and then refer to this sheet as they read.

from **Into**

Everest deals with trespassers harshly: The dead vanish beneath the snows, while the living struggle to explain what happened, and why. A survivor of the mountain's worst disaster examines the business of Mount Everest and the steep price of ambition.

352

DIFFERENTIATING INSTRUCTION

Learners Having Difficulty

Modeling. To help students read the excerpt from *Into Thin Air,* model the reading skill of understanding cause and effect. After students have read through the selection's second paragraph, say, "The narrator is exhausted, not elated, when reaching the summit. Why is this? The causes for his low enthusiasm are clear—lack of sleep, lack of food, weeks of coughing, injured ribs, oxygen deprivation. In this condition it would be difficult to relish the moment." Encourage students to look for further cause-and-effect relationships as they read.

English-Language Learners

Before students begin reading, you might discuss the idiom *into thin air.* Point out that it is usually used with the verb *vanish* or *disappear,* and it means "completely and mysteriously." When students finish reading Krakauer's report, ask them to explain the double meaning of the title.

Resources Reminder

For lessons designed for intermediate and advanced English-language learners, see

Thin Air

Jon Krakauer

Straddling the top of the world, one foot in Tibet and the other in Nepal, I cleared the ice from my oxygen mask, hunched a shoulder against the wind, and stared absently at the vast sweep of earth below. I understood on some dim, detached level that it was a spectacular sight. I'd been fantasizing about this moment, and the release of emotion that would accompany it, for many months. But now that I was finally here, standing on the summit of Mount Everest, I just couldn't summon the energy to care. **A**

It was the afternoon of May 10. I hadn't slept in 57 hours. The only food I'd been able to force down over the preceding three days was a bowl of Ramen soup and a handful of peanut M&M's. Weeks of violent coughing had left me with two separated ribs, making it excruciatingly painful to breathe. Twenty-nine thousand twenty-eight feet[1] up in the troposphere,[2] there was so little oxygen reaching my brain that my mental capacity was that of a slow child. Under the circumstances, I was incapable of feeling much of anything except cold and tired.

I'd arrived on the summit a few minutes after Anatoli Boukreev,[3] a Russian guide with an American expedition, and just ahead of Andy Harris, a guide with the New Zealand–based commercial team that I was a part of and someone with whom I'd grown to be friends during the last six weeks. I snapped four quick photos of Harris and Boukreev striking summit poses, and then turned and started down. My watch read 1:17 P.M. All told, I'd spent less than five minutes on the roof of the world.

1. In 1999, after this article was written, scientists using sophisticated equipment determined the elevation of Everest to be 29,035 feet, not 29,028 feet as previously believed.
2. **troposphere** (trō′pə·sfir′) *n.:* portion of the atmosphere directly below the stratosphere (it extends from 6 to 8 miles above the earth's surface).
3. **Anatoli Boukreev:** Boukreev (pictured at left on Mount Everest) was killed in an avalanche about a year and a half later, on December 25, 1997, while climbing Annapurna in the Himalayas.

DIRECT TEACHING

A Literary Focus
GRADE-LEVEL STANDARD

Ironies and contradictions. How does Krakauer feel after achieving something he has been fantasizing about for months? [emotionless, exhausted, numb] **Why is this ironic?** [Possible response: He and most people would probably expect that reaching the "top of the world" would bring a sense of euphoria or at least accomplishment. Unexpectedly, he feels nothing at all.]

Lesson Plans for Language Development, pp. 149–151, 165, 170.

Special Education Students

For lessons designed for special education students, see *Lesson Plans for Language Development,* pp. 152, 165, 170.

Advanced Learners

Acceleration. Use the following activity with advanced learners to move them toward the eleventh- and twelfth-grade Standard 3.3, for which they analyze the ways in which irony, tone, mood, and the author's style achieve specific rhetorical or aesthetic purpose or both.

Activity. Sir Edmund Hillary's *High in the Thin Cold Air* and Tenzing Norgay's *Tiger of the Snows* also report on the experience of climbing in the Himalayas. Ask students to read one or both of these accounts and to compare it with *Into Thin Air.* Encourage them to notice differences in the tone of each account and to consider how these differences relate to the purposes of each author.

Direct Teaching

A Reading Skills

Speculating. Why do you think the narrator mentions this change in the weather? [Possible responses: Weather may play an important role in what happens to the expeditions; at this altitude bad weather can be deadly.]

B Literary Focus
GRADE-LEVEL STANDARD

Ironies and contradictions. Why is it ironic that the clouds appeared "innocuous, wispy, insubstantial" to Krakauer? [Possible response: Apparently, these innocent-looking clouds turned into a "murderous" storm that claimed the lives of several people.]

C Vocabulary Development
GRADE-LEVEL STANDARD

Context clues. The terms *shank, corniced,* and *fin* have specialized meanings in mountaineering. Based on your reading of the paragraph, what do you think the three terms mean? [Possible responses: *shank*—segment of a ridge; *corniced*—with horizontal projections near the top; *fin*—a narrow vertical rock formation.]

D Reading Skills

Drawing conclusions. Time is critical for the ascending and descending mountaineers. What conclusion can you draw about this "traffic jam" at the Hillary Step? [Possible responses: It is a serious hazard that may have dire consequences; so many climbers should not attempt the summit at once.]

After a few steps, I paused to take another photo, this one looking down the Southeast Ridge, the route we had ascended. Training my lens on a pair of climbers approaching the summit, I saw something that until that moment had escaped my attention. To the south, where the sky had been perfectly clear just an hour earlier, a blanket of clouds now hid Pumori, Ama Dablam, and the other lesser peaks surrounding Everest.

Days later—after six bodies had been found, after a search for two others had been abandoned, after surgeons had amputated[4] the gangrenous[5] right hand of my teammate Beck Weathers—people would ask why, if the weather had begun to deteriorate, had climbers on the upper mountain not heeded the signs? Why did veteran Himalayan guides keep moving upward, leading a gaggle of amateurs, each of whom had paid as much as $65,000 to be ushered safely up Everest, into an apparent death trap?

Nobody can speak for the leaders of the two guided groups involved, for both men are now dead. But I can attest that nothing I saw early on the afternoon of May 10 suggested that a murderous storm was about to bear down on us. To my oxygen-depleted mind, the clouds drifting up the grand valley of ice known as the Western Cwm looked innocuous, wispy, insubstantial. Gleaming in the brilliant midday sun, they appeared no different from the harmless puffs of convection condensation that rose from the valley almost daily. As I began my descent, I was indeed anxious, but my concern had little to do with the weather. A check of the gauge on my oxygen tank had revealed that it was almost empty. I needed to get down, fast.

Nobody can speak for the leaders . . . for both men are now dead.

The uppermost shank of the Southeast Ridge is a slender, heavily corniced fin[6] of rock and wind-scoured snow that snakes for a quarter-mile toward a secondary pinnacle known as the South Summit. Negotiating the serrated[7] ridge presents few great technical hurdles, but the route is dreadfully exposed. After 15 minutes of cautious shuffling over a 7,000-foot abyss,[8] I arrived at the notorious Hillary Step, a pronounced notch in the ridge named after Sir Edmund Hillary, the first Westerner to climb the mountain, and a spot that does require a fair amount of technical maneuvering. As I clipped into a fixed rope and prepared to rappel[9] over the lip, I was greeted by an alarming sight.

Thirty feet below, some 20 people were queued up[10] at the base of the Step, and three climbers were hauling themselves up the rope that I was attempting to descend. I had no choice but to unclip from the line and step aside.

The traffic jam comprised climbers from three separate expeditions: the team I belonged to, a group of paying clients under the leadership of the celebrated New Zealand guide Rob Hall; another guided party headed by American Scott Fischer; and a nonguided team from Taiwan. Moving at the snail's pace that is the norm above 8,000 meters, the throng labored up the

4. **amputated** *v.:* cut off (a limb or body part) through surgery.
5. **gangrenous** (gaŋ′grə·nəs) *adj.:* affected by the decay of tissue resulting from a lack of blood supply.
6. **corniced** (kôr′nist) **fin:** curving and narrow ridge.
7. **serrated** *v.* used as *adj.:* notched like a saw.
8. **abyss** (ə·bis′) *n.:* deep crack or opening in the earth's surface.
9. **rappel** (ra·pel′) *v.:* descend a mountain by means of a double rope arranged around the climber's body so that he or she can control the slide downward.
10. **queued** (kyo͞o′d) **up:** lined up.

Vocabulary

deteriorate (dē·tir′ē·ə·rāt′) *v.:* worsen.

innocuous (i·näk′yo͞o·əs) *adj.:* harmless.

notorious (nō·tôr′ē·əs) *adj.:* famous, usually in an unfavorable sense.

354 Chapter 5 Irony and Ambiguity • Generating Research Questions and Evaluating Sources

Hillary Step one by one, while I nervously bided my time.

Harris, who left the summit shortly after I did, soon pulled up behind me. Wanting to conserve whatever oxygen remained in my tank, I asked him to reach inside my backpack and turn off the valve on my regulator, which he did. For the next ten minutes I felt surprisingly good. My head cleared. I actually seemed less tired than with the gas turned on. Then, abruptly, I felt like I was suffocating. My vision dimmed and my head began to spin. I was on the brink of losing consciousness.

Instead of turning my oxygen off, Harris, in his hypoxically[11] impaired state, had mistakenly cranked the valve open to full flow, draining the tank. I'd just squandered the last of my gas going nowhere. There was another tank waiting for me at the South Summit, 250 feet below, but to get there I would have to descend the most exposed terrain on the entire route without benefit of supplemental oxygen.

CAUSE AND EFFECT

1. What is the unexpected **result** of Krakauer's request of Harris?

But first I had to wait for the crowd to thin. I removed my now useless mask, planted my ice ax into the mountain's frozen hide, and hunkered on the ridge crest. As I exchanged banal[12] congratulations with the climbers filing past, inwardly I was frantic: "Hurry it up, hurry it up!" I silently pleaded. "While you guys are messing around here, I'm losing brain cells by the millions!"

Most of the passing crowd belonged to Fischer's group, but near the back of the parade two of my teammates eventually appeared: Hall and Yasuko Namba. Girlish and reserved, the 47-year-old Namba was 40 minutes away from becoming the oldest woman to climb Everest and the second Japanese woman to reach the highest point on each continent, the so-called Seven Summits.

Later still, Doug Hansen—another member of our expedition, a postal worker from Seattle who had become my closest friend on the mountain—arrived atop the Step. "It's in the bag!" I yelled over the wind, trying to sound more upbeat than I felt. Plainly exhausted, Doug mumbled something from behind his oxygen mask that I didn't catch, shook my hand weakly, and continued plodding upward.

The last climber up the rope was Fischer, whom I knew casually from Seattle, where we both lived. His strength and drive were legendary—in 1994 he'd climbed Everest without using bottled oxygen—so I was surprised at how slowly he was moving and how hammered he looked when he pulled his mask aside to say hello. "Bruuuuuuce!" he wheezed with forced cheer, employing his trademark, fratboyish greeting. When I asked how he was doing, Fischer insisted he was feeling fine: "Just dragging a little today for some reason. No big deal." With the Hillary Step finally clear, I clipped into the strand of orange rope, swung quickly around Fischer as he slumped over his ice ax, and rappelled over the edge.

It was after 2:30 when I made it down to the South Summit. By now tendrils of mist were wrapping across the top of 27,890-foot Lhotse and lapping at Everest's summit pyramid. No longer did the weather look so benign. I grabbed a fresh oxygen cylinder, jammed it onto my regulator, and hurried down into the gathering cloud.

Four hundred vertical feet above, where the summit was still washed in bright sunlight under an immaculate cobalt sky, my

---

11. **hypoxically** *adv.:* characterized by hypoxia, a condition resulting from a decrease in the oxygen reaching body tissues. Hypoxia is a common condition at very high altitudes.
12. **banal** *adj.:* everyday; commonplace.

Vocabulary
benign (bi·nīn′) *adj.:* here, favorable or harmless.

DIRECT TEACHING

E Reading Skills
Understanding cause and effect. [Possible response to question 1: Krakauer is trying to conserve oxygen, but instead he wastes the rest of his supply.]

F English-Language Learners
Slang and idioms. Explain to students learning English that when Krakauer says, "I'm losing brain cells by the millions," he is referring to the lack of oxygen reaching his brain, potentially causing damage. Also, point out that the idiom *It's in the bag* means "success is certain." In using this idiom, Krakauer is trying to encourage his fellow climbers.

G Literary Focus
GRADE-LEVEL STANDARD
Ironies and contradictions. Why is it incongruous and ominous that Fischer seems to be lagging? [Possible response: Fischer's "strength and drive were legendary" and, more importantly, he is the man responsible for the safety of his entire expedition. If he is having difficulty, it doesn't bode well for those in his care.]

CONTENT-AREA CONNECTIONS

Geography: Nepal
Nepal, a country of 25 million people, is the base for most Mount Everest expeditions. For years Nepal had little contact with the outside world. Then in the second half of the twentieth century, the country began to open up, encouraging tourism and exploiting its mountains as an attraction. Nepal has been deeply affected by the climbers who arrive in droves to attempt Nepal's Himalayan peaks. On the one hand, tourism brings millions of dollars into one of Asia's poorest countries. On the other hand, unfettered access to the country has brought extreme environmental degradation and profound cultural change.

Whole-class activity. Students can research the effects of tourism on the political, social, and environmental conditions in Nepal. Divide the class into two groups—one supporting Nepal's tourism industry and one opposing it. Have the class debate the issue, citing facts gathered during their research to support their positions.

DIRECT TEACHING

A Literary Focus
REVIEW STANDARD

Suspense. How does Krakauer build suspense in this paragraph?
[Possible responses: He uses the image of a ticking clock; he repeats the phrase "none of them"; he refers to ominous events to come.]

B Reading Skills

Speculating. What do you suppose caused Weathers to keep climbing despite his near blindness?
[Possible responses: desire to reach the peak; poor judgment caused by exhaustion and lack of oxygen; unwillingness to appear weaker than others who continued despite physical impairments, such as Krakauer with his separated ribs.]

compadres[13] were dallying,[14] memorializing their arrival at the apex of the planet with photos and high-fives—and using up precious ticks of the clock. None of them imagined that a horrible ordeal was drawing nigh. None of them suspected that by the end of that long day, every minute would matter. . . .

At 3 P.M., within minutes of leaving the South Summit, I descended into clouds ahead of the others. Snow started to fall. In the flat, diminishing light, it became hard to tell where the mountain ended and where the sky began. It would have been very easy to blunder off the edge of the ridge and never be heard from again. The lower I went, the worse the weather became.

When I reached the Balcony again, about 4 P.M., I encountered Beck Weathers standing alone, shivering violently. Years earlier, Weathers had undergone radial keratotomy to correct his vision. A side effect, which he discovered on Everest and consequently hid from Hall, was that in the low barometric pressure at high altitude, his eyesight failed. Nearly blind when he'd left Camp Four in the middle of the night but hopeful that his vision would improve at daybreak, he stuck close to the person in front of him and kept climbing.

Upon reaching the Southeast Ridge shortly after sunrise, Weathers had confessed to Hall that he was having trouble seeing, at which point Hall declared, "Sorry, pal, you're going down. I'll send one of the Sherpas[15] with you." Weathers countered that his vision was likely to improve as soon as the sun crept higher in the sky; Hall said he'd give Weathers 30 minutes to find out—after that, he'd have to wait there at 27,500 feet for Hall and the rest of the group to come back down. Hall didn't want Weathers descending alone. "I'm dead serious about this," Hall

13. **compadres** (kəm·pä′drāz′) *n.:* close friends; in this case, fellow members of the climbing team.
14. **dallying** *v.:* wasting time.

15. **Sherpas:** Tibetan people living on the southern slopes of the Himalayas. As experienced mountain climbers, the Sherpas are hired by expeditions to haul loads and set up camps and ropes.

Vocabulary
apex (ā′peks′) *n.:* highest point; top.

Doug Hansen approaching the summit.

STANDARD REVIEW

Using context clues. You may wish to use this activity to help prepare students for Practice 2 of Vocabulary Development on p. 365.

Activity. First, tell students that context clues may include definitions, examples, restatements (synonyms, for example), or contrast (antonyms). Then, have students use the context clues in the following numbered items to define the underlined terms.

1. Digging through the detritus on the ridge, the climber found an underlying layer of firm rock. [accumulated debris]
2. The peak, in its thick carapace of ice, gleamed white in the sun. [shell]
3. She used carabiners—metal clips—to attach the rope to her climbing harness. [metal clips]
4. Was he still on belay, or had he already unfastened the fixed rope bearing his weight? [suspended from a fixed rope]
5. The trek leader admonished everyone about the danger of wasting oxygen. [warned]

356 Chapter 5 Irony and Ambiguity • Generating Research Questions and Evaluating Sources

admonished his client. "Promise me that you'll sit right here until I return."

"I crossed my heart and hoped to die," Weathers recalls now, "and promised I wouldn't go anywhere." Shortly after noon, Hutchison, Taske, and Kasischke[16] passed by with their Sherpa escorts, but Weathers elected not to accompany them. "The weather was still good," he explains, "and I saw no reason to break my promise to Rob."

By the time I encountered Weathers, however, conditions were turning ugly. "Come down with me," I implored, "I'll get you down, no problem." He was nearly convinced, until I made the mistake of mentioning that Groom was on his way down, too. In a day of many mistakes, this would turn out to be a crucial one. "Thanks anyway," Weathers said. "I'll just wait for Mike. He's got a rope; he'll be able to short-rope[17] me." Secretly relieved, I hurried toward the South Col, 1,500 feet below.

CAUSE AND EFFECT

2. What is the **effect** of Weathers's promise to Hall?

These lower slopes proved to be the most difficult part of the descent. Six inches of powder snow blanketed outcroppings of loose shale. Climbing down them demanded unceasing concentration, an all but impossible feat in my current state. By 5:30, however, I was finally within 200 vertical feet of Camp Four, and only one obstacle stood between me and safety: a steep bulge of rock-hard ice that I'd have to descend without a rope. But the weather had deteriorated into a full-scale blizzard. Snow pellets born on 70-mph winds stung my face; any exposed skin was instantly frozen. The tents, no more than 200 horizontal yards away, were only intermittently visible through the whiteout. There was zero margin for error. Worried about making a critical blunder, I sat down to marshal my energy.

16. Stuart Hutchison, Dr. John Taske, and Lou Kasischke were three clients on Rob Hall's team.
17. **short-rope** *n.* used as *v.*: assist a weak or injured climber by hauling him or her.

Suddenly, Harris[18] appeared out of the gloom and sat beside me. At this point there was no mistaking that he was in appalling shape. His cheeks were coated with an armor of frost, one eye was frozen shut, and his speech was slurred. He was frantic to reach the tents. After briefly discussing the best way to negotiate the ice, Harris started scooting down on his butt, facing forward. "Andy," I yelled after him, "it's crazy to try it like that!" He yelled something back, but the words were carried off by the screaming wind. A second later he lost his purchase[19] and was rocketing down on his back.

Two hundred feet below, I could make out Harris's motionless form. I was sure he'd broken at least a leg, maybe his neck. But then he stood up, waved that he was OK, and started stumbling toward camp, which was for the moment in plain sight, 150 yards beyond.

I could see three or four people shining lights outside the tents. I watched Harris walk across the flats to the edge of camp, a distance he covered in less than ten minutes. When the clouds closed in a moment later, cutting off my view, he was within 30 yards of the tents. I didn't see him again after that, but I was certain that he'd reached the security of camp, where Sherpas would be waiting with hot tea. Sitting out in the storm, with the ice bulge still standing between me and the tents, I felt a pang of envy. I was angry that my guide hadn't waited for me.

Twenty minutes later I was in camp. I fell into my tent with my crampons still on, zipped the door tight, and sprawled across the frost-covered floor. I was drained, more exhausted than I'd ever

18. After writing this article, Krakauer discovered through conversations with Martin Adams (a client on Scott Fischer's team) that the person he thought was Harris was, in fact, Martin Adams.
19. **purchase** *n.*: firm hold.

Vocabulary
crucial (kro͞o′shəl) *adj.*: extremely important; decisive.

DIRECT TEACHING

C English-Language Learners

Cultural concepts. Explain that in some cultures, children draw an invisible X and say the words "Cross my heart and hope to die" when they want to seal a promise. Point out that in this dangerous situation, these words are ominous, possibly suggesting events to come.

D Reading Skills

Understanding cause and effect. [Possible response to question 2: Rather than trying to descend to safety with Krakauer, Weathers waits for Hall even as conditions deteriorate.]

E Advanced Learners

Acceleration. Direct students' attention to the bracketed text, and ask them to analyze Krakauer's style in this section. Ask students, "What purpose is Krakauer trying to achieve here?" [Possible responses: to describe his dangerous situation; to "put the reader there" with him on the mountain.] How does Krakauer achieve his purpose? [Possible response: He includes many sensory details and a vivid description of his situation and surroundings.]

F Literary Focus
GRADE-LEVEL STANDARD

Ironies and contradictions. Remind students that Harris is an expedition guide. A guide would be expected to survive a climb in good condition, to be concerned about his clients, and to make good decisions. What about Harris's behavior contradicts these facts? [Possible response: At this point, Harris does not meet these qualifications for a guide. He is physically battered by the climb; he's unconcerned with Krakauer's survival and is acting irrationally, as evidenced by the way he descends the ice bulge.]

DEVELOPING FLUENCY

Paired activity. Ask students to imagine that they have been hired to read the article aloud for an audio taping that will be broadcast to radio listeners. Have partners take turns reading sections of the article aloud, as though they are professional actors. Encourage students to read the text with as much expression as possible, modulating their voices to make the narrative suspenseful. You may wish to suggest that students actually tape their reading and then have pairs exchange tapes and listen to the other pair's reading.

DIRECT TEACHING

A Reading Skills
Understanding cause and effect. [Possible response to question 3: Hall is described as having a "conservative, systematic nature." Allowing Hansen to continue to the top, despite the man's weakened state (which was described earlier), contradicts Hall's nature. As a result, he and his client reached the summit "after the predetermined turnaround time" and are now in extreme danger from the growing storm.]

B Literary Focus
GRADE-LEVEL STANDARD
Ironies and contradictions. What is the ironic consequence of Harris breaking into Hall's radio call? [Harris is trying to aid Hall, but he actually harms him by feeding him inaccurate information about the availability of oxygen at the South Summit.]

been in my life. But I was safe. Andy was safe. The others would be coming into camp soon. We'd done it. We'd climbed Mount Everest.

It would be many hours before I learned that everyone had in fact not made it back to camp—that one teammate was already dead and that 23 other men and women were caught in a desperate struggle for their lives. . . .

Meanwhile, Hall and Hansen were still on the frightfully exposed summit ridge, engaged in a grim struggle of their own. The 46-year-old Hansen, whom Hall had turned back just below this spot exactly a year ago, had been determined to bag the summit this time around. "I want to get this thing done and out of my life," he'd told me a couple of days earlier. "I don't want to have to come back here."

Indeed Hansen had reached the top this time, though not until after 3 P.M., well after Hall's predetermined turnaround time. Given Hall's conservative, systematic nature, many people wonder why he didn't turn Hansen around when it became obvious that he was running late. It's not far-fetched to speculate that because Hall had talked Hansen into coming back to Everest this year, it would have been especially hard for him to deny Hansen the summit a second time—especially when all of Fischer's clients were still marching blithely toward the top.

"It's very difficult to turn someone around high on the mountain," cautions Guy Cotter, a New Zealand guide who summited Everest with Hall in 1992 and was guiding the peak for him in 1995 when Hansen made his first attempt. "If a client sees that the summit is close and they're dead set on getting there, they're going to laugh in your face and keep going up."

In any case, for whatever reason, Hall did not turn Hansen around. Instead, after reaching the summit at 2:10 P.M., Hall waited for more than an hour for Hansen to arrive and then headed down with him. Soon after they began their descent, just below the top, Hansen apparently ran out of oxygen and collapsed. "Pretty much the same thing happened to Doug in '95," says Ed Viesturs, an American who guided the peak for Hall that year. "He was fine during the ascent, but as soon as he started down he lost it mentally and physically. **A** He turned into a real zombie, like he'd used everything up."

CAUSE AND EFFECT
3. What **contradiction** is evident in Hall's behavior? What is the **result?**

B At 4:31 P.M., Hall radioed Base Camp to say that he and Hansen were above the Hillary Step and urgently needed oxygen. Two full bottles were waiting for them at the South Summit; if Hall had known this he could have retrieved the gas fairly quickly and then climbed back up to give Hansen a fresh tank. But Harris, in the throes of his oxygen-starved dementia,[20] overheard the 4:31 radio call while descending the Southeast Ridge and broke in to tell Hall that all the bottles at the South Summit were empty. So Hall stayed with Hansen and tried to bring the helpless client down without oxygen, but could get him no farther than the top of the Hillary Step.

Cotter, a very close friend of both Hall and Harris, happened to be a few miles from Everest Base Camp at the time, guiding an expedition on Pumori. Overhearing the radio conversations between Hall and Base Camp, he called Hall at 5:36 and again at 5:57, urging his mate to leave Hansen and come down alone. . . . Hall, however, wouldn't consider going down without Hansen.

20. **dementia** (di·men′shə) *n.:* mental impairment; madness.

Vocabulary
speculate (spek′yə·lāt′) *v.:* think; guess.

READING MINI-LESSON

Developing Word-Attack Skills
Write the following word pairs on the chalkboard. Have students read the words, compare their spellings and pronunciations, and tell the part of speech for each word. (In each pair, the first word is a noun, and the second word is a verb.)

breath	breathe
bath	bathe
cloth	clothe

Help students recognize that the final e affects the vowel sound and the sound of *th.* In the nouns *breath, bath,* and *cloth,* the vowel sound is short and *th* is unvoiced. When the final e is added to form the verbs *breathe, bathe,* and *clothe,* the vowel is long and *th* is voiced.

Explain that e after *th* usually indicates that the vowel sound is long and *th* is voiced, which means that the vocal cords vibrate to make the sound. Have students compare these examples: *lithograph, lithe; myth, scythe; path, swathe.*

Activity. Display these sentences. Ask students to identify the words in each sentence that have a long vowel sound and the voiced *th.* Answers are underlined.

1. She wrapped a moth-eaten shawl <u>blithely</u> around her shoulders.

There was no further word from Hall until the middle of the night. At 2:46 A.M. on May 11, Cotter woke up to hear a long, broken transmission, probably unintended: Hall was wearing a remote microphone clipped to the shoulder strap of his backpack, which was occasionally keyed on by mistake. In this instance, says Cotter, "I suspect Rob didn't even know he was transmitting. I could hear someone yelling—it might have been Rob, but I couldn't be sure because the wind was so loud in the background. He was saying something like 'Keep moving! Keep going!' presumably to Doug, urging him on."

If that was indeed the case, it meant that in the wee hours of the morning Hall and Hansen were still struggling from the Hillary Step toward the South Summit, taking more than 12 hours to traverse a stretch of ridge typically covered by descending climbers in half an hour.

CAUSE AND EFFECT

4. Why does it take them so long to traverse the ridge?

(C)

Hall's next call to Base Camp was at 4:43 A.M. He'd finally reached the South Summit but was unable to descend farther, and in a series of transmissions over the next two hours he sounded confused and irrational. "Harold[21] was with me last night," Hall insisted, when in fact Harris had reached the South Col at sunset. "But he doesn't seem to be with me now. He was very weak."

Mackenzie[22] asked him how Hansen was doing. "Doug," Hall replied, "is gone." That was all he said, and it was the last mention he ever made of Hansen.

On May 23, when Breashears and Viesturs, of the IMAX team,[23] reached the summit, they found no sign of Hansen's body but they did find an ice ax planted about 50 feet below the Hillary Step, along a highly exposed section of ridge where the fixed ropes came to an end. It is quite possible that Hall managed to get Hansen down the ropes to this point, only to have him lose his footing and fall 7,000 feet down the sheer Southwest Face, leaving his ice ax jammed into the ridge crest where he slipped.

During the radio calls to Base Camp early on May 11, Hall revealed that something was wrong with his legs, that he was no longer able to walk and was shaking uncontrollably. (D)

Guide Rob Hall.

21. **Harold:** Andy Harris's nickname.
22. **Mackenzie:** Dr. Caroline Mackenzie was Base Camp doctor for Rob Hall's team.
23. **IMAX team:** Another team of climbers, who were shooting a $5.5-million giant-screen movie about Mount Everest. The movie was released in 1998.

Vocabulary
traverse (trə·vʉrs′) *v.:* cross.

DIRECT TEACHING

(C) Reading Skills

Understanding cause and effect. [Possible responses to question 4: Hall and Hansen have no oxygen; Hansen is physically spent; they are trapped in a severe storm that hampers their movement and visibility.]

(D) Reading Skills

Understanding cause and effect. What might be causing Hall's uncontrollable shaking and loss of motor skills? [Possible responses: hypothermia; shock; exhaustion.] **How do you think his condition might affect his chances for survival?** [Possible responses: If he can't walk, his chances of making it to safety are minimal; if he can't use his legs, he can't move around to keep warm and is in danger of freezing to death.]

2. Her face was wreathed with light as she smiled a gap-toothed smile.
3. The soothsayer's smile soothed our fears as she began to speak.

STANDARD REVIEW

Distinguishing between fact and opinion. Remind students that facts are verifiable; they can be proved true or even by consulting reference sources by using the five senses. Opinions represent personal feelings and judgments. They can be supported, but they cannot be proved. "The expedition was a tragedy" is an opinion; "twelve people died" is a fact.

Activity. Direct students to re-read p. 355 and to locate facts as well as opinions in Krakauer's descriptions of Namba and Hansen.

Activity. Have students re-read Krakauer's final two paragraphs on p. 362 and decide which statements are facts and which are opinions.

Into Thin Air 359

DIRECT TEACHING

A Reading Skills

Understanding cause and effect. When Krakauer is at the summit, he de-ices his oxygen mask in less than five minutes. What could have caused Hall to take four hours to complete the same task? [Possible responses: Hall's fingers may be numb with cold or clumsy from exhaustion; his oxygen-starved brain keeps him from thinking clearly and working effectively.]

B Literary Focus
REVIEW STANDARD

Suspense. How does Krakauer let readers share the suspense that those at Camp Four felt about Hall? [Possible response: Krakauer raises readers' hopes with details about the oxygen and about Hall's preparations to descend, then lowers hopes with details about Hall's wavering and about the storm.]

C Literary Focus
GRADE-LEVEL STANDARD

Ironies and contradictions. Consider the technology that Hall is using. Why is it ironic that he is able to talk to his wife? [Possible response: At the brink of death, in the middle of a blizzard, near the top of Mount Everest, Hall is able to talk to his wife while she sits safely at home. Technology makes this possible, yet at the same time, it cannot help him survive.]

D Reading Skills

Understanding cause and effect. [Possible responses to question 5: frostbite; lack of oxygen; the unforeseen blizzard; errors in judgment such as allowing Hansen to attempt the summit; misinformation from Harris's phone call.]

This was very disturbing news to the people down below, but it was amazing that Hall was even alive after spending a night without shelter or oxygen at 28,700 feet in hurricane-force wind and minus-100-degree windchill.

At 5 A.M., Base Camp patched through a call on the satellite telephone to Jan Arnold, Hall's wife, seven months pregnant with their first child in Christchurch, New Zealand. Arnold, a respected physician, had summited Everest with Hall in 1993 and entertained no illusions about the gravity of her husband's predicament. "My heart really sank when I heard his voice," she recalls. "He was slurring his words markedly. He sounded like Major Tom[24] or something, like he was just floating away. I'd been up there; I knew what it could be like in bad weather. Rob and I had talked about the impossibility of being rescued from the summit ridge. As he himself had put it, 'You might as well be on the moon.' "

B **A** By that time, Hall had located two full oxygen bottles, and after struggling for four hours trying to de-ice his mask, around 8:30 A.M. he finally started breathing the life-sustaining gas. Several times he announced that he was preparing to descend, only to change his mind and remain at the South Summit. The day had started out sunny and clear, but the wind remained fierce, and by late morning the upper mountain was wrapped with thick clouds. Climbers at Camp Two reported that the wind over the summit sounded like a squadron of 747s, even from 8,000 feet below. . . .

Throughout that day, Hall's friends begged him to make an effort to descend from the South Summit under his own power. At 3:20 P.M., after one such transmission from Cotter, Hall began to sound annoyed. "Look," he said, "if I thought I could manage the knots on the fixed ropes with me frostbitten hands, I would have gone down six hours ago, pal. Just send a couple of the boys up with a big thermos of something hot—then I'll be fine."

C At 6:20 P.M., Hall was patched through a second time to Arnold in Christchurch. "Hi, my sweetheart," he said in a slow, painfully distorted voice. "I hope you're tucked up in a nice warm bed. How are you doing?"

"I can't tell you how much I'm thinking about you!" Arnold replied. "You sound so much better than I expected. . . . Are you warm, my darling?"

"In the context of the altitude, the setting, I'm reasonably comfortable," Hall answered, doing his best not to alarm her.

"How are your feet?"

"I haven't taken me boots off to check, but I think I may have a bit of frostbite."

"I'm looking forward to making you completely better when you come home," said Arnold. "I just know you're going to be rescued. Don't feel that you're alone. I'm sending all my positive energy your way!" Before signing off, Hall told his wife, "I love you. Sleep well, my sweetheart. Please don't worry too much."

These would be the last words anyone would hear him utter. Attempts to make radio contact with Hall later that night and the next day went unanswered. Twelve days later, when Breashears and Viesturs climbed over the South Summit on their way to the top, they found Hall lying on his right side in a shallow ice-hollow, his upper body buried beneath a drift of snow. **D**

CAUSE AND EFFECT

5. Name several of the **causes** that led to Hall's death.

Early on the morning of May 11, when I returned to Camp Four, Hutchison, standing in for Groom, who was unconscious in his tent, organized a team of four Sherpas to locate the bodies of our teammates Weathers and Namba. The Sherpa search party, headed by Lhakpa Chhiri, departed ahead of Hutchison,

24. **Major Tom:** reference to the David Bowie song "Space Oddity," which is about an astronaut, Major Tom, who is lost and floating in space.

CONTENT-AREA CONNECTIONS

Science: The Effects of High Altitude on the Human Body

High-altitude mountaineering places the human body under severe stress. One of the most common problems is altitude (or mountain) sickness. The disease is produced by the low atmospheric pressures and reduced oxygen found at high elevations. The sickness can occur anywhere above eight thousand feet. The higher the altitude, the lower the amount of oxygen in the air. At 25,000 feet, there is two thirds less oxygen in the air than there is at sea level. The symptoms of altitude sickness include headache, nausea, breathlessness, and exhaustion. In acute cases it can turn into a life-threatening condition when fluid floods the lungs or the brain. Climbers of Mount Everest try to lessen the effects of altitude

360 Chapter 5 Irony and Ambiguity • Generating Research Questions and Evaluating Sources

who was so exhausted and befuddled that he forgot to put his boots on and left camp in his light, smooth-soled liners. Only when Lhakpa Chhiri pointed out the blunder did Hutchison return for his boots. Following Boukreev's directions, the Sherpas had no trouble locating the two bodies at the edge of the Kangshung Face.

The first body turned out to be Namba, but Hutchison couldn't tell who it was until he knelt in the howling wind and chipped a three-inch-thick carapace of ice from her face. To his shock, he discovered that she was still breathing. Both her gloves were gone, and her bare hands appeared to be frozen solid. Her eyes were dilated.[25] The skin on her face was the color of porcelain. "It was terrible," Hutchison recalls. "I was overwhelmed. She was very near death. I didn't know what to do."

"He was as close to death as a person can be and still be breathing."

He turned his attention to Weathers, who lay 20 feet away. His face was also caked with a thick armor of frost. Balls of ice the size of grapes were matted to his hair and eyelids. After cleaning the frozen detritus[26] from his face, Hutchison discovered that he, too, was still alive: "Beck was mumbling something, I think, but I couldn't tell what he was trying to say. His right glove was missing and he had terrible frostbite. He was as close to death as a person can be and still be breathing."

Badly shaken, Hutchison went over to the Sherpas and asked Lhakpa Chhiri's advice. Lhakpa Chhiri, an Everest veteran respected by Sherpas and sahibs[27] alike for his mountain savvy, urged Hutchison to leave Weathers and Namba where they lay. Even if they survived long enough to be dragged back to Camp Four, they would certainly die before they could be carried down to Base Camp, and attempting a rescue would needlessly jeopardize the lives of the other climbers on the Col, most of whom were going to have enough trouble getting themselves down safely.

Hutchison decided that Chhiri was right. There was only one choice, however difficult: Let nature take its inevitable course with Weathers and Namba, and save the group's resources for those who could actually be helped. It was a classic act of triage.[28] When Hutchison returned to camp at 8:30 A.M. and told the rest of us of his decision, nobody doubted that it was the correct thing to do. **E**

Later that day a rescue team headed by two of Everest's most experienced guides, Pete Athans and Todd Burleson, who were on the mountain with their own clients, arrived at Camp Four. Burleson was standing outside the tents about 4:30 P.M. when he noticed someone lurching slowly toward camp. The person's bare right hand, naked to the wind and horribly frostbitten, was outstretched in a weird, frozen salute. Whoever it was reminded Athans of a mummy in a low-budget horror film. The mummy turned out to be none other than Beck Weathers, somehow risen from the dead. **F**

A couple of hours earlier, a light must have gone on in the reptilian core of Weathers' comatose[29] brain, and he regained consciousness. "Initially I thought I was in a dream," he recalls. "Then I saw how badly frozen my right hand was, and that helped bring me around to reality. Finally I woke up enough to recognize **G**

25. **dilated** *v.* used as *adj.:* made wider; here, referring to the pupil of the eye.
26. **detritus** (dē·trīt′əs) *n.:* debris.
27. **sahibs** (sä′ibz′) *n.:* term used by Sherpas to refer to the paying members of the expeditions.
28. **triage** (trē·äzh′) *n.:* assigning of priorities of medical care based on chances for survival.
29. **comatose** *adj.:* deeply unconscious due to injury or disease.

Vocabulary
jeopardize (jep′ər·dīz′) *v.:* endanger.

DIRECT TEACHING

E Reading Skills

Making judgments. Evaluate the decision made by Hutchison and Chhiri. Did they make the right choice? Explain. [Possible responses: The decision to leave Namba and Weathers was correct, because they had to consider the welfare of the whole group; the decision was incorrect, because leaving people to die is cruel. As long as Namba and Weathers were still breathing, every effort should have been made to save them.]

F Literary Focus GRADE-LEVEL STANDARD

Ironies and contradictions. What is incongruous about the arrival of Weathers? [It is completely unexpected. He had been left for dead by the rescue team.]

G Vocabulary Development

Context clues. *Comatose* is a medical term. How might the context clues help you uncover its meaning? [Possible responses: Weathers "regained consciousness" after "a light must have gone on in . . . [his] comatose brain," so *comatose* might mean "unconscious." Weathers's brain had been "comatose," but later he was "risen from the dead," so *comatose* might mean "in a deathlike state."]

sickness by acclimating themselves slowly to atmospheric conditions. Often they spend several weeks at Mount Everest Base Camp before moving on to higher elevations.

Culture: Sherpas

Individual activity. Invite interested students to conduct research to learn more about Sherpas. To help them begin their research, suggest that they find answers to questions such as these:

- How long have Sherpas been climbing the Himalayas?
- How does one hire and compensate Sherpas for their climbing guidance?
- What kind of life do Sherpas lead, living on the Himalayan slopes?

Suggest that students enter keywords such as *Sherpas, Himalayan guides, mountain-climbing guides,* or *Mount Everest guides* into an Internet search engine. Ask students to gather information from various sources and, if possible, give a multimedia presentation of their research to the class.

Direct Teaching

A Reading Skills

Understanding cause and effect. [Possible responses to question 6: Weathers saves his own life through an effort of sheer will. Abandoned by rescuers, he somehow summons up the energy to walk by himself into camp, overcoming frostbite, near blindness, and the storm.]

B Learners Having Difficulty

Summarizing. How would you summarize Krakauer's comments here? [Possible response: The same zeal that drives people to climb mountains can lead them to make bad decisions, leading to future tragedies like this one.]

Guided Practice

Monitoring students' progress. Guide the class in answering these comprehension questions. Direct students to locate passages in the text that support their responses.

Short Answer

1. How does Krakauer feel at the summit of Mount Everest? [ill, tired, and numb]
2. What does Krakauer notice when he first begins his descent? [A blanket of clouds is forming.]
3. Why does Krakauer have to wait at the Hillary Step? [Ascending climbers cause a "traffic jam."]
4. Why is it surprising that Beck Weathers survives? [Rescuers have already left him for dead.]
5. How do other climbers find out what is happening to Hall and Hansen? [Hall communicates via a small two-way radio.]

that the cavalry[30] wasn't coming so I better do something about it myself."

Although Weathers was blind in his right eye and able to focus his left eye within a radius of only three or four feet, he started walking into the teeth of the wind, deducing correctly that camp lay in that direction. If he'd been wrong he would have stumbled immediately down the Kangshung Face, the edge of which was a few yards in the opposite direction. Ninety minutes later he encountered "some unnaturally smooth, bluish-looking rocks," which turned out to be the tents of Camp Four. (A)

> **CAUSE AND EFFECT**
> 6. How did Weathers save his own life? What is **ironic** about his situation?

The next morning, May 12, Athans, Burleson, and climbers from the IMAX team short-roped Weathers down to Camp Two. On the morning of May 13, in a hazardous helicopter rescue, Weathers and Gau[31] were evacuated from the top of the icefall by Lieutenant Colonel Madan Khatri Chhetri of the Nepalese army. A month later, a team of Dallas surgeons would amputate Weathers' dead right hand just below the wrist and use skin grafts to reconstruct his left hand.

After helping to load Weathers and Gau into the rescue chopper, I sat in the snow for a long while, staring at my boots, trying to get some grip, however tenuous, on what had happened over the preceding 72 hours. Then, nervous as a cat, I headed down into the icefall for one last trip through the maze of decaying seracs.[32]

I'd always known, in the abstract, that climbing mountains was a dangerous pursuit. But until I climbed in the Himalayas this spring, I'd never actually seen death at close range. And there was so much of it: Including three members of an Indo-Tibetan team who died on the north side just below the summit in the same May 10 storm and an Austrian killed some days later, 11 men and women lost their lives on Everest in May 1996, a tie with 1982 for the worst single-season death toll in the peak's history. . . .[33]

Climbing mountains will never be a safe, predictable, rule-bound enterprise. It is an activity that idealizes risk-taking; its most celebrated figures have always been those who stuck their necks out the farthest and managed to get away (B) with it. Climbers, as a species, are simply not distinguished by an excess of common sense. And that holds especially true for Everest climbers: When presented with a chance to reach the planet's highest summit, people are surprisingly quick to abandon prudence altogether. "Eventually," warns Tom Hornbein, 33 years after his ascent of the West Ridge, "what happened on Everest this season is certain to happen again." ■

30. **cavalry** *n.:* soldiers on horseback or motorized transport; an allusion to the idea that troops were not coming to the rescue.
31. **Gau:** "Makalu" Gau Ming-Ho, leader of the Taiwanese National Expedition, another team climbing on Everest.
32. **seracs** *n.:* pointed masses of ice.
33. It actually was the worst death toll on record. After Krakauer wrote this article, a twelfth death was discovered.

Vocabulary
tenuous (ten′yo͞o·əs) *adj.:* weak; slight.

CONTENT-AREA CONNECTIONS

Culture: Extreme Sports
In this excerpt from *Into Thin Air,* Krakauer describes Mount Everest's powerful attraction and the dangers the mountain poses for those who try to scale it.

Whole-class activity. Use the information presented in the article as a jumping-off point for class discussion. Have students debate the following questions:

- What is the attraction of extreme sports such as mountain climbing, sky diving, scuba diving, and race car driving?
- Should inexperienced climbers be allowed to pay for the opportunity to climb Mount Everest?
- Does media attention encourage people to engage in risky, thrill-seeking activities?

Meet the Writer

Jon Krakauer

Journalist Climber

Jon Krakauer (1954–) had mountain climbers as boyhood heroes instead of baseball players or movie stars. He made his first climb when he was only eight and after college became a "climbing bum." During the 1980s, he began writing articles on outdoor subjects.

In 1996, when *Outside* magazine asked Krakauer to write about Everest, he was an experienced climber but had never been above 17,200 feet. He later said,

"If you don't understand Everest and appreciate its mystique, you're never going to understand this tragedy and why it's quite likely to be repeated."

After the disaster, Krakauer conducted dozens of interviews with other survivors. His article, completed five weeks after his return from Nepal, was published in September 1996. Krakauer still felt such a need to get the experience off his chest that he soon expanded the article into a book, *Into Thin Air,* which was an immediate bestseller. Despite that success, Krakauer has suffered grief and guilt over the disaster on Mount Everest and has said,

"I'm never climbing it again, never. . . . I wish I hadn't gone this time."

For Independent Reading

If you enjoyed reading this excerpt from Krakauer's magazine article, you might want to read the book *Into Thin Air* (1997), Krakauer's full-length account of the ill-fated Everest expeditions. You might also enjoy *Into the Wild* (1996), Krakauer's terrifying true account of a young man's fateful wilderness adventure.

Meet the Writer

Background. In 1996, when Krakauer joined the Everest trek, he had already won critical and public acclaim for his book *Into the Wild* (1996), an insightful report on an idealistic young loner whose dream of living deep in the Alaskan wilderness cost him his life.

For Independent Reading

Encourage students who read Krakauer's full narrative to share any new insights on the Mount Everest tragedy that they gain from their reading.

- To learn more about people who must take risks on a daily basis, students can read *Fighting Fire* by Caroline Paul. In it, Paul describes her challenges and experiences as an urban firefighter.
- Below-grade-level readers may enjoy Gary Paulsen's novel *Brian's Winter,* an account of a stranded teenage boy's struggle to survive a winter in the rugged Canadian wilderness.

DIFFERENTIATING INSTRUCTION

Advanced Learners

Enrichment. Some expedition participants and observers disagreed with aspects of Krakauer's account of the 1996 tragedy. The Russian climber Anatoli Boukreev, for example, was not pleased about Krakauer's description of his role in the events, and wrote his own account, *The Climb: Tragic Ambitions on Everest,* to express his own views. Even today, mountaineers continue to debate issues related to the 1996 events.

Activity. Invite students who read *Into Thin Air* to investigate the controversies that followed its publication. Ask them to share any new discoveries they make with the class.

Into Thin Air 363

INDEPENDENT PRACTICE

Literary Response and Analysis

Reading Check

1. Possible answer (underlining shows grave danger):
   Main events—Krakauer reaches summit and descends; Krakauer's oxygen runs out. *Outcome*—reaches South Summit; gets new tank; *Main event*—Weathers postpones descent. *Outcome*—trapped by storm; found but abandoned by rescuers; revives and reaches camp; loses right hand and sustains damage to his left hand. *Main event*—Other climbers linger at summit. *Outcome*—Several die. *Main event*—Hall lets Hansen go on to summit. *Outcome*—Hansen gives out after leaving summit, later dies; Hall dies. *Main event*—Krakauer and Harris stop above Camp Four. *Outcome*—Harris and Krakauer descend, and both arrive safely.

Interpretations

Possible Answers

2. The narrator reaches summit, yet feels no sense of triumph. Technology allows Hall to talk to his wife from the mountain but cannot save his life. Hall, a veteran, should survive any mountain ascent but dies. Weathers survives.
3. These ironies create a sense of surprise when expected outcomes fail to materialize.
4. *Effect*—death of Rob Hall. *Causes*—unwillingness to turn Hansen back; lingering at summit; false news about oxygen; the storm; refusal to leave Hansen; frostbite; exposure.
5. Hall, for giving his life, and Weathers, for saving himself, appear to be heroes; there are no heroes—they all took foolish risks and failed one another.
6. Climbing will always be risky; and people will always "abandon prudence" to reach higher summits.
7. Possible answers: Krakauer's feelings at the summit; the decision to leave Namba and Weathers; Weathers's survival; the conversations between Hall and his wife.
8. Possible answer: Everest symbolizes the unattainable and embodies the idea of being at the top of the world.

Evaluation

9. Students may say that subjectivity colors any first-person narrative but that Krakauer seems a reliable narrator. Some may say that a strictly factual account wouldn't affect readers in the same way.

Literary Response and Analysis

Reading Check

1. Make a list of the **main events** in this Everest story. Then, circle the events during which Krakauer or other climbers were in grave danger. Tell the outcome of each circled event.

Interpretations

2. Find and explain at least four examples of **situational irony, contradictions,** or **incongruities** in the article. (Hint: Consider what happens to Rob Hall and Beck Weathers for starters.)
3. **Situational irony** is a favorite device of short story writers. What impact does it have in this nonfiction narrative?
4. Choose one tragedy that happened on the mountain—for example, the death of Doug Hansen or the loss of Beck Weathers's right hand. Draw a **cause-and-effect diagram** similar to the one below to show the complex causes that led to the tragedy.

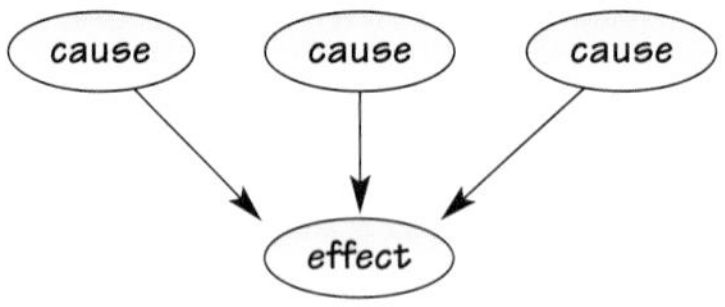

5. Are there any real-life heroes in this story? If so, who are they, and why do you think they are heroes?
6. What **conclusions** does Krakauer draw at the end of this selection? Do you think these conclusions apply to other "risk takers" as well? Explain.
7. What passages in this narrative impress you, puzzle you, shock you, or cause other strong reactions? Read those passages aloud in a group. Discuss how the events described affected your previous opinion of mountain climbing. (Check your Quickwrite notes.)
8. In an interview Krakauer gave about his experience in 1996 on Everest, he said, "We should think of Everest not as a mountain, but as the geologic embodiment of **myth.**" What do you think he means by that statement? In what way is Everest a "chunk of myth"?

Reading Standard 3.8
Interpret and evaluate the impact of contradictions, ironies, and incongruities in a text.

Evaluation

9. Evaluate the article in terms of its **subjectivity** and **objectivity.** Find some of the subjective details (thoughts, feelings, personal information) that Krakauer includes. Would you prefer reading a totally objective (factual) account? Explain.

Writing

Comparing Media Coverage

Today most important news events are covered in a variety of media genres—for example, newspapers, newsmagazines, TV news reports, TV newsmagazines, even TV talk shows. In 1996, the tragic Everest expedition was a hot news story for some time. Several of the survivors, such as Beck Weathers, became instant celebrities and appeared on TV talk shows.

Pick an event from today's news that interests you—any event that is widely covered in both newspapers and on television. Follow coverage of the event in different genres, and write a **brief report** comparing the coverage in those genres.

Use Comparing Media Genres, pages 382–389, for help with this assignment.

364 Chapter 5 Irony and Ambiguity • Generating Research Questions and Evaluating Sources

Vocabulary Development

Analogies: Parallel Word Pairs

PRACTICE 1

In an **analogy** the words in one pair relate to each other in the same way as the words in a second pair. Fill in each blank below with the word from the Word Bank that best completes the analogy. (Two words on the list are synonyms and may be used interchangeably.) For more help with analogies, see pages 29–30.

Word Bank
- deteriorate
- innocuous
- notorious
- benign
- apex
- crucial
- speculate
- traverse
- jeopardize
- tenuous

1. BASE : BOTTOM :: __________ : top.
2. SAFE : DANGEROUS :: __________ : harmful.
3. MISLEAD : DECEIVE :: _________ : endanger.
4. TRIVIAL : MINOR :: _______ : important.
5. TRY : ATTEMPT :: __________ : guess.
6. MINOR : MAJOR :: ___________ : malignant.
7. FAMOUS : STAR :: ________ : criminal.
8. WEAKEN : STRENGTHEN :: ________ : improve.
9. CLIMB : STAIRS :: ________ : bridge.
10. STRONG : POWERFUL :: _________ : weak.

Technical Vocabulary—Widgets, Whatsits, Thingamajigs

If you are a football fan, you know the meaning of *touchdown, off tackle,* and *scrimmage.* Before reading "Into Thin Air," did you know the meaning of *rappel* and *short-rope?*

"As I clipped into a fixed rope and prepared to rappel over the lip . . ." (page 354)

"He's got a rope; he'll be able to short-rope me." (page 357)

Almost every kind of work or play has its own special **technical vocabulary,** or **jargon.** When writers cover a technical subject for a general audience, they usually include **context clues** to help the reader guess the meaning, and sometimes they also provide footnotes. (Check the context clues and footnotes for *rappel* and *short-rope.* Can you explain these words to a friend?)

PRACTICE 2

1. Review the footnotes for these words from "Into Thin Air": *troposphere, dementia, triage, comatose.* List any context clues in the text that can help you determine the meanings of the words.
2. Write a list of technical terms for any field that you know well (perhaps a sport or a favorite hobby). Choose two of the most obscure terms, and write sentences using context clues that would enable a reader to understand the terms. See whether a classmate can guess the words' meanings.

Grade 8 Review Reading Standard 1.3 Use word meanings within the appropriate context and show ability to verify those meanings.

Reading Standard 1.1 Identify and use the literal meanings of words.

Vocabulary Development

Practice 1

1. apex
2. innocuous (or benign)
3. jeopardize
4. crucial
5. speculate
6. benign (or innocuous)
7. notorious
8. deteriorate
9. traverse
10. tenuous

Practice 2

Possible Answers

1. *troposphere. Context clues—* "Twenty-nine thousand twenty-eight feet up"; "there was so little oxygen reaching my brain."

   dementia. Context clues—"Two full bottles [of oxygen] were waiting"; "But Harris, in the throes of his oxygen-starved dementia . . . [told] Hall that all the bottles . . . were empty."

   triage. Context clues—"There was only one choice, however difficult: Let nature take its inevitable course with Weathers and Namba, and save the group's resources for those who could actually be helped. It was a classic act of triage."

   comatose. Context clue—"a light must have gone on in . . . Weathers' comatose brain, and he regained consciousness."
2. Sailing terms might include *leeward, windward, tack, come about, jibe, capsize, boom, stays, sheets, heel. Sentence—*We accidentally jibed, and this awkward turn brought the wind gusting from behind to play havoc with the sail.

ASSESSING

Assessment
- *Progress Assessment of Reading*
  - Selection Test

RETEACHING

For another selection to teach Standard 3.8, see *Interactive Reading,* Chapter 5.

Resources Reminder

Vocabulary
- *Vocabulary Development*
  - Vocabulary Worksheet, p. 28
- *Lesson Plans for Language Development*
  - Vocabulary, pp. 165, 170

STANDARDS FOCUS, pp. 366–373

(For grade-level and review standards taught in this lesson, see citations on Student Edition pages.)

Summary at grade level

Is the age of exploration over? Not to guests at the Explorers Club annual dinner. Club members dispute the idea that "all corners of the world have been explored." Some modern-day explorers, like Sylvia Earle and Robert Ballard, believe new treasures lie in the oceans' depths. Others, like astronaut Kathryn Sullivan, the first American female space walker, look to the stars. Many of the assembled explorers point to past heroes as inspiration, citing pioneers like Ernest Shackleton and Edmund Hillary. Although they respect these pioneering explorers, modern explorers believe that there are still many treasures to discover in the future. What sets these explorers apart? Some say it's the willingness to undertake difficult journeys and the heart to continue when the journey gets tough.

PRETEACHING

Standards Starter

Build prerequisite skills. Ask students to discuss information sources they could use to research great explorers from the past. Then, have students name sources they might use to investigate current explorers. Discuss the pros and cons of each type of resource.

Before You Read INFORMATIONAL MATERIALS

Explorers Say There's Still Lots to Look For

Generating Research Questions and Evaluating Sources

To research a topic, you need to generate specific, focused research questions. Then, you look for answers. Before you decide to use a source, evaluate it.

1. **Check relevance.** Always skim a source to make sure it has relevant information.
2. **Check the source's credentials.** Is the source a well-known newspaper, magazine, encyclopedia, or other reputable source? Does the writer seem qualified to speak on the subject? Has the writer written other books or articles on the topic?
3. **Check for bias.** Are you reading someone's subjective **opinion** or objective **facts**? If an opinion, ask whether the writer has any **bias,** or prejudice, toward the topic. This issue is especially important if you are researching a controversial topic.
4. **Check for accuracy.** Verify factual information in at least two reputable sources, such as encyclopedias or other reference sources.
5. **Check the source's timeliness.** Check publication dates. The most recent sources will have the most up-to-date information, but older information may provide historical details.

Reading Standard 2.3 Generate relevant questions about readings on issues that can be researched.

Be Wary of the Internet

Because the Internet is not monitored for accuracy as most publications are, you must carefully evaluate any information you find on it. The most accurate, reliable, and unbiased information can be found on sites that are affiliated with and created by reputable organizations, such as universities, government agencies, museums, and national news organizations. (The addresses for these sites usually include *edu, gov,* or *org.*) An individual's home page is not considered reliable. Always ask yourself:

- What qualifications does the Web site author have to speak on the topic?
- What is the purpose of the site?
- Does the site appear to be objective?
- When was the site created or updated?

Vocabulary Development

illusion (i·lo͞o′zhən) *n.:* misleading or inaccurate idea.

marooned (mə·ro͞ond′) *v.* used as *adj.:* left stranded, helpless, or isolated.

nudged (nujd) *v.:* lightly pushed; bumped.

whimsy (hwim′zē) *n.:* quaint or odd humor.

navigator (nav′ə·gāt′ər) *n.:* person who plots the course of a vehicle, usually a ship or plane.

Connecting to the Literature

Would you call the climbers on Mount Everest who are described in "Into Thin Air" adventurers or explorers? The following article discusses the difference between adventure and exploration and introduces you to some of the daring women and men who probe earth's unexplored regions.

RESOURCES: READING

Planning

- *One-Stop Planner* CD-ROM with Test Generator
- *On Course: Mapping Instruction*

Media

- *Audio CD Library*
  - disc 11

Reading

- *Interactive Reading,* Teacher's Edition
  - Graphic Organizer: 5 W's and H Chart

Differentiating Instruction

- *Lesson Plans for Language Development*
  - English-Language Learners, pp. 153–155, 166, 171
  - Special Education Students, pp. 156, 166, 171

366 Chapter 5 Irony and Ambiguity • Generating Research Questions and Evaluating Sources

NEWSPAPER ARTICLE

Explorers Say There's Still Lots to Look For

from *The Seattle Times,* May 21, 2000

Helen O'Neill

NEW YORK—The crickets were roasted to perfection. Baby scorpions adorned points of savory toast. And the saddle of beaver simmered gently in a decorative silver tureen.

Oceanographer[1] Sylvia Earle glided across the room in a shimmering red gown and golden shawl. She'd rather have been in her wet suit. She'd rather have been diving to the darkest corners of the abyss. Instead, "Her Deepness," as Earle is known, was busy in her role as honorary president of the Explorers Club, charming the cocktail crowd with her latest exploit: dancing a solitary dance with a giant octopus at the bottom of the Pacific.

Across the room, tuxedoed archaeologist[2] Johan Reinhard clutched his wineglass and chatted about his latest find—a 500-year-old Inca mummy unearthed atop a remote Andean peak. Next to him, Bertrand Piccard, first man to circumnavigate[3] earth in a balloon, engaged in intense debate about the future of solar-powered planes.

All around were people who have bushwhacked[4] through jungles, trekked across deserts, floated in space. Dripping medals and jewels and tales from afar, they gathered in the ballroom of the Waldorf-Astoria hotel for the annual Explorers Club banquet. Once a year they come here, to mingle with sponsors and troll[5] for support, to nibble on loin of kangaroo and explain to the world that there are still places to be discovered.

A Great Era of Exploration

A "There is a popular illusion that all corners of the earth have been explored," Earle says. "The greatest mountain ranges on the planet are underwater, where there is a whole continent waiting to be explored."

B In the past two years alone, Ian Baker reported discovering the fabled Shangri-La waterfall on Tibet's mighty Tsangpo River; Reinhard recovered three frozen Inca mummies from an Andean volcano; the body of English climber George Mallory,[6] who disappeared in 1924, was discovered on Mount Everest; and Robert Ballard located the world's oldest shipwrecks—two Phoenician cargo vessels in the Mediterranean. The same trip led him to uncover evidence of a giant flood about 7,000 years ago—perhaps the biblical flood of Noah.

1. **oceanographer** (ō′shə·näg′rə·fər) *n.:* scientist who studies the environment in the oceans.
2. **archaeologist** (är′kē·äl′ə·jist) *n.:* scientist who studies the life and cultures of the past, often through excavation of ancient sites and artifacts.
3. **circumnavigate** (sur′kəm·nav′ə·gāt′) *v.:* fly or sail completely around a geographic place.
4. **bushwhacked** *v.:* beat or cut one's way through bushes.
5. **troll** *v.:* literally, to fish with bait behind a slow-moving boat; in this instance it refers to "fishing" for funding.
6. **George Mallory:** In 1924, the British climbers George Mallory and Andrew Irvine disappeared in an attempt to reach Mount Everest's summit. In 1999, climbers discovered Mallory's frozen corpse near the summit.

Vocabulary

illusion (i·lo͞o′zhən) *n.:* misleading or inaccurate idea.

Vocabulary

- *Vocabulary Development*
  - Vocabulary Worksheet, p. 29

Assessment

- *Progress Assessment of Reading*
  - Selection Test
- *One-Stop Planner* CD-ROM with Test Generator

PRETEACHING

Preview Vocabulary

Have students read the definitions of the Vocabulary words on p. 366. Then, ask partners to work together on the following exercise. Possible responses are given.

1. Describe an illusion shared by many early seafarers. [the belief that the earth is flat]
2. Name someone who was marooned. [Robinson Crusoe]
3. What would happen if one car nudged another? [a minor accident]
4. Name someone known for a sense of whimsy. [Charlie Chaplin]
5. Identify someone you would trust as navigator on an expedition into the wilderness. [Jon Krakauer]

DIRECT TEACHING

A Learners Having Difficulty

Paraphrasing. Ask students to restate Earle's message in their own words. [Possible response: Although people might not think so, there is plenty left to explore, especially under the sea.]

B Reading Informational Materials

GRADE-LEVEL STANDARD

Generating research questions and evaluating sources. Which would be the better reference source to find out about Baker's most recent discovery, an encyclopedia or a magazine article? [Possible response: A magazine article would be a better source since magazines are more likely to have up-to-date information about recent archaeological finds.] Which would be the better source for information about Mallory's climbing career? [Possible response: an encyclopedia; Mallory is a historical figure whose achievements were made decades ago.]

DIRECT TEACHING

A Reading Informational Materials
GRADE-LEVEL STANDARD

Generating research questions and evaluating sources. Model for students several research questions that might be generated from this section of the article. Examples: "Which mountain peaks have never been climbed and what prevents people from climbing them?"; and "What equipment enables astronauts to walk in space?"

B Reading Informational Materials
GRADE-LEVEL STANDARD

? Generating research questions and evaluating sources. Point out Shackleton's advertisement for the *Endurance* expedition and the brief explanation of that adventure that follows. Ask students, "What else would you like to know about Shackleton's expedition?" [Possible responses: What did the men eat to survive? How long were they trapped on the ice floe?]

C Reading Skills

? Recognizing bias. Do you think Ballard would be an unbiased source to judge the importance of Shackleton's explorations? [Possible responses: Yes; Ballard is an accomplished explorer himself, so he would be a qualified judge of Shackleton's efforts. No; Ballard views Shackleton as a hero; therefore, his views might be biased by his personal admiration.]

A Explorers still scale peaks that never have been climbed, crawl through caves to the insides of earth, hurtle into space to walk among the stars. They find ancient tribes and ancient cities. They dig up dinosaurs. They journey to places where no one has reported being before: the jungles of central Congo, the Amazon and Peru, the deserts of Tibet and China, vast underwater caves in Mexico and Belize. They are only beginning to probe the oceans; 5 percent has been explored, though water covers 71 percent of the planet.

All of which makes Earle say, "I think the great era of exploration has just begun."

© Royal Geographical Society.

The ship from the Shackleton expedition, the *Endurance,* keeling over in the ice. Photo taken by expedition member Frank Hurley in 1915.

What Sets Them Apart

B "Men wanted for hazardous journey. Small wages, bitter cold, long months of complete darkness, constant danger, safe return doubtful. Honor and recognition in case of success."—Ernest Shackleton's 1914 advertisement for crew members for *Endurance.*

The ship was aptly named. Although Shackleton failed in his quest to cross the Antarctic,[7] his journey became one of the great epics of survival. Marooned for months on an ice floe, his ship crushed by pack ice, Shackleton managed to sail a lifeboat 800 miles, scale an unmapped mountain range, reach a Norwegian whaling station, and return to rescue all of his men.

Seventy-five years later, Robert Ballard wants to dig through the ice and find his hero's ship.

C Ballard is one of the most famous living explorers, and not just because he discovered the world's most famous shipwreck. Long before the lights of his little roaming robot lit up *Titanic*'s ghostly bow in 1985, the former naval officer and oceanographer dedicated his life to exploration. *Bismarck.* U.S.S. *Yorktown. Lusitania.*[8] Ballard has explored them all.

"When I die," Ballard says, "I want one word on my tombstone: Explorer."

7. **Antarctic:** ice-covered continent at the South Pole.

8. ***Bismarck.* U.S.S. *Yorktown. Lusitania:*** The *Bismarck* was an important German battleship that was sunk by the British navy during World War II. The U.S.S. *Yorktown* was an American aircraft carrier that was sunk by the Japanese navy during World War II. The *Lusitania* was a British ocean liner that was sunk by a German submarine during World War I.

Vocabulary
marooned (mə·ro͞ond') *v.* used as *adj.:* left stranded, helpless, or isolated.

DIFFERENTIATING INSTRUCTION

Learners Having Difficulty
Students may be unfamiliar with many of the places and historical events described in the exploration chart. On a world map, point out such locations as Mount Everest, the Northwest Passage, the Amazon region, Antarctica, the South Pole, and Amelia Earhart's flight path (Miami, Venezuela, Brazil, Africa, Calcutta, New Guinea, Nukumanu Islands). You might also wish to review map reading skills that students are likely to use in research, such as reading a legend, compass, and scale.

English-Language Learners
Before students read the article, review the chart of famous explorers on p. 371. Also, discuss with them the meanings of clichés ("having the heart to push on"; "thirst for adventure") and historical references (*Lusitania;* Hannibal) scattered throughout the article.

Resources Reminder
For lessons designed for intermediate and advanced English-language learners, see *Lesson Plans for Language Development,* pp. 153–155, 166, 171.

368 Chapter 5 Irony and Ambiguity • Generating Research Questions and Evaluating Sources

He is standing in his Institute of Exploration in Mystic, Connecticut, in a replica of the control room from which he discovered *Titanic.* The institute, which opened last year, is packed with videos and displays from Ballard's finds. On one wall, a large chart details his plans: searching for ancient wrecks in the Black Sea, the lost ships of the Franklin expedition[9] in the Canadian Arctic, Shackleton's *Endurance.*

"A lot of people do adventure," Ballard says. "They retrace Hannibal's route[10] in a Winnebago. They take a helicopter to the North Pole and have cocktails. That is not exploration."

True exploration, he says, is about having a vision and following it, about going where no one has dared go before, about bringing back scientific information and publishing it in journals.

"It's about having the heart to push on when you want to turn back," he says. "That is what sets explorers apart."

Seeking Knowledge

"Explorers are foragers,"[11] says Anna Roosevelt, curator of archaeology at the Field Museum of Natural History in Chicago and professor of anthropology at the University of Illinois. "They will seek until they find."

The great-granddaughter of Theodore Roosevelt spends much of her time foraging in the Amazon River basin, challenging conventional wisdom about early settlements there. She also challenges any notion that she is following in the footsteps of her famous ancestor, whose faded expedition photographs decorate the walls of the Explorers Club. Teddy Roosevelt, she says, was a great adventurer and a great president, but he wasn't an explorer in the true sense.

"People and animals died on his expeditions," she said of his legendary African safaris and canoe trips down the Amazon's River of Doubt. "They don't die on mine."

Roosevelt was one of the first women inducted into the Explorers Club after it opened its doors to women in 1981. Another was astronaut Kathryn Sullivan, first American woman to walk in space.

Sullivan didn't particularly feel like an explorer when she nudged her spaceship out of

Astronaut Kathryn Sullivan checks the antenna of the spaceship *Challenger.*

Vocabulary
nudged (nujd) *v.:* lightly pushed; bumped.

9. **Franklin expedition:** In 1845, the British explorer John Franklin led an expedition of two ships to the Arctic in search of a "northwest passage" linking the Atlantic and Pacific Oceans. The explorers and crew had to abandon ship and died one and a half years later in the Arctic wilderness. The ships were never found.
10. **Hannibal's route:** Hannibal (247–183 B.C.), a general in the ancient North African kingdom of Carthage, crossed the Alps to invade the Italian peninsula in 218 B.C.
11. **foragers** (fôr′ij·ərz) *n.:* those who search for what is needed or wanted.

DIRECT TEACHING

D English-Language Learners

Cultural concepts. Explain to students that a Winnebago is a type of recreational vehicle or motor home. Point out that here Ballard is making light of adventure in order to illustrate the difference between it and "real" exploration.

E Content-Area Connections

History: Theodore Roosevelt
Theodore Roosevelt (1858–1919), the twenty-sixth president of the United States, was known as an adventurer and avid outdoorsman. His presidency was notable for its early achievements in the realm of resource conservation. After his second term, he embarked on a yearlong African safari, collecting animals for the Smithsonian Institution and writing articles about his experiences. In 1913, Roosevelt traveled to South America to map the course of an unexplored river.

Special Education Students
For lessons designed for special education students, see *Lesson Plans for Language Development,* pp. 156, 166, 171.

Advanced Learners
Acceleration. Use this activity to move advanced learners toward the eleventh- and twelfth-grade Standard 2.3, for which they verify and clarify facts presented in a text by using a variety of consumer, workplace, and public documents.
Activity. Invite advanced learners to choose one fact presented in "Explorers Say There's Still Lots to Look For" and perform library and Internet research to verify that fact. Challenge students to consult four to six different types of informational sources and to present at least three different types of documents to corroborate the fact they chose to investigate.

DIRECT TEACHING

A Reading Informational Materials
GRADE-LEVEL STANDARD

? Generating research questions and evaluating sources. What are several sources that might be useful in researching the subject of February's Cameroon expedition? [Possible responses: a map of Cameroon; a book on the geography of Cameroon; a transcript of the phone interview in which February discusses his ascent of the Mandara Mountains.]

B Vocabulary Development
REVIEW STANDARD

? Greek and Latin root words. Explain to students that the word *technology* is derived from two Greek root words, *techne* (meaning "art or skill") and *–logy* (meaning "science or study of"). What are examples of other words that use one of these two root words? [Possible responses: *archaeology, psychology, technician, technical.*] You might discuss how each word's meaning relates to its root words.

Amelia Earhart in the cockpit of a small airplane.

the way so she could get a better view of earth. She was more amused by the whimsy of it all: Having trained for this moment so long, it actually felt normal. It wasn't until she got back to earth that she pondered its meaning.

"I think sometimes we learn more about ourselves and our place in society and in the universe than the places we thought we were going to explore."

A Clinging to a cliff in Cameroon, thirty-two-year-old South African climber Edmund February agreed. Sure it's an adventure, he said, in a phone interview from the mountain in December. But it's exploration, too.

"When we make these climbs, we are exploring a new dimension, a new theater," said February, who was pioneering a first ascent on the volcanic spires of the Mandara Mountains. "It's not with the same parameters as Scott or Amundsen. But it's more than just a thirst for adventure. It's a thirst for knowledge, too."

Much Still to Discover

"A few toes aren't much to give to achieve the pole," Peary exclaimed in 1898.

So what is left for modern-day explorers to achieve, or sacrifice? Plenty, says Bradford Washburn, a ninety-year-old cartographer[12] and mountaineer from Boston. Washburn was friends with Richard Byrd.[13] He interviewed for the position of navigator on Amelia Earhart's round-the-world flight, dropping out because he thought the radios were inadequate. In the 1930s he knocked out the door of a Lockheed Vega airplane and tied himself to the opposite bulkhead in order to map glaciers on Alaska's St. Elias Range. Last year, he directed an expedition that led to the discovery of a new altitude of Everest—29,035 feet, 7 feet higher than previously recorded.

"It was exciting," Washburn says, "but nothing as exciting as when Ed Hillary got to the top."

B Still, Washburn marvels at the technology that hurtles modern explorers toward new frontiers, and at the spirit propelling them.

12. **cartographer** (kär·täg′rə·fər) *n.:* person who makes maps or charts.
13. **Richard Byrd** (1888–1957): U.S. naval officer who pioneered the exploration of Arctic and Antarctic regions by air.

Vocabulary
whimsy (hwim′zē) *n.:* quaint or odd humor.
navigator (nav′ə·gāt′ər) *n.:* person who plots the course of a vehicle, usually a ship or plane.

CONTENT-AREA CONNECTIONS

History: Topics of Exploration
This article includes many references to historical events—events that help to motivate modern explorers into action.

Paired activity. Invite pairs of students to choose one of these references to explore further. For example, students might research Incan culture; the wrecks of the *Titanic, Lusitania, Bismarck,* or U.S.S. *Yorktown;* Shackleton's *Endurance* adventure; or Earhart's around-the-world flight. Have students generate relevant research questions, and remind them to evaluate the sources they are consulting. Finally, encourage pairs to report their findings to the class.

370 Chapter 5 Irony and Ambiguity • Generating Research Questions and Evaluating Sources

Ballard discovering the *Titanic,* Reinhard staring into the mummified face of an Inca child, Earle dancing with a giant octopus. All of them, Washburn says, are driven by the same spirit that drove Columbus and Peary and Byrd: to discover new worlds and document them.

At the Boston Museum of Science, where he is honorary director and where he still works several days a week, Washburn breaks into a poem.

"Something hidden. Go and find it. . . . Something lost behind the Ranges. Lost and waiting for you. Go!"

The poem is by Kipling.[14] It's one of Washburn's favorites. It's called "The Explorer."

C

14. **Rudyard Kipling** (1865–1936): British writer, poet, and Nobel Prize winner.

D

The following men and women, all mentioned in the article, make up a short list of some of the world's most famous explorers of the twentieth century.

Notable Explorers of the Twentieth Century

Roald Amundsen (1872–1928)	Norwegian explorer; first person to reach the South Pole and to sail through the Northwest Passage in the Arctic.
Robert Ballard (1942–)	American deep-sea explorer who discovered the wreck of the *Titanic* in 1985 and has pioneered use of underwater robots.
Amelia Earhart (1897–1937)	First woman to fly solo across the Atlantic. She disappeared over the Pacific Ocean during a round-the-world flight.
Sylvia Earle (1935–)	Pioneer researcher on marine ecosystems; has led over fifty deep-sea expeditions.
Edmund Hillary (1919–)	New Zealand mountain climber. He and Tenzing Norgay were the first to reach the top of Mount Everest, in 1953.
Robert Peary (1856–1920)	American explorer and naval officer credited with being first to reach the North Pole, in 1909.
Johan Reinhard (1943–)	High-altitude archaeologist specializing in ancient ceremonial sites in South America.
Anna Roosevelt (1946–)	Anthropologist and archaeologist who has documented civilization of the Amazon region dating back eleven thousand years.
Robert Scott (1868–1912)	British naval officer and explorer who died during an expedition that tried to reach the South Pole in 1912.
Ernest Shackleton (1874–1922)	British explorer and naval reserve officer whose third expedition to the Antarctic resulted in a heroic two-year struggle for survival.

DIRECT TEACHING

C Reading Skills

Finding the main idea. How does Kipling's poem relate to the main idea of this article? [Possible response: The poem challenges explorers to go out and discover new things. The article explains that explorers are doing just that and that there's still plenty to discover.]

D Reading Informational Materials

GRADE-LEVEL STANDARD

Generating research questions and evaluating sources. Ask students where they would turn to quickly find out more about the explorers listed. [Possible responses: an Internet search engine; a biographical dictionary.] What search engine keywords might you use to locate information about Sylvia Earle? [*Sylvia Earle, oceanography, Explorers Club president*] What types of Web sites might produce trustworthy, accurate information about her? [Possible responses: government sites; sites of oceanographic journals; and sites of magazines such as *National Geographic.*]

GUIDED PRACTICE

Guide the class in answering these comprehension questions.

True-False

1. Sylvia Earle believes there are whole new worlds to explore on the ocean floor. [T]
2. Robert Ballard plans to find Shackleton's *Endurance.* [T]
3. Explorer Anna Roosevelt is the great-granddaughter of Theodore Roosevelt. [T]
4. Veteran explorer Bradford Washburn believes that modern explorers do not compare to the great historical explorers. [F]

Explorers Say There's Still Lots to Look For 371

INDEPENDENT PRACTICE

Analyzing Informational Materials

Reading Check

1. Earle believes a continent is under the sea waiting to be explored.
2. The expedition to cross the Antarctic failed when Shackleton's ship became stuck in ice. To get help, he sailed eight hundred miles in a lifeboat and returned to rescue his men.
3. Ballard believes that true explorers follow a vision, go where no one has gone before, and report scientific information.

Test Practice

Answers and Model Rationales

1. **C** B is incorrect because it may not discuss Shackleton and his expedition. D is incorrect because Shackleton may not provide information about the *Endurance* in his testimony on the *Titanic.* A might be a reasonable source of information, but C is the best choice because the entire book is specifically focused on the *Endurance* expedition.
2. **F** As a dedicated oceanographer, Earle could hardly be expected to view the importance of deep-sea exploration objectively. The archaeologists Reinhard, Roosevelt, and Baker would likely be less biased, so G, H, and J are incorrect.
3. **D** Although the sources cited in A, B, and C may mention Ballard, a feature article that focuses specifically on Ballard is the best information source for the purpose.

Analyzing Informational Materials

Reading Check

1. According to Earle, where is there a "continent waiting to be explored"?
2. What happened on Ernest Shackleton's expedition?
3. According to Ballard, what defines true exploration?

Test Practice

1. If you were looking for the facts about the *Endurance* crew's months on the ice floe, which source would probably be *most* useful?
   - **A** "Sir Ernest Shackleton and the Antarctic," lecture at Explorers Club (May 7, 2001) by Dr. William Rom
   - **B** An entry on Antarctica in *The Columbia Encyclopedia*
   - **C** *The Endurance: Shackleton's Legendary Antarctic Expedition* by Caroline Alexander with photos of the expedition by Frank Hurley
   - **D** Ernest Shackleton's testimony (June 18, 1912) on the sinking of the *Titanic*
2. Who would probably have the *most* biased view of the importance of further deep-sea exploration?
   - **F** Sylvia Earle
   - **G** Anna Roosevelt
   - **H** Ian Baker
   - **J** Johan Reinhard
3. If you wanted to do further research on Ballard's career and his explorations, which source would be *most* useful?
   - **A** An article on robotics and exploration in *Time* magazine
   - **B** An encyclopedia article on deep-sea exploration
   - **C** A history of great shipwrecks of the Atlantic Ocean
   - **D** A feature article in a national newsmagazine on Ballard and his career
4. Which of the following sources would be *most* reliable if you were researching the history of the Explorers Club?
   - **F** The Web site of Explorers Club Lodge and Safaris, a lodge for backpackers in South Africa
   - **G** The Web site of the Explorers Club; its section on the club's history
   - **H** An interview with a friend whose grandfather was a member of the Explorers Club
   - **J** An entry on "Explorers Club" in a tour guide to New York City

Reading Standard 2.3 Generate relevant questions about readings on issues that can be researched.

Application

Think of several good **research questions** suggested by the article. Choose one question, and start your research. Evaluate all the sources you discover. Then, summarize your research experience in a few paragraphs.

4. **G** F is incorrect because this site provides information about a lodge. H might provide anecdotal information about the Explorers Club, and J might provide information for visitors, but these sources would not provide a complete picture of the club's history. The Explorers Club Web site (G), discussing the club's history, would be the best source of information—though one would need to assess its objectivity.

Test-Taking Tips

For more instruction on how to answer multiple-choice items, refer students to **Test Smarts.**

372 Chapter 5 Irony and Ambiguity • Generating Research Questions and Evaluating Sources

Vocabulary Development

Words in Context: Clues All Around

The words in the Word Bank are defined for you, but what if they weren't? Look back at the text, and see whether there are any **clues** in the surrounding words and sentences (the **context**) that tell you what each word means. Then, sharpen your understanding of these words with the practice below.

Word Bank
illusion
marooned
nudged
whimsy
navigator

PRACTICE 1

Write your answer to each of the following questions.

1. Why is an illusion different from the truth?
2. If you had to be marooned somewhere for a month, where would you choose to be, and what would you take with you?
3. If you nudged an object, what would happen to it? Have you nudged anything recently? Explain.
4. Is whimsy a quality that makes you laugh or not? Why?
5. A deep-sea research team has a job for a navigator. What responsibility does that position involve?

Word Clues: Greek and Latin Roots and Relations

What do a seismograph, an autobiography, and a telegraph have in common? Sound like a riddle? In fact, all three words share the Greek root *–graph–*, so they're related. Learning to recognize familiar Greek and Latin roots will help you fathom the meanings of many English words. Many of the roots in the chart below can be found in words in the selection.

Greek Root	Meaning	Example
–anthropo–	human being	anthropology
–auto–	self	autobiography
–bio–	life	biology
–graph–	to write	graphic
–photo–	light	photocopy
–psycho–	mind	psychoanalysis
Latin Root	**Meaning**	**Example**
–scrib–	write	script
–labor–	work	laboratory

PRACTICE 2

Think of at least one other word for each of the Greek and Latin roots listed above, and then write the word's meaning. Explain how knowing the meaning of the root helps you understand the word. Use a dictionary for help.

Grade 8 Review Reading Standard 1.3 Use word meanings within the appropriate context, and show ability to verify those meanings.

Reading Standard 1.1 Understand word derivations.

Vocabulary Development

Practice 1

Possible Answers

1. An illusion is what appears to be; the truth is what actually is.
2. I would like to be marooned on an island with pleasant weather, fruit trees, and beautiful beaches. I'd bring sunscreen.
3. If I nudged an object, it might fall over. Recently I nudged a vase, and it fell off a table and broke.
4. Whimsy is a quality that silly people possess; more often than not, they make me laugh.
5. The job of navigator probably involves steering the course of a robotic boat.

Practice 2

Possible Answers

Greek Roots

- *–anthropo–. Other word*—anthropomorphize. *Meaning*—attribute human characteristics to something.
- *auto–. Other word*—autonomy. *Meaning*—dependent only on oneself.
- *–bio–. Other word*—biometry. *Meaning*—the calculation of the human life span.
- *–graph–. Other word*—autograph. *Meaning*—a written signature.
- *–photo–. Other word*—photosynthesis. *Meaning*—the creation of chemical compounds aided by light.
- *–psycho–. Other word*—psychology. *Meaning*—the science that studies processes of the mind.

Latin Roots

- *–scrib–. Other word*—scribble. *Meaning*—to write carelessly.
- *–labor–. Other word*—laborer. *Meaning*—one who works.

Resources Reminder

Vocabulary

- *Vocabulary Development*
  - Vocabulary Worksheet, p. 29
- *Lesson Plans for Language Development*
  - Vocabulary, pp. 166, 171

ASSESSING

Assessment

- *Progress Assessment of Reading*
  - Selection Test

RETEACHING

For another selection to teach Standard 2.3, see *Interactive Reading,* Part 2.

STANDARDS FOCUS, pp. 374–380

(For the grade-level standards taught in this lesson, see the citations on Student Edition pages.)

Reading Skills

- Make inferences.

Summary ↔ *at grade level*

James Stevenson's mysterious disaster tale takes the form of a series of journal entries that wash ashore in a bottle on a South Atlantic island. According to these entries, the city of New York has been deluged by a massive flood, an event whose origins are cloaked in ambiguity. The narrator describes the scene from his high-rise apartment building. At first, the trapped residents seem bewildered. Some celebrate irrationally as the water moves ever higher, swallowing up one floor after another. In the final entry, the tenants congregate on the rooftop, straining against a bitter wind and watching the oncoming waves. The narrator has no hope of rescue; the reader must assume that he and his neighbors perish in the flood.

PRETEACHING

Preview Vocabulary

Have students read the Vocabulary words and then choose the word that matches the synonym below.

1. immersed [submerged]
2. retreat [recede]
3. conjecture [speculation]
4. movable [portable]
5. most likely [presumably]

Before You Read

Notes from a Bottle

Literary Focus

Ambiguities and Subtleties: Open to Interpretation

Often the stories we find most memorable are the ones that leave us thinking and guessing. Knowing this, writers sometimes challenge and baffle readers, presenting a kind of puzzle with important information omitted. They purposely make events or characters or even the theme of a work **ambiguous** or **subtle**—that is, unclear or open to different interpretations.

When we read such stories, we struggle to figure out what's happening, what has happened, what will happen—and why. It's up to each reader to piece things together and ponder the facts. The unusual story you're about to read focuses on a single apartment building in New York City; that much is clear. The rest—well, have fun figuring it out.

Reading Skills

Making Inferences

An **inference** is an educated guess—you make such guesses all the time. Suppose your friend, who's never late, doesn't appear at the usual time to pick you up for school. You infer that something's happened (like a traffic jam or an accident) to delay her, or maybe she's sick.

Similarly, when you read a story, you fill in missing information, reading between the lines to make guesses about what's left unsaid or unclear. In an ambiguous story like the one you are about to read, the writer has purposely left out important information. You must therefore work even harder to make inferences and decide what is happening and why.

Reading Standard 3.8 Interpret and evaluate the impact of ambiguities and subtleties in a text.

Make the Connection

Quickwrite

Attacking aliens, a giant asteroid, global warming, nuclear war—writers and scientists have made dire predictions about dangers that threaten to wipe out human life on earth. Choose one serious, life-threatening problem. Tell how you think you would react and what you would do in the three days before the dire prediction comes true.

Vocabulary Development

portable (pôr′tə·bəl) *adj.:* able to be carried.

presumably (prē·zo͞om′ə·blē) *adv.:* probably.

speculation (spek′yə·lā′shən) *n.:* thought; guesswork.

submerged (səb·mʉrjd′) *v.:* covered with water.

recede (ri·sēd′) *v.:* move back or away.

RESOURCES: READING

Planning

- *One-Stop Planner* CD-ROM with Test Generator
- *On Course: Mapping Instruction*

Media

- *Audio CD Library*
  - disc 11

- *Fine Art Transparencies*
  - Transparency 10

Reading

- *Interactive Reading,* Teacher's Edition
  - Graphic Organizer: Ambiguity Chart

374 Chapter 5 Irony and Ambiguity • Generating Research Questions and Evaluating Sources

Notes from a Bottle

James Stevenson

(A bottle containing the following notes was discovered on a mountainside on Ascension Island, in the South Atlantic.) **A**

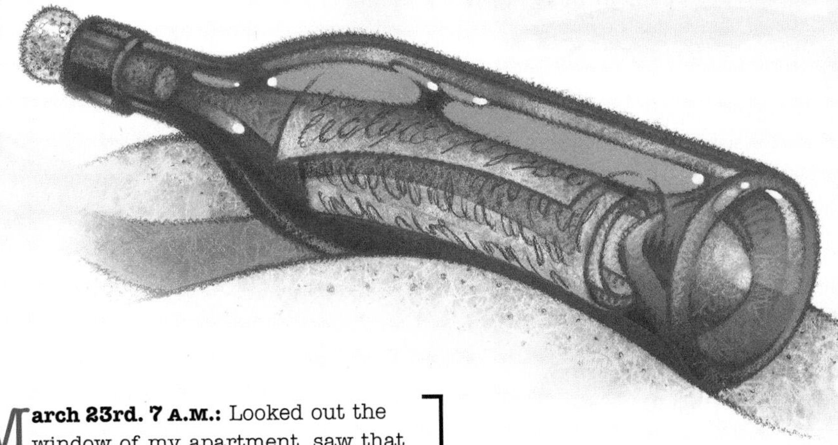

March 23rd. 7 A.M.: Looked out the window of my apartment, saw that the water was up to the second story all along Eighty-sixth Street. Yesterday, the movie marquees[1] toward Lexington were still visible at twilight, but this morning they are gone. There were, of course, no lights last night—there has been no electricity in the city for three days. (No telephones, no water, no heat, no television. Heat and telephone service had been gone for several days before that, owing to the fuel strike and the phone strike. Some portable radios still work, but they receive only the grainy sound of static.) A light snow is falling. **B**

4 P.M.: It is almost dark again, and the water is approaching the fourth floor. No planes or helicopters were seen today; the airports were probably the first to flood, and any planes that managed to get aloft would have run out of fuel by now. **C** It looks like another night of parties and celebrations. Across the street, candles and flashlight beams move about in the windows, and in our building loud, cheerful voices can be heard echoing in the fire stairs. There is a lot of shrieking and laughter. The children, as usual, are riding bicycles up and down the halls, as adults—bundled up in all manner of

1. **movie marquees:** structures projecting over the entrances to movie theaters that are usually lit up and display the name of the movie being shown.

Vocabulary
portable (pôr′tə·bəl) *adj.:* able to be carried.

PRETEACHING

Selection Starter

Motivate. Ask students to discuss the phrase *message in a bottle.* Who might send one? Why? Where might it wash up? Ask students if they have encountered other literary works or movies that include a message in a bottle.

DIRECT TEACHING

A Literary Focus
GRADE-LEVEL STANDARD

Ambiguities and subtleties. What questions does this statement create in the reader's mind? [Possible responses: Why did someone place these notes in a bottle? If the bottle was thrown into an ocean or river, how did it end up on a mountainside?]

B Learners Having Difficulty

Summarizing. What has occurred in New York City? [A great flood has besieged the city, knocking out utilities and services.]

C Literary Focus
GRADE-LEVEL STANDARD

Ambiguities and subtleties. Point out that here the author is subtly explaining the scope of the flood. Because planes taking off from New York airports would run out of fuel before finding a place to land, the flood must be widespread.

Differentiating Instruction
- *Lesson Plans for Language Development*
  - English-Language Learners, pp. 157–159, 167, 172
  - Special Education Students, pp. 160, 167, 172

Vocabulary
- *Vocabulary Development*
  - Vocabulary Worksheet, p. 30

Assessment
- *Progress Assessment of Reading*
  - Selection Test
- *One-Stop Planner* CD-ROM with Test Generator

DIRECT TEACHING

A Reading Skills

Making inferences. Why might people be reacting to the flood in such a festive way? [Possible responses: The children probably see the flood as a great adventure; they are probably happy because they do not have to go to school. The adults seem to be in denial; they cannot understand the events or do anything constructive about them. They may be trying to cover up their fear or to enjoy themselves because they believe they will not survive.]

B Vocabulary Development
GRADE-LEVEL STANDARD

Word roots. Draw students' attention to the word *dispensing.* Point out the word root *pens,* which means "to weigh" or "to pay." Then, discuss the meaning of *dispensing* ("to deal out in portions") and how its meaning relates to its word root. Challenge students to name other words that share the word root *pens.* [Possible responses: compensate, expensive, pension.]

C Reading Skills

Making inferences. How has the mood of the tenants changed? [Possible response: They no longer seem to be in a celebratory mood.] What can you infer about the reason for this change? [Possible response: With the water now up to the ninth floor, the tenants may realize that the situation is very serious and that their lives are at risk.]

---

clothing, and carrying drinks and candles—roam the building, going from one party to another. The Williamses, who were supposed to go on a cruise, have been dancing around in their vacation clothes—Audrey in a fur coat and bathing suit, Harold in a mask and flippers. A lot of things have been thrown out of windows; Ed Shea on 7 was tossing an orange back and forth to somebody in the building across the street; one group was **A** skimming L.P. records,[2] throwing them like Frisbees. There has been a good deal of horseplay. Carson on 8 would lean out his window and drop a paper bag full of flour on any head that was sticking out below. The biggest party last night was in the MacNeills' on 4—Alice played the piano, and everyone sang and danced until around three. (Today, a group of volunteers is moving the piano up to the Webers' on 6, just in case, and the Webers intend to have everybody in.) Phil Lewis amused everybody last night, saying that an ark[3] was on its way and that it was going to take two people from the Upper East Side. Martin, the doorman, has been drunk for a couple of days; he opened the Wenkers' apartment on 10—they're in Spain—and he has been holding court up **B** there, dispensing the Wenkers' liquor with a free hand. There is still no explanation for the flood, beyond rumors shouted from one building to another. A lot of activity on Eighty-sixth Street during the day. For a while, everyone was throwing piles of flaming newspapers out their windows and watching them float away, burning, and there was considerable boat traffic—outboards, rowboats, a Circle Line boat with a crowd aboard, a small tug,[4] a speedboat full of howling drunks towing a water skier in a black wet suit. An hour ago, the mayor went by, smiling grimly, in a large Chris-Craft cruiser with the city flag on the stern, the deck jammed with officials. Presumably, the water has reached Gracie Mansion[5] by now, although the mansion is on high ground.

> There is still no explanation for the flood . . .

C **March 24th. 3 P.M.:** The water is now just below my windows on the ninth floor. There is nothing to do but watch. The water is filthy—there had been the six-week garbage strike, and all the city's garbage is awash—and the seagulls are everywhere, feasting. A number of people came up to stay in my apartment during the night, but they have left now and gone to a higher floor. They all arrived with apologies and genial remarks, but when they left they did so without

2. **L.P. records:** long-playing phonograph records, playing at $33\frac{1}{3}$ revolutions per minute.
3. **ark** *n.:* large boat; reference to the Bible story of Noah's ark, which saved two of every creature from the great flood.
4. **tug** *n.:* small, powerful boat used to tow and push larger ships and barges.
5. **Gracie Mansion:** official residence of New York City's mayor.

Vocabulary
presumably (prē·zo͞om′ə·blē) *adv.:* probably.

DIFFERENTIATING INSTRUCTION

Learners Having Difficulty

Modeling. To help students read "Notes from a Bottle," model the reading skill of making inferences. After students have read the selection's first paragraph, say, "The largest city in the United States is without water, electricity, and television. From these details, I can infer that the water in the streets is not the result of a simple flood; the narrator is describing a disaster of extraordinary scope."

English-Language Learners

To help students who are unfamiliar with New York City to visualize the events of the story, share some images of the locations mentioned before they read. Photographs of Central Park, street scenes with theater marquees, avenues lined with high-rise buildings, Circle Line ferries, and Gracie Mansion will help students appreciate the magnitude of the event that the story describes.

Resources Reminder

For lessons designed for intermediate and advanced English-language learners, see *Lesson Plans for Language Development,* pp. 157–159, 167, 172.

376 Chapter 5 Irony and Ambiguity • Generating Research Questions and Evaluating Sources

fanfare[6]—simply disappeared, one or two at a time, when I wasn't looking. I'd hear the door click shut, and I'd know they'd gone upstairs. There has been constant speculation on the cause of the flood—an atomic test in the Arctic is a popular explanation—but no one has any information at all, and no one really expects any. Those of us who have lived here for any length of time have become hardened: One simply waits. Langford, the lawyer, who recently moved to New York and lives on 8, was furious at first. "Why haven't we been informed?" he kept demanding. "I have contacts in Washington. . . ." But when I saw him a few minutes ago—he was standing in the hall, eating a once-frozen TV dinner—he was brooding, and when others spoke to him he didn't reply.

5 P.M.: The strangest thing is the silence of the city. No car noises, honking, sirens. Bodies float by, tangled in wreckage—furniture, lumber, trash. Suddenly a boat's horn, but then it is silent again—extraordinary silence. The loudest sound, except when the gulls come near, is the slap of water just below the windowsill, or the scrape of something bumping the window air conditioner.

March 25th: We are on the roof now. I have no idea what time it is, but it is daylight. The lower buildings have been submerged, the tall office buildings stand like tombstones above the heaving waves. There are whitecaps[7] toward Central Park. An ocean liner stood by the Pan Am Building for a while, then moved out to sea. Our rooftop is packed with people; many huddle against the chimneys, trying to keep away from the bitter wind. Alice MacNeill—her piano was abandoned on 8—tried to get everyone to sing "Nearer My God to Thee,"[8] but there was little response. No one wants to accept the situation as final, and yet everyone is keeping to himself. Langford, I notice, has moved toward the tallest TV antenna and has stationed himself near its base. He dreams, I suppose, that when the water covers the roof and the skylights and the chimneys, he will shinny up the pole and cling to the top. In his mind, probably, the water will rise until it reaches his ankles, and then stop. That is his hope. Then the water will recede, go down, down, down—and he will be saved. The water is swirling around the skylights now. The wind shifts. The waves are coming straight in from the Atlantic. ■

The strangest thing is the silence of the city.

6. **fanfare** *n.:* showy display.

7. **whitecaps** *n.:* waves with white, foamy crests.

8. **"Nearer My God to Thee":** hymn reportedly played by the *Titanic*'s musicians as the ship was sinking.

Vocabulary

speculation (spek'yə·lā'shən) *n.:* thought; guesswork.

submerged (səb·murjd') *v.:* covered with water.

recede (ri·sēd') *v.:* move back or away.

DIRECT TEACHING

D Advanced Learners

Enrichment. Point out that the narrator cites nuclear arms as one possible cause of the flood. Explain to students that this story was written around 1969. Discuss with them how the historical events of that time, particularly the cold war, might have influenced this explanation of the flood and, on a larger scale, the entire story.

E Reading Skills

Making inferences. What situation do the building residents now find themselves in? [Possible response: . . . The narrator and his neighbors now face an imminent threat to their survival. . . . They have been forced to the roof by the floodwaters that now threaten to engulf their entire building.]

F Literary Focus GRADE-LEVEL STANDARD

Ambiguities and subtleties. The author leaves the reader with an ambiguous ending. In your opinion, what are the apartment dwellers' chances of survival? What are the chances that Langford's hopes, as hypothesized by the narrator, will be realized? [Possible response: It is probable that everyone on the roof is doomed because the author hints that the water has almost reached the rooftop and that the people will soon be engulfed by waves from the ocean.]

Special Education Students

For lessons designed for special education students, see *Lesson Plans for Language Development*, pp. 160, 167, 172.

Advanced Learners

Acceleration. Use the following activity with advanced learners to move them toward the eleventh- and twelfth-grade Standard 3.5, for which they evaluate the influences of the historical period that shaped the characters, plots, and settings of American literature.

Activity. Explain to students that through the end of the cold war, disaster scenarios involving nuclear-related tragedies that doomed the human race were common plotlines in literature and film. Challenge them to find and explore examples of these scenarios from the cold war era. Have students share the results of their research and discuss any common themes or plot elements of the examples.

GUIDED PRACTICE

Monitoring students' progress. Guide the class in answering these comprehension questions. Direct students to locate passages in the text that support their responses.

True-False

1. The narrator is trapped in his apartment building. [T]
2. The narrator explains the cause of the disaster that has struck New York City. [F]
3. The narrator sees the mayor of New York City. [T]
4. At the story's end, the building's residents retreat to the roof. [T]
5. Langford and the narrator escape in a boat. [F]

Meet the Writer

Background. James Stevenson's prolific career has included several series of books that each share characters or settings. His Mud Flat series tells of the adventures of a group of animals living in the Mud Flat community. Another series of books focuses on a witch named Emma, while yet another series revolves around a character named Grandpa. Most of these series books are picture books for young readers, but the stories and illustrations are enjoyed by readers of all ages.

Meet the Writer

James Stevenson

Writer, Illustrator, and Cartoonist

James Stevenson (1929–) works at two desks—one for writing and one for drawing. He's had an almost-fifty-year career as a cartoonist, reporter, and satirist on political and contemporary subjects. He is best known, however, as a writer and illustrator of whimsical, gently humorous books for young children.

Stevenson credits his elementary school in a suburb of New York City as a major influence on his creative life. His school, he recalls, encouraged its students to get involved in the social and political issues of the day and to express themselves artistically. It had a "policy of telling you that everybody could do everything. Everybody could sing, dance, act, play musical instruments, write stories, make pictures, and change the world."

By the time he was in college (and later, when he served as a U.S. Marine during the Korean War), Stevenson was selling cartoon ideas to *The New Yorker* magazine. He later worked as a reporter for *Life* magazine before joining *The New Yorker* as an editor, cartoonist, and staff writer.

Stevenson began his career by humorously depicting life in the suburbs, but by the 1960s, he was also satirizing political and national topics, such as the nuclear arms race and government bureaucracy. His major achievement, however, has been as a writer and illustrator of almost one hundred children's books, many of them winners of prestigious awards. Critics praised his ability to explore the difficulties of childhood with an insightful, lighthearted touch.

Stevenson credits movies and comic books, not the books he read as a child, with influencing his career:

> "I think that my experience and creative mind have been formed much more by movies and comic books. I like the idea of a storyboard, and I like the idea of a movie and all the different angles from which things can be viewed."

378 Chapter 5 Irony and Ambiguity • Generating Research Questions and Evaluating Sources

Literary Response and Analysis

Reading Check

1. **Summarize** what happens in the story by filling out a chart like the one below. Write a question mark next to items the story doesn't answer.

Where and when the story takes place	
What has happened before the story starts	
What happens during the story	
What happens as the story ends	

Interpretations

2. The story begins *in medias res* (in the middle of the action), with important information omitted. What **inferences** can you make about each of the following **ambiguities** in the story? What details help you make these inferences?
   - the cause of the flood
   - how widespread the flood is
   - the outcome for the narrator and his or her neighbors
3. What do the **title** and **subtitle** add to your knowledge of the story?
4. Trace the subtle changes in **mood,** or feeling, as the story progresses. Find sensory details and other details that help create the moods.
5. What do the **minor characters** (about whom we know almost nothing) add to the story?
6. What do the writer's choice of **point of view** and the story's **form** (journal entries) enable the writer to do?
7. An **allusion** is a reference to a real or literary character or event that's not explained—just mentioned. Find allusions to the biblical story of Noah and to the sinking of the *Titanic* (check the footnotes). What do these allusions add to the story?
8. What do you think is the author's **purpose** in this story? Explain. (Hint: The Meet the Writer feature on page 378 may give you some help.)

Evaluation

9. Evaluate the story's **credibility.** Which details seem credible and which incredible? Do you find the behavior of the characters credible? How does their behavior compare with what your own might be? (Check your Quickwrite notes.)

Writing

The Prequel or the Sequel

Write a brief **prequel** or **sequel**—a story that explains either what happens to cause the flood before Stevenson's story begins or what happens after the bottle is found. This is your chance to offer your interpretation of the story's **ambiguities** or **subtleties.** Make sure your details and interpretations are consistent with the details in Stevenson's story. For a challenge, make your story ambiguous as well.

Use "Writing a Short Story," pages 602–609, for help with this assignment.

Reading Standard 3.8 Interpret and evaluate the impact of ambiguities and subtleties in a text.

INDEPENDENT PRACTICE

Literary Response and Analysis

Reading Check

1. Possible summary chart: *Where and when story takes place*—a New York apartment building, from 7 A.M. on March 23 to sometime during the day of March 25. *What has happened before story starts*—Notes that make up the story have been found in a bottle on an island in the South Atlantic; labor strikes have cut off heat and phone service in New York City; there is no electricity and no water because floods have inundated the city. *What happens during story*—People react to the flood at first with partying and horseplay; they move to higher and higher floors of the building as the floodwaters rise. *What happens as story ends*—People flee to the roof; ocean waves threaten to overwhelm them; rescue seems unlikely.

Interpretations

Possible Answers

2. *Inference*—Melting ice caps cause the flood. *Detail*—A possible Arctic atomic test. *Inference*—The flood is global. *Detail*—Planes cannot land. *Inference*—The characters perish. *Detail*—The journal washes up in a bottle.
3. They indicate that the narrator placed his journal in a bottle. Discovery of the bottle on a distant mountain indicates that a flood raised sea levels worldwide.
4. An initial air of frivolity is seen in details like "cheerful voices" and "horseplay." The festive mood fades with descriptions of filthy water, brooding neighbors, and an eerie silence. Finally, the mood is dark and despondent.
5. The minor characters allow the author to show a variety of reactions to the disaster.
6. The first-person point of view limits the reader's knowledge to what the narrator knows, allowing the writer to make events ambiguous. The journal form allows the writer to provide an intimate firsthand account.
7. The allusions support the conjecture that few survive. Most of the *Titanic*'s passengers perished, and in the biblical flood, only two creatures of each species survive.
8. The purpose is to entertain the reader with a thought-provoking story. He is commenting on doomsday fears of the nuclear era.

Evaluation

9. It is not credible for people to be so festive during such a catastrophe or for them not to try to find a way to escape.

Vocabulary Development

Practice 1

- *portable.* –port– *Meaning*—able to be carried.
- *presumably.* –sum– *Meaning*—to take as true.
- *speculation.* –spec– *Meaning*—thought; the act of looking at or seeing a subject.
- *submerged.* –merg– *Meaning*—covered with water.
- *recede.* –ced– *Meaning*—move back or away.

Practice 2

1. *consumable.* –sum– *Meaning*—can be used up completely.
2. *emerge.* –merg– *Meaning*—to rise from.
3. *import.* –port– *Meaning*—to carry into.
4. *transport.* –port– *Meaning*—to carry to another place.
5. *intercede.* –ced– *Meaning*—to intervene.
6. *resume.* –sum– *Meaning*—to take action again.
7. *emergence.* –merg– *Meaning*—act of rising from something.
8. *proceed.* –ced– *Meaning*—to go forward.
9. *inspect.* –spec– *Meaning*—to see closely.
10. *prospect.* –spec– *Meaning*—the act of looking forward.

Resources Reminder

Vocabulary

- *Vocabulary Development*
  - Vocabulary Worksheet, p. 30
  - Cumulative Vocabulary Review, pp. 31–32
- *Lesson Plans for Language Development*
  - Vocabulary, pp. 167, 172

Grammar Link

Practice

(1) higher, (2) correct, (3) more resigned, (4) correct, (5) most maddening, (6) higher, (7) better, (8) worse

Vocabulary Development

Word Roots and Their Families

Some words have lots of relatives—other words that come from the same **root** (the part of the word that carries its core meaning). Knowing common roots can help you figure out the meanings of unfamiliar words.

Word Bank
portable
presumably
speculation
submerged
recede

PRACTICE 1

Using the chart, find the root of each Word Bank word. Then, explain how the root relates to the word's meaning.

Reading Standard 1.1 Understand word derivations.

Latin Root	Meaning	Example Word
–ced–	yield	precede
–merg–	plunge	merge
–port–	carry	export
–spec–	see	spectacle
–sum–	take	consume

PRACTICE 2

For each word below, indicate its Latin root from the chart at the left. Then, give the word's meaning. Use a dictionary for help. When you are done, group the words into "families"—words with the same root.

1. consumable
2. emerge
3. import
4. transport
5. intercede
6. resume
7. emergence
8. proceed
9. inspect
10. prospect

Grammar Link MINI-LESSON

Using Modifiers Correctly

Most **modifiers** (adjectives and adverbs) use the suffixes *–er* and *–est* or the words *more* and *most* or *less* and *least* to form their **degrees of comparison.**

1. Use the **comparative form** (*taller, more unusual, less patient*) to compare two things. Use the **superlative form** (*tallest, most unusual, least patient*) to compare more than two things.

   The building across the street is higher than ours. [comparative]

   That is the highest building on the block. [superlative]

2. Avoid **double comparisons.** Do not use both *–er* and *more/less* or both *–est* and *most/least* to modify the same word.

   INCORRECT The water rises more faster every hour.

   CORRECT The water rises faster every hour.

PRACTICE

For each underlined comparative or superlative modifier in the paragraph below, indicate whether it is correct, and if not, supply the correct form.

Every day the waters rise (1) more higher than the day before, and the city looks (2) stranger and stranger. Some people seem much (3) most resigned to their fate than others. They act (4) more calmly than their hysterical neighbors. The (5) more maddening thing of all is that no one knows the cause of the flooding. Do you suppose areas at (6) more higher elevations are (7) more better or (8) more worse off?

For more help, see Comparison of Modifiers in the *Holt Handbook,* pages 218–223.

ASSESSING

Assessment

- *Progress Assessment of Reading*
  - Selection Test

RETEACHING

For another selection to teach Standard 3.8, see *Interactive Reading,* Chapter 5.

Read On: FOR INDEPENDENT READING

FICTION

Expect the Unexpected

Roald Dahl's wicked imagination is showcased to perfection in ***Tales of the Unexpected.*** Here you'll encounter unusual characters and entertainingly horrible situations, from a long-suffering wife's revenge on an annoying husband to a "royal jelly" that has a startling effect on the baby who consumes it. These stories, collected from among Dahl's best, have only two things in common: All feature Dahl's dark sense of humor—and all will surprise you.

FICTION

The Other Side of the Mirror

Lewis Carroll's ***Alice's Adventures in Wonderland*** and ***Through the Looking-Glass*** follow its young heroine through the twists and turns of a strange new world where logic is turned completely on its head. After falling down a rabbit hole, Alice finds herself amid a host of odd characters who speak in baffling riddles. These tales are presented with further explanations in ***The Annotated Alice,*** which describes how the Alice stories were partly intended as witty social allegories.

NONFICTION

They Called It Unsinkable

Walter Lord's ***A Night to Remember,*** first published in 1955, is still regarded as one of the finest books about the *Titanic* disaster of 1912. Lord interviewed hundreds of the *Titanic*'s passengers to create a gripping, authentic narrative of what happened before and after the ship's fatal collision. Filled with deeply personal accounts of those who survived as well as tributes to those who didn't, ***A Night to Remember*** provides a fascinating look at an unforgettable event in history.

NONFICTION

Fearless Leader

In 1914, Sir Ernest Shackleton, a seasoned polar explorer, wanted to be the first man to cross the Antarctic continent. He assembled a team of experienced men to accompany him on what promised to be a career-making voyage. Little did Shackleton know that his ship, the *Endurance,* would be destroyed. Caroline Alexander's ***The Endurance: Shackleton's Legendary Antarctic Expedition*** uses journals, documents, and original photographs to reconstruct a historic voyage gone terribly wrong.

Read On

For Independent Reading

If students enjoyed the themes and topics explored in this chapter, you might recommend these titles for independent reading.

Assessment Options

The following projects can help you evaluate and assess your students' outside reading. Videotapes or audiotapes of completed projects may be included in student portfolios.

- **Translate the ending to the screen.** Have students work in small groups to rewrite as a movie script the last scene of a story selected from *Tales of the Unexpected.* Remind them that scripts focus more on dialogue and action than on description. Invite volunteers to perform the scripts for the class. Have them first summarize the events of the story up to the final scene. Then, invite students to discuss which medium—the story or the script—presents the ending more effectively.
- **Map an adventure.** Have students who chose *A Night to Remember* or *The Endurance: Shackleton's Legendary Antarctic Expedition* create a map that illustrates with words or symbols the key events described in the book.
- **Compare the book and the movie**. *Alice's Adventures in Wonderland* and *Through the Looking-Glass* and *A Night to Remember* have been adapted for the motion-picture screen. Suggest that students view a videotape of their selection and write an essay in which they compare the book with its film version. Ask students to discuss similarities and differences in setting, scenes, characterization, and dialogue. Finally, have students evaluate how well the film version conveys the content and spirit of the novel.

Toward Reading Two Million Words Annually

Estimated Word Counts and Reading Levels of Read On Books:

Fiction	Level	Words	Nonfiction	Level	Words
Tales of the Unexpected	at grade level	164,200	*A Night to Remember**	above grade level	54,800
*Alice's Adventures in Wonderland and Through the Looking-Glass**	below grade level	94,700	*The Endurance: Shackleton's Legendary Antarctic Expedition*	at grade level	66,300

*California Reading List Titles

KEY: ⇧ *above grade level* ⇔ *at grade level* ⇩ *below grade level*

PRETEACHING

Standards Starter

Motivate. Ask students to imagine they have just made news headlines by performing a heroic act, such as saving a drowning victim. What elements would the various news media include in their reports on students' heroic acts? Would the TV coverage of the event differ from the story in the newspaper? If so, in what ways? Allow students time to discuss how they would expect their stories to be reported in the media, and lead students to support with reasons and observations their answers on the differences among the various news media.

Resources Reminder

To introduce the workshop, you may want to use the journal starters in *Writing, Listening, & Speaking* Teaching Notes.

DIRECT TEACHING

Choose a News Event

You may want to bring to class several recent newspapers or newsmagazines for students to peruse in order to find a news event in which they are interested. Alternately, you might organize a trip to the school library during which students can research stories on the Internet. Students may also need help identifying reliable local sources of radio news—both the stations and the times at which the programs run.

If students do research on the Internet, you need to be aware that Internet resources often serve as public forums and their content can be unpredictable.

Comparing Media Genres

Writing Assignment
Listening and Speaking 1.2
Write an essay in which you compare and contrast the coverage of a single news event by two different news media.

As you know from reading the selections in the previous section, the truth is often ambiguous. Two characters may view the same event in wildly different—even opposite—ways. A similar ambiguity can be found in two different media accounts, or retellings, of the same event. For example, a news story in a newspaper may focus on one person's point of view of an event, whereas an Internet news story about the same event may provide several perspectives. In this workshop you will examine how news accounts vary and how different media shape those accounts.

Prewriting

go.hrw.com

GO TO: go.hrw.com
KEYWORD: HLLA 10-5
FOR: Professional Model, Writer's Guides, and Reference Sources

Choose a News Event

A Nose for News To find a news event for your comparison-contrast essay, scan the front section of a newspaper or watch a national news program. Once you've focused on one event that interests you, search for coverage in other news media, including news Web sites, magazines, and radio programs. If you have trouble finding an event covered in two different media, you may need to consider one that has greater appeal to a national or an international audience.

Compare Coverage

Two Roads, Same Destination News organizations share the same purpose—to provide accurate information about events that interest people. However, the ways news organizations report the information can be very different. Each story is molded into a unique account by the people involved in creating the story and by the technology used to present the story. Every word and picture you see in a news story has been chosen by a journalist, editor, or producer to fit the strengths of the medium in which the story appears. For example, television is uniquely suited to capture the roar of a crowd as a marathoner crosses the finish line, while a newspaper is better able to present a list of the runners and a map of the route.

As you compare the coverage of an event by two media, consider the **points of comparison** in the left-hand column of the chart on the next page. Answer the questions beside each point for both media. The answers will lead you to the specific ways the coverage of the two media is alike and different.

Listening and Speaking 1.2 Compare and contrast the ways in which media genres (e.g., televised news, news magazines, documentaries, online information) cover the same event.

CHAPTER 5 RESOURCES: WRITING

Planning
- *On Course: Mapping Instruction*
- *One-Stop Planner* CD-ROM
- *At Home: A Guide to Standards Mastery,* p. 19
- *At Home: In Spanish*
- *Writing, Listening, & Speaking,* Teaching Notes, p. 48

Differentiating Instruction
- *Lesson Plans for Language Development,* pp. 161–162
- *Supporting Instruction in Spanish*

Practice
- *Writing, Listening, & Speaking,* Ch. 5

382 Chapter 5 Irony and Ambiguity • Generating Research Questions and Evaluating Sources

COMPARING MEDIA: POINTS OF COMPARISON

Attention-getting techniques	• What words, sounds, and images are used to grab the audience's attention? • Does the story build suspense by slowly revealing the outcome of the event? Explain.
Structure	• What sequence does the information follow? • Does the story close with a neutral, positive, or negative view of the event?
Complexity	• How much information is given? • How many points of view are represented? • Is the event put in a broad enough context to explain most of its causes and consequences?
Objectivity	• Do the words in the story show an overtly positive or negative view of the subject? • Does the story seem to side with one person or group over another?
Emotional impact	• What feelings does the story arouse, if any? • What techniques are used to arouse these feelings?

A student used the questions in the chart above to compare the coverage of major Midwestern floods by a TV newsmagazine and a print newsmagazine. He organized his findings in the analysis log you see below, dividing information about the TV newsmagazine and the print newsmagazine into two columns. Then, he went back and underlined the similarities between the two stories. When he writes his essay, he will use the information in this log as evidence to support his thesis.

Analysis Log: TV Newsmagazine and Print Newsmagazine

Attention-getting techniques	TV: Used the words "horror," "heartbreak," and "terrible." Shots of the destruction and people crying.	Print: Used the words "horror," "tragedy," and "heartbreak in the heartland." Photos of rising floodwaters and upset people.
Structure	TV: Gave day-by-day accounts of the hardships two families must face. Ended with the families saying they would rebuild their homes and lives.	Print: Gave estimates of how many people lost property. Ended with a meteorologist's prediction of when flooding may occur again.
Complexity	TV: Focused on the points of view of two families. Included interviews with rescue workers.	Print: Gave many points of view—residents, rescue workers, government officials, meteorologists.

MODELING AND DEMONSTRATION

Comparing Media

Model for students the process of comparing coverage of a news event by showing students a brief video clip on a specific news event and by displaying a print story on the same event. Use the first four questions in the **Comparing Media: Points of Comparison** chart to guide your comparison of the coverage of the story. You may want to focus especially on questions about the story's complexity, as these questions may be most difficult for students to answer.

After you model the process for students, ask student volunteers to answer the remaining questions on the chart to compare coverage of the event.

DIRECT TEACHING

Integrating with Grammar, Usage, and Mechanics

As students start their comparison-contrast essays, they may have trouble using modifiers correctly or with general usage. You may want to review the corresponding chapters in the *Holt Handbook.*

Reinforcement

- *Daily Language Activities*

Evaluation and Assessment

- *Test Generator (One-Stop Planner CD-ROM)*
- *Progress Assessment of Writing, Listening, & Speaking,* Ch. 5
- *Diagnostic and Summative Assessments,* Midyear Test

Internet

- go.hrw.com (keyword: HLLA 10-5)
- Online assessments at go.hrw.com (keyword: HLLA)

DIRECT TEACHING

GRADE-LEVEL STANDARD

Develop a Thesis

Remind students that their thesis statements should reflect their understanding of the differences in media coverage. For example, an alternative to the thesis written by someone who favors TV coverage might read, "Although the magazine gave much more in-depth coverage of the floods, it could not begin to convey the shock and the enormity of the event as depicted on TV."

Remind students as well that their thesis statements should also provide specific characteristics of the differences and should also give some indication as to the effects of the differences—the TV coverage is more dramatic but less reliable, for example. You may want to offer students the following formula to follow for their theses:

> Unique characteristics and effects of Coverage 1 + Unique characteristics and effects of Coverage 2 + My judgment = Thesis

PRACTICE & APPLY 1

Guided and Independent Practice

Monitor students' understanding by asking them to complete the following steps:

1. Write your thesis statement on a sheet of paper.
2. Circle the unique characteristics of each medium mentioned in the thesis.
3. Draw a box around the judgment you make in your thesis.

If students have trouble choosing an event, you may want to assign the same event to a group. Group members could pool their resources and discuss their differing perspectives but each should write a paper individually. Then, have students complete **Practice and Apply 1** for independent practice.

Develop a Thesis

DO THIS

The Verdict Is . . . Just as judges pass judgment on legal cases, you will pass judgment on the coverage by the two news media. Did one story give more information? Was one story more dramatic? The conclusions or judgments you make will be the **thesis** of your essay. Write your thesis in a **clear and coherent** thesis statement, a sentence or two that tells your audience the conclusions you drew about each medium's coverage. An example of a thesis statement follows.

> While the television show could offer its audience a more vivid sense of the frightened families and enormous damage, the magazine ended up presenting a much more in-depth and informative account.

Organize Your Essay

What Goes Where? Everything has a place—even the details of a comparison-contrast essay. To write a **focused** comparison-contrast essay, use one of the organizational patterns below.

- **Block style—**If you organize your essay in block style you will either discuss all the similarities and then all the differences of the two media, or you will tell everything about one medium first before discussing the second medium. Block style works best for essays that contain few comparisons.
- **Point-by-point style—**If you organize your essay in point-by-point style, you will go back and forth between the two media. You will first explain how the media are alike and different for *one* point of comparison, then how they are alike and different for the *next* point of comparison, and so on. This style is best suited for essays that contain more comparisons.
- **Modified block style—**If you arrange your essay in modified block style, you will use a combination of block style and point-by-point style. The overall organization of the essay will be block: a discussion of similarities and then a discussion of differences. Within each section, though, the specific similarities and differences will be organized in point-by-point style. For example, the first section of the paper about the Midwestern floods would discuss the points of comparison that have similarities. The second section would discuss the points of comparison that have differences.

Writing 1.0 Students write coherent and focused essays. **1.1** Establish a coherent thesis that conveys a clear and distinctive perspective on the subject.

PRACTICE & APPLY 1 Use the instructions in this section to compare the coverage of a news event by two different media, write a thesis statement, and organize your ideas.

CRITICAL THINKING

Allow students time to brainstorm topics that would fit each of the three different organizational styles. Students should be able to give reasons for their choices. For example, an article discussing two models of skateboards made by the same company would likely use a point-by-point style because it would contain more comparisons than contrasts.

RESOURCES: WRITING

Practice & Apply 1

Guided Practice

- *Writing, Listening, & Speaking,* WS. pp. 49, 50

Reteaching and Modeling

- *Writing, Listening, & Speaking,* TP. 10
- *Writing, Listening, & Speaking,* WS. p. 51

Writing

Comparing Media Genres

A Writer's Framework

Introduction

- Start with an interesting opener.
- Provide background information about the news event.
- Introduce the two media you will compare and contrast.
- Present a clear thesis statement.

Body

- Organize your essay in block style, point-by-point style, or modified block style.
- Discuss the points of comparison.
- Include specific references to each news story as evidence for each point.

Conclusion

- Summarize your main points by restating your thesis.
- Offer ideas about how the two stories were shaped by the media that delivered them.
- Close with a final impression or insight.

A Writer's Model

More Than News

The weather is not what you usually think of as a fascinating news story. Sometimes, however, it grabs the attention of the entire country. Last month, several Midwestern states suffered the worst flooding in decades. One widely read newsmagazine published a long cover story on the flood, and a national weekly television newsmagazine devoted an entire broadcast to it. While the television show offered its audience a more vivid sense of the frightened families and enormous damage, the magazine ended up presenting a much more in-depth and informative account.

INTRODUCTION
Interesting opener
Background information
Reference to two media
Thesis statement

There were a number of similarities between the two stories. Both stories focused mostly on the human-interest angle, using similar shots of water rising over rooftops along with the worried or weeping faces of the newly homeless. In addition, both offered several interviews with residents who lost homes and with exhausted rescue workers. Perhaps because the event involved the kind of loss that everyone fears, both the television show and magazine also used a variety of attention-getting techniques to prompt an emotional response. Aside from the shocking visuals, both also used loaded words like "horror" and "tragedy" to describe the landscape.

BODY/Similarities:
1. Emotional impact
2. Complexity
3. Attention-getting techniques

(continued)

DIFFERENTIATING INSTRUCTION

Advanced Learners

Enrichment. You may have students find and cite at least one secondary source that comments on the coverage of the news event they choose. Since the media is frequently given to self-analysis, students can find appropriate commentary on newspaper editorial pages, TV news discussion shows, and in newsmagazines. In their conclusions especially, students should state whether they agree or disagree with the source or sources they cite. You may need to review with students the method of citation you prefer that they use.

DIFFERENTIATING INSTRUCTION

Learners Having Difficulty

If students have trouble developing an interesting, attention-grabbing opener for their papers, advise them to begin writing their drafts with the second step in the framework, providing necessary background about the news event. After students complete their drafts, they can then return to the beginning to create an opener that reflects what they discovered to be most interesting about their topics.

RETEACHING

A Writer's Model

If students are having difficulty choosing an organizational method for their papers, ask students to identify the organizational order used in **A Writer's Model** and to suggest reasons why the writer used that particular organization. [The model is written using the block method, with similarities first and differences second; the method allows the writer to concentrate on the media's many differences in coverage.]

Discuss with students how the model may have been written using another order [the point-by-point method, for example, might have focused on the common characteristics of the coverage of the two media but might not have as successfully emphasized the differences]. Make sure students have good reasons to support their choice of the best organizational method for the model. Analyzing the model will probably help students decide on an organizational method that will be best for their papers.

DIFFERENTIATING INSTRUCTION

English-Language Learners

As students read **A Writer's Model,** have them list on a separate sheet of paper any unfamiliar words they find. After students have finished reading the model, they can look up each word in the dictionary and write out the definition, along with a sample sentence of their own that uses the word correctly. Make sure students go back and compare their sentences to those in the model. Students should find that they have used not only the same definitions but that they have understood the context of the words as well.

Resources Reminder

For more help with English-Language Learners, see *Lesson Plans for Language Development.*

PRACTICE & APPLY 2

Guided and Independent Practice

Remind students that their thesis statements can be adjusted to reflect changes in focus, if the need arises during writing.

Encourage students to use the framework as a checklist as they write their drafts. This will help students see what elements, if any, still need to be supplied. You may circulate among students to spot-check checklists against their drafts for understanding.

(continued)

Differences:
1. Complexity

Despite their similarities, the two stories also had important differences. Among the most noticeable were the differing points of view each presented. The television show primarily focused on two families whose houses were in the path of the flood. This restricted point of view made the story quite personal. In contrast, the magazine article offered many points of view, including those of residents affected by the floods, rescue workers, government officials, and meteorologists. This number of different voices made the story less intimate, but provided readers with greater depth and clarity. By reading the magazine story, a reader understood more about how many people were in danger and how the flooding would affect the entire area.

2. Structure

Another major difference between the two stories was the way they structured their information. The TV report was structured like a mystery, suspensefully tracking the water as it rose day by day and concealing the fates of the two families' homes until the end of the program. In addition, despite the eventual ruin of both families' homes, the TV report offered a positive, storybook ending, with family members all pledging to rebuild their houses and lives. In contrast, the first paragraphs of the magazine story presented detailed estimates of how many people were affected by the flood. The magazine chose to close the article with a meteorologist's prediction about how soon the next round of flooding might occur in the region.

CONCLUSION
Restatement of thesis

Ideas about how stories were shaped

Final insight

It is true that the magazine and television stories both communicated the emotional impact of the story. However, the television story focused narrowly on the suffering of just a few people, while the print story provided a broader context and more factual information. Television has many strengths that make it appealing to viewers, especially the ways it can produce emotional responses with intimate interviews and dramatic visuals. However, television newsmagazine stories often stop there, failing to provide the context and depth that print newsmagazines can offer. The next time you think a television news story has given you the complete picture, you might check out a magazine article, too.

go.hrw.com

GO TO: go.hrw.com
KEYWORD: HLLA 10-5
FOR: Expanded Writer's Model and Student's Model

PRACTICE & APPLY 2 Use the framework on page 385 and the Writer's Model above to guide you as you write a first draft of your comparison-contrast essay.

RESOURCES: WRITING

Practice & Apply 2

Think Sheet

- *Writing, Listening, & Speaking,* WS. p. 52

Template

- *Writing, Listening, & Speaking,* WS. p. 53

- go.hrw.com (keyword: HLLA 10-5)

Revising

Evaluate and Revise Your Draft

Twice Is Nice Your job isn't done until you've given your essay at least two readings. Have you provided enough detail to show the strengths and weaknesses of the news stories you compared? Is your essay logically organized and smoothly written? As you revise, be sure to keep in mind your **audience** and the degree of **formality** your readers might expect in a comparison-contrast essay. Also, think about how the essay achieves your **purpose**—to provide information.

PEER REVIEW

Ask a classmate to read your paper and suggest ways you might improve your content, organization, or style. You might ask, for example, if you have provided enough specific references to the news stories to support your thesis.

First Reading: Content and Organization Use the guidelines in the chart below as a **think sheet.** The questions, tips, and revision techniques can help you revise the content and organization of your essay.

Guidelines: Comparing Media Genres

Evaluation Questions	Tips	Revision Techniques
1 Does the introduction engage the reader and include any necessary background information?	**Bracket** the sentences that capture the reader's attention. **Underline** the sentences that explain the event covered in the stories.	**Replace** the opening with one or two sentences that will grab the reader's attention. If necessary, **add** a few sentences that explain the event.
2 Does the introduction offer a clear thesis statement that presents the conclusions the writer drew about the media coverage?	**Draw a wavy line** under the thesis statement.	**Add** a statement that expresses the conclusions about the media coverage, or **revise** the existing statement to make it clearer.
3 Is the pattern of organization easy to follow?	**Label** the points of comparison, for example, structure, complexity, and so on. If the order is not logical, revise.	**Reorder** the points in a clear block style, point-by-point style, or modified block style.
4 Is each point of comparison supported by specific details and references to the news stories?	**Put a check** beside each detail or reference to a news story.	**Elaborate** on the points by offering examples, quotations, and other specific evidence from the two news stories.
5 Does the conclusion restate the thesis and reflect on how each story was shaped by the media? Does it offer a final impression?	**Draw a box** around the sentence that summarizes the thesis. **Highlight** the sentences that comment on how each story was shaped. **Star** any final impression or insight.	If necessary, **add** a brief restatement of the thesis. **Add** sentences that explain how media shaped the stories. **Add** a final impression of the media being compared.

DIRECT TEACHING

REVIEW STANDARD

Elaboration

To help students evaluate whether they have included ample support for the conclusions drawn in their essays, they might ask themselves *What additional proof will my audience require that my analysis is valid? How and where can I add details and examples that will strengthen the support in my paper?*

TECHNOLOGY TIP

Students working on their essays on computers can use the *Find* function of their word-processing software to make sure they maintain a consistent method of organization throughout their papers. Students can search for key words or phrases from their theses or support, such as *emotional impact, complexity,* and *structure,* to ensure that these topics are discussed in a specific location in the paper and in an organized fashion, instead of intermittently or haphazardly.

Second Reading: Style Now, focus on the style of your essay. Unvaried sentence length is a common problem in comparison-contrast essays. In comparing subject A to subject B, a writer's sentences often start to sound the same—either short and choppy or tongue-trippingly long. Consequently, the reader may become bored or confused. Use the chart below to help you **vary the sentence length** in your comparison-contrast essay.

Style Guidelines

Evaluation Question	Tip	Revision Technique
Is there a series of sentences that are all the same length?	**Put a jagged line** beneath three or more short sentences or long sentences in succession.	**Combine** a short sentence with another one, or **break** a longer sentence into two or more shorter ones.

ANALYZING THE REVISION PROCESS

Study these revisions, and answer the questions that follow.

> Another major difference between the two stories was the way they structured their information. The TV report was structured like a mystery~~. It suspensefully tracked~~ *, suspensefully tracking* the water as it rose day by day~~. It concealed~~ *and concealing* the fates of the two families' homes until the end of the program. (combine) In addition, despite the eventual ruin of both families' homes, the TV report offered a positive, storybook ending*, with family members all pledging to rebuild their houses and lives.* (add)

Responding to the Revision Process

1. Why did the writer combine the second, third, and fourth sentences?
2. How does the addition to the last sentence improve the passage?

Writing 1.9 Revise writing to improve the logic and coherence of the organization by taking into consideration the audience, purpose, and formality of the context.

PRACTICE & APPLY 3 Use the content, organization, and style guidelines on this page and the previous page to revise your draft. If a peer reviewed your essay, consider his or her comments as you revise.

GUIDED PRACTICE

Responding to the Revision Process

Answers

1. The writer combined the three sentences in order to vary sentence length within the passage.
2. The addition to the last sentence provides specific detail to support the writer's conclusion; without it, the writer's conclusion is unsupported.

PRACTICE & APPLY 3

Independent Practice

As students revise their essays, have them write their answers to the questions in the **Guidelines: Comparing Media Genres** chart on p. 387 as well as a brief description of any action taken. Students may benefit from revising their essays multiple times by focusing on different areas of revision with each pass.

RESOURCES: WRITING

Practice & Apply 3

Think Sheet

- *Writing, Listening, & Speaking,* WS. p. 55

Evaluation

- *Writing, Listening, & Speaking,* WS. p. 54

Practice & Apply 4

Assessment

- *Test Generator (One-Stop Planner* CD-ROM)
- *Progress Assessment of Writing, Listening, & Speaking,* pp. 15–18, 65–67

Internet

- Online assessments at go.hrw.com (keyword: HLLA)

388 Chapter 5 Irony and Ambiguity • Generating Research Questions and Evaluating Sources

Publishing

Proofread and Publish Your Essay

A Critical Eye Imagine finding a misspelled word or an ungrammatical sentence in a news article. Would it lead you to question the accuracy of the content, too? It probably would. The same is true of *your* readers. Show them that you have done a reliable job by carefully proofreading for grammar, usage, and mechanics errors. If you choose, ask a partner to help. Once you have found and corrected any mistakes, make a clean final copy of your essay.

Extra, Extra! Read All About It! You've thought deeply about how media messages shape events for readers, listeners, and viewers. Now, help others reflect on media by getting your essay to an audience of your own.

- Send your essay to the two news media you compared. (Look for an address within the publication or on the Web.) Ask for a response from the journalist or producer who created each story.
- Exchange essays with a group of classmates and then stage a discussion session. Perhaps this will lead you to form a group that monitors how different media present information.
- Working with a small group of classmates, turn your essay into a short multimedia presentation to teach younger children about the characteristics of different media.

TIP Proofreading will help you ensure that you follow the **conventions** of standard American English. In particular, watch for errors in parallel structure, which often occur when you are making comparisons and contrasts. For more on using **parallel structure,** see page 476 in the *Holt Handbook*.

Reflect on Your Essay

Analyze the Analysis What have you learned about news media —and about your own writing process—while drafting and polishing your essay? Use these questions to reflect on your experience.

- How was writing this essay similar to other essays you write in school? How was it different?
- How has writing this essay affected the way you understand and respond to news stories?
- Choose one of the stories you analyzed, and put yourself in the journalist's or producer's shoes. What would you have done differently in presenting the story? Explain your answer.

PRACTICE & APPLY 4 Proofread and publish your essay in one of the ways suggested on this page or in another interesting way. Then, reflect on news media and your writing process by answering the questions above.

DIRECT TEACHING

Proofread and Publish Your Essay

If students research the address of one of their chosen media publications on the Internet, you need to be aware that the World Wide Web often functions as a public forum and that its content may be unpredictable.

Resources Reminder

For help with writing assessment, see 6 Traits—Plus 1 in the "Scales and Sample Papers" section of *Progress Assessment of Writing, Listening, & Speaking.*

PRACTICE & APPLY 4

Guided and Independent Practice

You may want to guide students through the publishing stage by facilitating small round-table discussions on the topic of the characteristics of various news media.

Have students who are considering the same method of publishing their work meet in small groups to share strategies and ideas. Group members can also exchange papers to help each other with the task of proofreading. Students should complete **Practice and Apply 4** for independent practice.

Writing Workshop: Comparing Media Genres 389

Standards Review

Analyzing Informational Materials

STANDARDS FOCUS, pp. 390–393

(For the grade-level standard reviewed in this lesson, see Student Edition, p. 390.)

INTRODUCING THE STANDARDS REVIEW

Use this review to assess students' grasp of the standard taught in this chapter. If necessary, you can use the annotations to guide students in their reading before they answer the questions.

DIRECT TEACHING

A Analyzing Informational Materials
GRADE-LEVEL STANDARD

Generating research questions. Remind students to pause while reading to ask themselves questions about interesting or unclear information in the text. Later, they may wish to research the answers to these questions. Ask students, "What questions can you generate from this section?" [Possible responses: What do researchers hope to learn from exploring the oceans? Why might the different depths of the ocean offer different possibilities? Why is sea exploration so dangerous and expensive?]

STANDARDS REVIEW

Analyzing Informational Materials

Test Practice

Generating Research Questions and Evaluating Sources

DIRECTIONS: Read the following article. Then, read each multiple-choice question that follows, and write the letter of the best response.

The Last Frontier

Michael D. Lemonick

The irony of twentieth-century scientists venturing out to explore waters that have been navigated for thousands of years is not lost on oceanographers. More than one hundred expeditions have reached Everest, the 29,028-foot pinnacle of the Himalayas;[1] manned voyages to space have become commonplace; and robot probes have ventured to the outer reaches of the solar system. But only now are the deepest parts of the ocean coming within reach. "I think there's a perception that we have already explored the sea," says marine biologist Sylvia Earle, a former chief scientist at the National Oceanographic and Atmospheric Administration and a cofounder of Deep Ocean Engineering, the San Leandro, California, company where construction of *Deep Flight I*[2] began: "The reality is we know more about Mars than we know about the oceans."

That goes not only for the sea's uttermost depths but also for the still-mysterious middle waters three or four miles down, and even for the "shallows" a few hundred feet deep. For while the push to reach the very bottom of the sea has fired the imagination of some of the world's most daring explorers, it is just the most visible part of a broad international effort to probe the oceans' depths. It's a high-sea adventure fraught[3] with danger, and—because of the expense—with controversy as well.

But the rewards could be enormous: oil and mineral wealth to rival Alaska's North Slope and California's Gold Rush;[4] scientific discoveries that could change our view of how the planet—and the life-forms on it—evolved; natural substances that could yield new medicines and whole new classes of industrial chemicals. Beyond those practical benefits there is the intangible but real satisfaction that comes from exploring earth's last great frontier.

There's a lot to explore. Oceans cover nearly three quarters of the planet's surface—336 million cubic miles of water that reaches an average depth of 2.3 miles.

1. Since this article was written, the elevation of Mount Everest has been recalculated as 29,035 feet.
2. *Deep Flight I:* small, experimental submarine designed for deep-sea exploration.
3. **fraught** (frôt) *adj.:* filled.
4. **Alaska's North Slope and California's Gold Rush:** reference to the oil fields in Alaska's northern coast and the great California gold rush of 1849.

Pages 390–393 cover **Reading Standard 2.3** Generate relevant questions about readings on issues that can be researched.

READING MINI-LESSON

Reviewing Word-Attack Skills

Activity. Ask students to write the new word that is formed by combining each base word and suffix that are listed together below. Then, have them say the new word and underline any letter that is pronounced differently than it is in the base word. Encourage students to check pronunciations in a dictionary, if necessary.

1. introduce + –tion [introduction]
2. extreme + –ity [extremity]
3. practice + –able [practicable]
4. maniac + –al [maniacal]
5. logic + –ian [logician]
6. column + –ist [columnist]
7. oblige + –ation [obligation]
8. incise + –ive [incisive]
9. harmony + –ous [harmonious]

Activity. Display these pairs of related words. Have students read each word and underline the letters that spell the syllable that is said with the greatest stress. Answers are underlined.

The sea's intricate food webs support more life by weight and a greater diversity of animals than any other ecosystem,[5] from sulfur-eating bacteria clustered around deep-sea vents to fish that light up like Times Square billboards to lure their prey. Somewhere below, there even lurks the last certified sea monster left from prescientific times: the 64-foot-long giant squid.

The sea's economic potential is equally enormous. Majestically swirling ocean currents influence much of the world's weather patterns; figuring out how they operate could save trillions of dollars in weather-related disasters. The oceans also have vast reserves of commercially valuable minerals, including nickel, iron, manganese, copper, and cobalt. Pharmaceutical[6] and biotechnology[7] companies are already analyzing deep-sea bacteria, fish, and marine plants, looking for substances that they might someday turn into miracle drugs. Says Bruce Robison, of the Monterey Bay Aquarium Research Institute (MBARI) in California: "I can guarantee you that the discoveries beneficial to mankind will far outweigh those of the space program over the next couple of decades. If we can get to the abyss regularly, there will be immediate payoffs." **B**

5. **ecosystem** (ē′kō·sis′təm) *n.:* community of animals and plants related to each other and to their environment.
6. **pharmaceutical** (fär′mə·so͞ot′i·kəl) *adj.:* relating to drugs and medicines.
7. **biotechnology** (bī′ō·tek·näl′ə·jē) *n.* used as *adj.:* use of technology to study living organisms and solve problems involving them.

Getting there, though, will force explorers to cope with an environment just as perilous as outer space. Unaided, humans can't dive much more than 10 feet down—less than one three-thousandth of the way to the very bottom—before increasing pressure starts to build up painfully on the inner ear, sinuses, and lungs. Frigid subsurface water rapidly sucks away body heat. And even the most leathery of lungs can't hold a breath for more than two or three minutes.

For these reasons the modern age of deep-sea exploration had to wait for two key technological developments: engineer Otis Barton's 1930 invention of the bathysphere—essentially a deep-diving tethered steel ball—and the invention of scuba (short for "self-contained underwater breathing apparatus") by Jacques-Yves Cousteau and Emile Gagnan in 1943. Swimmers had been trying to figure out how to get oxygen underwater for thousands of years. Sponge divers in ancient Greece breathed from air-filled kettles; bulky-helmeted diving suits linked by hose to the surface first appeared in the 1800s. But it wasn't until scuba came along that humans, breathing compressed air, were able to move about freely underwater at depths of more than 100 feet. **C**

Even the most experienced scuba divers rarely venture below 150 feet, however, owing to increasingly crushing pressure and the laborious decompression process required to purge the blood of nitrogen (which can form bubbles as a diver returns to the surface and cause the excruciating and sometimes-fatal condition known as

DIRECT TEACHING

B Analyzing Informational Materials
GRADE-LEVEL STANDARD

Generating research questions. Ask students what research question or questions they might pose after reading this paragraph. [Possible responses: How do ocean currents influence the world's weather patterns? What weather disasters are caused by ocean currents? How might ocean life help cure diseases?]

C Analyzing Informational Materials
GRADE-LEVEL STANDARD

Generating research questions. What main idea or issue is dealt with in this paragraph? [Possible response: inventions that have enabled people to breathe underwater and to explore underseas.] What questions might you research related to this issue? [How do the bathysphere and the air-filled kettles work? How long can scuba divers stay underwater?]

1. moral	morality
2. medicine	medicinal
3. molecule	molecular
4. geometry	geometric
5. comedy	comedian

Activity. Display the following words on the chalkboard:

writhe	pithy	wrath
wreathed	toothsome	teethe
sheath	unsheathed	loathsome
loathe	lithe	mythical

Have students say the words and sort them according to the way the *th* sound is pronounced: Is it unvoiced as in *bath,* or is it voiced as in *bathe?* [*Unvoiced* th *as in* bath—pithy, wrath, toothsome, sheath, loathsome, mythical. *Voiced* th *as in* bathe—writhe, wreathed, teethe, unsheathed, loathe, lithe.]

Standards Review

DIRECT TEACHING

A Analyzing Informational Materials
GRADE-LEVEL STANDARD

Generating research questions. Model for students how different research questions might be posed about the same portion of text. Share with students the following examples of questions that might be generated from the bracketed section of text: "Why is deep-sea exploration so expensive?" "How much do submersibles cost?" "How many submersibles exist at this time?" and "What organizations currently finance deep-sea exploration?"

B Analyzing Informational Materials
GRADE-LEVEL STANDARD

? Generating research questions. What research question or questions can you generate about the information in this section of text? [Possible responses: Where are the deepest ocean trenches located? How deep are these trenches? What process did Robert Ballard follow to discover the wreck of the *Titanic*? What did he learn from his discovery?]

Test-Taking Tips

Remind students to carefully evaluate each answer to a multiple-choice item before selecting one of the choices. Explain that while an answer may appear to be correct, one of the remaining choices may be a better answer.

For more instruction on how to answer multiple-choice items, refer students to **Test Smarts.**

the bends). And pressurized diving suits make it possible for humans to descend only to 1,440 feet—far short of the deepest reaches of the oceans. . . .

Do scientists expect even more surprises as they venture farther below the surface? The question is a crucial one, as both scientists and policy makers debate the finances of deep-sea exploration. Most everyone acknowledges that there is some value in studying the oceans. It's expensive, though, and because of generally tight budgets, even the few existing manned submersibles[8] (which in any case are rated only for depths above 20,000 feet) often have to sit idle. Building more strikes some as a waste of money.

That includes some scientists. Although he has never been to the very deepest trenches, ocean explorer Robert Ballard of Woods Hole,[9] who is best known for discovering the wreck of the *Titanic* in 1985, is convinced that the action lies in the relative shallows. "I believe that the deep sea has very little to offer," he says. "I've been there. I've spent a career there. I don't see the future there." The French have decided not even to bother trying to break the 20,000-foot barrier—the range of their deepest-diving submersible, the three-person *Nautile.* Says Jean Jarry, director of the Toulon-sur-Mer research center of IFREMER, France's national oceanographic institute: "We think that's a good depth because it covers 97 percent of the ocean. To go beyond that is not very interesting and is very expensive."

But that attitude is far from universal. Biologist Greg Stone, of the New England Aquarium in Boston, compares reaching the deepest abyss with Christopher Columbus's search for the New World. "Why should we care about the deepest 3 percent of the oceans, and why do we need to reach it?" he asks rhetorically. "For one, we won't know what it holds until we've been there. There will certainly be new creatures. We'll be able to learn where gases from the atmosphere go in the ocean. We'll be able to get closest to where the geological action is. We know very little about the details of these processes. And once we're there, I'm sure studies will open up whole sets of new questions." . . .

—from *Time,* August 14, 1995

8. **submersibles** (səb•mʉr′sə•bəlz) *n.:* vessels that operate underwater, such as submarines.
9. **Woods Hole:** Woods Hole Oceanographic Institution, a research center located in Woods Hole, Massachusetts.

Using Academic Language

Review of Literary Terms
Reading Standard 3.8

Ask students to look back through the chapter to find the meanings of the terms listed at right. Then, have students show their grasp of Standard 3.8 by citing passages from the chapter that illustrate the meanings of those terms.

Verbal Irony (p. 314); **Situational Irony** (pp. 314, 316, 328, 349); **Dramatic Irony** (pp. 314, 316, 328); **Ambiguity** (pp. 315, 374); **Contradictions** (p. 349).

Review of Informational Terms
Reading Standard 2.3

Ask students to look back through the chapter to find the meanings of the terms listed

392 Chapter 5 Irony and Ambiguity • Generating Research Questions and Evaluating Sources

1. Which statement *best* expresses the **main idea** of "The Last Frontier"?
   - **A** Scuba divers are equipped to explore depths below 20,000 feet.
   - **B** Exploring the oceans could have many practical and scientific benefits.
   - **C** No scientist wants to explore the ocean below 20,000 feet.
   - **D** More than half of the earth's surface is covered by oceans.

2. Which research question will yield the *most* useful information for a report on deep-sea exploration?
   - **F** What is marine biology?
   - **G** What did Emile Gagnan invent?
   - **H** What percentage of the earth's oceans are below 20,000 feet?
   - **J** What deep-sea discoveries have been made using manned submersibles?

3. Which of the following research questions is *not* directly related to topics discussed in this article?
   - **A** What minerals have been discovered beneath the sea?
   - **B** What groups are currently exploring the ocean below 20,000 feet?
   - **C** What are the scientific benefits of exploring the frozen waters of the South Pole?
   - **D** How is deep-sea exploration funded?

4. If you were researching the invention of the bathysphere, which source would be *most* useful?
   - **F** A TV documentary about the life and work of Jacques-Yves Cousteau
   - **G** An article on Otis Barton in *Encyclopaedia Britannica,* published in 2002
   - **H** A Web page on deep-sea marine life maintained by the American Museum of Natural History
   - **J** A national magazine article on underwater volcanos

5. If you were researching the funding for exploration of the deepest parts of the ocean, who would you expect to be *most* biased against the funding?
   - **A** Jacques-Yves Cousteau
   - **B** Robert Ballard
   - **C** Greg Stone
   - **D** Bruce Robison

6. For a research paper on recently discovered deep-sea animals, which source would be *most* useful?
   - **F** The Web site of the National Oceanographic and Atmospheric Administration, updated February 2002
   - **G** The Web site of Jed Gaylin, a graduate-school student in oceanography; no update
   - **H** A 1985 interview with Jacques-Yves Cousteau in *The New Yorker* magazine
   - **J** A 1997 encyclopedia entry on plant and animal life in the oceans

below. Then, ask students to use those terms to explain how to generate relevant research questions.
Relevance (p. 366); **Credentials** (p. 366); **Bias** (p. 366); **Opinions** (p. 366); **Facts** (p. 366).

ASSESSING

Assessment

- *Progress Assessment of Reading*
  - Chapter Test
- *Diagnostic and Summative Assessments*
  - Midyear Test

TestPractice

Answers and Model Rationales

1. **B** Both A and C are false statements, and D is only one small detail from the selection. B is the best choice, succinctly capturing the most important idea in the article.
2. **J** F is too broad a topic, while H is too specific, yielding only one answer. G focuses the research on Gagnan, instead of on deep-sea exploration. Because submersibles are used in deep-sea exploration, learning about their discoveries will lead to a wealth of information.
3. **C** A, B, and D are all directly related to the content of the article. It seems likely that exploring the frozen waters of the South Pole would be a different kind of exploration than exploring the unfrozen ocean depths, so C is the correct answer.
4. **G** Since Otis Barton invented the bathysphere, a current *Encyclopaedia Brittanica* article about him would be a useful source of information. Documentaries, Web pages, and magazine articles might be useful sources, but in these choices, the topics do not relate to the invention of the bathysphere.
5. **B** Robert Ballard is the only individual listed in the choices who is quoted in the article as speaking *against* exploration of the deepest parts of the ocean. In fact, Greg Stone (C) is quoted as supporting such exploration.
6. **F** The most current information is the most useful for this purpose, eliminating H and J. The quality of information found on Web sites might be questioned unless the site is maintained by a government agency or other reputable organization, which is the case only in F.

Test Practice

Vocabulary Development

Context Clues

Modeling. Model the thoughts of a good reader answering item 1. Say: "The policeman's feelings and the grave situation are the main clues to the meaning of the word *consoling.* Humor would be completely inappropriate in this circumstance (A). C doesn't completely take into account the seriousness of the situation either. D is not appropriate to a police officer. Therefore, B is the best response."

Test Practice

Answers and Model Rationales

1. **B** See rationale above.
2. **G** J is wrong because *odd* has nothing to do with being the best, and F is wrong because luxury and speed are not qualities of safety. The word *rich* suggests luxury but not speed, so G is a better choice than H.
3. **D** In the sentence, *quelled* means the opposite of "causing upset," so *quieted* is the correct answer.
4. **H** *At first* and *but later* are clues that *innocuous* is an antonym of *deadly,* so H is correct. F and G mean something like *deadly. Wispy* does not fit the context.
5. **C** Based on the context clue, *traverse* means "cross over." A and D suggest different movements, and B makes no sense in the sentence.
6. **F** *Jeopardize* means "to risk," so F is correct. G and J do not make sense. H is incorrect because "the other climbers" do not need rescue.
7. **B** Based on the context clue "will soon flood," B is the only possible option.

TEST PRACTICE

Vocabulary Development

Test Practice

Context Clues

DIRECTIONS: Use context clues to help you choose the answer that gives the best definition for each underlined word.

1. The policemen felt sorry for Mary about her husband's death and tried to be consoling.
   Consoling means —
   A humorous
   B comforting
   C polite
   D religious
2. Built to be the very best ship of the era, the *Titanic* had several superlative qualities, including luxury and speed.
   Superlative means —
   F safety
   G supreme
   H rich
   J odd
3. Rather than causing upset, the shots the officers fired into the air quelled the panic among the passengers.
   Quelled means —
   A increased
   B repeated
   C renewed
   D quieted
4. In "Into Thin Air" the clouds drifting up the valley at first seemed completely innocuous, but later proved deadly.
   Innocuous means —
   F worrisome
   G dangerous
   H harmless
   J wispy
5. Because of the weather it took Hall and Hansen more than twelve hours to traverse a part of the ridge that climbers usually cross in half an hour.
   Traverse means —
   A retreat from
   B observe
   C cross over
   D go under
6. Following the Sherpas' advice, Hutchison decided not to jeopardize the other climbers' lives by making a risky effort to rescue Weathers and Namba, who were so close to death.
   Jeopardize means —
   F endanger
   G ensure
   H rescue
   J upset
7. In "Notes from a Bottle" the rising water has already submerged the lower buildings and will soon flood the city's tallest structures.
   Submerged means —
   A reacted to
   B covered with water
   C revealed
   D drawn attention to

Vocabulary Review

Use this activity to assess whether students have retained the chapter Vocabulary words. Ask students to use context clues to choose the Vocabulary word from the box that fits best in each sentence below.

presumably	crucial	ascertain	vainly
speculation			

1. My mother's approval is ______. I can go on the trip only if she agrees. [crucial]
2. ______ I pleaded my case. So far I have had no success. [Vainly]
3. Trying to guess what she will decide is pure ______. [speculation]
4. To ______ the right thing to do, she is talking with other parents. [ascertain]
5. Finally, she said, "We will see." ______ that means "Yes!" [Presumably]

STANDARDS REVIEW

Writing

Test Practice

DIRECTIONS: Read the following paragraph from a draft of a student's comparison-contrast essay. Then, read the questions below it. Choose the best answer to each question.

(1) Recently, two separate news sources carried articles about professional golfer Leon Dillard. (2) If you have access to the Web, you can read both articles online. (3) The newspaper article, "Young Egos Intruding on Sport," presents the opinion that Dillard is ruining the game by inspiring youths to take up the sport in hopes of making millions of dollars. (4) On the other hand, the magazine article, "Leon Dillard: On the Course and Off," presents a detailed account of Dillard's golfing career and the positive impact his sponsorship of urban golf leagues has had on the sport.

1. To present a clear, coherent thesis, which of these sentences could the writer add?
- **A** While both stories discuss Dillard's impact on the game, the newspaper conveys a more negative perspective.
- **B** Leon Dillard is an amazing golfer whose skills rival other greats.
- **C** Leon Dillard has been interviewed by media sources worldwide.
- **D** Newspaper articles are always more factual than magazine stories.

2. To support the ideas in sentence 3, which sentence could the writer add?
- **F** It gives a graphic diagram of Dillard's powerful golf swing.
- **G** It explains how Dillard began his golf career.
- **H** It focuses on Dillard's hobbies outside of golf.
- **J** It quotes youths who hope their golf lessons will lead to riches.

3. Which of the following sentences would elaborate on the ideas in sentence 4?
- **A** The newspaper article is biased, focusing on the writer's opinions.
- **B** The magazine article is part of a series of stories on Leon Dillard.
- **C** The article quotes a young golfer who admires Dillard's generosity.
- **D** Statistics in the newspaper show how much money Dillard has earned.

4. Which sentence should be deleted to improve the passage's organization?
- **F** 1
- **G** 2
- **H** 3
- **J** 4

5. To discuss the similarities between the two media, the writer could
- **A** explain that the newspaper is distributed only locally
- **B** defend the credibility of the sources quoted in each article
- **C** describe the photo of Dillard that accompanies the magazine article
- **D** discuss how both articles credit Dillard for influencing young golfers

RESOURCES: WRITING

Assessment
- *Test Generator (One-Stop Planner* CD-ROM)
- *Progress Assessment of Writing, Listening, & Speaking,* Ch. 5
- *Diagnostic and Summative Assessments,* Midyear Test

Internet
- Online assessments at go.hrw.com (keyword: HLLA)

Standards Review

Answers

1. A
2. J
3. C
4. G
5. D

APPLICATION

Consumer Report

For homework, have students apply the comparison-contrast skills they have learned in this workshop to report on a number of products in an area in which they have special knowledge. Students can write brief comparison-contrast articles evaluating the performance and value of different brands of golf balls, for example, or on the benefits and drawbacks of buying used books instead of new ones.

Homework

EXTENSION

Chart Your Future

To help students think about what they would like to do following high school, have them use what they know about comparison and contrast to evaluate some possibilities. Students should develop points of comparison for their subjects (careers, for example, or various colleges) and incorporate the information in a chart like the one on p. 383.

Then, have students write a paragraph that synthesizes the three most important points of comparison from their charts. Encourage students to gather information by consulting guidance counselors, individuals who have pursued the educational or career paths they are considering, or Internet college or career sites. *(You need to be aware that Internet resources are sometimes public forums and their content can be unpredictable.)*

Holt Literature and Language Arts: Mastering the California Standards

Chapter 6 Symbolism and Allegory

Synthesizing Sources

Program Organization

Holt Literature and Language Arts provides a complete curriculum for standards-based instruction in reading, literature, writing, listening and speaking, and language conventions. The instructional content is presented in quarters to enable teachers to anticipate and administer the quarterly assessments required by California.

About Chapter 6

Standards-based lesson plans and suggestions for pacing the presentation of Chapter 6, the related instructional material, and the recommended assessment are provided in *On Course: Mapping Instruction,* Chapter 6.

- In Chapter 6, students will identify and use words literally and figuratively; synthesize several sources on a single issue, paraphrase those sources and connect their ideas; recognize and understand various literary devices; and respond to literature both orally and in writing.

Language Arts Content

Which reading standards are taught in Chapter 6?

In this chapter, students will master the following Grade 10 standards and review standards from Grade 8. Selections or features marked with a ✔ constitute the minimum course of study that provides coverage of grade-level standards.

Grade 10 Standards

Word Analysis, Fluency, and Systematic Vocabulary Development

1.1 Identify and use the literal and figurative meanings of words, and understand word derivations.

✔ Analogies: Matching Relationships, p. 410

Word Mapping: Pinning Down Meaning, p. 417

Reading Comprehension (Focus on Informational Materials)

2.4 Synthesize the content from several sources or works by a single author dealing with a single issue; paraphrase the ideas, and connect them to other sources and related topics to demonstrate comprehension.

✔ "Coming of Age, Latino Style" (newspaper article)
✔ "Vision Quest" (encyclopedia entry)
"Crossing a Threshold to Adulthood" (op-ed article)
} pp. 411–416

Literary Response and Analysis

3.7 Recognize and understand the significance of various literary devices, including figurative language, imagery, allegory, and symbolism, and explain their appeal.

"Symbolism and Allegory: Signs of Something More"(standards essay), pp. 398–399

✔ "Through the Tunnel" (short story), pp. 400–409

"The Masque of the Red Death" (short story), pp. 418–431

"Stopping by Woods on a Snowy Evening" (poem)
"After Apple-Picking" (poem)
} pp. 433–438

"The Blue Stones" (standards review), pp. 450–451

(continued)

(continued)

Review Standard Grade 8

Reading 1.3 Use word meanings within the appropriate context, and show ability to verify those meanings by definition, restatement, example, comparison, or contrast.

Word Mapping: Pinning Down Meaning, p. 417

Context Clues: Filling in the Blanks, p. 432

Which writing, and listening and speaking standards are taught in Chapter 6?

Writing Strategies

1.1 Establish a controlling impression or coherent thesis that conveys a clear and distinctive perspective on the subject and maintain a consistent tone and focus throughout the piece of writing.

Analyze the Story and Develop a Thesis, pp. 440–441

Writing Applications

2.2 Write responses to literature.

a. Demonstrate a comprehensive grasp of the significant ideas of literature works.
Gather and Organize Support, pp. 441–442

b. Support important ideas and viewpoints through accurate and detailed references to the text or to other works.
Gather and Organize Support, pp. 441–442

c. Demonstrate awareness of the author's use of stylistic devices and an appreciation of the effects created.
Analyze the Story and Develop a Thesis, pp. 440–441

d. Identify and assess the impact of perceived ambiguities, nuances, and complexities within the text.
Gather and Organize Support, pp. 441–442

Listening and Speaking Strategies

1.4 Choose appropriate techniques for developing the introduction and conclusion.

Adapt Your Written Analysis, pp. 448–449

Listening and Speaking Applications

2.4 Deliver oral responses to literature.

a. Advance a judgment demonstrating a comprehensive grasp of the significant ideas of works or passages.
Adapt Your Written Analysis, pp. 448–449

b. Support important ideas and viewpoints through accurate and detailed references to the text or to other works.
Adapt Your Written Analysis, pp. 448–449

c. Demonstrate awareness of the author's use of stylistic devices and an appreciation of the effects created.
Adapt Your Written Analysis, pp. 448–449

d. Identify and assess the impact of perceived ambiguities, nuances, and complexities within the text.
Adapt Your Written Analysis, pp. 448–449

Review Standards Grade 8

Writing 2.2 Write research reports.

d. Support judgments through references to the text, other works, other authors, or to personal knowledge.
Supporting Details, p. 442

Speaking 2.2 Deliver research presentations.

d. Support judgments through references to the text, other works, other authors, or personal knowledge.
Adapt Your Written Analysis, pp. 448–449

Instructional Planning and Support

Where do I find lesson plans, additional resources, and other teaching aids?

- This Annotated Teacher's Edition and *On Course: Mapping Instruction* provide direction in planning and implementing a complete California standards–based curriculum. These components also include instructions for diagnostic, progress, and summative testing; for presenting direct instruction of the standards; for differentiating instruction to provide universal access; and for locating and using the program's ancillaries.
- Lesson and workshop resources are referenced at the beginning of each selection or workshop, in the bottom margin of this teacher's edition.
- Reminders for using additional resources appear in this teacher's edition at point of use.
- The *One-Stop Planner* CD-ROM contains editable lesson plans and all print ancillaries, available in PDF format.

What if I don't have time to teach all of Chapter 6?

- Most standards can be taught with a minimum number of selections and features. In the chart on the preceding page, the core lessons you need in order to provide complete coverage of the chapter standards are identified with a ✓.
- *On Course: Mapping Instruction,* Chapter 6, lists lessons and activities that provide minimum standards coverage.

What provisions have been made for students who have additional class time scheduled in language arts?

- *Interactive Reading* provides for alternative direct instruction and practice of the grade-level standards taught in Chapter 6.
- *Universal Access: Writing, Listening, and Speaking,* Chapter 6, contains worksheets and transparencies that provide practice in and reteaching and reinforcement of the writing and listening and speaking standards in Chapter 6.
- *Universal Access: Lesson Plans for Language Development,* Chapter 6 provides alternative teaching strategies and additional worksheets designed specifically for English-language learners and special education students. Many of the suggestions and activities in this ancillary will also be helpful to students in the regular classroom who are having difficulty with particular skills.

Universal Access

How do I differentiate instruction to ensure that all my students master the standards?

Holt Literature and Language Arts provides comprehensive, differentiated instruction for all types of students.

- Most of the general instruction and teaching strategies in the Annotated Teacher's Edition are at grade level. These instructions will work well with the majority of your students.
- Point-of-use suggestions are provided for advanced learners, learners having difficulty, English-language learners, and special education students.
- *Interactive Reading* is designed to anticipate and remediate problems that students may experience in achieving mastery of the reading standards. See *Interactive Reading,* Teacher's Edition, Chapter 6, for information on using the reader to differentiate instruction.
- *Universal Access: Writing, Listening, and Speaking,* Chapter 6, contains worksheets and transparencies that provide practice in and reteaching and reinforcement of the writing and listening and speaking standards in Chapter 6.
- *Universal Access: Lesson Plans for Language Development,* Chapter 6, offers teaching strategies and additional worksheets designed specifically for English-language learners and special education students.

Assessment

How do I determine whether my students are making progress in mastering the standards?

Progress Assessment

- Use the Standards Reviews at the end of Chapter 6 for an informal assessment of the informational reading and writing standards.
- Use Chapter 6 tests from the *Progress Assessment* booklets to assess comprehension and progress on mastering the standards taught in this chapter.

Summative Assessment

The content of *Holt Literature and Language Arts* has been divided into quarters to allow you to administer the four summative tests required by California. Chapters 6–8 and related instructional material constitute the third quarter of instruction. At the end of Chapter 8, you may ask students to take the Third-Quarter Test in *Diagnostic and Summative Assessments.*

Chapter 6

STANDARDS FOCUS

(For full text of standards taught in this chapter, see the Standards Correlation by Standard chart in the Student Edition.)

Grade-Level Standards

- Vocabulary Development 1.1
- Reading Comprehension 2.4
- Literary Response and Analysis 3.7
- Writing Strategies 1.1
- Writing Applications 2.2a–d
- Listening and Speaking Strategies 1.4
- Speaking Applications 2.4a–d

INTRODUCING THE CHAPTER

The stories and poems in this chapter share the capacity for suggesting meaning beyond what is obvious, for each selection makes use of symbols. For example, on the surface, Doris Lessing's "Through the Tunnel" is the tale of a boy taking on a physical challenge, but at a deeper level of meaning, it is a story of initiation into adulthood. Edgar Allan Poe's "The Masque of the Red Death" is superficially about people trying to escape a plague; symbolically, though, it's about the inevitability of death. Robert Frost's deceptively simple poems actually concern the complexities of life's work and life's choices.

In addition to the fiction and poetry, Chapter 6 provides an opportunity for students to synthesize information from more than one source. Three nonfiction selections deal with coming-of-age rituals in different cultures.

The chapter culminates with an opportunity for students to write an analysis of a short story and to present an oral response to literature.

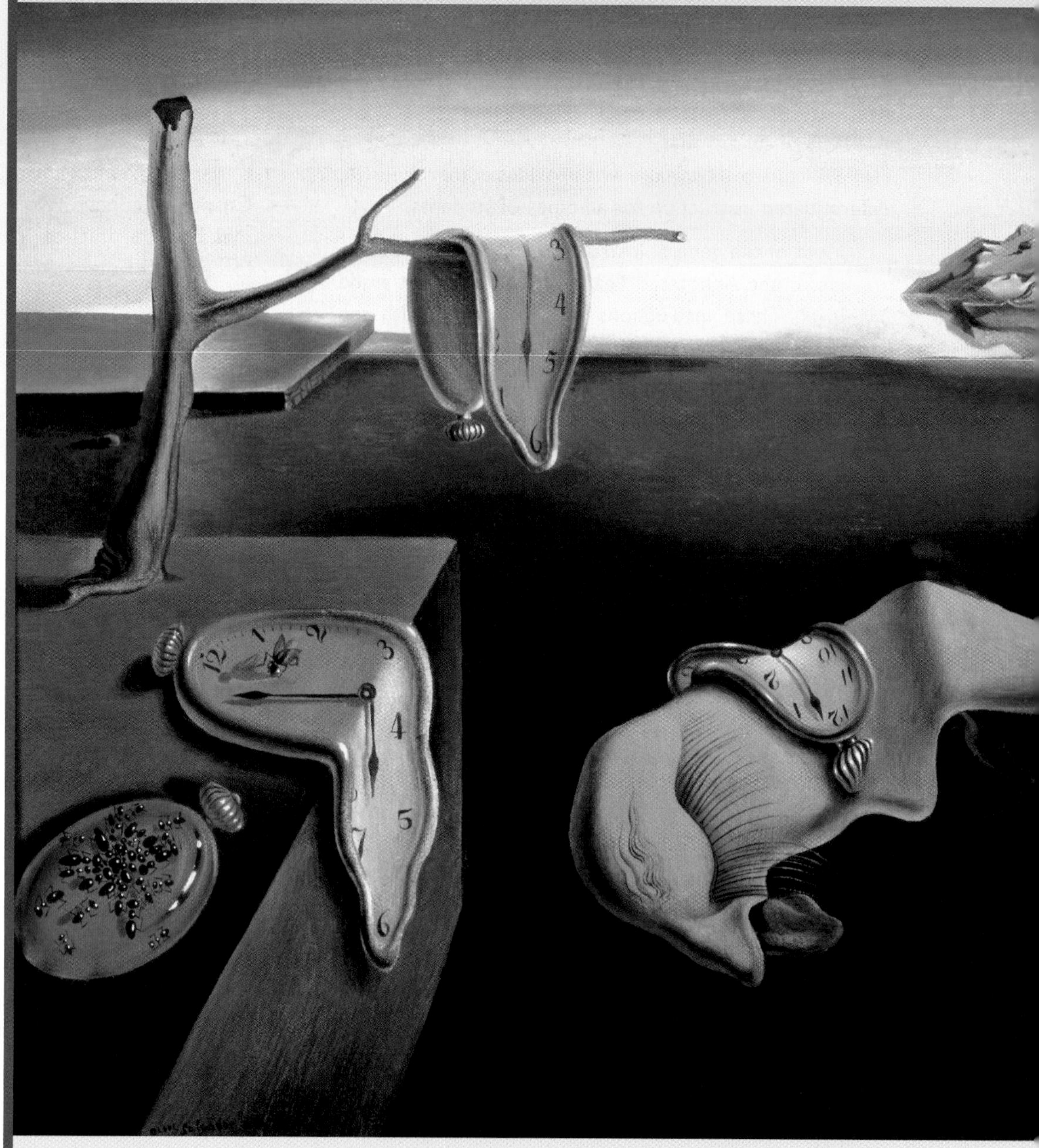

CHAPTER 6 RESOURCES: READING

Planning

- *One-Stop Planner* CD-ROM with Test Generator
- *On Course: Mapping Instruction*
- *At Home: A Guide to Standards Mastery*
- *At Home: In Spanish*
- *Supporting Instruction in Spanish*

Reading

- *Interactive Reading*

Differentiating Instruction

- *Lesson Plans for Language Development*

Vocabulary

- *Vocabulary Development*
    - Cumulative Vocabulary Review, pp. 36–37

Chapter 6

Symbolism and Allegory

SYNTHESIZING SOURCES

We are symbols, and inhabit symbols.

—Ralph Waldo Emerson

The Persistence of Memory (1931)
by Salvador Dali.
Oil on canvas (80.7 cm × 100.6 cm).

go.hrw.com
KEYWORD: HLLA 10-6

397

THE QUOTATION

Remind students that a symbol is something that represents something else by association, resemblance, or convention. For example, an A on a test is a symbol of high achievement. Invite students to suggest other symbols that are familiar to them. [Possible responses: Stars on the American flag represent each of the fifty states.]

VIEWING THE ART

The art of **Salvador Dali** (1904–1989) blurs the distinctions between object and subject and between dreams and reality. *The Persistence of Memory,* easily Dali's best-known work of art, presents an irrational landscape with painstaking detail. The disfigured clocks and barren vista are unconventional symbols that appear like objects in a dream. According to the theories of Sigmund Freud (1856–1939), which inspired Dali and other surrealists, the symbols of dreams express wishes and anxieties in an encoded form.

Activity. What does this painting suggest about memory's tendency to distort time? [The title and content of the painting imply that our memories can be altered over time and that memories of time can be inexact.]

Resources Reminder

Planning

- *At Home: A Guide to Standards Mastery*

Parent letters appear in this resource. Translations of these letters appear in *At Home: In Spanish.* Translations of selection summaries are found in *Supporting Instruction in Spanish.*

Reading

- *Interactive Reading*

The California framework requires students to read materials apart from in-class assignments. Additional reading suggestions are cited on the Read On page and on selected pages in the Student Edition.

Grammar

- *Holt Handbook*
  - Participle and the Participial Phrase, pp. 70–73

Assessment

- *Progress Assessment of Reading*
  - Chapter Test
- *One-Stop Planner* CD-ROM with Test Generator

Internet

- go.hrw.com
(Keyword: HLLA 10-6)

STANDARDS FOCUS, pp. 398–399

(For the grade-level standard taught in this lesson, see Student Edition, p. 398.)

Prerequisite Standard

- Grade 8, Literary Response and Analysis 3.6 **Identify significant literary devices (e.g., metaphor, symbolism, dialect, irony) that define a writer's style and use those elements to interpret the work.**

Literary Focus: Symbolism and Allegory

Remind students that a symbol has two levels of meaning, a literal level and a symbolic level. For example, on a literal level, a lamp in a window is simply an electric light, but on a symbolic level, it may mean "welcome." Symbols are found not only in literature, but also all around us. Objects associated with holidays are particularly rich in symbolic meaning. Choose a holiday, and ask students to name things associated with it. Then, ask them for the symbolic meanings of red roses, a ring, chocolates, and a heart.

Explain that allegory takes symbolism a step further in that most of the characters and events in an allegory stand for abstract qualities. Since people associate certain animals with certain qualities, animal characters are often used in one type of allegory called the fable. Explain that the animated cartoons of Disney and the comic strips of other artists are fables. You may wish to show a scene from a Disney cartoon and have students identify the qualities of the animal characters.

Literary Response and Analysis

Symbolism and Allegory *by* John Leggett

SIGNS OF SOMETHING MORE

Our everyday lives are full of symbols. The ring on your finger, though actually a piece of metal with a stone in it, may also be a symbol of something less concrete. For you it may symbolize love, calling to mind the special person who saved for months to buy it for you.

There are many symbols in our culture that we know and recognize at once. We automatically make the associations suggested by a cross, a six-pointed star, a crown, a skull and crossbones, and the Stars and Stripes. These commonly accepted symbols are **public symbols.**

Symbols in Literature: Making Associations

Writers of fiction, poetry, and drama create new, personal symbols in their work. Some literary symbols, like the great white whale in *Moby-Dick* and that stubborn spot of blood on Lady Macbeth's hand, become so widely known that eventually they too become a part of our public stockpile of symbols.

In literature a **symbol** is something (an object, a setting, an event, an animal, or even a person) that functions in a story the way you'd expect it to but also stands for something more than itself, usually something abstract. The white whale in *Moby-Dick* is a very real white whale in the novel, and Captain Ahab spends the whole book chasing it. Certain passages in that novel make clear to us that this whale is also associated with the mystery of evil in the world. That is how symbols work—by association. Most people associate the color green with new life and, therefore, with hope. In some cultures the color white is associated with innocence and purity; in others white is a color of death. We usually associate gardens with joy and wastelands with futility and despair. We associate winter with sterility and spring with fertility. We associate cooing doves with peace and pecking ravens with death, but these are associations, not equations.

A literary symbol isn't just a sign with one specific meaning. The picture of a cigarette in a circle with a diagonal line drawn through it is a sign meaning, precisely and specifically, "No Smoking." The white whale, on the other hand, doesn't mean, precisely and specifically, "the mystery of evil." Instead, the associations suggested by the writer, made by the characters in the story, and ultimately made by the reader evoke images of evil (and perhaps other elements), suggest aspects of the darker side of life, and hint at possible ways of seeing and thinking about the events portrayed.

Symbols invite the reader to participate in making sense of the text by building on the associations and connections that the symbols suggest.

Is It a Symbol?

However, you must be careful not to start looking for symbols in everything you read: They won't be there. Here are some hints to pay attention to when you sense that a story is operating on a symbolic level:

Reading Standard 3.7 Recognize and understand the significance of various literary devices, including figurative language, allegory, and symbolism, and explain their appeal.

DIFFERENTIATING INSTRUCTION

Learners Having Difficulty

Symbolism. To help students understand symbolism, you may wish to show them pictures of public symbols and elicit their meanings—for example, five interlocking rings (the Olympics), a cartoon elephant with stars and stripes on it (the Republican Party), or a bolt of lightning (danger or electricity). Have students work in small groups to come up with more public symbols and their meanings. Groups may share their results with the class. Emphasize that literary symbols often have less-precise meanings than public symbols. When they read a story, students should focus on recurring descriptions of a person, place, or object. The description may indicate that the item stands for something more than itself.

1 Symbols are often visual.

2 When some event or object or setting is used as a symbol, it often reappears throughout the story.

3 A symbol in literature is a form of **figurative language.** Like a metaphor a symbol is something that is identified with something else that is very *different* from it but that shares some quality. When you are thinking about whether something is used symbolically, ask yourself this: "Does this item also stand for something essentially different from itself?"

4 A symbol usually has something to do with a story's **theme.**

Why Use Symbols?

Why do writers use symbols? Why don't they just come out and tell us directly what they want to say? One answer is that symbols have the power to move us. When they fit a human emotion just right, they stir us and last for years in our imaginations. You may well find that you remember a story's symbol long after you have forgotten other parts of the story's plot.

Allegory: When Symbols Get Specific

Allegories are stories in which characters and places stand for virtues and vices. Characters in an allegory might even have names that describe what they symbolize: Ignorance, Mr. Worldly Wiseman, Little-Faith, Mrs. Bubble.

Years ago allegories were very popular. An allegory written in the seventeenth century by John Bunyan, called *The Pilgrim's Progress,* was at one time second only to the Bible in popularity in the English-speaking world. *The Pilgrim's Progress* is about a man named Christian and his progress through the world to the Celestial City. On the way he must conquer all kinds of dangers and temptations, such as the Giant Despair, the City of Destruction, and the Valley of Humiliation.

There are several types of allegory. In **fables,** animal characters that symbolize vices and virtues act out a story in order to teach a practical lesson about how to succeed in life. You might remember the sly fox, the slow-but-steady tortoise, the greedy crow.

Another kind of allegory is the parable. A **parable** is a brief story that is set in the ordinary everyday world and told to teach a lesson about ethics or morality. One of the most famous parables is that of the Good Samaritan (see page 278), who stops and helps a stranger who has been robbed and beaten. Today we still call caring strangers good Samaritans.

Practice

How many symbols can you find in public life? Try identifying what the following things stand for:

1. dove with an olive branch
2. blindfolded woman holding a pair of scales
3. yellow rose
4. yellow ribbon tied around a tree
5. dragon (dragons stand for different things in the East and the West)
6. pink ribbon in a lapel

Practice

1. A dove with an olive branch stands for peace.
2. A blindfolded woman holding a pair of scales stands for justice.
3. A yellow rose stands for friendship.
4. A yellow ribbon tied around a tree is a symbol of welcoming someone who has been away (often a military person who has been overseas).
5. In the East a dragon stands for good fortune or power. In the West a dragon stands for an enemy, the devil, or evil in general.
6. A pink ribbon in a lapel stands for remembering breast cancer victims.

Apply

Encourage students to think of other symbols that appear around them or in literature. Have each student draw pictures or write descriptions of their symbols. Pairs of students may then exchange papers and identify the meanings of each other's symbols.

Resources Reminder

Differentiating Instruction

- *Lesson Plans for Language Development*

For more instruction on symbolism and allegory for English-language learners and special education students, see *Lesson Plans for Language Development,* pp. 173, 174.

Advanced Learners

Acceleration. This activity can help to move students toward the eleventh- and twelfth-grade Standard 3.1, for which they analyze characteristics of subgenres such as allegory.

Activity. Encourage individual students to identify and analyze a short parable or fable, such as "The Parable of the Prodigal Son" from the Bible, Aesop's "The Lion and the Mouse," or La Fontaine's "The Fox and the Crow." Students should identify the work's characters, objects, and events that have both a literal and an allegorical meaning, and they should determine the lesson or moral conveyed. Then, have students work in small groups to share their analyses and to discuss characteristics that all the works have in common.

STANDARDS FOCUS, pp. 400–410

(For the grade-level standards taught in this lesson, see citations on Student Edition pages.)

Prerequisite Standard

- Grade 8, Literary Response and Analysis 3.6 **Identify significant literary devices (e.g., metaphor, symbolism, dialect, irony) that define a writer's style and use those elements to interpret the works.**

Reading Skills

- Re-read and read for details.

Summary *at grade level*

The protagonist of this initiation story is Jerry, a young British boy who is vacationing on a foreign coast with his widowed mother. Jerry longs to go to the "wild and rocky bay" but is uncomfortable leaving his mother on the "safe" beach; she worries about his encountering danger but worries more about babying him, so she lets him go off on his own. At the bay, Jerry is blissful when older local boys let him swim with them. He's terrified, though, as they swim through an underwater tunnel in the rock. When he clowns childishly instead of following their lead, the boys leave. Jerry then becomes determined to swim the tunnel. Suspense builds as he practices and prepares obsessively, enduring nosebleeds in order to increase his ability to hold his breath. Suspense peaks with Jerry's climactic swim through the dark, dangerous tunnel, which comes to symbolize his struggle for independence and maturity. After his accomplishment, Jerry no longer needs the boys' approval or the bay as a testing ground.

Before You Read

Through the Tunnel

Literary Focus

Symbolic Meaning: More Than Meets the Eye

When we read, we often sense that a story means more than what happens on its surface. For instance, if a young woman in a story is in serious conflict with her parents over her earrings (she loves them; they hate them), we should suspect that those earrings represent something important to her. A **symbol** is a person, place, thing, or event that stands both for itself and for something beyond itself. To the young woman the earrings may symbolize her independence or maturity. A large part of the appeal of symbols is that they often carry associations, connections, and powerful emotions.

The **symbolic meaning** of a story emerges from an overall interpretation of the story's symbols. As you read "Through the Tunnel," look for elements that could be symbolically significant. What might they mean?

Reading Skills

Re-reading and Reading for Details

Many stories need only one reading because everything seems perfectly clear the first time through. Other stories puzzle, nag, and tease us. They seem to have layers that invite peeling away to get at the story's core meaning. Once you finish reading such a story, you may want—or need—to go round again, **re-reading** the text to mine its subtler, deeper meanings.

As you re-read, you may be searching for answers to questions you've asked yourself at the story's end. You may also notice details that your eye jumped over during your first reading. Writers plant significant details as signposts or clues, but we often don't recognize their importance until we've read the story all the way to its end.

Plan to read this story twice. Ask yourself questions when you finish the first time: What puzzles you? What seems unclear? Then, re-read the story, looking for important details and answers to your questions.

Reading Standard 3.7 Recognize and understand the significance of various literary devices, including symbolism, and explain their appeal.

Make the Connection

Quickwrite

Think of a time when you felt you needed to prove yourself by achieving something that was difficult and challenging. What did you have to go through to reach your goal? Did you get or do what you wanted? How did you feel at the end? Freewrite for a few minutes about your experience.

Vocabulary Development

contrition (kən·trish′ən) *n.:* regret or sense of guilt at having done wrong.

supplication (sup′lə·kā′shən) *n.:* humble appeal or request.

defiant (dē·fī′ənt) *adj.:* challenging authority.

inquisitive (in·kwiz′ə·tiv) *adj.:* questioning; curious.

minute (mī·no͞ot′) *adj.:* small; tiny.

incredulous (in·krej′o͞o·ləs) *adj.:* disbelieving; skeptical.

RESOURCES: READING

Planning

- *One-Stop Planner* CD-ROM with Test Generator
- *On Course: Mapping Instruction*

Media

- *Audio CD Library*
  - disc 12

Reading

- *Interactive Reading*
  - Interactive version: "Through the Tunnel"
- *Interactive Reading,* Teacher's Edition
  - Graphic Organizer: Symbol Chart

Differentiating Instruction

- *Lesson Plans for Language Development*
  - English-Language Learners, pp. 175–177, 192, 196

Through the Tunnel

Doris Lessing

WATER SURGED INTO HIS MOUTH; HE CHOKED, SANK, CAME UP.

Going to the shore on the first morning of the vacation, the young English boy stopped at a turning of the path and looked down at a wild and rocky bay and then over to the crowded beach he knew so well from other years. His mother walked on in front of him, carrying a bright striped bag in one hand. Her other arm, swinging loose, was very white in the sun. The boy watched that white naked arm and turned his eyes, which had a frown behind them,

- Special Education Students, pp. 178, 192, 196
- *One-Stop Planner* CD-ROM with Test Generator

Vocabulary

- *Vocabulary Development*
  - Vocabulary Worksheet, p. 33

Assessment

- *Progress Assessment of Reading*
  - Selection Test

PRETEACHING

Selection Starter

Motivate. Many students will relate to the main character of this story, a young boy determined to accomplish a grueling physical task in order to prove himself. Trying out for a sports team or a part in a school play, mastering a difficult maneuver on a skateboard, or auditioning for a seat in the school band are just a few examples of what young people go through to be accepted into a group or to prove themselves. Invite students to share their experiences.

Build background. This story takes place at an unnamed seaside resort frequented by British tourists. This resort could be located on the Mediterranean Sea, perhaps along the coast of France or North Africa.

Preview Vocabulary

Have students take turns reading aloud the definitions of the Vocabulary words listed on p. 400. Then, have the partners reinforce their understanding of the words by having them choose the best word to complete each of the following sentences.

1. The refugee looked at the aid workers with ______ in his eyes. [supplication]
2. We understood that in the corporation's larger scheme, our role was ______. [minute]
3. She was ______ when he said that it was a counterfeit bill. [incredulous]
4. To be successful as an investigative reporter, it is good to have an ______ nature. [inquisitive]
5. He became ______ after destroying the fence, and the expression on his face showed that he felt no sense of ______. [defiant, contrition]

DIRECT TEACHING

A Literary Focus
GRADE-LEVEL STANDARD

Omniscient point of view. How do you know that this story is told by an omniscient narrator? [It is written in the third person; the narrator plays no part in the story but describes what each character is thinking and feeling.]

B Literary Focus
GRADE-LEVEL STANDARD

Symbolism. In this story, setting and symbolism are closely related. The "safe beach" symbolizes childhood and dependence; the "rocky bay," maturity and independence.

C Reading Skills

Reading for details. Which details in the passage suggest that Jerry and his mother have a close, caring relationship? [The mother's worry about Jerry; Jerry's familiarity with his mother's smile; Jerry's qualms about leaving his mother; the mother's determination to be caring but not overprotective.]

D Literary Focus
GRADE-LEVEL STANDARD

Figurative language. How does Lessing use figurative language to describe the rocks that Jerry sees? [She uses a simile, comparing the rocks to "discolored monsters."] Why is this effective? [Possible response: Jerry is taking a risk by venturing off in the "wild bay"; monsters are associated with the wild.]

E English-Language Learners

Interpreting idioms. Ask if students are familiar with the expression *a stone's throw,* meaning "a short distance."

---

toward the bay and back again to his mother. When she felt he was not with her, she swung around. "Oh, there you are, Jerry!" she said. She looked impatient, then smiled. "Why, darling, would you rather not come with me? Would you rather—" She frowned, conscientiously worrying over what amusements he might secretly be longing for, which she had been too busy or too careless to imagine. He was very familiar with that anxious, apologetic smile. Contrition sent him running after her. And yet, as he ran, he looked back over his shoulder at the wild bay; and all morning, as he played on the safe beach, he was thinking of it.

Next morning, when it was time for the routine of swimming and sunbathing, his mother said, "Are you tired of the usual beach, Jerry? Would you like to go somewhere else?"

"Oh, no!" he said quickly, smiling at her out of that unfailing impulse of contrition—a sort of chivalry.[1] Yet, walking down the path with her, he blurted out, "I'd like to go and have a look at those rocks down there."

She gave the idea her attention. It was a wild-looking place, and there was no one there, but she said, "Of course, Jerry. When you've had enough, come to the big beach. Or just go straight back to the villa, if you like." She walked away, that bare arm, now slightly reddened from yesterday's sun, swinging. And he almost ran after her again, feeling it unbearable that she should go by herself, but he did not.

She was thinking, Of course he's old enough to be safe without me. Have I been keeping him too close? He mustn't feel he ought to be with me. I must be careful.

He was an only child, eleven years old. She was a widow. She was determined to be neither possessive nor lacking in devotion. She went worrying off to her beach.

As for Jerry, once he saw that his mother had gained her beach, he began the steep descent to the bay. From where he was, high up among red-brown rocks, it was a scoop of moving bluish green fringed with white. As he went lower, he saw that it spread among small promontories and inlets of rough, sharp rock, and the crisping, lapping surface showed stains of purple and darker blue. Finally, as he ran sliding and scraping down the last few yards, he saw an edge of white surf and the shallow, luminous movement of water over white sand and, beyond that, a solid, heavy blue.

He ran straight into the water and began swimming. He was a good swimmer. He went out fast over the gleaming sand, over a middle region where rocks lay like discolored monsters under the surface, and then he was in the real sea—a warm sea where irregular cold currents from the deep water shocked his limbs.

When he was so far out that he could look back not only on the little bay but past the promontory that was between it and the big beach, he floated on the buoyant surface and looked for his mother. There she was, a speck of yellow under an umbrella that looked like a slice of orange peel. He swam back to shore, relieved at being sure she was there, but all at once very lonely.

On the edge of a small cape that marked the side of the bay away from the promontory was a loose scatter of rocks. Above them, some boys were stripping off their clothes. They came running, naked, down to the rocks. The English boy swam toward them but kept his distance at a stone's throw. They were of that coast; all of them were burned smooth dark brown and speaking a language he did not understand. To be with them, of them, was a craving that filled his whole body. He swam a little closer; they

1. **chivalry** (shiv′əl·rē) *n.:* here, an act of gentlemanly politeness.

Vocabulary
contrition (kən·trish′ən) *n.:* regret or sense of guilt at having done wrong.

DIFFERENTIATING INSTRUCTION

Learners Having Difficulty
Invite learners having difficulty to read "Through the Tunnel" in interactive format in *Interactive Reading* and to use the sidenotes as aids to understanding the selection. The interactive version provides additional instruction, practice, and assessment of the literature standard taught in the Student Edition. Monitor students' responses to the selection, and correct any misconceptions that arise.

Resources Reminder

Differentiating Instruction
- *Interactive Reading*
  - Interactive version: "Through the Tunnel"

English-Language Learners
Point out that since Lessing is a British writer, her style and use of language may have an unfamiliar quality. Have students try to restate

turned and watched him with narrowed, alert dark eyes. Then one smiled and waved. It was enough. In a minute, he had swum in and was on the rocks beside them, smiling with a desperate, nervous supplication. They shouted cheerful greetings at him; and then, as he preserved his nervous, uncomprehending smile, they understood that he was a foreigner strayed from his own beach, and they proceeded to forget him. But he was happy. He was with them.

They began diving again and again from a high point into a well of blue sea between rough, pointed rocks. After they had dived and come up, they swam around, hauled themselves up, and waited their turn to dive again. They were big boys—men, to Jerry. He dived, and they watched him; and when he swam around to take his place, they made way for him. He felt he was accepted and he dived again, carefully, proud of himself.

Soon the biggest of the boys poised himself, shot down into the water, and did not come up. The others stood about, watching. Jerry, after waiting for the sleek brown head to appear, let out a yell of warning; they looked at him idly and turned their eyes back toward the water. After a long time, the boy came up on the other side of a big dark rock, letting the air out of his lungs in a sputtering gasp and a shout of triumph. Immediately the rest of them dived in. One moment, the morning seemed full of chattering boys; the next, the air and the surface of the water were empty. But through the heavy blue, dark shapes could be seen moving and groping.

Jerry dived, shot past the school of underwater swimmers, saw a black wall of rock looming at him, touched it, and bobbed up at once to the surface, where the wall was a low barrier he could see across. There was no one visible; under him, in the water, the dim shapes of the swimmers had disappeared. Then one and then another of the boys came up on the far side of the barrier of rock, and he understood that they had swum through some gap or hole in it. He plunged down again. He could see nothing through the stinging salt water but the blank rock. When he came up, the boys were all on the diving rock, preparing to attempt the feat again. And now, in a panic of failure, he yelled up, in English, "Look at me! Look!" and he began splashing and kicking in the water like a foolish dog.

They looked down gravely, frowning. He knew the frown. At moments of failure, when he clowned to claim his mother's attention, it was with just this grave, embarrassed inspection that she rewarded him. Through his hot shame, feeling the pleading grin on his face like a scar that he could never remove, he looked up at the group of big brown boys on the rock and shouted, *"Bonjour! Merci! Au revoir! Monsieur, monsieur!"*[2] while he hooked his fingers round his ears and waggled them.

Water surged into his mouth; he choked, sank, came up. The rock, lately weighted with boys, seemed to rear up out of the water as their

2. ***Bonjour! Merci! Au revoir! Monsieur, monsieur!:*** French for "Hello! Thank you! Goodbye! Mister, mister!"—probably the only French words Jerry knows.

Vocabulary
supplication (sup'lə·kā'shən) *n.:* humble appeal or request.

DIRECT TEACHING

F Reading Skills

Reading for details. Which details show that even though Jerry appears to be accepted by the boys, he does not understand them and is still an outsider? [He yells out in warning when the boy does not reappear; the other boys are looking at the water unconcerned.]

G Literary Focus
REVIEW STANDARD

Setting. One function of setting is to create atmosphere. What atmosphere does Lessing create with the expressions *big dark rock; heavy blue, dark shapes; black wall of rock looming at him;* and *blank rock?* [Possible response: The words create a frightening, forbidding atmosphere.]

H Reading Skills

Drawing conclusions. Why is it important for Jerry to have the older boys' approval? [Possible response: He is lonely and wants to be accepted by these older boys as an equal.]

I Literary Focus
GRADE-LEVEL STANDARD

Figurative language. How does Lessing use figurative language to describe what Jerry is feeling? [She uses a simile to compare the expression on his face to a scar.] Why is this an effective comparison? [Possible response: A scar makes you look bad and is permanent. Jerry now appears foolish before the other boys, and there is nothing he can do about it.]

such sentences and phrases as "Why, darling, would you rather not come with me?"; "gained her beach"; "She gave the idea her attention"; and "He mustn't feel he ought to be with me." Also, explain the fact that in parts of Europe, a villa is a large vacation house.

Resources Reminder

For lessons designed for intermediate and advanced English-language learners, see *Lesson Plans for Language Development,* pp. 175–177, 192, 196.

Special Education Students

For lessons designed for special education students, see *Lesson Plans for Language Development,* pp. 178, 192, 196.

Advanced Learners

Enrichment. Ask students to identify some of the dangers that someone might face when swimming alone in the ocean, such as ocean currents, undertow, sharks, jellyfish, and so on.

Direct Teaching

A Reading Skills

Making inferences. Why do the older boys leave? [Jerry is acting like a child; he has not passed the test of performing and acting like one of them.]

B Literary Focus
REVIEW STANDARD

Setting. In this passage, Lessing contrasts the mother's landscape with Jerry's landscape. In the former she uses colors; in the latter she personifies the boulders and uses another metaphor to describe the rock. Ask students to identify specific words that create this contrast and to tell what effect is created. [Words and phrases for the mother's landscape are *yellow spot* and *orange umbrella;* for Jerry's landscape, *fanged and angry boulders* and *wall of rock.* One setting might be described as cheerful and the other as menacing.]

C Reading Skills

Reading for details. What details does the writer provide to help you visualize the scene in the water? [Details include the "clean, shining white sand, rippled firm and hard"; "two grayish shapes"; "a water dance"; "swimming in flaked silver"; and the rock that is "black, tufted lightly with greenish weed."]

weight was removed. They were flying down past him now, into the water; the air was full of falling bodies. Then the rock was empty in the hot sunlight. He counted one, two, three . . .

At fifty, he was terrified. They must all be drowning beneath him, in the watery caves of the rock! At a hundred, he stared around him at the empty hillside, wondering if he should yell for help. He counted faster, faster, to hurry them up, to bring them to the surface quickly, to drown them quickly—anything rather than the terror of counting on and on into the blue emptiness of the morning. And then, at a hundred and sixty, the water beyond the rock was full of boys blowing like brown whales. They swam back to the shore without a look at him.

He climbed back to the diving rock and sat down, feeling the hot roughness of it under his thighs. The boys were gathering up their bits of clothing and running off along the shore to another promontory. They were leaving to get away from him. He cried openly, fists in his eyes. There was no one to see him, and he cried himself out.

It seemed to him that a long time had passed, and he swam out to where he could see his mother. Yes, she was still there, a yellow spot under an orange umbrella. He swam back to the big rock, climbed up, and dived into the blue pool among the fanged and angry boulders. Down he went, until he touched the wall of rock again. But the salt was so painful in his eyes that he could not see.

He came to the surface, swam to shore, and went back to the villa to wait for his mother. Soon she walked slowly up the path, swinging her striped bag, the flushed, naked arm dangling beside her. "I want some swimming goggles," he panted, defiant and beseeching.

She gave him a patient, inquisitive look as she said casually, "Well, of course, darling."

But now, now, now! He must have them this minute, and no other time. He nagged and pestered until she went with him to a shop. As soon as she had bought the goggles, he grabbed them from her hand as if she were going to claim them for herself, and was off, running down the steep path to the bay.

Jerry swam out to the big barrier rock, adjusted the goggles, and dived. The impact of the water broke the rubber-enclosed vacuum, and the goggles came loose. He understood that he must swim down to the base of the rock from the surface of the water. He fixed the goggles tight and firm, filled his lungs, and floated, face down, on the water. Now he could see. It was as if he had eyes of a different kind—fish eyes that showed everything clear and delicate and wavering in the bright water.

Under him, six or seven feet down, was a floor of perfectly clean, shining white sand, rippled firm and hard by the tides. Two grayish shapes steered there, like long, rounded pieces of wood or slate. They were fish. He saw them nose toward each other, poise motionless, make a dart forward, swerve off, and come around again. It was like a water dance. A few inches above them the water sparkled as if sequins were dropping through it. Fish again—myriads of minute fish, the length of his fingernail—were drifting through the water, and in a moment he could feel the innumerable tiny touches of them against his limbs. It was like swimming in flaked silver. The great rock the big boys had swum through rose sheer out of the white sand—black, tufted lightly with greenish weed. He could see no gap in it. He swam down to its base.

Again and again he rose, took a big chestful of air, and went down. Again and again he groped over the surface of the rock, feeling it, almost hugging it in the desperate need to find the entrance. And then, once, while he was clinging

Vocabulary

defiant (dē·fī′ənt) *adj.:* challenging authority.

inquisitive (in·kwiz′ə·tiv) *adj.:* questioning; curious.

minute (mī·no͞ot′) *adj.:* small; tiny.

Content-Area Connections

Sports: Breath-Hold Diving

Tell students that diving without the benefit of oxygen tanks is called breath-hold diving. Whereas most people can dive thirty to forty feet underwater, some skilled divers have dived for approximately two minutes to depths greater than one hundred feet.

Individual activity. Ask interested students to investigate and report on breath-hold diving. They might research its history, techniques, and records, as well as the people who do it for a living.

Science: Geology

Individual activity. Underwater tunnels, caves, and other rock formations are not unusual. Encourage interested students to research information on how these natural features are created. Students might write a short report and include diagrams illustrating the process.

to the black wall, his knees came up and he shot his feet out forward and they met no obstacle. He had found the hole.

He gained the surface, clambered about the stones that littered the barrier rock until he found a big one, and with this in his arms, let himself down over the side of the rock. He dropped, with the weight, straight to the sandy floor. Clinging tight to the anchor of stone, he lay on his side and looked in under the dark shelf at the place where his feet had gone. He could see the hole. It was an irregular, dark gap; but he could not see deep into it. He let go of his anchor, clung with his hands to the edges of the hole, and tried to push himself in.

He got his head in, found his shoulders jammed, moved them in sidewise, and was inside as far as his wrist. He could see nothing ahead. Something soft and clammy touched his mouth; he saw a dark frond[3] moving against the grayish rock, and panic filled him. He thought of octopuses, of clinging weed. He pushed himself out backward and caught a glimpse, as he retreated, of a harmless tentacle of seaweed drifting in the mouth of the tunnel. But it was enough. He reached the sunlight, swam to shore, and lay on the diving rock. He looked down into the blue well of water. He knew he must find his way through that cave, or hole, or tunnel, and out the other side.

First, he thought, he must learn to control his breathing. He let himself down into the water with another big stone in his arms, so that he could lie effortlessly on the bottom of the sea. He counted. One, two, three. He counted steadily. He could hear the movement of blood in his chest. Fifty-one, fifty-two. . . . His chest was hurting. He let go of the rock and went up into the air. He saw that the sun was low. He rushed to the villa and found his mother at her supper. She said only, "Did you enjoy yourself?" and he said, "Yes."

All night the boy dreamed of the water-filled cave in the rock, and as soon as breakfast was over, he went to the bay.

That night, his nose bled badly. For hours he had been underwater, learning to hold his breath, and now he felt weak and dizzy. His mother said, "I shouldn't overdo things, darling, if I were you."

That day and the next, Jerry exercised his lungs as if everything, the whole of his life, all that he would become, depended upon it. Again his nose bled at night, and his mother insisted on his coming with her the next day. It was a torment to him to waste a day of his careful self-training, but he stayed with her on that other beach, which now seemed a place for small children, a place where his mother might lie safe in the sun. It was not his beach.

He did not ask for permission, on the following day, to go to his beach. He went, before his mother could consider the complicated rights and wrongs of the matter. A day's rest, he discovered, had improved his count by ten. The big boys had made the passage while he counted a hundred and sixty. He had been counting fast, in his fright. Probably now, if he tried, he could get through that long tunnel, but he was not going to try yet. A curious, most unchildlike persistence, a controlled impatience, made him wait. In the meantime, he lay underwater on the white sand, littered now by stones he had brought down from the upper air, and studied the entrance to the tunnel. He knew every jut and corner of it, as far as it was possible to see. It was as if he already felt its sharpness about his shoulders.

He sat by the clock in the villa, when his mother was not near, and checked his time. He was incredulous and then proud to find he could

3. **frond** (fränd) *n.:* large leaf or leaflike part of seaweed.

Vocabulary
incredulous (in·krej′o͞o·ləs) *adj.:* disbelieving; skeptical.

DIRECT TEACHING

D Literary Focus
GRADE-LEVEL STANDARD
Symbolism. Draw students' attention to the image of the dark hole in the underwater rock. What might this hole signify? [the unknown, danger, fear, and birth]

E Literary Focus
GRADE-LEVEL STANDARD
Symbolism. In addition to *hole,* Lessing uses the words *cave* and *tunnel* to characterize the place Jerry must go through. What might his journey mean on a symbolic level? [Possible responses: the journey from boyhood to manhood; a psychological breakthrough.] Why is a tunnel an appealing symbol? [Possible responses: A tunnel is a kind of passageway, and the journey from youth to maturity is often regarded as a type of passage.]

F Content-Area Connections
Science: Biology
The discomfort a person feels when holding his or her breath is largely caused by the buildup of carbon dioxide in the bloodstream.

G Reading Skills
Speculating. Why doesn't Jerry want his mother to find out what he is doing? [Possible responses: He is afraid she will tell him to stop; he is afraid of worrying her; he is acting on his own for the first time.]

DIRECT TEACHING

A Literary Focus
REVIEW STANDARD

Plot: Complication. What events are threatening to spoil Jerry's plan? [The end of the vacation, because Jerry now has a time limit for reaching his goal. The nosebleed, because Jerry worries that he might be incapable of making it through the tunnel.]

B Literary Focus
ADVANCED STANDARD

Style. Point out the author's use of parallel structure, repetition, and rhythm. You might want to have the passage read aloud (perhaps more than once). Then, ask students to describe the effects of these stylistic elements. [Possible response: These elements give the passage a heightened sense of drama and importance.]

C Literary Focus
GRADE-LEVEL STANDARD

Symbolism. What might the "tons of rock pressed down on where he would go" represent here? [Possible responses: the possibility of failure; the rock tunnel could become Jerry's grave.]

D Reading Skills

Reading for details. Which details contribute to the building of suspense? [Possible responses: Jerry's counting to himself; the mention of the pain he is feeling; the description of the physical changes he is experiencing; his beginning to lose count.]

hold his breath without strain for two minutes. The words "two minutes," authorized by the clock, brought close the adventure that was so necessary to him.

A In another four days, his mother said casually one morning, they must go home. On the day before they left, he would do it. He would do it if it killed him, he said defiantly to himself. But two days before they were to leave—a day of triumph when he increased his count by fifteen—his nose bled so badly that he turned dizzy and had to lie limply over the big rock like a bit of seaweed, watching the thick red blood flow onto the rock and trickle slowly down to the sea. He was frightened. Supposing he turned dizzy in the tunnel? Supposing he died there, trapped? Supposing—his head went around, in the hot sun, and he almost gave up. He thought he would return to the house and lie down, and next summer, perhaps, when he had another year's growth in him—then he would go through the hole.

B But even after he had made the decision, or thought he had, he found himself sitting up on the rock and looking down into the water; and he knew that now, this moment, when his nose had only just stopped bleeding, when his head was still sore and throbbing—this was the moment when he would try. If he did not do it now, he never would. He was trembling with fear that he would not go; and he was trembling with horror at the long, long tunnel under the rock, under the sea. Even in the open sunlight, the **C** barrier rock seemed very wide and very heavy; tons of rock pressed down on where he would go. If he died there, he would lie until one day—perhaps not before next year—those big boys would swim into it and find it blocked.

He put on his goggles, fitted them tight, tested the vacuum. His hands were shaking. Then he chose the biggest stone he could carry and slipped over the edge of the rock until half of him was in the cool enclosing water and half in the hot sun. He looked up once at the empty sky, filled his lungs once, twice, and then sank fast to the bottom with the stone. He let it go and began to count. He took the edges of the hole in his hands and drew himself into it, wriggling his shoulders in sidewise as he remembered he must, kicking himself along with his feet.

Soon he was clear inside. He was in a small rock-bound hole filled with yellowish-gray water. The water was pushing him up against the **D** roof. The roof was sharp and pained his back. He pulled himself along with his hands—fast, fast—and used his legs as levers. His head knocked against something; a sharp pain dizzied him. Fifty, fifty-one, fifty-two . . . He was without light, and the water seemed to press upon him with the weight of rock. Seventy-one, seventy-two . . . There was no strain on his lungs. He felt like an inflated balloon, his lungs were so light and easy, but his head was pulsing.

He was being continually pressed against the sharp roof, which felt slimy as well as sharp. Again he thought of octopuses, and wondered if the tunnel might be filled with weed that could tangle him. He gave himself a panicky, convulsive kick forward, ducked his head, and swam. His feet and hands moved freely, as if in open water. The hole must have widened out. He thought he must be swimming fast, and he was frightened of banging his head if the tunnel narrowed.

A hundred, a hundred and one . . . The water paled. Victory filled him. His lungs were beginning to hurt. A few more strokes and he would be out. He was counting wildly; he said a hundred and fifteen and then, a long time later, a hundred and fifteen again. The water was a clear jewel-green all around him. Then he saw, above his head, a crack running up through the rock. Sunlight was falling through it, showing the clean, dark rock of the tunnel, a single mussel[4] shell, and darkness ahead.

4. **mussel** *n.:* shellfish, similar to a clam or an oyster, that attaches itself to rocks.

READING MINI-LESSON

Developing Word-Attack Skills
Write this line from the selection on the chalkboard, underlining the adjective *minute:* "Fish again—myriads of minute fish, the length of his fingernail—were drifting through the water." Point out that in this context, the underlined word is not the word for a unit of time, *minute* (min′it). Instead, it is an adjective that means "very small," and it is pronounced "mī·noot′." Explain that *minute* (min′it) and *minute* (mī·noot′) are homographs—words that are spelled the same but have different meanings and often different pronunciations.

Next, have students discuss the meanings and compare the pronunciations of the homographs that appear in the following sentences:

- Present your report to everyone present.
- Does a male deer seek the company of does?
- They pine for the quiet of the pine forest.

He was at the end of what he could do. He looked up at the crack as if it were filled with air and not water, as if he could put his mouth to it to draw in air. A hundred and fifteen, he heard himself say inside his head—but he had said that long ago. He must go on into the blackness ahead, or he would drown. His head was swelling, his lungs cracking. A hundred and fifteen, a hundred and fifteen, pounded through his head, and he feebly clutched at rocks in the dark, pulling himself forward, leaving the brief space of sunlit water behind. He felt he was dying. He was no longer quite conscious. He struggled on in the darkness between lapses into unconsciousness. An immense, swelling pain filled his head, and then the darkness cracked with an explosion of green light. His hands, groping forward, met nothing; and his feet, kicking back, propelled him out into the open sea.

He drifted to the surface, his face turned up to the air. He was gasping like a fish. He felt he would sink now and drown; he could not swim the few feet back to the rock. Then he was clutching it and pulling himself up onto it. He lay face down, gasping. He could see nothing but a red-veined, clotted dark. His eyes must have burst, he thought; they were full of blood. He tore off his goggles and a gout[5] of blood went into the sea. His nose was bleeding, and the blood had filled the goggles.

He scooped up handfuls of water from the cool, salty sea, to splash on his face, and did not know whether it was blood or salt water he tasted. After a time, his heart quieted, his eyes cleared, and he sat up. He could see the local boys diving and playing half a mile away. He did not want them. He wanted nothing but to get back home and lie down.

In a short while, Jerry swam to shore and climbed slowly up the path to the villa. He flung himself on his bed and slept, waking at the sound of feet on the path outside. His mother was coming back. He rushed to the bathroom, thinking she must not see his face with bloodstains, or tearstains, on it. He came out of the bathroom and met her as she walked into the villa, smiling, her eyes lighting up.

5. **gout** (gout) *n.:* large glob.

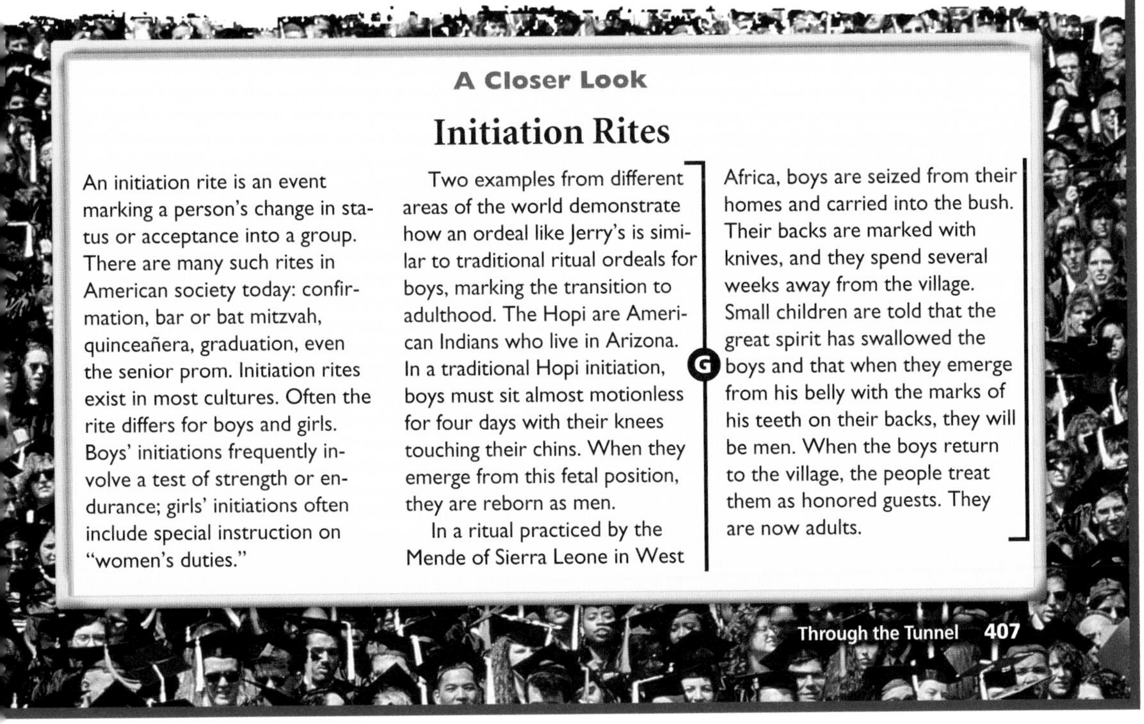

A Closer Look

Initiation Rites

An initiation rite is an event marking a person's change in status or acceptance into a group. There are many such rites in American society today: confirmation, bar or bat mitzvah, quinceañera, graduation, even the senior prom. Initiation rites exist in most cultures. Often the rite differs for boys and girls. Boys' initiations frequently involve a test of strength or endurance; girls' initiations often include special instruction on "women's duties."

Two examples from different areas of the world demonstrate how an ordeal like Jerry's is similar to traditional ritual ordeals for boys, marking the transition to adulthood. The Hopi are American Indians who live in Arizona. In a traditional Hopi initiation, boys must sit almost motionless for four days with their knees touching their chins. When they emerge from this fetal position, they are reborn as men.

In a ritual practiced by the Mende of Sierra Leone in West Africa, boys are seized from their homes and carried into the bush. Their backs are marked with knives, and they spend several weeks away from the village. Small children are told that the great spirit has swallowed the boys and that when they emerge from his belly with the marks of his teeth on their backs, they will be men. When the boys return to the village, the people treat them as honored guests. They are now adults.

DIRECT TEACHING

E Learners Having Difficulty

Clarifying. The water becomes clear, Jerry sees sunlight, and he is "at the end of what he could do." How do you know that Jerry still has not reached his goal? [The sunlight reveals "blackness ahead," and Jerry must "go on into the blackness." Apparently, the light Jerry sees is merely from a crack in the rock; he has not reached the end of the tunnel.]

F Reading Skills

Speculating. Why is Jerry no longer interested in the local boys? [Possible responses: His ordeal has left him exhausted physically and emotionally; play no longer seems important. His goal had become personal; he needed self-approval more than the approval of others.]

A CLOSER LOOK

This feature defines an initiation rite and provides two examples, one from the Hopi in New Mexico and Arizona and one from the Mende in Sierra Leone, West Africa.

G Reading Informational Materials

REVIEW STANDARD

Proving a point with evidence. What point is the writer trying to make by including the two examples of an initiation rite? [The writer is trying to make the point that most male initiation rites demand some kind of physical test and the ability to endure pain.]

Activity. Display these sentences. Call on volunteers to tell whether the homographs in each sentence have the same or different pronunciations.

1. They had a row over who would row. [different]
2. The second boat left a second later. [same]
3. Do not refuse to put refuse in the trash. [different]
4. Carrying a picnic hamper will hamper you on a hike. [same]
5. Did she ever intimate that they are intimate friends? [different]

DIRECT TEACHING

A Literary Focus
GRADE-LEVEL STANDARD

Irony. What is ironic about the mother's comment to Jerry about not overdoing it? [Possible response: She insists that he not swim anymore, unaware of the death-defying feat he has just accomplished.]

GUIDED PRACTICE

Monitoring students' progress. Guide the class in answering these comprehension questions.

Short Answer

1. Who is the protagonist? [Jerry, an eleven-year-old English boy]
2. Where is the story set? [along the coast of a foreign country]
3. How does Jerry reach the underwater tunnel? [by using rocks as anchors]
4. What piece of equipment does Jerry need for his adventure? [swimming goggles]
5. To whom does Jerry brag about finally swimming through the tunnel? [no one]

Meet the Writer

Background. Asked about the source of her characters, Doris Lessing has said, "Some people I write about come out of my life. Some, well, I don't know where they come from. They just spring from my own consciousness, perhaps the subconscious, and I'm surprised as they emerge. This is one of the excitements about writing. Someone says something, drops a phrase, and later you find that phrase turning into a character in a story, or a single, isolated, insignificant incident becomes the germ of a plot."

"Have a nice morning?" she asked, laying her hand on his warm brown shoulder a moment.

"Oh, yes, thank you," he said.

"You look a bit pale." And then, sharp and anxious, "How did you bang your head?"

"Oh, just banged it," he told her.

She looked at him closely. He was strained; his eyes were glazed-looking. She was worried. And then she said to herself, Oh, don't fuss! Nothing can happen. He can swim like a fish.

They sat down to lunch together.

"Mummy," he said, "I can stay underwater for two minutes—three minutes, at least." It came bursting out of him.

A "Can you, darling?" she said. "Well, I shouldn't overdo it. I don't think you ought to swim anymore today."

She was ready for a battle of wills, but he gave in at once. It was no longer of the least importance to go to the bay. ■

Meet the Writer

Doris Lessing

Out of Africa

Doris Lessing (1919–   ) was born in Persia (now Iran), where her father, who was British, was in charge of a bank. When she was five, her father, growing tired of the corruption around him and longing for a freer life, moved the family to a three-thousand-acre farm in Southern Rhodesia (now Zimbabwe). Life was extremely hard there. The farm's thirty to fifty African laborers lived in mud huts with no sanitation. Lessing's mother was homesick for England and often ill; her father was becoming increasingly unpredictable. The nearest neighbor was miles away. Lessing has described this childhood as "hellishly lonely." She has also acknowledged the advantage of such a childhood: Lacking company, she enriched her mind by reading classic European and American literature.

At the age of fourteen, Lessing quit school and went to work in Salisbury, the capital of Rhodesia, first as a nursemaid and then as a stenographer and telephone operator. Salisbury had a white population of about ten thousand and a larger black population that Lessing discovered "didn't count." During this period of her life, she became involved in radical politics and was twice married and twice divorced. In 1949, with her two-year-old son and the manuscript of her first novel, *The Grass Is Singing,* she fulfilled a lifelong wish by immigrating to England. The novel, about the complex relationship between a white farm wife and her African servant, was published in 1950, one of the earliest treatments in fiction of Africa's racial problems. From then on, Lessing supported herself by writing. Her powerful stories and novels are among the most admired writing of our day.

Lessing admits she writes to be "an instrument of change."

"It is not merely a question of preventing evil, but of strengthening a vision of good which may defeat the evil."

DIFFERENTIATING INSTRUCTION

Advanced Learners

Enrichment. Tell students that because of her radical political views, Lessing was expelled from Southern Rhodesia (now called Zimbabwe) and South Africa in the late 1950s. When she returned to South Africa forty years later, she was received as an honored and celebrated writer.

Activity. Have students find out more about the history of colonial Africa, in particular Zimbabwe and South Africa. Suggest that they enter *Doris Lessing, Rhodesia, Zimbabwe,* or *South Africa* as keywords in a search engine.

Literary Response and Analysis

Reading Check

1. Retell the **main events** of this story as Jerry might tell them to his best friend when he returns from vacation or to his own son later in life.

Interpretations

2. Why is it so important to Jerry to be with the boys on the wild beach? What significant details does the author provide to help us understand Jerry's feelings about the boys? (See pages 402–404.)

3. Identify the physical and mental "tortures" Jerry undergoes, first as he prepares for his ordeal and then as he swims through the tunnel. Which details suggest that Jerry's quest has great significance?

4. A ticking clock is usually good for creating **suspense.** What device does Lessing use to create a sort of "ticking clock" that increases our anxiety?

5. What breakthroughs has Jerry achieved by the story's end? Consider:
- Jerry's conquest of the tunnel
- his feelings about himself
- his dependence on his mother

6. What do you think is the main message, or **theme,** of this story? Consider:
- what the swim through the tunnel means to Jerry
- why Jerry no longer feels he has to go to the bay

7. Read the information in A Closer Look on page 407. Do you think Jerry's experience can be viewed as an initiation rite? What similarities and differences can you find in his experience and the coming-of-age rites in other cultures?

8. Check the text to see what you learn about the thoughts and feelings of Jerry's mother. How would the story be different if she, rather than the **omniscient narrator,** were telling it?

Evaluation

9. Have you ever taken great risks to prove yourself? (Check your Quickwrite notes.) Do you find it convincing that Jerry takes such a risk and survives? Explain.

Writing

Story Symbols

Symbols are appealing because they often carry powerful associations and emotional overtones. Write a brief **essay** analyzing the **symbolism** in "Through the Tunnel." First, consider the three **settings:** the wild beach, the safe beach, and the tunnel. Tell what you think each setting must symbolize for Jerry. Then, consider the larger **symbolic meaning** of Jerry's passage through the tunnel. What does his trip represent? Why is it a powerful symbol? Support your analysis, and elaborate with direct references to details in the story. (You can take notes in a chart like the one below.)

Symbol	Symbolic Meaning
Wild beach	
Safe beach	
Tunnel	
Trip through the tunnel	

► **Use "Analyzing a Short Story," pages 440–447, for help with this assignment.**

Reading Standard 3.7 Recognize and understand the significance of various literary devices, including symbolism, and explain their appeal.

Reading Check

1. The retelling should include the following events: Jerry's desire to go to the bay, his initial attempt at befriending the boys, his wonder at the boys' ability to stay underwater, his investigation of the gap they swim through, his use of goggles and of the large rock to reach the bottom, his self-training regimen and resulting nosebleeds, the announcement that the vacation would soon be ending, the climactic swim through the tunnel.

INDEPENDENT PRACTICE

Literary Response and Analysis

Interpretations

2. Jerry longs for company and acceptance. The author tells us that he is an only child and that after he swims away from his mother he is "all at once very lonely." When he sees the boys, "to be with them, of them, was a craving that filled his whole body." When they greet him, he is happy, and when they make room for him to dive, he feels accepted and proud.

3. To prepare for his ordeal, Jerry lies down on the sea floor, holding a rock, and counts until his chest hurts. Each night he has nosebleeds. As he goes through the tunnel, he feels pain when his back and head are pressed against the roof; his lungs hurt; his head swells; his lungs crack; his head aches; he nearly falls unconscious. Jerry's use of the rock as an anchor, his dreaming of the tunnel at night, and his checking his time by the clock suggest the significance of the quest.

4. Lessing allows us to hear Jerry's counting to himself.

5. Jerry achieved his goal as well as a sense of independence from his mother.

6. Possible answers: We have a need to set goals for ourselves and then to achieve them. Self-acceptance is more important than the approval of others.

7. Possible answers: Jerry's experience is similar in that it is a test of strength and endurance. It is different because Jerry is acting on his own.

8. Possible answers: The story might focus on her worries about Jerry and on her loneliness without him. The story would lack drama.

Evaluation

9. Students' responses will vary.

Vocabulary Development

Practice

1. minute
2. contrition
3. inquisitive
4. incredulous
5. supplication
6. defiant

Resources Reminder

Vocabulary

- *Vocabulary Development*
  - Vocabulary Worksheet, p. 33
- *Lesson Plans for Language Development*
  - Vocabulary, pp. 192, 196

Grammar Link

Practice

1. Possible Answers
   - The lapping water caused the small craft in the bay to rock unsteadily.
   - Jerry noticed how the ocean tides had created rippled sand.
   - The boys might have been members of a diving team.
   - The water teemed with myriads of tiny glittering fish.
2. Possible Answers
   - The water lapping at the black rocks had a purplish hue.
   - The sailors on the boats in the bay adjusted the mainsails rippled by the wind.
   - Diving deep down, Jerry managed to find the opening of the tunnel.
   - The sunlight glittering on the surface of the bay turned the water a deep green.

Vocabulary Development

Analogies: Matching Relationships

In an **analogy** the words in a first pair relate to each other in the same way as the words in a second pair. Many kinds of relationships are possible. For example, a pair of words can be synonyms (*timid : meek*) or antonyms (*timid : bold*), or one word can describe a characteristic of the other (*knife : sharp*) or express a degree of intensity (*whisper : scream*). Analogies are frequently written like this:

HUGE : ELEPHANT :: ___________ : gnat.

Word Bank
contrition
supplication
defiant
inquisitive
minute
incredulous

PRACTICE

Complete each analogy below with the word from the Word Bank that fits best. Begin by identifying the type of relationship in the first word pair. (For more help with analogies, see pages 29–30.)

Reading Standard 1.1 Identify and use the literal meanings of words.

1. HUGE : ELEPHANT :: ___________ : gnat
2. SADNESS : MOURNING :: ___________ : regretting
3. SECURE : SAFE :: ___________ : curious
4. NEEDY : BEGGAR :: ___________ : skeptic
5. WHISPER : SHOUT :: ___________ : demand
6. BRILLIANT : SMART :: ___________ : stubborn

Grammar Link MINI-LESSON

Powerful Participles

Participles are verb forms that can be used as adjectives to modify nouns and pronouns: *running* water, *cleared* land. Present participles always end in *–ing*, and most past participles end in *–ed* or *–d*. Because they combine the action of verbs and the descriptive power of adjectives, participles create vivid pictures in few words.

"He could see nothing through the stinging salt water but the blank rock."

"It was like swimming in flaked silver."

Participial phrases are participles with all their complements and modifiers.

"He was in a small rock-bound hole filled with yellowish-gray water."

PRACTICE

1. Write four sentences, using the following participles or any other participles you wish: *lapping, rippled, diving, glittering.* Make sure you use each participle as an adjective.
2. Now, write four more sentences, using the same participles in participial phrases. Compare your sentences with a partner's.

For more help, see The Participle and the Participial Phrase in the *Holt Handbook,* pages 70–74.

ASSESSING

Assessment

- *Progress Assessment of Reading*
  - Selection Test

RETEACHING

For a lesson reteaching Standard 3.7, see **Reteaching,** p. 939A. For another selection to teach Standard 3.7, see *Interactive Reading,* Chapter 6.

410 Chapter 6 Symbolism and Allegory • Synthesizing Sources

Before You Read INFORMATIONAL MATERIALS

Coming of Age, Latino Style ◆ Vision Quest ◆ Crossing a Threshold to Adulthood

Synthesizing Sources

When you research a topic, you often need to get a balanced view by looking at different sources. Then you can **synthesize** what you've read—pull it all together so that you can better understand the subject. The following guidelines will help:

- **Determine the message.** Look for the writer's **main ideas** and for **supporting details** in each source.
- **Paraphrase the ideas.** To help you understand a source, try paraphrasing its ideas, which means restating them *in your own words*. When you put a difficult or complex text in your own words, you'll understand it better. A paraphrase should be about the same length as the original source, and it should cover all the significant information in the original in the same order.
- **Determine the author's purpose and audience.** Was the piece written, for example, to tell a story, to change your opinion, or to give information?
- **Evaluate each source.** Determine the kinds and amount of support the writer gives. Is there enough support to make the ideas **credible**? Evaluate the tone and reliability too. Is the source **objective** (based solely on facts) or **subjective** (expressing the writer's opinions and feelings)?
- **Compare and contrast.** Compare sources in terms of the type of information in each one. What do they have in common? How do they differ?
- **Connect to other sources.** Connect the ideas to related topics and to stories and other articles you've read.

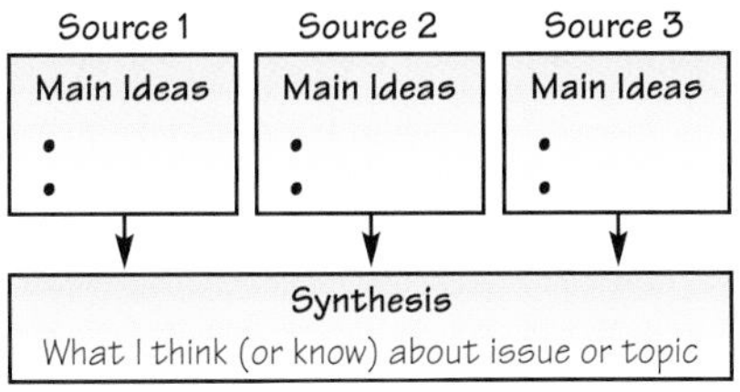

- **Synthesize.** Now, consider all your sources as a group. Do they work together to help you better understand a topic? Can you draw **conclusions** from the sources and form connections with other sources you have read?

Vocabulary Development

indigenous (in·dij′ə·nəs) *adj.:* native.

solitary (säl′ə·ter′ē) *adj.:* without others.

vigil (vij′əl) *n.:* watchful staying awake during the usual hours of sleep.

predominant (prē·däm′ə·nənt) *adj.:* most frequent or noticeable.

formidable (fôr′mə·də·bəl) *adj.:* remarkable; impressive.

inevitable (in·ev′i·tə·bəl) *adj.:* unavoidable; certain to happen.

Connecting to the Literature

In "Through the Tunnel," Jerry works hard to accomplish a difficult feat, and afterward he feels as if he's no longer a boy. The three articles that follow describe events that mark the passage to adulthood in various cultures.

Reading Standard 2.4
Synthesize the content from several sources dealing with a single issue; paraphrase the ideas and connect them to other sources and related topics.

STANDARDS FOCUS, pp. 411–417

(For grade-level and review standards taught in this lesson, see citations on Student Edition pages.)

Summary at grade level

Three articles describe initiation rituals in different cultures. "Coming of Age, Latino Style" describes a Hispanic celebration that marks a girl's entry into adulthood. "Vision Quest" tells how some American Indian boys reach manhood through a solitary quest. "Crossing a Threshold to Adulthood" describes wedding customs in Uzbekistan that signal becoming an adult.

PRETEACHING

Preview Vocabulary

To give students practice using the Vocabulary words listed on p. 411, have them respond to these questions. Possible responses are given.

1. If an unarmed band of rebels were fighting a formidable army, what would be the inevitable result? [The small band would be defeated.]
2. What was the predominant means of support used by the indigenous people of the Great Plains? [hunting]
3. Why might someone keep a solitary vigil in front of a candle? [to remember a loved one]

RESOURCES: READING

Planning
- *One-Stop Planner* CD-ROM with Test Generator
- *On-Course: Mapping Instruction*

Media
- *Audio CD Library*
  - disc 12

Reading
- *Interactive Reading,* Teacher's Edition
  - Graphic Organizer: Synthesis Chart

Differentiating Instruction
- *Lesson Plans for Language Development*
  - English-Language Learners, pp. 179–181, 193, 197
  - Special Education Students, pp. 182, 193, 197

Vocabulary
- *Vocabulary Development*
  - Vocabulary Worksheet, p. 34

Assessment
- *Progress Assessment of Reading*
  - Selection Test
- *One-Stop Planner* CD-ROM with Test Generator

DIRECT TEACHING

A Reading Informational Materials
GRADE-LEVEL STANDARD

Synthesizing sources: Author's purpose and audience. Have students scan the title, subtitle, and byline. Then, ask students, "Who is the intended audience for this article?" [readers of the *Boston Globe* newspaper] "Why do you think the author wrote this article?" [Possible response: to inform readers about a special ritual for Hispanic girls].

B Reading Informational Materials
GRADE-LEVEL STANDARD

Synthesizing sources: Paraphrase. Point out that the first two paragraphs of the article plunge the reader into an event. Only in the third paragraph does the writer begin to explain the event. Ask students to paraphrase the main idea in this paragraph. [Possible response: Glenda is celebrating her fifteenth birthday with a *quinceañera,* a Hispanic celebration of a girl becoming an adult.]

C Reading Informational Materials
GRADE-LEVEL STANDARD

Synthesizing sources: Evaluate. What sources is the author drawing upon for information about the *quinceañera?* [Possible responses: She cites experts and also the feelings and experiences of a family whose daughter celebrated her *quinceañera.*] Do you find these sources credible? Explain why or why not. [Possible responses: Yes, the author has reported information from both experts and ordinary people. No, the author does not tell who the experts are and only gives the opinions and experiences of one Hispanic family.]

NEWSPAPER ARTICLE

Coming of Age, Latino Style

Special Rite Ushers Girls into Adulthood

from *Boston Globe,* January 5, 1997

Cindy Rodriguez

LOWELL—Iris Cancel's eyes filled with pride, not tears, as she watched her daughter Glenda glide down the church aisle, her tiny frame covered by a white satin and lace dress that flared at the hips and trailed behind her. Small white flowers speckled the bodice,[1] and her long, dark hair, wrapped in baby's breath,[2] was encircled by a shimmery crown.

"I think it's an exciting day for her and everyone involved," Iris Cancel said. "Her father's a nervous wreck. I keep telling him, 'She's not getting married.'"

Glenda, a sophomore at Greater Lowell Vocational Technical School, did not celebrate her wedding a week ago Saturday, although the ceremony did resemble one. She celebrated a special birthday. She turned fifteen on December 26 and toasted it two days later with a *quinceañera,*[3] a custom in Hispanic communities that marks a girl's entrance into adulthood.

Experts of Hispanic culture disagree on the origin of the quinceañera. The word literally means "fifteen-year-old girl" but is also used to describe the entire celebration. Some say coming-of-age traditions in general, though not the quinceañera in particular, can be traced back to indigenous cultures. Then, it was a recognition that boys were ready to be warriors and girls were ready to bear children.

Some experts believe that for years the quinceañera was most often celebrated by upper-class Hispanics, who wrapped the social custom in religious symbolism and personal wealth. Elaborate celebrations similar to debutante balls[4] showed off a family's social status and daughter to possible suitors. A similar celebration for boys is uncommon among Hispanics.

Today the quinceañera is celebrated in the United States and abroad by Latinos of varied cultural backgrounds and economic classes. Glenda, one of six children, was born in Lowell to Puerto Rican parents. Iris, a mail handler at Holland Mark Martin in Burlington, and Marcos, a school-bus driver in Lowell, have lived in Massachusetts for twenty-nine years.

The celebration can be religious or secular,[5] inexpensive or costly. Some Hispanic families still host debutante-style balls that can cost up to $10,000, while others plan simple birthday parties.

1. **bodice** *n.:* upper part of a woman's dress.
2. **baby's breath** *n.:* a type of flower.
3. **quinceañera** (kēn′se · ä · nyer′ä).
4. **debutante balls** *n.:* formal dances held to introduce a group of young women into society.
5. **secular** (sek′yə · lər) *adj.:* worldly, as distinguished from religious.

Vocabulary
indigenous (in · dij′ə · nəs) *adj.:* native.

DIFFERENTIATING INSTRUCTION

Learners Having Difficulty

Modeling. Before students synthesize content from several sources, you may wish to have them review identifying main ideas and supporting details from a single source. To help students practice this skill, clip letters to the editor from a local newspaper and give one to each pair of students. Ask them to identify the writer's main idea and supporting details. Then, have them discuss and evaluate the credibility of the ideas. Students may exchange their letters and findings with another pair.

Resources Reminder

Reading

- *Interactive Reading,* Teacher's Edition
  - Graphic Organizer: Synthesis Chart

Still, the quinceañera in any form remains an important rite of passage for many Hispanic girls. For girls like Glenda, the purpose is not so much to find a future mate at the reception as to celebrate themselves.

"I feel like I deserve it," said Glenda, who gets good grades, has near-perfect school attendance, and attends church regularly. She plans to attend college to be a pediatrician[6] or a professional basketball player.

And, of course, it's fun to get dressed up for a celebration that in Glenda's case took a year to plan.

6. **pediatrician** (pē′dē·ə·trish′ən) *n.:* doctor who specializes in the care of children.

ENCYCLOPEDIA ARTICLE

Vision Quest

from *Encyclopaedia Britannica,* 1995

vision quest, among the American Indian hunters of the eastern woodlands and the Great Plains, an essential part of a young boy's (or, more rarely, a girl's) initiation into adulthood. The youth was sent out from the camp on a solitary vigil involving fasting[1] and prayer in order to gain some sign of the presence and nature of his guardian spirit (*q.v.*).[2] The specific techniques varied from tribe to tribe, as did the age at which the quest was to be undertaken, its length and intensity, and the nature of the sign.

In some traditions the youth would watch for an animal who behaved in a significant way; in others he discovered an object (usually a stone), which resembled some animal. In the predominant form, he had a dream in which his guardian appeared (usually in animal form), instructed him, took him on a visionary journey, and taught him songs. Upon receiving these signs and visions he returned to his home, indicated his success, and sought out a religious specialist for help in interpreting his visions.

The techniques of the vision quest are not confined only to those at puberty. They underlie every visionary experience of the Indian, from those of the ordinary man who seeks to gain contact with and advice from his guardian to the visions of the great prophets and shamans (religious personages with healing and psychic transformation powers). Among the South American Indians, the vision quest, like the guardian spirit, is confined exclusively to the shaman.

1. **fasting** *v.* used as *n.:* not eating.
2. ***q.v.:*** abbreviation for Latin *quod vide,* "which see." This abbreviation indicates that the encyclopedia from which this entry was taken contains a separate entry for *guardian spirit.*

Vocabulary

solitary (säl′ə·ter′ē) *adj.:* without others.

vigil (vij′əl) *n.:* watchful staying awake during the usual hours of sleep.

predominant (prē·däm′ə·nənt) *adj.:* most frequent or noticeable.

DIRECT TEACHING

D Reading Informational Materials
GRADE-LEVEL STANDARD

Synthesizing sources: Paraphrase. You may wish to point out that this article from an encyclopedia is written in a factual and objective style that offers a great deal of detailed information in a few sentences. Have students state the gist of the first sentence in their own words. [Possible response: Certain American Indians participated in vision quests as part of their rite of passage into adulthood.]

E Reading Informational Materials
GRADE-LEVEL STANDARD

Synthesizing sources: Compare and contrast. Ask students to compare and contrast the two articles they have just read. They should focus on the author's purpose, intended audience, tone, main idea, and the credibility of the information. [Students may say that both selections serve an informa-tional purpose and are intended for average readers. The newspaper article discusses a rite of passage for Hispanic girls; it has a lively tone and is credible because it uses experts and participants. The encyclopedia article discusses a rite of passage for some American Indians—usually boys. It is dry and factual and seems cred-ible although the sources of information are not revealed.]

English-Language Learners
Before students read these selections, review with them several words and phrases related to anthropology. You may wish to define and give examples of words such as *rite, ritual, celebration, ceremony, initiation,* and *quest.*

Special Education Students
For lessons designed for English-language learners and special education students, see *Lesson Plans for Language Development,* pp. 179–181, 182, 193, 197.

Advanced Learners
Enrichment. Ask students to work in small groups to identify various modern rites of passage. Examples might include getting a driver's license, voting in an election, or going to college. Invite students to discuss their own feelings and perspectives about the importance of rites of passage. Then, ask them to analyze ways in which these modern rites are similar to and different from the traditional rituals discussed in the three articles. Encourage them to discuss and debate the following question: Are young people in today's American society at an advantage or a disadvantage in not having clearly defined rites of passage that are the same for everyone?

DIRECT TEACHING

A Reading Informational Materials
GRADE-LEVEL STANDARD

? Synthesizing sources: Main idea and supporting details. The first few paragraphs of this op-ed article are full of details that will support the main idea, which becomes more explicit later in the piece. What are some of the supporting details? [Possible responses: In Uzbekistan, many people get married in September; marriage is an important ritual; weddings are always videotaped.]

B Reading Informational Materials
GRADE-LEVEL STANDARD

? Synthesizing sources: Connect. Remind students that they can draw on their own experiences when synthesizing information on a subject. How does Barnes's description of an Uzbekistan wedding compare with weddings you have attended? Are you familiar with wedding rituals in another culture that are similar to the ones Barnes describes? Encourage students to describe other wedding rituals they know.

C Reading Informational Materials
GRADE-LEVEL STANDARD

Synthesizing sources: Paraphrase. This sentence is crucial to the main point of the article. Ask students to paraphrase it. [Possible response: In Uzbekistan, marriage is the rite of passage that separates childhood from adulthood.]

OP-ED ARTICLE

Crossing a Threshold to Adulthood

from the *Times Union*, Albany, N.Y., September 24, 2000

Jessica Barnes

September is wedding season in Uzbekistan,[1] and every afternoon I hear the honking trumpet sound that announces the procession of men who accompany a groom to fetch his bride from her parents' home.

I go to a wedding almost every week now, and turn down invitations to several others. I'm surrounded by weddings. When I walk home from school, I'm passed by wedding processions; I go to sleep at night hearing the music from weddings in my neighborhood, occasionally interrupted by toasts spoken over a microphone.

The teachers at my school are more determined than ever to see me married in Uzbekistan; they can't bear the thought of sending me back to America next year as an old maid of twenty-five. I spend my lunch periods with them thinking up excuses for why I can't marry the Russian teacher's son or my director's cousin's neighbor.

When my local friends aren't attending weddings or plotting mine, they're watching the video from the latest wedding. Every wedding I've been to has been videotaped; the cameraman was such a formidable presence that when I think back on the wedding, I remember the married couple and the cameraman. We watch the videos over and over—or maybe we're not watching the same video more than once. Maybe I've seen a hundred different wedding videos. I can't tell because they're all the same. The same music, the same toasts, the same food. It's a ceremony with little room for variation.

Every video begins in the bride's home, just after the groom and his friends arrive. The bride is crying because she is about to leave the home where she grew up. Her girlfriends place a cloth over her head and lead her out of the house, where all the neighbors have gathered. The trumpets stop and the only sounds are the sobs of the bride and the murmured good wishes of her close family members.

The sadness of the moment always strikes me: How sad it is to grow up and leave others behind, and how inevitable. At the wedding, while everyone laughs and drinks and dances, the glum faces of the bride and groom preside over all. She is sad leaving her family and he is thinking of responsibilities that lie ahead as husband and father. Starting a family is no laughing matter in Uzbekistan.

Afterward, the whole thing is there, in one small, black cartridge, to be watched over and over. The day a bride leaves her parents' home, she crosses from childhood into adulthood in one neat step. This rite of

1. **Uzbekistan** (o͞oz·bek′i·stan′): central Asian country that became independent upon the breakup of the Soviet Union in 1991.

Vocabulary

formidable (fôr′mə·də·bəl) *adj.:* remarkable; impressive.

inevitable (in·ev′i·tə·bəl) *adj.:* unavoidable; certain to happen.

414 Chapter 6 Symbolism and Allegory • Synthesizing Sources

People celebrating at an Uzbeki wedding.

passage signifies the change in her role as clearly as if she were given a list of her job expectations.

I don't think I'll ever experience a rite of passage like that one. In America, we grow up in fits and starts. I got a driver's license at sixteen, the first step toward independence, but I was still a child. After I voted for the first time, I was still a child. I moved away from home to go to college, then moved back, a child with a degree.

After finishing with the Peace Corps,[2] I'll go back to my parents' home, and then eventually to an apartment of my own, and then, if I get married, to an apartment with my husband. At which of these points do I look in the mirror and say "childhood" is past and I am now an adult? I don't think it will happen in the few moments you can capture on videotape. I think, rather, one day I will realize that somewhere along the line it has happened. Or, worse, I'll never know.

In Uzbekistan, I've noticed the importance of these rites of passage for knowing yourself and what is expected of you. And there's comfort in the fact that everyone goes through them.

My Americanness wants to praise us all for growing up in different ways, at different paces. It's good to be different, but lonely and often confusing.

2. **Peace Corps:** U.S. agency that provides volunteers to assist people in underdeveloped countries.

DIRECT TEACHING

D Reading Informational Materials
GRADE-LEVEL STANDARD

Synthesizing sources: Evaluate. What support has Barnes given in the article for her conclusion about the importance of marriage in Uzbekistan culture? [She has given many examples from her personal experience.] Is her conclusion supported by objective or subjective details? Explain. [The details are both objective and subjective. Many of her observations are factual, but she also expresses her personal feelings and cultural biases.]

E Reading Informational Materials
GRADE-LEVEL STANDARD

Synthesizing sources: Connect. Barnes mentions some of her own modern "rites of passage"—driver's license, voting, moving away from home, going overseas, getting an apartment. What are some other modern rites of passage that you or people you know participate in? [Possible responses: going to a prom, buying a car, getting a part-time job, going to college.] How are these rites of passage different from those in Uzbekistan society? [Possible response: They are individual, not universal, and occur at different ages for different people, and sometimes not at all.]

F Reading Informational Materials
GRADE-LEVEL STANDARD

Synthesizing sources: Draw conclusions. Ask students to draw a conclusion that pulls together, or synthesizes, information about initiation rites from all three sources. [Possible response: Many cultures, traditional and modern, have rites of passage. The ceremonies vary greatly, but all mark in some way the important passage from childhood to adulthood.]

CONTENT-AREA CONNECTIONS

Culture: Rites of Passage
Tell students that rites of passage often contain three steps: separation from the community, indoctrination, and reentry into the community. The vision quest is an obvious example of these three steps.

Small-group activity. Ask students to consider how wedding and birthday rituals, bar and bat mitzvahs, fraternity hazing, and gang initiation rituals fit into the three-part pattern of separation, indoctrination, and reunion. Have each group choose a rite of passage—from their reading or from their life experience—to research further. After they have gathered information, students should discuss how the ritual fits or does not fit into the three-part structure. Students may report the results of their discussion to the class.

INDEPENDENT PRACTICE

Analyzing Informational Materials

Reading Check

1. It celebrates a Latino girl's fifteenth birthday and her entry into adulthood.
2. Its purpose is to gain information about one's guardian spirit and to pass from childhood to adulthood.
3. The rite is marriage.

Test Practice

Answers and Model Rationales

1. **A** B is incorrect because the articles are informative, not persuasive, and D is incorrect because only the third article compares rites of passage in two cultures. While the first and third articles provide eyewitness accounts (C), these accounts are supporting details, not the main purpose of each article.
2. **G** Only G is an inference you can make about "most societies" based on these selections. The other choices are too specific, providing an inference one might make based only on an American Indian rite of passage (F and J) or a Hispanic rite of passage (H).
3. **D** C is clearly wrong, as Barnes makes the opposite point. While a reader might infer A and B, Barnes does not make these statements. Students who recall Barnes's final paragraph will know that D is the correct answer.
4. **H** "Coming of Age . . ." (F) includes some of the author's personal thoughts but is largely objective. "Vision Quest" (G) is an encyclopedia article that is completely objective. J is incorrect because H contains mostly subjective impressions.

Analyzing Informational Materials

Reading Check

1. What special occasion does a quinceañera celebrate?
2. For certain American Indian tribes, what is the purpose of a vision quest?
3. What is the most typical rite of passage to adulthood in Uzbekistan?

Test Practice

1. What is the **purpose** of *each* of the three selections?
   - A To discuss one kind of initiation into adulthood
   - B To persuade readers of the importance of initiation rites
   - C To provide eyewitness accounts of coming-of-age rituals
   - D To compare initiation rites across cultures
2. From these three selections you can infer that in most societies the passage into adulthood is marked by some kind of —
   - F vision quest
   - G ceremony or ritual
   - H large party or dance
   - J painful ordeal
3. According to Jessica Barnes, American society —
   - A has a lower marriage rate than Uzbekistan
   - B places less emphasis on weddings than Uzbekistan
   - C demands that all its young people grow up at the same pace
   - D allows its young people to grow up at different paces
4. Which article is **subjective**? That is, in which does the writer express mostly personal thoughts?
   - F "Coming of Age, Latino Style"
   - G "Vision Quest"
   - H "Crossing a Threshold to Adulthood"
   - J None of the articles
5. Unlike Jerry's experience in "Through the Tunnel," the experiences described in these three articles —
   - A follow a cultural tradition
   - B are dangerous and life threatening
   - C take place indoors, surrounded by people
   - D take place when the individual is alone

Reading Standard 2.4 Synthesize the content from several sources dealing with a single issue; paraphrase the ideas and connect them to other sources and related topics.

Application

To **synthesize** what you've learned, write a brief essay about a ceremony you are familiar with or one that you've seen or read about that marks a passage into another phase of life. Give details about the ceremony (its purpose, what the person does, where and when the ceremony takes place). Then, **compare and contrast** your ceremony with those described in the three articles. You may **paraphrase** the main ideas in the articles.

5. **A** A is correct because the three articles describe rituals found in Hispanic, American Indian, and Uzbekistan cultural traditions, while Jerry devised his own personal coming-of-age ritual. Because Jerry's experience *was* dangerous (B) and solitary (D), these answers are incorrect. C is incorrect because the vision quest takes place outdoors.

Test-Taking Tips

Remind students to read each question slowly and carefully, paying particular attention to words such as *each, most, all, more, like,* or *unlike* in order to avoid incorrect answers.

For more information on how to answer multiple-choice items, refer students to **Test Smarts.**

Vocabulary Development

Word Mapping: Pinning Down Meaning

Sometimes you can figure out the meaning of a word from its **context.** Consider these two sentences from "Coming of Age, Latino Style":

> "Some say coming-of-age traditions in general, though not the quinceañera in particular, can be traced back to indigenous cultures. Then, it was a recognition that boys were ready to be warriors and girls were ready to bear children."

Word Bank
- indigenous
- solitary
- vigil
- predominant
- formidable
- inevitable

Does this context help you understand *indigenous?* Probably not. You'll have to use a dictionary to find the meaning that fits the context.

Creating a **word map,** or **semantic map,** will help you pin down the precise meaning of any unfamiliar word. Make up questions about the word, and then answer the questions. Here's how a student in Florida completed a word map for *indigenous*:

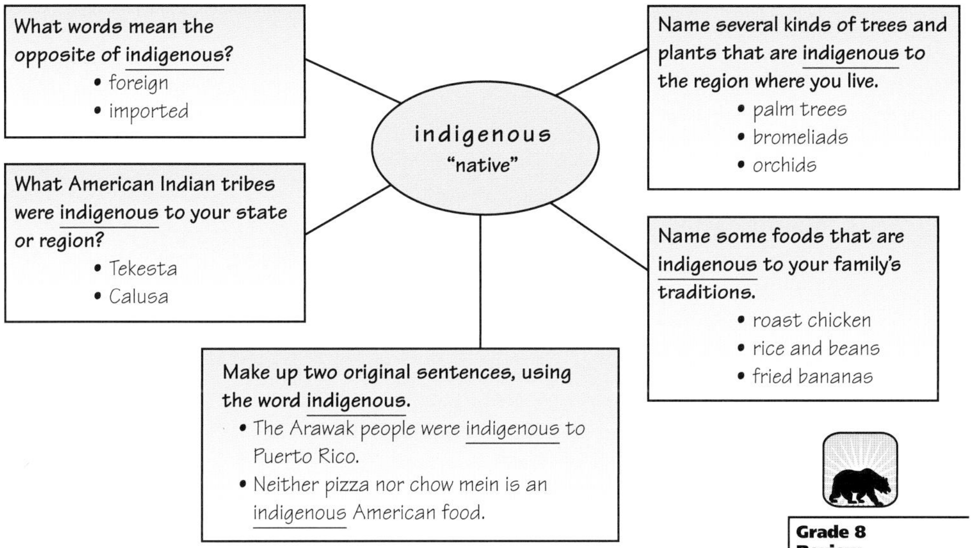

Grade 8 Review Reading Standard 1.3 Use word meanings within the appropriate context and show ability to verify those meanings.

Reading Standard 1.1 Identify and use the literal meanings of words.

PRACTICE

Work with a partner or small group to make a **word map** for each of the other words in the Word Bank. The questions you ask will vary, but in each map, try to include examples of times when you'd use the word and two original sentences. Exchange your finished word maps with another group.

Vocabulary Development

Practice

Possible Answers

- *solitary. Meaning*—alone. *Questions—Who has a solitary lifestyle?* [a single person] *What solitary game might you play?* [solitaire] *What solitary things might you see in nature?* [a lone tree, rock, or bird] *Sentence*—Reading a good book is a solitary pleasure.
- *vigil. Meaning*—a watch kept. *Questions—What kinds of vigils are there?* [prayer vigils; political protest vigils] *What vigils have you heard about in the news?* [vigils outside Congress, prisons, and churches] *Sentence*—The priest kept vigil with the prisoner on death row.
- *predominant. Meaning*—prevailing; most frequent. *Questions—What are the predominant religions of Indonesia, India, and Thailand?* [Islam; Hinduism; Buddhism] *Which nation is the predominant power in the world?* [the United States] *Sentence*—Green is one of the predominant colors in nature.
- *formidable. Meaning*—awe-inspiring. *Questions—What are synonyms for formidable?* [remarkable; impressive] *What words are antonyms?* [ordinary, weak] *Sentence*—The opera singer had a formidable presence onstage.
- *inevitable. Meaning*—unavoidable; certain to happen. *Questions—What things in life are inevitable?* [death and taxes] *What things are likely but not inevitable?* [global warming; overpopulation; war] *Sentence*—The chill of winter is inevitable in the Northeast.

Resources Reminder

Vocabulary
- *Vocabulary Development*
  - Vocabulary Worksheet, p. 34
- *Lesson Plans for Language Development*
  - Vocabulary, pp. 193, 197

ASSESSING

Assessment
- *Progress Assessment of Reading*
  - Selection Test

RETEACHING

For another selection to teach Standard 2.4, see *Interactive Reading,* Part 2.

Coming of Age . . . / Vision Quest / Crossing a Threshold . . . 417

STANDARDS FOCUS, pp. 418–432

(For grade-level and review standards taught in this lesson, see citations on Student Edition pages.)

Prerequisite Standard

- Grade 8, Literary Response and Analysis 3.6 **Identify significant literary devices (e.g., metaphor, symbolism, dialect, irony) that define a writer's style and use those elements to interpret the work.**

Reading Skills

- Monitor your reading: Ask questions.

Summary *above grade level*

Poe's tale of an eccentric nobleman and the Red Death ravaging his land can be read both as a chilling ghost story and as an allegory representing human folly and the inevitability of death. Prince Prospero invites a thousand lords and ladies to escape death by living luxuriously in his castle until the pestilence passes. To entertain his guests, Prospero hosts a masquerade party that takes place in seven halls, each a different color. At the stroke of midnight, a tall figure in a blood-spattered burial costume appears. Prospero demands that his friends seize the intruder, but everyone is frozen with fear as the stranger slowly walks through the rooms. Finally, Prospero rushes after him into the black seventh room. When the intruder turns, the host falls dead. The revelers then grab the stranger but find the costume empty. All soon die of the Red Death. The allegorical meaning of the story is found in such details as Prospero's name, the stranger's appearance, the arrangement of the seven halls (east to west, birth to death), and their colors, particularly the black (death) and red (blood) of the westernmost room with its ebony clock marking the inevitable passage of time.

Before You Read

The Masque of the Red Death

Literary Focus

Allegory: A Story Behind a Story

An **allegory** is a narrative that is really a double story. One story takes place on the surface. Under the surface the story's characters and events represent abstract ideas or states of being, things like love or freedom, evil or goodness, hell or heaven.

To work, an allegory must operate on two levels. On the level of pure storytelling, an allegory must hold our attention. Its characters must seem believable and interesting enough for us to care about them. On the allegorical level the ideas in the story must be accessible to us. As you read, you should find that the allegorical level of the story gradually begins to strike you.

See if you find that Poe's story of arrogance and death hooks you on both levels.

Reading Skills

Monitoring Your Reading: Asking Questions

As you read this story, you'll find questions at the open-book signs. The questions are designed to make you stop briefly and think about the text. They ask you to sum up what you have read. They ask you about the meanings of words. They remind you to visualize the action. These are issues that active readers think about all the time.

Reading Standard 3.7 Recognize and understand the significance of various literary devices, including allegory, and explain their appeal.

Make the Connection

Quickwrite

Rich and powerful people often build huge houses. They build high walls around their estates so that they can block out the upsetting parts of life. What realities of life must people face, no matter who they are? Write down your thoughts.

Background

Poe's fictional Red Death is probably based on the Black Death, which swept fourteenth-century Europe and Asia, killing as many as two thirds of the population in some regions in less than twenty years. (For more about the Black Death, see the ***Connection*** on page 429.) Poe calls the plague "the Red Death" because victims oozed blood from painful sores.

In this story a fourteenth-century prince gives a costume party, or masque, to try to forget about the epidemic raging all around him.

Vocabulary Development

profuse (prō·fyo͞os′) *adj.:* given or poured forth freely and abundantly; plentiful.

sagacious (sə·gā′shəs) *adj.:* wise; showing sound judgment.

contagion (kən·tā′jən) *n.:* spreading of disease.

imperial (im·pir′ē·əl) *adj.:* majestic; of great size or superior quality.

emanating (em′ə·nāt′iŋ) *v.:* coming forth; emerging, as from a source.

sedate (si·dāt′) *adj.* used as *n.:* calm; quiet.

pervaded (pər·vād′id) *v.:* spread throughout.

cessation (se·sā′shən) *n.:* ceasing or stopping.

propriety (prə·prī′ə·tē) *n.:* quality of being proper, fitting, or suitable.

tangible (tan′jə·bəl) *adj.:* that can be touched.

RESOURCES: READING

Planning

- *One-Stop Planner* CD-ROM with Test Generator
- *On Course: Mapping Instruction*

Media

- *Audio CD Library*
  - disc 12
- *Visual Connections*
  - Videocassette, Segment 5
- *Fine Art Transparencies*
  - Transparency 11

Reading

- *Interactive Reading,* Teacher's Edition
  - Graphic Organizer: Allegory Chart

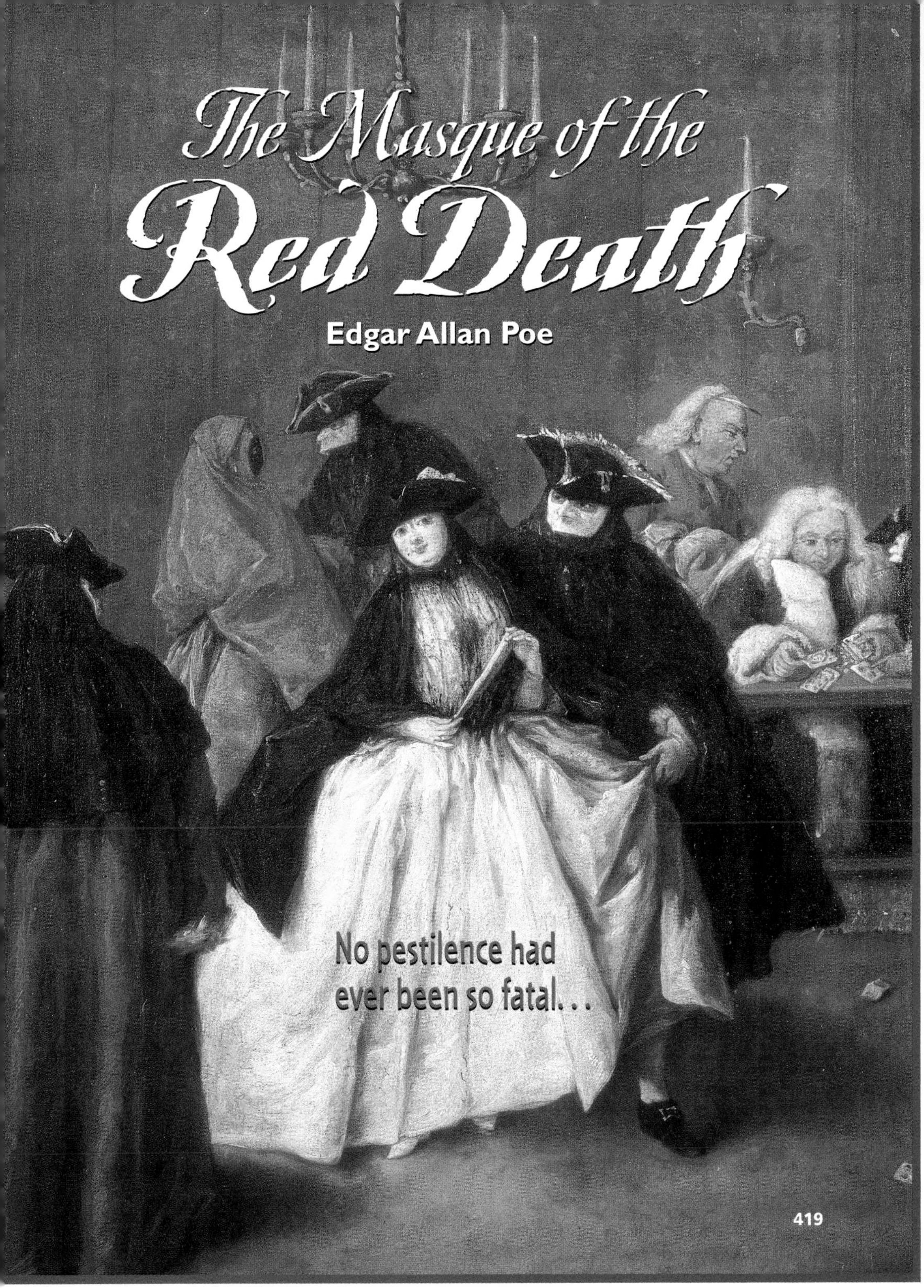

Differentiating Instruction

- *Lesson Plans for Language Development*
  - English-Language Learners, pp. 183–185, 194, 198
  - Special Education Students, pp. 186, 194, 198

Vocabulary

- *Vocabulary Development*
  - Vocabulary Worksheet, p. 35

Assessment

- *Progress Assessment of Reading*
  - Selection Test
- *One-Stop Planner* CD-ROM with Test Generator

PRETEACHING

Standards Starter

Build prerequisite skills. Remind students that an allegory is a literary work in which the characters, objects, and events stand for abstract qualities. An allegory can be read on one level for its literal meaning and on another for its symbolic, or allegorical, meaning. To review the concept, call on volunteers to read and analyze a simple example of an allegory, such as the fable of the tortoise and the hare.

Preview Vocabulary

Have students read the definitions of the Vocabulary words on p. 418. Then, ask students to match each Vocabulary word with its synonym below.

1. issuing forth [emanating]
2. termination [cessation]
3. serene [sedate]
4. plentiful [profuse]
5. infection [contagion]
6. correct behavior [propriety]
7. intelligent [sagacious]
8. touchable [tangible]
9. regal [imperial]
10. overspread [pervaded]

Assign the Reading

Homework

You may wish to assign the Quickwrite on p. 418 as homework and have students read Poe's tale in class. Learners who are having difficulty or who are not fluent in English might listen to the story being read aloud in the *Audio CD Library* while they follow along in their books. As students read the story, remind them to pause at the open-book signs to clarify what they have read. Advanced learners may wish to jot down their ideas about the possible allegorical meanings of Prince Prospero, Prospero's abbey, the black room, the red light in the black room, the clock, and the stranger.

DIRECT TEACHING

A Reading Skills

Monitoring your reading. Point out that this first paragraph introduces readers to the narrator's florid style and challenging vocabulary, as well as to the terrible symptoms and progress of the Red Death. To increase comprehension of difficult passages, encourage students to pause frequently to paraphrase. [Possible response to question A: The Red Death is a fatal disease in which victims feel pain and dizziness, bleed from their pores, and soon die.]

B Literary Focus
GRADE-LEVEL STANDARD

Allegory. Hints to the characters' allegorical meanings are often found in their names. For example, in John Bunyan's *Pilgrim's Progress,* characters include Mr. Worldly Wiseman, Faithful, and Hopeful. What does the name Prospero suggest about this character? [Possible response: He is prosperous (successful and rich).]

C Reading Skills

Monitoring your reading. [Possible response to question B: They lock themselves up in the prince's abbey with food and drink so they can survive comfortably while people outside the abbey suffer and die.]

The "Red Death" had long devastated the country. No pestilence had ever been so fatal, or so hideous. Blood was its Avatar[1] and its seal—the redness and the horror of blood. There were sharp pains, and sudden dizziness, and then profuse bleeding at the pores, with dissolution.[2] The scarlet stains upon the body and especially upon the face of the victim were the pest ban which shut him out from the aid and from the sympathy of his fellow men. And the whole seizure, progress, and termination of the disease were the incidents of half an hour.

A. MONITOR YOUR READING What is the Red Death?

But the Prince Prospero was happy and dauntless[3] and sagacious. When his dominions were half depopulated, he summoned to his presence a thousand hale and lighthearted friends from among the knights and dames of his court, and with these retired to the deep seclusion of one of his castellated abbeys.[4] This was an extensive and magnificent structure, the creation of the prince's own eccentric yet august[5] taste. A strong and lofty wall girdled it in. This wall had gates of iron. The courtiers, having entered, brought furnaces and massy hammers and welded the bolts. They resolved to leave means neither of ingress or egress[6] to the sudden impulses of despair or of frenzy from within. The abbey was amply provisioned. With such precautions the courtiers might bid defiance to contagion. The external world could take care of itself. In the meantime it was folly to grieve, or to think. The prince had provided all the appliances of pleasure. There were buffoons, there were improvisatori,[7] there were ballet dancers, there were musicians, there was Beauty, there was wine. All these and security were within. Without was the "Red Death."

B. MONITOR YOUR READING How do the prince and his friends try to escape the Red Death?

It was toward the close of the fifth or sixth month of his seclusion, and while the pestilence raged most furiously abroad, that the Prince Prospero entertained his thousand friends at a masked ball of the most unusual magnificence.

It was a voluptuous scene, that masquerade. But first let me tell of the rooms in which it was held. There were seven—an imperial suite. In many palaces, however, such suites form a long and straight vista, while the folding doors slide back nearly to the walls on either hand, so that the view of the whole extent is scarcely impeded. Here the case was very different; as might have been expected from the duke's love of the *bizarre.* The apartments were so irregularly disposed that the vision embraced

1. **Avatar** (av′ə·tär′) *n.:* embodiment; concrete expression of.
2. **dissolution** (dis′ə·lo͞o′shən) *n.:* here, death.
3. **dauntless** (dônt′lis) *adj.:* fearless.
4. **castellated** (kas′tə·lāt′id) **abbeys:** monasteries built with towers.
5. **august** *adj.:* grand.
6. **ingress or egress:** entrance or exit.
7. **improvisatori** (im·prä·və·zə·tôr′ē) *n.:* poets who make up a verse on the spur of the moment.

(Page 419)
Masked Ball in the Card Room (c. 1757–1760) by Pietro Longhi. Oil on canvas (62.5 cm × 51 cm).

Vocabulary

profuse (prō·fyo͞os′) *adj.:* given or poured forth freely and abundantly; plentiful.

sagacious (sə·gā′shəs) *adj.:* wise; showing sound judgment.

contagion (kən·tā′jən) *n.:* spreading of disease.

imperial (im·pir′ē·əl) *adj.:* majestic; of great size or superior quality.

DIFFERENTIATING INSTRUCTION

Learners Having Difficulty

Modeling. To help students read "The Masque of the Red Death," model the skill of monitoring your reading. Say, "Poe writes in a style full of description and allusion. When reading dense text like this, it is often useful to stop occasionally and ask myself questions and think about their answers." Encourage students as they read to visualize the action, summarize or paraphrase passages, or ask themselves questions about the text. The questions at the open-book signs will help students monitor their reading and lead to a deeper understanding of the story.

English-Language Learners

In order for students to fully understand this story, they must be able to grasp Poe's archaic vocabulary and complex sentences. To help clarify the meanings of words, you may wish to preview the sidenotes. Encourage students to use context clues to help figure out the meanings of other unfamiliar words. To clarify the meanings of sentences, suggest that students re-read difficult passages and then paraphrase them. If they but little more than one at a time. There was a sharp turn at every twenty or thirty yards, and at each turn a novel effect. To the right and left, in the middle of each wall, a tall and narrow Gothic window looked out upon a closed corridor which pursued the windings of the suite. These windows were of stained glass whose color varied in accordance with the prevailing hue of the decorations of the chamber into which it opened. That at the eastern extremity was hung, for example, in blue—and vividly blue were its windows. The second chamber was purple in its ornaments and tapestries, and here the panes were purple. The third was green throughout, and so were the casements. The fourth was furnished and lighted with orange—the fifth with white—the sixth with violet. The seventh apartment was closely shrouded in black velvet tapestries that hung all over the ceiling and down the walls, falling in heavy folds upon a carpet of the same material and hue. But in this chamber only, the color of the windows failed to correspond with the decorations. The panes here were scarlet—a deep blood color. Now in no one of the seven apartments was there any lamp or candelabrum, amid the profusion of golden ornaments that lay scattered to and fro or depended from the roof. There was no light of any kind emanating from lamp or candle within the suite of chambers. But in the corridors that followed the suite, there stood, opposite to each window, a heavy tripod, bearing a brazier of fire that projected its rays through the tinted glass and so glaringly illumined the room. And thus were produced a multitude of gaudy and fantastic appearances. But in the western or black chamber the effect of the firelight that streamed upon the dark hangings through the blood-tinted panes was ghastly in the extreme, and produced so wild a look upon the countenances of those who entered that there were few of the company bold enough to set foot within its precincts at all.

It was in this apartment, also, that there stood against the western wall a gigantic clock of ebony. Its pendulum swung to and fro with a dull, heavy, monotonous clang; and when the minute hand made the circuit of the face, and the hour was to be stricken, there came from the brazen lungs of the clock a sound which was clear and loud and deep and exceedingly musical, but of so peculiar a note and emphasis that, at each lapse of an hour, the musicians of the orchestra were constrained to pause, momentarily, in their performance, to hearken to the sound; and thus the waltzers perforce ceased their evolutions;[8] and there was a brief disconcert[9] of the whole gay company; and, while the chimes of the clock yet rang, it was observed that the giddiest grew pale, and the more

C. MONITOR YOUR READING Describe the seven rooms as you **visualize** them.

8. **evolutions** (ev′ə·lo͞o′shənz) *n.:* movements that are part of a pattern.
9. **disconcert** (dis′kən·surt′) *n.:* upset.

Vocabulary
emanating (em′ə·nāt′iŋ) *v.:* coming forth; emerging, as from a source.

listen as the story is read in the *Audio CD Library,* the reader's intonation may help students to better understand the story.

Resources Reminder

For lessons designed for intermediate and advanced English-language learners, see *Lesson Plans for Language Development,* pp. 183–185, 194, 198.

Special Education Students

For lessons designed for special education students, see *Lesson Plans for Language Development,* pp. 186, 194, 198.

DIRECT TEACHING

D Literary Focus
GRADE-LEVEL STANDARD

Symbol and allegory. What does Poe's description of the arrangement of the rooms suggest about their allegorical meaning? [Possible responses: The rooms may represent stages of life, because when you are in one stage of life, you can see only a little of the next stage ahead. Life is full of uncertainty and surprise.] **Which room is easternmost?** [the first, blue room] **Which is westernmost?** [the seventh, black room] **What do east and west often symbolize?** [Possible responses: East symbolizes sunrise, beginnings, life. West symbolizes sunset, endings, death.]

E Literary Focus
GRADE-LEVEL STANDARD

Setting and mood. How do the colors of the last room affect the mood, or emotional atmosphere, of the story? [Possible response: They are dark and ominous. The scarlet windows are a foreboding reminder of the Red Death.]

F Reading Skills

Monitoring your reading. [Possible response to question C: One cannot see from one room to another. Each room has its own color—blue, purple, green, orange, white, violet, and black—creating a brash, carnival-like fantasy. The last, westernmost room is black and scary because of the blood-red light cast by a fire on the other side of the tall red windows.]

G Literary Focus
GRADE-LEVEL STANDARD

Allegory. What is the literal meaning of a clock? [a time-telling device] **What might the giant clock symbolize?** [Possible response: the passing of time.] **Why is it allegorically appropriate for the clock to be in the seventh and final room?** [It is a reminder that death comes to every life.]

Direct Teaching

A Reading Skills

Monitoring your reading. [Possible response to question D: The chiming of the clock makes the partygoers pause and become confused and anxious.]

B Reading Skills

Expressing an opinion. In this paragraph the narrator brings Prospero's sanity into question. What is your opinion of Prince Prospero's mental state? [Possible responses: His obsession with the chambers and the masqueraders seems insane. He is eccentric but not mad.]

VIEWING THE ART

An eighteenth-century Venetian painter, **Francesco Guardi** (1712–1793) is best known for his architectural paintings depicting both scenes of Venice and *capricci,* or images of imaginary architecture. He also painted scenes of Venetian life, such as this one, which depicts the foyer of a theater. Venetians would gather in foyers to socialize, and the Venetian Senate issued numerous laws against the gambling that frequently occurred in them.

Activity. Ask students to comment on how this painting relates to the description of the masquerade in Poe's story. [Although fancily dressed and somewhat decadent in appearance, the group here is not as bizarre or macabre as that in Poe's story.]

aged and sedate passed their hands over their brows as if in confused reverie or meditation. But when the echoes had fully ceased, a light laughter at once pervaded the assembly; the musicians looked at each other and smiled as if at their own nervousness and folly, and made whispering vows, each to the other, that the next chiming of the clock should produce in them no similar emotion; and then, after the lapse of sixty minutes (which embrace three thousand and six hundred seconds of the Time that flies), there came yet another chiming of the clock, and then were the same disconcert and tremulousness[10] and meditation as before.

D. MONITOR YOUR READING What strange effect does the ebony clock have on the partygoers?

But, in spite of these things, it was a gay and magnificent revel. The tastes of the duke were peculiar. He had a fine eye for colors and effects. He disregarded the *decora*[11] of mere fashion. His plans were bold and

10. **tremulousness** (trem′yoo͞·ləs·nis) *n.:* trembling; fearfulness.

11. ***decora*** (də·kō′rə) *n.:* Latin for "accepted standards of good taste."

Vocabulary

sedate (si·dāt′) *adj.* used as *n.:* calm; quiet.

pervaded (pər·vād′id) *v.:* spread throughout.

The Redoute by Francesco Guardi (1712–1793).

422

DIFFERENTIATING INSTRUCTION

Advanced Learners

Acceleration. Use this activity to move advanced learners toward the eleventh- and twelfth-grade Standard 3.1, for which they analyze characteristics of subgenres such as allegory.

Activity. Have students review the story and find elements that they believe have allegorical meaning. Students should explain the meaning of each element they identify, as well as how Poe may have intended to use these allegorical elements to convey a moral lesson.

fiery, and his conceptions glowed with barbaric lustre. There are some who would have thought him mad. His followers felt that he was not. It was necessary to hear and see and touch him to be *sure* that he was not.

He had directed, in great part, the moveable embellishments of the seven chambers, upon occasion of this great *fête;*[12] and it was his own guiding taste which had given character to the masqueraders. Be sure they were grotesque. There were much glare and glitter and piquancy[13] and phantasm[14]—much of what has been since seen in *Hernani.*[15] There were arabesque[16] figures with unsuited limbs and appointments. There were delirious fancies such as the madman fashions. There was much of the beautiful, much of the wanton, much of the *bizarre,* something of the terrible, and not a little of that which might have excited disgust. To and fro in the seven chambers there stalked, in fact, a multitude of dreams. And these—the dreams—writhed in and about, taking hue[17] from the rooms, and causing the wild music of the orchestra to seem as the echo of their steps. And, anon,[18] there strikes the ebony clock which stands in the hall of the velvet. And then, for a moment, all is still, and all is silent

12. ***fête*** (fet′) *n.:* French for "celebration."
13. **piquancy** (pē′kən•sē) *n.:* quality of being pleasantly exciting.
14. **phantasm** (fan′taz′əm) *n.:* illusion.
15. ***Hernani:*** play by the French writer Victor Hugo.
16. **arabesque** (ar′ə•besk′) *adj.:* fantastic; elaborate.
17. **hue** (hyo͞o) *n.:* color or shade of color.
18. **anon** (ə•nän′) *adv.:* soon.

DIRECT TEACHING

C Vocabulary Development
REVIEW STANDARD

? Using context clues. Although Poe uses many unusual words, they can often be understood by using context clues. Poe uses the word *writhe* twice to describe the movements of the masked partygoers. From the context, what do you think *writhe* means? [Possible responses: to twist and turn; to be contorted.]

CONTENT-AREA CONNECTIONS

Boccaccio's History and Literature: *Decameron*

Throughout history, people have fled or hidden to avoid epidemic diseases. The writer Giovanni Boccaccio was living in Florence, Italy, when the plague killed roughly three out of every four people living there. Boccaccio survived and went on to write his masterpiece the *Decameron,* a collection of stories told by wealthy young Florentines who have retreated to a villa to escape the disease.

Mixed-ability group activity. Have groups of students imagine they are fleeing a modern epidemic and have holed up in a safe place. Have students entertain each other by taking turns telling stories of their own or stories they have read or heard.

Direct Teaching

A Reading Skills
Monitoring your reading.
[Possible responses to question E: The costumes are strange and sometimes disgusting or frightening. The partygoers take on the colors of the tinted windows. They avoid the seventh room because of its blackness, scary red glow, and the loud peal of its clock.]

B Reading Skills
Predicting. At midnight the music stops. What do you think might happen next? [Possible response: Poe is clearly setting the reader up for something scary or bizarre to happen at the stroke of midnight. Some students may say that the party will end or that the pestilence will invade the abbey.]

C Reading Skills
Monitoring your reading.
[Possible response to question F: At first people are surprised and disapproving; then they feel horror and disgust.]

D Literary Focus
GRADE-LEVEL STANDARD
Allegory. Poe devotes this long paragraph to a description of the stranger. What allegorical meaning might this tall, gaunt figure have? [Possible responses: evil, time, the Grim Reaper, the Red Death, death in general.]

---

save the voice of the clock. The dreams are stiff-frozen as they stand. But the echoes of the chime die away—they have endured but an instant—and a light, half-subdued laughter floats after them as they depart. And now again the music swells, and the dreams live, and writhe to and fro more merrily than ever, taking hue from the many-tinted windows through which stream the rays from the tripods. But to the chamber which lies most westwardly of the seven, there are now none of the maskers who venture; for the night is waning away; and there flows a ruddier light through the blood-colored panes; and the blackness of the sable drapery appalls;[19] and to him whose foot falls upon the sable carpet, there comes from the near clock of ebony a muffled peal more solemnly emphatic than any which reaches *their* ears who indulge in the more remote gaieties of the other apartments.

But these other apartments were densely crowded, and in them beat feverishly the heart of life. And the revel went whirlingly on, until at length there commenced the sounding of midnight upon the clock. And then the music ceased, as I have told; and the evolutions of the waltzers were quieted; and there was an uneasy cessation of all things as before. But now there were twelve strokes to be sounded by the bell of the clock; and thus it happened, perhaps, that more of thought crept, with more of time, into the meditations of the thoughtful among those who revelled. And thus, too, it happened, perhaps, that before the last echoes of the last chime had utterly sunk into silence, there were many individuals in the crowd who had found leisure to become aware of the presence of a masked figure which had arrested the attention of no single individual before. And the rumor of this new presence having spread itself whisperingly around, there arose at length from the whole company a buzz, or murmur, expressive of disapprobation[20] and surprise—then, finally, of terror, of horror, and of disgust.

In an assembly of phantasms such as I have painted, it may well be supposed that no ordinary appearance could have excited such sensation. In truth the masquerade license[21] of the night was nearly unlimited; but the figure in question had out-Heroded Herod,[22] and gone beyond the bounds of even the prince's indefinite decorum. There are chords in the hearts of the most reckless which cannot be touched without emotion. Even with the utterly lost, to whom life and death are equally jests, there are matters of which no jest can be made. The whole company, indeed, seemed now deeply to feel that in the costume and bearing of the stranger neither wit nor propriety existed. The figure was

E. MONITOR YOUR READING
What details suggest that the party is, as Poe says, grotesque and bizarre? Why don't the revelers go into the seventh room?

F. MONITOR YOUR READING
How does the masked figure affect the revelers?

19. **appalls** (ə·pôlz′) *v.:* fills with horror.

20. **disapprobation** (dis′ap′ rə·bā′shən) *n.:* disapproval.

21. **license** *n.:* here, excessive freedom.

22. **Herod:** evil biblical king who had baby boys slaughtered in his attempt to kill the infant Jesus. To "out-Herod Herod" is to be more evil than the worst tyrant.

Vocabulary
cessation (se·sā′shən) *n.:* ceasing or stopping.
propriety (prə·prī′ə·tē) *n.:* quality of being proper, fitting, or suitable.

Content-Area Connections

Literature: Biblical Allusions
Like many authors, Poe sometimes refers to people or passages from the Bible. Two such references that occur in "The Masque of the Red Death" are the phrases "out-Heroded Herod" and "like a thief in the night."
Individual activity. Have interested students research these allusions. Students may research the historical King Herod, as well as Biblical passages pertaining to Herod, and the first use of the phrase "to out-Herod Herod" in Shakespeare's *Hamlet.* Other students may research the biblical passages that refer to "a thief in the night" (I Thessalonians 5:2, Revelation 3:3, 2 Peter 3:10, Job 24:14).

Literature: Shakespeare and Poe
Although no one is sure of what literature or events influenced Poe as he wrote "The

424 Chapter 6 Symbolism and Allegory • Synthesizing Sources

tall and gaunt, and shrouded from head to foot in the habiliments[23] of the grave. The mask which concealed the visage was made so nearly to resemble the countenance of a stiffened corpse that the closest scrutiny must have had difficulty in detecting the cheat. And yet all this might have been endured, if not approved, by the mad revelers around. But the mummer[24] had gone so far as to assume the type of the Red Death. His vesture[25] was dabbled in *blood*—and his broad brow, with all the features of the face, was besprinkled with the scarlet horror.

When the eyes of Prince Prospero fell upon this spectral[26] image (which with a slow and solemn movement, as if more fully to sustain its *role,* stalked to and fro among the waltzers), he was seen to be convulsed, in the first moment with a strong shudder either of terror or distaste; but, in the next, his brow reddened with rage.

"Who dares?" he demanded hoarsely of the courtiers who stood near him—"who dares insult us with this blasphemous[27] mockery? Seize him and unmask him—that we may know whom we have to hang at sunrise, from the battlements!"

It was in the eastern or blue chamber in which stood the Prince Prospero as he uttered these words. They rang throughout the seven rooms loudly and clearly—for the prince was a bold and robust man, and the music had become hushed at the waving of his hand.

23. **habiliments** (hə·bil′ə·mənts) *n.:* clothing.
24. **mummer** *n.:* person who wears a mask or disguise.
25. **vesture** (ves′chər) *n.:* clothing.

G. MONITOR YOUR READING How is the masked guest costumed? Who do you **predict** this is?

26. **spectral** (spek′trəl) *adj.:* ghostly.
27. **blasphemous** (blas′fə·məs) *adj.:* here, highly disrespectful.

Masks and Death (1897) by James Ensor.

Masque of the Red Death," it is interesting that his main character has the same name as the main character in Shakespeare's *The Tempest.*

Individual activity. Have interested students read *The Tempest* and then analyze similarities and differences between Shakespeare's Prospero and Poe's Prospero. Invite volunteers to share their comparisons with the class.

DIRECT TEACHING

E Reading Skills

Monitoring your reading. [Possible response to question G: The guest is wearing a death shroud spattered in blood, and his mask looks like the face of a corpse, also dotted with blood. Some students may predict that this is a ghost of someone who has died of the Red Death.]

F Learners Having Difficulty

Finding details. What is the Prince's first reaction to the stranger? [fear or repulsion] What is his second reaction? [anger] Ask students whether the prince's response is appropriate. [Possible responses: Yes, because he has been trying to escape the Red Death; yes, because his escapist party is invaded by a figure that suggests disease and death.]

G English-Language Learners

Archaic language. Pause to check the reading comprehension of English-language learners. Elicit questions from students about difficult sentence structures and archaic language. Students might benefit from reviewing together any difficult words in the footnotes and from identifying synonyms for other unfamiliar words.

VIEWING THE ART

Belgian symbolist **James Ensor** (1860–1949) created art that portrayed people as grotesque and ridiculous. He created art that anticipated expressionism and surrealism. Ensor used masks to symbolize alienation, falseness, and the avoidance of reality, and he frequently portrayed skeletons together with living figures.

Activity. Ask students to speculate on the significance of this skull surrounded by grotesque masked figures. [Ensor may be commenting on how people behave foolishly despite the reality of death.]

VIEWING THE ART

John Byam Liston Shaw (1872–1919) was an English artist and illustrator. In addition to creating his own art, Shaw founded a school of art in Kensington, London. He created this illustration for *Selected Tales of Mystery,* a collection of Poe's stories published in 1909. Note how the artist emphasized the pile of bodies, the clock, and the shrouded figure of death by using a black background.

Activity. Ask students how Shaw's illustration responds to Poe's description of the colors of the seventh chamber. [Shaw shows velvet tapestries at right, with a blood red window, as described by Poe.]

426

READING MINI-LESSON

Developing Word-Attack Skills

Use words from the selection to explore the effect of *i* on consonants and the different sounds made when *i* precedes another vowel. Share these tips with students:

- When *i* follows *c*, as in *sagacious,* it creates the consonant sound /sh/.
- When *i* follows *g*, as in *contagious,* it creates the consonant sound /j/.
- When *i* follows *s*, as in *seclusion,* it creates the consonant sound /zh/.
- When *i* follows *t*, as in *precautions,* it creates the consonant sound /sh/.
- When *i* follows *l* or *n*, as it does in *peculiar* and *dominions,* it stands for the consonant sound /y/.
- The letter *i* stands for /ī/ in *defiance* and *propriety.*

It was in the blue room where stood the prince, with a group of pale courtiers by his side. At first, as he spoke, there was a slight rushing movement of this group in the direction of the intruder, who at the moment was also near at hand, and now, with deliberate and stately step, made closer approach to the speaker. But from a certain nameless awe with which the mad assumptions of the mummer had inspired the whole party, there were found none who put forth hand to seize him; so that, unimpeded, he passed within a yard of the prince's person; and, while the vast assembly, as if with one impulse, shrank from the centers of the rooms to the walls, he made his way uninterruptedly, but with the same solemn and measured step which had distinguished him from the first, through the blue chamber to the purple—through the purple to the green—through the green to the orange—through this again to the white—and even thence to the violet, ere a decided movement had been made to arrest him. **A** It was then, however, that the Prince Prospero, maddening with rage and the shame of his own momentary cowardice, rushed hurriedly through the six chambers, while none followed him on account of a deadly terror that had seized upon all. He bore aloft a drawn dagger, and had approached, in rapid impetuosity,[28] to within three or four feet of the retreating figure, when the latter, having attained the extremity of the velvet apartment, turned suddenly and confronted his pursuer. There was a sharp cry—and the dagger dropped gleaming upon the sable carpet, upon which, instantly afterwards, fell prostrate in death the Prince Prospero. Then, summoning the wild courage of despair, a throng of the revelers at once threw themselves into the black apartment, and, seizing the mummer, whose tall figure stood erect and motionless within the shadow of the ebony clock, gasped in unutterable horror at finding the grave cerements[29] and corpselike mask which they handled with so violent a rudeness, untenanted by any tangible form.

And now was acknowledged the presence of the Red Death. He had come like a thief in the night. And one by one dropped the revelers in the blood-bedewed halls of their revel, and died each in the despairing posture of his fall. And the life of the ebony clock went out with that of the last of the gay. And the flames of the tripods expired. And Darkness and Decay and the Red Death held illimitable dominion[30] over all. ■

28. **impetuosity** (im·pech′ o͞o·äs′i·tē) *n.:* rashness; impulsiveness.

29. **grave cerements** *n.:* shrouds; cloths that cover a body for burial.

H. MONITOR YOUR READING
What happens when the guest is unmasked? **B**

30. **dominion** *n.:* rule.

I. MONITOR YOUR READING
Who was the guest? What happens to the revelers? **C**

Vocabulary
tangible (tan′jə·bəl) *adj.:* that can be touched.

(Opposite) "And Darkness and Decay and the Red Death held illimitable dominion over all." Illustration (1909) by John Byam Liston Shaw for "The Masque of the Red Death."

DIRECT TEACHING

A Literary Focus
GRADE-LEVEL STANDARD

Allegory. As the story reaches its climax, Poe reiterates the sequence of chambers. What allegorical meaning can you conclude the rooms have? [Possible response: the stages of life.] What do you expect will happen when the prince reaches the last room? [Possible response: There will be a showdown between the stranger and the prince.]

B Reading Skills
Monitoring your reading.
[Possible response to question H: When the partygoers rip off the guest's costume, there is no one inside.]

C Reading Skills
Monitoring your reading.
[Possible response to question I: The guest was the Red Death. All the revelers die.]

GUIDED PRACTICE

Monitoring students' progress. Guide the class in answering these comprehension questions. Direct students to locate passages in the text that support their responses.

True-False

1. Each victim of the Red Death engaged in a lengthy struggle for survival. [F]
2. Prospero invited all subjects in his kingdom to stay in his abbey until the Red Death passed. [F]
3. The seventh room was completely black except for the red windows. [T]
4. The partygoers ignored the ringing of the ebony clock until it struck midnight. [F]
5. The uninvited guest was dressed like a corpse and his face was bloody. [T]

- The letter *i* stands for /ē/ in *imperial* and *delirious.*

Activity. Display these sets of words. Have volunteers identify the two words in which the underlined letter *i* has the same effect on another letter or stands for the same sound. Answers are in italics.

1. *delirious*	*furiously*	priority
2. *delusion*	extensive	*provisioned*
3. *appliances*	material	*propriety*
4. courtiers	*familiar*	*peculiar*
5. *especially*	*rapacious*	scientific

Meet the Writer

Background. Deprived of parental love, Edgar Allan Poe sought attention from women. His first engagement occurred when he was a teenager, but this secret engagement was canceled. Poe later married his cousin, but after her death he began living recklessly. He courted several women who admired his writing and helped him financially. Poe was engaged to poet Sarah Helen Whitman, who later canceled their engagement. Poe was later reunited with his first fiancée, but he died before they were married.

Meet the Writer

Edgar Allan Poe

Nightmare Worlds

Edgar Allan Poe (1809–1849) was a moody, sensitive person whose stories and poems dwell on the supernatural and on crime, torture, premature burial, and death. His writing, which brought him little comfort or security, reflects the dark, nightmare side of the imagination.

Poe's stormy personal history began when his father deserted his mother, a popular young actress, who died in 1811 in a theatrical rooming house in Richmond, Virginia, just before Edgar was three years old.

The Allans, a wealthy, childless couple, took him in and gave him a good education, expecting him to go into business eventually. Edgar wanted to be a writer, though, not a businessman. This disagreement and John Allan's persistent refusal to adopt Edgar legally led to frequent fights. John Allan had severed all connections with him by the time he was twenty-one. Eventually Poe entered upon a hectic, full-time literary career, working for a number of periodicals in Baltimore and New York.

In 1836, Poe married a thirteen-year-old cousin, Virginia Clemm. Although a drinking problem often got him into destructive fights with other writers and critics, Poe managed somehow to keep his household together. In 1845, he sold his poem "The Raven" to a newspaper for about fifteen dollars. "The Raven" was soon on everyone's lips, as popular as a top-ten song is today.

Poe was to know no peace, however. Virginia had already fallen victim to that plague of nineteenth-century life, tuberculosis. In 1847, she died, and Poe's loneliness and drinking increased. On October 3, 1849, when he was only forty years old, Poe was found, disoriented and suffering from exposure, outside a tavern in rainy, windswept Baltimore. He died in a Baltimore hospital from unspecified causes several days later.

Poe, a meticulous writer who was devoted to his craft, invented two genres: the mystery story and the horror story. Both forms have flourished ever since.

For Independent Reading

Poe's horror tales include "Hop-Frog" and "The Cask of Amontillado," two stories about cold-blooded revenge; "The Tell-Tale Heart," about an irrational murder; and "The Pit and the Pendulum," set in a prison in Toledo, Spain.

DIFFERENTIATING INSTRUCTION

Advanced Learners

Enrichment. Poe's life was haunted by disease and death. His father disappeared when Poe was young and his mother died soon after. At the time that Poe was writing "The Masque of the Red Death," he and his family had just lived through a devastating cholera epidemic in Baltimore, and his young wife Virginia had suffered a terrible hemorrhage. She soon died of tuberculosis.

Activity. Tell students that there are various theories as to what led Poe to create his fictional disease, the Red Death. Suggest that they enter *Edgar Allan Poe* plus one or more of the following keywords in a search engine: *Black Death, bubonic plague, Boccaccio* and *Decameron, Defoe* and *Journal of the Plague Year, Virginia Clemm* and *tuberculosis,* or *cholera epidemic* and *Baltimore.* Have students share their findings about the possible influences that led Poe to imagine the Red Death.

The Black Death

from When Plague Strikes

James Cross Giblin

The bubonic plague—the Black Death—arrived in Sicily in October 1347, carried by the crew of a fleet from the east. All the sailors on the ships were dead or dying. In the words of a contemporary historian, they had "sickness clinging to their very bones."

The harbor masters at the port of Messina ordered the sick sailors to remain on board, hoping in this way to prevent the disease from spreading to the town. They had no way of knowing that the actual carriers of the disease had already left the ships. Under cover of night, when no one could see them, they had scurried down the ropes that tied the ships to the dock and vanished into Messina.

The carriers were black rats and the fleas that lived in their hair. Driven by an unending search for food, the rats' ancestors had migrated slowly westward along the caravan routes. They had traveled in bolts of cloth and bales of hay, and the fleas had come with them.

Although it was only an eighth of an inch long, the rat flea was a tough, adaptable creature. It depended for nourishment on the blood of its host, which it obtained through a daggerlike snout that could pierce the rat's skin. And in its stomach the flea often carried thousands of the deadly bacteria that caused the bubonic plague.

The bacteria did no apparent harm to the flea, and a black rat could tolerate a moderate amount of them, too, without showing ill effects. But sometimes the flea contained so many bacteria that they invaded the rat's lungs or nervous system when the flea injected its snout. Then the rat died a swift and horrible death, and the flea had to find a new host.

Aiding the tiny flea in its search were its powerful legs, which could jump more than 150 times the creature's length. In most instances the flea landed on another black rat. Not always, though. If most of the rats in the vicinity were already dead or dying from the plague, the flea might leap to a human being instead. As soon as it had settled on the human's skin, the flea would begin to feed, and the whole process of infection would be repeated. . . .

From Sicily, trading ships loaded with infected flea-bearing rats carried the Black Death to ports on the mainland of Italy. Peddlers and other travelers helped spread it to inland cities such as Milan and Florence.

Conditions in these medieval cities provided a splendid breeding ground for all types of vermin, including rats. There were no regular garbage collections, and refuse accumulated in piles in the streets. Rushes from wet or marshy places, not rugs, covered the floors in most homes. After a meal, it was customary to throw bits of leftover food onto the rushes for the dog or cat to eat. Rats and mice often got their share, too.

Because the cities had no running water, even the wealthy seldom washed their heavy clothing, or their own bodies. As a result, both rich and poor were prime targets for lice and fleas and the diseases they carried—the most deadly being the bubonic plague. . . .

429

Connection

Summary at grade level

This Connection provides a detailed account of the origin, transmission, and results of the bubonic plague, or the Black Death. In 1347, rats with fleas that carry the plague bacillus first arrived in southern Europe at the port of Messina, Sicily. Before long, the thriving cities of northern Italy, such as Florence and Milan, were suffering from the plague. Boccaccio lived through the plague, and his masterwork the *Decameron* gives accounts of how various people reacted to the disease. Some isolated themselves in an effort to avoid the plague. Others ate, drank, and partied, figuring they would soon die. No matter what people did, many died. Some believed this was the end of the world.

A Reading Skills

Making predictions. Who do you think the "actual carriers of the disease" are? [Possible response: Based on the clue word *scurried,* it is likely that rats or other rodents were the carriers.]

B Reading Skills

Identifying cause and effect. Ask students to draw a simple diagram showing the cause-and-effect relationships that result in a person getting the plague. [Possible response: Fleas with deadly bacteria in their stomachs live on the blood of animals, especially rats → rats scurry around, moving the fleas from place to place → some fleas jump onto humans → a flea bite injects plague bacteria into a human → the human contracts the disease and is likely to die.]

Connecting and Comparing Texts

Many details from "The Masque of the Red Death"—from the symptoms and results of the disease to the way people reacted to it—are similar to details in this excerpt about the Black Death from Giblin's book. Have students re-read the story and the nonfiction Connection and then work in groups to make two lists—one with details about the Red Death and another with details about the Black Death. From these lists, students can create a Venn diagram showing the similarities and differences between the Black Death and Poe's Red Death.

DIRECT TEACHING

A Reading Skills

Comparing and contrasting. In what way did people respond to the Black Death as characters responded in Poe's story to the Red Death? [Possible responses: People of the time had no idea how the disease was spread or how to cure it. Like Prospero and his guests, some people isolated themselves from others in an attempt to avoid the disease. Other people, who expected to die soon, partied wildly, as did Prospero and his guests.]

B Reading Skills

Distinguishing between fact and opinion. Ask students to list some facts and opinions found in the eyewitness account of Agnolo di Tura. [*Facts*—People started dying in May; the dead were brought to a ditch without a priest or a bell; nobody wept. *Opinion*—people's belief that it was the end of the world.]

The most complete account of the Black Death in Italy was given by the writer Giovanni Boccaccio, who lived in the city of Florence. In the preface to his classic book the *Decameron,* Boccaccio wrote: "Some say that the plague descended upon the human race through the influence of the heavenly bodies, others that it was a punishment signifying God's righteous anger at our wicked way of life." . . .

The Plague (c. 1515–1516) by Marcantonio Raimondi.

A How did the people of Florence react to this mysterious and fatal disease? Some isolated themselves in their homes, according to Boccaccio. They ate lightly, saw no outsiders, and refused to receive reports of the dead or sick. Others adopted an attitude of "play today for we die tomorrow." They drank heavily, stayed out late, and roamed through the streets singing and dancing as if the Black Death were an enormous joke. Still others, if they were rich enough, abandoned their homes in the city and fled to villas in the countryside. They hoped in this way to escape the disease—but often it followed them.

Whatever steps they took, the same percentage of people in each group seemed to fall ill. So many died that the bodies piled up in the streets. A new occupation came into being: that of loading the bodies on carts and carrying them away for burial in mass graves.

"No more respect was accorded to dead people," Boccaccio wrote, "than would be shown toward dead goats."

The town of Siena, thirty miles south of Florence, suffered severe losses also. A man named Agnolo di Tura offered a vivid account of what happened there:

B "The mortality in Siena began in May. It was a horrible thing, and I do not know where to begin to tell of the cruelty . . . . Members of a household brought their dead to a ditch as best they could, without a priest, without any divine services. Nor did the death bell sound. . . . And as soon as those ditches were filled, more were dug. I, Agnolo di Tura, buried my five children with my own hands. . . . And no bells tolled, and nobody wept no matter what his loss because almost everyone expected death. . . . And people said and believed, 'This is the end of the world.'"

430

CONTENT-AREA CONNECTIONS

Science and History: Epidemics
Epidemic diseases have occurred throughout history and have sometimes even altered the course of human events. For example, because of the huge death toll due to the Black Death in Europe, the surviving peasants demanded more pay from landowners and the feudal system changed.

Mixed-ability group activity. Invite students to prepare and present oral reports about epidemic diseases that influenced history. Possible topics include the bubonic plague in the 1300s (in China or in Europe); smallpox, especially in the New World from the 1500s to the 1700s; or the flu epidemic of 1918–1919. Challenge students to explain in their reports exactly how the epidemic affected the course of history.

Literary Response and Analysis

Reading Check

1. How do Prince Prospero and his friends try to escape from the Red Death?
2. What kind of life do the prince and his guests lead in their world apart?
3. Describe the seven rooms of the prince's suite.
4. Why do the guests avoid the seventh room?
5. How do the guests respond to the chiming of the ebony clock?
6. How does the masked ball end?

Interpretations

7. In the long paragraph that describes the masquerade on pages 423–424, what details suggest madness?
8. What is the **climax** of this horror story—that moment of greatest suspense and emotion, when you know how the problem in the story is going to be resolved?
9. Most readers agree that this story can be interpreted as an **allegory.** What might each of the following characters, events, or colors, represent?
    - Prince Prospero (consider even the significance of his name)
    - the masked ball
    - the colors of the seven rooms
    - the seventh room itself
    - the ebony clock
    - the masked figure
10. In a sentence or two, summarize what you think is the story's **allegorical meaning**—the symbolic meaning behind the surface narrative. What does that additional level of meaning add to your appreciation of the story?
11. What unanswered questions do you have about this story?
12. Review the ***Connection*** on page 429. What parallels are there between the way Poe's characters react to the Red Death and the way people reacted to the Black Death in Europe?

Evaluation

13. According to Poe, every literary element in a story should be directed to achieve "a certain single effect." Decide what you think Poe's intended effect is in this story. Then, evaluate how well he achieves his goal. Support your evaluation with details from the story.

Writing

The Great Escape

Write a **story** of your own about a group of people who retreat to an isolated place in order to escape some danger. Before you write, decide what emotional effect you want to create in your story: horror? humor? irony? You might even consider writing your story so that it parodies Poe's story, or imitates it in a comical way. Refer to your Quickwrite notes for ideas. Filling out a story map like the one below before you write might help you.

Setting:
Characters:
Problem:
Main events:
Climax:

Reading Standard 3.7 Recognize and understand the significance of various literary devices, including allegory, and explain their appeal.

INDEPENDENT PRACTICE

Literary Response and Analysis

Interpretations

7. Possible answers: "grotesque" masqueraders; "glare and glitter"; "unsuited limbs and appointments"; "delirious fancies"; "madman fashions"; the people were "a multitude of dreams . . ." that "writhed"; they were the color of the rooms.
8. The climax occurs when Prospero rushes to kill the stranger, only to fall down dead himself.
9. Possible answers: *Prince Prospero*—worldly power; wealth; the good life. *The masked ball*—an escape from reality; illusion; fleeting life. *Colors of the seven rooms*—stages of life. *The seventh room itself*—death or the last stage of life. *The ebony clock*—inexorable passing of time. *The masked figure*—death.
10. Possible answers: Life is transient and death comes to everyone—neither wealth nor power can stop it. The allegorical level adds philosophical depth to a fanciful horror story.
11. Answers will vary.
12. Possible answer: Like some people in Europe, the characters in the story try to avoid the disease by having no contact with the outside world. Like others in Europe, Poe's characters eat, drink, and party while the epidemic rages.

Evaluation

13. Possible answer: The single effect may be a morbid melancholy. Supporting details include the many grim pathological details with which the story opens, as well as the grim conclusion.

Reading Check

1. They lock themselves up in Prospero's abbey.
2. They lead a life of wanton excess.
3. They are irregularly arranged, with each room having its own color. The first (easternmost) room is blue; the following rooms are purple, green, orange, white, and violet. The final (westernmost) room is black and scarlet.
4. They are frightened by the blackness of the seventh room, its scarlet windows lit by flickering fires, and its ebony clock marking the hour.
5. They stop what they are doing and feel anxious for a moment.
6. The ball ends when the guests rush to unmask the stranger and find no one in the costume; all then die of the Red Death.

Vocabulary Development

Context Clues: Filling In the Blanks

The **context,** the words and sentences that surround an unfamiliar word, may provide clues to its meaning. There are different kinds of context clues: **definition, restatement, synonym,** and **antonym.** The following sentences about "The Masque of the Red Death" contain context clues that will help you figure out the meaning of the underlined words. The context clues appear in *italic* type.

DEFINITION AND RESTATEMENT
The room's only light came from a brazier. *This metal pan filled with glowing coals* stood outside each window.

SYNONYM
The seventh room brought a ghastly look to the countenances, or *faces,* of all who entered it.

ANTONYM
Everyone at the ball viewed the masked stranger *not with approval* but with disapprobation.

Strategies for Using Context Clues

You've found a word you've never seen before, and you have no idea what it means.

- Think of that unfamiliar word as a blank that needs filling in.
- Determine the word's part of speech.
- Re-read the whole sentence, looking for context clues. Nothing in the sentence? Go back a couple of more sentences and forward one or two.
- Try a few synonyms (or definitions), and see if they make sense in the sentence.

Grade 8 Review Reading Standard 1.3 Use word meanings within the appropriate context and show ability to verify those meanings by definition, restatement, comparison, or contrast.

PRACTICE 1

List the context clues that help you guess the meaning of each underlined word in these sentences from the story. Write what you think each word means, and then check a dictionary.

1. "The 'Red Death' had long devastated the country. No pestilence had ever been so fatal, or so hideous."
2. "The seventh apartment was closely shrouded in black velvet tapestries that hung all over the ceiling and down the walls, falling in heavy folds upon a carpet of the same material and hue."
3. "There was no light of any kind emanating from lamp or candle within the suite of chambers."
4. "The figure was tall and gaunt, and shrouded from head to foot in the habiliments of the grave."
5. "The mask which concealed the visage was made so nearly to resemble the countenance of a stiffened corpse that the closest scrutiny must have had difficulty in detecting the cheat."
6. "And the whole seizure, progress, and termination of the disease were the incidents of half an hour."

PRACTICE 2

For each word in the **Word Bank,** write an original sentence that contains a **context clue**. Consider using definitions, restatements, synonyms, or antonyms. Exchange sentences with a partner, and underline the clues.

Word Bank
profuse
sagacious
contagion
imperial
emanating
sedate
pervaded
cessation
propriety
tangible

Vocabulary Development

Practice 1

1. *Context clue*—"devastated." *Word's meaning*—disease.
2. *Context clues*—"hung all over"; "falling . . . upon." *Word's meaning*—covered. *Context clues*—"black"; "same." *Word's meaning*—color.
3. *Context clue*—"from." *Word's meaning*—coming out.
4. *Context clue*—"shrouded." *Word's meaning*—clothing.
5. *Context clues*—"mask which concealed"; "countenance." *Word's meaning*—face.
6. *Context clues*—"seizure, progress"; "incidents of half an hour." *Word's meaning*—ending.

Practice 2

Possible Answers

1. The Red Death caused *profuse*, or abundant, bleeding.
2. The prince was a *sagacious* man; his wisdom was sound.
3. The Red Death spread; there was no avoiding the *contagion*.
4. One thousand guests were invited to the *imperial* palace.
5. There was merriment *emanating*, or coming from, the palace.
6. Some guests were *sedate*; others celebrated wildly.
7. Cheerfulness *pervaded* the festivities, spreading to everyone.
8. Each time the clock struck, there was a *cessation* of fun which began again afterward.
9. The crowd saw little *propriety* in the stranger's odd behavior.
10. The stranger took no *tangible* form—there was nothing to touch beneath his mask.

Resources Reminder

Vocabulary

- *Vocabulary Development*
  - Vocabulary Worksheet, p. 35
  - Cumulative Vocabulary Review, pp. 36–37
- *Lesson Plans for Language Development*
  - Vocabulary, pp. 194, 198

ASSESSING

Assessment

- *Progress Assessment of Reading*
  - Selection Test

RETEACHING

For a lesson reteaching Standard 3.7, see **Reteaching,** p. 939A. For another selection to teach Standard 3.7, see *Interactive Reading,* Chapter 6.

432 Chapter 6 Symbolism and Allegory • Synthesizing Sources

Before You Read

Stopping by Woods on a Snowy Evening
After Apple-Picking

Literary Focus

Symbolic Meaning: What Lies Beneath the Surface

Literally, snow is snow, a horse is a horse, woods are woods, and apples are apples. In the hands of a poet, however, ordinary things become **symbols**—that is, they stand for things other than themselves and suggest deeper layers of meaning. There's much more to these two poems by Robert Frost than a literal pause in a wintry journey and a rest after a hard day's apple picking.

So how can you tell when a poem has **symbolic meaning**? Be alert to clues the poet plants—repetition, emphasis, word associations, and mysterious images. Even though symbolic meanings in a poem may be difficult to pin down and express precisely, symbols appeal powerfully to our emotions and our imaginations.

Reading Skills

Monitoring Your Reading: Re-reading

Read each of these poems several times to understand them better.

As you re-read, take notes in a chart like the one at the top of the next column. Focus on one poem at a time, and follow these guidelines:

- On your second reading, jot down what you see in the poem—its visual images and what is happening.
- On your third reading of "Stopping by Woods on a Snowy Evening," jot down all the things you think are going through the traveler's mind as he gazes at the woods.
- On your third reading of "After Apple-Picking," jot down what you think "harvest" stands for on a deeper level.

Keep your notes.

	"Stopping by Woods on a Snowy Evening"	"After Apple-Picking"
Second Reading		
Third Reading		

Make the Connection

Quickwrite

Take a few minutes to jot down all of the **images, connotations,** and any other kinds of **associations** that occur to you for these words: *sleep, woods, dreaming, apples, apple-picking.* You can take notes in a chart like the one below:

	Images	Connotations/ Associations
Sleep		
Woods		
Dreaming		
Apples		
Apple-picking		

Reading Standard 3.7 Recognize and understand the significance of various literary devices, including symbolism, and explain their appeal.

STANDARDS FOCUS, pp. 433–438

(For the grade-level standard taught in this lesson, see citations on Student Edition pages.)

Summary *at grade level*

These two poems exhibit Frost's trademarks: rural settings, plain language with the natural rhythms of everyday speech, and images that invest the familiar with symbolic depth.

In "Stopping by Woods on a Snowy Evening," the speaker stops near an isolated wood. In a literal interpretation, he is tempted to stay because the woods are "lovely, dark, and deep," but he reminds himself of his "promises" and the miles still to go. Symbolically, however, the "sleep" the speaker mentions may stand for the peace found in death or an escape from his "promises"—the responsibilities that link him to his life.

Summary *above grade level*

On a literal level, "After Apple-Picking" is about a man who drifts off to sleep after a long, hard day of picking apples. He knows he will dream of the sight and the "rumbling sound / Of load on load of apples coming in." The poem is filled with images that may have symbolic meanings—from the ladder pointing toward heaven (a reminder of death) and the unfilled barrel (tasks yet to complete in life) to the "great harvest" (success in life) and the "Long sleep" (death).

RESOURCES: READING

Planning

- *One-Stop Planner* CD-ROM with Test Generator
- *On Course: Mapping Instruction*

Media

- *Audio CD Library*
  - disc 12
- *Visual Connections*
  - Videocassette, Segment 6

Reading

- *Interactive Reading,* Teacher's Edition
  - Graphic Organizer: Symbol Chart

Differentiating Instruction

- *Lesson Plans for Language Development*
  - English-Language Learners, pp. 187, 195, 198
  - Special Education Students, pp. 188, 195, 198

Assessment

- *Progress Assessment of Reading*
  - Selection Test
- *One-Stop Planner* CD-ROM with Test Generator

PRETEACHING

Standards Starter

Build prerequisite skills. Remind students that symbols are everyday things that have double meanings. An eagle, for example, is a powerful bird that is also used to represent the United States. Call on volunteers to quickly name other animals or objects that are used as symbols and to identify their literal and symbolic meanings.

DIRECT TEACHING

A Learners Having Difficulty

Reading inverted sentences. Remind students that poets often invert sentences to fit the rhyme and rhythm of a poem. Help students to clarify the meaning of the first line by locating the subject and restating the sentence in normal word order. [I think I know whose woods these are.]

B Literary Focus
GRADE-LEVEL STANDARD

Symbolism. What is the literal meaning of "the darkest evening of the year"? [Possible response: It is the winter solstice, the day that has the fewest hours of daylight.] What symbolic meaning might "the darkest evening" have? [Possible responses: mystery; sadness; a spiritual low point.]

C Literary Focus
GRADE-LEVEL STANDARD

Symbolism. On a symbolic level, what is attractive about the woods? [Possible response: They represent an escape from the responsibilities of human life.] The speaker rejects the woods, explaining that he has "miles to go before I sleep." What might "miles to go" symbolize? [Possible responses: duties to fulfill; the years before the speaker will die.]

Stopping by Woods on a Snowy Evening

Robert Frost

A
Whose woods these are I think I know.
His house is in the village, though;
He will not see me stopping here
To watch his woods fill up with snow.

My little horse must think it queer
To stop without a farmhouse near
Between the woods and frozen lake
B The darkest evening of the year.

He gives his harness bells a shake
To ask if there is some mistake.
The only other sound's the sweep
Of easy wind and downy flake.

C
The woods are lovely, dark, and deep,
But I have promises to keep,
And miles to go before I sleep,
And miles to go before I sleep.

DIFFERENTIATING INSTRUCTION

English-Language Learners

To help students hear the rhythm of the poems and visualize the images, have them listen to the recording in the *Audio CD Library.* Then, pair students with more proficient readers, and have the partners take turns reading the poems aloud. Pairs can then work together to break down difficult lines and discuss possible symbols.

Resources Reminder

For lessons designed for intermediate and advanced English-language learners, see *Lesson Plans for Language Development,* pp. 187, 195, 198.

Special Education Students

For lessons designed for special education students, see *Lesson Plans for Language Development,* pp. 188, 195, 198.

After Apple-Picking

Robert Frost

My long two-pointed ladder's sticking through a tree
Toward heaven still,
And there's a barrel that I didn't fill
Beside it, and there may be two or three
Apples I didn't pick upon some bough.
But I am done with apple-picking now.
Essence of winter sleep is on the night,
The scent of apples: I am drowsing off.
I cannot rub the strangeness from my sight
I got from looking through a pane of glass
I skimmed this morning from the drinking trough
And held against the world of hoary° grass.
It melted, and I let it fall and break.
But I was well
Upon my way to sleep before it fell,
And I could tell
What form my dreaming was about to take.
Magnified apples appear and disappear,
Stem end and blossom end,
And every fleck of russet showing clear.
My instep arch not only keeps the ache,
It keeps the pressure of a ladder-round.
I feel the ladder sway as the boughs bend.
And I keep hearing from the cellar bin
The rumbling sound
Of load on load of apples coming in.
For I have had too much
Of apple-picking: I am overtired
Of the great harvest I myself desired.
There were ten thousand thousand fruit to touch,
Cherish in hand, lift down, and not let fall.

Apples (1867) by Worthington Whittredge.

12. **hoary:** (hôr′ē) *adj.:* covered with hoarfrost, white crystals of ice. *Hoary* also means "very old; ancient."

DIRECT TEACHING

D Literary Focus GRADE-LEVEL STANDARD

Symbolism. On the literal level, what situation is described in these lines? [Possible response: The speaker's ladder is still in the tree; he missed a few apples; he left one barrel unfilled, but he is done picking apples.] **What might the ladder pointing toward heaven symbolize?** [Possible responses: thoughts of the afterlife; spiritual longings.] **What might the unfilled barrel and apples symbolize?** [Possible response: the unfinished tasks of life.]

E Learners Having Difficulty

Finding sequence of events. Point out that the poem is not in chronological order. What time of day is it in ll. 7–8, and what is the speaker doing? [It is night, and the speaker is getting ready to go to sleep.] **Do ll. 9–13 refer to a time before or after ll. 7–8? Explain.** [Before; ll. 9–13 refer to an incident that took place that morning.]

F Reading Skills

Interpreting. Literally speaking, what is the "pane of glass" that the speaker skimmed from the trough, and why did the world look strange through it? [Possible response: The pane is a layer of ice through which images appear indistinct.] **What symbolic meaning might this passage have?** [Possible responses: The speaker is hovering between two worlds—conscious wakefulness and the subconscious world of sleep and dreams. The ice might represent a window between these worlds.]

G Literary Focus GRADE-LEVEL STANDARD

Symbolism. The speaker reiterates that he is tired of apple-picking. What might "apple-picking" and "the great harvest" symbolize? [Possible responses: "Apple-picking" might symbolize everyday work. The "great harvest" might be a life's work or recognition for that work.]

Advanced Learners

Acceleration. Use this activity to move advanced learners toward the eleventh- and twelfth-grade Standard 3.2, for which they analyze the ways in which the theme of a selection represents a view or comment on life, using textual evidence to support the claim.

Activity. Tell students that Frost insisted that he did not repeat the last lines of "Stopping by Woods . . ." to invoke the journey toward death. Instead, he claimed the repetition was supposed to suggest the speaker's dreamlike state. Ask students whether they believe Frost's statement. Students should back up their opinions with words and lines from the poem.

After Apple-Picking 435

For all
That struck the earth,
No matter if not bruised or spiked with stubble,
Went surely to the cider-apple heap
As of no worth.
One can see what will trouble
This sleep of mine, whatever sleep it is.
Were he not gone,
The woodchuck could say whether it's like his
Long sleep, as I describe its coming on,
Or just some human sleep.

Apple Harvest by Levi Wells Prentice (1851–1935).

DIRECT TEACHING

A Literary Focus
GRADE-LEVEL STANDARD

Symbolism. What are the literal and symbolic meanings of the things troubling the speaker's sleep? [Possible response: On the literal level, the tasks and memories of the day are troubling his sleep. On the symbolic level, he is worrying about life tasks undone or not done well enough.]

B Content-Area Connections

Science: Woodchuck
The woodchuck's "Long sleep" is a reference to this animal's hibernation. Woodchucks, or groundhogs, hibernate for an extended period. They burrow deep underground in early fall and remain there until February or March.

VIEWING THE ART

While living in upstate New York, **Levi Wells Prentice** (1835–1935) began his career painting the Adirondack Mountains and the regions around Syracuse and Buffalo. When he moved to Brooklyn in 1883, however, Prentice preferred to paint still lifes. Most of the still lifes from this period depict fruit, especially apples.
Activity. Ask students to consider why Prentice turned to painting still lifes after he moved to Brooklyn. [Possible response: In his upstate environs, Prentice could paint the vast landscapes that surrounded him; living in the city, Prentice may have spent more of his time confined to the indoors where it was easier to depict natural subjects with still lifes.]

CONTENT-AREA CONNECTIONS

Science: Solstice and Equinox
Living among farmers, Frost would probably have been aware of the changing length of days throughout the year—from the longest day (summer solstice) to the shortest day (winter solstice). In between are the spring and fall equinoxes, when the hours of light and darkness are the same length.

Paired activity. Invite pairs of students to research the causes of varying day lengths. Students can report to the class, using diagrams or models to clarify the report.

Meet the Writer

Robert Frost

Beneath the Surface

Robert Frost (1874–1963), whom most Americans consider the voice of rural New England, was born in San Francisco and lived as a child in the industrial city of Lawrence, Massachusetts. He attended Dartmouth College for a few months but left to write poetry and work in a cotton mill. Years later, after he had become a husband and father, Frost returned to college but left after two years, again to write seriously.

In 1912, Frost moved his young family to England. During the three years he spent there, he wrote and published two books of poems—*A Boy's Will* (1913) and *North of Boston* (1914)—which were immediate successes on both sides of the Atlantic.

Frost went home to New England in 1915, finally able to make his living as a poet. During his long career he won four Pulitzer Prizes and often gave public readings and lectures. One of his last public appearances was at the 1961 inauguration of President John F. Kennedy, where he recited his poem "The Gift Outright."

Like the independent New England farmers he frequently wrote about, Frost went his own way. He refused to join his contemporaries in their experimental search for new poetic forms, finding all the freedom he needed within the bounds of traditional verse. Despite their apparently homespun subjects and traditional form, Frost's poems are only seemingly simple. Beneath their surface is a complex and often dark view of human life and personality. Frost said:

> "Like a piece of ice on a hot stove, the poem must ride on its own melting. . . . Read it a hundred times; it will forever keep its freshness as a metal keeps its fragrance. It can never lose its sense of a meaning that once unfolded by surprise as it went."

For Independent Reading

In a collection of Frost's poetry, read these all-time favorites: "The Road Not Taken," "Birches," "Acquainted with the Night," "Design," "Desert Places," and "The Gift Outright." Browse a little, and you'll discover favorites of your own to share with your classmates.

GUIDED PRACTICE

Monitoring students' progress. Guide the class in answering these comprehension questions.

True-False

1. The speaker in "Stopping by Woods . . ." does not know whose woods he is in. [F]
2. The speaker is frightened by the silence of the woods. [F]
3. The speaker leaves the woods regretfully. [T]
4. The speaker in "After Apple-Picking" sees various images from the day as he drifts to sleep. [T]
5. The speaker is at peace with the harvest. [F]

Meet the Writer

Background. At one point in his life Robert Frost was a farmer in Derry, New Hampshire. However, Frost himself declared he was too lazy to learn how to be a competent farmer. For instance, because he usually spent his evenings reading and writing poetry until late, Frost hated leaving his bed early in the morning to milk his only cow. His solution to this problem was to readjust his cow's schedule gradually so that he could milk her at noon and at midnight.

For Independent Reading

If students choose to read a collection of Frost's poetry, ask them to share a favorite poem with the class. Challenge students to explain why they enjoy the poem and, if applicable, how the poem's imagery, theme, or message relates to their own life.

DIFFERENTIATING INSTRUCTION

Advanced Learners

Enrichment. Dr. Donald J. Greiner, associate provost at the University of South Carolina, writes, "One might . . . consider that the greatness of ["Stopping by Woods . . ."] rests in part in its ambiguity and that the ambiguity derives from the speaker's hesitation. Literally, he has not moved at the end of the final stanza, and metaphorically he is frozen with indecision."

Small-group activity. Have small groups of students discuss this interpretation of the poem and decide whether they agree with it. They may wish to read other interpretations of the poem before they reach their final decision. Suggest that they enter the keywords *Robert Frost* or *Stopping by Woods on a Snowy Evening* plus *criticism* or *interpretation* in an Internet search engine. Have students share the results of their research and their final interpretation with their groups.

INDEPENDENT PRACTICE

Literary Response and Analysis

Reading Check

1. In "Stopping by Woods . . .," a person stops his horse to watch the snow fall in the woods and then moves on because he has things to do. In "After Apple-Picking," thoughts and images of the day and of the apple harvest float through the speaker's mind as he falls asleep after a hard day's work.

Interpretations

2. He may be thinking of the distance he must go before sleeping that night. He might be referring to the metaphorical sleep of death.
3. The woods may symbolize a peaceful place free of stress and responsibilities. The speaker has said no to lingering, to his desire to rest, to abandoning life's struggles.
4. The traveler has decided to return to the duties and demands of life. He wants to fulfill the "promises" he has made.
5. wealth, achievements, recognition
6. If apples symbolize earthly desires, the speaker may have gotten too much of what he thought he wanted. The speaker feels neither joy nor satisfaction, but exhaustion from his achievement.
7. The speaker seems to be referring to regular nightly sleep or to slipping away into the subconscious world of dreams, not to the sleep of death that the last line of "Stopping by Woods . . ." seems to invoke.
8. Answers will vary.
9. *"Stopping by Woods . . ."*—Powerful desires often pull people in one direction while daily responsibilities pull them in another. *"After Apple-Picking"*—People work hard to achieve worldly goals, only to find success less than satisfying.

Literary Response and Analysis

Stopping by Woods on a Snowy Evening
After Apple-Picking

Reading Check

1. For each poem, summarize what is **literally** happening in the poem. (Check your re-reading notes.)

Interpretations

2. In "Stopping by Woods on a Snowy Evening," the speaker says he has miles to go before he can sleep. What is he probably thinking of? What other, **metaphorical** sleep might he be referring to?
3. The big question set up by the poem is what those lovely, dark, and deep woods **symbolize** to the traveler. What do you think? What has the speaker said no to in passing them by?
4. Whatever the woods stand for, what has the speaker said yes to in deciding to go on? In other words, how has he resolved his **conflict**?
5. On a **symbolic** level, what do you think is "the great harvest" that the speaker in "After Apple-Picking" once valued (see lines 28–36)?
6. What is suggested by the speaker's statement that he is "overtired" of the great harvest he once wanted?
7. In "After Apple-Picking," trace the speaker's state of drowsiness and dreaming. (Note, for example, how many times the word *sleep* occurs and when a dream passage begins.) What kind of sleep do you think the speaker is talking about? **Compare** it to the sleep in lines 15–16 of "Stopping by Woods on a Snowy Evening."
8. Look at your Quickwrite notes. How have your associations with the words *sleep, woods,* and *apple-picking* changed after reading these poems?
9. The **theme** of a poem is an insight into life that the poet wants to convey. Try to express what you think is the theme of each poem.

Reading Standard 3.7 Recognize and understand the significance of various literary devices, including symbolism, and explain their appeal.

Comparing Poems

Alike yet Different

Write a brief **comparison-contrast essay** for these two poems. You might begin by taking notes in a chart like the one below. (See pages 254 and 283 for help with a comparison-contrast essay.)

	"Stopping by Woods on a Snowy Evening"	"After Apple-Picking"
Speaker		
Situation		
Setting/season		
Repeated words		
Symbols		
Theme		

Listening and Speaking

Oral Interpretation

Choose one of these poems to prepare for an **oral interpretation.** You'll have to make these decisions: Will you use a single voice or several? When will you slow down? speed up? pause for effect? Will you set the poem to music? Will you arrange it as a ballad? a hymn? a rock song? a rap song?

ASSESSING

Assessment

- *Progress Assessment of Reading*
  - Selection Test

RETEACHING

For a lesson reteaching Standard 3.7, see **Reteaching,** p. 939A. For another selection to teach Standard 3.7, see *Interactive Reading,* Chapter 6.

438 Chapter 6 Symbolism and Allegory • Synthesizing Sources

Read On: FOR INDEPENDENT READING

FICTION

A Rabbit Odyssey

When land developers begin to dig up the English countryside, they have no idea that their labor means life or death for a band of talking rabbits. Led by brave Hazel, eleven of the rabbits set off on a dangerous journey—battling illness, injuries, and evil animals—in search of a new place to live. If you're in the mood for an action-packed fantasy—one that also serves as a rich allegorical tale of human beings and nature—then Richard Adams's ***Watership Down*** is the book for you.

FICTION

Fateful Friendship

The Devon School, with its beautiful, tree-lined campus, seems a safe haven for boys during World War II. Gene, a lonely sixteen-year-old, is assigned the perfect roommate: athletic, fun-loving Finny, who drags Gene away from his schoolbooks and into the real world. Then friendship turns into rivalry, and rivalry turns into something far more sinister. ***A Separate Peace*** by John Knowles is the story of two boys whose struggle mirrors the terrible war being fought beyond campus walls.

This title is available in the HRW Library.

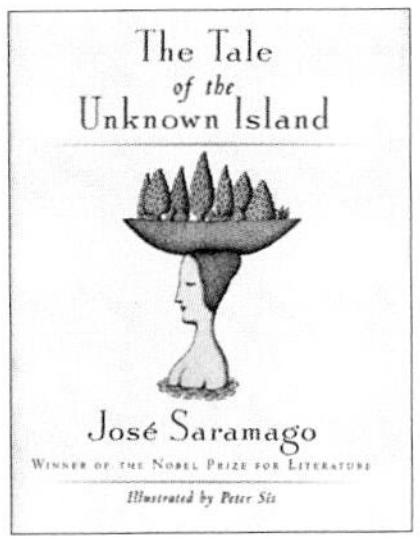

FICTION

In a Faraway Land

The Tale of the Unknown Island, by the Nobel Prize–winning author José Saramago, starts out as simply as a fairy tale: Wanting to discover an unknown island, a man goes to the king's door and asks for a boat. A palace cleaning woman overhears his request and follows the man, since she has never seen an unknown island herself. Their journey becomes a moving allegory of love and discovery, loss and gain—all revealed in a timeless story packed with substance, humor, and truth.

NONFICTION

Questions of Identity

In her autobiography, ***Black Ice,*** Lorene Cary tells of the difficult choices she had to make when she moved from her African American neighborhood in Philadelphia to an elite, formerly all-white prep school in New Hampshire. Thrust into an intimidating and unfamiliar setting, Cary began to question how to become a part of school life without sacrificing her own very distinct identity and values. Cary's struggle to succeed without seeming to betray her heritage is recorded with gutsy honesty.

Toward Reading Two Million Words Annually

Estimated Word Counts and Reading Levels of Read On Books:

Fiction			Nonfiction		
Watership Down	↓	191,200	*Black Ice**	↔	96,300
*A Separate Peace**	↔	88,200			
*The Tale of the Unknown Island**	↑	6,500			

***California Reading List Titles**

KEY: ↑ *above grade level* ↔ *at grade level* ↓ *below grade level*

Read On

For Independent Reading

If students enjoyed the themes and topics explored in this chapter, you might recommend these titles for independent reading.

Assessment Options

The following projects can help you evaluate and assess your students' outside reading. Videotapes or audiotapes of completed projects may be included in student portfolios.

- **Make a wall mural.** Have students create a mural showing the highlights of the rabbits' struggles in *Watership Down.* Students may work in groups to brainstorm ideas for images based on details from the novel. Assign each group a section of the mural. When the mural is complete, have each group explain to the class the action and events portrayed in their section.
- **Write a proposal.** Suggest that students who read *A Separate Peace* write a proposal of how they would adapt the novel to film. Students should focus on characterization (casting actors to portray Gene and Finny and giving reasons for their choices); setting (describing sets and props that would be needed); plot (outlining the conflict, major events, and the climax); and the themes of friendship, loyalty, jealousy, and betrayal. Students should conclude by making a strong case for filming the novel.
- **Interview the author.** Tell students to imagine that they have been granted an interview with Lorene Cary. Have pairs work together to list thought-provoking questions regarding Cary's life story as she relates it in *Black Ice.* Then, have partners create answers that she might give. Next, partners should perform the roles of Cary and the interviewer for the class. Then, have a question-and-answer session so that any student can ask "Cary" additional questions about her life.

Analyzing a Short Story

Writing Assignment
Writing 2.2 Write a response to literature in which you analyze the literary elements of a short story.

What makes a short story like Tom Godwin's "The Cold Equations" (page 164) compelling and memorable? One way to find out is through analysis. When you do a **literary analysis,** you take a critical and objective look at how a writer uses the elements of literature to create a unique work of literary art. A close analysis of a piece of literature gives you insight into how the author crafted the work and adds to your understanding of it.

Prewriting

GO TO: go.hrw.com
KEYWORD: HLLA 10-6
FOR: Professional Model, Writer's Guides, and Reference Sources

Choose a Story

The Choice Is Yours To choose an appropriate short story to analyze, consider stories you have already read and enjoyed as well as those recommended by others. Also consider stories by authors whose other works you have enjoyed. Your analysis will have to be 1,500 words long, so be sure to choose a story that is complex and rich in meaning.

Analyze the Story and Develop a Thesis

Take a Closer Look Read your story once to get an overall grasp of it. Then, discover what makes the story unique. To do that, analyze how the author uses the basic **elements of fiction.** The following chart defines these elements and provides questions you can answer about each one.

Quick guide

ANALYZING ELEMENTS OF FICTION

Element	Analysis Questions
Plot is the action or series of events depicted in the story.	• What is the **conflict,** or main problem, and who is involved in the story? • What is the story's **climax**—the most intense moment in the plot? • How is the conflict resolved? Is the **resolution** logical? • Do events happen in a predictable way, or does the writer build suspense by creating doubt about how the conflict will be resolved?
Setting is the time and place in which the story occurs.	• Where and when does the story take place? • Does the setting affect the plot, the characters, or the mood or atmosphere of the story? How?

(continued)

PRETEACHING

Standards Starter

Motivate. Ask students to think of a story or book they have read that they would recommend to others. Then, have students offer reasons why they recommend the work. Make a list of the reasons on the chalkboard. Point out that students have just engaged in a form of analysis.

Resources Reminder

To introduce the workshop, you may want to use the journal starters in *Writing, Listening, & Speaking* Teaching Notes.

TECHNOLOGY TIP

Remind students that each page of double-spaced, typed manuscript contains approximately 250 words. Therefore, a 1,500-word essay is usually between five and seven pages long. (The length will vary depending on which font and font size the student chooses.)

DIRECT TEACHING

GRADE-LEVEL STANDARD

Analyzing Elements of Fiction

Ask students to name television shows they enjoy watching. Ask them if the setting of each show is weak (not essential to the plot) or strong (strongly influences the plot), and have them explain their answers. Remind students that setting is also an important element in literature. In their essays, have students use specific textual references to evaluate and discuss the importance of a story's setting.

CHAPTER 6 RESOURCES: WRITING

Writing Workshop

Planning

- *On Course: Mapping Instruction*
- *One-Stop Planner* CD-ROM
- *Writing, Listening, & Speaking,* Teaching Notes, p. 56

Differentiating Instruction

- *Lesson Plans for Language Development,* pp. 189–190
- *Supporting Instruction in Spanish*

Practice

- *Writing, Listening, & Speaking,* Ch. 6

Reinforcement

- *Daily Language Activities*

(continued)

Characters are the individuals in a story.	• What are the major characters like? • What motivates the characters to behave as they do? • Do any of the characters change? If so, how and why?
Theme is an important idea about life.	• What important idea about life or human nature does the story reveal? • Do other elements, such as plot or characters, play a role in the development of the theme? If so, how?
Stylistic devices are the techniques a writer uses to create certain effects in a work.	• Does the writer's **diction,** or choice of important words, affect the tone of the story? How? • Does the writer use **imagery**—language that appeals to the senses? What is the effect of such imagery on the story? • Does the writer make imaginative comparisons through the use of **figurative language**—metaphor, simile, and personification?

Pick Your Target For your analysis, zero in on the element or elements that seem to dominate the story. Dominant elements will usually be the ones for which you have the most specific information. For example, based on his answers to the questions in the chart, one student analyzing "The Cold Equations" chose to focus on the story's plot.

Next, identify your main idea, or **thesis,** about the element or elements on which your analysis will focus. Draw a conclusion about the role of the focus element or elements in the story. Then, draft a thesis statement that includes the story's title and author and this conclusion. Here's one writer's working thesis statement, which he revised during drafting.

DO THIS

Focus element: plot
Conclusion: The story's powerful effect is a result of the suspense the writer builds into the plot.
Thesis statement: In "The Cold Equations," author Tom Godwin builds a plot tingling with suspense to create a memorable story.

Gather and Organize Support

Focusing In Support for a literary analysis includes **key points** to support your thesis, **details** from the story to provide evidence for the key points, and **elaboration** to link the details to the key points.

Key Points Key points are the aspects of the story that led you to the conclusion in your thesis statement. The student analyzing "The Cold Equations" decided that the suspense in the story came from the unknown identity of the stowaway, withheld information, and the question of whether Marilyn would contact her brother in time.

Writing 1.0 Students write essays that convey a tightly reasoned argument. **1.1** Establish a coherent thesis that conveys a clear and distinctive perspective on the subject. **2.0** Students produce texts of at least 1,500 words. **2.2** Write responses to literature. **2.2c** Demonstrate awareness of the author's use of stylistic devices and an appreciation of the effects created.

DIRECT TEACHING

Integrating with Grammar, Usage, and Mechanics

As students start their short story analyses, they may have trouble with capitalization and punctuation. You may want to review the corresponding chapters in the *Holt Handbook.*

Pick Your Target

Tell students that their thesis statements can focus on any short story element. They might create a thesis similar to one of the following examples.

1. In "A Short Story" by Jane Doe, a series of events causes the main character to change the views he has held since he was a child. [This thesis statement focuses on plot.]
2. In "A Short Story," author John Smith uses imagery to create a sense of tranquility for the reader in spite of the story's violent plot. [This thesis statement focuses on a stylistic device.]

Evaluation and Assessment

- *Test Generator (One-Stop Planner* CD-ROM)
- *Progress Assessment of Writing, Listening, & Speaking,* Ch. 6
- *Diagnostic and Summative Assessments,* Third-Quarter Test

Internet

- go.hrw.com (keyword: HLLA 10-6)
- Online assessments at go.hrw.com (keyword: HLLA)

DIRECT TEACHING

REVIEW STANDARD

Supporting Details

Encourage students to evaluate the relative value and significance of their textual support. Specifically, have them consider the quality of their evidence over the quantity. For example, a student might find fourteen similes in a story but only one example of a character that changes dramatically. Rather than simply choosing to write about figurative language because he or she has more examples, the student must decide which kind of textual support better interprets the story.

DIFFERENTIATING INSTRUCTION

English-Language Learners

Students who are learning English may find it difficult to read, comprehend, and successfully analyze a short story. You might want to have all English-Language Learners read the same short story aloud. You can sit in on the reading and lead frequent discussions about the literary elements in the story and also help students form thesis statements.

PRACTICE & APPLY 1

Guided and Independent Practice

Before students complete **Practice and Apply 1,** have them present to a small group the evidence from their stories that supports their thesis statements. The group should judge whether the evidence is sufficient and specific enough to prove each thesis. Students can also suggest ways for the presenters to strengthen their theses. Then, have students complete **Practice and Apply 1** as independent practice, taking into account the suggestions they have received.

Reference Note

For more on **direct quotations, paraphrases,** and **summaries,** see page 695.

Supporting Details To support your key points, use **references to the text**—details from the story in the form of direct quotations, paraphrases of passages, or summaries of ideas. You may also wish to consult professional works of literary analysis for support of your key points.

Elaboration Elaborate on supporting details to show that you have an understanding of the **significant ideas** in the short story. In other words, explain *how* your supporting details connect to key points.

Your elaboration might include a discussion of the **ambiguities, nuances,** and **complexities** of the work—three characteristics that give literature richness and depth.

- **Ambiguities** are situations that can be interpreted in more than one way.
- **Nuances** are slight variations in tone or meaning.
- **Complexities** exist when a story is rich in meaning but difficult to interpret.

Look at the partial chart below to see how the student writer started with a key point, found a detail to support that point, and then elaborated with an explanation. You can create a chart of your own to map out your key points, supporting details, and elaboration.

TIP When discussing events from a story, use the **literary present tense.** That is, refer to the events in the story as if they were happening right now. For example, write, "Marilyn hopes to visit her brother," not "Marilyn hoped to visit her brother."

Key Point	Supporting Detail	Elaboration
The author reveals the presence, but not the identity, of someone on the ship.	Quotation: "He was not alone. . . . There was something in the supply closet across the room . . . a living, human body."	The suspense comes from questions raised in the reader's mind: Why is the pilot supposed to be alone? Who is the stowaway in the closet? Is this person dangerous?

Get It in Order Your key points may suggest an **organizational pattern** for arranging your analysis. In an analysis of plot or character development, you might discuss key points in **chronological order**—the order in which they occurred in the story. For an analysis examining theme, you might use **order of importance,** explaining key points from most important to least important, or vice versa. Look at your key points. Which organizational pattern will you use?

Writing 2.2a Demonstrate a comprehensive grasp of the significant ideas of a literary work. **2.2b** Support important ideas and viewpoints through accurate and detailed references to the text or to other works. **2.2d** Identify and assess the impact of perceived ambiguities, nuances, and complexities within the text.

PRACTICE & APPLY 1 Use the instructions on pages 440–442 to choose and analyze a short story. Find a focus element, develop a thesis statement, and back up the thesis statement with key points, supporting details, and elaboration.

RESOURCES: WRITING

Practice & Apply 1

Guided Practice

- *Writing, Listening, & Speaking,* WS. pp. 57, 58

Reteaching and Modeling

- *Writing, Listening, & Speaking,* TP. 11
- *Writing, Listening, & Speaking,* WS. p. 59

442 Chapter 6 Symbolism and Allegory • Synthesizing Sources

Writing

Analyzing a Short Story

A Writer's Framework

Introduction

- Open with an interesting comment on the story, such as an observation related to your thesis.
- Include a thesis statement that names the story's title and author and states your conclusion about the element or elements your analysis focuses on.

Body

- Arrange your key points in chronological order or by order of importance.
- Back up key points with supporting details in the form of direct quotations, paraphrases, and summaries.
- Elaborate on supporting details by explaining how they support the key points.

Conclusion

- Summarize your key points.
- Restate your thesis, using different words.
- Leave readers with something to consider, such as a general comment about the story that relates to your thesis.

A Writer's Model

Suspense in "The Cold Equations"

Space is widely considered the last frontier, the last great challenge to human exploration. Because space exploration is dangerous, strict rules based on our understanding of the laws of nature must be made and followed. Can the dangers and demands of this final frontier also take human nature into account? In "The Cold Equations," author Tom Godwin uses plot developments to build suspense progressively as he explores this complex question.

INTRODUCTION
Interesting comment
Complexity suggested
Thesis statement

Godwin begins creating suspense in the very first scene by revealing the presence, but not the identity, of someone aboard the Emergency Dispatch Ship other than Barton, the pilot: "He was not alone. . . . There was something in the supply closet across the room . . . a living, human body." These statements raise questions in the reader's mind. Is Barton supposed to be alone? Who is the stowaway, and is the person dangerous? Barton considers the necessary fate of all stowaways—death—making the reader more anxious. Then, when Barton realizes that the intruder is an innocent teenager, it hits him—and the reader—"like a heavy and unexpected physical blow." Now the question is: Will Barton really kill a defenseless teenager?

BODY
Key point 1
Supporting detail
Elaboration

(continued)

CRITICAL THINKING

A Writer's Model

Begin a class discussion about **A Writer's Model,** encouraging students to think about how they might apply the answers to the following questions to their own analyses.

- How effectively do the writer's introductory comments lay a foundation for the thesis statement?
- Does the writer list key points in chronological order or order of importance? Is the writer's choice effective?
- How do you respond to the writer's conclusion? Can you think of a better conclusion?

MODELING AND DEMONSTRATION

A Writer's Model

To model the correct use and punctuation of the ellipsis, write on the chalkboard the first quote from "The Cold Equations" found in the second paragraph of **A Writer's Model.** Ask students to explain why the first and second ellipses are different. [The first example has a period because it ends a sentence, whereas the second example does not have a period because it joins two parts of a sentence.] Have volunteers demonstrate their understanding of the difference between the two by picking complete sentences from the same passage, removing parts of those sentences, and correctly punctuating the remaining parts with ellipses.

DIFFERENTIATING INSTRUCTION

Learners Having Difficulty

Students may have difficulty finding the best textual support for their ideas. To help them make sure they have expressed their ideas and adequately supported and elaborated on them, have them work with a partner. Partners can read each other's papers and determine whether points are clear and adequately supported. Points should be clear despite the students' not having read each other's stories.

RETEACHING

A Writer's Model

To help students avoid the words *I, me, my,* and *mine* when writing a literary analysis, remind them to reword statements or use the pronoun *one*. Provide students with the following examples.

Incorrect: The result is suspense, which kept me uncertain and anxious right up to the story's tragic end.

Correct: The result is suspense, which keeps the reader uncertain and anxious right up to the story's tragic end.

PRACTICE & APPLY 2

Guided and Independent Practice

To prevent students from becoming frustrated while beginning their drafts, guide them by alloting a half-hour to deal with any questions or difficulties that come up. Then, have students complete **Practice and Apply 2** as independent practice. Depending on student progress, you may want to schedule at least one more day in class for writing.

(continued)

Key point 2 Supporting details Elaboration Nuance explained	Godwin intensifies the suspense by withholding until nearly halfway through the story just how long Marilyn, the young stowaway, has to live. After Barton questions her about how and why she stowed away, he slows the rate of the ship's deceleration to conserve fuel. He does not believe that his action will change the outcome of events, but it is all he can do to postpone the unavoidable. Next, he calls Commander Delhart of the *Stardust*, the ship on which Marilyn had been traveling. He is sure this action is also "futile" since the spaceship will not be able to turn back for her. Still, he pursues this "one vain hope" to save Marilyn. Wanting to give her as much time as possible to accept her fate, he puts off calculating the deadline until Commander Delhart orders him to do so. All these delays create suspense by seeming to leave open the possibility that Marilyn may somehow be rescued. To add to this suspense, the author repeats both the cold rules of space travel and Marilyn's human, emotional pleas. Readers are forced to see the subtle difference in the tone created by the language of the rules and the tone created by Marilyn's language.
Key point 3 Supporting details Elaboration	With time running out for Marilyn, the author further increases the suspense by making her brother temporarily unreachable. When Barton contacts Gerry's base station on the planet Woden, Gerry is out in a helicopter that does not have a working radio. He is expected back at the camp soon—"in less than an hour at the most"—but Marilyn has less than an hour to live. Meanwhile, Woden is gradually turning, the camp slipping away from the range of the radio. The uncertainty about whether Gerry will return in time suggests that Marilyn may not even get to say goodbye to her beloved big brother.
CONCLUSION Summary of key points Restatement of thesis General comment	At important points in the story, Godwin deliberately holds back crucial information—who the stowaway is, when she must die, and whether she will be able to contact her brother. The result is suspense, which keeps the reader uncertain and anxious right up to the story's tragic conclusion. If Godwin's vision of the grim world of future space travel is accurate, we must consider whether exploring the final frontier is worth the price.

GO TO: go.hrw.com
KEYWORD: HLLA 10-6
FOR: Expanded Writer's Model and Student's Model

PRACTICE & APPLY 2 As you turn your prewriting notes into the first draft of your literary analysis, be sure to consult the framework on page 443 and the Writer's Model above. Return to the Prewriting section as necessary.

444 Chapter 6 Symbolism and Allegory • Synthesizing Sources

RESOURCES: WRITING

Practice & Apply 2

Think Sheet

- *Writing, Listening, & Speaking,* WS. p. 60

Template

- *Writing, Listening, & Speaking,* WS. p. 61

Internet

- go.hrw.com (keyword: HLLA 10-6)

Revising

Evaluate and Revise Your Draft

Check It Twice Carefully read your whole paper at least twice. First, examine the paper's content and organization, using the guidelines below. Then, use the guidelines on page 446 to help you focus on sentence style.

PEER REVIEW

Exchange your analysis with a peer. He or she may have ideas on how you can improve on your elaboration of supporting details.

First Reading: Content and Organization Use the following chart as a **think sheet** to help you evaluate and revise the content and organization of your analysis. You can use the chart either alone or during a peer review.

Guidelines: Analyzing a Short Story

Evaluation Questions	Tips	Revision Techniques
❶ Does the introduction grab the reader's attention with an interesting comment on the story?	**Put a star** beside the interesting comment.	**Add** an interesting comment about the story, such as an observation related to the thesis.
❷ Does the thesis statement identify the story's title and author, the literary element(s) discussed, and the conclusion about the element(s)?	**Circle** the title, the author, and the literary element(s) discussed. **Bracket** the writer's conclusion about the element(s).	If necessary, **add** any missing parts to the thesis statement: title and author, literary element(s), or conclusion about element(s).
❸ Are key points clearly identified and organized in the body of the analysis?	**Draw a wavy line** under each key point. **Number** each body paragraph for chronological order or order of importance.	**Add** a sentence clearly explaining the paragraph's key point. **Rearrange** paragraphs if they do not follow a clear order.
❹ Is each key point supported by details—direct quotations, summaries, and paraphrases—from the story?	**Highlight** each quotation, summary, and paraphrase from the story that is used as support.	**Add** supporting details to support your key points. **Delete** sentences that do not support a key point.
❺ Does elaboration connect key points and supporting details?	**Draw an arrow** to each sentence that elaborates a detail.	**Add** explanations that show how details relate to key points.
❻ Does the conclusion summarize the key points and restate the thesis? Does it include a comment about the story that relates to the thesis?	**Circle** the summary of the key points and **highlight** the restatement of the thesis. **Put a check mark** by the final comment.	**Add** a sentence that summarizes the key points or restates the thesis, if necessary. **Add** a final comment.

DIRECT TEACHING

Elaboration

To further elaborate in their essays, students might use the technique of questioning. Have students review each body paragraph of their essays and see whether a carefully worded question added to the paragraph might help focus the reader. This technique is used in the first and second paragraphs of **A Writer's Model** on p. 443.

Writing Workshop: Analyzing a Short Story 445

GUIDED PRACTICE

Responding to the Revision Process

Answers

1. The sentence does not further the explanation of how the author built suspense.
2. They were short, choppy sentences that were better combined.

DIFFERENTIATING INSTRUCTION

GRADE-LEVEL STANDARD

Advanced Learners

Enrichment. When they have finished their short story analyses, students might enjoy the challenge of selecting a novel and a film based on it and analyzing how the film represents the novel. When students have finished, have them share their analyses with the class.

PRACTICE & APPLY 3

Independent Practice

Warn students against the temptation to simply retell the short story. As they revise their content, they should look carefully for any sections in which they retold too much of the story without providing adequate analysis.

Second Reading: Style To keep readers interested, use a variety of sentence lengths. Avoid using several short, choppy sentences in a row. Instead, combine two or more such sentences by using **adjective clauses**—clauses that modify a noun or pronoun and are introduced by relative pronouns such as *who, whom, which,* and *that.* Notice how an adjective clause is used to combine the choppy sentences below.

Choppy Barton is the pilot of the EDS. He discovers a stowaway.

Combined Barton, who is the pilot of the EDS, discovers a stowaway.

Style Guidelines

Evaluation Question	Tip	Revision Technique
Does the paper include a variety of sentence lengths (some short, some long)?	**Underline** nouns and related pronouns that are repeated in short, back-to-back sentences.	**Replace** a repeated noun or pronoun with *who, whom, which,* or *that,* and **add** the clause to the related sentence.

ANALYZING THE REVISION PROCESS

Study these revisions, and answer the questions that follow.

With time running out for Marilyn, the author further increases the suspense by making her brother temporarily unreachable. ~~Marilyn explains that her sole reason for stowing away is to see her older brother.~~ When Barton contacts Gerry's base station on the planet Woden, Gerry is out in a helicopter ^that ~~. The helicopter~~ does not have a working radio.

delete

replace/add

Responding to the Revision Process

1. Why did the writer delete the second sentence?
2. Why did the writer combine the third and fourth sentences?

PRACTICE & APPLY 3 Use the guidelines on pages 445 and 446 to evaluate and revise the content, organization, and style of your draft. Consider peer comments, too.

Publishing

Proofread and Publish Your Analysis

A Last Look Before publishing your analysis, work with a classmate to proofread it at least twice for errors in grammar, spelling, and punctuation. Two sets of eyes and two minds are much better than one when it comes to spotting and correcting major and minor errors in these areas. Major errors can ruin an analysis with strong content and even minor errors can distract readers from an otherwise excellent analysis.

Share Your Work Other people may be interested in what you have to say about the short story you analyzed. To get your analysis in front of an audience, consider the following publishing options.

- Surf the Web to find the sites of high school literary magazines in different parts of the country and submit your analysis for publication and feedback.
- Submit your analysis to your school's newspaper or to a student literary magazine.
- With other students who analyzed short stories, create and bind a collection of analyses to be placed in the school library.
- Deliver your analysis as an oral response to literature. For more on **presenting a literary response,** see page 448.

TIP Proofreading will help you make sure that you follow the **conventions** of standard American English. Pay particular attention to your punctuation of the story's title and of direct quotations. For more on **punctuating quotations and titles,** see pages 341 and 345 in the *Holt Handbook.*

Reflect on Your Analysis

Looking Back Taking time to reflect on the process of writing a short story analysis will help you understand your strengths and weaknesses as a critical reader and writer. To think about what you have learned from this workshop, answer the following questions. If you add your analysis to your writing portfolio, include your written responses to these questions.

- How did you choose a story to analyze? Would you use this method to choose other stories or pieces of nonfiction to read for school or for enjoyment? Explain your response.
- How did your understanding of the story change as you wrote your analysis? Will this new understanding change how you approach reading other stories? Explain.

PRACTICE & APPLY 4 Proofread your short story analysis carefully for errors in language conventions. Then, publish your analysis, using one of the suggestions on this page. Finally, take stock of what you've learned by answering the reflection questions above.

CORRECTING MISCONCEPTIONS

Students may be under the assumption that content is separate from grammar, spelling, and punctuation. They may be accustomed to receiving separate grades for content and proper grammar on essays. Stress that grammatical errors in an essay affect the overall quality of the paper negatively; they indicate carelessness and will affect how a reader views the content.

DIRECT TEACHING

Share Your Work

You need to be aware that Internet resources are public forums, and their content can be unpredictable.

Resources Reminder

For help with the writing assessment, see 6 Traits—Plus 1 in the "Scales and Sample Papers" section of *Progress Assessment of Writing, Listening, & Speaking.*

PRACTICE & APPLY 4

Guided and Independent Practice

As students begin **Practice and Apply 4,** guide them by asking the following questions.

1. What was the most difficult part of writing your analysis? How did you overcome this difficulty?
2. What was the most important revision you made to your first draft? How did this change improve your analysis?

Point out to students that areas in which they had difficulty in earlier stages of writing might need special attention at the proofreading stage. Then, have students complete **Practice and Apply 4** as independent practice.

RESOURCES: WRITING

Practice & Apply 3

Think Sheet

- *Writing, Listening, & Speaking,* WS. p. 63

Evaluation

- *Writing, Listening, & Speaking,* WS. p. 62

Practice & Apply 4

Assessment

- *Test Generator* (*One-Stop Planner* CD-ROM)
- *Progress Assessment of Writing, Listening, & Speaking,* pp. 20–21, 68–70

Internet

- Online assessments at go.hrw.com (keyword: HLLA)

PRETEACHING

Motivate. Ask students to list stories or books that have been made into movies. You may want to write the list on the chalkboard. What changes are made when a book or story is adapted? Lead students to understand that the original story, which is communicated through written text, is simplified or otherwise changed to make it more effective in visual form. Point out to students that, in a way similar to how books and stories are adapted for the screen, their written analyses will be adapted for oral presentation.

DIFFERENTIATING INSTRUCTION

GRADE-LEVEL STANDARD

Learners Having Difficulty

Some students may not know how to inform the listening audience when lines are being quoted. Brainstorm with students possible ways to introduce quotes. Here are examples.

- The author writes . . .
- [Character's name] says . . .
- The story reads . . .
- Consider these lines from the story . . .

Presenting a Literary Response

Speaking Assignment

Listening and Speaking 2.4 Adapt your short story analysis for an oral response to literature, and present it to your class.

A literary analysis doesn't have to be a written presentation only; it can also make an effective oral presentation. In this workshop you will adapt your written literary analysis for delivery as an **oral response to literature.** Your purpose will be to show your audience that you have a firm grasp of the significant ideas of the story you are analyzing. A listening audience has very different needs than a reading audience, even if both groups contain your classmates and teacher. You have much to consider as you plan your adaptation and delivery.

Adapt Your Written Analysis

Consider the Ingredients Your written analysis consisted of an introduction, a body, and a conclusion. So should your oral presentation. However, you might need to make changes beyond simplified sentence structure and vocabulary to make the points of your paper interesting to listeners and easy to understand. Here are some things to consider.

Introduction The **introduction** to an oral presentation needs to be more dramatic and personal than a written introduction. Here are some ways you can adapt the introduction of your written response to grab your listeners' attention.

Quick guide!

DEVELOPING INTRODUCTIONS

Technique	Example
Begin with a quotation.	"It was the law, and there could be no appeal." The characters in Tom Godwin's "The Cold Equations" learn this lesson all too well. Despite the strong human concerns and emotions the author presents, the law is inescapable.
Begin with a personal observation or anecdote.	In my own experience, having a good reason for doing something I shouldn't has sometimes spared me the worst consequences. However, my experiences with human rules would not prepare me for the inescapable laws of space travel.
Begin with a reference to a familiar source.	According to Newton's laws of motion, the force of a planet's gravity is stronger on an object with more mass and increases the closer the object gets. It's one thing to read that in a science book, but it's completely different to think about how that law might affect human beings.

CHAPTER 6 RESOURCES: LISTENING & SPEAKING

Listening & Speaking Workshop

Planning

- *On Course: Mapping Instruction*
- *One-Stop Planner* CD-ROM
- *Writing, Listening, & Speaking*
  - Teaching Notes, p. 64
  - Project-Planning Guide, WS. p. 66

Think Sheet

- *Writing, Listening, & Speaking,* WS. p. 67

Differentiating Instruction

- *Lesson Plans for Language Development,* p. 191
- *Supporting Instruction in Spanish*

Evaluation and Assessment

- *Writing, Listening, & Speaking,* WS. p. 68

Your introduction should also identify the story's title and author and the conclusion about the story element or elements (plot, character, stylistic device, and so on) you plan to focus on. State this information in simple but strong language. That way your listeners will understand the basics of your presentation at the beginning, which will make the rest of your presentation easier to follow.

Body The **body** of your oral presentation is where you advance a **judgment** that shows you have a complete grasp of the important ideas in the short story. It will contain the same basic information your written analysis does. To adapt the written analysis, provide **extra elaboration** of the details that support your thesis. Extra elaboration makes an oral presentation easier to understand. If you need to provide **references to the text** (quotations, paraphrases, or summaries) to support a point, be sure you put the reference into context by explaining the circumstances or events that surround it.

Add plenty of **transitional words and phrases** to the body of your oral presentation to guide listeners through it. For chronological order, use words and phrases such as *after, then, next,* and *finally* to show the order of ideas. For order of importance, use words and phrases such as *mainly, to begin with,* and *more* (or *most*) *important.* Some transitional words such as *first, second, third,* and *last* can be used to show either order.

Conclusion The **conclusion** of your oral presentation should, like the introduction, be dramatic and personal. Summarize your key points and restate your thesis, all in simple but strong language. Then, close with a statement that shows your appreciation of the effects the author has created in the story.

Deliver Your Oral Response

Make a Note of It Make concise notes to guide you in delivering the ideas you have planned and organized. Your oral response will be **extemporaneous**—rehearsed extensively but not read or memorized. Your notes should contain clearly organized words and phrases to remind you of the ideas you will present. Write down word for word any quotations you will use from the story so that you will deliver them accurately.

Go Tell It Practice using your voice and body effectively. Speak loudly enough for everyone to hear and slowly enough for them to understand each word. Make eye contact with your audience, and vary your facial expressions to hold listener interest. Use both your voice and gestures to emphasize important ideas.

PRACTICE & APPLY 5 Adapt your written analysis as an oral presentation. Use your voice and gestures effectively as you deliver your oral response to literature.

TIP Don't forget to explain the **ambiguities, nuances,** and **complexities** that you discussed in your written analysis. Take extra care to explain how they are connected to your thesis statement. Also, be sure to point out **stylistic devices** that the author uses.

Listening and Speaking 1.4 Choose appropriate techniques for developing the introduction and conclusion. **2.0** Students deliver polished extemporaneous presentations. **2.4** Deliver oral responses to literature. **2.4a** Advance a judgment demonstrating a comprehensive grasp of the significant ideas of works. **2.4b** Support important ideas and viewpoints through references to the text. **2.4c** Demonstrate awareness of the author's use of stylistic devices. **2.4d** Identify and assess the impact of perceived ambiguities, nuances, and complexities within the text.

- *Progress Assessment of Writing, Listening, & Speaking,* p. 71
- *Diagnostic and Summative Assessments,* Third-Quarter Test

Extension

- *Writing, Listening, & Speaking,* Videocassette Segment 4
- *Writing, Listening, & Speaking,* WS. p. 69

Internet

- go.hrw.com (keyword: HLLA)

RETEACHING

REVIEW STANDARD

Make a Note of It

To help students deliver their presentations smoothly, suggest that they use both note cards and an outline. Have them put their note cards in order, and then have them create an outline that includes an entry for each card. With both an outline and their note cards on the podium, students will have a script to follow and a clear idea of where they are in their presentations.

CRITICAL THINKING

Have a volunteer deliver a portion of his or her analysis while hidden from view behind a screen or other object. Then, have the volunteer repeat the presentation in view of the class. Lead a discussion about which presentation was more effective, and emphasize the importance of nonverbal elements to the presentation.

PRACTICE & APPLY 5

Guided and Independent Practice

As students complete **Practice and Apply 5,** have them practice their speeches in small groups of two or three. As they listen to the speeches of others, have students consider the following questions.

- Is the speaker's introduction strong? What about the conclusion?
- Is the speaker's use of transitional words effective?
- Is the speaker's elaboration sufficient for an oral presentation?

After the discussion, group members can make recommendations for the final presentation. Then, have students complete **Practice and Apply 5** as independent practice.

Listening and Speaking Workshop: Presenting a Literary Response 449

Standards Review

Literary Response and Analysis

STANDARDS FOCUS, pp. 450–451

(For the grade-level standard reviewed in this lesson, see Student Edition, p. 450.)

INTRODUCING THE STANDARDS REVIEW

Use this review to test students' grasp of the standard taught in this chapter. You can use the annotations to guide students in their reading before they answer the questions.

DIRECT TEACHING

A Literary Focus
GRADE-LEVEL STANDARD

Symbolism. What does the figurehead symbolize? [the skipper's wife] What do the blue stones symbolize? [her eyes] How is the wife's reaction to her husband's putting the stones in the figurehead similar to her feelings when her husband names the ship after her? [She has negative emotions: She is greedy for the stones and jealous of the ship.]

B Literary Focus
GRADE-LEVEL STANDARD

Allegory. Allegories teach lessons. What is the lesson of this story? [Possible response: Jealousy and greed lead to distrust and deceit, which ultimately lead to bad results.]

Literary Response and Analysis

Test Practice

Symbolism and Allegory

DIRECTIONS: Read the following short story. Then, read each multiple-choice question that follows, and write the letter of the best response.

The Blue Stones

Isak Dinesen

There was once a skipper who named his ship after his wife. He had the figurehead of it beautifully carved, just like her, and the hair of it gilt. But his wife was jealous of the ship. "You think more of the figurehead than of me," she said to him. "No," he answered, "I think so highly of her because she is like you, yes, because she is you yourself. Is she not gallant, full-bosomed; does she not dance in the waves, like you at our wedding? In a way she is really even kinder to me than you are. She gallops along where I tell her to go, and she lets her long hair hang down freely, **(A)** while you put up yours under a cap. But she turns her back to me, so that when I want a kiss I come home to Elsinore." Now once, when this skipper was trading at Trankebar, he chanced to help an old native King to flee traitors in his own country. As they parted, the King gave him two big blue, precious stones, and these he had set into the face of his figurehead, like a pair of eyes to it. When he came home he told his wife of his adventure, and said: "Now she has your blue eyes too." "You had better give me the stones for a pair of earrings," said she. "No," he said again, "I cannot do that, and you would not ask me to if you understood." Still the wife could not stop fretting about the blue stones, and one day, when her husband was with the skippers' corporation, she had a glazier of the town take them out, and put two bits of blue glass into the figurehead instead, and the skipper did not find out, but sailed off to Portugal. But after some time the skipper's wife found that her eyesight was growing bad, and that she could not see to thread a needle. She went to a wise woman, who gave her ointments and waters, but they did not help her and in the end the old woman shook her head, and told her that this was a rare and incurable disease, and that she was going blind. "Oh, God," the wife then cried, "that the ship was back in the harbor of Elsinore. Then I should have the glass taken out, and the jewels put back. For did he not say that they were my eyes?" But the ship did not come back. **(B)** Instead the skipper's wife had a letter from the Consul of Portugal, who informed her that she had been wrecked, and gone to the bottom with all hands. And it was a very strange thing, the Consul wrote, that in broad daylight she had run straight into a tall rock, rising out of the sea.

Pages 450–451 cover **Reading Standard 3.7** Recognize and understand the significance of various literary devices, including allegory and symbolism, and explain their appeal.

READING MINI-LESSON

Reviewing Word-Attack Skills

Activity. Display these pairs of sentences. Have volunteers identify the homographs and tell if they are pronounced the same or differently.

1. A bandage was wound around his hand. What kind of wound did it conceal? [different]
2. My aunts cross the bridge every week. They visit and play bridge. [same]
3. The raptor spied a dove. It dove toward its prey, talons outstretched. [different]
4. The child read from a primer. We applied a primer before painting the wood. [different]
5. He joined a commune. He wanted to commune with nature. [different]

Activity. Display these sounds and words. Have volunteers identify the word in which the given sound is heard. Answers are underlined.

1.	/zh/	<u>occasion</u>	fashions
2.	/sh/	inquisitive	<u>impatient</u>
3.	/j/	<u>contagion</u>	gaieties
4.	/sh/	routine	<u>attention</u>

1. To the skipper the ship's figurehead represents —
   A freedom
   B his wife
   C his success as a captain
   D ideal feminine beauty

2. On a deeper level, what does the ship's figurehead seem to **symbolize** in the story?
   F The skipper's love for his wife
   G The uncertainty of human relationships
   H The wife's coldness toward her husband
   J Innocence

3. The **conflict** in the story between the skipper and his wife is caused by the wife's —
   A sadness and fear
   B compassion and understanding
   C worry and loneliness
   D jealousy and greed

4. In the story the big blue stones are a **symbol** of —
   F beauty
   G wealth and power
   H the wife's eyes
   J the sea

5. A clue that the stones are a **symbol** is their —
   A appearance throughout the story
   B unusual color and shape
   C strange history
   D great value

6. The story suggests that the wife goes blind and the ship sinks because —
   F the wife steals the figurehead's eyes
   G the skipper stops loving his wife
   H the skipper is cursed by the foreign king
   J the wife is an unlucky woman

7. Part of the appeal of reading "The Blue Stones" is that we realize that beneath the literal story lies —
   A a comic intent
   B an unhappy ending
   C a moral lesson
   D an allusion to the Bible

8. "The Blue Stones" can be interpreted as an **allegory** warning us about the dangers of —
   F jealousy and greed
   G loneliness
   H unhappy marriages
   J life at sea

5. /y/ violent valiant
6. /ī/ envious pious
7. /ē/ obsequious loquacious

ASSESSING

Assessment

- *Progress Assessment of Reading*
  - Chapter Test

TestPractice

Answers and Model Rationales

1. **B** The skipper tells his wife that "she [the figurehead] is you yourself." The figurehead is not related to freedom (A) or success (C). B is a better choice than D.
2. **F** The wife is cold toward her husband (H) and human relationships are uncertain (G), but the figurehead has nothing to do with these points. Innocence (J) plays no role in this story. Students can get the correct answer (F) by eliminating other choices.
3. **D** The wife shows no compassion or understanding (B). While she does exhibit some qualities of A and C, the conflict is caused by her jealousy and greed.
4. **H** After setting the blue stones into the figurehead's face, the skipper states that it now has his wife's eyes.
5. **A** The stones do have great value (D), but this doesn't make them a symbol. There is no mention of their history (C). There is no mention of the stones having an unusual shape (B). The recurrence of the stones (A) indicates that they function as a symbol.
6. **F** G is wrong because the skipper does not stop loving his wife, and H is wrong because there is no curse. The wife may be unlucky (J), but the cause of her misfortunes is the theft of the stones.
7. **C** A and D are wrong since the tale is not comic and has no biblical allusions. It does have a sad ending (B), but that is part of the literal story. The appeal of the story is partly that it conveys a moral lesson about honesty, trust, and love.
8. **F** The vices the story warns against are jealousy and greed (F). The other answers do not relate to the moral lesson of the allegory.

Test Practice

Vocabulary Development

Synonyms

Modeling. Model the process of determining the answer to item 1. Say, "Any of the answers might fit, but I think that a son who believes that his mother feels abandoned would feel guilty about leaving his mother alone. The noun *contrition* is related to the adjective *contrite*. A person who feels contrite feels sorry, so C, regret, is the correct answer."

Test Practice

Answers and Model Rationales

1. **C** See rationale above.
2. **J** *Inquisitive* and *inquiry* have the same root word. Someone who is inquisitive is questioning or curious. The other choices have nothing to do with questioning, so J is correct.
3. **B** Jerry might be happy, disappointed, or encouraged, but none of these is a synonym for *incredulous. Incredulous* is related to *incredible,* meaning "unbelievable"; *disbelieving* is correct.
4. **F** The only choice that fits with a ball, a prince, and the adjective *elegant* is *majestic.* Furthermore, both *imperial* and *majestic* allude to kingship.
5. **A** A sage is a wise person, so *sagacious* means "wise."
6. **F** Something that is tangible is concrete in its nature and can be touched.
7. **A** "Elderly and sedate" and "young, lively" contrast—a clue that *sedate* means "quiet."
8. **H** The word root of *propriety* is the same as *proper,* so *correctness* is the correct answer.
9. **B** *Foreign* (A) is an antonym of *indigenous.* Rituals and traditions are not limited to the cultures cited in C and D.

TEST PRACTICE

Vocabulary Development

Test Practice

Synonyms

DIRECTIONS: Choose the best synonym for the underlined word in each sentence.

1. Jerry feels contrition at first when he thinks his mother feels abandoned.
   - A worry
   - B anger
   - C regret
   - D sympathy
2. When he asks for swimming goggles, his mother gives him an inquisitive look.
   - F startled
   - G concerned
   - H frightened
   - J curious
3. Jerry times how long he can hold his breath and is incredulous at the results.
   - A disappointed
   - B disbelieving
   - C happy
   - D encouraged
4. The masked ball took place in the elegant imperial suite in Prince Prospero's palace.
   - F majestic
   - G unfinished
   - H colorful
   - J imaginary
5. Prospero thinks of himself as sagacious.
   - A wise
   - B brave
   - C cautious
   - D cheerful
6. The masked figure had no tangible form.
   - F touchable
   - G recognizable
   - H colorful
   - J remarkable
7. The elderly and the sedate watched the young, lively revelers dance.
   - A quiet
   - B rich
   - C restless
   - D worried
8. The stranger's appearance and actions showed a complete lack of propriety.
   - F refinement
   - G humor
   - H correctness
   - J awkwardness
9. Coming-of-age rituals and traditions are thought to be common to many indigenous cultures.
   - A foreign
   - B native
   - C agricultural
   - D religious

452 Chapter 6 Symbolism and Allegory • Synthesizing Sources

Using Academic Language

Review of Literary Terms
Reading Standard 3.7

Ask students to review the chapter to find the meanings of the terms listed below. Then, have students show their grasp of Standard 3.7 by citing passages from the chapter that illustrate the meanings of those terms. **Symbol** (pp. 398, 400, 433); **Allegory** (pp. 399, 418); **Fable** (p. 399); **Parable** (p. 399); **Symbolic Meaning** (p. 400).

Review of Informational Terms
Reading Standard 2.4

Ask students to use these terms to explain how to synthesize the content from several sources. **Synthesize** (p. 411); **Paraphrase** (p. 411); **Evaluate** (p. 411); **Objective** (p. 411); **Subjective** (p. 411); **Author's Purpose** (p. 411).

Writing

Test Practice

DIRECTIONS: Read the following paragraph from a draft of a student's analysis of a short story. Then, read the questions below it. Choose the best answer for each question.

(1) In "The Masque of the Red Death," Edgar Allan Poe creates a scene of nightmarish horror through his development of the story's setting. (2) Poe, a master of the Gothic story, is famous for his tales of horror and suspense. (3) He sets his story in a palace remarkable for its bizarre architecture, which gives the place an almost dreamlike quality. (4) The most frightening element of the setting, however, is the black room. (5) In it, "the effect of the firelight that streamed upon the dark hangings through the blood-tinted panes was ghastly in the extreme."

1. Which of the following statements containing direct quotations could be added to support the idea in sentence 3?
   - **A** "The 'Red Death' had long devastated the country," and people fled to the palace for protection.
   - **B** In the main corridor, "[t]here was a sharp turn at every twenty or thirty yards, and at each turn a novel effect."
   - **C** "Prince Prospero was happy and dauntless and sagacious" because he didn't believe that the plague could enter the palace.
   - **D** The uninvited guest's "broad brow, with all the features of the face, was besprinkled with the scarlet horror."

2. If the student wanted to elaborate sentence 4, which of the following would be the best way to do so?
   - **F** relate the gruesome symptoms of the "Red Death"
   - **G** explain the other frightening elements of the story
   - **H** describe how the masked figure looked
   - **J** speculate on the symbolism of the black room

3. Which sentence might be added to elaborate the direct quotation in sentence 5?
   - **A** The prince provides entertainers to keep his guests happy and occupied.
   - **B** Prince Prospero becomes angry with the uninvited guest.
   - **C** The description of the room foreshadows the horror that follows.
   - **D** The party guests grow quiet every time the great clock chimes.

4. Which sentence should be deleted to improve the passage's organization?
   - **F** 1
   - **G** 2
   - **H** 4
   - **J** 5

5. How could a student presenting this passage in an oral response to literature conclude the presentation?
   - **A** sum up and show appreciation for the effects created by the setting
   - **B** give details on Poe's life, including his childhood and marriage
   - **C** restate, word for word, the main idea of the paragraph
   - **D** describe how Poe also uses symbolism and tone in all his writings

Standards Review

Answers

1. B
2. J
3. C
4. G
5. A

APPLICATION

Story Time

For homework, have students create illustrated books that tell a story appropriate for children. As they work, have them focus on the basic elements of fiction: plot, setting, characters, theme, and stylistic devices. Once they have written the stories, have them draw or paint illustrations of the more interesting characters and events in the plot. If possible, have interested students share their stories with students in a local elementary school.

Homework

EXTENSION

On the Beat

Have students act as entertainment reporters and present a short oral review of either a live music performance they have recently seen or a music CD. The review should evaluate such elements as theme (many concerts and CDs have an overall theme) and mood, and it should be supported with specific evidence from the performance.

RESOURCES: WRITING, LISTENING, & SPEAKING

Assessment

- *Test Generator* (*One-Stop Planner* CD-ROM)
- *Progress Assessment of Writing, Listening, & Speaking*, Ch. 6
- *Diagnostic and Summative Assessments*, Third-Quarter Test

Internet

- Online assessments at go.hrw.com (keyword: HLLA)

Holt Literature and Language Arts: Mastering the California Standards

Chapter 7 Poetry

Program Organization

Holt Literature and Language Arts provides a complete curriculum for standards-based instruction in reading, literature, writing, listening and speaking, and language conventions. The instructional content is presented in quarters to enable teachers to anticipate and administer the quarterly assessments required by California.

About Chapter 7

Standards-based lesson plans and suggestions for pacing the presentation of Chapter 7, the related instructional material, and the recommended assessment are provided in *On Course: Mapping Instruction,* Chapter 7.

- In Chapter 7, students will identify and use words literally and figuratively; recognize and understand various literary devices; explain the way voice, persona, and narrator affect characterization; evaluate the aesthetic qualities of style; write a description of a person, and deliver a descriptive presentation.

Language Arts Content

Which reading standards are taught in Chapter 7?

In this chapter, students will master the following Grade 10 standards and review standards from Grade 8. Selections or features marked with a ✓ constitute the minimum course of study that provides coverage of grade-level standards.

Grade 10 Standards

Word Analysis, Fluency, and Systematic Vocabulary Development

1.1 Identify and use the literal and figurative meanings of words and understand word derivations.
Jargon: Job-Related Vocabulary, p. 526

Literary Response and Analysis

3.7 Recognize and understand the significance of various literary devices, including figurative language, imagery, allegory, and symbolism, and explain their appeal.
"Imagery: Seeing with Our Minds" (standards essay), pp. 456–457
✓ "Same Song" (poem), pp. 461–464
"Eating Together" (poem), "Grape Sherbet" (poem), p. 470
"The Legend" (elegy), p. 476
"Figurative Language: Language of the Imagination" (standards essay), pp. 477–478
"Simile" (poem), pp. 479–481
"I Am Offering This Poem" (poem), p. 486
"since feeling is first" (poem), pp. 484–486
✓ "Heart! We will forget him!" (poem), pp. 487, 492
✓ "Three Japanese Tankas" (tankas), p. 492
✓ "Shall I Compare Thee to a Summer's Day?" (sonnet), p. 495
"Ode to My Socks" (ode), pp. 497–502
"The Sounds of Poetry: Rhythm, Rhyme, and Other Sound Effects" (standards essay), pp. 503–505
✓ "Sea Fever" (poem), pp. 506–508
"Ex–Basketball Player" (poem), pp. 518–519, 524–525
"miss rosie" (poem), pp. 524–525
"Remember" (poem), pp. 527–530
"We Real Cool" (poem), pp. 531–534
"Jazz Fantasia" (poem), pp. 535–538
"Fireworks" (standards review), pp. 550–551

3.9 Explain how voice, persona, and the choice of a narrator affect characterization and the tone, plot, and credibility of a text.
"Eating Together" (poem), "Grape Sherbet" (poem), pp. 465–470

(continued)

(continued)

3.11 Evaluate the aesthetic qualities of style, including the impact of diction and figurative language on tone, mood, and theme, using the terminology of literary criticism.
"The Legend" (elegy), pp. 471–476

Review Standards Grade 8

Reading 1.1 Analyze idioms, analogies, metaphors, and similes to infer the literal and figurative meanings of phrases.
"miss rosie" (poem), pp. 521–525
"Ex–Basketball Player" (poem), pp. 524–525
Idioms All Around You, p. 525

Reading 1.2 Understand the most important points in the history of English language and use common word origins to determine the historical influences on English word meanings.
Archaic Words: Long Gone and Strange to Our Ears, p. 496

Reading 3.1 Determine and articulate the relationship between the purposes and characteristics of different forms of poetry.
"A Storm in the Mountains" (prose poem), pp. 458–460
"I Am Offering This Poem" (poem), pp. 482–483, 486
"since feeling is first" (poem), p. 486
"Three Japanese Tankas" (tankas), pp. 489–492
"Heart! We will forget him!" (poem), p. 492
"Shall I Compare Thee to a Summer's Day?" (sonnet), pp. 493–495
"Ode to My Socks" (ode), pp. 497–502
"Bonny Barbara Allan" (ballad), pp. 509–512
"The Flying Cat" (poem), pp. 513–517
"Fireworks" (standards review), pp. 550–551

Which writing, and listening and speaking standards are taught in Chapter 7?

Writing Strategies

1.1 Establish a controlling impression or coherent thesis that conveys a clear and distinctive perspective on the subject and maintain a consistent tone and focus throughout the piece of writing.
Taking in the View, p. 540
Determine a Controlling Impression, pp. 541–542

1.2 Use precise language, action verbs, sensory details, appropriate modifiers, and the active rather than the passive voice.
Gather Your Details, p. 541

1.9 Revise writing to improve the logic and coherence of the organization and controlling perspective, the precision of word choice, and the tone by taking into consideration the audience, purpose, and formality of the context.
Evaluate and Revise Your Essay, pp. 545–546

Writing Applications

2.1 Write biographical or autobiographical narratives or short stories.
c. Describe with concrete sensory details the sights, sounds, and smells of a scene and the specific actions, movements, gestures, and feelings of the characters; use interior monologue to depict the characters' feelings.
Gather Your Details, p. 541
e. Make effective use of descriptions of appearance, images, shifting perspectives, and sensory details.
Organize Your Description, p. 542

(continued)

(continued)

Listening and Speaking Strategies

1.7 Use props, visual aids, graphs, and electronic media to enhance the appeal and accuracy of presentations.
Make Note Cards, p. 549

1.8 Produce concise notes for extemporaneous delivery.
Make Note Cards, p. 549

1.9 Analyze the occasion and the interests of the audience and choose effective verbal and nonverbal techniques for presentations.
Speak Easy, p. 549

Speaking Applications

2.6 Deliver descriptive presentations.

a. Establish clearly the speaker's point of view on the subject of the presentation.
Attitude Check, p. 548

b. Establish clearly the speaker's relationship with that subject.
Attitude Check, p. 548

c. Use effective, factual descriptions of appearance, concrete images, shifting perspectives and vantage points, and sensory details.
Put It into Perspective, p. 548
More, or Less, the Same? p. 548

Review Standards Grade 8

Writing 1.1 Create compositions that establish a controlling impression, have a coherent thesis, and end with a clear and well-supported conclusion.
Describing a Person, pp. 540–547

Speaking 1.5 Use precise language, action verbs, sensory details, appropriate and colorful modifiers, and the active rather than the passive voice in ways that enliven oral presentations.
More, or Less, the Same? p. 548

Instructional Planning and Support

Where do I find lesson plans, additional resources, and other teaching aids?

- This Annotated Teacher's Edition and *On Course: Mapping Instruction* provide direction in planning and implementing a complete California standards–based curriculum. These components also include instructions for diagnostic, progress, and summative testing; for presenting direct instruction of the standards; for differentiating instruction to provide universal access; and for locating and using the program's ancillaries.
- Lesson and workshop resources are referenced at the beginning of each selection or workshop, in the bottom margin of this teacher's edition.
- Reminders for using additional resources appear in this teacher's edition at point of use.
- The *One-Stop Planner* CD-ROM contains editable lesson plans and all print ancillaries, available in PDF format.

What if I don't have time to teach all of Chapter 7?

- Most standards can be taught with a minimum number of selections and features. In the chart on the preceding page, the core lessons you need in order to provide complete coverage of the chapter standards are identified with a ✓.
- *On Course: Mapping Instruction,* Chapter 7, lists lessons and activities that provide minimum standards coverage.

What provisions have been made for students who have additional class time scheduled in language arts?

- *Interactive Reading* provides for alternative direct instruction and practice of the grade-level standards taught in Chapter 7.
- *Universal Access: Writing, Listening, and Speaking,* Chapter 7, contains worksheets and transparencies that provide practice in and reteaching and reinforcement of the writing and listening and speaking standards in Chapter 7.
- *Universal Access: Lesson Plans for Language Development,* Chapter 7, provides alternative teaching strategies and additional worksheets designed specifically for English-language learners and special education students. Many of the suggestions and activities in this ancillary will also be helpful to students in the regular classroom who are having difficulty with particular skills.

Universal Access

How do I differentiate instruction to ensure that all my students master the standards?

Holt Literature and Language Arts provides comprehensive, differentiated instruction for all types of students.

- Most of the general instruction and teaching strategies in the Annotated Teacher's Edition are at grade level. These instructions will work well with the majority of your students.
- Point-of-use suggestions are provided for advanced learners, learners having difficulty, English-language learners, and special education students.
- *Interactive Reading* is designed to anticipate and remediate problems that students may experience in achieving mastery of the reading standards. See *Interactive Reading,* Teacher's Edition, Chapter 7, for information on using the reader to differentiate instruction.
- *Universal Access: Writing, Listening, and Speaking,* Chapter 7, contains worksheets and transparencies that provide practice in and reteaching and reinforcement of the writing and listening and speaking standards in Chapter 7.
- *Universal Access: Lesson Plans for Language Development,* Chapter 7, offers teaching strategies and additional worksheets designed specifically for English-language learners and special education students.

Assessment

How do I determine whether my students are making progress in mastering the standards?

Progress Assessment

- Use the Standards Review at the end of Chapter 7 for an informal assessment of the informational reading and writing standards.
- Use Chapter 7 tests from the *Progress Assessment* booklets to assess comprehension and progress on mastering the standards taught in this chapter.

Summative Assessment

The content of *Holt Literature and Language Arts* has been divided into quarters to allow you to administer the four summative tests required by California. Chapters 6–8 and related instructional material constitute the third quarter of instruction. At the end of Chapter 8, you may ask students to take the Third-Quarter Test in *Diagnostic and Summative Assessments.*

Chapter 7

STANDARDS FOCUS

(For full text of standards taught in this chapter, see the Standards Correlation by Standard chart in the Student Edition.)

Grade-Level Standards

- Vocabulary Development 1.1
- Literary Response and Analysis 3.7
- Writing Strategies 1.1, 1.2, 1.9
- Writing Applications 2.1c, e
- Listening and Speaking Strategies 1.7, 1.8, 1.9
- Speaking Applications 2.6a–c

INTRODUCING THE CHAPTER

Through the poetry in this chapter, students will be invited to experience objects and ideas in fresh and unusual ways. They will discover how a poet can powerfully evoke images, sounds, and feelings with a few carefully chosen words. Pat Mora and Rita Dove, among others, illustrate the use of imagery in their poetry. A wide variety of poets—from William Shakespeare to N. Scott Momaday—exemplify the descriptive power of figurative language. Students can experience the sounds of poetry in a traditional ballad and in poems such as "We Real Cool," by Gwendolyn Brooks, and "Jazz Fantasia," by Carl Sandburg. The chapter culminates with an opportunity for students to use what they have learned about sensory language, imagery, and figurative language to write a description of a person and to present their work.

CHAPTER 7 RESOURCES: READING

Planning

- *One-Stop Planner* CD-ROM with Test Generator
- *On Course: Mapping Instruction*
- *At Home: A Guide to Standards Mastery*
- *At Home: In Spanish*
- *Supporting Instruction in Spanish*

Reading

- *Interactive Reading*

Differentiating Instruction

- *Lesson Plans for Language Development*

Assessment

- *Progress Assessment of Reading*
  - Chapter Test

Chapter 7

Poetry

Ink runs from the corners of my mouth.
There is no happiness like mine.
I have been eating poetry.

—Mark Strand

Poppies (late 17th century) by Yun Shouping.
Ink and color on silk.

go.hrw.com
KEYWORD:
HLLA 10-7

THE QUOTATION

Why do you think Mark Strand uses the metaphor of eating to express the pleasure he gets from reading poetry? [Possible response: Like eating food, reading poetry is a sensual experience that brings joy.]

VIEWING THE ART

Chinese painter, poet, and calligrapher **Yun Shouping** (1633–1690) is regarded as one the six greatest artists of the early Qing dynasty. Although he was not affiliated with the Emperor's court, his style was adopted as the official court painting style. Yun Shouping described two approaches to painting: one that uses outlines and one that doesn't use outlines, which was called "boneless." Yun Shouping felt that this latter style best captured the impression of nature.

Activity. One Chinese dictum about painting is: "Externally, learn from nature; internally, gain from the source of feeling." What do you think this means? [It suggests that Chinese art is concerned with understanding natural forms, but that its forms express inner emotions.]

Resources Reminder

Planning

- *At Home: A Guide to Standards Mastery*

Parent letters appear in this resource. Translations of these letters are found in *At Home: In Spanish.* Translations of selection summaries appear in *Supporting Instruction in Spanish.*

Reading

- *Interactive Reading*

The California framework requires students to read materials apart from in-class assignments. Additional readings are cited on the Read On page and on selected pages in the Student Edition.

- *One-Stop Planner* CD-ROM with Test Generator

Internet

- go.hrw.com (Keyword: HLLA 10-7)

STANDARDS FOCUS, pp. 456–457

(For the grade-level standard taught in this lesson, see Student Edition, p. 456.)

Prerequisite Standard

- Grade 6, Literary Response and Analysis 3.4 **Define how tone or meaning is conveyed in poetry through word choice, figurative language, sentence structure, line length, punctuation, rhythm, repetition, and rhyme.**

Literary Focus: Imagery

Ask students to suggest some popular song lyrics that contain sensory descriptions. Write each suggestion on the chalkboard and discuss the image evoked by the description. For example, "he swam like a shark through the crowded room" evokes an image of a dangerous, predatory person. After you have discussed several descriptions, have students categorize the images they evoke as positive or negative.

Literary Response and Analysis

Imagery *by* John Malcolm Brinnin

SEEING WITH OUR MINDS

An **image** is a representation of anything we can see, hear, taste, touch, or smell. A painter or sculptor can create an image of an apple so true to life that we'd like to eat it or feel its weight and roundness in our hands. A poet, using only words, can make us see and feel, taste and smell an apple by describing it as "rosy," "shiny," "heavy," "mushy," "sweet." The language that appeals to our five senses and creates images in our minds is called **imagery.**

Imagery and Feelings

To see how imagery works, look at the two poems about the moon on this page and the next one. The first poem, by John Haines, introduces many variations on the image of the moon. Can you find the image that tells us that the poem was written sometime after 1969, when humans first disturbed the dust of the moon and left their debris on its surface? The second poem, by Emily Dickinson, was written more than a hundred years earlier than Haines's poem.

These two "moon" poems show us something else that imagery can do: The poets, through their evocative imagery, tell us how they *feel* about the moon. Haines's images of the "moon of the poet" are ironic and violent. As we see this moon in our minds, we share his sadness and even his anger over the human capacity for destruction.

Dickinson, on the other hand, uses romantic images that help us see another moon and share other feelings. Her moon is personified as a beautiful woman, even a queen, dressed in all the beauties of the night sky. Images of gold, beryl, dew, amber, silver, trinkets, and dimities help us share her feelings of wonder, admiration, and perhaps playfulness.

Reading Standard 3.7 Recognize and understand the significance of various literary devices, including imagery, and explain their appeal.

Moons

There are moons like continents,
diminishing to a white stone
softly smoking
in a fog-bound ocean.

Equinoctial° moons,
immense rainbarrels spilling
their yellow water.

Moons like eyes turned inward,
hard and bulging
on the blue cheek of eternity.

And moons half-broken,
eaten by eagle shadows . . .

But the moon of the poet
is soiled and scratched, its seas
are flowing with dust.

And other moons are rising,
swollen like boils—

in their bloodshot depths
the warfare of planets
silently drips and festers.

—John Haines

5. **equinoctial** (ē′kwi·näk′shəl) *adj.:* of the spring and fall equinoxes, when day and night are of equal length.

DIFFERENTIATING INSTRUCTION

Learners Having Difficulty

Identifying imagery. Have small groups of students read several poems that you have selected. Ask them to identify in the poems descriptive phrases that appeal to one or more of the senses. Encourage a discussion of the image that each description evokes.

Advanced Learners

Acceleration. In order to move students toward the eleventh- and twelfth-grade Standard 3.4, have them consider how imagery evokes emotions and creates sensory impressions.

Activity. Tell students that poets often create vivid images by calling on senses that are not usually associated with the thing being described. Ask them to find in poems examples of sensory descriptions that evoke strong feelings. Invite students to read their examples aloud, and have the class categorize the examples by type of feeling, such as sadness, exuberance, and fear.

The Moon was but a Chin of Gold

The Moon was but a Chin of Gold
A Night or two ago—
And now she turns Her perfect Face
Upon the World below—

Her Forehead is of Amplest Blonde—
Her Cheek—a Beryl° hewn—
Her Eye unto the Summer Dew
The likest I have known—

Her Lips of Amber never part—
But what must be the smile
Upon Her Friend she could confer
Were such Her Silver Will—

And what a privilege to be
But the remotest Star—
For Certainty She takes Her Way
Beside Your Palace Door—

Her Bonnet is the Firmament°—
The Universe—Her Shoe—
The Stars—the Trinkets at Her Belt—
Her Dimities°—of Blue—

—Emily Dickinson

6. beryl *n.:* mineral that usually occurs in crystals of blue, green, pink, or yellow.
17. firmament *n.:* sky.
20. dimities *n.:* dresses made of dimity, a sheer, cool, cotton material.

Calvin and Hobbes © 1989 Watterson. Reprinted with permission of Universal Press Syndicate.

Practice

Think of an object or scene (perhaps a snowy winter night or a half-time performance), and then choose a particular **mood** (maybe peacefulness, joy, excitement). Jot down **imagery**—sensory words—that relates to your object or scene and mood. Your notes can be raw material for a poem.

Object or scene:
Mood:
Sights:
Smells:
Sounds:
Tastes:
Touch:

Thus, images are not made just for the eye. When we read poetry, we must arrive at that point where we can say to the poet not only "I see the picture you are creating" but also "I see what you are feeling. I see what you mean."

Practice

Students' responses will vary.
Sample Responses
Object or scene—a half-time performance
Mood—excitement, nervousness
Sights—colorful flags, flashing batons, glittering costumes, fireworks
Smells—freshly-mown grass, popcorn, smoke from fireworks
Sounds—drums beating, horns playing, fireworks popping, crowd cheering
Tastes—buttery popcorn, spicy hot dogs, fizzy soft drinks
Touch—soft blanket, rough wool overcoat, hard plastic benches

Apply

Direct students' attention to the cartoon on p. 457. Ask them how the cartoon relates to Brinnin's statement that "images are not made just for the eye." [Possible responses: Images can appeal to all the senses, including touch. Some images hit readers at a more primal level—like a snowball in the face.]

Resources Reminder

Differentiating Instruction

- *Lesson Plans for Language Development*

For more instruction on imagery for English-language learners and special education students, see *Lesson Plans for Language Development,* pp. 199, 200.

CONTENT-AREA CONNECTIONS

History: Staffed Lunar Flights

The first staffed craft to land on the moon, in 1969, was called *Eagle.* Its American astronauts retrieved samples from the lunar surface and left debris, such as boots and backpacks. Subsequent expeditions did the same. These facts sharpen Haines's images of "moons half-broken, / eaten by eagle shadows . . ." and "soiled and scratched."

STANDARDS FOCUS, pp. 458–460

(For the review standard taught in this lesson, see citations on Student Edition pages.)

Prerequisite Standard

- Grade 8, Literary Response and Analysis 3.6 **Identify significant literary devices (e.g., metaphor, symbolism, dialect, irony) that define a writer's style and use those elements to interpret the work.**

Summary *at grade level*

This prose poem re-creates the speaker's experience of a fierce nighttime lightning storm in a high mountain pass where he is camped. As the colors and sounds of the storm explode around him, he and his companions are first frightened, then awed, and finally grateful, feeling a deep sense of connection to the natural world.

VIEWING THE ART

Nikolai Roerich (1874–1947), born in St. Petersburg, Russia, was an artist with a wide range of talents. In addition to painting landscapes and imaginary historical scenes, Roerich designed sets for plays, furniture, and murals.

Activity. After students have read "A Storm in the Mountains," have them discuss how *Celestial Combat* captures the tone of the prose poem. [Possible response: The clouds in the landscape communicate the power of nature.]

Before You Read

A Storm in the Mountains

Literary Focus

Prose Poems: Prose Form, Poetic Language

The following **prose poem** is written in ordinary paragraph form, yet it uses the elements of poetry—especially very powerful **images** that make the speaker's world easy to see and feel. Like other poems, this prose poem, by a Russian novelist, allows us to enter the speaker's world and make our own meaning of it. After you've read Solzhenitsyn's work twice, read it aloud to yourself. Does it *sound* like a poem? Why?

Make the Connection

Quickwrite

Nature sometimes reminds us of how fragile we are (consider Jon Krakauer's harrowing experience on Mount Everest—see page 352). Can you think of a time when nature gave you a wake-up call? You might recall an earthquake, a bad storm, a tornado, a flood, or a forest fire. Use a chart like the one below to jot down the key details you remember about your experience with one of nature's dramatic events.

Where I was	
What happened	
What I saw and heard and touched	
What I thought/felt	

Grade 8 Review Reading Standard 3.1 Determine and articulate the relationship between the purposes and characteristics of different forms of poetry.

Russian State Museum, St. Petersburg, Russia.

Celestial Combat by Nikolai Roerich (1874–1947).

RESOURCES: READING

Planning

- *One-Stop Planner* CD-ROM with Test Generator
- *On Course: Mapping Instruction*

Media

- *Audio CD Library*
  - disc 13
- *Fine Art Transparencies*
  - Transparency 12

Reading

- *Interactive Reading*
  - Interactive version: "A Storm in the Mountains"
- *Interactive Reading,* Teacher's Edition
  - Graphic Organizer: Imagery Wheel

Differentiating Instruction

- *Lesson Plans for Language Development*
  - English-Language Learners, pp. 201, 234, 250
  - Special Education Students, pp. 201, 234, 250

Assessment

- *Progress Assessment of Reading*
  - Selection Test
- *One-Stop Planner* CD-ROM with Test Generator

A Storm in the Mountains

Aleksandr Solzhenitsyn

translated by Michael Glenny

It caught us one pitch-black night at the foot of the pass. We crawled out of our tents and ran **A** for shelter as it came towards us over the ridge.

Everything was black—no peaks, no valleys, no horizon to be seen, only the searing flashes of lightning separating darkness from light, and the gigantic peaks of Belaya-Kaya and Djuguturlyuchat[1] looming up out of the night. The huge black pine trees around us seemed as high as the mountains themselves. For a split second we felt ourselves on terra firma;[2] then once more everything would be plunged into darkness and chaos.

The lightning moved on, brilliant light alternating with pitch blackness, flashing white, then pink, then violet, the mountains and pines always springing back in the same place, their hugeness filling us with awe; yet when they disappeared we could not believe that they had ever existed.

The voice of the thunder filled the gorge, drowning the ceaseless roar of the rivers. **B** Like the arrows of Sabaoth,[3] the lightning flashes rained down on the peaks, **C** then split up into serpentine streams as though bursting into spray against the rock face, or striking and then shattering like a living thing.

As for us, we forgot to be afraid of the lightning, the thunder, and the downpour, just as a droplet in the ocean has no fear of a hurricane. Insignificant yet grateful, we became part of this world—a primal world in creation before our eyes. ■

1. **Belaya-Kaya** (bye·lī′ə kī′ə) **and Djuguturlyuchat** (djo͞o·go͞o·to͝or·lyo͞o′chət): two mountains in Russia.
2. **terra firma** (ter′ə fur′mə): Latin expression meaning "solid ground."
3. **Sabaoth** (sab′ā·äth′): biblical term meaning "armies."

PRETEACHING

Selection Starter

Build background. The lyrical appeal of this prose poem comes in part from the rhythm of the words. Encourage students to consider the task of the translator who, in translating the work from Russian to English, had to balance the piece's literal meaning against its lyrical flow.

DIRECT TEACHING

A Literary Focus
GRADE-LEVEL STANDARD

Imagery. What sense is appealed to in this passage? [sight] Which words or phrases help you "see"? [Possible response: "pitch-black night at the foot of the pass."]

B Literary Focus
GRADE-LEVEL STANDARD

Imagery. Have volunteers identify examples of imagery that appeal to the sense of hearing. ["voice of the thunder filled the gorge, drowning the ceaseless roar of the rivers"]

C Literary Focus
REVIEW STANDARD

Forms of poetry. Although "A Storm in the Mountains" is written in prose, what qualities does it exhibit that in part qualify it as poetry? [Its phrasing is lyrical, and it has vivid images.]

DIFFERENTIATING INSTRUCTION

Learners Having Difficulty

Invite learners having difficulty to read "A Storm in the Mountains" in interactive format in *Interactive Reading* and to use the sidenotes as aids to understanding the selection. The interactive version provides additional instruction, practice, and assessment of the literature standard taught in the Student Edition. Monitor students' responses to the selection, and correct any misconceptions that arise.

Resources Reminder

Reading

- *Interactive Reading*
  - Interactive version: "A Storm in the Mountains"

Advanced Learners

Enrichment. Challenge students to list at least four other literary works in which a storm brings an insight. They might list such works as *The Perfect Storm,* by Sebastian Junger, or "The Snow-Storm," by Ralph Waldo Emerson. Invite students to compare "A Storm in the Mountains" with these other works.

Meet the Writer

Background. In his Nobel Prize acceptance speech, Solzhenitsyn said, "Literature transmits condensed and irrefutable human experience. . . . It thus becomes the living memory of a nation. What has faded into history it thus keeps warm and preserves in a form that defies distortion and falsehood."

INDEPENDENT PRACTICE

Literary Response and Analysis

Reading Check

1. Possible answers: *Where I was*—I was in a tent at the foot of a pass. *What happened*—A storm rolled in. *What I saw and heard and touched*—Clouds rolled in, lightning flashed brilliantly, thunder roared, and rain pelted down. *What I thought/felt*—I was afraid at first; then I felt awed and grateful.

Interpretations

2. Possible answer: The rhythm of the phrases and the vivid imagery make it a prose poem instead of a news report, which would be more direct and straightforward. *Details*—"no peaks, no valleys, no horizon to be seen"; "brilliant light alternating with pitch blackness, flashing white, then pink, then violet."
3. Solzhenitsyn compared the lightning to arrows shot by a biblical army, creating an image of something potentially dangerous flying through the air.
4. He compared himself and his companions to droplets of ocean water not fearing a hurricane.
5. Solzhenitsyn gains a sense of nature's majesty and a sense of connection with the natural world. A person might achieve a similar sense of connectedness simply by enjoying a quiet moment in nature.

Meet the Writer

Aleksandr Solzhenitsyn

Russia's Nobel Laureate

Aleksandr Solzhenitsyn (sōl′zhə·nēt′sin) (1918–) spent many years in Soviet prisons. Solzhenitsyn catapulted to fame with the publication of his first novel, *One Day in the Life of Ivan Denisovich* (1962), which details the daily life of a political prisoner. Solzhenitsyn wrote from firsthand knowledge: In 1945, he was arrested for criticizing the Soviet leader Joseph Stalin and sentenced to eight years in prison and labor camps plus three years in exile. After his release he taught mathematics and physics and continued writing. After the publication of *The Gulag Archipelago* (1974), he was exiled from Russia. In 1976, Solzhenitsyn and his wife settled quietly in Vermont, where he continued to write and publish novels about Soviet life under the Communist regime.

In his acceptance speech for the 1970 Nobel Prize in literature, Solzhenitsyn commented on the relationship between life and literature:

"The sole substitute for an experience which we have not ourselves lived through is art and literature."

In 1994, with the cold war over and Russia's Communist regime out of power, Solzhenitsyn and his wife returned at last to their homeland.

Literary Response and Analysis

Grade 8 Review Reading Standard 3.1 Determine and articulate the relationship between the purposes and characteristics of different forms of poetry.

Reading Check

1. Fill out a chart like the one in the Quickwrite on page 458. Base it on the experience Solzhenitsyn describes.

Interpretations

2. What makes this description a **prose poem** rather than a news report—or some other kind of writing? Cite details from the poem.
3. Writers frequently use **allusions,** or references, to compare one thing to something else. What allusion to the Bible does Solzhenitsyn use to help us see the lightning as he saw it?
4. What **comparison** does Solzhenitsyn use to explain why he felt no fear?
5. What meaning or lesson does Solzhenitsyn draw from his experience? What other experience might also make a person feel "part of this world"?

Writing

An Encounter with Nature

Write a **prose poem** in which you describe the experience you recalled in your Quickwrite notes. Use images to help your readers share your experience. What meaning did you find in your encounter?

ASSESSING

Assessment

- *Progress Assessment of Reading*
  - Selection Test

Before You Read

Same Song

Literary Focus

Imagery: Words You Can See, Hear, Smell, Taste, and Touch

Imagery is language that appeals to the five senses. An **image** helps us re-create a person, a scene, or an object in our imaginations. When you hear the words "red wheelbarrow," for example, you form a picture in your mind's eye.

In this poem the speaker makes an **allusion,** or reference, to an old fairy tale most of us remember from childhood. When you come to this allusion, and if you recognize it, be aware of the image it instantly puts in your mind.

Make the Connection

Quickwrite

What are some of the things that high school students do to "look good"? How do they figure out what "looking good" should look like? How important is "looking good" anyway? Jot down your ideas.

Reading Standard 3.7 Recognize and understand the significance of various literary devices, including imagery, and explain their appeal.

STANDARDS FOCUS, pp. 461–464

(For the grade-level standard taught in this lesson, see citations on Student Edition pages.)

Prerequisite Standard

- Grade 6, Literary Response and Analysis 3.7 **Explain the effects of common literary devices (e.g., symbolism, imagery, metaphor) in a variety of fictional and nonfictional texts.**

Reading Skills

- Extend the text.

Summary *at grade level*

This speaker describes her twelve-year-old daughter's morning beauty ritual, performed while the speaker's sixteen-year-old son sleeps. At night the daughter goes to bed early while the son exercises. Both of the speaker's children are critical of their appearance.

RESOURCES: READING

Planning

- *One-Stop Planner* CD-ROM with Test Generator
- *On Course: Mapping Instruction*

Media

- *Audio CD Library*
  - disc 13

Reading

- *Interactive Reading,* Teacher's Edition
  - Graphic Organizer: Imagery Wheel

Differentiating Instruction

- *Lesson Plans for Language Development*
  - English-Language Learners, pp. 202, 235, 250
  - Special Education Students, pp. 202, 235, 250

Assessment

- *Progress Assessment of Reading*
  - Selection Test
- *One-Stop Planner* CD-ROM with Test Generator

PRETEACHING

Standards Starter

Build prerequisite skills. Explain to students that allusions are references to people, places, things, or events from history or culture. For example, when you say a woman is "a Cleopatra," readers know that she is a great beauty like the queen who ruled Egypt from 51 to 30 B.C. Allusions deepen the meaning of a work by suggesting comparison.

DIRECT TEACHING

Ⓐ Literary Focus GRADE-LEVEL STANDARD

Imagery. What words or phrases help create the images you "see" as you read this poem? [Possible responses: "stumbles"; "squeezes into faded jeans"; "strokes Aztec Blue shadow"; "cold dark"; "expanding biceps."]

Ⓑ Literary Focus ADVANCED STANDARD

Allusion. Why does the poet repeat the word *mirror* here and in l. 21? [to allude to the fairy tale "Snow White" in which the beauty-obsessed, wicked queen asks her magic mirror, "Mirror, mirror on the wall—who's the fairest of them all?"]

Ⓒ Reading Skills

Extending the text. This poem focuses on gender-based expectations. Have students discuss these questions: "Are boys and girls expected to meet equally tough standards of appearance?" and "Do both genders feel equal pressure to meet these standards in order to gain approval and self-esteem?"

Same Song

Pat Mora

While my sixteen-year-old son sleeps,
my twelve-year-old daughter
stumbles into the bathroom at six a.m.
plugs in the curling iron
squeezes into faded jeans
curls her hair carefully
strokes Aztec Blue shadow on her eyelids
smooths Frosted Mauve blusher on her cheeks
outlines her mouth in Neon Pink
peers into the mirror, mirror on the wall
frowns at her face, her eyes, her skin,
not fair.

At night this daughter
stumbles off to bed at nine
eyes half-shut while my son
jogs a mile in the cold dark
then lifts weights in the garage
curls and bench presses
expanding biceps, triceps, pectorals,
one-handed push-ups, one hundred sit-ups
peers into that mirror, mirror and frowns too.

for Libby

DIFFERENTIATING INSTRUCTION

Advanced Learners

Enrichment. Discuss with students the idea that standards of physical beauty vary over time and between regions.

Activity. Have small groups research standards of beauty in a particular region or during a particular time period and share their findings. Discuss the many differences in beauty standards and possible reasons for them.

Meet the Writer

Pat Mora

"Am I Lucky!"

If Pat Mora (1942–) has her way, every April 30 will be *Día de los niños/Día de los libros* (Children's Day/Book Day), a national celebration of language and literacy. Mora wants to bring to all children the power and pleasure of what she calls "bookjoy."

"I was born in El Paso, Texas, and grew up in a bilingual home where books were an important part of my life. I can speak and write in both English and Spanish—am I lucky! I've always enjoyed reading all kinds of books and now I get to write them too—to sit and play with words on my computer."

After receiving her master's degree from the University of Texas in El Paso, Mora taught in public schools and college. Her poetry has been collected in several volumes, including *Chants* (1984) and *Borders* (1986). Mora has also written *House of Houses* (1997), a memoir about her Mexican American ancestors, and she has written many children's books.

Meet the Writer

Background. Pat Mora wrote about her children in "Same Song." She says she enjoys writing about family members, "like my aunt who danced on her ninetieth birthday, and my mother who wanted to be a rainbow tulip when she was in grade school."

INDEPENDENT PRACTICE

Literary Response and Analysis

Reading Check

1. The speaker is a parent; the subject is gender-based beauty standards and expectations for young people.
2. The stanza break serves to move the focus from the daughter to the son.

Interpretations

3. Possible answer: The title refers to the children's behavior. Their actions differ but the motivation or "song" is the same—to achieve an ideal of physical beauty.
4. Images of a girl stumbling sleepily to a mirror where she curls her hair, applies colorful makeup, and squeezes into a pair of jeans help you visualize the daughter.
5. Images of a boy running in the cold dark and of his muscles expanding during weight lifting help you see what the son is doing.
6. The poem alludes to "Snow White." It creates an unpleasant image of the wicked queen demanding that her mirror answer her question, "Who is the fairest of them all?"
7. Both are unhappy with their looks. The word *frowns* gives a clue.
8. Possible answer: She is unhappy because she is not fair skinned; she feels it is unfair that she must live up to others' standards of beauty.
9. The message is that people, no matter how different they may appear, feel pressure to live up to societal ideals. It is true for everyone, but young people might feel it more intensely, since they often crave peer acceptance.

Literary Response and Analysis

Reading Check

1. Identify the speaker in the poem, and briefly describe the subject.
2. What purpose does the stanza break serve?

Interpretations

3. What does the poem's **title** mean?
4. What **images** does Mora use to help you visualize the speaker's daughter?
5. What **images** help you see what the son is doing?
6. What old fairy tale is the poem **alluding,** or referring, to in lines 10 and 21? What **image** does this reference put in your mind? (Is it a pleasant or unpleasant image?)
7. How do the son and daughter feel about the way they look? What word gives you a clue?
8. How do you interpret line 12—"not fair"? What two meanings could the word *fair* have here?
9. What **theme,** or message, do you think the poem conveys? Is that message true only for young people? Explain your responses.

Reading Standard 3.7 Recognize and understand the significance of various literary devices, including imagery, and explain their appeal.

Writing

Beautiful and Handsome—Who Decides?

Where, in your opinion, do women and men in our society get the standards for the way they think they should look? (Review your Quickwrite notes.) Write a brief **essay** giving your **opinion** on this question. Support your opinions with details, examples, or anecdotes from your own experience.

Use "Writing a Persuasive Essay," pages 294–301, for help with this assignment.

ASSESSING

Assessment

- *Progress Assessment of Reading*
  - Selection Test

RETEACHING

For a lesson reteaching Standard 3.7, see **Reteaching,** p. 939A. For another selection to teach Standard 3.7, see *Interactive Reading,* Chapter 7.

Before You Read

Eating Together
Grape Sherbet

Literary Focus

The Speaker in the Poem

The **speaker** in a poem is the voice that talks directly to us. It's a mistake to think that the writer and the speaker are always the same person. Sometimes we feel confident that the speaker is the poet. Often, however, the speaker is almost anyone (or anything) else—a fictional character, an animal, or even an object.

The choice of a speaker affects a poem's **tone,** the attitude expressed toward its subject or audience. The speaker's tone and his or her style of speaking create the speaker's **voice.**

Make the Connection

The next two speakers remember food and family. If you were asked to name one food you associate with your family or with your childhood, what would it be? Jot down some notes.

Reading Standard 3.9 Explain how voice and the choice of a narrator affect the tone of a text.

The Meal or *The Bananas* (1891) by Paul Gauguin.

STANDARDS FOCUS, pp. 465–470

(For the grade-level standards taught in this lesson, see citations on Student Edition pages.)

Summary *at grade level*

In "Eating Together," Li-Young Lee evokes vivid images as he describes a family sharing a dish of steamed trout. The mother tastes the meat, and the speaker notes that she eats the trout the same way his father did. He then compares his father's death to a snow-covered road.

Rita Dove's "Grape Sherbet" describes the speaker's memories of one Memorial Day. With other children the speaker romped through a family cemetery, unmindful of those buried there. Later, after her father's death, she savors these memories and her father's role in them.

VIEWING THE ART

French painter **Paul Gauguin** (1848–1903) developed a stylistically innovative style of painting characterized by non-naturalistic form, heightened color, and symbolic subject matter.

Activity. What might the subject matter of *The Meal* symbolize? [Possible response: By representing children of seemingly different ethnic backgrounds sitting at a table on which is displayed a variety of fruits and bowls, Gauguin seems to symbolize diversity while celebrating the subjects' similarities.]

RESOURCES: READING

Planning

- *One-Stop Planner* CD-ROM with Test Generator
- *On Course: Mapping Instruction*

Media

- *Audio CD Library*
  - disc 13

Reading

- *Interactive Reading,* Teacher's Edition
  - Graphic Organizer: Imagery Wheel

Differentiating Instruction

- *Lesson Plans for Language Development*
  - English-Language Learners, pp. 203, 236, 251
  - Special Education Students, pp. 204, 236, 251

Assessment

- *Progress Assessment of Reading*
  - Selection Test
- *One-Stop Planner* CD-ROM with Test Generator

PRETEACHING

Selection Starter

Motivate. Discuss with students the importance that many cultures place on sharing meals. How does eating together create a sense of family?

DIRECT TEACHING

A Literary Focus
GRADE-LEVEL STANDARD

Imagery. What images are created in these lines? What sense does each image appeal to? [Possible responses: *Sight*—the trout in the steamer with ginger and green onion arranged on it; the mother holding the fish-head meat between her fingers. *Smell and taste*—the smell and taste of the fish, the ginger, the green onion, and the sesame oil.]

B Literary Focus
GRADE-LEVEL STANDARD

Speaker. Who is the speaker? [Possible response: The speaker is probably a sensitive adolescent male, because it's implied that the father wasn't that old when he died.]

C Literary Focus
GRADE-LEVEL STANDARD

Imagery. Why might the poet have chosen this image to describe the father's death? [Possible response: Although the words describe a cold and isolated place, they also evoke an image of a beautiful and quiet place, suggesting peace and contentment.]

Eating Together

Li-Young Lee

In the steamer is the trout
A seasoned with slivers of ginger,
two sprigs of green onion, and sesame oil.
B We shall eat it with rice for lunch,
brothers, sister, my mother who will
taste the sweetest meat of the head,
holding it between her fingers
deftly, the way my father did
weeks ago. Then he lay down
to sleep like a snow-covered road
C winding through pines older than him,
without any travelers, and lonely for no one.

Meet the Writer

Li-Young Lee

"A Guest in the Language"

For Li-Young Lee (1957–   ), like many Americans, English is a second language; Chinese is his first.

"I'm highly aware that I'm a guest in the language. I'm wondering if that's not the truth for all of us, that somehow we're all guests in language, that once we start speaking any language somehow we bow to that language at the same time we bend that language to us."

Li-Young Lee was born in Jakarta, Indonesia, of Chinese parents who were political refugees. His father spent nineteen months in an Indonesian jail as a political prisoner. The family later fled to Hong Kong, Macau, and Japan. Lee was six years old when his family arrived in the United States. He grew up in a small town in western Pennsylvania, where his father was the Presbyterian minister. He remembers his father teaching him how to read from the Bible.

"On Sundays, if we weren't making rounds, we were at home observing silence. At least twice a week, our family kept a whole afternoon of quiet, neither speaking nor whispering, my father, my mother, my sister, three brothers, and I keeping everything to ourselves in the one house of three floors of square rooms and identical doors. It was clarifying, the quiet, and our stillness felt like a deep liberty. It was one more detail of my life with my father which made me feel strange in a world which found my family strange, with our accented speech and permanent bewilderment at meatloaf."

Ever since the publication of his first two books of poetry, *Rose* (1986) and *The City in Which I Love You* (1990), Lee has been widely acclaimed as a major new voice in American poetry. The poet Garrett Hongo (see page 475) calls Lee's poetic memoir, *The Winged Seed* (1995), "a memory palace of exile . . . and retribution."

Meet the Writer

Background. In an interview for *The Kenyon Review,* Li-Young Lee addressed his need to approach poetry as a whole-body experience: "I don't write poems with my mind only. I know there are a lot of poems that when you read them you say, 'Well, this is a mentality writing,' and it may be a very great one. But it seems to me that poetry comes from my elbow, the ache in my knee. My hip. The soles of my feet. Literally. And whether or not they ache will determine what kind of language I'm using. . . . You see, language for me isn't a mental thing; it's like your whole body."

DIRECT TEACHING

A Literary Focus
GRADE-LEVEL STANDARD

Imagery. Which phrases help you imagine this scene? [Possible responses: "swirled snow"; "gelled light"; "cap turned up so the bib resembles a duck."] Which sense do these phrases appeal to mostly? [sight]

B Literary Focus
GRADE-LEVEL STANDARD

Imagery. Which sense does the poet appeal to in describing the sherbet? [taste] Which words or phrases help you "taste" the sherbet? ["like salt on a melon that makes it sweeter"]

C Literary Focus
GRADE-LEVEL STANDARD

Speaker. A poem's images can help readers understand a speaker. Based on the imagery here, how has the speaker changed over time? [Possible response: As a child, she was carefree, giving little thought to those who had died. Now as an adult, she reflects on how she misses her father and owes him for these special memories.]

Grape Sherbet

Rita Dove

The day? Memorial.
After the grill
Dad appears with his masterpiece—
A swirled snow, gelled light.
We cheer. The recipe's
a secret and he fights
a smile, his cap turned up
so the bib resembles a duck.

That morning we galloped
through the grassed-over mounds
and named each stone
for a lost milk tooth. Each dollop
of sherbet, later,
B is a miracle,
like salt on a melon that makes it sweeter.

Everyone agrees—it's wonderful!
It's just how we imagined lavender
would taste. The diabetic grandmother
stares from the porch,
a torch
of pure refusal.

We thought no one was lying
there under our feet,
we thought it
was a joke. I've been trying
C to remember the taste,
but it doesn't exist.
Now I see why
you bothered,
father.

Spending Time by Jessie Coates (1950–).

DIFFERENTIATING INSTRUCTION

English-Language Learners
To help students understand some of the visual images in the poems, provide photographs from magazines of items such as a bamboo steamer, a trout, a piece of ginger root, green onions, a slice of melon, a dish of sherbet, and so forth. Then, read the poems aloud, pointing to the pictures as you mention each item.

Resources Reminder
For lessons designed for intermediate and advanced English-language learners, see *Lesson Plans for Language Development,* pp. 203, 236, 251.

Special Education Students
For lessons designed for special education students, see *Lesson Plans for Language Development,* pp. 204, 236, 251.

Meet the Writer

Rita Dove

"I Know What You Meant . . . I Felt That Too"

Rita Dove (1952–), an avid reader, remembers that when she was growing up—in Akron, Ohio—there was a feeling in the household "that the only ticket you have to a happy life is to do the best you can in whatever you do. And the one place we were allowed to go practically any time was the library, but we had to read all the books that we got. . . ." In 1970, Rita Dove was a Presidential Scholar, one of the top one hundred high school seniors in the nation.

"I know that every time that I write a poem . . . I try to remember or try to imagine that reader—the reader that I was—curled up on the couch, the moment of opening a book and absolutely having my world fall away and entering into another one and feeling there was one other voice that was almost inside of me, we were so close. In writing a poem, if the reader on the other end can come up and say: 'I know what you meant, I mean, I felt that too'—then we are a little less alone in the world, and that to me is worth an awful lot."

Rita Dove is the youngest person and the first African American to serve as poet laureate of the United States (1993–1995). She is now professor of English at the University of Virginia in Charlottesville.

GUIDED PRACTICE

Monitoring students' progress. Review "Eating Together" and "Grape Sherbet" with students. Then, arrange students in mixed-ability groups. Ask each group to compose a dialogue between the poems' speakers, dealing with the ideas in each poem. Invite volunteers from each group to read their dialogue for the class.

Meet the Writer

Background. About the poetry volume that includes "Grape Sherbet," Rita Dove said, "I suppose what I was trying to do in *Museum* was to deal with certain artifacts that we have in life, not the ordinary artifacts, the ones that you'd expect to find in a museum, but anything that becomes frozen by memory, or by circumstance or by history. . . . The other thing was to get the underside of the story, not to tell the big historical events, but in fact to talk about things which no one will remember but which are just as important in shaping our concept of ourselves and the world we live in."

VIEWING THE ART

Jessie Coates (1950–) is a folk artist from Louisiana who lives in Baton Rouge. Her paintings feature scenes of rural African American life. This painting depicts a small rustic house and a family enjoying the outdoors.

Advanced Learners

Enrichment. Discuss with students that both Li-Young Lee, of Chinese heritage, and Rita Dove, an African American, have expressed a desire to write poetry that speaks to all humanity—not just to those who share his or her cultural experience. Ask students to write a short paper about the universality of the experiences described in "Eating Together" and "Grape Sherbet."

INDEPENDENT PRACTICE

Literary Response and Analysis

Eating Together

Reading Check

1. Possible answer: The speaker is probably a thoughtful young male. The family members at the table are his mother, brothers, and sister. He also mentions his dead father. They are eating a trout and rice.

Interpretations

2. "he lay down to sleep like a snow-covered road winding through pines older than him"
3. The tone is wistful and sad, but accepting. Phrases such as "the way my father did weeks ago" and "snow-covered road winding through pines older than him . . . and lonely for no one" suggest this tone.

Grape Sherbet

Reading Check

1. The speaker is a woman recalling childhood memories. She remembers the look and taste of her father's grape sherbet, and the way her father looked in his cap.
2. They are running over grassed-over graves in a cemetery.

Interpretations

3. The grandmother is compared to a "torch of pure refusal." She is refusing to eat the sherbet.
4. The children thought death was a joke; they chose to not believe that people were buried in the cemetery.
5. The speaker's father is dead, and no one can re-create his recipe.
6. She now understands the small ways in which her father connected with her. The poem's tone is nostalgic.

Literary Response and Analysis

Eating Together

Reading Check

1. Who is the **speaker** of this poem? Identify the other family members who are mentioned. What are they eating?

Interpretations

2. A **simile** is a figure of speech that compares two unlike things using a specific word of comparison, such as *like, as,* or *resembles.* What simile tells you what has happened to the father?
3. What is the **tone** of this poem—the feeling or attitude the **speaker** takes toward the events he describes? What details especially suggest that tone to you?

Plate with Grapes and Peach (c. mid-1870s) by Paul Cezanne.

Grape Sherbet

Reading Check

1. Who is the **speaker** of "Grape Sherbet"? What details does the speaker remember about a family get-together on a Memorial Day in the past?
2. What are the speaker and the other children doing in lines 9–10?

Interpretations

3. A **metaphor** is a figure of speech that compares two unlike things. Unlike a simile, however, a metaphor makes the comparison without using a specific word of comparison. What metaphor describes the grandmother, in lines 18–21? What is she refusing?
4. What is the "joke" in line 25?
5. Why does the taste of the sherbet no longer exist (lines 25–27)?
6. What does the **speaker** mean when she says, "Now I see why you bothered, father"? What **tone** do you hear in this poem—what feeling does the speaker reveal toward this family memory?

Reading Standard 3.7 Recognize and understand the significance of various literary devices, including figurative language, and explain their appeal.

Reading Standard 3.9 Explain how voice and the choice of a narrator affect the tone of a text.

Writing

Comparing Memories

In an essay, **compare and contrast** Li-Young Lee's poem with Rita Dove's. Before you write, gather your details in a chart like the following one:

	Li-Young Lee	Rita Dove
Speaker		
Speaker's memory		
Setting		
Food		
Tone		
Message		

ASSESSING

Assessment

- *Progress Assessment of Reading*
  - Selection Test

RETEACHING

For a lesson reteaching Standard 3.9, see **Reteaching,** p. 939A.

Before You Read

The Legend

Literary Focus

Tone: An Attitude

When someone says, "I don't like your tone of voice," you know that person is complaining about your attitude. In the same way, **tone** in writing is the attitude the writer takes toward a subject, a character, or the reader. Tone may be sympathetic or critical, humorous or sarcastic, ironic or sentimental, bitter or sad—or any one of dozens of different feelings. In speech, tone is identified by voice. In writing, tone must be inferred from word choice, or **diction.**

Make the Connection

Quickwrite

What news story have you heard or seen lately that struck you as especially moving or inspiring or sad? Maybe it was a story buried on the newspaper's back page; maybe it was a front-page story or one that led the evening news on TV. Maybe the victim is someone you would like to memorialize. Whatever the story was, make a few notes about it. When you finish reading the poem and the ***Connection*** that follows, see whether you can use this incident as the basis of a poem of your own.

Background

One night, Garrett Hongo saw a TV news story about an Asian man who had been killed in an act of street violence. Much later, Hongo claims, this poem "just appeared."

Reading Standard 3.11 Evaluate the aesthetic qualities of style, including the impact of diction on tone.

STANDARDS FOCUS, pp. 471–476

(For the grade-level standards taught in this lesson, see citations on Student Edition pages.)

Prerequisite Standard

- Grade 8, Literary Response and Analysis 3.6 **Identify significant literary devices (e.g., metaphor, symbolism, dialect, irony) that define a writer's style and use those elements to interpret the work.**

Summary *at grade level*

This poem opens peacefully on a snowy street in Chicago, where a poor man of Asian descent is placing laundry in his car. Suddenly, he is shot by a boy who has just robbed a store. The speaker feels despair about the murder and shame at being "so distinct" from the victim. He ends his poem with a prayer for mercy. (See Connection on p. 474.)

RESOURCES: READING

Planning

- *One-Stop Planner* CD-ROM with Test Generator
- *On Course: Mapping Instruction*

Media

- *Audio CD Library*
  - disc 13

Reading

- *Interactive Reading,* Teacher's Edition
  - Graphic Organizer: Imagery Wheel

Differentiating Instruction

- *Lesson Plans for Language Development*
  - English-Language Learners, pp. 205, 237, 251
  - Special Education Students, pp. 206, 237, 251

Assessment

- *Progress Assessment of Reading*
  - Selection Test
- *One-Stop Planner* CD-ROM with Test Generator

PRETEACHING

Selection Starter

Motivate. Have students consider their emotional responses to violent events reported on broadcast news or in the newspaper.

Discuss with students how this poem is characterized as an elegy, which is a poem of mourning, usually for the dead. Explain that elegies are generally solemn, even melancholy, in tone. Have students watch for these characteristics as they read.

Assign the Reading

Homework

Assign the Quickwrite exercise as homework before students read the selection. Then, in class after students have read the Connection, ask them to re-read and discuss the poem, using what they have read to help them interpret ll. 44–46.

DIRECT TEACHING

A Literary Focus

GRADE-LEVEL STANDARD

Imagery. Which senses does the poet appeal to in this description? Explain. [He appeals to sight with words and phrases such as "snowing softly," "twilight," "wrinkled shopping bag," "neatly folded clothes," "gloveless hands," and "Rembrandt glow." He appeals to touch with phrases such as "warm laundry," "crinkled paper," and "flannellike."]

VIEWING THE ART

Dutch painter **Rembrandt van Rijn** (1606–1669) is known for his use of golden light to suggest emotion.

Activity. Ask students to explain how the artist's use of light in the portrait relates to the poet's reference in l. 9. [The poet sees the Asian man as glowing from an internal light, just as the old man in the painting is.]

Hermitage, St. Petersburg, Russia.

Portrait of an Old Man (c. 1652–1654) by Rembrandt. Oil on canvas (108 cm × 86 cm).

The Legend

Garrett Hongo

In Chicago, it is snowing softly
and a man has just done his wash for the week.
He steps into the twilight of early evening,
carrying a wrinkled shopping bag
full of neatly folded clothes,
and, for a moment, enjoys
the feel of warm laundry and crinkled paper,

DIFFERENTIATING INSTRUCTION

Learners Having Difficulty

Remind students that a good news story answers the *5W-How?* questions: *Who? What? When? Why? Where?* and *How?* Have students read "The Legend" while looking for and writing answers to each of these questions. Then, encourage a discussion of how the first part of the poem reads like a news story, while the end seems more personal and emotional.

English-Language Learners

Explain the meanings of the following unfamiliar words: *Slick* in l. 17 means "patch," and *Fairlane* in l. 19 refers to a Ford automobile that was popular in the 1970s.

Resources Reminder

For lessons designed for intermediate and

flannellike against his gloveless hands.
There's a Rembrandt° glow on his face,
a triangle of orange in the hollow of his cheek
as a last flash of sunset
blazes the storefronts and lit windows of the street.

He is Asian, Thai or Vietnamese,
and very skinny, dressed as one of the poor
in rumpled suit pants and a plaid mackinaw,°
dingy and too large.
He negotiates the slick of ice
on the sidewalk by his car,
opens the Fairlane's back door,
leans to place the laundry in,
and turns, for an instant,
toward the flurry of footsteps
and cries of pedestrians
as a boy—that's all he was—
backs from the corner package store°
shooting a pistol, firing it,
once, at the dumbfounded man
who falls forward,
grabbing at his chest.

A few sounds escape from his mouth,
a babbling no one understands
as people surround him
bewildered at his speech.
The noises he makes are nothing to them.
The boy has gone, lost
in the light array of foot traffic
dappling the snow with fresh prints.
Tonight, I read about Descartes' **C**
grand courage to doubt everything
except his own miraculous existence°
and I feel so distinct
from the wounded man lying on the concrete
I am ashamed.

Let the night sky cover him as he dies.
Let the weaver girl cross the bridge of heaven
and take up his cold hands.

IN MEMORY OF JAY KASHIWAMURA

B **D**

9. **Rembrandt:** Dutch painter (1606–1669), famous for his dramatic use of color and of light and shadow. (See the painting by Rembrandt on page 472.)

15. **mackinaw** *n.:* short, double-breasted coat made of heavy woolen cloth, usually plaid.

25. **package store:** retail store where alcohol is sold.

38–40. **Descartes' . . . existence:** René Descartes (1596–1650), a French philosopher and mathematician, attempted to explain the universe by reason alone. In his search for truth, he discarded all traditional ideas and doubted everything. The one thing he could not doubt was the fact that he was doubting, which led him to conclude, "I think; therefore I am" (in Latin, *Cogito, ergo sum*).

DIRECT TEACHING

B Literary Focus
GRADE-LEVEL STANDARD

Tone. What tone is expressed by the speaker in this part of the poem? Is it the tone you would expect to find in an elegy? Explain. [Possible response: The tone is direct and unemotional—much like the tone of a news report. It is not the mournful tone common to most elegies.]

C Reading Skills

Interpreting. How does the poem change, beginning at l. 38? [Lines 1–37 tell what the speaker sees. The rest of the poem describes what the speaker feels.] What are the speaker's feelings about the events? [Possible responses: The speaker feels ashamed of putting reason, as represented by Descartes's beliefs, over feeling; the speaker feels compassion for the victim, as shown by his vision of the man's being cared for in the spiritual world.]

D Literary Focus
GRADE-LEVEL STANDARD

Tone. How does the tone change in the poem's last six lines? What is the effect of the change? [Possible response: The tone becomes sorrowful and more elegiac in l. 41. Then in l. 44, the tone becomes mystical, perhaps religious. The effect is one of mourning and then benediction for the victim, and it provides closure to the tragic story.]

advanced English-language learners, see *Lesson Plans for Language Development,* pp. 205, 237, 251.

Special Education Students
For lessons designed for special education students, see *Lesson Plans for Language Development,* pp. 206, 237, 251.

Advanced Learners
Enrichment. Invite students to explore Descartes's beliefs and to contrast them with the spiritual ideas suggested in the poem.

Connection

Summary ⇔ *at grade level*

Garrett Hongo relates an Asian creation story about a Weaver Maid and a Herd Boy whose sacrifice holds the universe together. The maid and the boy labor in distant parts of the universe without companionship or love. Yet for one night of the year, the universe, in its compassion, builds a footbridge of stars so that the two can spend one night together. The legend offers a promise that the universe will respond to the human heart and that we will ultimately know the reason for our struggles and be given a reward for them.

DIRECT TEACHING

A Reading Skills

Speculating. Why do you think Hongo wants to believe that the universe is merciful? [Possible response: to give meaning to the events he has witnessed.]

B Reading Skills

Extending the text. Most people have felt the same need for mercy that Hongo feels. How do some of them meet their need? [Possible responses: They turn to a religion that allows for mercy; they turn to a philosophy for explanations.]

C Reading Skills

Making inferences. How might readers infer that the origin culture of this story was rural as well as ancient? [Possible response: The river of stars and the weaver and the shepherd suggest a rural setting.]

D English-Language Learners

Definitions. Tell students that the terms *web* and *warp* are used in weaving. A web is a whole piece of cloth being woven on a loom. Warp is the name for the lengthwise threads in a woven fabric.

Hongo Reflects on "The Legend"

When he was asked about "The Legend," here is what Hongo answered:

(A) What I wanted, the city could not give me. I wanted *mercy.* I wanted the universe to bend down and kiss its own creation, like a parent does to a child just after it's born, as (B) if a tenderness were the pure expression of the world for itself. I wanted to believe that what was not given could be given, that were a man or a woman to cry out for solace, that the world, for all of its steel plants and tire factories, for all of its liquor stores and razor wire, for all of its buses that belched carcinogenic poisons and people who passed you by on the freeway who cursed you with their eyes—for all of that, it would still lay its soft wings of blessing upon you if you cried out in need.

From time to time, I'd recollect a story I'd heard during childhood, probably in Hawaii, a legend about the creation of the universe. From an aunt baking *pan dulce*[1] or a cousin flinging stones with me into waves along Hau'ula Beach, into abandoned canefields or at the headboards of the Japanese graves on the promontory at the (C) Kahuku plantation, I'd heard that, in order for the stars to turn and remain where they were, it took two creatures and their sacrifice. It took a Weaver Maid to make the stars—Being—and a Herd Boy to make sure they all stayed together or apart as they should. The Weaver Maid and the Herd Boy lived on opposite sides of the Milky Way, that band of stars that is our galaxy and which Asians see as a mighty river of stars. They call it The River of Heaven. The Herd Boy and Weaver Maid are stars on its opposite banks, the one in a cluster around Antares,[2] the other far away and down along the flow, in a spot near Aldebaran.[3] (D) They labor, dutifully fabricating the web and warp of Being, herding the star bands in an eternal solitude, celibate, without love or companionship. Yet, for one night of the year, on an evening when the star sky is said to be clearest, the universe is supposed to succumb to an overwhelming pity for the two lovers, living out lives in exile from each other, lives in deprivation of passion, without emotional compass or root in material certainties. In the form of a flock of compassionate starlings or swallows in the

1. ***pan dulce*** (pän′ do͞ol′sā): sweet bread.

2. **Antares** (an • ter′ēz′): brightest star in the constellation Scorpius. Its name derives from the Greek for "rival of Ares" (Mars).
3. **Aldebaran** (al•deb′ə•rən): brightest star in the constellation Taurus.

CONTENT-AREA CONNECTIONS

Culture: Creation Legends

Small-group activity. Have students work in small groups to research creation legends from other cultures. Members of each group can do research, provide visual aids, and orally present the legends and give relevant background information. Encourage students to discuss whether the legends promote the idea of a merciful or at least a comprehensible universe.

Japanese or Chinese versions, in the folded and gigantic wing of Crow in the Tlingit and Haida versions of the North Coast Pacific Indians, the universe, *one turning,* responds by making a footbridge across the River of Heaven out of its own interlocking bodies, out of its own need to create mercy and requital in a night of love for the effortful sacrifices of two of its children.

It is a vision of the afterlife, in a sense, a promise that the world will provide for us a reward and a reason for our struggles. It is a parable[4] about mercy and fulfillment, the response of the universe to needs of the human heart. The poem is the story of the Weaver Girl and the Herd Boy, told in inner-city, contemporary terms. It is about my own needs for mercy, for a fulfillment to a broad, urban, and contemporary story that baffled me.

4. **parable** (par′ə·bəl) *n.:* brief story that teaches a moral or religious lesson.

Meet the Writer

Garrett Hongo

Looking for Mercy

Garrett Hongo (1951–) was born in Volcano, Hawaii, and grew up in Hawaii and Los Angeles. After graduating, with honors, from Pomona College, he toured Japan for a year and then returned to the United States to write and teach poetry. Hongo says he writes

"for my father in a very personal way. He was a great example to me of a man who refused to hate or, being different himself, to be afraid of difference. . . . I want my poems to be equal to his heart."

DIRECT TEACHING

E Content-Area Connections

Culture: Versions of the Legend

Why do you think Hongo mentions that this story exists in slightly different versions in these cultures? [Possible response: Hongo wants readers to know that this story is powerful enough to have migrated from one culture to another; he implies that the imagery of this story carries meaning for various cultures.]

F Learners Having Difficulty

Summarizing. **Who are the two lovers in the legend?** [the Weaver Maid and the Herd Boy] **What does the universe do for these lovers one night a year?** [It makes a footbridge across The River of Heaven so the lovers can be together.]

Meet the Writer

Background. Garrett Hongo attended high school with Japanese, Caucasian, Hispanic, and African American students. He credits this early multicultural exposure with teaching him about the importance of cultural links.

Connecting and Comparing Texts

At the end of this reflection, Hongo states that his poem "The Legend" is his rendition of the story of the Weaver Maid and the Herd Boy. Invite students to explain how the story of the Asian man's murder relates to the story of the celestial lovers. [Possible response: By mentioning the Weaver Maid at the end of the poem, Hongo hopes that in death the man might find the mercy he was not granted in life, just as the Weaver Maid and the Herd Boy are rewarded by a compassionate universe for their lives of sacrifice.]

INDEPENDENT PRACTICE

Literary Response and Analysis

Reading Check

1. The setting is snowy twilight on a sidewalk in Chicago.
2. An old man who is putting his freshly washed laundry in his car is randomly shot and killed by a young robber.

Interpretations

3. Possible answer: He is ashamed because he feels no connection with the dead man.
4. Possible answer: By connecting the man with the legend—that in death the man experiences the love and comfort promised in the story of the Weaver Maid and the Herd Boy—Hongo can hold onto the idea of a merciful universe.
5. Possible answers: *Images of setting*—"snowing softly"; "twilight"; "last flash of sunset blazes the storefronts and lit windows." *Images of characters*—"carrying a wrinkled shopping bag"; "gloveless hands"; "Rembrandt glow on his face"; "a boy—that's all he was—backs from the corner package store shooting a pistol." *Images of event*—"the dumbfounded man . . . falls forward, grabbing at his chest."
6. Possible answer: At first the tone is peaceful, created by words such as *snowing softly* and *glow.* Then the tone changes to one of alarm and dismay, created by words such as *slick, flurry,* and *cries.* At the end the tone becomes mystical, created by the phrase "Let the night sky cover him."

Literary Response and Analysis

Reading Check

1. Describe the poem's **setting,** or time and place.
2. In this poem an ordinary street scene is suddenly transformed by a tragic event. What happens?

Interpretations

3. Why do you suppose the speaker in the poem says he feels ashamed? (Re-read lines 38–43.)
4. Read Hongo's explanation of how he came to write "The Legend" (see the ***Connection*** on page 474). How do lines 38–46 of the poem relate to the legend and to the death?
5. What **images** does Hongo use to help you feel as if you were an eyewitness to the setting, the characters, and the event (lines 1–37)?
6. How would you describe the poem's **tone**? In other words, what is the poet's attitude toward the event he's made into a poem? List some of the details and words the poet uses to create the tone.

Reading Standard 3.7 Recognize and understand the significance of various literary devices, including imagery, and explain their appeal.

Reading Standard 3.11 Evaluate the aesthetic qualities of style, including the impact of diction on tone.

Writing

News Stories Are True Poems

"The true poem is the daily paper," wrote Walt Whitman in 1852. Write a **poem** that is based on a newspaper story or a television news report. (Check your Quickwrite notes.) Follow Hongo's pattern in "The Legend": Begin with a close observation of the scene, and focus on one or more unnamed characters. Then, tell what happens, using present-tense verbs. End your poem with a comment on your own feelings and thoughts about the event. Use your imagination to elaborate with **sensory images.** You might want to gather notes in a chart like the one below before you write your poem.

News story that poem will be about:
Description of scene:
Character(s):
What happened:
Important sensory images:
My thoughts and feelings about the event:

A Letter to the Writer

In his reflection on the poem (see the ***Connection*** on page 474), Garrett Hongo expresses a hope that the world will lay its soft wings of mercy upon him if he cries out in need. Write a **letter** to the poet responding to his comment. Tell him of an incident in which the world did "have mercy" on someone in need.

ASSESSING

Assessment

- *Progress Assessment of Reading*
  - Selection Test

RETEACHING

For a lesson reteaching Standard 3.11, see **Reteaching,** p. 939A.

Literary Response and Analysis

Figurative Language *by* John Malcolm Brinnin

LANGUAGE OF THE IMAGINATION

Long before people began to communicate through writing, they uttered combinations of words having the sound of poetry. Yet after thousands of years no one has produced a single definition of poetry that takes into account all the ways in which poetry makes itself heard.

Yet we all know poetry when we hear it—whether it's a passage from the Bible, the chorus of a song, or a striking phrase heard on a city street. Poetry is different from the plain prose we speak and from the flat language of a business report.

Speaking Figuratively

One of the elements that make poetry is **figurative language**—language based on some sort of **comparison** that is not literally true. Such language is so natural to us that we use it every day. Let's say you read this in the newspaper:

The Budget Committee hammered at the Treasury secretary for three hours.

You don't ask in horror, "Will they be charged with murder?" You understand immediately from the context that the writer is speaking figuratively. A **figure of speech** is language in which one thing (here, the continual questioning) is compared to something that seems to be entirely different (repeated blows with a hammer). A figure of speech is never literally true, but a good one always suggests a powerful truth to our imaginations.

Stated Likenesses: Similes

A **simile** is a figure of speech that uses the word *like, as, than,* or *resembles* to compare things that seem to have little or nothing in common. In a literal comparison, we might say, "His face was as red as his father's." But when we use a simile, the comparison becomes more striking and imaginative: "His face was as red as a ripe tomato," or "His face was like a stoplight."

Similes are part of every poet's equipment. In a good simile the comparison is unexpected but entirely reasonable. The English poet William Wordsworth opens a poem with this now-famous simile:

I wandered lonely as a cloud. . . .

This simile helps us see at once that the wandering speaker has no more sense of purpose than a cloud driven by the wind.

"Remorse sits in my stomach like a piece of stale bread. How does that *sound?"*

(continued)

Reading Standard 3.7 Recognize and understand the significance of various literary devices, including figurative language, and explain their appeal.

STANDARDS FOCUS, pp. 477–478

(For the grade-level standard taught in this lesson, see Student Edition, p. 477.)

Prerequisite Standard

- Grade 8, Literary Response and Analysis 3.6 **Identify significant literary devices (e.g., metaphor, symbolism, dialect, irony) that define a writer's style and use those elements to interpret the work.**

Literary Focus: Figurative Language

Point out to students that, as the essay suggests, we use figurative language every day. Explain that if students pay attention, they can find examples of simile, metaphor, and personification in the worlds of sports, film, and music, as well as literature. You may wish to share the following examples with students:

- A sportscaster says that a football player is "a charging bull." (metaphor)
- A student comments that a critic is like a wet blanket, snuffing out the bright hopes of young writers. (simile)
- A singer might croon, "My heart whispers, 'Let's go,' but my mind screams, 'No!'" (personification)

Then, have pairs of students work together to write down and discuss the lyrics of a few popular songs. Have each pair identify and list any lyrics that compare two dissimilar things in creative ways. Students can return to their lists once they have read the essay and identify each example of simile, metaphor, and personification.

DIFFERENTIATING INSTRUCTION

Learners Having Difficulty

Figurative language. The newspaper sports pages are rich in figurative language. Divide the class into mixed-ability groups of three students. Distribute sports pages, and have each group scan them for examples of metaphor, simile, and personification. Ask each group to list their findings and to share their list with the class.

English-Language Learners

Be sure students know how to pronounce the words *simile* and *metaphor.* After they read the article, have them list figures of speech that may have puzzled them. (Some of these may be idioms, such as "nip it in the bud" or "in the wink of an eye.") Challenge students to classify each example as simile, metaphor, or personification. Then, discuss the literal and figurative meanings of each expression.

Practice

Possible Answers

1. *backpack*—My backpack groaned in protest when I plopped my thick history textbook into it.
2. *toaster*—The toaster was a comforting campfire, warming my icy hands.
3. *quarterback*—Like a general commanding soldiers on the battlefield, the quarterback led his team to victory.
4. *drummer*—The drummer, hands and feet flying in all directions, was an animated octopus.
5. *schoolyard*—From the top floor of the building, the schoolyard looked like an ant farm, with children scurrying to and fro.
6. *beach*—Desolate and lonely in the cold winter months, the beach came alive in the summertime.

Apply

Homework

Encourage students to continue to look for examples of figurative language in their daily lives and to share those examples in a classwide collection. Suggest that they listen for figurative language in the dialogue of television sitcoms, in the lyrics of popular songs, and in sports newscasts. You may want to have students as homework, look for figures of speech as they read newspaper and magazine articles, and then present their examples to the class.

Making Identifications: Metaphors

A **metaphor** is another kind of comparison between unlike things, one in which some reasonable connection is instantly revealed. A metaphor is a more forceful version of a simile because the connective *like, as, resembles,* or *than* is not used. A **direct metaphor** says that something *is* something else: not "I wandered lonely as a cloud" but "I was a lonely cloud."

Metaphors, in fact, are basic to everyday conversation because they allow us to speak in a kind of imaginative shorthand. Suppose a man enters a diner and asks for two scrambled eggs on an English muffin. The waiter might call to the kitchen, "Two wrecks on a raft!" The waiter is using an **implied metaphor.**

Many of the metaphors we use in conversation are implied: "the long arm of the law," "this neck of the woods," "the foot of the mountain." All these metaphors suggest comparisons between parts of the body and things quite different from the body. Even single words can contain implied metaphors: "She *barked* her command" compares human speech to the sound a dog makes.

Metaphors in poetry can be startling. Here is how the American poet Robert Lowell uses metaphor to describe a construction site in Boston in a poem called "For the Union Dead":

> Behind their cage,
> yellow dinosaur steamshovels were
> grunting
> as they cropped up tons of mush
> and grass
> to gouge their underworld garage.

Metaphors are often **extended** over several lines of a poem and taken as far as they can logically go.

Humanizing the World: Personification

When we attribute human qualities to a nonhuman thing or to an abstract idea, we are using **personification.** We call computers "user-friendly," for example, or say that "misery loves company" or that "the future beckons." Personification is widely used by cartoonists, especially political cartoonists. You've probably seen justice personified as a blindfolded woman carrying scales and love personified as a chubby infant with a bow and arrow.

In poetry, figurative language is the most important means of imaginative expression. It is a tool that poets have used through the centuries to translate the experiences of their times into personal statements.

Practice

Turn up your imagination as you think about common objects, people, and places. Using each of the subjects listed below, write a **figure of speech**—a **simile,** a **metaphor,** or an instance of **personification.** Then, pick at least one subject of your own, and do the same. Here's an example: "The computer monitor stared back at her like an unfriendly, unblinking eye."

1. backpack
2. toaster
3. quarterback
4. drummer
5. schoolyard
6. beach

DIFFERENTIATING INSTRUCTION

English-Language Learners
For more instruction on figurative language for English-language learners and special education students, see *Lesson Plans for Language Development,* pp. 207, 208.

Advanced Learners
Acceleration. Use the following activity to move advanced learners toward the eleventh- and twelfth-grade Standard 3.4, for which they analyze ways in which poets use personification and figures of speech to evoke readers' emotions.
Activity. Point out that for any given thing, a variety of comparisons can be made, with dramatically different effects. For example, to say that something is "as red as blood" creates a different feeling than calling it "as red as a rose." Challenge students to invent their own contrasting sets of figurative comparisons, using at least one metaphor, one simile, and one example of personification.

Before You Read

Simile

Literary Focus

Simile: Extending the Comparison

A **simile** is a **figure of speech** that compares two unlike things by using a connecting word, such as *like, as, than,* or *resembles.* If you provide the missing words in the blanks below, you'll have four similes so overused that they're clichés: as quiet as a ____; like peas in a ____; as busy as a ____; as cold as ____. Poets hate clichés (you should too). They try to invent imaginative similes that no one's ever thought of before.

An **extended simile** continues the comparison for several lines or even through an entire poem.

Make the Connection

Quickwrite

How do you feel after you've had a serious argument with someone you love? What images or figures of speech can you think of to describe your feelings? Jot down whatever words and phrases come to mind, and keep your notes.

Reading Standard 3.7 Recognize and understand the significance of various literary devices, including figurative language, and explain their appeal.

Simile

N. Scott Momaday

What did we say to each other (A)
that now we are as the deer
who walk in single file (B)
with heads high
with ears forward (C)
with eyes watchful
with hooves always placed on firm ground
in whose limbs there is latent flight

STANDARDS FOCUS, pp. 479–481

(For the grade-level standard taught in this lesson, see citations on Student Edition pages.)

Summary *at grade level*

In this poem, Native American writer N. Scott Momaday uses an extended simile to compare the speaker and another person—someone with whom the speaker has recently quarreled—to silent, watchful deer.

DIRECT TEACHING

A Learners Having Difficulty

Interpreting. Point out that l. 1 suggests that the speaker has had a quarrel with the person whom he or she is addressing.

B Literary Focus
GRADE-LEVEL STANDARD

Simile. Why does the image of walking deer create an effective simile for this particular situation? [Possible response: We generally think of deer as silent, wary creatures. People often become silent and cautious following a quarrel.]

C Literary Focus
ADVANCED STANDARD

Style. Point out the writer's use of repetition and parallelism, as well as short lines, which combine to suggest silence and wariness.

RESOURCES: READING

Planning
- *One-Stop Planner* CD-ROM with Test Generator
- *On Course: Mapping Instruction*

Media
- *Audio CD Library*
  - disc 13

Reading
- *Interactive Reading,* Teacher's Edition
  - Graphic Organizer: Figures of Speech Chart

Differentiating Instruction
- *Lesson Plans for Language Development*
  - English-Language Learners, pp. 209, 238, 252
  - Special Education Students, pp. 209, 238, 252

Assessment
- *Progress Assessment of Reading*
  - Selection Test
- *One-Stop Planner* CD-ROM with Test Generator

GUIDED PRACTICE

Monitoring students' progress. Guide the class in answering these comprehension questions. Direct students to locate passages in the text that support their responses.

True-False

1. The speaker is addressing a person with whom he or she has quarreled. [T]
2. The speaker is observing deer in their natural habitat. [F]
3. The speaker uses personification to describe the deer. [F]
4. The speaker and another person are compared to deer that are ready for flight. [T]

Meet the Writer

Background. Along with other prominent Native American writers, N. Scott Momaday finds it troubling that many of today's young American Indians have little connection to the beliefs and traditions of their ancestors. This concern led Momaday to establish the Buffalo Trust, an organization dedicated to helping American Indians reclaim their cultural heritage and its spiritual values.

For Independent Reading

Encourage students who read *The Way to Rainy Mountain* to work together to organize a storytelling festival, during which they present to the class readings of their favorite excerpts from the book. Challenge students to present a variety of the genres represented in the book—legends, historical accounts, memoirs, and poems.

Meet the Writer

N. Scott Momaday

Rock-Tree Boy

When N. Scott Momaday (1934–   ) was six months old, his parents took him to a sacred place—Devils Tower in Wyoming, which the Kiowa people call Tsoai (Rock Tree). There an old storyteller gave Momaday the name Tsoai-talee, which means "Rock-Tree Boy." (Devils Tower looks like a steep-sided volcanic rock tower—it is 865 feet high.)

Momaday says that schooling was a problem at Jemez, in New Mexico, where he grew up, because there were no high schools nearby. He recalled his mother's influence:

"My mother has been the inspiration of many people . . . certainly she was mine at Jemez, when inspiration was the nourishment I needed most. I was at that age in which a boy flounders. I had not much sense of where I must go or of what I must do and be in my life, and there were for me moments of great, growing urgency, in which I felt that I was imprisoned in the narrow quarters of my time and place. I wanted, needed, to conceive of what my destiny might be, and my mother allowed me to believe that it might be worthwhile."

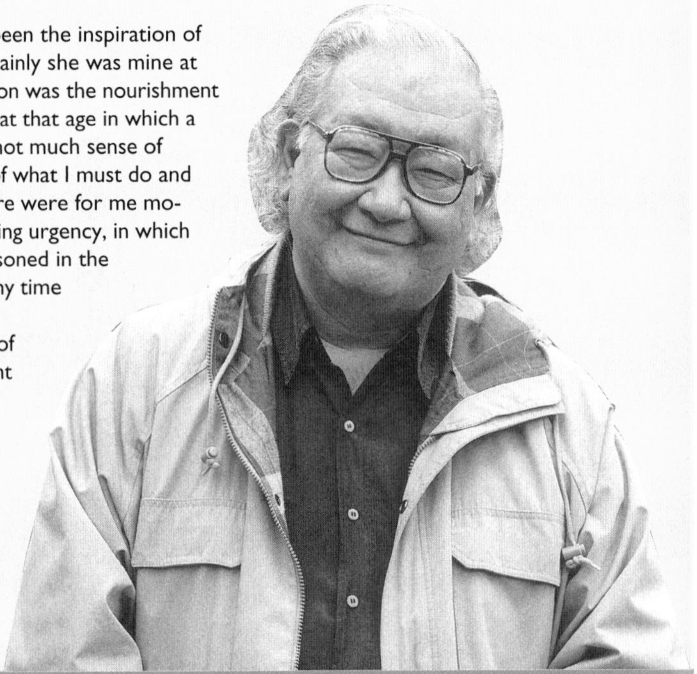

Momaday received his bachelor's degree from the University of New Mexico and his doctorate in English from Stanford University. While teaching at several universities, he has created novels, memoirs, poems, and paintings that draw upon his American Indian heritage.

For Independent Reading

House Made of Dawn (1968), Momaday's first novel, won the Pulitzer Prize in fiction. His memoir *The Way to Rainy Mountain* (1969) combines Kiowa legend, history, personal memories, and poetry.

DIFFERENTIATING INSTRUCTION

Advanced Learners

Acceleration. Use the following activity to move advanced learners toward the eleventh- and twelfth-grade Standard 3.4, for which they analyze ways in which poets use figures of speech to evoke readers' emotions.

Activity. Challenge students to characterize the tone and mood of the poem and to identify the emotions that the poem evokes in readers. Then, ask students to think of different tones, moods, and emotions that the subject of quarreling people might evoke. (For example: The humorous tone and lighthearted mood of sitcoms in which the characters' arguments evoke laughter from the audience.) Have students suggest two or three similes for quarreling people that are different in tone and mood—and, thus, in reader response—from that of "Simile."

Literary Response and Analysis

Interpretations

1. Whom is the **speaker** addressing? Before the poem begins, what has happened?
2. In the poem's **extended simile,** in what specific ways are the speaker and the person he or she is addressing like the deer?
3. What do you think is the special significance of the last line? (What is "latent flight"?)

Writing

"We Are Like . . ."

When two people who loved each other walk away from each other, what do they remind you of? You might think of something from the animal, vegetable, or mineral worlds. Write a poem in which you extend your comparison for at least three lines. (Check your Quickwrite notes.)

Comparing Similes

The poem below is by another American poet, Amy Lowell. Read the poem carefully, and then write a paragraph in which you **compare** this poem to Momaday's "Simile." First, summarize the text of each poem. Then, explain the terms of the comparison in the simile in each poem. Finally, tell which **simile** you think more powerfully describes the separation of lovers.

The Taxi

Amy Lowell

When I go away from you
The world beats dead
Like a slackened drum.
I call out for you against the jutted stars
And shout into the ridges of the wind.
Streets coming fast,
One after the other,
Wedge you away from me,
And the lamps of the city prick my eyes
So that I can no longer see your face.
Why should I leave you,
To wound myself upon the sharp edges
  of the night?

Reading Standard 3.7 Recognize and understand the significance of various literary devices, including figurative language, and explain their appeal.

INDEPENDENT PRACTICE

Literary Response and Analysis

Interpretations

1. Possible answers: The speaker is probably addressing a loved one or close friend. The speaker and the person being addressed have had a quarrel.
2. Possible answers: They are walking in single file. (Perhaps they had previously been side by side.) Their heads are high. They are alert to sounds and watchful, perhaps careful, about what to say next or about what action the other will take. Each is watching his or her step and is prepared to flee, if necessary.
3. Possible answers: The two people are prepared to bolt at the next sign of trouble; each is prepared to run from the other.

ASSESSING

Assessment

- *Progress Assessment of Reading*
  - Selection Test

RETEACHING

For a lesson reteaching Standard 3.7, see **Reteaching,** p. 939A. For another selection to teach Standard 3.7, see *Interactive Reading,* Chapter 7.

DIFFERENTIATING INSTRUCTION

Learners Having Difficulty

You may wish to have students work in small groups to answer the Interpretations questions and discuss the comparison of quarreling people to deer poised for flight. *Monitoring tip:* Before approaching question 3, have students offer definitions of the word *latent.* If necessary, define the word for them or refer them to a dictionary.

STANDARDS FOCUS, pp. 482–486

(For grade-level and review standards taught in this lesson, see citations on Student Edition pages.)

Summary ↔ *at grade level*

In this straightforward lyric, the speaker offers and expresses his love through a poem. The speaker's love is protective, comforting, and nurturing. It is described, in "homey" figures of speech, as a warm coat, a pot of corn, and a cabin in thick woods. The speaker's final message is that love is "all anyone needs" to protect one's inner life from an indifferent world.

PRETEACHING

Standards Starter

Motivate. Point out to students that they are probably already familiar with lyric poetry—from the popular music they listen to every day. Have them form small groups to prepare lists of popular songs that could be considered "lyric poetry." Then, have groups compare their lists and discuss the songs they have chosen.

Before You Read

I Am Offering This Poem

Literary Focus

Lyric Poetry: Singing Your Feelings

Lyric poetry owes its name to the ancient Greeks, who used the word *lyrikos* to refer to brief poems they sang to the accompaniment of the lyre, a stringed instrument. Today most lyrics are short, and they are still musical. Unlike a narrative poem, which tells a story, a lyric poem uses language to suggest (rather than state directly) a single, strong emotion. Most of the poems in this chapter are lyric poems.

Make the Connection

Quickwrite

Suppose someone says to you, "I have nothing to give you—except love." How would you feel? Is love enough? Jot down your ideas, and save your notes.

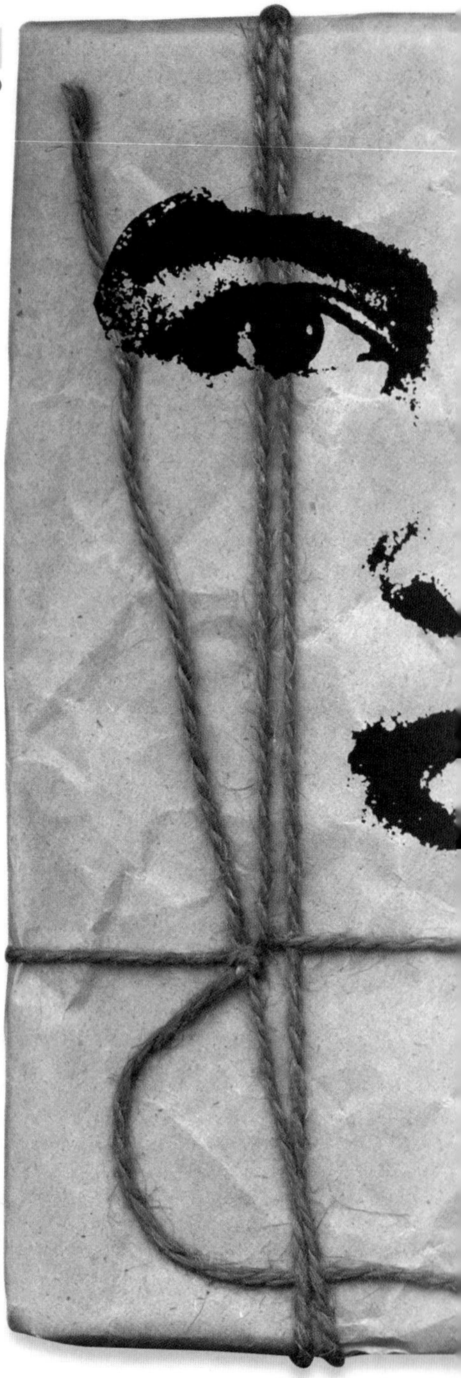

Grade 8 Review Reading Standard 3.1 Determine and articulate the relationship between the purposes and characteristics of different forms of poetry (e.g., lyric).

RESOURCES: READING

Planning
- *One-Stop Planner* CD-ROM with Test Generator
- *On Course: Mapping Instruction*

Media
- *Audio CD Library*
  - disc 13

Reading
- *Interactive Reading,* Teacher's Edition
  - Graphic Organizer: Figures of Speech Chart

Differentiating Instruction
- *Lesson Plans for Language Development*
  - English-Language Learners, pp. 210, 239, 252
  - Special Education Students, pp. 211, 239, 252

Assessment
- *Progress Assessment of Reading*
  - Selection Test
- *One-Stop Planner* CD-ROM with Test Generator

I Am Offering This Poem

Jimmy Santiago Baca

I am offering this poem to you,
since I have nothing else to give.
Keep it like a warm coat
when winter comes to cover you, **A**
or like a pair of thick socks
the cold cannot bite through,

I love you,

I have nothing else to give you,
so it is a pot full of yellow corn
to warm your belly in winter,
it is a scarf for your head, to wear
over your hair, to tie up around your face,

I love you,

Keep it, treasure this as you would
if you were lost, needing direction,
in the wilderness life becomes when mature;
and in the corner of your drawer,
tucked away like a cabin or hogan **B**
in dense trees, come knocking,
and I will answer, give you directions,
and let you warm yourself by this fire,
rest by this fire, and make you feel safe,

I love you,

It's all I have to give,
and all anyone needs to live,
and to go on living inside,
when the world outside **C**
no longer cares if you live or die;
remember,

I love you.

Meet the Writer

Jimmy Santiago Baca

To Prove That He Exists

Jimmy Santiago Baca (1952–) says he began to write so the world would know he existed. Born in New Mexico of Mexican American and Apache ancestry, he was abandoned by his parents when he was two. Baca's grandmother took care of him until he was sent to an orphanage at five. At eleven he ran away, living on the streets until he landed in prison at eighteen for possessing drugs. In prison, Baca felt sure he was going to die:

> "And I had to tell somebody that I was here. . . . It's unthinkable to come to a universe, to live as a human being, and then to die and not have anyone ever know you were there."

Baca taught himself to read and write in prison. He also began to keep a journal and eventually attended a poetry workshop. Then he "took a wild chance." He sent some poems to a magazine, and the magazine published them. Five books of poetry followed, along with essays, a screenplay, and a novel. Today Baca lives with his wife and sons in an old adobe house south of Albuquerque.

DIRECT TEACHING

A Literary Focus
GRADE-LEVEL STANDARD

Lyric poetry. Lyric poetry is a form for expressing strong feelings. What two strong feelings does this stanza suggest? [Possible responses: love, generosity]

B Reading Skills

Analyzing diction. Explain that a *hogan* is a traditional Navajo log home, hexagonal in shape, with a roof of packed earth and a doorway facing east. Why is the word *hogan* a better choice than, say, *home* would be? [Possible response: The word *hogan* gives a more precise visual image and extends the poem's cultural context.]

C Learners Having Difficulty

Paraphrasing. Ask students to explain in their own words the ideas in the poem's final stanza. [Possible response: Love is all I have to give you, and it's all you need to survive the difficult moments in your life. When things are tough, remember that I love you.]

Meet the Writer

Background. Jimmy Santiago Baca has said that "Real poetry comes from and expresses the common energy of the people. Those who divorce poetry from life rob it of its redemptive power." Although he is a highly acclaimed writer and the winner of many prestigious awards and prizes, Baca considers himself a "poet of the people." He conducts writing workshops at schools, colleges, reservations, barrio community centers, housing projects, and correctional facilities throughout the country.

DIFFERENTIATING INSTRUCTION

English-Language Learners

Although Baca's word choice should not present many problems for students, several sentence constructions might. Help students recognize the elliptical language in l. 16, and work with them to supply missing words in order to clarify the meaning. (For example, "in the wilderness [that] life becomes when [it is] mature. . . .")

Resources Reminder

For lessons designed for intermediate and advanced English-language learners, see *Lesson Plans for Language Development,* pp. 210, 239, 252.

Special Education Students

For lessons designed for special education students, see *Lesson Plans for Language Development,* pp. 211, 239, 252.

Summary at grade level

This lyric pits emotion against intellect, using grammar as a main metaphor. The speaker is trying to persuade his lover to join him in championing feeling over syntax, kisses over wisdom, a flutter of eyelids over an idea or thought, and life over a paragraph. The poem's often-quoted final line, "And death i think is no parenthesis," could be taken as saying that love is stronger than death or, on the contrary, that death is final and we must therefore enjoy life while it lasts.

PRETEACHING

Standards Starter

Build prerequisite skills. Provide several examples of similes and metaphors to help students understand the difference between the two figures of speech. For example, "My love is like a fire that burns out of control" (simile) and "My love is a fire burning out of control" (metaphor). Then, explain that Cummings uses both directly stated and implied metaphor in this poem. Point out that the poem's main metaphor, in which grammar and syntax stand for a too orderly approach to life, is not stated directly, but implied.

Before You Read

since feeling is first

Literary Focus

Metaphors: Grammar and Love

Lovers cannot bear to think of their love ending or of death separating them. Here a poet sings of love and puts down death, in two metaphors that only a writer would think of.

Like a simile, a **metaphor** is a surprising comparison between two unlike things, but a metaphor is more direct than a simile—it states that something *is* something else.

Make the Connection

Feeling Your Way

At first sight this poem might look difficult. Its lines break at unusual places; there is no capitalization; the punctuation isn't standard; and words are used in odd ways. If you read the poem silently a couple of times, however, and then read it aloud, you'll quickly "own" it—you'll be able to say, "I see what you mean. I understand how you feel."

Reading Standard 3.7 Recognize and understand the significance of various literary devices, including figurative language, and explain their appeal.

Lovers (1929) by Marc Chagall. Oil on canvas.

DIFFERENTIATING INSTRUCTION

Learners Having Difficulty

Explain that "since feeling is first" contrasts order and feelings. Invite students to create a two-column chart that displays these two aspects of the poem. Under the heading "Order," students should list such aspects as *syntax, wisdom, brain, paragraph,* and *parenthesis.* Under the heading "Emotion," students should add aspects related to feelings, such as *kiss, fool, kisses, flowers, cry, eyelids' flutter, laugh,* and *death.*

Resources Reminder

For lessons designed for intermediate and advanced English-language learners, see *Lesson Plans for Language Development,* pp. 210, 239, 252.

Special Education Students

For lessons designed for special education students, see *Lesson Plans for Language Development,* pp. 211, 239, 252.

Advanced Learners

Acceleration. Use the following activity to move advanced learners toward the eleventh- and twelfth-grade Standard 3.3, for

since feeling is first

E. E. Cummings

since feeling is first
who pays any attention
to the syntax° of things
will never wholly kiss you; **A**

wholly to be a fool
while Spring is in the world

my blood approves,
and kisses are a better fate
than wisdom **B**
lady i swear by all flowers. Don't cry
—the best gesture of my brain is less than
your eyelids' flutter which says

we are for each other:then
laugh,leaning back in my arms
for life's not a paragraph **C**

And death i think is no parenthesis **D**

---

3. **syntax** (sin'taks') *n.:* arrangement of words, phrases, and clauses in sentences; here, a systematic, orderly arrangement.

By permission of the Houghton Library, Harvard University (bMS Am 1892.11(92) folder 45).

Meet the Writer

E. E. Cummings

"Nobody Else Can Be Alive for You"

E. E. (Edward Estlin) Cummings (1894–1962) was born in Cambridge, Massachusetts. This son of a Unitarian minister grew up "only a butterfly's glide" from Harvard and "attended four Cambridge schools: the first, private—where everybody was extraordinarily kind; and where (in addition to learning nothing) I burst into tears and nosebleeds—the other three, public; where I flourished like the wicked and learned what the wicked learn, and where almost nobody cared about somebody else."

After graduating from Harvard, Cummings joined a volunteer U.S. ambulance corps in France. (The United States had not yet entered World War I.) A French censor decided that one of Cummings's odd-looking letters home was suspicious. So Cummings was arrested as a spy and held for three months in a prison camp, an experience he wrote about in a novel he called *The Enormous Room* (1922).

In his poetry, Cummings liked to use lowercase letters, space his words oddly across the page, and punctuate in his own style, although those oddities are only typographical. His themes are familiar: the joy, wonder, and mystery of life and the miracle of individual identity. He once advised young poets to be themselves:

> "... remember one thing only: that it's you—nobody else—who determines your destiny and decides your fate. Nobody else can be alive for you; nor can you be alive for anybody else."

which they analyze the ways in which the author's style achieves specific rhetorical or aesthetic purposes or both.

Activity. E. E. Cummings is famous for not following the rules of punctuation, capitalization, and other mechanics. Have students find examples in this poem of the poet's purposeful, playful disregard of conventional syntax and mechanics, including run-together words, missing capitals, and ambiguous constructions. Invite students to consider and explain how these stylistic devices reflect and reinforce the poem's message.

DIRECT TEACHING

A Reading Skills

Paraphrasing. How would you express ll. 1–4 in your own words? [Possible responses: In love, follow your heart, not your head.]

B Reading Skills

Interpreting. What does the speaker mean by the phrase, "kisses are a better fate / than wisdom"? [Possible responses: It's better to be in the world of love and emotion than in the world of ideas and knowledge; being able to love is better than being intellectual.]

C Literary Focus

GRADE-LEVEL STANDARD

Metaphor. Encourage students to explore this metaphor by identifying the features of a paragraph and noting how life differs from it. How is life not like a paragraph? [Possible responses: Life is more than an orderly, logical sequence; it is chaotic, joyous, unpredictable.]

D Vocabulary Development

REVIEW STANDARD

Multiple-meaning words. *Parenthesis* can have three distinct meanings: (1) a punctuation mark; (2) a word, phrase, or clause that adds an explanation or comment to a complete sentence; or (3) a literal interruption. Ask students to decide which meaning best fits the context of the poem, and why. [Possible response: A literal interruption, because the speaker is either saying that death can't stop love, or that death is a permanent, not a temporary break.]

Meet the Writer

Background. Poet Horace Gregory said that Cummings did not merely disregard conventional rules of mechanics. Rather, he devised new rules, "inflexible as laws in playing tennis, brilliantly stressed and pointed . . . orderly distortions and punctuations."

INDEPENDENT PRACTICE

Literary Response and Analysis

I Am Offering This Poem

Reading Check

1. He is offering the poem to someone he loves because "he has nothing else to give."
2. The refrain is "I love you."

Interpretations

3. *Similes*—"like a warm coat"; "like a pair of thick socks." *Direct metaphor*—"it is a pot full of yellow corn"; "it is a scarf." *Indirect metaphor*—"warm yourself by this fire."
4. Possible answers: Baca is right; as long as you have love, you can survive any circumstances. Millay is right; it is difficult to love when deprived of basic physical needs.
5. Any deeply loved person could be the recipient of the nurturing love described.

since feeling is first

Reading Check

1. *First sentence*—from "since feeling" to "kiss you." *Second*—from "wholly" to "wisdom." *Third*—from "lady" to "flowers." *Fourth*—from "Don't" to "each other." *Fifth*—"then laugh," to "no parenthesis."
2. Kisses are better than wisdom.
3. He insists that his greatest intellectual "gesture" does not have as much value as the smallest physical gesture that shows love.

Interpretations

4. Possible answers: In the last two lines, life is compared to a paragraph and death is compared to a parenthesis. The implication is that unlike these, life and death are not less orderly or rational. Cummings is contrasting emotion, life, and death with intellect and thought.
5. The speaker contrasts wisdom with kisses; a gesture of the brain with the eyelids' flutter; life with a paragraph. The speaker chooses kisses, fluttering eyelids, and life.

Literary Response and Analysis

I Am Offering This Poem

Reading Check

1. Why is the speaker offering this poem? To whom is he offering it?
2. What **refrain** does Baca keep repeating?

Interpretations

3. Throughout his poem, what **figures of speech** does Baca use to suggest what his love will do for the person he is addressing?
4. The speaker says that love is "all anyone needs to live." Another American poet, Edna St. Vincent Millay, has a poem that opens, "Love is not all; It is not meat nor drink / Nor slumber nor a roof against the rain. . . ." How do you feel about these two assessments of the importance of love? (Before you answer, check your Quickwrite notes.)
5. When we talk of "love poems," we usually think of romantic love. Could Baca's **lyric poem** be addressed to a child? to a good friend? to a parent? to anyone else? Discuss your responses.

Grade 8 Review Reading Standard 3.1 Determine and articulate the relationship between the purposes and characteristics of different forms of poetry (e.g., lyric).

Reading Standard 3.7 Recognize and understand the significance of various literary devices, including figurative language, and explain their appeal.

since feeling is first

Reading Check

1. Divide this poem into sentences that express complete thoughts. Where does each sentence begin and end?
2. According to the speaker of this poem, what is better than wisdom?
3. In lines 10–12, how does the speaker again contrast thinking with feeling?

Interpretations

4. In his **lyric poem,** Cummings expresses his feelings about love and death in two powerful **metaphors.** What are they, and how would you explain the comparisons they are based on?
5. Notice the **opposites** Cummings uses. A person who pays attention to the "syntax of things" (lines 2–3) is contrasted with someone who is "wholly . . . a fool" (line 5). What opposites does he pose to wisdom (line 9), the brain (line 11), and life (line 15)? In each case, which of the opposites does the speaker choose?

Writing

Twin Poems—Similar, Not Identical

In an essay, **compare and contrast** Baca's and Cummings's lyrics. For help finding the points of comparison between the poems, fill out a chart like the one below. At the end of your analysis, tell which of these love poems you would like to receive and why.

	Baca	Cummings
Speaker		
Person addressed		
Figures of speech		
Message		
Speaker's feelings		

RETEACHING

For a lesson reteaching Standard 3.7, see **Reteaching,** p. 939A. For another selection to teach Standard 3.7, see *Interactive Reading,* Chapter 7.

ASSESSING

Assessment

- *Progress Assessment of Reading*
  - Selection Test

Before You Read

Heart! We will forget him!

Literary Focus

Personification

Personification is a kind of metaphor in which a nonhuman thing or quality is talked about as if it were human. In "Heart! We will forget him!" Emily Dickinson addresses her heart as if it were a person who can listen, act, and feel.

Make the Connection

Trying to Forget

In this poem, Emily Dickinson tells the old, sad story of unrequited love—of love that is not returned. The poem is about conflict between will and emotion, between the thinking mind and the feeling heart.

Which do you think is more powerful—the mind or the heart? Does one control the other, or are they completely separate systems?

Reading Standard 3.7 Recognize and understand the significance of various literary devices, including figurative language, and explain their appeal.

Elvira Sitting at a Table (1919) by Amedeo Modigliani.

Heart! We will forget him!

Emily Dickinson

Heart! We will forget him!
You and I— tonight!
You may forget the warmth he gave—
I will forget the light! **A**

When you have done, pray tell me
That I may straight begin! **B**
Haste! lest while you're lagging
I remember him!

STANDARDS FOCUS, pp. 487–492

(For grade-level and review standards taught in this lesson, see citations on Student Edition pages.)

Summary at grade level

In this lyric about the pain of a love that has ended, the poet personifies her heart and instructs it to forget "the warmth he gave" while she forgets "the light." By separating the heart from the speaker, or emotion from reason, Dickinson implies that love cannot be easily tempered by rationality.

DIRECT TEACHING

A Literary Focus
GRADE-LEVEL STANDARD

Personification. Why do you think the speaker treats her heart as a being separate from herself? [Possible responses: She may feel that she's not strong enough to forget on her own and needs an ally; she may feel that her emotions function separately from her mind.]

B Learners Having Difficulty

Paraphrasing. Explain that *have done* means "have finished," *pray* means "please," and *straight* means "immediately."

RESOURCES: READING

Planning

- *One-Stop Planner* CD-ROM with Test Generator
- *On Course: Mapping Instruction*

Media

- *Audio CD Library*
  - disc 13

Reading

- *Interactive Reading,* Teacher's Edition
  - Graphic Organizer: Figures of Speech Chart

Differentiating Instruction

- *Lesson Plans for Language Development*
  - English-Language Learners, pp. 212, 240, 252
  - Special Education Students, pp. 213, 240, 252

Assessment

- *Progress Assessment of Reading*
  - Selection Test
- *One-Stop Planner* CD-ROM with Test Generator

GUIDED PRACTICE

Monitoring students' progress. Guide the class in answering these comprehension questions. Direct students to locate passages in the text to support their responses.

True-False

1. The speaker is talking to her former love in this poem. [F]
2. The speaker personifies her own heart. [T]
3. The speaker believes both she and her heart must work together to overcome lost love. [T]
4. By poem's close, the speaker has successfully forgotten her love. [F]

Meet the Writer

Background. In 1862, Dickinson wrote to a correspondent: "You ask of my companions. Hills, sir, and the sundown, and a dog as large as myself, that my father bought me. They are better than [human] beings because they know, but do not tell."

Dickinson did, however, reveal some part of her inner life in her writing. As editor Howard E. Hugo has said: "She could confide her poems to paper as if to a diary or journal, and therefore express and explore feelings too appalling to make public."

Meet the Writer

Emily Dickinson

Emily Dickinson (1848). Oil over a photograph.

The Granger Collection, New York.

Shy Genius

Emily Dickinson (1830–1886) rarely left Amherst, Massachusetts, her birthplace. There she lived unknown as a poet except to her family and a few friends, and there she produced almost eighteen hundred exquisite short poems that are now regarded as one of the great expressions of American genius.

She was the bright daughter of a well-to-do religious family; her father was a lawyer. As a girl at boarding school, she seemed high-spirited and happy. But something happened when she was a young woman (a love that was not, could not be requited, biographers speculate), and at thirty-one, she simply withdrew from the world. She dressed all in white, refused to leave her home or meet strangers, and devoted her life to her family—and to writing poetry. Of her own poetry, she wrote,

> "This is my letter to the World / That never wrote to Me. . . ."

She wrote her poems on little pieces of paper, tied them in neat packets, and occasionally gave them to relatives as valentine or birthday greetings or attached them to gifts of cookies or pies. In 1862, she sent four poems to the editor of *The Atlantic Monthly.* Only seven of her poems were published (anonymously) during her lifetime. When she died, at age fifty-six, she had no notion that one day she would be honored as one of America's greatest poets.

DIFFERENTIATING INSTRUCTION

English-Language Learners

Be sure that students know the meanings of some of the poem's less-familiar words: the imperative *Haste!* meaning "Hurry!" *lest,* meaning "for fear that," and *lagging,* which means "delaying" or "falling behind."

Resources Reminder

For lessons designed for English-language learners and special-education students, see *Lesson Plans for Language Development,* pp. 212, 213, 240, 252.

Advanced Learners

Acceleration. This activity can help to move students toward the eleventh- and twelfth-grade Standard 3.3, for which they analyze how tone and mood achieve specific purposes.

Activity. Have students identify and discuss the mood of the poem and the speaker's tone or attitude toward the subject. Point out that many poems about heartbreak are sad and mournful, but this poem is not.

Before You Read

Three Japanese Tankas

Literary Focus

Tanka Structure

The **tanka,** a Japanese poetic form, dates back to the seventh century and is written according to the strictest rules. In Japanese, tankas always have five unrhymed lines and a total of exactly thirty-one syllables. Lines 1 and 3 have five syllables each. Lines 2, 4, and 5 have seven each. (The English translations don't always follow this strict syllable count.) A tanka evokes a strong feeling with a single image.

Make the Connection

Quickwrite

A loves B more than B loves A; B used to love A but feared rejection and has decided to snub A. If you think you hear a lot of that kind of gossip in your cafeteria, take a look at love in Japan more than a thousand years ago. Jot down notes to fill out these metaphorical equations:
Love is . . . Life is . . .

Grade 8 Review Reading Standard 3.1 Determine and articulate the relationship between the purposes and characteristics of different forms of poetry.

A Closer Look

Poetry in the Golden Age of Japan

In the imperial court of Heian-era Japan (794–1185), poetry had both private and public functions. In private, poetry was the accepted language of love. A gentleman showed his interest in a lady of the court by sending her an admiring five-line poem (a tanka). If the poem she wrote in reply was encouraging, he paid her a visit. Their exchange of poems continued throughout their relationship, and each new message had to be original and intriguing.

Lovers also valued skillful calligraphy, exquisite paper, and a tasteful presentation. To match the mood of their poems, they covered tinted bamboo paper with scattered designs and tiny flecks of gold and silver foil. The final creation, carefully sealed with a twig or spray of flowers, was often lovely enough to decorate a folding screen.

Public poetry could be as romantic and beautiful as private poems, but it was presented and evaluated very differently. **A** At popular poetry contests (*uta-awase*), competitors grouped themselves into two teams, Right and Left. A judge gave the teams a topic, such as "spring" or "names of things," and awarded a point to the side that created and recited the more pleasing composition. The team that had the most points after several rounds won. The government Office of Poetry preserved exceptional spoken poems in written anthologies.

Summary ↔ *at grade level*

Each of these Japanese tankas is prefaced with a one-line context and is built on a single image. The first might be paraphrased, "Should we pass by the opportunity to light up each other's life through love?" Its image is the night sky, which can be flooded with light when the clouds suddenly part for the moon. The second poem evokes the image of the speaker aboard a "drifting ship." Every day since falling in love, she's been drenched in painful, cold water. The third poem was sent attached to a rice stalk with empty husks that are likened to the speaker's life. This life has "emptied itself," presumably after the loss of a loved one. In these poems, love is a wistful, often disappointed longing.

A CLOSER LOOK

DIRECT TEACHING

A Reading Informational Materials
REVIEW STANDARD

? Determining the adequacy of evidence. How does the author support the conclusion that public and private poems are equally romantic and beautiful? [The author provides no evidence to support this claim.] How might the claim have been supported? [by providing examples of public poems]

DIFFERENTIATING INSTRUCTION

Learners Having Difficulty

Suggest that students isolate these tankas' images—darkness, cold waves, an empty seed husk—and ask themselves, "How is living without love like this image?" Have students answer in their own words from their experiences or from their reading. Such reflection may provide enough context for students to identify with Komachi's speakers.

Advanced Learners

Acceleration. Use the following activity to move advanced learners toward the eleventh- and twelfth-grade Standard 3.7a, for which they contrast the major literary forms, techniques, and characteristics of the major literary periods.

Activity. Many cultures have produced their own forms of traditional love poetry. Have interested students research one culture or literary period, such as Persia, ancient Greece or medieval and romantic, and find examples of love poetry. Then students should write a brief essay comparing and contrasting a love poem of their choice with Komachi's tanka poetry.

PRETEACHING

Standards Starter

Motivate. Share with students this quotation by E. B. White: "I think there is no such thing as a long poem. . . . Poetry is intensity, and nothing is intense for long." Ask students to think about this idea in the context of the poetry form they are about to read, the tanka. How does the shortness of the form intensify images and feelings?

DIRECT TEACHING

A Literary Focus
GRADE-LEVEL STANDARD

Tanka structure. A tanka's five lines usually focus on a single image. As you read this tanka, what image emerges in your mind? [Possible responses: a cloudy night sky with moon breaking through; a man and woman looking at the night sky together.]

B Reading Skills

Interpreting. In this tanka, what might the "drifting ship" refer to? [Possible responses: The lover's indecisiveness or indifference; the speaker's insecurities.]

C Literary Focus
GRADE-LEVEL STANDARD

Tanka structure. Ask students to review the structure of this third tanka and identify the ways this English translation has remained true to tanka's strict rules. [The poem is unrhymed; there are five lines; l. 1 has five syllables, and there are thirty-one syllables.]

D Reading Skills

Expressing an opinion. It was traditional to attach a tanka to a spray of flowers or colorful autumn leaves. How would you feel if someone sent you an empty grain stalk instead? [Possible responses: puzzled; upset; insulted.]

Three Japanese Tankas

Ono Komachi

translated by Jane Hirshfield
with Mariko Aratani

1

Sent anonymously to a man who had passed in front of the screens of my room

A
Should the world of love
end in darkness,
without our glimpsing
that cloud-gap
where the moon's light fills the sky?

2

Sent to a man who seemed to have changed his mind

B
Since my heart placed me
on board your drifting ship,
not one day has passed
that I haven't been drenched
in cold waves.

3

C
Sent in a letter attached to a rice stalk with an empty seed husk

D
How sad that I hope
to see you even now,
after my life has emptied itself
like this stalk of grain
into the autumn wind.

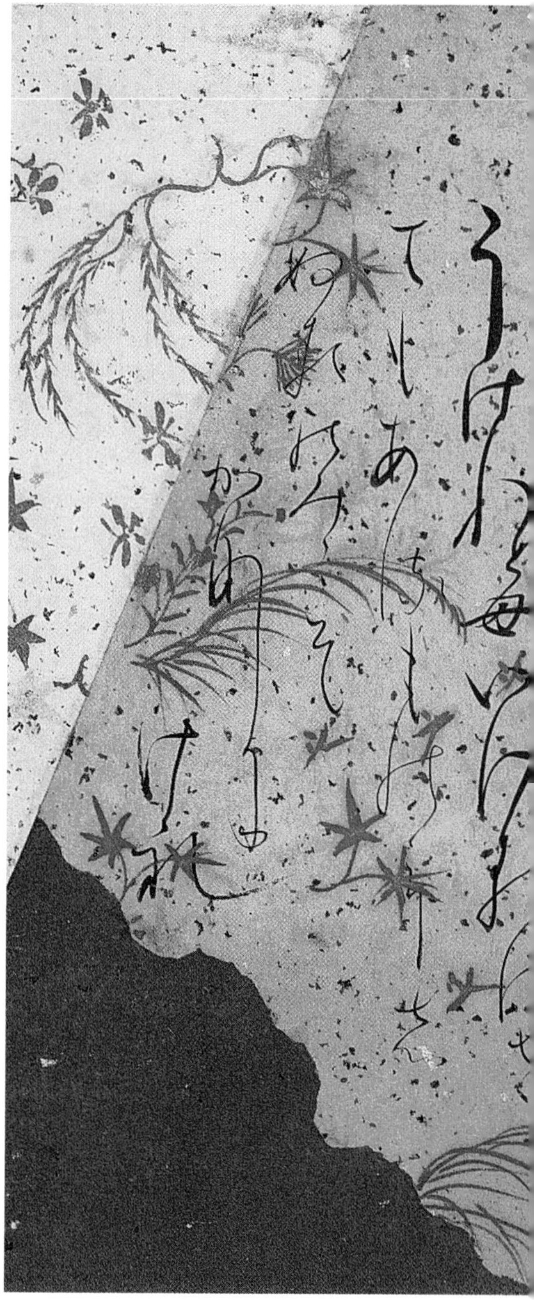

Page from Ishiyamagire: Poems of Ki no Tsurayuki (872?–c. 946). Calligraphy on paper.

Courtesy of the Freer Gallery of Art/Smithsonian Institution, Washington, D.C. (69.4).

DIFFERENTIATING INSTRUCTION

English-Language Learners

Help these students interpret the compound construction *cloud-gap* in the first tanka. Explain that it means "gap in the clouds," and that its brevity gives it greater poetic force.

Resources Reminder

For lessons designed for intermediate and advanced English-language learners, see *Lesson Plans for Language Development,* pp. 212, 240, 252.

Special Education Students

For lessons designed for special education students, see *Lesson Plans for Language Development,* pp. 213, 240, 252.

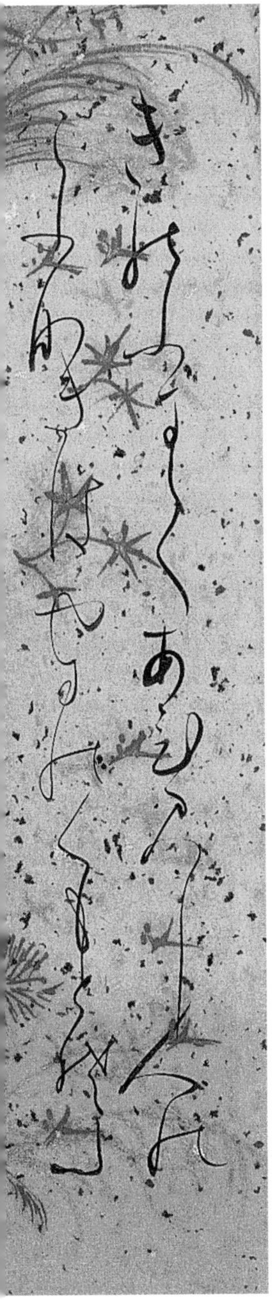

Meet the Writer

Ono Komachi

A Leading Lady and Poet

Ono Komachi (834–?) may have been the daughter of a ninth-century Japanese lord and may have served at the imperial court. Though little is known about her life, she is believed to have had at least one child and one grandchild. She was supposed to have been one of the most beautiful women of her time but is said to have died in poverty—aged and forgotten but still writing poetry.

Whatever the facts of her life, it is indisputable that Komachi was one of the great figures in an age when women dominated Japanese society and literature. In her hundred or so short poems that survive, she illuminates the subject of love through her understanding of Buddhist ideas about the fleeting nature of existence.

The Poetess Ono Komachi (c. 1820) by Hokkei. Surimono print (20 cm × 17 cm).
Spencer Museum of Art: The William Bridges Thayer Memorial (00.1561).

GUIDED PRACTICE

Monitoring students' progress. Guide the class in answering these comprehension questions. Direct students to locate passages in the text to support their responses.

True-False

1. One tanka focuses on an image of cherry blossoms in the moonlight. [F]
2. The speaker's heart, in one tanka, places her on a drifting ship. [T]
3. In one tanka, the speaker compares her jealousy to the green leaves of a flower. [F]
4. In these tankas, love is disappointing. [T]

Meet the Writer

Background. Among her contemporaries Ono Komachi's poetry was regarded as intense and passionate. Because of the reputation of her work and her beauty, she became the subject of many legends. More than five centuries after her death, the classical No dramatist Kan'ami Kiyotsugu wrote a play about her, presenting her life as a Buddhist allegory and describing her as "the brightest flower long ago."

CONTENT-AREA CONNECTIONS

Culture and History: The Heian Era
Share this quotation about the Heian era from Jerrold M. Packard: "[In] that long-ago Japan, beauty was measured in extraordinarily precise degrees of social refinement, in subtle nuances of life that was lived, at its height, in . . . observed niceties."

Individual activity. Call on students to point out evidence in the tankas that would support this quotation. [Possible response: The prose introduction to each tanka reflects the etiquette for writing and "presenting" poetry. The strictness of the structure of a tanka supports the idea of beauty "measured in extraordinarily precise degrees."]

INDEPENDENT PRACTICE

Literary Response and Analysis

Heart! We will forget him! Three Japanese Tankas

Reading Check

1. The speaker is a woman. She is talking to her heart.
2. The speaker is trying to overcome heartbreak by breaking free of the memories of the man she was in love with.
3. Possible answer: The speakers have all been disappointed in love.

Interpretations

4. She tells Heart to help her get over a lost love: Heart is to forget the man's warmth and to let her know as soon as that's done. Possible paraphrases: *warmth*—love, kindness; *light*—knowledge, wisdom.
5. Possible answers: *Night clouds*—gloom with a slim chance of joy; *the wave-washed, drifting ship*—loss and hopelessness; *the empty husk*—hollowness.
6. Possible answer: Dickinson's poem leaves readers with a feeling of determination, strength, and purpose, whereas the tankas leave a feeling of hopelessness.
7. Possible answers: The poems still touch basic emotions that transcend time; Dickinson's language and the tankas' customs are too outdated for modern readers.

Literary Response and Analysis

Heart! We will forget him! Three Japanese Tankas

Reading Check

1. Who is the **speaker** of Dickinson's poem, and whom is the speaker talking to?
2. What does the speaker in Dickinson's poem want to do?
3. Describe the situation of the speaker in each of the three tankas.

Interpretations

4. Dickinson **personifies** her heart by telling it to do things that only a person can do. What does she tell her heart? How would you paraphrase what she means by "warmth" and "light" (lines 3–4)?
5. Look back at the **images** and the **figures of speech** in the three **tankas.** What feelings do they suggest to you?
6. How does the **mood,** or feeling, in Dickinson's poem **compare** to the mood in Komachi's tankas?
7. All of these poems were written many years ago—the tankas are centuries old. Are they dated? Do they still apply to people's feelings and experiences today? Explain your responses to the lyrics.

Grade 8 Review Reading Standard 3.1 Determine and articulate the relationship between the purposes and characteristics of different forms of poetry.

Reading Standard 3.7 Recognize and understand the significance of various literary devices, including figurative language, and explain their appeal.

Writing

The Hidden Character

All of these poems contain hidden, unidentified characters—the men in Komachi's poems and the lost love in Dickinson's poem. If any one of these hidden characters could speak, what do you think he would say? Write a **letter** or **journal entry** in the character's voice (using the first-person pronoun *I*). Respond to what the speaker in the poem has written about you and about your love.

Try a Tanka

Review the information about the **tanka form** on page 489. Then, in tanka style, write a series of **poems** that trace a relationship. (You don't have to get exactly the right number of syllables in each line.) Try to use the **images** or **figures of speech** that you created for the Quickwrite on page 489. Finally, describe a symbolic object you might send with your tanka.

Bridge Across the Moon (1834) by Yashima Gakutei. Woodblock print.
Janette Ostier Gallery, Paris, France/Giraudon, Paris/SuperStock.

ASSESSING

Assessment

- *Progress Assessment of Reading*
  - Selection Test

RETEACHING

For a lesson reteaching Standard 3.7, see **Reteaching,** p. 939A. For another lesson to teach Standard 3.7, see *Interactive Reading,* Chapter 7.

DIFFERENTIATING INSTRUCTION

Learners Having Difficulty

If students have difficulty answering question 3, ask them to consider what idea all three tankas have in common. If necessary, encourage students to reflect on each speaker's feelings toward love in these tankas.

Advanced Learners

Enrichment. Challenge students to extend their responses to question 7 by writing a few paragraphs to defend their opinions on the timelessness of these poems. Remind students that when expressing their opinions about literature, they should provide examples from the actual text to support their ideas.

Before You Read

Shall I Compare Thee to a Summer's Day?

Literary Focus

The Sonnet: Strict Structure

The sonnet form favored (but not invented) by William Shakespeare is the **English sonnet** (also called, because he perfected the form, the **Shakespearean sonnet**). Its fourteen lines are divided into three **quatrains** (rhyming four-line stanzas) and a concluding **couplet** (pair of rhyming lines). Each quatrain makes a point or gives an example, and the couplet sums it all up.

For a biography of William Shakespeare, see page 741.

Make the Connection

Quickwrite

In Shakespeare's day every gentleman was expected to write sonnets in praise of his beloved. Writing a sonnet was a challenge, a kind of game. The speaker of this sonnet expresses passionate feelings within very strict rules—not an easy task.

Before you read this poem, write your response to this question: Why would someone want to compare the person he or she loves to a summer's day?

Alice Hilliard (end of the 16th century) by Nicholas Hilliard. Body color on vellum.
Victoria and Albert Museum, London/Art Resource, New York.

Grade 8 Review Reading Standard 3.1
Determine and articulate the relationship between the purposes and characteristics of different forms of poetry (e.g., sonnet).

STANDARDS FOCUS, pp. 493–496

(For grade-level and review standards taught in this lesson, see citations on Student Edition pages.)

Summary *above grade level*

In this Shakespearean sonnet, the speaker proclaims his beloved is "more lovely and more temperate" than a summer day. The first two quatrains argue that summer is fickle and fleeting. In the third quatrain and the final couplet, the beloved's qualities are presented as an "eternal summer," even defying death through the poem's "eternal lines." While clearly a tribute to a loved one, the poem also celebrates the immortalizing power of art, a characteristic Renaissance conceit.

PRETEACHING

Standards Starter

Motivate. Before students read the poem for themselves, have them listen to the recording of it in the *Audio CD Library*. This can help them with both the pronunciation of words and the meaning of the lines.

RESOURCES: READING

Planning

- *One-Stop Planner* CD-ROM with Test Generator
- *On Course: Mapping Instruction*

Media

- *Audio CD Library*
  - disc 13
- *Fine Art Transparencies*
  - Transparency 13

Reading

- *Interactive Reading,* Teacher's Edition
  - Graphic Organizer: Figures of Speech Chart

Differentiating Instruction

- *Lesson Plans for Language Development*
  - English-Language Learners, pp. 214, 241, 253
  - Special Education Students, pp. 215, 241, 253

Assessment

- *Progress Assessment of Reading*
  - Selection Test
- *One-Stop Planner* CD-ROM with Test Generator

DIRECT TEACHING

A Literary Focus
REVIEW STANDARD

Sonnet. Ask students to examine the poem's structure. Have them identify where each quatrain begins and ends and which words rhyme in each quatrain. Then, ask a volunteer to point out and read aloud the concluding couplet. Discuss the challenge that this strict structure might present to a poet.

B English-Language Learners

Multiple-meaning words. Help students understand that *temperate* means both "mild" and "constant" and that England's summer may be neither.

C Literary Focus
REVIEW STANDARD

Sonnet. How does this quatrain differ from the first two quatrains? [Possible response: In the first two quatrains, the speaker asks and answers a question focusing on summer's failings; here, he turns his attention to his beloved's eternal qualities.]

D Learners Having Difficulty

Paraphrasing. Point out the concluding couplet, and remind students that its function is to sum up the main message of the poem. Ask students to paraphrase the couplet in their own words. [Possible response: As long as men live and this poem lives, you will live too.]

Shall I Compare Thee to a Summer's Day?

William Shakespeare

Shall I compare thee to a summer's day?
(B) Thou art more lovely and more temperate.
Rough winds do shake the darling buds of May,
And summer's lease hath all too short a date.
Sometime too hot the eye of heaven shines,
And often is his gold complexion dimmed;
(A) And every fair from fair sometime declines,
By chance, or nature's changing course, untrimmed;°
But thy eternal summer shall not fade,
Nor lose possession of that fair thou ow'st,°
(C) Nor shall Death brag thou wand'rest in his shade,
When in eternal lines to time thou grow'st:
(D) So long as men can breathe or eyes can see,
So long lives this, and this gives life to thee.

---

8. untrimmed *v.* used as *adj.:* without trimmings (decorations).
10. thou ow'st: you own.

DIFFERENTIATING INSTRUCTION

Learners Having Difficulty
Guide students in paraphrasing ll. 3–4. (For example, "Stormy winds shake flower buds in May, and summer is too short" is a possible paraphrase.) Then, have students work in small groups to paraphrase the rest of the sonnet, two lines at a time, as an aid to comprehension. To help students understand ll. 7–8, tell them that *fair* (l. 7) is a noun meaning "beauty."

English-Language Learners
Students will benefit from a review of Shakespeare's language before they begin reading the poem. You might review archaic language (*thee, thou, hath,* and *ow'st*); inverted sentence structures (l. 5, "Sometime too hot the eye of heaven shines"); and unfamiliar meanings of words (*fair* meaning "beauty").

Resources Reminder
For lessons designed for intermediate and advanced English-language learners, see *Lesson Plans for Language Development,* pp. 214, 241, 253.

Special Education Students
For lessons designed for special education students, see *Lesson Plans for Language Development,* pp. 215, 241, 253.

Literary Response and Analysis

Reading Check

1. The **speaker** opens the sonnet by wondering if he should compare his beloved to a summer's day. How does he answer his own question? What reasons does he give in line 2 for rejecting the comparison?

Interpretations

2. In lines 3–8, the speaker continues to think about his comparison. What **image** does he use to show that summer weather is unpredictable?
3. Explain the **metaphor** and **personification** in lines 5–8. Why is the "eye of heaven" neither constant nor trustworthy?
4. According to lines 7–8, what can happen to any kind of beauty?
5. In the third **quatrain** (lines 9–12), the speaker makes a daring statement to his beloved. What does he claim will never happen?
6. What does the speaker mean by "eternal lines to time" (line 12)? What is the connection between those eternal lines and the prediction he makes in lines 9–11?
7. Would you say that this sonnet is a love poem, or is it really about something else? Explain your interpretation.
8. If you were going to describe someone you love, what would you **compare** him or her to? (See what you thought of the speaker's suggested comparison in your Quickwrite.)
9. Has the poet's bold assertion in his **couplet** proved true? In what ways can other kinds of art immortalize someone? Give as many examples as you can think of.

Writing

Are You Flattered—or Annoyed?

Imagine that you are the person addressed in Shakespeare's sonnet. Prepare a written or an oral **response** to this poem. What do you think of Shakespeare's rejection of the summer-day comparison? What do you think of the speaker's saying you'll never get old or die because of his poem? Decide what **tone** you'll take: flattered, irritated, sarcastic, confused, loving—something else? Meet with a classmate to present your responses.

William Shakespeare by David Levine.

Reprinted with permission from *The New York Review of Books.* Copyright ©1967 NYREV, Inc.

How Is It Made?

In an **essay,** take the sonnet apart to see how well Shakespeare has followed the blueprint for an English sonnet. Before you write, gather your notes in a chart like the following one:

Quatrain 1	Main point:
Quatrain 2	Main point:
Quatrain 3	Main point:
Couplet	Summation:

Grade 8 Review Reading Standard 3.1 Determine and articulate the relationship between the purposes and characteristics of different forms of poetry (e.g., sonnet).

Reading Standard 3.7 Recognize and understand the significance of various literary devices, including figurative language, and explain their appeal.

INDEPENDENT PRACTICE

Literary Response and Analysis

Reading Check

1. The speaker tries out the comparison and then rejects it, saying that his beloved is even better than a summer's day. In l. 2, the speaker explains that his beloved is "more lovely and more temperate" than a summer's day.

Interpretations

2. The speaker describes rough winds shaking the buds of flowers.
3. Possible answer: The "eye of heaven" is the sun, which is unreliable because it may be dimmed by clouds, fog, or rain.
4. Possible answer: Chance events or the passage of time can cause beauty to fade.
5. The speaker claims that his beloved—and the beloved's beauty—will never die.
6. Possible answer: The "eternal lines" are the lines of the poem. These lines will immortalize the beloved.
7. Possible answers: It is a love poem because it shows the speaker's strong, loving emotions; the poem is about poetry's power to endure as much as it is about love.
8. Possible answers: a song; the stars; the sea; a comfortable shirt.
9. Possible answers: Yes, because we are reading the poem centuries later; no, it has immortalized only the poet—we don't even know his beloved's name. Great art—be it poetry, prose, painting, or song—lasts through time, immortalizing its creators and subjects.

DIFFERENTIATING INSTRUCTION

Learners Having Difficulty

If students need help answering some of these questions, have them work in a small, mixed-ability group. *Monitoring tip:* If students have difficulty with question 3, review the definitions of metaphor and personification, providing examples for each.

Advanced Learners

Acceleration. This activity can help to move students toward the eleventh- and twelfth-grade Standard 3.7b, for which they relate literary works to the major issues of their eras.

Activity. To extend answers to question 7, have students share their knowledge of the Renaissance and its concerns, including issues of romance, humans' place in the world, and the immortal nature of art. Encourage them to discuss these issues in the context of Shakespeare's poem.

Vocabulary Development

Practice

thee: you
thou: you
art: are
hath: has
thy: your
ow'st: own
wand'rest: wander
grow'st: grow

Resources Reminder

Vocabulary

- *Lesson Plans for Language Development*
  - Vocabulary, pp. 241, 253

Grammar Link

Practice

Possible Answers

1. The eye of heaven sometime(s) shines too hot, and his gold complexion is often dimmed.
2. It would be placed after *declines.*
3. when thou grow'st in eternal lines to time

ASSESSING

Assessment

- *Progress Assessment of Reading*
  - Selection Test

RETEACHING

For a lesson reteaching Standard 3.7, see **Reteaching,** p. 939A. For another selection to teach Standard 3.7, see *Interactive Reading,* Chapter 7.

Vocabulary Development

Archaic Words: Long Gone and Strange to Our Ears

Shakespeare's plays are sometimes presented in modern dress, set in the present or in the recent past. In a contemporary movie version of *Hamlet,* for example, young Hamlet works in a high-tech firm and intones his "To be or not to be" soliloquy (speech to himself) while browsing in a video store.

The English language has been through many changes and is changing still, adding new words and meanings, letting others drift out of use. For example, in Shakespeare's day the pronouns *thee* and *thou,* along with the other *th–* pronouns, *thy* and *thine,* were used to address people whom the speaker was familiar with or intimate with (wife, husband, close friend). *You,* on the other hand, and the other *y–* pronouns, *your* and *yours,* were used with people who were not intimate friends or who were the speaker's superior (parents, bosses, kings). Shakespeare also used the verb endings *–st* and *–th* (as in *didst* and *goeth*), which are no longer used today. In fact, even in Shakespeare's day these verb endings sounded a little old-fashioned. Today all these words are **archaic,** which means they are no longer used. (For more about archaic words in Shakespeare's plays, see pages 752–753.)

Grade 8 Review Reading Standard 1.2 Determine the historical influences on English word meanings.

PRACTICE

What happens when you bring Shakespeare's language up to date?

Find all of the archaic words in this sonnet, and replace each one with its modern equivalent. Then, try reading the sonnet aloud—first with the archaic words and then with the modern ones. Does a "translation" work?

Grammar Link MINI-LESSON

Inverted Sentences—Variety and Challenge

Syntax refers to sentence structure, to the way words, phrases, and clauses are arranged to show their relationships. In his poem on page 485, E. E. Cummings lightly mocks people who worry about syntax, but without rules of syntax, language would be unintelligible.

English sentences usually begin with the **subject,** followed by the **verb** and, if there is one, a **complement.** Modifiers are placed near the words they modify. Some writers choose to wrench this syntax out of its usual order. Shakespeare, for example, in order to keep his rhymes and meter going, uses what we call **inverted sentences** (sentences in which the order is *not* subject-verb-complement and in which modifiers sometimes appear in unexpected places).

PRACTICE

1. What other word order could you use within lines 5 and 6 of the Shakespeare sonnet?
2. In line 7, where would the prepositional phrase "from fair" ordinarily be placed?
3. What other word order could you propose for line 12?

DIFFERENTIATING INSTRUCTION

Learners Having Difficulty

Some students may need additional practice in changing the word order of sentences. Write the following sentences on the chalkboard. Have students invert the syntax in any way that makes sense.

1. The summer sun shone all day. [Possible answer: All day the summer sun shone.]
2. The clouds rolled in, gray and cold. [Possible answer: In rolled the clouds, gray and cold.]
3. Love is rarely perfect. [Possible answer: Rarely is love perfect.]
4. My beloved, how might I find her? [Possible answer: How might I find her, my beloved?]
5. The flowers displayed their beauty in the rain. [Possible answer: In the rain the flowers displayed their beauty.]

Before You Read

Ode to My Socks

Literary Focus

Ode: A Lofty Lyric

A traditional **ode** is a long lyric poem about a serious subject, written in a dignified style. In ancient Greece and Rome, odes were recited or sung in public, often to celebrate a triumph in the Olympic Games.

From 1954 to 1959, the Chilean poet Pablo Neruda published four volumes of odes to such unconventional everyday objects and experiences as soap, onions, love, summer, the color green, French fries, corn, bees—and a pair of socks.

Extended Metaphor and Simile: Continuing Comparisons

Who would think that a pair of socks could inspire an outpouring of **metaphors** and **similes** in which the poet sees his new socks as rabbits, fish, blackbirds, cannons—and even more. Many of these similes and metaphors are **extended** throughout the poem, which means that the poet continues to develop points of comparison between his socks and other things.

Make the Connection

Quickwrite

If you could talk directly to a beloved article of clothing (a pair of jeans, say, or sneakers or a T-shirt), what might you say? Jot down some ideas, and save your notes.

Grade 8 Review Reading Standard 3.1 Determine and articulate the relationship between the purposes and characteristics of different forms of poetry (e.g., ode).

Reading Standard 3.7 Recognize and understand the significance of various literary devices, including figurative language, and explain their appeal.

STANDARDS FOCUS, pp. 497–502

(For grade-level and review standards taught in this lesson, see citations on Student Edition pages.)

Summary *at grade level*

Neruda chooses a lofty poetry form, the ode, to explore an ordinary, everyday subject—a gift of woolen socks. The speaker uses a variety of similes and metaphors to describe his socks and his feet while wearing them, likening them to animals and sea creatures, among other things. By celebrating the virtues of these mundane objects, Neruda illustrates the emotional richness attached to life's simple things.

PRETEACHING

Standards Starter

Build prerequisite skills. Remind students that a metaphor is a comparison between two unlike things that does not use a connecting word. Have volunteers provide examples of metaphors. Then, challenge students to create an extended metaphor by building on one of the examples, finding many points of comparison. [Possible example: Life is a roller coaster—it has ups and downs; it moves slowly at first and then speeds up; and, at times, it can seem like it is moving out of control.]

RESOURCES: READING

Planning

- *One-Stop Planner* CD-ROM with Test Generator
- *On Course: Mapping Instruction*

Media

- *Audio CD Library*
  - disc 13

Reading

- *Interactive Reading,* Teacher's Edition
  - Graphic Organizer: Figures of Speech Chart

Differentiating Instruction

- *Lesson Plans for Language Development*
  - English-Language Learners, pp. 216, 242, 253
  - Special Education Students, pp. 217, 242, 253

Assessment

- *Progress Assessment of Reading*
  - Selection Test
- *One-Stop Planner* CD-ROM with Test Generator

DIRECT TEACHING

A Literary Focus
REVIEW STANDARD

? Ode. Why is a pair of socks an unusual choice for the subject of an ode? [Possible response: Odes usually involve serious subjects, and socks would not normally be considered items of sufficient dignity to be the subject of an ode.]

B Literary Focus
GRADE-LEVEL STANDARD

? Metaphor. What qualities are suggested by the images of sharks, blackbirds, and cannons? [Possible responses: power; strength; sleekness; military bearing.]

Ode to My Socks

Pablo Neruda

translated by Robert Bly

Maru Mori brought me
a pair
of socks
which she knitted herself
with her sheepherder's hands,
two socks as soft
as rabbits.
I slipped my feet
into them
as though into
two
cases
knitted
with threads of
twilight
and goatskin.
Violent socks,
my feet were
two fish made
of wool,
two long sharks
sea-blue, shot
through
by one golden thread,
two immense blackbirds,
two cannons:
my feet
were honored
in this way
by

498

DIFFERENTIATING INSTRUCTION

Learners Having Difficulty
You may wish to group students in pairs or small groups to read and analyze the poem. Students can work together to identify and categorize the examples of figurative language used by the speaker to describe the socks and his relationship to them.

English-Language Learners
Ask volunteers who speak Spanish to read aloud a copy of Neruda's poem in Spanish (easily available from online sources—search for "Oda a los Calcetines"). Have them comment on any differences they find between the original version and its translation.

Resources Reminder
For lessons designed for intermediate and advanced English-language learners, see *Lesson Plans for Language Development,* pp. 216, 242, 253.

Special Education Students
For lessons designed for special education students, see *Lesson Plans for Language Development,* pp. 217, 242, 253.

these
heavenly
socks.
They were
so handsome
for the first time
my feet seemed to me
unacceptable
like two decrepit
firemen, firemen
unworthy
of that woven
fire,
of those glowing
socks.

Nevertheless
I resisted
the sharp temptation
to save them somewhere
as schoolboys
keep
fireflies,
as learned men
collect
sacred texts,
I resisted
the mad impulse
to put them
into a golden
cage
and each day give them
birdseed
and pieces of pink melon.
Like explorers
in the jungle who hand
over the very rare
green deer
to the spit°
and eat it
with remorse,
I stretched out
my feet
and pulled on
the magnificent
socks
and then my shoes.

The moral
of my ode is this:
beauty is twice
beauty
and what is good is doubly
good
when it is a matter of two socks
made of wool
in winter.

68. spit *n.:* thin rod or stick on which meat is roasted.

DIRECT TEACHING

C Literary Focus
GRADE-LEVEL STANDARD

? Extended metaphor and simile. In ll. 46–63, what images does the speaker use to build an extended comparison between the socks and treasured collectibles? [The speaker likens them to fireflies collected by schoolboys, sacred texts collected by wise men, and pet birds collected in golden cages.]

D Learners Having Difficulty

Summarizing. Ask students to summarize the speaker's moral, or the main message of the poem. [Possible response: Some people might be tempted to save and preserve such wonderful gifts, but it is better to use and enjoy them.]

Ode to My Socks 499

GUIDED PRACTICE

Monitoring students' progress. Guide the class in answering these comprehension questions. Direct students to locate passages in the text that support their responses.

True-False

1. Maru Mori knitted socks as a gift for the speaker. [T]
2. The speaker compares his feet to two firemen. [T]
3. The speaker decides not to wear the socks. [F]
4. The speaker wears the socks on a journey into the jungle. [F]
5. The speaker believes that beautiful things should be enjoyed, not preserved. [T]

Meet the Writer

Background. Neruda was in Spain during the outbreak of the Spanish Civil War in 1936. A staunch supporter of the anti-fascist cause, he wrote numerous poems about the war in support of the Republicans (collected in *España en el Corazón*). Neruda was a good friend of the Spanish writer Federico Garcia Lorca, who was executed by the fascists in 1937.

For Independent Reading

Students who appreciated Neruda's unconventional ode might enjoy *Odes to Common Things* translated by Kenneth Krabbenhoft. The collection includes twenty-five translated odes by Neruda that address everyday objects like loaves of bread and boxes of tea.

Meet the Writer

Pablo Neruda

"To Roam, to Go Singing Through the World"

Pablo Neruda (1904–1973), the most important Latin American poet of the twentieth century, was baptized Neftalí Ricardo Reyes Basoalto. He changed his name when he began writing poetry, to avoid embarrassing his father, who frowned on his literary ambitions. Even as a child, Neruda observed nature closely—"birds, beetles, partridge eggs" and "the perfection of insects." In his *Memoirs* he writes,

> "Anyone who hasn't been in the Chilean forest doesn't know this planet. I have come out of that landscape, that mud, that silence, to roam, to go singing through the world."

Neruda wrote his first poems when he was very young, and by fifteen he'd had several poems published. He enrolled in the University of Chile in Santiago, Chile's capital, planning to become a French professor, but he took a detour to serve as Chile's consul to Rangoon, Burma, the first of several diplomatic postings in Asia. Throughout his diplomatic career in Spain, France, and Mexico, Neruda continued publishing prize-winning volumes of poetry. A lifelong political activist, he wrote and spoke eloquently in support of Chile's poor Indians and workers. He was elected to Chile's senate, but a speech highly critical of Chile's repressive government led to an order for his arrest. In 1949, Neruda fled Chile for three years until the order for his arrest was dropped.

Pablo Neruda (1970) by Sofia Gandarias.

Neruda was awarded the Nobel Prize in literature in 1971 "for a poetry that with the action of an elemental force brings alive a continent's destiny and dreams." In his acceptance speech he wrote,

> "I have always maintained that the writer's task has nothing to do with mystery or magic, and that the poet's, at least, must be a personal effort for the benefit of all. The closest thing to poetry is a loaf of bread or a ceramic dish or a piece of wood lovingly carved, even if by clumsy hands."

DIFFERENTIATING INSTRUCTION

Advanced Learners

Enrichment. Explain to students that the Chilean landscape that so influenced Neruda is among the most fascinating and diverse in the world. The country, which spans an immense stretch of South America's Pacific coastline, includes the forbidding Atacama desert (the world's driest) in the north, portions of the world's second highest mountain range (the Andes) in the east, and thousands of square miles of lush forest in the central and southern regions.

Activity. Have students research the Chilean environment and work in groups to create a bulletin board featuring nature images from the country. Have students choose poems by Neruda to accompany the images they select.

CONNECTION / MEMOIR

The Word

Pablo Neruda

What a great language I have, it's a fine language we inherited from the fierce conquistadors[1] . . . They strode over the giant *cordilleras,*[2] over the rugged Americas, hunting for potatoes, sausages, beans, black tobacco, gold, corn, fried eggs, with a voracious appetite not found in the world since then . . . They swallowed up everything, religions, pyramids, tribes, idolatries[3] just like the ones they brought along in their huge sacks . . . Wherever they went, they razed the land . . . But words fell like pebbles out of the boots of the barbarians,[4] out of their beards, their helmets, their horseshoes, luminous words that were left glittering here . . . our language. We came up losers . . . We came up winners . . . They carried off the gold and left us the gold . . . They carried everything off and left us everything . . . They left us the words.

—from *Memoirs*

1. **conquistadors** (kän·kwis′tə·dôrz′) *n.:* sixteenth-century Spanish conquerors of much of Central and South America.
2. ***cordilleras*** (kôr·di·yer′äs) *n.:* mountain system of western South America.
3. **idolatries** (ī·däl′ə·trēz) *n.:* devotions to or worship of idols, or images of gods.
4. **barbarians** (bär·ber′ē·ənz) *n.:* here, foreigners; aliens.

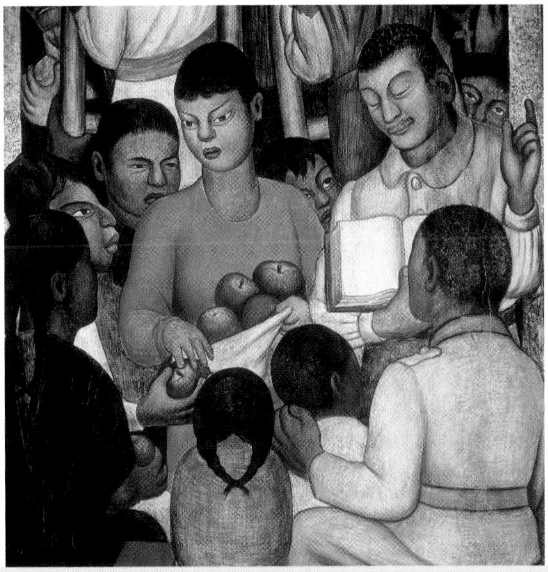

Fruit of the Earth (*Los Frutos*) (detail) (1926) by Diego Rivera. Mural in Mexico City.

Connection

Summary *at grade level*

In an excerpt from his memoirs, Pablo Neruda discusses the two-sided legacy of the Spanish conquistadors who pillaged South America in the sixteenth century. While noting that these invaders devastated the landscape and destroyed native cultures, Neruda maintains that they also left behind an invaluable gift—the gift of the Spanish language.

A Reading Skills

Drawing conclusions. What language is Neruda referring to? [Spanish]

B Learners Having Difficulty

Summarizing. How does Neruda describe the conquistadors? [Possible response: greedy, devouring all they encounter.]

C Reading Skills

Interpreting. Who is the "We" referred to by Neruda? Why are "We" both "winners" and "losers"? [Possible responses: "We" refers to the people of the countries invaded by the conquistadors. They are losers because their natural resources were stolen and their native religions and cultures destroyed. They are winners because they have been left the riches of the Spanish language.]

VIEWING THE ART

Mexico's most famous artist, **Diego Rivera** (1886–1957) was a preeminent mural painter of the twentieth century. Rivera used his art to represent Mexico's rich cultural past and to help the country build its future.

Activity. How does Rivera link literacy with prosperity in his painting? [A man presenting an open book is placed next to a woman bearing fruits.]

Connecting and Comparing Texts

Use the following questions to stimulate a discussion of the memoir excerpt and its relationship to "Ode to My Socks":

- How does Neruda feel about the Spanish language? Support your answer with details from the excerpt. [Possible response: He values it greatly, regarding it as a kind of treasure. He describes its words as "luminous" and the language as a kind of "gold," of equal value to the actual gold taken by the conquistadors.]
- What kind of "treasure" does Neruda exalt in "Ode to My Socks"? [a pair of woolen socks—an ordinary, everyday item]
- How are the socks of the poem and the Spanish language, as described in the memoir, similar? [Possible responses: Both are things that are used every day; both are described as "gifts" and "treasures."]

INDEPENDENT PRACTICE

Literary Response and Analysis

Reading Check

1. The speaker received the socks as a gift from Maru Mori.
2. The socks are blue with single golden stripes.
3. The speaker resists the impulse to store the socks away as some kind of valuable treasure.
4. The speaker wears the socks.
5. The speaker seems to say that the best way to honor the lovely socks is to wear them.

Interpretations

6. *Similes*—Socks "soft as rabbits," "two cases knitted with threads of twilight and goatskin"; Feet "like two decrepit firemen." *Extended simile*—The speaker is tempted to save his socks "as schoolboys keep fireflies, as learned men collect sacred texts." *Metaphors*—Feet "fish," "sharks," "blackbirds," and "cannons." *Extended metaphor*—The socks are compared to prized birds.
7. The speaker is clearly overjoyed at his new possessions; he views the socks as things of wonder.
8. Beauty is found in everyday things, not just in abstract ideas like truth. The physical comfort of wool socks in winter can be just as beautiful as works of art.
9. While praising socks in an ode is humorous, Neruda is sincere about it. By using a lofty form to celebrate a mundane object, he suggests that beauty, joy, and wonder can be found anywhere.

Evaluation

10. Neruda's use of fresh, playful similes and metaphors suggests he loves what words can do.

Literary Response and Analysis

Reading Check

1. Where did the socks come from?
2. If the socks were lost or stolen, what factual description could you give someone searching for them?
3. What temptation and what mad impulse does the speaker resist?
4. What does the speaker end up doing with the pair of socks?
5. What does the speaker say is the "moral" of his ode?

Interpretations

6. Make a list of all of the poem's **similes** and **metaphors.** Which ones are **extended** over several or more lines? Which ones do you think are the most interesting or the most fun?

Similes	
Extended similes	
Metaphors	
Extended metaphors	

Grade 8 Review Reading Standard 3.1 Determine and articulate the relationship between the purposes and characteristics of different forms of poetry (e.g., ode).

Reading Standard 3.7 Recognize and understand the significance of various literary devices, including figurative language, and explain their appeal.

7. Based on how the **speaker** talks about his socks, describe how he feels about his gift.
8. John Keats's famous poem "Ode on a Grecian Urn" ends with these lines: "'Beauty is truth, truth beauty.' That is all / Ye know on earth, and all ye need to know." What do you think Neruda's stated moral in lines 77–85 means? How might it relate to Keats's lines?
9. How credible is it that anyone would be so passionate about a pair of socks? Do you think Neruda intends this ode to be taken seriously, or is he writing a **parody** of an ode? (A **parody** is a humorous imitation of a serious work of literature, art, or music.) Support your opinion with references to the poem and to the way it demonstrates the qualities of an ode (see page 497).

Evaluation

10. In the selection from his memoir (see the ***Connection*** on page 501), Neruda says that words are "everything." Do you think his love of language is evident in the similes and metaphors he uses in "Ode to My Socks"? Explain your opinion.

Writing

Ode to a Common Thing

Write an **ode** to an object you see every day. Start by observing the object closely and making some notes about how it looks, what it resembles, and how it makes you feel. (Look back at your Quickwrite notes for ideas.) What **tone** will you give your ode?

Ode to My . . .
How it looks:
What it resembles:
How it makes me feel:

ASSESSING

Assessment

- *Progress Assessment of Reading*
  - Selection Test

RETEACHING

For a lesson reteaching Standard 3.7, see **Reteaching,** p. 939A. For another selection to teach Standard 3.7, see *Interactive Reading,* Chapter 7.

Literary Response and Analysis

The Sounds of Poetry

RHYTHM, RHYME, AND OTHER SOUND EFFECTS

by John Malcolm Brinnin

Rhythm: Music in Speech

Poetry is a musical kind of speech. Like music, poetry is based on **rhythm**—that is, on the alternation of stressed and unstressed sounds that makes the voice rise and fall.

Poets have a choice of the kind of rhythm they can use. They can use **meter**—a strict rhythmic pattern of stressed and unstressed syllables in each line, or they can write in **free verse**—a loose kind of rhythm that sounds more like natural speech than like formal poetry.

Meter: Patterns of Sound

In **metrical poetry** (poetry that has a meter), stressed and unstressed syllables are arranged in a regular pattern. Here's a famous stanza from *The Rime of the Ancient Mariner* by Samuel Taylor Coleridge:

˘ ´ ˘ ´ ˘ ´ ˘ ´
He prayeth best, who loveth best

˘ ´ ˘ ´ ˘ ´
All things both great and small;

˘ ˘ ´ ´ ˘ ´ ˘ ´
For the dear God who loveth us,

˘ ´ ˘ ´ ˘ ´
He made and loveth all.

The stress (´) indicates a stressed syllable. The breve (˘) indicates an unstressed syllable. Indicating the stresses this way is called **scanning** a poem.

In metrical poetry, variation is important. Without any variation at all, meter becomes mechanical and monotonous, like the steady ticktock of a clock. An occasional change in rhythm, as in the third line of the stanza from *The Rime of the Ancient Mariner,* also allows the poet to draw attention to key words in the poem.

Five Kinds of Feet

A line of metrical poetry is made up of metrical units called feet. A **foot** is a unit consisting of at least one stressed syllable and usually one or more unstressed syllables. Here are the five common types of feet used by poets in English and an example of a single word that matches each pattern:

˘ ´
iamb (insist)

´ ˘
trochee (double)

˘ ˘ ´
anapest (understand)

´ ˘ ˘
dactyl (excellent)

´ ´
spondee (football)

(For more about these feet, see Meter in the Handbook of Literary Terms.)

(continued)

Reading Standard 3.7 Recognize and understand the significance of various literary devices, and explain their appeal.

STANDARDS FOCUS, pp. 503–505

(For the grade-level standard taught in this lesson, see Student Edition, p. 503.)

Literary Focus: The Sounds of Poetry

Introduce the section on rhythm by asking students to name some art forms in which rhythm is important. [Possible responses: music, dance, poetry.] Then, focus on rhythmic patterns in music. Ask students with musical experience to name some different rhythmic forms used in music, such as three-four time, four-four time, and stressed and unstressed beats. Have them demonstrate one or more of these forms by tapping the rhythms on a table or desk. Explain that like musicians, poets have a variety of established rhythm patterns to choose from when writing poetry. They can also decide not to use established rhythm patterns at all.

Introduce the section on meter by reminding students that meter can be produced by different patterns of sound. Share the following mnemonic devices to help students remember these patterns. The first letter of each name and of each foot begin with the same letter.

An-toi-nette—anapest
Dor-o-thy—dactyl
I-rene—iamb
Says-who—spondee
Tra-cy—trochee

Introduce the section on rhyme by pointing out that in poetry, as in music, rhythm is just one aspect of sound. Sound effects such as rhyme, alliteration, and onomatopoeia add an essential musical quality to many poems.

DIFFERENTIATING INSTRUCTION

Learners Having Difficulty

The section on meter and metrical poetry may be especially challenging for some students. You may wish to have these students listen to several metrical poems on audiotape. If possible, provide at least one poem in iambic meter and others in anapestic or dactylic meter. On the first playing, direct students to listen for content. On the second playing, have students tap out the meters as they listen. You might provide the students with copies of the poems and encourage students to read along as they listen to the audiotapes.

Because songs often feature exaggerated stresses, you might have students review one or more simple songs, such as "Yankee Doodle." Then, encourage students to review poems. Point out that recognizing meter can help them correctly pronounce new vocabulary words in metrical poems.

Free Verse: No Rules

Early in the twentieth century some American and English poets decided that they would rid poetry of its prettiness, sentimentality, and artificiality by concentrating on a new kind of poetry. Calling themselves **imagists,** they declared that imagery alone—without any elaborate metrics or stanza patterns—could carry the full emotional message of a poem. They called their poetry **free verse** because it is free from the old metric rules.

Robert Frost, who disliked free verse, said that writing without the metric rules was "like playing tennis with the net down." What he meant was that the net on the tennis court is like meter in poetry—the essential part of the game, which players must both respect and overcome. Nevertheless, more and more poets write in free-verse cadences that follow "curves of thought" or "shapes of speech."

Rhyme: Chiming Sounds

Rhyme is the repetition of the accented vowel sound and all subsequent sounds in a word (*time/dime, history/mystery, lobster/mobster*).

Chiming sounds that punctuate the rhythm of a poem also give the poem structure and make it easy to remember. In the cartoon on this page, Edgar Allan Poe searches for words to rhyme with the refrain "Nevermore" in his poem "The Raven."

In poetry the chiming sounds of rhymes may occur at the ends of lines—**end rhyme**—or within a line—**internal rhyme.** A perfect rhyme, like *cat/mat* or *verging/merging,* is called an **exact rhyme.** When sounds are similar but not exact, as in *fellow/follow* or *mystery/mastery*, the rhyme is called **approximate rhyme.** Approximate rhymes are also called half rhymes, slant rhymes, or imperfect rhymes. The following verse from "Father William," a comic poem by Lewis Carroll, contains exact rhymes:

"You are old, Father William," the young
    man said,
"And your hair has become very white;
And yet you incessantly stand on your
    head—
Do you think, at your age, it is right?"

Drawing by Chas. Addams. ©1983 The New Yorker Magazine, Inc.

DIFFERENTIATING INSTRUCTION

Advanced Learners

Acceleration. Use the following activity to move advanced learners toward the eleventh- and twelfth-grade Standard 3.4, for which they analyze ways in which poets use sounds to evoke readers' emotions.

Activity. Have students select poems that they feel demonstrate the use of one or more of the sound effects discussed in the essay (for example, metrical patterns or internal rhyme). Invite each student to read the chosen poem to the class. After each reading, the reader should lead a discussion focusing on the featured sound effect and reflecting on its contribution to the poem's overall emotional impact.

504 Chapter 7 Poetry

In the next poem the rhymes are both approximate (*washes/rushes, bales/orioles*) and exact (*sea/mystery*):

This is the land the Sunset washes

This is the land the Sunset washes—
These are the banks of the Yellow Sea—
Where it rose—or whither it rushes—
There are the Western Mystery!

Night after night her purple traffic
Strews the landing with Opal Bales—
Merchantmen poise upon horizons—
Dip—and vanish like Orioles!

—Emily Dickinson

Alliteration: Repeated Beginning Sounds

Alliteration is the repetition of consonant sounds in words that appear close together; strictly speaking, alliteration occurs at the beginnings of words or on accented syllables. Alliteration used with restraint can result in lines as memorable as this one from Percy Bysshe Shelley's "Ode to the West Wind":

O Wild West Wind, thou breath of
Autumn's being

Or this one from Robert Frost's "Acquainted with the Night":

I have stood still and stopped the sound
of feet

Onomatopoeia: Sounds into Words

Onomatopoeia (än′ō·mat′ō·pē′ə) is the use of words that sound like what they mean (*snap, crackle, pop*). *Onomatopoeia,* Greek for "making of words," has come to refer to the making of words by imitating or suggesting sounds.

In its most basic form, onomatopoeia is a single word (*gurgle, bang, rattle, boom, hiss, buzz*) that echoes a natural or mechanical sound. For the poet, onomatopoeia is a way of conveying meaning through evocative words that also provide musical accompaniment—as background music in a movie can affect the mood of a scene.

In this famous example from Tennyson's *The Princess,* onomatopoeia is used with such exactness that the sounds of the poem voice a particular feeling that words alone could only approximate:

The moan of doves in immemorial elms
And murmuring of innumerable bees

Practice

As in ancient days, when poetry was not written but only spoken or sung, poetry today is addressed to the ear. You can't really say that you know a poem until you've heard it read aloud.

Choose one of the poems you've already read in this chapter (or any favorite poem), and **read it aloud** to yourself and then to a partner or a small group.

Then, write a paragraph or two discussing the poem's **rhythm, rhyme,** or other **sound effects.**

Practice

Encourage students to rehearse their readings before reciting their poems to other students. Paragraphs will vary depending upon the poems that students choose.

Apply

Homework

Point out to students that songwriters as well as poets make use of sound effects such as exact rhyme, approximate rhyme, internal rhyme, alliteration, and onomatopoeia in their compositions. You may want to assign the following activity as homework. Have students choose a favorite song and write a paragraph analyzing its use of one or more of these effects in its lyrics. You may wish to have students share their songs with the class.

For additional work on rhythm, direct students to the metrical poems in this chapter: Shakespeare's "Shall I Compare Thee to a Summer's Day?"; the anonymous ballad "Bonny Barbara Allan"; and Dickinson's "Heart! We will forget him!" For each poem, have students identify a dominant meter. Also, guide students in analyzing the free-verse poems in this chapter, helping them to note the subtle rhythms created by balancing longer and shorter phrases and by following "curves of thought."

Resources Reminder

Differentiating Instruction

- *Lesson Plans for Language Development*

For more instruction on the sounds of poetry for English-language learners and special education students, see *Lesson Plans for Language Development,* pp. 218, 219.

The Sounds of Poetry: Rhythm, Rhyme, and Other Sound Effects 505

STANDARDS FOCUS, pp. 506–508

(For the grade-level standard taught in this lesson, see citations on Student Edition pages.)

Summary *at grade level*

In this hypnotic poem, the speaker hears "the call of the turning tide" luring him back to the sea. By using vivid imagery—from gray mist to blown spume to crying gulls—Masefield conveys the speaker's feverish longing for the adventurous life he left behind. Pairs of rhymed lines built predominantly in iambic meter help reproduce the rolling rhythm of the sea.

PRETEACHING

Selection Starter

Motivate. Make an imagery chart on the chalkboard with the column headings "Sight," "Sound," "Taste," "Touch," and "Smell." For each sense, have students name images that come to mind when they think of the sea. List students' responses on the chart. Then, ask students, "How does this imagery of the sea make you feel?" Have each student write a word or phrase in response. Then, read the poem aloud to the class, and ask students to discuss how the imagery in the poem compares with the imagery listed in the chart. Have students discuss how the poem's imagery made them feel.

Before You Read

Sea Fever

Literary Focus

Meter: Rhythms of the Sea

Meter is a pattern of stressed and unstressed syllables in poetry. Read this famous poem aloud to hear how the poet's use of meter suggests the motion of a ship on the high seas. Where do you hear and feel the rolling rhythm of the sea swells? Where do you hear and feel the slap of waves against the ship?

Rhyme

Rhyme is probably the one feature most people identify with poetry, especially rhyme at the ends of lines in a poem. (Of course, many poems, especially modern ones, do not rhyme.) **Rhyme** is the repetition of vowel sounds and all sounds following them in words that are close together (*sky/by, shaking/breaking*). Usually rhymes create a particular pattern in a poem, called a **rhyme scheme.** Poetry owes much of its music to the effect of rhyme. As you read, notice the rhymes in "Sea Fever." How do they contribute to the music of the poem?

Make the Connection

Feverish

What do you think this poem's title means? Does the title remind you of any other fever?

Reading Standard 3.7 Recognize and understand the significance of various literary devices, and explain their appeal.

Background

Although supertankers and cruise ships are much taller than sailing ships, the term *tall ship* is still used for a sailing vessel with high masts. For millions of landlubbers, the image of a tall ship triggers dreams of romance, freedom, and adventure, just as it did for Masefield.

"The wheel's kick" in line 3 is a reference to what can happen when a sudden shift in the wind or tide causes a ship's steering wheel to "kick over"—to spin out of control until the person at the helm can grab it and put the ship back on course. "Trick" (line 12) is a sailing term for a round-trip voyage. Years ago a "long trick" might have involved a voyage from England to China and back, a trip that could last for more than a year.

RESOURCES: READING

Planning

- *One-Stop Planner* CD-ROM with Test Generator
- *On Course: Mapping Instruction*

Media

- *Audio CD Library*
  - disc 13

Reading

- *Interactive Reading,* Teacher's Edition
  - Graphic Organizer: Sounds of Poetry Chart

Differentiating Instruction

- *Lesson Plans for Language Development*
  - English-Language Learners, pp. 220, 243, 254
  - Special Education Students, pp. 221, 243, 254

Assessment

- *Progress Assessment of Reading*
  - Selection Test
- *One Stop Planner* CD-ROM with Test Generator

Sea Fever

John Masefield

I must go down to the seas again, to the lonely sea and the sky, **A**
And all I ask is a tall ship and a star to steer her by;
And the wheel's kick and the wind's song and the white sail's shaking,
And a gray mist on the sea's face and a gray dawn breaking.

I must go down to the seas again, for the call of the running tide
Is a wild call and a clear call that may not be denied;
And all I ask is a windy day with the white clouds flying,
And the flung spray and the blown spume,° and the sea gulls crying. **B**

I must go down to the seas again, to the vagrant gypsy life, **C**
To the gull's way and the whale's way where the wind's like a whetted knife; **D**
And all I ask is a merry yarn from a laughing fellow-rover.
And a quiet sleep and a sweet dream when the long trick's over.

8. spume (spyo͞om) *n.:* foam or froth.

Meet the Writer

John Masefield

Sailor-Poet

John Masefield (1878–1967), born in England, was orphaned by the time he was thirteen years old. At once, as boys could do in those days, he joined the merchant navy and shipped around the world for several years. On a trip to New York, he jumped ship and lived for a time in the city as what we'd call today a homeless person. He began to write poetry after coming across a collection of Chaucer's *Canterbury Tales* in a New York bookstore.

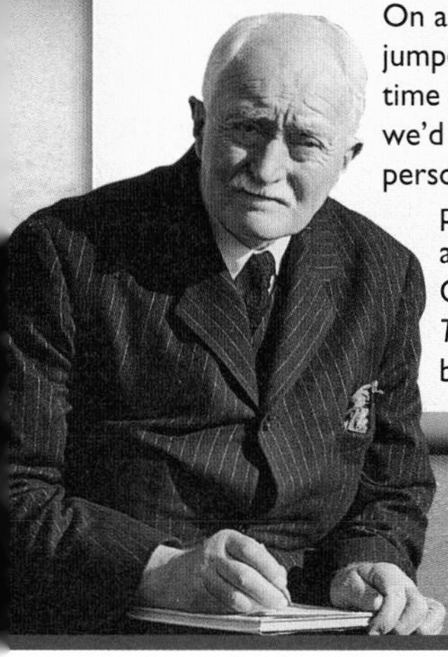

Masefield is best remembered today for poems inspired by the years he spent as a seaman, first on windjammers in the last days of the sailing ships and then on tramp steamers and ocean liners. No one has better evoked for the landlubber the sense of freedom and adventure, the taste of salt and spray associated with sailing "before the mast," or the pride that marked the crews of even the rustiest and dingiest of freighters.

For more than thirty years, Masefield served as Britain's poet laureate. Of his passion for sailing ships, the poet said:

"They were the only youth I had, and the only beauty I knew in my youth, and now that I am old, not many greater beauties seem to be in the world."

DIRECT TEACHING

A Literary Focus
REVIEW STANDARD

Rhythm and meter. Read the first line of the poem aloud, and then scan it on the chalkboard so students can hear and then see the pattern of stressed and unstressed syllables:
"I must go down to the seas again, to the lonely sea and the sky."

B Literary Focus
REVIEW STANDARD

Rhyme. What are the end rhymes in this stanza? [*tide/denied, flying/crying*] What is the stanza's rhyme scheme? [*aabb*]

C Vocabulary Development
REVIEW STANDARD

Using context clues. Ask students to figure out the meaning of *vagrant* using context clues, such as the nearby word *gypsy* and in l. 11 *fellow-rover.* [Both a rover and a gypsy are roamers or wanderers. *Vagrant* means "wandering."] Why is this word important to the poem's meaning? [Possible response: The speaker dreams of recapturing the carefree life he once led.]

D Literary Focus
REVIEW STANDARD

Alliteration. What aspect of life at sea is suggested by the repeated *w* and *wh* sounds? [Possible response: the sound of the wind.]

DIFFERENTIATING INSTRUCTION

English-Language Learners
Explain that *spume* refers specifically to the froth and foam of waves. A *rover* is a "wanderer." *Whetted* means "sharpened," as if on an old-fashioned whetstone. Finally, make sure students realize that in the context of l. 11, *yarn* means "exaggerated story or tall tale."

Resources Reminder
For lessons designed for intermediate and advanced English-language learners, see *Lesson Plans for Language Development,* pp. 220, 243, 254.

Special Education Students
For lessons designed for special education students, see *Lesson Plans for Language Development,* pp. 221, 243, 254.

Advanced Learners
Acceleration. Use the following activity to move advanced learners toward the eleventh- and twelfth-grade Standard 3.4, for which they analyze ways in which poets use imagery, personification, figures of speech, and sounds to evoke readers' emotions.

Activity. Ask students to discuss how Masefield uses each of the literary elements listed above (imagery, personification, and so on) to create a vivid picture of the ocean's emotional pull on the sailor.

INDEPENDENT PRACTICE

Literary Response and Analysis

Reading Check

1. The speaker asks for a tall ship and a star to navigate by; to experience the sensations of being at sea (ll. 2–4, 7–9); to hear a "merry yarn"; and to have a "quiet sleep and a sweet dream."
2. The speaker hears the call of the running tide or the sea.
3. The speaker yearns for the "vagrant" seafaring life.

Interpretations

4. Possible answers: The "long trick" might refer to an extended journey at sea, or it might serve as a metaphor for a seafarer's entire life. The "quiet sleep" and "sweet dream" may be literal, or they may refer to death and an afterlife.
5. Possible answers: "Sea fever" is an intense longing to be at sea, which is what the poem describes. Other "fevers" might be intense feelings of love and homesickness.
6. Possible answers: *See*—tall ship, a solitary star, a gray dawn, white clouds. *Hear*—wind, the shaking sail, sea gulls' crying. *Feel*—the wheel's spinning, the sea spray, the cold wind.
7. There are seven strong beats in each line. Lines 3, 4, 6, 8, and 10 show examples of variation in the meter.
8. Answers will vary. Many students will choose ll. 1, 3, and 8.
9. The poem uses an *aabb* rhyme scheme. Students may say that the end-rhymed pairs contribute a singsong quality that evokes the rhythmic feel of the tides or of a ship at sea.
10. Possible answer: Masefield repeats *w* and *wh* sounds in ll. 3 and 5 in the words *wheel, wind, white,* and *windy.*

Literary Response and Analysis

Reading Check

1. What does the speaker ask for?
2. What call does the speaker hear?
3. What kind of life does the speaker yearn for?

Interpretations

4. What do you think the "long trick" and the "quiet sleep" and "sweet dream" stand for in the last line?
5. You are probably familiar with a variety of expressions that use *fever* **metaphorically**—for example, "spring fever" and "gold-rush fever." What exactly is "sea fever," and why is it a good **title** for the poem? What other "fevers" might grip someone the way the sea has gripped this speaker?
6. What specific **images** in the poem help you see, hear, and even feel the kind of life the speaker longs for?
7. Read the poem aloud, and scan it line by line, marking the stressed syllables (′) and the unstressed syllables (˘). How many strong beats do you hear in each line? Where do you hear variations in the **meter**?
8. After you have scanned the poem, read it aloud again. Where does the **meter** reinforce the sense of the poem—the kick of the wheel and the roll of the sea?
9. What pattern of **rhyme** is used in the poem? How does the **rhyme scheme** contribute to the overall sound and music of the poem?
10. Masefield uses **alliteration** throughout the poem to create his sea song. Where is alliteration especially strong?

Reading Standard 3.7 Recognize and understand the significance of various literary devices, including figurative language and imagery, and explain their appeal.

Writing

What's *Your* "Fever"?

Write a **poem** in imitation of Masefield's that opens "I must go . . ." Give your poem a title that uses the word *fever.* Describe the place you long to go back to. Try to find **images** that help your readers share what you can see, smell, taste, hear, and touch in this special place. You might enjoy imitating Masefield's **meter.**

ASSESSING

Assessment

- *Progress Assessment of Reading*
  - Selection Test

RETEACHING

For lessons reteaching Standard 3.7, see **Reteaching,** p. 939A. For another selection to teach Standard 3.7, see *Interactive Reading,* Chapter 7.

Before You Read

Bonny Barbara Allan

Literary Focus

The Ballad

"Bonny Barbara Allan" is a **ballad,** a story that is told in song. Most ballads use simple language and two of the oldest elements of poetry: a strong **meter** and a **refrain** (whole lines or stanzas repeated at regular intervals).

Folk ballads such as this one, which have been passed down orally from generation to generation, often tell tales of true love or domestic violence. Folk ballads also use certain formulas—phrases such as "white as milk," "red, red lips," "red-roan steed," and "true, true love." The images of trees and rosebushes growing on lovers' graves is also a formula. All of these formulas were part of the ballad singer's repertoire; whenever the singer needed to describe a woman's skin, for example, a formula was available. The formulas also made the song easy to memorize.

As you read this old ballad, think about whether its love story is timely or out of date. Could it happen today?

Make the Connection

Some Things Never Change

Write down the titles of some songs popular today. Then, think about the content of the songs. Are they happy or tragic? Are any songs about love? about betrayal? What are their refrains?

Background

The tragic story of Barbara Allan and her fickle lover originated in Scotland in the seventeenth century. Like many Scottish ballads, this one traveled to America in the eighteenth century with the Scots-Irish who settled in the mountains of Appalachia. There the song of Barbara Allan continued to be sung, often with changes that made it a local love story.

Grade 8 Review Reading Standard 3.1 Determine and articulate the relationship between the purposes and characteristics of different forms of poetry (e.g., ballad).

A hunting party (14th century), School of Paris. Ivory.

Victoria and Albert Museum, London/Art Resource, New York.

STANDARDS FOCUS, pp. 509–512

(For the review standard taught in this lesson, see citations on Student Edition pages.)

Summary *at grade level*

In this folk ballad of unrequited and tragic love, William, a young man, becomes ill and requests a healing kiss from Barbara Allan, but she refuses. Barbara Allan claims that William has slighted her, to which he responds, "Hardhearted Barbara Allan," and soon dies. Haunted by his final words, a refrain she seems to hear everywhere, Barbara Allan too succumbs to sudden death and is buried next to him. In an unexpected turn of events, a "red, red rose" grows from William's grave and entwines itself around a briar growing from Barbara Allan's grave, becoming a "truelove knot," which suggests the redemptive power of love.

RESOURCES: READING

Planning

- *One-Stop Planner* CD-ROM with Test Generator
- *On Course: Mapping Instruction*

Media

- *Audio CD Library*
  - disc 13

Reading

- *Interactive Reading,* Teacher's Edition
  - Graphic Organizer: Sounds of Poetry Chart

Differentiating Instruction

- *Lesson Plans for Language Development*
  - English-Language Learners, pp. 222, 244, 254
  - Special Education Students, pp. 223, 244, 254

Assessment

- *Progress Assessment of Reading*
  - Selection Test
- *One-Stop Planner* CD-ROM with Test Generator

DIRECT TEACHING

A Literary Focus
REVIEW STANDARD

Ballad. Point out "the merry month of May" as an example of a formulaic phrase found in many folk ballads.

B Learners Having Difficulty

Changing your reading strategy. Read aloud the ballad's first few stanzas so that students can hear the meter. Then, ask them to listen for the meter as they read the rest of the poem silently. Suggest that when they lose track of the meter, they re-read and try various stress patterns on the lines in question.

C Reading Skills

? Expressing an opinion. What do you think of Barbara's response? [Possible response: She seems petty and self-centered.]

VIEWING THE ART

This medieval illuminated manuscript from France illustrates the idea of courtly love. Within this ideal, a couple's relationship was based on the feudal relationship between a knight and his nobleman.

Activity. Does the couple in this illuminated manuscript appear to be of the same social class as William and Barbara Allan? [No. The couple in the illustration appear to be of the aristocracy, whereas the couple in the folk ballad are not.]

British Library, London/Bridgeman Art Library, London/SuperStock.

Lovers in a garden (c. 1487–1495). Painting from a French illuminated manuscript.

Bonny Barbara Allan

Anonymous

A Oh, in the merry month of May,
When all things were a-blooming,
Sweet William came from the Western states
And courted Barbara Allan.

B But he took sick, and very sick
And he sent for Barbara Allan,
And all she said when she got there,
"Young man, you are a-dying."

"Oh yes, I'm sick, and I'm very sick,
And I think that death's upon me;
But one sweet kiss from Barbara's lips
Will save me from my dying."

C "But don't you remember the other day
You were down in town a-drinking?
You drank your health to the ladies all around,
And slighted Barbara Allan."

DIFFERENTIATING INSTRUCTION

Learners Having Difficulty
To help students focus on the story told in this ballad, pair them with more fluent readers. Together, pairs can work through the poem stanza by stanza, summarizing the story details in each. Once pairs have completed their summaries, they can read the ballad aloud and discuss how sound and repetition are used.

English-Language Learners
Explain that the *a* is used in the following words for the sake of meter: *a-blooming, a-dying, a-drinking, a-ringing, a-singing,* and *a-coming.* Also, help students distinguish possessives ("Barbara's lips") from contractions ("death's upon me," "don't," "hadn't," "I'll").

Resources Reminder
For lessons designed for English-language learners, see *Lesson Plans for Language Development,* pp. 222, 244, 254.

Special Education Students
For lessons designed for special education students, see *Lesson Plans for Language Development,* pp. 223, 244, 254.

510 Chapter 7 Poetry

"Oh yes, I remember the other day
I was down in town a-drinking;
I drank my health to the ladies all 'round.
But my love to Barbara Allan."

He turned his face to the wall;
She turned her back upon him;
The very last word she heard him say,
"Hardhearted Barbara Allan."

As she passed on through London Town,
She heard some bells a-ringing,
And every bell, it seemed to say,
"Hardhearted Barbara Allan."

She then passed on to the country road,
And heard some birds a-singing;
And every bird, it seemed to say,
"Hardhearted Barbara Allan."

She hadn't got more than a mile from town
When she saw his corpse a-coming;
"O bring him here, and ease him down,
And let me look upon him.

"Oh, take him away! Oh, take him away!
For I am sick and dying!
His death-cold features say to me,
'Hardhearted Barbara Allan.'

"O Father, O Father, go dig my grave,
And dig it long and narrow;
Sweet William died for me today;
I'll die for him tomorrow."

They buried them both in the old graveyard,
All side and side each other.
A red, red rose grew out of his grave,
And a green briar out of hers.

They grew and grew so very high
That they could grow no higher;
They lapped, they tied in a truelove knot—
The rose ran 'round the briar.

A Choral Reading: The Balladeers

As far as we know, ballads were sung by individuals. Even so, here are some ideas for a choral reading of a ballad—no instruments required!

- First, examine the ballad: How many people are speaking? Which lines could be recited by a chorus? (Refrains are often a good choice for several speakers.)
- Next, think of how the speakers are feeling. (Usually in a ballad, feelings run pretty strong.) How can you express those feelings, using volume, pitch, and tone of voice? Where do feelings change?
- Will you use gestures? props? How will you dress?
- Finally, mark up a copy of your choral reading to use as a script. Watch the punctuation, and let it guide you in deciding where to pause and when to speed up. Indicate words to emphasize.
- Practice. Evaluate and adjust your performance before you present it to an audience. Have you and your fellow balladeers caught the texture of this sad story of love and betrayal?

DIRECT TEACHING

D Literary Focus
REVIEW STANDARD
Ballad. How are the first five stanzas typical of the ballad? [Possible responses: strong meter; simple language; a love story; repetition.]

E Literary Focus
REVIEW STANDARD
Ballad. How does the repetition of vowel sounds in the refrain "Hardhearted Barbara Allan" affect the ballad's mood? [Possible response: It creates the effect of groans or sighs, creating a melancholy mood.]

F Literary Focus
REVIEW STANDARD
Ballad. What might the red rose and the briar symbolize? [Possible responses: The red rose might symbolize William's loving heart. Green often stands for jealousy, and the green briar could symbolize Barbara's jealous heart.]

G Reading Skills
Drawing conclusions. What does the ballad's closing image suggest about love? [Possible response: True love can conquer even a hard heart.]

GUIDED PRACTICE

Monitoring students' progress. Guide the class in answering these comprehension questions.

Short Answer

1. Why does William send for Barbara Allan? [He is dying and hopes her kiss will revive him.]
2. Why does she refuse his request? [She feels that he has slighted her.]
3. What words haunt Barbara Allan? ["Hardhearted Barbara Allan"]
4. What grows above the graves? [a red rose and a green briar]

Advanced Learners

Acceleration. Use the following activity to move advanced learners toward the eleventh- and twelfth-grade Standard 3.4, for which they analyze ways in which the "sound" of language achieves specific purposes.

Activity. Remind students that this folk ballad has endured for generations, and ask them to identify reasons for its lasting appeal. Have them consider questions like these:

- How would readers respond if this story were told in a different genre, such as a short story or a play?
- How does the folk song use sounds to evoke readers' emotions?
- What are the effects of the ballad's strong metric pattern on the mood and tone?

INDEPENDENT PRACTICE

Literary Response and Analysis

Reading Check

1. William, who loves Barbara Allan, is dying, and Barbara doesn't seem to care.
2. William asks Barbara Allan for a kiss. She refuses him because she believes he has slighted her.
3. William explains that he did not slight her. He claims that he expressed his love for her by singling her out from other women.
4. Barbara is haunted by William's words; she seems to hear "Hardhearted Barbara Allan" everywhere she goes.
5. William and Barbara are united by the rose and briar, which grow out of their graves and entwine.

Interpretations

6. Possible answers: William's death may have been caused by disease; Barbara died of a broken heart, grief, or remorse. The ballad also omits details about the couple's relationship before William's illness and about why Barbara refuses to accept William's explanation.
7. Possible answer: Barbara's refusal to accept William's explanation of his behavior, even as he is dying, is evidence of her hardheartedness. Her sadness after his death indicates that there is a compassionate side to her character.
8. Possible answers: The rose entwines itself around the more aggressive briar. In death, William's love—symbolized by the rose—has finally conquered the prickly, hardhearted nature of Barbara.
9. Types of repetition include meter, rhyme, and alliteration. The ballad's refrain is "Hardhearted Barbara Allan."

Literary Response and Analysis

Reading Check

1. What problem does the ballad set up in stanzas 1 and 2?
2. In stanza 3, what favor does William ask of Barbara Allan? According to the next stanza, why does she refuse him?
3. How does William explain his "insult" to Barbara Allan?
4. What happens to Barbara Allan after William calls her "hardhearted"?
5. How are William and Barbara Allan united after death?

Interpretations

6. **Ballads** are **narrative poems,** but they never tell the whole story. What details are left out of this one? For example, what caused William's death? How about Barbara Allan's?
7. What evidence shows that Barbara Allan is indeed hardhearted? Does anything indicate that she is *not* hardhearted? Explain.
8. We'd expect the aggressive vines of a briar to grow around any nearby plant. Which plant entwines the other in this story? Which character and which emotion have triumphed?
9. Note all the different kinds of **repetition** you can find in this ballad. What is the **refrain**?

Grade 8 Review Reading Standard 3.1 Determine and articulate the relationship between the purposes and characteristics of different forms of poetry (e.g., ballad).

Writing

In a News Flash

Ballads often took their subjects from stories of domestic tragedy that would today be featured on the evening news. Write your own version of this ballad as if it were tomorrow's **news story.** Remember that a good reporter answers the *5W-How?* questions—*who? what? when? where? why?* and *how?* You might also want to invent interviews with relatives and friends of Barbara Allan and Sweet William. Write a news report for the morning paper, or record your story on videotape or audiotape for a TV or radio news broadcast. Even though reporters don't usually create their own headlines, you'll have to create your headline for this story.

Songs Yesterday and Today

In a brief **essay, compare and contrast** this popular old ballad with the kinds of songs popular today, such as country-and-western songs. Before you write, gather your details in a chart like the following one:

	Ballad	Today's Songs
Subjects		
Rhythms (musical effects)		
Refrains		
Level of violence		

ASSESSING

Assessment

- *Progress Assessment of Reading*
  - Selection Test

Before You Read

The Flying Cat

Literary Focus

Free Verse: The Rhythms of Everyday Speech

Like many contemporary poets, Naomi Shihab Nye writes in **free verse.** Free verse uses no regular meter or rhyme scheme but instead attempts to imitate the natural rhythms of speech. Nye's poem has a distinct rhythm, created by the use of long and short sentences and many run-on lines (lines that do not end with any mark of punctuation). Read the poem aloud to hear its conversational rhythm.

Make the Connection

Quickwrite

Do animals have feelings? Can they, for example, feel love or fear? Do they have thoughts and memories? Jot down your opinions, and save your notes.

Grade 8 Review Reading Standard 3.1 Determine and articulate the relationship between the purposes and characteristics of different forms of poetry.

STANDARDS FOCUS, pp. 513–517

(For the review standard taught in this lesson, see citations on Student Edition pages.)

Summary *at grade level*

In Nye's free-verse poem, the speaker addresses herself in the second person as she reveals her nervousness about shipping her cat in an airplane's cargo hold. Beset by a variety of fears, the speaker goes so far as to disguise her own voice in order to repeatedly query the airline about how the pet will fare. The airline's reassurances fail to assuage her fears, and at the moment of departure, the speaker hugs the cat, soaking in the animal's trust. The animal itself has no concept of what lies ahead and remains blissfully unaware of the speaker's concerns.

PRETEACHING

Selection Starter

Build background. Remind students that when animals travel by air, they often travel in an airplane's cargo hold along with the luggage. Cargo holds are pressurized and usually temperature controlled and ventilated.

RESOURCES: READING

Planning

- *One-Stop Planner* CD-ROM with Test Generator
- *On Course: Mapping Instruction*

Media

- *Audio CD Library*
  - disc 13

Reading

- *Interactive Reading,* Teacher's Edition
  - Graphic Organizer: Sounds of Poetry Chart

Differentiating Instruction

- *Lesson Plans for Language Development*
  - English-Language Learners, pp. 224, 245, 255
  - Special Education Students, pp. 225, 245, 255

Assessment

- *Progress Assessment of Reading*
  - Selection Test
- *One-Stop Planner* CD-ROM with Test Generator

DIRECT TEACHING

(A) Literary Focus
REVIEW STANDARD

Free verse. Who is the "you" that the speaker is addressing? [Possible response: herself.] What kind of conversation is she having? [She is talking to herself.]

(B) Literary Focus
REVIEW STANDARD

Free verse. How does this stanza differ structurally from the first stanza? [Possible response: The first stanza consists of three sentences of varying lengths; this one consists of three parallel questions.]

(C) Learners Having Difficulty

Questioning. What is the speaker doing, and why is she using "different voices"? [Possible response: She is calling the airline repeatedly, disguising her voice so they won't know it is the same caller.]

(D) Literary Focus
REVIEW STANDARD

Free verse. How does the punctuation and the rhythm of this sentence help to enhance the meaning? [Possible response: The clause that ends with a comma, expressing the idea that the speaker gets an answer, is longer than the second clause, in which the speaker is cut off. The end punctuation helps the reader experience the finality of the speaker's being cut off.]

(E) Reading Skills

Making inferences. How does the speaker feel about the airline's response to her questions? [Possible responses: She feels they aren't taking her concerns seriously. She feels they don't care.]

The Flying Cat

Naomi Shihab Nye

(A) Never, in all your career of worrying, did you imagine
what worries could occur concerning the flying cat.
You are traveling to a distant city.
The cat must travel in a small box with holes.

(B) Will the baggage compartment be pressurized?
Will a soldier's footlocker fall on the cat during take-off?
Will the cat freeze?

(C) (D) You ask these questions one by one, in different voices
over the phone. Sometimes you get an answer,
sometimes a click.
Now it's affecting everything you do.
At dinner you feel nauseous, like you're swallowing
at twenty thousand feet.
In dreams you wave fish-heads, but the cat has grown propellers,
the cat is spinning out of sight!

Will he faint when the plane lands?
Is the baggage compartment soundproofed?
Will the cat go deaf?

(E) "Ma'am, if the cabin weren't pressurized, your cat would explode."
And spoken in a droll impersonal tone, as if
the explosion of cats were another statistic!

Hugging the cat before departure, you realize again
the private language of pain. He purrs. He trusts you.
He knows little of planets or satellites,
black holes in space or the weightless rise of fear.

DIFFERENTIATING INSTRUCTION

Learners Having Difficulty

You may wish to model the process of reading free-verse poetry by reading the first stanza aloud. Remind students to pay attention to the poem's punctuation and pause briefly at commas, make full stops at periods, and read through lines that lack end punctuation.

English-Language Learners

Before reading, be sure to discuss with students the characteristics of free verse described on p. 513. You may wish to pair students with more fluent readers and have them read the poem aloud to each other as if they were simply having a conversation.

Meet the Writer

Naomi Shihab Nye

Stories in Everyday Objects

Naomi Shihab Nye (1952–   ) is a poet, a storyteller, an anthologist, an essayist, a teacher, and a songwriter. She also works in schools, encouraging students to find the poet in themselves. In her first two collections of poetry, *Different Ways to Pray* (1980) and *Hugging the Jukebox* (1982), Nye was writing on a topic she still feels passionately about: the experiences people from different cultures share. In *Yellow Glove* (1986), several poems deal with small, everyday objects—which are a recurring focus of her work.

"Since I was a small child, I've felt that little inanimate things were very wise, that they had their own kind of wisdom, something to teach me if I would only pay the right kind of attention to them."

She thinks that poems about such objects say, "Pause. Take note. A story is being told through this thing."

For Independent Reading

Nye's young-adult novel *Habibi* (1997) draws on her experience as an American teenager of half-Palestinian descent as she describes a visit made by a Palestinian American teenager to her father's homeland in the 1970s.

Meet the Writer

Naomi Shihab Nye's love for poetry blossomed at an early age. "I wrote my first poem at age six, about visiting Chicago. I still remember the way the words felt coming out of my pencil, big and round and brave. My teacher at Central School let me hang it in the hall and a girl from an upper grade mentioned weeks later that she 'knew what I meant.' Boom—I was hooked. Words were magic wands. I felt powerful and satisfied when I used them. Somehow it felt even better using them on paper than just saying them. I could stand back and look at my life."

Resources Reminder

For lessons designed for intermediate and advanced English-language learners, see *Lesson Plans for Language Development,* pp. 224, 245, 255.

Special Education Students

For lessons designed for special education students, see *Lesson Plans for Language Development,* pp. 225, 245, 255.

Connection

Summary ⬌ *at grade level*

In an interview with Bill Moyers, Naomi Shihab Nye describes poetry as a conversation and advises students to approach poetry with this idea in mind. Since students probably don't fear everyday conversation, neither should they fear "talking" to the words they read or write on a page. To Nye, reading and writing poetry is a different kind of talk than the chatter of everyday life; it provides an opportunity to slow down, savor a phrase, and focus on individual images and words.

DIRECT TEACHING

A Learners Having Difficulty

Paraphrasing. According to Nye, how does poetry resemble a conversation? [Possible response: Poetry is a dialogue between the reader and the words on the page.]

B Reading Skills

Drawing conclusions. What are the students Nye meets wary of? [Possible response: They are nervous about reading or writing poetry.]

C Content-Area Connections

Literature: Haiku

Remind students that haiku is a form of short poetry that originated in Japan. Traditional haiku have seventeen syllables divided between three lines. Because of this structure, haiku usually focus on a single image, often related to nature.

Interview with Naomi Shihab Nye

Bill Moyers

The journalist Bill Moyers talked to Naomi Shihab Nye about writing, poetry, language, and life. Here is an excerpt from their conversation.

Moyers. Poetry is a form of conversation for you, isn't it?

Nye. Absolutely. Poetry is a conversation with the world; poetry is a conversation with the words on the page in which you allow those words to speak back to you; and poetry is a conversation with yourself. Many times I meet students and see a little look of wariness in their faces—"I'm not sure I *want* to do this or I'm not sure I *can* do this"—I like to say, "Wait a minute. How nervous are you about the conversation you're going to have at lunch today with your friends?" And they say, "Oh, we're not nervous at all about *that*. We do *that* every day." Then I tell them they can come to feel the same way about writing. Writing doesn't have to be an exotic or stressful experience. You can just sit down with a piece of paper and begin talking and see what speaks back.

Moyers. Talking out loud? When you're alone?

Nye. Well, sometimes, I often begin talking out loud, whether I'm alone or not. My son will say, "You were talking to yourself right now." And I say, "That's what I was doing; but I was so comfortable with you and I didn't notice it." I often just repeat a phrase I've heard or some words I want to write down so I won't forget them. In our culture especially I think we need to talk to ourselves more, and we also need to *listen* to ourselves more.

Moyers. Some people think there's so much talk in America—the talk shows, call-in shows, interviews, . . . press conferences, TV commercials—that it's all just a babble.

Nye. Maybe what I mean is a different kind of talk, because the kind I'm thinking about is a very slow and deliberate, delighted kind of talk. My favorite quote comes from Thailand: "Life is so short we must move very slowly." I think that poems help us to do that by allowing us to savor a single image, a single phrase. Think about haiku—those little seventeen-syllable poems—how many people have savored a single haiku poem over hundreds of years? Reading a poem slows you down, and when you slow down, you are likely to read it more than one time. You read it more slowly than you would speak to somebody in a store, and we *need* that slow experience with words, as well as those quick and jazzy ones.

—from *The Language of Life*

Connecting and Comparing Texts

In the interview, Nye focuses on the idea of poetry as a conversation. Invite students to discuss Nye's poem in the context of the views she reveals. You may wish to use the following prompts to stimulate discussion:

- In the interview, Nye discusses talking to herself out loud. What aspect of "The Flying Cat" does this seem to echo? [Possible response: By speaking to "you," the speaker seems to be talking to herself, addressing her own fears and anxieties.]
- What kinds of conversation take place in "The Flying Cat"? [Possible responses: A conversation between the speaker and herself; a conversation between the speaker and the reader; a conversation between the poet and the world.]

516 Chapter 7 Poetry

Literary Response and Analysis

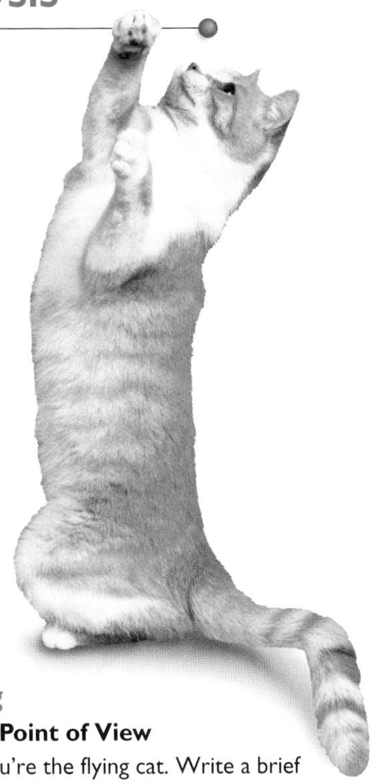

Reading Check

1. What anxiety is the speaker sharing with you?
2. What horrible things does the speaker ask you to imagine in regard to her cat?
3. What does she ask you to realize about the cat at the end of the poem?

Interpretations

4. Explain what you think the speaker means by "the private language of pain" (line 23). What significance do you see in the fact that she says she realizes that pain "again"?
5. Is this poem about more than the cat? How does the last stanza extend the meaning of the poem?
6. Although this poem is written without rhyme or meter—it is written in **free verse**—it is designed with care. What structural element do you notice immediately as you look at the poem on the page? What examples of **parallelism**—words, phrases, or sentences with a similar grammatical structure—can you find?

Evaluation

7. In Bill Moyers's interview of Nye (see the ***Connection*** on page 516), she says that reading poetry is important because we need "the slow experience with words" that poems give us. Do you agree with Nye? Are there words or phrases in "The Flying Cat" that had a special impact on you as you read the poem? Explain your answers.

Writing

A Feline Point of View

Imagine you're the flying cat. Write a brief **free-verse** poem (or a few paragraphs of prose) describing the plane trip from your point of view. You might describe how you feel about your worried owner, what happens during the trip, what you think about during the trip, and how you feel when you arrive at your destination. (Check your Quickwrite notes before beginning.)

Listening and Speaking

Different Voices

Prepare Nye's poem for performance. First, determine whether you want to use more than one speaker. Then, decide how you'll read the questions. Will you do as the poet says she did and ask them in different voices? Rehearse your poem, and perform it for a small group or your class.

Grade 8 Review Reading Standard 3.1 Determine and articulate the relationship between the purposes and characteristics of different forms of poetry.

INDEPENDENT PRACTICE

Literary Response and Analysis

Reading Check

1. The speaker is anxious about shipping her cat by plane.
2. She asks readers to imagine the cat in an unpressurized baggage compartment, luggage falling on the cat, the cat freezing, the cat fainting, the cat being scared by noise, the cat going deaf.
3. The cat trusts the speaker and does not share her fears.

Interpretations

4. Possible answers: The deep anxiety she feels for the cat is intensely personal; by saying "again," the speaker emphasizes that she has felt this before.
5. Possible answer: The poem is about the speaker's anxieties, her "career of worrying," embodied by her fear of entrusting her cat to an airline. The last stanza expands the poem's themes to include the nature of trust, the relationship between ignorance and bliss, and the pain of letting go despite fear.
6. One immediately notices the six-stanza structure of the poem, as well as the two indented stanzas. These indented stanzas are examples of parallelism: Each contains three questions with similar grammatical structures.

Evaluation

7. Students answers will vary. Some may point out that l. 19 had a special impact because another voice is introduced that breaks the poem's rhythm.

ASSESSING

Assessment

- *Progress Assessment of Reading*
  - Selection Test

DIFFERENTIATING INSTRUCTION

Learners Having Difficulty

You may wish to have students work individually on the Reading Check questions and discuss the Interpretations questions in small groups. *Monitoring tip:* If students have difficulty with question 6, ask them to look for examples of repetition, which can signal parallel sentence structures.

Advanced Learners

Enrichment. Extend question 6 by challenging students to write a paragraph or two analyzing the entire poem. Students might comment on how the poem's structural elements contribute to its sound and rhythm patterns. Students might also comment on line lengths and line breaks, punctuation, and sound effects.

STANDARDS FOCUS, pp. 518–526

(For grade-level and review standards taught in this lesson, see citations on Student Edition pages.)

Summary ↔ *at grade level*

This lyric poem depicts the drab life of a former high school basketball star. Stuck in a dead-end job as a gas station attendant, Flick Webb lives in the past with only the memories of his glory days to sustain him. The speaker senses an air of regret around Webb, who now clowns with an inner tube or loiters in a luncheonette.

PRETEACHING

Selection Starter

Motivate. Invite students to discuss where they imagine themselves to be ten years, or even twenty years, after graduating from high school. What can they do to help make sure their ambitions are realized?

Before You Read

Ex–Basketball Player

Literary Focus

Sound Effects

Even though Updike's poem sounds free and conversational, it's written within a tight **structure.** The basic beat is **iambic pentameter**—five iambs (˘ ′) to a line. This meter is closest to the rhythm of everyday English speech, and its use gives the poem an informal, conversational sound. You'll find the same meter providing the beat in a poem written centuries before Updike's: Shakespeare's sonnet on page 494. Updike uses other sound devices: **Internal rhymes** and **alliteration** lend his unrhymed poem verbal music. Read it aloud.

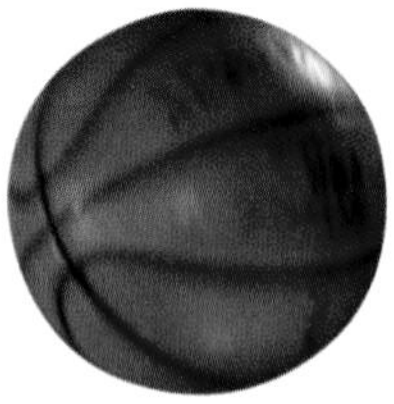

Make the Connection

Sports and Life

Almost every school has a sports hero, someone who is a natural at the game. Like the glittering stars whose brilliance fades overnight, some of these bright heroes seem to dim after graduation.

How important are school athletics to you? Do you think they prepare young people for life? Why?

Reading Standard 3.7 Recognize and understand the significance of various literary devices, and explain their appeal.

RESOURCES: READING

Planning

- *One-Stop Planner* CD-ROM with Test Generator
- *On Course: Mapping Instruction*

Media

- *Audio CD Library*
  - disc 13

Reading

- *Interactive Reading,* Teacher's Edition
  - Graphic Organizer: Sounds of Poetry Chart

Differentiating Instruction

- *Lesson Plans for Language Development*
  - English-Language Learners, pp. 226, 246, 255
  - Special Education Students, pp. 227, 246, 255

Assessment

- *Progress Assessment of Reading*
  - Selection Test
- *One-Stop Planner* CD-ROM with Test Generator

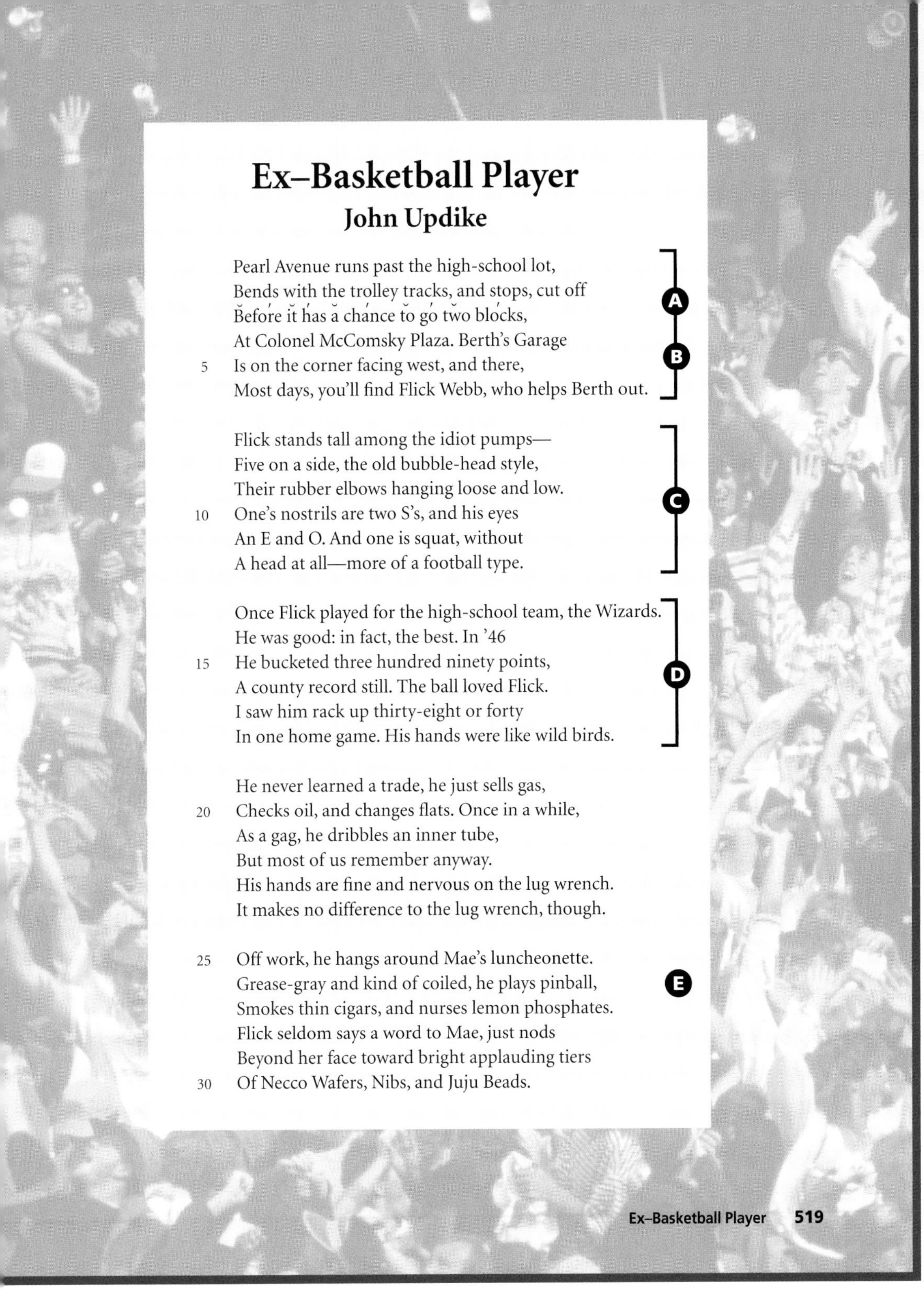

Ex–Basketball Player

John Updike

Pearl Avenue runs past the high-school lot,
Bends with the trolley tracks, and stops, cut off
Before it has a chance to go two blocks,
At Colonel McComsky Plaza. Berth's Garage
Is on the corner facing west, and there,
Most days, you'll find Flick Webb, who helps Berth out.

Flick stands tall among the idiot pumps—
Five on a side, the old bubble-head style,
Their rubber elbows hanging loose and low.
One's nostrils are two S's, and his eyes
An E and O. And one is squat, without
A head at all—more of a football type.

Once Flick played for the high-school team, the Wizards.
He was good: in fact, the best. In '46
He bucketed three hundred ninety points,
A county record still. The ball loved Flick.
I saw him rack up thirty-eight or forty
In one home game. His hands were like wild birds.

He never learned a trade, he just sells gas,
Checks oil, and changes flats. Once in a while,
As a gag, he dribbles an inner tube,
But most of us remember anyway.
His hands are fine and nervous on the lug wrench.
It makes no difference to the lug wrench, though.

Off work, he hangs around Mae's luncheonette.
Grease-gray and kind of coiled, he plays pinball,
Smokes thin cigars, and nurses lemon phosphates.
Flick seldom says a word to Mae, just nods
Beyond her face toward bright applauding tiers
Of Necco Wafers, Nibs, and Juju Beads.

DIRECT TEACHING

A Literary Focus
REVIEW STANDARD

Sound effects: Iambic pentameter. Help students scan the third line and identify the five iambs: "Before it has a chance to go two blocks,"

Then, ask the class to identify the lines in the first stanza that deviate from the meter. [ll. 1, 2, and 4]

B Literary Focus
REVIEW STANDARD

Sound effects: Rhymes. Ask students to point out rhyming words and alliteration in ll. 1–3. [The words *past* and *tracks* are internal near rhymes; *lot, stops,* and *blocks* are rhymes or near rhymes; *trolley tracks* is an example of alliteration.]

C Content-Area Connections

History: Pump styles
Students may be unfamiliar with the rounded "bubble-head style" of gas pumps. To help students understand the metaphor, have them search the Internet or other sources for photographs of old gas pumps. Also point out that the letters *E-S-S-O* refer to Esso, the former name of Exxon.

D Vocabulary Development
GRADE-LEVEL STANDARD

Jargon. What sports jargon is used in this stanza? [*bucketed, rack up*] What do these terms mean? [*Bucketed* means "scored baskets," and *rack up* means "collect points."]

E Literary Focus
REVIEW STANDARD

Sound effects: Alliteration. Remind students that alliteration is the repetition of consonant sounds. What examples of alliteration do you notice in l. 26? [*Grease* and *gray, kind* and *coiled,* and *plays* and *pinball* are examples of alliteration.]

DIFFERENTIATING INSTRUCTION

English-Language Learners
For students unfamiliar with the game of basketball, play a videotape of a recent game. Have students who are familiar with basketball explain the game's rules and scoring system and demonstrate moves such as dribbling and dunking. In addition, be sure that students know that tires had inner tubes until fairly recently and that the brand names referred to in the last line are types of candy.

Resources Reminder
For lessons designed for intermediate and advanced English-language learners, see *Lesson Plans for Language Development,* pp. 226, 246, 255.

Special Education Students
For lessons designed for special education students, see *Lesson Plans for Language Development,* pp. 227, 246, 255.

GUIDED PRACTICE

Monitoring students' progress. Guide the class in answering these comprehension questions.

Short Answer

1. What is Flick Webb's claim to fame? [He was an outstanding high school basketball player.]
2. Where does Flick work? [at a gas station]
3. How does Flick remind people of his past fame? [He sometimes dribbles an inner tube.]
4. What does Flick do when he's not working? [He hangs out at a luncheonette.]

Meet the Writer

Background. One of America's great contemporary writers, John Updike has written more than fifty books since his volume of poems *The Carpentered Hen and Other Tame Creatures* appeared in 1958. Both "Ex–Basketball Player" and "Ace in the Hole"—a short story collected in *The Same Door* in 1959—can be seen as early sketches of Harry "Rabbit" Angstrom, Updike's most famous former high school athlete. About his subjects, Updike writes, "The idea of a hero is aristocratic. Now either nobody is a hero or everyone is. I vote for everyone. My subject is the American Protestant small-town middle class."

Meet the Writer

John Updike

Observer of American Life

John Updike (1932–   ) was born in the small town of Shillington, Pennsylvania. A year after he graduated from Harvard University, he got a job on the staff of *The New Yorker* magazine, which has published much of his writing ever since.

Though he has won fame for his novels and short stories, Updike is also a poet of great wit and craft. He is particularly drawn to occasional poetry—pieces inspired by odd or funny incidents reported in the newspapers or observed in the American suburban landscape of housing developments, service stations, and supermarkets. Despite his humorous approach, Updike is a sharp social observer and a serious moralist.

Among the most successful of Updike's novels are the Rabbit tales (the last two of which won Pulitzer Prizes): *Rabbit, Run* (1960), *Rabbit Redux* (1971), *Rabbit Is Rich* (1981), and *Rabbit at Rest* (1990). These novels chronicle the life of Harry "Rabbit" Angstrom, an ex–basketball player. Rabbit lives an outwardly conventional life in a small Pennsylvania town, but his hidden yearnings and disappointing relationships reveal the uncertainties of contemporary American life.

In accepting the American Book Award in 1982, Updike spoke these words to young writers:

"Have faith. May you surround yourselves with parents, editors, mates, and children as supportive as mine have been. But the essential support and encouragement of course comes from within, arising out of the mad notion that your society needs to know what only you can tell it."

DIFFERENTIATING INSTRUCTION

Advanced Learners

Enrichment. Discussing Updike's early work, the critic Richard Rupp noted: "One reason for Updike's success rests on his celebrated style, a restless, exhaustive exploration of minute physical detail."

Activity. Invite students to evaluate this comment in light of "Ex–Basketball Player." How does Updike employ a "restless, exhaustive exploration of minute physical detail" in this poem?

520 Chapter 7 Poetry

Before You Read

miss rosie

Literary Focus

Idioms—Not Literally True

An **idiom** is an expression that is peculiar to a certain language and cannot be understood by a mere literal definition of its individual words. For example, the literal meaning of "to fall in love" would be absurd. Like many idioms, this one implies a comparison. The experience of love can be so overwhelming that it feels like losing your footing or falling into a trap, although not necessarily an unpleasant one.

Idioms are so common in English that you probably use them all the time. Here are a few more common examples: "raining cats and dogs," "to have the upper hand," "to jump out of my skin." Can you think of others? Idioms present a particular difficulty for people learning a new language.

If an idiom is unfamiliar to you—as the idiom "i stand up" in "miss rosie" might be—the context might help you understand it.

Make the Connection

Portrait of a Woman

No one can say that Clifton's portrait of Miss Rosie is very pretty. Yet beauty—and what can happen to it—is the subject of the poem. Notice how figures of speech help you see contrasting pictures, past and present, of Miss Rosie.

Grade 8 Review Reading Standard 1.1 Analyze idioms to infer the literal and figurative meanings of phrases.

Mirage (1993) by Catherine Howe. Oil on canvas. Collection Alan P. Power, Venice, California.

Summary at grade level

This poem's speaker uses strong figures of speech—"wrapped up like garbage" and "wet brown bag of a woman"—to depict the degradation of a once strong and beautiful woman. With the repeated idiom "I stand up," however, the speaker declares her respect for Miss Rosie.

PRETEACHING

Selection Starter

Motivate. Have students discuss how they feel when they see homeless people or panhandlers on the street. Do they ever imagine the stories behind these people's lives? Do they wonder what the person was like when he or she was their age?

VIEWING THE ART

Catherine Howe (1959–), a figurative painter, is known for her powerful paintings of women. Howe uses bold expressionist brush strokes and often reflects colors from a background onto the bodies of her subjects.

Activity. Ask students to describe how the subject of *Mirage* resembles Miss Rosie, both in her youth and in her present state. [Possible response: The subject of the painting is pretty and well-dressed and carries a hat that a young southern woman might wear, but her posture and facial expression make her seem isolated and possibly troubled.]

READING SKILLS REVIEW

Adjusting reading strategies. Tell students that they can benefit from reading a poem several times and adjusting their reading strategy each time according to their purpose. Model this skill with "Ex–Basketball Player," using the following steps:

1. Read the poem aloud at a normal conversational rate, and have students give their initial responses to Updike's poem.
2. Read the poem aloud slowly, with an emphasis on its meter. Tell students that this type of second reading helps one to recognize and analyze a poem's rhyme and meter.
3. Point out that a careful silent reading is often necessary to interpret a poem's meaning. In this third reading, encourage students to pause, re-read, and start again in order to glean as much meaning as possible.
4. Finally, invite students to read the poem aloud again for their own enjoyment.

DIRECT TEACHING

(A) Literary Focus
GRADE-LEVEL STANDARD

? Figurative language. What does the speaker mean when she says that Miss Rosie is "waiting for" her mind "like next week's grocery"? [Possible responses: Miss Rosie is not always mentally present; Miss Rosie is waiting for mental clarity to come to her, which—like next week's groceries—may not come at all.]

(B) Reading Skills

? Drawing conclusions. Why does the speaker refer twice to Miss Rosie's past? [Possible responses: She wants to emphasize the contrast between the past and the present; she wants to emphasize that Miss Rosie is an individual worthy of respect.]

(C) Literary Focus
REVIEW STANDARD

? Idiom. What are the literal and idiomatic meanings of "i stand up"? [The literal meaning is "i get to my feet." The idiomatic meaning could be "I represent or defend" or "I honor and respect."]

miss rosie
Lucille Clifton

when i watch you
wrapped up like garbage
sitting, surrounded by the smell
of too old potato peels
or
when i watch you
in your old man's shoes
with the little toe cut out
(A) sitting, waiting for your mind
like next week's grocery
i say
when i watch you
you wet brown bag of a woman
(B) who used to be the best looking gal in georgi
used to be called the Georgia Rose
i stand up
through your destruction
(C) i stand up

DIFFERENTIATING INSTRUCTION

Learners Having Difficulty
Have pairs of students work through the poem and identify the sensory details that Clifton uses to create her images. Suggest that students use a chart to organize words that appeal to the senses of sight, smell, and touch. Students can use the chart to write brief descriptions of Miss Rosie as the speaker sees her.

English-Language Learners
Students might not know the denotative and connotative meanings of the word *gal.* Explain that the word means "girl" and that it connotes a woman who is lively and fun loving.

Resources Reminder
For lessons designed for intermediate and advanced English-language learners, see *Lesson Plans for Language Development,* pp. 226, 246, 255.

Special Education Students
For lessons designed for special education students, see *Lesson Plans for Language Development,* pp. 227, 246, 255.

Meet the Writer

Lucille Clifton

Celebrating Survival

Lucille Clifton (1936–) writes both fiction and poetry and has published many books for children. One of Clifton's best-known works is *Generations* (1976), a poetic memoir composed of portraits of five generations of her family. It begins with her great-great-grandmother, who was brought from Africa to New Orleans and sold into slavery. Like all of Clifton's work, *Generations* is honest but rarely bitter. As one critic observed, her purpose is perpetuation and celebration, not judgment.

Clifton says that family stories are part of the ingredients that make us who we are. She remembers hearing her own family's stories when she was growing up.

"My father told those stories to me over and over. That made them seem important. He told the stories to whoever was present, but I was the only person who listened. I think there is a matter of preserving the past for the future's sake. I think if we see our lives as an ongoing story, it's important to include all the ingredients of it and not have it in little compartments. I like to think of it as not just that was then, this is now, but that they all connect. For some reason, I've always been a person who found more interesting the stories between the stories. I've always wondered the hows and the whys to things. Why is this like this? What has gone into making us who we are? Is it good or not so good? What is destroying us? What will keep us warm?"

GUIDED PRACTICE

Monitoring students' progress. Guide the class in answering these comprehension questions.

Short Answer

1. Whom is the speaker watching? [Miss Rosie]
2. What is Miss Rosie like now? [She seems to be a street person.]
3. What was Miss Rosie once like? [She was "the best looking gal in Georgia."]
4. What does the speaker vow to do through Miss Rosie's destruction? [stand up]

Meet the Writer

Background. As a young adult in the 1950s, Clifton attended Howard University to study theater. It was there that Clifton discovered "that one could write and take it seriously and have it matter." Nearly fifty years later, Clifton was reminded again how her words "matter" when she was awarded the National Book Award for poetry in 2000 for *Blessing the Boats: New and Selected Poems, 1988–2000.*

DEVELOPING FLUENCY

Mixed-ability group activity. Divide the class into mixed-ability groups, and ask them to practice reading aloud both "Ex–Basketball Player" and "miss rosie." You might suggest that students copy each poem on a piece of paper, marking pauses and other cues that will help them develop fluency in reading the poems aloud. Remind students to pay attention to each poem's punctuation—to pause briefly at commas, make full stops at periods, and to read through lines that lack end punctuation. Because "miss rosie" does not contain much punctuation, suggest that students be alert to the rhythms of natural speech in their readings.

INDEPENDENT PRACTICE

Literary Response and Analysis

Ex-Basketball Player

Reading Check

1. Possible answers: ll. 19–20, 25–27
2. Possible answers: ll. 13–18

Interpretations

3. *Internal rhyme*—"loose and low" and "E and O." *Alliteration*—"trolley tracks," "Colonel McComsky," "find Flick," "loose and low," "Checks oil, and changes flats," "Grease-gray," "kind of coiled," and "plays pinball."
4. The street is cut off by a plaza, just as Flick's stardom was cut off after high school; the street doesn't go very far, just as Flick's life never went very far.
5. The pumps are "Five on a side" and hold their "elbows hanging loose and low" like basketball players. The word *idiot* modifies *pumps,* which may be an unkind comment on Flick and athletes. Flick "stands tall" among them, however, suggesting that he has the ability to accomplish more.
6. Flick sees the candy as a crowd at a basketball game. The personification suggests that Flick still fantasizes about being a star. Perhaps his old dreams are all he has left.
7. Lines 1, 2, and 4 in the first stanza and ll. 7, 8, and 12 in the second stanza vary the iambic pentameter.

miss rosie

Reading Check

1. Possible answers: ll. 2, 7, 9, 13
2. Possible answers: ll. 14–15

Interpretations

3. Possible answers: "wrapped up like garbage"; "waiting for your mind / like next week's grocery"; "wet brown bag of a woman." Each image creates a picture of sadness, wasted potential, and diminished capacity.
4. Possible answers: "Stand up" in the poem's context could mean "to protect, defend, salute." The image is of someone standing tall in the midst of disaster and Miss Rosie's refusal to be conquered. The speaker feels a link with Miss Rosie and remembers that she was once a beautiful and vital young woman. The speaker is standing up for Miss Rosie by recognizing Miss Rosie's life through poetry.
5. Possible answers: Miss Rosie may symbolize all the people lost to poverty, homelessness, and mental illness. She may symbolize the human capacity to endure.

Literary Response and Analysis

Ex–Basketball Player

Reading Check

1. Find details in the poem that tell us how Flick spends his time now.
2. Find details that tell us about Flick's past.

Interpretations

3. What different kinds of **sound effects** can you identify? Look especially for **internal rhyme** and **alliteration.** Note them all, and give examples.
4. Look back at the opening description of Pearl Avenue. How can this street be seen as a **metaphor** for Flick's life?
5. In the second stanza, find words that **personify** the gas pumps—that make them seem as if they were alive. Do you think Flick is similar to the pumps? Why or why not?
6. In the last stanza, what is the candy **compared** to, and who sees it that way? What do you think this suggests about Flick's fantasies—or dreams?
7. Scan the first and second stanzas of the poem. Which lines vary the **iambic pentameter** to avoid a mechanical sound? Which lines are in regular iambic pentameter?

Grade 8 Review Reading Standard 1.1 Analyze idioms to infer the literal and figurative meanings of phrases.

Reading Standard 3.7 Recognize and understand the significance of various literary devices, including figurative language, and explain their appeal.

miss rosie

Reading Check

1. What details tell you how Miss Rosie looks now?
2. What details tell you how Miss Rosie used to look?

Interpretations

3. Which **figure of speech** in "miss rosie" do you think is the most powerful? What picture of Miss Rosie does it create for you?
4. The **idiom** "i stand up," used twice, gives the most important clue to how the writer wants us to feel about Miss Rosie. What does standing up in the face of Miss Rosie's destruction mean? Why might the speaker be moved to "stand up" for Miss Rosie?
5. In a way, Miss Rosie seems to represent something more than herself, something never named. What do you think she might **symbolize**?

Writing

Portrait of a Person

In their poems, Updike and Clifton paint a memorable portrait of a person who has lost the glory of former times. Think of someone you know or someone famous (or create a character of your own). Write a **description** of that person in either the heyday of success or past his or her prime. Be sure to use vivid **sensory images** as you describe what the person looks like and what he or she does.

► **Use "Describing a Person," pages 540–547, for help with this assignment.**

The Poet in You

Here's what Lucille Clifton says about how she writes poetry:

> I have a feeling that sometimes rather than wrestle and look for words, you have to be still and let them come. I was not trained as a poet, and I've never taken poetry lessons or had workshops. Nobody taught me anything much, really. So I learned how to learn, and what I learned is that I could be still and allow the world and the impressions and the feelings—I'm very good with feelings—to come to me, and I could use our language to write them down.

Try it. Plant yourself in front of something that you love (or merely like)—or something that disturbs you. Jot down all of the feelings and words and phrases as they occur to you. When you're finished taking notes, see whether you've got the makings of a poem. Work on it until you're satisfied, adding whatever sound effects seem natural and easy.

Comparing Poems

In an **essay, compare and contrast** Updike's poem about Flick with Clifton's poem about Miss Rosie. Before you begin writing, take notes on the points of comparison between the two poems, using a chart like this one:

	"Ex-Basketball Player"	"miss rosie"
What character is like today		
What character was once like		
Speaker's attitude toward character		

Vocabulary Development

Idioms All Around You

PRACTICE 1

1. Look over both poems, and note all of the expressions that you'd classify as **idioms** (see page 521). Get together with classmates, and see whether you agree.
2. With a small group, survey students in your school, or survey your family or neighbors. Ask them to think of as many idioms as they can, in English or other languages. Read a few idioms to get them started—for example, "big shot," "go in one ear and out the other." You might prepare a dictionary of idioms to share with the class.

Grade 8 Review Reading Standard 1.1 Analyze idioms to infer the literal and figurative meanings of phrases.

Reading Standard 1.1 Identify and use the literal and figurative meanings of words.

(continued)

Vocabulary Development

Practice 1

1. "*Ex–Basketball Player" idioms*—"runs past," "cut off," "helps Berth out," "hangs around," "nurses." *"miss rosie" idiom*—"i stand up."
2. Lists and dictionaries will vary.

DIFFERENTIATING INSTRUCTION

Learners Having Difficulty

If students have trouble answering question 4 (p. 524) about "miss rosie," encourage them to think about other things for which people "stand up." For example, one might stand up for a friend who is being teased by others. *Monitoring tip:* You might discuss with students a few examples of similes and metaphors before they answer the Literary Response and Analysis questions on p. 524.

Vocabulary Development

Practice 2

Possible Word Maps

- *bucketed. Context Clues*—"In '46 / He bucketed three hundred ninety points, / A county record still. The ball loved Flick."

  Technical Meaning—scored points in a basketball game by putting the ball through the basket.

  Other Meanings—placed something in a bucket.

- *rack up. Context Clues*—"He bucketed three hundred ninety points, / A county record still." "I saw him rack up thirty-eight or forty / In one home game."

  Technical Meaning—accumulate or score points in a game.

  Other Meanings—prepare the balls for a game of pool.

- *dribbles. Context Clues*—"His hands were like wild birds," ". . . he dribbles an inner tube."

  Technical Meaning—bounces the ball between one hand and the floor while moving on the basketball court.

  Other Meanings—drools; trickles or leaks slowly.

Resources Reminder

Vocabulary

- *Lesson Plans for Language Development*
  - Vocabulary, pp. 246, 255

ASSESSING

Assessment

- *Progress Assessment of Reading*
  - Selection Test

RETEACHING

For a lesson reteaching Standard 3.7, see **Reteaching,** p. 939A. For another lesson to teach Standard 3.7, see *Interactive Reading,* Chapter 7.

Jargon: Job-Related Vocabulary

Jargon is the specialized vocabulary used by people in particular jobs or sharing particular interests. Doctors have jargon, as do athletes, actors, computer users, and sailors.

PRACTICE 2

Set up a word map similar to the one below for *dunk,* in order to study each of the basketball terms Updike uses in his poem. If you're hooked on sports jargon, do the same for other sports terms, or make charts for technical terms associated with your hobby or special interest.

dunk

Context Clues
Poised under the rim,
she leapt and dunked the ball
for the winning points.

Technical Meaning
thrust a ball into the
net while leaping above
the basket

Other Meanings
plunge into; dip a
doughnut into coffee

Before You Read

Remember

Literary Focus

Repetition and Refrain: Singing Sounds

Both poets and songwriters use **repetition** to create emotional effects. When certain words or phrases or sentences occur repeatedly in a kind of pattern, they're called a **refrain.** You can probably sing dozens of refrains (the part everyone remembers best) from your favorite songs. Refrains create musical effects because they repeat the exact sounds and sentence patterns again and again. Refrains also give emphasis to certain ideas. Sometimes a refrain can so draw out a story that it builds up tension and creates suspense.

Make the Connection

Quickwrite

One of George and Ira Gershwin's most popular ballads list a series of memories. The second stanza goes like this: "The way you wear your hat / The way you sip your tea / The memory of all that / No, they can't take that away from me."

On a piece of paper, list some of the events, objects, people, and places you can remember most vividly.

Reading Standard 3.7 Recognize and understand the significance of various literary devices, and explain their appeal.

The Sun Dance (c. 1880s). Native American Plains Indian (probably Sioux) painting on animal hide.

STANDARDS FOCUS, pp. 527–530

(For the grade-level standard taught in this lesson, see citations on Student Edition pages.)

Summary *at grade level*

In this lyric poem by Native American poet Joy Harjo, the speaker reminds us to remember the important things in life, such as the moon, the sun, one's parents, the earth, and the animals and people who populate it. The word *remember* serves as a gentle refrain.

PRETEACHING

Selection Starter

Motivate. Ask students to name their favorite songs. Do they have refrains? Would the songs be different without them? Discuss what refrains add to songs or poems.

RESOURCES: READING

Planning
- *One-Stop Planner* CD-ROM with Test Generator
- *On Course: Mapping Instruction*

Media
- *Audio CD Library*
  - disc 13

Reading
- *Interactive Reading,* Teacher's Edition
  - Graphic Organizer: Sounds of Poetry Chart

Differentiating Instruction
- *Lesson Plans for Language Development*
  - English-Language Learners, pp. 228, 247, 256
  - Special Education Students, pp. 228, 247, 256

Assessment
- *Progress Assessment of Reading*
  - Selection Test
- *One-Stop Planner* CD-ROM with Test Generator

DIRECT TEACHING

A Literary Focus
GRADE-LEVEL STANDARD

? Personification. How is the moon personified here? [as a woman]

B Literary Focus
REVIEW STANDARD

? Repetition. What emotional effect does the repetition of the word *remember* create in this poem? [Possible responses: The repetition of *remember* lends the poem's message a sense of urgency and importance; it emphasizes the emotional bond between the speaker and whomever the speaker is addressing.]

VIEWING THE ART

Beginning in 1910, **Arthur Dove** (1880–1946) was the first American to paint entirely abstract pictures. Dove's paintings use bright colors, curving shapes, and abstract forms to suggest that objects are not separate entities, but active forces within an environment of constant change. Dove believed that by slowly arriving at abstract forms as he studied the natural world, he could reveal "essences"—shapes that symbolized the forces of nature and the spiritual reality behind them. *Sun* illustrates Dove's use of simplified forms to suggest movement, rhythm, and the flux and harmony of nature.

Activity. Ask students to compare the effects that Harjo strives for in "Remember" with the effects that Dove seeks in *Sun.* [Possible response: Both Harjo and Dove seek to explain fundamental truths about nature by repeating simple, bold patterns with minor variations.]

Remember

Joy Harjo

Remember the sky that you were born under,
know each of the star's stories.
(A) Remember the moon, know who she is.
Remember the sun's birth at dawn, that is the
strongest point of time. Remember sundown
and the giving away to night.
Remember your birth, how your mother struggled
to give you form and breath. You are evidence of
her life, and her mother's, and hers.
(B) Remember your father. He is your life, also.
Remember the earth whose skin you are:
red earth, black earth, yellow earth, white earth
brown earth, we are earth.

Sun (1943) by Arthur G. Dove. Wax emulsion on canvas (24″ × 32″).

DIFFERENTIATING INSTRUCTION

Learners Having Difficulty
As they read the poem, have students make lists of what the speaker says to remember. Then, have them work in small groups to read the poem aloud and discuss why the speaker urges them to remember these things. Groups should use the lists and their discussions to create a prose summary of the poem.

English-Language Learners
For lessons designed for intermediate and advanced English-language learners and for special education students, see *Lesson Plans for Language Development,* pp. 228, 247, 256.

Remember the plants, trees, animal life who all have their
tribes, their families, their histories, too. Talk to them,
listen to them. They are alive poems. **C**
Remember the wind. Remember her voice. She knows the
origin of this universe.
Remember that you are all people and that all people
are you.
Remember that you are this universe and that this
universe is you.
Remember that all is in motion, is growing, is you.
Remember that language comes from this.
Remember the dance that language is, that life is.
Remember. **D**

Meet the Writer

Joy Harjo

"Enter the Poet's World"

Many of the poems of Joy Harjo (1951–) deal with her mixed Muscogee Creek and Cherokee heritage and the themes of personal survival and mythic space. Harjo performs her poetry and plays the saxophone with a band, Poetic Justice.

When she writes, Harjo says, she often feels the presence of her ancestors, and sometimes an old Creek Indian within her acts as her muse.

Here's what she tells her college students about how to read a poem:

"First of all, it's important to read the poem out loud. Poetry is an oral art—it's *meant* to be spoken and to be read out loud. I have my students memorize at least two poems a semester, which they usually don't like doing, but they come to see why it's important. I've given thought to having everyone memorize a poem a week—for which I'm sure I would not be very popular—but there's such magic in doing that. Then it's important to be willing to let go of your immediate reality and enter the poet's world."

DIRECT TEACHING

C Learners Having Difficulty

Questioning. What might the speaker mean when she calls plants, trees, and animals "alive poems"? [Possible response: The speaker is comparing plants, trees, and animals to poems, perhaps implying that like poems, plants and animals tell stories and can teach people about life.]

D English-Language Learners

Multiple-meaning words. Point out that the word *remember* can mean two distinct things: an instance of calling to mind something specific from the past or the state of constantly keeping certain things in mind. Which meaning of *remember* is the speaker using in this poem? [Possible response: The speaker wants her audience to constantly keep in mind the things she is saying.]

Meet the Writer

Background. Joy Harjo does not consider music to be a hobby or sideline to her writing. Rather, she says, each feeds the other. "I am asked often about how music has informed my poetry, changed it. It's difficult to say exactly, except to acknowledge that of course it has all along. The first poetry I heard and recognized as pure poetry was the improvised line of a trumpet player on a jazz tune on the radio when I was four-years-old. That was it. I've been trying to get it right ever since."

INDEPENDENT PRACTICE

Literary Response and Analysis

Reading Check

1. The word *remember* acts as a kind of refrain.

Interpretations

2. Possible answers: a child, a family member, a friend, a student.
3. The elements of nature the speaker personifies include the moon and the wind. The speaker personifies both as women to be remembered as one remembers one's mother.
4. The speaker compares our skin to the earth's surface and all the different colors that can be found on it. She compares plants and animals to people and poems, and she compares language to a dance.
5. Possible answers: While the statements are not logical, they are true in the sense that everyone is connected to each other and the universe; the statements are not logical or true because most people are very different from one another and the universe is made up of a lot more than just one person.
6. Possible answers: This poem is a guide for how to live your life; this poem is one person's opinion about what is important in life.
7. Possible answer: The last seven lines of the poem are the most important because they deliver the speaker's message that the entire universe is connected and that what we say and do is important.
8. Possible answer: The refrain gives the poem a gentle yet urgent tone and emphasizes the importance and immediacy of the message.

Literary Response and Analysis

Reading Check

1. What single word, piled up throughout the poem, acts as a kind of **refrain**?

Interpretations

2. Whom do you suppose this **speaker** is talking to?
3. What elements of nature does the speaker **personify**—that is, in what way does she talk about them as if they were human?
4. What **metaphors** does the speaker use to describe our skin, which comes in all colors; the plants; animal life; and language itself?
5. What do you make of lines 19–22? Are these two statements logical? Do they sound true to you?
6. Someone has asked you what this poem is about. What will you say?
7. What lines from the poem do you think are especially important in delivering the speaker's message?
8. How does the **refrain** contribute to the poem's **tone** and message?

Writing

Memories

Re-read your Quickwrite notes, and choose a number of the memories that are most meaningful to you. Then, imitate Harjo's poem by writing a series of sentences that begin "I remember . . ."

Orders

Harjo's poem is like a series of instructions to someone the poet addresses as "you." Write a series of **instructions** to a person *you* know: a child or a friend or an older person. Keep repeating one **verb** in your series of instructions (such as *love* or *read* or *hope*). You should include at least three things that you want the person to do.

Reading Standard 3.7 Recognize and understand the significance of various literary devices, including figurative language, and explain their appeal.

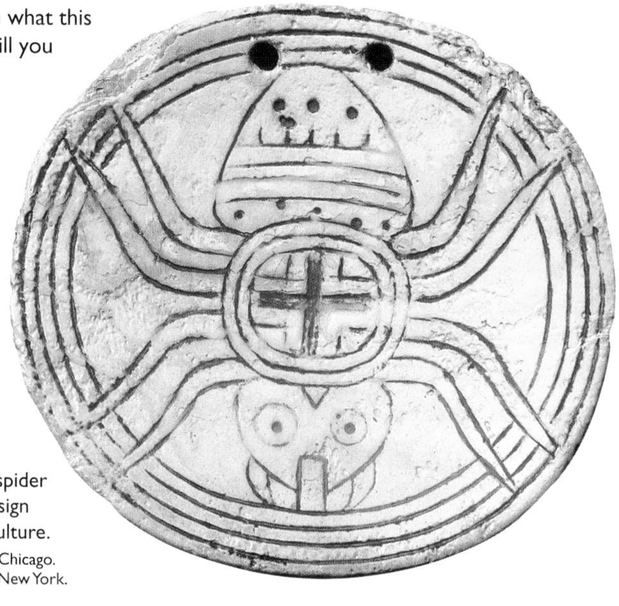

Shell disc inscribed with a spider and sacred-cross-of-fire design (c. 1000 A.D.). Mississippi culture.
Field Museum of Natural History, Chicago.
© Werner Forman/Art Resource, New York.

ASSESSING

Assessment

- *Progress Assessment of Reading*
  - Selection Test

RETEACHING

For a lesson reteaching Standard 3.7, see **Reteaching,** p. 939A. For another lesson to teach Standard 3.7, see *Interactive Reading,* Chapter 7.

Before You Read

We Real Cool

Literary Focus

Alliteration: Repeated Consonant Sounds

Remember the old tongue twisters "*P*eter *P*iper *p*icked a *p*eck of *p*ickled *p*e*pp*ers" and "*Sh*e sells sea*sh*ells by the sea*sh*ore"? Both of those contain examples of **alliteration**—the repetition of the same or similar consonant sounds at the beginning (usually) of words that are close together. (A consonant is any letter or combination of letters that is not a vowel.)

By carefully choosing and arranging ordinary, everyday English words, poets make music with the sounds of words. The literary devices of rhyme, rhythm, repetition, onomatopoeia, and alliteration provide the special sound effects.

Make the Connection

Quickwrite

Read Brooks's poem aloud several times, and imagine how the young people look, dress, and move. Jot down a description of what you visualize. Keep your notes to use on page 534.

Reading Standard 3.7 Recognize and understand the significance of various literary devices, and explain their appeal.

STANDARDS FOCUS, pp. 531–534

(For the grade-level standard taught in this lesson, see citations on Student Edition pages.)

Summary *at grade level*

The speakers of "We Real Cool" are young pool players. Although these young people boast about dropping out of school and doing "cool" things, such as staying out late and drinking, they know they are going to die soon.

PRETEACHING

Standards Starter

Motivate. Help students grasp the power of alliteration by having them replace some of the words in old tongue twisters with less alliterative ones; for example, "John markets seashells at the beach."

RESOURCES: READING

Planning

- *One-Stop Planner* CD-ROM with Test Generator
- *On Course: Mapping Instruction*

Media

- *Audio CD Library*
  - disc 13
- *Visual Connections*
  - Videocassette, Segment 7

Reading

- *Interactive Reading,* Teacher's Edition
  - Graphic Organizer: Sounds of Poetry Chart

Differentiating Instruction

- *Lesson Plans for Language Development*
  - English-Language Learners, pp. 229, 248, 256
  - Special Education Students, pp. 229, 248, 256

Assessment

- *Progress Assessmet of Reading*
  - Selection Test
- *One-Stop Planner* CD-ROM with Test Generator

DIRECT TEACHING

A Literary Focus
REVIEW STANDARD

Sound effects: Rhyme and alliteration. Brooks writes free verse "dotting a little rhyme here and there." In this stanza, have students find the internal rhyme ["late," "straight"] and the alliteration ["Lurk late," "Strike straight"].

B Reading Skills

Determining author's purpose. What message is Brooks sending to young people with this poem? [Possible responses: She is suggesting that a "cool" lifestyle can end in early death; she hopes to convince other "pool players" to change their ways.]

VIEWING THE ART

Jacob Lawrence (1917–2000) used his art to investigate and celebrate African American life and culture. Living in Harlem, he depicted the activities of his community, including pool halls where he enjoyed playing. Lawrence adopts an unusual point of view above the pool table, capturing the poses of those playing the game.

Activity. Do you think that Lawrence's attitude toward the game is the same as that expressed by Brooks? [Lawrence's painting seems positive or neutral toward the game, whereas Brooks seems to view pool halls as places where lives are wasted.]

We Real Cool

The Pool Players.
Seven at The Golden Shovel.

We real cool. We
Left school. We

(A) Lurk late. We
Strike straight. We

Sing sin. We
Thin gin. We

(B) Jazz June. We
Die soon.

—Gwendolyn Brooks

Pool (1954) by Jacob Lawrence. Tempera on hardboard ($9\frac{7}{8}$″ × $13\frac{7}{8}$″).
Hirshhorn Museum and Sculpture Garden, Smithsonian Institution. Artwork © 2002 Gwendolyn Knight Lawrence, courtesy of The Jacob and Gwendolyn Lawrence Foundation.

DIFFERENTIATING INSTRUCTION

Learners Having Difficulty
Make sure students understand that the subtitle refers to the poem's speakers. If necessary, pair students having difficulty with more proficient readers to identify the alliteration and internal rhyme in the poem.

English-Language Learners
Point out that the expression "strike straight" refers to striking the pool ball with a cue, or pool stick. However, some students might note that the phrase may have other, more threatening connotations. Students may not recognize the use of *jazz* as a verb. Explain that in this context, *jazz* means "acting cool or livening things up."

Meet the Writer

Gwendolyn Brooks

Chicago's Voice

Gwendolyn Brooks (1917–2000) was born in Topeka, Kansas, but for most of her life she was associated with Chicago, especially with its large African American population. Skilled in many different kinds of poetry, Brooks wrote with both formal elegance and an ear for the natural speech rhythms of the people of Chicago's South Side. In an interview, Brooks gave the following answers to questions about her work:

Q. Why do you write poetry?

Brooks. I like the concentration, the crush; I like working with language, as others like working with paints and clay or notes.

Q. Has much of your poetry a racial element?

Brooks. Yes. It is organic, not imposed. It is my privilege to state "Negroes" not as curios but as people.

Q. What is your poet's premise [basic principle]?

Brooks. "Vivify the contemporary fact," said Whitman. I like to vivify the *universal* fact, when it occurs to me. But the universal wears contemporary clothing very well.

For Independent Reading

You might enjoy Brooks's novel *Maud Martha* (1953), which follows a young African American girl as she grows up and finds her dream.

Meet the Writer

Background. In 1950, Gwendolyn Brooks became the first African American writer to win a Pulitzer Prize. Her poetry focuses on ordinary people living ordinary lives. As Brooks points out, however, she discovered early in life that "what was common could also be a flower." The idea that something common can be beautiful was essential to developing what Brooks calls her "G.B. voice." That voice has reached readers, young and old, for almost fifty years.

For Independent Reading

Suggest that students who enjoyed "We Real Cool" explore more of Brooks's poetry in her *Selected Poems.* This book collects nearly one hundred poems, including "We Real Cool," "The Bean Eaters," and "Langston Hughes."

Resources Reminder

For lessons designed for intermediate and advanced English-language learners, see *Lesson Plans for Language Development,* pp. 229, 248, 256.

Special Education Students

For lessons designed for special education students, see *Lesson Plans for Language Development,* pp. 229, 248, 256.

INDEPENDENT PRACTICE

Literary Response and Analysis

Reading Check

1. The *we* are seven young pool players at the Golden Shovel.
2. We learn that they have dropped out of school, stay out late, play pool, drink, and will die young.

Interpretations

3. The subtitle's two lines function like stage directions, supplying the speakers and setting. Students may associate the word *golden* with glamour or wealth, and they may associate the word *shovel* with graves or gardens.
4. Possible answers: A life in the fast lane has no future.
5. Alliterative phrases include "Lurk late," "Strike straight," "Sing sin," "Jazz June," and "real cool" (the ending consonants). Students may say that the alliteration gives the poem the sound of a chant.
6. Possible answer: The poem uses a lot of internal rhyme, such as *cool/school, late/straight,* and *sin/Thin/gin.* Because the poem's lines are so short, the internal rhymes stand out and enhance the poem's rhythm.
7. Every syllable is stressed.
8. Possible answer: The speakers' tone is defiant. The poem's tone, however, is ironic and almost regretful at the wasted lives of these youths.

Evaluation

9. Most students will think the poem still applies to life today, since many kids are still dropping out of school, getting into trouble, and dying young. Others might feel that the references, such as to jazz, are a little outdated.

Literary Response and Analysis

Reading Check

1. Who is the *we* in this poem?
2. What important facts do we learn about the speaker or speakers?

Interpretations

3. What purpose do the two lines immediately below the title serve? What **connotations,** or associations, do you have with the words *golden* and *shovel*?
4. What do you think is the poem's **theme,** or message?
5. Where does the poet use **alliteration**? When you read the poem aloud, how does the unusual repetition affect the sound of the poem?
6. Describe the poem's unusual use of **rhymes.**
7. The poem's **meter,** or pattern of stressed and unstressed syllables, is extremely unusual. It is clearly the work of a skilled poet. Scan the poem. What meter does Brooks use to pound out her story?
8. How would you describe the poem's **tone,** the poet's attitude toward the characters and subject? What words would you use to describe the speaker's tone?

Evaluation

9. Brooks wrote "We Real Cool" in 1960—more than forty years ago. Do you think the poem is outdated, or does it still apply to life today? Explain, referring to details in the poem and to your Quickwrite notes.

Reading Standard 3.7 Recognize and understand the significance of various literary devices, and explain their appeal.

Writing

A Poem with Sound Effects

Try to write your own **poem** in imitation of "We Real Cool." You could open with Brooks's title, or you could choose one of your own. You might build your poem on a series of statements that begin "I am . . ." or "We are . . ." Who will be the **speaker** (or speakers) of your poem? Work in as many examples of **alliteration** as you can.

Listening and Speaking

An Oral Interpretation

Here's what Brooks said about reading her poem aloud:

> The *We's* in "We Real Cool" are tiny, wispy, weakly argumentative "Kilroy-is-here" announcements. The boys have no accented sense of themselves, yet they are aware of a semi-defined personal importance. Say the *We* softly.

With a group, prepare and present an **oral interpretation** of this poem. Decide whether you'll use a single voice or several voices or even a chorus. Will you use background music, and if so, what piece will you choose? Be sure to prepare scripts indicating where your speakers will pause and how they'll vary their volume. Ask the audience to evaluate the class performances.

ASSESSING

Assessment

- *Progress Assessment of Reading*
  - Selection Test

RETEACHING

For a lesson reteaching Standard 3.7, see **Reteaching,** p. 939A. For another selection to teach Standard 3.7, see *Interactive Reading,* Chapter 7.

Before You Read

Jazz Fantasia

Literary Focus

Onomatopoeia: Sound Echoes Sense

How do we create language to communicate? No one is certain about the origins of language, but we do know that a few words in our languages are *echoic* in origin. That means that the words echo, or imitate, the sounds they name. Both nouns and verbs —such as *hush, buzz, whoosh, hiss,* and *hiccup*—can have echoic origins. The literary device that uses such words is called **onomatopoeia** (än′ō·mat′ō·pē′ə). Poets choose and place such words carefully to achieve a very special sound effect—the unity of sound and meaning.

"Jazz Fantasia" is about jazz, so it's not surprising that the poet has used some words that echo the sounds of jazz. Read the poem once silently, and then read it aloud more than once. Listen to its sounds.

Bass by Gil Mayers (1947–). Mixed media. Private collection.

Make the Connection

Quickwrite

Choose a kind of music that you know and like. What sounds do you associate with that music? Jot down some ideas, and save your notes.

Background

During the late nineteenth century small groups of African Americans in the South created a unique kind of music—jazz. Their music was improvised and unrehearsed, with a syncopated, irregular beat and many melodic variations. Jazz soloists wail and croon on the clarinet, saxophone, trumpet, and trombone. In the early days of jazz, though, musicians often played any object that could make a sound—for example, tin pans (see line 5 of the poem), coconuts, and sandpaper (line 6). Traps (line 9) are percussion instruments: drums, cymbals, blocks, and bells.

Jazz was born in New Orleans, then quickly spread throughout the South and on to Chicago, Kansas City, New York, and California. By the time Carl Sandburg wrote "Jazz Fantasia" (published in 1920), Americans and Europeans had discovered jazz and were enjoying what came to be known as the Jazz Age.

A **fantasia** is an unrehearsed, spontaneous musical composition with a structure determined by the composer's fancy. The word can also apply to a similarly constructed literary work.

Reading Standard 3.7 Recognize and understand the significance of various literary devices, and explain their appeal.

STANDARDS FOCUS, pp. 535–538

(For the grade-level standard taught in this lesson, see citations on Student Edition pages.)

Summary *at grade level*

In this lyric tribute to jazz, poet Carl Sandburg uses onomatopoeia and other sound effects to capture the magic of jazz music. The poem has two distinct parts. In the first, the intensity of the music leads Sandburg to compare it to a moaning autumn wind, a racing car, and two people fighting. In the second part of the poem, the music's transition to a gentler sound leads to metaphorical comparisons with a steamboat traveling quietly at night. The poem concludes with the refrain "Go to it, O jazzmen."

PRETEACHING

Standards Starter

Motivate. To help students more fully appreciate the concept of onomatopoeia, have them say aloud the words listed in the Literary Focus. Then, discuss why these sounds are echoic. About each word, ask: What does the word mean? How does the way it sounds echo its meaning?

RESOURCES: READING

Planning
- *One-Stop Planner* CD-ROM with Test Generator
- *On Course: Mapping Instruction*

Media
- *Audio CD Library*
  - disc 13

Reading
- *Interactive Reading,* Teacher's Edition
  - Graphic Organizer: Sounds of Poetry Chart

Differentiating Instruction
- *Lesson Plans for Language Development*
  - English-Language Learners, pp. 230, 249, 256
  - Special Education Students, pp. 230, 249, 256

Assessment
- *Progress Assessment of Reading*
  - Selection Test
- *One-Stop Planner* CD-ROM with Test Generator

DIRECT TEACHING

VIEWING THE ART

This print is a part of a series dedicated to jazz, which greatly inspired **Romare Bearden** (1914–1988). Its title, *Tenor Sermon,* calls to mind jazz's roots in gospel music. Bearden's style is loose and calligraphic, capturing the spirit of jazz.

A Literary Focus
REVIEW STANDARD

Sound effects. What sound effects does Sandburg use in this first stanza? [*Repetition*—"Drum on your drums." *Alliteration*—"batter/banjoes"; "sob/saxophones."]

B Literary Focus
REVIEW STANDARD

Onomatopoeia. Where does Sandburg use onomatopoeia in these lines? [The "husha-husha-hush" imitates the sound of sandpaper.]

C Literary Focus
REVIEW STANDARD

Speaker. The poem's speaker addresses the jazz players directly. What effect does this have on the poem? [Possible responses: It makes the poem feel more immediate because it implies that the speaker is listening to the musicians at that moment; it adds to the poem's spoken quality.]

D English-Language Learners

Slang. Some students may be puzzled by the meaning of the word *Can* here. Explain that *can* in this context is slang for "stop."

E Literary Focus
GRADE-LEVEL STANDARD

Imagery. How does this stanza convey that the mood of the music has changed? [Possible response: Unlike images in the previous stanza, these images are calm and beautiful. This implies that the music has grown calmer.]

Gift of Mr. Eugene Ivan Schuster. Smithsonian American Art Museum, Washington, D.C./Art Resource, New York. © Romare Bearden Foundation/Licensed by VAGA, New York, NY.

Jazz Series: Tenor Sermon (1979) by Romare Bearden. Color lithograph on paper (24¾″ × 34¾″).

Jazz Fantasia

Carl Sandburg

(A) Drum on your drums, batter on your banjoes,
sob on the long cool winding saxophones.
Go to it, O jazzmen.

Sling your knuckles on the bottoms of the happy
(B) tin pans, let your trombones ooze, and go husha-
husha-hush with the slippery sand-paper.

Moan like an autumn wind high in the lonesome treetops, moan soft like
you wanted somebody terrible, cry like a racing car slipping away from a
(C) motorcycle cop, bang-bang! you jazzmen, bang altogether drums, traps,
banjoes, horns, tin cans—make two people fight on the top of a stairway
and scratch each other's eyes in a clinch tumbling down the stairs.

(D) Can the rough stuff . . . now a Mississippi steamboat pushes up the night
river with a hoo-hoo-hoo-oo . . . and the green lanterns calling to the high
(E) soft stars . . . a red moon rides on the humps of the low river hills . . .
go to it, O jazzmen.

536 Chapter 7 Poetry

DIFFERENTIATING INSTRUCTION

Learners Having Difficulty
The informal structure and rhythms of this poem may pose problems for some students. Suggest that they work in small groups to break down and list the poem's images one by one. They should identify each image as belonging in one of two categories: "images of musicians playing" and "figurative images of the music."

English-Language Learners
The slang, the names of musical instruments, and other specialized vocabulary may pose problems for English-language learners. If possible, bring in pictures of some of the instruments, such as drums, banjoes, saxophones, tin pans, trombones, and sandpaper. Then, as a class, go over the meanings of words and phrases such as "sling your knuckles,"

Meet the Writer

Carl Sandburg

Poet of the Prairies

Carl Sandburg (1878–1967) wrote just about everything—poetry, history, biography, songs, newspaper articles, a novel, and children's books. He was a school dropout at thirteen, but he had a love of reading and writing from the time he was a little boy, and that love never left him. Like Walt Whitman, whose poetry influenced him greatly, the common man and America's history were the main focus of Sandburg's writings.

Sandburg was born and grew up in Galesburg, Illinois, a small town not far from the Mississippi River. He was one of seven children of poor Swedish immigrants. To supplement the family income, he left school at thirteen and began a series of odd jobs: driving a milk wagon, working in a barbershop, and serving as an apprentice tinsmith. At eighteen he traveled throughout the Midwest as a hobo. After a brief stint in the army during the Spanish-American War, Sandburg attended college in Galesburg. The big city—first Milwaukee, then Chicago—drew him, and he worked as a journalist from 1912 until the early 1930s.

Sandburg got his first break as a poet in 1914 when Harriet Monroe published six of his poems in *Poetry: A Magazine of Verse.* Monroe said of his early work: "One feels in all these poems a true and deep emotion of love as the central controlling motive—love of the prairie country, the prairie towns and city, and the people who struggle through toilsome lives there."

For many years, from the early 1920s to 1939, Sandburg also labored on a six-volume biography of his hero, Abraham Lincoln, a work that won Sandburg the Pulitzer Prize in history in 1940.

In his introduction to *Good Morning, America* (1928), a collection of poems, Sandburg lists thirty-eight definitions of poetry. Here are four of them:

> "Poetry is the report of a nuance between two moments, when people say, 'Listen!' and 'Did you see it?' 'Did you hear it? What was it?'
>
> Poetry is a sliver of the moon lost in the belly of a golden frog.
>
> Poetry is a packsack of invisible keepsakes.
>
> Poetry is an echo asking a shadow dancer to be a partner."

Meet the Writer

Background. Sandburg's love of music went beyond jazz. He also loved collecting and performing American folk music. He would often close one of his poetry readings with a folk song. In 1927, Sandburg published *American Songbag,* a collection of 280 folk songs, ballads, and ditties. However, his fascination with ordinary people and their lives surpassed his interest in music. Sandburg's attitude can be summed up in a quote taken from an ad for a lecture he gave on the poet Walt Whitman: "Books are but empty nothings compared with living, pulsing men and women. Life is stranger and greater than anything ever written about it."

For Independent Reading

If students enjoyed Sandburg's poem about jazz, they may wish to look at other poems by famous American poets in the collection *Americans' Favorite Poems: The Favorite Poem Project Anthology,* edited by Robert Pinsky and Maggie Dietz.

"motorcycle cop," "clinch," "Mississippi steamboat," and "humps."

Resources Reminder

For lessons designed for intermediate and advanced English-language learners, see *Lesson Plans for Language Development,* pp. 230, 249, 256.

Special Education Students

For lessons designed for special education students, see *Lesson Plans for Language Development,* pp. 230, 249, 256.

Advanced Learners

Enrichment. Point out that, like "Jazz Fantasia," Sandburg's definitions of poetry are a combination of actual and metaphorical images. The first definition describes something actual; the others are metaphorical.

Activity. Have students examine the ways in which "Jazz Fantasia" fits the four definitions of poetry. For instance, what makes "Jazz Fantasia" a "packsack of invisible keepsakes"?

INDEPENDENT PRACTICE

Literary Response and Analysis

Reading Check

1. The speaker of the poem addresses the jazz musicians he is listening to.
2. The speaker tells the musicians to "go to it"—improvise, make noise, express themselves.

Interpretations

3. Other sound effects include repetition, such as "Drum on your drums," and alliteration, such as "batter on your banjoes."
4. The poem's irregular rhythm is appropriate because the rhythms of jazz are often irregular. The rhythm changes by slowing down in l. 11, "Can the rough stuff."
5. Images such as an autumn wind moaning, a car pursued by cops, or two fighters tumbling down the stairs convey jazz's roughness and power. Images such as the steamboat sounding its horn, lanterns calling to the stars, or a red moon lying low on the hills create a gentler mood and testify to jazz's softer side.
6. The verbs Sandburg uses, such as "batter," "sob," "sling," "moan," and "cry," are vivid and help the jazz music come alive. He chose these verbs to convey the sounds of the music. Substitutes may not be as vivid and may not convey the power of jazz in the same way.
7. Similes include "moan like an autumn wind" and "cry like a racing car." Metaphors include "a Mississippi steamboat pushes up the night" and "a red moon rides on the humps of the low river hills." Instances of personification include "happy tin pans" and "the green lanterns calling to the high soft stars."

Literary Response and Analysis

Reading Check

1. Whom does the **speaker** of the poem address?
2. What message does the speaker give?

Interpretations

3. Point out the uses of **onomatopoeia** in the poem. What other **sound effects** can you identify?
4. Why is the poem's irregular **rhythm** appropriate? At what point in the poem does the rhythm change?
5. Which **images** convey the roughness and power of jazz? Which images create an altogether different **mood**?
6. Notice Sandburg's use of vivid **verbs** throughout the poem. Why do you think he chose these particular verbs? (Try substituting synonyms, and notice how the poem changes.)
7. Where does the poet use **similes, metaphors,** and **personification** to describe the jazzmen and their music?

Writing

Playing Another Kind of Tune

Do what Carl Sandburg did: Write a **free-verse poem** that imitates a specific kind of music or sound. (Before you begin to write, look back at your Quickwrite notes for page 535. If you haven't settled on a subject yet, brainstorm ideas with a small group of classmates.) In your poem, include **sensory details, figurative language, onomatopoeia,** and all the **sound effects** you can think of.

Listening and Speaking

Oral Interpretation

Here's a poem that *must* be read aloud. Practice your interpretation. Where will your voice rise and fall? What words will you emphasize? Which ones will you speak softly? Where will you take a breath? Practice reading the poem aloud until it sounds right to you, and then read it aloud to a small group or to a partner.

Reading Standard 3.7 Recognize and understand the significance of various literary devices, including figurative language and imagery, and explain their appeal.

Cherry Rouge (1976) by Bernard Rancillac. (1.6 m × 1.3 m).

Giraudon/Art Resource, New York.

ASSESSING

Assessment

- *Progress Assessment of Reading*
  - Selection Test

RETEACHING

For a lesson reteaching Standard 3.7, see **Reteaching,** p. 939A. For another selection to teach Standard 3.7, see *Interactive Reading,* Chapter 7.

Read On: FOR INDEPENDENT READING

POETRY

Now Hear This

You may think of poetry as a quiet pursuit, but ***Poetry Out Loud,*** edited by Robert Alden Rubin, reminds us that poems are meant to be heard as well as seen. You'll find more than one hundred poems suited for reading aloud in this collection—from Shakespeare's songs to Lewis Carroll's "Jabberwocky" to the American classic "Casey at the Bat." Limericks, lyrics, and rap are also featured in this collection of poems you'll want to read aloud.

POETRY

From East to West

One hundred and twenty-nine poets from sixty-eight countries are featured in ***This Same Sky: A Collection of Poems from Around the World,*** edited by Naomi Shahib Nye. These poems—many of which are translated here for the first time—address such universal yet individual subjects as dreamers and dreams, families, nature, loss, and the power of language and words. With titles like "A New Dress," "Bicycles," and "At the Ferry," ***This Same Sky*** shows us just how closely connected the entire world really is, despite great cultural differences.

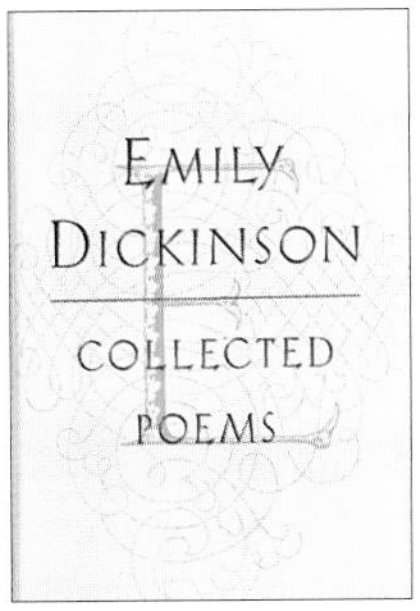

POETRY

Add a Dash of Dickinson

The reclusive nineteenth-century poet Emily Dickinson may have inspired more contemporary American poets than any other writer. To find out what all the fuss is about, take a look at ***Emily Dickinson: Collected Poems,*** with an insightful introduction by Martha Dickinson Bianchi. This collection includes poems that are alternately playful ("I'm nobody!"), exhilarating ("Wild nights!"), and reflective ("I felt a funeral in my brain").

POETRY

Through Neruda's Eyes

Pablo Neruda is regarded as one of the greatest poets of the twentieth century. His poems tackle a range of universal themes, including love, peace, war, and the beauty and mystery of the natural world. For a sampling of his best works, read ***Selected Poems,*** a bilingual edition that allows you to read his poetry in English translation and Neruda's native Spanish. These soulful, impassioned, and humane works may change the way you view poetry . . . and life.

Toward Reading Two Million Words Annually

Estimated Word Counts and Reading Levels of Read On Books:

Poetry	Level	Words	Poetry	Level	Words
Poetry Out Loud	at grade level	40,300	*Emily Dickinson: The Collected Poems*	at grade level	34,400
*This Same Sky**	below grade level	24,300	*Pablo Neruda: Selected Poems*	above grade level	108,400

*California Reading List Title

KEY: above grade level · at grade level · below grade level

Read On

For Independent Reading

If students enjoyed the poems presented in this chapter, you might recommend the following titles for independent reading.

Assessment Options

The following projects can help you evaluate and assess your students' outside reading. Videotapes or audiotapes of student projects may be included in their portfolios.

- **Give a reading.** As the name implies, the poems in *Poetry Out Loud* are perfect for a poetry reading. Ask students who read this book to present two poems from the collection to the class. As they practice reading, have them keep these questions in mind: What tone of voice should I use? Which words shall I emphasize? How fast should I speak? Where shall I pause?
- **Create a collage.** Suggest that students who read *This Same Sky* create a collage based on one poem from the collection. The collage should have the poem at its center and include images and information about the country and culture of the poet. Post all the collages on a bulletin board titled "World Poetry."
- **Discover Dickinson.** Invite students who read *Emily Dickinson: The Collected Poems* to prepare an oral presentation on this fascinating poet and her poetry. Students might choose several poems or an aspect of Dickinson's life for their focus.
- **Pair bilingual partners for poetry.** Pair up Spanish-speaking and English-speaking students who read *Pablo Neruda: Selected Poems.* Have each pair give a reading of one of Neruda's poems in both Spanish and English. Students may pass out copies of both versions for the class to follow along. After the paired readings, you may wish to hold a discussion about translating poetry.

Read On 539

PRETEACHING

Standards Starter

Motivate. Ask students to imagine their class will be corresponding with foreign students who have never visited the United States. What details can students give their pen pals to paint an accurate picture of the place in which they live? Write on the chalkboard the sensory detail headings *Sight, Hearing, Smell, Touch, Taste,* and have volunteers give vivid examples for each heading. Point out that putting the right details together in a well-written paragraph can be more descriptive than a photograph.

DIRECT TEACHING

Consider Purpose and Audience

You may want to remind students that there is more than one form in which to present a description. The appropriate form depends on a student's purpose and audience. For example, if a student's purpose is to celebrate a friend's birthday or recent achievement, a letter might be a good choice. If the purpose is to remember a deceased family member, a journal entry might be more appropriate. For the purpose of this assignment, an essay is probably the better choice.

Resources Reminder

To introduce the workshop, you may want to use the journal starters in *Writing, Listening, & Speaking* Teaching Notes.

Describing a Person

Writing Assignment
Writing 2.0 Write a description of a specific person that you know well or that you can learn more about.

In this chapter you've read descriptive poetry that allowed you to experience the moments the poets wished to share with you. Did you find the people, places, and events described somewhat familiar or entirely new? Could you envision what the poets described? Good **description** uses words to create a picture. Now it's your turn to learn new strategies for creating vivid descriptions to share with others.

Prewriting

go.hrw.com

GO TO: go.hrw.com
KEYWORD: HLLA 10-7
FOR: Professional Model, Writer's Guides, and Reference Sources

Choose a Subject

Snapshots Memorable photographs, such as those you have seen in calendars, in books and magazines, or on the Internet, compose a scene using light and shapes. When you describe a subject through writing, you use only words to compose a mental picture for your audience. Through words, you define your subject and highlight its importance to you. For this workshop you will describe a person. To find a suitable subject that will leave a lasting impression on your audience, consider the following.

- The person should be someone that you know well or someone that you can talk to and learn more about as you prepare to write.
- The person should be either someone that will immediately interest your essay's readers or someone that you can make interesting through your description.

Consider Purpose and Audience

Taking in the View Think about your **purpose,** or reason for writing. Knowing this can help you communicate a **clear and distinctive perspective,** or point of view—your unique thoughts and feelings about the subject. You will describe the subject and explain your relationship with him or her. Think of this purpose throughout the writing process to ensure that you maintain a consistent and focused perspective in your essay.

Next, think about who your **audience** will be. Who is likely to read your essay? What do they already know about your subject? What kind of details about the subject will they find interesting and appealing? Write with your audience in mind at all times.

Writing 1.1 Establish a controlling impression that conveys a clear and distinctive perspective on the subject. **2.0** Students combine the rhetorical strategies of narration, exposition, persuasion, and description.

CHAPTER 7 RESOURCES: WRITING

Writing Workshop

Planning

- *On Course: Mapping Instruction*
- *One-Stop Planner* CD-ROM
- *At Home: A Guide to Standards Mastery,* p. 21
- *At Home: In Spanish*
- *Writing, Listening, & Speaking,* Teaching Notes, p. 70

Differentiating Instruction

- *Lesson Plans for Language Development,* pp. 231–232
- *Supporting Instruction in Spanish*

Practice

- *Writing, Listening, & Speaking,* Ch. 7

Gather Your Details

Hunting and Gathering When you describe your subject, include details that will help your readers mentally create a complete portrait of the person—not just a visual re-creation of the person.

- Include details that give your readers a real sense of *knowing* the whole person, not just his or her physical **appearance.**
- Gather details by searching your memory, by observing your subject directly, or by talking with or interviewing the subject.
- Use **precise language** and **concrete details** rather than vague, general descriptions.
- Use a combination of the main kinds of details in your description, as shown in the following chart.

Quick guide

KINDS OF DETAILS

Type	Use
sensory details—words and phrases that appeal to the five senses: sight, hearing, touch, smell, and taste	to describe the **sights, sounds,** and **smells** associated with your subject and the **actions, movements,** and **gestures** that make that person unique
factual details—names, dates, numbers, and quotations, as well as true statements	to provide details about your subject that you can't relate through the senses
figurative details—similes, metaphors, and examples of **personification**	to create imaginative comparisons between something unfamiliar and something familiar (For more on **similes, metaphors,** and **personification,** see pages 477–478.)
details of thoughts and feelings	to allow the audience to know what you think and how you feel about the subject

Determine a Controlling Impression

Mission Control Once you've gathered details, you must determine your **controlling impression**—the particular idea or feeling you are trying to communicate about your subject. Follow these steps to determine your controlling impression.

DO THIS

- Begin by looking at the details you've gathered.
- Next, write down a handful of nouns or adjectives that best sum up the majority of these details. Ignore details that seem out of place; they may not support your controlling impression.
- Finally, circle one or two of the best nouns or adjectives to use in a statement of the controlling impression.

On the next page is an example that shows how a student writing about his uncle developed a statement of his controlling impression.

Writing 1.2 Use precise language. **2.1c** Describe with concrete sensory details the sights, sounds, and smells and the specific actions, movements, gestures, and feelings of the characters. **2.1e** Make effective use of descriptions of appearance and sensory details.

DIRECT TEACHING

Integrating with Grammar, Usage, and Mechanics

As students start their descriptions, they might have trouble with capitalization and punctuation. You may want to review the corresponding chapters in the *Holt Handbook.*

MODELING AND DEMONSTRATION

Kinds of Details

Model for students the gathering of sufficient details on the subject by asking students for the name of a celebrity they all know and then using students' comments to fill out a chart on the chalkboard like the **Kinds of Details** chart given. You may need to prompt students to include movements and gestures or help them to create figurative details about the person. Once the chart is complete, ask a volunteer to demonstrate using the same steps to gather details on a subject of his or her choice.

DIFFERENTIATING INSTRUCTION

Learners Having Difficulty

Students may have difficulty finding details about their subjects that are not abstract or general, and they may not understand why words such as *nice* and *happy* are not particularly good choices in a descriptive essay. You can help students by giving them the following challenge: *If you can use the detail to describe several people other than your subject, delete it.* Such a challenge will force students to strive for vivid, individual details and concrete examples in their descriptions.

Reinforcement

- *Daily Language Activities*

Evaluation and Assessment

- *Test Generator (One-Stop Planner* CD-ROM)
- *Progress Assessment of Writing, Listening, & Speaking,* Ch. 7
- *Diagnostic and Summative Assessments,* Third-Quarter Test

Internet

- go.hrw.com (keyword: HLLA 10-7)
- Online assessments at go.hrw.com (keyword: HLLA)

TECHNOLOGY TIP

Students can use the cut-and-paste functions of a word-processing program to shuffle and rearrange the details they have gathered on their subjects. They might choose to create pictures, in which the words and phrases have a distinctive shape—the silhouette of a person (with the details arranged from head to foot), for example; or, if the subject is always wearing a particular hat, the shape of that hat. This fun activity will help students decide on a method of organization for their descriptive essays.

DIRECT TEACHING

Organize Your Description

Explain to students that they should consider the tone they use in their descriptions. In a subjective description, they should aim for an informal, personal tone. They should also use that tone consistently throughout the essay.

PRACTICE & APPLY 1

Guided and Independent Practice

1. Have students make a list of steps for completing **Practice and Apply 1,** and then check their work.
2. Students should use this brief guide when writing and revising.
3. Assign **Practice and Apply 1** for independent practice.

TIP Keep in mind that you can fine-tune your statement of the controlling impression as you progress through the stages of the writing process.

Subject: Uncle Samir
Details: proud of his unruly hair, smiling deep blue eyes, his dog smells, always looks you in the eye, smiles often, neatly groomed, graceful, stirring voice, physically fit, dresses nicely
Impression details give: kindness, pride, respect, cleanliness
Statement of controlling impression: From top to bottom, Uncle Samir is all pride and respect.

Once you've determined your controlling impression, discard any details that do not support it. For example, the description of Uncle Samir on page 543 is meant to impress readers, so the writer left out information about his uncle's dog smelling.

Organize Your Description

DO THIS

Making It All Make Sense Next, arrange your details in a clear and **logical order** that will make sense to your audience.

- **Spatial order** is the arrangement of details in space. You can describe your subject from near to far, from far to near, from top to bottom, from bottom to top, or from side to side. This order primarily uses sight details. For example, the Writer's Model describes Uncle Samir from his head to his feet. Give your readers transition clues as you shift attention from one detail to another. For example, write "**beneath** his nose," "**over** by his left ear," or "as you move **closer,** you notice. . . ."
- **Order of importance** presents details from most important to least important, or vice versa. For example, if Uncle Samir's shockingly blue eyes were his most outstanding characteristic, then the Writer's Model might have begun by focusing on those eyes and then giving less important details last, or vice versa. Begin with the most important detail if you want to capture your reader's attention right away. Finish with the most important detail if you want to create a strong final impression.

You can easily use a combination of spatial order and order of importance, too. Just begin your description by dividing your subject into rough areas—for example, head, body, and feet. Then, describe by order of importance the individual details of each area—for example, moving from the eyes to the ears to the nose, depending on each feature's importance.

PRACTICE & APPLY 1 Using the prewriting instructions on pages 540–542, select a subject, gather details, write a statement of your controlling impression, and logically organize your descriptive essay.

RESOURCES: WRITING

Practice & Apply 1

Guided Practice

- *Writing, Listening, & Speaking,* WS. pp. 71, 72

Reteaching and Modeling

- *Writing, Listening, & Speaking,* TP. 12
- *Writing, Listening, & Speaking,* WS. p. 73

Writing

Describing a Person

A Writer's Framework

Introduction

- Attract your readers' attention.
- Introduce the person you will describe.
- Make a clear statement of your controlling impression.

Body

- Use sensory, factual, and figurative details; include your thoughts and feelings.
- Use only details that support your controlling impression.
- Arrange your details spatially or by order of importance.

Conclusion

- Sum up the details you have related.
- Restate your controlling impression, expressing it in different words.
- Make a final comment about your subject.

A Writer's Model

Samir of the Kingdom of Jordan

Last summer, my father's brother, Samir, immigrated to the United States. Samir had lived his whole life in Amman, Jordan, and had spent his last eleven years there practicing dentistry. Because my father had immigrated to America before I was born, I had never met my uncle before. He is currently living in our house while he is looking for a place of his own. Getting to know him, I have found that from top to bottom, Uncle Samir is all pride and respect.

INTRODUCTION — Factual details; Controlling impression

Uncle Samir is forty-five years old with a mass of tangled, dark brown hair (with some gray) that looks more like a bird's nest than a head of hair. He told me one morning, "This hair is impossible. The harder I try to tame it, the worse it fights back." I think he is proud that his hair has as much spirit as he does.

BODY — Spatial order—top; Figurative detail; Thoughts

His eyes really seem to smile. They are shockingly blue—deeper than any eyes I have ever seen. They are certainly unique for our family, who all have brown eyes. When Uncle Samir speaks to you, he always looks you in the eye, which makes you feel that what you have to say is very important to him and draws your respect, too.

Sensory details—sight; Feelings

Since Uncle Samir came to stay, I've rarely seen him without a smile beneath his well-groomed mustache. He often emphasizes what he says with sweeping flourishes of his graceful hands. When he is in the shower or when he is cooking, you can hear Uncle Samir singing in Arabic with a voice like a great opera star—low, loud, and clear. I

Sensory details—sight; Sensory details—hearing

(continued)

DIFFERENTIATING INSTRUCTION

GRADE-LEVEL STANDARD

Advanced Learners

Enrichment. Point out to students that in a descriptive essay, a controlling impression is often a first impression thoughtfully broadened and deepened to touch on the person's unique personality. For example, in describing a person, one's first impression may be the person's good posture, which can be linked, in an essay, to his or her honest, upright nature. Challenge students to make such connections (or contrasts) between the subject's appearance and his or her nature. Students can read **A Writer's Model** and answer the following questions to review the concept of a controlling impression:

- What connections or contrasts does the writer make about the subject's appearance and nature? [The writer links the subject's neat appearance—and contrasts his unkempt hair—with the subject's dignified bearing and respect.]
- Are all of the details relevant to the controlling impression? [Yes; also, key words and concepts such as *respect* and *pride* are repeated throughout.]
- How does the model's final comment expand on the controlling impression? [The comment expresses the writer's wish that he or she become like the subject.]

RETEACHING

A Writer's Model

To help students write their own descriptive essays, refer them to **A Writer's Model.** Have them note in the margins of their drafts the elements of description (factual details, controlling impression, types of descriptive details, and conclusion) like those noted alongside the model. The notes allow students to scan their drafts to make sure they include and recognize concepts explained in the workshop.

(continued)

do not always know what he is singing about, but his voice is emotionally stirring.

Spatial order—middle

My uncle stands tall and walks with a confident stride. He is more physically fit than my father, who is actually the younger of the two brothers. He says that physical fitness is the fastest way to mental fitness. My father and he work out regularly at the community center, or as Uncle Samir says "I work out, your father tries to catch up!"

Factual details

It's hard for me to imagine my uncle at the community center because I have never seen Uncle Samir dressed in a T-shirt and shorts, or even blue jeans. Each morning when I wake up, he is already wearing freshly pressed clothing. His slacks always have a sharp crease, and he's never without his tie—even at the dinner table, which is unusual for my family. Though immaculate looking, his clothes do always smell like a dentist's office. I guess that's just one of the downsides to being a dentist.

Sensory detail—smell

Thoughts

Spatial order—bottom

When your eyes travel down Uncle Samir from head to toe, the journey ends with his shoes, shining with a clean, dark black radiance. He takes great care each day that these shoes are shiny enough he can see himself in them. Those shiny shoes are the ultimate contrast to his hurricane of hair.

Figurative detail

CONCLUSION

Restatement of controlling impression

Summary of details

Final comment

If I could describe my uncle in two words, they would be *proud* and *respectful.* I have only known him for a short time, but in that time I've come to truly admire him. You can sense that Uncle Samir is a quality person by the way he stands, walks, dresses, and talks. He has pride in who he is, where he's come from, and where he's going in life. I hope some of that will rub off on me as we get to know each other better in the future.

GO TO: go.hrw.com
KEYWORD: HLLA 10-7
FOR: Expanded Writer's Model and Student's Model

PRACTICE & APPLY 2 Using the framework and Writer's Model on pages 543–544 as guides, write the first draft of your descriptive essay. Be sure to include a variety of details as you work to create a distinct controlling impression of your subject.

PRACTICE & APPLY 2

Guided and Independent Practice

Check to see that students are following **A Writer's Framework,** making sure they are using enough descriptive details to support the main idea. If details are lacking, ask the following questions to help them think of more details:

- How did you engage the reader in the introduction?
- Which details are most effective in helping the reader sense what you are describing?

RESOURCES: WRITING

Practice & Apply 2

Think Sheet

- *Writing, Listening, & Speaking,* WS. p. 74

Template

- *Writing, Listening, & Speaking,* WS. p. 75

Internet

- go.hrw.com (keyword: HLLA 10-7)

Revising

Evaluate and Revise Your Essay

The Finishing Touches Re-read your draft. First, evaluate and revise its content and organization by using the guidelines in the chart below. Then, focus on its style by using the chart on the next page. Think about your **audience,** your **purpose,** and the **formality** of the essay's context when revising.

PEER REVIEW

Exchange your essay with a peer before you revise. He or she may have ideas on how you can more clearly order the details in your description.

First Reading: Content and Organization Answer the questions in the left-hand column of the following chart. If you need help, use the tips in the middle column. To make any needed changes, use the revision techniques in the right-hand column.

Guidelines: Describing a Person

Evaluation Questions	Tips	Revision Techniques
1 Does the introduction contain a statement of the controlling impression?	**Bracket** the sentence in the introduction that expresses thoughts and feelings on the subject.	If needed, **add** a sentence that includes the controlling impression of the subject.
2 Are body details arranged logically by spatial order or by order of importance?	**Number** the details, with details about the top of the subject as *1,* middle as *2,* and bottom as *3* to ensure correct spatial order. For order of importance, **underline** the most important detail to make sure it is either presented first or last.	**Rearrange** a spatial presentation in correct spatial order, or **rearrange** a presentation done by order of importance by putting the most important detail either first or last.
3 Does the description contain a variety of concrete sensory details?	**Label** each sensory detail according to the sense to which it appeals. If the description does not have at least three different types of sensory details, revise.	**Add** additional details that appeal to a sense not yet used in your essay.
4 Does the description relate thoughts and feelings about the subject?	**Label** thoughts with a *T* and feelings with an *F*. If there aren't at least three examples, revise.	**Elaborate** on details by providing your thoughts and feelings about the subject.
5 Do all details relate to the controlling impression?	**Cross out** any details that do not directly relate to your controlling impression.	**Cut** or **replace** any details that do not relate to your controlling impression.
6 Does the conclusion restate the controlling impression and summarize the points of the description?	**Bracket** the sentence or sentences that restate the controlling impression and sum up main points.	**Add** a sentence that restates the thesis or summarizes the main points, if necessary.

DIRECT TEACHING

REVIEW STANDARD

Elaboration

Students may have trouble giving a detailed description because they do not realize how much their word banks must be expanded in order to give an accurate picture of things. You can illustrate the point by bringing to the classroom color samples for paint or by pointing out two similar colors on objects in the classroom. Tell students that though both colors are blue, for example, they are not the same, and that the difference can be expressed in one of two ways. One can expand one's vocabulary, to find words such as *cerulean,* or one can expand one's imagination, to create phrases such as *as sharp as sapphires.* Have students review in particular the visual details in their essays in order to expand both their vocabularies and their imaginations.

Writing Workshop: Describing a Person 545

Second Reading: Style During the second reading, you should focus on style—*how* you express your ideas. Just as your choice of clothing can be an expression of your style of dress, your choice of words can be an expression of your writing style. You can both dress up your essay and ensure that your readers get a crystal-clear image of the person you've described by replacing vague nouns, verbs, and adjectives with more **precise language.** For example, replace "ran" with "sprinted," "jogged," or "scampered." Replace "happy" with "exhilarated," "inspired," or "perky." Use the following style guidelines to find and fix any fuzzy language in your description.

editor in charge

Style Guidelines

Evaluation Question	Tip	Revision Technique
Are the ideas in this essay made clear with precise nouns, verbs, and adjectives?	**Circle** any vague nouns, verbs, and adjectives that do not give a crystal-clear picture of the subject.	**Replace** vague nouns, verbs, and adjectives with more precise language.

ANALYZING THE REVISION PROCESS

Study these revisions, and answer the questions that follow.

Since Uncle Samir came to stay, I've rarely seen him without a smile ~~on his lips.~~ *beneath his well-groomed mustache.* ~~I've seen mustache trimmers on sale at the department store.~~ He often emphasizes what he says with ~~hand gestures.~~ *sweeping flourishes of his graceful hands.*

replace, delete

replace

Responding to the Revision Process

1. How did the replacement in line one improve this passage?
2. Why did the writer delete the second sentence?
3. Why did the writer replace "hand gestures" with "sweeping flourishes of his graceful hands"?

Writing 1.2 Use precise language. **1.9** Revise writing to improve the controlling perspective by taking into consideration the audience, purpose, and formality of the context.

PRACTICE & APPLY 3 Using the revising instructions on pages 545–546 and the Analyzing the Revision Process example above as a model, evaluate and revise the content, organization, and style of your descriptive essay.

GUIDED PRACTICE

Responding to the Revision Process

Answers

1. The replacement is a more particular, individual detail that gives a fuller picture of the subject; every person has lips, but not everyone has a "well-groomed mustache."
2. The second sentence gives irrelevant information.
3. The replacement is more detailed and unique to the subject.

PRACTICE & APPLY 3

Independent Practice

As students revise their papers, encourage them to study closely even those passages in which they are satisfied they have given a good description. Tell students that the difference between a good and a great description is a very small one, maybe even the matter of one key word. If students expect to awe their readers, they must first surprise themselves.

Publishing

Proofread and Publish Your Essay

Get It Right Writers often hurry to get their ideas down on paper. Not surprisingly, first drafts usually contain many mistakes—and often these mistakes are carried over into later drafts. Consequently, it is vital that you re-read your description and exchange essays with a classmate for peer proofreading. Make sure the essay uses correct grammar, punctuation, and spelling.

Share and Share Alike Keep in mind that your descriptive essay is more than just a listing of the details you have gathered about a person. It also includes your perspective, or insights, on that person. Share this perspective with others by doing one of the following.

- With your classmates, create a collection of descriptive essays to use as a class reference source showing the different ways you've all described your subjects.
- If you described a person that you admire, such as a parent, teacher, or friend, enter your essay in a contest looking for "America's best."
- If your description is of a teacher or student at your school, ask if you may post it on your school's Web page. Browsers or future students may be interested to hear about the people at your school.
- Adapt your essay and deliver it as an oral descriptive presentation to your class, your family, or another interested audience. For more on **presenting a description,** see page 548.

Reflect on Your Essay

Seeking Closure After publishing your description, take some time to reflect on the processes you went through to create it. Answer the following questions on your own paper.

- What did writing about your subject teach you about yourself? What new insights did you gain about your relationship with your subject?
- How did you decide which sensory details to include about your subject and which to exclude?
- How did you decide the order in which you organized your details? How could you use this same organizational structure for other types of writing or for other classes?

PRACTICE & APPLY 4 Following the instructions on this page, proofread your description and correct any mistakes you find. Consider your publishing options; then, reflect on what you have learned in writing this essay.

TIP Proofreading will help ensure that your essay follows the **conventions** of standard American English. For example, you may find that your description compares your subject to someone or something else. Be sure that you use comparative and superlative forms correctly. For more on **comparative and superlative forms,** see page 221 of the *Holt Handbook.*

RESOURCES: WRITING

Practice & Apply 3

Think Sheet

- *Writing, Listening, & Speaking,* WS. p. 77

Evaluation

- *Writing, Listening, & Speaking,* WS. p. 76

Practice & Apply 4

Assessment

- *Test Generator (One-Stop Planner* CD-ROM)
- *Progress Assessment of Writing, Listening, & Speaking,* pp. 22–25, 72–74

Internet

- Online assessments at go.hrw.com (keyword: HLLA)

DIFFERENTIATING INSTRUCTION

English-Language Learners

Some students settle for general adjectives, such as *tall, happy, big,* and *nice,* to describe people. As a remedy, have students work with a partner, using a thesaurus to find synonyms to replace such vague adjectives with words such as *lanky, elated, immense,* and *delightful.*

Resources Reminder

For more help with English-Language Learners, see *Lesson Plans for Language Development.*

DIRECT TEACHING

Proofread and Publish Your Essay

If students decide to publish their essays on an online site, you need to be aware that Internet resources are sometimes public forums, and their content can be unpredictable.

Resources Reminder

For help with writing assessment, see 6 Traits—Plus 1 in the "Scales and Sample Papers" section of *Progress Assessment of Writing, Listening, & Speaking.*

PRACTICE & APPLY 4

Guided and Independent Practice

Monitor students' progress by doing the following:

1. Ask students to write a short list of grammar, usage, and mechanics errors they commonly find when proofreading their papers.
2. Have them list strategies for correcting these errors.
3. After briefly checking students' lists, take a quick poll to make sure each student has an idea for publishing his or her essay.

Then, have students complete **Practice and Apply 4** for independent practice.

PRETEACHING

Motivate. Ask students if they have ever listened to a biography of someone famous. Then, have students answer the following questions:

- How did the narrator try to bring the facts to life for his or her listeners?
- Did the narrator succeed? Why or why not?

Brainstorm with students some strategies that would be useful for presenting an oral description, and tell students that this workshop will give them the opportunity to try out the strategies they suggest.

CRITICAL THINKING

Arrange students in small groups, and have group members read their essays to one another. Though students will not read their essays aloud for their presentations, feedback from the group can help students determine which parts of their essays are the most interesting when presented aloud.

Have the listeners consider the following guidelines for feedback:

- Which sensory details make the description come alive?
- Which places in the essay would benefit from more sensory detail?
- Which parts of the essay do you consider essential? Which parts could be left out of an oral presentation?

Presenting a Description

Speaking Assignment
Listening and Speaking 2.6 Adapt a descriptive essay for an oral presentation and deliver the presentation to your class.

You can add a whole new dimension to your description by presenting it orally. **Descriptive presentations** allow you to use your voice, gestures, and visuals to help your audience create a vivid mental image of your subject. Reading your essay aloud, however, would likely be dry and uninteresting to your audience. Instead, adapt your essay to make it more suited for oral delivery.

Adapt Your Presentation

A Reason for Everything Before you begin planning your presentation, consider your **purpose**—your reason for giving the presentation. As with your written essay, your purpose will be to describe a person and to convey your thoughts and feelings about him or her. However, in your descriptive presentation, you can also use your voice, body, and visuals to achieve your purpose.

Attitude Check Much of the audience's interest in your oral description will center on your relationship with the subject. Your subjective description will show your **personal involvement** with your subject to let your audience see why he or she is important to you. Be sure to provide a unique **point of view**—your thoughts and feelings about your subject.

Put It into Perspective Another way to adapt your description is to shift your **perspective,** or **vantage point**—the physical position from which you observe the subject. For example, the captain of the school's soccer team may appear small and ordinary from your seat in the bleachers, but your point of view could change drastically if you were to play next to her, or even meet her face to face after the game. Presenting details from more than one vantage point will allow your audience to form a more complete picture of your subject.

More, or Less, the Same? After you know how much time you'll have for your presentation, you may need to cut or add details. If you don't have time to include all of the **sensory, factual,** and **figurative details** from your written essay, be sure that you don't cut details that are essential to your **controlling impression.** The details you keep should not only provide **concrete imagery** to help your listeners picture the subject's appearance, but should also convey your thoughts and feelings about him or her. If you must add to your description, consider additional research, such as interviewing your subject or the people who know him or her.

Speaking 2.6 Deliver descriptive presentations. **2.6a** Establish clearly the speaker's point of view on the subject of the presentation. **2.6b** Establish clearly the speaker's relationship with that subject (e.g., dispassionate observation, personal involvement). **2.6c** Use effective, factual descriptions of appearance, concrete images, shifting perspectives and vantage points, and sensory details.

CHAPTER 7 RESOURCES: LISTENING & SPEAKING

Listening & Speaking Workshop

Planning
- *On Course: Mapping Instruction*
- *One-Stop Planner* CD-ROM
- *Writing, Listening, & Speaking*
  - — Teaching Notes, p. 78
  - — Project-Planning Guide, WS. p. 80

Think Sheet
- *Writing, Listening, & Speaking,* WS. p. 81

Differentiating Instruction
- *Lesson Plans for Language Development,* p. 233
- *Supporting Instruction in Spanish*

Evaluation and Assessment
- *Writing, Listening, & Speaking,* WS. p. 82

Plan Your Presentation

Organize Your Ideas In a written essay, it's easy for readers to follow the flow of your ideas from paragraph to paragraph because they can go back and re-read if they get confused. However, in an oral presentation, listeners cannot go back and catch anything that they missed. Reexamine the **organizational pattern** of your written essay. Ask yourself whether the same pattern will be effective when presented aloud. Will the details you present first grab your audience's attention? Will the details you discuss in your conclusion leave a lasting impression? If your answer to either of these questions is no, then you may need to consider reorganizing your essay to suit your new audience.

Make Note Cards Next, put your ideas onto **note cards.** Make an introductory note card containing information to draw your audience into your presentation. Then, make one note card for the controlling impression, one for each supporting detail, and one for your concluding thoughts. Each card should include **summaries,** or brief notes about the key ideas you want to share, rather than word-for-word explanations. Number your cards to keep them in order.

Once your cards are complete, look for places to employ **visuals,** such as photos, props, or electronic media, in your presentation. For example, if you were describing your grandmother, you could bring in a picture of her or something else that's closely associated with her, such as her favorite book or a CD of the music that she listened to when she was your age.

Practice Your Presentation

Speak Easy While your note cards may be a convenient backup if you forget what to say, reading directly from them during the presentation may put your audience to sleep. Use verbal and nonverbal techniques to keep your listeners alert and to make your points clear.

- **Verbal techniques** include speaking clearly, loudly, and slowly so that everyone in the room can understand you.
- **Nonverbal techniques** include maintaining eye contact with audience members, making appropriate gestures, and occasionally changing your facial expressions to match your message. For example, you might raise your eyebrows to show surprise or scrunch your nose to indicate a feeling of disgust.

PRACTICE & APPLY 5 Adapt the descriptive essay you wrote in the Writing Workshop, and practice your verbal and nonverbal delivery techniques. Finally, present your description orally to your class.

Reference Note

For more on **spatial order** and **order of importance,** see page 542.

TIP When presenting your description, avoid using an overly formal tone or using gestures that might distract or offend your audience. Your vocabulary should suit your audience and purpose. For example, if your audience contains many children, do not use complex vocabulary.

Speaking 1.0 Students use gestures, tone, and vocabulary tailored to the audience and purpose. **1.7** Use props, visual aids, and electronic media to enhance the appeal and accuracy of presentations. **1.8** Produce concise notes. **1.9** Analyze the occasion and the interests of the audience and choose effective verbal and nonverbal techniques (e.g., voice, gestures, eye contact) for presentations.

RETEACHING

GRADE-LEVEL STANDARDS

Practice Your Presentation

If students need more help with nonverbal communication, show them a videotaped oral presentation with the sound muted, and ask what they can determine about the topic and the import of the speech. Periodically pause the videotape to solicit student input, and then discuss with students the importance of nonverbal communication such as eye contact and gestures. Emphasize that any visuals students use should complement and amplify their presentations rather than distract from them.

DIFFERENTIATING INSTRUCTION

Learners Having Difficulty

Allow time in class for students to practice giving their oral presentations to small groups. Give students the following set of questions with which they can constructively critique one another's rehearsals:

- What was the strongest part of the presentation?
- Was the description clear, interesting, and well organized? Why or why not?
- What verbal techniques did the speaker use to good effect?
- What nonverbal techniques did the speaker use?
- What areas need some improvement, and what are your suggestions?

PRACTICE & APPLY 5

Guided and Independent Practice

Monitor students' understanding by discussing with students the elements that make a successful presentation. Write students' suggestions on the chalkboard, and leave the remarks there so students will have reminders as they begin work on their presentations.

- *Progress Assessment of Writing, Listening, & Speaking,* p. 75
- *Diagnostic and Summative Assessments,* Third-Quarter Test

Extension

- *Writing, Listening, & Speaking,* Videocassette Segment 5
- *Writing, Listening, & Speaking,* WS. p. 83

Internet

- go.hrw.com (keyword: HLLA)

Standards Review

Literary Response and Analysis

STANDARDS FOCUS, pp. 550–551

(For the grade-level and review standards reviewed in this lesson, see Student Edition, p. 550.)

INTRODUCING THE STANDARDS REVIEW

Use this review to assess students' understanding of the standards taught in this chapter. If necessary, use the annotations to guide students before they answer the questions.

DIRECT TEACHING

(A) Literary Focus
REVIEW STANDARD

Lyric poetry. Unlike narrative poems, which tell a story, lyric poems are concerned with the speaker's thoughts and emotions. How do these lines hint that this is a lyric poem? [Their subject is hatred.]

(B) Literary Focus
GRADE-LEVEL STANDARD

Figures of speech. What type of comparison is made in ll. 3–6? [a metaphor] What are being compared? [The speaker's emotion is compared to fireworks.]

(C) Literary Focus
GRADE-LEVEL STANDARD

Imagery. What is the poet conveying through these vivid, colorful images? [Possible response: the intense emotions that the speaker feels when seeing the other person.]

(D) Literary Focus
REVIEW STANDARD

Sound effects. What poetic sound effects do these lines contain? [*Alliteration*—"meet me," "cubes, and crimson." *End rhyme*—"asunder"/ "wonder," "moons"/"maroons."]

Literary Response and Analysis

Test Practice

DIRECTIONS: Read the following poem. Then, read each multiple-choice question that follows, and write the letter of the best response.

Fireworks

Amy Lowell

(A) You hate me and I hate you,
And we are so polite, we two!

(B) But whenever I see you, I burst apart
And scatter the sky with my blazing heart.
It spits and sparkles in stars and balls,
Buds into roses—and flares, and falls.

Scarlet buttons, and pale green disks,
Silver spirals and asterisks,
Shoot and tremble in a mist
Peppered with mauve and amethyst.

I shine in the windows and light up the trees,
And all because I hate you, if you please.

(C) And when you meet me, you rend asunder
And go up in a flaming wonder
Of saffron cubes, and crimson moons,
(D) And wheels all amaranths° and maroons.

Golden lozenges° and spades,
Arrows of malachites° and jades,
Patens° of copper, azure sheaves.
As you mount, you flash in the glossy leaves.

Such fireworks as we make, we two!
Because you hate me and I hate you.

Grade 8 Review Reading Standard 3.1 Determine and articulate the relationship between the purposes and characteristics of different forms of poetry.

Reading Standard 3.7 Recognize and understand the significance of various literary devices, including figurative language and imagery, and explain their appeal.

---

16. **amaranths** (am′ə·ranths′) *n.:* dark purplish reds similar to the color of the amaranth flower.
17. **lozenges** (läz′ ənj·əz) *n.:* diamond shapes.
18. **malachites** (mal′ə·kīts′) *n.:* gems made of a green mineral used in ornamental objects or as a source of copper ore.
19. **patens** (pat′'ns) *n.:* metal disks or plates.

Using Academic Language

Review of Literary Terms
Reading Standard 3.7 and Grade 8 Review Reading Standard 3.1

Ask students to look back through the chapter to find the meanings of the terms listed at right. Then, have students show their grasp of the standards by citing passages from the chapter that illustrate the meanings of those terms.

Meter (p. 506); **Rhyme** (p. 506); **Rhyme Scheme** (p. 506); **Ballad** (p. 509); **Refrain** (pp. 509, 527); **Free Verse** (p. 513); **Iambic Pentameter** (p. 518); **Repetition** (p. 527); **Alliteration** (p. 531); **Onomatopoeia** (p. 535).

1. "Fireworks" can be classified as —
   A a lyric poem
   B a narrative poem
   C an elegy
   D a ballad

2. From the poem, we can tell —
   F that the speaker is a man
   G that the speaker is a woman
   H that the speaker is a child
   J nothing about the speaker's sex or age

3. What has happened to cause the speaker's "blazing heart" (line 4)?
   A The speaker has been insulted.
   B The speaker has lost an argument.
   C The speaker has been jilted.
   D We never find out.

4. The **repetition** of the *s, b,* and *f* sounds in lines 5 and 6 is an example of —
   F onomatopoeia
   G alliteration
   H simile
   J free verse

5. How does Lowell use **meter** and **rhyme** in "Fireworks"?
   A She uses four stresses per line with a strict rhyme scheme.
   B She uses five stresses per line with no end rhyme.
   C She uses free verse with a strict rhyme scheme.
   D She uses free verse with no end rhyme.

6. The poem contains an **extended metaphor,** which begins in —
   F the first stanza
   G the second stanza
   H the third stanza
   J the fourth stanza

7. The fireworks in the poem describe —
   A a relationship between two people
   B a holiday celebration
   C a family get-together
   D a war scene

8. Most of the poem's **imagery** deals with —
   F natural landscapes
   G urban scenes
   H colors and smells
   J colors and shapes

9. The poem's first line, repeated twice (with variations), becomes a kind of —
   A stanza
   B refrain
   C simile
   D metaphor

10. The **rhymes** in the poem can be defined as —
   F free verse
   G internal only
   H exact
   J approximate

Test-Taking Tips

Remind students to always return to the passage when a question refers to a quotation from a selection or a specific line (for example, in questions 3 and 4). For more instruction on how to answer multiple-choice items, refer students to **Test Smarts.**

TestPractice

Answers and Model Rationales

1. **A** The poem expresses the speaker's feelings. It neither mourns a subject (C) nor tells a story (B and D).
2. **J** The speaker makes no reference to age or gender, so F, G, and H are incorrect.
3. **D** The specific cause is not revealed in the poem.
4. **G** Alliteration is the repetition of consonant sounds as in "spits and sparkles in stars." Onomatopoeia (F) has nothing to do with sound repetition. H is wrong because simile is a figure of speech, and J is incorrect because free verse is a poetry form.
5. **C** The poem is written with regular end rhyme, but a varied number of stresses per line.
6. **G** The extended fireworks metaphor begins in the second stanza.
7. **A** The fireworks describe the speaker's relationship with someone addressed as "you."
8. **J** Colors include scarlet, green, silver, mauve, amethyst, and crimson. Shapes include lozenges, spades, cubes, moons, disks, and spirals.
9. **B** The repeated line serves as a refrain. It is not a complete stanza (A), and it makes no comparison (C and D).
10. **H** The rhymes are paired, exact end rhymes.

ASSESSING

Assessment

- *Progress Assessment of Reading*
  - Chapter Test

Writing

Test Practice

DIRECTIONS: Read the following paragraph from a draft of a student's descriptive essay. Then, read the questions below it. Choose the best answer to each question, and mark your answers on your own paper.

(1) When I was young, I lived next door to a kind, elderly man named Mr. Osborne. (2) He was like the grandfather I never had. (3) Mr. Osborne was 76, had never married, and lived alone with his golden retriever. (4) His house was small and was within walking distance of the park. (5) He had gleaming white teeth and a smile that charmed all his neighbors. (6) Every day I would see him trimming the bushes outside his house, and if he saw me he would always pick the prettiest flower in his garden for me. (7) In school, I would paint pictures to give him in return, and later he would look at them with his deep blue eyes lined with melancholy creases, and tell me in his wavering voice that they were the best he'd ever seen. (8) When he died years later, he left in his house a brown portfolio containing all of the artwork I had ever given him.

552 Chapter 7 Poetry

1. Which sentence should be deleted to improve the controlling impression of the passage?
   - **A** 1
   - **B** 2
   - **C** 4
   - **D** 7

2. Which of the following phrases would be a more precise replacement for the phrase "trimming the bushes outside his house" in sentence 6?
   - **F** trimming all of the plants in his big, beautiful yard
   - **G** working on the landscape outside his house
   - **H** cutting each one of the plants in his front yard
   - **J** carefully pruning the rose bushes in front of his house

3. Which sentence would be most appropriate if the writer wanted to add sensory details to the passage?
   - **A** His hands were always gnarled, scratched, and deeply tanned from working in his flower beds all day.
   - **B** Mr. Osborne was a flower expert and knew of more than twenty different types of roses that grew in our area.
   - **C** The first thing I did after school each day was hurry over to visit with Mr. Osborne and talk about our day.
   - **D** Mr. Osborne's dog was named Rocky, and I often took him on long walks around the neighborhood.

4. Which of the following sentences, if added to the end of the paragraph, would reinforce its controlling impression?
   - **F** Mr. Osborne was famous all over the community for his flower gardens and won several local contests.
   - **G** I realized then that we had shared a common bond—I had been the granddaughter he had never had.
   - **H** Mr. Osborne was the only person who thought that my artwork was worth anything.
   - **J** Having close friendships with your neighbors is a good way to build community spirit.

5. If you were listening to an oral presentation of this description, what tone would you expect the speaker to use?
   - **A** humorous
   - **B** angry
   - **C** sentimental
   - **D** smug

Standards Review

Answers

1. C
2. J
3. A
4. G
5. C

APPLICATION

Write a Poem

Have each student create as homework a poem based on his or her description or on another subject. Tell students that vivid details, precise diction, and inventive figurative language are essential in a poem. Students may or may not choose to rhyme the lines in their poems, but encourage them to pay attention to the rhythm of their words by reading their drafts aloud as they write and revise. Volunteers can share their poems with the class by presenting them orally.

Homework

EXTENSION

Imagined Places

Ask students to find a vivid description of a place in a novel or short story they have read recently and analyze the writer's style. For example, does the writer use vivid verbs, series of adjectives, or a particular type of sentence structure? Then, have students create imagined descriptions of their own, using the short story or novel description as a model. Remind them to choose a place each really wants to describe, whether it be a space station in the future or a city in the past.

RESOURCES: WRITING, LISTENING, & SPEAKING

Assessment

- *Test Generator (One-Stop Planner* CD-ROM)
- *Progress Assessment of Writing, Listening, & Speaking,* Ch. 7
- *Diagnostic and Summative Assessments,* Third-Quarter Test

Internet

- Online assessments at go.hrw.com (keyword: HLLA)

Holt Literature and Language Arts: Mastering the California Standards

Chapter 8 Literary Criticism: Evaluating Style
Evaluating an Argument

Program Organization

Holt Literature and Language Arts provides a complete curriculum for standards-based instruction in reading, literature, writing, listening and speaking, and language conventions. The instructional content is presented in quarters to enable teachers to anticipate and administer the quarterly assessments required by California.

About Chapter 8

Standards-based lesson plans and suggestions for pacing the presentation of Chapter 8, the related instructional material, and the recommended assessment are provided in *On Course: Mapping Instruction*, Chapter 8.

- In Chapter 8, students will identify and use words literally and figuratively; evaluate the credibility of an author's argument; evaluate the aesthetic qualities of style; use precise language, sensory details, and active voice; and write a short story.

Language Arts Content

Which reading standards are taught in Chapter 8?

In this chapter, students will master the following Grade 10 standards and review standards from Grade 8. Selections or features marked with a ✓ constitute the minimum course of study that provides coverage of grade-level standards.

Grade 10 Standards

Word Analysis, Fluency, and Systematic Vocabulary Development

1.1 Identify and use the literal and figurative meanings of words and understand word derivations.
- Words from Spanish, p. 563
- ✓ Literal and Figurative Use of Words, p. 585
- Roots and Relations, p. 599

Reading Comprehension (Focus on Informational Materials)

2.8 Evaluate the credibility of an author's argument or defense of a claim by critiquing the relationship between generalizations and evidence, the comprehensiveness of evidence, and the way in which the author's intent affects the structure and tone of the text.
- ✓ "Call of the Wild—Save Us!" (magazine article), pp. 577–584

Literary Response and Analysis

3.11 Evaluate the aesthetic qualities of style, including the impact of diction and figurative language on tone, mood, and theme, using the terminology of literary criticism.
- "Evaluating Style: *How* It's Said" (standards essay), pp. 556–557
- "Geraldo No Last Name" (short story), pp. 558–562
- ✓ "Night Calls" (short story), pp. 564–575
- "A Very Old Man with Enormous Wings" (short story), pp. 586–598
- "My Lucy Friend Who Smells Like Corn" (standards review), pp. 610–612

(*continued*)

(continued)

Review Standards Grade 8

Reading 1.1 Analyze idioms, analogies, metaphors, and similes to infer the literal and figurative meanings of phrases.
Literal and Figurative Language: Imagery, p. 599

Reading 1.3 Use word meanings within the appropriate context, and show ability to verify those meanings by definition, restatement, example, comparison, or contrast.
Verifying Meanings by Examples, p. 576
Using Contexts, p. 585

Which writing standards are taught in Chapter 8?

Writing Strategies

1.2 Use precise language, action verbs, sensory details, appropriate modifiers, and the active rather than the passive voice.
Plot, pp. 603–604
Second Reading, p. 608

Writing Applications

2.1 Write biographical or autobiographical narratives or short stories.

a. Relate a sequence of events and communicate the significance of the events to the audience.
Plot, pp. 603–604

b. Locate scenes and incidents in specific places.
Setting, p. 604

c. Describe with concrete sensory details the sights, sounds, and smells of a scene and the specific actions, movements, gestures, and feelings of the characters; use interior monologue to depict the characters' feelings.
Characters, pp. 602–603
Plot, pp. 603–604
Tip, p. 603

d. Pace the presentation of actions to accommodate changes in time and mood.
Plot, pp. 603–604

e. Make effective use of descriptions of appearance, images, shifting perspectives, and sensory details.
Point of View, p. 604

Review Standard Grade 8

Writing 2.1 Write biographies, autobiographies, short stories, or narratives.

c. Employ narrative and descriptive strategies.
Finding an Idea, pp. 602–604

Instructional Planning and Support

Where do I find lesson plans, additional resources, and other teaching aids?

- This Annotated Teacher's Edition and *On Course: Mapping Instruction* provide direction in planning and implementing a complete California standards–based curriculum. These components also include instructions for diagnostic, progress, and summative testing; for presenting direct instruction of the standards; for differentiating instruction to provide universal access; and for locating and using the program's ancillaries.
- Lesson and workshop resources are referenced at the beginning of each selection or workshop, in the bottom margin of this teacher's edition.
- Reminders for using additional resources appear in this teacher's edition at point of use.
- The *One-Stop Planner* CD-ROM contains editable lesson plans and all print ancillaries, available in PDF format.

What if I don't have time to teach all of Chapter 8?

- Most standards can be taught with a minimum number of selections and features. In the chart on the preceding page, the core lessons you need in order to provide complete coverage of the chapter standards are identified with a ✓.
- *On Course: Mapping Instruction,* Chapter 8, lists lessons and activities that provide minimum standards coverage.

What provisions have been made for students who have additional class time scheduled in language arts?

- *Interactive Reading* provides for alternative direct instruction and practice of the grade-level standards taught in Chapter 8.
- *Universal Access: Writing, Listening, and Speaking,* Chapter 8, contains worksheets and transparencies that provide practice in and reteaching and reinforcement of the writing and listening and speaking standards in Chapter 8.
- *Universal Access: Lesson Plans for Language Development,* Chapter 8, provides alternative teaching strategies and additional worksheets designed specifically for English-language learners and special education students. Many of the suggestions and activities in this ancillary will also be helpful to students in the regular classroom who are having difficulty with particular skills.

Universal Access

How do I differentiate instruction to ensure that all my students master the standards?

Holt Literature and Language Arts provides comprehensive, differentiated instruction for all types of students.

- Most of the general instruction and teaching strategies in the Annotated Teacher's Edition are at grade level. These instructions will work well with the majority of your students.
- Point-of-use suggestions are provided for advanced learners, learners having difficulty, English-language learners, and special education students.
- *Interactive Reading* is designed to anticipate and remediate problems that students may experience in achieving mastery of the reading standards. See *Interactive Reading,* Teacher's Edition, Chapter 8, for information on using the reader to differentiate instruction.
- *Universal Access: Writing, Listening, and Speaking,* Chapter 8, contains worksheets and transparencies that provide practice in and reteaching and reinforcement of the writing and listening and speaking standards in Chapter 8.
- *Universal Access: Lesson Plans for Language Development,* Chapter 8, offers teaching strategies and additional worksheets designed specifically for English-language learners and special education students.

Assessment

How do I determine whether my students are making progress in mastering the standards?

Progress Assessment

- Use the Standards Review at the end of Chapter 8 for an informal assessment of the informational reading and writing standards.
- Use Chapter 8 tests from the *Progress Assessment* booklets to assess comprehension and progress on mastering the standards taught in this chapter.

Summative Assessment

The content of *Holt Literature and Language Arts* has been divided into quarters to allow you to administer the four summative tests required by California. Chapters 6–8 and related instructional material constitute the third quarter of instruction. At the end of Chapter 8, you may ask students to take the Third-Quarter Test in *Diagnostic and Summative Assessments.*

Chapter 8

STANDARDS FOCUS

(For full text of standards taught in this chapter, see the Standards Correlation by Standard chart in the Student Edition.)

Grade-Level Standards

- Vocabulary Development 1.1
- Reading Comprehension 2.8
- Literary Response and Analysis 3.11
- Writing Strategies 1.2
- Writing Applications 2.1a–e

INTRODUCING THE CHAPTER

The selections in this chapter illustrate a wide variety of literary styles. In "Geraldo No Last Name," Sandra Cisneros paints a vivid picture of life, using a simple, true-to-life conversational style. In "Night Calls," Lisa Fugard evokes a poignant, melancholic mood, using a poetic style filled with imagery and figurative language. In "A Very Old Man with Enormous Wings," Gabriel García Márquez casually and comically mixes the everyday with bizarre fantasy to create magic realism, his trademark style. With each selection, students will discuss aspects of style. By the end of the chapter, they should emerge with a good grasp of the literary elements that contribute to a writer's style.

Students will also read and evaluate the argument of "Call of the Wild—Save Us!" This persuasive article alerts readers to the many species that are endangered by human actions.

The chapter closes with an opportunity for students to develop individual styles while writing their own short stories.

CHAPTER 8 RESOURCES: READING

Planning

- *One-Stop Planner* CD-ROM with Test Generator
- *On-Course: Mapping Instruction*
- *At Home: A Guide to Standards Mastery*
- *At Home: In Spanish*
- *Supporting Instruction in Spanish*

Reading

- *Interactive Reading*

Differentiating Instruction

- *Lesson Plans for Language Development*

Vocabulary

- *Vocabulary Development*
  - Cumulative Vocabulary Review, pp. 41–42

Chapter 8

LITERARY CRITICISM

Evaluating Style

EVALUATING AN ARGUMENT

Proper words in proper places, make the true definition of a style.

—Jonathan Swift

Three Musicians (1921) by Pablo Picasso.
Oil on canvas (201 cm × 223 cm).
Museum of Modern Art, New York.

go.hrw.com
KEYWORD:
HLLA 10-8

THE QUOTATION

Ask students to read and discuss the quotation about literary style by the great satirist Jonathan Swift. Tell students that "proper" in this context does not mean "respectable" or "genteel," but "right" or "exact." Have students paraphrase the quotation. [Possible paraphrase: The right words in the right places is the true meaning of style.] Point out that as the quotation sums up, a writing style depends upon just two things: the writer's choice of words and how he or she places these words in sentences.

VIEWING THE ART

Throughout his career, **Pablo Picasso** (1881–1973) was inspired by the way music can build meaning through abstract forms, and his work often depicted musicians and musical instruments. The phase of Picasso's career represented by this painting is known as synthetic cubism, which is characterized by decorative patterning, collage, and bright colors.

Activity. Judging from the colors and forms in *Three Musicians,* what sort of music do you imagine they are playing? [Possible response: Perhaps they are playing lively or frenetic music.]

Resources Reminder

Planning

- *At Home: A Guide to Standards Mastery*

Parent letters appear in this resource. Translations of these letters are found in *At Home: In Spanish.* Translations of selection and connection summaries are found in *Supporting Instruction in Spanish.*

Reading

- *Interactive Reading*
  - Reading Log

The California framework requires students to read materials apart from in-class assignments. Additional readings are cited on the Read On page and in the Student Edition.

Assessment

- *Progress Assessment of Reading*
  - Chapter Test
- *Diagnostic and Summative Assessments*
  - Third-Quarter Test
- *One-Stop Planner* CD-ROM with Test Generator

Internet

- go.hrw.com (Keyword: HLLA 10-8)

STANDARDS FOCUS, pp. 556–557

(For the grade-level standard taught in this lesson, see Student Edition, p. 556.)

Prerequisite Standard

- Grade 8, Literary Response and Analysis 3.6 **Identify significant literary devices (e.g., metaphor, symbolism, dialect, irony) that define a writer's style and use those elements to interpret the work.**

Literary Focus: Style

Ask students to think of particular public figures and to characterize their personal styles with adjectives such as *formal, informal; vivid, dull; imaginative, ordinary; plain, fancy; serious, comic*; and so on. Point out that a writer's style can be characterized in much the same way. Literary style is created by the words a writer uses (diction), the way the words are put together (sentence structure), the way figurative language is used, and the overall tone and mood of the work. Explain to students that although this may sound complicated, a writer's style is as immediately apparent as someone's personal style. To illustrate this point, read a few sentences from various writers with very different styles, such as Sandra Cisneros and Edgar Allan Poe. Ask students for specific words that characterize each writer's style.

Evaluating Style *by* Mara Rockliff

HOW IT'S SAID

Reading Standard 3.11 Evaluate the aesthetic qualities of style, including the impact of diction and figurative language on tone, mood, and theme, using the terminology of literary criticism. (Aesthetic approach)

Style: Everybody's Got It

Suppose a friend sends you an e-mail from her dad's address. Chances are you wouldn't read too far before you realized who was really writing to you. *What* your friend said would clue you in, but *how* she said it—the words she picked and the way she put those words together—would also tell you a lot. That is, her **style** would be a giveaway.

Every piece of writing has a style—a special way of using words—though not all styles are equally distinct. If you pick up a city newspaper, all the front-page articles will sound alike, even though different reporters may have written them. Their style could be called straightforward news reporting—no frills, no fancy words. Flip to columns by Dave Barry or Miss Manners, and you'll find two different styles. Dave Barry is flip and funny. Miss Manners is, well, a little fussy.

Diction: The Power of a Word

Style starts with **diction**—the words a writer chooses. If you want a research paper to sound serious and scientific, will you use the expression *busted leg* or *fractured femur*? If you write a story for young children, will you call the hero *pertinacious, obdurate,* or simply *stubborn*?

Long words with Latin roots (like *pertinacious*) tend to come across as formal and intellectual. They might make the writer sound like a showoff. Shorter Anglo-Saxon words (like *stubborn*) sound plain and to the point. Even more casual are slang words (*pigheaded* or *die-hard*) and contractions (*He's stubborn, isn't he?* instead of *He is stubborn, is he not?*).

Formal diction is what makes many classic novels sound old-fashioned to contemporary readers. Take, for example, the first sentence of *Washington Square* by Henry James, published in 1880:

> During a portion of the first half of the present century, and more particularly during the latter part of it, there flourished and practiced in the city of New York a physician who enjoyed perhaps an exceptional share of the consideration which, in the United States, has always been bestowed upon distinguished members of the medical profession.

A writer today might say:

> Americans respect doctors, and in New York fifty years ago Dr. Sloper was respected even more than most.

Sentence Structure: Putting It All Together

Of course, the second version uses not just simpler words but fewer words. That's another aspect of style—**sentence structure,** or the way words are put together. A writer can use mostly long, elaborate sentences (as Henry James did) or simple, direct sentences, as the contemporary writer Gary Paulsen does:

> He had to fly it somehow. Had to fly the plane. He had to help himself.

DIFFERENTIATING INSTRUCTION

Learners Having Difficulty

Style. Suggest to students that the most important thing to remember about style is that "it's not *what* you say; it's *how* you say it." To help students understand what style means, you might write on the chalkboard and read aloud the following examples on the subject of love:

- William Shakespeare—"Shall I compare thee to a summer's day? / Thou art more lovely and more temperate: / Rough winds do shake the darling buds of May, / And summer's lease hath all too short a date."
- Robert Burns—"O my luve's like a red, red rose, / That's newly sprung in June: / Oh my luve's like the melody / That's sweetly played in tune."

Compare Shakespeare's formal diction, elaborate grammar, and indirect comparison to Burns's simple words, simple sentence structure, and direct similes.

One Irish writer, James Joyce, wrote long run-on sentences that sound exactly like thoughts racing through a person's mind. One sentence in his novel *Ulysses* runs on for forty pages!

Ernest Hemingway wrote sentences so straightforward and plain that several generations of novelists have tried to copy his style; William Faulkner wrote sentences so elaborate and ornate that several generations of novelists have tried to copy *his* style.

Figures of Speech: Plain Style Versus Ornate Style

Figures of speech are expressions that are based on unusual comparisons and are not literally true.

Some writers prefer a plain style and so don't use many figures of speech. Those who favor a more ornate or poetic style use a great number of them. You might not realize it, but nonfiction writers often use figurative language. Here is a scientific writer, Lewis Thomas, using a simile to explain warts:

> Warts are wonderful structures. They can appear overnight on any part of the skin, like mushrooms on a damp lawn.

Tone: An Attitude

Another aspect of a writer's style is tone. **Tone** is the attitude a writer takes toward the subject of a work, its characters, or the audience. Some writers, for example, convey a tone of pessimism: "I can't read another one of his books," someone might say. "They are so *depressing.*" Other writers may use language that creates a tone of humor or joy. Some writers have a satiric tone (think of TV sitcoms). Some have tragic tones (think of a Shakespeare play like *Romeo and Juliet*).

Mood: An Atmosphere

Mood, which is the atmosphere a writer creates in a work, is also an aspect of style. Many writers become famous for the moods or atmospheres they create. Some readers buy every Stephen King novel that comes out because they love to enter his spooky settings.

Theme

A writer's style might not actually create his or her **theme,** the idea about life that a story is expressing. Style does have a powerful influence on theme, though. A story that presents a dark and sad worldview, for example, will almost certainly be written in a somber style.

Practice

Here is a simple sentence:

The boy walked through the woods.

1. Rewrite the sentence using **figurative language** to create an atmosphere of gloom.
2. Rewrite the sentence using an ornate style.
3. Rewrite the sentence to indicate a **tone** of affection for the boy.

Practice

1. Possible answer: The dejected boy dragged his feet through the murky shadows of the forest, like a prisoner on his way to the firing squad.
2. Possible answer: Though he was over six feet tall and handsome as the day was long, the boy was still a boy and so he strolled aimlessly along the sun-dappled, leafy forest path with not a crease on his brow, nor a misgiving on his mind.
3. Possible answer: The golden-haired lad scampered through the woods like a sprite, stopping here and there to examine an unusual stone or insect before continuing on his sunlit path.

Apply

Encourage students to work in small groups to practice writing in different styles. One student may come up with a simple sentence, and then each student may propose a different style for that sentence. Students may read their sentences aloud before moving to the next style.

Resources Reminder

Differentiating Instruction

For more instruction on style for English-language learners and special education students, see *Lesson Plans for Language Development,* pp. 257, 258.

Advanced Learners

Acceleration. Use the following activity to help move students toward the eleventh- and twelfth-grade Standard 3.3, which requires that they analyze the ways in which irony, tone, mood, the author's style, and the "sound" of language achieve specific rhetorical and aesthetic purposes.

Activity. Have groups of students analyze a short story or poem that has a distinctive style. First, have them characterize the style. Then, have them create a chart that lists certain literary elements (diction, mood, figurative language) and explains how each element contributes to the style. Finally, have students analyze the impact of the style on the author's rhetorical and aesthetic purposes.

STANDARDS FOCUS, pp. 558–563

(For the grade-level standards taught with this selection, see citations on Student Edition pages.)

Prerequisite Standard

- Grade 8, Literary Response and Analysis 3.6 **Identify significant literary devices (e.g., metaphor, symbolism, dialect, irony) that define a writer's style and use those elements to interpret the work.**

Reading Skills

- Monitor your reading: Question.

Summary *at grade level*

This very brief story centers on a young Mexican American woman named Marin and the man she met at a dance, Geraldo. Although the action of the plot has occurred before the story begins, the reader is hooked when the narrator reveals that Marin was the last person to see Geraldo alive. She danced with him and then he was struck by a hit-and-run driver as he was leaving the dance. Because Geraldo spoke only Spanish, carried no identification, and didn't mention his last name, Marin cannot help the hospital staff or police identify him. Moreover, she cannot explain her motivation for maintaining a long vigil in the emergency room. Although Marin herself is confused about her feelings and actions regarding a man she barely knows, the story points to the theme of the preciousness of every human life—whether the person speaks English or Spanish, is wealthy or poor, has a last name or not. In the end, the omniscient narrator fills in a few details about Geraldo and people like him—their poverty, their loneliness, their responsibilities, and the tragic anonymity of their lives and deaths.

Before You Read

Geraldo No Last Name

Literary Focus

Style: The Personal Stamp

Just as no two people in the world have the same fingerprints, so does everyone have a unique style. Your style is your own mode of expression. The way you dress is a style. So is the way you shape your sentences. Are they short and simple, or long and complicated? When you read your writing aloud, does it have the rhythm of poetry, or does it sound plain?

In literary works, **style** refers to the particular way writers use language to express their feelings and ideas. Style is largely created through sentence length and word choice. Some writers' styles are so famous that people can read a single sentence and know they are reading, for example, a short story by Ernest Hemingway. A Cisneros story has that kind of distinctive style. Listen for it.

Diction and Tone

Diction, or word choice, is one of the main ingredients of style. Writers carefully select particular words to express their thoughts and feelings and their attitude. For example, diction can be formal (*remove yourself*) or informal (*get a move on*). Diction can be plain (*clothing*) or fancy (*apparel*). Diction can also be colloquial, full of slang, poetic, and so on.

Diction has a powerful effect on creating tone in a piece of writing. **Tone,** which is not easy to define, can be described as the writer's attitude toward the subject or audience. The tone of a work can be, for example, serious, playful, sarcastic, or angry. Sometimes changing a single word can change the tone (*isn't/aint, worker/brazer*). As you read, notice the diction Cisneros uses. What tone does she create?

Reading Standard 3.11 Evaluate the aesthetic qualities of style, including the impact of diction on tone, using the terminology of literary criticism. (Aesthetic approach)

Reading Skills

Monitoring Your Reading: Questioning

Good readers **ask questions** as they read—perhaps about unfamiliar vocabulary, a confusing description, or a character's behavior. Good writers, like Cisneros, sometimes invite questions by purposely leaving some things unanswered. Jot down your questions as you read this story.

Make the Connection

Quickwrite

Sometimes our paths cross with other people's unexpectedly, and all too briefly. Have you ever wondered what might have happened if you had gotten to know that person better? Complete a chart like the one below with notes about someone you met briefly whom you wish you could have known better.

What do you remember most about the person?		
How did you meet the person?	Where?	When?
Characteristics/Traits of the person:		

RESOURCES: READING

Planning

- *One-Stop Planner* CD-ROM with Test Generator
- *On Course: Mapping Instruction*

Media

- *Audio CD Library*
  - disc 14

- *Fine Art Transparencies*
  - Transparency 14

Reading

- *Interactive Reading*
  - Interactive version: "Geraldo No Last Name"
- *Interactive Reading,* Teacher's Edition
  - Graphic Organizer: Style Chart

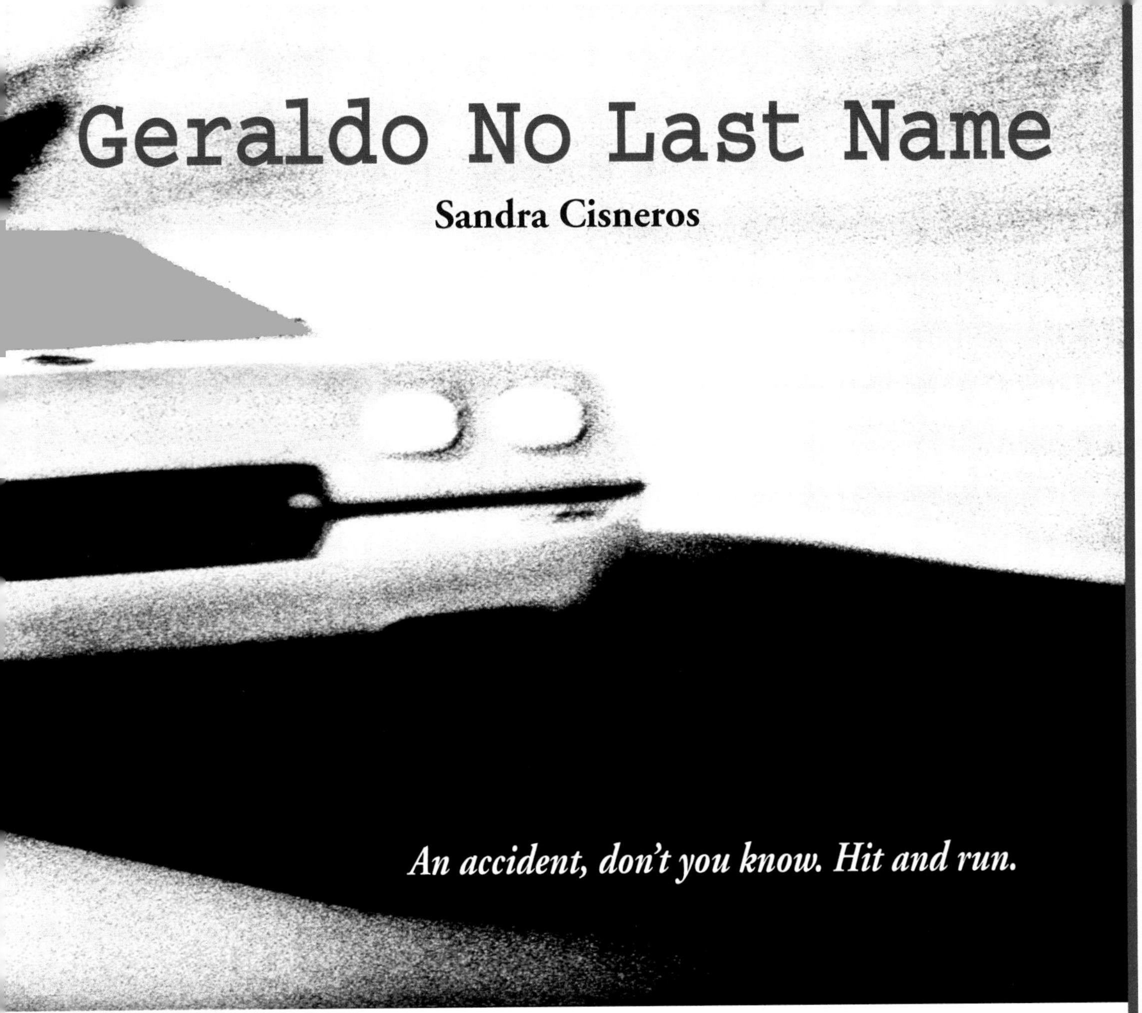

Geraldo No Last Name

Sandra Cisneros

An accident, don't you know. Hit and run.

She met him at a dance. Pretty too, and young. Said he worked in a restaurant, (A) but she can't remember which one. Geraldo. (B) That's all. Green pants and Saturday shirt. Geraldo. That's what he told her.

Differentiating Instruction

- *Lesson Plans for Language Development*
  - English-Language Learners, pp. 259–261, 277, 281
  - Special Education Students, pp. 262, 277, 281

Assessment

- *Progress Assessment of Reading*
  - Selection Test
- *One-Stop Planner* CD-ROM with Test Generator

PRETEACHING

Standards Starter

Build prerequisite skills. Remind students that words and sentences are the only tools a writer has to craft a work of literature. Invite students to suggest styles that may be created by these combinations of words and sentences:

- simple words and short declarative sentences [Possible response: a direct, no-nonsense style.]
- dialect, contractions, and meandering sentences [Possible responses: a comic, informal style; a conversational style.]
- a challenging vocabulary and elaborate, convoluted sentences [Possible response: a formal style.]

DIRECT TEACHING

(A) Literary Focus
GRADE-LEVEL STANDARD

Style: Diction. Remind students that diction refers to a writer's choice of words and is an essential element of style. What sort of words does Cisneros use? [Possible response: simple, informal ones.] Based on this first paragraph, how would you characterize Cisneros's style? [Possible responses: direct; fragmentary; conversational.]

(B) Reading Skills

Monitoring your reading: Questioning. After reading this short paragraph, what questions do you have about the two characters? [Possible responses: Who is "she"? Why did she learn so little about Geraldo? Is something going to happen to him? Are they going to be friends?]

DIRECT TEACHING

VIEWING THE ART

Nick Quijano (1953–) depicts a dance in a Hispanic community. **Activity.** Have students look at the art carefully and identify as many instruments as they can. [congas, timbales, maracas, guiro ("fish"), bongos, trumpets, saxophones, cymbals, cowbells, flute, string bass] Based on the instruments, have students speculate about the type of music the band is playing. [probably Afro-Cuban or Latin jazz] You may wish to have students bring in a recording of music suggested by the painting.

A Learners Having Difficulty

Summarizing. "That's the story," Marin told the hospital people and police. Restate her story in your own words. [Possible response: I went to a dance and danced with Geraldo, the guy who got hit by a car. I don't know anything else about him.]

B Reading Skills

Monitoring your reading: Questioning. If students question what this sentence means, point out that the narrator is following Marin's thoughts, which are sometimes fragmentary or confused, or leap to conclusions. Call on a volunteer to express the complete meaning of her sentence. [Possible response: If a surgeon had come, he could have stopped the bleeding and saved Geraldo's life so that Geraldo himself could have told people who his family and friends were and where they were.]

Permanent Collection, Puerto Rico Tourism Museum, Old San Juan, Puerto Rico.

El Club (1990) by Nick Quijano. Gouache on paper (22″ × 30″).

And how was she to know she'd be the last one to see him alive. An accident, don't you know. Hit and run. Marin, she goes to all those dances. Uptown. Logan. Embassy. Palmer. Aragon. Fontana. The manor. She likes to dance. She knows how to do cumbias and salsas and rancheras even. And he was just someone she danced with. Somebody she met that night. That's right.

That's the story. That's what she said again and again. Once to the hospital people and twice to the police. No address. No name. Nothing in his pockets. Ain't it a shame.

Only Marin can't explain why it mattered, the hours and hours, for somebody she didn't even know. The hospital emergency room. Nobody but an intern working all alone. And maybe if the surgeon would've come, maybe if he hadn't lost so much blood, if the surgeon had only come, they would know who to notify and where.

But what difference does it make? He wasn't anything to her. He wasn't her boyfriend or

DIFFERENTIATING INSTRUCTION

Learners Having Difficulty

Modeling. Invite learners having difficulty to read "Geraldo No Last Name" in *Interactive Reading* and to use the sidenotes as aids to understanding the story. The interactive version provides additional instruction, practice, and assessment of the literature standard. Monitor students' responses to the story, and correct any misconceptions.

Resources Reminder

Differentiating Instruction

- *Interactive Reading*
  - Interactive version: "Geraldo No Last Name"

English-Language Learners

To fully understand this story, students must be able to grasp Cisneros's fragmentary and

560 Chapter 8 Evaluating Style • Evaluating an Argument

anything like that. Just another brazer[1] who didn't speak English. Just another wetback.[2] You know the kind. The ones who always look ashamed. And what was she doing out at 3:00 A.M. anyway? Marin who was sent home with her coat and some aspirin. How does she explain?

She met him at a dance. Geraldo in his shiny shirt and green pants. Geraldo going to a dance.

What does it matter?

They never saw the kitchenettes. They never knew about the two-room flats[3] and sleeping rooms he rented, the weekly money orders sent home, the currency exchange. How could they?

His name was Geraldo. And his home is in another country. The ones he left behind are far away, will wonder, shrug, remember. Geraldo—he went north . . . we never heard from him again. ■

1. **brazer** (brā′zer) *n.:* Americanization of the Spanish word *bracero,* used in the United States to refer to a Mexican laborer allowed into the United States temporarily to work.
2. **wetback** *n.:* offensive term for a Mexican laborer who illegally enters the United States, often by swimming or wading the Rio Grande.
3. **flats** *n.:* apartments.

Meet the Writer

Sandra Cisneros

"Unforgettable as a First Kiss"

Sandra Cisneros (1954–   ) spent her childhood moving back and forth between Chicago, where she was born, and Mexico, where her father was born. She currently lives in San Antonio, Texas.

Cisneros's first full-length work, *The House on Mango Street,* appeared in 1984. The narrator of this series of connected stories is a lively and thoughtful girl named Esperanza. (Her name means "hope" in Spanish.) Cisneros has also published collections of her poetry, including *My Wicked Wicked Ways* (1987), and another collection of stories, *Woman Hollering Creek* (1991). One critic has said that her stories "invite us into the souls of characters as unforgettable as a first kiss."

Cisneros did not find her unique voice as a writer until she attended the Writers' Workshop at the University of Iowa.

"Everyone seemed to have some communal knowledge which I did not have. It was not until [the] moment when I separated myself, when I considered myself truly distinct, that my writing acquired a voice. I knew I was a Mexican woman, but I didn't think it had anything to do with why I felt so much imbalance in my life, whereas it had everything to do with it! My race, my gender, my class! That's when I decided I would write about something my classmates couldn't write about."

For Independent Reading

"Geraldo No Last Name" is from Cisneros's first book, *The House on Mango Street,* a series of stories about Esperanza Cordero that range from Esperanza's first kiss to dreams of her own home. This coming-of-age classic is set in a Spanish-speaking area of Chicago.

elliptical style. Encourage students to listen to the story being read aloud in the *Audio CD Library* before they read it for themselves. This will help accustom them to the conversational style and will help them understand the story better.

Resources Reminder

For lessons designed for intermediate and advanced English-language learners, see *Lesson Plans for Language Development,* pp. 259–261, 277, 281.

Special Education Students

For lessons designed for special education students, see *Lesson Plans for Language Development,* pp. 262, 277, 281.

DIRECT TEACHING

C Literary Focus
GRADE-LEVEL STANDARD

Style. Ask students to characterize Cisneros's style, choosing from the following possibilities: *spare, simple, formal, informal, down-to-earth, official, scholarly,* or *conversational.* Then, ask students to back up their answers with excerpts from the text. [Possible response: Cisneros's simple, conversational style is evident in phrases such as "or anything like that," "just another," and "You know the kind."]

D Literary Focus
GRADE-LEVEL STANDARD

Style: Sentence structure and theme. Ask students how the style of the last two paragraphs differs from that of the rest of the story. [Possible response: The sentences are complete, longer, and have a higher level of diction, creating a serious, more formal style and a didactic tone.] Ask students how this shift in style points toward the theme of the story. [Possible response: It prompts the reader to take Geraldo seriously and points to a theme about the preciousness of every human life and every human interaction, no matter how brief or seemingly insignificant.]

GUIDED PRACTICE

Monitoring students' progress. Guide the class in answering these comprehension questions.

Short Answer

1. Where does Geraldo work? [in a restaurant]
2. Where does Marin meet Geraldo? [at a dance]
3. What kind of doctor does Marin think might have been able to save Geraldo? [a surgeon]
4. Where is Geraldo's family? ["in another country," perhaps Mexico]

INDEPENDENT PRACTICE

Literary Response and Analysis

Reading Check

1. I met Geraldo at a dance, but I did not find out his last name or the name of the restaurant where he works. He was struck in a hit-and-run accident. That's all I know.

Interpretations

2. Possible answers: Does Geraldo have a family? friends? Will they find out what happened to him? The writer wants to make the reader care about Geraldo even though we know almost nothing about him.
3. He worked and enjoyed dancing. We might infer that he was kind and responsible and was willing to live in poor conditions to save money to help his family.
4. Possible answers: Marin may be trying to "fill in the blanks" about a person she happened to meet on the last day of his life; she may be trying to make sense of a senseless tragedy.
5. "They" are the police, the hospital staff, and society in general. The story has an omniscient point of view.
6. Possible answers: Yes, it is about love for our fellow human beings; no, Marin and Geraldo didn't know each other long enough to love each other.
7. Possible answer: Every life is precious and so every death is tragic, even when the person is seemingly insignificant and anonymous.
8. Answers will vary, but many may reveal the existence of regrets, unanswered questions, or musings about what might have been.

Literary Response and Analysis

Reading Check

1. Retell the **main events** of this story to a classmate as you imagine Marin told them to the police.

Interpretations

2. What questions do you still have about the story? Why do you think the writer has not provided this information?
3. Exactly what do you know about the **character** of Geraldo? What **inferences,** or guesses, can you make about the kind of person he was?
4. After Geraldo dies, Marin can't understand why their meeting mattered and why she spent so many hours in the hospital waiting room. Why do you think she keeps thinking about the meeting and wondering what it meant?
5. At the end of the story, Cisneros says "they" never saw certain aspects of Geraldo's life. Who are "they"? What is the story's **point of view**?
6. Do you think this is a story about love? Talk about your responses in class.
7. In just a few broad strokes, Cisneros sketches two characters and one tragic event. How would you express the **theme,** or central idea, of this very short story?
8. Look back at your Quickwrite notes. Are there any similarities between the "brief encounter" you described and the one in the story? Explain.

Reading Standard 3.11 Evaluate the aesthetic qualities of style, including the impact of diction on tone and theme, using the terminology of literary criticism. (Aesthetic approach)

Literary Criticism

9. How would you describe Cisneros's **diction** in this story? How does it affect the story's **tone**? Try rewriting a few sentences, changing the diction (words, expressions) to create an altogether different tone.
10. Cisneros uses many short sentences and sentence fragments in her story. How does this aspect of her **style** contribute to the story's impact? Do you think it affects the **theme**? Explain your answer.
11. Cisneros consciously chose words to create touches of poetry. Find examples of **rhyme, rhythm,** or other **sound effects.** Do you think these aspects of her **style** add to the story or detract from its power? Explain.

Writing

Whose Story Is It?

Who is the **protagonist,** the central **character** in this story—Geraldo or Marin? In a brief **essay,** cite details from the story to support your view.

Listening and Speaking

Hearing a Style

Present an **oral interpretation** of the story. Decide how you should use your voice to emphasize Cisneros's unusual **style.** Think of when you should pause, read slowly, read quickly, and raise or lower your voice. Ask your audience for feedback.

562 Chapter 8 Evaluating Style • Evaluating an Argument

Literary Criticism

9. The diction is simple, colloquial, and true to life. The tone is detached on the surface, but serious and deeply felt beneath.
10. The short sentences and fragments make the story more real and so heighten its impact. The realism of the style affects the theme by making the reader believe in and care about two "insignificant" characters, just as Marin cared about Geraldo.
11. *Poetic touches*—"Somebody she met that night. That's right"; "No address. No name. Nothing in his pockets. Ain't it a shame." Most students will find that the poetic effects enhance the story by giving it greater vitality and distinctiveness.

Vocabulary Development

Words from Spanish

Peppering her stories with Spanish is part of Cisneros's unique **style.**

> "She knows how to do cumbias and salsas and rancheras even."

PRACTICE

Even if you don't understand Spanish, you probably use many common English words that came originally from Spanish. Fill in each blank with one of the words from Spanish listed in the box at the right. Before you begin, look up any unfamiliar words in a dictionary.

1. Maya prepared her special recipe for Texas _____.
2. The hikers enjoyed the view from the top of the steep _____.
3. Many buildings in the Southwest are constructed from _____.
4. When we visited the hundred-acre _____, we saw a black _____ running in the distance.
5. They decided to eat their dinner outdoors on the _____.

Words from Spanish

adobe
barbecue
bonanza
canyon
mustang
patio
poncho
ranch

Grammar Link MINI-LESSON

Revising Sentence Fragments

A **sentence** is a group of words that contains a subject and a verb and expresses a complete thought. A **sentence fragment** is a group of words that does not contain the basic parts of a complete sentence. If you answer no to any of the following questions, the word group is a fragment:

1. Does the group of words have a subject?
2. Does it have a verb?
3. Does it express a complete thought?

FRAGMENT	Was her dancing partner. [subject missing]
SENTENCE	Geraldo was her dancing partner.
FRAGMENT	Marin at the hospital. [verb missing]
SENTENCE	Marin waited at the hospital.
FRAGMENT	When she was asked. [not a complete thought]
SENTENCE	She could not give his full name when she was asked.

Why do you think Cisneros uses so many sentence fragments in this story? Writers often use fragments for emphasis or to make dialogue sound authentic. To revise a sentence fragment, add, subtract, or change words so that the group of words has all three essential sentence parts.

PRACTICE

Turn the following fragments into complete sentences. Exchange your sentences with a partner to be sure you've left no "frags."

Cisneros's *The House on Mango Street* (1984) a beautiful book. Consists of stories, sketches, and vignettes about family, friends, houses, and neighborhood. A young girl (Esperanza Cordero) the narrator. Deals with Chicano (Mexican American) culture in Chicago neighborhood. Although they are Americans. Many of the characters like outsiders in their own land.

Reading Standard 1.1
Identify and use the literal meanings of words and understand word derivations.

Vocabulary Development

Practice

1. barbecue
2. canyon
3. adobe
4. ranch; mustang
5. patio

Resources Reminder

Vocabulary

- *Lesson Plans for Language Development*
  - Vocabulary, pp. 277, 281

Grammar Link

Practice

Cisneros's *The House on Mango Street* (1984) is a beautiful book. It consists of stories, sketches, and vignettes about family, friends, houses, and neighborhoods. A young girl (Esperanza Cordero) is the narrator. The story deals with Chicano (Mexican American) culture in a Chicago neighborhood. Although they are Americans, many of the characters feel like outsiders in their own land.

ASSESSING

Assessment

- *Progress Assessment of Reading*
  - Selection Test

RETEACHING

For a lesson reteaching style, see **Reteaching,** p. 939A. For another selection to teach Standard 3.11, see *Interactive Reading,* Chapter 8.

STANDARDS FOCUS, pp. 564–576

(For grade-level and review standards taught with this selection, see citations on Student Edition pages.)

Reading Skills

- Monitor your reading.

Summary above grade level

The melancholy mood of this story is established by its setting, a remote part of South Africa where the narrator's father lives alone in a run-down compound on a neglected wildlife sanctuary. The narrator, Marlene, grew up on the sanctuary and can imitate the calls of wild animals. She has been attending boarding school since she was eight, when her mother was killed in a car accident. Soon after the accident, park officials brought a rare red-crested night heron to the sanctuary. Although her father had been on the verge of resigning and leaving the park, he stayed on to take care of the heron in the hope that a mate might be found. But five years have passed, and that hope has died. One night during the narrator's visit, she hears her father go out and release the heron. The next morning his mood is light as he explains that a hyena must have gotten the heron. Then, father and daughter begin fixing up the house and the compound. At night, they both hear the heron's call by the river and Marlene hears her father go down to the river. Then, one night there is no call and Marlene sees her father's eyes go "dull like a dead animal's." When Marlene comes across the bird's remains, she buries them but does not tell her father. That evening, Marlene goes down to the river and hides. When she hears her father, she makes the call of the heron and her father moves toward the sound. The poignant mood of the story is enhanced by the author's use of evocative language and figures of speech.

Before You Read

Night Calls

Literary Focus

Mood: A Feeling or Atmosphere

One of the important elements of fiction is mood. **Mood** is the feeling or atmosphere evoked by a piece of writing. Mood is created by language.

Some writers—Edgar Allan Poe is a good example—are famous for stories that evoke moods. (For a story by Poe, see page 419.) Poe's moods are created in part by his settings. His pits, blood-red rooms, and haunted houses create atmospheres of dread. Poe's stories have sent generations of readers to check their locks.

But suppose a writer wants to create a mood of joy. That writer might put us in sunlit gardens or flower-filled meadows, rather than in a prison or a pit. That writer's images would create a peaceful atmosphere—not the nightmare moods created by Poe's images of rat-filled pits.

Lisa Fugard, who wrote the next story, creates a powerful mood with her vivid descriptions and **sensory images** of a neglected South African wildlife sanctuary. Her **figures of speech,** or unusual comparisons, also help create the mood. (For more about figures of speech, see pages 477–478.)

The mood of her story is also affected by an event we learn about in a **flashback** near the start of the story. How does the neglected setting reflect the lives of Marlene and her grieving father?

Pages 564–572 cover **Reading Standard 3.11** Evaluate the aesthetic qualities of style, including the impact of diction and figurative language on mood, using the terminology of literary criticism. (Aesthetic approach)

Reading Skills

Monitor Your Reading

As you read this story, stop from time to time to think about what you have just read. Consider what is revealed about the characters. Think about the **mood** created by the setting. Notice the writer's use of language, especially her **figures of speech.** Be aware of **flashbacks,** and be sure you know why they are necessary to your understanding of the story. (The questions at the open-book signs will help you.)

Make the Connection

Quickwrite

When we love someone, we often perform very small acts of deception to make our loved one happy, or to keep bad news from him or her. Think of how children, in particular, can be affected by the loss of a parent and the grief of a survivor. What will those children do to help their parent feel happy again? Jot down your thoughts.

Vocabulary Development

inevitably (in·ev′i·tə·blē) *adv.:* unavoidably.

avid (av′id) *adj.:* eager and enthusiastic.

indigenous (in·dij′ə·nəs) *adj.:* native; growing naturally in a region or country.

opulent (äp′yo͞o·lənt) *adj.:* rich; luxuriant.

adamant (ad′ə·mənt) *adj.:* unyielding; firm.

abutting (ə·but′iŋ) *v.* used as *adj.:* bordering upon; next to.

lauding (lôd′iŋ) *v.* used as *adj.:* praising.

tremulous (trem′yo͞o·ləs) *adj.:* trembling; quivering.

patina (pat′′n·ə) *n.:* color change resulting from age, as on old wood or silver.

RESOURCES: READING

Planning

- *One-Stop Planner* CD-ROM with Test Generator
- *On Course: Mapping Instruction*

Media

- *Audio CD Library*
  - disc 14

Reading

- *Interactive Reading,* Teacher's Edition
  - Graphic Organizer: Style Chart

Night Calls

Lisa Fugard

I saw that my father's eyes had gone dull like a dead animal's.

Landscape with Monkeys (c. 1910) by Henri Rousseau. Oil on canvas.
Barnes Foundation, Merion, Pennsylvania. © Barnes Foundation/SuperStock.

PRETEACHING

Standards Starter

Build prerequisite skills. Remind students that they can determine the mood of "Night Calls" by noticing how they feel as they read the story.

Preview Vocabulary

Use the following sentences to reinforce students' understanding of the Vocabulary words on p. 564.

1. The ______ on the silver vase made it more valuable as an antique, but Aunt Clara was ______ that we polish it anyway. [patina, adamant]
2. Plants that are ______ to a region ______ disappear after the area is developed. [indigenous, inevitably]
3. A(n) ______ bird-watcher, John identifies birds by their ______ calls. [avid, tremulous]
4. The town was a jumble of houses, with ______ homes of the wealthy ______ run-down shacks of the poor. [opulent, abutting]
5. To build their self-confidence, the teacher was constantly ______ her students. [lauding]

VIEWING THE ART

The fanciful paintings of **Henri Rousseau** (1844–1910) earned him the admiration of modernist artists and critics, despite being an outsider to their groups. Rousseau's art frequently features exotic settings such as deserts and jungles—habitats that he likely never saw, since he never left France.

Activity. This painting seems exotic and dreamlike; its plants and animals suggest mystery. Have students study the painting and then write about how this atmosphere is created and what might take place in a scene like this one.

Differentiating Instruction

- *Lesson Plans for Language Development*
  - English-Language Learners, pp. 263–265, 278, 281
  - Special Education Students, pp. 266, 278, 281

Vocabulary

- *Vocabulary Development*
  - Vocabulary Worksheet, p. 38

Assessment

- *Progress Assessment of Reading*
  - Selection Test
- *One-Stop Planner* CD-ROM with Test Generator

DIRECT TEACHING

A Literary Focus
GRADE-LEVEL STANDARD

Mood. What images are used to describe the father? [hands that are "slablike," "like two chunks of meat"] What mood does this description create? [Possible responses: fear; horror; melancholy.]

B Reading Skills

Making inferences. What can you infer about the narrator's father from these sensory details? [He smokes and drinks and might not bathe often.] What mood do the details help to create? [Possible responses: unease; fear; discomfort.]

C Reading Skills

Monitoring your reading: Character. [Possible responses to question 1: The narrator is thirteen, lives away from home, and is uncomfortable around her father. Her father is large, unkempt, and uncomfortable around his daughter.]

D Reading Skills

Monitoring your reading: Making inferences. [Possible responses to question 2: She desperately wanted to be liked—by the girls at school and by her father. Her performance of animal calls gained her popularity with the "in crowd" at school, so she hoped to gain her father's esteem by doing the calls for him.]

A My father's hands were huge. Slablike. When he was idle, they seemed to hang off the ends of his arms like two chunks of meat. He sat on his hands during the months he courted my mother.

When I was thirteen, I watched my thin hand disappear into his. It was at the train station at Modder River. I'd come home for the September holidays. It was hot, and the only other car at the small station pulled away. The siding at Modder River, 150 miles north of Johannesburg, was never busy. I remember it all clearly, standing in the dust, watching him get out of the truck and walk toward me, noticing that there was no smile on his face but still feeling my body move toward him, my arms opening for an embrace, something rising in my throat. My father stopped and held out his right hand.

Once in the truck, I was filled with anxiety about how close to him I could sit. I settled in the middle of my half of the bench seat and watched his large, brown hand move from the steering wheel to the gearshift and back. I B breathed deeply. Suddenly I was filled with the smell of him: Borkum Riff tobacco, sweat, the sweet odor of cheap Cape brandy. Filled with his secrets, I felt like a thief and moved a little closer to the window.

Then we were at the entrance to the Modder River Wildlife Sanctuary, and I jumped out of the car to open the gate. It swung easily, once I unlatched it, and banged against the wooden fence post, startling several guinea fowl that scampered into the veld.[1] "Krrdll . . . krrdll . . . krrdll," I called, and they slowed down. I mimicked their rattling cry again, and they stopped. Again, and a few of them stepped hesitantly toward me. Laughingly, I turned to find my father's smile, but his face was gone, blotted out by the expanse of blue sky reflected in the windshield. C

> **CHARACTER**
> 1. What have you learned so far about the narrator and her father?

I have a gift for mimicking bird and animal calls.

I have a gift for mimicking bird and animal calls. During my third year at boarding school I'd finally made myself popular and gained the respect of Wendy Venter, the bully of our dorm, by doing several calls late one night. It became a ritual, and every couple of weeks, around midnight, I'd hear rustling and whispering from the eleven other girls in the dormitory; then a balled-up sock would land on my bed, usually right next to my head, and Wendy would call my name in a sly whisper, "Marlene." The dorm would fall silent. Lying back in the darkness I'd start with the deep moan of the spotted eagle owl; then the high-pitched yip of the black-backed jackal; the low snuffle and violent laugh of the hyena; and then a deadly combination: the rasping, half-swallowed growl of the leopard, followed by the wild scream of the chacma baboon. Inevitably one of the younger girls would begin to cry, and I'd hear Wendy snickering in the darkness.

I'd told my father about this during my next trip home, about how much the other girls had enjoyed it, and I offered to do it for him one evening, offered to steal into his room at midnight, crouch at the foot of his bed, and D make the calls for him. He'd shaken his head ever so slightly. "I've got the real thing right outside my window," he said.

> **MAKING INFERENCES**
> 2. What do you learn about the narrator from this **flashback** to her early years at boarding school?

1. **veld** *n.:* in South Africa, open grassy country with few bushes and almost no trees.

Vocabulary
inevitably (in·ev′i·tə·blē) *adv.:* unavoidably.

DIFFERENTIATING INSTRUCTION

Learners Having Difficulty

Modeling. To help students read "Night Calls," model the skill of monitoring your reading. Say: "From the very beginning of this story, we know that the two main characters are a thirteen-year-old girl and her father. But the author only gradually reveals additional information about these characters. Every page or so, pause and ask yourself, 'What have I learned so far about the narrator? About her father? How does the setting affect the mood?'"

English-Language Learners

Encourage students to use context clues to guess the meanings of unfamiliar words, particularly those relating to the land and wildlife of South Africa. Point out, for example, that in the first paragraph on p. 567, students need

As we drove up to our house now, I noticed the shabby state of the compound. The road was rutted and washed-out in many places by the spring rains. The visitors' kiosk was boarded up, and the map of the sanctuary had been knocked off its post and lay on the ground. Even the pond had been neglected. When my parents had first come to Modder River, five years before I was born, my father had had the pond dug out for my mother. An avid botanist,[2] she'd planted it with indigenous water lilies that she collected, along with bulrushes, seven-weeks ferns, and floating hearts. During the two years when the Modder River was reduced to a trickle by the drought, the local farmers had been astonished to hear that my father was actually pumping precious water from our borehole into the pond to prevent it from drying up. An opulent jewel in the dusty, cracked landscape, it became a haven for birds, being visited by pied kingfishers, mountain chats, spoonbills, bokmakieries, a pair of black-shouldered kites—all told, my mother counted 107 different species. Now a thick layer of brown scum covered the shallow, stagnant water. I remembered a letter that I'd received from my father several months before. The scrawled handwriting hadn't even looked like his. I'd read it once and then hidden it away, scared by the loneliness that the words hinted at.

IMAGES

3. Which **images** of the setting create a **mood** of sadness and a sense of decay?

None of this seemed to matter, however, when I stood among our dogs, being pelted with paws and tails and long pink tongues: King, with his tail plumed like an ostrich feather, and Blitz, a lean, black shadow. They clattered behind me as I went into my bedroom. The room was still and dark and smelled musty. Quickly I opened the wooden shutters. I moved to the chest of drawers and found the large framed photograph of my mother, frozen at age thirty-two. She was laughing, and her head was turned slightly as a lock of hair blew across her face. I traced her jaw line with my finger and moved to the mirror with the photograph, but the dogs were demanding, barking and pawing at my legs.

> I stopped, panting, trying to catch my breath.

I ran outside with them and chased them up and down the cool stone lengths of the veranda, flying past the living room and the dining room, screeching past my father's study and back again with the dogs racing behind me. Back and forth I went, until the force of motion made me round the corner past my parents' old bedroom. I stopped, panting, trying to catch my breath. I stared at the large fenced-in area under the blue gum tree. It was where my father kept the red-crested night heron, one of the last of its kind.

The year that the park officials brought the bird to Modder River had been a difficult one. My mother was killed in a car accident just before my eighth birthday. Numbly, I watched my father make funeral arrangements with the help of his sister, Annette, who drove up from Johannesburg. She was adamant: There was no way I could stay at Modder River. It was too remote, and there was my schooling to consider; my mother had been my tutor. As for my father,

Vocabulary

avid (av′id) *adj.:* eager and enthusiastic.

indigenous (in·dij′ə·nəs) *adj.:* native; growing naturally in a region or country.

opulent (äp′yo͞o·lənt) *adj.:* rich; luxuriant.

adamant (ad′ə·mənt) *adj.:* unyielding; firm.

2. **botanist** *n.:* scientist who studies plant life.

not turn to a dictionary to understand that *pied kingfishers, mountain chats, spoonbills, bokmakieries,* and *black-shouldered kites* are the names of various birds. The context clues "a haven for birds" and "107 different species" make this clear.

Resources Reminder

For lessons designed for intermediate and advanced English-language learners, see *Lesson Plans for Language Development,* pp. 263–265, 278, 281.

Special Education Students

For lessons designed for special education students, see *Lesson Plans for Language Development,* pp. 266, 278, 281.

Direct Teaching

E Literary Focus
GRADE-LEVEL STANDARD

Setting and mood. Setting is crucial to a story's mood. What evocative words does the author use to establish the setting? [Possible responses: "shabby"; "neglected"; "brown scum"; "stagnant."] What mood is created by this setting? [Possible response: The mood is depressing.]

F Vocabulary Development
REVIEW STANDARD

Context clues. How does the context reveal the meaning of *botanist*—"someone who studies plants"? [The words "she'd planted it with indigenous water lilies that she collected, along with bulrushes, seven-weeks ferns, and floating hearts" shows the narrator's mother's knowledge of plants.]

G Reading Skills

Monitoring your reading: Images. [Possible responses to question 3: Images that create the mood of sadness and decay include the rutted, washed-out road; the boarded-up kiosk; the map knocked off its post; the neglected, scum-covered pond; the letter revealing the father's loneliness.]

H Literary Focus
GRADE-LEVEL STANDARD

Figurative language. What figures of speech does the author use to describe the dogs? [One has a "tail plumed like an ostrich feather" (simile) and the other is "a lean, black shadow" (metaphor).]

I Literary Focus
GRADE-LEVEL STANDARD

Flashback. What time change has occurred between this paragraph and the previous ones? [The narrator has moved back five years in time, from being thirteen to being about eight, when her mother died.]

DIRECT TEACHING

VIEWING THE ART

Virginian artist **William H. Turner** (1935–) makes sculptures of animals out of bronze. Bronze sculptures are made by first creating a clay or wax model, which is then used to create a mold. Once a mold is made, molten bronze can be poured into it in order to make as many copies of the original model as the sculptor desires. Because Turner is interested in creating sculptures that appear as much as possible like the animals they are based on, he then applies color to them.

A Reading Skills

Monitoring your reading: Plot. [Possible responses to question 4: The flashback reveals that the narrator's mother was killed in a car accident, leaving her father alone at the place that reminded him of his wife. Then, when he was about to resign, he agreed to look after a red-crested heron and stay at Modder River while the narrator went away to boarding school.]

it made no sense for him to remain, grieving, in a place so closely associated with his wife. My father was on the verge of resigning as warden of the small sanctuary when park officials telephoned about the bird. The red-crested night heron had been captured at the vlei[3] on Nie Te Ver, the farm abutting the sanctuary's eastern border, and the National Parks Board wanted the heron kept at Modder River on the slim chance that they might find a mate for it.

A Mr. Vanjaarsveld arrived with the bird. "We had to tie the bugger's beak up, otherwise he'd have cut us to ribbons," he said, as he placed a large burlap bag in the pen that my father had hastily constructed. He opened the bag and then quickly stepped out and shut the gate. A few moments of silence—then a wild flurry of wings, the sound of the air being thumped, and the heron hit the wire at the top of the pen and came crashing down. Again and again, till the bird lay in the dust exhausted, its wings useless. Quietly my father opened the gate and stepped inside the pen. For several minutes he squatted on his haunches in the corner and then slowly he inched his way toward the bird. Kneeling alongside it, he checked the feathers for damage, spreading the wings on the ground in front of him, like a fan. Then, making soft noises in the back of his throat, he untied the strip of burlap around the heron's beak. My father stayed on at Modder River, and arrangements were made for me to go to boarding school.

A PLOT
4. What two important events does this **flashback** reveal?

During holidays I came home, and my father would share the latest news about the heron

3. **vlei** *n.*: in South Africa, a temporary lake formed in a marshy area during the rainy season.

Vocabulary
abutting (ə·but′iŋ) *v.* used as *adj.*: bordering upon; next to.

Preening Heron by William H. Turner.

DIFFERENTIATING INSTRUCTION

Advanced Learners

Acceleration. Use this activity to move advanced learners toward the eleventh- and twelfth-grade Standard 3.3, for which they analyze the ways in which irony, tone, mood, the author's style, and the "sound" of language achieve specific rhetorical or aesthetic purposes or both.

Activity. Have students review the story and analyze the ways in which Fugard uses language to create mood. Suggest that they then look at a specific passage of the story and discuss questions like these:

- How does the mood fit with the characterizations and the theme of the story?
- What different word choices might be made to change the mood of the passage?

568 Chapter 8 Evaluating Style • Evaluating an Argument

with me. He showed me articles from the local papers lauding the conservation efforts surrounding the bird, as well as articles from foreign countries in languages we couldn't understand. He showed me the stamp that the South African government issued—a thirty-seven-cent stamp with the heron's lean profile and brilliant crest. And once he gave me a feather, a long, steel-gray feather from the tip of the heron's wing, a flight feather, and it was smooth as I stroked it against my cheek during the overnight train ride back to boarding school. But after two or three years, interest in the heron faded. The articles died down, and in private the National Parks Board expressed their doubts to my father that they would ever find a mate for the bird. The sanctuary was small, and apart from a secretive leopard we didn't have any of the Big Five—animals like elephants and lions that attracted tourists. Modder River returned to the way it used to be, a trickle of visitors on the occasional weekend. **B**

> I lay in bed and let the night overtake me . . .

I stared at the pen for a long time now. I knew what was in there. A large gray bird, with ugly hooked feet, a long slithery neck that gave me nightmares, and a red crest that was raised during the courtship ritual. I had never seen the crest, but once I'd caught a glimpse of a small red feather that had escaped from the heron's crown. There was no need to walk through the dust to look at the bird under the swaying blue gum tree branches. I went anyway. Effortlessly, I climbed the blue gum tree, but now it was difficult for me to squeeze into the small fork halfway up. The heron pecked listlessly at a dried-out fish, and I noticed that the pen hadn't been cleaned in quite a while. I'd spent many school holidays in the tree watching my father as he fed the bird, collected the feathers during the molt,[4] and proudly chatted with visitors. Maybe he'd known that I was up there all the time. **C** **D**

CHARACTER
5. What details seem to reveal the narrator's attitude toward the heron?

I shivered. The sun had set, taking all the warmth with it, and a thin veil of light pressed against our house and the Modder River as it crawled like a fat brown snake out of the mountains. **E**

Walking back down the length of the veranda, I peered through the windows of the rooms we'd stopped using, the dining room with its yellow wood table, the living room where my mother's desk was still piled high with the field guides and books she'd used to identify unknown plants she'd come across. The outside light flickered on, and I found my father in the kitchen, heating up a tin of curry. We ate our dinner in silence, and then he read a book and I listened to the radio. I felt uncomfortable in the house and longed for the morning, when I could go racing through the veld with the dogs, go out looking for tracks and walk far into the sanctuary. At 10 P.M., as was custom, my father switched off the electricity generator and went to his study, where he slept.

The low hum now gone, I lay in bed and let the night overtake me, hungrily following the calls in the darkness. A jackal marking his territory, the rhythmic eruptions of spring bullfrogs, the steady breath of King at the foot of my bed. And then I heard another familiar sound, the

4. **molt** *n.:* shedding of feathers at certain intervals, prior to replacement by new growth.

Vocabulary
lauding (lôd′iŋ) *v.* used as *adj.:* praising.

DIRECT TEACHING

B Reading Skills

Speculating. What role does the heron play in the father's life for the first few years following the mother's death? [The heron gives the father a project to be involved with and a way to lessen his grief. Perhaps he identifies with the bird, who is alone and without a mate.] What do you think will happen to the heron and the father as interest in the heron wanes and the possibility of finding a mate decreases? [Possible responses: The bird may die; the father may get depressed.]

C Learners Having Difficulty

Finding details. How old is the narrator in this paragraph, and how do you know? [She is thirteen. The word "now" indicates that she is back in the time frame in which the story began.] How much time has passed since her mother died and her father began looking after the heron? [five years]

D Reading Skills

Monitoring your reading: Character. [Possible responses to question 5: Details that reveal the narrator's dislike of the heron include "ugly hooked feet" and "long slithery neck that gave me nightmares." But because the narrator spent many school holidays in the tree watching her father take care of the bird, she also seems to be intrigued by it.]

E Literary Focus
GRADE-LEVEL STANDARD

Figurative language and mood. What simile does the writer use to describe the river? [The river "crawled like a fat brown snake out of the mountains."] What mood does this simile create? [Possible responses: disgust; unease.]

READING MINI-LESSON

Developing Word-Attack Skills
Explain that in many words, *a–* is a prefix and stands for the unaccented vowel sound schwa (/ə/). In this selection we find *across, abutting, alongside, apart, alone, asleep, away,* and *abruptly.* In other words, *a–* is part of a stressed first syllable. The selection word *adamant* is an example of this: /ad′ə • mənt/.
Activity. Display these words. Have students identify words in which *a–* stands for /ə/ (answers are underlined) and words in which *a–* is part of an accented first syllable (answers are checked).

abandon	abalone	aberration
academic	ascent	accent ✓
adapt	adage ✓	affable ✓
afford	aground	agony ✓
amend	avid ✓	avenge

Direct Teaching

A Reading Skills

Monitoring your reading: Images. [Possible responses to question 6: "A jackal marking his territory"; "the rhythmic eruptions of spring bullfrogs"; "the creaking of the gate"; the heron's neck was "liquid in the moonlight, curving and swaying"; its beak "glinted like a dagger"; the father's hand "was sunk deep into the heron's soft breast"; "a tremulous wail."]

B Reading Skills

Monitoring your reading: Making inferences. [Possible responses to question 7: The father wants to give the heron its freedom and a chance to find a mate on its own; he may also want his own freedom from the responsibility of caring for the bird. He lies about letting the bird go because he doesn't realize his true motivations or doesn't want to reveal them to his daughter.] **Why do you think the narrator goes along with her father's lie?** [Possible responses: She doesn't want to confront him; she senses that he is happier now that the bird is free, and she wants him to stay happy.]

C Literary Focus
GRADE-LEVEL STANDARD

? Symbol. The recurrence of an animal or object may indicate that it has symbolic meaning. On the literal level, what do you know about the heron and its history? [The heron is an endangered species; the father got it just after his wife died; he stayed at the sanctuary because of the bird; he let the bird go; the bird calls and the father goes down to the river.] **What abstract idea might the heron symbolize?** [Possible response: the father's grief, loneliness, and longing for his wife.]

creaking of the gate on the heron's pen. Gently I felt my way down the hall and into my parents' old bedroom. I hid behind the soft lace curtains, and as my eyes grew accustomed to the night, I saw my father move slowly across the compound carrying the heron gently under his arm, its long legs dangling at his side. The heron's neck was liquid in the moonlight, curving and swaying, at times seeming to entwine my father. Its beak glinted like a dagger. One of my father's hands followed the bird's neck, lightly touching it at times, while the other was sunk deep into the heron's soft breast, pale gray feathers around his wrist. My father slipped by with the heron, and I went back to bed and stared into the darkness. Later on I heard a tremulous wail repeated several times. It came from the river. I knew it was the red-crested night heron, even though I'd never heard its call before, **A** and I thought about my father in the darkness on the banks of the Modder River with the bird.

IMAGES

6. Which **images** and **figures of speech** in this passage help you hear and see the setting and the heron?

Detail of *Landscape with Monkeys* (c. 1910) by Henri Rousseau. Oil on canvas.

Barnes Foundation, Merion, Pennsylvania. © Barnes Foundation/SuperStock.

At breakfast the next morning, my father told me that a hyena had gotten the best of us, had finally broken into the heron's pen, because the bird had disappeared. Under the blue gum tree we examined a huge hole in the fence. "Yes, I think so, Dad," I said, and nodded in agreement as we watched King and Blitz sniff inside the pen. He seemed lighter and chatted with me about school as I helped him dismantle the fence. "Hyena," he had said with such authority. He told me that now he might even be able to come to the end-of-the-year recital at my school. That night I made fried bananas and ice cream for dessert, and we listened to a radio play together. At **B** ten, just before he switched off the generator, I looked in the mirror and thought, I have his eyes.

MAKING INFERENCES

7. Why do you think the father releases the heron and lies about what he did?

In bed, in the blackness, I listened to the night again. The jackal that had been barking the previous night had moved on, and it seemed quiet out there. It wasn't long before I heard the heron calling. I knew my father heard it as well, and I tried to picture him in his bed. I wondered if his heart beat like mine, an urgent knocking in my chest. I rolled over and thought of the red-crested night **C** heron, alone by the river, the last of its kind, and I imagined that its crest was raised and that it picked its way delicately through the muddy water, lifting its feet up like wet handkerchiefs.

The following night I heard the heron's call again, and I also heard footsteps leaving our house. I knew it was my father going down to the river. For ten nights the heron called and my father followed. During the days we worked on repairing things around the compound. We cleaned up the pond and made a day trip to the

Vocabulary
tremulous (trem′yo͞o·ləs) *adj.:* trembling; quivering.

CONTENT-AREA CONNECTIONS

Geography/History: South Africa
Have volunteers identify South Africa on a map and share what they know about it. Point out that we hear more about the social and political turmoil of South Africa than about its beauty and abundant wildlife.

Small-group activity. Have small groups of students research and report on aspects of South Africa's history or geography.

Science: Endangered Species
The red-crested night heron is imaginary, but today many real animals are very nearly "the last of their kind."

Individual activity. Have each student research an endangered species, focusing on causes of endangerment and ways in which people are trying to help.

570 Chapter 8 Evaluating Style • Evaluating an Argument

western corner of the sanctuary, where the Modder River dropped abruptly into a densely forested ravine—gnarled trees hung with a thick gray moss that I called "old man's beard." We collected water lilies from the dappled pools, wrapping their roots in damp newspaper and placing them in our packs. Baboons barked from the rocky ledges. We saw the spoor of the leopard, two pugmarks[5] in the rich black mud. For the drive home I sat in the back of the truck. As my father shifted to low gear and negotiated the sandy part of the road that ran alongside the river, I scanned the banks, hoping to catch a glimpse of the heron roosting, waiting for nightfall. I spent a day repairing the signs along the Succulent Trail, a one-mile loop that wound through an area that my father had filled with rare plants—aloe albida, aloe monotropa, a lydenberg cycad. We put the map back on its post and touched it up with small pots of paint, the Modder River a blue vein in the brown landscape.

IMAGES
8. What **images** help you visualize the sanctuary?

D

Then, one long night, I didn't hear the heron's call. The bird had disappeared, and when I got out of bed the next morning, I saw that my father's eyes had gone dull like a dead animal's. I knew why but couldn't say anything. Then he started walking all the time, often coming home only for an hour or two in the early dawn. I'd hear the creak of the floorboards near the kitchen and the thud of Blitz's tail on the floor. I'd hear my father pacing, and then, eventually, stillness. He's lying on the sofa in his study, he's asleep now, I'd say to myself. Then the pacing again and the soft slam of the screen door. From the blue gum tree I'd see him crisscrossing the veld, like a rabid dog, always coming back to touch the river. Straining my eyes, I'd watch him walk farther and farther away, until he vanished into the landscape.

FIGURES OF SPEECH
9. What **similes** describe the father in this paragraph?

E

Accidentally, I found the heron's remains. I was out late one afternoon, looking for a snakeskin for my next school biology project. I had chosen a rocky area, where I'd seen cobras and puff adders sunning themselves, and as I moved slowly through it, poking into crevices with a stick, I came across a broken fan of bloodied feathers. The steel-gray patina was unmistakable, and I knew it was part of the heron's wing. I scratched out a hole with my stick and buried the feathers, pushing a large rock over the small grave.

F

I made sandwiches for supper that night. I made extra ones for my father, but he didn't come home. I sat on the veranda with King and Blitz until ten o'clock, when I switched off the generator. Swiftly, silently, I followed the footpath down to the far bank of the river, pushing my way through the warm water that came up to my waist. I hid in the reeds and waited.

An hour later I saw my father on the opposite bank, looking, listening. He sat down on the dark sand and rolled a pebble in his large palms. I crouched even lower. Slowly I tilted my head back until my throat was wide open and a tremulous wail slid out. My father stood up and looked across the water to where I was crouched. Again I made the sound, again and again. He took three more small steps toward my side of the river and his hands fluttered like giant, tawny moths in the moonlight. ■

G

FIGURES OF SPEECH
10. How did the narrator view her father's hands at the start of the story? How does she see them now?

H

5. **spoor . . . pugmarks:** *Spoor* is the track or trail of a wild animal. *Pugmarks* are the footprints or trail of an animal.

Vocabulary
patina (pat′'n·ə) *n.:* color change resulting from age, as on old wood or silver.

DIRECT TEACHING

D Reading Skills
Monitoring your reading: Images. [Possible responses to question 8: "densely forested ravine"; "gnarled trees hung with . . . 'Old man's beard' "; "dappled pools"; "rocky ledges"; "rich black mud"; "rare plants"; "the Modder River a blue vein in the brown landscape."]

E Reading Skills
Monitoring your reading: Figures of speech. [Possible responses to question 9: His eyes are "dull like a dead animal's"; he moves "like a rabid dog."] **What mood do these similes create?** [Possible response: distress and anguish.]

F Reading Skills
? Drawing conclusions. How do you think the heron died? [It was probably killed by snakes.] **Why does the narrator bury the bird?** [Possible responses: She doesn't want the father to find it; she is sorry about the heron's death and wants to pay it her respects.]

G Reading Skills
? Comparing and contrasting. What is the difference in the narrator's motivation for making the animal calls in her school dorm and for making the heron's call here? [Possible response: She used her skill selfishly to become more popular at school. Now, she uses it selflessly to give her father hope.]

H Reading Skills
Monitoring your reading: Figures of speech. [Possible response to question 10: Instead of being heavy like slabs of meat, her father's hands are light now, like moths' wings in the moonlight.] **What theme might this imagery point toward?** [Possible responses: Hope can raise the spirits and make the heart light; drawing someone to a false hope, like a moth to a flame, is ultimately destructive.]

DEVELOPING FLUENCY

Mixed-ability group activity. Combine students of different abilities into groups. Have each group choose a passage of the story that they particularly like. Have students practice reading through the passage a sentence at a time, changing the reader after each sentence. Then, have students perform their reading for the class.

GUIDED PRACTICE

Monitoring students' progress. Guide the class in answering these comprehension questions. Direct students to locate passages in the text that support their responses.

True-False

1. The nature sanctuary is in the outback of Australia. [F]
2. The narrator's mother died of cancer. [F]
3. The narrator's father dislikes the heron, so he lets it out of its cage. [F]
4. The narrator finds the dead heron but tells no one. [T]
5. At the end, the narrator's father thinks the heron is alive. [T]

Meet the Writer

Lisa Fugard

Writing About Home

Lisa Fugard (1961–) grew up in South Africa, the daughter of the playwright, director, and actor Athol Fugard and Sheila Fugard, a novelist and poet. Fugard chose acting as her first career and performed in many stage productions, including a tour of black townships as the female lead in her father's play *My Children! My Africa!*

Eventually, Fugard says, she "let theater and acting go away." She turned instead to writing and discovered that her acting experience, especially its deep study of characters and motivations, helped her create believable fictional characters.

Fugard recalls how she came to write "Night Calls" and how the story changed as she revised it:

"'Night Calls' actually evolved from watching a program on public television about a pair of Japanese cranes. They were the last of their kind and they were being tended to by this Japanese man. I remember watching the program and being terribly moved by the idea of these two birds—that after they were gone, there was nothing left."

She set her story in Japan and recalls that she struggled to use unfamiliar Japanese names, plants, and animals. Halfway through her rewrite, she moved the story to South Africa—and felt completely at home. Through several drafts, "Night Calls" explored the relationship between a father and son, but in her final draft Fugard changed the main character to a daughter. The red-crested night heron, she says, is fictional too; no such bird has ever existed.

Fugard says that the source of writer's block is a desire to write down only perfect sentences and stories. She feels that writers need to learn how to

"outfox the censor we all have, how to tap into the imagination, and how to take the risk to write from the heart."

DIFFERENTIATING INSTRUCTION

Advanced Learners

Enrichment. Fugard's parents were quite involved in the political and racial turmoil of apartheid in South Africa, and she was influenced by their activities.

Activity. Suggest that students enter *Lisa Fugard, South Africa, apartheid,* and *Athol Fugard* as keywords in an Internet search engine. Have students share information about the possible influences that South African politics had on Lisa Fugard's writing.

572 Chapter 8 Evaluating Style • Evaluating an Argument

CONNECTION / POEM

Waiting for *E. gularis*

Linda Pastan

"An African heron was found on the northeast end of Nantucket Island. . . ."
—news release

"The sighting of the century . . ."
—Roger Tory Peterson

Exile
by accident
he came

against
all instinct
to this watery place,

mistaking it
perhaps
as the explorers did

for some
new
Orient.

This morning,
dreaming
of the inexplicable

I rise from sleep, smoothing
the sheets behind me
to match

the water smoothed sand
silk
under my bare feet.

I walk past morning joggers
who worship in pain
the crucible of breath,

past dune and marsh
stockaded with eel grass
to this pond,

just as a breeze comes up
like rumors
of his appearance.

Young people in bathing suits
lounge here, fans
waiting for their rock star

E. gularis—even his name
becomes
an incantation.

The pond
is all surface
this cloudy day,

the dark side of the mirror
where nothing shows
until you stare enough

Connection

Summary at grade level

This Connection presents a poem based on an actual occurrence, the sighting of a rare African heron on the East Coast of the United States. Two quotations precede the poem: One is from a news release, the other from the famous bird-guide author Roger Tory Peterson. The poem begins with the speaker identifying the heron as an "exile." She gets up and takes a morning walk along the beach and finds people looking for *E. gularis*. She does not see the rare bird, but notes other wildlife around the pond and the bird-watchers with their "binoculars raised like pistols."

DIRECT TEACHING

A Learners Having Difficulty

Reading aloud. Have students read the first twelve lines aloud. Remind them that poets often break lines to emphasize certain words. Why might Pastan begin her poem with the single word "Exile"? [Possible response: to emphasize that the bird is alone, far from home.]

B Literary Focus GRADE-LEVEL STANDARD

Figurative language. What is the heron compared to? [a rock star] What is the pond compared to? [the back of a mirror] What do these metaphors suggest thematically? [Possible response: People are more concerned with surfaces than real things.]

Connecting and Comparing Texts

Invite students to compare and contrast this poem with the story "Night Calls." Have them consider similarities and differences between

- the speaker in the poem and the narrator of the story
- the two herons
- the relationships between the two birds and the other characters
- the moods and themes of the two selections

[Students may say that on a surface level, "Night Calls" and "Waiting for *E. gularis*" are similar. Both authors have written about a rare species of bird that interests people. Yet, the moods and themes of the two works are different. Pastan's poem ends with the almost violent image of binoculars as pistols, creating a rough, hard-edged mood and a theme of the heartlessness of humans who see animals as just another thing to tick off their lists. Fugard's story, on the other hand, deals with complex human emotions. The red-crested night heron becomes a symbol of the narrator's father's longing for his wife. The mood of "Night Calls" is poignant and heartfelt without being tragic. Its theme is about complicated relationships and emotions and the hopes that connect people to life.]

DIRECT TEACHING

A Literary Focus
GRADE-LEVEL STANDARD

? Figurative language. **How is the surface of the pond like childhood puzzles?** [First, you can't see anything except the surface; then you make out faces (in the puzzle) or wildlife (around the pond).]

B Reading Skills

? Making inferences. **State in your own words the question that the speaker imagines the little blue herons asking.** [Possible response: "Why don't the bird-watchers care about us?"] **How might the speaker answer that question?** [Possible response: "You are ordinary, not a 'rock star' rarity like *E. gularis.*"]

C Literary Focus
GRADE-LEVEL STANDARD

? Figurative language. **What does the speaker compare the bird-watchers' binoculars to?** [pistols] **What does this simile reveal about the speaker's feelings toward the bird-watchers?** [She thinks they are heartless, caring only to add another bird to their lists.] **What does this final simile reveal about the poem's theme?** [People need to realize that birds, like all life-forms, have lives of their own and do not exist merely for humans' entertainment.]

VIEWING THE ART

John James Audubon (1785–1851) published extensive illustrated studies of the birds of North America. He increased the public knowledge of and appreciation for wildlife. The Audubon Society, one of the first conservation groups, was named in his honor when it was formed in 1888.

Activity. **How does Audubon emphasize the large size of the Heron?** [The tall bird is bent over, filling the rectangular composition.]

A
as at those childhood puzzles—
how many faces can you find
concealed here?

And there moving towards us
is the turtle's miniature
face,

and there the mask
the wild duck wears, stitching
a ruffle

B
at the pond's far edge
where now
the Little Blue herons

curve their necks
to question marks
(why not me?)

C
where in a semi-circle
ornithologists
wait

to add another notch
to their life
lists,

binoculars
raised
like pistols.

Great Blue Heron by John James Audubon.

574 Chapter 8 Evaluating Style • Evaluating an Argument

Literary Response and Analysis

Reading Check

1. How does the narrator's life change just before her eighth birthday?
2. What is Marlene's special talent?
3. Why is the red-crested night heron sent to the Modder River sanctuary?
4. What happens to the plan to find a mate for the bird? What happens to the sanctuary as a result?
5. How does Marlene's father explain what happened to the heron when it disappeared from the sanctuary?

Interpretations

6. What details show that the father, narrator, and sanctuary are suffering from the loss of the narrator's mother?
7. To answer the following questions, you will have to **infer** the character's **motivation.** Give evidence from the story to support your inferences. Remember that a character's motivations may be purposely **ambiguous,** or open to several interpretations. (Check your Quickwrite notes also.)
   - What do you think the heron meant to the father?
   - Why does the father release it?
   - Why does the father lie to Marlene about how the heron escaped?
   - Why doesn't the narrator tell her father that the heron is dead?
   - Why does the narrator imitate the heron's call at the story's end?

Literary Criticism

8. When the narrator returns for the September holidays, she notices changes in the **setting.** How has the setting changed? What **mood** do these changes create?

9. One aspect of Fugard's **diction** and **style** is her use of words that help us hear the sounds made by various animals. Expain how each sound below helps you imagine the animal that makes it.

yip	wail	scream
growl	moan	snuffle

Comparing Literature

10. The poem by Linda Pastan (see the *Connection* on page 573) is also about a heron. How many similarities can you find between the poem and the story? In what important ways are the **moods** of the two pieces different?

Writing

Analyzing Style

In a brief essay, analyze Fugard's **style.** Before you write, collect your details in a chart like the one below. Conclude your essay with a statement explaining your response to the story.

Elements of Style	Examples	My Comments
Imagery		
Figurative language		
Creation of mood		
Use of flashbacks		

Creating a Mood

A wildlife sanctuary and a lonely home are settings that create a strong mood in this story. Write a paragraph describing a setting that creates a **mood.** Word choice, or **diction,** will be important. Tell how the setting looks, smells, sounds, perhaps even tastes and feels.

Reading Standard 3.11 Evaluate the aesthetic qualities of style, including the impact of diction and figurative language on mood, using the terminology of literary criticism. (Aesthetic approach)

INDEPENDENT PRACTICE

Literary Response and Analysis

7. Possible answers:
   - The heron represented hope, a reason to live after his wife's death. *Evidence*—the father's staying at the sanctuary for the heron's sake; his care of the bird; his pride in it; his eyes going "dead" when the heron disappears.
   - He releases the heron to give it freedom and a chance to find a mate. *Evidence*—He feels freer after the heron is free. He follows its call.
   - He lies because he cannot reveal his feelings. *Evidence*—He does not embrace her; he is silent at dinner.
   - The narrator knows how much the bird meant to her father and cannot bear to tell him it is dead. *Evidence*—She saw his eyes go "dead" when the heron disappeared.
   - She imitates the heron's call to give her father hope—for the bird and for himself. *Evidence*—After the call, she sees his hands fluttering.

Literary Criticism

8. The sanctuary is run-down and neglected. This creates a mood of sadness, decay, and abandonment.
9. *Yip*—call of black-backed jackal. *Growl*—call of leopard. *Wail*—call of the heron. *Moan*—call of spotted owl. *Scream*—call of chacma baboon. *Snuffle*—sound of hyena.

Comparing Literature

10. Both the story and the poem deal with one heron, with a rare bird, with humans interested in the bird. Students may say that the story's mood is touching or sad, while the poem's mood is bitter or scornful.

Reading Check

1. Her mother dies.
2. She imitates animal calls.
3. to protect it while waiting for a mate to be found
4. The plan fails and people lose interest in the sanctuary, which becomes run-down.
5. He says that a hyena must have broken into the heron's cage.

Interpretations

6. Possible details: the father's withdrawn nature, unsmiling face; the narrator's discomfort around her father; rutted road, boarded-up kiosk, fallen post, stagnant pond; the narrator's musty bedroom; the unused rooms.

Vocabulary Development

Practice 1

1. Thunder inevitably follows lightning. Night inevitably follows day.
2. As an avid reader, I love books.
3. Oak trees, raccoons, and deer are indigenous to this region.
4. My friend's opulent wedding featured gourmet food.
5. I adamantly support that ban because drivers should focus.
6. Canada and Mexico abut the United States.
7. I laud *Into Thin Air* as a brilliant book!
8. Singing or speaking to an audience might make one tremulous.
9. I'd leave the patina on copper; it might protect the metal.

Practice 2

Possible Answers

- What is an idle friend doing?
- When do you often feel anxiety?
- What kind of animal could have scampered through the forest?
- What would I be doing if I mimicked your speech?
- How might a stagnant pond smell?
- How would a stream look if it moved listlessly?
- Who is a school authority?

Practice 3

1. "Train station" and "the only other car at the small station pulled away" help you guess that a "siding" is a short railroad track that connects with the main track and allows the train to come up to the station.
2. The "map of the sanctuary" on the ground helps you know that the "kiosk" is a small information booth.
3. "Drought" and "pumping precious water" help you guess that the "borehole" is a well.

Vocabulary Development

Verifying Meanings by Examples

Word Bank
inevitably
avid
indigenous
opulent
adamant
abutting
lauding
tremulous
patina

PRACTICE 1

You can own a new word (that is, add it to your working vocabulary) by using it, especially by giving examples of the word in action. Use complete sentences to write your answers to the questions that follow:

1. What inevitably follows lightning? Think of another example of something that inevitably follows something else.
2. If you are an avid reader, how do you feel about reading?
3. Name three things that are indigenous to your community.
4. You've been to an opulent wedding. Describe the wedding.
5. You are adamant about a proposed law banning the use of cell phones by drivers. Explain why.
6. Name two countries abutting the United States.
7. Write a sentence lauding a book you've read recently.
8. Describe two situations that might make a person feel tremulous.
9. Which of the following has a patina: tarnished silverware, a sunset, a hard-boiled egg, a copper statue that's turned green? Would you try to get rid of the patina? Explain.

PRACTICE 2

For each of the following words, make up a question like those in Practice 1 above: *idle* (page 566), *anxiety* (page 566), *scampered* (page 566), *mimicked* (page 566), *stagnant* (page 567), *listlessly* (page 569), and *authority* (page 570). Try out your questions on a classmate.

PRACTICE 3

Grade 8 Review Reading Standard 1.3 Use word meanings within the appropriate context, and show ability to verify those meanings by definition, restatement, or example.

Even when you've never seen a word before, the **context** may provide clues that help you accurately guess the word's meaning. What context clues would help you define the underlined words in these sentences?

1. "It was at the train station at Modder River. . . . It was hot, and the only other car at the small station pulled away. The siding at Modder River . . . was never busy." (page 566)
2. "The visitors' kiosk was boarded up, and the map of the sanctuary had been knocked off its post and lay on the ground." (page 567)
3. "During the two years when the Modder River was reduced to a trickle by the drought, the local farmers had been astonished to hear that my father was actually pumping precious water from our borehole into the pond to prevent it from drying up." (page 567)

Resources Reminder

Vocabulary

- *Vocabulary Development*
  - Vocabulary Worksheet, p. 38
- *Lesson Plans for Language Development*
  - Vocabulary, pp. 278, 281

ASSESSING

Assessment

- *Progress Assessment of Reading*
  - Selection Test

RETEACHING

For a lesson reteaching mood, see **Reteaching,** p. 939A. For another selection to teach Standard 3.11, see *Interactive Reading,* Chapter 8.

576 Chapter 8 Evaluating Style • Evaluating an Argument

Before You Read INFORMATIONAL MATERIALS

Call of the Wild—Save Us!

Evaluating an Author's Argument

Persuasive writing tries to persuade you to believe an idea or take an action. You'll find persuasive writing in editorials, letters to the editor, speeches, position papers, advertisements, and magazine articles like the one you are about to read. To make up your mind about whether or not a writer's argument is **credible** and should persuade you, take these steps:

1. **Follow the author's argument.** An **argument** is a series of statements designed to persuade you. Usually it begins with a clear statement of the writer's **opinion** or **claim.** Then, to persuade you, the writer provides **reasons** as well as **evidence** to back up those reasons.

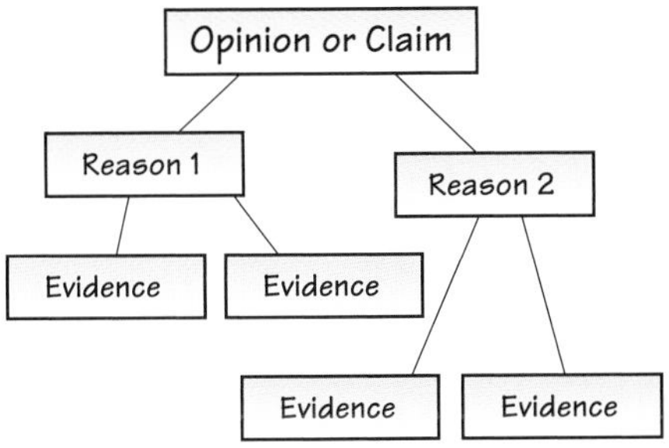

2. **Evaluate the support.** Don't believe anyone who tries to convince you by saying, "Because I say so." Make sure the author's opinions and generalizations are supported with enough **evidence** to be convincing. Evidence includes **logical appeals,** such as facts, statistics, examples, and expert opinions. Be on the lookout for **emotional appeals.** Emotional appeals can support an argument, but they are not evidence. (For more about logical and emotional appeals, see pages 284–285.) Be sure to distinguish **facts** (statements that can be proved true) from **opinions** (statements that can't be proved).

3. **Look at structure.** When you're analyzing a piece of persuasive writing, it's important to identify the writer's **main ideas** and the order in which they are presented. Are the main ideas convincing? Are they presented in a logical order?

   A good writer carefully orders an argument to be the most persuasive. Readers generally remember the beginning and the end of a piece the most. Therefore, a common way to structure an argument is from least important idea to most important idea—or the reverse. An effective variation on this is to start with the second most important idea and end with the most important one. (Other common ways in which writers structure their arguments are with comparison and contrast and with cause and effect.)

   Also look at **text organizers.** In a printed text, subheads help convey the writer's argument; so do important terms in boldface type. Photos and graphics may add new information—so be sure to read the captions.

4. **Identify the author's intent.** In a persuasive piece the author's **intent** is clearly to persuade you, but of what exactly? Sometimes the writer's goal is just to change your thinking, but often it is a **call to action,** asking you to go

Pages 577–582 cover **Reading Standard 2.8** Evaluate the credibility of an author's argument or defense of a claim by critiquing the relationship between generalizations and evidence, the comprehensiveness of evidence, and the way in which the author's intent affects the structure and tone of the text.

STANDARDS FOCUS, pp. 577–585

(For grade-level and review standards taught in this lesson, see citations on Student Edition pages.)

Prerequisite Standards

- Grade 7, Reading Comprehension 2.6 **Assess the adequacy, accuracy, and appropriateness of the author's evidence to support claims and assertions, noting instances of bias and stereotyping.**
- Grade 8, Reading Comprehension 2.7 **Evaluate the unity, coherence, logic, internal consistency, and structural patterns of text.**

Summary *at grade level*

This magazine article urges Americans to save endangered species. The author first explains why we are losing dozens of species every day: Human beings are crowding wild plants and animals off the planet by destroying their habitats as we develop land for human use.

The author gives reasons for saving endangered species and supports his arguments with evidence. The first reason is based on our own self-interest: Half of all our medications and toiletries, the author asserts, are derived from wild plants and animals.

The author then presents an ethical reason, claiming that human beings do not have the moral right to destroy other species. He acknowledges that protecting wildlife will cost billions of dollars a year, but he argues that the expense is a good investment in the future.

Finally, he issues a call to action, explaining the steps each individual can take to support conservation efforts worldwide. These efforts, he urges, will be an important part of our legacy to future generations.

RESOURCES: READING

Media

- *Audio CD Library*
  - disc 14
- *Interactive Reading,* Teacher's Edition
  - Graphic Organizer: Argument-Evaluation Chart

Differentiating Instruction

- *Lesson Plans for Language Development*
  - English-Language Learners, pp. 267–269, 279, 282
  - Special Education Students, pp. 270, 279, 282

Vocabulary

- *Vocabulary Development*
  - Vocabulary Worksheet, p. 39

PRETEACHING

Standards Starter

Motivate. Bring in copies of your local newspaper's "Letters to the Editor" page. Have students meet in small groups to evaluate the letters dealing with a single issue. Ask them which letter presents the most convincing argument and why they think so. Afterward, have students compare their evaluations in a class discussion. Use the discussion to introduce the terms *reasons, arguments, evidence, fact, opinion, logical appeal, emotional appeal,* and *tone.*

Preview Vocabulary

To reinforce students' understanding of the Vocabulary words on p. 578, have students write or discuss their responses to the following questions. Possible answers are given.

1. Why might animals become extinct if their habitats suffer degradation? [Animals depend on certain types of environments for their food, shelter, and reproduction. If an area decreases, so will the animal population that depends on it.]
2. Do you consider conservation to be an ethical issue? [Yes, preserving natural resources is a moral issue because the survival and living quality of people and other species depend on the environment. To destroy these resources would be morally wrong.]
3. What kinds of impoverishment might result from excess consumerism? [People may go into debt by overusing credit to buy things that they don't really need. People may overuse natural resources to produce luxury consumer goods. People's values may become impoverished by an overemphasis on buying and selling.]
4. Is it a veritable tragedy when people with a terminal illness are bereft of companionship and support? [Yes, it is truly tragic when a dying person lacks companionship and support.]

out and *do* something. Are you being asked to buy a certain product, vote in a certain way, write a letter, send money? Look for a call to action; if you find one, it's an important part of the argument.

5. **Identify the author's tone.** An author's **intent** directly affects a work's **tone,** the writer's attitude toward the subject or audience. Identifying the tone may help you evaluate the credibility of an argument. If the intent is to persuade, the tone might be serious, sincere, concerned, or objective. If a writer uses a highly emotional tone for an argument that is meant to be objective—based on facts—then the argument is not credible. If you are not sure of the author's intent, the tone may clue you in.
6. **Evaluate the author's credentials.** You know by now not to believe everything you read. Before you decide how to respond to the persuasion, evaluate the writer's **credibility.** How knowledgeable is the writer about the subject being discussed? Is the writer an expert and currently working in the field? What are his or her qualifications? Sometimes this information is right there for you to read; sometimes you have to hunt for it.

▶ **For more about persuasive writing, see "Writing a Persuasive Essay," pages 294–301.**

Vocabulary Development

habitats (hab′i·tats′) *n.:* places where plants or animals normally grow or live.

extinct (ek·stiŋkt′) *adj.:* no longer in existence.

impoverishment (im·päv′ər·ish·mənt) *n.:* reducing to poverty or taking away of resources.

degradation (deg′rə·dā′shən) *n.:* decline.

ethical (eth′i·kəl) *adj.:* moral; having to do with goodness or rightness in conduct.

conservation (kän′sər·vā′shən) *n.* used as *adj.:* protection and preservation of natural resources.

bereft (bē·reft′) *adj.:* not having something needed or expected.

consumerism (kən·so͞om′ər·iz′əm) *n.:* buying and using of goods or services.

terminal (tʉr′mə·nəl) *adj.:* of or relating to an end, often an end to life.

veritable (ver′i·tə·bəl) *adj.:* actual; true.

Connecting to the Literature

In "Night Calls" the narrator's father, the warden of a small wildlife preserve, cares for the last of a species of heron. In the next article you'll read about how each of us can help save species from extinction. The danger of extinction is becoming all too common in our modern, industrialized world.

578 Chapter 8 Evaluating Style • Evaluating an Argument

MAGAZINE ARTICLE

Call of the Wild—Save Us!

from *Good Housekeeping*, April 1991

Norman Myers

A garbage-filled swamp near Marseilles, France.

Each day we lose roughly fifty to one hundred wildlife species. They are crowded off the planet by human beings, who are deciding that there isn't enough room on the earth for them and us too. **A**

We don't do it deliberately. We simply destroy their habitats. We chop down their forests, dig up their grasslands, drain their marshes, pollute their rivers and lakes, pave over their other habitats, and generally jump on whatever corners of the earth they have chosen to make their last stand. We certainly don't drive them extinct with malice aforethought.[1] Very few species are eliminated through overhunting and other direct forms of assault. ❶

❶ EVALUATING AN ARGUMENT
According to the writer, why are we losing wildlife species? **B**

1. **malice aforethought:** deliberate intention to do something unlawful.

Vocabulary

habitats (hab′i·tats′) *n.:* places where plants or animals normally grow or live.

extinct (ek·stiŋkt′) *adj.:* no longer in existence.

DIRECT TEACHING

A Reading Informational Materials
GRADE-LEVEL STANDARD

? Evaluating an argument: Facts and opinions. With what alarming fact does the author begin his argument? ["Each day we lose roughly fifty to one hundred wildlife species."]

B Reading Skills

Evaluating an argument.
[Possible response to question 1: We are losing wildlife species because we inadvertently destroy animal habitats as we develop land for our own uses.]

DIFFERENTIATING INSTRUCTION

English-Language Learners

These students may find the article difficult to read because it includes an unusual mixture of abstract language, slang, idioms, and cultural references. Use the Vocabulary list and footnotes to preview abstract concepts discussed in the article. Before students start reading, you might also introduce the following idioms used in the article: *gone for good, carries weight, pay its way, knock them off, get a move on, tread more lightly, get our conservation act together,* and *measured up to the challenge.*

Resources Reminder

For lessons designed for intermediate and advanced English-language learners, see *Lesson Plans for Language Development,* pp. 267–269, 279, 282.

Special Education Students

For lessons designed for special education students, see *Lesson Plans for Language Development,* pp. 270, 279, 282.

DIRECT TEACHING

A English-Language Learners

Interpreting figurative language. Make sure students understand that the phrase "By the time readers of this magazine climb into their rocking chairs" means "by the time readers are elderly." If the author assumes that the average age of his readers is about thirty, then he is referring to forty or fifty years in the future.

B Reading Informational Materials

GRADE-LEVEL STANDARD

? Evaluating an argument: Reason. What reason for preserving wildlife species does the author present in this paragraph? [Many important medicines are derived from wild plants and animals, and more may still be discovered.]

C Reading Skills

Evaluating evidence. [Possible response to question 2: Facts in the paragraph include the statements that there is about "one chance in two" that a drugstore item is derived from wild plants and animals; that the commercial value of such products is $400 million a year; and that the rosy periwinkle of Madagascar is an ingredient in medication for treating Hodgkin's disease, leukemia, and other blood cancers.]

But effectively and increasingly, we are denying living space to thousands of fellow **(A)** species, animals and plants, each year. By the time readers of this magazine climb into their rocking chairs, the total may well become millions, in fact a whopping half of *all* species. This is a holocaust[2]—a rending of the very fabric of life on earth—because mass extinction will impose a longer-lasting impoverishment on the planetary ecosystem[3] than any other environmental problem. All other kinds of environmental degradation are reversible. But when a species is gone, it is gone for good.

We Are All Losers

(B) All too often we shall find that will be "for bad" in terms of our everyday welfare. When we visit our neighborhood drugstore, there is one chance in two that our purchase—an antibiotic, an antiviral, a diuretic, a laxative, an analgesic,[4] or a host of other items—would not be available for us without raw materials from wild plants and animals. The commercial value of all these products worldwide is more than $400 million a year. The rosy periwinkle of Madagascar provided one of the most significant breakthroughs against cancer in recent decades. It has led to the manufacture of two potent therapies against Hodgkin's disease, leukemia, and other blood cancers. Cancer specialists believe there could be at least another ten tropical forest plants with capacity to generate similar superstar drugs against other forms of cancer—provided the scientist can get to them **(C)** before the chainsaw devastates their habitats. ❷

❷ EVALUATING EVIDENCE
What **facts** are stated in this paragraph?

The economic argument in support of species carries weight with politicians and planners. If wildlife can pay its way in the marketplace, they will listen; if not, then they won't. But should we not consider a further

Rosy Periwinkle, a tropical dry-forest plant from Madagascar.

2. **holocaust** *n.:* great or total destruction of life.
3. **ecosystem** *n.:* community of living things and its physical environment.
4. **antibiotic, . . . analgesic:** types of medication. An antibiotic fights infection; an analgesic relieves pain.

Vocabulary

impoverishment (im·päv′ər·ish·mənt) *n.:* reducing to poverty or taking away of resources.

degradation (deg′rə·dā′shən) *n.:* decline.

DIFFERENTIATING INSTRUCTION

Learners Having Difficulty

To help students analyze the argument presented in the article, suggest that they copy the graphic organizer shown on p. 577 before reading, making the boxes big enough to write notes in. Read aloud the first page of the article with students, and help them fill in the top box with a statement of the author's opinion or claim. Then, have students fill in the other boxes as they read on, identifying the reasons that the author presents for his claim and the evidence he gives to support them.

Advanced Learners

Acceleration. Use this activity to move advanced learners toward the eleventh- and twelfth-grade Standard 2.3, for which they verify and clarify facts presented in a text by using a variety of consumer, workplace, and public documents.

Activity. Have students do research on the Internet to verify at least two facts presented in the article. For example, can they confirm, using a reliable source, that the world is losing fifty to one hundred wildlife species per day? Two possible research sources are the Web sites for the World Wildlife Fund and the United Nations.

580 Chapter 8 Evaluating Style • Evaluating an Argument

argument as well—the ethical aspect? What right have we, a single species, to eliminate even a single other species, let alone to knock them off in vast numbers? Shouldn't our fellow passengers on planet Earth, many of them like us, the refined outcome of evolution, enjoy as much right to continued existence as we do? **D**

Therein lies another irony. We are the sole species with the capacity to wantonly[5] snuff out the life of other species—yet we are also the sole species with the capacity to save other creatures. Fortunately, and at long glorious last, we are starting to realize this fundamental truth. The UN is putting together a global treaty to safeguard wildlife. This will mean an effort on the part of nations to preserve wildlife wherever it occurs; in practice it will entail a campaign on the part of the rich nations to finance conservation activities in developing, mainly tropical nations where species are most abundant—and where conservation resources are scarcest. **E**

What Will It Cost?

Probably several billions of dollars a year. But it will be a sound investment. **F** Suppose we save those anticancer plants: That alone would generate health benefits worth several billion annually.

Suppose, moreover, the entire bill were to be picked up by people in the world's rich nations. There are 1.2 billion of us. If the bill were, say, $2.5 billion a year, we would each pay just over $2 per year. For the cost of a beer or a hamburger, we could do it.

A rich-nation couple spends $175,000 to bring up a child from cradle through college. For the sake of a *tiny* additional investment, that child will grow up into a world deprived of millions of wildlife species and bereft of much of what makes the world diverse and interesting, spectacular and special. The question is not "Can we afford to do it eventually?" It is "How can we possibly afford *not* to do it now?" ❸ **G**

> **❸ EVALUATING AN ARGUMENT**
> In the last three paragraphs, where does the writer appeal to **logic**? Where does he appeal to **emotion**?

What You Can Do

I am often asked what individuals can do while waiting for political leaders to get a move on. Lots of specific things. They can support their conservation group of choice, perhaps bearing in mind that the longest established is the World Wildlife Fund (1250 24th Street, N.W., Washington, D.C. 20037). After writing that check, they can write on another piece of paper, one that costs less yet seems to cost more, given the relatively small number of conservationists who do it! They can write to their senator and congressperson, urging support for the legislative initiative in behalf of global wildlife. **H**

More importantly still, they can figure out ways to tread more lightly on the planet, notably by cutting back on excessive forms of consumerism and waste. This helps environments generally and habitats for wildlife specifically. There will ultimately be no healthy place for wildlife except on a planet

Vocabulary

ethical (eth′i·kəl) *adj.:* moral; having to do with goodness or rightness in conduct.

conservation (kän′sər·vā′shən) *n.* used as *adj.:* protection and preservation of natural resources.

bereft (bē·reft′) *adj.:* not having something needed or expected.

consumerism (kən·so͞om′ər·iz′əm) *n.:* buying and using of goods or services.

5. **wantonly** *adv.:* senselessly; in a deliberately cruel way.

DIRECT TEACHING

D Reading Informational Materials

GRADE-LEVEL STANDARD

? Evaluating an argument: Reason. What additional reason for preserving wildlife species does the author present here? [Possible responses: Humans have an ethical responsibility to protect other species; we have no moral right to destroy them.]

E Learners Having Difficulty

Paraphrasing. Help students to paraphrase the ideas in this passage. [Possible response: Rich nations will have to pay the cost for programs to save the wildlife in poorer nations. This is because most endangered species live in tropical areas where money to use for conservation is scarce.]

F English-Language Learners

Multiple-meaning word. Point out that, in this context, the word *sound* means "financially wise or secure."

G Reading Skills

Evaluating an argument. [Possible response to question 3: Appeals to logic include a reference to the financial benefits of saving anti-cancer plants and the calculation that conservation efforts would cost each individual only $2 per year. Appeals to emotion include the loaded words used to describe a world "bereft of much of what makes the world diverse and interesting, spectacular and special" and the urgent final question, "How can we possibly afford *not* to do it now?"]

H Reading Informational Materials

GRADE-LEVEL STANDARD

? Evaluating an argument. Does the article include a call to action? Explain. [Yes, after explaining the problem, the author urges readers to take specific steps to help solve the problem.]

CONTENT-AREA CONNECTIONS

Science: Rainforest Remedies

Many of the plants from which we derive medications are found in tropical rainforests.
Individual activity. Have students research and report on specific medications with ingredients that come from the rainforest and the plants from which these medications are derived. One good starting point for their research is the Web site for the Rainforest Action Network (RAN).

Social Science: Preserving Wetlands

Many American communities witness political battles between conservationists who want to protect shrinking wetland habitats and real-estate developers who oppose restrictions on where they can build.
Individual activity. Have students research both sides of such controversies in their own community.

DIRECT TEACHING

A Content-Area Connections
Culture: Environmental Activism

"Think globally, act locally" is a popular slogan among conservation activists. It encourages individuals to consider the global consequences of their behavior and then to act by making appropriate changes in their own communities that will help make the world a better place for all people.

B Reading Skills
Tone. [Possible response to question 4: The tone might be described as urgent, pleading, and tentatively hopeful.]

C Reading Informational Materials
GRADE-LEVEL STANDARD

Evaluating an author's credentials. What qualifies the author to speak out on environmental issues? [Possible response: He teaches at a university and is an environmental consultant to important organizations such as the United Nations.]

GUIDED PRACTICE

Monitoring students' progress. To check students' comprehension of the article, guide the class in the following activity.

Activity. On the chalkboard, copy the graphic organizer shown on p. 577. Invite volunteers to complete the organizer by identifying the author's claim, the reasons he presents to support the claim, and the evidence he gives to support his reasons.

The Bengal tiger is native to South Asia. It is an endangered species whose numbers decreased dramatically during the twentieth century.

A that is healthy all 'round. So: more recycling, fewer gas-guzzling cars, and all the other "think globally, act locally" measures.

Above all, remember that not only our children will look back upon this time of gathering shadows for the wildlife world. Their children and thousands of generations into the future will wonder why more was not done to tackle the terminal threat to wildlife. Alternatively, if we get our conservation act together, our successors will marvel at how we measured up to the challenge and how we saved species in their veritable millions. We still have time, though only *just* time. Those species out there—they are waiting to hear from us. **B** 4

C *Norman Myers is a university lecturer, an author, and an environmental consultant to many organizations, including the United Nations.*

4 TONE How would you describe the **tone** of the last paragraph?

Vocabulary

terminal (tʉr′mə·nəl) *adj.:* of or relating to an end, often an end to life.

veritable (ver′i·tə·bəl) *adj.:* actual; true.

582 Chapter 8 Evaluating Style • Evaluating an Argument

FAMILY/COMMUNITY ACTIVITY

Encourage students to find specific actions that they and their families can take to "think globally, act locally." These might include organizing family or community recycling efforts, protecting endangered habitats in the community, reducing consumption of products with wasteful packaging, joining environmental organizations, or writing to their representatives in Congress about environmental issues. Specific suggestions for citizen action can be found at the Web site for the National Wildlife Federation.

Analyzing Informational Materials

Reading Check

1. According to the author, how are we losing fifty to one hundred species of wildlife a day?
2. Why does the author mention the rosy periwinkle of Madagascar?
3. What three things does the author say that individuals can do to help solve the problem of endangered species?

Test Practice

1. The **opinion** or **claim** expressed in this article is that something must be done now to —
   - A bring back extinct species
   - B prevent more species from becoming extinct
   - C increase the number of species
   - D stop the destruction of rain forests

2. The *first* **reason** the writer gives to support his opinion is that —
   - F politicians and planners don't care
   - G tropical nations are already preserving wildlife
   - H rich nations have a moral duty to provide aid
   - J wild plants and animals are the source of medications

3. The *second* **reason** the writer gives to support his opinion is that —
   - A humans have an ethical obligation to preserve other species
   - B the United Nations has ignored the problem
   - C every nation is already doing its best
   - D the United States is funding the efforts of tropical nations

4. Next, the writer considers how to cope with the —
   - F politicians' objections
   - G public's lack of interest
   - H cost of conservation efforts
   - J worldwide economic problems

5. Under which heading is the **call-to-action** section found?
   - A "We Are All Losers"
   - B "What Will It Cost"
   - C "What You Can Do"
   - D "Call of the Wild—Save Us!"

6. Which of these sentences expresses an **opinion**?
   - F "Each day we lose roughly fifty to one hundred wildlife species."
   - G "What right have we, a single species, to eliminate even a single other species . . . ?"
   - H "The UN is putting together a global treaty to safeguard wildlife."
   - J "There are 1.2 billion of us."

(*continued*)

Reading Standard 2.8 Evaluate the credibility of an author's argument or defense of a claim by critiquing the relationship between generalizations and evidence, the comprehensiveness of evidence, and the way in which the author's intent affects the structure and tone of the text.

Reading Check

1. By developing formerly wild land for human use, we are destroying the habitats that wildlife need to survive.
2. It is an example that supports his claim that rare tropical plants can be the source of lifesaving medications and must be saved.
3. He says that individuals should give money to conservation organizations, write to their representatives in Congress about environmental issues, and cut back on their own consumption and waste.

INDEPENDENT PRACTICE

Analyzing Informational Materials

Test Practice

Answers and Model Rationales

1. **B** The author claims that we must "preserve wildlife wherever it occurs." A is wrong because "when a species is gone, it is gone for good"; C is wrong because he does not discuss increasing the number of species; D is wrong because the rainforest is one of many habitats that must be preserved.
2. **J** J is discussed in the first paragraph of "We Are All Losers." The author claims that politicians and planners *do* care about the economic costs of losing species (F). He says that most tropical nations are too poor to spend on conservation (G). H is the author's *second* reason.
3. **A** A is stated in the second paragraph of "We Are All Losers." The author states that the United Nations is preparing a treaty to safeguard wildlife (B). He states that rich nations need to do more (C). He asks rich nations such as the United States to fund efforts in tropical nations (D).
4. **H** This issue, "What Will It Cost?" is the only one discussed.
5. **C** Suggestions are given under the subhead "What You Can Do." The need for action is only implied elsewhere.
6. **G** An opinion is a judgment or feeling that cannot be proved. No one can prove whether we have the right to eliminate other species. F, H, and J are verifiable facts.

Call of the Wild—Save Us! 583

7. D Only D states information that can be proved true. A, B, and C are all opinions, statements of the author's feelings or judgments about the issue. They cannot be proved.

8. J The author is clearly concerned about what he considers to be an urgent problem. Some students may choose H, but it is not the best answer because the article combines emotional appeals with many logical appeals and statements of fact. F and G are wrong because the author is very serious about the problem and does not dwell on contrasts between expectations and reality.

9. D According to the biographical information at the end of the article, the author teaches at a university and is an environmental consultant to many organizations, including the United Nations, so he is clearly an expert on the topic. Some students may feel that the author is biased, but important organizations would not hire a consultant who was biased, so A is incorrect. The author clearly has more credentials than the average citizen, so B is wrong. The author may well be sincere and honest, but these qualities in themselves do not make him credible, so C is wrong.

Test-Taking Tips

Urge students to make certain that they understand the questions before they choose an answer. Suggest that they read each question slowly and pay particular attention to any words that are in italics.

For more information on how to answer multiple-choice questions, refer students to **Test Smarts.**

Analyzing Informational Materials

7. Which of the following states a **fact**?
   - **A** "But should we not consider a further argument as well—the ethical aspect?"
   - **B** "Those species out there—they are waiting to hear from us."
   - **C** "Alternatively, if we get our conservation act together, our successors will marvel at how we measured up to the challenge. . . ."
   - **D** "The commercial value of all these products worldwide is more than $400 million a year."

8. The **tone** of this article is *best* described as —
   - **F** humorous
   - **G** ironic
   - **H** highly emotional
   - **J** concerned

9. How **credible** is the writer, according to the information given about him at the end of the article?
   - **A** Not very, because he is biased
   - **B** Not very, because he is an ordinary citizen
   - **C** Very, because he sincerely believes his opinions and is honest
   - **D** Very, because he is an expert on the topic

Application

Analyze *either* Myers's essay or another short piece of persuasive writing (an editorial, a letter to the editor, or a newspaper or magazine column) about a specific issue.

First, outline the writer's **argument** in a graphic like the one on the right. Then, evaluate how **credible,** or convincing, you find the argument. Do you find enough **evidence** and support for the writer's opinion or claim? How do the **structure** and **tone** of the text contribute to its effectiveness?

Writer's opinion or claim:
Reason 1:
Supporting evidence:
Supporting evidence:
Reason 2:
Supporting evidence:
Supporting evidence:
Structure:
Tone:

584 Chapter 8 Evaluating Style • Evaluating an Argument

Vocabulary Development

Using Contexts

PRACTICE 1

Use **context clues** in the following sentences to help you choose the correct Word Bank word for each blank.

Word Bank
habitats
extinct
impoverishment
degradation
ethical
conservation
bereft
consumerism
terminal
veritable

1. There are no dinosaurs today since they are _______.
2. He was concerned about the _______ of standards and values.
3. Her illness had grown severe and was now in a _______ stage.
4. Both law and religion deal with _______ questions and issues.
5. The charity was completely _______ of needed funds.
6. The _______ of many animals can be found in the rain forest.
7. Some critics feel too much _______ is highly wasteful.
8. The drought had turned the countryside into a _______ desert.
9. The careful _______ of resources is vital for our economy.
10. The economic decline has caused _______ of workers.

Literal and Figurative Use of Words

When you use a word or phrase **literally,** you mean it to be understood in its literal sense, the way the word or words are defined in a dictionary. Sometimes, though, you use words **figuratively**—you don't *really* mean what you say. You expect that the reader or listener will understand that you are using some quality or aspect of the word or phrase to express an idea more colorfully or to create an original image.

> "By the time readers of this magazine climb into their rocking chairs, the total may well become millions, in fact a whopping half of *all* species."

Does the writer mean that the readers of the magazine will literally climb into rocking chairs, or is he using this phrase figuratively, to mean "reach old age"?

PRACTICE 2

Rewrite each sentence from the selection, translating the underlined **figurative** expressions into **literal** ones.

1. "We chop down their forests, dig up their grasslands, . . . and generally jump on whatever corners of the earth they have chosen to make their last stand."
2. "This is a holocaust—a rending of the very fabric of life on earth. . . ."
3. "If wildlife can pay its way in the marketplace, they will listen. . . ."
4. "Above all, remember that not only our children will look back upon this time of gathering shadows for the wildlife world."

Grade 8 Review Reading Standard 1.3 Use word meanings within the appropriate context.

Reading Standard 1.1 Identify and use the literal and figurative meanings of words.

Vocabulary Development

Practice 1

1. extinct
2. degradation
3. terminal
4. ethical
5. bereft
6. habitats
7. consumerism
8. veritable
9. conservation
10. impoverishment

Practice 2

Possible Answers

1. "We chop down their forests, dig up their grasslands, . . . and generally take over whatever geographic areas they have chosen to make their last stand."
2. "This is a holocaust—a destruction of the complex interdependency of life on earth. . . ."
3. "If wildlife can bring economic benefits to society, they will listen. . . ."
4. "Above all, remember that not only our children will look back upon this increasingly dangerous time for the wildlife world."

Resources Reminder

Vocabulary

- *Vocabulary Development*
  - Vocabulary Worksheet, p. 39
- *Lesson Plans for Language Development*
  - Vocabulary, pp. 279, 282

ASSESSING

Assessment

- *Progress Assessment of Reading*
  - Selection Test

RETEACHING

For a lesson reteaching evaluating an author's argument, see **Reteaching,** p. 939A. For another selection to teach Standard 2.8, see *Interactive Reading,* Part 2.

Call of the Wild—Save Us! **585**

STANDARDS FOCUS, pp. 586–600

(For grade-level and review standards taught in this lesson, see citations on Student Edition pages.)

Prerequisite Standard

- Grade 8, Literary Response and Analysis 3.6 **Identify significant literary devices (e.g., metaphor, symbolism, dialect, irony) that define a writer's style and use those elements to interpret the work.**

Reading Skills

- Appreciate a writer's style.

Summary *above grade level*

One night when Pelayo and Elisenda's baby is very ill, they discover an elderly, dirty, pitiful winged man in their courtyard. Because of his dialect and "sailor's voice," they guess he is a castaway, but a neighbor claims he is an angel sent for the child. The couple locks the man in a chicken coop, the child recovers, the villagers come to gawk at and torment the creature, and the priest begins an interminable investigation into his angelic authenticity. Meanwhile, Pelayo and Elisenda become rich by charging admission to see the angel. Although bizarre miracles occur, the angel eventually loses his audience to a traveling spider woman. The angel, now a nuisance, roams through Pelayo and Elisenda's new house. Soon the couple discovers that the angel is ill, but his health improves as winter comes to an end. Recovered, he begins to grow new feathers and to sing sea chanteys. One day, while Elisenda watches from her kitchen window, the old angel flaps awkwardly away.

Before You Read

A Very Old Man with Enormous Wings

Literary Focus

Magic Realism

Like many contemporary South American writers, García Márquez writes a kind of fiction called **magic realism.** This **style** of writing is characterized by elements of fantasy (often borrowed from mythology) that are casually inserted into the most earthy, realistic settings. The magic realists often suspend the laws of nature. In using this bizarre mixture of the commonplace and the outlandish, the magic realists can force us to think about our fixed notions of "reality" and "normality." This blurring of fantasy and reality is often an important part of the **themes,** or main ideas about life, that the magic realists want to convey.

Reading Skills

Appreciating a Writer's Style

One of the great pleasures of reading is appreciating a writer's style—especially the writer's choice of words and images that help create a work's **tone, mood,** and theme. As you read this story by García Márquez, notice the way he tosses together the offbeat, the commonplace, and the sublime into that strange mix known as **magic realism.**

Notice, too, his unusual, even startling combinations of **images,** and be aware of the things they help you to see. Try to decide why some of his images seem funny, some sad, and some—appropriately enough—magical.

Reading Standard 3.11 Evaluate the aesthetic qualities of style, including the impact of diction on tone, mood, and theme, using the terminology of literary criticism. (Aesthetic approach)

Make the Connection

Quickwrite

Brainstorm a list of characters from myth and legend who have wings. What happens to each of those characters? Then, brainstorm a list of modern stories or movies in which an alien visits the ordinary world on earth. What usually happens to those strangers visiting a strange land?

Vocabulary Development

stench (stench) *n.:* offensive smell.

impeded (im·pēd′id) *v.* used as *adj.:* held back or blocked, as by an obstacle.

magnanimous (mag·nan′ə·məs) *adj.:* generous; noble.

reverence (rev′ə·rəns) *n.:* attitude or display of deep respect and awe.

frivolous (friv′ə·ləs) *adj.:* not properly serious; silly. *Frivolous* also means "trivial; of little value or importance."

impertinences (im·purt′'n·ən·siz) *n.:* insults; disrespectful acts or remarks.

ingenuous (in·jen′yo͞o·əs) *adj.:* too trusting; tending to believe too readily.

prudence (pro͞o′dəns) *n.:* cautiousness; sound judgment.

cataclysm (kat′ə·kliz′əm) *n.:* disaster; sudden, violent event.

providential (präv′ə·den′shəl) *adj.:* fortunate; like something caused by a divine act.

affliction (ə·flik′shən) *n.:* suffering; distress.

lament (lə·ment′) *v.:* feel very sorry.

RESOURCES: READING

Planning

- *One-Stop Planner* CD-ROM with Test Generator
- *On Course: Mapping Instruction*

Reading

- *Interactive Reading,* Teacher's Edition
  - Graphic Organizer: Style Chart

Differentiating Instruction

- *Lesson Plans for Language Development*
  - English-Language Learners, pp. 271–273, 280, 282
  - Special Education Students, pp. 274, 280, 282

A flesh-and-blood angel was held captive in Pelayo's house.

A Very Old Man with Enormous WINGS

A Tale for Children

Gabriel García Márquez
translated by Gregory Rabassa

On the third day of rain they had killed so many crabs inside the house that Pelayo had to

Vocabulary

- *Vocabulary Development*
  - Vocabulary Worksheet, p. 40

Assessment

- *Progress Assessment of Reading*
  - Selection Test
- *One-Stop Planner* CD-ROM with Test Generator

PRETEACHING

Selection Starter

Build background. "A Very Old Man with Enormous Wings" was published with six other stories in a book called *The Incredible and Sad Story of Innocent Eréndira and Her Heartless Grandmother.* In this story collection, García Márquez seems to be responding to his still-new celebrity status. This story about the old man and other stories in the volume hint at his discomfort with fame. All the stories deal with public figures, and some, like the old angel in this story, would prefer to escape that public exposure.

Preview Vocabulary

Have student pairs review the Vocabulary words on p. 586 and write two possible answers for each of the following questions.

1. What would you do if a millionaire became magnanimous toward you?
2. How would an ingenuous person fare in a bargaining situation?
3. What providential things do you wish for?
4. What might cause a stench in a vacant lot?
5. What would happen if you didn't use prudence in budgeting your money?
6. What kinds of events might you lament?
7. How could you be impeded by wings?
8. What could happen if your senator was frivolous?
9. What might happen if parents ignored their children's impertinences?
10. What affliction might keep a person from competing in a race?
11. What kind of cataclysm might occur in your town?
12. What would happen if reverence for tradition were abandoned?

DIRECT TEACHING

A Literary Focus
GRADE-LEVEL STANDARD

? Magic realism. What elements of magic realism do you find in this paragraph? [Possible response: Up to the final phrase, the paragraph describes common people and events in an ordinary place, using everyday speech. Into this setting, a fantastic element, the wings, is casually introduced.]

B Vocabulary Development
GRADE-LEVEL STANDARD

Understanding word derivations. Point out the word *fugitive.* Tell students that the word comes from the Latin root word *fugere,* meaning "to flee." Discuss how knowledge of the root, along with context clues, can help them determine that *fugitive* means "fleeing" or "vagabond." Then, ask students to identify other words that are related to the root word *fugere.* [Possible responses: refugee, refuge, centrifugal.]

C Reading Skills

? Appreciating a writer's style. How does this description make you feel about the angel? [Possible responses: sorry, sympathetic, sad.] How does the writer evoke this response? [He places the angel in a degrading situation, which contrasts with the pure, clean, ethereal conditions in which we expect to find an angel.]

---

cross his drenched courtyard and throw them into the sea, because the newborn child had a temperature all night and they thought it was due to the stench. The world had been sad since Tuesday. Sea and sky were a single ash-gray thing, and the sands of the beach, which on March nights glimmered like powdered light, had become a stew of mud and rotten shellfish. The light was so weak at noon that when Pelayo was coming back to the house after throwing away the crabs, it was hard for him to see what it was that was moving and groaning in the rear of the courtyard. He had to go very close to see that it was an old man, a very old man, lying face down in the mud, who, in spite of his tremendous efforts, couldn't get up, impeded by his enormous wings. **A**

Frightened by that nightmare, Pelayo ran to get Elisenda, his wife, who was putting compresses on the sick child, and he took her to the rear of the courtyard. They both looked at the fallen body with mute stupor.[1] He was dressed like a ragpicker. There were only a few faded hairs left on his bald skull and very few teeth in his mouth, and his pitiful condition of a drenched great-grandfather had taken away any sense of grandeur he might have had. His huge buzzard wings, dirty and half plucked, were forever entangled in the mud. They looked at him so long and so closely that Pelayo and Elisenda very soon overcame their surprise and in the end found him familiar. Then they dared speak to him, and he answered in an incomprehensible dialect with a strong sailor's voice. That was how they skipped over the inconvenience of the wings and quite intelligently concluded that he was a lonely castaway from some foreign ship wrecked by the storm. And yet, they called in a neighbor woman who knew everything about life and death to see him, and all she needed was one look to show them their mistake.

"He's an angel," she told them. "He must have been coming for the child, but the poor fellow is so old that the rain knocked him down."

On the following day everyone knew that a flesh-and-blood angel was held captive in Pelayo's house. Against the judgment of the wise neighbor woman, for whom angels in those **B** times were the fugitive survivors of a celestial conspiracy,[2] they did not have the heart to club him to death. Pelayo watched over him all afternoon from the kitchen, armed with his bailiff's[3] club, and before going to bed, he dragged him out of the mud and locked him up with the hens in the wire chicken coop. In the middle of the night, when the rain stopped, Pelayo and Elisenda were still killing crabs. A short time afterward the child woke up without a fever and with a desire to eat. Then they felt magnanimous and decided to put the angel on a raft with fresh water and provisions for three days and leave him to his fate on the high seas. But when they went out into the courtyard with the first light of dawn, they found the whole neighborhood in front of the chicken coop having fun with the angel, without the slightest reverence, tossing him things to eat through the openings in the wire as if he weren't a supernatural creature but a circus animal. **C**

1. **stupor** (sto͞o′pər) *n.:* dullness of the mind and senses.

2. **celestial conspiracy:** According to the Book of Revelation in the Bible (12:7–9), Satan originally was an angel who led a rebellion in Heaven. As a result, he and his followers, called the fallen angels, were cast out of Heaven.

3. **bailiff's:** A bailiff is a minor local official.

Vocabulary

stench (stench) *n.:* offensive smell.

impeded (im·pēd′id) *v.* used as *adj.:* held back or blocked, as by an obstacle.

magnanimous (mag·nan′ə·məs) *adj.:* generous; noble.

reverence (rev′ə·rəns) *n.:* attitude or display of deep respect and awe.

DIFFERENTIATING INSTRUCTION

Learners Having Difficulty

Modeling. To help students read "A Very Old Man with Enormous Wings," model the reading skill of appreciating the writer's style. Say: "When García Márquez writes 'Sea and sky were a single ash-gray thing, and the sands of the beach . . . had become a stew of mud and rotten shellfish,' he creates a dark mood by crafting startling images that help me see and smell an unpleasant scene." Encourage students as they read to ask themselves, "What is the mood or tone at this point in the story, and how has the writer created it?"

Resources Reminder

Reading

- *Interactive Reading,* Teacher's Edition
  - Graphic Organizer: Style Chart

English-Language Learners

For students to grasp the irony of the story, they will need to understand how the old man with wings completely contradicts the conventional images of angels in Western literature and art. You might bring in reproductions of paintings (by Renaissance Italian painters, for example) and even discuss the role of angels in modern-day television shows and movies.

588 Chapter 8 Evaluating Style • Evaluating an Argument

Father Gonzaga arrived before seven o'clock, alarmed at the strange news. By that time onlookers less frivolous than those at dawn had already arrived and they were making all kinds of conjectures[4] concerning the captive's future. The simplest among them thought that he should be named mayor of the world. Others of sterner mind felt that he should be promoted to the rank of five-star general in order to win all wars. Some visionaries hoped that he could be put to stud in order to implant on earth a race of winged wise men who could take charge of the universe. But Father Gonzaga, before becoming a priest, had been a robust woodcutter. Standing by the wire, he reviewed his catechism[5] in an instant and asked them to open the door so that he could take a close look at that pitiful man who looked more like a huge decrepit hen among the fascinated chickens. He was lying in a corner drying his open wings in the sunlight among the fruit peels and breakfast leftovers that the early risers had thrown him. Alien to the impertinences of the world, he only lifted his antiquarian[6] eyes and murmured something in his dialect when Father Gonzaga went into the chicken coop and said good morning to him in Latin. The parish priest had his first suspicion of an impostor when he saw that he did not

4. **conjectures** (kən·jek′chərz) *n.:* guesses not completely supported by evidence.
5. **catechism** (kat′ə·kiz′əm) *n.:* book of religious principles consisting of a series of questions and answers.

6. **antiquarian** (an′ti·kwer′ē·ən) *adj.:* ancient.

Vocabulary

frivolous (friv′ə·ləs) *adj.:* not properly serious; silly. *Frivolous* also means "trivial; of little value or importance."

impertinences (im·purt′'n·ən·siz) *n.:* insults; disrespectful acts or remarks.

DIRECT TEACHING

D Reading Skills

Making inferences. What do these details reveal about the people's expectations of angels? [Possible responses: They expect angels to be strong, powerful, and wise; they expect angels to help them in some way.]

E Reading Skills

Appreciating a writer's style. What is the effect of this image of the winged man in the chicken coop? [Possible responses: The image is surprising, funny, disgusting, and deflating; the image contradicts the expectations of viewers who predict great things from the angel.]

Resources Reminder

For lessons designed for intermediate and advanced English-language learners, see *Lesson Plans for Language Development,* pp. 271–273, 280, 282.

Special Education Students

For lessons designed for special education students, see *Lesson Plans for Language Development,* pp. 274, 280, 282.

Advanced Learners

Enrichment. As students read, ask them to think about how the photographs connect to the story. How do the images by themselves suggest magic realism? What could be the photographer's purpose in combining reality and fantasy? How does this purpose compare with the writer's purpose in doing the same?

A Very Old Man with Enormous Wings 589

VIEWING THE ART

Clint Clemens traveled to Mexico to take photographs of **Sergio Bustamante**'s fantastic sculptures for a book collaboration. Be sure students notice how Bustamante has combined disparate elements to create unexpected forms.

Sergio Bustamante was born in Mexico and has lived for many years in Guadalajara. He was trained as an architect but found the profession too restricting. He started making sculptures from papier-mâché, and later he began working in bronze and ceramic. His sculptures mix human and animal forms.

Activity. Discuss similarities between the artwork and the story in their mixing of earthy realistic elements with outlandish fantasy. [Just as one would not expect to see fingers with faces or people riding a fish in real life, one would also be caught off guard by a man with wings.]

The artwork displayed throughout the story can inspire students to do some writing of their own. You might suggest that they write a fairy tale or myth based on any of the photos of Bustamante's work that accompany this selection.

DIFFERENTIATING INSTRUCTION

Advanced Learners

Enrichment. Invite students to view artworks by several twentieth-century Mexican artists who incorporate elements of magic realism in their work. Students might select works by Mario Martín del Campo, Rodolfo Morales, Frieda Kahlo, and others they discover through research. Encourage students to identify examples of magic and realism juxtaposed in the artworks. Then, have small groups discuss cultural influences that might lead to an emphasis on magic realism in works by certain Latin American visual artists and writers during the modern period.

understand the language of God or know how to greet His ministers. Then he noticed that seen close up, he was much too human: He had an unbearable smell of the outdoors, the back side of his wings was strewn with parasites[7] and his main feathers had been mistreated by terrestrial[8] winds, and nothing about him measured up to the proud dignity of angels. Then he came out of the chicken coop and in a brief sermon warned the curious against the risks of being ingenuous. He reminded them that the devil had the bad habit of making use of carnival tricks in order to confuse the unwary. He argued that if wings were not the essential element in determining the difference between a hawk and an airplane, they were even less so in the recognition of angels. Nevertheless, he promised to write a letter to his bishop so that the latter would write to his primate[9] so that the latter would write to the Supreme Pontiff[10] in order to get the final verdict from the highest courts.

His prudence fell on sterile hearts. The news of the captive angel spread with such rapidity that after a few hours the courtyard had the bustle of a marketplace, and they had to call in troops with fixed bayonets to disperse the mob that was about to knock the house down. Elisenda, her spine all twisted from sweeping up so much marketplace trash, then got the idea of fencing in the yard and charging five cents admission to see the angel.

The curious came from far away. A traveling carnival arrived with a flying acrobat, who buzzed over the crowd several times, but no one paid any attention to him because his wings were not those of an angel but, rather, those of a sidereal[11] bat. The most unfortunate invalids on earth came in search of health: a poor woman who since childhood had been counting her heartbeats and had run out of numbers; a Portuguese man who couldn't sleep because the noise of the stars disturbed him; a sleepwalker who got up at night to undo the things he had done while awake; and many others with less serious ailments. In the midst of that shipwreck disorder that made the earth tremble, Pelayo and Elisenda were happy with fatigue, for in less than a week they had crammed their rooms with money and the line of pilgrims waiting their turn to enter still reached beyond the horizon.

The angel was the only one who took no part in his own act. He spent his time trying to get comfortable in his borrowed nest, befuddled by the hellish heat of the oil lamps and sacramental candles that had been placed along the wire. At first they tried to make him eat some mothballs, which, according to the wisdom of the wise neighbor woman, were the food prescribed for angels. But he turned them down, just as he turned down the papal[12] lunches that the penitents brought him, and they never found out whether it was because he was an angel or because he was an old man that in the end he ate nothing but eggplant mush. His only supernatural virtue seemed to be patience. Especially during the first days, when the hens pecked at him, searching for stellar parasites that proliferated[13] in his wings, and the cripples pulled out feathers to touch their defective parts

7. **parasites** *n.:* plants or animals that live on or in other living things, on which they feed.
8. **terrestrial** *adj.:* earthly.
9. **primate** (prī′mit) *n.:* archbishop or highest-ranking bishop in an area.
10. **Supreme Pontiff:** pope, head of the Roman Catholic Church.

11. **sidereal** (sī·dir′ē·əl) *adj.:* of the stars.
12. **papal** (pā′pəl) *adj.:* here, fit for the pope.
13. **proliferated** (prō·lif′ə·rāt′id) *v.:* quickly increased in number.

Vocabulary

ingenuous (in·jen′yo͞o·əs) *adj.:* too trusting; tending to believe too readily.

prudence (pro͞o′dəns) *n.:* cautiousness; sound judgment.

CONTENT-AREA CONNECTIONS

Science: Wings

Point out to students Father Gonzaga's argument that wings are not the essential element in determining the difference between hawks and airplanes.

Small-group activity. Have small groups of students research and discuss similarities and differences between bird wings and airplane wings. Invite volunteers to share what they have learned with the class.

Culture: Carnivals

Sideshows were a regular feature of traveling carnivals and circuses. They included such acts as sword swallowers, fire eaters, and individuals, like the spider woman, whose physical conditions made them curiosities.

DIRECT TEACHING

A Literary Focus
GRADE-LEVEL STANDARD

Magic realism. What senses are appealed to in this description of the angel? [sound, smell, sight] What details that are not normally linked are placed together in these images? [angel "wings" that are "strewn with parasites"]

B Vocabulary Development
GRADE-LEVEL STANDARD

Understanding word derivations. Point out the word *verdict,* which means "the finding of a jury." Explain that *verdict* shares the Latin root word *dicere,* meaning "to say," with other words such as *predict, dictate, contradict,* and *diction.* Discuss the meaning of each of these words, focusing on the connection to the Latin root word.

C Literary Focus
REVIEW STANDARD

Irony. What is ironic about this scene? [Possible responses: Angels are spiritual beings, but the scene has "the bustle of a marketplace." Angels are believed to be spiritual, peaceful, and kindly, inspiring the reverse of mob violence and military force.]

D Reading Skills

Expressing an opinion. What do you think of Elisenda's decision? [Possible responses: She has worked hard and deserves the money. It is cruel to put the man on display. Elisenda is merely an entrepreneur with an opportunity.]

E Literary Focus
GRADE-LEVEL STANDARD

Magic realism. What elements of magic realism do you find here? [Possible responses: the fact that an angel makes a nest; the notion that angels eat mothballs; the casual acceptance of all this as being real.]

Direct Teaching

A Literary Focus
REVIEW STANDARD

Character. What can you conclude about the angel's disposition? [Possible responses: He is not angry or dangerous, but uninterested in the crowds and their petty curiosity. He feels physical pain when the crowd brands him. He weeps. He is patient.]

B Reading Skills

Appreciating a writer's style. In a few words, García Márquez characterizes the angel by using an interesting oxymoron. What would a "cataclysm in repose" be like? [Possible response: dangerous, powerful, like a sleeping volcano.]

C Content-Area Connections

Culture: Angels

These matters are being investigated to determine if the stranger is an angel. A navel indicates that a person was born from a mother. In medieval times, theologians debated how many angels would fit on the head of a pin. Finally, there is a down-to-earth suggestion (maybe he's "just a Norwegian with wings"). García Márquez is satirizing heated theological disputes of past eras.

with, and even the most merciful threw stones at him, trying to get him to rise so they could see him standing. The only time they succeeded in arousing him was when they burned his side with an iron for branding steers, for he had been motionless for so many hours that they thought he was dead. He awoke with a start, ranting in his hermetic[14] language and with tears in his eyes, and he flapped his wings a couple of times, which brought on a whirlwind of chicken dung and lunar dust and a gale of panic that did not seem to be of this world. Although many thought that his reaction had been one not of rage but of pain, from then on they were careful not to annoy him, because the majority understood that his passivity was not that of a hero taking his ease but that of a cataclysm in repose.

Father Gonzaga held back the crowd's frivolity with formulas of maidservant inspiration while awaiting the arrival of a final judgment on the nature of the captive. But the mail from Rome showed no sense of urgency. They spent their time finding out if the prisoner had a navel, if his dialect had any connection with Aramaic,[15] how many times he could fit on the head of a pin, or whether he wasn't just a Norwegian with wings. Those meager letters might have come and gone until the end of time if a providential event had not put an end to the priest's tribulations.[16]

It so happened that during those days, among so many other carnival attractions, there arrived in town the traveling show of the woman who had been changed into a spider for having disobeyed her parents. The admission to see her was not only less than the admission to see the angel, but people were permitted to ask her all manner of questions about her absurd state and to examine her up and down so that no one would ever doubt the truth of her horror. She was a frightful tarantula the size of a ram and with the head of a sad maiden. What was most heart-rending, however, was not her outlandish shape but the sincere affliction with which she

14. **hermetic** *adj.:* difficult to understand; mysterious.
15. **Aramaic** (ar′ə·mā′ik) *n.:* ancient Middle Eastern language spoken by Jesus and his disciples.
16. **tribulations** (trib′yə·lā′shənz) *n.:* conditions of great unhappiness, such as oppression causes.

Vocabulary

cataclysm (kat′ə·kliz′əm) *n.:* disaster; sudden, violent event.

providential (präv′ə·den′shəl) *adj.:* fortunate; like something caused by a divine act.

affliction (ə·flik′shən) *n.:* suffering; distress.

Developing Fluency

Remind students that this story is subtitled "A Tale for Children." Point out that, like most children's stories, this one might best be appreciated when read aloud.

Mixed-ability group activity. Arrange students into mixed-ability groups. Have them divide the story into approximately equal parts, one part for each group member. Then, invite group members to take turns reading their parts of the story aloud. Encourage students to read slowly, clearly, and expressively.

recounted the details of her misfortune. While still practically a child, she had sneaked out of her parents' house to go to a dance, and while she was coming back through the woods after having danced all night without permission, a fearful thunderclap rent the sky in two and through the crack came the lightning bolt of brimstone[17] that changed her into a spider. Her only nourishment came from the meatballs that charitable souls chose to toss into her mouth. A spectacle like that, full of so much human truth and with such a fearful lesson, was bound to defeat without even trying that of a haughty angel who scarcely deigned to look at mortals. Besides, the few miracles attributed to the angel showed a certain mental disorder, like the blind man who didn't recover his sight but grew three new teeth, or the paralytic who didn't get to walk but almost won the lottery, or the leper whose sores sprouted sunflowers. Those consolation miracles, which were more like mocking fun,

17. **brimstone** *n.:* sulfur, a pale-yellow element that burns with a blue flame and a suffocating odor.

Direct Teaching

D Literary Focus
GRADE-LEVEL STANDARD

Imagery. What senses are appealed to in this description? [sight (lightning), sound (thunderclap), smell (brimstone), taste (meatballs)]

E Reading Skills

Analyzing. What is unusual about these miracles? [Possible responses: They are incongruent with the ailments. They are unexpected. While bizarre and even cruel, they are also comical.]

Content-Area Connections

Literature: A Pair of Stories

"A Very Old Man with Enormous Wings" appears in a book of short stories called *The Incredible and Sad Story of Innocent Eréndira and Her Heartless Grandmother,* in which it is paired with "The Handsomest Drowned Man in the World." Each story is subtitled "A Tale for Children."

Small-group activity. Have students find "The Handsomest Drowned Man in the World" in a library. (This story is also included in a collection titled *Leaf Storm and Other Stories.*) After students read the story, have them hold a panel discussion to compare it with the story about the angel. Ask students to give reasons why each of these stories might be subtitled "A Tale for Children."

A Very Old Man with Enormous Wings **593**

DIRECT TEACHING

A Literary Focus
REVIEW STANDARD

Character. How would you characterize Pelayo and Elisenda, based on their actions since the old man's arrival? [Possible response: They are hardworking, practical, self-centered people who take advantage of a chance to make money. They are ungrateful to the angel, who makes them rich, and cruel to force him to live in a dung heap.]

B Literary Focus
GRADE-LEVEL STANDARD

Magic realism. How do the doctor's findings challenge us to rethink our fixed ideas about reality? [Possible response: The doctor, presumably a man of science, finds the wings perfectly natural and wonders why everyone doesn't have them.]

C English-Language Learners

Idioms. Tell students that *here and there* is an idiom meaning "to various places."

D Literary Focus
GRADE-LEVEL STANDARD

Paradox. Notice the paradox here—angels are usually assumed to be immortal. Elisenda and Pelayo are not upset by the thought of the old man dying; they just don't know what to do with deceased angels.

had already ruined the angel's reputation when the woman who had been changed into a spider finally crushed him completely. That was how Father Gonzaga was cured forever of his insomnia and Pelayo's courtyard went back to being as empty as during the time it had rained for three days and crabs walked through the bedrooms.

The owners of the house had no reason to lament. With the money they saved they built a two-story mansion with balconies and gardens and high netting so that crabs wouldn't get in during the winter, and with iron bars on the windows so that angels wouldn't get in. Pelayo also set up a rabbit warren close to town and gave up his job as bailiff for good, and Elisenda bought some satin pumps with high heels and many dresses of iridescent silk, the kind worn on Sunday by the most desirable women in those times. The chicken coop was the only thing that didn't receive any attention. If they washed it down with creolin and burned tears of myrrh[18] inside it every so often, it was not in homage[19] to the angel but to drive away the dung-heap stench that still hung everywhere like a ghost and was turning the new house into an old one. At first, when the child learned to walk, they were careful that he not get too close to the chicken coop. But then they began to lose their fears and got used to the smell, and before the child got his second teeth, he'd gone inside the chicken coop to play, where the wires were falling apart. The angel was no less standoffish with him than with other mortals, but he tolerated the most ingenious infamies[20] with the patience of a dog who had no illusions. They both came down with chickenpox at the same time. The doctor who took care of the child couldn't resist the temptation to listen to the angel's heart, and he found so much whistling in the heart and so many sounds in his kidneys that it seemed impossible for him to be alive. What surprised him most, however, was the logic of his wings. They seemed so natural on that completely human organism that he couldn't understand why other men didn't have them too.

When the child began school, it had been some time since the sun and rain had caused the collapse of the chicken coop. The angel went dragging himself about here and there like a stray dying man. They would drive him out of the bedroom with a broom and a moment later find him in the kitchen. He seemed to be in so many places at the same time that they grew to think that he'd been duplicated, that he was reproducing himself all through the house, and the exasperated and unhinged Elisenda shouted that it was awful living in that hell full of angels. He could scarcely eat and his antiquarian eyes had also become so foggy that he went about bumping into posts. All he had left were the bare cannulae[21] of his last feathers. Pelayo threw a blanket over him and extended him the charity of letting him sleep in the shed, and only then did they notice that he had a temperature at night and was delirious with the tongue twisters of an old Norwegian. That was one of the few times they became alarmed, for they thought he was going to die and not even the wise neighbor woman had been able to tell them what to do with dead angels.

And yet he not only survived his worst winter but seemed improved with the first sunny days. He remained motionless for several days in the farthest corner of the courtyard, where no one would see him, and at the beginning of December some large, stiff feathers began to grow on his wings, the feathers of a

18. **myrrh** (mʉr) *n.:* sweet-smelling substance used in making perfume.
19. **homage** (häm′ij) *n.:* any gift or action that shows reverence, honor, or respect.
20. **infamies** *n.:* here, disrespectful acts; insults.
21. **cannulae** (kan′yo͞o·lē′) *n.:* tubes.

Vocabulary
lament (lə·ment′) *v.:* feel very sorry.

READING MINI-LESSON

Developing Word-Attack Skills
This story contains examples of words with similar sounds and different letters, as well as words with different sounds and similar letters. Use them to explore letter-sound relationships.

Write the words *catechism* (p. 589) and *cataclysm* (p. 592) on the chalkboard. Explain that the sounds of the words are identical with one exception: the *l* in *cataclysm* does not occur in *catechism.* Explore the different letter-sound relationships: /ə/ is spelled *e* in *catechism,* but *a* in *cataclysm;* /k/ is spelled *ch* in *catechism,* but *c* in *cataclysm;* /i/ is spelled *i* in *catechism,* but *y* in *cataclysm.*

Write the words *ingenuous* (p. 591) and *ingenious* (p. 594) on the chalkboard. Note that the words are spelled the same except for the sixth letter. Then, compare the pronunciations: *ingenuous* has four syllables scarecrow, which looked more like another misfortune of decrepitude.[22] But he must have known the reason for those changes, for he was quite careful that no one should notice them, that no one should hear the sea chanteys[23] that he sometimes sang under the stars. One morning Elisenda was cutting some bunches of onions for lunch when a wind that seemed to come from the high seas blew into the kitchen. Then she went to the window and caught the angel in his first attempts at flight. They were so clumsy that his fingernails opened a furrow in the vegetable patch and he was on the point of knocking the shed down with the ungainly flapping that slipped on the light and couldn't get a grip on the air. But he did manage to gain altitude. Elisenda let out a sigh of relief, for herself and for him, when she saw him pass over the last houses, holding himself up in some way with the risky flapping of a senile[24] vulture. She kept watching him even when she was through cutting the onions and she kept on watching until it was no longer possible for her to see him, because then he was no longer an annoyance in her life but an imaginary dot on the horizon of the sea. ■ **E**

22. **decrepitude** *n.:* feebleness; weakness.
23. **chanteys** (shan′tēz) *n.:* songs sung by sailors to set a rhythm for their work.
24. **senile** (sē′nīl′) *adj.:* showing confusion, loss of memory, and other signs of mental weakness or damage because of old age.

DIRECT TEACHING

E Reading Skills

Appreciating a writer's style. How do you visualize the winged creature based on the image of "the risky flapping of a senile vulture"? [Possible responses: He seems very old, slightly crazy, awkward, and at risk of falling. Calling him a "vulture" suggests both his nearly hairless skull and also the spiritual death of the townspeople.] What does the woman's watching until he is "an imaginary dot on the horizon" rather than "an annoyance in her life" suggest about people? [Possible response: People prefer to imagine a spiritual presence rather than to actually experience one.]

(in·jen′yo͞o·əs); *ingenious* has three syllables (in·jēn′yəs).

Activity. Display these pairs of words. Have volunteers read each pair aloud and tell if the words have similar sounds but different spellings or similar spellings but different sounds.

1. deprecate — depreciate
   [dep′rə·kāt′; dē·prē′shē·āt′; similar spellings, different sounds]
2. pleasance — malfeasance
   [plez′əns; mal·fē′zəns; similar spellings, different sounds]
3. hypercritical — hypocritical
   [hī′pər·krit′i·kəl; hip′ə·krit′i·kəl; similar spellings, different sounds]
4. cynical — pinnacle
   [sin′i·kəl; pin′ə·kəl; similar sounds, different spellings]
5. denial — menial
   [dē·nī′əl; mē′nē·əl; similar spellings, different sounds]
6. perpetrate — perpetuate
   [pur′pə·trāt′; pər·pech′o͞o·āt′; similar spellings, different sounds]
7. linear — skinnier
   [lin′ē·ər; skin′ē·ər; similar sounds, different spellings]

GUIDED PRACTICE

Monitoring students' progress. Guide the class in answering these true-false questions. Direct students to locate passages in the text that support their answers.

True-False

1. The townspeople treat the man with wings with respect because they believe he is an angel. [F]
2. The people finally lose interest in the man with wings. [T]
3. Pelayo and Elisenda resent the presence of the man with wings in their new mansion. [T]
4. The doctor discovers that the man's wings are pasted on. [F]
5. The man with wings eventually sprouts new feathers and flies away. [T]

Meet the Writer

Background. Gabriel García Márquez began making up stories while very young. "My earliest recollection is of drawing 'comics,'" he said, "and I realize now that this may have been because I couldn't yet write. I've always tried to find ways of telling stories and I've stuck to literature as the most accessible. But I think my vocation is not so much to be a writer as a storyteller."

Critic Regina Janes, among others, has noted that an essential element in the delight created by the story is the contrast between our perceptions of what angels are like and García Márquez's angel who talks like a sailor, is smelly and parasite ridden, and is not very good at flying.

Meet the Writer

Gabriel García Márquez

Memory's Magician

Gabriel García Márquez (1928–) sets much of his fiction in the imaginary town of Macondo, which in many ways resembles the sleepy, decaying, backwater town of Aracataca, Colombia, where he was born. Because his parents were poor, young Gabriel was raised by his maternal grandparents, in a large old house crowded with relatives and relics of the family's past. His grandmother told him tales of ancestors, spirits, and ghosts; and his grandfather, a retired colonel (whom García Márquez has called "the most important figure of my life"), spoke continually of a past so vivid that it became as real to the young boy as the present.

After studying law and working abroad as a journalist for many years, García Márquez became an international celebrity with the publication of his novel *One Hundred Years of Solitude* (1967). This epic masterpiece tells the comic and tragic saga of seven generations of Macondo's founding family. The Chilean poet Pablo Neruda called the novel "the greatest revelation in the Spanish language since *Don Quixote*." García Márquez won the Nobel Prize for literature in 1982.

He says this about writing when you are young:

"When you are young, you write almost—well, every writer is different, I'm talking about myself—almost like writing a poem. You write on impulses and inspiration. You have so much inspiration that you are not concerned with technique. You just see what comes out, without worrying much about what you are going to say and how. On the other hand, later, you know exactly what you are going to say and what you want to say. And you have a lot to tell. Even if all of your life you continue to tell about your childhood, later you are better able to interpret it, or at least interpret it in a different way."

For Independent Reading

García Márquez's many works of magic realism have delighted and intrigued readers around the world. You might enjoy his book of short stories, *Strange Pilgrims*.

DIFFERENTIATING INSTRUCTION

Advanced Learners

Enrichment. Inform students that García Márquez was inspired by his grandmother, who told compelling stories laced with supernatural events that she described vividly, without changing the tone of her voice or the expression on her face.

Activity. Have students write a short essay describing how the tone of the writing in "A Very Old Man with Enormous Wings" reflects the storytelling technique that García Márquez learned from his grandmother. Invite volunteers to read their essays aloud for the class.

Like Gabriel García Márquez, Jack Agüeros transforms ordinary realities with a touch of fantasy. In this poem he presents a startling vision of the homeless people who use the subways of New York City for shelter. Agüeros roots his images in the everyday through realistic details—references to Calcutta, a city in India where hundreds of thousands live on the streets, and the Gowanus Canal, a polluted body of water in Brooklyn, New York. But he also includes an ***allusion*** *(a reference) to Macondo, an imaginary village that is the setting for much of García Márquez's fiction.*

Sonnet for Heaven Below

Jack Agüeros

No, it wasn't Macondo, and it wasn't Calcutta in time past.
But subway magic turned the tunnels into Beautyrest mattresses **A**
And plenty of God's children started sleeping there. Some
Were actually Angels fatigued from long hours and no pay.

This is an aside, but I have to alert you. Angels run
Around, don't shave or bathe; acid rain fractures their
Feathers, and french fries and coca cola corrupt
The color of their skin and make them sing hoarsely.
The gossamer shoes so perfect for kicking clouds
Stain and tear on the concrete and in the hard light
Of the city they start to look like abandoned barges
Foundering in the cancerous waters of the Gowanus Canal.

Shabby gossamer shoes always arouse the derision of smart New Yorkers.
Mercifully, Angels aren't tourists, so they are spared total disdain.

Connection

Summary above grade level

This sonnet is about the homeless people who sleep in New York City's subways—or who used to. Be sure students read the italicized headnote before they read the poem. In his first line, Agüeros alludes to two famous practitioners of magic realism: García Márquez, whose stories are set in the fictional town of Macondo, and Salman Rushdie, who writes about India. Agüeros also alludes to magic realism when he says that magic has transformed the subway tunnels into mattresses. Like the old man with wings, these Angels are not what you would think of as being angelic. They don't shave or bathe; they eat bad food; their gossamer shoes tear on the concrete. In the last two lines the poet notes, almost as an aside, that the Angels' "shabby gossamer shoes" are looked down on by fashionable, street-smart New Yorkers, but at least the Angels are not tourists.

DIRECT TEACHING

A Literary Focus
GRADE-LEVEL STANDARD

Magic realism. What is the poet's style of writing? How do you know? [Possible response: The style is magic realism. The poet combines the grim reality of homeless people sleeping in New York City's subways with the fantasy that they are angels and the tunnels where they sleep are mattresses.]

Connecting and Comparing Texts

Guide a discussion comparing "Sonnet for Heaven Below" with "A Very Old Man with Enormous Wings." Ask the following questions:

- How are the angels in the two pieces similar and different? [The angels in both pieces are earthy and even downtrodden—not pure, clean, or ethereal. The angel in the story has wings and eventually flies; we're not sure if the subway angels fly, but the speaker does refer to their fractured feathers.]
- What elements of magic realism do you find in the two pieces? [Both pieces include many ordinary, realistic details that are casually blended with magical elements, including the angels, subways turned into mattresses, and gossamer shoes.]
- How do the speaker of the poem and the narrator of the story feel about their angels? [They describe them in ways that arouse our sympathy. Most readers will identify with the poor angels and not with the disdainful New Yorkers or the self-centered villagers who are indifferent to the miracle in their midst.]

INDEPENDENT PRACTICE

Literary Response and Analysis

Reading Check

1. Pelayo and Elisenda conclude that he is a castaway, shipwrecked by a storm. The neighbor thinks he is an angel. Father Gonzaga fears he may be a fraud.
2. Pelayo and Elisenda charge admission to see him. The money helps them build a mansion and live well.
3. A blind man grows three new teeth, a person who cannot walk almost wins the lottery, and a person with leprosy sprouts sunflowers from the sores.
4. People lose interest in the angel.

Interpretations

5. Possible answers: lack of humility or compassion; selfishness; gullibility; suspiciousness; fickleness; ignorance.
6. Possible answers: His actions give few clues to either a divine or evil origin. He might be mythical, but there is little evidence of it. He might be from another universe, but his many human qualities argue against that.
7. It certainly has a deeper meaning. It may mean that when we meet something unusual, we may try to make the situation fit our expectations rather than accepting it as it is. It may mean that even when the miraculous falls into our backyard, we won't recognize it.
8. They are alike in that they suffer as humans do. Agüeros seems to be talking about people, whereas García Márquez's angel has supernatural qualities. Unlike García Márquez's angel, Argüeros's angels do not have another place where they belong. Both New Yorkers in the poem and the townspeople in García Márquez's story treat their angels with contempt, indifference, and annoyance.

Literary Criticism

9. Possible answers: the existence of a flesh-and-blood man with wings; the miracles; the story of the spider woman.
10. Possible answers: the description of the old man in the chicken coop; the angel's response to the branding iron; the spider woman. Bizarre, often painful images such as these dropped casually into the story help create a darkly comical tone.
11. Possible answers: The story seems based more on the underlying reality, because the feelings and behavior of the characters are true to human nature. The story seems based more on fantasy because the only meaningful events involve supernatural characters such as the winged man and the spider woman.

Literary Response and Analysis

Reading Check

1. The townspeople have various ideas about what the winged old man is. What do Pelayo and Elisenda think he is? What does their neighbor think? and Father Gonzaga?
2. How does the winged old man change the lives of Pelayo and Elisenda?
3. What miracles are attributed to the old man?
4. What happens when another novelty, a spider-woman, comes to town?

Interpretations

5. Writing that ridicules human behaviors is called **satire.** What human shortcomings might García Márquez be satirizing in this story? Consider:
   - how Pelayo and Elisenda treat the old man
   - Father Gonzaga's reactions to him
   - how the townspeople react
6. Do you think the old man is a divine figure or an evil one, or neither? Explain your view. What other possibilities might explain his identity? (Check your Quickwrite notes.)
7. Do you think this story is intended merely to amuse us, or does it have a deeper **theme**? Do you think the old man might **symbolize,** or represent, the miracles we wish for but cannot accept when they happen or the misunderstood artist whose imagination longs to soar?
8. How are the "angels" in "Sonnet for Heaven Below" (see the ***Connection*** on page 597) similar to the old man with enormous wings? Compare how "smart New Yorkers" treat the angels with the way the old man is treated.

Reading Standard 3.11
Evaluate the aesthetic qualities of style, including the impact of diction on tone, mood, and theme, using the terminology of literary criticism. (Aesthetic approach)

Literary Criticism

9. What details in this story illustrate the **style** of **magic realism**—that is, elements of fantasy mixed in with the commonplace?
10. Which of García Márquez's **images** did you find most startling and memorable? How does the author use these images to create the story's **mood** and **tone**?
11. García Márquez has said:

> It always amuses me that the biggest praise for my work comes for the imagination while the truth is there is not a single line in all my work that does not have a basis in reality.

Does the story seem based more on fantasy than on an underlying reality? Explain.

Writing

Create Your Own Magic Realism

Write a **fantastic story** of your own about a character from folklore, mythology, or popular culture who falls into our world. Consider these possibilities:

- Hercules, the strongest teenager in the world, enrolls at your school
- a fairy godmother visits a poor girl in New York City
- a dragon asks to be admitted to the local zoo

▶ **Use "Writing a Short Story," pages 602–609, for help with this assignment.**

598 Chapter 8 Evaluating Style • Evaluating an Argument

Vocabulary Development

Roots and Relations

Knowing a word's **root word** will help you to understand its related forms. For example, *antique, antiquated, antiquarian,* and *antiquity* come from the Latin root word *antiquus,* which means "ancient; old."

Word Bank
- stench
- impeded
- magnanimous
- reverence
- frivolous
- impertinences
- ingenuous
- prudence
- cataclysm
- providential
- affliction
- lament

PRACTICE 1

Using a dictionary, trace the origin of each word in the Word Bank to find its **root word.** Also note its **part of speech.** Then, look for related forms and their parts of speech. (Some of the words have many related forms; one word has none.) Note that adding or changing a **suffix** often changes a word's part of speech. Summarize your findings for each word in a graphic like the one below for the word *impeded.*

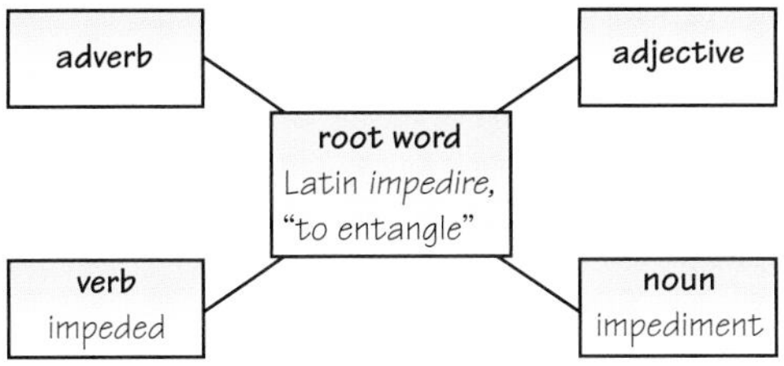

Literal and Figurative Language: Imagery

García Márquez's story is filled with **imagery,** language that appeals directly to our senses as well as to our imagination. When an image uses words in their **literal** (dictionary) sense, the words mean exactly what they say. But when an image uses **figurative language,** the words are not meant to be understood literally. That's because figurative language always involves an imaginative **comparison** of two basically unlike things.

LITERAL "There were only a few faded hairs left on his bald skull and very few teeth in his mouth. . . ."

FIGURATIVE "And the sands of the beach, which on March nights glimmered like powdered light, had become a stew of mud and rotten shellfish."

Grade 8 Review Reading Standard 1.1 Analyze metaphors and similies to infer the figurative meanings of phrases.

Reading Standard 1.1 Identify and use the literal and figurative meanings of words and understand word derivations.

PRACTICE 2

1. Look back at the story, and find at least three examples of unusual imagery. Do the images use **literal** or **figurative** language?
2. Write a description of a person or group of people in a specific setting. Use both literal and figurative language in your description and images that appeal to the senses.

Vocabulary Development

Practice 1

Possible Answers

- *stench, n.; root word*—Old English *stincan,* "to stink"; no related words.
- *magnanimous, adj.; root word*—Latin *magnanimus,* "great mind"; *related words*—magnanimity, *n.,* magnificent, *adj.,* magnate, *n.*
- *reverence, n.; root word*—Latin *reverentia,* "feeling of awe"; *related words*—revere, *v.,* reverend, *n.,* reverent, *adj.*
- *frivolous, adj.; root word*—Latin *frivolus,* "silly"; *related word*—frivolity, *n.*
- *impertinences, n.; root word*—Latin *impertinens,* "not to hold"; *related words*—impertinent, *adj.,* pertain, *v.*
- *ingenuous, adj.; root word*—Latin *ingenuus,* "naive, honest"; *related words*—ingenuity, *n.,* ingénue, *n.*
- *prudence, n.; root word*—Latin *prudens,* "wise, foreseeing"; *related words*—prudential, *adj.,* prudent, *adj.*
- *cataclysm, n.; root word*—Greek *kataklysmos,* "deluge"; *related word*—cataclysmic, *adj.*
- *providential, adj.; root word*—Latin *providens,* "to foresee"; *related words*—providence, *n.,* provident, *adj.*
- *affliction, n.; root word*—Latin *afflictus,* "to put down"; *related words*—afflict, *v.,* afflictive, *adj.*
- *lament, v.; root word*—Latin *lamentum,* "to mourn aloud"; *related words*—lamentation, *n.,* lamentable, *adj.*

Practice 2

1. Possible answer: *Figurative*—"a stew of mud and rotten shellfish"; "that pitiful man who looked more like a huge decrepit hen among the fascinated chickens." *Literal*—"There were only a few faded hairs left on his bald skull and very few teeth in his mouth. . . ."
2. Descriptions will vary.

Resources Reminder

Vocabulary

- *Vocabulary Development*
  - Vocabulary Worksheet, p. 40
  - Cumulative Vocabulary Review, pp. 41–42
- *Lesson Plans for Language Development*
  - Vocabulary, pp. 280, 282

Grammar Link

Practice

Possible Answer

Pelayo was frightened by that nightmare, so he ran to get Elisenda, his wife, who was putting compresses on the sick child. He took her to the rear of the courtyard, where they both looked at the fallen body with mute stupor. He was dressed like a ragpicker. There were only a few faded hairs left on his bald skull and very few teeth in his mouth. His huge buzzard wings were dirty, half plucked, and forever tangled in the mud.

ASSESSING

Assessment

- *Progress Assessment of Reading*
  - Selection Test

RETEACHING

For a lesson reteaching Standard 3.11, see **Reteaching,** p. 939A. For another selection to teach Standard 3.11, see *Interactive Reading,* Chapter 8.

Grammar Link MINI-LESSON

Varying Sentence Length and Structure

Experienced writers use a variety of sentence structures and sentence lengths so that their paragraphs don't have the singsong sound of beginning-readers' books. To vary your sentences, you'll first need to recall how to distinguish independent and subordinate clauses.

An **independent clause** expresses a complete thought and can stand by itself as a sentence.

"The curious came from far away."

A **subordinate clause** does not express a complete thought and cannot stand alone.

"when the rain stopped"
"that a flesh-and-blood angel was held captive in Pelayo's house"

Every English sentence can be placed in one of the four categories in the chart below:

Type of Sentence	Example
A **simple sentence** has one independent clause and no subordinate clauses. Its subject or verb or both may be compound.	"He was dressed like a ragpicker."
A **compound sentence** has two or more independent clauses but no subordinate clause.	"Then they dared speak to him, and he answered in an incomprehensible dialect with a strong sailor's voice."
A **complex sentence** has one independent clause and at least one subordinate clause.	"The simplest among them thought that he should be named mayor of the world."
A **compound-complex sentence** has two or more independent clauses and at least one subordinate clause.	"Sea and sky were a single ash-gray thing, and the sands of the beach, which on March nights glimmered like powdered light, had become a stew of mud and rotten shellfish."

PRACTICE

Edit this choppy paragraph by combining some sentences into compound, complex, or compound-complex sentences. Then, check page 588 to see how García Márquez wrote this paragraph:

Pelayo was frightened by that nightmare. Pelayo ran to get Elisenda. She was his wife. She was putting compresses on the sick child. He took her to the rear of the courtyard. They both looked at the fallen body with mute stupor. He was dressed like a ragpicker. There were only a few faded hairs left on his bald skull. There were very few teeth in his mouth. His huge buzzard wings were dirty. They were also half plucked. They were forever tangled in the mud.

Read On: FOR INDEPENDENT READING

FICTION

Masters of Style

A man pursued by a headless horseman, two mothers sharing a dark secret in Rome, and an awkward waltz that never seems to end—these are just a few of the characters and situations you'll encounter in ***Great American Stories.*** This collection features the best of such admired authors as Nathaniel Hawthorne, Mark Twain, Edgar Allan Poe, and Willa Cather—all masters of style who helped change the shape of American literature.

This title is available in the HRW Library.

FICTION

High Seas Struggle

Ernest Hemingway earned his fame from his spare, powerful writing style and his ability to make words come alive on the page. In his novella ***The Old Man and the Sea,*** Hemingway's talents were in their finest form. This is the story of Santiago, an aging Cuban fisherman who glimpses an irresistible catch from his boat: a magnificent marlin that bobs to the surface of the Gulf Stream. Amazingly, the great fish takes the hook into its mouth—and then continues to swim for his life. A classic conflict of man versus nature ensues.

NONFICTION

Between Two Cultures

Ernesto Galarza, a teacher and political activist, is probably best known for his autobiography, ***Barrio Boy.*** Galarza first describes his early boyhood in western Mexico—a beautiful rural setting rich in song, folklore, and customs. Then the Mexican Revolution begins, and Galarza's family flees to a very different place: a barrio in Sacramento, California. *Barrio Boy* tells the story of a family caught between their heritage and their adopted land.

This title is available in the HRW Library.

NONFICTION

Life with Wolves

For most people, living near a den of wolves is a less than appealing prospect. Scientist Farley Mowat had no choice. The government's Wildlife Service sent him to northern Canada to investigate the wolves' killing of the endangered arctic caribou. Mowat found something he had never expected—sympathy for the noble wolf families—and a companionship with local Inuit people. Farley Mowat's ***Never Cry Wolf*** is the true story of his life-changing experience.

This title is available in the HRW Library.

Read On

For Independent Reading

If students enjoyed the themes and topics explored in this chapter, you might recommend these titles for independent reading.

Assessment Options

The following projects can help you evaluate and assess your students' outside reading. Videotapes or audiotapes of completed projects may be included in student portfolios.

- **Write a how-to article.** Have students write a how-to article explaining the steps of a process they learned about in the book they read. For example, students who read *Never Cry Wolf* can explain how to track a wolf or how to eat a mouse; readers of *The Old Man and the Sea* can explain how to catch a giant marlin, using simple equipment; and readers of *Barrio Boy* can explain how to prepare a Mexican food, how to celebrate a Mexican holiday, or how to adjust to life in a new country.
- **Evaluate the author's style.** Have students analyze and evaluate the style used by the author of the book they read. Students who read *Great American Stories* can compare and contrast the styles of two different writers. Students should evaluate diction, sentence structure, figurative language, and other distinctive stylistic features.
- **Compare and contrast themes.** *Barrio Boy, The Old Man and the Sea,* and *Never Cry Wolf* all convey important ideas about courage, persistence, and self-reliance. Have students who read different books meet in small groups to discuss similarities and differences in how the three authors view these important human qualities.

Toward Reading Two Million Words Annually

Estimated Word Counts and Reading Levels of Read On Books:

Fiction			Nonfiction		
Great American Stories	↑	109,600	*Barrio Boy*	↓	125,200
The Old Man and the Sea	↔	30,200	*Never Cry Wolf**	↔	48,100

*California Reading List Titles

KEY: ↑ *above grade level* ↔ *at grade level* ↓ *below grade level*

PRETEACHING

Standards Starter

Motivate. Ask students to name their favorite stories and to give reasons why they like the stories they mention. Write students' suggestions on the chalkboard, and point out that what they like about a story—the elements that make it effective—can be placed in one or more clearly defined categories. Show students how their suggestions fit into the categories (character, setting, plot), and tell them they will study these categories before writing their own stories.

Resources Reminder

To introduce the workshop, you may want to use the journal starters in *Writing, Listening, & Speaking* Teaching Notes.

DIRECT TEACHING

Finding an Idea

Explain that authors sometimes use their own experiences as a basis for their short stories. Students may choose to write short stories that reflect personal experience, but remind them that short stories are a form of fiction: They may reflect, but should not actually represent, a real person, event, or setting. If students choose to base their stories on actual events, suggest that they change some elements to serve their individual writing purposes.

Integrating with Grammar, Usage, and Mechanics

As students begin their stories, they might have trouble using punctuation correctly. You may want to review the corresponding chapters in the *Holt Handbook*.

Writing a Short Story

Writing Assignment
Writing 2.1 Use your creative talent to write an effective short story.

Have you ever admired the style of a short story like Sandra Cisneros's "Geraldo No Last Name"? Have you wished that you could put an event from your imagination into words that would captivate your audience as Gabriel García Márquez does in his short story, "A Very Old Man with Enormous Wings"? In this workshop you can create a **short story** with style and imagination.

Prewriting

GO TO: go.hrw.com
KEYWORD: HLLA 10-8
FOR: Professional Model, Writer's Guides, and Reference Sources

Finding an Idea

Where to Start? A short story is a work of fiction that usually has a single idea as its starting point. That idea may arise from any source. From that point, the story evolves from the writer's imagination. If you are struggling for an idea for a story, brainstorm your personal experiences, dreams, ambitions, and interests.

Begin at the Beginning The main ingredients of any short story are **characters, plot, point of view, setting,** and **theme.** A writer can, of course, emphasize one or more elements more than others. As the writer, you decide which elements are most important in your story.

DO THIS

Characters Short stories usually fully develop only the main character. Supporting characters are developed as thoroughly as their roles in the story require; minor characters, for example, might be characterized in a single sentence. Examine the questions and one writer's responses to those questions about his main character in the chart below. Then, create a chart of your own to record details about your main and supporting characters.

Quick guide

RECORDING CHARACTER DETAILS

Questions	Character
How does the character think, act, and feel?	*Jesse—intensely moody 15-year-old; slouches and pouts; respectful and cooperative, at times grudgingly*
What motivates the character?	*Jesse is motivated by his desire to be a great basketball player. When he's not playing basketball, he's thinking about it.*

(continued)

Writing 2.1 Write short stories.

CHAPTER 8 RESOURCES: WRITING

Writing Workshop

Planning
- *On Course: Mapping Instruction*
- *One-Stop Planner* CD-ROM
- *Writing, Listening, & Speaking,* Teaching Notes, p. 84

Differentiating Instruction
- *Lesson Plans for Language Development,* pp. 275–276
- *Supporting Instruction in Spanish*

Practice
- *Writing, Listening, & Speaking,* Ch. 8

(continued)

What does the character look like? What is his or her voice like?	*Jesse—tall and lanky, not yet filled out. Black hair, dark complexion; voice changes from low to high when excited.*
What distinct or unique mannerisms or habits does the character have?	*Jesse—frequently interrupts whatever he's doing by going through the motions of a jump shot.*

TIP An effective way to develop believable characters is to involve them in **dialogue,** conversation between characters. You can also reveal what a character is thinking or feeling through **interior monologue,** talk that goes on inside a character's head.

Plot **Plot** is what happens in a story—the actions or sequence of events. The events occur as the result of a **conflict,** or struggle between opposing forces. Conflicts are **external** when a character struggles against an outside force and **internal** when the struggle is within a character. Look at the types of conflicts in the chart below.

TYPES OF CONFLICT

Conflict	Definition	Example
Character vs. character (external)	The main character is in conflict with another character in the story.	*Jesse struggles against the established star of the basketball team of his new team in Florida.*
Character vs. the environment (external)	The main character is in conflict with an aspect of his or her environment.	*Jesse struggles to keep up with his new teammates in the unfamiliar heat and humidity of Florida.*
Character vs. a situation (external)	The main character is in conflict with a situation or circumstance outside him- or herself.	*Jesse struggles against what he perceives as his new basketball coaches' prejudice against players new to the school.*
Character vs. him- or herself (internal)	The main character struggles with conflicting desires, ideas, or feelings within him- or herself.	*Jesse is torn between his resentment at being moved from his familiar life and his need to adjust to his new surroundings.*

The plot of your story unfolds through a series of events, called the **rising action,** to the **climax,** or high point, of the story. Each plot event builds on the previous event until the climax. After the climax the **resolution,** or denouement, settles the conflict and ends the story. The resolution may also make clear the significance of the story's events. Here are some techniques you can use to construct your plot.

- Narrate the events of your plot in **chronological order,** the order in which the events occur. Consider using **flashbacks** to provide background information that is important to understanding your plot.
- **Pace** the action of your plot. For example, create a frantic mood by narrating events quickly, using short sentences. Create a leisurely mood by narrating events slowly, using longer sentences.

Writing 2.1a Relate a sequence of events and communicate the significance of the events to the audience. **2.1c** Use interior monologue to depict the characters' feelings. **2.1d** Pace the presentation of actions to accommodate changes in time and mood.

MODELING AND DEMONSTRATION

Plot

To be sure that students understand how sensory details can help them construct their plots, model how to use the following cluster diagram.

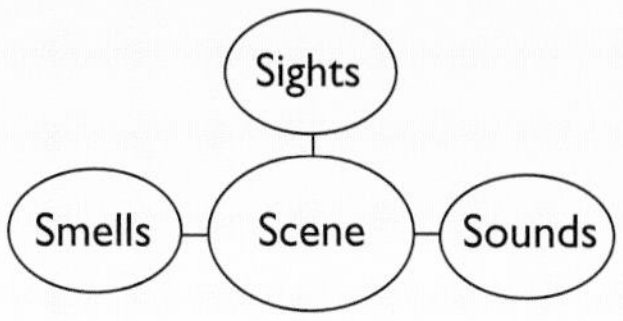

Using the first two paragraphs from **A Writer's Model** on p. 605, show students how a scene or event is described by means of sensory details. Then, ask for volunteers to demonstrate and explain a cluster diagram based on scenes or events in their own stories.

DIFFERENTIATING INSTRUCTION

Learners Having Difficulty

To help students get started with the writing assignment, remind them that writing problems frequently resolve themselves during the writing process. Also, their stories may take a different direction from the original plan.Tell students not to be too critical of their work until they finish their first drafts. Then, they can cut, add, and replace, building on and developing interesting aspects of the various story elements.

English-Language Learners

Students who are learning English may find it difficult to write a short story. Encourage these students to simplify the steps in this workshop; they could tell a lightly fictionalized story from their own lives, stick to first-person point of view, and use only two or three characters. You may want to assign a partner to help answer any questions students might have. When students have finished writing, have their partners read their stories to discover and help them correct any errors in spelling or grammar, usage, and mechanics.

Reinforcement

- *Daily Language Activities*

Evaluation and Assessment

- *Test Generator (One-Stop Planner* CD-ROM)
- *Progress Assessment of Writing, Listening, & Speaking,* Ch. 8
- *Diagnostic and Summative Assessments,* Third-Quarter Test

Internet

- go.hrw.com (keyword: HLLA 10-8)
- Online assessments at go.hrw.com (keyword: HLLA)

- Provide abundant **sensory details** and **figurative language** (such as metaphor, simile, and personification) to create effective **images.** Help your readers imagine the sights, smells, and sounds of a scene or event and the actions, movements, gestures, and feelings of your characters.
- Locate scenes and incidents in **specific places.**

Point of View The **point of view** of a short story is the vantage point of the story's narrator. Each point of view has advantages and disadvantages. Once you decide on a point of view, stick to it. Shifting points of view can ruin your story's coherence and confuse your readers. Here are your choices.

Quick guide!

POINTS OF VIEW

Points of View	Advantages	Disadvantages
First person: The main character or a supporting character tells the story using the pronoun *I*.	This point of view gives the reader a sense of hearing from the primary participant directly or from an eyewitness.	The narrator can't reveal everything. For example, he or she can't reveal the thoughts of other characters.
Third person omniscient: An outsider (rather than a character in the story) tells the story, using third-person pronouns—*he, she,* and *they.*	Omniscient narrators know all and can tell all. For example, they can use **shifting perspectives** to show the same event from the perspectives of several characters.	Stories with omniscient narrators often make readers feel far removed from the characters and action, as in a fairy tale.
Third person limited: An outsider tells the story through the eyes and mind of the main character, using third-person pronouns.	The third-person-limited narrator focuses attention on the thoughts and feelings of the main character, making it easy for the reader to identify with him or her.	Limited narrators may have trouble making minor characters seem real. The writer could slip into the omniscient point of view without being aware of it.

Setting The **setting** of your story is the time and location in which it takes place. Setting can be insignificant in a short story or vitally important. If, for example, you want to use the setting to help establish the mood or atmosphere of your story, or if the setting is important to the conflict of your story, describe it thoroughly.

Theme The **theme** of your story expresses an idea about what it means to be human. Themes usually have to do with basic human needs and emotions. You can directly state your story's theme, but most modern stories suggest, or imply, the theme. The reader pieces together the clues you provide and from them infers the story's theme.

Writing 1.2 Use sensory details. **2.1b** Locate scenes and incidents in specific places. **2.1c** Describe with concrete sensory details the sights, sounds, and smells of a scene and the specific actions, movements, gestures, and feelings of the characters. **2.1e** Make effective use of descriptions of appearance, images, shifting perspectives, and sensory details.

PRACTICE & APPLY 1 Using the guidelines provided on the preceding pages, choose an idea for your story. Then, select a point of view, and plan your story.

PRACTICE & APPLY 1

Guided and Independent Practice

Guide students' progress by having them complete a simple chart, such as the one below, of the elements in their stories.

Element	My Choice
point of view	
character(s)	
conflict	
setting	
theme	

Then, have them complete **Practice and Apply 1** as independent practice.

RESOURCES: WRITING

Practice & Apply 1

Guided Practice

- *Writing, Listening, & Speaking,* WS. p. 85

Reteaching and Modeling

- *Writing, Listening, & Speaking,* TP. 13
- *Writing, Listening, & Speaking,* WS. p. 87

604 Chapter 8 Evaluating Style • Evaluating an Argument

Writing

Writing a Short Story

A Writer's Framework

Beginning
- Begin with an exciting event, or introduce the main character in an intriguing way.
- Establish the setting and point of view.
- Introduce the story's conflict.

Middle
- Narrate the events in chronological order, and pace the action.
- Use dialogue, interior monologue, sensory details, and figurative language to develop characters.
- Locate scenes in specific places.

End
- Resolve the conflict in a logical and believable way.
- State or clearly imply the theme through changes in the main character or through the resolution of the conflict.

A Writer's Model

Finding a Friend

BEGINNING
Main character
Point of view/ Interior monologue
Interior conflict
Metaphor

Jesse, a tall and lanky fifteen-year-old, slouched on the edge of his bed, his expression sullen, pouting. He had been moping around his new house for the entire week he had been there. How could his father have moved the family away from sunny, warm, and beautiful California, home of the Hoopsters and Dunk Martin? They had moved to hot, rainy Florida, home of hurricanes and uh . . . who? Oh, yeah, the Sharks and the Keys were Florida's pro basketball teams. Big deal! He had to adjust, he knew, but he couldn't stop the movies of his California life from running in his head.

MIDDLE
Rising action
Flashback/Sensory details

Jesse was upstairs unpacking his sizable collection of basketball souvenirs. He savored the feel of his miniature autographed basketball, which he had caught from a Hoopsters cheerleader who had tossed the autographed balls into the stands where he happened to be sitting. He could almost hear the roar of the crowd at that game as Dunk power-dunked over three helpless defenders. The last piece he unwrapped was a small gold medal, his greatest source of pride. He had received the medal when his team won first place in their division in last summer's basketball league—the same team now playing without him.

Interior monologue

Jesse rose, put up a phantom jump shot, and slouched toward the window. Would he ever find anyone to shoot baskets with? Through

(continued)

RETEACHING

GRADE-LEVEL STANDARD

A Writer's Framework

If students are having trouble understanding what the steps listed in **A Writer's Framework** accomplish, draw on the chalkboard a visual depiction such as the one given here.

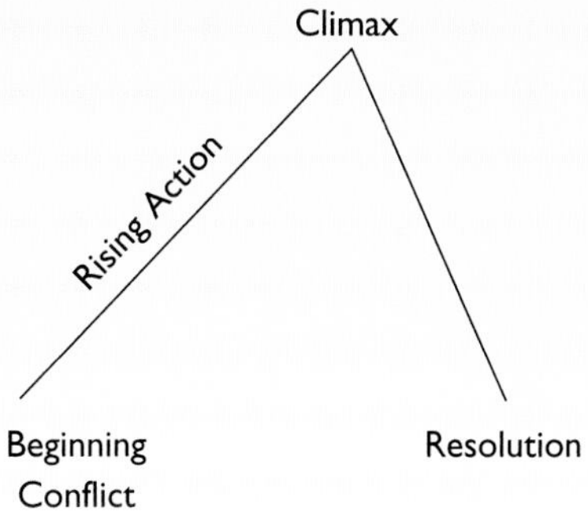

Point out that the beginning of a story depicts the main character in everyday life or before a life-changing event. Through rising action, the main character usually pursues something he or she wants; by the climax, however, the character sees events in a different light. The resolution of a story suggests how the character's life has changed even as he or she gets back to a normal state of events.

DIRECT TEACHING

GRADE-LEVEL STANDARD

A Writer's Model

Students who write a story using a first-person or a third-person omniscient narrator may choose to include interior monologue to reveal the characters' feelings and thoughts. For an example of this technique, you may wish to examine with students the first and third paragraphs of **A Writer's Model.**

DIFFERENTIATING INSTRUCTION

Advanced Learners

Enrichment. Students can be challenged to write their short stories in the style of an author whose work they admire. First, have them follow the steps outlined in this workshop. Then, coach students to spend a few minutes jotting down the key elements of the style they would like to emulate. Finally, have students list ways they can re-create the style within their own stories.

CRITICAL THINKING

Begin a class analysis of **A Writer's Model,** encouraging students to think also about how they might apply the answers to the following questions to their own stories.

1. **How effective is the portrayal of the character Jesse? Compare the story to the questions in the chart on pp. 602–603.** [Students will probably say that A Writer's Model effectively portrays Jesse as he is described in the chart. Some students may say that the story does not use all of the details given in the chart.]
2. **How would the story change if it were written in the first-person point of view?** [The story would be told only from Jesse's point of view. The writer would have to find other ways to present details about Jesse's appearance and the thoughts of other characters. On the other hand, Jesse's feelings and reactions might have a stronger impact if presented directly by him.]
3. **What is the theme of this story?** [One possible theme: *Change can bring opportunity as well as sacrifice.*] **Do you think the theme is too obvious, too hidden, or effectively clear?** [Student answers will vary.]

PRACTICE & APPLY 2

Guided and Independent Practice

Guide student progress by having students meet with a partner to share the beginnings of their essays. Students should check to make sure their partners are following **A Writer's Framework.** Spot-check several pairs' work. Then, have students complete **Practice and Apply 2** as independent practice.

(continued)

Sensory details

the window he saw an older man wearing ragged shorts and basketball shoes. Jesse watched as his next-door neighbor, limping noticeably on his left leg, pushed a lawn mower slowly across the wide green expanse in front of his house. He was surprised to see his mother scurrying

Simile

toward the neighbor with a tall glass in her hand, like a waitress at a busy restaurant. The man drank the lemonade Mrs. Estrada had brought him, pausing between swallows to talk.

Dialogue

"Jesse, the man next door shouldn't have to mow his own lawn with that bad leg of his. You should mow his lawn when you mow ours," Jesse's mom said that night at dinner.

"Mom! His yard's bigger than ours!" Jesse whined.

"Jesse," she responded, "don't be so thoughtless."

Metaphor

Jesse, still irritated at his mom, remembered the man's limp and felt his anger slip quietly through him and away, a basketball swishing through the rim, hardly touching the net.

Sensory details

The next weekend, Jesse pulled on his favorite sneakers, so old and full of holes they could hardly be called shoes. He slowly headed out to mow his lawn—and his neighbor's. As he was finishing, the neighbor walked up to him. Jesse hadn't noticed before how tall the man was.

Dialogue

"Hi, Jesse. I'm Dan. Thanks for a very nice job. Come on in and have a cold glass of tea." Jesse smiled and followed Dan into the house.

"Sit down while I get our drinks," Dan said. Jesse sat and began to look around the room. His eye caught sight of an ornate glass case in the far corner. Curious, he got up and crossed to the case for a closer look. On the top shelf was a large bronze trophy. It was surrounded by

Sensory details

old photographs, framed newspaper articles, and smaller trophies. Jesse leaned in closer and read aloud the plaque attached to the trophy—"Dan Casey, Most Valuable Player, 1968 All-Star Game."

END
Climax

As Dan walked back into the room, Jesse wheeled around, sputtering, voice high, "Dan Casey! You're Dan Casey! I've got your 1968 All-Star card!"

Resolution

"I saw your goal yesterday, Jesse. Mind if I come over and shoot a few baskets with you now and then? I was pretty good at it before I

Theme (implied)

blew out this old knee," Dan said. Later that afternoon, Jesse put up a shot from the top of the key—nothin' but net—and thought how great Florida was.

GO TO: go.hrw.com
KEYWORD: HLLA 10-8
FOR: Expanded Writer's Model and Student's Model

PRACTICE & APPLY 2 Refer to the framework on page 605 and the Writer's Model above as you write the first draft of the short story you planned earlier.

RESOURCES: WRITING

Practice & Apply 2

Think Sheet

- *Writing, Listening, & Speaking,* WS. p. 88

Template

- *Writing, Listening, & Speaking,* WS. p. 89

Internet

- go.hrw.com (keyword: HLLA 10-8)

606 Chapter 8 Evaluating Style • Evaluating an Argument

Revising

Evaluate and Revise Your Short Story

Fresh Eyes Writing a short story requires a significant expenditure of time, energy, and imagination, so you want it to be as good as it can be, which usually requires revision. If you have time, put the draft of your short story aside for a day or two to give your eyes and mind a break. Then, read it very carefully two more times, first to evaluate the content and organization and second to evaluate the style.

PEER REVIEW

Before you revise your work, exchange stories with a classmate. He or she will bring a fresh eye to the story, and may have ideas about how you can improve the dialogue.

First Reading Use the following chart to help you evaluate and revise the content and organization of your short story. To use the chart, ask yourself the questions in the left-hand column. Use the tips in the middle column to help you answer the questions. Then, use the revision techniques in the right-hand column to make needed changes.

Guidelines: Writing a Short Story

Evaluation Questions	Tips	Revision Techniques
1 Does the story open with an exciting event or intriguing introduction to the main character?	▶ **Underline** the event or introduction to the main character that seizes readers' attention.	▶ To draw readers in, **add** an exciting event or intriguing introduction to the main character.
2 Is the point of view, or vantage point, from which the story is told consistent?	▶ **Circle** all the pronouns in the story that reveal the point of view.	▶ **Reword** any instances of inconsistent point of view.
3 Is the conflict clear? Do the events in the story lead to a climax? Are all events relevant to the plot?	▶ **Double underline** the sentence(s) that makes the conflict clear. **Bracket** the sentence(s) containing the climax. **Draw a line** through irrelevant events.	▶ **Add** or **elaborate** on events to develop the plot. **Delete** events that do not contribute to the development of the plot.
4 Does the story contain sensory details and figurative language that develop the events, characters, and setting?	▶ **Put a check mark** next to sensory details and figurative language that describe events, characters, and setting.	▶ **Add** sensory details and figurative language as necessary to describe vividly events, characters, and setting.
5 Does the story contain dialogue?	▶ **Put a star** by conversations between characters.	▶ **Add** correctly punctuated dialogue.
6 Is the conflict resolved logically? Is the theme directly stated or implied?	▶ **Highlight** the resolution of the conflict. **Put two stars** by the sentence(s) stating or implying the theme.	▶ **Elaborate** upon the resolution, the statement of theme, or the sentences that imply the theme.

DIRECT TEACHING

REVIEW STANDARD

Elaboration

Point out to students that when writing a short story, they are trying to convince their readers that the view of the world they are presenting is real. You may want to use an object from the room—for example, a dog-eared paperback book with marginal notes, a favorite coat, or a notebook covered in a student's writing—to point out that what creates interest is the concrete and individual, which makes one object or person different from another. Challenge students to replace generic language (the word *sound,* for example) with words that reflect an individual, concrete reality (for example, *gong* or *crash*).

Writing Workshop: Writing a Short Story 607

TECHNOLOGY TIP

You may want to remind students that some word-processing applications allow the import of clip art, pictures, and other graphics. If students have access to a digital scanner, they can use it to convert their illustrations into computer graphics.

GUIDED PRACTICE

Responding to the Revision Process

Answers

1. The change improves the sentence by introducing a more precise, vivid action verb.
2. The addition strongly implies that Jesse has solved his problem of being angry because of his family's move. It also brings the action of the story to a satisfying close by implying a theme.

PRACTICE & APPLY 3

Independent Practice

Have pairs of students read their stories aloud to one another and answer the following questions.

1. Did the narrative hold your interest? Why or why not?
2. What words seem awkward or vague?

Have students use feedback from this peer review to help in the revision process.

Second Reading Sophisticated writers of fiction are always conscious of their use of language, including the verbs they use in their stories. They often choose vivid **action verbs** to express the physical or mental activity of their characters. Take a look at the difference between weak verbs and vivid ones in the examples below.

Weak Verbs Maria **walked** into her sister's room and **took** her new sweater.

Vivid Verbs Maria **tiptoed** into her sister's room and **snatched** her new sweater.

Now, take a look at the verbs you've used in your short story. Are they vivid, precise, and powerful? Use the chart below to evaluate and revise your style.

editor in charge

Style Guidelines

Evaluation Question	Tip	Revision Technique
Does the story contain vivid action verbs?	**Circle** all the action verbs in the story.	**Replace** weak action verbs with vivid ones.

ANALYZING THE REVISION PROCESS

Study these revisions, and answer the questions that follow.

> "I saw your goal yesterday, Jesse. Mind if I come over and shoot a few baskets with you now and then? I was pretty good at it before I ~~hurt~~ *blew out* this old knee," Dan said. *Later that afternoon, Jesse put up a shot from the top of the key—nothin' but net—and thought how great Florida was.*

replace

elaborate

Responding to the Revision Process

1. Does the change the writer made to the third sentence improve the sentence? Why?
2. Why did the writer add a sentence?

PRACTICE & APPLY 3 Using the guidelines in this section, first evaluate and revise the content and organization of your story. Then, evaluate and revise the style of your story. Examine the Writer's Model and the revisions shown in the example paragraph above as models for your own revisions. If possible, work with a peer throughout the revision process.

Writing 1.2 Use action verbs.

608 Chapter 8 Evaluating Style • Evaluating an Argument

Publishing

Proofread and Publish Your Short Story

Be Conventional Writing a short story is a creative endeavor; nevertheless, you should follow the basic rules of grammar, usage, and mechanics when you write one. Minor errors in these areas can be annoying for readers. Major errors can cause them to deposit your story in the nearest recycling bin. The one exception is dialogue, where the rules of grammar and usage do not apply because dialogue should reflect the way people really talk. Proofread your short story to eliminate errors in grammar, usage, and mechanics.

Who Will Read My Story? Now that you've got your story in good form, it's time to let others read it. There are many ways that you can make your story available to a wider audience. Here are some ideas.

- Put your story together with your other writings to create a small collection of your work, and distribute it to family members and close friends.
- Submit your story to the school newspaper or any other publication that accepts work from young writers. Ask your teacher or your school librarian to help you find a list of publications that you can contact, or conduct an Internet search.
- Put your short story on the Internet, either on your own Web page, your school's Web site, or on one of the many sites that accept work from young writers.

Reflect on Your Short Story

Consider the Process Now think back about what you've done, and mull over what you've learned in the process of writing a short story. Here are some questions to consider.

- How did writing this short story help you understand and appreciate the process that professional authors go through?
- How do you think your story stacks up against some of the stories you've read during your study of literature? Compare your development of specific elements to the development of the same elements by authors whose stories you've read.

PRACTICE & APPLY 4 Using the guidelines on this page, first proofread your essay for errors in standard American grammar, usage, and mechanics. Then, publish your story for a wider audience. Finally, reflect on the process you went through in writing your story by answering the reflection questions above.

TIP Be sure that you observe the **conventions** of standard American English as you proofread. For example, check for errors in subject-verb agreement. Eliminate them unless you purposefully use them in dialogue. For more on **subject-verb agreement,** see page 110 in the *Holt Handbook.*

DIRECT TEACHING

Proofread and Publish Your Short Story

If students choose to publish their stories on the Web, keep in mind that Internet resources are sometimes public forums, and their content can be unpredictable.

Resources Reminder

For help with writing assessment, see 6 Traits—Plus 1 in the "Scales and Sample Papers" section of *Progress Assessment of Writing, Listening, & Speaking.*

PRACTICE & APPLY 4

Guided and Independent Practice

Guide the proofreading process by writing on the chalkboard the second bulleted question under **Consider the Process** ("How do you think your story stacks up against some of the stories you've read during your study of literature?") and brainstorming possible responses with students. Encourage students to look for ways to improve their own stories based on what they like in other stories. Then, have them complete **Practice and Apply 4** as independent practice.

RESOURCES: WRITING

Practice & Apply 3

Think Sheet

- *Writing, Listening, & Speaking,* WS. p. 91

Evaluation

- *Writing, Listening, & Speaking,* WS. p. 90

Practice & Apply 4

Assessment

- *Test Generator* (*One-Stop Planner* CD-ROM)
- *Progress Assessment of Writing, Listening, & Speaking,* pp. 26–28, 76–78

Internet

- Online assessments at go.hrw.com (keyword: HLLA)

Standards Review

Literary Response and Analysis

STANDARDS FOCUS, pp. 610–612

(For the grade-level standard reviewed in this lesson, see Student Edition, p. 610.)

INTRODUCING THE STANDARDS REVIEW

Use this review to assess students' grasp of the standard taught in this chapter. If necessary, you can use the annotations to guide students in their reading before they answer the questions.

DIRECT TEACHING

A Literary Focus GRADE-LEVEL STANDARD

Style: Figurative language. What kind of figurative language does the author use when she describes Lucy's tongue as "rolling around in there like a blind worm"? [She uses a simile.]

B Literary Focus GRADE-LEVEL STANDARD

Style: Diction and sentence structure. Find examples of sentence fragments and nonstandard usage in this passage. [*Sentence fragments*—"Screen door with no screen"; "Little black dog biting his fur"; "Fat couch on the porch." *Nonstandard usage*—"she didn't cry neither"; "so it don't stretch out"] How well does this style suit the story's narrator? Explain. [The narrator is a young girl talking about her best friend. The diction and sentence structure are realistic and help readers hear the voice of a young girl talking in her own words about someone she cares about.]

Literary Response and Analysis

Test Practice

Literary Criticism: Evaluating Style

DIRECTIONS: Read the short-short story that follows. Then, read each multiple-choice question, and write the letter of the best response.

My Lucy Friend Who Smells Like Corn

Sandra Cisneros

Lucy Anguiano, Texas girl who smells like corn, like Frito Bandito chips, like tortillas, something like that warm smell of nixtamal[1] or bread the way her head smells when she's leaning close to you over a paper cut-out doll or on the porch when we are squatting over marbles trading this pretty crystal that leaves a blue star on your hand for that giant cat-eye with a grasshopper green spiral in the center like the juice of bugs on the windshield when you drive to the border, like the yellow blood of butterflies. *Have you ever eated dog food? I have.* After crunching like ice, she opens her big mouth to prove it, only a pink tongue rolling around in there like a blind worm, and Janey looking in because she said show me. But me I like that Lucy, corn smell hair and aqua flip flops just like mine which we bought at K-mart for only 79¢ same time. I'm going to sit in the sun, don't care if it's a million trillion degrees outside, so my skin can get so dark it's blue where it bends like Lucy's. Her whole family like that. Eyes like knife slits. Lucy and her sisters. Norma, Margarita, Ofelia, Herminia, Nancy, Olivia, Cheli, y la Amber Sue.

Screen door with no screen. BANG! Little black dog biting his fur. Fat couch on the porch. Some of the windows painted blue, some pink because her Daddy got tired that day or forgot. Mama in the kitchen feeding clothes into the wringer washer[2] and clothes rolling out all stiff and twisted and flat like paper. Lucy got her arm stuck once and had to yell Maaa! and her Mama had to put the machine in reverse and then her hand rolled back, the finger black and later, the nail fell off. *But did your arm get flat like the clothes? What happened to your arm? Did they have to pump it with air?* No, only the finger, and she didn't cry neither.

Lean across the porch rail and pin the pink sock of the baby Amber Sue on top of Cheli's flowered t-shirt, and the blue jeans of la Ofelia over the inside seam of Olivia's blouse, over the flannel nightgown of

Pages 610–612 cover **Reading Standard 3.11** Evaluate the aesthetic qualities of style, including the impact of diction and figurative language on tone, mood, and theme, using the terminology of literary criticism. (Aesthetic approach)

1. **nixtamal** (niks•tä•mäl′) *n.:* partially cooked corn that has been boiled with lime in preparation for making corn tortillas.
2. **wringer washer:** old-fashioned washing machine in which clothing, after being washed, is rolled through a device (the wringer) that squeezes out the water.

READING MINI-LESSON

Reviewing Word-Attack Skills

Activity. Display these pairs of words. Have students identify the word in each pair in which the initial *a* does not stand for /ə/.

1. avenge	avenue	[avenue]
2. avid	avow	[avid]
3. alien	align	[alien]
4. aback	abacus	[abacus]
5. abominate	aborigine	[aborigine]
6. adjust	adjutant	[adjutant]
7. adulate	adopt	[adulate]
8. abysmal	abstract	[abstract]
9. acclaim	acclamation	[acclamation]
10. acquiesce	acquire	[acquiesce]
11. aghast	agile	[agile]
12. amorous	among	[amorous]

Margarita so it don't stretch out, and then you take the workshirts of their Daddy and hang them upside down like this, and this way all the clothes don't get so wrinkled and take up less space and you don't waste pins. The girls all wear each other's clothes, except Olivia who is stingy, because there ain't no boys here. Only girls and one father who is never home hardly and one mother who says *Ay! I'm real tired* and so many sisters there's no time to count them.

I'm sitting in the sun even though it's the hottest part of the day, the part that makes the streets dizzy, when the heat makes a little hat on the top of your head and bakes the dust and weed grass and sweat up good, all steamy and smelling like sweet corn.

I want to rub heads and sleep in a bed with little sisters, some at the top and some at the feets. I think it would be fun to sleep with sisters you could yell at one at a time or all together, instead of alone on the fold-out chair in the living room.

When I get home Abuelita[3] will say *Didn't I tell you?* and I'll get it because I was supposed to wear this dress again tomorrow. But first I'm going to jump off an old pissy mattress in the Anguiano yard. I'm going to scratch your mosquito bites, Lucy, so they'll itch you, then put mercurochrome[4] smiley faces on them. We're going to trade shoes and wear them on our hands. We're going to walk over to Janey Ortiz's house and say *We're never ever going to be your friend again forever!* We're going to run home backwards and we're going to run home frontwards, look twice **C** under the house where the rats hide and I'll stick one foot in there because you dared me, sky so blue and heaven inside those white clouds. I'm going to peel a scab from my knee and eat it, sneeze on the cat, give you three M&M's I've been saving for you since yesterday, comb your hair with my fingers and braid it into teeny-tiny braids real pretty. We're going to wave to a lady we don't know on the bus. Hello! I'm going to somersault on the rail of the front porch even though my chones[5] show. And cut paper dolls we draw ourselves, and color in their clothes with crayons, my arm around your neck. And when we look at each other, our arms gummy from an orange popsicle we split, we could be sisters right? **D** We could be, you and me waiting for our teeths to fall and money. You laughing something into my ear that tickles, and me going Ha Ha Ha Ha. Her and me, my Lucy friend who smells like corn.

3. **Abuelita** (ä·bwel·ē′tä): affectionate Spanish word for "Grandma."
4. **mercurochrome** (mər·kyoor′ə·krōm′) *n.:* reddish solution painted on cuts and scrapes to prevent infection.
5. **chones** (chō′nes) *n.:* Spanish slang for "pants."

DIRECT TEACHING

C Literary Focus
GRADE-LEVEL STANDARD

Style: Imagery and tone. What imagery does the author use to help readers imagine the fun that two close childhood friends can have together? [Imagery includes "jump off an old pissy mattress," "scratch your mosquito bites, Lucy, so they'll itch," "mercurochrome smile face," "trade shoes and wear them on our hands," "run home backwards," "sky so blue," "peel a scab from my knee and eat it," "sneeze on the cat," "braid it into teeny-tiny braids," and "somersault on the rail of the front porch."] **What tone, or attitude, does this imagery create?** [The tone may be described as affectionate, upbeat, or fun loving.]

D Literary Focus
GRADE-LEVEL STANDARD

Style and theme. **Based on how the narrator describes Lucy, how important is Lucy to her?** [Possible responses: Lucy is an important friend to whom the narrator feels very close. She wishes that she and Lucy could be sisters.] **What message about childhood friendships do you think the author wants to convey?** [Possible responses: Children are capable of very intense feelings for their friends. Close friendships are an important part of childhood.]

Test-Taking Tips

Remind students to use the process of elimination to answer questions that include the word *except*. They should go back to the story and look for examples of each option until they identify one that *cannot* be found in the selection.

For more instruction on how to answer multiple-choice items, refer students to **Test Smarts.**

Activity. Display these pairs of words without the underlines. Have students either (1) underline the letters that are different in the words but stand for the same sounds or (2) underline the letters that are the same but stand for different sounds. Answers are underlined.

1.	hearse	curse
2.	hostage	postage
3.	dossier	glossier
4.	emasculate	immaculate
5.	factitive	factitious
6.	misery	miserly
7.	arsonist	arsenic
8.	sickle	icicle
9.	autonomous	anonymous
10.	peregrine	paraffin

Standards Review

TestPractice

Answers and Model Rationales

1. **D** Lucy is the subject of the story, so A is wrong. The narrator wishes she were Lucy's sister, so B is wrong. Janey Ortiz (C) is mentioned briefly.
2. **H** A simile is a figure of speech, often introduced by the word *like,* that makes an imaginative comparison.
3. **C** Among the images and similes that create a lively, upbeat mood are "like Frito Bandito chips" and "aqua flip-flops."
4. **F** The affectionate tone prevails throughout the story, most clearly at the end.
5. **D** Conflict is not an element of style, so D is correct.
6. **H** Sentence fragments are conversational. Formal writing (A) uses only complete sentences. The use of fragments is intentional, so G is wrong. Most people speak in fragments, so J is wrong.
7. **D** The narrator's diction makes it clear that she is a child *now,* so D the answer.
8. **F** Lucy is important to the narrator. The story does not tell what becomes of their friendship, so G and H do not apply. The liveliness and sincerity of the tone seem to contradict J.

1. Who is the **narrator** of this story?
   - A Lucy Anguiano
   - B One of Lucy's sisters
   - C Janey Ortiz
   - D An unnamed girl
2. In the first sentence of the story, Cisneros's description of a marble's center as being "like the juice of bugs on the windshield" is an example of which kind of **figurative language**?
   - F Extended metaphor
   - G Metaphor
   - H Simile
   - J Personification
3. The **images** and **figurative language** in the first paragraph help to create which of the following **moods**?
   - A Sad and somber
   - B Quiet and thoughtful
   - C Upbeat and lively
   - D Detached and cold
4. The writer's **tone,** or attitude, is best described as —
   - F affectionate
   - G critical
   - H fearful
   - J mocking
5. All of the following contribute to the story's unique **style** *except* —
   - A the diction, or word choice
   - B the figurative language
   - C the length of the sentences
   - D the story's conflicts
6. What is the effect of the author's use of sentence fragments?
   - F They create a formal tone.
   - G They remind us of the importance of using good grammar.
   - H They create a friendly, informal tone.
   - J They show us that the narrator is unusual.
7. The author's **diction,** or word choice, suggests all of the following about the narrator *except* that she —
   - A is observant
   - B loves life
   - C is young
   - D is looking back on her childhood
8. Which statement *best* describes the story's **theme**?
   - F Friendship is important, especially to children.
   - G Friendships fade as you get older.
   - H True friendship lasts forever.
   - J Childhood friendships are not very deep.

Using Academic Language

Review of Literary Terms
Reading Standard 3.11

Ask students to look back through the chapter to find the meanings of the terms listed at right. Then, have students show their grasp of Standard 3.11 by citing passages from the chapter that illustrate the meanings of those terms.

Style (pp. 556, 558); **Diction** (pp. 556, 558); **Sentence Structure** (p. 556); **Figures of Speech** (pp. 557, 564); **Tone** (pp. 557, 558, 578); **Mood** (pp. 557, 564); **Theme** (p. 557); **Magic Realism** (p. 586).

Review of Informational Terms
Reading Standard 2.8

Ask students to use these terms to explain how to evaluate the credibility of an author's argument.

Persuasive Writing (p. 577); **Credibility** (pp. 577, 578); **Argument** (p. 577); **Logical Appeals** (p. 577); **Emotional Appeals** (p. 577); **Facts** (p. 577); **Opinions** (p. 577); **Intent** (p. 577).

Vocabulary Development

Multiple-Meaning Words

Test Practice

DIRECTIONS: Choose the answer in which the underlined word is used in the same way as it is used in the numbered sentence.

1. "What does it matter?"
   - A The scientist looked for foreign matter.
   - B I have a personal matter to discuss.
   - C In a matter of minutes, everything changed.
   - D His election will matter a great deal to the country.

2. "As we drove up to our house now, I noticed the shabby state of the compound."
   - F Ferric oxide, a chemical compound, is commonly known as rust.
   - G A high fence surrounds the three buildings in the government compound.
   - H *Scarecrow* is a compound word.
   - J There's no need to compound the problem.

3. "It so happened that during those days, among so many other carnival attractions, there arrived in town . . . the woman who had been changed into a spider. . . ."
   - A Kindness and loyalty are just two of his many attractions.
   - B What are your favorite theme park attractions?
   - C He demonstrated the attractions of different magnets to various metals.
   - D I saw the coming attractions for a movie that looked interesting.

4. "A fearful thunderclap rent the sky in two. . . ."
   - F She plans to rent a convertible.
   - G The house was available for rent.
   - H Her rejection rent his heart apart.
   - J Rent on an apartment is due the first of the month.

5. "They can support their conservation group of choice, perhaps bearing in mind that the longest established is the World Wildlife Fund."
   - A A bearing fell out of his skate wheel.
   - B He had a proud bearing.
   - C The pressure was bearing down on her.
   - D All summer long he was bearing a secret grudge.

6. "But it will be a sound investment."
   - F The sound of the phone awakened her.
   - G She gives very sound advice.
   - H The waters in the sound were calm and smooth.
   - J It didn't sound like a good idea.

Test Practice

Vocabulary Development

Multiple-Meaning Words

Modeling. Model the answer to item 1. Say: "In the sentence, *matter* is used as a verb meaning 'to be important.' The only option that uses *matter* as a verb is D, and it has the same meaning. In A, *matter* means 'substance'; in B, 'issue'; and in C, 'time period.'"

TestPractice

Answers and Model Rationales

1. **D** See rationale above.
2. **G** In the example, and in G, *compound* is a noun meaning "area containing a group of buildings." In F, it means "a combination of chemical elements." In H, it identifies a word made by combining two smaller words. In J, it is a verb meaning "to add to."
3. **B** In the example, and in B, *attractions* refers to entertainment features. In A, it refers to appealing personal qualities; in C, to a physical property; and in D, to promotional movie excerpts.
4. **H** In the example, as in H, *rent* is a verb meaning "tore." In F, *rent* is a verb meaning "pay to use for a time." In G and J, it is a noun meaning "payments made by tenants to a landlord."
5. **D** In the example, as in D, *bearing* is a verb meaning "keeping." In A, it is a noun referring to a machine part. In B, it is a noun meaning "body posture." In C, it is a verb meaning "exerting pressure."
6. **G** In the example and in G, *sound* is an adjective meaning "wise." In F, it is a noun referring to audible vibrations; in H, it is a noun that refers to a body of water. In J, it is a verb meaning "seem."

Vocabulary Review

Use this activity to assess whether students have retained the chapter Vocabulary. Ask students to complete each sentence with the correct word from the box.

indigenous	prudence	magnanimous
degradation	terminal	

1. We should all lament the ______ we have caused to our environment. [degradation]
2. Different types of animals are ______ to different habitats. [indigenous]
3. He is naive and rash, totally bereft of common sense and ______. [prudence]
4. There is no known cure for that disease; it is inevitably ______. [terminal]
5. He is revered for his ethical, ______ treatment of other people. [magnanimous]

STANDARDS REVIEW

Writing

Test Practice

DIRECTIONS: Read the following paragraph from a draft of a student's short story. Then, read the questions below it. Choose the best answer to each question, and mark your answers on your own paper.

(1) Julia's heart sank as she saw the red and blue squad car lights dance in her rearview mirror. (2) Why had she been driving so fast? (3) She'd been in a hurry to pick up her best friend, who had two expensive concert tickets for that evening, but now she was on the side of the road, stopped for speeding. (4) The officer, grim-faced, took her information very deliberately and walked slowly back to the squad car to check it. (5) Julia's palms were sweating as she clutched the hot steering wheel, fearful of doing anything the officer might think was disrespectful but wishing he would get on with it—give her the citation and let her go—before it was too late for the concert. (6) The officer returned and, frowning severely, returned her license and registration. (7) "Slow down, young lady," he growled, "because the next one won't be a warning."

1. To describe the setting with sensory details, which of the following sentences could the writer add?

- **A** The asphalt of the highway emitted a steamy heat that engulfed her car.
- **B** A wide, black belt cinched the officer's girth tightly.
- **C** She pictured herself in prison stripes weeding her parents' garden.
- **D** She was painfully aware of passing cars slowing to see the criminal.

2. What sentence could the writer add to include effective details about the main character's physical appearance?

- **F** Her dirty car put a smudge on the officer's uniform as he leaned against it.
- **G** She could just imagine her dad's face, contorted with anger, when he got the news.
- **H** Her face burned red with embarrassment as the officer walked toward her.
- **J** She had no idea that the stern police officer would think of taking pity on her.

3. To shift the perspective of the passage, which of the following sentences could the writer add?

- **A** She knew her mother would make her feel guilty for a month.
- **B** She wondered how her older brother had felt when he got his first ticket.
- **C** As Julia drove off, the officer smiled, remembering his first ticket.
- **D** She knew her mother would make her promise to be more careful.

614 Chapter 8 Evaluating Style • Evaluating an Argument

4. Which of the following sentences best describes the conflict of the passage?
   - **F** Students believed that the police in that area ticketed young drivers for any sort of minor traffic infraction.
   - **G** Julia was faced with a traffic ticket and a fine as well as potentially harsher consequences from her parents.
   - **H** Now Julia would have to give up a Saturday and take a defensive driving course to keep her insurance rates from going up.
   - **J** Julia was torn by her fear of appearing disrespectful of the officer and her desire to pick up her friend and get to the concert on time.

5. If the following sentence were added to the passage, how would it change the point of view of the passage? "As Julia drove away, the officer shook his head sadly, hoping the warning would be enough to slow the girl down."
   - **A** from third-person omniscient to third-person limited
   - **B** from first-person main character to first-person supporting character
   - **C** from third-person limited to third-person omniscient
   - **D** from first-person supporting character to first-person main character

FOR BETTER OR FOR WORSE

RESOURCES: WRITING

Assessment

- *Test Generator* (*One-Stop Planner* CD-ROM)
- *Progress Assessment of Writing, Listening, & Speaking*, Ch. 8
- *Diagnostic and Summative Assessments*, Third-Quarter Test

Internet

- Online assessments at go.hrw.com (keyword: HLLA)

Standards Review

Answers

1. A
2. H
3. C
4. J
5. C

APPLICATION

Narrative Poem

Have students work at home to adapt their short stories into narrative poems. Point out that a narrative poem tells a story in a very precise, colorful manner, in much fewer words than a short story. However, a narrative poem will use many of the elements found in a short story (character, plot, setting). Students may or may not choose to use rhyme, but they should pay attention to the rhythm of their lines and choose line breaks accordingly. Ask volunteers to share their poems with the class.

Homework

EXTENSION

Giving an Eyewitness Account

Tell students that narratives, in the form of eyewitness accounts, are frequently used in resolving legal or business conflicts or problems. Point out to students that such accounts differ from a short story in many obvious ways, but one thing remains the same: the importance of presenting a chronologically ordered series of events with clear, precise, vivid description and an accurate sense of character. Ask students to imagine that they have witnessed the commission of a crime and have been asked to provide an eyewitness account. Have each present the eyewitness account orally or as a skit with a partner.

Holt Literature and Language Arts: Mastering the California Standards

Chapter 9 Literary Criticism: Biographical and Historical Approach
Using Primary and Secondary Sources

Program Organization

Holt Literature and Language Arts provides a complete curriculum for standards-based instruction in reading, literature, writing, listening and speaking, and language conventions. The instructional content is presented in quarters to enable teachers to anticipate and administer the quarterly assessments required by California.

About Chapter 9

Standards-based lesson plans and suggestions for pacing the presentation of Chapter 9, the related instructional material, and the recommended assessment are provided in *On Course: Mapping Instruction,* Chapter 9.

- In Chapter 9, students will identify and use words literally and figuratively; distinguish between denotative and connotative meanings of words; use words from mythology; extend ideas from primary and secondary sources; analyze the way a work is related to its historical period; write a research report and deliver an oral presentation.

Language Arts Content

Which reading standards are taught in Chapter 9?

In this chapter, students will master the following Grade 10 standards and review standards from Grade 8. Selections or features marked with a ✔ constitute the minimum course of study that provides coverage of grade-level standards.

Grade 10 Standards
Word Analysis, Fluency, and Systematic Vocabulary Development

1.1 Identify and use the literal and figurative meanings of words and understand word derivations.
✔ Meaning Maps, p. 631
Clarifying Word Meanings, p. 643
Analogies: Matching Word Pairs, p. 650
Demonstrating Word Knowledge, p. 659
Words from Old Norse and Anglo-Saxon, p. 688

1.2 Distinguish between the denotative and connotative meanings of words and interpret the connotative power of words.
Synonyms and Connotations, p. 631

1.3 Identify Greek, Roman, and Norse mythology and use the knowledge to understand the origin and meaning of new words.
Words Derived from Greek and Roman Myths, p. 672
Words from Old Norse and Anglo-Saxon, p. 688

Reading Comprehension (Focus on Informational Materials)

2.5 Extend ideas presented in primary or secondary sources through original analysis, evaluation, and elaboration.
"The War Escalates" (textbook), "Dear Folks" (letter)
✔ from "Declaration of Independence from the War in Vietnam" (speech) } pp. 632–643
"The Media and the War" (standards review)
from "The Vietnam War: An Eyewitness History" (standards review) } pp. 712–715

(continued)

(continued)

Literary Response and Analysis

3.12 Analyze the way in which a work of literature is related to the themes and issues of its historical period.
"Biography and History: How the Two Affect Literary Criticism" (standards essay), pp. 618–619
✔ "Where Have You Gone, Charming Billy?" (short story), pp. 620–630
"The Sword in the Stone" (legend), pp. 644–649
"The Tale of Sir Launcelot du Lake" (legend), pp. 651–658
"Theseus" (Greek myth), pp. 660–671; "Sigurd, the Dragon Slayer" (Norse myth), pp. 673–687

Review Standards Grade 8

Reading 1.2 Understand the most important points in the history of the English language and use common word origins to determine the historical influences on English word meaning.
A Changing Language: English Word Origins, p. 659
Words from Old Norse and Anglo-Saxon, p. 688

Reading 3.7 Analyze a work of literature, showing how it reflects the heritage, traditions, attitudes, and beliefs of its author.
"Biography and History: How the Two Affect Literary Criticism" (standards essay), pp. 618–619
"Where Have You Gone, Charming Billy?" (short story), pp. 620–630

Which writing, and listening and speaking standards are taught in Chapter 9?

Writing Strategies

1.3 Use clear research questions and suitable research methods to elicit and present evidence from primary and secondary sources.
Develop Research Questions, pp. 691–692; Answer Research Questions, pp. 692–693

1.4 Develop the main ideas within the body of the composition through supporting evidence.
Record Information, pp. 693–696

1.5 Synthesize information from multiple sources and identify complexities and discrepancies in the information and the different perspectives found in each medium.
Analyze the Information, pp. 696–697

1.6 Integrate quotations and citations into a written text while maintaining the flow of ideas.
Credit Your Sources, pp. 698–699; Integrate Direct Quotations into Your Paper, p. 700

1.7 Use appropriate conventions for documentation in the text, notes, and bibliographies by adhering to those in style manuals.
Record Information, pp. 693–696; Credit Your Sources, pp. 698–699

Writing Applications

2.3 Write expository compositions, including analytical essays and research reports.

a. Marshal evidence in support of a thesis and related claims, including information on all relevant perspectives.
Write a Thesis Statement, p. 697; Organize Your Ideas, pp. 697–698

b. Convey information and ideas from primary and secondary sources accurately and coherently.
Record Information, pp. 693–696; Credit Your Sources, pp. 698–699

c. Make distinctions between the relative value and significance of specific data, facts, and ideas.
Weighing Different Kinds of Answers, p. 693

d. Include visual aids by employing appropriate technology to organize and record information on charts, maps, and graphs.
In an Orderly Fashion, p. 697

e. Anticipate and address readers' potential misunderstandings, biases, and expectations.
Think About Purpose, Audience, and Tone, p. 691

f. Use technical terms and notations accurately.
Credit Your Sources, pp. 698–699

(continued)

(continued)

Listening and Speaking Strategies

1.3 Choose logical patterns of organization to inform and to persuade, by soliciting agreement or action, or to unite audiences behind a common belief or cause.
Adapt Your Research Paper, pp. 710–711

1.7 Use props, visual aids, graphs, and electronic media to enhance the appeal and accuracy of presentations.
Main Points, p. 710

1.8 Produce concise notes for extemporaneous delivery.
Off the Cuff, p. 711

1.9 Analyze the occasion and the interests of the audience and choose effective verbal and nonverbal techniques for presentations.
Sounds and Silence, p. 711

Speaking Applications

2.2 Deliver expository presentations.
- a. Marshal evidence in support of a thesis and related claims, including information on all relevant perspectives.
Simplify, Simplify, Simplify, pp. 710–711
- b. Convey information and ideas from primary and secondary sources accurately and coherently.
Primary and Secondary Sources, p. 711
- c. Make distinctions between the relative value and significance of specific data, facts, and ideas.
Evidence, p. 710
- d. Include visual aids by employing appropriate technology to organize and display information on charts, maps, and graphs.
Main Points, p. 710
- e. Anticipate and address the listener's potential misunderstandings, biases, and expectations.
Your Listening Audience, p. 710
- f. Use technical terms and notations accurately.
Tip, p. 711

2.3 Apply appropriate interviewing techniques.
- a. Prepare and ask relevant questions: Getting a Second Opinion, p. 711
- b. Make notes of responses: Getting a Second Opinion, p. 711
- d. Use language that conveys maturity, sensitivity, and respect: Getting a Second Opinion, p. 711
- f. Compile and report responses: Getting a Second Opinion, p. 711

Review Standards Grade 8

Writing 2.3 Write research reports.
- c. Use a variety of primary and secondary sources and distinguish the nature and value of each.
Finding Different Kinds of Answers, p. 693

Speaking 2.3 Deliver research presentations.
- c. Use a variety of primary and secondary sources and distinguish the nature and value of each.
Primary and Secondary Sources, p. 711

Instructional Planning and Support

Where do I find lesson plans, additional resources, and other teaching aids?

- This Annotated Teacher's Edition and *On Course: Mapping Instruction* provide direction in planning and implementing a complete California standards–based curriculum. These components also include instructions for diagnostic, progress, and summative testing; for presenting direct instruction of the standards; for differentiating instruction to provide universal access; and for locating and using the program's ancillaries.
- Lesson and workshop resources are referenced at the beginning of each selection or workshop, in the bottom margin of this teacher's edition.
- Reminders for using additional resources appear in this teacher's edition at point of use.
- The *One-Stop Planner* CD-ROM contains editable lesson plans and all print ancillaries, available in PDF format.

What if I don't have time to teach all of Chapter 9?

- Most standards can be taught with a minimum number of selections and features. In the chart on the preceding page, the core lessons you need in order to provide complete coverage of the chapter standards are identified with a ✔.
- *On Course: Mapping Instruction,* Chapter 9, lists lessons and activities that provide minimum standards coverage.

What provisions have been made for students who have additional class time scheduled in language arts?

- *Interactive Reading* provides for alternative direct instruction and practice of the grade-level standards taught in Chapter 9.
- *Universal Access: Writing, Listening, and Speaking,* Chapter 9, contains worksheets and transparencies that provide practice in and reteaching and reinforcement of the writing and listening and speaking standards in Chapter 9.
- *Universal Access: Lesson Plans for Language Development,* Chapter 9, provides alternative teaching strategies and additional worksheets designed specifically for English-language learners and special education students. Many of the suggestions and activities in this ancillary will also be helpful to students in the regular classroom who are having difficulty with particular skills.

Universal Access

How do I differentiate instruction to ensure that all my students master the standards?

Holt Literature and Language Arts provides comprehensive, differentiated instruction for all types of students.

- Most of the general instruction and teaching strategies in the Annotated Teacher's Edition are at grade level. These instructions will work well with the majority of your students.
- Point-of-use suggestions are provided for advanced learners, learners having difficulty, English-language learners, and special education students.
- *Interactive Reading* is designed to anticipate and remediate problems that students may experience in achieving mastery of the reading standards. See *Interactive Reading,* Teacher's Edition, Chapter 9, for information on using the reader to differentiate instruction.
- *Universal Access: Writing, Listening, and Speaking,* Chapter 9, contains worksheets and transparencies that provide practice in and reteaching and reinforcement of the writing and listening and speaking standards lessons in Chapter 9.
- *Universal Access: Lesson Plans for Language Development,* Chapter 9, offers teaching strategies and additional worksheets designed specifically for English-language learners and special education students.

Assessment

How do I determine whether my students are making progress in mastering the standards?

Progress Assessment

- Use the Standards Review at the end of Chapter 9 for an informal assessment of the informational reading and writing standards.
- Use Chapter 9 tests from the *Progress Assessment* booklets to assess comprehension and progress on mastering the standards taught in this chapter.

Summative Assessment

The content of *Holt Literature and Language Arts* has been divided into quarters to allow you to administer the four summative tests required by California. Chapters 9–10 and related instructional material constitute the fourth quarter of instruction. At the end of Chapter 11, you may ask students to take the End-of-Year Test in *Diagnostic and Summative Assessments.*

Chapter 9

STANDARDS FOCUS

(For full text of standards taught in this chapter, see Standards Correlation by Standard chart in the Student Edition.)

Grade-Level Standards

- Vocabulary Development 1.1, 1.2, 1.3
- Reading Comprehension 2.5
- Literary Response and Analysis 3.12
- Writing Strategies 1.3, 1.4, 1.5, 1.6, 1.7
- Writing Applications 2.3a–f
- Written and Oral English-Language Conventions 1.5
- Listening and Speaking Strategies 1.3, 1.7, 1.8, 1.9
- Speaking Applications 2.2a–f, 2.3a–g

INTRODUCING THE CHAPTER

In Chapter 9, students analyze the ways that writers' lives and times are reflected in their work.

The chapter opens with views of the Vietnam War. Students will be introduced to a short story about a young soldier facing his first day of combat, a story that echoes the writer's own experience. Then, students will read a variety of primary and secondary sources—including a textbook excerpt, a letter, and a speech—that express differing views about the war.

The chapter next takes readers on a journey to the days of the British King Arthur and the knights of the Roundtable, and then still further back, to the time of Greek and Norse myths. Students will encounter retellings of some of the world's most beloved legends and myths.

Finally, the chapter concludes with an opportunity for students to increase their understanding of primary and secondary sources as they use such sources to write a research paper.

CHAPTER 9 RESOURCES: READING

Planning

- *One-Stop Planner* CD-ROM with Test Generator
- *On Course: Mapping Instruction*
- *At Home: A Guide to Standards Mastery*
- *At Home: In Spanish*
- *Supporting Instruction in Spanish*

Reading

- *Interactive Reading*

Differentiating Instruction

- *Lesson Plans for Language Development*

Vocabulary

- *Vocabulary Development*
  - Cumulative Vocabulary Review, pp. 47–48

Chapter 9

LITERARY CRITICISM

Biographical and Historical Approach

USING PRIMARY AND SECONDARY SOURCES

Literature is the memory of humanity.

—Isaac Bashevis Singer

"It hung upon a thorn and there he blew three deadly notes."
Illustration by N. C. Wyeth for the *Boy's King Arthur* (1917).
Oil on canvas.

go.hrw.com
KEYWORD:
HLLA 10-9

617

THE QUOTATION

Isaac Bashevis Singer (1904–1991) was a Polish American writer best known for his stories of life in Eastern Europe. He was awarded the Nobel Prize in literature in 1978. The quotation refers to the way literature reveals what is important in the lives of humans. Throughout the ages, literature—both oral and written—has recorded our traditions, cultures, and beliefs, our wars and conflicts, our victories and achievements.

VIEWING THE ART

American illustrator **Newell Convers Wyeth** (1882–1945) was a prolific artist, creating more than three thousand illustrations for books, magazines, advertisements, and posters, as well as paintings and murals. Wyeth made this illustration for a retelling of the Arthurian legends by American poet Sidney Lanier (1842–1881).
Activity. What can you observe about this knight, based on his appearance and actions? [The knight is large, well armored, richly attired, and somewhat ominous. He is sounding a horn, perhaps as a warning or other signal.]

Resources Reminder

Planning

- *At Home: A Guide to Standards Mastery*

Parent letters appear in this resource. Translations of these letters are found in *At Home: In Spanish.* Translations of selection summaries appear in *Supporting Instruction in Spanish.*

Reading

- *Interactive Reading*

The California framework requires students to read materials apart from in-class assignments. Additional readings are cited on the Read On page and on selected pages in the Student Edition.

Grammar

- *Holt Handbook*
  - Misplaced Modifiers, pp. 225–230

Assessment

- *Progress Assessment of Reading*
  - Chapter Test
- *One-Stop Planner* CD-ROM with Test Generator

Internet

- go.hrw.com (Keyword: HLLA10-9)

STANDARDS FOCUS, pp. 618–619

(For the grade-level standard taught in this lesson, see Student Edition, p. 618.)

Prerequisite Standards

- Grade 8, Literary Response and Analysis 3.3 **Compare and contrast motivations and reactions of literary characters from different historical eras confronting similar situations or conflicts.**
- Grade 8, Literary Response and Analysis 3.4 **Analyze the relevance of the setting (e.g., place, time, customs) to the mood, tone, and meaning of the text.**

Literary Focus: Biographical and Historical Approaches

Ask students to imagine watching a favorite movie or television program with a person from a different period in history. What would that person find confusing? What elements of our society and culture would need to be explained? A person from the eighteenth century, for example, would be surprised to see people writing with a computer rather than with ink and quill and to find so many women engaged in professional careers. Discuss the fact that any work, whether on film or in literature, must first be understood in relation to its time and place in history.

Literary Response and Analysis

Biography and History *by* Kylene Beers

HOW THE TWO AFFECT LITERARY CRITICISM

If you put on a pair of sunglasses whose lenses have a reddish tint, suddenly all the colors of the world are slightly different. Green leaves are greener. Yellow sunlight bouncing off the sidewalk is less harsh. Sunsets are more spectacular. Wearing those rose-colored lenses does indeed affect the way you see the world.

Writers, too, are looking at the world through "lenses." Writers live in particular times and places. Each writer brings to a work a family background, an educational background, a work background. All of these backgrounds of the writer—biographical and historical—affect his or her work.

Two Approaches to a Text: Biographical and Historical

Here we will talk about two ways of approaching a text: through biographical lenses and through historical lenses.

Grade 8 Review Reading Standard 3.7 Analyze a work of literature, showing how it reflects the heritage, traditions, attitudes, and beliefs of its author. (Biographical approach)

Reading Standard 3.12 Analyze the way in which a work of literature is related to the themes and issues of its historical period. (Historical approach)

A **biographical approach** means that you use the writer's life experiences as you analyze and respond to a text. In other words, you look for ways in which the writer's personal experiences are revealed in the text. You might even find ways in which the writer's prejudices are reflected in the work.

In the story by Alice Walker on page 77, for example, you read about a simple woman in the rural South who is visited one day by a daughter who talks down to her. If you know that Walker herself grew up in the rural South and that, furthermore, she left home to attend a fine school in the North, you might decide that the story reflects some of Walker's personal history. In the same way, if you know that Saki grew up with two strict aunts, you will have an insight into the character of the disapproving aunt in "The Storyteller" (page 155).

A **historical approach** means that you use the time period in which a text was written as a help in analyzing and responding to the work. Ray Bradbury's "The Pedestrian" (page 47), for example, was written during the 1950s, a time when people thought that technology, and especially television, would limit their freedom. You see those concerns as you read that story. Furthermore, if you know that during the 1950s (a time marked by events known as the cold war), Americans feared the Soviet Union and the rise of totalitarianism, then you will read the story with even greater insight.

Try It Out: Biographical and Historical Criticism

Read the following poem as if you do not know anything about its author or the time when it was written:

I, Too

I, too, sing America.

I am the darker brother.
They send me to eat in the kitchen
When company comes,
But I laugh,
And eat well,
And grow strong.

DIFFERENTIATING INSTRUCTION

Learners Having Difficulty

Biographical and historical approach. To help students understand these approaches to a text, have them choose a familiar sitcom. Ask them to think about how the writers of the program come up with their ideas—for example, how they draw upon their own personal experiences of family, work, school, and life in the world around them. You might have students contrast the issues in a sitcom from thirty years ago with those of today.

English-Language Learners

For more instruction on biographical and historical approaches to a text for English-language learners and special education students, see *Lesson Plans for Language Development,* pp. 283–284.

Tomorrow,
I'll be at the table
When company comes.
Nobody'll dare
Say to me,
"Eat in the kitchen,"
Then.

Besides,
They'll see how beautiful I am
And be ashamed—

I, too, am America.

Think about what this poem means. Now, think about it again knowing that it was written by Langston Hughes, one of the most respected African American poets. How does having **biographical** knowledge about the writer shape your understanding of the poem? Suppose that you also know that Walt Whitman (1819–1892), a poet who strongly influenced Hughes, wrote a poem called "I Hear America Singing." What more can you now say about Hughes's poem?

Let's add another dimension—the **historical dimension.** Comments Hughes makes in "I, Too" are shaped by the historical period in which he lived. When Hughes wrote this poem, in 1924, segregation and discrimination were the norm in the United States. Laws kept African Americans attending separate schools, drinking from separate water fountains, riding at the backs of buses, eating in separate restaurants. Most professions were not open to African Americans, so many worked as "domestics" and as such were obliged to eat in the kitchen, not at the dining-room table. You quickly see that understanding history helps you understand a poem.

A historical lens is also helpful when you read myths and legends. **Myths** are stories that are closely linked to a particular society, that are basically religious in nature, and that reflect the values of the society that tells them. **Legends** are stories based on real historical events. As they are told and retold, they tend to take on many fantastic, even supernatural elements.

In this chapter you will read myths and legends from three historical periods: late medieval Britain, ancient Greece, and medieval Scandinavia. The King Arthur stories were told in England by a people nostalgic for a glorious past, when knights roamed the land using might for right. The ancient Greek myths were told by a people who believed that the gods involved themselves in human affairs. The Scandinavian myths were told by a people with a pessimistic view of the world, seeing valor as the only certainty. Understanding that history will enrich your understanding of these works.

Practice

As you read the selections in this chapter, make a chart like the one below. Use it to see the selections in terms of biography and in terms of history.

Selection:
Author:
Topic of selection:
What I know about the author's life:
What I know about the historical times in which the selection was told or written:

Practice

Students' responses will vary. Possible response:

Selection—from "Declaration of Independence from the War in Vietnam"

Author—Martin Luther King, Jr.

Topic of selection—the devastating effects of the costs and the violence of the Vietnam War on the poor

What I know about the author's life—Martin Luther King, Jr., was a leader in the civil rights movement of the 1950s and 1960s.

What I know about the historical times in which the selection was told or written—The civil rights movement was taking place; there was a great deal of controversy over the United States' involvement in the Vietnam War.

Apply

You may wish to encourage student pairs to exchange and read some examples of their own creative writing. Have the partners look for reflections in the works of the writer's life experiences and of issues and themes of the times. If they prefer, have the partners choose a story or poem from this book that they have already read and study it again through the lens of history and biography.

Advanced Learners

Acceleration. Help move students toward the eleventh- and twelfth-grade Standard 3.7b, for which they relate literary works and authors to the major themes and issues of their eras.

Activity. Have students choose one of the selections in this chapter as the subject of background research. Those who choose the modern works should focus on the lives of the writers and on the political issues of the day. Those who prefer the myths and legends should focus on such aspects of the past as religion, cultural history, and social conventions. As students read the work, have them pay close attention to how it fits with the major themes and issues of its era.

STANDARDS FOCUS, pp. 620–631

(For grade-level and review standards taught in this lesson, see citations on Student Edition pages.)

Prerequisite Standard

- Grade 8, Literary Response and Analysis 3.4 **Analyze the relevance of the setting (e.g., place, time, customs) to the mood, tone, and meaning of the text.**

Summary *at grade level*

The story is told from a limited-third-person viewpoint, focusing on Paul Berlin's mental struggle to conquer his fear in Vietnam. After his first day in combat (during which he watched Billy Boy Watkins die of a heart attack), Paul Berlin is on a tense night march to the sea. To quell his fear, he thinks about home, his childhood, and his father. Flashbacks reveal the details of Billy Boy's death: After a mine blows off his foot, Billy's fear of dying brings on a heart attack. In further ironic ignominy, his body later falls from the helicopter lifting it and is fished from the rice paddy by his platoon, who sing the children's song of the title. Recalling these events, Paul cracks: He giggles so hysterically that another soldier must smother him into silence so the noise does not alert the Vietcong to their position. The patrol finally gets to the sea, their objective, but Paul's fear remains.

Before You Read

Where Have You Gone, Charming Billy?

Literary Focus

Understanding Historical Context

"Where Have You Gone, Charming Billy?" re-creates a young soldier's fears on his first night in the field during the Vietnam War. To appreciate the details in the story, you need to understand its **historical context.** There were no "front lines" in the war, and fighting took the form of unexpected guerrilla skirmishes. From moment to moment, the main character doesn't know what to expect—from his strange surroundings or from his own heart.

Seeing an Author in His Work

Tim O'Brien lived through the events he writes about. His experiences as a soldier in Vietnam have served as the focus of his fiction and nonfiction.

The Vietnam War divided the United States with particular bitterness. Although the war had a profound effect on our nation, for many years not many fiction writers dealt with it. O'Brien has written about it almost exclusively. Fact and fiction are interwoven in his work, and his attitudes about the war are reflected in the themes and issues that recur throughout his works—fear, courage, violence, and the constant threat of death. In the story that follows, he focuses on one soldier's feelings during his initiation into combat.

For more about O'Brien, see page 628.

Grade 8 Review Reading Standard 3.7 Analyze a work of literature, showing how it reflects the heritage, traditions, attitudes, and beliefs of its author. (Biographical approach)

Reading Standard 3.12 Analyze the way in which a work of literature is related to the themes and issues of its historical period. (Historical approach)

Make the Connection

Quickwrite

When you hear the word *war,* what do you think of? Why do people watch war movies? Why is war such a powerful subject? Jot down your thoughts about war.

Background

After many centuries of independence from China, Vietnam became a colony of France in the nineteenth century. In 1954, Vietnam was divided in two after a bitter war for independence from France, with a Communist government set up in the north and a pro-Western one in the south.

Feeling threatened by the spread of communism in Asia, the United States began sending military advisors to South Vietnam in 1955 to help defend it against the north. U.S. combat troops began arriving in 1965. Inevitably South Vietnam began to depend on the United States to fight the war with North Vietnam, and by 1969 more than half a million U.S. troops were fighting in South Vietnam. The government of North Vietnam eventually prevailed, however. In 1973, a peace agreement was signed, and U.S. troops withdrew from Vietnam.

Vocabulary Development

stealth (stelth) *n.:* secretiveness; sly behavior.

diffuse (di·fyo͞os′) *adj.:* spread out; unfocused.

skirted (skʉrt′id) *v.:* passed around rather than through. *Skirted* also means "missed narrowly; avoided."

agile (aj′əl) *adj.:* lively; moving easily and quickly.

inertia (in·ʉr′shə) *n.:* tendency to remain either at rest or in motion.

valiantly (val′yənt·lē) *adv.:* bravely.

consolation (kän′sə·lā′shən) *n.:* act of comforting.

RESOURCES: READING

Planning

- *One-Stop Planner* CD-ROM with Test Generator
- *On Course: Mapping Instruction*

Media

- *Audio CD Library*
  - disc 15
- *Fine Art Transparencies*
  - Transparency 15

Reading

- *Interactive Reading*
  - Interactive version: "Where Have You Gone, Charming Billy?"
- *Interactive Reading,* Teacher's Edition
  - Graphic Organizer: Historical/Biographical Analysis Chart

PRETEACHING

Selection Starter

Build background. To prepare students for the historical context of this story, play "Watching a War: Vietnam on Television" (Videocassette, Segment 8, *Visual Connections*).

Standards Starter

Build prerequisite skills. Point out that one way of getting at the theme of any story is to look at how the main character changes over the course of the story. Often, what this character discovers about life is what the writer wants to reveal to the reader.

Preview Vocabulary

To familiarize students with the Vocabulary words on p. 620, have them complete each of these sentences with the word that fits the context.

1. Rescuers ______ swam across the swollen stream to help the trapped family. [valiantly]
2. The losing team found little ______ in the second-place trophy. [consolation]
3. Although its engine was stalled, the car's ______ allowed us to coast into the station. [inertia]
4. We carefully ______ the pasture where the bull grazed. [skirted]
5. The dance teacher admired the routine performed by the ______ ballerina. [agile]
6. The cat crept with ______ toward the pigeon. [stealth]
7. The ______ spray from the broken sprinkler created puddles on the walk. [diffuse]

Assign the Reading

Homework

You may wish to have students read Meet the Writer (p. 628) as homework before reading the story.

Differentiating Instruction

- *Lesson Plans for Language Development*
  - English-Language Learners, pp. 285–287, 312, 318
  - Special Education Students, pp. 288, 312, 318

Vocabulary

- *Vocabulary Development*
  - Vocabulary Worksheet, p. 43

Assessment

- *Progress Assessment of Reading*
  - Selection Test
- *One-Stop Planner* CD-ROM with Test Generator

DIRECT TEACHING

A Literary Focus
GRADE-LEVEL STANDARD

Understanding historical context. How does the silent, single-file march of the soldiers at night reflect a pattern of fighting in the Vietnam War? [Possible response: To combat America's superior military force, our adversaries in Vietnam avoided open warfare and used guerilla tactics, concealing land mines and planning surprise attacks in the jungle. The soldiers' silent march in the dark shows they are guarding against an enemy ambush.]

B Literary Focus
GRADE-LEVEL STANDARD

Understanding historical context. Like the fictional Paul Berlin, some of the U.S. soldiers who fought in Vietnam did not wish to be there. They were drafted into military service by the government. Other soldiers volunteered and were proud to serve their country in Vietnam. Among soldiers as among other Americans, there were bitter disagreements about U.S. involvement in the war.

C Vocabulary Development
GRADE-LEVEL STANDARD

Connotations. Why is the word *pinched* a good choice to describe the way in which Berlin's eyes were shut? [Possible response: *Pinched* connotes a forced movement; the word choice shows that Berlin is working hard to shut out the harsh reality of his situation.]

D Reading Skills

Making inferences. Why do you think the other soldier speaks so harshly to Paul Berlin? [Possible answer: The soldier knows his survival depends partly on Berlin. If Berlin is not alert to danger, his carelessness could affect the safety of those around him.]

The platoon of twenty-six soldiers moved slowly in the dark, single file, not talking. One by one, like sheep in a dream, they passed through the hedgerow, crossed quietly over a meadow, and came down to the rice paddy.[1] There they stopped. Their leader knelt down, motioning with his hand, and one by one the other soldiers squatted in the shadows, vanishing in the primitive stealth of warfare. For a long time they did not move. Except for the sounds of their breathing, the twenty-six men were very quiet: some of them excited by the adventure, some of them afraid, some of them exhausted from the long night march, some of them looking forward to reaching the sea, where they would be safe. At the rear of the column, Private First Class Paul Berlin lay quietly with his forehead resting on the black plastic stock of his rifle, his eyes closed. He was pretending he was not in the war, pretending he had not watched Billy Boy Watkins die of a heart attack that afternoon. He was pretending he was a boy again, camping with his father in the midnight summer along the Des Moines River.[2] In the dark, with his eyes pinched shut, he pretended. He pretended that when he opened his eyes, his father would be there by the campfire and they would talk softly about whatever came to mind and then roll into their sleeping bags, and that later they'd wake up and it would be morning and there would not be a war, and that Billy Boy Watkins had not died of a heart attack that afternoon. He pretended he was not a soldier.

In the morning, when they reached the sea, it would be better.

In the morning, when they reached the sea, it would be better. The hot afternoon would be over, he would bathe in the sea, and he would forget how frightened he had been on his first day at the war. The second day would not be so bad. He would learn.

There was a sound beside him, a movement, and then a breathed "Hey!"

He opened his eyes, shivering as if emerging from a deep nightmare.

"Hey!" a shadow whispered. "We're *moving*. Get up."

"Okay."

"You sleepin', or something?"

"No." He could not make out the soldier's face. With clumsy, concrete hands he clawed for his rifle, found it, found his helmet.

The soldier shadow grunted. "You got a lot to learn, buddy. I'd shoot you if I thought you was sleepin'. Let's go."

Private First Class Paul Berlin blinked.

Ahead of him, silhouetted against the sky, he saw the string of soldiers wading into the flat paddy, the black outline of their shoulders and packs and weapons. He was comfortable. He did not want to move. But he was afraid, for it was his first night at the war, so he hurried to catch up, stumbling once, scraping his knee, groping as though blind; his boots sank into the thick paddy water, and he smelled it all around him. He would tell his mother how it smelled: mud and algae and cattle manure and chlorophyll;[3] decay, breeding mosquitoes and leeches as big as mice; the fecund[4] warmth of the paddy waters rising up to his cut knee. But he would not tell how frightened he had been.

1. **rice paddy:** flooded field for growing rice.
2. **Des Moines River:** river in Des Moines, Iowa.
3. **chlorophyll** (klôr′ə·fil′) *n.:* green substance found in plant cells.
4. **fecund** (fē′kənd) *adj.:* fertile; producing abundantly.

Vocabulary
stealth (stelth) *n.:* secretiveness; sly behavior.

DIFFERENTIATING INSTRUCTION

Learners Having Difficulty
Invite learners having difficulty to read "Where Have You Gone, Charming Billy?" in interactive format in *Interactive Reading.* The interactive version provides additional instruction, practice, and assessment of the literature standard taught in the Student Edition. Monitor students' responses to the selection, and correct any misconceptions that arise.

Resources Reminder

Differentiating Instruction

- *Interactive Reading*
  - Interactive version: "Where Have You Gone, Charming Billy?"

English-Language Learners
Preview some of the military terms, such as *machine gun, breech, muzzle,* and *ammunition.*

622 Chapter 9 Biographical and Historical Approach • Using Primary and Secondary Sources

Once they reached the sea, things would be better. They would have their rear guarded by three thousand miles of ocean, and they would swim and dive into the breakers and hunt crayfish and smell the salt, and they would be safe.

He followed the shadow of the man in front of him. It was a clear night. Already the Southern Cross[5] was out. And other stars he could not yet name—soon, he thought, he would learn their names. And puffy night clouds. There was not yet a moon. Wading through the paddy, his boots made sleepy, sloshing sounds, like a lullaby, and he tried not to think. Though he was afraid, he now knew that fear came in many degrees and types and peculiar categories, and he knew that his fear now was not so bad as it had been in the hot afternoon, when poor Billy Boy Watkins got killed by a heart attack. His fear now was diffuse and unformed: ghosts in the tree line, nighttime fears of a child, a boogeyman in the closet that his father would open to show empty, saying, "See? Nothing there, champ. Now you can sleep." In the afternoon it had been worse: The fear had been bundled and tight and he'd been on his hands and knees, crawling like an insect, an ant escaping a giant's footsteps, and thinking nothing, brain flopping like wet cement in a mixer, not thinking at all, watching while Billy Boy Watkins died.

Now, as he stepped out of the paddy onto a narrow dirt path, now the fear was mostly the fear of being so terribly afraid again.

He tried not to think.

There were tricks he'd learned to keep from thinking. Counting: He counted his steps, concentrating on the numbers, pretending that the steps were dollar bills and that each step through the night made him richer and richer, so that soon he would become a wealthy man, and he kept counting and considered the ways he might spend the money after the war and what he would do. He would look his father in the eye and shrug and say, "It was pretty bad at first, but I learned a lot and I got used to it." Then he would tell his father the story of Billy Boy Watkins. But he would never let on how frightened he had been. "Not so bad," he would say instead, making his father feel proud.

Songs, another trick to stop from thinking: *Where have you gone, Billy Boy, Billy Boy, oh, where have you gone, charming Billy? I have gone to seek a wife, she's the joy of my life, but she's a young thing and cannot leave her mother,* and other songs that he sang in his thoughts as he walked toward the sea. And when he reached the sea, he would dig a deep hole in the sand and he would sleep like the high clouds and he would not be afraid anymore.

The moon came out. Pale and shrunken to the size of a dime.

The helmet was heavy on his head. In the morning he would adjust the leather binding. He would clean his rifle, too. Even though he had been frightened to shoot it during the hot afternoon, he would carefully clean the breech and the muzzle and the ammunition so that next time he would be ready and not so afraid. In the morning, when they reached the sea, he would begin to make friends with some of the other soldiers. He would learn their names and laugh at their jokes. Then when the war was over, he would have war buddies, and he would write to them once in a while and exchange memories.

Walking, sleeping in his walking, he felt better. He watched the moon come higher.

Once they skirted a sleeping village. The smells again—straw, cattle, mildew. The men

5. **Southern Cross:** constellation, or group of stars, in the Southern Hemisphere.

Vocabulary

diffuse (di·fyo͞os′) *adj.:* spread out; unfocused.

skirted (skurt′id) *v.:* passed around rather than through. *Skirted* also means "missed narrowly; avoided."

DIRECT TEACHING

E Literary Focus
REVIEW STANDARD

Seeing an author in his work. How does the author create the feeling that "you are there"? [Possible response: The sensory images, such as "the shadow of the man in front of him" and the sights of the sky and the sound of boots, put us inside the soldier's mind, making the experience vivid and real.] **Why is this scene so believable?** [It may reflect the author's own experience.]

F Learners Having Difficulty

Understanding figurative language. Be sure students know what a cement mixer is and how its turning mixes the wet materials that will be cement. The image suggests a terrifying cycle of "not thinking."

G Literary Focus
REVIEW STANDARD

Theme. Based on what you have learned about the character so far, what do you predict the theme of the story will be? [Possible response: It will have something to do with fear and being afraid of fear.]

H Literary Focus
GRADE-LEVEL STANDARD

Tone. How does the tone change when Berlin imagines how things will be when they reach the coast? [Possible response: The dark tone of fear becomes upbeat, almost lighthearted.]

Resources Reminder

For lessons designed for intermediate and advanced English-language learners, see *Lesson Plans for Language Development,* pp. 285–287, 312, 318.

Special Education Students

For lessons designed for special education students, see *Lesson Plans for Language Development,* pp. 288, 312, 318.

Advanced Learners

Acceleration. Use this activity to move advanced learners toward the eleventh- and twelfth-grade Standard 3.9, for which they analyze a literary work to determine how the author's philosophical position has contributed to the quality of the work and the credibility of the characters.

Activity. Have students discuss the selection in light of O'Brien's experience and views. Spark discussion with questions like these:

- What do you think the author wants you to understand about war? How does he lead you to this understanding?
- What might be the author's philosophical position regarding U.S. involvement in the Vietnam War?
- How do O'Brien's views and experiences affect the credibility of the characters?

DIRECT TEACHING

A Literary Focus
GRADE-LEVEL STANDARD

Understanding historical context. Explain to students that most Vietnamese are Buddhist and Taoist. Buddhists burn incense during religious ceremonies to honor their ancestors. The "perfumy" smell Paul notices is probably incense burned at the tiny altars in the graveyard.

B Reading Skills

Making a generalization. What generalization can you make about a change in the popularity of the Vietnam War with the American public? [Possible response: As the war progressed, it became increasingly unpopular with Americans, as shown by the fact that the numbers who rallied for peace jumped from 20,000 to 300,000 in four years.] Which of the statistics might help to explain the unpopularity of the war? [Possible response: The war's unpopularity may be, in part, because it lasted so long, it cost so many Americans their lives, it took years from the lives of the millions of young men and women who served, and it cost the taxpayers many billions of dollars.]

C Reading Skills

Making inferences. How influential do you think this war was on the events of the time? [Possible response: Considering that the war went on for twenty years, that millions of Americans served and thousands died, and that $150 billion was spent, the Vietnam War had an enormous influence on events.] What statistic suggests that the war remains of great importance to many Americans? [the fact that 2.5 million people visit the Vietnam War Memorial each year] You might point out that the photo in the background of "A Closer Look" shows a small section of the Vietnam War Memorial in Washington, D.C.

were quiet. On the far side of the village, buried in the dark smells, a dog barked. The column stopped until the barking died away; then they marched fast away from the village, through a graveyard filled with conical-shaped[6] burial mounds and tiny altars made of clay and stone. (A) The graveyard had a perfumy smell. A nice place to spend the night, he thought. The mounds would make fine battlements,[7] and the smell was nice and the place was quiet. But they went on, passing through a hedgerow and across another paddy and east toward the sea.

He walked carefully. He remembered what he'd been taught: Stay off the center of the path, for that was where the land mines and booby traps were planted, where stupid and lazy soldiers like to walk. Stay alert, he'd been taught. Better alert than inert.[8] Ag-ile, mo-bile, hos-tile. He wished he'd paid better attention to the training. He could not remember what they'd said about how to stop being afraid; they hadn't given any lessons in courage—not that he could remember—and they hadn't mentioned how

6. **conical-** (kän′i·kəl) **shaped** *adj.:* shaped like a cone.
7. **battlements** *n.:* fortifications from which to shoot.
8. **inert** (in·urt′) *adj.:* without movement; here, dead.

Vocabulary
agile (aj′əl) *adj.:* lively; moving easily and quickly.

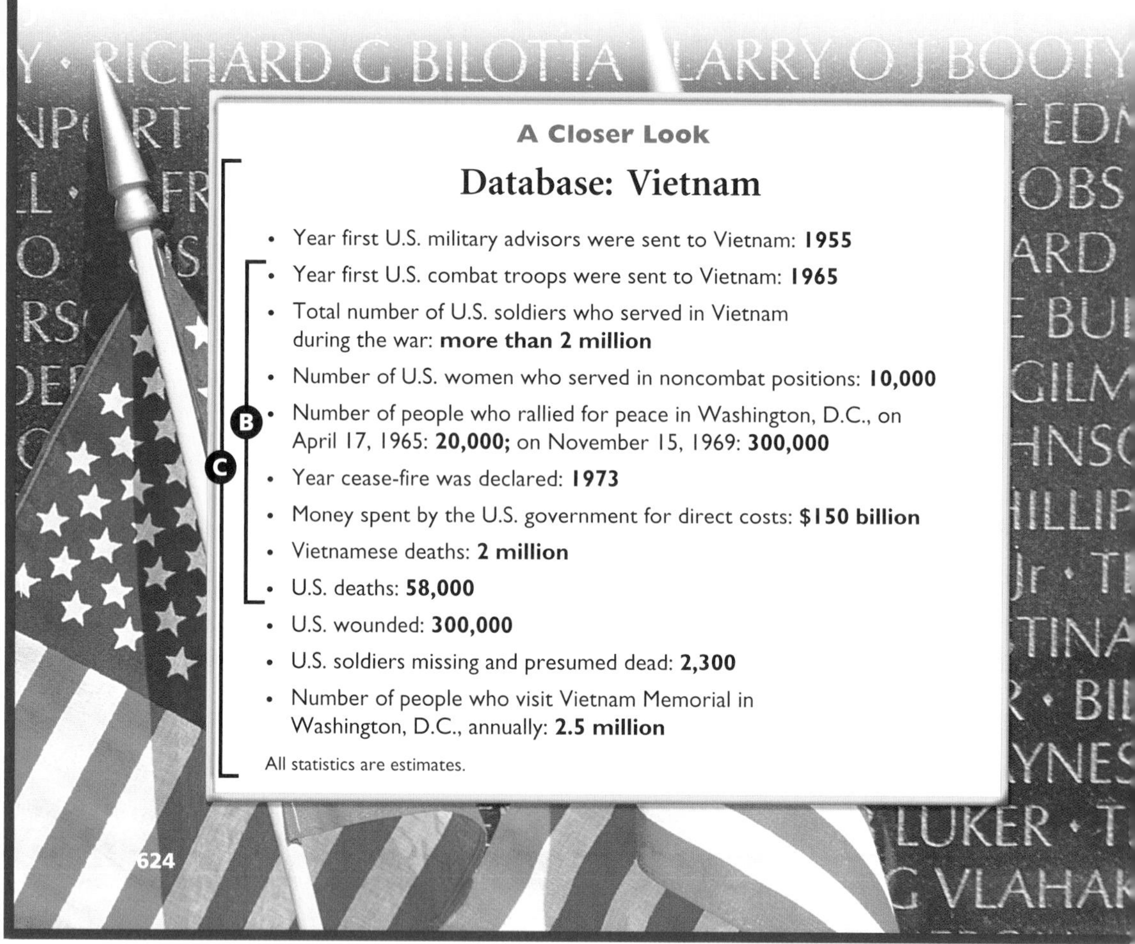

A Closer Look

Database: Vietnam

- Year first U.S. military advisors were sent to Vietnam: **1955**
- Year first U.S. combat troops were sent to Vietnam: **1965**
- Total number of U.S. soldiers who served in Vietnam during the war: **more than 2 million**
- Number of U.S. women who served in noncombat positions: **10,000**
- (B) Number of people who rallied for peace in Washington, D.C., on April 17, 1965: **20,000;** on November 15, 1969: **300,000**
- (C) Year cease-fire was declared: **1973**
- Money spent by the U.S. government for direct costs: **$150 billion**
- Vietnamese deaths: **2 million**
- U.S. deaths: **58,000**
- U.S. wounded: **300,000**
- U.S. soldiers missing and presumed dead: **2,300**
- Number of people who visit Vietnam Memorial in Washington, D.C., annually: **2.5 million**

All statistics are estimates.

CONTENT-AREA CONNECTIONS

History: American Wars
The Vietnam War was the longest war in American history. In what other ways does it compare and contrast with various wars that Americans have fought?
Individual activity. Have each student create a graphic organizer, such as a bar graph, line graph, or table, to compare the Vietnam War with another war in American history: American Revolution, Civil War, World War I, World War II, Korean War, Persian Gulf War, War on Terrorism. Encourage students to research and then present the information on graphic organizers. Have students show their graphic organizers to the class and discuss the stories told by the statistics.

Billy Boy Watkins would die of a heart attack, his face turning pale and the veins popping out.

Private First Class Paul Berlin walked carefully. Stretching ahead of him like dark beads on an invisible chain, the string of shadow soldiers whose names he did not yet know moved with the silence and slow grace of smoke. Now and again moonlight was reflected off a machine gun or a wristwatch. But mostly the soldiers were quiet and hidden and faraway-seeming in a peaceful night, strangers on a long street, and he felt quite separate from them, as if trailing behind like the caboose on a night train, pulled along by inertia, sleepwalking, an afterthought to the war.

D

Better alert than inert.
Ag-ile, mo-bile, hos-tile.

So he walked carefully, counting his steps. When he had counted to 3,485, the column stopped.

One by one the soldiers knelt or squatted down.

The grass along the path was wet. Private First Class Paul Berlin lay back and turned his head so that he could lick at the dew with his eyes closed, another trick to forget the war. He might have slept. "I *wasn't* afraid," he was screaming or dreaming, facing his father's stern eyes. "I wasn't afraid," he was saying. When he opened his eyes, a soldier was sitting beside him, quietly chewing a stick of Doublemint gum.

E

"You sleepin' again?" the soldier whispered.

"No," said Private First Class Paul Berlin. "Hell, no."

The soldier grunted, chewing his gum. Then he twisted the cap off his canteen, took a swallow, and handed it through the dark.

"Take some," he whispered.

"Thanks."

"You're the new guy?"

"Yes." He did not want to admit it, being new to the war.

The soldier grunted and handed him a stick of gum. "Chew it quiet—OK? Don't blow no bubbles or nothing."

"Thanks. I won't." He could not make out the man's face in the shadows.

They sat still and Private First Class Paul Berlin chewed the gum until all the sugars were gone; then the soldier said, "Bad day today, buddy."

Private First Class Paul Berlin nodded wisely, but he did not speak.

"Don't think it's always so bad," the soldier whispered. "I don't wanna scare you. You'll get used to it soon enough. . . . They been fighting wars a long time, and you get used to it."

"Yeah."

"You will."

They were quiet awhile. And the night was quiet, no crickets or birds, and it was hard to imagine it was truly a war. He searched for the soldier's face but could not find it. It did not matter much. Even if he saw the fellow's face, he would not know the name; and even if he knew the name, it would not matter much.

F

"Haven't got the time?" the soldier whispered.

"No."

"Rats. . . . Don't matter, really. Goes faster if you don't know the time, anyhow."

"Sure."

"What's your name, buddy?"

"Paul."

"Nice to meet ya," he said, and in the dark beside the path, they shook hands. "Mine's Toby. Everybody calls me Buffalo, though." The soldier's hand was strangely warm and soft. But it was a very big hand. "Sometimes they just call me Buff," he said.

G

Vocabulary

inertia (in·ʉr′shə) *n.:* tendency to remain either at rest or in motion.

DIRECT TEACHING

D Literary Focus
REVIEW STANDARD

Seeing an author in his work. What does this passage reveal about Paul? [Possible response: He feels separate from the war and from his patrol. He might be deliberately isolating himself mentally and emotionally from the situation. He may, perhaps, be so confused and frightened that he can't accept his real situation.] Do you think this passage is based on an experience of the author's? Why or why not? [Possible response: Yes, because the description is so vivid and real; yes, because it seems as if the author is recalling these feelings.]

E Reading Skills

Interpreting. According to this passage, what is Paul anxious about? [Possible response: He seems to fear his father's "stern" eyes, perhaps accusing his son of cowardice—as if fear is a sign of cowardice.]

F Reading Skills

Drawing conclusions. Why do you think the soldier's name and what he looks like are not important to Paul? [Possible response: Paul is wary of intimacy because the man might be killed.]

G English-Language Learners

Idioms and slang. Explain that "got the time?" is an idiom meaning "What time is it?" Point out, too, in the text that follows, that the word *croaking* is used to mean "dying." In the same paragraph the word *bloody* is a British slang intensifier meaning very. (In England, *bloody* is considered vulgar.)

DEVELOPING FLUENCY

Mixed-ability group activity. Arrange students in mixed-ability groups of three. Explain to them that each group will read the story aloud, with each student taking one of these roles: Paul Berlin, Toby, and narrator. Have a more fluent reader in each group assume the role of narrator. Then, have students practice reading the story aloud. Point out that those students reading the men's dialogue should aim to read naturally, as if they were having a conversation. Also point out that students can use descriptions like "he whispered" or "he snorted" as cues for reading with proper expression.

DIRECT TEACHING

A Reading Skills

Determining author's purpose. Point out to students that the author constantly refers to the character Paul as "Private First Class Paul Berlin." What idea might the author be trying to reinforce by repeating this formal name each time? [Possible response: The author might be trying to emphasize Paul's status as the new guy who has no nickname, in sharp contrast to Toby, who is affectionately called "Buffalo" or simply "Buff" by his fellow soldiers.]

B Literary Focus
GRADE-LEVEL STANDARD

Imagery. This long single sentence contains a series of events linked by *and,* with imagery that helps us experience the terrifying scene almost as if we were there ourselves. What images does the writer use? What senses does each image evoke? ["hissed," sound; "giggling," sound; "drinking Coca-Cola from bright-red aluminum cans," sight, taste, touch; "it made a tiny little sound—*poof*," sound; "his foot lying behind him, most of it still in the boot," sight.]

And again they were quiet. They lay in the grass and waited. The moon was very high now and very bright, and they were waiting for cloud cover. The soldier suddenly snorted.

"What is it?"

"Nothin'," he said, but then he snorted again. "A bloody *heart attack*!" the soldier said. "Can't get over it—old Billy Boy croaking from a lousy heart attack. . . . A heart attack—can you believe it?"

The idea of it made Private First Class Paul Berlin smile. He couldn't help it.

"Ever hear of such a thing?"

"Not till now," said Private First Class Paul Berlin, still smiling.

"Me neither," said the soldier in the dark. "Gawd, dying of a heart attack. Didn't know him, did you."

"No."

"Tough as nails."

"Yeah."

"And what happens? A heart attack. Can you imagine it?"

"Yes," said Private First Class Paul Berlin. He wanted to laugh. "I can imagine it." And he imagined it clearly. He giggled—he couldn't help it. He imagined Billy's father opening the telegram: SORRY TO INFORM YOU THAT YOUR SON BILLY BOY WAS YESTERDAY SCARED TO DEATH IN ACTION IN THE REPUBLIC OF VIETNAM, VALIANTLY SUCCUMBING[9] TO A HEART ATTACK SUFFERED WHILE UNDER ENORMOUS STRESS, AND IT IS WITH GREATEST SYMPATHY THAT . . . He giggled again. He rolled onto his belly and pressed his face into his arms. His body was shaking with giggles.

The big soldier hissed at him to shut up, but he could not stop giggling and remembering the hot afternoon, and poor Billy Boy, and how they'd been drinking Coca-Cola from bright-red aluminum cans, and how they'd started on the day's march, and how a little while later poor Billy Boy stepped on the mine, and how it made a tiny little sound—*poof*—and how Billy Boy stood there with his mouth wide open, looking down at where his foot had been blown off, and how finally Billy Boy sat down very casually, not saying a word, with his foot lying behind him, most of it still in the boot.

He giggled louder—he could not stop. He bit his arm, trying to stifle it, but remembering:

9. **succumbing** *v.* used as *adj.* (used with *to*): here, dying from.

Vocabulary
valiantly (val′yənt·lē) *adv.:* bravely.

READING MINI-LESSON

Developing Word-Attack Skills
Point out the chant Paul remembers from basic training, found on p. 624: *Ag-ile, mo-bile, hos-tile.* Most often, these words are pronounced with an unaccented vowel sound in the final syllable: /a′jəl/, /mō′bəl/, /häs′təl/. Here, however, the words are written in syllables to show the reader that they should be pronounced as they are spelled, with a long *i* sound in the final syllable: /aj′īl′/, /mō′bīl′/, /hos′tīl′/.

Display the words below. Have students tell if the syllable spelled with the *i*-consonant-e pattern has a long *i* sound.

reptile	archive	fertile
inventive	bibliophile	

[*Inventive* and *fertile* do not have syllables with the long *i* sound.]

Activity. Have students group these words by whether long *i* is or is not heard in the *i*-consonant-e syllable. Answers are underlined.

fragile	<u>appetite</u>	<u>parasite</u>
favorite	<u>misfile</u>	lattice
<u>entice</u>	<u>reconcile</u>	pumice
<u>supine</u>	<u>turpentine</u>	determine
<u>porcupine</u>	discipline	<u>undermine</u>

"War's over, Billy," the men had said in consolation, but Billy Boy got scared and started crying and said he was about to die. "Nonsense," the medic said, Doc Peret, but Billy Boy kept bawling, tightening up, his face going pale and transparent and his veins popping out. Scared stiff. Even when Doc Peret stuck him with morphine, Billy Boy kept crying.

"Shut up!" the big soldier hissed, but Private First Class Paul Berlin could not stop. Giggling and remembering, he covered his mouth. His eyes stung, remembering how it was when Billy Boy died of fright.

"Shut up!"

But he could not stop giggling, the same way Billy Boy could not stop bawling that afternoon.

Afterward Doc Peret had explained: "You see, Billy Boy really died of a heart attack. He was scared he was gonna die—so scared he had himself a heart attack—and that's what really killed him. I seen it before."

So they wrapped Billy in a plastic poncho, his eyes still wide open and scared stiff, and they carried him over the meadow to a rice paddy, and then when the medevac helicopter[10] arrived, they carried him through the paddy and put him aboard, and the mortar rounds were falling everywhere, and the helicopter pulled up, and Billy Boy came tumbling out, falling slowly and then faster, and the paddy water sprayed up as if Billy Boy had just executed a long and dangerous dive, as if trying to escape Graves Registration, where he would be tagged and sent home under a flag, dead of a heart attack.

"Shut up!" the soldier hissed, but Paul Berlin could not stop giggling, remembering: scared to death.

Later they waded in after him, probing for Billy Boy with their rifle butts, elegantly and delicately probing for Billy Boy in the stinking paddy, singing—some of them—*Where have you gone, Billy Boy, Billy Boy, oh, where have you gone, charming Billy?* Then they found him. Green and covered with algae, his eyes still wide open and scared stiff, dead of a heart attack suffered while—

"Shut up!" the soldier said loudly, shaking him.

But Private First Class Paul Berlin could not stop. The giggles were caught in his throat, drowning him in his own laughter: scared to death like Billy Boy.

Giggling, lying on his back, he saw the moon move, or the clouds moving across the moon. Wounded in action, dead of fright. A fine war story. He would tell it to his father, how Billy Boy had been scared to death, never letting on . . . He could not stop.

The soldier smothered him. He tried to fight back, but he was weak from the giggles.

The moon was under the clouds and the column was moving. The soldier helped him up. "You OK now, buddy?"

"Sure."

"What was so bloody funny?"

"Nothing."

"You can get killed, laughing that way."

"I know. I know that."

"You got to stay calm, buddy." The soldier handed him his rifle. "Half the battle, just staying calm. You'll get better at it," he said. "Come on, now."

He turned away and Private First Class Paul Berlin hurried after him. He was still shivering.

He would do better once he reached the sea, he thought, still smiling a little. A funny war story that he would tell to his father, how Billy Boy Watkins was scared to death. A good joke. But even when he smelled salt and heard the sea, he could not stop being afraid. ■

10. **medevac** (med'i·vak') **helicopter:** helicopter used to evacuate wounded soldiers to hospitals and medical care.

Vocabulary
consolation (kän'sə·lā'shən) *n.:* act of comforting.

DIRECT TEACHING

C English-Language Learners

Idioms. "Scared stiff" is an idiom suggesting the paralysis that may accompany intense fear. Suggest that students watch for the repetition of "scared stiff" after Billy Boy literally has been scared to death.

D Vocabulary Development

Connotations. What do the words *bawling* and *giggling* connote that *crying* and *laughing* do not? [Possible response: Both words connote behavior more appropriate for children than adult soldiers. The words emphasize the childlike fear that Billy Boy and Paul Berlin feel.]

E Literary Focus
GRADE-LEVEL STANDARD

Conflict. What two conflicts are going on here? [Possible response: the external conflict between the soldier and Paul and the internal conflict within Paul, as he tries to stifle his hysteria]

F Literary Focus
GRADE-LEVEL STANDARD

Understanding historical context. In the movies, war is often portrayed as a heroic adventure. For many people this notion was punctured by the reality of the Vietnam War. How does Billy's fate contrast with romantic portrayals of soldiers at war? [Possible response: Billy's bawling, his fear-caused heart attack, and his fall from the helicopter are ironic contrasts to portrayals of soldiers as stoic and heroic in combat and to the military honors accorded the dead.]

G Literary Focus
GRADE-LEVEL STANDARD

Conflict and theme. What is the principal conflict in this story? [the conflict within Paul to overcome his fear] What has Paul learned about war? [Possible response: The fear is constant; he won't get over it.]

FAMILY/COMMUNITY ACTIVITY

Invite students to interview Vietnam veterans in their family or in their community. Have them prepare questions ahead of time, focusing the interview on the stresses of war and the techniques soldiers used in dealing with those stresses. With the permission of the veteran being interviewed, some students may want to record their interview on audiotape or videotape and then share it with the class.

GUIDED PRACTICE

Monitoring students' progress. Guide the class in answering these comprehension questions. Direct students to locate passages in the text that support their answers.

True-False

1. Paul Berlin is in his first day of combat. [T]
2. Billy Boy dies of loss of blood after he steps on a land mine. [F]
3. Paul focuses on reaching the sea. [T]
4. Toby offers Paul advice on how to be a good soldier. [T]
5. By the end of the story, Paul has overcome his fear. [F]

Meet the Writer

Background. When Tim O'Brien was at Fort Lewis, receiving his advanced infantry training, he decided that he wanted to desert to Sweden rather than serve in Vietnam. Then, on the eve of his planned desertion, having already written the letters explaining the flight to those close to him, he got his order to go to Vietnam—and he went. He was honorably discharged in 1970 and attended graduate school at Harvard University upon his return.

"It's kind of a semantic game: lying versus truth-telling," O'Brien said while talking about his approach to writing. "But I think it's an important game that writers and readers and anyone interested in art in general should be fully aware of. One doesn't lie for the sake of lying; one does not invent merely for the sake of inventing. One does it for a particular purpose and that purpose always is to arrive at some kind of spiritual truth that one can't discover simply by recording the world-as-it-is. We're inventing and using imagination for sublime reasons—to get at the essence of things, not merely at the surface."

Meet the Writer

Tim O'Brien

The Power of the Heart

It was the Vietnam War that made Tim O'Brien (1946–) a writer. He was drafted immediately after graduating from Macalester College in St. Paul, Minnesota, in 1968. He then spent two years as an infantryman in Vietnam.

When he returned from Vietnam, O'Brien used his imagination to cope with memories of the war. Many of his stories are told from the point of view of a young soldier named Paul Berlin. These stories eventually grew into a novel, *Going After Cacciato,* which won the National Book Award in 1979. "Where Have You Gone, Charming Billy?" was used, with some changes, as Chapter 31 of that novel.

In 1990, O'Brien published *The Things They Carried,* referring to the burdens, both material and emotional, carried by the U.S. soldiers in Vietnam—the M-16 rifles, the comic books, the flak jackets, and the fear. In 1994, he published *In the Lake of the Woods,* another novel about his persistent theme—the lingering memory of Vietnam.

The following passage is from O'Brien's autobiographical account of his experiences in Vietnam, *If I Die in a Combat Zone, Box Me Up and Ship Me Home.* Mad Mark was the platoon leader.

"One of the most persistent and appalling thoughts which lumbers through your mind as you walk through Vietnam at night is the fear of getting lost, of becoming detached from the others, of spending the night alone in that frightening and haunted countryside. It was dark. We walked in a single file, perhaps three yards apart. Mad Mark took us along a crazy, wavering course. We veered off the road, through clumps of trees, through tangles of bamboo and grass, zigzagging through graveyards of dead Vietnamese who lay there under conical mounds of dirt and clay. The man to the front and the man to the rear were the only holds on security and sanity. We followed the man in front like a blind man after his dog, like Dante following Virgil through the Inferno, and we prayed that the man had not lost his way, that he hadn't lost contact with the man to his front. We tensed the muscles around our eyeballs and peered straight ahead. We hurt ourselves staring at the man's back. We strained. We dared not look away for fear the man might fade and dissipate and turn into absent shadow. Sometimes, when the jungle closed in, we reached out to him, touched his shirt.

The man to the front is civilization. He is the United States of America and every friend you have ever known; he is Erik and blond girls and a mother and a father. He is your life, and he is your altar and God combined. And, for the man stumbling along behind you, you alone are his torch."

DIFFERENTIATING INSTRUCTION

Advanced Learners

Enrichment. Reviewer Celia Betsky has observed that "the simplicity of O'Brien's language and statements, the dry remoteness of his tone, are deceptive, for they encompass a range of private emotions and universal conditions. He strips words of their ordinary meanings like a plane spraying defoliant and then pumps new life into them."

Activity. Ask students to use what they know about the Vietnam War to explain the allusion to "a plane spraying defoliant." Then, have groups of students discuss Betsky's observation, and challenge them to find examples in the story that support it.

628 Chapter 9 Biographical and Historical Approach • Using Primary and Secondary Sources

For centuries, women have gone to war, but their contributions have rarely been acknowledged. Lily Lee Adams was one of the thousands of women who cared for wounded and dying soldiers in Vietnam. She served with the Army Nurse Corps at the Twelfth Evacuation Hospital in Cu Chi from 1969 to 1970.

The Friendship Only Lasted a Few Seconds

Lily Lee Adams

He said "Mom,"
And I responded
And became her.
I never lied
to him.
And I couldn't
Explain that to others.
I got all and more back.
But the friendship
Only lasted a few seconds.

And he called me Mary.
I wished she could
Be there for him.
I felt I was in
Second place,
But I did the
Best I could
And the friendship
Only lasted a few seconds.

And he told me,
"I don't believe this,
I'm dying for nothing."
Then he died.
Again, the friendship
Only lasted a few seconds.

How can the World
Understand any of this?
How can I keep the
World from forgetting?
After all the friendship
Only lasted a few seconds.

Vietnam Women's Memorial in Washington, D.C.

Connection

Summary below grade level

This poem describes a brief encounter during the Vietnam War between a nurse and a dying soldier.

DIRECT TEACHING

A Reading Skills

Hypothesizing. What do you think the speaker means in saying that she became someone else but wasn't lying? [Possible response: To the soldier, she was his mother, so she was not lying.]

B Reading Skills

Making inferences. What does the speaker mean in saying, "the friendship / Only lasted a few seconds"? [Possible response: The soldier quickly dies but the encounter was meaningful.]

C Reading Skills

Hypothesizing. Who could Mary be? [Possible response: the soldier's wife or girlfriend back home]

D Reading Skills

Interpreting. Why does the speaker say she was in "Second place"? [She was not Mary.]

E Literary Focus
GRADE-LEVEL STANDARD

Understanding historical context. Why does the soldier feel he is "dying for nothing"? [Possible response: Many people felt that the United States had no reason to be fighting in Vietnam; even among soldiers, there was limited support.]

F Reading Skills

Hypothesizing. What does the speaker appear to want in the last stanza of the poem? [Possible response: She wants the complex but brief experience of trying to comfort a dying soldier to be acknowledged as important.]

Connecting and Comparing Texts

Encourage students to discuss and compare these two selections. You may wish to use the following prompts to stimulate discussion:

- How is Paul's relationship to Billy like the relationship between the speaker of this poem and the dying soldier? [Possible response: Both relationships were brief but left a deep impression on the person who lived.]
- How are the dying soldier's final thoughts similar to the thoughts Paul Berlin experienced on his first day in combat? [Possible response: Both soldiers think of their families or the things they associate with home.]
- How do the story and the poem differ in tone? [Possible response: The tone of the story moves back and forth between terror and unrealistic cheerfulness; the tone of the poem is one of sad acceptance.]

INDEPENDENT PRACTICE

Literary Response and Analysis

Reading Check

1. Possible answer: In Vietnam today, William Watkins died of a heart attack after experiencing severe trauma to his lower extremities from a land mine. His body was evacuated by helicopter to be returned to his family.

Interpretations

2. Possible answers: It is ironic that Billy dies from fear, not from his terrible wound, and that instead of being taken away with dignity, his body falls from the helicopter.
3. Possible answers:
   - The song provides a macabre contrast to Billy's death; the song's cheery tone helps the soldiers maintain an emotional distance from the event.
   - Flashbacks to camping trips contrast Paul's peacetime life with his war experiences.
   - Paul's uncontrollable giggling shows that he is terrified to the point of hysteria.
   - Toby represents camaraderie and the wisdom of experience.
4. Possible answer: He has discovered that war is terrifying, brutal, and indifferent to life, and that he can be made hysterical with fear. Possible themes: War is hell. Fear can be as destructive as the cause of the fear.
5. Possible answer: The tone is dark and threatening. ("fear had been bundled and tight and he'd been on his hands and knees crawling…thinking nothing, brain flopping like wet cement in a mixer…"; "…like dark beads on an invisible chain, the string of shadow soldiers…")
6. He expects the sea to bring him safety and an end to fear. Instead, his fear is still with him.

Literary Response and Analysis

Reading Check

1. Tell the story of Billy Boy's death to a partner as you imagine a TV news reporter based in Vietnam might have reported it on the day it happened. Tell **what** happened, **whom** it happened to, **where** it happened, **why** it happened, and **how** it happened.

Interpretations

2. There is a central irony in warfare, which has to do with the fact that soldiers kill people they do not even know. What is **ironic,** or contrary to what we would expect, about how Billy Boy dies? about how his body is removed?
3. Explain the significance of each of these story elements:
   - the song "Where Have You Gone, Billy Boy?"
   - the **flashbacks** to camping trips
   - Paul's fit of uncontrollable giggling
   - the **minor character** Toby
4. What do you think Paul has discovered about war and about himself on his first day of combat? What **theme,** or central idea, relating to war is O'Brien expressing in this story?
5. **Tone** is the writer's attitude toward the subject. How would you describe this story's tone? Analyze the way in which O'Brien creates that tone. Cite lines and incidents from the story.
6. In a sense this is a story about a hero's journey. Such journeys often take the form of a **quest,** a search for something of great value. What is it that Paul expects to find at the sea, the endpoint on his journey? Ironically, what does he find instead?

Grade 8 Review Reading Standard 3.7 Analyze a work of literature, showing how it reflects the heritage, traditions, attitudes, and beliefs of its author. (Biographical approach)

Reading Standard 3.12 Analyze the way in which a work of literature is related to the themes and issues of its historical period. (Historical approach)

Literary Criticism

7. Think about the story's **historical context**—the 1960s and the period of U.S. involvement in the Vietnam War. (You will find some nonfiction accounts of the war on pages 634–641.) How does O'Brien's story reflect its historical period and the **themes** and **issues** of that time?
8. Having read this story and the biographical information about the author (see Meet the Writer on page 628), explain how the story likely reflects O'Brien's attitudes toward the Vietnam War. Give examples from the story to support your interpretation. Remember that the **tone** of a work is a good clue to the writer's attitude.
9. Look back at the poem written by a nurse in Vietnam (see the ***Connection*** on page 629). How does that poem affect your understanding of O'Brien's story and of the Vietnam War?

Writing

Why War?

War is a recurring subject in literature and movies. Why do you think writers and moviemakers so often choose war as their subject? Write an **essay** proposing answers to this question. To support your **opinion,** give reasons why some people *write* about war and its violence and others *read* about it. At the end of your essay, explain how war stories like this one affect *you.* (Check your Quickwrite notes before you begin.)

Literary Criticism

7. Possible answer: Soldiers who fought in the Vietnam War had little sense of common purpose. When the United States finally pulled troops out of Vietnam, it had not met its goals. Like the war, O'Brien's story does not have an obvious hero or a victory.
8. Possible answer: O'Brien probably experienced much of the horror witnessed by Paul in the story, since his writing helped him "cope with the memories of the war." O'Brien's dark and fearful tone in describing Paul's experience, along with the irony and pointlessness of Billy's death, suggest that O'Brien views the Vietnam War as meaningless, the cause of needless suffering.
9. Possible answer: The poem, like the story, emphasizes the fragility of life, the need for contact, and the fear of dying.

Vocabulary Development

Meaning Maps

On page 625, Tim O'Brien uses the word *inertia* to describe a feeling of being pulled as if by a train. Many people think of *inertia* only as laziness or inactivity, but the dictionary refers to it as the "tendency of an object in motion to keep moving in the same direction or of an object at rest to remain at rest, unless the object is affected by another force." Look at the meaning map one student made to understand this word:

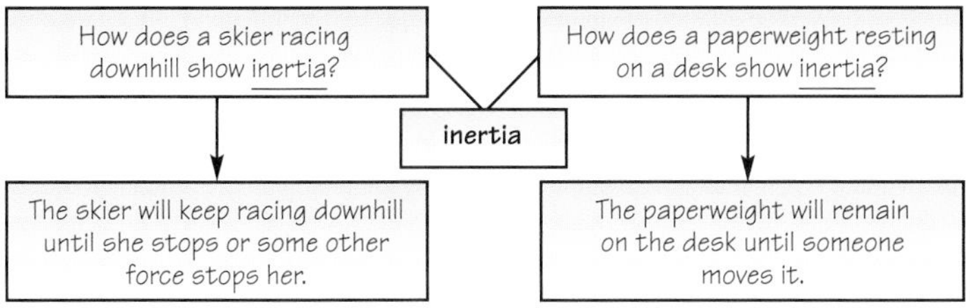

Word Bank
- stealth
- diffuse
- skirted
- agile
- inertia
- valiantly
- consolation

PRACTICE 1

Make your own meaning maps for the remaining Word Bank words. You will have to think of your own questions and answers. Compare your maps with a classmate's when you're done.

Synonyms and Connotations

Most English words have several **synonyms,** words with the same or similar meanings. Synonyms usually have different **connotations,** or emotional associations. O'Brien carefully chooses words with connotations that create the effects he wants.

PRACTICE 2

Answer the questions below about connotations:

1. "With clumsy, concrete hands he clawed for his rifle. . . ."
   Try substituting *heavy* for *concrete* and *reached* for *clawed.* How does the image change?
2. "The moon came out. Pale and shrunken to the size of a dime."
   What are the connotations of *shrunken?* Why wouldn't *as big as a dime* have the same effect?
3. "But Billy Boy kept bawling, tightening up, his face going pale. . . ."
   What does *bawling* suggest that *crying* doesn't? Who might *bawl?*
4. " 'Shut up!' the big soldier hissed. . . ."
   Why do you think O'Brien uses *hissed* instead of *whispered* or *said?*
5. "Later they waded in after him, probing for Billy Boy with their rifle butts, elegantly and delicately probing for Billy Boy in the stinking paddy. . . ."
   Explain why the words *elegantly* and *delicately* in this context are ironic. What are their connotations?

Reading Standard 1.1
Identify and use the literal meanings of words.

Reading Standard 1.2
Distinguish between the denotative and connotative meanings of words and interpret the connotative power of words.

ASSESSING

Assessment
- *Progress Assessment of Reading*
  - Selection Test

Vocabulary Development

Practice 1

Possible Answers

- *diffuse. Map entries*—What produces light that is not diffuse? A spotlight and a flashlight produces light that is not diffuse.
- *skirted. Map entries*—What situations are often skirted? Traffic jams, sensitive issues, and dangerous situations are often skirted.
- *agile. Map entries*—What professions might require you to be agile? Being a professional dancer, gymnast, or basketball player would require you to be agile.
- *consolation. Map entries*—To whom might you offer consolation? You might offer consolation to someone who has lost a loved one or to someone who has lost a job.

Practice 2

Possible Answers

1. The hands seem less disembodied and uncontrollable.
2. The connotations of *shrunken* are that the thing described is diminished and less vital than it once was. *Big as a dime* does not offer a sense that something has been lost, such as the full impact of the moon's light.
3. *Bawling* suggests something that a baby might do. It makes Billy Boy's behavior seem childish, as if he has emotionally regressed.
4. *Hissed* makes the soldier seem dangerous, like a snake.
5. *Elegantly* and *delicately* connote something done in a refined and proper setting. The words are ironic because they are out of place in this context—the reader expects the situation to be anything but elegant.

Resources Reminder

Vocabulary
- *Vocabulary Development*
  - Vocabulary Worksheet, p. 43
- *Lesson Plans for Language Development*
  - Vocabulary, pp. 312, 318

STANDARDS FOCUS, pp. 632–643

(For the grade-level standards taught in this lesson, see citations on Student Edition pages.)

Prerequisite Standard

- Grade 8, Literary Response and Analysis 2.3 **Find similarities and differences between texts in the treatment, scope, or organization of ideas.**

Summary *at grade level*

This feature presents one secondary source and two primary sources dealing with different aspects of the Vietnam War.

The secondary source is an excerpt from a history textbook, written decades after the end of the war. The authors have had time to weigh a great deal of information. They present the crucial Gulf of Tonkin incident, revealing that President Johnson misinformed the American people and Congress in order to justify greater U.S. involvement in Vietnam. The textbook excerpt also reveals that the troops included disproportionate numbers of the young, the poor, the uneducated, and people of color.

The two primary sources were written during the war itself and illustrate some of the passionate feelings that the war aroused. Students will read a letter written by a soldier who has just watched many of his friends die and has narrowly escaped death himself. The other primary source, a speech by Martin Luther King, is concerned with the injustices and violence of the U.S. government abroad and at home.

Read together, these three sources reveal the complexities of the Vietnam War and people's reactions to it. Students have the opportunity to analyze and evaluate the sources and to connect them with one another and with other selections, such as "Where Have You Gone, Charming Billy?" and "The Friendship Only Lasted a Few Seconds."

Before You Read INFORMATIONAL MATERIALS

The War Escalates ◆ Dear Folks ◆ *from* Declaration of Independence from the War in Vietnam

Using Primary and Secondary Sources: Balancing Viewpoints

Research materials can be classified according to two main groups: primary sources and secondary sources. (The chart on this page shows examples of each.) Each type of source has advantages and limitations.

- A **primary source** is a firsthand account, original material that has not been interpreted or edited by any other writers. Good examples of primary sources are letters, speeches, oral histories, and interviews (you've already seen examples of the latter two on pages 89–92). Primary sources are valuable because they include details and feelings that only an eyewitness can provide. Their drawback is that they are usually highly subjective and limited to one person's viewpoint.
- A **secondary source** contains information (often researched in primary sources) that is retold, summarized, or interpreted by a writer. A secondary source is written by someone who did not participate in the events that are written about, and it is often written after the events occurred. The history textbooks you use in school are good examples of secondary sources. (You'll find an example on pages 634–636.) Other common secondary sources are encyclopedia articles and biographies.

Most magazine and newspaper articles are secondary sources. It is important to note, though, that newspaper and magazine articles are primary sources if they are eyewitness reports, editorials, or opinion pieces. (Also, a historian researching a past time would consider any newspaper article from that time a primary-source document of the era.)

Secondary sources are generally more objective and cover a broader range of information than primary sources.

Pages 632–641 cover **Reading Standard 2.5** Extend ideas presented in primary or secondary sources through original analysis, evaluation, and elaboration.

Primary Sources	Secondary Sources
Letters	Encyclopedia articles
Speeches	Reference books
Oral histories	Biographies
Interviews	Textbooks
Diaries	Most newspaper articles
Autobiographies	Most magazine articles
Editorials	History books
Eyewitness news reports	Literary criticism
Literary works	
Public documents	

Using the Sources

Good researchers consult many sources and carefully balance the information found in them before drawing any conclusions. The following checklist can help you use both primary and secondary sources:

1. Analyze. Focus on what the text says and how the ideas are expressed.
- Find the writer's **main idea,** and see how it's supported.
- Determine the writer's **purpose.** For example, is the writer giving information, expressing feelings, describing an event or a person, or persuading you to do or to believe something? Texts may have several purposes, but one is usually dominant.

632 Chapter 9 Biographical and Historical Approach • Using Primary and Secondary Sources

RESOURCES: READING

Planning
- *One-Stop Planner* CD-ROM with Test Generator
- *On Course: Mapping Instruction*

Media
- *Audio CD Library*
  - disc 15
- *Visual Connections*
  - Videocassette, Segment 8

Differentiating Instruction
- *Lesson Plans for Language Development*
  - English-Language Learners, pp. 289–291, 313, 319
  - Special Education Students, pp. 292, 313, 319

- Look for the text's **structure** or special features. For example, a textbook has subheads, key terms, quotations, photos, and illustrations that provide information and help guide you.
- Check for **facts** (which can be proved) and **opinions** (which can't). Both primary and secondary sources are likely to have a mixture of both.
- Determine the writer's **tone,** or attitude. A text may be totally **objective** (including only facts), or it may be **subjective** (expressing the writer's thoughts, feelings, and opinions). It may be written in formal or informal language. A personal letter, for example, usually uses informal language. A speech may use special techniques, such as **repetition** and **rhetorical questions** (questions that are not meant to be answered). Look for both of these techniques in the speech that follows.

2. Evaluate. Decide how much you should believe—and why.

- How **credible** is the source? How knowledgeable is the writer about the subject? This question is important for both primary and secondary sources. When using a secondary source, check the bibliography and other notes to evaluate the research the writer has done.
- Does the writer seem to have a **bias,** or prejudice toward the topic? Watch for words or phrases that present a one-sided view.
- When was the text written? A recent date may be better for a secondary source on a topic, but primary sources from the time of the event can be more valuable.
- What is the writer's **audience**? If the piece was written for a particular audience, it may affect the text's credibility.
- Is the source **accurate**? You should always try to check for accuracy.

3. Elaborate. Connect what you read in one source to information in other sources.

- Never make a generalization or draw conclusions based on reading a single source. Compare facts and details from several sources.
- When you finish researching, figure out your own thoughts, opinions, and feelings on the subject.

Vocabulary Development

facile (fas′il) *adj.:* easy.

rehabilitation (rē′hə·bil′ə·tā′shən) *n.:* bringing or restoring to a good condition.

manipulation (mə·nip′yo͞o·lā′shən) *n.:* skillful, often unfair management or control.

compassion (kəm·pash′ən) *n.:* deep sympathy; pity.

aghast (ə·gast′) *adj.:* horrified.

initiative (i·nish′ə·tiv) *n.:* action of taking the first step or movement.

Connecting to the Literature

You've just read Tim O'Brien's fictional picture of the Vietnam War. The nonfiction accounts that follow—a textbook excerpt, a soldier's letter, and a speech—will help you evaluate O'Brien's story and expand your knowledge of the war.

PRETEACHING

Standards Starter

Motivate. Before exploring the information on primary and secondary sources in the Before You Read section, ask students to recall some recent assignments for which they performed research. Have volunteers give examples of the different resources they used to find particular information and list each example on the board. Then, after reviewing the information in the Before You Read section, students can identify the sources listed on the board as primary or secondary.

Preview Vocabulary

Have pairs of students take turns reading aloud the definitions of the Vocabulary Development words on p. 633. Then, have them work together on the following exercise to reinforce understanding of the words. (Possible answers are given.)

1. Suggest a facile solution for teachers needing transportation when their cars are being repaired. [They can take the bus.]
2. Describe one instance in which a person might need to undergo rehabilitation. [A player who sprains an ankle in a basketball game would need rehabilitation.]
3. Explain one way manipulation is used in advertising. [Advertisers hire celebrities to tout a product, hoping this will persuade consumers to buy the product.]
4. Tell about a time when someone you know acted with compassion. [When my dog died, my best friend listened all night long to stories about my dog.]
5. Recall an experience that made you feel aghast. [While driving one winter morning, I hit a patch of ice and almost had an accident.]
6. Tell about a time when you took the initiative to get something done. [Last year I organized a surprise anniversary party for my parents.]

Vocabulary

- *Vocabulary Development*
  - Vocabulary Worksheet, p. 44

Assessment

- *Progress Assessment of Reading*
  - Selection Test
- *One-Stop Planner* CD-ROM with Test Generator

DIRECT TEACHING

A Reading Informational Materials
GRADE-LEVEL STANDARD

Using secondary sources: Text structures. Have students identify the text structures on this page. [head, subheads, illustration, caption, quotation, text] **Given the text structures, what is the likely subject of this page?** [the escalation of the war due to the Gulf of Tonkin incident]

B Reading Skills

Analyzing. [Possible response to question 2: The paragraph at the bottom of this page takes up the first of the key questions, regarding the constitutional issue raised by the Tonkin Gulf Resolution. The Constitution stipulates that an American president has war-making powers only by the consent of Congress. In 1964, President Johnson misrepresented a naval incident that had occurred in the Gulf of Tonkin, off the coast of North Vietnam, and won from Congress the authority to increase American military involvement in the Vietnam War.]

C Reading Skills

Analyzing. [Possible response to question 3: The excerpt from Johnson's speech is the primary source on this page.]

D Reading Informational Materials
GRADE-LEVEL STANDARD

Using secondary sources: Analyze. What did the Secretary of Defense advise in 1963? [increased U.S. involvement in Vietnam] **How did the Gulf of Tonkin incident enable Johnson to escalate the war in 1964?** [Congress authorized the president to use "all necessary measures" to defend the United States.]

SECONDARY SOURCE | TEXTBOOK

SECTION 2

The War Escalates

1. These pages are taken from a history textbook titled *The American Nation* by Paul Boyer.

READ TO DISCOVER

1. What constitutional issue did the Tonkin Gulf Resolution raise?
2. What strategies did U.S. forces use in the Vietnam War?
3. What role did the media play in the Vietnam War?
4. Why did some Americans oppose the war, and how did the government respond?

ANALYZE
2. Chapters or sections in textbooks often begin with lists of **key questions, terms, and vocabulary.** *Which of the key questions under Read to Discover does this page answer?* **B**

DEFINE
escalation
defoliants
search-and-destroy missions
pacification
doves
hawks

IDENTIFY
Robert S. McNamara
Tonkin Gulf Resolution
Operation Rolling Thunder
Ho Chi Minh Trail
Students for a Democratic Society
J. William Fulbright

ANALYZE
3. Although history textbooks are **secondary sources,** they may include some **primary sources.** *What is the primary source on this page?* **C**

EYEWITNESSES TO History

A ***"Renewed hostile actions against United States ships on the high seas in the Gulf of Tonkin have today required me to order the military forces of the United States to take action in reply. The initial attack on the destroyer Maddox, on August 2, was repeated today by a number of hostile vessels attacking two U.S. destroyers with torpedoes. . . . We believe at least two of the attacking boats were sunk. There were no U.S. losses. . . . But repeated acts of violence against the Armed Forces of the United States must be met not only with alert defense, but with positive reply. That reply is being given as I speak to you tonight. Air action is now in execution against gunboats and certain supporting facilities in North Vietnam which have been used in these hostile operations."***

—Lyndon B. Johnson, nationally televised speech, August 4, 1964

The Gulf of Tonkin incident drew the United States deeper into the Vietnam War.

Near midnight on August 4, 1964, President Lyndon B. Johnson appeared on national television. His announcement to the American people that night marked a new stage in U.S. involvement in the war in Vietnam.

The Tonkin Gulf Resolution

D In 1963 Secretary of Defense **Robert S. McNamara** had advised President Johnson that he would have to increase the U.S. military commitment to South Vietnam to prevent a Communist victory. Before increasing the U.S. commitment, Johnson needed to get congressional backing. The events in the Gulf of Tonkin gave him the opportunity. Johnson asked Congress to authorize the use of military force "to prevent further aggression." In response, both houses of Congress overwhelmingly passed the **Tonkin Gulf Resolution.** This gave the president authority to take "all necessary measures to repel any armed attack against forces of the United States."

DIFFERENTIATING INSTRUCTION

Learners Having Difficulty

Preview these three selections with students, and guide them in identifying the characteristics of each that determines whether it is a primary or secondary source. Then, ask students to reiterate the general characteristics of each type of source. [*Primary*—eyewitness details, feelings, immediacy, subjectivity. *Secondary*—research, comprehensive overview, balance, objectivity.]

English-Language Learners

In order for students to understand these selections, they must be familiar with certain words and phrases related to war. You may wish to review such terms as *hostile vessels, destroyer, radar, sonar, torpedoes, guerrillas,* and *mortars* before students begin reading.

634 Chapter 9 Biographical and Historical Approach • Using Primary and Secondary Sources

Johnson claimed that the attacks in the Gulf of Tonkin were unprovoked. In reality, however, the U.S. destroyer *Maddox* had been spying in support of South Vietnamese raids against North Vietnam and had fired first. The second attack, moreover, probably never occurred. Some U.S. sailors apparently misinterpreted interference on their radar and sonar as enemy ships and torpedoes. Nonetheless, Johnson and his advisers got what they wanted: authority to expand the war.

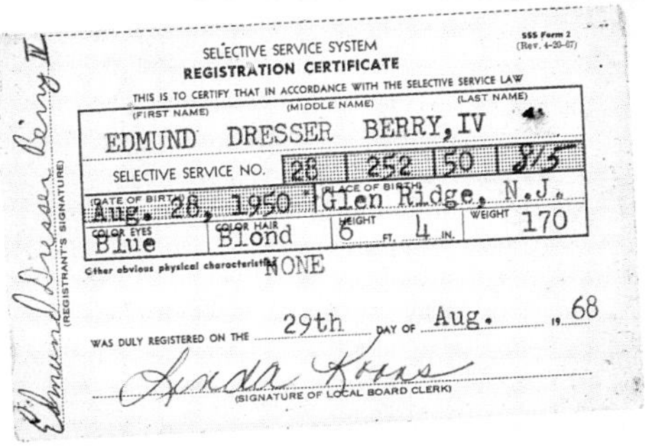
SSS Form 2 (Rev. 4-20-67)

SELECTIVE SERVICE SYSTEM
REGISTRATION CERTIFICATE

THIS IS TO CERTIFY THAT IN ACCORDANCE WITH THE SELECTIVE SERVICE LAW

(FIRST NAME) EDMUND (MIDDLE NAME) DRESSER (LAST NAME) BERRY, IV

SELECTIVE SERVICE NO. 28 | 252 | 50 | 315

DATE OF BIRTH Aug. 28, 1950 PLACE OF BIRTH Glen Ridge, N.J.

COLOR EYES Blue COLOR HAIR Blond HEIGHT 6 FT. 4 IN. WEIGHT 170

Other obvious physical characteristics NONE

WAS DULY REGISTERED ON THE 29th DAY OF Aug. 19 68

(SIGNATURE OF LOCAL BOARD CLERK)

(REGISTRANT'S SIGNATURE)

During the Vietnam War millions of American men received draft registration certificates like this one.

Wayne Morse of Oregon was one of just two senators who voted against the Tonkin Gulf Resolution. He warned, "I believe that history will record we have made a great mistake. . . . We are in effect giving the President war-making powers in the absence of a declaration of war." In other words, by passing the resolution, Congress had essentially given up its constitutional power to declare war. **E**

READING CHECK: Analyzing Information How did President Johnson mislead the American public?

F
ANALYZE
4. Reading checks are often provided to help you review or analyze the material.
What is the answer to the reading-check question on this page?

U.S. Forces in Vietnam

President Johnson soon called for an **escalation,** or buildup, of U.S. military forces in Vietnam. He ordered the Selective Service, the agency charged with carrying out the military draft, to begin calling up young men to serve in the armed forces. In April 1965 the Selective Service notified 13,700 draftees.

G
ANALYZE
5. Notice the levels of major **headings** and **subheadings** that help organize the material.
What is the main heading on this page?

The troops. During the war more than 2 million Americans served in Vietnam. In the beginning most were professional soldiers who were already enlisted in the armed forces. As the demand for troops grew, however, more and more draftees were shipped to Vietnam. The average U.S. soldier in Vietnam was younger, poorer, and less educated than those who had served in World War II or in the Korean War.

One out of four young men who registered for the draft was excused from service for health reasons. Another 30 percent received non-health-related exemptions or deferments—postponements of service. Most of these were for college enrollment. Mainly because of college deferments, young men from higher-income families were the least likely to be drafted. As a result, poor Americans served in numbers far greater than their proportion in the general population.

H
EVALUATE
6. Textbooks should have an objective, unbiased **tone,** which is the writer's attitude.
What is the tone of the subsection "The troops"?

DIRECT TEACHING

E Reading Informational Materials
GRADE-LEVEL STANDARD

Using secondary sources: Analyze. Given that only two out of one hundred senators voted against the Tonkin Gulf Resolution, why did the authors devote a whole paragraph to this one dissenting vote? [Possible response: The quotation—a primary source—describes Congress's mistake in giving the president the power to wage war without a declaration of war. The quotation also illustrates the idea that the majority is not always right.]

F Reading Skills
Analyzing. [Possible response to question 4: Johnson misled the public by telling them that U.S. ships had been attacked when in fact it was the U.S. spy ship that had fired first.]

G Reading Skills
Analyzing. [Possible response to question 5: The main topic is the Americans who served in the military in Vietnam.]

H Reading Skills
Evaluating. [Possible response to question 6: The tone is even, calm, and objective.]

Resources Reminder
For lessons designed for intermediate and advanced English-language learners, see *Lesson Plans for Language Development,* pp. 289–291, 313, 319.

Special Education Students
For lessons designed for special education students, see *Lesson Plans for Language Development,* pp. 292, 313, 319.

Advanced Learners
Acceleration. Use the following activity to move advanced learners toward the eleventh- and twelfth-grade Standard 2.1, for which they analyze the rhetorical devices of different types of public documents and the way in which authors use those devices.
Activity. Have students focus on the speech excerpt by Martin Luther King, Jr., and identify King's main idea or his purpose for giving the speech. What rhetorical devices does King use to propel his message? (Students might note such factors as emotional appeals, facts, opinions, repetition, and parallelism.) Students should relate their findings in an essay in which they explain how King uses these devices in his speech to achieve his goal.

DIRECT TEACHING

A Reading Skills

Elaborating. [Possible response to question 7: The quotation and the poem are similar in that each is a sorrowful representation of a female nurse's experience with the war. They are different in that the poem's speaker is able to offer some comfort to the dying soldier, a fact that comforts her as well. Meeks, however, is consumed with despair and a sense of outrage at the human cost of war.]

B Reading Skills

Analyzing. [Possible response to question 8: The lieutenant is bandaging an injured soldier's foot and leg.]

C Reading Informational Materials

GRADE-LEVEL STANDARD

Using secondary sources: Evaluate. Point out to students that this quotation from Meeks is a primary source. How does including this quotation help support the claim in the previous paragraph that "nurses faced the horrors of combat on a daily basis"? [Possible response: The quotation provides first-hand evidence that nurses did encounter war horrors each day.]

African Americans and Hispanics served in combat in very high numbers, particularly during the early years of the war. Many served in the most dangerous ground units. As a result, they experienced very high casualty rates. In 1965, for example, African Americans accounted for almost 24 percent of all battle deaths, even though they made up just 11 percent of the U.S. population. **A**

ELABORATE

7. Compare Edie Meeks's quote with the poem on page 629. How are they alike, and how are they different?

The most vivid images of the war show soldiers facing the hardships and terrors of battle. Some confronted the enemy in well-defined battles in the highlands. Others cut their way through the jungle, where they heard but seldom saw the enemy. Still others waded through rice paddies and searched rural villages for guerrillas. Most Americans who went to Vietnam, however, served in support positions such as administration, communications, engineering, medical care, and supply and transportation. They were rarely safe. Enemy rockets and mortars could—and did—strike anywhere. **B**

ANALYZE

8. Captions that accompany photographs and illustrations provide further information and sometimes pose a question.

What is the answer to the question in the caption on this page?

Some 10,000 servicewomen filled noncombat positions in Vietnam, mostly as nurses. Although they did not carry guns into battle, nurses faced the horrors of combat on a daily basis. Edie Meeks described the experience of working as a nurse at a field hospital.

History Makers Speak **C**

"We really saw the worst of it, because the nurses never saw any of the victories. If the Army took a hill, we saw what was left over. I remember one boy who was brought in missing two legs and an arm, and his eyes were bandaged. A general came in later and pinned a Purple Heart on the boy's hospital gown, and the horror of it all was so amazing that it just took my breath away. You thought, was this supposed to be an even trade?"

—Edie Meeks, quoted in *Newsweek,* March 8, 1999

Another 20,000 to 45,000 women worked in civilian capacities, many as volunteers for humanitarian organizations such as the Red Cross.

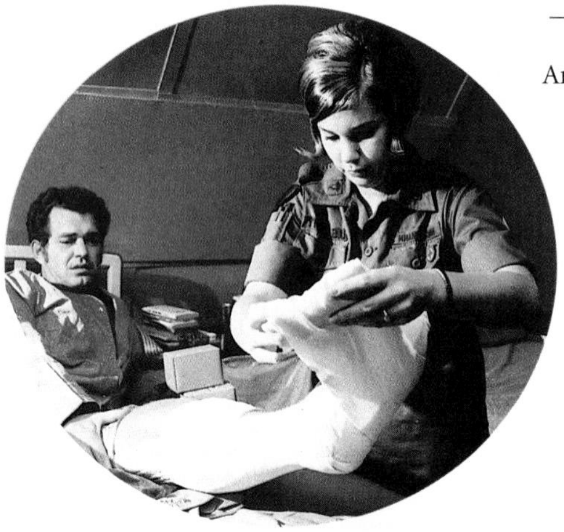

INTERPRETING THE VISUAL RECORD

Nurses. First Lieutenant Elaine Niggemann served at the 24th EVAC Hospital. ***What is the lieutenant doing?***

CONTENT-AREA CONNECTIONS

History: The Antiwar Movement

U.S. combat troops were involved in the Vietnam War for eight years. The war claimed about 2 million Vietnamese lives and 58,000 American lives. Antiwar demonstrations in the United States attracted enormous crowds of protesters; in 1969, for example, more than a quarter million people assembled peacefully at the Washington Monument to demonstrate their opposition to the war.

Individual activity. Encourage interested students to research aspects of the antiwar movement. They may focus on particular events, such as the demonstrations in Washington or on college campuses, or on larger themes, such as the interaction of the civil rights movement and the antiwar movement. Have students form a panel to discuss the results of their research for the class.

PRIMARY SOURCE

LETTER

Dear Folks

Kenneth W. Bagby

The battle of the Ia Drang Valley, which took place in mid-November of 1965, was one of the hardest fought and most bloody of the entire war. The letter which follows is Sp4c[1] Kenneth W. Bagby's personal account of the action during that fierce encounter, written soon afterward to his parents in Winchester, Virginia. **D**

Plei-Ku, Vietnam
Nov. 17, 1965

Dear Folks,

I met a boy on the ship coming over to Vietnam. He was a good guy from the State of Missouri. He was my friend. We lived in the same tent together, went into An Khe together, and spent most of our free time together. I got to know this boy well, and he was my best friend. His name was Dan Davis. **E**

On Monday morning, the 15th of November, he died in my arms of two bullet wounds in the chest. He said, "Ken, I can't breathe." There was nothing I could do.

To the right of me another friend, whose last name was Balango, died of a wound in the throat. Up front Sergeant Brown, my squad leader, was hit in the chest and leg. To my left Sp4c A. Learn was hit in the ankle.

We were crossing a field and were pinned down by automatic weapons fire from the enemy. We were pinned down for about 45 minutes before the rest of the platoon could get to us, and save the rest of us.

So went the biggest and worst battle that any American force has had in Vietnam. We outdone the Marines and Airborne by a long shot. Estimated V.C.[2] killed, 2,000. Our casualties, I cannot give the information out. The battle took place on the Cambodian border. . . . **F**

Our battalion, the 1st Bn. 7th Cav., is completely inactive due to the killed and wounded of its men. My squad which consists of nine men, three came out, myself, Sergeant Scott, and a boy named Stidell.

1. **Sp4c:** specialist, fourth class.
2. **V.C.:** abbreviation for "Viet Cong," a North Vietnamese guerrilla force that sought to overthrow the South Vietnamese government (1954–1975).

DIRECT TEACHING

D Reading Informational Materials
GRADE-LEVEL STANDARD

Using primary sources: Evaluate. One way to evaluate the credibility of a source is to determine who the audience is. Who is Bagby writing to? [his parents and family back home] Given this audience, how would you evaluate the credibility of Bagby's letter? [Possible responses: The letter provides honest feelings and relates details as Bagby experienced them. Because Bagby is under mental and emotional strain, his letter may not be accurate or objective in some ways.]

E Reading Informational Materials
GRADE-LEVEL STANDARD

Using primary sources: Analyzing tone. Remind students that tone is conveyed through a writer's choice of words and details. Is the tone of these paragraphs objective or subjective, formal or informal? [Possible response: The tone is informal and subjective, conveying the writer's thoughts and feelings.]

F Reading Informational Materials
GRADE-LEVEL STANDARD

Using primary sources: Determining author purpose. Why did Bagby write this letter? [Possible responses: to express his feelings and describe events; to persuade his parents and others to support the war; to inform his family of what had happened and to let them know that he is OK.]

CONTENT-AREA CONNECTIONS

History/Culture: War and the Media
Vietnam was the first war in which television journalists could send shocking images of combat scenes and the resulting death and destruction into nearly every American living room each evening. The images stirred up deep feelings about the war and split Americans like no other issue. They also influenced the way future administrations would allow wars to be covered by the media.

Individual activity. Interested students may research the media coverage of the Vietnam War. Some students may focus on the war years and the media's effect on the prosecution of the war. Other students might examine how the media was given or denied access to subsequent wars and conflicts, such as the Gulf War and the war in Afghanistan.

Direct Teaching

A Reading Skills

Analyzing. [Possible responses to question 1: The tone is emotional, horrified, subjective, distraught, distressed, anguished, haunted.] You may point out that this paragraph is given greater emotional resonance by the repetition of such phrases as "I will never forget" and such words as "never." What is the effect of this repetition? [Possible response: It emphasizes the writer's thoughts and feelings of anguish and conveys these feelings to the reader.]

B Reading Skills

Analyzing. [Possible response to question 2: to protect U.S. citizens and to prevent the enemy from harming anyone else] Ask students to explain Bagby's bias as revealed in this paragraph. [Possible responses: Bagby believes that the U.S. forces in Vietnam are protecting the American people. He seems to believe the government rationale that the fighting in Southeast Asia will protect the free world from Communism.]

C Reading Skills

Elaborating. [Possible responses to question 3: Bagby believes the war is just and necessary. He loves his country and is willing to die for it. Berlin has a more detached and ironic view of the war. He doesn't discuss patriotic feelings; he just wants to survive and return home.]

Folks, by all rights I should be dead. The good Lord evidently saw fit to spare me, for some reason. I prayed, and prayed and prayed some more, the three days we were in battle.

The many men that died, I will never forget. The odor of blood and decayed bodies, I will never forget. I am all right. I will never be the same though, never, never, never. If I have to go into battle again, if I am not killed, I will come out insane. I cannot see and go through it again. I know I can't. The friends I lost and the many bodies I carried back to the helicopters to be lifted out, I will never forget. **(A)** ❶

> **❶ ANALYZE** What words would you use to describe the letter's **tone,** especially in this paragraph?

The pen that I am writing this letter with belongs to Stash Arrows, the boy that rode up to Winchester with me, on my emergency leave. Pop, remember him. He was hit three times in the back. I don't know if he is still alive or not. I hope and pray he is. God, I hope so.

Folks, don't let these men die in vain. Appreciate what they are doing over here in Vietnam. They died protecting you all, and all the people in the United States. We just cannot have the enemy get to the folks back home. We have got to stop them here, before that happens. If it is God's will, we will do it. Tell the people back home to pray for us, as we need their prayers. . . . **(B)** ❷

> **❷ ANALYZE** What are Bagby's reasons for fighting in Vietnam?

We raised the American flag on the grounds. We were fighting on Tuesday, the 16th of November. It waved proudly for the Armed Forces and the people of America, as it did in so many battles won in World War II and Korea. I sat beside a tree and looked at it, and hoped I would never see the day it would be torn down and destroyed.

Folks, I am glad Eddy is not here and my son Kenny is not here. I hope they never have to see or experience the horrors of war. I will give my life to see that they don't. . . . **(C)** ❸

> **❸ ELABORATE** How does Bagby's view of the war compare with Paul Berlin's in "Where Have You Gone, Charming Billy?" (page 621)?

As always,

Your son,

Kenneth

CONTENT-AREA CONNECTIONS

History: The Domino Theory

One of the main rationales for U.S. involvement in South Vietnam was the domino theory. This theory held that countries are like a row of dominoes: Once you knock over the first one, all the rest will fall in quick succession. In other words, if South Vietnam were to fall to communism, then all of Southeast Asia would soon follow. The fear was that eventually such nations as India, Australia, and even the United States would come under Communist rule.

Small-group activity. Have students work in small groups to research the domino theory and record any important facts and expert opinions they find. Then, pair groups or have students within each group debate the ideas and principles associated with the domino theory. You might use the following questions to stimulate discussion:

- Does the domino theory contain fallacies or lapses in logic? What are they?
- Why was the theory nevertheless so effective as a rationale for the war?
- What are some examples that either support or refute the domino theory?

You may wish to close the activity with a whole-class discussion on the topic.

SPEECH

PRIMARY SOURCE

from Declaration of Independence from the War in Vietnam

D

Martin Luther King, Jr.

Martin Luther King, Jr., in Atlanta on April 30, 1967, speaking against U.S. involvement in Vietnam.

Since I am a preacher by trade, I suppose it is not surprising that I have . . . major reasons for bringing Vietnam into the field of my moral vision. There is at the outset a very obvious and almost facile connection between the war in Vietnam and the struggle I, and others, have been waging in America. E A few years ago there was a shining moment in that struggle. It seemed as if there was a real promise of hope for the poor—both black and white—through the Poverty Program.[1] Then came the buildup in Vietnam, and I watched the program broken and eviscerated[2] as if it were some idle political plaything or a society gone mad on war, and I knew that America would never invest the necessary funds or energies in rehabilitation of its poor so long as Vietnam continued to draw men and skills and money like some demonic, destructive suction tube. So I was increasingly compelled to see the war as an enemy of the poor and to attack it as such. 1

1 ANALYZE
What is the first reason King gives for opposing the Vietnam War?

F

1. **Poverty Program:** In May 1964, President Lyndon B. Johnson declared a nationwide war on poverty. He announced a number of federal programs to aid the nation's poor and to create what he called the Great Society.

2. **eviscerated** (ē·vis′ər·āt′id) *v.* used as *adj.:* gutted; having its force or significance taken away.

Vocabulary
facile (fas′il) *adj.:* easy.
rehabilitation (rē′hə·bil′ə·tā′shən) *n.:* bringing or restoring to a good condition.

DIRECT TEACHING

D Reading Informational Materials
GRADE-LEVEL STANDARD

Using primary sources: Analyze. What does the title of this speech allude to? [the U.S. Declaration of Independence] **What implicit comparison is King making with this title?** [Possible response: He is comparing his actions to those of the American colonists.] **What declaration is King making?** [Possible response: He is declaring that he will not go along with the actions of those in power, but will disagree openly, just as the colonists did.] **How does the title alone begin to convince readers of the rightness of King's point of view?** [Possible response: By linking himself to the respected and admired Declaration of Independence, King is declaring his patriotism and moral rectitude at the same time.]

E Reading Informational Materials
GRADE-LEVEL STANDARD

Using primary sources: Evaluate. At the outset, King states who he is and where he is coming from. How does this declaration of his bias affect the content of what he is about to say? [Possible response: By stating upfront that he is a preacher, he gives legitimacy to his views on injustice, poverty, and war.]

F Reading Skills

Analyzing. [Possible response to question 1: King opposes the war because it takes men, skills, and money away from the struggle against poverty in the United States.]

Direct Teaching

A Reading Informational Materials
GRADE-LEVEL STANDARD

Using primary sources: Elaborate. Remind students that because a primary source is usually subjective, it is a good idea to compare any primary-source assertions with information from a secondary source. What is King's assertion here? [Soldiers from poor and black families were being sent in disproportionately high numbers to Vietnam.] Is King's assertion backed up by a secondary source? [yes, by "The War Escalates," the textbook excerpt]

B Reading Informational Materials
GRADE-LEVEL STANDARD

Using primary sources: Analyze. What comparisons is King making between the situation at home and in Vietnam? [Possible responses: Young blacks with few liberties in the United States are sent to guarantee those liberties in Southeast Asia. Black and white boys fight and die together in Vietnam but can't sit together in U.S. schools or live in the same U.S. neighborhood.] What main idea is King conveying with these comparisons? [Possible response: Poor blacks are mistreated at home and exploited in the war effort.]

C Reading Informational Materials
GRADE-LEVEL STANDARD

Using primary sources: Elaborate and analyze. King is well-known for his devotion to the principle of nonviolence, yet here he says he had to reexamine his commitment. Does King condone violence? [Possible response: No, but he feels he cannot preach nonviolence to young blacks without first condemning the U.S. government-sponsored violence against the people of Vietnam.]

A wounded U.S. soldier being helped by fellow soldiers during the Vietnam War.

Perhaps the more tragic recognition of reality took place when it became clear to me that the war was doing far more than devastating the hopes of the poor at home. It was sending their sons and their brothers and their husbands to fight and to die in extraordinarily high proportions relative to the rest of the population. We were taking the young black men who had been crippled by our society and sending them eight thousand miles away to guarantee liberties in Southeast Asia which they had not found in southwest Georgia and East Harlem. So we have been repeatedly faced with the cruel irony of watching Negro and white boys on TV screens as they kill and die together for a nation that has been unable to seat them together in the same schools. So we watch them in brutal solidarity[3] burning the huts of a poor village, but we realize that they would never live on the same block in Detroit. I could not be silent in the face of such cruel manipulation of the poor.

My third reason grows out of my experience in the ghettos of the North over the last three years—especially the last three summers. As I have walked among the desperate, rejected, and angry young men, I have told them that Molotov cocktails[4] and rifles would not solve their problems. I have tried to offer them my deepest compassion while maintaining my conviction that social change comes most meaningfully through nonviolent action. But, they asked, what about Vietnam? They asked if our own nation wasn't using massive doses of violence to solve its problems, to bring about the changes it wanted. Their questions hit home, and I knew that I

3. **solidarity** n.: complete unity.
4. **Molotov cocktails:** makeshift explosives.

Vocabulary

manipulation (mə·nip′yo͞o·lā′shən) *n.:* skillful, often unfair management or control.

compassion (kəm·pash′ən) *n.:* deep sympathy; pity.

Family/Community Activity

Encourage students to identify a passage in King's speech or Bagby's letter that they find particularly compelling. Have them read this passage to friends or family members and record their reactions. Students might also ask their subjects to share some of their memories or knowledge about the Vietnam War, if appropriate. Finally, ask students to share their friends' and family members' reactions to their passages with the class.

could never again raise my voice against the violence of the oppressed in the ghettos without having first spoken clearly to the greatest purveyor[5] of violence in the world today—my own government. . . .

Somehow this madness must cease. I speak as a child of God and a brother to the suffering poor of Vietnam and the poor of America who are paying the double price of smashed hopes at home and death and corruption in Vietnam. I speak as a citizen of the world, for the world as it stands aghast at the path we have taken. I speak as an American to the leaders of my own nation. The great initiative in this war is ours. The initiative to stop must be ours. . . .

We must move past indecision to action. We must find new ways to speak for peace in Vietnam and justice throughout the developing world—a world that borders on our doors. If we do not act, we shall surely be dragged down the long, dark, and shameful corridors of time reserved for those who possess power without compassion, might without morality, and strength without sight. ❷

Now let us begin. Now let us rededicate ourselves to the long and bitter—but beautiful—struggle for a new world. This is the calling of the sons of God, and our brothers wait eagerly for our response. Shall we say the odds are too great? Shall we tell them the struggle is too hard? Will our message be that the forces of American life militate[6] against their arrival as full men, and we send our deepest regrets? Or will there be another message, of longing, of hope, of solidarity with their yearnings, of commitment to their cause, whatever the cost? The choice is ours, and though we might prefer it otherwise, we *must* choose in this crucial moment of human history. ❸

—April 4, 1967

❷ ANALYZE What does King want the listener to do or believe?

❸ EVALUATE What effect do the **rhetorical questions** have in this paragraph? How convincing do you find King's speech? Why?

Vocabulary

aghast (ə·gast′) *adj.:* horrified.

initiative (i·nish′ə·tiv) *n.:* action of taking the first step or movement.

Children playing in the shadow of high-rise buildings in a North Carolina city in the mid-1960s.

5. **purveyor** (pər·vā′ər) *n.:* provider; supplier.
6. **militate** *v.* (used with *against*): work to prohibit.

DIRECT TEACHING

D Reading Informational Materials
GRADE-LEVEL STANDARD

Using primary and secondary sources: Elaborate. Who was the initiator or aggressor in the Vietnam War? Compare the facts and assertions made here by King, by President Johnson in his speech, and by the authors of the history textbook. What informed, balanced conclusion can you draw? [Possible response: King's assertion that the United States was the initiator and the conclusion of the textbook authors that the United States misled the American people to escalate the war are more credible and accurate than Johnson's assertion that the United States had to defend itself against unprovoked attacks.]

E Reading Informational Materials
GRADE-LEVEL STANDARD

Using primary sources: Analyze. [Possible responses to question 2: King wants his listeners to unite against U.S. military involvement in Vietnam. King wants the U.S. government to take action and stop what it has started: the war in Vietnam.]

F Reading Informational Materials
GRADE-LEVEL STANDARD

Using primary and secondary sources: Evaluate. [Possible response to question 3: The rhetorical questions challenge listeners to think about their own answers to the questions, and, in the process, about their own opinions and beliefs. Most students will find the speech convincing in its heartfelt conviction and powerful language, and in the fact that historians have shown King's assertions to be valid.]

INDEPENDENT PRACTICE

Analyzing Informational Materials

Reading Check

1. It allowed the president to expand U.S. military action in Vietnam, in effect allowing him to wage war without having Congress declare war.
2. Two million American troops served in Vietnam, including 10,000 women.
3. Two thirds of them were killed.
4. The war diverted money and attention from the programs that were helping the poor, while sending their young men to fight and die in disproportionate numbers.

Test Practice

Answers and Model Rationales

1. **C** Bagby's letter and King's speech do not address A, B, or D, so C is the only possible correct answer.
2. **F** G is clearly incorrect, as the resolution was important enough to include in a textbook. H is also incorrect, as the resolution actually took away Congress's power to declare war. J is a little tricky, but the resolution had more to do with taking away Congress's constitutional powers than confirming the president's powers.
3. **D** The letter is mostly a way for Bagby to express his feelings (C), but it also has passages that inform and that persuade (A and B).
4. **G** F is incorrect because Bagby is very subjective. Bagby was just a soldier, not an expert on the war, so J is incorrect. While the letter is impassioned (H), that is not its main value as a research source. Rather, it is important because it provides a firsthand eyewitness account (G).

Analyzing Informational Materials

Reading Check

1. What power did the Tonkin Gulf Resolution give to the president?
2. How many American troops served in the Vietnam War? How many women served in the armed forces?
3. According to "Dear Folks," what happened to the men in Kenneth Bagby's squad?
4. According to King, why was the Vietnam War an enemy of poor Americans?

Test Practice

1. All three of the sources concern —
   - **A** the history of Vietnam
   - **B** the causes of the Vietnam War
   - **C** the U.S. armed forces in Vietnam
   - **D** the U.S. Congress and president
2. From what you've read in "The War Escalates," you can infer that the Tonkin Gulf Resolution —
   - **F** was a turning point in U.S. involvement in the war
   - **G** was an unimportant piece of legislation
   - **H** gave unusual powers to Congress
   - **J** confirmed the president's constitutional powers
3. Which is *not* a **purpose** of Kenneth Bagby's letter, "Dear Folks"?
   - **A** To inform
   - **B** To persuade
   - **C** To express feelings
   - **D** To entertain
4. The value of "Dear Folks" as a research source is that it —
   - **F** is objective and factual
   - **G** relates a firsthand experience of the war
   - **H** is impassioned and sincere
   - **J** is written by an expert
5. Which source seems to support King's claim that an extraordinarily high proportion of the poor were sent to fight in Vietnam?
   - **A** "Dear Folks"
   - **B** "The War Escalates"
   - **C** "Where Have You Gone, Charming Billy?" (page 621)
   - **D** "The Friendship Only Lasted a Few Seconds" (page 629)
6. The primary **purpose** of the excerpt from "Declaration of Independence from the War in Vietnam" is to —
   - **F** give information about the war
   - **G** give information about the Viet Cong
   - **H** persuade listeners of King's point of view about the war
   - **J** describe specific events in the war
7. Which source has the *most* credibility as a history of the Vietnam War?
   - **A** "Dear Folks"
   - **B** The excerpt from "Declaration of Independence from the War in Vietnam"
   - **C** "The War Escalates"
   - **D** "Where Have You Gone, Charming Billy?" (page 621)

Reading Standard 2.5 Extend ideas presented in primary or secondary sources through original analysis, evaluation, and elaboration.

5. **B** The soldiers written about in A, C, and D may or may not have been poor. Only the textbook excerpt (B) addresses the issue of the high proportion of the poor being sent to Vietnam.
6. **H** King does not mention the Viet Cong by name (G), or mention specific events in the war (J), or even give information about the war itself (F). Rather, his speech tries to convince listeners of King's views on the war and its effects.
7. **C** "Dear Folks" and King's speech (A and B) are too subjective and emotional or impassioned to be credible. The short story (D) is not credible as history because it is fiction. The secondary source (C) has the greatest credibility because it synthesizes information that has been validated over time.

Test Practice

8. The source that most closely resembles the point of view and content of "Where Have You Gone, Charming Billy?" (page 621) is —

F the section "U.S. Forces in Vietnam" from "The War Escalates"

G Kenneth Bagby's letter, "Dear Folks"

H the excerpt from King's speech, "Declaration of Independence from the War in Vietnam"

J Lyndon Johnson's August 4, 1964, speech, which appears in "The War Escalates"

Application

In a brief essay, write your own analysis and evaluation of these primary and secondary sources about the Vietnam War. For each piece, first summarize its **main ideas.** Then, consider how **credible,** biased, or accurate each piece seems to be. Assess the value of each piece as a primary or secondary source. Finally, explain how these sources connect to what you already know about the Vietnam War, including the information about Tim O'Brien and his story "Where Have You Gone, Charming Billy?" (see page 621). Before you write, you can take notes in a chart like the one on the right:

Primary ❑
Secondary ❑
Title:
Analyze (main ideas):
Evaluate (accuracy, reliability, bias):
Elaborate (connections to other sources):

Vocabulary Development

Clarifying Word Meanings

PRACTICE

Word Bank
facile
rehabilitation
manipulation
compassion
aghast
initiative

You reinforce your understanding of an unfamiliar word's meaning each time you use it in a sentence or think about how it should be used. Answer the following questions about each of the words from the Word Bank. Then, write an original sentence for each word. Check your original sentences with a partner or small group.

1. Identify several local, national, or world problems for which you think there is no facile solution.
2. What should be done for the rehabilitation of a person who has broken a leg?
3. How did Lyndon Johnson's actions demonstrate a manipulation of events during the Tonkin Gulf crisis?
4. How would you show your compassion for someone who has suffered a great loss?
5. What might someone do or say that would leave you aghast?
6. If you could take the initiative for a new project or organization at your school, what would you do?

Reading Standard 1.1 Identify and use the literal meanings of words.

8. G Only Bagby's letter (G) is similar to "Where Have You Gone, Charming Billy?" in both content and point of view (first-person account by a soldier in Vietnam). King's speech (H) is from the point of view of a nonviolent activist. The textbook excerpt (F) has the objective point of view of a historian. Johnson's speech (J) has the point of view and stentorian tones of a powerful man.

Test-Taking Tips

For more instruction on how to answer multiple-choice items, refer students to **Test Smarts.**

Vocabulary Development

Practice

Possible Answers

1. There is no facile solution to the complex problem of global warming.
2. Rest is important for the rehabilitation of a broken leg.
3. Johnson's claim that U.S. ships were attacked when, in fact, the U.S. spy ship fired first was a manipulation of the Gulf of Tonkin situation.
4. One way to show compassion for a person who has suffered a great loss is by listening to her as she expresses her feelings.
5. If someone claimed he had killed a person, that would leave the listener aghast.
6. If I could take the initiative for a new organization, I would start an extreme-sports club.

Resources Reminder

Vocabulary

- *Vocabulary Development*
  - Vocabulary Worksheet, p. 44
- *Lesson Plans for Language Development*
  - Vocabulary, pp. 313, 319

ASSESSING

Assessment

- *Progress Assessment of Reading*
  - Selection Test

RETEACHING

For a lesson reteaching Standard 2.5, see **Reteaching,** p. 939A. For another selection to teach Standard 2.5, see *Interactive Reading,* Part 2.

STANDARDS FOCUS, pp. 644–650

(For the grade-level standards taught in this lesson, see citations on Student Edition pages.)

Prerequisite Standard

- Grade 8, Literary Response and Analysis 3.7 **Analyze a work of literature, showing how it reflects the heritage, traditions, attitudes, and beliefs of its author. (Biographical approach)**

Summary *at grade level*

After King Uther dies, leaving the nobility battling for the throne, Merlin advises the archbishop of Canterbury to call the nobles together in London on Christmas Day with the promise that the true successor to the throne will be miraculously revealed. The archbishop leads the nobles to the churchyard, where a large stone has appeared. In it is embedded a sword, passing through an anvil; its inscription proclaims that he who removes the sword is the rightful king of Britain. When all fail at this task, a tournament is set. At the joust, Sir Kay, Arthur's foster brother, finds his sword missing. To help him, Arthur (unobserved and ignoring the inscription) pulls the sword from the stone. Sir Kay, recognizing the sword, claims the throne for himself, but his father, Sir Ector, demands a full account of what has happened. This leads Arthur to repeat the feat, causing Ector and Kay to kneel before him. The other nobles refuse to believe Arthur's birthright, even though he frees the sword three more times. When he succeeds again at Pentecost, the commoners force his coronation.

Before You Read

The Sword in the Stone

Literary Focus

Arthurian Legend

A **legend** is a story about extraordinary deeds that has been told and retold for generations among a group of people. Legends, which are often about a particular person, are thought to have a historical basis but may also contain some elements of magic and myth. You can think of them as lying somewhere between historical fact and myth.

The King Arthur legends are probably based on a fifth- or sixth-century Celtic (kel′tik) chieftain, or warlord, who lived in Wales and led his people to victory against Saxon invaders from northern Germany. The chieftain was said to have been fatally wounded in battle and buried in the abbey of Glastonbury, where a gravestone can still be seen bearing his name.

Arthurian legend as we know it today emerged gradually over centuries as storytellers told and retold popular tales about a great chief who mysteriously disappeared but promised to return when his people needed him.

When Sir Thomas Malory wrote *Le Morte d'Arthur,* toward the end of the fifteenth century, the days of knights were over. Nonetheless, something in Malory's portrayal of those days seems to have answered a longing in his audience for the more orderly time of knights and lords and castles—a time when "might fought for right."

Reading Standard 3.12 Analyze the way in which a work of literature is related to the themes and issues of its historical period. (Historical approach)

Make the Connection

Quickwrite

Jot down five or six qualities that you associate with the word *hero.*

Background

Legendary heroes like King Arthur are born in dangerous times, when heroes are most needed. Here is the story of Arthur's birth: King Uther of England, who was unmarried, loved Igraine (ē′grān), another man's wife. In disguise the king deceived Igraine into thinking he was her husband. Arthur was the child born to Igraine as a result of that trick.

The wise man Merlin knew the baby was in danger because many men wanted Uther's throne, so he asked Sir Ector and his wife to raise the infant Arthur with their own son, Kay.

When King Uther died, no one except Merlin knew Arthur's true identity, which would be revealed when Arthur completed a task that only the rightful king could perform.

Vocabulary Development

confronted (kən·frunt′id) *v.:* faced.

inscription (in·skrip′shən) *n.:* something inscribed or engraved, as on a coin or monument.

oath (ōth) *n.:* solemn promise or declaration; vow.

ignoble (ig·nō′bəl) *adj.:* not noble in birth or position.

tumultuous (to͞o·mul′cho͞o·əs) *adj.:* wild; noisy.

realm (relm) *n.:* kingdom.

coronation (kôr′ə·nā′shən) *n.:* act or ceremony of crowning a sovereign.

RESOURCES: READING

Planning

- *One-Stop Planner* CD-ROM with Test Generator
- *On Course: Mapping Instruction*

Media

- *Audio CD Library*
  - disc 15

- *Visual Connections*
  - Videocassette, Segment 9
- *Fine Art Transparencies*
  - Transparency 16

Reading

- *Interactive Reading,* Teacher's Edition
  - Graphic Organizer: Hero Chart

644 Chapter 9 Biographical and Historical Approach • Using Primary and Secondary Sources

THE SWORD IN THE STONE

from **Le Morte d'Arthur**
Sir Thomas Malory
retold by **Keith Baines**

ERD OF THIS STONE AND ANVYLD IS RIGHT

During the years that followed the death of King Uther, while Arthur was still a child, the ambitious barons fought one another for the throne, and the whole of Britain stood in jeopardy. Finally the day came when the Archbishop of Canterbury, on the advice of Merlin, summoned the nobility to London for Christmas morning. In his message the archbishop promised that the true succession to the British throne would be miraculously revealed. Many of the nobles purified themselves during their journey, in the hope that it would be to them that the succession would fall.

PRETEACHING

Standards Starter

Build background. To introduce the historical setting of "The Sword and the Stone," play "For Love and Honor" (Videocassette, Segment 9, in *Visual Connections*). This video will give students insight into the concept of chivalry, which preoccupied the historical period reflected in the story.

Preview Vocabulary

To familiarize students with the Vocabulary Development words on p. 644, have them complete each sentence below with the word that best fits the context.

1. Everyone who lived in the evil king's ______ feared him. [realm]
2. The haughty countess ignored the ______ commoners who worked in the kitchen. [ignoble]
3. The knights swore an ______ of loyalty to one another. [oath]
4. A gala ball was held at the palace following the queen's ______. [coronation]
5. The boy bravely ______ his fear of the bucking horse and leapt onto its back. [confronted]
6. The ______ on the base of the statue revealed the hero's name and accomplishments. [inscription]
7. The quiet stream became a ______ torrent after the rains. [tumultuous]

Differentiating Instruction

- *Lesson Plans for Language Development*
  - English-Language Learners, pp. 293–295, 314, 320
  - Special Education Students, pp. 296, 314, 320

Vocabulary

- *Vocabulary Development*
  - Vocabulary Worksheet, p. 45

Assessment

- *Progress Assessment of Reading*
  - Selection Test
- *One-Stop Planner* CD-ROM with Test Generator

DIRECT TEACHING

A Learners Having Difficulty

Paraphrasing. Ask a volunteer to restate this inscription in modern English. [Possible response: Whoever pulls out this sword from this stone is the rightfully born king of all Britain.]

B Literary Focus
GRADE-LEVEL STANDARD

Arthurian legend. Why might a sword be used as a symbol of leadership? [Possible response: Long ago, it was important for kings to be able to lead their people into battle and to defend them from attack by others. The sword would represent a king's ability to fulfill such military duties.]

C Reading Skills

Analyzing. What is the significance of Arthur freeing the sword from the stone without effort or forethought? [Possible responses: It shows that he is Britain's rightful king and that he is unaware of his great destiny.]

D Literary Focus
GRADE-LEVEL STANDARD

Character traits. A character who highlights another character's personality by displaying contrasting traits is called a character foil. How is Sir Kay a foil to Arthur's heroic character traits? [Possible response: By being selfish, demanding, and dishonest, Sir Kay allows us to recognize Arthur's heroic traits of humility, obedience, and honesty.]

The archbishop held his service in the city's greatest church (St. Paul's), and when matins[1] were done, the congregation filed out to the yard. They were confronted by a marble block into which had been thrust a beautiful sword. The block was four feet square, and the sword passed through a steel anvil[2] which had been struck in the stone and which projected a foot from it. The anvil had been inscribed with letters of gold:

WHOSO PULLETH OUTE THIS SWERD
OF THIS STONE AND ANVYLD IS
RIGHTWYS KYNGE BORNE OF ALL
BRYTAYGNE

The congregation was awed by this miraculous sight, but the archbishop forbade anyone to touch the sword before Mass had been heard. After Mass, many of the nobles tried to pull the sword out of the stone, but none was able to, so a watch of ten knights was set over the sword, and a tournament[3] proclaimed for New Year's Day, to provide men of noble blood with the opportunity of proving their right to the succession.

Sir Ector, who had been living on an estate near London, rode to the tournament with Arthur and his own son Sir Kay, who had been recently knighted. When they arrived at the tournament, Sir Kay found to his annoyance that his sword was missing from its sheath, so he begged Arthur to ride back and fetch it from their lodging.

Arthur found the door of the lodging locked and bolted, the landlord and his wife having left for the tournament. In order not to disappoint his brother, he rode on to St. Paul's, determined to get for him the sword which was lodged in the stone. The yard was empty, the guard also having slipped off to see the tournament, so Arthur strode up to the sword and, without troubling to read the inscription, tugged it free. He then rode straight back to Sir Kay and presented him with it.

Sir Kay recognized the sword and, taking it to Sir Ector, said, "Father, the succession falls to me, for I have here the sword that was lodged in the stone." But Sir Ector insisted that they should all ride to the churchyard, and once there, bound Sir Kay by oath to tell how he had come by the sword. Sir Kay then admitted that Arthur had given it to him. Sir Ector turned to Arthur and said, "Was the sword not guarded?"

"It was not," Arthur replied.

"Would you please thrust it into the stone again?" said Sir Ector. Arthur did so, and first Sir Ector and then Sir Kay tried to remove it, but both were unable to. Then Arthur, for the second time, pulled it out. Sir Ector and Sir Kay both knelt before him.

"Why," said Arthur, "do you both kneel before me?"

"My lord," Sir Ector replied, "there is only one man living who can draw the sword from the stone, and he is the true-born king of Britain." Sir Ector then told Arthur the story of his birth and upbringing.

"My dear father," said Arthur, "for so I shall always think of you—if, as you say, I am to be king, please know that any request you have to make is already granted."

Sir Ector asked that Sir Kay should be made royal seneschal,[4] and Arthur declared that while they both lived it should be so. Then the three of them visited the archbishop and told him what had taken place.

1. **matins** (mat'’nz) *n.:* morning prayers.
2. **anvil** *n.:* iron or steel block on which metal objects are hammered into shape.
3. **tournament** *n.:* sport in which two knights compete on horseback, trying to unseat each other with long polelike weapons called lances.
4. **royal seneschal** (sen'ə·shəl): person in charge of the king's household. This was a powerful and respected position.

Vocabulary

confronted (kən·frunt'id) *v.:* faced.

inscription (in·skrip'shən) *n.:* something inscribed or engraved, as on a coin or monument.

oath (ōth) *n.:* solemn promise or declaration; vow.

DIFFERENTIATING INSTRUCTION

Learners Having Difficulty

Encourage pairs of students to read the selection aloud, pausing now and then to summarize and discuss the events.

English-Language Learners

Before reading, you may familiarize students with the language of the legend, discussing such words and concepts as *nobility, archbishop, duke, baron,* and *commoners.*

Resources Reminder

For lessons designed for special education, intermediate, and advanced English-language learners, see *Lesson Plans for Language Development,* pp. 293–296, 314, 320.

Advanced Learners

Acceleration. Use the following activity to move advanced learners toward the eleventh- and twelfth-grade Standard 3.7a, contrasting characteristics of literary periods.

Small-group activity. Have students define *hero* based on the depiction of Arthur in *Le Morte d'Arthur.* Then, have them explore the concept of heroism in ancient, romantic, and modern works, and contrast the characteristics of a hero in different periods.

All those dukes and barons with ambitions to rule were present at the tournament on New Year's Day. But when all of them had failed, and Arthur alone had succeeded in drawing the sword from the stone, they protested against one so young, and of ignoble blood, succeeding to the throne.

The secret of Arthur's birth was known to only a few of the nobles surviving from the days of King Uther. The archbishop urged them to make Arthur's cause their own; but their support proved ineffective. The tournament was repeated at Candlemas[5] and at Easter, with the same outcome as before.

Finally, at Pentecost,[6] when once more Arthur alone had been able to remove the sword, the commoners arose with a tumultuous cry and demanded that Arthur should at once be made king. The nobles, knowing in their hearts that the commoners were right, all knelt before Arthur and begged forgiveness for having delayed his succession for so long. Arthur forgave them and then, offering his sword at the high altar, was dubbed[7] first knight of the realm. The coronation took place a few days later, when Arthur swore to rule justly, and the nobles swore him their allegiance. ■

5. **Candlemas:** Christian festival that honors the purification of the Virgin Mary after the birth of Jesus. It falls on February 2.
6. **Pentecost:** Christian festival celebrated on the seventh Sunday after Easter, commemorating the descent of the Holy Spirit upon the Apostles.
7. **dubbed** *v.:* conferred knighthood on by tapping on the shoulder with a sword.

Vocabulary

ignoble (ig·nō′bəl) *adj.:* not noble in birth or position.

tumultuous (to͞o·mul′cho͞o·əs) *adj.:* wild and noisy.

realm (relm) *n.:* kingdom.

coronation (kôr′ə·nā′shən) *n.:* act or ceremony of crowning a sovereign.

Meet the Writer

Sir Thomas Malory

A Master of Escape

We know only a little about the life of Sir Thomas Malory (1405?–1471). His title indicates that he was a knight, and we know that he was a soldier and a member of Parliament for a brief time. We also know that he spent most of the last twenty years of his life in prison, accused of some very unchivalrous crimes: assault, extortion, cattle rustling, poaching, jail breaking, plundering an abbey, and "waylaying the duke of Buckingham." Malory pleaded innocent to all charges, and it is likely that he was framed by political enemies. (It is also possible that Malory was something of a scoundrel.) During those miserable years in jail, Malory wrote his great romance.

The twelfth-century world of chivalrous knights in shining armor was almost as foreign to Malory as it is to us today. (For more about knights and chivalry, see page 651.) The invention of gunpowder and the rise of the middle class had already broken down the feudal order. While Malory scribbled heroic tales in a dark jail cell, English political and social life was in a state of turmoil that no amount of chivalry seemed likely to cure. Perhaps Malory yearned for a return to chivalry, to a simpler way of life with established codes of behavior. He might also have been trying to create a romantic escape from the grim realities of his personal life.

(For another knightly adventure from Malory's *Le Morte d'Arthur,* see page 652.)

DIRECT TEACHING

E Literary Focus
GRADE-LEVEL STANDARD

Arthurian legend. Whom do the nobles want as king? [someone of their own class] What does their behavior indicate about the society of the time? [Possible responses: There was a line between upper and lower classes that could not be crossed; people were not free to move out of their stations in life.] In this retelling of the legend, how is this balance of power redressed? [Possible response: Arthur is crowned when the commoners demand that he be made king despite his supposedly low status.]

GUIDED PRACTICE

Monitoring students' progress. Guide students in answering these questions. Have them support their answers with passages from the text.

True-False

1. Arthur was the son of King Uther. [T]
2. Arthur could not compete because he lost his sword. [F]
3. Arthur pulled the sword from the stone for Sir Kay to use. [T]
4. In the end the nobles joined in pledging allegiance to Arthur. [T]

Meet the Writer

Background. According to documents unearthed in the 1890s, Malory seems to have backed the losing Duke of Lancaster in the English civil strife known as the Wars of the Roses (1455–1485), an action that led to his imprisonment by factions loyal to the victorious Duke of York.

Le Morte d'Arthur did not appear in print until 1485, some fourteen years after Malory's death. The printer William Caxton took upon himself the role of editor, arranging Malory's manuscript into 507 chapters and 21 books and supplying the title.

READING MINI-LESSON

Developing Word-Attack Skills

Write the selection word *jeopardy* on the chalkboard. Point out that the vowels *eo* together stand here for a short *e* sound: /jep′ər·dē/. Write the words *leopard* and *leotard.* Note the different pronunciations of these words that are spelled alike except for one letter:

leopard /lep′ərd/
leotard /lē′ə·tärd′/

The *eo* combination may stand for one sound but more often stands for two sounds.

Activity. Have students tell what sound or sounds the letters *eo* stand for in each word.

geography	jeopardize	neophyte
peony	people	preoccupy
theology	theory	yeoman

[geography /ē o/; jeopardize /e/; neophyte /ē ə/; peony /ē ə/; people /ē/; preoccupy /ē o/; theology /ē o/; theory /ē ə/ or /i/; yeoman /ō/]

Connection

Summary ↔ *at grade level*

In this essay, John Steinbeck reveals how *Le Morte d'Arthur* affected him as a child. Malory's stories of courage, sadness, frustration, and gallantry gave Steinbeck a new view of the world. In particular, the strange language of the text instilled in him a passionate love for the English language. Steinbeck also credits the book with forming his sense of right and wrong and his hatred of injustice and oppression.

A Reading Skills

Making inferences. What does John Steinbeck imply about his feelings toward reading in this statement? Why is this attitude ironic? [Possible responses: Steinbeck implies that as a child he thought reading was torture. This attitude is ironic because Steinbeck became one of America's most respected authors.]

B English-Language Learners

Archaic language. Explore with students the meanings of the archaic terms: both *yclept* (ē·klept′) and *hyght* (hīt) mean "called" or "named"; *wist* means "knew."

C Learners Having Difficulty

Breaking down difficult text. Help students to translate archaic lines into modern English. [Possible responses: "And when the child is born, let it be delivered unbaptized to me over there at the secret back gate." "The strangeness of the language enchanted me and carried me into the ancient setting."]

The American novelist John Steinbeck (1902–1968), author of The Grapes of Wrath, Of Mice and Men, *and* The Pearl, *was nine years old when he first read an abridged version of Malory's King Arthur tales.*

"The Magic Happened"

John Steinbeck

A Books were printed demons—the tongs and thumbscrews of outrageous persecution. And then, one day, an aunt gave me a book and fatuously ignored my resentment. I stared at the black print with hatred, and then, gradually, the pages opened and let me in. The magic happened. The Bible and Shakespeare and *Pilgrim's Progress*[1] belonged to everyone. But this was mine—it was a cut version of the Caxton *Morte d'Arthur* of Thomas Malory. I loved the old spelling of the words—and the words no longer used. Perhaps a passionate love for the English language opened to me from this one book. **B** I was delighted to find out paradoxes[2]—that *cleave* means both "to stick together" and "to cut apart"; that *host* means both "an enemy" and "a welcoming friend"; that *king* and *gens* (people) stem from the same root. For a long time, I had a secret language—*yclept* and *hyght, wist*—and *accord* meaning "peace," and *entente* meaning "purpose," and *fyaunce* meaning "promise.". . . But beyond the glorious and secret words—"And when the chylde is borne lete it be delyvered to me at yonder privy posterne uncrystened"—oddly enough **C** I knew the words from whispering them to myself. The very strangeness of the language dyd me enchante, and vaulted me into an ancient scene.

King Arthur (detail), from tapestry of the "Nine Worthies" (c. 1490).
Historisches Museum, Basel, Switzerland.

And in that scene were all the vices that ever were—and courage and sadness and frustration, but particularly gallantry[3]—perhaps the only single quality of man that the West has invented. I think my sense of right and wrong, my feeling of noblesse oblige,[4] and any thought I may have against the oppressor and for the oppressed came from this secret book. It did not outrage my sensibilities as nearly all the children's books did. It did not seem strange to me that Uther Pendragon wanted the wife of his vassal[5] and took her by trickery. I was not frightened to find that there were evil knights, as well as noble ones. In my own town there were men who wore the clothes of virtue whom I knew to be bad. In pain or sorrow or confusion, I went back to my magic book. Children are violent and cruel—and good—and I was all of these—and all of these were in the secret book.

1. ***Pilgrim's Progress*** *n.:* famous allegory written by John Bunyan in 1678.
2. **paradoxes** *n.:* apparent contradictions that are actually true.
3. **gallantry** *n.:* act of great courtesy or bravery.
4. **noblesse oblige** (nō·bles′ ō·blēzh′) *n.:* obligation of people of high position to behave nobly.
5. **vassal** *n.:* medieval tenant or servant.

Connecting and Comparing Texts

Have students work in small groups to summarize the aspects of Malory's tales that appealed most to the young Steinbeck, based on Steinbeck's essay. [Possible responses: The archaic words sparked Steinbeck's love of the English language; the knights' gallantry awakened his concern for the oppressed; the awareness that knights had both virtues and vices rang true for him.] Then, ask students to return to "The Sword in the Stone" to identify these features in this excerpt from Malory's legend.

Literary Response and Analysis

Reading Check

1. Make a **time line** showing the **main events** that take place in this part of Arthur's story. (You don't need to show the dates; just put the events in **chronological order.**) Start with the death of King Uther (before the story begins), and end with Arthur's coronation.

Interpretations

2. In what ways does Arthur, even as a young boy, show that he is a **hero**? How does Sir Kay, his foster brother, show signs that he is definitely *not* heroic material?
3. **Legends** often have both a historical basis and some element of exaggeration or fantasy. What elements of magic in this tale move it out of the realm of the ordinary and into that of legend?
4. What heroic values does this story teach? Which of these values are still important today? (Be sure to refer to your Quickwrite notes.)

Literary Criticism

5. During Arthur's time, England, like the rest of Europe, operated on a **feudal system** with three distinct social classes: the nobility, the commoners, and the clergy. What role does each class play in this story? Why would the tale have special appeal to the commoners?
6. "England's green and pleasant land" tempted invaders and conquerors—first the Celts, then Romans (first century), Saxons (beginning in the fifth century), Danes (eighth to eleventh centuries), and Normans (1066). Why would the question of succession to the throne have been of paramount importance to the people who first heard these tales recited?
7. In a typical **romance** (for more about romance, see page 651), the hero's origins are mysterious. He is frequently raised in obscurity before taking his rightful place as leader. How does the story of Arthur reflect this pattern?

Evaluation

8. Even today, Arthur lives. For example, T. H. White's novel based on the Arthurian legends, *The Once and Future King*, became a bestseller and the basis of the long-running Broadway musical *Camelot* (1960). There are even computer games retelling Arthur's story. Why do you suppose the story of King Arthur has had lasting appeal?

Writing

Remembering "Magic"

"The magic happened" for John Steinbeck at the age of nine when he first read Malory's *Morte d'Arthur* (see the ***Connection*** on page 648). Think of a book, movie, or TV show that made a strong, almost "magical," impression on you at a young age. In a brief essay, explain how you felt about the work then, why it was important to you, and how you feel about the work now.

Reading Standard 3.12 Analyze the way in which a work of literature is related to the themes and issues of its historical period. (Historical approach)

INDEPENDENT PRACTICE

Literary Response and Analysis

3. The fact that the sword has mysteriously been thrust into a stone and that only one person—the true king—can pull it out moves the tale out of the ordinary and into legend.
4. Possible answers: The story teaches loyalty, humility, generosity, and forgiveness. Some students may say these traits remain important; others may say that displaying these traits can make a person vulnerable, for example, in business.

Literary Criticism

5. Possible answers: The nobility insists that one of their own be king. The commoners force the nobles to accept Arthur. The clergy acts as a go-between, indirectly supporting Arthur. The tale would have special appeal to commoners because Arthur, at first, seemed to be one of them and because they held a pivotal role in selecting the new king.
6. Possible answers: They would have wanted to ensure that the throne fell legitimately to one of their own, rather than to a usurper, and to be sure that the new king was strong and brave, able to protect them from invaders.
7. Arthur was not publicly acknowledged by his father and, as the adopted son of Sir Ector, lived in obscurity, unaware of his royal birthright.

Reading Check

1. The time line should include the arrival of the nobility in London; the presentation of the sword in the stone and the reading of the inscription; the failed attempts by the nobles to withdraw the sword; Arthur's withdrawal of the sword for Sir Kay; the revelation of the truth about what happened; the attempts to deny Arthur the throne; and the final acceptance of Arthur as king.

Interpretations

2. As a boy, Arthur displays virtue—a heroic quality. He is willing to do anything for Sir Kay, even though Sir Kay lies and tries to steal the throne. Arthur is also generous to his adopted father, Sir Ector. Sir Kay behaves unheroically in concealing how he got the sword.

Evaluation

8. Possible answers: Stories about the success of an underdog are popular because most of us sometimes feel like underdogs; people today are still drawn to stories of kings, heroes, and pageantry.

Vocabulary Development

Practice

1. confronted
2. coronation
3. tumultuous
4. inscription
5. oath
6. ignoble
7. realm

Resources Reminder

Vocabulary

- *Vocabulary Development*
  - Vocabulary Worksheet, p. 45
- *Lesson Plans for Language Development*
  - Vocabulary, pp. 314, 320

Grammar Link

Practice

Possible answers:

1. Returning to St. Paul's, Arthur found the sword in the stone.
2. Arthur could not get into the locked door of the lodging.
3. Telling a lie, Sir Kay tried to become the king.
4. Sir Kay, bound by oath, finally told the true story of how he had gotten the sword.
5. With a great cry, the commoners demanded that Arthur be made king.

ASSESSING

Assessment

- *Progress Assessment of Reading*
  - Selection Test

Vocabulary Development

Analogies: Matching Word Pairs

On pages 29–30 and 410, review the steps for completing analogy test questions and the different types of relationships that may appear in an analogy.

Word Bank
confronted
inscription
oath
ignoble
tumultuous
realm
coronation

PRACTICE

Reading Standard 1.1 Identify and use the literal meanings of words.

Complete each analogy with a word from the Word Bank.

1. REPAIR : FIX ::__________ : faced
2. FOOTBALL : SPORT :: __________ : ceremony
3. BOLD : CAUTIOUS :: __________ : quiet
4. HARVESTED : CROP :: written : __________
5. JOKE : HUMOROUS :: __________ : solemn
6. WEAK : POWERFUL :: __________ : noble
7. CONCLUSION : ENDING :: __________ : kingdom

Grammar Link MINI-LESSON

Misplaced Modifiers: Keep Them Close

A word, phrase, or clause that seems to modify the wrong word in a sentence is called a **misplaced modifier.** Place modifiers as close as possible to the words they modify. When they're separated, the meaning is unclear and often funny.

MISPLACED Miraculous, the congregation was awed by the appearance of the sword in the stone. [Was the congregation miraculous?]

CLEAR The congregation was awed by the miraculous appearance of the sword in the stone.

MISPLACED Stuck in the anvil, Arthur pulled out the sword. [Was Arthur stuck in the anvil?]

CLEAR Arthur pulled out the sword stuck in the anvil.

PRACTICE

Rewrite these sentences, correcting every misplaced modifier:

1. Arthur found the sword in the stone returning to St. Paul's.
2. Locked, Arthur could not get into the door of the lodging.
3. Sir Kay tried to become the king telling a lie.
4. Sir Kay finally told the true story of how he had gotten the sword bound by oath.
5. The commoners demanded that Arthur with a great cry be made king.

For more help, see Misplaced Modifiers in the *Holt Handbook,* pages 225–230.

DIFFERENTIATING INSTRUCTION

Learners Having Difficulty
Have students rewrite the following sentences, correcting each misplaced modifier.

1. Still a child, the throne was not something Arthur dreamed of. [Still a child, Arthur did not dream of the throne.]
2. Arthur took the sword to Sir Kay pulled from the stone. [Arthur took the sword, pulled from the stone, to Sir Kay.]
3. Kneeling, Arthur was recognized by Sir Ector as true-born king. [Kneeling, Sir Ector recognized Arthur as true-born king.]
4. Arthur was able to remove the sword alone. [Arthur alone was able to remove the sword.]
5. The commoners at once demanded that Arthur be crowned. [The commoners demanded that Arthur be crowned at once.]

650 Chapter 9 Biographical and Historical Approach • Using Primary and Secondary Sources

Before You Read

The Tale of Sir Launcelot du Lake

Literary Focus

The Literature of Romance

During the Middle Ages a new form of literature, called the **romance,** developed in France and spread like a firestorm throughout Europe. Romances got their name because they were first told in Old French and Provençal, which are Romance languages (languages derived from Latin, the language of the Romans).

Romances began in the twelfth century as popular narratives describing the adventures of knights and other heroes. Wandering story singers collected these stories and recited them as they traveled from town to town. By the fourteenth century, romances had been taken over by the upper classes. As old oral storytellers gradually disappeared, the romances were passed on as written stories, polished and professional.

The primary purpose of romances was to celebrate the ideals of **chivalry,** the code of behavior the medieval knight was supposed to follow. He was to be brave, honorable, loyal, pious, and generous to foes, ready to help the weak and to protect women. The typical knight sought quests to prove his courage. The **knightly quest** (see page 657) typically involved saving maidens, slaying dragons, and battling less noble persons. Adventure was the call; heroism, the role.

Reading Skills

Summarizing: Just What's Important

A good **plot summary** tells only the main characters and events, omitting all the delicious details. The summary states the plot's bare bones: what the main character wants (**motivation**), what prevents him or her from getting it (**conflict**), and how the conflict is resolved (**resolution**).

When you're reading a story, it often helps to stop at key points to summarize what is happening. The questions at the open-book signs will help you do that as you read about Sir Launcelot.

Make the Connection

Quickwrite

Now that the days of knightly quests are gone, how can someone in today's world prove his or her heroism? Jot down your ideas, and save your notes.

Background

Of the 150 knights who sit at King Arthur's Round Table, Sir Launcelot is Arthur's favorite—and the bravest too. Although Launcelot is devoted to Arthur, he falls in love with Arthur's wife, Queen Gwynevere, causing great suffering for the unfortunate trio. In this tale, as Launcelot goes searching for adventure, he runs into Morgan le Fay, Arthur's evil half sister. Famous for her enchantments, Morgan continually plots to destroy Arthur.

Vocabulary Development

diverted (də·vʉrt'id) *v.:* amused; entertained.

fidelity (fə·del'ə·tē) *n.:* loyalty; devotion.

oblige (ə·blīj') *v.:* compel by moral, legal, or physical force.

champion (cham'pē·ən) *v.:* fight for; defend; support.

adversary (ad'vər·ser'ē) *n.:* opponent; enemy.

sovereign (säv'rən) *n.:* king; ruler.

wrath (rath) *n.:* great anger.

Reading Standard 3.12 Analyze the way in which a work of literature is related to the themes and issues of its historical period. (Historical approach)

STANDARDS FOCUS, pp. 651–659

(For the grade-level and review standards taught in this lesson, see citations on Student Edition pages.)

Prerequisite Standard

- Grade 8, Literary Response and Analysis 3.7 **Analyze a work of literature, showing how it reflects the heritage, traditions, attitudes, and beliefs of its author. (Biographical approach)**

Reading Skills

- Summarize.

Summary *at grade level*

Bored with life in Camelot, Sir Launcelot, the most accomplished knight of the Round Table, rides out in search of adventure. Four queens, including the sorceress Morgan le Fay, find Sir Launcelot sleeping, cast a spell on him, and imprison him in a castle. Morgan le Fay explains that Sir Launcelot must take one of the queens as his paramour or forfeit his life. Loyal to Queen Gwynevere, Sir Launcelot boldly refuses. A young noblewoman in the castle secretly agrees to release Sir Launcelot on the condition that he will champion her father, King Bagdemagus, at an upcoming tournament. He proceeds to the tournament at the castle of King Bagdemagus where he proves himself invincible, repaying his debt to the king's daughter.

RESOURCES: READING

Media

- *Audio CD Library*
  - disc 15

Reading

- *Interactive Reading,* Teacher's Edition
  - Graphic Organizer: Hero Chart

Differentiating Instruction

- *Lesson Plans for Language Development*
  - English-Language Learners, pp. 297–299, 315, 321
  - Special Education Students, pp. 300, 315, 321

Vocabulary

- *Vocabulary Development*
  - Vocabulary Worksheet, p. 46

Assessment

- *Progress Assessment of Reading*
  - Selection Test
- *One-Stop Planner* CD-ROM with Test Generator

PRETEACHING

Selection Starter

Build background. This excerpt begins with the words "When King Arthur returned from Rome . . ." Tell students that, according to legend, Arthur fought a war against the Roman emperor Lucius and conquered much of western Europe. Early accounts claim he was called home before completing this conquest because Modred, either his son or nephew, had seized his kingdom and queen. Later accounts state that Arthur did complete his victory over the Romans and returned home to begin the quest for the Holy Grail.

Preview Vocabulary

Ask students to review the Vocabulary Development words on p. 651. Then, have them write their responses to the following questions. (Possible responses are given.)

1. What are some ways in which small children might be diverted? [by hearing stories read to them; by playing games]
2. Why is fidelity important among friends? [Friends must feel that they can trust one another.]
3. What might a police officer oblige you to do? [show your driver's license]
4. If you champion a cause, what are some actions you might take? [work to raise funds; write to representatives; make speeches]
5. Name at least one adversary faced by Batman. [the Riddler, Catwoman]
6. What might you do first if you were introduced to a sovereign? [bow and show respect]
7. How might a worker avoid the wrath of a stern supervisor? [by doing all tasks well and on time]

The Tale of Sir Launcelot du Lake

"Of all his knights one was supreme."

***from* Le Morte d'Arthur**

Sir Thomas Malory

***retold by* Keith Baines**

When King Arthur returned from Rome he settled his court at Camelot, and there gathered about him his knights of the Round Table, who diverted themselves with jousting[1] and tournaments. Of all his knights one was supreme, both in prowess[2] at arms and in nobility of bearing, and this was Sir Launcelot, who was also the favorite of Queen Gwynevere, to whom he had sworn oaths of fidelity.

1. **jousting** (joust′iŋ) *v.* used as *n.:* form of combat between two knights on horseback. Each used a long lance to try to knock the other from his horse.
2. **prowess** (prou′is) *n.:* superior ability.

Vocabulary

diverted (də·vurt′id) *v.:* amused; entertained.

fidelity (fə·del′ə·tē) *n.:* loyalty; devotion.

652

DIFFERENTIATING INSTRUCTION

Learners Having Difficulty

Modeling. To help students read "The Tale of Sir Launcelot du Lake," use the first paragraph to model the reading skill of summarizing. [Possible summary: King Arthur assembled the knights of the Round Table at Camelot. Sir Launcelot, a favorite of Queen Gwynevere, was the finest of the knights.]

English-Language Learners

Define words that are related to the story: *sorceress* ("a woman skilled in magic"), *abbey* ("a monastery or convent"), a medieval *tournament* ("a contest in which knights match their skills at jousting and swordplay.")

Resources Reminder

For lessons designed for intermediate and advanced English-language learners, see *Lesson Plans for Language Development,* pp. 297–299, 315, 321.

One day Sir Launcelot, feeling weary of his life at the court, and of only playing at arms,[3] decided to set forth in search of adventure. He asked his nephew Sir Lyonel to accompany him, and when both were suitably armed and mounted, they rode off together through the forest.

At noon they started across a plain, but the intensity of the sun made Sir Launcelot feel sleepy, so Sir Lyonel suggested that they should rest beneath the shade of an apple tree that grew by a hedge not far from the road. They dismounted, tethered their horses, and settled down.

"Not for seven years have I felt so sleepy," said Sir Launcelot, and with that fell fast asleep, while Sir Lyonel watched over him.

While Sir Launcelot still slept beneath the apple tree, four queens started across the plain. They were riding white mules and accompanied by four knights who held above them, at the tips of their spears, a green silk canopy, to protect them from the sun. The party was startled by the neighing of Sir Launcelot's horse and, changing direction, rode up to the apple tree, where they discovered the sleeping knight. And as each of the queens gazed at the handsome Sir Launcelot, so each wanted him for her own.

"Let us not quarrel," said Morgan le Fay. "Instead, I will cast a spell over him so that he remains asleep while we take him to my castle and make him our prisoner. We can then oblige him to choose one of us for his paramour."[4]

Sir Launcelot was laid on his shield and borne by two of the knights to the Castle Charyot, which was Morgan le Fay's stronghold. He awoke to find himself in a cold cell, where a young noblewoman was serving him supper.

"What cheer?" she asked.

"My lady, I hardly know, except that I must have been brought here by means of an enchantment."

"Sir, if you are the knight you appear to be, you will learn your fate at dawn tomorrow." And with that the young noblewoman left him. Sir Launcelot spent an uncomfortable night but at dawn the four queens presented themselves and Morgan le Fay spoke to him:

"Sir Launcelot, I know that Queen Gwynevere loves you, and you her. But now you are my prisoner, and you will have to choose: either to take one of us for your paramour, or to die miserably in this cell—just as you please. Now I will tell you who we are: I am Morgan le Fay, Queen of Gore; my companions are the Queens of North Galys, of Estelonde, and of the Outer Isles. So make your choice."

"A hard choice! Understand that I choose none of you, lewd sorceresses that you are; rather will I die in this cell. But were I free, I would take pleasure in proving it against any who would champion you that Queen Gwynevere is the finest lady of this land."

"So, you refuse us?" asked Morgan le Fay.

"On my life, I do," Sir Launcelot said finally, and so the queens departed.

SUMMARIZING

1. Summarize Launcelot's adventure with the four queens.

Sometime later, the young noblewoman who had served Sir Launcelot's supper reappeared.

"What news?" she asked.

"It is the end," Sir Launcelot replied.

"Sir Launcelot, I know that you have refused

3. **playing at arms:** fighting with weapons as a sport only.
4. **paramour** (par′ə·mo͝or′) *n.:* sweetheart; from Old French, meaning "with love." Today the term refers to an illicit lover.

Vocabulary

oblige (ə·blīj′) *v.:* compel by moral, legal, or physical force.

champion (cham′pē·ən) *v.:* fight for; defend; support.

DIRECT TEACHING

A Literary Focus
GRADE-LEVEL STANDARD

The literature of romance. What typical element of romantic literature does this decision of Sir Launcelot illustrate? [Possible response: Sir Launcelot's decision to seek adventure is typical of the knightly quest, the call to a heroic adventure.]

B Content-Area Connections

Literature

Students might wonder why Sir Lyonel did not alert Sir Launcelot to the approaching queens. Tell them that some events from the original story have been omitted. Sir Lyonel was awakened by the sound of galloping horses and watched as a lone knight captured three other knights. Hoping to show off his own fighting prowess, Sir Lyonel left Launcelot's side to battle the lone knight. He, too, was captured, and the conquering knight rode off with him and the other prisoners.

C Literary Focus
GRADE-LEVEL STANDARD

The literature of romance. What characteristics of chivalry does Sir Launcelot display here? [Possible response: loyalty to Queen Gwynevere and bravery in offering to fight for her honor]

D Reading Skills

Summarizing. [Possible response to question 1: Morgan le Fay places a spell on Launcelot, and he is taken to her castle. There, four queens demand that he choose one of them as his paramour—or die. He rejects them, proclaiming his loyalty to Queen Gwynevere.]

Special Education Students

For lessons designed for special education students, see *Lesson Plans for Language Development,* pp. 300, 315, 321.

Advanced Learners

Acceleration. Use the following activity to move advanced learners toward the eleventh- and twelfth-grade Standard 3.6, for which they analyze how authors have drawn upon archetypes from myth and tradition.

Activity. Ask students to choose two works, from different historical periods, that include romantic heroes, and then write an essay comparing Launcelot with the other heroes. Encourage students to explore what is constant about the romantic ideal even though characters and problems vary according to a work's time period.

DIRECT TEACHING

A Literary Focus
GRADE-LEVEL STANDARD

The literature of romance. What typical elements of a romance have already occurred in this tale? [Possible responses: Launcelot has ridden out on a quest for adventure; he has experienced a magical enchantment; he has outsmarted the evil Morgan le Fay with the aid of a helper; he has agreed to champion the good King Bagdemagus against his opponents.]

B Literary Focus
REVIEW STANDARD

Style. How does the author's style here and elsewhere help suggest a medieval setting? [Possible responses: The knights' conversation is very formal, even courtly, suggesting their noble background. The speakers use somewhat archaic words and phrases, such as *sorely wounded* and *staunch,* to suggest the medieval setting.]

C English-Language Learners

Special terms. Make sure students realize that *rounded* means "turned against" or "assailed." Also, *yielded* in this context means "surrendered."

the four queens, and that they wish to kill you out of spite. But if you will be ruled by me, I can save you. I ask that you will champion my father at a tournament next Tuesday, when he has to combat the King of North Galys, and three knights of the Round Table, who last Tuesday defeated him ignominiously."[5]

"My lady, pray tell me, what is your father's name?"

"King Bagdemagus."

"Excellent, my lady, I know him for a good king and a true knight, so I shall be happy to serve him."

"May God reward you! And tomorrow at dawn I will release you, and direct you to an abbey[6] which is ten miles from here, and where the good monks will care for you while I fetch my father."

"I am at your service, my lady."

As promised, the young noblewoman released Sir Launcelot at dawn. When she had led him through the twelve doors to the castle entrance, she gave him his horse and armor, and directions for finding the abbey.

"God bless you, my lady; and when the time comes I promise I shall not fail you."

Sir Launcelot rode through the forest in search of the abbey, but at dusk had still failed to find it, and coming upon a red silk pavilion,[7] apparently unoccupied, decided to rest there overnight, and continue his search in the morning.

He had not been asleep for more than an hour, however, when the knight who owned the pavilion returned, and got straight into bed with him. Having made an assignation[8] with his paramour, the knight supposed at first that Sir Launcelot was she, and taking him into his arms, started kissing him. Sir Launcelot awoke with a start, and seizing his sword, leaped out of bed and out of the pavilion, pursued closely by the other knight. Once in the open they set to with their swords, and before long Sir Launcelot had wounded his unknown adversary so seriously that he was obliged to yield.

The knight, whose name was Sir Belleus, now asked Sir Launcelot how he came to be sleeping in his bed, and then explained how he had an assignation with his lover, adding:

"But now I am so sorely wounded that I shall consider myself fortunate to escape with my life."

"Sir, please forgive me for wounding you; but lately I escaped from an enchantment, and I was afraid that once more I had been betrayed. Let us go into the pavilion and I will staunch your wound."

Sir Launcelot had just finished binding the wound when the young noblewoman who was Sir Belleus' paramour arrived, and seeing the wound, at once rounded in fury on Sir Launcelot.

"Peace, my love," said Sir Belleus. "This is a noble knight, and as soon as I yielded to him he treated my wound with the greatest care." Sir Belleus then described the events which had led up to the duel.

"Sir, pray tell me your name, and whose knight you are," the young noblewoman asked Sir Launcelot.

"My lady, I am called Sir Launcelot du Lake."

"As I guessed, both from your appearance and from your speech; and indeed I know you better than you realize. But I ask you, in recompense

5. **ignominiously** (ig′nə·min′ē·əs·lē) *adv.:* dishonorably; disgracefully.
6. **abbey** (ab′ē) *n.:* place where monks or nuns live.
7. **pavilion** (pə·vil′yən) *n.:* large tent, often with a peaked top.
8. **assignation** (as′ig·nā′shən) *n.:* appointment, often made secretly.

Vocabulary
adversary (ad′vər·ser′ē) *n.:* opponent; enemy.

for[9] the injury you have done my lord, and out of the courtesy for which you are famous, to recommend Sir Belleus to King Arthur, and suggest that he be made one of the knights of the Round Table. I can assure you that my lord deserves it, being only less than yourself as a man-at-arms, and sovereign of many of the Outer Isles."

"My lady, let Sir Belleus come to Arthur's court at the next Pentecost.[10] Make sure that you come with him, and I promise I will do what I can for him; and if he is as good a man-at-arms as you say he is, I am sure Arthur will accept him."

Launcelot Enters a Tournament

As soon as it was daylight, Sir Launcelot armed, mounted, and rode away in search of the abbey, which he found in less than two hours. King Bagdemagus' daughter was waiting for him, and as soon as she heard his horse's footsteps in the yard, ran to the window, and, seeing that it was Sir Launcelot, herself ordered the servants to stable his horse. She then led him to her chamber, disarmed him, and gave him a long gown to wear, welcoming him warmly as she did so.

King Bagdemagus' castle was twelve miles away, and his daughter sent for him as soon as she had settled Sir Launcelot. The king arrived with his retinue[11] and embraced Sir Launcelot, who then described his recent enchantment, and the great obligation he was under to his daughter for releasing him.

"Sir, you will fight for me on Tuesday next?"

"Sire, I shall not fail you; but please tell me the names of the three Round Table knights whom I shall be fighting."

"Sir Modred, Sir Madore de la Porte, and Sir Gahalantyne. I must admit that last Tuesday they defeated me and my knights completely."

"Sire, I hear that the tournament is to be fought within three miles of the abbey. Could you send me three of your most trustworthy knights, clad in plain armor, and with no device,[12] and a fourth suit of armor which I myself shall wear? We will take up our position just outside the tournament field and watch while you and the King of North Galys enter into combat with your followers; and then, as soon as you are in difficulties, we will come to your rescue, and show your opponents what kind of knights you command."

This was arranged on Sunday, and on the following Tuesday Sir Launcelot and the three knights of King Bagdemagus waited in a copse,[13] not far from the pavilion which had been erected for the lords and ladies who were to judge the tournament and award the prizes.

SUMMARIZING
2. Summarize the way in which Launcelot ends up fighting in the tournament.

The King of North Galys was the first on the field, with a company of ninescore[14] knights; he was followed by King Bagdemagus with fourscore knights, and then by the three knights of the Round Table, who remained apart from both companies. At the first encounter King Bagdemagus lost twelve knights, all killed, and the King of North Galys six.

9. **in recompense** (rek′əm·pens′) **for:** in compensation for; make up for.
10. **Pentecost** (pen′tə·kôst′): Christian holiday that falls seven weeks after Easter.
11. **retinue** (ret′'n·o͞o′) *n.:* servants; attendants serving someone of importance.
12. **device** *n.:* design on a coat of arms. In a tournament, knights wore or carried a coat of arms to identify the noble for whom they were fighting.
13. **copse** (käps) *n.:* thicket of small trees or shrubs.
14. **ninescore** *n.:* 180. A *score* is 20.

Vocabulary
sovereign (säv′rən) *n.:* king; ruler.

DIRECT TEACHING

D Literary Focus
GRADE-LEVEL STANDARD
The literature of romance. What chivalric ideals are illustrated by this incident at the pavilion? [Possible response: The scene enables Launcelot to display his skill as a man-at-arms, his compassion for the wounded knight, and his courteous deference to the lady.]

E Learners Having Difficulty
Re-reading. Students may benefit from re-reading this paragraph to clarify who is being referred to by the various uses of the pronoun *his*.

F Reading Skills
Making inferences. Why do you think Launcelot wants to fight in plain armor with no device (a coat of arms or identifying symbol)? [Possible response: He wants his identity to remain anonymous since he is fighting against three of his fellow knights from the Round Table.]

G Reading Skills
Summarizing. [Possible response to question 2: The daughter of King Bagdemagus helps Launcelot escape from Morgan le Fay's castle. In return, she asks Launcelot to fight as her father's knight at an upcoming tournament. After a long ride, Launcelot stops to rest at a pavilion. Later, a knight climbs into bed with Launcelot, mistaking him for his lover. A fight ensues and Launcelot wounds the other knight. When the misunderstanding is explained, Launcelot binds the knight's wounds and promises to introduce him to King Arthur. Finally, Launcelot meets King Bagdemagus's daughter at the abbey. The king arrives, and Launcelot learns he will be fighting members of the Round Table. He then asks the king to provide him with three knights and unmarked armor.]

CONTENT-AREA CONNECTIONS

Literature: Sir Launcelot
Sir Launcelot first appeared as an important character in a French story written around 1180 by Chrétien de Troyes. The son of the king of Brittany, Launcelot was taken as an infant and raised by the Lady of the Lake, a sorceress whose castle stood at the bottom of a lake. Later in life, Launcelot fathered Sir Galahad, the morally perfect knight who found the Holy Grail.

DIRECT TEACHING

Ⓐ Reading Skills

Summarizing. [Possible response to question 3: After the first encounter, in which King Bagdemagus loses twelve knights, Launcelot rides onto the field and wounds the king of North Galys and five of his knights. Next, the three Round Table knights join the fray, and Launcelot wounds them also. Then he defeats so many of King Galys's knights that the king is forced to admit defeat.]

GUIDED PRACTICE

Monitoring students' progress. Guide the class in answering these comprehension questions. Direct students to locate passages in the text that support their responses. (Possible answers are given in brackets.)

Short Answer

1. Why does Launcelot decide to leave Camelot? [He is tired of court life and wants to find some real adventure.]
2. What is the first adventure Launcelot finds himself involved in? [He is taken captive by Morgan le Fay and three other queens.]
3. How does King Bagdemagus's daughter help Launcelot? [She frees him from the four witches' prison in exchange for his helping her father.]
4. Why does Launcelot injure the knight Sir Belleus? [A misunderstanding causes Sir Belleus to embrace Launcelot while he is sleeping, and Launcelot is compelled to protect himself.]
5. How does Launcelot repay his debt to King Bagdemagus's daughter? [Launcelot helps King Bagdemagus win a tournament.]

With that, Sir Launcelot galloped on to the field, and with his first spear unhorsed five of the King of North Galys' knights, breaking the backs of four of them. With his next spear he charged the king, and wounded him deeply in the thigh.

"That was a shrewd blow," commented Sir Madore, and galloped onto the field to challenge Sir Launcelot. But he too was tumbled from his horse, and with such violence that his shoulder was broken.

Sir Modred was the next to challenge Sir Launcelot, and he was sent spinning over his horse's tail. He landed head first, his helmet became buried in the soil, and he nearly broke his neck, and for a long time lay stunned.

Finally, Sir Gahalantyne tried; at the first encounter both he and Sir Launcelot broke their spears, so both drew their swords and hacked vehemently at each other. But Sir Launcelot, with mounting wrath, soon struck his opponent a blow on the helmet which brought the blood streaming from eyes, ears, and mouth. Sir Gahalantyne slumped forward in the saddle, his horse panicked, and he was thrown to the ground, useless for further combat.

Sir Launcelot took another spear, and unhorsed sixteen more of the King of North Galys' knights, and with his next, unhorsed another twelve; and in each case with such violence that none of the knights ever fully recovered. The King of North Galys was forced to admit defeat, and the prize was awarded to King Bagdemagus.

SUMMARIZING

Ⓐ 3. In two or three sentences, tell what happens at the tournament.

That night Sir Launcelot was entertained as the guest of honor by King Bagdemagus and his daughter at their castle, and before leaving was loaded with gifts.

"He rode his way with the queen unto Joyous Gard." Illustration by N. C. Wyeth for *The Boy's King Arthur* (1917).

"My lady, please, if ever again you should need my services, remember that I shall not fail you." ■

Vocabulary
wrath (rath) *n.:* great anger.

Arthur's kingdom thrived while the Round Table existed, but "might for right" did not last. Several knights told King Arthur about the relationship between his wife and Launcelot. Gwynevere was judged guilty of adultery and sentenced to burn at the stake. At the last moment, Launcelot, charging through the guards, snatched Gwynevere from the flames and took her back to his castle. The resulting hostility between Arthur and Launcelot split the knights' allegiance. Thus, sexual immorality brought an end to the fellowship of the Round Table.

656

DEVELOPING FLUENCY

Small-group activity. Remind students that legends such as this one were often included in works by troubadours, or poet-musicians, who performed in royal courts. Suggest that students imagine how the troubadours might have told the tale to their early audiences. Then, ask students working in small groups to take turns reading parts of the story aloud with feeling—as if they were trying to entertain a large crowd. If possible, allow them to record their readings to produce a storytelling festival on tape.

Connection

Summary at grade level

In this essay, David Adams Leeming examines the role of the hero in the romance plot. He notes similarities between heroes in medieval stories and those in modern genres, such as westerns, science fiction, and fantasy, and even in computer games. Leeming also discusses the changing role of women in the genre. He explains that in medieval romances women often played villainous or passive roles, while in modern romances, women can take on the role of hero.

CONNECTION / ESSAY

The world of romance was—and still is today—an ideal world of exaggeration and wish fulfillment, a world where the forces of good always triumph over the forces of evil.

The Romance: WHERE GOOD ALWAYS TRIUMPHS

David Adams Leeming

The hero's quest. A typical romance plot consists of a series of marvelous adventures with many magical events. The hero's adventures usually assume the form of a **quest,** a long, perilous journey in search of something of value: a kingdom, the rescue of a maiden, the destruction of a devouring beast, a treasure trove.

Joseph Campbell, author of *The Hero with a Thousand Faces,* writes that the hero's journey underlies the literature of all cultures. Typically the hero leaves the safety of home to cross into strange lands where he must prove that he has the wit, will, and strength to survive. During his quest the hero comes into conflict with a host of enemies—evil knights, monsters, and dragons—that he must fight or outsmart. He may be aided in his quest by a faithful companion or by a magic weapon. He often has a mysterious connection to the world of nature and is sometimes aided by animals. (In the modern quest trilogy *The Lord of the Rings* by J.R.R. Tolkien, the hero is aided by trees.) By the end of a typical romance, the hero has passed all the tests, suffered losses, gained what he had sought, and earned a measure of wisdom. In its purest form the hero's quest is a struggle between good and evil. Interpreted metaphorically, the quest is a journey into and out of the evil side of human nature. **B**

Romances are still alive and well. Western novels and movies, science fiction and fantasy, adventure tales, mysteries, even some computer and video games—all use elements of the old romances. Good is still pitted against evil as the modern hero confronts new-age monsters. The hero still has incredible luck and strength, but his or her magical powers have disappeared.

Something new: The women step up. In medieval romances, women were usually betrayers, seducers, victims, or rewards. Today, especially in science fiction and fantasy, women pursue the hero's journey; they go on their own quests, take risks, and slay their own dragons. **C** No matter who the questing hero is, modern romance stories continue to reveal our dreams of an ideal human community. Whether they were written yesterday or will be written tomorrow, romances show us the best that humans are capable of.

B Reading Skills

Making inferences. Why is it important for the hero to encounter enemies such as evil knights, sorceresses, and dragons in romance stories? [Possible response: Enemies are needed to illustrate the struggle between good and evil and to highlight the many strengths and virtues of the hero.]

C Reading Skills

Drawing conclusions. How does the way women have been portrayed in literature over time reflect their changing roles in society? [Possible response: In medieval times and for centuries afterward, women's roles in society were considered to be less important than those of men. Today in Western culture, women have come closer to equal status with men and so they are sometimes portrayed as heroes in stories.]

Connecting and Comparing Texts

Invite students to discuss "The Tale of Sir Launcelot du Lake" in the context of Leeming's essay on the romance genre. You may wish to use the following prompts to stimulate discussion:

- Leeming discusses the importance of "the hero's quest." How would you describe Launcelot's quest in this selection? [Possible response: At first, Launcelot was simply on a quest for adventure; then his goal was to escape imprisonment. Finally, his quest compelled him to repay his debt to King Bagdemagus's daughter.]
- Leeming explains that the hero comes into conflict with "a host of enemies" during his quest. What enemies does Launcelot face in this selection? [Possible responses: the four queens, including Morgan le Fay; Sir Belleus, although this was a misunderstanding; the knights of the tournament, including Modred, Madore de la Porte, and Gahalantyne.]
- Leeming points out that women were often portrayed negatively in medieval romances. What evidence can you find in the selection to support this claim? [Possible response: Morgan le Fay and the three other queens were evildoers who enchanted Launcelot and took him prisoner.]

INDEPENDENT PRACTICE

Literary Response and Analysis

Reading Check

1. Possible answer: After I left Camelot, Morgan le Fay cast a spell over me while I slept. Later, at her castle, she demanded that I choose one of four queens as my paramour—or be killed. I refused. A noblewoman released me when I agreed to support her father in a joust. Secretly leaving the castle, I lost my way. Due to a case of mistaken identity, I injured Sir Belleus. In the end, however, I kept my promise to champion the noblewoman's father, King Bagdemagus, against the king of North Galys and defeated all my opponents in a tournament.

Interpretations

2. Possible answers: Launcelot resists the advances of Morgan le Fay; he aids the noblewoman and champions her father; in the tournament, he shows extraordinary skill. Some students might find his relationship with Gwynevere unchivalrous.
3. Possible answers: Sir Launcelot has a quest; Morgan le Fay is a wicked adversary who uses magic; the hero has further adventures in a case of mistaken identity and at the tournament. The shows students cite will vary.
4. Possible answers: *Settings. Arthurian Legend*—castles; British countryside; medieval times. *Westerns*—the American West; ranches; the late nineteenth century. *Characters. Arthurian Legend*—good and evil knights and kings; lords and ladies. *Westerns*—lawmen; robbers; rustlers; ranchers. *Plots. Arthurian Legend*—hero fights evil knight, sorceress, or monster. *Westerns*—hero fights robber or rustler. *Themes. Arthurian Legend* and *Westerns*—good versus evil.

Literary Response and Analysis

Reading Check

1. You are Sir Launcelot, reporting to King Arthur about your adventures. Using the first person, briefly **summarize the main events** that befell you on your journey.

Interpretations

2. Identify at least three of Launcelot's actions that are worthy of a chivalric **hero.** What, if anything, does he do that seems unheroic?
3. A **romance** usually includes these motifs: adventure, quests, wicked adversaries, even magic (see the ***Connection*** on page 657). Describe the typical elements of a romance that you find in this tale. Are any of these elements found in TV shows and movies today? Explain.
4. John Steinbeck, who was captivated by Malory's tales as a boy (see the ***Connection*** on page 648), once compared the Arthurian legends to the American western movie. Take notes in the form of a chart, **comparing and contrasting** these two kinds of stories. Then, tell which you prefer and why.

	Arthurian Legend	Westerns
Settings		
Characters		
Plots		
Themes		

Reading Standard 3.12 Analyze the way in which a work of literature is related to the themes and issues of its historical period. (Historical approach)

Literary Criticism

5. Based on this tale, what can you say about the **character traits** medieval culture valued in its heroes?
6. **Compare and contrast** the medieval hero with your own ideas about heroes. (Where do your own ideas about heroes come from?) Be sure to refer to your Quickwrite notes.
7. The Arthurian stories are not dull; they are full of violence, betrayals, romantic intrigues, and even comedy. Which of these elements did you find in this tale and in "The Sword in the Stone" (page 645)? Cite details.
8. Knights really existed in twelfth-century England. Why do you think a romance such as this one would captivate a twelfth-century peasant, who struggled to survive, or a nobleperson?

Writing

Stay Tuned for More About Arthur

What became of Gwynevere and Morgan le Fay? What special powers did Merlin have? What was medieval combat like? Make a list of Arthur-related questions. Do some research, and narrow your list to one topic about which you will write a **research paper.** Use both print and Internet sources for your report.

▶ **Use "Writing a Research Paper," pages 690–709, for help with this assignment.**

"Very good, Gary: 'A hero is a celebrity who did something real.' "

Literary Criticism

5. Possible answer: The culture valued loyalty, chivalry, and physical prowess.
6. Students' heroes might embody independence of mind and action, more than loyalty. Also, mental ability and insight might be valued more than physical strength.
7. In "The Sword in the Stone," Sir Kay betrays Arthur. In "Sir Launcelot du Lake," there is violence in the jousts, betrayal of Arthur by Gwynevere, romantic intrigue when Morgan le Fay attempts to ensnare Launcelot, and comedy when Launcelot is mistaken for Sir Belleus' paramour.
8. Possible answer: A romance might allow peasants to escape from the daily drudgery of their lives and might entertain nobles with exciting stories of appealing men and women of their own class.

Vocabulary Development

Demonstrating Word Knowledge

PRACTICE 1

Word Bank
diverted
fidelity
oblige
champion
adversary
sovereign
wrath

Reinforce your understanding of the Word Bank words by writing an answer to each of the following questions.

1. When you've been very tense, what has diverted you?
2. Why is fidelity to a cause an admired quality?
3. What are some things that a dog owner is obliged to do to take good care of his or her pet?
4. What sports team do you champion?
5. How should a team member treat an adversary during a sporting event? afterward?
6. Why does a sovereign have power over his or her country?
7. What is something that could cause you to feel wrath?

A Changing Language: English Word Origins

All languages change over time. English vocabulary, grammar, spelling, and pronunciation have changed a great deal since the fifteenth century, when Sir Thomas Malory wrote in the Midland dialect then spoken in London. For example, consider the **derivation** and the original **meaning** of *worship:* When Malory called a brave knight "a knight of much worship," he meant "a knight well-known for his worth." In Old English the word for this concept was *weorthscipe,* or *worthship,* that is, "worthy of honor, dignity, or rank." Gradually the word acquired religious connotations and lost its secular meaning, as well as its *th* sound. Today the meaning of *worship* is almost wholly religious.

PRACTICE 2

Translate this passage from *Le Morte d'Arthur* into the kind of English spoken in the United States today. First, read the passage aloud. Then, take a guess at the meanings of unfamiliar-looking words. Check your guesses in a dictionary's **etymologies,** or word origins. Do you find the Middle English spellings included in the word's **etymology**?

"A, Launcelot!" he sayd, "thou were hede of al Crysten knyghtes! And now I dare say," sayd syr Ector, "thou sir Launcelot, there thou lyest, that thou were never matched of erthely knyghtes hande. And thou werre the curtest knyght that ever bare shelde!"

—Sir Thomas Malory

Grade 8 Review Reading Standard 1.2 Understand the most important points in the history of the English language and use common word origins to determine the historical influences on English word meanings.

Reading Standard 1.1 Identify and use the literal meanings of words.

Vocabulary Development

Practice 1

Possible answers:

1. I am diverted by listening to quiet music.
2. Fidelity to a cause shows that a person has the strength of his or her convictions and can be counted on.
3. A pet owner is obliged to give the animal its required vaccinations and keep the animal clean and well fed.
4. I champion the Giants, the Athletics, the Dodgers, the Angels, and the Padres.
5. A team member should treat the adversary as an opponent during the event but as a friend afterward.
6. A sovereign has power because the citizens accept him or her as their ruler.
7. A thief stealing my belongings may make me feel wrath.

Practice 2

Possible answer: "Ah, Lancelot!" he said, "you were the best of all Christian knights! And now I dare say," said Sir Hector, "you Sir Lancelot, there you lie, you who were never defeated by the hand of any earthly knight. And you were the most courteous knight who ever bore a shield."

Resources Reminder

Vocabulary

- *Vocabulary Development*
  - Vocabulary Worksheet, p. 46
- *Lesson Plans for Language Development*
  - Vocabulary, pp. 315, 321

ASSESSING

Assessment

- *Progress Assessment of Reading*
  - Selection Test

STANDARDS FOCUS, pp. 660–672

(For the grade-level standards taught in this lesson, see citations on Student Edition pages.)

Summary *at grade level*

The myth opens as Theseus learns that he is the son of Aegeus, the king of Athens. As proof of his identity, Theseus claims the sword and shoes that Aegeus has buried for him. Setting out for Athens, Theseus chooses a dangerous land route to prove his courage. He slays many villains on the way.

News of this mysterious hero precedes him to Athens, where Aegeus, abetted by Medea, prepares to poison the young man whose popularity threatens the throne. When Theseus arrives in Athens, Aegeus invites him to a banquet with the idea of poisoning him. As Medea hands him the poisoned cup, Theseus draws his sword, eager to reveal his identity, and is saved.

King Minos of Crete is demanding a terrible tribute from Athens: Seven young women and seven young men must be sent to the Labyrinth in Crete, home of the brutal Minotaur. Theseus volunteers to go. In Crete, Ariadne, the daughter of King Minos, falls in love with Theseus. She asks Daedalus, the creator of the Labyrinth, to show her a way out of the maze, so she can save Theseus and marry him. Daedalus gives her a ball of thread, which Theseus is to unwind as he travels through the maze. Theseus slays the Minotaur and, using the thread, leads the Athenian youths out. On the return to Athens, Ariadne is either deserted by Theseus or dies on the island of Naxos. Her exact fate is not known.

Nearing Athens, Theseus forgets to raise the white sail, to signal his father that he is alive. Believing his son is dead, Aegeus jumps to his own death into the sea. Theseus becomes king of Athens but resigns in order to establish the world's first democracy.

Before You Read

Theseus

Literary Focus

Myths and Society

In ancient Greece, as elsewhere, **myths**—traditional stories about gods and heroes—were much more than entertaining tales. Myths were part of the Greek religion, and like all myths they defined the culture of the people who believed in them. The myths—the word is from *mythos,* Greek for "story"—told the people who they were, where they came from, and what they should value in life.

By means of myths, people were also able to deal with the mysteries they encountered in life—mysteries they saw in the outside world and in their own inner worlds as well.

Though they often have supernatural powers, the heroes in the Greek myths are recognizably human. They are not divine, even though some of them were fathered by gods. They are not humanized animals, the way trickster heroes are in some mythologies (Coyote in North America and Spider in Africa).

In a typical hero myth, a young man is sent on a quest to find something of great value, including self-knowledge and self-control. These hero stories reveal the human qualities that the ancient Greeks valued and taught to their children. The Greek hero stories tell of people who are not always noble. Like all of us, the characters are often selfish or stubborn or even cruel. They sometimes disobey the gods, with grave, even tragic consequences. Some of them are even pawns of the gods. Their worth is measured in how they respond to adversities.

Theseus, whose story you are about to read, was the hero particularly identified with the city of Athens. Theseus is an example of a hero who uses his might to do right—though even he sometimes fails.

Reading Standard 3.12 Analyze the way in which a work of literature is related to the themes and issues of its historical period. (Historical approach)

Make the Connection

Quickwrite

Stories about heroes who embark on perilous journeys to fulfill a quest are still told today. Think about examples of perilous journeys in movies and video games as well as print material. Does the questing hero undertake the journey to use might for right or for some other purpose? Jot down some examples of modern heroes and quests.

Background

Ancient Greek Culture: The Context for the Myths

Ancient Greek civilization gave us the Olympic Games, drama, the concept of democracy—and much more.

From its earliest history, Greece was a land of small, independent city-states. Greece is mostly mountainous, with small valleys; off its coasts are numerous islands. Thus, the people lived in isolated mountain or island communities, each with its own government. The city of Athens, for instance, had its own king, who ruled the city and immediate surrounding countryside. There were many other separate kingdoms, including neighboring Salamis, Eleusis, and Sparta.

Though some Athenians today believe that the myths about Theseus are based on the life of an actual early king, scholars believe Theseus is totally mythic. According to legend, when Theseus became king of Athens, he united the small independent

RESOURCES: READING

Planning

- *One-Stop Planner* CD-ROM with Test Generator
- *On Course: Mapping Instruction*

Media

- *Audio CD Library*
  - disc 16

Reading

- *Interactive Reading,* Teacher's Edition
  - Graphic Organizer: Hero Chart

Differentiating Instruction

- *Lesson Plans for Language Development*
  - English-Language Learners, pp. 301–303, 316, 322
  - Special Education Students, pp. 304, 316, 322

660 Chapter 9 Biographical and Historical Approach • Using Primary and Secondary Sources

kingdoms scattered across Attica (see the map below) into a single federation—the great city-state of Athens. Theseus is thus credited with beginning the first people's democracy. Athens became the home of liberty, at least for free males, the first place in the world where people governed themselves.

How much of this myth is true? It is hard to answer that question, but certainly some episodes had a basis in reality. For example, if you go to the beautiful island of Crete today, you can see the ruins of King Minos's palace. You can even see a painting on the wall that shows a young man leaping over a great bull that is flanked by two women.

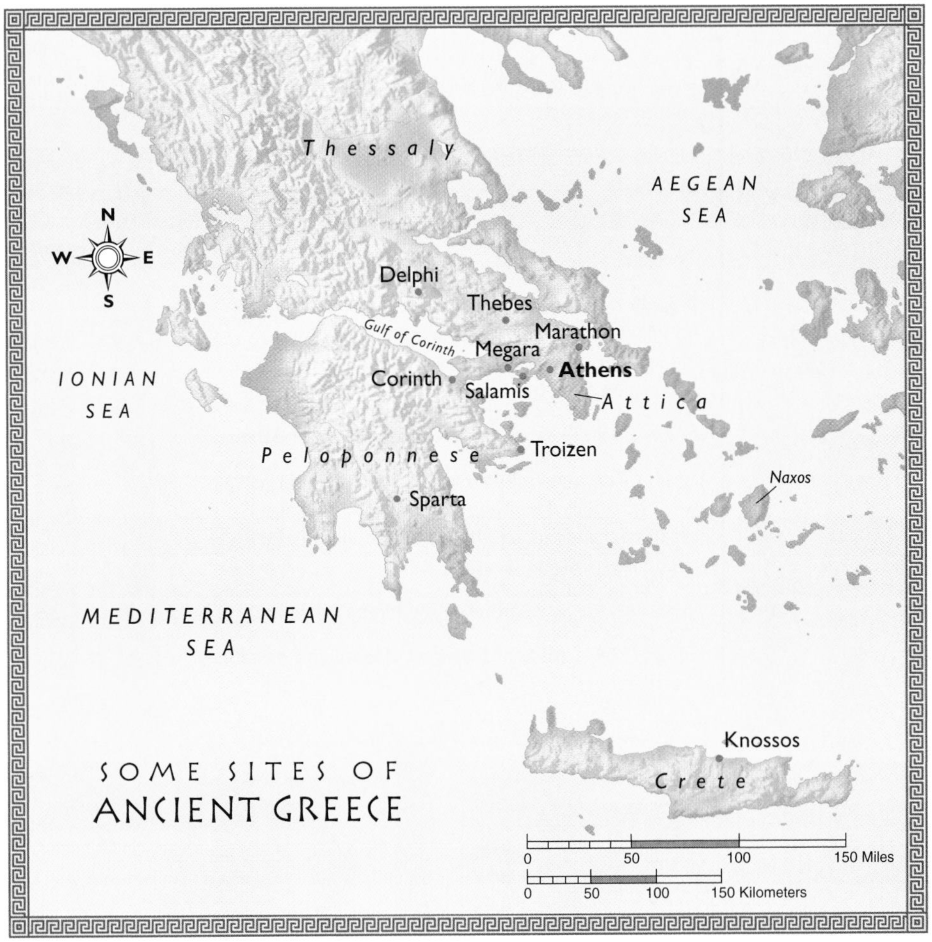

Assessment

- *Progress Assessment of Reading*
  - Selection Test
- *One-Stop Planner* CD-ROM with Test Generator

PRETEACHING

Selection Starter

Motivate. Use the Quickwrite activity on the Before You Read page to help students appreciate the universal appeal of tales of heroic quests. Encourage students to recognize elements of the heroic quest in movies such as in fantasies (*Star Wars* and *Lord of the Rings),* as well as in detective stories, biographies (*Erin Brockovich*), and tales of people forced to cope with life-threatening diseases. As students discuss these movies, ask the following questions. What is the hero searching for or trying to achieve? What adversities or challenges does the hero face? What virtues and values does the hero demonstrate in the quest? What character flaws show that the hero is human?

Standards Starter

Build background. Call students' attention to the map of ancient Greece, and explain that it offers a graphic depiction of Theseus's world during the historical period in which he lived. Have students locate Troizen, the home of Theseus's mother and the place where Theseus was raised, and Athens, the city-state that King Aegeus ruled. Then, ask students to discuss how the geographical features of Greece led to their being many small, independent kingdoms rather than one unified state.

Assign the Reading

You may wish to have proficient readers read the myth on their own, while other students read the myth together in small groups. Because the plot of the myth is so compressed, complicated, and episodic, you may wish to have group members take turns reading sections aloud. Ask the groups to pause after each section and summarize and discuss what has happened thus far.

DIRECT TEACHING

Ⓐ Reading Skills

Reading aloud. You may wish to call on volunteers to pronounce the names of the characters, and then have all students repeat the names in unison. To further familiarize students with the names, you might draw family trees on the board, showing that Theseus is the offspring of Aethra and of Aegeus, king of Athens, and that Ariadne is the daughter of Minos, king of Crete.

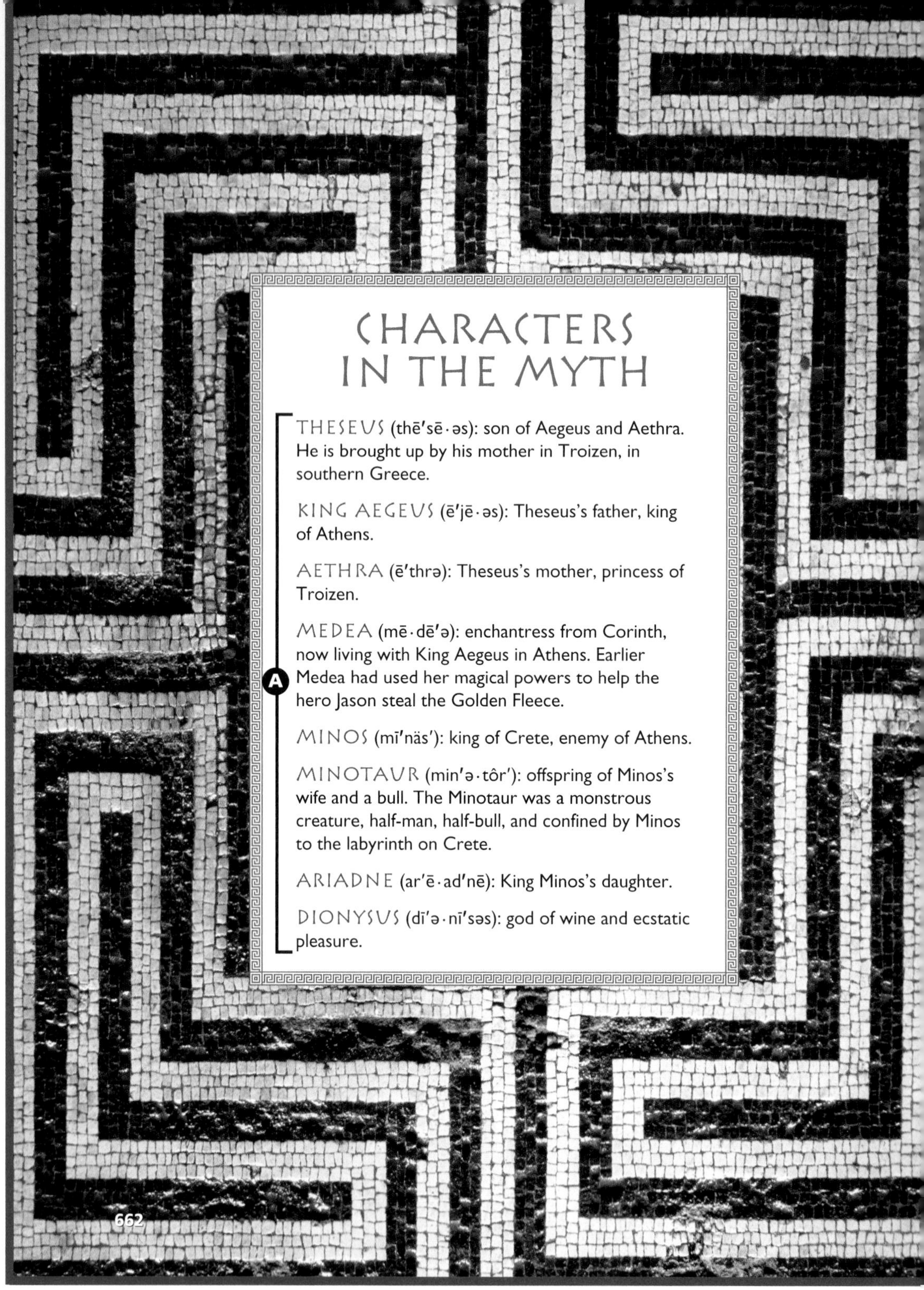

CHARACTERS IN THE MYTH

Ⓐ

THESEUS (thē′sē·əs): son of Aegeus and Aethra. He is brought up by his mother in Troizen, in southern Greece.

KING AEGEUS (ē′jē·əs): Theseus's father, king of Athens.

AETHRA (ē′thrə): Theseus's mother, princess of Troizen.

MEDEA (mē·dē′ə): enchantress from Corinth, now living with King Aegeus in Athens. Earlier Medea had used her magical powers to help the hero Jason steal the Golden Fleece.

MINOS (mī′näs′): king of Crete, enemy of Athens.

MINOTAUR (min′ə·tôr′): offspring of Minos's wife and a bull. The Minotaur was a monstrous creature, half-man, half-bull, and confined by Minos to the labyrinth on Crete.

ARIADNE (ar′ē·ad′nē): King Minos's daughter.

DIONYSUS (dī′ə·nī′səs): god of wine and ecstatic pleasure.

DIFFERENTIATING INSTRUCTION

Learners Having Difficulty

To help students follow the myth's episodic plot, write on the chalkboard its eight major episodes, which students will be asked to summarize in the Reading Check on page 670: (1) Theseus's childhood, (2) his perilous journey to Athens, (3) recognition by his father, (4) trial in the Labyrinth, (5) loss of Ariadne, (6) mistake with sails, (7) triumph in Athens, (8) war against Thebes. As students read, have them note when each new episode begins and what major events occur in each one.

English-Language Learners

Edith Hamilton's style includes many long, complex sentences and diction that is formal and somewhat archaic. You may wish to have English-language learners first listen to the myth being read aloud on the *Audio CD Library* disc while they follow along in their books.

Resources Reminder

For lessons designed for intermediate and advanced English-language learners, see *Lesson Plans for Language Development,* pp. 301–303, 316, 322.

THESEUS

***retold by* Edith Hamilton**

Head of Theseus. Detail of a mural from Herculaneum, Italy.

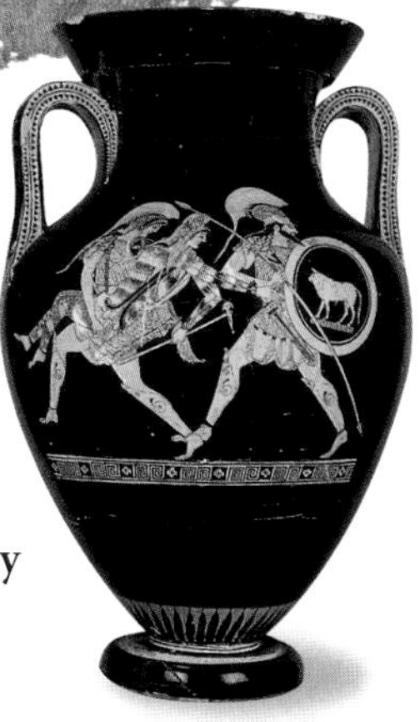

Theseus pictured on a Greek amphora, a type of jar (5th century B.C.).

The great Athenian hero was Theseus. He had so many adventures and took part in so many great enterprises that there grew up a saying in Athens, "Nothing without Theseus."

DIRECT TEACHING

VIEWING THE ART

The myth of Theseus was created by the Greeks and adopted by the Romans, who derived much of their religion and culture from the Greeks. Here the head of Theseus is a detail of a fresco found in Herculaneum, a town in southern Italy that was destroyed by the eruption of Mount Vesuvius in A.D. 79 along with the city of Pompeii. Because these towns were buried in ash, much in them was preserved and unearthed by archaeologists.

Many Greek amphorae, such as this one picturing Theseus, have been uncovered and pieced together, as terra-cotta pottery is quite durable. Since both pottery and walls were often decorated in classical times, we have been able to learn a great deal about the art and culture of these civilizations. **Activity.** Compare the style of the Roman mural with that of the Greek amphora. [The Roman painting depicts details of Theseus's head with some realism, whereas the Greek painting offers less detail, is flat in appearance, and emphasizes action rather than psychological motivation.]

Special Education Students
For lessons designed for special education students, see *Lesson Plans for Language Development,* pp. 304, 316, 322.

Advanced Learners
Acceleration. Use the following activity to move advanced learners toward the eleventh- and twelfth-grade standard 3.7c, for which they evaluate the philosophical, political, religious, ethical, and social influences of the historical period that shaped the characters, plots, and settings of literary works.
Activity. Tell students that the words *ethics* and *ethical* are derived from the Greek root *ethos,* meaning "character." Greek philosophers wrote in depth about ethics, the study that defines and evaluates moral and immoral behavior, duty, and obligation. Have students analyze the actions of Theseus and evaluate how ethical his behavior was at different points in the story's plot. Ask them what other clues in the story hint that the ancient Greeks were concerned about the ethics of their heroes.

Painted figure of the Minotaur, on a Greek cup (c. 515 B.C.).

He was the son of the Athenian king, Aegeus. He spent his youth, however, in his mother's home, a city in southern Greece. Aegeus went back to Athens before the child was born, but first he placed in a hollow a sword and a pair of shoes and covered them with a great stone. He did this with the knowledge of his wife and told her that whenever the boy—if it was a boy—grew strong enough to roll away the stone and get the things beneath it, she could send him to Athens to claim him as his father. The child was a boy, and he grew up strong far beyond others, so that when his mother finally took him to the stone he lifted it with no trouble at all. She told him then that the time had come for him to seek his father, and a ship was placed at his disposal by his grandfather. But Theseus refused to go by water, because the voyage was safe and easy. His idea was to become a great hero as quickly as possible, and easy safety was certainly not the way to do that. Hercules, who was the most magnificent of all the heroes of Greece, was always in his mind, and the determination to be just as magnificent himself. This was quite natural, since the two were cousins.

He steadfastly refused, therefore, the ship his mother and grandfather urged on him, telling them that to sail on it would be a contemptible[1] flight from danger, and he set forth to go to Athens by land. The journey was long and very hazardous because of the bandits that beset the road. He killed them all, however; he left not one alive to trouble future travelers. His idea of dealing justice was simple but effective: What each had done to others, Theseus did to him. Sciron,[2] for instance, who had made those he captured kneel to wash his feet and then kicked them down into the sea, Theseus hurled over a precipice. Sinir, who killed people by fastening them to two pine trees bent down to the ground and letting the trees go, died in that way himself. Procrustes[3] was placed upon the iron bed which he used for his victims, tying them to it and then making them the right length for it by stretching those who were too short and

1. **contemptible** (kən·tempt′ə·bəl) *adj.:* hateful; worthy of contempt; disgraceful.
2. **Sciron** (sī′rōn′).
3. **Procrustes** (prō·krus′tēz).

DIRECT TEACHING

A English-Language Learners

Interpreting idioms. Point out that although the word *disposal* usually means "the act of getting rid of something," the phrase *at his disposal* has a special meaning. It means "ready for his use or service; under his control."

B Literary Focus
GRADE-LEVEL STANDARD

Myths and society. What virtues does this passage suggest that the ancient Greeks valued highly? How can you tell? [Possible response: The passage suggests that ancient Greeks valued courage, risk-taking, strength, and a disregard for personal safety, as shown by Theseus considering it "contemptible" to choose the easy route to Athens and by his taking the most dangerous way in order to prove his courage and heroism.]

C Content-Area Connections

History: Ancient Justice
Theseus's idea of justice—that the punishment should exactly match the crime—was very common in the ancient world. It was first stated in the Code of Hammurabi, a Babylonian code of laws compiled around 1750 B.C. Its most famous provision was that criminals should lose "an eye for an eye, a tooth for a tooth." Although this provision sounds harsh to us today, it was actually intended to limit retaliation, to ensure that the punishment of criminals did not exceed their crimes.

D Vocabulary Development
GRADE-LEVEL STANDARD

Words from Greek myths. The legend of Procrustes gave rise to the English word *procrustean.* This adjective means "producing conformity by arbitrary or ruthless means" or "having a cruel disregard for individual differences."

CONTENT-AREA CONNECTIONS

History: The Rise of Democracy
Although Greek mythology attributes the establishment of Athenian democracy to Theseus, historians say that democracy was established in Athens by a statesman named Cleisthenes in the 6th century B.C.

Small-group activity. Have students research the basic structure of Athenian democracy, including the following elements: how Athenian citizenship was determined; how laws were made; how leaders were chosen; and how the justice system worked. Then, have students make a chart comparing and contrasting the basic elements of Athenian democracy with those of representative government in the United States today.

664 Chapter 9 Biographical and Historical Approach • Using Primary and Secondary Sources

cutting off as much as was necessary from those who were too long. The story does not say which of the two methods was used in his case, but there was not much to choose between them and in one way or the other Procrustes' career ended.

It can be imagined how Greece rang with the praises of the young man who had cleared the land of these banes[4] to travelers. When he reached Athens, he was an acknowledged hero, and he was invited to a banquet by the King, **E** who of course was unaware that Theseus was his son. In fact, he was afraid of the young man's great popularity, thinking that he might win the people over to make him king, and he invited him with the idea of poisoning him. The plan was not his, but Medea's, the heroine of the Quest of the Golden Fleece, who knew through her sorcery who Theseus was. She had fled to Athens when she left Corinth in her winged car, and she had acquired great influence over Aegeus, which she did not want disturbed by the appearance of a son. But as she handed him the poisoned cup, Theseus, wishing to make himself known at once to his father, drew his sword. The King instantly recognized it and dashed the cup to the ground. Medea escaped, as she always did, and got safely away to Asia.

THE MINOTAUR WAS A MONSTER, HALF BULL, HALF HUMAN.

Aegeus then proclaimed to the country that Theseus was his son and heir. The new heir apparent soon had an opportunity to endear him- **F** self to the Athenians.

Years before his arrival in Athens, a terrible misfortune had happened to the city. Minos, the powerful ruler of Crete, had lost his only son, **G** Androgenes,[5] while the young man was visiting the Athenian king. King Aegeus had done what no host should do: He had sent his guest on an expedition full of peril—to kill a dangerous bull. Instead, the bull had killed the youth. Minos invaded the country, captured Athens and declared that he would raze it to the ground unless every nine years the people sent him a tribute[6] of seven maidens and seven youths. A horrible fate awaited these young creatures. When they reached Crete they were given to the Minotaur to devour.

The Minotaur was a monster, half bull, half human, the offspring of Minos's wife Pasiphaë[7] and a wonderfully beautiful bull. Poseidon[8] had given this bull to Minos in order that he should sacrifice it to him, but Minos could not bear to slay it and kept it for himself. To punish him, Poseidon had made Pasiphaë fall madly in love with it.

When the Minotaur was born, Minos did not kill him. He had Daedalus,[9] a great architect and inventor, construct a place of confinement for him from which escape was impossible. Daedalus built the Labyrinth, famous throughout the world. Once inside, one would go endlessly along its twisting paths without ever finding the exit. To this place the young Athenians were each time taken and left to the Minotaur. There was no possible way to escape. In whatever direction they ran, they might be running straight to the monster; if they stood still, he might at any moment emerge from the maze. Such was the doom which awaited fourteen youths and maidens a few days after Theseus reached Athens. The time had come for the next installment of the tribute.

4. **banes** *n.:* causes of destruction or ruin.
5. **Androgenes** (an·drä′jə·nēz).
6. **tribute** *n.:* something paid by one nation or ruler to another as an acknowledgment of submission.
7. **Pasiphaë** (pə·sif′ā·ē′).
8. **Poseidon** (pō·sī′dən): god of horses and of the sea; brother of Zeus.
9. **Daedalus** (ded′'l·əs).

DIRECT TEACHING

E Reading Skills

Making predictions. What might Theseus do at dinner that could save his own life? [He might show his father his sword, the proof of his true identity, before Aegeus and Medea have a chance to poison him.]

F English-Language Learners

Interpreting homonyms. Tell students that the word *heir* is pronounced the same as *air.* An heir is someone who is entitled to inherit another person's wealth or title. *Heir apparent* is a legal term, meaning that the person's right to inherit cannot be legally denied or overturned.

G Literary Focus
GRADE-LEVEL STANDARD

Flashback. For what purpose does the author include the long flashback about King Minos of Crete? [The flashback gives background information to explain the ongoing tragedy in Athens, which Theseus will help to resolve.]

CONTENT-AREA CONNECTIONS

Topology: The Mathematics of Mazes
Today, a branch of mathematics called topology can be used to analyze mazes such as the labyrinth and determine the most efficient path through them. The principles of topology also apply to the design of networks such as electrical lines, phone lines, and computer systems.

Paired activity. Have partners research the basic principles of topology and use them to design both a unicursal maze and a multicursal maze. Then, have the pairs exchange their mazes and solve them.

Theseus 665

DIRECT TEACHING

A Learners Having Difficulty

Monitoring students' progress. Ask the following questions to make sure students are following the plot: Why does Theseus offer himself as one of the victims to be sent to Crete? [He wants to slay the Minotaur, free his father's kingdom from the fate decreed by King Minos, and prove himself a hero.]

B Learners Having Difficulty

Breaking down difficult text. This passage condenses the climax of the story into a few long compound and complex sentences with many clauses, appositives, and parenthetical phrases. Have volunteers read each sentence aloud, and list the events described in each one. Then, have students summarize the events in their own words.

VIEWING THE ART

This Greek black-figure cup depicts Theseus and the Minotaur in combat. Like any motif that was represented many times within a visual tradition, there are differences in the way it is represented. Here the Minotaur looks less ferocious than the one on the painted cup on p. 664.
Activity. What indications are there that Theseus will defeat the Minotaur? [Theseus has his sword at the monster's back and is clearly in a superior fighting position.]

Theseus and the Minotaur pictured on a black-figured cup from Athens (c. 550–540 B.C.).

At once Theseus came forward and offered to be one of the victims. All loved him for his goodness and admired him for his nobility, but they had no idea that he intended to try to kill the Minotaur. He told his father, however, and promised him that if he succeeded, he would have the black sail which the ship with its cargo of misery always carried changed to a white one, so that Aegeus could know long before it came to land that his son was safe.

When the young victims arrived in Crete, they were paraded before the inhabitants on their way to the Labyrinth. Minos' daughter Ariadne was among the spectators, and she fell in love with Theseus at first sight as he marched past her. She sent for Daedalus and told him he must show her a way to get out of the Labyrinth, and she sent for Theseus and told him she would bring about his escape if he would promise to take her back to Athens and marry her. As may be imagined, he made no difficulty about that, and she gave him the clue she had got from Daedalus, a ball of thread which he was to fasten at one end to the inside of the door and unwind as he went on. This he did and, certain that he could retrace his steps whenever he chose, he walked boldly into the maze, looking for the Minotaur. He came upon him asleep and fell upon him, pinning him to the ground; and with his fists—he had no other weapon—he battered the monster to death.

As an oak tree falls on the hillside
Crushing all that lies beneath,
So Theseus. He presses out the life,
The brute's savage life, and now it lies dead.
Only the head sways slowly, but the horns are useless now.

When Theseus lifted himself up from that terrific struggle, the ball of thread lay where he had dropped it. With it in his hands, the way out was clear. The others followed, and taking Ariadne with them they fled to the ship and over the sea toward Athens.

FAMILY/COMMUNITY ACTIVITY

Like Theseus, most mythological heroes perform acts of courage that benefit an entire community. Have students poll their families, friends, and neighbors, asking what people in American society today best display this kind of heroism. In their poll, students may wish to include choices such as firefighters and other emergency workers, police officers, community activists, government leaders, scientists, journalists, teachers, and religious leaders. Have the class compile all their results and present them in a graph.

On the way there they put in at the island of Naxos, and what happened then is differently reported. One story says that Theseus deserted Ariadne. She was asleep, and he sailed away without her, but Dionysus found her and comforted her. The other story is much more favorable to Theseus. She was extremely seasick, and he set her ashore to recover while he returned to the ship to do some necessary work. A violent wind carried him out to sea and kept him there a long time. On his return he found that Ariadne had died, and he was deeply afflicted.[10]

Both stories agree that when they drew near to Athens, he forgot to hoist the white sail. Either his joy at the success of his voyage put every other thought out of his head, or his grief for Ariadne. The black sail was seen by his father, King Aegeus, from the Acropolis,[11] where for days he had watched the sea with straining eyes. It was to him the sign of his son's death, and he threw himself down from a rocky height into the sea and was killed. The sea into which he fell was called the Aegean ever after.

So Theseus became King of Athens, a most wise and disinterested[12] king. He declared to the people that he did not wish to rule over them; he wanted a people's government where all would be equal. He resigned his royal power and organized a commonwealth, building a council hall where the citizens should gather and vote. The only office he kept for himself was that of commander in chief. Thus Athens became, of all earth's cities, the happiest and most prosperous, the only true home of liberty, the one place in the world where the people governed themselves. It was for this reason that in the great War of the Seven against Thebes,[13] when the victorious Thebans refused burial to those of the enemy who had died, the vanquished[14] turned to Theseus and Athens for help, believing that free men under such a leader would never consent to having the helpless dead wronged. They did not turn in vain. Theseus led his army against Thebes, conquered her, and forced her to allow the dead to be buried. But when he was victor, he did not return evil to the Thebans for the evil they had done. He showed himself the perfect knight. He refused to let his army enter and loot the city. He had come not to harm Thebes, but to bury the Argive[15] dead, and that duty done he led his soldiers back to Athens. ■

10. **afflicted** *adj.:* distressed; upset.
11. **Acropolis** (ə·kräp′ə·lis): fortified heights in Athens. A huge temple to Athena stands on top of the hill.
12. **disinterested** *adj.:* fair; impartial. (*Disinterested* should not be confused with *uninterested,* which means "not interested.")
13. **Thebes** (thēbz): chief city of Boeotia, a region in ancient Greece.
14. **vanquished** *v.* used as *n.:* conquered; defeated.
15. **Argive** (är′gīv): another word for "Greek." All of these people were Greek, but they gave allegiance to their separate small kingdoms.

Ariadne (15th century) by Antico (Pier Jacopo Alari Bonacolsi). Partially gilded bronze statue.

DIRECT TEACHING

C Literary Focus
GRADE-LEVEL STANDARD

Myths and society. In what sense might Theseus be described as a flawed hero? [Even though he is brave and willing to put himself at risk for the sake of others, he sometimes makes mistakes and may even be disloyal to the young woman who saved his life.] **Why do you think the author includes two different versions of what happened at Naxos and two possible explanations for why Theseus forgot to raise the white sail?** [Possible response: The alternative explanations show that the Greeks did not consider their heroes perfect.]

D Vocabulary Development
GRADE-LEVEL STANDARD

Words from Greek myths. How did the Aegean Sea, off the coast of Greece, get its name? [It is named after King Aegeus, who is said to have thrown himself into the sea when he thought his son was dead.]

E Literary Focus
GRADE-LEVEL STANDARD

Myths and society. What character trait, demonstrated by Theseus, was clearly valued by the Athenians? [The Athenians must have valued self-restraint, which Theseus demonstrates by not returning evil for the evil that the Thebans had done.] **How has this trait grown in Theseus since the beginning of the myth?** [At the beginning he returned "evil for evil" in dealing with the bandits along the road to Athens.]

DEVELOPING FLUENCY

Whole-class activity. The long sentences in this selection offer good practice for students to develop their skills in breaking down difficult text. Have them choose a paragraph in the selection and practice reading each long sentence aloud, noting where they should pause and which words they should emphasize in order to make the meaning of the sentence clear to listeners. Then, have them read the entire paragraph aloud for an audience.

GUIDED PRACTICE

Monitoring students' progress. Guide the class in answering these comprehension questions.

True or False

1. Theseus is the son of King Aegeus of Athens. [T]
2. Theseus asks Daedalus for a map of the Labyrinth. [F]
3. Theseus slays a monster called the Minotaur. [T]
4. Theseus and Ariadne get married and return to Athens together. [F]
5. As king of Athens, Theseus refuses to help fight the Thebans. [F]

Meet the Writer

Background. Even though she did not attend school until she was sixteen, Edith Hamilton was well educated by her parents at home. By the time she was eight, she could read French, German, Latin, and Greek, as well as English. Her love of Greece was a lifelong passion. When she was named an honorary citizen of Athens, four days before her ninetieth birthday, she said that it was the proudest moment of her life.

For Independent Reading

- Edith Hamilton's *The Greek Way* remains one of the best introductions to the culture and achievements of ancient Greece.
- Students who enjoyed the myth of Theseus can read more Greek myths in both Edith Hamilton's *Mythology* and *Bulfinch's Mythology: The Age of Fable,* by Thomas Bulfinch.
- Students interested in learning more about the heroic quest in literature might enjoy *Greek Gods and Heroes,* by Robert Graves, as well as *Mythology: The Voyage of the Hero,* by David Adams Leeming.

Meet the Writer

Edith Hamilton

A Passion for Ancient Greece

The retellings of the Greek myths that many people first encounter as children are probably those by Edith Hamilton (1867–1963). When Hamilton retired from teaching the classics at Bryn Mawr School in Baltimore, she decided she wanted to share her knowledge with a wider audience. Thus, she began writing *Mythology,* which soon became a bestseller. The miracle of Greek mythology, Hamilton said, is

"a humanized world. . . . All the art and all the thought of Greece centered in human beings."

The classics—the literature of ancient Greece and Rome—had been part of Hamilton's life from the time she was seven years old. She became so identified with Greece that in 1957 she was named an honorary citizen of Athens.

For Independent Reading

If you, like Hamilton, enjoy learning about the ancient world, try these Hamilton classics:

- *The Greek Way*
- *The Roman Way*

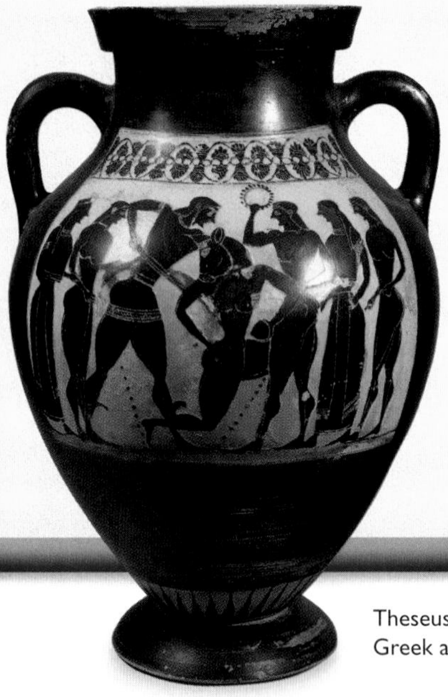

Theseus and the Minotaur pictured on a Greek amphora (c. 550–500 B.C.).

668 Chapter 9 Biographical and Historical Approach • Using Primary and Secondary Sources

Joseph Campbell wrote many books on the importance of mythology in our everyday lives. Here is a portion of an interview with Campbell, done for a six-hour PBS series. The interviewer is the journalist Bill Moyers.

"All We Need Is That Piece of String"

Moyers. What's the significance of the trials, and tests, and ordeals of the hero?

Campbell. If you want to put it in terms of intentions, the trials are designed to see to it that the intending hero should be really a hero. Is he really a match for this task? Can he overcome the dangers? Does he have the courage, the knowledge, the capacity, to enable to serve? . . .

Moyers. I like what you say about the old myth of Theseus and Ariadne. Theseus says to Ariadne, "I'll love you forever if you can show me a way to come out of the labyrinth." So she gives him a ball of string, which he unwinds as he goes into the labyrinth, and then follows to find the way out. You say, "All he had was the string. That's all you need."

Campbell. That's all you need—an Ariadne thread.

Moyers. Sometimes we look for great wealth to save us, a great power to save us, or great ideas to save us, when all we need is that piece of string.

Campbell. That's not always easy to find. But it's nice to have someone who can give you a clue. That's the teacher's job, to help you find your Ariadne thread.

◎ ◎ ◎

Campbell. The big question is whether you are going to be able to say a hearty yes to your adventure.

Moyers. The adventure of the hero?

Campbell. Yes, the adventure of the hero—the adventure of being alive.

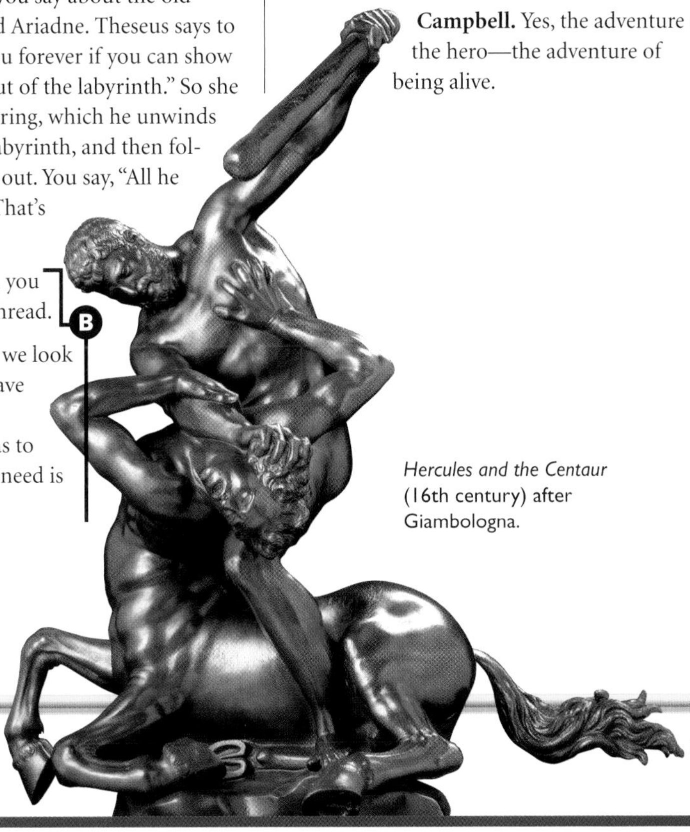

Hercules and the Centaur (16th century) after Giambologna.

669

Connection

Summary at grade level

In this excerpt from *The Power of Myth,* journalist Bill Moyers and scholar Joseph Campbell discuss the metaphorical significance of the ball of string that helps Theseus find his way out of the labyrinth. Campbell says that the labyrinth represents the journey, or "adventure," of life—full of trials, twists and turns, and blind alleys. The piece of string represents the individual's faith in, and acceptance of, the journey—the belief that enables individuals to persevere and become the heroes of their own quest for meaning and understanding.

DIRECT TEACHING

A Reading Skills

Finding the main idea. Why does every hero have to endure trials or perform difficult tasks? [The trials prove that he or she has the character traits needed to lead and serve others. These traits might include courage, intelligence, skill, and perseverance.]

B Literary Focus GRADE-LEVEL STANDARD

Myth and metaphor. If the labyrinth is a metaphor for life, what might the piece of string be a metaphor for? [Possible response: The piece of string represents a guide to finding our way through life, a faith or belief that helps us discover what will bring us peace, success, and a feeling of accomplishment.]

Connecting and Comparing Texts

The scholar Joseph Campbell believes that every person's life can be seen as a heroic quest and that we can study the experiences of mythological heroes to find guidance on how to live our own lives.

Ask students if they agree with Campbell's view of the connection between mythology and life. Have them give reasons and examples from the Theseus myth and from their own lives to support their point of view.

Literary Response and Analysis

Reading Check

1. This myth can be divided into eight episodes. **Summarize** in a few sentences the **main events** in each episode:

a. Theseus's childhood

b. his perilous journey to Athens

c. recognition by his father

d. trial in the labyrinth

e. loss of Ariadne

f. mistake with sails

g. triumph in Athens

h. war against Thebes

Interpretations

2. What is revealed about the **character** of Theseus when he insists on taking the land route to Athens?

3. In many **quest** stories the hero must descend into an underworld before the quest can be successfully completed. How could the labyrinth be seen as that underworld?

4. In Greek myths the hero is fully human. He is never part beast, part human. How is the Minotaur, then, the evil opposite of the ideal hero?

5. Explain the ways in which Theseus fits Joseph Campbell's definition of the hero (see the ***Connection*** on page 669).

6. What stories today are organized around a perilous journey? What are the goals of these modern questing heroes? How does the level of violence in these stories compare with the violence in the Theseus myth? (Check your Quickwrite notes.)

7. Explain what you think Joseph Campbell means by an "Ariadne thread." Have you had an Ariadne thread in your life? What was it?

Literary Criticism

8. What can you infer about the ancient Greek concept of justice by the way Theseus deals with the bandits he meets on his perilous journey?

9. What threatens Theseus at the moment of his reunion with his father? Since the ancient Greeks valued hospitality and courtesy to strangers, how would they have responded to this part of Theseus's story?

10. What other detail reveals the importance of kindness to strangers in ancient Greece?

11. From this myth, what can you infer about the relationship between Athens and Crete, two powerful Greek city-states? How does Theseus change the situation between the two cities?

12. An important Greek value is underscored in the Thebans' refusal to allow the burial of their slain enemies. One of the holiest laws of the Greeks demanded that certain rites be performed for the dead and that the body be buried. If the body was allowed to rot in the sun, the dead person would be condemned to eternal unrest. How did Theseus show respect for that religious principle?

13. What do Theseus's actions after the conquest of Thebes reveal about the Athenian code of honor in war? How does this code compare with the way wars are conducted today?

Reading Standard 3.12 Analyze the way in which a work of literature is related to the themes and issues of its historical period. (Historical approach)

INDEPENDENT PRACTICE

Literary Response and Analysis

Reading Check

1. a. Theseus grows up with his mother, unaware that he is King Aegeus's son. When he is strong enough, he lifts the stone under which Aegeus has buried a sword and shoes that prove his identity.

b. Theseus takes the perilous land route to Athens. He kills all the bandits along the way, using their own methods against them.

c. Not knowing who Theseus is, Aegeus fears the new hero's popularity. Inspired by Medea, he plans to poison the young man; however, Theseus draws his sword, and his father recognizes him.

d. Ariadne, daughter of King Minos, loves Theseus and asks the creator of the Labyrinth for a way to escape it. Daedalus gives her a ball of thread for Theseus to use to mark his trail. Theseus slays the Minotaur and escapes.

e. On the way home, the ship stops at the Island of Naxos. Ariadne dies there, either because Theseus abandoned her or because she was sick.

f. As he nears Athens, Theseus forgets to raise a white sail as a signal to his father that he is alive. Seeing a black sail, Aegeus jumps to his death in grief.

g. Theseus becomes king of Athens but gives it up to establish the world's first democracy.

h. Theseus forces the Thebans to allow vanquished armies to bury their dead. He refuses to allow his soldiers to loot the now conquered city of Thebes.

Interpretations

2. Possible answers: Theseus shows his courage and eagerness to prove himself a hero; Theseus shows that he is foolish and reckless.

3. The Labyrinth is a place of doom, which has a terrifying monster and from which, seemingly, there is no escape.

4. The Minotaur is half bull and half human.

5. Possible answer: Theseus chooses to confront danger to prove that he is a great hero.

6. Students may cite books or movies with quest themes. The goals of modern heroes are usually either altruistic or purely personal. Students' answers may vary regarding levels of violence in modern heroic stories.

7. Possible answer: To Campbell, an "Ariadne thread" is knowledge or information that guides us through difficult situations.

670 Chapter 9 Biographical and Historical Approach • Using Primary and Secondary Sources

Writing

Comparing Heroes

Both the Arthurian legend and the Theseus myths are about heroes who claim their rightful kingdom. In an essay, **compare and contrast** Theseus's story with Arthur's. Before you write, collect your details in a chart like the one below:

	Theseus	Arthur
Parentage		
Childhood		
Search for father		
Test to prove identity		
Quest		
Savior of a people		

Researching Heroes

According to Edith Hamilton, there were four great Greek heroes before the Trojan War. Theseus was one. Two others were men (Perseus and Herakles—also known as Hercules) and one was a woman (Atalanta). Choose one of these three other heroes, and research versions of his or her story. Consult at least two collections of Greek myths in your research. Use your findings as the basis of a **research paper.** Before you write, you will have to focus your research so that you have one main topic to present in your thesis statement.

Use "Writing a Research Paper," pages 690–709, for help with this assignment.

Theseus in Panels

The Greek myths have provided rich subject matter for illustrators. Try your hand at reformulating the Theseus story into a series of cartoon panels. First, divide the story into discrete episodes, and assign one event to a panel. Put the characters' dialogue (you will have to make it up) in balloons, and provide a caption for each panel that explains what is happening. If you want to limit your story, you could focus on the adventure in the labyrinth.

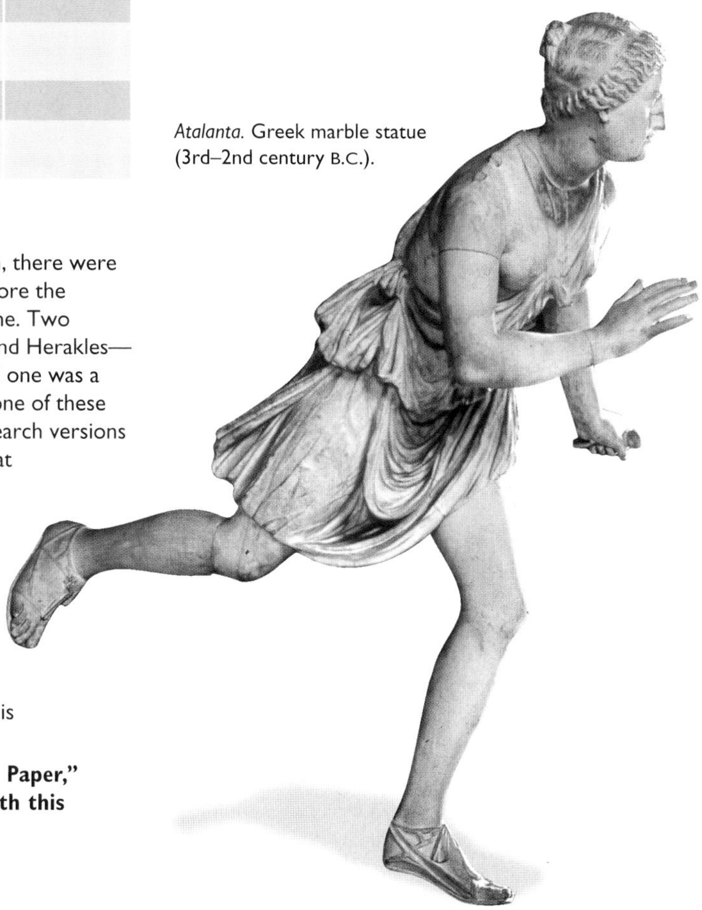

Atalanta. Greek marble statue (3rd–2nd century B.C.).

Literary Criticism

8. Readers can infer that the Greeks believed that punishment should be swift and proportional to the crime.
9. Not knowing Theseus's true identity, his father intends to kill him. The ancient Greeks would likely have felt outraged at such behavior.
10. When Androgenes, son of King Minos, visited Aegeus, the king did not protect his guest but sent him on a perilous quest. Androgenes was killed. As a result, Minos invaded Athens and demands the sacrifice of Athenian youths every nine years.
11. Possible answer: There was conflict and hostility between Athens and Crete. Theseus shifts the balance of power in Athens' favor, after many years during which Crete had dominated Athens.
12. When the Thebans refuse to let their enemies bury their war dead, Theseus intervenes, conquering the Thebans to make sure that the dead can be buried.
13. Possible response: Theseus's not allowing his armies to burn and loot Thebes suggests that the Athenian code of honor prohibited soldiers from harming civilians. Wartime codes today vary widely.

Vocabulary Development

Practice

1. Early books of maps featured an opening illustration showing Atlas holding the earth on his shoulders, with outlines of the continents drawn on the globe. Over time, a book of maps came to be called an *atlas.*
2. People who are *furious* might behave like the Furies. They might be eager for vengeance and strike out at those who make them angry.
3. The *Olympic* mountain range, in the state of Washington, is named after Mount Olympus. The highest mountain in this range is itself named Mount Olympus.
4. A *nemesis* is a person or thing that causes someone's downfall; a formidable opponent.
5. An *odyssey* is any long journey full of trials and adventures or any long, challenging intellectual or spiritual quest.
6. A *volcano* erupts in fiery rocks and forges mountains.
7. A person with a *mercurial* personality has quickly changing moods. The person may also be eloquent and clever.
8. A *herculean* task is one so difficult that it seems impossible to achieve. Examples might include achieving peace between long-warring nations or overcoming great hardships in order to achieve success.
9. The *Amazons* were a legendary race of women warriors who fought against the Greeks, according to Greek mythology.
10. A *labyrinth* is a maze or any place with a complicated series of passageways. The adjective *labyrinthine* describes anything intricate or complicated.

Resources Reminder

Vocabulary

- *Lesson Plans for Language Development*
  - Vocabulary, pp. 316, 322

Vocabulary Development

Words Derived from Greek and Roman Myths

Greek or Roman Word	English Word
Amazons	amazon
Atlas	atlas
Europa	Europe
Furies	fury
Hercules	herculean
Janus	January
Juno	June
Labyrinth	labyrinth
Mars	martial
Mercury	mercurial
Mount Olympus	olympic
Nemesis	nemesis
Oceanus	ocean
Odysseus	odyssey
Vulcan	volcano

PRACTICE

Read the information, and answer the questions that follow about words from the Greek and Roman myths. To answer the questions, you might need to look up the derivation of each underlined word in a college or unabridged dictionary.

Reading Standard 1.3 Identify Greek and Roman mythology and use the knowledge to understand the origin and meaning of new words.

1. A god called **Atlas** held up the whole earth and heavens on his shoulders.
   Why is a book of maps called an atlas?
2. The **Furies** were wild female spirits, with snakes for hair, who punished wrongdoers and avenged crimes.
   How is our word furious related to the Furies?
3. The Greek gods were said to live atop **Mount Olympus** in Greece.
   What northwestern U.S. mountain range is named for this home of the Greek gods?
4. **Nemesis** (nem′ə·sis) was the goddess who handed out justice or vengeance to wrongdoers.
   What do we mean when we make remarks like "That test was my nemesis"?
5. **Odysseus,** the hero of Homer's epic the *Odyssey,* took ten years to travel home from the Trojan War.
   How is the word odyssey related to Odysseus's journey?
6. **Vulcan** was the Roman god of fire, forges, and metalworking.
   How do you think the word volcano is related to this god's name?
7. **Mercury** was the messenger of the Roman gods. Mercury is identified with manual skill, eloquence, cleverness, travel, and thievery.
   What is meant when a person is described as mercurial?
8. The Greek hero Herakles is called **Hercules** by the Romans. He was renowned for his twelve labors, which required great strength and courage.
   Give an example of a herculean task someone today might be asked to perform.
9. Who were the Amazons, for whom the South American river was named?
10. You have read about the famous labyrinth on Crete.
    How is the word labyrinth used today?

ASSESSING

Assessment

- *Progress Assessment of Reading*
  - Selection Test

672 Chapter 9 Biographical and Historical Approach • Using Primary and Secondary Sources

Before You Read

Sigurd, the Dragon Slayer

Literary Focus

Norse Myths and the Monster Slayer

A **myth** is a traditional story that is basically religious in nature. Myths usually explain a belief, a ritual, or a mysterious natural phenomenon. In almost all cultures, for example, you will find myths that explain why the seasons change, how humankind learned to make fire, and why we have to die.

Many myths have dragons and other monsters as characters. Traditionally the dragon guards a treasure hoard that was acquired through deceit or violence. "Sigurd, the Dragon Slayer," a Norse myth, features what might be the **archetypal** dragon slayer—the model of the hero who descends to the underworld to slay a monster.

Make the Connection

Quickwrite

Descendants of these dragons and monsters can be found even in the stories we tell today. Can you think of any stories you have read or seen in the movies that feature a loathsome creature as the villain? What usually are the powers of these creatures? What makes them a threat? Who or what are today's dragon slayers?

Background

Norse mythology consists of stories that were told in Scandinavia and Germany for thousands of years. The oldest surviving written versions of these ancient tales, called *Eddas,* came from Iceland in the thirteenth century.

Norse mythology also includes great hero tales, called *sagas,* which are part of an oral storytelling tradition. The story of Sigurd is part of the Volsunga saga.

Unlike the Greek myths, the Norse myths foretell a day of doom when the entire world will be consumed by fire and all life ended. Not only will human life end on that day (called Ragnarok) but the gods will also perish. It is a tragic outlook—nothing will be able to change it. (The myths do contain a remote glimpse of hope, however—a prophecy of a new world to come after Ragnarok.)

In her introduction to *Legends of the North,* Olivia Coolidge writes this about the Norse myths:

> The violent history of the northern peoples and the harsh conditions of their lives have helped to form a body of legend which is highly individual. The gods of Asgard [home of the Norse gods and slain heroes], like the men who believed in them, were engaged in a constant struggle in which goodness warred against evil, light against darkness, warmth against cold. Boisterous humor was seen in contrast to shadowy forces at whose hands the earth was fated to perish at last on the Day of Doom.
>
> Such being the religion of the Norsemen, it is not surprising to find that the human heroes of legend are people who have much to endure. Happy endings are rare. Life is short. The pathos is heightened by every man's intense love of life and interest in human affairs. Courage chiefly elevates these stories, since in them the hero accepts with a fine exultation every test of his power to endure.

Reading Standard 3.12 Analyze the way in which a work of literature is related to the themes and issues of its historical period. (Historical approach)

STANDARDS FOCUS, pp. 673–688

(For the grade-level and review standards taught in this lesson, see citations on Student Edition pages.)

Summary *at grade level*

When Sigurd, son of the great warrior Sigmund, is born, the dwarf Regin knows that the boy will become a dragon slayer.

When Sigurd is grown, Regin taunts him, saying that he has neither his own horse nor his own sword. The god Odin gives Sigurd a powerful horse named Grayfell. Regin then tells Sigurd about the dragon Fafnir, who guards a treasure. Regin offers Sigurd most of the treasure if he will slay the dragon and roast its heart for him to eat. Sigurd agrees and asks Regin to make him a sword. Regin makes two swords, but both break. Finally, Regin reforges the pieces of Sigurd's dead father's sword, and this sword passes Sigurd's test.

Regin and Sigurd travel to the mansion in which Fafnir guards his treasure. Sigurd slays the dragon. While roasting the dragon's heart for Regin to eat, Sigurd accidentally tastes the fat from the meat and becomes wise. He hears two birds chattering and understands their language. The birds say that the dragon's heart will make Regin strong as well as wise, and that Regin plans to use his new strength to kill Sigurd, so that he can take all the treasure for himself. Sigurd slays the dwarf and claims the treasure.

RESOURCES: READING

Planning

- *One-Stop Planner* CD-ROM with Test Generator
- *On Course: Mapping Instruction*

Media

- *Audio CD Library*
  - disc 16

Reading

- *Interactive Reading,* Teacher's Edition
  - Graphic Organizer: Hero Chart

Differentiating Instruction

- *Lesson Plans for Language Development*
  - English-Language Learners, pp. 305–307, 317, 323
  - Special Education Students, pp. 308, 317, 323

Assessment

- *Progress Assessment of Reading*
  - Selection Test
- *One-Stop Planner* CD-ROM with Test Generator

PRETEACHING

Selection Starter

Motivate. Use the Quickwrite activity on the Before You Read page to stir up interest in the dragon-slayer theme of the selection. Students may mention fantasy movies that actually feature dragons, as well as traditional monster movies about vampires, zombies, and mummies. Other possibilities are science fiction movies in the *Star Wars, Star Trek, Jurassic Park,* and *Godzilla* series. Students might also mention films about nature gone berserk, such as *Jaws, The Birds,* and *The Andromeda Strain.*

Assign the Reading

Read aloud the cast of characters on p. 674 and the Introduction on p. 676, so that students understand how all of the characters are related and what sequence of events has preceded the adventure of Sigurd. To allow everyone a chance to read, you may wish to assign students to read the parts of King Alf, Odin, and Hiordis and have other students take turns reading the narration and the parts of Sigurd and Regin.

CHARACTERS IN THE MYTH

REGIN: a dwarf, brother of Fafnir. In Norse mythology, dwarfs are a race of ugly, deceitful creatures who live under the earth and work as master craftsmen. The word *dwarf* probably comes from an Indo-European base meaning "trick or injure."

SIGURD (sig′ərd): the most famous hero in Norse mythology, the last of the Volsung family.

SIGMUND (sig′mənd): Sigurd's father, who was killed in battle before Sigurd's birth.

HIORDIS (hē·ôr′dis): Sigurd's mother, who married King Alf after Sigmund's death.

FAFNIR (fäv′nir′): an evil dwarf who was turned into a dragon. Fafnir is Regin's brother.

REIDMAR (rēd′mär): the dwarf king, father of Regin, Otter, and Fafnir.

ODIN: the leader of the gods, and the god of war and wisdom.

Sigurd killing the dragon Fafnir. Carved portal from the Hylestad church, Norway (12th century).

DIFFERENTIATING INSTRUCTION

Learners Having Difficulty

To help students follow the plot of the myth, have students copy the chart on p. 687 to use as a graphic aid. Then, read aloud the Introduction, and help students fill in the *Characters* and *Setting* sections of the chart. Ask them to predict what conflicts the characters will face and confirm or revise their predictions as they read. Also have students fill in the *Main events, Climax,* and *Resolution* sections. Use the completed charts as a Reading Check to make sure that students have grasped the plot.

English-Language Learners

The diction used in this retelling includes words that students are not likely to encounter in everyday speech and reading. These include *whither* (where), *whence* (from where), *lest* (for fear that), *borne* (given birth to), *wielding* (holding and using), *grant* (give), *wooed* (sought to marry), *against this day* (in preparation for this day), and *smite* (kill). Introduce these words before students read, and encourage them to use context clues to help them figure out the meanings of any other old-fashioned words.

674 Chapter 9 Biographical and Historical Approach • Using Primary and Secondary Sources

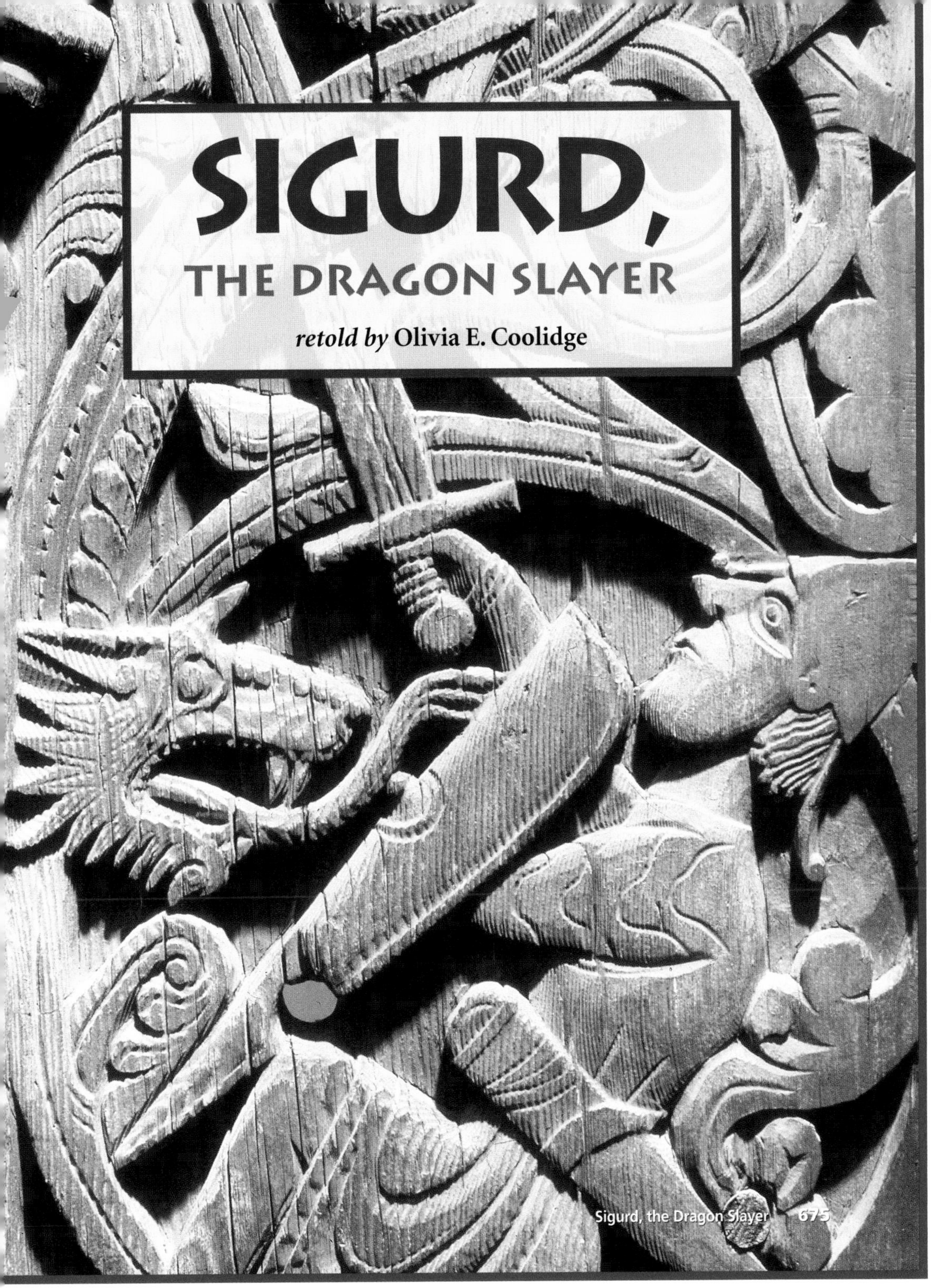

SIGURD, THE DRAGON SLAYER

retold by Olivia E. Coolidge

DIRECT TEACHING

VIEWING THE ART

This picture is a detail of a doorway that was originally carved in the Hylestad church in Setesdal, Norway. Carved around the year 1200, the doorway is decorated with scenes from the myth of Sigurd the dragon slayer. The episodes of this myth are interwoven in plant patterns, integrating them into a whole while maintaining the scenes as discrete moments in the narrative. This doorway is an example of a *bas-relief,* a term for sculpture that protrudes only slightly from its background surface. See another part of the carved doorway on p. 679.

Activity. What part of the story is depicted in this detail of the portal? [It shows Sigurd killing the dragon.]

Resources Reminder

For lessons designed for intermediate and advanced English-language learners, see *Lesson Plans for Language Development,* pp. 305–307, 317, 323.

Special Education Students

For lessons designed for special education students, see *Lesson Plans for Language Development,* pp. 308, 317, 323.

Advanced Learners

Acceleration. Use the following activity with advanced learners to move them toward the eleventh- and twelfth-grade Standard 3.6, for which they analyze the way in which authors through the centuries have used archetypes drawn from myth and tradition in literature and film.

Activity. Tell students that writer J.R.R. Tolkien was greatly influenced by Norse mythology when he wrote his Lord of the Rings trilogy of fantasy novels: *The Fellowship of the Ring, The Two Towers,* and *The Return of the King.* Encourage students to either read novels in the series or to view the recent films that are based on them. Then, have students identify similarities between Tolkien's characters, plots, and themes and those of "Sigurd, the Dragon Slayer."

DIRECT TEACHING

(A) Content-Area Connections

Literature: The Volsunga Saga The warrior Volsung was the grandson of the god Odin and the father of Sigmund, Sigurd's father. The cycle of myths about this family of warriors is known as the Volsunga saga. In German, Sigurd is known as Siegfried, and his story inspired Richard Wagner to compose his operas *Siegfried* and *Götterdämmerung,* parts of the famous *Ring* cycle of operas.

(B) English-Language Learners

Idioms. Help students understand the phrase *kept his own counsel,* which means "kept his plan secret," or "told no one of his intentions." Then, encourage students to use context clues to figure out the meaning of the phrase *draws to a close* ("is coming to an end").

Viking coin minted in England (10th–11th century).

INTRODUCTION

Sigurd's story is part of a cycle of hero sagas. Before this particular story opens, Loki, the cunning god of fire, thoughtlessly kills an otter sunning itself—but the otter is actually the son of Reidmar, the king of the dwarfs.

That night, Reidmar captures Loki and Odin, king of the gods. Furious, the dwarf king threatens to kill both of them in revenge for his son's death. Odin suggests a ransom instead. So Loki is sent off to steal the famous gold hoard of the elf Andvari.

When Reidmar receives the gold, he frees his hostages—but the lust for gold can result in evil. That night the dwarf king's son, Fafnir, kills his own father and seizes the elfin treasure for himself. The third son of the dwarf king, Regin, flees, terrified for his own life.

Many years pass. Fafnir, the brother who stole his father's gold, has changed his shape into that of a dragon. Fafnir now lies coiled jealously around his golden treasure in his dead father's crumbling hall. Meanwhile Regin, the third son, has wandered the world looking for a hero who can slay Fafnir and seize the treasure for Regin.

One day a royal child is born in a peaceful kingdom. Regin recognizes the child as the one who will slay the dragon and get the gold. The baby, Sigurd, is the son of the great warrior Sigmund, who died in battle.

Now starts Sigurd's story.

THE DRAGON SLAYER

(A) Regin saw the baby, Sigurd, and his heart was wonderfully stirred, for he knew the dragon slayer was born after ages of time. He said nothing to Hiordis, who had borne this son to Sigmund, the Volsung, after that great hero had died. (B) He kept his own counsel while the child was an infant, but he burned with secret desire. Years passed more slowly than ever, but at last he saw Sigurd had become a tall, golden-haired lad. Then finally he went to King Alf, who had wedded the widowed Hiordis. "My long life draws to a close," he said. "Grant me a pupil before I die, that I may teach him the skill of my hands, the words of my songs, and my herbs of healing, lest my wisdom perish with me and be forgotten."

"It is a good request," answered Alf, "and I grant it. Whom will you have?"

"Give me Sigurd," answered Regin quickly.

"It is done," declared the king, marveling at the beautiful boy who seemed to have touched the heart of this dark, secretive old man.

After this time the aged Regin appeared to recover the fire of his earlier days. The hand of Sigurd became cunning with the harp strings. His strong, young voice delighted the feasters with the legends of ancient time. He worked also with Regin in the smithy,[1] but there he could never rival his master, though among men he was a notable smith. He learned much of strange herbs and of the ways of the woodlands. Of the evil workings of Regin's mind, he understood nothing at all. Yet though other people spoke of the old man's love for his pupil, Sigurd felt the cold craft behind it. Though he admired his wise master, he had no affection for him.

Sigurd was wielding the hammer in the smithy one day when Regin, studying his mighty form, judged the awaited time was near.

1. **smithy** *n.:* workplace of a smith, one who makes or repairs metal objects in a fiery forge. In former times, smiths used their hammers to shape the hot metal into armor, weapons, and shoes for horses.

676 Chapter 9 Biographical and Historical Approach • Using Primary and Secondary Sources

"Sigurd," he said when the din[2] ceased and the iron was thrust back in the fire, "you are the last of the Volsungs, who were a great warrior race. Are you content in this tame little country where Alf's sons, your brothers, grow up to be kings?"

Sigurd turned from the fire toward him. "I would ride into the world tomorrow," he answered, "were it not for my mother, and for King Alf, who has treated me well."

"So well," replied Regin drily, "that you have neither horse nor sword."

"I ride what horse I please," retorted Sigurd, "as do the king's own sons."

"Your brothers are children. When they are men like you, they will have their own."

"I can have any horse for the asking," persisted Sigurd. This was true, for Alf was pleased by the youth's request.

"The horses are in the pasture at the head of the valley," said he. "Go up and choose which you will. It is time you had one of your own."

As Sigurd ran lightly toward the pasture, many a head turned after him. His bright hair shone in the sun, and in spite of his great size, he moved with the grace of a deer. "What will become of him," thought the elders. "Surely there was never before a young man so handsome and strong."

"SURELY THERE WAS NEVER BEFORE A YOUNG MAN SO HANDSOME AND STRONG."

Odin himself stood in the way near the pasture, watching the young runner approach. The god seemed an old man in tattered garments of gray which stirred, as if in a breeze, though the air was perfectly still. "Greetings," said he, fixing the youth with his one bright eye of blue. "Greetings, Sigurd. Why do you run?"

"To choose me a horse," panted Sigurd. "Are you the herdsman?"

"Do I look like a herdsman?"

"No. Like a warrior."

"You say well," said the god. "I am indeed a warrior, and I knew your father, Sigmund, all his days. Come with me, and let us test the strength of these horses by driving them through the stream."

The river was running in flood, for the snows had melted. Here at the head of the valley it came foaming down from the mountains with a roar. Sigurd and Odin collected the horses and drove them at a gallop down to the riverbank. Some wheeled to right or left when they saw the boiling water, and fled splashing along the shallows, whinnying with alarm. Some plunged full into the torrent, which carried them away, tossing, kicking, rolling, now under and now up. A few swam steadily, though these too were carried down. Only one great gray horse leapt far out into the water and made for the opposite bank. They saw him reach the shallows, climb up, and stand in the flowering meadow to shake his silvery sides. Finally with a snort he plunged back into the water to return.

"I gave your father a sword," said Odin as they watched the great creature breasting the flood. "Now I give you this horse. Ride out and win fame. When you come to the shield-roofed hall of Odin where your father sits, the heroes shall rise to greet you as the greatest one of them all. Look now how Grayfell stands in the shallows. He is of the tireless strain of Sleipner, the horse that Odin rides."

Sigurd leapt down into the water and swung himself onto Grayfell's back. Air whistled past them as they raced down the meadow. Drops sprayed from the mane of Grayfell. Turf flew up behind his heels. The two came thundering down the valley like an avalanche from the hills, huge horse and huge rider gleaming in the light of the evening sun.

2. **din** *n.:* noise.

DIRECT TEACHING

C Reading Skills

Analyzing dialogue. How does Regin persuade Sigurd to acquire his own horse? [He suggests that Sigurd is being treated unfairly by his stepfather and is being prevented from pursuing his destiny as a warrior. These accusations persuade Sigurd to prove Regin wrong by asking his stepfather for a horse.] **What is Regin's real motive for goading Sigurd?** [He wants Sigurd to ride out and slay the dragon for him.]

D Literary Focus
GRADE-LEVEL STANDARD

Norse myths. Because Scandinavia is a part of the world that endures long, dark winters with very few hours of daylight, its mythology focuses on the contrasting symbols of light and darkness, which represent good and evil. Sigurd, the virtuous hero, is described as "golden," "bright," and shining like the sun. In contrast, Regin, the evil dwarf, is described as "dark" and secretive.

E Literary Focus
GRADE-LEVEL STANDARD

Myths and archetypes. The god Odin comes to earth to help the hero Sigurd begin his quest. This theme of divine or magical assistance to the hero is an archetype that appears in many myths around the world.

F Literary Focus
GRADE-LEVEL STANDARD

Norse myths. How does the image of horse and rider "gleaming in the light of the evening sun" reflect the symbolism of Norse mythology? [To the Norse, images of light were symbols of virtue and were often used to describe heroes.]

DIRECT TEACHING

A Reading Skills

Making inferences. Why does Regin complain about Odin's interaction with Sigurd? [Regin may fear that Odin will oppose his own plans to use Sigurd. Students may point out that Regin's father once threatened to kill Odin (see the Introduction on page 676).]

B Learners Having Difficulty

Re-reading. Tell students that this passage shows an important change in the relationship between Regin and Sigurd. Have them re-read the passage and identify examples of Sigurd's growing mistrust of Regin and growing confidence in his own power. [As Regin tells the tale of the gold, Sigurd looks at him "with a half-formed feeling of doubt." When Regin offers him a sword, Sigurd studies and tests it, using all his strength. When the sword breaks, Sigurd laughs "at his master's frightened face" and mocks Regin. Finally, Sigurd says "from this time on nobody is master to me."]

C Vocabulary Development

GRADE-LEVEL STANDARD

Words from Old Norse and Anglo-Saxon. The word *smith,* meaning "a worker in metals," is derived from Old English and is related to the German root *smid.* It is used to make compound words such as *blacksmith, silversmith,* and *goldsmith.* The surname *Smith* was given to those who were engaged in these occupations. The ending *–smith* has come to be applied to anyone who makes or works with a specific material, in words such as *locksmith, wordsmith,* and *tunesmith.*

"Who gave you that horse?" asked Regin when the young man slid off at his door.

A "An old man with the wind in his garments and a single, bright blue eye. He spoke to me of my father."

"I know that old man," said Regin sourly. "He knew my father too. Why must he meddle now? But tell me, where will you ride with your fine horse?"

"Into the world."

"But whither? Will you serve some other king?"

"Never that!" cried Sigurd hotly. "I will win my own wealth and fame."

"I have an adventure for you," said Regin. "No man could achieve it till now. It is the winning of a fabulous treasure, enough to make both of us kings."

"What is the deed?"

"Come into the smithy," said Regin. "Blow up the fire, for my tale is long. Sit down by the bench while I tell you who I am, whence came the treasure, and where lies the hideous dragon who was my brother once. Kill him, for he is utterly evil, and take what you will. All I ask is the wisdom which he has stored in his heart for ages on ages, while I squandered[3] mine on men. Roast me the heart of the dragon, that I may eat, and be wise. Then take your fill of the treasure, and leave me what little you please."

B Sigurd listened long to the tale of Reidmar and of the curse on Andvari's gold.[4] The fire grew low. The moon came up, as the quiet voice of Regin poured forth his long-stored hate. Each to the other in the darkness seemed only a vague, black shape, but the eyes of Regin gloated[5] on Sigurd, who peered back at his master with a half-formed feeling of doubt. At last silence fell. Sigurd burned for adventure, but Regin burned for the gold. "I will slay the dragon," said Sigurd slowly. "But first, you must make me a sword."

"Get up and light me the torches," answered Regin. "I have made you a sword against this day. Open my chest there, and take it. All my skill went into the work."

Sigurd opened the chest by the wall and took out a gold-hilted sword. Down the dark blade ran strange signs of magic, and the hilt was studded with gems. He turned it over in his hands and scanned it, but the great blade had never a flaw. "Let us prove your skill, master of smiths," said he. With that, he swung it high and brought it down on the anvil with all his force. The blade broke with a fearful crash, and the point quivered past Regin's ear. Sigurd laughed at his master's frightened face as he threw the hilt on the floor. "I see this adventure is not for us, since your skill is too poor," he mocked.

"I will make you another," cried Regin. "This time it will never break, though you drive the anvil into the floor."

"When it is done, I will come back," said the hero, "but from this time on nobody is master to me."

It was many days later before Regin was ready. His eyes were red from peering into the fire, as they had been in the workshop of Reidmar. "Come into the smithy," said he. "I have your sword."

The sword lay on the bench dully shining. From hilt to point it was of bare steel unadorned. **C** "Try this on the anvil," said Regin. "I am the master smith, and I tell you that if you break this, no steel that is forged on earth will serve your turn."

Again Sigurd lifted the sword. Again he swung it. Again he brought it down. There was a crack, and the shattered pieces lay strewn at

3. **squandered** *v.:* used wastefully or extravagantly.
4. **curse . . . gold:** Loki, the Norse fire god and master of cunning, forced the elf Andvari to give him all of his golden treasure hoard. Andvari placed a curse on his gold, saying that it would bring sorrow to anyone who owned it.
5. **gloated** *v.:* looked at with spiteful pleasure.

CONTENT-AREA CONNECTIONS

History: Viking and Anglo-Saxon Cultures

During the Viking Age, from about A.D. 800 to 1050, Scandinavian warriors raided and colonized large areas of the British Isles. The Viking expeditions had a significant impact on the language, social structure, commerce, and culture of England and Ireland.

Activity. Have students research the history of interactions between Vikings and Anglo-Saxons from A.D. 800 to 1050. Ask them to list specific ways that each culture made a lasting impression on the other during that period.

The forging of the sword Gram, from the Sigurd myth. Carved portal from the Hylestad church, Norway (12th century).

Sigurd's feet. Regin stood astonished, for even he had never suspected the young man's giant strength. Sigurd laughed. "You say truly," he cried. "No sword will serve my turn but one which was not forged in an earthly fire." He cast the pieces from him and strode out.

Queen Hiordis was in the dairy, where the women were making cheese. "Mother," said Sigurd coming to her as she carried a pail of whey. "Mother, where is my father's sword?"

Hiordis started, and a great splash of whey fell from the pan onto the dairy floor. "What need do you have of a sword?" asked she, putting her burden down.

"I am a man," said Sigurd, "and a mighty hero's son. This land is too quiet for me. I will go out and win fame."

"Before you were even born," said Hiordis, "I knew that this day would come. Two months after I was wed, great Sigmund fell, and with him my father and all the men of my house. I alone hid in a thicket so that the plundering **D**

DIRECT TEACHING

VIEWING THE ART

Another part of the carved doorway from the Hylestad church, this detail illustrates the forging of Sigurd's sword by Regin. Note how the sword appears broken and how the two men appear to be confronting one another.

D Learners Having Difficulty

Monitoring students' progress. Hiordis's diction and manner of speaking may make this passage difficult for some students to read. To assess their understanding, ask, "Why did Hiordis save the pieces of Sigmund's shattered sword after he died?" [She knew that she would give birth to Sigmund's son and that he would grow up to be a great hero who would need his father's sword.]

CONTENT-AREA CONNECTIONS

Music: Richard Wagner's Ring Cycle
The nineteenth-century German composer Richard Wagner used Norse and German legends as sources for his famous cycle of operas *The Ring of the Nibelung.* One of the operas concerns the heroic quest of Siegfried, the German name for Sigurd.

Activity. Students who are interested in music may listen to a portion of a recording of the opera *Siegfried.* Encourage them to listen specifically for leitmotifs, the symbolic musical phrases used to represent different characters, emotions, and themes in the Siegfried story. Then, have students evaluate how well the music conveys the emotions and ideas of the heroic quest.

Direct Teaching

A Advanced Learners

Acceleration. Mythic heroes are often the offspring of great heroes, although some of them, such as Arthur and Theseus, may not realize their true heritage at first. The hero's quest is presented as his destiny, a great objective that no one can prevent him from pursuing. Have groups of advanced learners identify other works that include this archetype of the son of a heroic figure pursuing his destiny.

B Literary Focus
GRADE-LEVEL STANDARD

Myths and archetypes. The sword endowed with magical powers given to the hero by the gods is a recurring pattern in heroic quests. Ask students to cite examples of such swords from other works of literature or from popular fantasy movies.

C Vocabulary Development
GRADE-LEVEL STANDARD

Words from Old Norse and Anglo-Saxon. The word *threshold* is derived from the Old English word *threscwald* and is related to the Old Norse word *threskjoldr.* In Old English the root *threscan* means "to thresh" or "to stamp." The threshold of a house is the place where a person stamps his feet before entering. Today, the meaning of *threshold* has been expanded to include any boundary or beginning. In science, it indicates a level or value above which an event will occur and below which it will not occur (for example, *a pain threshold*).

Viking pendant from Sweden.

hosts of the enemy passed me by. Then I crept into the moonlight and found where my father lay, and mighty Sigmund with the dead heaped up before him like a wall. In his hand was the hilt of the sword that Odin gave, but the pieces of the shattered blade lay shining around him on the grass. Then I foresaw this day and gathered them up to be your inheritance."

Hiordis went to her room and opened the chest where her clothes were always stored. There, under stiff mantles and robes of silver and blue lay a long piece of gold tissue with something heavy within.

"Your father was old when I wedded him," said she. "His sons had grown up, and won fame, and were dead. Then he wooed me, and I chose him gladly, for I thought, 'What woman will bear a greater hero than the wife of the most famous warrior alive?'"

A "My stepfather is no warrior, however," remarked Sigurd.

"Alf is a good man and kind. This is a peaceful land, and I am happy here, but it is not the place for which you were born."

"That is true," said her son, "and I will say farewell, for when I go, I shall never return."

"Your fame will come back," she answered. "It will ring in my ears till I die." She gave him the sword, and he went down the stair and out over the flowering meadow. His mother watched him out of her window till the path hid him from sight.

Regin still sat in the smithy when Sigurd strode in and laid the bundle before him. "There is my sword," he said.

Regin opened the bundle and looked at the pieces, which glowed with a strange, pale light. "This was forged in heavenly fires," he said slowly, "and I am of the dwarf people. There is death to me in the steel."

"There is death to the dragon," replied Sigurd.

"Be it so. Leave me the pieces. I will remake B the blade."

When Sigurd came again to the smithy, the great sword lay on the bench, and a pale light ran down the center from the hilt to the end of the blade. The edges, however, were dark and sharpened fine as a hair. Sigurd looked at the magic symbols which were carved in the steel. He fitted his hand to the jeweled hilt, and the sword stirred in his grip. He lifted it high and swung it. Suddenly he brought it down. With a crash the anvil fell shattered, while the blade sprung back unharmed. Then he cried, "I name this sword 'the Wrath of Sigurd.' No man shall feel it and live."

Regin said, "The long day is done. It is now a month that I have toiled for you. Tonight let us sleep. Tomorrow we will ride out against Fafnir, and the treasure shall be your own."

Fafnir's End

The hall of the dwarf king, Reidmar, no longer blazed in the sun. The gilt[6] had washed off its beams, the wide door was fallen from its hinges, and grass grew on the roof. "Look!" said Regin, pointing where a great track ran from the C threshold[7] down to the riverbank. It was

6. **gilt** *n.:* thin covering of gold.
7. **threshold** *n.:* entrance; doorway.

FAMILY/COMMUNITY ACTIVITY

An important theme of hero myths is the need for young adults to leave home in order to discover who they really are and what they are meant to do in life. Encourage students to discuss this theme with an adult family member or older friend. In the older person's experience, how important was the process of leaving home and becoming independent? What difficulties and rewards did the process involve? Is the search for one's true self and one's destiny only for the young, or is it a lifelong process?

ground through the dirt of the hillside to the depth of a tall man.

"That path must be made by Fafnir," said Sigurd, "and he uses it often, for no grass grows in it."

"Men say," answered Regin, "that the treasure still lies where my father piled it on the ground before his seat. Around it coils Fafnir, the serpent, gloating over it all day long. But when the moon shines down on him through the rents[8] in the ruined hall, he dreams of his youth, and the spring in the woodlands, and of the great gods he saw when the world was young. The gray morning wakens him early, and at that hour he loathes what he has become. He leaves his treasure and goes out to drink of the river, yet by dawn desire overcomes him once more, so that he returns to the gold."

THE SCALES OF THE MONSTER RATTLED.

"When he goes down the path in the morning before it is yet quite light, I will meet him and smite[9] him," said Sigurd.

D "His scales are as tough as steel, and it does no good to strike unless you can kill at a blow. Wound him, and he will crush you as you might step on an ant."

"I will dig a pit in the pathway and crouch there in the dark. When he comes, his eyes will be on the river and his mind still full of his dreams. Perhaps he will not see where I lie. Then as he rolls over me, I will thrust up through his belly where the scales are not so strong. This way I may reach his heart."

E "But if he sees you?"

Sigurd laughed. "You will wait another thousand years for a dragon slayer. That is all."

The moon was full and rose early. It took little time to dig the pit. Sigurd wrapped himself in his cloak and went to sleep while Regin stood on guard. He never stirred until Regin, weary of watching, touched his shoulder and whispered, "Hush! It is time."

F Overhead at the edge of the mountains, the sky was pale gray by now, but a river mist hung in the valley and clung to the grassy slope, so that low in the depths of Fafnir's track, it was still dark as the grave.

G Sigurd crouched, his sword under his cloak, for he feared lest its gleam should be seen. No wind stirred in the trees by the river. A fox barked. The little clouds overhead turned white with the approach of day.

Something moved in the house. There was a scraping sound as though a log were being pushed over the floor. The scales of the monster rattled. A stone rolled down the track. The sounds came closer, and with them a strong, damp, musty smell. Sigurd saw through the thinning mist that a dark shape was filling the sunken pathway from side to side. The dawn was very close. He could see the huge head now almost on the edge of his hole. It was flat and scaly like a snake's, but the weary eyes were human, though of monstrous size. They stared straight through the gloom at Sigurd, whose grip tightened on his sword. For a moment the two seemed to look at each other, eye to eye, yet the monster moved on, dull and unseeing, heavy with sleep.

Black darkness rolled over Sigurd. Stench stifled[10] him. Loose earth filled up the pit. Inch by inch the creature slid over him. Sigurd shut his eyes, set his teeth, and waited. He dared not strike too soon.

After what seemed minutes, he thought, I must risk it now. With that he straightened his knees and drove the sword upward with all his force. It tore up through the cloak, through the loose earth, and on with the force of his arm

8. **rents** *n.:* holes; gaps.
9. **smite** *v.:* kill.
10. **stifled** *v.:* smothered; suffocated.

DIRECT TEACHING

D Literary Focus
GRADE-LEVEL STANDARD

? Figurative language. How does Regin convey the size and strength of Fafnir? [He uses two similes, comparing Fafnir's scales to the toughness of steel and saying that Fafnir can "crush you as you might step on an ant."]

E Literary Focus
GRADE-LEVEL STANDARD

? Mythic heroes. What traits does Sigurd reveal as the moment of his great trial approaches? [By laughing, making a joke about the possibility that he may die, and sleeping soundly, he reveals that he is fearless and relaxed.]

F Literary Focus
GRADE-LEVEL STANDARD

Myths and archetypes. The simile "as dark as the grave" suggests that Sigurd, like many mythic heroes, has descended into a dark underworld, or land of the dead, in order to pursue his quest. This impression is strengthened in the last paragraph on this page, as the dragon passes over the pit and "black darkness" covers Sigurd.

G Literary Focus
GRADE-LEVEL STANDARD

? Imagery and mood. How does vivid imagery create a suspenseful mood? [As Sigurd waits, the imagery "No wind stirred" and "a fox barked" show how quiet it is. Then, as the dragon awakens, there is a "scraping" and rattling. With the sounds comes a "damp, musty smell." At first, Sigurd sees only a "dark shape" but then gets a close-up look at the dragon's head.]

DEVELOPING FLUENCY

Whole-class activity. You may wish to have students read aloud the suspenseful final section of the myth, "Fafnir's End" (pp. 680–683). Assign students to read the parts of Sigurd, Regin, and the talking birds. Then, have volunteers audition for the role of the narrator. Have them read from p. 681 for their audition, beginning with the paragraph that opens, "Sigurd crouched, his sword under his cloak. . . ." Ask the readers to modulate their voices to create a vivid impression of the sights and sounds described and to create a growing feeling of suspense, or tension. When you have selected a narrator, have students rehearse reading together and then perform for the class. You may wish to have more than one group try this activity.

DIRECT TEACHING

VIEWING THE ART

Another part of the carved doorway from the Hylestad church, this detail shows Sigurd roasting Fafnir's heart.

Activity. What does tasting the fat from Fafnir's heart do for Sigurd? [It gives him strength and knowledge and allows him to understand the birds.]

Sigurd roasting the dragon Fafnir's heart. Carved portal from the Hylestad church, Norway (12th century).

READING MINI-LESSON

Developing Word-Attack Skills

Tell students that when a two-syllable word has one consonant letter between two vowel letters, it often indicates that the vowel sound in the first syllable is long. The following selection words illustrate this: *pupil, rival, evil, waken, human,* and *moment.*

Point out that although the vowel-consonant-vowel pattern is a good indicator of long vowel sounds, it doesn't work every time. It is particularly unreliable when the middle consonant letter is *v*. Cite the selection word *covet* as an example. *Covet* has the vowel-consonant-vowel pattern, but it does not have a long vowel sound in the first syllable. In *covet,* the *o* stands for short *u*: /kuv'it/. Compare these words, all of which have the letters *cove.* Have students tell which *o* stands for long *o* or short *u* in each word.

cove cover covet covey

[Only the word *cove* is pronounced with the long *o.* The words *cover, covet,* and *covey* are pronounced with the short *u.*]

Activity. Have students compare the vowel sounds in each series of words and identify

682 Chapter 9 Biographical and Historical Approach • Using Primary and Secondary Sources

until it buried itself to the hilt. A great cry came from the monster. The echoing hills threw back and forth to each another a long succession of cries. Fafnir writhed. His huge body arched like a bow. Sigurd leapt from the pit. The tail lashed wildly after its slayer. Blood rolled down the track to the stream.

The sun was up behind the mountains, but the valley was still cold and gray. When the long death struggles were over, Regin crept from the bushes to look at the endless monster, the color of weathered stone. He gave a great sigh. "You have killed him," he said to Sigurd. "He was my brother once."

Sigurd laughed shortly. "It is late to think of that."

"Yet he was my brother, and you killed him. The fire which burned within me is quenched now in his blood. The long years of my waiting are over, the days of work and the endless wakeful nights. Now let me sleep for an hour, since I watched all this night for you. Kindle me a fire while I rest, and roast me Fafnir's heart. I will eat it and be wise, and after that, we will look on the ancient treasure which has waited so long for us."

"I will gladly do that," replied Sigurd. "You are old, and our journey was long."

Regin lay on the bank by the river. Sigurd lighted a fire in the glade.[11] He spitted[12] the monster's heart on a stick and thrust it into the flame. It hissed and crackled as he turned it from side to side. The sun came over the hills. Two woodpeckers sat in the trees calling to each other over his head. The meat blackened a little at the edges, and Sigurd thought it was nearly done. He put out his hand to turn it. It sputtered, and the hot fat seared[13] his finger.

Sigurd put his hand to his mouth. As he tasted the fat with his tongue, all kinds of knowledge leapt suddenly into his head. The birds still chattered in the trees. Sigurd heard the first one say, "See how the hero, Sigurd, sits roasting Fafnir's heart."

"He roasts it for Regin," answered the other. "Does he not know that the wisdom and strength of the dragon go to him who eats?"

"Sigurd needs no strength from Fafnir, and he cares nothing for the wisdom of the dwarfs."

"Regin cares, but he covets[14] the wisdom, and he needs the strength to slay."

"To slay?"

"Fool! To slay Sigurd. Is not Sigurd his tool to kill Fafnir? Is not his use over? Regin planned this murder when he first saw the dragon slayer as a child in his mother's arms."

Sigurd turned from the fire to look at Regin. For the first time he understood the master of cunning who had reared him to this end. He saw how the love of gold burned in Regin, who must kill lest he have to divide. He understood the cold dwarfs who knew neither conscience nor pity, and who despised mankind for feeling these things.

Regin opened his eyes. The two stared a moment, and the truth was open to each. Regin snatched at his belt for a dagger and leapt at the young man, who sprang up and away, fumbling for his long sword. The dwarf struck too soon, and his dagger whistled savagely through the air. Again he jumped, like a wildcat, but this time the sword met him halfway. He gave a great cry as it pierced him, and he dropped twisting on the grass.

Sigurd looked soberly down on the two evil brothers, great serpent and scheming dwarf. He left them on the grass by the river and turned up to the hill to the crumbling house which hid the treasure he had won. ■

11. **glade** *n.:* open space in a forest.
12. **spitted** *v.:* roasted on a thin, pointed rod or bar that is turned over a fire.
13. **seared** *v.:* burned the surface of.
14. **covets** *v.:* envies.

the words with long vowel sounds. Words with the long vowel sound are underlined.

1.	drive	drivel	driven	driver
2.	rave	ravage	raven	ravenous
3.	have	haven	haversack	havoc
4.	rival	riven	rivet	river
5.	snide	sniper	snivel	sliver
6.	cloven	covenant	woven	slovenly
7.	gavel	gravel	navel	travel
8.	lover	clover	hover	drover

DIRECT TEACHING

A Literary Focus
REVIEW STANDARD

Plot: Climax. What imagery helps you imagine the story's climax, the death of Fafnir? [The force Sigurd uses as his sword "tore up . . . until it buried itself to the hilt"; the "echoing hills" throwing Fafnir's death cries back and forth; Fafnir's body that "writhed" and "arched like a bow" and its tail that "lashed wildly after its slayer"; blood that "rolled down the track to the stream"]

B Literary Focus
GRADE-LEVEL STANDARD

Mythic heroes. What knowledge does Sigurd acquire at the end of his quest, after he tastes a bit of fat from the dragon's heart? [Possible response: He learns about the powers of good and evil. Although he has been suspicious of Regin, he only now realizes that Regin has been planning to kill him all along. He understands the depth of Regin's cunning, evil, and greed. He sees the distinction between humans and dwarfs: Human beings have a conscience and feel pity, but dwarfs do not.]

GUIDED PRACTICE

Monitoring students' practice. Guide the class in answering these comprehension questions. Direct students to locate passages in the text that support their responses.

True or False

1. Sigurd is the son of the god Odin. [F]
2. Sigurd is trained by a dwarf named Regin. [T]
3. Sigurd's mother tries to prevent him from leaving on his quest. [F]
4. Sigurd's sword is made from the shattered pieces of his father's sword. [T]
5. At the end of the story, Sigurd kills both the dragon and Regin. [T]

DIRECT TEACHING

A Learners Having Difficulty

Finding details. Why does Odin have only one eye? [He had to give up one of his eyes to pay for the gift of wisdom.]

B Learners Having Difficulty

Summarizing. How are Frigga, Balder, and Thor related to Odin? [Frigga is Odin's wife; Balder and Thor are his sons.]

C Reading Skills

Making inferences. Myths were often created to explain natural phenomena. What sound in nature is explained by Thor's throwing his mighty hammer? [the sound of thunder]

A Closer Look

THE NORSE GODS

ODIN (or **Woden**) is the leader of the Norse gods. His job is to keep the world safe from destruction for as long as he can. Odin knows that eventually he and his race of gods and all the world will perish at the hands of the Giants. Two wolves crouch at Odin's feet. Two ravens perch on his shoulders and each day bring him news from earth. (A) Odin once went to the Well of Wisdom to beg for wisdom; he was granted the gift, but he had to pay for it with one eye. He lives in **Asgard,** the golden home of the gods. **Wednesday** is named for him.

Odin. Hand-colored engraving.

Frigga escorted by Valkyries in the sky. Lithograph.

FRIGGA (or **Frigg**) is the wife of Odin and the goddess of the clouds. Frigga can see into the future. (**Friday** is generally believed to be named for Frigga.)

THOR is the god of (B) thunder, the eldest son of Odin. Thor protects humans from the dangerous Giants in the underworld. His main weapon is his mighty (C) hammer, which returns on its own to Thor's iron-gloved hand after it is thrown. **Thursday** is named for Thor.

Thor swinging his mighty hammer. Illustration by Arthur Rackham (c. 1900).

Viking amber figurine, possibly representing Thor.

FREY and **FREYA**, brother and sister, are beloved gods. Frey is the god of weather and the harvest. Freya is the goddess of love and beauty. **Friday** is sometimes considered to be named after Freya.

Freya, the most lovely of the gods. Illustration by J. Doyle Penrose.

A romantic portrayal of Balder by B. Fogelberg. Marble statue (1840).

BALDER (or **Baldur**) is the beloved son of Frigga and Odin. Frigga tried to save Balder from the curse of death. She extracted promises from all living things not to harm Balder—except that she ignored the humble mistletoe. The tricky Loki, jealous of Balder, discovered that Frigga had forgotten to extract a promise from mistletoe. Loki arranged for a branch of mistletoe to kill the god. After Balder's death, grief and sadness came to Asgard. **D**

The god Tiu losing his hand to Fenris, from a manuscript page.

LOKI is one of the evil Giants. He is a trickster and a schemer. The **GIANTS** are the enemies of all that is good. **E**

Loki bound to a rock in punishment for the death of Balder. Illustration by J. Doyle Penrose (c. 1870).

FENRIS is a wolf, another of Loki's unpleasant brood of children. Fenris was chained at last by the god **TIU** (or **Tyr**), who was left with only one hand after Fenris attacked him. **Tuesday** is named for Tiu. **F**

Direct Teaching

D Content-Area Connections

Science: Mistletoe

Although the mistletoe plant is a traditional Christmas decoration, its berries are actually poisonous and can be fatal to children. The small plants are semiparasitic: The leaves make food by photosynthesis, but the plant also attaches itself to trees and extracts additional nutrients from its hosts. Native Americans believed that the mistletoe had medicinal value, and in some ancient European cultures the plant was thought to have magical powers.

E Reading Skills

Making inferences. How do the Norse myths help to explain the existence of good and evil? [Possible response: The gods, led by Odin, are forces for good and they protect human beings. The giants, led by Loki, are evil—the enemies of all goodness.]

F Reading Skills

Making generalizations. What generalization can you make about the Norse gods and the days of the week? [Many days of the week are named after Norse gods.]

Sigurd, the Dragon Slayer 685

Meet the Writer

Background. Olivia Coolidge believed that studying history and mythology was one of the best ways to learn about life, especially about the timeless values that concern people of every age, including ours. Her work has been praised for its vivid descriptive details that bring faraway places and exotic characters to life.

For Independent Reading

- In addition to Coolidge's *Legends of the North,* students interested in Norse mythology might enjoy *Nordic Gods and Heroes,* a retelling of the ancient legends by Padraic Colum.
- Students who are fascinated by dragons and the dragon-slaying motif in mythology will enjoy Anne McCaffrey's *A Diversity of Dragons,* a survey of dragon lore throughout history, from the time of the ancient Babylonians to the fantasy novels of today.

Meet the Writer

Olivia Coolidge

Storyteller and Teacher

Olivia Coolidge (1908–   ) grew up in the English countryside midway between London and Oxford in a somewhat Spartan household, with no car, gas, electricity, central heating, or even hot water. From an early age, as she made up fairy stories with her sister that they would tell each other in bed, she knew that she was interested in writing.

Coolidge grew up to become a teacher. After she came to the United States for a long visit in the 1930s, she decided to stay on, eventually marrying and raising four children here. Finally she began writing the stories that had always interested her:

"Because my own childhood was different from most people's here, I got in the habit of telling stories to groups of children around a fire, sometimes about things I had read. During World War II, I was teaching, and at the same time I was learning about what American children read, and what they don't like to read, and what they are missing. After the war, like all of us, I had time for myself. The very first thing I did with it was to write a children's book."

Coolidge has written more than two dozen books, most of them for young readers. They include biographies of Abraham Lincoln and the Indian leader Mohandas K. Gandhi. She is probably best known, however, for her collections of myths and legends, including *Legends of the North,* her book of Norse myths.

For Independent Reading

You'll find more myths and hero stories in Olivia Coolidge's *Greek Myths* and *The Trojan War.*

686 Chapter 9 Biographical and Historical Approach • Using Primary and Secondary Sources

Literary Response and Analysis

Reading Check

1. To review the **plot** structure of this myth, fill out a story map like the one that follows:

Characters:
Setting:
Problems or conflicts:
Main events:
Climax:
Resolution:

2. What is Regin's **motive,** or reason, for taking Sigurd on as a pupil?
3. Why does Regin want the dragon's heart?

Interpretations

4. In Sigurd's story, as in Arthur's (page 645) and Theseus's (page 663), a sword plays an important role. What similarities and differences do you find in the roles a sword plays in each story?
5. In hero stories there is often a prophecy of the hero's destiny. What does Odin say about Sigurd's future? What prophecy does Hiordis make?
6. What **images** help you imagine what Fafnir looks, smells, and feels like? How does Fafnir's appearance and character contrast with Sigurd's?
7. Describe Fafnir's **setting**—the hall in which he lives. What details in the setting suggest decay?
8. Describe Sigurd's plan to kill Fafnir. Heroes often must descend into a dark underworld to fulfill their quest. In what ways is Sigurd in a kind of underworld as he awaits the dragon?
9. What accident saves Sigurd's life?

Literary Criticism

10. What details in the story tell you that Sigurd is a hero who is favored by the gods? Based on your answer, explain the qualities that the Norse seem to value in their heroes.
11. The Norse hero sagas are full of magic. What examples of magic can you find in Sigurd's story?
12. Edith Hamilton writes,

> Like the early Christians, the Norsemen measured their life by heroic standards. The Christian, however, looked forward to a heaven of eternal joy. The Norseman did not. But it would appear that for unknown centuries, until the Christian missionaries came, heroism was enough.

How is this outlook on life mirrored in the Sigurd myth?

Writing

A Modern Monster

This storyteller uses vivid **imagery** to help us see and even smell the monster. Write a **description** of your own monster that might appear in a modern hero story. Decide what your monster will look like, smell like, feel like, sound like. What treasure trove will your monster guard? (Check your Quickwrite notes.)

Listening and Speaking

A Tale to Tell

Research another Norse myth, and retell it in your own words to a small group. Try one of these myths: the death of Balder, the apples of Idun, part of the story of Beowulf. How will you use your voice to capture your audience's attention?

Reading Standard 3.12 Analyze the way in which a work of literature is related to the themes and issues of its historical period. (Historical approach)

INDEPENDENT PRACTICE

Literary Response and Analysis

Reading Check

1. Possible answers: *Characters*—Sigurd, Regin, King Alf, Odin, Hiordis, Fafnir. *Setting*—a kingdom in old Scandinavia. *Problems or conflicts*—Regin wants treasure; Sigurd wants horse, sword, hero's fame; Sigurd fights dragon; Regin schemes to kill Sigurd. *Main events*—Regin gets permission to train Sigurd; Odin gives Sigurd the horse Grayfell; Regin asks Sigurd to slay Fafnir; Sigurd gets his father's magic sword; Sigurd makes a plan and slays the dragon; Sigurd learns of Regin's plan; Sigurd slays Regin and claims treasure. *Climax*—Sigurd slays the dragon. *Resolution*—Sigurd learns of Regin's plan, slays Regin, and claims the treasure.
2. Regin wants to claim the treasure by Sigurd's defeat of Fafnir.
3. The dragon's heart will give Regin the strength to kill Sigurd and to take all of the treasure.

Interpretations

4. They all confirm their heroic status by claiming their fathers' swords. Arthur and Theseus use the swords to prove their identities. Theseus and Sigurd slay a monster.
5. Odin says he will be hailed as the greatest hero of all. Hiordis says his fame will ring in her ears until she dies.
6. Possible answers: *Sight*—"flat and scaly like a snake's"; "eyes . . . of monstrous size"; "huge body arched like a bow." *Smell*—"a strong . . . smell"; "Stench stifled him." *Touch*—scales "tough as steel." Fafnir is huge, weary, repulsive, and evil. Sigurd is young, handsome, adventurous, and virtuous.
7. The hall is crumbling. Details include "washed off" gilt, fallen door, and grass on the roof.
8. Sigurd plans to lie in a pit along Fafnir's path and stab it as it travels over him. Sigurd's pit is under the earth's surface, dark, and threatening.
9. Sigurd accidentally tastes Fafnir's fat, which makes him wise. He learns of Regin's plot from two birds, whose language he now understands.

Literary Criticism

10. Odin gives Sigurd Grayfell, the strongest horse of all. Qualities include strength, daring, grace, and courage.
11. a dragon; eating dragon's heart confers wisdom and strength; a curse on the gold; Sigmund's sword; talking birds
12. Possible answer: Sigurd's hopes for the future are focused on earthly glory.

Sigurd, the Dragon Slayer 687

Vocabulary Development

Practice 1

1. The word *hell* is derived from the name *Hela.*
2. The word *saga* usually refers to a long chronicle of events, either fiction or nonfiction, sometimes of heroic proportions, such as "the saga of westward expansion in frontier America" or "the saga of one man's quest for freedom." A "family saga" is a long novel chronicling characters and events in a single family over several generations.
3. The expression *to go berserk* means "to become crazed" or "to lose emotional control and become violently agitated." A person might go berserk after being abused mentally or physically or after being given disturbing news.

Practice 2

Modern English Word	Old English Word
1. *bird*	*brid*
2. *blood*	*blod*
3. *brother*	*brothor*
4. *dwarf*	*dwergh*
5. *gold*	*geolu*
6. *grass*	*grœs*
7. *hill*	*hyll*
8. *moon*	*mona*
9. *morning*	*morn*
10. *sword*	*sweord*
11. *truth*	*treowth*

Resources Reminder

Vocabulary

- Cumulative Vocabulary Review, pp. 47–48
- *Lesson Plans for Language Development*
  - Vocabulary, pp. 317, 323

Vocabulary Development

Words from Old Norse and Anglo-Saxon

The Vikings were highly skilled sailors and warriors from Scandinavia who raided the coasts of Europe and the British Isles from the eighth to the tenth centuries. They even sailed as far as the New World. Many everyday words (such as *freckle, guess, sky, skirt,* and *ugly*) came into English from Old Norse, courtesy of the Vikings. A few of those words are directly tied to the Old Norse myths, as are our names for several of the days of the week (see ***A Closer Look,*** page 684).

PRACTICE 1

Read the information in each item, and answer the questions. Use a college or unabridged dictionary to look up the **derivation,** or **etymology,** of the English words.

1. What common English word comes from the name of *Hela,* the Norse goddess of death and the underworld?
2. The English word *saga* comes from an Old Norse word that means "thing said; story or tale." What are some examples of the way we use the word *saga* today?
3. *Berserkers* were Norse warriors (real warriors, not mythical ones) who wore bearskins and were known for their great ferocity in battle. What does our modern expression *to go berserk* mean? What might cause someone to go berserk?

Grade 8 Review Reading Standard 1.2 Understand the most important points in the history of the English language.

Reading Standard 1.1 Understand word derivations.

Reading Standard 1.3 Identify Norse mythology and use the knowledge to understand the origin and meaning of new words.

PRACTICE 2

As the chart at the right shows, some of our most basic English words come from the Anglo-Saxon tribes that invaded England during the fifth and sixth centuries. They were Germanic peoples from various parts of northern Europe, and their language, which we call Old English, had a lasting impact on English. Old English was spoken in England from about A.D. 450 to about 1100.

Use a college or unabridged dictionary to look up and list the original forms (labeled *OE*) of the following words from "Sigurd, the Dragon Slayer." Which words have changed most?

1. bird
2. blood
3. brother
4. dwarf
5. gold
6. grass
7. hill
8. moon
9. morning
10. sword
11. truth

Modern English Word	Old English Word
go	*gan*
fight	*feohtan*
sleep	*slæp*
eat	*etan*
father	*fæder*
mother	*modor*
land	*land*
house	*hus*
home	*hām*
water	*wæter*

ASSESSING

Assessment

- *Progress Assessment of Reading*
  - Selection Test

688 Chapter 9 Biographical and Historical Approach • Using Primary and Secondary Sources

Read On: FOR INDEPENDENT READING

FICTION

Before the Minotaur

Mary Renault's mythical novel ***The King Must Die*** takes us through the boyhood and early life of the Greek hero Theseus, who would one day be famous for slaying the Minotaur. Bored with his uneventful life and filled with dreams of glory, young Theseus sets out on a journey to find his fate. He encounters a series of challenges beyond his expectations and returns to Athens a great hero.

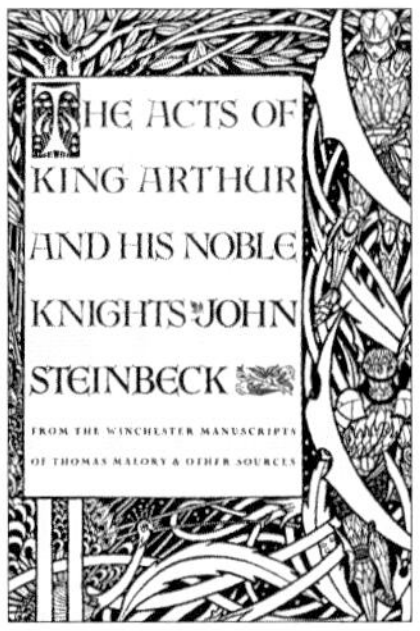

FICTION

Visiting Camelot

If you'd like to know more about the Arthurian legend, then John Steinbeck's ***The Acts of King Arthur and His Noble Knights*** is sure to please. Although this volume is focused on Arthur—older and more seasoned than he was when he first plucked the sword from the stone—it also features the adventures of such famous figures as Launcelot, Guinevere, and Gawain. John Steinbeck has converted their stories into clear, modern prose that opens the doors to the legendary city of Camelot.

FICTION

Tour of Duty

Richie Parry wants nothing more than to attend college and become a great writer someday. When his hopes for college are dashed, he makes a choice that will define the rest of his life: He signs up to fight in the Vietnam War. Walter Dean Myers's novel ***Fallen Angels*** is the gritty story of an African American private who finds himself in an atmosphere of violence, prejudice, and fear—yet somehow manages to form lasting friendships through it all.

This title is available in the HRW Library.

NONFICTION

Vietnam Legacy

The Vietnam Veterans Memorial in Washington, D.C., is a place of remembrance for thousands of people who lost a loved one in the Vietnam War. Heartfelt letters, poems, and notes appear at the granite wall each year—some mourning a death, others celebrating a life. Journalist Laura Palmer tracked down the authors of these tributes and asked them to share more memories about the missing and the dead. The end product is ***Shrapnel in the Heart: Letters and Remembrances from the Vietnam Veterans Memorial,*** a moving book that gives faces and stories to the names engraved on the wall.

Read On

For Independent Reading

If students enjoyed the themes and topics explored in this chapter, you might recommend these titles for independent reading.

Assessment Options

The following projects can help you evaluate and assess your students' outside reading. Videotapes or audiotapes of completed projects may be included in student portfolios.

- **Create comic strips.** Have students of mixed abilities create comic strips that depict scenes from *The King Must Die* or *Acts of King Arthur and His Noble Knights.* The group should agree on the scenes to depict. Some students can lay out the action for each panel, others can compose the dialogue, and those with artistic ability can draw the scenes.
- **Compare and contrast.** How is the Theseus of *The King Must Die* like and unlike the Theseus in Edith Hamilton's retelling of the myth? How are Steinbeck's Arthur and Launcelot like and unlike the characters students have already encountered in this chapter? Ask students who have read *The King Must Die* or *The Acts of King Arthur* to compare and contrast the different versions of these heroes for the class.
- **Keep a journal.** If Richard Parry had kept a journal, what would he have written? Students who have read *Fallen Angels* or any of the other novels can take the role of a character and capture his or her thoughts and feelings in the form of journal entries.
- **Design a medal or award.** Invite students who have read *Shrapnel in the Heart* to choose one special person to honor. Ask them to design a medal or award for the person and to write a speech of tribute. You may wish to hold a memorial for the heroes of the Vietnam War, and have each student give his or her speech and display the medal or award.

Toward Reading Two Million Words Annually

Estimated Word Counts and Reading Levels of Read On Books:

Fiction	Level	Words	Nonfiction	Level	Words
*The King Must Die**	above grade level	150,500	*Shrapnel in the Heart: Letters and Remembrances from the Vietnam Veterans Memorial*	at grade level	112,900
The Acts of King Arthur and His Noble Knights	at grade level	129,500			
*Fallen Angels**	below grade level	42,100			

***California Reading List Titles**

KEY: ⬆ *above grade level* ⬌ *at grade level* ⬇ *below grade level*

Writing a Research Paper

Writing Assignment
Writing 2.3 Write a research paper of at least 1,500 words in which you present and document information about the historical or biographical background of a literary topic.

What is the historical background for Sigurd, the heroic character in Norse mythology? Why is Medea's nationality important in the Greek account of King Theseus? Is the figure of King Arthur based on a historical person? Finding the answers to these questions means you may have to dig for information—or do **research.** Doing research is the process by which you uncover treasures; that is, you unearth information that will help you answer complex questions like the ones above. Just as treasure hunters show off their finds, in this workshop you will also share your discoveries with others in a research paper.

Prewriting

go.hrw.com

GO TO: go.hrw.com
KEYWORD: HLLA 10-9
FOR: Professional Model, Writer's Guides, and Reference Sources

Choose a Subject and Refine a Topic

When, What, or Who? The task—selecting a subject based on the historical or biographical background of a literary topic—at first may seem overwhelming, when you consider the amount of literature and history available. To help you find a direction for your investigation, consider the following areas for research.

- a historical event depicted in literature—for example, the Vietnam War used as background in a short story by Tim O'Brien
- a historical figure appearing in literature—such as Julius Caesar, dramatized in Shakespeare's *Julius Caesar*
- an author's interests as revealed through literature—for example, Emily Dickinson's interest in nature as shown in her poems
- the background of a piece of literature—such as a description of the Norse culture that created the myth of Sigurd

Scout It Out After you have selected an area for research, scout out possible subjects by browsing through your textbook, your school's library, or a bookstore. Skim newspapers and magazines for mention of connections between history and literature. Watch documentaries or films that explore biographical or historical connections between a piece of literature and the writer's world. Pick a search engine and search the Internet for key references to literature and history or biography. Then, choose a subject to research.

Survey the Landscape Once you've chosen a subject, get an overview of its possibilities by looking for the kinds of information

Writing 2.0 Students produce texts of at least 1,500 words each. **2.3** Write expository compositions, including analytical essays and research reports.

PRETEACHING

Standards Starter

Motivate. Have students brainstorm lists of everyday questions (for example, the location of a business or how much a CD costs) that they have answered during the past week by using research methods. Have students explain how they found the answers to their questions (for example, calling information, using the phone book, searching on the World Wide Web). Point out that students will be using similar types of strategies as they complete this workshop.

Resources Reminder

To introduce the workshop, you may want to use the journal starters in *Writing, Listening, & Speaking* Teaching Notes.

DIRECT TEACHING

Choose a Subject and Define a Topic

Please be aware that Internet resources are sometimes public forums and that their content may be unpredictable.

CHAPTER 9 RESOURCES: WRITING

Writing Workshop

Planning

- *On Course: Mapping Instruction*
- *One-Stop Planner* CD-ROM
- *At Home: A Guide to Standards Mastery,* p. 23
- *At Home: In Spanish*
- *Writing, Listening, & Speaking,* Teaching Notes, p. 92

Differentiating Instruction

- *Lesson Plans for Language Development,* pp. 309–310
- *Supporting Instruction in Spanish*

Practice

- *Writing, Listening, & Speaking,* Ch. 9

690 Chapter 9 Biographical and Historical Approach • Using Primary and Secondary Sources

available on it. Then, you can telescope in on a topic that you can manage. For example, one student who began with "King Arthur" as a possible subject narrowed her subject to the topic "the development of the legend of King Arthur." Here are some ideas for narrowing your broad subject to a more specific topic.

- **Read two or three general articles** about your subject in reference books such as encyclopedias. Notice headings and subheadings in the articles and consider using one of these as the topic of your paper.
- **Search the World Wide Web** for pages or sites containing key words related to your subject.
- **Look up your subject** in the *Readers' Guide to Periodical Literature* or in your library's card catalog or online catalog. Note the topics listed under subject headings.
- **Discuss your subject with someone** (a teacher or librarian, for example) who might have knowledge about it. See if your discussion gives you ideas for narrowing your subject.

Think About Purpose, Audience, and Tone

Setting Out on Your Mission . . . The basic **purpose** of a research paper is expository, or informational. As you research your topic, you'll uncover information and develop your own ideas about it. When you write your paper, you'll explain what you've learned.

As you plan your research, consider the needs and interests of your potential **audience**—your readers. To help your readers understand your topic, ask yourself, "What might my readers already know about the topic? How might I increase their understanding?" Make some notes about responses you could make to their questions. Keep in mind that your readers may already have some **expectations** about your topic, especially if you have chosen one as well known as King Arthur. If your research uncovers new ideas about the topic, you will want to address any **potential misunderstandings** that your readers may have.

Think also about your **tone**—your attitude toward your topic and readers. The typical research paper is formal in tone; that is, you'll use third-person pronouns, such as *he, she,* and *they,* to reflect your objective stance. You'll also avoid casual and informal language, such as slang, colloquial expressions, and contractions, to maintain a formal tone.

Develop Research Questions

Where Are You Going Next? Remember that a research paper should ask and answer good questions. Before you look for

Writing 1.0 The writing demonstrates students' awareness of the audience and purpose. **1.3** Use clear research questions and suitable research methods to elicit and present evidence from primary and secondary sources. **2.3e** Anticipate and address readers' potential misunderstandings and expectations.

DIFFERENTIATING INSTRUCTION

English-Language Learners

You may want to encourage students to choose a topic related to their native countries. For example, they might research authors or particular literary forms native to their home countries. This strategy reinforces the links between students and their native cultures and offers them topics that may be of personal interest.

Resources Reminder

For more help with English-Language Learners, see *Lesson Plans for Language Development.*

CRITICAL THINKING

To help students analyze the various uses of purpose, audience, and tone, you may want to provide articles both from magazines written primarily to entertain and from magazines written primarily to inform. Have students skim the articles, looking for clues that illustrate the purpose, audience, and tone of each article. For example, the tone of an entertainment magazine is likely to be less formal than that of a newsmagazine.

DIRECT TEACHING

Think About Purpose, Audience, and Tone

You may want to remind students that there is more than one form in which to present research. For example, professional writers sometimes choose colloquial language or a less formal tone for effect. Some forms may be more appropriate depending on students' purpose and audience. Remind students that a more formal tone is more appropriate for them, particularly if their writing will have an adult audience (such as a teacher).

Reinforcement

- *Daily Language Activities*

Evaluation and Assessment

- *Test Generator (One-Stop Planner* CD-ROM)
- *Progress Assessment of Writing, Listening, & Speaking,* Ch. 9
- *Diagnostic and Summative Assessments,* End-of-Year Test

Internet

- go.hrw.com (keyword: HLLA 10-9)
- Online assessments at go.hrw.com (keyword: HLLA)

DIRECT TEACHING

Integrating with Grammar, Usage, and Mechanics

As students begin their research papers, they may have trouble with spelling and with writing effective sentences. You may want to review these chapters in the *Holt Handbook.*

information on your topic, jot down some specific questions to explore. Working with a list of **research questions** will make it easier for you to sort through the information you find. Look at the following questions one student asked about her topic.

- Who is the real King Arthur, and how did the stories about him develop?
- Were the Knights of the Round Table real people? How did the Quest for the Holy Grail come to be a part of the story?
- Have the stories about King Arthur always been the same, or have they changed?

Answer Research Questions

Looking for Answers The first step in finding information on your topic is knowing where to look. The following chart lists some library and community resources you can use to get started on your research investigation.

Quick guide!

LIBRARY AND COMMUNITY RESOURCES

Resource	Source of Information
Card catalog or online catalog	Books listed by title, author, and subject (most libraries also list audiovisual materials)
***Readers' Guide to Periodical Literature* or *National Newspaper Index* (online and print versions)**	Subject and author index to magazine and journal articles; index to major newspapers
Microfilm or microfiche	Indexes to major newspapers such as *The LA Times,* back issues of newspapers and magazines
General reference books or CD-ROMs	Encyclopedias, encyclopedia yearbooks, dictionaries
Specialized reference books or CD-ROMs	Biographical reference sources, encyclopedias of special subjects, atlases, almanacs
Videotapes and audiotapes	Movies, documentaries, filmstrips, audiotapes of books
The librarian	Help in finding and using sources
World Wide Web and online services	Articles, interviews, bibliographies, pictures, videos, sound recordings
Museums and historical societies	Special exhibits, libraries and bookstores, experts on various subjects
Schools and colleges	Libraries, experts on various subjects

692 Chapter 9 Biographical and Historical Approach • Using Primary and Secondary Sources

Finding Different Kinds of Answers The information you find in your resources may be either primary or secondary. A **primary source** is firsthand information, such as a historical document, a letter, a speech, or an oral history. A **secondary source** contains information derived from or about a primary source, such as an encyclopedia article, a documentary, or a history book. For example, the student researching King Arthur found primary source information in the various legends of King Arthur and secondary source information in books and articles about the legends.

Weighing Different Kinds of Answers Sometimes you'll have to judge the relative value and significance of information. To determine what information to include in your research, ask yourself, "Is the information from a *reliable* source? Is the information *relevant* to my limited topic? Is the information *recently* published?"

Record Information

Who Said What? Keeping track of all your sources is essential for giving credit within your paper as well as for preparing the *Works Cited* list that accompanies your final version. For each of the sources you find, record the author, title, publication information, and location on an index card (sometimes called a bibliography card) or sheet of paper or in a computer file. Then, assign each source a number. The following example shows how one student listed source information on an index card.

TIP The *Works Cited* list includes all the sources that you refer to in your paper; it allows readers a quick way to find out all the publication information about the specific sources.

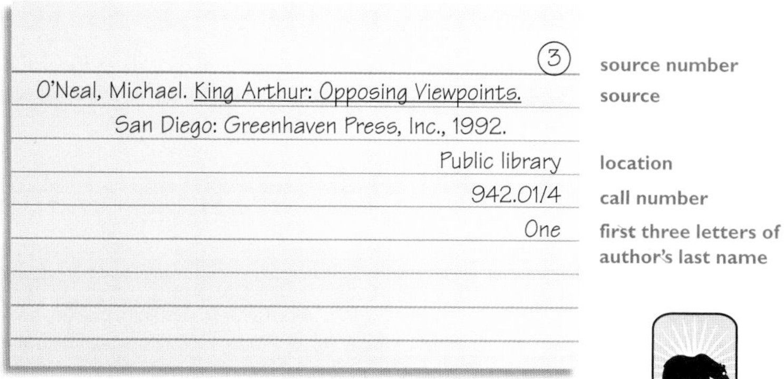

The format for recording source information shown above and on the following pages is the one recommended by the **Modern Language Association of America (MLA).** Your teacher may ask you to use a different format, such as that of the **American Psychological Association (APA).** Be sure you know which format your teacher requires. Then, follow the style conventions of the required format for all your documentation.

Writing 1.7 Use appropriate conventions for documentation in the text, notes, and bibliographies by adhering to those in style manuals. **2.3b** Convey information and ideas from primary and secondary sources accurately and coherently. **2.3c** Make distinctions between the relative value and significance of specific data, facts, and ideas.

MODELING AND DEMONSTRATION

Who Said What?

Model the process of creating a bibliography card for students. Select a magazine article, and show students where to find the author's name, the title, and the publication information. Using the chart on pp. 694–695, show students how to record the source information accurately. Then, have a volunteer demonstrate understanding by selecting a book and placing the correct information on the chalkboard or overhead projector. Remind students to refer to the chart on these pages as they fill out their source cards.

Writing Workshop: Writing a Research Paper 693

RETEACHING

GRADE-LEVEL STANDARD

Helpful Signs Along the Way

If students have difficulty understanding the importance of recording source information accurately, have them follow the steps below.

1. Whisper a one-sentence message to a student on one side of the room.
2. Have that student whisper it to the next student in the row or line.
3. Continue until each student has heard the message.
4. Ask the last student to speak the message aloud.

The message will probably be greatly distorted from the original. Explain that even a small error can become magnified, especially as students copy information from an original source to a note card to a rough draft, which will hinder others from locating the sources on their own.

Helpful Signs Along the Way Record information from your sources accurately—not only for yourself but also for your readers. If you have included complete information from your sources, then your readers will be able to do research into your topic themselves. The following guidelines tell you how to record information from different types of sources for a *Works Cited* list. Use this guide to help you complete your own *Works Cited* list.

GUIDELINES FOR RECORDING SOURCE INFORMATION

1. **Source by One Author.** Write the author's or editor's last name first (follow the names of editors with a comma and the abbreviation *ed.*); the title of the book; the place of publication; the publishing company's name; and the year of publication. (To make it easier to locate a book later, put its call number in the lower right-hand part of the index card, paper, or computer file.)

   Day, David. The Search for King Arthur. New York: Facts on File, 1995.

2. **Source by More Than One Author.** For the first listed author, write the last name first. For all other authors, write the first name first. Then, follow the format for books with one author to complete the record.

   Matthews, John, and Michael J. Stead. King Arthur's Britain: A Photographic Odyssey. New York: Sterling, 1995.

3. **Magazine or Newspaper Article.** Write the author's name (if given), last name first; the title of the article; the name of the magazine or newspaper; the day (if given), month, and year of publication; and page numbers on which the article begins and ends. For an article in a newspaper that has different editors or multiple sections, specify the editions (use *ed.*) or sections before the page number.

   Menon, Shanti. "King Arthnou was here." Discover. Jan. 1999: 30.

4. **Encyclopedia Article.** Write the author's name (if given), last name first; the title of the article; the name of the encyclopedia; the edition (if given); and the year of publication. (Use the abbreviation *ed.* for *edition.*)

   Reiss, Edmund. "Arthur, King." The World Book Encyclopedia. 2001 ed.

5. **Radio or TV Program.** Write the program title; the name of the network; the call letters and city of the local station (if any); and the broadcast date.

   ABC Nightly News. ABC. KABC, Los Angeles. 14 June 2001.

6. **Movie or Video Recording.** Write the title of the work (and other pertinent information) and the director or producer's name (use *Dir.* for *Director* and *Prod.* for *Producer*); for movies, write the original distributor's name (for movies not available on video) and the year of release; for video recordings, write the word *Videocassette* or *Videodisc,* the distributor's name, and the year the video recording was released.

   Le Morte D'Arthur: The Legend of the King. Great Books Ser. Dir. Dale Minor. Videocassette. Discovery Communications, 1993.

7. **Interview.** Write the interviewee's name, last name first; the type of interview (personal or telephone, for example); and the day, month, and year of the interview.

   Morris, Sandy. Telephone interview. 22 June 2001.

694 Chapter 9 Biographical and Historical Approach • Using Primary and Secondary Sources

8. CD-ROM. Write the author's name (if given), last name first; title (include print publisher, date, and page numbers if material was first in a print source); the term *CD-ROM;* city (if given); distributor; date of publication.

"Arthurian Legend." Compton's Interactive Encyclopedia. 1998 ed. CD-ROM. Compton's NewMedia, Inc. 1995.

9. Online Source. Write the author's name (if given), last name first; title of work; title of the site; volume number, issue number, or other identifying number; posting date; name of any institution or organization associated with the site; date of access; and Internet address.

Snell, Melissa. "The Truth of Arthur." Medieval History. 1999. About.com Inc. 21 June 2001 <http://historymedren.about.com/library/weekly/aa031099.htm>.

Words, Words, Words Begin gathering information by skimming a source. Look over the Table of Contents, or browse through the Index. Use self-adhesive notes or slips of paper to mark pages with answers to your research questions. Bookmark Web sites that look promising. Then, take notes using the following techniques.

DO THIS

- A **direct quotation** uses the author's exact words. Copy the material word for word, and put quotation marks around it.
- A **paraphrase** restates a passage from the source in your own words, with your own sentence structure. Your restatement is about the same length as the original.
- A **summary** is a highly condensed passage—usually one fourth to one third the length of the original—in which you record only the most important ideas from the source.

The following is an example of how one student practiced using the three techniques in taking notes from a passage in John Matthews and Michael J. Stead's book *King Arthur's Britain: A Photographic Odyssey.*

Direct quotation: "It is not possible to state, with any final certainty, whether or not such a person called Arthur ever lived. If he did, he most certainly was not a king, did not wear shining armour, and in all probability was not accompanied by a band of noble knights who sat together at a round table."

Paraphrase: Scholars don't know for sure whether Arthur was a real person, but they are almost positive that the real Arthur was not a king. He probably didn't even wear a suit of armor or go to battle with the Knights of the Round Table.

Summary: If a real Arthur did actually live, he probably was not the popular King Arthur most people think of today.

Writing 2.3b Convey information and ideas from primary and secondary sources accurately and coherently.

TECHNOLOGY TIP

Students using CD-ROM or online sources should record the source on the copy of the article immediately after printing the article. Finding the source material later may be difficult without this information. For example, some Web sites may be unavailable at a later date.

You need to be aware that Internet resources are sometimes public forums and that their content may be unpredictable.

DIRECT TEACHING

REVIEW STANDARD

Words, Words, Words

Suggest that, as they paraphrase material, students read a sentence and then cover it with a sheet of paper while paraphrasing. Often, students find it easier to be original if they work from memory rather than look at the actual material.

Writing Workshop: Writing a Research Paper 695

DIFFERENTIATING INSTRUCTION

GRADE-LEVEL STANDARD

Advanced Learners

Enrichment. Encourage students to think about why using someone else's words or ideas without giving them credit, an act called plagiarism, is a serious academic offense. Provide this example:

> A researcher uses her co-worker's ideas to help her discover a cure for a disease. The researcher publishes her findings but does not give her co-worker credit for his ideas.

Students may say that by not giving her co-worker credit, the researcher has effectively "stolen" his ideas. Students may liken this behavior to cheating. Point out that if the researcher had given her co-worker credit for his ideas by mentioning his name in her article, she would not have been plagiarizing.

Learners Having Difficulty

Some students may be more successful assessing their note cards in this way: After they have organized their note cards into subject piles, point out that they should have relatively equal "piles" of note cards for each of their major headings. If students find that one of their piles contains few note cards, encourage them to rethink their organizational plan or to do more research to ensure adequate support for each idea.

TIP Unless you want to quote a source directly, always take notes in your own words. To avoid plagiarism, a serious academic offense, always credit your sources—even when restating the author's ideas.

Card Collecting As you write down direct quotations, paraphrases, and summaries from your sources, you gather facts and details—the **evidence** that you will use as you begin to develop your ideas. To keep track of all the information you gather when you take notes, use a separate note card, sheet of paper, or computer file for each item of information. Make a heading at the top of the card by recording a key word or phrase about the information, and write down the source number. Write the direct quotation, paraphrase, or summary, and be sure to include the page number. The following shows a note card one student made about the Saxon invasions into Britain, events that led to Arthur's leadership.

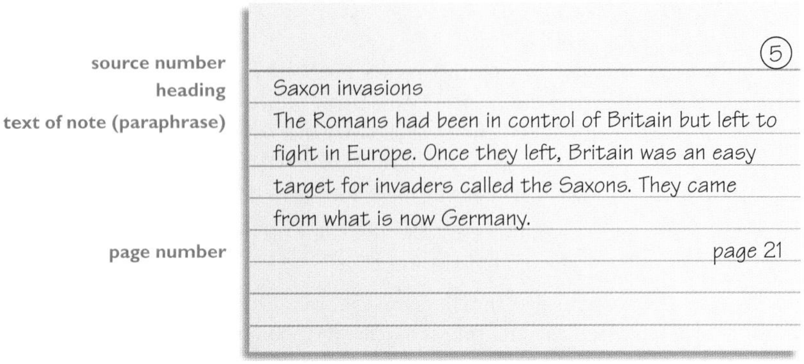

Analyze the Information

Weighing the Differences Now, analyze the information you've gathered. Begin by separating your note cards, using the headings to group all cards with similar information. As you sort through your research information, you may find that some sources disagree about issues or facts or that some of the information you've collected may be surprising to you and your readers. For example, the student writing about Arthur discovered that Arthur is not considered an exclusively English hero and that some scholars in fact disagree on whether Arthur was a real person.

To give an accurate picture of the complexity of your topic, follow these steps.

1. **Bring together—or *synthesize*—all the information from the multiple sources you've consulted.** Look over your information, and compare the sources' interpretations of your topic. Look for ways that your sources agree on the facts and details of your research and for ways they disagree.
2. **Identify different interpretations about any significant points of your research.** Mentioning the differing points of view about your topic shows that you have been an objective investigator.

Writing 1.4 Develop the main ideas within the body of the composition through supporting evidence. **1.5** Synthesize information from multiple sources and identify complexities and discrepancies in the information and the different perspectives found in each medium.

696 Chapter 9 Biographical and Historical Approach • Using Primary and Secondary Sources

3. **Explain the importance of each interpretation.** In your explanation, you may offer your judgment about which interpretation seems most valuable or accurate to you. You should also explain why and how you arrived at that conclusion.

Write a Thesis Statement

What's It All About? The thesis statement for a research paper states your main idea about your topic and lets your readers know what main points you plan to cover. You may first draft a preliminary thesis statement that acts as a guidepost, and then revise your thesis, perhaps more than once, as you continue shaping your paper. The writer who chose "the development of the legend of King Arthur" for a topic drafted this preliminary thesis statement based on her research findings.

> Legends about King Arthur developed because of history, storytellers, and writers who changed the story.

Organize Your Ideas

In an Orderly Fashion Review your notes, and divide them into different groups based on the headings of your note cards. Arrange the cards within each group according to your main idea and main points. Sorting your notes in this way helps you organize your main points and plan how you will support your thesis statement with your research and evidence. To show adequate development for each idea, use a coherent order by following one of the methods below or a combination of all three methods.

- **Chronological order** gives events in the order they happen.
- **Logical order** groups related ideas together.
- **Order of importance** begins with the most important detail and moves to the least important (or the reverse).

Sometimes you may need to include complicated material in your research paper. In order to maintain a coherent organization, consider using **visuals** such as charts, maps, and graphs in your paper to present information that is technical or complicated. Provide a key to explain any technical terms or notations on your visuals.

Where's the Map? An outline is like a map for your research paper. It helps you see where your paper is headed and how you'll get there. A **formal outline** is divided into main points and subpoints, and is strictly balanced. Use the groups of cards that you have sorted as a basis for developing your outline. Look at the following example from an outline developed for a student's research paper on the legend of King Arthur.

Writing 2.3a Marshal evidence in support of a thesis and related claims, including information on all relevant perspectives. **2.3d** Include visual aids by employing appropriate technology to organize and record information on charts, maps, and graphs. **2.3f** Use technical terms and notations accurately.

DIRECT TEACHING

Write a Thesis Statement

These three steps can help students as they draft their thesis statements:

1. Review the information you have gathered, especially the main ideas on each note card.
2. Think about what possible approaches your notes suggest.
3. Draw conclusions by writing a sentence that concisely illustrates the approach supported by the information in your notes.

By following these steps, students can develop thesis statements like this.

> Although the politics and technology depicted in *Ender's Game* might seem unrealistic, Orson Scott Card's descriptions of human actions, thoughts, and feelings ring remarkably true.

Organize Your Ideas

As students plan their reports, have them use a visual organizer such as the one below to help them shape their body paragraphs.

Subtopic:
#1 Support:
Conclusion:
Conclusion:
#2 Support:
Conclusion:
Conclusion:
Concluding Sentence:

Writing Workshop: Writing a Research Paper 697

DIFFERENTIATING INSTRUCTION

Learners Having Difficulty

If students find creating a formal outline daunting, you may want to have them create a working outline first, which will allow them to arrange details in groups without using numbers or letters. Have students follow these steps:

- Use the key word or phrase from each note card to group all notes with similar information.
- Use the key words or phrases as the main section headings of the informal outline.
- Order the ideas within each group of cards, and write them down as subsection headings.
- Determine which supporting details to include, and list them under the subsection headings.

When their notes are organized satisfactorily, students can create a formal outline from the working outline.

DIRECT TEACHING

Credit Your Sources

Determining when to give credit to a source may be difficult for some students. To help them distinguish between common knowledge and material that should be credited, give students these examples. Ask them to determine whether the material should be credited or not.

1. George Washington was the first president of the United States. [common knowledge]
2. Cancer is the second-leading cause of death in children under fourteen years of age. [material that should be credited]
3. There is enough concrete in Hoover Dam to pave a standard highway, sixteen feet wide, from San Francisco to New York City. [material that should be credited]
4. The United States has a representative form of government. [common knowledge]

TIP The outline shows that the third main point is "Key writers." That main point will include at least four paragraphs to cover the subpoints listed next to the capital letters.

III. Key writers
  A. Geoffrey of Monmouth
    1. Created The History of the Kings of Britain
    2. Established medieval time period for legend
  B. French writers
    1. Altered legend and translated into French (Robert Wace)
    2. Introduced chivalry and courtly love (Chrétien de Troyes)
  C. Cistercian monks
    1. Rearranged legend chronologically in The Vulgate Cycle
    2. Introduced Sir Galahad
  D. Sir Thomas Malory
    1. Changed legend again to focus on adventure
    2. Created epic masterpiece Le Morte D'Arthur

Credit Your Sources

Credit Where Credit Is Due When you draft your essay, you need to give credit to any writer from whose work you have gathered specific information. The challenge is deciding when and how to do this. The following questions and answers should help you.

TIP Some teachers prefer **footnotes** (citations placed at the bottom of the same page on which they occur). Some prefer **endnotes** (citations identical to footnotes, but gathered at the end of the paper).

- **When?** Give credit for specific data (facts, dates, and so on), original ideas, opinions, insights, or any other information that you found in the work of another writer.
- **How?** Give credit within the body of your paper using MLA-style parenthetical citations, like those in the chart on the next page, unless your teacher gives you other directions.

Parenthetical citations are simply credits given within parentheses immediately following borrowed information. For example, the sentence below includes a parenthetical citation.

> The Saxon attacks, along with those of other invaders, devastated the civilization of Britain (Day 11–12).

Writing 1.6 Integrate quotations and citations into a written text while maintaining the flow of ideas. **1.7** Use appropriate conventions for documentation in the text, notes, and bibliographies by adhering to those in style manuals. **2.3b** Convey information and ideas from primary and secondary sources accurately and coherently.

You need to give only enough information in the parenthetical citation to enable the reader to find the full citation on the *Works Cited* page and to show exactly where in that source you found the information. (A *Works Cited* list that refers to books only is called a *Bibliography*.)

The chart on the next page provides specific guidelines for citing sources within your report, using MLA-style parenthetical citations.

698 Chapter 9 Biographical and Historical Approach • Using Primary and Secondary Sources

GUIDELINES FOR GIVING CREDIT WITHIN A PAPER

Quick guide

Place the information in parentheses at the end of the sentence in which you used someone else's words or ideas.

1. **Source with one author.** Author's last name followed by page number(s). (Andronik 12)
2. **Sources by authors with the same last name.** First initial and last name of each author followed by page number(s). (J. Smith 38) and (L. Smith 72)
3. **Source with more than one author.** All authors' last names followed by page number(s). (Matthews and Stead 11)
4. **Source with no author given.** Title or a shortened form of it and page number(s). ("Arthur the King" 48)
5. **One-page source, unpaginated source, CD-ROM or online source, or article from an encyclopedia or other work arranged alphabetically.** Author's name only. If no author's name is given, title only. (Alexander)
6. **More than one source by the same author.** Author's last name and the title or shortened form of it followed by page number(s). (Ashe, "The Legend" 7; Ashe, "King Arthur" 23)
7. **Author's name given in paragraph.** Page number only. (144)
8. **Indirect source.** *Qtd. in* ("quoted in") before the source and page number. (qtd. in O'Neal 49)

Identifying Sources You will list on a *Works Cited* page all those sources whose words or ideas you used in your paper. To prepare the *Works Cited* page, refer to the guidelines on pages 694–695 that you followed for preparing source cards. In addition, also use the following basic guidelines.

1. **Center the words *Works Cited*** one inch from the top. Use a separate sheet of paper for your *Works Cited* list.
2. **Follow the format** you used in listing the source on your source cards (page 693) for each entry on your *Works Cited* list.
3. **List your sources alphabetically** by authors' last names. If no author is given, alphabetize by the first important word in the title.
4. **Begin each listing at the left margin** and **indent all other lines** for the same listing one-half inch, or five spaces if you are using a computer. Remember to double-space each entry.

Writing 1.7 Use appropriate conventions for documentation in the text, notes, and bibliographies by adhering to those in style manuals.

DIRECT TEACHING

Guidelines for Giving Credit Within a Paper

Explain to students that a primary source may be included in another primary source or a secondary source. If the student uses or quotes this sort of primary source—for example, a letter from Thomas Jefferson quoted in a biography about him—he or she is actually using an indirect source for the citation and therefore must use "qtd. in."

Writing Workshop: Writing a Research Paper 699

Integrate Direct Quotations into Your Paper

And I Quote . . . Using direct quotations in your research paper adds credibility to your writing. However, be sure to avoid using too many long quotations. If you overuse quotations, your paper will look like a cut-and-paste version of other authors' works. In the following example, one student experimented with various ways to weave quotations from Michael O'Neal's book *King Arthur: Opposing Viewpoints* into a paper.

- Use a phrase or a clause within the sentence and enclose it in quotation marks.

> O'Neal says the book was the "first organized version" of Arthur's life and victories (39).

- Include a short quotation (four lines or less) with your own words. Enclose the quotation within quotation marks.

> According to O'Neal, "Geoffrey devotes about one-fifth of his book to Arthur" (39).

- Set off a long quotation (more than four typed lines) by indenting each line ten spaces from the left margin, or one inch if you are using a computer. Introduce it in your own words, followed by a colon. Do not use quotation marks.

> The book The History of the Kings of Britain focuses extensively on Arthur:
>
> > Geoffrey devotes about one-fifth of his book to Arthur. In contrast to the piecemeal accounts of traveling storytellers, Geoffrey provides the first organized version of the story, giving it a beginning, middle, and end. Many of the elements found in later Arthurian legends, however, are missing (O'Neal 39).

Writing 1.6 Integrate quotations and citations into a written text while maintaining the flow of ideas.

PRACTICE & APPLY 1 Use the information above to select a topic and research sources. Be sure to take notes and analyze the information. Then, write a thesis statement and develop an outline, organizing the information for a research paper.

PRACTICE & APPLY 1

Guided and Independent Practice

Before they proceed with their research, guide students by making sure they have:

- Chosen a general subject and gained an overview of it
- Narrowed the subject to a suitable, refined topic
- Considered purpose, audience, and tone
- Compiled a list of research questions to direct their research

Conference with students individually as they complete these steps. Help them develop research questions if they have not done so. Then, have them complete **Practice and Apply 1** as independent practice.

RESOURCES: WRITING

Practice & Apply 1

Guided Practice

- *Writing, Listening, & Speaking,* WS. pp. 93, 94, 95

Reteaching and Modeling

- *Writing, Listening, & Speaking,* TP. 14
- *Writing, Listening, & Speaking,* WS. p. 96

700 Chapter 9 Biographical and Historical Approach • Using Primary and Secondary Sources

Writing

Writing a Research Paper

A Writer's Framework

Introduction

- Create interest in your topic with an attention getter.
- Include a thesis statement that states your main idea about your topic and includes your main points.
- Indicate the order in which you will present your main points about the topic.
- Include background information, if necessary.

Body

- Develop each main point from your outline with subpoints in separate body paragraphs.
- Support each main point and subpoint with facts and details in the form of direct quotations, paraphrases, and summaries.
- Synthesize the different perspectives found in the research.
- Integrate quotations and citations smoothly.

Conclusion

- Summarize the main points of your research.
- Restate your thesis in a new way.
- Leave readers with an insight or a dramatic statement related to your topic.

A Writer's Model

A Legend Is Born

Stories of King Arthur and his glorious kingdom of Camelot have been enchanting listeners for over 1,000 years. Scholars still cannot agree, however, whether Arthur was a real person. Most scholars believe that if a real Arthur lived, "he most certainly was not a king, did not wear shining armour, and in all probability was not accompanied by a band of noble knights who sat together at a round table" (Matthews and Stead 11). Yet an elaborate and enduring legend developed around Arthur by the combination of a bit of history, a strong oral tradition, and writers who picked up and expanded the story.

The legend has many forms and variations, but the story that readers recognize tells of a young boy who pulls a sword from a stone, becomes king, forms a fellowship of knights known as the Round Table, and lives in a kingdom called Camelot with his queen Guinevere and his advisor, the wizard Merlin. Arthur's knights devote themselves to good deeds and to the quest of finding the Holy Grail. Trouble befalls the kingdom when one of Arthur's closest knights,

INTRODUCTION
Attention getter
Direct quotation
Source with two authors
Thesis statement
Background information: Paraphrase
Summary

(continued)

Writing Workshop: Writing a Research Paper **701**

TECHNOLOGY TIP

Point out to students that the writer of this model defined terms that might be unfamiliar to the typical reader: *Britons, Celts,* and *Saxons.* Students should do the same in their papers. If online or CD-ROM dictionaries are available, have students use them to define technical terms.

You need to be aware that Internet resources are sometimes public forums and that their content may be unpredictable.

(continued)

Lancelot, falls in love with Guinevere and Arthur is betrayed by Mordred, his rebellious son. Betrayal of loyalty and trust destroy Camelot and its golden age in a great final battle between Arthur and Mordred (Alexander).

Online source

BODY

First main point: History

The historical foundation for the Arthurian legend comes from the struggles of the people of Britain against first the Romans and then the Saxons. The Britons, as the people in Britain were known, came to appreciate the culture and protection that the Romans brought to their land during their long occupation (Andronik 5, 19). The Britons were from a race of Celtic people that had occupied the island of Britain for 1,000 years, but who in the first century A.D. thought of themselves as both Roman and Christian (Day 10). However, when the Roman soldiers began leaving Britain to fight for the Roman Empire in Europe, the Britons, or Celts as they were also called, were vulnerable to attack by Saxon invaders, who came from an area now called Germany (Andronik 21). The Saxon attacks, along with those of other invaders, devastated the civilization of Britain (Day 11–12).

Source with one author

Summary

Desperate not to lose their way of life and their land, the Britons fought back, and in a decisive battle around 500 A.D. at Badon Hill, a military leader named Arthur—veteran of thirteen battles against the Saxons—led the Britons to victory. Their land and their culture had been saved, thanks to the military prowess of Arthur. The victory led to a period of peace (Alexander). Historians and writers disagree about how long the period of peace lasted. While writer David Day reports that this golden time lasted three decades (15), historian Michael O'Neal lists it as fifty years (32), and writer Caroline Alexander reports that it was forty. No matter how long it was, this time of peace meant the Britons were no longer under Roman rule nor under attack by invaders. For the Britons, "It was their heroic age and Arthur was their greatest hero" (Day 15).

Discussion of different interpretations

Evaluating comment

Second main point: Oral tradition

This tiny historical seed, which may or may not be accurate, was watered and nurtured by the oral tradition. Andronik points out that very few people could read or write during the time of the Dark Ages, roughly 400–800 A.D., but that "the oral tradition was very strong among the Celts" (5–6). When Britain finally succumbed to Anglo-Saxon rule, many Celts fled overland to Wales and overseas to Europe. There they told stories and sang songs for centuries about their great leader, Arthur (Alexander). O'Neal explains that as England and France came out of the Dark Ages, the aristocrats

Direct quotation

Author named in sentence

702 Chapter 9 Biographical and Historical Approach • Using Primary and Secondary Sources

became hungry for learning and history (14). This hunger was satisfied by traveling storytellers, or minstrels, who told stories called "The Matter of Britain," which recapped Arthur's great victory and Britain's golden age (O'Neal 14–15). The oral tradition, however, is prone to exaggeration, so the stories about Arthur may have been changed by storytellers to please their listeners. New details, characters, and events no doubt crept into the story, and many versions of Arthur's deeds probably existed (O'Neal 16–17).

Third main point: Key writers

Despite his popularity, Arthur may have remained a minor hero of folklore if not for key writers who picked up and changed the legend. In 1135, the Welsh monk Geoffrey of Monmouth published The History of the Kings of Britain. He transformed Arthur into a king and included a full-length account of Arthur's life:

Long quotation

> Geoffrey devotes about one-fifth of his book to Arthur. In contrast to the piecemeal accounts of traveling storytellers, Geoffrey provides the first organized version of the story, giving it a beginning, middle, and end. Many of the elements found in later Arthurian legends, however, are missing (O'Neal 39).

Most scholars agree that Geoffrey's work is not real history, but "a bizarre combination of fact and fiction" (Day 39). The hand-lettered book, however, was a huge success similar to "an international best seller . . . that put Arthur on the map" (Alexander). O'Neal says the book also "established Arthur as a prominent historical figure," giving credibility to the portrayal of Arthur as a king (39).

Geoffrey's work also established an enduring framework by setting the time period for the Arthurian legend as medieval (Snell). Although the real Arthur would have lived and conquered in the Dark Ages—some 600 years before Geoffrey's history was written—Geoffrey portrays Arthur and his court using the monk's medieval culture of the twelfth century. Arthur is "usually imagined as living in the Middle Ages, and going around in castles with knights in armour and magnificently dressed ladies. But he certainly didn't," Arthurian expert Geoffrey Ashe explains ("A Conversation"). Geoffrey of Monmouth was simply following the practice of many medieval writers, who updated settings and customs in their works ("A Conversation"). Despite its inaccuracy, the medieval setting remained a central part of Arthurian legend.

Source with no author given

French writers expanded the legend next, transforming Geoffrey's history into romances about knights in shining armor. Many of these changes were made to please an aristocratic female audience who dominated the courts of Europe (Day 113–114). The

(continued)

Writing Workshop: Writing a Research Paper 703

DIRECT TEACHING

GRADE-LEVEL STANDARDS

A Writer's Model

It may help students to see how the source information they are recording on their index cards will be used later in their research papers. Point out that the citations in the body of **A Writer's Model** on pp. 701–706 include information from the writer's source cards. Then, show students the **Works Cited** section at the end of the model. Point out that the sources in the list are the same sources that students recorded on their cards, and they should appear in the same format.

Remind students that because the information they write down on their source cards will be used later, they should record it accurately and follow the punctuation set forth in the chart on pp. 694–695.

(continued)

French poet Robert Wace translated Geoffrey's book into French and altered the original story (White xvii). According to O'Neal, Wace made his stories less violent and emphasized the pageantry of Arthur's court to appeal to the British queen Eleanor, who was French by birth (51). Even more significant, he introduced the Round Table, which immediately became a central part of Arthurian stories (White xvii; O'Neal 51).

Information found in two sources

The French poet Chrétien de Troyes made even more changes to the legend by writing romances that focused on chivalry and courtly love. Arthur became more interested in courtly pursuits than in fighting battles. In addition, the focus shifted to the Knights of the Round Table and their adventures, loves, and quests (White xviii). Chrétien's knight was "well-mannered, well-spoken, educated, generous, brave, gifted as an artist and musician, courteous and above all, without equal in battle" (Day 114). Chrétien's stories of courtly love and Arthur's knights with their "elaborate conventions of courtly love—the hidden messages, the midnight meetings, the violent emotions—provided a romantic escape" for Chrétien's patroness, Countess Marie, and her female companions (O'Neal 59–60). Chrétien's wildly popular romances produced three lasting additions to the legend: the love affair between Lancelot and Guinevere, Camelot, and the Quest for the Holy Grail (White xix, xx, 162). Although Chrétien introduced the Holy Grail, he did not say specifically what it was. That was left to another French writer, Robert De Boron, who described the Grail as the cup used by Christ during the Last Supper (O'Neal 76, 80).

Summary

The next evolution in the legend came when the French romances changed back into historical works, but this time with "a serious religious purpose" (Conlee). A group of Cistercian monks collected and arranged all the stories about Arthur and his knights into a chronological history, titled The Vulgate Cycle. The stories focus heavily on the Quest for the Holy Grail and "a great effort is made to bestow upon the events of the Arthur story a fundamentally religious purpose" (Conlee). The Vulgate Cycle introduced the knight Sir Galahad, reinforced the Christian symbolism of the Grail, and would serve as the basis for Sir Thomas Malory to create his masterpiece, Le Morte d'Arthur (Matthews and Stead 107).

Paraphrase

Thomas Malory took the vast jumble of stories in The Vulgate Cycle and peeled away everything that made the stories hard to understand (Matthews and Stead 107). He rearranged the events,

704 Chapter 9 Biographical and Historical Approach • Using Primary and Secondary Sources

focused on the drama and action, added realistic dialogue, and cut religious commentary that took away from the adventure and characters of the story (Matthews, Le Morte xvii). The result was an epic masterpiece that would ensure Arthur's popularity for centuries and serve as the "basis for all the modern versions of the story" (Andronik 12). Good timing also played a part in the success of Le Morte d'Arthur. The printing press was a new invention, and the English printer William Caxton published it in 1485, making it "one of the first printed secular books in the English language" (Day 143).

Author of more than one source

Over five hundred years after Le Morte d'Arthur was published, King Arthur and his legends remain popular. Malory's work inspired other great works by literary giants in both England and the United States, including Alfred Lord Tennyson, Sir Walter Scott, William Wordsworth, Henry Wadsworth Longfellow, Mark Twain, and T. S. Eliot (Day 163). Just as writers have done through the centuries, filmmakers have also found find new ways to portray Arthur and his kingdom. He is spoofed in Monty Python and the Holy Grail, romanticized in the Broadway musical and film Camelot, and transformed into a space cowboy in the form of Luke Skywalker in Star Wars (Le Morte). Day points out that Luke's mentor Obi-wan Kenobe is a Merlin-inspired character (60).

Videocassette

CONCLUSION

Restatement of thesis

Summarizing statement

The enduring appeal of Arthurian legend highlights both the adaptability and timelessness of the legend. Tracing the evolution of the legend shows the way the story was easily adapted and changed to fit the time, interests, and ideals of the tellers and listeners. Despite the changes, however, the basic story maintained its universal appeal by portraying the timeless themes of love, loyalty, loss, commitment to lofty ideals, and the frailty of human nature. Richard Barber says that in many ways the Arthurian legend has replaced classical myths for modern writers and readers (3). The names Arthur, Guinevere, Lancelot, and Merlin are "as familiar in our literature as the gods of ancient Greece" (Barber 3). Whatever his form and however his story is cast, King Arthur has certainly proven that he "is truly a hero for all ages" (Day 157). Long live the King!

Final insight

Writing Workshop: Writing a Research Paper 705

DIRECT TEACHING

Works Cited

Remind students that online databases can have unusual or varying capitalizations. For example, the online database in the first item under the **Works Cited** head can also appear as MasterFILE ELITE. EBSCOHost.

Works Cited

Explain to students that the capitalization of words from other languages can sometimes vary. For example, in the **Works Cited** section the title *Le Morte D'Arthur* appears with a capital D because that is how the primary source uses it. However, the title also can acceptably appear as *Le Morte d'Arthur*, as it does in **A Writer's Model.**

PRACTICE & APPLY 2

Guided and Independent Practice

Guide the writing process by reminding students to refer to **A Writer's Framework** and **A Writer's Model** on pp. 701–706 for examples of how to craft an effective paper. Walk about the classroom as students work, and help them find appropriate examples as needed. Then, have students complete **Practice and Apply 2** as independent practice.

TIP Research papers and their *Works Cited* lists are normally double-spaced. Because of limited space on these pages, A Writer's Model is single-spaced. To see a double-spaced version of a paper, go to page 509 in the *Holt Handbook*.

Works Cited

Alexander, Caroline. "A Pilgrim's Search for Relics of the Once and Future King." Smithsonian Feb. 1996: 32–41. MasterFILE Elite. EBSCOhost. Long Beach Public Library, Long Beach, CA. 28 May 2001.

Andronik, Catherine M. Quest for a King: Searching for the Real King Arthur. New York: Atheneum, 1989.

Barber, Richard. The Arthurian Legends: An Illustrated Anthology. New York: Dorset Press, 1985.

Conlee, John, ed. "Prose Merlin: Introduction." Prose Merlin. Kalamazoo, Michigan: Western Michigan University for TEAMS, 1998. TEAMS Middle English Texts. Ed. Russell Peck. The Medieval Institute at Western Michigan University. 20 June 2001 <http://www.lib.rochester.edu/camelot/teams/pmint.htm>.

"A Conversation with Geoffrey Ashe." Britannia. 23 May 2001 <http://www.britannia.com/history/arthur1html>.

Day, David. The Search for King Arthur. New York: Facts on File, 1995.

Le Morte D'Arthur: The Legend of the King. Great Books Ser. Dir. Dale Minor. Videocassette. Discovery Communications, 1993.

Matthews, John, ed. Le Morte D'Arthur. By Thomas Malory. New York: Sterling, 2000. xvi–xx.

Matthews, John, and Michael J. Stead. King Arthur's Britain: A Photographic Odyssey. New York: Sterling, 1995.

O'Neal, Michael. King Arthur: Opposing Viewpoints. San Diego: Greenhaven Press, Inc., 1992.

Snell, Melissa. "The Truth of Arthur." Medieval History. 1999. About.com Inc. 21 June 2001 <http://historymedren.about.com/library/weekly/aa031099.htm>.

White, Richard, ed. King Arthur: In Legend and History. New York: Routledge, 1998.

GO TO: go.hrw.com
KEYWORD: HLLA 10-9
FOR: Student's Model

Language Conventions 1.5 Reflect appropriate manuscript requirements, including title page presentation, pagination, spacing and margins, and integration of source and support material with appropriate citations.

PRACTICE & APPLY 2 Use the Writer's Framework and the Writer's Model as guides to draft your research paper. Remember to include a thesis statement and develop each main idea with evidence from primary and secondary sources.

RESOURCES: WRITING

Practice & Apply 2

Think Sheet

- *Writing, Listening, & Speaking*, WS. p. 97

Template

- *Writing, Listening, & Speaking*, WS. p. 98

Internet

- go.hrw.com (keyword: HLLA 10-9)

706 Chapter 9 Biographical and Historical Approach • Using Primary and Secondary Sources

Revising

Evaluate and Revise Your Draft

Read and Read Again You might think at this point in the writing process that you've been shuffling information from pile to pile and from paragraph to paragraph. You probably need to step back and let your paper rest a day, if possible, so that you can look at it again with new insight. After all, you've made a great effort to be accurate in your research. Now check for accuracy in your writing. To make sure that your efforts show themselves in the best light, read your draft at least twice. The first time, focus on content and organization. The second time, concentrate on style.

PEER REVIEW

Exchange research papers with a classmate. Each of you should check to make sure that parenthetical citations document all direct quotations, paraphrases, and summaries.

First Reading: Content and Organization Use the guidelines below to help you examine the content and organization of your research paper. If you need help in answering the questions in the left-hand column, use the tips in the middle column. Then, make revisions by following the revision techniques suggested in the right-hand column.

Guidelines: Writing a Research Paper

Evaluation Questions	Tips	Revision Techniques
1 Does the introduction create interest in the topic? Does it include a clear thesis statement and the main points the paper covers?	**Bracket** the sentence(s) that may interest the reader. **Underline** the thesis statement. **Double underline** the main points.	**Add** an interesting opening sentence. **Add** a clear thesis statement. **Elaborate** by stating which main points the research paper covers.
2 Does the body of the paper develop each main point included in the thesis statement?	**Number** in the margin of the paper each main point that develops the thesis.	**Add** main points by using your own ideas or information from your sources.
3 Does the paper use direct quotations, paraphrases, or summaries to support each main point and subpoint?	**Write** ***DQ, P,*** or ***S*** in the margin to identify the kinds of information used as supporting evidence.	**Elaborate** on each point by adding direct quotations, paraphrases, or summaries from your sources.
4 Do parenthetical citations document source information within sentences or paragraphs?	**Highlight** the information inside parentheses. **Draw an arrow** to the information it documents.	**Add** parenthetical citations for any information requiring documentation.
5 Does the conclusion summarize the research, restate the paper's thesis, and include a final insight?	**Draw a wavy line** under the summary of the research. **Circle** the restatement of the thesis. **Star** the final insight.	**Add** a summary of the research, a restatement of thesis, or a final insight if any of these is missing.

DIRECT TEACHING

Guidelines: Writing a Research Paper

Advise students to use the **Guidelines** chart on this page as a think sheet by answering the questions in their notebooks. Explain that using think sheets to summarize their notes allows students to place their thoughts, observations, and questions on paper, which in turn helps improve the content and organization of their research papers.

Elaboration

Suggest that students needing to gather more information from sources make an appointment with a school librarian or media specialist. This person has been trained to assist in research needs and can help students locate information, including obscure facts.

CORRECTING MISCONCEPTIONS

Students might mistakenly attempt to remove all simple sentences from their essays, thinking that complex sentences are preferred in all cases. Stress to students that they should avoid having too many of one type of sentence, whether it be simple or complex. Sentence variety is the preferred goal.

GUIDED PRACTICE

Responding to the Revision Process

Answers

1. The three sentences were short and choppy; combining them creates smoother, more effective writing.
2. The writer added page numbers in order to document sources.
3. The writer added information to bring together the differing details and to add insight to them.

PRACTICE & APPLY 3

Independent Practice

Have pairs of students analyze the sentences in each other's papers, looking for short, choppy sentences that could be combined. To help with this activity, suggest these steps:

1. Draw a slash at the end of every sentence.
2. Make a quick visual check to find short sentences in isolation or in groups.
3. Using the guidelines on this page, determine if the sentences you have found should be revised.

Have students use feedback from this peer review to help in the revision process.

Second Reading: Style Sometimes in writing a long research paper, you may find that your sentences begin to have the same short and choppy pattern. To make your ideas flow smoothly and increase sentence variety, look for short, choppy sentences that could be combined into **complex sentences.** For example, you may add words such as *after, as, because, that,* and *when* to the beginning of a short sentence and combine it with other short sentences to form a complex sentence.

Style Guidelines

Evaluation Question	Tip	Revision Technique
Does the paper use several short, choppy sentences in a row?	**Highlight** any short sentences. **Bracket** any two or three sentences that could be combined into a complex sentence.	**Combine** short sentences into complex sentences to make sure that the ideas flow smoothly from one another.

ANALYZING THE REVISION PROCESS

Study these revisions, and answer the questions that follow.

add — *While* ^Writer David Day reports that this golden time lasted

add, combine — three decade*s (15),* ~~.~~ ~~H~~*h*istorian Michael O'Neal lists it as fifty years *(32), and*

add — Writer Caroline Alexander reports that it was forty. *No matter how long it was, this time of peace meant the Britons were no longer under Roman rule nor under attack by invaders.*

Responding to the Revision Process

1. Why did the writer combine the three sentences? What is the effect of this change?
2. What information did the writer add in parentheses? Why is the information important?
3. Why do you think the writer added information to the end of this passage?

PRACTICE & APPLY 3 Revise the content and organization of your research paper, using the guidelines on page 707. Then, use the guidelines above to see whether you need to combine choppy sentences into longer, complex ones.

708 Chapter 9 Biographical and Historical Approach • Using Primary and Secondary Sources

Publishing

Proofread and Publish Your Paper

Perfect It When the Cistercian monks were hand copying the legends of King Arthur into *The Vulgate Cycle,* they probably made a mistake or two in the transcriptions. You, however, are doing more than rote copying, and your final paper should be worthy of all the time you have spent researching and writing. Before you submit your final copy, proofread your paper, checking for errors in grammar, spelling, and mechanics.

Spread the Word After all your research, you probably are a local authority on your topic. Don't let all that work go to waste. Instead, share the results of your research with an audience, perhaps using one of the following suggestions.

- Present the results of your research to your classmates in an oral report.
- Ask a media specialist in your school if you can set up a multimedia display, showcasing the results of your research about literature.
- Find a Web site dedicated to information about literature, and ask permission to create a hyperlink to a Web publication of your research paper.
- Submit a portion of your paper to your school's literary magazine for possible publication.
- Dress as the subject of your research paper or in a costume appropriate to that time period for your literature class. In small groups, or on a panel, discuss the information you have learned.

Reflect on Your Paper

Learning from Experience You are nearing the end of a complex project requiring persistence and skill. Reflect on your experience with the research paper by answering the following questions.

- How did researching and writing about your topic affect your understanding of the literature on which it was based?
- How did researching and writing about your topic affect your understanding of the time period you chose?
- What advice would you give a student a year or two younger than you about the process you used for this kind of research paper?

PRACTICE & APPLY 4 Using the guidelines on this page, proofread, publish, and reflect on your research paper. Make sure that your parenthetical citations and your *Works Cited* list adhere to the required format.

TIP Proofreading will help ensure that your paper follows the **conventions** of standard American English. Correct any dangling modifiers—modifiers that do not clearly and sensibly modify a group of words in a sentence. For more on **dangling modifiers,** see page 224 in the *Holt Handbook.*

Writing 2.0 Student writing demonstrates a command of standard American English.

DIRECT TEACHING

Spread the Word

You need to be aware that Internet resources are sometimes public forums and that their content may be unpredictable.

Resources Reminder

For help with writing assessment, see 6 Traits—Plus 1 in the "Scales and Sample Papers" section of *Progress Assessment of Writing, Listening, & Speaking.*

PRACTICE & APPLY 4

Guided and Independent Practice

Guide the proofreading process by writing on the chalkboard the question from the third bulleted question in **Learning from Experience:** "What advice would you give a student a year or two younger than you about the process you used for this kind of research paper?" Then, brainstorm possible responses with students. Encourage them to keep useful suggestions in mind as they complete their papers. Finally, have them complete **Practice and Apply 4** as independent practice.

RESOURCES: WRITING

Practice & Apply 3

Think Sheet

- *Writing, Listening, & Speaking,* WS. p. 100

Evaluation

- *Writing, Listening, & Speaking,* WS. p. 99

Practice & Apply 4

Assessment

- *Test Generator (One-Stop Planner* CD-ROM)
- *Progress Assessment of Writing, Listening, & Speaking,* pp. 29–34, 79–82

Internet

- Online assessments at go.hrw.com (keyword: HLLA)

Writing Workshop: Writing a Research Paper 709

PRETEACHING

Motivate. Ask students to recall recent instances when they have listened to a speaker who shared information. [Possibilities include lectures, demonstrations, or political speeches.] Ask them to think about which speakers were most effective at conveying their information. What made them effective? On the chalkboard, place student responses into categories, such as *voice, visuals,* and *graphics.* Tell students to keep these points of effective delivery in mind as they prepare to deliver their research papers orally.

DIFFERENTIATING INSTRUCTION

Learners Having Difficulty

As a class, watch broadcasts of local or national news. As they watch, have students jot down notes about the different techniques the newscasters use to enhance their delivery. Afterward, lead a discussion in which students share their notes and discuss which techniques can be incorporated into their presentations.

Advanced Learners

Enrichment. Have students contact a local television station to request an interview with a news anchor. Students should seek information about how the anchor has researched various news stories and what research resources are available to television reporters. Volunteers could present their findings to the class.

Presenting Research

Speaking Assignment
Listening and Speaking 2.2
Adapt your research paper for a focused and coherent oral presentation to an audience of your classmates.

A research paper can be a complex, lengthy essay, filled with documentation. Reading a 1,500-word research paper aloud to your classmates would be a time-consuming activity, and the depth of your research might be lost on an audience with flagging interest. To adapt your research paper for an oral presentation, use the strategies in this workshop.

Adapt Your Research Paper

Your Listening Audience Generally, the **purpose** of both a written and an oral presentation of research is the same—expository, or informational. Unlike your reading audience, your listening **audience** may be your classmates, who probably have not read your research paper. Therefore, skim through your research paper and highlight any information that you think will be important to convey at the beginning of the oral presentation. Remember to catch your listening audience's attention early with an opening gambit—a clever anecdote, wise saying, or sage quote from your research.

TIP Remember to address briefly your audience's **expectations** or **misunderstandings** at the beginning of your oral presentation.

Simplify, Simplify, Simplify If you had world enough and time, presenting all the results of your research to your classmates could be sublime. However, you probably will find it necessary to limit your paper's range. Use the following suggestions about the elements of your research paper to help you make adjustments.

Thesis Statement Re-examine your thesis statement. Select the most important and most interesting main points from your thesis statement to guide you as you adapt the rest of your research paper.

Main Points Develop only one or two main points for your oral presentation, although you may briefly refer to other aspects of your topic. To supplement your presentation of your main points, to highlight the complexity of your additional research, or to convey additional information while you are speaking, consider using **visuals,** such as maps, pictures, photographs, or video clips; **graphics,** such as charts, outlines, or carefully drawn posters; or **electronic media,** such as a computer-generated presentation.

Evidence For your oral presentation, include the most important supporting evidence for each of the main points you have selected. Review your written research to determine the **relative value and significance** of your evidence. Ask yourself, "What evidence is necessary to support this main point?"

Listening and Speaking 1.0 Students deliver focused and coherent presentations. **1.7** Use props, visual aids, graphs, and electronic media to enhance the appeal and accuracy of presentations. **2.2** Deliver expository presentations. **2.2a** Marshal evidence in support of a thesis and related claims, including information on all relevant perspectives. **2.2c** Make distinctions between the relative value and significance of specific data, facts, and ideas. **2.2d** Include visual aids by employing appropriate technology to organize and display information on charts, maps, and graphs. **2.2e** Anticipate and address the listener's potential misunderstandings and expectations.

CHAPTER 9 RESOURCES: LISTENING & SPEAKING

Listening & Speaking Workshop

Planning

- *On Course: Mapping Instruction*
- *One-Stop Planner* CD-ROM
- *Writing, Listening, & Speaking*
  - — Teaching Notes, p. 101
  - — Project-Planning Guide, WS. p. 103

Think Sheet

- *Writing, Listening, & Speaking,* WS. p. 104

Differentiating Instruction

- *Lesson Plans for Language Development,* p. 311
- *Supporting Instruction in Spanish*

Evaluation and Assessment

- *Writing, Listening, & Speaking,* WS. p.105

Primary and Secondary Sources When you select evidence to support your main points, use information from both primary and secondary sources. Since your presentation will not include a *Works Cited* list, tell your audience your sources within the text of your speech. Be **accurate** by correctly citing the author and source, and be **coherent** by inserting the source information into your text either directly before or after your evidence as in the following example.

Written version	For the Britons, "It was their heroic age and Arthur was their greatest hero" (Day 15).
Spoken version	In The Search for King Arthur, writer David Day writes about the Britons, "It was their heroic age and Arthur was their greatest hero."

TIP Refer to your sources in your written research paper to double-check that any **technical terms** or **notations**—documented sources of information—that you use for your speech are accurate.

Finally, Then The last thing you say is probably what your audience will remember most. Review the conclusion in your written research paper. Plan to restate your thesis and end your oral presentation with a dramatic turn of phrase.

Off the Cuff You will deliver an **extemporaneous** speech—that is, a speech outlined and rehearsed, but not memorized. To help you sound natural, use note cards. Put one main point, possibly accompanied by a brief example or detail, on each card. Use colored cards for any special material you plan to read word for word, such as a quotation. Arrange your cards in a logical organizational pattern to help your audience follow your ideas.

Deliver Your Presentation

Sounds and Silence Use standard American English in your presentation. To enhance your delivery further, use a combination of the following **verbal** and **nonverbal techniques.** Speak slowly, clearly, distinctly, and loudly enough to be heard by the people in the back of the room. Emphasize important words or phrases by pausing after them. Finally, look directly at the audience, occasionally glancing at your notes to prompt your memory or to read a quotation.

Getting a Second Opinion Rehearse your oral presentation before a family member, friend, or teacher. Then, respectfully **interview** the person about your performance. Ask questions about your performance, such as "Was the source citation clear in my oral presentation?" Take notes on the responses. Compile the information and use it to adjust your oral presentation, according to the suggestions.

PRACTICE & APPLY 5 Use the instruction above to adapt your research paper for an oral presentation. Rehearse your presentation, using note cards. Deliver your polished presentation to an audience.

Listening and Speaking 1.3 Choose logical patterns of organization. **1.8** Produce concise notes for extemporaneous delivery. **1.9** Analyze the occasion and the interests of the audience and choose effective verbal and nonverbal techniques for presentations. **2.0** Student speaking demonstrates a command of standard American English. **2.2b** Convey information and ideas from primary and secondary sources accurately and coherently. **2.2f** Use technical terms and notations accurately. **2.3** Apply appropriate interviewing techniques. **2.3a** Prepare and ask relevant questions. **2.3b** Make notes of responses. **2.3c** Use language that conveys respect. **2.3f** Compile and report responses.

DIRECT TEACHING

Off the Cuff

As students prepare their speeches, give them a mini-lesson on the skillful use of language and rhetorical strategies. You may wish to discuss topics such as the appropriate blend of formal and informal language and the use of inclusive personal pronouns, figurative language, or alliteration.

RETEACHING

REVIEW STANDARD

Sounds and Silence

To reteach the concept of pacing in delivering a speech, have the class watch appropriate situation comedies or stand-up comic routines. After students have viewed the shows, have them discuss the effectiveness of timing in the delivery of lines. How effective is a well-placed pause? Why is it effective? Explain that well-placed pauses will allow their audience to process information before hearing new information.

PRACTICE & APPLY 5

Guided and Independent Practice

To guide students in using their rehearsal time productively, have them use this checklist to evaluate their own or a peer's delivery.

- The purpose is clearly defined.
- The ideas are tailored to the audience.
- The introduction is engaging.
- The thesis statement has been revised successfully.
- The main ideas have been simplified effectively.
- The supporting evidence has been simplified effectively.
- The conclusion is memorable.

- *Progress Assessment of Writing, Listening, & Speaking,* p. 83
- *Diagnostic and Summative Assessments,* End-of-Year Test

Extension

- *Writing, Listening, & Speaking,* Videocassette Segment 6
- *Writing, Listening, & Speaking,* WS. p. 106

Internet

- go.hrw.com (keyword: HLLA)

Standards Review

Analyzing Informational Materials

STANDARDS FOCUS, pp. 712–715

(For the grade-level standard reviewed in this lesson, see Student Edition, p. 712.)

INTRODUCING THE STANDARDS REVIEW

Use this review to test students' grasp of the use of primary and secondary sources.

DIRECT TEACHING

A Reading Informational Materials
GRADE-LEVEL STANDARD

? Extending ideas presented in primary or secondary sources. What effect do the news media seem to have on the government's credibility? [The news media provide people with information that contradicts official reports. As a result, people are more likely to mistrust the government.]

B Reading Informational Materials
GRADE-LEVEL STANDARD

? Extending ideas presented in primary or secondary sources. Upon reading that the news media criticized the government's policies, what questions might a thoughtful reader ask about the media? [Possible responses: Were the media completely accurate in their reporting? Were the journalists' reports completely objective and free from bias?]

STANDARDS REVIEW

Analyzing Informational Materials

Test Practice

Using Primary and Secondary Sources

DIRECTIONS: Read the following excerpts from a variety of primary and secondary sources. Then, read each multiple-choice question that follows, and write the letter of the best response.

The Media and the War

Paul Boyer

By the end of 1967 more than 16,000 Americans had been killed in Vietnam. Thousands more had been injured or disabled. Despite the government's optimistic forecasts, a U.S. victory seemed increasingly distant. American television news programs showed gruesome images of terrified Vietnamese civilians and dead or injured soldiers. Some Americans responded by demanding that the military be allowed to do whatever it took to win. Others wanted the United States to pull out of Vietnam. **A**

The Vietnam War invaded American homes in a way that no previous conflict had. During previous wars the military had imposed tight press restrictions. In this war, reporters, photographers, and TV camera crews accompanied soldiers on patrol and interviewed people throughout South Vietnam. Television beamed footage and reports of the war into people's homes on a nightly basis. As a result, Americans saw images that seemed to contradict the government's reports.

Reporters such as David Halberstam of *The New York Times* and Neil Sheehan of United Press International criticized the government's optimism. As early as 1962 they argued that the war could not be won as long as the United States supported the unpopular and corrupt regime[1] of Ngo Dinh Diem. Journalists also reported on the ineffectiveness of South Vietnam's troops and accused the U.S. government of inflating[2] enemy body counts to give the appearance of progress. **B**

As the gap between official government reports and media accounts grew wider, doubts at home increased. The administration found itself criticized by both **doves**—people who opposed the war—and **hawks**—people who supported the war's goals. Hawks criticized the way the war was being fought. They argued for more U.S. troops and heavier bombing. Air Force General Curtis LeMay expressed the frustration of many hawks. "Here we are at the height of our power. The most powerful nation in the world. And yet we're afraid to use that power."

1. **regime** (rə·zhēm′) *n.:* government; rule.
2. **inflating** *v.* used as *n.:* increasing beyond what is accurate.

Pages 712–715 cover **Reading Standard 2.5** Extend ideas presented in primary or secondary sources through original analysis, evaluation, and elaboration.

READING MINI-LESSON

Reviewing Word-Attack Skills

Activity. Display these pairs of words. All or most of the letters of the first word appear in the second word. Have students tell if the sounds of the first word are also heard in the second.

1. mice, pumice [no]
2. site, parasite [yes]
3. rite, favorite [no]
4. vile, rile [yes]
5. nine, asinine [yes]
6. rite, meteorite [yes]
7. bile, tile [yes]
8. site, composite [no]
9. mine, determine [no]

Activity. Display these sets of words. Have students identify the two words in which *eo* stands for the same sound(s). Answers are underlined.

Doves opposed the war for many reasons. Pacifists[3] such as Martin Luther King, Jr., believed that all war was wrong. Some doves, such as diplomat George Kennan, were convinced that Vietnam was not crucial to national security. Others feared that the United States might use nuclear weapons. Pediatrician and author Dr. Benjamin Spock and others argued that the United States was fighting against the wishes of a majority of Vietnamese.

—from *The American Nation* **(history textbook)**

3. **pacifists** (pas′ə·fists′) *n.:* people who oppose war for moral reasons.

from The Vietnam War: An Eyewitness History

edited by Sanford Wexler

JOHN M. G. BROWN

Thanks a lot for the Christmas presents. They were great. Yesterday I went up Thunder Road on a guarded truck convoy to see the Bob Hope USO Christmas show. It was really a good time and very moving. One of **C** the girls started crying while she was singing "Silent Night" to us and got interrupted by a barrage of artillery going off nearby. If you see **D** pictures of it, I'll be sitting just to the left of two tanks with "Merry Christmas" painted on them.

—Pfc. John M. G. Brown, U.S.A., First Aviation Battalion from a **letter** to his family of December 25, 1967, from *Rice Paddy Grunt* (1986)

DICKEY CHAPPELLE

As I fell into the hypnotic rhythm of the patrol—we were moving between trees and cane fields, stepping high so we would not trip and clatter on the uneven ground—I was obsessed by a question that had plagued me on other walks in other wars: Why?

Why was it that humans still got along so badly that conflicts were settled like this, by young men betting their lives at hide-and-seek? Did **E** I truly think I could, with the camera around my neck, help end the need

DIRECT TEACHING

C Reading Informational Materials
GRADE-LEVEL STANDARD

Extending ideas presented in primary or secondary sources. In this excerpt from his letter, Private Brown offers no direct opinion about the war. What two episodes does he describe that clearly show ironic contrast? [The song "Silent Night" is interrupted by the sound of artillery; the tanks, symbols of war and destruction, have "Merry Christmas" painted on them.]

D Reading Informational Materials
GRADE-LEVEL STANDARD

Extending ideas presented in primary or secondary sources. How does this excerpt give support to the point made in the second paragraph of the first selection? [When used as footage in news broadcasts, scenes of the war shot by photographers had an emotional impact on viewers at home.]

E Reading Informational Materials
GRADE-LEVEL STANDARD

Extending ideas presented in primary or secondary sources. "The Media and the War" discusses the categories of "hawks," those who supported the war, and "doves," those who opposed it. What category does this writer fall into? [Most likely she is a pacifist; she has moral and philosophical grounds for opposing all war.]

1. people	<u>peonage</u>	<u>peonies</u>
2. geometric	<u>geometry</u>	<u>geography</u>
3. <u>rheostat</u>	<u>stereotype</u>	yeoman
4. <u>theorem</u>	<u>theory</u>	theology
5. <u>eons</u>	<u>neon</u>	neophyte
6. <u>leopard</u>	<u>jeopardize</u>	leotard

Activity. Have students identify the word in each set that has the long vowel sound shown. Answers are underlined.

1. /ā/	ravel	<u>raven</u>	ravenous
2. /ē/	<u>evil</u>	devil	level
3. /ī/	civil	snivel	<u>rival</u>
4. /ō/	oven	<u>cloven</u>	proven
5. /ā/	satin	Latin	<u>latent</u>
6. /ē/	seven	sever	<u>fever</u>
7. /ō/	novel	<u>nova</u>	novice
8. /ī/	trivia	<u>tribal</u>	trivet

DIRECT TEACHING

A Reading Informational Materials
GRADE-LEVEL STANDARD
Extending ideas presented in primary or secondary sources. Which argument made by some of the "doves" would find support in this diary entry? [That, in fighting the Vietnam War, the United States was opposing the wishes of some of the Vietnamese people.]

B Reading Informational Materials
GRADE-LEVEL STANDARD
Extending ideas presented in primary or secondary sources. In this brief excerpt, how does Ron Kovic indirectly offer an opinion on war? [He shows how war can take away the lives of even those who survive the battlefield.]

C Reading Informational Materials
GRADE-LEVEL STANDARD
Extending ideas presented in primary or secondary sources. In what important ways does "The Media and the War" differ from the other selections in this lesson? [Possible response: "The Media and the War" informs readers that people had strong feelings about the war, while the others show what some people were feeling. "The Media and the War" discusses the attitudes of the people at home in the United States, whereas the others reveal the thoughts of those actually on the battlefield.]

for the carbine[1] on my shoulder? Did I think I could make plain how warring really was, how quickly the cutting edge of fear excised[2] every human virtue, leaving only the need to live? Here, now, the supreme virtue was the ability to shoot fast. Or first.

—Dickey Chappelle, journalist with a U.S. and Vietnamese River Assault Group in the Mekong Delta in 1965, **eyewitness account** in *National Geographic,* February 1966 [Chappelle, who died on November 4, 1965, was the first American correspondent to be killed in action in South Vietnam.]

DU LUC

A For the third time my life turned to war again. For the liberation of our compatriots[3] in the south, a situation of boiling oil and burning fire is necessary! A situation in which husband is separated from wife, father from son, brother from brother is necessary. Now, my life is full of hardship. Not enough rice to eat, not enough salt to give taste to my tongue, not enough clothing to keep myself warm. But, in my heart, I keep loyal to the [Communist] Party and to the people.

—Du Luc, Vietcong soldier
diary entry of December 1960, from *Time,* December 15, 1961

RON KOVIC

B C In one big bang they have taken it all from me, in one clean sweep, and now I am in this place around all the others like me, and though I keep trying not to feel sorry for myself, I want to cry. There is no shortcut around this thing. It is too soon to die even for a man who has died once already.

I try to keep telling myself it is good to still be alive, to be back home. I remember thinking on the ambulance ride to the hospital that this was the Bronx, the place where Yankee Stadium was, where Mickey Mantle played. I think I realized then also that my feet would never touch the stadium grass; I would never play a game in that place.

—Sgt. Ron Kovic, U.S.M.C., on being severely wounded in action in 1967, from his **autobiography,** *Born on the Fourth of July* (1976)

1. **carbine** (kär′bīn′) *n.:* light semiautomatic or automatic rifle.
2. **excised** (ek·sīzd′) *v.:* cut out, as if surgically removed.
3. **compatriots** (kəm·pā′trē·əts) *n.:* citizens of one's own country.

Using Academic Language

Review of Literary Terms
Reading Standard 3.12 and Grade 8 Review Standard 3.7

Ask students to look back through the chapter to find the meanings of the terms listed below. Then, have students show their grasp of the standards by citing passages from the chapter that illustrate the meanings of those terms. **Biographical Approach** (p. 618); **Historical Approach** (p. 618); **Historical Dimension** (p. 619); **Myths** (pp. 619, 660, 673); **Legends** (pp. 619, 644); **Historical Context** (p. 620); **Romance** (p. 651).

Review of Informational Terms
Reading Standard 2.5

Ask students to use these terms to explain how to extend ideas presented in primary or secondary sources.

Primary Source (p. 632); **Secondary Source** (p. 632); **Analyze** (p. 632); **Main Idea** (p. 632); **Writer's Purpose** (p. 632); **Structure** (p. 633); **Facts** (p. 633); **Opinions** (p. 633); **Tone** (p. 633); **Objective** (p. 633); **Subjective** (p. 633); **Evaluate** (p. 633); **Credibility** (p. 633); **Bias** (p. 633); **Audience** (p. 633); **Accuracy** (p. 633); **Elaborate** (p. 633).

1. Which of these informational readings is a **secondary source**?
   A The textbook excerpt "The Media and the War"
   B Du Luc's diary entry
   C The excerpt from Ron Kovic's autobiography
   D John M. G. Brown's letter

2. The writer's **purpose** in the excerpts by Du Luc, Ron Kovic, and Dickey Chappelle is to —
   F express strong personal feelings
   G give detailed information about combat
   H persuade the reader to support the war
   J persuade the reader to oppose the war

3. "The Media and the War" presents information that helps us to understand —
   A the reasons for U.S. involvement in the war
   B the U.S. military strategy for the war
   C the reasons for Americans' antiwar feelings
   D the history of Vietnam before the war

4. Which writer's source would be *most* useful in researching the war as seen from the Vietnamese point of view?
   F Ron Kovic
   G Du Luc
   H Dickey Chappelle
   J The textbook writer, Paul Boyer

5. The sources by John M. G. Brown, Du Luc, and Ron Kovic are *alike* in that they —
   A are antiwar
   B strongly support the war
   C are based on other sources of information
   D provide an eyewitness point of view

6. What kind of source would you expect to provide the *most* objective reporting about the war?
   F An autobiography
   G A newspaper or magazine article
   H A diary entry
   J A letter home

7. The two texts that are private and personal (that the writers never intended to publish) are the ones by John M. G. Brown and —
   A the textbook writer, Paul Boyer
   B Du Luc
   C Ron Kovic
   D Dickey Chappelle

8. The writer who expresses despair over humankind's seeming dependence on war and the fate of humankind is —
   F Dickey Chappelle
   G Du Luc
   H Ron Kovic
   J the textbook writer, Paul Boyer

9. Which of the following sources would be *least* helpful if you wanted to extend and elaborate on the ideas presented in these selections?
   A An interview with someone who served in combat in the Vietnam War
   B An encyclopedia entry about the Vietnam War
   C A map of Vietnam
   D A 1967 television news report about the Vietnam War

TestPractice

Answers and Model Rationales

1. **A** Textbooks are generally secondary sources. The selections listed in B, C, and D are eyewitness accounts, which are always primary sources.
2. **F** None of the excerpts gives detailed information about combat (G). One writer supports the war whereas another opposes it (H, J). As eyewitness accounts, all express strong personal feelings.
3. **C** The writer gives neither the reasons for U.S. involvement in the war nor the history of Vietnam before the war. Although he mentions criticisms of the military strategy, he does not explain it. The subject of the excerpt is the antiwar feelings of many Americans.
4. **G** Du Luc's diary entry is the only excerpt written by a person who is Vietnamese.
5. **D** Only one of the sources of the excerpts strongly supports the war, so A and B are incorrect. All are primary sources, so C is incorrect. D is the correct answer because all are first-person accounts by eyewitnesses.
6. **G** F, H, and J are examples of writing that are very personal and subjective in nature.
7. **B** A, C, and D are incorrect because textbooks, autobiographies, and articles by correspondents are all intended for publication. Personal diaries are not.
8. **F** Chappelle says that she is "plagued" by the question of why humans need to settle their conflicts by war.
9. **C** A map gives information on geography and political boundaries, not ideas such as those presented in the selections.

Test-Taking Tips

For information on how to answer multiple-choice items, refer students to **Test Smarts.**

Test Practice

Vocabulary Development

Context Clues

Modeling. Model the thought process of a good reader answering item 1. Say, "If they went directly through a sleeping village or defended it, someone would be alerted to their presence, so options A and C are incorrect. If they went in the opposite direction, their presence would be pointless, so D is incorrect. If they went around it, they would remain unnoticed, so B is correct."

Test Practice

Answers and Model Rationales

1. **B** See rationale above.
2. **J** If someone dies while purposefully defending his country, it is not comical (F), unexpected (G), or a mistake (H), so J is correct.
3. **C** Words of anger (A) and warning (D) would not calm a fearful person. C is better than B because words of love do not seem appropriate to the situation.
4. **J** A new king would not necessarily rescue a country's economy (F), stability (G), or church (H). J is the most logical choice.
5. **B** A and C do not fit the context. B is a better choice than D because usually a person makes a *promise* to tell the truth.
6. **H** F and J do not describe a cry of protest. Since the cry was "kept up," G is incorrect. The words *loud* and *cry of protest* are clues that H is correct.
7. **B** The words *challenging, tournament,* and *powerful* are clues that B is correct. A, C, and D do not describe a strong person who is engaged in a contest.
8. **F** You would not speak of someone matching another in fear (G), attention (H), or pity (J). F is, therefore, correct.

STANDARDS REVIEW

Vocabulary Development

Test Practice

Context Clues

DIRECTIONS: Use context clues to help you choose the answer that gives the best definition for the underlined word.

1. They skirted a sleeping village so that no one would be alerted to their presence.
Skirted means —
- **A** went directly through
- **B** went around
- **C** defended
- **D** went in the opposite direction of

2. The telegram would say that he died valiantly while dutifully defending his country.
Valiantly means —
- **F** comically
- **G** unexpectedly
- **H** mistakenly
- **J** bravely

3. To ease his fear, the men offered Billy words of consolation, but nothing could calm him.
Consolation means —
- **A** anger
- **B** love
- **C** comfort
- **D** warning

4. The realm of Britain was in danger until a new king could be placed on the throne.
Realm means —
- **F** economy
- **G** stability
- **H** church
- **J** kingdom

5. Sir Kay made an oath to tell the truth.
Oath means —
- **A** test
- **B** promise
- **C** curse
- **D** opportunity

6. The commoners kept up their loud, tumultuous cry of protest when the nobles disputed Arthur's right to be king of Britain.
Tumultuous means —
- **F** sad and tearful
- **G** extremely brief
- **H** noisy and wild
- **J** weak and uncertain

7. The knights challenging Launcelot at the tournament found him to be a powerful adversary.
Adversary means —
- **A** negotiator
- **B** opponent
- **C** personality
- **D** friend

8. During the tournament, Sir Gahalantyne was no match for Launcelot's increasing wrath.
Wrath means —
- **F** anger
- **G** fear
- **H** attention
- **J** pity

Vocabulary Review

Use this activity to assess whether students have retained the chapter Vocabulary. Ask students to complete each of the sentences below with the Vocabulary word from the box that best fits the context.

agile	champion	diverted	initiative
confronted			

1. We applauded the students' ______ in starting a fund for the new library. [initiative]
2. He ______ the consequences of not preparing for the exam. [confronted]
3. Our senator would ______ legislation favoring health-care reform. [champion]
4. The children were ______ with small toys and candy. [diverted]
5. Someone so strong and ______ will be a great asset to the basketball team. [agile]

Writing

Test Practice

DIRECTIONS: Read the following paragraph from a draft of a student's research paper. Then, read the questions below it. Choose the best answer to each question, and mark your answers on your own paper.

(1) Senator at age thirty-two, Julius Caesar was a historical figure who accomplished many things. (2) Known as "one of Rome's greatest generals and statesmen," Caesar used his brilliant leadership and "helped make Rome the center of an empire that stretched across Europe." (3) After studying oratory—the art of making speeches—in Greece, Caesar worked his way up through various political positions. (4) He first became the quaestor of Spain, then the aedile of Rome, then the pontifex maximus under the Consul (McGill 51). (5) Caesar was assassinated on March 15, 44 B.C. (6) Caesar's sharp political instincts greatly advanced his economic and military power, allowing him to become the sole dictator of Rome in 44 B.C. (McGill 52).

1. Which of the following sentences based on a secondary source could the student add to support the thesis?
   - A Caesar was captured by pirates on his way to study in Greece (McGill 51).
   - B Caesar's marriage to Cornelia, against the wishes of his family, put his career at risk (Duggan 36).
   - C Caesar had a secret alliance with the First Triumvirate (McGill 52).
   - D Caesar won military prestige, losing only two battles in nine years (Gruen 12).
2. What should the student do to give credit for the quotations in sentence 2?
   - F omit the quotation marks since they are unnecessary
   - G use appropriate documentation in the text and in the *Works Cited* list
   - H expand the quotation to include the entire sentence from the source
   - J cite the source in the text but do not include it in the *Works Cited* list
3. To make sentence 4 more understandable for the reader, the student could
   - A define the technical terms naming Caesar's political positions
   - B include visuals by employing appropriate technology
   - C relate whether the facts came from a primary or secondary source
   - D cite more examples of Caesar's political aspirations
4. Which sentence should be deleted or moved to another paragraph?
   - F 2
   - G 4
   - H 5
   - J 6
5. To present the information in a research presentation, the student should
   - A read aloud the *Works Cited* list to prove her research
   - B answer listeners' potential questions by reading the entire paper aloud
   - C include props and visuals, such as a representation of Caesar or a map
   - D avoid citing primary or secondary sources altogether

Standards Review

Answers

1. D
2. G
3. A
4. H
5. C

APPLICATION

Documentary

Have students select a peer's research paper and create a 15- to 20-minute documentary on the subject. Since the research is of a literary nature, students will probably use many video images of photographs and documents in addition to a narrator. If possible, have students use the paper's author as a consultant. Remind students to run appropriate credits at the end of the documentary.

EXTENSION

Media Comparison

For homework, have students compare two different kinds of media messages that contain research. For example, you might have them consider a nightly news report and a Web site, or a newsmagazine and a documentary film. As students view or read each media message, have them identify at least three pieces of researched information, including the sources used. Students may organize their findings in a chart.

Homework

You need to be aware that Internet resources are sometimes public forums and that their content may be unpredictable.

RESOURCES: WRITING, LISTENING, & SPEAKING

Assessment

- *Test Generator (One-Stop Planner* CD-ROM)
- *Progress Assessment of Writing, Listening, & Speaking,* Ch. 9
- *Diagnostic and Summative Assessments,* End-of-Year Test

Internet

- Online assessments at go.hrw.com (keyword: HLLA)

Holt Literature and Language Arts: Mastering the California Standards

Chapter 10 Drama
Evaluating an Argument

Program Organization

Holt Literature and Language Arts provides a complete curriculum for standards-based instruction in reading, literature, writing, listening and speaking, and language conventions. The instructional content is presented in quarters to enable teachers to anticipate and administer the quarterly assessments required by California.

About Chapter 10

Standards-based lesson plans and suggestions for pacing the presentation of Chapter 10, the related instructional material, and the recommended assessment are provided in *On Course: Mapping Instruction,* Chapter 10.

- In Chapter 10, students will identify and use words literally and figuratively; evaluate the credibility of a claim; articulate the relationship between the characteristics of different dramatic literature; identify and describe different functions of dialogue; design and publish documents using software and graphics; analyze historically significant speeches; assess language and delivery and their affect on a speech; evaluate the quality, effectiveness, and type of argument used by a speaker; and identify the aesthetic effects of a media presentation.

Language Arts Content

Which reading standards are taught in Chapter 10?

In this chapter, students will master the following Grade 10 standards and review standards from Grade 8. Selections or features marked with a ✓ constitute the minimum course of study that provides coverage of grade-level standards.

Grade 10 Standards
Word Analysis, Fluency, and Systematic Vocabulary Development

1.1 Identify and use the literal and figurative meanings of words and understand word derivations.
Word Analogies: Word Pairs with the Same Relationship, p. 739
✓ Multiple Meanings: Recognizing Puns, p. 781
Understanding Elizabethan English, p. 805
Clarifying Meanings: Words in Context, p. 888

1.2 Distinguish between the denotative and connotative meanings of words and interpret the connotative power of words.
Word Connotations: Powerful Associations, p. 739

Reading Comprehension (Focus on Informational Materials)

2.8 Evaluate the credibility of an author's argument or defense of a claim by critiquing the relationship between generalizations and evidence, the comprehensiveness of evidence, and the way in which the author's intent affects the structure and tone of the text.
✓ "*Julius Caesar* in an Absorbing Production" (play review), pp. 881–887
"Brutus's Funeral Speech" (standards review), pp. 902–903

(*continued*)

(continued)

Literary Response and Analysis

3.1 Articulate the relationship between the expressed purposes and the characteristics of different forms of dramatic literature.

"Drama: Forms and Stagecraft" (standards essay), pp. 720–723
The Brute (comedy), pp. 724–738
The Tragedy of Julius Caesar (tragedy), pp. 754–755
✓ *The Tragedy of Julius Caesar, Act I* (tragedy), pp. 758–780
The Tragedy of Julius Caesar, Act II (tragedy), pp. 782–804
The Tragedy of Julius Caesar, Act III (tragedy), pp. 806–832
The Tragedy of Julius Caesar, Act IV (tragedy), pp. 834–852
The Tragedy of Julius Caesar, Act V (tragedy), pp. 854–879

3.10 Identify and describe the function of dialogue, scene designs, soliloquies, asides, and character foils in dramatic literature.

"Drama: Forms and Stagecraft" (standards essay), pp. 720–723
✓ "The Elizabethan Stage," pp. 745–749
The Tragedy of Julius Caesar (tragedy), pp. 754–755
✓ *The Tragedy of Julius Caesar, Act I* (tragedy), pp. 758–780
The Tragedy of Julius Caesar, Act II (tragedy), pp. 782–804
The Tragedy of Julius Caesar, Act III (tragedy), pp. 806–832
The Tragedy of Julius Caesar, Act IV (tragedy), pp. 834–852
The Tragedy of Julius Caesar, Act V (tragedy), pp. 854–879

Review Standards Grade 8

Reading 1.2 Understand the most important points in the history of the English language and use common word origins to determine the historical influences on English word meanings.

"How to Read Shakespeare," pp. 752–753

Reading 1.3 Use word meanings within the appropriate context, and show ability to verify those meanings by definition, restatement, example, comparison, or contrast.

Clarifying Meanings: Words in Context, p. 888

Which writing, and listening and speaking standards are taught in Chapter 10?

Writing Strategies

1.1 Establish a controlling impression or coherent thesis that conveys a clear and distinctive perspective on the subject and maintain a consistent tone and focus throughout the piece of writing.

Write Your Thesis Statement, p. 892

1.2 Use precise language, action verbs, sensory details, appropriate modifiers, and the active rather than the passive voice.

Second Reading: Style, p. 896

1.4 Develop the main ideas within the body of the composition through supporting evidence.

Gather Evidence and Organize, p. 892

1.8 Design and publish documents by using advanced publishing software and graphic programs.

Tell It to the World, p. 897

1.9 Revise writing to improve the logic and coherence of the organization and controlling perspective, the precision of word choice, and the tone by taking into consideration the audience, purpose, and formality of the context.

Revise Your Essay, pp. 895–896

(continued)

(continued)

Listening and Speaking Strategies

1.1 Formulate judgments about the ideas under discussion and support those judgments with convincing evidence.
Analyze Content, pp. 898–899

1.10 Analyze historically significant speeches to find the rhetorical devices and features that make them memorable.
Analyze Content! pp. 898–899
Analyze Organization, pp. 899–900
Analyze Delivery, pp. 900–901

1.11 Assess how language and delivery affect the mood and tone of the oral communication and make an impact on the audience.
Rhetorical Devices, p. 899
Analyze Delivery, pp. 900–901

1.12 Evaluate the clarity, quality, effectiveness, and general coherence of a speaker's important points, arguments, evidence, organization of ideas, delivery, diction, and syntax.
Evaluate a Speech, p. 901

1.13 Analyze the types of arguments used by the speaker, including argument by causation, analogy, authority, emotion, and logic.
Arguments, pp. 898–899

1.14 Identify the aesthetic effects of a media presentation and evaluate the techniques used to create them.
Compare the Film to the Play, pp. 890–892

Review Standards Grade 8

Writing 1.1 Create compositions that establish a controlling impression, have a coherent thesis, and end with a clear and well-supported conclusion.
Write Your Thesis Statement, p. 892

Speaking 1.0 Students deliver focused, coherent presentations that convey ideas clearly and relate to the background and interests of the audience. They evaluate the content of oral communication.
Evaluate a Speech, p. 901

Instructional Planning and Support

Where do I find lesson plans, additional resources, and other teaching aids?

- This Annotated Teacher's Edition and *On Course: Mapping Instruction* provide direction in planning and implementing a complete California standards–based curriculum. These components also include instructions for diagnostic, progress, and summative testing; for presenting direct instruction of the standards; for differentiating instruction to provide universal access; and for locating and using the program's ancillaries.
- Lesson and workshop resources are referenced at the beginning of each selection or workshop, in the bottom margin of this teacher's edition.
- Reminders for using additional resources appear in this teacher's edition at point of use.
- The *One-Stop Planner* CD-ROM contains editable lesson plans and all print ancillaries, available in PDF format.

What if I don't have time to teach all of Chapter 10?

- Most standards can be taught with a minimum number of selections and features. In the chart on the preceding page, the core lessons you need in order to provide complete coverage of the chapter standards are identified with a ✓.
- *On Course: Mapping Instruction,* Chapter 10, lists lessons and activities that provide minimum standards coverage.

What provisions have been made for students who have additional class time scheduled in language arts?

- *Interactive Reading* provides for alternative direct instruction and practice of the grade-level standards taught in Chapter 10.
- *Universal Access: Writing, Listening, and Speaking,* Chapter 10, contains worksheets and transparencies that provide practice in and reteaching and reinforcement of the writing and listening and speaking standards in Chapter 10.
- *Universal Access: Lesson Plans for Language Development,* Chapter 10, provides alternative teaching strategies and additional worksheets designed specifically for English-language learners and special education students. Many of the suggestions and activities in this ancillary will also be helpful to students in the regular classroom who are having difficulty with particular skills.

Universal Access

How do I differentiate instruction to ensure that all my students master the standards?

Holt Literature and Language Arts provides comprehensive, differentiated instruction for all types of students.

- Most of the general instruction and teaching strategies in the Annotated Teacher's Edition are at grade level. These instructions will work well with the majority of your students.
- Point-of-use suggestions are provided for advanced learners, learners having difficulty, English-language learners, and special education students.
- *Interactive Reading* is designed to anticipate and remediate problems that students may experience in achieving mastery of the reading standards. See *Interactive Reading,* Teacher's Edition, Chapter 10, for information on using the reader to differentiate instruction.
- *Universal Access: Writing, Listening, and Speaking,* Chapter 10, contains worksheets and transparencies that provide practice in and reteaching and reinforcement of the writing and listening and speaking standards in Chapter 10.
- *Universal Access: Lesson Plans for Language Development,* Chapter 10, offers teaching strategies and additional worksheets designed specifically for English-language learners and special education students.

Assessment

How do I determine whether my students are making progress in mastering the standards?

Progress Assessment

- Use the Standards Reviews at the end of Chapter 10 for an informal assessment of the informational reading and writing standards.
- Use Chapter 10 tests from the *Progress Assessment* booklets to assess comprehension and progress on mastering the standards taught in this chapter.

Summative Assessment

The content of *Holt Literature and Language Arts* has been divided into quarters to allow you to administer the four summative tests required by California. Chapters 9–10 and related instructional material constitute the fourth quarter of instruction. At the end of Chapter 11, you may ask students to take the End-of-Year Test in *Diagnostic and Summative Assessments.*

Chapter 10

STANDARDS FOCUS

(For full text of standards taught in this chapter, see the Standards Correlation by Standard chart in the Student Edition.)

Grade-Level Standards

- Vocabulary Development 1.1, 1.2
- Reading Comprehension 2.8
- Literary Response and Analysis 3.1, 3.10
- Writing Strategies 1.1, 1.2, 1.4, 1.8, 1.9
- Listening and Speaking Strategies 1.1, 1.10, 1.11, 1.12, 1.13, 1.14

INTRODUCING THE CHAPTER

This chapter contains two dramatic selections that illustrate the scope of the theater. The chapter includes both Anton Chekhov's *The Brute,* a nineteenth-century Russian comedy in one act, and William Shakespeare's classic tragedy *Julius Caesar.* Drama is the form of literature with which your students, having grown up on television and movies, are perhaps most familiar. Although students have already absorbed many of the conventions and techniques of drama, bringing the literature to life through dramatic readings and interpretations may be a new experience for them. Explain to the class that the scripts they will be investigating are meant to be performed, not read silently. Encourge students to read the plays aloud and to envision the action as they read. At the end of the chapter, students will be asked to compare a scene from a film to the play from which it was adapted and analyze the film techniques the director uses. In addition, students will be given an opportunity to analyze and evaluate a historically significant speech.

CHAPTER 10 RESOURCES: READING

Planning

- *One-Stop Planner* CD-ROM with Test Generator
- *On Course: Mapping Instruction*
- *At Home: A Guide to Standards Mastery*
- *At Home: In Spanish*
- *Supporting Instruction in Spanish*

Reading

- *Interactive Reading*

Differentiating Instruction

- *Lesson Plans for Language Development*

Vocabulary

- *Vocabulary Development*
    - Cumulative Vocabulary Review, pp. 51–52

Chapter 10

DRAMA

EVALUATING AN ARGUMENT

Drama began as the act of a whole community. Ideally, there would be no spectators. In practice, every member of the audience should feel like an understudy.

—W. H. Auden

David Hockney's stage set for the opera *Tristan and Isolde.*
Courtesy of the artist.

go.hrw.com
KEYWORD: HLLA 10-10

THE QUOTATION

Drama grew out of rituals and ceremonial occasions that many of the world's early societies used to mark events such as the start of a new growing season, a successful hunt, or an important triumph over a much-feared enemy. Discuss with students whether they think modern societies have similar ceremonies.

VIEWING THE ART

This expansive, otherworldly set was created by **David Hockney** (1937–), a versatile British artist who lives in Los Angeles. The set was designed for the Los Angeles Opera's production of *Tristan and Isolde,* an opera by Richard Wagner. Hockney also directed and produced the opera. The large curving panels, together with the complex lighting, create an environment that is far from everyday life.

Activity. After reading a play from this unit, draw a design for a set which you feel is appropriate to its content and style. Consider the characters, setting, and mood of the dramatic work when designing your set.

Resources Reminder

Planning

- *At Home: A Guide to Standards Mastery*

Parent letters appear in this resource. Translations of these letters appear in *At Home: In Spanish.* Translations of selection summaries appear in *Supporting Instruction in Spanish.*

Reading

- *Interactive Reading*

The California framework requires students to read materials apart from in-class assignments. Additional readings are cited on the Read On page and on selected pages in the Student Edition.

Assessment

- *Progress Assessment of Reading*
  - Chapter Test
- *One-Stop Planner* CD-ROM with Test Generator

Internet

- go.hrw.com
(Keyword: HLLA 10-1)

STANDARDS FOCUS, pp. 720–723

(For the grade level standards taught in this lesson, see Student Edition, p. 720.)

Prerequisite Standard

- Grade 8, Literary Response and Analysis 3.6 **Identify significant literary devices (e.g., metaphor, symbolism, dialect, irony) that define a writer's style and use those elements to interpret the work.**

Literary Focus: Drama

This essay outlines the general structure of drama, as well as the special characteristics of comedy and tragedy. Special emphasis is paid to conflict, scene design, and dialogue. The basic elements of drama, the framework upon which most plays are built, are similar to those of other literary forms: characters, conflict, and suspense. In drama, however, all information must be conveyed through the characters' dialogue, their physical actions, and the play's visual elements (set, costume, sound effects). Conflict must be shown, not merely summarized. But most plays do not focus solely on physical action. They are concerned with more subtle conflicts between characters, which must be worked out through speech. Present a basic conflict to students, for example, going to a movie versus going to a sporting event. Divide the class into pairs or small groups and ask them to resolve the conflict. Groups should then transform their conversation into a short dramatic scene that can be presented to the class.

Literary Response and Analysis

Drama *by* Diane Tasca

FORMS AND STAGECRAFT

Reading Standard 3.1 Articulate the relationship between the expressed purposes and the characteristics of different forms of dramatic literature (e.g., comedy, tragedy, drama, dramatic monologue).

Reading Standard 3.10 Identify and describe the function of dialogue, scene designs, soliloquies, and asides in dramatic literature.

A **drama** is a story that is enacted in real space and time by live actors for a live audience. The word *drama* is based on the Greek verb *dran,* which means "to do." It could be said, then, that a drama, or play, is something that involves people "doing things": Words are spoken, actions are taken, minds are changed.

The earliest plays that we have copies of were written in about the fifth century B.C. in ancient Greece. These plays were produced for festivals to honor Dionysus, the god of wine and fertility. Playwrights wrote new works each year to compete for top honors at this festival. The comedies and tragedies written for these competitions thousands of years ago established conventions in structure that are still followed by many playwrights today.

Dramatic Structure

Like stories, plays involve characters who take action to resolve a problem or **conflict** of some sort. The conflict in a play can take many forms. A conflict can develop between characters who want different things or the same thing. A conflict can develop between a character and his or her circumstances (perhaps he is imprisoned, or she is about to lose her job). A conflict can also exist *within* a character who is torn by competing desires (a son wants to know the truth about his father, but he is afraid to take the steps to find it). The important fact about any conflict is that it means a great deal to the person involved. No conflict is interesting for very long unless the playwright makes us *care about* that person.

As the character in a play takes steps to resolve a conflict—to get what he or she wants—**complications** keep arising. Eventually the events of the play build to a **climax,** an action that determines how the conflict will be resolved. The climax may be an argument, a love scene, a talk with a stranger. The **resolution** of the play follows, as the conflict is resolved and the action ends.

> *Those tragedies written long ago in ancient Greece follow the fortunes of a protagonist known as the tragic hero.*

Tragedy: A Fatal Fall

A **tragedy** is a play that ends unhappily. Those tragedies written long ago in ancient Greece follow the fortunes of a protagonist known as the **tragic hero.** This hero is a noble figure who is admirable in many ways, but he or she has a **tragic flaw,** a personal failing, such as pride, rebelliousness, or jealousy. This flaw results in a choice that ultimately leads the hero to a tragic end, usually death.

Though the classic Greek tragedies deal with elevated figures, the problems they portray speak directly to their audiences: What is right and wrong, just and unjust?

DIFFERENTIATING INSTRUCTION

Learners Having Difficulty

Have students work in pairs to summarize what the essay says about conflict in drama. Their summaries should be divided into three sections: dramatic structure, tragedy, and comedy. In the first section, they should briefly explain the different types of conflict and the various stages of a conflict. The second and third sections should tell what conflicts are presented in tragedy and comedy respectively.

Advanced Learners

Enrichment. Have small groups of students conduct research into the origins of theater. Then, ask them to create a large, visually striking time line, notating significant developments, for display in the classroom.

What is the relationship between the individual and a higher power, such as the state or the gods? Why do we live, and how should we die? This is what tragedy does: It pits human limitations against the larger forces of destiny—an almighty power or an indifferent universe.

Comedy: The Happy Landing

A **comedy** is a play that ends happily. Comedies have their own typical conflicts and plot patterns. The most common plot in comedy involves boy-meets-girl, boy-loses-girl, boy-wins-girl. The genders in this pattern have sometimes been reversed in contemporary comedies. Whereas the principal characters in classical tragedies were noble, the central characters in a comedy could be anyone—princes, townspeople, servants.

The conflict in comedy usually hinges on a problem of the heart, such as a thwarted courtship or a romantic misunderstanding.

The **conflict** in comedy usually hinges on a problem of the heart, such as a thwarted courtship or a romantic misunderstanding. This conflict is resolved happily in a comedy, but there are always comical complications along the way. Shakespeare's comedies often toss people of different backgrounds together, resulting in funny mismatches. The comedy *As You Like It,* for example, involves four sets of lovers, a young woman disguised as a boy, and nobles who have been banished from their palaces to a forest.

Like most comedies, *As You Like It* ends in a wedding—four weddings, in fact. Even today many comedies end in weddings, suggesting that life continues despite all of our problems, that each wedding presents the possibility of creating a whole new society.

Modern Drama: Moving in Many Directions

Dramas today, both tragedies and comedies, usually focus on personal issues. The psychological development of the characters often takes center stage, even when the play deals with a larger social or ethical issue. Americans live in a democracy, not a monarchy, so it's not surprising that our contemporary protagonists are seldom kings and queens. The people in plays written today—whether tragic or comic—are usually ordinary people much like the rest of us.

Contemporary dramas also tend to be less bound by conventional structures than plays from earlier times. Many modern playwrights like to experiment with structure. Modern plays might include long flashbacks to an earlier time. They might include visual projections of a character's fantasies. They might include music. One experimental playwright had his main characters act out the entire play while buried up to their necks in sand.

Scene Design: Setting the Stage

Plays are meant to be performed. As you read the text of a play, remember that the playwright wrote those words to be acted

Drama: Forms and Stagecraft 721

out on a stage. Theater artists—actors, directors, designers, lighting technicians, and stage crew—help the playwright's vision become an actuality on the stage.

Stages today vary greatly in dimension and layout. In Shakespeare's time the stage extended out into the viewing area, and the audience stood around (or sat in balconies) on three sides. Many modern theaters still use this type of "thrust" stage. Another type of stage is "in the round": The playing area is surrounded on all sides by the audience. In the most common type of modern stage, however, the playing area extends behind an opening called a *proscenium arch.* The audience sits on one side looking into the action, much as if they were looking into a window. The stage behind the arch has its own directions: *upstage* (away from the audience), *downstage* (toward the audience), *stage right* and *stage left* (to the actors' right and left when facing the audience).

Scene design—sets, lights, costumes, and props—can transform a bare stage into ancient Rome, a Russian drawing room, or a South African farm. The **set** for one play might be so realistic and detailed that the audience feels they are peering into someone's actual home. For another play the set might be abstract, consisting of a few platforms painted black.

Lighting also adds to the transformation of the stage. The mood and appearance of the set can be totally changed by a skilled lighting director.

The actors, of course, wear **costumes.** These are the responsibility of the costume designer, who works closely with the director of the play (and sometimes with the playwright). Like sets, costumes can be very specific to a particular historical period, or they can be abstract and minimal. In one famous production of *Hamlet,* for example, actor Richard Burton wore black leotards—no princely satins or crown.

Finally, **props** (short for *properties*) are portable items—handbags, phones, letters—that actors carry or handle onstage in order to perform the actions of the play. A person in charge of props must be certain the right props are available at the right moments in the play. If they are missing, the result can be unintentionally funny or can ruin a moment of high suspense.

Words and Action: Characters Onstage

The conversations of the characters onstage are called **dialogue.** Long speeches by individual characters are monologues or soliloquies. A **monologue** is spoken by one character to other characters onstage. A **soliloquy** is spoken by a character who is alone onstage, speaking to himself or herself or to the audience. Soliloquies often express a character's deepest feelings and may signal an important change in the character's thinking.

Sometimes characters, especially in Shakespeare's plays, comment on the action of the play, using asides. **Asides** are spoken to the audience or to one character; the other characters onstage do not hear an aside.

Written texts of plays also include **stage directions,** which describe the setting and the characters' actions. They often describe how a character should deliver a particular line (*angrily, stupidly,*

722 Chapter 10 Drama • Evaluating an Argument

sweetly). While modern playwrights often include detailed stage directions, Shakespeare and other early dramatists provided hardly any.

The Audience

Robert Anderson, the author of *Tea and Sympathy* and *I Never Sang for My Father,* writes about another "collaborator" who helps bring a play to life.

"The playwright's final collaborator is the audience. The play exists somewhere between the stage and the spectator. In a sense, we get out of a play only what we bring to it. Out of some deep feeling of joy or sadness or excitement, a playwright writes a story, sounds a note, hoping to evoke a responsive chord from the audience. This response is what might be called the 'Oh, yes!' reaction. Playwrights write about particular experiences or observations. Enhancing these particulars with their imagination, they hope to reach something universal, something in everyone's experience. If they succeed, then members of the audience might ask, 'How did you know what my family is like?' The playwright, of course, did not know about the audience's families, but he knew his own, and in some ways all families are the same.

One of the special qualities of the theater is that when we respond, we respond as a group. This mass response of laughter or tears or excitement gives us a reassuring feeling that we are not alone, that we are one with the people sitting around us, with everyone in the theater, and in a sense, with our community and the world."

Practice

Choose a play or movie that you remember seeing, and discuss its dramatic elements. Start out by describing the **stage set** or sets. Next, indicate who the **characters** are and what their relationship is. Evaluate the characters' **dialogue.** Does it make clear what the characters want and why they are having trouble getting it? Finally, try your hand at writing a few of the **stage directions,** based on what you imagine them to have been.

Robert Anderson

Practice

Possible Answer

Death of a Salesman by Arthur Miller

Stage set—Kitchen at center stage with table, chairs, and refrigerator; stage at right is raised to suggest a bedroom; another part of the stage is raised even higher to suggest another bedroom. The entire setting is wholly or partially transparent.

Characters—Willy Loman, an aging traveling salesman too tired to continue life on the road, asks for a desk job and is refused. He fears losing the respect of his family (Biff and Happy, his sons, and Linda, his wife) and of society as he confronts the gap between his dreams and the dismal reality of his life.

Dialogue—It becomes clear from Willy's speeches that he wants to be admired and respected and that he wants the same things for his sons, particularly Biff.

Sample stage directions—Policeman enters stage left and adjusts his equipment belt. Boys immediately stop what they're doing as if frozen.

Resources Reminder

Differentiating Instruction

- *Lesson Plans for Langage Development*

For additional instruction on drama for English-language learners and special education students, see *Lesson Plans for Language Development,* pp. 325, 326.

Drama: Forms and Stagecraft 723

STANDARDS FOCUS, pp. 724–740

(For the grade-level standards taught in this lesson, see citations on Student Edition pages.)

Prerequisite Standard

- Grade 8, Literary Response and Analysis 3.6 **Identify significant literary devices (e.g., metaphor, symbolism, dialect, irony) that define a writer's style and use those elements to interpret the work.**

Reading Skills

- Make predictions.

Summary *at grade level*

Grigory S. Smirnov, gentleman farmer, comes to collect a debt from Mrs. Popov, a young widow. Smirnov is a confirmed bachelor who has vowed never to marry. Mrs. Popov, whose late husband was often unfaithful to her, has vowed to remain faithful to him forever in order to demonstrate her love. The two discover a fiery attraction as their stubborn argument over the debt leads to a confrontation that almost results in a duel. The play ends not with gunshots, but with a passionate kiss.

Before You Read

The Brute

Literary Focus

Comedy: It Ends Happily

In both structure and characterization, a comedy is the opposite of a tragedy. A **comedy** is a story that ends happily—often with a marriage. Many comedies have a **plot** structured around boy-meets-girl (or, today, girl-meets-boy), in which the lovers must overcome obstacles so they can fall into each other's arms at the play's end. In the most typical example of a comedy, the plot is a celebration of the renewal of life and the power of love.

Farce: Exaggerated Comedy

A **farce** is a type of comedy in which exaggerated and often stereotyped characters are involved in ridiculous situations. The humor in farce is based on crude physical actions, or slapstick, and clowning. Characters may slip on banana peels, walk into doors, or disguise themselves in clothes of the opposite sex.

The word *farce* is a French word meaning "stuffing." Years ago farces were used as "stuffing" during the interludes of a serious play. Even tragedies, however, may include farcical elements, for comic relief. Today farce is often the basic ingredient in comic TV sitcoms.

Reading Standard 3.1 Articulate the relationship between the expressed purposes and the characteristics of different forms of dramatic literature (e.g., comedy).

Reading Skills

Making Predictions

Chekhov's play spotlights two "battling lovers," Mrs. Popov and Smirnov. This basic dramatic situation—the meeting of two characters who are wildly antagonistic to each other at first—has been used in thousands of Hollywood comedies. The audience *knows* that the two are going to end up together eventually. The question that keeps us in suspense is: "*When* and *how* is that going to happen?"

Part of the fun of watching these stories is in seeing if we can predict when that moment of realization will take place. If the storyteller is clever, we find that our predictions are not always exactly right.

As you read the play, note the places where you make **predictions** about these characters and their future. How accurate are your predictions?

Make the Connection

Quickwrite

Two people meet. One person is shy; the other is loud and aggressive. They hate each other on sight. They argue. Soon, however, they find themselves attracted to each other. What do you think of the expression "Opposites attract"? Can you think of any movies, TV shows, or novels that are based on that idea? Do you see opposites attracting in real life?

Vocabulary Development

indisposed (in′di·spōzd′) *adj.:* slightly ill.

emancipation (ē·man′sə·pā′shən) *n.:* liberation; the act of setting free from restraint or control or being set free.

malicious (mə·lish′əs) *adj.:* intentionally harmful.

insinuate (in·sin′yo͞o·āt′) *v.:* suggest.

incoherent (in′kō·hir′ənt) *adj.:* rambling; disjointed.

impudence (im′pyo͞o·dəns) *n.:* quality of being disrespectful.

impunity (im·pyo͞o′ni·tē) *n.:* freedom from punishment.

RESOURCES: READING

Planning

- *One-Stop Planner* CD-ROM with Test Generator
- *On Course: Mapping Instruction*

Reading

- *Interactive Reading,* Teacher's Edition
  - Graphic Organizer: Elements of Comedy Chart

Differentiating Instruction

- *Lesson Plans for Language Development*
  - English-Language Learners, pp. 327–329, 360, 367
  - Special Education Students, pp. 330, 360, 367

724 Chapter 10 Drama • Evaluating an Argument

THE BRUTE
A Joke in One Act

Anton Chekhov
translated by Eric Bentley

Characters

Mrs. Popov, widow and landowner, small, with dimpled cheeks

Mr. Grigory S. Smirnov, gentleman farmer, middle-aged

Luka, Mrs. Popov's footman, an old man

Gardener

Coachman

Hired Men

The photographs throughout the play are from the 2002 production by the Expression Theater Ensemble.

Preteaching

Selection Starter

Motivate. Students have seen many comedies on stage, screen, and television. Have them retell the plots of their favorite comedies, and then discuss what elements make them funny. Ask students if any of the following elements of farce appear in the comedy: stereotyped characters, exaggeration, noisy activity, broad physical humor, or repetition. Explain that extreme characters and situations are the staples of comedy in general and farce in particular. Discuss the following questions: Are there some aspects of these comedies that are realistic? Beneath the surface, do the characters remind you of actual people?

Preview Vocabulary

Have students review the Vocabulary words on p. 724. Then, have pairs of students write a paragraph in which they incorporate all the Vocabulary words. The paragraph can take the form of a news item or a short-short story. Encourage students to be creative and humorous.

Assign the Reading

Students could first read this short, one-act play silently in class. You might want to divide the play into sections, divide the class into small groups, and have groups discuss each section after they read it.

Vocabulary

- *Vocabulary Development*
  - Vocabulary Worksheet, p. 49

Assessment

- *Progress Assessment of Reading*
  - Selection Test
- *One-Stop Planner* CD-ROM with Test Generator

DIRECT TEACHING

A Content-Area Connections

Culture: Nineteenth-Century Lifestyles

Make sure students know that a drawing room was a formal living room in upper-class homes. "In deep mourning" refers to the traditional dress of black worn for a period after the death of a loved one. What do the set and costume indicate? [Possible responses: The play is set in the past; Mrs. Popov is wealthy.]

B Literary Focus

GRADE-LEVEL STANDARD

Comedy. Mrs. Popov's exaggerated manner of speaking and her excessive period of mourning establishes the play's comic (farcical) tone. Ask students to pay special attention to Mrs. Popov's words and actions and how they reflect stereotypes of feminine behavior.

C Reading Skills

Making predictions. Since this play is a comedy, do you think Mrs. Popov will remain loyal to her late husband's memory or not? [Probably not, because comedies are structured around falling in love and usually end with a marriage.]

D Reading Skills

Interpreting. Why does Mrs. Popov want Toby to have extra oats? [She is making a sentimental gesture in memory of her husband, who adored Toby.]

A *The drawing room of a country house.* MRS. POPOV, *in deep mourning, is staring hard at a photograph.* LUKA *is with her.*

B **Luka.** It's not right, ma'am, you're killing yourself. The cook has gone off with the maid to pick berries. The cat's having a high old time in the yard catching birds. Every living thing is happy. But you stay moping here in the house like it was a convent,[1] taking no pleasure in nothing. I mean it, ma'am! It must be a full year since you set foot out of doors.

Mrs. Popov. I must never set foot out of doors again, Luka. Never! I have nothing to set foot out of doors *for.* My life is done. *He* is in his grave. I have buried myself alive in this house. We are *both* in our graves.

Luka. You're off again, ma'am. I just won't listen to you no more. Mr. Popov is dead, but what can we do about that? It's God's doing. God's will be done. You've cried over him, you've done your share of mourning, haven't you? There's a limit to everything. You can't go on weeping and wailing forever. My old lady died, for that matter, and I wept and wailed over her a whole month long. Well, that was it. I couldn't weep and wail all my life, she just wasn't worth it. (*He sighs.*) As for the neighbors, you've forgotten all about them, ma'am. You don't visit them and you don't let them visit you. You and I are like a pair of spiders—excuse the expression, ma'am—here we are in this house like a pair of spiders, we never see the light of day. And it isn't like there was no nice people around either. The whole county's swarming with 'em. There's a regiment quartered at Riblov, and the officers are so good-looking! The girls can't take their eyes off them.—There's a ball at the camp every Friday.—The military band plays most every day of the week.—What do you say, ma'am? You're young, you're pretty, you could enjoy yourself! Ten years from now you may want to strut and show your feathers to the officers, and it'll be too late.

Mrs. Popov (*firmly*). You must never bring this subject up again, Luka. Since Popov died, life has been an empty dream to me, you know that. *You* may think I am alive. Poor ignorant Luka! You are wrong. I am dead. I'm in my grave. Never more shall I see the light of day, never strip from my body this . . . raiment[2] of death! Are you listening, Luka? Let his ghost learn how I love him! C Yes, *I* know, and *you* know, he was often unfair to me, he was cruel to me, and he was unfaithful to me. What of it? *I* shall be faithful to *him,* that's all. I will show him how *I* can love. Hereafter, in a better world than this, he will welcome me back, the same loyal girl I always was—

"Since Popov died, life has been an empty dream to me."

Luka. Instead of carrying on this way, ma'am, you should go out in the garden and take a bit of a walk, ma'am. Or why not harness Toby and take a drive? Call on a couple of the neighbors, ma'am?

Mrs. Popov (*breaking down*). Oh, Luka!

Luka. Yes, ma'am? What have I said, ma'am? Oh dear!

Mrs. Popov. Toby! You said Toby! He adored that horse. When he drove me out to the Korchagins and the Vlasovs, it was always with Toby! He was a wonderful driver, do you remember, Luka? So graceful! So strong! I can see him now, pulling at those reins with all his might and D main! Toby! Luka, tell them to give Toby an extra portion of oats today.

Luka. Yes, ma'am.

1. **convent** *n.:* religious home for nuns.

2. **raiment** (rā′mənt) *n.:* clothing.

DIFFERENTIATING INSTRUCTION

Learners Having Difficulty

Invite learners having difficulty to read *The Brute* silently to themselves for homework or with a partner in a private setting. Encourage these students to focus on passages in the play that make the most sense for them. A chart may be employed to help students remember the clear sections. Once they have completed the reading, they should meet with other students to form a small group and share their findings, focusing specifically on areas where there isn't any overlap. In this way, students will help bridge difficulties for each other.

English-Language Learners

A good deal of the comedy in this opening section is derived from the contrast between Luka's down-to-earth, sometimes ungrammatical language and Mrs. Popov's overwrought, highly sentimental, formal language. Help students notice this contrast by identifying examples.

Resources Reminder

For lessons designed for intermediate and advanced English-language learners, see *Lesson Plans for Language Development,* pp. 327–329, 360, 367.

[*A bell rings.*]

Mrs. Popov. Who is that? Tell them I'm not home.

Luka. Very good, ma'am. (*Exit.*)

Mrs. Popov (*gazing again at the photograph*). You shall see, my Popov, how a wife can love and forgive. Till death do us part. Longer than that. Till death reunite us forever! (*Suddenly a titter breaks through her tears.*) Aren't you ashamed of yourself, Popov? Here's your little wife, being good, being faithful, so faithful she's locked up here waiting for her own funeral, while you—doesn't it make you ashamed, you naughty boy? You were terrible, you know. You were unfaithful, and you made those awful scenes about it, you stormed out and left me alone for weeks—

[*Enter* LUKA.]

Luka (*upset*). There's someone asking for you, ma'am. Says he must—

Mrs. Popov. I suppose you told him that since my husband's death I see no one?

Luka. Yes, ma'am. I did, ma'am. But he wouldn't listen, ma'am. He says it's urgent.

Mrs. Popov (*shrilly*). I see no one!!

Luka. He won't take no for an answer, ma'am. He just curses and swears and comes in anyway. He's a perfect monster, ma'am. He's in the dining room right now. **E** **F**

Mrs. Popov. In the dining room, is he? I'll give him his comeuppance. Bring him in here this minute. (*Exit* LUKA. *Suddenly sad again*) Why do they do this to me? Why? Insulting my grief, intruding on my solitude? (*She sighs.*) I'm afraid I'll have to enter a convent. I will, I *must* enter a convent.

[*Enter* MR. SMIRNOV *and* LUKA.]

Smirnov (*to* LUKA). Dolt! Idiot! You talk too much! (*Seeing* MRS. POPOV. *With dignity*) May I have the honor of introducing myself, madam? Grigory S. Smirnov, landowner and lieutenant of artillery, retired. Forgive me, madam, if I disturb your peace and quiet, but my business is both urgent and weighty. **G**

Mrs. Popov (*declining to offer him her hand*). What is it you wish, sir?

Smirnov. At the time of his death, your late husband—with whom I had the honor to be acquainted, ma'am—was in my debt to the tune of twelve hundred rubles. I have two notes to prove it. Tomorrow, ma'am, I must pay the interest on a bank loan. I have therefore no alternative, ma'am, but to ask you to pay me the money today.

Mrs. Popov. Twelve hundred rubles? But what did my husband owe it to you for?

Smirnov. He used to buy his oats from me, madam.

Mrs. Popov (*to* LUKA, *with a sigh*). Remember what I said, Luka: Tell them to give Toby an extra portion of oats today! (*Exit* LUKA.) My dear Mr.—what was that name again?

Smirnov. Smirnov, ma'am.

Mrs. Popov. My dear Mr. Smirnov, if Mr. Popov owed you money, you shall be paid—to the last ruble, to the last kopeck. But today—you must excuse me, Mr.—what was it?

DIRECT TEACHING

E Literary Focus
GRADE-LEVEL STANDARD

Comedy. Luka's comments are our first introduction to the play's other main character. What elements of exaggeration do you note in this description? [Possible responses: The character is described as a "monster." He sounds more like some kind of wild animal than a man. His loud and rude behavior is extremely obnoxious.]

F Reading Skills

Making predictions. Can you predict a conflict ahead? [Mrs. Popov is likely to tangle with this rude "monster."]

G Learners Having Difficulty

Reading aloud. The dialogue that begins with this speech and ends on p. 728, when Mrs. Popov exits, is especially fun for students to read aloud. An oral reading will help them recognize the conflict between the two characters and their exaggerated responses to the situation.

Special Education Students

For lessons designed for special education students, see *Lesson Plans for Language Development*, pp. 330, 360, 367.

Advanced Learners

Enrichment. Have students research the period in which the play is set—Czarist Russia in the latter half of the nineteenth century. As they read the play, have them discuss periodically how the setting contributes to the play's theme and viewpoint.

DIRECT TEACHING

A Literary Focus
GRADE-LEVEL STANDARD

Conflict. What conflict has developed here? [An external conflict over money has developed between the two main characters.] Are you more inclined at this point to side with Mrs. Popov or with Smirnov? [Possible responses: Smirnov, because he really needs the money; Mrs. Popov, because she is only asking him to wait two days.]

B Literary Focus
GRADE-LEVEL STANDARD

Comedy. In this comic monologue, Smirnov's rage builds up to a humorously exaggerated level. The humor is heightened by the fact that he is speaking to himself, rather than Mrs. Popov, whose abrupt exit has elicited the outburst. Repetition is a frequently used element of comedy. Ask students to identify instances of repetition. Did you find these funny? Why or why not? [Smirnov repeats "not in the mood" several times and his question about the interest.] What other element of farce is found in Smirnov's monologue? [Possible response: Smirnov works himself into a physical rage; at the end of the monologue, he is shuddering with rage and gasping for breath. His crude physical actions are an element of farce.]

Smirnov. Smirnov, ma'am.

A **Mrs. Popov.** Today, Mr. Smirnov, I have no ready cash in the house. (SMIRNOV *starts to speak.*) Tomorrow, Mr. Smirnov, no, the day after tomorrow, all will be well. My steward[3] will be back from town. I shall see that he pays what is owing. Today, no. In any case, today is exactly seven months from Mr. Popov's death. On such a day you will understand that I am in no mood to think of money.

Smirnov. Madam, if you don't pay up now, you can carry me out feet foremost. They'll seize my estate.

Mrs. Popov. You can have your money. (*He starts to thank her.*) Tomorrow. (*He again starts to speak.*) That is: the day after tomorrow.

Smirnov. I don't need the money the day after tomorrow. I need it today.

Mrs. Popov. I'm sorry, Mr.—

Smirnov (*shouting*). Smirnov!

Mrs. Popov (*sweetly*). Yes, of course. But you can't have it today.

Smirnov. But I can't wait for it any longer!

Mrs. Popov. Be sensible, Mr. Smirnov. How can I pay you if I don't have it?

Smirnov. You don't have it?

Mrs. Popov. I don't have it.

Smirnov. Sure?

Mrs. Popov. Positive.

Smirnov. Very well. I'll make a note to that effect. (*Shrugging*) And then they want me to keep cool. I meet the tax commissioner on the street, and he says, "Why are you always in such a bad humor, Smirnov?" Bad humor! How can I help it, in God's name? I need money, I need it desperately. Take yesterday: I leave home at the crack of dawn; I call on all my debtors. Not a one of them pays up. Footsore and weary, I creep at midnight into some little dive and try to snatch a few winks of sleep on the floor by the vodka barrel. Then today, I come here, fifty miles from home, saying to myself, "At last, at last, I can be sure of something," and you're not in the mood! You give me a mood! How the devil can I help getting all worked up?

"I'm in a rage! I'm in a positively towering rage!"

Mrs. Popov. I thought I'd made it clear, Mr. Smirnov, that you'll get your money the minute my steward is back from town?

Smirnov. What the hell do I care about your steward? Pardon the expression, ma'am. But it was you I came to see.

Mrs. Popov. What language! What a tone to take to a lady! I refuse to hear another word. (*Quickly, exit.*)

B **Smirnov.** Not in the mood, huh? "Exactly seven months since Popov's death," huh? How about me? (*Shouting after her*) Is there this interest to pay, or isn't there? I'm asking you a question: Is there this interest to pay, or isn't there? So your husband died, and you're not in the mood, and your steward's gone off someplace, and so forth and so on, but what can *I* do about all that, huh? What do *you* think I should do? Take a running jump and shove my head through the wall? Take off in a balloon? You don't know my *other* debtors. I call on Gruzdeff. Not at home. I look for Yaroshevitch. He's hiding out. I find Kooritsin. He kicks up a row, and I have to throw him through the window. I work my way right down the list. Not a kopeck. Then I come to you, and damn it, if you'll pardon the expression, you're not in the mood! (*Quietly, as he realizes he's talking to air*) I've spoiled them all, that's what; I've let them play me for a sucker. Well, I'll show them. I'll show this one. I'll stay right here

3. **steward** (stōō'ərd) *n.:* person in charge of running an estate.

DIFFERENTIATING INSTRUCTION

Learners Having Difficulty

Paraphrasing. Smirnov's long speech on p. 728 may be difficult for some students to fully comprehend and appreciate. Just seeing the long blocks of uninterrupted text can be daunting for them. Smirnov is basically reiterating what he has gone through to collect the money people owe him. Have students identify and paraphrase each of the episodes described.

English-Language Learners

Mrs. Popov's explanation of why she cannot repay the debt immediately ("I am in no mood to think of money") infuriates Smirnov. He repeats this phrase many times during his outbursts, growing angrier with each repetition of it. Make sure that students are familiar with the common English expression "I'm not in the mood." It is often used as a trivial excuse for not doing something.

till she pays up. Ugh! (*He shudders with rage.*) I'm in a rage! I'm in a positively towering rage! Every nerve in my body is trembling at forty to the dozen! I can't breathe, I feel ill, I think I'm going to faint, hey, you there!

[*Enter* LUKA.]

Luka. Yes, sir? Is there anything you wish, sir?
Smirnov. Water! Water!! No, make it vodka. (*Exit* LUKA.) Consider the logic of it. A fellow creature is desperately in need of cash, so desperately in need that he has to seriously contemplate hanging himself, and this woman, this mere chit of a girl, won't pay up, and why not? Because, forsooth, she isn't in the mood! Oh, the logic of women! Come to that, I never have liked them, I could do without the whole sex. Talk to a woman? I'd rather sit on a barrel of dynamite, the very thought gives me gooseflesh. Women! Creatures of poetry and romance! Just to see one in the distance gets me mad. My legs start twitching with rage. I feel like yelling for help.

[*Enter* LUKA, *handing* SMIRNOV *a glass of water.*]

Luka. Mrs. Popov is indisposed, sir. She is seeing no one.
Smirnov. Get out. (*Exit* LUKA.) Indisposed, is she? Seeing no one, huh? Well, she can see me or not, but I'll be here, I'll be right here till she pays up. If you're sick for a week, I'll be here for a week. If you're sick for a year, I'll be here for a year. You won't get around *me* with your widow's weeds[4] and your schoolgirl dimples. I know all about dimples. (*Shouting through the window*) Semyon, let the horses out of those shafts, we're not leaving, we're staying, and tell them to give the horses some oats, yes, oats, you fool, what do you think? (*Walking away from the window*) What a mess, what an unholy mess! I didn't sleep last night, the heat is terrific today, not a one of 'em has paid up, and here's this—this skirt in mourning that's not in the mood! My head aches, where's that— (*He drinks from the glass.*) Water, ugh! You there!

[*Enter* LUKA.]

Luka. Yes, sir. You wish for something, sir?
Smirnov. Where's that confounded vodka I asked for? (*Exit* LUKA. SMIRNOV *sits and looks himself over.*) Oof! A fine figure of a man *I* am! Unwashed, uncombed, unshaven, straw on my vest, dust all over me. The little woman must've taken me for a highwayman. (*Yawns*) I suppose it wouldn't be considered polite to barge into a drawing room in this state, but who cares? I'm not a visitor, I'm a creditor—most unwelcome of guests, second only to Death.

[*Enter* LUKA.]

Luka (*handing him the vodka*). If I may say so, sir, you take too many liberties, sir.
Smirnov. What?!
Luka. Oh, nothing, sir, nothing.
Smirnov. Who do you think you're talking to? Shut your mouth!
Luka (*aside*). There's an evil spirit abroad. The devil must have sent him. Oh! (*Exit* LUKA.)
Smirnov. What a rage I'm in! I'll grind the whole world to powder. Oh, I feel ill again. You there!

4. **widow's weeds:** black clothing worn by a widow to mourn a husband's death.

Vocabulary
indisposed (in'di·spōzd') *adj.:* slightly ill.

DIRECT TEACHING

C Literary Focus
GRADE-LEVEL STANDARD
Conflict. What new basis for a conflict between Smirnov and Mrs. Popov is established in this speech? [Smirnov announces that he hates all women.]

D Reading Skills
Making predictions. Do you think Smirnov will really live up to his words? What do you think will happen next? [Possible responses: Smirnov will probably wait for Mrs. Popov to return, but he still might not get the money because she is as stubborn as he is. The fact that he has noticed Mrs. Popov's "schoolgirl dimples" indicates that he is noticing her physical appearance; this might be a sign that he is starting to develop a romantic attraction. Since comedies generally end in marriage, Smirnov and Mrs. Popov will probably fall in love.]

E Advanced Learners
Enrichment. What subtle change in Smirnov's character occurs here? What might this change indicate? [Possible response: Smirnov pays attention to how he might appear to Mrs. Popov. He is beginning to care about her opinion of him.]

Advanced Learners
Acceleration. In order to move students towards eleventh- and twelfth-grade standard 3.1, point out that a character in a farce cannot be too sensitive or sympathetic or that much of the humor the character generates will be lost.
Activity. Have students identify several clear examples of Smirnov's coarseness in his dealings with Mrs. Popov or Luka and encourage them to rewrite one of those examples as realistic drama.

DIRECT TEACHING

A English-Language Learners

Understanding diction. Help students recognize that Mrs. Popov's overly formal diction is very old-fashioned, even by the nineteenth-century standards of the play's setting. What effect does her diction have? [Possible responses: Mrs. Popov's overly formal diction is humorous. Her extreme modesty here contradicts her previous assertiveness.]

[*Enter* MRS. POPOV.]

A **Mrs. Popov** (*looking at the floor*). In the solitude of my rural retreat, Mr. Smirnov, I've long since grown unaccustomed to the sound of the human voice. Above all, I cannot bear shouting. I must beg you not to break the silence.

Smirnov. Very well. Pay me my money and I'll go.

Mrs. Popov. I told you before, and I tell you again, Mr. Smirnov: I have no cash; you'll have to wait till the day after tomorrow. Can I express myself more plainly?

Smirnov. And *I* told *you* before, and *I* tell *you* again, that I need the money today, that the day after tomorrow is too late, and that if you don't pay, and pay now, I'll have to hang myself in the morning!

Mrs. Popov. But I have no cash. This is quite a puzzle.

Smirnov. You won't pay, huh?

Mrs. Popov. I *can't* pay, Mr. Smirnov.

Smirnov. In that case, I'm going to sit here and wait. (*Sits down*) You'll pay up the day after tomorrow? Very good. Till the day after tomorrow, here I sit. (*Pause. He jumps up.*) Now look, do I have to pay that interest tomorrow, or don't I? Or do you think I'm joking?

Mrs. Popov. I must ask you not to raise your voice, Mr. Smirnov. This is not a stable.

Smirnov. Who said it was? Do I have to pay the interest tomorrow or not?

Mrs. Popov. Mr. Smirnov, do you know how to behave in the presence of a lady?

Smirnov. No, madam, I do not know how to behave in the presence of a lady.

READING MINI-LESSON

Developing Word-Attack Skills

Explain that new words are added to the English language all the time. New words are created in different ways, but two important ways are *derivation,* adding prefixes and suffixes to an existing word, and *compounding,* putting existing words together to form new words. The selection word *comeuppance* is an example of both word-making techniques. First the two words *come* and *up* are put together. Then the noun-forming suffix *–ance* is added. Point out that reading unfamiliar words formed by derivation and compounding requires recognizing the smaller words that make up the words. Write the selection word *playacting* on the chalkboard. Have students identify the elements that make up the word: *play* + *act* + *–ing.* Invite students to suggest other words they know that were created by adding affixes to an existing word and adding two existing words together.

Activity. Have students identify the existing words and affixes that make up each of these words. Answers appear in brackets.

1. stick-to-itiveness
2. neoimpressionism
3. micrometeorology

Mrs. Popov. Just what I thought. I look at you, and I say: ugh! I hear you talk, and I say to myself: "That man doesn't know how to talk to a lady."

Smirnov. You'd like me to come simpering[5] to you in French, I suppose. "*Enchanté, madame! Merci beaucoup* for not paying zee money, *madame! Pardonnez-moi* if I 'ave disturbed you, *madame!* How *charmante* you look in mourning, *madame!*"

Mrs. Popov. Now you're being silly, Mr. Smirnov.

Smirnov (*mimicking*). "Now you're being silly, Mr. Smirnov." "You don't know how to talk to a lady, Mr. Smirnov." Look here, Mrs. Popov, I've known more women than you've known kitty cats. I've fought three duels on their account. I've jilted twelve and been jilted by nine others. Oh, yes, Mrs. Popov, I've played the fool in my time, whispered sweet nothings, bowed and scraped and endeavored to please. Don't tell me I don't know what it is to love, to pine away with longing, to have the blues, to melt like butter, to be weak as water. I was full of tender emotion. I was carried away with passion. I squandered half my fortune on the sex. I chattered about women's emancipation. But there's an end to everything, dear madam. Burning eyes, dark eyelashes, ripe, red lips, dimpled cheeks, heaving bosoms, soft whisperings, the moon above, the lake below—I don't give a rap for that sort of nonsense any more, Mrs. Popov. I've found out about women. Present company excepted, they're liars. Their behavior is mere playacting; their conversation is sheer gossip. Yes, dear lady, women, young or old, are false, petty, vain, cruel, malicious, unreasonable. As for intelligence, any sparrow could give them points. Appearances, I admit, can be deceptive. In appearance, a woman may be all poetry and romance, goddess and angel, muslin[6] and fluff. To look at her exterior is to be transported to heaven. But I have looked at her interior, Mrs. Popov, and what did I find there—in her very soul? A crocodile. (*He has gripped the back of the chair so firmly that it snaps.*) And, what is more revolting, a crocodile with an illusion, a crocodile that imagines tender sentiments are its own special province, a crocodile that thinks itself queen of the realm of love! Whereas, in sober fact, dear madam, if a woman can love anything except a lap dog, you can hang me by the feet on that nail. For a man, love is suffering, love is sacrifice. A woman just swishes her train around and tightens her grip on your nose. Now, you're a woman, aren't you, Mrs. Popov? You must be an expert on some of this. Tell me, quite frankly, did you ever know a woman to be—faithful, for instance? Or even sincere? Only old hags, huh? Though some women are old hags from birth. But as for the others? You're right: A faithful woman is a freak of nature—like a cat with horns.

> "Mr. Smirnov, do you know how to behave in the presence of a lady?"

Mrs. Popov. Who *is* faithful, then? Who *have* you cast for the faithful lover? Not man?

Smirnov. Right first time, Mrs. Popov: man.

Mrs. Popov (*going off into a peal of bitter laughter*). Man! Man is faithful! That's a new one! (*Fiercely*) What right do you have to say this, Mr. Smirnov? Men faithful? Let me tell you something. Of all the men I have ever known, my late husband Popov was the best. I loved him, and

5. **simpering** *v.:* speaking in a silly, affected way.

6. **muslin** *n.:* a kind of cotton fabric.

Vocabulary

emancipation (ē·man′sə·pā′shən) *n.:* liberation; the act of setting free from restraint or control or being set free.

malicious (mə·lish′əs) *adj.:* intentionally harmful.

DIRECT TEACHING

B Content-Area Connections

Culture: The French Connection Smirnov is deliberately mocking the affectations of the Russian upper classes, who considered it refined to converse in French. The Russian aristocracy looked down on their own language until Aleksandr Pushkin, the great national poet, helped to popularize its use.

C English-Language Learners

Understanding figurative language. Point out Smirnov's extravagant use of figures of speech. Help students understand the comparison being made in each. Explain that the figures of speech Smirnov uses are clichés because they are unoriginal and overused. Ask students to create some original ones.

D Reading Skills

Interpreting. Smirnov and Mrs. Popov are more alike than they first appear. Can you find any parallel between Smirnov's past experience and Mrs. Popov's? [Both have been hurt by their experiences with the opposite sex.]

E Literary Focus

GRADE-LEVEL STANDARD

Comedy. What element of farce does Chekhov use here? [Smirnov's breaking the chair adds a touch of slapstick, or exaggerated physical humor.]

4. futuristic
5. open-mindedness
6. landownership
7. postmodernism
8. unsportsmanlike
9. counterclockwise
10. echolocation
11. ideographic
12. interplanetary
13. perfectionist
14. hypersensitivity

1. stick + to + it + *–ive* + *–ness*
2. *neo–* + impress + *–ion* + *–ism*
3. *micro–* + meteor + *–ology*
4. futur(e) + *–ist* + *–ic*
5. open + minded + *–ness*
6. land + owner + *–ship*
7. *post–* + modern + *–ism*
8. *un–* + sports + man + *–like*
9. *counter–* + clock + *–wise*
10. echo + locat(e) + *–ion*
11. *ideo–* + graph + *–ic*
12. *inter–* + planet + *–ary*
13. perfect + *–ion* + *–ist*
14. *hyper–* + sensitiv(e) + *–ity*

Direct Teaching

A Literary Focus
GRADE-LEVEL STANDARD

Character. Since Mrs. Popov had an unfaithful husband, why do you think she intends to remain faithful to him even after his death? [Possible response: Mrs. Popov is doing this for herself rather than for her late husband—she seems to enjoy cultivating a suffering yet self-righteous image of herself.]

B Reading Skills

Making predictions. Smirnov's comment reveals that Mrs. Popov is taking care to appear attractive and also that Smirnov is looking closely enough to notice. Why is Mrs. Popov so outraged by Smirnov's insinuation? How do you predict their relationship will develop? [Possible responses: Mrs. Popov is outraged because Smirnov has exposed an inconsistency in the image she wants to cultivate. They will probably continue to fight for a while more before some resolution is reached. Since they are not being honest with each other, they won't be able to admit their mutual attraction.]

C Literary Focus
GRADE-LEVEL STANDARD

Comedy. This is a classic farcical situation—a weak character panicking at a stronger character's threats. What other element of farce is used here? [the exaggerated physical responses of both Smirnov and Luka; the surprisingly strong language Smirnov uses, especially when compared to Luka's weak pleading for Smirnov to go]

---

there are women who know how to love, Mr. Smirnov. I gave him my youth, my happiness, my life, my fortune. I worshipped the ground he trod on—and what happened? The best of men was unfaithful to me, Mr. Smirnov. Not once in a while. All the time. After he died, I found his desk drawer full of love letters. While he was alive, he was always going away for the weekend. He squandered my money. He flirted with other women before my very eyes. But, in spite of all, Mr. Smirnov, *I* was faithful. Unto death. And beyond. I am *still* faithful, Mr. Smirnov! Buried alive in this house, I shall wear mourning till the day I, too, am called to my eternal rest.

Smirnov (*laughing scornfully*). Expect me to believe that? As if I couldn't see through all this hocus-pocus. Buried alive! Till you're called to your eternal rest! Till when? Till some little poet—or some little subaltern[7] with his first moustache—comes riding by and asks: "Can that be the house of the mysterious Tamara, who for love of her late husband has buried herself alive, vowing to see no man?" Ha!

Mrs. Popov (*flaring up*). How dare you? How dare you insinuate—?

Smirnov. You may have buried yourself alive, Mrs. Popov, but you haven't forgotten to powder your nose.

Mrs. Popov (*incoherent*). How dare you? How—?

Smirnov. Who's raising his voice now? Just because I call a spade a spade. Because I shoot straight from the shoulder. Well, don't shout at me, I'm not your steward.

Mrs. Popov. I'm not shouting, you're shouting! Oh, leave me alone!

Smirnov. Pay me the money, and I will.

Mrs. Popov. You'll get no money out of me!

Smirnov. Oh, so that's it!

Mrs. Popov. Not a ruble, not a kopeck. Get out! Leave me alone!

Smirnov. Not being your husband, I must ask you not to make scenes with me. (*He sits.*) I don't like scenes.

> "I'm not shouting, you're shouting! Oh, leave me alone!"

Mrs. Popov (*choking with rage*). You're sitting down?

Smirnov. Correct, I'm sitting down.

Mrs. Popov. I asked you to leave!

Smirnov. Then give me the money. (*Aside*) Oh, what a rage I'm in, what a rage!

Mrs. Popov. The impudence of the man! I won't talk to you a moment longer. Get out. (*Pause*) Are you going?

Smirnov. No.

Mrs. Popov. No?!

Smirnov. No.

Mrs. Popov. On your head be it. Luka! (*Enter* LUKA.) Show the gentleman out, Luka.

Luka (*approaching*). I'm afraid, sir, I'll have to ask you, um, to leave, sir, now, um—

Smirnov (*jumping up*). Shut your mouth, you old idiot! Who do you think you're talking to? I'll make mincemeat of you.

Luka (*clutching his heart*). Mercy on us! Holy saints above! (*He falls into an armchair.*) I'm taken sick! I can't breathe!

Mrs. Popov. Then where's Dasha? Dasha! Dasha! Come here at once! (*She rings.*)

Luka. They gone picking berries, ma'am, I'm alone here—Water, water, I'm taken sick!

Vocabulary

insinuate (in·sin′yo͞o·āt′) *v.:* suggest.

incoherent (in′kō·hir′ənt) *adj.:* rambling; disjointed.

impudence (im′pyo͞o·dəns) *n.:* quality of being disrespectful.

7. **subaltern** (səb·ôl′tərn) *n.:* a person of low rank.

Differentiating Instruction

Learners Having Difficulty

Students may have difficulty understanding why Mrs. Popov claims to be so loyal to her husband even though she quite readily admits that he was unfaithful to her. Have students form small groups and brainstorm plausible reasons for Mrs. Popov's behavior. Remind them that sometimes people say one thing but really believe something else.

English-Language Learners

Smirnov peppers his speech with a number of idioms. Have students guess at the meaning of the following sentences and then explain any they are still unable to grasp. They should then paraphrase each one.

- "As if I couldn't see through all this hocus-pocus."
- "Just because I call a spade a spade."
- "Because I shoot straight from the shoulder."
- "I'll make mincemeat out of you."

Mrs. Popov (*to* SMIRNOV). Get out, you!

Smirnov. Can't you even be polite with me, Mrs. Popov?

Mrs. Popov (*clenching her fists and stamping her feet*). With you? You're a wild animal, you were never housebroken!

Smirnov. What? What did you say?

Mrs. Popov. I said you were a wild animal, you were never housebroken.

Smirnov (*advancing upon her*). And what right do you have to talk to me like that?

Mrs. Popov. Like what?

Smirnov. You have insulted me, madam.

Mrs. Popov. What of it? Do you think I'm scared of you?

"What of it? Do you think I'm scared of you?"

Smirnov. So you think you can get away with it because you're a woman. A creature of poetry and romance, huh? Well, it doesn't go down with me. I hereby challenge you to a duel.

Luka. Mercy on us! Holy saints alive! Water!

Smirnov. I propose we shoot it out.

Mrs. Popov. Trying to scare me again? Just because you have big fists and a voice like a bull? You're a brute.

Smirnov. No one insults Grigory S. Smirnov with impunity! And I don't care if you *are* a female.

Mrs. Popov (*trying to outshout him*). Brute, brute, brute! **D**

Smirnov. The sexes are equal, are they? Fine: Then it's just prejudice to expect men alone to pay for insults. I hereby challenge—

Mrs. Popov (*screaming*). All right! You want to shoot it out? All right! Let's shoot it out! **E**

Smirnov. And let it be here and now!

Mrs. Popov. Here and now! All right! I'll have Popov's pistols here in one minute! (*Walks away, then turns*) Putting one of Popov's bullets through your silly head will be a pleasure! *Au revoir.* (*Exit.*)

Smirnov. I'll bring her down like a duck, a sitting duck. I'm not one of your little poets, I'm no little subaltern with his first moustache. No, sir, there's no weaker sex where I'm concerned!

Luka. Sir! Master! (*He goes down on his knees.*) Take pity on a poor old man, and do me a favor: Go away. It was

Vocabulary
impunity (im·pyo͞o'ni·tē) *n.:* freedom from punishment.

DIRECT TEACHING

D Literary Focus
GRADE-LEVEL STANDARD

Character. How has Mrs. Popov's behavior changed? [She is no longer the refined, suffering lady but has become noisy and vehement.] **Is the change believable? Why or why not?** [Possible responses: Yes, Mrs. Popov has been confrontational and slightly aggressive throughout the play, so it is a logical extension of her character. No, even though she is upset, it is incongruent with her being a widow in mourning.]

E Content-Area Connections

Culture: Dueling Differences
Women did not traditionally fight duels; therefore, Chekhov's audience would have found Mrs. Popov's readiness to "shoot it out" highly comical.

DEVELOPING FLUENCY

Small-group activity. Have students work in small groups to develop a dramatic reading of a favorite section of *The Brute*. For an effective oral interpretation and smooth delivery, students need to be thoroughly familiar with all the vocabulary and expressions in the play.

DIRECT TEACHING

A Literary Focus
GRADE-LEVEL STANDARD

Character. How does Smirnov's attitude toward Mrs. Popov appear to be changing? [He is favorably struck by her spirit.] **Is the change believable?** [Possible responses: Yes, he has said all along that he doesn't like traditional women. No, he doesn't appear to like women in general, no matter what.]

B Reading Skills

Making predictions. Luka seems convinced that the battle between Mrs. Popov and Smirnov will culminate in a duel. Do you predict there will be a duel? Why or why not? [Possible responses: Yes, Mrs. Popov seems determined to go through with it. No, Smirnov is no longer angry with her; he's just humoring her at this point.]

C Literary Focus
GRADE-LEVEL STANDARD

Comedy. How does the tone of the dialogue here humorously contrast with its subject? [Possible response: In calm, matter-of-fact tones, the two characters are discussing their plan to try and kill one another.]

D Literary Focus
GRADE-LEVEL STANDARD

Comedy. A touch of slapstick helps this scene remain farcical rather than becoming melodramatic. In the middle of a serious speech, Smirnov ludicrously breaks another chair.

bad enough before, you nearly scared me to death. But a duel—!

Smirnov (*ignoring him*). A duel! That's equality of the sexes for you! That's women's emancipation! Just as a matter of principle I'll bring her down like a duck. But what a woman! "Putting one of Popov's bullets through your silly head . . ." Her cheeks were flushed, her eyes were gleaming! And, by Heaven, she's accepted the challenge! I never knew a woman like this before!

Luka. Sir! Master! Please go away! I'll always pray for you!

A **Smirnov** (*again ignoring him*). What a woman! Phew!! *She's* no sourpuss; *she's* no crybaby. She's fire-and-brimstone.[8] She's a human cannonball. What a shame I have to kill her!

Luka (*weeping*). Please, kind sir, please, go away!

Smirnov (*as before*). I like her, isn't that funny? With those dimples and all? I like her. I'm even prepared to consider letting her off that debt. And where's my rage? It's gone. I never knew a woman like this before.

[*Enter* MRS. POPOV *with pistols.*]

Mrs. Popov (*boldly*). Pistols, Mr. Smirnov! (*Matter of fact*) But before we start, you'd better show me how it's done, I'm not too familiar with these things. In fact I never gave a pistol a second look.

B **Luka.** Lord, have mercy on us, I must go hunt up the gardener and the coachman. Why has this catastrophe fallen upon us, O Lord? (*Exit.*)

Smirnov (*examining the pistols*). Well, it's like this. There are several makes: One is the Mortimer, with capsules, especially constructed for dueling. What you have here are Smith and Wesson triple-action revolvers, with extractor, first-rate job, worth ninety rubles at the very least. You hold it this way. (*Aside*) My Lord, what eyes she has! They're setting me on fire.

Mrs. Popov. This way?

C **Smirnov.** Yes, that's right. You cock the trigger, take aim like this, head up, arm out like this. Then you just press with this finger here, and it's all over. The main thing is, keep cool, take slow aim, and don't let your arm jump.

Mrs. Popov. I see. And if it's inconvenient to do the job here, we can go out in the garden.

Smirnov. Very good. Of course, I should warn you: I'll be firing in the air.

Mrs. Popov. What? This is the end. Why?

Smirnov. Oh, well—because—for private reasons.

Mrs. Popov. Scared, huh? (*She laughs heartily.*) Now don't you try to get out of it, Mr. Smirnov. My blood is up. I won't be happy till I've drilled a hole through that skull of yours. Follow me. What's the matter? Scared?

Smirnov. That's right. I'm scared.

Mrs. Popov. Oh, come on, what's the matter with you?

Smirnov. Well, um, Mrs. Popov, I um, I like you.

Mrs. Popov (*laughing bitterly*). Good Lord! He likes me, does he? The gall[9] of the man. (*Showing him the door*) You may leave, Mr. Smirnov.

Smirnov (*Quietly puts the gun down, takes his hat, and walks to the door. Then he stops, and the pair look at each other without a word. Then, approaching gingerly*). D Listen, Mrs. Popov. Are you still mad at me? I'm in the devil of a temper myself, of course. But then, you see—what I mean is—it's this way—the fact is—(*roaring*) Well, is it my fault if I like you? (*Clutches the back of a chair. It breaks.*) What fragile furniture you have here! I like you. Know what I mean? I could fall in love with you.

Mrs. Popov. I hate you. Get out!

Smirnov. What a woman! I never saw anything

8. **fire-and-brimstone** *adj.:* often refers to eternal punishment in hell or describes fiery religious sermons; here, extremely lively.

9. **gall** (gôl) *n.:* nerve; rude boldness.

DIFFERENTIATING INSTRUCTION

Learners Having Difficulty

Have students consider the comic effect the two main characters have on an audience as they discuss the duel in such matter-of-fact tones. Remind them that if the duel takes place, the result will be fatal for one of the characters. Tell students that humor is sometimes generated from serious topics when they are handled in an understated way.

English-Language Learners

Smirnov uses several colorful expressions to describe what Mrs. Popov is and what she is not. Have students guess at the meaning of the following phrases and then explain any they are still unable to grasp: *sourpuss, crybaby,* and a *human cannonball.* Also point out the footnote that explains "fire and brimstone."

Advanced Learners

Enrichment. Have students read one of Chekhov's more serious plays: *The Seagull, Uncle Vanya, The Three Sisters,* or *The Cherry Orchard.*

Activity. Have students write an essay analyzing the relationship between two or more of the characters in the play.

DEVELOPING FLUENCY

Individual activity. Smirnov and Mrs. Popov go through many emotional changes. Have students re-read this scene, paying special attention to the stage directions. Then, have them choose other ways the characters might respond to one another, and have students rewrite the dialogue accordingly.

DIRECT TEACHING

A Literary Focus GRADE-LEVEL STANDARD

Character. Mrs. Popov is still furious at Smirnov, but she is also falling in love with him; her behavior reaches heights of absurdity as she contradicts herself. Is her behavior believable or is it purely exaggeration? [Possible responses: Believable, because she's confused by her changing emotions and doesn't realize what she's saying; exaggerated, because her ambivalence about Smirnov is too far-fetched.]

B Literary Focus GRADE-LEVEL STANDARD

Conflict. This is the play's climax—the most intense moment at which the central conflict is about to be resolved. How is the conflict resolved? [Possible response: with an embrace and a kiss.]

C Literary Focus GRADE-LEVEL STANDARD

Comedy. What elements of farce are evident in the play's ending? [Possible response: Instead of a duel, the play ends with a loving embrace—this sudden reversal of action is an element of farce. The kiss that resolves the lovers' conflict occurs right after Mrs. Popov tells Smirnov she hates him—and just as her servants arrive with weapons to protect her from the "brute."]

D Reading Skills

Interpreting. What is the significance of Mrs. Popov's comment? [At the beginning of the play, Mrs. Popov instructs her servants to give Toby oats, as a sentimental remembrance of her late husband. The reversal signifies that she has lost interest in being faithful to his memory.]

---

like it. Oh, I'm lost, I'm done for, I'm a mouse in a trap.

Mrs. Popov. Leave this house, or I shoot!

Smirnov. Shoot away! What bliss to die of a shot that was fired by that little velvet hand! To die gazing into those enchanting eyes. I'm out of my mind. I know: You must decide at once. Think for one second, then decide. Because if I leave now, I'll never be back. Decide! I'm a pretty decent chap. Landed gentleman, I should say. Ten thousand a year. Good stable. Throw a kopeck up in the air, and I'll put a bullet through it. Will you marry me?

Mrs. Popov (*indignant, brandishing*[10] *the gun*). We'll shoot it out! Get going! Take your pistol!

Smirnov. I'm out of my mind. I don't understand anything any more. (*Shouting*) You there! That vodka!

Mrs. Popov. No excuses! No delays! We'll shoot it out!

Smirnov. I'm out of my mind. I'm falling in love. I *have* fallen in love. (*He takes her hand vigorously; she squeals.*) I love you. (*He goes down on his knees.*) I love you as I've never loved before. I jilted twelve and was jilted by nine others. But I didn't love a one of them as I love you. I'm full of tender emotion. I'm melting like butter. I'm weak as water. I'm on my knees like a fool, and I offer you my hand. It's a shame; it's a disgrace. I haven't been in love in five years. I took a vow against it. And now, all of a sudden, to be swept off my feet, it's a scandal. I offer you my hand, dear lady. Will you or won't you? You won't? Then don't! (*He rises and walks toward the door.*)

Mrs. Popov. I didn't say anything.

Smirnov (*stopping*). What?

Mrs. Popov. Oh nothing, you can go. Well, no, just a minute. No, you can go. Go! I detest you! But, just a moment. Oh, if you knew how furious I feel! (*Throws the gun on the table*) My fingers have gone to sleep holding that horrid thing. (*She is tearing her handkerchief to shreds.*) And what are you standing around for? Get out of here!

Smirnov. Goodbye.

Mrs. Popov. Go, go, go! (*Shouting*) Where are you going? Wait a minute! No, no, it's all right, just go. I'm fighting mad. Don't come near me, don't come near me!

> "I love you. But it doesn't make sense."

Smirnov (*who is coming near her*). I'm pretty disgusted with myself—falling in love like a kid, going down on my knees like some moon-gazing whippersnapper, the very thought gives me gooseflesh. (*Rudely*) I love you. But it doesn't make sense. Tomorrow, I have to pay that interest, and we've already started mowing. (*He puts his arm about her waist.*) I shall never forgive myself for this.

Mrs. Popov. Take your hands off me, I hate you! Let's shoot it out!

[*A long kiss. Enter* LUKA *with an axe, the* GARDENER *with a rake, the* COACHMAN *with a pitchfork,* HIRED MEN *with sticks.*]

Luka (*seeing the kiss*). Mercy on us! Holy saints above!

Mrs. Popov (*dropping her eyes*). Luka, tell them in the stable that Toby is *not* to have any oats today.

Curtain

---

10. **brandishing** *v.:* waving about in a challenging way.

736 Chapter 10 Drama • Evaluating an Argument

Meet the Writer

Anton Chekhov

"Slice-of-Life" Playwright

Anton Chekhov (1860–1904) is one of the two playwrights who have most influenced modern drama. The other is the Norwegian writer Henrik Ibsen (1828–1906), whose plays often deal with contemporary social problems and are called well-made plays because they have a well-crafted plot. Chekhov's major plays, on the other hand, are often called slices of life. Rather than focusing on plot, they are more concerned with psychological insights, with the slow ebb and flow of moods, and with subtly shifting relationships.

Chekhov was born in a small seaport in southern Russia, the son of an unsuccessful shopkeeper. His family was poor and totally dependent on young Anton's support. The money came in from short stories and sketches that Chekhov churned out for humor magazines. At the same time, he was studying medicine at the University of Moscow.

Chekhov became a doctor but did not practice long. Instead, he developed his skills in writing and produced hundreds of short stories and five major plays over the course of his tragically short life.

In one of his many letters, Chekhov gave this writing advice to Maxim Gorky, another famous Russian writer:

"When you read proof, take out adjectives and adverbs wherever you can. You use so many of them that the reader finds it hard to concentrate and he gets tired. You understand what I mean when I say, 'The man sat on the grass.' You understand because the sentence is clear and there is nothing to distract your attention. Conversely, the brain has trouble understanding me if I say, 'A tall, narrow-chested man of medium height with a red beard sat on green grass trampled by passersby, sat mutely, looking about timidly and fearfully.' This doesn't get its meaning through to the brain immediately, which is what good writing must do, and fast."

In his last years, ill with the tuberculosis that would soon kill him, Chekhov wrote five full-length serious plays, four of which are masterpieces that are still produced in theaters all over the world: *The Seagull, Uncle Vanya, The Three Sisters,* and *The Cherry Orchard.*

For Independent Reading

In *The Cherry Orchard,* as in his other full-length dramas, Chekhov lets "the things that happen on stage be as complex and yet as simple as they are in life. For instance, people are having a meal at the table, just having a meal, but at the same time their happiness is being created, or their lives are being smashed up."

GUIDED PRACTICE

Monitoring students' progress. To check students' comprehension of the play, ask them to respond to the following questions. Direct students to locate passages in the text that support their responses.

Short Answer

1. How does Mrs. Popov respond to her husband's death? [She overreacts by going into excessive mourning.]
2. When Smirnov demands that Mrs. Popov pay the debt her husband owed him, what does she do at first? [She tells him that she will pay him.]
3. Why does Smirnov challenge Mrs. Popov to a duel? [He challenges her to a duel, because she insults him.]
4. How does Mrs. Popov react to Smirnov's challenge? [She enthusiastically agrees to the duel.]
5. What happens after Smirnov and Mrs. Popov prepare for the duel? [They admit their attraction for each other and fall into each other's arms.]

Meet the Writer

Background. Over the course of his relatively short life, Chekhov wrote hundreds of short stories and several one-act comedies, among them *The Brute.* These little comedies were written early in his career. Though they do not match the achievement of his later great plays—and Chekhov himself considered them unimportant "vaudevilles"—the public loved them. The humor in these plays is based on exaggeration and stereotypes, but the characters do exhibit psychological complexity.

INDEPENDENT PRACTICE

Literary Response and Analysis

Reading Check

1. Mrs. Popov wants to remain in mourning. Smirnov wants to collect on a debt owed him. Luka wants to rejoin community life.
2. Both Mrs. Popov and Smirnov want to be with each other. Luka wants peace and quiet.

Interpretations

3. The play's title refers to Smirnov, who first appears as an angry, demanding character. Students might prefer *The Brute* because of its irony. Others might choose *The Bear* if they know that this animal is a Russian symbol.
4. Early in the play, when she thinks of Popov fondly, she orders Toby, her dead husband's horse, to be given an extra portion of oats. At the end, when she has fallen in love with Smirnov, she cancels this order.
5. All of these characteristics of a farce apply to *The Brute* except the first one; the main characters do exhibit some psychological complexity.
6. Mrs. Popov displays ridiculous behavior in her excessive mourning. Smirnov's greed makes him appear rude and boorish. As the play progresses, their ideas of feminine and masculine behavior are ridiculed.
7. He changes his mind because she accepts his challenge to a duel. She changes her mind when she begins to waver in her insistence that he leave.

Literary Response and Analysis

Reading Check

1. Complete this **character web,** telling what each of the three characters wants at the beginning of the play:

2. By the end of the play, how have these wants changed?

Interpretations

3. Explain the play's **title.** Who or what is the brute? This title is sometimes translated as *The Bear.* Which title do you feel is more interesting?
4. What is the significance of Mrs. Popov's last line?
5. A **farce** is a kind of **comedy** that most of us are familiar with, since farces are standard fare in movies and on television. Here are some of the characteristics of a farce:
   - A farce is a knockabout comedy without complex characters.
   - A farce intends to make us laugh by using a lot of physical action.
   - Nothing tragic happens in a farce.
   - The characters in a farce make a lot of noise; the stage is busy with action.

   Which of these characteristics apply to *The Brute*? Be sure to cite specific situations in the play.
6. If the writer's **purpose** in a farce is to ridicule human behavior, when and how are the two **main characters** first shown to be ridiculous? As the play develops, what new behaviors does Chekhov ridicule?
7. Why does Smirnov begin to change his mind about Mrs. Popov? At what **climactic** moment in the play do we know that she has changed her mind too? (Were you able to **predict** when this reversal would occur?)
8. **Repetition** is frequently used in comedies—people seem to find something funny in repeated patterns of speech or behavior. Find two examples of repetition in this play. Did you find the repetition funny? Explain your responses.
9. **Compare and contrast** Mrs. Popov and Smirnov. How are they alike, and how do they differ?

Evaluation

10. Do you find Chekhov's battling lovers to be **credible,** or believable? Do you think they would finally be attracted to each other? (Refer to your Quickwrite notes.)

Writing

The Next Act

A **comedy** often ends with a marriage or with the promise of one, but comedies almost never follow the couple beyond their marriage. What do you think will happen to Smirnov and Mrs. Popov after they are married? Imagine a day in their lives ten years later, and write the **dialogue** for this next act. To get your dialogue going, have the characters face a decision—for example, how to spend some money; what to do about Luka, who still dislikes Smirnov; what to do about the photographs of Mrs. Popov's first husband, which are still around the house.

Reading Standard 3.1 Articulate the relationship between the expressed purposes and the characteristics of different forms of dramatic literature (e.g., comedy).

8. Possible examples: Luka repeatedly begs Smirnov to go away; Mrs. Popov repeats "Let's shoot it out!"; Smirnov repeats in exasperation that Mrs. Popov is "not in the mood."
9. Both have been faithful and loving, but both have suffered in their relationships. Smirnov has become angry and embittered; Mrs. Popov has retreated into romantic notions of undying loyalty.

Evaluation

10. Although students may feel Chekhov's characters are exaggerated, most will recognize that the exaggerations are based on a truth—that people with extreme attitudes are often highly susceptible to change.

738 Chapter 10 Drama • Evaluating an Argument

Vocabulary Development

Word Analogies: Word Pairs with the Same Relationship

In an **analogy** test item you have to choose the word that will give the second word pair the same relationship as the first word pair. The word pairs may be synonyms or antonyms, or they may have other relationships. (For more on analogies, see pages 29–30.)

Word Bank
- indisposed
- emancipation
- malicious
- insinuate
- incoherent
- impudence
- impunity

PRACTICE 1

Write the word from the Word Bank that completes each analogy. Hint: Try reading the analogy item aloud: *Energetic* is to *vigorous* as *mean* is to which word in the Word Bank?

1. ENERGETIC : VIGOROUS :: mean : ____________
2. ACCEPTANCE : REJECTION :: ____________ : enslavement
3. JOYOUS : HAPPY :: ill : ____________
4. CALM : DISQUIET :: ____________ : respect
5. DEFY : RESIST :: assert : ____________
6. OPTIMISM : HOPE :: protection : ____________
7. ORDERLY : CHAOTIC :: clear : ____________

Word Connotations: Powerful Associations

Every word has a **denotation,** or dictionary meaning, but many words also have **connotations,** powerful emotional overtones and associations. These passages from *The Brute* have words with rich connotations:

> "In appearance, a woman may be all poetry and romance, goddess and angel, muslin and fluff."

> "What a woman! Phew!! *She's* no sourpuss; *she's* no crybaby. She's fire and brimstone. She's a human cannonball."

PRACTICE 2

1. In each passage above, identify words that you think have strong connotations. Describe what the word or phrase suggests to you.
2. Rewrite each passage, substituting words with altogether different connotations. For example, *romance* might become *kindness.*

Reading Standard 1.1 Identify and use the literal meanings of words.

Reading Standard 1.2 Distinguish between the denotative and connotative meanings of words and interpret the connotative power of words.

Vocabulary Development

Practice 1

1. malicious
2. emancipation
3. indisposed
4. impudence
5. insinuate
6. impunity
7. incoherent

Practice 2

Possible Answers

1. In the first passage, "poetry and romance" connote beauty and gentleness; "goddess and angel" connote ethereal, or otherworldly, qualities; and "muslin and fluff" suggest plain and simple characteristics.

   In the second passage, "sourpuss" and "crybaby" bring to mind a childish, fretful, whining person with an extremely unpleasant expression. "Fire and brimstone" connotes anger, and "human cannonball" connotes movement and speed with the ability to destroy things in her path.
2. Rewritten passages will vary. Have students explain the connotations.

Resources Reminder

Vocabulary

- *Vocabulary Development*
  - Vocabulary Worksheet, p. 49
- *Lesson Plans for Language Development*
  - Vocabulary, pp. 360, 367

Grammar Link

Practice

Possible Answer

Mrs. Popov remains faithful to her dead husband although he was a cad. For instance, he deceived her, made terrible scenes, then left her alone for weeks at a time. One day Smirnov enters, and he demands payment for money he lent to Mr. Popov. Smirnov needs the cash, because he owes the bank interest. Since he hasn't paid the interest, he will surely lose his land.

ASSESSING

Assessment

- *Progress Assessment of Reading*
  - Selection Test

RETEACHING

For a lesson reteaching Standard 3.1, see **Reteaching,** p. 939A. For another selection to teach Standard 3.1, see *Interactive Reading,* Chapter 10.

Grammar Link MINI-LESSON

Using Transitions to Connect Related Ideas

Transitional words and **phrases,** such as those in the chart below, serve as signposts to help readers follow your thoughts. When you write, choose appropriate transitional words and phrases to connect related ideas. With these helpful transitions, you can combine short, choppy sentences that sound like a telegram to form smoother-sounding sentences that flow together and make more sense to the reader:

Transitional Words and Phrases	
Comparing	also, similarly, too, and, in addition
Contrasting	but, however, in contrast, even though, although
Cause and effect	for, since, so, as a result, so that, because
Example	for instance, for example, in fact, in other words
Chronological order	after, then, first, finally, next, when
Order of importance	first, last, mainly, then
Spatial order	next, into, there, behind, before, above, over, down

Notice how the underlined transitional words and phrases connect closely related ideas in the paragraph below:

> Anton Chekhov wrote hundreds of short stories and several hilarious one-act comedies, but he is best remembered for his serious full-length dramas. When *The Sea Gull* was first performed, in 1896 in St. Petersburg, it was very badly received. As a result, Chekhov left the theater after the performance and vowed never to write another play. However, the Moscow Art Theater's 1898 production of *The Sea Gull* was a tremendous success and established Chekhov as a leading playwright.

PRACTICE

Revise the paragraph below using **transitional words** and **phrases** to connect closely related ideas. (You will be combining sentences.) In a small group, discuss your revised paragraphs.

Mrs. Popov remains faithful to her dead husband. He was a cad. He deceived her. He made terrible scenes. He left her alone for weeks at a time. One day, Smirnov enters. He demands payment for money he lent to Mr. Popov. Smirnov needs the cash. He owes the bank interest. He hasn't paid the interest. He will surely lose his land.

William Shakespeare's Life
A Biographical Sketch
by Robert Anderson

Compared with what we know about writers today, we know very little about William Shakespeare's life. In the early 1600s, nobody realized that this actor and writer would one day become known as the world's greatest playwright and poet. In the 1600s, there were no talk show-hosts to interview Shakespeare, no Sunday supplements to feature all the intimate details of his life. This neglect, however, has been corrected. By now more material has been written about Shakespeare and his works than about any other writer in the world. **A**

William Shakespeare.
Popperfoto/Archive Photos.

What we do know about Shakespeare comes mainly from public records. We know that he was baptized on April 26, 1564, in Stratford-on-Avon, a market town about one hundred miles northwest of London. It is assumed he was born a few days before his baptism, and so his birthday is celebrated on April 23, possibly only because he died on that date in 1616. He was one of eight children.

DIRECT TEACHING

A Reading Informational Materials
GRADE-LEVEL STANDARD

Secondary sources. What special difficulties would biographers of Shakespeare face? [Possible responses: The limited amount of historical records would make it very difficult to reconstruct Shakespeare's personal life. Separating facts from unsubstantiated anecdotal and legendary material would be an enormous challenge.]

VIEWING THE ART

This portrait is a much later engraving after the Chandos portrait of Shakespeare. The Chandos portrait, in oil, is not authenticated as a life portrait. The engraving made for the First Folio of 1623, called The Flower Portrait, is the one most likely to have been drawn from life.

DIFFERENTIATING INSTRUCTION

Learners Having Difficulty

Generalizing. Have students note some of the author biographies in their *Holt Literature and Language Arts* text and identify features that are typical of biographies. Next, have students note how autobiographies differ from biographies. Remind them that biographies are usually narrated from the third-person point of view, while autobiographies are narrated from the first-person point of view.

English-Language Learners

Help students draw up a list of basic questions that they think should be answered in a brief biographical sketch. Then, have students interview a partner and write a paragraph or two presenting the information they have gathered.

Resources Reminder

For lessons designed for English-language learners and special education students, see *Lesson Plans for Language Development*, pp. 331, 332.

Advanced Learners

Enrichment. Encourage students to discuss why biography is one of the most popular forms of nonfiction. If they've read the selection from *Angela's Ashes* beginning on p. 194, ask them whether they think it can be considered a biography. Small groups of students can informally debate this question.

DIRECT TEACHING

A English-Language Learners

Explain that in the United States today, the term *grammar school* refers to elementary school, which includes the first four to eight grades and often a kindergarten.

B Content-Area Connections

History: Ovid

Born after Julius Caesar's assassination, Publius Ovidius Naso, or Ovid (43 B.C.–A.D. 17), was the first major writer of the Roman Empire. His greatest work, the mythological epic the *Metamorphoses,* traces the history of the world from its origins to the deification of Julius Caesar.

C Vocabulary Development

REVIEW STANDARD

A playwright is a person who writes plays. This compound word combines *play* and *wright,* an obsolete word derived from the Old English *wyrhta* or *wryhta,* meaning "worker" or "maker."

The Photo Works/Photo Researchers.

Shakespeare's birthplace on Henly Street in Stratford, England.

His father, John Shakespeare, was a merchant and a man of some importance in the town, serving at various times as alderman and high bailiff—the equivalent of a mayor today.

A William went to the local grammar school, which was very different from grammar schools today. In those days it was rare for students to move on to a university; the Stratford grammar school provided Shakespeare and other boys of Stratford (no girls went to school) with all their formal education. What they learned in this school was Latin—Latin grammar and Latin literature, including the schoolboys' B favorite: Ovid's amorous retelling of the Greek and Roman myths.

In 1582, Shakespeare married Anne Hathaway, who was eight years older than he was, and in 1583, their first child, Susanna, was born. In 1585, Anne gave birth to twins, Hamnet and Judith. Then, from 1585 until 1592, Shakespeare's history goes blank.

C Many people believe that Shakespeare went to London to seek his fortune the year after the twins were born. We know that by 1592 he had become an actor and a playwright, because that year a rival playwright, Robert Greene, scathingly warned other playwrights against the actor who had become a writer:

CONTENT-AREA CONNECTIONS

History: Elizabethan Education

No Elizabethan had to attend school; getting an education was a voluntary matter. Shakespeare attended the King's New School. As with all grammar schools of the era, it was nothing like grammar schools in the United States today. A boy who attended grammar school (if his parents could afford it) was in class for about ten hours a day, six days a week. The curriculum emphasized Latin, a good foundation for a career in the church or the law. A boy who finished grammar school at the age of twelve or thirteen had probably spent five years studying Latin. History, modern foreign languages, and other subjects that we consider essential today were optional. Students had to work hard, and teachers used corporal punishment to enforce discipline.

742 Chapter 10 Drama • Evaluating an Argument

There is an upstart crow, beautified with our feathers . . .
that supposes he is as well able to bombast out a blank verse
as the best of you. . . .

Greene refers to a fable in which a crow struts about in another bird's feathers—as an actor can only recite others' words. Greene was insulting an upstart, a mere actor who dared to *write*.

Actors were held in disrepute at the time. In fact, they were often lumped together with other unsavory groups: "rogues, vagabonds, sturdy beggars, and common players." Local officials frequently tried to close the theaters because they felt clerks and apprentices wasted time there (performances were in the daytime). They also felt that disease was too easily spread among the members of the audience. In fact, the London theaters were closed for long periods during the plague years of 1592–1594. **D**

Thus, actors sought the protection and support of noblemen with the power to speak for their rights against critical town authorities. It appears that in 1594, Shakespeare became a charter member of a theatrical group called the Lord Chamberlain's Men, which became the King's Men in 1603. (The patron of the group was none other than King James himself.) Shakespeare acted and wrote for this company until he retired to Stratford in 1612. By that time he had written thirty-seven plays—**comedies, histories, tragedies,** and **romances**—including his tragic masterpieces *Hamlet, Othello, King Lear,* and *Macbeth.*

It is sometimes difficult to fix the dates of Shakespeare's works because plays were not routinely published after production,

Patrick Stewart and Anjanue Ellis in Shakespeare's *The Tempest* in a 1995 New York Shakespeare Festival Production.

DIRECT TEACHING

D Reading Informational Materials
GRADE-LEVEL STANDARD

? Secondary sources. It is interesting to note that plays were not considered serious literature during Shakespeare's time. Instead, they were regarded in the same way that many people today regard (or disregard) television and film scripts. Why do you think people didn't think of plays as literature? [Possible responses: If something is entertaining, many people think that it can't have artistic value. To be truly appreciated, a play has to be seen, and relatively few people were able to attend plays. Most plays were not published.]

CONTENT-AREA CONNECTIONS

Literature: Academic Controversy

Whole-class activity. Shakespeare was a young man living in the country with a wife and three children in 1585. By 1592, he was a recognized poet in England, writing sophisticated sonnets for an aristocratic audience. This metamorphosis during "the lost years" seems too unlikely for some literary researchers, who suggest that the plays and poems were written by someone other than Shakespeare, perhaps a nobleman who desired anonymity. This "anti-Stratfordian" position has had many adherents over the last century. Nevertheless, most Shakespearean scholars maintain the orthodox view that the man from Stratford, despite his humble origins, was indeed the genius who created the plays and sonnets.

Have students research and report on the various theories of authorship proposed by "anti-Stratfordian" scholars.

Direct Teaching

A Content-Area Connections

Literature: Publishing Plays
There were no copyright laws in Shakespeare's day, and publishing a play made it open to use by rival theater companies. Thus, plays were rarely published unless they were flops or so out-of-date as to be unprofitable. The printed versions of Shakespeare's individual plays were called quartos.

B Reading Informational Materials

GRADE-LEVEL STANDARD

Primary sources. The Swiss visitor was Thomas Platter, a doctor from Basel, and his *Travels in England* provides a fascinating firsthand account of life in Shakespeare's day. The dance he mentions, a lively, often farcical, afterpiece called a jig, was a common way to conclude Elizabethan drama and was meant to appeal to the less sophisticated audience members. Why might primary sources, such as this one, be more reliable than secondary sources? Why might they be less reliable?
[Possible response: The details might be more accurate, as well as more colorful, because the writer actually witnessed them. However, the writer is more likely to give his or her own opinion, sometimes without much supporting evidence.]

C Learners Having Difficulty

Chronological order. Ask students to identify the major events in Shakespeare's life and theatrical career that are mentioned in this introductory material. Then, have them present the dates and details in a time line.

A as they generally are now. In Shakespeare's day, plays became the property of the theaters, and the theaters were not eager to have copies made available for rival theaters to use. Some of Shakespeare's plays were published during his lifetime, but often in versions of dubious authenticity. It was not until 1623 that two men who had been with Shakespeare in the King's Men brought out what they called "True Original Copies" of all the plays. This volume is called the First Folio.

B It is believed that *Julius Caesar* was written in 1599, because of what a Swiss traveler who was in England in September 1599 wrote about a visit to the Globe. The Swiss visitor was most impressed, for good reason, with the intricate and vigorous Elizabethan dancing:

> After dinner on the twenty-first of September, at about two o'clock, I went with my companions over the water, and in the strewn-roof house [the playhouse with a thatched roof] saw the tragedy of the first Emperor Julius with at least fifteen characters very well acted. At the end of the comedy they danced according to their custom with extreme elegance. Two men in men's clothes and two in women's gave this performance, in wonderful combination with each other.

C Shakespeare died on April 23, 1616, at the age of fifty-two. He was buried in the Holy Trinity Church at Stratford, where his grave can still be seen today. A bequest he made in his will has attracted almost as much interest and curiosity as anything in his plays—he left his wife his "second-best bed."

Poster featuring Denzel Washington in Shakespeare's *Richard III* in a 1990 New York Shakespeare Festival production.

Content-Area Connections

Literature: Shakespeare's Epitaph
Shakespeare's famous epitaph is rendered below in modern English. It may have been an attempt to keep his remains from being removed later to make way for those of someone else—a common practice of the day:

Good friend, for Jesus' sake forbear
To dig the dust enclosèd here.
Blessed be the man that spares these stones,
And cursed be he that moves my bones.

Shakespeare's instruction about the "second-best bed" has been given a wide range of interpretations. It seems that his daughter Susanna Hall, who inherited most of Shakespeare's estate and whom Shakespeare's wife, Anne, lived with after William's death, got the best bed.

The Elizabethan Stage

by Robert Anderson

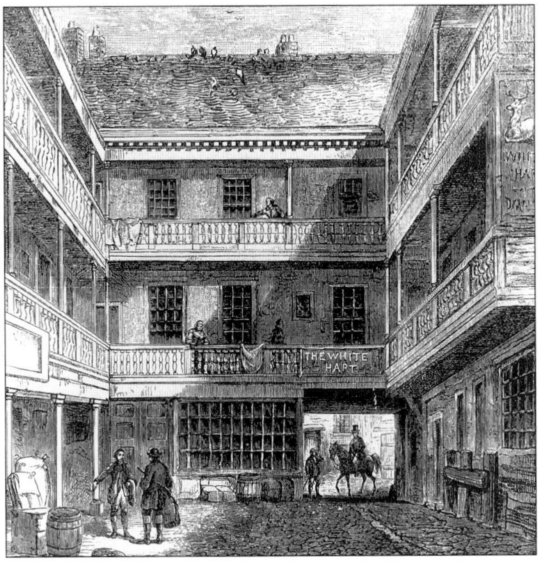

The White Hart Inn, London. Engraving.

By permission of The Folger Shakespeare Library.

The Elizabethan stage would have seemed very strange to **D** American theatergoers of fifty or sixty years ago, who were accustomed to elaborate and realistic settings placed on a stage separated from the audience by a huge velvet curtain. This is called a proscenium stage, and though it's still more or less standard today, the newer arena stages, thrust stages, and open stages have made us much more at home with Shakespeare's theater. The use of these simpler stages, which make the audience feel they're a part of the action, recalls the saying that all you need for a theater is "a platform and a passion or two."

As with Shakespeare's life, we have only sketchy information about the early English theaters. It appears that the wandering acting companies in England had originally set up their stages—mere platforms—wherever they could find space, often in the courtyards of inns. The audience stood around three sides of the stage, or if they paid more, they sat in chairs on the balconies surrounding the inn yard.

pages 745–749 cover **Reading Standard 3.10** Identify and describe the function of scene designs in dramatic literature.

DIRECT TEACHING

D Content-Area Connections

History: Queen Elizabeth I
Late sixteenth- and early seventeenth-century England is called Elizabethan England after Queen Elizabeth I, who reigned from 1558 to 1603. During this time, England flourished as a nation. It became a political, industrial, and commercial power and enjoyed vigorous growth in the areas of art and science.

DEVELOPING FLUENCY

Whole-class activity. If you read this material in class, pause after each section and have students orally summarize the information they have just read. Encourage them to use this strategy frequently while reading on their own, especially with informational texts. Before they continue reading the next section, have students read the head and make predictions about what will be covered in that section.

DIRECT TEACHING

(A) Reading Informational Materials
GRADE-LEVEL STANDARD

Author's argument. The author does not give his opinion about this incident directly. However, he does so indirectly through his choice of words and tone of voice. Have students re-read this paragraph and evaluate its overall tone. Do you think the author approves or disapproves of the company's actions? What words or phrases led to your conclusion? [Possible response: The author seems to approve—he inserts the qualifying phrase "somewhat behind" when he mentions the rent payments; he uses the word "threatened" to describe the landlord's reaction; he concludes with a complimentary statement about Shakespeare.]

Courtesy Chris Beetles Ltd., London.

The Globe Theatre, a view of Shoreditch in 1590, by Cyril Walter Hodges. Watercolor with pen, ink, and body color (9″ × 6½″).

When James Burbage (the father of Richard Burbage, the actor who was to perform most of Shakespeare's great tragic parts) decided in 1576 to build the first permanent theater just outside the city of London, it was natural that he should duplicate the courtyard theaters in which his company had been performing. Burbage called his new playhouse simply "The Theatre."

The Globe—The "Wooden O"

(A) In 1599, the owner of the land on which Burbage had built his theater apparently decided to raise the rent. Because the theater was somewhat behind in its rent payments, the landlord threatened to take it over. On

In *Henry V*, Shakespeare ca the theater "thi wooden O."

CONTENT-AREA CONNECTIONS

History: Ticket Prices
Basic admission to the Globe was a penny, which gave a viewer standing room in the open pit around the stage. The Globe was thus a popular playhouse affordable to the masses. In 1596, James Burbage built his Blackfriars playhouse, which catered to wealthier theatergoers. At Blackfriars, six-pence (*pence* is the plural of *penny*) bought a viewer a bench far from the stage, three times that amount got the viewer a seat in the "pit," and five times that amount put the viewer in a box seat next to the stage. That seating plan has survived in many theaters to this day.

746 Chapter 10 Drama • Evaluating an Argument

the night of January 20, 1599, James Burbage's son Cuthbert and others in the company stealthily took their theater apart timber by timber and rowed the pieces across the river, where they later reconstructed the theater and called it the Globe. This was the theater where Shakespeare's greatest plays were performed.

In *Henry V,* Shakespeare calls the theater "this wooden O." It consisted of an open space, perhaps sixty-five feet in diameter, surrounded by a more or less circular building thirty feet high and consisting of three tiers of seats for spectators. As in the inn courtyards, the stage, which was forty feet by thirty feet and five feet off the ground, projected into the open space. **B**

The interesting part of the stage was at the rear, where there was a small curtained inner stage flanked by two entrances, with an upper stage above it. Stout pillars held up a narrow roof over the rear part of the stage. This was called the Heavens. The front part of the stage was equipped with a trapdoor, which could be used for burial scenes, surprise entrances, and mysterious exits. **C**

A replica of the Globe Theatre has been constructed very near its former location in London. The queen of England attended its opening in 1997, and Shakespeare's plays are still performed there today.

The Sets: Mostly Imagination

Shakespeare trusted his audience's imagination. He knew he did not need elaborate sets to re-create a battle scene or a bedroom or the Roman Forum. The audience members could do it for themselves. Moreover, without elaborate sets to move on and off the stage, Shakespeare could change scenes with the kind of fluidity we see in movies today. **D**

Here is how Shakespeare prompted his audience to see hundreds of horsemen (and to costume his kings) in lines from the Prologue to *Henry V:*

> Let us . . .
> On your imaginary forces work. . . .
> Think, when we talk of horses, that you see them
> Printing their proud hoofs i' th' receiving earth;
> For 'tis your thoughts that now must deck our kings. . . .

Though Shakespeare made no attempt to use realistic settings, it appears that his kings and other characters were splendidly decked out. He also called for flags and banners and musicians, and the

DIRECT TEACHING

B Reading Informational Materials
GRADE-LEVEL STANDARD

Secondary sources. The octagonal or roughly circular design of Burbage's theater was inspired to some degree by the bull- and bear-baiting rings that were popular along the Thames at this time. The advantage of these circular arenas, where chained bulls or bears were attacked by fierce dogs, was that many spectators could gather around the center of the action. What advantage(s) would a circular design have for theatergoers? [Possible response: They could similarly see and hear the play's action better in a circular theater.]

C Reading Skills

Visualizing. What are some basic visual differences between the Globe Theatre and most present-day movie theaters? [Possible responses: The Globe was an open-air theater, whereas most movie theaters are enclosed by walls and a ceiling. The Globe was octagonal, whereas movie theaters today are usually rectangular.]

D Reading Informational Materials
GRADE-LEVEL STANDARD

Secondary sources. What are some advantages of imagining the scenery rather than having it provided onstage? [Possible responses: The audience is not limited by the props and scenery. The mind has the freedom to visualize the scene in a more grand and fitting way than a set designer could provide.]

DIFFERENTIATING INSTRUCTION

Advanced Learners

Enrichment. Shakespeare's Globe Theatre was reconstructed in the mid-1990s in London close to the site of the old Globe Theatre, which burned down in 1613. Ask interested students to research how architects and builders figured out how the old Globe looked, what building materials and methods were used in the original construction, and what materials and methods were used in reconstructing the theater.

Direct Teaching

A Reading Informational Materials
GRADE-LEVEL STANDARD

Secondary sources. Many sound effects used today could have been used in Shakespeare's time. Can you think of ways of imitating sounds of thunder or horses' hooves on stage? [Possible responses: Thunder might be simulated by hitting a large drum and horses' hooves by clapping blocks of wood together.]

B Reading Informational Materials
GRADE-LEVEL STANDARD

Secondary sources. Why do you think women did not perform onstage during Shakespeare's time? [Possible responses: The theater seems like a rowdy, even slightly dangerous place during this time period. Traditionally, many occupations and professions have been denied to women.]

C Reading Informational Materials
GRADE-LEVEL STANDARD

Author's argument. Does the author give enough evidence to support his generalization that boy actors playing female roles were "not that unbelievable"? [Possible response: The evidence the author presents helps us visualize how this transformation was possible, but his argument might be more persuasive if he included a firsthand account of the audience's reaction.]

multilayered stage could produce special effects. Characters could be **A** lowered from the Heavens by cranes, and there were sound effects as well. In fact, these special effects caused the destruction of the Globe. In 1613, during the battle scene of *Henry VIII,* a stagehand was lighting the fuse of a cannon. A spark flew up and started a fire in the thatched roof of the Heavens, and the theater burned down.

Because the plays were performed during the day in the open air, there was no need for stage illumination. Shakespeare had to convey the idea of night by having characters carry torches. (Today, to shoot a night scene in the daytime, movie directors darken the scene by using filters on their cameras.)

The Actors: All Males

B In Shakespeare's time all actors were male. (It wasn't until 1660, when the exiled King Charles II was restored to the English throne and the repressive Puritan dominance ended, that women played in professional theaters.) Boys who had been recruited from the choir schools and trained professionally played the female roles. **C** It was not too difficult to create the illusion that these boys were women. Shakespeare's plays were performed in contemporary Elizabethan costumes, and women's clothing of the day was very elaborate and concealing, with long, full skirts flowing from extremely narrow waists. Women of the time also wore elaborate wigs and powdered their faces heavily. So, all in all, the transformation of boys into women characters was not so unbelievable.

In yet another reversal of roles, the mezzo-soprano Tatiana Troyanos, a woman, portrays Caesar in Handel's opera *Julius Caesar.*
The Bettmann Archive.

CONTENT-AREA CONNECTIONS

Culture: Costumes
Actors on Shakespeare's stage dressed like Elizabethans, but their costuming was controversial just the same. England had Clothing Acts, which spelled out quite clearly what certain classes of people could and could not wear. (For example, no one lower than a knight could wear a velvet cloak.) So for an actor—a person of the lower classes—to dress as a nobleman or a king was something of a scandal. It violated the "natural" order of things, and there was fear that it would put dreams of grandeur into the heads of lower-class audiences.

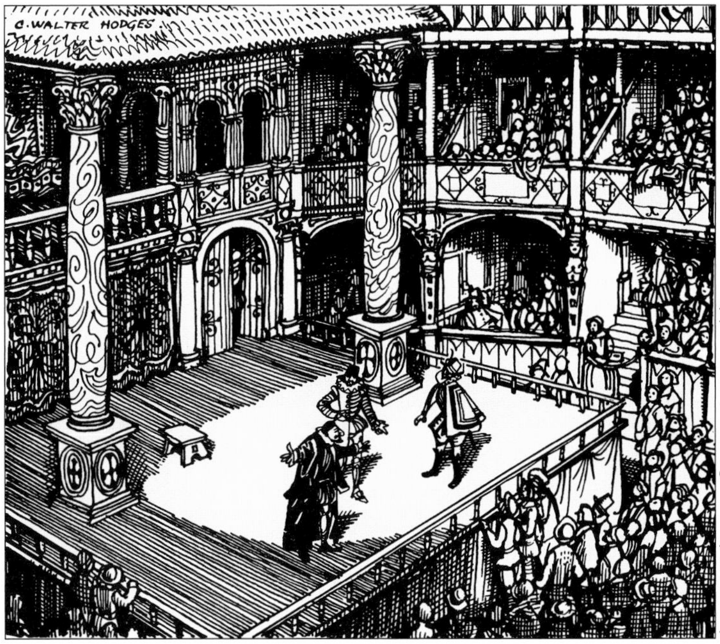

Drawing of a Globe Theatre performance.

By permission of The Folger Shakespeare Library.

Hooking the Audience's Attention

The Elizabethan theater was a convivial place where people arrived early, visited with friends, made new acquaintances, moved around freely, and ate and drank before and during the performance. (The occasion might have had something of the feeling of a Saturday matinee at a local shopping-mall movie theater.) Playwrights had to write scenes that would catch the attention of this audience, and many actors held their attention by vigorous and flamboyant acting. By comparison, today's movie cameras are so sensitive that sometimes all an actor has to do is think the right thoughts, and that is enough. Elizabethan actors had to do more than that since they were trying to hold the interest of three thousand restless people who were also busy eating, drinking, and talking. We get the impression that, like actors working on modern thrust or arena stages, the Elizabethan players had to keep on the move so that spectators on all three sides could catch their expressions and hear their voices. **D**

> The occasion might have had something of the feeling of a Saturday matinee at a local shopping-mall movie theater.

DIRECT TEACHING

D Reading Informational Materials
GRADE-LEVEL STANDARD

? Secondary sources. How might the realities of the Elizabethan theater have influenced Shakespeare's and his fellow playwrights' writing? [Possible response: They might have included more physical action in their plays, such as sword fights, as well as farcical humor that relied on slapstick and clowning. It was noted earlier in this feature, in the firsthand account of the Swiss traveler who visited the Globe, that dancing was a common way of concluding an Elizabethan drama.]

CONTENT-AREA CONNECTIONS

History: Theatrical Performances
Elizabethan theater companies performed an incredible number of plays each year by today's standards. In *Shakespeare Alive!*, Joseph Papp and Elizabeth Kirkland note: "In a typical season—indoor, outdoor, and touring—a company might play six days a week, forty-nine weeks a year, and perform around forty plays, over half of them brand new. . . . In two weeks a single company might typically put on eleven performances of ten different plays—some new ones, some old ones, without batting an eye. . . . New plays were introduced frequently usually about every two weeks. Old plays could be revived on extremely short notice. Most plays ran for seven or eight performances, spread out over the season. A 'long run' was defined as any play that was performed more than twenty times over a period of years."

History: A New Globe
In 1997, a new Globe theater opened on London's South Bank, just two hundred yards from the original site, with a production of *Henry V*. The new theater is an almost exact reproduction of the old Globe; it is round and timbered and open to the air. It even includes an area for groundlings.

The Elizabethan Stage 749

Direct Teaching

A Vocabulary Development
REVIEW STANDARD

Dictator has come to be synonymous with *tyrant,* but the word originally referred to any leader who was given supreme authority by the Roman Senate on a temporary basis in times of emergency.

B Content-Area Connections

Literature: Plutarch

Shakespeare used Plutarch's basic historical information but changed the timing and sequence of some events; he invented others for dramatic purposes. In Act I, for instance, the victory over Pompey's sons and the Feast of Lupercal are celebrated on the same day, but according to Plutarch, these events occurred on separate days.

C English-Language Learners

Political jargon. The following words relate to the political structure of the Roman republic: *consul, Forum, governor, patrician, plebeian, province, Senate, tribune.* Have students use a dictionary or book about ancient Rome to discover their meanings.

D Content-Area Connections

History: Roman Rule

Pompey and Crassus were already jockeying for positions of power when Caesar, eager to become a consul, arrived in Rome after a year in Spain. Secretly, the three agreed to combine forces: Pompey and Crassus would make sure that Caesar became a consul; in return, Caesar would use his influence (possibly including his army) to promote the causes that suited the trio best.

The Play: The Results of Violence

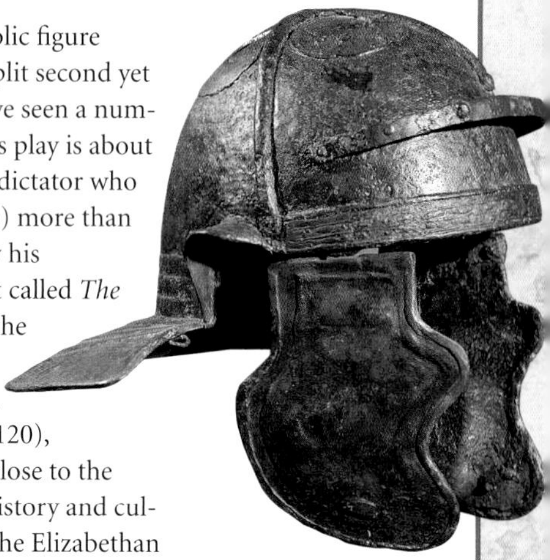

Roman helmet from Judea.

Assassination. The murder of a public figure is an act that can take place in a split second yet change the course of history. We've seen a number of assassinations in recent history. This play is about the assassination of a Roman general and dictator who lived and died (an extremely violent death) more than two thousand years ago. Shakespeare drew his material from an ancient biographical text called *The Parallel Lives,* which first appeared under the title *The Lives of the Noble Grecians and Romans* in translation in England in 1579. This work was written by Plutarch (46–c. 120), a Greek writer and biographer who lived close to the time of Julius Caesar. Greek and Roman history and culture had a great appeal for the English of the Elizabethan Age. They tended to see their own age mirrored in those great ancient civilizations.

Rome in Caesar's Day: Continuous War

We get the impression that the Roman world in Caesar's time was continuously at war. Today the generals of the U.S. Army are ultimately responsible to the president, who is their commander in chief. But two thousand years ago in Rome, the generals had enormous individual power. Powerful generals like Caesar moved with their plundering armies over the entire Mediterranean world. After these "private armies" subdued weaker countries, the territories were then ruled by Roman governors who exacted cruel taxes from the conquered people.

Sometimes the generals turned on one another, because they were strong men battling for power. This is what happened when the generals Caesar and Pompey clashed in the civil war that began in 49 B.C.

Caesar and Pompey: Jealousy and Murder

Caesar and Pompey were friends. Pompey married Caesar's daughter by his first wife. In 60 B.C., the two generals helped bring order to a weakened government, when they, along with Crassus, formed the First Triumvirate (three-man government).

Differentiating Instruction

Advanced Learners

Enrichment. People of the Elizabethan age saw a parallel to their own age in Greek and Roman history. Have students identify a prior period in North American, European, African, Latin American, or Asian history that they think has parallels to the current period in U.S. history. Students can prepare charts and graphs to represent similarities and present their findings to the class.

750 Chapter 10 Drama • Evaluating an Argument

Eager for still more power and realizing that he could achieve it only with conquests and money, Caesar departed for what has been called the Gallic Wars. For eight years he and his armies roamed Europe, subjugating France, Belgium, and parts of Holland, Germany, and Switzerland. Caesar amassed huge sums of money, which he sent back to Rome to gain favor among the people. **E**

Caesar's daughter died in 54 B.C., and in 49 B.C. Pompey, jealous of Caesar's growing power and favor among the people, threw his weight to the Senate, which was also wary of Caesar's ambitions.

Caesar considered himself a defender of the people, but critics said that he gained the people's support with bribes and handouts. His enemies said he deprived the Romans of their liberty.

Caesar refused the Senate's order to give up his command and return to Rome as a private citizen. Instead, he marched his army on Rome, took control, and chased Pompey all the way to Egypt. There Pompey was murdered before Caesar could capture him. Caesar lingered in Egypt for nine months, bewitched by the twenty-two-year-old Cleopatra. Establishing her on the throne of Egypt under his protection, Caesar went to Spain, where he defeated an army led by Pompey's sons. **F**

The Unconquerable God

When he returned to Rome, Caesar was invincible. He was declared dictator for ten years and saw to it that his supporters, including Brutus, became senators. As his desire for power grew obsessive, he had a statue of himself, bearing the inscription "To the Unconquerable God," erected in the temple of Quirinus. The common people loved him; later Caesar was declared dictator for life.

However, to a number of Romans, Caesar's ambition was deplorable. The last Roman king had been overthrown 450 years before, when the Romans set up a republican government. The idea of another king ruling the "free Romans" was unthinkable. As Caesar's arrogance and power became unbearable to certain senators, they made plans to assassinate him on March 15, 44 B.C. Shakespeare's play opens a month before the murder.

Bust of Julius Caesar (date unknown).
National Museum, Naples. The Bettmann Archive.

DIRECT TEACHING

E Reading Informational Materials
GRADE-LEVEL STANDARD

Primary sources. During this lengthy campaign, Caesar kept a journal—*Commentaries on the Gallic Wars.* Intended as a publicity tool to demonstrate his leadership qualities to the Roman people, the journal has survived as an excellent eyewitness account of life in the Roman army.

F Literary Focus
ADVANCED STANDARD

Allusions. The expression *crossing the Rubicon*—taking a decisive or momentous step—is an allusion to this event. Camped along the Rubicon River, the boundary between Gaul and Italy, Caesar had to decide whether he would obey the Senate's order or take his troops back to Rome. According to the Roman biographer Suetonius, Caesar "paused for a while, and realizing what a step he was taking, he turned to those about him and said: 'Even yet we may turn back; but once cross yon little bridge, and the whole issue is with the sword. . . . Take we the course which the signs of the gods and the false dealings of our foes point out. The die is cast!'"

DIRECT TEACHING

A Content-Area Connections

Literature: Blank Verse and Prose

Point out that most of the dialogue in *Julius Caesar,* as in most of Shakespeare's plays, is in blank verse rather than prose. Characters speaking verse are usually noble, whereas those characters speaking in prose are common folk, or at least are acting like common folk. Prince Hal, in *Henry IV, Part I,* for instance, speaks prose in the tavern and verse at court.

B Vocabulary Development

REVIEW STANDARD

Make sure students understand that *archaic* means "having to do with an earlier or more primitive time" and is taken from a Greek word meaning "ancient."

C Reading Informational Materials

GRADE-LEVEL STANDARD

Secondary sources. Can you suggest some words that were in use by your parents, say, thirty years ago that now might sound somewhat archaic? [Students might suggest terms for outdated technology, such as *mimeograph* and *typewriter,* or they might cite out-of-date slang words, such as *groovy, cool,* or *hip.*]

How to Read Shakespeare

Hear the Beat

A As with all of Shakespeare's plays, *Julius Caesar* is written in blank verse. **Blank verse** duplicates the natural rhythms of English speech. Blank verse is unrhymed **iambic pentameter,** which means that each line of poetry in the play is built on five iambs. An **iamb** consists of an unstressed syllable followed by a stressed syllable, as in the word *prepáre*. In this case, **pentameter** means that there are five iambs in a line. Read these lines aloud to feel the beat, or rhythm. Better yet, strike the strong and weak beats with your fingers (try it!):

The evil that men do lives after them,
The good is oft interrèd with their bones.

A whole play written in this pattern would have a singsong effect. To break the monotony and alter the emphasis, Shakespeare sometimes reverses the stressed and unstressed syllables.

Actors don't always read speeches with the same emphasis. You'll probably find variations in reading these lines in your own group. (Read this aloud.)

This was the noblest Roman of them all.
All the conspirators save only he
Did that they did in envy of great Caesar.

Shakespeare doesn't let all his characters speak in blank verse. You'll notice that the commoners speak, as we all do, in ordinary prose. (So does Brutus in his funeral oration.)

Pauses and Stops for Breath

Follow the punctuation marks, and resist the temptation to stop at the end of each line. Thus, in the first passage on this page ("The evil . . ."), you pause at the end of the first line and come to a full stop at the end of the second. (Try it.) In the next passage, you make a full stop for breath at the end of the first line but not at the end of the second line. The second line has no end punctuation, and sense requires that you move on. (Try it.) Lines that end with a punctuation mark are called **end-stopped** lines. Lines that do not end with a punctuation mark are called **run-on** lines. (To determine the complete meaning, you must "run on" to the next line.)

B Archaic Words

C One character in the play is a soothsayer. In Shakespeare's day the word *sooth* meant "truth." Today we'd call such a person a fortuneteller. Here, from *Julius Caesar,* are some other words that are now archaic:

ague: fever.
alarum: call to arms, such as a trumpet blast.
an: if.
betimes: from time to time.
fleering: flattering.
hence, whence, thence: here, where, there.
hie: hurry.
knave: servant, or person of humble birth.
prithee: pray thee (beg thee).
smatch: small amount.

Grade 8 Review Reading Standard 1.2 Determine the historical influences on English word meanings.

DEVELOPING FLUENCY

Whole-class activity. As you dicuss the information in "Hear the Beat" and "Pauses and Stops for Breath," ask students to emphasize the sounds of words and the music that results when phrasing is combined with pitch, rate, and volume. Encourage students to offer a variety of readings for the second set of lines in the text. You might also have these students choose a brief speech from Act I to present orally and to follow with an explanation of the musicality of its language.

752 Chapter 10 Drama • Evaluating an Argument

Words with Different Meanings

The most troublesome words in Shakespeare's plays are those that are still in use but now have different meanings. When Flavius calls the cobbler "thou naughty knave," he seems to be merely scolding the man. However, *naughty* here means "worthless," so the sense of Flavius's line is different from what you might have thought. Here are other familiar words from *Julius Caesar* that had different meanings in Shakespeare's day:

closet: small room, often a private study.

exhalations: meteors.

gentle: noble. *Gentleman* once referred to a man who had a title.

ghastly: ghostly.

humor: temper or disposition.

indifferently: impartially.

just: true.

merely: wholly; entirely.

repair: go.

sad: serious.

saucy: presumptuous.

soft: slowly; "wait a minute."

wit: intelligence.

Act It Out!

Don't forget that this play was created for an ordinary audience—people just like the ones who flock to movies or rock concerts today. To get a feel for the play as action, plan to perform as much of it as possible.

You might begin with the first scene—a brief street scene in which a group of working people encounter two military officers. Here are some suggestions for **oral interpretation:**

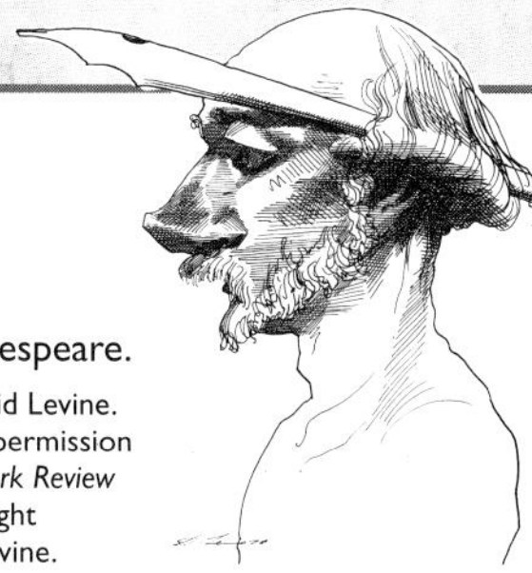

William Shakespeare.

Drawing by David Levine. Reprinted with permission from *The New York Review of Books*. Copyright ©1978 David Levine.

1. In small groups, assign a part to each group member.
2. For this first scene especially, you could do **choral readings.** Again, break into groups. Then, split your group into two smaller groups. Let one small group read the commoners' lines and the other small group read the speeches of the tribunes. Then, have the groups switch roles: The commoners become the tribunes, and the tribunes become the commoners.

As you read the scene, don't worry about the way the archaic words are pronounced. Don't worry about the poetry either: Read all the lines in the scene as if they were prose. Read for sense only: At this point, don't worry about acting out the scene.

After your reading, discuss with the members of your group what happens in the scene and how you feel about it. Who are these people? What is going on?

Now, give a **dramatic performance** of the scene. Some of you will be the **actors,** at least one will be the **director,** and some of you will be the **audience.** How will you set the scene? What are the characters doing as they speak? What props will you need, if any? How will you get audience feedback after your performance?

Beginnings and endings are important in Shakespeare. What did you learn from performing this opening scene?

DIRECT TEACHING

D English-Language Learners

Multiple meanings. Make sure students are familiar with the modern meanings of the listed words. [*closet:* a cabinet or recess for hanging clothes; *exhalations:* emissions of breath; *gentle:* kind, not violent or harsh; *ghastly:* horrible; *humor:* the ability to express or appreciate something funny; *indifferently:* without passion or interest; *just:* fair; *merely:* simply; *repair:* fix; *sad:* unhappy; *saucy:* exhibiting boldness or disregard of others; *soft:* the opposite of hard; *wit:* clever humor]

VIEWING THE ART

David Levine (1926–) is one of America's most gifted and esteemed caricaturists. Explain that a caricature is an exaggerated, usually satirical portrait of a real person or a kind of person (such as a grande dame or a VIP). A caricature may also satirize an event or a situation. Caricatures have been popular forms of satire since the time of the ancient Egyptians.

Activity. Have students compare David Levine's caricature of Shakespeare with the portrait of Shakespeare on p. 741. Have students identify the features that Levine has exaggerated.

DIFFERENTIATING INSTRUCTION

Learners Having Difficulty

Explain that new words and new meanings for words often result from new ideas, new styles, and new technology. Such words often enter a language as slang or jargon and may eventually become a fixed part of the language. Ask students to choose an area of interest and to identify five to ten words that are specific to that area. Students should explain the meaning of each word and any multiple meanings that a word may have. Students may share or exchange words and compile a class lexicon.

Advanced Learners

Enrichment. Encourage students who show an interest in word meanings as described in "Archaic Words" or "Words with Different Meanings" to extend the study in the text. Suggest that they research additional words with archaic or different meanings to share with the class. Invite them to present these words in an in-class activity, such as a game of charades or another word game of their own making.

How to Read Shakespeare 753

STANDARDS FOCUS, pp. 754–880

(For the grade-level standards taught in this lesson, see citations on Student Edition pages.)

Prerequisite Standard

- Grade 8, Literary Response and Analysis 3.6 **Identify significant literary devices (e.g., metaphor, symbolism, dialect, irony) that define a writer's style and use those elements to interpret the work.**

Summary *at grade level*

Act I

Scene 1 establishes the main political conflict of the tragedy: Is Julius Caesar the defender or manipulator of the people?

In Scene 2, as Caesar and his retinue walk to the Lupercal games, a soothsayer warns Caesar to beware the ides of March. When Brutus, remaining behind with Cassius, expresses his fears that the people have crowned Caesar, Cassius seizes the moment to paint Caesar as a dangerous, unworthy tyrant and to push Brutus toward conspiracy. Brutus is swayed by Cassius's arguments and agrees to consider joining a conspiracy. Casca, detained by Brutus and Cassius, reports that Antony indeed offered Caesar a crown three times, which Caesar refused before a cheering crowd. Cassius plots to write anonymous letters to Brutus, praising Brutus's honor and hinting at Caesar's ambition.

Scene 3 opens a month later, on the night of March 14. Terrifying unnatural occurrences set an ominous tone. Knowing that other senators intend to crown Caesar the next day, Cassius calls together his fellow conspirators, writes further inflammatory letters to Brutus, and sets out to visit him with a last appeal.

Before You Read

The Tragedy of Julius Caesar

Literary Focus

Tragedy: Alas, an Unhappy Ending

Lest we wonder, Shakespeare tells us in the title that *Julius Caesar* is a tragedy. A **tragedy** is a play, novel, or other narrative that depicts serious and important events and ends unhappily for the main character. Like the tragedies of the ancient Greeks, Shakespeare's tragedies share these characteristics:

- The main character is often high ranking and dignified, not an ordinary man or woman.
- The main character has a **tragic flaw**—a defect in character or judgment—that directly causes the character's downfall.
- The work ends unhappily, with the death of the main character.

All of Shakespeare's tragedies (for example, *Julius Caesar, Hamlet, King Lear, Macbeth,* and *Romeo and Juliet*) share a similar five-part structure.

1. In **Act I,** the **exposition** introduces the main characters and their conflicts, establishes the setting, and provides background information.
2. In **Act II,** suspense builds as plot events create a **rising action,** a series of complications caused by the main characters when they try to resolve their conflicts.
3. In **Act III,** the **crisis,** or **turning point,** occurs. This is the dramatic and tense moment when the main character makes a choice that determines the rest of the play's action. (In a **comedy** the turning point lifts the play upward to a happy ending; in a **tragedy,** events spiral downward to an inevitable unhappy ending.)
4. **Act IV** presents the **falling action**—the consequences, or results, of actions taken during the **turning point.** This act propels the main character deeper and deeper into disaster; the tragic ending seems inevitable.
5. In **Act V,** near the end of the play, the **climax,** or moment of greatest tension, occurs. In a tragedy the climax is usually the death of the tragic hero. A brief **resolution** (or **denouement**) closely follows the climax, tying up any loose ends in the plot, and the play ends.

Reading Standard 3.1 Articulate the relationship between the expressed purposes and the characteristics of different forms of dramatic literature (e.g., tragedy).

Sidenotes throughout the play cover **Reading Standard 3.10** Identify and describe the function of dialogue, scene designs, soliloquies, asides, and character foils in dramatic literature.

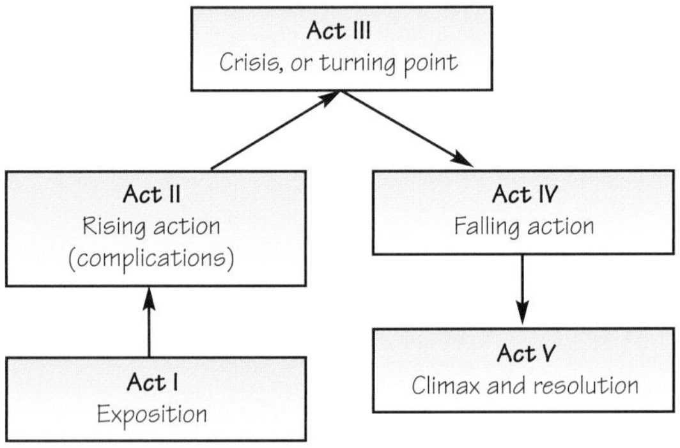

RESOURCES: READING

Planning

- *One-Stop Planner* CD-ROM with Test Generator
- *On Course: Mapping Instruction*
- *Visual Connections*
  - Videocassette, Segment 10
- *Fine Art Transparencies*
  - Transparency 17

Reading

- *Interactive Reading,* Teacher's Edition
  - Graphic Organizer: Dramatic Elements Chart

754 Chapter 10 Drama • Evaluating an Argument

Background

In all of Shakespeare's plays the characters (no matter what historical period they live in) inhabit a world that is run by a just God who ultimately rewards good and punishes evil. In Shakespeare's day, people believed that the universe was essentially good and orderly. All order stemmed from the authority of God, the supreme ruler. The monarch's right to rule came from God too, and so opposition to the anointed ruler was considered opposition to God. When the chain of authority was snapped, the heavens would be offended, and a whole society could be plunged into disorder.

When Shakespeare wrote this play, Queen Elizabeth was old and in failing health. She had no children. When she died, what would become of the country she had ruled so peacefully for nearly forty years? Would there be a bloody struggle for the throne? Would the country slip back into the violence that had preceded Elizabeth's reign? These questions show that the story of Julius Caesar had immediate connections for the Elizabethans—it tapped into their own desire for stability in government, into their dread of civil war.

Make the Connection

Quickwrite

Before you read *Julius Caesar*, think about the Elizabethan view of the universe. How is it different from our ideas about government? Write your responses to the following statements. Do you agree? disagree? Why? Are you unsure about some of them? Are any of them disturbing?

1. Chaos results when the lawful social order is broken.
2. The best intentions of good, noble people can lead to tragedy.
3. Language is a powerful weapon, and in the hands of a skilled person, it can be used to manipulate others.
4. Violence and bloodshed can never have morally good results.
5. Orderliness and stable rule, even rule by a dictator, are preferable to chaos.

(Save your notes.)

The **Staging the Play** sidenotes, which appear throughout the play, will help you visualize the performance of the play—including the way the stage is set, the way the actors move and interact onstage, and the way they say their lines.

PRETEACHING

Selection Starter

Motivate. William Shakespeare's *The Tragedy of Julius Caesar* is the story of a political assassination, an exploration of political, psychological, and moral turmoil that might remind students of some movies they have seen. The play also contains compelling political parallels to twentieth-century history, revealing how power can corrupt even the seemingly incorruptible. Write the following quotation on the chalkboard: "Power corrupts and absolute power corrupts absolutely." Ask students to name some political figures who abused their power. Discuss what psychological or practical reasons might have motivated the figure to do so. How did people respond to this abuse of power? What other ways could they have responded?

Assign the Reading

Homework

You might want to have students read some sections of the play in class, and assign other sections as homework. It might also be helpful for students to keep a notebook as they read. They can summarize each scene, draw pictures to help them visualize the action, write down their own thoughts and ideas, and take note of any words or points in the play that they found confusing. Divide the class into pairs, and have partners share their responses and questions.

Differentiating Instruction

- *Lesson Plans for Language Development*
  - English-Language Learners, pp. 333–335, 361, 368
  - Special Education Students, pp. 336, 361, 368

Assessment

- *Progress Assessment of Reading*
  - Selection Test
- *One-Stop Planner* CD-ROM with Test Generator

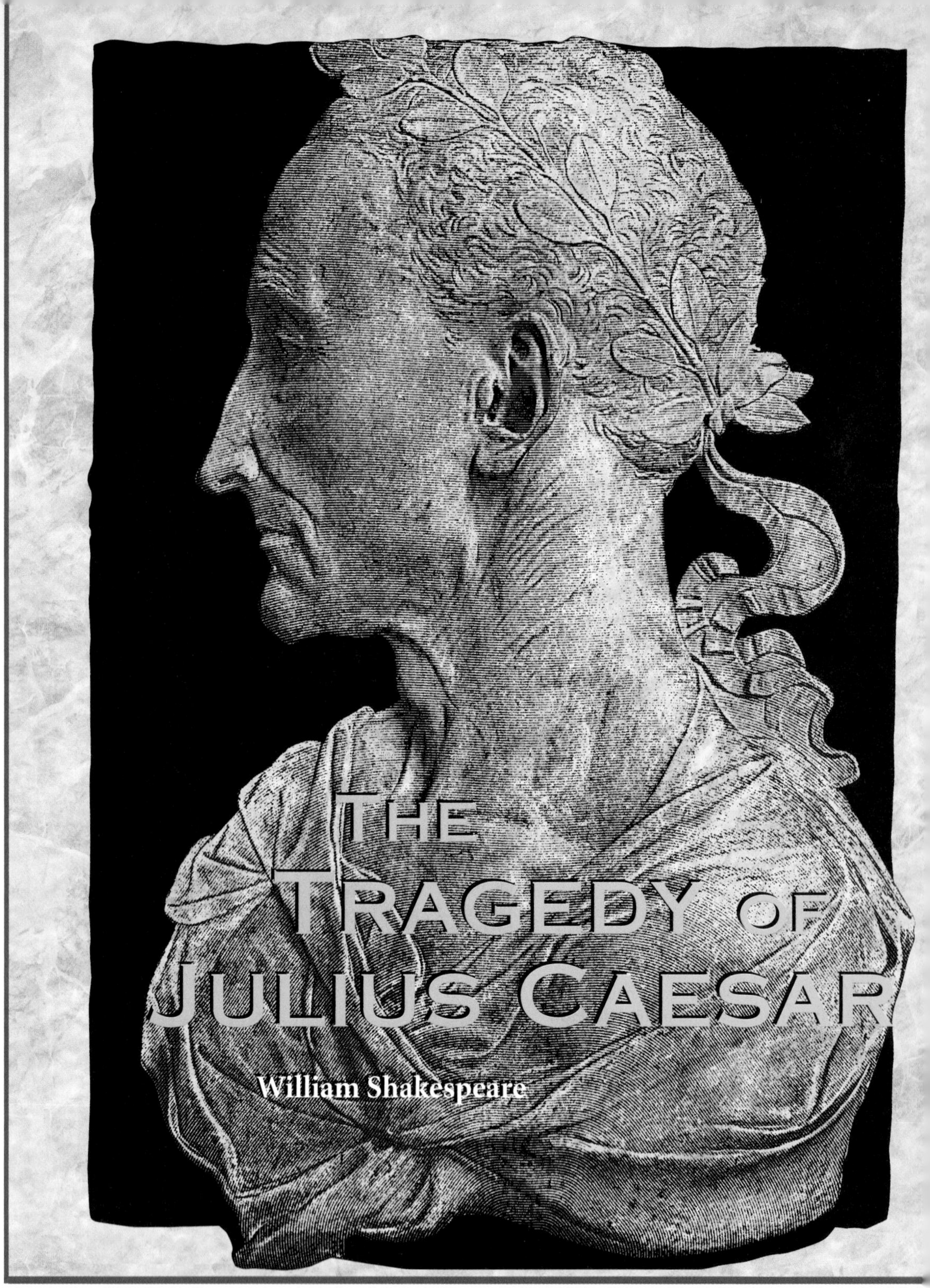

The Tragedy of Julius Caesar

William Shakespeare

CHARACTERS

Julius Caesar

Octavius Caesar
Marcus Antonius
M. Aemilius Lepidus
triumvirs (three officials who share power) after the death of Julius Caesar

Cicero
Publius
Popilius Lena
senators

Marcus Brutus
Cassius
Casca
Trebonius
Ligarius
Decius Brutus
Metellus Cimber
Cinna
conspirators against Julius Caesar

Flavius
Marullus
tribunes (officials appointed to administer the law)

Artemidorus of Cnidos, a teacher of rhetoric
A Soothsayer
Cinna, a poet
Another Poet

Lucilius
Titinius
Messala
Young Cato
Volumnius
friends of Brutus and Cassius

Varro
Clitus
Claudius
Strato
Lucius
Dardanius
servants of Brutus

Pindarus, servant of Cassius
Calphurnia, wife of Caesar
Portia, wife to Brutus
Senators, Citizens, Guards, Attendants, etc.

Scene: During most of the play, at Rome; later, near Sardis, and near Philippi.

Note: The text of this play is taken in entirety from the *Signet Classic Shakespeare.* The editors of the *Signet Classic Shakespeare* have refrained from making abundant changes in the text, but they have added line numbers and act and scene divisions, as well as indications of locale at the beginning of scenes.

(Background) The ruins of the Roman Forum.

DIRECT TEACHING

A Literary Focus
GRADE-LEVEL STANDARD

Tragedy. The opening scenes are the exposition of the play; they present information about the main characters and their conflicts. Explain that the first scene does not introduce a major character but does outline the relationship between the plebeians, or common people, and Caesar and the attitude of soldiers toward the plebeians. As students read, encourage them to make note of characters and events.

B Vocabulary Development
GRADE-LEVEL STANDARD

Recognizing puns. This strategy is presented in the Vocabulary feature on p. 781. Sidenotes throughout Act I help students recognize Shakespeare's puns. When students think they spot a pun, suggest they read the lines aloud. The sounds of the words can help them recognize puns. What puns are there in this passage? ["with the awl" and "withal, I am indeed . . . a surgeon" (ll. 21–23); *cobbler* meaning "shoemaker" and "bungler"; *souls* and *soles*; and the double meaning of *recover*]

Responses to Margin Questions

Stage direction. Flavius's imperious speech brings a confrontational tone to the play, foreshadowing conflicts to come.

Line 16. The men are outwardly respectful, but they are bold and mocking.

ACT I

SCENE 1. *Rome. A street.*

A *Enter* FLAVIUS, MARULLUS, *and certain* COMMONERS *over the stage.*

Flavius.
Hence! Home, you idle creatures, get you home!
Is this a holiday? What, know you not,
Being mechanical,° you ought not walk
Upon a laboring day without the sign
Of your profession?° Speak, what trade art thou?

Carpenter. Why, sir, a carpenter.

Marullus.
Where is thy leather apron and thy rule?
What dost thou with thy best apparel on?
You, sir, what trade are you?

Cobbler. Truly, sir, in respect of a fine workman,° I am but, as you would say, a cobbler.°

Marullus.
But what trade art thou? Answer me directly.

Cobbler. A trade, sir, that, I hope, I may use with a safe conscience, which is indeed, sir, a mender of bad soles.

Flavius.
What trade, thou knave? Thou naughty° knave, what trade?

Cobbler. Nay, I beseech you, sir, be not out with me: yet, if you be out, sir, I can mend you.

B **Marullus.**
What mean'st thou by that? Mend me, thou saucy fellow?

Cobbler. Why, sir, cobble you.

Flavius.
Thou art a cobbler, art thou?

Cobbler. Truly, sir, all that I live by is with the awl:° I meddle with no tradesman's matters, nor women's matters; but withal,° I am indeed, sir, a surgeon to old shoes: when they are in great danger, I recover them. As proper men as ever trod upon neat's leather° have gone upon my handiwork.

Flavius.
But wherefore art not in thy shop today?
Why dost thou lead these men about the streets?

Staging the Play
Stage direction. *We are on a crowded street in Rome. It is lined with statues near what is today known as the Palatine Hill (which is where the palaces, or* palatia, *were). A joyous, peaceful crowd is milling about. Two tribunes—military men—enter with the noisy mob of commoners. What tone does Flavius's first speech bring immediately to the play?*

3. mechanical: working class.

5. sign of your profession: your work clothes and tools.

10. In other words, in comparison with a skilled laborer.
11. cobbler: In Shakespeare's day the word meant both "shoemaker" and "bungler."

15. naughty: worthless.

Staging the Play
16. *It is important in this play to watch the moods of the crowd. Do you think these commoners are afraid of the military men, or are they acting comically and boldly?*

21. awl: sharp, pointed tool for making holes in wood or leather.

23. withal: nevertheless.

25. neat's leather: leather from cattle.

DIFFERENTIATING INSTRUCTION

Learners Having Difficulty
Remind learners having difficulty that Shakespeare's drama has fascinated audiences for centuries. His plays are not meant to be easy to grasp; rather, they are meant to be dazzling. A play by Shakespeare is so rich with action, characterization, wordplay, and poetry that a single reading or production can never reveal all that is there. Yet Shakespeare's plays *are* accessible; they have something to delight and intrigue everyone.

English-Language Learners
Emphasize use of the sidenotes, especially for definitions of archaic words and idioms. Review iambic pentameter so that students will recognize the basic pattern of Shakespeare's language. In addition, have students pause frequently when reading to answer basic questions, such as "Who is speaking?" "To whom is the character speaking?" "What is the character speaking about?"

Resources Reminder
For lessons designed for intermediate and advanced English-language learners, see

758 Chapter 10 Drama • Evaluating an Argument

Cobbler. Truly, sir, to wear out their shoes, to get myself into more work. But indeed, sir, we make holiday to see Caesar and to rejoice in his triumph.

Marullus.
Wherefore rejoice? What conquest brings he home?
What tributaries° follow him to Rome,
To grace in captive bonds his chariot wheels?
You blocks, you stones, you worse than senseless things!
O you hard hearts, you cruel men of Rome,
Knew you not Pompey?° Many a time and oft
Have you climbed up to walls and battlements,
To tow'rs and windows, yea, to chimney tops,
Your infants in your arms, and there have sat
The livelong day, with patient expectation,
To see great Pompey pass the streets of Rome.
And when you saw his chariot but appear,
Have you not made an universal shout,
That Tiber trembled underneath her banks
To hear the replication° of your sounds
Made in her concave shores?°
And do you now put on your best attire?
And do you now cull out a holiday?
And do you now strew flowers in his way
That comes in triumph over Pompey's blood?
Be gone!
Run to your houses, fall upon your knees,
Pray to the gods to intermit° the plague
That needs must light on this ingratitude.

Flavius.
Go, go, good countrymen, and, for this fault,
Assemble all the poor men of your sort;
Draw them to Tiber banks and weep your tears
Into the channel, till the lowest stream
Do kiss the most exalted shores of all.

[*Exeunt all the* COMMONERS.]

See, whe'r their basest mettle° be not moved;
They vanish tongue-tied in their guiltiness.
Go you down that way towards the Capitol;
This way will I. Disrobe the images,°
If you do find them decked with ceremonies.

? **30.** *Why might Shakespeare begin his tragedy on a comic note? What important facts does the cobbler reveal?*

33. tributaries: captives (captive enemies who have to pay tribute, or tax, to Rome).

? **Staging the Play**
A ***monologue*** *is a long speech that a character directs to other characters onstage. What might Marullus be doing as he speaks this monologue?*

37. Pompey: Roman politician and general who was defeated by Caesar in 48 B.C. and later murdered.

46. replication: echo; copy.

47. concave shores: carved-out banks of the river.

? **Staging the Play**
52. *How should this short line be spoken?*

54. intermit: hold back.

? **55.** *What is the key word in the last line of this speech? Why is Marullus angry at the mob?*

? **Staging the Play**
Stage direction. *Pay attention to the movements of the crowd. What mood has taken over these commoners as they leave the stage? Would you have them leave in a defiant mood, or are they ashamed?*

61. basest mettle: basic substance; their "stuff."

64. images: statues.

DIRECT TEACHING

C Reading Skills

Interpreting. Explain that Shakespeare depicts the plebeians throughout the play as a gullible and easily led group. Why do you think Flavius and Marullus are anxious to change their point of view? [Possible response: Since the commoners make up most of the population, their support is essential if the republic is to be maintained.]

D Learners Having Difficulty

Finding details. What details tell you that the crowd once supported Pompey? [They once sat all day to see Pompey and cheered loudly for him.]

E Reading Skills

Iambic pentameter. Which of these five lines is not in iambic pentameter? What effect does it have? ["Be gone!" is not in iambic pentameter. The effect is meant to startle the Romans.]

Responses to Margin Questions

Line 30. He might do so to attract the attention of the audience or to provide irony. The cobbler reveals that Caesar is returning from a victory and that the plebeians are happy with him.
Monologue. Marullus could be using threatening gestures, pushing the men or striking them.
Line 52. This angry command should be issued with great force.
Line 55. The key word is "ingratitude," which reveals that Marullus is angry at the people's fickleness.
Stage direction. Because the men exit silently and quickly, defiance is an unlikely mood. The tribunes have made the men ashamed of forgetting Pompey.

Lesson Plans for Language Development, pp. 333–335, 361, 368.

Special Education Students
For lessons designed for special education students, see *Lesson Plans for Language Development,* pp. 336, 361, 368.

Advanced Learners
Enrichment. Have students use library resources to find information about some aspect of Caesar's life or career—his family background, his rise to power, his accomplishments. Then, ask students to prepare a brief feature article that might appear in a weekly newsmagazine.

Direct Teaching

A Content-Area Connections

Culture: Roman Gods

As a Roman god of agriculture, Lupercus, the Lycean Pan, or Faunus, was associated with fertility. Since belief in this god's powers was widespread, Caesar should not necessarily be faulted as superstitious for hoping that the ritual will help Calphurnia shake off her "sterile curse." This hope takes on new meaning when we consider that Caesar may soon be crowned king and will need an heir to carry on his dynasty.

B Reading Skills

Drawing inferences. What does this interaction between Caesar and Mark Antony tell you about their relationship? [Possible responses: Caesar has great authority and position, as evidenced by how Antony leaps to do his bidding. Antony is devoted and loyal to Caesar.]

Responses to Margin Questions

Line 75. Flavius fears Caesar will use his popularity with the masses to increase his power and rule Rome as a dictator.

Stage direction. In contrast with the mob, Marullus and Flavius would be in a sour mood, resenting the celebration and scorning the masses.

Line 10. Antony is loyal.

Line 12. The soothsayer should be visible to the audience but not to Caesar. He should be positioned to step out and stand alone. Caesar might react with mixed emotions, both irritated and disturbed.

Marullus.
May we do so?
You know it is the feast of Lupercal.°

Flavius.
It is no matter; let no images
Be hung with Caesar's trophies. I'll about
And drive away the vulgar° from the streets;
So do you too, where you perceive them thick.
These growing feathers plucked from Caesar's wing
Will make him fly an ordinary pitch,°
Who else would soar above the view of men
And keep us all in servile fearfulness. *[Exeunt.]*

Scene 2. *A public place.*

Enter CAESAR, ANTONY *(dressed for the race),* CALPHURNIA, PORTIA, DECIUS, CICERO, BRUTUS, CASSIUS, CASCA, *a* SOOTHSAYER; *after them,* MARULLUS *and* FLAVIUS.

Caesar.
Calphurnia!

Casca. Peace, ho! Caesar speaks.

Caesar. Calphurnia!

Calphurnia. Here, my lord.

Caesar.
Stand you directly in Antonius' way
When he doth run his course. Antonius!

Antony. Caesar, my lord?

Caesar.
Forget not in your speed, Antonius,
To touch Calphurnia; for our elders say
The barren, touchèd in this holy chase,
Shake off their sterile curse. **A** **B**

Antony. I shall remember:
When Caesar says "Do this," it is performed.

Caesar.
Set on, and leave no ceremony out.

Soothsayer. Caesar!

Caesar. Ha! Who calls?

Casca.
Bid every noise be still; peace yet again!

67. Lupercal: old Roman fertility festival celebrated on February 15. In the ceremony young men raced around the Palatine Hill (at the base of which is the Lupercal cave) and whipped bystanders with strips of goatskin. Those who were whipped were assured of fertility. The Lupercal cave is believed to be where the twins Romulus and Remus, the founders of Rome, were suckled by a wolf.

70. vulgar: common people.

73. an ordinary pitch: at an ordinary height.

? *75. What does Flavius fear about Caesar?*

? **Staging the Play**
Stage direction. *As Caesar and his retinue enter, the crowd makes way for them. Antony is dressed for the race held on the Feast of Lupercal, which this year also celebrates Caesar's latest victory. Caesar would be richly dressed—perhaps too richly. What mood would Marullus and Flavius be in?*

? **10.** *This speech suggests something important about Antony. What is it?*

? **Staging the Play**
12. *A lot of ceremonial music and ritual have opened this scene, so our attention has been focused on Caesar and his followers. Now the soothsayer, or foreteller of the future, is suddenly visible. This is a dramatic moment, for it foreshadows what will happen. Where would you place the soothsayer? How should Caesar react to his call?*

Differentiating Instruction

Learners Having Difficulty

Summarizing. Have students work in small groups to contribute ideas and information in order to produce a summary of a scene. One student can record the summary; another student can illustrate the scene; a third can read the summary and describe the illustration.

English-Language Learners

Have students work in small groups to create a sociogram that shows the complex relationships among the main characters. One student in the group can identify the main characters and write their names on a chart. Another student can write a few words describing each character and draw arrows between the char-

"BEWARE THE IDES OF MARCH."

The performance photographs illustrating this play are from the 1988 New York Shakespeare Festival production, starring Al Pacino as Antony and Martin Sheen as Brutus.

DIRECT TEACHING

VIEWING THE ART

Draw students' attention to the source of the photograph—a production of the play by the New York Shakespeare Festival.
Activity. Have students identify the main characters in the photograph. Then, have students describe the emotions each character is showing, based on the character's posture and facial expression.

acters' names, indicating their relationships. A third can summarize the relationships. The chart can be added to as students continue to read the play.

Advanced Learners

Enrichment. Point out to students that the first line of Scene 2 is divided between two characters—Caesar and Casca. The division of a line is not an uncommon occurrence in Shakespeare. Here, it adds a sense of importance and urgency to Caesar's words.
Activity. Encourage students to identify and analyze other instances of this technique as they read the play.

DIRECT TEACHING

A Vocabulary Development
REVIEW STANDARD

Word origins. The word *soothsayer* comes from the Old English word *sooth,* meaning "truth." Some possible synonyms are *fortuneteller* and *seer.*

B Literary Focus
GRADE-LEVEL STANDARD

Foreshadowing. Although the soothsayer has an extremely minor role, his few words have great implications. What simple dramatic technique does Shakespeare use to focus the audience's attention on the soothsayer's words? [Repetition—Brutus repeats the soothsayer's warning; the soothsayer will also repeat his warning in l. 23.] How does the soothsayer's repeated warning serve as foreshadowing? [Possible response: It alerts the audience to the fact that Caesar faces serious danger and identifies when the danger will occur.]

C Reading Skills

Analyzing. Why do you think Caesar dismisses the soothsayer's warning so quickly? [Possible response: Caesar is very self-confident; he is so sure of his popularity and power that he can't imagine that he might be in danger.]

Responses to Margin Questions

Line 17. Caesar is deaf in one ear.
Line 18. The line could be sinister, forceful, prophetic, fearful, or mysterious.
Stage direction. Brutus's answer should show that he is preoccupied, perhaps deliberately separating himself from the celebrants.

Caesar.
Who is it in the press° that calls on me?
I hear a tongue, shriller than all the music,
Cry "Caesar." Speak; Caesar is turned to hear.

Soothsayer.
Beware the ides of March.

Caesar. What man is that?

Brutus.
A soothsayer bids you beware the ides of March.

Caesar.
Set him before me; let me see his face.

Cassius.
Fellow, come from the throng; look upon Caesar.

Caesar.
What say'st thou to me now? Speak once again.

Soothsayer.
Beware the ides of March.

Caesar.
He is a dreamer, let us leave him. Pass.

[*Sennet.*° *Exeunt all except* BRUTUS *and* CASSIUS.]

Cassius.
Will you go see the order of the course?

Brutus. Not I.

Cassius. I pray you do.

Brutus.
I am not gamesome: I do lack some part
Of that quick spirit that is in Antony.
Let me not hinder, Cassius, your desires;
I'll leave you.

Cassius.
Brutus, I do observe you now of late;
I have not from your eyes that gentleness
And show of love as I was wont to have;
You bear too stubborn and too strange a hand°
Over your friend that loves you.

Brutus. Cassius,
Be not deceived: if I have veiled my look,
I turn the trouble of my countenance
Merely° upon myself. Vexèd I am
Of late with passions of some difference,°
Conceptions only proper to myself,
Which give some soil,° perhaps, to my behaviors;

15. press: crowd.

17. *What physical disability might this line suggest?*

Staging the Play
18. *The ides of March are March 15. In some productions this warning is heard as an ominous and disembodied cry. In what different ways could the line be spoken?*

Sennet: flourish, or fanfare of trumpets announcing a ceremonial entrance or exit.

Staging the Play
Stage direction. *Except for Brutus and Cassius, the stage is empty for a few moments as they stand looking at the departing Caesar. The action line of the play—the assassination—begins now with Cassius's rather casual question (line 25). How should Brutus speak his answer?*

35. You . . . hand: Cassius is comparing Brutus's treatment of him with the way a trainer treats a horse.

39. Merely: wholly.

40. passions of some difference: conflicting feelings or emotions.

42. give some soil: stain or mar.

CONTENT-AREA CONNECTIONS

History: The Roman Calendar

The first Roman calendar, borrowed from the Greeks, consisted of 10 months divided into 304 days. The remaining sixty days, which fell in the middle of winter, seemed to have been ignored by the Romans. By the time of Julius Caesar, the accumulated error caused by the incorrect length of the Roman year had made the calendar about three months ahead of the seasons. On the advice of his astronomer, in 46 B.C., Julius Caesar divided the year into 12 months of 30 or 31 days, except for February, which had 29 days. To realign the calendar, he ruled that the first year of the new calendar would have 445 days, leading the Romans to call it "the year of confusion."

But let not therefore my good friends be grieved
(Among which number, Cassius, be you one)
Nor construe° any further my neglect
Than that poor Brutus, with himself at war,
Forgets the shows of love to other men.

Cassius.
Then, Brutus, I have much mistook your passion,°
By means whereof this breast of mine hath buried
Thoughts of great value, worthy cogitations.°
Tell me, good Brutus, can you see your face?

Brutus.
No, Cassius; for the eye sees not itself
But by reflection, by some other things.

Cassius.
'Tis just:°
And it is very much lamented, Brutus,
That you have no such mirrors as will turn
Your hidden worthiness into your eye,
That you might see your shadow.° I have heard
Where many of the best respect° in Rome
(Except immortal Caesar), speaking of Brutus,
And groaning underneath this age's yoke,
Have wished that noble Brutus had his eyes.

Brutus.
Into what dangers would you lead me, Cassius,
That you would have me seek into myself
For that which is not in me?

Cassius.
Therefore, good Brutus, be prepared to hear;
And since you know you cannot see yourself
So well as by reflection, I, your glass°
Will modestly discover to yourself
That of yourself which you yet know not of.
And be not jealous on° me, gentle Brutus:
Were I a common laughter,° or did use
To stale with ordinary oaths my love
To every new protester,° if you know
That I do fawn on men and hug them hard,
And after scandal them;° or if you know
That I profess myself in banqueting
To all the rout,° then hold me dangerous.

45. construe: interpret.

? **47.** *How does Brutus explain his behavior?*

48. passion: feeling.

50. worthy cogitations: reflections of great value.

54. just: true.

58. shadow: reflection (of what others think of him).
59. respect: reputation.

? **Staging the Play**
60. *How would Cassius say the parenthetical remark?*

68. glass: mirror.

71. jealous on: suspicious of.

72. common laughter: butt of a joke; object of mockery.

74. In other words, if he swore to love everyone who came along.

76. scandal them: ruin them by gossip.

78. rout (rout): common people; the mob.

? **78.** *What, in sum, is Cassius telling Brutus here?*

DIRECT TEACHING

D Reading Skills

? Interpreting. What does Brutus mean when he says he is "with himself at war"? [Possible response: Brutus's feelings about Caesar are causing an internal conflict: Although Brutus loves and admires Caesar, he does not want him to assume absolute power and shatter the Roman republic.]

E Learners Having Difficulty

? Paraphrasing. What is Cassius telling Brutus? [Possible response: Cassius regrets that Brutus does not have a mirror that could show him how highly others think of him. Cassius states that many respected citizens wish that Brutus could see himself as they do.]

F Literary Focus
GRADE-LEVEL STANDARD

? Tragedy. Explain that in all Shakespearean tragedies the center of the drama is the protagonist, or main character, someone with a highly sensitive moral conscience who suffers and dies because of having a tragic character flaw or being unsuited to the role he or she must play. Who is the protagonist? [Brutus] What weakness does the protagonist show in relation to Cassius and the idea of a conspiracy? [Possible response: Brutus's high-minded traits and concern with honor make it hard for him to recognize the personal jealousy and ambitions that motivate Cassius in the conspiracy.]

DEVELOPING FLUENCY

Individual activity. Tell students that Shakespeare often used words as different parts of speech from the way they are normally used today. For example, we think of *vulgar* as an adjective, but Shakespeare uses it as a noun. The difference is partly a result of the changing usage of words over time and of the demands of writing in iambic pentameter. Write the line below on the chalkboard.

Have students identify the part of speech of the underlined word and rewrite the line with the word changed into the part of speech we would most often use today. "I have heard / Where many of the best <u>respect</u> in Rome . . ." (ll. 58–59) [noun; I have heard that many of the most respected people in Rome . . .]

Responses to Margin Questions

Line 47. Brutus says that he has been troubled and has turned inward, trying to sort out his conflicting emotions.
Line 60. Cassius would speak sarcastically.
Line 78. Cassius says that he can be trusted.

DIRECT TEACHING

A Reading Skills

? Interpreting. Why do you think the major historical scene of Caesar being received by the Roman people occurs offstage while the drama focuses on the interaction of Brutus and Cassius? [Possible response: Shakespeare wants us to focus on the interaction between Cassius and Brutus.]

B Literary Focus GRADE-LEVEL STANDARD

? Scene design. Where are the opening acts of the play set? [in the streets near the Roman Capitol and Forum] What might be the scene design? [many buildings close together; narrow, cobblestone streets] What effect might this scene design have? [Possible response: It reinforces the secrecy of the conspirators.]

C Reading Skills

Iambic pentameter. Ask students to explain the apostrophe in *accout'red* and the accent on the second syllable of *plungèd* in l. 105. [They are necessary to maintain the iambic pentameter.] Have students read the line aloud and note which syllables are stressed.

Responses to Margin Questions

Stage direction. They should show concern.

Line 80. Cassius should speak quickly, with energy and passion. He might also show his joy that Brutus agrees with him.

Line 89. Students could support either interpretation but should see that Brutus has so far shown himself to be thoughtful and not so foolishly idealistic that Cassius does not desire his aid.

Line 97. Cassius complains that Caesar, an ordinary human being, has set himself up as a god.

[*Flourish*° *and shout.*]

A **Brutus.**
What means this shouting? I do fear the people
B Choose Caesar for their king.

Cassius. Ay, do you fear it?
Then must I think you would not have it so.

Brutus.
I would not, Cassius, yet I love him well.
But wherefore do you hold me here so long?
What is it that you would impart to me?
If it be aught toward the general good,
Set honor in one eye and death i' th' other,
And I will look on both indifferently;°
For let the gods so speed me, as I love
The name of honor more than I fear death.

Cassius.
I know that virtue to be in you, Brutus,
As well as I do know your outward favor.°
Well, honor is the subject of my story.
I cannot tell what you and other men
Think of this life, but for my single self,
I had as lief° not be, as live to be
In awe of such a thing as I myself.
I was born free as Caesar; so were you:
We both have fed as well, and we can both
Endure the winter's cold as well as he:
For once, upon a raw and gusty day,
The troubled Tiber chafing with° her shores,
Caesar said to me "Dar'st thou, Cassius, now
Leap in with me into this angry flood,
C And swim to yonder point?" Upon the word,
Accout'red as I was, I plungèd in
And bade him follow: so indeed he did.
The torrent roared, and we did buffet it
With lusty sinews, throwing it aside
And stemming it with hearts of controversy.°
But ere we could arrive the point proposed,
Caesar cried "Help me, Cassius, or I sink!"
I, as Aeneas,° our great ancestor,
Did from the flames of Troy upon his shoulder
The old Anchises bear, so from the waves of Tiber
Did I the tired Caesar. And this man
Is now become a god, and Cassius is

Flourish: brief, elaborate music played by trumpets.

? Staging the Play
Stage direction. *The trumpet sounds offstage, and the crowd's roar is heard again. How would Cassius and Brutus react?*

? Staging the Play
80. *This is what Cassius has wanted to hear. How should he deliver this speech?*

87. indifferently: impartially; fairly.

? Staging the Play
89. *Brutus could sound noble here, or he could be played as foolishly idealistic, even priggish. How would you deliver this speech?*

91. outward favor: appearance.

95. as lief (lēf): just as soon.

? 97. *This is a long and important* ***monologue.*** *What is Cassius's chief complaint about Caesar?*

101. chafing with: raging against (the river was rough with waves and currents).

109. hearts of controversy: hearts full of aggressive feelings, or fighting spirit.

112. Aeneas (i • nē′ əs): legendary forefather of the Roman people who, in Virgil's *Aeneid,* fled the burning city of Troy carrying his aged father on his back. (In many accounts of the legend, Romulus and Remus are descendants of Aeneas.)

CONTENT-AREA CONNECTIONS

Social Science: Roman Government
As in modern democracies, the officials of ancient Rome were elected by the general public in a political system that included checks and balances to prevent any one leader from becoming too powerful. The governing body in Rome in Caesar's time was the Senate, and all the main characters in the play (Brutus, Cassius, Mark Antony) were senators.

Two powerful officials, called consuls, were elected by the general public each year. The power of the consuls was checked by having them share power. The consuls' short term of office was another check on their power.

Julius Caesar was able to achieve a level of power exceeding that of a consul because the Roman republic was caught in a series of civil wars. In the interests of military expediency, a

764 Chapter 10 Drama • Evaluating an Argument

A wretched creature, and must bend his body
If Caesar carelessly but nod on him.
He had a fever when he was in Spain,
And when the fit was on him, I did mark
How he did shake; 'tis true, this god did shake.
His coward lips did from their color fly, **D**
And that same eye whose bend doth awe the world
Did lose his luster; I did hear him groan;
Ay, and that tongue of his, that bade the Romans
Mark him and write his speeches in their books,
Alas, it cried, "Give me some drink, Titinius,"
As a sick girl. Ye gods! It doth amaze me,
A man of such a feeble temper should
So get the start of the majestic world,
And bear the palm° alone.

[*Shout. Flourish.*]

Brutus.
Another general shout?
I do believe that these applauses are
For some new honors that are heaped on Caesar.

Cassius.
Why, man, he doth bestride the narrow world
Like a Colossus,° and we petty men
Walk under his huge legs and peep about
To find ourselves dishonorable graves.
Men at some time are masters of their fates:
The fault, dear Brutus, is not in our stars,°
But in ourselves, that we are underlings.
Brutus and Caesar: what should be in that "Caesar"?
Why should that name be sounded more than yours?
Write them together, yours is as fair a name;
Sound them, it doth become the mouth as well;
Weigh them, it is as heavy; conjure with 'em,
"Brutus" will start a spirit as soon as "Caesar."
Now, in the names of all the gods at once,
Upon what meat doth this our Caesar feed,
That he is grown so great? Age, thou art shamed!
Rome, thou hast lost the breed of noble bloods!
When went there by an age, since the great flood,°
But it was famed with more than with one man?
When could they say (till now) that talked of Rome,

Staging the Play
118. *How should Cassius say this last sentence?*

Staging the Play
121. *What word should be stressed here?*

131. bear the palm: hold the palm branch, an award given to a victorious general.

131. *Why has Cassius told Brutus these anecdotes about Caesar? What is his point?*

136. Colossus: huge statue of Helios that was said to straddle the entrance to the harbor at Rhodes, an island in the Aegean Sea. The statue, so huge that ships passed under its legs, was one of the Seven Wonders of the ancient world. It was destroyed by an earthquake in 224 B.C.

140. stars: Elizabethans believed that one's life was governed by the stars, or constellation, one was born under.

Staging the Play
142. *There is often a pause here, after the Colossus metaphor. How would Cassius say the names Brutus and Caesar?*

152. the great flood: flood sent by Zeus to drown all the wicked people on earth. Only the faithful couple Deucalion and Pyrrha were saved.

DIRECT TEACHING

D Vocabulary Development
GRADE-LEVEL STANDARD

Recognizing puns. Point out that "color" or "colors" can mean one's flag or the banner to which one owes allegiance. How does "color" become a pun in l. 122? [Caesar's pale lips are compared to a coward fleeing his colors, suggesting that Caesar is a traitor.]

E Learners Having Difficulty

Comparing and contrasting. These students might benefit from making a Venn diagram comparing and contrasting Cassius and Brutus. Have them note the personal traits and political beliefs that are unique to each character, as well as those that the characters share.

F Reading Skills

Recognizing persuasive techniques. Does Cassius rely on facts or on eloquent language in his efforts to persuade Brutus to join the conspiracy? [Possible response: Cassius doesn't really provide any facts to justify his plan to assassinate Caesar; his flowery rhetoric is, however, very persuasive.]

Responses to Margin Questions

Line 118. Cassius could speak with bitterness, outrage, or sarcasm.
Line 121. Cassius would stress "god" sarcastically.
Line 131. His stories show that Caesar, a mere mortal who has no right to proclaim himself a god, is unworthy to rule Rome. He wants to convince Brutus to join the conspiracy.
Line 142. Cassius would articulate these words because he is presenting the names for consideration and comparison. He could pronounce them with equal weight, or his pronunciation could show a preference.

number of exceptions to the rule of law were made. Also, the Senate honored Caesar for his successful military exploits by awarding him additional honors and powers.

Culture: Astrology
The practice of astrology was widespread throughout the Middle East, Asia, and Europe in ancient times. With the rise of Christianity and its emphasis on free will, astrology fell out of official favor to some degree. But in the late Middle Ages, partly through Muslim influence, belief in astrology grew. In 1585, Pope Sixtus V officially condemned astrology for religious, not scientific reasons. Eventually, scientific discoveries and changing concepts of the universe further undermined widespread belief in astrology.

The Tragedy of Julius Caesar, Act I, Scene 2 765

DIRECT TEACHING

A Vocabulary Development
GRADE-LEVEL STANDARD

Recognizing puns. Remind students that changes in pronunciation have rendered some of Shakespeare's puns less obvious to modern readers. After reading the note for l. 156, have students explain Cassius's intent in punning on Rome and room. [Possible response: Cassius humorously suggests that Rome has a great deal of room in it now, since there is only one great man, Caesar, and everyone else is small.]

B English-Language Learners

Inverted word order. Shakespeare frequently uses inverted word order in his sentences, either to emphasize certain words and phrases or to maintain the rhythm of iambic pentameter. For example, in ll. 162–170, Brutus begins several sentences with a subordinate clause that in normal word order would follow the main clause. How could the first line in the passage be reordered in normal word order? [I am nothing jealous that you do love me.] Work with students to reorder the rest of the passage.

Response to Margin Question

Line 161. Cassius is appealing to Brutus's sense of pride and honor.

A That her wide walks encompassed but one man?
Now is it Rome indeed, and room° enough,
When there is in it but one only man.
O, you and I have heard our fathers say,
There was a Brutus once that would have brooked°
Th' eternal devil to keep his state in Rome
As easily as a king.°

Brutus.
B That you do love me, I am nothing jealous;
What you would work me to, I have some aim;°
How I have thought of this, and of these times,

156. Rome . . . room: a pun; both words were pronounced rōōm in Shakespeare's day.

159. brooked: put up with.

161. This refers to an ancestor of Brutus's who, in the sixth century B.C., helped to expel the last king from Rome and set up the republic.

? **161.** *Why does Cassius mention Brutus's famous ancestor?*

163. aim: idea.

DIFFERENTIATING INSTRUCTION

Advanced Learners

Enrichment. Point out that Cassius's claims about Caesar's weaknesses are not borne out by Roman historians. According to Suetonius, "Caesar was a most skilled swordsman and horseman, and showed surprising powers of endurance. He always led his army, more often on foot than in the saddle. . . . If he reached an unfordable river he would either swim or propel himself across it on an inflated skin, and often arrived at his destination before his messengers whom he had sent ahead to announce his approach." Similarly, Plutarch wrote: "[Caesar] used warfare as a tonic to his health. By long, hard journeys, simple diet, sleeping night after night in the open, and rough living he . . . made his body strong enough to resist all attacks."

Activity. Have students research evidence that supports the view of Caesar as either brave or cowardly. They can share their research with the rest of the class and then lead a discussion based on the following questions:

- Why might Caesar have been deliberately misrepresented in ll. 100–130?
- What conclusions can be drawn about Cassius?

I shall recount hereafter. For this present,
I would not so (with love I might entreat you)
Be any further moved. What you have said
I will consider; what you have to say
I will with patience hear, and find a time
Both meet° to hear and answer such high things.
Till then, my noble friend, chew upon this:
Brutus had rather be a villager
Than to repute himself a son of Rome
Under these hard conditions as this time
Is like to lay upon us.

Cassius. I am glad
That my weak words have struck but thus much show
Of fire from Brutus.

[*Enter* CAESAR *and his* TRAIN.]

Brutus.
The games are done, and Caesar is returning.

Cassius.
As they pass by, pluck Casca by the sleeve,
And he will (after his sour fashion) tell you
What hath proceeded worthy note today.

Brutus.
I will do so. But look you, Cassius,
The angry spot doth glow on Caesar's brow,
And all the rest look like a chidden° train:
Calphurnia's cheek is pale, and Cicero
Looks with such ferret° and such fiery eyes
As we have seen him in the Capitol,
Being crossed in conference by some senators.

Cassius.
Casca will tell us what the matter is.

Caesar. Antonius.

Antony. Caesar?

Caesar.
Let me have men about me that are fat,
Sleek-headed men, and such as sleep a-nights.
Yond Cassius has a lean and hungry look;
He thinks too much: such men are dangerous.

Antony.
Fear him not, Caesar, he's not dangerous;
He is a noble Roman, and well given.°

170. meet: appropriate.

? 175. *A* ***character foil*** *is a character who serves as a contrast to another character, so that each one stands out vividly. How is Cassius a foil to Brutus?*

C

? 177. *According to Cassius's speech, how has Brutus delivered his previous line? Has Cassius gotten what he wants?*

? **Staging the Play**
Stage direction. *Cassius and Brutus move downstage left to allow the procession (Caesar's train) to pass across the width of the backstage area to an entrance down right. In this way the audience sees two acting areas at one time—one for the conspirators and their growing intimacy and one for the pompous world of public ceremony. Would the two actors next speak openly, or are they already acting secretively?*

184. chidden (chid′n): rebuked; corrected.

186. ferret: weasellike animal, usually considered crafty.

? 188. *Cicero at this time is sixty-two years old, famous as a great advocate of the republic. Though he had supported Pompey and opposed Caesar, Cicero liked Caesar personally and had nothing to do with the assassination. What does Brutus think of Cicero?*

? **Staging the Play**
190. *Cassius and Brutus move away, and we focus on Caesar, who casts a suspicious look at Cassius, now downstage left. What does Caesar's next speech tell you about Cassius's physical appearance?*

D

197. well given: well disposed to support Caesar.

DIRECT TEACHING

C Reading Skills

? Making inferences. Do you think Brutus is aware that Cassius is hinting at a conspiracy against Caesar? Do you think Brutus understands that Cassius is trying to flatter and manipulate him? [Possible response: Brutus's previous comment that he has "some aim" at what Cassius would "work" him to seems to indicate that he understands what Cassius is plotting and is contemplating getting involved. However, Brutus seems unaware that he is being manipulated.]

D Literary Focus
GRADE-LEVEL STANDARD

? Character. What do Caesar's remarks about Cassius tell you about the Roman leader? [Possible response: Caesar's remarks reveal that he is very perceptive; he intuitively recognizes that Cassius presents a danger to him.]

Responses to Margin Questions

Line 175. Cassius's self-interest is apparent while Brutus more obviously upholds the interests of the republic.

Line 177. Brutus has spoken with spirit and determination. Cassius has achieved a first step.

Stage direction. They are already secretive, keenly observing Caesar and his followers.

Line 188. Brutus characterizes Cicero as a sly person (a weasel) who reacts violently when crossed.

Line 190. Cassius is a thin and intense man.

DEVELOPING FLUENCY

Whole-class activity. Re-reading is crucial for gaining a deeper understanding of a text, especially one as complicated as *Julius Caesar.* Have students re-read the following passages and discuss the questions.

1. Re-read Scene 2, ll. 142–147. Why does Cassius compare Brutus with Caesar? Why does Cassius deliberately find no difference between them? [Cassius wants to show Brutus that there is no substantive difference between him (Brutus) and Caesar; therefore, there is no reason why Caesar should be king.]
2. Re-read ll. 158–161. Why does Cassius contrast Brutus with his ancestor, also named Brutus? [He wants to suggest that Brutus should be bolder, like his ancestor, who would have done anything to defend the Roman republic.]

DIRECT TEACHING

(A) Literary Focus
GRADE-LEVEL STANDARD

? Character. Caesar's first observation about Cassius revealed impressive insight. What less favorable side of Caesar's character do these lines show? [Possible response: Caesar reveals his vanity and egotism here; he arrogantly places himself above the rest of humanity and dismisses Cassius as someone others, but not Caesar, might fear.]

(B) Reading Skills

? Hypothesizing. The real Caesar was not deaf in one ear, as he suggests in l. 213. Why do you think Shakespeare might have invented this detail about the Roman leader? [Possible responses: to suggest that Caesar is vulnerable; to show that he is a mere mortal.]

(C) Reading Skills

? Iambic pentameter. Point out that Casca's lines are written in prose, not iambic pentameter. Shakespeare usually reserves prose for the speech of comical or minor characters. Why do you think Shakespeare has Casca speak in prose here, not blank verse? [Possible responses: Shakespeare might be indicating that Casca is a lesser character among the conspirators. Casca, a senator, affects the demeanor of a plebeian in order to show sarcasm.]

Responses to Margin Questions

Line 212. Caesar fears Cassius's insightfulness and his hunger for power, which he believes is fueled by envy. Caesar himself is too vain to admit to fear and assumes a heroic public stance.

Stage direction. Casca shows sarcasm by not answering Brutus's questions directly and by using the descriptions "gentler" and "honest" in ll. 229–230.

Caesar.
(A) Would he were fatter! But I fear him not.
Yet if my name were liable to fear,
I do not know the man I should avoid
So soon as that spare Cassius. He reads much,
He is a great observer, and he looks
Quite through the deeds of men.° He loves no plays,
As thou dost, Antony; he hears no music;
Seldom he smiles, and smiles in such a sort°
As if he mocked himself, and scorned his spirit
That could be moved to smile at anything.
Such men as he be never at heart's ease
Whiles they behold a greater than themselves,
And therefore are they very dangerous.
I rather tell thee what is to be feared
Than what I fear; for always I am Caesar.
(B) Come on my right hand, for this ear is deaf,
And tell me truly what thou think'st of him.

[*Sennet. Exeunt* CAESAR *and his* TRAIN.]

Casca.
You pulled me by the cloak; would you speak with me?

Brutus.
Ay, Casca; tell us what hath chanced today,
That Caesar looks so sad.°

Casca.
Why, you were with him, were you not?

Brutus.
I should not then ask Casca what had chanced.

(C) **Casca.** Why, there was a crown offered him; and being offered him, he put it by° with the back of his hand, thus; and then the people fell a-shouting.

Brutus. What was the second noise for?

Casca. Why, for that too.

Cassius.
They shouted thrice; what was the last cry for?

Casca. Why, for that too.

Brutus. Was the crown offered him thrice?

Casca. Ay, marry,° was't, and he put it by thrice, every time gentler than other; and at every putting-by mine honest neighbors shouted.

Cassius.
Who offered him the crown?

---

203. In other words, he looks through what men *do* to search out their feelings and motives.
205. sort: manner.

? 212. *Caesar's analysis of Cassius is accurate. Why does he fear Cassius? What does the speech tell us about Caesar himself?*

? Staging the Play
Stage direction. *As the procession leaves through an upstage portal at left, Brutus pulls on the toga of Casca as he passes. Casca is rough and sarcastic. How is his sarcasm suggested in the following lines?*

217. sad: serious.

221. put it by: pushed it aside.

228. marry: mild oath meaning "by the Virgin Mary."

DEVELOPING FLUENCY

Individual activity. Have students choose one of the major speeches or soliloquies in Act I to memorize. Before they begin to memorize, students should make sure they thoroughly understand the ideas and the vocabulary in the passage. Encourage them to present their speeches to the class.

768 Chapter 10 Drama • Evaluating an Argument

Casca. Why, Antony.

Brutus.
Tell us the manner of it, gentle Casca.

Casca. I can as well be hanged as tell the manner of it: it was mere foolery; I did not mark it. I saw Mark Antony offer him a crown—yet 'twas not a crown neither, 'twas one of these coronets°—and, as I told you, he put it by once; but for all that, to my thinking, he would fain° have had it. Then he offered it to him again; then he put it by again; but to my thinking, he was very loath to lay his fingers off it. And then he offered it the third time. He put it the third time by; and still as he refused it, the rabblement hooted, and clapped their chopt° hands, and threw up their sweaty nightcaps,° and uttered such a deal of stinking breath because Caesar refused the crown, that it had, almost, choked Caesar; for he swounded° and fell down at it. And for mine own part, I durst not laugh, for fear of opening my lips and receiving the bad air. **D**

Cassius.
But, soft,° I pray you; what, did Caesar swound?

Casca. He fell down in the market place, and foamed at mouth, and was speechless.

Brutus.
'Tis very like he hath the falling-sickness.°

Cassius.
No, Caesar hath it not; but you, and I,
And honest Casca, we have the falling-sickness. **E**

Casca. I know not what you mean by that, but I am sure Caesar fell down. If the tag-rag people° did not clap him and hiss him, according as he pleased and displeased them, as they use to do the players in the theater, I am no true man.

Brutus.
What said he when he came unto himself?

Casca. Marry, before he fell down, when he perceived the common herd was glad he refused the crown, he plucked me ope° his doublet° and offered them his throat to cut. **F** An° I had been a man of any occupation,° if I would not have taken him at a word, I would I might go to hell among the rogues. And so he fell. When he came to himself again, he said, if he had done or said anything amiss, he desired their worships to think it was his infirmity. Three or four wenches,° where I stood, cried "Alas, good soul!" and forgave him with all their hearts;

? Staging the Play
233. *How would Brutus respond to this news about the crown?*

237. coronets: small crowns.

238. fain: happily.

243. chopt: chapped (raw and rough from hard work and the weather).

244. nightcaps: Casca is mockingly referring to the hats of the workingmen.

246. swounded: swooned; fainted.

? 248. *How does Casca feel about the Roman mob?*

249. soft: wait a minute.

252. falling-sickness: old term for the disease we now call epilepsy, which is marked by seizures and momentary loss of consciousness.

? 254. *What do you think Cassius means here?*

256. tag-rag people: contemptuous reference to the commoners in the crowd.

262. plucked me ope: plucked open. **doublet:** close-fitting jacket.

263. An: if. **man of any occupation:** working man.

268. wenches: girls or young women.

DIRECT TEACHING

D Literary Focus
GRADE-LEVEL STANDARD

? Dialogue. After the serious speeches of Cassius and Brutus, Shakespeare provides some humor with Casca's lively prose narration. What details in Casca's delivery and speech might appeal to the audience? [Possible responses: He gives a colorful and cynical account of Caesar's refusal of the crown. He gives an exaggerated account of the odor of the crowd and how it caused Caesar to faint.]

E Vocabulary Development
GRADE-LEVEL STANDARD

? Recognizing puns. How does Cassius pun on the term *falling-sickness?* [Possible responses: He suggests that he and other Romans, through their own weakness, are falling in status. As they fall under Caesar's imperial rule, they will not stand as honorably as they did in the republic.]

F Vocabulary Development
ADVANCED STANDARD

Anachronisms. Tell students that an anachronism is an event or detail in a literary work that is chronologically out of place. A doublet is an Elizabethan form of dress, not something Caesar would have worn.

Responses to Margin Questions

Line 233. Brutus is seriously concerned and apprehensive.

Line 248. Casca finds them repulsive and laughable.

Line 254. Cassius could be punning on several meanings of *fall* and *falling* to justify the conspiracy and its possible failure.

DIFFERENTIATING INSTRUCTION

Advanced Learners

Enrichment. As part of his portrayal of Caesar, Shakespeare presents the great Roman through the eyes of a conspirator, the cynical Casca, who views Caesar's actions in the Forum as a bit of crude playacting.

Activity. In small groups, have students discuss the following questions:

- What is Shakespeare's purpose in doing so?
- Why does he present Caesar in such an unflattering light in the initial act?

Then, have them imagine the same scene told from the point of view of either Cassius or Brutus. Students should rewrite the scene from that character's viewpoint. As they continue to read the play, ask them to cite examples that show how Shakespeare's attitude toward Caesar slowly changes.

DIRECT TEACHING

Ⓐ English-Language Learners

Interpreting colloquialisms. Explain the colloquialism "It's all Greek to me." There are several variations of this basic expression, but they all mean the same thing: that something doesn't make sense or that it's confusing. For example, people might say this when confronted with an extremely difficult text or in response to hearing complicated professional jargon. Another expression with a similar meaning is "I don't get it." Ask students for examples of expressions from their own language that might be used in similar circumstances.

Ⓑ Reading Skill

Speculating. Why do you think Cicero expressed himself in Greek at the Forum? What might he have said? [Possible response: He may have been making disparaging remarks about Caesar that he wanted only his like-minded, educated acquaintances to hear.]

Responses to Margin Questions

Line 271. Casca believes Caesar is an insincere showman courting the favor of the crowd and secretly desiring to be king.

Line 282. They are silenced for removing decorations from Caesar's statues that celebrate his triumphs. Caesar acts swiftly and harshly against those who oppose him.

**". . . THEREFORE IT IS MEET
THAT NOBLE MINDS KEEP EVER
WITH THEIR LIKES;
FOR WHO SO FIRM THAT CANNOT
BE SEDUCED?"**

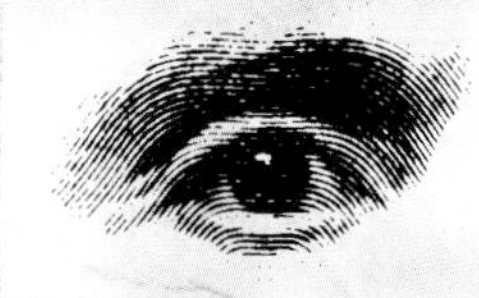

but there's no heed to be taken of them; if Caesar had stabbed their mothers, they would have done no less.

Brutus.
And after that, he came thus sad away?

Casca. Ay.

Cassius.
Ⓐ Did Cicero say anything?

Casca. Ay, he spoke Greek.

Cassius. To what effect?

Casca. Ⓑ Nay, an I tell you that, I'll ne'er look you i' th' face again. But those that understood him smiled at one another and shook their heads; but for mine own part, it was Greek to me. I could tell you more news too: Marullus and Flavius, for pulling scarfs off Caesar's images, are put to silence.° Fare you well. There was more foolery yet, if I could remember it.

Cassius. Will you sup with me tonight, Casca?

Casca. No, I am promised forth.°

Cassius. Will you dine with me tomorrow?

Casca. Ay, if I be alive, and your mind hold, and your dinner worth the eating.

Cassius. Good; I will expect you.

Casca. Do so. Farewell, both. *[Exit.]*

Brutus.
What a blunt fellow is this grown to be!
He was quick mettle° when he went to school.

Cassius.
So is he now in execution
Of any bold or noble enterprise,
However he puts on this tardy form.°
This rudeness° is a sauce to his good wit,°
Which gives men stomach to disgest° his words
With better appetite.

? **271.** *Casca gets very sarcastic here. What does he think of Caesar?*

282. put to silence: silenced, perhaps by dismissal from their positions as tribunes or by exile.

? **282.** *Why are Marullus and Flavius silenced? What does this tell you about Caesar?*

285. forth: previously. (He has other plans.)

292. quick mettle: lively of disposition.

295. tardy form: sluggish appearance.

296. rudeness: rough manner. **wit:** intelligence.

297. disgest: digest.

CONTENT-AREA CONNECTIONS

History: Roman Statesman
Cicero (106–43 B.C.) was the greatest Roman orator, as well as a leading politician and philosopher. He was the foremost exponent of republican principles in the Senate and had previously saved the republic from a plot to overthrow it. An ally of Pompey, Cicero strongly opposed Caesar and was a bitter enemy of Mark Antony. After Pompey's death, Caesar forgave Cicero. Although Cicero did not take part in Caesar's assassination, he strongly applauded it.

Culture: Medieval Hierarchy
According to medieval ideas still prevalent in England at the time of Shakespeare, the universe was organized in what critic Arthur O. Lovejoy has called "the great chain of being." God in heaven was at the top of the hierarchy. Between heaven and earth were nine orders of angels. On earth, humans stood below God and the angels and above animals, plants, and inanimate matter. The state, the Church, and the family modeled themselves after the heavenly hierarchy. Thus, the head

Brutus.

And so it is. For this time I will leave you.
Tomorrow, if you please to speak with me,
I will come home to you; or if you will,
Come home to me, and I will wait for you.

Cassius.

I will do so. Till then, think of the world.°

[*Exit* BRUTUS.]

Well, Brutus, thou art noble; yet I see
Thy honorable mettle may be wrought
From that it is disposed;° therefore it is meet
That noble minds keep ever with their likes;
For who so firm that cannot be seduced?
Caesar doth bear me hard,° but he loves Brutus.
If I were Brutus now and he were Cassius,
He should not humor° me. I will this night,
In several hands,° in at his windows throw,
As if they came from several citizens,
Writings, all tending to the great opinion
That Rome holds of his name; wherein obscurely
Caesar's ambition shall be glancèd at.°
And after this, let Caesar seat him sure;°
For we will shake him, or worse days endure. [*Exit.*]

SCENE 3. *A street.*

Thunder and lightning. Enter from opposite sides CASCA *and* CICERO.

Cicero.

Good even, Casca; brought you Caesar home?
Why are you breathless? And why stare you so?

Casca.

Are not you moved, when all the sway of earth°
Shakes like a thing unfirm? O Cicero,
I have seen tempests,° when the scolding winds
Have rived° the knotty oaks, and I have seen
Th' ambitious ocean swell and rage and foam,
To be exalted with° the threat'ning clouds;
But never till tonight, never till now,
Did I go through a tempest dropping fire.
Either there is a civil strife in heaven,

303. the world: the state of affairs in Rome.

304. *Cassius delivers a* ***soliloquy****—a speech in which a character (who is usually alone onstage) expresses aloud thoughts and feelings that the audience overhears. How does Cassius feel about Brutus?*

306. In other words, he may be persuaded against his better nature to join the conspirators.

309. bear me hard: has a grudge (hard feelings) against me.

311. humor: influence by flattery.

312. hands: varieties of handwriting.

316. glancèd at: touched on.

317. seat him sure: make his position secure.

318. *What is Cassius going to write in the letters to Brutus? What does he hope these letters will accomplish?*

Staging the Play

Stage direction. *In Shakespeare's day, other than a drum roll or "thunder sheet," there was no way to reproduce the drama of nature onstage. How might the actors themselves suggest the threatening weather?*

3. all the sway of earth: all the principles that govern earth.

5. tempests: storms.

6. rived (rīvd): split.

8. exalted with: elevated to.

DIRECT TEACHING

C Literary Focus
GRADE-LEVEL STANDARD

Soliloquy. Explain that Cassius's speech is a soliloquy, a long speech by a character who is alone onstage, in which he expresses his innermost thoughts and feelings. What do you learn from Cassius's soliloquy? [Possible responses: He admires the high-mindedness of Brutus. He gloats over the effect he has had on Brutus. He is fundamentally selfish.]

D Literary Focus
GRADE-LEVEL STANDARD

Tragedy. Explain that Cassius's soliloquy marks the end of Scene 2 and the end of the exposition, the introductory explanation of the characters and the situation in a story. Ask students to give a full summary of the basic facts of the play from the exposition.

E Literary Focus
GRADE-LEVEL STANDARD

Imagery. In Shakespeare's time, the dramatist used imagery to do what is now done by special effects. What does Shakespeare's imagery suggest about Rome? [Possible response: Rome is in a state of upheaval and chaos.]

Responses to Margin Questions

Line 304. Cassius has less regard for Brutus, now that he realizes his friend can be flattered into joining the conspiracy.

Line 318. Cassius will write that Brutus is respected and will hint at Caesar's dangerous ambition. Cassius is using the letters to flatter Brutus and convince him that the conspirators' cause is honorable and widely supported.

Stage direction. The actors could cower in reaction to thunder and lightning; they could also shout to be heard over the storm.

of the state was viewed as God's appointed deputy on earth, ruling in accordance with a divine plan. Any attempt to overturn the monarch was an act of disobedience against God and would disturb the harmony of the universe.

Individual activity. As students read, ask them to look for evidence of this medieval idea that chaos results when the prescribed social order is broken.

The Tragedy of Julius Caesar, Act I, Scene 3 771

DIRECT TEACHING

A Reading Skills

Analyzing. Cicero believes that people interpret supernatural signs according to their own purposes or points of view. How might Caesar and his allies interpret the signs described by Casca in ll. 3–13? How would the interpretation of the conspirators differ? [Possible response: Caesar and his allies might claim the heavens are angry with the conspirators, who threaten to disrupt the divinely ordered scheme of things; the conspirators would say that the gods are angry with Caesar for planning to become an all-powerful king.]

B Reading Skills

Iambic pentameter. A playwright writing in strict iambic pentameter runs the risk of having the lines take on a singsong and monotonous quality. Draw attention to instances in which Shakespeare varies the rhythm, as in ll. 35–40. In l. 38, there is an extra syllable; in ll. 39–40, the five pairs of stressed and unstressed syllables are shared between Cicero and Casca.

Responses to Margin Questions

Line 13. Casca now speaks in blank verse, not prose, indicating that he is no longer affecting the manner of a plebeian.

Line 32. Casca believes that the events are a sign that the gods are angry and will visit destruction on Rome.

Line 35. Cicero agrees that the events are unusual but states that people often misinterpret natural occurrences.

Or else the world, too saucy° with the gods,
Incenses them to send destruction.

Cicero.
Why, saw you anything more wonderful?

Casca.
A common slave—you know him well by sight—
Held up his left hand, which did flame and burn
Like twenty torches joined, and yet his hand,
Not sensible of° fire, remained unscorched.
Besides—I ha' not since put up my sword—
Against° the Capitol I met a lion,
Who glazed° upon me and went surly by
Without annoying me. And there were drawn
Upon a heap a hundred ghastly° women,
Transformèd with their fear, who swore they saw
Men, all in fire, walk up and down the streets.
And yesterday the bird of night° did sit
Even at noonday upon the market place,
Hooting and shrieking. When these prodigies°
Do so conjointly meet, let not men say,
"These are their reasons, they are natural,"
For I believe they are portentous° things
Unto the climate° that they point upon.

Cicero.
Indeed, it is a strange-disposèd time:
But men may construe things after their fashion,
Clean from the purpose° of the things themselves.
Comes Caesar to the Capitol tomorrow?

Casca.
He doth; for he did bid Antonius
Send word to you he would be there tomorrow.

Cicero.
Good night then, Casca; this disturbèd sky
Is not to walk in.

Casca. Farewell, Cicero. [*Exit* CICERO.]

[*Enter* CASSIUS.]

Cassius.
Who's there?

Casca. A Roman.

Cassius. Casca, by your voice.

Casca.
Your ear is good. Cassius, what night is this?

12. saucy: disrespectful; presumptuous.

? **13.** *How is Casca different here from the way he was depicted earlier?*

18. not sensible of: not sensitive to.

20. Against: opposite or near.

21. glazed: stared.

23. ghastly: ghostly; pale.

26. bird of night: owl (believed to be a bad omen).

28. prodigies (präd′ə•jēs): extraordinary happenings.

31. portentous (pôr•ten′təs): ominous.

32. climate: region or place.

? **32.** *Shakespeare often uses disorder in nature to suggest a nation's disorder. What does Casca think?*

35. Clean from the purpose: contrary to the real meaning.

? **35.** *How does the aged Cicero respond to Casca's report?*

DIFFERENTIATING INSTRUCTION

Learners Having Difficulty

Generalizing. Remind students that a generalization is a type of inference in which the reader combines information in a text with information that he or she already knows in order to make a judgment that extends beyond a specific text to the general world. Ask students to use Cicero's observation in ll. 33–35 to make a generalization about how people interpret and understand events. [Possible response: People often interpret any event that occurs in a way that reinforces their own beliefs and viewpoints.]

Advanced Learners

Enrichment. Have students discuss how "spin doctors," official spokespersons, and pundits in current politics illustrate Cicero's observation about interpreting events.

Cassius.
A very pleasing night to honest men.
Casca.
Who ever knew the heavens menace so?
Cassius.
Those that have known the earth so full of faults.
For my part, I have walked about the streets,
Submitting me unto the perilous night,
And thus unbracèd,° Casca, as you see,
Have bared my bosom to the thunder-stone, **C**
And when the cross° blue lightning seemed to open
The breast of heaven, I did present myself
Even in the aim and very flash of it.
Casca.
But wherefore did you so much tempt the heavens?
It is the part° of men to fear and tremble
When the most mighty gods by tokens° send
Such dreadful heralds to astonish us.
Cassius.
You are dull, Casca, and those sparks of life
That should be in a Roman you do want,°
Or else you use not. You look pale, and gaze,
And put on fear, and cast yourself in wonder,
To see the strange impatience of the heavens;
But if you would consider the true cause
Why all these fires, why all these gliding ghosts,
Why birds and beasts from quality and kind,°
Why old men, fools, and children calculate,°
Why all these things change from their ordinance,° **D**
Their natures and preformèd faculties,°
To monstrous quality,° why, you shall find
That heaven hath infused them with these spirits°
To make them instruments of fear and warning
Unto some monstrous state.
Now could I, Casca, name to thee a man
Most like this dreadful night,
That thunders, lightens, opens graves, and roars
As doth the lion in the Capitol; **E**
A man no mightier than thyself, or me,
In personal action, yet prodigious° grown
And fearful, as these strange eruptions are.
Casca.
'Tis Caesar that you mean, is it not, Cassius?

? **43.** *Can you explain Cassius's response to the disordered night?*

48. unbracèd: *with his jacket unfastened.*

50. cross: jagged.

54. part: role.

55. tokens: signs.

58. want: lack.

64. from quality and kind: act against their natures.

65. calculate: prophesy; try to predict the future.

66. ordinance: natural behavior.

67. preformèd faculties: natural or normal qualities.

68. monstrous quality: unnatural condition.

69. spirits: supernatural powers.

? **Staging the Play**
72. *How might Cassius's tone of voice change here?*

77. prodigious (prō·dij′əs): monstrous.

DIRECT TEACHING

C English-Language Learners

Synonyms. Explain that the word *thunder-stone* in l. 49 is a synonym for *thunderbolt* and emphasizes the idea that the angry gods are hurling projectiles at the people of Rome. Help students use a thesaurus to find a synonym for the word *bared* in the same line. [exposed]

D Reading Skills

? **Drawing conclusions.** How does Cassius interpret these strange occurrences? [Possible response: Cassius views the "monstrous quality" of the disturbances as a warning from the gods that Caesar has grown to some "monstrous state"—unnaturally powerful and fearsome.]

E Literary Focus
GRADE-LEVEL STANDARD

? **Figurative language.** What two things are being compared in this passage? [Caesar and the stormy night] What effect does this comparison have? [Possible response: It makes Caesar sound violent and dangerous. It makes Caesar sound powerful, yet irrational.]

Responses to Margin Questions

Line 43. Cassius interprets the events as a sign that Caesar is wicked and must be stopped. As an "honest" man, Cassius feels he is safe.

Line 72. Cassius could lower his voice to make a confidential statement.

Activity. Ask students to find examples in editorials and op-ed page columns in newspapers that illustrate how commentators often interpret the same event differently.

CONTENT-AREA CONNECTIONS

History: Abraham Lincoln

In April 1865, Abraham Lincoln was assassinated by John Wilkes Booth, a Shakespearean actor. A member of one of the most famous acting families in the United States, Booth's father, Junius Brutus Booth, was named after Brutus, the noble-minded conspirator against Caesar. Booth's older brother, Edwin Thomas Booth, excelled in tragic Shakespearean roles and became one of the greatest actors in American history. On November 25, 1864, Edwin and his brothers staged a well-received benefit performance of *Julius Caesar* to raise money for a statue of Shakespeare in Central Park in New York City. Five months later, Booth shot and killed Lincoln during a theatrical performance. In a final dramatic gesture, Booth leaped from a balcony, shouting *"Sic semper tyrannis,"* a Latin motto meaning "Thus be it ever to tyrants."

Shakespeare was Lincoln's favorite author, and guests at the White House were often treated to Shakespearean recitations by the

Cassius.
Let it be who it is; for Romans now
Have thews° and limbs like to their ancestors;
But, woe the while!° Our fathers' minds are dead,
And we are governed with our mothers' spirits;
Our yoke and sufferance° show us womanish.
Casca.
Indeed, they say the senators tomorrow
Mean to establish Caesar as a king;
And he shall wear his crown by sea and land,
In every place save here in Italy.
Cassius.
I know where I will wear this dagger then;
Cassius from bondage will deliver Cassius.
Therein,° ye gods, you make the weak most strong;
Therein, ye gods, you tyrants do defeat.
Nor stony tower, nor walls of beaten brass,
Nor airless dungeon, nor strong links of iron,
Can be retentive to° the strength of spirit;
But life, being weary of these worldly bars,
Never lacks power to dismiss itself.
If I know this, know all the world besides,
That part of tyranny that I do bear
I can shake off at pleasure. [*Thunder still.*°]
Casca. So can I;
So every bondman in his own hand bears
The power to cancel his captivity.
Cassius.
And why should Caesar be a tyrant then?
Poor man, I know he would not be a wolf
But that he sees the Romans are but sheep;
He were no lion, were not Romans hinds.°
Those that with haste will make a mighty fire
Begin it with weak straws. What trash is Rome,
What rubbish and what offal,° when it serves
For the base matter to illuminate
So vile a thing as Caesar! But, O grief,
Where hast thou led me? I, perhaps, speak this
Before a willing bondman; then I know
My answer must be made.° But I am armed,
And dangers are to me indifferent.
Casca.
You speak to Casca, and to such a man

81. thews (thyo͞oz): sinews or muscles.

82. woe the while: too bad for our times.

84. Our yoke and sufferance: our burden and our timid acceptance of it.

Staging the Play
89. *Cassius's response to this news is usually played as one of anger. What is he probably holding in his hand?*

91. Therein: in other words, in the act of suicide.

95. be retentive to: restrain.

100. *What is Cassius threatening to do?*

100. still: continues.

106. hinds: female deer. (The word also means "peasants" and "servants".)

109. offal: garbage, especially the parts of a butchered animal that are considered inedible or rotten.

114. My answer must be made: I must later answer for my words.

115. *Does Cassius seriously mean that Casca is a willing slave of Caesar's? What reaction is he looking for?*

DIRECT TEACHING

A Literary Focus GRADE-LEVEL STANDARD

Character. How does Cassius use this scene of storm and terror to advance his own agenda? What does this tell you about him? [Possible response: Cassius reveals himself to be a cunning manipulator of other people. Cassius uses Casca's terror of the storm to suggest that he, like many of his contemporaries and unlike their forefathers, is a coward.]

B English-Language Learners

Archaic language. Point out the phrase "ye gods" in l. 91, and explain that in archaic English *ye* was used as the second-person plural pronoun—that is, *ye* was the plural of *thou*.

C Content-Area Connections

Culture: Suicide
Although suicide is expressly forbidden in Judaism, Christianity, and Islam, it was not so in ancient Rome. For example, for high-ranking Romans accused of capital crimes, suicide was offered as an alternative to execution, as a way to resolve otherwise unresolvable issues of personal honor.

Responses to Margin Questions

Line 89. He is probably holding a dagger.
Line 100. He is threatening to commit suicide.
Line 115. No. Cassius hopes Casca will angrily declare himself against Caesar.

president. Lincoln, who suffered from depression, turned to Shakespeare for consolation and wisdom.

Culture: Greek Philosophy
Two classical philosophies help us better appreciate the characters of Brutus and Cassius. Brutus believed in Stoicism, a philosophy that saw virtue, as expressed in action, as the supreme purpose of life. Stoicism also taught that the result of wisdom is the performance of duty and that joy and grief should not be outwardly shown. Furthermore, in doing one's duty, the Stoic must spare neither him- or herself nor others.

Cassius believed in Epicureanism, though he seems too bitter to be an Epicurean. Epicurus taught that pleasure is the chief good, and pleasure was defined as freedom of the body from pain and of the soul from anxiety. Prudence was the means to these ends. To the Epicureans, who did not believe in divine intervention or an afterlife, fear, especially fear of death, was the greatest evil.

DIRECT TEACHING

A Reading Skills

Critical thinking. Why is Pompey's porch an appropriate place for the conspirators to meet? [Possible response: Pompey had been Caesar's enemy and was defeated by him; meeting there is a way to pay homage to Pompey and perhaps plan to avenge him.]

B Literary Focus
GRADE-LEVEL STANDARD

Figurative language. What does Cassius compare the appearance of the sky to? [He compares the "bloody, fiery, and most terrible" sky to the "work" that must be done by the conspirators.]

C Reading Skills

Drawing conclusions. Why do you think Cassius wants the letter posted on the statue of Brutus's ancestor? [Possible response: Brutus's ancestor was instrumental in establishing the republic in the first place; finding the letter on the statue will remind the present Brutus of his duty to preserve the republic out of respect for his ancestor.]

Responses to Margin Questions

Line 130. Cassius gives hints of rebellious thoughts when he exclaims, "But, O grief, / Where has thou led me?" (ll. 111–112). Cunningly, he lets Casca first mention a faction "for redress of all these griefs." (l. 118)

Line 139. Cassius is impatient, anxious, perhaps about both his plans and the conspirators' loyalty.

That is no fleering° tell-tale. Hold, my hand.
Be factious° for redress of all these griefs,
And I will set this foot of mine as far
As who goes farthest. [*They clasp hands.*]

Cassius. There's a bargain made.
Now know you, Casca, I have moved already
Some certain of the noblest-minded Romans
To undergo with me an enterprise
Of honorable dangerous consequence;
And I do know, by this° they stay for me
In Pompey's porch,° for now, this fearful night,
There is no stir or walking in the streets,
And the complexion of the element°
In favor's like° the work we have in hand,
Most bloody, fiery, and most terrible.

[*Enter* CINNA.]

Casca.
Stand close° awhile, for here comes one in haste.

Cassius.
'Tis Cinna; I do know him by his gait;
He is a friend. Cinna, where haste you so?

Cinna.
To find out you. Who's that? Metellus Cimber?

Cassius.
No, it is Casca, one incorporate
To° our attempts. Am I not stayed for,° Cinna?

Cinna.
I am glad on't. What a fearful night is this!
There's two or three of us have seen strange sights.

Cassius.
Am I not stayed for? Tell me.

Cinna. Yes, you are.
O Cassius, if you could
But win the noble Brutus to our party—

Cassius.
Be you content. Good Cinna, take this paper,
And look you lay it in the praetor's chair,°
Where Brutus may but find it; and throw this
In at his window; set this up with wax
Upon old Brutus' statue.° All this done,
Repair° to Pompey's porch, where you shall find us.

117. fleering: flattering.
118. Be factious (fak′shəs): Go ahead and organize a faction, or group, opposed to Caesar.

125. by this: by this time.

126. Pompey's porch: the entrance to a theater built by Pompey.

128. complexion of the element: appearance of the sky.
129. In favor's like: in appearance is like.

? **130.** *Cassius has begun his conversation with Casca by showing him his dagger and threatening suicide as a way to free himself from bondage. At what point does the conversation shift to an altogether different method of freeing himself?*
131. close: hidden.

136. incorporate to: bound up with. **stayed for:** waited for.

? **139.** *What is Cassius's mood?*

143. praetor's (prē′tərz) **chair:** chief magistrate's chair; Brutus's chair.

146. old Brutus' statue: statue of Brutus's heroic ancestor.
147. Repair: go.

DEVELOPING FLUENCY

Whole-class activity. After students complete Act I, discuss the theme of the play. You might begin by asking students to re-read the dialogue between Cassius and Brutus (Scene 2, ll. 135–177). Have students discuss how Cassius veils his ambition by making appeals to Brutus's sense of honor. Also, discuss whether Caesar's actions strike them as those of an ambitious person or those of an honorable person. Have students re-read Casca's description of the attempted crowning of Caesar (ll. 220–287) and suggest reasons why Shakespeare keeps the big ceremonial scene offstage and relates it only in comic prose. [Possible response: He wants to depict Caesar as dishonorable and ambitious.] Point out that this view of Caesar will change as events progress.

776 Chapter 10 Drama • Evaluating an Argument

Is Decius° Brutus and Trebonius there?

Cinna.

All but Metellus Cimber, and he's gone
To seek you at your house. Well, I will hie,°
And so bestow these papers as you bade me.

Cassius.

That done, repair to Pompey's Theater.

[*Exit* CINNA.]

Come, Casca, you and I will yet ere day
See Brutus at his house; three parts of him
Is ours already, and the man entire
Upon the next encounter yields him ours.

Casca.

O, he sits high in all the people's hearts;
And that which would appear offense in us,
His countenance,° like richest alchemy,°
Will change to virtue and to worthiness.

Cassius.

Him, and his worth, and our great need of him,
You have right well conceited.° Let us go,
For it is after midnight, and ere day
We will awake him and be sure of him.

[*Exeunt.*]

148. Decius: Decimus, a relative of Brutus.

D ? **148.** *What is Cassius asking Cinna to do?*

150. hie: hurry.

159. countenance: approval. **alchemy:** "science" that was supposed to change ordinary metals into gold.

E **162. conceited:** Cassius is punning here. The word means both "understood" and "described in an elaborate metaphor" (called a *conceit*).

"MEN AT SOME TIME ARE MASTERS OF THEIR FATES: THE FAULT, DEAR BRUTUS, IS NOT IN OUR STARS, BUT IN OURSELVES, THAT WE ARE UNDERLINGS."

—CASSIUS, ACT I, SCENE 2 (LINES 139–141)

DIRECT TEACHING

D Reading Skills

? Making inferences. The conspirator Cinna is a minor character who appears only briefly in this scene. What do his behavior and comments suggest about those who support the conspiracy? [Possible responses: Cinna's breathlessness suggests the excited mood of the conspirators. Cinna's concern that Brutus should join the conspiracy shows the high regard in which the conspirators hold Brutus.]

E Vocabulary Development

GRADE-LEVEL STANDARD

Recognizing puns. Make sure students understand that *conceited* comes from the same word root as *conceived,* meaning "thought." Also, point out that a conceit is an elaborate metaphor, such as Casca's description of Brutus as an alchemist who changes offense to virtue. Ask students what third possible play on *conceited* might be intended. [Casca regards himself too highly—that is, he is conceited.]

Response to Margin Question

Line 148. Cassius asks Cinna to deliver three anonymous letters to places where Brutus will discover them.

Check Test: Short Answer

Monitoring students' progress To check students' comprehension of the story, ask them to respond to the following questions. Direct students to locate passages in the text that support their responses.

1. In the opening scene, what two events are the workers celebrating? [They are celebrating the feast of Lupercal and Caesar's triumph.]
2. During the celebration, what warning does the soothsayer give to Caesar? [He warns Caesar to beware the ides of March.]
3. Who does Caesar feel is dangerous? [He feels that Cassius is dangerous.]
4. What does Casca report that Mark Antony did after the Lupercal games? [Antony offered Caesar a crown.]
5. At the end of Act I, how is Cassius planning to win Brutus to the conspiracy? [He has written anonymous inflammatory letters to Brutus and plans to visit him at home.]

The Tragedy of Julius Caesar, Act I, Scene 3 777

A CLOSER LOOK

This article describes the prominent role that superstition played in the lives of all Romans. Natural events, such as lightning or an eclipse, were often interpreted as omens. Animals, especially birds, also played a special role in the divination of the future. Even dreams were seen as messages from the gods.

DIRECT TEACHING

A Reading Informational Materials
GRADE-LEVEL STANDARD

Author's argument. Why does the author insert the qualifying phrase "just about everyone"? [The author uses this phrase to make his generalization more believable.]

B Reading Informational Materials
GRADE-LEVEL STANDARD

Author's argument. What persuasive technique does the author use here to support the claim that most Romans were superstitious? [The author supports the generalization with anecdotes.]

C Content-Area Connection

Why might the Roman people have been so superstitious? [Possible response: Their superstitions helped them perceive some kind of order in an otherwise chaotic world.]

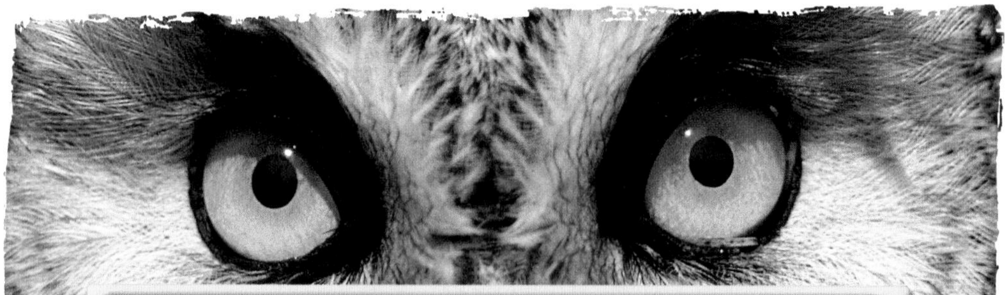

A Closer Look

Roman Superstitions

(A) At the time of Julius Caesar, just about everyone believed in magic, omens, and revelations.

The Romans examined everyday occurrences for warnings of good and evil. For example, they believed that the sound of a distant storm or a rooster crowing in the night could affect the outcome of a personal matter or even a political event. Politicians believed so strongly in signs that they created a site in Rome's Capitol where they could consult specialists.

Many people thought that animals were the spirits of their dead ancestors. Therefore, the physical characteristics and actions of certain animals were seen as signs of protection and warning. Ravens, owls, and crows supposedly revealed signs through their calls. Other meanings were taken from the flight of eagles, vultures, and buzzards.

Animals were killed and offered as sacrifices to the gods. Their entrails were examined by a haruspex (hə·rus′peks′), a soothsayer who specialized in foretelling events by studying internal organs. Abnormalities—imperfections and deformities in color, shape, or position—indicated the anger of a particular god.

The commanders of Roman military fleets counted on "sacred" chickens to predict success in battle. If the chickens ate vigorously and dropped food from their beaks on the morning of battle, all would go well in combat. If the chickens (B) did not eat, the signs were unfavorable. One commander whose sacred chickens refused to eat at sea threw them overboard. "If they won't eat, let them drink!" he said. The commander lost the battle.

The owl was considered a bad omen. Once when an owl flew into Rome's Capitol, the Romans carefully scrubbed the building with water and sulfur to drive out the owl's supposed evil influences.

Solar eclipses were interpreted as supernatural and as omens of disaster. Speaking about an eclipse as a natural occurrence was against the law. Lightning was also seen as a bad omen. Even dreams were seen as messages from the gods.

(C) As odd as all of this may seem to us today, during Julius Caesar's time these superstitions were held by everyone from the ruling classes to the common people.

778 Chapter 10 Drama • Evaluating an Argument

DIFFERENTIATING INSTRUCTION

Learners Having Difficulty

Help students identify resources on the pages of Act I that can help them obtain a better understanding of the play. Resources include sidenote annotations and margin questions, as well as photographs, highlighted quotations, and the Closer Look feature on p. 778. Ask them to identify specific lines that are more easily understood as a result of having read this article.

Advanced Learners

Enrichment. Ask students to discuss why people—then and now—want to know what the future holds. Conclude the discussion by pointing out that Shakespeare knew that members of his Elizabethan audience were interested in the subject and that they would respond to the elements of superstition that underscore the ideas in his play.

Literary Response and Analysis

Act I

Reading Check

1. Why are the workers celebrating in Scene 1? Why does Marullus scold them?
2. What does the soothsayer tell Caesar in Scene 2? How does Caesar respond?
3. What happens when Caesar is offered the crown?
4. At the end of Scene 2, what is Cassius planning to do to persuade Brutus to join the conspiracy against Caesar?
5. At the beginning of Scene 3, what do Cicero and Casca discuss? Why are they disturbed?
6. What happens at the end of Scene 3 to move the conspiracy plot forward?

Interpretations

7. Shakespeare uses nature to mirror the disorders in human lives. What details in Scene 3 do you think evoke a sense of danger and terror?
8. What is your impression of Cassius, the **protagonist,** or main character, who drives the action in Act I? By the act's end, what steps has he taken toward his goal?
9. The **exposition** of Act I introduces the characters and conflict. How would you describe the tragedy's **conflict** as it is established in Act I?
10. A healthy republic requires a reasonably intelligent and responsive citizenry. How do the nobles in the play speak of the citizens of Rome? What do you learn from this act about the moods and loyalties of the Roman people?
11. How would you evaluate the **character** of Brutus? Is he strong, weak, or something in between? (Do all readers agree?)
12. A **character foil** is a character who serves as a contrast to another character. Throughout the play, Cassius serves as a **character foil** to Brutus. In what ways is Cassius a foil to Brutus in this act?
13. Do you have conflicting feelings about Caesar during this act? Explain. Describe your impressions of his **character,** based on your responses to his speeches and actions and on what other characters say about him.

Evaluation

14. Does the play deal with issues that no longer concern us, or is it relevant to our lives today? Explain. Share with others some lines in this act that you think could be used to comment on current politics or politicians. (You might want to look back at your Quickwrite notes for page 755.)

Writing

A Wily Persuader

Persuasion is the use of language to influence people to behave or think in certain ways. (For more on persuasion and its strategies, see pages 284–285.) You'll get a good idea of the power of persuasion if you examine Cassius's speeches in Act I, Scene 2, when he tries to persuade Brutus to turn against his friend and join the conspiracy to overthrow Caesar. Take notes on where the clever Cassius uses these **persuasive techniques:** specific **evidence** (facts, examples), **loaded words** (words with

Reading Standard 3.1 Articulate the relationship between the expressed purposes and the characteristics of different forms of dramatic literature (e.g., tragedy).

Reading Standard 3.10 Identify and describe the function of dialogue and character foils in dramatic literature.

INDEPENDENT PRACTICE

Literary Response and Analysis

Act I

Reading Check

1. The workers are celebrating the feast of Lupercal and Caesar's return to Rome after defeating Pompey's sons. Marullus rebukes them for ignoring their debt of gratitude to Pompey, their former hero, and for supporting Caesar.
2. The soothsayer twice warns Caesar, "Beware the ides of March," but Caesar ignores him.
3. According to Casca, Caesar reluctantly turns down all three offers of the crown.
4. Cassius plans to throw letters supposedly written by other citizens into Brutus's house.
5. Cicero and Casca discuss the supernatural events that occur on a stormy night in Rome. They are disturbed that these events might foreshadow Caesar's tyranny.
6. Cassius instructs Cinna to place forged letters urging Brutus to oppose Caesar in Brutus's house, in his chair, and on the statue of his ancestor. He also arranges a meeting of the conspirators.

Interpretations

7. The violent storm, with its thunder, lightning, and eerie fire, is dangerous and foreboding. Shakespeare also uses reports of supernatural phenomena—burning men, a lion at the Capitol, an owl shrieking at noon, open graves, ghosts—to build a sinister mood.
8. Cassius seems cunning and persuasive. By the end of Act I, he has persuaded Brutus to consider the plot, recruited Casca, forged letters to Brutus, and called a meeting of the conspirators.
9. Possible answer: The main conflict is between those Romans who believe Caesar to be a strong, effective leader who should be king and those who view him as a tyrant who should be deposed as a threat to the republic.
10. In general, the nobles view the commoners with contempt. Flavius describes the commoners as "idle creatures," and Marullus rails against their ingratitude and fickleness. Casca's speeches are filled with venomous descriptions of the people. Cassius characterizes the populace as "womanish" (l. 84) and as servile "trash" (ll. 108–111).

(Continued)

The Tragedy of Julius Caesar, Act I 779

Independent Practice

Interpretations

11. Possible answers: Brutus's dialogue with Cassius in Scene 2 of Act I reveals both positive and negative traits. Brutus is selfless and idealistic, genuinely concerned with the welfare of the Roman populace. On the other hand, Brutus's weaknesses are his gullibility and pride. Brutus seems to be rapidly falling for Cassius's mainly emotional arguments against Caesar.
12. Possible answer: Cassius thinks that people are generally weak and should be manipulated for one's own benefit, whereas Brutus wants to believe the best about people. These characters balance each other: Brutus is pure idealism while Cassius is pure pragmatism.
13. Possible answer: Caesar is revered by the populace and by some senators as a strong, successful leader. He is accessible to the masses, and he is a keen judge of character. At the same time, Caesar is impetuous, power hungry, vain, and calculating.

Evaluation

14. Most students will see the current relevance of the play. Shifting loyalties are a part of today's political scene, perhaps even more so because of the media. Students may suggest that any large crowd, in ancient Rome or the modern United States, can react on the inspiration of the moment. Even highly educated people are susceptible to charismatic leaders. Some lines might be: Scene 2, l. 10; Scene 2, ll. 140–141; and Scene 2, ll. 312–318.

emotional overtones), **repetition** for effect, **emotional appeals** to self-interest. Then, in a brief essay, analyze Cassius's persuasive techniques.

Listening and Speaking

By Their Words You Will Know Them

Cassius and Brutus are clearly going to be important figures in the play. What kind of men are they? With a partner, choose a section of their **dialogue** (their conversation with other characters) that reveals the character of each man. Then, prepare an **oral interpretation** of the conversation. Present your dramatic reading to the class, and be sure to ask for feedback.

Bust of Julius Caesar.
© Art Resource, New York.

Vocabulary Development

Multiple Meanings: Recognizing Puns

Some people call puns juvenile humor, but Shakespeare's audiences enjoyed them. A **pun** is a word or phrase that means two different things at the same time. (Here's an old pun: What is black and white and read all over? Answer: a newspaper.)

In the first scene of *Julius Caesar*, when the cobbler says he is a cobbler, he plays on two meanings of the word. In Shakespeare's day the word could mean either "shoemaker" or "bungler." When he calls himself "a mender of bad soles," the cobbler also puns on the meaning of *soles*. *Soles* refers to parts of shoes but also sounds exactly like *souls*.

Some puns are based on two meanings of a word (*cobbler*). Others involve **homophones,** words that sound alike but have different spellings and meanings (*soles/souls*).

Here are two of Shakespeare's puns in Act I:

"All that I live by is with the awl. . . ." (Scene 1, line 21)

"I am . . . a surgeon to old shoes: when they are in great danger, I recover them." (Scene 1, lines 23–24)

PRACTICE

You could map the puns used by the cobbler and show the jokes like this:

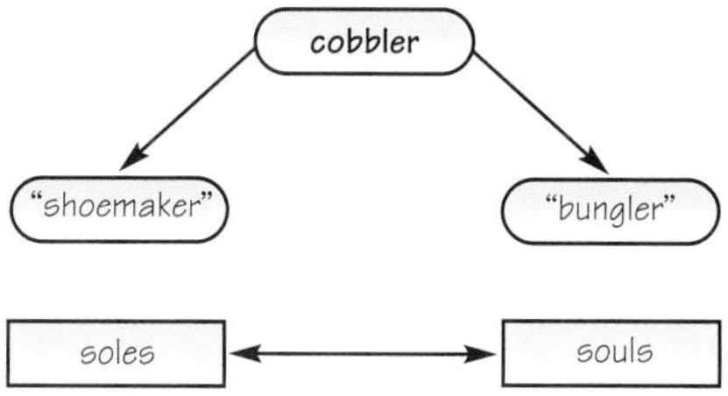

1. Make maps that explain the puns on *awl* and *recover* in the lines above.
2. Use two of the words below (or words of your choice) to create original puns. Do a pun map for each one.

break **flour** **son**

Reading Standard 1.1 Identify and use the literal meanings of words.

Vocabulary Development

Practice

Possible Answers

1. The cobbler jokes that his entire (or *all* of his) livelihood is dependent on a single tool, the *awl*. He then explains that he makes shoes better (*recovers* them) by putting new *covers* on them.
2. Pun maps created by students should either indicate the dual meaning of a single word or point out the homophonic relationship between two different words. Examples might include *son,* "a male child," and *sun,* "the star that provides light and heat for the earth" and *flour,* "the basic ingredient for bread," and *flower,* "a basic natural element."

ASSESSING

Assessment

- *Progress Assessment of Reading*
  - Selection Test

RETEACHING

For a lesson reteaching Standard 3.1, see **Reteaching,** 939A. For another selection to teach Standard 3.1, see *Interactive Reading,* Chapter 10.

Summary ↔ *at grade level*

Act II

Scene I finds Brutus at home before dawn on March 15, struggling to persuade himself that Caesar must die. When Cassius and his faction arrive, Brutus joins the conspiracy but rejects Cassius's plan to kill Mark Antony. Brutus can see Caesar's death as a sacrifice; Antony's death seems like unnecessary butchery. After the men go, Portia chides Brutus for not sharing his internal conflicts, and he reluctantly agrees to do so.

Scene 2 opens with Caesar at home, restless after a night that disturbed all Rome. He plans to go to the Senate, despite the warnings of his fortunetellers and his wife Calphurnia's dream. At Calphurnia's pleading, Caesar changes his mind, but the conspirator Decius Brutus goads Caesar about his weakness, interprets the dream favorably, and reports that the Senate will crown Caesar that day. The other conspirators arrive, and Caesar prepares to accompany them to the Senate.

Scenes 3 and 4, both brief, are set in a street leading to the Capitol. Artemidorus has written a warning of the plot, which he hopes to give to Caesar as he passes. In the final scene, Portia, greatly agitated, is obviously burdened by her knowledge of the assassination. Her distress deepens when she meets the soothsayer, who is also waiting to warn Caesar of danger.

PRETEACHING

Standards Starter

Before students begin to read Act II, review the previous act with them. Students might find Act II (the rising action) more exciting to read, since there is a greater focus on plot events, which result in various complications and a growing sense of suspense.

ACT II

SCENE 1.
Rome.

"HE WOULD BE CROWNED.
HOW THAT MIGHT CHANGE HIS NATURE,
THERE'S THE QUESTION."

RESOURCES: READING

Media

- *Audio CD Library*
  - disc 18
- *Visual Connections*
  - Videocassette, Segment 10
- *Fine Art Transparencies*
  - Transparency 17

Reading

- *Interactive Reading,* Teacher's Edition
  - Graphic Organizer: Dramatic Elements Chart

Differentiating Instruction

- *Lesson Plans for Language Development*
  - English-Language Learners, pp. 337–339, 362, 369
  - Special Education Students, pp. 340, 362, 369

Enter BRUTUS *in his orchard.*

Brutus.
What, Lucius, ho!
I cannot, by the progress of the stars,
Give guess how near to day. Lucius, I say!
I would it were my fault to sleep so soundly.
When, Lucius, when? Awake, I say! What, Lucius!

[*Enter* LUCIUS.]

Lucius. Called you, my lord?
Brutus.
Get me a taper° in my study, Lucius.
When it is lighted, come and call me here.
Lucius. I will, my lord. [*Exit.*]
Brutus.
It must be by his death; and for my part,
I know no personal cause to spurn at° him,
But for the general.° He would be crowned.
How that might change his nature, there's the question. **(A)**
It is the bright day that brings forth the adder,
And that craves° wary walking. Crown him that,
And then I grant we put a sting in him
That at his will he may do danger with.
Th' abuse of greatness is when it disjoins
Remorse° from power; and, to speak truth of Caesar,
I have not known when his affections swayed°
More than his reason. But 'tis a common proof°
That lowliness° is young ambition's ladder,
Whereto the climber upward turns his face;
But when he once attains the upmost round, **(B)**
He then unto the ladder turns his back,
Looks in the clouds, scorning the base degrees°
By which he did ascend. So Caesar may;
Then lest he may, prevent.° And, since the quarrel°
Will bear no color° for the thing he is,
Fashion it thus:° that what he is, augmented,
Would run to these and these extremities;
And therefore think him as a serpent's egg
Which hatched, would as his kind grow mischievous,
And kill him in the shell.

? Staging the Play
Stage direction. *Brutus's garden often has a set of steps in the back, set in a half circle. Below the steps is a stone bench. On the right and left are the doorways of an impressive residence. The door to the left is the servants' entrance, where Brutus directs his call to Lucius. Why is Brutus so anxious about the time?*

7. taper: candle.

? 10. *In this* ***soliloquy****, what is Brutus trying to convince himself of?*

11. spurn at: rebel against.
12. the general: the general good.
15. craves: demands.
19. Remorse: compassion.
20. affections swayed: emotions ruled.
21. common proof: matter of common experience.
22. lowliness: humility.
26. base degrees: low rungs of the ladder; also lower government offices and lower classes of people.
28. prevent: We must prevent it.
quarrel: argument.
29. bear no color: bear no weight.
30. Fashion it thus: state the case this way.

? 34. *According to Brutus, who is like a serpent's egg and why?*

DIRECT TEACHING

(A) Literary Focus GRADE-LEVEL STANDARD

Soliloquy. In this soliloquy, Brutus wrestles with a difficult decision. How does Brutus begin to justify joining the conspiracy against Caesar? [Possible responses: Brutus thinks that he must consider the good of the people. He decides that a crowned Caesar would become dangerous.]

(B) Literary Focus GRADE-LEVEL STANDARD

Figurative language. What extended metaphor does Brutus use to describe how Caesar may act if crowned king? [Brutus compares Caesar to someone of low standing who climbs "ambition's ladder," reaches the top rung, and then turns his back on those below.]

Responses to Margin Questions

Stage direction. He is struggling with the decision of whether or not Caesar should die, and he knows Cassius will be arriving to hear his decision.
Line 10. He is trying to convince himself that Caesar should be assassinated.
Line 34. Brutus compares Caesar to a serpent's egg; crowning him will unleash his evil nature, as hatching sets free a "mischievous" snake.

DIFFERENTIATING INSTRUCTION

Learners Having Difficulty

Before beginning Act II, ask students to summarize the major events that occurred in Act I. Answer any lingering questions they may have about those events. Then, ask students to make some predictions about what they think will happen next. Encourage the use of sidenotes to help students understand Elizabethan English.

English-Language Learners

Remind these students that Act II, like Act I, is heavily annotated, with definitions and paraphrases of words and phrases in the margins. Continue to encourage students to use the notes consistently, especially to help them understand Elizabethan English.

Resources Reminder

For lessons designed for English-language learners and special education students, see *Lesson Plans for Language Development,* pp. 337–339, 340, 362, 369.

Advanced Learners

Acceleration. In order to move students towards eleventh- and twelfth-grade standard 3.7c, have students examine Brutus's soliloquy on p. 783 with respect to the philosophical, political, religious, ethical, and social influences relevant to the period.

DIRECT TEACHING

A Literary Focus
GRADE-LEVEL STANDARD

Soliloquy. Soliloquies often provide direct insight into character. Brutus never suspects that the letters might be forgeries. Also, the letters lead him to think about historical events and abstract ideals, not the crisis facing Rome. What does his reaction to the letters suggest about him? [Possible responses: He is an idealist, not a man of practical affairs. He is too trusting.]

B Reading Skills
GRADE-LEVEL STANDARD

Understanding Elizabethan English. What does Lucius mean when he says, "March is wasted fifteen days"? [The fifteenth day of March has begun.]

Responses to Margin Questions

Stage direction. This is the letter that Cassius wrote and had Cinna deliver.
Line 40. Yes, he heard it delivered.
Line 58. Brutus would probably read contemplatively but react more passionately. At the end, his voice may become fervent.

[*Enter* LUCIUS.]

Lucius.
The taper burneth in your closet,° sir.
Searching the window for a flint, I found
This paper thus sealed up, and I am sure
It did not lie there when I went to bed.

[*Gives him the letter.*]

Brutus.
Get you to bed again; it is not day.
Is not tomorrow, boy, the ides of March?
Lucius. I know not, sir.
Brutus.
Look in the calendar and bring me word.
Lucius. I will, sir. [*Exit.*]
Brutus.
The exhalations° whizzing in the air
Give so much light that I may read by them.

[*Opens the letter and reads.*]

"Brutus, thou sleep'st; awake, and see thyself.
Shall Rome, &c.° Speak, strike, redress.°
Brutus, thou sleep'st; awake."

A Such instigations have been often dropped
Where I have took them up.
"Shall Rome, &c." Thus must I piece it out:
Shall Rome stand under one man's awe? What, Rome?
My ancestors did from the streets of Rome
The Tarquin° drive, when he was called a king.
"Speak, strike, redress." Am I entreated
To speak and strike? O Rome, I make thee promise,
If the redress will follow, thou receivest
Thy full petition at the hand of Brutus!

[*Enter* LUCIUS.]

Lucius.
B Sir, March is wasted fifteen days.

[*Knock within.*]

Brutus.
'Tis good. Go to the gate; somebody knocks.

35. closet: small private room; study.

? ***Stage direction.*** *Whose letter is this?*

? **40.** *Does Brutus know of the soothsayer's warning?*

44. exhalations: meteors.

47. &c.: read "et cetera."
redress: correct a wrong.

54. Tarquin: Tarquinius Superbus, the last king of Rome.

? **Staging the Play**
58. *What actions might Brutus engage in as he reads this message? What is his tone of voice at the end?*

DIFFERENTIATING INSTRUCTION

Learners Having Difficulty
As they read through Act II, ask students to note lines that are difficult to comprehend. Then, have them form groups to share their notes and work together to analyze and interpret the lines. One group member can read the lines aloud; another can use resources such as sidenotes and a dictionary to specify meanings. A third student can paraphrase the passages, and a fourth can record the paraphrases.

Advanced Learners
Enrichment. Have students research the assassinations of major political figures in history, including Julius Caesar, Abraham Lincoln, Archduke Francis Ferdinand of Austria, Mohandas (Mahatma) Gandhi, John F. Kennedy, Martin Luther King, Jr., Anwar Sadat, Indira Gandhi, and Yitzhak Rabin. Ask students to trace the aftermath of one such assassination to determine whether it led to greater political stability or to turmoil.

784 Chapter 10 Drama • Evaluating an Argument

[*Exit* LUCIUS.]

Since Cassius first did whet me against Caesar,
I have not slept.
Between the acting of a dreadful thing
And the first motion, all the interim is
Like a phantasma,° or a hideous dream.
The genius and the mortal instruments°
Are then in council, and the state of a man,
Like to a little kingdom, suffers then
The nature of an insurrection.

[*Enter* LUCIUS.]

Lucius.
Sir, 'tis your brother° Cassius at the door,
Who doth desire to see you.

Brutus. Is he alone?

Lucius.
No, sir, there are moe° with him.

Brutus. Do you know them?

Lucius.
No, sir; their hats are plucked about their ears,
And half their faces buried in their cloaks,
That by no means I may discover them
By any mark of favor.°

Brutus. Let 'em enter. [*Exit* LUCIUS.]
They are the faction. O conspiracy,
Sham'st thou to show thy dang'rous brow by night,
When evils are most free? O, then by day
Where wilt thou find a cavern dark enough
To mask thy monstrous visage? Seek none, conspiracy;
Hide it in smiles and affability:
For if thou path, thy native semblance on,°
Not Erebus° itself were dim enough
To hide thee from prevention.

65. phantasma: apparition; hallucination.

66. The genius and the mortal instruments: the mind (genius) and the emotions and physical powers of the body.

70. brother: brother-in-law; Cassius is married to Brutus's sister.

72. moe: more.

76. favor: appearance.

83. In other words, if you walk (path) in your true way.

84. Erebus (er′ə·bəs): dark region of the Underworld.

"BETWEEN THE ACTING OF A DREADFUL THING AND THE FIRST MOTION, ALL THE INTERIM IS LIKE A PHANTASMA, OR A HIDEOUS DREAM."

DIRECT TEACHING

C English-Language Learners

Legal jargon. Brutus, a political man, uses legal terms to describe his internal conflict. What words in this passage (ll. 64–69) sound like they might be used in a legal or political context? [*motion, interim, instruments, council, state, kingdom,* and *insurrection*] Encourage students to look up any words they are unfamiliar with in a dictionary. They can then paraphrase the lines in which the words appear.

D Advanced Learners

Interpreting personification. What does Brutus's personification of the conspiracy imply about the guilt of the conspirators? [Possible response: By personifying the conspiracy as a monstrous being with a mind and momentum of its own, Brutus implies that the plot to kill Caesar is now beyond the control of the conspirators.]

E Learners Having Difficulty

Paraphrasing. Have students work together to restate the gist of Brutus's observations about the conspiracy. [Possible paraphrase: If the conspirators must sneak around at night to keep their plot secret, there will be no way to hide it in the light of day; so the conspirators should put on bright, friendly faces and give the appearance that all is normal.]

DEVELOPING FLUENCY

Individual activity. Have students choose a favorite speech of ten or more lines from Act II, Scene I; practice it; and read it aloud with feeling, paying special attention to the nuances and rhythm of the language. If possible, record students' readings so that they can work on polishing their pronunciation and delivery.

The Tragedy of Julius Caesar, Act II, Scene 1 785

DIRECT TEACHING

A Reading Skills
GRADE-LEVEL STANDARD

? Understanding Elizabethan English. It was common in Elizabethan English to form questions without a helping verb. In l. 89, for example, Brutus asks, "Know I these men . . . ?" What would he ask, using modern English? ["Do I know these men . . . ?"] Encourage students to notice other questions without helping verbs as they read on.

B Reading Skills

? Making inferences. Do you think Cassius is being completely sincere? Besides admiration, what else might motivate his compliment to Brutus? [Possible response: He wants to calm Brutus and allay his fears.]

C Literary Focus
GRADE-LEVEL STANDARD

? Dramatic dialogue. This conversation occurs while Cassius and Brutus are whispering to each other. What two different purposes might the conversation serve? [Possible responses: It heightens suspense about what Brutus and Cassius might be whispering in the background. It draws attention to the day on which Caesar will be murdered and to the Capitol, where he will meet his fate.]

Responses to Margin Questions

Stage direction. The six conspirators are probably grouped opposite Brutus, with Cassius standing in front of his five accomplices. Their faces are apparently hidden by hats and cloaks.

Line 100. Possible response: The actors who are speaking would likely stand downstage (toward the front). Brutus and Cassius would probably move upstage (toward the rear).

[*Enter the conspirators,* CASSIUS, CASCA, DECIUS, CINNA, METELLUS CIMBER, *and* TREBONIUS.]

Cassius.
I think we are too bold upon° your rest.
Good morrow, Brutus; do we trouble you?

Brutus.
I have been up this hour, awake all night.
Know I these men that come along with you?

Cassius.
Yes, every man of them; and no man here
But honors you; and every one doth wish
You had but that opinion of yourself
Which every noble Roman bears of you.
This is Trebonius.

Brutus. He is welcome hither.

Cassius.
This, Decius Brutus.

Brutus. He is welcome too.

Cassius.
This, Casca; this, Cinna; and this, Metellus Cimber.

Brutus.
They are all welcome.
What watchful cares° do interpose themselves
Betwixt your eyes and night?

Cassius. Shall I entreat a word?

[*They whisper.*]

Decius.
Here lies the east; doth not the day break here?

Casca. No.

Cinna.
O, pardon, sir, it doth; and yon gray lines
That fret° the clouds are messengers of day.

Casca.
You shall confess that you are both deceived.
Here, as I point my sword, the sun arises,
Which is a great way growing on° the south,
Weighing the youthful season of the year.
Some two months hence, up higher toward the north
He first presents his fire; and the high east
Stands as the Capitol, directly here.

Brutus.
Give me your hands all over, one by one.

? Staging the Play
Stage direction. *Describe what the stage looks like right now. From what is said of the conspirators, how would you imagine they are dressed?*

86. too bold upon: too bold in intruding on.

98. watchful cares: cares that keep you awake.

? Staging the Play
100. *How would you have the actors placed onstage as Brutus and Cassius huddle and the others talk?*

104. fret: interlace.

107. growing on: tending toward.

READING SKILLS REVIEW

Chronological order. Review with students that chronological order is the order in which events occur. Point out that a work based on historical events usually follows the actual sequence of those events. Explain, however, that Shakespeare tended to reorder events to tell a more coherent story.

Activity. Point out that Caesar's victory celebration over Pompey's sons actually occurred in October of 45 B.C., while Shakespeare sets it in February of 44 B.C. Have students discuss why this change helps make the play more compact.

786 Chapter 10 Drama • Evaluating an Argument

Cassius.
And let us swear our resolution.
Brutus.
No, not an oath. If not the face of men,°
The sufferance° of our souls, the time's abuse°—
If these be motives weak, break off betimes,°
And every man hence to his idle bed.
So let high-sighted tyranny range on
Till each man drop by lottery. But if these
(As I am sure they do) bear fire enough
To kindle cowards and to steel with valor
The melting spirits of women, then, countrymen,
What need we any spur but our own cause
To prick° us to redress? What other bond
Than secret Romans that have spoke the word,
And will not palter?° And what other oath
Than honesty to honesty engaged
That this shall be, or we will fall for it?
Swear priests and cowards and men cautelous,°
Old feeble carrions° and such suffering souls
That welcome wrongs; unto bad causes swear
Such creatures as men doubt; but do not stain
The even virtue of our enterprise,
Nor th' insuppressive mettle of our spirits,
To think that or our cause or our performance
Did need an oath; when every drop of blood
That every Roman bears, and nobly bears,
Is guilty of a several bastardy°
If he do break the smallest particle
Of any promise that hath passed from him.
Cassius.
But what of Cicero? Shall we sound him?
I think he will stand very strong with us.
Casca.
Let us not leave him out.
Cinna. No, by no means.
Metellus.
O, let us have him, for his silver hairs
Will purchase us a good opinion,
And buy men's voices to commend our deeds.
It shall be said his judgment ruled our hands;
Our youths and wildness shall no whit appear,
But all be buried in his gravity.°

114. If not the face of men: Our honest faces should be enough.
115. sufferance: endurance. **time's abuse:** abuses of the times.
116. betimes: at once.
124. prick: urge.
126. palter: deceive.
129. cautelous: deceitful.
130. carrions: people so old or sick they are almost dead and rotting.
138. of a several bastardy: of several acts that are not truly "Roman."
149. gravity: seriousness and stability.

DIRECT TEACHING

D Reading Skills

Finding the main idea. According to Brutus, why do the conspirators have no need to swear an oath? [Brutus states that as honorable Romans engaged in a virtuous cause, the conspirators have no need of an oath; only those involved in dubious causes swear allegiance.]

E Literary Focus GRADE-LEVEL STANDARD

Character. Cassius suggests an oath, but Brutus says no, and the rest accept his decision. What does this incident reveal about the leadership of the conspiracy? [Possible responses: Brutus is now the leader of the conspiracy. Cassius and the rest seem impressed by Brutus's high-minded argument.]

F Literary Focus GRADE-LEVEL STANDARD

Character foil. Throughout this scene and the next, the politically astute Cassius makes practical suggestions to ensure the conspirators' success, including swearing the oath, bringing in Cicero, and killing Mark Antony. The high-minded Brutus rejects the suggestions because they're not in keeping with his ideals. Why does Cassius acquiesce? [He needs Brutus's support.]

G Learners Having Difficulty

Paraphrasing. How would you paraphrase Metellus's comment? [Possible paraphrase: Cicero is well-respected, and if he joins us, people will think favorably of the conspiracy.]

Activity. As students read, make them aware of the instances in which Shakespeare changed historical chronology: Mark Antony gave his funeral oration in the days following Caesar's death, not immediately after it; the triumvirs did not meet until a year and a half after the assassination; the battles of Philippi weren't fought until 42 B.C. Have students discuss how changing the chronology adds dramatic impact.

Activity. Suggest that students create a time line to record events in the play, dividing the time line into increments appropriate to each act. As students continue reading, have them record key events on the time line.

The Tragedy of Julius Caesar, Act II, Scene 1 787

DIRECT TEACHING

A Literary Focus
GRADE-LEVEL STANDARD

Rising action. As tension builds around the assassination plot, Brutus grows more decisive. How does his comment and Cassius's reply reflect his new position as leader of the conspiracy? [Possible response: Brutus forcefully rejects Cassius's suggestion that Cicero join the conspiracy. Cassius immediately acquiesces, an indication that he is relinquishing his role as leader.]

B Learners Having Difficulty

Summarizing. Why does Brutus feel that the conspirators should not murder both Caesar and Antony? [Possible response: He feels that the conspirators' actions will be seen as too brutal and malicious if they kill both men.]

C Literary Focus
GRADE-LEVEL STANDARD

Figurative language. Brutus uses hunting metaphors to describe how Caesar should be stabbed. What does the metaphor show about Brutus's regard for Caesar? [Possible response: He honors and respects Caesar.]

Responses to Margin Questions

Line 152. Brutus says Cicero will not follow a plan that someone else begins.
Line 153. He is easily swayed by others.
Line 162. Possible response: Cassius seems like a coldblooded killer compared to Brutus, who is more humane.
Line 170. Brutus speaks with anguish.
Line 180. He wants people to think he acted out of a love of liberty, not malice.

Brutus.
O, name him not! Let us not break with him,°
For he will never follow anything
That other men begin.
Cassius. Then leave him out.
Casca.
Indeed, he is not fit.
Decius.
Shall no man else be touched but only Caesar?
Cassius.
Decius, well urged. I think it is not meet
Mark Antony, so well beloved of Caesar,
Should outlive Caesar; we shall find of° him
A shrewd contriver;° and you know, his means,
If he improve° them, may well stretch so far
As to annoy° us all; which to prevent,
Let Antony and Caesar fall together.
Brutus.
Our course will seem too bloody, Caius Cassius,
To cut the head off and then hack the limbs,
Like wrath in death and envy° afterwards;
For Antony is but a limb of Caesar.
Let's be sacrificers, but not butchers, Caius.
We all stand up against the spirit of Caesar,
And in the spirit of men there is no blood.
O, that we then could come by Caesar's spirit,
And not dismember Caesar! But, alas,
Caesar must bleed for it. And, gentle friends,
Let's kill him boldly, but not wrathfully;
Let's carve him as a dish fit for the gods,
Not hew him as a carcass fit for hounds.
And let our hearts, as subtle masters do,
Stir up their servants° to an act of rage,
And after seem to chide 'em. This shall make
Our purpose necessary, and not envious;
Which so appearing to the common eyes,
We shall be called purgers,° not murderers.
And for Mark Antony, think not of him;
For he can do no more than Caesar's arm
When Caesar's head is off.
Cassius. Yet I fear him;
For in the ingrafted° love he bears to Caesar——

150. break with him: break our news to him, reveal our plan.

152. *Why do they decide not to ask Cicero to join them?*

153. *What kind of person does Casca seem to be?*

157. of: in.
158. shrewd contriver: cunning and dangerous schemer.
159. improve: make good use of.
160. annoy: harm.

162. *This is the second time that Brutus contradicts Cassius. How does Cassius serve as a **foil** to Brutus?*
164. envy: malice.

Staging the Play
170. *How might the actor playing Brutus look when he speaks this sentence?*

176. servants: hands or emotions.

180. purgers: healers.
180. *What does Brutus want the public, or history, to think of him?*

184. ingrafted: firmly rooted.

CONTENT-AREA CONNECTIONS

History: Shakespeare's Details
The Greek biographer Plutarch, who died around A.D. 120, is the source for most of Shakespeare's story of *Julius Caesar.* Interestingly, however, Shakespeare chose not to use certain details about Brutus found in Plutarch. For example, he doesn't mention that Caesar pardoned Brutus's life at the battle of Pharsalus. Nor does Shakespeare reveal that Brutus was unusually malicious in stabbing Caesar. Most interestingly, there is no mention of the widespread belief that Brutus was Caesar's illegitimate son.

Small-group activity. Have small groups of students discuss the following question: Why might Shakespeare have omitted or changed certain biographical facts about Brutus? Help students realize that Shakespeare probably omitted these details in order to portray Brutus as sympathetically as possible.

788 Chapter 10 Drama • Evaluating an Argument

Brutus.
Alas, good Cassius, do not think of him.
If he love Caesar, all that he can do
Is to himself—take thought° and die for Caesar.
And that were much he should,° for he is given
To sports, to wildness, and much company.

Trebonius.
There is no fear in him;° let him not die,
For he will live and laugh at this hereafter.

[*Clock strikes.*]

Brutus.
Peace! Count the clock.

Cassius. The clock hath stricken three.

Trebonius.
'Tis time to part.

Cassius. But it is doubtful yet
Whether Caesar will come forth today or no;
For he is superstitious grown of late,
Quite from the main° opinion he held once
Of fantasy, of dreams, and ceremonies.°
It may be these apparent prodigies,°
The unaccustomed terror of this night,
And the persuasion of his augurers°
May hold him from the Capitol today.

Decius.
Never fear that. If he be so resolved,
I can o'ersway him; for he loves to hear
That unicorns may be betrayed with trees,
And bears with glasses, elephants with holes,
Lions with toils, and men with flatterers;
But when I tell him he hates flatterers,
He says he does, being then most flatterèd.

187. take thought: take to thinking too much and become depressed.
188. In other words, that is too much to expect of him.

190. no fear in him: nothing to fear in him.

191. *What do Brutus, Cassius, and Trebonius think of Antony?*

196. main: strong.

197. ceremonies: ceremonial rituals undertaken to determine the future, usually from the examination of signs in the entrails of slaughtered animals.
198. prodigies: disasters.
200. augurers (ô′gər·ərz): those who foretell the future.

"LET'S KILL HIM BOLDLY, BUT NOT WRATHFULLY;
LET'S CARVE HIM AS A DISH FIT FOR THE GODS,
NOT HEW HIM AS A CARCASS
FIT FOR HOUNDS."

DIRECT TEACHING

D Literary Focus
GRADE-LEVEL STANDARD

Tragedy. A tragic hero is usually a man of greatness who has a vulnerability that leads to his downfall. According to Aristotle, the hero's downfall is caused by "some error of judgment." Brutus's error in judgment is allowing Mark Antony to live, a high-minded decision that will eventually cost the conspirators their lives. Why do you think Brutus makes this decision? [Possible response: Brutus apparently feels that Antony will be powerless without Caesar.]

E Literary Focus
GRADE-LEVEL STANDARD

Anachronism. Point out that in the setting of the play (ancient Rome) mechanical clocks had not yet been invented. People of ancient Rome relied on sundials and water clocks to keep track of time.

F Literary Focus
GRADE-LEVEL STANDARD

Tragedy. Dramatic irony occurs when the audience knows something that one or more characters in the play do not. Who else has been manipulated by flattery? [Brutus has been manipulated by Cassius.]

Response to Margin Question

Line 191. Brutus thinks Antony is ineffective without Caesar; Cassius fears him and his devotion to Caesar; Trebonius believes he is a survivor, a man without deep feelings.

Direct Teaching

A Advanced Learners

Making connections. How does this passage compare with Brutus's earlier comments about the "monstrous visage" of the conspiracy in ll. 77–85 and the honest faces of the conspirators in ll. 114–140? [Possible responses: In his earlier remarks, Brutus sees the conspiracy as shameful and in need of hiding behind "smiles and affability." In this later remark, he is encouraging the conspirators to indeed put on a happy face. He seems to believe that the plot is both monstrous and virtuous.]

B Literary Focus
REVIEW STANDARD

Character. What side of Brutus does this passage about Lucius reveal? [Possible response: In allowing his servant Lucius to sleep and in gently remarking on how much he envies the "honey-heavy dew of slumber," Brutus shows himself capable of warmth and tenderness.]

Responses to Margin Questions

Line 211. Decius says that Caesar delights in other people's weaknesses, but he shares these faults and is easily manipulated. Some may see Decius as manipulative; others may view him as pragmatic.
Line 221. The light could be brought up gradually to suggest the dawning of a new day.

Let me work;
For I can give his humor° the true bent,
And I will bring him to the Capitol.

Cassius.
Nay, we will all of us be there to fetch him.

Brutus.
By the eighth hour; is that the uttermost?°

Cinna.
Be that the uttermost, and fail not then.

Metellus.
Caius Ligarius doth bear Caesar hard,
Who rated° him for speaking well of Pompey.
I wonder none of you have thought of him.

Brutus.
Now, good Metellus, go along by him.°
He loves me well, and I have given him reasons;
Send him but hither, and I'll fashion him.

Cassius.
The morning comes upon 's; we'll leave you, Brutus.
And, friends, disperse yourselves; but all remember
What you have said, and show yourselves true Romans.

A

Brutus.
Good gentlemen, look fresh and merrily.
Let not our looks put on° our purposes,
But bear it as our Roman actors do,
With untired spirits and formal constancy.°
And so good morrow to you every one.

[*Exeunt all except* BRUTUS.]

B

Boy! Lucius! Fast asleep? It is no matter;
Enjoy the honey-heavy dew of slumber.
Thou hast no figures nor no fantasies°
Which busy care draws in the brains of men;
Therefore thou sleep'st so sound.

[*Enter* PORTIA.]

Portia. Brutus, my lord.

Brutus.
Portia, what mean you? Wherefore rise you now?
It is not for your health thus to commit
Your weak condition to the raw cold morning.

210. humor: mood.

211. *According to Decius, what sort of man is Caesar? (What do you think of people like Decius?)*

213. uttermost: latest.

216. rated: berated; scolded.

218. him: his house.

Staging the Play
221. *How would you use lighting here to suggest the time?*

225. put on: display.

227. formal constancy: consistent good conduct.

231. figures . . . fantasies: figments of the imagination.

790 Chapter 10 Drama • Evaluating an Argument

"DEAR MY LORD, MAKE ME ACQUAINTED WITH YOUR CAUSE OF GRIEF."

Portia.
Nor for yours neither. Y'have ungently, Brutus,
Stole from my bed; and yesternight at supper
You suddenly arose and walked about,
Musing and sighing, with your arms across;°
And when I asked you what the matter was,
You stared upon me with ungentle looks.
I urged you further; then you scratched your head,
And too impatiently stamped with your foot.
Yet I insisted, yet you answered not,
But with an angry wafter° of your hand
Gave sign for me to leave you. So I did,
Fearing to strengthen that impatience
Which seemed too much enkindled, and withal°
Hoping it was but an effect of humor,°
Which sometime hath his hour with every man.
It will not let you eat, nor talk, nor sleep,
And could it work so much upon your shape
As it hath much prevailed on your condition,
I should not know you Brutus. Dear my lord,
Make me acquainted with your cause of grief.

Brutus.
I am not well in health, and that is all.

Portia.
Brutus is wise and, were he not in health,
He would embrace the means to come by it.

Brutus.
Why, so I do. Good Portia, go to bed.

Portia.
Is Brutus sick, and is it physical°
To walk unbracèd° and suck up the humors°
Of the dank morning? What, is Brutus sick,
And will he steal out of his wholesome bed,
To dare the vile contagion of the night,

240. arms across: crossed arms, a sign of melancholy or depression in Shakespeare's day.

246. wafter: wave.

249. withal: also.

250. humor: moodiness.

Staging the Play
256. *Where would Portia be standing?*

Staging the Play
260. *Some directors have Portia come too close to Brutus, physically and emotionally, and have him break away here. What would Portia's actions be?*

261. physical: healthy.

262. unbracèd: with his jacket opened. **humors:** Here the word means "dampness (of the air)."

DIRECT TEACHING

C Learners Having Difficulty

Finding details. What actions of Brutus lead Portia to conclude that he is upset? [Brutus got up in the middle of the night; he rose from the dinner table and walked around muttering and sighing; when Portia asked about his troubles, Brutus stamped his foot and waved her away.]

D Literary Focus GRADE-LEVEL STANDARD

Figurative language. What is personified in these lines? [Moodiness is personified.]

E Literary Focus GRADE-LEVEL STANDARD

Monologue. What does Portia's monologue reveal to Brutus? [Possible response: She shows that she cares very deeply about him and wants him to tell her what is wrong.]

Responses to Margin Questions

Line 256. By the end of this line, Portia is probably standing close to Brutus.

Line 260. Portia could show her concern by following Brutus and grasping his toga.

CONTENT-AREA CONNECTIONS

Culture: The Four Humors
When Portia blames her mood on a "humor," she refers to one of the four humors of Elizabethan physiology—phlegm, yellow bile, blood, and black bile. Each of these elemental bodily fluids supposedly related to a specific temperament or mood. Diseases and emotions were determined by the balance of the humors, and the ideal state occurred when all four were in proper proportion. A person with an excess of phlegm is phlegmatic, pale and sluggish; too much yellow bile produces a choleric person, who is quick to anger and unmerciful. A sanguine person, with blood predominating, is excessively jovial and passionate, and black bile supposedly produces a melancholic individual, often maudlin or lovesick.

Individual activity. Have students choose the character that they most identify with and write a short psychological profile of that character taking into account the information they just learned.

The Tragedy of Julius Caesar, Act II, Scene 1 **791**

Direct Teaching

A Literary Focus
GRADE-LEVEL STANDARD

Figurative language. Explain that although Elizabethans used the word *suburbs* as we do to describe communities near cities, Portia uses the word figuratively to denote a place outside or far away from the center of her husband's affections.

A "DWELL I BUT IN THE SUBURBS OF YOUR GOOD PLEASURE? IF IT BE NO MORE, PORTIA IS BRUTUS' HARLOT, NOT HIS WIFE."

CONTENT-AREA CONNECTIONS

Culture: Attitudes Toward Marriage
In ll. 272–274 on p. 793, Portia reflects an Elizabethan view on marriage, not one that was typically held in ancient Rome. That is, as a result of her marriage vow, Portia sees herself as one with her husband. This is in keeping with the Christian belief: "[T]hey twain shall be one flesh" (Matthew 19:5).

Most Romans had a less idealized view of marriage. In general, only men who had the responsibility of continuing the family line tended to marry, and economic and political considerations were all-important in the matchmaking. Once married, a couple thought it irrelevant whether their marriage was loving or loveless. Any public display of affection between husband and wife—even a hug or a kiss—was deemed indecent, and divorce rates were high.

And tempt the rheumy and unpurgèd air°
To add unto his sickness? No, my Brutus;
You have some sick offense within your mind,
Which by the right and virtue of my place
I ought to know of; and upon my knees
I charm° you, by my once commended beauty,
By all your vows of love, and that great vow
Which did incorporate and make us one,
That you unfold to me, your self, your half,
Why you are heavy,° and what men tonight
Have had resort to you; for here have been
Some six or seven, who did hide their faces
Even from darkness.

Brutus. Kneel not, gentle Portia.

Portia.
I should not need, if you were gentle Brutus.
Within the bond of marriage, tell me, Brutus,
Is it excepted° I should know no secrets
That appertain to you? Am I your self
But, as it were, in sort or limitation,
To keep with you at meals, comfort your bed,
And talk to you sometimes? Dwell I but in the suburbs
Of your good pleasure? If it be no more,
Portia is Brutus' harlot, not his wife.

Brutus.
You are my true and honorable wife,
As dear to me as are the ruddy drops
That visit my sad heart.

Portia.
If this were true, then should I know this secret.
I grant I am a woman; but withal
A woman that Lord Brutus took to wife.
I grant I am a woman; but withal
A woman well reputed, Cato's° daughter.
Think you I am no stronger than my sex,
Being so fathered and so husbanded?
Tell me your counsels, I will not disclose 'em.
I have made strong proof of my constancy,
Giving myself a voluntary wound
Here in the thigh; can I bear that with patience,
And not my husband's secrets?

Brutus. O ye gods,
Render me worthy of this noble wife!

266. The night was supposed to be unhealthy, since the air was not purified (purged) by the sun.

B

Staging the Play
270. *What clue tells us what Portia does here? Is she becoming calmer or more agitated?*

271. charm: beg.

275. heavy: depressed (heavyhearted).

Staging the Play
278. *What is Brutus doing here?*

281. excepted: made an exception that.

295. Cato joined Pompey against Caesar and killed himself at the end to avoid living under the rule of a tyrant. He was a most respected man, famous for his integrity.

C

Staging the Play
300. *What does Portia suddenly do to prove her loyalty and strength of character? How do you think Brutus should respond?*

D

DIRECT TEACHING

B Literary Focus
GRADE-LEVEL STANDARD

Complications. What complications are being caused by Brutus's part in the assassination conspiracy? [Possible response: A rift between husband and wife is developing. Brutus must choose between his loyalty to the conspiracy, which means keeping their secret, and his loyalty to Portia.]

C Literary Focus
REVIEW STANDARD

Character. What does Portia really want when she begs Brutus, "Tell me your counsels"? [Possible response: She is asking not only for specific information but also for an exchange based on the trust between a husband and wife.]

D Reading Skills

Interpreting. How do Portia and Brutus seem alike and well suited to each other? [Possible response: Both show nobility, strength of character, and concern for others.]

Responses to Margin Questions

Line 270. "[U]pon my knees" shows that Portia is kneeling. She becomes more agitated.
Line 278. He helps Portia rise.
Line 300. She shows Brutus a self-inflicted wound. Brutus is greatly moved. He could embrace her or turn away, overcome by emotion.

CONTENT-AREA CONNECTIONS

Literature: Critical Comment
According to Coppélia Kahn in *Julius Caesar: A Modern Perspective,* "In his other plays based on Roman history, Shakespeare gives women much more prominence than in *Julius Caesar,* where both Portia and Calphurnia speak in only two scenes. In this play Rome is more intensely a man's world than in Shakespeare's main sources, Plutarch's biographies of Caesar, Brutus, and Mark Antony. While Plutarch notes the intermarriages among patricians that held their political alliances together and recounts with relish anecdotes in which women figure prominently, Shakespeare focuses dramatic interest on relations among men.

Indeed, in terms of the Republic, to be a Roman means to be gendered male. Our word "virtue" comes from the Latin word *virtus,* meaning both manliness and valor, which is derived from Latin *vir,* man. The virtues promoted by the social and political life of the Republic are also gendered masculine and considered proper to men alone, as is made clear in the two scenes in which Portia is onstage."

CONTENT-AREA CONNECTIONS

Literature: Critical Comment
According to Paul A. Jorgensen in *William Shakespeare: The Tragedies,* Portia in this scene provides us with "a unique vision of the very human Brutus that only a wife can know. In this view he lacks the proud control that he manages with men. He scratches his head, impatiently stamps his foot, and angrily waves her away. Yet he loves her tenderly and immediately redeems himself in our eyes when he protests to Portia: 'You are my true and honorable wife, / As dear to me as are the ruddy drops / That visit my sad heart' (Act II, Scene 1, ll. 288–290). Brutus has, one might say, chosen a life of the 'sad heart.' . . . He has no sense of humor. . . . He has no small talk and no small interests. What he loves about Portia is her courage . . . and her nobility. . . ."

[*Knock.*]

Hark, hark! One knocks. Portia, go in a while,
And by and by thy bosom shall partake
The secrets of my heart.
All my engagements I will construe to thee,
All the charactery of my sad brows.°
Leave me with haste. [*Exit* PORTIA.]

[*Enter* LUCIUS *and* CAIUS LIGARIUS.]

Lucius, who's that knocks?

Lucius.
Here is a sick man that would speak with you.

Brutus.
Caius Ligarius, that Metellus spake of.
Boy, stand aside. Caius Ligarius! How?

Ligarius.
Vouchsafe° good morrow from a feeble tongue.

Brutus.
O, what a time have you chose out, brave Caius,
To wear a kerchief!° Would you were not sick!

Ligarius.
I am not sick, if Brutus have in hand
Any exploit worthy the name of honor.

Brutus.
Such an exploit have I in hand, Ligarius,
Had you a healthful ear to hear of it.

Ligarius.
By all the gods that Romans bow before,
I here discard my sickness! Soul of Rome,
Brave son, derived from honorable loins,
Thou, like an exorcist, hast conjured up
My mortifièd° spirit. Now bid me run,
And I will strive with things impossible,
Yea, get the better of them. What's to do?

Brutus.
A piece of work that will make sick men whole.

Ligarius.
But are not some whole that we must make sick?

Brutus.
That must we also. What it is, my Caius,
I shall unfold to thee, as we are going
To whom° it must be done.

308. In other words, the meaning of all the lines written in his forehead (from worry).

313. Vouchsafe: please accept.

315. kerchief: scarf (it shows he is sick).

Staging the Play
321. *What action might he make with this line?*

324. mortifièd: deadened.

331. To whom: to the house of whom.

DIRECT TEACHING

A Reading Skills

Iambic pentameter. What word has Shakespeare omitted in l. 317? Why do you think he left it out? [He has omitted the word *of* after *worthy* to maintain the rhythm of the line.]

B Advanced Learners

Speculating. Why is Ligarius, despite his illness, so willing to follow Brutus? [Possible response: Brutus has the reputation of being the noblest man in Rome. At a word from Brutus, Ligarius ignores his illness and is ready to serve his country.]

C Vocabulary Development
GRADE-LEVEL STANDARD

Recognizing puns. Ask students to explain the pun that Brutus and Ligarius use in these lines. [Both Brutus and Ligarius are punning on Ligarius's sickness. Brutus is talking about a cure for those ailing under the sickness of tyranny; Ligarius is talking about murdering the tyrant.]

Response to Margin Question

Line 321. He could remove his scarf.

READING SKILLS REVIEW

Analyzing cause-and-effect relationships. Remind students that a cause is an event or circumstance that produces a result, or effect. As an example, explain that in Act II of *Julius Caesar,* Calphurnia's dreams cause her to cry out three times in her sleep: Her dreams are the cause; her cries are the effect.

Activity. Have students prepare a story map, using cause-and-effect relationships, to identify critical events in Acts I and II. Student maps could be in the form of two vertical columns labeled "Cause" and "Effect," or the maps could be in the form of a series of paired horizontal boxes, one box containing the cause and the other box containing the related effect. Encourage students to add to the story map for Acts III and IV.

The Tragedy of Julius Caesar, Act II, Scene 1 795

DIRECT TEACHING

A Reading Skills
GRADE-LEVEL STANDARD

Understanding Elizabethan English. Point out the word *sufficeth* in l. 333. Explain that the final *th* is an archaic verb ending that corresponds to the modern s ending that we add to present-tense verbs in the third-person singular.

B Advanced Learners

? Analyzing. Why do you think Shakespeare adds a clap of thunder at the close of this scene? [Possible responses: The thunder might suggest that the gods are angry that Ligarius is blindly following Brutus in an assault on the established order. The thunder suggests the sealed fate of Caesar, now that Ligarius is the last to join the conspirators.]

C Literary Focus
GRADE-LEVEL STANDARD

? Character. What flaws in Caesar's character are most evident in this comment? [Possible responses: pomposity; arrogance.]

D English-Language Learners

Interpreting idioms. Point out that this line is the origin of the idiom *stand on ceremony,* which now means "proceed in an overly formal fashion." Have students compare the modern meaning to the original one found in the margin note.

Response to Margin Question

Stage direction. Thunder portends weighty actions and signals disturbance. Sounding alone, it would be a dramatic coda to the action; as background noise, it would heighten the urgency of the scene.

Ligarius. Set on° your foot,
And with a heart new-fired I follow you,
A To do I know not what; but it sufficeth
B That Brutus leads me on. [*Thunder.*]
Brutus. Follow me, then. [*Exeunt.*]

SCENE 2. *Caesar's house.*

Thunder and lightning. Enter JULIUS CAESAR *in his nightgown.*

Caesar.
Nor heaven nor earth have been at peace tonight:
Thrice hath Calphurnia in her sleep cried out,
"Help, ho! They murder Caesar!" Who's within?

[*Enter a* SERVANT.]

Servant. My lord?
Caesar.
Go bid the priests do present° sacrifice,
And bring me their opinions of success.°
Servant. I will, my lord. [*Exit.*]

[*Enter* CALPHURNIA.]

Calphurnia.
What mean you, Caesar? Think you to walk forth?
You shall not stir out of your house today.
Caesar.
C Caesar shall forth. The things that threatened me
Ne'er looked but on my back; when they shall see
The face of Caesar, they are vanishèd.
Calphurnia.
D Caesar, I never stood on ceremonies,°
Yet now they fright me. There is one within,
Besides the things that we have heard and seen,
Recounts most horrid sights seen by the watch.°
A lioness hath whelpèd° in the streets,
And graves have yawned, and yielded up their dead;
Fierce fiery warriors fought upon the clouds
In ranks and squadrons and right form of war,
Which drizzled blood upon the Capitol;
The noise of battle hurtled in the air,

331. Set on: set off on.

? Staging the Play
Stage direction. *Thunder is a kind of actor in Shakespeare's plays. What mood does it evoke? Would you have this thunder sound alone, or would you have it serve as background noise for these speeches?*

5. present (prez′ənt): immediate.

6. opinions of success: opinions about the course of events.

13. ceremonies: again, a reference to the rituals of priests that were supposed to reveal omens.

16. watch: watchman.

17. whelpèd: given birth.

DEVELOPING FLUENCY

Paired activity. Have pairs of students read aloud the dialogues between Portia and Brutus in Scene 1 and between Caesar and Calphurnia in Scene 2. Before they practice reading aloud, students should contrast the two marriages, noting their strengths or weaknesses, and analyze how these are reflected in the dialogues.

796 Chapter 10 Drama • Evaluating an Argument

DIRECT TEACHING

VIEWING THE ART

Activity. Have students describe the content and mood of the photograph. Ask them to discuss similarities and differences between this photograph and those on pp. 792 and 794.

DIRECT TEACHING

A Reading Skills

? Making judgments. Do you agree with the attitude toward death that Caesar expresses in these famous lines? Why or why not? [Possible responses: I agree with Caesar; most people are so afraid of dying that their fear keeps them from having adventures that would add excitement to their lives. I disagree with Caesar; many people grow accustomed to facing danger during their lifetime, and death is merely one of the dangers to be avoided as long as possible.]

B Literary Focus
GRADE-LEVEL STANDARD

? Figurative language. What metaphor does Caesar use to describe himself in ll. 42–48? [He likens himself to a beast: He says he would be a beast without a heart not to go to the Senate; he then describes himself and danger as twin lions, with Caesar being the elder and more terrible of the two.]

Responses to Margin Questions

Line 26. Responses will vary. You might ask volunteers to read Calphurnia's speech in at least two different ways.
Line 31. She believes that the horrors are omens of Caesar's death.
Line 37. Caesar maintains that he is one of the brave few who are unafraid of death, because he knows that death is inevitable. Caesar might become more arrogant when the servant enters.
Line 37. Caesar says he is unafraid, but he may be disturbed and unsettled by the ominous thunder and lightning and by Calphurnia's dream.
Line 48. Responses will vary. Ask students to defend their interpretations and discuss how each would affect the rest of the scene.
Line 54. She is kneeling.

Horses did neigh and dying men did groan,
And ghosts did shriek and squeal about the streets.
O Caesar, these things are beyond all use,°
And I do fear them.

Caesar. What can be avoided
Whose end is purposed by the mighty gods?
Yet Caesar shall go forth; for these predictions
Are to° the world in general as to Caesar.

Calphurnia.
When beggars die, there are no comets seen;
The heavens themselves blaze forth the death of princes.

Caesar.
Cowards die many times before their deaths;
The valiant never taste of death but once.
Of all the wonders that I yet have heard,
It seems to me most strange that men should fear,
Seeing that death, a necessary end,
Will come when it will come.

[*Enter a* SERVANT.]

What say the augurers?

Servant.
They would not have you to stir forth today.
Plucking the entrails of an offering forth,
They could not find a heart within the beast.

Caesar.
The gods do this in shame of cowardice:
Caesar should be a beast without a heart
If he should stay at home today for fear.
No, Caesar shall not. Danger knows full well
That Caesar is more dangerous than he.
We are two lions littered in one day,
And I the elder and more terrible.
And Caesar shall go forth.

Calphurnia. Alas, my lord,
Your wisdom is consumed in confidence.
Do not go forth today. Call it my fear
That keeps you in the house and not your own.
We'll send Mark Antony to the Senate House,
And he shall say you are not well today.
Let me, upon my knee, prevail in this.

Caesar.
Mark Antony shall say I am not well,

25. beyond all use: beyond all we are used to in our normal experience.

? Staging the Play
26. *Calphurnia can be played here as hysterical and overly emotional or as truly frightened for her husband. Which way do you think the part should be played?*

29. Are to: apply to.

? 31. *What does Calphurnia mean?*

? 37. *How does Caesar feel about death? How does his tone change when he addresses the servant?*

? 37. *The augurers were very important in ancient Rome. Their duty was to tell from certain signs whether some action was favored by the gods. Signs were read in the flights of birds, in thunder, in the way sacred chickens ate their food, and in the conditions of the organs of a sacrificial animal. What is Caesar's mood as he hears of the augury this morning?*

? Staging the Play
48. *Caesar could end this speech with pomposity, dignity, or even humor. How do you interpret his tone?*

? Staging the Play
54. *What is Calphurnia doing?*

READING SKILLS REVIEW

Paraphrasing. Remind students that paraphrasing, or rephrasing a passage in their own words, is a good way to test their understanding of a text. Point out that this is especially true with passages in Shakespeare's Elizabethan English, which not only contain archaic words but also invert the order of words in sentences to meet the demands of blank verse.

Activity. Have students paraphrase the following lines in their own words. Possible paraphrases are given in brackets.

1. Brutus: "Peace! Count the clock." (Act II, Scene 1, l. 192) [Be quiet! Listen to how many times the clock strikes.]
2. Portia: "Brutus is wise and, were he not in health, / He would embrace the means to

And for thy humor,° I will stay at home.

[*Enter* DECIUS.]

Here's Decius Brutus, he shall tell them so.

Decius.
Caesar, all hail! Good morrow, worthy Caesar;
I come to fetch you to the Senate House.

Caesar.
And you are come in very happy° time
To bear my greeting to the senators,
And tell them that I will not come today.
Cannot, is false; and that I dare not, falser:
I will not come today. Tell them so, Decius.

Calphurnia.
Say he is sick.

Caesar. Shall Caesar send a lie?
Have I in conquest stretched mine arm so far
To be afeard to tell graybeards the truth?
Decius, go tell them Caesar will not come.

Decius.
Most mighty Caesar, let me know some cause,
Lest I be laughed at when I tell them so.

Caesar.
The cause is in my will: I will not come.
That is enough to satisfy the Senate.
But for your private satisfaction,
Because I love you, I will let you know.
Calphurnia here, my wife, stays° me at home.
She dreamt tonight she saw my statue,°
Which, like a fountain with an hundred spouts,
Did run pure blood, and many lusty Romans
Came smiling and did bathe their hands in it.
And these does she apply for° warnings and portents

56. humor: mood.

Staging the Play
56. *Here is a sudden change. Would a kiss between lines 54 and 55 explain it?*

60. happy: lucky.

Staging the Play
65. *Is Caesar angry or gentle?*

75. stays: keeps.

76. statue: pronounced here in three syllables (stat • yo͞o • ə) for the meter.

80. apply for: explain as.

"COWARDS DIE MANY TIMES BEFORE THEIR DEATHS; THE VALIANT NEVER TASTE OF DEATH BUT ONCE."

DIRECT TEACHING

C Vocabulary Development
REVIEW STANDARD

Word origins. *Hail* is an archaic salutation used to express acclamation. It is generally delivered as a loud eager expression of approval, praise, or assent.

D Literary Focus
GRADE-LEVEL STANDARD

Character. What previous evidence in Scene 2 shows that Caesar is not afraid to go to the Senate? Why does he tell Decius he will not go? [Students may cite ll. 26–29 and 41–48 as evidence of Caesar's fearlessness. He has decided not to go because of Calphurnia's fears.]

Responses to Margin Questions

Line 56. Yes. However, Calphurnia's distress could have risen to such a pitch, especially on her knees, that Caesar is truly moved by her concern.

Line 65. His speech indicates he may be angry.

come by it." (Act II, Scene 1, ll. 258–259) [Brutus is smart, and if he were sick, he would find a way to get better.]

3. Decius: "This dream is all amiss interpreted. . . ." (Act II, Scene 2, l. 83) [This dream has been misinterpreted.]

4. Portia: "I would have had thee there and here again / Ere I can tell thee what thou shouldst do there." (Act II, Scene 4, ll. 4–5) [I wish you could have gone there and come back again before I can tell you what you should do there.]

DIRECT TEACHING

A Advanced Learners

Making connections. In Act I, Cicero says that people "construe things after their fashion." How does this discussion illustrate Cicero's statement? [Possible response: Calphurnia interprets the dream in a way that will keep her husband safe, while Decius suggests a meaning that will lead Caesar into danger.]

B Literary Focus GRADE-LEVEL STANDARD

Rising action / dramatic irony. How do these lines add tension to the play's rising action? [Possible response: They make us wonder if Decius's lie will convince Caesar.] What is ironic about Decius's speech? [Possible response: He claims he has a dear love for Caesar, when he is actually plotting to kill him.]

Responses to Margin Questions

Line 83. Decius, accustomed to manipulating Caesar, is likely to be confident and smooth.
Line 91. He is probably relieved.
Line 99. Decius hopes Caesar, who does not want to appear cowardly, will bridle at the suggestion that he is ruled by his wife's whims.
Line 107. She may react with horror or anger. Responses will vary as to why Caesar goes. Ask students to support their interpretations.
Stage direction. The conspirators are no doubt resolute, but they may express some fear or nervousness.
Line 113. In Act I, Scene 2, l. 194, Caesar says, "Yond Cassius has a lean and hungry look."

And evils imminent, and on her knee
Hath begged that I will stay at home today.

Decius.
This dream is all amiss interpreted;
It was a vision fair and fortunate:
Your statue spouting blood in many pipes,
In which so many smiling Romans bathed,
Signifies that from you great Rome shall suck
Reviving blood, and that great men shall press
For tinctures, stains, relics, and cognizance.°
This by Calphurnia's dream is signified.

Caesar.
And this way have you well expounded it.

Decius.
I have, when you have heard what I can say;
And know it now, the Senate have concluded
To give this day a crown to mighty Caesar.
If you shall send them word you will not come,
Their minds may change. Besides, it were a mock
Apt to be rendered, for someone to say
"Break up the Senate till another time,
When Caesar's wife shall meet with better dreams."
If Caesar hide himself, shall they not whisper
"Lo, Caesar is afraid"?
Pardon me, Caesar, for my dear dear love
To your proceeding° bids me tell you this,
And reason to my love is liable.°

Caesar.
How foolish do your fears seem now, Calphurnia!
I am ashamèd I did yield to them.
Give me my robe, for I will go.

[*Enter* BRUTUS, LIGARIUS, METELLUS CIMBER, CASCA, TREBONIUS, CINNA, *and* PUBLIUS.]

And look where Publius is come to fetch me.

Publius.
Good morrow, Caesar.

Caesar. Welcome, Publius.
What, Brutus, are you stirred so early too?
Good morrow, Casca. Caius Ligarius,
Caesar was ne'er so much your enemy°
As that same ague° which hath made you lean.
What is't o'clock?

Staging the Play
83. *Remember what Decius is here for. We should sense his hungry absorption of Caesar's dream. How should he explain the dream—is he confident, fawning, awed, nervous?*

89. cognizance: identifying emblems worn by a nobleman's followers.

Staging the Play
91. *There should be a pause here. Caesar's fate is about to be sealed. Does he seem relieved or amused?*

99. *What reaction from Caesar is Decius seeking when he refers to "Caesar's wife"? How is Decius playing on Caesar's fears?*

103. proceeding: advancement.

104. liable: subordinate.

107. *Suddenly Caesar changes his mind. Decius has succeeded. How would Calphurnia react now? Do you think Caesar concedes because he foolishly believes Decius, or because he heroically accepts his fate?*

Staging the Play
Stage direction. *What mood would the conspirators be in as they approach their victim?*

112. enemy: Ligarius had supported Pompey in the civil war and had recently been pardoned.

113. ague (ā′gyo͞o′): fever.

113. *Where else has Caesar mentioned that a character is lean?*

DIFFERENTIATING INSTRUCTION

Learners Having Difficulty

Making inferences. Remind students that they can make inferences, or intelligent guesses, about what characters are like on the basis of evidence in the text. This evidence includes what a character says and does, as well as what others say and think about the character.

Activity. Have students re-read the interactions between Caesar and Decius on pp. 799–800 in order to draw some inferences about the kind of character Decius is. Make sure they point out specific lines that helped shape their thoughts. Have students also make inferences about Trebonius and Brutus on the basis of their reactions to Caesar's hospitality at the end of Scene 2.

Brutus. Caesar, 'tis strucken eight.

Caesar.
I thank you for your pains and courtesy.

[*Enter* ANTONY.]

See! Antony, that revels long a-nights,
Is notwithstanding up. Good morrow, Antony.

Antony.
So to most noble Caesar.

Caesar. Bid them prepare within.
I am to blame to be thus waited for.
Now, Cinna; now, Metellus; what, Trebonius,
I have an hour's talk in store for you;
Remember that you call on me today;
Be near me, that I may remember you.

Trebonius.
Caesar, I will (*aside*) and so near will I be,
That your best friends shall wish I had been further.

Caesar.
Good friends, go in and taste some wine with me,
And we (like friends) will straightway go together.

Brutus (*aside*).
That every like is not the same,° O Caesar,
The heart of Brutus earns° to think upon. [*Exeunt.*]

Staging the Play
117. *How can the actors playing Antony and Caesar establish the fact that a deep friendship exists between them?*

Staging the Play
124. *An **aside** is a speech addressed to one other character or to the audience, out of hearing of the other actors onstage. How would this aside be spoken?*

127. *What **irony** do you feel here? (What do we know that Caesar is ignorant of?)*

128. In other words, that those who appear to be friends are not really friends at all.

129. earns: grieves.

SCENE 3. *A street near the Capitol, close to Brutus's house.*

Enter ARTEMIDORUS *reading a paper.*

Artemidorus. "Caesar, beware of Brutus; take heed of Cassius; come not near Casca; have an eye to Cinna; trust not Trebonius; mark well Metellus Cimber; Decius Brutus loves thee not; thou hast wronged Caius Ligarius. There is but one mind in all these men, and it is bent against Caesar. If thou beest not immortal, look about you: security gives way to conspiracy.° The mighty gods defend thee!
Thy lover,° Artemidorus."
Here will I stand till Caesar pass along,
And as a suitor° will I give him this.
My heart laments that virtue cannot live
Out of the teeth of emulation.°
If thou read this, O Caesar, thou mayest live;
If not, the Fates with traitors do contrive.° [*Exit.*]

7. In other words, a feeling of security gives the conspirators their opportunity.
8. lover: friend (one who loves you).
10. suitor: one who seeks a favor.

12. Out of the teeth of emulation: beyond the reach of envy.
14. contrive: plot or scheme.

DIRECT TEACHING

C Literary Focus
GRADE-LEVEL STANDARD

Asides. Trebonius assures Caesar that he will stand by him and then continues to speak, not to Caesar however, but to the audience. What actual intention does he express in this aside? [Trebonius will stand near Caesar, not to talk to him, but in order to be able to stab him better.]

D Reading Skills

Interpreting. Why do you think Shakespeare has Caesar repeatedly express his friendship for the conspirators here? [Possible responses: Shakespeare wants to build sympathy for Caesar just before his assassination. Caesar's friendliness toward the conspirators builds irony and tension, making their actions more dramatic and awful.]

Responses to Margin Questions

Line 117. Possible responses: They can show delight in seeing each other; they can clasp hands warmly; they can speak in familiar tones; they can embrace.
Line 124. Trebonius probably speaks maliciously.
Line 127. We feel dramatic irony because we realize, but Caesar does not, that his friends are really his most dangerous enemies.

Advanced Learners

Enrichment. Ask students to research ancient sites of Rome, several of which are mentioned in the play. Some suggestions are the Roman Forum, the Colosseum, the Pantheon, and the Capitol. Encourage students to use a variety of resources, such as history books, art books, the Internet, travel guide books, and travel brochures. Are all of these sites able to be visited today? Students might use maps and pictures to prepare an architectural "walking tour" of the city.

The Tragedy of Julius Caesar, Act II, Scene 3 801

DIRECT TEACHING

A Reading Skills

Making inferences. In this scene, Portia is terribly upset and wants Lucius to run to the Capitol for news. What can we infer has happened? [It appears that Brutus has finally told her about his involvement in the assassination plot.]

Response to Margin Question

Line 9. Yes, she is struggling not to reveal a secret. No. Although toward the end of Scene I, Brutus promises Portia that he will tell her everything, he leaves with Ligarius (l. 330), and the two arrive early the next morning with the other conspirators at Caesar's house. In stage time, therefore, it would seem that he has not had time to speak to Portia.

SCENE 4. *Another part of the street.*

Enter PORTIA *and* LUCIUS.

Portia.
I prithee, boy, run to the Senate House;
Stay not to answer me, but get thee gone.
Why dost thou stay?

Lucius. To know my errand, madam.

Portia.
I would have had thee there and here again
Ere I can tell thee what thou shouldst do there.
O constancy,° be strong upon my side;
Set a huge mountain 'tween my heart and tongue!
I have a man's mind, but a woman's might.
How hard it is for women to keep counsel!°
Art thou here yet?

Lucius. Madam, what should I do?
Run to the Capitol, and nothing else?
And so return to you, and nothing else?

A

Portia.
Yes, bring me word, boy, if thy lord look well,
For he went sickly forth; and take good note
What Caesar doth, what suitors press to him.
Hark, boy, what noise is that?

Lucius.
I hear none, madam.

Portia. Prithee, listen well.
I hear a bustling rumor° like a fray,°
And the wind brings it from the Capitol.

Lucius.
Sooth,° madam, I hear nothing.

[*Enter the* SOOTHSAYER.]

Portia.
Come hither, fellow. Which way hast thou been?

Soothsayer.
At mine own house, good lady.

Portia.
What is't o'clock?

Soothsayer. About the ninth hour, lady.

6. **constancy:** determination.

9. **counsel:** a secret.

? 9. *Is there a clue in this speech that Brutus has told Portia of the conspiracy to murder Caesar? Does the script provide an opportunity for him to tell her after their conversation in Scene 1? In "stage time" (the time at which the play's events take place), could he have told Portia of the plot?*

18. **rumor:** noise. **fray:** fight.

20. **Sooth:** in truth.

STANDARD REVIEW

Activity. Begin a discussion about the play's theme by asking whether Brutus's motives for joining the conspiracy are honorable. [Some students will contend that Brutus's motives are honorable, in that he is genuinely concerned with the welfare of Rome. Others will assert that killing Caesar is an ambitious act, one that will give himself and the other conspirators power.] Explain that in *Julius Caesar,* the conflicting motivations of honor and ambition are juxtaposed in such a way that it is difficult to determine which is predominant.

Students might also discuss the question of whether Caesar is motivated more by ambition or by honor.

802 Chapter 10 Drama • Evaluating an Argument

"Ay me, how weak a thing the heart of woman is!"

Portia.
Is Caesar yet gone to the Capitol?
Soothsayer.
Madam, not yet; I go to take my stand,
To see him pass on to the Capitol.
Portia.
Thou hast some suit to Caesar, hast thou not?
Soothsayer.
That I have, lady; if it will please Caesar
To be so good to Caesar as to hear me,
I shall beseech him to befriend himself.
Portia.
Why, know'st thou any harm's intended towards him?
Soothsayer.
None that I know will be, much that I fear may chance.
Good morrow to you. Here the street is narrow;
The throng that follows Caesar at the heels,
Of senators, of praetors,° common suitors,
Will crowd a feeble man almost to death.
I'll get me to a place more void,° and there
Speak to great Caesar as he comes along. *[Exit.]*
Portia.
I must go in. Ay me, how weak a thing
The heart of woman is! O Brutus,
The heavens speed thee in thine enterprise!
Sure, the boy heard me—Brutus hath a suit
That Caesar will not grant—O, I grow faint.
Run, Lucius, and commend me to my lord;
Say I am merry; come to me again,
And bring me word what he doth say to thee.
[Exeunt severally.]

35. praetors (prē′tərz): magistrates; city officials.

37. void: empty.

Staging the Play
46. *What does this* ***soliloquy*** *reveal about Portia's state of mind? Why might she deliver line 45 after a pause?*

Direct Teaching

B Reading Skills

Analyzing. Why do you think Portia asks the soothsayer whether he knows of any harm that is intended against Caesar? [Possible response: She is afraid that news of the plot has leaked out. She is worried that Brutus might be caught during the assassination.]

C Literary Focus
REVIEW STANDARD

Character. How does Portia in this last scene seem different from the Portia in Scene 1? [Possible response: In the first scene, Portia revealed great strength, a devotion to her husband, and a stoical willingness to endure any suffering for him. In this scene, she reflects on her weakness and is afraid that because she is a woman, she might not be able to control her feelings or keep the important secret.]

D Literary Focus
REVIEW STANDARD

Dramatic irony. Why is it ironic that Portia wants Brutus to hear that she is merry? [She is actually anything but merry; she is very worried and confused.]

Response to Margin Question

Line 46. Portia may be torn between devotion to Brutus and fear of the murder. She could pause as she tries to devise a message Brutus will understand and Lucius will not.

Check Test: True-False

Monitoring students' progress. To check students' comprehension of the story, ask them to respond to the following questions. Direct students to locate passages in the text that support their responses.

1. Brutus decides that Caesar should not die but then changes his mind. [F]
2. Brutus immediately tells Portia about the conspiracy. [F]
3. Calphurnia convinces Caesar to stay home, but when Decius reinterprets her dream, Caesar decides to go to the Senate. [T]
4. Artemidorus knows about the murder plot but is afraid to warn Caesar. [F]
5. The soothsayer is waiting near the Capitol to warn Caesar again of danger. [T]

The Tragedy of Julius Caesar, Act II, Scene 4 **803**

INDEPENDENT PRACTICE

Literary Response and Analysis

Act II

Reading Check

1. Brutus claims that he is acting for the public good, that Caesar's ambition and love of power will become tyranny.
2. Cassius proposes the murder of Antony; Brutus argues that it is too vicious and unnecessary.
3. Portia wants to know why Brutus is troubled.
4. Calphurnia urges Caesar to say he is too ill to go to the Senate; she dreamed he was murdered.
5. Decius favorably reinterprets the dream and tells Caesar he will be crowned.

Interpretations

6. The pace in Act II is slower than in Act I, but the characters are more agitated. Act II is dominated by fearful waiting and anxiety. Brutus and the conspirators spend a sleepless night as does Calphurnia. Portia, too, is agitated and upset.
7. Brutus says taking an oath would show weakness and invite dishonor. This view shows Brutus to be very high-minded, as well as concerned with appearances.
8. Caesar's character is marked by contradictions. He is confident yet indecisive, fearful yet courageous, arrogant yet docile, and superstitious yet rational. Caesar is not a monster, but he is not a sympathetic character either.
9. At the end of Scene 1, thunder underscores the momentum of the conspiracy; at the start of Scene 2, thunder suggests dangerous foreboding.

Literary Response and Analysis

Act II

Reading Check

1. A **soliloquy** is a speech given by a character alone onstage. Look at Brutus's soliloquy at the beginning of Act II. What reasons does he give for killing Caesar?
2. Who proposes the murder of Antony? Why does Brutus oppose it?
3. What does Portia demand in the **dialogue,** or conversation, with Brutus in Scene 1?
4. In Scene 2, what does Calphurnia try to persuade Caesar to do? Why?
5. How does Decius persuade Caesar to attend the Senate?

Interpretations

6. When you read rather than watch a play, you have to stage it in your imagination, to visualize the movements of characters and the sounds of voices. As you imagine Act II, tell how it compares with Act I—is the pace faster or slower? Are the characters calmer or more agitated? Which scenes make you think so?
7. Why won't Brutus swear an oath (Scene 1, lines 114–140)? What **character traits** does this speech reveal?
8. Describe the complexities of Caesar's **character.** How do you feel about him—is he a monstrous tyrant or a sympathetic man? Explain.
9. Where does Shakespeare use thunder and other storm sounds in the **setting** to suggest cosmic disorder? How does this weather make you feel?
10. In the **rising action** of Act II, describe how Shakespeare creates and builds **suspense** during Scenes 3 and 4. What questions are you left with as the second act of this **tragedy** ends?

Reading Standard 3.1 Articulate the relationship between the expressed purposes and the characteristics of different forms of dramatic literature (e.g., tragedy).

Reading Standard 3.10 Identify and describe the function of dialogue, scene designs, and soliloquies.

Evaluation

11. In Scene 4, Portia appears to know that Brutus is involved in a plot to kill Caesar, although the play does not include a scene in which Brutus gives her this information. Is this omission a weakness in the play? If you were writing such a scene, how would you have Portia react to her husband's news?

Writing

Women's Work

How do you feel about Portia's lament in her soliloquy in Scene 4, lines 39–40: "Ay me, how weak a thing / The heart of woman is!"? In a brief essay, **compare and contrast** the characters of Portia and Calphurnia, and analyze their function in this act.

Listening and Speaking

A Play Within a Play

Caesar's scene with Calphurnia and later with Decius (Scene 2) is a perfect play-within-a-play. Prepare the scene for **dramatic performance.** Before you rehearse, be sure you understand the characters' **motivations.**

10. In Scene 3, Shakespeare introduces Artemidorus, whose letter could prevent the assassination; in Scene 4, the soothsayer also has knowledge that could prevent the attack. These characters build suspense and raise the question of whether or not the attack will go as planned.

Evaluation

11. Some may feel the omission is not a problem, since Brutus promises to tell her (Act II, Scene 1, ll. 305–308). Others may notice that Brutus leaves with Ligarius for Caesar's house without telling Portia anything about the plot. Students' scenes may show Portia opposing Brutus's decision, or they may show her lending her support.

Vocabulary Development

Understanding Elizabethan English

The English language classifies words as nouns, verbs, and so on. When someone mixes up the parts of speech, purists are outraged. (Today, for example, purists deplore the use of the noun *network* as a verb.) Shakespeare freely used the same words as different parts of speech.

1. Here he makes a verb out of the noun *conceit*:

> "You have right well conceited."
> —Act I, Scene 3, line 162

2. Here he uses an adjective (*vulgar*) as a noun (we'd say *vulgar people*):

> ". . . drive away the vulgar from the streets. . . ."
> —Act I, Scene 1, line 70

3. In some passages he omits words:

> "So Caesar may;
> Then lest he may, prevent."
> —Act II, Scene 1, lines 27–28

What's understood here is "prevent him from doing it."

PRACTICE

Use the notes alongside the text of Act II for help with these questions:

1. In Scene 1, line 3 (page 783), Brutus says he cannot "Give guess how near to day." How would you expand this phrase?

2. What word does Brutus omit after the word *general* in line 12 of Scene 1 (page 783)?

3. What do you think Lucius means in Scene 1, line 73 (page 785), when he says the conspirators' "hats are plucked about their ears"?

4. In Scene 1, line 83 (page 785), what noun does Shakespeare use as a verb?

Reading Standard 1.1
Identify and use the literal meanings of words.

Marlon Brando plays Mark Antony in a 1953 film version of *Julius Caesar.*

Vocabulary Development

Practice

1. Give a guess how near to day it is.

2. He omits the word *good.*

3. Their hats are pulled down low so as to conceal their faces.

4. Shakespeare uses the noun *path,* meaning "to walk."

ASSESSING

Assessment

- *Progress Assessment of Reading*
  - Selection Test

RETEACHING

For a lesson reteaching Standard 3.1, see **Reteaching,** p. 939A. For another selection to teach Standard 3.1, see *Interactive Reading,* Chapter 10.

Summary at grade level

Act III

In Scene 1, Caesar, on his way to the Capitol, discounts the soothsayer's warning. He accepts Artemidorus's written warning but is diverted from reading it. At the Capitol, Metellus occupies Caesar's attention while the others surround him. Casca strikes the first blow; the others stab their leader in turn. Shocked and angered, Antony pretends to swear allegiance to the deposers. He asks to bear the body to the Forum and to give a eulogy. Brutus agrees, but Cassius correctly fears Antony's motives. In a soliloquy, Antony reveals that he will avenge Caesar's death.

Scene 2 shifts to the forum, where Brutus and Antony address the public at Caesar's funeral. The people first accept Brutus's reason for the murder. However, Antony's more powerful oration persuades them of the conspirators' treachery. When Antony shows Caesar's wounds and reads his public-spirited will, the furious mob rushes off to burn the assassins' homes.

In the brief Scene 3, Cinna, a poet, is attacked by the angry mob because he has the same name as the conspirator Cinna. The scene shows the breakdown of social order.

PRETEACHING

Selection Starter

Motivate. Remind students that Act II unfolded the play's rising action, which was the forming conspiracy. Explain that in Act III, the rising action will reach a turning point, a defining event that will precipitate the rest of the play's action. Ask students to list possible turning points the plot may take in Act III.

ACT III

SCENE 1.
Rome. Before the Capitol.

"FRIENDS, ROMANS, COUNTRYMEN, LEND ME YOUR EARS . . ."
—ANTONY, ACT III, SCENE 2
(LINE 73)

RESOURCES: READING

Planning

- *One-Stop Planner* CD-ROM with Test Generator
- *On Course: Mapping Instruction*
- *Visual Connections*
  - Videocassette, Segment 10
- *Fine Art Transparencies*
  - Transparency 17

Reading

- *Interactive Reading*
  - Interactive version: *Julius Caesar,* Act III, Scene 2

Flourish. Enter CAESAR, BRUTUS, CASSIUS, CASCA, DECIUS, METELLUS CIMBER, TREBONIUS, CINNA, ANTONY, LEPIDUS, ARTEMIDORUS, PUBLIUS, POPILIUS, *and the* SOOTHSAYER.

Caesar.
The ides of March are come.

Soothsayer.
Ay, Caesar, but not gone.

Artemidorus.
Hail, Caesar! Read this schedule.° **(A)**

Decius.
Trebonius doth desire you to o'er-read,
At your best leisure, this his humble suit. **(B)**

Artemidorus.
O Caesar, read mine first; for mine's a suit
That touches° Caesar nearer. Read it, great Caesar.

Caesar.
What touches us ourself shall be last served.

Artemidorus.
Delay not, Caesar; read it instantly.

Caesar.
What, is the fellow mad?

Publius. Sirrah,° give place.

Cassius.
What, urge you your petitions in the street?
Come to the Capitol.

[CAESAR *goes to the Capitol, the rest following.*]

Popilius.
I wish your enterprise today may thrive. **(C)**

Cassius.
What enterprise, Popilius?

Popilius. Fare you well.

[*Advances to* CAESAR.]

Brutus.
What said Popilius Lena?

? **Staging the Play**
Stage direction. *This scene takes place on the Capitol Hill, where the temple of Jupiter is located. A half circle of steps is seen at the back of the stage, with a throne on top. A statue of Pompey—the enemy Caesar defeated in the recent civil war—is seen to the side. Caesar walks to center stage, and the others flank him. How should Caesar regard the soothsayer and Artemidorus? Should he address his first remark to the soothsayer or to the crowd in general?*

3. schedule: scroll of paper.

7. touches: concerns.

? **8.** *Is this sincerity or false humility?*

10. Sirrah (sir′ə): like *sir,* but used to address an inferior, often intending disrespect or anger.

? **Staging the Play**
10. *Publius speaks to Artemidorus, and the conspirators rush the petitioner away from Caesar. Whom is Cassius addressing in the next speech?*

? **13.** *Popilius speaks to Cassius. Do you think he knows about the conspiracy?*

DIRECT TEACHING

(A) Reading Skills

Paraphrasing. This skill is presented on p. 833. Opportunities to apply the skill occur throughout Act III. Point out that the paper Artemidorus holds is referred to by three words on this page. Ask students to identify the words and to describe the paper and its contents. [The words are *schedule* (l. 3), *suit* (l. 6), and *petitions* (l. 11). It is a rolled piece of paper that contains a plea or a warning.]

(B) Literary Focus
GRADE-LEVEL STANDARD

? **Rising action.** Why does Decius mention Trebonius's suit at this point? [Possible response: Decius quickly intervenes to draw attention away from Artemidorus, who wants to warn Caesar of the danger.]

(C) Reading Skills

? **Paraphrasing.** How would you paraphrase Popilius's words? [Possible response: I hope your plan succeeds today.]

Responses to Margin Questions

Stage direction. Caesar should pay attention to them.
Line 8. Caesar is falsely humble.
Line 11. He addresses Artemidorus.
Line 13. Popilius seems to know at this point.

- *Interactive Reading,* Teacher's Edition
  - Graphic Organizer: Dramatic Elements Chart

Differentiating Instruction

- *Lesson Plans for Language Development*
  - English-Language Learners, pp. 341–343, 363, 370
  - Special Education Students, pp. 344, 363, 370

Assessment

- *Progress Assessment of Reading*
  - Selection Test
- *One-Stop Planner* CD-ROM with Test Generator

The Tragedy of Julius Caesar, Act III, Scene 1 807

DIRECT TEACHING

A Literary Focus GRADE-LEVEL STANDARD

Character foils. How do Brutus and Cassius respond differently to the threat that Popilius might represent? [Possible response: Cassius is panic-stricken and almost loses control of himself; Brutus is cool and maintains his composure.]

B Learners Having Difficulty

Finding sequence of events. Why do the conspirators at this point send Metellus to "prefer his suit to Caesar"? [Possible response: Pretending to speak on Metellus's behalf, the conspirators can close in around Caesar and murder him.]

C Reading Skills

Paraphrasing. How would you state Caesar's reply to Metellus in your own words? [Possible response: There's no sense bowing and acting humble, Cimber, to get Caesar to change his mind about your brother. Since Caesar is too noble to make mistakes, I will not change my original decision.]

Responses to Margin Questions

Line 26. Antony could hinder the murder.
Line 29. The conspirators are arranging themselves around Caesar as planned.

Cassius.
He wished today our enterprise might thrive.
I fear our purpose is discoverèd.
Brutus.
Look how he makes to° Caesar; mark him.
(A) Cassius.
Casca, be sudden, for we fear prevention.°
Brutus, what shall be done? If this be known,
Cassius or Caesar never shall turn back,°
For I will slay myself.
Brutus. Cassius, be constant.°
Popilius Lena speaks not of our purposes;
For look, he smiles, and Caesar doth not change.
Cassius.
Trebonius knows his time; for look you, Brutus,
He draws Mark Antony out of the way.

[*Exeunt* ANTONY *and* TREBONIUS.]

Decius.
Where is Metellus Cimber? Let him go
(B) And presently prefer his suit to Caesar.
Brutus.
He is addressed.° Press near and second him.
Cinna.
Casca, you are the first that rears your hand.
Caesar.
Are we all ready? What is now amiss
That Caesar and his Senate must redress?
Metellus.
Most high, most mighty, and most puissant° Caesar,
Metellus Cimber throws before thy seat
An humble heart. [*Kneeling.*]
Caesar. I must prevent thee, Cimber.
These couchings° and these lowly courtesies
Might fire the blood of ordinary men,
And turn preordinance and first decree°
(C) Into the law of children. Be not fond°
To think that Caesar bears such rebel blood
That will be thawed from the true quality°
With that which melteth fools—I mean sweet words,
Low-crookèd curtsies, and base spaniel fawning.
Thy brother by decree is banishèd.
If thou dost bend and pray and fawn for him,

18. makes to: makes his way toward.

19. prevention: being prevented from carrying out their deed.

21. turn back: come out alive.

22. constant: calm.

? **26.** *Why is Trebonius getting Antony out of the way?*

29. addressed: ready.

? **Staging the Play**
29. *What is happening near Caesar now?*

33. puissant (pyo͞o′i·sənt): powerful.

36. couchings: very low bows.

38. These were old Roman laws. Caesar warns that the laws might be changed at whim if they are not vigilant (just as the laws of children can be changed).
39. fond: so foolish as.
41. true quality: that is, firmness.

DIFFERENTIATING INSTRUCTION

Learners Having Difficulty

Modeling. To help students read Act III, model the reading skill of paraphrasing. Say, "Read ll. 35–39 at the bottom of p. 808. If you look at the context, you'll see that the stage direction shows the character Cimber is kneeling. Combining this knowledge with the sidenotes, you can paraphrase Caesar's words. He is saying, 'I have to stop you, Cimber. These very low bows and cheap flattery might get to ordinary men and turn the rule of law into children's laws.' Now you might also guess that Caesar will say he, Caesar, is not one of these ordinary men." Urge students to use the sidenotes to help them paraphrase as they read.

English-Language Learners

For lessons designed for English-language learners and special education students, see *Lesson Plans for Language Development*, pp. 341–343, 344, 363, 370.

Advanced Learners

Acceleration. In anticipation of Antony's famous funeral oration (Scene 2, ll. 73–107, 118–137, 169–197, 210–230), explain that persuasive arguments may be logical or faulty. Facts, statistics, and other information support a logical argument. A faulty argu-

I spurn thee like a cur out of my way.
Know, Caesar doth not wrong, nor without cause
Will he be satisfied.

Metellus.
Is there no voice more worthy than my own,
To sound more sweetly in great Caesar's ear
For the repealing of my banished brother?

Brutus.
I kiss thy hand, but not in flattery, Caesar,
Desiring thee that Publius Cimber may
Have an immediate freedom of repeal.°

Caesar.
What, Brutus?

Cassius. Pardon, Caesar; Caesar, pardon!
As low as to thy foot doth Cassius fall
To beg enfranchisement° for Publius Cimber.

Caesar.
I could be well moved, if I were as you;
If I could pray to move,° prayers would move me;
But I am constant as the Northern Star,
Of whose true-fixed and resting° quality
There is no fellow° in the firmament.
The skies are painted with unnumb'red sparks,
They are all fire and every one doth shine;
But there's but one in all doth hold his place.
So in the world; 'tis furnished well with men,
And men are flesh and blood, and apprehensive;
Yet in the number I do know but one
That unassailable holds on his rank,°
Unshaked of motion; and that I am he,
Let me a little show it, even in this—
That I was constant° Cimber should be banished,
And constant do remain to keep him so.

Cinna.
O Caesar——

Caesar. Hence! Wilt thou lift up Olympus?°

Decius.
Great Caesar——

Caesar. Doth not Brutus bootless° kneel?

Casca.
Speak hands for me!

[*They stab* CAESAR.]

Staging the Play
48. *What is Caesar doing during this speech? What is Metellus doing in response to Caesar's words?*

51. *Whom is Metellus addressing here?*

Staging the Play
52. *Brutus steps forward; notice that he uses the pronoun* thy *in an insulting way, since Caesar is not his social inferior, nor is the situation intimate. How might Caesar react to Brutus's surprising words?*

54. freedom of repeal: permission to return from exile.

57. enfranchisement: restoration of the rights of citizenship.

59. pray to move: beg others to change their minds.

61. resting: changeless.

62. fellow: equal.

69. rank: position.

Staging the Play
70. *At what point in this speech would Caesar rise from his throne? The senators now rush in around Caesar and, in most productions, kneel before him. Casca has worked his way in back of Caesar.*

72. constant: firmly determined.

74. Olympus: in Greek mythology, the mountain where the gods lived.

75. bootless: in vain.

Staging the Play
75. *This line is often spoken to show Caesar's great fondness for Brutus. How else might it be spoken?*

Staging the Play
76. *What does this line mean? What is Casca doing?*

DIRECT TEACHING

D Reading Skills

Understanding Elizabethan English. In ll. 52 and 53, Brutus uses the familiar pronouns *thy* and *thee,* usually reserved for an intimate or inferior, instead of the formal *your* and *you,* which would be appropriate here. What does this show about Brutus's intent? [Possible responses: Brutus is showing false intimacy to conceal his intent to kill Caesar; since Brutus intends to kill Caesar, he no longer bothers to address him with respect.]

E Literary Focus
GRADE-LEVEL STANDARD

Dramatic dialogue. Ask students if they agree with critic T. S. Dorsch, who said that Caesar makes "such extravagant expressions of arrogance that all sympathy for him is alienated, and the action of the assassins is for the moment almost accepted as justifiable." [Possible responses: Yes, Caesar is so vain and arrogant that he would be disastrous for Rome; no, nothing justifies murder.]

Responses to Margin Questions

Line 48. Caesar commands Metellus to rise. Metellus perhaps continues bowing and fawning, provoking Caesar to push him away.
Line 51. He is appealing to the senators.
Line 52. He might be taken aback.
Line 70. Caesar could rise at "and that I am he" (l. 70) or on the earlier words "but one" (l. 68).
Line 75. An actor might emphasize Caesar's arrogance and anger.
Line 76. Casca means that his actions speak for him. Casca is the first to stab Caesar.

ment uses hasty generalizations, circular reasoning, ad hominem arguments (directed at the person rather than the person's logic), or false analogies. Explain that an author or speaker may also use anecdote and appeals to emotion.

Activity. After students have read Act III through Antony's funeral oration, have them identify where he uses the following techniques: anecdote [ll. 171–173]; and ad hominem argument [l. 197, in which Antony calls the conspirators "traitors"].

The Tragedy of Julius Caesar, Act III, Scene 1 809

DIRECT TEACHING

A Literary Focus
GRADE-LEVEL STANDARD

Dramatic dialogue. You may have heard this line quoted before, as it is among the most famous in Shakespeare's plays. What is Caesar expressing here? [Possible response: Caesar is expressing profound disappointment—that is, if Brutus could betray him like this, then he doesn't want to live.]

B Literary Focus
GRADE-LEVEL STANDARD

Turning point. Most critics view the death of Caesar as the turning point of the play. Why might this be the turning point? [Possible response: Planning the assassination has been the focus of the first two acts; now the action must take its inexorable course.]

Response to Margin Question

Line 77. He sees Brutus as one of the assassins. One interpretation of Caesar's words is "if this friend is now my enemy, my death is certain."

"LIBERTY, FREEDOM, AND ENFRANCHISEMENT!"

A **Caesar.**
Et tu, Brutè?° Then fall Caesar. [*Dies.*]

Cinna.
Liberty! Freedom! Tyranny is dead!
Run hence, proclaim, cry it about the streets.

Cassius.
B Some to the common pulpits, and cry out
"Liberty, freedom, and enfranchisement!"

Brutus.
People, and senators, be not affrighted.
Fly not; stand still; ambition's debt is paid.

Casca.
Go to the pulpit, Brutus.

Decius. And Cassius too.

77. ***Et tu, Brutè?:*** Latin for "And you also, Brutus?"

Staging the Play
77. *The murder of Caesar has been staged in many ways. Low-budget productions have to worry about laundry bills for stained togas, but most productions show blood. In some productions each dagger has attached to it a plastic capsule, which the actors break with their fingernails. In other productions, Caesar has a "blood" bag concealed under his toga. To stage the murder, directors often have the conspirators standing at different places onstage—all points to which Caesar runs in his attempt to escape. The last point is Brutus's. What does Caesar see as he utters his last words? Why does he say, "Then fall Caesar"?*

CONTENT-AREA CONNECTIONS

Art: Paintings of Caesar

Individual activity. Italian artists of the Renaissance and later periods created extraordinary canvases that depicted scenes from Caesar's life. Refer students to reproductions of such paintings as *The Triumph of Caesar* by Andrea Mantegna and *The Death of Caesar* by Vincenza Camuccini. Students may do a report on these paintings or use them as models for their own illustrations.

History: Shakespeare's England

Small-group activity. Have small groups of students do presentations on Shakespeare's England. Topics might include the following items:

- the struggle between Queen Elizabeth and Mary, Queen of Scots
- the Church of England and Queen Elizabeth
- theater in Elizabethan England
- Shakespeare's life

810 Chapter 10 Drama • Evaluating an Argument

Brutus.
Where's Publius?°
Cinna.
Here, quite confounded with this mutiny.
Metellus.
Stand fast together, lest some friend of Caesar's
Should chance——
Brutus.
Talk not of standing. Publius, good cheer;
There is no harm intended to your person,
Nor to no Roman else. So tell them, Publius.
Cassius.
And leave us, Publius, lest that the people
Rushing on us should do your age some mischief.
Brutus.
Do so; and let no man abide° this deed
But we the doers.

[*Enter* TREBONIUS.]

Cassius.
Where is Antony?
Trebonius. Fled to his house amazed.
Men, wives, and children stare, cry out and run,
As it were doomsday.
Brutus. Fates, we will know your pleasures.
That we shall die, we know; 'tis but the time,
And drawing days out, that men stand upon.°
Casca.
Why, he that cuts off twenty years of life
Cuts off so many years of fearing death.
Brutus.
Grant that, and then is death a benefit.
So are we Caesar's friends, that have abridged
His time of fearing death. Stoop, Romans, stoop,
And let us bathe our hands in Caesar's blood
Up to the elbows, and besmear our swords.
Then walk we forth, even to the market place,°
And waving our red weapons o'er our heads,
Let's all cry "Peace, freedom, and liberty!"

85. Publius is a very old senator, too old to flee.

94. abide: take the consequences of.

100. stand upon: wait for.

Staging the Play
107. *What are the conspirators doing now?*

108. market place: Forum, center of public and commercial life in Rome.

DIRECT TEACHING

C Literary Focus
GRADE-LEVEL STANDARD

Foreshadowing. What earlier events foreshadowed this scene of "doomsday" that now occurs in the Roman streets? [Possible response: the strange portents of the previous night—meteors, fires, roaming lions, and so on.]

D Content-Area Connections
Culture: Mythology
In Greek and Roman mythology, the Fates are the three goddesses of destiny. The Roman Fates were called Nona, Decuma, and Morta. Nona spins the thread of life, Decuma determines its length, and Morta cuts the thread at death.

E Literary Focus
REVIEW STANDARD

Symbol. Why does Brutus ask the conspirators to join him in bathing his hands in Caesar's blood? What might the blood symbolize? [Possible response: Brutus hopes to transform the gruesome murder into a purifying ritual that makes Caesar's blood a symbol of "Peace, freedom, and liberty."]

Response to Margin Question
Line 107. They are staining their hands and swords with Caesar's blood.

DIFFERENTIATING INSTRUCTION

Learners Having Difficulty
Review the numbering system used to identify lines in the play. Explain that a split line is numbered once, even though it includes the speech of two characters. (The two parts form one full line of five iambs.) Note that acts are represented by capital Roman numerals and the scenes and line numbers by Arabic numerals. Encourage students to use the sidenotes as they read.

Advanced Learners
Activity. Have students practice scanning lines of *Julius Caesar* to get used to the beats of iambic pentameter. Then, suggest that they use iambic pentameter to write a brief account of a current event in the news or a description of something that happened at school or in the community. You might suggest that students use a few words from Elizabethan English in their iambic accounts.

The Tragedy of Julius Caesar, Act III, Scene 1 **811**

Direct Teaching

A Literary Focus
GRADE-LEVEL STANDARD
? Turning point. In ll. 111–113, Cassius says that this scene will be "acted over" throughout the ages. How does Brutus react to this idea? [He agrees that they have accomplished a historical feat.] At this turning point, or crisis, in the plot, what attitude does Brutus express toward the dead Caesar? [Possible response: He now regards Caesar as insignificant, no more important than "dust."]

B Reading Skills
Paraphrasing. Ask students to paraphrase the message that Antony sends. [Possible response: Antony says that although he loved Caesar, he also loves and honors Brutus and is willing to follow him through the difficult times ahead as long as Brutus guarantees his safety.]

C Literary Focus
GRADE-LEVEL STANDARD
? Turning point. In the aftermath of violence, how does Brutus plan to proceed as Rome's leader? [Possible response: Brutus intends to be peaceful and diplomatic, assuring the safety of Antony, Caesar's chief supporter.]

Responses to Margin Questions

Line 118. As students offer ideas, ask them how each delivery (sincere idealism or self-righteous fervor) could affect the upcoming dramatic conflict between Brutus's faction and Caesar's loyalists.
Line 137. Antony asks for a promise of safety if he comes to the Capitol.

Cassius.
Stoop then, and wash. How many ages hence
Shall this our lofty scene be acted over
In states unborn and accents yet unknown!

Brutus. (A)
How many times shall Caesar bleed in sport,
That now on Pompey's basis° lies along°
No worthier than the dust!

Cassius. So oft as that shall be,
So often shall the knot of us be called
The men that gave their country liberty.

Decius.
What, shall we forth?

Cassius. Ay, every man away.
Brutus shall lead, and we will grace his heels
With the most boldest and best hearts of Rome.

[*Enter a* SERVANT.]

Brutus.
Soft, who comes here? A friend of Antony's.

Servant. (B)
Thus, Brutus, did my master bid me kneel;
Thus did Mark Antony bid me fall down;
And, being prostrate, thus he bade me say:
Brutus is noble, wise, valiant, and honest;
Caesar was mighty, bold, royal, and loving.
Say I love Brutus, and I honor him;
Say I feared Caesar, honored him, and loved him.
If Brutus will vouchsafe that Antony
May safely come to him and be resolved°
How Caesar hath deserved to lie in death,
Mark Antony shall not love Caesar dead
So well as Brutus living; but will follow
The fortunes and affairs of noble Brutus
Thorough° the hazards of this untrod state
With all true faith. So says my master Antony.

Brutus. (C)
Thy master is a wise and valiant Roman;
I never thought him worse.
Tell him, so please him come unto this place,
He shall be satisfied and, by my honor,
Depart untouched.

Servant. I'll fetch him presently.°
[*Exit* SERVANT.]

115. basis: base (of Pompey's statue). **lies along:** stretches out.

? Staging the Play
118. *These speeches can be delivered in various ways. Would you emphasize the self-righteousness of the conspirators or their idealism?*

131. resolved: satisfied.

136. Thorough: through.

? 137. *What does Antony ask of Brutus?*

142. presently: immediately.

Developing Fluency

Mixed-ability group activity. As students read Act III, ask them to note lines that they find particularly hard to understand. After students have finished reading each scene, divide the class into mixed-ability groups, and have group members share their notes with each other. They can work together to analyze difficult or confusing lines for meaning. Remind students that paraphrasing will help them better comprehend Shakespeare's verse and prose. Then, have students re-read aloud dialogue containing the lines they previously found difficult.

"HOW MANY AGES HENCE
SHALL THIS OUR LOFTY SCENE
BE ACTED OVER
IN STATES UNBORN AND
ACCENTS YET UNKNOWN!"

Brutus.
I know that we shall have him well to friend.

Cassius.
I wish we may. But yet have I a mind
That fears him much; and my misgiving still
Falls shrewdly to the purpose.°

[*Enter* ANTONY.] **D**

Brutus.
But here comes Antony. Welcome, Mark Antony.

Antony.
O mighty Caesar! Dost thou lie so low?
Are all thy conquests, glories, triumphs, spoils,
Shrunk to this little measure? Fare thee well.
I know not, gentlemen, what you intend,
Who else must be let blood,° who else is rank.°
If I myself, there is no hour so fit
As Caesar's death's hour, nor no instrument
Of half that worth as those your swords, made rich
With the most noble blood of all this world.
I do beseech ye, if you bear me hard,°
Now, whilst your purpled hands do reek and smoke,
Fulfill your pleasure. Live a thousand years,
I shall not find myself so apt to die;
No place will please me so, no mean of death,
As here by Caesar, and by you cut off,
The choice and master spirits of this age.

E

Brutus.
O Antony, beg not your death of us! **F**
Though now we must appear bloody and cruel,
As by our hands and this our present act
You see we do, yet see you but our hands
And this the bleeding business they have done.

146. In other words, my misgivings, or doubts, are usually justified.

Staging the Play
146. *How does Cassius say this line? Notice that at this moment the play takes a turn and that the hunters now become the hunted.*

Staging the Play
148. *Where should Antony position himself? In this speech, where would you have the actor playing Antony pause? What movements or gestures would he make?*

152. Antony is punning here: "Let blood" can mean "bleed a sick person in order to cure the illness," or it can mean "shed blood (kill)." **rank:** another pun—swollen with disease (and thus in need of bleeding) or swollen with power.

157. bear me hard: bear a grudge against me.

163–253. *We've had a glimpse of Antony earlier in the play, but this scene is the first time he speaks at length. What is the purpose of this **dialogue,** or conversation, between Brutus, Antony, and Cassius?*

DIRECT TEACHING

D Literary Focus
GRADE-LEVEL STANDARD

Turning point. Some critics view the arrival of Antony at the assassination scene as the turning point because it is at this juncture that the fortunes of the conspirators begin to decline. Why might the conspirators fail? [Possible response: The conspirators lack direction; they have no plan to deal with the ensuing political chaos in Rome.]

E Literary Focus
REVIEW STANDARD

Character. Until now, Antony has been presented as Caesar's lightweight sidekick. What different traits does Antony reveal in this speech? [Possible responses: Antony seems more imposing here; he is capable of sincere feeling and subtle psychology.]

F Reading Skills

Interpreting. What does Antony imply by offering his life to the conspirators? [Possible response: Antony implies that he will pose no threat to them.]

Responses to Margin Questions

Line 146. Cassius says this line worriedly.

Line 148. Antony is near Caesar's body. A natural break occurs at the end of l. 150. Antony could stoop to Caesar's body and then rise to face the conspirators. He could point out their swords and gesture pleadingly.

Line 163–253. This dialogue will help establish Antony's fate in the wake of Caesar's murder.

CONTENT-AREA CONNECTIONS

History: Oratory in Ancient Rome

Individual activity. Explain to students that oratory, the art of swaying an audience by eloquent speech, was important in many areas of life in ancient Rome and Greece. Point out that the three greatest orators in ancient Rome were Cato, Cicero, and Mark Antony. Invite students to find out more about these early orators and their artfulness with language.

DIRECT TEACHING

A Literary Focus
GRADE-LEVEL STANDARD

? Character foils. How would you contrast the responses of Brutus and Cassius to Antony? [Possible response: Brutus, earnest and idealistic, assures Antony at length of the conspirators' "kind love, good thoughts, and reverence." Cassius, the shrewd politician, is distrustful and, with fewer words, quick to appeal to Antony's self-interest regarding the granting of titles in the future.]

B English-Language Learners

? Appreciating puns. What is the double meaning of "slippery ground" in l. 191? [Antony may be referring not only to his current political standing but also to the ground he is literally standing on, which could be slippery with blood.]

Responses to Margin Questions

Line 178. Brutus reveals his idealism and deep feeling, while Cassius shows his political pragmatism and insight.
Line 185. Antony shakes hands with each man. He doesn't want to appear to be a threat to the deposers. Also, by having the blood on their hands rub off on his, he appears to be sharing in (and approving of) their act.
Line 194. Antony is near the corpse but could be standing or kneeling.

Our hearts you see not; they are pitiful;°
And pity to the general wrong of Rome—
As fire drives out fire, so pity pity—
Hath done this deed on Caesar. For your part,
To you our swords have leaden° points, Mark Antony:
Our arms in strength of malice, and our hearts
Of brothers' temper, do receive you in
A With all kind love, good thoughts, and reverence.

Cassius.
Your voice shall be as strong as any man's
In the disposing of new dignities.°

Brutus.
Only be patient till we have appeased
The multitude, beside themselves with fear,
And then we will deliver you the cause
Why I, that did love Caesar when I struck him,
Have thus proceeded.

Antony. I doubt not of your wisdom.
Let each man render me his bloody hand.
First, Marcus Brutus, will I shake with you;
Next, Caius Cassius, do I take your hand;
Now, Decius Brutus, yours; now yours, Metellus;
Yours, Cinna; and, my valiant Casca, yours;
Though last, not least in love, yours, good Trebonius.
Gentlemen all—alas, what shall I say?
B My credit° now stands on such slippery ground
That one of two bad ways you must conceit° me,
Either a coward or a flatterer.
That I did love thee, Caesar, O, 'tis true!
If then thy spirit look upon us now,
Shall it not grieve thee dearer than thy death
To see thy Antony making his peace,
Shaking the bloody fingers of thy foes,
Most noble, in the presence of thy corse?°
Had I as many eyes as thou hast wounds,

169. pitiful: full of pity.

173. leaden: blunt (not made of steel).

178. dignities: titles.

? 178. *Again, Cassius serves as **foil** to Brutus. What differences in character do Brutus and Cassius reveal here in replying to Antony?*

? Staging the Play
185. *This is a rather bold step on Antony's part. What is he doing? What is his motive?*

191. credit: reputation.
192. conceit: judge.

? Staging the Play
194. *What is Antony's position on stage now—is he standing or kneeling? Is he near the corpse or far away from it?*

199. corse (kôrs): corpse.

"THAT I DID LOVE THEE, CAESAR, O, 'TIS TRUE!"

DEVELOPING FLUENCY

Paired activity. Have students identify the few run-on lines in Antony's speech (ll. 183–210) and practice reading them so that the meaning flows smoothly from line to line. Then, have one student in a pair read Antony's entire speech aloud, pausing appropriately at the end of punctuated lines. The other student should listen carefully and paraphrase and summarize the content of the speech, using everyday language. Then, partners should reverse roles. When students have enhanced their fluency with this speech, ask them to assess Antony's skills as an orator. They should consider the strength of his imagery, his ability to express his emotions, and his persuasiveness. After students have assessed Antony's oration skills, explain that his most brilliant speech is coming up soon in Scene 2 and that the same pairs can take on the reading and paraphrasing of that famous address.

Weeping as fast as they stream forth thy blood,
It would become me better than to close
In terms of friendship with thine enemies.
Pardon me, Julius! Here wast thou bayed, brave hart;°
Here didst thou fall, and here thy hunters stand,
Signed in thy spoil and crimsoned in thy lethe.°
O world, thou wast the forest to this hart;
And this indeed, O world, the heart of thee.
How like a deer, stroken by many princes,
Dost thou here lie!

Cassius.
Mark Antony—

Antony. Pardon me, Caius Cassius.
The enemies of Caesar shall say this;
Then, in a friend, it is cold modesty.°

Cassius.
I blame you not for praising Caesar so;
But what compact mean you to have with us?
Will you be pricked in number of° our friends,
Or shall we on, and not depend on you?

Antony.
Therefore I took your hands, but was indeed
Swayed from the point by looking down on Caesar.
Friends am I with you all, and love you all,
Upon this hope, that you shall give me reasons
Why, and wherein, Caesar was dangerous.

Brutus.
Or else were this a savage spectacle.
Our reasons are so full of good regard
That were you, Antony, the son of Caesar,
You should be satisfied.

Antony. That's all I seek;
And am moreover suitor that I may
Produce° his body to the market place,
And in the pulpit, as becomes a friend,
Speak in the order of his funeral.

Brutus.
You shall, Mark Antony.

Cassius. Brutus, a word with you.
(*Aside to* BRUTUS.) You know not what you do; do not consent
That Antony speak in his funeral.
Know you how much the people may be moved

204. Antony compares Caesar to a deer (hart) hunted down by barking (baying) hounds. "Brave hart" is also a pun on "brave heart."

206. In other words, marked with the wounds of your slaughter and reddened by your blood (compared to the river Lethe in the underworld).

210. *Why is the imagery of the hunted deer (hart) so appropriate here? How does it make you feel about Caesar?*

213. modesty: moderation.

216. pricked in number of: counted with. In counting off a list of people, the Romans would prick a hole in a wax-covered tablet.

228. Produce: take.

232. *An **aside** is words spoken by one character to another character, or to the audience, that others onstage are not supposed to hear. What is the function of Cassius's aside to Brutus?*

DIRECT TEACHING

C Reading Skills

Making connections. Who else used an image of the hunt to describe the murder of Caesar? [Brutus did in Act II, Scene 1, ll. 173–174: "Let's carve him as a dish fit for the gods, / Not hew him as a carcass fit for hounds."]

D Reading Skills

Reading Shakespeare. What word does Shakespeare omit in l. 217 for the sake of rhythm? [He omits *go* or *move.* ("Or shall we *go / move* on . . . ?")] What inverted word order is used in l. 220? [Antony says "Friends am I with you all," an inverted form of "I am friends with you all."]

Responses to Margin Questions

Line 210. Like a lone deer trapped by organized hunters, Caesar was defenseless and unsuspecting. Antony's image arouses pity and gives Caesar a natural majesty.
Line 232. Cassius is warning Brutus not to allow Antony to speak at Caesar's funeral. The aside contrasts these character foils (Brutus and Cassius) and adds suspense and tension to the play's turning point.

DIFFERENTIATING INSTRUCTION

English-Language Learners

Make sure students understand that an aside can be spoken by a character as if speaking to himself or herself, to the audience, or to just one or more characters—but not all characters—present onstage (as in Cassius's aside to Brutus, on this page). Other characters don't hear the aside. Also, review that in a soliloquy a character alone onstage describes an inner conflict, showing her or his innermost feelings.

Advanced Learners

Enrichment. Since the accomplishments of ancestors played a key role in a Roman's self-image, a funeral in ancient Rome offered an opportunity to honor not only the deceased person but his or her forebears. Each family kept wax death masks of their ancestors, and during funerals these masks were worn as the grieving family headed to the service in the Forum. There a young relative of the decedent would mount the speaker's platform and deliver an oration. Although the speech began by honoring the deceased person, the address would lead up to a recounting of the glorious achievements of the dead man or woman's ancestors. The ritual gave the family the occasion to honor its past and reinforce the behavior and attitudes it regarded as exemplary.

READING SKILLS REVIEW

Ask students to recall some of the reading skills that can help them gain a better understanding of a text. [Students should mention re-reading, using resources, and questioning.] Emphasize that forming questions while reading helps readers retain information that interests them. Remind students that they may find answers by re-reading text, drawing conclusions, making inferences, using resources, and discussing ideas with other students.

Activity. Have students form questions regarding Act III, such as these: Why did Casca strike the first blow against Caesar? Where were the senators, besides Antony, who loved Caesar and might have fought the conspirators at the assassination? Why (later in Act III) does Brutus allow Antony to give his funeral oration, and why doesn't he or a trusted co-conspirator remain at the Forum to oversee Antony's speech?

By that which he will utter?

Brutus. By your pardon:
I will myself into the pulpit first,
And show the reason of our Caesar's death.
What Antony shall speak, I will protest
He speaks by leave and by permission,
And that we are contented Caesar shall
Have all true rites and lawful ceremonies.
It shall advantage more than do us wrong.

Cassius.
I know not what may fall;° I like it not. **A**

Brutus.
Mark Antony, here, take you Caesar's body.
You shall not in your funeral speech blame us,
But speak all good you can devise of Caesar,
And say you do't by our permission;
Else shall you not have any hand at all
About his funeral. And you shall speak
In the same pulpit whereto I am going,
After my speech is ended. **B**

Antony. Be it so;
I do desire no more.

Brutus.
Prepare the body then, and follow us.

[*Exeunt all except* ANTONY.]

Antony.
O pardon me, thou bleeding piece of earth,
That I am meek and gentle with these butchers! **C**
Thou art the ruins of the noblest man
That ever livèd in the tide of times.
Woe to the hand that shed this costly blood!
Over thy wounds now do I prophesy
(Which like dumb mouths do ope their ruby lips
To beg the voice and utterance of my tongue),
A curse shall light upon the limbs of men;
Domestic fury and fierce civil strife
Shall cumber° all the parts of Italy;
Blood and destruction shall be so in use,
And dreadful objects so familiar,
That mothers shall but smile when they behold
Their infants quartered° with the hands of war,

243. fall: befall; happen.

Staging the Play
254. *How should Antony immediately change his tone? Whom is he talking to?*

Staging the Play
263. *During this speech some directors let us hear the offstage noise of the crowd. At what moments in this speech would the offstage cries of the mob and even other street noises be appropriate?*

264. cumber: burden.
268. quartered: butchered (cut in four parts).

DIRECT TEACHING

A Literary Focus
REVIEW STANDARD

Foreshadowing. What turn of events does Cassius foreshadow when he murmurs, "I like it not"? [Possible response: Cassius's comment hints that Antony will use his funeral oration to turn the public against the conspirators.]

B Reading Skills

Paraphrasing. In your own words, what does Brutus tell Antony to do? [Possible response: Brutus tells Antony that he can speak after Brutus at the funeral if he agrees not to blame the conspirators in his speech. He is to honor Caesar and must point out that the deposers have given him permission to speak.]

C Literary Focus
GRADE-LEVEL STANDARD

Falling action. How does the beginning of Antony's soliloquy show that the play's turning point will now precipitate its falling action? [Possible response: Antony reveals his deep grief over Caesar's death and his desire for revenge, revealing that he has deceived Brutus and that the falling action will involve great conflict.]

Responses to Margin Questions

Line 254. Antony's tone should change to grief and rage. He is now speaking to Caesar.
Line 263. The noise could begin at l. 260 and continue through the speech, or it could punctuate ll. 260–261, 265–268, and 272–275.

CONTENT-AREA CONNECTIONS

Literature: The Mark Antony Character

In a study of the style of *Julius Caesar,* critic Vivian Thomas makes the following comment about Mark Antony: "In contrast [to Brutus], Mark Antony manifests no sign of internal doubts and is absolutely clear-eyed about the power of language and gesture. Despite being genuinely moved by Caesar's death, he plots his course with calculated guile, cynically taking the bloodied hands of the assassins in apparent friendship while mentally placing them on a death list. To Antony, Caesar's wounds 'like dumb mouths do ope their ruby lips, / To beg the voice and utterance of my tongue' (ll. 260–261)."

The Tragedy of Julius Caesar, Act III, Scene 1 817

DIRECT TEACHING

A Literary Focus
REVIEW STANDARD

Character. What traits does Antony reveal about himself in his soliloquy? [Possible responses: He is passionately loyal to Caesar; he is boldly determined, even ruthless.]

B Reading Skills

Paraphrasing. How would you restate Antony's words? [Possible response: You have a big heart, and you're sad. Find a place alone to cry. Seeing your tears brings tears to my eyes. Is your boss on his way here?]

C Reading Skills

Speculating. In ll. 290–296 why does Antony tell Octavius's servant to await the outcome of his oration before reporting to Octavius? [Possible response: The people's reaction to Antony's impassioned appeal will determine Octavius's action. If the reaction proves favorable, Octavius will most likely advance to Rome to back Antony with military force.]

Responses to Margin Questions

Line 284. He might touch his shoulder or gently move him away from the body.

Line 297. Ask students to describe what is conveyed if Antony stands alone at Caesar's feet or if he lifts the body, embracing it. Crowd noises would heighten Antony's plotting and prepare for the mob in the Forum.

All pity choked with custom of fell° deeds,
And Caesar's spirit, ranging for revenge,
With Atè° by his side come hot from hell,
Shall in these confines with a monarch's voice
Cry "Havoc,"° and let slip the dogs of war,
That this foul deed shall smell above the earth
With carrion° men, groaning for burial.

[*Enter Octavius's* SERVANT.]

You serve Octavius Caesar, do you not?

Servant.
I do, Mark Antony.

Antony.
Caesar did write for him to come to Rome.

Servant.
He did receive his letters and is coming,
And bid me say to you by word of mouth—
O Caesar! [*Seeing the body.*]

Antony.
Thy heart is big;° get thee apart and weep.
Passion, I see, is catching, for mine eyes,
Seeing those beads of sorrow stand in thine,
Began to water. Is thy master coming?

Servant.
He lies tonight within seven leagues° of Rome.

Antony.
Post° back with speed, and tell him what hath chanced.
Here is a mourning Rome, a dangerous Rome,
No Rome of safety for Octavius yet.
Hie° hence and tell him so. Yet stay awhile;
Thou shalt not back till I have borne this corse
Into the market place; there shall I try°
In my oration how the people take
The cruel issue° of these bloody men;
According to the which, thou shalt discourse
To young Octavius of the state of things.
Lend me your hand. [*Exeunt.*]

269. fell: evil.

271. Atè (ā'tē): Greek goddess of revenge.

273. Cry "Havoc": give the signal for the devastation and disorder to begin.

275. carrion: dead and rotting.

282. big: full of grief.

Staging the Play
284. *What might Antony do to the servant to make us feel his compassion?*

286. seven leagues: about twenty-one miles.

287. Post: ride on horseback (changing horses along the way).

290. Hie: hurry.

292. try: test.

294. cruel issue: cruel deed; also, the outcome or result of cruelty.

Staging the Play
297. *Would you end this scene with Antony raising the body in his arms, or would you have him stand over it? Would the noise of the crowd be heard from offstage?*

DIFFERENTIATING INSTRUCTION

Learners Having Difficulty

Struggling learners will benefit from identifying and discussing archaic words and allusions in Antony's soliloquy. Refer students to the sidenotes, and suggest that partners or small groups discuss parts of the speech that are unclear to them. Then, suggest that students paraphrase the soliloquy and compare their paraphrase with that of another group.

Invite learners having difficulty to read *Julius Caesar* in interactive format in *Interactive Reading* and to use the sidenotes as aids to understanding the selection. The interactive version provides additional instruction, practice, and assessment of the literature standard taught in the Student Edition. Monitor students' responses to the selection, and correct any misconceptions that arise.

English-Language Learners

For lessons designed for English-language learners and special education students, see *Lesson Plans for Language Development,* pp. 341–343, 344, 363, 370.

Advanced Learners

Activity. Remind students that the art of oratory involves the use of figures of speech, well-chosen vocabulary (diction), and excel-

818 Chapter 10 Drama • Evaluating an Argument

SCENE 2. *The Forum.*

Enter BRUTUS *and goes into the pulpit, and* CASSIUS, *with the* PLEBEIANS.°

Plebeians.
We will be satisfied! Let us be satisfied!

Brutus.
Then follow me, and give me audience, friends.
Cassius, go you into the other street
And part the numbers.
Those that will hear me speak, let 'em stay here;
Those that will follow Cassius, go with him;
And public reasons shall be renderèd
Of Caesar's death.

First Plebeian. I will hear Brutus speak.

Second Plebeian.
I will hear Cassius, and compare their reasons,
When severally we hear them renderèd.

[*Exit* CASSIUS, *with some of the* PLEBEIANS.]

Third Plebeian.
The noble Brutus is ascended. Silence!

Brutus. Be patient till the last.
Romans, countrymen, and lovers, hear me for my cause, and be silent, that you may hear. Believe me for mine honor, and have respect to mine honor, that you may believe. Censure° me in your wisdom, and awake your senses,° that you may the better judge. If there be any in this assembly, any dear friend of Caesar's, to him I say that Brutus' love to Caesar was no less than his. If then that friend demand why Brutus rose against Caesar, this

Plebeians: the common people.

Staging the Play
Stage direction. *The Roman Forum was a busy, crowded, open area. At one end of the Forum was the Rostrum, a "pulpit" from which Rome's great public figures spoke. In stage sets the pulpit is usually set on a semicircular platform with steps leading up to it. This scene is wild and noisy. What is Brutus's mood as he fights free of the mob and goes up to the pulpit?*

16. Censure: judge.
17. senses: reasoning powers.

"ROMANS, COUNTRYMEN, AND LOVERS, HEAR ME FOR MY CAUSE . . ."

DIRECT TEACHING

D Reading Skills

Reading Shakespeare. Why do you think Shakespeare has Brutus deliver his speech in prose, not in blank verse? [Possible response: The prose suggests Brutus's directness and sincerity, as he is expressing his ideas simply and without artifice.]

E Literary Focus
REVIEW STANDARD

Style. Point out that Brutus's oration is composed in sets of clauses elaborately balanced against one another. Shakespeare also creates a pleasing rhythm with parallelism, or the repetition of words and phrases that have the same grammatical structure. Have students find examples of parallelism in Brutus's speech. [Possible example: "Believe me . . . and have respect to mine honor. . . . Censure me . . . and awake your senses. . . ."]

Response to Margin Question

Stage direction. Brutus is impatient to confront and appease the people.

READING SKILLS REVIEW

lent phrasing and sentence structure. Challenge students to analyze Antony's soliloquy or another speech earlier in the play, identifying the oratorical components that Shakespeare includes to give resonance to his speechmaker's words.

Persuasive techniques. Review the fact that persuasive techniques are often used in speeches to persuade or convince audiences to take action or to believe or think in a given way about a subject, idea, event, person, and so on. Review the point that logical appeals are made up of reasons and evidence, while emotional appeals persuade by working on the audience's emotions.
Activity. Have students analyze Brutus's use of logical appeals in his funeral oration for Caesar. Ask them to assess whether he offers adequate evidence and reasons to support his claims and thus justify the assassination.
Activity. Remind students that some of the plebeians follow Cassius to hear his reasons for the assassination. Have students compose a speech that Cassius might give, including any inadequate reasons and faulty logic that would be appropriate to Cassius's point of view.

The Tragedy of Julius Caesar, Act III, Scene 2 819

Direct Teaching

A **Reading Skills**

Analyzing. What flaw can you detect in Brutus's argument? [Possible response: Brutus assumes the point that he should prove—that Caesar had to die rests on the unproved assumption that Caesar was ambitious.]

B **Literary Focus**
GRADE-LEVEL STANDARD

Turning point. Why might it have been a mistake to allow Antony to bear Caesar's body to the funeral? [Possible responses: The bloody body could be used to inflame the crowd; by carrying the body, Antony can imply that he had a special connection to Caesar, which he could use to his advantage with the plebeians at the funeral.]

C **Reading Skills**

Making judgments. What do you think of Brutus's decision to leave the Forum before Antony gives his speech? [Possible response: The decision seems unwise since he is placing too much trust in Antony, a possible enemy.]

Responses to Margin Questions

Line 22. Brutus says he killed Caesar for the good of Rome. He says that Caesar was too ambitious.
Line 33. Brutus assumes the people value plain-spoken, simple speech.
Line 50. The cry is ironic because Brutus assassinated Caesar to free the people from monarchy. It is clear that the crowd has not grasped Brutus's earnest explanation of his motives.
Line 52. Antony would probably stand respectfully near the body, but he would be watching closely, sizing up the crowd.

A is my answer: Not that I loved Caesar less, but that I loved Rome more. Had you rather Caesar were living, and die all slaves, than that Caesar were dead, to live all free men? As Caesar loved me, I weep for him; as he was fortunate, I rejoice at it; as he was valiant, I honor him; but, as he was ambitious, I slew him. There is tears, for his love; joy, for his fortune; honor, for his valor; and death, for his ambition. Who is here so base, that would be a bondman?° If any, speak; for him have I offended. Who is here so rude,° that would not be a Roman? If any, speak; for him have I offended. Who is here so vile, that will not love his country? If any, speak; for him have I offended. I pause for a reply.

All. None, Brutus, none!

Brutus. Then none have I offended. I have done no more to Caesar than you shall do to Brutus. The question of his death is enrolled° in the Capitol; his glory not extenuated,° wherein he was worthy, nor his offenses enforced,° for which he suffered death.

B [*Enter* MARK ANTONY, *with Caesar's body.*]

Here comes his body, mourned by Mark Antony, who, though he had no hand in his death, shall receive the benefit of his dying, a place in the commonwealth, as **C** which of you shall not? With this I depart, that, as I slew my best lover for the good of Rome, I have the same dagger for myself, when it shall please my country to need my death.

All. Live, Brutus! Live, live!

First Plebeian.
Bring him with triumph home unto his house.

Second Plebeian.
Give him a statue with his ancestors.

Third Plebeian.
Let him be Caesar.

Fourth Plebeian. Caesar's better parts°
Shall be crowned in Brutus.

First Plebeian.
We'll bring him to his house with shouts and clamors.

Brutus. My countrymen—

Second Plebeian. Peace! Silence! Brutus speaks.

First Plebeian. Peace, ho!

? **22.** *In this important* ***monologue,*** *what reasons does Brutus give for killing Caesar?*

29. bondman: slave.

30. rude: rough and uncivilized.

? **33.** *Notice that Brutus's speech is in prose, not poetry. What value does Brutus presume the people cherish—as he cherishes it?*

37. In other words, there is a record of the reasons he was killed. **extenuated:** lessened.

38. enforced: exaggerated.

50. better parts: better qualities.

? **50.** *Why is this cry from the mob, in lines 50–51, ironic? Has the crowd understood Brutus's motives at all?*

? **Staging the Play**
52. *What would you have Antony doing while the mob is talking? (Remember: He has brought Caesar's body to the Forum.)*

Content-Area Connections

Literature: Rhetoric in *Julius Caesar*
In *Shakespeare: A Life in Drama,* Stanley Wells discusses the funeral orations this way: "The most conspicuously rhetorical scene in the play occurs in the Forum. . . . In a sense this scene not merely uses rhetoric but is about rhetoric—about the power of emotively structured speech to sway men, to turn a crowd into a mob, to overwhelm reason with passion. Brutus's speech is in prose, excellent and effective in its laconic way: he has the crowd shouting 'Live, Brutus, live!' . . ."

Mixed-ability group activity. Divide the class into small groups of mixed ability. Have groups examine the rhetoric that Brutus uses in his speech, such as his appeal to his reputation for honorable behavior and his protests of great love for Caesar. Then, invite students to take turns reading the speech as other group members identify the rhetorical flourishes.

820 Chapter 10 Drama • Evaluating an Argument

Brutus.
Good countrymen, let me depart alone,
And, for my sake, stay here with Antony.
Do grace to Caesar's corpse, and grace his speech°
Tending to Caesar's glories, which Mark Antony
By our permission, is allowed to make.
I do entreat you, not a man depart,
Save I alone, till Antony have spoke. [*Exit.*]

First Plebeian.
Stay, ho! And let us hear Mark Antony.

Third Plebeian.
Let him go up into the public chair;°
We'll hear him. Noble Antony, go up.

Antony.
For Brutus' sake, I am beholding to you. **D**

57. grace his speech: listen respectfully to Antony's funeral oration.

63. public chair: pulpit or rostrum.

DIRECT TEACHING

D Literary Focus
REVIEW STANDARD

Theme. One of Shakespeare's themes in *Julius Caesar* is that political success often precludes straightforwardness, or at least idealistic virtue. Ask students to explain the insincerity of Antony's line. [Antony is not "beholding" to them for Brutus's sake but for his own motives of revenge and perhaps power.] Then, invite students to respond to this theme. [Students' responses will vary.]

DEVELOPING FLUENCY

Paired activity. Provide students with an opportunity to appreciate the rhythmic quality of Shakespeare's blank verse. Pick a block of dialogue in Act III, such as that between Brutus and Antony in Scene 1 or Antony's funeral oration in Scene 2. Group students in pairs for echo readings. First, one partner should read a section of dialogue aloud, then the other partner should repeat what the first partner has read. Have different students experiment by stressing different words and stretching or condensing pauses. After students have done varied oral interpretations of the dialogue, have them discuss how Shakespeare's use of iambic pentameter affected their readings.

Direct Teaching

A Reading Skills

Reading Shakespeare. How would you describe the difference between Brutus's prose speech and Antony's blank verse? [Possible response: Brutus's down-to-earth prose seems less eloquent and passionate than Antony's verse.]

B Reading Skills

Analyzing. How does Antony attack Brutus's argument? [Possible response: Antony isolates Brutus's unproved assumption—that Caesar was ambitious—and sets out to disprove it. If he can do this, Brutus's argument falls apart.]

C Reading Skills

Appreciating language. How does Antony use repetition effectively in this speech? [Possible response: By repeatedly calling Brutus an "honorable man" while undermining his assertion that Caesar was ambitious, Antony casts doubt on Brutus's character.] Point out that this rhetoric is also one of the most famous examples of verbal irony, the use of words to suggest the opposite of their literal meaning.

Responses to Margin Questions

Line 73. By moving the body to the pulpit, Antony will keep it in the people's view as he speaks. Ironic or sympathetic tones may be heard in the prologue.
Line 93. The crowd could repeat his phrases, gesture and shout in agreement, and draw their neighbor's attention to certain points.

Fourth Plebeian.
What does he say of Brutus?
Third Plebeian. He says, for Brutus' sake,
He finds himself beholding to us all.
Fourth Plebeian.
'Twere best he speak no harm of Brutus here!
First Plebeian.
This Caesar was a tyrant.
Third Plebeian. Nay, that's certain.
We are blest that Rome is rid of him.
Second Plebeian.
Peace! Let us hear what Antony can say.
Antony.
You gentle Romans—
All. Peace, ho! Let us hear him.
Antony.
Friends, Romans, countrymen, lend me your ears;
I come to bury Caesar, not to praise him.
The evil that men do lives after them,
The good is oft interrèd with their bones;
So let it be with Caesar. The noble Brutus
Hath told you Caesar was ambitious.
If it were so, it was a grievous fault,
And grievously hath Caesar answered° it.
Here, under leave of Brutus and the rest
(For Brutus is an honorable man,
So are they all, all honorable men),
Come I to speak in Caesar's funeral.
He was my friend, faithful and just to me;
But Brutus says he was ambitious,
And Brutus is an honorable man.
He hath brought many captives home to Rome,
Whose ransoms did the general coffers° fill;
Did this in Caesar seem ambitious?
When that the poor have cried, Caesar hath wept;
Ambition should be made of sterner stuff.
Yet Brutus says he was ambitious;
And Brutus is an honorable man.
You all did see that on the Lupercal

? Staging the Play
73. *An important question: Where would you place Caesar's body so that Antony can use it most effectively? Be sure to perform this famous funeral oration. What different tones do you hear in Antony's* ***monologue****?*

80. answered: paid the penalty for.

89. general coffers: public funds.

? Staging the Play
93. *Remember that the crowd is pressing in on Antony. What movements or sounds would they make as Antony says things that are meant to sway their feelings?*

Content-Area Connections

Social Science: Political Oratory
Critic Rosalie L. Colie sums up the political oratory of Brutus and Antony: "[Antony's] rhetoric is active, emotional, moving and ultimately victorious over the relatively more neutral, more correct rhetoric of his opponent. The tricks of irony and sensationalism in Antony's repertory win over the fickle, casual populace, with important political results. But we must realize how *political* both men are, how they both use forensic oratory as a political weapon . . . Brutus seeking to damp down, Antony to stoke the potential fires of popular wrath."
Individual activity. Invite students to respond in an essay to this analysis of the funeral orations. As to the success of each speech, ask them to consider the order of the speakers, reminding them that crowds often are most roused by what they hear last.

822 Chapter 10 Drama • Evaluating an Argument

I thrice presented him a kingly crown,
Which he did thrice refuse. Was this ambition?
Yet Brutus says he was ambitious;
And sure he is an honorable man.
I speak not to disprove what Brutus spoke,
But here I am to speak what I do know.
You all did love him once, not without cause;
What cause withholds you then to mourn for him?
O judgment, thou art fled to brutish beasts,
And men have lost their reason! Bear with me;
My heart is in the coffin there with Caesar,
And I must pause till it come back to me.

First Plebeian.
Methinks there is much reason in his sayings.

Second Plebeian.
If thou consider rightly of the matter,
Caesar has had great wrong.

Third Plebeian. Has he, masters?
I fear there will a worse come in his place.

Fourth Plebeian.
Marked ye his words? He would not take the crown,
Therefore 'tis certain he was not ambitious.

First Plebeian.
If it be found so, some will dear abide it.°

Second Plebeian.
Poor soul, his eyes are red as fire with weeping.

Third Plebeian.
There's not a nobler man in Rome than Antony.

Fourth Plebeian.
Now mark him, he begins again to speak.

Antony.
But yesterday the word of Caesar might
Have stood against the world; now lies he there,
And none so poor to° do him reverence.
O masters! If I were disposed to stir
Your hearts and minds to mutiny and rage,
I should do Brutus wrong and Cassius wrong,
Who, you all know, are honorable men.

Staging the Play
107. *What do lines 106–107 mean? What could Antony be doing at this point, as our attention is drawn again to the crowd?*

114. dear abide it: pay dearly for it.

120. so poor to: so low in rank as to.

DIRECT TEACHING

D Reading Skills

Analyzing. Why do you think Antony singles out Brutus and not Cassius or others as the target of his attack? [Possible response: Antony targets Brutus for the same reason that Cassius chose him to lead the coup—because the coup's success rests on Brutus's reputation.]

E Literary Focus
GRADE-LEVEL STANDARD

Turning point. What do the plebeians' comments suggest about how the play's turning point will affect its falling action? [Possible response: The comments suggest that the populace will side with Antony and against Brutus, thus putting Brutus and the conspirators on the defensive in the play's falling action.]

F Literary Focus
GRADE-LEVEL STANDARD

Turning point. Why does Antony say that he will not wrong Brutus and Cassius? [He has promised Brutus not to blame the conspirators.] What does he intend to do at this dramatic turning point? [His strategy is to pretend to honor the conspirators while insinuating that they are murdering traitors.]

Response to Margin Question

Line 107. Antony has supposedly been overcome with grief and must regain his composure. He could weep, turn his back, or lean against the coffin.

DIFFERENTIATING INSTRUCTION

Advanced Learners
Enrichment. Encourage students to find out more about significant persuasive oratory from history. Suggest they investigate speeches by Sojourner Truth, Susan B. Anthony, Mohandas (Mahatma) Gandhi, Winston Churchill, Franklin D. Roosevelt, John F. Kennedy, Barbara Jordan, and Martin Luther King, Jr. In analyzing these speeches, students should identify elements that made the speech important, such as appeals to emotion, imagery, allusions, rhetorical repetition, and figures of speech.
Activity. Invite individual students or pairs of students to present a historic speech to the class. Students should first introduce the speech by giving some information about its historical context. Then, they can read the speech (or recite it from memory) and describe some of the effects the speech had on its audience and on events in its historical period.

DIRECT TEACHING

Ⓐ Learners Having Difficulty

Questioning. Why does Antony mention the will if he does not mean to read it? [Clearly, Antony wants to read the will, and by mentioning its contents, he hopes to raise the people's curiosity and provoke them to make him read it.]

Ⓑ Reading Skills

Paraphrasing. How would you paraphrase Antony's words? [Possible response: It's not wise that you know how much Caesar loved you. You're humans, not sticks or stones. If you knew Caesar's will, you'd go crazy. It's better that you don't know what he left you. If you did, what would happen?]

Ⓒ Literary Focus GRADE-LEVEL STANDARD

Dramatic action. What is suggested by Antony's coming down to join the plebeians in a ring around Caesar's corpse? [Possible response: It shows that Antony and the commoners are uniting around their fallen leader and against the conspirators.]

Responses to Margin Questions

Line 137. Antony has implied that Caesar's will contains evidence of his love for the people.

Line 146. Antony primes the mob to react with anger after hearing Caesar's bequest. An actor could show Antony's scheming by overacting the "sincerity." He could also make his pauses long so that the mob begs him to continue.

Line 152. Responses will vary. Have students consider how the choice affects the remainder of Antony's speech in this scene and the audience's opinion of Antony for the rest of the play.

I will not do them wrong; I rather choose
To wrong the dead, to wrong myself and you,
Than I will wrong such honorable men.
But here's a parchment with the seal of Caesar; Ⓐ
I found it in his closet; 'tis his will.
Let but the commons hear this testament,
Which, pardon me, I do not mean to read,
And they would go and kiss dead Caesar's wounds,
And dip their napkins° in his sacred blood;
Yea, beg a hair of him for memory,
And dying, mention it within their wills,
Bequeathing it as a rich legacy
Unto their issue.°

Fourth Plebeian.
We'll hear the will; read it, Mark Antony.

All. The will, the will! We will hear Caesar's will!

Antony.
Have patience, gentle friends, I must not read it.
It is not meet you know how Caesar loved you. Ⓑ
You are not wood, you are not stones, but men;
And being men, hearing the will of Caesar,
It will inflame you, it will make you mad.
'Tis good you know not that you are his heirs;
For if you should, O, what would come of it?

Fourth Plebeian.
Read the will! We'll hear it, Antony!
You shall read us the will, Caesar's will!

Antony.
Will you be patient? Will you stay awhile?
I have o'ershot myself° to tell you of it.
I fear I wrong the honorable men
Whose daggers have stabbed Caesar; I do fear it.

Fourth Plebeian.
They were traitors. Honorable men!

All. The will! The testament!

Second Plebeian. They were villains, murderers! The will!
Read the will!

Antony.
You will compel me then to read the will? Ⓒ
Then make a ring about the corpse of Caesar,
And let me show you him that made the will.
Shall I descend? And will you give me leave?

All. Come down.

---

133. napkins: handkerchiefs.

137. issue: children; heirs.

? **137.** *Antony says he is not going to read the will, but what has he already implied about its contents?*

? **Staging the Play**
146. *Again, how has Antony scored his point indirectly? How could an actor play Antony in this scene to make him seem manipulative?*

150. o'ershot myself: gone farther than I intended.

? **Staging the Play**
152. *The irony here is so obvious that an actor playing Antony must make a choice about how to say these lines: Will he continue his pretense of honoring Caesar's assassins, or will he finally drop this pose and speak with obviously scathing sarcasm?*

CONTENT-AREA CONNECTIONS

History/Architecture: The Roman Forum

Small-group activity. The Roman Forum was a place of architectural grandeur, political action, and public importance. Encourage groups of three or four students to research and report on the Forum, the setting for most of Act III. Ask them to describe its purpose in Roman life and some of the activities and events that occurred there. Some groups might also draw a picture or make a scale model of the Forum, while others might design a kind of U.S. Forum that would serve the needs of a contemporary community in this country.

824 Chapter 10 Drama • Evaluating an Argument

Second Plebeian. Descend.

[ANTONY *comes down.*]

Third Plebeian. You shall have leave.
Fourth Plebeian. A ring! Stand round.
First Plebeian.
Stand from the hearse, stand from the body!
Second Plebeian.
Room for Antony, most noble Antony!
Antony.
Nay, press not so upon me; stand far off.
All. Stand back! Room! Bear back.
Antony.
If you have tears, prepare to shed them now.
You all do know this mantle; I remember
The first time ever Caesar put it on:
'Twas on a summer's evening, in his tent,
That day he overcame the Nervii.°
Look, in this place ran Cassius' dagger through;
See what a rent the envious° Casca made;

Staging the Play
168. *How do you visualize the placement of the actors at this point? Where is Caesar's body?*

Staging the Play
169. *Watch for clues that tell what Antony is doing for effect as he delivers this speech. What is he holding in line 170?*

173. Nervii: one of the tribes conquered by Caesar, in 57 B.C.

175. envious: spiteful.

DIRECT TEACHING

D Reading Skills

Evaluating. How do you know Antony is making up this information about the stab wounds to further vilify the conspirators? [Antony was not present at the assassination, so he would have no way of knowing this information.]

Responses to Margin Questions

Line 168. The actors are ringed about Antony and the corpse. Caesar's body is now center stage.
Line 169. Antony is holding Caesar's cloak or toga.

DIFFERENTIATING INSTRUCTION

Learners Having Difficulty

If you are showing a video of a movie version of *Julius Caesar,* many learners might benefit from seeing Act III of the tragedy at this time. Point out actor's gestures, delivery of lines, staging, and so on to help students get a grasp on the meaning of the play, especially the drama stemming from its turning point. Then, have students continue reading Act III, and ask them to compare the film version to images they had formed in their imagination.

The Tragedy of Julius Caesar, Act III, Scene 2 825

Direct Teaching

A Literary Focus
GRADE-LEVEL STANDARD

? Dramatic dialogue. What shift has Antony made in the style and tone of his verbal attack on Brutus? [Possible response: Antony has gone from veiled implications and verbal irony to bluntly defaming Brutus as heartless and ungrateful.]

B Literary Focus
GRADE-LEVEL STANDARD

? Turning point. Some critics view the moment in Antony's speech when the mob turns on the conspirators as the turning point. Why might this be the turning point? [The people are excited to the point of frenzy against the conspirators, and the fortunes of Brutus and Cassius are going to fall.]

C Reading Skills

? Recognizing persuasive techniques. Brutus has already given his reasons for assassinating Caesar. Why does Antony say he doesn't know "what private griefs" motivated the conspirators? [With this comment, Antony reduces Brutus's high-minded civic principles to mere personal animosity toward Caesar.]

Responses to Margin Questions

Line 193. The people are crying.
Line 197. Antony may be pointing to the wounds on Caesar's body.
Line 215. Yes. Brutus has given his reasons, but Antony implies that the conspirators have "private griefs."

Through this the well-belovèd Brutus stabbed,
And as he plucked his cursèd steel away,
Mark how the blood of Caesar followed it,
As rushing out of doors, to be resolved
If Brutus so unkindly knocked, or no;
For Brutus, as you know, was Caesar's angel.
Judge, O you gods, how dearly Caesar loved him!
This was the most unkindest cut of all;
For when the noble Caesar saw him stab,
Ingratitude, more strong than traitors' arms,
Quite vanquished him. Then burst his mighty heart;
And, in his mantle muffling up his face,
Even at the base of Pompey's statue°
(Which all the while ran blood) great Caesar fell.
O, what a fall was there, my countrymen!
Then I, and you, and all of us fell down,
Whilst bloody treason flourished over us.
O, now you weep, and I perceive you feel
The dint° of pity; these are gracious drops.
Kind souls, what weep you when you but behold
Our Caesar's vesture° wounded? Look you here,
Here is himself, marred as you see with traitors.

First Plebeian. O piteous spectacle!
Second Plebeian. O noble Caesar!
Third Plebeian. O woeful day!
Fourth Plebeian. O traitors, villains!
First Plebeian. O most bloody sight!
Second Plebeian. We will be revenged.
All. Revenge! About! Seek! Burn! Fire! Kill! Slay! Let not a traitor live!
Antony. Stay, countrymen.
First Plebeian. Peace there! Hear the noble Antony.
Second Plebeian. We'll hear him, we'll follow him, we'll die with him!

Antony.
Good friends, sweet friends, let me not stir you up
To such a sudden flood of mutiny.
They that have done this deed are honorable.
What private griefs° they have, alas, I know not,
That made them do it. They are wise and honorable,
And will, no doubt, with reasons answer you.
I come not, friends, to steal away your hearts;
I am no orator, as Brutus is;

188. statue: pronounced in three syllables.

? Staging the Play
193. *What is the crowd doing as Antony speaks?*

194. dint: stroke.

196. vesture: clothing.

? Staging the Play
197. *What has Antony done with the body now?*

213. griefs: grievances.

? 215. *Notice that Antony implies that reasons have not already been given. Have they?*

826 Chapter 10 Drama • Evaluating an Argument

CONTENT-AREA CONNECTIONS

History: Caesar's Funeral

In devising the great Forum scene, Shakespeare had only the slightest information of what actually occurred at Caesar's funeral. The historian Plutarch described the funeral this way: "Afterwards, when Caesar's body was brought into the market place, Antonius making his funeral oration in praise of the dead, according to the ancient custom of Rome, and perceiving that his words moved the common people to compassion, he framed his eloquence to make their hearts yearn the more; and taking Caesar's gown all bloody in his hand, he laid it open to the sight of them all, showing what a number of cuts and holes it had upon it. Therewithal the people fell presently into such a rage and mutiny, that there was no more order kept among the common people."

Direct Teaching

A Literary Focus
GRADE-LEVEL STANDARD

Dramatic dialogue. Would you agree with Antony that he is someone who does not have "the power of speech / To stir men's blood"? [Possible response: No, he knows he is doing just that, having proved himself a skillful orator able to move people to action.]

B Literary Focus
GRADE-LEVEL STANDARD

Turning point. The play's rising action has reached a crisis. What does this turning point suggest for the fortunes of Brutus and the conspirators in the play's falling action? [The plebeians' violent anger suggests that Brutus and company will face great odds in the play's falling action.]

C Reading Skills

Analyzing. Why does Antony remind the crowd about the will? [Possible responses: Antony has already won over the crowd, but he wants to make absolutely certain they are devoted to him and his cause; he wants to further incite their anger.]

Responses to Margin Questions

Line 223. Antony characterizes himself as a plain speaker and Brutus as an orator. Because his motive is, in fact, to "stir men's blood," he wants the mob to believe that Brutus is devious and self-serving.
Line 230. The key word is *mutiny.*
Line 238. Possible responses: Antony sees them as gullible, as a tool for his ends. Some students may also think he shares some of Caesar's warm feeling for the populace.

But (as you know me all) a plain blunt man
That love my friend, and that they know full well
That gave me public leave to speak of him.
A For I have neither writ, nor words, nor worth,
Action, nor utterance, nor the power of speech
To stir men's blood; I only speak right on.
I tell you that which you yourselves do know,
Show you sweet Caesar's wounds, poor poor dumb mouths,
And bid them speak for me. But were I Brutus,
And Brutus Antony, there were an Antony
Would ruffle up your spirits, and put a tongue
In every wound of Caesar that would move
The stones of Rome to rise and mutiny.

All.
We'll mutiny.

B **First Plebeian.** We'll burn the house of Brutus.

Third Plebeian.
Away, then! Come, seek the conspirators.

Antony.
Yet hear me, countrymen. Yet hear me speak.

All.
Peace, ho! Hear Antony, most noble Antony!

Antony.
Why, friends, you go to do you know not what:
Wherein hath Caesar thus deserved your loves?
Alas, you know not; I must tell you then:
C You have forgot the will I told you of.

All.
Most true, the will! Let's stay and hear the will.

Antony.
Here is the will, and under Caesar's seal.
To every Roman citizen he gives,
To every several° man, seventy-five drachmas.°

Second Plebeian.
Most noble Caesar! We'll revenge his death!

Third Plebeian. O royal Caesar!

Antony. Hear me with patience.

All. Peace, ho!

Antony.
Moreover, he hath left you all his walks,
His private arbors, and new-planted orchards,
On this side Tiber; he hath left them you,
And to your heirs forever: common pleasures,°

? **223.** *How does Antony characterize himself, as compared with Brutus? What is his motive?*

? **230.** *Again, the irony is obvious here. What is the key word in Antony's* ***monologue****?*

? **238.** *Notice how many times the mob goes to run off and how Antony pulls it back again. How do you think Antony feels about this herd of people he has so cleverly manipulated?*

242. several: individual. **drachmas** (drak′məs): silver coins (Greek currency).

250. common pleasures: public recreation areas.

Content-Area Connections

Mathematics: Roman Currency

Individual activity. As part of his will, Caesar bequeathed each free Roman seventy-five drachmas. Ask interested students to research the value of the drachma and its history as a unit of currency. Students should try to find out, for example, whether Rome had its own currency and why the Greek drachma would be the preferred form of currency.

Geography: The Tiber River

Individual activity. In his will, Caesar also bequeathed to the Romans land along the Tiber. Invite interested students to research the path of the Tiber River and describe its importance to life in central Italy and specifically Rome. Students may compare statistics on the Tiber with those of a U.S. river, such as the Mississippi, the Missouri, the Ohio, or the Hudson.

828 Chapter 10 Drama • Evaluating an Argument

To walk abroad and recreate yourselves.
Here was a Caesar! When comes such another?

First Plebeian.
Never, never! Come, away, away!
We'll burn his body in the holy place,
And with the brands fire the traitors' houses.
Take up the body.

Second Plebeian. Go fetch fire.

Third Plebeian. Pluck down benches.

Fourth Plebeian. Pluck down forms, windows,° anything!

[*Exeunt* PLEBEIANS *with the body.*]

Antony.
Now let it work: Mischief, thou art afoot,
Take thou what course thou wilt.

[*Enter* SERVANT.]

How now, fellow?

Servant.
Sir, Octavius is already come to Rome.

Antony. Where is he?

Servant.
He and Lepidus are at Caesar's house.

Antony.
And thither will I straight to visit him;
He comes upon a wish. Fortune is merry,
And in this mood will give us anything.

Servant.
I heard him say, Brutus and Cassius
Are rid° like madmen through the gates of Rome.

Antony.
Belike° they had some notice of the people,
How I had moved them. Bring me to Octavius.

[*Exeunt.*]

SCENE 3. *A street.*

Enter CINNA *the poet, and after him the* PLEBEIANS.

Cinna.
I dreamt tonight that I did feast with Caesar,
And things unluckily charge my fantasy.°

259. forms, windows: long benches and shutters.

Staging the Play
260. *Antony is alone onstage. The noise of the mob dies off in the distance. We might in some productions see the reflection of flames and hear the sounds of rioting. How should Antony speak these lines?*

269. Are rid: have ridden.

269. *What have Brutus and Cassius done?*

270. Belike: probably.

2. That is, events unluckily fill his imagination (with ominous ideas).

DIRECT TEACHING

D Literary Focus
GRADE-LEVEL STANDARD

Dramatic dialogue. What is Mark Antony saying here? [Possible response: I've set this turmoil in motion. Now let it take its own course.] **What does the couplet reveal about Antony's motives?** [He wanted all along to incite the mob against the conspirators.]

E Reading Skills

Evaluating. Do you think the oratorical methods Antony used to move the people were unscrupulous? Why or why not? [Possible responses: Yes, Antony was unscrupulous because he did not follow the spirit of the rules that he and Brutus discussed; like a demagogue, Antony manipulated the Romans to advance his own agenda. No, he was not unscrupulous because he loved Caesar and could not have persuaded the people within the limitations forced on him by Brutus.]

F Content-Area Connections

History: Cinna
The poet Gains Helvius Cinna, some of whose verse survives today, was actually a friend of Caesar's and was in the street leading to the funeral. The conspirator's name was Lucius Cornelius Cinna.

Responses to Margin Questions

Line 260. He should sound triumphant and ready for action.
Line 269. They have fled the city.

The Tragedy of Julius Caesar, Act III, Scene 3 829

DIRECT TEACHING

A Literary Focus
GRADE-LEVEL STANDARD

Dramatic dialogue. With this dialogue, how does Shakespeare begin to show the breakdown in Rome's social order? [Possible response: He has plebeians, now a vigilante mob, threateningly questioning citizens in the street.]

B Literary Focus
REVIEW STANDARD

Symbol. What might the horrible death of Cinna the poet symbolize? [Possible response: Rome's fall into moral chaos and its loss of unity and integrity.]

C Reading Skills

Reading Shakespeare. What dramatic purpose does this brief final scene in Act III achieve? [Possible responses: The scene builds up excitement; it provides a sense of the immediate consequences of the assassination; it foreshadows the fall of the conspirators.]

Responses to Margin Questions

Line 31. Possible responses: The comedy relieves some of the tension that has been building through the play; by using the poet as the butt of a joke, Shakespeare shows self-mocking wit.
Line 38. They have killed Cinna.

I have no will to wander forth of doors,
Yet something leads me forth.

First Plebeian. What is your name?

Second Plebeian. Whither are you going?

Third Plebeian. Where do you dwell?

Fourth Plebeian. Are you a married man or a bachelor?

Second Plebeian. Answer every man directly.

First Plebeian. Ay, and briefly.

Fourth Plebeian. Ay, and wisely.

Third Plebeian. Ay, and truly, you were best.

Cinna. What is my name? Whither am I going? Where do I dwell? Am I a married man or a bachelor? Then, to answer every man directly and briefly, wisely and truly: wisely I say, I am a bachelor.

Second Plebeian. That's as much as to say, they are fools that marry; you'll bear me a bang° for that, I fear. Proceed directly.

Cinna. Directly, I am going to Caesar's funeral.

First Plebeian. As a friend or an enemy?

Cinna. As a friend.

Second Plebeian. That matter is answered directly.

Fourth Plebeian. For your dwelling, briefly.

Cinna. Briefly, I dwell by the Capitol.

Third Plebeian. Your name, sir, truly.

Cinna. Truly, my name is Cinna.

First Plebeian. Tear him to pieces! He's a conspirator.

Cinna. I am Cinna the poet! I am Cinna the poet!

Fourth Plebeian. Tear him for his bad verses! Tear him for his bad verses!

Cinna. I am not Cinna the conspirator.

Fourth Plebeian. It is no matter, his name's Cinna; pluck but his name out of his heart, and turn him going.°

Third Plebeian. Tear him, tear him!

[They attack him.]

Come, brands, ho! Firebrands! To Brutus', to Cassius'! Burn all! Some to Decius' house, and some to Casca's; some to Ligarius'! Away, go!

[Exeunt all the PLEBEIANS *with* CINNA.*]*

18. bear me a bang: get a blow from me.

31. *What is the function of this scene, with its bit of* ***comedy*** *at this point in the play?*

34. turn him going: send him packing.

Staging the Play
38. *What has the mob done to the innocent poet Cinna? Try performing this chilling mob scene, perhaps using a chorus for the plebeians' lines.*

FAMILY/COMMUNITY ACTIVITY

Try to involve the whole class in conducting a forum called "Political Instability: The Relevance of *Julius Caesar.*" Begin by assigning a group of students the task of rendering dramatic readings of key speeches surrounding the planning of the assassination, the assassination itself, and the ensuing political conflict in the play. Have another group offer analysis of the speeches, focusing on paraphrasing and character motivation, such as the desire for power, manipulation of the masses, and so on. Invite a third group to research nations in the world that have recently experienced violent coups and political instability. Ask them to look for parallels to the Rome of *Julius Caesar* and to focus on one or two countries where political problems have resulted in significant human suffering. Each group should then rehearse the oral presentation of their material. You might stage-manage the forum so that the material is presented in a logical order that best connects the political drama of the play to the real-life current events. Stage the forum in the school auditorium, and invite parents and other members of the community. Encourage students to offer a question-and-answer period in which solutions to world political problems are explored.

A Closer Look

Roman Government: Rule by the Rich

Roman politics often resembled a theatrical production, complete with performers and an audience. The Forum was the stage, the politicians were the actors, and citizens from all social classes came to watch the show. Assemblies, elections, and trials were held outdoors. Noisy crowds often booed and heckled the politicians.

With the abolition of the monarchy in 509 B.C., the Roman republic was established. (A *republic* is a state in which power is vested in the citizens, who are entitled to vote; they elect representatives, who govern on behalf of the citizens.) Yet a huge gap continued to exist between rich and poor, and for centuries only the rich were allowed to hold public office. Some of the wealthiest members of society were members of the Senate, which controlled Rome's domestic and foreign affairs. Not until more than two hundred years after the Roman republic was established were a select few from the lower classes allowed to enter politics.

D According to Marcus Cicero (106–43 B.C.), orator, philosopher, and senator, "the difficulty of devising policy has caused the transfer of power from a king to a group, and the ignorance and rashness of the masses have caused its transfer from the many to the few." His words affirm his belief in the ignorance of the "lower classes," a prejudice common among members of the privileged classes at the time.

The United States is a representative democracy, or a republic, in which citizens elect others to make public-policy decisions for them in assemblies instead of attending the assemblies and making their own decisions, as Roman citizens did. The Roman republic, however, was a direct democracy, not an indirect or representative one. In Rome eligible voters could attend assemblies, vote on legislation, and elect government officials. However, Rome was the only place where voting was authorized, so many citizens could not exercise their voting rights because they had neither the time nor the money to travel from their homes to Rome.

E In Rome, legislation was proposed, formulated, and discussed by the Senate and then presented to the assemblies for approval. Because the upper classes controlled the Senate, they controlled all legislation. Even though each citizen had the right to vote on every issue, the Roman republic wasn't an ideal democracy. Lacking the guiding principle of government of the people, for the people, and by the people, it amounted to rule by the aristocracy, which served the interests of the elite while pretending to give voice to the populace.

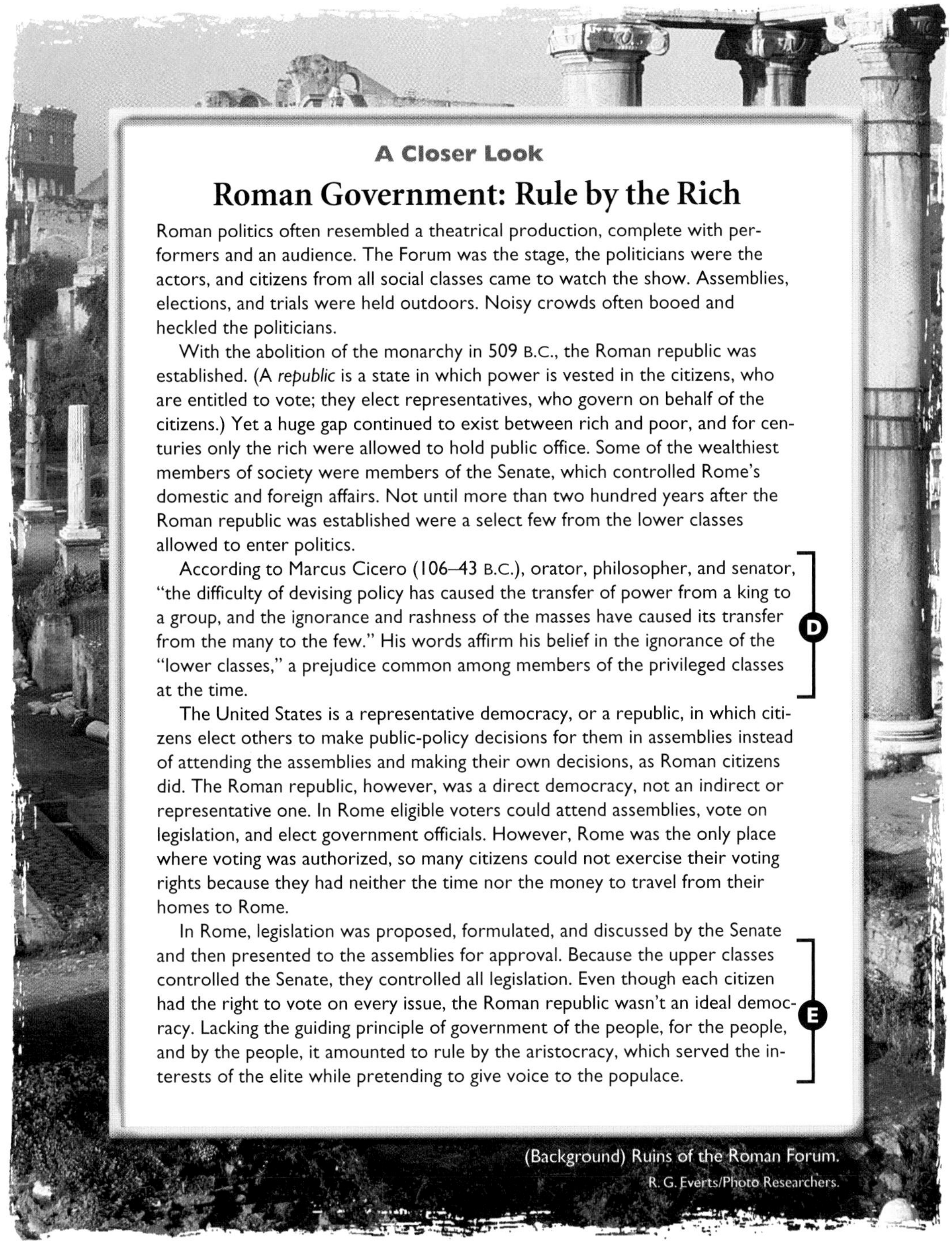

(Background) Ruins of the Roman Forum.
R. G. Everts/Photo Researchers.

A CLOSER LOOK

Roman politics unfolded at the Forum, where leaders legislated before lively crowds from all social classes. From 509 B.C., Rome was a republic, with power vested in its citizens. For centuries, however, only the wealthiest citizens could be senators, and a huge gap persisted between rich and poor. Marcus Cicero, the Roman statesman, attributed this classist inequity to the "ignorance and rashness of the masses." Unlike the United States, a representative democracy, the Roman republic was a direct democracy in which eligible citizens could vote on legislation. But this privilege occurred only in Rome, excluding most citizens from outside the city. Still, the major inequity stemmed from control of the Senate by the wealthy, which made Rome an aristocracy posing as a republic.

DIRECT TEACHING

D Reading Skills

Making connections. How is this attitude of Rome's ruling class toward commoners reflected in *Julius Caesar*? [Possible response: in Antony's manipulation of the masses in Act III, which results in their rash and violent outburst.]

E Reading Skills

Finding the main idea. What is the main idea of this paragraph and of the essay? [Rome was ruled by the rich.] Where else is this idea conveyed? [in the title and in the second and third paragraphs]

DIFFERENTIATING INSTRUCTION

Learners Having Difficulty

Write the word *republic* on the chalkboard, and ask students what images and ideas the word brings to mind. [Possible responses: the U.S. flag; the Pledge of Allegiance; voting.] Review the fact that representative government is a key characteristic of a republic. Then, have students read the feature and write a paragraph stating the aspects of ancient Roman rule that did not uphold the principles of a republic.

Advanced Learners

Individual activity. Students may wish to research information about the role of lobbyists on Washington's Capitol Hill and the considerable influence that campaign contributors have sometimes been able to wield in the nation's political arenas. Research should include descriptions of legislation that limits the behavior of lobbyists and the legal amounts of campaign contributions.

The Tragedy of Julius Caesar, Act III 831

INDEPENDENT PRACTICE

Literary Response and Analysis

Act III

Reading Check

1. Caesar makes a show of saying he will read Artemidorus's message last.
2. Cassius is afraid Antony will turn the people against them. Brutus says that he will justify the killing first and then allow Antony only to honor Caesar.
3. Antony is the protagonist, and he wants to avenge Caesar. Cassius's warning prepares us for this development.
4. He willed each citizen seventy-five drachmas and land. They turn on the conspirators.
5. The plebeians kill the poet Cinna for having the same name as the conspirator Cinna.

Interpretations

6. Brutus treats Antony with high-minded dignity and naive trust; Cassius shows skepticism.
7. Antony vows the assassins will pay with their lives. The speech foreshadows conflict.
8. Cassius warns Brutus not to allow Antony to speak at Caesar's funeral, but Brutus fails to heed the advice.
9. Loaded words include "my friend, faithful and just to me" (l. 85); "the poor have cried, Caesar hath wept" (l. 91); "My heart is in the coffin there with Caesar" (l. 106). The appeal built on repetition is Antony's ironic refrain about Brutus claiming Caesar was "ambitious" and Brutus being an "honorable man."
10. According to Brutus, Antony is given "to wildness, and much company" and lacks Caesar's drive and intelligence. Caesar admires Antony's carousing but also values his opinion. Only Cassius sees Antony as shrewd, devious, and dangerously loyal to Caesar. Most students will agree with Cassius, given Antony's behavior in Act III.
11. Some students may say the assassination, since it could have failed; others may point to Brutus's decision, since it allowed Antony to turn the people against the conspirators.
12. The lines suggest that this event will be dramatized often—as Shakespeare himself is doing.

Evaluation

13. Students who agree with Antony may say that Brutus overreacted; students who identify with Brutus might suggest that Antony has little regard for the republic and, like Caesar, is power hungry. Most will deem Antony's speech more persuasive.

Literary Response and Analysis

Act III

Reading Check

1. In Scene I, a chance still exists that the conspiracy might be foiled. Why does Artemidorus fail to get Caesar to read his warning?
2. In Scene I, why does Cassius argue against allowing Antony to speak at Caesar's funeral? What reasons does Brutus give for overruling him?
3. After the assassination the **protagonist** appears—the main character, who drives the rest of the play. Who is this person, and what does he want? How have we been prepared for his appearance?
4. What information concerning Caesar's will does Antony disclose to the crowd in Scene 2? How does the crowd react?
5. What do the plebeians do in Scene 3?

Reading Standard 3.1 Articulate the relationship between the expressed purposes and the characteristics of different forms of dramatic literature (e.g., tragedy).

Reading Standard 3.10 Identify and describe the function of dialogue, soliloquies, asides, and character foils in dramatic literature.

Interpretations

6. Explain how Brutus and Cassius act as **character foils** (contrasting characters) in their responses to Antony in Scene I.
7. How does Antony's **soliloquy** at the end of Scene I (lines 254–275) indicate his intentions regarding the assassins? What could this speech **foreshadow,** or hint at?
8. An **aside** is a speech or remark spoken by a character to the audience or to another character onstage that others onstage are not supposed to hear. Why is the aside that Cassius makes to Brutus in Scene I before Antony's speech important?
9. One of the great examples of **persuasive oratory** is found in Act III, Scene 2, lines 73–107, in which Antony changes the mood of the mob. What specific **emotional appeals** does Antony use? Find, for example, uses of **loaded words** (words with strong emotional overtones) and **repetition.**
10. Until Act III, Antony has barely figured in the play. How have others **characterized** him? Do you agree? Why?
11. The third act of a Shakespearean **tragedy** usually contains the **turning point,** the moment when all the action of the play begins to spiral toward the **tragic ending.** Which of the following events do you think is the turning point in this **tragedy**? Why?
    - the assassination of Caesar
    - Brutus's decision to allow Antony to address the crowd
12. Lines 111–118 of Scene I suggest that the conspirators' deed will be "acted over," or repeated, "many ages hence." What meaning do you think Shakespeare intended in these lines?

Evaluation

13. Whose funeral speech—Brutus's or Antony's—comes closer to expressing your own thoughts about Caesar's death? Whose speech is more powerfully persuasive? Support your view.

Writing

Behind the Scenes

We never again see the cobbler from Act I. Suppose the shoemaker is in the crowd that listens to Brutus and Antony, carries away Caesar's body, and then attacks the poet Cinna. Write a **new scene** in which the shoemaker and another character talk about the events of the ides of March. Perform your **dialogue.**

832 Chapter 10 Drama • Evaluating an Argument

Reading Skills

Paraphrasing: Your Own Words

When you **paraphrase** a passage, you express all of its ideas in your own words. (A paraphrase is different from a **summary,** which expresses only the main ideas.) Look at Caesar's speech and its paraphrase:

SPEECH

Caesar.
Thy brother by decree is banishèd.
If thou dost bend and pray and fawn for him,
I spurn thee like a cur out of my way.
—Act III, Scene 1, lines 44–46

PARAPHRASE

Your brother is banished by law. If you lower yourself to grovel and beg for him, I'll treat you like a dog and kick you out of my way.

PRACTICE

Read the following passages in their contexts in the play. Then, **paraphrase** every idea in each passage below:

1. **Antony.**
That I did love thee, Caesar, O, 'tis true!
If then thy spirit look upon us now,
Shall it not grieve thee dearer than thy death
To see thy Antony making his peace,
Shaking the bloody fingers of thy foes,
Most noble, in the presence of thy corse?
—Act III, Scene 1, lines 194–199

2. **Antony.**
Friends, Romans, countrymen, lend me your ears;
I come to bury Caesar, not to praise him.
The evil that men do lives after them,
The good is oft interrèd with their bones . . .
—Act III, Scene 2, lines 73–76

Mark Antony.
Roman sculpture.
Museum of the Vatican, Rome, Italy.

Reading Skills

Practice

Possible Answers

1. I loved you Caesar—that's true. If your spirit sees me now, making peace with your noble enemies and shaking their bloody hands in the presence of your corpse, won't my betrayal hurt you even more than your death?
2. Friends, Romans, fellow citizens, please listen to me. I'm here to bury Caesar, not to praise him. When people die, it's their bad deeds that are remembered; their good deeds are often forgotten.

ASSESSING

Assessment

- *Progress Assessment of Reading*
  - Selection Test

RETEACHING

For a lesson reteaching Standard 3.1, see **Reteaching,** p. 939A. For another selection to teach Standard 3.1, see *Interactive Reading,* Chapter 10.

READING SKILLS REVIEW

Activity. Have students read and paraphrase the following passages from Act III: (1) Caesar's words to the senators in Scene 1, ll. 58–62, and (2) Antony's address to the plebeians in Scene 2, ll. 224–230. [Possible responses: (1) Your pleas might affect me if I were as emotional as you; but I am as unchangeable as the Northern Star, which, unlike any other star in the sky, keeps to its fixed position. (2) I am only telling you what you already know and asking Caesar's pitiful wounds—silent as they are—to speak for themselves. But if I were a smooth-tongued orator like Brutus, I could stir you! I could make the very wounds on Caesar's body shout so loudly that even the stones of Rome would rise and mutiny!]

ACT IV

SCENE 1. *A house in Rome.*

Enter ANTONY, OCTAVIUS, *and* LEPIDUS.

Antony.
These many then shall die; their names are pricked.

Octavius.
Your brother too must die; consent you, Lepidus?

Lepidus.
I do consent—

Octavius. Prick him down, Antony.

Lepidus.
Upon condition Publius shall not live,
Who is your sister's son, Mark Antony.

Antony.
He shall not live; look, with a spot I damn him.
But, Lepidus, go you to Caesar's house;
Fetch the will hither, and we shall determine
How to cut off some charge in legacies.°

Lepidus.
What, shall I find you here?

Octavius.
Or here or at the Capitol. [*Exit* LEPIDUS.]

Antony.
This is a slight unmeritable man,
Meet to be sent on errands; is it fit,
The threefold world° divided, he should stand
One of the three to share it?°

Octavius. So you thought him,

9. In other words, cut down on some of the expenses by changing the legacies.

14. threefold world: three parts of the Roman Empire: Europe, Asia, and Africa.

15. Antony, Octavius, and Lepidus now govern the Roman Empire as a triumvirate, or three-member ruling body.

"... WE ARE AT THE STAKE,
AND BAYED ABOUT WITH
MANY ENEMIES ..."

Summary at grade level

Act IV

Scene 1 opens in Rome. Antony, Octavius, and Lepidus now rule as a triumvirate, but not without conflict. When Antony and Octavius learn that the exiled Brutus and Cassius have raised armies, they combine forces to meet the challengers.

In the brief Scene 2, Brutus and Cassius exchange grievances. Brutus suggests they go to his tent to avoid arguing before their soldiers.

In Scene 3, both men unleash a flood of emotions that charges the scene and the play's falling action with dramatic intensity. The quarrel, in which Brutus accuses Cassius of corruption, is eventually reconciled. Brutus then dumbfounds Cassius by revealing that Portia's suicide has troubled his mind. Brutus devises a plan to advance to Philippi to meet the forces of Antony and Octavius. Before the night ends, however, Caesar's Ghost appears to Brutus chillingly warning, "thou shalt see me at Philippi."

DIRECT TEACHING

A Literary Focus
GRADE-LEVEL STANDARD

Dramatic dialogue. How does Shakespeare's dialogue dramatize the power of these three rulers? [Possible response: It shows the casual brutality with which the three men decide on who is to die.]

RESOURCES: READING

Media
- *Visual Connections*
  - Videocassette, Segment 10
- *Fine Art Transparencies*
  - Transparency 17

Reading
- *Interactive Reading,* Teacher's Edition
  - Graphic Organizer: Dramatic Elements Chart

Differentiating Instruction
- *Lesson Plans for Language Development*
  - English-Language Learners, pp. 345–347, 364, 371
  - Special Education Students, pp. 348, 364, 371

Assessment
- *Progress Assessment of Reading*
  - Selection Test
- *One-Stop Planner* CD-ROM with Test Generator

And took his voice° who should be pricked to die
In our black sentence and proscription.°

Antony.
Octavius, I have seen more days than you;
And though we lay these honors on this man,
To ease ourselves of divers sland'rous loads,°
He shall but bear them as the ass bears gold,
To groan and sweat under the business,
Either led or driven, as we point the way;
And having brought our treasure where we will,
Then take we down his load, and turn him off,
(Like to the empty ass) to shake his ears
And graze in commons.°

Octavius. You may do your will;
But he's a tried and valiant soldier.

Antony.
So is my horse, Octavius, and for that
I do appoint him store of provender.°
It is a creature that I teach to fight,
To wind, to stop, to run directly on,
His corporal motion governed by my spirit.
And, in some taste,° is Lepidus but so.
He must be taught, and trained, and bid go forth.
A barren-spirited fellow; one that feeds
On objects, arts, and imitations,
Which, out of use and staled by other men,
Begin his fashion.° Do not talk of him
But as a property.° And now, Octavius,
Listen great things. Brutus and Cassius
Are levying powers;° we must straight make head.°
Therefore let our alliance be combined,
Our best friends made, our means stretched;
And let us presently go sit in council
How covert matters may be best disclosed,
And open perils surest answerèd.

Octavius.
Let us do so; for we are at the stake,
And bayed about with many enemies;°
And some that smile have in their hearts, I fear,
Millions of mischiefs. [*Exeunt.*]

16. voice: vote.
17. proscription: death sentence. In Roman law a person under proscription could be killed by anyone, and the killer had no fear of murder charges being brought against him.

? **17.** *What details in this **dialogue** suggest that this triumvirate is showing signs of strain? How has Antony changed from the person we saw in Act III?*

20. divers sland'rous loads: blame that will be laid against them.

? **26.** *Who is compared to the ass?*

27. in commons: on pasture land that is commonly held, or shared by everyone.

30. appoint . . . provender: allot him a supply of food.

34. in some taste: in some measure.

39. In other words, he is always behind the times.
40. property: tool.

42. levying powers: gathering armies. **straight make head:** immediately gather troops.

49. A metaphor referring to the Elizabethan sport of bearbaiting, in which a bear was chained to a stake and attacked by dogs.

DIRECT TEACHING

B Literary Focus
REVIEW STANDARD

? **Character.** In Act III, Antony's guile and ruthlessness could be seen as the behavior of a vengeful man upset at the murder of his friend. What does this exchange suggest about Antony? [He can be backbiting, arrogant, and mean.] **How does Octavius come off in comparison?** [In defending Lepidus, Octavius seems more honorable.]

C Advanced Learners

? **Enrichment.** What earlier speech reflects this idea of using a person to enhance the moral appearance of a faction? [In Act II, Scene 1, ll. 144–149, Metellus suggests enlisting Cicero in the conspiracy, so "his silver hairs will purchase" the assassins a "good opinion."]

D Literary Focus
REVIEW STANDARD

? **Mood.** What mood do the triumvirate's discussions create in Scene 1? [Antony's decision to execute his relative, violate Caesar's will, and take advantage of Lepidus create a sinister mood.]

Responses to Margin Questions

Line 17. Antony insults Lepidus, and Octavius disagrees. Antony now seems disloyal and power hungry.
Line 26. Lepidus is compared to the ass.

DIFFERENTIATING INSTRUCTION

Learners Having Difficulty
Point out that Act IV will contain the play's falling action, the events that proceed from the turning point and lead us toward the resolution. To help students grasp this structure, say, "Imagine that the play's events are rising toward a peak called the turning point. In many movies this might be a heist, a kidnapping, or a murder. After this key act, nothing is the same. All the following events stem from that act, and often they head toward a kind of payback or justice. These subsequent events are the falling action."
Activity. Ask students to write a brief prediction of the falling action in Act IV.

English-Language Learners
For lessons designed for English-language learners and special education students, see *Lesson Plans for Language Development,* pp. 345–347, 348, 364, 371.

Advanced Learners
Acceleration. To move students toward the eleventh- and twelfth-grade Standard 3.3, have them analyze the effect of mood in Julius Caesar. They can write a brief essay that looks at how Shakespeare changes the mood on the falling action of Act IV.

The Tragedy of Julius Caesar, Act IV, Scene 1 835

DIRECT TEACHING

A Reading Skills

Paraphrasing. How would you paraphrase ll. 7–10? [Possible response: Because of some change in himself or people below him, Cassius has done some things that he shouldn't have. But since he is nearby, he will be able to justify these actions.]

B Reading Skills

Finding the main idea. What is the main point that Brutus makes in ll. 18–27? [Possible response: Brutus remarks that the formality that Cassius shows toward Lucius is a mask to hide the fact that Cassius no longer feels friendly toward him or Brutus. Brutus suggests that people who feign formality are hollow and will fail when challenged.]

Responses to Margin Questions

Stage direction. Antony turned the Roman masses against the assassins, so Brutus and Cassius had to flee for their life.

Line 18. Brutus is displeased with something that Cassius has done, and Cassius is only distantly courteous to Lucilius.

SCENE 2. *Camp near Sardis.*

Drum. Enter BRUTUS, LUCILIUS, LUCIUS, *and the* ARMY. TITINIUS *and* PINDARUS *meet them.*

Brutus. Stand ho!
Lucilius. Give the word, ho! and stand.
Brutus.
What now, Lucilius, is Cassius near?
Lucilius.
He is at hand, and Pindarus is come
To do you salutation from his master.
Brutus.
He greets me well.° Your master, Pindarus,
In his own change, or by ill officers,°
Hath given me some worthy cause to wish
Things done undone; but if he be at hand,
I shall be satisfied.°
Pindarus. I do not doubt
But that my noble master will appear
Such as he is, full of regard and honor.
Brutus.
He is not doubted. A word, Lucilius,
How he received you; let me be resolved.°
Lucilius.
With courtesy and with respect enough,
But not with such familiar instances,°
Nor with such free and friendly conference
As he hath used of old.
Brutus. Thou hast described
A hot friend cooling. Ever note, Lucilius,
When love begins to sicken and decay
It useth an enforcèd ceremony.
There are no tricks in plain and simple faith;
But hollow men, like horses hot at hand,°
Make gallant show and promise of their mettle;

[*Low march within.*]

But when they should endure the bloody spur,
They fall their crests, and like deceitful jades°
Sink in the trial. Comes his army on?

? *Stage direction. Several months have passed since the assassination. Brutus and Cassius are in Sardis, the capital of ancient Lydia, a kingdom in Asia Minor. Why did Brutus and Cassius flee from Rome with their armies?*

6. **He greets me well:** He sends greetings with a good man.
7. In other words, either from a change of feelings or because of the bad advice or the bad deeds of subordinates.
10. **be satisfied:** get a satisfactory explanation.
14. **resolved:** informed.
16. **familiar instances:** friendly behavior.

? 18. *What details show that a split might be taking place in the conspirators' ranks?*

23. **hot at hand:** very energetic at the start of the race.
26. **jades:** old horses.

CONTENT-AREA CONNECTIONS

Art: Battle Gear in Caesar's Time
Individual activity. Mention that battle scenes have long been a favorite subject of painters and sculptors. Suggest that students draw or paint scenes of the rival camps. They can use the library or the Internet to research the clothing and equipment used at the time. You might also suggest they watch Joseph Mankiewicz's 1953 film of *Julius Caesar,* which won an Oscar for best art direction.

History: Horses in Ancient Rome
Small-group activity. Horses are mentioned several times in this act, both as metaphor and as military transportation. Suggest that small groups of students research the importance of horses in battle. Ask them to offer information on where the Romans obtained horses and how they used them. Groups can then offer an oral presentation for the whole class.

836 Chapter 10 Drama • Evaluating an Argument

**"JUDGE ME, YOU GODS!
WRONG I MINE ENEMIES?
AND IF NOT SO, HOW SHOULD
I WRONG A BROTHER?"**

Lucilius.
They mean this night in Sardis to be quartered;
The greater part, the horse in general,°
Are come with Cassius.

[*Enter* CASSIUS *and his* POWERS.]

Brutus. Hark! He is arrived.
March gently on to meet him.
Cassius. Stand, ho!
Brutus. Stand, ho! Speak the word along.
First Soldier. Stand!
Second Soldier. Stand!
Third Soldier. Stand!
Cassius.
Most noble brother, you have done me wrong.
Brutus.
Judge me, you gods! Wrong I mine enemies?
And if not so, how should I wrong a brother?
Cassius.
Brutus, this sober form of yours hides wrongs;
And when you do them—
Brutus. Cassius, be content.°
Speak your griefs softly; I do know you well.
Before the eyes of both our armies here
(Which should perceive nothing but love from us)
Let us not wrangle. Bid them move away;
Then in my tent, Cassius, enlarge° your griefs,
And I will give you audience.
Cassius. Pindarus,
Bid our commanders lead their charges off
A little from this ground.

29. the horse in general: all the cavalry.

Staging the Play
36. *What do you picture happening on stage here?*

41. content: calm.

46. enlarge: express in greater detail.

DIRECT TEACHING

C Reading Skills

Reading Shakespeare. Note the inverted word order that Shakespeare uses here. How would you restate these lines in modern English? [Possible response: The gods can judge me! Do I wrong my enemies? If I don't, then how could I wrong a brother?]

D Literary Focus
GRADE-LEVEL STANDARD

Falling action. What does this dialogue show about the prospects for Brutus and Cassius in the play's falling action? [Possible response: The bickering shows that the fortunes of the conspirators are in decline.] Why is Brutus's advice to move inside the tents sound? [Possible responses: Arguing in front of the soldiers would have a negative effect on their morale; soldiers need to know that their leaders are united.]

Response to Margin Question

Line 36. As Brutus and Cassius meet, the soldiers pass the order to halt along the line.

STANDARD REVIEW

Character. One key to understanding *Julius Caesar* is a firm grasp of character and character motivation. The interactions between characters in the play underpin its dramatic structure, directly affect the tragic plot, and provide insight into Shakespeare's themes. The following activity can help students gain a better insight into the characters and enhance their comprehension of the play.

Activity. Divide the class into groups of four. Each group should brainstorm information about each of four main characters in the play. One student may act as a recorder, or the information may be recorded on tape. Next the group should develop questions for each character—what the character thinks about another character or situation, or what the character knows about life in Rome or his or her personal life. Then, each group member should take one of the roles and pretend to be that character. Finally, using its list of questions, each group interviews characters from another group, with the answers recorded to form a class bank of character insight.

The Tragedy of Julius Caesar, Act IV, Scene 2 **837**

DIRECT TEACHING

A Literary Focus
GRADE-LEVEL STANDARD

Falling action. In Act IV, Shakespeare accelerates the falling action, reinforcing his theme that assassination, a violent transfer of power, causes disorder. What has happened to Brutus and Cassius? [They have descended into bitter conflict.] Why is Cassius upset with Brutus? [Brutus condemned Lucius for taking bribes even after Cassius wrote a letter on Lucius's behalf; Cassius sees Brutus as too ethical when the conspirators need money to defend themselves.]

B English-Language Learners

Interpreting idioms. Make sure students understand that *to have an itching palm* is an idiom meaning "to be greedy for money."

C Reading Skills

Making connections. What event in Act III does Brutus seem to refer to in l. 24? [He refers to the conspirators' act of bathing their hands in Caesar's blood as a way to purify themselves in their cause of liberty and freedom.]

Response to Margin Question

Line 12. Brutus has accused Cassius of taking bribes.

Brutus.
Lucilius, do you the like, and let no man
Come to our tent till we have done our conference.
Let Lucius and Titinius guard our door.

[*Exeunt all except* BRUTUS *and* CASSIUS.]

SCENE 3. *Brutus' tent.*

Cassius.
That you have wronged me doth appear in this:
You have condemned and noted° Lucius Pella
For taking bribes here of the Sardians;
Wherein my letters, praying on his side,
Because I knew the man, was slighted off.

Brutus.
You wronged yourself to write in such a case.

Cassius.
In such a time as this it is not meet
That every nice offense should bear his comment.°

Brutus.
Let me tell you, Cassius, you yourself
Are much condemned to have an itching palm,
To sell and mart° your offices for gold
To undeservers.

Cassius. I an itching palm?
You know that you are Brutus that speaks this,
Or, by the gods, this speech were else your last.

Brutus.
The name of Cassius honors° this corruption,
And chastisement doth therefore hide his head.

Cassius. Chastisement!

Brutus.
Remember March, the ides of March remember.
Did not great Julius bleed for justice' sake?
What villain touched his body, that did stab,
And not for justice? What, shall one of us,
That struck the foremost man of all this world
But for supporting robbers,° shall we now
Contaminate our fingers with base bribes,
And sell the mighty space of our large honors°
For so much trash as may be graspèd thus?
I had rather be a dog, and bay the moon,
Than such a Roman.

2. noted: publicly disgraced.

8. That . . . comment: that every trivial offense should be criticized.

11. mart: trade; traffic in.

? 12. *What has Brutus accused Cassius of?*

15. honors: gives an air of respectability to.

23. supporting robbers: supporting or protecting dishonest public officials.
25. our large honors: capacity to be honorable and generous.

DIFFERENTIATING INSTRUCTION

Learners Having Difficulty

Activity. If students have difficulty with the quarrel between Brutus and Cassius in Scene 3, try a paired reading and summarizing activity. One student can read and summarize the lines of Cassius; the other can read and summarize the lines of Brutus.

English-Language Learners

Encourage students to use context clues to figure out the meaning of unfamiliar words. On pp. 838–839, for example, the words *slighted* (l. 5), *condemned* (l. 10), *chastisement* (l. 16), *endure* (l. 29), and *testy* (l. 46) may be new to some readers. Suggest that they use a dictionary when the context clues are inadequate.

Advanced Learners

Enrichment. Invite students to identify and analyze examples of figurative language in Act IV. Suggest that they begin by looking at the metaphors and similes in Scene 2, ll. 23–27; Scene 3, l. 24; and Scene 3, ll. 100–101.

838 Chapter 10 Drama • Evaluating an Argument

Cassius. Brutus, bait not me;
I'll not endure it. You forget yourself
To hedge me in. I am a soldier, I,
Older in practice, abler than yourself
To make conditions.
Brutus. Go to! You are not, Cassius.
Cassius. I am.
Brutus. I say you are not.
Cassius.
Urge° me no more, I shall forget myself;
Have mind upon your health, tempt me no farther.
Brutus. Away, slight man!
Cassius.
Is't possible?
Brutus. Hear me, for I will speak.
Must I give way and room to your rash choler?°
Shall I be frighted when a madman stares?
Cassius.
O ye gods, ye gods! Must I endure all this?
Brutus.
All this? Ay, more: fret till your proud heart break.
Go show your slaves how choleric you are,
And make your bondmen tremble. Must I budge?°
Must I observe° you? Must I stand and crouch
Under your testy humor? By the gods,
You shall digest the venom of your spleen,°
Though it do split you; for, from this day forth,
I'll use you for my mirth, yea, for my laughter,
When you are waspish.
Cassius. Is it come to this?
Brutus.
You say you are a better soldier:
Let it appear so; make your vaunting° true,
And it shall please me well. For mine own part,
I shall be glad to learn of noble men.
Cassius.
You wrong me every way; you wrong me, Brutus;
I said, an elder soldier, not a better.
Did I say, better?
Brutus. If you did, I care not.
Cassius.
When Caesar lived, he durst° not thus have moved° me.

35. Urge: goad; bully.

? **36.** *What threat is Cassius making to Brutus?*

39. choler: anger.

44. budge: defer.

45. observe: wait on.

47. spleen: fiery temper. (The spleen was believed to be the seat of the emotions.)

52. vaunting: boasting.

? **57.** *What did Cassius say?*

58. durst: dared. **moved:** exasperated.

DIRECT TEACHING

D Reading Skills

Comparing and contrasting. How is the conflict between Cassius and Brutus similar to that between Antony and Octavius? [Possible responses: Cassius points out that he is more experienced than Brutus, and Antony implied the same thing to Octavius.]

E Reading Skills

Reading Shakespeare. Notice how Shakespeare splits the line of iambic pentameter between two characters in ll. 38 and 50. What effect does this have? [Possible response: It stresses the intensity of the quarrel, allowing rapid-fire retorts by each character.]

F Literary Focus
GRADE-LEVEL STANDARD

Character foils. Heated arguments can reveal character traits. How does this quarrel highlight the contrast between these character foils? [Possible response: The argument shows that Brutus can be self-righteous and petulant, while Cassius is incredulous but contained.]

G Literary Focus
REVIEW STANDARD

Falling action. Besides Cassius's alleged bribe taking, what current and past events might explain the very tense mood in Brutus's tent? [Possible responses: The two men are nervous about the upcoming battle; they have lost their homes and connections in Rome and realize their position is shaky.]

Responses to Margin Questions

Line 36. Cassius is prepared to fight.
Line 57. Cassius said he was "older in practice" and thus "abler" to make military decisions.

CONTENT-AREA CONNECTIONS

History: Slavery in Ancient Rome
Brutus refers to Cassius's slaves and bondsmen. Slavery was a common practice in ancient Rome, as it had been in Greece and in other ancient cultures. Most slaves were citizens of countries and territories conquered by Rome in war. People who failed to pay their debts or who were convicted of serious crimes were also sentenced to slavery. Wealthy masters used slaves to maintain their homes and work their farms. When Roman citizens went off to war, the government used slaves to maintain the urban labor force as well as the agricultural labor force. Roman slaves had few rights—in fact, the masters had the power of life and death over slaves. In the end, Rome's increasing dependence on slaves is considered to have contributed to the empire's downfall.

The Tragedy of Julius Caesar, Act IV, Scene 3 839

DIRECT TEACHING

Ⓐ Literary Focus
GRADE-LEVEL STANDARD

Character foils. How does this dialogue point to a contrast between Brutus and Cassius that was evident in the play's rising action? [Possible response: The dialogue shows Brutus's idealism, which sometimes has a morally superior tone, and Cassius's pragmatism, which can seem shady at times.]

Ⓑ Reading Skills

Reading Shakespeare. What meaning for *trash* might Shakespeare have intended in ll. 26 and 74? ["money"]

Ⓒ Reading Skills

Extending the text. When is it appropriate to find fault in a friend? When is it better to overlook faults? [Possible response: It's useful to point out faults in a friend when those faults cause or seem likely to cause a great deal of harm. It's usually better to overlook a friend's minor faults, since addressing them could cause unnecessary conflict and hostility.]

Response to Margin Question

Line 75. Students may or may not think that Brutus is hypocritical. Perhaps Brutus is thinking unclearly and may not see the inconsistency in refusing to raise money by "vile means" while being eager to benefit by such money.

Brutus.
Peace, peace, you durst not so have tempted him.
Cassius. I durst not?
Brutus. No.
Cassius.
What? Durst not tempt him?
Brutus. For your life you durst not.
Cassius.
Do not presume too much upon my love;
I may do that I shall be sorry for.
Brutus.
You have done that you should be sorry for.
There is no terror, Cassius, in your threats;
For I am armed so strong in honesty
That they pass by me as the idle wind,
Which I respect not. I did send to you
For certain sums of gold, which you denied me;
For I can raise no money by vile means.
By heaven, I had rather coin my heart
And drop my blood for drachmas than to wring
From the hard hands of peasants their vile trash
By any indirection.° I did send
To you for gold to pay my legions,
Which you denied me. Was that done like Cassius?
Should I have answered Caius Cassius so?
When Marcus Brutus grows so covetous
To lock such rascal counters° from his friends,
Be ready, gods, with all your thunderbolts,
Dash him to pieces!
Cassius. I denied you not.
Brutus.
You did.
Cassius. I did not. He was but a fool
That brought my answer back. Brutus hath rived° my heart.
A friend should bear his friend's infirmities;
But Brutus makes mine greater than they are.
Brutus.
I do not, till you practice them on me.
Cassius.
You love me not.
Brutus. I do not like your faults.

75. indirection: illegal methods.

? 75. *What do you think of Brutus's moral position here? Does it seem honorable or hypocritical?*

80. counters: coins.

84. rived: broken.

DEVELOPING FLUENCY

Mixed-ability group activity. Create mixed-ability groups with four to five students in a group. Then, read all or part of Act IV aloud as a class, having each group share the role of one character. Encourage group members to figure out equitable and comfortable ways to divide up their character's lines. They may decide that they will take turns in a certain order, that each group member will read a certain number of lines, or that members will use a preset signal when they are ready for the next member to take over. Suggest that groups meet in a prereading practice period in which readers having difficulty can get help reading their allotted lines from other group members. In the read-aloud, encourage students to inflect their lines with drama when the dialogue invites it.

Cassius.
A friendly eye could never see such faults.
Brutus.
A flatterer's would not, though they do appear
As huge as high Olympus.
Cassius.
Come, Antony, and young Octavius, come,
Revenge yourselves alone on Cassius,
For Cassius is aweary of the world:
Hated by one he loves; braved° by his brother;
Checked like a bondman; all his faults observed,
Set in a notebook, learned and conned by rote°
To cast into my teeth. O, I could weep
My spirit from mine eyes! There is my dagger,
And here my naked breast; within, a heart
Dearer than Pluto's mine,° richer than gold;
If that thou be'st a Roman, take it forth.
I, that denied thee gold,° will give my heart.
Strike as thou didst at Caesar; for I know,
When thou didst hate him worst, thou lovedst him better
Than ever thou lovedst Cassius.
Brutus. Sheathe your dagger.
Be angry when you will, it shall have scope.
Do what you will, dishonor shall be humor.°
O Cassius, you are yokèd with a lamb
That carries anger as the flint bears fire,
Who, much enforcèd, shows a hasty spark,
And straight is cold again.
Cassius. Hath Cassius lived
To be but mirth and laughter to his Brutus
When grief and blood ill-tempered vexeth him?
Brutus.
When I spoke that, I was ill-tempered too.
Cassius.
Do you confess so much? Give me your hand.
Brutus.
And my heart too.
Cassius. O Brutus!
Brutus. What's the matter?

D

? **91.** *We haven't seen Brutus and Cassius alone together since the assassination. What does this* ***dialogue*** *reveal about their characters? their feelings?*

95. braved: defied.

97. conned by rote: learned by heart.

E

? **Staging the Play**
99. *What is Cassius doing, and why?*

101. Pluto's mine: the riches under the earth. Pluto was the Roman god of the underworld (akin to the Greek god Hades); Shakespeare confuses him with Plutus, god of riches.

103. that . . . gold: that *you say* denied you gold.

108. In other words, dishonor or insults will be seen merely as the result of eccentric personality traits.

F

? **112.** *Have Brutus's feelings changed? Why or why not?*

? **Staging the Play**
117. *What actions could mark the change in feelings now?*

DIRECT TEACHING

D Literary Focus
REVIEW STANDARD

? **Character.** What does this argument suggest about the kind of person that each man is? [Possible response: The argument suggests that both men are inclined to pettiness and fault finding.] **What do these traits suggest about the possible fate of Rome?** [Possible response: Their character traits raise the question of whether their weaknesses may prove more dangerous to Rome than Caesar's.]

E Reading Skills

? **Making connections.** In ll. 92–106, Cassius expresses a death wish—to die at the hands of Antony and Octavius or Brutus. How does this wish echo earlier threats? [In Act I, Scene 3, l. 90, Cassius threatens suicide to escape Caesar's tyranny. In Act III, Scene 1, l. 22, he threatens suicide if the assassination plot is exposed.]

F Literary Focus
REVIEW STANDARD

? **Conflict.** How does the quarrel between Brutus and Cassius end? Have they resolved their original grievance? [Possible responses: To end the quarrel, Cassius yields, out of despair, and asks Brutus to kill him. Brutus recognizes Cassius's ill temper and acknowledges his own. The original grievance, bribe taking, is not mentioned in the reconciliation.]

Responses to Margin Questions

Line 91. Both men can be petty and easily wounded. Both are tense.
Line 99. Cassius tells Brutus to kill him because Cassius wants to prove his love for Brutus and shame him.
Line 112. Brutus's fondness for Cassius has won out. He is no longer angry, even if he cannot condone Cassius's actions.
Line 117. Brutus and Cassius could embrace.

CONTENT-AREA CONNECTIONS

Literature: The Dark Side of Brutus
Regarding the character traits that Brutus reveals in this scene, critic T. S. Dorsch says: "It is during his quarrel with Cassius that Brutus shows to least advantage. No one who reads the first hundred lines of Act IV, Scene 3, could feel that Shakespeare meant us to have any sympathy for Brutus during this exchange. . . . [H]is demeanor is intolerable. He adopts the tone of an Olympian god chiding an erring mortal and at the same time lapses into the language of a squabbling schoolboy. Caesar himself is no more arrogant than Brutus when he says, for example: 'There is no terror, Cassius, in your threats; / For I am armed so strong in honesty / That they pass me by as the idle wind, / Which I respect not . . .' (ll. 66–69)."

DIFFERENTIATING INSTRUCTION

Learners Having Difficulty

Activity. Ask students to view a popular movie, such as *Star Wars* or *Titanic.* After students select the movie, have small groups watch it together. Ask them to identify the work's exposition, rising action, crisis or turning point, falling action, and finally its climax and resolution. They should also identify the mood of each of these five dramatic-structure parts, the protagonist and antagonist, and the central conflict. Explain that Shakespeare's plays are greatly responsible for the refinement of the classical dramatic structure that still serves as the basis for many movies, plays, and TV shows.

Advanced Learners

Move students toward the eleventh- and twelfth-grade Standard 3.2 by having them explore *Julius Caesar* for Shakespeare's theme that social disorder is a probable result of violent political coups. Have students supply textual evidence that supports Shakespeare's social commentary.

Cassius.
Have not you love enough to bear with me
When that rash humor which my mother gave me
Makes me forgetful?

Brutus. Yes, Cassius, and from henceforth,
When you are over-earnest with your Brutus,
He'll think your mother chides, and leave you so.

[*Enter a* POET, *followed by* LUCILIUS, TITINIUS, *and* LUCIUS.]

Poet.
Let me go in to see the generals;
There is some grudge between 'em; 'tis not meet
They be alone.

Lucilius. You shall not come to them.

Poet. Nothing but death shall stay me.

Cassius. How now. What's the matter?

Poet.
For shame, you generals! What do you mean?
Love, and be friends, as two such men should be;
For I have seen more years, I'm sure, than ye.

Cassius.
Ha, ha! How vilely doth this cynic° rhyme!

Brutus.
Get you hence, sirrah! Saucy fellow, hence!

Cassius.
Bear with him, Brutus, 'tis his fashion.

Brutus.
I'll know his humor when he knows his time.°
What should the wars do with these jigging° fools?
Companion,° hence!

Cassius. Away, away, be gone!

[*Exit* POET.]

Brutus.
Lucilius and Titinius, bid the commanders
Prepare to lodge their companies tonight.

Cassius.
And come yourselves, and bring Messala with you
Immediately to us. [*Exeunt* LUCILIUS *and* TITINIUS.]

Brutus. Lucius, a bowl of wine.

[*Exit* LUCIUS.]

Staging the Play
122. *How could a humorous note be sounded here?*

131. cynic: rude person.

134. his time: the right time to speak.
135. jigging: rhyming.
136. Companion: lower-class fellow.

136. *Remember that Shakespeare himself was a "jigging fool." What is the point of this scene with the poet?*

DIRECT TEACHING

A Literary Focus GRADE-LEVEL STANDARD

Dramatic dialogue. How does this dialogue dramatize Cassius's dependence on Brutus? [Possible responses: It shows how Cassius needs Brutus's approval, even though Brutus is a man of inferior political judgment; he is willing to demean himself to get Brutus's approval.]

B Literary Focus GRADE-LEVEL STANDARD

Character foils. How does this exchange highlight the difference in these character foils? [Possible response: Cassius urges Brutus to humor the colorful poet, while Brutus, offended, stands on ceremony.] How might Brutus's leadership of the failed coup have affected him? [Possible response: The new power he felt after the assassination may have gone to his head a bit.]

Responses to Margin Questions

Line 122. Brutus could act out the chiding by shaking his finger at Cassius.

Line 136. It is as if the author has walked into the play, a joke sure to amuse the audience, at least the Elizabethan audience. The scene also serves as comic relief after the tense argument.

READING SKILLS REVIEW

Review how the use of graphic organizers, such as Venn diagrams, cluster maps, and charts, can help readers record important ideas and details from a text. Emphasize that a cluster map connects ideas and shows the relationship between ideas and supporting details. Encourage students to recall and explain cluster maps they've made in the past. Then, explain that cluster maps can also help readers better understand characters.

Activity. Have students create character-attribute cluster maps for Antony, Cassius, and Brutus, using the model at right. Ask students to add attributes to their maps as they read Acts IV and V. Point out that they may also revise clusters as new character attributes comes to light. For instance, if they decide as they read that Antony is not really spiteful, they might delete that attribute and substitute another.

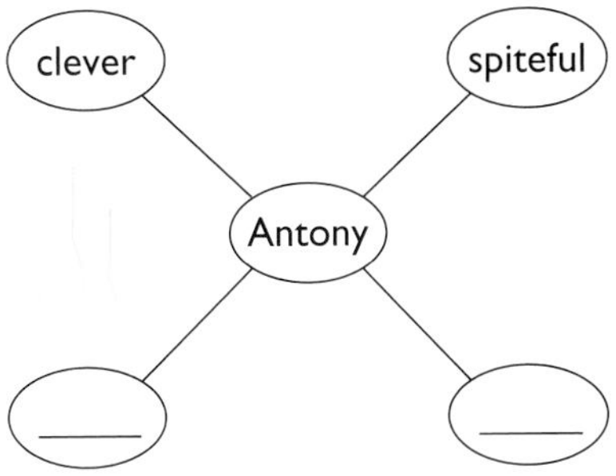

The Tragedy of Julius Caesar, Act IV, Scene 3 **843**

DIRECT TEACHING

A Literary Focus
GRADE-LEVEL STANDARD

Falling action. How does the news of Portia's death contribute to the falling action of the play, which leads to the resolution? [Possible responses: Portia's anxiety over Brutus was a complication in the rising action of Act II; with her death, the issue is resolved, and Brutus has less to live for. Her suicide, prompted by the growing strength of the triumvirate, does not bode well for the conspirators.]

B Reading Skills

Responding to the text. Is Brutus's restraint about Portia's death admirable, or is he carrying self-control too far? [Possible responses: Brutus is too unemotional and should be grieving; Brutus must focus on the imminent battle and cannot wallow in grief.]

C Reading Skills

Comparing and contrasting. How would you contrast Cassius's emotional state with Brutus's at this point? [Cassius is overflowing with emotion, while Brutus shows a subdued and passionless state of mind.]

Responses to Margin Questions

Line 144. Brutus should probably speak impassively.
Lines 145–160. Cassius is more emotional.

Cassius.
I did not think you could have been so angry.
Brutus.
O Cassius, I am sick of many griefs.
Cassius.
Of your philosophy you make no use,
If you give place to accidental evils.
Brutus.
No man bears sorrow better. Portia is dead.
Cassius. Ha? Portia?
Brutus. She is dead.
Cassius.
How scaped I killing when I crossed you so?
O insupportable and touching loss!
Upon what sickness?
Brutus. Impatient of my absence,
And grief that young Octavius with Mark Antony
Have made themselves so strong—for with her death
That tidings came—with this she fell distract,°
And (her attendants absent) swallowed fire.°
Cassius.
And died so?
Brutus. Even so.
Cassius. O ye immortal gods!

[*Enter* LUCIUS, *with wine and tapers.*]

Brutus.
Speak no more of her. Give me a bowl of wine.
In this I bury all unkindness, Cassius.

[*Drinks.*]

Cassius.
My heart is thirsty for that noble pledge.
Fill, Lucius, till the wine o'erswell the cup;
I cannot drink too much of Brutus' love.

[*Drinks. Exit* LUCIUS.]

[*Enter* TITINIUS *and* MESSALA.]

Brutus.
Come in, Titinius! Welcome, good Messala.
Now sit we close about this taper here,
And call in question° our necessities.

Staging the Play **144.** *This reference is to Brutus's philosophy of Stoicism, which taught that we should master our emotions, lead lives dictated by reason and duty, and submit to fate. How might Brutus deliver his next shocking line?*

Staging the Play **145–160.** *Who is probably more emotional in this scene—Brutus or Cassius? (Many fine actors have shown no emotion as they played Brutus in this scene.)*

153. fell distract: became distraught.
154. According to Plutarch, Portia killed herself by putting hot coals in her mouth.

163. call in question: consider.

STANDARD REVIEW

Figurative language. Review the principal kinds of figurative language—simile, metaphor, and personification—and ask students to provide examples of each.
Activity. Have students analyze the following excerpts from Act IV to see how Shakespeare uses figurative language. For each excerpt, ask students what kind of figurative language is used and what image each figure of speech brings to mind.

- "But hollow men, like horses hot at hand, / Make gallant show and promise of their mettle. . . ." (Scene 2, ll. 23–24) [simile; battle or horses rearing up]
- "For I am armed so strong in honesty" (Scene 3, l. 67) [metaphor; weapons or battle]
- "And here my naked breast; within, a heart / Dearer than Pluto's mine, richer than gold. . . ." (Scene 3, ll. 100–101) [simile; valuable metal or rich treasure]

Activity. Challenge students to find an example of figurative language on p. 844. Ask them to identify its type and the point it makes. [l. 158: My heart is thirsty for that noble pledge"—personification shows how a heart yearns for something.]

Cassius.
Portia, art thou gone?
Brutus. No more, I pray you.
Messala, I have here receivèd letters
That young Octavius and Mark Antony
Come down upon us with a mighty power,
Bending their expedition toward Philippi.°
Messala.
Myself have letters of the selfsame tenure.°
Brutus.
With what addition?
Messala.
That by proscription and bills of outlawry°
Octavius, Antony, and Lepidus
Have put to death an hundred senators.
Brutus.
Therein our letters do not well agree.
Mine speak of seventy senators that died
By their proscriptions, Cicero being one.
Cassius.
Cicero one?
Messala. Cicero is dead,
And by that order of proscription.
Had you your letters from your wife, my lord?
Brutus. No, Messala.
Messala.
Nor nothing in your letters writ of her?
Brutus.
Nothing, Messala.
Messala. That methinks is strange.
Brutus.
Why ask you? Hear you aught of her in yours?
Messala. No, my lord.
Brutus.
Now as you are a Roman, tell me true.
Messala.
Then like a Roman bear the truth I tell,
For certain she is dead, and by strange manner.
Brutus.
Why, farewell, Portia. We must die, Messala.
With meditating that she must die once,°
I have the patience to endure it now.

168. Philippi: ancient city in northern Greece.

169. tenure: tenor; meaning.

171. bills of outlawry: lists of proscribed people.

Staging the Play
179. *A peculiar scene now takes place, in which Brutus seems again to hear for the first time the news of his wife's death. Some scholars believe that the original account of Portia's death was told in lines 179–193 and that Shakespeare later rewrote the scene, which is now lines 141–155. A production might not use both scenes. Which would you use, and why? (If a director did decide to use both scenes, how should Brutus act in the second one?)*

189. once: at some time.

Staging the Play
190. *The actor playing Brutus must be careful not to make him seem cold and unfeeling. How could this scene be played to suggest Brutus's humanity, as well as his Stoicism?*

DIRECT TEACHING

D Content-Area Connections

History: Rule After Caesar
After the assassination, Mark Antony threatened to become even more dictatorial than Caesar. So Cicero, as the leading senator, persuaded many colleagues to back Octavius as a short-term figurehead and alternative to Antony. Octavius vowed to save Rome from anarchy and dictatorship. To undermine Antony, Cicero's camp mounted a vicious propaganda war and tried to block Antony's appointment as a provincial governor. Later, Octavius joined forces with Antony in the Second Triumvirate and did nothing to stop Antony from eliminating Cicero and as many as two thousand other political opponents.

E Content-Area Connections

Literature: Shakespeare's Revisions
Some critics believe these lines about Portia's death were written earlier and intended by Shakespeare to replace the previous discussion of her death in ll. 141–155. However, these earlier lines were incompletely deleted from the manuscript and so appeared in the First Folio in 1623.

Responses to Margin Questions

Line 179. Possible responses: The version in ll. 141–155 is better because it connects Portia's death to Brutus's previous burst of anger, shows more of his sorrow, and presents Cassius's grief more fully. The second version has an advantage in that it shows Brutus's Stoical reaction as he learns of the death. (If a director used both scenes, Brutus could be feigning ignorance in ll. 180 and 182 in order to avoid discussing his private sorrow.)
Line 190. Brutus could be struggling to control his feelings.

CONTENT-AREA CONNECTIONS

Literature: Is Brutus's Virtue Absurd?
Critic Sir Mungo MacCallum says about Brutus: "[He] has brought about an upturn of society by assassinating the one man who could organize that society. His own motives were honorable, though not so unimpeachable as he assumed. . . . Now in the confusions that ensue, he finds, to his horror, that revolutions are not made with rose water. . . . So he condemns [Lucius] Pella for bribery. Cassius judges the case better. He sees that Pella is an efficient officer of whose services he does not wish to be deprived. He sees that in domestic broils the leaders must not be too particular about their instruments, that, according to the proverb, you must go into the water to catch fish. But Brutus will not go into the water. He thinks that an assassin should only have Galahads in his troops. And sometimes his offended virtue becomes even a little absurd. . . ."

DIRECT TEACHING

A Reading Skills

Evaluation. Whose plan would you be more likely to follow? Why? [Some students may choose Cassius's plan because it is logical and because Cassius has proved a shrewder judge of people and situations than Brutus; others may choose Brutus's plan because his argument is persuasive and supported by facts about the "people 'twixt Philippi and this ground."]

Response to Margin Question

Line 200. Cassius wants to force Antony's troops to march to Sardis, a journey that will tire and weaken them.

Messala.
Even so great men great losses should endure.

Cassius.
I have as much of this in art° as you,
But yet my nature could not bear it so.

Brutus.
Well, to our work alive. What do you think
Of marching to Philippi presently?

Cassius.
I do not think it good.

Brutus. Your reason?

Cassius. This it is:
'Tis better that the enemy seek us;
So shall he waste his means, weary his soldiers,
Doing himself offense, whilst we, lying still,
Are full of rest, defense, and nimbleness.

Brutus.
Good reasons must of force° give place to better.
The people 'twixt Philippi and this ground
Do stand but in a forced affection;°
For they have grudged us contribution.
The enemy, marching along by them,
By them shall make a fuller number up,
Come on refreshed, new-added and encouraged;
From which advantage shall we cut him off
If at Philippi we do face him there,
These people at our back.

Cassius. Hear me, good brother.

Brutus.
Under your pardon. You must note beside
That we have tried the utmost of our friends,
Our legions are brimful, our cause is ripe.
The enemy increaseth every day;

192. in art: the art of being a Stoic.

? **200.** *What plan does Cassius propose regarding Antony's forces at Philippi?*

201. of force: of necessity.

203. That is, they support us only grudgingly.

"THERE IS A TIDE IN THE AFFAIRS OF MEN
WHICH, TAKEN AT THE FLOOD, LEADS ON
TO FORTUNE;
OMITTED, ALL THE VOYAGE OF THEIR LIFE
IS BOUND IN SHALLOWS AND IN
MISERIES."

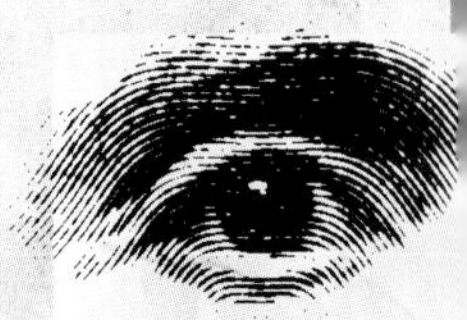

CONTENT-AREA CONNECTIONS

History: Military Service in Ancient Rome

Joining the military was the main way in which members of the peasant class in ancient Rome were able to rise in the civic hierarchy. By demonstrating the all-important quality of *virtus,* or manly valor, on the battlefield, a man gained the acknowledgment of the entire city. In addition to the significant rise in social status brought by being a veteran of a successful campaign, every soldier also received a share of the spoils of war. Additional rewards of land from grateful generals were also not uncommon. These inducements of higher social status and wealth proved sufficient to attract a more than adequate supply of soldiers, and Roman leaders generally faced little difficulty in filling their ranks.

846 Chapter 10 Drama • Evaluating an Argument

We, at the height, are ready to decline.
There is a tide in the affairs of men
Which, taken at the flood, leads on to fortune;
Omitted,° all the voyage of their life
Is bound in shallows and in miseries.
On such a full sea are we now afloat,
And we must take the current when it serves,
Or lose our ventures.

Cassius. Then, with your will,° go on;
We'll along ourselves and meet them at Philippi.

Brutus.
The deep of night is crept upon our talk,
And nature must obey necessity,
Which we will niggard with a little rest.°
There is no more to say?

Cassius. No more. Good night.
Early tomorrow will we rise and hence.

[*Enter* LUCIUS.]

Brutus.
Lucius, my gown. [*Exit* LUCIUS.]
Farewell, good Messala.
Good night, Titinius. Noble, noble Cassius,
Good night, and good repose.

Cassius. O my dear brother,
This was an ill beginning of the night.
Never come such division 'tween our souls!
Let it not, Brutus.

[*Enter* LUCIUS, *with the gown.*]

Brutus. Everything is well.

Cassius.
Good night, my lord.

Brutus. Good night, good brother.

Titinius, Messala.
Good night, Lord Brutus.

Brutus. Farewell, every one.

[*Exeunt.*]

Give me the gown. Where is thy instrument?°

Lucius.
Here in the tent.

B **218. Omitted:** neglected.

C ? 222. *Where does Brutus want to fight Antony, and why?*

222. with your will: as you wish.

? 223. *Which man seems to dominate the action now?*

D **226. niggard with a little rest:** cheat with a short period of sleep.

? **Staging the Play**
231. *In some productions at this point in the scene, Brutus takes a letter out of his pocket and burns it. What letter are we to assume he is destroying, and what does his action demonstrate?*

237. instrument: probably a lute.

DIRECT TEACHING

B Reading Skills

? Paraphrasing. **How would you paraphrase Brutus's extended metaphor (ll. 216–222)?** [Possible response: There comes a time in our life when we must seize opportunities. The seizing of such opportunities leads to good fortune. But if we ignore them, we'll regret it. We're now at such a point. We must jump at our chance, or we'll fail.] **Why might these lines often be quoted?** [Possible responses: The language is beautiful; the idea expressed in them can apply to many decisions that arise in life.]

C Reading Skills

? Drawing conclusions. **Why doesn't Cassius argue more strenuously for his plan?** [Possible responses: Maybe Cassius feels he can't win in a confrontation with Brutus; after the fierce quarrel and the news of Portia's death, he may want to placate Brutus.]

D Literary Focus
GRADE-LEVEL STANDARD

? Falling action. **How does Brutus's decision to advance to Philippi contribute to the falling action of the play?** [Possible response: Brutus's decision to advance rather than wait suggests a desire to get it over with. We have the sense that events are hurtling to the final catastrophe.]

Responses to Margin Questions

Line 222. Brutus wants to fight at Philippi. He's afraid that if Antony marches on Sardis, men along the way will join his forces.
Line 223. Cassius yields to Brutus.
Line 231. Brutus is burning the letter that announced Portia's suicide. His action shows that he will put aside his grief and move on to battle.

The Tragedy of Julius Caesar, Act IV, Scene 3 847

DIRECT TEACHING

A Literary Focus
GRADE-LEVEL STANDARD

Dramatic dialogue. In Act IV so far, Brutus has been rigid, self-righteousness, and sharp-tongued. What purpose might this dialogue serve? [Possible response: Shakespeare may have included this dialogue, in which Brutus shows a fatherly kindness and understanding, to elicit sympathy for the Brutus character.]

B Reading Skills

Recognizing anachronisms. This skill is presented on p. 853. An opportunity to apply the skill occurs here in Act IV. Ask students to find an anachronism in these lines. [Brutus would have been reading from a scroll, not a book, since bound books weren't produced until about the second century A.D.]

"HA! WHO COMES HERE?
I THINK IT IS THE WEAKNESS OF MINE EYES
THAT SHAPES THIS MONSTROUS APPARITION."

Brutus. What, thou speak'st drowsily?
Poor knave, I blame thee not; thou art o'erwatched.°
Call Claudius and some other of my men;
I'll have them sleep on cushions in my tent.
Lucius. Varro and Claudius!

[*Enter* VARRO *and* CLAUDIUS.]

Varro. Calls my lord?
Brutus.
I pray you, sirs, lie in my tent and sleep.
It may be I shall raise you by and by
On business to my brother Cassius.
Varro.
So please you, we will stand and watch your pleasure.°
Brutus.
I will not have it so; lie down, good sirs;
It may be I shall otherwise bethink me.

[VARRO *and* CLAUDIUS *lie down.*]

Look, Lucius, here's the book I sought for so;
I put it in the pocket of my gown.
Lucius.
I was sure your lordship did not give it me.
Brutus.
Bear with me, good boy, I am much forgetful.
Canst thou hold up thy heavy eyes awhile,
And touch thy instrument a strain or two?
Lucius.
Ay, my lord, an't please you.

239. o'erwatched: exhausted.

247. watch your pleasure: wait for your orders.

DEVELOPING FLUENCY

Whole-class activity. To help students better understand the emotional pitch of drama, conduct an oral reading from ll. 224 through the end of Act IV. Assign the roles of Brutus, Cassius, Titinius, Lucius, Varro, Claudius, and the Ghost, and have readers practice any lines they find difficult. After the oral reading, involve the whole class in a discussion of this part of the play. Ask students what they think is the purpose of this quiet, nocturnal scene. [Possible responses: It provides a calm after the tension of the first half of the act; it shows Brutus's tender side; it introduces Caesar's Ghost, which foreshadows Brutus's death.] Then, point out that great drama rises and falls in emotional pitch, cresting in waves of conflict that ebb into small scenes of calm. Remind students that this quiet but ominous section is part of the play's falling action—that these events, especially the Ghost's warning, will directly lead to the climax. Finally, ask them to predict what kind of mood and action that the opening of Act V might contain, keeping in mind that it follows this period of spooky calm.

848 Chapter 10 Drama • Evaluating an Argument

Brutus. It does, my boy.
I trouble thee too much, but thou art willing.
Lucius. It is my duty, sir.
Brutus.
I should not urge thy duty past thy might;
I know young bloods look for a time of rest.
Lucius. I have slept, my lord, already.
Brutus.
It was well done, and thou shalt sleep again;
I will not hold thee long. If I do live,
I will be good to thee.

[Music, and a song.]

This is a sleepy tune. O murd'rous° slumber!
Layest thou thy leaden mace° upon my boy,
That plays thee music? Gentle knave, good night;
I will not do thee so much wrong to wake thee.
If thou dost nod, thou break'st thy instrument;
I'll take it from thee; and, good boy, good night.
Let me see, let me see; is not the leaf turned down
Where I left reading? Here it is, I think.

[Enter the GHOST *of Caesar.]*

How ill this taper burns. Ha! Who comes here?
I think it is the weakness of mine eyes
That shapes this monstrous apparition.
It comes upon° me. Art thou anything?
Art thou some god, some angel, or some devil,
That mak'st my blood cold, and my hair to stare?°
Speak to me what thou art.
Ghost.
Thy evil spirit, Brutus.
Brutus. Why com'st thou?
Ghost.
To tell thee thou shalt see me at Philippi.
Brutus. Well; then I shall see thee again?
Ghost. Ay, at Philippi.
Brutus.
Why, I will see thee at Philippi then.

[Exit GHOST.*]*

? **Staging the Play**
Stage direction. *How could lighting be used to suggest an intimate, drowsy, and nonmilitaristic scene?*

265. murd'rous: deathlike.

266. mace: heavy club carried by public officials.

276. upon: toward.

278. stare: stand on end.

? **Staging the Play**
279. *How would you "stage" the Ghost? Would you have him in military dress? in his bloodied toga? Would you not show the Ghost at all, but merely project his voice onstage?*

? **281.** *What does the Ghost's appearance* ***foreshadow,*** *or hint at?*

DIRECT TEACHING

C Literary Focus
REVIEW STANDARD

Mood. When Brutus is alone with Lucius, how does this scene's mood change? [Possible response: It becomes tender and mellow.]

D Reading Skills

Reading Shakespeare. Why does Shakespeare continue this scene between Brutus and Lucius? [Possible response: After thoroughly showing the caustic and pompous Brutus, he wants to assure that we appreciate Brutus's gentle, compassionate side; he may have added music to enhance the scene's mood.]

E Literary Focus
GRADE-LEVEL STANDARD

Falling action. How does the Ghost contribute to the falling action and prepare us for resolution? [Possible response: The Ghost's veiled threat increases the sense of decline in Brutus's fortunes and foreshadows the doom that awaits him and Cassius in the play's resolution.]

Responses to Margin Questions

Stage direction. The lights could fade or change to warmer colors. A director or lighting designer might also use candles or focus dim spotlights in certain places.
Line 279. Ask students to give reasons for each staging approach.
Line 281. The Ghost foreshadows Brutus's death.

CONTENT-AREA CONNECTIONS

Literature: Shakespeare's Supernatural World

Elizabethan England was a good place for ghosts—so Shakespeare's plays abound with supernatural beings. According to critic Kristian Smidt, Shakespeare "seems to have found it tempting" to tap his audience's belief in witches and ghosts. The ghosts, Smidt says, aren't the "vulgar, screeching kind" of folklore, but "dignified, stately presences." In writing these apparitions, Shakespeare helped to create many features that still inform portrayals of ghosts today. The critic also notes that Shakespeare did not invent all these beings, finding some in his sources (as he did in Plutarch for *Julius Caesar*) and others in earlier plays. In any case, types of supernatural beings in Shakespeare's work, Smidt explains, assume a pattern: Spirits mainly show up in his early plays, ghosts prevail in his middle period, and gods dominate later work.

The Tragedy of Julius Caesar, Act IV, Scene 3 **849**

DIRECT TEACHING

(A) Reading Skills

Making judgments. In the falling action of Act IV, Shakespeare has made a tense, eerie mood. Suppose Brutus only imagines he sees the Ghost. What might this suggest about his mental and emotional state? [Possible responses: Caesar holds great sway in Brutus's imagination; Brutus feels guilt about having stabbed Caesar; Brutus is under extreme strain resulting from his wife's suicide and the pressure of the upcoming battle.]

Response to Margin Question

Line 293. Brutus would be much relieved if Lucius's dream were the source of the ghostly words.

Now I have taken heart thou vanishest.
Ill spirit, I would hold more talk with thee.
Boy! Lucius! Varro! Claudius! Sirs, awake!
Claudius!
Lucius. The strings, my lord, are false.°
Brutus.
He thinks he still is at his instrument.
Lucius awake!
Lucius. My lord?
Brutus.
Didst thou dream, Lucius, that thou so criedst out?
Lucius.
My lord, I do not know that I did cry.
Brutus.
Yes, that thou didst. Didst thou see anything?
Lucius. Nothing, my lord.
Brutus.
Sleep again, Lucius. Sirrah Claudius!
(*To* VARRO.) Fellow thou, awake!
(A) **Varro.** My lord?
Claudius. My lord?
Brutus.
Why did you so cry out, sirs, in your sleep?
Both.
Did we, my lord?
Brutus. Ay. Saw you anything?
Varro.
No, my lord, I saw nothing.
Claudius. Nor I, my lord.
Brutus.
Go and commend me to my brother Cassius;
Bid him set on his pow'rs betimes before,°
And we will follow.
Both. It shall be done, my lord.
[*Exeunt.*]

289. Lucius sleepily supposes that his instrument is out of tune.

Staging the Play
293. *In one production the Ghost scene was staged so that the Ghost's words seemed to come from the mouth of the sleeping Lucius. How would this explain Brutus's question to Lucius about "crying out"?*

305. That is, lead his forces out early in the morning, ahead of Brutus and his troops.

DIFFERENTIATING INSTRUCTION

Learners Having Difficulty
To help assess students' comprehension of the basic plot events in Act IV, use the following questions:

1. Who are the three men ruling Rome? [Antony, Octavius, and Lepidus]
2. Where are Brutus and Cassius when they meet in Scene 2? [They are in a camp near Sardis, in Asia Minor.]
3. What reports about Cassius have angered Brutus? [Cassius is rumored to have taken bribes.]
4. After the two men quarrel, what personal trouble does Brutus reveal to Cassius? [Portia, Brutus's wife, has committed suicide.]
5. What is Brutus and Cassius's military plan, and who suggests it? [They will fight the enemy's forces at Philippi, as Brutus suggested.]

850 Chapter 10 Drama • Evaluating an Argument

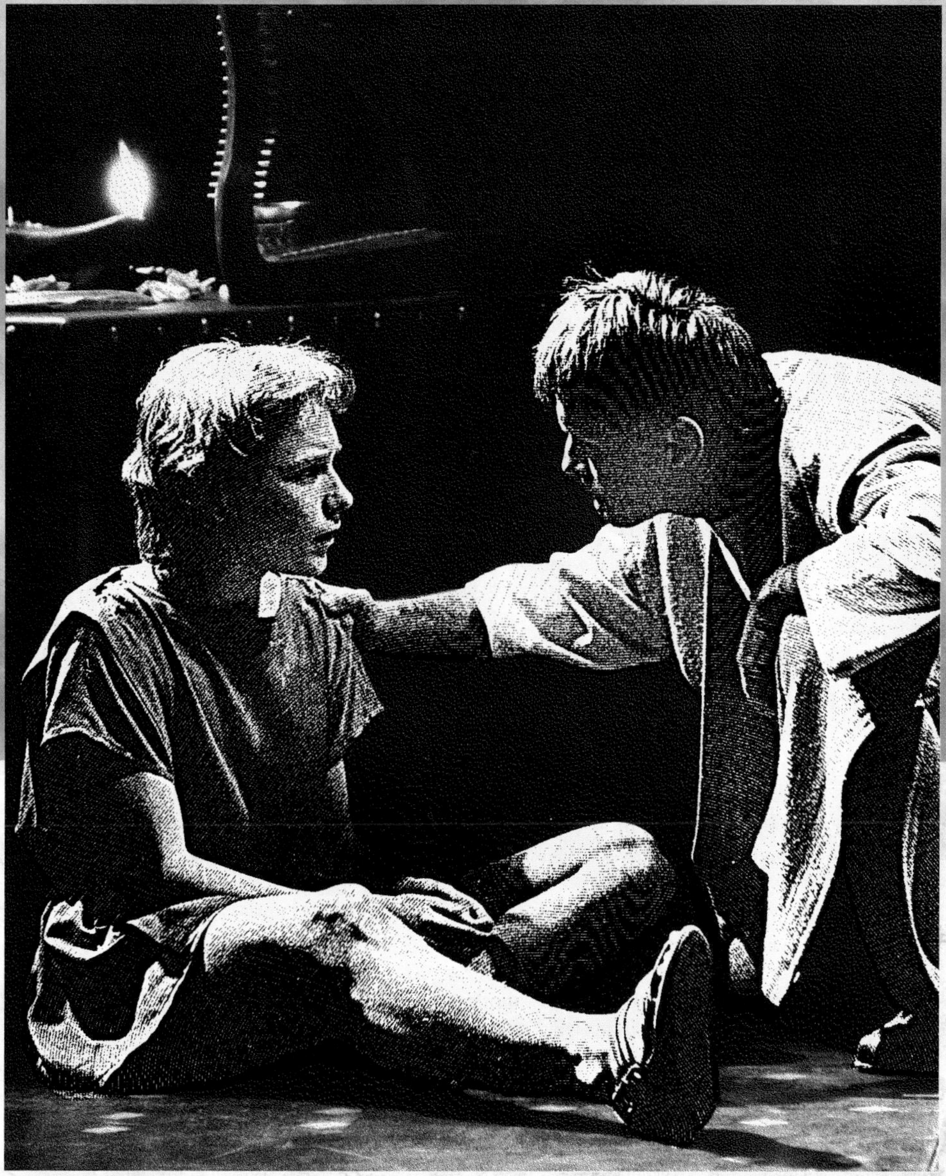

"DIDST THOU DREAM, LUCIUS,
THAT THOU SO CRIEDST OUT?"

FAMILY/COMMUNITY ACTIVITY

Organize a forum called "Brutus and Cassius: Unsettling Differences," and invite parents and other members of the community. If possible, bring in at least one therapist, family counselor, or other professional in the field of human relations or behavior. Start by staging a spirited dramatic reading of the argument between Brutus and Cassius (Scene 3, ll. 1–122). Hold auditions for the two parts, allowing all interested students to try out. For those who don't land the parts, assign other roles, such as directing, dialogue coaching, paraphrasing, and so on. The readers should rehearse their lines. Paraphrasers can translate the scene into contemporary English and then reproduce the paraphrase to give to attendees of the forum. Invite another group of students to write an introduction to the forum. The introduction should set the scene and explain the purpose of the reading: to examine a dramatic argument from *Julius Caesar* as a springboard for exploring constructive ways of settling differences. Assign a speaker from this group to read the introduction. After the dramatic reading, invite the therapist or counselor to comment on Brutus and Cassius's argument. To foster discussion, encourage attendees to comment on Brutus and Cassius's behavior in the argument.

Literary Response and Analysis

Act IV

Reading Check

1. Brutus and Cassius, in exile, have raised armies to challenge the triumvirate. In turn, Antony, Octavius, and Lepidus are preparing to fight.
2. They are deciding whom to sentence to death. Antony wants to drop Lepidus when his usefulness runs out, and Octavius disagrees but will not stop Antony.
3. Brutus doubts Cassius's honesty.
4. Cassius is angry that Brutus ignored his appeals and publicly condemned Lucius Pella for taking bribes. Brutus has heard that Cassius has also taken bribes and is incensed that Cassius refused to send him gold to pay his soldiers.
5. Portia, upset at the triumvirate's power, killed herself by swallowing fire (coals). Brutus bears her death unemotionally, admitting sorrow but refusing to dwell on it.
6. Brutus sees Caesar's Ghost.

Interpretations

7. Antony proves treacherous, dishonest, and cruel. Some students may feel the contrast is too extreme with earlier characterization. Others will disagree, pointing to Antony's cunning in the Act III funeral speech.
8. Students' answers will vary. They may suggest low lighting, with a spotlight on only the action at center stage. They may have soldiers standing behind the main action.
9. The conflict is resolved when both men calm down and admit to bad moods. Brutus apologizes to Cassius for his "ill-tempered" words. Cassius asks Brutus's pardon when Cassius is cranky. By scene's end, they've reaffirmed their friendship.
10. In both meetings the leaders are in conflict. Both Antony and Cassius reveal their greed, and each argues that he, as a seasoned soldier, knows war's realities better than his partner. Octavius and Brutus seem more principled. One difference is that Brutus and Cassius's conflict is more emotional but is finally settled, whereas the conflict between Antony and Octavius is less intense and is not resolved.
11. Brutus is kind, gentle, compassionate, and fatherly toward Lucius.
12. Possible answer: If an actor plays the Ghost, it takes on more significance in the action; a voice representing the Ghost could imply that it is a figment of Brutus's imagination, signifying his guilt or anguish.

Literary Response and Analysis

Act IV

Reading Check

1. Describe the military situation presented in Act IV. What is going on between the conspirators and the triumvirate?
2. As Scene 1 opens, what are Antony, Octavius, and Lepidus doing? What breach has opened among them?
3. Why is Brutus uneasy at the beginning of Scene 2?
4. Throughout the play, Brutus and Cassius have been **foils,** or contrasting characters. What are the issues that cause them to quarrel in their **dialogue,** or conversation, in Scene 3?
5. According to Brutus, what were the reasons for Portia's death? How does he respond to her death?
6. What vision does Brutus see at the end of Act IV?

Interpretations

Reading Standard 3.1 Articulate the relationship between the expressed purposes and the characteristics of different forms of dramatic literature (e.g., tragedy).

Reading Standard 3.10 Identify and describe the function of dialogue, scene designs, and character foils in dramatic literature.

7. How is Antony **characterized** by his words and actions in Scene 1? In your opinion, is the Antony we see in this scene consistent with the Antony we saw earlier? Explain.
8. If you were **staging** the play, how would you let your audience know that in Scene 2 the **setting,** or **scene design,** has changed—instead of a house in Rome, the setting is now a battlefield?
9. In **drama,** relationships burst open under pressure and reveal certain truths. After the burst the relationship is either renewed or ended. Brutus and Cassius have been friends throughout the play, with Cassius clearly the subordinate. In Scene 3, they quarrel. How is their **conflict** resolved? What has become of their relationship by the end of the scene?
10. **Compare and contrast** the meeting of the conspirators in Scene 3 with the meeting of the triumvirate in Scene 1. In what ways are the scenes parallel? In what ways do they differ?
11. The scene with Cassius shows a harsh Brutus. What kind of Brutus appears with Lucius and the guards?
12. As the director of the play, you would have to decide how to **stage** the Ghost. You could have an actor play the Ghost, or you could use just a voice. What would each choice suggest about whether the Ghost is real? What might the Ghost represent to Brutus?
13. In lines 141–160 of Scene 3, Brutus and Cassius display different reactions to Portia's death. Why are their reactions different? How do you feel about these men now?
14. Which **character** do you sympathize with most by the end of Act IV? Why?
15. In Act IV of this **tragedy,** what consequences of the turning point in Act III do we see? How does Brutus's situation worsen?

Evaluation

16. Think about the two groups preparing for war here. Which side would you want to be on? Why?

Writing

A Boy's View

If you were young Lucius, what would you think about the events you've observed? How would you feel about Brutus? Write Lucius's thoughts and fears in a **journal entry.** Read your entry aloud to the class.

Reading Skills

Recognizing Anachronisms

An **anachronism** (from *ana–*, "against," and *chronos*, "time") is an event or a detail that is inappropriate for the time period. For example, a car in a story about the Civil War would be an anachronism; cars had not yet been invented. In a play set in the 1920s, the word *nerd* would be an anachronism. *Nerd* wasn't used as slang until much later in the twentieth century.

Remember that *Julius Caesar* is set in 44–42 B.C. in ancient Rome. Do you see anachronisms in these passages?

1. ". . . he plucked me ope his doublet and offered them his throat to cut."

   —Act I, Scene 2, lines 261–262

2. "Peace! Count the clock."
   "The clock hath stricken three."

   —Act II, Scene 1, line 192

3. "Look, Lucius, here's the book I sought for so;
   I put it in the pocket of my gown."

   —Act IV, Scene 3, lines 250–251

PRACTICE

1. Find the one word in each passage at the left that is out of its time. Suppose Shakespeare wanted to correct his errors. How could he eliminate the anachronisms? Rewrite each passage, and then compare the changes you made with your classmates' versions.
2. Make a class list of other situations that would be anachronistic. An example might be the conspirators' use of guns instead of daggers to kill Caesar or Brutus's receipt of a telegram telling him of Portia's death.

Roman Forum, Rome, Italy.

Reading Skills

Practice

1. Anachronistic words in passages 1–3: *doublet, clock, book.* Students' rewritten passages will probably use, respectively, *robe* or *toga, sundial, scroll.*
2. Answers will vary. Aspects of Act I, for example, that might lend themselves well to anachronism include the occupations of the workers at the beginning of the play or the circumstances under which Cassius saved Caesar from drowning.

ASSESSING

Assessment

- *Progress Assessment of Reading*
  - Selection Test

RETEACHING

For a lesson reteaching Standard 3.1, see **Reteaching,** p. 939A. For another selection to teach Standard 3.1, see *Interactive Reading,* Chapter 10.

13. Cassius seems to take Portia's death harder than Brutus does. Cassius's words are more emotional, while Brutus's matter-of-fact tone reflects his stoicism. Students will probably identify more closely with Cassius.
14. Students will probably sympathize with Brutus or Cassius, who show warmth in their reconciliation, rather than Antony, who shows only ruthlessness.
15. Possible answer: The conspirators' exile, the conflict between Brutus and Cassius, and the triumvirate's relative power are all consequences of the turning point. Other consequences include Portia's death and the appearance of the Ghost, which worsen Brutus's situation.

Evaluation

16. Answers will vary. Some students might prefer to be on Brutus's side because they agree with his republican views. Others might side with Antony since he seems destined to win.

Summary at grade level

Act V

In Scene I, the opposing armies face each other on the plains of Philippi. In Scene 2, Brutus gains an advantage over Octavius's army and orders reinforcements.

Scene 3 opens elsewhere on the battlefield, where Cassius learns that his army is surrounded by Antony's men and that Brutus's soldiers are occupied with looting. After receiving an inaccurate report about his troops' loyalty, Cassius believes himself to be defeated and orders Pindarus to kill him with the sword that stabbed Caesar.

In the final scene, Brutus, who has seen Caesar's Ghost again, believes defeat inescapable and, in effect, commits suicide, leaving Octavius and Antony triumphant.

PRETEACHING

Selection Starter

Motivate. Review the events of each of the previous four acts and discuss how the Shakespearean five-part dramatic structure has so far been reflected in each act.

DIRECT TEACHING

A Literary Focus
GRADE-LEVEL STANDARD

Dramatic dialogue. What function does this speech serve? [Possible responses: It helps recap the events for the audience. It helps the audience visualize the setting.]

Responses to Margin Questions

Stage direction. Flags, tents, and other equipment could indicate a military encampment.

Line 20. There is friction or rivalry between them.

Stage direction. Although all four men make taunts, Octavius and Brutus are more restrained than Antony and Cassius.

ACT V

SCENE 1. *The plains of Philippi.*

Enter OCTAVIUS, ANTONY, *and their* ARMY.

Octavius.
Now, Antony, our hopes are answerèd;
You said the enemy would not come down,
But keep the hills and upper regions.
It proves not so; their battles° are at hand;
They mean to warn us at Philippi here,
Answering before we do demand of them.

Antony.
Tut, I am in their bosoms,° and I know
Wherefore they do it. They could be content
To visit other places, and come down
With fearful bravery, thinking by this face
To fasten in our thoughts that they have courage;
But 'tis not so.

[*Enter a* MESSENGER.]

Messenger. Prepare you, generals,
The enemy comes on in gallant show;
Their bloody sign° of battle is hung out,
And something to be done immediately.

Antony.
Octavius, lead your battle softly on
Upon the left hand of the even° field.

Octavius.
Upon the right hand I; keep thou the left.

Antony.
Why do you cross me in this exigent?°

Octavius.
I do not cross you; but I will do so.

[*March. Drum. Enter* BRUTUS, CASSIUS, *and their* ARMY; LUCILIUS, TITINIUS, MESSALA, *and others.*]

Brutus.
They stand, and would have parley.

Cassius.
Stand fast, Titinius, we must out and talk.

Staging the Play
Stage direction. *This act is crammed with action and could be confusing to follow. As you read, you might take notes about the movements of the armies. What props might be used to indicate that we are now on the plains of Philippi with Antony's and Octavius's army?*

4. battles: armies.

7. am in their bosoms: know their secret thoughts.

14. sign: flag.

17. even: level.

19. exigent (ek'sə·jent): critical moment.

20. *What does this **dialogue** reveal about the relationship between Antony and Octavius?*

Staging the Play
Stage direction. *The armies should be placed at opposite sides of the stage, with a kind of no man's land between them. In the next lines, notice which man in which army speaks. They are taunting one another across the short distance that separates them.*

RESOURCES: READING

Media
- *Audio CD Library*
  - disc 18
- *Visual Connections*
  - Videocassette, Segment 10
- *Fine Art Transparencies*
  - Transparency 17

Reading
- *Interactive Reading,* Teacher's Edition
  - Graphic Organizer: Dramatic Elements Chart

Differentiating Instruction
- *Lesson Plans for Language Development*
  - English-Language Learners, pp. 349–351, 365, 372
  - Special Education Students, pp. 352, 365, 372

854 Chapter 10 Drama • Evaluating an Argument

Octavius.
Mark Antony, shall we give sign of battle?
Antony.
No, Caesar, we will answer on their charge.
Make forth, the generals would have some words.
Octavius.
Stir not until the signal.
Brutus.
Words before blows; is it so, countrymen?
Octavius.
Not that we love words better, as you do.
Brutus.
Good words are better than bad strokes, Octavius.
Antony.
In your bad strokes, Brutus, you give good words;
Witness the hole you made in Caesar's heart,
Crying "Long live! Hail, Caesar!"
Cassius. Antony,
The posture of your blows are yet unknown;
But for your words, they rob the Hybla° bees,
And leave them honeyless.
Antony. Not stingless too.
Brutus.
O, yes, and soundless too;
For you have stol'n their buzzing, Antony,
And very wisely threat before you sting.
Antony.
Villains! You did not so, when your vile daggers
Hacked one another in the sides of Caesar.
You showed your teeth like apes, and fawned like hounds,
And bowed like bondmen, kissing Caesar's feet;
Whilst damnèd Casca, like a cur, behind
Struck Caesar on the neck. O you flatterers!
Cassius.
Flatterers! Now, Brutus, thank yourself;
This tongue had not offended so today,
If Cassius might have ruled.°
Octavius.
Come, come, the cause. If arguing make us sweat,
The proof of it will turn to redder drops.

34. Hybla: town in Sicily famous for its honey.

47. ruled: gotten his way.

? **47.** *What is Cassius referring to?*

DIRECT TEACHING

B Content-Area Connections

History / Literature: Taunts The ritual prebattle exchange of recriminations, taunts, and challenges was an ancient custom that was probably used to incite the warring parties to fight hard. This type of parley became a convention of Elizabethan plays (good examples occur in Christopher Marlowe's *Tamburlaine the Great*) and helped recap the conflicts for the audience.

C Reading Skills

? Making inferences. What words are Antony and Cassius referring to? [Possible responses: Antony refers to the words he thinks (erroneously) that Brutus spoke as Brutus stabbed Caesar. Cassius refers to the sweet words Antony used to assure the conspirators of his friendship after the assassination.]

D Learners Having Difficulty

? Paraphrasing. How would you express the meaning of Antony's speech in your own words? [Possible response: Rather than threaten Caesar, the conspirators smiled and flattered him, pretending to be his friends until they could secretly stab him from behind.]

Response to Margin Question

Line 47. Cassius wanted to kill Antony at the time of the assassination.

DIFFERENTIATING INSTRUCTION

Learners Having Difficulty

Before beginning Act V, ask students to summarize the major events that occurred in Act IV. Answer any lingering questions they may have about those events. Ask students to make some predictions about what they think will happen next.

English-Language Learners

Review some of the battle-related terminology that appears in this act. Possible words to review that are not defined in the margins include *[battle]field, parley, charge, foe, wing, legion, hilt,* and *camp.* Continue to encourage students to use the sidenotes consistently, especially to help understand Elizabethan English.

Advanced Learners

Acceleration. Have small groups of students research how Roman legions were organized and financed. Suggest that students find examples of how "the spoils of war" were used to motivate soldiers and enrich Rome. Then, have them evaluate, either in discussion or in writing, how this historical background information shapes the plot of Act V.

The Tragedy of Julius Caesar, Act V, Scene 1 855

Look,
I draw a sword against conspirators.
When think you that the sword goes up again?
Never, till Caesar's three and thirty wounds
Be well avenged; or till another Caesar°
Have added slaughter to the sword of traitors.

Brutus.
Caesar, thou canst not die by traitors' hands,
Unless thou bring'st them with thee.

54. another Caesar: meaning Octavius himself.

STANDARD REVIEW

Plot structure. Have students identify the five-part Shakespearean structure and the corresponding events in the plot.

I. Exposition—presentation of political scene; introduction of Brutus, Cassius, Caesar (Act I)
II. Rising Action—formation of conspiracy (Act II)
III. Turning Point—assassination (Act III)
IV. Falling Action—Brutus and Antony vie for the allegiance of the Romans; Antony wins the favor of the Romans (Act III); Brutus sees Caesar's Ghost (Act IV); Antony's forces gain the upper hand (Act V)
V. Final Climax and Resolution—the deaths of Cassius and Brutus (Act V)

In Shakespeare's plays the turning point almost always comes in Act III, when something happens that turns the action inexorably downward toward tragedy. This moment also marks a climax of the play, but not the final one or the most powerful one. Traditionally, this climax comes near the end of the action: Here, it occurs when Cassius and Brutus die. At this moment the conflicts in the play are resolved and the tragedy is completed.

856 Chapter 10 Drama • Evaluating an Argument

Octavius. So I hope.
I was not born to die on Brutus' sword.

Brutus.
O, if thou wert the noblest of thy strain,
Young man, thou couldst not die more honorable.

Cassius.
A peevish schoolboy, worthless° of such honor, **A**
Joined with a masker and a reveler. **B**

Antony.
Old Cassius still!

61. **worthless:** unworthy.

? 62. *Whom is Cassius taunting here? What does he think of this "new Caesar"?*

DIRECT TEACHING

A Learners Having Difficulty

Finding details. Octavius was twenty-one years old at the time of the battle and had seen several years of military life. How does Cassius offend Octavius? [He refers to him as a peevish, or irritable, schoolboy.]

B Content-Area Connections

History: Roman Reveler
Explain that a masker is someone who participates in a masque (a type of dramatic pageant) or masquerade ball. Cassius is referring to Antony's reputation as a lover of plays and wild parties. In his biography of Antony, Plutarch notes that the Roman noblemen "did abhor his [Antony's] banquets and drunken feasts [that] he made at unseasonable times, and his extreme wasteful expenses. . . . In his house they did nothing but feast, dance, and mask. And [he] himself passed away the time in hearing of foolish plays. . . ."

Response to Margin Question

Line 62. Cassius is taunting first Octavius and then Antony. Cassius thinks Octavius is whining, immature, and unequal to his title. Also, Antony's comment about Cassius echoes Caesar's estimation of Cassius in Act I.

DIFFERENTIATING INSTRUCTION

Learners Having Difficulty

Chronological order. Ask students to work individually or in groups to create storyboards that graphically depict six to eight major events in the play's plot in chronological order. They should select events from the beginning of Act I through Act V, Scene 1. Students should identify and label the characters, indicate elements of the setting, and provide a written synopsis of each event.

Advanced Learners

Enrichment. Have groups develop a television or newspaper report on the emerging battle between the conspirators and the triumvirate. Students should summarize the background and current situation, interview the key members of the two opposing groups, analyze the situation, and suggest possibilities that might occur in the next few hours or days.

The Tragedy of Julius Caesar, Act V, Scene 1 857

DIRECT TEACHING

A English-Language Learners

Idioms. Explain that the idiom *not have the stomach for* means "being unwilling or disinclined to do something."

B Literary Focus
ADVANCED STANDARD

? Alliteration and assonance. What examples of alliteration occur in this line? [*w, b, sw,* and *l*] What examples of assonance? [long *o* and short *i*] What is their effect? [Possible response: They add momentum.]

C Literary Focus
GRADE-LEVEL STANDARD

? Conflict. By using the term *on the hazard* (a term originally used in gambling), what does Shakespeare suggest about Cassius's inner conflict concerning the coming battle? [Cassius struggles with the idea that fighting is a gamble and all could be lost.]

D Advanced Learners

Symbolism. Challenge students to cite instances in folklore, literature, and art in which eagles have been used as a symbol of power and authority.

E Literary Focus
GRADE-LEVEL STANDARD

? Climax / resolution. What does Cassius's change of mind about the significance of omens suggest about the battle's outcome? [Possible responses: He is afraid that the gods, angry about the assassination, will avenge Caesar.]

Response to Margin Question

Line 88. Ravens, crows, and kites are carrion eaters; a canopy of shadows suggests the darkness of death; the expression *give up the ghost* means "to die."

Octavius. Come, Antony; away!
Defiance, traitors, hurl we in your teeth.
A If you dare fight today, come to the field;
If not, when you have stomachs.

[*Exeunt* OCTAVIUS, ANTONY, *and* ARMY.]

Cassius.
B Why, now blow wind, swell billow, and swim bark!
C The storm is up, and all is on the hazard.°

Brutus.
Ho, Lucilius, hark, a word with you.

[LUCILIUS *and* MESSALA *stand forth.*]

Lucilius. My lord?

[BRUTUS *and* LUCILIUS *converse apart.*]

Cassius.
Messala.

Messala. What says my general?

Cassius. Messala,
This is my birthday; as this very day
Was Cassius born. Give me thy hand, Messala:
Be thou my witness that against my will
(As Pompey was) am I compelled to set
Upon one battle all our liberties.
You know that I held Epicurus strong,°
And his opinion; now I change my mind,
And partly credit things that do presage.°
D Coming from Sardis, on our former ensign°
Two mighty eagles fell, and there they perched,
Gorging and feeding from our soldiers' hands,
Who to Philippi here consorted° us.
E This morning are they fled away and gone,
And in their steads do ravens, crows, and kites
Fly o'er our heads and downward look on us
As we were sickly prey; their shadows seem
A canopy most fatal, under which
Our army lies, ready to give up the ghost.

Messala.
Believe not so.

Cassius. I but believe it partly,
For I am fresh of spirit and resolved
To meet all perils very constantly.

68. on the hazard: at risk.

76. held Epicurus strong: believed in the philosophy of Epicurus, a philosopher of the third century B.C. who held that omens were worthless.

78. presage (prē • sāj′): foretell.

79. former ensign: foremost flag.

82. consorted: accompanied.

? **88.** *What images in this* ***monologue*** *suggest death and decay?*

CONTENT-AREA CONNECTIONS

Culture: Signs of Nature

A notable and probably unhealthy aspect of Roman culture was a deep dread of beginnings. The success of any undertaking was determined by the way it began, so Romans looked for as many guarantees as possible before starting. The gods supplied the best guarantees, and at least half of Roman religion was devoted to the quest for and interpretation of divine portents. Roman portents took the form of natural signs, such as the crows and ravens that appear to Cassius. The most common portents were called auspices and were considered signs from Jupiter. Since the sky was Jupiter's domain, the auspices usually appeared in the sky in the form of birds or lightning. (The word *auspices* literally means "bird observation.") A major responsibility of every Roman magistrate was to consult the auspices.

Brutus.
Even so, Lucilius.
Cassius. Now, most noble Brutus,
The gods today stand friendly, that we may,
Lovers in peace, lead on our days to age!
But since the affairs of men rests still incertain,
Let's reason with the worst that may befall.
If we do lose this battle, then is this
The very last time we shall speak together.
What are you then determinèd to do?
Brutus.
Even by the rule of that philosophy
By which I did blame Cato for the death
Which he did give himself; I know not how,
But I do find it cowardly and vile,
For fear of what might fall, so to prevent
The time° of life, arming myself with patience
To stay the providence of some high powers
That govern us below.
Cassius. Then, if we lose this battle,
You are contented to be led in triumph°
Thorough the streets of Rome?
Brutus.
No, Cassius, no; think not, thou noble Roman,
That ever Brutus will go bound to Rome;
He bears too great a mind. But this same day
Must end that work the ides of March begun;
And whether we shall meet again I know not.
Therefore our everlasting farewell take.
Forever, and forever, farewell, Cassius!
If we do meet again, why, we shall smile;
If not, why then this parting was well made.
Cassius.
Forever, and forever, farewell, Brutus!
If we do meet again, we'll smile indeed;
If not, 'tis true this parting was well made.
Brutus.
Why then, lead on. O, that a man might know
The end of this day's business ere it come!
But it sufficeth that the day will end,
And then the end is known. Come, ho! Away!

[*Exeunt.*]

? Staging the Play
92. *Remember that the two pairs of men have been talking separately. What action should now take place onstage?*

105. time: term, or natural span.

? 107. *Brutus refers again to his Stoic philosophy, which taught that he should be ruled by reason, not by emotion. What is Brutus saying about suicide?*

108. in triumph: as a captive in the victor's procession.

? 109. *According to this speech, what will happen to the losing armies?*

DIRECT TEACHING

F Content-Area Connections

History: Cato
Cato was Portia's father and thus Brutus's father-in-law. He was also Brutus's uncle; thus, Brutus and Portia were cousins. Cato fought on Pompey's side against Caesar and committed suicide rather than be captured.

G Literary Focus
GRADE-LEVEL STANDARD

? Internal conflict. How might you explain Brutus's thinking here? [Possible responses: Brutus seems to be against suicide merely to avoid uncertain danger or disgrace. He seems resolved to fight until he is killed. He experiences a crisis of faith as his former beliefs are overruled by his current fears.]

H Reading Skills

? Making predictions. What do you predict the outcome of the battle will be? [Possible responses: Some students may predict victory for the conspirators because Antony has been exposed as a corrupt leader. Others may say that the conspirators will lose because of the omens or because they are fighting for an unjust cause.]

Responses to Margin Questions

Line 92. Brutus and Cassius come together for a final parting before each exits with his army.
Line 107. He believes it is cowardly to end one's life in order to avoid hardship.
Line 109. They will be paraded through the streets of Rome.

The Tragedy of Julius Caesar, Act V, Scene 1 **859**

DIRECT TEACHING

A Literary Focus
GRADE-LEVEL STANDARD

Scene design. Shakespeare's method of suggesting that a battle is in progress is to offer a sequence of quick little scenes to show what is occurring in various sectors of the battle area. In what previous parts of the play has Shakespeare used short scenes to show rapid action? [Act II, Scenes 3 and 4; Act III, Scene 3; Act IV, Scenes 1 and 2]

B Reading Skills

Drawing conclusions. Who are the "villains" that Cassius refers to? [They are his own men, who are retreating.]

C Learners Having Difficulty

Summarizing. What does Cassius ask Titinius to do? [He asks him to gallop at top speed to the camp below to discover whether Brutus's men or Antony's men have overtaken the site.]

Responses to Margin Questions

Line 6. Brutus is ordering a sudden attack on Octavius's troops.
Line 8. Cassius's men have run from the enemy. Brutus's men, flushed with success over Octavius, have begun looting. Cassius's troops are now surrounded by Antony's.

SCENE 2. *The field of battle.*

Alarum.° *Enter* BRUTUS *and* MESSALA.

Brutus.
Ride, ride, Messala, ride, and give these bills°
Unto the legions on the other side.

[*Loud alarum.*]

Let them set on at once; for I perceive
But cold demeanor° in Octavius' wing,
And sudden push° gives them the overthrow.
Ride, ride, Messala! Let them all come down.

[*Exeunt.*]

Alarum: call to arms by drum or trumpet.

1. **bills:** orders.

4. **cold demeanor:** lack of fighting spirit.
5. **push:** attack.

? 6. *What orders has Brutus given his army?*

SCENE 3. *The field of battle.*

Alarums. Enter CASSIUS *and* TITINIUS.

Cassius.
O, look, Titinius, look, the villains fly!
Myself have to mine own turned enemy.
This ensign° here of mine was turning back;
I slew the coward, and did take it° from him.

Titinius.
O Cassius, Brutus gave the word too early,
Who, having some advantage on Octavius,
Took it too eagerly; his soldiers fell to spoil,°
Whilst we by Antony are all enclosed.

[*Enter* PINDARUS.]

Pindarus.
Fly further off, my lord, fly further off!
Mark Antony is in your tents, my lord.
Fly, therefore, noble Cassius, fly far off!

Cassius.
This hill is far enough. Look, look, Titinius!
Are those my tents where I perceive the fire?

Titinius.
They are, my lord.

Cassius. Titinius, if thou lovest me,
Mount thou my horse and hide thy spurs in him°
Till he have brought thee up to yonder troops

3. **ensign:** standard-bearer.
4. **it:** the flag (standard).

7. **spoil:** loot.

? 8. *What have Brutus's and Cassius's armies done?*

15. In other words, dig your spurs into him to make him go at top speed.

DIFFERENTIATING INSTRUCTION

English-Language Learners
Encourage students to return to earlier acts and identify lines that they understand differently now that they are more accustomed to Shakespearean language. Students might also list words that seem to have several different meanings.

Advanced Learners
Acceleration. Have students work individually or in pairs to adapt a portion of *Julius Caesar* into an excerpt from a novel. Ask them to read their prose aloud and note some of the problems they faced in the writing.

860 Chapter 10 Drama • Evaluating an Argument

And here again, that I may rest assured
Whether yond troops are friend or enemy.

Titinius.
I will be here again even with a thought.° [*Exit.*]

Cassius.
Go, Pindarus, get higher on that hill;
My sight was ever thick. Regard Titinius,
And tell me what thou not'st about the field.

[*Exit* PINDARUS.]

This day I breathèd first. Time is come round,
And where I did begin, there shall I end.
My life is run his compass.° Sirrah, what news?

Pindarus (*above*). O my lord!

Cassius. What news?

Pindarus (*above*).
Titinius is enclosèd round about
With horsemen that make to him on the spur;°
Yet he spurs on. Now they are almost on him.
Now, Titinius! Now some light. O, he lights too!
He's ta'en! (*Shout.*) And, hark! They shout for joy.

Cassius.
Come down; behold no more.
O, coward that I am, to live so long,
To see my best friend ta'en before my face!

[*Enter* PINDARUS.]

Come hither, sirrah.

19. even with a thought: immediately.

? 24. *What is Cassius referring to here?*

25. is run his compass: has completed its appointed span.

? **Staging the Play**
26. *Pindarus stands on the upper stage, suggesting that he is on the hilltop, looking over the field of battle. What does he report to Cassius, who stands below?*

29. on the spur: at top speed.

"O, COWARD THAT I AM,
TO LIVE SO LONG,
TO SEE MY BEST FRIEND
TA'EN BEFORE MY FACE!"

DIRECT TEACHING

D Vocabulary Development
GRADE-LEVEL STANDARD

Understanding Shakespeare. The word *thick* in l. 21 has the archaic meaning of "dull" or "dim." Why might Shakespeare have Cassius suffer from poor vision? [Possible response: The playwright suggests Cassius is shortsighted—both literally and figuratively—about the prospects of the battle.]

E Reading Skills

Main idea. What does Pindarus think he sees? [Titinius being overtaken and seized by Antony's troops.]

Responses to Margin Questions

Line 24. Cassius predicts he will die on that day, his birthday.

Line 26. Pindarus reports that Titinius is surrounded by horsemen who overtake him, seize him as he dismounts, and shout for joy.

READING SKILLS REVIEW

Questioning. Remind students that asking questions about the text as they read will help them to think deeply about what they are reading. Emphasize that in addition to asking questions that begin with *who, what, when, where, why,* and *how* about specific aspects of the text, students should also pose more global questions: What exactly don't I understand? What do I know that will help me with this? What should I do to understand it better? Students should also use questions to determine which element—language, plot, or character—is giving them the most difficulty.

Activity. Ask students to write five *5W-How?* questions about events or characters in the play that are unclear to them. Then, have them work with a partner to re-read parts of the play, discuss the questions, and provide responses.

The Tragedy of Julius Caesar, Act V, Scene 3 **861**

DIRECT TEACHING

A Literary Focus
GRADE-LEVEL STANDARD

Climax / resolution. Why is it significant that Cassius dies with Caesar's name on his lips? [Possible responses: Cassius's dying words suggest that Caesar's spirit has won the battle and still dominates the play. It's ironic that Cassius killed Caesar to free himself and his country from tyranny, but only with his own death can Cassius truly escape Caesar.]

B Literary Focus
GRADE-LEVEL STANDARD

Figurative language. Why do you think Shakespeare compares Cassius's death to the sunset? [Possible responses: The redness of the setting sun suggests the redness of blood. The end of the day suggests the end of a life. Cassius's death is the end of an era.]

Responses to Margin Questions

Line 46. Cassius has Pindarus kill him, using the sword that Cassius used to kill Caesar. Cassius believes Titinius has been taken by the enemy.

Line 54. Titinius is free, not captured, as Cassius believed. The audience may feel sad that Cassius has mistakenly sacrificed his life.

Line 65. Titinius thinks Cassius did not believe in his success in carrying out the order or in the success of Brutus's army.

In Parthia° did I take thee prisoner;
And then I swore thee, saving of° thy life,
That whatsoever I did bid thee do,
Thou shouldst attempt it. Come now, keep thine oath.
A Now be a freeman, and with this good sword,
That ran through Caesar's bowels, search this bosom.
Stand not to answer. Here, take thou the hilts,
And when my face is covered, as 'tis now,
Guide thou the sword—Caesar, thou art revenged,
Even with the sword that killed thee. [*Dies.*]

Pindarus.
So, I am free; yet would not so have been,
Durst I have done my will. O Cassius!
Far from this country Pindarus shall run,
Where never Roman shall take note of him. [*Exit.*]

[*Enter* TITINIUS *and* MESSALA.]

Messala.
It is but change,° Titinius; for Octavius
Is overthrown by noble Brutus' power,
As Cassius' legions are by Antony.

Titinius.
These tidings will well comfort Cassius.

Messala.
Where did you leave him?

Titinius. All disconsolate,
With Pindarus his bondman, on this hill.

Messala.
Is not that he that lies upon the ground?

Titinius.
He lies not like the living. O my heart!

Messala.
Is not that he?

Titinius. No, this was he, Messala,
But Cassius is no more. O setting sun,
B As in thy red rays thou dost sink to night,
So in his red blood Cassius' day is set.
The sun of Rome is set. Our day is gone;
Clouds, dews, and dangers come; our deeds are done!
Mistrust of° my success hath done this deed.

Messala.
Mistrust of good success hath done this deed.
O hateful Error, Melancholy's child,

37. Parthia: ancient country (corresponding to part of modern Iran) that was the site of many Roman military campaigns.
38. saving of: sparing.

Staging the Play
46. *What does Cassius have Pindarus do for him? What does he believe has happened?*

51. change: exchange of fortune.

Staging the Play
54. *Titinius and Messala enter from the wings and do not see Cassius's body at first. What irony do we in the audience feel when we hear their conversation?*

65. Mistrust of: disbelief in.

65. *What does Titinius think caused Cassius to kill himself?*

DIFFERENTIATING INSTRUCTION

Learners Having Difficulty
Have students complete plot charts that present the main events of the play. The charts should briefly describe the introduction, rising action, climax, falling action, and resolution. Have students compare and discuss their charts.

Advanced Learners
Enrichment. Have small groups of students discuss alternative courses of action that Cassius and Brutus might have taken in the final act, actions that would probably have resulted in a more positive outcome. Have students explain why each alternative scenario might be in keeping with each character's traits.

862 Chapter 10 Drama • Evaluating an Argument

"THE SUN OF ROME IS SET."

CONTENT-AREA CONNECTIONS

Literature: A Critical Comment

According to G. B. Harrison in *Shakespeare's Tragedies,* "*Julius Caesar* in several ways marks a transition in the development of Shakespeare's dramatic art. In his early plays, in *Romeo and Juliet,* for instance, he cared more for the story than for the motives. In *Julius Caesar,* Shakespeare begins to be interested in the workings of the minds of two or three selected individuals; for the play is less concerned with the fate of the Dictator than with the motives which led Brutus to join the conspirators, the action and reaction of Cassius upon Brutus and Brutus upon Cassius, and their moral degeneration after the murder. The story is thus shown not objectively, but from the points of view of certain individuals."

DIRECT TEACHING

A Literary Focus
ADVANCED STANDARD

Apostrophe. An apostrophe is a figure of speech in which something nonhuman is addressed as if it were capable of responding to the speaker. What example of apostrophe do you find in Messala's speech? [Messala addresses Error as if it were capable of hearing him.]

B Literary Focus
REVIEW STANDARD

Theme. How does Titinius's statement develop the thematic statement made by Cicero in Act I: "But men may construe things after their fashion"? [Possible response: The play has come full circle with Titinius's agonized lament, "Alas, thou hast misconstrued everything!" The course of people's lives is determined by how they interpret or construe the events around them.]

C Advanced Learners

Making connections. Who else in this act makes a similar cry? [Before he dies, Cassius cries, "Caesar, thou art revenged, / Even with the sword that killed thee" (Scene 3, ll. 45–46).] What central concept in the play does Brutus's statement point to? [Caesar remains the most powerful force throughout the play, even after his death; in attacking Caesar, the conspirators made a major misjudgment.]

Response to Margin Question

Line 96. Caesar's assassination led them to this battlefield. Brutus also seems to be remembering the Ghost's message in Act IV, Scene 3, ll. 279–284.

A
Why dost thou show to the apt° thoughts of men
The things that are not? O Error, soon conceived,
Thou never com'st unto a happy birth,
But kill'st the mother° that engend'red thee!

Titinius.
What, Pindarus! Where art thou, Pindarus?

Messala.
Seek him, Titinius, whilst I go to meet
The noble Brutus, thrusting this report
Into his ears. I may say "thrusting" it;
For piercing steel and darts envenomèd
Shall be as welcome to the ears of Brutus
As tidings of this sight.

Titinius. Hie you, Messala,
And I will seek for Pindarus the while.

[*Exit* MESSALA.]

B
Why didst thou send me forth, brave Cassius?
Did I not meet thy friends, and did not they
Put on my brows this wreath of victory,
And bid me give it thee? Didst thou not hear their shouts?
Alas, thou hast misconstrued everything!
But hold thee, take this garland on thy brow;
Thy Brutus bid me give it thee, and I
Will do his bidding. Brutus, come apace,°
And see how I regarded Caius Cassius.
By your leave, gods.° This is a Roman's part:°
Come, Cassius' sword, and find Titinius' heart.

[*Dies.*]

[*Alarum. Enter* BRUTUS, MESSALA, YOUNG CATO, STRATO, VOLUMNIUS, *and* LUCILIUS.]

Brutus.
Where, where, Messala, doth his body lie?

Messala.
Lo, yonder, and Titinius mourning it.

Brutus.
Titinius' face is upward.

Cato. He is slain.

C
Brutus.
O Julius Caesar, thou art mighty yet!
Thy spirit walks abroad, and turns our swords
In our own proper entrails. [*Low alarums.*]

68. apt: credulous; easily impressed.

71. the mother: that is, Cassius, who conceived the error.

87. apace: quickly.

89. He asks the gods' permission to end his life before the time they have allotted to him. **part:** role; duty.

? **96.** *Why does Brutus invoke Caesar's name?*

READING SKILLS REVIEW

Making inferences about character. Review the fact that making an inference involves making a guess about something on the basis of information in the text and the reader's prior knowledge and experience. Point out that students have made inferences about the characters Caesar, Antony, Brutus, and Portia in previous acts.

Activity. Ask students to review information about Lucilius and Cato from this scene. (You may also want to provide the information from the Content-Area Connections annotation A, in the side column on p. 866.) Ask students to make inferences about the traits that these two characters share. Ask students to speculate about the reasons for the two

864 Chapter 10 Drama • Evaluating an Argument

Cato. Brave Titinius!
Look, whe'r° he have not crowned dead Cassius.

Brutus.
Are yet two Romans living such as these?
The last of all the Romans, fare thee well!
It is impossible that ever Rome
Should breed thy fellow.° Friends, I owe moe tears
To this dead man than you shall see me pay.
I shall find time, Cassius; I shall find time.
Come, therefore, and to Thasos° send his body;
His funerals shall not be in our camp,
Lest it discomfort° us. Lucilius, come,
And come, young Cato; let us to the field.
Labeo and Flavius set our battles on.
'Tis three o'clock; and, Romans, yet ere night
We shall try fortune in a second fight. *[Exeunt.]*

97. **whe'r:** whether.

101. **fellow:** equal.

104. **Thasos:** island in the Aegean Sea, near Philippi.

106. **discomfort:** discourage.

SCENE 4. *The field of battle.*

Alarum. Enter BRUTUS, MESSALA, YOUNG CATO, LUCILIUS, *and* FLAVIUS.

Brutus.
Yet, countrymen, O, yet hold up your heads!
[Exit, with followers.]

Cato.
What bastard° doth not? Who will go with me?
I will proclaim my name about the field.
I am the son of Marcus Cato,° ho!
A foe to tyrants, and my country's friend.
I am the son of Marcus Cato, ho!

[Enter SOLDIERS *and fight.]*

2. **bastard:** low fellow.

4. Thus he is Portia's brother.

"O, JULIUS CAESAR, THOU ART MIGHTY YET!
THY SPIRIT WALKS ABROAD, AND TURNS OUR SWORDS
IN OUR OWN PROPER ENTRAILS."

DIRECT TEACHING

D Reading Skills

Memorizing famous passages. This skill is presented on p. 880. Opportunities to apply the skill occur in Act V. **How would you break up this speech into segments if you wanted to memorize it?** [Possible response: ll. 98–99; ll. 100–102; l. 103; l. 104 to the middle of l. 106; the middle of l. 106 to 108; ll. 109–110.]

E Literary Focus
GRADE-LEVEL STANDARD

Scene design. **What does Shakespeare emphasize by having each scene in this act open with alarums?** [Possible responses: They indicate scenes of battle. The low-beating drum rolls and trumpet calls underscore the inevitably advancing doom.]

F Literary Focus
GRADE-LEVEL STANDARD

Climax / resolution. **Why do you think Shakespeare has Brutus hurry out at the beginning of Scene 4 surrounded by his men?** [Possible response: It suggests that Brutus is rushing here and there on the battlefield, rallying his troops for the climactic final battle. It shows that Brutus is still in control of loyal troops, adding a sense of suspense to the approaching climax and resolution.]

soldiers' extraordinary selflessness. Ask students what generalization they can make about Shakespeare's depiction of Roman soldiers on the basis of the information he provides about Lucilius, Cato, Titinius, and Pindarus.

The Tragedy of Julius Caesar, Act V, Scene 4 865

DIRECT TEACHING

A Content-Area Connections

History: Plutarch's Account

According to Plutarch, Lucilius impersonated Brutus in the hope of saving him. ". . . one of Brutus's friends called Lucilius, who seeing a troop of barbarous men . . . going all together right against Brutus, he determined to stay them with the hazard of his life, and, being left behind, told them that he was Brutus; and, because they should believe him, he prayed them to bring him to Antonius. . . . "

B Reading Skills

Making inferences. What does Lucilius's willingness to die in Brutus's place reveal? [Possible responses: Brutus's officers are totally devoted to their leader; Brutus's nobility inspires extraordinary loyalty.]

C Advanced Learners

Speculating. Why do you think the soldiers would be unwilling to kill "a noble prisoner"? [Possible responses: Killing Brutus could have major political implications. The choice to kill Brutus should rightfully be left to Antony. Noble prisoners could be ransomed for large sums of money.]

Responses to Margin Questions

Line 7. Their actions may be a diversionary tactic to protect Brutus and to divide Antony's troops.

Line 32. Antony seems more compassionate. He commands that a brave enemy be spared. However, his behavior is also a strategic change: "I had rather have / Such men my friends than enemies" (ll. 28–29).

A
Lucilius.
And I am Brutus, Marcus Brutus, I;
Brutus, my country's friend, know me for Brutus!

[YOUNG CATO *falls.*]

O young and noble Cato, art thou down?
Why, now thou diest as bravely as Titinius,
And mayst be honored, being Cato's son.

First Soldier.
Yield, or thou diest.

B
Lucilius. Only I yield to die.
There is so much that thou wilt kill me straight;°
Kill Brutus, and be honored in his death.

First Soldier.
C
We must not. A noble prisoner!

[*Enter* ANTONY.]

Second Soldier.
Room, ho! Tell Antony, Brutus is ta'en.

First Soldier.
I'll tell the news. Here comes the general.
Brutus is ta'en, Brutus is ta'en, my lord.

Antony.
Where is he?

Lucilius.
Safe, Antony; Brutus is safe enough.
I dare assure thee that no enemy
Shall ever take alive the noble Brutus.
The gods defend him from so great a shame!
When you do find him, or alive or dead,
He will be found like Brutus, like himself.°

Antony.
This is not Brutus, friend, but, I assure you,
A prize no less in worth. Keep this man safe;
Give him all kindness. I had rather have
Such men my friends than enemies. Go on,
And see whe'r Brutus be alive or dead,
And bring us word unto Octavius' tent
How everything is chanced.° [*Exeunt.*]

Staging the Play 7. *Lucilius is impersonating Brutus. What are these young men doing, and why?*

13. That is, there is so much inducement to kill me that you will surely do so right away. (Some editors have interpreted this line to mean that Lucilius is offering his captors money to kill him rather than take him prisoner.)

25. like himself: true to his own noble nature.

32. chanced: turned out.

32. *Not long ago Antony was compiling a list of the enemies he was to have murdered. How does he seem to have changed?*

CONTENT-AREA CONNECTIONS

Literature: A Critical Comment

In a critical treatise on *Julius Caesar,* Vivian Thomas writes: "Despite his immensely sympathetic appeal, the treatment of Marcus Brutus is too ironic to bear the full weight of tragic hero. He never gains a clear understanding of his own mistakes and of what went wrong and why. His dying reflection:—'Countrymen, / My heart doth joy that yet in all my life / I found no man but he was true to me.' (ll. 33–35) is no doubt true and is truly moving but it is undercut by his seeming failure to realize that in order to fulfill what he saw as his public duty he betrayed Julius Caesar. . . . Likewise, Brutus reveals no understanding of the political inheritance he bequeaths to Rome; he remains confident that he has acted rightly and that history will vindicate him."

SCENE 5. *The field of battle.*

Enter BRUTUS, DARDANIUS, CLITUS, STRATO, *and* VOLUMNIUS.

Brutus.
Come, poor remains of friends, rest on this rock.

Clitus.
Statilius showed the torchlight, but, my lord,
He came not back; he is or ta'en or slain.°

Brutus.
Sit thee down, Clitus. Slaying is the word;
It is a deed in fashion. Hark thee, Clitus.

[*Whispers.*]

Clitus.
What, I, my lord? No, not for all the world!

Brutus.
Peace then, no words.

Clitus. I'll rather kill myself.

Brutus.
Hark thee, Dardanius. [*Whispers.*]

Dardanius. Shall I do such a deed?

Clitus. O Dardanius!

Dardanius. O Clitus!

Clitus.
What ill request did Brutus make to thee?

Dardanius.
To kill him, Clitus. Look, he meditates.

Clitus.
Now is that noble vessel° full of grief,
That it runs over even at his eyes.

Brutus.
Come hither, good Volumnius; list° a word.

Volumnius.
What says my lord?

Brutus. Why, this, Volumnius:
The ghost of Caesar hath appeared to me
Two several° times by night; at Sardis once,
And this last night here in Philippi fields.
I know my hour is come.

Volumnius. Not so, my lord.

3. According to Plutarch, Statilius volunteered to see what was happening at Cassius's camp. If all was well, he was to signal with his torchlight. He did signal but then was killed while returning to Brutus's camp.

? **5.** *What is Brutus's mood?*

13. vessel: figure of speech meaning "human being."

15. list: listen to.

18. several: separate.

DIRECT TEACHING

D Literary Focus
GRADE-LEVEL STANDARD

? Climax / resolution. How would you contrast the state of Brutus's army with the state of Antony's? [Possible response: As conditions deteriorate, Brutus's army crumbles and becomes demoralized; by contrast, Antony's soldiers remain well organized and disciplined.] What does this suggest about the battle's outcome? [Antony's men seem almost certain to win the battle.]

E Reading Skills

? Making inferences. What is Brutus asking his devoted men to do? [Brutus asks his men to help him commit suicide by holding his sword while he runs onto it.]

Response to Margin Question

Line 5. Brutus's cynical remark shows his hopelessness.

The Tragedy of Julius Caesar, Act V, Scene 5 **867**

Direct Teaching

A Literary Focus
GRADE-LEVEL STANDARD

Conflict. Look back at Brutus's comments to Cassius about suicide in Scene 1, ll. 100–112. How do you think Brutus has reconciled his internal conflict? [Possible response: Although Brutus found suicide in battle cowardly and vile, he also stated that he would never allow himself to be taken back to Rome as a prisoner; in his mind, suicide seems to be the lesser of the two evils.]

B Literary Focus
GRADE-LEVEL STANDARD

Irony. Why is it ironic that everyone in Brutus's life has been true to him? [Although no one ever betrayed him, he betrayed Caesar by leading the conspiracy.]

C Literary Focus
GRADE-LEVEL STANDARD

Climax / resolution. Does Brutus's speech suggest anything about the play's resolution? [Possible responses: Brutus still believes that his cause has been just even though Octavius and Mark Antony have attained victory. He suggests that under the rule of these men, there will be an end to Roman freedom.]

D Literary Focus
REVIEW STANDARD

Theme. Why is it important that the man who holds the sword has some "smatch of honor"? [Possible response: Honor is all-important to Brutus; it is the principle for which he has lived and for which he dies.]

Response to Margin Question

Line 41. Brutus means that his death is waiting for him.

Brutus.
Nay, I am sure it is, Volumnius.
Thou seest the world, Volumnius, how it goes;
Our enemies have beat us to the pit.°

[*Low alarums.*]

(A)
It is more worthy to leap in ourselves
Than tarry till they push us. Good Volumnius,
Thou know'st that we two went to school together;
Even for that our love of old, I prithee
Hold thou my sword-hilts whilst I run on it.

Volumnius.
That's not an office for a friend, my lord.

[*Alarum still.*]

Clitus.
Fly, fly, my lord, there is no tarrying here.

Brutus.
Farewell to you; and you; and you, Volumnius.
Strato, thou hast been all this while asleep;
Farewell to thee too, Strato. Countrymen,
(B)
My heart doth joy that yet in all my life
I found no man but he was true to me.
(C)
I shall have glory by this losing day
More than Octavius and Mark Antony
By this vile conquest shall attain unto.
So fare you well at once, for Brutus' tongue
Hath almost ended his life's history.
Night hangs upon mine eyes; my bones would rest,
That have but labored to attain this hour.

[*Alarum. Cry within,* "Fly, fly, fly!"]

Clitus.
Fly, my lord, fly!

Brutus. Hence! I will follow.

[*Exeunt* CLITUS, DARDANIUS, *and* VOLUMNIUS.]

(D)
I prithee, Strato, stay thou by thy lord,
Thou art a fellow of a good respect.°
Thy life hath had some smatch° of honor in it;
Hold then my sword, and turn away thy face,
While I do run upon it. Wilt thou, Strato?

23. pit: trap for capturing wild animals; also, a grave.

41. *What does he mean by saying that "night hangs upon" his eyes?*

45. respect: reputation.

46. smatch: trace; taste.

Content-Area Connections

Literature: A Critical Comment
According to Coppélia Kahn in *Julius Caesar: A Modern Prespective,* ". . . [B]oth [Cassius and Brutus] imply in their last words that Caesar's spirit has taken revenge on them, and many critics have adopted this interpretation, which provides a certain kind of moral closure typical of Elizabethan revenge plays. But we need not seek explanations only in the supernatural realm. Brutus and Cassius, in effect, help to bring about their own downfall through their moral blindness and tactical errors, and Mark Antony foments civil war to serve his own interests. Curiously, the 'monstrous apparition' that appears to Brutus in his tent on the eve of battle calls itself not Caesar but 'Thy evil spirit' and says only 'thou shalt see me at Philippi.' Perhaps Shakespeare

Strato.
Give me your hand first. Fare you well, my lord.

Brutus.
Farewell, good Strato—Caesar, now be still;
I killed not thee with half so good a will. [*Dies.*]

[*Alarum. Retreat. Enter* ANTONY, OCTAVIUS, MESSALA, LUCILIUS, *and the* ARMY.]

Octavius. What man is that?

Messala.
My master's man. Strato, where is thy master?

Staging the Play
51. *How many bodies now lie on the stage? It is important for a director of a Shakespearean tragedy to remember how many bodies are onstage. Getting rid of them is often a challenge.*

DIRECT TEACHING

E Reading Skills

Paraphrasing. How would you paraphrase Brutus's final words? [Possible response: Caesar, your spirit may rest. I go to my own death more willingly than I carried out your assassination.]

F Literary Focus
GRADE-LEVEL STANDARD

Climax / resolution. The play's climax, or moment of greatest tension, is the deaths of Cassius and Brutus. With Brutus's death, the play's action now turns to the resolution, which ties up any loose ends in the plot.

Response to Margin Question

Line 51. There are four bodies—those of Cassius, Titinius, Cato, and Brutus.

is implying that Brutus's own fatal error of judgment in thinking that republican liberty could be achieved only by killing Caesar has resulted, quite contrary to his intentions, in evil. Brutus himself is not evil, though his uncompromising idealism carries with it a subtle vanity. We might say that he only carries to a misguided extreme the values and expectations implied in the republican ideals he inherited. As Cicero states, 'Men may construe many things after their fashion, / Clean from the purpose of the things themselves.'"

DIRECT TEACHING

A Literary Focus
GRADE-LEVEL STANDARD

? Dramatic dialogue. Strato's words eulogize Brutus. They also reinforce the play's theme of honor. What role did honor play in Brutus's life? [Possible response: Honor was the ultimate focus and literally the undoing of Brutus's life.]

B Literary Focus
GRADE-LEVEL STANDARD

? Climax / resolution. How do Octavius's words help the play move to completion? [Possible response: Octavius restores peace, ends the bloodshed, and attempts to heal the wounds.]

C Reading Skills

? Memorizing famous passages. How might you divide this speech in order to memorize it? [Possible response: l. 68; ll. 69–70; ll. 71–72; ll. 73–75.]

D Advanced Learners

Enrichment. Ask students to name other individuals from history whom Nature might describe by saying to all the world, "This was a man!" or "This was a woman!" Ask them to focus on individuals who seem to embody a harmonious mixture of traits.

Response to Margin Question

Line 61. He offers to take Brutus's men into his service.

"THIS WAS THE NOBLEST ROMAN OF THEM ALL. . . .
HIS LIFE WAS GENTLE, AND THE ELEMENTS
SO MIXED IN HIM THAT NATURE
MIGHT STAND UP
AND SAY TO ALL THE WORLD,
'THIS WAS A MAN!'"

Strato.
(A) Free from the bondage you are in, Messala;
The conquerors can but make a fire of him.
For Brutus only overcame himself,
And no man else hath honor by his death.

Lucilius.
So Brutus should be found. I thank thee, Brutus,
That thou hast proved Lucilius' saying true.

Octavius.
All that served Brutus, I will entertain them.
(B) Fellow, wilt thou bestow° thy time with me?

Strato.
Ay, if Messala will prefer° me to you.

Octavius. Do so, good Messala.

Messala. How died my master, Strato?

Strato.
I held the sword, and he did run on it.

Messala.
Octavius, then take him to follow thee,
That did the latest service to my master.

Antony.
This was the noblest Roman of them all.
All the conspirators save only he
Did that they did in envy of great Caesar;
(C) He, only in a general honest thought
And common good to all, made one of them.°
(D) His life was gentle, and the elements
So mixed in him that Nature might stand up
And say to all the world, "This was a man!"

61. bestow: spend.

? **61.** *How does Octavius indicate by his words to his former enemies that the strife is finally over?*

62. prefer: recommend.

72. made one of them: joined their group.

STANDARD REVIEW

Theme. Have the class discuss possible themes of *Julius Caesar.* Suggest that one possible theme is the struggle between ambition and honor.

Activity. After students have read Act V, ask them to paraphrase Antony's words in Scene 5, ll. 68–72, using some form of the words *honor and ambition.* [Possible response: Of all the conspirators, only Brutus acted purely for honorable reasons; the others were moved by ambition or envy.] **Ask students to suggest why someone acting out of honor would meet such a tragic end.** [Possible response: The tragedy has been the failure of an idealist to survive in a world where his honor and other noble qualities force him into destruction even as they show him in the most favorable light.]

870 Chapter 10 Drama • Evaluating an Argument

Octavius.
According to his virtue, let us use° him
With all respect and rites of burial. **E**
Within my tent his bones tonight shall lie,
Most like a soldier ordered honorably.
So call the field to rest, and let's away
To part° the glories of this happy day. **F**

[Exeunt omnes.]

76. **use:** treat.

81. **part:** divide.

Staging the Play
81. *Order has been restored; healing will begin. Which actor would you have exit last?*

DIRECT TEACHING

E Content-Area Connections

History / Culture: Honoring the Dead

The Roman practice was to cremate bodies in a sacred place, not bury them. In fact, it was Antony, not Octavius, who extended honors to the dead Brutus. After finding Brutus's dead body, Antony covered it with his scarlet mantle, another detail changed by Shakespeare.

F Literary Focus

GRADE-LEVEL STANDARD

Climax / resolution. In Shakespearean tragedy, the dominant leader always utters the final hopeful lines. What do these lines tell us? [Possible response: In the inevitable struggle for power that will arise between Octavius and Antony, Octavius will emerge victorious.]

Response to Margin Question

Line 81. Since Shakespeare makes Octavius the authority figure at the end of the play, a final exit for Octavius would best support the values embodied in the play.

Check Test: True-False

Monitoring students' progress. Ask students to answer the following questions.

1. Before the battle, Antony, Octavius, Brutus, and Cassius meet in a tent to shake hands and pledge an honorable fight. [F]
2. During the battle, Pindarus mistakes Brutus's troops for the enemy and reports to Cassius that Titinius is captured. [T]
3. Cassius commits suicide by recklessly going into the battle unarmed. [F]
4. Brutus is captured by Antony and commits suicide out of shame. [F]
5. At the end of the play, Antony is the sole ruler of Rome. [F]

The Tragedy of Julius Caesar, Act V, Scene 5 871

Connection

Summary ↔ *at grade level*

This theory describes the elements of tragedy as observed by Aristotle, who was the first to define it. Key elements of tragedy are the presence of a hero from a high station and a tragic character flaw in that hero that leads to his or her downfall. The overall effect of tragedy is to induce a catharsis in the audience—to purge them of pity and terror.

DIRECT TEACHING

A Reading Informational Materials
GRADE-LEVEL STANDARD

Extending sources. Think about a movie or television program that involved you so completely that you felt a release when its issues were finally resolved. Would it be accurate to describe what you saw as a tragedy? Why or why not? [Responses will vary. Be sure students measure the movie or TV show against Aristotle's criteria.]

B Advanced Learners

Speculating. In theory, a tragic hero in Aristotle's day needed to belong to the royal family. What kinds of circumstances would fulfill Aristotle's requirements today? [Today a fall from good fortune could involve a character who starts out very rich, powerful, or famous in almost any field.]

C Literary Focus
GRADE-LEVEL STANDARD

Tragic hero. On the basis of the information given so far, how would you define *tragic hero*? [A tragic hero is a fortunate or privileged person who is nevertheless brought down by a personal weakness or an error in judgment.]

CONNECTION / THEORY

Tragedy was first defined by the Greek philosopher Aristotle (384–322 B.C.), and critics have been arguing about it ever since. Aristotle's definition is not a rule for what tragedy should be; *it is a description of what he believed tragedy* was, *based on his observations of Greek drama, particularly the works of Sophocles.*

Aristotle. Hellenic sculpture. (32 cm high).
Louvre, Paris.

What Is a Tragic Hero?

According to Aristotle, the function of **tragedy** is to arouse pity and fear in the audience so that we may be purged, or cleansed, of these unsettling emotions. Aristotle's term for this emotional purging is the Greek word *catharsis.* **A** Although no one is exactly sure what Aristotle meant by *cartharsis,* it seems clear that he was referring to that strangely pleasurable sense of emotional release we experience after watching a great tragedy. For some reason, we usually feel exhilarated, not depressed, at the end.

According to Aristotle, a tragedy can arouse these twin emotions of pity and fear only if it presents a certain type of hero, who is neither completely good nor completely bad.

B Aristotle also says that the **tragic hero** should be someone "highly renowned and prosperous," which in Aristotle's day meant a member of the royalty. Why not an ordinary working person? we might ask. The answer is simply that the hero must fall from tremendous good fortune. Otherwise, we wouldn't feel such pity and fear.

> . . . the change of fortune presented must not be the spectacle of a virtuous man brought from prosperity to adversity: For this moves neither pity nor fear; it merely shocks us. Nor again, that of a bad man passing from adversity to prosperity: For nothing can be more alien to the spirit of tragedy; . . . it neither satisfies the moral sense nor calls forth pity or fear. Nor, again, should the downfall of the utter villain be exhibited. A plot of this kind would, doubtless, satisfy the moral sense, but it would inspire neither pity nor fear; for pity is aroused by unmerited misfortune, fear by the misfortune of a man like ourselves. . . . **C** There remains, then, the character between these two extremes—that of a man who is not eminently good and just, yet whose misfortune is brought about not by vice or depravity, but by some error or frailty. . . .
>
> —Aristotle, the *Poetics,* translated by S. H. Butcher

Connecting and Comparing Texts

After reading the Connection feature, have students explain how *Julius Caesar* demonstrates the principles of tragedy outlined by Aristotle. Who do they consider the tragic hero in this play and why? Then, ask why themes such as "doing the right thing" or "ambition versus honor" might turn up in many tragedies. To conclude the discussion, ask students if they would use the term *catharsis* to describe the experience of reading *Julius Caesar.*

Critics have argued over what Aristotle meant by the tragic hero's "error or frailty." Is the hero defeated because of a single error of judgment, or is the cause of the hero's downfall a **tragic flaw**—a fundamental character weakness, such as destructive pride, ruthless ambition, or obsessive jealousy? In either interpretation the key point is that the hero is on some level responsible for his or her own downfall. The hero is not the mere plaything of the gods—the helpless victim of fate or of someone else's villainy. By the end of the play, the tragic hero comes to recognize his or her own error and to accept its tragic consequences. The real hero does not curse fate or the gods. The real hero is humbled—and enlightened—by the tragedy.

Yet we, the audience, feel that the hero's punishment exceeds the crime, that the hero gets more than he or she deserves. We feel pity because the hero is a suffering human being who is flawed like us. We also feel fear because the hero is *better* than we are, and *still* he failed. What hope can there be for us? **D**

Melpomene, muse of tragedy. Detail from the Mosaic of the Nine Muses, Rome.

DIRECT TEACHING

D Reading Informational Materials
GRADE-LEVEL STANDARD

Extending sources. Do you think that Aristotle's view of tragedy assumes that life is essentially hopeless? Explain. [Possible responses: No, because in Aristotle's world, only a few of the highborn suffered tragedy. No, because hope lies in accepting the lesson that the gods teach by way of the tragedy.]

DIFFERENTIATING INSTRUCTION

Learners Having Difficulty

Outlining. Have students work in small groups to outline the essay as they read it. Urge them to pause to reread, ask questions, and discuss paragraphs as necessary. Remind them to summarize the main idea of each paragraph in a single sentence, if possible. Their outlines should consist of these key ideas plus important supporting details and examples.

Connection

Summary ↔ *at grade level*

This newspaper article by journalist Jimmy Breslin was written in the days following the assassination of Martin Luther King, Jr., a tension filled time when there was rioting in the streets of many American cities and the threat of anarchy was imminent.

Breslin reports on events in Washington, D.C. The city he describes is more like a battlefield than the capitol of a powerful nation. Fires light the sky, wreckage is everywhere, and troops wearing gas masks walk the streets.

DIRECT TEACHING

A Reading Skills

Making connections. How does the assassination of Martin Luther King, Jr., relate to *Julius Caesar*? [Possible response: A prominent political leader is brutally murdered, the public responds with violent emotion, and there is the threat of anarchy.]

B Reading Informational Materials
GRADE-LEVEL STANDARD

Author's argument. What purpose does this paragraph serve? [Possible response: It provides sensory details that help the reader envision the chaos.]

CONNECTION / FEATURE ARTICLE

THE FEAR AND THE FLAMES

Jimmy Breslin

The 1960s was a time of great unrest and change in this country. Two situations contributed to the social and political upheavals: The United States was involved in an increasingly unpopular and bloody war in Vietnam, and African Americans were organizing a powerful movement to demand their civil rights, which had been denied them for decades. At the head of the nonviolent civil rights movement was Martin Luther King, Jr. A popular and respected leader, King had helped organize the Montgomery, Alabama, bus boycott in 1955 and later spoke out against U.S. involvement in Vietnam. In 1963, more than 250,000 Americans gathered to hear King deliver his now famous "I Have a Dream" speech at the Lincoln Memorial.

On April 4, 1968, this preacher of nonviolent resistance was assassinated by a sniper in Memphis, Tennessee. As news of King's murder took hold, the cities of the United States erupted in violence. Rioters attacked others, set fires, and stole goods from stores.

Here is journalist Jimmy Breslin's powerful feature article describing the scene in Washington, D.C., following King's assassination.

A WASHINGTON, April 6—In the end, in the fear and the smoke there seems to be no society at all. A Nobel Peace Prize–winner is dead in an assassination, and the cities that make up the country are dotted with flames. Last night, America became a place where you could understand the meaning of the word *anarchy*.[1]

When the traffic light on the corner of Thirteenth and V turned red, the body on the sidewalk could be seen. It was a man in his thirties, lying on his back. One leg was drawn up under him. People walked through the smoke from the fires and went past the man without bothering to look at him.

B Two dogs that had been rooting at spoiled garbage came up and were sniffing at the man. Two Army trucks, staying close to the curb, came rushing past. The dogs jumped back and went away.

The man was in a brown suit and had on a shirt and tie. Blood ran from his nose and mouth. In the dark you couldn't tell whether there was dirt or blood from a chest wound on his shirt. "He's dead," somebody said.

"No, I think he's just about breathing," somebody else said.

1. ***anarchy*** (an′ər•kē) *n.:* absence of government; lawlessness; chaos.

Connecting and Comparing Texts

Julius Caesar dramatizes a historical event, the assassination of an extremely popular and charismatic Roman political leader. However, Caesar's death, which occurs about midway though the play, is not the play's climax. In the subsequent two acts, Shakespeare focuses on the aftermath of the assassination—its psychological effect on the conspirators and the reaction of the Roman populace to their beloved hero's death. Breslin's article was written just days after Martin Luther King, Jr., arguably the most prominent political figure in the civil rights movement, was brutally murdered. Yet King is barely mentioned in the article. Instead, Breslin, like Shakespeare, focuses on the effects of the assassination—the violent emotional response of disillusioned African Americans and the threat of anarchy.

874 Chapter 10 Drama • Evaluating an Argument

❦

A hospital was in the middle of the block. The man probably had been dumped on the corner with the idea that the hospital would come out and get him. The hospital has a circular driveway in front of it. It is five stories high. The sign says "Children's Hospital, Founded in 1870." Glass entrance doors were locked. A guard opened them, but only grumpily.

"You've got a man dying up on the corner," he was told.

The guard turned and walked into the dimly lit lobby. A short man in a business suit came out from an office behind the reception counter. "I'm the administrator,"[2] he said.

"There's a man dying on the corner," he was told.

"What do you want us to do?" the administrator said.

"Help him."

The man shook his head. "I'm not sending anybody from this place outside tonight for any reason," he said. "Let somebody else come and do it. We're not taking any chances."

❦

Outside, people kept walking past the body on the street. The police finally came and took the man away to a hospital emergency ward. Washington, D.C., the capital of the nation, was like this last night.

2. **administrator** *n.:* manager or director.

Martin Luther King, Jr., speaking in Memphis, Tennessee, on April 3, 1968, the day before he was assassinated.
AP photo/Charles Kelly.

DIRECT TEACHING

C Reading Informational Materials
GRADE-LEVEL STANDARD

Extending sources. Have students evaluate Breslin's choice of words in these sentences. How objective or subjective is his writing? [Possible response: When he describes the sign and the locked doors, Breslin uses words that don't have strong connotations. However, the adverb *grumpily,* used to describe the guard's reluctance to open the door, indicates an interpretation or opinion.]

D Reading Informational Materials
GRADE-LEVEL STANDARD

Extending sources. The person speaking to the hospital guard and administrator is not identified. Why might Breslin not have identified the speaker? [Possible responses: The speaker might not have given his name or Breslin might not have asked for it. The speaker, like the dying man, remains an anonymous figure, symbolizing a general rather than individual tragedy.]

E Reading Informational Materials
GRADE-LEVEL STANDARD

Extending sources. There is a structural break between the previous dialogue and this scene. What might have been the author's intention in inserting the break? [Possible response: Breslin might want to indicate that a significant amount of time has elapsed between the two events or he might want to show that he has moved on to a new vantage point.]

DIFFERENTIATING INSTRUCTION

Learners Having Difficulty

Creating a mood. Although this piece by Breslin is a nonfiction article, it employs many literary devices usually associated with fictional writing. Have partners examine each of the scenes described by Breslin and identify examples of imagery. Partners should then discuss how Breslin uses imagery to create an overall mood.

Advanced Learners

Enrichment. Invite groups or individuals to research the history of the civil rights movement and to express their findings in a time line. If several individuals or groups work on this project, they might agree to research different eras and then combine their findings into a master time line that runs through 1963 and up to the present.

DIRECT TEACHING

A Reading Skills

Visualizing. Read this passage out loud or have a volunteer do so. Ask students to close their eyes and visualize the scene. What paradox is evident here? [The images of flames and the light being reflected in the jets of water is unexpectedly beautiful, a stark contrast to the actual horror of the situation.]

B Reading Informational Materials
GRADE-LEVEL STANDARD

Author's argument. How does the anecdote about Jimmy Flood support the author's claim about black Americans made in the last sentence of the first paragraph on p. 876? [Possible response: Flood's reaction to the situation is ambiguous; his smile could express ironical acceptance or grim satisfaction. However, his reaction might upset many white Americans.]

On Fourteenth Street, firetrucks were parked in the middle of the street for blocks. Firemen and soldiers from the Sixth Cavalry, who had fixed bayonets,[3] walked through the broken glass that covered the streets of all Washington last night. The firemen threw water high into the air at buildings that were burning out of control. The water streams caught the light of the fire, and the water cascaded off the tops of the burning buildings and went high into the air in an orange spray. Smoke covered the street and the sky over the street. The Capitol of the United States was gray and dim behind a shroud of smoke from fires set by people who are black and who no longer will live in this country as white people want them to.

Jimmy Flood stood on the corner of Fourteenth and Gerard and watched the water run under the broken furniture piled in the gutter. Jimmy Flood

3. **fixed bayonets** *n.:* guns with blades attached to the barrels.

Smoke obscures the traffic of city streets in Washington, D.C., after the rioting that followed the assassination of Martin Luther King, Jr., in April 1968.

CONTENT-AREA CONNECTIONS

History: The Turbulent '60s

According to the editors of *Newsweek,* "The '60s were, as they said in those days, a trip—frantic, turbulent and more than a bit scary. . . .

". . . The civil rights movement had found its voice in King's 'I have a dream' speech, which awed a quarter of a million marchers massed around the Reflecting Pool in Washington in 1963. But the reality of white intransigence prevailed; Birmingham reverberated with the snarl of Bull Connor's police dogs and then shuddered as a bomb ripped through the black Baptist church, killing four young girls. Solid successes in voter-registration drives and boycotts only kindled the hatred of segregationists, who murdered three courageous civil rights workers in Mississippi. . . .

"A growing number of blacks also came to reject the white man's values and legal niceties. Dashikis and afros blossomed in inner-city neighborhoods, and militants . . . emerged as folk heroes. The strains of 'We Shall Overcome' were drowned out by the chant of 'black power.' . . ."

876 Chapter 10 Drama • Evaluating an Argument

stared at the fire, which was turning a six-story corner apartment house into a shell. His eyes brightened and his teeth showed in a smile. The smile of Detroit and Newark and Watts and Chicago[4] and all the other places that should have shown us how bad it would be.

"It's hard to believe this is Washington," somebody said.

"Washington's just another town to me," Jimmy Flood said. "I live in Atlantic City. I live in Washington. It makes no difference. I get sixty dollars a week whether I'm here or some other place."

Smoke blew with the wind and billowed low along Fourteenth Street, and he had to duck into the doorway of a smashed shoe store to breathe. Smoke was everywhere in the city. It was hanging in front of the brilliant television lights they had set up in front of the West Wing of the White House.

The living part of the White House was dark, except for light showing through drapes on the second floor.

A building destroyed by fire during riots in Washington, D.C., following the assassination of Martin Luther King, Jr.

At Fourteenth and F in the city's main business district, a business district that has been looted,[5] shattered, and set afire, troops walked eight and ten abreast with both hands on their weapons. They wore helmets and gas masks and their voices were muffled while they talked to each other through the gas masks.

A captain with the name Rhodes sewed to his fatigues stood alongside a parked jeep and listened to a radio.

"The gas masks?" he was saying. "Oh, that's because we're going to use a chemical deployment if anything happens. It's better to do that than a straight show of force."

"I see. What do you use, Mace?"

"No. We'll just use gas," he said.

This was Washington, D.C., the place the world looks at, on Friday night, April 6, 1968. And this was for all of the past and for Martin Luther King, who now is all of the present. . . .

4. **Detroit . . . Chicago:** cities that experienced civil rights problems in the 1960s.
5. **looted** *v.:* robbed.

DIRECT TEACHING

C Advanced Learners

Interpreting. How might you interpret this exchange? [The first speaker suggests violence is more unthinkable in Washington than in other cities. Jimmy's response deflates the idea that Washington is unique; Washington is no better than other cities in how it treats minorities.]

D Reading Informational Materials
GRADE-LEVEL STANDARD

Extending secondary sources. How might the smoke hanging over the city be interpreted in a figurative sense? [The smoke is like racism, because both keep people from perceiving things clearly.]

E Reading Informational Materials
GRADE-LEVEL STANDARD

Author's argument. This is the first time that Breslin has mentioned King since the beginning of the article. What is the effect? [Possible response: The invoking of King's name and his nonviolent mission are in sharp and shocking contrast to the warlike images presented in the article.]

Activity. Students who are interested in this time period might want to research the assassinations of other prominent American political figures: John F. Kennedy, Robert Kennedy, and Malcolm X. What effect did these deaths have on the nation? Students can present their research to the class.

INDEPENDENT PRACTICE

Literary Response and Analysis

Act V

Reading Check

1. The four characters are Brutus, Cassius, Antony, and Octavius.
2. In the first battle, Antony takes Cassius's army, and Brutus overthrows the troops of Octavius. After Cassius's suicide, Antony and Octavius defeat the conspirators' forces.
3. Cassius, on a hill, sends Titinius to determine whether distant troops are friends or enemies. He then asks Pindarus to climb higher, observe Titinius, and report. Pindarus mistakes Brutus's jubilant troops for the enemy and reports that Titinius is captured. Cassius, thinking he sent Titinius to his doom, asks Pindarus to kill him.
4. Brutus sees the two visions of Caesar as a sign that he must die. Defeated in battle, he finds it more honorable to take his life than to wait for capture.
5. Antony proclaims that Brutus was the only conspirator who acted from pure motives. Octavius orders that he be buried with full military honors.

Interpretations

6. The play's climax is the deaths of Cassius and Brutus.
7. Octavius emerges as the character who can restore order to Rome.
8. Ironies include: Cassius claims that his sight is "ever thick" (l. 21), but Pindarus's clear sight does no better in revealing the truth; the wreath of victory becomes a funeral wreath (ll. 81–83 and 97); Cassius indirectly causes Titinius's death ll. 87–90).
9. Both men use their last words to acknowledge that they die in retribution for Caesar's death. Cassius, however, expresses no regret for the murder, while Brutus again expresses sorrow, implying that he acted out of necessity rather than desire. Taking into account the play's cultural context and the characters of the two men, their suicides seem inevitable, but some students may argue otherwise.
10. In Act II, Brutus decides to spare Antony. In Act III, he allows Antony to give a funeral oration. Brutus brings about his own downfall by sparing Antony and giving him an opportunity to unite the Romans against the conspirators.
11. Some students may feel that Brutus made a grave error; others may argue that his choice was right—or at least necessary.

Literary Response and Analysis

Act V

Reading Check

1. Which four characters finally confront one another in Scene 1 of Act V?
2. What are the results of the first round of battle at Philippi? In the end, who triumphs over whom?
3. What mistaken assumptions lead to Cassius's death?
4. Why does Brutus think he must commit suicide?
5. How do Antony and Octavius react to Brutus's death?

Interpretations

6. In this **tragedy** the plot's rising action peaks at the **climax,** the moment of greatest tension, when we find out how the **conflict** will be resolved. Identify the play's climax.
7. In the **resolution,** the last scene, why is it significant that Octavius delivers the play's final speech?
8. In Scene 3, Cassius's death scene, identify at least three examples of **irony,** a turn of events that is contrary to our expectations. How do these ironies make you feel?
9. Look at Scenes 3 and 5 and the dying words of Cassius and Brutus. How does each man view Caesar's murder? Do you think each man had a choice other than suicide? Explain.
10. Brutus makes two mistakes—one in Act II and one in Act III—that stem from his idealized vision of the assassination and his self-image as an "honorable man." What are these errors, and how do they lead to Brutus's **tragic** downfall?
11. Describe your final view of Brutus and the choices he made. Did he misread the evidence that Caesar might become king? Should he have betrayed a friend for the public good? Was he wrong to kill the only man who could bring order out of chaos? Support your responses with evidence from the play.
12. Critics argue that Julius Caesar dominates the play (Cassius says in Act I that he "doth bestride the narrow world / Like a Colossus."). How would you defend this view? How is Caesar present in the second half of the play?
13. In Aristotle's essay the *Poetics* (see the ***Connection*** on page 872), he describes the **tragic hero** as a person more noble than evil, whose fortunes go from good to bad, someone with a character flaw that leads to his downfall. Does Brutus fit this description, or is the tragic hero someone else—perhaps Caesar? Do you think, instead, that the play lacks a tragic hero? Defend your answer.

Evaluation

14. Few words inspired such anxiety in the ancient Romans as the word *king.* Consider these questions about kingship: Were the anxieties of Brutus and others about Caesar's potential "kingship" justified? How do you think Shakespeare's audience, living under the strong and stable monarchy of the aging Queen Elizabeth I, might have felt about choosing between dictatorship and anarchy? How do you think American audiences of today feel about this issue? (Look back at your Quickwrite notes for page 755.)

Reading Standard 3.1 Articulate the relationship between the expressed purposes and the characteristics of different forms of dramatic literature (e.g., comedy, tragedy, drama).

Reading Standard 3.10 Identify and describe the function of dialogue and scene designs in dramatic literature.

878 Chapter 10 Drama • Evaluating an Argument

Writing

Choose from among the following assignments to respond to the play:

1. Comparing a Play and a Movie

In a video store or a library, look for a movie version of *Julius Caesar.* You might find the 1953 version, starring James Mason as Brutus, or the 1970 version, starring Charlton Heston as Antony. After you watch the movie, compare it with Shakespeare's play. How closely does the movie stick to the original? Which of Shakespeare's scenes are dropped? Which ones are "opened up"—moved offstage into different settings? Write a brief essay **comparing and contrasting** the movie and the play. Consider what a movie has that a play does not—realistic settings, closeups, fadeouts, additional stage movements, and a musical score.

Use "Comparing a Play and a Film," pages 890–897, for help with this assignment.

2. Comparing Caesar and King

In a brief **essay, compare** Jimmy Breslin's account of events in Washington, D.C., following the assassination of Martin Luther King, Jr. (see the ***Connection*** on page 874), with Shakespeare's depiction of events following Julius Caesar's assassination (see Act III, Scenes 2 and 3). What similarities can you find in these two accounts? What, if anything, do they reveal about human nature?

3. You Be the Critic

Using what you've learned in this chapter about the purposes and characteristics of drama, write a **critical review** of a movie or TV drama you've watched recently. Begin by identifying the work's genre (tragedy, comedy, drama), and think about the criteria you will use to evaluate the work. Are the characters and plot believable? Is the action suspenseful, the ending satisfying? How effective are the dialogue, scene designs, and costumes? Cite details to support any general statements you make about the work. (Before you begin, you might want to read the review on page 882 of a production of *Julius Caesar.*)

4. Analyzing a Character

In a brief essay, write a **character analysis** of Brutus. First, read the following critical comments. Then, become a critic yourself. Evaluate the comments, and use them as you form your own **thesis statement,** a clear statement of your main idea or argument. Be sure to include details from the play to elaborate and to support your statements about Brutus.

> Brutus is humorlessly good. If his duty is to know himself, his performance fails. Nobility has numbed him until he cannot see himself for his principles. . . . He is not mad or haunted or inspired or perplexed in the extreme. He is simply confused.
>
> —Mark Van Doren

> Brutus is an intellectual who can do things, who is not . . . hampered by doubts. . . . He cannot realize that men seek their own interests, for he has never sought his own, he has lived nobly among noble thoughts, wedded to a noble wife.
>
> —E. M. Forster

Writing

1. **Comparing a play and a movie.** Students may want to work together on this activity or at least watch the movie together in small groups. If possible, make available the equipment and space for students to work on this assignment in school.
2. **Comparing Caesar and King.** Remind students to take into account the historical and cultural context of each event. To what extent did the standards and mores of the time period influence the reactions of the people?

   You might have students work together to create Venn diagrams or comparison-and-contrast charts to develop points to use in their essay.
3. **You be the critic.** You might want to discuss students' movie or TV drama choices with them before they begin to write to make sure that their choices are appropriate and substantial enough for a critical evaluation.
4. **Analyzing a character.** Suggest that students follow this structure when they write their essays: introductory paragraph (clear statement of thesis); three supporting paragraphs (three main points in support of thesis statement), concluding paragraph (restatement of thesis). If students use one of the critical comments, suggest that they summarize it for their thesis statement. You might have volunteers suggest one-sentence summaries.

12. Caesar sets in motion all the events of the play, and he remains the acknowledged force behind everyone's actions, even after his death. Not only do the characters continually refer to Caesar, but Shakespeare also keeps the ruler in the action—by using his corpse on stage, by introducing the Ghost, and by having Cassius kill himself with the same sword that stabbed Caesar.

13. No character in *Julius Caesar* exactly fits Aristotle's definition of a tragic hero, but Brutus certainly exhibits some of the characteristics: He is noble, honorable in intent, flawed, and doomed through his own character and actions. Caesar may more nearly fit the role theoretically but not dramatically, since he doesn't behave like a tragic hero.

Evaluation

14. The Elizabethans did not have a horror of monarchy or consider a king or queen to be by definition a tyrant. The prevailing view was that monarchs ruled by divine right. Having endured violent civil wars, the English valued the peace of Elizabeth's strong reign. People today would probably fear both dictatorship and anarchy.

Reading Skills

Practice

This feature provides students with a basic strategy for memorizing well-known speeches. Ask the class to suggest additional methods of memorizing.

Don't allow students to wait until the presentation date to give their memorized speeches a first hearing. Have students memorize with a partner (preferably someone who has chosen the same speech) and meet with that partner at least twice. Partners may give each other pointers about presentation and test each other's technical accuracy

Encourage students not to be too severe or judgmental when they evaluate their peers. Remind them that constructive criticism consists of pointing out good points as well as aspects that could be improved upon. Students should try to balance negative comments with positive ones, and be extremely careful how they word their responses.

If possible, audio or videotape students' presentations, so that they can evaluate and perfect their own deliveries.

ASSESSING

Assessment

- *Progress Assessment of Reading*
  - Selection Test

RETEACHING

For a lesson reteaching Standard 3.1, see **Reteaching,** p. 939A. For another selection to teach Standard 3.1, see *Interactive Reading,* Chapter 10.

Reading Skills

Memorizing Famous Passages: Making Them Yours

If you memorize some of Shakespeare's famous speeches now, you'll find yourself remembering them years later. One way to memorize speeches easily is to use the "bricklayer" method. Like a bricklayer who lays down row upon row of bricks, an actor memorizes lines by building one line upon another. Read the first line of a speech until you can say it without looking at it. Then, read that line and the next line until you can say the first two lines without looking at them. Continue until you can say the whole speech without looking at it. Then, you can work on your **interpretation** and **dramatic presentation.**

1. Why, man, he doth bestride the narrow world
   Like a Colossus, and we petty men
   Walk under his huge legs and peep about
   To find ourselves dishonorable graves.
   Men at some time are masters of their fates:
   The fault, dear Brutus, is not in our stars,
   But in ourselves, that we are underlings.
   —Act I, Scene 2, lines 135–141
2. Cowards die many times before their deaths;
   The valiant never taste of death but once.
   Of all the wonders that I yet have heard,
   It seems to me most strange that men should fear,
   Seeing that death, a necessary end,
   Will come when it will come.
   —Act II, Scene 2, lines 32–37
3. The evil that men do lives after them,
   The good is oft interrèd with their bones. . . .
   —Act III, Scene 2, lines 75–76
4. There is a tide in the affairs of men
   Which, taken at the flood, leads on to fortune;
   Omitted, all the voyage of their life
   Is bound in shallows and in miseries.
   On such a full sea are we now afloat,
   And we must take the current when it serves,
   Or lose our ventures.
   —Act IV, Scene 3, lines 216–222

PRACTICE

Choose at least two of the speeches above. Using the bricklayer technique, memorize the speeches. Then, in a small group, **evaluate** one another's dramatic presentations. How did they differ? Does your group have a favorite one?

880 Chapter 10 Drama • Evaluating an Argument

Before You Read INFORMATIONAL MATERIALS

Julius Caesar in an Absorbing Production

Evaluating an Author's Argument: A Critical Review

How do you choose which new movie or TV show to watch? You might listen to friends' recommendations. You might also turn to a professional review.

What to Look for in a Review

1. **What is the intent, or purpose?** In a review the author's **purpose** is **persuasive.** The writer's argument includes an **opinion statement** (usually worded as a **generalization**) followed by support to convince you that the opinion is right. Ask yourself: "What is the writer trying to get me to *believe?* How does the writer's purpose affect the **structure** of the argument and the **tone**? Does the tone seem appropriate for the **audience**?"
2. **What are the criteria?** Whenever you make a judgment about how good or bad something is (from fajitas to TV comedies), you base your evaluation on **criteria,** or standards of excellence. For example, what are the qualities that make a screenplay or an actor's performance outstanding?
3. **What's the evidence?** A critical review of a play would probably include the following types of **evidence:** critical judgments, examples, and facts. The reviewer would discuss the **elements of drama** (plot, characters, conflict, theme) as well as the **staging** (acting, sets, costumes, lighting).
4. **Is the evidence comprehensive?** Remember that you can't *prove* an opinion (as you can a fact). You can only support it—and the more support you give, the more convincing you are. Is the reviewer's evidence comprehensive, or has something important been omitted?
5. **Who is the writer?** To decide how **credible** and convincing a review is, you need to know whose opinion you are reading. Is the writer experienced and qualified to write about this topic? Is the author biased in some way? How can you tell?

Vocabulary Development

gaunt (gônt) *adj.:* here, grim and forbidding.

vitality (vī · tal′ə · tē) *n.:* energy; vigor.

surly (sʉr′lē) *adj.:* bad-tempered; rude.

unorthodox (un · ôr′thə · däks′) *adj.:* unusual; not conforming to usual norms.

sinister (sin′is · tər) *adj.:* evil.

reticent (ret′ə·sənt) *adj.:* silent; reserved.

perplexed (pər · plekst′) *adj.:* uncertain.

idealist (ī · dē′əl · ist) *n.:* someone who is guided by ideals, or standards of perfection.

Connecting to the Literature

In 1937, with dictators such as Adolf Hitler in power, the American director Orson Welles staged a modern-dress production of *Julius Caesar* at the Mercury Theater in New York City. In this version, Brutus was viewed as a hero for killing the tyrant Caesar. One critic's review of the production follows.

Pages 882–885 cover **Reading Standard 2.8** Evaluate the credibility of an author's argument or defense of a claim by critiquing the relationship between generalizations and evidence, the comprehensiveness of evidence, and the way in which the author's intent affects the structure and tone of the text.

STANDARDS FOCUS, pp. 881–888

(For grade-level and review standards taught in this lesson, see citations on Student Edition pages.)

Prerequisite Standard

- Grade 7, Reading comprehension 2.4 **Identify and trace the development of an author's argument, point of view, or perspective in text.**

Summary *at grade level*

This review from the *New York Post* praises Orson Welles's 1937 modern-dress production of *Julius Caesar.*

PRETEACHING

Selection Starter

Build background. Orson Welles (1915–1985) was an influential figure in theater and film. His best-known work, *Citizen Kane* (1941), has been called the most influential film in American movie history. John Mason Brown gave Welles's *Julius Caesar* a wonderful review, but not all critics shared his enthusiasm. Still, Welles's production ran for 157 performances in New York City—a record for a production of that play in the United States.

Preview Vocabulary

Activity. Have students write a humorous job posting or personal ad incorporating all the vocabulary words.

RESOURCES: READING

Planning

- *One-Stop Planner* CD-ROM with Test Generator
- *On Course: Mapping Instruction*

Media

- *Audio CD Library*
  - disc 18

Reading

- *Interactive Reading,* Teacher's Edition
  - Graphic Organizer: Argument-Evaluation Chart

Differentiating Instruction

- *Lesson Plans for Language Development*
  - English-Language Learners, pp. 353–355, 366, 373
  - Special Education Students, pp. 356, 366, 373

Vocabulary

- *Vocabulary Development*
  - Vocabulary Worksheet, p. 50

Assessment

- *Progress Assessment of Reading*
  - Selection Test
- *One-Stop Planner* CD-ROM with Test Generator

DIRECT TEACHING

A Advanced Learners

? Allusion. Brown is alluding to the beginning of Mark Antony's funeral oration (Act III, Scene 2, l. 74). How is Brown's phrasing different from the original and why? [Brown switches "praise" and "bury"; and by *bury,* he means "give the production a bad review." On the previous day, he "buried" a production of *Antony and Cleopatra* by panning it; now Brown has come before his readers to praise *Julius Caesar,* not to put it out of business with an unfavorable review.]

B Reading Skills

Evaluating an argument. [Possible response for question 1: Brown claims that Orson Wells's production of *Julius Caesar* is the best play of the season. Have students gather evidence as they read that supports Brown's claim.]

C Reading Informational Materials

GRADE-LEVEL STANDARD

? Author's argument. Brown doesn't begin to describe specific aspects of the production quite yet. Instead, he talks about the production's general impact on the audience. What is his purpose in doing so? [Brown is making his first main point here in support of his claim.]

D Reading Informational Materials

GRADE-LEVEL STANDARD

? Extending sources. What do you think would be the value of taking a Shakespearean play set long ago and reworking it to fit a modern time and place? [Possible responses: The reworked version might help a modern audience understand better the issues that Shakespeare was addressing; the new version might enable the audience to see contemporary issues in a new light and to rethink their own beliefs and values.]

PLAY REVIEW

Julius Caesar in an Absorbing Production

from the *New York Post,* November 12, 1937

John Mason Brown

(A) This is no funeral oration such as Miss Bankhead and Mr. Tearle forced me to deliver yesterday when they interred *Antony and Cleopatra.*[1] I come to praise *Caesar* at the Mercury, not to bury it. Of all the many new plays and productions the season has so far revealed, this modern-dress version of the mob mischief and demagoguery[2] which can follow the assassination of a dictator is by all odds the most exciting, the most imaginative, the most topical, (B) the most awesome, and the most absorbing. ❶

❶ EVALUATING AN ARGUMENT
Paraphrase Brown's **opinion,** or **claim,** about the production.

(C) The astonishing, all-impressive virtue of Mr. Welles's *Julius Caesar* is that, magnificent as it is as theater, it is far larger than its medium. Something deathless and dangerous in the world sweeps past you down the darkened aisles at the Mercury and takes possession of the proud, gaunt stage. . . . It is an ageless warning, made in such arresting terms that it not only gives a new vitality to an ancient story but unrolls in your mind's eye a map of the world which is increasingly splotched with sickening colors.

Mr. Welles does not dress his conspirators and his Storm Troopers in Black Shirts or in Brown.[3] He does not have to. The antique Rome, which we had thought was securely Roman in Shakespeare's tragedy, he shows us to be a dateless state of mind. . . . To an extent no other director in our day and country has equaled, (D) Mr. Welles proves in his production that Shakespeare was indeed not of an age but for all time. After this surly modern Caesar, dressed in a green uniform and scowling behind the mask-like face of a contemporary dictator, has fallen at the Mercury and new mischief is (E) afoot, we cannot but shudder before the prophet's wisdom of those lines which read:

"How many ages hence
Shall this our lofty scene be acted over
In states unborn and accents yet unknown!"[4] ❷

❷ EVALUATING EVIDENCE
In the second paragraph, Brown cites his *first* main point about the production—"it is an ageless warning." What **evidence** does he then give to support this view?

1. The movie actress Tallulah Bankhead opened in *Antony and Cleopatra* on November 10, 1937. Mr. Brown gave the production an unfavorable review.
2. **demagoguery** (dem′ə · gäg′ər · ē) *n.:* appealing to the emotions and prejudices of people in order to stir up discontent and gain power.
3. **Storm . . . Brown:** Storm troopers, members of Hitler's Nazi-party militia, wore brown shirts. In Italy, Mussolini's Fascist party members wore uniforms with black shirts.
4. Lines 111–113, spoken by Cassius in Act III, Scene 1.

Vocabulary
gaunt (gônt) *adj.:* here, grim and forbidding.
vitality (vī · tal′ə · tē) *n.:* energy; vigor.
surly (sʉr′lē) *adj.:* bad-tempered; rude.

DIFFERENTIATING INSTRUCTION

Learners Having Difficulty

Visualizing. Have students re-read the essay, paying careful attention to the changes Welles made in his production. Then, working in small groups, have students plan a modern-dress version of *Julius Caesar.* As an example, have them discuss how the conflicts and themes of the play would change if it were set in the world of professional sports or any other area of today's culture. They should consider how they would present the following elements of the play: setting, lights, props, music, sound effects, costumes, murders, funerals, battles, and women's roles.

The Bettmann Archive.

The Orson Welles production of *Julius Caesar* (Mercury Theater, New York, 1937).

To fit the play into modern dress and give it its fullest implication,[5] Mr. Welles has not hesitated to take his liberties with the script. Unlike Professor Strunk, however, who attempted to improve upon *Antony and Cleopatra,* he has not stabbed it through the heart. He has only chopped away at its body. You may miss a few fingers, even an arm and leg in the *Julius Caesar* you thought you knew. But the heart of the drama beats more vigorously in this production than it has in years. If the play ceases to be Shakespeare's tragedy, it does manage to become ours. **F**

5. **implication** *n.:* suggested meaning.

That is the whole point and glory of Mr. Welles's unorthodox, but welcome, restatement of it. ❸

He places it upon a bare stage, the brick walls of which are crimson[6] and naked. A few steps and a platform and an abyss[7] beyond are the setting. A few steps—and the miracle of enveloping shadows, knifelike rays, and superbly changing lights. . . .

❸ EVALUATING AN ARGUMENT
What is Brown's **opinion** of what Welles has done to Shakespeare's text? **G**

6. **crimson** *adj.:* deep red.
7. **abyss** (ə · bis′) *n.:* deep gulf or pit.

Vocabulary
unorthodox (un · ôr′thə · däks′) *adj.:* unusual; not conforming to usual norms.

DIRECT TEACHING

E Reading Skills

Evaluating evidence. [Possible response to question 2: As evidence, Brown notes that Welles does not set his play in any specific time period; he also notes the audience's strong reaction to Cassius's prophetic lines in Act III.]

F Reading Skills

Making judgments. Because Welles wanted to highlight the character of Brutus, he made cuts in the play accordingly, including deleting most of Act V. As a result, his production ran only 109 minutes. Do you think that such heavy reworking does Shakespeare's writing a disservice? Explain. [Possible responses: Yes, cutting large portions out of a Shakespearean play is inexcusable; every scene in his plays serves a definite purpose, or else he would not have included it. No, Shakespeare's ideas can come through clearly in a reworked version, as happens in movie and television adaptations. The changes that a director makes are justified if the audience understands the new format better than the traditional one.]

G Reading Skills

Evaluating an argument. [Possible response to question 3: Brown is enthusiastic about Welles's changes; he thinks the cuts help the audience focus on the play's main message.]

English-Language Learners
For lessons designed for English-language learners and special education students, see *Lesson Plans for Language Development,* pp. 353–355, 356, 366, 373.

Advanced Learners
Acceleration. Have students choose a movie or play that they have recently seen. Then, have students write a review of it, using the same tone and style that John Mason Brown employs in his review. Remind students of the key elements of an effective review: a clear statement of opinion, supporting details, description of the basic plot, comments about how effective various actors were in their roles, and an explanation of how the work affects or is meant to affect the audience.

DIRECT TEACHING

DIRECT TEACHING

Ⓐ Reading Skills

Analyzing structure. [Possible response to question 4: Brown discusses the play's setting, lighting, and staging.] **What does Brown think about the staging?** [Possible response: Brown thinks that Welles's direction is very effective and that it helps reinforce Shakespeare's ideas.]

Ⓑ Reading Informational Materials
GRADE-LEVEL STANDARD

Author's argument. What generalization does Brown make about Welles's acting ability? [Welles has a quiet and simple acting style that is very effective.] **How does Brown support his generalization?** [Possible response: He notes that Welles plays Brutus as a "reticent" character, and he commends Welles's reading of the funeral oration.]

His direction, which is constantly creative, is never more so than in its first revelation of Caesar hearing the warning of the soothsayer, or in the fine scene in which Cinna, the poet, is engulfed by a sinister crowd of ruffians.[8] Even when one misses Shakespeare's lines, Mr. Welles keeps drumming the meaning of his play into our minds by the scuffling of his mobs when they prowl in the shadows, or the herd-like thunder of their feet when they run as one threatening body. It is a memorable device. Like the setting in which it is used, it is pure theater: vibrant, unashamed, and enormously effective. ❹

> **❹ ANALYZING STRUCTURE** Ⓐ
> In the previous two paragraphs, what aspects of the play does Brown discuss?

The theatrical virtues of this modern-dress *Julius Caesar* do not stop with its excitements as a stunt in showmanship. They extend to the performances. As Brutus Mr. Welles shows once again how uncommon is his gift for speaking great words simply. His tones are conversational. His manner is quiet. The deliberation of his speech is the mark of the honesty which flames within him. His reticent Brutus is at once a foil to the staginess of the production as a whole and to the oratory[9] of Caesar and Antony. He is a perplexed liberal, this Brutus; an idealist who is swept by bad events into actions which have no less dangerous consequences for the state. His simple reading of the funeral oration is in happy contrast to what is usually done with the speech. Ⓑ

8. **ruffians** *n.:* toughs; hoodlums.
9. **oratory** *n.:* skilled public speaking.

American Theatre
LEADING THEATRE OF ST. LOUIS
Direction: AMERICAN THEATRICAL COMPANY
UNITED BOOKING OFFICE, Inc., Booking Managers
PAUL BEISMAN, Resident Manager

BEGINNING MONDAY EVENING, APRIL 4, 1938
Matinees Wednesday and Saturday

ALEX YOKEL
PRESENTS
ORSON WELLES' MODERN PRODUCTION
— OF —
THE TRAGEDY OF
"JULIUS CAESAR"
— BY —
WILLIAM SHAKESPEARE
STAGED BY ORSON WELLES

DRAMATIS PERSONAE
JULIUS CAESAR ....
MARCUS ANTONIUS .... LAWRENCE FLETCHER
PUBLIUS .... EDMOND O'BRIEN
MARCUS BRUTUS .... EDWIN BLAKE
CASSIUS .... TOM POWERS
CASCA .... MORGAN FARLEY
TREBONIUS .... EDGAR BARRIER
LIGARIUS .... GREGORY ROBINS
DECIUS BRUTUS .... McGREGOR GIBB
METELLUS CIMBER .... ERIC MANSFIELD
CINNA, the Conspirator .... BERNARD SAVAGE
FLAVIUS .... JOHN STRAUB
MARULLUS .... NORMAN WESS
ARTEMIDORUS .... EDWARD STANSBURY
CINNA, the Poet .... ARTHUR WILLIAM ROW
LUCIUS .... VINCENT J. DONEHUE
CALPURNIA, wife to Caesar .... FRED THOMPSON
PORTIA, wife to Brutus .... HELEN CRAIG
STATILLIUS .... MURIEL BRASSLER
CARPENTER .... HAROLD J. KENNEDY
COBBLER .... STANLEY POSS
.... ROBERT EARLE
AND
Fred Heider, Robert Geake, Gene Yell, Arthur Hoffe, Seymour Milbert,
Citizens, Soldiers, Attendants.
Continued on Other Side

Orson Welles's popular production of *Julius Caesar* toured the country. This playbill is for a performance in St. Louis.

Bettmann/CORBIS.

George Coulouris is an admirable Antony. So fresh is his characterization, so intelligent his performance that even "Friends, Romans, countrymen" sounds on his tongue as if it

Vocabulary

sinister (sin′is · tər) *adj.:* evil.

reticent (ret′ə · sənt) *adj.:* silent; reserved.

perplexed (pər · plekst′) *v.* used as *adj.:* uncertain.

idealist (ī · dē′əl · ist) *n.:* someone who is guided by ideals, or standards of perfection.

CONTENT-AREA CONNECTIONS

Drama: Global Shakespeare

Ben Jonson once wrote of Shakespeare, "He was not of an age but for all time." That saying has been proven true in light of the success that Shakespeare's work still enjoys in practically every country and language in the world. Each year productions of *Julius Caesar* are seen by thousands of people; the comedies have been presented in African villages and in the barrios of Mexico City. As further evidence of the aptness of Jonson's saying, Shakespeare is performed more often today than in his own time. Indeed, the further we get from the time Shakespeare lived the more popular his plays become.

Cast members of *Julius Caesar* gather for a toast on January 4, 1938. Orson Welles is toward the center, holding a pipe.
Bettmann/CORBIS.

were a rabble-rousing harangue[10] which he is uttering for the first time. Joseph Holland's Caesar is an imperious[11] dictator who could be found frowning at you in this week's newsreels. He is excellently conceived and excellently projected. Some mention, however inadequate, must be made of Martin Gabel's capable Cassius, of John Hoysradt's Decius Brutus, of the conspirators whose black hats are pluck'd about their ears, and Norman Lloyd's humorous yet deeply affecting Cinna. ⑤

⑤ EVALUATING EVIDENCE
List several examples Brown gives as **evidence** to support his opinion of the acting.

It would be easy to find faults here and there: to wonder about the wisdom of some of the textual changes even in terms of the present production's aims; to complain that the whole tragedy does not fit with equal ease into its modern treatment; and to wish this or that scene had been played a little differently. But such faultfindings strike me in the case of this *Julius Caesar* as being as picayune[12] as they are ungrateful. What Mr. Welles and his associates at the Mercury have achieved is a triumph that is exceptional from almost every point of view. ⑥

⑥ EVALUATING AN ARGUMENT
How does the last paragraph affect the **credibility** of Brown's argument?

10. **rabble-rousing harangue:** scolding speech designed to arouse people to anger.
11. **imperious** (im • pir′ē • əs) *adj.:* arrogant; domineering.
12. **picayune** *adj.:* trivial; unimportant.

DIRECT TEACHING

C Advanced Learners

Allusions. What specific line in the play does Brown allude to here? [In Act II, Scene 1, l.73, Lucius describes the conspirators as having their hats "plucked about their ears."]

D Reading Skills

Evaluating evidence. [Possible response to question 5: Besides paying special attention to Welles's Brutus, Brown also praises the actors that play each of the other main characters (Antony, Caesar, Cassius, Decius, Cinna).]

E Reading Skills

Evaluating an argument. [Possible response to question 6: Brown admits that the production does have some weak points. This acknowledgment ultimately makes his review more credible.]

GUIDED PRACTICE

True-False

Monitoring students' progress. To check students' comprehension of the story, ask them to respond to the following questions and to support their responses.

1. Brown states his opinion of Welles's production of *Julius Caesar* at the very beginning of the review. [T]
2. Brown says that Welles's cuts add a new vitality to the play. [T]
3. For his production, Welles's rewrote a couple of Brutus's main speeches. [F]
4. Brown tells the reader how he would have staged the play. [F]
5. Brown has several strong reservations about Welles's production. [F]

INDEPENDENT PRACTICE

Analyzing Informational Materials

Reading Check

1. The costumes are modern dress. Caesar wears a green uniform.
2. Brown discusses all of the following elements: directing, acting, staging, sets, lighting, and costumes.

Test Practice

Answers and Model Rationales

1. **B** Brown's claim is that the play is the season's best. In the first sentence of paragraph 1 (A), Brown only hints that his opinion of the play will be favorable, but he does not actually give it. In the last sentence of paragraph 2 (C), he supports his opinion by speaking of the play's relevance. In the first sentence of the last paragraph (D), he acknowledges the production's shortcomings.
2. **F** Brown never mentions the history of the play, Shakespeare's biography, or Welles's previous successes as a director (G, H, and J).
3. **D** Brown briefly mentions the costumes on p. 882 and describes the set on p. 883; he talks extensively about Welles's and the other actors' performances on pp. 884–885.
4. **H** Brown's point-by-point discussion of the play is a typical way of structuring a review. Although Brown does anticipate readers' objections (J), he does not do so until p. 885, and this is not an important structuring point.
5. **C** Even though students might disagree with Brown's extremely favorable opinion of the production, he does present extensive evidence to back his claim.
6. **J** F and H include adjectives (*memorable* and *admirable*) that have favorable connotations, and G includes a metaphor that expresses subjectivity.

Analyzing Informational Materials

Reading Check

1. What type of costumes does Welles use in his production of *Julius Caesar*?
2. Name four aspects of the play that Brown discusses in his review.

Test Practice

Reading Standard 2.8 Evaluate the credibility of an author's argument or defense of a claim by critiquing the relationship between generalizations and evidence, the comprehensiveness of evidence, and the way in which the author's intent affects the structure and tone of the text.

1. The writer's **opinion statement** about the play is best stated in —
   - **A** the first sentence of paragraph 1
   - **B** the last sentence of paragraph 1
   - **C** the last sentence of paragraph 2
   - **D** the first sentence of the last paragraph

2. To support his **opinion,** Brown discusses —
   - **F** the staging of the production
   - **G** the history of the play
   - **H** Shakespeare's biography
   - **J** Welles's previous successes as a director

3. One aspect of the production that Brown does *not* discuss in this review is the —
   - **A** actors' performances
   - **B** set
   - **C** costumes
   - **D** audience's reaction

4. How does Brown **structure** his review?
   - **F** He uses a cause-and-effect structure.
   - **G** He uses a comparison-contrast structure.
   - **H** He discusses different aspects of the production, one at a time.
   - **J** He opens by anticipating readers' objections.

5. Which of the following statements about the writer of this review is accurate?
   - **A** He is biased against the play.
   - **B** He is biased against modern-dress productions of Shakespeare.
   - **C** He presents a great deal of evidence to support his opinion.
   - **D** He does not give enough evidence to be convincing.

6. Which of these statements is *not* an **opinion**?
   - **F** "It is a memorable device."
   - **G** "But the heart of the drama beats more vigorously in this production than it has in years."
   - **H** "George Coulouris is an admirable Antony."
   - **J** "He places it upon a bare stage, the brick walls of which are crimson and naked."

886 Chapter 10 Drama • Evaluating an Argument

7. The **tone** of this article is best described as —
   - **A** humorous
   - **B** sarcastic
   - **C** informal
   - **D** admiring

8. Brown tailors his argument to fit his **audience,** who are —
   - **F** high school students
   - **G** professional actors and directors
   - **H** readers of a New York newspaper
   - **J** listeners of a radio program

9. Before you decide whether you find Brown's critical review **credible,** you'd want to know more about —
   - **A** Orson Welles's movies
   - **B** William Shakespeare's comedies
   - **C** Julius Caesar's life and death
   - **D** Brown's qualifications as a reviewer

Application

Brown clearly gives a thumbs-up to Orson Welles's production of *Julius Caesar.* Do you give a thumbs-up to Brown's review? In a brief essay, evaluate Brown's review. First, summarize Brown's **opinion statement.** Then, discuss the **structure** and **tone** Brown uses for his review. Next, evaluate the types of **evidence** he uses and decide whether the evidence is sufficiently convincing. Finally, discuss how **credible** you find his argument—in other words, if you were able to see Welles's production, would you want to? (A chart like the one below will help you gather your notes.)

Evaluating a Review
Opinion statement:
Structure:
Tone:
Evidence:
Credibility:

7. D Some students might argue for C, since Brown is expressing an opinion. However, his diction and sentence structure are fairly formal.

8. H The review originally appeared in the *New York Post;* this information is found right below the title.

9. D Although finding out more about the subjects listed in A, B, and C would be interesting, it is ultimately Brown's credentials as a reviewer that add credibility to his opinions.

Test-Taking Tips

For more information on how to answer multiple-choice items, refer students to **Test Smarts.**

Application

Possible answer: The thesis of John Mason Brown's review—that is, his opinion statement—is the long second sentence of the first paragraph, in which he claims that the Mercury Theater's *Julius Caesar* is the finest production of the 1937 season. Brown structures his review in a simple point-by-point analysis of the production's dramatic elements: the costumes, the text, the staging, the direction, and the performances. Throughout the review Brown's tone is one of lavish praise, as indicated by phrases such as "most absorbing," "superbly changing lights," and "a triumph." Brown supports all his claims with ample evidence. In the discussion of the costumes, for example, he describes the modern dress as perfectly suited to showing the "fullest implication" of the play's relevance to our own time. Brown gives particular attention to the various performances, praising each of the principle actors in turn: Orson Welles, George Coulouris, and Joseph Holland. On the whole, Brown's review is very credible: He displays a deep knowledge and love of the theater, and he adds a few words of "fault-finding" to temper all the praise. After reading Brown's review, any fan of Shakespeare would want to see this Mercury production of *Julius Caesar*—"a triumph that is exceptional from almost every point of view."

Vocabulary Development

Practice

Possible Answers

1. *Gaunt* would mean "harsh" or "grim" in this context. It implies that the stage setting is minimal or sparse and ominously suggestive.
2. Descriptions will vary. A *vital organ* is one that is necessary to the maintenance of life.
3. Students might mention such behavior as angry outbursts, a lack of communication skills, frequent moodiness, and obstinacy.
4. Welles treats Shakespeare's text in an *unorthodox* manner—he makes deep cuts in the text and stages the play in modern dress. *Unorthodox* has religious and political connotations; it suggests a person who deliberately rejects an established way of doing things.
5. Since *sinister* suggests a situation that is not only mysterious but also slightly dangerous, students would probably not be comfortable in such a situation. Literary examples will vary.
6. Since a *reticent* person is silent and reserved, they are not likely to gossip or run for political office.
7. Examples will vary; some students might mention situations in which they were faced with a difficult moral or ethical decision.
8. An idealist tends to see things as they should be, not as they are. Political or social causes might attract an idealistic person.

Resources Reminder

Vocabulary

- *Vocabulary Development*
  - Vocabulary Worksheet, p. 50
  - Cumulative Vocabulary Review, pp. 51–52
- *Lesson Plans for Language Development*
  - Vocabulary, pp. 366, 373

Vocabulary Development

Clarifying Meanings: Words in Context

PRACTICE

Word Bank

gaunt
vitality
surly
unorthodox
sinister
reticent
perplexed
idealist

Answer the following questions for help clarifying the meanings of the Word Bank words.

1. *Gaunt* can mean "harsh; forbidding; grim"—or, when describing a person, "very thin; worn out." Why would Brown describe the stage setting as gaunt and proud? How do you imagine such a setting?
2. *Vitality, vital, revitalize,* even *vitamin*—all share a common Latin root word, *vita,* meaning "life." Describe a person or a situation that is full of vitality. What do you think is meant by a *vital organ,* such as the heart?
3. Is surly high on your list of favorite character traits? Think of someone you know or have observed who is frequently surly. What don't you like about his or her behavior?
4. What is it about Orson Welles's production of *Julius Caesar* that's unorthodox? What connotations does the word unorthodox have that *unusual* does not have?
5. Would you be comfortable in a situation that seemed sinister? Why? Can you think of a sinister character in literature?
6. Is an extremely reticent person likely to gossip or run for political office? Explain why or why not.
7. Some people find themselves perplexed when faced with a difficult situation or a confusing issue. What kind of problem might make you perplexed? Why?
8. In the play review, the character of Brutus is described as an idealist. What kind of person is an idealist? What kinds of activities might he or she get involved with?

Grade 8 Review Reading Standard 1.3 Use word meanings within the appropriate context and show ability to verify those meanings.

Reading Standard 1.1 Identify and use the literal meanings of words.

The director and actor Orson Welles in 1951.

ASSESSING

Assessment

- *Progress Assessment of Reading*
  - Selection Test

RETEACHING

For a lesson reteaching Standard 2.8, see **Reteaching,** p. 939A. For another selection to teach Standard 2.8, see *Interactive Reading,* Part 2.

888 Chapter 10 Drama • Evaluating an Argument

Read On: FOR INDEPENDENT READING

PLAY

Scottish Tragedy

Julius Caesar is not the only assassinated leader featured in a Shakespearean tragedy. In 1040, a Scottish chieftain named Macbeth killed King Duncan I and seized the throne of Scotland. Shakespeare dramatized this story in his tragedy ***Macbeth***—a play whose characters grapple with family loyalties, greed, and the price of ambition. You may find that this tale of medieval intrigue provides shocking contrasts to *The Tragedy of Julius Caesar.*
This title is available in the HRW Library.

PLAY

Chasing the Dream

Lorraine Hansberry's stirring drama ***A Raisin in the Sun*** takes us inside the home of the Younger family—five larger-than-life personalities cramped but not crushed by their small, shabby living space. Each of the Youngers has big dreams—and no one's dreams are bigger than Walter's, who thinks that money will solve his family's problems. You'll be moved by this story of an African American family's fortunes, losses, and hopes.
This title is available in the HRW Library.

PLAY

Uninvited Guest

Major General Tom Powers is a man who commands respect. As a dyed-in-the-wool army man and a proud husband and father, he enjoys all the comforts of suburban life. Then the impossible happens: A flying saucer lands in his backyard, and from it emerges a visitor named Kreton—a distinguished alien in an 1860s costume who is looking for Robert E. Lee. Gore Vidal's comedy ***Visit to a Small Planet*** is a wildly funny study of what happens when worlds collide—and unite.

PLAYS

All the World's a Stage

Some of the greatest plays ever to hit the stage are compiled in ***A Book of Plays.*** Here you'll have a front-row seat to drama that is astonishing in scope—featuring everything from a heartbreaking family story (Tennessee Williams's *The Glass Menagerie)* to a witty dialogue (Dorothy Parker's *Here We Are*) to a page-turning whodunit (Susan Glaspell's *Trifles*). The Russian playwright Anton Chekhov and the Irish playwright John Millington Synge add a distinguished international flavor to the collection.
This title is available in the HRW Library.

Toward Reading Two Million Words Annually

Estimated Word Counts and Reading Levels of Read On Books:

Drama

*Macbeth**	above grade level	112,400
*A Raisin in the Sun**	at grade level	52,300
Visit to a Small Planet	below grade level	18,600
A Book of Plays	at grade level	122,400

***California Reading List Titles**

KEY: *above grade level* *at grade level* *below grade level*

Read On

For Independent Reading

If students enjoyed the themes and topics explored in this chapter, you might recommend these titles for independent reading.

Assessment Options

The following projects can help you evaluate and assess your students' outside reading. Videotapes or audiotapes of completed projects may be included in student portfolios.

- **Compare two Shakespeare plays.** Invite students to compare *Macbeth* and *Julius Caesar* in relation to the theme of "ambition or honor." Questions students might address in their essays include: How are the main characters alike? How are they different? How are the circumstances different in each play? What seems to be Shakespeare's attitude toward the main characters? What elements make each play a tragedy?
- **Production proposal.** Students who have read *Visit to a Small Planet* can get together and discuss how it could be produced as a television movie or major motion picture. They should consider any changes that might need to be made, such as cuts, updating certain scenes, special effects, and the addition or omission of certain characters. Students should then write a proposal to the network or film company presenting their ideas.
- **Talk show.** Invite students who have read *A Raisin in the Sun* to hold a radio or television talk show focusing on the subject of the American dream. They can discuss questions such as: Is the dream an illusion or does it help people to attain goals they might not otherwise attempt? Students may assume the persona of characters in the play. If possible, video or audiotape their show.

PRETEACHING

Standards Starter

Motivate. Ask students if they have ever been disappointed in a movie based on a book they've enjoyed. Ask them to share the reasons they were disappointed. [Answers will probably include that they disliked the casting, sets, or changes to the original story line.] Tell students that in this lesson they will learn a method for comparing and contrasting a written work with its film adaptation.

Resources Reminder

To introduce the workshop, you may want to use the journal starters in *Writing, Listening, & Speaking* Teaching Notes.

DIRECT TEACHING

On with the Show

If students read a film review online, *you need to be aware that Internet resources are public forums, and their content may be unpredictable.*

Integrating with Grammar, Usage, and Mechanics

As students begin their essays, they may have trouble with writing complete or effective sentences. You may want to review the corresponding chapters in the *Holt Handbook*.

DIFFERENTIATING INSTRUCTION

Learners Having Difficulty

Some students may have difficulty taking accurate and helpful notes while viewing the film. Encourage them to speak their notes into a cassette recorder and transcribe them later.

Writing Workshop

Comparing a Play and a Film

Writing Assignment
Listening and Speaking 1.14
Write an essay in which you compare a scene from a film to the play from which it was adapted and analyze the film techniques the director uses.

Imagine that you're watching a film adaptation of *The Tragedy of Julius Caesar,* the play you read earlier in this chapter. Early in the movie, you notice that Cassius is missing and lines that he speaks in the play are instead showing up in Brutus's dialogue. Filmmakers often alter plays in order to convey personal visions, appeal to specific audiences, or create certain reactions in viewers. It's little wonder that adaptations can look and feel radically different from the plays that inspired them. In this workshop you will compare a scene from a film adaptation of a play with the same scene in the written play, and then you will analyze and evaluate some of the techniques used in the film.

Prewriting

GO TO: go.hrw.com
KEYWORD: HLLA 10-10
FOR: Professional Model, Writer's Guides, and Reference Sources

Choose a Film and Focus on One Scene

On with the Show To begin, find a video of a film adaptation of a play you've read or one you'll read before watching the film. If you have trouble finding an adaptation, try one of the following suggestions.

- Browse a video store, looking for movies with familiar play titles.
- Read film reviews online and in newspapers and magazines.
- Ask a friend, teacher, or family member for a recommendation.
- Borrow a couple of videos from your school or public library. The librarian should be able to direct you toward film adaptations of plays.

Tunnel Vision Limit the scope of your evaluation by focusing on one important scene in the film. To find that scene, first sit down and **watch the video actively.** Pay close attention to each scene, and take notes on your reactions. Does a scene bring out a strong emotional response in you? Do you see a connection between the themes or issues in a scene and in your life? After watching the video, review your notes and select the scene to which you had the strongest reaction.

Listening and Speaking 1.14 Identify the aesthetic effects of a media presentation and evaluate the techniques used to create them (e.g., compare Shakespeare's *Henry V* with Kenneth Branagh's 1990 film version).

Compare the Film to the Play

What's New? Once you've chosen a scene from the film, re-read the same scene from the play and take notes on any differences. Specifically, write down ways in which the film scene's **narrative techniques** differ from the written scenes. Narrative techniques in the film will involve changes to the story itself, such as changes in

CHAPTER 10 RESOURCES: WRITING

Writing Workshop

Planning
- *On Course: Mapping Instruction*
- *One-Stop Planner* CD-ROM
- *Writing, Listening, & Speaking,* Teaching Notes, p. 107

Differentiating Instruction
- *Lesson Plans for Language Development,* pp. 357–358
- *Supporting Instruction in Spanish*

Practice
- *Writing, Listening, & Speaking,* Ch. 10

Reinforcement
- *Daily Language Activities*

890 Chapter 10 Drama • Evaluating an Argument

characters, setting, plot, dialogue, or theme. Ask yourself the following questions to analyze the film's narrative techniques.

ANALYZING NARRATIVE TECHNIQUES	
Characters, setting, and plot	Has the filmmaker eliminated, added, combined, or otherwise changed characters? Has the filmmaker changed the setting or plot? If so, how do the changes affect the story?
Dialogue	Are there differences in dialogue between the play and the film? For example, are lines added or cut in the film? Does a character in the film deliver lines that were spoken by another in the play?
Theme	Did the filmmaker alter the theme, or message, of the original story? How does the change affect the viewer's reaction to the story?

TIP Keep in mind that you'll probably need to view the film scene and read the play version several times as you make your comparisons. You should add new observations to your notes each time you view the film or read the play.

Pictures Speak? In addition to narrative techniques, filmmakers use film techniques to make a film from a play. **Film techniques** include using lighting, camera shots and angles, sound and music, and special effects to bring out a reaction in the viewer. For example, a filmmaker might combine ominous music, dramatic lighting, and a tilted camera angle to create suspense and make an audience worry that something bad is about to happen. Answer the following questions to analyze the filmmaker's use of film techniques.

ANALYZING FILM TECHNIQUES	
Lighting	How is lighting used in the scene? Does it affect the mood of the scene?
Camera shots and angles	What types of camera shots are used—long shots, medium shots, close-ups? Why might the filmmaker use different shots? From what angles does the camera shoot the scene's characters and actions? How do the angles affect your reactions to the scene?
Sound and music	What music and sound effects are included? What effect do they create?
Special effects	Are there special effects that you wouldn't expect to see in a stage presentation of the play? If so, do they enhance your appreciation of the story or distract you from it?

One student took the notes on the following page while viewing Franco Zeffirelli's 1990 production of *Hamlet*. She will later look back at these notes to find specific **references** to the play and the film to support her thesis statement.

CORRECTING MISCONCEPTIONS

Students may mistakenly believe that filmmakers have an obligation to incorporate all of a playwright's stage directions into a film adaptation. Explain that filmmakers may liberally change not only a play's staging but also any of the elements on this chart. The effectiveness of these changes is part of what earns praise for the movie.

DIRECT TEACHING

GRADE-LEVEL STANDARD

Analyzing Narrative Techniques

An additional narrative technique that students may recognize within the text of the play is stage direction. Ask students the following question:

- Did the filmmaker follow the stage directions given in the play?

If there are changes, follow up with this question:

- What differences do the changes make to the play's meaning?

Have students brainstorm possible answers, and lead students to understand that film's use of cameras and editing provides a greater variety of staging options.

MODELING AND DEMONSTRATION

Analyzing Film Techniques

Play for the class a scene from a film (preferably the Zeffirelli film *Hamlet*, which is treated in **A Writer's Model** on p. 893), and discuss the elements listed in the **Analyzing Film Techniques** chart. Point out that not every question will apply to the scenes they choose—not every scene will have special effects, for example—but that they should be aware of the filmmaker's and actors' unique interpretations of the play. After you have modeled answering the questions in the chart, have volunteers demonstrate answering similar questions about the films they have chosen.

Evaluation and Assessment

- *Test Generator (One-Stop Planner* CD-ROM)
- *Progress Assessment of Writing, Listening, & Speaking,* Ch. 10
- *Diagnostic and Summative Assessments,* End-of-Year Test

Internet

- go.hrw.com (keyword: HLLA 10-10)
- Online assessments at go.hrw.com (keyword: HLLA)

DIFFERENTIATING INSTRUCTION

REVIEW STANDARD

English-Language Learners

As students begin including quotations in their writing, model ways to introduce quotations smoothly. Ask students to keep the following points in mind:

- **Do not** use an obvious phrase such as "As this quotation shows…" to introduce a quotation.
- **Do** explain how the quotation supports the thesis sentence (for example, "Hamlet expresses his sadness by saying...").

Resources Reminder

For more help with English-Language Learners, see *Lesson Plans for Language Development.*

PRACTICE & APPLY 1

Guided and Independent Practice

Guide student analyses of the original play by providing this list of steps:

1. Read stage directions to find descriptions of characters, props, costumes, and sets.
2. Notice lines of dialogue that reveal characterization.
3. Jot down observations about literary elements (setting, conflict, figurative language) that impress you.
4. Look for patterns and repetition within literary elements.

Then, have students complete **Practice and Apply 1** as independent practice.

> **Plot:** Act 1, scene 1, is cut. The audience doesn't learn the significance of the ghost's armor.
> **Setting:** Film viewers see and hear the banquet, which is only described in the play.
> **Sound:** Footsteps, soft music, and a moaning wind add to the suspenseful atmosphere.
> **Lighting:** The battlements are moonlit with areas that are very dark. The lighting allows us to see the cold temperature through the icy breath coming from the characters.
> **Camera shots and angles:** Camera angles show the characters on the battlements looking down on the celebration. Close-ups of Hamlet's face show that he's sweating and troubled.

Write Your Thesis Statement

DO THIS

What's It All About? Narrative and film techniques result from specific choices made by the filmmaker to create certain **aesthetic effects,** or emotional and intellectual responses, in the viewer. Look back at your viewing notes to see how you responded to the scene. Then, look at the notes you took on narrative and film techniques to see what the filmmaker did to create those responses. Write a **thesis statement** that identifies your reponses, as shown in this student example.

TIP Because you want to convey a serious and knowledgeable **tone,** choose your words carefully when writing your thesis statement.

> In reworking Shakespeare's ghost scenes, director Franco Zeffirelli uses narrative and film techniques to create a suspenseful atmosphere and to generate feelings of empathy for Hamlet.

Gather Evidence and Organize

Picking Up the Pieces Once you've written your thesis statement, look at the text of the original play and your notes on the film to find **evidence**—quotations or examples—to support it. For example, the Writer's Model on page 893 gives specific examples of how lighting and sound create the film's suspenseful atmosphere.

Putting It All Together Your essay combines a comparison of the narrative techniques with an analysis and evaluation of the film techniques. Because of this, you will use two organizational patterns.

- First, arrange your comparison of narrative techniques in **point-by-point order,** comparing points until you've covered them all.
- Next, arrange the film techniques by **order of importance,** discussing the most important technique either first or last.

Writing 1.1 Establish a coherent thesis that conveys a clear and distinctive perspective on the subject and maintain a consistent tone and focus throughout the piece of writing. **1.4** Develop the main ideas within the body of the composition through supporting evidence.

PRACTICE & APPLY 1 Compare a play to its film adaptation by analyzing the narrative and film techniques the filmmaker used. Then, write your thesis statement, gather evidence, and organize your essay.

RESOURCES: WRITING

Practice & Apply 1

Guided Practice

- *Writing, Listening, & Speaking,* WS. p. 108

Reteaching and Modeling

- *Writing, Listening, & Speaking,* TP. 15
- *Writing, Listening, & Speaking,* WS. p. 110

892 Chapter 10 Drama • Evaluating an Argument

Comparing a Play and a Film

A Writer's Framework

Introduction	Body	Conclusion
• Provide an interesting opener. • Introduce the original play and playwright, and the film adaptation and filmmaker. • Clearly state your thesis.	• Compare narrative techniques in point-by-point order. • Analyze film techniques by order of importance. • Use evidence to support your ideas.	• Remind readers of your thesis by restating it in different words. • End with a closing thought or question that readers can ponder after they've finished reading.

A Writer's Model

Zeffirelli's *Hamlet:* A Ghost of the Original?

INTRODUCTION
Interesting opener

Are you the kind of person who thinks nothing can surpass the genius of Shakespeare, or do you wish someone would update the language and add effects to make his plays more interesting to a twenty-first-century audience? Sometimes you can get the best of both worlds. William Shakespeare's *Hamlet* and Franco Zeffirelli's film version of the play share the same characters and the same basic story. However, in reworking Shakespeare's ghost scenes, Zeffirelli uses narrative and film techniques to create a suspenseful atmosphere and to generate feelings of empathy for Hamlet.

Play and playwright, film and filmmaker

Thesis statement

Comparison of narrative techniques:

1. Plot—play

Zeffirelli changes the plot of *Hamlet* to get straight to the main action and characters. In the play, the audience first encounters the ghost in Act 1, Scene 1. Audience members learn that the king, Hamlet's father, is dead and that a ghost in his armor is walking the castle's battlements at night. The characters in the scene think that the ghost's appearance may be an omen that hints at Denmark's troubled political situation, which includes a possible Norwegian invasion.

Plot—film

In the film, however, this scene is replaced by one of the king's funeral—a scene that is not in the play. By making this replacement, Zeffirelli has chosen to focus his film on the personal, rather than political, side of the story. As in the play, when Horatio and Hamlet first meet, Horatio tells Hamlet about the ghost on the battlements. Zeffirelli moves this exchange from Act 1, Scene 2 of the play to the beginning of his suspense-filled ghost scene.

(continued)

DIRECT TEACHING

A Writer's Model

Point out the title of **A Writer's Model,** which uses a combination title separated by a colon; the first half is straightforward, and the second is catchy or inviting. Encourage students to use this strategy—quite common with essays of this type—with their titles if they are having trouble creating one on their own.

DIFFERENTIATING INSTRUCTION

Advanced Learners

Enrichment. Have students identify a living filmmaker whose work they admire. Then, have them create a short list of questions asking how the filmmaker approaches filming an adaptation of an existing play or novel. Encourage students to focus on how the filmmaker makes decisions about major narrative changes. Finally, have students do research to see if they can find answers to some of their questions in interviews with, or articles by or about, the filmmaker.

Writing Workshop: Comparing a Play and a Film 893

DIRECT TEACHING

GRADE-LEVEL STANDARDS

Point out to students the parenthetical citation that appears in **A Writer's Model.** Explain that the writer is citing his source—in this case, the text of *Hamlet*—indicating where in the play he found this quotation: Act 1, Scene 4, line 7.

CRITICAL THINKING

Ask students to evaluate which kind of performance is generally more entertaining to watch: a play or a film? Have students do a five-minute timed exercise in their journals, writing their reasons for preferring one more than the other. Encourage students to consider taking a position opposite the one they might usually take.

PRACTICE & APPLY 2

Guided and Independent Practice

Guide student preparations by asking them to answer the following questions:

1. What is your thesis statement?
2. What main points support the thesis?
3. What evidence supports each main point?
4. How will you organize your paper?

After students have answered the questions, hold individual conferences with them to discuss their responses. Encourage them to explore areas that might need strengthening as they prepare to write their first drafts. Then, have them complete **Practice and Apply 2** on their own.

(continued)

2. Setting—play / **Quotation** / **Setting—film**

Zeffirelli also adds to his story's setting. In the play, while Horatio, Hamlet, and friends await the ghost on the battlements, stage directions indicate "A flourish of trumpets, and ordinance shot off, within" (I.iv.7). Hamlet indicates that this is a part of the new king's custom of staying up late and carousing. The play's audience doesn't see the celebration; however, Zeffirelli's film does show it—full of warmth, color, music, and laughter. The celebration acts as a sharp contrast to the cold, dark, suspenseful atmosphere on the battlements where Hamlet encounters the ghost.

Evaluation of film techniques: / **1. Sound effects**

The film techniques Zeffirelli uses are as important as his narrative techniques. His ghost scene incorporates subtle yet important sound effects. Footsteps on the battlements, quiet notes of soft music, and the moaning wind add to the suspenseful atmosphere. They differ greatly from the lively music and laughter of the celebration.

2. Lighting / **3. Camera angles**

Visually, the battlements are bathed in fog, harsh moonlight, and shadows. Icy clouds of breath float through the shot, chilling the viewer. The empty sky creates a sense of being up very high in a stony, isolated place. To create the visual contrast with the celebration, the camera angle shows Hamlet and the others standing on the battlements, looking down into the banquet hall through an opening in the roof.

4. Camera shots

When Hamlet and the ghost go off on their own, the camera follows Hamlet as he climbs a steep circular stairway to a higher portion of the battlements. Once Hamlet is there, the camera cuts back and forth from close-ups of the ghost as it tells its tale of horror to close-ups of Hamlet's face reacting. The audience sees every detail of Hamlet's sweating, pain-wracked face as he listens. This creates empathy for Hamlet, since we can vividly see his emotions and understand what is going on inside him.

CONCLUSION / **Restatement of thesis** / **Closing thought**

Franco Zeffirelli's film version of *Hamlet* is interesting, dramatic, and entertaining. Although the play shares these qualities, viewers also benefit from Zeffirelli's gifted use of film techniques. The filmmaker has created a charged, suspenseful atmosphere in which the viewer feels empathy for Hamlet. While movie audiences miss out on the complexity of the original play, they may still enjoy sitting back and taking in the thrill of this suspenseful, fast-moving adaptation.

GO TO: go.hrw.com
KEYWORD: HLLA 10-10
FOR: Expanded Writer's Model and Student's Model

PRACTICE & APPLY 2 Refer to the framework on page 893 and the Writer's Model above as you write the first draft of your essay. Include citations whenever you quote sources. For more on **crediting your sources,** see page 698.

RESOURCES: WRITING

Practice & Apply 2

Think Sheet

- *Writing, Listening, & Speaking,* WS. p. 111

Template

- *Writing, Listening, & Speaking,* WS. p. 112

Internet

- go.hrw.com (keyword: HLLA 10-10)

Revising

Revise Your Essay

The Big Picture Writing that hasn't gone through the revision process is much like a piece of unfinished furniture. It will serve its purpose just fine in its rough state, but it's not until the final touches are done that the piece becomes truly beautiful. When you revise, you shape your ideas and their expression so that they can best achieve their desired effect. Read through your draft at least twice to evaluate and revise it, first for content and organization and then for style.

PEER REVIEW

Exchange your essay with a peer before you revise. He or she can help ensure that you discuss the narrative techniques in point-by-point order and the film techniques by order of importance.

First Reading: Content and Organization Evaluate the content and organization of your essay, using the guidelines below as a **think sheet.** First, answer the questions in the left-hand column. If you need help answering them, refer to the tips in the middle column. Then, make the changes suggested in the right-hand column.

Guidelines: Comparing a Play and a Film

Evaluation Questions	Tips	Revision Techniques
1 Is the opening engaging? Does the first paragraph introduce the play and its film adaptation? Does it include their creators?	**Underline** the engaging opening. **Bracket** the introduction of the play, the film adaptation, and their creators.	**Add** an intriguing question or an interesting quotation from the play or movie. **Add** a sentence that introduces the play, the film, and their creators.
2 Does the thesis statement identify the responses of the viewer?	**Highlight** the thesis statement.	**Add** a thesis that identifies your responses to the film's narrative and film techniques.
3 Is the essay well organized?	**Label** the narrative and film techniques discussed in the essay.	**Rearrange** the techniques so that all the narrative techniques are discussed first in point-by-point order, followed by all the film techniques organized by order of importance.
4 Is the discussion of each technique supported with evidence?	**Put a check mark** by each quotation and example from the play or film.	**Add** evidence or **elaborate** on existing evidence.
5 Does the conclusion restate the thesis? Does it leave the audience with a closing thought or question?	**Underline** the sentence restating the thesis. **Double-underline** the closing thought or question.	**Add** a restatement of the thesis. If necessary, **add** a sentence or two that gives the essay's readers something to consider after they finish reading.

DIRECT TEACHING

Elaboration

One way for students to elaborate in their essays is to carry each comparison or contrast to its logical conclusion. This means that students do not stop after presenting one or two points. They must set up the comparison or contrast, explain it, and then comment upon its significance.

Writing Workshop: Comparing a Play and a Film 895

RETEACHING

GRADE-LEVEL STANDARD

Second Reading: Style

To help students provide adequate sensory details, bring in several photographs of different scenes. Place students in random groups of five, and give each group one picture. Tell students that they will have thirty seconds to individually record all of the sight words that the picture brings to mind. After thirty seconds, let students share their responses within their groups. Then, have students do the same for two other senses (hearing, smell, taste, or touch). Finally, have the groups discuss which words provide the most effective descriptions of the scenes in the pictures.

GUIDED PRACTICE

Responding to the Revision Process

Answers

1. *Dark* and *cold* are relative terms; the specific descriptions increase the sentence's effectiveness.
2. The last sentence does not fit with the section on lighting and camera angles; it addresses narrative techniques, not film techniques.

PRACTICE & APPLY 3

Independent Practice

Have students exchange papers with a partner. After reading each other's essays, have them answer these two questions on a separate sheet of paper and share their responses with their partners:

1. Which section of the essay was most effective? Why?
2. Do you feel you need more information or explanation to understand the paper fully?

Have students incorporate their partner's comments as they make their final revisions.

Second Reading: Style Once you've revised the content and organization of your essay, you can then concentrate on your **style**—the unique way that you use language to express yourself and your ideas. One way to improve your style is to use vivid **sensory details** that appeal to the senses of sight, hearing, smell, taste, and touch. Try to add a variety of these details to your discussions of narrative and film techniques so that your readers can picture the scenes you're describing.

editor in charge

Style Guidelines

Evaluation Question	Tip	Revision Technique
Does the essay include vivid details that appeal to the five senses in its discussions of narrative and film techniques?	**Put a check mark** next to sensory details that describe the techniques, which you have already labeled.	If necessary, **add** sensory details to the descriptions that lack them, or **reword** existing details to make them more vivid.

ANALYZING THE REVISION PROCESS

Study these revisions, and answer the questions that follow.

reword: Visually, the battlements are ~~dark and cold~~ *bathed in fog, harsh moonlight, and shadows. Icy clouds of breath float through the shot, chilling the viewer.* The empty sky creates a sense of being up very high in a stony, isolated place.

rearrange: The play's audience doesn't see the celebration; however, Zeffirelli's film does show it—full of warmth, color, music, and laughter. *move up*

Responding to the Revision Process

1. How does rewording the first sentence improve the description of the film technique?
2. Why do you think the writer moved the last sentence to an earlier part of the paper?

Writing 1.2 Use sensory details. **1.9** Revise writing to improve the logic and coherence of the organization.

PRACTICE & APPLY 3 Revise the content and organization of your draft by following the guidelines on page 895. Then, use the guidelines on this page to evaluate and revise the style of your essay.

896 Chapter 10 Drama • Evaluating an Argument

Publishing

Proofread and Publish Your Essay

Make It Shine! After you've revised your essay, be sure to proofread it. Check for and correct any errors in grammar, usage, and mechanics. Have someone else—a classmate, parent, or friend—proofread your paper, too. Two sets of eyes are better than one when it comes to proofreading.

Tell It to the World Now that you have written, revised, and proofread your essay, it's time for others to read it. Here are some suggestions for publication.

- Post your essay to an online bookstore or video outlet that invites people to submit comments on various videos.
- With a group of classmates, compile your essays into a classroom reference book. Future classes doing similar projects can then read your essays to get ideas for their own.
- Using **publishing software** and **graphic programs,** jazz up your essay to create a Web site dedicated to the play or film you have chosen. Ask for feedback from visitors to your site.

Reflect on Your Essay

The Final Take Finally, take a look back on what you have learned in the process of writing this essay. Closely examining your progress through each step of the process can help you recognize your strengths and weaknesses as a writer as well as your understanding of media presentations. Use these questions to focus your thoughts.

- Which stage of the writing process—prewriting, writing, revising, or publishing—was the most difficult for you? Why? Which skills do you need to sharpen to make that stage easier the next time you write?
- How did writing this essay help you understand the choices made by filmmakers?
- How will your knowledge of narrative and film techniques influence the way you view other films that are based on plays? other films in general?
- How has viewing the film influenced your reading of the play?

PRACTICE & APPLY 4 Take time to proofread your paper carefully. Then, look over the publishing options given above and select one to get your essay in front of an audience. Finally, answer the reflection questions.

TIP Proofreading will help ensure that your essay follows English **conventions.** As you proofread, check that you have correctly punctuated items in a series, such as a list of narrative techniques. For more on **serial commas,** see page 298 of the *Holt Handbook*.

COMPUTER TIP

To create a well-designed Web site, see *Designing Your Writing* in the *Writer's Handbook*.

Writing 1.8 Design and publish documents by using advanced publishing software and graphic programs.

TECHNOLOGY TIP

If students prepare their analyses on a word processor, have them check spelling with the spellchecker. However, remind students that they must still proofread their final copies; spellchecking programs highlight only misspellings, not homonyms or words spelled correctly but misused.

DIRECT TEACHING

Tell It to the World

If students post their essays online, *you need to be aware that Internet resources are sometimes public forums, and their content may be unpredictable.*

Resources Reminder

For help with writing assessment, see 6 Traits—Plus 1 in the "Scales and Sample Papers" section of *Progress Assessment of Writing, Listening, and Speaking.*

PRACTICE & APPLY 4

Guided and Independent Practice

Guide the proofreading process by pairing students. Have each group take turns reading aloud random sentences from each other's papers. Hearing sentences this way will allow the writer to concentrate on the construction and effectiveness of individual sentences. Then, have students complete **Practice and Apply 4** as independent practice.

RESOURCES: WRITING

Practice & Apply 3

Think Sheet

- *Writing, Listening, & Speaking,* WS. p. 114

Evaluation

- *Writing, Listening, & Speaking,* WS. p. 113

Practice & Apply 4

Assessment

- *Test Generator (One-Stop Planner* CD-ROM)
- *Progress Assessment of Writing, Listening, & Speaking,* pp. 35–38, 84–86

Internet

- Online assessments at go.hrw.com (keyword: HLLA)

Writing Workshop: Comparing a Play and a Film 897

Analyzing and Evaluating Speeches

Speaking Assignment
Listening and Speaking 1.10
Analyze a historically significant speech to discover what makes it effective and memorable.

Earlier in this chapter you read Mark Antony's powerful eulogy presented at the funeral of Julius Caesar. Although his speech was full of sound reasoning, Antony turned the crowd into an angry mob through his passion and eloquent speaking style. Rhetoric—the art of speaking well—has played an important role in history as well as literature. Throughout history, speakers have used rhetoric to change people's minds, to sway their hearts, and to spur them to action. In this workshop you will have the opportunity to evaluate the impact of rhetoric in a **historically significant speech.**

Select a Speech

go.hrw.com

GO TO: go.hrw.com
KEYWORD: HLLA 10-10
FOR: Historical Speeches

Lend Me Your Ears Your school and public libraries, history textbook, and the Internet are all good places to begin your search for a speech to analyze. Look for written texts, audio recordings, and videotapes of historically significant speeches. Think about topics that interest you, such as environmental protection, freedom of speech, or civil rights, and do a little research for speeches that have been made on those topics. You might also want to consider historical events, such as the fall of the Berlin Wall (1989), and find important speeches that were given during that time period. If possible, find a speech that you can watch on video. While the words and ideas expressed in a great speech are important, the speaker's voice, gestures, and body posture also add to the speech's effectiveness.

Analyze Content

Tricks of the Trade Most speeches—unless they are purely informational, like research presentations—contain elements of persuasion. That is, the speaker is trying to convince his or her listeners to believe an idea, support a cause, or take an action. Therefore, any analysis of a speech must include a look at the types of **arguments** and **rhetorical devices** a speaker can use to be persuasive. Examine the speech you've chosen for examples of each.

Listening and Speaking 1.10 Analyze historically significant speeches (e.g., Abraham Lincoln's "Gettysburg Address," Martin Luther King, Jr.'s "I Have a Dream") to find the rhetorical devices and features that make them memorable. **1.13** Analyze the types of arguments used by the speaker, including argument by causation, analogy, authority, emotion, and logic.

Arguments In order to persuade an audience, a speaker must provide **arguments**—reasons and evidence (facts, statistics, examples, and expert testimony) that show why listeners should change their minds or take action on an issue. Some common types of arguments used in persuasive speaking are listed on the next page.

Preteaching

Motivate. Write the following phrases on the chalkboard and ask students if they can identify the speakers.

- I have a dream... [Martin Luther King, Jr.]
- Four score and seven years ago... [Abraham Lincoln]
- And a'n't I a woman? [Sojourner Truth]

After students have identified the speakers, ask why these phrases are so well known. [Possible answers include the celebrity of the speaker or the importance of the speech.] Tell students that in this lesson they will learn to analyze a speech and decide for themselves why some speeches endure.

Technology Tip

Many CD-ROM resources, such as encyclopedias and periodical archives, offer audio clips of famous speeches. Students can identify a significant figure from a particular time period, then look under the person's name. An audio icon will probably indicate available audio.

Differentiating Instruction

Grade-Level Standard

Advanced Learners

Enrichment. Have students check out from the school or public library a videotape of a speech and identify in it one of the common arguments used by orators. (If students don't have access to a videocassette player at home, arrange for them to use the school's resources.) Ask the students to rewrite the argument in two different ways, making sure to adhere to the original tone and purpose of the speech.

Chapter 10 Resources: Listening & Speaking

Listening & Speaking Workshop

Planning
- *On Course: Mapping Instruction*
- *One-Stop Planner* CD-ROM
- *Writing, Listening, & Speaking*
  —Teaching Notes, p. 115
  —Project-Planning Guide, WS. p. 117

Think Sheet
- *Writing, Listening, & Speaking,* WS. p. 118

Differentiating Instruction
- *Lesson Plans for Language Development,* p. 359
- *Supporting Instruction in Spanish*

Evaluation and Assessment
- *Writing, Listening, & Speaking,* WS. p. 120

- **argument by causation:** demonstrates how a cause-and-effect relationship supports the speaker's point
- **analogy:** explains or illustrates a point by making a literal comparison between two unlike things
- **appeal to authority:** cites an expert on a subject to support a point
- **appeal to emotion:** uses examples or language that appeals to the audience's emotional needs and values
- **appeal to logic:** gives facts, statistics, and examples that appeal to the listeners' minds

Rhetorical Devices Good speakers use **rhetorical devices**—certain ways of using language to persuade listeners or get their attention. Look for these common rhetorical devices in the speech you analyze.

- **allusion:** referring to literature or to an actual event, person, or place
- **diction:** choosing words to create a certain **tone** (the attitude the speaker expresses toward the subject) or **mood** (the speech's overall impression on the audience)
- **metaphor:** imaginatively comparing unlike things
- **repetition:** repeating important words or phrases
- **rhetorical question:** posing a question without expecting an answer
- **parallelism:** using the same **syntax,** or sentence structure, to point out a similarity in ideas

TIP Some speakers misuse rhetoric to cover up a lack of meaning or to mislead listeners. Be sure the speaker's arguments are sound and logical before making up your mind about any issue.

Analyze Organization

Taking Orders You should also look at how a speech is organized. Good speeches are **coherent**—logically organized and showing a clear connection between ideas. Which of the following organizational patterns can you find in the speech you're analyzing?

- **deductive pattern:** The speaker states the thesis at the beginning of the speech, then gives arguments and reasons to support the thesis. Speakers organize their material **deductively** to move their audiences from general ideas to more specific ones.
- **inductive pattern:** The speaker first presents arguments and reasons, then states the thesis later in the speech. Speakers organize their material **inductively** to move their audiences from specific ideas to more general ones.

Analyze This! Read the excerpt on the next page from a speech given in Washington, D.C., by Chief Joseph of the Nez Perce. In 1879, Chief Joseph traveled to the nation's capital to speak with the country's

Listening and Speaking 1.1 Formulate judgments about the ideas under discussion. **1.11** Assess how language and delivery affect the mood and tone of the oral communication and make an impact on the audience.

DIRECT TEACHING

GRADE-LEVEL STANDARD

Analyze This!

Point out to students that Chief Joseph uses the inductive approach. He begins his series of arguments with an emotional appeal, saying that he is heartsick thinking of the government's broken promises. He concludes his speech by presenting his thesis.

- *Progress Assessment of Writing, Listening, & Speaking,* p. 87
- *Diagnostic and Summative Assessments,* End-of-Year Test

Internet

- go.hrw.com (keyword: HLLA)

Listening & Speaking Workshop: Analyzing and Evaluating Speeches 899 leaders. Although he was given assurances that his people would have justice, Chief Joseph didn't believe in words not supported by actions. The annotations on the left side illustrate the arguments and rhetorical devices Chief Joseph used in his speech.

Parallelism and Repetition

Appeal to emotions

Appeal to logic

Analogy

Metaphor and rhetorical question

Appeal to authority

Thesis

Appeal to emotions

. . . Good words do not last long unless they amount to something. Words do not pay for my dead people. They do not pay for my country now overrun by white men. They do not protect my father's grave. They do not pay for my horses and cattle. Good words do not give me back my children. Good words will not make good the promise of your war chief, General Miles. Good words will not give my people a home where they can live in peace and take care of themselves. I am tired of talk that comes to nothing. It makes my heart sick when I remember all the good words and all the broken promises. . . . If the white man wants to live in peace with the Indian he can live in peace. There need be no trouble. Treat all men alike. Give them the same laws. Give them all an even chance to live and grow. All men were made by the same Great Spirit Chief. They are all brothers. The earth is the mother of all people, and all people should have equal rights upon it. You might as well expect rivers to run backward as that any man who was born a free man should be contented penned up and denied liberty to go where he pleases. If you tie a horse to a stake, do you expect he will grow fat? If you pen an Indian up on a small spot of earth and compel him to stay there, he will not be contented nor will he grow and prosper. I have asked some of the Great White Chiefs where they get their authority to say to the Indian that he shall stay in one place, while he sees white men going where they please. They cannot tell me.

I only ask of the Government to be treated as all other men are treated. If I cannot go to my own home, let me have a home in a country where my people will not die so fast. . . .

Analyze Delivery

Not What but How Often, *how* a speaker delivers his or her message is as important as the message itself. When you view or listen to a speech, pay close attention to the speaker's **delivery**—how he or she uses voice and body. Delivery reinforces the speaker's tone and the speech's mood. For example, speakers who stand tall, speak clearly, use natural gestures, and make direct eye contact with audience members show that they care about their subject and audience. When listeners can feel the speaker's respect, they are more receptive to the speaker's message, which creates a positive mood.

RETEACHING

Analyze Delivery

If students have trouble analyzing the arguments, rhetorical devices, and delivery techniques in Chief Joseph's speech, you may want to play a videotape of another speech. Ask students to respond in their own words to the following questions. As they respond, point out to them whenever they are using a concept given a specific name in their book.

- What does the speaker say to make the ideas sound more appealing? [rhetorical devices]
- Does the speaker back up what he or she says? If so, how? [evidence]
- What surprising connections does the speaker make? [coherence and clarity]
- How does the speaker feel about the subject of the speech? How can you tell? [gestures, tone, and mood]

After students have answered the questions and discussed the terms, review with them the questions given in the **Evaluating Speeches** chart on p. 901 and point out their similarity to the questions they have just answered.

Speakers who slouch, mumble, use no gestures, and stare directly at their papers show audience members that either they're uninterested in the subject or care little about what the audience thinks. This indifference from the speaker makes for an uninterested, unfriendly mood.

Evaluate a Speech

What's It Worth? The most important test of a good persuasive speech is your own reaction. As you evaluate a speech, use the questions in the following chart to form your own **judgments** and to support them with evidence.

Quick guide

EVALUATING SPEECHES

CONTENT

- **Arguments:** What kinds of arguments did the speaker use? Which were most effective? Why?
- **Evidence:** What kinds of evidence did the speaker provide (facts, statistics, examples, expert testimony)? What evidence did you find most effective? Why?
- **Rhetorical Devices:** What rhetorical devices did the speaker use? Which had the greatest effect?
- **Tone and Mood:** How did the speaker's language affect the tone and mood of the speech?

ORGANIZATION

- **Coherence and Clarity:** How was the speech organized (deductively or inductively)? Did the speaker make and support one point at a time? How clearly were the speaker's points connected to each other and to the speech's main idea?

DELIVERY

- **Voice:** Did the speaker speak clearly? Could you understand him or her without straining?
- **Gestures:** What kinds of gestures did the speaker use? Were they appropriate and effective? What important points did they reinforce?
- **Tone and Mood:** How did the speaker's voice and gestures express his or her attitude toward the audience and the speech's subject? How did the speaker's delivery affect the mood of the speech?

GENERAL

- **Effectiveness:** Did the speech broaden your view of the issue? Did it change your mind? Explain.

PRACTICE & APPLY 5 Depending on your access to audiovisual resources, choose one of these options to analyze a historically significant speech.

- If the speech is available on video and you have access to a player, answer all the questions in the above chart.
- If the speech is not available on video or you do not have access to a player, use the written text to answer only the questions about its content, organization, and general effectiveness.

Use your responses to the questions in the chart to write a one-paragraph evaluation of the speech.

Listening and Speaking 1.0 Students formulate adroit judgments about oral communication. **1.12** Evaluate the clarity, quality, effectiveness, and general coherence of a speaker's important points, arguments, evidence, organization of ideas, delivery, diction, and syntax.

DIRECT TEACHING

GRADE-LEVEL STANDARD

Evaluate a Speech

Remind students that it is often up to them to *infer,* or make an educated guess about, the thesis of a speech.

DIFFERENTIATING INSTRUCTION

REVIEW STANDARD

Learners Having Difficulty

Many students will have difficulty evaluating all the different aspects of a speech. Remind them to separate the elements (as indicated on the **Evaluating Speeches** chart) and focus on one at a time. If they are viewing a recorded speech, they should listen multiple times, each time with a different purpose. If they are hearing a speech live, they should focus on different elements at different points in the speech.

PRACTICE & APPLY 5

Guided and Independent Practice

To guide students as they organize their evaluation notes into a paragraph, briefly review the order of importance. Then, have them complete **Practice and Apply 5** on their own.

Standards Review

Analyzing Informational Materials

STANDARDS FOCUS, pp. 902–903

(For the grade-level standard reviewed in this lesson, see Student Edition, p. 902)

INTRODUCING THE STANDARDS REVIEW

Use this review to assess students' grasp of the standards taught in this chapter. If necessary, you can use the annotations to guide students in their reading before they answer the questions.

DIRECT TEACHING

A Analyzing Informational Materials
GRADE-LEVEL STANDARD

? Author's argument. What is the author's claim? [She claims that Brutus's funeral speech to the Romans in Act III, Scene 2, of *Julius Caesar* is faulty.]

B Analyzing Informational Materials
GRADE-LEVEL STANDARD

? Author's argument. Why does the author paraphrase Brutus's argument? [Possible response: She paraphrases Brutus's speech in order to show how vague it is.]

C Analyzing Informational Materials
GRADE-LEVEL STANDARD

? Author's argument. What evidence does the author give to support her claim that Brutus's logic is faulty? [She cites specific lines from the speech and explains why they are examples of the either-or fallacy.]

STANDARDS REVIEW

Analyzing Informational Materials

Test Practice

Evaluating an Author's Argument

DIRECTIONS: Read the following essay. Then, read each multiple-choice question that follows, and write the letter of the best response.

The following essay discusses Brutus's speech to the Romans in Act III, Scene 2, of Julius Caesar.

Brutus's Funeral Speech

Phyllis Goldenberg

When Brutus speaks to the Romans, he has two purposes. His first (and surely more important) purpose is to convince his listeners that Caesar's murder was justified.[1] His second purpose is to introduce Mark Antony. Brutus gets a D– on his speech, while Antony walks away with an A+. Brutus's speech is practically a failure. **A**

The most serious flaw in Brutus's speech is that his evidence is too vague. This is the essence of Brutus's argument: You know that I am an honorable man. (Is it honorable to assassinate a leader for the reasons Brutus offers?) I loved Caesar as much as you did, but Caesar was a threat to Rome because he was ambitious. Brutus is vague about Caesar's "crimes"; he never tells exactly how Caesar was ambitious or why his ambition was bad. **B** In fact, the word *ambitious* is a poor choice because it has favorable connotations as well as negative ones. For example, we admire someone for being ambitious and striving to achieve a high goal. Yet Brutus assumes that ambition is all bad. He doesn't give any convincing evidence to prove that Caesar deserved to die.

Brutus's logic is faulty also. As part of his justification of Caesar's murder, he says, "Had you rather Caesar were living, and die all slaves, than that Caesar were dead, to live all free men?" (Act III, Scene 2, lines 22–24). This is an example of the either-or fallacy,[2] one kind of faulty reasoning. Brutus says that only two positions are possible: Either Caesar is allowed to live and all Rome is in slavery, or Caesar is killed and all Rome is free. In reality there are many other possibilities between these two extremes. **C** Why should we believe Brutus anyway? He doesn't substantiate[3] either of the claims he makes: Why does Caesar alive mean slavery? Why does Caesar dead mean freedom?

Brutus uses a powerful emotional appeal when he appeals to his listeners' patriotism, but it's not enough to justify Caesar's murder. He says, "Who is here so rude,[4] that would not be a Roman? . . . Who is here so vile,[5] that will not love his country?" (Act III, Scene 2, lines 30–32). He pauses for effect, knowing full well that no one will publicly admit to being unpatriotic. *Vile,* of course, is a loaded word, and it's "vile" not to love one's country.

1. **justified** *v.*: shown to be just, or right.
2. **either-or fallacy:** type of faulty reasoning in which a situation is described as if there were only two choices when there may be several.
3. **substantiate** *v.*: confirm; show to be true.
4. **rude** *adj.*: rough; uncivilized.
5. **vile** *adj.*: evil.

Pages 902–903 cover **Reading Standard 2.8** Evaluate the credibility of an author's argument or defense of a claim by critiquing the relationship between generalizations and evidence, the comprehensiveness of evidence, and the way in which the author's intent affects the structure and tone of the text.

READING MINI-LESSON

Reviewing Word-Attack Skills

Activity. Have students identify the component parts of these words formed by derivation or compounding.

1. protohistorian [proto– + histor(y) + –ian]
2. ultraconservative [ultra– + conserv(e) + –ative]
3. bioregionalism [bio– + region + –al + –ism]
4. antitakeover [anti– + take + over]
5. autoradiography [auto– + radio + graph + –y]
6. unidirectional [uni– + direct + –ion + –al]
7. telestereoscope [tele– + stereo + –scope]
8. semiopaque [semi– + opaque]
9. happenstance [happen + stance]
10. psychodrama [psycho– + drama]

If we had only Brutus's speech in this act, we'd probably think it wasn't bad. He is very sincere. Yet Brutus is far less passionate and thus far less convincing to the mob than Antony is. Brutus doesn't use any of the persuasive devices that Antony uses. He also ignores rule 1 of persuasive speaking: Nobody believes anybody without proof. Brutus is vague and illogical, and his appeal to patriotism isn't enough to save his speech. Brutus may or may not be an honorable man, but he is certainly a terrible orator.[6]

D

6. **orator** (ôr′ət•ər) *n.:* public speaker.

1. The writer's **opinion statement,** or **claim,** appears in —
   - A the first sentence of the first paragraph
   - B the last sentence of the first paragraph
   - C the first sentence of the second paragraph
   - D the last sentence of the second paragraph

2. The author's **intent,** or **purpose,** is to —
   - F prove that Brutus is honorable
   - G persuade us that Brutus is a hero
   - H evaluate Brutus's character
   - J persuade us that Brutus's funeral speech is a failure

3. The writer's **purpose** controls the essay's **structure,** since each of the second through the fifth paragraphs deals with flaws in —
   - A Shakespeare's logic
   - B Brutus's character
   - C Brutus's funeral speech
   - D the play's plot

4. The essay's **evidence** consists of —
   - F quotations from the play and references to specific events in the play
   - G quotations from literary critics about the play
   - H quotations from Shakespeare about the play
   - J facts about the historical Brutus

5. The writer discusses Brutus's either-or fallacy as **evidence** to support which statement?
   - A Brutus's evidence is too vague.
   - B Brutus uses an emotional appeal.
   - C Brutus's logic is faulty.
   - D Brutus is insincere.

6. Which word *best* describes the essay's overall **tone?**
   - F sympathetic
   - G angry
   - H persuasive
   - J passionate

7. From the first sentence of the second paragraph, we can infer that the writer has **structured** her argument with —
   - A the least important reason first
   - B the most important reason first
   - C the most important reason last
   - D no apparent order

8. Which statement is *not* true?
   - F The essay is clearly structured.
   - G The argument includes statistics.
   - H Each reason is supported by evidence.
   - J The argument includes opinion.

Using Academic Language

Review of Literary Terms
Reading Standards 3.1 and 3.10

Have students show their grasp of the standards by citing passages from the chapter that illustrate the meanings of these terms: **Drama** (p. 720); **Conflict** (p. 720); **Complications** (p. 720); **Climax** (p. 720); **Resolution** (pp. 720, 754); **Tragedy** (pp. 720, 754, 872); **Tragic Hero, Tragic Flaw** (pp. 720, 754, 872); **Comedy** (pp. 721, 724); **Stages, Dialogue, Monologue, Soliloquy, Asides, Stage Directions, Farce** (p. 724).

Review of Informational Terms
Reading Standard 2.8

Ask students to use the following terms to explain how to evaluate the credibility of an author's argument or defense of a claim. **Author's Intent, Generalization, Structure, Tone, Evidence, Credibility,** (p. 881).

DIRECT TEACHING

D Analyzing Informational Materials
GRADE-LEVEL STANDARD

? Author's argument. Why doesn't the author discuss any of the persuasive devices that Antony uses? [Possible response: Her argument is that Brutus's speech is faulty, not that Antony's speech is effective.]

Test-Taking Tips

For more instruction on how to answer multiple-choice items, refer students to **Test Smarts.**

TestPractice

Answers and Model Rationales

1. **B** The author's claim, that Brutus's speech is faulty, is explicitly stated at the end of the first paragraph. A mentions Brutus's purpose in giving the speech. C and D present evidence to support the author's claim.
2. **J** The author is only concerned about the effectiveness of Brutus's speech.
3. **C** The author is not concerned with the wider issues of character and plot, nor with faulty logic on Shakespeare's part.
4. **F** The author decided to use only the speech itself, a primary source, rather than using secondary sources (G, H, and J).
5. **C** The author discusses the either-or fallacy in paragraph 3 to explain Brutus's faulty logic.
6. **H** The author uses logic, rather than emotion to convince the reader. F, G, and J are indicative of emotional appeals.
7. **B** The sentence contains the key phrase "the most serious flaw."
8. **G** The argument includes textual, but not numerical, evidence. Since the author's claim is basically a well-supported opinion, H and J are wrong.

Test Practice

Vocabulary Development

Synonyms

Modeling. Model the thought process of a good reader answering item 1. Say, "Mrs. Popov mourns for her dead husband and refuses to leave the house. Since grief causes suffering, *ill* works best."

Test Practice

Answers and Model Rationales

1. **B** See rationale above.
2. **J** Smirnov does not have a high opinion of women, so he would be most scornful by the idea of women's liberation.
3. **C** Since Smirnov's remarks are described as being harsh, they must be extremely negative.
4. **F** Only F and H are offenses. If Smirnov was evil Mrs. Popov would probably be more than offended.
5. **D** When we are upset we are in less control. To ramble (D) means to be without aim or focus.
6. **F** The adjective *vital* describes something that is necessary to maintain life. *Vitality* is simply the noun form of this word.
7. **C** Brutus is a serious (D) character; he must be played that way. While not everyone would play him as reserved (C), playing Brutus as bold (A) or fearful (B), however, would go against character.
8. **F** The sentence includes another synonym for *unorthodox*—the word *new*. Something new is something that is not usual.
9. **C** Brutus is also depicted as "swepted by bad events," suggesting a state of confusion and uncertainty (C).

TEST PRACTICE

Vocabulary Development

Test Practice

Synonyms

DIRECTIONS: Choose the best synonym for the underlined word in each sentence.

1. Luka says that Mrs. Popov is <u>indisposed</u>.
   - **A** busy
   - **B** ill
   - **C** away
   - **D** forgetful
2. Smirnov seems to sneer at the idea of the <u>emancipation</u> of women.
   - **F** kindness
   - **G** restriction
   - **H** respectability
   - **J** liberation
3. Smirnov's harsh remarks about women sound <u>malicious</u>.
   - **A** lighthearted
   - **B** logical
   - **C** spiteful
   - **D** confused
4. Mrs. Popov is offended by Smirnov's <u>impudence</u>.
   - **F** disrespect
   - **G** stupidity
   - **H** evilness
   - **J** unattractiveness
5. Mrs. Popov's <u>incoherent</u> response to Smirnov's remark shows how upset she is.
   - **A** humorous
   - **B** insincere
   - **C** rapid
   - **D** rambling
6. John Mason Brown says that Orson Welles's production of *Julius Caesar* brings new <u>vitality</u> to the story.
   - **F** energy
   - **G** color
   - **H** hope
   - **J** insight
7. Orson Welles plays Brutus as a <u>reticent</u> character.
   - **A** bold
   - **B** fearful
   - **C** reserved
   - **D** serious
8. Brown considers this version of *Julius Caesar* to be new and <u>unorthodox</u>.
   - **F** unusual
   - **G** unremarkable
   - **H** unclear
   - **J** unsuccessful
9. In Welles's production, Brutus is depicted as a <u>perplexed</u> individual.
   - **A** political
   - **B** complex
   - **C** uncertain
   - **D** selfish

Vocabulary Review

Ask students to match the synonym below with a Vocabulary word from the box.

idealist	surly	sinister
insinuate	impunity	

1. hint [insinuate]
2. gruff [surly]
3. immunity [impunity]
4. wicked [sinister]
5. dreamer [idealist]

ASSESSING

Assessment

- *Progress Assessment of Reading*
  - Chapter Test

Writing

Test Practice

DIRECTIONS: Read the following paragraph from a draft of a student's comparison of a scene from the film and play versions of *The Crucible.* Then, answer the questions below it.

(1) The action in the film version of Arthur Miller's play *The Crucible* continues long after the play's curtain falls. (2) The final scene is shot with the camera behind three nooses, ominously observing the arrival of the prisoner cart. (3) The background music is sad and slow, and no other sound can be heard until the prisoners begin praying in unison as the ropes are placed around their necks. (4) Fortunately, this form of punishment is no longer commonly used in this country. (5) After a noise, the camera cuts to a shot showing only the top of the rope against the sky. (6) The viewer is left stunned by this sharp final image.

1. Which sentence could the writer add after sentence 1 to provide a clear thesis?

- **A** The film version is much shorter than the written play.
- **B** The movie uses sound and visual effects to show the exciting landscape.
- **C** The movie uses visual and sound effects to create a sense of tragedy.
- **D** In the film version, conversation is more important than action.

2. Which of the following should be added to sentence 1?

- **F** the name of the film's lead actor
- **G** the name of the filmmaker
- **H** the setting of the film
- **J** the film's distributor

3. Which sentence could be added to elaborate on sentence 3?

- **A** The soft music contrasts with the growing volume of the prayers to create a tense atmosphere.
- **B** The sound techniques make the viewer feel happy that John Proctor is getting the punishment he deserves.
- **C** The sounds in the film scene are no more effective than the stage directions found in the play's original text.
- **D** This use of gentle sound makes the viewer feel relieved that the witch hunt is finally over.

4. Which sentence should replace sentence 5 in order to add sensory details?

- **F** After a scary noise, the camera cuts to a shot showing only the rope.
- **G** The camera cuts to a shot showing only a rope against a blue sky.
- **H** After a thump, the camera cuts to a shot showing only a taut rope against a blue sky.
- **J** After a terrible noise, the camera cuts to a shot showing only the hangman's rope.

5. Which sentence should be deleted to improve the organization?

- **A** 1
- **B** 3
- **C** 4
- **D** 6

Standards Review

Answers

1. C
2. G
3. A
4. H
5. C

APPLICATION

Create a Film Adaptation

Divide the class into groups of four or five, and have each group select a scene from a play. Have them modify the scene as if they were filmmakers creating an adaptation. Encourage them to use lighting and sound wherever possible to create the effects they desire.

EXTENSION

Write a Speech

For homework, have students select both a famous person and an important event (for example, Abraham Lincoln and the occasion of the first humans on the moon). Instruct them to write a speech for the person and the event (for example, Lincoln congratulating the crew of *Apollo 11* upon their return to earth). Emphasize that students should not re-create an actual speech by the famous person but should place the person in a different era or situation.

Homework

RESOURCES: WRITING, LISTENING, & SPEAKING

Assessment

- *Test Generator (One-Stop Planner* CD-ROM)
- *Progress Assessment of Writing, Listening, & Speaking,* Ch. 10
- *Diagnostic and Summative Assessments,* End-of-Year Test

Internet

- Online assessments at go.hrw.com (keyword: HLLA)

Holt Literature and Language Arts: Mastering the California Standards

Chapter 11 Consumer and Workplace Documents
Music on the E-frontier

Program Organization

Holt Literature and Language Arts provides a complete curriculum for standards-based instruction in reading, literature, writing, listening and speaking, and language conventions. The instructional content is presented in quarters to enable teachers to anticipate and administer the quarterly assessments required by California.

About Chapter 11

Standards-based lesson plans and suggestions for pacing the presentation of Chapter 11, the related instructional material, and the recommended assessment are provided in *On Course: Mapping Instruction,* Chapter 11.

- In Chapter 11, students will analyze workplace documents; prepare a bibliography of reference materials; follow technical directions; critique the logic of functional documents; and write business letters and technical documents.

Language Arts Content

Which reading standards are taught in Chapter 11?

In this chapter, students will master the following Grade 10 standards and review a standard from Grade 8. Selections or features marked with a ✔ constitute the minimum course of study that provides coverage of grade-level standards.

Grade 10 Standards
Word Analysis, Fluency, and Systematic Vocabulary Development

2.1 Analyze the structure and format of functional workplace documents, including the graphics and headers, and explain how authors use the features to achieve their purposes.
Analyzing Functional Workplace Documents (contract), pp. 916–920
✔ Analyzing Informational Materials (standards review), pp. 938–939

2.2 Prepare a bibliography of reference materials for a report using a variety of consumer, workplace, and public documents.
Citing Internet Sources (sample citations), pp. 921–926
✔ Analyzing Informational Materials (standards review), pp. 938–939

2.6 Demonstrate use of sophisticated learning tools by following technical directions.
Following Technical Directions (instruction manual), pp. 913–915
✔ Analyzing Informational Materials (standards review), pp. 938–939

2.7 Critique the logic of functional documents by examining the sequence of information and procedures in anticipation of possible reader misunderstandings.
Evaluating the Logic of Functional Documents (magazine article, product review), pp. 909–912
✔ Analyzing Informational Materials (standards review), pp. 938–939

Review Standard Grade 8

Reading 2.1 Compare and contrast the features and elements of consumer materials to gain meaning from documents.
Reading Consumer Documents (contract, instruction manual, product information), pp. 927–931
Analyzing Informational Materials (standards review), pp. 938–939

Which writing standards are taught in Chapter 11?

Writing Applications

2.5 Write business letters.
Analyzing Informational Materials (standards review), pp. 938–939
- a. Provide clear and purposeful information and address the intended audience appropriately.
Writing Business Letters (business letters), pp. 934–937
- b. Use appropriate vocabulary, tone, and style to take into account the nature of the relationship with, and the knowledge and interests of, the recipients.
Writing Business Letters (business letters), pp. 934–937
- c. Highlight central ideas or images.
Writing Business Letters (business letters), pp. 934–937
- d. Follow a conventional style with page formats, fonts, and spacing that contribute to the documents' readability and impact.
Writing Business Letters (business letters), pp. 934–935

2.6 Write technical documents.
- a. Report information and convey ideas logically and correctly.
Writing Technical Documents (technical document), pp. 932–933
- b. Offer detailed and accurate specifications.
Writing Technical Documents (technical document), pp. 932–933
- c. Include scenarios, definitions, and examples to aid comprehension.
Writing Technical Documents (technical document), pp. 932–933
- d. Anticipate readers' problems, mistakes, and misunderstandings.
Writing Technical Documents (technical document), pp. 932–933

Instructional Planning and Support

Where do I find lesson plans, additional resources, and other teaching aids?

- This Annotated Teacher's Edition and *On Course: Mapping Instruction* provide direction in planning and implementing a complete California standards–based curriculum. These components also include instructions for diagnostic, progress, and summative testing; for presenting direct instruction of the standards; for differentiating instruction to provide universal access; and for locating and using the program's ancillaries.
- Lesson and workshop resources are referenced at the beginning of each selection or workshop, in the bottom margin of this teacher's edition.
- Reminders for using additional resources appear in this teacher's edition at point of use.
- The *One-Stop Planner* CD-ROM contains editable lesson plans and all print ancillaries, available in PDF format.

What if I don't have time to teach all of Chapter 11?

- Most standards can be taught with a minimum number of selections and features. In the chart on the preceding page, the core lessons you need in order to provide complete coverage of the chapter standards are identified with a ✔.
- *On Course: Mapping Instruction,* Chapter 11, lists lessons and activities that provide minimum standards coverage.

What provisions have been made for students who have additional class time scheduled in language arts?

- *Interactive Reading* provides for alternative direct instruction and practice of the grade-level standards taught in Chapter 11.
- *Universal Access: Writing, Listening, and Speaking,* Chapter 11, contains worksheets and transparencies that provide practice in and reteaching and reinforcement of the writing and listening and speaking standards in Chapter 11.
- *Universal Access: Lesson Plans for Language Development,* Chapter 11, provides alternative teaching strategies and additional worksheets designed specifically for English-language learners and special education students. Many of the suggestions and activities in this ancillary will also be helpful to students in the regular classroom who are having difficulty with particular skills.

Universal Access

How do I differentiate instruction to ensure that all my students master the standards?

Holt Literature and Language Arts provides comprehensive, differentiated instruction for all types of students.

- Most of the general instruction and teaching strategies in the Annotated Teacher's Edition are at grade level. These instructions will work well with the majority of your students.
- Point-of-use suggestions are provided for advanced learners, learners having difficulty, English-language learners, and special education students.
- *Interactive Reading* is designed to anticipate and remediate problems that students may experience in achieving mastery of the reading standards. See *Interactive Reading,* Teacher's Edition, Chapter 11, for information on using the reader to differentiate instruction.
- *Universal Access: Writing, Listening, and Speaking,* Chapter 11, contains worksheets and transparencies that provide practice in and reteaching and reinforcement of the writing and listening and speaking standards in Chapter 11.
- *Universal Access: Lesson Plans for Language Development,* Chapter 11, offers teaching strategies and additional worksheets designed specifically for English-language learners and special education students.

Assessment

How do I determine whether my students are making progress in mastering the standards?

Progress Assessment

- Use the Standards Review at the end of Chapter 11 for an informal assessment of the informational reading and writing standards.
- Use Chapter 11 tests from the *Progress Assessment* booklets to assess comprehension and progress on mastering the standards taught in this chapter.

Summative Assessment

The content of *Holt Literature and Language Arts* has been divided into quarters to allow you to administer the four summative tests required by California. Chapters 9–10 and related instructional material constitute the fourth quarter of instruction. At the end of Chapter 11, you may ask students to take the End-of-Year Test in *Diagnostic and Summative Assessments.*

Chapter 11

STANDARDS FOCUS

(For full text of standards taught in this chapter, see the Standards Correlation by Standard chart in the Student Edition.)

Grade-Level Standards

- Reading Comprehension 2.1, 2.2, 2.6, 2.7
- Writing Applications 2.5a–d, 2.6a–d

CHAPTER 11 RESOURCES: READING, WRITING

Planning

- *One-Stop Planner* CD-ROM with Test Generator
- *On Course: Mapping Instruction*
- *At Home: A Guide to Standards Mastery*
- *At Home: In Spanish*
- *Supporting Instruction in Spanish*

Differentiating Instruction

- *Lesson Plans for Language Development*

Assessment

- *Progress Assessment of Reading*
  - Chapter Test
- *Progress Assessment of Writing, Listening, & Speaking*
  - Chapter Test
- *Diagnostic and Summative Assessment*
  - End-of-Year Test
- *One-Stop Planner* CD-ROM with Test Generator

Chapter 11

CONSUMER AND WORKPLACE DOCUMENTS

Music on the E-frontier

by Flo Ota De Lange
and Sheri Henderson

INTRODUCING THE CHAPTER

Chapter 11 represents a departure from literature and drama and takes students into a world of documents that they will encounter in their everyday lives.

A glance at the Table of Contents reveals that the reading students will do in this chapter is challenging. Students should find it well worth their time and attention, however, because the documents represent the kind of careful reading they need to do to become informed when buying and using technical products. The documents include an informational article and product reviews that can help consumers make an informed purchasing decision. A troubleshooting guide and a service contract will also help users of electronic products meet their needs.

Students will also learn how to create a bibliography of Internet sources. In addition, they will focus on writing skills, learning how to write clear, concise technical directions and business letters.

Resources Reminder

Planning

- *At Home: A Guide to Standards Mastery*

Parent letters appear in this resource. Translations of these letters are found in *At Home: In Spanish.* Translations of selection summaries appear in *Supporting Instruction in Spanish.*

THE QUOTATION

Born in Kansas City, Kansas, in 1920, Charlie Parker was one of the giants of modern jazz. An alto-saxophonist, he was a pioneer in the art of jazz improvisation, creating new chord patterns and unexpected rhythms in his highly original saxophone solos. At first, listeners found this new, individualistic sound jarring, and Parker was widely criticized, even by fellow musicians. Eventually, however, he won many disciples and imitators in the jazz world, and his influence spread to popular music in general. Parker died in 1955, before reaching his thirty-fifth birthday.

Focus: Consumer and Workplace Documents

This chapter teaches students how to analyze, interpret, and evaluate a variety of consumer and workplace documents, as well as how to write their own technical documents and business letters. All of the informational materials are linked to the Internet music revolution. If you consult "Using Informational Materials" on p. 908 of the Student Edition, you will find more detailed descriptions of the documents students will read.

DIRECT TEACHING

A Content-Area Connections

Science: MP3 Technology

This technology compresses audio signals into a very small computer file, by removing parts of the signal that are redundant or irrelevant. MP3 files can be quickly downloaded from a Web site and then played back with no loss of the original sound quality. The research that created this new technology was begun in Germany in 1987 by the Fraunhofer Institute, which received a patent for the process in 1989. It wasn't until 1997, however, that the first practical MP3 player was developed.

Introduction

Music on the E-frontier

Music is your own experience, your own thoughts, your wisdom. If you don't live it, it won't come out of your horn.

—Charlie Parker

Joining the E-music Revolution

In this chapter you'll step into the e-music revolution as you imagine you're part of a garage band composing and recording its songs.

Not so many years ago portable music was a person shoeing the sidewalk, shouldering a boombox some four cinderblocks large and just about as heavy. Flash forward in time, and the portable music scene has been radically transformed. It's almost as if someone had taken that old boombox, sent it down a rabbit hole, and pulled it out the other side as an MP3 player.

A With the arrival of MP3 music files, almost any kind of music has become little more than a mouse click away. You need to be careful about what is legal on the music e-frontier, though. It is **legal** to rip tracks from a CD you own to a computer or to the Internet as long as they are for your own use and not for the use of other people. You may download free promotional tracks from the Internet; they are clearly marked, usually under the heading "Free Music." You may buy a track for your own use. It is ***not* legal** to download music that someone other than the copyright holder has put on the Internet.

Using Informational Materials

In this chapter you'll be relating **informational materials** to different aspects of the e-music revolution. You'll work with various kinds of documents—**workplace, consumer, public,** and **technical documents,** as well as **business letters.**

For example, you'll critique a magazine article on audio-speaker information, learn how to install a sound card, and review the consumer documents that come with a digital multitrack recorder. You'll also learn how to write conflict-resolution rules to settle conflicts that might arise in a garage band, and you'll learn how to write a business letter to promote that band.

In this section, you'll learn a great deal about reading consumer, public, workplace, and technical documents. You'll also become a more informed participant in the e-music revolution.

Some Types of Informational Materials

Consumer documents
- contracts
- instruction manuals
- product information
- warranties

Public documents
- government regulations
- schedules of events and services

Workplace documents
- business letters
- contracts
- instruction manuals
- memorandums

Technical documents
- how-to instructions
- installation instructions
- scientific procedures

Before You Read INFORMATIONAL MATERIALS

Evaluating the Logic of Functional Documents

Computer Sounds

Think about how excited people must have been to hear a computer make its first beep and chirp. Back then few people thought of combining computers and music. Why would anyone do that? What kind of song could be made out of chirps and beeps?

Since then computer sound engineers have gotten so good at deciphering the tricks of 3-D sound that they can convince us a meteorite is hurtling at us from behind and cause us to duck!

In its broadest sense, *e-music* refers to any sound a computer can produce. It includes not only the latest CDs but also the sound of that meteorite, streaming audio, sound bites, and so on. So how does one get the best out of the e-music revolution? A good place to start is with your sound equipment.

Criteria for Functional Documents

In this lesson you'll have a chance to critique a magazine article that reviews computer speakers and sound cards. Such a **product review** is one type of **functional document.** Other types include **instructions, contracts,** and **warranties.** All functional documents share a basic goal: to help get things done. To be successful, they must meet two criteria:

- They must be **clearly organized** and **easily understood.**
- They must present information, procedures, or both in a **logical sequence.**

Failure to meet either of these criteria can cause serious misunderstandings. When documents confuse rather than inform a reader, a product is likely to get sent back. No matter how good a product may be, what good is it to you if you can't figure out how to make it work?

Logical Sequence

Here are three types of **logical sequences** and the kinds of functional documents that use them:

- **step by step**—recipes and other instructions (such as the directions for installing a sound card on page 914)
- **point by point**—legal documents (such as the Collaboration Agreement on page 918) and articles (such as "First Things First" on page 910)
- **highest to lowest (or lowest to highest),** which may be based on price or quality—product reviews (such as those on page 911)

Evaluating a Functional Document

As you read the following document, ask yourself these questions:

- Is each section clear and easy to understand?
- Is the sequence of information logical?

Read carefully. Can you spot any errors in logical sequence?

In the first part of the article, the marginal notes suggest the kinds of questions you might ask yourself. After that you're on your own.

Pages 909–911 cover **Reading Standard 2.7** Critique the logic of functional documents by examining the sequence of information and procedures in anticipation of possible reader misunderstandings.

STANDARDS FOCUS, pp. 909–912

(For the grade-level standard taught with this lesson, see citations on Student Edition pages.)

Prerequisite Standard

- Grade 8, Reading Comprehension 2.7 **Evaluate the unity, coherence, logic, internal consistency, and structural patterns of text.**

Summary above grade level

This lesson offers an article of the type that might appear in a consumer electronics magazine. Its technical language may be familiar to some students but confusing to others. The first section of the article explains how to evaluate your computer before you decide to spend money on a new sound card and speakers. This section gives guidelines about matching the expansion slots, speed, and power of your computer to the different types of sound cards and speakers available. The second section of the aticle is a product review chart that evaluates a range of speakers and sound cards of varying power, quality, and price.

PRETEACHING

Selection Starter

Build background. Students' technical knowledge of, and practical experience with, the sound capabilities of computers are likely to vary widely. If your class includes students familiar with this technology, divide the class into small groups with at least one computer-savvy member per group. Have this member explain what he or she knows about sound cards and speakers, and ask the rest of the group to make a list of questions about information they would like to learn from the selection.

RESOURCES: READING

Planning

- *One-Stop Planner* CD-ROM with Test Generator
- *On Course: Mapping Instruction*

Differentiating Instruction

- *Lesson Plans for Language Development*
  - English-Language Learners, pp. 376, 388, 395
  - Special Education Students, pp. 377, 388, 395

Assessment

- *Progress Assessment of Reading*
  - Selection Test

DIRECT TEACHING

A Reading Informational Materials
GRADE-LEVEL STANDARD

Evaluating functional documents. In item 1, what prior knowledge of computers does the writer assume that readers have? [The writer assumes that readers know what an expansion slot is and how to locate it and that readers can identify a sound card.]

B Reading Informational Materials
GRADE-LEVEL STANDARD

Evaluating functional documents. What two types of information about your computer's expansion slots must you know before you can choose the right type of sound card? [You need to know whether the slot accepts cards with a PCI bus or an ISA bus. You also need to know whether the slot can run cards at 33 MHz or 66 MHz.] Where can you find out this information about your computer? [in the user manual]

C Reading Informational Materials
GRADE-LEVEL STANDARD

Evaluating functional documents. How could the writer have made this section of the article easier to understand? [Possible response: The writer could have defined the technical terms *sampling rates, signal-to-noise ratio, voice, wavetable synthesis, MIDI.*]

D Reading Informational Materials
GRADE-LEVEL STANDARD

Evaluating functional documents. Where in the article should this information be moved in order to be most helpful to readers? [Possible response: It should follow the first sentence of the article, before the information now in item 1.]

MAGAZINE ARTICLE

AUDIO ASSERTIONS the expert audio magazine

Multimedia Sound Card and Speakers: Buying Guide and Reviews

First Things First

Before you plunk down your hard-earned cash on a new sound card and speakers, know what you already own:

1. If your computer has expansion slots, check to see if one slot is free. If all your slots are in use, check to see if one of them is housing your current sound card. You can probably use that slot for a new card.

I'd better check my slots.

2. Your computer's user's manual will tell you its specific requirements, but here are some tips:
   A. Most of the newer sound cards use a PCI (peripheral component interface) bus, but some use an ISA (industry standard architecture) bus. Be sure that the card you choose fits the slot you have free. Also be sure that the new card can run at the speed required by your computer's free slot. PCI can run at clock speed of 33 or 66 MHz (megahertz). If the card you install will run at only 66 MHz and your computer requires 33MHz, your computer can be damaged. Most cards run at both speeds, but check it out to be sure.
   B. Power consumption is important. Your computer has a maximum that all slots combined may use—for example, 45 watts. You risk damaging your computer if you exceed this limit by plugging power-hungry cards into all of your slots.

Whew! PCI or ISA? 33 or 66 MHz? Watts? I'll need my user's manual.

3. Regarding sound-card quality, keep the following points in mind:
   - **sampling rates:** Higher rates produce better quality sound.
   - **signal-to-noise ratio:** Higher ratios (decibels, or dBs) produce clearer sound.
   - **voices:** More voices produce richer sound.
   - **wave-table synthesis:** This method produces sound that is far superior to the older FM synthesis.
   - **MIDI** (musical-instrument digital interface) **input/output jacks:** These are necessary if you want to write or perform music and record your work.

Signal-to-noise ratios, dBs, MIDI—I'd better look these technical terms up before I buy anything.

4. Does your computer have expansion slots? Some computers of the all-in-one variety come with fixed sound capabilities pre-installed. If you own such a model, your best option for improved sound is to upgrade your speakers.

Wait a minute. Th item is out of order. If I don't have any slots, I could have skipped items 1–3!

5. Finally, it's important to remember that your sound card and your speakers must work together. It will be useless to purchase top-of-the-line speakers if you do not have a sound card that can deliver the sound the speakers were built to accommodate, and the same goes the other way around. In general, the more you spend on speakers and sound cards, the more powerful your system will be. On the other hand, how much power do you *really* need?

Need? We I guess I *want* more than I reall *need.* I'll have to think hard about that one.

DIFFERENTIATING INSTRUCTION

Learners Having Difficulty

Modeling. Even students who are adept at reading most other kinds of texts may find this technical material difficult and frustrating to read. To increase their comfort level, read aloud p. 910, stopping when necessary to share your own questions and frustrations and thinking aloud about how you might cope with them if you really wanted to buy a sound card. For example, as you read item 2A, you might say, "What in the world are a PCI bus and an ISA bus, and how would I know which one my computer has? I guess I'd have to check my user's manual. For now, I'll just make a list of the things I need to check."

Then, on the chalkboard, write *Things to Check Before Buying a Sound Card: 1. PCI or ISA bus?* Ask students to help you complete the list as you read.

Buying Guide and Reviews

PRODUCT REVIEW

Multimedia Speakers	Price	Date*	Review
Scornucopia	$299	9/01	Best sub + satellite system to be heard, with an ultra-clean sound that's a bit cerebral and bass light. A thinking-person's choice.
Infinite-space	$180	10/00	Worthwhile midprice system with clean, if hygienic sound. A can't-go-wrong choice.
Aurllogic	$142	12/99	Great value with a tight, punchy sound. Knockout bass.
Airtight	$80	8/99	Nicely built and nice musical sound. Nice choice.

E

Sound Cards	Price	Date*	Review
SonicBombardier	$249.95	8/01	Excellent package, including almost everything you'll need to record your own music: SonicBoltblaster sound card (see below); full GS-compliant instrument set; great software bundle with award-winning MIDI sequencing software; cables.
SonicBoltblaster	$189.99	8/01	One of the best consumer-oriented cards on the market today, with MIDI input/output; headphone jack; 5.1-channel output; 1,024 wave-table voices, 64 of them hardware accelerated; > 96-dB signal-to-noise ratio; sample at 2, 4, and 8 megabytes; wave-table or FM synthesis; minimal software bundle.
SonicBonanza	$99.95	6/00	Surprisingly affordable for its features: card supporting 2, 4, or 6 speakers; wave-table synthesizer with capacity to support 64 hardware-accelerated voices and 1,240 software voices; > 96-dB signal-to-noise ratio; sample at 2, 4, and 8 megabytes. Good software bundle for MP3, MIDI, and WAV file conversion, playback, and rip to CD.
TD3S200	$24.95	2/98	Bargain-basement 3-D sound. Card supporting 2 speakers; samples up to 48 kHz; > 96-dB signal-to-noise ratio; 320 voices; wave-table or FM synthesis, software limited to drivers. Look for a used model at auction for an even better price.

F G

*The date indicates the month and year in which a full review of the product appeared in *Audio Assertions.*

Understanding the Document

You may not understand all of the **technical language** in this article, but you can probably follow the writer's main ideas. Using the information in the article and the product reviews, you can pick out speakers and a sound card that meet your needs and your wallet.

DIRECT TEACHING

E Reading Informational Materials
GRADE-LEVEL STANDARD

Evaluating functional documents. In what order does the writer list the speakers? [They are listed from most expensive to least expensive.] How does the quality of the speakers relate to their prices? [Possible response: The more expensive speakers seem to be of better quality: The most expensive one is "the best." The least expensive one is merely "nice."]

F Reading Informational Materials
GRADE-LEVEL STANDARD

Evaluating functional documents. How helpful would this review be to the average consumer? Explain. [Possible response: The claim "one of the best" is helpful, but the details used to support the claim are written in technical terms that the average consumer would not understand, terms that the writer has not defined or explained in the article.]

G Reading Informational Materials
GRADE-LEVEL STANDARD

Evaluating functional documents. Why does the writer list the TD3S200 sound card last? [It is the least expensive.] How do its features compare with those of the other sound cards? [Possible response: It comes with very little software, whereas the SonicBombardier pack includes "a great software bundle" and the SonicBonanza includes "a good software bundle." The TD3S200 includes only 320 voices, whereas the SonicBonanza includes 1,240 voices.]

Advanced Learners

Enrichment. Use the following activity to challenge computer-savvy students and to put their knowledge and experience to good use. **Activity.** Have these students read the manual for a computer in your classroom or computer lab. Ask them to find out whether the computer has expansion slots and, if so, what type of sound card it will accept. These students might also research such technical terms as *PCI bus* and *ISA bus.* Then they can use diagrams and colloquial language to orally explain to the class what the terms mean.

INDEPENDENT PRACTICE

Analyzing Informational Materials

Reading Check

1. in an available expansion slot
2. They should be of comparable quality and power.
3. It can damage the computer if its speed does not match that of the computer's expansion slot or if adding a new card takes more power than your computer can support.
4. Higher rates produce better quality sound.

Test Practice

Answers and Model Rationales

1. **A** Item 4 should be listed first because if your computer does not have expansion slots, then its sound capability is fixed and you cannot add a sound card.
2. **H** Item 2A does not tell how to find expansion slots.
3. **B** A and C are incorrect because the article includes many technical terms. The article is accessible to anyone familiar with these terms, so D is incorrect.
4. **H** The items are arranged in a "highest to lowest" sequence—the opposite of J. The reviews do not list a series of steps or give point-by-point comparisons (F and G).
5. **D** The signal-to-noise ratio is a feature of the sound card, not the consumer's computer.
6. **F** The most expensive items are best in quality—the opposite of H. G is wrong because you can't determine quality by sight, and J is not mentioned.

Test-Taking Tips

For more instruction on how to answer multiple-choice questions, refer students to **Test Smarts.**

Analyzing Informational Materials

Reading Check

1. According to "First Things First," where in your computer do you put a new sound card?
2. What does the article say about matching sound cards to speakers?
3. Under what conditions can a sound card damage your computer?
4. Why should a sound card have high sampling-rate capability?

Test Practice

1. To correct the error in **logical sequence** in the article "First Things First," where should step 4 be moved?
   - **A** Directly before step 1
   - **B** Between steps 1 and 2
   - **C** Between steps 2 and 3
   - **D** After step 5

2. "First Things First" item 2A covers all of the following topics *except* —
   - **F** PCI and ISA buses
   - **G** 33 and 66 MHz
   - **H** finding your slot
   - **J** matching sound-card and slot capabilities

3. The product reviews in "Buying Guide and Reviews" are written in language that is —
   - **A** informal yet informative
   - **B** vague and imprecise
   - **C** too simplistic
   - **D** understandable only by an expert sound engineer

4. In "Buying Guide and Reviews," the speakers are arranged in which **logical sequence**?
   - **F** Step by step
   - **G** Point by point
   - **H** Highest to lowest
   - **J** Lowest to highest

5. Before buying one of the sound cards that are reviewed, readers will need to investigate all of the following aspects of their computer *except* its —
   - **A** MHz
   - **B** expansion slots
   - **C** wattage
   - **D** signal-to-noise ratio

6. The general relationship of price to quality shown in the "Buying Guide and Reviews" can *best* be expressed by which of the following statements?
   - **F** You get what you pay for.
   - **G** What you see is what you get.
   - **H** Cheaper products are better.
   - **J** Products are cheaper by the dozen.

Reading Standard 2.7
Critique the logic of functional documents by examining the sequence of information and procedures in anticipation of possible reader misunderstandings.

Application

Is it a **logical sequence** to place "First Things First" before "Buying Guide and Reviews"? Explain why or why not. What possible **reader misunderstandings** are created or avoided by the order of these two sections?

ASSESSING

Assessment

- *Progress Assessment of Reading*
  - Selection Test

RETEACHING

For a lesson reteaching Standard 2.7, see **Reteaching,** p. 939A. For another selection to teach Standard 2.7, see *Interactive Reading,* Part 2.

Before You Read INFORMATIONAL MATERIALS

Following Technical Directions

How to Install a Sound Card

Early personal computers only beeped and chirped because they had no sound cards. Now, however, advances in computer-sound capabilities are so rapid that there is a practical value in knowing how to install a sound-card upgrade. Let's take a look at the directions for doing that.

Reading Technical Directions

The directions for using electronic, mechanical, and scientific products and procedures are called **technical directions.** You follow technical directions whenever you

- program your friends' numbers in your cell phone
- install a TV satellite dish on your roof
- do an experiment in biology lab

When you first look at them, technical directions may seem hard to understand. How will you ever be able to sort through all that information? All you have to do is **pay attention** and **follow each step carefully in the sequence presented.** Technical directions will teach you how to do whatever you want to do—for instance, install that sound-card upgrade. When you're finished, you can sit back, relax, and listen to awesome new sounds.

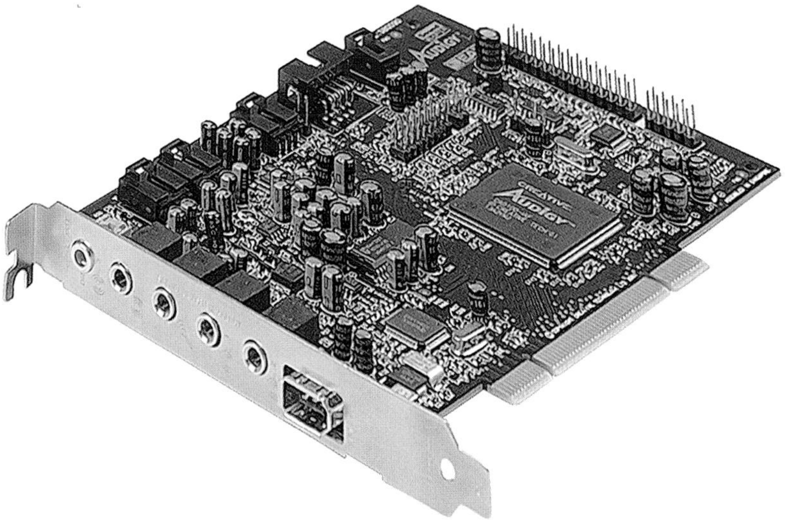

Reading Standard 2.6 Demonstrate use of sophisticated learning tools by following technical directions (e.g., those found with graphic calculators and specialized software programs and in access guides to World Wide Web sites on the Internet).

STANDARDS FOCUS, pp. 913–915

(For the grade-level standard taught with this lesson, see citations on Student Edition pages.)

Prerequisite Standard

- Grade 8, Reading Comprehension 2.5 **Understand and explain the use of a complex mechanical device by following technical directions.**

Summary *at grade level*

This lesson gives students practice in following the type of technical directions one might find in a computer manual or in a manual accompanying electronic equipment. In twelve detailed steps, the directions lead students through the process of installing a computer sound card. Readers are told not only what to do but also when, how, and why to perform each step.

PRETEACHING

Standards Starter

Build background. Ask students to recall a time when they had to follow instructions in order to do something new on a computer. Were the directions easy to follow? Were students able to follow the directions and accomplish the task? What tips would they give to other computer users about following directions? Have students discuss these questions in small groups and then share their tips with the class.

RESOURCES: READING

Planning

- *One-Stop Planner* CD-ROM with Test Generator
- *On Course: Mapping Instruction*

Differentiating Instruction

- *Lesson Plans for Language Development*
  - English-Language Learners, pp. 378, 389, 395
  - Special Education Students, pp. 379, 389, 395

Assessment

- *Progress Assessment of Reading*
  - Selection Test

DIRECT TEACHING

A Reading Informational Materials
GRADE-LEVEL STANDARD

? Following technical directions. Why do you think you must perform step 2 before step 3? [Possible response: If you don't discharge the static electricity in your body before opening the computer, the static might be discharged into the internal workings of your computer and damage its parts.]

B Reading Informational Materials
GRADE-LEVEL STANDARD

? Following technical directions. Do readers need to perform the tasks in *both* 5a and 5b? Explain. [No, they need to perform only 5a *or* 5b. If the slot is empty, they follow 5a. If there is already a card in the slot, they follow 5b.]

C Reading Informational Materials
GRADE-LEVEL STANDARD

? Following technical directions. In your own words, summarize what you need to do in step 9. [Possible response: You need to plug one end of the audio cable into the sound card and the other end of the cable into the CD-ROM or DVD-ROM drive.]

D Reading Informational Materials
GRADE-LEVEL STANDARD

? Following technical directions. What should you be able to do after you have completed step 12? [You should be able to put a CD or DVD in the drive and play music or watch a movie, which you will hear through the computer speakers.]

INSTRUCTION MANUAL

Installing a Computer Sound Card*

1. Be sure the computer is switched off.

A

2. To avoid damaging your computer, touch something metal on the outside of your computer with your fingers to discharge static electricity. Then, unplug your computer.
3. Open the computer case.
4. Locate the slot you want on the motherboard. See the user's manual for specific instructions on the location and types of slots on the computer.

B

5a. If the slot is empty, remove the screw that holds the metal slot cover in place, slide the cover out, and set both the screw and the cover aside for later.

5b. If the slot currently contains the old sound card, remove the screw that holds the card in place, and gently pull the card from the slot. It may need a firm yet careful tug. CAUTION: If rocked against the sides of the slot, the card might snap off in the slot or pry the slot from the motherboard. You will see an audio cable attached at one end to the sound card and at the other end to the CD- or DVD-ROM drive. Disconnect this cable from the drive by pulling gently.

6. Plug the new sound card into the prepared slot by pressing down firmly until the connector is fully inserted. It should be a tight fit, but do not use undue force. If you encounter resistance, take the card out, check for alignment and possible obstructions, and try again.
7. To be sure the card is in place, give it a gentle tug. It should resist and stay in place. The connector strip's metal conductors should also be just barely visible when viewed at eye level.
8. Find the screw and the slot cover that were removed in step 5a. Both may need to be replaced. If the card is built with an integrated slot cover, only the screw that will hold the new card in place will need to be replaced. Be sure the slot is covered. Then, tighten the screw to hold the new sound card in place.

C

9. Connect the audio cable to the sound card and to the CD- or DVD-ROM drive. Find connector pins on the sound card and on the back of the disk drive that correspond to the plugs on each end of the audio cable. Be sure to line these pins up carefully and press gently. As in step 6, if you encounter resistance, check to see that all pins are straight and that there are no other obstructions. Then, try again.
10. Close the computer case.
11. Connect the external speakers to their appropriate jacks.

D

12. Plug in the power cord, and turn on the computer and monitor. Once the computer is up and running, insert the CD that accompanies the sound card, and complete the software driver installation by following the on-screen instructions.

* Instructions for PC users.

DIFFERENTIATING INSTRUCTION

Learners Having Difficulty
Students with little technical knowledge or experience may need help interpreting the following terms in the directions: *powered down, static electricity, motherboard, audio cable, CD-ROM drive, DVD-ROM drive, connector strip, metal conductors, integrated slot cover, connector pins, external speakers, jacks, software driver.* Pair these students with computer-savvy partners who can explain these terms to them.

Advanced Learners
Enrichment. Students adept at following technical directions might enjoy demonstrating or actually teaching other students how to install new software or perform a new function on their computers.

914 Chapter 11 Consumer and Workplace Documents

Analyzing Informational Materials

Reading Check

1. Why should you touch something metal before opening the computer case?
2. Describe the dangers involved in removing a sound card, according to step 5b. What precautions must be taken with the card, and what could go wrong?
3. How will you know when the sound card is properly in place?
4. How does the sound card connect to the CD- or DVD-ROM drive?
5. What information will you need to look up in the user's manual? At what point in the project should you get this information?

Test Practice

1. Which of the following steps should be broken into several steps for improved clarity?
   - **A** Step 3
   - **B** Step 4
   - **C** Step 5a
   - **D** Step 5b

2. How can you find out where to install the new sound card?
   - **F** Look in the user's manual that came with your computer.
   - **G** Find the location of the old sound card, if there is one.
   - **H** Follow the audio cable from the CD- or DVD-ROM.
   - **J** Do all of the above.

3. Users whose computers already have an old sound card installed will complete which step *first*?
   - **A** Turn the computer on.
   - **B** Remove the old card.
   - **C** Install the new card.
   - **D** Install the new software driver.

4. Where will you find the instructions for installing the software driver for the sound card?
   - **F** Elsewhere in the instruction manual
   - **G** In step 12
   - **H** In step 9
   - **J** On the CD that accompanies the sound card

Reading Standard 2.6 Demonstrate use of sophisticated learning tools by following technical directions (e.g., those found with graphic calculators and specialized software programs and in access guides to World Wide Web sites on the Internet).

Application

Challenge yourself by learning how to do something that requires following **technical directions.** Browse through the user's manual of a computer or software program until you find a skill you'd like to master. Before you start, carefully read *all* the directions to get the big picture. Then, follow each instruction step by step. When you finish, try it out—to check that you've accomplished what you set out to do.

Reading Check

1. to discharge the static electricity from your body to avoid damaging the computer
2. When removing an old sound card, one must be careful not to damage the old sound card, the motherboard, or the new sound card.
3. You can give the card a gentle tug, and it will stay in place. Also, the connector strip's metal conductors will be just barely visible when viewed at eye level.
4. The sound card comes with an audio cable.
5. Before beginning the installation process, find out which slot on the motherboard is used for the sound card.

INDEPENDENT PRACTICE

Analyzing Informational Materials

Test Practice

Answers and Model Rationales

1. **D** Step 5b is very long and discusses two separate tasks: removing the old sound card and disconnecting the audio cable. Steps 3, 4, and 5a (A, B, C) are short and each involves a single task.
2. **J** Options F, G, and H describe three different ways to find the slot for the sound card. Option F is referred to in step 4, G is implied in step 5b, and H is implied in step 9.
3. **B** You must remove the old card (step 5b) before you can install the new one (step 6). Turning on the computer is done in step 12, as is installing the software driver.
4. **J** There is no reference to instructions elsewhere in the manual. Neither step 9 nor step 12 provides instructions, but step 12 refers to instructions on the CD.

Test-Taking Tips

For more information on how to answer multiple-choice questions, refer students to **Test Smarts.**

ASSESSING

Assessment

- *Progress Assessment of Reading*
  - Selection Test

RETEACHING

For another selection to teach Standard 2.6, see *Interactive Reading,* Part 2.

STANDARDS FOCUS, pp. 916–920

(For the grade-level standard taught with this lesson, see citations on Student Edition pages.)

Prerequisite Standard

- Grade 7, Reading Comprehension 2.1 **Understand and analyze the differences in structure and purpose between various categories of informational materials (e.g., textbooks, newspapers, instructional manuals, signs).**

Summary *at grade level*

In this lesson, students analyze the structure, format, and purposes of two workplace documents relating to the music industry. The first is a lead sheet for musicians, which concisely provides vital information about a song. The second is a simple legal document, a collaboration agreement between two songwriters.

PRETEACHING

Selection Starter

Build background. Invite students to share their prior knowledge of music-related documents. You may prompt them with such questions as: "What do band members look at when they play a song?" [a musical score or lead sheet] "What do recording artists sign with producers?" [a contract]

DIRECT TEACHING

A Reading Informational Materials
GRADE-LEVEL STANDARD

Analyzing workplace documents. Explain that a lead sheet does not look like an average workplace document, but it functions in a similar way—to help people get something done. Can you identify who a lead sheet helps and what it helps them do? [It helps musicians learn a piece of music and play it together.]

Before You Read INFORMATIONAL MATERIALS

Analyzing Functional Workplace Documents

A Workplace Document for Musicians

A time of great change is usually also a time of great opportunity. For example, the unparalleled growth of the Internet has contributed to the e-music revolution, and the e-music revolution combined with the advent of the World Wide Web has given songwriters and musicians new ways of reaching their audience. What does all this mean to you?

Let's say you've written a song. Since the process by which a songwriter develops the germ of an idea into a full-blown song varies with the individual, we'll pick up on the life of your song at the point when your band is playing it for the very first time. You enter the rehearsal studio. Your fellow musicians are tuning up their instruments. What happens then?

A You pull out a functional workplace document. A what? A **functional workplace** document can be defined as any document that helps people get things done effectively. One of the workplace documents that help a songwriter and a band get things done is a **music lead sheet.** Let's take a look at one.

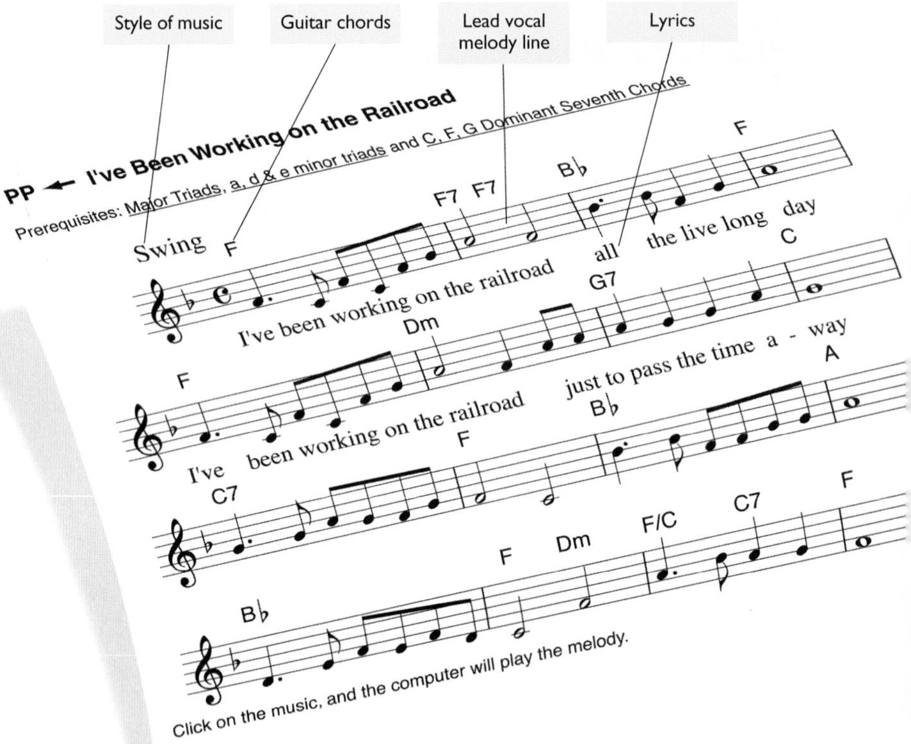

Reading Standard 2.1 Analyze the structure and format of functional workplace documents, including the graphics and headers and explain how authors use the features to achieve their purposes.

916

RESOURCES: READING

Planning

- *One-Stop Planner* CD-ROM with Test Generator
- *On Course: Mapping Instruction*

Differentiating Instruction

- *Lesson Plans for Language Development*
  - English-Language Learners, pp. 380, 390, 396
  - Special Education Students, pp. 381, 390, 396

Assessment

- *Progress Assessment of Reading*
  - Selection Test

Analyzing a Lead Sheet

As you can see, a lead sheet includes several types of information about a musical piece:

- style of music **B**
- guitar chords
- lead vocal melody line
- lyrics **C**

The lead sheet provides this information clearly and concisely. It enables band members to learn a song quickly and efficiently, thus cutting down on rehearsal time and on recording time and costs.

Emphasizing Important Points

Most workplace documents rely on elements such as **font style, headers,** and **graphics** to emphasize important points and present information clearly. Lead sheets, in contrast, rely on the traditions of music notation. Music is formatted on a five-line staff begun with a clef. Even people who are not musicians often know what treble and bass clefs look like because those symbols have come to stand for music, as in the cartoon below.

Analyzing a Collaboration Agreement

Another type of workplace document in the field of music is one that specifies who owns a work and how royalties will be divided. **D** Say you and your fellow band members have written a song that you want to publish yourselves. You have created something of potential value. How will you divide up the royalties that you are sure will come rolling in? You can prepare for this eventuality by signing a **collaboration agreement,** a kind of **contract.**

Let's look at how two musicians handled this problem. Sara Songster wrote the lyrics and Mike Melodic wrote the music to "All Day," a song they published themselves. They agreed to split any royalties fifty-fifty, and they signed the collaboration agreement that appears on the next page.

DIRECT TEACHING

B Reading Informational Materials
GRADE-LEVEL STANDARD

? Analyzing workplace documents. Why is the style designation *Swing* important to users of this document? [Possible response: It lets musicians know how the music should be played.] How does this designation help the composer achieve his or her purpose? [Possible response: It conveys the style the composer has in mind so that musicians can interpret the song correctly.]

C Reading Informational Materials
GRADE-LEVEL STANDARD

? Analyzing workplace documents. Lyrics of a song are like lines of a poem. They often exhibit rhyme and rhythm and help to establish the mood of the piece. Can you identify an example of rhyme in these lyrics? [day/away] What overall mood do the lyrics convey? [Possible response: a feeling of weariness, melancholy, and perhaps despair]

D Reading Informational Materials
GRADE-LEVEL STANDARD

? Analyzing workplace documents. Have students list all the types of information provided on the lead sheet. [Style, guitar chords, lead vocal line, lyrics, key, time signature, tones, and rhythms] What does all this information allow band members to do? [Possible response: Play the song easily and accurately.]

DIFFERENTIATING INSTRUCTION

Learners Having Difficulty
To help students understand these documents, you may wish to preview some musical and legal terms. Call on a student musician to draw on the board a simple five-line musical staff, along with the clef, the key, the time signature, and the notes of a simple melody. Ask the student to explain each element and to sing or play the melody while pointing to each note. Also point out that a legal document may contain archaic words, such as *whereas* and *thereof.* Assure students that they will be able to guess the meanings from the context.

English-Language Learners
For lessons designed for intermediate and advanced English-language learners, see *Lesson Plans for Language Development,* pp. 380, 390, 396.

Analyzing Functional Workplace Documents 917

DIRECT TEACHING

A Reading Informational Materials
GRADE-LEVEL STANDARD

? Analyzing workplace documents. What purpose does the title of this document serve? [Possible response: It immediately conveys the general purpose or content of the document.]

B Reading Informational Materials
GRADE-LEVEL STANDARD

? Analyzing workplace documents. What important data does the first paragraph contain? [the date, names of the people involved, name of the song, and proportion of authorship]

C Reading Informational Materials
GRADE-LEVEL STANDARD

? Analyzing workplace documents. What formatting has been used to make the different parts of the agreement easy to separate and understand? [numerical headings, paragraph breaks, and spaces between paragraphs]

A COLLABORATION AGREEMENT

CONTRACT

Self-published Musical Composition

Date: 2/8/02

B In a Collaboration Agreement dated February 8, 2002, Sara Songster and Mike Melodic have agreed that they are equal co-authors of both the words and the music of the song titled "All Day," hereinafter called the Composition.

C
I. The worldwide copyrights for the Composition, and any and all extensions and renewals thereof, are owned as follows:

Sara Songster: undivided 50 percent
Mike Melodic: undivided 50 percent

II. Sara Songster and Mike Melodic are entitled to administer their respective copyright shares in the Composition.

III. The Composition is to be registered with the U.S. Copyright Office, ASCAP, BMI, and/or SESAC, and other U.S. and foreign music agencies, in accordance with the provisions of this Agreement.

IV. The Authors' share of all royalties and other earnings derived from the Composition are to be apportioned and paid as follows:

Sara Songster: undivided 50 percent
Mike Melodic: undivided 50 percent

V. The Publishers' share of all royalties and other earnings derived from the Composition are to be apportioned and paid as follows:

Sara Songster: undivided 50 percent
Mike Melodic: undivided 50 percent

Signed:

Sara Songster *Sara Songster* Date 2-8-02

Mike Melodic *Mike Melodic* Date 2/8/02

Analyzing the Document

This collaboration agreement is based on a straight-down-the-middle, fifty-fifty split. There are, of course, other ways to split proceeds from a self-published song. For example, if Sara Songster had written not only the lyrics but also parts of the melody, her share might be 60 percent and Mike Melodic's, 40 percent. Royalty income can be split in a variety of ways, depending on the number of people involved and each

DIFFERENTIATING INSTRUCTION

Special Education Students
For lessons designed for special education students, see *Lesson Plans for Language Development,* pp. 381, 390, 396.

Advanced Learners
Enrichment. Use the following activity to reinforce students' understanding of the format and function of a musical lead sheet.

Activity. Ask students to choose a favorite song for this activity. Have students analyze the song closely, noting such features of the song as the style of music and the lyrics. Then, challenge students to create a lead sheet for the song, using the sample lead sheet on p. 916 as a model. If necessary, encourage students to use Internet and library resources to identify the song's guitar chords and lead vocal melody line. Invite volunteers to share their lead sheets with the class and play the songs on which they are based.

person's contribution. A collaboration agreement is important because it is a **legally binding document** (assuming the parties are old enough to enter a binding contract). It eliminates surprises by settling the matter of shares before there is any royalty income to pay out.

The collaboration agreement on page 918 makes effective use of **structure** and **format** to achieve its purpose. Some of its features are

- a centered **title,** or **header,** clearly stating the purpose of the document
- a **new section** for each major point
- **numerical headers** for each major section
- **spacing** between each major section
- **indentation**

The information in the collaboration agreement also follows a **logical sequence:**

1. It first lists copyright shares (I).
2. In the next two steps (II, III), it defines issues related to copyright.
3. It defines royalty shares of each signer as author (IV) and publisher (V).

Analyzing the Elements of Workplace Documents

Let's take a closer look at common elements of many effective workplace documents.

Structure

Written text is often daunting to the human eye when black type stretches on with nary a white space in sight. By the time a reader gets to the end, the beginning might be long forgotten. To remedy this problem, writers break text into sections. The **sections** in a functional document might be a short paragraph or maybe only a sentence.

In a legal document like the one on page 918, each **main idea** is given its own **section,** separated by a line of **space.** This format makes it simple to locate a particular point among many. Separating points in this way also increases the likelihood that the entire text will be both read and understood.

Sections are often introduced by **headers,** such as **titles** and **subtitles.** In this document the section headers are **roman numerals.** The numbers help readers locate information easily. A person who wants to talk about a particular point can simply cite the number of the section and begin the discussion.

Sequence

The **sequence,** or order, in which ideas are presented makes a big difference to a reader's understanding. Sequence governs the flow of a document and facilitates comprehension. Some common types of sequencing are

- chronological
- alphabetical
- spatial
- logical

Most functional documents follow a **logical sequence,** such as the **point-by-point** (numbered) sequence used in the collaboration agreement (page 918) or the **step-by-step sequence** used in technical directions, as in "Installing a Computer Sound Card" (page 914).

Format

The **format,** or design, of a document highlights important information and focuses the reader's attention on key words, sections, and ideas. To format a document, a designer draws on

- **formatting elements**—bold or italic type, margin width, indentation, line spacing
- **graphic elements**—drawings, photographs, and other artwork
- **design elements**—placement of the text and graphics on the page, use of white space, choice of color

DIRECT TEACHING

D Content-Area Connections

Culture: Contracts and the Law
Some students may think that Sara and Mike did not need to bother with a written document; they could have simply made a verbal agreement to split their royalties 50-50. You may wish to tell students that often the point of legal documents is to put on paper what people have agreed to in order to prevent confusion or conflict in the future. This is especially important in the United States, which has become a very litigious society. People who make verbal agreements often run into trouble when, months or years later, one of the parties "remembers" the agreement differently and demands something that wasn't originally agreed to. Once Mike and Sara sign this agreement, the chance that they will get into a future conflict and be involved in a lawsuit is greatly reduced.

E Learners Having Difficulty

Finding details. You may wish to have learners who are having difficulty form into small groups, and have them identify in the Collaboration Agreement on p. 918 each of the elements outlined here and in the next column.

F English-Language Learners

Dialect. Explain to students that *nary* is a regional term used by some speakers of English to mean "no" or "not one." The word *nary* derives from *ne'er a,* which, in turn means "never a." Point out that the text could be worded "with never a white space in sight" or "with no white space in sight." If necessary, advise students that white space means any place on the page that has no type or graphic element.

CONTENT-AREA CONNECTIONS

Science: Recording Technology
Until sound recording technology came into widespread use in approximately 1940, the only way a composer could convey how a song should sound was through such musical documents as a score or a lead sheet. Now composers and singer-songwriters make recordings of their compositions. Other musicians can listen to these recordings and understand the composer's intentions for the way a piece should be played.

Paired activity. Encourage pairs of students to find a variety of recordings of a particular song. They should compare and contrast the composer's original recording with those of other artists who recorded, or "covered," the original. Have students write a comparison-contrast essay and read it to the class. Students may illustrate their points by playing excerpts of each recording.

Analyzing Functional Workplace Documents 919

INDEPENDENT PRACTICE

Analyzing Informational Materials

Reading Check

1. It helps musicians learn a new song quickly and efficiently.
2. short numbered sections with spacing between sections and indentation to set off important information
3. a logical sequence
4. They have divided their royalties equally (50%-50%).

Test Practice

Answers and Model Rationales

1. **C** Options A and B are clearly wrong. Answer D may at times be true, but that would be an incidental side effect, not the main purpose of the document.
2. **G** Options F, H, and J are ways that ordinary documents may be formatted, but the lead sheet is formatted on a musical staff.
3. **A** The collaboration agreement has roman numerals (A) that indicate main points.
4. **H** A scan of the agreement shows that it uses indentations (F), sections (G), and spaces (J) but no graphics (H).
5. **A** The agreement is not ordered according to the alphabet or by spatial arrangement, so C and D are wrong. There is not a clear step-by-step sequence such as one finds in instructions (B). The best answer is point-by-point (A).

Test-Taking Tips

For more instruction on how to answer multiple-choice items, refer students to **Test Smarts.**

Analyzing Informational Materials

Reading Check

1. What does the music lead sheet help musicians do?
2. What are some of the most common **structural elements** of functional workplace documents?
3. What type of **sequence** does the collaboration agreement use?
4. How have Sara Songster and Mike Melodic divided their royalties?

Test Practice

1. The purpose of a **functional workplace document** is to —
   - **A** increase paperwork
   - **B** have something to download
   - **C** help people get things done
   - **D** reduce work
2. A music lead sheet is formatted —
   - **F** in paragraphs
   - **G** on a five-line staff
   - **H** with colored headers
   - **J** by indentations
3. The **main points** in the collaboration agreement are indicated by —
   - **A** roman numerals
   - **B** italic type and a line of space
   - **C** boldface key words
   - **D** titles that summarize each main idea
4. The collaboration agreement uses all of the following **elements** *except* —
   - **F** indentations
   - **G** sections
   - **H** graphics
   - **J** spaces
5. The collaboration agreement follows which type of **sequence**?
   - **A** Point by point
   - **B** Step by step
   - **C** Alphabetical
   - **D** Spatial

Reading Standard 2.1 Analyze the structure and format of functional workplace documents, including the graphics and headers and explain how authors use the features to achieve their purposes.

Application

A Web site can be considered a functional document. Log on to the Internet, and go to the home page of a Web site you visit regularly. Analyze the structure and format of that page. Then, see if you can identify a sequence used to present information to the viewer. How effectively has the page designer used graphic, design, and formatting elements? How could the page be improved? If you don't have access to the Internet, use the Web site shown on page 207.

ASSESSING

Assessment

- *Progress Assessment of Reading*
  - Selection Test

RETEACHING

For a lesson reteaching Standard 2.1, see **Reteaching,** p. 939A. For another selection to teach Standard 2.1, see *Interactive Reading,* Part 2.

920 Chapter 11 Consumer and Workplace Documents

Before You Read INFORMATIONAL MATERIALS

Citing Internet Sources

Following Your Research Trail

The Internet is what made the e-music revolution possible, and any information on the e-music world you might want to research is only a mouse click away—whether it is how to use your computer as a composing device or how to understand 3-D sound.

When you prepare a report on e-music (or any other topic) using information you find on the Internet, you must include an orderly list of the sources you used. This list, which appears at the end of the report, is called a *Works Cited* list. Its purpose is to allow your readers to follow your research trail.

Documenting Internet Sources

When you cite a printed book, you can usually assume your reader will be able to find the book in a library. But online information is frequently updated, daily in some cases. Therefore, Internet sources require more documentation than print sources do.

You cannot, of course, be expected to document changes made in a Web site between the time you make your notation and the time your reader goes to the site to find the work. You should, though, give your reader as much information as you have. In particular, it is crucial to reproduce exactly the **URL** (uniform resource locator), or Internet address.

How do you cite sources you find on the Internet? Do you do it as if you were citing a book, or do you do something else? In the sections that follow, you'll learn how to cite works from the World Wide Web.

The box below shows the general format for an online source. The chart on page 922 lists in greater detail the **order** in which items should appear in your citations. It is a long list, and your *Works Cited* list will not likely include every item on the list.

The conventional punctuation marks that you should use appear in boldface within brackets. For example, a period will be noted as "[**.**]." Where no punctuation appears in brackets (as in item 14), simply insert a space and go on.

GENERAL FORMAT FOR AN ONLINE SOURCE

Author's Last Name**,** Author's First Name (if known)**.** **"**Title of Work**."** Title of Web Site or Database**.** Date of electronic publication**.** Name of Sponsoring Institution**.** Date information was accessed <URL>**.**

Note: Enclose an electronic address, or URL, in angled brackets. If the URL must continue on a new line, divide the address immediately after one of the slash marks within it. Do not use a hyphen or any other mark of punctuation to divide the address.

Pages 921–926 cover **Reading Standard 2.2** Prepare a bibliography of reference materials for a report using a variety of consumer, workplace, and public documents.

STANDARDS FOCUS, pp. 921–926

(For the grade-level standard taught with this lesson, see citations on Student Edition pages.)

Summary *at grade level*

This lesson leads students through the process of preparing a bibliography of Internet sources. Topics include: the order in which to list information in a bibliographic citation; choosing a bibliographic style; examples of bibliographic citations; using note cards to record information about sources; and formatting the bibliography. Students learn that a bibliography is important because it lets readers know the writer's sources and allows readers to refer to those sources. Students also learn to be specific when citing Internet sources because the information on Web pages changes frequently.

PRETEACHING

Selection Starter

Build background. Most students have had experience preparing bibliographies of print materials. Explain that Internet citations are similar but often more complex. They include such items as posting dates; names of Web sites, subscription services, and discussion forums; and many other detailed pieces of information.

RESOURCES: READING

Planning

- *One-Stop Planner* CD-ROM with Test Generator
- *On Course: Mapping Instruction*

Differentiating Instruction

- *Lesson Plans for Language Development*
  - English-Language Learners, pp. 382, 391, 396
  - Special Education Students, pp. 383, 391, 396

Assessment

- *Progress Assessment of Reading*
  - Selection Test

DIRECT TEACHING

A Reading Informational Materials

GRADE-LEVEL STANDARD

Citing works in Internet sources. You may wish to form small groups of students of mixed abilities to read and review the material on this chart. Suggest that they work together to identify an example of the information in each numbered entry from the bibliographic citations on p. 923. To make this easier, you may wish to give a copy of p. 923 to each student so they can mark it up. They might, for example, circle the title of a work and then write “Title” in the margin beside it.

Order in Which Information Is Presented in an Internet Citation

1. Author’s Last Name [,] Author’s First Name and Middle Initial (if given) [,] abbreviation such as Ed. (if appropriate) [.]
2. [“] Title of Work Found in Online Scholarly Project, on Database, or in Periodical [”] *or* [“] Title of Posting to Discussion List or Forum (taken from the subject line) [.] [”] followed by the description Online posting [.]
3. Title of Book (underlined) [.]
4. The abbreviation Ed. followed by Name of Editor (if relevant and not cited earlier, as in Ed. Susan Smith) [.]
5. Publication information for any print version of the source: City of Publication [:] Name of Publisher [,] year of publication [.]
6. Title of Scholarly Project, Database, Magazine, Professional Site, or Personal Site (underlined) [.]
7. Name of Editor of Scholarly Project or Database (if available) [.]
8. Volume number, issue number, or other identifying number of the source (if available) [.]
9. Date of electronic publication, posting, or latest update (often found at the bottom of the site’s home page) [.]
10. Name of Subscription Service [,] and, if a library, Name of Library [,] Name of City [,] and Abbreviation of State in which library is located [.]
11. For a posting to a discussion list or forum, Name of List or Forum [.]
12. If sections are numbered, number range or total number of pages, paragraphs, or other sections (if information is available) [.]
13. Name of Institution or Organization Sponsoring or Associated with the Web Site [.]
14. Date on which source was accessed
15. [<] Electronic address (URL) of source [>] *or,* if a subscription service, [<] URL of service’s main page (if known) [>] and [[] Keyword: Keyword Assigned by Service []] *or* [[] Path: sequence of topics followed to reach the page cited, as in first topic [;] second topic [;] third topic [;] and so on, ending with the page you are citing []] [.]

Sample Citations

Let’s look now at some citations for **consumer, public, and workplace sites**—sources you might find when surfing the Internet for information about e-music. (Some of these are made-up sources.)

All of the sample citations in this chapter follow the style of the Modern Language Association (MLA). You can look at the MLA’s stylebook in the library for more information on how to prepare citations. Other styles for documenting sources are also available and acceptable. The style you use is less important than choosing one and sticking to it. Be sure to ask your teacher whether he or she wants you to follow a particular style.

DIFFERENTIATING INSTRUCTION

Learners Having Difficulty
Explain to students that the best way for them to learn how to create a bibliography is through practice. You might distribute several printouts of different Web pages to small groups of students, and work with them to identify the information that should be included in a bibliographic citation, using the list on p. 922. Assure students that they need not memorize this list; they are free to use such reference sources as they compile their bibliographies. Point out that not all information on the list will be available from a Web site and that some information will be difficult to find, but that they should always try to provide as much information as possible.

English-Language Learners
Students who are learning English may find the bibliography-related vocabulary and abbreviations challenging. You may wish to pair these students with more fluent English

922 Chapter 11 Consumer and Workplace Documents

Sample Works Cited Citations for Consumer, Public, and Workplace Documents

Product Information from a Commercial Site

"About the Latest Sound Cards." Sound Cards Update Page. 10 Aug. 2001. New Sounds 4 Sept. 2001 <http://www.NewSoundstoday.com/article/index.asp>.

Article from an Online Nonprofit Magazine Dedicated to Protecting Consumers

Sleuthing, I. B. "Sound Cards and Speakers: Buying Guide and Reviews." Audio Assertions 8 Aug. 2001. 7 Sept. 2001 <http://www.audioassertions.org/main/article/soundcard/1.html>. **B**

Article from a Reference Database (Encyclopedia)

"Musical Notation." Electric Library Presents: Encyclopedia.Com. The Columbia Electronic Encyclopedia, Sixth Ed. 2000. Columbia UP. 15 July 2001 <http://www.encyclopedia.com/articles/08892.html>.

Online Information from a University Library Site

The Hoagy Carmichael Collection. 1 Nov. 1999. Digital Library Program and The Archives of Traditional Music at Indiana U. 4 Sept. 2001 <http://www.dlib.indiana.edu/collections/hoagy/index.html>. **C**

Copyright Forms from the Library of Congress (Government Office)

United States. Library of Congress. US Copyright Office. Form PA—For a Work of the Performing Arts. Washington: GPO, 1999. 30 Sept. 2001 <http://www.loc.gov/copyright/forms/formpa.pdf>.

Information from a Company's FAQ Page

"Supermusicnotation Software." The Music's Muse, Inc. 3 Jan. 2001 <http://www.themusicsmuse.com/corp/faqs/faqslist.html>.

Posting to a Discussion List (Message Board)

Chart Climbers. "Why Surfers Pause and Pass." Online posting. 3 June 2001. Way Kool Net. 19 Sept. 2001 <http://www.waykoolnet.com/mboards/boards.cgi?board=prgm&read=9218>. **D**

Quotation from an E-mail Communication

Nguyen, W. "Re: 3-D sound, how to do it cheaply." E-mail to the author. 21 Aug. 2001.

speakers to review both the bibliographic samples and the note cards. Have students list any new or difficult terms in a glossary that they can use for reference while completing this lesson and future bibliographies.

Resources Reminder

For lessons designed for intermediate and advanced English-language learners, see *Lesson Plans for Language Development,* pp. 382, 391, 396.

Special Education Students

For lessons designed for special education students, see *Lesson Plans for Language Development,* pp. 383, 391, 396.

DIRECT TEACHING

B Reading Informational Materials
GRADE-LEVEL STANDARD

Citing works in Internet sources. Emphasize to students that the order of information in an Internet citation is very important. To illustrate this importance, ask: When did the writer access this source? [Sept. 7, 2001] When was the page posted or updated? [August 8, 2001] Point out that a reader can differentiate between the dates listed in the citation by knowing the order in which information should appear.

C Reading Informational Materials
GRADE-LEVEL STANDARD

Citing works in Internet sources. Point out to students that the collections of many libraries are now available on the Internet. What did the author find on this library site? [a collection of material relating to Hoagy Carmichael] How would a reader find Carmichael's song lyrics from this bibliographic reference? [The reader would follow the path listed: Go to the Indiana University Library home page, browse the collections, and find the index page for the Hoagy Carmicheal collection.]

D Reading Informational Materials
GRADE-LEVEL STANDARD

Citing works in Internet sources. What is the name of the discussion list that the writer accessed? [Chart Climbers] What organization sponsors the discussion list? [Way Kool Net] You may wish to tell students that information from a discussion list may not always be accurate. What might be a better source of that information? [Possible response: an accredited Web page, such as those from a site sponsored by a university or government.]

DIRECT TEACHING

A Reading Informational Materials
GRADE-LEVEL STANDARD

? Citing works in Internet sources. If the student taking these notes needs to get more information about Nick Hornby, where could he or she go? [The student could look for biographical information or links at the Experience Music Project site or search the name *Nick Hornby* with an internet search engine.]

B Reading Informational Materials
GRADE-LEVEL STANDARD

Citing works in Internet sources. You may wish to remind students that taking notes from Internet sources is very similar to taking notes from print sources. Point out that even though students may find it tedious to write down bibliographic information as they surf Web sites, they will find it easier and quicker than trying to remember the information a few weeks later.

Using Note Cards

As you find sources on the Internet, it is a good idea to record the information you will need for your *Works Cited* list on three-by-five inch note cards. You can also include other important information about your sources on these cards. Here are some examples. (Some of these are made-up sources.)

Source type: Public document
What it is: Online interview
Author(s): none listed
Title: EMP Interviews: Nick Hornby
Other Information: Experience Music Project is a museum in (A) Seattle, Washington, devoted completely to music. The site had last been updated on Sept. 4, 2001. That was the day I visited. A lot of what the site has is digital, so it's very useful for doing research. You could spend days on this site.
URL: http://www.emplive.com — I went to the home page, then to archives, then EMP Interviews, then Nick Hornby.

Source type: Consumer document
What it is: Online consumer newsletter
Author(s): Stewart Cheifet
Title: Hardware Damage from Incorrect Clock Speed in PCI Cards
(B) **Other information:** from Inside the Internet newsletter, June 1999 [vol. 6, issue 8], page 3. Published by Superior Technical Data, Inc. A really clear explanation of the problem and how to avoid it. Accessed on Sept. 3, 2001.
URL: http://www.suptechdata.com/text/press/letter.html

DIFFERENTIATING INSTRUCTION

Advanced Learners

Enrichment. Use the following activity with advanced learners to extend their knowledge of bibliographies.

Activity. Have students work in small groups to compile a general checklist for creating a bibliography. Students should explain how to cite not only various types of electronic sources but also various types of standard print media (books, magazines, newspapers) and other media (films and documentaries). Suggest that students provide a sample bibliography illustrating how the items on their checklists should appear in a bibliography. Once you've reviewed the information, you might distribute these checklists to the class for reference.

Source type: Workplace document
What it is: Reference source
Author(s): none listed; published by Mpeg.TV and edited by Tristan Savatier
Title: MPEG Audio Resources and Software
Other Information: A good overview of MPEG audio and a place to start getting other resources. The page had been last updated May 31, 2000. I accessed it on August 31, 2001.
URL: http://www.mpeg.org/MPEG/audio.html

C

Formatting a Works Cited List

The final step in writing your report is compiling all the sources you have used in a *Works Cited* list. Follow these formatting steps:

- Begin a new page. At the top of the page, center the title Works Cited.
- Alphabetize your sources by the last name of each entry's author (or first author listed if there are more than one). If no author is cited, alphabetize the source by the first two words in the title, ignoring *A, An,* and *The.*
- If you used two or more sources by the same author, use the author's full name in the first entry only. For the other entries, type three dashes in place of the name, followed by a period and the rest of the citation.
- Double-space the list, and begin each entry at the left margin. If an entry runs longer than one line, indent the succeeding lines five spaces.

DIRECT TEACHING

C Reading Informational Materials
GRADE-LEVEL STANDARD

? Citing works in Internet sources. What two aspects of this site did the researcher find noteworthy? [Possible response: It provided a good overview of MPEG audio and a good place to start accessing other resources.]

CONTENT-AREA CONNECTIONS

Science: E-music Technology
Information about music and musicians is abundantly available on the Internet. Use the following activity to pique students' interest in Internet research and to offer them more practice with preparing a bibliography.

Paired activity. Have pairs of students choose one of their favorite musicians or music groups to research. Then, have them search the Internet for information about the musician. Ask students to locate at least five sources of information. Encourage students to fill out note cards like those on pp. 924–925 as they perform their research. Finally, have students practice preparing a bibliography of the sources they located.

INDEPENDENT PRACTICE

Analyzing Informational Materials

Reading Check

1. It helps others to follow your research trail.
2. Internet citations contain more information.
3. the style of the Modern Language Association (MLA)
4. the style that your teacher, employer, or publisher requests

Test Practice

Answers and Model Rationales

1. **D** The sample entries on p. 923 show that the URL comes last. The author's name (A), date of access (B), and publisher (C) always appear before the URL.
2. **H** The author and title come first; nothing further appears after the URL.
3. **D** Answers A and C left off the "http://" designation, and B omitted the brackets. Only D is a complete, correct entry.
4. **G** F is wrong; neither the sample entries nor the order of information suggests this answer. H is wrong; *three* dashes and a period are used when citing more than one entry by the same author. J is wrong; the URL always comes last. The formatting section on p. 925 clearly states the information in option G.
5. **D** Bibliographies should be typed, so A is wrong. The MLA style (B) is a good style, but others are acceptable. One's own personal style (C) is not acceptable. The section on style on p. 922 explains that D is the correct answer.

Analyzing Informational Materials

Reading Check

1. How does a *Works Cited* list help others?
2. How do Internet citations differ from citations for printed materials?
3. What style is followed in the sample citations on page 923?
4. What style should you follow in preparing your *Works Cited* list?

Test Practice

1. According to MLA style, when you cite an Internet source, what is the *last* item mentioned?
   - **A** The author's first name
   - **B** The date you accessed the source
   - **C** The publisher
   - **D** The URL
2. According to MLA style, when you cite an Internet source, where should you put the date that you accessed the site?
   - **F** At the very end of the citation
   - **G** At the very beginning of the citation
   - **H** Just before the URL
   - **J** Just after the URL
3. According to MLA style, which is the correct way to cite a URL ?
   - **A** www.hrw.com
   - **B** http://www.hrw.com
   - **C** //www.hrw.com
   - **D** <http://www.hrw.com>.
4. How would a work with no author be alphabetized in a *Works Cited* list?
   - **F** Use Anonymous as the author.
   - **G** Alphabetize by the first two words in the title, excluding *A, An,* or *The.*
   - **H** Place two dashes and a period; then, alphabetize by the title, as above.
   - **J** Alphabetize by the first word in the URL.
5. In preparing your *Works Cited* list, you should —
   - **A** use cursive handwriting
   - **B** always follow MLA style
   - **C** not be concerned about the style you use
   - **D** follow the style your teacher requests

Reading Standard 2.2 Prepare a bibliography of reference materials for a report using a variety of consumer, workplace, and public documents.

Application

Prepare a *Works Cited* list using the sources listed on the note cards shown on pages 924–925. Follow the MLA style used in the examples listed on pages 921–923. Then, if you have access to a computer, find three other *credible* Internet sources dealing with e-music, and add them to the *Works Cited* list.

Test-Taking Tips

For instruction on how to answer multiple-choice items, refer students to **Test Smarts.**

RETEACHING

For another selection to teach Standard 2.2, see *Interactive Reading,* Part 2.

ASSESSING

Assessment

- *Progress Assessment of Reading*
  - Selection Test

Before You Read INFORMATIONAL MATERIALS

Reading Consumer Documents

Messages from the Manufacturer

The band has learned your song, and now you are ready to record it. You are standing in a working studio, surrounded by the latest in digital recording equipment. When a recording studio makes an investment in digital electronic equipment, it pays attention to the **consumer documents** that come with the equipment. Why? Because the studio's owners know from experience that the **contract, warranty, product information,** and **instruction manual** contain information vital to the smooth operation of the equipment.

Elements Versus Features

They have learned the difference between the elements and the features of a warranty, for example. What is the difference between elements and features, you ask?

For a moment, think of cars. You know that all cars have engines, transmissions, accelerators, and brakes. These are **elements**—the basic parts—of all cars. But not all cars have leather upholstery. Leather seats are a feature of some makes and models. **Features** are what make a model distinct from other models out there.

Similarly, all **warranties** contain certain **elements:** They all exist to assure the buyer (you) that the product will live up to the claims of the manufacturer. They also specify what the manufacturer will do if the product fails to deliver as promised. These elements are basic to all warranties.

The **features** of a warranty, on the other hand, are what make some warranties better than others. For example, say you are looking at two MP3 players that appear identical except for their names. How do you decide which one to buy? Try looking at the warranties. Which warranty offers you a better deal if you need to have the item repaired? Which provides longer coverage? In other words, which warranty has better features?

Elements of Consumer Documents

Here are some different types of consumer documents and the **elements** each type of document contains:

- **product information**—descriptions of the product and what it will do for you
- **contract**—a legal agreement spelling out the rights and obligations of the purchaser and the manufacturer, seller, or service agency
- **warranty**—a legal document stating what the manufacturer will do if the product fails to live up to the manufacturer's claims and what the buyer must do to obtain service
- **instruction manual**—instructions on how to use the product and how to troubleshoot problems
- **technical directions**—directions for installation and use

The next three pages show examples of consumer documents. For the contract on page 928, boxed notes help you identify key elements and some features. As you read the documents, look for other elements and features.

Pages 927–930 cover **Grade 8 Review Reading Standard 2.1** Compare and contrast the features and elements of consumer materials to gain meaning from documents (e.g., warranties, contracts, product information, instruction manuals).

STANDARDS FOCUS, pp. 927–931

(For the review standard taught with this lesson, see citations on Student Edition pages.)

Summary *at grade level*

In this lesson, students analyze three consumer documents: a manufacturer's service contract, a troubleshooting guide from an instruction manual, and product information from the FCC (Federal Communications Commission). The information—in this case, about a digital recorder—is classified under the terms: *element,* or the standard parts of each type of document; and *features,* or the aspects that make a particular document distinct. By understanding these types of consumer documents, students can become more savvy buyers and users of consumer goods.

PRETEACHING

Selection Starter

Build background. Ask students to tell what they or their families have done when an appliance or electronic product failed to function properly. Has a product such as a fax machine, printer, CD player, or dishwasher broken down? Did students consult an instruction manual or use a warranty for the product? To prompt a classroom discussion, you might share a time when you used such a document.

RESOURCES: READING

Planning
- *One-Stop Planner* CD-ROM with Test Generator
- *On Course: Mapping Instruction*

Differentiating Instruction
- *Lesson Plans for Language Development*
  - English-Language Learners, pp. 384, 392, 396
  - Special Education Students, pp. 385, 392, 396

Assessment
- *Progress Assessment of Reading*
  - Selection Test

DIRECT TEACHING

A Reading Informational Materials
GRADE-LEVEL STANDARD

Analyzing consumer documents. What is covered by this contract? [parts and labor for two years] How can warranty coverage be considered both an element and a feature of this contract? [Possible response: The coverage is an element because all warranties explain what the manufacturer will cover if problems arise. It is a feature because the specific details of coverage—parts and labor for two years—are what makes this warranty different from another warranty.]

B Reading Informational Materials
GRADE-LEVEL STANDARD

Analyzing consumer documents. Name one limitation spelled out in this contract. [Possible responses: damage caused by misuse, by unauthorized repair, or by improper installation or electrical connections]

C Reading Informational Materials
GRADE-LEVEL STANDARD

Analyzing consumer documents. Ask students why the unauthorized repair clause of this contract is an element rather than a feature. [Possible response: It is a type of disclaimer that is likely to appear in all similar service contracts.]

D Reading Informational Materials
GRADE-LEVEL STANDARD

Analyzing consumer documents. How might a different manufacturer "outdo" this feature in its service contract? [Possible answer: A different manufacturer might allow transfer of the service contract without a fee.]

Element: offers repair when warranty expires.

Aulsound Extended Service Contract

CONTRACT

ADMINISTRATOR
Aulsound Warranty Service Corporation
P.O. Box 840001
Century City, CA 90067

SERVICE CONTRACT AGREEMENT
Digital Multitrack Recorder DMR88

TERMS AND CONDITIONS

Element: details of coverage. **Feature:** two years parts *and* labor.

Details of coverage. This Service Contract provides coverage of any operating parts or labor required for the product listed above, for two years from date of original purchase. There will be no cost to the Purchaser for any authorized covered repair that is performed by one of our highly skilled service associates. **A**

Element: limitations.

Limitations. This Service Contract covers product failures occurring during normal use. It does not cover misuse or abuse of the product during delivery, installation, or setup adjustments. It does not cover damage that occurs while adjusting consumer controls, loss of data or programming support, unauthorized repair, **B** customer-sponsored specification changes, cosmetic damage, or simple maintenance as recommended in the product owner's guide. It also does not cover repairs that are necessary because of improper installation or improper electrical connections. Consequential or incidental damages are not covered. Damage due to acts of God are not covered.

Element: maintenance requirement.

Maintenance requirement. The Purchaser must maintain the product in accordance with the requirements or recommendations set forth by the manufacturer to keep this Service Contract in force. Evidence of proper maintenance and/or service, when required by Administrator, must be submitted to validate a claim.

Element: unauthorized-repair clause.

Unauthorized-repair clause. IMPORTANT: Unauthorized repairs may void **C** this Service Contract. The cost of unauthorized repairs will be the responsibility of the Purchaser.

Element: transfer of ownership. **Features:** twenty-five-dollar fee and registration within fifteen days.

Transfer of ownership. This Service Contract is transferable with ownership of the product. Transfer may be accomplished only if the Purchaser **D** mails or delivers to the Administrator a twenty-five dollar [$25.00] transfer fee and registers the name and address of the new owner within fifteen [15] days of change of ownership.

Element: cancellation clause. **Features:** cancel any time for prorated refund; 100 percent if within thirty days.

Cancellation clause. This Service Contract may be canceled by the Purchaser at any time, for any reason. In event of cancellation, we will provide a prorated refund minus reasonable handling costs and any claims that may have been paid. Any cancellation requested by the Purchaser within thirty [30] days of the Service Contract application date will be 100 percent canceled by the Administrator.

Element: contract insurance.

Contract insurance. Your Service Contract is fully insured by Aulquiet Insurance Company, 80 Sampler Way, Los Angeles, CA 90017. Purchasers who do not receive payment within sixty [60] days of submitting a pre-authorized covered claim may submit the claim directly to Aulquiet Insurance Company, Contractual Liability Claims Department, at the above address.

Element: renewal clause.

Renewal clause. This Service Contract may be renewed at the discretion of the Administrator. The renewal premium will be based on the age of the covered product, current service costs, the covered product's repair history, and actuarial data.

928 Chapter 11 Consumer and Workplace Documents

DIFFERENTIATING INSTRUCTION

Learners Having Difficulty
To help students understand the difference between workplace documents and consumer documents, explain that consumer documents are included with the purchase of various consumer goods. Ask students to recall the documents that they have seen with telephones, CD players, food processors, and similar products. You may wish to distribute some examples of consumer documents to groups of students. Have each group glance over each document and then tell the class what it is and what its purpose is.

English-Language Learners
Make sure that students are familiar with terms commonly found in consumer documents, particularly in technical manuals. You

Elements: list of problems and possible solutions.

INSTRUCTION MANUAL

Troubleshooting Guide

E If you encounter problems operating your Aulsound DMR88 or if the product does not work as expected, look up the problem in this table, and follow the advice provided.

PROBLEM	ADVICE
The DMR88 does not turn on.	• Make sure that the power cord is plugged into an AC wall outlet. • Check the AC IN connector at the rear of DMR88. • Make sure that the DMR88 power switch is in the ON position. • If there is still no power, contact your Aulsound dealer.
F No sound is coming from a connected music source.	• Make sure that the MONITOR LEVEL control is raised. • Make sure that the FLIP and MONITOR SELECT switches are set correctly.
The DMR88 does not record.	• Make sure that the disc's write-protect tab is set to UNPROTECT. • Make sure that the PLAY function is not on. Press a REC SELECT button, and make sure that the track is ready to record. • Make sure that the signal you wish to record has been selected at the recording source for the appropriate track. Use the CUE LEVEL control to determine whether the signal is being sent to the track.
Lever meters do not indicate signal levels.	• Make sure that the track you wish to record has been selected. • Press the REC button, and make sure that the DMR88 is in RECORD-PAUSE mode.
Recordings play back at the wrong pitch.	• Make sure that the PITCH function is not set at VARIABLE. • Make sure that the 1/2 PLAY function is turned off.

DIRECT TEACHING

E Reading Informational Materials

GRADE-LEVEL STANDARD

? Analyzing consumer documents. Troubleshooting guides are one of the most useful consumer documents because they provide solutions to the most common problems. Have students look at the general format of this document. What is in the left-hand column? [common problems, or symptoms] What is in the right-hand column? [possible solutions to each problem] Why is this chart format better than a plain text format? [Possible response: It makes the document easier to understand and easier to use; the user can scan the left-hand column for a specific problem and quickly find the solutions.]

F Reading Informational Materials

GRADE-LEVEL STANDARD

? Analyzing consumer documents. What should owners of the DMR88 do if they cannot hear a connected music source? [Make sure that the MONITOR LEVEL control is raised and that the FLIP and MONITOR SELECT switches are set correctly.]

may wish to define and give examples of some words from the troubleshooting guide that may be unfamiliar, such as *AC wall outlet, power-up, write-protect tab, track, signal,* and *pitch.*

Resources Reminder

For lessons designed for intermediate and advanced English-language learners, see *Lesson Plans for Language Development,* pp. 384, 392, 396.

Special Education Students

For lessons designed for special education students, see *Lesson Plans for Language Development,* pp. 385, 392, 396.

DIRECT TEACHING

A Reading Informational Materials
GRADE-LEVEL STANDARD

? Analyzing consumer documents. Why do you think the FCC Information (included in the Instruction Manual) is classified as an element rather than a feature? [Possible response: because the FCC is responsible for setting standards for products and making sure that all manufacturers meet them.]

B Reading Informational Materials
GRADE-LEVEL STANDARD

? Analyzing consumer documents. How did the designer use type style and formatting to structure this document for ease of use? [Possible response: The designer began each major point with all capitals and separated the three points with space.] What logical sequence does the information in this document follow? [It begins with the most important point and moves to the least important.] Explain why this is a good way to sequence a document. [Possible response: Most readers start at the beginning of a document. Even if they do not read the entire document, they do read the most important part.]

C Reading Informational Materials
GRADE-LEVEL STANDARD

? Analyzing consumer documents. What would you say is the overall purpose of the FCC Information document? [Possible response: To inform the buyer of important information about the use and characteristics of the product.]

A FCC* Information (USA)

PRODUCT INFORMATION

1. **IMPORTANT NOTICE: DO NOT MODIFY THIS UNIT!**
This unit, when installed as indicated in the instructions contained in this manual, meets FCC requirements. Modifications not expressly approved by Aulsound may void your authority, granted by the FCC, to use this product.

B 2. **IMPORTANT:** When connecting this product to accessories and/or another product, the high-quality shielded cables supplied with this product MUST be used. Follow all installation instructions. Failure to follow instructions could void your FCC authorization to use this product in the United States.

3. **NOTE:** This product has been tested and found to comply with the requirements listed in FCC Regulations, Part 15 for Class "B" digital devices. Compliance with these requirements provides a reasonable level of assurance that your use of this product in a residential environment will not result in harmful interference with other electronic devices. This equipment generates and uses radio frequencies and, if not installed and used according to the instructions found in the user's manual, may cause interference harmful to the operation of other electronic devices. Compliance with FCC regulations does not guarantee that interference will not occur in all installations. If this product is found to be the source of interference, which can be determined by turning the unit OFF and ON, try to eliminate the problem by using one of the following measures:
   - Relocate either this product or the device that is being affected by the interference.
   - Utilize other outlets that are on different branch (circuit breaker or fuse) circuits, or install AC line filter(s). In the case of radio or TV interference, relocate or reorient the antenna.
   - If the antenna lead-in is a 300-ohm ribbon lead, change the lead-in to a coaxial type cable.

If these corrective measures do not produce satisfactory results, contact the local retailer authorized to distribute this type of product. If you cannot locate the appropriate retailer, contact Aulsound Corporation of America, Electronic Service Division, 1000 Wilshire Blvd., Los Angeles, CA 90017.

*FCC: Federal Communications Commission, U.S. agency that regulates communication by telegraph, telephone, radio, TV, cable TV, and satellite.

Purpose of Consumer Documents

C By now you probably have a pretty good understanding of what consumer documents are meant to do—serve you. They are a source of information that makes it easier for you to operate and enjoy the products you use.

Since you are using a good digital-recording system, your new CD is sure to sound great when your friends—and strangers all over the world—listen to it on the Internet. Congratulations!

CONTENT-AREA CONNECTIONS

Social Science: Government Agencies
Paired activity. Invite interested students to perform research to learn more about the Federal Communications Commission. Ask students to find out when the agency was founded, which section of the federal government it is a part of, and exactly which public or consumer segments it regulates. They can then compile this information in an FCC fact sheet. Encourage students to find examples of official FCC information from products they use and to present these examples to the class with their fact sheets.

930 Chapter 11 Consumer and Workplace Documents

Analyzing Informational Materials

Reading Check

1. List three **elements** of an extended service contract.

2. What are some **features** of the limitations clause of Aulsound's extended-service contract (on page 928)?

3. What are the common **elements** of a troubleshooting guide?

4. Why does the FCC have jurisdiction over a digital multisound recorder?

Test Practice

1. An element common to all **consumer documents** is —
   - A a product warranty
   - B legal information
   - C instructions
   - D useful information

2. The **features** of a particular consumer document —
   - F are what the document shares with all other consumer documents
   - G distinguish it from other documents of the same type
   - H make the product extremely desirable to the consumer
   - J describe the limitations of the document

3. To make sure repairs to a digital multitrack recorder are covered beyond the period specified in the warranty, you would obtain a(n) —
   - A extensive instruction manual
   - B FCC information sheet
   - C installation guide
   - D extended-service contract

4. A **troubleshooting guide** is designed to help you —
   - F install a product
   - G solve problems operating the product
   - H customize the product
   - J change the product's specifications

5. The FCC-information document (page 930) and the troubleshooting guide (page 929) *both* provide information on —
   - A what to do when something doesn't work right
   - B the legal responsibilities of the purchaser and the manufacturer
   - C product specifications
   - D warranty coverage when the product breaks down

Grade 8 Review Reading Standard 2.1 Compare and contrast the features and elements of consumer materials to gain meaning from documents (e.g., warranties, contracts, product information, instruction manuals).

Application

Examine some consumer documents (production information, instruction manuals, warranties, and so on). Find the documents for at least one product in your home (anything from a TV to a toaster), and identify their features and elements. Then, bring the documents to class. In a small group, compare and contrast the documents you and the other members of your group have found. How many elements can you find in common? What types of features do you find?

INDEPENDENT PRACTICE

Analyzing Informational Materials

Reading Check

1. details of coverage; limitations; maintenance requirement
2. misuse or abuse of the product, loss of data, unauthorized repair, improper installation.
3. a list of common problems and a list of their likely solutions
4. The FCC has jurisdiction over any device that might cause electronic interference.

Test Practice

Answers and Model Rationales

1. **D** A product warranty (A) is a consumer document, not an element of one. Not every consumer document has legal information and useful instructions (B and C).
2. **G** Answer F defines elements, not features. A description of limitations is an element, so J is also incorrect. Option H might be a byproduct of a feature, but it does not define *features.*
3. **D** Choices A, B, and C have nothing to do with coverage of repairs.
4. **G** Installation (F), customization (H), and changing the specifications (J) are generally covered in an instruction manual.
5. **A** The Troubleshooting Guide does not discuss legal responsibilities (B) or product specifications (C). Neither document deals with product repairs (D).

Test-Taking Tips

For more instruction on how to answer multiple-choice items, refer students to **Test Smarts.**

ASSESSING

Assessment

- *Progress Assessment of Reading*
  - Selection Test

RETEACHING

For a lesson reteaching Standard 2.1, see **Reteaching,** p. 939A. For another selection to teach Standard 2.1, see *Interactive Reading,* Part 2.

Reading Consumer Documents 931

STANDARDS FOCUS, pp. 932–933

(For the grade-level standard taught with this lesson, see the citations on Student Edition pages.)

Writing

Prerequisite Standard

- Grade 8, Writing Applications 2.6a–b **Write technical documents. Identify the sequence of activities needed to design a system, operate a tool, or explain the bylaws of an organization. Include all the factors and variables that need to be considered.**

PRETEACHING

Selection Starter

Build background. Remind students that Aristotle (384–322 B.C.) was an ancient Greek philosopher whose thinking has greatly influenced our modern world.

Motivate. Use the quotation as the basis for a class discussion about the importance of conflict resolution. Point out that most people have been involved in a conflict that got out of control for precisely the reasons described by the great philosopher. Ask students to apply the quotation to a dispute they have observed or been involved in. For example, Was someone angry with the wrong person, or enraged over a minor incident? Ask students how having a plan to deal with the conflict might have helped.

Writing Technical Documents

Anyone can become angry. That is easy. But to be angry with the right person, in the right degree, at the right time, for the right reason, and in the right way—that is not easy.

—Aristotle

Writing Rules for Conflict Resolution

When you're just getting started in music and hoping to make a splash in the world, how do you and your bandmates arrive at decisions that will further the group's efforts? How do you turn your inevitable conflicts into productive discussions?

It is better to deal with conflict before it reaches a crisis than to let it get so far out of hand that you cannot control it. This means that you deal with a problem as soon as you sense there is a problem. It is easier to do this if you have worked out beforehand some rules for **conflict resolution** that the group can refer to and use when problems arise. See, for example, the rules below.

Writing Standard 2.6 Write technical documents (e.g., a manual on rules of behavior for conflict resolution). **2.6a.** Report information and convey ideas logically and correctly. **2.6b.** Offer detailed and accurate specifications. **2.6c.** Include scenarios, definitions, and examples to aid comprehension. **2.6d.** Anticipate readers' problems, mistakes, and misunderstandings.

Six Rules for Conflict Resolution

The word *candor* refers to the quality of being fair and unprejudiced. It also refers to expressing yourself honestly and frankly. Here are six rules for conflict resolution based on the word *candor:*

Cease what you're doing. Count to ten. Take a walk. Do whatever you do to cool down.

Ask yourself what is going on. Try to figure out what the conflict is all about.

Name the problem as you see it. Describe it to the other persons involved without blaming anyone, without adding fuel to the fire.

Discover a problem-solving plan by talking things out with those involved. Often this involves some sort of **compromise,** in which each person gives in a little in order to reach an agreement.

Operate that plan. Put it into effect by cooperating with the others involved.

Reevaluate the plan. Quite often people do not complete the process of putting a plan of action in place because they feel better after talking things over or they get distracted. When the problem reoccurs, they think their problem-solving efforts have been wasted. Instead, resolve to use the plan.

RESOURCES: WRITING

Planning

- *One-Stop Planner* CD-ROM with Test Generator
- *On Course: Mapping Instruction*

Differentiating Instruction

- *Lesson Plans for Language Development*
  - English-Language Learners, pp. 386, 393, 397
  - Special Education Students, pp. 386, 393, 397

Assessment

- *Progress Assessment of Writing, Listening, & Speaking*
  - Selection Test
- *One-Stop Planner* CD-ROM with Test Generator

Some Useful Technical Documents

Conflict-resolution rules constitute a type of **technical document,** as do **procedures for conducting a meeting** and **minutes of a meeting.** You will probably find the ability to write such documents useful at some time or other in your life.

Minutes are usually taken at every official meeting in order to keep track of what has been decided, and you probably go to lots of meetings. Your band is not likely to be the only organization you belong to. You might also be a member of your school government or on the committee to decorate the gym for the class prom, for instance. If any of the organizations you belong to do not already have written rules for conflict resolution and procedures for conducting a meeting, you might want to form a committee to write them.

Tips for Writing Technical Documents

Here are some tips for writing a successful technical document:

- Convey all information **clearly, concisely,** and **correctly.**
- Arrange information in a **logical order.**
- Be **specific.**
- Include **definitions** and **examples** to aid comprehension.
- Anticipate possible reader misunderstandings.

PRACTICE

When people in a group are trying to work together toward a common goal, many problems can arise. Pick one of the situations described below, and write some **conflict-resolution rules** to help solve the group's problems. Be clear and specific, and include **definitions, examples,** and **scenarios** (specific situations) if they will help make the rules clear.

1. Julie thinks that John isn't doing his fair share of the work. John was supposed to have the band fliers printed before their next gig, but he hasn't done it, and now time is running out. Julie has stepped in for John before when he has slacked off, but now she is angry. She thinks John should do what he said he would do. Write some conflict-resolution rules that would help Julie and John resolve this problem.

2. Gary is the band's treasurer. There isn't enough money for everything the band would like to do, so Gary wants to set budget priorities. Write some budget rules that would help prevent conflicts about money in the band.

3. Ted believes the band's drummer is taking up too much rehearsal time tuning her drums. He says Sari should get her drums in shape before rehearsals begin. Sari argues that her drumheads go out of tune because other people are fooling around with her equipment when she isn't there. Write some rules that would help resolve this conflict.

DIRECT TEACHING

Tips for Writing Technical Documents

As you discuss these tips with the class, you may wish to have students apply them to the Six Rules for Conflict Resolution on p. 932.

- **Ask students if anything in the Six Rules seems unclear or incorrect.** [Most students will find the rules easy to understand.] **Then, call on volunteers to point out examples of concise writing.** [Possible response: Each rule but the last is written as several very short imperative sentences.]
- **How is the information organized?** [It is arranged in a logical step-by-step order—each step must be accomplished before the next.]
- **How specific are the rules?** [Possible response: Very specific. The rules tell exactly what to do.]
- **Which tip for writing technical documents is not applied in the Six Rules?** [include definitions and examples] **How might using this tip either improve or weaken the Six Rules?** [Possible response: Adding examples would lengthen the rules, perhaps thereby making them less effective. Adding examples from real life would show that the rules work.]
- **How do the Six Rules deal with possible misunderstandings?** [The last rule explains that not completing the plan of action can spoil problem-solving efforts.]

DIFFERENTIATING INSTRUCTION

English-Language Learners

Understanding idioms. On p. 932, several common expressions may puzzle students who are learning English. You may wish to explain that *make a splash* means "do something to be noticed," *cool down under your collar* means "get your anger under control," and *adding fuel to the fire* means "saying something that makes things worse." Point out that these expressions plus the sentence fragment at the end of the Six Rules are examples of informal writing.

STANDARDS FOCUS, pp. 934–937

(For the grade-level standard taught with this lesson, see citations on Student Edition pages.)

Writing

Prerequisite Standard

- Grade 8, Writing Applications 2.5a–b **Write documents related to career development, including simple business letters and job applications. Present information purposefully and succinctly and meet the needs of the intended audience. Follow the conventional format for the type of document (e.g., letter of inquiry, memorandum).**

Standards Coming Up in the Next Level

Grades 11–12, Writing Applications 2.5a–d **Write job applications and resumes. Provide clear and purposeful information and address the intended audience appropriately. Use varied levels, patterns, and types of language to achieve intended effects and aid comprehension. Modify the tone to fit the purpose and audience. Follow the conventional style for that type of document (e.g., resumé, memorandum) and use page formats, fonts, and spacing that contribute to the readability and impact of the document.**

PRETEACHING

Motivate. Ask students to think about situations they encounter in which writing a business letter might be helpful. For example, have they ever purchased defective merchandise, wished their town would sponsor a hockey team, or looked for an after-school job? In each of these cases, a business letter might help them get the results they want.

Writing Business Letters

A Request Letter

You and your band are giving a performance in the public-library auditorium to help raise money for the children's bookmobile. You are in charge of publicizing the event. You've noticed that your local newspaper runs a public-announcement column. To submit your listing, you'll write a business letter.

Business letters require a **style** of writing that is different from the one you use to write your song lyrics. ("Don't be cruel" is a great lyric, but in a business letter . . . Well, you get the point.) Often the purpose of a business letter is to **request** that someone do something for you: hire you, donate money to your cause, provide you with information, fix your problem, or as in this case, promote your band. Therefore, you want to make the best possible impression. One way to make a good impression is to pay attention to the elements of a proper business letter.

Writing Standard 2.5 Write business letters. **2.5a.** Provide clear and purposeful information and address the intended audience appropriately. **2.5b.** Use appropriate vocabulary, tone, and style to take into account the nature of the relationship with, and the knowledge and interests of, the recipients. **2.5c.** Highlight central ideas or images. **2.5d.** Follow a conventional style with page formats, fonts, and spacing that contribute to the documents' readability and impact.

Elements of a Business Letter

The style, tone, and vocabulary of a business letter should be appropriate to the subject matter and audience. A **personal letter** to your uncle Pete asking for a loan to buy a new amp for your band will have a very different style from a business letter making the same request of a bank. The **style** and **tone** of a business letter are **formal.** Focus on these elements whenever you write a business letter:

- **Clarity**—clarity and conciseness are extremely important in business letters. The recipient should not have to sift through irrelevant details or poor organization to find your main points.
- **Courtesy**—all business letters should be polite. Even if you are writing a **complaint letter,** there is little to be gained from discourtesy. Remember: You want to gain the reader's cooperation.
- **Tone**—the **tone** of a business letter, although friendly, is usually **formal**—as if you were talking to your principal or to the interview committee at the college you hope to attend.
- **Style**—the **style** of a business letter is **formal.** That means it contains no slang, no contractions, and no sentence fragments.
- **Vocabulary**—your vocabulary should take into account the knowledge and interest of the reader. You may wish to try on some of those not-so-everyday vocabulary words you are constantly studying in books like this one. However, don't overdo it. Your letter should reflect your own personality.

Format of a Business Letter

Business letters are expected to follow a conventional **format,** or style, as shown in the example on the next page. Note that every business letter has these six parts:

- heading
- inside address
- salutation
- body
- closing
- signature

The example letters on pages 935 and 936 use a **block-style format.** Notice that all six parts of the business letter (heading, inside address, salutation, body, closing, and signature) align at the left margin.

In a **modified-block-style format** the heading, closing, and signature are indented, as is every paragraph in the body of the letter. See the letter on page 937 for an example of the modified block style.

RESOURCES: WRITING

Planning

- *One-Stop Planner* CD-ROM with Test Generator
- *On Course: Mapping Instruction*

Differentiating Instruction

- *Lesson Plans for Language Development*
  - English-Language Learners, pp. 387, 394, 397
  - Special Education Students, pp. 387, 394, 397

Assessment

- *Progress Assessment of Writing, Listening, & Speaking*
  - Selection Test
- *One-Stop Planner* CD-ROM with Test Generator

BUSINESS LETTER

Business Letter Format

Heading.	Your Street Address Your City, State, and ZIP code Date on which letter is written
Inside address.	Recipient's Title [Mr., Miss, Dr., Professor, Rev., etc.] and First and Last Name Recipient's business title Company Name Street Address City, State, and ZIP code
Salutation, followed by a colon.	Dear [Title and Last Name of Recipient]:
Body: paragraph 1.	In this paragraph, tell the recipient why you are writing, stating what you are requesting in clear and concise language.
Body: paragraph 2.	In this paragraph, include information relevant to your goal, such as relevant facts about your background or questions you have for the recipient.
Body: paragraph 3.	Here you thank the recipient in advance for whatever actions he or she may take in regard to your request in the first paragraph.
Closing, followed by a comma.	Sincerely,
Four blank lines for signature—followed by your typed name.	*Your Signature* Your Full Name

DIRECT TEACHING

Business Letter Format

Advise students that in business writing, things like appearance and first impressions count. A letter that shows respect for form and convention is more likely to be taken seriously than a letter showing little regard for form.

Point out that in the heading and inside address, the only abbreviation should be the name of the state. Explain that it is correct to use the two-letter state abbreviations established by the U.S. Post Office. These abbreviations are listed in many telephone books and dictionaries. However, designations such as "Street," "Avenue," "Lane," "Drive," and "Boulevard" should be spelled out. The date should be presented with the month spelled out and the year shown with all four digits.

If students are not sure whether they are addressing a man or a woman, they should write "Mr. or Ms. . . ." If they do not have a person's name at all, they should write "Dear Sir or Madam."

DIRECT TEACHING

Two Sample Business Letters

Ask students to point out in the first sample letter the elements of a business letter that are referred to on p. 934. Students should notice that the writing in the body of the letter is clear and concise, and that no extraneous information is included. The style, tone, and vocabulary are appropriate to the subject and audience. In paragraph 1, the request is stated clearly. In paragraph 2, all relevant facts are included; and in paragraph 3, the recipient is thanked in advance.

Have students show how the sample follows the format of a business letter. They should point out that all six parts of the business letter are included: heading, inside address, salutation, body, closing, and signature.

Two Sample Business Letters

You've learned the format. Now, see what some business letters look like.

BUSINESS LETTER

440 Melody Lane
Rockville, CA 91112
June 2, 2002

Ms. Bettina Johnson
Editor, "Doings in Town"
The Rockville Observer
1 Main Street
Rockville, CA 91111

Dear Ms. Johnson:

I am writing to submit a news item for inclusion in your column, "Doings in Town," for the June 17 edition of *The Rockville Observer.* I understand that you list town events that are open to the public.

Our band, The DumpStar Gang, is giving a benefit performance to raise funds for the public library's children's bookmobile. The performance will take place in the public-library auditorium on June 21 at 7:30 P.M. Admission is free, but a ten-dollar donation is requested. Refreshments will be served after the performance.

Thank you in advance for including our performance in your column. The publicity should make it possible for us to raise additional funds for the children's bookmobile.

Sincerely yours,

Mike Musicano

Mike Musicano
The DumpStar Gang

BUSINESS LETTER

THE ROCKVILLE OBSERVER
1 MAIN STREET, ROCKVILLE, CA 91111

June 4, 2002

Mr. Mike Musicano
440 Melody Lane
Rockville, CA 91112

Dear Mr. Musicano:

We received your letter and will be happy to list your benefit performance in the "Doings in Town" column in our June 17 edition. In addition, in order to further support the library's children's bookmobile, we would like to help publicize your event with a feature article on your band.

Our reporter Ritsa Lott will call you this Friday to arrange an interview. Since time is short, I am requesting now that you send us some photographs and information about the DumpStar Gang. Please address these materials to Ritsa Lott, Staff Reporter.

Thank you for your prompt attention to our request and for your good work in support of the library.

Sincerely,

Bettina Johnson

Bettina Johnson
Editor, "Doings in Town"

PRACTICE

What a great reply! The extra publicity should give both the library and the band a big boost. Your assignment is to write Mike Musicano's reply to Bettina Johnson's letter. To do so, it might help you to know that when you enclose materials such as photographs and press releases in an envelope along with a business letter, it is customary to leave a space below your name and then type "enc." (short for *enclosure*).

GUIDED PRACTICE

Monitoring students' progress. Ask students to explain how the second sample letter follows the elements and format of a business letter.

INDEPENDENT PRACTICE

Assign the Practice activity. It will help you assess students' understanding of both the proper form for a business letter and the elements of clarity, conciseness, style, tone, vocabulary, and courtesy that are essential in a business letter.

DIFFERENTIATING INSTRUCTION

Learners Having Difficulty
If students are having difficulty composing a business letter for the Practice activity, you may wish to offer them a few suggestions. Point out that, except for the date, they can simply copy the heading, inside address, salutation, closing, and signature of the letter on p. 936. Note that the body of the letter should reply to the information in Bettina Johnson's letter. There should be a "thank you" for the listing of the benefit performance in the "Doings in Town" column; an expression of Mike Musicano's gratitude and delight that the *Rockville Observer* wants to do a feature article on the band; and a mention of photographs and information that Mike is sending separately to Ritsa Lott.

Writing Business Letters 937

Standards Review

Analyzing Informational Materials

STANDARDS FOCUS, pp. 938–939

(For grade-level and review standards reviewed in this lesson, see Student Edition, p. 938.)

INTRODUCING THE STANDARDS REVIEW

Use this review to assess students' grasp of consumer and workplace documents.

Test Practice

Answers and Model Rationales

1. **C** Skimming beforehand (A), calculating time (D), and finishing in one session (B) are not essential.
2. **G** Functional documents are designed to help get things done, so a logical sequence is usually best.
3. **C** Since products differ in price, a highest-to-lowest ranking is most useful in a product review.
4. **G** Step-by-step order is the most logical sequence for completing a task.
5. **C** Either omitting a step (A) or putting a step in the wrong order (B) can produce a faulty result.
6. **H** F and J are possible goals of specific workplace documents, but not all. G is not a likely goal.
7. **B** A collaboration agreement specifies the rights and obligations of parties to a collaboration, or legal contract.
8. **H** A site is most reliably accessed through its URL.

STANDARDS REVIEW

Analyzing Informational Materials

Test Practice

Grade 8 Review Reading Standard 2.1 Compare and contrast the features and elements of consumer materials.
Reading Standard 2.1 Analyze the structure and format of functional workplace documents.
Reading Standard 2.2 Prepare a bibliography of reference materials for a report using a variety of consumer, workplace, and public documents.
Reading Standard 2.6 Demonstrate use of sophisticated learning tools by following technical directions.
Reading Standard 2.7 Critique the logic of functional documents by examining the sequence of information and procedures.
Writing Standard 2.5 Write business letters.

Consumer and Workplace Documents

DIRECTIONS: Read each question about consumer and workplace documents that follows, and write the letter of the best response.

1. What is the *most* important thing to do when following **technical directions**?
   - **A** Read all the directions quickly to get the big picture.
   - **B** Complete the project in one uninterrupted session.
   - **C** Follow each step carefully and in the correct sequence.
   - **D** Decide ahead of time how much time to allow for the project.

2. Which type of **sequence** do most **functional documents** follow?
   - **F** Alphabetical
   - **G** Logical
   - **H** Spatial
   - **J** Chronological

3. Which type of **functional document** is *most* suited to a **logical sequence** that progresses from highest to lowest?
   - **A** A contract
   - **B** A recipe
   - **C** A product review
   - **D** A set of directions

4. The *most* **logical order** for presenting a set of **instructions** is —
   - **F** chronological order
   - **G** step-by-step order
   - **H** order of importance
   - **J** spatial order

5. A set of **technical directions** is badly flawed if it —
   - **A** omits a step
   - **B** puts a step in the wrong order
   - **C** does either of the above
   - **D** does none of the above

6. The **purpose** of a **functional workplace document** is to —
   - **F** eliminate some jobs
   - **G** increase paperwork
   - **H** help people get things done
   - **J** lessen people's dependence on computers

7. Which type of document is a **collaboration agreement**?
   - **A** A warranty
   - **B** A contract
   - **C** Technical directions
   - **D** U.S. Copyright Office registration

8. In an **Internet citation** the *most* crucial piece of information to reproduce accurately is the —
   - **F** author's name
   - **G** title of the site
   - **H** URL
   - **J** date the site was accessed

Using Academic Language

Review of Informational Terms
Reading Standards 2.2, 2.6, 2.7, and Grade 8 Review Reading Standard 2.1
Ask students to look back through the chapter to find the meanings of the terms listed below. Then, have students show their grasp of the standards by citing passages from the chapter that show the meanings of those terms.
Functional Document (p. 909); **Logical Sequence** (p. 909); **Technical Directions** (pp. 913, 927); **Functional Workplace Document** (p. 916); **Collaboration Agreement** (p. 917); **Contract** (pp. 917, 927); **Sequence** (p. 919); **Structure** (p. 919); **Format** (p. 919); **URL** (p. 921); **Order** (p. 921); **Consumer Documents** (p. 927); **Elements** (p. 927); **Features** (p. 927); **Product Information** (p. 927); **Warranty** (p. 927); **Instruction Manual** (p. 927).

9. According to MLA style, where in an **Internet citation** do you place the date a site was accessed?
   - A Right after the URL
   - B Just before the URL
   - C At the beginning of the entry
   - D At the end of the entry

10. According to MLA style, which of the following citations of a URL is correct?
   - F <http.www.yourschool.edu
   - G www.yourschool.edu
   - H <http://www.yourschool.edu>.
   - J http://www.yourschool.edu

11. In a ***Works Cited*** **list,** in what order are the entries listed?
   - A Alphabetically by the title of the work
   - B Alphabetically by the author's last name (when known)
   - C Alphabetically by the URL
   - D Chronologically by the date the source was accessed

12. Which **consumer document** is *most* likely to help you if you encounter problems operating a product?
   - F A contract
   - G A troubleshooting guide
   - H A warranty
   - J Product information

13. What is the **purpose** of an **extended-service contract**?
   - A To provide a basic warranty for a product
   - B To give advice on how to repair a product
   - C To provide coverage for repairs to a product after the warranty expires
   - D To provide a money-back guarantee of a product

14. FCC (Federal Communications Commission) information is included with some products to —
   - F provide a U.S. government warranty for the product
   - G teach consumers how to use the product
   - H warn consumers against tampering with the product
   - J offer government advice for repairing the product

15. In which of these **consumer documents** are you *most* likely to find out how powerful a new computer is?
   - A A warranty
   - B Product information
   - C Safety guide
   - D Instruction manual

16. Which of the following elements is *not* part of a **business letter**?
   - F The salutation
   - G The signature
   - H The inside address
   - J The outside address

9. D The author and title come first; the URL comes last.

10. H G lacks the http:// prefix; F and J are missing one or more angle brackets. All but H lack the final period.

11. B Works are arranged alphabetically by title (A) only if the author is not known.

12. G A troubleshooting guide lists the most common problems with their solutions. Warranties and extended service contracts are useful only if the product must be serviced.

13. C An extended-service contract pays for service to a product, but does not tell how to repair it, and is not needed as long as the product is covered by a warranty.

14. H The FCC is not responsible for warranties or teaching consumers how to use or repair products, but for making sure products are not altered in a way that might cause electronic interference to communications.

15. B Warranties do not describe a product's features; safety guides and instruction manuals only describe features relevant to safety and use.

16. J The outside address appears on the envelope; the salutation, signature, and inside address appear on the letter itself.

ASSESSING

Assessment

- *Progress Assessment of Reading*
  - Chapter Test
- *Progress Assessment of Writing, Listening, & Speaking*
  - Chapter Test
- *Diagnostic and Summative Assessment*
  - End-of-Year Test

DIFFERENTIATING INSTRUCTION

Advanced Learners

Enrichment. Ask students to choose a device used in the classroom, such as an overhead projector or a CD player, and have students familiar with the device briefly jot down instructions for its use, breaking down instructions into clear steps.

Activity. Have students form small groups to write instruction manuals for classroom devices of their choosing. They should determine which sets of instructions to put first, how to title the instructions, and in what order the steps should be presented. If original manuals for the devices that students chose are available, have the groups exchange manuals and review the student-written manuals against the manufacturers' manuals.

Reteaching Lessons

Analyzing Workplace Documents

Reading Standard 2.1 Analyze the structure and format of functional workplace documents, including the graphics and headers, and explain how authors use the features to achieve their purposes.

Objective: To analyze the structure and format of functional workplace documents, including the graphics and headers, and explain how authors use the features to achieve their purposes.

Direct Teaching: Share the following information with students.

What do these types of information have in common: the diagram a plumber uses to install a sink, the warranty for a DVD player, the instructions to operate a fax machine, and the contracts that lawyers draw up when two large companies merge? They are all types of functional documents; their common purpose is to present information, procedures, or both in a logical sequence.

The designers and writers of printed functional documents routinely use certain structures and formats to help users understand and apply the information contained in the documents. For instance, writers often use headings and subheadings to label the main topic and subtopics. (It is a good idea to scan these headings to see what the document covers before getting into the details.) Writers also frequently divide the text of functional documents into short, manageable sections by the use of subheads (set off by special typefaces), line spacing, indentation, and numbering. The most effective documents present these text sections in a logical order or sequence, often step by step or point by point. In many cases, diagrams and other graphics are included along with the text because they can convey certain types of complex information far more efficiently than words alone.

Guided Practice: **Analyzing workplace documents.** Explain that writers of effective workplace documents arrange information logically to suit the content and purpose of the document. Review the types of sequencing often used in functional documents—step by step, point by point, and order of importance—and discuss when each method might be used. (Step-by-step sequencing is used for how-to instructions; point-by-point sequencing is used for showing the relationship between separate items of information, as in a legal document; and order of importance is used for summaries of points of interest or things to do.)

Make available for analysis functional workplace documents from the school environment, such as memoranda about holidays, testing schedules, and staff meetings; instructions on fire safety; and statements of school policy. Have students discuss how structural and formatting elements are used in these documents to present information.

Independent Practice: **Evaluating workplace documents.** As homework, students should locate examples of functional workplace documents—such as contracts, leases, insurance policies, memoranda—using library or Internet resources. Ask students to analyze the documents they find and to explain how the writers use structural and formatting features to help convey information. Encourage them to organize their analyses on a chart like the one below. (Example features relevant to the collaboration agreement on p. 918 are included in the first column of the chart.) Remind students to identify and list the specific features of the documents they are examining and not to limit their analyses to the list of features in the sample chart. Have a follow-up discussion in which students compare and contrast similar types of documents and evaluate how well or poorly the writers make use of structural and formatting features.

Feature	Example from Document	Purpose of Feature
headers	flush-left head at top	announces the purpose of document
logical sequence		
numbered sections		
indentation		
font style		

Reteaching the Standards

Reading Standard 2.5
Extend ideas presented in primary or secondary sources through original analysis, evaluation, and elaboration.

Extending Ideas

Objective: To extend ideas presented in primary or secondary sources through original analysis, evaluation, and elaboration.

Direct Teaching: Share the following thoughts with students.

Imagine you're conducting research for a report, and the author of one of the articles you read expresses ideas that are radically different from your own. Do you automatically change your opinion? No, there is no need to accept an author's ideas just because they are in print. It is always wise to analyze, evaluate, and extend the ideas, reasons, and explanations that writers use to support their conclusions. That means asking questions like these: Who is the author's intended audience? What does the author want the audience to learn or believe? What are the topic and main ideas? What details support the topic and develop the main ideas? Are the author's facts accurate? Do I agree with what the author proposes or believes? What do I already know about this topic? What more do I want to find out? Analyzing, evaluating, and elaborating (or connecting the author's ideas with their own knowledge and experience) can be done in any order during the reading process. In fact, the best readers usually begin elaborating as soon as they start reading.

Guided Practice: **Creating a chain of ideas.** Have students read the first paragraph of "The Child's View of Working Parents" (p. 26). Draw a chain on the chalkboard as follows:

Analyze	+	Evaluate	+	Elaborate

Brainstorm with students to develop questions about the first paragraph. Work together to decide the category—analyze, evaluate, or elaborate—to which each question belongs. [Possible responses: *Analyze*—Based on the title and opening paragraph, what is the topic of the article? For what audience and purpose is the author writing? What facts does she include? What opinions does she offer? *Evaluate*—Does the article make sense so far? Does it suit its intended audience and purpose? Are the facts correct? *Elaborate*—What do I already know about the topic? What personal experience or knowledge can shed more light on the topic? What more do I want to know?] Then, have students read the rest of "The Child's View of Working Parents." Ask student partners to fill in the chain of ideas by answering the questions that the class developed with reference to the article as a whole.

As a group the class should discuss Cora Daniels's ideas on the child's view of working parents and their own ideas on the same topic. Encourage students to refer to their charts during the discussion. Conclude by asking students if they think that Daniels does a good job of supporting her ideas and informing readers on her topic. Ask students how the ideas and experiences of their classmates helped them to form their own ideas and opinions on the topic and to evaluate the article.

Independent Practice: **Evaluating informational writing.** Ask groups of three students to choose an informational article from a classroom magazine or local newspaper. After they read the article, each group should analyze and evaluate the material and decide if it would make a good source of information for its topic. Remind students to use their own ideas and experiences as they discuss the merits of the selection. Ask the groups to write a short paragraph that states and explains their opinion.

Reading Standard 2.7
Critique the logic of functional documents by examining the sequence of information and procedures in anticipation of possible reader misunderstandings.

Evaluating Functional Documents

Objective: To evaluate the sequence of information and procedures in functional documents in anticipation of possible reader misunderstandings.

Direct Teaching: Share the following ideas with students.

How good are you at following directions? How good are the directions you follow? Writing instructions, whether for use at home or in the workplace, is a challenging task, and the results range in quality from excellent to awful. Therefore, when you are faced with a set of directions, it is smart to read carefully through the steps in the process before you start doing anything. Look especially for two frequently occurring problems: missing steps or steps presented in the wrong order. If undetected, mistakes like these can waste your time, try your patience, and cause damage to materials—in some cases, ruining the outcome.

As you read how-to instructions, it is helpful also to visualize the process being described. In other words, complete a dry run in your mind. If the instructions are for assembling or making something, check the list of materials against what you already have. Do you anticipate needing something the list has left out? Pay attention to any diagrams. Think about each step, and ask yourself if its place in the overall sequence makes sense. Think about any steps that might be missing. Finding one mistake doesn't necessarily mean that you will find another, but reading instructions carefully and visualizing what needs to be done will help you to spot and solve problems before they happen.

Guided Practice: **Evaluating functional documents.** Share with students your experiences using instructions that were badly written, and relate what happened as a result. Then, ask students to share similar experiences. Together, discuss what can be learned from such mishaps.

On the chalkboard, write the following instructions for assembling a pet carrier, or provide individual copies of the instructions to students.

Assembling a Pet Carrier

Materials:

top section with handle
bottom section
door
package of nuts (7) and bolts (7)

Directions:

1. Place top section, with the handle raised, on top of the bottom section. Align door opening and bolt holes.
2. Hold the top section by the handle with one hand. Raise the front (the door end) far enough to insert the bottom hinge post of the door into the hole in the bottom section.
3. Lower the top section. Make sure the hinge post goes into the hole in the top section.
4. Fasten the top and bottom sections together by inserting a bolt through each matched pair of holes and securing with a nut.
5. Make sure the door is positioned so the latch is on the outside.

Have students read the instructions and then analyze them in pairs. Begin by asking students to identify and evaluate the type of sequence used. [It is a step-by-step, chronological sequence, which is a logical way to present instructions for assembling an item.] Point out that although the instructions are generally straightforward and easy to follow, the last step is out of order. Ask students to discuss what would happen if the user of the functional document had not discovered the mistake beforehand and began assembling the pet carrier according to these directions. [Possible response: The user would assemble the door with the latch inside and would have to remove all the bolts to correct the problem.] Next, ask students where in the process the fifth step should have been included. [Possible response: The last step should have come after the second step or have been included as part of the second step.] Finally, discuss other ways that the instructions could be improved. [Possible response: A diagram or photograph of each step in the process (including a picture of the completely assembled carrier) would be helpful.]

Independent Practice: **Evaluating functional documents.** As homework, have students evaluate a set of step-by-step instructions. For example, they might evaluate instructions for installing virus-protection software on a computer, for programming a portable CD player, for assembling a toy, or for putting up a fence. Ask students to evaluate how user-friendly their instructional documents are. Have them consider such questions as

- Are the steps clear and logically arranged?
- Are any steps missing or out of order?
- What questions or problems might arise for someone using these instructions?
- Does the process require any materials or equipment not listed in the directions?
- What could the writer have done to make the instructions more helpful or user-friendly?

Have a follow-up discussion in which students point out the strengths and weaknesses of the instructional materials they evaluated. You may want to challenge more advanced or technically confident students to rewrite faulty instructions, making them clearer and easier to use.

Evaluating an Argument

Reading Standard 2.8
Evaluate the credibility of an author's argument or defense of a claim by critiquing the relationship between generalizations and evidence, the comprehensiveness of evidence, and the way in which the author's intent affects the structure and tone of the text (e.g., in professional journals, editorials, political speeches, primary source material).

Objective: To evaluate the credibility of an author's argument by critiquing the relationship between the generalizations and the evidence, the comprehensiveness of the evidence, and the way in which the author's intent affects the tone.

Direct Teaching: Share the following information with students.

Every day you are bombarded with other people's ideas, arguments, and opinions about a wide range of topics—from movies to political causes or candidates. How should you evaluate these opinions? As you read or listen to persuasive material, such as movie reviews and newspaper editorials, first identify the writer's argument or claim. This is the generalization—what he or she is trying to convince you to think or to do. Then, pay attention to the facts, examples, and reasons the writer uses to support the generalization. Remember that besides provable facts, supportive evidence can come in the form of an anecdote, or story based on personal experience; an opinion from someone the writer views as an expert; and an analogy or comparison to a similar situation or issue. After you've identified the generalization and the evidence that supports it, decide whether the evidence offered is comprehensive and convincing. You may ask these types of questions:

- **Does the evidence relate to the claim?**
- **Does the evidence make sense?**
- **Is there enough evidence to prove the generalization?**
- **Does the evidence address all aspects of the claim and anticipate possible counterarguments?**

A writer's tone can also influence how seriously you take her or his arguments. If the issue is an important one, a reasonable or logical tone may be more persuasive than a lighthearted one, although passionate appeals to emotion sometimes sway an audience more effectively than reason alone.

Guided Practice: **Evaluating an argument.** Have students read the first two paragraphs of Sue Shellenbarger's essay "Diary of a Mad Blender" (p. 24). Ask students what the essay is about. [integrating work and personal life] On the chalkboard, draw a step chart like the one below, including the headers in the form of questions. Continue reading the essay with students. Ask students to tell you when Shellenbarger's position on integrating work and personal roles becomes clear. [Her claim or generalization about the topic does not crystallize until the last three paragraphs.] Have students state Shellenbarger's position in the form of a generalization, and write it on the chart. Then, have students go back and look for the specific evidence Shellenbarger uses to support her claim. Add the evidence that students cite to the chart. Next, ask students to identify the nature of the evidence presented and to consider whether or not it is comprehensive. Finally, ask students how

Step 3: **Is the evidence comprehensive and convincing? Why or why not?** [Possible responses: Since the evidence is based entirely on the personal experiences and values of the author, it will be convincing only to the extent that it corresponds with readers' own experiences and values. Since the evidence is all anecdotal, it is not comprehensive. Corroborating evidence from scientific studies, for instance, is lacking.]

Step 2: **What evidence is given to support the claim?** [Possible responses: Personal anecdotes show that following the advice of experts on using pockets of time more productively does result in the author getting more work done. Additional personal experiences—such as missing her son's accomplishment on the snowboard, forgetting an editor's request, losing the company of her daughter while watching television, and temporarily losing her creativity—show the personal price she pays for the gains.]

Step 1: **What is the author's claim?** [Possible response: Attempts to integrate work and one's personal life result in work gains and personal losses.]

they would describe the tone of the article and on what evidence they base their conclusion. [Possible response: The tone is light; the title and the use of images such as a "chronic stretcher of deadlines" and an office that "looks like a landfill" exemplify this tone.] Ask students why they think the author used this tone and how it affects the strength of her argument. [Possible response: The light tone makes the article amusing to read and the author easy to like and identify with. As a result, it is more likely that the reader will accept the author's personal experience as convincing evidence of her claim.]

Independent Practice: **Evaluating an argument.** Have pairs of students read a political column in a newspaper or magazine and evaluate the credibility of the commentator's argument by using a step chart. If more than one pair chooses an article on the same topic or issue, encourage students to compare and then discuss their evaluations. When they have finished, ask pairs to display their charts and share their evaluations with the class.

You may want to ask advanced students to write their own persuasive articles or essays, countering the arguments made in one of the opinion pieces that they evaluated. They could then submit their persuasive essay to the class for evaluation of their evidence and counterarguments.

Grade 8 Review Reading Standard 2.1
Compare and contrast the features and elements of consumer materials to gain meaning from documents (e.g., warranties, contracts, product information, instruction manuals).

Comparing Consumer Documents

Objective: To compare and contrast the features and elements of consumer materials to gain meaning from the documents.

Direct Teaching: Share the following ideas with students.

Imagine that it's Saturday, and your uncle drops you at the grocery store to buy some unscented soap while he goes to the appliance store to shop for a new refrigerator. You grab a three-pack of soap, check the label to be sure it's unscented, and quickly pay for your purchase. When you meet your uncle at the local appliance store, he is comparing the product information of two different models of refrigerators. You realize that buying a major appliance or a piece of electronic equipment is much more complicated than buying soap. It calls for a thorough check of all the information available on the product. Being an informed consumer is especially important today because the number of features on the latest appliances and electronic devices can be bewildering, and making a poor decision that leads to the purchase of an expensive product can be very costly.

One source of consumer information is the manufacturer of the product. Most companies supply printed or online product information that you can examine before making a purchase, as well as some sort of purchase agreement, guarantee, or warranty that protects you from defective workmanship for a period of time after your date of purchase. Service agreements for repairs (often offered by the retailer) are another option that requires careful scrutiny before signing. You don't want to agree to pay for services that you are unlikely to need. Also, manufacturers often provide instruction manuals or other technical directions that can help you decide if a particular model is the one that meets your needs. For example, by reading product information on a variety of refrigerators, your uncle can find out which models will fit in the space available in his kitchen and which have the storage capacity that he needs. If he were buying a power tool or computer component, he would be wise to evaluate the technical directions or instruction manual to see if these materials are clear and easy to read. A product, no matter how fine, is not very desirable if you can't figure out how to use it. Reading consumer documents helps you to make wise purchasing decisions.

Guided Practice: **Comparing consumer documents.** Use the following information to review the different types of consumer documents with students.

Product information: physical description of a product (including its components), as well as a description of what a tool, machine, and so on can do; also includes use requirements, such as power, memory (for computer software), size, capacity

Contract: information on the legal uses of the product

Warranty: guarantees a level of performance for a specified period of time and usually details what happens if the product fails during that period, including how it can be serviced and at whose expense

Instruction manual: instructions for using the product and its features; usually includes how to troubleshoot common problems

Technical directions: directions for how to install or assemble the product

Review the Aulsound extended service contract (p. 928). Discuss the various clauses, and have students identify what each one promises the consumer and under what conditions. Then, on the chalkboard, copy the excerpt from the limited warranty (p. 939I of the Annotated Teacher's Edition), or provide individual copies to students.

The Viberight Recorder

Limited Warranty Agreement

For a period of one (1) year from the date of purchase, Viberight warrants that the materials used in the product will be defect-free under normal use and service and will perform in accordance with the description in the product user's guide. The customer accepts all responsibility for validation and compatibility with other equipment used with the product. The product is sold as is with no warranty expressed or implied and has no return privilege unless it is deemed by Viberight to be defective.

Guide students as they compare and contrast features in the Viberight limited warranty agreement with those in the Aulsound extended service contract. Use a comparison chart like the one below to organize the differences that students identify between the two kinds of consumer documents. (Possible responses appear in brackets.)

Aulsound Extended Service Contract	Viberight Limited Warranty Agreement
Period Covered: [2 years with possibility of renewal]	**Period Covered:** [1 year]
Cost: [no cost to consumer for authorized repairs, but consumer must pay to maintain the insurance]	**Cost:** [no cost to consumer, but manufacturer has made no explicit promises to pay for any repairs]
Extent of Coverage: [parts and labor]	**Extent of Coverage:** [does not specify either parts or labor]
Conditions: [covers product failures during normal use; repairs must be done by authorized service associates]	**Conditions:** [manufacturer reserves right to judge whether a product is defective and whether or not to pay for its repair]

When students have finished their comparisons, lead a discussion about which plan offers consumers the best protection on their purchase: the Viberight limited warranty agreement or the Aulsound extended service contract. Make sure students understand that a service contract is a type of insurance that consumers must pay for; a warranty merely states what, if any, level of performance the manufacturer is prepared to guarantee and what, if anything, it will do if the product fails to perform as promised. Remind students to cite specific clauses from both documents to support their conclusions. [Possible response: The Viberight limited warranty agreement guarantees the consumer next to nothing but also costs the consumer nothing; the Aulsound extended service contract offers no-cost repairs when needed but requires consumers to pay to maintain the insurance.]

Independent Practice: **Comparing product features.** As homework, students should compare the features of two products, such as two brands or models of cameras, calculators, or portable CD players. Have them base their comparisons on information obtained from warranties; instruction manuals; and product information from manufacturers, retailers, or consumer advocacy organizations. Tell students that they can also obtain product information from local appliance, electronics, or department stores. Other sources of information may include the Internet and print reviews of new products in special-interest magazines that focus on consumer goods, such as cars, computer technology, or photography. Encourage students to make a chart similar to the one used in the Guided Practice to organize their points of comparison.

During a follow-up discussion, have students discuss what they discovered by making the comparison charts and how this type of information could help them make wise purchases and guide them to use products successfully after their purchase.

Reading Standard 3.1
Articulate the relationship between the expressed purposes and the characteristics of different forms of dramatic literature (e.g., comedy, tragedy, drama, dramatic monologue).

Analyzing Dramatic Literature

Objective: To articulate the relationship between the expressed purposes and the characteristics of tragedy and comedy.

Direct Teaching: Share the following ideas with students.

Think about the plays you have seen or read. What emotions did they stir up in you? Did they make you laugh or cry? Did they make you reflect on the meaning of life? Plays can produce a variety of responses because playwrights explore the range of human emotions. Like movies, plays come in a variety of types, which have different characteristics, depending on the effect that the playwright wishes to have on the audience. The author of a comedy, for example, may wish to emphasize that characters and societies can overcome obstacles and be restored to happiness and good order. In other words, things turn out all right in the end. (Comedies, by the way, don't have to make us laugh, although they often do.) The author of a tragedy, on the other hand, might want to remind us that individuals—even those with great gifts and high social standing—can make fateful choices that destroy themselves and others. Plays consist mostly of dialogue, or conversation between characters, but dramatists also have unique ways of revealing the innermost feelings of their characters. These include the soliloquy (when a character alone onstage speaks directly to the audience) and the aside (when a character turns to the audience or to another character and says something that the other characters onstage cannot hear). Understanding these characteristics will enrich your appreciation for reading dramatic literature and for seeing it performed.

Guided Practice: Analyzing the characteristics of tragedy. Discuss with students the characteristics and purposes of comedy and tragedy. You may want to direct them to the Handbook of Literary Terms (p. 979). Then, have students review the characters and plot of *The Tragedy of Julius Caesar* (p. 754). Point out that the play is a Shakespearean tragedy, a type of drama in which the main character or characters suffer great misfortune, often death, both due to character flaws and the workings of fate or chance. Copy the concept web below on the chalkboard. Discuss each of the elements of tragedy shown on the web. Then, work with students to give examples of each element from *Julius Caesar.* (Possible responses appear in brackets.)

You may want to tell students that there is some disagreement about who is the central character or tragic hero of *Julius Caesar:* Caesar or Brutus. Most critics agree that Brutus, despite the title, is the play's central focus and its true tragic hero.

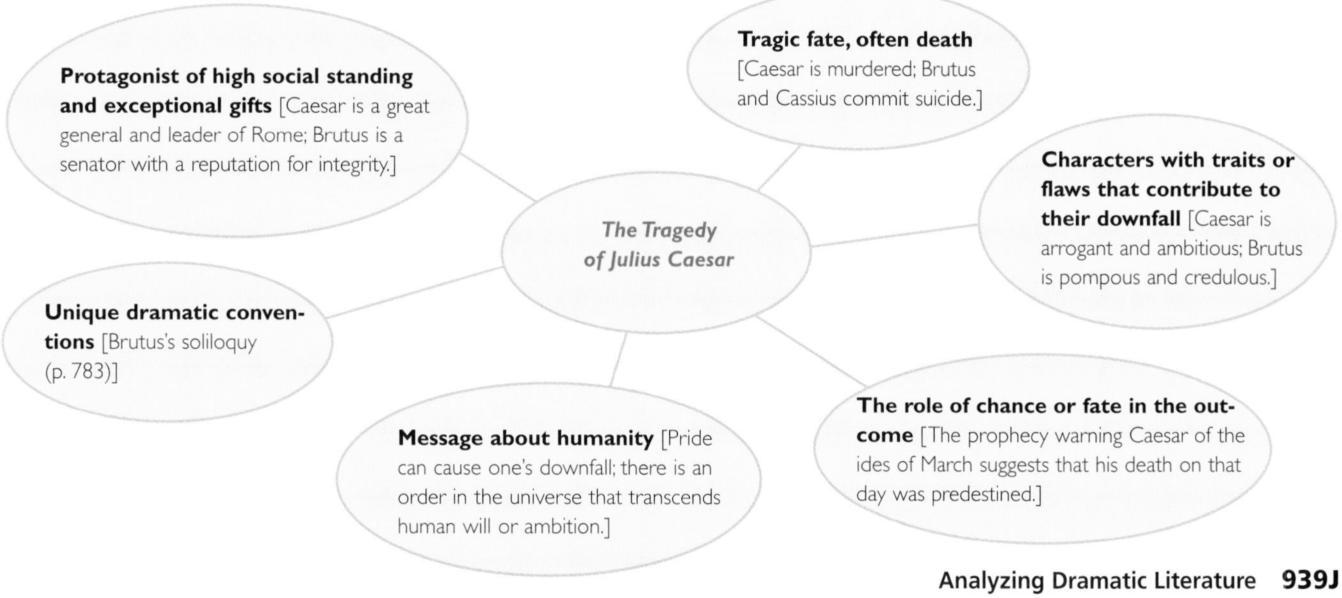

Independent Practice: Analyzing the characteristics of comedy. Have students complete a similar web for a comedy that they have read, seen, or performed. They may want to analyze Chekhov's *The Brute,* (p. 724). On the chalkboard, draw a web like the one below, or make copies you can distribute to students. (Possible responses appear in brackets.) Review the elements of comedy with students. Then, have students complete the web as homework. Follow up with a classroom discussion, comparing and contrasting the plays the students analyzed.

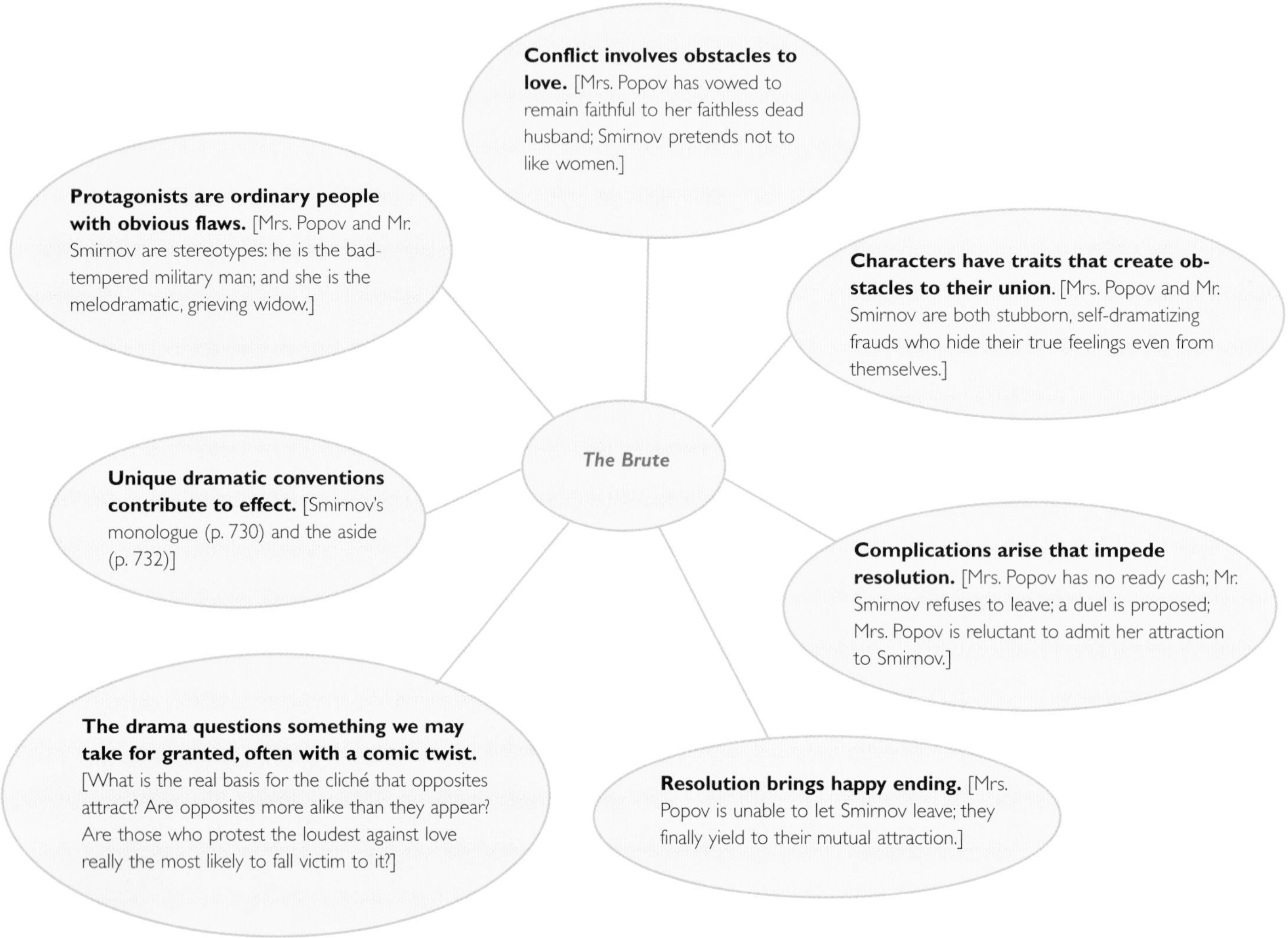

Reading Standard 3.4 Determine characters' traits by what the characters say about themselves in narration, dialogue, dramatic monologue, and soliloquy

Character Traits

Objective: To determine characters' traits by what the characters say about themselves in narration and dialogue.

Direct Teaching: Share the following ideas with students.

Writers want you to get to know the characters they create and to form opinions about them. That is why writers sometimes use narration to tell you directly what a character is like. More often, authors reveal a character's traits or qualities indirectly by showing the character thinking, feeling, talking, and doing things. Readers interpret these clues and figure out what they tell about the character's traits. Analyzing dialogue, or conversation between characters, is a particularly effective way to learn about a character because it provides an opportunity not only to see how that character speaks and behaves toward others but also how others see that character.

Guided Practice: **Charting character traits.** Make sure students understand the differences between direct and indirect characterization and between narration and dialogue. If necessary, provide examples of each. Then, have students read the first three paragraphs of "The Pedestrian" (p. 46), looking for examples of indirect characterization. On the chalkboard, copy the chart on the right and ask students to identify any information the narrator provides about what Leonard Mead thinks, does, or says. Write students' responses on the chart and then help them figure out what each clue implies about Leonard Mead's character traits. (Possible responses appear in brackets.)

Next, have students read the dialogue between Leonard Mead and the police (or the automated police car) on pp. 49–51. As they read, encourage students to jot down some exact quotations from the dialogue that give clues to Mead's character traits. Write some of these responses on the chart, and discuss what each piece of dialogue suggests about Mead's character. Write students' inferences in the second column. Remind them that what Mead says is just one set of clues to his character. What he *does* is also very important, and even what he *doesn't* say or do sheds light on his personality. End with a general class discussion of Leonard Mead's character, based on students' work interpreting traits from clues in the text.

Character Trait in Narration	Character Trait Implied
[Leonard Mead likes to walk outside on wintry nights through deserted streets.]	[adventurous; hardy]
[He makes his own decisions on which way to walk, striding purposefully.]	[independent; decisive]
[He is used to being alone but sometimes looks into the windows of homes.]	[lonely; reflective]
Character-Trait Clues in Dialogue	**Character Trait Implied**
["Put up your hands!" "But—" he said.]	[reluctantly compliant]
["Not married"; "Nobody wanted me."]	[lonely; sad; without illusions]
["Get in." "I protest!"]	[defiant; courageous]

Independent Practice: **Determining character traits.** Have pairs of students choose another short story they have read either in *Holt Literature and Language Arts* or in some other source. Ask them to review the story and complete a character-trait chart for the main character, like the one used in the Guided Practice. Before students begin, remind them to look for revealing clues to the main character's traits in both narration and dialogue. Remind students that in some stories the main character is also the narrator. In those cases, what the character reveals about himself or herself in the narration has to be evaluated in light of other evidence, including how other characters view the narrator and what the narrator actually does. After completing their charts, ask pairs to develop a short paragraph, describing their character's traits and explaining why they do or do not admire the character.

Reading Standard 3.5
Compare works that express a universal theme and provide evidence to support the ideas expressed in each work.

Universal Themes

Objective: To compare works that express a universal theme and to provide evidence to support the ideas expressed in each work.

Direct Teaching: Share the following ideas with students.

The best writers are interested in exploring issues and questions that concern us all. They explore, for example, what true friendship is, how love can change a person's life, or how the loss of something or someone special can profoundly affect us. These subjects have universal interest because people of all ages, times, and cultures face similar challenges and have similar desires and limitations. The subject of a work of literature, however, is not its theme. The theme is the particular slant the writer takes on the subject, and it can usually be expressed with a theme statement. The theme statement is a generalization that sums up the writer's "take," or slant, on the subject. For example, the theme of a story on the subject of loss could be summarized in this theme statement: "Denying the importance of what we've lost doesn't really make us feel any better." Another writer may offer a similar or different take on the same subject. In order to discover the theme of a literary work, readers must consider all its elements and how they interact. Focusing on how the main character faces conflict and how he or she changes over the course of the story can be particularly helpful in getting insight into the theme.

Guided Practice: **Comparing universal themes.** Ask students to read "Catch the Moon" (p. 233) and "The Bass, the River, and Sheila Mant" (p. 243). Draw on the chalkboard a flowchart like the one below. After students have finished reading, discuss with them the common subject that both stories address. (Possible responses appear in brackets.) Guide them as they determine which slant each writer takes on the subject, noting similarities and differences in the writers' approaches. Help students to shape their insights into a statement of a universal theme that could apply to both stories, and add this theme statement to the chart. Then, have students work together to identify an important difference in the two writers' treatments of the universal theme. Make sure students cite specific evidence from the stories, placing emphasis on how each character changes by the end of the story.

Common Subject: [the effects of romantic attraction]

Universal Theme: [Under the powerful influence of romantic attraction, people behave in surprising or uncharacteristic ways.]

Difference: [Luis in "Catch the Moon" is softened and humanized by his attraction to Naomi; the feelings she awakens in him turn him in a more positive direction.]

Difference: [The narrator of "The Bass, the River, and Sheila Mant" betrays himself and his own values under the influence of a powerful attraction. As a result of his encounter with Sheila Mant, the narrator grows in understanding and acceptance of himself.]

Independent Practice: Comparing universal themes. After students have completed their group work, ask them to use their comparison charts to write brief essays, explaining which writer they think is more effective in expressing his or her take on the effects of romantic attraction. Remind students that their analyses should consider elements of character, setting, conflict, and resolution. Remind them also that you are not asking them which variation on the common theme they agree with but which author they think created the more convincing characters and plot.

As an alternative, you may want to ask advanced students to choose and compare two other works—from their textbook or from another source—that share a universal theme. Encourage them to use a flowchart to organize their ideas.

Reading Standard 3.7 Recognize and understand the significance of various literary devices, including figurative language, imagery, allegory, and symbolism, and explain their appeal.

Literary Devices

Objective: To recognize and understand the significance of various literary devices, including imagery and symbolism, and explain their appeal.

Direct Teaching: Share the following information with students.

Anyone can retell a simple series of events or give a straightforward description of something they have seen or heard. What sets gifted writers apart, however, is their ability to go beyond the obvious and excite readers with new sensations, ideas, and feelings. (In Saki's "The Storyteller," the ability to excite is what makes the bachelor's tale so effective.) Writers can achieve amazing effects with words alone, making use of a variety of literary devices, including imagery and symbolism. Imagery is the use of words to make vivid sense impressions on readers' imaginations. Imagery makes it possible for readers to see, hear, smell, and feel what the writer wants them to experience. Symbols are people, places, events, and objects that have meaning in and of themselves but also represent larger ideas. For example, the character of Job in the Bible story is both an individual who lives in a particular time and place and a symbol, or representation, of the suffering of humanity. Symbols and imagery add richness to a text and help readers make connections with their own experience, visualize the events and characters being presented, and see familiar things in new ways.

Guided Practice: **Interpreting symbols.** Have students read the excerpt from "Hands: For Mother's Day" (p. 84). On the chalkboard, draw a chart like the one below. Ask students to think about Giovanni's quilt as a symbol, an object that has concrete meaning in this literary work as well as more abstract or broader significance. Begin by asking students to identify some of the concrete qualities of this quilt. After you have written these in the first column of the chart, lead students in a discussion of what these concrete qualities suggest about the quilt's meaning. Add students' ideas to the chart. (Possible responses appear in brackets.) Then, have students discuss how the symbol of the quilt helped them reach a deeper understanding of the lives of the women Giovanni is writing about.

Symbol: Quilt	
Concrete Qualities	**Abstract Meanings**
[blanket]	[warmth, security]
[quaint museum piece]	[tradition, beauty]
[scraps and leftovers from a richer culture]	[the virtues of simplicity and "making do"]
[difficult job]	[industry, creativity, self-sufficiency]
[lovable and worthwhile]	[true value]

Independent Practice: Evaluating imagery and symbolism. Have students review "The Storyteller" (p. 154). Remind them that in the story, a bachelor quiets three irksome children with a story about the rewards of "goodness." Ask students to read the story the bachelor tells, which begins with the last paragraph on p. 156. Have small groups of students choose examples of vivid imagery that excites the children's imagination. [the descriptions of the park and of the wolf] Then, have them identify people, places, and objects that have symbolic significance. [the pigs, the park, the white pinafore, the clinking medals] Have the groups discuss the effects of the images and symbols they identify, using charts to help them organize their ideas. Finally, lead a class discussion on why the bachelor's story is so much more interesting than the story the aunt tells.

Reading Standard 3.9 Explain how voice, persona, and the choice of a narrator affect characterization and the tone, plot, and credibility of a text.

Choice of Narrator

Objective: To explain how voice, persona, and the choice of a narrator affect the tone, plot, and credibility of a text.

Direct Teaching: Share the following ideas with students.

The voice that tells the story in a literary work is called the narrator. This narrative voice is not the voice of the author per se but of a persona, or character, created by the author to tell the story. This narrator tells the story from a particular point of view, or vantage point, which the author chooses. Narrators can tell stories from the perspective of someone removed from the action. Such narrators refer to the characters in the third person, by name or as "he" or "she." These narrators can be omniscient (all-knowing) or limited in what they know. Omniscient narrators have a godlike vantage point. They see and know what is happening in all the characters' minds and understand all the aspects of the story. Generally, third-person-limited narrators are only aware of the thoughts and feelings of one character. They describe only what that one character knows, observes, or believes to be true. The other characters in the story are seen from their perspective only.

A writer can also create a narrator who tells the story from a singular point of view, using the pronoun *I*. These first-person narrators are usually characters in the story, and everything they describe about the action and the other characters is filtered through their perspective. Therefore, readers must make judgments about a first-person narrator's credibility or reliability.

Obviously, the writer's choice of narrator affects which events will be included in a story and the tone, or attitude, with which those events will be told. Omniscient narration tends toward a more objective, or impersonal, tone, while first-person narration is generally more subjective, or personal.

Guided Practice: **Analyzing point of view, tone, and plot.** Review with students the differences between omniscient, third-person-limited, and first-person narration, or point of view. You may want to help them by telling a simple story, such as an account of a soccer game, from two points of view. First, recount the game from an omniscient narrator's point of view and then from a first-person (or insider's) point of view—from that of a team member, for example. When you are finished, ask students to talk about how the tone and coverage of the events changed when you switched from an omniscient to a first-person narrator.

Next, have students read "Contents of the Dead Man's Pocket" (p. 4). On the chalkboard, draw a web like the one on p. 939R. Ask students to identify the point of view of the story and cite examples from the text that support their conclusion. Write their responses on the chalkboard. (Possible responses appear in brackets.) Students will probably have little trouble identifying the third-person narrator, but they will need to read the whole story to be sure that the narration is limited to Tom's experience. The strongest evidence for the third-person-limited point of view is that we are told nothing about Tom's wife except what he knows, sees, or hears.

After students have identified textual clues indicating third-person-limited narration, ask them how the tone of the story might have differed had it been told from the first-person point of view. [Possible responses: It might have been more emotional and less controlled if Tom, as the first-person narrator, spoke directly to the reader from his ledge outside his high-rise apartment; although it might seem more immediate and scarier, the first-person narrator might lessen the suspense, since the reader might assume he lives to tell the story.]

Point of View
[third-person limited]
Textual Clues
[The pronouns *he* and *she* and proper nouns, such as *Tom,* are used to refer to the characters; only the inner life of and the events experienced by one character, Tom, are presented.]

Tone
[detached, objective, precise]
Textual Clues
[Example: "Very slowly, sliding his forehead down the trough of the brick corner and bending his knees, he lowered his body toward the paper lying between his outstretched feet." (p. 9)]

"Contents of the Dead Man's Pocket"

Plot Coverage
[limited to Tom's feelings and the events he experiences]
Textual Clues
[Nothing is told of the wife's feelings or of what happens to her after she leaves the apartment.]

Independent Practice: **Evaluating the choice of narrator.** Have students choose another short story from *Holt Literature and Language Arts* or from a collection of stories they have at home or can borrow from the library. Urge them to organize their thinking about the author's choice of narrator on a web like the one used for the Guided Practice. Then, have them use their webs to write a short essay, explaining how the author's choice of narrator affects the work's tone and its plot. Encourage students to also evaluate the credibility of the narrator, determining if he or she is presented by the author as generally credible or not. Remind students to cite specific examples from the text to support their conclusions.

Reading Standard 3.11
Evaluate the aesthetic qualities of style, including the impact of diction and figurative language on tone, mood, and theme, using the terminology of literary criticism. (Aesthetic approach)

Author's Style

Objective: To evaluate the aesthetic qualities of style, including the impact of diction and figurative language on tone and mood.

Direct Teaching: Share the following information with students.

Literary critics often use terms such as diction, figurative language, tone, and mood in discussing a writer's style. If you understand these terms, you will be better prepared to read literary criticism and to write your own.

Style is the distinctive manner in which writers present their ideas—their way with words. One of the principal ways that writers create a style is through their diction, their choice of words. For example, a writer can choose to use a simple, plain word such as *rich* or a more ornate one like *opulent,* as Lisa Fugard does on p. 567 of "Night Calls." Writers can also choose between words that are formal or informal, modern or old-fashioned, factual or fanciful—to name just a few of the many choices open to them. Writers often choose words based on their connotations—that is, on the emotions, images, and ideas associated with the words. On p. 567 of "Night Calls," the author chooses the word *adamant* rather than *firm* to describe Aunt Annette's attitude about where the narrator should live after her mother's death. By choosing the word *adamant,* with its connotations of solidity and immovability, the writer is conveying not just that the aunt has made up her mind but also that she is as set and unshakable in her conviction as a stone.

Other important components of style include the use of figurative comparisons and sensory language. Figurative comparisons make connections between things or experiences that seem at first to be utterly unlike yet turn out to have unexpected similarities or affinities. The most common forms of these comparisons are similes and metaphors. Sensory language appeals to one of the five senses, and writers use it to help readers see, hear, smell, touch, and feel what the characters are experiencing.

The choice of words affects the tone, the attitude the writer takes toward the subject, and the mood, the feeling created in the reader. Often, these two are very similar. As you read, pay careful attention to the writer's word choices and think about how those particular choices affect the tone and mood of the work as a whole. Ask yourself questions like the following items:

- **Are most of the words simple or elaborate, formal or informal, logical or emotional?**
- **What attitude toward the characters and the subject matter do the word choices convey?**
- **What is the emotional effect of the words the writer chooses?**
- **Do the words create strong sensory images?**
- **Does the writer use original and imaginative comparisons that give the work a unique style or personal flair?**

Guided Practice: Diction, sensory language, and figurative comparisons. Ask students to read the story "Night Calls" (p. 564). Then, read the following passages aloud to students and discuss with them the word choices accented in boldface. Help them to identify the words with strong connotations and the examples of sensory language and figurative comparisons. (Possible responses appear in brackets.) Then, lead them in a discussion of how these word choices affect the overall feel or mood of the passage.

"Suddenly I was filled with the smell of him: Borkum Riff **tobacco, sweat, the sweet odor** [sensory language appealing to sense of smell] of **cheap** [connotative word suggesting the father's meager, deprived way of living] Cape brandy. Filled with his secrets, I felt **like a thief** [simile comparing narrator's secretive observation of her father to stealing] and moved a little closer to the window." (p. 566) [Overall effect: sadness, shame, longing.]

"The heron's **neck was liquid** [metaphor] in the **moonlight, curving and swaying** [sensory language appealing to senses of sight and touch], at times **seeming to entwine my father** [figurative comparison]. Its beak glinted **like a dagger** [simile]. (p. 571)
[Overall effect: poignant, painful beauty; tortured love.]

Next, draw on the chalkboard a chart like the one below and ask students to make a copy for themselves. Then, have student pairs work together to find additional examples from "Night Calls" of Fugard's distinctive style of diction. Have the pairs fill in their charts and then share their examples with the rest of the class. (The first row in the chart has been filled in with additional examples of unique diction from the story.) Finally, work with the whole class to discuss the effect of Fugard's word choices on the tone and mood of the story as a whole. [The overall mood and tone is one of tender sadness, loss, and unexpressed love.]

Independent Practice: Comparing word choice, tone, and mood. As homework students might read the magazine article "Call of the Wild—Save Us!" (p. 577) or another nonfiction article of their choice. Have students write a short essay comparing and contrasting the author's style in the nonfiction piece with Lisa Fugard's in "Night Calls." Have them begin by identifying the purpose of each work. They should then focus primarily on the word choice, looking first in the nonfiction article for the kinds of language they identified as characteristic of "Night Calls." If students choose to analyze "Call of the Wild—Save Us!" they will quickly discover that there is very little connotative, figurative, or sensory language in the article. On the contrary, the language is generally denotative, literal, and precise. The diction is meant to appeal to reason and logic rather than to emotion and imagination. Remind students to include specific examples from both works to illustrate their points and to conclude by comparing and contrasting the overall style and effects of the two works.

Advanced students may want to experiment with creating a writing style of their own. Suggest that they write a paragraph or two on an endangered species. Urge them to be clear about the purpose of their writing (to persuade, describe, inspire, move, or entertain, for example) and to decide what tone and mood they wish to create. Then they can carefully choose their words to achieve the purpose and effects they desire.

Connotative Words	Sensory Language	Figurative Comparisons
["I'd hear my father *pacing*." (p. 571)]	["water lilies from the *dappled* pools" (p. 571)]	["lifting its feet up *like wet handkerchiefs*" (p. 570)]

Grade 8 Review Reading Standard 3.7 Analyze a work of literature, showing how it reflects the heritage, traditions, attitudes, and beliefs of its author. (Biographical approach)

Biographical Approach

Objective: To analyze a work of literature, showing how it reflects the heritage, traditions, attitudes, and beliefs of its author.

Direct Teaching: Share the following ideas with students.

One way of deepening your understanding of what you read is to recognize the connections that exist between writers' lives and what they write. Good writers draw from their own knowledge, experiences, and interests. Their writing reflects what they understand and believe about the world and the people in it. Biographical factors that can influence a writer's work include cultural or religious background, ethnic or racial heritage, education, work, hobbies, and personal experiences of all kinds. A writer born in India, for example, would probably write differently about his or her native land than a person who spent time there as a tourist. A writer with experience working as a police officer would bring a different perspective and vocabulary to a work of crime fiction than would someone who had no firsthand experience with law enforcement. Racial discrimination, poverty, or the discovery of a special interest or talent are only some examples of personal experiences that can have a shaping influence on a writer's subject matter and themes. Because these connections between an author's life and work can be so revealing, it is sometimes helpful to get some biographical information about an author before reading a literary work and to look for connections during and after your reading.

Guided Practice: Connecting an author's life and work. Have students read the story "Everyday Use" (p. 76), as well as the Meet the Writer feature (p. 83) and the interview with Alice Walker (p. 88). Then, as you read aloud the following passages from "Everyday Use," have students discuss how each passage reflects what they learned from the biographical sketch and the interview with Walker. Urge them to consider Walker's heritage, experience, attitudes, and beliefs. (Possible responses appear in brackets.)

- **"Maggie will be nervous until after her sister goes: She will stand hopelessly in corners, homely and ashamed of the burn scars down her arms and legs. . . ."**
  [This reflects Walker's own childhood experience of traumatic injury. She was blinded in one eye by a shot from a BB gun and was very shy and solitary as a result.]

- **"We raised the money . . . to send her to Augusta to school. She used to read to us without pity, forcing words, lies, other folks' habits, whole lives upon us two. . . ."**
  [This reflects Walker's own scholarship, education, and childhood love of reading and writing.]

- **"'No, Mama,' she says. 'Not "Dee," Wangero Leewanika Kemanjo!'"**
  [This reflects Walker's and other African Americans' interest in their African ethnic heritage, an interest that was particularly intense in the 1960s and 1970s, when the story is set.]

- **"'You was named after your aunt Dicie,' I said. . . . We called her 'Big Dee' after Dee was born."**
  [This reflects the importance to Walker of her female forebears, of the cultural heritage that came down from her mother and grandmothers.]

- **"'She can always make some more,' I said. 'Maggie knows how to quilt.'"**
  [This reflects Walker's belief, expressed in the interview, that making a quilt is more meaningful than collecting or displaying it.]

After you have discussed the individual passages with students, lead them in a general discussion of the connections between Alice Walker's life and values and her story "Everyday Use." As students make connections, summarize them on a chart like the one on the following page.

Alice Walker	"Everyday Use"
[grew up poor in the rural segregated South]	[Mama's family comes from same background.]
[blinded in one eye]	[Maggie has burn scars.]
[shy and self-conscious]	[Maggie is quiet and shy.]
[attended college in Atlanta and became a writer]	[Dee went away to school, left town, and "made it."]
[Women in her family give her sense of self.]	[A strong woman is at the center of the story.]
[Quilt-making is part of her heritage]	[Old quilts are central to story.]
[made quilts from her own clothes to preserve important memories]	[Memories of Grandma are attached to story quilts.]
[believes it's important to create own quilt and use it]	[Mama gives quilts to Maggie since, unlike Dee, she will use them.]

Independent Practice: **Connecting life and work.** Ask students to read "Lamb to the Slaughter" (p. 316), and the Meet the Writer feature (p. 325) on Roald Dahl that follows it. After students have finished reading, point out (in the middle of the first column on p. 325) where Dahl says that boarding schools were "just rules, rules and still more rules that had to be obeyed." Ask students how they think this statement relates to Dahl's story. Then, for homework, have students write an essay, analyzing the connections between the quotations from Dahl in the biographical sketch and the story. For instance, do they consider "Lamb to the Slaughter" one of Dahl's more realistic stories or one of his more fantastic stories? What about this story might give the writer a sense of "absolute freedom"? Encourage students to read other short stories by Dahl and to find out more about his life. They can use this information to broaden their essays, making more connections between Dahl's life and his literary work.

Resource Center

Introduction to Reading Matters

Why Reading Matters

I read good enough. I mean, most of the time I don't know the answers to the questions that are at the end of the chapter like in my science book or even at the end of stories we read in English, but that's okay, because those questions are hard. Right? Anyway, how are those questions going to help me in real life, you know, when I'm out of school and working?

—Collin, grade 10

Collin takes driver's ed, plays basketball, works at a bagel shop on weekends, and struggles in school. He'd like to make better grades, but because he doesn't read well, he has problems doing his homework and studying for tests. But when you ask (as I did) how he reads, he says, "Good enough." It's good enough for him because he doesn't see the connection between being able to read well and doing well in school and in the job he'll someday have as an adult.

He asks how answering the questions in his social studies, science, and literature books is going to help him in "real life." Well, being able to answer questions in school helps in two ways. First, answering questions is a quick way to show yourself and your teachers what you understand about content. Second, since most of the questions you answer either force you to recall specific information or push you to figure out more complex problems, answering questions can help you become a better thinker. Being a better thinker is helpful in any job.

It all starts with reading. If you can't read the stories and essays in your textbooks or the questions or the tests, then all sorts of negative things begin to happen. That's because no matter where you live, no matter what you do, you are surrounded by print—from textbooks, e-mail messages, and Web pages to how-to instruction manuals and magazines. In a literate society, reading is critical.

The following section is designed to help you with reading. In it you'll find strategies that will help you better comprehend the texts you read. Take some time right now to flip through the pages of this section. You'll see that each lesson is brief—so you can learn a lot in a little bit of time. You can return to this section as often as you need to. Use the strategies suggested here with the selections in this book. Then, try them as you read other texts. The more you think about the topics covered in this section and practice what's suggested here, the better you'll be at reading.

That's important because, after all, *reading matters.*

—Kylene Beers

Using Reading Matters

Reading Matters contains practical, easy-to-use lessons and strategies designed to improve students' reading comprehension and reading rate. Think of this section as a handbook that students can use throughout the year—on their own, with a partner, or with the class as a whole. Like any handbook, Reading Matters can be read in any order, accessed at any point, and referred to frequently.

Some of your students may not require all of the instruction in these lessons, but most will benefit from the reading tips and strategies. Students can apply these strategies to the selections in *Holt Literature and Language Arts* and to any other literary and informational texts they encounter. Each lesson teaches a set of skills that students can use throughout their lives.

Using Reading Matters with the Student Edition

Introduce students to Reading Matters early in the school year.

- Preview the section with students, noting the lesson content, headings, and boxes.
- Introduce each lesson in class and model each reading strategy.
- Emphasize that these lessons and strategies can help students with both literary and informational texts.
- Advise students that in order to be a proficient reader, they must acquire skills that will enable them to understand difficult texts.

Throughout the year, you might use a particular reading strategy as preteaching instruction for a selection or chapter. Or you may choose to target only those students who need remediation. You can also use strategy lessons for reteaching and review.

Reading Up Close

To make sure that students know how to use Reading Matters, review the Reading Up Close box. Ask a volunteer to read aloud each bulleted item. Then, stop to discuss questions students may have. Point out to students that Reading Matters is a resource that they can use on their own. Its purpose is simply to introduce strategies that will help them improve their reading skills.

A Reading Log

You might ask students to dedicate a section of their notebook for maintaining a reading log. Ask them to take brief notes about the experiences of applying the strategies described in Reading Matters. Ask students to record whether the strategies improved both their comprehension and reading rate. Explain that by looking over the year's entries, they should be able to chart their progress toward becoming more proficient readers.

Reading Matters

When the Text Is Tough

Remember the reading you did back in first, second, and third grades? Big print. Short texts. Easy words. Now in high school, however, the texts you read are often filled with small print, long chapters, and complicated plots or topics. Also, you now find yourself reading a variety of material—from your driver's-ed handbook to college applications, from job applications to income-tax forms, from e-mail to e-zines, from classics to comics, from textbooks to checkbooks.

Doing something every day that you find difficult and tedious isn't much fun—and that includes reading. So, this section of this book is designed for you, to show you what to do when the text gets tough. Let's begin by looking at some *reading* matters.

READING UP CLOSE

How to Use This Section

- **This section is for you.** Turn to it whenever you need to remind yourself about what to do when the text gets tough. Don't wait for your teacher to assign this section for you to read. It's your handbook. Use it.
- **Read the sections that you need.** You don't have to read every word. Skim the headings, and find the information you need.
- **Use this information for help with reading for other classes,** not just for the reading you do in this book.
- **Don't be afraid to re-read the information you find in Reading Matters.** The best readers constantly re-read information.
- **If you need more help, then check the index.** The index will direct you to other pages in this book with information on reading skills and strategies.

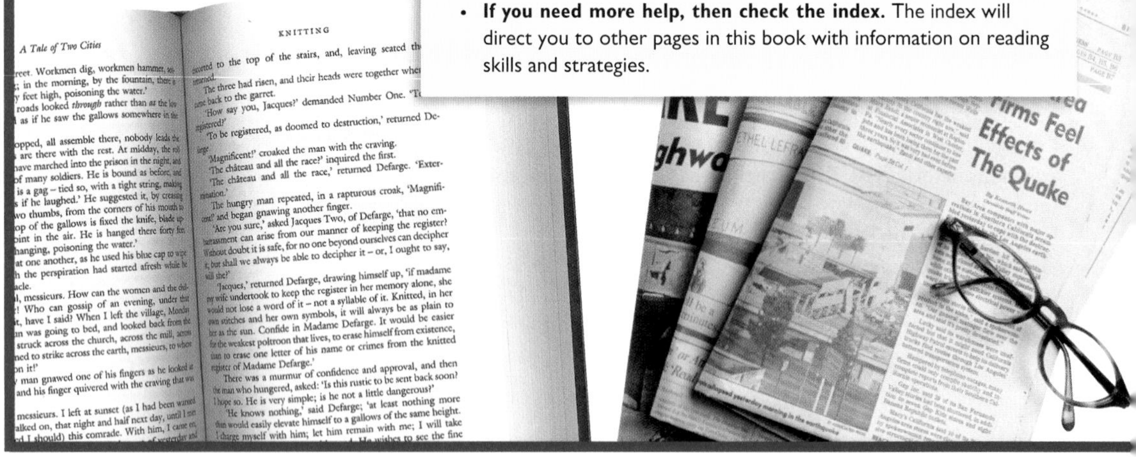

Improving Your Comprehension

Have you seen the reruns of an old weekly television show called *Lost in Space*? Perhaps you saw the more recent movie version of it? If so, you probably remember the robot that constantly tried to warn the young boy, Will Robinson, when danger was near by waving his robot arms and announcing loudly, "Danger approaching, Will Robinson!" Then Will would look up from whatever he was doing, notice whatever evil was moments away, and take action. But until the robot warned him, Will would ignore all warning signs that danger was at hand.

Wouldn't it be nice if something would warn us as we were about to enter a dangerous area when we were reading—a part of the text that we might not understand? Perhaps our own little robots could pop up in books, saying, "Danger, reader! Misunderstandings approaching!" Then we'd know to slow down, pay attention, and carefully study the text we were reading.

Actually those signs do appear, but not as arm-waving robots in the margins of books. Instead, the signs appear in our minds as we are reading. However, unless we are paying attention, we often read on past them, not noticing the warnings they offer. What we need to do is learn to recognize the danger signs so that like Will Robinson, we will know when to look up and take action.

READING UP CLOSE

▸ Looking for the Danger Signs

Study each of the signs to the right, and decide what type of danger each could signify when you read. You might want to copy these signs onto stick-on notes to put on your texts as you read.

Improving Your Comprehension

This lesson contains strategies that students can use to improve their comprehension of both literary and informational texts.

Reading Up Close

Have students speculate on what the danger signs might signal on the road to understanding and completing a text.

Possible Responses

1. A fork-in-the-road sign might mark the point in a text where the reader recognizes that the story's plot, or the writer's argument, might take two or more paths.
2. A dead-end sign might indicate a point at which the reader doesn't understand the text.
3. A winding-road sign might indicate that the text requires special attention.
4. The no-U-turn sign might indicate a point where the reader resists the temptation to re-read but continues with the hope of better understanding the text after completing it.
5. A yield sign might indicate a point where the reader has to change the predictions that were made earlier in the text.
6. A U-turn sign might indicate a point in the text where the reader has to re-read a passage to improve comprehension.
7. A falling-rocks sign might indicate a part of the text that contains difficult vocabulary words or complex ideas.
8. A stop sign might indicate the point where the reader pauses to note questions.
9. The people-working sign might indicate a point where the writer needs to clarify some aspect of the text.
10. The railroad-crossing sign might indicate a point in the text that requires re-reading and rewording (p. 948).

Using This Lesson

When students choose novels to read for pleasure, they select ones with characters and plots that interest them. As a result, students stay focused and engaged as they read. The stories in the Student Edition have been chosen both for their literary quality and with the interests of student readers in mind. However, students will still find some of the literary selections difficult to follow and will have difficulty focusing and staying engaged by the text.

Many students' attention wanders while reading informational texts, such as textbook, newspaper, magazine, or articles on the Internet. So, you might find it helpful to use this lesson before students read the first set of informational materials in Chapter 1.

Reading Up Close

Point out that "When I read," is a broad, general clause encompassing all types of reading. Students will quickly realize that their responses will vary according to the type of text they are reading. You might ask students to complete this survey with a specific kind of text in mind—"When I read a science textbook," for instance, or "When I read poetry . . ." Even when the genre is made more specific, "When I read" is a broad generalization that doesn't necessarily apply to all texts of a particular genre. Students find some poems easy to read and some difficult.

Focus on the Tips

Take time in class to explain the tips for staying focused. Tip 1 helps students: become active readers; monitor their reading, pausing to ask themselves questions about the text; and answer their own questions. Tip 2 encourages them to take notes as they read. Both strategies apply to literary and informational texts.

Danger Sign 1

You can't remember what you read.

This happens to all readers occasionally. You read something, and your attention wanders for a moment, but your eyes don't quit moving from word to word. In a few minutes you realize you are several pages beyond the last point where you can remember thinking about what you were reading. Then you know you need to back up and start over.

Forgetting what you've read is a danger sign only if it happens to you frequently. If you constantly complete a reading assignment but don't remember anything that you've been reading, then you probably are in the habit of letting your mind focus on something else while your eyes are focusing on the words. That's a habit you need to break.

READING UP CLOSE

Measure Your Attention Quotient

Take the following survey to see what your attention quotient is. The lower the score, the less attention you pay to what you are reading.

When I read, I . . .

1. let my mind wander
- **a.** most of the time
- **b.** sometimes
- **c.** almost never

2. forget what I'm reading
- **a.** most of the time
- **b.** sometimes
- **c.** almost never

3. get confused and stay confused
- **a.** most of the time
- **b.** sometimes
- **c.** almost never

4. discover I've turned lots of pages and don't have a clue as to what I've read
- **a.** most of the time
- **b.** sometimes
- **c.** almost never

5. rarely finish whatever I'm supposed to be reading
- **a.** most of the time
- **b.** sometimes
- **c.** almost never

Tips for Staying Focused

1. Don't read from the beginning of the assignment to the end without pausing. Set up checkpoints for yourself, either every few pages or every five minutes. At those checkpoints, stop reading and ask yourself some basic questions—"What's happening now? What do I not understand?"
2. As you read, keep paper and pen close by. Take notes as you read, in particular jotting down questions you have about what confuses you, interests you, or perhaps even surprises you.

Danger Sign 2

You don't "see" what you are reading.

The ability to visualize—or see in your mind—what you are reading is important for comprehension. To understand how visualizing makes a difference, try this quick test. When you get home, turn on a television to a program you enjoy. Then, turn your back to the television set. How long will you keep "watching" the program that way? Probably not long. Why not? Because it would be boring if you couldn't see what was happening. The same is true of reading: If you can't see in your mind what is happening on the page, then you probably will tune out quickly. You can improve your ability to visualize a text by practicing the following strategies:

1. **Read a few sentences; then, pause, and describe what is happening on the page.** Forcing yourself to describe the scene will take some time at first, but it will help in the long run.
2. **On a sheet of paper or a stick-on note, make a graphic representation of what is happening as you are reading.** For instance, if two characters are talking, draw two stick figures with arrows pointing between them to show yourself that they are talking.
3. **Discuss a scene or a part of a chapter with a buddy.** Talk about what you "saw" as you were reading.
4. **Read aloud.** If you are having trouble visualizing the text, it might be because you aren't really "hearing" it. Try reading a portion of your text aloud, using good expression and phrasing. As you hear the words, you may find it easier to see the scenes.

READING UP CLOSE

Visualizing What You Read

Read this scene from "Where Have You Gone, Charming Billy?" (p. 622), and discuss what you see:

> "The platoon of twenty-six soldiers moved slowly in the dark, single file, not talking. One by one, like sheep in a dream, they passed through the hedgerow, crossed quietly over a meadow, and came down to the rice paddy. There they stopped. Their leader knelt down, motioning with his hand, and one by one the other soldiers squatted in the shadows, vanishing in the primitive stealth of warfare. For a long time they did not move. Except for the sounds of their breathing, the twenty-six men were very quiet. . . ."

Using This Lesson

At first glance, **Visualization** might seem to apply better to literary texts than to informational ones, but Visualization can also enhance the comprehension of nonfiction and informational texts, such as news reports, how-to instructions, and biographical texts.

After discussing the passage from Tim O'Brien's "Where Have You Gone, Charming Billy?" (p. 622), you might encourage students to practice the reading strategy with a passage from a short story, poem, novel, or play of their choice. Ask students to read aloud the passage they have chosen and discuss what they "see."

Although the word *visualize* refers to the sense of sight, note that this strategy covers all kinds of sensory details, not just those that appeal to the sense of sight. You might introduce this strategy with Jack Finney's "Contents of the Dead Man's Pocket" (p. 5) and Louise Erdrich's "The Leap" (p. 31).

Focus on the Tips

Have students practice visualization in class, working with partners or in small groups. After students have practiced each of the four strategies for visualizing, have them discuss their reading experience and whether the strategies helped them comprehend the text. Encourage students to frequently use the strategies that they find most helpful.

Reading Up Close

As students read the passage from "Where Have You Gone, Charming Billy?" encourage them to note the details that appeal to the senses. [Possible responses: *Sight*—"dark"; "hedgerow"; "meadow"; "rice paddy"; "motioning with his hand." *Sound*—"not talking"; "sounds of their breathing."]

Using This Lesson

This lesson introduces five reading strategies that apply to both literary and informational texts. These strategies appear in earlier grades of the *Holt Literature and Language Arts* program, so for some students this will be a review.

Using the Think-Aloud Strategy

The **Think-Aloud strategy** helps students remain focused as they read. However, some students may be intimidated by trying to classify their comments. (Note that the Reading Up Close box provides examples of the different types of comments.) Emphasize that classifying their comments isn't important. The goal of this reading strategy is to monitor their understanding and to make students active readers who will comment on and ask questions about a text.

Be sure to model Think-Aloud in class. You might read a difficult poem or a passage from a challenging informational text to demonstrate a variety of comments and the fact that not every sentence or line of text deserves a comment.

Reading Up Close

Emphasize that there is no limit to the number of Think-Aloud comments students can make. Explain that Jarred made several dozen comments about "Everyday Use," but only five are provided as examples of the different types of comments in the bulleted list.

You might have students work with a partner to practice the Think-Aloud strategy with a selection such as Edgar Lee Masters's "Lucinda Matlock" (p. 85) or Santha Rama Rau's "By Any Other Name" (p. 113).

Danger Sign 3

You constantly answer "I don't know" to questions at the end of reading selections.

If you consistently don't know the answers to questions about what you've been reading, then you probably would benefit from the following strategies:

Think-Aloud. Comprehension problems don't appear only after you *finish* reading. Confusion occurs *as* you read. Therefore, don't wait until you complete your reading assignment to try to understand the text; instead, work on comprehending while reading by becoming an active reader.

Active readers **predict, connect, clarify, question,** and **visualize** as they read. If you don't do those things, then you need to pause while you read to

- make predictions
- make connections
- clarify in your own thoughts what you are reading
- question what you don't understand
- visualize the text and observe key details

Use the Think-Aloud strategy to practice your active-reading skills. Read a selection of text aloud to a partner. As you read, pause to make comments and ask questions. Your partner's job is to tally your comments and classify each according to the list above.

READING UP CLOSE

One Student's Think-Aloud

Here's Jarred's Think-Aloud for "Everyday Use," by Alice Walker (p. 77):

Page 77, first sentence: "What in the world is this talking about when it says they made the yard so wavy? How do you make a yard wavy?" **(Question)**

Page 77, fifth sentence: "Okay, I get it. It's not a grass yard, but like clay and sand." **(Clarification)**

Page 79, top of second column: "Maggie and Dee remind me of my two sisters. My older sister thinks she is so much better than the other one." **(Connection)**

Page 79 bottom and top 80: "I can just imagine what Dee and her boyfriend look like with their bright clothes and long hair." **(Visualization)**

946 Resource Center Reading Matters

Retelling. While the Think-Aloud strategy keeps you focused as you read, the Retelling strategy helps you after reading. Read the tips for retelling on this page, and then practice retelling small portions of your reading assignments. You might ask a friend to listen to you retell what you have read, or you might record yourself as you retell a selection.

READING UP CLOSE

Evaluate Your Retelling

Listen to your retelling, and ask yourself:

1. Does my retelling make sense?
2. Does it have enough information?
3. Is the information in the correct order?
4. Could a drawing or a diagram help my retelling?
5. If someone listening to my retelling hadn't read the text, what would that person visualize?
6. To improve my next retelling, should I focus on characters, sequence of events, amount of detail, or general conclusions?

Retelling Prompts for Fiction

1. State what text you are retelling.
2. Give characters' names, and explain who they are.
3. Sequence the events using words like *first, second, third, then, later, next,* and *last.*
4. Identify the conflict in the story.
5. Explain the resolution of the conflict.
6. Tell what you enjoyed or did not enjoy about the text.

Retelling Prompts for Informational Texts

State what text you are retelling, and identify the structure of the text.

- If the structure is a **sequence** (the water cycle), use words like *first, second, third, then, later, afterwards, following that, before,* and *last.*
- If the structure is **comparison and contrast** (the differences between World War I and World War II), use words or phrases such as *by comparison, by contrast, on the other hand, yet, but, however, nevertheless, conversely, then again,* or *in opposition.*
- If showing **cause-and-effect relationships,** use words like *reason, motive, basis,* and *grounds* to discuss **causes,** and use words like *outcome, consequence, result,* and *product* to discuss **effects.**

Using the Retelling Strategy

The **Retelling strategy** works well with literary and informational texts. Creating this kind of oral summary requires that students recall specific details and organize their thoughts. In addition, both of these skills will improve their writing.

You may wish to model the Retelling strategy in class so that students recognize the importance of sequencing events and identifying main ideas. Model retelling a passage from a short story students have already read, and then model a passage from an informational text. Alert students to listen carefully for words that indicate sequence (*first, second, then,* and *next*) or relationships of ideas, such as comparison and contrast and cause and effect.

If you use this strategy with learners having difficulty or special education students, have students work with a partner or in small groups as they listen to and comment on each other's retellings.

Reading Up Close

Students can use the criteria in the Reading Up Close box to plan their retellings as well as to evaluate them. Have students use this strategy on a long short story, such as Amy Tan's "Two Kinds" (p. 98), or a long nonfiction text, such as Hanson W. Baldwin's article "R.M.S. Titanic" (p. 330).

Using the Re-reading and Rewording Strategies

Re-reading. Assure students that everyone has had the experience of having to re-read a difficult text. Note that the **Re-reading strategy** is especially helpful with challenging informational texts (such as technical instructions, journal articles, and science and history textbooks) and with ambiguous or "archaic" literary texts.

You might model the Re-reading strategy in class by reading aloud a passage from a difficult selection—for example, a computer instruction manual or one of Shakespeare's plays. Use the Think-Aloud strategy as you read, emphasizing that there are questions and sentences that puzzle you. Re-read the selection, using the Think-Aloud strategy a second time to demonstrate how re-reading the passage helps answer your questions.

Have students practice the Re-reading strategy on one of selections such as Jon Krakauer's "Into Thin Air" (p. 352) or James Stevenson's "Notes from a Bottle" (p. 375).

Rewording. Over the years, students have probably had much practice with paraphrasing, so **Rewording** will not be a new concept for most students. You can give them additional practice by occasionally providing informational or literary passages (one or two paragraphs) that contain difficult words and complex ideas. Let students choose the sentences they want to reword.

Reading Up Close

Discuss with students the example in the Reading Up Close feature. Point out that Katie used two word tools—a dictionary and a thesaurus. Some students may benefit from a quick review of how to use a dictionary and thesaurus.

Re-reading and Rewording. The best way to improve your comprehension is simply to **re-read.** The first time you read something, you get the basic idea of the text. The next time you read it, you revise your understanding. Try thinking of your first reading as a draft—just like the first draft of an essay. As you revise your essay, you are improving your writing. As you revise your reading, you are improving your comprehension.

Sometimes, as you re-read, you find some specific sentences or even passages that you just don't understand. When that's the case, you need to spend some time closely studying those sentences. One effective way to tackle tough text is to **reword** it:

1. On a sheet of paper, write the sentences that are confusing you.
2. Leave a few blank lines between each line you write.
3. Then, choose the difficult words, and replace them in the space above.
4. While you wouldn't want to reword every line of a text, this is a powerful way to help you understand key sentences.

READING UP CLOSE

One Student's Rewording

After tenth-grader Katie read "The Masque of the Red Death" (p. 419), she copied a few sentences she didn't understand. After re-reading them, she reworded them, using a thesaurus and a dictionary. Later she explained that "rewording helps me understand what the author is trying to say."

decided ways entrance or exit
1. They ~~resolved~~ to leave ~~means~~ neither of ~~ingress or egress~~ to the
urges desperation or unrest
sudden ~~impulses~~ of ~~despair or of frenzy~~ from within. (page 420)

thin covered
2. The figure was tall and ~~gaunt,~~ and ~~shrouded~~ from head to foot
clothing
in the ~~habiliments~~ of the grave. (pages 424–425)

Summarizing Narrative Text. Understanding a long piece of text is easier if you can summarize chunks of it. If you are reading a **narrative,** or story, then use a strategy called **Somebody Wanted But So (SWBS)** to help you write a summary of what you are reading. SWBS is a powerful way to think about the characters in a story and note what each did, what conflict each faced, and what the resolution was. As you write an SWBS statement for different characters in the same story, you are forcing yourself to rethink the story from different **points of view.** By analyzing point of view in this way, you get a better understanding of the impact of the author's choice of narrator.

Here are the steps for writing SWBS statements:

1. Write the words *Somebody, Wanted, But,* and *So* at the top of four columns.
2. In the "Somebody" column, write a character's name.
3. Then, in the "Wanted" column, write what that character wanted to do.
4. Next, in the "But" column, explain what happened that kept the character from doing what he or she wanted.
5. Finally, in the "So" column, explain the eventual outcome.
6. If you're making an SWBS chart for a long story or novel, you'll need to write several statements at different points in the story.

READING UP CLOSE

One Student's SWBS Chart

Here's Josh's SWBS chart for "Through the Tunnel" (p. 401). He's written an SWBS statement for Jerry up to where he gets swimming goggles (page 404). Write another for the same character from page 404 to the end. Then, write an SWBS statement for his mother.

Somebody	Wanted	But	So
Jerry	wanted to swim through the rock,	but he couldn't hold his breath long enough,	so he has to practice holding his breath.

Summarizing Expository Text. If summarizing the information in **expository,** or informational, texts is difficult, try a strategy called GIST.

Steps for GIST

1. Divide the text you want to summarize into three or four sections.
2. Read the first section.
3. Draw twenty blank lines on a sheet of paper.
4. Write a summary of the first section of text using exactly twenty words—one word for each blank.

Using the SWBS Strategy: Summarizing Narrative Texts

The **Somebody Wanted But So (SWBS) strategy** helps students focus on the literary elements of character, conflict, and point of view. Using this strategy will help students clarify and organize their thinking about a narrative text. By design, the SWBS statement omits details and focuses on a single character's conflict. Therefore, a long or complex narrative may require several SWBS statements.

Reading Up Close

Note that the sample SWBS chart provides only a partial summary for Doris Lessing's "Through the Tunnel" (p. 401). [A sample SWBS chart for Jerry's mother might be: *Somebody*—Jerry's mother. *Wanted*—wanted to protect her son. *But*—but she also wanted him to be independent. *So*—so she let him go off on his own.] For further practice, ask students to use the SWBS strategy with any of the short stories and plays in the Student Edition.

Using the GIST Strategy: Summarizing Expository Texts

Students who use this strategy must create a summarizing statement that is exactly twenty words long. Explain to students that practicing the **GIST (Generating Interactions between Schemata and Text) strategy** is not easy and that it is a bit like solving a word puzzle. Each GIST statement summarizes the main idea of its section as well as all preceding sections.

Suggest that students work in pairs or in small groups and compare their statements. Encourage them to continue trying out different summarizing statements until they find one that is both reasonable and accurate. Point out that if a statement runs too long or too short, they should restate their summary using different words.

Reading Up Close

Turn to p. 413 and ask students to compare the text with Tony's GIST statements. Have them suggest improvements or alternative ways of wording the statements.

Remind students that they can use the GIST strategy on any of the informational materials texts in the Student Edition.

Using the Key Words Strategy

This **Key Words strategy** helps students compare and contrast important elements in literary texts (such as the character traits of two different characters) and in informational materials (such as events during two different wars).

5. Read the next section of text. In your next set of twenty blanks, write a new summary statement that combines your first summary with whatever you want to add from this second section of text. It's important to note that even though you've now got two sections of text to cover, you still have only twenty blanks to fill, not forty.
6. Repeat this one or two more times, depending on how much more text you have. When you are finished, you'll have a twenty-word statement that gives you the gist, or overall idea, of what the entire text is about.

READING UP CLOSE

One Student's GIST

After reading "Vision Quest" (p. 413), Tony wrote the following GIST statements:

GIST 1 (first paragraph)
To reach adulthood, boys in some American Indian tribes underwent a vision quest—a solitary vigil of prayer and fasting.

GIST 2 (for paragraphs 1 and 2)
During their vision quest initiation rites, American Indian boys prayed and fasted until they received a significant sign or vision.

GIST 3 (complete article)
Vision quests of prayer and fasting are important to American Indian adults as well as to boys undergoing initiation rites.

Key Words. Sometimes you don't want to write a summary or outline of what you've been reading. Sometimes you just want to jot down some key words to remind yourself about a specific topic. To keep your key words organized, don't forget your ABCs. Just make yourself a copy of a page filled with boxes, as in the following example. You can use your computer to make this page or just grab a pencil and notebook paper. Once your boxes are drawn, all you have to do is decide what information to include.

For instance, Amy uses her Key Word chart while reading "Two Kinds" (page 99). She puts "Mother" in blue at the top of the page and "*Ni kan*" in red. As she reads the story and thinks of words to describe each character, she puts those key character-description words in the correct box in the correct color. So, she writes "demanding" in blue (because she thinks that word describes Mother) in the C–D box. She writes "angry" in red (because this word is for *Ni kan*) in the A–B box. Amy's completed Key Word chart can serve as a starting point for writing a comparison-contrast essay.

950 Resource Center Reading Matters

READING UP CLOSE

▸ Using a Key Word Chart

Here is Amy's partially filled-out Key Word chart for "Two Kinds." Read the story, and find more key words to describe the two main characters.

Mother Ni Kan

A–B	C–D	E–F	G–H	I–J	K–L
angry	demanding				
M–N	**O–P**	**Q–R**	**S–T**	**U–V–W**	**X–Y–Z**

Kwan used his Key Word chart in history class as he was reading the chapter on World War II. He used it to keep up with countries (*Allies* written in red, *Axis* in blue), military leaders, and major battles.

Improving Your Reading Rate

If your reading concerns are more about getting through the words than figuring out the meaning, then this part of Reading Matters is for you.

If you think you are a slow reader, then reading can seem overwhelming. But you can change your reading rate—the pace at which you read. All you have to do is practice. The point isn't to read so fast that you just rush over words—the I'mgoingtoreadsofastthat-allthewordsruntogether approach. Instead, the goal is to find a pace that keeps you moving comfortably through the pages. Why is it important to establish a good reading rate? Let's do a little math to see why your silent reading rate counts.

MATH PROBLEM!

If you read 40 words per minute (WPM) and there are 400 words on a page, then how long will it take you to read 1 page? 5 pages? 10 pages? How long will it take if you read 80 WPM? 100 WPM? 200 WPM?

Reading Up Close

You might ask students to apply the Key Words strategy to each of the topics in the following selections:

- the English and Indian cultures in Santha Rama Rau's "By Any Other Name" (p. 112)
- the main characters and events in Isabel Allende's "And of Clay Are We Created" (p. 257) and Roger Rosenblatt's "The Man in the Water" (p. 273)
- the hero quests of "Theseus" (p. 660) and "Sigurd, the Dragon Slayer" (p. 673)

Improving Your Reading Rate

You may wish to have students determine a baseline reading rate score at the beginning of the school year. Then, have students retest themselves at the middle and end of the year to calculate how much their speed has increased. Remind them to use similar kinds of texts every time they retest their speed.

Most students already recognize that their reading rate varies according to their purpose for reading. When they read a novel or a magazine for pure entertainment, for example, they will read much more quickly than when they are studying a lesson in their science textbooks.

Reading Rate and Homework

The math problem (p. 951) and the chart (p. 952) should convince students that an improvement in their reading rate will result in more free time for fun.

Reading Up Close

Emphasize that reading comprehension must not be sacrificed to increase reading speed. Explain that the speed at which they read does not matter if they do not understand what they are reading.

Review with students these three types of reading:

- A **close reading** is reading at a slower speed when it is important to understand and remember what you have read. Students should use a close reading when they are studying for a test, following directions, reading technical information, or analyzing a literary text.
- **Skimming** is reading at a very rapid rate in order to search for specific information: a telephone number, a name, a place, or a date. While skimming, you move very quickly over the lines, and you do not pause to understand everything that you are reading.
- **Scanning** is an even faster type of reading. You scan a text when you preview it, glancing at chapter headings, boldface words, text organizers, and graphics.

Figuring Out Your Reading Rate

Choose a passage from a selection in the Student Edition (such as, "Julius Caesar in an Absorbing Production," p. 882). Time students as they read the passage and let them determine their own reading rates. Ask a few simple questions to assess students' comprehension. For example:

- Did the writer like this production of *Julius Caesar* or dislike it?
- What kinds of costumes do the actors wear?

As you figure out the problem, you see that it takes 100 minutes to read 10 pages at the slowest pace and only 20 minutes at the fastest pace. See the chart for all the times:

	1 page @400 words/page	5 pages @400 words/page	10 pages @400 words/page
40 WPM	10 minutes	50 minutes	100 minutes
80 WPM	5 minutes	25 minutes	50 minutes
100 WPM	4 minutes	20 minutes	40 minutes
200 WPM	2 minutes	10 minutes	20 minutes

Reading Rate and Homework

Now, assume that with literature homework, science homework, and social studies homework, in one night you have 40 pages to read. If you are reading at 40 WPM, you are spending over 6 *hours* just reading the information; but at 100 WPM, you would spend only about 2 hours and 45 minutes. And at 200 WPM, you'd finish in 1 hour and 20 minutes.

READING UP CLOSE

Tips on Varying Your Reading Rate

- Increasing your rate doesn't help if your comprehension goes down.
- Remember that your rate will vary as your purpose for reading varies. You'll read more slowly when you are studying for a test than when you are skimming a text.

Figuring Out Your Reading Rate

To determine your silent-reading rate, you'll need three things: a watch or clock with a second hand, a book, and someone who will watch the time for you. Then, follow these steps:

Example

1st minute	180 words
2nd minute	215 words
3rd minute	190 words
	585 words ÷ 3 = 195 WPM

1. Have your friend time you as you begin reading to yourself.
2. Read at your normal rate. Don't speed just because you're being timed.
3. Stop when your friend tells you one minute is up.
4. Count the number of words you read.
5. Repeat this process several more times using different passages.
6. Then, add the number of words together, and divide by the number of times you timed yourself. That's your average rate.

Reading Rate Reminders

You can improve your reading rate by using the following strategies:

1. **Make sure you aren't reading just one word at a time, with a pause between each word.** Practice phrasing words in your mind as you read. For instance, look at the sample sentence, and pause only where you see the slash marks. One slash (/) means pause a bit. Two slashes (//) mean pause a bit longer.

   Jack and Jill/ went up the hill/ to fetch a pail of water.// Jack fell down/ and broke his crown/ and Jill came tumbling after.//

   Now, read it again, pausing after each word:

   Jack/ and/ Jill/ went/ up/ the/ hill/ to/ fetch/ a/ pail/ of/ water.// Jack/ fell/ down/ and/ broke/ his/ crown/ and/ Jill/ came/ tumbling/ after.//

   Hear the difference? Word-at-a-time reading is much slower than phrase reading. You can hear good phrasing by listening to a book on tape.
2. **Make sure you aren't sounding out each word.** At this point in school, you need to be able to recognize whole words and save the sounding-out strategy for words you haven't seen before. In other words, you ought to be able to read *material* as "material" and not as "ma-ter-i-al," but you might need to move more slowly through *metacognition* so that you read that word as "met-a-cog-ni-tion."
3. **Make sure when you are reading silently that you really are reading silently.** Don't move your lips or read aloud very softly when reading. These habits slow you down. Remember, if you need to slow down (for instance, when the information you are reading is confusing you), then reading aloud to yourself is a smart thing to do. But generally, silent reading means reading silently!
4. **Don't use your finger to point to words as you read.** If you find that you always use your finger to point to words as you read (instead of just occasionally, when you are really concentrating), then you are probably reading one word at a time. Instead, use a bookmark to help yourself stay on the right line, and practice your phrase reading.
5. **As you practice your fluency, remember that the single best way to improve your reading rate is simply to read more!** You won't get better at what you never do. So start reading more, and remember these tips. Soon you'll find that reading too slowly isn't a problem anymore.

Reading Rate Reminders

Review these five essential steps to faster reading. Assure students that it is possible, but not easy, to rid themselves of the bad reading habits (numbers 1–4) that tend to slow readers. Hard work and practice are necessary to improve reading skills, but well worth the time and effort.

Writer's Handbook

The Writing Process

There may be as many ways to write as there are kinds of texts. While individual writers' techniques may vary, successful writers do have one thing in common: the writing process. The writing process is made up of four stages, and each stage involves certain activities. The chart below summarizes what happens during each stage of the writing process.

Quick guide!

STAGES OF THE WRITING PROCESS

Prewriting	• Choose your topic.
	• Identify your purpose and audience, and select a form.
	• Generate ideas and gather information about the topic.
	• Begin to organize the information.
	• Decide the main point you want to express.
Writing	• Grab your readers' attention in the introduction.
	• Provide background information.
	• State your main points, support, and elaboration.
	• Follow a plan of organization.
	• Wrap up with a conclusion.
Revising	• Evaluate your draft.
	• Revise the draft's content, organization, and style.
Publishing	• Proofread, or edit, your final draft.
	• Publish, or share your finished writing with readers.
	• Reflect on your writing experience.

TIP The writing process is **recursive,** meaning that writers go back and forth between the stages as necessary. For example, as you revise an essay you may realize that one paragraph contains no details to support your main idea. You can go back to the prewriting and drafting stages, gathering and adding more information to the paragraph.

At every stage of the writing process, you'll need to stay focused on your goal for the piece of writing and on your specific audience. Use the following suggestions to keep your writing on track.

The Writing Process 955

- **Keep your ideas focused.** Every idea in a piece must clearly support your thesis or the controlling impression you want to create. Those ideas must also be **coherent,** or strongly connected to one another. Keep your thesis and purpose in mind every step of the way, eliminating any ideas that might take the reader's attention away from your distinct perspective or from a tightly reasoned argument.
- **Use a consistent tone.** Using the same tone throughout a piece will help to unify the ideas you present. Consider what tone—from slangy and joking to serious and formal—will best fit your audience and your topic, and stick with that tone.
- **Plan to publish.** Make publishing a piece—sharing it with an audience—easier by carefully revising and proofreading. Enlist the help of classmates to catch errors you might miss because you know the piece too well, and use the following proofreading guidelines. The numbers in parentheses indicate the pages in the *Holt Handbook* on which instruction on each skill begins.

Quick guide

GUIDELINES FOR PROOFREADING

1. Is every sentence complete, not a fragment or run-on? (444)
2. Are punctuation marks used correctly? (290, 320, 336, 354)
3. Are the first letters of sentences and proper nouns and adjectives capitalized? (264)
4. Does each verb agree in number with its subject? (110) Are verb forms and tenses used correctly? (170)
5. Are subject and object forms of personal pronouns used correctly? (144) Do pronouns agree with clear antecedents in number and in gender? (130)

Quick guide

As you proofread, mark corrections using the symbols below.

SYMBOLS FOR REVISING AND PROOFREADING

Symbol	Example	Meaning of Symbol
≡	Maple High school (≡ under s)	Capitalize a lowercase letter.
/	the First person (/ through F)	Lowercase a capital letter.
^	on the fourth ^of May	Insert a missing word, letter, or punctuation mark.
^——	in the ~~East~~ West	Replace a word.
ℯ/	tell me the ~~the~~ plan	Delete a word, letter, or punctuation mark.
∪∩	recieve	Change the order of letters.
¶	¶ "Help!" someone cried.	Begin a new paragraph.

956 Resource Center Writer's Handbook

Paragraphs

A **paragraph** is made up of sentences grouped together for a reason—usually to present and support a single main idea, or central focus. In the same way, a composition is made up of a group of paragraphs working together to develop and support a thesis or controlling idea that makes the composition work as a whole.

Parts of a Body Paragraph

While paragraphs in narrative writing don't always have a central focus, paragraphs in most other types of compositions do usually emphasize a main idea. These **body paragraphs** usually include a **topic sentence, supporting sentences,** and, sometimes, a **clincher sentence.**

PARTS OF PARAGRAPHS

Topic Sentence	• directly states the paragraph's main idea • often is the first sentence in the paragraph, but may occur at the end for emphasis or variety
Supporting Sentences	• support the main idea of a paragraph • use the following kinds of details *sensory details:* information collected using sight, hearing, smell, touch, or taste *facts:* information that can be proved *statistics:* information in number form *examples:* specific instances or illustrations of a general idea *anecdotes:* extended examples or brief personal stories *scenarios:* general descriptions of potential events or common situations *commonly held beliefs:* ideas on which most people agree *hypotheses:* unproven theories that serve as the basis for investigation *definitions:* explanations of a concept
Clincher Sentence	• sometimes (but not always) found at the end of longer paragraphs • emphasizes or summarizes the main idea

TIP You can provide many other types of information as supporting evidence, including descriptions, expert opinions, reasons, and personal experience. Use a combination of types of support to give your writing variety.

Paragraphs 957

Putting the Parts Together A typical paragraph that includes the parts listed in the chart on page 957 uses the following structure. Be aware, though, that you can use a different structure for effect—for example, you might occasionally leave out the clincher sentence and place your topic sentence at the end of the paragraph to drive home your point.

Typical Body Paragraph Structure

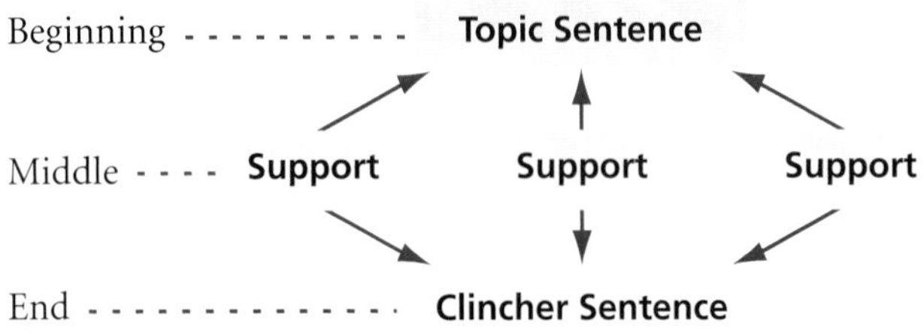

The following passage from an online magazine article shows how the parts of a paragraph work together to support a main idea—in this case, the idea that electric "bug zappers" do a poor job of protecting humans from insect bites.

Topic sentence

Supporting sentences

(Facts and statistics)

Clincher sentence

> Electric insect traps, or "bug zappers," are effective killing machines, but they kill the wrong kind of insects, claims University of Delaware entomologist Doug Tallamy. Over the course of a summer, Tallamy and a high school student, Tim Frick, analyzed the victims of the electric traps installed in six yards in Newark, Delaware. Of the 13,789 insects killed, just 31—less than one-quarter of one percent—were biting insects. Tallamy and Frick estimate that the millions of traps employed in the U.S. needlessly kill 71 billion to 350 billion "nontarget insects" each year, causing untold damage to ecosystems. Bug zappers, they conclude, are "worthless" as well as "counterproductive."
>
> Steve Nadis, "Bug Zappers Miss Their Mark," *Omni Online*

Notice that the topic sentence immediately calls the reader's attention to the paragraph's main idea: These traps kill the wrong insects. The rest of the paragraph maintains a consistent focus on this idea. Each supporting sentence contains evidence that supports this main idea, including facts and statistics. The final sentence, a clincher sentence, emphasizes the main idea by presenting a judgment based on the facts and statistics in the supporting sentences.

958 Resource Center Writer's Handbook

Qualities of Paragraphs

Having the parts of a paragraph in place is just the beginning of developing a good paragraph. The next step is to consider the **unity** and **coherence** of the ideas within the paragraph. Think of these qualities as the strong glue that holds the parts of a well-written paragraph together.

Unity Unity is the quality achieved when all of the sentences in a paragraph work together as a unit to express or support one main idea and to maintain a consistent focus. Unrelated ideas spoil unity and distract the reader. Unity is present in a paragraph when all sentences relate to an implied or stated main idea or to a sequence of events. In a narrative paragraph, unity is achieved when all the sentences work together to narrate the event.

Coherence Along with unity, good paragraphs have coherence. Coherence is achieved when all of the details and ideas in a paragraph are both logically arranged and clearly connected.

To ensure that the ideas in a paragraph are arranged in a way that makes sense, pay attention to the structure or organizational pattern of the ideas. You will usually use one of the orders described in the chart below; in some cases, though, you may use a combination of two or even more of these orders.

TYPES OF ORDER Quick guide

Order	When To Use	How It Works
Chronological	• to tell a story • to explain a process	presents actions and events according to the order in which they occur
Spatial	• to describe a place or object	arranges details or ideas according to their location in space
Logical	• to explain or classify (by defining, dividing a subject into parts, or comparing and contrasting)	groups related details or ideas together to show their relationship
Order of Importance	• to inform or to persuade	arranges details or ideas from the most important to the least important, or vice versa

Paragraphs 959

In addition to presenting details in an order that makes sense, a paragraph that has coherence should also show readers how those details are connected. You can show connections between ideas by using direct references or transitional expressions. **Direct references** refer to an idea presented earlier. **Transitional expressions** are words or phrases that take readers from one idea to the next, signaling the relationship between the ideas. The following chart explains how to use these two strategies for connecting ideas.

Quick guide

CONNECTING IDEAS

Connecting Strategy	How To Use It
Direct References	• Use a noun or pronoun that refers to a noun or pronoun used earlier. • Repeat a word used earlier. • Use a word or phrase that means the same thing as a noun or pronoun used earlier.
Transitional Expressions	• Compare ideas (*also, and, besides, in addition, similarly, too*). • Contrast ideas (*although, but, however, instead, nevertheless, otherwise, yet*). • Show cause and effect (*as a result, be-cause, consequently, so, therefore, thus*). • Show time (*after, before, eventually, finally, first, meanwhile, then, when*). • Show place (*above, across, around, beyond, from, here, in, on, over, there, to, under*). • Show importance (*first, last, mainly, then, to begin with*).

PRACTICE & APPLY Develop a paragraph on the topic of your choice. After identifying the main idea you will present, take the following steps to draft your paragraph.

- Plan your topic sentence, supporting sentences with a variety of types of support, and clincher sentence.
- Create unity and coherence to maintain a consistent focus in your paragraph. Use an appropriate order, and connect your ideas using direct references and transitional expressions.

960 Resource Center Writer's Handbook

The Writer's Language

As part of revising a draft, fine-tune its **style** so that it will grab readers. To improve your paper's style, consider your **word choice** and use the **active voice.** Also, analyze the **tone** of your writing to make your style not only engaging but also appropriate.

Give It Flair! Consider what is missing from the following passage.

> As I hiked around a bend, I saw a snake smack in the middle of the path. Its skin was being shed. It moved against the rocks. Eventually it got out of its old skin. Now it looked real different. It was smooth. There was a lot of sun. My forehead was covered with sweat. I couldn't hear nothing. I looked at the snake's eyes. They were black.

The passage poorly shares the writer's experience. The writer must improve word choice, using **precise language, sensory details, action verbs,** and **appropriate modifiers,** and use the **active voice** when possible.

Precise Language The passage above describes the snake in a vague way. Changing *moved* to *wriggled* or *slithered* would vividly show the snake's movement. Also, what kind of snake is it? What does the snake look like before, during, and after shedding its skin? Revise your own writing to show your subject vividly through precise language.

Sensory Details The statement "It was smooth" doesn't give readers much information about the snake. The description "smooth as silk" or "smooth as a stone" would explain how it feels to touch the snake. Words like *stone* and *silk* are the building blocks of sensory details, details that tell how things look, feel, taste, sound, or smell.

Action Verbs Which is more interesting—"They were black" or "They glittered like black stones"? Generally, *be* verbs (such as *were*) and other dull verbs such as *go, have,* and *do* don't tell readers much. Action verbs such as *glittered* and *sparkled* bring a subject to life.

Appropriate Modifiers An appropriate modifier clearly relates to the correct word or phrase. For example, the word *real* in the passage is an adjective used incorrectly to modify the adjective *different*. The writer should use the adverb *really* or, even better, eliminate the tired word *really* altogether. Check that each modifier you use is both necessary and correct.

Active Voice In the **passive** voice, the action happens to the subject. For example, "Its skin was being shed" uses the passive voice. In the

The Writer's Language 961

active voice, the subject does the action. The more forceful sentence "The snake was shedding its skin" uses the active voice.

TIP Word choice directly affects tone and level of formality. For example, consider the difference between "A veggie burrito packs a nutritious punch" and "A vegetarian burrito provides many nutrients."

Toning Up Your **tone** expresses your attitude toward your audience and topic and comes through in the formality of your language, including your word choice. Consider these points.

- **Who is my audience?** When you speak, you adjust your tone based on listener reactions. For example, if listeners frown at a joke, you probably turn more serious. In writing, imagine your readers' attitude toward your topic and adopt a tone reflecting that attitude.
- **Why am I writing?** Your tone must fit your **purpose.** For example, if your purpose is to inform, avoid a sarcastic tone—even if your readers enjoy sarcasm—because irony could interfere with your goal.
- **For what context, or occasion, am I writing?** Are you writing for a school assignment or to share a story with a friend? The occasion that prompts your writing determines its formality. For a formal occasion, use standard English, avoiding contractions and slang.

Read the following revision of the passage on page 961. Notice how revisions in word choice, voice, and tone bring the passage to life.

A Writer's Model

Precise language
Active voice
Action verbs
Appropriate modifiers
Sensory details
Precise language
Sensory detail

As I hiked around a bend, I saw a gopher snake right in the middle of the path. The snake was shedding its skin. It wriggled and rubbed itself against the rough rocks. Eventually it slithered out of the flaky, dead layer of skin. Now it was as smooth as a polished apple, black and brown like shiny shoes. The morning sun was hot, and beads of sweat ran down my forehead. The world was silent—even the birds had stopped chirping. I looked right into the snake's eyes. They glittered like tiny chips of black stone.

PRACTICE & APPLY Revise the following paragraph for style, and use your imagination to add details.

Roosevelt Park is nice. People play softball there. Kids play on the playground, sliding down the slides and swinging on the swings. There's a petting zoo, too, with different kinds of animals that can be touched. There's a merry-go-round that first goes around slow and then fast. If you are hungry, there are places to eat. Or you can do nothing. I'm glad there's a place to go with my friends on weekends.

962 Resource Center Writer's Handbook

Designing Your Writing

If you've ever tried to read a messy, confusing flier or a scientific report filled with statistics, you know how important design and visuals are in making documents readable. A document's design should help to communicate its information clearly and effectively. Visuals, such as a photograph or chart, should be used when needed to help readers grasp a point.

Page Design

Eye Appeal Your page design, or **layout,** can influence your audience's desire and ability to read your document. When you design a document, make it as appealing and easy to read as possible, whether you create it by hand or using word-processing or publishing software. Use the following design elements to improve readability.

- **Columns** arrange text in separate sections printed side by side. Text in reference books and newspapers usually appears in columns. A **block** is a rectangle of text shorter than a page, such as a single newspaper story. Blocks are separated by white space.
- A **bullet** (•) is a dot or symbol used to make information stand out. Bullets often separate information into lists like this one. They attract attention and help readers remember the ideas listed.
- A **callout** is an important sentence from the text printed in a large font. Many magazine articles catch readers' attention with callouts.
- A **heading** tells what a section of text, such as a chapter, will be about. Headings appear at the beginning of a section of text. A **subheading** indicates a new idea or section within a heading. Several subheadings may appear under one heading. Headings and subheadings are often set in large letters, boldface type, or a different font.
- **White space** is any area on a page where there is little or no text or visuals. Usually, white space is limited to the margins and the spaces between words, lines, and columns. Advertisements have more white space than books or articles in newspapers or magazines.
- **Contrast** refers to the balance of light and dark areas on a page. Dark areas are those that contain blocks of text or graphics. Light areas have little type and few graphics. A page with high contrast, or balanced light and dark areas, is easier to read than a page with low contrast, such as one that is mostly light or one that is filled with text and images.

Designing Your Writing 963

- **Emphasis** is how a page designer indicates to a reader which information on a page is most important. For example, the front page of a newspaper uses photographs and bold or large headlines to place emphasis on a particular story.

Type

Bold and Beautiful To enhance the readability of your documents, choose type carefully, considering especially the **case** and **font** of letters.

Case Most texts you read use mostly lowercase letters with capital letters at the beginnings of sentences. However, you can use all capital letters and small capitals for specific purposes within a document.

- **Uppercase letters** All uppercase, or capital, letters may be used in headings or titles. Because words in all capitals can be difficult to read, use all caps only for emphasis, not for large bodies of text.
- **Small caps** Small capitals are uppercase letters that are reduced in size. They appear in abbreviations of time, such as 9:00 A.M. and A.D. 1500.

Font A **font** is one complete set of characters (such as letters, numbers, and punctuation marks) of a given size and design.

- **Types of fonts** All fonts belong to one of three categories:

Quick guide

FONT CATEGORIES

Category	Explanation	How It Is Used
decorative, or **script,** fonts	elaborately designed characters that convey a distinct mood or feeling	Decorative fonts are difficult to read and should be used in small amounts for an artistic effect.
serif fonts	characters with small strokes (serifs) attached at each end	Because the strokes on serif characters help guide the reader's eyes from letter to letter, serif type is often used for large bodies of text.
sans serif fonts	characters formed of neat straight lines, with no serifs at the ends of letters	Sans serif fonts are easy to read and are used for headings, subheadings, callouts, and captions.

- **Font size** The size of type is called the font size or point size. Most newspapers and textbooks use type measured at 12 points, with larger type for headings and headlines and smaller type for captions.
- **Font styles** Most text is set in roman type (not slanted). *Italic,* or slanted, type has special uses, as for captions or book titles. Underscored or boldface type can be used for emphasis.

964 Resource Center Writer's Handbook

Visuals

Get the Picture? Some information can be communicated much more effectively visually than in writing. Your visuals must meet the same standards of accuracy as your text, and their design must also be uncluttered. Use only one or two colors for emphasis to keep your visuals clear. Here are some visuals you might find useful.

Charts Charts show relationships among ideas or data. A **flowchart** uses geometric shapes linked by arrows to show the sequence of events in a process. A **pie chart** is a circle divided into wedges, with each wedge representing a certain percentage of the total. As in the example below, a legend usually notes the concept each wedge color represents.

EXAMPLE

Where Old Tires Go

What happens to the 242 million scrap tires that are disposed of each year?

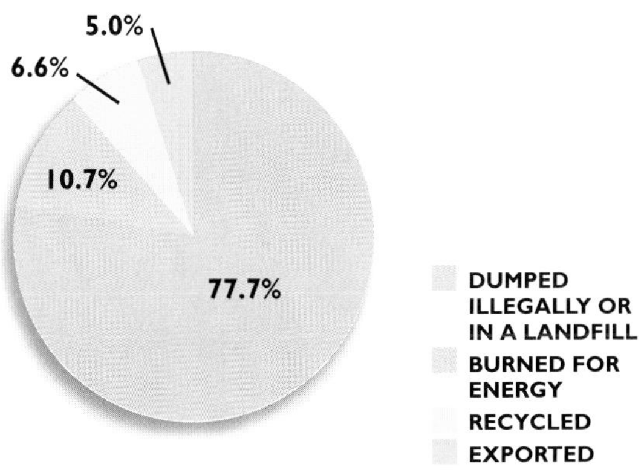

Diagrams Diagrams are simple drawings that show what something looks like, how something works, or how to do something. This diagram shows how water moves to create an ocean swell.

EXAMPLE

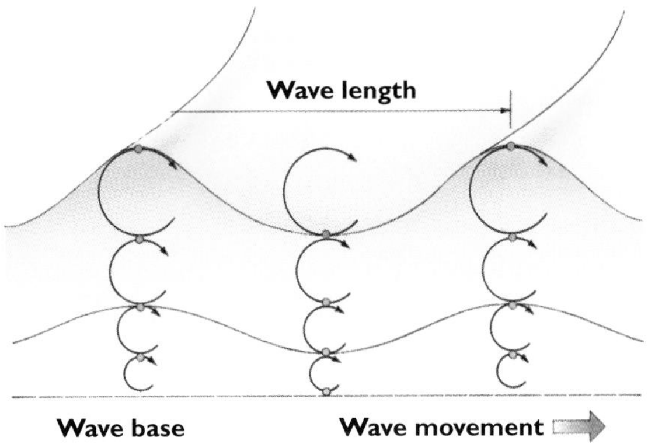

Designing Your Writing 965

Graphs Graphs present numeric information visually and can show how one thing changes in relation to another. A **line graph** can show changes or trends over time, compare trends, or show how two or more variables interact. A **bar graph,** such as the one below, can compare quantities at a glance, show trends or changes over time, or indicate the parts of a whole.

EXAMPLE

Top Five Longest North American Rivers

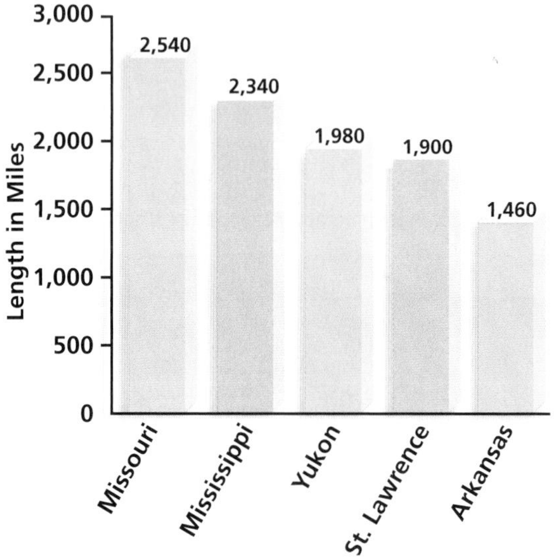

Other Visuals Other visuals you might use in your documents include illustrations, time lines, and maps.

- **Illustrations** include drawings, photographs, and other artwork.
- **Time lines** identify events that have taken place over a given period of time. Usually, events are identified or described above the time line, and the time demarcations are indicated below it.
- **Maps** represent part of the earth or space. Maps of the earth may show geographical features, roads, cities, and other important locations.

PRACTICE & APPLY Choose a visual to effectively communicate the following information. Then, use the guidelines in this section to create the visual.

One hundred students at Chavez High School are involved in team sports. Thirty-five students play soccer, twenty-three students play softball, twenty-seven play football, and fifteen play volleyball.

966 Resource Center Writer's Handbook

Test Smarts *by* Flo Ota De Lange *and* Sheri Henderson

Strategies for Taking Multiple-Choice Tests

Whatever you choose to do in the future, a high school diploma can open doors for you. It is a basic requirement for many, many jobs as well as for getting into college. But to get that diploma, you'll have to pass a lot of tests—pop quizzes in class, midterm exams, finals, your state's standardized tests required for graduation, and the SAT or ACT if you are thinking about college.

Taking tests doesn't have to be the scary nightmare many students make it out to be. With some preparation you'll do just fine. The first thing you have to do, of course, is study. Yes, study, study, study! Read all your assignments at least once, and make sure you have mastered the skills being taught.

Even when you know all the material, however, you might not do well on a test if you get nervous or are not familiar with the kinds of questions being asked. This chapter will give you some strategies that will help you approach your tests with confidence—and let your abilities shine through.

Stay Calm

It's test time. You have studied the material, and you know your stuff, but you're still nervous. That's OK. A little nervousness will help you focus, but so will a calm body. Take a few deep breaths—five slow counts in, five slow counts out. Now you're ready to begin the test.

Track Your Time

First, take a few minutes to estimate how much time you have for each question. Then, set checkpoints for yourself—the number of questions that should be completed at a quarter of the time, half of the time, and so on. That way you can **pace yourself** throughout the test. If you're behind, you can speed up. If you're ahead, you can—and should—slow down.

Master the Directions

Read the directions carefully to be sure you know exactly what to do and how to do it. If you are supposed to fill in an oval, fill it in cleanly and carefully. Don't make a checkmark in it or scribble outside the lines. Be careful also to match the number of the question to the number on the answer sheet. Do just what the directions say to do.

Study the Questions

Read each question once, twice, three times—until you are certain you know what the question is asking. Watch for words like *not* and *except;* they tell you to look for choices that are false, different, or opposite in some way.

Anticipate Answers

Once you are sure you understand the question, **anticipate the answer.** Then, read the choices. If the answer you gave is there, it is probably correct. To be sure, though, check out each choice. If you don't know the answer, eliminate any choices you think are wrong. Then, make an educated—not a wild—guess about the choices that remain. Be careful to **avoid distracters,** answers that are true but don't fit the question.

Don't Give Up

If you are having a hard time with a test, take a deep breath and **keep on going.** On most tests the questions do not get more difficult as you go, and an easier question is probably coming up soon. Remember: The last question on a test is worth just as many points as the first, so give it your all—all the way to the end.

Types of Test Questions

You will feel a lot more confident taking a test if you are familiar with the kinds of questions

Test Smarts 967

given. The following pages describe and give examples of the different types of multiple-choice questions you'll find on many of your tests. Tips on how to approach the questions are also included.

Reading Comprehension Questions

Reading comprehension questions seek to determine not only whether you have gotten the facts straight but also how well you can think critically about what you have read. You have to make accurate **inferences** and **predictions** as well as determine the author's attitude, purpose, and meaning.

The readings and the questions may be long and complicated or short and easy. Pay attention to the purpose of the question, and you will have a good chance of selecting the correct answer.

Following the informational reading below, you will find examples of some of the most common types of reading comprehension questions.

DIRECTIONS: Read the following selection. Then, choose the best answer for each question that follows.

E-Music Appreciation

There you are, back in the time when the usual way of packaging music albums was on long-playing vinyl records. Sharing a song discovery with a friend meant either having that friend over to your house or schlepping your new album over to the friend's house. And as for moving your album collection—it meant getting specially constructed packing boxes from a local moving-van company and preparing yourself to do a lot of hefting. Then the advent of audio on compact discs cut the size and weight of one's music collection by some 75 percent and relieved a lot of aching backs. But what's that your friend just tossed you? Her music collection on a one-ounce hard drive? Well, well, well. Talk about downsizing.

How did a person's music collection make the trip from pounds-heavy long-playing vinyl records to a one-ounce hard drive? Before 1987, compact-disc-quality sound files were so big and cumbersome and computer modems and processors were so slo-o—o—ow that the idea of downloading and uploading music files on a PC seemed an impossibility, something outside the realm of the practical. Then, in 1987, a German engineering firm devised a compression standard known as mpeg-1 Audio Layer 3—a standard that in the vernacular would be known as MP3.

What the MP3 standard accomplished was the compression of a digital audio file from, say, the size of a one-hundred-page book to the size of a ten-page book. So compressed, an audio file could now be cost effectively stored and carried on computers, and just as important, it could be played without significant loss in sound quality. How to play an MP3 music file?

MP3 audio files had significant software problems when it came to playability. The few players available were not user friendly and lacked several of the features of home stereo hardware.

What now? Enter one Justin Frankel, a teenager who wanted a better player. For months, Justin Frankel wrote code twelve hours a day. When his mother suggested he spend some time outdoors, he observed that outdoors was "overrated." And when he had completed his code-writing marathon, Justin Frankel had fulfilled his longtime dream of having compact-disc-quality music on his personal computer.

(continued)

968 Resource Center Test Smarts

Did the software he wrote have the features people wanted? Frankel uploaded his freeware onto his Web site. He had forty thousand visitors a day during his first month. In the following seventeen months his MP3-player software had been downloaded fifteen million times. Talk about building a better mousetrap.

FACTUAL-RECALL QUESTIONS ask you to do a close reading to find **details** or **facts** straight from the selection. Search carefully. The words may not be identical, but the answer will be there.

1. The article provides the *most* information on —

A e-mail

B technology

C personal computers

D e-music

Answer: **The correct answer is D.** Although choices **A, B,** and **C** are all mentioned, the *most* information is about e-music.

2. Which of the following is *not* discussed in this article?

A Vinyl records

B Audiocassettes

C Justin Frankel

D MP3

Answer: Did you spot the word *not*? **The correct answer is B.** This is a detail, or close-reading, question. Audiocassettes are not mentioned in this selection; choices **A, B,** and **C** are all discussed in the selection.

INFERENCE QUESTIONS ask you to connect **clues.** You read between the lines to make an **educated guess.** An inference question sometimes requires you to apply what you already know.

3. Based on this selection, which of the following is the most important characteristic of a successful software programmer?

A Self-motivation

B Love of music

C Scattered interests

D Desire to keep things as they are

Answer: This question requires a careful reading. **The correct answer is A.** Frankel had to be highly self-motivated to sit in his room writing code for month after month with no guarantee of success. Choice **B** is consistent with Frankel's interest in music, but it is not a characteristic that is essential for a computer programmer. **C** is incorrect because it suggests an inability to focus on one thing—not true of Frankel. **D** is incorrect because this is certainly not one of Frankel's goals or a goal of anyone creating new computer software.

MAIN-IDEA QUESTIONS ask you to state the selection's **main idea** or **draw a conclusion.** Sometimes a main-idea question asks you to choose the **best title** for a selection.

4. The main idea of this article is —

A clever inventions can make life more fun

B music is big business

C the popularity of personal computers has grown as they have become smaller, faster, and less expensive

D big sound and small size have fueled the explosion of MP3 onto the music scene

Answer: **D is the correct answer** because it makes a statement that reflects the entire selection. **A** and **B** are way too broad and reflect only part of the selection—if at all. **C** is a true statement but doesn't have anything to do with this article.

Test Smarts 969

EVALUATION QUESTIONS ask you to use your own knowledge and life experience to give an **opinion** about the selection. Sometimes an evaluation question asks about the writer's purpose or style of writing.

5. The factual information in this article seems to be —

A reliable because it mentions facts and dates that can be checked in other sources

B reliable because the writer is a well-known expert on e-music

C unreliable because the writer is clearly biased against e-music

D unreliable because the tone is informal and somewhat humorous

Answer: **A is the correct answer** to this tough question. **B** is incorrect but could trick you because we don't know who wrote this selection; the writer isn't identified. **C** is incorrect because the article contains no evidence of the writer's bias against e-music. **D** has a **distracter** designed to make you think. The tone of the article *is* informal and somewhat humorous, but that wouldn't necessarily make the information unreliable.

Vocabulary Questions

Vocabulary questions test your understanding of word meanings—both in and out of context. Some are simple and some are tricky. Read each question carefully.

After the excerpt from a novel below, you will find examples of some of the most common types of vocabulary questions:

DIRECTIONS: Read the following novel excerpt about a cat named Stripey that lives on a small ship anchored offshore. Then, choose the best answer for each question.

Through years of attempting to lick herself clean, for she had never quite lost her self-respect, Stripey had become as thickly coated with mud inside as out. She was in a perpetual process of readjustment, not only to tides and seasons, but to the rats she encountered on the wharf. Up to a certain size, that is to say the size attained by rats at a few weeks old, she caught and ate them, and, with a sure instinct for authority, brought in their tails to lay them at the feet of Martha. Any rats in excess of this size chased Stripey. The resulting uncertainty as to whether she was coming or going had made her, to some extent, mentally unstable.

—from *Offshore* by Penelope Fitzgerald

DEFINITION OR SYNONYM QUESTIONS are the simplest type of vocabulary question. They ask for a definition or synonym of a word. There are no clues to help you. You are expected to know the word's meaning.

6. Instinct means —

A respect

B hatred

C relating to cats

D inborn tendency

Answer: **D is the correct answer.** You just plain have to know the word's meaning.

CONTEXT-CLUE QUESTIONS ask you to define an unfamiliar word. You will find clues to the word's meaning in the sentence in which the word appears or in the sentences immediately before or after it. You choose the answer that best defines the underlined word.

970 Resource Center Test Smarts

7. "She was in a perpetual process of re-adjustment, not only to tides and seasons, but to the rats she encountered on the wharf."

   Perpetual means —

   A important

   B humorous

   C continual

   D immediate

Answer: **C is the correct answer.** The context clues ("tides and seasons" that are continually changing and "rats" that are always around) indicate that Stripey is continually having to re-adjust. **A** is incorrect but may at first seem like a possible answer. It does not fit the full context of change over time. **B** is incorrect. Mention of rats in the sentence is clearly not humorous. **D** is incorrect. The mention of tides and seasons indicates something that happens over time and not just immediately.

MULTIPLE-MEANING QUESTIONS ask you to recognize which meaning of a familiar word is the one being used in a sentence. You choose the sentence that uses the underlined word in the same way it is used in the original sentence.

8. Stripey moved in a kind of crawl.

   A Fia moved that the meeting be adjourned.

   B Sean's family moved to Los Angeles from Chicago.

   C Carla moved quickly to send the fly ball to the infield.

   D The movie's ending moved her to tears.

Answer: **The correct answer is C.** Stripey isn't (**A**) putting an idea up for a vote, (**B**) changing where she lives, or (**D**) tugging at people's heart-strings. You need a sentence using *moved* in a way that involves motion or changing position, which is choice **C.**

SENTENCE-COMPLETION OR FILL-IN-THE-BLANK QUESTIONS ask you to use the appropriate vocabulary word to complete a sentence. Sometimes questions have two blanks, but these aren't any harder than one-blank questions. The trick is to find the choice that fits both blanks correctly. As a short-cut, determine which choices contain a word that fits the first blank. Then, consider only those choices when filling in the second blank. Be sure to notice words that indicate similarity (*and, because*) or difference (*but, although, though*).

9. The paragraph about Stripey is ________, but it is also ________.

   A funny, comic

   B sad, somber

   C autobiographical, funny

   D comic, ironic

Answer: First, eliminate choices that will not work in the first blank. Answer **C** will not work in the first blank: The passage is not autobiographical. Then, review the possibilities for the second blank in the remaining choices—**A, B,** and **D.** The question includes *but,* a word that indicates a difference, so you know that the choices must be different in some way. Since the two words in choices **A** and **B** are synonyms, **the correct answer is D:** comic, ironic.

ANALOGY QUESTIONS ask you to recognize the relationship between a pair of words and to identify a second pair of words that has the same relationship. An analogy question is written in this form: A : B :: C : D, which can be read as "A is to B as C is to D."

The tricky part of these questions is figuring out the relationship. There are many types of relationships, including the following ones:

- **degree** (*pink : red :: beige : brown*)
- **size** (*hummingbird : ostrich :: house cat : tiger*)
- **part to whole** (*leg : lion :: fin : fish*)
- **cause and effect** (*cold : shiver :: hot : sweat*)

Test Smarts

Test Smarts 971

- **synonyms** (*happy : cheery :: sad : glum*)
- **antonyms** (*happy : sad :: nice : mean*)

Once you figure out the relationship between the first pair of words, try expressing it as a sentence—for example, *A leg is a part of a lion.* Then, pick from the choices the pair of words that has the same relationship—for example, *A fin is a part of a fish.* (For more about analogies, see pages 29–30.)

10. Stripey : cat ::

A rats : wharf

B Martha : character

C mud : season

D Martha : rat

Answer: **The correct answer is B.** Try turning the incomplete analogy into a sentence, as in, *Stripey is the name of a cat.* Now, try out each answer in the same sentence: *Rats are the name of a wharf? Martha is the name of a character? Mud is the name of a season? Martha is the name of a rat?* Only one answer, **B,** fits this sentence.

Multiple-Choice Writing Questions

Multiple-choice writing questions are designed to test your knowledge of **standard written English.** To answer them, you will need to know the rules of punctuation, such as when and how to use commas, quotation marks, end marks, italics, and so on. You will also need to know some basic rules of grammar: active versus passive voice, subject-verb agreement, correct verb tense, correct sentence structure, correct diction, parallel construction in sentences and paragraphs, to name a few. Here are the three most common types of multiple-choice writing questions:

IDENTIFYING-SENTENCE-ERRORS QUESTIONS ask you to look at underlined sections of a sentence and choose the section that includes an error. You are not expected to correct the error.

11. A widely distributed memo from a telegraph company in 1876 reportedly stated, "This (A) 'telephone' (B) has too many shortcomings to be seriously considered as a means of communication. The (C) device is inherently of no value to us." (D) No error. (E)

Answer: **The correct answer is E.** Sentences with no error may be the hardest to figure out because you keep looking for an error. But this answer is sometimes used, so look carefully, and then trust yourself when you find nothing wrong.

IMPROVING-SENTENCES QUESTIONS may ask you to choose the correct version of an underlined section:

12. A big record company is said to have rejected the Beatles in 1962, stating as a reason "we don't like their sound, and guitar music is on the way out."

A stating as a reason, "we

B stating as a reason, "We

C stating as a reason, We

D stating as a reason "We

Answer: **B is the correct answer.** A direct quotation that's a sentence begins with a capital letter and is enclosed in quotation marks. A comma follows the introductory part of the sentence—right before the quotation begins.

972 Resource Center Test Smarts

13. <u>The head of a major movie studio, he said in 1927, "Who</u> wants to hear actors talk?"

A The head of a major movie studio, said in 1927, "Who

B The head of a major movie studio said in 1927, Who

C The head of a major movie studio said in 1927, "Who

D The Head of a major movie studio said in 1927, "Who

Answer: **C is the correct answer.** You have to read the choices very carefully to see that **A** is wrong because of the comma before *said.* **B** is incorrect because there's no quotation mark before *Who,* and **D** is incorrect because the word *head* should not be capitalized.

IMPROVING-THE-PARAGRAPH QUESTIONS are preceded by a paragraph. You may be asked to pick a choice that combines or rewrites portions of sentences. You may be asked to decide which sentences could be added or removed from the paragraph. You may be asked which sentence could be used to strengthen the writer's argument, or you could be asked to pick a thesis statement for the paragraph.

DIRECTIONS: Re-read the last paragraph of the informational reading "E-Music Appreciation" on pages 968–969. Then, choose the best answer for each question based on that paragraph.

14. Which is the *best* way to combine the second and third sentences in the last paragraph of "E-Music Appreciation" without omitting important information?

A In the first month of having uploaded his freeware for distribution from his Web site, Frankel was getting forty thousand visitors a day.

B Frankel had more than thirty thousand visitors a day when his software was distributed on the Internet.

C In the first month, Frankel was swamped with visitors.

D Frankel's Web site had more than forty thousand visitors a day, and he distributed his software, which was free, from his Web site.

Answer: **A is the best answer.** All of the choices are punctuated correctly. You are looking for the sentence that contains all of the important information and says it smoothly without repetition. **B** leaves out important information (in the first month) and gets the number of visitors wrong. **C** uses the vague word *swamped* without giving any idea of how many visitors the Web site had. **D** contains the appropriate information, but it's awkwardly worded.

Test Smarts 973

Strategies for Taking Writing Tests

Writing a Response to Literature

On a test, you may be asked to respond in writing to an autobiographical narrative. To do so effectively, you must draw conclusions that show your understanding of the ideas in the text as well as the author's purpose and style. Follow the steps below. The sample responses provided are based on the prompt to the right. ("By Any Other Name" begins on page 113.)

Prompt

In the autobiographical narrative "By Any Other Name," Indian students are given English names. In an essay, analyze the effect the English had on Indian students' identities, and note the author's point about this episode in her life.

THINKING IT THROUGH

Writing a Response to Literature

STEP 1 **First, read the prompt carefully; then, read the selection.** Decide what tasks the prompt calls for, and get an overview of the selection.

The essay relates experiences the author had while attending an English school in India. I have to explain what effect the English doing things like changing students' names had on the Indian students' identities and what the author's point is.

STEP 2 **Choose a topic, and identify your main points.** Skim the selection to identify and support the main points you will make.

My topic is assigned in this case. My main points will be that the writer felt that "Cynthia" (her English name) was not herself but a separate person, that there was pressure on the Indian students to change their culture as well as their names, and that despite those changes, the English people were still prejudiced against the Indian students.

STEP 3 **Develop a thesis for your essay.** Your thesis will sum up your main points and draw a conclusion about your topic.

My thesis will be: The teachers tried to make the Indian students more "English" by changing their names and their culture, but nothing could change the teachers' prejudice against the Indian students.

STEP 4 **Gather support for your thesis.** Choose details and examples that will provide strong support, and elaborate on those details and examples by drawing on your own knowledge and experience.

Along with other support, I'll explain that the girl with the braids became like the English students, but she clearly missed her own identity and culture.

STEP 5 **Write your essay.** Arrange your ideas to show how they relate to each other and to your thesis. As you draft your essay, maintain a serious, objective tone, vary your sentence types, and use precise language. Revise your essay to grab readers' interest from the very beginning. Finally, proofread carefully.

974 Resource Center Test Smarts

Writing a Response to Expository Text

Sometimes, you read an informative selection and immediately forget the important ideas. However, when you are asked to *respond* to expository text, you not only remember the ideas but draw conclusions based on them, developing a deeper understanding of the selection. To write a response to expository text, follow the steps below. ("An Ancient Enemy Gets Tougher" begins on page 207.)

Prompt

In the informative Web site article, "An Ancient Enemy Gets Tougher," the writer uses an informal tone, including contractions and slang. Write an essay in which you analyze this tone and the content of the article to determine the writer's intended audience. Support your points with relevant examples.

THINKING IT THROUGH

Writing a Response to Expository Text

STEP 1 **First, read the prompt carefully; then, read the selection.** Decide what tasks the prompt calls for, and get an overview of the selection.

I need to read looking for clues about the audience for this article.

STEP 2 **Decide on your general answer, and identify your main supporting points.** Skim the selection to identify the main points you will make to support your answer to the prompt.

This article seems to be written for kids, based on the word choice and overall sentence style. The content is fairly simple, too—it doesn't get into scientific detail but just explains the big concept.

STEP 3 **Develop a thesis statement for your essay.** Your thesis statement will sum up your main points and draw a conclusion about your topic.

My thesis statement will be: The article's sentence style, tone, and content make it clear that it was written for an audience of younger readers.

STEP 4 **Gather support for your thesis.** Choose details and examples that will provide strong support, and elaborate on those details and examples by drawing on your own knowledge and experience.

Word choices like "the little guy that packs a TB wallop," the use of simple sentences and lots of questions, and not explaining things like exactly how TB affects the body's functions are all evidence supporting my thesis. My experience in reading about diseases in my biology textbook tells me there's more to explain and a more adult way to explain it than what is shown here.

STEP 5 **Write your essay.** Begin with an introduction that grabs attention and clearly states your thesis. Using examples from the text, explain your conclusions about the piece. End by restating your thesis. Finally, proofread and correct any errors in grammar, usage, and mechanics.

Test Smarts 975

Writing a Biographical Narrative

A **biographical narrative** shares true events experienced by a person, describing not only *what* happened, but also *how* and *why* these events occurred. If you are asked to write a biographical narrative for a test, follow the steps below. The sample responses provided are based on the prompt to the right.

Prompt

Choose an older person who has been a positive influence on your life. Relate an incident from that person's life that involved you, and explain why you think this event was important.

THINKING IT THROUGH

Writing a Biographical Narrative

STEP 1 **Carefully read the prompt, and choose a subject.** You must address all parts of the prompt in your narrative.

I'll write about my grandfather because he's important to me and we do lots of things together.

STEP 2 **Choose an incident to relate, and identify its parts.** Outline in sequence the smaller events that make up your chosen experience.

I'll describe the time my grandfather came to talk to my middle school social studies class about growing up in Laos.

1. He was looking forward to speaking to the class.
2. I had to tell him the English words for a couple of things, and he mispronounced some words.
3. One kid laughed at him, but the rest of the class was more respectful.
4. After class he went and talked to the boy who laughed, and they became friends.

STEP 3 **Identify important details about the people, events, and setting.** Details should be relevant and specific to bring the incident to life.

I'll describe my grandfather's appearance and the way he talked, the classroom, and the sound of the boy's laughter. I'll also explain how the boy's tone and facial expressions changed as he and my grandfather talked.

STEP 4 **Draw a conclusion based on the events.** Decide why the incident is significant; this conclusion will be the basis for your narrative's thesis.

This incident is important because I got to see my grandfather confront and eliminate prejudice in a kind and courageous way.

STEP 5 **Write a draft of your biographical narrative.** Include an introduction to provide context for readers. Revise your draft to use a consistent tone and point of view and appropriate pacing. Then, proofread and correct any errors in grammar, usage, and mechanics.

976 Resource Center Test Smarts

Writing an Expository Composition

The purpose of an **expository composition** is to inform readers. You must clearly explain ideas new to your audience, anticipating their questions, misunderstandings, and biases about the topic. Follow these steps to write an expository composition for a test. The sample responses provided below are based on the prompt to the right.

Prompt

Consider a hobby or extracurricular activity in which you participate. Explain the essential information—for example, rules, definitions, or techniques—to help a reader unfamiliar with this activity to understand it.

Test Smarts

THINKING IT THROUGH

Writing an Expository Composition

STEP 1 Carefully read the prompt, and choose a topic. Make sure you address all parts of the prompt and choose a topic you know well.

I need to explain the important information about an activity. I'll write about the video productions we do in the school media club.

STEP 2 Divide the topic into parts. Outline the main categories of information you will provide about your topic.

The essential information is about the equipment we use, the techniques we use in creating a production, and the planning process. My body paragraphs will cover those three parts.

STEP 3 Brainstorm details about each part of the topic you have identified. Details should keep readers interested and answer the *5W-How?* questions *(Who? What? Where? When? Why? How?).*

I'll focus on the details that most people don't know, such as how certain effects are achieved and everything that goes into planning and creating our daily school newscast.

STEP 4 Synthesize your ideas to plan a thesis and conclusion. Decide what point the information about your topic makes. Draft a thesis sentence based on this point, and plan to drive that point home in your conclusion.

I want to emphasize that a lot more goes into creating a video production than most people realize. That will be my thesis. I'll restate that idea in my conclusion while pointing out that despite all the work, video production is really fun and rewarding.

STEP 5 Write a draft of your expository composition. Grab readers' attention from the beginning, and keep them interested by doing more than stringing together obvious information about your topic. Instead, point out more intriguing ideas and explain how they support your thesis. Revise your draft to use an authoritative voice and to make clear connections between ideas. Then, proofread to correct any errors in grammar, usage, and mechanics.

Test Smarts 977

Writing a Persuasive Composition

Often on tests you will be asked to write a **persuasive composition** on an assigned topic. Although you might think you have little to say about an issue you didn't choose, you can explore your ideas to develop a convincing argument using the strategy below. The sample responses provided are based on the prompt to the right.

Prompt

Imagine that your school district is debating whether to hold athletics practices only during the school day or only after school. Choose a position on this issue, and write a letter to the school board in which you support that position.

THINKING IT THROUGH

Writing a Persuasive Composition

STEP 1 Carefully read the prompt, and identify your point of view.

The options are to hold practices only during the school day or only after school. If practices are held only after school, students who ride the bus and students who have jobs or other responsibilities won't be able to participate. I think practices should be during the school day so everyone has a chance to participate.

STEP 2 Identify reasons and evidence in favor of your position. Brainstorm a variety of reasons and evidence based on your knowledge and experience. Choose only the strongest support to use in your essay.

1. *After-school practices might exclude good athletes. My friend Paloma is a great runner but has to take care of her little brother after school.*
2. *It might keep students from developing their skills. I tried volleyball just for fun and wound up getting good at it and learning teamwork.*
3. *It might discourage students from exercising. Studies show that people who don't exercise have more health problems than people who do.*

STEP 3 Draft a thesis statement, and arrange ideas in order of importance.

My thesis statement will preview the order of my reasons: After-school practices would deny some students the opportunity to participate in athletics, preventing them from discovering their skills, shortchanging our teams, and most important, endangering the health of our student body.

STEP 4 Consider and address a possible counterargument. Decide why a reader might oppose your position on the issue, and plan a response to that reason.

Some people might say that practicing after school will allow more time for developing skills, but if athletics is a class, athletes can have "homework" to practice those skills.

STEP 5 Draft your essay. Use a respectful and serious tone to show readers you mean business. Develop your reasons in the order you have chosen, and conclude by addressing a counterargument and restating your opinion. Finally, check that your spelling, punctuation, grammar, and usage are correct.

978 Resource Center Test Smarts

Handbook of Literary Terms

For more information about a topic, turn to the page(s) in this book indicated on a separate line at the end of most entries. For example, to learn more about *Alliteration,* turn to pages 505 and 531.

On another line are cross-references to entries in this handbook that provide closely related information. For instance, at the end of *Alliteration* are cross-references to *Assonance* and *Rhythm.*

ALLEGORY **Narrative in which characters and settings stand for abstract ideas or moral qualities.** In addition to the literal meaning of the story, an allegory contains a symbolic, or **allegorical,** meaning. Characters and places in allegories often have names that indicate the abstract ideas they stand for: Justice, Deceit, Vanity. Many of Edgar Allan Poe's stories are allegories, including "The Masque of the Red Death" (page 419).

See pages 399, 418.

ALLITERATION **Repetition of the same or similar consonant sounds in words that are close together.** Although alliteration most often consists of sounds that begin words, it may also involve sounds that occur within words:

> Where the quail is whistling betwixt the woods
>   and the wheat-lot.
>
> —Walt Whitman, from "Song of Myself"

See pages 505, 531.
See also *Assonance, Rhythm.*

ALLUSION **Reference to a statement, a person, a place, an event, or a thing that is known from literature, history, religion, myth, politics, sports, science, or the arts.** Can you identify the literary allusion in the cartoon at the top of the next column? If not, turn to page 810.

See pages 140, 316, 597.

"Et tu, Baxter?"

AMBIGUITY **Element of uncertainty in a text, in which something can be interpreted in a number of different ways.** Ambiguity adds a layer of complexity to a story, for it presents us with a variety of possible interpretations, all of which are valid. The ending of "Night Calls" by Lisa Fugard (page 565) is a good example of ambiguity. That ending is open to several interpretations. **Subtleties,** or fine distinctions, help create ambiguity.

See pages 315, 374.

ANALOGY **Comparison made between two things to show how they are alike.** In "The Man in the Water" (page 273), the writer draws an analogy between a man's struggle to stay alive in freezing water and a battle against "an implacable, impersonal enemy."

See also *Metaphor, Simile.*

ANECDOTE **Very brief account of a particular incident.** Like **parables,** anecdotes are often used by philosophers and teachers of religion to point out truths about life.

See also *Fable, Folk Tale, Parable.*

Handbook of Literary Terms 979

ASIDE **In a play, words spoken by a character directly to the audience or to another character but not overheard by others onstage.** In Act II, Scene 2 (page 801) of *Julius Caesar,* Trebonius and Brutus speak ominous asides that Caesar cannot hear.

See page 815.

ASSONANCE **Repetition of similar vowel sounds followed by different consonant sounds in words that are close together.** Like alliteration, assonance creates musical and rhythmic effects:

> And so all the night-tide, I lie down by the side,
> Of my darling, my darling, my life and my bride
>
> —Edgar Allan Poe, from "Annabel Lee"

See also *Alliteration, Rhythm.*

ATMOSPHERE See Mood.

AUTOBIOGRAPHY **Account by a writer of his or her own life.** "Typhoid Fever" (page 194) is a selection from a famous autobiography by Frank McCourt. "By Any Other Name" (page 113) by Santha Rama Rau is an example of a short autobiographical essay.

See also *Biography.*

BALLAD **Song or songlike poem that tells a story.** Ballads often tell stories that have tragic endings. Most ballads have a regular pattern of **rhythm** and **rhyme** and use simple language and repetition. Generally they have a **refrain**—lines or words repeated at regular intervals. **Folk ballads** (such as "Bonny Barbara Allan," page 510) were composed by unknown singers and passed on orally for generations before being written down. **Literary ballads** and some country-and-western songs imitate folk ballads.

See page 509.

BIOGRAPHY **Account of a person's life written or told by another person.** A classic American biography is Carl Sandburg's multivolume work about Abraham Lincoln. Today biographies of writers, actors, sports stars, and TV personalities are often bestsellers.

See also *Autobiography.*

BLANK VERSE **Poetry written in unrhymed iambic pentameter.** *Blank verse* means that the poetry is unrhymed. *Iambic pentameter* means that each line contains five iambs; an **iamb** is a type of **metrical foot** that consists of an unstressed syllable followed by a stressed syllable (˘ ′). Blank verse is the most important metrical form in English dramatic and epic poetry and the major verse line in Shakespeare's plays. One reason blank verse has been popular, even with some modern poets, is that it combines the naturalness of unrhymed verse and the structure of metrical verse.

> When I see birches bend to left and right
> Across the line of straighter darker trees,
> I like to think some boy's been swinging them.
>
> —Robert Frost, from "Birches"

See page 752.
See also *Iambic Pentameter, Meter.*

CHARACTER **Individual in a story, poem, or play.** A character always has human traits, even if the character is an animal, as in Aesop's fables. In myths the characters are divinities or heroes with superhuman powers, such as the hero Theseus in "Theseus" (page 662) or Sigurd in "Sigurd, the Dragon Slayer" (page 674). Most characters are ordinary human beings, however.

A writer can reveal a character's personality by

1. telling us directly what the character is like (generous, deceitful, timid, and so on)
2. describing how the character looks and dresses
3. letting us hear the character speak
4. letting us listen to the character's inner thoughts and feelings
5. revealing what other people think or say about the character
6. showing the character's actions

The first method listed above is called **direct characterization:** The writer tells us directly what the character is like. The other five methods are **indirect characterization.** We have to put clues together to figure out what a character is like, just as we do in real life when we are getting to know someone.

Static and flat characters often function as **subordinate characters** in a story. This means that they

980 Resource Center Handbook of Literary Terms

may play important roles in a story, but they are not the main actors in the plot.

A **static character** does not change much in the course of a story. A **dynamic character,** on the other hand, changes in some important ways as a result of the story's action. **Flat characters** have only one or two personality traits and can be summed up in a single phrase. In contrast, **round characters** are complex and have many different traits. The needs or conflicts that drive a character are called **motivation.**

See pages 45, 74–75, 76, 96–97, 112.
See also *Protagonist.*

COMEDY **In general, a story that ends happily.** The hero of a comedy is usually an ordinary character who overcomes a series of obstacles that block what he or she wants. Many comedies have a boy-meets-girl (or girl-meets-boy) plot, in which young lovers must face figures from the older generation who do not want them to marry. At the end of such comedies, the lovers marry, and everyone celebrates the renewal of life and love, as in Shakespeare's play *A Midsummer Night's Dream.* In structure and characterization a comedy is the opposite of a **tragedy.**

In a serious literary work a humorous scene is said to provide **comic relief.**

See pages 721, 724.
See also *Drama, Tragedy.*

CONFLICT **Struggle or clash between opposing characters, forces, or emotions.** In an **external conflict** a character struggles against an outside force, which may be another character, society as a whole, or something in nature. In "The Cold Equations" (page 164), Barton and Cross find themselves in a fight with the harsh laws of nature.

An **internal conflict** is a struggle between opposing needs, desires, or emotions within a single character. The main character in W. D. Wetherell's "The Bass, the River, and Sheila Mant" (page 244) is torn between his desire to land a fish and his desire to impress a girl. Many works, especially longer ones, contain both internal and external conflicts, and an external conflict often leads to internal problems.

See pages 2–3, 45, 96, 98, 243.

CONNOTATIONS **All the meanings, associations, or emotions that a word suggests.** For example, an expensive restaurant might advertise its delicious "cuisine" rather than its delicious "cooking." *Cuisine* and *cooking* have the same **denotation** (literal meaning): "prepared food." However, *cuisine,* a word from French, has connotations of elegance and sophistication; *cooking,* a plain English word, suggests the plainness of everyday food. Connotations play an important role in creating **diction, mood,** and **tone.**

See pages 54, 282, 631.
See also *Diction, Mood, Tone.*

COUPLET **Two consecutive lines of poetry that form a unit, often emphasized by rhythm or rhyme.** Since the Middle Ages the couplet has been used to express a completed thought or to provide a sense of closure, as in this final speech from Shakespeare's play *Julius Caesar:*

> So call the field to rest, and let's away
> To part the glories of this happy day.

See page 493.

DESCRIPTION **Type of writing intended to create a mood or an emotion or to re-create a person, a place, a thing, an event, or an experience.** Description uses **images** that appeal to the senses, helping us imagine how a subject looks, sounds, smells, tastes, or feels. Description is used in fiction, nonfiction, drama, and poetry.

See also *Imagery.*

DIALECT **Way of speaking that is characteristic of a particular region or group of people.** A dialect may have a distinct vocabulary, pronunciation system, and grammar. In the United States the dialect used in formal writing and spoken by most TV and radio announcers is known as standard English. This is the dialect taught in schools. To bring characters to life, writers often use dialects.

See page 95.

DIALOGUE **Conversation between two or more characters.** Dramas are made up of dialogue, which is also important in novels and stories and in some poems and nonfiction.

See pages 74, 76, 722.

Handbook of Literary Terms 981

DICTION **Writer's or speaker's choice of words.** Diction is an essential element of a writer's **style.** A writer can choose words that are simple or flowery *(clothing/apparel),* modern or old-fashioned *(dress/frock),* general or specific *(pants/designer jeans).* Writers choose words for their connotations (emotional associations) as well as their literal meanings, or denotations.

See pages 139, 556, 558.
See also *Connotations, Tone.*

DRAMA **Story that is written to be acted for an audience.** The action of a drama is driven by a character who wants something and who takes steps to get it. The major elements of a dramatic plot are **exposition, complications, climax,** and **resolution.** The term *drama* is also used to refer to a serious play that is neither a **comedy** nor a **tragedy.**

See pages 720–723, 745–749, 754.

DRAMATIC MONOLOGUE **A poem in which a speaker addresses one or more silent listeners, often reflecting on a specific problem or situation.** Though the person addressed in a dramatic monologue does not speak, we often can discover something about the listener or listeners by paying close attention to the speaker's words. The most famous dramatic monologues in English literature are those written by Robert Browning. Here are the opening lines of "My Last Duchess," spoken by a duke to his agent. The agent remains silent. As the monologue continues, we learn the duke's dark secret:

> That's my last Duchess painted on the wall,
> Looking as if she were alive. I call
> That piece a wonder, now: Frà Pandolf's hands
> Worked busily a day, and there she stands.
> Will 't please you sit and look at her?
>
> —Robert Browning, from
> "My Last Duchess"

See pages 75, 85.

EPIC **Long narrative poem that relates the great deeds of a larger-than-life hero who embodies the values of a particular society.** Most epics include elements of myth, legend, folklore, and history; their tone is serious and their language grand. Epic heroes undertake quests to achieve something of tremendous value to themselves or their society. Homer's *Odyssey* and *Iliad* and Virgil's *Aeneid* are the best-known epics in the Western tradition. The great epic of India is the *Mahabharata;* Japan's is *The Tale of the Heike;* and Mali's is *Sundiata.*

ESSAY **Short piece of nonfiction that examines a single subject from a limited point of view.** Most essays can be classified as personal or formal. A **personal essay** (sometimes called **informal**) is generally subjective, revealing a great deal about the writer's personality and feelings. Its tone is conversational, sometimes even humorous.

A **formal essay** is usually serious, objective, and impersonal in tone. Because formal essays are often written to inform or persuade, they are expected to be factual, logical, and tightly organized.

See pages 254, 272.

EXPOSITION **Type of writing that explains, gives information, or clarifies an idea.** Exposition is generally objective and formal in tone (as in a magazine article on nutrition).

Exposition is also the term for the first part of a plot (also called the **basic situation**), which presents the main characters and their conflicts.

See page 2.
See also *Plot.*

FABLE **Brief story in prose or verse that teaches a moral, or a practical lesson about life.** The characters of most fables are animals that behave and speak like humans. Some of the most popular fables are those attributed to Aesop, who scholars believe was a slave in ancient Greece. Other widely read fables are those in the *Panchatantra,* ancient Indian tales about the art of ruling wisely.

See page 399.
See also *Folk Tale, Parable.*

FIGURE OF SPEECH **Word or phrase that describes one thing in terms of another and that is not meant to be understood on a literal level.** Figures of speech, or **figurative language,** always involve some sort of imaginative comparison between seemingly unlike things. The most common

982 Resource Center Handbook of Literary Terms

are the **simile** ("My heart is like a singing bird"), the **metaphor** ("Life's but a walking shadow"), and **personification** ("Death has reared himself a throne").

See pages 242, 557, 564, 585, 599.
See also *Metaphor, Personification, Simile, Symbol.*

FLASHBACK Scene in a movie, play, short story, novel, or narrative poem that interrupts the present action of the plot to show events that happened at an earlier time. In "Everyday Use" (page 77), the narrator uses a flashback to a house fire to explain family conflicts. Flashbacks are commonly used in movies.

See pages 3, 31, 564.

FLASH-FORWARD Scene in a movie, play, short story, novel, or narrative poem that interrupts the present action of the plot to shift into the future. Writers may use a flash-forward to create dramatic irony. By means of the flash-forward, we know the future, but the story characters do not.

See page 3.

FOIL Character who serves as a contrast to another character. Writers use a foil to emphasize differences between two characters. In *Julius Caesar,* the solemn, self-controlled Octavius is a foil for the excitable, impetuous Antony.

See pages 767, 779, 788.

FOLK TALE Anonymous traditional story originally passed down orally from generation to generation. Folk tales are told in every culture, and similar tales are told throughout the world. Many of these stories have been written down. Scholars draw a sharp distinction between folk tales and myths. **Myths,** unlike folk tales, are stories about humans and gods and are basically religious in nature. Examples of folk tales are fairy tales, fables, legends, ghost stories, tall tales, anecdotes, and even jokes. Folk tales tend to travel, so the same plot often appears in several cultures. For example, there are said to be nine hundred versions of the folk tale about Cinderella.

See also *Fable, Myth, Tall Tale.*

FORESHADOWING The use of clues to hint at events that will occur later in the plot. Foreshadowing arouses the reader's curiosity and increases **suspense.** In Act I, Scene 3, of *Julius Caesar* (page 771), references to violent disturbances in the heavens foreshadow the turbulence and violence that will soon occur in the human world.

See pages 3, 31.
See also *Plot, Suspense.*

FREE VERSE Poetry that does not have a regular meter or rhyme scheme. Poets writing in free verse try to capture the natural rhythms of ordinary speech. To create musical effects, they may use **alliteration, assonance, internal rhyme,** and **onomatopoeia.** They also often repeat words or grammatical structures.

> Women sit or move to and fro, some old,
> some young,
> The young are beautiful—but the old are more
> beautiful than the young.
>
> —Walt Whitman, from "Beautiful Women"

See pages 504, 513.
See also *Alliteration, Assonance, Meter, Onomatopoeia, Rhythm.*

GENRE (zhän′rə) **The category that a work of literature is classified under. Five major genres in literature are nonfiction, fiction, poetry, drama, and myth.** Chapters 7 and 10 of this book are organized by genre: by poetry and by drama.

See pages 255, 256.

HAIKU Japanese verse form consisting of three lines and usually seventeen syllables (five in the first line, seven in the second, and five in the third). The writer of a haiku uses association and suggestion to describe a particular moment of discovery or enlightenment. A haiku often presents an image of daily life that relates to a particular season. Many modern American poets (such as William Carlos Williams, Amy Lowell, Ezra Pound, Richard Wright, and Gary Snyder) have tried to capture the spirit of haiku, though they have not always followed the form strictly.

Handbook of Literary Terms 983

HYPERBOLE Figure of speech that uses exaggeration to express strong emotion or create a comic effect. Writers often use hyperbole (hī·pʉr′bə·lē), also called **overstatement,** to intensify a description or to emphasize the essential nature of something. If you say that a limousine is as long as an ocean liner, you are using hyperbole.

IAMBIC PENTAMETER Line of poetry made up of five iambs. An **iamb** is a metrical foot consisting of an unstressed syllable followed by a stressed syllable, as in dĕný and ĕxpéct. Iambic pentameter is by far the most common meter in English poetry.

See pages 518, 752.
See also *Blank Verse, Meter.*

IDIOM Expression peculiar to a particular language that means something different from the literal meaning of the words. "It's raining cats and dogs" and "We heard it straight from the horse's mouth" are idioms of American English. One of the difficulties of translating a work from another language is translating idioms.

See page 521.

IMAGERY Language that appeals to the senses. Imagery is used in all types of writing but is especially important in poetry. Most images are visual—that is, they create in the reader's mind pictures that appeal to the sense of sight. Imagery may also appeal to the senses of sound, smell, touch, and taste, as in the following lines about winter. (*Saw* in line 2 is a wise saying; *crabs* in line 5 are crab apples; and to *keel* is to cool by stirring.)

> When all aloud the wind doth blow,
>   And coughing drowns the parson's saw,
> And birds sit brooding in the snow,
>   And Marian's nose looks red and raw,
> When roasted crabs hiss in the bowl,
> Then nightly sings the staring owl—Tu whit,
> Tu-who, a merry note,
> While greasy Joan doth keel the pot.
>
> —William Shakespeare
> from *Love's Labor's Lost*

See pages 456–457, 564, 599.

INCONGRUITY (in′kän·gro͞o′i·tē) **A lack of fitness or appropriateness.** When someone goes to a formal dinner party dressed in a bathing suit, the situation is incongruous. Incongruity is often used to create situational irony in literature.

See page 349.
See also *Irony.*

INVERSION Reversal of normal word order in a sentence. The normal word order in an English sentence is subject-verb-complement (if there is a complement). Modifiers are usually placed immediately before or after the word they modify. Poets use inversion to give emphasis and variety and to create rhymes or accommodate a meter.

> Open here I flung the shutter, when, with
>   many a flirt and flutter,
> In there stepped a stately Raven of the
>   saintly days of yore;
> Not the least obeisance made he; not a
>   minute stopped or stayed he. . . .
>
> —Edgar Allan Poe, from "The Raven"

See page 162.

IRONY Contrast or discrepancy between expectation and reality. In **verbal irony** a speaker says one thing but means the opposite. In Shakespeare's *Julius Caesar,* Antony uses **verbal irony** during his funeral oration for Caesar. When he insists that "Brutus is an honorable man," he means precisely the opposite.

In **situational irony** what actually happens is the opposite of what is expected or appropriate. In Tim O'Brien's story "Where Have You Gone, Charming Billy?" (page 621), we feel a strong sense of irony when Paul Berlin is overcome with laughter upon being told of the death of his fellow soldier, Billy Boy Watkins.

Dramatic irony occurs when the reader or the audience knows something important that a character does not know. In "The Cold Equations" by Tom Godwin (page 164), when Marilyn mischievously asks what her punishment will be, she expects simply to be fined; we know that her fate will be much graver.

See pages 314–315, 316, 328, 349.
See also *Tone.*

984 Resource Center Handbook of Literary Terms

LYRIC POETRY Poetry that expresses a speaker's emotions or thoughts and does not tell a story. The term **lyric** comes from ancient Greece, where such poems were recited to the accompaniment of a stringed instrument called a lyre. Most lyric poems are short, and they imply, rather than state directly, a single strong emotion. Li-Young Lee's "Eating Together" (page 466) and John Masefield's "Sea Fever" (page 507) are lyric poems.

See page 482.
See also *Sonnet.*

MAGIC REALISM Style of fiction, commonly associated with contemporary Latin American writers, in which fantasy and reality are casually combined, producing humorous and thought-provoking results. "A Very Old Man with Enormous Wings" (page 587), in which an old, winged, humanlike creature lands in a poor family's backyard, is an example of magic realism.

See page 586.

METAPHOR Figure of speech that makes a comparison between two unlike things without using a connective word such as *like, as, than,* or *resembles.* Some metaphors, such as Gerard Manley Hopkins's comparison "I am soft sift / In an hourglass," are **direct.** (If he had written, "I am *like* soft sift . . . ," he would have been using a **simile.**) Other metaphors are **implied,** such as the one in Walt Whitman's lines "O Captain! my Captain! our fearful trip is done, / The ship has weather'd every rack, the prize we sought is won." The images imply a comparison between a captain commanding his ship and a president leading his country (in this case, the president was Lincoln).

An **extended metaphor** is developed over several lines or throughout an entire poem. In the poem "Fireworks" (page 550), Amy Lowell uses an extended metaphor when, over many lines of poetry, she compares strong feelings to fireworks.

A **mixed metaphor** is the inconsistent combination of two or more metaphors. Mixed metaphors are usually unintentional and often humorous: "It's no use closing the barn door after the milk has been spilled."

See pages 478, 484.
See also *Analogy, Figure of Speech, Personification, Simile, Symbol.*

METER A generally regular pattern of stressed and unstressed syllables in poetry. To indicate the metrical pattern of a poem, we mark the stressed syllables with the symbol (ʹ) and the unstressed syllables with the symbol (˘). Analyzing the metrical pattern of a poem in this way is called **scanning** the poem, or **scansion** (skan′shən).

Meter is measured in units called feet. A **foot** usually consists of one stressed syllable and one or more unstressed syllables. Here are examples of the standard feet in English poetry:

1. **iamb** (iambic): an unstressed syllable followed by a stressed syllable, as in *forget, deceive.* This line from "The Eagle" by Alfred, Lord Tennyson, has four iambic feet:

   The wrinkled sea beneath him crawls

2. **trochee** (trochaic): a stressed syllable followed by an unstressed syllable, as in *listen, lonely.* This line from William Shakespeare's *Macbeth* is in trochees:

   Double, double, toil and trouble

3. **anapest** (anapestic): two unstressed syllables followed by one stressed syllable, as in *understand, luncheonette.* This line from "The Destruction of Sennacherib" by George Gordon, Lord Byron, is in anapests:

   The Assyrian came down like the wolf on the fold

4. **dactyl** (dactylic): one stressed syllable followed by two unstressed syllables, as in *excellent, temperate.* This extract from Shakespeare's *Macbeth* contains dactyls:

   . . . you murdering ministers . . .

5. **spondee** (spondaic): two stressed syllables, as in *heartbeat* and *football.* This foot is used for emphasis, as in these lines from *Leaves of Grass* by Walt Whitman:

   Come up here, bard, bard,
   Come up here, soul, soul. . . .

A metrical line is named for the type of foot and the number of feet in the line. (*Dimeter* is two feet, *trimeter* three feet, *tetrameter* four feet, and *pentameter* five feet.) Thus a line of five iambs is called *iambic pentameter;* a line of four trochees is *trochaic tetrameter.*

See pages 503, 506.
See also *Blank Verse, Iambic Pentameter.*

Handbook of Literary Terms 985

MOOD **A story's atmosphere or the feeling it evokes.** Mood is often created by the story's setting. A story set on a dreary moor where cold water seeps into the hero's boots will probably convey a mood of suspense and uneasiness. A story set in a garden full of sunlight and the chirps of birds will probably create a mood of peace. Edgar Allan Poe's bizarre setting of "The Masque of the Red Death" (page 419) creates a dizzying atmosphere of horror.

See pages 44–45, 46, 140.
See also *Setting.*

MYTH **Traditional story that is rooted in a particular culture, is basically religious, and usually serves to explain a belief, a ritual, or a mysterious natural phenomenon.** Most myths grew out of religious rituals; almost all of them involve the influence of gods on human affairs. Every culture has its own mythology. For centuries the myths of ancient Greece and Rome were influential in the Western world.

See pages 619, 660–661, 673.

NARRATION **Type of writing that tells about a series of related events.** Narration can be long (an entire book) or short (a brief anecdote). Narration is most often found in fiction, drama, and narrative poetry (such as epics and ballads), but it also is used in nonfiction works (such as biographies and essays).

NARRATOR **The voice telling a story.** The choice of a narrator is very important in storytelling. For example, in "By the Waters of Babylon" (page 141), we know only what the narrator knows, and like him, we must figure out the mysteries of the Place of the Gods.

See also *Point of View.*

NONFICTION **Prose writing that deals with real people, things, events, and places.** The most popular forms are biography and autobiography. Essays, newspaper stories, magazine articles, historical accounts, scientific reports, and even personal diaries and letters are also nonfiction.

See page 255.

NOVEL **Long fictional prose narrative, usually of more than fifty thousand words.** In general, the novel uses the same basic literary elements as the short story **(plot, character, setting, theme, and point of view),** but these elements are usually more fully developed in the novel. Many novels have several subplots, for instance. Some modern novels are basically character studies, with only the barest plot. Others concentrate on setting, tone, or even language itself.

ONOMATOPOEIA (än′ō·mat′ō·pē′ə) **Use of a word whose sound imitates or suggests its meaning.** *Buzz, splash,* and *bark* are examples of onomatopoeia. In poetry, onomatopoeia reinforces meaning and creates evocative and musical sound effects.

See pages 505, 535.

PARABLE **Brief story that teaches a lesson about life.** A parable has human characters, and its events are drawn from the stuff of everyday life. Parables usually illustrate moral or religious lessons. A fable, in contrast, usually has animal characters and teaches a practical lesson about how to succeed in life. The most famous parables in Western literature are found in the Bible.

See pages 278, 399.
See also *Fable, Folk Tale.*

PARADOX **A statement or a situation that seems to be a contradiction but that reveals a truth.** Paradoxes are designed to make readers stop and think. They often express aspects of life that are mysterious, surprising, or difficult to describe. When the ancient Mariner in Samuel Taylor Coleridge's poem cries, "Water, water everywhere, / Nor any drop to drink," he is expressing a paradox. He is dying of thirst adrift in the ocean, the water from which he cannot drink.

PARALLELISM **Repetition of words, phrases, or sentences that have the same grammatical structure or that state a similar idea.** Parallelism, or parallel structure, helps make lines rhythmic and memorable and heightens their emotional effect:

> Bring me my bow of burning gold!
> Bring me my arrows of desire!
> Bring me my spear! O clouds, unfold!
> Bring me my chariot of fire!
>
> —William Blake, from "Jerusalem"

986 Resource Center Handbook of Literary Terms

PERSONA Mask or voice assumed by a writer. Authors often take on other identities in their works. In a short story a writer may assume a persona by using a first-person narrator. When a poet is not the speaker of a poem, the poet is creating a persona.

See pages 138, 140.
See also *Point of View, Speaker.*

PERSONIFICATION Type of metaphor in which a nonhuman thing or quality is talked about as if it were human. In the example below, trees are personified as women throwing off their robes.

> The trees are undressing, and fling in many
> places—
> On the gray road, the roof, the window sill—
> Their radiant robes and ribbons and yellow laces.
>
> —Thomas Hardy
> from "Last Week in October"

See pages 478, 487.
See also *Figure of Speech, Metaphor.*

PERSUASION Type of writing designed to change the way a reader or listener thinks or acts. Persuasive writing can be found in speeches, newspaper editorials, essays, and advertisements.

See pages 284–285.

PLOT Series of related events that make up a story or drama. Plot is "what happens" in a story, novel, or play. A story map shows the parts of a plot.

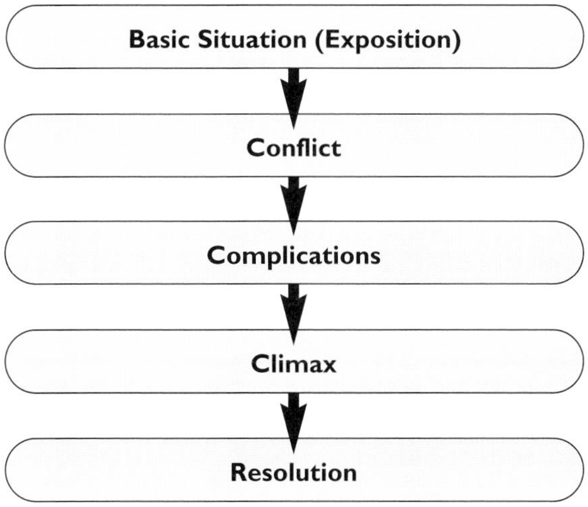

The **climax** is the most intense moment in the plot, the moment at which something happens that reveals how the conflict will turn out. In the **resolution,** or denouement (dā′no͞o·män′), all the problems in the story are resolved, and the story is brought to a close.

See pages 2–3, 4.

POETRY Type of rhythmic, compressed language that uses figures of speech and imagery to appeal to the reader's emotions and imagination. The major forms of poetry are **lyric** and **narrative.** A popular type of lyric is the **sonnet.** Two major types of narrative are the **epic** and the **ballad.** Though poetry is one of the oldest forms of human expression, it is extremely difficult to define.

See pages 456–457, 477–478, 503–505.
See also *Ballad, Epic, Lyric Poetry, Sonnet.*

POINT OF VIEW Vantage point from which a writer narrates, or tells, a story. The three main points of view are omniscient, third-person-limited, and first-person.

In the **omniscient** (or "all-knowing") **point of view,** the narrator plays no part in the story but can tell us what all the characters are thinking and feeling as well as what is happening in other places. For example, in "Through the Tunnel" (page 401), the storyteller can tell us what both Jerry and his mother are thinking and feeling.

In the **third-person-limited point of view,** the narrator, who plays no part in the story, zooms in on the thoughts and feelings of one character. In "Catch the Moon" by Judith Ortiz Cofer (page 234), we know Luis's thoughts and feelings but the emotions of his father and of Naomi are revealed only through their words and Luis's observations.

In the **first-person point of view,** the narrator (using the first-person pronoun *I*) is a character in the story. When we read a story told in the first person, we hear and see only what the narrator hears and sees. We must ask ourselves if the narrator is **credible,** or **reliable.** An **unreliable narrator** does not always know what is happening in the story, or he or she might be lying or telling us only part of the story. For example, in "By the Waters of Babylon" (see page 141), we cannot rely on the narrator to tell us the mystery of the Place of the Gods because he does not know it.

See pages 138–139, 140, 154, 163.
See also *Narrator.*

Handbook of Literary Terms 987

PROTAGONIST Main character in fiction or drama. The protagonist is the character we focus our attention on, the person who sets the plot in motion. The character or force that blocks the protagonist is called the **antagonist.** Most protagonists are rounded, dynamic characters who change in some important way by the end of the story, novel, or play. The antagonist is often, but not always, the villain in a story. Similarly, the protagonist is often, but not always, the hero.

See page 96.
See also *Character.*

PUN Play on the multiple meanings of a word or on two words that sound alike but have different meanings. Many jokes and riddles are based on puns. ("When is a doctor most annoyed?" Answer: "When he runs out of patients.") Shakespeare was one of the greatest punsters of all time. In Antony's speech to the conspirators after Caesar's murder in Act III (page 813), Antony puns on the expression "to let blood." Doctors used to draw, or let, blood from sick people to cure them; murderers also "let blood."

See page 781.

REFRAIN Repeated word, phrase, line, or group of lines. Though refrains are usually associated with poetry and songs, they are sometimes used in prose, especially in speeches. Refrains create rhythm and may also build suspense or emphasize important words or ideas.

See page 527.

RHYME Repetition of accented vowel sounds and all sounds following them in words that are close together in a poem. *Heart* and *start* rhyme, as do *plaster* and *faster.* The most common type of rhyme, **end rhyme,** occurs at the ends of lines.

> When she I loved looked every day
> Fresh as a rose in June,
> I to her cottage bent my way,
> Beneath the evening moon.
>
> —William Wordsworth
> from "Strange Fits of Passion
> Have I Known"

The pattern of rhymed lines in a poem is called its **rhyme scheme.** You indicate a rhyme scheme by giving each new end rhyme a new letter of the alphabet. For example, the rhyme scheme in Wordsworth's stanza is *abab.*

Internal rhymes occur within lines.

> The warm sun is failing, the bleak wind is
> wailing,
> The bare boughs are sighing, the pale flowers
> are dying . . .
>
> —Percy Bysshe Shelley
> from "Autumn: A Dirge"

Words that sound similar but do not rhyme exactly are called **approximate rhymes** (or **half rhymes, slant rhymes,** or **imperfect rhymes**). The approximate rhymes at the ends of lines in this stanza from a poem about war keep the reader off balance and even uneasy, in keeping with the poem's subject:

> Let the boy try along this bayonet blade
> How cold steel is, and keen with hunger of
> blood;
> Blue with all malice, like a madman's flash;
> And thinly drawn with famishing for flesh.
>
> —Wilfred Owen, from "Arms and the Boy"

See pages 504–505, 506.

RHYTHM Musical quality in language, produced by repetition. Rhythm occurs naturally in all forms of spoken and written language. Poems written in **meter** create rhythm by a strict pattern of stressed and unstressed syllables. Writers can also create rhythm by repeating grammatical structures, by using pauses, by varying line lengths, and by balancing long and short words or phrases.

See page 503.
See also *Meter.*

ROMANCE Centuries ago, in France and England, a romance was a verse narrative about the adventures of a hero who undertakes a quest for a high ideal. The tales of King Arthur are

988 Resource Center Handbook of Literary Terms

typical romances. The term *romance* later came to mean any story set in a world of wish fulfillment, with larger-than-life characters having superhuman powers. Romances usually involve a series of adventures that end with good triumphing over evil. Fairy tales and western movies are often built on the old romance plots and use the characters typical of romance literature.

See pages 651, 657.

SATIRE Type of writing that ridicules human weakness, vice, or folly in order to reveal a weakness or to bring about social reform. Satires often try to persuade the reader to do or believe something by showing the opposite view as absurd—or even as vicious and inhumane. One of the favorite techniques of the satirist is **exaggeration**—overstating something to make it look worse than it is.

See page 154.
See also *Hyperbole, Irony.*

SCENE DESIGN Sets, lights, costumes, and props, which bring a play to life onstage. Sets are the furnishings and scenery that suggest the time and place of the action. **Props** (short for *properties*) are all the objects that the actors use onstage, such as books, telephones, suitcases.

See pages 721–722.

SETTING Time and place of a story or play. Setting can function in several ways in a story. It can provide atmosphere, as the ice-coated world does in Jim Heynen's "What Happened During the Ice Storm" (page 306). Setting may provide conflict in a story, as it does in Tim O'Brien's "Where Have You Gone, Charming Billy?" (page 621). One of the most important functions of setting is to reveal character. In Alice Walker's "Everyday Use" (page 77), the narrator's home helps show us who she is and what her life is like.

See pages 44–45, 46, 140.
See also *Mood.*

SHORT STORY Short piece of narrative fiction. Edgar Allan Poe (see page 428), who lived and wrote during the first half of the nineteenth century, is often credited with writing the first short stories. He defined the short story (which he called the "prose tale") as a narrative that can be read in a single sitting and that creates a "single effect."

SIMILE Figure of speech that makes a comparison between two seemingly unlike things by using a connective word such as *like, as, than,* or *resembles.* Here is a simile that creates a dramatic visual image; like any good figure of speech, Hardy's simile is original and vivid:

> The Roman Road runs straight and bare
> As the pale parting-line in hair
>
> —Thomas Hardy
> from "The Roman Road"

See pages 477, 479.
See also *Analogy, Figure of Speech, Metaphor.*

SOLILOQUY Long speech in which a character who is alone onstage expresses private thoughts or feelings. The soliloquy (sə·lil′ə·kwē), especially popular in Shakespeare's day, is an old dramatic convention. Near the beginning of Act II in *Julius Caesar* (page 783), Brutus's speech in which he decides to join the conspiracy against Caesar is a soliloquy.

See pages 75, 722.

SONNET Fourteen-line lyric poem, usually written in iambic pentameter. There are two major types of sonnets. The **Italian sonnet,** also called the **Petrarchan sonnet,** is named after the fourteenth-century Italian poet Francesco Petrarch, who popularized the form. The Petrarchan sonnet has two parts: an eight-line **octave** with the rhyme scheme *abbaabba,* and a six-line **sestet** with the rhyme scheme *cdecde.* The octave usually presents a problem, poses a question, or expresses an idea, which the sestet then resolves, answers, or drives home. A modern variation on the Italian sonnet, by E. E. Cummings, can be found on page 485. Like many sonnets, Cummings's poem is about love.

The other major sonnet form is called the **Shakespearean sonnet,** or the **English sonnet.** It has three **quatrains** (four-line units) followed by a concluding **couplet** (two-line unit). The three quatrains often express related ideas or examples; the couplet sums up the poet's conclusion or message. The most common rhyme scheme for the Shakespearean sonnet is *abab cdcd efef gg.* A Shakespearean sonnet—also about love—can be found on page 494.

See page 493.
See also *Lyric Poetry.*

Handbook of Literary Terms 989

SPEAKER The voice that is talking to us in a poem. Sometimes the speaker is the same as the poet, but the poet may also create a different voice, speaking as a child, a woman, a man, a nation, an animal, or even an object.

See page 465.
See also *Dramatic Monologue, Persona.*

STANZA Group of consecutive lines that form a single unit in a poem. A stanza in a poem is something like a paragraph in prose: It often expresses a unit of thought. A stanza may consist of only one line or of any number of lines beyond that. John Updike's "Ex–Basketball Player" (page 519) consists of five six-line stanzas, each expressing a unit of thought.

See also *Sonnet.*

STYLE The particular way in which a writer uses language. Style is created mainly through **diction** (word choice), use of **figurative language,** and sentence patterns. Style can be described as plain, ornate, formal, ironic, conversational, sentimental, and so on.

See pages 556–557, 558, 586.

SUSPENSE The uncertainty or anxiety we feel about what is going to happen next in a story. Writers often create suspense by dropping hints or clues foreshadowing something—especially something bad—that is going to happen later. Writers also create suspense by setting up time limits, as in "R.M.S. Titanic" (page 330), where our suspense builds as we are shown the minutes ticking away.

See page 3.
See also *Foreshadowing, Plot.*

SYMBOL Person, place, thing, or event that stands both for itself and for something beyond itself. Many symbols have become so widely recognized that they are **public symbols:** In Western cultures, for example, most people recognize the heart as a symbol of love and the snake as a symbol of evil. Writers often invent new, personal symbols. For example, in this mysterious poem, "The Sick Rose," what might the rose and the worm symbolize?

O Rose, thou art sick!
The invisible worm,
That flies in the night,
In the howling storm,
Has found out thy bed
Of crimson joy:
And his dark secret love
Does thy life destroy.

—William Blake

See pages 398–399, 400, 433.
See also *Figure of Speech.*

TALL TALE An outrageously exaggerated and obviously unbelievable humorous story. In pre-TV days, the tall tale was a kind of oral entertainment. In the Southwest, cowboys sat around their campfires telling stories about Pecos Bill, who invented the lariat, rode a bucking Kansas tornado, and dug the Rio Grande river. Other tall tale heroes include the Northwest logger Paul Bunyan (and Babe, his gigantic blue ox), the Pennsylvania steel man Joe Magarac, and the New England fisherman Captain Stormalong. Tall tales were told about real-life figures, too, such as Tennessee frontiersman Davy Crockett and sharpshooter Annie Oakley.

A modern **urban tall tale**—perennially rumored to be true—tells of a baby pet alligator someone flushed down a toilet in New York City. The result, according to this tale, is that monster alligators populate the sewers beneath the city.

See *Folk Tale.*

THEME The central idea or insight about human life revealed by a work of literature. A theme is not the same as a work's subject, which can usually be expressed in a word or two: old age, ambition, love. The theme is the revelation the writer wishes us to discover about that subject. There is no single correct way to express a theme, and sometimes a work has several themes. Many works have **ambiguous themes;** that is, they have no clear single meaning but are open to a variety of interpretations, even

990 Resource Center Handbook of Literary Terms

opposing ones. Some themes are so commonly found in the literature of all cultures and all ages that they are called **universal themes.** Here are some universal themes found in stories throughout the ages: "Heroes must undergo trials and endure losses before they can claim their rightful kingdom." "Arrogance and pride can bring destruction." "When the rule of law is broken, chaos and anarchy will result." "Love will endure and triumph over evil."

Although a few stories, poems, and plays have themes that are stated directly, most themes are implied. The reader must piece together all the clues the writer has provided to arrive at a discovery of the work's total meaning. Two of the most important clues to consider are the way the main character has changed and the way the conflict has been resolved.

See pages 230–231, 232, 233, 243, 255, 256.

TONE **The attitude a writer takes toward a subject, a character, or the reader.** Tone is conveyed through the writer's choice of words and details. For example, Tim O'Brien's story "Where Have You Gone, Charming Billy?" (page 621) is ironic in tone. John Masefield's "Sea-Fever" (page 507) has a nostalgic tone for a life that is now past.

See pages 44, 139, 193, 557, 558.
See also *Connotations, Diction, Irony.*

TRAGEDY **Play, novel, or other narrative, depicting serious and important events, in which the main character comes to an unhappy end.** In a tragedy, the main character is usually dignified and courageous and often high ranking. This character's downfall may be caused by a **tragic flaw** (a serious character weakness) or by forces beyond the hero's control. The tragic hero usually wins self-knowledge and wisdom, even though he or she suffers defeat, possibly even death. Shakespeare's *The Tragedy of Julius Caesar* (page 756) is a tragedy. Tragedy is distinct from **comedy,** in which an ordinary character overcomes obstacles to get what he or she wants. At the end of most comedies, the characters are all happily integrated into society (comedies often end with weddings). Tragedies often end with death or separation or alienation.

See pages 720, 754.
See also *Comedy, Drama.*

VOICE **The writer's or speaker's distinctive use of language in a text.** Voice is created by a writer's **tone** and **diction,** or choice of words. Some writers have such a distinctive voice that you can identify their works on the basis of voice alone. Frank McCourt creates a distinctive voice in his memoir about growing up in Ireland, "Typhoid Fever" (see page 194).

See pages 139, 193, 205, 465.

Handbook of Literary Terms 991

Handbook of Reading and Informational Terms

For more information about a topic, turn to the page(s) in this book indicated on a separate line at the end of most entries. To learn more about *Inference,* for example, turn to page 76.

The words in **boldface** are other key terms, with definitions provided in context. On another line there are cross-references to entries in this Handbook that provide closely related information. For instance, *Logic* contains a cross-reference to *Logical Order.*

ARGUMENT **A series of statements in a text designed to convince us of something.** What the writer or speaker wants to prove is called the **claim** (or the **opinion**). An argument might appeal to both our reason and our emotions. An argument in a scientific or historical journal, for instance, would probably present only **logical appeals,** which include sound reasons and factual evidence. An argument in a political text would probably also include emotional appeals, which are directed more to our "hearts" than to our minds. Some arguments use **loaded words** (words loaded with emotional connotations) and **anecdotes** (brief, personal stories) that also appeal to our feelings. It is important to be able to recognize emotional appeals used in arguments—and to be aware of how they can trick an audience.

Arguments may be found in editorials, magazine articles, political speeches, professional journals, and primary source material.

See pages 284–285, 577–578, 881.

CAUSE AND EFFECT **A text structure that shows how or why one thing leads to another.** The **cause** is the reason that an action takes place. The **effect** is the result or consequence of the cause. A cause can have more than one effect, and an effect may have several causes. Writers may explain causes only or effects only.

A text may be organized in a cause-effect chain. One cause leads to an effect, which causes another effect, and so on. Notice the cause-effect chain in the following paragraph from "An Ancient Enemy Gets Tougher" (page 207):

> But if there's a glitch in the body's defense system, and it doesn't work quite right, these once tiny balls can grow, some to the size of a baseball, as the bacteria inside them reproduce. These balls can erupt, spreading bacteria to other parts of the body through the blood. More balls, or "tubercles," grow, eventually clogging up the way the body does its daily business.

Cause:
There's a glitch in the body's defense system.

↓

Effect:
Those tiny balls grow, even to the size of a baseball.

↓

Cause:
The bacteria reproduce.

↓

Effect/Cause:
The balls erupt. They spread bacteria through the blood.

↓

Effect/Cause:
More balls grow, clogging the way the body does business.

Handbook of Reading and Informational Terms 993

Writers use the cause-and-effect pattern in both narrative and informational texts. In most short stories, events in the plot are connected in a cause-effect chain. Some words and phrases that signal the cause-effect pattern are *because, depended on, inspired, produced, resulting in, led to,* and *outcome.* Never assume, either in your reading or in real life, that one event causes another just because it happened before it.

See pages 4, 349.
See also *Text Structures.*

CHRONOLOGICAL ORDER **The arrangement of details in time order, that is, in the order in which they occurred.** Chronological order is used in a narrative, which describes a series of events, and in texts that explain the steps in a process.

See page 4.
See also *Text Structures.*

CLAIM **The idea or opinion that a writer tries to prove or defend in an argument.** The claim is stated as a **generalization,** a broad statement or conclusion that covers many situations (or follows from the evidence). The following statements are examples of claims stated as generalizations.

> Everyone should feel a moral responsibility to come to the aid of others in need. ("If Decency Doesn't, Law Should Make Us Samaritans," page 286)
>
> Nations must preserve wildlife species wherever they occur. ("Call of the Wild—Save Us!" page 579)

The author of the argument then supports the claim with either logical appeals (reasons backed by factual evidence), emotional appeals, or both.

See pages 284, 577.
See also *Argument, Generalization.*

COHERENT **Logically integrated, consistent, and understandable.** A text is **coherent** (kō·hir′ənt) when its ideas are arranged in an order that makes sense to the reader. To aid in coherence, writers help readers follow a text by using **transitions,** words and phrases that show how ideas are connected.

Common Transitional Words and Phrases

Comparing Ideas also, and, too, moreover, similarly, another	**Contrasting Ideas** although, still, yet, but, on the other hand, instead
Showing Cause-Effect for, since, as a result, therefore, so that, because	**Showing Importance** first, last, to begin with, mainly, more important
Showing Location above, across, over, there, inside, behind, next to, through, near	**Showing Time** before, at last, now, when, eventually, at once, finally

See page 740.

COMPARISON AND CONTRAST **A method of organizing information by showing similarities and differences among various groups of details.**

See pages 112, 254, 283.
See also *Text Structures.*

CONSUMER DOCUMENTS **Informative texts directed to consumers, such as warranties, contracts, or instruction manuals.** Here are some points to keep in mind when you read consumer documents:

994 Resource Center Handbook of Reading and Informational Terms

1. Try to read the consumer document before you buy the product. Then you can ask the clerk to explain anything you don't understand.

2. Read all of the pages in whatever language comes most easily to you. (Many documents are printed in two or three languages.) You will often find important information where you least expect it, such as at the end of the document.

3. Read the fine print. *Fine* here means "tiny and barely readable." Some fine-print statements in documents are required by law. They are designed to protect you, the consumer, so the company may not be interested in emphasizing these points.

4. Don't expect the document to be interesting or easy to read. If you don't understand a statement, and you can't ask someone at the store that sold you the product, call or write to the company that made it. You should complain to the company if you find its consumer document confusing.

5. Before you sign anything, read everything on the page, and be sure you understand what you're agreeing to. Ask to take the document home, and have your parent or guardian read it. If you are not of legal age, an adult may be responsible for whatever you've signed. Make a copy of any document that you've signed—and keep the copy in a place where you can find it.

See pages 927–930.

CONTEXT CLUES **The words and sentences surrounding a word.** Context clues can sometimes help you guess at the meaning of an unfamiliar word. You will find examples below of three types of context clues. In the examples, the unfamiliar word appears in **boldface.** The context clue is underlined.

Definition: Look for words that define the unfamiliar word, often by giving a synonym or a definition for it.

> He was an EDS pilot, **inured** to the sight of death, long since accustomed to it.

Example: Look for examples that reveal the meaning of the unfamiliar word.

> . . . I performed **listlessly,** my head propped on one arm. I pretended to be bored. And I was.

Contrast: Find words that contrast the unfamiliar word with a word or phrase you already know.

> But when they went out into the courtyard with the first light of dawn, they found the whole neighborhood in front of the chicken coop having fun with the angel, without the slightest **reverence,** tossing him things to eat through the openings in the wire as if he weren't a supernatural creature but a circus animal.

See pages 87, 432.

CREDIBILITY **The believability of a writer's argument.** To evaluate credibility, you first need to determine the author's claim, or opinion. Then you need to look at the **reasons** (statements that explain *why* the author holds the opinion) and the **evidence** (information that supports each reason). To be credible, evidence must be **relevant,** that is, directly related to the argument; **comprehensive,** that is, sufficient to be convincing; and **accurate,** that is, from a source that can be trusted as factually correct or otherwise reliable.

The writer's **intent** should also be considered. If you're reading an opinion essay, for instance, be sure to note any credentials or background information about the writer. Does the writer work for

Handbook of Reading and Informational Terms 995

an institution that represents a particular point of view? Has the writer published a book on the same topic? Do emotional appeals and fallacious reasoning reveal a bias even though the writer pretends to be fair to both sides of the argument?

Notice the **tone** of the text. An argument that is based on logical appeals will usually have a serious, sincere tone. An angry or self-righteous tone might make you question the credibility of the argument.

See pages 284–285, 577–578, 881.
See also *Argument.*

DICTIONARY You use a dictionary to find the precise meaning and usage of words. The elements of a typical entry are explained below.

Sample Dictionary Entry

(1) (2) (3) (4) (5)

in·dulge (in dulj′) ***vt.*** **-dulged′, -dulg′ing** [L *indulgere,* to be kind to, yield to < *in-* + base prob. akin to Gr *dolichos,* long & Goth *tulgus,* firm] (5) **1** to yield to or satisfy (a desire); (6) give oneself up to [to *indulge* a craving for sweets] (7) **2** to gratify the wishes of; be very lenient with; humor **3** [Archaic] (8) to grant as a kindness, favor, or privilege **—*vi.*** to give way to one's own desires; indulge oneself (*in* something) **—in·dulg′er *n.*** (9)
***SYN.*—indulge** implies a yielding to the wishes or desires of oneself or another, as because of a weak will or an amiable nature; **humor** suggests compliance with the mood or whim of another [they *humored* the dying man]; **pamper** implies overindulgence or excessive gratification; **spoil** emphasizes the harm done to the personality or character by overindulgence or excessive attention [grandparents often *spoil* children]; **baby** suggests the sort of pampering and devoted care lavished on infants and connotes a potential loss of self-reliance [because he was sickly, his mother continued to *baby* him] **—*ANT.* discipline, restrain** (10)

©1999 *Webster's New World College Dictionary,* Fourth Edition.

1. **Entry word.** The entry word shows how the word is spelled and divided into syllables. It may also show capitalization and other spellings.
2. **Pronunciation. Phonetic symbols** (such as the *schwa,* ə) and **diacritical marks** (such as the *dieresis,* ä) show how to pronounce the entry word. A key to these symbols and marks usually appears at the bottom of every other page of a dictionary. In this book a pronunciation guide appears at the bottom of every other page of the Glossary (pages 1009–1114).
3. **Part-of-speech label.** This label tells how the entry word is used. When a word can be used as more than one part of speech, definitions are grouped by part of speech. The sample entry shows three definitions of *indulge* as a transitive verb *(vt.)* and one as an intransitive verb *(vi.).*
4. **Other forms.** Sometimes the spellings of plural forms of nouns, principal parts of verbs, and comparative and superlative forms of adjectives and adverbs are shown.
5. **Word origin.** A word's origin, or **etymology** (et′ə·mäl′ə·jē), shows where the word comes from. *Indulge* comes from the Latin *indulgere,* which probably comes from the prefix *in–,* meaning "not," added to the Greek *dolichos,* "long," and the Gothic *tulgus,* "firm."
6. **Examples.** Phrases or sentences show how the entry word is used.
7. **Definitions.** If a word has more than one meaning, the meanings are numbered or lettered.
8. **Special-usage labels.** These labels identify special meanings or special uses of the word. Here, *Archaic* indicates an outdated meaning.
9. **Related word forms.** Other forms of the entry word are listed. Usually these are created by the addition of suffixes.
10. **Synonyms and antonyms. Synonyms** (words similar in meaning) and **antonyms** (words opposite in meaning) may appear at the end of the entry.

996 Resource Center Handbook of Reading and Informational Terms

A dictionary is available as a book or a CD-ROM or as part of a word-processing program or Web site.

EVIDENCE Specific information or proof that backs up the reasons in an argument. Factual evidence includes statements that can be proved by direct observation or by checking reliable reference sources. **Statistics** (facts in the form of numbers) and **expert testimony,** statements from people who are recognized as experts or authorities on an issue, may all be considered factual evidence.

In fields where discoveries are constantly being made, such as in astronomy and genetics, facts need to be checked in a recently published source. Remember that a Web site on the Internet may be current, but it may not be reliable because anybody can post a statement on the Internet. If you suspect that a statement presented as a fact is not true, try to find the same fact in another source.

See pages 206, 284.

FALLACIOUS (fə·lā′shəs) **REASONING Faulty reasoning, or mistakes in logical thinking.** (The word *fallacious* comes from a Latin word meaning "deceptive; tricky." The word *false* comes from the same root word as does the word *fallacy*.) Fallacious reasoning leads to false or incorrect conclusions. Here are some types of fallacious reasoning:

1. **Begging the question,** also called **circular reasoning,** assumes the truth of a statement before it has been proved. You appear to be giving a reason to support your opinion, but all you're doing is restating your opinion in different words.

> College graduates are financially successful because they can get high-paying jobs.

2. **Name-calling** uses labels to attack a person who holds an opposing view, instead of giving reasons or evidence to attack the opposing view itself. This fallacy includes criticizing the person's character, situation, or background.

> Computer geeks are out of touch with the real world.

3. **Stereotyping** gives all members of a group the same (usually undesirable) characteristics. It assumes that everyone (or everything) in that group is alike. (The word *stereotype* comes from the word for a metal plate that was used to print the same image over and over.) Stereotypes are often based on misconceptions about racial, social, religious, gender, or ethnic groups.

> Teenagers are too self-centered to participate in service programs.

4. **Hasty generalization** is a broad, general statement or conclusion that is made without sufficient evidence to back it up. A hasty generalization is often made on the basis of only one or two experiences or observations.

> **Insufficient evidence:** Jenna's cat has fleas, and she spends a lot of money on cat food.
>
> **Hasty generalization:** Cats don't make good pets.

If any exceptions to the conclusion can be found, the generalization is *not* true.

5. **Either-or fallacy** assumes that there are only two possible choices or solutions (usually extremes), even though there may be many.

> I have to get a driver's license, or I'll lose all my friends.

Handbook of Reading and Informational Terms 997

6. **False cause and effect** occurs when one event is said to be the cause of another event just because the two events happened in sequence. You cannot assume that an event caused whatever happened afterward.

> As soon as I started jogging, my grades improved.

GENERALIZATION **A broad statement that applies to or covers many individuals, experiences, situations, observations, or texts.** A **valid generalization** is a type of conclusion that is drawn after considering as many of the facts as possible. Here are some specific facts from "Ill-Equipped Rescuers Dig Out Volcano Victims" (page 267) and a generalization based on them. Notice that each fact is one piece of evidence. The generalization then states what the evidence adds up to, drawing a conclusion that applies to all members of the group.

> **Specific facts:** Thousands of people were trapped alive in the ruins. There was no organization or plan to search for the living and help the survivors. There were few helicopters available to carry the victims to a nearby town. Emergency vehicles could not be brought in because the roads were not passable.
>
> **Generalization:** More victims of the volcanic eruption could have been saved if the relief effort had been better organized.

A generalization jumps from your own specific experiences and observations to a larger, general understanding.

See page 233.

GRAPHS **Graphic depiction of information.** **Line graphs** generally show changes in quantity over time. **Bar graphs** usually compare quantities within categories. **Pie graphs,** or **circle graphs,** show proportions by dividing a circle into different-sized sections, like slices of a pie.

How to Read a Graph

1. **Read the title.** The title will tell you the subject and purpose of the graph.
2. **Read the headings and labels.** These will help you determine the types of information presented.
3. **Analyze the details.** Read numbers carefully. Note increases or decreases. Look for the direction or order of events and trends and for relationships.

INFERENCE **A guess based on observation and prior experience.** When you make inferences about a literary work, you use evidence from the text, from other texts you have read, and from your own prior experience. One way to analyze a character, for instance, is to consider what the person says and how he or she interacts with other characters. In the short story "The Leap" (page 36), the narrator says:

> Since my father's recent death, there is no one to read to her, which is why I returned, in fact, from my failed life where the land is flat. I came home to read to my mother, to read out loud, to read long into the dark if I must, to read all night.

Here are some clues to look for when making inferences:

Character. In a work of literature, look at a character's speech, actions, thoughts, and appearance. What do others think and say about the character?

Tone (the writer's attitude). In both literary and informational texts, look at the writer's choice of words and details.

Theme or **main idea.** Look for the writer's most important point, opinion, or message. What idea can you take from the text that extends beyond it to the world at large?

998 Resource Center Handbook of Reading and Informational Terms

You infer, or predict, what will happen next in the plot of a story based on what the writer has already told you. You change your inferences as the writer gives you more information. Sometimes a writer will deliberately drop a clue that leads you, for a short time, to an incorrect inference. That's part of the fun of reading. Until you get to the end of a suspenseful story, you can never be sure how the plot will turn out.

When you're writing about a story or an informational text, you must be sure your inferences are supported by details in the text.

Supported inferences are based directly on evidence in a text that you can point to and on reasonable prior knowledge. Some interpretation of the evidence is possible, but you cannot ignore or contradict facts that the writer gives you.

Unsupported inferences are conclusions that are not logical. They ignore the facts in the text or misinterpret them. Whenever you're asked to write an essay about a text, it's a good idea to re-read the text before and after you write your essay. Check each inference you make against the text to make sure you can find evidence for it. For example, if you write an analysis of a character and you say that the character never answers a question directly, you should cite details from the text to support your inference.

See pages 76, 98, 374.

INFORMATIVE TEXTS **Texts that communicate information and data.** When you're reading informative texts, you need to read slowly, looking for main ideas and important details. Slow and careful reading is especially important when you're trying to get meaning from consumer, workplace, and public documents. These documents are often not written by professional writers, so they may be difficult to read.

See also *Consumer Documents, Public Documents, Workplace Documents.*

LOGIC **Correct reasoning.** A logical text presents reasons supported by evidence (facts and examples). A text is illogical when it does not provide reasons backed by evidence. Notice how each sentence in this paragraph from "Explorers Say There's Still Lots to Look For" (page 368) gives evidence that supports the writer's main idea that there are still many places to explore.

> Explorers still scale peaks that have never been climbed, crawl through caves to the insides of earth, hurtle into space to walk among the stars. They find ancient tribes and ancient cities. They dig up dinosaurs. They journey to places where no one has reported being before: the jungles of central Congo, the Amazon and Peru, the deserts of Tibet and China, vast underwater caves in Mexico and Belize. They are only beginning to probe the oceans; 5 percent has been explored, though water covers 71 percent of the planet.

See pages 284–285.
See also *Logical Order.*

LOGICAL ORDER **A method of organizing information by putting details into related groupings.** Writers use logical order most often when they want to classify information, that is, to examine a subject and its relationship to other subjects. For example, when you classify, you can divide a subject into its parts (considering men's responsibilities at work and at home, "Double Daddy," page 22). You can also use the comparison-contrast pattern to show similarities and differences among various groups (comparing laws that protect good Samaritans in various states, "Good Samaritans U.S.A. Are Afraid to Act," page 288).

See pages 254, 283, 542, 959.
See also *Text Structures.*

Handbook of Reading and Informational Terms 999

MAIN IDEA The writer's most important point, opinion, or message. The main idea may be stated directly, or it may be only suggested or implied. If the idea is not stated directly, it's up to you to look at the details and decide on the idea that they all seem to support. Try to restate the writer's main idea in your own words.

In an argument the main idea (the generalization that the writer is trying to prove) is called the **claim,** or **opinion.**

> **Main idea of an essay:** A book can change a child's life ("The Magic Happened," page 648).
>
> **Claim of an argument:** The Vietnam War must be stopped ("Declaration of Independence from the War in Vietnam," page 639).

See page 272.

MAP A drawing showing all or part of the earth's surface or of bodies in the sky. Physical maps illustrate the natural landscape of an area, using shading, lines, and color to show landforms and elevation. **Political maps** show political units, such as states and nations. They usually also show borders and capitals and other major cities. **Special-purpose maps** present specific information, such as the locations of Annapurna and Everest in the Himalayas ("Into Thin Air," page 351), and the Roman Empire at the death of Caesar (*Julius Caesar,* page 871).

How to Read a Map

1. **Determine the focus of the map.** The map's title and labels tell you its focus—its subject and the geographical area it covers.
2. **Study the legend.** The **legend,** or **key,** explains the symbols, lines, colors, and shadings used in the map.
3. **Check directions and distances.** Maps often include a **compass rose,** a diagram that shows north, south, east, and west. If there isn't one, assume that north is at the top, west to the left, and so on. Many maps also include a scale that relates distances on the map to actual distances.
4. **Look at the larger context.** The **absolute location** of any place on earth is given by its **latitude** (the number of degrees north or south of the equator) and its **longitude** (the number of degrees east or west of the **prime meridian,** or 0 degrees longitude). Some maps also include **locator maps,** which show the area depicted in relation to a larger area.

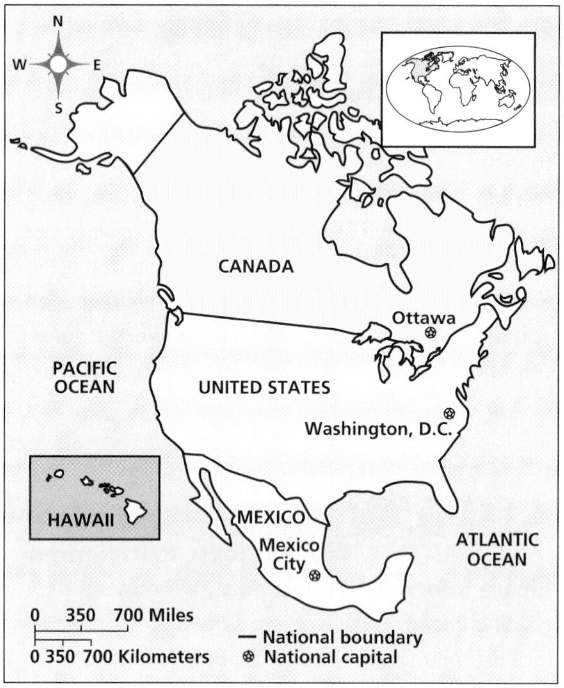

OPINION A statement of a person's belief, idea, or attitude. A **fact** is something that can be verified or proved by direct observation or by checking a reliable reference source. An **opinion** cannot be proved to be either true or false—even when it is supported by facts. The following statement is an unsupported opinion.

1000 Resource Center Handbook of Reading and Informational Terms

Julius Caesar is an outstanding play.

A **valid opinion** is an opinion that is supported by verifiable facts. In the following example, the verifiable facts are underlined.

Julius Caesar is an outstanding play because it contains moral conflicts as well as ideas about power and politics that are still important today.

When you read a persuasive text, remember that statements of opinion can't be proved, but they can and should be supported by facts and logical reasoning.

See pages 284, 577.

ORDER OF IMPORTANCE **A means of organizing information by ranking details in the order of their importance.** Writers of persuasive texts have to decide whether to give the strongest reason first or to present the weakest reason first and end with the strongest point. Informational texts such as news articles always begin with the most important details because they want to grab the reader's attention immediately. The structure of a news article looks like an upside-down triangle, with the least important details at the bottom.

See pages 296, 542.
See also *Text Structures*.

OUTLINING **A way of organizing information to show relationships among key details in a text.** You can use outlining as a writer and as a reader.

Outlining puts main ideas and details in a form that you can review quickly. An **informal outline,** sometimes called a working outline, should have at least three main ideas. You put supporting details under each main idea, like this:

Informal Outline

I. First main idea
 A. Detail supporting first main idea
 B. Another detail supporting first main idea
 C. Third detail supporting first main idea
II. Second main idea
 [etc.]

A **formal outline** is especially useful if you're writing a research paper. You might start with a working outline and then revise it into a formal one. Your teacher may ask you to submit a formal outline with your completed research paper.

Formal outlines use Roman numerals (I, II, III), capital letters (A, B, C), and Arabic numerals (1, 2, 3) to show order, relationship, and relative importance of ideas. The headings in a formal outline should have the same grammatical structure, and you must be consistent in your use of either phrases or sentences. (You can't switch back and forth between them.) There should always be at least two divisions under each heading or none at all.

Here is the beginning of a formal outline of a textbook chapter on the Vietnam War (page 634):

Formal Outline

I. TV speech by Lyndon B. Johnson, 8/4/64
 A. Destroyer *Maddox* attacked on 8/2 in Gulf of Tonkin
 B. U.S. military forces ordered to take action against gunboats
II. The Tonkin Gulf Resolution
 A. In 1963, Johnson advised by McNamara to increase U.S. commitment to South Vietnam

(continued)

Handbook of Reading and Informational Terms 1001

(continued)

> B. Johnson's need for congressional support
>   1. The Gulf of Tonkin events an opportunity
>   2. Request for authorization of military force overwhelmingly passed

See pages 697–698.

PARAPHRASING Restating each sentence of a text in your own words. Paraphrasing is usually used only for difficult texts. Paraphrasing a text helps you to be certain you understand it. When you paraphrase, you follow the author's sequence of ideas. You carefully reword each line (if it's a poem) or sentence (if it's prose) without changing the author's ideas or leaving anything out. You restate each figure of speech to be sure you understand the basis of the comparison. If sentences are missing words or if the words are wrenched out of the usual order, you rephrase the sentence.

A paraphrase is longer than a **summary,** which is a brief statement of the main ideas in a text. Here are a paraphrase and a summary of a paragraph from the Parable of the Good Samaritan (page 278):

> **Paraphrase:** A man traveling from Jerusalem to Jericho was attacked by robbers who tore off his clothes, injured him, and left him half dead. When a priest passed that way and saw the wounded man, he crossed to the other side of the road. A Levite did the same thing; he looked at the victim and ignored his need for help. But when a Samaritan encountered the wounded man, he pitied him. He treated the man's wounds with oil and wine. Then he put him on the animal he had been riding and took him to an inn, where he continued to treat his wounds. The next day, before he left, he gave the innkeeper money and told him to take care of the wounded man. "If you spend more money taking care of him," he said, "I'll pay you back when I return."
>
> Which of the three travelers acted as a neighbor to the man attacked by robbers?
>
> **Summary:** On the road from Jerusalem to Jericho, robbers attacked a traveler and left him half dead. A priest and a Levite passed the victim and ignored him, but a Samaritan gave him the help he needed. Which of the three behaved as if he were the victim's neighbor?

See pages 411, 833.

PRIMARY SOURCE An original, firsthand account. Primary sources may include an autobiography; an eyewitness testimony; a letter, speech, or literary work; a historical document; and information gathered from firsthand surveys or interviews. "A Fireman's Story" (page 345) is an example of a primary source. It's important to use primary sources whenever they are available on a topic, but you need to research widely to make sure that a primary source is not biased.

Be sure to keep track of your primary sources by numbering each source and recording the necessary publishing information. If you quote directly from the primary source, be sure to use quotation marks and to give credit to your source.

See pages 88, 632–633.
See also *Secondary Source.*

PUBLIC DOCUMENTS Informative texts put out by the government or public agencies. Public documents include political

1002 Resource Center Handbook of Reading and Informational Terms

platforms, public policy statements, speeches, and debates. These documents inform the public about government policy, laws, municipal codes, records, schedules, and the like.

See pages 639, 908.

RESEARCH QUESTIONS **Questions that are focused on a specific subject, which the researcher searches to answer.** Questions are essential tools for focusing your research.

One way to generate research questions is to use a KWL chart as a research guide. This kind of chart is an easy way to organize questions and answers, especially if you know how to set up columns and rows on your computer. In the K column, you note what you already know about the subject. In the W column, you note what you'd like to find out. As you do your research, complete the L column by answering the questions you've asked in the W column.

Research questions can also be generated by brainstorming or by using the *5W-How* questions: *Who? What? When? Where? Why?* and *How?* As you seek primary and secondary source information at libraries and museums, in various electronic media (Internet, films, tapes), and from personal interviews, you will come up with more research questions. Always remember to keep your questions focused on the specific subject you have chosen.

See page 187.

ROOTS, PREFIXES, SUFFIXES

English words are often made up of two or more word parts. These words parts include

- **roots, which carry a word's core meaning**
- **prefixes, added onto the beginning of a word or in front of a word root to form a new word**
- **suffixes, added onto the end of a word or after a word root to form a new word**

Most word roots come from Greek and Latin. Prefixes and suffixes come from Greek, Latin, and Anglo-Saxon.

Greek Roots	Meaning	Examples
–astro–, –aster–	star	**astro**nomy, **aster**isk
–cosmo–	world; order	**cosmo**logy, **cosmo**politan
–eu–	good; well	**eu**phoria, **eu**phemism
–gno–, –kno–	know	**kno**wledge, a**gno**stic
–hypno–	sleep	**hypno**tize, **hypno**tic
–mis–	hatred of	**mis**anthrope, **mis**ology
–ortho–	straight	**ortho**pedics, **ortho**dontics
–pseudo–	false	**pseudo**nym, **pseudo**morph
–the–, –them–, –thet–	place; put	epi**thet**, anti**the**sis
–theo–	god	**theo**logy, **theo**cracy

Handbook of Reading and Informational Terms 1003

Latin Roots	Meaning	Examples
–anima–, –anim–	life; mind	**animal**, **animat**e
–aqua–	water	**aqua**rium, **aqua**naut
–cid–, –cis–	cut off; kill	homi**cide**, con**cis**e
–cor–, –card–	heart	**cor**onary, **card**iac
–fum–	smoke; scent	**fum**igate, per**fum**e
–gen–	race; family	**gen**ealogy, pro**gen**itor
–leg–	law	**leg**al, **leg**islate
–noc–, –nox–	night	equi**nox**, **noc**turne
–tract–	pull; draw	at**tract**, sub**tract**ion
–voc–, –vok–	voice; call	**voc**al, re**vok**e

Greek Prefixes	Meaning	Examples
anti–	against	**anti**body, **anti**social
dia–	through; across	**dia**gram, **dia**lectic
hypo–	under; below	**hypo**dermic, **hypo**allergenic
para–	beside; beyond	**para**legal, **para**llel
peri–	around	**peri**scope, **peri**phery

Latin Prefixes	Meaning	Examples
bene–	good	**bene**fit, **bene**diction
contra–	against	**contra**dict, **contra**st
extra–	outside	**extra**curricular, **extra**ordinary
intra–	within	**intra**venous, **intra**mural
trans–	across; over	**trans**atlantic, **trans**cend

Anglo-Saxon/Old English Prefixes	Meaning	Examples
be–	around	**be**dew, **be**get
for–	away; off; from	**for**get, **for**go
mis–	badly; not	**mis**hap, **mis**take
over–	above	**over**look, **over**coat
un–	not; reverse of	**un**sound, **un**kempt

1004 Resource Center Handbook of Reading and Informational Terms

Greek Suffixes	Meaning	Examples
–ess	female	poet**ess**, lion**ess**
–ic	having; showing	parapleg**ic**, ton**ic**
–ize	resemble; cause to be	American**ize**, ostrac**ize**
–meter	measure	thermo**meter**, baro**meter**
–oid	like; resembling	fact**oid**, andr**oid**

Latin Suffixes	Meaning	Examples
–age	act; result of	marri**age**, voy**age**
–fic	making; creating	horri**fic**, scienti**fic**
–ive	relating to; belonging to	inquisit**ive**, sport**ive**
–let	small	pig**let**, rivu**let**
–ure	act; state of being	leis**ure**, compos**ure**

Anglo-Saxon/Old English Suffixes	Meaning	Examples
–en	become	bright**en**, sull**en**
–ful	full of; marked by	cheer**ful**, fear**ful**
–ness	quality; state	kind**ness**, crazi**ness**
–ship	quality of	kin**ship**, relation**ship**
–ward	in the direction	for**ward**, sky**ward**

Handbook of Reading and Informational Terms 1005

SECONDARY SOURCE A secondhand account written by a writer who did not participate directly in the events he or she interprets, relates, or analyzes. Secondary sources may include encyclopedias, magazine articles, textbooks, biographies, and technical journals. The historical article "The Day the Clowns Cried" (page 40) is an example of a secondary source that was found on a Web site. A research paper may include both primary and secondary sources.

See pages 88, 632–633.

SPATIAL (spā'shəl) ORDER A means of organizing information by showing where things are located. (The word *spatial* is related to the word *space*. Spatial order shows where things are located in space.) Spatial order is often used in descriptive writing. Here is an example from the beginning of "Through the Tunnel" (page 401). Phrases showing spatial order are underlined.

> Going <u>to the shore</u> on the first morning of the vacation, the young English boy stopped <u>at a turning of the path</u> and looked <u>down at a wild and rocky bay</u> and then <u>over to the crowded beach</u> he knew so well from other years.

See page 542.
See also *Text Structures.*

SYNTHESIZING Putting all the different sources of information together in a process that gives you a better understanding of the whole subject. In order to synthesize information, you first gather information about a topic from several sources. Then, you find each writer's main ideas. Paraphrasing ideas, restating them in your own words, can help you understand difficult texts. Next, you examine the ideas in each source. You compare and contrast the ideas you've found. To synthesize what you have learned, you draw conclusions about the information you have gathered.

See pages 21, 411.
See also *Generalization.*

TEXT STRUCTURES Any organizational patterns that writers use to make their meaning clear. In imaginative literature text structures range from the plot structures in stories and dramas to the sonnet structure in poetry.

In nonfiction and informational texts, the writer's **intent** or **purpose** in creating the text determines how the text will be organized. Don't expect writers of informational texts and nonfiction to use the same structure throughout an entire text. Most writers switch from one type of structure to another and may even combine structures. Four basic ways of arranging ideas or details in nonfiction and informational texts are

1. **Chronological order, time order,** or **sequence**—putting events or steps in the order in which they occur. For an example of chronological order, see "Diary of a Mad Blender" (page 24). Most narrative and historical texts are written in chronological order. Chronological order is also found in writing that explains a process, such as in technical directions and in recipes. This type of chronological order is called **step-by-step order.**
2. **Spatial order**—the order that shows where things are located. This pattern is used in descriptive writing. It is especially useful in helping readers visualize setting. See the first paragraph of "From a Lifeboat" (page 346).
3. **Order of importance**—ranking details from most important to least important, or from least important to most important. Writers of persuasive texts in particular have to decide which order makes the strongest impact: putting the strongest reason first, and the weaker ones later, or saving the strongest reason for

1006 Resource Center Handbook of Reading and Informational Terms

last. For an example of a text that uses order of importance, see the concluding section of "R.M.S. Titanic" (pages 342–343). News articles always begin with the most important details because they want to grab the reader's attention immediately.

4. **Logical order**—classifying details into related groups. One type of logical order is the **comparison and contrast** text structure, which shows similarities and differences among various groups. See "Crossing a Threshold to Adulthood" (page 414), in which growing up in Uzbekistan is contrasted with growing up in America.

   Other methods used to organize texts include
   - **enumeration** (ē·nōō′mər·ā·shen)—also called **listing**—citing a list of details: first, second, and so on. See the alphabetical list of noted explorers in "Explorers Say There's Still Lots to Look for" (page 367).
   - **cause-and-effect**—showing how events happen as a result of other events. See "'Thinkin' on Marryin''" (page 91).
   - **problem-solution**—explaining how a problem may be solved. See "Taste—the Final Frontier" (page 188).
   - **question-answer**—asking questions, then giving the answers. See "The Child's View of Working Parents" (page 26).

Recognizing these structures will help you understand the ideas in a text. The following guidelines can help you recognize text structures:

1. Search the text for the main idea. Look for clue words (**transitions**) that signal a specific pattern of organization. Also note colors, special type, headers, numbered lists, and icons that may be used to highlight terms or indicate text structure.
2. Analyze the text for other important ideas. Think about how the ideas connect, and look for an obvious pattern.
3. Remember that a writer might use one organizational pattern throughout a text or combine two or more patterns.
4. Draw a graphic organizer that maps how the text is structured. Some common graphic organizers are a **causal chain** (for the cause-effect text structure), a **flowchart** (showing chronological sequence), and a **Venn diagram** (showing similarities and differences).

See pages 296, 542, 577, 919.
See also *Chronological Order, Logical Order, Order of Importance, Spatial Order.*

WORKPLACE DOCUMENTS **Job-related texts, such as job applications, memos, instructional manuals, and employee handbooks.** When you read workplace documents, keep these points in mind (in addition to the points about reading consumer documents, cited on pages 994–995):

1. Take all the time you need to read and understand the document. Don't let anyone rush you or tell you that a document is unimportant or just a formality.
2. Read technical directions carefully, even if they're just posted on the side of a device you're supposed to operate. Read all of the directions before you start. Ask questions if you're not sure how to proceed. Don't try anything out before you know what will happen next.
3. The employee handbook contains the "rules of the game" at that particular business. It tells you about holidays, work hours, break times, and vacations as well as other important company policies. Read the employee handbook from cover to cover.

See page 919.
See also *Consumer Documents.*

Handbook of Reading and Informational Terms 1007

Glossary

The glossary that follows is an alphabetical list of words found in the selections in this book. Use this glossary just as you would use a dictionary—to find out the meanings of unfamiliar words. (Some technical, foreign, and more obscure words in this book are not listed here but instead are defined for you in the footnotes that accompany many of the selections.)

Many words in the English language have more than one meaning. This glossary gives the meanings that apply to the words as they are used in the selections in this book. Words closely related in form and meaning are usually listed together in one entry (for instance, *compassion* and *compassionate*), and the definition is given for the first form.

The following abbreviations are used:

adj.	adjective
adv.	adverb
n.	noun
v.	verb

Each word's pronunciation is given in parentheses. A guide to the pronunciation symbols appears at the bottom of this page. For more information about the words in this glossary or for information about words not listed here, consult a dictionary.

A

abiding (ə·bīd′iŋ) *adj.:* continuing; lasting.
abut (ə·but′) *adj.:* border upon; lie next to. —**abutting** *v.* used as *adj.*
adamant (ad′ə·mənt) *adj.:* unyielding; firm.
administer (ad·min′is·tər) *v.:* give; apply. —**administered** *v.* used as *adj.*
adversary (ad′vər·ser′ē) *n.:* opponent; enemy.
affliction (ə·flik′shən) *n.:* suffering; distress.
aghast (ə·gast′) *adj.:* horrified.
agile (aj′əl) *adj.:* lively; moving easily and quickly.
allegation (al′ə·gā′shən) *n.:* in law, assertion, or positive statement, made without proof.
annihilate (ə·nī′ə·lāt′) *v.:* destroy; demolish.
antipathy (an·tip′ə·thē) *n.:* feeling of hatred; powerful and deep dislike.
antiseptic (an′tə·sep′tik) *n.:* substance used to sterilize or to prevent infection.
anxiety (aŋ·zī′ə·tē) *n.:* state of being worried or uneasy.
apex (ā′peks′) *n.:* highest point; top.
apprehension (ap′rē·hen′shən) *n.:* dread; fear of a future event.
arresting (ə·rest′iŋ) *adj.:* interesting; striking.
ascertain (as′ər·tān′) *v.:* find out with certainty; determine.
assail (ə·sāl′) *v.:* attack.
autonomy (ô·tän′ə·mē) *n.:* independence.
avid (av′id) *adj.:* eager and enthusiastic.

B

benign (bi·nīn′) *adj.:* here, favorable or harmless.
bereft (bē·reft′) *adj.:* not having something needed or expected.
betrayal (bē·trā′əl) *n.:* **1.** failure to fulfill another's hopes. **2.** act of disloyalty; deception.
breach (brēch) *v.:* break through.

C

callous (kal′əs) *adj.:* unfeeling.
cataclysm (kat′ə·kliz′əm) *n.:* disaster; sudden, violent event.

at, āte, cär; ten, ēve; is, īce; gō, hôrn, look, tōōl; oil, out; up, fur; ə *for unstressed vowels, as* a *in* ago, u *in* focus; ′ *as in* Latin (lat′'n); chin; she; thin; *the*; zh *as in* azure (azh′ər); ŋ *as in* ring (riŋ)

Glossary

Glossary 1009

cessation (se·sā′shən) *n.:* ceasing or stopping.
champion (cham′pē·ən) *v.:* fight for; defend; support.
chronic (krän′ik) *adj.:* constant; habitual.
clamor (klam′ər) *v.:* cry out; ask. —**clamoring** *v.* used as *adj.*
colleague (käl′ēg′) *n.:* fellow worker.
commemorate (kə·mem′ə·rāt′) *v.:* serve as a reminder of.
commiserate (kə·miz′ər·āt′) *v.:* show or express sympathy.
compassion (kəm·pash′ən) *n.:* deep sympathy; pity.
concussion (kən·kush′ən) *n.:* powerful shock or impact.
confirmation (kän′fər·mā′shən) *n.:* proof.
confront (kən·frunt′) *v.:* face.
conservation (kän′sər·vā′shən) *n.:* protection and preservation of natural resources. —**conservation** *n.* used as *adj.*
consolation (kän′sə·lā′shən) *n.:* act of comforting.
console (kən·sōl′) *v.:* comfort. —**consoling** *v.* used as *adj.*
conspicuous (kən·spik′yo͞o·əs) *adj.:* obvious or easy to see.
constrict (kən·strikt′) *v.:* limit; confine. —**constricting** *v.* used as *adj.*
construe (kən·stro͞o′) *v.:* interpret.
consumerism (kən·so͞om′ər·iz′əm) *n.:* buying and using of goods or services.
contagion (kən·tā′jən) *n.:* spreading of disease.
contrition (kən·trish′ən) *n.:* regret or sense of guilt at having done wrong.
conviction (kən·vik′shən) *n.:* strong belief; certainty.
coronation (kôr′ə·nā′shən) *n.:* act or ceremony of crowning a sovereign.
corroborate (kə·räb′ə·rāt′) *v.:* support; uphold the truth of.
cower (kou′ər) *v.:* draw back or huddle in fear. —**cowering** *v.* used as *adj.*
crucial (kro͞o′shəl) *adj.:* extremely important; decisive.

D

dawdle (dôd′′l) *v.:* waste time; linger.
defiant (dē·fī′ənt) *adj.:* challenging authority.
degradation (deg′rə·dā′shən) *n.:* decline.
denizen (den′ə·zen) *n.:* inhabitant or occupant.
deplorable (dē·plôr′ə·bəl) *adj.:* very bad. —**deplorably** *adv.*
depraved (dē·prāvd′) *adj.:* immoral.
deteriorate (dē·tir′ē·ə·rāt′) *v.:* worsen.
diffuse (di·fyo͞os′) *adj.:* spread out; unfocused.
discard (dis·kärd′) *v.:* abandon; get rid of. —**discarding** *v.* used as *adj.*
discordant (dis·kôrd′′nt) *adj.:* clashing; not in harmony.
dismantle (dis·mant′′l) *v.:* take apart.
diversion (də·vur′zhən) *n.:* something that distracts the attention.
divert (də·vurt′) *v.:* amuse; entertain.
doctrine (däk′trin) *n.:* principle; teaching; belief.
dubious (do͞o′bē·əs) *adj.:* doubtful; not sure.

E

ebb (eb) *v.:* lessen or weaken. The ebb is the flow of water away from the land as the tide falls.
ebony (eb′ə·nē) *adj.:* dark or black.
emanate (em′ə·nāt′) *v.:* come forth; emerge, as from a source.
emancipation (ē·man′sə·pā′shən) *n.:* liberation; the act of setting free from restraint or control or being set free.
encroach (en·krōch′) *v.:* advance. —**encroaching** *v.* used as *adj.*
equanimity (ek′wə·nim′ə·tē) *n.:* calmness; composure.
ethical (eth′i·kəl) *adj.:* moral; having to do with goodness or rightness in conduct.
exhalation (eks′hə·lā′shən) *n.:* something breathed out; breath.
extinct (ek·stiŋkt′) *adj.:* no longer in existence.
extravagant (ek·strav′ə·gənt) *adj.:* excessive; showy.
extricate (eks′tri·kāt′) *v.:* release; disentangle. —**extricating** *v.* used as *n.*

F

facile (fas′il) *adj.:* easy.
feign (fān) *v.:* pretend.
fiasco (fē·as′kō) *n.:* total failure.
fidelity (fə·del′·ə·tē) *n.:* loyalty; devotion.
filial (fil′ē·əl) *adj.:* pertaining to or due from a son or a daughter.
flail (flāl) *v.:* wave wildly. —**flailing** *v.* used as *adj.*

1010 Resource Center Glossary

formidable (fôr′mə·də·bəl) *adj.:* remarkable; impressive.

fortitude (fôrt′ə·to͞od′) *n.:* firm courage; strength to endure pain or danger.

frivolous (friv′ə·ləs) *adj.:* **1.** not properly serious; silly. **2.** trivial; of little value or importance.

furtive (fʉr′tiv) *adj.:* **1.** acting as if trying not to be seen. **2.** done secretly.

G

garble (gär′bəl) *v.:* confuse; mix up. —**garbled** *v.* used as *adj.*

gaunt (gônt) *adj.:* here, grim and forbidding.

generate (jen′ər·āt′) *v.:* arise; come into being.

H

habitat (hab′i·tat′) *n.:* person's environment or living space; place where plants or animals normally grow or live.

harass (har′əs) *v.:* bother; trouble. —**harassing** *v.* used as *n.*

hospitality (häs′pi·tal′ə·tē) *n.:* friendly, caring treatment of guests.

I

idealist (ī·dē′əl·ist) *n.:* someone who is guided by ideals, or standards of perfection.

ignoble (ig·nō′bəl) *adj.:* not noble in birth or position.

illiterate (i·lit′ər·it) *adj.:* uneducated; unable to read or write.

illusion (i·lo͞o′zhən) *n.:* misleading or inaccurate idea.

immunity (i·myo͞on′ə·tē) *n.:* freedom from a legal obligation.

immutable (i·myo͞ot′ə·bəl) *adj.:* unchangeable; never changing or varying.

impede (im·pēd′) *v.:* hold back or block, as by an obstacle. —**impeded** *v.* used as *adj.*

imperceptible (im′pər·sep′tə·bəl) *adj.:* so slight as to be almost unnoticeable. —**imperceptibly** *adv.*

imperial (im·pir′ē·əl) *adj.:* majestic; of great size or superior quality.

impertinence (im·pʉrt′′n·əns) *n.:* insult; disrespectful act or remark.

implacable (im·plak′ə·bəl) *adj.:* relentless; not affected by attempts at change.

impoverish (im·päv′ər·ish) *v.:* make poor. —**impoverished** *v.* used as *adj.*

impoverishment (im·päv′ər·ish·mənt) *n.:* reducing to poverty or taking away of resources.

impudence (im′pyo͞o·dəns) *n.:* quality of being disrespectful.

impunity (im·pyo͞o′ni·tē) *n.:* freedom from punishment.

incoherent (in′kō·hir′ənt) *adj.:* rambling; disjointed.

incomprehensible (in·käm′prē·hen′sə·bəl) *adj.:* not understandable.

incredulous (in·krej′o͝o·ləs) *adj.:* disbelieving; skeptical.

increment (in′krə·mənt) *n.:* small increase.

indemnify (in·dem′ni·fī′) *v.:* in a legal sense, protect.

indigenous (in·dij′ə·nəs) *adj.:* native; growing naturally in a region or country.

indisposed (in′di·spōzd′) *adj.:* slightly ill.

induce (in·do͞os′) *v.:* persuade; lead on.

ineffable (in·ef′ə·bəl) *adj.:* indescribable; inexpressible. —**ineffably** *adv.*

inertia (in·ʉr′shə) *n.:* tendency to remain either at rest or in motion.

inevitable (in·ev′i·tə·bəl) *adj.:* unavoidable; certain to happen. —**inevitably** *adv.*

ingenuity (in′jə·no͞o′ə·tē) *n.:* cleverness; originality; skill.

ingenuous (in·jen′yo͞o·əs) *adj.:* too trusting; tending to believe too readily.

initiative (i·nish′ə·tiv) *n.:* action of taking the first step or movement.

innocuous (i·näk′yo͞o·əs) *adj.:* harmless.

inquisitive (in·kwiz′ə·tiv) *adj.:* questioning; curious.

inscription (in·skrip′shən) *n.:* something inscribed or engraved, as on a coin or monument.

insinuate (in·sin′yo͞o·āt′) *v.:* suggest.

at, āte, cär; ten, ēve; is, īce; gō, hôrn, lo͝ok, to͞ol; oil, out; up, fʉr; ə *for unstressed vowels, as* a *in* ago, u *in* focus; ′ *as in* Latin (lat′′n); chin; she; thin; *th*e; zh *as in* azure (azh′ər); ŋ *as in* ring (riŋ)

Glossary

Glossary 1011

insular (in′sə·lər) *adj.:* isolated from one's surroundings; narrow-minded.
integrate (in′tə·grāt′) *v.:* combine; unify.
interminable (in·tur′mi·nə·bəl) *adj.:* endless.
intermittent (in′tər·mit′′nt) *adj.:* appearing or occurring from time to time.
intimidate (in·tim′ə·dāt′) *v.:* make afraid.
inure (in·yo͞or′) *v.:* make accustomed to something difficult or painful. —**inured** *v.* used as *adj.*
irrelevant (i·rel′ə·vənt) *adj.:* not relating to the point or situation. —**irrelevantly** *adv.*
irrevocable (i·rev′ə·kə·bəl) *adj.:* irreversible; incapable of being canceled or undone.

J

jeopardize (jep′ər·dīz′) *v.:* endanger.
jeopardy (jep′ər·dē) *n.:* great danger; peril.
judicious (jo͞o·dish′əs) *adj.:* wise and careful.

L

lament (lə·ment′) *v.:* **1.** say with regret or sorrow. **2.** feel very sorry.
laud (lôd) *v.:* praise. —**lauding** *v.* used as *adj.*
liability (lī′ə·bil′ə·tē) *n.:* legal obligation or responsibility to make good a damage or loss.
listless (list′lis) *adj.:* without energy or interest. —**listlessly** *adv.*
luminous (lo͞o′mə·nəs) *adj.:* glowing; giving off light.
luxuriate (lug·zhoor′ē·āt′) *v.* (used with *in*): take great pleasure.

M

magnanimous (mag·nan′ə·məs) *adj.:* generous; noble.
magnitude (mag′nə·to͞od′) *n.:* greatness or size.
malicious (mə·lish′əs) *adj.:* intentionally harmful.
manifest (man′ə·fest′) *v.:* **1.** appear; become evident. **2.** show; reveal.
manipulation (mə·nip′yo͞o·lā′shən) *n.:* skillful, often unfair management or control.
maroon (mə·ro͞on′) *v.:* leave stranded, helpless, or isolated. —**marooned** *v.* used as *adj.*
maximize (mak′sə·mīz′) *v.:* increase as much as possible.
mesmerize (mez′mər·īz′) *v.:* spellbind; fascinate. —**mesmerizing** *v.* used as *adj.*
metabolism (mə·tab′ə·liz′əm) *n.:* process by which living organisms turn food into energy and living tissue.
minute (mī·no͞ot′) *adj.:* small; tiny.
mutiny (myo͞ot′′n·ē) *n.:* rebellion or revolt against authority.

N

navigator (nav′ə·gāt′ər) *n.:* person who plots the course of a vehicle, usually a ship or plane.
nonchalant (nän′shə·länt′) *adj.:* without interest or concern; indifferent. —**nonchalantly** *adv.*
notorious (nō·tôr′ē·əs) *adj.:* famous, usually in an unfavorable sense.
nudge (nuj) *v.:* push lightly; bump.

O

oath (ōth) *n.:* solemn promise or declaration; vow.
oblige (ə·blīj′) *v.:* compel by moral, legal, or physical force.
oppress (ə·pres′) *v.:* persecute; keep down by unjust use of power.
opulent (äp′yo͞o·lənt) *adj.:* rich; luxuriant.

P

palatable (pal′it·ə·bəl) *adj.:* tasty; fit to be eaten or drunk.
palpitate (pal′pə·tāt′) *v.:* throb; quiver. —**palpitating** *v.* used as *adj.*
pandemonium (pan′də·mō′nē·əm) *n.:* wildly noisy, chaotic scene.

1012 Resource Center Glossary

paramount (par′ə·mount′) *adj.:* supreme; dominant.
patina (pat′′n·ə) *n.:* color change resulting from age, as on old wood or silver.
peevishness (pē′vish·nis) *n.:* irritability.
pensive (pen′siv) *adj.:* dreamily thoughtful.
perfunctory (pər·fuŋk′tə·rē) *adj.:* not exerting much effort; unconcerned.
perplexed (pər·plekst′) *adj.:* uncertain.
persistent (pər·sist′ənt) *adj.:* continuing.
pertinent (purt′′n·ənt) *adj.:* having some connection with the subject.
pervade (pər·vād′) *v.:* spread throughout.
petulant (pech′ə·lənt) *adj.:* impatient; irritable; peevish.
phenomenon (fə·näm′ə·nən) *n.:* observable event, fact, or circumstance.
pit (pit) *v.:* place in competition.
placid (plas′id) *adj.:* calm; tranquil.
poignant (poin′yənt) *adj.:* emotionally moving; touching.
poise (poiz) *v.:* balance; keep steady. —**poised** *v.* used as *adj.*
ponderous (pän′dər·əs) *adj.:* heavy and slow moving.
portable (pôr′tə·bəl) *adj.:* able to be carried.
potent (pōt′′nt) *adj.:* powerful; convincing.
precarious (pri·ker′ē·əs) *adj.:* in danger of falling down; unstable.
predominant (prē·däm′ə·nənt) *adj.:* most frequent or noticeable.
premises (prem′is·iz) *n.:* house or building and its surrounding property.
presentiment (prē·zent′ə·mənt) *n.:* foreboding; feeling that something bad is about to happen.
presumable (prē·zo͞om′ə·bəl) *adj.:* probable. —**presumably** *adv.*
prodigy (präd′ə·jē) *n.:* child of highly unusual talent or genius.
profuse (prō·fyo͞os′) *adj.:* given or poured forth freely and abundantly; plentiful.
projection (prō·jek′shən) *n.:* something that juts out from a surface.
propriety (prə·prī′ə·tē) *n.:* quality of being proper, fitting, or suitable.
providential (präv′ə·den′shəl) *adj.:* fortunate; like something caused by a divine act.
provincial (prə·vin′shəl) *adj.:* belonging to a province, especially a rural one; also, unsophisticated.
prudence (pro͞o′dəns) *n.:* cautiousness; sound judgment.

Q

quell (kwel) *v.:* quiet; subdue.
quizzical (kwiz′i·kəl) *adj.:* puzzled; questioning.

R

radiance (rā′dē·əns) *n.:* brightness; light.
rancid (ran′sid) *adj.:* stale or spoiled.
rationalization (rash′ən·ə·lə·zā′shən) *n.:* seemingly reasonable excuse or explanation for one's behavior—but not the real reason.
realm (relm) *n.:* kingdom.
rebound (ri·bound′) *v.:* bounce back.
recede (ri·sēd′) *v.:* move back or away.
recoil (ri·koil′) *v.:* draw back in fear, surprise, or disgust.
recrimination (ri·krim′ə·nā′shən) *n.:* accusation against an accuser; countercharge.
regressive (ri·gres′iv) *adj.:* moving backward or returning to an earlier or less advanced condition.
rehabilitation (rē′hə·bil′ə·tā′shən) *n.:* bringing or restoring to a good condition.
relic (rel′ik) *n.:* object or thing from the past that may have a special meaning or association, sometimes a religious one.
resignation (rez′ig·nā′shən) *n.:* passive acceptance; submission.
resolute (rez′ə·lo͞ot′) *adj.:* determined.
reticent (ret′ə·sənt) *adj.:* silent; reserved.
retort (ri·tôrt′) *n.:* sharp reply.
reverence (rev′ə·rəns) *n.:* attitude or display of deep respect and awe.
rifle (rī′fəl) *v.:* search thoroughly or in a rough manner. —**rifling** *v.* used as *n.*

Glossary

at, āte, cär; ten, ēve; is, īce; gō, hôrn, look, to͞ol; oil, out; up, fur; ə *for unstressed vowels, as* a *in* ago, u *in* focus; ′ *as in* Latin (lat′′n); chin; she; thin; *the*; zh *as in* azure (azh′ər); ŋ *as in* ring (riŋ)

Glossary 1013

S

sagacious (sə·gā′shəs) *adj.:* wise; showing sound judgment.
sarcastic (sär·kas′tik) *adj.:* mocking; taunting; in a manner that makes fun of something or someone.
sedate (si·dāt′) *adj.:* calm and dignified; quiet. —**sedately** *adv.*
sidle (sīd″l) *v.:* move sideways, especially in a shy or sneaky manner.
sinister (sin′is·tər) *adj.:* evil.
skirt (skurt) *v.:* **1.** pass around rather than through. **2.** miss narrowly; avoid.
solidarity (säl′ə·dar′ə·tē) *n.:* complete unity in a group or organization.
solitary (säl′ə·ter′ē) *adj.:* without others.
sovereign (säv′rən) *n.:* king; ruler.
speculate (spek′yə·lāt′) *v.:* think; guess.
speculation (spek′yə·lā′shən) *n.:* thought; guesswork.
splice (splīs) *v.:* join by inserting and binding together. —**splicing** *v.* used as *n.*
stealth (stelth) *n.:* secretiveness; sly behavior.
stench (stench) *n.:* offensive smell.
stricken (strik′ən) *adj.:* heartbroken; affected by or suffering from something painful or distressing.
submerge (səb·murj′) *v.:* cover with water.
subterranean (sub′tə·rā′nē·ən) *adj.:* underground.
sultry (sul′trē) *adj.:* hot and humid; sweltering.
superlative (sə·pur′lə·tiv) *adj.:* supreme; better than all others.
supplication (sup′lə·kā′shən) *n.:* humble appeal or request.
surly (sur′lē) *adj.:* bad-tempered; rude.
surreptitious (sur′əp·tish′əs) *adj.:* stealthy; sneaky. —**surreptitiously** *adv.*

T

tangible (tan′jə·bəl) *adj.:* that can be touched.
tenacity (tə·nas′ə·tē) *n.:* stubborn persistence and determination.
tentative (ten′tə·tiv) *adj.:* timid; hesitant.
tenuous (ten′yo͞o·əs) *adj.:* weak; slight.
tepid (tep′id) *adj.:* neither hot nor cold; lukewarm.
terminal (tur′mə·nəl) *adj.:* of or relating to an end, often an end to life.
torrent (tôr′ənt) *n.:* violent, forceful rush.
traverse (trə·vurs′) *v.:* cross.
trek (trek) *v.:* journey.
tremulous (trem′yo͞o·ləs) *adj.:* trembling; quivering.
tumultuous (to͞o·mul′cho͞o·əs) *adj.:* wild; noisy.

U

unimpeded (un′im·pēd′id) *adj.:* not blocked; unobstructed.
unorthodox (un·ôr′thə·däks′) *adj.:* unusual; not conforming to usual norms.

V

vain (vān) *adj.:* without success; fruitless. —**vainly** *adv.*
valiant (val′yənt) *adj.:* brave. —**valiantly** *adv.*
valid (val′id) *adj.:* meeting the requirements of established standards.
veritable (ver′i·tə·bəl) *adj.:* actual; true.
vigil (vij′əl) *n.:* watchful staying awake during the usual hours of sleep.
vintage (vin′tij) *adj.:* dating from a time long past.
vitality (vī·tal′ə·tē) *n.:* energy; vigor.

W

whimsy (hwim′zē) *n.:* quaint or odd humor.
wizened (wiz′ənd) *adj.:* wrinkled and dried up.
wrath (rath) *n.:* great anger.

1014 Resource Center Glossary

Acknowledgments

For permission to reprint copyrighted material, grateful acknowledgment is made to the following sources:

Lily Lee Adams: "The Friendship Only Lasted a Few Seconds" by Lily Lee Adams from *Connections,* newsletter of the William Joiner Center at University of Massachusetts, Boston, Spring 1990. Copyright © 1990 by Lily Lee Adams.
Bill Adler Books Inc.: From "Dear Folks" by Kenneth W. Bagby from *Letters from Vietnam,* edited by Bill Adler. Copyright © 1967 by Bill Adler.
Norma Bradley Allen: From *The Quilters: Women and Domestic Art* by Norma Bradley Allen and Patricia Cooper. Copyright © 1977 by Patricia Cooper Baker and Norma Allen.
Gloria Allred and Lisa Bloom: From "If Decency Doesn't, Law Should Make Us Samaritans" by Gloria Allred and Lisa Bloom from *Houston Chronicle,* September 18, 1997. Copyright © 1997 by Gloria Allred and Lisa Bloom.
Arte Público Press: "Same Song" from *Borders* by Pat Mora. Copyright © 1986 by Pat Mora. Published by Arte Público Press–University of Houston, Houston, TX, 1986.
The Associated Press: From "Jack Finney, 84; His Novel Became Cult Classic 'Body Snatchers'" from *Boston Globe,* November 17, 1995. Copyright © 1995 by The Associated Press. From "Explorers Say There's Still Lots to Look For" by Helen O'Neill from *The Seattle Times,* May 21, 2000. Copyright © 2000 by The Associated Press.
Jessica Barnes: "Crossing a Threshold into Adulthood" by Jessica Barnes from *Times Union,* September 24, 2000. Copyright © 2000 by Jessica Barnes.
Elizabeth Barnett, Literary Executor: From "Sonnet XXX" of *Fatal Interview* from *Collected Poems* by Edna St. Vincent Millay. Copyright © 1931, 1958 by Edna St. Vincent Millay and Norma Millay Ellis. Published by HarperCollins Publishers.
Applause Theatre & Cinema Books: *The Brute* by Anton Chekhov, English version by Eric Bentley. Copyright 1956 and renewed © 1984 by Eric Bentley. Published by Samuel French, Inc.
Susan Bergholz Literary Services, New York: "Geraldo No Last Name" from *The House on Mango Street* by Sandra Cisneros. Copyright © 1984 by Sandra Cisneros. Published by Vintage Books, a division of Random House, Inc., and in hardcover by Alfred A. Knopf in 1994. All rights reserved. "My Lucy Friend Who Smells Like Corn" from *Woman Hollering Creek* by Sandra Cisneros. Copyright © 1991 by Sandra Cisneros. Published by Vintage Books, a division of Random House, Inc., New York, and originally in hardcover by Random House, Inc. All rights reserved.
Robert Bly: From "Ode to My Socks" by Pablo Neruda from *Neruda and Vallejo: Selected Poems,* edited and translated by Robert Bly. Copyright © 1971 by Robert Bly. Published by Beacon Press.
BOA Editions, Ltd.: "miss rosie" from *good woman: poems and a memoir 1969–1980* by Lucille Clifton. Copyright © 1987 by Lucille Clifton. "Eating Together" from *Rose: Poems* by Li-Young Lee. Copyright © 1986 by Li-Young Lee.
The Book Report, Inc.: From "Exclusive TBR Interview with Frank McCourt" by Jesse Kornbluth from "Author Transcripts," accessed September 11, 1998, at http://www.bookwire.com/TBR/transcripts.article$3259.
The Boston Globe: From "Coming of Age, Latino Style, Special Rite Ushers Girls into Adulthood" by Cindy Rodriguez from *The Boston Globe,* January 5, 1997. Copyright © 1997 by The Boston Globe.
Brandt & Brandt Literary Agents, Inc.: "By the Waters of Babylon" from *The Selected Works of Stephen Vincent Benét.* Copyright © 1937 by Stephen Vincent Benét; copyright renewed © 1964 by Thomas C. Benét, Stephanie P. Mahin, and Rachel Benét Lewis.
Jimmy Breslin: "The Fear and the Flames" by Jimmy Breslin from *New York Post,* April 6, 1968. Copyright © 1968 by Jimmy Breslin.
Broadside Press: From *Report from Part One* by Gwendolyn Brooks. Copyright © 1972 by Gwendolyn Brooks. Published by Broadside Press, Detroit.
The Estate of Gwendolyn Brooks: "We Real Cool" from *Blacks* by Gwendolyn Brooks. Copyright © 1991 by Gwendolyn Brooks. Published by Third World Press, Chicago, 1991.
Curtis Brown, Ltd.: "R.M.S. Titanic" by Hanson W. Baldwin from *Harper's Magazine,* January 1934. Copyright © 1934 by Hanson W. Baldwin.
Rick J. Brown: From "The Day the Clowns Cried" by Rick Brown from *History Buff,* accessed October 31, 2000, at http://www.discovery.com/guides/history/historybuff/library/reffire.html.
The Christian Science Monitor: "A State Championship vs. Runner's Conscience" by John Christian Hoyle from *The Christian Science Monitor,* February 5, 1999. Copyright © 1999 by The Christian Science Monitor. Online at csmonitor.com. "Deprived of Parent Time? Not Most Kids" by Kim Campbell from *The Christian Science Monitor,* April 5, 2000. Copyright © 2000 by The Christian Science Monitor. All rights reserved. Online at csmonitor.com.
Judith Ortiz Cofer: Quotes by Judith Ortiz Cofer from *The Global Education Project,* accessed January 10, 2001, at http://ultrix.ramapo.edu/global/cofer.html, January 10, 2001.
Don Congdon Associates, Inc.: From "Drunk and in Charge of a Bicycle" from *The Stories of Ray Bradbury.* Copyright © 1980 by Ray Bradbury. "The Pedestrian" by Ray Bradbury from *The Reporter,* August 7, 1951. Copyright © 1951 by the Fortnightly Publishing Co.; copyright renewed © 1979 by Ray Bradbury. "Contents of the Dead Man's Pocket" by Jack Finney. Copyright © 1956 by Crowell-Collier Co.; copyright renewed © 1984 by Jack Finney.
The Dallas Morning News: From "Alice in Wonderland" by Toni Y. Joseph from *The Dallas Morning News,* May 27, 1992. Copyright © 1992 by The Dallas Morning News.
Dell Publishing, a division of Random House, Inc.: "Where Have You Gone, Charming Billy?" slightly adapted from *Going After Cacciato* by Tim O'Brien. Copyright © 1975, 1976, 1977, 1978 by Tim O'Brien. From *If I Die in a Combat Zone, Box Me Up and Ship Me Home* by Tim O'Brien. Copyright © 1973 by Tim O'Brien.
The Denver Post: From "Double Daddy" by Penny Parker from *The Denver Post,* September 5, 1999. Copyright © 1999 by The Denver Post.
Barbara Sande Dimmitt: From "The Education of Frank McCourt" by Barbara Sande Dimmitt from *Reader's Digest,* November 1997. Copyright © 1997 by Barbara Sande Dimmitt.
Discovery Communications, Inc.: "Epidemic! On the Trail of Killer Diseases" by Karen Watson from *Discovery Channel* Web site, accessed March 9, 2001, at http://www.discovery.com/exp/epidemic/tb/tb.html. Copyright © by Discovery Communications, Inc.
Doubleday, a division of Random House, Inc.: From *The Language of Life: A Festival of Poets* by Bill Moyers. Copyright © 1995 by Public Affairs Television, Inc., and David Grubin Productions, Inc. From *The Power of Myth* by Joseph Campbell with Bill Moyers. Copyright © 1988 by Apostrophe S Productions, Inc., and Alfred van der Marck Editions.

Acknowledgments 1015

Rita Dove: "Grape Sherbet" from *Museum* by Rita Dove. Copyright © 1983 by Rita Dove. Published by Carnegie-Mellon University Press.
Dutton Signet, a division of Penguin Putnam Inc.: "The Tale of Sir Launcelot du Lake" and "The Sword in the Stone" from *Le Morte D'Arthur* by Sir Thomas Malory, translated by Keith Baines. Translation copyright © 1962 by Keith Baines; copyright renewed © 1990 by Francesca Evans.
Encyclopaedia Britannica, Inc.: Entry for "Vision Quest" from *The New Encyclopaedia Britannica,* 15th Edition, vol. 12. Copyright © 1995 by Encyclopaedia Britannica, Inc.
Farrar, Straus & Giroux, LLC: From "The Country Boy" and "Lost in the City" from *Memoirs* by Pablo Neruda, translated by Hardie St. Martin. Translation copyright © 1976, 1977 by Farrar, Straus & Giroux, LLC. "A Storm in the Mountains" from *Stories and Prose Poems* by Alexander Solzhenitsyn, translated by Michael Glenny. Translation copyright © 1971 by Michael Glenny. From Introduction from *The Acts of King Arthur and His Noble Knights* by John Steinbeck, edited by Chase Horton. Copyright © 1976 by Elaine Steinbeck.
Fortune Magazine: From "The Child's View of Working Parents" by Cora Daniels from *Fortune,* vol. 140, no. 9, November 8, 1999. Copyright © 1999 by Time, Inc.
Lisa Fugard: "Night Calls" by Lisa Fugard from *Outside,* vol. XX, no. 5, May 1995, Copyright © 1995 by Lisa Fugard. Quotes by Lisa Fugard from *Selected Shorts* radio inverview. Copyright © by Lisa Fugard.
The Estate of Ira Gershwin: From "They Can't Take That Away from Me" by George and Ira Gershwin.
Tom Godwin and Scott Meredith Literary Agency, 845 Third Avenue, New York, NY 10022: From *The Cold Equations* by Tom Godwin. Copyright 1954 by Tom Godwin.
Greenhaven Press, Inc.: From *Great Mysteries: King Arthur, Opposing Viewpoints®* by Michael O'Neal. Copyright © 1992 by Greenhaven Press, Inc.
Guardian Newspapers Limited: From "Taste—The Final Frontier" by Esther Addley from *The Guardian,* April 21, 2000. Copyright © by Guardian Newspapers Limited.
Hanging Loose Press: "Sonnet for Heaven Below" from *Correspondence Between the Stonehaulers* by Jack Agüeros. Copyright © 1991 by Jack Agüeros.
Harcourt Inc.: From "Tentative (First Model) Definitions of Poetry" from *Good Morning, America* by Carl Sandburg. Copyright 1928 and renewed © 1956 by by Carl Sandburg. "Everyday Use" from *In Love & Trouble: Stories of Black Women* by Alice Walker. Copyright © 1973 by Alice Walker.
HarperCollins Publishers: From *Paula* by Isabel Allende, translated by Margaret Sayers Peden. Copyright © 1994 by Isabel Allende; translation copyright © 1995 by HarperCollins Publishers. "The Black Death" from *When Plague Strikes: The Black Death, Smallpox, AIDS* by James Cross Giblin. Copyright © 1995 by James Cross Giblin. From "Hands: For Mother's Day" from *The Selected Poems of Nikki Giovanni.* Compilation copyright © 1996 by Nikki Giovanni. "A Very Old Man with Enormous Wings" from *Leaf Storm and Other Stories* by Gabriel García Márquez. Copyright © 1971 by Gabriel García Márquez. "By Any Other Name" from *Gifts of Passage* by Santha Rama Rau. Copyright 1951 and renewed © 1979 by Santha Rama Rau. Originally appeared in *The New Yorker.*
Harper's Magazine: "The Leap" by Louise Erdrich from *Harper's Magazine,* March 1990. Copyright © 1990 by Harper's Magazine. All rights reserved.
Harvard University Press and the Trustees of Amherst College: "Heart! We will forget him!," from "This is my letter to the World," "This is the land the Sunset washes," and "The Moon was but a Chin of Gold" from *The Poems of Emily Dickinson,* edited by Thomas H. Johnson. Copyright © 1951, 1955, 1979 by the President and Fellows of Harvard College. Published by The Belknap Press of Harvard University Press, Cambridge, MA.
David Higham Associates Limited: "Lamb to the Slaughter" from *Someone Like You* by Roald Dahl. Copyright © 1961 by Roald Dahl.
Henry Holt and Company, LLC: "Stopping by Woods on a Snowy Evening" from *The Poetry of Robert Frost,* edited by Edward Connery Lathem. Copyright 1923, © 1969 by Henry Holt and Company, LLC; copyright 1951 by Robert Frost.
Garrett Hongo: Comment on "The Legend" by Garrett Hongo. Copyright © 1997 by Garrett Hongo.
Houghton Mifflin Company: "All Watched Over by Machines of Loving Grace" and "It's Raining in Love" from *The Pill Versus the Springhill Mine Disaster* by Richard Brautigan. Copyright © 1965 by Richard Brautigan. All rights reserved. From Introduction and from "The Dragon Slayer" and "Fafnir's End" from *Legends of the North* by Olivia E. Coolidge. Copyright 1951 by Olivia E. Coolidge. From *Offshore* by Penelope Fitzgerald. Copyright © 1979 by Penelope Fitzgerald. All rights reserved.
The Estate of Martin Luther King, Jr., c/o Writers House as agent for the proprietor: From "Declaration of Independence from the War in Vietnam" by Martin Luther King, Jr. Copyright © 1963 by Martin Luther King; copyright renewed © 1991 by Coretta Scott King.
Alfred A. Knopf, a division of Random House, Inc.: "What Happened During the Ice Storm" from *The One Room Schoolhouse* by Jim Heynen. Copyright © 1993 by Jim Heynen. "The Legend" from *The River of Heaven* by Garrett Hongo. Copyright © 1988 by Garrett Hongo. "I, Too" from *The Collected Poems of Langston Hughes.* Copyright © 1994 by The Estate of Langston Hughes. "Through the Tunnel" from *Stories* by Doris Lessing. Copyright © 1978 by Doris Lessing. "Gracious Goodness" from *Circles on the Water* by Marge Piercy. Copyright © 1982 by Marge Piercy. "Ex–Basketball Player" from *The Carpentered Hen and Other Tame Creatures* by John Updike. Copyright © 1982 by John Updike. "Powder" from *The Night in Question: Stories* by Tobias Wolff. Copyright © 1996 by Tobias Wolff.
Kenneth Koch: "You want a social life, with friends" from *Straits: Poems* by Kenneth Koch. Copyright © 1998 by Kenneth Koch.
Barbara S. Kouts, Literary Agent: From "Whatever Is Really Yours: An Interview with Louise Erdrich" from *Survival This Way* by Joseph Bruchac. Copyright © 1987 by Joseph Bruchac.
Li-Young Lee: Quote by Li-Young Lee from *San Diego Union-Tribune,* April 11, 1996. Copyright © 1996 by Li-Young Lee.
Little, Brown and Company (Inc.): From "Theseus" from *Mythology* by Edith Hamilton. Copyright © 1942 by Edith Hamilton; copyright renewed © 1969 by Dorian Fielding Reid and Doris Fielding Reid.
Liveright Publishing Corporation: "since feeling is first" from *Complete Poems, 1904–1962* by E. E. Cummings, edited by George J. Firmage. Copyright 1926, 1954, © 1991 by the Trustees for the E. E. Cummings Trust; copyright © 1985 by George James Firmage.
Los Angeles Times: From "Baca: A Poet Emerges from Prison of His Past" by Beth Ann Krier from *Los Angeles Times,* February 15, 1989. Copyright © 1989 by the Los Angeles Times. "Local Hands on a New Space Project" by Seema Mehta from *Los Angeles Times,* September 8, 2000. Copyright © 2000 by Los Angeles Times.
The McGraw-Hill Book Companies: From *Born on the Fourth of July* by Ron Kovic. Copyright © 1976 by Ron Kovic.
Marion C. Meyer: "As I Fell . . ." by Dickey Chappelle from *National Geographic,* February 1966. Copyright © 1966 by Dickey Chappelle.
N. Scott Momaday: "Simile" from *The Gourd Dancer* by N. Scott Momaday. Copyright © 1976 by N. Scott Momaday. From *The Names: A Memoir* by N. Scott Momaday. Copyright © 1976 by N. Scott Momaday.
Norman Myers: From "Call of the Wild—Save Us!" by Norman Myers from *Good Housekeeping,* vol. 212, April 1991. Copyright © 1991 by Norman Myers.

1016 Acknowledgments

Thomas Nelson Inc.: From *Rice Paddy Grunt* by John M. G. Brown. Copyright © 1986 by John M. G. Brown.

New Directions Publishing Corporation: "I Am Offering This Poem" from *Immigrants in Our Own Land* by Jimmy Santiago Baca. Copyright © 1982 by Jimmy Santiago Baca. From "The Walls Do Not Fall [9]" from *Trilogy* by Hilda Doolittle. Copyright © 1944 by Oxford University Press; copyright renewed © 1972 by Norman Holmes Pearson.

New York Post: "*Julius Caesar* in an Absorbing Production" by John Mason Brown from *New York Post,* November 12, 1937. Copyright 1937 by NYP Holdings, Inc.

The New York Times Company: From "Love and Age: A Talk with García Márquez" by Marlise Simons from *The New York Times Book Review,* April 7, 1985. Copyright © 1985 by The New York Times Company. Quote by Jack Finney from "Some Time Later, a Sequel to 'Time and Again'" by Lawrence Van Gelder from *The New York Times,* December 13, 1994. Copyright © 1994 by The New York Times Company. From "A Baby's Quilt to Sew Up the Generations" by Felicia R. Lee from *The New York Times,* July 9, 2000. Copyright © 2000 by The New York Times Company.

Newsweek, Inc.: From "Nursing the Dying" by Edie Meeks from *Newsweek,* March 8, 1999, p. 61. Copyright © 1999 by Newsweek, Inc. All rights reserved.

W. W. Norton & Company, Inc.: "Waiting for *E. gularis*" from *A Fraction of Darkness* by Linda Pastan. Copyright © 1985 by Linda Pastan.

Naomi Shihab Nye: "The Flying Cat" from *Hugging the Jukebox* by Naomi Shihab Nye. Copyright © 1982 by Naomi Shihab Nye.

OMNI Publications International Ltd.: From "Bug Zappers Miss Their Mark" by Steve Nadis from Omni Online, 1996. Copyright © 1996 by Omni Publications International, Ltd.

Progressive Grocer Magazine, Bill Communications Inc., a VNU Company: From "What Price Glory?" by Len Lewis from *Progressive Grocer,* vol. 79, no. 5, May 2000. Copyright © 2000 by Progressive Grocer Magazine.

G. P. Putnam's Sons, a division of Penguin Putnam Inc.: "Two Kinds" from *The Joy Luck Club* by Amy Tan. Copyright © 1989 by Amy Tan.

Random House, Inc.: From "Peter and Rosa" (retitled "The Blue Stones") from *Winter's Tales* by Isak Dinesen. Copyright 1942 by Random House, Inc.; copyright renewed © 1970 by Johan Philip Thomas Ingerslev, c/o The Rungstedlund Foundation.

Steven Ratiner: From "Rita Dove: Chorus of Voices" from *Giving Their Word—Conversations with Contemporary Poets* by Steven Ratiner. Copyright © 1993 by Steven Ratiner. Published by University of Massachusetts Press, 2002.

Rutledge Hill Press, Nashville, Tennessee: From *A Communion of Spirits* by Roland L. Freeman. Copyright © 1996 by Roland L. Freeman.

Jim Sagel and Publishers Weekly®: From "Sandra Cisneros," an interview by Jim Sagel, from *Publishers Weekly®,* vol. 238, no. 15, March 29, 1991. Copyright © 1991 by Publishers Weekly®.

Scholastic Inc.: "Catch the Moon" from *An Island Like You: Stories from the Barrio* by Judith Ortiz Cofer. Copyright © 1995 by Judith Ortiz Cofer. Published by Orchard Books, an imprint of Scholastic Inc. From "Pat Mora's Biography" from *Authors Online Library,* accessed July 17, 2001, at http://teacher.scholastic.com/authorsandbooks/authors/mora/bio.htm. Copyright © 2002 by Scholastic Inc.

Scribner, a division of Simon & Schuster: "And of Clay Are We Created" from *The Stories of Eva Luna* by Isabel Allende, translated by Margaret Sayers Peden. Copyright © 1989 by Isabel Allende; translation © 1991 by Macmillan Publishing Company. From *Angela's Ashes* by Frank McCourt. Copyright © 1996 by Frank McCourt.

Simon & Schuster Inc.: From *The Winged Seed: A Remembrance* by Li-Young Lee. Copyright © 1995 by Li-Young Lee.

The Society of Authors as the Literary Representative of the Estate of John Masefield: "Sea Fever" from *Poems* by John Masefield. Published by Macmillan Publishing Company, New York, 1953.

James Stevenson: "Notes from a Bottle" by James Stevenson from *The New Yorker,* 1969. Copyright © 1969 by James Stevenson.

Mark Strand: From "Eating Poetry" from *Reasons for Moving* by Mark Strand. Copyright © 1968 by Mark Strand.

Amy Tan and Sandra Dijkstra Literary Agency: From "Mother Tongue" by Amy Tan. Copyright © 1990 by Amy Tan. First appeared in *The Threepenny Review.*

Thunder's Mouth Press: "Remember" from *She Had Some Horses* by Joy Harjo. Copyright © 1983, 1997 by Thunder's Mouth Press.

Time Inc.: "For the Third Time" by Du Luc, from diary entry of December 1960, from *Time,* December 15, 1961. Copyright © 1961 by Time Inc. "The Man in the Water" by Roger Rosenblatt from *Time,* January 26, 1982. Copyright © 1982 by Time Inc. From "The Last Frontier" by Michael D. Lemonick from *Time,* August 14, 1995. Copyright © 1995 by Time Inc.

University of Pittsburgh Press: "The Bass, the River, and Sheila Mant" from *The Man Who Loved Levittown* by W. D. Wetherell. Copyright © 1985 by W. D. Wetherell.

Villard Books, a division of Random House, Inc.: From *Into Thin Air* by Jon Krakauer. Copyright © 1997 by Jon Krakauer.

Vintage Books, a division of Random House, Inc.: "How sad that I hope . . . ," "Should the world of love . . . ," and "Since my heart placed me . . ." from *The Ink Dark Moon: Love Poems* by Ono No Komachi and Izumi Shikibu, translated by Jane Hirshfield and Mariko Aratani. Copyright © 1990 by Jane Hirshfield and Mariko Aratani.

The Virginian-Pilot: "Good Samaritans U.S.A. Are Afraid to Act" by Ann Sjoerdsma from *The Virginian-Pilot,* September 15, 1997. Copyright © 1997 by The Virginian-Pilot.

The Wall Street Journal: From "Diary of a Mad Blender: A Week of Managing Every Spare Minute" by Sue Shellenbarger from *The Wall Street Journal,* March 22, 2000. Copyright © 2000 by Down Jones & Company, Inc.

The Washington Post: From "Ill-Equipped Rescuers Dig Out Volcano Victims: Aid Slow to Reach Columbian Town" by Bradley Graham from *The Washington Post,* November 16, 1985. Copyright © 1985 by The Washington Post.

Wesleyan University Press: "Moons" from *The Stone Harp* by John Haines. Copyright © 1971 by John Haines.

W. D. Wetherell: From "A Trout for Celeste" from *Vermont River* by W. D. Wetherell. Copyright © 1984 by W. D. Wetherell.

Wiley Publishing, Inc.: Entry for "indulge" and pronunciation keys from *Webster's New World™ College Dictionary,* Fourth Edition. Copyright © 2000, 1999 by Wiley Publishing, Inc. All rights reserved.

The H. W. Wilson Company: Quote from "Olivia Coolidge" from *More Junior Authors,* accessed November 19, 2001, at http://vweb.hwwilsonweb.com/cgi-bin/webspirs.cgi. Copyright © 2001 by The H. W. Wilson Company.

Sources Cited

From letter to Maxim Gorki from *The Selected Letters of Anton Chekhov,* edited by Lillian Hellman, translated by Sidonie Lederer. Published by Farrar, Straus & Company, New York, 1955.

From "James Stevenson" from *Contemporary Authors,* January 10, 2001. Published by The Gale Group, Farmington Hills, MI, 2001.

Quote by Roald Dahl from *The New York Times Book Review.*

Quote by Frank McCourt from "From 'Ashes' to Stardom" by Malcolm Jones, Jr., from *Newsweek,* August 25, 1997. Published by Newsweek.

Acknowledgments 1017

Picture Credits

The illustrations and/or photographs on the Contents pages are picked up from pages in the textbook. Credits for those can be found either on the textbook page on which they appear or in the listing below.

Page 2: © cartoonbank.com; **5:** © Pete Seaward/Getty Images; **9:** © Nat Norman/Getty Images; **10:** © Pete Seaward/Getty Images; **13:** © Lawrence Thornton/Getty Images; **14:** © Euan Myles/Getty Images; **17:** Kim Komenich/TimePix; **18:** © Amos Morgan/Getty Images; **27:** © Bruce Ayres/Getty Images; **32:** © Sarto/Lund/Getty Images; **34:** © Dewitt Jones/CORBIS; **36–37:** © Frank Herholdt/Getty Images; **39:** Keri Pickett/TimePix; **40:** AP/Associated Press; **47:** © Getty Images; **52:** © Syndicated Features Limited/The Image Works; **55:** (top left) Cover photo: Lambert Studios/Archive Photos; (top right) Cover from *Nectar in a Sieve* by Kamala Markandaya, copyright © 1954 by The John Day Company. Used by permission of Signet, a division of Penguin Putnam, Inc.; (bottom left) From *Fahrenheit 451* by Ray Bradbury. Used with permission of Ballantine Books, a division of Random House, Inc.; (bottom right) From *The Hot Zone* (jacket cover) by Richard Preston, copyright. Used by permission of Doubleday, a division of Random House, Inc.; **78–82** (borders): Detail of *His Grandmother's Quilt.* Courtesy of the artist; **83:** © Anthony Barboza/Buddha Studio; **84:** Romare Howard Bearden Foundation. Licensed by VAGA, New York; **85:** © Baron/Getty Images; **89:** © 2001 Roland L. Freeman, Washington, D.C.; **97:** © cartoonbank.com; **99:** © Stephanie Dalton Cowan/Getty Images; **101:** © Lake County Museum/CORBIS; **105:** © David Perry/Getty Images; **108:** © Reuters/CORBIS; **113:** Copyright © 1977 by Santha Rama Rau. Reprinted by permission of William Morris Agency, Inc., on behalf of the author; **117:** © Lindsay Hebberd/CORBIS; **118:** © Elliot Erwitt/Magnum Photos; **121:** (top left) Cover from *Washington Square* by Henry James. Courtesy of the Oxford University Press/National Gallery of London; (top right) Cover from *Fences* by August Wilson, copyright © 1986 by August Wilson. Used by permission of Dutton Signet, a division of Penguin Putnam, Inc.; (bottom left) Cover used by permission of University Press of New England; (bottom right) Cover from *Fifth Chinese Daughter* by Jade Snow Wong, courtesy University of Washington Press; **139:** Reprinted courtesy of The Saturday Evening Post; **141:** © Getty Images; **149:** Fisk University Galleries, Nashville, Tenn.; **151:** Culver Pictures, Inc.; **160:** E. O. Hoppé/TimePix; **164:** (top right) © WY/Getty Images; (center) John Lei, Omni–Photo Communications, Inc.; (bottom left) © Joe Sohm/The Stock Market/CORBIS; **166:** (background) © NASA/Getty Images; (inset) John Lei, Omni–Photo Communications, Inc.; **168:** (top) © Stephen Simpson/Getty Images; (bottom) Jon Davison/The Image Bank; **171:** © Aram Gesar/Getty Images; **177:** (background) Chris Butler/Science Photo Library/Photo Researchers, Inc.; (inset) John Lei, Omni–Photo Communications, Inc.; **180–181:** © Stephen Simpson/Getty Images; **184:** Morgan-Cain & Associates; **188, 189, 190:** NASA; **194–195** (background): © Bettmann/CORBIS; **195** (inset): From *Angela's Ashes* by Frank McCourt. © 1996 by Frank McCourt. Reproduced by permission of Scribner's, a division of Simon & Schuster. All rights reserved; **196–199** (background): © CORBIS; **196** (inset): © Bettmann/CORBIS; **200:** AP/Wide World Photos; **201, 202–203:** Morgan-Cain & Associates; **207:** (top left) Kwangshin Kim/Photo Researchers, Inc.; (top right) S. Camazine/Photo Researchers, Inc.; (bottom right) © S. Lowry/University of Ulster/Getty Images; **208:** (top) © Barts Hospital/Getty Images; (bottom) Richard Falco/Black Star Publishing/PictureQuest; **209:** © Hulton-Deutsch Collection/CORBIS; **211:** (top left) Cover photo: A. P. Allenson, E. O. Hoppé. Courtesy of Royal Photographic Society; (top right) From *Dune* by Frank Herbert. Used by permission of G. P. Putnam's Sons, a division of Penguin Putnam, Inc.; (bottom left) Cover from *Platero and I* by Juan Ramón Jiménez. Jacket illustration copyright © 1994 by Antonio Frasconi. Reprinted by permission of Clarion Books/Houghton Mifflin Company. All rights reserved; (bottom right) Cover from *Hiroshima* by John Hersey. Illustrated by Wendell Minor. Used by permission of Vintage Books, a division of Random House, Inc.; **222:** University of California at Irvine/NASA; **223:** NASA Marshall Space Flight Center, photo by Dennis Olive; **233:** © Getty Images; (background) Timothy Fuller/PhotoSpin; **234:** (left, right, middle center, background) © Getty Images; (top center) PhotoSpin; (bottom center) Timothy Fuller; **236:** Timothy Fuller; **239:** © Getty Images; (background) Timothy Fuller/PhotoSpin; **240:** Photo of Judith Ortiz Cofer is reprinted with permission from the publisher, Arte Público Press; **243:** © Burton McNeely/Getty Images; **244:** (top) © Burton McNeeley/Getty Images; (bottom) © Gerald Brimacombe; **244–245:** Kirchoff/Wohlberg; **246:** © Gerald Brimacombe; **249:** © Burton McNeeley/Getty Images; **250:** Francois Camoin; **257:** © Getty Images; **259:** J. N. Marso/USGS; **265:** © Getty Images; **266:** © Ed Kashi/CORBIS; **267:** Frank Fournier/Contact Press Images; **273, 274, 276:** © Terry Ashe/Getty Images; **277:** Bernard Gotfryd/Woodfin Camp & Associates; **278:** © Todd Gipstein/CORBIS; **279:** © Dennis O'Clair/Getty Images; **287:** Ellis Herwig/Stock Boston Inc./PictureQuest; **293:** (top left) From *A Tale of Two Cities* by Charles Dickens. Cover art © HRW, cover design Chris Smith, background © CORBIS/Owen Franken/Jeremy Homer; (top right) Cover from *The Sound of Waves* by Yukio Mishima. Used by permission of Vintage Books, a division of Random House, Inc.; (bottom left) Cover from *Laughing Boy* by Oliver La Farge, copyright © 1929 by Oliver La Farge. Used by permission of Dutton Signet, a division of Penguin Putnam, Inc.; (bottom right) Cover from *The Perfect Storm* by Sebastian Junger. Cover photo by Th. D.A. DeLange/FPG. Copyright © 1997 by Sebastian Junger. Used by permission of W. W. Norton & Company; **306:** Walter Geiersperger/Index Stock Photography; **307:** Stephen John Krasemann/Photo Researchers, Inc.; **325:** Nancy Crampton; **328:** (left) Courtesy Ken Marschall Collection; (right) © CORBIS/Sygma; **329:** (left) Titanic Historical Society, Don Lynch Collection, Indian Orchard (MA); (right) The Illustrated London News Picture Library; **330–331:** Illustrations by Ken Marschall © 1992 from *Titanic: An Illustrated History*, a Hyperion/Madison Press Book; **333:** (background) Color Box/FPG International; (left) Reproduced by courtesy of White Star Publications; (right) The Illustrated London News Picture Library; **334:** (background) Color Box/FPG International; (top) Hulton-Deutsch Collection, London; (bottom) Titanic Historical Society, Indian Orchard (MA); **337:** (background) Color Box/FPG International; (top)

Picture Credits **1019**

Titanic Historical Society, Indian Orchard (MA); (bottom) © Bettmann/CORBIS; **338–339:** Illustrations by Ken Marschall © 1992 from *Titanic: An Illustrated History,* a Hyperion/Madison Press Book; **344:** (top) AP/Wide World Photos; (bottom) Detail of an illustration by Ken Marschall © 1992 from *Titanic: An Illustrated History,* a Hyperion/Madison Press Book; **345:** (left) © Bettmann/CORBIS; (top right) The Illustrated London News Picture Library; (bottom right) AP/Wide World Photos; **346:** (top) Titanic Historical Society, Don Lynch Collection, Indian Orchard (MA); (bottom) Titanic Historical Society, Indian Orchard (MA); **349–351** (background): © Gordon Wiltsie/Alpenimage Ltd.; **351:** (top) © Ed Viesturs/Ethereal, Inc.; (bottom) Caroline Mackenzie/Woodfin Camp & Associates; **352–353:** © Neil Beidleman/Woodfin Camp & Associates; **354–363** (background): © Gordon Wiltsie; **356:** © Neil Beidleman/Woodfin Camp & Associates; **359:** Scott Fischer/ Woodfin Camp & Associates; **362:** © Chris Noble/Getty Images; **363:** © Andrew Eccles/CORBIS Outline; **368:** Royal Geographical Society, London; **369:** NASA; **370:** © Bettmann/CORBIS; **378:** Courtesy of Harper Collins; **381:** (top left) *Tales of the Unexpected;* (top right) *Alice's Adventures in Wonderland & Through the Looking-Glass;* (bottom left) *A Night to Remember;* (bottom right) *The Endurance: Shackleton's Legendary Antarctic Expedition;* **396–397:** AKG Berlin/SuperStock; **400–401:** M. Rubio/West Stock; **401:** Jerry Jones/Photo Researchers, Inc.; **403:** (top) John Neubauer/PhotoEdit; (bottom) M. Rubio/West Stock; **407:** © Andy Sacks/Getty Images; **408:** © Bettmann/CORBIS; **415:** Shamil Zhumatov/Reuters/TimePix; **422–423:** © Erich Lessing/ Art Resource, NY; **425:** © Erich Lessing/Art Resource, NY; **426:** Julian Hartnoll, London/Private collection/Bridgeman Art Library; **428:** Mansell/TimePix; **429–430** (background): Planet Art; **430:** © Historical Picture Archive/CORBIS; **434:** © David Muench/ CORBIS; **435:** © Burstein Collection/CORBIS; **436:** © Christie's Images/CORBIS; **437:** Eric Schaal/TimePix; **439:** (top left) *Watership Down;* (top right) *A Separate Peace* by John Knowles. Cover © HRW; (bottom left) *The Tale of the Unknown Island* (book jacket) by José Saramago. Jacket illustration by Peter Sis. Used by permission of Harcourt; (bottom right) *Black Ice;* **454–455:** © Christie's Images, Inc.; **458:** AGE/FotoStock/ SuperStock; **459:** © Craig Aurness/CORBIS; **460:** AP/Wide World Photos; **461:** (left) John Henley/The Stock Market; (right) Paul Simcock/The Image Bank; **462:** Stockbyte/PictureQuest; **463:** Arte Público Press/University of Houston; **464:** (top) © EyeWire/Getty Images; (bottom) © CORBIS; **465:** Réunion des Musées Nationaux/Art Resource, NY; **466:** (background) Honeychurch Antiques, Ltd./CORBIS; (inset) © Getty Images; **467:** Arthur Furst; **468–469:** Private collection/Jessie Coates/Super-Stock; **469:** © Tim Wright/CORBIS; **470:** © The Barnes Foundation, Merion Station, Penn./CORBIS; **471:** © John Johnson/Getty Images; **472:** © Scala/Art Resource, NY; **475:** Charles Wright; **476:** © Jayme Thornton/Getty Images; **479:** Manfred Danegger/ Photo Researchers, Inc.; **480:** Nancy Crampton; **481:** Pictor International, Ltd./PictureQuest; **483:** Alexandria King/ Albuquerque Journal; **485:** Joe Travers/Liaison International; **487:** © Francis G. Mayer/CORBIS; **489:** Morgan-Cain & Associates; **494:** Kaoru Mikami/Photonica; **497:** © Kim Sayer/CORBIS; **500:** © Archivo Iconografico, S.A./CORBIS; **501:** 2002 Banco de México, Diego Rivera and Frida Kahlo Museums Trust, Av. Cinco de Mayo No. 2, Col. Centro, Del Cuauhtémoc 06059, México, D.F. Schalkwijk/Art Resource, NY; **506:** M. P. Kahl/Photo Researchers, Inc.; **507:** (background) © Harold Sund/Getty Images; (inset) © Bettmann/CORBIS; **508:** Picture Images; **509:** © Victoria and Albert Museum, London/Art Resource, NY; **513:** Renee Purse/Photo Researchers, Inc.; **514–515:** © G. K. & Vikki Hart/Getty Images; **515:** James H. Evans; **516:** Lynn Saville; **517:** © Getty Images; **518:** © Alan Thornton/Getty Images; **519:** © Pascal Rondeau/Getty Images; **520:** Rick Friedman/Black Star Publishing/PictureQuest; **522:** © Sean Ellis/Getty Images; **523:** Nancy Crampton; **526:** © Getty Images; © Paul Abdoo; **530:** Werner Forman/Art Resource, NY; **531:** © Janet Century; **532:** Artwork © 2002 Gwendolyn Knight Lawrence, courtesy of The Jacob and Gwendolyn Lawrence Foundation; **533:** (top) © Getty Images; (bottom) © Bettmann/CORBIS; **535:** Private collection/ Gil Mayers/SuperStock; **537:** Archive Photos/PictureQuest; **539:** (top left) From *Poetry Out Loud,* edited by Robert A. Rubin. Copyright © 1993 by Algonquin Books of Chapel Hill. Reprinted by permission of Algonquin Books of Chapel Hill, a division of Workman Publishing; (top right) *This Same Sky: A Collection of Poems from Around the World.* Cover illustration © 1992 by Deborah Maverick Kelley; (bottom left) Cover from *Emily Dickinson: Collected Poems.* Jacket design by Leah Lococo. Courtesy of Barnes & Noble, Inc.; (bottom right) Cover from *Neruda: Selected Poems* (Boston: Houghton Mifflin, 1990). Reprinted by permission of Houghton Mifflin Company. All rights reserved; **552:** © Getty Images; **559:** © Donald Johnson/Getty Images; **561:** © 1994 Rubén Guzmán; **565** (background): Morgan-Cain & Associates, Inc.; **568:** Turner Sculpture; **572:** © John Scranton; **573:** © Getty Images; **574:** © Francis G. Mayer/CORBIS; (feather) © Getty Images; **579:** © Getty Images; **580:** Richard Shiell/Earth Scenes; **582:** © Alan and Sandy Carey/Getty Images; **587, 589, 590, 592, 593, 595:** Art by Sergio Bustamante/photographs © Clint Clemens. All rights reserved; **596:** © Ulf Andersen/Gamma Press, Inc.; **597:** Sepp Seitz/ Woodfin Camp & Associates; **601:** (top left) *Great American Stories,* cover © HRW, art by Sabra Field © 1991; (top right) Cover from *The Old Man and the Sea* by Ernest Hemingway, Hemingway Century Edition (New York: Scribner, a division of Simon & Schuster, Inc., 1999). Cover illustration © 1999 Production Pascal Blais, Inc., Imagica Corp., Panorama Film Studio of Yaroslav; (bottom left) *Barrio Boy* by Ernesto Galarza. Cover © HRW, photo by Rick Williams; (bottom right) *Never Cry Wolf* by Farley Mowat. Cover art by Bob Ziering. Used by permission of HRW; **621:** Philip Jones Griffiths/Magnum Photos, Inc.; (background) © Dirck Halstead/Getty Images; **624:** © B. Hemphill/Photo Researchers, Inc.; **626:** © Dirck Halstead/Getty Images; **628:** AP/Wide World Photos; **629:** © Paul S. Conklin/UNIPHOTO; **634:** The News Archive/PRC Archive; **635:** PRC Archive; **636:** The National Archives; **639:** AP/Wide World Photos; **640:** Charles Bonnay/Black Star Publishing/PictureQuest; **641:** © CORBIS; **645:** © Chapman & Perry/The Image Works; **648:** Art Resources, NY; **656:** Reprinted with the permission of Atheneum Books for Young Readers, an imprint of Simon and Schuster Children's Publishing Division, from *The Boy's King Arthur* by Sydney Lanier, illustrated by N. C. Wyeth. Copyright 1917, 1924 Charles Scribner's Sons, copyright renewed 1945 N. C. Wyeth and 1952 John Lanier, David Lanier, and Sterling Lanier; **661:** Morgan-Cain & Associates; **662:** © Mimmo Jodice/CORBIS; **667:** © Erich Lessing/Art Resource, NY; **668:** (top) James Whitmore/TimePix; (bottom) © Gianni Dagli Orti/CORBIS; **669:** © Arte & Immagini SRL/CORBIS; **671:** Louvre, Paris/Bridgeman Art Library; **674:** Ronald Sheridan, Ancient Art & Architecture Collection; **676:** Werner Forman/Art Resource, NY; **676–685** (border): Morgan-Cain & Associates; **679, 680, 682:** © Werner Forman/CORBIS; **684:** (top) Ny Carlsberg Glyptotek, Copenhagen/North Wind Picture Archives; (center) © Bettmann/CORBIS; (bottom right) Arthur Rackham/Wood River Gallery/PictureQuest; (bottom left) Werner Forman/Art Resource, NY; **685:** (top left) Mary Evans Picture Library; (top right) Fogelberg, BE NM 394 Balder. Photo: The National Museum of Fine Arts, Stockholm; (bottom left) Royal Library, Copenhagen/Bridgeman Art Library; (bottom right) Mary Evans Picture Library;

1020 Picture Credits

686: Houghton Mifflin Company, Boston; **689:** (top left) From *The King Must Die* (book cover) by Mary Renault, copyright © 1958 by Mary Renault. Used by permission of Vintage Books, a division of Random House, Inc.; (top right) Jacket design by Louise Fili from *The Acts of King Arthur and His Noble Knights* by John Steinbeck. Jacket design copyright © 1993 by Louise Fili. Reprinted by permission of Farrar, Strauss and Giroux; (bottom left) *Fallen Angels* by Walter Dean Myers. Cover art © HRW, cover photo by Steve Harris, cover design by Scott Stricker; (bottom right) *Shrapnel in the Heart: Letters and Remembrances from the Vietnam Veterans Memorial;* **718:** 1997 Production of *Tristan and Isolde* performed at the Los Angeles Opera. Production conceived and directed by David Hockney. Photo by Robert Millard; **723:** © Nancy Crampton; **725; 727; 730; 733, 735:** 2002 production of *The Brute* performed by The Expression Theatre Ensemble. Photos by Rade Vranesh; **737:** © Bettmann/CORBIS; **741:** Popperfoto Ltd.; **742:** © The Photo Works/Photo Researchers, Inc.; **743:** © Michal Daniel/New York Shakespeare Festival; **744:** © Paul Davis. Courtesy of the artist; **748:** © Bettmann/CORBIS; **749:** The Shakespeare Centre Library, Stratford-on-Avon, England; **750:** © Erich Lessing/Art Resource, NY; **751:** © Bettmann/CORBIS; **755:** Photofest; **756:** © Giraudon/Art Resource, NY; **757:** © Ray Manley/SuperStock, Florida; **761, 766, 774:** © George E. Joseph; **778:** Rod Planck/Photo Researchers, Inc.; **780:** Art Resource, NY; **782:** © Martha Swope/TimePix; **792, 794, 797:** © George E. Joseph; **805:** Courtesy MGM/Ronald Grant Archive; **806, 810, 816, 821, 825, 827:** © George E. Joseph; **831:** © R. G. Everts/Photo Researchers, Inc.; **833:** © Bettmann/CORBIS; **842, 851, 856–857, 863, 869:** © George E. Joseph; **872:** Réunion des Musées Nationaux/Art Resource, NY; **873:** Gilles Mermet/Art Resource, NY; **875:** AP/Wide World Photos; **876, 877:** Dennis Brack/Black Star Publishing/PictureQuest; **883, 884, 885:** © Bettmann/CORBIS; **888:** © Hulton-Deutsch Collection/CORBIS; **889:** (top left) *Macbeth;* (top right) *A Raisin in the Sun;* (bottom left) *Visit to a Small Planet;* (bottom right) *A Book of Plays;* **906–907:** Mark Richards/PhotoEdit; **913:** Creative Labs; **916:** Morgan-Cain & Associates; **917:** PEANUTS © United Features Syndicate. Reprinted by Permission; **924–925, 936:** © Getty Images.

Illustrations

Dykes, John, 23, 25
Forkan, Joe, 66, 68
Hargreaves, Greg, 375
High, Richard, 652–657
Lopez, Rafael, 43, 498–499
Newbold, Greg, 154–155, 156–157, 158–159
Reagan, Mike, 871
Steinberg, James, 317, 319, 320, 321, 323, 324

Maps

Nepal, Tibet, and India, 351
Some Sites of Ancient Greece, 661
Rome at the Death of Caesar, 871
North America, 1000

Picture Credits / Illustrations

Picture Credits / Illustrations / Maps 1021

Index of Skills

The boldface page numbers indicate an extensive treatment of the topic.

LITERARY RESPONSE AND ANALYSIS

Index of Skills

Index of Skills **1023**

1024 Index of Skills

READING COMPREHENSION (INFORMATIONAL MATERIALS)

Index of Skills

Index of Skills **1025**

1026 Index of Skills

READING: WORD ANALYSIS, FLUENCY, AND SYSTEMATIC VOCABULARY DEVELOPMENT

READING SKILLS AND STRATEGIES

Index of Skills

Index of Skills **1027**

WRITING STRATEGIES AND APPLICATIONS

1028 Index of Skills

Index of Skills 1029

1030 Index of Skills

Index of Skills

Index of Skills 1031

1032 Index of Skills

WRITTEN AND ORAL ENGLISH-LANGUAGE CONVENTIONS

Index of Skills **1033**

LISTENING AND SPEAKING STRATEGIES AND APPLICATIONS / MEDIA ANALYSIS

1034 Index of Skills

INDEPENDENT READING

Index of Skills **1035**

1036 Index of Skills

Index of Art

Index of Art

Index of Art 1037

1038 Index of Art

Index of Authors and Titles

Page numbers in italic type refer to the pages on which author biographies appear.

Index of Authors and Titles 1039

1040 Index of Authors and Titles

For permission to reprint copyrighted material, grateful acknowledgment is made to the following sources:

American Heritage: Quote by Roger Rosenblatt from "How Have We Changed?" from *American Heritage,* vol. 45, no. 8, December 1994. Copyright © 1994 by American Heritage.

Brandt & Hochman Literary Agents, Inc.: From "Litany for Dicatorships" by Stephen Vincent Benét. Copyright © 1935 by Stephen Vincent Benét; copyright renewed © 1963 by Thomas C. Benét, Stephanie B. Mahin, and Rachel Benét Lewis.

Don Congdon Associates, Inc.: Quote, "You can't have 'plot' . . ." by Ray Bradbury.

Barbara Sande Dimmitt: From telephone interview with Barbara Sande Dimmitt conducted on October 21, 1998 by Holt, Rinehart and Winston.

The Gale Group: Quote by Tim O'Brien from *Contemporary Authors,* New Revision Series, vol. 58, edited by Daniel Jones and John D. Jorgenson. Copyright © 1997 by Gale Research Inc.

Harcourt, Inc.: From "Study of the Text" from *Shakespeare: Major Plays and the Sonnets,* edited by G. B. Harrison. Copyright © 1948 by Harcourt Brace & Company; copyright renewed © 1975 by G. B. Harrison.

Devon McNamara: From Devon McNamara's review of *Angela's Ashes* by Frank McCourt from *The Christian Science Monitor,* 1996. Copyright © 1996 by Devon McNamara. First published in *The Christian Science Monitor*.

NEA Today: Quote by Amy Tan from "Meet:" from *NEA Today,* vol. 10, no. 3, October 1991. Copyright © 1991 by the National Education Association of the United States.

Thomas Nelson and Sons Ltd.: From the Introduction and Footnotes to *Julius Caesar, the Arden Edition of the Works of William Shakespeare,* edited by T. S. Dorsch. First published in 1955 by Methuen & Co. Ltd.

W. W. Norton & Company, Inc.: From *Shakespeare: A Life in Drama* by Stanley Wells. Copyright © 1995 by Stanley Wells.

Pocket Books, a division of Simon & Schuster, Inc.: From "Julius Caesar: A Modern Perspective" by Coppelia Kahn from *The Tragedy of Julius Caesar* by William Shakespeare. Copyright © 1992 by The Folger Shakespeare Library.

Red Crane Books, Sante Fe, NM: From *Working in the Dark: Reflections of a Poet of the Barrio* by Jimmy Santiago Baca. Copyright © 1992 by Jimmy Santiago Baca.

Simon & Schuster, Inc.: From "Notes, Chapter 1" from *Admiral Death* by Hanson W. Baldwin. Copyright © 1938 by Hanson W. Baldwin.

Sources Cited

From appendix to *Cancer Ward* by Aleksandr Solzhenitsyn. Published by Farrar, Straus and Giroux, Inc., New York, 1969.

Quote from "Puerto Rican Literature in Georgia? An Interview with Judith Ortiz Cofer" by Rafael Ocasio from *Kenyon Review,* vol. 14, no. 4, Fall 1992.

From a review of *The Unexpected Salami* by Laurie Gwen Shapiro from *Kirkus Reviews,* vol. LXVI, no. 6, March 15, 1998. Published by Kirkus Associates, LP, New York, 1998.

Quote by Pat Mora from "Conserving Natural and Cultural Diversity: The Prose and Poetry of Pat Mora" by Patrick D. Murphy from *MELUS,* Spring 1996. Published by MELUS, Amherst, MA, 1996.

From "Amy Tan Walks in Two Worlds" by Sarah Lyall from *The New York Times.*

From "Viewing the Visual Arts," book review of *You Can't Keep a Good Woman Down* by Alice Walker, by Katha Pollitt from The *New York Times*, May 24, 1981.

From *Shakespeare's Living Art* by Rosalie L. Colie. Published by Princeton University Press, Princeton, NJ, 1974.

From interview with Doris Lessing from *Counterpoint* by Roy Newquist. Published by Rand McNally, Chicago, 1964.

From "From the Dark Carnival to the Machineries of Joy" by Orson Scott Card from *The Washington Post,* Book World, November 2, 1980.